# Legislation for
# Business Law

Rachel E. Cooper

Solicitor
Lecturer in Legal Practice, University of Sheffield

OXFORD
UNIVERSITY PRESS

# OXFORD
UNIVERSITY PRESS

Great Clarendon Street, Oxford OX2 6DP

Oxford University Press is a department of the University of Oxford.
It furthers the University's objective of excellence in research, scholarship,
and education by publishing worldwide in

Oxford  New York

Auckland  Cape Town  Dar es Salaam  Hong Kong  Karachi
Kuala Lumpur  Madrid  Melbourne  Mexico City  Nairobi
New Delhi  Shanghai  Taipei  Toronto

With offices in

Argentina  Austria  Brazil  Chile  Czech Republic  France  Greece
Guatemala  Hungary  Italy  Japan  Poland  Portugal  Singapore
South Korea  Switzerland  Thailand  Turkey  Ukraine  Vietnam

Oxford is a registered trade mark of Oxford University Press
in the UK and in certain other countries

Published in the United States
by Oxford University Press Inc., New York

British Library Cataloguing in Publication Data

Data available

Typeset by Newgen Imaging Systems (P) Ltd., Chennai, India
Printed in Great Britain
on acid-free paper by
Ashford Colour Press Ltd., Gosport, Hampshire

ISBN  978–0–19–958065–1

10 9 8 7 6 5 4 3 2 1

# Preface

This legislation book has been compiled specifically for students studying Business Law and Practice on the Legal Practice Course. The content of the book has been determined by reference to the Legal Practice Course Outcomes 2007 so is tailored to meet the requirements of the 'new' Legal Practice Course which will be run by many Legal Practice Course providers from 2009.

The legislation contained in the text is as in force at 1 May 2009 with the exception of the Companies Act 2006 and the Companies (Model Articles) Regulations 2008 which are set out as in force with effect from 1 October 2009. All other pending amendments are printed in italics and footnoted. Repeals and provisions that are omitted by amendment are shown by ellipses.

*REC*
May 2009

# Contents list

| | | |
|---|---|---|
| *Alphabetical contents* | | *ix* |
| *Chronological contents* | | *xi* |

**Part I**     **Company Law**     **1**

| | |
|---|---|
| Companies Act 2006 | 1 |
| Company Directors Disqualification Act 1986 | 434 |
| Companies (Tables A to F) Regulations 1985 (SI 1985/805) | 447 |
| Companies (Model Articles) Regulations 2008 (SI 2008/3229) | 463 |

**Part II**     **Company and Business Names**     **499**

| | |
|---|---|
| Company and Business Names Regulations 1981 (SI 1981/1685) | 499 |
| Companies (Trading Disclosures) Regulations 2008 (SI 2008/495) | 502 |

**Part III**     **Partnership Law**     **505**

| | |
|---|---|
| Partnership Act 1890 | 505 |
| Limited Liability Partnerships Act 2000 | 511 |
| Limited Liability Partnerships Regulations 2001 (SI 2001/1090) | 521 |

**Part IV**     **Insolvency Law**     **558**

| | |
|---|---|
| Insolvency Act 1986 | 558 |

**Part V**     **Financial Services**     **787**

| | |
|---|---|
| Financial Services and Markets Act 2000 | 787 |
| Financial Services and Markets Act 2000 (Regulated Activities) Order 2001 (SI 2001/544) | 1016 |
| Financial Services and Markets Act 2000 (Professions) (Non-Exempt Activities) Order 2001 (SI 2001/1227) | 1066 |

**Part VI**     **Sale of Goods**     **1069**

| | |
|---|---|
| Sale of Goods Act 1979 | 1069 |
| Unfair Contract Terms Act 1977 | 1089 |
| Unfair Terms in Consumer Contracts Regulations 1999 (SI 1999/2083) | 1098 |

# Alphabetical contents list

C   Companies Act 2006 ... 1
    Company and Business Names Regulations
        1981 (SI 1981/1685) ... 499
    Company Directors Disqualification Act
        1986 ... 434
    Companies (Model Articles) Regulations
        2008 (SI 2008/3229) ... 463
    Companies (Tables A to F) Regulations 1985
        (SI 1985/805) ... 447
    Companies (Trading Disclosures)
        Regulations 2008 (SI 2008/495) ... 502
F   Financial Services and Markets Act
        2000 ... 787
    Financial Services and Markets Act 2000
        (Professions) (Non-Exempt Activities)
        Order 2001 (SI 2001/1227) ... 1066

    Financial Services and Markets Act 2000
        (Regulated Activities) Order 2001 (SI
        2001/544) ... 1016
I   Insolvency Act 1986 ... 558
L   Limited Liability Partnerships Act
        2000 ... 511
    Limited Liability Partnerships Regulations
        2001 (SI 2001/1090) ... 521
P   Partnership Act 1890 ... 505
S   Sale of Goods Act 1979 ... 1069
U   Unfair Contract Terms Act 1977 ... 1089
    Unfair Terms in Consumer Contracts
        Regulations 1999 (SI 1999/2083) ... 1098

# Chronological contents list

Partnership Act 1890 ... 505
Unfair Contract Terms Act 1977 ... 1089
Sale of Goods Act 1979 ... 1069
Company and Business Names Regulations
    1981 (SI 1981/1685) ... 499
Companies (Tables A to F) Regulations 1985
    (SI 1985/805) ... 447
Insolvency Act 1986 ... 558
Company Directors Disqualification Act
    1986 ... 434
Unfair Terms in Consumer Contracts
    Regulations 1999 (SI 1999/2083) ... 1098
Financial Services and Markets Act
    2000 ... 787
Limited Liability Partnerships Act
    2000 ... 511

Financial Services and Markets Act 2000
    (Regulated Activities) Order 2001 (SI
    2001/544) ... 1016
Limited Liability Partnerships Regulations
    2001 (SI 2001/1090) ... 521
Financial Services and Markets Act 2000
    (Professions) (Non-Exempt Activities)
    Order 2001 (SI 2001/1227) ... 1066
Companies Act 2006 ... 1
Companies (Trading Disclosures)
    Regulations 2008 (SI 2008/495) ... 502
Companies (Model Articles) Regulations
    2008 (SI 2008/3229) ... 463

# Company Law

## Companies Act 2006

(2006, c. 46)

**PART 1  GENERAL INTRODUCTORY PROVISIONS**

*Companies and Companies Acts*
1 Companies
2 The Companies Acts

*Types of company*
3 Limited and unlimited companies
4 Private and public companies
5 Companies limited by guarantee and having share capital
6 Community interest companies

**PART 2  COMPANY FORMATION**

*General*
7 Method of forming company
8 Memorandum of association

*Requirements for registration*
9 Registration documents
10 Statement of capital and initial shareholdings
11 Statement of guarantee
12 Statement of proposed officers
13 Statement of compliance

*Registration and its effect*
14 Registration
15 Issue of certificate of incorporation
16 Effect of registration

**PART 3  A COMPANY'S CONSTITUTION**

**CHAPTER 1  INTRODUCTORY**
17 A company's constitution

**CHAPTER 2  ARTICLES OF ASSOCIATION**

*General*
18 Articles of association
19 Power of Secretary of State to prescribe model articles
20 Default application of model articles

*Alteration of articles*
21 Amendment of articles
22 Entrenched provisions of the articles
23 Notice to registrar of existence of restriction on amendment of articles
24 Statement of compliance where amendment of articles restricted
25 Effect of alteration of articles on company's members
26 Registrar to be sent copy of amended articles
27 Registrar's notice to comply in case of failure with respect to amended articles

*Supplementary*
28 Existing companies: provisions of memorandum treated as provisions of articles

**CHAPTER 3  RESOLUTIONS AND AGREEMENTS AFFECTING A COMPANY'S CONSTITUTION**
29 Resolutions and agreements affecting a company's constitution

30 Copies of resolutions or agreements to be forwarded to registrar

**CHAPTER 4  MISCELLANEOUS AND SUPPLEMENTARY PROVISIONS**

*Statement of company's objects*
31 Statement of company's objects

*Other provisions with respect to a company's constitution*
32 Constitutional documents to be provided to members
33 Effect of company's constitution
34 Notice to registrar where company's constitution altered by enactment
35 Notice to registrar where company's constitution altered by order
36 Documents to be incorporated in or accompany copies of articles issued by company

*Supplementary provisions*
37 Right to participate in profits otherwise than as member void
38 Application to single member companies of enactments and rules of law

**PART 4  A COMPANY'S CAPACITY AND RELATED MATTERS**

*Capacity of company and power of directors to bind it*
39 A company's capacity
40 Power of directors to bind the company
41 Constitutional limitations: transactions involving directors or their associates
42 Constitutional limitations: companies that are charities

*Formalities of doing business under the law of England and Wales or Northern Ireland*
43 Company contracts
44 Execution of documents
45 Common seal
46 Execution of deeds
47 Execution of deeds or other documents by attorney

*Formalities of doing business under the law of Scotland*
48 Execution of documents by companies

*Other matters*
49 Official seal for use abroad
50 Official seal for share certificates etc.
51 Pre-incorporation contracts, deeds and obligations
52 Bills of exchange and promissory notes

**PART 5  A COMPANY'S NAME**

**CHAPTER 1  GENERAL REQUIREMENTS**

*Prohibited names*
53 Prohibited names

*Sensitive words and expressions*
54 Names suggesting connection with government or public authority
55 Other sensitive words or expressions

56 Duty to seek comments of government department or other specified body

*Permitted characters etc.*

57 Permitted characters etc.

### CHAPTER 2 INDICATIONS OF COMPANY TYPE OR LEGAL FORM

*Required indications for limited companies*

58 Public limited companies
59 Private limited companies
60 Exemption from requirement as to use of 'limited'
61 Continuation of existing exemption: companies limited by shares
62 Continuation of existing exemption: companies limited by guarantee
63 Exempt company: restriction on amendment of articles
64 Power to direct change of name in case of company ceasing to be entitled to exemption

*Inappropriate use of indications of company type or legal form*

65 Inappropriate use of indications of company type or legal form

### CHAPTER 3 SIMILARITY TO OTHER NAMES

*Similarity to other name on registrar's index*

66 Name not to be the same as another in the index
67 Power to direct change of name in case of similarity to existing name
68 Direction to change name: supplementary provisions

*Similarity to other name in which person has goodwill*

69 Objection to company's registered name
70 Company names adjudicators
71 Procedural rules
72 Decision of adjudicator to be made available to public
73 Order requiring name to be changed
74 Appeal from adjudicator's decision

### CHAPTER 4 OTHER POWERS OF THE SECRETARY OF STATE

75 Provision of misleading information etc.
76 Misleading indication of activities

### CHAPTER 5 CHANGE OF NAME

77 Change of name
78 Change of name by special resolution
79 Change of name by means provided for in company's articles
80 Change of name: registration and issue of new certificate of incorporation
81 Change of name: effect

### CHAPTER 6 TRADING DISCLOSURES

82 Requirement to disclose company name etc.
83 Civil consequences of failure to make required disclosure
84 Criminal consequences of failure to make required disclosures
85 Minor variations in form of name to be left out of account

### PART 6 A COMPANY'S REGISTERED OFFICE

*General*

86 A company's registered office
87 Change of address of registered office

*Welsh companies*

88 Welsh companies

### PART 7 RE-REGISTRATION AS A MEANS OF ALTERING A COMPANY'S STATUS

*Introductory*

89 Alteration of status by re-registration

*Private company becoming public*

90 Re-registration of private company as public

91 Requirements as to share capital
92 Requirements as to net assets
93 Recent allotment of shares for non-cash consideration
94 Application and accompanying documents
95 Statement of proposed secretary
96 Issue of certificate of incorporation on re-registration

*Public company becoming private*

97 Re-registration of public company as private limited company
98 Application to court to cancel resolution
99 Notice to registrar of court application or order
100 Application and accompanying documents
101 Issue of certificate of incorporation on re-registration

*Private limited company becoming unlimited*

102 Re-registration of private limited company as unlimited
103 Application and accompanying documents
104 Issue of certificate of incorporation on re-registration

*Unlimited private company becoming limited*

105 Re-registration of unlimited company as limited
106 Application and accompanying documents
107 Issue of certificate of incorporation on re-registration
108 Statement of capital required where company already has share capital

*Public company becoming private and unlimited*

109 Re-registration of public company as private and unlimited
110 Application and accompanying documents
111 Issue of certificate of incorporation on re-registration

### PART 8 A COMPANY'S MEMBERS

### CHAPTER 1 THE MEMBERS OF A COMPANY

112 The members of a company

### CHAPTER 2 REGISTER OF MEMBERS

*General*

113 Register of members
114 Register to be kept available for inspection
115 Index of members
116 Rights to inspect and require copies
117 Register of members: response to request for inspection or copy
118 Register of members: refusal of inspection or default in providing copy
119 Register of members: offences in connection with request for or disclosure of information
120 Information as to state of register and index
121 Removal of entries relating to former members

*Special cases*

122 Share warrants
123 Single member companies
124 Company holding its own shares as treasury shares

*Supplementary*

125 Power of court to rectify register
126 Trusts not to be entered on register
127 Register to be evidence
128 Time limit for claims arising from entry in register

### CHAPTER 3 OVERSEAS BRANCH REGISTERS

129 Overseas branch registers
130 Notice of opening of overseas branch register
131 Keeping of overseas branch register
132 Register or duplicate to be kept available for inspection in UK
133 Transactions in shares registered in overseas branch
134 Jurisdiction of local courts
135 Discontinuance of overseas branch register

CHAPTER 4 PROHIBITION ON SUBSIDIARY BEING
MEMBER OF ITS HOLDING COMPANY
*General prohibition*
136 Prohibition on subsidiary being a member of its
holding company
137 Shares acquired before prohibition became
applicable
*Subsidiary acting as personal representative or trustee*
138 Subsidiary acting as personal representative or
trustee
139 Interests to be disregarded: residual interest under
pension scheme or employees' share scheme
140 Interests to be disregarded: employer's rights of
recovery under pension scheme or employees'
share scheme
*Subsidiary acting as dealer in securities*
141 Subsidiary acting as authorised dealer in
securities
142 Protection of third parties in other cases where
subsidiary acting as dealer in securities
*Supplementary*
143 Application of provisions to companies not limited
by shares
144 Application of provisions to nominees

PART 9 EXERCISE OF MEMBERS' RIGHTS
*Effect of provisions in company's articles*
145 Effect of provisions of articles as to enjoyment or
exercise of members' rights
*Information rights*
146 Traded companies: nomination of persons to enjoy
information rights
147 Information rights: form in which copies to be
provided
148 Termination or suspension of nomination
149 Information as to possible rights in relation to
voting
150 Information rights: status of rights
151 Information rights: power to amend
*Exercise of rights where shares held on behalf of others*
152 Exercise of rights where shares held on behalf of
others: exercise in different ways
153 Exercise of rights where shares held on behalf of
others: members' requests

PART 10 A COMPANY'S DIRECTORS
CHAPTER 1 APPOINTMENT AND REMOVAL
OF DIRECTORS
*Requirement to have directors*
154 Companies required to have directors
155 Companies required to have at least one director
who is a natural person
156 Direction requiring company to make appointment
*Appointment*
157 Minimum age for appointment as director
158 Power to provide for exceptions from minimum
age requirement
159 Existing under-age directors
160 Appointment of directors of public company to be
voted on individually
161 Validity of acts of directors
*Register of directors, etc.*
162 Register of directors
163 Particulars of directors to be registered: individuals
164 Particulars of directors to be registered: corporate
directors and firms
165 Register of directors' residential addresses
166 Particulars of directors to be registered: power to
make regulations
167 Duty to notify registrar of changes
*Removal*
168 Resolution to remove director
169 Director's right to protest against removal

CHAPTER 2 GENERAL DUTIES OF DIRECTORS
*Introductory*
170 Scope and nature of general duties
*The general duties*
171 Duty to act within powers
172 Duty to promote the success of the company
173 Duty to exercise independent judgment
174 Duty to exercise reasonable care, skill and
diligence
175 Duty to avoid conflicts of interest
176 Duty not to accept benefits from third parties
177 Duty to declare interest in proposed transaction or
arrangement
*Supplementary provisions*
178 Civil consequences of breach of general duties
179 Cases within more than one of the general duties
180 Consent, approval or authorisation by members
181 Modification of provisions in relation to charitable
companies

CHAPTER 3 DECLARATION OF INTEREST IN
EXISTING TRANSACTION OR ARRANGEMENT
182 Declaration of interest in existing transaction or
arrangement
183 Offence of failure to declare interest
184 Declaration made by notice in writing
185 General notice treated as sufficient declaration
186 Declaration of interest in case of company with
sole director
187 Declaration of interest in existing transaction by
shadow director

CHAPTER 4 TRANSACTIONS WITH DIRECTORS
REQUIRING APPROVAL OF MEMBERS
*Service contracts*
188 Directors' long-term service contracts: requirement
of members' approval
189 Directors' long-term service contracts: civil
consequences of contravention
*Substantial property transactions*
190 Substantial property transactions: requirement of
members' approval
191 Meaning of 'substantial'
192 Exception for transactions with members or other
group companies
193 Exception in case of company in winding up or
administration
194 Exception for transactions on recognised
investment exchange
195 Property transactions: civil consequences of
contravention
196 Property transactions: effect of subsequent
affirmation
*Loans, quasi-loans and credit transactions*
197 Loans to directors: requirement of members'
approval
198 Quasi-loans to directors: requirement of members'
approval
199 Meaning of 'quasi-loan' and related expressions
200 Loans or quasi-loans to persons connected with
directors: requirement of members' approval
201 Credit transactions: requirement of members'
approval
202 Meaning of 'credit transaction'
203 Related arrangements: requirement of members'
approval
204 Exception for expenditure on company business
205 Exception for expenditure on defending
proceedings etc.
206 Exception for expenditure in connection with
regulatory action or investigation
207 Exceptions for minor and business transactions
208 Exceptions for intra-group transactions
209 Exceptions for money-lending companies
210 Other relevant transactions or arrangements
211 The value of transactions and arrangements

212 The person for whom a transaction or arrangement is entered into
213 Loans etc.: civil consequences of contravention
214 Loans etc.: effect of subsequent affirmation

*Payments for loss of office*
215 Payments for loss of office
216 Amounts taken to be payments for loss of office
217 Payment by company: requirement of members' approval
218 Payment in connection with transfer of undertaking etc. requirement of members' approval
219 Payment in connection with share transfer: requirement of members' approval
220 Exception for payments in discharge of legal obligations etc.
221 Exception for small payments
222 Payments made without approval: civil consequences

*Supplementary*
223 Transactions requiring members' approval: application of provisions to shadow directors
224 Approval by written resolution: accidental failure to send memorandum
225 Cases where approval is required under more than one provision
226 Requirement of consent of Charity Commission: companies that are charities

**CHAPTER 5  DIRECTORS' SERVICE CONTRACTS**
227 Directors' service contracts
228 Copy of contract or memorandum of terms to be available for inspection
229 Right of member to inspect and request copy
230 Directors' service contracts: application of provisions to shadow directors

**CHAPTER 6  CONTRACTS WITH SOLE MEMBERS WHO ARE DIRECTORS**
231 Contract with sole member who is also a director

**CHAPTER 7 DIRECTORS' LIABILITIES**

*Provision protecting directors from liability*
232 Provisions protecting directors from liability
233 Provision of insurance
234 Qualifying third party indemnity provision
235 Qualifying pension scheme indemnity provision
236 Qualifying indemnity provision to be disclosed in directors' report
237 Copy of qualifying indemnity provision to be available for inspection
238 Right of member to inspect and request copy

*Ratification of acts giving rise to liability*
239 Ratification of acts of directors

**CHAPTER 8  DIRECTORS' RESIDENTIAL ADDRESSES: PROTECTION FROM DISCLOSURE**
240 Protected information
241 Protected information: restriction on use or disclosure by company
242 Protected information: restriction on use or disclosure by registrar
243 Permitted use or disclosure by the registrar
244 Disclosure under court order
245 Circumstances in which registrar may put address on the public record
246 Putting the address on the public record

**CHAPTER 9  SUPPLEMENTARY PROVISIONS**

*Provision for employees on cessation or transfer of business*
247 Power to make provision for employees on cessation or transfer of business

*Records of meetings of directors*
248 Minutes of directors' meetings
249 Minutes as evidence

*Meaning of 'director' and 'shadow director'*
250 'Director'
251 'Shadow director'

*Other definitions*
252 Persons connected with a director
253 Members of a director's family
254 Director 'connected with' a body corporate
255 Director 'controlling' a body corporate
256 Associated bodies corporate
257 References to company's constitution

*General*
258 Power to increase financial limits
259 Transactions under foreign law

**PART 11  DERIVATIVE CLAIMS AND PROCEEDINGS BY MEMBERS**

**CHAPTER 1  DERIVATIVE CLAIMS IN ENGLAND AND WALES OR NORTHERN IRELAND**
260 Derivative claims
261 Application for permission to continue derivative claim
262 Application for permission to continue claim as a derivative claim
263 Whether permission to be given
264 Application for permission to continue derivative claim brought by another member

**CHAPTER 2  DERIVATIVE PROCEEDINGS IN SCOTLAND**
265 Derivative proceedings
266 Requirement for leave and notice
267 Application to continue proceedings as derivative proceedings
268 Granting of leave
269 Application by member to be substituted for member pursuing derivative proceedings

**PART 12  COMPANY SECRETARIES**

*Private companies*
270 Private company not required to have secretary

*Public companies*
271 Public company required to have secretary
272 Direction requiring public company to appoint secretary
273 Qualifications of secretaries of public companies

*Provisions applying to private companies with a secretary and to public companies*
274 Discharge of functions where office vacant or secretary unable to act
275 Duty to keep register of secretaries
276 Duty to notify registrar of changes
277 Particulars of secretaries to be registered: individuals
278 Particulars of secretaries to be registered: corporate secretaries and firms
279 Particulars of secretaries to be registered: power to make regulations
280 Acts done by person in dual capacity

**PART 13  RESOLUTIONS AND MEETINGS**

**CHAPTER 1  GENERAL PROVISIONS ABOUT RESOLUTIONS**
281 Resolutions
282 Ordinary resolutions
283 Special resolutions
284 Votes: general rules
285 Votes: specific requirements
286 Votes of joint holders of shares
287 Saving for provisions of articles as to determination of entitlement to vote

**CHAPTER 2  WRITTEN RESOLUTIONS**

*General provisions about written resolutions*
288 Written resolutions of private companies
289 Eligible members

*Circulation of written resolutions*

290 Circulation date

291 Circulation of written resolutions proposed by directors

292 Members' power to require circulation of written resolution

293 Circulation of written resolution proposed by members

294 Expenses of circulation

295 Application not to circulate members' statement

*Agreeing to written resolutions*

296 Procedure for signifying agreement to written resolution

297 Period for agreeing to written resolution

*Supplementary*

298 Sending documents relating to written resolutions by electronic means

299 Publication of written resolution on website

300 Relationship between this Chapter and provisions of company's articles

**CHAPTER 3  RESOLUTIONS AT MEETINGS**

*General provisions about resolutions at meetings*

301 Resolutions at general meetings

*Calling meetings*

302 Directors' power to call general meetings

303 Members' power to require directors to call general meeting

304 Directors' duty to call meetings required by members

305 Power of members to call meeting at company's expense

306 Power of court to order meeting

*Notice of meetings*

307 Notice required of general meeting

308 Manner in which notice to be given

309 Publication of notice of meeting on website

310 Persons entitled to receive notice of meetings

311 Contents of notices of meetings

312 Resolution requiring special notice

313 Accidental failure to give notice of resolution or meeting

*Members' statements*

314 Members' power to require circulation of statements

315 Company's duty to circulate members' statement

316 Expenses of circulating members' statement

317 Application not to circulate members' statement

*Procedure at meetings*

318 Quorum at meetings

319 Chairman of meeting

320 Declaration by chairman on a show of hands

321 Right to demand a poll

322 Voting on a poll

323 Representation of corporations at meetings

*Proxies*

324 Rights to appoint proxies

325 Notice of meeting to contain statement of rights

326 Company-sponsored invitations to appoint proxies

327 Notice required of appointment of proxy etc.

328 Chairing meetings

329 Right of proxy to demand a poll

330 Notice required of termination of proxy's authority

331 Saving for more extensive rights conferred by articles

*Adjourned meetings*

332 Resolution passed at adjourned meeting

*Electronic communications*

333 Sending documents relating to meetings etc. in electronic form

*Application to class meetings*

334 Application to class meetings

335 Application to class meetings: companies without a share capital

**CHAPTER 4  PUBLIC COMPANIES: ADDITIONAL REQUIREMENTS FOR AGMS**

336 Public companies: annual general meeting

337 Public companies: notice of AGM

338 Public companies: members' power to require circulation of resolutions for AGMs

339 Public companies: company's duty to circulate members' resolutions for AGMs

340 Public companies: expenses of circulating members' resolutions for AGM

**CHAPTER 5  ADDITIONAL REQUIREMENTS FOR QUOTED COMPANIES**

*Website publication of poll results*

341 Results of poll to be made available on website

*Independent report on poll*

342 Members' power to require independent report on poll

343 Appointment of independent assessor

344 Independence requirement

345 Meaning of 'associate'

346 Effect of appointment of a partnership

347 The independent assessor's report

348 Rights of independent assessor: right to attend meeting etc.

349 Rights of independent assessor: right to information

350 Offences relating to provision of information

351 Information to be made available on website

*Supplementary*

352 Application of provisions to class meetings

353 Requirements as to website availability

354 Power to limit or extend the types of company to which provisions of this Chapter apply

**CHAPTER 6  RECORDS OF RESOLUTIONS AND MEETINGS**

355 Records of resolutions and meetings etc.

356 Records as evidence of resolutions etc.

357 Records of decisions by sole member

358 Inspection of records of resolutions and meetings

359 Records of resolutions and meetings of class of members

**CHAPTER 7  SUPPLEMENTARY PROVISIONS**

360 Computation of periods of notice etc.: clear day rule

361 Meaning of 'quoted company'

**PART 14  CONTROL OF POLITICAL DONATIONS AND EXPENDITURE**

*Introductory*

362 Introductory

*Donations and expenditure to which this Part applies*

363 Political parties, organisations etc. to which this Part applies

364 Meaning of 'political donation'

365 Meaning of 'political expenditure'

*Authorisation required for donations or expenditure*

366 Authorisation required for donations or expenditure

367 Form of authorising resolution

368 Period for which resolution has effect

*Remedies in case of unauthorised donations or expenditure*

369 Liability of directors in case of unauthorised donation or expenditure

370 Enforcement of directors' liabilities by shareholder action

371 Enforcement of directors' liabilities by shareholder action: supplementary

372 Costs of shareholder action

373 Information for purposes of shareholder action

*Exemptions*

374 Trade unions

375 Subscription for membership of trade association

376  All-party parliamentary groups
377  Political expenditure exempted by order
378  Donations not amounting to more than £5,000 in
     any twelve month period

*Supplementary provisions*
379  Minor definitions

## PART 15  ACCOUNTS AND REPORTS

### CHAPTER 1 INTRODUCTION
*General*
380  Scheme of this Part

*Companies subject to the small companies regime*
381  Companies subject to the small companies regime
382  Companies qualifying as small: general
383  Companies qualifying as small: parent
     companies
384  Companies excluded from the small companies
     regime

*Quoted and unquoted companies*
385  Quoted and unquoted companies

### CHAPTER 2  ACCOUNTING RECORDS
386  Duty to keep accounting records
387  Duty to keep accounting records: offence
388  Where and for how long records to be kept
389  Where and for how long records to be kept:
     offences

### CHAPTER 3  A COMPANY'S FINANCIAL YEAR
390  A company's financial year
391  Accounting reference periods and accounting
     reference date
392  Alteration of accounting reference date .

### CHAPTER 4  ANNUAL ACCOUNTS
*General*
393  Accounts to give true and fair view

*Individual accounts*
394  Duty to prepare individual accounts
395  Individual accounts: applicable accounting
     framework
396  Companies Act individual accounts
397  IAS individual accounts

*Group accounts: small companies*
398  Option to prepare group accounts

*Group accounts: other companies*
399  Duty to prepare group accounts
400  Exemption for company included in EEA group
     accounts of larger group
401  Exemption for company included in non-EEA
     group accounts of larger group
402  Exemption if no subsidiary undertakings need be
     included in the consolidation

*Group accounts: general*
403  Group accounts: applicable accounting
     framework
404  Companies Act group accounts
405  Companies Act group accounts: subsidiary
     undertakings included in the consolidation
406  IAS group accounts
407  Consistency of financial reporting
     within group
408  Individual profit and loss account where group
     accounts prepared

*Information to be given in notes to the accounts*
409  Information about related undertakings
410  Information about related undertakings:
     alternative compliance
410A Information about off-balance sheet
     arrangements
411  Information about employee numbers and costs
412  Information about directors' benefits:
     remuneration
413  Information about directors' benefits: advances,
     credit and guarantees

*Approval and signing of accounts*
414  Approval and signing of accounts

### CHAPTER 5  DIRECTORS' REPORT
*Directors' report*
415  Duty to prepare directors' report
415A Directors' report: small companies exemption
416  Contents of directors' report: general
417  Contents of directors' report: business review
418  Contents of directors' report: statement as to
     disclosure to auditors
419  Approval and signing of directors' report

### CHAPTER 6  QUOTED COMPANIES: DIRECTORS' REMUNERATION REPORT
420  Duty to prepare directors' remuneration report
421  Contents of directors' remuneration report
422  Approval and signing of directors' remuneration
     report

### CHAPTER 7  PUBLICATION OF ACCOUNTS AND REPORTS
*Duty to circulate copies of accounts and reports*
423  Duty to circulate copies of annual accounts and
     reports
424  Time allowed for sending out copies of accounts
     and reports
425  Default in sending out copies of accounts and
     reports: offences

*Option to provide summary financial statement*
426  Option to provide summary financial statement
427  Form and contents of summary financial
     statement: unquoted companies
428  Form and contents of summary financial
     statement: quoted companies
429  Summary financial statements: offences

*Quoted companies: requirements as to website publication*
430  Quoted companies: annual accounts and reports
     to be made available on website

*Right of member or debenture holder to demand copies of
accounts and reports*
431  Right of member or debenture holder to copies of
     accounts and reports: unquoted companies
432  Right of member or debenture holder to copies of
     accounts and reports: quoted companies

*Requirements in connection with publication of accounts
and reports*
433  Name of signatory to be stated in published
     copies of accounts and reports
434  Requirements in connection with publication of
     statutory accounts
435  Requirements in connection with publication of
     non-statutory accounts
436  Meaning of 'publication' in relation to accounts
     and reports

### CHAPTER 8  PUBLIC COMPANIES: LAYING OF ACCOUNTS AND REPORTS BEFORE GENERAL MEETING
437  Public companies: laying of accounts and reports
     before general meeting
438  Public companies: offence of failure to lay
     accounts and reports

### CHAPTER 9  QUOTED COMPANIES: MEMBERS' APPROVAL OF DIRECTORS' REMUNERATION REPORT
439  Quoted companies: members' approval of
     directors' remuneration report
440  Quoted companies: offences in connection with
     procedure for approval

### CHAPTER 10  FILING OF ACCOUNTS AND REPORTS
*Duty to file accounts and reports*
441  Duty to file accounts and reports with the
     registrar
442  Period allowed for filing accounts
443  Calculation of period allowed

*Filing obligations of different descriptions of company*
444 Filing obligations of companies subject to small companies regime
444A Filing obligations of companies entitled to small companies exemption in relation to directors' report
445 Filing obligations of medium-sized companies
446 Filing obligations of unquoted companies
447 Filing obligations of quoted companies
448 Unlimited companies exempt from obligation to file accounts

*Requirements where abbreviated accounts delivered*
449 Special auditor's report where abbreviated accounts delivered
450 Approval and signing of abbreviated accounts

*Failure to file accounts and reports*
451 Default in filing accounts and reports: offences
452 Default in filing accounts and reports: court order
453 Civil penalty for failure to file accounts and reports

**CHAPTER 11 REVISION OF DEFECTIVE ACCOUNTS AND REPORTS**
*Voluntary revision*
454 Voluntary revision of accounts etc.

*Secretary of State's notice*
455 Secretary of State's notice in respect of accounts or reports

*Application to court*
456 Application to court in respect of defective accounts or reports
457 Other persons authorised to apply to the court
458 Disclosure of information by tax authorities

*Power of authorised person to require documents etc.*
459 Power of authorised person to require documents, information and explanations
460 Restrictions on disclosure of information obtained under compulsory powers
461 Permitted disclosure of information obtained under compulsory powers
462 Power to amend categories of permitted disclosure

**CHAPTER 12 SUPPLEMENTARY PROVISIONS**
*Liability for false or misleading statements in reports*
463 Liability for false or misleading statements in reports

*Accounting and reporting standards*
464 Accounting standards

*Companies qualifying as medium-sized*
465 Companies qualifying as medium-sized: general
466 Companies qualifying as medium-sized: parent companies
467 Companies excluded from being treated as medium-sized

*General power to make further provision about accounts and reports*
468 General power to make further provision about accounts and reports

*Other supplementary provisions*
469 Preparation and filing of accounts in euros
470 Power to apply provisions to banking partnerships
471 Meaning of 'annual accounts' and related expressions
472 Notes to the accounts
473 Parliamentary procedure for certain regulations under this Part
474 Minor definitions

**PART 16 AUDIT**

**CHAPTER 1 REQUIREMENT FOR AUDITED ACCOUNTS**
*Requirement for audited accounts*
475 Requirement for audited accounts
476 Right of members to require audit

*Exemption from audit: small companies*
477 Small companies: conditions for exemption from audit

478 Companies excluded from small companies exemption
479 Availability of small companies exemption in case of group company

*Exemption from audit: dormant companies*
480 Dormant companies: conditions for exemption from audit
481 Companies excluded from dormant companies exemption

*Companies subject to private sector audit*
482 Non-profit-making companies subject to public sector audit
483 Scottish public sector companies: audit by Auditor General for Scotland

*General power of amendment by regulations*
484 General power of amendment by regulations

**CHAPTER 2 APPOINTMENT OF AUDITORS**
*Private companies*
485 Appointment of auditors of private company: general
486 Appointment of auditors of private company: default power of Secretary of State
487 Term of office of auditors of private company
488 Prevention by members of deemed reappointment of auditor

*Public companies*
489 Appointment of auditors of public company: general
490 Appointment of auditors of public company: default power of Secretary of State
491 Term of office of auditors of public company

*General provisions*
492 Fixing of auditor's remuneration
493 Disclosure of terms of audit appointment
494 Disclosure of services provided by auditor or associates and related remuneration

**CHAPTER 3 FUNCTIONS OF AUDITOR**
*Auditor's report*
495 Auditor's report on company's annual accounts
496 Auditor's report on directors' report
497 Auditor's report on auditable part of directors' remuneration report

*Duties and rights of auditors*
498 Duties of auditor
499 Auditor's general right to information
500 Auditor's right to information from overseas subsidiaries
501 Auditor's rights to information: offences
502 Auditor's rights in relation to resolutions and meetings

*Signature of auditor's report*
503 Signature of auditor's report
504 Senior statutory auditor
505 Names to be stated in published copies of auditor's report
506 Circumstances in which names may be omitted

*Offences in connection with auditor's report*
507 Offences in connection with auditor's report
508 Guidance for regulatory and prosecuting authorities: England, Wales and Northern Ireland
509 Guidance for regulatory authorities: Scotland

**CHAPTER 4 REMOVAL, RESIGNATION, ETC. OF AUDITORS**
*Removal of auditor*
510 Resolution removing auditor from office
511 Special notice required for resolution removing auditor from office
512 Notice to registrar of resolution removing auditor from office
513 Rights of auditor who has been removed from office

*Failure to re-appoint auditor*
514 Failure to re-appoint auditor: special procedure required for written resolution

515 Failure to re-appoint auditor: special notice
required for resolution at general meeting

*Resignation of auditor*

516 Resignation of auditor
517 Notice to registrar of resignation of auditor
518 Rights of resigning auditor

*Statement by auditor on ceasing to hold office*

519 Statement by auditor to be deposited with company
520 Company's duties in relation to statement
521 Copy of statement to be sent to registrar
522 Duty of auditor to notify appropriate audit authority
523 Duty of company to notify appropriate audit
authority
524 Information to be given to accounting authorities
525 Meaning of 'appropriate audit authority' and
'major audit'

*Supplementary*

526 Effect of casual vacancies

**CHAPTER 5  QUOTED COMPANIES: RIGHT OF
MEMBERS TO RAISE AUDIT CONCERNS AT
ACCOUNTS MEETING**

527 Members' power to require website publication of
audit concerns
528 Requirements as to website availability
529 Website publication: company's supplementary
duties
530 Website publication: offences
531 Meaning of 'quoted company'

**CHAPTER 6  AUDITORS' LIABILITY**

*Voidness of provisions protecting
auditors from liability*

532 Voidness of provisions protecting auditors from
liability

*Indemnity for costs of defending proceedings*

533 Indemnity for costs of successfully defending
proceedings

*Liability limitation agreements*

534 Liability limitation agreements
535 Terms of liability limitation agreement
536 Authorisation of agreement by members of the
company
537 Effect of liability limitation agreement
538 Disclosure of agreement by company

**CHAPTER 7  SUPPLEMENTARY PROVISIONS**

539 Minor definitions

**PART 17  A COMPANY'S SHARE CAPITAL**

**CHAPTER 1  SHARES AND SHARE CAPITAL
OF A COMPANY**

*Shares*

540 Shares
541 Nature of shares
542 Nominal value of shares
543 Numbering of shares
544 Transferability of shares
545 Companies having a share capital
546 Issued and allotted share capital

*Share capital*

547 Called-up share capital
548 Equity share capital

**CHAPTER 2  ALLOTMENT OF SHARES:
GENERAL PROVISIONS**

*Power of directors to allot shares*

549 Exercise by directors of power to allot shares etc.
550 Power of directors to allot shares etc.: private
company with only one class of shares
551 Power of directors to allot shares etc.:
authorisation by company

*Prohibition of commissions, discounts
and allowances*

552 General prohibition of commissions, discounts
and allowances

553 Permitted commission

*Registration of allotment*

554 Registration of allotment

*Return of allotment*

555 Return of allotment by limited company
556 Return of allotment by unlimited company
allotting new class of shares
557 Offence of failure to make return

*Supplementary provisions*

558 When shares are allotted
559 Provisions about allotment not applicable to
shares taken on formation

**CHAPTER 3  ALLOTMENT OF EQUITY SECURITIES:
EXISTING SHAREHOLDERS' RIGHT OF
PRE-EMPTION**

*Introductory*

560 Meaning of 'equity securities' and related
expressions

*Existing shareholders' right of pre-emption*

561 Existing shareholders' right of pre-emption
562 Communication of pre-emption offers to
shareholders
563 Liability of company and officers in case of
contravention

*Exceptions to right of pre-emption*

564 Exception to pre-emption right: bonus shares
565 Exception to pre-emption right: issue for non-cash
consideration
566 Exception to pre-emption right: securities held
under employees' share scheme

*Exclusion of right of pre-emption*

567 Exclusion of requirements by private companies
568 Exclusion of pre-emption right: articles conferring
corresponding right

*Disapplication of pre-emption rights*

569 Disapplication of pre-emption rights: private
company with only one class of shares
570 Disapplication of pre-emption rights: directors
acting under general authorisation
571 Disapplication of pre-emption rights by special
resolution
572 Liability for false statement in directors' statement
573 Disapplication of pre-emption rights: sale of
treasury shares

*Supplementary*

574 References to holder of shares in relation to offer
575 Saving for other restrictions on offer or allotment
576 Saving for certain older pre-emption requirements
577 Provisions about pre-emption not applicable to
shares taken on formation

**CHAPTER 4  PUBLIC COMPANIES: ALLOTMENT
WHERE ISSUE NOT FULLY SUBSCRIBED**

578 Public companies: allotment where issue not fully
subscribed
579 Public companies: effect of irregular allotment
where issue not fully subscribed

**CHAPTER 5  PAYMENT FOR SHARES**

*General rules*

580 Shares not to be allotted at a discount
581 Provision for different amounts to be paid on shares
582 General rule as to means of payment
583 Meaning of payment in cash

*Additional rules for public companies*

584 Public companies: shares taken by subscribers of
memorandum
585 Public companies: must not accept undertaking to
do work or perform services
586 Public companies: shares must be at least one-
quarter paid up
587 Public companies: payment by long-term
undertaking

*Supplementary provisions*

588 Liability of subsequent holders of shares

589  Power of court to grant relief
590  Penalty for contravention of this Chapter
591  Enforceability of undertakings to do work etc.
592  The appropriate rate of interest

### CHAPTER 6  PUBLIC COMPANIES: INDEPENDENT VALUATION OF NON-CASH CONSIDERATION

*Non-cash consideration for shares*
593  Public company: valuation of non-cash consideration for shares
594  Exception to valuation requirement: arrangement with another company
595  Exception to valuation requirement: merger
596  Non-cash consideration for shares: requirements as to valuation and report
597  Copy of report to be delivered to registrar

*Transfer of non-cash asset in initial period*
598  Public company: agreement for transfer of non-cash asset in initial period
599  Agreement for transfer of non-cash asset: requirement of independent valuation
600  Agreement for transfer of non-cash asset: requirements as to valuation and report
601  Agreement for transfer of non-cash asset: requirement of approval by members
602  Copy of resolution to be delivered to registrar
603  Adaptation of provisions in relation to company re-registering as public
604  Agreement for transfer of non-cash asset: effect of contravention

*Supplementary provisions*
605  Liability of subsequent holders of shares
606  Power of court to grant relief
607  Penalty for contravention of this Chapter
608  Enforceability of undertakings to do work etc.
609  The appropriate rate of interest

### CHAPTER 7  SHARE PREMIUMS

*The share premium account*
610  Application of share premiums

*Relief from requirements as to share premiums*
611  Group reconstruction relief
612  Merger relief
613  Merger relief: meaning of 90% equity holding
614  Power to make further provision by regulations
615  Relief may be reflected in company's balance sheet

*Supplementary provisions*
616  Interpretation of this Chapter

### CHAPTER 8  ALTERATION OF SHARE CAPITAL

*How share capital may be altered*
617  Alteration of share capital of limited company

*Sub–division or consolidation of shares*
618  Sub-division or consolidation of shares
619  Notice to registrar of sub-division or consolidation

*Reconversion of stock into shares*
620  Reconversion of stock into shares
621  Notice to registrar of reconversion of stock into shares

*Redenomination of share capital*
622  Redenomination of share capital
623  Calculation of new nominal values
624  Effect of redenomination
625  Notice to registrar of redenomination
626  Reduction of capital in connection with redenomination
627  Notice to registrar of reduction of capital in connection with redenomination
628  Redenomination reserve

### CHAPTER 9  CLASSES OF SHARE AND CLASS RIGHTS

*Introductory*
629  Classes of shares

*Variation of class rights*
630  Variation of class rights: companies having a share capital
631  Variation of class rights: companies without a share capital
632  Variation of class rights: saving for court's powers under other provisions
633  Right to object to variation: companies having a share capital
634  Right to object to variation: companies without a share capital
635  Copy of court order to be forwarded to the registrar

*Matters to be notified to the registrar*
636  Notice of name or other designation of class of shares
637  Notice of particulars of variation of rights attached to shares
638  Notice of new class of members
639  Notice of name or other designation of class of members
640  Notice of particulars of variation of class rights

### CHAPTER 10  REDUCTION OF SHARE CAPITAL

*Introductory*
641  Circumstances in which a company may reduce its share capital

*Private companies: reduction of capital supported by solvency statement*
642  Reduction of capital supported by solvency statement
643  Solvency statement
644  Registration of resolution and supporting documents

*Reduction of capital confirmed by the court*
645  Application to court for order of confirmation
646  Creditors entitled to object to reduction
647  Offences in connection with list of creditors
648  Court order confirming reduction
649  Registration of order and statement of capital

*Public company reducing capital below authorised minimum*
650  Public company reducing capital below authorised minimum
651  Expedited procedure for re-registration as a private company

*Effect of reduction of capital*
652  Liability of members following reduction of capital
653  Liability to creditor in case of omission from list of creditors

### CHAPTER 11  MISCELLANEOUS AND SUPPLEMENTARY PROVISIONS

654  Treatment of reserve arising from reduction of capital
655  Shares no bar to damages against company
656  Public companies: duty of directors to call meeting on serious loss of capital
657  General power to make further provision by regulations

### PART 18  ACQUISITION BY LIMITED COMPANY OF ITS OWN SHARES

### CHAPTER 1  GENERAL PROVISIONS

*Introductory*
658  General rule against limited company acquiring its own shares
659  Exceptions to general rule

*Shares held by company's nominee*
660  Treatment of shares held by nominee
661  Liability of others where nominee fails to make payment in respect of shares

*Shares held by or for public company*
662  Duty to cancel shares in public company held by or for the company
663  Notice of cancellation of shares
664  Re-registration as private company in consequence of cancellation
665  Issue of certificate of incorporation on re-registration

666  Effect of failure to re-register
667  Offence in case of failure to cancel shares or re-register
668  Application of provisions to company re-registering as public company
669  Transfer to reserve on acquisition of shares by public company or nominee

*Charges of public company on own shares*

670  Public companies: general rule against lien or charge on own shares

*Supplementary provisions*

671  Interests to be disregarded in determining whether company has beneficial interest
672  Residual interest under pension scheme or employees' share scheme
673  Employer's charges and other rights of recovery
674  Rights as personal representative or trustee
675  Meaning of 'pension scheme'
676  Application of provisions to directors

**CHAPTER 2  FINANCIAL ASSISTANCE FOR PURCHASE OF OWN SHARES**

*Introductory*

677  Meaning of 'financial assistance'

*Circumstances in which financial assistance prohibited*

678  Assistance for acquisition of shares in public company
679  Assistance by public company for acquisition of shares in its private holding company
680  Prohibited financial assistance an offence

*Exceptions from prohibition*

681  Unconditional exceptions
682  Conditional exceptions

*Supplementary*

683  Definitions for this Chapter

**CHAPTER 3  REDEEMABLE SHARES**

684  Power of limited company to issue redeemable shares
685  Terms and manner of redemption
686  Payment for redeemable shares
687  Financing of redemption
688  Redeemed shares treated as cancelled
689  Notice to registrar of redemption

**CHAPTER 4  PURCHASE OF OWN SHARES**

*General provisions*

690  Power of limited company to purchase own shares
691  Payment for purchase of own shares
692  Financing of purchase of own shares

*Authority for purchase of own shares*

693  Authority for purchase of own shares

*Authority for off-market purchase*

694  Authority for off-market purchase
695  Resolution authorising off-market purchase: exercise of voting rights
696  Resolution authorising off-market purchase: disclosure of details of contract
697  Variation of contract for off-market purchase
698  Resolution authorising variation: exercise of voting rights
699  Resolution authorising variation: disclosure of details of variation
700  Release of company's rights under contract for off-market purchase

*Authority for market purchase*

701  Authority for market purchase

*Supplementary provisions*

702  Copy of contract or memorandum to be available for inspection
703  Enforcement of right to inspect copy or memorandum
704  No assignment of company's right to purchase own shares
705  Payments apart from purchase price to be made out of distributable profits

706  Treatment of shares purchased
707  Return to registrar of purchase of own shares
708  Notice to registrar of cancellation of shares

**CHAPTER 5  REDEMPTION OR PURCHASE BY PRIVATE COMPANY OUT OF CAPITAL**

*Introductory*

709  Power of private limited company to redeem or purchase own shares out of capital

*The permissible capital payment*

710  The permissible capital payment
711  Available profits
712  Determination of available profits

*Requirements for payment out of capital*

713  Requirements for payment out of capital
714  Directors' statement and auditor's report
715  Directors' statement: offence if no reasonable grounds for opinion
716  Payment to be approved by special resolution
717  Resolution authorising payment: exercise of voting rights
718  Resolution authorising payment: disclosure of directors' statement and auditor's report
719  Public notice of proposed payment
720  Directors' statement and auditor's report to be available for inspection

*Objection to payment by members or creditors*

721  Application to court to cancel resolution
722  Notice to registrar of court application or order

*Supplementary provisions*

723  When payment out of capital to be made

**CHAPTER 6  TREASURY SHARES**

724  Treasury shares
725  Treasury shares: maximum holdings
726  Treasury shares: exercise of rights
727  Treasury shares: disposal
728  Treasury shares: notice of disposal
729  Treasury shares: cancellation
730  Treasury shares: notice of cancellation
731  Treasury shares: treatment of proceeds of sale
732  Treasury shares: offences

**CHAPTER 7  SUPPLEMENTARY PROVISIONS**

733  The capital redemption reserve
734  Accounting consequences of payment out of capital
735  Effect of company's failure to redeem or purchase
736  Meaning of 'distributable profits'
737  General power to make further provision by regulations

**PART 19  DEBENTURES**

*General provisions*

738  Meaning of 'debenture'
739  Perpetual debentures
740  Enforcement of contract to subscribe for debentures
741  Registration of allotment of debentures
742  Debentures to bearer (Scotland)

*Register of debenture holders*

743  Register of debenture holders
744  Register of debenture holders: right to inspect and require copy
745  Register of debenture holders: response to request for inspection or copy
746  Register of debenture holders: refusal of inspection or default in providing copy
747  Register of debenture holders: offences in connection with request for or disclosure of information
748  Time limit for claims arising from entry in register

*Supplementary provisions*

749  Right of debenture holder to copy of deed
750  Liability of trustees of debentures
751  Liability of trustees of debentures: saving for certain older provisions
752  Power to re-issue redeemed debentures

753 Deposit of debentures to secure advances
754 Priorities where debentures secured by floating charge

## PART 20  PRIVATE AND PUBLIC COMPANIES

### CHAPTER 1  PROHIBITION OF PUBLIC OFFERS BY PRIVATE COMPANIES

755 Prohibition of public offers by private company
756 Meaning of 'offer to the public'
757 Enforcement of prohibition: order restraining proposed contravention
758 Enforcement of prohibition: orders available to the court after contravention
759 Enforcement of prohibition: remedial order
760 Validity of allotment etc. not affected

### CHAPTER 2  MINIMUM SHARE CAPITAL REQUIREMENT FOR PUBLIC COMPANIES

761 Public company: requirement as to minimum share capital
762 Procedure for obtaining certificate
763 The authorised minimum
764 Power to alter authorised minimum
765 Authorised minimum: application of initial requirement
766 Authorised minimum: application where shares denominated in different currencies etc.
767 Consequences of doing business etc. without a trading certificate

## PART 21  CERTIFICATION AND TRANSFER OF SECURITIES

### CHAPTER 1  CERTIFICATION AND TRANSFER OF SECURITIES: GENERAL

*Share certificates*
768 Share certificate to be evidence of title

*Issue of certificates etc on allotment*
769 Duty of company as to issue of certificates etc. on allotment

*Transfer of securities*
770 Registration of transfer
771 Procedure on transfer being lodged
772 Transfer of shares on application of transferor
773 Execution of share transfer by personal representative
774 Evidence of grant of probate etc.
775 Certification of instrument of transfer

*Issue of certificates etc. on transfer*
776 Duty of company as to issue of certificates etc. on transfer
777 Issue of certificates etc.: cases within the Stock Transfer Act 1982

*Issue of certificates etc. on allotment or transfer to financial institution*
778 Issue of certificates etc.: allotment or transfer to financial institution

*Share warrants*
779 Issue and effect of share warrant to bearer
780 Duty of company as to issue of certificates on surrender of share warrant
781 Offences in connection with share warrants (Scotland)

*Supplementary provisions*
782 Issue of certificates etc.: court order to make good default

### CHAPTER 2  EVIDENCING AND TRANSFER OF TITLE TO SECURITIES WITHOUT WRITTEN INSTRUMENT

*Introductory*
783 Scope of this Chapter
784 Power to make regulations

*Powers exercisable*
785 Provision enabling procedures for evidencing and transferring title

786 Provision enabling or requiring arrangements to be adopted
787 Provision enabling or requiring arrangements to be adopted: order-making powers

*Supplementary*
788 Provision that may be included in regulations
789 Duty to consult
790 Resolutions to be forwarded to registrar

## PART 22  INFORMATION ABOUT INTERESTS IN A COMPANY'S SHARES

*Introductory*
791 Companies to which this Part applies
792 Shares to which this Part applies

*Notice requiring information about interests in shares*
793 Notice by company requiring information about interests in its shares
794 Notice requiring information: order imposing restrictions on shares
795 Notice requiring information: offences
796 Notice requiring information: persons exempted from obligation to comply

*Orders imposing restrictions on shares*
797 Consequences of order imposing restrictions
798 Penalty for attempted evasion of restrictions
799 Relaxation of restrictions
800 Removal of restrictions
801 Order for sale of shares
802 Application of proceeds of sale under court order

*Power of members to require company to act*
803 Power of members to require company to act
804 Duty of company to comply with requirement
805 Report to members on outcome of investigation
806 Report to members: offences
807 Right to inspect and request copy of reports

*Register of interests disclosed*
808 Register of interests disclosed
809 Register to be kept available for inspection
810 Associated index
811 Rights to inspect and require copy of entries
812 Court supervision of purpose for which rights may be exercised
813 Register of interests disclosed: refusal of inspection or default in providing copy
814 Register of interests disclosed: offences in connection with request for or disclosure of information
815 Entries not to be removed from register
816 Removal of entries from register: old entries
817 Removal of entries from register: incorrect entry relating to third party
818 Adjustment of entry relating to share acquisition agreement
819 Duty of company ceasing to be public company

*Meaning of interest in shares*
820 Interest in shares: general
821 Interest in shares: right to subscribe for shares
822 Interest in shares: family interests
823 Interest in shares: corporate interests
824 Interest in shares: agreement to acquire interests in a particular company
825 Extent of obligation in case of share acquisition agreement

*Other supplementary provisions*
826 Information protected from wider disclosure
827 Reckoning of periods for fulfilling obligations
828 Power to make further provision by regulations

## PART 23  DISTRIBUTIONS

### CHAPTER 1  RESTRICTIONS ON WHEN DISTRIBUTIONS MAY BE MADE

*Introductory*
829 Meaning of 'distribution'

*General rules*

830 Distributions to be made only out of profits available for the purpose
831 Net asset restriction on distributions by public companies

*Distributions by investment companies*

832 Distributions by investment companies out of accumulated revenue profits
833 Meaning of 'investment company'
834 Investment company: condition as to holdings in other companies
835 Power to extend provisions relating to investment companies

**CHAPTER 2  JUSTIFICATION OF DISTRIBUTION BY REFERENCE TO ACCOUNTS**

*Justification of distribution by reference to accounts*

836 Justification of distribution by reference to relevant accounts

*Requirements applicable in relation to relevant accounts*

837 Requirements where last annual accounts used
838 Requirements where interim accounts used
839 Requirements where initial accounts used

*Application of provisions to successive distributions etc.*

840 Successive distributions etc. by reference to the same accounts

**CHAPTER 3  SUPPLEMENTARY PROVISIONS**

*Accounting matters*

841 Realised losses and profits and revaluation of fixed assets
842 Determination of profit or loss in respect of asset where records incomplete
843 Realised profits and losses of long term insurance business
844 Treatment of development costs

*Distributions in kind*

845 Distributions in kind: determination of amount
846 Distributions in kind: treatment of unrealised profits

*Consequences of unlawful distribution*

847 Consequences of unlawful distribution

*Other matters*

848 Saving for certain older provisions in articles
849 Restriction on application of unrealised profits
850 Treatment of certain older profits or losses
851 Application of rules of law restricting distributions
852 Saving for other restrictions on distributions
853 Minor definitions

**PART 24  A COMPANY'S ANNUAL RETURN**

854 Duty to deliver annual returns
855 Contents of annual return: general
855A Required particulars of directors and secretaries
856 Contents of annual return: information about share capital and shareholders
856A Contents of annual return: information about shareholders: non-traded companies
856B Contents of annual return: information about shareholders: traded companies
857 Contents of annual return: power to make further provision by regulations
858 Failure to deliver annual return

**PART 25  COMPANY CHARGES**

**CHAPTER 1  COMPANIES REGISTERED IN ENGLAND AND WALES OR IN NORTHERN IRELAND**

*Requirement to register company charges*

860 Charges created by a company
861 Charges which have to be registered: supplementary
862 Charges existing on property acquired

*Special rules about debentures*

863 Charge in series of debentures

864 Additional registration requirement for commission etc. in relation to debentures
865 Endorsement of certificate on debentures

*Charges in other jurisdictions*

866 Charges created in, or over property in, jurisdictions outside the United Kingdom
867 Charges created in, or over property in, another United Kingdom jurisdiction

*Orders charging land: Northern Ireland*

868 Northern Ireland: registration of certain charges etc. affecting land

*The register of charges*

869 Register of charges to be kept by registrar
870 The period allowed for registration
871 Registration of enforcement of security
872 Entries of satisfaction and release
873 Rectification of register of charges

*Avoidance of certain charges*

874 Consequence of failure to register charges created by a company

*Companies' records and registers*

875 Companies to keep copies of instruments creating charges
876 Company's register of charges
877 Instruments creating charges and register of charges to be available for inspection

**CHAPTER 2  COMPANIES REGISTERED IN SCOTLAND**

*Charges requiring registration*

878 Charges created by a company
879 Charges which have to be registered: supplementary
880 Duty to register charges existing on property acquired
881 Charge by way of *ex facie* absolute disposition, etc.

*Special rules about debentures*

882 Charge in series of debentures
883 Additional registration requirement for commission etc. in relation to debentures

*Charges on property outside the United Kingdom*

884 Charges on property outside the United Kingdom

*The register of charges*

885 Register of charges to be kept by registrar
886 The period allowed for registration
887 Entries of satisfaction and relief
888 Rectification of register of charges

*Avoidance of certain charges*

889 Charges void unless registered

*Companies' records and registers*

890 Copies of instruments creating charges to be kept by company
891 Company's register of charges
892 Instruments creating charges and register of charges to be available for inspection

**CHAPTER 3  POWERS OF THE SECRETARY OF STATE**

893 Power to make provision for effect of registration in special register
894 General power to make amendments to this Part

**PART 26  ARRANGEMENTS AND RECONSTRUCTIONS**

*Application of this Part*

895 Application of this Part

*Meeting of creditors or members*

896 Court order for holding of meeting
897 Statement to be circulated or made available
898 Duty of directors and trustees to provide information

*Court sanction for compromise or arrangement*

899 Court sanction for compromise or arrangement

*Reconstructions and amalgamations*

900 Powers of court to facilitate reconstruction or amalgamation

*Obligations of company with respect to articles etc*
901 Obligations of company with respect to articles etc

## PART 27

### CHAPTER 1 MERGERS AND DIVISIONS OF PUBLIC COMPANIES

*Introductory*
902 Application of this Part
903 Relationship of this Part to Part 26

### CHAPTER 2 MERGER

*Introductory*
904 Mergers and merging companies

*Requirements applicable to merger*
905 Draft terms of scheme (merger)
906 Publication of draft terms (merger)
907 Approval of members of merging companies
908 Directors' explanatory report (merger)
909 Expert's report (merger)
910 Supplementary accounting statement (merger)
911 Inspection of documents (merger)
912 Approval of articles of new transferee company (merger)
913 Protection of holders of securities to which special rights attached (merger)
914 No allotment of shares to transferor company or its nominee (merger)

*Exceptions where shares of transferor company held by transferee company*
915 Circumstances in which certain particulars and reports not required (merger)
916 Circumstances in which meeting of members of transferee company not required (merger)
917 Circumstances in which no meetings required (merger)

*Other exceptions*
918 Other circumstances in which meeting of members of transferee company not required (merger)
918A Agreement to dispense with expert's report (merger)

### CHAPTER 3 DIVISION

*Introductory*
919 Divisions and companies involved in a division

*Requirements to be complied with in case of division*
920 Draft terms of scheme (division)
921 Publication of draft terms (division)
922 Approval of members of companies involved in the division
923 Directors' explanatory report (division)
924 Expert's report (division)
925 Supplementary accounting statement (division)
926 Inspection of documents (division)
927 Report on material changes of assets of transferor company (division)
928 Approval of articles of new transferee company (division)
929 Protection of holders of securities to which special rights attached (division)
930 No allotment of shares to transferor company or its nominee (division)

*Exceptions where shares of transferor company held by transferee company*
931 Circumstances in which meeting of members of transferor company not required (division)

*Other exceptions*
932 Circumstances in which meeting of members of transferee company not required (division)
933 Agreement to dispense with reports etc (division)
934 Power of court to exclude certain requirements (division)

### CHAPTER 4 SUPPLEMENTARY PROVISIONS

*Expert's report and related matters*
935 Expert's report: valuation by another person
936 Experts and valuers: independence requirement

937 Experts and valuers: meaning of 'associate'

*Powers of the court*
938 Power of court to summon meeting of members or creditors of existing transferee company
939 Court to fix date for transfer of undertaking etc of transferor company

*Liability of transferee companies*
940 Liability of transferee companies for each other's defaults

*Interpretation*
941 Meaning of 'liabilities' and 'property'

## PART 28 TAKEOVERS ETC.

### CHAPTER 1 THE TAKEOVER PANEL

*The Panel and its rules*
942 The Panel
943 Rules
944 Further provisions about rules
945 Rulings
946 Directions

*Information*
947 Power to require documents and information
948 Restrictions on disclosure
949 Offence of disclosure in contravention of section 948

*Co-operation*
950 Panel's duty of co-operation

*Hearings and appeals*
951 Hearings and appeals

*Contravention of rules etc*
952 Sanctions
953 Failure to comply with rules about bid documentation
954 Compensation
955 Enforcement by the court
956 No action for breach of statutory duty etc

*Funding*
957 Fees and charges
958 Levy
959 Recovery of fees, charges or levy

*Miscellaneous and supplementary*
960 Panel as party to proceedings
961 Exemption from liability in damages
962 Privilege against self-incrimination
963 Annual reports
964 Amendments to the Financial Services and Markets Act 2000

### CHAPTER 2 IMPEDIMENTS TO TAKEOVERS

*Opting in and opting out*
966 Opting in and opting out
967 Further provision about opting-in and opting-out resolutions

*Consequences of opting in*
968 Effect on contractual restrictions
969 Power of offeror to require general meeting to be called

*Supplementary*
970 Communication of decisions
971 Interpretation of Chapter
972 Transitory provision
973 Power to extend to Isle of Man and Channel Islands

### CHAPTER 3 'SQUEEZE-OUT' AND 'SELL-OUT'

*Takeover offers*
974 Meaning of 'takeover offer'
975 Shares already held by the offeror etc.
976 Cases where offer treated as being on same terms
977 Shares to which an offer relates
978 Effect of impossibility etc. of communicating or accepting offer

*'Squeeze-out'*
979 Right of offeror to buy out minority shareholder

980  Further provision about notices given under
     section 979
981  Effect of notice under section 979
982  Further provision about consideration held on
     trust under section 981(9)

                    *'Sell-out'*

983  Right of minority shareholder to be bought out by
     offeror
984  Further provision about rights conferred by
     section 983
985  Effect of requirement under section 983

                  *Supplementary*

986  Applications to the court
987  Joint offers

                  *Interpretation*

988  Associates
989  Convertible securities
990  Debentures carrying voting rights
991  Interpretation

#### CHAPTER 4  AMENDMENTS TO PART 7 OF THE
#### COMPANIES ACT 1985

992  Matters to be dealt with in directors' report

### PART 29  FRAUDULENT TRADING

993  Offence of fraudulent trading

### PART 30  PROTECTION OF MEMBERS AGAINST
### UNFAIR PREJUDICE

                  *Main provisions*

994  Petition by company member
995  Petition by Secretary of State
996  Powers of the court under this Part

              *Supplementary provisions*

998  Copy of order affecting company's constitution to
     be delivered to registrar
997  Application of general rule making powers
999  Supplementary provisions where company's
     constitution altered

### PART 31  DISSOLUTION AND RESTORATION TO
### THE REGISTER

#### CHAPTER 1  STRIKING OFF

        *Registrar's power to strike off defunct company*

1000 Power to strike off company not carrying on
     business or in operation
1001 Duty to act in case of company being wound up
1002 Supplementary provisions as to service of letter
     or notice

                *Voluntary striking off*

1003 Striking off on application by company
1004 Circumstances in which application not to be
     made: activities of company
1005 Circumstances in which application not to be
     made: other proceedings not concluded
1006 Copy of application to be given to members,
     employees, etc.
1007 Copy of application to be given to new members,
     employees, etc.
1008 Copy of application: provisions as to service of
     documents
1009 Circumstances in which application to be
     withdrawn
1010 Withdrawal of application
1011 Meaning of 'creditor'

#### CHAPTER 2  PROPERTY OF DISSOLVED COMPANY

            *Property vesting as bona vacantia*

1012 Property of dissolved company to be bona vacantia
1013 Crown disclaimer of property vesting as bona
     vacantia
1014 Effect of Crown disclaimer

        *Effect of Crown disclaimer: England and Wales
                and Northern Ireland*

1015 General effect of disclaimer

1016 Disclaimer of leaseholds
1017 Power of court to make vesting order
1018 Protection of persons holding under a lease
1019 Land subject to rentcharge

            *Effect of Crown disclaimer: Scotland*

1020 General effect of disclaimer
1021 Power of court to make vesting order
1022 Protection of persons holding under a lease

                *Supplementary provisions*

1023 Liability for rentcharge on company's land after
     dissolution

#### CHAPTER 3  RESTORATION TO THE REGISTER

        *Administrative restoration to the register*

1024 Application for administrative restoration to the
     register
1025 Requirements for administrative restoration
1026 Application to be accompanied by statement of
     compliance
1027 Registrar's decision on application for
     administrative restoration
1028 Effect of administrative restoration

        *Restoration to the register by the court*

1029 Application to court for restoration to the register
1030 When application to the court may be made
1031 Decision on application for restoration by the court
1032 Effect of court order for restoration to the register

                *Supplementary provisions*

1033 Company's name on restoration
1034 Effect of restoration to the register where
     property has vested as bona vacantia

### PART 32  COMPANY INVESTIGATIONS:
### AMENDMENTS

1035 Powers of Secretary of State to give directions to
     inspectors
1036 Resignation, removal and replacement of
     inspectors
1037 Power to obtain information from former
     inspectors etc
1038 Power to require production of documents
1039 Disqualification orders: consequential amendments

### PART 33  UK COMPANIES NOT FORMED UNDER
### COMPANIES LEGISLATION

#### CHAPTER 1  COMPANIES NOT FORMED UNDER
#### COMPANIES LEGISLATION BUT AUTHORISED TO
#### REGISTER

1040 Companies authorised to register under this Act
1041 Definition of "joint stock company"
1042 Power to make provision by regulations

#### CHAPTER 2  UNREGISTERED COMPANIES

1043 Unregistered companies

### PART 34  OVERSEAS COMPANIES

                    *Introductory*

1044 Overseas companies
1045 Company contracts and execution of documents
     by companies

              *Registration of particulars*

1046 Duty to register particulars
1047 Registered name of overseas company
1048 Registration under alternative name

                *Other requirements*

1049 Accounts and reports: general
1050 Accounts and reports: credit or financial
     institutions
1051 Trading disclosures
1052 Company charges
1053 Other returns etc

                  *Supplementary*

1054 Offences
1055 Disclosure of individual's residential address:
     protection from disclosure

1056  Requirement to identify persons authorised to accept service of documents
1057  Registrar to whom returns, notices etc to be delivered
1058  Duty to give notice of ceasing to have registrable presence
1059  Application of provisions in case of relocation of branch

### PART 35  THE REGISTRAR OF COMPANIES
*The registrar*
1060  The registrar
1061  The registrar's functions
1062  The registrar's official seal
1063  Fees payable to registrar

*Certificates of incorporation*
1064  Public notice of issue of certificate of incorporation1065  Right to certificate of incorporation
1065  Right to certificate of incorporation

*Registered numbers*
1066  Company's registered numbers
1067  Registered numbers of branches of overseas company

*Delivery of documents to the registrar*
1068  Registrar's requirements as to form, authentication and manner of delivery
1069  Power to require delivery by electronic means
1070  Agreement for delivery by electronic means
1071  Document not delivered until received

*Requirements for proper delivery*
1072  Requirements for proper delivery
1073  Power to accept documents not meeting requirements for proper delivery
1074  Documents containing unnecessary material
1075  Informal correction of document
1076  Replacement of document not meeting requirements for proper delivery

*Public notice of receipt of certain documents*
1077  Public notice of receipt of certain documents
1078  Documents subject to Directive disclosure requirements
1079  Effect of failure to give public notice

*The register*
1080  The register
1081  Annotation of the register
1082  Allocation of unique identifiers
1083  Preservation of original documents
1084  Records relating to companies that have not been dissolved etc

*Inspection etc. of the register*
1085  Inspection of the register
1086  Right to copy of material on the register
1087  Material not available for public inspection
1088  Application to registrar to make addresses unavailable for public inspection
1089  Form of application for inspection on copy
1090  Form and manner in which copies to be provided
1091  Certification of copies as accurate
1092  Issue of process for production of records kept be registrar

*Correction or removal of material on the register*
1093  Registrar's notice to resolve inconsistency on the register
1094  Administrative removal of material from the register
1095  Rectification of register on application to registrar
1096  Rectification of the register under court order
1097  Powers of court on ordering removal of material from the register
1098  Public notice of removal of certain material from the register

*The registrar's index of company names*
1099  The registrar's index of company names
1100  Right to inspect index

1101  Power to amend enactments relating to bodies other than corporate bodies

*Language requirements: translation*
1102  Application of language requirements
1103  Documents to be drawn up and delivered in English
1104  Documents relating to Welsh companies
1105  Documents that may be drawn up and delivered in other languages
1106  Voluntary filing of translations
1107  Certified translations

*Supplementary provisions*
1108  Transliteration of names and addresses: permitted characters
1109  Transliteration of names and addresses: voluntary transliteration into Roman characters
1110  Transliteration of names and addresses: certification
1111  Registrar's requirement as to certification or verification
1112  General false statement offence
1113  Enforcement of company's filing obligations
1114  Application of provisions about documents and delivery
1115  Supplementary provisions relating to electronic documents
1116  Alterntaive to publication on the Gazette
1117  Registrar's rules
1118  Payments into the Consolidated Fund
1119  Contracting out of registrar's functions
1120  Application of this Part to overseas companies

### PART 36  OFFENCES UNDER THE COMPANIES ACTS
*Liability of officer in default*
1121  Liability of officer in default
1122  Liability of company as officer in default
1123  Application to bodies other than companies

*Offences under the Companies Act 1985*
1124  Amendments of the Companies Act 1985

*General provisions*
1125  Meaning of 'daily default fine'
1126  Consents required for certain prosecutions
1127  Summary proceedings: venue
1128  Summary proceedings: time limit for proceedings
1129  Legal professional privilege
1130  Proceedings against unincorporated bodies
1131  Imprisonment on summary conviction in England and Wales: transitory provision

*Production and inspection of documents*
1132  Production and inspection of documents where offence suspected

*Supplementary*
1133  Transitional provision

### PART 37  COMPANIES: SUPPLEMENTARY PROVISIONS
*Company records*
1134  Meaning of 'company records'
1135  Form of company records
1136  Regulations about where certain company records to be kept available for inspection
1137  Regulations about inspection of records and provision of copies
1138  Duty to take precautions against falsification

*Service addresses*
1139  Service of documents on company
1140  Service of documents on directors, secretaries and others
1141  Service addresses
1142  Requirement to give service address

*Sending or supplying documents or information*
1143  The company communications provisions
1144  Sending or supplying documents or information
1145  Right to hard copy version
1146  Requirement of authentication

1147 Deemed delivery of documents and information
1148 Interpretation of company communications provisions

*Requirements as to independent valuation*
1149 Application of valuation requirements
1150 Valuation by qualified independent person
1151 The independence requirement
1152 Meaning of 'associate'
1153 Valuer entitled to full disclosure

*Notice of appointment of certain officers*
1154 Duty to notify registrar of certain appointments etc
1155 Offence of failure to give notice

*Courts and legal proceedings*
1156 Meaning of 'the court'
1157 Power of court to grant relief in certain cases

**PART 38  COMPANIES: INTERPRETATION**

*Meaning of 'UK-registered company'*
1158 Meaning of 'UK-registered company'

*Meaning of 'subsidiary' and related expressions*
1159 Meaning of 'subsidiary' etc.
1160 Meaning of 'subsidiary' etc.: power to amend

*Meaning of 'undertaking' and related expressions*
1161 Meaning of 'undertaking' and related expressions
1162 Parent and subsidiary undertakings

*Other definitions*
1163 'Non-cash asset'
1164 Meaning of 'banking company' and 'banking group'
1165 Meaning of 'insurance company' and related expressions
1166 'Employees' share scheme'
1167 Meaning of 'prescribed'
1168 Hard copy and electronic form and related expressions
1169 Dormant companies
1170 Meaning of 'EEA State' and related expressions
1171 The former Companies Acts

*General*
1172 References to requirements of this Act
1173 Minor definitions: general
1174 Index of defined expressions

**PART 39  COMPANIES: MINOR AMENDMENTS**

1175 Removal of special provisions about accounts and audit of charitable companies
1176 Power of Secretary of State to bring civil proceedings on company's behalf
1177 Repeal of certain provisions about company directors
1178 Repeal of requirement that certain companies publish periodical statement
1179 Repeal of requirement that Secretary of State prepare annual report
1180 Repeal of certain provisions about company charges
1181 Access to constitutional documents of RTE and RTM companies

**PART 40  COMPANY DIRECTORS: FOREIGN DISQUALIFICATION ETC.**

*Introductory*
1182 Persons subject to foreign restrictions
1183 Meaning of 'the court' and 'UK company'

*Power to disqualify*
1184 Disqualification of persons subject to foreign restrictions
1185 Disqualification regulations: supplementary
1186 Offence of breach of disqualification

*Power to make persons liable for company's debts*
1187 Personal liability for debts of company

*Power to require statements to be sent to the registrar of companies*
1188 Statements from persons subject to foreign restrictions

1189 Statements from persons disqualified
1190 Statements: whether to be made public
1191 Offences

**PART 41  BUSINESS NAMES**

**CHAPTER 1  RESTRICTED OR PROHIBITED NAMES**

*Introductory*
1192 Application of this Chapter

*Sensitive words or expressions*
1193 Name suggesting connection with government or public authority
1194 Other sensitive words or expressions
1195 Requirement to seek comments of government department or other relevant body
1196 Withdrawal of Secretary of State's approval

*Misleading names*
1197 Name containing inappropriate indication of company type or legal form
1198 Name giving misleading indication of activities

*Supplementary*
1199 Savings for existing lawful business names

**CHAPTER 2  DISCLOSURE REQUIRED IN CASE OF INDIVIDUAL OR PARTNERSHIP**

*Introductory*
1200 Application of this Chapter
1201 Information required to be disclosed

*Disclosure requirements*
1202 Disclosure required: business documents etc
1203 Exemption for large partnerships if certain conditions met
1204 Disclosure required: business premises

*Consequences of failure to make required disclosure*
1205 Criminal consequences of failure to make required disclosure
1206 Civil consequences of failure to make required disclosure

**CHAPTER 3  SUPPLEMENTARY**

1207 Application of general provisions about offences
1208 Interpretation

**PART 42  STATUTORY AUDITORS**

**CHAPTER 1  INTRODUCTORY**

1209 Main purposes of Part
1210 Meaning of 'statutory auditor' etc
1211 Eligibility for appointment as a statutory auditor: overview

**CHAPTER 2  INDIVIDUALS AND FIRMS**

*Eligibility for appointment*
1212 Individuals and firms: eligibility for appointment as a statutory auditor
1213 Effect of ineligibility

*Independence requirement*
1214 Independence requirement
1215 Effect of lack of independence

*Effect of appointment of a partnership*
1216 Effect of appointment of a partnership

*Supervisory bodies*
1217 Supervisory bodies
1218 Exemption from liability for damages

*Professional qualifications*
1219 Appropriate qualifications
1220 Qualifying bodies and recognised professional qualifications
1221 Approval of overseas qualifications
1222 Eligibility of individuals retaining only 1967 Act authorisation

*Information*
1223 Matters to be notified to the Secretary of State
1223A Notification of matters relevant to other EEA States
1224 The Secretary of State's power to call for information

1224A  Restrictions on disclosure
1224B  Offence of disclosure in contravention of
section 1224A
*Enforcement*
1225  Compliance orders

### CHAPTER 3 AUDITORS GENERAL

*Eligibility for appointment*
1226  Auditors General: eligibility for appointment
as a statutory auditor

*Conduct of audits*
1227  Individuals responsible for audit work on behalf
of Auditors General

*The Independent Supervisor*
1228  Appointment of the Independent Supervisor

*Supervision of Auditors General*
1229  Supervision of Auditors General by the
Independent Supervisor
1230  Duties of Auditors General in relation to
supervision arrangements

*Reporting requirement*
1231  Reports by the Independent Supervisor

*Information*
1232  Matters to be notified to the Independent
Supervisor
1233  The Independent Supervisor's power to call for
information

*Enforcement*
1234  Suspension notices
1235  Effect of suspension notices
1236  Compliance orders

*Proceedings*
1237  Proceedings involving the Independent
Supervisor

*Grants*
1238  Grants to the Independent Supervisor

### CHAPTER 4 THE REGISTER OF AUDITORS ETC

1239  The register of auditors
1240  Information to be made available to public

### CHAPTER 5 REGISTERED THIRD COUNTRY AUDITORS

*Introductory*
1241  Meaning of 'third country auditor', 'registered
third country auditor' etc

*Duties*
1242  Duties of registered third country auditors

*Information*
1243  Matters to be notified to the Secretary of State
1244  The Secretary of State's power to call for
information

*Enforcement*
1245  Compliance orders
1246  Removal of third country auditors from the
register of auditors
1247  Grants to bodies concerned with arrangements
under Schedule 12

### CHAPTER 6 SUPPLEMENTARY AND GENERAL

*Power to require second company audit*
1248  Secretary of State's power to require second audit
of a company
1249  Supplementary provision about second audits

*False and misleading statements*
1250  Misleading, false and deceptive statements

*Fees*
1251  Fees

*Duty of Secretary of State to report on inspections*
1251A  Duty of the Secretary of State to report on
inspections

*Delegation of Secretary of State's functions*
1252  Delegation of the Secretary of State's functions
1253  Delegation of functions to an existing body

*Cooperation with foreign competent authorities*
1253A  Requests to foreign competent authorities
1253B  Requests from EEA competent authorities
1253C  Notification to competent authorities of other
EEA States

*Transfer of papers to third countries*
1253D  Restriction on transfer of audit working papers
to third countries
1253E  Working arrangements for transfer of papers
1253F  Publication of working arrangements

*International obligations*
1254  Directions to comply with international
obligations

*General provision relating to offences*
1255  Offences by bodies corporate, partnerships and
unincorporated associations
1256  Time limits for prosecution of offences
1257  Jurisdiction and procedure in respect of offences

*Notices etc*
1258  Service of notices
1259  Documents in electronic form

*Interpretation*
1260  Meaning of 'associate'
1261  Minor definitions
1262  Index of defined expressions

*Miscellaneous and general*
1263  Power to make provision in consequence of
changes affecting accountancy bodies
1264  Consequential amendments

### PART 43 TRANSPARENCY OBLIGATIONS AND RELATED MATTERS

*Introductory*
1265  The transparency obligations directive

*Transparency obligations*
1266  Transparency rules
1267  Competent authority's power to call for
information
1268  Powers exercisable in case of infringement of
transparency obligation

*Other matters*
1269  Corporate governance rules
1270  Liability for false or misleading statements in
certain publications
1271  Exercise of powers where UK is host member
State
1272  Transparency obligations and related matters:
minor and consequential amendments
1273  Corporate governance regulations

### PART 44 MISCELLANEOUS PROVISIONS

*Regulation of actuaries etc*
1274  Grants to bodies concerned with actuarial
standards etc
1275  Levy to pay expenses of bodies concerned with
actuarial standards etc
1276  Application of provisions to Scotland and
Northern Ireland

*Information as to exercise of voting rights by institutional
investors*
1277  Power to require information about exercise of
voting rights
1278  Institutions to which information provisions apply
1279  Shares to which information provisions apply
1280  Obligations with respect to provision of
information

*Disclosure of information under the Enterprise Act 2002*
1281  Disclosure of information under the Enterprise
Act 2002

*Expenses of winding up*
1282  Payment of expenses of winding up

*Commonhold Associations*
1283  Amendment of memorandum or articles of
commonhold associations

### PART 45  NORTHERN IRELAND
1284  Extension of Companies Acts to Northern Ireland
1285  Extension of GB enactments relating to SEs
1286  Extension of GB enactments relating to certain other forms of business organisation
1287  Extension of enactments relating to business names

### PART 46  GENERAL SUPPLEMENTARY PROVISIONS
*Regulations and orders*
1288  Regulations and orders: statutory instrument
1289  Regulations and orders: negative resolution procedure
1290  Regulations and orders: affirmative resolution procedure
1291  Regulations and orders: approval after being made
1292  Regulations and orders: supplementary
*Meaning of 'enactment'*
1293  Meaning of 'enactment'
*Consequential and transitional provisions*
1294  Power to make consequential amendments etc
1295  Repeals
1296  Power to make transitional provisions and savings
1297  Continuity of the law

### PART 47  FINAL PROVISIONS
1298  Short title
1299  Extent
1300  Commencement

### SCHEDULE 1 — CONNECTED PERSONS: REFERENCES TO AN INTEREST IN SHARES OR DEBENTURES

### SCHEDULE 2 — SPECIFIED PERSONS, DESCRIPTIONS OF DISCLOSURES ETC FOR THE PURPOSES OF SECTION 948
Part 1 — Specified persons
Part 2 — Specified descriptions of disclosures
Part 3 — Overseas regulatory bodies

### SCHEDULE 3 — AMENDMENTS OF REMAINING PROVISIONS OF THE COMPANIES ACT 1985 RELATING TO OFFENCES

### SCHEDULE 4 — DOCUMENTS AND INFORMATION SENT OR SUPPLIED TO A COMPANY
Part 1 — Introduction
Part 2 — Communications in hard copy form
Part 3 — Communications in electronic form
Part 4 — Other agreed forms of communication

### SCHEDULE 5 — COMMUNICATIONS BY A COMPANY
Part 1 — Introduction
Part 2 — Communications in hard copy form
Part 3 — Communications in electronic form
Part 4 — Communications by means of a website
Part 5 — Other agreed forms of communication
Part 6 — Supplementary provisions

### SCHEDULE 6 — MEANING OF 'SUBSIDIARY' ETC.: SUPPLEMENTARY PROVISIONS

### SCHEDULE 7 — PARENT AND SUBSIDIARY UNDERTAKINGS: SUPPLEMENTARY PROVISIONS

### SCHEDULE 8 — INDEX OF DEFINED EXPRESSIONS

### SCHEDULE 9 — REMOVAL OF SPECIAL PROVISIONS ABOUT ACCOUNTS AND AUDIT OF CHARITABLE COMPANIES
Part 1 — The Companies Act 1985 (c. 6)
Part 2 — The Companies (Northern Ireland) Order 1986 (S.I. 1986/1032 (N.I. 6)

### SCHEDULE 10 — RECOGNISED SUPERVISORY BODIES
Part 1 — Grant and revocation of recognition of a supervisory body
Part 2 — Requirements for recognition of a supervisory body
Part 3 — Arrangements in which recognised supervisory bodies are required to participate

### SCHEDULE 11 — RECOGNISED PROFESSIONAL QUALIFICATIONS
Part 1 — Grant and revocation of recognition of a professional qualification
Part 2 — Requirements for recognition of a professional qualification

### SCHEDULE 11A — SPECIFIED PERSONS, DESCRIPTIONS, DISCLOSURES ETC FOR THE PURPOSES OF SECTION 1224A

### SCHEDULE 12 — ARRANGEMENTS IN WHICH REGISTERED THIRD COUNTRY AUDITORS ARE REQUIRED TO PARTICIPATE

### SCHEDULE 13 — SUPPLEMENTARY PROVISIONS WITH RESPECT TO DELEGATION ORDER

### SCHEDULE 14 — STATUTORY AUDITORS: CONSEQUENTIAL AMENDMENTS

### SCHEDULE 15 — TRANSPARENCY OBLIGATIONS AND RELATED MATTERS: MINOR AND CONSEQUENTIAL AMENDMENTS
Part 1 — Amendments of the Financial Services and Markets Act 2000
Part 2 — Amendments of the Companies (Audit, Investigations and Community Enterprise) Act 2004

### SCHEDULE 16 — REPEALS

*An Act to reform company law and restate the greater part of the enactments relating to companies; to make other provision relating to companies and other forms of business organisation; to make provision about directors' disqualification, business names, auditors and actuaries; to amend Part 9 of the Enterprise Act 2002; and for connected purposes.* [8th November 2006]

# PART 1 GENERAL INTRODUCTORY PROVISIONS

*Companies and Companies Acts*

**1 Companies**

(1) In the Companies Acts, unless the context otherwise requires—

'company' means a company formed and registered under this Act, that is—

(a) a company so formed and registered after the commencement of this Part, or

(b) a company that immediately before the commencement of this Part—

(i) was formed and registered under the Companies Act 1985 (c. 6) or the Companies (Northern Ireland) Order 1986 (S.I. 1986/1032 (N.I. 6)), or

(ii) was an existing company for the purposes of that Act or that Order,

(which is to be treated on commencement as if formed and registered under this Act).

(2) Certain provisions of the Companies Acts apply to—

(a) companies registered, but not formed, under this Act (see Chapter 1 of Part 33), and

(b) bodies incorporated in the United Kingdom but not registered under this Act (see Chapter 2 of that Part).

(3) For provisions applying to companies incorporated outside the United Kingdom, see Part 34 (overseas companies).

**2 The Companies Acts**

(1) In this Act 'the Companies Acts' means—

(a) the company law provisions of this Act,

(b) Part 2 of the Companies (Audit, Investigations and Community Enterprise) Act 2004 (c. 27) (community interest companies), and

(c) the provisions of the Companies Act 1985 (c. 6) and the Companies Consolidation (Consequential Provisions) Act 1985 (c. 9) that remain in force.

(2) The company law provisions of this Act are—

(a) the provisions of Parts 1 to 39 of this Act, and

(b) the provisions of Parts 45 to 47 of this Act so far as they apply for the purposes of those Parts.

*Types of company*

**3 Limited and unlimited companies**

(1) A company is a 'limited company' if the liability of its members is limited by its constitution. It may be limited by shares or limited by guarantee.

(2) If their liability is limited to the amount, if any, unpaid on the shares held by them, the company is 'limited by shares'.

(3) If their liability is limited to such amount as the members undertake to contribute to the assets of the company in the event of its being wound up, the company is 'limited by guarantee'.

(4) If there is no limit on the liability of its members, the company is an 'unlimited company'.

**4 Private and public companies**

(1) A 'private company' is any company that is not a public company.

(2) A 'public company' is a company limited by shares or limited by guarantee and having a share capital—

(a) whose certificate of incorporation states that it is a public company, and

(b) in relation to which the requirements of this Act, or the former Companies Acts, as to registration or re-registration as a public company have been complied with on or after the relevant date.

(3) For the purposes of subsection (2)(b) the relevant date is—

(a) in relation to registration or re-registration in Great Britain, 22nd December 1980;

(b) in relation to registration or re-registration in Northern Ireland, 1st July 1983.

(4) For the two major differences between private and public companies, see Part 20.

**5 Companies limited by guarantee and having share capital**

(1) A company cannot be formed as, or become, a company limited by guarantee with a share capital.

(2) Provision to this effect has been in force—

(a) in Great Britain since 22nd December 1980, and

(b) in Northern Ireland since 1st July 1983.

(3) Any provision in the constitution of a company limited by guarantee that purports to divide the company's undertaking into shares or interests is a provision for a share capital.

This applies whether or not the nominal value or number of the shares or interests is specified by the provision.

**6    Community interest companies**

(1) In accordance with Part 2 of the Companies (Audit, Investigations and Community Enterprise) Act 2004 (c. 27)—

    (a) a company limited by shares or a company limited by guarantee and not having a share capital may be formed as or become a community interest company, and

    (b) a company limited by guarantee and having a share capital may become a community interest company.

(2) The other provisions of the Companies Acts have effect subject to that Part.

# PART 2   COMPANY FORMATION

## *General*

**7    Method of forming company**

(1) A company is formed under this Act by one or more persons—

    (a) subscribing their names to a memorandum of association (see section 8), and

    (b) complying with the requirements of this Act as to registration (see sections 9 to 13).

(2) A company may not be so formed for an unlawful purpose.

**8    Memorandum of association**

(1) A memorandum of association is a memorandum stating that the subscribers—

    (a) wish to form a company under this Act, and

    (b) agree to become members of the company and, in the case of a company that is to have a share capital, to take at least one share each.

(2) The memorandum must be in the prescribed form and must be authenticated by each subscriber.

## *Requirements for registration*

**9    Registration documents**

(1) The memorandum of association must be delivered to the registrar together with an application for registration of the company, the documents required by this section and a statement of compliance.

(2) The application for registration must state—

    (a) the company's proposed name,

    (b) whether the company's registered office is to be situated in England and Wales (or in Wales), in Scotland or in Northern Ireland,

    (c) whether the liability of the members of the company is to be limited, and if so whether it is to be limited by shares or by guarantee, and

    (d) whether the company is to be a private or a public company.

(3) If the application is delivered by a person as agent for the subscribers to the memorandum of association, it must state his name and address.

(4) The application must contain—

    (a) in the case of a company that is to have a share capital, a statement of capital and initial shareholdings (see section 10);

    (b) in the case of a company that is to be limited by guarantee, a statement of guarantee (see section 11);

    (c) a statement of the company's proposed officers (see section 12).

(5) The application must also contain—

    (a) a statement of the intended address of the company's registered office; and

    (b) a copy of any proposed articles of association (to the extent that these are not supplied by the default application of model articles: see section 20).

(6) The application must be delivered—

    (a) to the registrar of companies for England and Wales, if the registered office of the company is to be situated in England and Wales (or in Wales);

    (b) to the registrar of companies for Scotland, if the registered office of the company is to be situated in Scotland;

    (c) to the registrar of companies for Northern Ireland, if the registered office of the company is to be situated in Northern Ireland.

**10    Statement of capital and initial shareholdings**

(1) The statement of capital and initial shareholdings required to be delivered in the case of a company that is to have a share capital must comply with this section.

(2) It must state—

    (a) the total number of shares of the company to be taken on formation by the subscribers to the memorandum of association,

    (b) the aggregate nominal value of those shares,

    (c) for each class of shares—
        (i)   prescribed particulars of the rights attached to the shares,
        (ii)  the total number of shares of that class, and
        (iii) the aggregate nominal value of shares of that class, and
    (d) the amount to be paid up and the amount (if any) to be unpaid on each share (whether on account of the nominal value of the share or by way of premium).

(3) It must contain such information as may be prescribed for the purpose of identifying the subscribers to the memorandum of association.

(4) It must state, with respect to each subscriber to the memorandum—
    (a) the number, nominal value (of each share) and class of shares to be taken by him on formation, and
    (b) the amount to be paid up and the amount (if any) to be unpaid on each share (whether on account of the nominal value of the share or by way of premium).

(5) Where a subscriber to the memorandum is to take shares of more than one class, the information required under subsection (4)(a) is required for each class.

## 11  Statement of guarantee

(1) The statement of guarantee required to be delivered in the case of a company that is to be limited by guarantee must comply with this section.

(2) It must contain such information as may be prescribed for the purpose of identifying the subscribers to the memorandum of association.

(3) It must state that each member undertakes that, if the company is wound up while he is a member, or within one year after he ceases to be a member, he will contribute to the assets of the company such amount as may be required for—
    (a) payment of the debts and liabilities of the company contracted before he ceases to be a member,
    (b) payment of the costs, charges and expenses of winding up, and
    (c) adjustment of the rights of the contributories among themselves,
not exceeding a specified amount.

## 12  Statement of proposed officers

(1) The statement of the company's proposed officers required to be delivered to the registrar must contain the required particulars of—
    (a) the person who is, or persons who are, to be the first director or directors of the company;
    (b) in the case of a company that is to be a private company, any person who is (or any persons who are) to be the first secretary (or joint secretaries) of the company;
    (c) in the case of a company that is to be a public company, the person who is (or the persons who are) to be the first secretary (or joint secretaries) of the company.

(2) The required particulars are the particulars that will be required to be stated—
    (a) in the case of a director, in the company's register of directors and register of directors' residential addresses (see sections 162 to 166);
    (b) in the case of a secretary, in the company's register of secretaries (see sections 277 to 279).

(3) The statement must also contain a consent by each of the persons named as a director, as secretary or as one of joint secretaries, to act in the relevant capacity.

If all the partners in a firm are to be joint secretaries, consent may be given by one partner on behalf of all of them.

## 13  Statement of compliance

(1) The statement of compliance required to be delivered to the registrar is a statement that the requirements of this Act as to registration have been complied with.

(2) The registrar may accept the statement of compliance as sufficient evidence of compliance.

*Registration and its effect*

## 14  Registration

If the registrar is satisfied that the requirements of this Act as to registration are complied with, he shall register the documents delivered to him.

## 15  Issue of certificate of incorporation

(1) On the registration of a company, the registrar of companies shall give a certificate that the company is incorporated.

(2) The certificate must state—
    (a) the name and registered number of the company,
    (b) the date of its incorporation,
    (c) whether it is a limited or unlimited company, and if it is limited whether it is limited by shares or limited by guarantee,
    (d) whether it is a private or a public company, and
    (e) whether the company's registered office is situated in England and Wales (or in Wales), in Scotland or in Northern Ireland.

(3) The certificate must be signed by the registrar or authenticated by the registrar's official seal.

(4) The certificate is conclusive evidence that the requirements of this Act as to registration have been complied with and that the company is duly registered under this Act.

### 16  Effect of registration

(1) The registration of a company has the following effects as from the date of incorporation.

(2) The subscribers to the memorandum, together with such other persons as may from time to time become members of the company, are a body corporate by the name stated in the certificate of incorporation.

(3) That body corporate is capable of exercising all the functions of an incorporated company.

(4) The status and registered office of the company are as stated in, or in connection with, the application for registration.

(5) In the case of a company having a share capital, the subscribers to the memorandum become holders of the shares specified in the statement of capital and initial shareholdings.

(6) The persons named in the statement of proposed officers—

(a) as director, or

(b) as secretary or joint secretary of the company,

are deemed to have been appointed to that office.

# PART 3  A COMPANY'S CONSTITUTION

## Chapter 1  Introductory

### 17  A company's constitution

Unless the context otherwise requires, references in the Companies Acts to a company's constitution include—

(a) the company's articles, and

(b) any resolutions and agreements to which Chapter 3 applies (see section 29).

## Chapter 2  Articles of association

### *General*

### 18  Articles of association

(1) A company must have articles of association prescribing regulations for the company.

(2) Unless it is a company to which model articles apply by virtue of section 20 (default application of model articles in case of limited company), it must register articles of association.

(3) Articles of association registered by a company must—

(a) be contained in a single document, and

(b) be divided into paragraphs numbered consecutively.

(4) References in the Companies Acts to a company's 'articles' are to its articles of association.

### 19  Power of Secretary of State to prescribe model articles

(1) The Secretary of State may by regulations prescribe model articles of association for companies.

(2) Different model articles may be prescribed for different descriptions of company.

(3) A company may adopt all or any of the provisions of model articles.

(4) Any amendment of model articles by regulations under this section does not affect a company registered before the amendment takes effect.

'Amendment' here includes addition, alteration or repeal.

(5) Regulations under this section are subject to negative resolution procedure.

### 20  Default application of model articles

(1) On the formation of a limited company—

(a) if articles are not registered, or

(b) if articles are registered, in so far as they do not exclude or modify the relevant model articles,

the relevant model articles (so far as applicable) form part of the company's articles in the same manner and to the same extent as if articles in the form of those articles had been duly registered.

(2) The 'relevant model articles' means the model articles prescribed for a company of that description as in force at the date on which the company is registered.

### *Alteration of articles*

### 21  Amendment of articles

(1) A company may amend its articles by special resolution.

(2) In the case of a company that is a charity, this is subject to—

(a) in England and Wales, section 64 of the Charities Act 1993 (c. 10);

(b) in Northern Ireland, section 96 of the Charities Act (Northern Ireland) 2008.

(3) In the case of a company that is registered in the Scottish Charity Register, this is subject to—

    (a) section 112 of the Companies Act 1989 (c. 40), and

    (b) section 16 of the Charities and Trustee Investment (Scotland) Act 2005 (asp 10).

## 22   Entrenched provisions of the articles

(1) A company's articles may contain provision ('provision for entrenchment') to the effect that specified provisions of the articles may be amended or repealed only if conditions are met, or procedures are complied with, that are more restrictive than those applicable in the case of a special resolution.

(2) Provision for entrenchment may only be made—

    (a) in the company's articles on formation, or

    (b) by an amendment of the company's articles agreed to by all the members of the company.

(3) Provision for entrenchment does not prevent amendment of the company's articles—

    (a) by agreement of all the members of the company,

    (b) by order of a court or other authority having power to alter the company's articles.

(4) Nothing in this section affects any power of a court or other authority to alter a company's articles.

## 23   Notice to registrar of existence of restriction on amendment of articles

(1) Where a company's articles—

    (a) on formation contain provision for entrenchment,

    (b) are amended so as to include such provision, or

    (c) are altered by order of a court or other authority so as to restrict or exclude the power of the company to amend its articles,

the company must give notice of that fact to the registrar.

(2) Where a company's articles—

    (a) are amended so as to remove provision for entrenchment, or

    (b) are altered by order of a court or other authority—

        (i) so as to remove such provision, or

        (ii) so as to remove any other restriction on, or any exclusion of, the power of the company to amend its articles,

the company must give notice of that fact to the registrar.

## 24   Statement of compliance where amendment of articles restricted

(1) This section applies where a company's articles are subject—

    (a) to provision for entrenchment, or

    (b) to an order of a court or other authority restricting or excluding the company's power to amend the articles.

(2) If the company—

    (a) amends its articles, and

    (b) is required to send to the registrar a document making or evidencing the amendment,

the company must deliver with that document a statement of compliance.

(3) The statement of compliance required is a statement certifying that the amendment has been made in accordance with the company's articles and, where relevant, any applicable order of a court or other authority.

(4) The registrar may rely on the statement of compliance as sufficient evidence of the matters stated in it.

## 25   Effect of alteration of articles on company's members

(1) A member of a company is not bound by an alteration to its articles after the date on which he became a member, if and so far as the alteration—

    (a) requires him to take or subscribe for more shares than the number held by him at the date on which the alteration is made, or

    (b) in any way increases his liability as at that date to contribute to the company's share capital or otherwise to pay money to the company.

(2) Subsection (1) does not apply in a case where the member agrees in writing, either before or after the alteration is made, to be bound by the alteration.

## 26   Registrar to be sent copy of amended articles

(1) Where a company amends its articles it must send to the registrar a copy of the articles as amended not later than 15 days after the amendment takes effect.

(2) This section does not require a company to set out in its articles any provisions of model articles that—

    (a) are applied by the articles, or

    (b) apply by virtue of section 20 (default application of model articles).

(3) If a company fails to comply with this section an offence is committed by—

    (a) the company, and

    (b) every officer of the company who is in default.

(4) A person guilty of an offence under this section is liable on summary conviction to a fine not exceeding level 3 on the standard scale and, for continued contravention, a daily default fine not exceeding one-tenth of level 3 on the standard scale.

### 27    Registrar's notice to comply in case of failure with respect to amended articles

(1) If it appears to the registrar that a company has failed to comply with any enactment requiring it—

    (a) to send to the registrar a document making or evidencing an alteration in the company's articles, or

    (b) to send to the registrar a copy of the company's articles as amended,

the registrar may give notice to the company requiring it to comply.

(2) The notice must—

    (a) state the date on which it is issued, and

    (b) require the company to comply within 28 days from that date.

(3) If the company complies with the notice within the specified time, no criminal proceedings may be brought in respect of the failure to comply with the enactment mentioned in subsection (1).

(4) If the company does not comply with the notice within the specified time, it is liable to a civil penalty of £200.

This is in addition to any liability to criminal proceedings in respect of the failure mentioned in subsection (1).

(5) The penalty may be recovered by the registrar and is to be paid into the Consolidated Fund.

*Supplementary*

### 28    Existing companies: provisions of memorandum treated as provisions of articles

(1) Provisions that immediately before the commencement of this Part were contained in a company's memorandum but are not provisions of the kind mentioned in section 8 (provisions of new-style memorandum) are to be treated after the commencement of this Part as provisions of the company's articles.

(2) This applies not only to substantive provisions but also to provision for entrenchment (as defined in section 22).

(3) The provisions of this Part about provision for entrenchment apply to such provision as they apply to provision made on the company's formation, except that the duty under section 23(1)(a) to give notice to the registrar does not apply.

## Chapter 3  Resolutions and agreements affecting a company's constitution

### 29    Resolutions and agreements affecting a company's constitution

(1) This Chapter applies to—

    (a) any special resolution;

    (b) any resolution or agreement agreed to by all the members of a company that, if not so agreed to, would not have been effective for its purpose unless passed as a special resolution;

    (c) any resolution or agreement agreed to by all the members of a class of shareholders that, if not so agreed to, would not have been effective for its purpose unless passed by some particular majority or otherwise in some particular manner;

    (d) any resolution or agreement that effectively binds all members of a class of shareholders though not agreed to by all those members;

    (e) any other resolution or agreement to which this Chapter applies by virtue of any enactment.

(2) References in subsection (1) to a member of a company, or of a class of members of a company, do not include the company itself where it is such a member by virtue only of its holding shares as treasury shares.

### 30    Copies of resolutions or agreements to be forwarded to registrar

(1) A copy of every resolution or agreement to which this Chapter applies, or (in the case of a resolution or agreement that is not in writing) a written memorandum setting out its terms, must be forwarded to the registrar within 15 days after it is passed or made.

(2) If a company fails to comply with this section, an offence is committed by—

    (a) the company, and

    (b) every officer of it who is in default.

(3) A person guilty of an offence under this section is liable on summary conviction to a fine not exceeding level 3 on the standard scale and, for continued contravention, a daily default fine not exceeding one-tenth of level 3 on the standard scale.

(4) For the purposes of this section, a liquidator of the company is treated as an officer of it.

## Chapter 4  Miscellaneous and supplementary provisions

*Statement of company's objects*

### 31  Statement of company's objects

(1) Unless a company's articles specifically restrict the objects of the company, its objects are unrestricted.

(2) Where a company amends its articles so as to add, remove or alter a statement of the company's objects—

    (a) it must give notice to the registrar,

    (b) on receipt of the notice, the registrar shall register it, and

    (c) the amendment is not effective until entry of that notice on the register.

(3) Any such amendment does not affect any rights or obligations of the company or render defective any legal proceedings by or against it.

(4) In the case of a company that is a charity, the provisions of this section have effect subject to—

    (a) in England and Wales, section 64 of the Charities Act 1993 (c. 10);

    (b) in Northern Ireland, section 96 of the Charities Act (Northern Ireland) 2008.

(5) In the case of a company that is entered in the Scottish Charity Register, the provisions of this section have effect subject to the provisions of the Charities and Trustee Investment (Scotland) Act 2005 (asp 10).

*Other provisions with respect to a company's constitution*

### 32  Constitutional documents to be provided to members

(1) A company must, on request by any member, send to him the following documents—

    (a) an up-to-date copy of the company's articles;

    (b) a copy of any resolution or agreement relating to the company to which Chapter 3 applies (resolutions and agreements affecting a company's constitution) and that is for the time being in force;

    (c) a copy of any document required to be sent to the registrar under—

        (i) section 34(2) (notice where company's constitution altered by enactment), or

        (ii) section 35(2)(a) (notice where order of court or other authority alters company's constitution);

    (d) a copy of any court order under section 899 (order sanctioning compromise or arrangement) or section 900 (order facilitating reconstruction or amalgamation);

    (e) a copy of any court order under section 996 (protection of members against unfair prejudice: powers of the court) that alters the company's constitution;

    (f) a copy of the company's current certificate of incorporation, and of any past certificates of incorporation;

    (g) in the case of a company with a share capital, a current statement of capital;

    (h) in the case of a company limited by guarantee, a copy of the statement of guarantee.

(2) The statement of capital required by subsection (1)(g) is a statement of—

    (a) the total number of shares of the company,

    (b) the aggregate nominal value of those shares,

    (c) for each class of shares—

        (i) prescribed particulars of the rights attached to the shares,

        (ii) the total number of shares of that class, and

        (iii) the aggregate nominal value of shares of that class, and

    (d) the amount paid up and the amount (if any) unpaid on each share (whether on account of the nominal value of the share or by way of premium).

(3) If a company makes default in complying with this section, an offence is committed by every officer of the company who is in default.

(4) A person guilty of an offence under this section is liable on summary conviction to a fine not exceeding level 3 on the standard scale.

### 33  Effect of company's constitution

(1) The provisions of a company's constitution bind the company and its members to the same extent as if there were covenants on the part of the company and of each member to observe those provisions.

(2) Money payable by a member to the company under its constitution is a debt due from him to the company.

In England and Wales and Northern Ireland it is of the nature of an ordinary contract debt.

### 34  Notice to registrar where company's constitution altered by enactment

(1) This section applies where a company's constitution is altered by an enactment, other than an enactment amending the general law.

(2) The company must give notice of the alteration to the registrar, specifying the enactment, not later than 15 days after the enactment comes into force.

In the case of a special enactment the notice must be accompanied by a copy of the enactment.

(3) If the enactment amends—

(a) the company's articles, or

(b) a resolution or agreement to which Chapter 3 applies (resolutions and agreements affecting a company's constitution),

the notice must be accompanied by a copy of the company's articles, or the resolution or agreement in question, as amended.

(4) A 'special enactment' means an enactment that is not a public general enactment, and includes—

(a) an Act for confirming a provisional order,

(b) any provision of a public general Act in relation to the passing of which any of the standing orders of the House of Lords or the House of Commons relating to Private Business applied, or

(c) any enactment to the extent that it is incorporated in or applied for the purposes of a special enactment.

(5) If a company fails to comply with this section an offence is committed by—

(a) the company, and

(b) every officer of the company who is in default.

(6) A person guilty of an offence under this section is liable on summary conviction to a fine not exceeding level 3 on the standard scale and, for continued contravention, a daily default fine not exceeding one-tenth of level 3 on the standard scale.

### 35   Notice to registrar where company's constitution altered by order

(1) Where a company's constitution is altered by an order of a court or other authority, the company must give notice to the registrar of the alteration not later than 15 days after the alteration takes effect.

(2) The notice must be accompanied by—

(a) a copy of the order, and

(b) if the order amends—

(i)   the company's articles, or

(ii)  a resolution or agreement to which Chapter 3 applies (resolutions and agreements affecting the company's constitution),

a copy of the company's articles, or the resolution or agreement in question, as amended.

(3) If a company fails to comply with this section an offence is committed by—

(a) the company, and

(b) every officer of the company who is in default.

(4) A person guilty of an offence under this section is liable on summary conviction to a fine not exceeding level 3 on the standard scale and, for continued contravention, a daily default fine not exceeding one-tenth of level 3 on the standard scale.

(5) This section does not apply where provision is made by another enactment for the delivery to the registrar of a copy of the order in question.

### 36   Documents to be incorporated in or accompany copies of articles issued by company

(1) Every copy of a company's articles issued by the company must be accompanied by—

(a) a copy of any resolution or agreement relating to the company to which Chapter 3 applies (resolutions and agreements affecting a company's constitution),

(b) where the company has been required to give notice to the registrar under section 34(2) (notice where company's constitution altered by enactment), a statement that the enactment in question alters the effect of the company's constitution,

(c) where the company's constitution is altered by a special enactment (see section 34(4)), a copy of the enactment, and

(d) a copy of any order required to be sent to the registrar under section 35(2)(a) (order of court or other authority altering company's constitution).

(2) This does not require the articles to be accompanied by a copy of a document or by a statement if—

(a) the effect of the resolution, agreement, enactment or order (as the case may be) on the company's constitution has been incorporated into the articles by amendment, or

(b) the resolution, agreement, enactment or order (as the case may be) is not for the time being in force.

(3) If the company fails to comply with this section, an offence is committed by every officer of the company who is in default.

(4) A person guilty of an offence under this section is liable on summary conviction to a fine not exceeding level 3 on the standard scale for each occasion on which copies are issued, or, as the case may be, requested.

(5) For the purposes of this section, a liquidator of the company is treated as an officer of it.

### 37  Right to participate in profits otherwise than as member void

In the case of a company limited by guarantee and not having a share capital any provision in the company's articles, or in any resolution of the company, purporting to give a person a right to participate in the divisible profits of the company otherwise than as a member is void.

### 38  Application to single member companies of enactments and rules of law

Any enactment or rule of law applicable to companies formed by two or more persons or having two or more members applies with any necessary modification in relation to a company formed by one person or having only one person as a member.

## PART 4  A COMPANY'S CAPACITY AND RELATED MATTERS

*Capacity of company and power of directors to bind it*

### 39  A company's capacity

(1)  The validity of an act done by a company shall not be called into question on the ground of lack of capacity by reason of anything in the company's constitution.

(2)  This section has effect subject to section 42 (companies that are charities).

### 40  Power of directors to bind the company

(1)  In favour of a person dealing with a company in good faith, the power of the directors to bind the company, or authorise others to do so, is deemed to be free of any limitation under the company's constitution.

(2)  For this purpose—

(a)  a person 'deals with' a company if he is a party to any transaction or other act to which the company is a party,

(b)  a person dealing with a company—

(i)   is not bound to enquire as to any limitation on the powers of the directors to bind the company or authorise others to do so,

(ii)  is presumed to have acted in good faith unless the contrary is proved, and

(iii) is not to be regarded as acting in bad faith by reason only of his knowing that an act is beyond the powers of the directors under the company's constitution.

(3)  The references above to limitations on the directors' powers under the company's constitution include limitations deriving—

(a)  from a resolution of the company or of any class of shareholders, or

(b)  from any agreement between the members of the company or of any class of shareholders.

(4)  This section does not affect any right of a member of the company to bring proceedings to restrain the doing of an action that is beyond the powers of the directors.

But no such proceedings lie in respect of an act to be done in fulfilment of a legal obligation arising from a previous act of the company.

(5)  This section does not affect any liability incurred by the directors, or any other person, by reason of the directors' exceeding their powers.

(6)  This section has effect subject to—

section 41 (transactions with directors or their associates), and

section 42 (companies that are charities).

### 41  Constitutional limitations: transactions involving directors or their associates

(1)  This section applies to a transaction if or to the extent that its validity depends on section 40 (power of directors deemed to be free of limitations under company's constitution in favour of person dealing with company in good faith).

Nothing in this section shall be read as excluding the operation of any other enactment or rule of law by virtue of which the transaction may be called in question or any liability to the company may arise.

(2)  Where—

(a)  a company enters into such a transaction, and

(b)  the parties to the transaction include—

(i)   a director of the company or of its holding company, or

(ii)  a person connected with any such director,

the transaction is voidable at the instance of the company.

(3)  Whether or not it is avoided, any such party to the transaction as is mentioned in subsection (2)(b)(i) or (ii), and any director of the company who authorised the transaction, is liable—

(a)  to account to the company for any gain he has made directly or indirectly by the transaction, and

(b)  to indemnify the company for any loss or damage resulting from the transaction.

(4)  The transaction ceases to be voidable if—

(a)  restitution of any money or other asset which was the subject matter of the transaction is no longer possible, or

(b) the company is indemnified for any loss or damage resulting from the transaction, or

(c) rights acquired bona fide for value and without actual notice of the directors' exceeding their powers by a person who is not party to the transaction would be affected by the avoidance, or

(d) the transaction is affirmed by the company.

(5) A person other than a director of the company is not liable under subsection (3) if he shows that at the time the transaction was entered into he did not know that the directors were exceeding their powers.

(6) Nothing in the preceding provisions of this section affects the rights of any party to the transaction not within subsection (2)(b)(i) or (ii).

But the court may, on the application of the company or any such party, make an order affirming, severing or setting aside the transaction on such terms as appear to the court to be just.

(7) In this section—

(a) 'transaction' includes any act; and

(b) the reference to a person connected with a director has the same meaning as in Part 10 (company directors).

## 42  Constitutional limitations: companies that are charities

(1) Sections 39 and 40 (company's capacity and power of directors to bind company) do not apply to the acts of a company that is a charity except in favour of a person who—

(a) does not know at the time the act is done that the company is a charity, or

(b) gives full consideration in money or money's worth in relation to the act in question and does not know (as the case may be)—

(i)   that the act is not permitted by the company's constitution, or

(ii)  that the act is beyond the powers of the directors.

(2) Where a company that is a charity purports to transfer or grant an interest in property, the fact that (as the case may be)—

(a) the act was not permitted by the company's constitution, or

(b) the directors in connection with the act exceeded any limitation on their powers under the company's constitution,

does not affect the title of a person who subsequently acquires the property or any interest in it for full consideration without actual notice of any such circumstances affecting the validity of the company's act.

(3) In any proceedings arising out of subsection (1) or (2) the burden of proving—

(a) that a person knew that the company was a charity, or

(b) that a person knew that an act was not permitted by the company's constitution or was beyond the powers of the directors,

lies on the person asserting that fact.

(4) In the case of a company that is a charity the affirmation of a transaction to which section 41 applies (transactions with directors or their associates) is ineffective without the prior written consent of—

(a) in England and Wales, the Charity Commission;

(b) in Northern Ireland, the Department for Social Development.

(5) This section does not extend to Scotland (but see section 112 of the Companies Act 1989(c. 40)).

### *Formalities of doing business under the law of England and Wales or Northern Ireland*

## 43  Company contracts

(1) Under the law of England and Wales or Northern Ireland a contract may be made—

(a) by a company, by writing under its common seal, or

(b) on behalf of a company, by a person acting under its authority, express or implied.

(2) Any formalities required by law in the case of a contract made by an individual also apply, unless a contrary intention appears, to a contract made by or on behalf of a company.

## 44  Execution of documents

(1) Under the law of England and Wales or Northern Ireland a document is executed by a company—

(a) by the affixing of its common seal, or

(b) by signature in accordance with the following provisions.

(2) A document is validly executed by a company if it is signed on behalf of the company—

(a) by two authorised signatories, or

(b) by a director of the company in the presence of a witness who attests the signature.

(3) The following are 'authorised signatories' for the purposes of subsection (2)—

(a) every director of the company, and

(b) in the case of a private company with a secretary or a public company, the secretary (or any joint secretary) of the company.

(4) A document signed in accordance with subsection (2) and expressed, in whatever words, to be executed by the company has the same effect as if executed under the common seal of the company.

(5) In favour of a purchaser a document is deemed to have been duly executed by a company if it purports to be signed in accordance with subsection (2).

A 'purchaser' means a purchaser in good faith for valuable consideration and includes a lessee, mortgagee or other person who for valuable consideration acquires an interest in property.

(6) Where a document is to be signed by a person on behalf of more than one company, it is not duly signed by that person for the purposes of this section unless he signs it separately in each capacity.

(7) References in this section to a document being (or purporting to be) signed by a director or secretary are to be read, in a case where that office is held by a firm, as references to its being (or purporting to be) signed by an individual authorised by the firm to sign on its behalf.

(8) This section applies to a document that is (or purports to be) executed by a company in the name of or on behalf of another person whether or not that person is also a company.

### 45  Common seal

(1) A company may have a common seal, but need not have one.

(2) A company which has a common seal shall have its name engraved in legible characters on the seal.

(3) If a company fails to comply with subsection (2) an offence is committed by—

(a) the company, and

(b) every officer of the company who is in default.

(4) An officer of a company, or a person acting on behalf of a company, commits an offence if he uses, or authorises the use of, a seal purporting to be a seal of the company on which its name is not engraved as required by subsection (2).

(5) A person guilty of an offence under this section is liable on summary conviction to a fine not exceeding level 3 on the standard scale.

(6) This section does not form part of the law of Scotland.

### 46  Execution of deeds

(1) A document is validly executed by a company as a deed for the purposes of section 1(2)(b) of the Law of Property (Miscellaneous Provisions) Act 1989 (c. 34) and for the purposes of the law of Northern Ireland if, and only if—

(a) it is duly executed by the company, and

(b) it is delivered as a deed.

(2) For the purposes of subsection (1)(b) a document is presumed to be delivered upon its being executed, unless a contrary intention is proved.

### 47  Execution of deeds or other documents by attorney

(1) Under the law of England and Wales or Northern Ireland a company may, by instrument executed as a deed, empower a person, either generally or in respect of specified matters, as its attorney to execute deeds or other documents on its behalf.

(2) A deed or other document so executed, whether in the United Kingdom or elsewhere, has effect as if executed by the company.

*Formalities of doing business under the law of Scotland*

### 48  Execution of documents by companies

(1) The following provisions form part of the law of Scotland only.

(2) Notwithstanding the provisions of any enactment, a company need not have a company seal.

(3) For the purposes of any enactment—

(a) providing for a document to be executed by a company by affixing its common seal, or

(b) referring (in whatever terms) to a document so executed,

a document signed or subscribed by or on behalf of the company in accordance with the provisions of the Requirements of Writing (Scotland) Act 1995 (c. 7) has effect as if so executed.

*Other matters*

### 49  Official seal for use abroad

(1) A company that has a common seal may have an official seal for use outside the United Kingdom.

(2) The official seal must be a facsimile of the company's common seal, with the addition on its face of the place or places where it is to be used.

(3) The official seal when duly affixed to a document has the same effect as the company's common seal.

This subsection does not extend to Scotland.

(4) A company having an official seal for use outside the United Kingdom may—

(a) by writing under its common seal, or

(b) as respects Scotland, by writing subscribed in accordance with the Requirements of Writing (Scotland) Act 1995,

authorise any person appointed for the purpose to affix the official seal to any deed or other document to which the company is party.

(5) As between the company and a person dealing with such an agent, the agent's authority continues—

    (a) during the period mentioned in the instrument conferring the authority, or

    (b) if no period is mentioned, until notice of the revocation or termination of the agent's authority has been given to the person dealing with him.

(6) The person affixing the official seal must certify in writing on the deed or other document to which the seal is affixed the date on which, and place at which, it is affixed.

### 50 Official seal for share certificates etc.

(1) A company that has a common seal may have an official seal for use—

    (a) for sealing securities issued by the company, or

    (b) for sealing documents creating or evidencing securities so issued.

(2) The official seal—

    (a) must be a facsimile of the company's common seal, with the addition on its face of the word 'Securities', and

    (b) when duly affixed to the document has the same effect as the company's common seal.

### 51 Pre-incorporation contracts, deeds and obligations

(1) A contract that purports to be made by or on behalf of a company at a time when the company has not been formed has effect, subject to any agreement to the contrary, as one made with the person purporting to act for the company or as agent for it, and he is personally liable on the contract accordingly.

(2) Subsection (1) applies—

    (a) to the making of a deed under the law of England and Wales or Northern Ireland, and

    (b) to the undertaking of an obligation under the law of Scotland,

as it applies to the making of a contract.

### 52 Bills of exchange and promissory notes

A bill of exchange or promissory note is deemed to have been made, accepted or endorsed on behalf of a company if made, accepted or endorsed in the name of, or by or on behalf or on account of, the company by a person acting under its authority.

# PART 5  A COMPANY'S NAME

## Chapter 1  General requirements

### *Prohibited names*

### 53 Prohibited names

A company must not be registered under this Act by a name if, in the opinion of the Secretary of State—

    (a) its use by the company would constitute an offence, or

    (b) it is offensive.

### *Sensitive words and expressions*

### 54 Names suggesting connection with government or public authority

(1) The approval of the Secretary of State is required for a company to be registered under this Act by a name that would be likely to give the impression that the company is connected with—

    (a) Her Majesty's Government, any part of the Scottish administration or Her Majesty's Government in Northern Ireland,

    (b) a local authority, or

    (c) any public authority specified for the purposes of this section by regulations made by the Secretary of State.

(2) For the purposes of this section—

'local authority' means—

    (a) a local authority within the meaning of the Local Government Act 1972 (c. 70), the Common Council of the City of London or the Council of the Isles of Scilly,

    (b) a council constituted under section 2 of the Local Government etc. (Scotland) Act 1994 (c. 39), or

    (c) a district council in Northern Ireland;

'public authority' includes any person or body having functions of a public nature.

(3) Regulations under this section are subject to affirmative resolution procedure.

### 55 Other sensitive words or expressions

(1) The approval of the Secretary of State is required for a company to be registered under this Act by a name that includes a word or expression for the time being specified in regulations made by the Secretary of State under this section.

(2) Regulations under this section are subject to approval after being made.

**56  Duty to seek comments of government department or other specified body**

(1) The Secretary of State may by regulations under—

    (a) section 54 (name suggesting connection with government or public authority), or

    (b) section 55 (other sensitive words or expressions),

require that, in connection with an application for the approval of the Secretary of State under that section, the applicant must seek the view of a specified Government department or other body.

(2) Where such a requirement applies, the applicant must request the specified department or other body (in writing) to indicate whether (and if so why) it has any objections to the proposed name.

(3) Where a request under this section is made in connection with an application for the registration of a company under this Act, the application must—

    (a) include a statement that a request under this section has been made, and

    (b) be accompanied by a copy of any response received.

(4) Where a request under this section is made in connection with a change in a company's name, the notice of the change sent to the registrar must be accompanied by—

    (a) a statement by a director or secretary of the company that a request under this section has been made, and

    (b) a copy of any response received.

(5) In this section 'specified' means specified in the regulations.

*Permitted characters etc.*

**57  Permitted characters etc.**

(1) The Secretary of State may make provision by regulations—

    (a) as to the letters or other characters, signs or symbols (including accents and other diacritical marks) and punctuation that may be used in the name of a company registered under this Act; and

    (b) specifying a standard style or format for the name of a company for the purposes of registration.

(2) The regulations may prohibit the use of specified characters, signs or symbols when appearing in a specified position (in particular, at the beginning of a name).

(3) A company may not be registered under this Act by a name that consists of or includes anything that is not permitted in accordance with regulations under this section.

(4) Regulations under this section are subject to negative resolution procedure.

(5) In this section 'specified' means specified in the regulations.

## Chapter 2  Indications of company type or legal form

*Required indications for limited companies*

**58  Public limited companies**

(1) The name of a limited company that is a public company must end with 'public limited company' or 'p.l.c.'.

(2) In the case of a Welsh company, its name may instead end with 'cwmni cyfyngedig cyhoeddus' or 'c.c.c.'.

(3) This section does not apply to community interest companies (but see section 33(3) and (4) of the Companies (Audit, Investigations and Community Enterprise) Act 2004 (c. 27)).

**59  Private limited companies**

(1) The name of a limited company that is a private company must end with 'limited' or 'ltd.'.

(2) In the case of a Welsh company, its name may instead end with 'cyfyngedig' or 'cyf.'.

(3) Certain companies are exempt from this requirement (see section 60).

(4) This section does not apply to community interest companies (but see section 33(1) and (2) of the Companies (Audit, Investigations and Community Enterprise) Act 2004).

**60  Exemption from requirement as to use of 'limited'**

(1) A private company is exempt from section 59 (requirement to have name ending with 'limited' or permitted alternative) if—

    (a) it is a charity,

    (b) it is exempted from the requirement of that section by regulations made by the Secretary of State, or

    (c) it meets the conditions specified in—

        section 61 (continuation of existing exemption: companies limited by shares), or

        section 62 (continuation of existing exemption: companies limited by guarantee).

(2) The registrar may refuse to register a private limited company by a name that does not include the word 'limited' (or a permitted alternative) unless a statement has been delivered to him that the company meets the conditions for exemption.

(3) The registrar may accept the statement as sufficient evidence of the matters stated in it.

(4) Regulations under this section are subject to negative resolution procedure.

### 61 Continuation of existing exemption: companies limited by shares

(1) This section applies to a private company limited by shares—

    (a) that on 25th February 1982—

        (i) was registered in Great Britain, and

        (ii) had a name that, by virtue of a licence under section 19 of the Companies Act 1948 (c. 38) (or corresponding earlier legislation), did not include the word 'limited' or any of the permitted alternatives, or

    (b) that on 30th June 1983—

        (i) was registered in Northern Ireland, and

        (ii) had a name that, by virtue of a licence under section 19 of the Companies Act (Northern Ireland) 1960 (c. 22 (N.I.)) (or corresponding earlier legislation), did not include the word 'limited' or any of the permitted alternatives.

(2) A company to which this section applies is exempt from section 59 (requirement to have name ending with 'limited' or permitted alternative) so long as—

    (a) it continues to meet the following two conditions, and

    (b) it does not change its name.

(3) The first condition is that the objects of the company are the promotion of commerce, art, science, education, religion, charity or any profession, and anything incidental or conducive to any of those objects.

(4) The second condition is that the company's articles—

    (a) require its income to be applied in promoting its objects,

    (b) prohibit the payment of dividends, or any return of capital, to its members, and

    (c) require all the assets that would otherwise be available to its members generally to be transferred on its winding up either—

        (i) to another body with objects similar to its own, or

        (ii) to another body the objects of which are the promotion of charity and anything incidental or conducive thereto,

    (whether or not the body is a member of the company).

### 62 Continuation of existing exemption: companies limited by guarantee

(1) A private company limited by guarantee that immediately before the commencement of this Part—

    (a) was exempt by virtue of section 30 of the Companies Act 1985 (c. 6) or Article 40 of the Companies (Northern Ireland) Order 1986 (S.I. 1986/1032 (N.I. 6)) from the requirement to have a name including the word 'limited' or a permitted alternative, and

    (b) had a name that did not include the word 'limited' or any of the permitted alternatives,

is exempt from section 59 (requirement to have name ending with 'limited' or permitted alternative) so long as it continues to meet the following two conditions and does not change its name.

(2) The first condition is that the objects of the company are the promotion of commerce, art, science, education, religion, charity or any profession, and anything incidental or conducive to any of those objects.

(3) The second condition is that the company's articles—

    (a) require its income to be applied in promoting its objects,

    (b) prohibit the payment of dividends to its members, and

    (c) require all the assets that would otherwise be available to its members generally to be transferred on its winding up either—

        (i) to another body with objects similar to its own, or

        (ii) to another body the objects of which are the promotion of charity and anything incidental or conducive thereto,

    (whether or not the body is a member of the company).

### 63 Exempt company: restriction on amendment of articles

(1) A private company—

    (a) that is exempt under section 61 or 62 from the requirement to use 'limited' (or a permitted alternative) as part of its name, and

    (b) whose name does not include 'limited' or any of the permitted alternatives,

must not amend its articles so that it ceases to comply with the conditions for exemption under that section.

(2) If subsection (1) above is contravened an offence is committed by—

    (a) the company, and

    (b) every officer of the company who is in default.

For this purpose a shadow director is treated as an officer of the company.

(3) A person guilty of an offence under this section is liable on summary conviction to a fine not exceeding level 5 on the standard scale and, for continued contravention, a daily default fine not exceeding one-tenth of level 5 on the standard scale.

(4) Where immediately before the commencement of this section—

(a) a company was exempt by virtue of section 30 of the Companies Act 1985 (c. 6) or Article 40 of the Companies (Northern Ireland) Order 1986 (S.I. 1986/1032 (N.I. 6)) from the requirement to have a name including the word 'limited' (or a permitted alternative), and

(b) the company's memorandum or articles contained provision preventing an alteration of them without the approval of—

    (i)   the Board of Trade or a Northern Ireland department (or any other department or Minister), or

    (ii)  the Charity Commission,

that provision, and any condition of any such licence as is mentioned in section 61(1)(a)(ii) or (b)(ii) requiring such provision, shall cease to have effect. This does not apply if, or to the extent that, the provision is required by or under any other enactment.

(5) It is hereby declared that any such provision as is mentioned in subsection (4)(b) formerly contained in a company's memorandum was at all material times capable, with the appropriate approval, of being altered or removed under section 17 of the Companies Act 1985 or Article 28 of the Companies (Northern Ireland) Order 1986 (S.I. 1986/1032 (N.I. 6)) (or corresponding earlier enactments).

## 64 Power to direct change of name in case of company ceasing to be entitled to exemption

(1) If it appears to the Secretary of State that a company whose name does not include 'limited' or any of the permitted alternatives—

(a) has ceased to be entitled to exemption under section 60(1)(a) or (b), or

(b) in the case of a company within section 61 or 62 (which impose conditions as to the objects and articles of the company)—

    (i)   has carried on any business other than the promotion of any of the objects mentioned in subsection (3) of section 61 or, as the case may be, subsection (2) of section 62, or

    (ii)  has acted inconsistently with the provision required by subsection (4)(a) or (b) of section 61 or, as the case may be, subsection (3)(a) or (b) of section 62,

the Secretary of State may direct the company to change its name so that it ends with 'limited' or one of the permitted alternatives.

(2) The direction must be in writing and must specify the period within which the company is to change its name.

(3) A change of name in order to comply with a direction under this section may be made by resolution of the directors.

This is without prejudice to any other method of changing the company's name.

(4) Where a resolution of the directors is passed in accordance with subsection (3), the company must give notice to the registrar of the change.

Sections 80 and 81 apply as regards the registration and effect of the change.

(5) If the company fails to comply with a direction under this section an offence is committed by—

(a) the company, and

(b) every officer of the company who is in default.

(6) A person guilty of an offence under this section is liable on summary conviction to a fine not exceeding level 5 on the standard scale and, for continued contravention, a daily default fine not exceeding one-tenth of level 5 on the standard scale.

(7) A company that has been directed to change its name under this section may not, without the approval of the Secretary of State, subsequently change its name so that it does not include 'limited' or one of the permitted alternatives.

This does not apply to a change of name on re-registration or on conversion to a community interest company.

*Inappropriate use of indications of company type or legal form*

## 65 Inappropriate use of indications of company type or legal form

(1) The Secretary of State may make provision by regulations prohibiting the use in a company name of specified words, expressions or other indications—

(a) that are associated with a particular type of company or form of organisation, or

(b) that are similar to words, expressions or other indications associated with a particular type of company or form of organisation.

(2) The regulations may prohibit the use of words, expressions or other indications—

(a) in a specified part, or otherwise than in a specified part, of a company's name;

(b) in conjunction with, or otherwise than in conjunction with, such other words, expressions or indications as may be specified.

(3) A company must not be registered under this Act by a name that consists of or includes anything prohibited by regulations under this section.

(4) In this section 'specified' means specified in the regulations.

(5) Regulations under this section are subject to negative resolution procedure.

## Chapter 3  Similarity to other names

*Similarity to other name on registrar's index*

### 66   Name not to be the same as another in the index

(1)  A company must not be registered under this Act by a name that is the same as another name appearing in the registrar's index of company names.

(2)  The Secretary of State may make provision by regulations supplementing this section.

(3)  The regulations may make provision—

  (a)  as to matters that are to be disregarded, and

  (b)  as to words, expressions, signs or symbols that are, or are not, to be regarded as the same,

for the purposes of this section.

(4)  The regulations may provide—

  (a)  that registration by a name that would otherwise be prohibited under this section is permitted—

    (i)   in specified circumstances, or

    (ii)  with specified consent, and

  (b)  that if those circumstances obtain or that consent is given at the time a company is registered by a name, a subsequent change of circumstances or withdrawal of consent does not affect the registration.

(5)  Regulations under this section are subject to negative resolution procedure.

(6)  In this section 'specified' means specified in the regulations.

### 67   Power to direct change of name in case of similarity to existing name

(1)  The Secretary of State may direct a company to change its name if it has been registered in a name that is the same as or, in the opinion of the Secretary of State, too like—

  (a)  a name appearing at the time of the registration in the registrar's index of company names, or

  (b)  a name that should have appeared in that index at that time.

(2)  The Secretary of State may make provision by regulations supplementing this section.

(3)  The regulations may make provision—

  (a)  as to matters that are to be disregarded, and

  (b)  as to words, expressions, signs or symbols that are, or are not, to be regarded as the same,

for the purposes of this section.

(4)  The regulations may provide—

  (a)  that no direction is to be given under this section in respect of a name—

    (i)   in specified circumstances, or

    (ii)  if specified consent is given, and

  (b)  that a subsequent change of circumstances or withdrawal of consent does not give rise to grounds for a direction under this section.

(5)  Regulations under this section are subject to negative resolution procedure.

(6)  In this section 'specified' means specified in the regulations.

### 68   Direction to change name: supplementary provisions

(1)  The following provisions have effect in relation to a direction under section 67 (power to direct change of name in case of similarity to existing name).

(2)  Any such direction—

  (a)  must be given within twelve months of the company's registration by the name in question, and

  (b)  must specify the period within which the company is to change its name.

(3)  The Secretary of State may by a further direction extend that period.

Any such direction must be given before the end of the period for the time being specified.

(4)  A direction under section 67 or this section must be in writing.

(5)  If a company fails to comply with the direction, an offence is committed by—

  (a)  the company, and

  (b)  every officer of the company who is in default.

For this purpose a shadow director is treated as an officer of the company.

(6)  A person guilty of an offence under this section is liable on summary conviction to a fine not exceeding level 3 on the standard scale and, for continued contravention, a daily default fine not exceeding one-tenth of level 3 on the standard scale.

*Similarity to other name in which person has goodwill*

### 69   Objection to company's registered name

(1)  A person ('the applicant') may object to a company's registered name on the ground—

  (a)  that it is the same as a name associated with the applicant in which he has goodwill, or

  (b)  that it is sufficiently similar to such a name that its use in the United Kingdom would be likely to mislead by suggesting a connection between the company and the applicant.

(2) The objection must be made by application to a company names adjudicator (see section 70).

(3) The company concerned shall be the primary respondent to the application.
Any of its members or directors may be joined as respondents.

(4) If the ground specified in subsection (1)(a) or (b) is established, it is for the respondents to show—

  (a) that the name was registered before the commencement of the activities on which the applicant relies to show goodwill; or

  (b) that the company—

      (i) is operating under the name, or

      (ii) is proposing to do so and has incurred substantial start-up costs in preparation, or

      (iii) was formerly operating under the name and is now dormant; or

  (c) that the name was registered in the ordinary course of a company formation business and the company is available for sale to the applicant on the standard terms of that business; or

  (d) that the name was adopted in good faith; or

  (e) that the interests of the applicant are not adversely affected to any significant extent.

If none of those is shown, the objection shall be upheld.

(5) If the facts mentioned in subsection (4)(a), (b) or (c) are established, the objection shall nevertheless be upheld if the applicant shows that the main purpose of the respondents (or any of them) in registering the name was to obtain money (or other consideration) from the applicant or prevent him from registering the name.

(6) If the objection is not upheld under subsection (4) or (5), it shall be dismissed.

(7) In this section 'goodwill' includes reputation of any description.

## 70  Company names adjudicators

(1) The Secretary of State shall appoint persons to be company names adjudicators.

(2) The persons appointed must have such legal or other experience as, in the Secretary of State's opinion, makes them suitable for appointment.

(3) An adjudicator—

  (a) holds office in accordance with the terms of his appointment,

  (b) is eligible for re-appointment when his term of office ends,

  (c) may resign at any time by notice in writing given to the Secretary of State, and

  (d) may be dismissed by the Secretary of State on the ground of incapacity or misconduct.

(4) One of the adjudicators shall be appointed Chief Adjudicator.
He shall perform such functions as the Secretary of State may assign to him.

(5) The other adjudicators shall undertake such duties as the Chief Adjudicator may determine.

(6) The Secretary of State may—

  (a) appoint staff for the adjudicators;

  (b) pay remuneration and expenses to the adjudicators and their staff;

  (c) defray other costs arising in relation to the performance by the adjudicators of their functions;

  (d) compensate persons for ceasing to be adjudicators.

## 71  Procedural rules

(1) The Secretary of State may make rules about proceedings before a company names adjudicator.

(2) The rules may, in particular, make provision—

  (a) as to how an application is to be made and the form and content of an application or other documents;

  (b) for fees to be charged;

  (c) about the service of documents and the consequences of failure to serve them;

  (d) as to the form and manner in which evidence is to be given;

  (e) for circumstances in which hearings are required and those in which they are not;

  (f) for cases to be heard by more than one adjudicator;

  (g) setting time limits for anything required to be done in connection with the proceedings (and allowing for such limits to be extended, even if they have expired);

  (h) enabling the adjudicator to strike out an application, or any defence, in whole or in part—

      (i) on the ground that it is vexatious, has no reasonable prospect of success or is otherwise misconceived, or

      (ii) for failure to comply with the requirements of the rules;

  (i) conferring power to order security for costs (in Scotland, caution for expenses);

  (j) as to how far proceedings are to be held in public;

  (k) requiring one party to bear the costs (in Scotland, expenses) of another and as to the taxing (or settling) the amount of such costs (or expenses).

(3) The rules may confer on the Chief Adjudicator power to determine any matter that could be the subject of provision in the rules.

(4) Rules under this section shall be made by statutory instrument which shall be subject to annulment in pursuance of a resolution of either House of Parliament.

### 72   Decision of adjudicator to be made available to public

(1) A company names adjudicator must, within 90 days of determining an application under section 69, make his decision and his reasons for it available to the public.

(2) He may do so by means of a website or by such other means as appear to him to be appropriate.

### 73   Order requiring name to be changed

(1) If an application under section 69 is upheld, the adjudicator shall make an order—

    (a) requiring the respondent company to change its name to one that is not an offending name, and

    (b) requiring all the respondents—

        (i) to take all such steps as are within their power to make, or facilitate the making, of that change, and

        (ii) not to cause or permit any steps to be taken calculated to result in another company being registered with a name that is an offending name.

(2) An 'offending name' means a name that, by reason of its similarity to the name associated with the applicant in which he claims goodwill, would be likely—

    (a) to be the subject of a direction under section 67 (power of Secretary of State to direct change of name), or

    (b) to give rise to a further application under section 69.

(3) The order must specify a date by which the respondent company's name is to be changed and may be enforced—

    (a) in England and Wales or Northern Ireland, in the same way as an order of the High Court;

    (b) in Scotland, in the same way as a decree of the Court of Session.

(4) If the respondent company's name is not changed in accordance with the order by the specified date, the adjudicator may determine a new name for the company.

(5) If the adjudicator determines a new name for the respondent company he must give notice of his determination—

    (a) to the applicant,

    (b) to the respondents, and

    (c) to the registrar.

(6) For the purposes of this section a company's name is changed when the change takes effect in accordance with section 81(1) (on the issue of the new certification of incorporation).

### 74   Appeal from adjudicator's decision

(1) An appeal lies to the court from any decision of a company names adjudicator to uphold or dismiss an application under section 69.

(2) Notice of appeal against a decision upholding an application must be given before the date specified in the adjudicator's order by which the respondent company's name is to be changed.

(3) If notice of appeal is given against a decision upholding an application, the effect of the adjudicator's order is suspended.

(4) If on appeal the court—

    (a) affirms the decision of the adjudicator to uphold the application, or

    (b) reverses the decision of the adjudicator to dismiss the application,

the court may (as the case may require) specify the date by which the adjudicator's order is to be complied with, remit the matter to the adjudicator or make any order or determination that the adjudicator might have made.

(5) If the court determines a new name for the company it must give notice of the determination—

    (a) to the parties to the appeal, and

    (b) to the registrar.

## Chapter 4   Other powers of the Secretary of State

### 75   Provision of misleading information etc.

(1) If it appears to the Secretary of State—

    (a) that misleading information has been given for the purposes of a company's registration by a particular name, or

    (b) that an undertaking or assurance has been given for that purpose and has not been fulfilled,

the Secretary of State may direct the company to change its name.

(2) Any such direction—

    (b) must specify the period within which the company is to change its name.

(3) The Secretary of State may by a further direction extend the period within which the company is to change its name.

Any such direction must be given before the end of the period for the time being specified.

(4) A direction under this section must be in writing.

(5) If a company fails to comply with a direction under this section, an offence is committed by—

    (a) the company, and

    (b) every officer of the company who is in default.

For this purpose a shadow director is treated as an officer of the company.

(6) A person guilty of an offence under this section is liable on summary conviction to a fine not exceeding level 3 on the standard scale and, for continued contravention, a daily default fine not exceeding one-tenth of level 3 on the standard scale.

### 76  Misleading indication of activities

(1) If in the opinion of the Secretary of State the name by which a company is registered gives so misleading an indication of the nature of its activities as to be likely to cause harm to the public, the Secretary of State may direct the company to change its name.

(2) The direction must be in writing.

(3) The direction must be complied with within a period of six weeks from the date of the direction or such longer period as the Secretary of State may think fit to allow.

This does not apply if an application is duly made to the court under the following provisions.

(4) The company may apply to the court to set the direction aside.

The application must be made within the period of three weeks from the date of the direction.

(5) The court may set the direction aside or confirm it.

If the direction is confirmed, the court shall specify the period within which the direction is to be complied with.

(6) If a company fails to comply with a direction under this section, an offence is committed by—

    (a) the company, and

    (b) every officer of the company who is in default.

For this purpose a shadow director is treated as an officer of the company.

(7) A person guilty of an offence under this section is liable on summary conviction to a fine not exceeding level 3 on the standard scale and, for continued contravention, a daily default fine not exceeding one-tenth of level 3 on the standard scale.

## Chapter 5  Change of name

### 77  Change of name

(1) A company may change its name—

    (a) by special resolution (see section 78), or

    (b) by other means provided for by the company's articles (see section 79).

(2) The name of a company may also be changed—

    (a) by resolution of the directors acting under section 64 (change of name to comply with direction of Secretary of State under that section);

    (b) on the determination of a new name by a company names adjudicator under section 73 (powers of adjudicator on upholding objection to company name);

    (c) on the determination of a new name by the court under section 74 (appeal against decision of company names adjudicator);

    (d) under section 1033 (company's name on restoration to the register).

### 78  Change of name by special resolution

(1) Where a change of name has been agreed to by a company by special resolution, the company must give notice to the registrar.

This is in addition to the obligation to forward a copy of the resolution to the registrar.

(2) Where a change of name by special resolution is conditional on the occurrence of an event, the notice given to the registrar of the change must—

    (a) specify that the change is conditional, and

    (b) state whether the event has occurred.

(3) If the notice states that the event has not occurred—

    (a) the registrar is not required to act under section 80 (registration and issue of new certificate of incorporation) until further notice,

    (b) when the event occurs, the company must give notice to the registrar stating that it has occurred, and

    (c) the registrar may rely on the statement as sufficient evidence of the matters stated in it.

### 79  Change of name by means provided for in company's articles

(1) Where a change of a company's name has been made by other means provided for by its articles—

    (a) the company must give notice to the registrar, and

    (b) the notice must be accompanied by a statement that the change of name has been made by means provided for by the company's articles.

(2) The registrar may rely on the statement as sufficient evidence of the matters stated in it.

### 80  Change of name: registration and issue of new certificate of incorporation

(1) This section applies where the registrar receives notice of a change of a company's name.

(2) If the registrar is satisfied—

    (a) that the new name complies with the requirements of this Part, and

(b) that the requirements of the Companies Acts, and any relevant requirements of the company's articles, with respect to a change of name are complied with,

the registrar must enter the new name on the register in place of the former name.

(3) On the registration of the new name, the registrar must issue a certificate of incorporation altered to meet the circumstances of the case.

### 81 Change of name: effect

(1) A change of a company's name has effect from the date on which the new certificate of incorporation is issued.

(2) The change does not affect any rights or obligations of the company or render defective any legal proceedings by or against it.

(3) Any legal proceedings that might have been continued or commenced against it by its former name may be continued or commenced against it by its new name.

## Chapter 6  Trading disclosures

### 82 Requirement to disclose company name etc.

(1) The Secretary of State may by regulations make provision requiring companies—
  (a) to display specified information in specified locations,
  (b) to state specified information in specified descriptions of document or communication, and
  (c) to provide specified information on request to those they deal with in the course of their business.

(2) The regulations—
  (a) must in every case require disclosure of the name of the company, and
  (b) may make provision as to the manner in which any specified information is to be displayed, stated or provided.

(3) The regulations may provide that, for the purposes of any requirement to disclose a company's name, any variation between a word or words required to be part of the name and a permitted abbreviation of that word or those words (or vice versa) shall be disregarded.

(4) In this section 'specified' means specified in the regulations.

(5) Regulations under this section are subject to affirmative resolution procedure.

### 83 Civil consequences of failure to make required disclosure

(1) This section applies to any legal proceedings brought by a company to which section 82 applies (requirement to disclose company name etc) to enforce a right arising out of a contract made in the course of a business in respect of which the company was, at the time the contract was made, in breach of regulations under that section.

(2) The proceedings shall be dismissed if the defendant (in Scotland, the defender) to the proceedings shows—
  (a) that he has a claim against the claimant (pursuer) arising out of the contract that he has been unable to pursue by reason of the latter's breach of the regulations, or
  (b) that he has suffered some financial loss in connection with the contract by reason of the claimant's (pursuer's) breach of the regulations,

unless the court before which the proceedings are brought is satisfied that it is just and equitable to permit the proceedings to continue.

(3) This section does not affect the right of any person to enforce such rights as he may have against another person in any proceedings brought by that person.

### 84 Criminal consequences of failure to make required disclosures

(1) Regulations under section 82 may provide—
  (a) that where a company fails, without reasonable excuse, to comply with any specified requirement of regulations under that section an offence is committed by—
    (i) the company, and
    (ii) every officer of the company who is in default;
  (b) that a person guilty of such an offence is liable on summary conviction to a fine not exceeding level 3 on the standard scale and, for continued contravention, a daily default fine not exceeding one-tenth of level 3 on the standard scale.

(2) The regulations may provide that, for the purposes of any provision made under subsection (1), a shadow director of the company is to be treated as an officer of the company.

(3) In subsection (1)(a) 'specified' means specified in the regulations.

### 85 Minor variations in form of name to be left out of account

(1) For the purposes of this Chapter, in considering a company's name no account is to be taken of—
  (a) whether upper or lower case characters (or a combination of the two) are used,
  (b) whether diacritical marks or punctuation are present or absent,
  (c) whether the name is in the same format or style as is specified under section 57(1)(b) for the purposes of registration,

provided there is no real likelihood of names differing only in those respects being taken to be different names.

(2)  This does not affect the operation of regulations under section 57(1)(a) permitting only speci-fied characters, diacritical marks or punctuation.

# PART 6  A COMPANY'S REGISTERED OFFICE

## *General*

### 86  A company's registered office

A company must at all times have a registered office to which all communications and notices may be addressed.

### 87  Change of address of registered office

(1)  A company may change the address of its registered office by giving notice to the registrar.

(2)  The change takes effect upon the notice being registered by the registrar, but until the end of the period of 14 days beginning with the date on which it is registered a person may validly serve any document on the company at the address previously registered.

(3)  For the purposes of any duty of a company—

    (a)  to keep available for inspection at its registered office any register, index or other document, or

    (b)  to mention the address of its registered office in any document,

a company that has given notice to the registrar of a change in the address of its registered office may act on the change as from such date, not more than 14 days after the notice is given, as it may determine.

(4)  Where a company unavoidably ceases to perform at its registered office any such duty as is mentioned in subsection (3)(a) in circumstances in which it was not practicable to give prior notice to the registrar of a change in the address of its registered office, but—

    (a)  resumes performance of that duty at other premises as soon as practicable, and

    (b)  gives notice accordingly to the registrar of a change in the situation of its registered office within 14 days of doing so,

it is not to be treated as having failed to comply with that duty.

## *Welsh companies*

### 88  Welsh companies

(1)  In the Companies Acts a 'Welsh company' means a company as to which it is stated in the regis-ter that its registered office is to be situated in Wales.

(2)  A company—

    (a)  whose registered office is in Wales, and

    (b)  as to which it is stated in the register that its registered office is to be situated in England and Wales,

may by special resolution require the register to be amended so that it states that the company's regis-tered office is to be situated in Wales.

(3)  A company—

    (a)  whose registered office is in Wales, and

    (b)  as to which it is stated in the register that its registered office is to be situated in Wales,

may by special resolution require the register to be amended so that it states that the company's regis-tered office is to be situated in England and Wales.

(4)  Where a company passes a resolution under this section it must give notice to the registrar, who shall—

    (a)  amend the register accordingly, and

    (b)  issue a new certificate of incorporation altered to meet the circumstances of the case.

# PART 7  RE-REGISTRATION AS A MEANS OF ALTERING A COMPANY'S STATUS

## *Introductory*

### 89  Alteration of status by re-registration

A company may by re-registration under this Part alter its status—

    (a)  from a private company to a public company (see sections 90 to 96);

    (b)  from a public company to a private company (see sections 97 to 101);

    (c)  from a private limited company to an unlimited company (see sections 102 to 104);

    (d)  from an unlimited private company to a limited company (see sections 105 to 108);

    (e)  from a public company to an unlimited private company (see sections 109 to 111).

## *Private company becoming public*

### 90  Re-registration of private company as public

(1)  A private company (whether limited or unlimited) may be re-registered as a public company limited by shares if—

(a) a special resolution that it should be so re-registered is passed,

(b) the conditions specified below are met, and

(c) an application for re-registration is delivered to the registrar in accordance with section 94, together with—

    (i) the other documents required by that section, and

    (ii) a statement of compliance.

(2) The conditions are—

(a) that the company has a share capital;

(b) that the requirements of section 91 are met as regards its share capital;

(c) that the requirements of section 92 are met as regards its net assets;

(d) if section 93 applies (recent allotment of shares for non-cash consideration), that the requirements of that section are met; and

(e) that the company has not previously been re-registered as unlimited.

(3) The company must make such changes—

(a) in its name, and

(b) in its articles,

as are necessary in connection with its becoming a public company.

(4) If the company is unlimited it must also make such changes in its articles as are necessary in connection with its becoming a company limited by shares.

## 91   Requirements as to share capital

(1) The following requirements must be met at the time the special resolution is passed that the company should be re-registered as a public company—

(a) the nominal value of the company's allotted share capital must be not less than the authorised minimum;

(b) each of the company's allotted shares must be paid up at least as to one-quarter of the nominal value of that share and the whole of any premium on it;

(c) if any shares in the company or any premium on them have been fully or partly paid up by an undertaking given by any person that he or another should do work or perform services (whether for the company or any other person), the undertaking must have been performed or otherwise discharged;

(d) if shares have been allotted as fully or partly paid up as to their nominal value or any premium on them otherwise than in cash, and the consideration for the allotment consists of or includes an undertaking to the company (other than one to which paragraph (c) applies), then either—

    (i) the undertaking must have been performed or otherwise discharged, or

    (ii) there must be a contract between the company and some person pursuant to which the undertaking is to be performed within five years from the time the special resolution is passed.

(2) For the purpose of determining whether the requirements in subsection (1)(b), (c) and (d) are met, the following may be disregarded—

(a) shares allotted—

    (i) before 22nd June 1982 in the case of a company then registered in Great Britain, or

    (ii) before 31st December 1984 in the case of a company then registered in Northern Ireland;

(b) shares allotted in pursuance of an employees' share scheme by reason of which the company would, but for this subsection, be precluded under subsection (1)(b) (but not otherwise) from being re-registered as a public company.

(3) No more than one-tenth of the nominal value of the company's allotted share capital is to be disregarded under subsection (2)(a).

For this purpose the allotted share capital is treated as not including shares disregarded under subsection (2)(b).

(4) Shares disregarded under subsection (2) are treated as not forming part of the allotted share capital for the purposes of subsection (1)(a).

(5) A company must not be re-registered as a public company if it appears to the registrar that—

(a) the company has resolved to reduce its share capital,

(b) the reduction—

    (i) is made under section 626 (reduction in connection with redenomination of share capital),

    (ii) is supported by a solvency statement in accordance with section 643, or

    (iii) has been confirmed by an order of the court under section 648, and

(c) the effect of the reduction is, or will be, that the nominal value of the company's allotted share capital is below the authorised minimum.

## 92   Requirements as to net assets

(1) A company applying to re-register as a public company must obtain—

(a) a balance sheet prepared as at a date not more than seven months before the date on which the application is delivered to the registrar,

(b) an unqualified report by the company's auditor on that balance sheet, and

(c) a written statement by the company's auditor that in his opinion at the balance sheet date the amount of the company's net assets was not less than the aggregate of its called-up share capital and undistributable reserves.

(2) Between the balance sheet date and the date on which the application for re-registration is delivered to the registrar, there must be no change in the company's financial position that results in the amount of its net assets becoming less than the aggregate of its called-up share capital and undistributable reserves.

(3) In subsection (1)(b) an 'unqualified report' means—

(a) if the balance sheet was prepared for a financial year of the company, a report stating without material qualification the auditor's opinion that the balance sheet has been properly prepared in accordance with the requirements of this Act;

(b) if the balance sheet was not prepared for a financial year of the company, a report stating without material qualification the auditor's opinion that the balance sheet has been properly prepared in accordance with the provisions of this Act which would have applied if it had been prepared for a financial year of the company.

(4) For the purposes of an auditor's report on a balance sheet that was not prepared for a financial year of the company, the provisions of this Act apply with such modifications as are necessary by reason of that fact.

(5) For the purposes of subsection (3) a qualification is material unless the auditor states in his report that the matter giving rise to the qualification is not material for the purpose of determining (by reference to the company's balance sheet) whether at the balance sheet date the amount of the company's net assets was not less than the aggregate of its called-up share capital and undistributable reserves.

(6) In this Part 'net assets' and 'undistributable reserves' have the same meaning as in section 831 (net asset restriction on distributions by public companies).

## 93　Recent allotment of shares for non-cash consideration

(1) This section applies where—

(a) shares are allotted by the company in the period between the date as at which the balance sheet required by section 92 is prepared and the passing of the resolution that the company should re-register as a public company, and

(b) the shares are allotted as fully or partly paid up as to their nominal value or any premium on them otherwise than in cash.

(2) The registrar shall not entertain an application by the company for re-registration as a public company unless—

(a) the requirements of section 593(1)(a) and (b) have been complied with (independent valuation of non-cash consideration; valuer's report to company not more than six months before allotment), or

(b) the allotment is in connection with—

　(i) a share exchange (see subsections (3) to (5) below), or

　(ii) a proposed merger with another company (see subsection (6) below).

(3) An allotment is in connection with a share exchange if—

(a) the shares are allotted in connection with an arrangement under which the whole or part of the consideration for the shares allotted is provided by—

　(i) the transfer to the company allotting the shares of shares (or shares of a particular class) in another company, or

　(ii) the cancellation of shares (or shares of a particular class) in another company; and

(b) the allotment is open to all the holders of the shares of the other company in question (or, where the arrangement applies only to shares of a particular class, to all the holders of the company's shares of that class) to take part in the arrangement in connection with which the shares are allotted.

(4) In determining whether a person is a holder of shares for the purposes of subsection (3), there shall be disregarded—

(a) shares held by, or by a nominee of, the company allotting the shares;

(b) shares held by, or by a nominee of—

　(i) the holding company of the company allotting the shares,

　(ii) a subsidiary of the company allotting the shares, or

　(iii) a subsidiary of the holding company of the company allotting the shares.

(5) It is immaterial, for the purposes of deciding whether an allotment is in connection with a share exchange, whether or not the arrangement in connection with which the shares are allotted involves the issue to the company allotting the shares of shares (or shares of a particular class) in the other company.

(6) There is a proposed merger with another company if one of the companies concerned proposes to acquire all the assets and liabilities of the other in exchange for the issue of its shares or other securities to shareholders of the other (whether or not accompanied by a cash payment).

'Another company' includes any body corporate.

(7) For the purposes of this section—

(a) the consideration for an allotment does not include any amount standing to the credit of any of the company's reserve accounts, or of its profit and loss account, that has been applied in paying up (to any extent) any of the shares allotted or any premium on those shares; and

(b) 'arrangement' means any agreement, scheme or arrangement, (including an arrangement sanctioned in accordance with—

(i) Part 26 of this Act (arrangements and reconstructions), or

(ii) section 110 of the Insolvency Act 1986 (c. 45) or Article 96 of the Insolvency (Northern Ireland) Order 1989 (S.I. 1989/2405 (N.I. 19)) (liquidator in winding up accepting shares as consideration for sale of company's property).

## 94   Application and accompanying documents

(1) An application for re-registration as a public company must contain—

(a) a statement of the company's proposed name on re-registration; and

(b) in the case of a company without a secretary, a statement of the company's proposed secretary (see section 95).

(2) The application must be accompanied by—

(a) a copy of the special resolution that the company should re-register as a public company (unless a copy has already been forwarded to the registrar under Chapter 3 of Part 3);

(b) a copy of the company's articles as proposed to be amended;

(c) a copy of the balance sheet and other documents referred to in section 92(1); and

(d) if section 93 applies (recent allotment of shares for non-cash consideration), a copy of the valuation report (if any) under subsection (2)(a) of that section.

(3) The statement of compliance required to be delivered together with the application is a statement that the requirements of this Part as to re-registration as a public company have been complied with.

(4) The registrar may accept the statement of compliance as sufficient evidence that the company is entitled to be re-registered as a public company.

## 95   Statement of proposed secretary

(1) The statement of the company's proposed secretary must contain the required particulars of the person who is or the persons who are to be the secretary or joint secretaries of the company.

(2) The required particulars are the particulars that will be required to be stated in the company's register of secretaries (see sections 277 to 279).

(3) The statement must also contain a consent by the person named as secretary, or each of the persons named as joint secretaries, to act in the relevant capacity.

If all the partners in a firm are to be joint secretaries, consent may be given by one partner on behalf of all of them.

## 96   Issue of certificate of incorporation on re-registration

(1) If on an application for re-registration as a public company the registrar is satisfied that the company is entitled to be so re-registered, the company shall be re-registered accordingly.

(2) The registrar must issue a certificate of incorporation altered to meet the circumstances of the case.

(3) The certificate must state that it is issued on re-registration and the date on which it is issued.

(4) On the issue of the certificate—

(a) the company by virtue of the issue of the certificate becomes a public company,

(b) the changes in the company's name and articles take effect, and

(c) where the application contained a statement under section 95 (statement of proposed secretary), the person or persons named in the statement as secretary or joint secretary of the company are deemed to have been appointed to that office.

(5) The certificate is conclusive evidence that the requirements of this Act as to re-registration have been complied with.

*Public company becoming private*

## 97   Re-registration of public company as private limited company

(1) A public company may be re-registered as a private limited company if—

(a) a special resolution that it should be so re-registered is passed,

(b) the conditions specified below are met, and

(c) an application for re-registration is delivered to the registrar in accordance with section 100, together with—

(i) the other documents required by that section, and

(ii) a statement of compliance.

(2) The conditions are that—

    (a) where no application under section 98 for cancellation of the resolution has been made—

        (i) having regard to the number of members who consented to or voted in favour of the resolution, no such application may be made, or

        (ii) the period within which such an application could be made has expired, or

    (b) where such an application has been made—

        (i) the application has been withdrawn, or

        (ii) an order has been made confirming the resolution and a copy of that order has been delivered to the registrar.

(3) The company must make such changes—

    (a) in its name, and

    (b) in its articles,

as are necessary in connection with its becoming a private company limited by shares or, as the case may be, by guarantee.

## 98   Application to court to cancel resolution

(1) Where a special resolution by a public company to be re-registered as a private limited company has been passed, an application to the court for the cancellation of the resolution may be made—

    (a) by the holders of not less in the aggregate than 5% in nominal value of the company's issued share capital or any class of the company's issued share capital (disregarding any shares held by the company as treasury shares);

    (b) if the company is not limited by shares, by not less than 5% of its members; or

    (c) by not less than 50 of the company's members;

but not by a person who has consented to or voted in favour of the resolution.

(2) The application must be made within 28 days after the passing of the resolution and may be made on behalf of the persons entitled to make it by such one or more of their number as they may appoint for the purpose.

(3) On the hearing of the application the court shall make an order either cancelling or confirming the resolution.

(4) The court may—

    (a) make that order on such terms and conditions as it thinks fit,

    (b) if it thinks fit adjourn the proceedings in order that an arrangement may be made to the satisfaction of the court for the purchase of the interests of dissentient members, and

    (c) give such directions, and make such orders, as it thinks expedient for facilitating or carrying into effect any such arrangement.

(5) The court's order may, if the court thinks fit—

    (a) provide for the purchase by the company of the shares of any of its members and for the reduction accordingly of the company's capital; and

    (b) make such alteration in the company's articles as may be required in consequence of that provision.

(6) The court's order may, if the court thinks fit, require the company not to make any, or any specified, amendments to its articles without the leave of the court.

## 99   Notice to registrar of court application or order

(1) On making an application under section 98 (application to court to cancel resolution) the applicants, or the person making the application on their behalf, must immediately give notice to the registrar.

This is without prejudice to any provision of rules of court as to service of notice of the application.

(2) On being served with notice of any such application, the company must immediately give notice to the registrar.

(3) Within 15 days of the making of the court's order on the application, or such longer period as the court may at any time direct, the company must deliver to the registrar a copy of the order.

(4) If a company fails to comply with subsection (2) or (3) an offence is committed by—

    (a) the company, and

    (b) every officer of the company who is in default.

(5) A person guilty of an offence under this section is liable on summary conviction to a fine not exceeding level 3 on the standard scale and, for continued contravention, a daily default fine not exceeding one-tenth of level 3 on the standard scale.

## 100   Application and accompanying documents

(1) An application for re-registration as a private limited company must contain a statement of the company's proposed name on re-registration.

(2) The application must be accompanied by—

    (a) a copy of the resolution that the company should re-register as a private limited company (unless a copy has already been forwarded to the registrar under Chapter 3 of Part 3); and

    (b) a copy of the company's articles as proposed to be amended.

(3) The statement of compliance required to be delivered together with the application is a statement that the requirements of this Part as to re-registration as a private limited company have been complied with.

(4) The registrar may accept the statement of compliance as sufficient evidence that the company is entitled to be re-registered as a private limited company.

### 101    Issue of certificate of incorporation on re-registration

(1) If on an application for re-registration as a private limited company the registrar is satisfied that the company is entitled to be so re-registered, the company shall be re-registered accordingly.

(2) The registrar must issue a certificate of incorporation altered to meet the circumstances of the case.

(3) The certificate must state that it is issued on re-registration and the date on which it is issued.

(4) On the issue of the certificate—

(a) the company by virtue of the issue of the certificate becomes a private limited company, and

(b) the changes in the company's name and articles take effect.

(5) The certificate is conclusive evidence that the requirements of this Act as to re-registration have been complied with.

### *Private limited company becoming unlimited*

### 102    Re-registration of private limited company as unlimited

(1) A private limited company may be re-registered as an unlimited company if—

(a) all the members of the company have assented to its being so reregistered,

(b) the condition specified below is met, and

(c) an application for re-registration is delivered to the registrar in accordance with section 103, together with—

(i)    the other documents required by that section, and

(ii)    a statement of compliance.

(2) The condition is that the company has not previously been re-registered as limited.

(3) The company must make such changes in its name and its articles—

(a) as are necessary in connection with its becoming an unlimited company; and

(b) if it is to have a share capital, as are necessary in connection with its becoming an unlimited company having a share capital.

(4) For the purposes of this section—

(a) a trustee in bankruptcy of a member of the company is entitled, to the exclusion of the member, to assent to the company's becoming unlimited; and

(b) the personal representative of a deceased member of the company may assent on behalf of the deceased.

(5) In subsection (4)(a), 'a trustee in bankruptcy of a member of the company' includes—

(a) a permanent trustee or an interim trustee (within the meaning of the Bankruptcy (Scotland) Act 1985 (c. 66)) on the sequestrated estate of a member of the company;

(b) a trustee under a protected trustee deed (within the meaning of the Bankruptcy (Scotland) Act 1985) granted by a member of the company.

### 103    Application and accompanying documents

(1) An application for re-registration as an unlimited company must contain a statement of the company's proposed name on re-registration.

(2) The application must be accompanied by—

(a) the prescribed form of assent to the company's being registered as an unlimited company, authenticated by or on behalf of all the members of the company;

(b) a copy of the company's articles as proposed to be amended.

(3) The statement of compliance required to be delivered together with the application is a statement that the requirements of this Part as to re-registration as an unlimited company have been complied with.

(4) The statement must contain a statement by the directors of the company—

(a) that the persons by whom or on whose behalf the form of assent is authenticated constitute the whole membership of the company, and

(b) if any of the members have not authenticated that form themselves, that the directors have taken all reasonable steps to satisfy themselves that each person who authenticated it on behalf of a member was lawfully empowered to do so.

(5) The registrar may accept the statement of compliance as sufficient evidence that the company is entitled to be re-registered as an unlimited company.

### 104    Issue of certificate of incorporation on re-registration

(1) If on an application for re-registration of a private limited company as an unlimited company the registrar is satisfied that the company is entitled to be so re-registered, the company shall be re-registered accordingly.

(2) The registrar must issue a certificate of incorporation altered to meet the circumstances of the case.

(3) The certificate must state that it is issued on re-registration and the date on which it is issued.

(4) On the issue of the certificate—

(a) the company by virtue of the issue of the certificate becomes an unlimited company, and

(b) the changes in the company's name and articles take effect.

(5) The certificate is conclusive evidence that the requirements of this Act as to re-registration have been complied with.

### *Unlimited private company becoming limited*

### 105   Re-registration of unlimited company as limited

(1) An unlimited company may be re-registered as a private limited company if—

(a) a special resolution that it should be so re-registered is passed,

(b) the condition specified below is met, and

(c) an application for re-registration is delivered to the registrar in accordance with section 106, together with—

(i)   the other documents required by that section, and

(ii)   a statement of compliance.

(2) The condition is that the company·has not previously been re-registered as unlimited.

(3) The special resolution must state whether the company is to be limited by shares or by guarantee.

(4) The company must make such changes—

(a) in its name, and

(b) in its articles,

as are necessary in connection with its becoming a company limited by shares or, as the case may be, by guarantee.

### 106   Application and accompanying documents

(1) An application for re-registration as a limited company must contain a statement of the company's proposed name on re-registration.

(2) The application must be accompanied by—

(a) a copy of the resolution that the company should re-register as a private limited company (unless a copy has already been forwarded to the registrar under Chapter 3 of Part 3);

(b) if the company is to be limited by guarantee, a statement of guarantee;

(c) a copy of the company's articles as proposed to be amended.

(3) The statement of guarantee required to be delivered in the case of a company that is to be limited by guarantee must state that each member undertakes that, if the company is wound up while he is a member, or within one year after he ceases to be a member, he will contribute to the assets of the company such amount as may be required for—

(a) payment of the debts and liabilities of the company contracted before he ceases to be a member,

(b) payment of the costs, charges and expenses of winding up, and

(c) adjustment of the rights of the contributories among themselves,

not exceeding a specified amount.

(4) The statement of compliance required to be delivered together with the application is a statement that the requirements of this Part as to re-registration as a limited company have been complied with.

(5) The registrar may accept the statement of compliance as sufficient evidence that the company is entitled to be re-registered as a limited company.

### 107   Issue of certificate of incorporation on re-registration

(1) If on an application for re-registration of an unlimited company as a limited company the registrar is satisfied that the company is entitled to be so reregistered, the company shall be reregistered accordingly.

(2) The registrar must issue a certificate of incorporation altered to meet the circumstances of the case.

(3) The certificate must state that it is issued on re-registration and the date on which it is so issued.

(4) On the issue of the certificate—

(a) the company by virtue of the issue of the certificate becomes a limited company, and

(b) the changes in the company's name and articles take effect.

(5) The certificate is conclusive evidence that the requirements of this Act as to re-registration have been complied with.

### 108   Statement of capital required where company already has share capital

(1) A company which on re-registration under section 107 already has allotted share capital must within 15 days after the re-registration deliver a statement of capital to the registrar.

(2) This does not apply if the information which would be included in the statement has already been sent to the registrar in—

    (a) a statement of capital and initial shareholdings (see section 10), or

    (b) a statement of capital contained in an annual return (see section 856(2)).

(3) The statement of capital must state with respect to the company's share capital on re registration—

    (a) the total number of shares of the company,

    (b) the aggregate nominal value of those shares,

    (c) for each class of shares—

        (i) prescribed particulars of the rights attached to the shares,

        (ii) the total number of shares of that class, and

        (iii) the aggregate nominal value of shares of that class, and

    (d) the amount paid up and the amount (if any) unpaid on each share (whether on account of the nominal value of the share or by way of premium).

(4) If default is made in complying with this section, an offence is committed by—

    (a) the company, and

    (b) every officer of the company who is in default.

(5) A person guilty of an offence under this section is liable on summary conviction to a fine not exceeding level 3 on the standard scale and, for continued contravention, a daily default fine not exceeding one-tenth of level 3 on the standard scale.

### Public company becoming private and unlimited

### 109   Re-registration of public company as private and unlimited

(1) A public company limited by shares may be re-registered as an unlimited private company with a share capital if—

    (a) all the members of the company have assented to its being so reregistered,

    (b) the condition specified below is met, and

    (c) an application for re-registration is delivered to the registrar in accordance with section 110, together with—

        (i) the other documents required by that section, and

        (ii) a statement of compliance.

(2) The condition is that the company has not previously been re-registered—

    (a) as limited, or

    (b) as unlimited.

(3) The company must make such changes—

    (a) in its name, and

    (b) in its articles,

as are necessary in connection with its becoming an unlimited private company.

(4) For the purposes of this section—

    (a) a trustee in bankruptcy of a member of the company is entitled, to the exclusion of the member, to assent to the company's re-registration; and

    (b) the personal representative of a deceased member of the company may assent on behalf of the deceased.

(5) In subsection (4)(a), 'a trustee in bankruptcy of a member of the company' includes—

    (a) a permanent trustee or an interim trustee (within the meaning of the Bankruptcy (Scotland) Act 1985 (c. 66)) on the sequestrated estate of a member of the company;

    (b) a trustee under a protected trustee deed (within the meaning of the Bankruptcy (Scotland) Act 1985) granted by a member of the company.

### 110   Application and accompanying documents

(1) An application for re-registration of a public company as an unlimited private company must contain a statement of the company's proposed name on re-registration.

(2) The application must be accompanied by—

    (a) the prescribed form of assent to the company's being registered as an unlimited company, authenticated by or on behalf of all the members of the company, and

    (b) a copy of the company's articles as proposed to be amended.

(3) The statement of compliance required to be delivered together with the application is a statement that the requirements of this Part as to re-registration as an unlimited private company have been complied with.

(4) The statement must contain a statement by the directors of the company—

    (a) that the persons by whom or on whose behalf the form of assent is authenticated constitute the whole membership of the company, and

    (b) if any of the members have not authenticated that form themselves, that the directors have taken all reasonable steps to satisfy themselves that each person who authenticated it on behalf of a member was lawfully empowered to do so.

(5)  The registrar may accept the statement of compliance as sufficient evidence that the company is entitled to be re-registered as an unlimited private company.

### 111  Issue of certificate of incorporation on re-registration

(1)  If on an application for re-registration of a public company as an unlimited private company the registrar is satisfied that the company is entitled to be so re-registered, the company shall be re-registered accordingly.

(2)  The registrar must issue a certificate of incorporation altered to meet the circumstances of the case.

(3)  The certificate must state that it is issued on re-registration and the date on which it is so issued.

(4)  On the issue of the certificate—

   (a)  the company by virtue of the issue of the certificate becomes an unlimited private company, and

   (b)  the changes in the company's name and articles take effect.

(5)  The certificate is conclusive evidence that the requirements of this Act as to re-registration have been complied with.

# PART 8  A COMPANY'S MEMBERS

## Chapter 1  The members of a company

### 112  The members of a company

(1)  The subscribers of a company's memorandum are deemed to have agreed to become members of the company, and on its registration become members and must be entered as such in its register of members.

(2)  Every other person who agrees to become a member of a company, and whose name is entered in its register of members, is a member of the company.

## Chapter 2  Register of members

### *General*

### 113  Register of members

(1)  Every company must keep a register of its members.

(2)  There must be entered in the register—

   (a)  the names and addresses of the members,

   (b)  the date on which each person was registered as a member, and

   (c)  the date at which any person ceased to be a member.

(3)  In the case of a company having a share capital, there must be entered in the register, with the names and addresses of the members, a statement of—

   (a)  the shares held by each member, distinguishing each share—

      (i)   by its number (so long as the share has a number), and

      (ii)  where the company has more than one class of issued shares, by its class, and

   (b)  the amount paid or agreed to be considered as paid on the shares of each member.

(4)  If the company has converted any of its shares into stock, and given notice of the conversion to the registrar, the register of members must show the amount and class of stock held by each member instead of the amount of shares and the particulars relating to shares specified above.

(5)  In the case of joint holders of shares or stock in a company, the company's register of members must state the names of each joint holder.

In other respects joint holders are regarded for the purposes of this Chapter as a single member (so that the register must show a single address).

(6)  In the case of a company that does not have a share capital but has more than one class of members, there must be entered in the register, with the names and addresses of the members, a statement of the class to which each member belongs.

(7)  If a company makes default in complying with this section an offence is committed by—

   (a)  the company, and

   (b)  every officer of the company who is in default.

(8)  A person guilty of an offence under this section is liable on summary conviction to a fine not exceeding level 3 on the standard scale and, for continued contravention, a daily default fine not exceeding one-tenth of level 3 on the standard scale.

### 114  Register to be kept available for inspection

(1)  A company's register of members must be kept available for inspection—

   (a)  at its registered office, or

   (b)  at a place specified in regulations under section 1136.

(2) A company must give notice to the registrar of the place where its register of members is kept available for inspection and of any change in that place.

(3) No such notice is required if the register has, at all times since it came into existence (or, in the case of a register in existence on the relevant date, at all times since then) been kept available for inspection at the company's registered office.

(4) The relevant date for the purposes of subsection (3) is—

    (a) 1st July 1948 in the case of a company registered in Great Britain, and

    (b) 1st April 1961 in the case of a company registered in Northern Ireland.

(5) If a company makes default for 14 days in complying with subsection (2), an offence is committed by—

    (a) the company, and

    (b) every officer of the company who is in default.

(6) A person guilty of an offence under this section is liable on summary conviction to a fine not exceeding level 3 on the standard scale and, for continued contravention, a daily default fine not exceeding one-tenth of level 3 on the standard scale.

### 115  Index of members

(1) Every company having more than 50 members must keep an index of the names of the members of the company, unless the register of members is in such a form as to constitute in itself an index.

(2) The company must make any necessary alteration in the index within 14 days after the date on which any alteration is made in the register of members.

(3) The index must contain, in respect of each member, a sufficient indication to enable the account of that member in the register to be readily found.

(4) The index must be at all times kept available for inspection at the same place as the register of members.

(5) If default is made in complying with this section, an offence is committed by—

    (a) the company, and

    (b) every officer of the company who is in default.

(6) A person guilty of an offence under this section is liable on summary conviction to a fine not exceeding level 3 on the standard scale and, for continued contravention, a daily default fine not exceeding one-tenth of level 3 on the standard scale.

### 116  Rights to inspect and require copies

(1) The register and the index of members' names must be open to the inspection—

    (a) of any member of the company without charge, and

    (b) of any other person on payment of such fee as may be prescribed.

(2) Any person may require a copy of a company's register of members, or of any part of it, on payment of such fee as may be prescribed.

(3) A person seeking to exercise either of the rights conferred by this section must make a request to the company to that effect.

(4) The request must contain the following information—

    (a) in the case of an individual, his name and address;

    (b) in the case of an organisation, the name and address of an individual responsible for making the request on behalf of the organisation;

    (c) the purpose for which the information is to be used; and

    (d) whether the information will be disclosed to any other person, and if so—

        (i) where that person is an individual, his name and address,

        (ii) where that person is an organisation, the name and address of an individual responsible for receiving the information on its behalf, and

        (iii) the purpose for which the information is to be used by that person.

### 117  Register of members: response to request for inspection or copy

(1) Where a company receives a request under section 116 (register of members: right to inspect and require copy), it must within five working days either—

    (a) comply with the request, or

    (b) apply to the court.

(2) If it applies to the court it must notify the person making the request.

(3) If on an application under this section the court is satisfied that the inspection or copy is not sought for a proper purpose—

    (a) it shall direct the company not to comply with the request, and

    (b) it may further order that the company's costs (in Scotland, expenses) on the application be paid in whole or in part by the person who made the request, even if he is not a party to the application.

(4) If the court makes such a direction and it appears to the court that the company is or may be subject to other requests made for a similar purpose (whether made by the same person or different persons), it may direct that the company is not to comply with any such request.

The order must contain such provision as appears to the court appropriate to identify the requests to which it applies.

(5) If on an application under this section the court does not direct the company not to comply with the request, the company must comply with the request immediately upon the court giving its decision or, as the case may be, the proceedings being discontinued.

## 118  Register of members: refusal of inspection or default in providing copy

(1) If an inspection required under section 116 (register of members: right to inspect and require copy) is refused or default is made in providing a copy required under that section, otherwise than in accordance with an order of the court, an offence is committed by—

    (a) the company, and

    (b) every officer of the company who is in default.

(2) A person guilty of an offence under this section is liable on summary conviction to a fine not exceeding level 3 on the standard scale and, for continued contravention, a daily default fine not exceeding one-tenth of level 3 on the standard scale.

(3) In the case of any such refusal or default the court may by order compel an immediate inspection or, as the case may be, direct that the copy required be sent to the person requesting it.

## 119  Register of members: offences in connection with request for or disclosure of information

(1) It is an offence for a person knowingly or recklessly to make in a request under section 116 (register of members: right to inspect or require copy) a statement that is misleading, false or deceptive in a material particular.

(2) It is an offence for a person in possession of information obtained by exercise of either of the rights conferred by that section—

    (a) to do anything that results in the information being disclosed to another person, or

    (b) to fail to do anything with the result that the information is disclosed to another person,

knowing, or having reason to suspect, that person may use the information for a purpose that is not a proper purpose.

(3) A person guilty of an offence under this section is liable—

    (a) on conviction on indictment, to imprisonment for a term not exceeding two years or a fine (or both);

    (b) on summary conviction—

        (i) in England and Wales, to imprisonment for a term not exceeding twelve months or to a fine not exceeding the statutory maximum (or both);

        (ii) in Scotland or Northern Ireland, to imprisonment for a term not exceeding six months, or to a fine not exceeding the statutory maximum (or both).

## 120  Information as to state of register and index

(1) When a person inspects the register, or the company provides him with a copy of the register or any part of it, the company must inform him of the most recent date (if any) on which alterations were made to the register and there were no further alterations to be made.

(2) When a person inspects the index of members' names, the company must inform him whether there is any alteration to the register that is not reflected in the index.

(3) If a company fails to provide the information required under subsection (1) or (2), an offence is committed by—

    (a) the company, and

    (b) every officer of the company who is in default.

(4) A person guilty of an offence under this section is liable on summary conviction to a fine not exceeding level 3 on the standard scale.

## 121  Removal of entries relating to former members

An entry relating to a former member of the company may be removed from the register after the expiration of ten years from the date on which he ceased to be a member.

### *Special cases*

## 122  Share warrants

(1) On the issue of a share warrant the company must—

    (a) enter in the register of members—

        (i) the fact of the issue of the warrant,

        (ii) a statement of the shares included in the warrant, distinguishing each share by its number so long as the share has a number, and

        (iii) the date of the issue of the warrant, and

    (b) amend the register, if necessary, so that no person is named on the register as the holder of the shares specified in the warrant.

(2) Until the warrant is surrendered, the particulars specified in subsection (1)(a) are deemed to be those required by this Act to be entered in the register of members.

(3)  The bearer of a share warrant may, if the articles of the company so provide, be deemed a member of the company within the meaning of this Act, either to the full extent or for any purposes defined in the articles.

(4)  Subject to the company's articles, the bearer of a share warrant is entitled, on surrendering it for cancellation, to have his name entered as a member in the register of members.

(5)  The company is responsible for any loss incurred by any person by reason of the company entering in the register the name of a bearer of a share warrant in respect of the shares specified in it without the warrant being surrendered and cancelled.

(6)  On the surrender of a share warrant, the date of the surrender must be entered in the register.

### 123    Single member companies

(1)  If a limited company is formed under this Act with only one member there shall be entered in the company's register of members, with the name and address of the sole member, a statement that the company has only one member.

(2)  If the number of members of a limited company falls to one, or if an unlimited company with only one member becomes a limited company on re-registration, there shall upon the occurrence of that event be entered in the company's register of members, with the name and address of the sole member—

(a)  a statement that the company has only one member, and

(b)  the date on which the company became a company having only one member.

(3)  If the membership of a limited company increases from one to two or more members, there shall upon the occurrence of that event be entered in the company's register of members, with the name and address of the person who was formerly the sole member—

(a)  a statement that the company has ceased to have only one member, and

(b)  the date on which that event occurred.

(4)  If a company makes default in complying with this section, an offence is committed by—

(a)  the company, and

(b)  every officer of the company who is in default.

(5)  A person guilty of an offence under this section is liable on summary conviction to a fine not exceeding level 3 on the standard scale and, for continued contravention, a daily default fine not exceeding one-tenth of level 3 on the standard scale.

### 124    Company holding its own shares as treasury shares

(1)  Where a company purchases its own shares in circumstances in which section 724 (treasury shares) applies—

(a)  the requirements of section 113 (register of members) need not be complied with if the company cancels all of the shares forthwith after the purchase, and

(b)  if the company does not cancel all of the shares forthwith after the purchase, any share that is so cancelled shall be disregarded for the purposes of that section.

(2)  Subject to subsection (1), where a company holds shares as treasury shares the company must be entered in the register as the member holding those shares.

*Supplementary*

### 125    Power of court to rectify register

(1)  If—

(a)  the name of any person is, without sufficient cause, entered in or omitted from a company's register of members, or

(b)  default is made or unnecessary delay takes place in entering on the register the fact of any person having ceased to be a member,

the person aggrieved, or any member of the company, or the company, may apply to the court for rectification of the register.

(2)  The court may either refuse the application or may order rectification of the register and payment by the company of any damages sustained by any party aggrieved.

(3)  On such an application the court may decide any question relating to the title of a person who is a party to the application to have his name entered in or omitted from the register, whether the question arises between members or alleged members, or between members or alleged members on the one hand and the company on the other hand, and generally may decide any question necessary or expedient to be decided for rectification of the register.

(4)  In the case of a company required by this Act to send a list of its members to the registrar of companies, the court, when making an order for rectification of the register, shall by its order direct notice of the rectification to be given to the registrar.

### 126    Trusts not to be entered on register

No notice of any trust, expressed, implied or constructive, shall be entered on the register of members of a company registered in England and Wales or Northern Ireland, or be receivable by the registrar.

### 127  Register to be evidence

The register of members is prima facie evidence of any matters which are by this Act directed or authorised to be inserted in it.

### 128  Time limit for claims arising from entry in register

(1)  Liability incurred by a company—

    (a)  from the making or deletion of an entry in the register of members, or

    (b)  from a failure to make or delete any such entry,

is not enforceable more than ten years after the date on which the entry was made or deleted or, as the case may be, the failure first occurred.

(2)  This is without prejudice to any lesser period of limitation (and, in Scotland, to any rule that the obligation giving rise to the liability prescribes before the expiry of that period).

## Chapter 3  Overseas branch registers

### 129  Overseas branch registers

(1)  A company having a share capital may, if it transacts business in a country or territory to which this Chapter applies, cause to be kept there a branch register of members resident there (an 'overseas branch register').

(2)  This Chapter applies to—

    (a)  any part of Her Majesty's dominions outside the United Kingdom, the Channel Islands and the Isle of Man, and

    (b)  the countries or territories listed below.

| | |
|---|---|
| Bangladesh | Malaysia |
| Cyprus | Malta |
| Dominica | Nigeria |
| The Gambia | Pakistan |
| Ghana | Seychelles |
| Guyana | Sierra Leone |
| The Hong Kong Special Administrative Region of the People's Republic of China | Singapore |
| India | South Africa |
| Ireland | Sri Lanka |
| Kenya | Swaziland |
| Kiribati | Trinidad and Tobago |
| Lesotho | Uganda |
| Malawi | Zimbabwe |

(3)  The Secretary of State may make provision by regulations as to the circumstances in which a company is to be regarded as keeping a register in a particular country or territory.

(4)  Regulations under this section are subject to negative resolution procedure.

(5)  References—

    (a)  in any Act or instrument (including, in particular, a company's articles) to a dominion register, or

    (b)  in articles registered before 1st November 1929 to a colonial register,

are to be read (unless the context otherwise requires) as a reference to an overseas branch register kept under this section.

### 130  Notice of opening of overseas branch register

(1)  A company that begins to keep an overseas branch register must give notice to the registrar within 14 days of doing so, stating the country or territory in which the register is kept.

(2)  If default is made in complying with subsection (1), an offence is committed by—

    (a)  the company, and

    (b)  every officer of the company who is in default.

(3)  A person guilty of an offence under subsection (2) is liable on summary conviction to a fine not exceeding level 3 on the standard scale and, for continued contravention, a daily default fine not exceeding one-tenth of level 3 on the standard scale.

### 131  Keeping of overseas branch register

(1)  An overseas branch register is regarded as part of the company's register of members ('the main register').

(2)  The Secretary of State may make provision by regulations modifying any provision of Chapter 2 (register of members) as it applies in relation to an overseas branch register.

(3) Regulations under this section are subject to negative resolution procedure.

(4) Subject to the provisions of this Act, a company may by its articles make such provision as it thinks fit as to the keeping of overseas branch registers.

### 132   Register or duplicate to be kept available for inspection in UK

(1) A company that keeps an overseas branch register must keep available for inspection—
  (a) the register, or
  (b) a duplicate of the register duly entered up from time to time,
at the place in the United Kingdom where the company's main register is kept available for inspection.

(2) Any such duplicate is treated for all purposes of this Act as part of the main register.

(3) If default is made in complying with subsection (1), an offence is committed by—
  (a) the company, and
  (b) every officer of the company who is in default.

(4) A person guilty of an offence under subsection (3) is liable on summary conviction to a fine not exceeding level 3 on the standard scale and, for continued contravention, a daily default fine not exceeding one-tenth of level 3 on the standard scale.

### 133   Transactions in shares registered in overseas branch register

(1) Shares registered in an overseas branch register must be distinguished from those registered in the main register.

(2) No transaction with respect to shares registered in an overseas branch register may be registered in any other register.

(3) An instrument of transfer of a share registered in an overseas branch register—
  (a) is regarded as a transfer of property situated outside the United Kingdom, and
  (b) unless executed in a part of the United Kingdom, is exempt from stamp duty.

### 134   Jurisdiction of local courts

(1) A competent court in a country or territory where an overseas branch register is kept may exercise the same jurisdiction as is exercisable by a court in the United Kingdom—
  (a) to rectify the register (see section 125), or
  (b) in relation to a request for inspection or a copy of the register (see section 117).

(2) The offences—
  (a) of refusing inspection or failing to provide a copy of the register (see section 118), and
  (b) of making a false, misleading or deceptive statement in a request for inspection or a copy (see section 119), may be prosecuted summarily before any tribunal having summary criminal jurisdiction in the country or territory where the register is kept.

(3) This section extends only to those countries and territories to which paragraph 3 of Schedule 14 to the Companies Act 1985 (c. 6)(which made similar provision) extended immediately before the coming into force of this Chapter.

### 135   Discontinuance of overseas branch register

(1) A company may discontinue an overseas branch register.

(2) If it does so all the entries in that register must be transferred—
  (a) to some other overseas branch register kept in the same country or territory, or
  (b) to the main register.

(3) The company must give notice to the registrar within 14 days of the discontinuance.

(4) If default is made in complying with subsection (3), an offence is committed by—
  (a) the company, and
  (b) every officer of the company who is in default.

(5) A person guilty of an offence under subsection (4) is liable on summary conviction to a fine not exceeding level 3 on the standard scale and, for continued contravention, a daily default fine not exceeding one-tenth of level 3 on the standard scale.

## Chapter 4   Prohibition on subsidiary being member of its holding company

*General prohibition*

### 136   Prohibition on subsidiary being a member of its holding company

(1) Except as provided by this Chapter—
  (a) a body corporate cannot be a member of a company that is its holding company, and
  (b) any allotment or transfer of shares in a company to its subsidiary is void.

(2) The exceptions are provided for in—
 section 138 (subsidiary acting as personal representative or trustee), and
 section 141 (subsidiary acting as authorised dealer in securities).

### 137   Shares acquired before prohibition became applicable

(1) Where a body corporate became a holder of shares in a company—
  (a) before the relevant date, or

(b) on or after that date and before the commencement of this Chapter in circumstances in which the prohibition in section 23(1) of the Companies Act 1985 or Article 33(1) of the Companies (Northern Ireland) Order 1986 (S.I. 1986/1032 (N.I. 6)) (or any corresponding earlier enactment), as it then had effect, did not apply, or

(c) on or after the commencement of this Chapter in circumstances in which the prohibition in section 136 did not apply,

it may continue to be a member of the company.

(2) The relevant date for the purposes of subsection (1)(a) is—

(a) 1st July 1948 in the case of a company registered in Great Britain, and

(b) 1st April 1961 in the case of a company registered in Northern Ireland.

(3) So long as it is permitted to continue as a member of a company by virtue of this section, an allotment to it of fully paid shares in the company may be validly made by way of capitalisation of reserves of the company.

(4) But, so long as the prohibition in section 136 would (apart from this section) apply, it has no right to vote in respect of the shares mentioned in subsection (1) above, or any shares allotted as mentioned in subsection (3) above, on a written resolution or at meetings of the company or of any class of its members.

### *Subsidiary acting as personal representative or trustee*

### 138 Subsidiary acting as personal representative or trustee

(1) The prohibition in section 136 (prohibition on subsidiary being a member of its holding company) does not apply where the subsidiary is concerned only—

(a) as personal representative, or

(b) as trustee,

unless, in the latter case, the holding company or a subsidiary of it is beneficially interested under the trust.

(2) For the purpose of ascertaining whether the holding company or a subsidiary is so interested, there shall be disregarded—

(a) any interest held only by way of security for the purposes of a transaction entered into by the holding company or subsidiary in the ordinary course of a business that includes the lending of money;

(b) any interest within—

section 139 (interests to be disregarded: residual interest under pension scheme or employees' share scheme), or

section 140 (interests to be disregarded: employer's rights of recovery under pension scheme or employees' share scheme);

(c) any rights that the company or subsidiary has in its capacity as trustee, including in particular—

(i) any right to recover its expenses or be remunerated out of the trust property, and

(ii) any right to be indemnified out of the trust property for any liability incurred by reason of any act or omission in the performance of its duties as trustee.

### 139 Interests to be disregarded: residual interest under pension scheme or employees' share scheme

(1) Where shares in a company are held on trust for the purposes of a pension scheme or employees' share scheme, there shall be disregarded for the purposes of section 138 any residual interest that has not vested in possession.

(2) A 'residual interest' means a right of the company or subsidiary ('the residual beneficiary') to receive any of the trust property in the event of—

(a) all the liabilities arising under the scheme having been satisfied or provided for, or

(b) the residual beneficiary ceasing to participate in the scheme, or

(c) the trust property at any time exceeding what is necessary for satisfying the liabilities arising or expected to arise under the scheme.

(3) In subsection (2)—

(a) the reference to a right includes a right dependent on the exercise of a discretion vested by the scheme in the trustee or another person, and

(b) the reference to liabilities arising under a scheme includes liabilities that have resulted, or may result, from the exercise of any such discretion.

(4) For the purposes of this section a residual interest vests in possession—

(a) in a case within subsection (2)(a), on the occurrence of the event mentioned there (whether or not the amount of the property receivable pursuant to the right is ascertained);

(b) in a case within subsection (2)(b) or (c), when the residual beneficiary becomes entitled to require the trustee to transfer to him any of the property receivable pursuant to the right.

(5) In this section 'pension scheme' means a scheme for the provision of benefits consisting of or including relevant benefits for or in respect of employees or former employees.

(6) In subsection (5)—

    (a) 'relevant benefits' means any pension, lump sum, gratuity or other like benefit given or to be given on retirement or on death or in anticipation of retirement or, in connection with past service, after retirement or death; and

    (b) 'employee' shall be read as if a director of a company were employed by it.

## 140    Interests to be disregarded: employer's rights of recovery under pension scheme or employees' share scheme

(1) Where shares in a company are held on trust for the purposes of a pension scheme or employees' share scheme, there shall be disregarded for the purposes of section 138 any charge or lien on, or set-off against, any benefit or other right or interest under the scheme for the purpose of enabling the employer or former employer of a member of the scheme to obtain the discharge of a monetary obligation due to him from the member.

(2) In the case of a trust for the purposes of a pension scheme there shall also be disregarded any right to receive from the trustee of the scheme, or as trustee of the scheme to retain, an amount that can be recovered or retained, under section 61 of the Pension Schemes Act 1993 (c. 48) or section 57 of the Pension Schemes (Northern Ireland) Act 1993 (c. 49) (deduction of contributions equivalent premium from refund of scheme contributions) or otherwise, as reimbursement or partial reimbursement for any contributions equivalent premium paid in connection with the scheme under Part 3 of that Act.

(3) In this section 'pension scheme' means a scheme for the provision of benefits consisting of or including relevant benefits for or in respect of employees or former employees.

'Relevant benefits' here means any pension, lump sum, gratuity or other like benefit given or to be given on retirement or on death or in anticipation of retirement or, in connection with past service, after retirement or death.

(4) In this section 'employer' and 'employee' shall be read as if a director of a company were employed by it.

### *Subsidiary acting as dealer in securities*

## 141    Subsidiary acting as authorised dealer in securities

(1) The prohibition in section 136 (prohibition on subsidiary being a member of its holding company) does not apply where the shares are held by the subsidiary in the ordinary course of its business as an intermediary.

(2) For this purpose a person is an intermediary if he—

    (a) carries on a bona fide business of dealing in securities,

    (b) is a member of or has access to a regulated market, and

    (c) does not carry on an excluded business.

(3) The following are excluded businesses—

    (a) a business that consists wholly or mainly in the making or managing of investments;

    (b) a business that consists wholly or mainly in, or is carried on wholly or mainly for the purposes of, providing services to persons who are connected with the person carrying on the business;

    (c) a business that consists in insurance business;

    (d) a business that consists in managing or acting as trustee in relation to a pension scheme, or that is carried on by the manager or trustee of such a scheme in connection with or for the purposes of the scheme;

    (e) a business that consists in operating or acting as trustee in relation to a collective investment scheme, or that is carried on by the operator or trustee of such a scheme in connection with and for the purposes of the scheme.

(4) For the purposes of this section—

    (a) the question whether a person is connected with another shall be determined in accordance with section 839 of the Income and Corporation Taxes Act 1988 (c. 1);

    (b) 'collective investment scheme' has the meaning given in section 235 of the Financial Services and Markets Act 2000 (c. 8);

    (c) 'insurance business' means business that consists in the effecting or carrying out of contracts of insurance;

    (d) 'securities' includes—

        (i)  options,

        (ii) futures, and

        (iii) contracts for differences,

        and rights or interests in those investments;

    (e) 'trustee' and 'the operator' in relation to a collective investment scheme shall be construed in accordance with section 237(2) of the Financial Services and Markets Act 2000 (c. 8).

(5) Expressions used in this section that are also used in the provisions regulating activities under the Financial Services and Markets Act 2000 have the same meaning here as they do in those provisions.

See section 22 of that Act, orders made under that section and Schedule 2 to that Act.

**142  Protection of third parties in other cases where subsidiary acting as dealer in securities**

(1)  This section applies where—

(a)  a subsidiary that is a dealer in securities has purportedly acquired shares in its holding company in contravention of the prohibition in section 136, and

(b)  a person acting in good faith has agreed, for value and without notice of the contravention, to acquire shares in the holding company—

(i)  from the subsidiary, or

(ii)  from someone who has purportedly acquired the shares after their disposal by the subsidiary.

(2)  A transfer to that person of the shares mentioned in subsection (1)(a) has the same effect as it would have had if their original acquisition by the subsidiary had not been in contravention of the prohibition.

*Supplementary*

**143  Application of provisions to companies not limited by shares**

In relation to a company other than a company limited by shares, the references in this Chapter to shares shall be read as references to the interest of its members as such, whatever the form of that interest.

**144  Application of provisions to nominees**

The provisions of this Chapter apply to a nominee acting on behalf of a subsidiary as to the subsidiary itself.

# PART 9  EXERCISE OF MEMBERS' RIGHTS

*Effect of provisions in company's articles*

**145  Effect of provisions of articles as to enjoyment or exercise of members' rights**

(1)  This section applies where provision is made by a company's articles enabling a member to nominate another person or persons as entitled to enjoy or exercise all or any specified rights of the member in relation to the company.

(2)  So far as is necessary to give effect to that provision, anything required or authorised by any provision of the Companies Acts to be done by or in relation to the member shall instead be done, or (as the case may be) may instead be done, by or in relation to the nominated person (or each of them) as if he were a member of the company.

(3)  This applies, in particular, to the rights conferred by—

(a)  sections 291 and 293 (right to be sent proposed written resolution);

(b)  section 292 (right to require circulation of written resolution);

(c)  section 303 (right to require directors to call general meeting);

(d)  section 310 (right to notice of general meetings);

(e)  section 314 (right to require circulation of a statement);

(f)  section 324 (right to appoint proxy to act at meeting);

(g)  section 338 (right to require circulation of resolution for AGM of public company); and

(h)  section 423 (right to be sent a copy of annual accounts and reports).

(4)  This section and any such provision as is mentioned in subsection (1)—

(a)  do not confer rights enforceable against the company by anyone other than the member, and

(b)  do not affect the requirements for an effective transfer or other disposition of the whole or part of a member's interest in the company.

*Information rights*

**146  Traded companies: nomination of persons to enjoy information rights**

(1)  This section applies to a company whose shares are admitted to trading on a regulated market.

(2)  A member of such a company who holds shares on behalf of another person may nominate that person to enjoy information rights.

(3)  'Information rights' means—

(a)  the right to receive a copy of all communications that the company sends to its members generally or to any class of its members that includes the person making the nomination, and

(b)  the rights conferred by—

(i)  section 431 or 432 (right to require copies of accounts and reports), and

(ii)  section 1145 (right to require hard copy version of document or information provided in another form).

(4)  The reference in subsection (3)(a) to communications that a company sends to its members generally includes the company's annual accounts and reports.

For the application of section 426 (option to provide summary financial statement) in relation to a person nominated to enjoy information rights, see subsection (5) of that section.

(5) A company need not act on a nomination purporting to relate to certain information rights only.

### 147 Information rights: form in which copies to be provided

(1) This section applies as regards the form in which copies are to be provided to a person nominated under section 146 (nomination of person to enjoy information rights).

(2) If the person to be nominated wishes to receive hard copy communications, he must—

(a) request the person making the nomination to notify the company of that fact, and

(b) provide an address to which such copies may be sent.

This must be done before the nomination is made.

(3) If having received such a request the person making the nomination—

(a) notifies the company that the nominated person wishes to receive hard copy communications, and

(b) provides the company with that address,

the right of the nominated person is to receive hard copy communications accordingly.

(4) This is subject to the provisions of Parts 3 and 4 of Schedule 5 (communications by company) under which the company may take steps to enable it to communicate in electronic form or by means of a website.

(5) If no such notification is given (or no address is provided), the nominated person is taken to have agreed that documents or information may be sent or supplied to him by the company by means of a website.

(6) That agreement—

(a) may be revoked by the nominated person, and

(b) does not affect his right under section 1145 to require a hard copy version of a document or information provided in any other form.

### 148 Termination or suspension of nomination

(1) The following provisions have effect in relation to a nomination under section 146 (nomination of person to enjoy information rights).

(2) The nomination may be terminated at the request of the member or of the nominated person.

(3) The nomination ceases to have effect on the occurrence in relation to the member or the nominated person of any of the following—

(a) in the case of an individual, death or bankruptcy;

(b) in the case of a body corporate, dissolution or the making of an order for the winding up of the body otherwise than for the purposes of reconstruction.

(4) In subsection (3)—

(a) the reference to bankruptcy includes—

(i) the sequestration of a person's estate, and

(ii) a person's estate being the subject of a protected trust deed (within the meaning of the Bankruptcy (Scotland) Act 1985 (c. 66)); and

(b) the reference to the making of an order for winding up is to—

(i) the making of such an order under the Insolvency Act 1986 (c. 45) or the Insolvency (Northern Ireland) Order 1989 (S.I. 1989/2405 (N.I. 19)), or

(ii) any corresponding proceeding under the law of a country or territory outside the United Kingdom.

(5) The effect of any nominations made by a member is suspended at any time when there are more nominated persons than the member has shares in the company.

(6) Where—

(a) the member holds different classes of shares with different information rights, and

(b) there are more nominated persons than he has shares conferring a particular right,

the effect of any nominations made by him is suspended to the extent that they confer that right.

(7) Where the company—

(a) enquires of a nominated person whether he wishes to retain information rights, and

(b) does not receive a response within the period of 28 days beginning with the date on which the company's enquiry was sent,

the nomination ceases to have effect at the end of that period.

Such an enquiry is not to be made of a person more than once in any twelve-month period.

(8) The termination or suspension of a nomination means that the company is not required to act on it.

It does not prevent the company from continuing to do so, to such extent or for such period as it thinks fit.

### 149 Information as to possible rights in relation to voting

(1) This section applies where a company sends a copy of a notice of a meeting to a person nominated under section 146 (nomination of person to enjoy information rights).

(2) The copy of the notice must be accompanied by a statement that—

    (a) he may have a right under an agreement between him and the member by whom he was nominated to be appointed, or to have someone else appointed, as a proxy for the meeting, and

    (b) if he has no such right or does not wish to exercise it, he may have a right under such an agreement to give instructions to the member as to the exercise of voting rights.

(3) Section 325 (notice of meeting to contain statement of member's rights in relation to appointment of proxy) does not apply to the copy, and the company must either—

    (a) omit the notice required by that section, or

    (b) include it but state that it does not apply to the nominated person.

### 150 Information rights: status of rights

(1) This section has effect as regards the rights conferred by a nomination under section 146 (nomination of person to enjoy information rights).

(2) Enjoyment by the nominated person of the rights conferred by the nomination is enforceable against the company by the member as if they were rights conferred by the company's articles.

(3) Any enactment, and any provision of the company's articles, having effect in relation to communications with members has a corresponding effect (subject to any necessary adaptations) in relation to communications with the nominated person.

(4) In particular—

    (a) where under any enactment, or any provision of the company's articles, the members of a company entitled to receive a document or information are determined as at a date or time before it is sent or supplied, the company need not send or supply it to a nominated person—

        (i) whose nomination was received by the company after that date or time, or

        (ii) if that date or time falls in a period of suspension of his nomination; and

    (b) where under any enactment, or any provision of the company's articles, the right of a member to receive a document or information depends on the company having a current address for him, the same applies to any person nominated by him.

(5) The rights conferred by the nomination—

    (a) are in addition to the rights of the member himself, and

    (b) do not affect any rights exercisable by virtue of any such provision as is mentioned in section 145 (provisions of company's articles as to enjoyment or exercise of members' rights).

(6) A failure to give effect to the rights conferred by the nomination does not affect the validity of anything done by or on behalf of the company.

(7) References in this section to the rights conferred by the nomination are to—

    (a) the rights referred to in section 146(3) (information rights), and

    (b) where applicable, the rights conferred by section 147(3) (right to hard copy communications) and section 149 (information as to possible voting rights).

### 151 Information rights: power to amend

(1) The Secretary of State may by regulations amend the provisions of sections 146 to 150 (information rights) so as to—

    (a) extend or restrict the classes of companies to which section 146 applies,

    (b) make other provision as to the circumstances in which a nomination may be made under that section, or

    (c) extend or restrict the rights conferred by such a nomination.

(2) The regulations may make such consequential modifications of any other provisions of this Part, or of any other enactment, as appear to the Secretary of State to be necessary.

(3) Regulations under this section are subject to affirmative resolution procedure.

*Exercise of rights where shares held on behalf of others*

### 152 Exercise of rights where shares held on behalf of others: exercise in different ways

(1) Where a member holds shares in a company on behalf of more than one person—

    (a) rights attached to the shares, and

    (b) rights under any enactment exercisable by virtue of holding the shares, need not all be exercised, and if exercised, need not all be exercised in the same way.

(2) A member who exercises such rights but does not exercise all his rights, must inform the company to what extent he is exercising the rights.

(3) A member who exercises such rights in different ways must inform the company of the ways in which he is exercising them and to what extent they are exercised in each way.

(4) If a member exercises such rights without informing the company—

    (a) that he is not exercising all his rights, or

    (b) that he is exercising his rights in different ways,

the company is entitled to assume that he is exercising all his rights and is exercising them in the same way.

**153    Exercise of rights where shares held on behalf of others: members' requests**

(1) This section applies for the purposes of—

    (a) section 314 (power to require circulation of statement),

    (b) section 338 (public companies: power to require circulation of resolution for AGM),

    (c) section 342 (power to require independent report on poll), and

    (d) section 527 (power to require website publication of audit concerns).

(2) A company is required to act under any of those sections if it receives a request in relation to which the following conditions are met—

    (a) it is made by at least 100 persons;

    (b) it is authenticated by all the persons making it;

    (c) in the case of any of those persons who is not a member of the company, it is accompanied by a statement—

        (i) of the full name and address of a person ('the member') who is a member of the company and holds shares on behalf of that person,

        (ii) that the member is holding those shares on behalf of that person in the course of a business,

        (iii) of the number of shares in the company that the member holds on behalf of that person,

        (iv) of the total amount paid up on those shares,

        (v) that those shares are not held on behalf of anyone else or, if they are, that the other person or persons are not among the other persons making the request,

        (vi) that some or all of those shares confer voting rights that are relevant for the purposes of making a request under the section in question, and

        (vii) that the person has the right to instruct the member how to exercise those rights;

    (d) in the case of any of those persons who is a member of the company, it is accompanied by a statement—

        (i) that he holds shares otherwise than on behalf of another person, or

        (ii) that he holds shares on behalf of one or more other persons but those persons are not among the other persons making the request;

    (e) it is accompanied by such evidence as the company may reasonably require of the matters mentioned in paragraph (c) and (d);

    (f) the total amount of the sums paid up on—

        (i) shares held as mentioned in paragraph (c), and

        (ii) shares held as mentioned in paragraph (d),

        (iii) divided by the number of persons making the request, is not less than £100;

    (g) the request complies with any other requirements of the section in question as to contents, timing and otherwise.

# PART 10  A COMPANY'S DIRECTORS

## Chapter 1  Appointment and removal of directors

### *Requirement to have directors*

**154    Companies required to have directors**

(1) A private company must have at least one director.

(2) A public company must have at least two directors.

**155    Companies required to have at least one director who is a natural person**

(1) A company must have at least one director who is a natural person.

(2) This requirement is met if the office of director is held by a natural person as a corporation sole or otherwise by virtue of an office.

**156    Direction requiring company to make appointment**

(1) If it appears to the Secretary of State that a company is in breach of—

section 154 (requirements as to number of directors), or

section 155 (requirement to have at least one director who is a natural person),

the Secretary of State may give the company a direction under this section.

(2) The direction must specify—

    (a) the statutory requirement the company appears to be in breach of,

    (b) what the company must do in order to comply with the direction, and

    (c) the period within which it must do so.

That period must be not less than one month or more than three months after the date on which the direction is given.

(3) The direction must also inform the company of the consequences of failing to comply.

(4)  Where the company is in breach of section 154 or 155 it must comply with the direction by—

    (a)  making the necessary appointment or appointments, and

    (b)  giving notice of them under section 167,

before the end of the period specified in the direction.

(5)  If the company has already made the necessary appointment or appointments (or so far as it has done so), it must comply with the direction by giving notice of them under section 167 before the end of the period specified in the direction.

(6)  If a company fails to comply with a direction under this section, an offence is committed by—

    (a)  the company, and

    (b)  every officer of the company who is in default.

For this purpose a shadow director is treated as an officer of the company.

(7)  A person guilty of an offence under this section is liable on summary conviction to a fine not exceeding level 5 on the standard scale and, for continued contravention, a daily default fine not exceeding one-tenth of level 5 on the standard scale.

### *Appointment*

### 157  Minimum age for appointment as director

(1)  A person may not be appointed a director of a company unless he has attained the age of 16 years.

(2)  This does not affect the validity of an appointment that is not to take effect until the person appointed attains that age.

(3)  Where the office of director of a company is held by a corporation sole, or otherwise by virtue of another office, the appointment to that other office of a person who has not attained the age of 16 years is not effective also to make him a director of the company until he attains the age of 16 years.

(4)  An appointment made in contravention of this section is void.

(5)  Nothing in this section affects any liability of a person under any provision of the Companies Acts if he—

    (a)  purports to act as director, or

    (b)  acts as a shadow director,

although he could not, by virtue of this section, be validly appointed as a director.

(6)  This section has effect subject to section 158 (power to provide for exceptions from minimum age requirement).

### 158  Power to provide for exceptions from minimum age requirement

(1)  The Secretary of State may make provision by regulations for cases in which a person who has not attained the age of 16 years may be appointed a director of a company.

(2)  The regulations must specify the circumstances in which, and any conditions subject to which, the appointment may be made.

(3)  If the specified circumstances cease to obtain, or any specified conditions cease to be met, a person who was appointed by virtue of the regulations and who has not since attained the age of 16 years ceases to hold office.

(4)  The regulations may make different provision for different parts of the United Kingdom.

This is without prejudice to the general power to make different provision for different cases.

(5)  Regulations under this section are subject to negative resolution procedure.

### 159  Existing under-age directors

(1)  This section applies where—

    (a)  a person appointed a director of a company before section 157 (minimum age for appointment as director) comes into force has not attained the age of 16 when that section comes into force, or

    (b)  the office of director of a company is held by a corporation sole, or otherwise by virtue of another office, and the person appointed to that other office has not attained the age of 16 years when that section comes into force,

and the case is not one excepted from that section by regulations under section 158.

(2)  That person ceases to be a director on section 157 coming into force.

(3)  The company must make the necessary consequential alteration in its register of directors but need not give notice to the registrar of the change.

(4)  If it appears to the registrar (from other information) that a person has ceased by virtue of this section to be a director of a company, the registrar shall note that fact on the register.

### 160  Appointment of directors of public company to be voted on individually

(1)  At a general meeting of a public company a motion for the appointment of two or more persons as directors of the company by a single resolution must not be made unless a resolution that it should be so made has first been agreed to by the meeting without any vote being given against it.

(2)  A resolution moved in contravention of this section is void, whether or not its being so moved was objected to at the time.

But where a resolution so moved is passed, no provision for the automatic reappointment of retiring directors in default of another appointment applies.

(3) For the purposes of this section a motion for approving a person's appointment, or for nominating a person for appointment, is treated as a motion for his appointment.

(4) Nothing in this section applies to a resolution amending the company's articles.

### 161 Validity of acts of directors

(1) The acts of a person acting as a director are valid notwithstanding that it is afterwards discovered—

(a) that there was a defect in his appointment;

(b) that he was disqualified from holding office;

(c) that he had ceased to hold office;

(d) that he was not entitled to vote on the matter in question.

(2) This applies even if the resolution for his appointment is void under section 160 (appointment of directors of public company to be voted on individually).

*Register of directors, etc.*

### 162 Register of directors

(1) Every company must keep a register of its directors.

(2) The register must contain the required particulars (see sections 163, 164 and 166) of each person who is a director of the company.

(3) The register must be kept available for inspection—

(a) at the company's registered office, or

(b) at a place specified in regulations under section 1136.

(4) The company must give notice to the registrar—

(a) of the place at which the register is kept available for inspection, and

(b) of any change in that place,

unless it has at all times been kept at the company's registered office.

(5) The register must be open to the inspection—

(a) of any member of the company without charge, and

(b) of any other person on payment of such fee as may be prescribed.

(6) If default is made in complying with subsection (1), (2) or (3) or if default is made for 14 days in complying with subsection (4), or if an inspection required under subsection (5) is refused, an offence is committed by—

(a) the company, and

(b) every officer of the company who is in default.

For this purpose a shadow director is treated as an officer of the company.

(7) A person guilty of an offence under this section is liable on summary conviction to a fine not exceeding level 5 on the standard scale and, for continued contravention, a daily default fine not exceeding one-tenth of level 5 on the standard scale.

(8) In the case of a refusal of inspection of the register, the court may by order compel an immediate inspection of it.

### 163 Particulars of directors to be registered: individuals

(1) A company's register of directors must contain the following particulars in the case of an individual—

(a) name and any former name;

(b) a service address;

(c) the country or state (or part of the United Kingdom) in which he is usually resident;

(d) nationality;

(e) business occupation (if any);

(f) date of birth.

(2) For the purposes of this section 'name' means a person's Christian name (or other forename) and surname, except that in the case of—

(a) a peer, or

(b) an individual usually known by a title,

the title may be stated instead of his Christian name (or other forename) and surname or in addition to either or both of them.

(3) For the purposes of this section a 'former name' means a name by which the individual was formerly known for business purposes.

Where a person is or was formerly known by more than one such name, each of them must be stated.

(4) It is not necessary for the register to contain particulars of a former name in the following cases—

(a) in the case of a peer or an individual normally known by a British title, where the name is one by which the person was known previous to the adoption of or succession to the title;

(b) in the case of any person, where the former name—
    (i)   was changed or disused before the person attained the age of 16 years, or
    (ii)  has been changed or disused for 20 years or more.
(5)  A person's service address may be stated to be 'The company's registered office'.

### 164   Particulars of directors to be registered: corporate directors and firms

A company's register of directors must contain the following particulars in the case of a body corporate, or a firm that is a legal person under the law by which it is governed—
    (a)  corporate or firm name;
    (b)  registered or principal office;
    (c)  in the case of an EEA company to which the First Company Law Directive (68/151/ EEC) applies, particulars of—
        (i)   the register in which the company file mentioned in Article 3 of that Directive is kept (including details of the relevant state), and
        (ii)  the registration number in that register;
    (d)  in any other case, particulars of—
        (i)   the legal form of the company or firm and the law by which it is governed, and
        (ii)  if applicable, the register in which it is entered (including details of the state) and its registration number in that register.

### 165   Register of directors' residential addresses

(1)  Every company must keep a register of directors' residential addresses.
(2)  The register must state the usual residential address of each of the company's directors.
(3)  If a director's usual residential address is the same as his service address (as stated in the company's register of directors), the register of directors' residential addresses need only contain an entry to that effect.
This does not apply if his service address is stated to be 'The company's registered office'.
(4)  If default is made in complying with this section, an offence is committed by—
    (a)  the company, and
    (b)  every officer of the company who is in default.
For this purpose a shadow director is treated as an officer of the company.
(5)  A person guilty of an offence under this section is liable on summary conviction to a fine not exceeding level 5 on the standard scale and, for continued contravention, a daily default fine not exceeding one-tenth of level 5 on the standard scale.
(6)  This section applies only to directors who are individuals, not where the director is a body corporate or a firm that is a legal person under the law by which it is governed.

### 166   Particulars of directors to be registered: power to make regulations

(1)  The Secretary of State may make provision by regulations amending—
section 163 (particulars of directors to be registered: individuals),
section 164 (particulars of directors to be registered: corporate directors and firms), or
section 165 (register of directors' residential addresses),
so as to add to or remove items from the particulars required to be contained in a company's register of directors or register of directors' residential addresses.
(2)  Regulations under this section are subject to affirmative resolution procedure.

### 167   Duty to notify registrar of changes

(1)  A company must, within the period of 14 days from—
    (a)  a person becoming or ceasing to be a director, or
    (b)  the occurrence of any change in the particulars contained in its register of directors or its register of directors' residential addresses,
give notice to the registrar of the change and of the date on which it occurred.
(2)  Notice of a person having become a director of the company must—
    (a)  contain a statement of the particulars of the new director that are required to be included in the company's register of directors and its register of directors' residential addresses, and
    (b)  be accompanied by a consent, by that person, to act in that capacity.
(3)  Where—
    (a)  a company gives notice of a change of a director's service address as stated in the company's register of directors, and
    (b)  the notice is not accompanied by notice of any resulting change in the particulars contained in the company's register of directors' residential addresses,
the notice must be accompanied by a statement that no such change is required.
(4)  If default is made in complying with this section, an offence is committed by—
    (a)  the company, and
    (b)  every officer of the company who is in default.
For this purpose a shadow director is treated as an officer of the company.

(5)  A person guilty of an offence under this section is liable on summary conviction to a fine not exceeding level 5 on the standard scale and, for continued contravention, a daily default fine not exceeding one-tenth of level 5 on the standard scale.

*Removal*

### 168   Resolution to remove director

(1)  A company may by ordinary resolution at a meeting remove a director before the expiration of his period of office, notwithstanding anything in any agreement between it and him.

(2)  Special notice is required of a resolution to remove a director under this section or to appoint somebody instead of a director so removed at the meeting at which he is removed.

(3)  A vacancy created by the removal of a director under this section, if not filled at the meeting at which he is removed, may be filled as a casual vacancy.

(4)  A person appointed director in place of a person removed under this section is treated, for the purpose of determining the time at which he or any other director is to retire, as if he had become director on the day on which the person in whose place he is appointed was last appointed a director.

(5)  This section is not to be taken—

> (a)  as depriving a person removed under it of compensation or damages payable to him in respect of the termination of his appointment as director or of any appointment terminating with that as director, or
>
> (b)  as derogating from any power to remove a director that may exist apart from this section.

### 169   Director's right to protest against removal

(1)  On receipt of notice of an intended resolution to remove a director under section 168, the company must forthwith send a copy of the notice to the director concerned.

(2)  The director (whether or not a member of the company) is entitled to be heard on the resolution at the meeting.

(3)  Where notice is given of an intended resolution to remove a director under that section, and the director concerned makes with respect to it representations in writing to the company (not exceeding a reasonable length) and requests their notification to members of the company, the company shall, unless the representations are received by it too late for it to do so—

> (a)  in any notice of the resolution given to members of the company state the fact of the representations having been made; and
>
> (b)  send a copy of the representations to every member of the company to whom notice of the meeting is sent (whether before or after receipt of the representations by the company).

(4)  If a copy of the representations is not sent as required by subsection (3) because received too late or because of the company's default, the director may (without prejudice to his right to be heard orally) require that the representations shall be read out at the meeting.

(5)  Copies of the representations need not be sent out and the representations need not be read out at the meeting if, on the application either of the company or of any other person who claims to be aggrieved, the court is satisfied that the rights conferred by this section are being abused.

(6)  The court may order the company's costs (in Scotland, expenses) on an application under subsection (5) to be paid in whole or in part by the director, notwithstanding that he is not a party to the application.

## Chapter 2  General duties of directors

*Introductory*

### 170   Scope and nature of general duties

(1)  The general duties specified in sections 171 to 177 are owed by a director of a company to the company.

(2)  A person who ceases to be a director continues to be subject—

> (a)  to the duty in section 175 (duty to avoid conflicts of interest) as regards the exploitation of any property, information or opportunity of which he became aware at a time when he was a director, and
>
> (b)  to the duty in section 176 (duty not to accept benefits from third parties) as regards things done or omitted by him before he ceased to be a director.

To that extent those duties apply to a former director as to a director, subject to any necessary adaptations.

(3)  The general duties are based on certain common law rules and equitable principles as they apply in relation to directors and have effect in place of those rules and principles as regards the duties owed to a company by a director.

(4)  The general duties shall be interpreted and applied in the same way as common law rules or equitable principles, and regard shall be had to the corresponding common law rules and equitable principles in interpreting and applying the general duties.

(5) The general duties apply to shadow directors where, and to the extent that, the corresponding common law rules or equitable principles so apply.

*The general duties*

## 171  Duty to act within powers

A director of a company must—

    (a)  act in accordance with the company's constitution, and

    (b)  only exercise powers for the purposes for which they are conferred.

## 172  Duty to promote the success of the company

(1) A director of a company must act in the way he considers, in good faith, would be most likely to promote the success of the company for the benefit of its members as a whole, and in doing so have regard (amongst other matters) to—

    (a)  the likely consequences of any decision in the long term,

    (b)  the interests of the company's employees,

    (c)  the need to foster the company's business relationships with suppliers, customers and others,

    (d)  the impact of the company's operations on the community and the environment,

    (e)  the desirability of the company maintaining a reputation for high standards of business conduct, and

    (f)  the need to act fairly as between members of the company.

(2) Where or to the extent that the purposes of the company consist of or include purposes other than the benefit of its members, subsection (1) has effect as if the reference to promoting the success of the company for the benefit of its members were to achieving those purposes.

(3) The duty imposed by this section has effect subject to any enactment or rule of law requiring directors, in certain circumstances, to consider or act in the interests of creditors of the company.

## 173  Duty to exercise independent judgment

(1) A director of a company must exercise independent judgment.

(2) This duty is not infringed by his acting—

    (a)  in accordance with an agreement duly entered into by the company that restricts the future exercise of discretion by its directors, or

    (b)  in a way authorised by the company's constitution.

## 174  Duty to exercise reasonable care, skill and diligence

(1) A director of a company must exercise reasonable care, skill and diligence.

(2) This means the care, skill and diligence that would be exercised by a reasonably diligent person with—

    (a)  the general knowledge, skill and experience that may reasonably be expected of a person carrying out the functions carried out by the director in relation to the company, and

    (b)  the general knowledge, skill and experience that the director has.

## 175  Duty to avoid conflicts of interest

(1) A director of a company must avoid a situation in which he has, or can have, a direct or indirect interest that conflicts, or possibly may conflict, with the interests of the company.

(2) This applies in particular to the exploitation of any property, information or opportunity (and it is immaterial whether the company could take advantage of the property, information or opportunity).

(3) This duty does not apply to a conflict of interest arising in relation to a transaction or arrangement with the company.

(4) This duty is not infringed—

    (a)  if the situation cannot reasonably be regarded as likely to give rise to a conflict of interest; or

    (b)  if the matter has been authorised by the directors.

(5) Authorisation may be given by the directors—

    (a)  where the company is a private company and nothing in the company's constitution invalidates such authorisation, by the matter being proposed to and authorised by the directors; or

    (b)  where the company is a public company and its constitution includes provision enabling the directors to authorise the matter, by the matter being proposed to and authorised by them in accordance with the constitution.

(6) The authorisation is effective only if—

    (a)  any requirement as to the quorum at the meeting at which the matter is considered is met without counting the director in question or any other interested director, and

    (b)  the matter was agreed to without their voting or would have been agreed to if their votes had not been counted.

(7) Any reference in this section to a conflict of interest includes a conflict of interest and duty and a conflict of duties.

### 176    Duty not to accept benefits from third parties

(1)  A director of a company must not accept a benefit from a third party conferred by reason of—

(a)  his being a director, or

(b)  his doing (or not doing) anything as director.

(2)  A 'third party' means a person other than the company, an associated body corporate or a person acting on behalf of the company or an associated body corporate.

(3)  Benefits received by a director from a person by whom his services (as a director or otherwise) are provided to the company are not regarded as conferred by a third party.

(4)  This duty is not infringed if the acceptance of the benefit cannot reasonably be regarded as likely to give rise to a conflict of interest.

(5)  Any reference in this section to a conflict of interest includes a conflict of interest and duty and a conflict of duties.

### 177    Duty to declare interest in proposed transaction or arrangement

(1)  If a director of a company is in any way, directly or indirectly, interested in a proposed transaction or arrangement with the company, he must declare the nature and extent of that interest to the other directors.

(2)  The declaration may (but need not) be made—

(a)  at a meeting of the directors, or

(b)  by notice to the directors in accordance with—

(i)    section 184 (notice in writing), or

(ii)   section 185 (general notice).

(3)  If a declaration of interest under this section proves to be, or becomes, inaccurate or incomplete, a further declaration must be made.

(4)  Any declaration required by this section must be made before the company enters into the transaction or arrangement.

(5)  This section does not require a declaration of an interest of which the director is not aware or where the director is not aware of the transaction or arrangement in question.

For this purpose a director is treated as being aware of matters of which he ought reasonably to be aware.

(6)  A director need not declare an interest—

(a)  if it cannot reasonably be regarded as likely to give rise to a conflict of interest;

(b)  if, or to the extent that, the other directors are already aware of it (and for this purpose the other directors are treated as aware of anything of which they ought reasonably to be aware); or

(c)  if, or to the extent that, it concerns terms of his service contract that have been or are to be considered—

(i)    by a meeting of the directors, or

(ii)   by a committee of the directors appointed for the purpose under the company's constitution.

*Supplementary provisions*

### 178    Civil consequences of breach of general duties

(1)  The consequences of breach (or threatened breach) of sections 171 to 177 are the same as would apply if the corresponding common law rule or equitable principle applied.

(2)  The duties in those sections (with the exception of section 174 (duty to exercise reasonable care, skill and diligence)) are, accordingly, enforceable in the same way as any other fiduciary duty owed to a company by its directors.

### 179    Cases within more than one of the general duties

Except as otherwise provided, more than one of the general duties may apply in any given case.

### 180    Consent, approval or authorisation by members

(1)  In a case where—

(a)  section 175 (duty to avoid conflicts of interest) is complied with by authorisation by the directors, or

(b)  section 177 (duty to declare interest in proposed transaction or arrangement) is complied with,

the transaction or arrangement is not liable to be set aside by virtue of any common law rule or equitable principle requiring the consent or approval of the members of the company.

This is without prejudice to any enactment, or provision of the company's constitution, requiring such consent or approval.

(2)  The application of the general duties is not affected by the fact that the case also falls within Chapter 4 (transactions requiring approval of members), except that where that Chapter applies and—

(a)  approval is given under that Chapter, or

(b)  the matter is one as to which it is provided that approval is not needed, it is not necessary also to comply with section 175 (duty to avoid conflicts of interest) or section 176 (duty not to accept benefits from third parties).

(3) Compliance with the general duties does not remove the need for approval under any applicable provision of Chapter 4 (transactions requiring approval of members).

(4) The general duties—

(a) have effect subject to any rule of law enabling the company to give authority, specifically or generally, for anything to be done (or omitted) by the directors, or any of them, that would otherwise be a breach of duty, and

(b) where the company's articles contain provisions for dealing with conflicts of interest, are not infringed by anything done (or omitted) by the directors, or any of them, in accordance with those provisions.

(5) Otherwise, the general duties have effect (except as otherwise provided or the context otherwise requires) notwithstanding any enactment or rule of law.

**181    Modification of provisions in relation to charitable companies**

(1) In their application to a company that is a charity, the provisions of this Chapter have effect subject to this section.

(2) Section 175 (duty to avoid conflicts of interest) has effect as if—

(a) for subsection (3) (which disapplies the duty to avoid conflicts of interest in the case of a transaction or arrangement with the company) there were substituted—

'(3) This duty does not apply to a conflict of interest arising in relation to a transaction or arrangement with the company if or to the extent that the company's articles allow that duty to be so disapplied, which they may do only in relation to descriptions of transaction or arrangement specified in the company's articles.';

(b) for subsection (5) (which specifies how directors of a company may give authority under that section for a transaction or arrangement) there were substituted—

'(4) Authorisation may be given by the directors where the company's constitution includes provision enabling them to authorise the matter, by the matter being proposed to and authorised by them in accordance with the constitution.'.

(3) Section 180(2)(b) (which disapplies certain duties under this Chapter in relation to cases excepted from requirement to obtain approval by members under Chapter 4) applies only if or to the extent that the company's articles allow those duties to be so disapplied, which they may do only in relation to descriptions of transaction or arrangement specified in the company's articles.

(4) After section 26(5) of the Charities Act 1993 (c. 10) (power of Charity Commission to authorise dealings with charity property etc) insert—

'(5A) In the case of a charity that is a company, an order under this section may authorise an act notwithstanding that it involves the breach of a duty imposed on a director of the company under Chapter 2 of Part 10 of the Companies Act 2006 (general duties of directors).'.

(5) This section does not extend to Scotland.

## Chapter 3   Declaration of interest in existing transaction or arrangement

**182    Declaration of interest in existing transaction or arrangement**

(1) Where a director of a company is in any way, directly or indirectly, interested in a transaction or arrangement that has been entered into by the company, he must declare the nature and extent of the interest to the other directors in accordance with this section.

This section does not apply if or to the extent that the interest has been declared under section 177 (duty to declare interest in proposed transaction or arrangement).

(2) The declaration must be made—

(a) at a meeting of the directors, or

(b) by notice in writing (see section 184), or

(c) by general notice (see section 185).

(3) If a declaration of interest under this section proves to be, or becomes, inaccurate or incomplete, a further declaration must be made.

(4) Any declaration required by this section must be made as soon as is reasonably practicable.

Failure to comply with this requirement does not affect the underlying duty to make the declaration.

(5) This section does not require a declaration of an interest of which the director is not aware or where the director is not aware of the transaction or arrangement in question.

For this purpose a director is treated as being aware of matters of which he ought reasonably to be aware.

(6) A director need not declare an interest under this section—

(a) if it cannot reasonably be regarded as likely to give rise to a conflict of interest;

(b) if, or to the extent that, the other directors are already aware of it (and for this purpose the other directors are treated as aware of anything of which they ought reasonably to be aware); or

    (c) if, or to the extent that, it concerns terms of his service contract that have been or are to be considered—
        (i) by a meeting of the directors, or
        (ii) by a committee of the directors appointed for the purpose under the company's constitution.

### 183   Offence of failure to declare interest

(1) A director who fails to comply with the requirements of section 182 (declaration of interest in existing transaction or arrangement) commits an offence.

(2) A person guilty of an offence under this section is liable—
    (a) on conviction on indictment, to a fine;
    (b) on summary conviction, to a fine not exceeding the statutory maximum.

### 184   Declaration made by notice in writing

(1) This section applies to a declaration of interest made by notice in writing.

(2) The director must send the notice to the other directors.

(3) The notice may be sent in hard copy form or, if the recipient has agreed to receive it in electronic form, in an agreed electronic form.

(4) The notice may be sent—
    (a) by hand or by post, or
    (b) if the recipient has agreed to receive it by electronic means, by agreed electronic means.

(5) Where a director declares an interest by notice in writing in accordance with this section—
    (a) the making of the declaration is deemed to form part of the proceedings at the next meeting of the directors after the notice is given, and
    (b) the provisions of section 248 (minutes of meetings of directors) apply as if the declaration had been made at that meeting.

### 185   General notice treated as sufficient declaration

(1) General notice in accordance with this section is a sufficient declaration of interest in relation to the matters to which it relates.

(2) General notice is notice given to the directors of a company to the effect that the director—
    (a) has an interest (as member, officer, employee or otherwise) in a specified body corporate or firm and is to be regarded as interested in any transaction or arrangement that may, after the date of the notice, be made with that body corporate or firm, or
    (b) is connected with a specified person (other than a body corporate or firm) and is to be regarded as interested in any transaction or arrangement that may, after the date of the notice, be made with that person.

(3) The notice must state the nature and extent of the director's interest in the body corporate or firm or, as the case may be, the nature of his connection with the person.

(4) General notice is not effective unless—
    (a) it is given at a meeting of the directors, or
    (b) the director takes reasonable steps to secure that it is brought up and read at the next meeting of the directors after it is given.

### 186   Declaration of interest in case of company with sole director

(1) Where a declaration of interest under section 182 (duty to declare interest in existing transaction or arrangement) is required of a sole director of a company that is required to have more than one director—
    (a) the declaration must be recorded in writing,
    (b) the making of the declaration is deemed to form part of the proceedings at the next meeting of the directors after the notice is given, and
    (c) the provisions of section 248 (minutes of meetings of directors) apply as if the declaration had been made at that meeting.

(2) Nothing in this section affects the operation of section 231 (contract with sole member who is also a director: terms to be set out in writing or recorded in minutes).

### 187   Declaration of interest in existing transaction by shadow director

(1) The provisions of this Chapter relating to the duty under section 182 (duty to declare interest in existing transaction or arrangement) apply to a shadow director as to a director, but with the following adaptations.

(2) Subsection (2)(a) of that section (declaration at meeting of directors) does not apply.

(3) In section 185 (general notice treated as sufficient declaration), subsection (4) (notice to be given at or brought up and read at meeting of directors) does not apply.

(4) General notice by a shadow director is not effective unless given by notice in writing in accordance with section 184.

## Chapter 4 Transactions with directors requiring approval of members

*Service contracts*

**188 Directors' long-term service contracts: requirement of members' approval**

(1) This section applies to provision under which the guaranteed term of a director's employment—

(a) with the company of which he is a director, or

(b) where he is the director of a holding company, within the group consisting of that company and its subsidiaries,

is, or may be, longer than two years.

(2) A company may not agree to such provision unless it has been approved—

(a) by resolution of the members of the company, and

(b) in the case of a director of a holding company, by resolution of the members of that company.

(3) The guaranteed term of a director's employment is—

(a) the period (if any) during which the director's employment—

(i) is to continue, or may be continued otherwise than at the instance of the company (whether under the original agreement or under a new agreement entered into in pursuance of it), and

(ii) cannot be terminated by the company by notice, or can be so terminated only in specified circumstances, or

(b) in the case of employment terminable by the company by notice, the period of notice required to be given,

or, in the case of employment having a period within paragraph (a) and a period within paragraph (b), the aggregate of those periods.

(4) If more than six months before the end of the guaranteed term of a director's employment the company enters into a further service contract (otherwise than in pursuance of a right conferred, by or under the original contract, on the other party to it), this section applies as if there were added to the guaranteed term of the new contract the unexpired period of the guaranteed term of the original contract.

(5) A resolution approving provision to which this section applies must not be passed unless a memorandum setting out the proposed contract incorporating the provision is made available to members—

(a) in the case of a written resolution, by being sent or submitted to every eligible member at or before the time at which the proposed resolution is sent or submitted to him;

(b) in the case of a resolution at a meeting, by being made available for inspection by members of the company both—

(i) at the company's registered office for not less than 15 days ending with the date of the meeting, and

(ii) at the meeting itself.

(6) No approval is required under this section on the part of the members of a body corporate that—

(a) is not a UK-registered company, or

(b) is a wholly-owned subsidiary of another body corporate.

(7) In this section 'employment' means any employment under a director's service contract.

**189 Directors' long-term service contracts: civil consequences of contravention**

If a company agrees to provision in contravention of section 188 (directors' long-term service contracts: requirement of members' approval)—

(a) the provision is void, to the extent of the contravention, and

(b) the contract is deemed to contain a term entitling the company to terminate it at any time by the giving of reasonable notice.

*Substantial property transactions*

**190 Substantial property transactions: requirement of members' approval**

(1) A company may not enter into an arrangement under which—

(a) a director of the company or of its holding company, or a person connected with such a director, acquires or is to acquire from the company (directly or indirectly) a substantial non-cash asset, or

(b) the company acquires or is to acquire a substantial non-cash asset (directly or indirectly) from such a director or a person so connected,

unless the arrangement has been approved by a resolution of the members of the company or is conditional on such approval being obtained.

For the meaning of 'substantial non-cash asset' see section 191.

(2) If the director or connected person is a director of the company's holding company or a person connected with such a director, the arrangement must also have been approved by a resolution of the members of the holding company or be conditional on such approval being obtained.

(3) A company shall not be subject to any liability by reason of a failure to obtain approval required by this section.

(4) No approval is required under this section on the part of the members of a body corporate that—

    (a) is not a UK-registered company, or

    (b) is a wholly-owned subsidiary of another body corporate.

(5) For the purposes of this section—

    (a) an arrangement involving more than one non-cash asset, or

    (b) an arrangement that is one of a series involving non-cash assets,

shall be treated as if they involved a non-cash asset of a value equal to the aggregate value of all the non-cash assets involved in the arrangement or, as the case may be, the series.

(6) This section does not apply to a transaction so far as it relates—

    (a) to anything to which a director of a company is entitled under his service contract, or

    (b) to payment for loss of office as defined in section 215 (payments requiring members' approval).

### 191 Meaning of 'substantial'

(1) This section explains what is meant in section 190 (requirement of approval for substantial property transactions) by a 'substantial' non-cash asset.

(2) An asset is a substantial asset in relation to a company if its value—

    (a) exceeds 10% of the company's asset value and is more than £5,000, or

    (b) exceeds £100,000.

(3) For this purpose a company's 'asset value' at any time is—

    (a) the value of the company's net assets determined by reference to its most recent statutory accounts, or

    (b) if no statutory accounts have been prepared, the amount of the company's called-up share capital.

(4) A company's 'statutory accounts' means its annual accounts prepared in accordance with Part 15, and its 'most recent' statutory accounts means those in relation to which the time for sending them out to members (see section 424) is most recent.

(5) Whether an asset is a substantial asset shall be determined as at the time the arrangement is entered into.

### 192 Exception for transactions with members or other group companies

Approval is not required under section 190 (requirement of members' approval for substantial property transactions)—

    (a) for a transaction between a company and a person in his character as a member of that company, or

    (b) for a transaction between—

        (i) a holding company and its wholly-owned subsidiary, or

        (ii) two wholly-owned subsidiaries of the same holding company.

### 193 Exception in case of company in winding up or administration

(1) This section applies to a company—

    (a) that is being wound up (unless the winding up is a members' voluntary winding up), or

    (b) that is in administration within the meaning of Schedule B1 to the Insolvency Act 1986 (c. 45) or the Insolvency (Northern Ireland) Order 1989 (S.I. 1989/2405 (N.I. 19)).

(2) Approval is not required under section 190 (requirement of members' approval for substantial property transactions)—

    (a) on the part of the members of a company to which this section applies, or

    (b) for an arrangement entered into by a company to which this section applies.

### 194 Exception for transactions on recognised investment exchange

(1) Approval is not required under section 190 (requirement of members' approval for substantial property transactions) for a transaction on a recognised investment exchange effected by a director, or a person connected with him, through the agency of a person who in relation to the transaction acts as an independent broker.

(2) For this purpose—

    (a) 'independent broker' means a person who, independently of the director or any person connected with him, selects the person with whom the transaction is to be effected; and

    (b) 'recognised investment exchange' has the same meaning as in Part 18 of the Financial Services and Markets Act 2000 (c. 8).

### 195   Property transactions: civil consequences of contravention

(1)  This section applies where a company enters into an arrangement in contravention of section 190 (requirement of members' approval for substantial property transactions).

(2)  The arrangement, and any transaction entered into in pursuance of the arrangement (whether by the company or any other person), is voidable at the instance of the company, unless—

   (a)  restitution of any money or other asset that was the subject matter of the arrangement or transaction is no longer possible,

   (b)  the company has been indemnified in pursuance of this section by any other persons for the loss or damage suffered by it, or

   (c)  rights acquired in good faith, for value and without actual notice of the contravention by a person who is not a party to the arrangement or transaction would be affected by the avoidance.

(3)  Whether or not the arrangement or any such transaction has been avoided, each of the persons specified in subsection (4) is liable—

   (a)  to account to the company for any gain that he has made directly or indirectly by the arrangement or transaction, and

   (b)  (jointly and severally with any other person so liable under this section) to indemnify the company for any loss or damage resulting from the arrangement or transaction.

(4)  The persons so liable are—

   (a)  any director of the company or of its holding company with whom the company entered into the arrangement in contravention of section 190,

   (b)  any person with whom the company entered into the arrangement in contravention of that section who is connected with a director of the company or of its holding company,

   (c)  the director of the company or of its holding company with whom any such person is connected, and

   (d)  any other director of the company who authorised the arrangement or any transaction entered into in pursuance of such an arrangement.

(5)  Subsections(3) and(4) are subject to the following two subsections.

(6)  In the case of an arrangement entered into by a company in contravention of section 190 with a person connected with a director of the company or of its holding company, that director is not liable by virtue of subsection (4)(c) if he shows that he took all reasonable steps to secure the company's compliance with that section.

(7)  In any case—

   (a)  a person so connected is not liable by virtue of subsection (4)(b), and

   (b)  a director is not liable by virtue of subsection (4)(d),

if he shows that, at the time the arrangement was entered into, he did not know the relevant circumstances constituting the contravention.

(8)  Nothing in this section shall be read as excluding the operation of any other enactment or rule of law by virtue of which the arrangement or transaction may be called in question or any liability to the company may arise.

### 196   Property transactions: effect of subsequent affirmation

Where a transaction or arrangement is entered into by a company in contravention of section 190 (requirement of members' approval) but, within a reasonable period, it is affirmed—

   (a)  in the case of a contravention of subsection (1) of that section, by resolution of the members of the company, and

   (b)  in the case of a contravention of subsection (2) of that section, by resolution of the members of the holding company,

the transaction or arrangement may no longer be avoided under section 195.

*Loans, quasi-loans and credit transactions*

### 197   Loans to directors: requirement of members' approval

(1)  A company may not—

   (a)  make a loan to a director of the company or of its holding company, or

   (b)  give a guarantee or provide security in connection with a loan made by any person to such a director,

unless the transaction has been approved by a resolution of the members of the company.

(2)  If the director is a director of the company's holding company, the transaction must also have been approved by a resolution of the members of the holding company.

(3)  A resolution approving a transaction to which this section applies must not be passed unless a memorandum setting out the matters mentioned in subsection (4) is made available to members—

   (a)  in the case of a written resolution, by being sent or submitted to every eligible member at or before the time at which the proposed resolution is sent or submitted to him;

   (b)  in the case of a resolution at a meeting, by being made available for inspection by members of the company both—

(i)   at the company's registered office for not less than 15 days ending with the date of the meeting, and

(ii)  at the meeting itself.

(4) The matters to be disclosed are—

(a) the nature of the transaction,

(b) the amount of the loan and the purpose for which it is required, and

(c) the extent of the company's liability under any transaction connected with the loan.

(5) No approval is required under this section on the part of the members of a body corporate that—

(a) is not a UK-registered company, or

(b) is a wholly-owned subsidiary of another body corporate.

### 198   Quasi-loans to directors: requirement of members' approval

(1) This section applies to a company if it is—

(a) a public company, or

(b) a company associated with a public company.

(2) A company to which this section applies may not—

(a) make a quasi-loan to a director of the company or of its holding company, or

(b) give a guarantee or provide security in connection with a quasi-loan made by any person to such a director,

unless the transaction has been approved by a resolution of the members of the company.

(3) If the director is a director of the company's holding company, the transaction must also have been approved by a resolution of the members of the holding company.

(4) A resolution approving a transaction to which this section applies must not be passed unless a memorandum setting out the matters mentioned in subsection (5) is made available to members—

(a) in the case of a written resolution, by being sent or submitted to every eligible member at or before the time at which the proposed resolution is sent or submitted to him;

(b) in the case of a resolution at a meeting, by being made available for inspection by members of the company both—

(i)   at the company's registered office for not less than 15 days ending with the date of the meeting, and

(ii)  at the meeting itself.

(5) The matters to be disclosed are—

(a) the nature of the transaction,

(b) the amount of the quasi-loan and the purpose for which it is required, and

(c) the extent of the company's liability under any transaction connected with the quasi-loan.

(6) No approval is required under this section on the part of the members of a body corporate that—

(a) is not a UK-registered company, or

(b) is a wholly-owned subsidiary of another body corporate.

### 199   Meaning of 'quasi-loan' and related expressions

(1) A 'quasi-loan' is a transaction under which one party ('the creditor') agrees to pay, or pays otherwise than in pursuance of an agreement, a sum for another ('the borrower') or agrees to reimburse, or reimburses otherwise than in pursuance of an agreement, expenditure incurred by another party for another ('the borrower')—

(a) on terms that the borrower (or a person on his behalf) will reimburse the creditor; or

(b) in circumstances giving rise to a liability on the borrower to reimburse the creditor.

(2) Any reference to the person to whom a quasi-loan is made is a reference to the borrower.

(3) The liabilities of the borrower under a quasi-loan include the liabilities of any person who has agreed to reimburse the creditor on behalf of the borrower.

### 200   Loans or quasi-loans to persons connected with directors: requirement of members' approval

(1) This section applies to a company if it is—

(a) a public company, or

(b) a company associated with a public company.

(2) A company to which this section applies may not—

(a) make a loan or quasi-loan to a person connected with a director of the company or of its holding company, or

(b) give a guarantee or provide security in connection with a loan or quasi-loan made by any person to a person connected with such a director,

unless the transaction has been approved by a resolution of the members of the company.

(3) If the connected person is a person connected with a director of the company's holding company, the transaction must also have been approved by a resolution of the members of the holding company.

(4) A resolution approving a transaction to which this section applies must not be passed unless a memorandum setting out the matters mentioned in subsection (5) is made available to members—

    (a) in the case of a written resolution, by being sent or submitted to every eligible member at or before the time at which the proposed resolution is sent or submitted to him;

    (b) in the case of a resolution at a meeting, by being made available for inspection by members of the company both—

        (i) at the company's registered office for not less than 15 days ending with the date of the meeting, and

        (ii) at the meeting itself.

(5) The matters to be disclosed are—

    (a) the nature of the transaction,

    (b) the amount of the loan or quasi-loan and the purpose for which it is required, and

    (c) the extent of the company's liability under any transaction connected with the loan or quasi-loan.

(6) No approval is required under this section on the part of the members of a body corporate that—

    (a) is not a UK-registered company, or

    (b) is a wholly-owned subsidiary of another body corporate.

### 201 Credit transactions: requirement of members' approval

(1) This section applies to a company if it is—

    (a) a public company, or

    (b) a company associated with a public company.

(2) A company to which this section applies may not—

    (a) enter into a credit transaction as creditor for the benefit of a director of the company or of its holding company, or a person connected with such a director, or

    (b) give a guarantee or provide security in connection with a credit transaction entered into by any person for the benefit of such a director, or a person connected with such a director,

unless the transaction (that is, the credit transaction, the giving of the guarantee or the provision of security, as the case may be) has been approved by a resolution of the members of the company.

(3) If the director or connected person is a director of its holding company or a person connected with such a director, the transaction must also have been approved by a resolution of the members of the holding company.

(4) A resolution approving a transaction to which this section applies must not be passed unless a memorandum setting out the matters mentioned in subsection (5) is made available to members—

    (a) in the case of a written resolution, by being sent or submitted to every eligible member at or before the time at which the proposed resolution is sent or submitted to him;

    (b) in the case of a resolution at a meeting, by being made available for inspection by members of the company both—

        (i) at the company's registered office for not less than 15 days ending with the date of the meeting, and

        (ii) at the meeting itself.

(5) The matters to be disclosed are—

    (a) the nature of the transaction,

    (b) the value of the credit transaction and the purpose for which the land, goods or services sold or otherwise disposed of, leased, hired or supplied under the credit transaction are required, and

    (c) the extent of the company's liability under any transaction connected with the credit transaction.

(6) No approval is required under this section on the part of the members of a body corporate that—

    (a) is not a UK-registered company, or

    (b) is a wholly-owned subsidiary of another body corporate.

### 202 Meaning of 'credit transaction'

(1) A 'credit transaction' is a transaction under which one party ('the creditor')—

    (a) supplies any goods or sells any land under a hire-purchase agreement or a conditional sale agreement,

    (b) leases or hires any land or goods in return for periodical payments, or

    (c) otherwise disposes of land or supplies goods or services on the understanding that payment (whether in a lump sum or instalments or by way of periodical payments or otherwise) is to be deferred.

(2) Any reference to the person for whose benefit a credit transaction is entered into is to the person to whom goods, land or services are supplied, sold, leased, hired or otherwise disposed of under the transaction.

(3) In this section—

'conditional sale agreement' has the same meaning as in the Consumer Credit Act 1974 (c.39); and

'services' means anything other than goods or land.

### 203   Related arrangements: requirement of members' approval

(1)  A company may not—

    (a)  take part in an arrangement under which—

        (i)   another person enters into a transaction that, if it had been entered into by the company, would have required approval under section 197, 198, 200 or 201, and

        (ii)  that person, in pursuance of the arrangement, obtains a benefit from the company or a body corporate associated with it, or

    (b)  arrange for the assignment to it, or assumption by it, of any rights, obligations or liabilities under a transaction that, if it had been entered into by the company, would have required such approval,

unless the arrangement in question has been approved by a resolution of the members of the company.

(2)  If the director or connected person for whom the transaction is entered into is a director of its holding company or a person connected with such a director, the arrangement must also have been approved by a resolution of the members of the holding company.

(3)  A resolution approving an arrangement to which this section applies must not be passed unless a memorandum setting out the matters mentioned in subsection (4) is made available to members—

    (a)  in the case of a written resolution, by being sent or submitted to every eligible member at or before the time at which the proposed resolution is sent or submitted to him;

    (b)  in the case of a resolution at a meeting, by being made available for inspection by members of the company both—

        (i)   at the company's registered office for not less than 15 days ending with the date of the meeting, and

        (ii)  at the meeting itself.

(4)  The matters to be disclosed are—

    (a)  the matters that would have to be disclosed if the company were seeking approval of the transaction to which the arrangement relates,

    (b)  the nature of the arrangement, and

    (c)  the extent of the company's liability under the arrangement or any transaction connected with it.

(5)  No approval is required under this section on the part of the members of a body corporate that—

    (a)  is not a UK-registered company, or

    (b)  is a wholly-owned subsidiary of another body corporate.

(6)  In determining for the purposes of this section whether a transaction is one that would have required approval under section 197, 198, 200 or 201 if it had been entered into by the company, the transaction shall be treated as having been entered into on the date of the arrangement.

### 204   Exception for expenditure on company business

(1)  Approval is not required under section 197, 198, 200 or 201 (requirement of members' approval for loans etc) for anything done by a company—

    (a)  to provide a director of the company or of its holding company, or a person connected with any such director, with funds to meet expenditure incurred or to be incurred by him—

        (i)   for the purposes of the company, or

        (ii)  for the purpose of enabling him properly to perform his duties as an officer of the company, or

    (b)  to enable any such person to avoid incurring such expenditure.

(2)  This section does not authorise a company to enter into a transaction if the aggregate of—

    (a)  the value of the transaction in question, and

    (b)  the value of any other relevant transactions or arrangements,

exceeds £50,000.

### 205   Exception for expenditure on defending proceedings etc.

(1)  Approval is not required under section 197, 198, 200 or 201 (requirement of members' approval for loans etc) for anything done by a company—

    (a)  to provide a director of the company or of its holding company with funds to meet expenditure incurred or to be incurred by him—

        (i)   in defending any criminal or civil proceedings in connection with any alleged negligence, default, breach of duty or breach of trust by him in relation to the company or an associated company, or

        (ii)  in connection with an application for relief (see subsection (5)), or

    (b)  to enable any such director to avoid incurring such expenditure,

if it is done on the following terms.

(2)  The terms are—

    (a)  that the loan is to be repaid, or (as the case may be) any liability of the company incurred under any transaction connected with the thing done is to be discharged, in the event of—

    (i) the director being convicted in the proceedings,

    (ii) judgment being given against him in the proceedings, or

    (iii) the court refusing to grant him relief on the application; and

   (b) that it is to be so repaid or discharged not later than—

    (i) the date when the conviction becomes final,

    (ii) the date when the judgment becomes final, or

    (iii) the date when the refusal of relief becomes final.

 (3) For this purpose a conviction, judgment or refusal of relief becomes final—

   (a) if not appealed against, at the end of the period for bringing an appeal;

   (b) if appealed against, when the appeal (or any further appeal) is disposed of.

 (4) An appeal is disposed of—

   (a) if it is determined and the period for bringing any further appeal has ended, or

   (b) if it is abandoned or otherwise ceases to have effect.

 (5) The reference in subsection (1)(a)(ii) to an application for relief is to an application for relief under—

  section 661(3) or (4) (power of court to grant relief in case of acquisition of shares by innocent nominee), or

  section 1157 (general power of court to grant relief in case of honest and reasonable conduct).

## 206 Exception for expenditure in connection with regulatory action or investigation

Approval is not required under section 197, 198, 200 or 201 (requirement of members' approval for loans etc) for anything done by a company—

   (a) to provide a director of the company or of its holding company with funds to meet expenditure incurred or to be incurred by him in defending himself—

    (i) in an investigation by a regulatory authority, or

    (ii) against action proposed to be taken by a regulatory authority,

    in connection with any alleged negligence, default, breach of duty or breach of trust by him in relation to the company or an associated company, or

   (b) to enable any such director to avoid incurring such expenditure.

## 207 Exceptions for minor and business transactions

 (1) Approval is not required under section 197, 198 or 200 for a company to make a loan or quasi-loan, or to give a guarantee or provide security in connection with a loan or quasi-loan, if the aggregate of—

   (a) the value of the transaction, and

   (b) the value of any other relevant transactions or arrangements,

does not exceed £10,000.

 (2) Approval is not required under section 201 for a company to enter into a credit transaction, or to give a guarantee or provide security in connection with a credit transaction, if the aggregate of—

   (a) the value of the transaction (that is, of the credit transaction, guarantee or security), and

   (b) the value of any other relevant transactions or arrangements,

does not exceed £15,000.

 (3) Approval is not required under section 201 for a company to enter into a credit transaction, or to give a guarantee or provide security in connection with a credit transaction, if—

   (a) the transaction is entered into by the company in the ordinary course of the company's business, and

   (b) the value of the transaction is not greater, and the terms on which it is entered into are not more favourable, than it is reasonable to expect the company would have offered to, or in respect of, a person of the same financial standing but unconnected with the company.

## 208 Exceptions for intra-group transactions

 (1) Approval is not required under section 197, 198 or 200 for—

   (a) the making of a loan or quasi-loan to an associated body corporate, or

   (b) the giving of a guarantee or provision of security in connection with a loan or quasi-loan made to an associated body corporate.

 (2) Approval is not required under section 201—

   (a) to enter into a credit transaction as creditor for the benefit of an associated body corporate, or

   (b) to give a guarantee or provide security in connection with a credit transaction entered into by any person for the benefit of an associated body corporate.

## 209 Exceptions for money-lending companies

 (1) Approval is not required under section 197, 198 or 200 for the making of a loan or quasi-loan, or the giving of a guarantee or provision of security in connection with a loan or quasi-loan, by a money-lending company if—

   (a) the transaction (that is, the loan, quasi-loan, guarantee or security) is entered into by the company in the ordinary course of the company's business, and

(b) the value of the transaction is not greater, and its terms are not more favourable, than it is reasonable to expect the company would have offered to a person of the same financial standing but unconnected with the company.

(2) A 'money-lending company' means a company whose ordinary business includes the making of loans or quasi-loans, or the giving of guarantees or provision of security in connection with loans or quasi-loans.

(3) The condition specified in subsection (1)(b) does not of itself prevent a company from making a home loan—

(a) to a director of the company or of its holding company, or

(b) to an employee of the company,

if loans of that description are ordinarily made by the company to its employees and the terms of the loan in question are no more favourable than those on which such loans are ordinarily made.

(4) For the purposes of subsection (3) a 'home loan' means a loan—

(a) for the purpose of facilitating the purchase, for use as the only or main residence of the person to whom the loan is made, of the whole or part of any dwelling-house together with any land to be occupied and enjoyed with it,

(b) for the purpose of improving a dwelling-house or part of a dwelling-house so used or any land occupied and enjoyed with it, or

(c) in substitution for any loan made by any person and falling within paragraph (a) or (b).

## 210    Other relevant transactions or arrangements

(1) This section has effect for determining what are 'other relevant transactions or arrangements' for the purposes of any exception to section 197, 198, 200 or 201.

In the following provisions 'the relevant exception' means the exception for the purposes of which that falls to be determined.

(2) Other relevant transactions or arrangements are those previously entered into, or entered into at the same time as the transaction or arrangement in question in relation to which the following conditions are met.

(3) Where the transaction or arrangement in question is entered into—

(a) for a director of the company entering into it, or

(b) for a person connected with such a director,

the conditions are that the transaction or arrangement was (or is) entered into for that director, or a person connected with him, by virtue of the relevant exception by that company or by any of its subsidiaries.

(4) Where the transaction or arrangement in question is entered into—

(a) for a director of the holding company of the company entering into it, or

(b) for a person connected with such a director,

the conditions are that the transaction or arrangement was (or is) entered into for that director, or a person connected with him, by virtue of the relevant exception by the holding company or by any of its subsidiaries.

(5) A transaction or arrangement entered into by a company that at the time it was entered into—

(a) was a subsidiary of the company entering into the transaction or arrangement in question, or

(b) was a subsidiary of that company's holding company,

is not a relevant transaction or arrangement if, at the time the question arises whether the transaction or arrangement in question falls within a relevant exception, it is no longer such a subsidiary.

## 211    The value of transactions and arrangements

(1) For the purposes of sections 197 to 214 (loans etc.)—

(a) the value of a transaction or arrangement is determined as follows, and

(b) the value of any other relevant transaction or arrangement is taken to be the value so determined reduced by any amount by which the liabilities of the person for whom the transaction or arrangement was made have been reduced.

(2) The value of a loan is the amount of its principal.

(3) The value of a quasi-loan is the amount, or maximum amount, that the person to whom the quasi-loan is made is liable to reimburse the creditor.

(4) The value of a credit transaction is the price that it is reasonable to expect could be obtained for the goods, services or land to which the transaction relates if they had been supplied (at the time the transaction is entered into) in the ordinary course of business and on the same terms (apart from price) as they have been supplied, or are to be supplied, under the transaction in question.

(5) The value of a guarantee or security is the amount guaranteed or secured.

(6) The value of an arrangement to which section 203 (related arrangements) applies is the value of the transaction to which the arrangement relates.

(7) If the value of a transaction or arrangement is not capable of being expressed as a specific sum of money—

(a) whether because the amount of any liability arising under the transaction or arrangement is unascertainable, or for any other reason, and

(b) whether or not any liability under the transaction or arrangement has been reduced,

its value is deemed to exceed £50,000.

### 212  The person for whom a transaction or arrangement is entered into

For the purposes of sections 197 to 214 (loans etc) the person for whom a transaction or arrangement is entered into is—

(a) in the case of a loan or quasi-loan, the person to whom it is made;

(b) in the case of a credit transaction, the person to whom goods, land or services are supplied, sold, hired, leased or otherwise disposed of under the transaction;

(c) in the case of a guarantee or security, the person for whom the transaction is made in connection with which the guarantee or security is entered into;

(d) in the case of an arrangement within section 203 (related arrangements), the person for whom the transaction is made to which the arrangement relates.

### 213  Loans etc.: civil consequences of contravention

(1) This section applies where a company enters into a transaction or arrangement in contravention of section 197, 198, 200, 201 or 203 (requirement of members' approval for loans etc).

(2) The transaction or arrangement is voidable at the instance of the company, unless—

(a) restitution of any money or other asset that was the subject matter of the transaction or arrangement is no longer possible,

(b) the company has been indemnified for any loss or damage resulting from the transaction or arrangement, or

(c) rights acquired in good faith, for value and without actual notice of the contravention by a person who is not a party to the transaction or arrangement would be affected by the avoidance.

(3) Whether or not the transaction or arrangement has been avoided, each of the persons specified in subsection (4) is liable—

(a) to account to the company for any gain that he has made directly or indirectly by the transaction or arrangement, and

(b) (jointly and severally with any other person so liable under this section) to indemnify the company for any loss or damage resulting from the transaction or arrangement.

(4) The persons so liable are—

(a) any director of the company or of its holding company with whom the company entered into the transaction or arrangement in contravention of section 197, 198, 201 or 203,

(b) any person with whom the company entered into the transaction or arrangement in contravention of any of those sections who is connected with a director of the company or of its holding company,

(c) the director of the company or of its holding company with whom any such person is connected, and

(d) any other director of the company who authorised the transaction or arrangement.

(5) Subsections (3) and (4) are subject to the following two subsections.

(6) In the case of a transaction or arrangement entered into by a company in contravention of section 200, 201 or 203 with a person connected with a director of the company or of its holding company, that director is not liable by virtue of subsection (4)(c) if he shows that he took all reasonable steps to secure the company's compliance with the section concerned.

(7) In any case—

(a) a person so connected is not liable by virtue of subsection (4)(b), and

(b) a director is not liable by virtue of subsection (4)(d),

if he shows that, at the time the transaction or arrangement was entered into, he did not know the relevant circumstances constituting the contravention.

(8) Nothing in this section shall be read as excluding the operation of any other enactment or rule of law by virtue of which the transaction or arrangement may be called in question or any liability to the company may arise.

### 214  Loans etc.: effect of subsequent affirmation

Where a transaction or arrangement is entered into by a company in contravention of section 197, 198, 200, 201 or 203 (requirement of members' approval for loans etc.) but, within a reasonable period, it is affirmed—

(a) in the case of a contravention of the requirement for a resolution of the members of the company, by a resolution of the members of the company, and

(b) in the case of a contravention of the requirement for a resolution of the members of the company's holding company, by a resolution of the members of the holding company,

the transaction or arrangement may no longer be avoided under section 213.

*Payments for loss of office*

### 215    Payments for loss of office

(1)  In this Chapter a 'payment for loss of office' means a payment made to a director or past director of a company—

    (a)  by way of compensation for loss of office as director of the company,

    (b)  by way of compensation for loss, while director of the company or in connection with his ceasing to be a director of it, of—

        (i)   any other office or employment in connection with the management of the affairs of the company, or

        (ii)  any office (as director or otherwise) or employment in connection with the management of the affairs of any subsidiary undertaking of the company,

    (c)  as consideration for or in connection with his retirement from his office as director of the company, or

    (d)  as consideration for or in connection with his retirement, while director of the company or in connection with his ceasing to be a director of it, from—

        (i)   any other office or employment in connection with the management of the affairs of the company, or

        (ii)  any office (as director or otherwise) or employment in connection with the management of the affairs of any subsidiary undertaking of the company.

(2)  The references to compensation and consideration include benefits otherwise than in cash and references in this Chapter to payment have a corresponding meaning.

(3)  For the purposes of sections 217 to 221 (payments requiring members' approval)—

    (a)  payment to a person connected with a director, or

    (b)  payment to any person at the direction of, or for the benefit of, a director or a person connected with him,

is treated as payment to the director.

(4)  References in those sections to payment by a person include payment by another person at the direction of, or on behalf of, the person referred to.

### 216    Amounts taken to be payments for loss of office

(1)  This section applies where in connection with any such transfer as is mentioned in section 218 or 219 (payment in connection with transfer of undertaking, property or shares) a director of the company—

    (a)  is to cease to hold office, or

    (b)  is to cease to be the holder of—

        (i)   any other office or employment in connection with the management of the affairs of the company, or

        (ii)  any office (as director or otherwise) or employment in connection with the management of the affairs of any subsidiary undertaking of the company.

(2)  If in connection with any such transfer—

    (a)  the price to be paid to the director for any shares in the company held by him is in excess of the price which could at the time have been obtained by other holders of like shares, or

    (b)  any valuable consideration is given to the director by a person other than the company,

the excess or, as the case may be, the money value of the consideration is taken for the purposes of those sections to have been a payment for loss of office.

### 217    Payment by company: requirement of members' approval

(1)  A company may not make a payment for loss of office to a director of the company unless the payment has been approved by a resolution of the members of the company.

(2)  A company may not make a payment for loss of office to a director of its holding company unless the payment has been approved by a resolution of the members of each of those companies.

(3)  A resolution approving a payment to which this section applies must not be passed unless a memorandum setting out particulars of the proposed payment (including its amount) is made available to the members of the company whose approval is sought—

    (a)  in the case of a written resolution, by being sent or submitted to every eligible member at or before the time at which the proposed resolution is sent or submitted to him;

    (b)  in the case of a resolution at a meeting, by being made available for inspection by the members both—

        (i)   at the company's registered office for not less than 15 days ending with the date of the meeting, and

        (ii)  at the meeting itself.

(4)  No approval is required under this section on the part of the members of a body corporate that—

    (a)  is not a UK-registered company, or

    (b)  is a wholly-owned subsidiary of another body corporate.

### 218 Payment in connection with transfer of undertaking etc.: requirement of members' approval

(1) No payment for loss of office may be made by any person to a director of a company in connection with the transfer of the whole or any part of the undertaking or property of the company unless the payment has been approved by a resolution of the members of the company.

(2) No payment for loss of office may be made by any person to a director of a company in connection with the transfer of the whole or any part of the undertaking or property of a subsidiary of the company unless the payment has been approved by a resolution of the members of each of the companies.

(3) A resolution approving a payment to which this section applies must not be passed unless a memorandum setting out particulars of the proposed payment (including its amount) is made available to the members of the company whose approval is sought—

(a) in the case of a written resolution, by being sent or submitted to every eligible member at or before the time at which the proposed resolution is sent or submitted to him;

(b) in the case of a resolution at a meeting, by being made available for inspection by the members both—

(i) at the company's registered office for not less than 15 days ending with the date of the meeting, and

(ii) at the meeting itself.

(4) No approval is required under this section on the part of the members of a body corporate that—

(a) is not a UK-registered company, or

(b) is a wholly-owned subsidiary of another body corporate.

(5) A payment made in pursuance of an arrangement—

(a) entered into as part of the agreement for the transfer in question, or within one year before or two years after that agreement, and

(b) to which the company whose undertaking or property is transferred, or any person to whom the transfer is made, is privy,

is presumed, except in so far as the contrary is shown, to be a payment to which this section applies.

### 219 Payment in connection with share transfer: requirement of members' approval

(1) No payment for loss of office may be made by any person to a director of a company in connection with a transfer of shares in the company, or in a subsidiary of the company, resulting from a takeover bid unless the payment has been approved by a resolution of the relevant shareholders.

(2) The relevant shareholders are the holders of the shares to which the bid relates and any holders of shares of the same class as any of those shares.

(3) A resolution approving a payment to which this section applies must not be passed unless a memorandum setting out particulars of the proposed payment (including its amount) is made available to the members of the company whose approval is sought—

(a) in the case of a written resolution, by being sent or submitted to every eligible member at or before the time at which the proposed resolution is sent or submitted to him;

(b) in the case of a resolution at a meeting, by being made available for inspection by the members both—

(i) at the company's registered office for not less than 15 days ending with the date of the meeting, and

(ii) at the meeting itself.

(4) Neither the person making the offer, nor any associate of his (as defined in section 988), is entitled to vote on the resolution, but—

(a) where the resolution is proposed as a written resolution, they are entitled (if they would otherwise be so entitled) to be sent a copy of it, and

(b) at any meeting to consider the resolution they are entitled (if they would otherwise be so entitled) to be given notice of the meeting, to attend and speak and if present (in person or by proxy) to count towards the quorum.

(5) If at a meeting to consider the resolution a quorum is not present, and after the meeting has been adjourned to a later date a quorum is again not present, the payment is (for the purposes of this section) deemed to have been approved.

(6) No approval is required under this section on the part of shareholders in a body corporate that—

(a) is not a UK-registered company, or

(b) is a wholly-owned subsidiary of another body corporate.

(7) A payment made in pursuance of an arrangement—

(a) entered into as part of the agreement for the transfer in question, or within one year before or two years after that agreement, and

(b) to which the company whose shares are the subject of the bid, or any person to whom the transfer is made, is privy,

is presumed, except in so far as the contrary is shown, to be a payment to which this section applies.

### 220   Exception for payments in discharge of legal obligations etc.

(1) Approval is not required under section 217, 218 or 219 (payments requiring members' approval) for a payment made in good faith—

    (a) in discharge of an existing legal obligation (as defined below),

    (b) by way of damages for breach of such an obligation,

    (c) by way of settlement or compromise of any claim arising in connection with the termination of a person's office or employment, or

    (d) by way of pension in respect of past services.

(2) In relation to a payment within section 217 (payment by company) an existing legal obligation means an obligation of the company, or any body corporate associated with it, that was not entered into in connection with, or in consequence of, the event giving rise to the payment for loss of office.

(3) In relation to a payment within section 218 or 219 (payment in connection with transfer of undertaking, property or shares) an existing legal obligation means an obligation of the person making the payment that was not entered into for the purposes of, in connection with or in consequence of, the transfer in question.

(4) In the case of a payment within both section 217 and section 218, or within both section 217 and section 219, subsection (2) above applies and not subsection (3).

(5) A payment part of which falls within subsection (1) above and part of which does not is treated as if the parts were separate payments.

### 221   Exception for small payments

(1) Approval is not required under section 217, 218 or 219 (payments requiring members' approval) if—

    (a) the payment in question is made by the company or any of its subsidiaries, and

    (b) the amount or value of the payment, together with the amount or value of any other relevant payments, does not exceed £200.

(2) For this purpose 'other relevant payments' are payments for loss of office in relation to which the following conditions are met.

(3) Where the payment in question is one to which section 217 (payment by company) applies, the conditions are that the other payment was or is paid—

    (a) by the company making the payment in question or any of its subsidiaries,

    (b) to the director to whom that payment is made, and

    (c) in connection with the same event.

(4) Where the payment in question is one to which section 218 or 219 applies (payment in connection with transfer of undertaking, property or shares), the conditions are that the other payment was (or is) paid in connection with the same transfer—

    (a) to the director to whom the payment in question was made, and

    (b) by the company making the payment or any of its subsidiaries.

### 222   Payments made without approval: civil consequences

(1) If a payment is made in contravention of section 217 (payment by company)—

    (a) it is held by the recipient on trust for the company making the payment, and

    (b) any director who authorised the payment is jointly and severally liable to indemnify the company that made the payment for any loss resulting from it.

(2) If a payment is made in contravention of section 218 (payment in connection with transfer of undertaking etc), it is held by the recipient on trust for the company whose undertaking or property is or is proposed to be transferred.

(3) If a payment is made in contravention of section 219 (payment in connection with share transfer)—

    (a) it is held by the recipient on trust for persons who have sold their shares as a result of the offer made, and

    (b) the expenses incurred by the recipient in distributing that sum amongst those persons shall be borne by him and not retained out of that sum.

(4) If a payment is in contravention of section 217 and section 218, subsection (2) of this section applies rather than subsection (1).

(5) If a payment is in contravention of section 217 and section 219, subsection (3) of this section applies rather than subsection (1), unless the court directs otherwise.

*Supplementary*

### 223   Transactions requiring members' approval: application of provisions to shadow directors

(1) For the purposes of—

    (a) sections 188 and 189 (directors' service contracts),

    (b) sections 190 to 196 (property transactions),

    (c) sections 197 to 214 (loans etc.), and

    (d) sections 215 to 222 (payments for loss of office),

a shadow director is treated as a director.

(2) Any reference in those provisions to loss of office as a director does not apply in relation to loss of a person's status as a shadow director.

### 224 Approval by written resolution: accidental failure to send memorandum

(1) Where—

(a) approval under this Chapter is sought by written resolution, and

(b) a memorandum is required under this Chapter to be sent or submitted to every eligible member before the resolution is passed,

any accidental failure to send or submit the memorandum to one or more members shall be disregarded for the purpose of determining whether the requirement has been met.

(2) Subsection (1) has effect subject to any provision of the company's articles.

### 225 Cases where approval is required under more than one provision

(1) Approval may be required under more than one provision of this Chapter.

(2) If so, the requirements of each applicable provision must be met.

(3) This does not require a separate resolution for the purposes of each provision.

### 226 Requirement of consent of Charity Commission: companies that are charities

For section 66 of the Charities Act 1993 (c. 10) substitute—

### '66 Consent of Commission required for approval etc by members of charitable companies

(1) Where a company is a charity—

(a) any approval given by the members of the company under any provision of Chapter 4 of Part 10 of the Companies Act 2006 (transactions with directors requiring approval by members) listed in subsection (2) below, and

(b) any affirmation given by members of the company under section 196 or 214 of that Act (affirmation of unapproved property transactions and loans), is ineffective without the prior written consent of the Commission.

(2) The provisions are—

(a) section 188 (directors' long-term service contracts);

(b) section 190 (substantial property transactions with directors etc);

(c) section 197, 198 or 200 (loans and quasi-loans to directors etc);

(d) section 201 (credit transactions for benefit of directors etc);

(e) section 203 (related arrangements);

(f) section 217 (payments to directors for loss of office);

(g) section 218 (payments to directors for loss of office: transfer of undertaking etc).

### 66A Consent of Commission required for certain acts of charitable company

(1) A company that is a charity may not do an act to which this section applies without the prior written consent of the Commission.

(2) This section applies to an act that—

(a) does not require approval under a listed provision of Chapter 4 of Part 10 of the Companies Act 2006 (transactions with directors) by the members of the company, but

(b) would require such approval but for an exemption in the provision in question that disapplies the need for approval on the part of the members of a body corporate which is a wholly-owned subsidiary of another body corporate.

(3) The reference to a listed provision is a reference to a provision listed in section 66(2) above.

(4) If a company acts in contravention of this section, the exemption referred to in subsection (2)(b) shall be treated as of no effect in relation to the act.'.

## Chapter 5 Directors' service contracts

### 227 Directors' service contracts

(1) For the purposes of this Part a director's 'service contract', in relation to a company, means a contract under which—

(a) a director of the company undertakes personally to perform services (as director or otherwise) for the company, or for a subsidiary of the company, or

(b) services (as director or otherwise) that a director of the company undertakes personally to perform are made available by a third party to the company, or to a subsidiary of the company.

(2) The provisions of this Part relating to directors' service contracts apply to the terms of a person's appointment as a director of a company.

They are not restricted to contracts for the performance of services outside the scope of the ordinary duties of a director.

### 228 Copy of contract or memorandum of terms to be available for inspection

(1) A company must keep available for inspection—

(a) a copy of every director's service contract with the company or with a subsidiary of the company, or

(b) if the contract is not in writing, a written memorandum setting out the terms of the contract.

(2) All the copies and memoranda must be kept available for inspection at—

(a) the company's registered office, or

(b) a place specified in regulations under section 1136.

(3) The copies and memoranda must be retained by the company for at least one year from the date of termination or expiry of the contract and must be kept available for inspection during that time.

(4) The company must give notice to the registrar—

(a) of the place at which the copies and memoranda are kept available for inspection, and

(b) of any change in that place,

unless they have at all times been kept at the company's registered office.

(5) If default is made in complying with subsection (1), (2) or (3), or default is made for 14 days in complying with subsection (4), an offence is committed by every officer of the company who is in default.

(6) A person guilty of an offence under this section is liable on summary conviction to a fine not exceeding level 3 on the standard scale and, for continued contravention, a daily default fine not exceeding one-tenth of level 3 on the standard scale.

(7) The provisions of this section apply to a variation of a director's service contract as they apply to the original contract.

### 229   Right of member to inspect and request copy

(1) Every copy or memorandum required to be kept under section 228 must be open to inspection by any member of the company without charge.

(2) Any member of the company is entitled, on request and on payment of such fee as may be prescribed, to be provided with a copy of any such copy or memorandum.

The copy must be provided within seven days after the request is received by the company.

(3) If an inspection required under subsection (1) is refused, or default is made in complying with subsection (2), an offence is committed by every officer of the company who is in default.

(4) A person guilty of an offence under this section is liable on summary conviction to a fine not exceeding level 3 on the standard scale and, for continued contravention, a daily default fine not exceeding one-tenth of level 3 on the standard scale.

(5) In the case of any such refusal or default the court may by order compel an immediate inspection or, as the case may be, direct that the copy required be sent to the person requiring it.

### 230   Directors' service contracts: application of provisions to shadow directors

A shadow director is treated as a director for the purposes of the provisions of this Chapter.

## Chapter 6   Contracts with sole members who are directors

### 231   Contract with sole member who is also a director

(1) This section applies where—

(a) a limited company having only one member enters into a contract with the sole member,

(b) the sole member is also a director of the company, and

(c) the contract is not entered into in the ordinary course of the company's business.

(2) The company must, unless the contract is in writing, ensure that the terms of the contract are either—

(a) set out in a written memorandum, or

(b) recorded in the minutes of the first meeting of the directors of the company following the making of the contract.

(3) If a company fails to comply with this section an offence is committed by every officer of the company who is in default.

(4) A person guilty of an offence under this section is liable on summary conviction to a fine not exceeding level 5 on the standard scale.

(5) For the purposes of this section a shadow director is treated as a director.

(6) Failure to comply with this section in relation to a contract does not affect the validity of the contract.

(7) Nothing in this section shall be read as excluding the operation of any other enactment or rule of law applying to contracts between a company and a director of the company.

## Chapter 7   Directors' liabilities

*Provision protecting directors from liability*

### 232   Provisions protecting directors from liability

(1) Any provision that purports to exempt a director of a company (to any extent) from any liability that would otherwise attach to him in connection with any negligence, default, breach of duty or breach of trust in relation to the company is void.

(2) Any provision by which a company directly or indirectly provides an indemnity (to any extent) for a director of the company, or of an associated company, against any liability attaching to him in connection with any negligence, default, breach of duty or breach of trust in relation to the company of which he is a director is void, except as permitted by—

    (a) section 233 (provision of insurance),

    (b) section 234 (qualifying third party indemnity provision), or

    (c) section 235 (qualifying pension scheme indemnity provision).

(3) This section applies to any provision, whether contained in a company's articles or in any contract with the company or otherwise.

(4) Nothing in this section prevents a company's articles from making such provision as has previously been lawful for dealing with conflicts of interest.

### 233 Provision of insurance

Section 232(2) (voidness of provisions for indemnifying directors) does not prevent a company from purchasing and maintaining for a director of the company, or of an associated company, insurance against any such liability as is mentioned in that subsection.

### 234 Qualifying third party indemnity provision

(1) Section 232(2) (voidness of provisions for indemnifying directors) does not apply to qualifying third party indemnity provision.

(2) Third party indemnity provision means provision for indemnity against liability incurred by the director to a person other than the company or an associated company.

Such provision is qualifying third party indemnity provision if the following requirements are met.

(3) The provision must not provide any indemnity against—

    (a) any liability of the director to pay—

        (i) a fine imposed in criminal proceedings, or

        (ii) a sum payable to a regulatory authority by way of a penalty in respect of non-compliance with any requirement of a regulatory nature (however arising); or

    (b) any liability incurred by the director—

        (i) in defending criminal proceedings in which he is convicted, or

        (ii) in defending civil proceedings brought by the company, or an associated company, in which judgment is given against him, or

        (iii) in connection with an application for relief (see subsection (6)) in which the court refuses to grant him relief.

(4) The references in subsection (3)(b) to a conviction, judgment or refusal of relief are to the final decision in the proceedings.

(5) For this purpose—

    (a) a conviction, judgment or refusal of relief becomes final—

        (i) if not appealed against, at the end of the period for bringing an appeal, or

        (ii) if appealed against, at the time when the appeal (or any further appeal) is disposed of; and

    (b) an appeal is disposed of—

        (i) if it is determined and the period for bringing any further appeal has ended, or

        (ii) if it is abandoned or otherwise ceases to have effect.

(6) The reference in subsection (3)(b)(iii) to an application for relief is to an application for relief under—

section 661(3) or (4) (power of court to grant relief in case of acquisition of shares by innocent nominee), or

section 1157 (general power of court to grant relief in case of honest and reasonable conduct).

### 235 Qualifying pension scheme indemnity provision

(1) Section 232(2) (voidness of provisions for indemnifying directors) does not apply to qualifying pension scheme indemnity provision.

(2) Pension scheme indemnity provision means provision indemnifying a director of a company that is a trustee of an occupational pension scheme against liability incurred in connection with the company's activities as trustee of the scheme.

Such provision is qualifying pension scheme indemnity provision if the following requirements are met.

(3) The provision must not provide any indemnity against—

    (a) any liability of the director to pay—

        (i) a fine imposed in criminal proceedings, or

        (ii) a sum payable to a regulatory authority by way of a penalty in respect of non-compliance with any requirement of a regulatory nature (however arising); or

    (b) any liability incurred by the director in defending criminal proceedings in which he is convicted.

(4) The reference in subsection (3)(b) to a conviction is to the final decision in the proceedings.

(5) For this purpose—

    (a) a conviction becomes final—

        (i)   if not appealed against, at the end of the period for bringing an appeal, or

        (ii)  if appealed against, at the time when the appeal (or any further appeal) is disposed of; and

    (b) an appeal is disposed of—

        (i)   if it is determined and the period for bringing any further appeal has ended, or

        (ii)  if it is abandoned or otherwise ceases to have effect.

(6) In this section 'occupational pension scheme' means an occupational pension scheme as defined in section 150(5) of the Finance Act 2004 (c. 12) that is established under a trust.

### 236   Qualifying indemnity provision to be disclosed in directors' report

(1) This section requires disclosure in the directors' report of—

    (a) qualifying third party indemnity provision, and

    (b) qualifying pension scheme indemnity provision.

Such provision is referred to in this section as 'qualifying indemnity provision'.

(2) If when a directors' report is approved any qualifying indemnity provision (whether made by the company or otherwise) is in force for the benefit of one or more directors of the company, the report must state that such provision is in force.

(3) If at any time during the financial year to which a directors' report relates any such provision was in force for the benefit of one or more persons who were then directors of the company, the report must state that such provision was in force.

(4) If when a directors' report is approved qualifying indemnity provision made by the company is in force for the benefit of one or more directors of an associated company, the report must state that such provision is in force.

(5) If at any time during the financial year to which a directors' report relates any such provision was in force for the benefit of one or more persons who were then directors of an associated company, the report must state that such provision was in force.

### 237   Copy of qualifying indemnity provision to be available for inspection

(1) This section has effect where qualifying indemnity provision is made for a director of a company, and applies—

    (a) to the company of which he is a director (whether the provision is made by that company or an associated company), and

    (b) where the provision is made by an associated company, to that company.

(2) That company or, as the case may be, each of them must keep available for inspection—

    (a) a copy of the qualifying indemnity provision, or

    (b) if the provision is not in writing, a written memorandum setting out its terms.

(3) The copy or memorandum must be kept available for inspection at—

    (a) the company's registered office, or

    (b) a place specified in regulations under section 1136.

(4) The copy or memorandum must be retained by the company for at least one year from the date of termination or expiry of the provision and must be kept available for inspection during that time.

(5) The company must give notice to the registrar—

    (a) of the place at which the copy or memorandum is kept available for inspection, and

    (b) of any change in that place,

unless it has at all times been kept at the company's registered office.

(6) If default is made in complying with subsection (2), (3) or (4), or default is made for 14 days in complying with subsection (5), an offence is committed by every officer of the company who is in default.

(7) A person guilty of an offence under this section is liable on summary conviction to a fine not exceeding level 3 on the standard scale and, for continued contravention, a daily default fine not exceeding one-tenth of level 3 on the standard scale.

(8) The provisions of this section apply to a variation of a qualifying indemnity provision as they apply to the original provision.

(9) In this section 'qualifying indemnity provision' means—

    (a) qualifying third party indemnity provision, and

    (b) qualifying pension scheme indemnity provision.

### 238   Right of member to inspect and request copy

(1) Every copy or memorandum required to be kept by a company under section 237 must be open to inspection by any member of the company without charge.

(2) Any member of the company is entitled, on request and on payment of such fee as may be prescribed, to be provided with a copy of any such copy or memorandum.

The copy must be provided within seven days after the request is received by the company.

(3) If an inspection required under subsection (1) is refused, or default is made in complying with subsection (2), an offence is committed by every officer of the company who is in default.

(4) A person guilty of an offence under this section is liable on summary conviction to a fine not exceeding level 3 on the standard scale and, for continued contravention, a daily default fine not exceeding one-tenth of level 3 on the standard scale.

(5) In the case of any such refusal or default the court may by order compel an immediate inspection or, as the case may be, direct that the copy required be sent to the person requiring it.

*Ratification of acts giving rise to liability*

### 239   Ratification of acts of directors

(1) This section applies to the ratification by a company of conduct by a director amounting to negligence, default, breach of duty or breach of trust in relation to the company.

(2) The decision of the company to ratify such conduct must be made by resolution of the members of the company.

(3) Where the resolution is proposed as a written resolution neither the director (if a member of the company) nor any member connected with him is an eligible member.

(4) Where the resolution is proposed at a meeting, it is passed only if the necessary majority is obtained disregarding votes in favour of the resolution by the director (if a member of the company) and any member connected with him.

This does not prevent the director or any such member from attending, being counted towards the quorum and taking part in the proceedings at any meeting at which the decision is considered.

(5) For the purposes of this section—

(a) 'conduct' includes acts and omissions;

(b) 'director' includes a former director;

(c) a shadow director is treated as a director; and

(d) in section 252 (meaning of 'connected person'), subsection (3) does not apply (exclusion of person who is himself a director).

(6) Nothing in this section affects—

(a) the validity of a decision taken by unanimous consent of the members of the company, or

(b) any power of the directors to agree not to sue, or to settle or release a claim made by them on behalf of the company.

(7) This section does not affect any other enactment or rule of law imposing additional requirements for valid ratification or any rule of law as to acts that are incapable of being ratified by the company.

## Chapter 8  Directors' residential addresses: protection from disclosure

### 240   Protected information

(1) This Chapter makes provision for protecting, in the case of a company director who is an individual—

(a) information as to his usual residential address;

(b) the information that his service address is his usual residential address.

(2) That information is referred to in this Chapter as 'protected information'.

(3) Information does not cease to be protected information on the individual ceasing to be a director of the company.

References in this Chapter to a director include, to that extent, a former director.

### 241   Protected information: restriction on use or disclosure by company

(1) A company must not use or disclose protected information about any of its directors, except—

(a) for communicating with the director concerned,

(b) in order to comply with any requirement of the Companies Acts as to particulars to be sent to the registrar, or

(c) in accordance with section 244 (disclosure under court order).

(2) Subsection (1) does not prohibit any use or disclosure of protected information with the consent of the director concerned.

### 242   Protected information: restriction on use or disclosure by registrar

(1) The registrar must omit protected information from the material on the register that is available for inspection where—

(a) it is contained in a document delivered to him in which such information is required to be stated, and

(b) in the case of a document having more than one part, it is contained in a part of the document in which such information is required to be stated.

(2) The registrar is not obliged—

(a) to check other documents or (as the case may be) other parts of the document to ensure the absence of protected information, or

(b) to omit from the material that is available for public inspection anything registered before this Chapter comes into force.

(3) The registrar must not use or disclose protected information except—

    (a) as permitted by section 243 (permitted use or disclosure by registrar), or

    (b) in accordance with section 244 (disclosure under court order).

### 243 Permitted use or disclosure by the registrar

(1) The registrar may use protected information for communicating with the director in question.

(2) The registrar may disclose protected information—

    (a) to a public authority specified for the purposes of this section by regulations made by the Secretary of State, or

    (b) to a credit reference agency.

(3) The Secretary of State may make provision by regulations—

    (a) specifying conditions for the disclosure of protected information in accordance with this section, and

    (b) providing for the charging of fees.

(4) The Secretary of State may make provision by regulations requiring the registrar, on application, to refrain from disclosing protected information relating to a director to a credit reference agency.

(5) Regulations under subsection (4) may make provision as to—

    (a) who may make an application,

    (b) the grounds on which an application may be made,

    (c) the information to be included in and documents to accompany an application, and

    (d) how an application is to be determined.

(6) Provision under subsection (5)(d) may in particular—

    (a) confer a discretion on the registrar;

    (b) provide for a question to be referred to a person other than the registrar for the purposes of determining the application.

(7) In this section—

'credit reference agency' means a person carrying on a business comprising the furnishing of information relevant to the financial standing of individuals, being information collected by the agency for that purpose; and

'public authority' includes any person or body having functions of a public nature.

(8) Regulations under this section are subject to negative resolution procedure.

### 244 Disclosure under court order

(1) The court may make an order for the disclosure of protected information by the company or by the registrar if—

    (a) there is evidence that service of documents at a service address other than the director's usual residential address is not effective to bring them to the notice of the director, or

    (b) it is necessary or expedient for the information to be provided in connection with the enforcement of an order or decree of the court,

and the court is otherwise satisfied that it is appropriate to make the order.

(2) An order for disclosure by the registrar is to be made only if the company—

    (a) does not have the director's usual residential address, or

    (b) has been dissolved.

(3) The order may be made on the application of a liquidator, creditor or member of the company, or any other person appearing to the court to have a sufficient interest.

(4) The order must specify the persons to whom, and purposes for which, disclosure is authorised.

### 245 Circumstances in which registrar may put address on the public record

(1) The registrar may put a director's usual residential address on the public record if—

    (a) communications sent by the registrar to the director and requiring a response within a specified period remain unanswered, or

    (b) there is evidence that service of documents at a service address provided in place of the director's usual residential address is not effective to bring them to the notice of the director.

(2) The registrar must give notice of the proposal—

    (a) to the director, and

    (b) to every company of which the registrar has been notified that the individual is a director.

(3) The notice must—

    (a) state the grounds on which it is proposed to put the director's usual residential address on the public record, and

    (b) specify a period within which representations may be made before that is done.

(4) It must be sent to the director at his usual residential address, unless it appears to the registrar that service at that address may be ineffective to bring it to the individual's notice, in which case it may be sent to any service address provided in place of that address.

(5) The registrar must take account of any representations received within the specified period.

(6) What is meant by putting the address on the public record is explained in section 246.

### 246 Putting the address on the public record

(1) The registrar, on deciding in accordance with section 245 that a director's usual residential address is to be put on the public record, shall proceed as if notice of a change of registered particulars had been given—

(a) stating that address as the director's service address, and

(b) stating that the director's usual residential address is the same as his service address.

(2) The registrar must give notice of having done so—

(a) to the director, and

(b) to the company.

(3) On receipt of the notice the company must—

(a) enter the director's usual residential address in its register of directors as his service address, and

(b) state in its register of directors' residential addresses that his usual residential address is the same as his service address.

(4) If the company has been notified by the director in question of a more recent address as his usual residential address, it must—

(a) enter that address in its register of directors as the director's service address, and

(b) give notice to the registrar as on a change of registered particulars.

(5) If a company fails to comply with subsection (3) or (4), an offence is committed by—

(a) the company, and

(b) every officer of the company who is in default.

(6) A person guilty of an offence under subsection (5) is liable on summary conviction to a fine not exceeding level 5 on the standard scale and, for continued contravention, a daily default fine not exceeding one-tenth of level 5 on the standard scale.

(7) A director whose usual residential address has been put on the public record by the registrar under this section may not register a service address other than his usual residential address for a period of five years from the date of the registrar's decision.

## Chapter 9 Supplementary provisions

*Provision for employees on cessation or transfer of business*

### 247 Power to make provision for employees on cessation or transfer of business

(1) The powers of the directors of a company include (if they would not otherwise do so) power to make provision for the benefit of persons employed or formerly employed by the company, or any of its subsidiaries, in connection with the cessation or the transfer to any person of the whole or part of the undertaking of the company or that subsidiary.

(2) This power is exercisable notwithstanding the general duty imposed by section 172 (duty to promote the success of the company).

(3) In the case of a company that is a charity it is exercisable notwithstanding any restrictions on the directors' powers (or the company's capacity) flowing from the objects of the company.

(4) The power may only be exercised if sanctioned—

(a) by a resolution of the company, or

(b) by a resolution of the directors,

in accordance with the following provisions.

(5) A resolution of the directors—

(a) must be authorised by the company's articles, and

(b) is not sufficient sanction for payments to or for the benefit of directors, former directors or shadow directors.

(6) Any other requirements of the company's articles as to the exercise of the power conferred by this section must be complied with.

(7) Any payment under this section must be made—

(a) before the commencement of any winding up of the company, and

(b) out of profits of the company that are available for dividend.

*Records of meetings of directors*

### 248 Minutes of directors' meetings

(1) Every company must cause minutes of all proceedings at meetings of its directors to be recorded.

(2) The records must be kept for at least ten years from the date of the meeting.

(3) If a company fails to comply with this section, an offence is committed by every officer of the company who is in default.

(4) A person guilty of an offence under this section is liable on summary conviction to a fine not exceeding level 3 on the standard scale and, for continued contravention, a daily default fine not exceeding one-tenth of level 3 on the standard scale.

### 249   Minutes as evidence

(1) Minutes recorded in accordance with section 248, if purporting to be authenticated by the chairman of the meeting or by the chairman of the next directors' meeting, are evidence (in Scotland, sufficient evidence) of the proceedings at the meeting.

(2) Where minutes have been made in accordance with that section of the proceedings of a meeting of directors, then, until the contrary is proved—

    (a) the meeting is deemed duly held and convened,

    (b) all proceedings at the meeting are deemed to have duly taken place, and

    (c) all appointments at the meeting are deemed valid.

*Meaning of 'director' and 'shadow director'*

### 250   'Director'

In the Companies Acts 'director' includes any person occupying the position of director, by whatever name called.

### 251   'Shadow director'

(1) In the Companies Acts 'shadow director', in relation to a company, means a person in accordance with whose directions or instructions the directors of the company are accustomed to act.

(2) A person is not to be regarded as a shadow director by reason only that the directors act on advice given by him in a professional capacity.

(3) A body corporate is not to be regarded as a shadow director of any of its subsidiary companies for the purposes of—

Chapter 2 (general duties of directors),

Chapter 4 (transactions requiring members' approval), or

Chapter 6 (contract with sole member who is also a director),

by reason only that the directors of the subsidiary are accustomed to act in accordance with its directions or instructions.

*Other definitions*

### 252   Persons connected with a director

(1) This section defines what is meant by references in this Part to a person being 'connected' with a director of a company (or a director being 'connected' with a person).

(2) The following persons (and only those persons) are connected with a director of a company—

    (a) members of the director's family (see section 253);

    (b) a body corporate with which the director is connected (as defined in section 254);

    (c) a person acting in his capacity as trustee of a trust—

        (i) the beneficiaries of which include the director or a person who by virtue of paragraph (a) or (b) is connected with him, or

        (ii) the terms of which confer a power on the trustees that may be exercised for the benefit of the director or any such person,

    other than a trust for the purposes of an employees' share scheme or a pension scheme;

    (d) a person acting in his capacity as partner—

        (i) of the director, or

        (ii) of a person who, by virtue of paragraph (a), (b) or (c), is connected with that director;

    (e) a firm that is a legal person under the law by which it is governed and in which—

        (i) the director is a partner,

        (ii) a partner is a person who, by virtue of paragraph (a), (b) or (c) is connected with the director, or

        (iii) a partner is a firm in which the director is a partner or in which there is a partner who, by virtue of paragraph (a), (b) or (c), is connected with the director.

(3) References in this Part to a person connected with a director of a company do not include a person who is himself a director of the company.

### 253   Members of a director's family

(1) This section defines what is meant by references in this Part to members of a director's family.

(2) For the purposes of this Part the members of a director's family are—

    (a) the director's spouse or civil partner;

    (b) any other person (whether of a different sex or the same sex) with whom the director lives as partner in an enduring family relationship;

    (c) the director's children or step-children;

    (d) any children or step-children of a person within paragraph (b) (and who are not children or step-children of the director) who live with the director and have not attained the age of 18;

    (e) the director's parents.

(3) Subsection (2)(b) does not apply if the other person is the director's grandparent or grandchild, sister, brother, aunt or uncle, or nephew or niece.

### 254  Director 'connected with' a body corporate

(1) This section defines what is meant by references in this Part to a director being 'connected with' a body corporate.

(2) A director is connected with a body corporate if, but only if, he and the persons connected with him together—

    (a) are interested in shares comprised in the equity share capital of that body corporate of a nominal value equal to at least 20% of that share capital, or

    (b) are entitled to exercise or control the exercise of more than 20% of the voting power at any general meeting of that body.

(3) The rules set out in Schedule 1 (references to interest in shares or debentures) apply for the purposes of this section.

(4) References in this section to voting power the exercise of which is controlled by a director include voting power whose exercise is controlled by a body corporate controlled by him.

(5) Shares in a company held as treasury shares, and any voting rights attached to such shares, are disregarded for the purposes of this section.

(6) For the avoidance of circularity in the application of section 252 (meaning of 'connected person')—

    (a) a body corporate with which a director is connected is not treated for the purposes of this section as connected with him unless it is also connected with him by virtue of subsection (2)(c) or (d) of that section (connection as trustee or partner); and

    (b) a trustee of a trust the beneficiaries of which include (or may include) a body corporate with which a director is connected is not treated for the purposes of this section as connected with a director by reason only of that fact.

### 255  Director 'controlling' a body corporate

(1) This section defines what is meant by references in this Part to a director 'controlling' a body corporate.

(2) A director of a company is taken to control a body corporate if, but only if—

    (a) he or any person connected with him—

        (i) is interested in any part of the equity share capital of that body, or

        (ii) is entitled to exercise or control the exercise of any part of the voting power at any general meeting of that body, and

    (b) he, the persons connected with him and the other directors of that company, together—

        (i) are interested in more than 50% of that share capital, or

        (ii) are entitled to exercise or control the exercise of more than 50% of that voting power.

(3) The rules set out in Schedule 1 (references to interest in shares or debentures) apply for the purposes of this section.

(4) References in this section to voting power the exercise of which is controlled by a director include voting power whose exercise is controlled by a body corporate controlled by him.

(5) Shares in a company held as treasury shares, and any voting rights attached to such shares, are disregarded for the purposes of this section.

(6) For the avoidance of circularity in the application of section 252 (meaning of 'connected person')—

    (a) a body corporate with which a director is connected is not treated for the purposes of this section as connected with him unless it is also connected with him by virtue of subsection (2) (c) or (d) of that section (connection as trustee or partner); and

    (b) a trustee of a trust the beneficiaries of which include (or may include) a body corporate with which a director is connected is not treated for the purposes of this section as connected with a director by reason only of that fact.

### 256  Associated bodies corporate

For the purposes of this Part—

    (a) bodies corporate are associated if one is a subsidiary of the other or both are subsidiaries of the same body corporate, and

    (b) companies are associated if one is a subsidiary of the other or both are subsidiaries of the same body corporate.

### 257  References to company's constitution

(1) References in this Part to a company's constitution include—

    (a) any resolution or other decision come to in accordance with the constitution, and

    (b) any decision by the members of the company, or a class of members, that is treated by virtue of any enactment or rule of law as equivalent to a decision by the company.

(2) This is in addition to the matters mentioned in section 17 (general provision as to matters contained in company's constitution).

*General*

### 258 Power to increase financial limits

(1) The Secretary of State may by order substitute for any sum of money specified in this Part a larger sum specified in the order.

(2) An order under this section is subject to negative resolution procedure.

(3) An order does not have effect in relation to anything done or not done before it comes into force.

Accordingly, proceedings in respect of any liability incurred before that time may be continued or instituted as if the order had not been made.

### 259 Transactions under foreign law

For the purposes of this Part it is immaterial whether the law that (apart from this Act) governs an arrangement or transaction is the law of the United Kingdom, or a part of it, or not.

# PART 11 DERIVATIVE CLAIMS AND PROCEEDINGS BY MEMBERS

## Chapter 1 Derivative claims in England and Wales or Northern Ireland

### 260 Derivative claims

(1) This Chapter applies to proceedings in England and Wales or Northern Ireland by a member of a company—

    (a) in respect of a cause of action vested in the company, and

    (b) seeking relief on behalf of the company.

This is referred to in this Chapter as a 'derivative claim'.

(2) A derivative claim may only be brought—

    (a) under this Chapter, or

    (b) in pursuance of an order of the court in proceedings under section 994 (proceedings for protection of members against unfair prejudice).

(3) A derivative claim under this Chapter may be brought only in respect of a cause of action arising from an actual or proposed act or omission involving negligence, default, breach of duty or breach of trust by a director of the company.

The cause of action may be against the director or another person (or both).

(4) It is immaterial whether the cause of action arose before or after the person seeking to bring or continue the derivative claim became a member of the company.

(5) For the purposes of this Chapter—

    (a) 'director' includes a former director;

    (b) a shadow director is treated as a director; and

    (c) references to a member of a company include a person who is not a member but to whom shares in the company have been transferred or transmitted by operation of law.

### 261 Application for permission to continue derivative claim

(1) A member of a company who brings a derivative claim under this Chapter must apply to the court for permission (in Northern Ireland, leave) to continue it.

(2) If it appears to the court that the application and the evidence filed by the applicant in support of it do not disclose a prima facie case for giving permission (or leave), the court—

    (a) must dismiss the application, and

    (b) may make any consequential order it considers appropriate.

(3) If the application is not dismissed under subsection (2), the court—

    (a) may give directions as to the evidence to be provided by the company, and

    (b) may adjourn the proceedings to enable the evidence to be obtained.

(4) On hearing the application, the court may—

    (a) give permission (or leave) to continue the claim on such terms as it thinks fit,

    (b) refuse permission (or leave) and dismiss the claim, or

    (c) adjourn the proceedings on the application and give such directions as it thinks fit.

### 262 Application for permission to continue claim as a derivative claim

(1) This section applies where—

    (a) a company has brought a claim, and

    (b) the cause of action on which the claim is based could be pursued as a derivative claim under this Chapter.

(2) A member of the company may apply to the court for permission (in Northern Ireland, leave) to continue the claim as a derivative claim on the ground that—

    (a) the manner in which the company commenced or continued the claim amounts to an abuse of the process of the court,

    (b) the company has failed to prosecute the claim diligently, and

    (c) it is appropriate for the member to continue the claim as a derivative claim.

(3) If it appears to the court that the application and the evidence filed by the applicant in support of it do not disclose a prima facie case for giving permission (or leave), the court—

    (a) must dismiss the application, and

    (b) may make any consequential order it considers appropriate.

(4) If the application is not dismissed under subsection (3), the court—

    (a) may give directions as to the evidence to be provided by the company, and

    (b) may adjourn the proceedings to enable the evidence to be obtained.

(5) On hearing the application, the court may—

    (a) give permission (or leave) to continue the claim as a derivative claim on such terms as it thinks fit,

    (b) refuse permission (or leave) and dismiss the application, or

    (c) adjourn the proceedings on the application and give such directions as it thinks fit.

### 263 Whether permission to be given

(1) The following provisions have effect where a member of a company applies for permission (in Northern Ireland, leave) under section 261 or 262.

(2) Permission (or leave) must be refused if the court is satisfied—

    (a) that a person acting in accordance with section 172 (duty to promote the success of the company) would not seek to continue the claim, or

    (b) where the cause of action arises from an act or omission that is yet to occur, that the act or omission has been authorised by the company, or

    (c) where the cause of action arises from an act or omission that has already occurred, that the act or omission—

      (i) was authorised by the company before it occurred, or

      (ii) has been ratified by the company since it occurred.

(3) In considering whether to give permission (or leave) the court must take into account, in particular—

    (a) whether the member is acting in good faith in seeking to continue the claim;

    (b) the importance that a person acting in accordance with section 172 (duty to promote the success of the company) would attach to continuing it;

    (c) where the cause of action results from an act or omission that is yet to occur, whether the act or omission could be, and in the circumstances would be likely to be—

      (i) authorised by the company before it occurs, or

      (ii) ratified by the company after it occurs;

    (d) where the cause of action arises from an act or omission that has already occurred, whether the act or omission could be, and in the circumstances would be likely to be, ratified by the company;

    (e) whether the company has decided not to pursue the claim;

    (f) whether the act or omission in respect of which the claim is brought gives rise to a cause of action that the member could pursue in his own right rather than on behalf of the company.

(4) In considering whether to give permission (or leave) the court shall have particular regard to any evidence before it as to the views of members of the company who have no personal interest, direct or indirect, in the matter.

(5) The Secretary of State may by regulations—

    (a) amend subsection (2) so as to alter or add to the circumstances in which permission (or leave) is to be refused;

    (b) amend subsection (3) so as to alter or add to the matters that the court is required to take into account in considering whether to give permission (or leave).

(6) Before making any such regulations the Secretary of State shall consult such persons as he considers appropriate.

(7) Regulations under this section are subject to affirmative resolution procedure.

### 264 Application for permission to continue derivative claim brought by another member

(1) This section applies where a member of a company ('the claimant')—

    (a) has brought a derivative claim,

    (b) has continued as a derivative claim a claim brought by the company, or

    (c) has continued a derivative claim under this section.

(2) Another member of the company ('the applicant') may apply to the court for permission (in Northern Ireland, leave) to continue the claim on the ground that—

    (a) the manner in which the proceedings have been commenced or continued by the claimant amounts to an abuse of the process of the court,

    (b) the claimant has failed to prosecute the claim diligently, and

    (c) it is appropriate for the applicant to continue the claim as a derivative claim.

(3) If it appears to the court that the application and the evidence filed by the applicant in support of it do not disclose a prima facie case for giving permission (or leave), the court—

    (a) must dismiss the application, and

    (b) may make any consequential order it considers appropriate.

(4) If the application is not dismissed under subsection (3), the court—

    (a) may give directions as to the evidence to be provided by the company, and

    (b) may adjourn the proceedings to enable the evidence to be obtained.

(5) On hearing the application, the court may—

    (a) give permission (or leave) to continue the claim on such terms as it thinks fit,

    (b) refuse permission (or leave) and dismiss the application, or

    (c) adjourn the proceedings on the application and give such directions as it thinks fit.

## Chapter 2  Derivative proceedings in Scotland

### 265    Derivative proceedings

(1) In Scotland, a member of a company may raise proceedings in respect of an act or omission specified in subsection (3) in order to protect the interests of the company and obtain a remedy on its behalf.

(2) A member of a company may raise such proceedings only under subsection (1).

(3) The act or omission referred to in subsection (1) is any actual or proposed act or omission involving negligence, default, breach of duty or breach of trust by a director of the company.

(4) Proceedings may be raised under subsection (1) against (either or both)—

    (a) the director referred to in subsection (3), or

    (b) another person.

(5) It is immaterial whether the act or omission in respect of which the proceedings are to be raised or, in the case of continuing proceedings under section 267 or 269, are raised, arose before or after the person seeking to raise or continue them became a member of the company.

(6) This section does not affect—

    (a) any right of a member of a company to raise proceedings in respect of an act or omission specified in subsection (3) in order to protect his own interests and obtain a remedy on his own behalf, or

    (b) the court's power to make an order under section 996(2)(c) or anything done under such an order.

(7) In this Chapter—

    (a) proceedings raised under subsection (1) are referred to as 'derivative proceedings',

    (b) the act or omission in respect of which they are raised is referred to as the 'cause of action',

    (c) 'director' includes a former director,

    (d) references to a director include a shadow director, and

    (e) references to a member of a company include a person who is not a member but to whom shares in the company have been transferred or transmitted by operation of law.

### 266    Requirement for leave and notice

(1) Derivative proceedings may be raised by a member of a company only with the leave of the court.

(2) An application for leave must—

    (a) specify the cause of action, and

    (b) summarise the facts on which the derivative proceedings are to be based.

(3) If it appears to the court that the application and the evidence produced by the applicant in support of it do not disclose a prima facie case for granting it, the court—

    (a) must refuse the application, and

    (b) may make any consequential order it considers appropriate.

(4) If the application is not refused under subsection (3)—

    (a) the applicant must serve the application on the company,

    (b) the court—

        (i)  may make an order requiring evidence to be produced by the company, and

        (ii) may adjourn the proceedings on the application to enable the evidence to be obtained, and

    (c) the company is entitled to take part in the further proceedings on the application.

(5) On hearing the application, the court may—

    (a) grant the application on such terms as it thinks fit,

    (b) refuse the application, or

    (c) adjourn the proceedings on the application and make such order as to further procedure as it thinks fit.

**267   Application to continue proceedings as derivative proceedings**

  (1) This section applies where—

    (a) a company has raised proceedings, and

    (b) the proceedings are in respect of an act or omission which could be the basis for derivative proceedings.

  (2) A member of the company may apply to the court to be substituted for the company in the proceedings, and for the proceedings to continue in consequence as derivative proceedings, on the ground that—

    (a) the manner in which the company commenced or continued the proceedings amounts to an abuse of the process of the court,

    (b) the company has failed to prosecute the proceedings diligently, and

    (c) it is appropriate for the member to be substituted for the company in the proceedings.

  (3) If it appears to the court that the application and the evidence produced by the applicant in support of it do not disclose a prima facie case for granting it, the court—

    (a) must refuse the application, and

    (b) may make any consequential order it considers appropriate.

  (4) If the application is not refused under subsection (3)—

    (a) the applicant must serve the application on the company,

    (b) the court—

      (i) may make an order requiring evidence to be produced by the company, and

      (ii) may adjourn the proceedings on the application to enable the evidence to be obtained, and

    (c) the company is entitled to take part in the further proceedings on the application.

  (5) On hearing the application, the court may—

    (a) grant the application on such terms as it thinks fit,

    (b) refuse the application, or

    (c) adjourn the proceedings on the application and make such order as to further procedure as it thinks fit.

**268   Granting of leave**

  (1) The court must refuse leave to raise derivative proceedings or an application under section 267 if satisfied—

    (a) that a person acting in accordance with section 172 (duty to promote the success of the company) would not seek to raise or continue the proceedings (as the case may be), or

    (b) where the cause of action is an act or omission that is yet to occur, that the act or omission has been authorised by the company, or

    (c) where the cause of action is an act or omission that has already occurred, that the act or omission—

      (i) was authorised by the company before it occurred, or

      (ii) has been ratified by the company since it occurred.

  (2) In considering whether to grant leave to raise derivative proceedings or an application under section 267, the court must take into account, in particular—

    (a) whether the member is acting in good faith in seeking to raise or continue the proceedings (as the case may be),

    (b) the importance that a person acting in accordance with section 172 (duty to promote the success of the company) would attach to raising or continuing them (as the case may be),

    (c) where the cause of action is an act or omission that is yet to occur, whether the act or omission could be, and in the circumstances would be likely to be—

      (i) authorised by the company before it occurs, or

      (ii) ratified by the company after it occurs,

    (d) where the cause of action is an act or omission that has already occurred, whether the act or omission could be, and in the circumstances would be likely to be, ratified by the company,

    (e) whether the company has decided not to raise proceedings in respect of the same cause of action or to persist in the proceedings (as the case may be),

    (f) whether the cause of action is one which the member could pursue in his own right rather than on behalf of the company.

  (3) In considering whether to grant leave to raise derivative proceedings or an application under section 267, the court shall have particular regard to any evidence before it as to the views of members of the company who have no personal interest, direct or indirect, in the matter.

  (4) The Secretary of State may by regulations—

    (a) amend subsection (1) so as to alter or add to the circumstances in which leave or an application is to be refused,

    (b) amend subsection (2) so as to alter or add to the matters that the court is required to take into account in considering whether to grant leave or an application.

(5) Before making any such regulations the Secretary of State shall consult such persons as he considers appropriate.

(6) Regulations under this section are subject to affirmative resolution procedure.

## 269 Application by member to be substituted for member pursuing derivative proceedings

(1) This section applies where a member of a company ('the claimant')—

(a) has raised derivative proceedings,

(b) has continued as derivative proceedings raised by the company, or

(c) has continued derivative proceedings under this section.

(2) Another member of the company ('the applicant') may apply to the court to be substituted for the claimant in the action on the ground that—

(a) the manner in which the proceedings have been commenced or continued by the claimant amounts to an abuse of the process of the court,

(b) the claimant has failed to prosecute the proceedings diligently, and

(c) it is appropriate for the applicant to be substituted for the claimant in the proceedings.

(3) If it appears to the court that the application and the evidence produced by the applicant in support of it do not disclose a prima facie case for granting it, the court—

(a) must refuse the application, and

(b) may make any consequential order it considers appropriate.

(4) If the application is not refused under subsection (3)—

(a) the applicant must serve the application on the company,

(b) the court—

(i) may make an order requiring evidence to be produced by the company, and

(ii) may adjourn the proceedings on the application to enable the evidence to be obtained, and

(c) the company is entitled to take part in the further proceedings on the application.

(5) On hearing the application, the court may—

(a) grant the application on such terms as it thinks fit,

(b) refuse the application, or

(c) adjourn the proceedings on the application and make such order as to further procedure as it thinks fit.

# PART 12  COMPANY SECRETARIES

### Private companies

## 270 Private company not required to have secretary

(1) A private company is not required to have a secretary.

(2) References in the Companies Acts to a private company 'without a secretary' are to a private company that for the time being is taking advantage of the exemption in subsection (1); and references to a private company 'with a secretary' shall be construed accordingly.

(3) In the case of a private company without a secretary—

(a) anything authorised or required to be given or sent to, or served on, the company by being sent to its secretary—

(i) may be given or sent to, or served on, the company itself, and

(ii) if addressed to the secretary shall be treated as addressed to the company; and

(b) anything else required or authorised to be done by or to the secretary of the company may be done by or to—

(i) a director, or

(ii) a person authorised generally or specifically in that behalf by the directors.

### Public companies

## 271 Public company required to have secretary

A public company must have a secretary.

## 272 Direction requiring public company to appoint secretary

(1) If it appears to the Secretary of State that a public company is in breach of section 271 (requirement to have secretary), the Secretary of State may give the company a direction under this section.

(2) The direction must state that the company appears to be in breach of that section and specify—

(a) what the company must do in order to comply with the direction, and

(b) the period within which it must do so.

That period must be not less than one month or more than three months after the date on which the direction is given.

(3) The direction must also inform the company of the consequences of failing to comply.

(4) Where the company is in breach of section 271 it must comply with the direction by—

(a) making the necessary appointment, and

(b) giving notice of it under section 276,

before the end of the period specified in the direction.

(5) If the company has already made the necessary appointment, it must comply with the direction by giving notice of it under section 276 before the end of the period specified in the direction.

(6) If a company fails to comply with a direction under this section, an offence is committed by—

(a) the company, and

(b) every officer of the company who is in default.

For this purpose a shadow director is treated as an officer of the company.

(7) A person guilty of an offence under this section is liable on summary conviction to a fine not exceeding level 5 on the standard scale and, for continued contravention, a daily default fine not exceeding one-tenth of level 5 on the standard scale.

### 273  Qualifications of secretaries of public companies

(1) It is the duty of the directors of a public company to take all reasonable steps to secure that the secretary (or each joint secretary) of the company—

(a) is a person who appears to them to have the requisite knowledge and experience to discharge the functions of secretary of the company, and

(b) has one or more of the following qualifications.

(2) The qualifications are—

(a) that he has held the office of secretary of a public company for at least three of the five years immediately preceding his appointment as secretary;

(b) that he is a member of any of the bodies specified in subsection (3);

(c) that he is a barrister, advocate or solicitor called or admitted in any part of the United Kingdom;

(d) that he is a person who, by virtue of his holding or having held any other position or his being a member of any other body, appears to the directors to be capable of discharging the functions of secretary of the company.

(3) The bodies referred to in subsection (2)(b) are—

(a) the Institute of Chartered Accountants in England and Wales;

(b) the Institute of Chartered Accountants of Scotland;

(c) the Association of Chartered Certified Accountants;

(d) the Institute of Chartered Accountants in Ireland;

(e) the Institute of Chartered Secretaries and Administrators;

(f) the Chartered Institute of Management Accountants;

(g) the Chartered Institute of Public Finance and Accountancy.

*Provisions applying to private companies with a
secretary and to public companies*

### 274  Discharge of functions where office vacant or secretary unable to act

Where in the case of any company the office of secretary is vacant, or there is for any other reason no secretary capable of acting, anything required or authorised to be done by or to the secretary may be done—

(a) by or to an assistant or deputy secretary (if any), or

(b) if there is no assistant or deputy secretary or none capable of acting, by or to any person authorised generally or specifically in that behalf by the directors.

### 275  Duty to keep register of secretaries

(1) A company must keep a register of its secretaries.

(2) The register must contain the required particulars (see sections 277 to 279) of the person who is, or persons who are, the secretary or joint secretaries of the company.

(3) The register must be kept available for inspection—

(a) at the company's registered office, or

(b) at a place specified in regulations under section 1136.

(4) The company must give notice to the registrar—

(a) of the place at which the register is kept available for inspection, and

(b) of any change in that place,

unless it has at all times been kept at the company's registered office.

(5) The register must be open to the inspection—

(a) of any member of the company without charge, and

(b) of any other person on payment of such fee as may be prescribed.

(6) If default is made in complying with subsection (1), (2) or (3), or if default is made for 14 days in complying with subsection (4), or if an inspection required under subsection (5) is refused, an offence is committed by—

(a) the company, and

(b) every officer of the company who is in default.

For this purpose a shadow director is treated as an officer of the company.

(7) A person guilty of an offence under this section is liable on summary conviction to a fine not exceeding level 5 on the standard scale and, for continued contravention, a daily default fine not exceeding one-tenth of level 5 on the standard scale.

(8) In the case of a refusal of inspection of the register, the court may by order compel an immediate inspection of it.

### 276  Duty to notify registrar of changes

(1) A company must, within the period of 14 days from—

(a) a person becoming or ceasing to be its secretary or one of its joint secretaries, or

(b) the occurrence of any change in the particulars contained in its register of secretaries,

give notice to the registrar of the change and of the date on which it occurred.

(2) Notice of a person having become secretary, or one of joint secretaries, of the company must be accompanied by a consent by that person to act in the relevant capacity.

(3) If default is made in complying with this section, an offence is committed by every officer of the company who is in default.

For this purpose a shadow director is treated as an officer of the company.

(4) A person guilty of an offence under this section is liable on summary conviction to a fine not exceeding level 5 on the standard scale and, for continued contravention, a daily default fine not exceeding one-tenth of level 5 on the standard scale.

### 277  Particulars of secretaries to be registered: individuals

(1) A company's register of secretaries must contain the following particulars in the case of an individual—

(a) name and any former name;

(b) address.

(2) For the purposes of this section 'name' means a person's Christian name (or other forename) and surname, except that in the case of—

(a) a peer, or

(b) an individual usually known by a title,

the title may be stated instead of his Christian name (or other forename) and surname or in addition to either or both of them.

(3) For the purposes of this section a 'former name' means a name by which the individual was formerly known for business purposes.

Where a person is or was formerly known by more than one such name, each of them must be stated.

(4) It is not necessary for the register to contain particulars of a former name in the following cases—

(a) in the case of a peer or an individual normally known by a British title, where the name is one by which the person was known previous to the adoption of or succession to the title;

(b) in the case of any person, where the former name—

(i)  was changed or disused before the person attained the age of 16 years, or

(ii)  has been changed or disused for 20 years or more.

(5) The address required to be stated in the register is a service address.

This may be stated to be 'The company's registered office'.

### 278  Particulars of secretaries to be registered: corporate secretaries and firms

(1) A company's register of secretaries must contain the following particulars in the case of a body corporate, or a firm that is a legal person under the law by which it is governed—

(a) corporate or firm name;

(b) registered or principal office;

(c) in the case of an EEA company to which the First Company Law Directive (68/151/EEC) applies, particulars of—

(i)  the register in which the company file mentioned in Article 3 of that Directive is kept (including details of the relevant state), and

(ii)  the registration number in that register;

(d) in any other case, particulars of—

(i)  the legal form of the company or firm and the law by which it is governed, and

(ii)  if applicable, the register in which it is entered (including details of the state) and its registration number in that register.

(2) If all the partners in a firm are joint secretaries it is sufficient to state the particulars that would be required if the firm were a legal person and the firm had been appointed secretary.

### 279  Particulars of secretaries to be registered: power to make regulations

(1) The Secretary of State may make provision by regulations amending—

section 277 (particulars of secretaries to be registered: individuals), or

section 278 (particulars of secretaries to be registered: corporate secretaries and firms),

so as to add to or remove items from the particulars required to be contained in a company's register of secretaries.

(2) Regulations under this section are subject to affirmative resolution procedure.

**280   Acts done by person in dual capacity**

A provision requiring or authorising a thing to be done by or to a director and the secretary of a company is not satisfied by its being done by or to the same person acting both as director and as, or in place of, the secretary.

# PART 13  RESOLUTIONS AND MEETINGS

## Chapter 1  General provisions about resolutions

### 281   Resolutions

(1)  A resolution of the members (or of a class of members) of a private company must be passed—

   (a)  as a written resolution in accordance with Chapter 2, or

   (b)  at a meeting of the members (to which the provisions of Chapter 3 apply).

(2)  A resolution of the members (or of a class of members) of a public company must be passed at a meeting of the members (to which the provisions of Chapter 3 and, where relevant, Chapter 4 apply).

(3)  Where a provision of the Companies Acts—

   (a)  requires a resolution of a company, or of the members (or a class of members) of a company, and

   (b)  does not specify what kind of resolution is required,

what is required is an ordinary resolution unless the company's articles require a higher majority (or unanimity).

(4)  Nothing in this Part affects any enactment or rule of law as to—

   (a)  things done otherwise than by passing a resolution,

   (b)  circumstances in which a resolution is or is not treated as having been passed, or

   (c)  cases in which a person is precluded from alleging that a resolution has not been duly passed.

### 282   Ordinary resolutions

(1)  An ordinary resolution of the members (or of a class of members) of a company means a resolution that is passed by a simple majority.

(2)  A written resolution is passed by a simple majority if it is passed by members representing a simple majority of the total voting rights of eligible members (see Chapter 2).

(3)  A resolution passed at a meeting on a show of hands is passed by a simple majority if it is passed by a simple majority of—

   (a)  the members who, being entitled to do so, vote in person on the resolution, and

   (b)  the persons who vote on the resolution as duly appointed proxies of members entitled to vote on it.

(4)  A resolution passed on a poll taken at a meeting is passed by a simple majority if it is passed by members representing a simple majority of the total voting rights of members who (being entitled to do so) vote in person or by proxy on the resolution.

(5)  Anything that may be done by ordinary resolution may also be done by special resolution.

### 283   Special resolutions

(1)  A special resolution of the members (or of a class of members) of a company means a resolution passed by a majority of not less than 75%.

(2)  A written resolution is passed by a majority of not less than 75% if it is passed by members representing not less than 75% of the total voting rights of eligible members (see Chapter 2).

(3)  Where a resolution of a private company is passed as a written resolution—

   (a)  the resolution is not a special resolution unless it stated that it was proposed as a special resolution, and

   (b)  if the resolution so stated, it may only be passed as a special resolution.

(4)  A resolution passed at a meeting on a show of hands is passed by a majority of not less than 75% if it is passed by not less than 75% of—

   (a)  the members who, being entitled to do so, vote in person on the resolution, and

   (b)  the persons who vote on the resolution as duly appointed proxies of members entitled to vote on it.

(5)  A resolution passed on a poll taken at a meeting is passed by a majority of not less than 75% if it is passed by members representing not less than 75% of the total voting rights of the members who (being entitled to do so) vote in person or by proxy on the resolution.

(6)  Where a resolution is passed at a meeting—

   (a)  the resolution is not a special resolution unless the notice of the meeting included the text of the resolution and specified the intention to propose the resolution as a special resolution, and

   (b)  if the notice of the meeting so specified, the resolution may only be passed as a special resolution.

### 284   Votes: general rules

(1)  On a vote on a written resolution—

(a) in the case of a company having a share capital, every member has one vote in respect of each share or each £10 of stock held by him, and

(b) in any other case, every member has one vote.

(2) On a vote on a resolution on a show of hands at a meeting—

(a) every member present in person has one vote, and

(b) every proxy present who has been duly appointed by a member entitled to vote on the resolution has one vote.

(3) On a vote on a resolution on a poll taken at a meeting—

(a) in the case of a company having a share capital, every member has one vote in respect of each share or each £10 of stock held by him, and

(b) in any other case, every member has one vote.

(4) The provisions of this section have effect subject to any provision of the company's articles.

**285   Votes: specific requirements**

(1) Where a member entitled to vote on a resolution has appointed one proxy only, and the company's articles provide that the proxy has fewer votes in a vote on a resolution on a show of hands taken at a meeting than the member would have if he were present in person—

(a) the provision about how many votes the proxy has on a show of hands is void, and

(b) the proxy has the same number of votes on a show of hands as the member who appointed him would have if he were present at the meeting.

(2) Where a member entitled to vote on a resolution has appointed more than one proxy, subsection (1) applies as if the references to the proxy were references to the proxies taken together.

(3) In relation to a resolution required or authorised by an enactment, if a private company's articles provide that a member has a different number of votes in relation to a resolution when it is passed as a written resolution and when it is passed on a poll taken at a meeting—

(a) the provision about how many votes a member has in relation to the resolution passed on a poll is void, and

(b) a member has the same number of votes in relation to the resolution when it is passed on a poll as he has when it is passed as a written resolution.

**286   Votes of joint holders of shares**

(1) In the case of joint holders of shares of a company, only the vote of the senior holder who votes (and any proxies duly authorised by him) may be counted by the company.

(2) For the purposes of this section, the senior holder of a share is determined by the order in which the names of the joint holders appear in the register of members.

(3) Subsections (1) and (2) have effect subject to any provision of the company's articles.

**287   Saving for provisions of articles as to determination of entitlement to vote**

Nothing in this Chapter affects—

(a) any provision of a company's articles—

(i)   requiring an objection to a person's entitlement to vote on a resolution to be made in accordance with the articles, and

(ii)  for the determination of any such objection to be final and conclusive, or

(b) the grounds on which such a determination may be questioned in legal proceedings.

## Chapter 2   Written resolutions

*General provisions about written resolutions*

**288   Written resolutions of private companies**

(1) In the Companies Acts a 'written resolution' means a resolution of a private company proposed and passed in accordance with this Chapter.

(2) The following may not be passed as a written resolution—

(a) a resolution under section 168 removing a director before the expiration of his period of office;

(b) a resolution under section 510 removing an auditor before the expiration of his term of office.

(3) A resolution may be proposed as a written resolution—

(a) by the directors of a private company (see section 291), or

(b) by the members of a private company (see sections 292 to 295).

(4) References in enactments passed or made before this Chapter comes into force to—

(a) a resolution of a company in general meeting, or

(b) a resolution of a meeting of a class of members of the company,

have effect as if they included references to a written resolution of the members, or of a class of members, of a private company (as appropriate).

(5) A written resolution of a private company has effect as if passed (as the case may be)—

(a) by the company in general meeting, or

(b) by a meeting of a class of members of the company,

and references in enactments passed or made before this section comes into force to a meeting at which a resolution is passed or to members voting in favour of a resolution shall be construed accordingly.

**289  Eligible members**

(1) In relation to a resolution proposed as a written resolution of a private company, the eligible members are the members who would have been entitled to vote on the resolution on the circulation date of the resolution (see section 290).

(2) If the persons entitled to vote on a written resolution change during the course of the day that is the circulation date of the resolution, the eligible members are the persons entitled to vote on the resolution at the time that the first copy of the resolution is sent or submitted to a member for his agreement.

*Circulation of written resolutions*

**290  Circulation date**

References in this Part to the circulation date of a written resolution are to the date on which copies of it are sent or submitted to members in accordance with this Chapter (or if copies are sent or submitted to members on different days, to the first of those days).

**291  Circulation of written resolutions proposed by directors**

(1) This section applies to a resolution proposed as a written resolution by the directors of the company.

(2) The company must send or submit a copy of the resolution to every eligible member.

(3) The company must do so—

(a) by sending copies at the same time (so far as reasonably practicable) to all eligible members in hard copy form, in electronic form or by means of a website, or

(b) if it is possible to do so without undue delay, by submitting the same copy to each eligible member in turn (or different copies to each of a number of eligible members in turn),

or by sending copies to some members in accordance with paragraph (a) and submitting a copy or copies to other members in accordance with paragraph (b).

(4) The copy of the resolution must be accompanied by a statement informing the member—

(a) how to signify agreement to the resolution (see section 296), and

(b) as to the date by which the resolution must be passed if it is not to lapse (see section 297).

(5) In the event of default in complying with this section, an offence is committed by every officer of the company who is in default.

(6) A person guilty of an offence under this section is liable—

(a) on conviction on indictment, to a fine;

(b) on summary conviction, to a fine not exceeding the statutory maximum.

(7) The validity of the resolution, if passed, is not affected by a failure to comply with this section.

**292  Members' power to require circulation of written resolution**

(1) The members of a private company may require the company to circulate a resolution that may properly be moved and is proposed to be moved as a written resolution.

(2) Any resolution may properly be moved as a written resolution unless—

(a) it would, if passed, be ineffective (whether by reason of inconsistency with any enactment or the company's constitution or otherwise),

(b) it is defamatory of any person, or

(c) it is frivolous or vexatious.

(3) Where the members require a company to circulate a resolution they may require the company to circulate with it a statement of not more than 1,000 words on the subject matter of the resolution.

(4) A company is required to circulate the resolution and any accompanying statement once it has received requests that it do so from members representing not less than the requisite percentage of the total voting rights of all members entitled to vote on the resolution.

(5) The 'requisite percentage' is 5% or such lower percentage as is specified for this purpose in the company's articles.

(6) A request—

(a) may be in hard copy form or in electronic form,

(b) must identify the resolution and any accompanying statement, and

(c) must be authenticated by the person or persons making it.

**293  Circulation of written resolution proposed by members**

(1) A company that is required under section 292 to circulate a resolution must send or submit to every eligible member—

(a) a copy of the resolution, and

(b) a copy of any accompanying statement.

This is subject to section 294(2) (deposit or tender of sum in respect of expenses of circulation) and section 295 (application not to circulate members' statement).

(2) The company must do so—

    (a) by sending copies at the same time (so far as reasonably practicable) to all eligible members in hard copy form, in electronic form or by means of a website, or

    (b) if it is possible to do so without undue delay, by submitting the same copy to each eligible member in turn (or different copies to each of a number of eligible members in turn),

or by sending copies to some members in accordance with paragraph (a) and submitting a copy or copies to other members in accordance with paragraph (b).

(3) The company must send or submit the copies (or, if copies are sent or submitted to members on different days, the first of those copies) not more than 21 days after it becomes subject to the requirement under section 292 to circulate the resolution.

(4) The copy of the resolution must be accompanied by guidance as to—

    (a) how to signify agreement to the resolution (see section 296), and

    (b) the date by which the resolution must be passed if it is not to lapse (see section 297).

(5) In the event of default in complying with this section, an offence is committed by every officer of the company who is in default.

(6) A person guilty of an offence under this section is liable—

    (a) on conviction on indictment, to a fine;

    (b) on summary conviction, to a fine not exceeding the statutory maximum.

(7) The validity of the resolution, if passed, is not affected by a failure to comply with this section.

### 294  Expenses of circulation

(1) The expenses of the company in complying with section 293 must be paid by the members who requested the circulation of the resolution unless the company resolves otherwise.

(2) Unless the company has previously so resolved, it is not bound to comply with that section unless there is deposited with or tendered to it a sum reasonably sufficient to meet its expenses in doing so.

### 295  Application not to circulate members' statement

(1) A company is not required to circulate a members' statement under section 293 if, on an application by the company or another person who claims to be aggrieved, the court is satisfied that the rights conferred by section 292 and that section are being abused.

(2) The court may order the members who requested the circulation of the statement to pay the whole or part of the company's costs (in Scotland, expenses) on such an application, even if they are not parties to the application.

*Agreeing to written resolutions*

### 296  Procedure for signifying agreement to written resolution

(1) A member signifies his agreement to a proposed written resolution when the company receives from him (or from someone acting on his behalf) an authenticated document—

    (a) identifying the resolution to which it relates, and

    (b) indicating his agreement to the resolution.

(2) The document must be sent to the company in hard copy form or in electronic form.

(3) A member's agreement to a written resolution, once signified, may not be revoked.

(4) A written resolution is passed when the required majority of eligible members have signified their agreement to it.

### 297  Period for agreeing to written resolution

(1) A proposed written resolution lapses if it is not passed before the end of—

    (a) the period specified for this purpose in the company's articles, or

    (b) if none is specified, the period of 28 days beginning with the circulation date.

(2) The agreement of a member to a written resolution is ineffective if signified after the expiry of that period.

*Supplementary*

### 298  Sending documents relating to written resolutions by electronic means

(1) Where a company has given an electronic address in any document containing or accompanying a proposed written resolution, it is deemed to have agreed that any document or information relating to that resolution may be sent by electronic means to that address (subject to any conditions or limitations specified in the document).

(2) In this section 'electronic address' means any address or number used for the purposes of sending or receiving documents or information by electronic means.

### 299  Publication of written resolution on website

(1) This section applies where a company sends—

    (a) a written resolution, or

    (b) a statement relating to a written resolution,

to a person by means of a website.

(2) The resolution or statement is not validly sent for the purposes of this Chapter unless the resolution is available on the website throughout the period beginning with the circulation date and ending on the date on which the resolution lapses under section 297.

### 300   Relationship between this Chapter and provisions of company's articles

A provision of the articles of a private company is void in so far as it would have the effect that a resolution that is required by or otherwise provided for in an enactment could not be proposed and passed as a written resolution.

## Chapter 3  Resolutions at meetings

### *General provisions about resolutions at meetings*

### 301   Resolutions at general meetings

A resolution of the members of a company is validly passed at a general meeting if—

      (a) notice of the meeting and of the resolution is given, and

      (b) the meeting is held and conducted,

in accordance with the provisions of this Chapter (and, where relevant, Chapter 4) and the company's articles.

### *Calling meetings*

### 302   Directors' power to call general meetings

The directors of a company may call a general meeting of the company.

### 303   Members' power to require directors to call general meeting

(1) The members of a company may require the directors to call a general meeting of the company.

(2) The directors are required to call a general meeting once the company has received requests to do so from—

      (a) members representing at least the required percentage of such of the paid-up capital of the company as carries the right of voting at general meetings of the company (excluding any paid-up capital held as treasury shares); or

      (b) in the case of a company not having a share capital, members who represent at least the required percentage of the total voting rights of all the members having a right to vote at general meetings.

(3) The required percentage is 10% unless, in the case of a private company, more than twelve months has elapsed since the end of the last general meeting—

      (a) called in pursuance of a requirement under this section, or

      (b) in relation to which any members of the company had (by virtue of an enactment, the company's articles or otherwise) rights with respect to the circulation of a resolution no less extensive than they would have had if the meeting had been so called at their request,

in which case the required percentage is 5%.

(4) A request—

      (a) must state the general nature of the business to be dealt with at the meeting, and

      (b) may include the text of a resolution that may properly be moved and is intended to be moved at the meeting.

(5) A resolution may properly be moved at a meeting unless—

      (a) it would, if passed, be ineffective (whether by reason of inconsistency with any enactment or the company's constitution or otherwise),

      (b) it is defamatory of any person, or

      (c) it is frivolous or vexatious.

(6) A request—

      (a) may be in hard copy form or in electronic form, and

      (b) must be authenticated by the person or persons making it.

### 304   Directors' duty to call meetings required by members

(1) Directors required under section 303 to call a general meeting of the company must call a meeting—

      (a) within 21 days from the date on which they become subject to the requirement, and

      (b) to be held on a date not more than 28 days after the date of the notice convening the meeting.

(2) If the requests received by the company identify a resolution intended to be moved at the meeting, the notice of the meeting must include notice of the resolution.

(3) The business that may be dealt with at the meeting includes a resolution of which notice is given in accordance with this section.

(4) If the resolution is to be proposed as a special resolution, the directors are treated as not having duly called the meeting if they do not give the required notice of the resolution in accordance with section 283.

### 305   Power of members to call meeting at company's expense

(1) If the directors—

(a) are required under section 303 to call a meeting, and

(b) do not do so in accordance with section 304,

the members who requested the meeting, or any of them representing more than one half of the total voting rights of all of them, may themselves call a general meeting.

(2) Where the requests received by the company included the text of a resolution intended to be moved at the meeting, the notice of the meeting must include notice of the resolution.

(3) The meeting must be called for a date not more than three months after the date on which the directors become subject to the requirement to call a meeting.

(4) The meeting must be called in the same manner, as nearly as possible, as that in which meetings are required to be called by directors of the company.

(5) The business which may be dealt with at the meeting includes a resolution of which notice is given in accordance with this section.

(6) Any reasonable expenses incurred by the members requesting the meeting by reason of the failure of the directors duly to call a meeting must be reimbursed by the company.

(7) Any sum so reimbursed shall be retained by the company out of any sums due or to become due from the company by way of fees or other remuneration in respect of the services of such of the directors as were in default.

### 306   Power of court to order meeting

(1) This section applies if for any reason it is impracticable—

(a) to call a meeting of a company in any manner in which meetings of that company may be called, or

(b) to conduct the meeting in the manner prescribed by the company's articles or this Act.

(2) The court may, either of its own motion or on the application—

(a) of a director of the company, or

(b) of a member of the company who would be entitled to vote at the meeting,

order a meeting to be called, held and conducted in any manner the court thinks fit.

(3) Where such an order is made, the court may give such ancillary or consequential directions as it thinks expedient.

(4) Such directions may include a direction that one member of the company present at the meeting be deemed to constitute a quorum.

(5) A meeting called, held and conducted in accordance with an order under this section is deemed for all purposes to be a meeting of the company duly called, held and conducted.

*Notice of meetings*

### 307   Notice required of general meeting

(1) A general meeting of a private company (other than an adjourned meeting) must be called by notice of at least 14 days.

(2) A general meeting of a public company (other than an adjourned meeting) must be called by notice of—

(a) in the case of an annual general meeting, at least 21 days, and

(b) in any other case, at least 14 days.

(3) The company's articles may require a longer period of notice than that specified in subsection (1) or (2).

(4) A general meeting may be called by shorter notice than that otherwise required if shorter notice is agreed by the members.

(5) The shorter notice must be agreed to by a majority in number of the members having a right to attend and vote at the meeting, being a majority who—

(a) together hold not less than the requisite percentage in nominal value of the shares giving a right to attend and vote at the meeting (excluding any shares in the company held as treasury shares), or

(b) in the case of a company not having a share capital, together represent not less than the requisite percentage of the total voting rights at that meeting of all the members.

(6) The requisite percentage is—

(a) in the case of a private company, 90% or such higher percentage (not exceeding 95%) as may be specified in the company's articles;

(b) in the case of a public company, 95%.

(7) Subsections (5) and (6) do not apply to an annual general meeting of a public company (see instead section 337(2)).

### 308   Manner in which notice to be given

Notice of a general meeting of a company must be given—

(a) in hard copy form,

(b) in electronic form, or

(c) by means of a website (see section 309),

or partly by one such means and partly by another.

### 309 Publication of notice of meeting on website

(1) Notice of a meeting is not validly given by a company by means of a website unless it is given in accordance with this section.

(2) When the company notifies a member of the presence of the notice on the website the notification must—

(a) state that it concerns a notice of a company meeting,

(b) specify the place, date and time of the meeting, and

(c) in the case of a public company, state whether the meeting will be an annual general meeting.

(3) The notice must be available on the website throughout the period beginning with the date of that notification and ending with the conclusion of the meeting.

### 310 Persons entitled to receive notice of meetings

(1) Notice of a general meeting of a company must be sent to—

(a) every member of the company, and

(b) every director.

(2) In subsection (1), the reference to members includes any person who is entitled to a share in consequence of the death or bankruptcy of a member, if the company has been notified of their entitlement.

(3) In subsection (2), the reference to the bankruptcy of a member includes—

(a) the sequestration of the estate of a member;

(b) a member's estate being the subject of a protected trust deed (within the meaning of the Bankruptcy (Scotland) Act 1985 (c. 66)).

(4) This section has effect subject to—

(a) any enactment, and

(b) any provision of the company's articles.

### 311 Contents of notices of meetings

(1) Notice of a general meeting of a company must state—

(a) the time and date of the meeting, and

(b) the place of the meeting.

(2) Notice of a general meeting of a company must state the general nature of the business to be dealt with at the meeting.

This subsection has effect subject to any provision of the company's articles.

### 312 Resolution requiring special notice

(1) Where by any provision of the Companies Acts special notice is required of a resolution, the resolution is not effective unless notice of the intention to move it has been given to the company at least 28 days before the meeting at which it is moved.

(2) The company must, where practicable, give its members notice of any such resolution in the same manner and at the same time as it gives notice of the meeting.

(3) Where that is not practicable, the company must give its members notice at least 14 days before the meeting—

(a) by advertisement in a newspaper having an appropriate circulation, or

(b) in any other manner allowed by the company's articles.

(4) If, after notice of the intention to move such a resolution has been given to the company, a meeting is called for a date 28 days or less after the notice has been given, the notice is deemed to have been properly given, though not given within the time required.

### 313 Accidental failure to give notice of resolution or meeting

(1) Where a company gives notice of—

(a) a general meeting, or

(b) a resolution intended to be moved at a general meeting,

any accidental failure to give notice to one or more persons shall be disregarded for the purpose of determining whether notice of the meeting or resolution (as the case may be) is duly given.

(2) Except in relation to notice given under—

(a) section 304 (notice of meetings required by members),

(b) section 305 (notice of meetings called by members), or

(c) section 339 (notice of resolutions at AGMs proposed by members),

subsection (1) has effect subject to any provision of the company's articles.

*Members' statements*

### 314 Members' power to require circulation of statements

(1) The members of a company may require the company to circulate, to members of the company entitled to receive notice of a general meeting, a statement of not more than 1,000 words with respect to—

    (a) a matter referred to in a proposed resolution to be dealt with at that meeting, or

    (b) other business to be dealt with at that meeting.

(2) A company is required to circulate a statement once it has received requests to do so from—

    (a) members representing at least 5% of the total voting rights of all the members who have a relevant right to vote (excluding any voting rights attached to any shares in the company held as treasury shares), or

    (b) at least 100 members who have a relevant right to vote and hold shares in the company on which there has been paid up an average sum, per member, of at least £100.

See also section 153 (exercise of rights where shares held on behalf of others).

(3) In subsection (2), a 'relevant right to vote' means—

    (a) in relation to a statement with respect to a matter referred to in a proposed resolution, a right to vote on that resolution at the meeting to which the requests relate, and

    (b) in relation to any other statement, a right to vote at the meeting to which the requests relate.

(4) A request—

    (a) may be in hard copy form or in electronic form,

    (b) must identify the statement to be circulated,

    (c) must be authenticated by the person or persons making it, and

    (d) must be received by the company at least one week before the meeting to which it relates.

### 315 Company's duty to circulate members' statement

(1) A company that is required under section 314, to circulate a statement must send a copy of it to each member of the company entitled to receive notice of the meeting—

    (a) in the same manner as the notice of the meeting, and

    (b) at the same time as, or as soon as reasonably practicable after, it gives notice of the meeting.

(2) Subsection (1) has effect subject to section 316(2) (deposit or tender of sum in respect of expenses of circulation) and section 317 (application not to circulate members' statement).

(3) In the event of default in complying with this section, an offence is committed by every officer of the company who is in default.

(4) A person guilty of an offence under this section is liable—

    (a) on conviction on indictment, to a fine;

    (b) on summary conviction, to a fine not exceeding the statutory maximum.

### 316 Expenses of circulating members' statement

(1) The expenses of the company in complying with section 315 need not be paid by the members who requested the circulation of the statement if—

    (a) the meeting to which the requests relate is an annual general meeting of a public company, and

    (b) requests sufficient to require the company to circulate the statement are received before the end of the financial year preceding the meeting.

(2) Otherwise—

    (a) the expenses of the company in complying with that section must be paid by the members who requested the circulation of the statement unless the company resolves otherwise, and

    (b) unless the company has previously so resolved, it is not bound to comply with that section unless there is deposited with or tendered to it, not later than one week before the meeting, a sum reasonably sufficient to meet its expenses in doing so.

### 317 Application not to circulate members' statement

(1) A company is not required to circulate a members' statement under section 315 if, on an application by the company or another person who claims to be aggrieved, the court is satisfied that the rights conferred by section 314 and that section are being abused.

(2) The court may order the members who requested the circulation of the statement to pay the whole or part of the company's costs (in Scotland, expenses) on such an application, even if they are not parties to the application.

*Procedure at meetings*

### 318 Quorum at meetings

(1) In the case of a company limited by shares or guarantee and having only one member, one qualifying person present at a meeting is a quorum.

(2) In any other case, subject to the provisions of the company's articles, two qualifying persons present at a meeting are a quorum, unless—

    (a) each is a qualifying person only because he is authorised under section 323 to act as the representative of a corporation in relation to the meeting, and they are representatives of the same corporation; or

    (b) each is a qualifying person only because he is appointed as proxy of a member in relation to the meeting, and they are proxies of the same member.

(3)  For the purposes of this section a 'qualifying person' means—

    (a)  an individual who is a member of the company,

    (b)  a person authorised under section 323 (representation of corporations at meetings) to act as the representative of a corporation in relation to the meeting, or

    (c)  a person appointed as proxy of a member in relation to the meeting.

### 319  Chairman of meeting

(1)  A member may be elected to be the chairman of a general meeting by a resolution of the company passed at the meeting.

(2)  Subsection (1) is subject to any provision of the company's articles that states who may or may not be chairman.

### 320  Declaration by chairman on a show of hands

(1)  On a vote on a resolution at a meeting on a show of hands, a declaration by the chairman that the resolution—

    (a)  has or has not been passed, or

    (b)  passed with a particular majority,

is conclusive evidence of that fact without proof of the number or proportion of the votes recorded in favour of or against the resolution.

(2)  An entry in respect of such a declaration in minutes of the meeting recorded in accordance with section 355 is also conclusive evidence of that fact without such proof.

(3)  This section does not have effect if a poll is demanded in respect of the resolution (and the demand is not subsequently withdrawn).

### 321  Right to demand a poll

(1)  A provision of a company's articles is void in so far as it would have the effect of excluding the right to demand a poll at a general meeting on any question other than—

    (a)  the election of the chairman of the meeting, or

    (b)  the adjournment of the meeting.

(2)  A provision of a company's articles is void in so far as it would have the effect of making ineffective a demand for a poll on any such question which is made—

    (a)  by not less than 5 members having the right to vote on the resolution; or

    (b)  by a member or members representing not less than 10% of the total voting rights of all the members having the right to vote on the resolution (excluding any voting rights attached to any shares in the company held as treasury shares); or

    (c)  by a member or members holding shares in the company conferring a right to vote on the resolution, being shares on which an aggregate sum has been paid up equal to not less than 10% of the total sum paid up on all the shares conferring that right (excluding shares in the company conferring a right to vote on the resolution which are held as treasury shares).

### 322  Voting on a poll

On a poll taken at a general meeting of a company, a member entitled to more than one vote need not, if he votes, use all his votes or cast all the votes he uses in the same way.

### 323  Representation of corporations at meetings

(1)  If a corporation (whether or not a company within the meaning of this Act) is a member of a company, it may by resolution of its directors or other governing body authorise a person or persons to act as its representative or representatives at any meeting of the company.

(2)  Where the corporation authorises only one person, he is entitled to exercise the same powers on behalf of the corporation as the corporation could exercise if it were an individual member of the company.

(3)  Where the corporation authorises more than one person, any one of them is entitled to exercise the same powers on behalf of the corporation as the corporation could exercise if it were an individual member of the company.

(4)  Where the corporation authorises more than one person and more than one of them purport to exercise a power under subsection (3)—

    (a)  if they purport to exercise the power in the same way, the power is treated as exercised in that way,

    (b)  if they do not purport to exercise the power in the same way, the power is treated as not exercised.

*Proxies*

### 324  Rights to appoint proxies

(1)  A member of a company is entitled to appoint another person as his proxy to exercise all or any of his rights to attend and to speak and vote at a meeting of the company.

(2)  In the case of a company having a share capital, a member may appoint more than one proxy in relation to a meeting, provided that each proxy is appointed to exercise the rights attached to a different

share or shares held by him, or (as the case may be) to a different £10, or multiple of £10, of stock held by him.

### 325   Notice of meeting to contain statement of rights

(1) In every notice calling a meeting of a company there must appear, with reasonable prominence, a statement informing the member of—

(a) his rights under section 324, and

(b) any more extensive rights conferred by the company's articles to appoint more than one proxy.

(2) Failure to comply with this section does not affect the validity of the meeting or of anything done at the meeting.

(3) If this section is not complied with as respects any meeting, an offence is committed by every officer of the company who is in default.

(4) A person guilty of an offence under this section is liable on summary conviction to a fine not exceeding level 3 on the standard scale.

### 326   Company-sponsored invitations to appoint proxies

(1) If for the purposes of a meeting there are issued at the company's expense invitations to members to appoint as proxy a specified person or a number of specified persons, the invitations must be issued to all members entitled to vote at the meeting.

(2) Subsection (1) is not contravened if—

(a) there is issued to a member at his request a form of appointment naming the proxy or a list of persons willing to act as proxy, and

(b) the form or list is available on request to all members entitled to vote at the meeting.

(3) If subsection (1) is contravened as respects a meeting, an offence is committed by every officer of the company who is in default.

(4) A person guilty of an offence under this section is liable on summary conviction to a fine not exceeding level 3 on the standard scale.

### 327   Notice required of appointment of proxy etc.

(1) This section applies to—

(a) the appointment of a proxy, and

(b) any document necessary to show the validity of, or otherwise relating to, the appointment of a proxy.

(2) Any provision of the company's articles is void in so far as it would have the effect of requiring any such appointment or document to be received by the company or another person earlier than the following time—

(a) in the case of a meeting or adjourned meeting, 48 hours before the time for holding the meeting or adjourned meeting;

(b) in the case of a poll taken more than 48 hours after it was demanded, 24 hours before the time appointed for the taking of the poll;

(c) in the case of a poll taken not more than 48 hours after it was demanded, the time at which it was demanded.

(3) In calculating the periods mentioned in subsection (2) no account shall be taken of any part of a day that is not a working day.

### 328   Chairing meetings

(1) A proxy may be elected to be the chairman of a general meeting by a resolution of the company passed at the meeting.

(2) Subsection (1) is subject to any provision of the company's articles that states who may or who may not be chairman.

### 329   Right of proxy to demand a poll

(1) The appointment of a proxy to vote on a matter at a meeting of a company authorises the proxy to demand, or join in demanding, a poll on that matter.

(2) In applying the provisions of section 321(2) (requirements for effective demand), a demand by a proxy counts—

(a) for the purposes of paragraph (a), as a demand by the member;

(b) for the purposes of paragraph (b), as a demand by a member representing the voting rights that the proxy is authorised to exercise;

(c) for the purposes of paragraph (c), as a demand by a member holding the shares to which those rights are attached.

### 330   Notice required of termination of proxy's authority

(1) This section applies to notice that the authority of a person to act as proxy is terminated ('notice of termination').

(2) The termination of the authority of a person to act as proxy does not affect—

(a) whether he counts in deciding whether there is a quorum at a meeting,

(b) the validity of anything he does as chairman of a meeting, or

(c)  the validity of a poll demanded by him at a meeting,

unless the company receives notice of the termination before the commencement of the meeting.

(3)  The termination of the authority of a person to act as proxy does not affect the validity of a vote given by that person unless the company receives notice of the termination—

(a)  before the commencement of the meeting or adjourned meeting at which the vote is given, or

(b)  in the case of a poll taken more than 48 hours after it is demanded, before the time appointed for taking the poll.

(4)  If the company's articles require or permit members to give notice of termination to a person other than the company, the references above to the company receiving notice have effect as if they were or (as the case may be) included a reference to that person.

(5)  Subsections (2) and (3) have effect subject to any provision of the company's articles which has the effect of requiring notice of termination to be received by the company or another person at a time earlier than that specified in those subsections.

This is subject to subsection (6).

(6)  Any provision of the company's articles is void in so far as it would have the effect of requiring notice of termination to be received by the company or another person earlier than the following time—

(a)  in the case of a meeting or adjourned meeting, 48 hours before the time for holding the meeting or adjourned meeting;

(b)  in the case of a poll taken more than 48 hours after it was demanded, 24 hours before the time appointed for the taking of the poll;

(c)  in the case of a poll taken not more than 48 hours after it was demanded, the time at which it was demanded.

(7)  In calculating the periods mentioned in subsections (3)(b) and (6) no account shall be taken of any part of a day that is not a working day.

### 331   Saving for more extensive rights conferred by articles

Nothing in sections 324 to 330 (proxies) prevents a company's articles from conferring more extensive rights on members or proxies than are conferred by those sections.

*Adjourned meetings*

### 332   Resolution passed at adjourned meeting

Where a resolution is passed at an adjourned meeting of a company, the resolution is for all purposes to be treated as having been passed on the date on which it was in fact passed, and is not to be deemed passed on any earlier date.

*Electronic communications*

### 333   Sending documents relating to meetings etc. in electronic form

(1)  Where a company has given an electronic address in a notice calling a meeting, it is deemed to have agreed that any document or information relating to proceedings at the meeting may be sent by electronic means to that address (subject to any conditions or limitations specified in the notice).

(2)  Where a company has given an electronic address—

(a)  in an instrument of proxy sent out by the company in relation to the meeting, or

(b)  in an invitation to appoint a proxy issued by the company in relation to the meeting,

it is deemed to have agreed that any document or information relating to proxies for that meeting may be sent by electronic means to that address (subject to any conditions or limitations specified in the notice).

(3)  In subsection (2), documents relating to proxies include—

(a)  the appointment of a proxy in relation to a meeting,

(b)  any document necessary to show the validity of, or otherwise relating to, the appointment of a proxy, and

(c)  notice of the termination of the authority of a proxy.

(4)  In this section 'electronic address' means any address or number used for the purposes of sending or receiving documents or information by electronic means.

*Application to class meetings*

### 334   Application to class meetings

(1)  The provisions of this Chapter apply (with necessary modifications) in relation to a meeting of holders of a class of shares as they apply in relation to a general meeting.

This is subject to subsections (2) and (3).

(2)  The following provisions of this Chapter do not apply in relation to a meeting of holders of a class of shares—

(a)  sections 303 to 305 (members' power to require directors to call general meeting), and

(b)  section 306 (power of court to order meeting).

(3) The following provisions (in addition to those mentioned in subsection (2)) do not apply in relation to a meeting in connection with the variation of rights attached to a class of shares (a 'variation of class rights meeting')—

    (a) section 318 (quorum), and

    (b) section 321 (right to demand a poll).

(4) The quorum for a variation of class rights meeting is—

    (a) for a meeting other than an adjourned meeting, two persons present holding at least one-third in nominal value of the issued shares of the class in question (excluding any shares of that class held as treasury shares);

    (b) for an adjourned meeting, one person present holding shares of the class in question.

(5) For the purposes of subsection (4), where a person is present by proxy or proxies, he is treated as holding only the shares in respect of which those proxies are authorised to exercise voting rights.

(6) At a variation of class rights meeting, any holder of shares of the class in question present may demand a poll.

(7) For the purposes of this section—

    (a) any amendment of a provision contained in a company's articles for the variation of the rights attached to a class of shares, or the insertion of any such provision into the articles, is itself to be treated as a variation of those rights, and

    (b) references to the variation of rights attached to a class of shares include references to their abrogation.

### 335 Application to class meetings: companies without a share capital

(1) The provisions of this Chapter apply (with necessary modifications) in relation to a meeting of a class of members of a company without a share capital as they apply in relation to a general meeting.

  This is subject to subsections (2) and (3).

(2) The following provisions of this Chapter do not apply in relation to a meeting of a class of members—

    (a) sections 303 to 305 (members' power to require directors to call general meeting), and

    (b) section 306 (power of court to order meeting).

(3) The following provisions (in addition to those mentioned in subsection (2)) do not apply in relation to a meeting in connection with the variation of the rights of a class of members (a 'variation of class rights meeting')—

    (a) section 318 (quorum), and

    (b) section 321 (right to demand a poll).

(4) The quorum for a variation of class rights meeting is—

    (a) for a meeting other than an adjourned meeting, two members of the class present (in person or by proxy) who together represent at least one-third of the voting rights of the class;

    (b) for an adjourned meeting, one member of the class present (in person or by proxy).

(5) At a variation of class rights meeting, any member present (in person or by proxy) may demand a poll.

(6) For the purposes of this section—

    (a) any amendment of a provision contained in a company's articles for the variation of the rights of a class of members, or the insertion of any such provision into the articles, is itself to be treated as a variation of those rights, and

    (b) references to the variation of rights of a class of members include references to their abrogation.

## Chapter 4 Public companies: additional requirements for AGMs

### 336 Public companies: annual general meeting

(1) Every public company must hold a general meeting as its annual general meeting in each period of 6 months beginning with the day following its accounting reference date (in addition to any other meetings held during that period).

(2) A company that fails to comply with subsection (1) as a result of giving notice under section 392 (alteration of accounting reference date)—

    (a) specifying a new accounting reference date, and

    (b) stating that the current accounting reference period or the previous accounting reference period is to be shortened,

shall be treated as if it had complied with subsection (1) if it holds a general meeting as its annual general meeting within 3 months of giving that notice.

(3) If a company fails to comply with subsection (1), an offence is committed by every officer of the company who is in default.

(4) A person guilty of an offence under this section is liable—

    (a) on conviction on indictment, to a fine;

(b) on summary conviction, to a fine not exceeding the statutory maximum.

### 337  Public companies: notice of AGM

(1)  A notice calling an annual general meeting of a public company must state that the meeting is an annual general meeting.

(2)  An annual general meeting may be called by shorter notice than that required by section 307(2) or by the company's articles (as the case may be), if all the members entitled to attend and vote at the meeting agree to the shorter notice.

### 338  Public companies: members' power to require circulation of resolutions for AGMs

(1)  The members of a public company may require the company to give, to members of the company entitled to receive notice of the next annual general meeting, notice of a resolution which may properly be moved and is intended to be moved at that meeting.

(2)  A resolution may properly be moved at an annual general meeting unless—

  (a)  it would, if passed, be ineffective (whether by reason of inconsistency with any enactment or the company's constitution or otherwise),

  (b)  it is defamatory of any person, or

  (c)  it is frivolous or vexatious.

(3)  A company is required to give notice of a resolution once it has received requests that it do so from—

  (a)  members representing at least 5% of the total voting rights of all the members who have a right to vote on the resolution at the annual general meeting to which the requests relate (excluding any voting rights attached to any shares in the company held as treasury shares), or

  (b)  at least 100 members who have a right to vote on the resolution at the annual general meeting to which the requests relate and hold shares in the company on which there has been paid up an average sum, per member, of at least £100.

See also section 153 (exercise of rights where shares held on behalf of others).

(4)  A request—

  (a)  may be in hard copy form or in electronic form,

  (b)  must identify the resolution of which notice is to be given,

  (c)  must be authenticated by the person or persons making it, and

  (d)  must be received by the company not later than—

    (i)  6 weeks before the annual general meeting to which the requests relate, or

    (ii)  if later, the time at which notice is given of that meeting.

### 339  Public companies: company's duty to circulate members' resolutions for AGMs

(1)  A company that is required under section 338 to give notice of a resolution must send a copy of it to each member of the company entitled to receive notice of the annual general meeting—

  (a)  in the same manner as notice of the meeting, and

  (b)  at the same time as, or as soon as reasonably practicable after, it gives notice of the meeting.

(2)  Subsection (1) has effect subject to section 340(2) (deposit or tender of sum in respect of expenses of circulation).

(3)  The business which may be dealt with at an annual general meeting includes a resolution of which notice is given in accordance with this section.

(4)  In the event of default in complying with this section, an offence is committed by every officer of the company who is in default.

(5)  A person guilty of an offence under this section is liable—

  (a)  on conviction on indictment, to a fine;

  (b)  on summary conviction, to a fine not exceeding the statutory maximum.

### 340  Public companies: expenses of circulating members' resolutions for AGM

(1)  The expenses of the company in complying with section 339 need not be paid by the members who requested the circulation of the resolution if requests sufficient to require the company to circulate it are received before the end of the financial year preceding the meeting.

(2)  Otherwise—

  (a)  the expenses of the company in complying with that section must be paid by the members who requested the circulation of the resolution unless the company resolves otherwise, and

  (b)  unless the company has previously so resolved, it is not bound to comply with that section unless there is deposited with or tendered to it, not later than—

    (i)  six weeks before the annual general meeting to which the requests relate, or

    (ii)  if later, the time at which notice is given of that meeting,

    a sum reasonably sufficient to meet its expenses in complying with that section.

# Chapter 5  Additional requirements for quoted companies

*Website publication of poll results*

### 341  Results of poll to be made available on website

(1)  Where a poll is taken at a general meeting of a quoted company, the company must ensure that the following information is made available on a website—

(a)  the date of the meeting,

(b)  the text of the resolution or, as the case may be, a description of the subject matter of the poll,

(c)  the number of votes cast in favour, and

(d)  the number of votes cast against.

(2)  The provisions of section 353 (requirements as to website availability) apply.

(3)  In the event of default in complying with this section (or with the requirements of section 353 as it applies for the purposes of this section), an offence is committed by every officer of the company who is in default.

(4)  A person guilty of an offence under subsection (3) is liable on summary conviction to a fine not exceeding level 3 on the standard scale.

(5)  Failure to comply with this section (or the requirements of section 353) does not affect the validity of—

(a)  the poll, or

(b)  the resolution or other business (if passed or agreed to) to which the poll relates.

(6)  This section only applies to polls taken after this section comes into force.

*Independent report on poll*

### 342  Members' power to require independent report on poll

(1)  The members of a quoted company may require the directors to obtain an independent report on any poll taken, or to be taken, at a general meeting of the company.

(2)  The directors are required to obtain an independent report if they receive requests to do so from—

(a)  members representing not less than 5% of the total voting rights of all the members who have a right to vote on the matter to which the poll relates (excluding any voting rights attached to any shares in the company held as treasury shares), or

(b)  not less than 100 members who have a right to vote on the matter to which the poll relates and hold shares in the company on which there has been paid up an average sum, per member, of not less than £100.

See also section 153 (exercise of rights where shares held on behalf of others).

(3)  Where the requests relate to more than one poll, subsection (2) must be satisfied in relation to each of them.

(4)  A request—

(a)  may be in hard copy form or in electronic form,

(b)  must identify the poll or polls to which it relates,

(c)  must be authenticated by the person or persons making it, and

(d)  must be received by the company not later than one week after the date on which the poll is taken.

### 343  Appointment of independent assessor

(1)  Directors who are required under section 342 to obtain an independent report on a poll or polls must appoint a person they consider to be appropriate (an 'independent assessor') to prepare a report for the company on it or them.

(2)  The appointment must be made within one week after the company being required to obtain the report.

(3)  The directors must not appoint a person who—

(a)  does not meet the independence requirement in section 344, or

(b)  has another role in relation to any poll on which he is to report (including, in particular, a role in connection with collecting or counting votes or with the appointment of proxies).

(4)  In the event of default in complying with this section, an offence is committed by every officer of the company who is in default.

(5)  A person guilty of an offence under this section is liable on summary conviction to a fine not exceeding level 5 on the standard scale.

(6)  If at the meeting no poll on which a report is required is taken—

(a)  the directors are not required to obtain a report from the independent assessor, and

(b)  his appointment ceases (but without prejudice to any right to be paid for work done before the appointment ceased).

### 344  Independence requirement

(1)  A person may not be appointed as an independent assessor—

    (a) if he is—
        (i) an officer or employee of the company, or
        (ii) a partner or employee of such a person, or a partnership of which such a person is a partner;
    (b) if he is—
        (i) an officer or employee of an associated undertaking of the company, or
        (ii) a partner or employee of such a person, or a partnership of which such a person is a partner;
    (c) if there exists between—
        (i) the person or an associate of his, and
        (ii) the company or an associated undertaking of the company,
a connection of any such description as may be specified by regulations made by the Secretary of State.

    (2) An auditor of the company is not regarded as an officer or employee of the company for this purpose.

    (3) In this section—
'associated undertaking' means—
    (a) a parent undertaking or subsidiary undertaking of the company, or
    (b) a subsidiary undertaking of a parent undertaking of the company; and
'associate' has the meaning given by section 345.

    (4) Regulations under this section are subject to negative resolution procedure.

## 345 Meaning of 'associate'

    (1) This section defines 'associate' for the purposes of section 344 (independence requirement).
    (2) In relation to an individual, 'associate' means—
    (a) that individual's spouse or civil partner or minor child or step-child,
    (b) any body corporate of which that individual is a director, and
    (c) any employee or partner of that individual.
    (3) In relation to a body corporate, 'associate' means—
    (a) any body corporate of which that body is a director,
    (b) any body corporate in the same group as that body, and
    (c) any employee or partner of that body or of any body corporate in the same group.
    (4) In relation to a partnership that is a legal person under the law by which it is governed, 'associate' means—
    (a) any body corporate of which that partnership is a director,
    (b) any employee of or partner in that partnership, and
    (c) any person who is an associate of a partner in that partnership.
    (5) In relation to a partnership that is not a legal person under the law by which it is governed, 'associate' means any person who is an associate of any of the partners.
    (6) In this section, in relation to a limited liability partnership, for 'director' read 'member'.

## 346 Effect of appointment of a partnership

    (1) This section applies where a partnership that is not a legal person under the law by which it is governed is appointed as an independent assessor.
    (2) Unless a contrary intention appears, the appointment is of the partnership as such and not of the partners.
    (3) Where the partnership ceases, the appointment is to be treated as extending to—
    (a) any partnership that succeeds to the practice of that partnership, or
    (b) any other person who succeeds to that practice having previously carried it on in partnership.
    (4) For the purposes of subsection (3)—
    (a) a partnership is regarded as succeeding to the practice of another partnership only if the members of the successor partnership are substantially the same as those of the former partnership, and
    (b) a partnership or other person is regarded as succeeding to the practice of a partnership only if it or he succeeds to the whole or substantially the whole of the business of the former partnership.
    (5) Where the partnership ceases and the appointment is not treated under subsection (3) as extending to any partnership or other person, the appointment may with the consent of the company be treated as extending to a partnership, or other person, who succeeds to—
    (a) the business of the former partnership, or
    (b) such part of it as is agreed by the company is to be treated as comprising the appointment.

## 347 The independent assessor's report

    (1) The report of the independent assessor must state his opinion whether—
    (a) the procedures adopted in connection with the poll or polls were adequate;

(b) the votes cast (including proxy votes) were fairly and accurately recorded and counted;

(c) the validity of members' appointments of proxies was fairly assessed;

(d) the notice of the meeting complied with section 325 (notice of meeting to contain statement of rights to appoint proxy);

(e) section 326 (company-sponsored invitations to appoint proxies) was complied with in relation to the meeting.

(2) The report must give his reasons for the opinions stated.

(3) If he is unable to form an opinion on any of those matters, the report must record that fact and state the reasons for it.

(4) The report must state the name of the independent assessor.

### 348  Rights of independent assessor: right to attend meeting etc.

(1) Where an independent assessor has been appointed to report on a poll, he is entitled to attend—

(a) the meeting at which the poll may be taken, and

(b) any subsequent proceedings in connection with the poll.

(2) He is also entitled to be provided by the company with a copy of—

(a) the notice of the meeting, and

(b) any other communication provided by the company in connection with the meeting to persons who have a right to vote on the matter to which the poll relates.

(3) The rights conferred by this section are only to be exercised to the extent that the independent assessor considers necessary for the preparation of his report.

(4) If the independent assessor is a firm, the right under subsection (1) to attend the meeting and any subsequent proceedings in connection with the poll is exercisable by an individual authorised by the firm in writing to act as its representative for that purpose.

### 349  Rights of independent assessor: right to information

(1) The independent assessor is entitled to access to the company's records relating to—

(a) any poll on which he is to report;

(b) the meeting at which the poll or polls may be, or were, taken.

(2) The independent assessor may require anyone who at any material time was—

(a) a director or secretary of the company,

(b) an employee of the company,

(c) a person holding or accountable for any of the company's records,

(d) a member of the company, or

(e) an agent of the company,

to provide him with information or explanations for the purpose of preparing his report.

(3) For this purpose 'agent' includes the company's bankers, solicitors and auditor.

(4) A statement made by a person in response to a requirement under this section may not be used in evidence against him in criminal proceedings except proceedings for an offence under section 350 (offences relating to provision of information).

(5) A person is not required by this section to disclose information in respect of which a claim to legal professional privilege (in Scotland, to confidentiality of communications) could be maintained in legal proceedings.

### 350  Offences relating to provision of information

(1) A person who fails to comply with a requirement under section 349 without delay commits an offence unless it was not reasonably practicable for him to provide the required information or explanation.

(2) A person guilty of an offence under subsection (1) is liable on summary conviction to a fine not exceeding level 3 on the standard scale.

(3) A person commits an offence who knowingly or recklessly makes to an independent assessor a statement (oral or written) that—

(a) conveys or purports to convey any information or explanations which the independent assessor requires, or is entitled to require, under section 349, and

(b) is misleading, false or deceptive in a material particular.

(4) A person guilty of an offence under subsection (3) is liable—

(a) on conviction on indictment, to imprisonment for a term not exceeding two years or a fine (or both);

(b) on summary conviction—

(i) in England and Wales, to imprisonment for a term not exceeding twelve months or to a fine not exceeding the statutory maximum (or both);

(ii) in Scotland or Northern Ireland, to imprisonment for a term not exceeding six months, or to a fine not exceeding the statutory maximum (or both).

(5) Nothing in this section affects any right of an independent assessor to apply for an injunction (in Scotland, an interdict or an order for specific performance) to enforce any of his rights under section 348 or 349.

### 351   Information to be made available on website

(1)  Where an independent assessor has been appointed to report on a poll, the company must ensure that the following information is made available on a website—

    (a)  the fact of his appointment,

    (b)  his identity,

    (c)  the text of the resolution or, as the case may be, a description of the subject matter of the poll to which his appointment relates, and

    (d)  a copy of a report by him which complies with section 347.

(2)  The provisions of section 353 (requirements as to website availability) apply.

(3)  In the event of default in complying with this section (or with the requirements of section 353 as it applies for the purposes of this section), an offence is committed by every officer of the company who is in default.

(4)  A person guilty of an offence under subsection (3) is liable on summary conviction to a fine not exceeding level 3 on the standard scale.

(5)  Failure to comply with this section (or the requirements of section 353) does not affect the validity of—

    (a)  the poll, or

    (b)  the resolution or other business (if passed or agreed to) to which the poll relates.

*Supplementary*

### 352   Application of provisions to class meetings

(1)  The provisions of—

section 341 (results of poll to be made available on website), and

sections 342 to 351 (independent report on poll),

apply (with any necessary modifications) in relation to a meeting of holders of a class of shares of a quoted company in connection with the variation of the rights attached to such shares as they apply in relation to a general meeting of the company.

(2)  For the purposes of this section—

    (a)  any amendment of a provision contained in a company's articles for the variation of the rights attached to a class of shares, or the insertion of any such provision into the articles, is itself to be treated as a variation of those rights, and

    (b)  references to the variation of rights attached to a class of shares include references to their abrogation.

### 353   Requirements as to website availability

(1)  The following provisions apply for the purposes of—

section 341 (results of poll to be made available on website), and

section 351 (report of independent observer to be made available on website).

(2)  The information must be made available on a website that—

    (a)  is maintained by or on behalf of the company, and

    (b)  identifies the company in question.

(3)  Access to the information on the website, and the ability to obtain a hard copy of the information from the website, must not be conditional on the payment of a fee or otherwise restricted.

(4)  The information—

    (a)  must be made available as soon as reasonably practicable, and

    (b)  must be kept available throughout the period of two years beginning with the date on which it is first made available on a website in accordance with this section.

(5)  A failure to make information available on a website throughout the period specified in subsection (4)(b) is disregarded if—

    (a)  the information is made available on the website for part of that period, and

    (b)  the failure is wholly attributable to circumstances that it would not be reasonable to have expected the company to prevent or avoid.

### 354   Power to limit or extend the types of company to which provisions of this Chapter apply

(1)  The Secretary of State may by regulations—

    (a)  limit the types of company to which some or all of the provisions of this Chapter apply, or

    (b)  extend some or all of the provisions of this Chapter to additional types of company.

(2)  Regulations under this section extending the application of any provision of this Chapter are subject to affirmative resolution procedure.

(3)  Any other regulations under this section are subject to negative resolution procedure.

(4)  Regulations under this section may—

    (a)  amend the provisions of this Chapter (apart from this section);

    (b)  repeal and re-enact provisions of this Chapter with modifications of form or arrangement, whether or not they are modified in substance;

    (c)  contain such consequential, incidental and supplementary provisions (including provisions amending, repealing or revoking enactments) as the Secretary of State thinks fit.

## Chapter 6 Records of resolutions and meetings

### 355 Records of resolutions and meetings etc.

(1) Every company must keep records comprising—

    (a) copies of all resolutions of members passed otherwise than at general meetings,

    (b) minutes of all proceedings of general meetings, and

    (c) details provided to the company in accordance with section 357 (decisions of sole member).

(2) The records must be kept for at least ten years from the date of the resolution, meeting or decision (as appropriate).

(3) If a company fails to comply with this section, an offence is committed by every officer of the company who is in default.

(4) A person guilty of an offence under this section is liable on summary conviction to a fine not exceeding level 3 on the standard scale and, for continued contravention, a daily default fine not exceeding one-tenth of level 3 on the standard scale.

### 356 Records as evidence of resolutions etc.

(1) This section applies to the records kept in accordance with section 355.

(2) The record of a resolution passed otherwise than at a general meeting, if purporting to be signed by a director of the company or by the company secretary, is evidence (in Scotland, sufficient evidence) of the passing of the resolution.

(3) Where there is a record of a written resolution of a private company, the requirements of this Act with respect to the passing of the resolution are deemed to be complied with unless the contrary is proved.

(4) The minutes of proceedings of a general meeting, if purporting to be signed by the chairman of that meeting or by the chairman of the next general meeting, are evidence (in Scotland, sufficient evidence) of the proceedings at the meeting.

(5) Where there is a record of proceedings of a general meeting of a company, then, until the contrary is proved—

    (a) the meeting is deemed duly held and convened,

    (b) all proceedings at the meeting are deemed to have duly taken place, and

    (c) all appointments at the meeting are deemed valid.

### 357 Records of decisions by sole member

(1) This section applies to a company limited by shares or by guarantee that has only one member.

(2) Where the member takes any decision that—

    (a) may be taken by the company in general meeting, and

    (b) has effect as if agreed by the company in general meeting,

he must (unless that decision is taken by way of a written resolution) provide the company with details of that decision.

(3) If a person fails to comply with this section he commits an offence.

(4) A person guilty of an offence under this section is liable on summary conviction to a fine not exceeding level 2 on the standard scale.

(5) Failure to comply with this section does not affect the validity of any decision referred to in subsection (2).

### 358 Inspection of records of resolutions and meetings

(1) The records referred to in section 355 (records of resolutions etc.) relating to the previous ten years must be kept available for inspection—

    (a) at the company's registered office, or

    (b) at a place specified in regulations under section 1136.

(2) The company must give notice to the registrar—

    (a) of the place at which the records are kept available for inspection, and

    (b) of any change in that place,

unless they have at all times been kept at the company's registered office.

(3) The records must be open to the inspection of any member of the company without charge.

(4) Any member may require a copy of any of the records on payment of such fee as may be prescribed.

(5) If default is made for 14 days in complying with subsection (2) or an inspection required under subsection (3) is refused, or a copy requested under subsection (4) is not sent, an offence is committed by every officer of the company who is in default.

(6) A person guilty of an offence under this section is liable on summary conviction to a fine not exceeding level 3 on the standard scale and, for continued contravention, a daily default fine not exceeding one-tenth of level 3 on the standard scale.

(7) In a case in which an inspection required under subsection (3) is refused or a copy requested under subsection (4) is not sent, the court may by order compel an immediate inspection of the records or direct that the copies required be sent to the persons who requested them.

**359   Records of resolutions and meetings of class of members**

The provisions of this Chapter apply (with necessary modifications) in relation to resolutions and meetings of—

    (a) holders of a class of shares, and

    (b) in the case of a company without a share capital, a class of members,

as they apply in relation to resolutions of members generally and to general meetings.

## Chapter 7  Supplementary provisions

**360   Computation of periods of notice etc.: clear day rule**

    (1) This section applies for the purposes of the following provisions of this Part—

section 307(1) and (2) (notice required of general meeting),

section 312(1) and (3) (resolution requiring special notice),

section 314(4)(d) (request to circulate members' statement),

section 316(2)(b) (expenses of circulating statement to be deposited or tendered before meeting),

section 338(4)(d)(i) (request to circulate member's resolution at AGM of public company), and

section 340(2)(b)(i) (expenses of circulating statement to be deposited or tendered before meeting).

    (2) Any reference in those provisions to a period of notice, or to a period before a meeting by which a request must be received or sum deposited or tendered, is to a period of the specified length excluding—

    (a) the day of the meeting, and

    (b) the day on which the notice is given, the request received or the sum deposited or tendered.

**361   Meaning of 'quoted company'**

In this Part 'quoted company' has the same meaning as in Part 15 of this Act.

# PART 14  CONTROL OF POLITICAL DONATIONS AND EXPENDITURE

*Introductory*

**362   Introductory**

This Part has effect for controlling—

    (a) political donations made by companies to political parties, to other political organisations and to independent election candidates, and

    (b) political expenditure incurred by companies.

*Donations and expenditure to which this Part applies*

**363   Political parties, organisations etc. to which this Part applies**

    (1) This Part applies to a political party if—

    (a) it is registered under Part 2 of the Political Parties, Elections and Referendums Act 2000 (c. 41), or

    (b) it carries on, or proposes to carry on, activities for the purposes of or in connection with the participation of the party in any election or elections to public office held in a member State other than the United Kingdom.

    (2) This Part applies to an organisation (a 'political organisation') if it carries on, or proposes to carry on, activities that are capable of being reasonably regarded as intended—

    (a) to affect public support for a political party to which, or an independent election candidate to whom, this Part applies, or

    (b) to influence voters in relation to any national or regional referendum held under the law of the United Kingdom or another member State.

    (3) This Part applies to an independent election candidate at any election to public office held in the United Kingdom or another member State.

    (4) Any reference in the following provisions of this Part to a political party, political organisation or independent election candidate, or to political expenditure, is to a party, organisation, independent candidate or expenditure to which this Part applies.

**364   Meaning of 'political donation'**

    (1) The following provisions have effect for the purposes of this Part as regards the meaning of 'political donation'.

    (2) In relation to a political party or other political organisation—

    (a) 'political donation' means anything that in accordance with sections 50 to 52 of the Political Parties, Elections and Referendums Act 2000—

(i)   constitutes a donation for the purposes of Chapter 1 of Part 4 of that Act (control of donations to registered parties), or

(ii)   would constitute such a donation reading references in those sections to a registered party as references to any political party or other political organisation, and

(b) section 53 of that Act applies, in the same way, for the purpose of determining the value of a donation.

(3)  In relation to an independent election candidate—

(a) 'political donation' means anything that, in accordance with sections 50 to 52 of that Act, would constitute a donation for the purposes of Chapter 1 of Part 4 of that Act (control of donations to registered parties) reading references in those sections to a registered party as references to the independent election candidate, and

(b) section 53 of that Act applies, in the same way, for the purpose of determining the value of a donation.

(4)  For the purposes of this section, sections 50 and 53 of the Political Parties, Elections and Referendums Act 2000 (c. 41) (definition of 'donation' and value of donations) shall be treated as if the amendments to those sections made by the Electoral Administration Act 2006 (which remove from the definition of 'donation' loans made otherwise than on commercial terms) had not been made.

### 365   Meaning of 'political expenditure'

(1)  In this Part 'political expenditure', in relation to a company, means expenditure incurred by the company on—

(a) the preparation, publication or dissemination of advertising or other promotional or publicity material—

(i)   of whatever nature, and

(ii)   however published or otherwise disseminated,

that, at the time of publication or dissemination, is capable of being reasonably regarded as intended to affect public support for a political party or other political organisation, or an independent election candidate, or

(b) activities on the part of the company that are capable of being reasonably regarded as intended—

(i)   to affect public support for a political party or other political organisation, or an independent election candidate, or

(ii)   to influence voters in relation to any national or regional referendum held under the law of a member State.

(2)  For the purposes of this Part a political donation does not count as political expenditure.

*Authorisation required for donations or expenditure*

### 366   Authorisation required for donations or expenditure

(1)  A company must not—

(a) make a political donation to a political party or other political organisation, or to an independent election candidate, or

(b) incur any political expenditure,

unless the donation or expenditure is authorised in accordance with the following provisions.

(2)  The donation or expenditure must be authorised—

(a) in the case of a company that is not a subsidiary of another company, by a resolution of the members of the company;

(b) in the case of a company that is a subsidiary of another company by—

(i)   a resolution of the members of the company, and

(ii)   a resolution of the members of any relevant holding company.

(3)  No resolution is required on the part of a company that is a wholly-owned subsidiary of a UK-registered company.

(4)  For the purposes of subsection (2)(b)(ii) a 'relevant holding company' means a company that, at the time the donation was made or the expenditure was incurred—

(a) was a holding company of the company by which the donation was made or the expenditure was incurred,

(b) was a UK-registered company, and

(c) was not a subsidiary of another UK-registered company.

(5)  The resolution or resolutions required by this section—

(a) must comply with section 367 (form of authorising resolution), and

(b) must be passed before the donation is made or the expenditure incurred.

(6)  Nothing in this section enables a company to be authorised to do anything that it could not lawfully do apart from this section.

### 367   Form of authorising resolution

(1)  A resolution conferring authorisation for the purposes of this Part may relate to—

(a) the company passing the resolution,

(b) one or more subsidiaries of that company, or

(c) the company passing the resolution and one or more subsidiaries of that company.

(2) A resolution may be expressed to relate to all companies that are subsidiaries of the company passing the resolution—

(a) at the time the resolution is passed, or

(b) at any time during the period for which the resolution has effect,

without identifying them individually.

(3) The resolution may authorise donations or expenditure under one or more of the following heads—

(a) donations to political parties or independent election candidates;

(b) donations to political organisations other than political parties;

(c) political expenditure.

(4) The resolution must specify a head or heads—

(a) in the case of a resolution under subsection (2), for all of the companies to which it relates taken together;

(b) in the case of any other resolution, for each company to which it relates.

(5) The resolution must be expressed in general terms conforming with subsection (2) and must not purport to authorise particular donations or expenditure.

(6) For each of the specified heads the resolution must authorise donations or, as the case may be, expenditure up to a specified amount in the period for which the resolution has effect (see section 368).

(7) The resolution must specify such amounts—

(a) in the case of a resolution under subsection (2), for all of the companies to which it relates taken together;

(b) in the case of any other resolution, for each company to which it relates.

### 368 Period for which resolution has effect

(1) A resolution conferring authorisation for the purposes of this Part has effect for a period of four years beginning with the date on which it is passed unless the directors determine, or the articles require, that it is to have effect for a shorter period beginning with that date.

(2) The power of the directors to make a determination under this section is subject to any provision of the articles that operates to prevent them from doing so.

*Remedies in case of unauthorised donations or expenditure*

### 369 Liability of directors in case of unauthorised donation or expenditure

(1) This section applies where a company has made a political donation or incurred political expenditure without the authorisation required by this Part.

(2) The directors in default are jointly and severally liable—

(a) to make good to the company the amount of the unauthorised donation or expenditure, with interest, and

(b) to compensate the company for any loss or damage sustained by it as a result of the unauthorised donation or expenditure having been made.

(3) The directors in default are—

(a) those who, at the time the unauthorised donation was made or the unauthorised expenditure was incurred, were directors of the company by which the donation was made or the expenditure was incurred, and

(b) where—

(i) that company was a subsidiary of a relevant holding company, and

(ii) the directors of the relevant holding company failed to take all reasonable steps to prevent the donation being made or the expenditure being incurred,

the directors of the relevant holding company.

(4) For the purposes of subsection (3)(b) a 'relevant holding company' means a company that, at the time the donation was made or the expenditure was incurred—

(a) was a holding company of the company by which the donation was made or the expenditure was incurred,

(b) was a UK-registered company, and

(c) was not a subsidiary of another UK-registered company.

(5) The interest referred to in subsection (2)(a) is interest on the amount of the unauthorised donation or expenditure, so far as not made good to the company—

(a) in respect of the period beginning with the date when the donation was made or the expenditure was incurred, and

(b) at such rate as the Secretary of State may prescribe by regulations.

Section 379(2) (construction of references to date when donation made or expenditure incurred) does not apply for the purposes of this subsection.

(6) Where only part of a donation or expenditure was unauthorised, this section applies only to so much of it as was unauthorised.

**370  Enforcement of directors' liabilities by shareholder action**

(1) Any liability of a director under section 369 is enforceable—

(a) in the case of a liability of a director of a company to that company, by proceedings brought under this section in the name of the company by an authorised group of its members;

(b) in the case of a liability of a director of a holding company to a subsidiary, by proceedings brought under this section in the name of the subsidiary by—

(i) an authorised group of members of the subsidiary, or

(ii) an authorised group of members of the holding company.

(2) This is in addition to the right of the company to which the liability is owed to bring proceedings itself to enforce the liability.

(3) An 'authorised group' of members of a company means—

(a) the holders of not less than 5% in nominal value of the company's issued share capital,

(b) if the company is not limited by shares, not less than 5% of its members, or

(c) not less than 50 of the company's members.

(4) The right to bring proceedings under this section is subject to the provisions of section 371.

(5) Nothing in this section affects any right of a member of a company to bring or continue proceedings under Part 11 (derivative claims or proceedings).

**371  Enforcement of directors' liabilities by shareholder action: supplementary**

(1) A group of members may not bring proceedings under section 370 in the name of a company unless—

(a) the group has given written notice to the company stating—

(i) the cause of action and a summary of the facts on which the proceedings are to be based,

(ii) the names and addresses of the members comprising the group, and

(iii) the grounds on which it is alleged that those members constitute an authorised group; and

(b) not less than 28 days have elapsed between the date of the giving of the notice to the company and the bringing of the proceedings.

(2) Where such a notice is given to a company, any director of the company may apply to the court within the period of 28 days beginning with the date of the giving of the notice for an order directing that the proposed proceedings shall not be brought, on one or more of the following grounds—

(a) that the unauthorised amount has been made good to the company;

(b) that proceedings to enforce the liability have been brought, and are being pursued with due diligence, by the company;

(c) that the members proposing to bring proceedings under this section do not constitute an authorised group.

(3) Where an application is made on the ground mentioned in subsection (2)(b), the court may as an alternative to directing that the proposed proceedings under section 370 are not to be brought, direct—

(a) that such proceedings may be brought on such terms and conditions as the court thinks fit, and

(b) that the proceedings brought by the company—

(i) shall be discontinued, or

(ii) may be continued on such terms and conditions as the court thinks fit.

(4) The members by whom proceedings are brought under section 370 owe to the company in whose name they are brought the same duties in relation to the proceedings as would be owed by the company's directors if the proceedings were being brought by the company.

But proceedings to enforce any such duty may be brought by the company only with the permission of the court.

(5) Proceedings brought under section 370 may not be discontinued or settled by the group except with the permission of the court, which may be given on such terms as the court thinks fit.

**372  Costs of shareholder action**

(1) This section applies in relation to proceedings brought under section 370 in the name of a company ('the company') by an authorised group ('the group').

(2) The group may apply to the court for an order directing the company to indemnify the group in respect of costs incurred or to be incurred by the group in connection with the proceedings.

The court may make such an order on such terms as it thinks fit.

(3) The group is not entitled to be paid any such costs out of the assets of the company except by virtue of such an order.

(4) If no such order has been made with respect to the proceedings, then—

(a) if the company is awarded costs in connection with the proceedings, or it is agreed that costs incurred by the company in connection with the proceedings should be paid by any defendant, the costs shall be paid to the group; and

(b) if any defendant is awarded costs in connection with the proceedings, or it is agreed that any defendant should be paid costs incurred by him in connection with the proceedings, the costs shall be paid by the group.

(5) In the application of this section to Scotland for 'costs' read 'expenses' and for 'defendant' read 'defender'.

### 373    Information for purposes of shareholder action

(1) Where proceedings have been brought under section 370 in the name of a company by an authorised group, the group is entitled to require the company to provide it with all information relating to the subject matter of the proceedings that is in the company's possession or under its control or which is reasonably obtainable by it.

(2) If the company, having been required by the group to do so, refuses to provide the group with all or any of that information, the court may, on an application made by the group, make an order directing—

(a) the company, and

(b) any of its officers or employees specified in the application,

to provide the group with the information in question in such form and by such means as the court may direct.

*Exemptions*

### 374    Trade unions

(1) A donation to a trade union, other than a contribution to the union's political fund, is not a political donation for the purposes of this Part.

(2) A trade union is not a political organisation for the purposes of section 365 (meaning of 'political expenditure').

(3) In this section—

'trade union' has the meaning given by section 1 of Trade Union and Labour Relations (Consolidation) Act 1992 (c. 52) or Article 3 of the Industrial Relations (Northern Ireland) Order 1992 (S.I. 1992/807 (N.I. 5));

'political fund' means the fund from which payments by a trade union in the furtherance of political objects are required to be made by virtue of section 82(1)(a) of that Act or Article 57(2)(a) of that Order.

### 375    Subscription for membership of trade association

(1) A subscription paid to a trade association for membership of the association is not a political donation for the purposes of this Part.

(2) For this purpose—

'trade association' means an organisation formed for the purpose of furthering the trade interests of its members, or of persons represented by its members, and

'subscription' does not include a payment to the association to the extent that it is made for the purpose of financing any particular activity of the association.

### 376    All-party parliamentary groups

(1) An all-party parliamentary group is not a political organisation for the purposes of this Part.

(2) An 'all-party parliamentary group' means an all-party group composed of members of one or both of the Houses of Parliament (or of such members and other persons).

### 377    Political expenditure exempted by order

(1) Authorisation under this Part is not needed for political expenditure that is exempt by virtue of an order of the Secretary of State under this section.

(2) An order may confer an exemption in relation to—

(a) companies of any description or category specified in the order, or

(b) expenditure of any description or category so specified (whether framed by reference to goods, services or other matters in respect of which such expenditure is incurred or otherwise),

or both.

(3) If or to the extent that expenditure is exempt from the requirement of authorisation under this Part by virtue of an order under this section, it shall be disregarded in determining what donations are authorised by any resolution of the company passed for the purposes of this Part.

(4) An order under this section is subject to affirmative resolution procedure.

### 378    Donations not amounting to more than £5,000 in any twelve month period

(1) Authorisation under this Part is not needed for a donation except to the extent that the total amount of—

(a) that donation, and

(b) other relevant donations made in the period of 12 months ending with the date on which that donation is made,

exceeds £5,000.

(2) In this section—

'donation' means a donation to a political party or other political organisation or to an independent election candidate; and

'other relevant donations' means—

(a) in relation to a donation made by a company that is not a subsidiary, any other donations made by that company or by any of its subsidiaries;

(b) in relation to a donation made by a company that is a subsidiary, any other donations made by that company, by any holding company of that company or by any other subsidiary of any such holding company.

(3) If or to the extent that a donation is exempt by virtue of this section from the requirement of authorisation under this Part, it shall be disregarded in determining what donations are authorised by any resolution passed for the purposes of this Part.

*Supplementary provisions*

### 379  Minor definitions

(1) In this Part—

'director' includes shadow director; and

'organisation' includes any body corporate or unincorporated association and any combination of persons.

(2) Except as otherwise provided, any reference in this Part to the time at which a donation is made or expenditure is incurred is, in a case where the donation is made or expenditure incurred in pursuance of a contract, any earlier time at which that contract is entered into by the company.

# PART 15  ACCOUNTS AND REPORTS

## Chapter 1  Introduction

### *General*

### 380  Scheme of this Part

(1) The requirements of this Part as to accounts and reports apply in relation to each financial year of a company.

(2) In certain respects different provisions apply to different kinds of company.

(3) The main distinctions for this purpose are—

(a) between companies subject to the small companies regime (see section 381) and companies that are not subject to that regime; and

(b) between quoted companies (see section 385) and companies that are not quoted.

(4) In this Part, where provisions do not apply to all kinds of company—

(a) provisions applying to companies subject to the small companies regime appear before the provisions applying to other companies,

(b) provisions applying to private companies appear before the provisions applying to public companies, and

(c) provisions applying to quoted companies appear after the provisions applying to other companies.

### *Companies subject to the small companies regime*

### 381  Companies subject to the small companies regime

The small companies regime applies to a company for a financial year in relation to which the company—

(a) qualifies as small (see sections 382 and 383), and

(b) is not excluded from the regime (see section 384).

### 382  Companies qualifying as small: general

(1) A company qualifies as small in relation to its first financial year if the qualifying conditions are met in that year.

(2) A company qualifies as small in relation to a subsequent financial year—

(a) if the qualifying conditions are met in that year and the preceding financial year;

(b) if the qualifying conditions are met in that year and the company qualified as small in relation to the preceding financial year;

(c) if the qualifying conditions were met in the preceding financial year and the company qualified as small in relation to that year.

(3) The qualifying conditions are met by a company in a year in which it satisfies two or more of the following requirements—

| Turnover | Not more than £6.5 million |
|---|---|
| Balance sheet total | Not more than £3.26 million |
| Number of employees | Not more than 50 |

(4)  For a period that is a company's financial year but not in fact a year the maximum figures for turnover must be proportionately adjusted.

(5)  The balance sheet total means the aggregate of the amounts shown as assets in the company's balance sheet.

(6)  The number of employees means the average number of persons employed by the company in the year, determined as follows—

    (a)  find for each month in the financial year the number of persons employed under contracts of service by the company in that month (whether throughout the month or not),

    (b)  add together the monthly totals, and

    (c)  divide by the number of months in the financial year.

(7)  This section is subject to section 383 (companies qualifying as small: parent companies).

### 383  Companies qualifying as small: parent companies

(1)  A parent company qualifies as a small company in relation to a financial year only if the group headed by it qualifies as a small group.

(2)  A group qualifies as small in relation to the parent company's first financial year if the qualifying conditions are met in that year.

(3)  A group qualifies as small in relation to a subsequent financial year of the parent company—

    (a)  if the qualifying conditions are met in that year and the preceding financial year;

    (b)  if the qualifying conditions are met in that year and the group qualified as small in relation to the preceding financial year;

    (c)  if the qualifying conditions were met in the preceding financial year and the group qualified as small in relation to that year.

(4)  The qualifying conditions are met by a group in a year in which it satisfies two or more of the following requirements—

| 1. | Aggregate turnover | Not more than £6.5 million net (or £7.8 million gross) |
|---|---|---|
| 2. | Aggregate balance sheet total | Not more than £3.26 million net (or £3.9 million gross) |
| 3. | Aggregate number of employees | Not more than 50 |

(5)  The aggregate figures are ascertained by aggregating the relevant figures determined in accordance with section 382 for each member of the group.

(6)  In relation to the aggregate figures for turnover and balance sheet total—

'net' means after any set-offs and other adjustments made to eliminate group transactions—

    (a)  in the case of Companies Act accounts, in accordance with regulations under section 404,

    (b)  in the case of IAS accounts, in accordance with international accounting standards; and

'gross' means without those set-offs and other adjustments.

A company may satisfy any relevant requirement on the basis of either the net or the gross figure.

(7)  The figures for each subsidiary undertaking shall be those included in its individual accounts for the relevant financial year, that is—

    (a)  if its financial year ends with that of the parent company, that financial year, and

    (b)  if not, its financial year ending last before the end of the financial year of the parent company.

If those figures cannot be obtained without disproportionate expense or undue delay, the latest available figures shall be taken.

### 384  Companies excluded from the small companies regime

(1)  The small companies regime does not apply to a company that is, or was at any time within the financial year to which the accounts relate—

    (a)  a public company,

    (b)  a company that—

      (i)   is an authorised insurance company, a banking company, an e-money issuer, a MiFID investment firm or a UCITS management company, or

      (ii)  carries on insurance market activity, or

    (c)  a member of an ineligible group.

(2)  A group is ineligible if any of its members is—

    (a)  a public company,

    (b)  a body corporate (other than a company) whose shares are admitted to trading on a regulated market in an EEA State,

    (c)  a person (other than a small company) who has permission under Part 4 of the Financial Services and Markets Act 2000 (c. 8) to carry on a regulated activity,

    (d)  a small company that is an authorised insurance company, a banking company, an e-money issuer, a MiFID investment firm or a UCITS management company, or

    (e)  a person who carries on insurance market activity.

(3)  A company is a small company for the purposes of subsection (2) if it qualified as small in relation to its last financial year ending on or before the end of the financial year to which the accounts relate.

*Quoted and unquoted companies*

### 385 Quoted and unquoted companies

(1) For the purposes of this Part a company is a quoted company in relation to a financial year if it is a quoted company immediately before the end of the accounting reference period by reference to which that financial year was determined.

(2) A 'quoted company' means a company whose equity share capital—

(a) has been included in the official list in accordance with the provisions of Part 6 of the Financial Services and Markets Act 2000 (c. 8), or

(b) is officially listed in an EEA State, or

(c) is admitted to dealing on either the New York Stock Exchange or the exchange known as Nasdaq.

In paragraph (a) 'the official list' has the meaning given by section 103(1) of the Financial Services and Markets Act 2000.

(3) An 'unquoted company' means a company that is not a quoted company.

(4) The Secretary of State may by regulations amend or replace the provisions of subsections (1) to (2) so as to limit or extend the application of some or all of the provisions of this Part that are expressed to apply to quoted companies.

(5) Regulations under this section extending the application of any such provision of this Part are subject to affirmative resolution procedure.

(6) Any other regulations under this section are subject to negative resolution procedure.

## Chapter 2  Accounting records

### 386 Duty to keep accounting records

(1) Every company must keep adequate accounting records.

(2) Adequate accounting records means records that are sufficient—

(a) to show and explain the company's transactions,

(b) to disclose with reasonable accuracy, at any time, the financial position of the company at that time, and

(c) to enable the directors to ensure that any accounts required to be prepared comply with the requirements of this Act (and, where applicable, of Article 4 of the IAS Regulation).

(3) Accounting records must, in particular, contain—

(a) entries from day to day of all sums of money received and expended by the company and the matters in respect of which the receipt and expenditure takes place, and

(b) a record of the assets and liabilities of the company.

(4) If the company's business involves dealing in goods, the accounting records must contain—

(a) statements of stock held by the company at the end of each financial year of the company,

(b) all statements of stocktakings from which any statement of stock as is mentioned in paragraph (a) has been or is to be prepared, and

(c) except in the case of goods sold by way of ordinary retail trade, statements of all goods sold and purchased, showing the goods and the buyers and sellers in sufficient detail to enable all these to be identified.

(5) A parent company that has a subsidiary undertaking in relation to which the above requirements do not apply must take reasonable steps to secure that the undertaking keeps such accounting records as to enable the directors of the parent company to ensure that any accounts required to be prepared under this Part comply with the requirements of this Act (and, where applicable, of Article 4 of the IAS Regulation).

### 387 Duty to keep accounting records: offence

(1) If a company fails to comply with any provision of section 386 (duty to keep accounting records), an offence is committed by every officer of the company who is in default.

(2) It is a defence for a person charged with such an offence to show that he acted honestly and that in the circumstances in which the company's business was carried on the default was excusable.

(3) A person guilty of an offence under this section is liable—

(a) on conviction on indictment, to imprisonment for a term not exceeding two years or a fine (or both);

(b) on summary conviction—

(i) in England and Wales, to imprisonment for a term not exceeding twelve months or to a fine not exceeding the statutory maximum (or both);

(ii) in Scotland or Northern Ireland, to imprisonment for a term not exceeding six months, or to a fine not exceeding the statutory maximum (or both).

### 388 Where and for how long records to be kept

(1) A company's accounting records—

(a) must be kept at its registered office or such other place as the directors think fit, and

(b) must at all times be open to inspection by the company's officers.

(2)  If accounting records are kept at a place outside the United Kingdom, accounts and returns with respect to the business dealt with in the accounting records so kept must be sent to, and kept at, a place in the United Kingdom, and must at all times be open to such inspection.

(3)  The accounts and returns to be sent to the United Kingdom must be such as to—

(a)  disclose with reasonable accuracy the financial position of the business in question at intervals of not more than six months, and

(b)  enable the directors to ensure that the accounts required to be prepared under this Part comply with the requirements of this Act (and, where applicable, of Article 4 of the IAS Regulation).

(4)  Accounting records that a company is required by section 386 to keep must be preserved by it—

(a)  in the case of a private company, for three years from the date on which they are made;

(b)  in the case of a public company, for six years from the date on which they are made.

(5)  Subsection (4) is subject to any provision contained in rules made under section 411 of the Insolvency Act 1986 (c. 45) (company insolvency rules) or Article 359 of the Insolvency (Northern Ireland) Order 1989 (S.I. 1989/2405 (N.I. 19)).

### 389  Where and for how long records to be kept: offences

(1)  If a company fails to comply with any provision of subsections (1) to (3) of section 388 (requirements as to keeping of accounting records), an offence is committed by every officer of the company who is in default.

(2)  It is a defence for a person charged with such an offence to show that he acted honestly and that in the circumstances in which the company's business was carried on the default was excusable.

(3)  An officer of a company commits an offence if he—

(a)  fails to take all reasonable steps for securing compliance by the company with subsection (4) of that section (period for which records to be preserved), or

(b)  intentionally causes any default by the company under that subsection.

(4)  A person guilty of an offence under this section is liable—

(a)  on conviction on indictment, to imprisonment for a term not exceeding two years or a fine (or both);

(b)  on summary conviction—

(i)  in England and Wales, to imprisonment for a term not exceeding twelve months or to a fine not exceeding the statutory maximum (or both);

(ii)  in Scotland or Northern Ireland, to imprisonment for a term not exceeding six months, or to a fine not exceeding the statutory maximum (or both).

## Chapter 3  A company's financial year

### 390  A company's financial year

(1)  A company's financial year is determined as follows.

(2)  Its first financial year—

(a)  begins with the first day of its first accounting reference period, and

(b)  ends with the last day of that period or such other date, not more than seven days before or after the end of that period, as the directors may determine.

(3)  Subsequent financial years—

(a)  begin with the day immediately following the end of the company's previous financial year, and

(b)  end with the last day of its next accounting reference period or such other date, not more than seven days before or after the end of that period, as the directors may determine.

(4)  In relation to an undertaking that is not a company, references in this Act to its financial year are to any period in respect of which a profit and loss account of the undertaking is required to be made up (by its constitution or by the law under which it is established), whether that period is a year or not.

(5)  The directors of a parent company must secure that, except where in their opinion there are good reasons against it, the financial year of each of its subsidiary undertakings coincides with the company's own financial year.

### 391  Accounting reference periods and accounting reference date

(1)  A company's accounting reference periods are determined according to its accounting reference date in each calendar year.

(2)  The accounting reference date of a company incorporated in Great Britain before 1st April 1996 is—

(a)  the date specified by notice to the registrar in accordance with section 224(2) of the Companies Act 1985 (c. 6) (notice specifying accounting reference date given within nine months of incorporation), or

(b)  failing such notice—

(i)  in the case of a company incorporated before 1st April 1990, 31st March, and

(ii)  in the case of a company incorporated on or after 1st April 1990, the last day of the month in which the anniversary of its incorporation falls.

(3) The accounting reference date of a company incorporated in Northern Ireland before 22nd August 1997 is—

  (a) the date specified by notice to the registrar in accordance with article 232(2) of the Companies (Northern Ireland) Order 1986 (S.I. 1986/1032 (N.I. 6)) (notice specifying accounting reference date given within nine months of incorporation), or

  (b) failing such notice—

    (i)  in the case of a company incorporated before the coming into operation of Article 5 of the Companies (Northern Ireland) Order 1990 (S.I. 1990/593 (N.I. 5)), 31st March, and

    (ii) in the case of a company incorporated after the coming into operation of that Article, the last day of the month in which the anniversary of its incorporation falls.

(4) The accounting reference date of a company incorporated—

  (a) in Great Britain on or after 1st April 1996 and before the commencement of this Act,

  (b) in Northern Ireland on or after 22nd August 1997 and before the commencement of this Act, or

  (c) after the commencement of this Act,

is the last day of the month in which the anniversary of its incorporation falls.

(5) A company's first accounting reference period is the period of more than six months, but not more than 18 months, beginning with the date of its incorporation and ending with its accounting reference date.

(6) Its subsequent accounting reference periods are successive periods of twelve months beginning immediately after the end of the previous accounting reference period and ending with its accounting reference date.

(7) This section has effect subject to the provisions of section 392 (alteration of accounting reference date).

### 392  Alteration of accounting reference date

(1) A company may by notice given to the registrar specify a new accounting reference date having effect in relation to—

  (a) the company's current accounting reference period and subsequent periods, or

  (b) the company's previous accounting reference period and subsequent periods.

A company's 'previous accounting reference period' means the one immediately preceding its current accounting reference period.

(2) The notice must state whether the current or previous accounting reference period—

  (a) is to be shortened, so as to come to an end on the first occasion on which the new accounting reference date falls or fell after the beginning of the period, or

  (b) is to be extended, so as to come to an end on the second occasion on which that date falls or fell after the beginning of the period.

(3) A notice extending a company's current or previous accounting reference period is not effective if given less than five years after the end of an earlier accounting reference period of the company that was extended under this section.

This does not apply—

  (a) to a notice given by a company that is a subsidiary undertaking or parent undertaking of another EEA undertaking if the new accounting reference date coincides with that of the other EEA undertaking or, where that undertaking is not a company, with the last day of its financial year, or

  (b) where the company is in administration under Part 2 of the Insolvency Act 1986 (c. 45) or Part 3 of the Insolvency (Northern Ireland) Order 1989 (S.I. 1989/2405 (N.I. 19)), or

  (c) where the Secretary of State directs that it should not apply, which he may do with respect to a notice that has been given or that may be given.

(4) A notice under this section may not be given in respect of a previous accounting reference period if the period for filing accounts and reports for the financial year determined by reference to that accounting reference period has already expired.

(5) An accounting reference period may not be extended so as to exceed 18 months and a notice under this section is ineffective if the current or previous accounting reference period as extended in accordance with the notice would exceed that limit.

This does not apply where the company is in administration under Part 2 of the Insolvency Act 1986 (c. 45) or Part 3 of the Insolvency (Northern Ireland) Order 1989 (S.I. 1989/2405 (N.I. 19)).

(6) In this section 'EEA undertaking' means an undertaking established under the law of any part of the United Kingdom or the law of any other EEA State.

## Chapter 4  Annual accounts

### *General*

### 393  Accounts to give true and fair view

(1) The directors of a company must not approve accounts for the purposes of this Chapter unless they are satisfied that they give a true and fair view of the assets, liabilities, financial position and profit or loss—

(a) in the case of the company's individual accounts, of the company;

(b) in the case of the company's group accounts, of the undertakings included in the consolidation as a whole, so far as concerns members of the company.

(2) The auditor of a company in carrying out his functions under this Act in relation to the company's annual accounts must have regard to the directors' duty under subsection (1).

*Individual accounts*

### 394 Duty to prepare individual accounts

The directors of every company must prepare accounts for the company for each of its financial years.

Those accounts are referred to as the company's 'individual accounts'.

### 395 Individual accounts: applicable accounting framework

(1) A company's individual accounts may be prepared—

(a) in accordance with section 396 ('Companies Act individual accounts'), or

(b) in accordance with international accounting standards ('IAS individual accounts').

This is subject to the following provisions of this section and to section 407 (consistency of financial reporting within group).

(2) The individual accounts of a company that is a charity must be Companies Act individual accounts.

(3) After the first financial year in which the directors of a company prepare IAS individual accounts ('the first IAS year'), all subsequent individual accounts of the company must be prepared in accordance with international accounting standards unless there is a relevant change of circumstance.

(4) There is a relevant change of circumstance if, at any time during or after the first IAS year—

(a) the company becomes a subsidiary undertaking of another undertaking that does not prepare IAS individual accounts,

(aa) the company ceases to be a subsidiary undertaking,

(b) the company ceases to be a company with securities admitted to trading on a regulated market in an EEA State, or

(c) a parent undertaking of the company ceases to be an undertaking with securities admitted to trading on a regulated market in an EEA State.

(5) If, having changed to preparing Companies Act individual accounts following a relevant change of circumstance, the directors again prepare IAS individual accounts for the company, subsections (3) and (4) apply again as if the first financial year for which such accounts are again prepared were the first IAS year.

### 396 Companies Act individual accounts

(1) Companies Act individual accounts must comprise—

(a) a balance sheet as at the last day of the financial year, and

(b) a profit and loss account.

(2) The accounts must—

(a) in the case of the balance sheet, give a true and fair view of the state of affairs of the company as at the end of the financial year, and

(b) in the case of the profit and loss account, give a true and fair view of the profit or loss of the company for the financial year.

(3) The accounts must comply with provision made by the Secretary of State by regulations as to—

(a) the form and content of the balance sheet and profit and loss account, and

(b) additional information to be provided by way of notes to the accounts.

(4) If compliance with the regulations, and any other provision made by or under this Act as to the matters to be included in a company's individual accounts or in notes to those accounts, would not be sufficient to give a true and fair view, the necessary additional information must be given in the accounts or in a note to them.

(5) If in special circumstances compliance with any of those provisions is inconsistent with the requirement to give a true and fair view, the directors must depart from that provision to the extent necessary to give a true and fair view.

Particulars of any such departure, the reasons for it and its effect must be given in a note to the accounts.

### 397 IAS individual accounts

Where the directors of a company prepare IAS individual accounts, they must state in the notes to the accounts that the accounts have been prepared in accordance with international accounting standards.

*Group accounts: small companies*

### 398 Option to prepare group accounts

If at the end of a financial year a company subject to the small companies regime is a parent company the directors, as well as preparing individual accounts for the year, may prepare group accounts for the year.

*Group accounts: other companies*

### 399 Duty to prepare group accounts

(1) This section applies to companies that are not subject to the small companies regime.

(2) If at the end of a financial year the company is a parent company the directors, as well as preparing individual accounts for the year, must prepare group accounts for the year unless the company is exempt from that requirement.

(3) There are exemptions under—

section 400 (company included in EEA accounts of larger group),

section 401 (company included in non-EEA accounts of larger group), and

section 402 (company none of whose subsidiary undertakings need be included in the consolidation).

(4) A company to which this section applies but which is exempt from the requirement to prepare group accounts, may do so.

### 400 Exemption for company included in EEA group accounts of larger group

(1) A company is exempt from the requirement to prepare group accounts if it is itself a subsidiary undertaking and its immediate parent undertaking is established under the law of an EEA State, in the following cases—

   (a) where the company is a wholly-owned subsidiary of that parent undertaking;

   (b) where that parent undertaking holds more than 50% of the allotted shares in the company and notice requesting the preparation of group accounts has not been served on the company by shareholders holding in aggregate—

      (i)   more than half of the remaining allotted shares in the company, or

      (ii)  5% of the total allotted shares in the company.

Such notice must be served not later than six months after the end of the financial year before that to which it relates.

(2) Exemption is conditional upon compliance with all of the following conditions—

   (a) the company must be included in consolidated accounts for a larger group drawn up to the same date, or to an earlier date in the same financial year, by a parent undertaking established under the law of an EEA State;

   (b) those accounts must be drawn up and audited, and that parent undertaking's annual report must be drawn up, according to that law—

      (i)   in accordance with the provisions of the Seventh Directive (83/349/EEC) (as modified, where relevant, by the provisions of the Bank Accounts Directive (86/635/EEC) or the Insurance Accounts Directive (91/674/EEC)), or

      (ii)  in accordance with international accounting standards;

   (c) the company must disclose in its individual accounts that it is exempt from the obligation to prepare and deliver group accounts;

   (d) the company must state in its individual accounts the name of the parent undertaking that draws up the group accounts referred to above and—

      (i)   if it is incorporated outside the United Kingdom, the country in which it is incorporated, or

      (ii)  if it is unincorporated, the address of its principal place of business;

   (e) the company must deliver to the registrar, within the period for filing its accounts and reports for the financial year in question, copies of—

      (i)   those group accounts, and

      (ii)  the parent undertaking's annual report,

      (iii) together with the auditor's report on them;

   (f) any requirement of Part 35 of this Act as to the delivery to the registrar of a certified translation into English must be met in relation to any document comprised in the accounts and reports delivered in accordance with paragraph (e).

(3) For the purposes of subsection (1)(b) shares held by a wholly-owned subsidiary of the parent undertaking, or held on behalf of the parent undertaking or a wholly-owned subsidiary, shall be attributed to the parent undertaking.

(4) The exemption does not apply to a company any of whose securities are admitted to trading on a regulated market in an EEA State.

(5) Shares held by directors of a company for the purpose of complying with any share qualification requirement shall be disregarded in determining for the purposes of this section whether the company is a wholly-owned subsidiary.

(6) In subsection (4) 'securities' includes—

   (a) shares and stock,

   (b) debentures, including debenture stock, loan stock, bonds, certificates of deposit and other instruments creating or acknowledging indebtedness,

   (c) warrants or other instruments entitling the holder to subscribe for securities falling within paragraph (a) or (b), and

   (d) certificates or other instruments that confer—

      (i)   property rights in respect of a security falling within paragraph (a), (b) or (c),

(ii) any right to acquire, dispose of, underwrite or convert a security, being a right to which the holder would be entitled if he held any such security to which the certificate or other instrument relates, or

(iii) a contractual right (other than an option) to acquire any such security otherwise than by subscription.

### 401 Exemption for company included in non-EEA group accounts of larger group

(1) A company is exempt from the requirement to prepare group accounts if it is itself a subsidiary undertaking and its parent undertaking is not established under the law of an EEA State, in the following cases—

(a) where the company is a wholly-owned subsidiary of that parent undertaking;

(b) where that parent undertaking holds more than 50% of the allotted shares in the company and notice requesting the preparation of group accounts has not been served on the company by shareholders holding in aggregate—

(i) more than half of the remaining allotted shares in the company, or

(ii) 5% of the total allotted shares in the company.

Such notice must be served not later than six months after the end of the financial year before that to which it relates.

(2) Exemption is conditional upon compliance with all of the following conditions—

(a) the company and all of its subsidiary undertakings must be included in consolidated accounts for a larger group drawn up to the same date, or to an earlier date in the same financial year, by a parent undertaking;

(b) those accounts and, where appropriate, the group's annual report, must be drawn up—

(i) in accordance with the provisions of the Seventh Directive (83/349/EEC) (as modified, where relevant, by the provisions of the Bank Accounts Directive (86/635/EEC) or the Insurance Accounts Directive (91/674/EEC)), or

(ii) in a manner equivalent to consolidated accounts and consolidated annual reports so drawn up;

(c) the group accounts must be audited by one or more persons authorised to audit accounts under the law under which the parent undertaking which draws them up is established;

(d) the company must disclose in its individual accounts that it is exempt from the obligation to prepare and deliver group accounts;

(e) the company must state in its individual accounts the name of the parent undertaking which draws up the group accounts referred to above and—

(i) if it is incorporated outside the United Kingdom, the country in which it is incorporated, or

(ii) if it is unincorporated, the address of its principal place of business;

(f) the company must deliver to the registrar, within the period for filing its accounts and reports for the financial year in question, copies of—

(i) the group accounts, and

(ii) where appropriate, the consolidated annual report,

together with the auditor's report on them;

(g) any requirement of Part 35 of this Act as to the delivery to the registrar of a certified translation into English must be met in relation to any document comprised in the accounts and reports delivered in accordance with paragraph (f).

(3) For the purposes of subsection (1)(b), shares held by a wholly-owned subsidiary of the parent undertaking, or held on behalf of the parent undertaking or a wholly-owned subsidiary, are attributed to the parent undertaking.

(4) The exemption does not apply to a company any of whose securities are admitted to trading on a regulated market in an EEA State.

(5) Shares held by directors of a company for the purpose of complying with any share qualification requirement shall be disregarded in determining for the purposes of this section whether the company is a wholly-owned subsidiary.

(6) In subsection (4) 'securities' includes—

(a) shares and stock,

(b) debentures, including debenture stock, loan stock, bonds, certificates of deposit and other instruments creating or acknowledging indebtedness,

(c) warrants or other instruments entitling the holder to subscribe for securities falling within paragraph (a) or (b), and

(d) certificates or other instruments that confer—

(i) property rights in respect of a security falling within paragraph (a), (b) or (c),

(ii) any right to acquire, dispose of, underwrite or convert a security, being a right to which the holder would be entitled if he held any such security to which the certificate or other instrument relates, or

(iii) a contractual right (other than an option) to acquire any such security otherwise than by subscription.

### 402   Exemption if no subsidiary undertakings need be included in the consolidation

A parent company is exempt from the requirement to prepare group accounts if under section 405 all of its subsidiary undertakings could be excluded from consolidation in Companies Act group accounts.

*Group accounts: general*

### 403   Group accounts: applicable accounting framework

(1) The group accounts of certain parent companies are required by Article 4 of the IAS Regulation to be prepared in accordance with international accounting standards ('IAS group accounts').

(2) The group accounts of other companies may be prepared—

(a) in accordance with section 404 ('Companies Act group accounts'), or

(b) in accordance with international accounting standards ('IAS group accounts').

This is subject to the following provisions of this section.

(3) The group accounts of a parent company that is a charity must be Companies Act group accounts.

(4) After the first financial year in which the directors of a parent company prepare IAS group accounts ('the first IAS year'), all subsequent group accounts of the company must be prepared in accordance with international accounting standards unless there is a relevant change of circumstance.

(5) There is a relevant change of circumstance if, at any time during or after the first IAS year—

(a) the company becomes a subsidiary undertaking of another undertaking that does not prepare IAS group accounts,

(b) the company ceases to be a company with securities admitted to trading on a regulated market in an EEA State, or

(c) a parent undertaking of the company ceases to be an undertaking with securities admitted to trading on a regulated market in an EEA State.

(6) If, having changed to preparing Companies Act group accounts following a relevant change of circumstance, the directors again prepare IAS group accounts for the company, subsections (4) and (5) apply again as if the first financial year for which such accounts are again prepared were the first IAS year.

### 404   Companies Act group accounts

(1) Companies Act group accounts must comprise—

(a) a consolidated balance sheet dealing with the state of affairs of the parent company and its subsidiary undertakings, and

(b) a consolidated profit and loss account dealing with the profit or loss of the parent company and its subsidiary undertakings.

(2) The accounts must give a true and fair view of the state of affairs as at the end of the financial year, and the profit or loss for the financial year, of the undertakings included in the consolidation as a whole, so far as concerns members of the company.

(3) The accounts must comply with provision made by the Secretary of State by regulations as to—

(a) the form and content of the consolidated balance sheet and consolidated profit and loss account, and

(b) additional information to be provided by way of notes to the accounts.

(4) If compliance with the regulations, and any other provision made by or under this Act as to the matters to be included in a company's group accounts or in notes to those accounts, would not be sufficient to give a true and fair view, the necessary additional information must be given in the accounts or in a note to them.

(5) If in special circumstances compliance with any of those provisions is inconsistent with the requirement to give a true and fair view, the directors must depart from that provision to the extent necessary to give a true and fair view.

Particulars of any such departure, the reasons for it and its effect must be given in a note to the accounts.

### 405   Companies Act group accounts: subsidiary undertakings included in the consolidation

(1) Where a parent company prepares Companies Act group accounts, all the subsidiary undertakings of the company must be included in the consolidation, subject to the following exceptions.

(2) A subsidiary undertaking may be excluded from consolidation if its inclusion is not material for the purpose of giving a true and fair view (but two or more undertakings may be excluded only if they are not material taken together).

(3) A subsidiary undertaking may be excluded from consolidation where—

(a) severe long-term restrictions substantially hinder the exercise of the rights of the parent company over the assets or management of that undertaking, or

(b) the information necessary for the preparation of group accounts cannot be obtained without disproportionate expense or undue delay, or

(c) the interest of the parent company is held exclusively with a view to subsequent resale.

(4)  The reference in subsection (3)(a) to the rights of the parent company and the reference in subsection (3)(c) to the interest of the parent company are, respectively, to rights and interests held by or attributed to the company for the purposes of the definition of 'parent undertaking' (see section 1162) in the absence of which it would not be the parent company.

### 406  IAS group accounts

Where the directors of a company prepare IAS group accounts, they must state in the notes to those accounts that the accounts have been prepared in accordance with international accounting standards.

### 407  Consistency of financial reporting within group

(1)  The directors of a parent company must secure that the individual accounts of—
  (a)  the parent company, and
  (b)  each of its subsidiary undertakings,
are all prepared using the same financial reporting framework, except to the extent that in their opinion there are good reasons for not doing so.

(2)  Subsection (1) does not apply if the directors do not prepare group accounts for the parent company.

(3)  Subsection (1) only applies to accounts of subsidiary undertakings that are required to be prepared under this Part.

(4)  Subsection (1) does not require accounts of undertakings that are charities to be prepared using the same financial reporting framework as accounts of undertakings which are not charities.

(5)  Subsection (1)(a) does not apply where the directors of a parent company prepare IAS group accounts and IAS individual accounts.

### 408  Individual profit and loss account where group accounts prepared

(1)  This section applies where—
  (a)  a company prepares group accounts in accordance with this Act, and
  (b)  the notes to the company's individual balance sheet show the company's profit or loss for the financial year determined in accordance with this Act.

(2)  The company's individual profit and loss account need not contain the information specified in section 411 (information about employee numbers and costs).

(3)  The company's individual profit and loss account must be approved in accordance with section 414(1) (approval by directors) but may be omitted from the company's annual accounts for the purposes of the other provisions of the Companies Acts.

(4)  The exemption conferred by this section is conditional upon its being disclosed in the company's annual accounts that the exemption applies.

*Information to be given in notes to the accounts*

### 409  Information about related undertakings

(1)  The Secretary of State may make provision by regulations requiring information about related undertakings to be given in notes to a company's annual accounts.

(2)  The regulations—
  (a)  may make different provision according to whether or not the company prepares group accounts, and
  (b)  may specify the descriptions of undertaking in relation to which they apply, and make different provision in relation to different descriptions of related undertaking.

(3)  The regulations may provide that information need not be disclosed with respect to an undertaking that—
  (a)  is established under the law of a country outside the United Kingdom, or
  (b)  carries on business outside the United Kingdom,
if the following conditions are met.

(4)  The conditions are—
  (a)  that in the opinion of the directors of the company the disclosure would be seriously prejudicial to the business of—
    (i)   that undertaking,
    (ii)  the company,
    (iii) any of the company's subsidiary undertakings, or
    (iv)  any other undertaking which is included in the consolidation;
  (b)  that the Secretary of State agrees that the information need not be disclosed.

(5)  Where advantage is taken of any such exemption, that fact must be stated in a note to the company's annual accounts.

### 410  Information about related undertakings: alternative compliance

(1)  This section applies where the directors of a company are of the opinion that the number of undertakings in respect of which the company is required to disclose information under any provision of regulations under section 409 (related undertakings) is such that compliance with that provision would result in information of excessive length being given in notes to the company's annual accounts.

(2)  The information need only be given in respect of—

    (a)  the undertakings whose results or financial position, in the opinion of the directors, principally affected the figures shown in the company's annual accounts, and

    (b)  where the company prepares group accounts, undertakings excluded from consolidation under section 405(3) (undertakings excluded on grounds other than materiality).

(3)  If advantage is taken of subsection (2)—

    (a)  there must be included in the notes to the company's annual accounts a statement that the information is given only with respect to such undertakings as are mentioned in that subsection, and

    (b)  the full information (both that which is disclosed in the notes to the accounts and that which is not) must be annexed to the company's next annual return.

For this purpose the 'next annual return' means that next delivered to the registrar after the accounts in question have been approved under section 414.

(4)  If a company fails to comply with subsection (3)(b), an offence is committed by—

    (a)  the company, and

    (b)  every officer of the company who is in default.

(5)  A person guilty of an offence under subsection (4) is liable on summary conviction to a fine not exceeding level 3 on the standard scale and, for continued contravention, a daily default fine not exceeding one-tenth of level 3 on the standard scale.

## 410A  Information about off-balance sheet arrangements

(1)  In the case of a company that is not subject to the small companies regime, if in any financial year—

    (a)  the company is or has been party to arrangements that are not reflected in its balance sheet, and

    (b)  at the balance sheet date the risks or benefits arising from those arrangements are material,

the information required by this section must be given in notes to the company's annual accounts.

(2)  The information required is—

    (a)  the nature and business purpose of the arrangements, and

    (b)  the financial impact of the arrangements on the company.

(3)  The information need only be given to the extent necessary for enabling the financial position of the company to be assessed.

(4)  If the company qualifies as medium-sized in relation to the financial year (see sections 465 to 467) it need not comply with subsection (2)(b).

(5)  This section applies in relation to group accounts as if the undertakings included in the consolidation were a single company.

## 411  Information about employee numbers and costs

(1)  In the case of a company not subject to the small companies regime, the following information with respect to the employees of the company must be given in notes to the company's annual accounts—

    (a)  the average number of persons employed by the company in the financial year, and

    (b)  the average number of persons so employed within each category of persons employed by the company.

(2)  The categories by reference to which the number required to be disclosed by subsection (1)(b) is to be determined must be such as the directors may select having regard to the manner in which the company's activities are organised.

(3)  The average number required by subsection (1)(a) or (b) is determined by dividing the relevant annual number by the number of months in the financial year.

(4)  The relevant annual number is determined by ascertaining for each month in the financial year—

    (a)  for the purposes of subsection (1)(a), the number of persons employed under contracts of service by the company in that month (whether throughout the month or not);

    (b)  for the purposes of subsection (1)(b), the number of persons in the category in question of persons so employed;

and adding together all the monthly numbers.

(5)  In respect of all persons employed by the company during the financial year who are taken into account in determining the relevant annual number for the purposes of subsection (1)(a) there must also be stated the aggregate amounts respectively of—

    (a)  wages and salaries paid or payable in respect of that year to those persons;

    (b)  social security costs incurred by the company on their behalf; and

    (c)  other pension costs so incurred.

This does not apply in so far as those amounts, or any of them, are stated elsewhere in the company's accounts.

(6)  In subsection (5)—

'pension costs' includes any costs incurred by the company in respect of—

(a) any pension scheme established for the purpose of providing pensions for persons currently or formerly employed by the company,

(b) any sums set aside for the future payment of pensions directly by the company to current or former employees, and

(c) any pensions paid directly to such persons without having first been set aside;

'social security costs' means any contributions by the company to any state social security or pension scheme, fund or arrangement.

(7) This section applies in relation to group accounts as if the undertakings included in the consolidation were a single company.

**412    Information about directors' benefits: remuneration**

(1) The Secretary of State may make provision by regulations requiring information to be given in notes to a company's annual accounts about directors' remuneration.

(2) The matters about which information may be required include—

(a) gains made by directors on the exercise of share options;

(b) benefits received or receivable by directors under long-term incentive schemes;

(c) payments for loss of office (as defined in section 215);

(d) benefits receivable, and contributions for the purpose of providing benefits, in respect of past services of a person as director or in any other capacity while director;

(e) consideration paid to or receivable by third parties for making available the services of a person as director or in any other capacity while director.

(3) Without prejudice to the generality of subsection (1), regulations under this section may make any such provision as was made immediately before the commencement of this Part by Part 1 of Schedule 6 to the Companies Act 1985 (c. 6).

(4) For the purposes of this section, and regulations made under it, amounts paid to or receivable by—

(a) a person connected with a director, or

(b) a body corporate controlled by a director,

are treated as paid to or receivable by the director.

The expressions 'connected with' and 'controlled by' in this subsection have the same meaning as in Part 10 (company directors).

(5) It is the duty of—

(a) any director of a company, and

(b) any person who is or has at any time in the preceding five years been a director of the company,

to give notice to the company of such matters relating to himself as may be necessary for the purposes of regulations under this section.

(6) A person who makes default in complying with subsection (5) commits an offence and is liable on summary conviction to a fine not exceeding level 3 on the standard scale.

**413    Information about directors' benefits: advances, credit and guarantees**

(1) In the case of a company that does not prepare group accounts, details of—

(a) advances and credits granted by the company to its directors, and

(b) guarantees of any kind entered into by the company on behalf of its directors,

must be shown in the notes to its individual accounts.

(2) In the case of a parent company that prepares group accounts, details of—

(a) advances and credits granted to the directors of the parent company, by that company or by any of its subsidiary undertakings, and

(b) guarantees of any kind entered into on behalf of the directors of the parent company, by that company or by any of its subsidiary undertakings,

must be shown in the notes to the group accounts.

(3) The details required of an advance or credit are—

(a) its amount,

(b) an indication of the interest rate,

(c) its main conditions, and

(d) any amounts repaid.

(4) The details required of a guarantee are—

(a) its main terms,

(b) the amount of the maximum liability that may be incurred by the company (or its subsidiary), and

(c) any amount paid and any liability incurred by the company (or its subsidiary) for the purpose of fulfilling the guarantee (including any loss incurred by reason of enforcement of the guarantee).

(5) There must also be stated in the notes to the accounts the totals—

(a) of amounts stated under subsection (3)(a),

(b) of amounts stated under subsection (3)(d),

(c) of amounts stated under subsection (4)(b), and

(d) of amounts stated under subsection (4)(c).

(6) References in this section to the directors of a company are to the persons who were a director at any time in the financial year to which the accounts relate.

(7) The requirements of this section apply in relation to every advance, credit or guarantee subsisting at any time in the financial year to which the accounts relate—

(a) whenever it was entered into,

(b) whether or not the person concerned was a director of the company in question at the time it was entered into, and

(c) in the case of an advance, credit or guarantee involving a subsidiary undertaking of that company, whether or not that undertaking was such a subsidiary undertaking at the time it was entered into.

(8) Banking companies and the holding companies of credit institutions need only state the details required by subsections (3)(a) and (4)(b).

### *Approval and signing of accounts*

### 414   Approval and signing of accounts

(1) A company's annual accounts must be approved by the board of directors and signed on behalf of the board by a director of the company.

(2) The signature must be on the company's balance sheet.

(3) If the accounts are prepared in accordance with the provisions applicable to companies subject to the small companies regime, the balance sheet must contain a statement to that effect in a prominent position above the signature.

(4) If annual accounts are approved that do not comply with the requirements of this Act (and, where applicable, of Article 4 of the IAS Regulation), every director of the company who—

(a) knew that they did not comply, or was reckless as to whether they complied, and

(b) failed to take reasonable steps to secure compliance with those requirements or, as the case may be, to prevent the accounts from being approved,

commits an offence.

(5) A person guilty of an offence under this section is liable—

(a) on conviction on indictment, to a fine;

(b) on summary conviction, to a fine not exceeding the statutory maximum.

## Chapter 5   Directors' report

### *Directors' report*

### 415   Duty to prepare directors' report

(1) The directors of a company must prepare a directors' report for each financial year of the company.

(2) For a financial year in which—

(a) the company is a parent company, and

(b) the directors of the company prepare group accounts,

the directors' report must be a consolidated report (a 'group directors' report') relating to the undertakings included in the consolidation.

(3) A group directors' report may, where appropriate, give greater emphasis to the matters that are significant to the undertakings included in the consolidation, taken as a whole.

(4) In the case of failure to comply with the requirement to prepare a directors' report, an offence is committed by every person who—

(a) was a director of the company immediately before the end of the period for filing accounts and reports for the financial year in question, and

(b) failed to take all reasonable steps for securing compliance with that requirement.

(5) A person guilty of an offence under this section is liable—

(a) on conviction on indictment, to a fine;

(b) on summary conviction, to a fine not exceeding the statutory maximum.

### 415A   Directors' report: small companies exemption

(1) A company is entitled to small companies exemption in relation to the directors' report for a financial year if—

(a) it is entitled to prepare accounts for the year in accordance with the small companies regime, or

(b) it would be so entitled but for being or having been a member of an ineligible group.

(2) The exemption is relevant to—

section 416(3) (contents of report: statement of amount recommended by way of dividend),

section 417 (contents of report: business review), and

sections 444 to 446 (filing obligations of different descriptions of company).

### 416   Contents of directors' report: general

(1)  The directors' report for a financial year must state—

(a)  the names of the persons who, at any time during the financial year, were directors of the company, and

(b)  the principal activities of the company in the course of the year.

(2)  In relation to a group directors' report subsection (1)(b) has effect as if the reference to the company was to the undertakings included in the consolidation.

(3)  Except in the case of a company entitled to the small companies exemption, the report must state the amount (if any) that the directors recommend should be paid by way of dividend.

(4)  The Secretary of State may make provision by regulations as to other matters that must be disclosed in a directors' report.

Without prejudice to the generality of this power, the regulations may make any such provision as was formerly made by Schedule 7 to the Companies Act 1985.

### 417   Contents of directors' report: business review

(1)  Unless the company is entitled to the small companies exemption, the directors' report must contain a business review.

(2)  The purpose of the business review is to inform members of the company and help them assess how the directors have performed their duty under section 172 (duty to promote the success of the company).

(3)  The business review must contain—

(a)  a fair review of the company's business, and

(b)  a description of the principal risks and uncertainties facing the company.

(4)  The review required is a balanced and comprehensive analysis of—

(a)  the development and performance of the company's business during the financial year, and

(b)  the position of the company's business at the end of that year,

consistent with the size and complexity of the business.

(5)  In the case of a quoted company the business review must, to the extent necessary for an understanding of the development, performance or position of the company's business, include—

(a)  the main trends and factors likely to affect the future development, performance and position of the company's business; and

(b)  information about—

(i)   environmental matters (including the impact of the company's business on the environment),

(ii)  the company's employees, and

(iii) social and community issues,

including information about any policies of the company in relation to those matters and the effectiveness of those policies; and

(c)  subject to subsection (11), information about persons with whom the company has contractual or other arrangements which are essential to the business of the company.

If the review does not contain information of each kind mentioned in paragraphs (b)(i), (ii) and (iii) and (c), it must state which of those kinds of information it does not contain.

(6)  The review must, to the extent necessary for an understanding of the development, performance or position of the company's business, include—

(a)  analysis using financial key performance indicators, and

(b)  where appropriate, analysis using other key performance indicators, including information relating to environmental matters and employee matters.

'Key performance indicators' means factors by reference to which the development, performance or position of the company's business can be measured effectively.

(7)  Where a company qualifies as medium-sized in relation to a financial year (see sections 465 to 467), the directors' report for the year need not comply with the requirements of subsection (6) so far as they relate to non-financial information.

(8)  The review must, where appropriate, include references to, and additional explanations of, amounts included in the company's annual accounts.

(9)  In relation to a group directors' report this section has effect as if the references to the company were references to the undertakings included in the consolidation.

(10)  Nothing in this section requires the disclosure of information about impending developments or matters in the course of negotiation if the disclosure would, in the opinion of the directors, be seriously prejudicial to the interests of the company.

(11)  Nothing in subsection (5)(c) requires the disclosure of information about a person if the disclosure would, in the opinion of the directors, be seriously prejudicial to that person and contrary to the public interest.

### 418   Contents of directors' report: statement as to disclosure to auditors

(1)  This section applies to a company unless—

(a)  it is exempt for the financial year in question from the requirements of Part 16 as to audit of accounts, and

(b)  the directors take advantage of that exemption.

(2)  The directors' report must contain a statement to the effect that, in the case of each of the persons who are directors at the time the report is approved—

(a)  so far as the director is aware, there is no relevant audit information of which the company's auditor is unaware, and

(b)  he has taken all the steps that he ought to have taken as a director in order to make himself aware of any relevant audit information and to establish that the company's auditor is aware of that information.

(3)  'Relevant audit information' means information needed by the company's auditor in connection with preparing his report.

(4)  A director is regarded as having taken all the steps that he ought to have taken as a director in order to do the things mentioned in subsection (2)(b) if he has—

(a)  made such enquiries of his fellow directors and of the company's auditors for that purpose, and

(b)  taken such other steps (if any) for that purpose,

as are required by his duty as a director of the company to exercise reasonable care, skill and diligence.

(5)  Where a directors' report containing the statement required by this section is approved but the statement is false, every director of the company who—

(a)  knew that the statement was false, or was reckless as to whether it was false, and

(b)  failed to take reasonable steps to prevent the report from being approved,

commits an offence.

(6)  A person guilty of an offence under subsection (5) is liable—

(a)  on conviction on indictment, to imprisonment for a term not exceeding two years or a fine (or both);

(b)  on summary conviction—

(i)   in England and Wales, to imprisonment for a term not exceeding twelve months or to a fine not exceeding the statutory maximum (or both);

(ii)  in Scotland or Northern Ireland, to imprisonment for a term not exceeding six months, or to a fine not exceeding the statutory maximum (or both).

### 419   Approval and signing of directors' report

(1)  The directors' report must be approved by the board of directors and signed on behalf of the board by a director or the secretary of the company.

(2)  If in preparing the report advantage is taken of the small companies exemption, it must contain a statement to that effect in a prominent position above the signature.

(3)  If a directors' report is approved that does not comply with the requirements of this Act, every director of the company who—

(a)  knew that it did not comply, or was reckless as to whether it complied, and

(b)  failed to take reasonable steps to secure compliance with those requirements or, as the case may be, to prevent the report from being approved,

commits an offence.

(4)  A person guilty of an offence under this section is liable—

(a)  on conviction on indictment, to a fine;

(b)  on summary conviction, to a fine not exceeding the statutory maximum.

## Chapter 6  Quoted companies: directors' remuneration report

### 420   Duty to prepare directors' remuneration report

(1)  The directors of a quoted company must prepare a directors' remuneration report for each financial year of the company.

(2)  In the case of failure to comply with the requirement to prepare a directors' remuneration report, every person who—

(a)  was a director of the company immediately before the end of the period for filing accounts and reports for the financial year in question, and

(b)  failed to take all reasonable steps for securing compliance with that requirement,

commits an offence.

(3)  A person guilty of an offence under this section is liable—

(a)  on conviction on indictment, to a fine;

(b)  on summary conviction, to a fine not exceeding the statutory maximum.

### 421   Contents of directors' remuneration report

(1)  The Secretary of State may make provision by regulations as to—

(a)  the information that must be contained in a directors' remuneration report,

(b)  how information is to be set out in the report, and

(c)  what is to be the auditable part of the report.

(2)  Without prejudice to the generality of this power, the regulations may make any such provision as was made, immediately before the commencement of this Part, by Schedule 7A to the Companies Act 1985 (c. 6).

(3)  It is the duty of—

(a)  any director of a company, and

(b)  any person who is or has at any time in the preceding five years been a director of the company,

to give notice to the company of such matters relating to himself as may be necessary for the purposes of regulations under this section.

(4)  A person who makes default in complying with subsection (3) commits an offence and is liable on summary conviction to a fine not exceeding level 3 on the standard scale.

## 422  Approval and signing of directors' remuneration report

(1)  The directors' remuneration report must be approved by the board of directors and signed on behalf of the board by a director or the secretary of the company.

(2)  If a directors' remuneration report is approved that does not comply with the requirements of this Act, every director of the company who—

(a)  knew that it did not comply, or was reckless as to whether it complied, and

(b)  failed to take reasonable steps to secure compliance with those requirements or, as the case may be, to prevent the report from being approved,

commits an offence.

(3)  A person guilty of an offence under this section is liable—

(a)  on conviction on indictment, to a fine;

(b)  on summary conviction, to a fine not exceeding the statutory maximum.

## Chapter 7  Publication of accounts and reports

### *Duty to circulate copies of accounts and reports*

## 423  Duty to circulate copies of annual accounts and reports

(1)  Every company must send a copy of its annual accounts and reports for each financial year to—

(a)  every member of the company,

(b)  every holder of the company's debentures, and

(c)  every person who is entitled to receive notice of general meetings.

(2)  Copies need not be sent to a person for whom the company does not have a current address.

(3)  A company has a 'current address' for a person if—

(a)  an address has been notified to the company by the person as one at which documents may be sent to him, and

(b)  the company has no reason to believe that documents sent to him at that address will not reach him.

(4)  In the case of a company not having a share capital, copies need not be sent to anyone who is not entitled to receive notices of general meetings of the company.

(5)  Where copies are sent out over a period of days, references in the Companies Acts to the day on which copies are sent out shall be read as references to the last day of that period.

(6)  This section has effect subject to section 426 (option to provide summary financial statement).

## 424  Time allowed for sending out copies of accounts and reports

(1)  The time allowed for sending out copies of the company's annual accounts and reports is as follows.

(2)  A private company must comply with section 423 not later than—

(a)  the end of the period for filing accounts and reports, or

(b)  if earlier, the date on which it actually delivers its accounts and reports to the registrar.

(3)  A public company must comply with section 423 at least 21 days before the date of the relevant accounts meeting.

(4)  If in the case of a public company copies are sent out later than is required by subsection (3), they shall, despite that, be deemed to have been duly sent if it is so agreed by all the members entitled to attend and vote at the relevant accounts meeting.

(5)  Whether the time allowed is that for a private company or a public company is determined by reference to the company's status immediately before the end of the accounting reference period by reference to which the financial year for the accounts in question was determined.

(6)  In this section the 'relevant accounts meeting' means the accounts meeting of the company at which the accounts and reports in question are to be laid.

## 425  Default in sending out copies of accounts and reports: offences

(1)  If default is made in complying with section 423 or 424, an offence is committed by—

(a)  the company, and

      (b)  every officer of the company who is in default.

   (2)  A person guilty of an offence under this section is liable—

      (a)  on conviction on indictment, to a fine;

      (b)  on summary conviction, to a fine not exceeding the statutory maximum.

*Option to provide summary financial statement*

### 426  Option to provide summary financial statement

   (1)  A company may—

      (a)  in such cases as may be specified by regulations made by the Secretary of State, and

      (b)  provided any conditions so specified are complied with,

provide a summary financial statement instead of copies of the accounts and reports required to be sent out in accordance with section 423.

   (2)  Copies of those accounts and reports must, however, be sent to any person entitled to be sent them in accordance with that section and who wishes to receive them.

   (3)  The Secretary of State may make provision by regulations as to the manner in which it is to be ascertained, whether before or after a person becomes entitled to be sent a copy of those accounts and reports, whether he wishes to receive them.

   (4)  A summary financial statement must comply with the requirements of—

section 427 (form and contents of summary financial statement: unquoted companies), or

section 428 (form and contents of summary financial statement: quoted companies).

   (5)  This section applies to copies of accounts and reports required to be sent out by virtue of section 146 to a person nominated to enjoy information rights as it applies to copies of accounts and reports required to be sent out in accordance with section 423 to a member of the company.

   (6)  Regulations under this section are subject to negative resolution procedure.

### 427  Form and contents of summary financial statement: unquoted companies

   (1)  A summary financial statement by a company that is not a quoted company must—

      (a)  be derived from the company's annual accounts, and

      (b)  be prepared in accordance with this section and regulations made under it.

   (2)  The summary financial statement must be in such form, and contain such information, as the Secretary of State may specify by regulations.

The regulations may require the statement to include information derived from the directors' report.

   (3)  Nothing in this section or regulations made under it prevents a company from including in a summary financial statement additional information derived from the company's annual accounts or the directors' report.

   (4)  The summary financial statement must—

      (a)  state that it is only a summary of information derived from the company's annual accounts;

      (b)  state whether it contains additional information derived from the directors' report and, if so, that it does not contain the full text of that report;

      (c)  state how a person entitled to them can obtain a full copy of the company's annual accounts and the directors' report;

      (d)  contain a statement by the company's auditor of his opinion as to whether the summary financial statement—

         (i)  is consistent with the company's annual accounts and, where information derived from the directors' report is included in the statement, with that report, and

        (ii)  complies with the requirements of this section and regulations made under it;

      (e)  state whether the auditor's report on the annual accounts was unqualified or qualified and, if it was qualified, set out the report in full together with any further material needed to understand the qualification;

      (f)  state whether, in that report, the auditor's statement under section 496 (whether directors' report consistent with accounts) was qualified or unqualified and, if it was qualified, set out the qualified statement in full together with any further material needed to understand the qualification;

      (g)  state whether that auditor's report contained a statement under—

         (i)  section 498(2)(a) or (b) (accounting records or returns inadequate or accounts not agreeing with records and returns), or

        (ii)  section 498(3) (failure to obtain necessary information and explanations),

           and if so, set out the statement in full.

   (5)  Regulations under this section may provide that any specified material may, instead of being included in the summary financial statement, be sent separately at the same time as the statement.

   (6)  Regulations under this section are subject to negative resolution procedure.

### 428  Form and contents of summary financial statement: quoted companies

   (1)  A summary financial statement by a quoted company must—

(a) be derived from the company's annual accounts and the directors' remuneration report, and

(b) be prepared in accordance with this section and regulations made under it.

(2) The summary financial statement must be in such form, and contain such information, as the Secretary of State may specify by regulations.

The regulations may require the statement to include information derived from the directors' report.

(3) Nothing in this section or regulations made under it prevents a company from including in a summary financial statement additional information derived from the company's annual accounts, the directors' remuneration report or the directors' report.

(4) The summary financial statement must—

(a) state that it is only a summary of information derived from the company's annual accounts and the directors' remuneration report;

(b) state whether it contains additional information derived from the directors' report and, if so, that it does not contain the full text of that report;

(c) state how a person entitled to them can obtain a full copy of the company's annual accounts, the directors' remuneration report or the directors' report;

(d) contain a statement by the company's auditor of his opinion as to whether the summary financial statement—

(i) is consistent with the company's annual accounts and the directors' remuneration report and, where information derived from the directors' report is included in the statement, with that report, and

(ii) complies with the requirements of this section and regulations made under it;

(e) state whether the auditor's report on the annual accounts and the auditable part of the directors' remuneration report was unqualified or qualified and, if it was qualified, set out the report in full together with any further material needed to understand the qualification;

(f) state whether that auditor's report contained a statement under—

(i) section 498(2) (accounting records or returns inadequate or accounts or directors' remuneration report not agreeing with records and returns), or

(ii) section 498(3) (failure to obtain necessary information and explanations), and if so, set out the statement in full;

(g) state whether, in that report, the auditor's statement under section 496 (whether directors' report consistent with accounts) was qualified or unqualified and, if it was qualified, set out the qualified statement in full together with any further material needed to understand the qualification.

(5) Regulations under this section may provide that any specified material may, instead of being included in the summary financial statement, be sent separately at the same time as the statement.

(6) Regulations under this section are subject to negative resolution procedure.

### 429  Summary financial statements: offences

(1) If default is made in complying with any provision of section 426, 427 or 428, or of regulations under any of those sections, an offence is committed by—

(a) the company, and

(b) every officer of the company who is in default.

(2) A person guilty of an offence under this section is liable on summary conviction to a fine not exceeding level 3 on the standard scale.

*Quoted companies: requirements as to website publication*

### 430  Quoted companies: annual accounts and reports to be made available on website

(1) A quoted company must ensure that its annual accounts and reports—

(a) are made available on a website, and

(b) remain so available until the annual accounts and reports for the company's next financial year are made available in accordance with this section.

(2) The annual accounts and reports must be made available on a website that—

(a) is maintained by or on behalf of the company, and

(b) identifies the company in question.

(3) Access to the annual accounts and reports on the website, and the ability to obtain a hard copy of the annual accounts and reports from the website, must not be—

(a) conditional on the payment of a fee, or

(b) otherwise restricted, except so far as necessary to comply with any enactment or regulatory requirement (in the United Kingdom or elsewhere).

(4) The annual accounts and reports—

(a) must be made available as soon as reasonably practicable, and

(b) must be kept available throughout the period specified in subsection (1)(b).

(5) A failure to make the annual accounts and reports available on a website throughout that period is disregarded if—

    (a) the annual accounts and reports are made available on the website for part of that period, and

    (b) the failure is wholly attributable to circumstances that it would not be reasonable to have expected the company to prevent or avoid.

(6) In the event of default in complying with this section, an offence is committed by every officer of the company who is in default.

(7) A person guilty of an offence under subsection (6) is liable on summary conviction to a fine not exceeding level 3 on the standard scale.

*Right of member or debenture holder to demand copies of accounts and reports*

### 431 Right of member or debenture holder to copies of accounts and reports: unquoted companies

(1) A member of, or holder of debentures of, an unquoted company is entitled to be provided, on demand and without charge, with a copy of—

    (a) the company's last annual accounts,

    (b) the last directors' report, and

    (c) the auditor's report on those accounts (including the statement on that report).

(2) The entitlement under this section is to a single copy of those documents, but that is in addition to any copy to which a person may be entitled under section 423.

(3) If a demand made under this section is not complied with within seven days of receipt by the company, an offence is committed by—

    (a) the company, and

    (b) every officer of the company who is in default.

(4) A person guilty of an offence under this section is liable on summary conviction to a fine not exceeding level 3 on the standard scale and, for continued contravention, a daily default fine not exceeding one-tenth of level 3 on the standard scale.

### 432 Right of member or debenture holder to copies of accounts and reports: quoted companies

(1) A member of, or holder of debentures of, a quoted company is entitled to be provided, on demand and without charge, with a copy of—

    (a) the company's last annual accounts,

    (b) the last directors' remuneration report,

    (c) the last directors' report, and

    (d) the auditor's report on those accounts (including the report on the directors' remuneration report and on the directors' report).

(2) The entitlement under this section is to a single copy of those documents, but that is in addition to any copy to which a person may be entitled under section 423.

(3) If a demand made under this section is not complied with within seven days of receipt by the company, an offence is committed by—

    (a) the company, and

    (b) every officer of the company who is in default.

(4) A person guilty of an offence under this section is liable on summary conviction to a fine not exceeding level 3 on the standard scale and, for continued contravention, a daily default fine not exceeding one-tenth of level 3 on the standard scale.

*Requirements in connection with publication of accounts and reports*

### 433 Name of signatory to be stated in published copies of accounts and reports

(1) Every copy of a document to which this section applies that is published by or on behalf of the company must state the name of the person who signed it on behalf of the board.

(2) In the case of an unquoted company, this section applies to copies of—

    (a) the company's balance sheet, and

    (b) the directors' report.

(3) In the case of a quoted company, this section applies to copies of—

    (a) the company's balance sheet,

    (b) the directors' remuneration report, and

    (c) the directors' report.

(4) If a copy is published without the required statement of the signatory's name, an offence is committed by—

    (a) the company, and

    (b) every officer of the company who is in default.

(5) A person guilty of an offence under this section is liable on summary conviction to a fine not exceeding level 3 on the standard scale.

### 434  Requirements in connection with publication of statutory accounts

(1)  If a company publishes any of its statutory accounts, they must be accompanied by the auditor's report on those accounts (unless the company is exempt from audit and the directors have taken advantage of that exemption).

(2)  A company that prepares statutory group accounts for a financial year must not publish its statutory individual accounts for that year without also publishing with them its statutory group accounts.

(3)  A company's 'statutory accounts' are its accounts for a financial year as required to be delivered to the registrar under section 441.

(4)  If a company contravenes any provision of this section, an offence is committed by—
  (a)  the company, and
  (b)  every officer of the company who is in default.

(5)  A person guilty of an offence under this section is liable on summary conviction to a fine not exceeding level 3 on the standard scale.

(6)  This section does not apply in relation to the provision by a company of a summary financial statement (see section 426).

### 435  Requirements in connection with publication of non-statutory accounts

(1)  If a company publishes non-statutory accounts, it must publish with them a statement indicating—
  (a)  that they are not the company's statutory accounts,
  (b)  whether statutory accounts dealing with any financial year with which the non-statutory accounts purport to deal have been delivered to the registrar, and
  (c)  whether an auditor's report has been made on the company's statutory accounts for any such financial year, and if so whether the report—
    (i)  was qualified or unqualified, or included a reference to any matters to which the auditor drew attention by way of emphasis without qualifying the report, or
    (ii)  contained a statement under section 498(2) (accounting records or returns inadequate or accounts or directors' remuneration report not agreeing with records and returns), or section 498(3) (failure to obtain necessary information and explanations).

(2)  The company must not publish with non-statutory accounts the auditor's report on the company's statutory accounts.

(3)  References in this section to the publication by a company of 'non-statutory accounts' are to the publication of—
  (a)  any balance sheet or profit and loss account relating to, or purporting to deal with, a financial year of the company, or
  (b)  an account in any form purporting to be a balance sheet or profit and loss account for a group headed by the company relating to, or purporting to deal with, a financial year of the company,
otherwise than as part of the company's statutory accounts.

(4)  In subsection (3)(b) 'a group headed by the company' means a group consisting of the company and any other undertaking (regardless of whether it is a subsidiary undertaking of the company) other than a parent undertaking of the company.

(5)  If a company contravenes any provision of this section, an offence is committed by—
  (a)  the company, and
  (b)  every officer of the company who is in default.

(6)  A person guilty of an offence under this section is liable on summary conviction to a fine not exceeding level 3 on the standard scale.

(7)  This section does not apply in relation to the provision by a company of a summary financial statement (see section 426).

### 436  Meaning of 'publication' in relation to accounts and reports

(1)  This section has effect for the purposes of—
section 433 (name of signatory to be stated in published copies of accounts and reports),
section 434 (requirements in connection with publication of statutory accounts), and
section 435 (requirements in connection with publication of non-statutory accounts).

(2)  For the purposes of those sections a company is regarded as publishing a document if it publishes, issues or circulates it or otherwise makes it available for public inspection in a manner calculated to invite members of the public generally, or any class of members of the public, to read it.

## Chapter 8  Public companies: laying of accounts and reports before general meeting

### 437  Public companies: laying of accounts and reports before general meeting

(1)  The directors of a public company must lay before the company in general meeting copies of its annual accounts and reports.

(2) This section must be complied with not later than the end of the period for filing the accounts and reports in question.

(3) In the Companies Acts 'accounts meeting', in relation to a public company, means a general meeting of the company at which the company's annual accounts and reports are (or are to be) laid in accordance with this section.

### 438   Public companies: offence of failure to lay accounts and reports

(1) If the requirements of section 437 (public companies: laying of accounts and reports before general meeting) are not complied with before the end of the period allowed, every person who immediately before the end of that period was a director of the company commits an offence.

(2) It is a defence for a person charged with such an offence to prove that he took all reasonable steps for securing that those requirements would be complied with before the end of that period.

(3) It is not a defence to prove that the documents in question were not in fact prepared as required by this Part.

(4) A person guilty of an offence under this section is liable on summary conviction to a fine not exceeding level 5 on the standard scale and, for continued contravention, a daily default fine not exceeding one-tenth of level 5 on the standard scale.

## Chapter 9  Quoted companies: members' approval of directors' remuneration report

### 439   Quoted companies: members' approval of directors' remuneration report

(1) A quoted company must, prior to the accounts meeting, give to the members of the company entitled to be sent notice of the meeting notice of the intention to move at the meeting, as an ordinary resolution, a resolution approving the directors' remuneration report for the financial year.

(2) The notice may be given in any manner permitted for the service on the member of notice of the meeting.

(3) The business that may be dealt with at the accounts meeting includes the resolution.
This is so notwithstanding any default in complying with subsection (1) or (2).

(4) The existing directors must ensure that the resolution is put to the vote of the meeting.

(5) No entitlement of a person to remuneration is made conditional on the resolution being passed by reason only of the provision made by this section.

(6) In this section—
'the accounts meeting' means the general meeting of the company before which the company's annual accounts for the financial year are to be laid; and
'existing director' means a person who is a director of the company immediately before that meeting.

### 440   Quoted companies: offences in connection with procedure for approval

(1) In the event of default in complying with section 439(1) (notice to be given of resolution for approval of directors' remuneration report), an offence is committed by every officer of the company who is in default.

(2) If the resolution is not put to the vote of the accounts meeting, an offence is committed by each existing director.

(3) It is a defence for a person charged with an offence under subsection (2) to prove that he took all reasonable steps for securing that the resolution was put to the vote of the meeting.

(4) A person guilty of an offence under this section is liable on summary conviction to a fine not exceeding level 3 on the standard scale.

(5) In this section—
'the accounts meeting' means the general meeting of the company before which the company's annual accounts for the financial year are to be laid; and
'existing director' means a person who is a director of the company immediately before that meeting.

## Chapter 10  Filing of accounts and reports

*Duty to file accounts and reports*

### 441   Duty to file accounts and reports with the registrar

(1) The directors of a company must deliver to the registrar for each financial year the accounts and reports required by—
section 444 (filing obligations of companies subject to small companies regime),
section 444A (filing obligations of companies entitled to small companies exemption in relation to directors' report),
section 445 (filing obligations of medium-sized companies),
section 446 (filing obligations of unquoted companies), or
section 447 (filing obligations of quoted companies).

(2) This is subject to section 448 (unlimited companies exempt from filing obligations).

**442    Period allowed for filing accounts**

(1)  This section specifies the period allowed for the directors of a company to comply with their obligation under section 441 to deliver accounts and reports for a financial year to the registrar.

This is referred to in the Companies Acts as the 'period for filing' those accounts and reports.

(2)  The period is—

(a)  for a private company, nine months after the end of the relevant accounting reference period, and

(b)  for a public company, six months after the end of that period.

This is subject to the following provisions of this section.

(3)  If the relevant accounting reference period is the company's first and is a period of more than twelve months, the period is—

(a)  nine months or six months, as the case may be, from the first anniversary of the incorporation of the company, or

(b)  three months after the end of the accounting reference period,

whichever last expires.

(4)  If the relevant accounting reference period is treated as shortened by virtue of a notice given by the company under section 392 (alteration of accounting reference date), the period is—

(a)  that applicable in accordance with the above provisions, or

(b)  three months from the date of the notice under that section,

whichever last expires.

(5)  If for any special reason the Secretary of State thinks fit he may, on an application made before the expiry of the period otherwise allowed, by notice in writing to a company extend that period by such further period as may be specified in the notice.

(6)  Whether the period allowed is that for a private company or a public company is determined by reference to the company's status immediately before the end of the relevant accounting reference period.

(7)  In this section 'the relevant accounting reference period' means the accounting reference period by reference to which the financial year for the accounts in question was determined.

**443    Calculation of period allowed**

(1)  This section applies for the purposes of calculating the period for filing a company's accounts and reports which is expressed as a specified number of months from a specified date or after the end of a specified previous period.

(2)  Subject to the following provisions, the period ends with the date in the appropriate month corresponding to the specified date or the last day of the specified previous period.

(3)  If the specified date, or the last day of the specified previous period, is the last day of a month, the period ends with the last day of the appropriate month (whether or not that is the corresponding date).

(4)  If—

(a)  the specified date, or the last day of the specified previous period, is not the last day of a month but is the 29th or 30th, and

(b)  the appropriate month is February,

the period ends with the last day of February.

(5)  'The appropriate month' means the month that is the specified number of months after the month in which the specified date, or the end of the specified previous period, falls.

*Filing obligations of different descriptions of company*

**444    Filing obligations of companies subject to small companies regime**

(1)  The directors of a company subject to the small companies regime—

(a)  must deliver to the registrar for each financial year a copy of a balance sheet drawn up as at the last day of that year, and

(b)  may also deliver to the registrar—

(i)    a copy of the company's profit and loss account for that year, and

(ii)   a copy of the directors' report for that year.

(2)  The directors must also deliver to the registrar a copy of the auditor's report on the accounts (and any directors' report) that it delivers.

This does not apply if the company is exempt from audit and the directors have taken advantage of that exemption.

(3)  The copies of accounts and reports delivered to the registrar must be copies of the company's annual accounts and reports, except that where the company prepares Companies Act accounts—

(a)  the directors may deliver to the registrar a copy of a balance sheet drawn up in accordance with regulations made by the Secretary of State, and

(b)  there may be omitted from the copy profit and loss account delivered to the registrar such items as may be specified by the regulations.

These are referred to in this Part as 'abbreviated accounts'.

(4)  If abbreviated accounts are delivered to the registrar the obligation to deliver a copy of the auditor's report on the accounts is to deliver a copy of the special auditor's report required by section 449.

(5) Where the directors of a company subject to the small companies regime deliver to the registrar IAS accounts, or Companies Act accounts that are not abbreviated accounts, and in accordance with this section—

(a) do not deliver to the registrar a copy of the company's profit and loss account, or

(b) do not deliver to the registrar a copy of the directors' report,

the copy of the balance sheet delivered to the registrar must contain in a prominent position a statement that the company's annual accounts and reports have been delivered in accordance with the provisions applicable to companies subject to the small companies regime.

(6) The copies of the balance sheet and any directors' report delivered to the registrar under this section must state the name of the person who signed it on behalf of the board.

(7) The copy of the auditor's report delivered to the registrar under this section must—

(a) state the name of the auditor and (where the auditor is a firm) the name of the person who signed it as senior statutory auditor, or

(b) if the conditions in section 506 (circumstances in which names may be omitted) are met, state that a resolution has been passed and notified to the Secretary of State in accordance with that section.

### 444A  Filing obligations of companies entitled to small companies exemption in relation to directors' report

(1) The directors of a company that is entitled to small companies exemption in relation to the directors' report for a financial year—

(a) must deliver to the registrar a copy of the company's annual accounts for that year, and

(b) may also deliver to the registrar a copy of the directors' report.

(2) The directors must also deliver to the registrar a copy of the auditor's report on the accounts (and any directors' report) that it delivers.

This does not apply if the company is exempt from audit and the directors have taken advantage of that exception.

(3) The copies of the balance sheet and directors' report delivered to the registrar under this section must state the name of the person who signed it on behalf of the board.

(4) The copy of the auditor's report delivered to the registrar under this section must—

(a) state the name of the auditor and (where the auditor is a firm) the name of the person who signed it as senior statutory auditor, and

(b) be signed by the auditor or (where the auditor is a firm) in the name of the firm by a person authorised to sign on its behalf,

or, if the conditions in section 506 (circumstances in which names may be omitted) are met, state that a resolution has been passed and notified to the Secretary of State in accordance with that section.

(5) This section does not apply to companies within section 444 (filing obligations of companies subject to the small companies regime).

### 445  Filing obligations of medium-sized companies

(1) The directors of a company that qualifies as a medium-sized company in relation to a financial year (see sections 465 to 467) must deliver to the registrar a copy of—

(a) the company's annual accounts, and

(b) the directors' report.

(2) They must also deliver to the registrar a copy of the auditor's report on those accounts (and on the directors' report).

This does not apply if the company is exempt from audit and the directors have taken advantage of that exemption.

(3) Where the company prepares Companies Act accounts, the directors may deliver to the registrar a copy of the company's annual accounts for the financial year—

(a) that includes a profit and loss account in which items are combined in accordance with regulations made by the Secretary of State, and

(b) that does not contain items whose omission is authorised by the regulations.

These are referred to in this Part as 'abbreviated accounts'.

(4) If abbreviated accounts are delivered to the registrar the obligation to deliver a copy of the auditor's report on the accounts is to deliver a copy of the special auditor's report required by section 449.

(5) The copies of the balance sheet and directors' report delivered to the registrar under this section must state the name of the person who signed it on behalf of the board.

(6) The copy of the auditor's report delivered to the registrar under this section must—

(a) state the name of the auditor and (where the auditor is a firm) the name of the person who signed it as senior statutory auditor, or

(b) if the conditions in section 506 (circumstances in which names may be omitted) are met, state that a resolution has been passed and notified to the Secretary of State in accordance with that section.

(7) This section does not apply to companies within—

    (a)  section 444 (filing obligations of companies subject to the small companies regime), or

    (b)  section 444A (filing obligations of companies entitled to small companies exemption in relation to directors' report).

## 446   Filing obligations of unquoted companies

    (1)  The directors of an unquoted company must deliver to the registrar for each financial year of the company a copy of—

      (a)  the company's annual accounts, and

      (b)  the directors' report.

    (2)  The directors must also deliver to the registrar a copy of the auditor's report on those accounts (and the directors' report).

This does not apply if the company is exempt from audit and the directors have taken advantage of that exemption.

    (3)  The copies of the balance sheet and directors' report delivered to the registrar under this section must state the name of the person who signed it on behalf of the board.

    (4)  The copy of the auditor's report delivered to the registrar under this section must—

      (a)  state the name of the auditor and (where the auditor is a firm) the name of the person who signed it as senior statutory auditor, or

      (b)  if the conditions in section 506 (circumstances in which names may be omitted) are met, state that a resolution has been passed and notified to the Secretary of State in accordance with that section.

    (5)  This section does not apply to companies within—

      (a)  section 444 (filing obligations of companies subject to the small companies regime),

      (aa)  section 444A (filing obligations of companies entitled to small companies exemption in relation to directors' report), or

      (b)  section 445 (filing obligations of medium-sized companies).

## 447   Filing obligations of quoted companies

    (1)  The directors of a quoted company must deliver to the registrar for each financial year of the company a copy of—

      (a)  the company's annual accounts,

      (b)  the directors' remuneration report, and

      (c)  the directors' report.

    (2)  They must also deliver a copy of the auditor's report on those accounts (and on the directors' remuneration report and the directors' report).

    (3)  The copies of the balance sheet, the directors' remuneration report and the directors' report delivered to the registrar under this section must state the name of the person who signed it on behalf of the board.

    (4)  The copy of the auditor's report delivered to the registrar under this section must—

      (a)  state the name of the auditor and (where the auditor is a firm) the name of the person who signed it as senior statutory auditor, or

      (b)  if the conditions in section 506 (circumstances in which names may be omitted) are met, state that a resolution has been passed and notified to the Secretary of State in accordance with that section.

## 448   Unlimited companies exempt from obligation to file accounts

    (1)  The directors of an unlimited company are not required to deliver accounts and reports to the registrar in respect of a financial year if the following conditions are met.

    (2)  The conditions are that at no time during the relevant accounting reference period—

      (a)  has the company been, to its knowledge, a subsidiary undertaking of an undertaking which was then limited, or

      (b)  have there been, to its knowledge, exercisable by or on behalf of two or more undertakings which were then limited, rights which if exercisable by one of them would have made the company a subsidiary undertaking of it, or

      (c)  has the company been a parent company of an undertaking which was then limited.

The references above to an undertaking being limited at a particular time are to an undertaking (under whatever law established) the liability of whose members is at that time limited.

    (3)  The exemption conferred by this section does not apply if—

      (a)  the company is a banking or insurance company or the parent company of a banking or insurance group, or

      (b)  each of the members of the company is—

        (i)  a limited company,

        (ii)  another unlimited company each of whose members is a limited company, or

        (iii)  a Scottish partnership each of whose members is a limited company.

The references in paragraph (b) to a limited company, another unlimited company or a Scottish partnership include a comparable undertaking incorporated in or formed under the law of a country or territory outside the United Kingdom.

(4) Where a company is exempt by virtue of this section from the obligation to deliver accounts—

    (a) section 434(3) (requirements in connection with publication of statutory accounts: meaning of 'statutory accounts') has effect with the substitution for the words 'as required to be delivered to the registrar under section 441' of the words 'as prepared in accordance with this Part and approved by the board of directors'; and

    (b) section 435(1)(b) (requirements in connection with publication of non-statutory accounts: statement whether statutory accounts delivered) has effect with the substitution for the words from 'whether statutory accounts' to 'have been delivered to the registrar' of the words 'that the company is exempt from the requirement to deliver statutory accounts'.

(5) In this section the 'relevant accounting reference period', in relation to a financial year, means the accounting reference period by reference to which that financial year was determined.

### *Requirements where abbreviated accounts delivered*

### 449 Special auditor's report where abbreviated accounts delivered

(1) This section applies where—

    (a) the directors of a company deliver abbreviated accounts to the registrar, and

    (b) the company is not exempt from audit (or the directors have not taken advantage of any such exemption).

(2) The directors must also deliver to the registrar a copy of a special report of the company's auditor stating that in his opinion—

    (a) the company is entitled to deliver abbreviated accounts in accordance with the section in question, and

    (b) the abbreviated accounts to be delivered are properly prepared in accordance with regulations under that section.

(3) The auditor's report on the company's annual accounts need not be delivered, but—

    (a) if that report was qualified, the special report must set out that report in full together with any further material necessary to understand the qualification, and

    (b) if that report contained a statement under—

        (i) section 498(2)(a) or (b) (accounts, records or returns inadequate or accounts not agreeing with records and returns), or

        (ii) section 498(3) (failure to obtain necessary information and explanations),

        the special report must set out that statement in full.

(4) The provisions of—

sections 503 to 506 (signature of auditor's report), and

sections 507 to 509 (offences in connection with auditor's report),

apply to a special report under this section as they apply to an auditor's report on the company's annual accounts prepared under Part 16.

(5) If abbreviated accounts are delivered to the registrar, the references in section 434 or 435 (requirements in connection with publication of accounts) to the auditor's report on the company's annual accounts shall be read as references to the special auditor's report required by this section.

### 450 Approval and signing of abbreviated accounts

(1) Abbreviated accounts must be approved by the board of directors and signed on behalf of the board by a director of the company.

(2) The signature must be on the balance sheet.

(3) The balance sheet must contain in a prominent position above the signature a statement to the effect that it is prepared in accordance with the special provisions of this Act relating (as the case may be) to companies subject to the small companies regime or to medium-sized companies.

(4) If abbreviated accounts are approved that do not comply with the requirements of regulations under the relevant section, every director of the company who—

    (a) knew that they did not comply, or was reckless as to whether they complied, and

    (b) failed to take reasonable steps to prevent them from being approved,

commits an offence.

(5) A person guilty of an offence under subsection (4) is liable—

    (a) on conviction on indictment, to a fine;

    (b) on summary conviction, to a fine not exceeding the statutory maximum.

### *Failure to file accounts and reports*

### 451 Default in filing accounts and reports: offences

(1) If the requirements of section 441 (duty to file accounts and reports) are not complied with in relation to a company's accounts and reports for a financial year before the end of the period for filing those accounts and reports, every person who immediately before the end of that period was a director of the company commits an offence.

(2) It is a defence for a person charged with such an offence to prove that he took all reasonable steps for securing that those requirements would be complied with before the end of that period.

(3) It is not a defence to prove that the documents in question were not in fact prepared as required by this Part.

(4) A person guilty of an offence under this section is liable on summary conviction to a fine not exceeding level 5 on the standard scale and, for continued contravention, a daily default fine not exceeding one-tenth of level 5 on the standard scale.

### 452 Default in filing accounts and reports: court order

(1) If—

    (a) the requirements of section 441 (duty to file accounts and reports) are not complied with in relation to a company's accounts and reports for a financial year before the end of the period for filing those accounts and reports, and

    (b) the directors of the company fail to make good the default within 14 days after the service of a notice on them requiring compliance,

the court may, on the application of any member or creditor of the company or of the registrar, make an order directing the directors (or any of them) to make good the default within such time as may be specified in the order.

(2) The court's order may provide that all costs (in Scotland, expenses) of and incidental to the application are to be borne by the directors.

### 453 Civil penalty for failure to file accounts and reports

(1) Where the requirements of section 441 are not complied with in relation to a company's accounts and reports for a financial year before the end of the period for filing those accounts and reports, the company is liable to a civil penalty.

This is in addition to any liability of the directors under section 451.

(2) The amount of the penalty shall be determined in accordance with regulations made by the Secretary of State by reference to—

    (a) the length of the period between the end of the period for filing the accounts and reports in question and the day on which the requirements are complied with, and

    (b) whether the company is a private or public company.

(3) The penalty may be recovered by the registrar and is to be paid into the Consolidated Fund.

(4) It is not a defence in proceedings under this section to prove that the documents in question were not in fact prepared as required by this Part.

(5) Regulations under this section having the effect of increasing the penalty payable in any case are subject to affirmative resolution procedure.

Otherwise, the regulations are subject to negative resolution procedure.

# Chapter 11 Revision of defective accounts and reports

*Voluntary revision*

### 454 Voluntary revision of accounts etc.

(1) If it appears to the directors of a company that—

    (a) the company's annual accounts,

    (b) the directors' remuneration report or the directors' report, or

    (c) a summary financial statement of the company,

did not comply with the requirements of this Act (or, where applicable, of Article 4 of the IAS Regulation), they may prepare revised accounts or a revised report or statement.

(2) Where copies of the previous accounts or report have been sent out to members, delivered to the registrar or (in the case of a public company) laid before the company in general meeting, the revisions must be confined to—

    (a) the correction of those respects in which the previous accounts or report did not comply with the requirements of this Act (or, where applicable, of Article 4 of the IAS Regulation), and

    (b) the making of any necessary consequential alterations.

(3) The Secretary of State may make provision by regulations as to the application of the provisions of this Act in relation to—

    (a) revised annual accounts,

    (b) a revised directors' remuneration report or directors' report, or

    (c) a revised summary financial statement.

(4) The regulations may, in particular—

    (a) make different provision according to whether the previous accounts, report or statement are replaced or are supplemented by a document indicating the corrections to be made;

    (b) make provision with respect to the functions of the company's auditor in relation to the revised accounts, report or statement;

    (c) require the directors to take such steps as may be specified in the regulations where the previous accounts or report have been—

        (i) sent out to members and others under section 423,

    (ii)  laid before the company in general meeting, or

    (iii)  delivered to the registrar,

or where a summary financial statement containing information derived from the previous accounts or report has been sent to members under section 426;

    (d)  apply the provisions of this Act (including those creating criminal offences) subject to such additions, exceptions and modifications as are specified in the regulations.

  (5)  Regulations under this section are subject to negative resolution procedure.

*Secretary of State's notice*

### 455  Secretary of State's notice in respect of accounts or reports

  (1)  This section applies where—

    (a)  copies of a company's annual accounts or directors' report have been sent out under section 423, or

    (b)  a copy of a company's annual accounts or directors' report has been delivered to the registrar or (in the case of a public company) laid before the company in general meeting,

and it appears to the Secretary of State that there is, or may be, a question whether the accounts or report comply with the requirements of this Act (or, where applicable, of Article 4 of the IAS Regulation).

  (2)  The Secretary of State may give notice to the directors of the company indicating the respects in which it appears that such a question arises or may arise.

  (3)  The notice must specify a period of not less than one month for the directors to give an explanation of the accounts or report or prepare revised accounts or a revised report.

  (4)  If at the end of the specified period, or such longer period as the Secretary of State may allow, it appears to the Secretary of State that the directors have not—

    (a)  given a satisfactory explanation of the accounts or report, or

    (b)  revised the accounts or report so as to comply with the requirements of this Act (or, where applicable, of Article 4 of the IAS Regulation),

the Secretary of State may apply to the court.

  (5)  The provisions of this section apply equally to revised annual accounts and revised directors' reports, in which case they have effect as if the references to revised accounts or reports were references to further revised accounts or reports.

*Application to court*

### 456  Application to court in respect of defective accounts or reports

  (1)  An application may be made to the court—

    (a)  by the Secretary of State, after having complied with section 455, or

    (b)  by a person authorised by the Secretary of State for the purposes of this section,

for a declaration (in Scotland, a declarator) that the annual accounts of a company do not comply, or a directors' report does not comply, with the requirements of this Act (or, where applicable, of Article 4 of the IAS Regulation) and for an order requiring the directors of the company to prepare revised accounts or a revised report.

  (2)  Notice of the application, together with a general statement of the matters at issue in the proceedings, shall be given by the applicant to the registrar for registration.

  (3)  If the court orders the preparation of revised accounts, it may give directions as to—

    (a)  the auditing of the accounts,

    (b)  the revision of any directors' remuneration report, directors' report or summary financial statement, and

    (c)  the taking of steps by the directors to bring the making of the order to the notice of persons likely to rely on the previous accounts,

and such other matters as the court thinks fit.

  (4)  If the court orders the preparation of a revised directors' report it may give directions as to—

    (a)  the review of the report by the auditors,

    (b)  the revision of any summary financial statement,

    (c)  the taking of steps by the directors to bring the making of the order to the notice of persons likely to rely on the previous report, and

    (d)  such other matters as the court thinks fit.

  (5)  If the court finds that the accounts or report did not comply with the requirements of this Act (or, where applicable, of Article 4 of the IAS Regulation) it may order that all or part of—

    (a)  the costs (in Scotland, expenses) of and incidental to the application, and

    (b)  any reasonable expenses incurred by the company in connection with or in consequence of the preparation of revised accounts or a revised report,

are to be borne by such of the directors as were party to the approval of the defective accounts or report.

For this purpose every director of the company at the time of the approval of the accounts or report shall be taken to have been a party to the approval unless he shows that he took all reasonable steps to prevent that approval.

(6) Where the court makes an order under subsection (5) it shall have regard to whether the directors party to the approval of the defective accounts or report knew or ought to have known that the accounts or report did not comply with the requirements of this Act (or, where applicable, of Article 4 of the IAS Regulation), and it may exclude one or more directors from the order or order the payment of different amounts by different directors.

(7) On the conclusion of proceedings on an application under this section, the applicant must send to the registrar for registration a copy of the court order or, as the case may be, give notice to the registrar that the application has failed or been withdrawn.

(8) The provisions of this section apply equally to revised annual accounts and revised directors' reports, in which case they have effect as if the references to revised accounts or reports were references to further revised accounts or reports.

### 457   Other persons authorised to apply to the court

(1) The Secretary of State may by order (an 'authorisation order') authorise for the purposes of section 456 any person appearing to him—

   (a) to have an interest in, and to have satisfactory procedures directed to securing, compliance by companies with the requirements of this Act (or, where applicable, of Article 4 of the IAS Regulation) relating to accounts and directors' reports,
   (b) to have satisfactory procedures for receiving and investing complaints about companies' annual accounts and directors' reports, and
   (c) otherwise to be a fit and proper person to be authorised.

(2) A person may be authorised generally or in respect of particular classes of case, and different persons may be authorised in respect of different classes of case.

(3) The Secretary of State may refuse to authorise a person if he considers that his authorisation is unnecessary having regard to the fact that there are one or more other persons who have been or are likely to be authorised.

(4) If the authorised person is an unincorporated association, proceedings brought in, or in connection with, the exercise of any function by the association as an authorised person may be brought by or against the association in the name of a body corporate whose constitution provides for the establishment of the association.

(5) An authorisation order may contain such requirements or other provisions relating to the exercise of functions by the authorised person as appear to the Secretary of State to be appropriate.

No such order is to be made unless it appears to the Secretary of State that the person would, if authorised, exercise his functions as an authorised person in accordance with the provisions proposed.

(6) Where authorisation is revoked, the revoking order may make such provision as the Secretary of State thinks fit with respect to pending proceedings.

(7) An order under this section is subject to negative resolution procedure.

### 458   Disclosure of information by tax authorities

(1) The Commissioners for Her Majesty's Revenue and Customs may disclose information to a person authorised under section 457 for the purpose of facilitating—

   (a) the taking of steps by that person to discover whether there are grounds for an application to the court under section 456 (application in respect of defective accounts etc), or
   (b) a decision by the authorised person whether to make such an application.

(2) This section applies despite any statutory or other restriction on the disclosure of information.

Provided that, in the case of personal data within the meaning of the Data Protection Act 1998 (c. 29), information is not to be disclosed in contravention of that Act.

(3) Information disclosed to an authorised person under this section—

   (a) may not be used except in or in connection with—
      (i) taking steps to discover whether there are grounds for an application to the court under section 456, or
      (ii) deciding whether or not to make such an application,
         or in, or in connection with, proceedings on such an application; and
   (b) must not be further disclosed except—
      (i) to the person to whom the information relates, or
      (ii) in, or in connection with, proceedings on any such application to the court.

(4) A person who contravenes subsection (3) commits an offence unless—

   (a) he did not know, and had no reason to suspect, that the information had been disclosed under this section, or
   (b) he took all reasonable steps and exercised all due diligence to avoid the commission of the offence.

(5) A person guilty of an offence under subsection (4) is liable—

   (a) on conviction on indictment, to imprisonment for a term not exceeding two years or a fine (or both);
   (b) on summary conviction—

(i)    in England and Wales, to imprisonment for a term not exceeding twelve months or to a
fine not exceeding the statutory maximum (or both);

(ii)    in Scotland or Northern Ireland, to imprisonment for a term not exceeding six months,
or to a fine not exceeding the statutory maximum (or both).

(6)  Where an offence under this section is committed by a body corporate, every officer of the body
who is in default also commits the offence.

For this purpose—

(a)  any person who purports to act as director, manager or secretary of the body is treated as an
officer of the body, and

(b)  if the body is a company, any shadow director is treated as an officer of the company.

*Power of authorised person to require documents etc.*

### 459  Power of authorised person to require documents, information and explanations

(1)  This section applies where it appears to a person who is authorised under section 457 that there
is, or may be, a question whether a company's annual accounts or directors' report comply with the
requirements of this Act (or, where applicable, of Article 4 of the IAS Regulation).

(2)  The authorised person may require any of the persons mentioned in subsection (3) to produce
any document, or to provide him with any information or explanations, that he may reasonably require
for the purpose of—

(a)  discovering whether there are grounds for an application to the court under section 456, or

(b)  deciding whether to make such an application.

(3)  Those persons are—

(a)  the company;

(b)  any officer, employee, or auditor of the company;

(c)  any persons who fell within paragraph (b) at a time to which the document or information
required by the authorised person relates.

(4)  If a person fails to comply with such a requirement, the authorised person may apply to the court.

(5)  If it appears to the court that the person has failed to comply with a requirement under subsection (2), it may order the person to take such steps as it directs for securing that the documents are
produced or the information or explanations are provided.

(6)  A statement made by a person in response to a requirement under subsection (2) or an order
under subsection (5) may not be used in evidence against him in any criminal proceedings.

(7)  Nothing in this section compels any person to disclose documents or information in respect of
which a claim to legal professional privilege (in Scotland, to confidentiality of communications) could
be maintained in legal proceedings.

(8)  In this section 'document' includes information recorded in any form.

### 460  Restrictions on disclosure of information obtained under compulsory powers

(1)  This section applies to information (in whatever form) obtained in pursuance of a requirement
or order under section 459 (power of authorised person to require documents etc.) that relates to the
private affairs of an individual or to any particular business.

(2)  No such information may, during the lifetime of that individual or so long as that business continues to be carried on, be disclosed without the consent of that individual or the person for the time
being carrying on that business.

(3)  This does not apply—

(a)  to disclosure permitted by section 461 (permitted disclosure of information obtained under
compulsory powers), or

(b)  to the disclosure of information that is or has been available to the public from another
source.

(4)  A person who discloses information in contravention of this section commits an offence,
unless—

(a)  he did not know, and had no reason to suspect, that the information had been disclosed
under section 459, or

(b)  he took all reasonable steps and exercised all due diligence to avoid the commission of the
offence.

(5)  A person guilty of an offence under this section is liable—

(a)  on conviction on indictment, to imprisonment for a term not exceeding two years or a fine
(or both);

(b)  on summary conviction—

(i)    in England and Wales, to imprisonment for a term not exceeding twelve months or to a
fine not exceeding the statutory maximum (or both);

(ii)    in Scotland or Northern Ireland, to imprisonment for a term not exceeding six months,
or to a fine not exceeding the statutory maximum (or both).

(6) Where an offence under this section is committed by a body corporate, every officer of the body who is in default also commits the offence.

For this purpose—

    (a) any person who purports to act as director, manager or secretary of the body is treated as an officer of the body, and

    (b) if the body is a company, any shadow director is treated as an officer of the company.

### 461 Permitted disclosure of information obtained under compulsory powers

(1) The prohibition in section 460 of the disclosure of information obtained in pursuance of a requirement or order under section 459 (power of authorised person to require documents etc.) that relates to the private affairs of an individual or to any particular business has effect subject to the following exceptions.

(2) It does not apply to the disclosure of information for the purpose of facilitating the carrying out by the authorised person of his functions under section 456.

(3) It does not apply to disclosure to—

    (a) the Secretary of State,

    (b) the Department of Enterprise, Trade and Investment for Northern Ireland,

    (c) the Treasury,

    (d) the Bank of England,

    (e) the Financial Services Authority, or

    (f) the Commissioners for Her Majesty's Revenue and Customs.

(4) It does not apply to disclosure—

    (a) for the purpose of assisting a body designated by an order under section 1252 (delegation of functions of the Secretary of State) to exercise its functions under Part 42;

    (b) with a view to the institution of, or otherwise for the purposes of, disciplinary proceedings relating to the performance by an accountant or auditor of his professional duties;

    (c) for the purpose of enabling or assisting the Secretary of State or the Treasury to exercise any of their functions under any of the following—

        (i) the Companies Acts,

        (ii) Part 5 of the Criminal Justice Act 1993 (c. 36) (insider dealing),

        (iii) the Insolvency Act 1986 (c. 45) or the Insolvency (Northern Ireland) Order 1989 (S.I. 1989/2405 (N.I. 19)),

        (iv) the Company Directors Disqualification Act 1986 (c. 46) or the Company Directors Disqualification (Northern Ireland) Order 2002 (S.I. 2002/3150 (N.I. 4)),

        (v) the Financial Services and Markets Act 2000 (c. 8);

    (d) for the purpose of enabling or assisting the Department of Enterprise, Trade and Investment for Northern Ireland to exercise any powers conferred on it by the enactments relating to companies, directors' disqualification or insolvency;

    (e) for the purpose of enabling or assisting the Bank of England to exercise its functions;

    (f) for the purpose of enabling or assisting the Commissioners for Her Majesty's Revenue and Customs to exercise their functions;

    (g) for the purpose of enabling or assisting the Financial Services Authority to exercise its functions under any of the following—

        (i) the legislation relating to friendly societies or to industrial and provident societies,

        (ii) the Building Societies Act 1986 (c. 53),

        (iii) Part 7 of the Companies Act 1989 (c. 40),

        (iv) the Financial Services and Markets Act 2000; or

    (h) in pursuance of any Community obligation.

(5) It does not apply to disclosure to a body exercising functions of a public nature under legislation in any country or territory outside the United Kingdom that appear to the authorised person to be similar to his functions under section 456 for the purpose of enabling or assisting that body to exercise those functions.

(6) In determining whether to disclose information to a body in accordance with subsection (5), the authorised person must have regard to the following considerations—

    (a) whether the use which the body is likely to make of the information is sufficiently important to justify making the disclosure;

    (b) whether the body has adequate arrangements to prevent the information from being used or further disclosed other than—

        (i) for the purposes of carrying out the functions mentioned in that subsection, or

        (ii) for other purposes substantially similar to those for which information disclosed to the authorised person could be used or further disclosed.

(7) Nothing in this section authorises the making of a disclosure in contravention of the Data Protection Act 1998 (c. 29).

### 462 Power to amend categories of permitted disclosure

(1) The Secretary of State may by order amend section 461(3), (4) and (5).

(2) An order under this section must not—

    (a) amend subsection (3) of that section (UK public authorities) by specifying a person unless the person exercises functions of a public nature (whether or not he exercises any other function);

    (b) amend subsection (4) of that section (purposes for which disclosure permitted) by adding or modifying a description of disclosure unless the purpose for which the disclosure is permitted is likely to facilitate the exercise of a function of a public nature;

    (c) amend subsection (5) of that section (overseas regulatory authorities) so as to have the effect of permitting disclosures to be made to a body other than one that exercises functions of a public nature in a country or territory outside the United Kingdom.

(3) An order under this section is subject to negative resolution procedure.

## Chapter 12 Supplementary provisions

*Liability for false or misleading statements in reports*

### 463 Liability for false or misleading statements in reports

(1) The reports to which this section applies are—

    (a) the directors' report,

    (b) the directors' remuneration report, and

    (c) a summary financial statement so far as it is derived from either of those reports.

(2) A director of a company is liable to compensate the company for any loss suffered by it as a result of—

    (a) any untrue or misleading statement in a report to which this section applies, or

    (b) the omission from a report to which this section applies of anything required to be included in it.

(3) He is so liable only if—

    (a) he knew the statement to be untrue or misleading or was reckless as to whether it was untrue or misleading, or

    (b) he knew the omission to be dishonest concealment of a material fact.

(4) No person shall be subject to any liability to a person other than the company resulting from reliance, by that person or another, on information in a report to which this section applies.

(5) The reference in subsection (4) to a person being subject to a liability includes a reference to another person being entitled as against him to be granted any civil remedy or to rescind or repudiate an agreement.

(6) This section does not affect—

    (a) liability for a civil penalty, or

    (b) liability for a criminal offence.

*Accounting and reporting standards*

### 464 Accounting standards

(1) In this Part 'accounting standards' means statements of standard accounting practice issued by such body or bodies as may be prescribed by regulations.

(2) References in this Part to accounting standards applicable to a company's annual accounts are to such standards as are, in accordance with their terms, relevant to the company's circumstances and to the accounts.

(3) Regulations under this section may contain such transitional and other supplementary and incidental provisions as appear to the Secretary of State to be appropriate.

*Companies qualifying as medium-sized*

### 465 Companies qualifying as medium-sized: general

(1) A company qualifies as medium-sized in relation to its first financial year if the qualifying conditions are met in that year.

(2) A company qualifies as medium-sized in relation to a subsequent financial year—

    (a) if the qualifying conditions are met in that year and the preceding financial year;

    (b) if the qualifying conditions are met in that year and the company qualified as medium-sized in relation to the preceding financial year;

    (c) if the qualifying conditions were met in the preceding financial year and the company qualified as medium-sized in relation to that year.

(3) The qualifying conditions are met by a company in a year in which it satisfies two or more of the following requirements—

| Turnover | Not more than £25.9 million |
|---|---|
| Balance sheet total | Not more than £12.9 million |
| Number of employees | Not more than 250 |

(4) For a period that is a company's financial year but not in fact a year the maximum figures for turnover must be proportionately adjusted.

(5) The balance sheet total means the aggregate of the amounts shown as assets in the company's balance sheet.

(6) The number of employees means the average number of persons employed by the company in the year, determined as follows—

    (a) find for each month in the financial year the number of persons employed under contracts of service by the company in that month (whether throughout the month or not),

    (b) add together the monthly totals, and

    (c) divide by the number of months in the financial year.

(7) This section is subject to section 466 (companies qualifying as medium-sized: parent companies).

### 466    Companies qualifying as medium-sized: parent companies

(1) A parent company qualifies as a medium-sized company in relation to a financial year only if the group headed by it qualifies as a medium-sized group.

(2) A group qualifies as medium-sized in relation to the parent company's first financial year if the qualifying conditions are met in that year.

(3) A group qualifies as medium-sized in relation to a subsequent financial year of the parent company—

    (a) if the qualifying conditions are met in that year and the preceding financial year;

    (b) if the qualifying conditions are met in that year and the group qualified as medium-sized in relation to the preceding financial year;

    (c) if the qualifying conditions were met in the preceding financial year and the group qualified as medium-sized in relation to that year.

(4) The qualifying conditions are met by a group in a year in which it satisfies two or more of the following requirements—

| Aggregate turnover | Not more than £25.9 million net (or £31.1 million gross) |
|---|---|
| Aggregate balance sheet total | Not more than £12.9 million net (or £15.5 million gross) |
| Aggregate number of employees | Not more than 250 |

(5) The aggregate figures are ascertained by aggregating the relevant figures determined in accordance with section 465 for each member of the group.

(6) In relation to the aggregate figures for turnover and balance sheet total—

'net' means after any set-offs and other adjustments made to eliminate group transactions—

    (a) in the case of Companies Act accounts, in accordance with regulations under section 404,

    (b) in the case of IAS accounts, in accordance with international accounting standards; and

'gross' means without those set-offs and other adjustments.

A company may satisfy any relevant requirement on the basis of either the net or the gross figure.

(7) The figures for each subsidiary undertaking shall be those included in its individual accounts for the relevant financial year, that is—

    (a) if its financial year ends with that of the parent company, that financial year, and

    (b) if not, its financial year ending last before the end of the financial year of the parent company.

If those figures cannot be obtained without disproportionate expense or undue delay, the latest available figures shall be taken.

### 467    Companies excluded from being treated as medium-sized

(1) A company is not entitled to take advantage of any of the provisions of this Part relating to companies qualifying as medium-sized if it was at any time within the financial year in question—

    (a) a public company,

    (b) a company that—

        (i) has permission under Part 4 of the Financial Services and Markets Act 2000 (c. 8) to carry on a regulated activity, or

        (ii) carries on insurance market activity, or

    (c) a member of an ineligible group.

(2) A group is ineligible if any of its members is—

    (a) a public company,

    (b) a body corporate (other than a company) whose shares are admitted to trading on a regulated market,

    (c) a person (other than a small company) who has permission under Part 4 of the Financial Services and Markets Act 2000 to carry on a regulated activity,

    (d) a small company that is an authorised insurance company, a banking company, an e-money issuer, a MiFID investment firm or a UCITS management company, or

    (e) a person who carries on insurance market activity.

(3) A company is a small company for the purposes of subsection (2) if it qualified as small in relation to its last financial year ending on or before the end of the financial year in question.

(4)  This section does not prevent a company from taking advantage of section 417(7) (business review: non-financial information) by reason only of its having been a member of an ineligible group at any time within the financial year in question.

*General power to make further provision about accounts and reports*

### 468   General power to make further provision about accounts and reports

(1)  The Secretary of State may make provision by regulations about—

(a)  the accounts and reports that companies are required to prepare;

(b)  the categories of companies required to prepare accounts and reports of any description;

(c)  the form and content of the accounts and reports that companies are required to prepare;

(d)  the obligations of companies and others as regards—

(i)   the approval of accounts and reports,

(ii)   the sending of accounts and reports to members and others,

(iii)   the laying of accounts and reports before the company in general meeting,

(iv)   the delivery of copies of accounts and reports to the registrar, and

(v)   the publication of accounts and reports.

(2)  The regulations may amend this Part by adding, altering or repealing provisions.

(3)  But they must not amend (other than consequentially)—

(a)  section 393 (accounts to give true and fair view), or

(b)  the provisions of Chapter 11 (revision of defective accounts and reports).

(4)  The regulations may create criminal offences in cases corresponding to those in which an offence is created by an existing provision of this Part.

The maximum penalty for any such offence may not be greater than is provided in relation to an offence under the existing provision.

(5)  The regulations may provide for civil penalties in circumstances corresponding to those within section 453(1) (civil penalty for failure to file accounts and reports).

The provisions of section 453(2) to (5) apply in relation to any such penalty.

*Other supplementary provisions*

### 469   Preparation and filing of accounts in euros

(1)  The amounts set out in the annual accounts of a company may also be shown in the same accounts translated into euros.

(2)  When complying with section 441 (duty to file accounts and reports), the directors of a company may deliver to the registrar an additional copy of the company's annual accounts in which the amounts have been translated into euros.

(3)  In both cases—

(a)  the amounts must have been translated at the exchange rate prevailing on the date to which the balance sheet is made up, and

(b)  that rate must be disclosed in the notes to the accounts.

(4)  For the purposes of sections 434 and 435 (requirements in connection with published accounts) any additional copy of the company's annual accounts delivered to the registrar under subsection (2) above shall be treated as statutory accounts of the company.

In the case of such a copy, references in those sections to the auditor's report on the company's annual accounts shall be read as references to the auditor's report on the annual accounts of which it is a copy.

### 470   Power to apply provisions to banking partnerships

(1)  The Secretary of State may by regulations apply to banking partnerships, subject to such exceptions, adaptations and modifications as he considers appropriate, the provisions of this Part (and of regulations made under this Part) applying to banking companies.

(2)  A 'banking partnership' means a partnership which has permission under Part 4 of the Financial Services and Markets Act 2000 (c. 8).

But a partnership is not a banking partnership if it has permission to accept deposits only for the purpose of carrying on another regulated activity in accordance with that permission.

(3)  Expressions used in this section that are also used in the provisions regulating activities under the Financial Services and Markets Act 2000 have the same meaning here as they do in those provisions.

See section 22 of that Act, orders made under that section and Schedule 2 to that Act.

(4)  Regulations under this section are subject to affirmative resolution procedure.

### 471   Meaning of 'annual accounts' and related expressions

(1)  In this Part a company's 'annual accounts', in relation to a financial year, means—

(a)  the company's individual accounts for that year (see section 394), and

(b)  any group accounts prepared by the company for that year (see sections 398 and 399).

This is subject to section 408 (option to omit individual profit and loss account from annual accounts where information given in group accounts).

(2) In the case of an unquoted company, its 'annual accounts and reports' for a financial year are—
(a) its annual accounts,
(b) the directors' report, and
(c) the auditor's report on those accounts and the directors' report (unless the company is exempt from audit).
(3) In the case of a quoted company, its 'annual accounts and reports' for a financial year are—
(a) its annual accounts,
(b) the directors' remuneration report,
(c) the directors' report, and
(d) the auditor's report on those accounts, on the auditable part of the directors' remuneration report and on the directors' report.

### 472  Notes to the accounts

(1) Information required by this Part to be given in notes to a company's annual accounts may be contained in the accounts or in a separate document annexed to the accounts.

(2) References in this Part to a company's annual accounts, or to a balance sheet or profit and loss account, include notes to the accounts giving information which is required by any provision of this Act or international accounting standards, and required or allowed by any such provision to be given in a note to company accounts.

### 473  Parliamentary procedure for certain regulations under this Part

(1) This section applies to regulations under the following provisions of this Part—
section 396 (Companies Act individual accounts),
section 404 (Companies Act group accounts),
section 409 (information about related undertakings),
section 412 (information about directors' benefits: remuneration, pensions and compensation for loss of office),
section 416 (contents of directors' report: general),
section 421 (contents of directors' remuneration report),
section 444 (filing obligations of companies subject to small companies regime),
section 445 (filing obligations of medium-sized companies),
section 468 (general power to make further provision about accounts and reports).

(2) Any such regulations may make consequential amendments or repeals in other provisions of this Act, or in other enactments.

(3) Regulations that—
(a) restrict the classes of company which have the benefit of any exemption, exception or special provision,
(b) require additional matter to be included in a document of any class, or
(c) otherwise render the requirements of this Part more onerous,
are subject to affirmative resolution procedure.

(4) Otherwise, the regulations are subject to negative resolution procedure.

### 474  Minor definitions

(1) In this Part—
'e-money issuer' means a person who has permission under Part 4 of the Financial Services and Markets Act 2000 (c. 8) to carry on the activity of issuing electronic money within the meaning of article 9B of the Financial Services and Markets Act 2000 (Regulated Activities) Order 2001 (S.I. 2001/544);
'group' means a parent undertaking and its subsidiary undertakings;
'IAS Regulation' means EC Regulation No. 1606/2002 of the European Parliament and of the Council of 19 July 2002 on the application of international accounting standards;
'included in the consolidation', in relation to group accounts, or 'included in consolidated group accounts', means that the undertaking is included in the accounts by the method of full (and not proportional) consolidation, and references to an undertaking excluded from consolidation shall be construed accordingly;
'international accounting standards' means the international accounting standards, within the meaning of the IAS Regulation, adopted from time to time by the European Commission in accordance with that Regulation;
'MiFID investment firm' means an investment firm within the meaning of Article 4.1.1 of Directive 2004/39/EC of the European Parliament and of the Council of 21 April 2004 on markets in financial instruments, other than—
(a) a company to which that Directive does not apply by virtue of Article 2 of that Directive,
(b) a company which is an exempt investment firm within the meaning of regulation 4A(3) of the Financial Services and Markets Act 2000 (Markets in Financial Instruments) Regulations 2007, and
(c) any other company which fulfils all the requirements set out in regulation 4C(3) of those Regulations;

'profit and loss account', in relation to a company that prepares IAS accounts, includes an income statement or other equivalent financial statement required to be prepared by international accounting standards;

'regulated activity' has the meaning given in section 22 of the Financial Services and Markets Act 2000, except that it does not include activities of the kind specified in any of the following provisions of the Financial Services and Markets Act 2000 (Regulated Activities) Order 2001 (S.I. 2001/544)—

    (a) article 25A (arranging regulated mortgage contracts),

    (b) article 25B (arranging regulated home reversion plans),

    (c) article 25C (arranging regulated home purchase plans),

    (d) article 39A (assisting administration and performance of a contract of insurance),

    (e) article 53A (advising on regulated mortgage contracts),

    (f) article 53B (advising on regulated home reversion plans),

    (g) article 53C (advising on regulated home purchase plans),

    (h) article 21 (dealing as agent), article 25 (arranging deals in investments) or article 53 (advising on investments) where the activity concerns relevant investments that are not contractually based investments (within the meaning of article 3 of that Order), or

    (i) article 64 (agreeing to carry on a regulated activity of the kind mentioned in paragraphs (a) to (h));

'turnover', in relation to a company, means the amounts derived from the provision of goods and services falling within the company's ordinary activities, after deduction of—

    (a) trade discounts,

    (b) value added tax, and

    (c) any other taxes based on the amounts so derived;

'UCITS management company' has the meaning given by the Glossary forming part of the Handbook made by the Financial Services Authority under the Financial Services and Markets Act 2000 (c. 8).

(2) In the case of an undertaking not trading for profit, any reference in this Part to a profit and loss account is to an income and expenditure account.

References to profit and loss and, in relation to group accounts, to a consolidated profit and loss account shall be construed accordingly.

# PART 16  AUDIT

## Chapter 1  Requirement for audited accounts

### *Requirement for audited accounts*

### 475  Requirement for audited accounts

(1) A company's annual accounts for a financial year must be audited in accordance with this Part unless the company—

    (a) is exempt from audit under—

        section 477 (small companies), or

        section 480 (dormant companies); or

    (b) is exempt from the requirements of this Part under section 482 (non-profit-making companies subject to public sector audit).

(2) A company is not entitled to any such exemption unless its balance sheet contains a statement by the directors to that effect.

(3) A company is not entitled to exemption under any of the provisions mentioned in subsection (1)(a) unless its balance sheet contains a statement by the directors to the effect that—

    (a) the members have not required the company to obtain an audit of its accounts for the year in question in accordance with section 476, and

    (b) the directors acknowledge their responsibilities for complying with the requirements of this Act with respect to accounting records and the preparation of accounts.

(4) The statement required by subsection (2) or (3) must appear on the balance sheet above the signature required by section 414.

### 476  Right of members to require audit

(1) The members of a company that would otherwise be entitled to exemption from audit under any of the provisions mentioned in section 475(1)(a) may by notice under this section require it to obtain an audit of its accounts for a financial year.

(2) The notice must be given by—

    (a) members representing not less in total than 10% in nominal value of the company's issued share capital, or any class of it, or

    (b) if the company does not have a share capital, not less than 10% in number of the members of the company.

(3) The notice may not be given before the financial year to which it relates and must be given not later than one month before the end of that year.

*Exemption from audit: small companies*

### 477 Small companies: conditions for exemption from audit

(1) A company that meets the following conditions in respect of a financial year is exempt from the requirements of this Act relating to the audit of accounts for that year.

(2) The conditions are—

(a) that the company qualifies as a small company in relation to that year,

(b) that its turnover in that year is not more than £6.5 million, and

(c) that its balance sheet total for that year is not more than £3.26 million.

(3) For a period which is a company's financial year but not in fact a year the maximum figure for turnover shall be proportionately adjusted.

(4) For the purposes of this section—

(a) whether a company qualifies as a small company shall be determined in accordance with section 382(1) to (6), and

(b) 'balance sheet total' has the same meaning as in that section.

(5) This section has effect subject to—

section 475(2) and (3) (requirements as to statements to be contained in balance sheet),

section 476 (right of members to require audit),

section 478 (companies excluded from small companies exemption), and

section 479 (availability of small companies exemption in case of group company).

### 478 Companies excluded from small companies exemption

A company is not entitled to the exemption conferred by section 477 (small companies) if it was at any time within the financial year in question—

(a) a public company,

(b) a company that—

(i) is an authorised insurance company, a banking company, an e-money issuer, a MiFID investment firm or a UCITS management company, or

(ii) carries on insurance market activity, or

(c) a special register body as defined in section 117(1) of the Trade Union and Labour Relations (Consolidation) Act 1992 (c. 52) or an employers' association as defined in section 122 of that Act or Article 4 of the Industrial Relations (Northern Ireland) Order 1992 (S.I. 1992/807 (N.I.5)).

### 479 Availability of small companies exemption in case of group company

(1) A company is not entitled to the exemption conferred by section 477 (small companies) in respect of a financial year during any part of which it was a group company unless—

(a) the conditions specified in subsection (2) below are met, or

(b) subsection (3) applies.

(2) The conditions are—

(a) that the group—

(i) qualifies as a small group in relation to that financial year, and

(ii) was not at any time in that year an ineligible group;

(b) that the group's aggregate turnover in that year is not more than £6.5 million net (or £7.8 million gross);

(c) that the group's aggregate balance sheet total for that year is not more than £3.26 million net (or £3.9 million gross).

(3) A company is not excluded by subsection (1) if, throughout the whole of the period or periods during the financial year when it was a group company, it was both a subsidiary undertaking and dormant.

(4) In this section—

(a) 'group company' means a company that is a parent company or a subsidiary undertaking, and

(b) 'the group', in relation to a group company, means that company together with all its associated undertakings.

For this purpose undertakings are associated if one is a subsidiary undertaking of the other or both are subsidiary undertakings of a third undertaking.

(5) For the purposes of this section—

(a) whether a group qualifies as small shall be determined in accordance with section 383 (companies qualifying as small: parent companies);

(b) 'ineligible group' has the meaning given by section 384(2) and (3);

(c) a group's aggregate turnover and aggregate balance sheet total shall be determined as for the purposes of section 383;

(d) 'net' and 'gross' have the same meaning as in that section;

(e) a company may meet any relevant requirement on the basis of either the gross or the net figure.

(6) The provisions mentioned in subsection (5) apply for the purposes of this section as if all the bodies corporate in the group were companies.

*Exemption from audit: dormant companies*

### 480   Dormant companies: conditions for exemption from audit

(1) A company is exempt from the requirements of this Act relating to the audit of accounts in respect of a financial year if—

  (a) it has been dormant since its formation, or

  (b) it has been dormant since the end of the previous financial year and the following conditions are met.

(2) The conditions are that the company—

  (a) as regards its individual accounts for the financial year in question—

   (i) is entitled to prepare accounts in accordance with the small companies regime (see sections 381 to 384), or

   (ii) would be so entitled but for having been a public company or a member of an ineligible group, and

  (b) is not required to prepare group accounts for that year.

(3) This section has effect subject to—

section 475(2) and (3) (requirements as to statements to be contained in balance sheet),

section 476 (right of members to require audit), and

section 481 (companies excluded from dormant companies exemption).

### 481   Companies excluded from dormant companies exemption

A company is not entitled to the exemption conferred by section 480 (dormant companies) if it was at any time within the financial year in question a company that—

  (a) is an authorised insurance company, a banking company, an e-money issuer, a MiFID investment firm or a UCITS management company, or

  (b) carries on insurance market activity.

*Companies subject to public sector audit*

### 482   Non-profit-making companies subject to public sector audit

(1) The requirements of this Part as to audit of accounts do not apply to a company for a financial year if it is non-profit-making and its accounts—

  (a) are subject to audit—

   (i) by the Comptroller and Auditor General by virtue of an order under section 25(6) of the Government Resources and Accounts Act 2000 (c. 20), or

   (ii) by the Auditor General for Wales by virtue of section 96, or an order under section 144, of the Government of Wales Act 1998 (c. 38);

  (b) are accounts—

   (i) in relation to which section 21 of the Public Finance and Accountability (Scotland) Act 2000 (asp 1) (audit of accounts: Auditor General for Scotland) applies, or

   (ii) that are subject to audit by the Auditor General for Scotland by virtue of an order under section 483 (Scottish public sector companies: audit by Auditor General for Scotland); or

  (c) are subject to audit by the Comptroller and Auditor General for Northern Ireland by virtue of an order under Article 5(3) of the Audit and Accountability (Northern Ireland) Order 2003 (S.I. 2003/418 (N.I. 5)).

(2) In the case of a company that is a parent company or a subsidiary undertaking, subsection (1) applies only if every group undertaking is non-profit-making.

(3) In this section 'non-profit-making' has the same meaning as in Article 48 of the Treaty establishing the European Community.

(4) This section has effect subject to section 475(2) (balance sheet to contain statement that company entitled to exemption under this section).

### 483   Scottish public sector companies: audit by Auditor General for Scotland

(1) The Scottish Ministers may by order provide for the accounts of a company having its registered office in Scotland to be audited by the Auditor General for Scotland.

(2) An order under subsection (1) may be made in relation to a company only if it appears to the Scottish Ministers that the company—

  (a) exercises in or as regards Scotland functions of a public nature none of which relate to reserved matters (within the meaning of the Scotland Act 1998 (c. 46)), or

  (b) is entirely or substantially funded from a body having accounts falling within paragraph (a) or (b) of subsection (3).

(3) Those accounts are—

  (a) accounts in relation to which section 21 of the Public Finance and Accountability (Scotland) Act 2000 (asp 1) (audit of accounts: Auditor General for Scotland) applies,

(b) accounts which are subject to audit by the Auditor General for Scotland by virtue of an order under this section.

(4) An order under subsection (1) may make such supplementary or consequential provision (including provision amending an enactment) as the Scottish Ministers think expedient.

(5) An order under subsection (1) shall not be made unless a draft of the statutory instrument containing it has been laid before, and approved by resolution of, the Scottish Parliament.

*General power of amendment by regulations*

### 484   General power of amendment by regulations

(1) The Secretary of State may by regulations amend this Chapter or section 539 (minor definitions) so far as applying to this Chapter by adding, altering or repealing provisions.

(2) The regulations may make consequential amendments or repeals in other provisions of this Act, or in other enactments.

(3) Regulations under this section imposing new requirements, or rendering existing requirements more onerous, are subject to affirmative resolution procedure.

(4) Other regulations under this section are subject to negative resolution procedure.

## Chapter 2  Appointment of auditors

*Private companies*

### 485   Appointment of auditors of private company: general

(1) An auditor or auditors of a private company must be appointed for each financial year of the company, unless the directors reasonably resolve otherwise on the ground that audited accounts are unlikely to be required.

(2) For each financial year for which an auditor or auditors is or are to be appointed (other than the company's first financial year), the appointment must be made before the end of the period of 28 days beginning with—

(a) the end of the time allowed for sending out copies of the company's annual accounts and reports for the previous financial year (see section 424), or

(b) if earlier, the day on which copies of the company's annual accounts and reports for the previous financial year are sent out under section 423.

This is the 'period for appointing auditors'.

(3) The directors may appoint an auditor or auditors of the company—

(a) at any time before the company's first period for appointing auditors,

(b) following a period during which the company (being exempt from audit) did not have any auditor, at any time before the company's next period for appointing auditors, or

(c) to fill a casual vacancy in the office of auditor.

(4) The members may appoint an auditor or auditors by ordinary resolution—

(a) during a period for appointing auditors,

(b) if the company should have appointed an auditor or auditors during a period for appointing auditors but failed to do so, or

(c) where the directors had power to appoint under subsection (3) but have failed to make an appointment.

(5) An auditor or auditors of a private company may only be appointed—

(a) in accordance with this section, or

(b) in accordance with section 486 (default power of Secretary of State).

This is without prejudice to any deemed re-appointment under section 487.

### 486   Appointment of auditors of private company: default power of Secretary of State

(1) If a private company fails to appoint an auditor or auditors in accordance with section 485, the Secretary of State may appoint one or more persons to fill the vacancy.

(2) Where subsection (2) of that section applies and the company fails to make the necessary appointment before the end of the period for appointing auditors, the company must within one week of the end of that period give notice to the Secretary of State of his power having become exercisable.

(3) If a company fails to give the notice required by this section, an offence is committed by—

(a) the company, and

(b) every officer of the company who is in default.

(4) A person guilty of an offence under this section is liable on summary conviction to a fine not exceeding level 3 on the standard scale and, for continued contravention, a daily default fine not exceeding one-tenth of level 3 on the standard scale.

### 487   Term of office of auditors of private company

(1) An auditor or auditors of a private company hold office in accordance with the terms of their appointment, subject to the requirements that—

(a) they do not take office until any previous auditor or auditors cease to hold office, and

(b) they cease to hold office at the end of the next period for appointing auditors unless re-appointed.

(2) Where no auditor has been appointed by the end of the next period for appointing auditors, any auditor in office immediately before that time is deemed to be re-appointed at that time, unless—

(a) he was appointed by the directors, or

(b) the company's articles require actual re-appointment, or

(c) the deemed re-appointment is prevented by the members under section 488, or

(d) the members have resolved that he should not be re-appointed, or

(e) the directors have resolved that no auditor or auditors should be appointed for the financial year in question.

(3) This is without prejudice to the provisions of this Part as to removal and resignation of auditors.

(4) No account shall be taken of any loss of the opportunity of deemed re-appointment under this section in ascertaining the amount of any compensation or damages payable to an auditor on his ceasing to hold office for any reason.

### 488 Prevention by members of deemed re-appointment of auditor

(1) An auditor of a private company is not deemed to be re-appointed under section 487(2) if the company has received notices under this section from members representing at least the requisite percentage of the total voting rights of all members who would be entitled to vote on a resolution that the auditor should not be re-appointed.

(2) The 'requisite percentage' is 5%, or such lower percentage as is specified for this purpose in the company's articles.

(3) A notice under this section—

(a) may be in hard copy or electronic form,

(b) must be authenticated by the person or persons giving it, and

(c) must be received by the company before the end of the accounting reference period immediately preceding the time when the deemed reappointment would have effect.

*Public companies*

### 489 Appointment of auditors of public company: general

(1) An auditor or auditors of a public company must be appointed for each financial year of the company, unless the directors reasonably resolve otherwise on the ground that audited accounts are unlikely to be required.

(2) For each financial year for which an auditor or auditors is or are to be appointed (other than the company's first financial year), the appointment must be made before the end of the accounts meeting of the company at which the company's annual accounts and reports for the previous financial year are laid.

(3) The directors may appoint an auditor or auditors of the company—

(a) at any time before the company's first accounts meeting;

(b) following a period during which the company (being exempt from audit) did not have any auditor, at any time before the company's next accounts meeting;

(c) to fill a casual vacancy in the office of auditor.

(4) The members may appoint an auditor or auditors by ordinary resolution—

(a) at an accounts meeting;

(b) if the company should have appointed an auditor or auditors at an accounts meeting but failed to do so;

(c) where the directors had power to appoint under subsection (3) but have failed to make an appointment.

(5) An auditor or auditors of a public company may only be appointed—

(a) in accordance with this section, or

(b) in accordance with section 490 (default power of Secretary of State).

### 490 Appointment of auditors of public company: default power of Secretary of State

(1) If a public company fails to appoint an auditor or auditors in accordance with section 489, the Secretary of State may appoint one or more persons to fill the vacancy.

(2) Where subsection (2) of that section applies and the company fails to make the necessary appointment before the end of the accounts meeting, the company must within one week of the end of that meeting give notice to the Secretary of State of his power having become exercisable.

(3) If a company fails to give the notice required by this section, an offence is committed by—

(a) the company, and

(b) every officer of the company who is in default.

(4) A person guilty of an offence under this section is liable on summary conviction to a fine not exceeding level 3 on the standard scale and, for continued contravention, a daily default fine not exceeding one-tenth of level 3 on the standard scale.

**491  Term of office of auditors of public company**

(1) The auditor or auditors of a public company hold office in accordance with the terms of their appointment, subject to the requirements that—

(a) they do not take office until the previous auditor or auditors have ceased to hold office, and

(b) they cease to hold office at the conclusion of the accounts meeting next following their appointment, unless re-appointed.

(2) This is without prejudice to the provisions of this Part as to removal and resignation of auditors.

*General provisions*

**492  Fixing of auditor's remuneration**

(1) The remuneration of an auditor appointed by the members of a company must be fixed by the members by ordinary resolution or in such manner as the members may by ordinary resolution determine.

(2) The remuneration of an auditor appointed by the directors of a company must be fixed by the directors.

(3) The remuneration of an auditor appointed by the Secretary of State must be fixed by the Secretary of State.

(4) For the purposes of this section 'remuneration' includes sums paid in respect of expenses.

(5) This section applies in relation to benefits in kind as to payments of money.

**493  Disclosure of terms of audit appointment**

(1) The Secretary of State may make provision by regulations for securing the disclosure of the terms on which a company's auditor is appointed, remunerated or performs his duties.

Nothing in the following provisions of this section affects the generality of this power.

(2) The regulations may—

(a) require disclosure of—

(i) a copy of any terms that are in writing, and

(ii) a written memorandum setting out any terms that are not in writing;

(b) require disclosure to be at such times, in such places and by such means as are specified in the regulations;

(c) require the place and means of disclosure to be stated—

(i) in a note to the company's annual accounts (in the case of its individual accounts) or in such manner as is specified in the regulations (in the case of group accounts),

(ii) in the directors' report, or

(iii) in the auditor's report on the company's annual accounts.

(3) The provisions of this section apply to a variation of the terms mentioned in subsection (1) as they apply to the original terms.

(4) Regulations under this section are subject to affirmative resolution procedure.

**494  Disclosure of services provided by auditor or associates and related remuneration**

(1) The Secretary of State may make provision by regulations for securing the disclosure of—

(a) the nature of any services provided for a company by the company's auditor (whether in his capacity as auditor or otherwise) or by his associates;

(b) the amount of any remuneration received or receivable by a company's auditor, or his associates, in respect of any such services.

Nothing in the following provisions of this section affects the generality of this power.

(2) The regulations may provide—

(a) for disclosure of the nature of any services provided to be made by reference to any class or description of services specified in the regulations (or any combination of services, however described);

(b) for the disclosure of amounts of remuneration received or receivable in respect of services of any class or description specified in the regulations (or any combination of services, however described);

(c) for the disclosure of separate amounts so received or receivable by the company's auditor or any of his associates, or of aggregate amounts so received or receivable by all or any of those persons.

(3) The regulations may—

(a) provide that 'remuneration' includes sums paid in respect of expenses;

(b) apply to benefits in kind as well as to payments of money, and require the disclosure of the nature of any such benefits and their estimated money value;

(c) apply to services provided for associates of a company as well as to those provided for a company;

(d) define 'associate' in relation to an auditor and a company respectively.

(4) The regulations may provide that any disclosure required by the regulations is to be made—

    (a) in a note to the company's annual accounts (in the case of its individual accounts) or in such manner as is specified in the regulations (in the case of group accounts),

    (b) in the directors' report, or

    (c) in the auditor's report on the company's annual accounts.

  (5) If the regulations provide that any such disclosure is to be made as mentioned in subsection (4) (a) or (b), the regulations may require the auditor to supply the directors of the company with any information necessary to enable the disclosure to be made.

  (6) Regulations under this section are subject to negative resolution procedure.

## Chapter 3  Functions of auditor

### *Auditor's report*

### 495  Auditor's report on company's annual accounts

  (1) A company's auditor must make a report to the company's members on all annual accounts of the company of which copies are, during his tenure of office—

    (a) in the case of a private company, to be sent out to members under section 423;

    (b) in the case of a public company, to be laid before the company in general meeting under section 437.

  (2) The auditor's report must include—

    (a) an introduction identifying the annual accounts that are the subject of the audit and the financial reporting framework that has been applied in their preparation, and

    (b) a description of the scope of the audit identifying the auditing standards in accordance with which the audit was conducted.

  (3) The report must state clearly whether, in the auditor's opinion, the annual accounts—

    (a) give a true and fair view—

      (i) in the case of an individual balance sheet, of the state of affairs of the company as at the end of the financial year,

      (ii) in the case of an individual profit and loss account, of the profit or loss of the company for the financial year,

      (iii) in the case of group accounts, of the state of affairs as at the end of the financial year and of the profit or loss for the financial year of the undertakings included in the consolidation as a whole, so far as concerns members of the company;

    (b) have been properly prepared in accordance with the relevant financial reporting framework; and

    (c) have been prepared in accordance with the requirements of this Act (and, where applicable, Article 4 of the IAS Regulation).

Expressions used in this subsection that are defined for the purposes of Part 15 (see section 474) have the same meaning as in that Part.

  (4) The auditor's report—

    (a) must be either unqualified or qualified, and

    (b) must include a reference to any matters to which the auditor wishes to draw attention by way of emphasis without qualifying the report.

### 496  Auditor's report on directors' report

The auditor must state in his report on the company's annual accounts whether in his opinion the information given in the directors' report for the financial year for which the accounts are prepared is consistent with those accounts.

### 497  Auditor's report on auditable part of directors' remuneration report

  (1) If the company is a quoted company, the auditor, in his report on the company's annual accounts for the financial year, must—

    (a) report to the company's members on the auditable part of the directors' remuneration report, and

    (b) state whether in his opinion that part of the directors' remuneration report has been properly prepared in accordance with this Act.

  (2) For the purposes of this Part, 'the auditable part' of a directors' remuneration report is the part identified as such by regulations under section 421.

### *Duties and rights of auditors*

### 498  Duties of auditor

  (1) A company's auditor, in preparing his report, must carry out such investigations as will enable him to form an opinion as to—

    (a) whether adequate accounting records have been kept by the company and returns adequate for their audit have been received from branches not visited by him, and

    (b) whether the company's individual accounts are in agreement with the accounting records and returns, and

(c) in the case of a quoted company, whether the auditable part of the company's directors' remuneration report is in agreement with the accounting records and returns.

(2) If the auditor is of the opinion—

(a) that adequate accounting records have not been kept, or that returns adequate for their audit have not been received from branches not visited by him, or

(b) that the company's individual accounts are not in agreement with the accounting records and returns, or

(c) in the case of a quoted company, that the auditable part of its directors' remuneration report is not in agreement with the accounting records and returns,

the auditor shall state that fact in his report.

(3) If the auditor fails to obtain all the information and explanations which, to the best of his knowledge and belief, are necessary for the purposes of his audit, he shall state that fact in his report.

(4) If—

(a) the requirements of regulations under section 412 (disclosure of directors' benefits: remuneration, pensions and compensation for loss of office) are not complied with in the annual accounts, or

(b) in the case of a quoted company, the requirements of regulations under section 421 as to information forming the auditable part of the directors' remuneration report are not complied with in that report,

the auditor must include in his report, so far as he is reasonably able to do so, a statement giving the required particulars.

(5) If the directors of the company—

(a) have prepared accounts in accordance with the small companies regime, or

(b) have taken advantage of the small companies exemption in preparing the directors' report,

and in the auditor's opinion they were not entitled to do so, the auditor shall state that fact in his report.

## 499  Auditor's general right to information

(1) An auditor of a company—

(a) has a right of access at all times to the company's books, accounts and vouchers (in whatever form they are held), and

(b) may require any of the following persons to provide him with such information or explanations as he thinks necessary for the performance of his duties as auditor.

(2) Those persons are—

(a) any officer or employee of the company;

(b) any person holding or accountable for any of the company's books, accounts or vouchers;

(c) any subsidiary undertaking of the company which is a body corporate incorporated in the United Kingdom;

(d) any officer, employee or auditor of any such subsidiary undertaking or any person holding or accountable for any books, accounts or vouchers of any such subsidiary undertaking;

(e) any person who fell within any of paragraphs (a) to (d) at a time to which the information or explanations required by the auditor relates or relate.

(3) A statement made by a person in response to a requirement under this section may not be used in evidence against him in criminal proceedings except proceedings for an offence under section 501.

(4) Nothing in this section compels a person to disclose information in respect of which a claim to legal professional privilege (in Scotland, to confidentiality of communications) could be maintained in legal proceedings.

## 500  Auditor's right to information from overseas subsidiaries

(1) Where a parent company has a subsidiary undertaking that is not a body corporate incorporated in the United Kingdom, the auditor of the parent company may require it to obtain from any of the following persons such information or explanations as he may reasonably require for the purposes of his duties as auditor.

(2) Those persons are—

(a) the undertaking;

(b) any officer, employee or auditor of the undertaking;

(c) any person holding or accountable for any of the undertaking's books, accounts or vouchers;

(d) any person who fell within paragraph (b) or (c) at a time to which the information or explanations relates or relate.

(3) If so required, the parent company must take all such steps as are reasonably open to it to obtain the information or explanations from the person concerned.

(4) A statement made by a person in response to a requirement under this section may not be used in evidence against him in criminal proceedings except proceedings for an offence under section 501.

(5) Nothing in this section compels a person to disclose information in respect of which a claim to legal professional privilege (in Scotland, to confidentiality of communications) could be maintained in legal proceedings.

### 501    Auditor's rights to information: offences

(1) A person commits an offence who knowingly or recklessly makes to an auditor of a company a statement (oral or written) that—

(a) conveys or purports to convey any information or explanations which the auditor requires, or is entitled to require, under section 499, and

(b) is misleading, false or deceptive in a material particular.

(2) A person guilty of an offence under subsection (1) is liable—

(a) on conviction on indictment, to imprisonment for a term not exceeding two years or a fine (or both);

(b) on summary conviction—

(i) in England and Wales, to imprisonment for a term not exceeding twelve months or to a fine not exceeding the statutory maximum (or both);

(ii) in Scotland or Northern Ireland, to imprisonment for a term not exceeding six months or to a fine not exceeding the statutory maximum (or both).

(3) A person who fails to comply with a requirement under section 499 without delay commits an offence unless it was not reasonably practicable for him to provide the required information or explanations.

(4) If a parent company fails to comply with section 500, an offence is committed by—

(a) the company, and

(b) every officer of the company who is in default.

(5) A person guilty of an offence under subsection (3) or (4) is liable on summary conviction to a fine not exceeding level 3 on the standard scale.

(6) Nothing in this section affects any right of an auditor to apply for an injunction (in Scotland, an interdict or an order for specific performance) to enforce any of his rights under section 499 or 500.

### 502    Auditor's rights in relation to resolutions and meetings

(1) In relation to a written resolution proposed to be agreed to by a private company, the company's auditor is entitled to receive all such communications relating to the resolution as, by virtue of any provision of Chapter 2 of Part 13 of this Act, are required to be supplied to a member of the company.

(2) A company's auditor is entitled—

(a) to receive all notices of, and other communications relating to, any general meeting which a member of the company is entitled to receive,

(b) to attend any general meeting of the company, and

(c) to be heard at any general meeting which he attends on any part of the business of the meeting which concerns him as auditor.

(3) Where the auditor is a firm, the right to attend or be heard at a meeting is exercisable by an individual authorised by the firm in writing to act as its representative at the meeting.

*Signature of auditor's report*

### 503    Signature of auditor's report

(1) The auditor's report must state the name of the auditor and be signed and dated.

(2) Where the auditor is an individual, the report must be signed by him.

(3) Where the auditor is a firm, the report must be signed by the senior statutory auditor in his own name, for and on behalf of the auditor.

### 504    Senior statutory auditor

(1) The senior statutory auditor means the individual identified by the firm as senior statutory auditor in relation to the audit in accordance with—

(a) standards issued by the European Commission, or

(b) if there is no applicable standard so issued, any relevant guidance issued by—

(i) the Secretary of State, or

(ii) a body appointed by order of the Secretary of State.

(2) The person identified as senior statutory auditor must be eligible for appointment as auditor of the company in question (see Chapter 2 of Part 42 of this Act).

(3) The senior statutory auditor is not, by reason of being named or identified as senior statutory auditor or by reason of his having signed the auditor's report, subject to any civil liability to which he would not otherwise be subject.

(4) An order appointing a body for the purpose of subsection (1)(b)(ii) is subject to negative resolution procedure.

### 505    Names to be stated in published copies of auditor's report

(1) Every copy of the auditor's report that is published by or on behalf of the company must—

(a) state the name of the auditor and (where the auditor is a firm) the name of the person who signed it as senior statutory auditor, or

(b) if the conditions in section 506 (circumstances in which names may be omitted) are met, state that a resolution has been passed and notified to the Secretary of State in accordance with that section.

(2) For the purposes of this section a company is regarded as publishing the report if it publishes, issues or circulates it or otherwise makes it available for public inspection in a manner calculated to invite members of the public generally, or any class of members of the public, to read it.

(3) If a copy of the auditor's report is published without the statement required by this section, an offence is committed by—

(a) the company, and

(b) every officer of the company who is in default.

(4) A person guilty of an offence under this section is liable on summary conviction to a fine not exceeding level 3 on the standard scale.

### 506  Circumstances in which names may be omitted

(1) The auditor's name and, where the auditor is a firm, the name of the person who signed the report as senior statutory auditor, may be omitted from—

(a) published copies of the report, and

(b) the copy of the report delivered to the registrar under Chapter 10 of Part 15 (filing of accounts and reports),

if the following conditions are met.

(2) The conditions are that the company—

(a) considering on reasonable grounds that statement of the name would create or be likely to create a serious risk that the auditor or senior statutory auditor, or any other person, would be subject to violence or intimidation, has resolved that the name should not be stated, and

(b) has given notice of the resolution to the Secretary of State, stating—

(i) the name and registered number of the company,

(ii) the financial year of the company to which the report relates, and

(iii) the name of the auditor and (where the auditor is a firm) the name of the person who signed the report as senior statutory auditor.

*Offences in connection with auditor's report*

### 507  Offences in connection with auditor's report

(1) A person to whom this section applies commits an offence if he knowingly or recklessly causes a report under section 495 (auditor's report on company's annual accounts) to include any matter that is misleading, false or deceptive in a material particular.

(2) A person to whom this section applies commits an offence if he knowingly or recklessly causes such a report to omit a statement required by—

(a) section 498(2)(b) (statement that company's accounts do not agree with accounting records and returns),

(b) section 498(3) (statement that necessary information and explanations not obtained), or

(c) section 498(5) (statement that directors wrongly took advantage of exemption from obligation to prepare group accounts).

(3) This section applies to—

(a) where the auditor is an individual, that individual and any employee or agent of his who is eligible for appointment as auditor of the company;

(b) where the auditor is a firm, any director, member, employee or agent of the firm who is eligible for appointment as auditor of the company.

(4) A person guilty of an offence under this section is liable—

(a) on conviction on indictment, to a fine;

(b) on summary conviction, to a fine not exceeding the statutory maximum.

### 508  Guidance for regulatory and prosecuting authorities: England, Wales and Northern Ireland

(1) The Secretary of State may issue guidance for the purpose of helping relevant regulatory and prosecuting authorities to determine how they should carry out their functions in cases where behaviour occurs that—

(a) appears to involve the commission of an offence under section 507 (offences in connection with auditor's report), and

(b) has been, is being or may be investigated pursuant to arrangements—

(i) under paragraph 15 of Schedule 10 (investigation of complaints against auditors and supervisory bodies), or

(ii) of a kind mentioned in paragraph 24 of that Schedule (independent investigation for disciplinary purposes of public interest cases).

(2) The Secretary of State must obtain the consent of the Attorney General before issuing any such guidance.

(3) In this section 'relevant regulatory and prosecuting authorities' means—

(a) supervisory bodies within the meaning of Part 42 of this Act,

(b) bodies to which the Secretary of State may make grants under section 16(1) of the Companies (Audit, Investigations and Community Enterprise) Act 2004 (c. 27) (bodies concerned with accounting standards etc.),

(c) the Director of the Serious Fraud Office,

(d) the Director of Public Prosecutions or the Director of Public Prosecutions for Northern Ireland, and

(e) the Secretary of State.

(4) This section does not apply to Scotland.

### 509    Guidance for regulatory authorities: Scotland

(1) The Lord Advocate may issue guidance for the purpose of helping relevant regulatory authorities to determine how they should carry out their functions in cases where behaviour occurs that—

(a) appears to involve the commission of an offence under section 507 (offences in connection with auditor's report), and

(b) has been, is being or may be investigated pursuant to arrangements—

(i) under paragraph 15 of Schedule 10 (investigation of complaints against auditors and supervisory bodies), or

(ii) of a kind mentioned in paragraph 24 of that Schedule (independent investigation for disciplinary purposes of public interest cases).

(2) The Lord Advocate must consult the Secretary of State before issuing any such guidance.

(3) In this section 'relevant regulatory authorities' means—

(a) supervisory bodies within the meaning of Part 42 of this Act,

(b) bodies to which the Secretary of State may make grants under section 16(1) of the Companies (Audit, Investigations and Community Enterprise) Act 2004 (c. 27) (bodies concerned with accounting standards etc.), and

(c) the Secretary of State.

(4) This section applies only to Scotland.

## Chapter 4  Removal, resignation, etc. of auditors

### *Removal of auditor*

### 510    Resolution removing auditor from office

(1) The members of a company may remove an auditor from office at any time.

(2) This power is exercisable only—

(a) by ordinary resolution at a meeting, and

(b) in accordance with section 511 (special notice of resolution to remove auditor).

(3) Nothing in this section is to be taken as depriving the person removed of compensation or damages payable to him in respect of the termination—

(a) of his appointment as auditor, or

(b) of any appointment terminating with that as auditor.

(4) An auditor may not be removed from office before the expiration of his term of office except by resolution under this section.

### 511    Special notice required for resolution removing auditor from office

(1) Special notice is required for a resolution at a general meeting of a company removing an auditor from office.

(2) On receipt of notice of such an intended resolution the company must immediately send a copy of it to the auditor proposed to be removed.

(3) The auditor proposed to be removed may make with respect to the intended resolution representations in writing to the company (not exceeding a reasonable length) and request their notification to members of the company.

(4) The company must (unless the representations are received by it too late for it to do so)—

(a) in any notice of the resolution given to members of the company, state the fact of the representations having been made, and

(b) send a copy of the representations to every member of the company to whom notice of the meeting is or has been sent.

(5) If a copy of any such representations is not sent out as required because received too late or because of the company's default, the auditor may (without prejudice to his right to be heard orally) require that the representations be read out at the meeting.

(6) Copies of the representations need not be sent out and the representations need not be read at the meeting if, on the application either of the company or of any other person claiming to be aggrieved, the court is satisfied that the auditor is using the provisions of this section to secure needless publicity for defamatory matter.

The court may order the company's costs (in Scotland, expenses) on the application to be paid in whole or in part by the auditor, notwithstanding that he is not a party to the application.

### 512    Notice to registrar of resolution removing auditor from office

(1) Where a resolution is passed under section 510 (resolution removing auditor from office), the company must give notice of that fact to the registrar within 14 days.

(2) If a company fails to give the notice required by this section, an offence is committed by—

(a) the company, and

(b) every officer of it who is in default.

(3) A person guilty of an offence under this section is liable on summary conviction to a fine not exceeding level 3 on the standard scale and, for continued contravention, a daily default fine not exceeding one-tenth of level 3 on the standard scale.

### 513    Rights of auditor who has been removed from office

(1) An auditor who has been removed by resolution under section 510 has, notwithstanding his removal, the rights conferred by section 502(2) in relation to any general meeting of the company—

(a) at which his term of office would otherwise have expired, or

(b) at which it is proposed to fill the vacancy caused by his removal.

(2) In such a case the references in that section to matters concerning the auditor as auditor shall be construed as references to matters concerning him as a former auditor.

*Failure to re-appoint auditor*

### 514    Failure to re-appoint auditor: special procedure required for written resolution

(1) This section applies where a resolution is proposed as a written resolution of a private company whose effect would be to appoint a person as auditor in place of a person (the 'outgoing auditor') whose term of office has expired, or is to expire, at the end of the period for appointing auditors.

(2) The following provisions apply if—

(a) no period for appointing auditors has ended since the outgoing auditor ceased to hold office, or

(b) such a period has ended and an auditor or auditors should have been appointed but were not.

(3) The company must send a copy of the proposed resolution to the person proposed to be appointed and to the outgoing auditor.

(4) The outgoing auditor may, within 14 days after receiving the notice, make with respect to the proposed resolution representations in writing to the company (not exceeding a reasonable length) and request their circulation to members of the company.

(5) The company must circulate the representations together with the copy or copies of the resolution circulated in accordance with section 291 (resolution proposed by directors) or section 293 (resolution proposed by members).

(6) Where subsection (5) applies—

(a) the period allowed under section 293(3) for service of copies of the proposed resolution is 28 days instead of 21 days, and

(b) the provisions of section 293(5) and (6) (offences) apply in relation to a failure to comply with that subsection as in relation to a default in complying with that section.

(7) Copies of the representations need not be circulated if, on the application either of the company or of any other person claiming to be aggrieved, the court is satisfied that the auditor is using the provisions of this section to secure needless publicity for defamatory matter.

The court may order the company's costs (in Scotland, expenses) on the application to be paid in whole or in part by the auditor, notwithstanding that he is not a party to the application.

(8) If any requirement of this section is not complied with, the resolution is ineffective.

### 515    Failure to re-appoint auditor: special notice required for resolution at general meeting

(1) This section applies to a resolution at a general meeting of a company whose effect would be to appoint a person as auditor in place of a person (the 'outgoing auditor') whose term of office has ended, or is to end—

(a) in the case of a private company, at the end of the period for appointing auditors;

(b) in the case of a public company, at the end of the next accounts meeting.

(2) Special notice is required of such a resolution if—

(a) in the case of a private company—

(i) no period for appointing auditors has ended since the outgoing auditor ceased to hold office, or

(ii) such a period has ended and an auditor or auditors should have been appointed but were not;

(b) in the case of a public company—

(i) there has been no accounts meeting of the company since the outgoing auditor ceased to hold office, or

(ii) there has been an accounts meeting at which an auditor or auditors should have been appointed but were not.

(3) On receipt of notice of such an intended resolution the company shall forthwith send a copy of it to the person proposed to be appointed and to the outgoing auditor.

(4) The outgoing auditor may make with respect to the intended resolution representations in writing to the company (not exceeding a reasonable length) and request their notification to members of the company.

(5) The company must (unless the representations are received by it too late for it to do so)—

(a) in any notice of the resolution given to members of the company, state the fact of the representations having been made, and

(b) send a copy of the representations to every member of the company to whom notice of the meeting is or has been sent.

(6) If a copy of any such representations is not sent out as required because received too late or because of the company's default, the outgoing auditor may (without prejudice to his right to be heard orally) require that the representations be read out at the meeting.

(7) Copies of the representations need not be sent out and the representations need not be read at the meeting if, on the application either of the company or of any other person claiming to be aggrieved, the court is satisfied that the auditor is using the provisions of this section to secure needless publicity for defamatory matter.

The court may order the company's costs (in Scotland, expenses) on the application to be paid in whole or in part by the outgoing auditor, notwithstanding that he is not a party to the application.

### *Resignation of auditor*

### 516   Resignation of auditor

(1) An auditor of a company may resign his office by depositing a notice in writing to that effect at the company's registered office.

(2) The notice is not effective unless it is accompanied by the statement required by section 519.

(3) An effective notice of resignation operates to bring the auditor's term of office to an end as of the date on which the notice is deposited or on such later date as may be specified in it.

### 517   Notice to registrar of resignation of auditor

(1) Where an auditor resigns the company must within 14 days of the deposit of a notice of resignation send a copy of the notice to the registrar of companies.

(2) If default is made in complying with this section, an offence is committed by—

(a) the company, and

(b) every officer of the company who is in default.

(3) A person guilty of an offence under this section is liable—

(a) on conviction on indictment, to a fine;

(b) on summary conviction, to a fine not exceeding the statutory maximum and, for continued contravention, a daily default fine not exceeding one-tenth of the statutory maximum.

### 518   Rights of resigning auditor

(1) This section applies where an auditor's notice of resignation is accompanied by a statement of the circumstances connected with his resignation (see section 519).

(2) He may deposit with the notice a signed requisition calling on the directors of the company forthwith duly to convene a general meeting of the company for the purpose of receiving and considering such explanation of the circumstances connected with his resignation as he may wish to place before the meeting.

(3) He may request the company to circulate to its members—

(a) before the meeting convened on his requisition, or

(b) before any general meeting at which his term of office would otherwise have expired or at which it is proposed to fill the vacancy caused by his resignation,

a statement in writing (not exceeding a reasonable length) of the circumstances connected with his resignation.

(4) The company must (unless the statement is received too late for it to comply)—

(a) in any notice of the meeting given to members of the company, state the fact of the statement having been made, and

(b) send a copy of the statement to every member of the company to whom notice of the meeting is or has been sent.

(5) The directors must within 21 days from the date of the deposit of a requisition under this section proceed duly to convene a meeting for a day not more than 28 days after the date on which the notice convening the meeting is given.

(6) If default is made in complying with subsection (5), every director who failed to take all reasonable steps to secure that a meeting was convened commits an offence.

(7) A person guilty of an offence under this section is liable—

(a) on conviction on indictment, to a fine;

(b) on summary conviction to a fine not exceeding the statutory maximum.

(8) If a copy of the statement mentioned above is not sent out as required because received too late or because of the company's default, the auditor may (without prejudice to his right to be heard orally) require that the statement be read out at the meeting.

(9) Copies of a statement need not be sent out and the statement need not be read out at the meeting if, on the application either of the company or of any other person who claims to be aggrieved, the

court is satisfied that the auditor is using the provisions of this section to secure needless publicity for defamatory matter.

The court may order the company's costs (in Scotland, expenses) on such an application to be paid in whole or in part by the auditor, notwithstanding that he is not a party to the application.

(10) An auditor who has resigned has, notwithstanding his resignation, the rights conferred by section 502(2) in relation to any such general meeting of the company as is mentioned in subsection (3)(a) or (b) above.

In such a case the references in that section to matters concerning the auditor as auditor shall be construed as references to matters concerning him as a former auditor.

### Statement by auditor on ceasing to hold office

### 519 Statement by auditor to be deposited with company

(1) Where an auditor of an unquoted company ceases for any reason to hold office, he must deposit at the company's registered office a statement of the circumstances connected with his ceasing to hold office, unless he considers that there are no circumstances in connection with his ceasing to hold office that need to be brought to the attention of members or creditors of the company.

(2) If he considers that there are no circumstances in connection with his ceasing to hold office that need to be brought to the attention of members or creditors of the company, he must deposit at the company's registered office a statement to that effect.

(3) Where an auditor of a quoted company ceases for any reason to hold office, he must deposit at the company's registered office a statement of the circumstances connected with his ceasing to hold office.

(4) The statement required by this section must be deposited—

(a) in the case of resignation, along with the notice of resignation;

(b) in the case of failure to seek re-appointment, not less than 14 days before the end of the time allowed for next appointing an auditor;

(c) in any other case, not later than the end of the period of 14 days beginning with the date on which he ceases to hold office.

(5) A person ceasing to hold office as auditor who fails to comply with this section commits an offence.

(6) In proceedings for such an offence it is a defence for the person charged to show that he took all reasonable steps and exercised all due diligence to avoid the commission of the offence.

(7) A person guilty of an offence under this section is liable—

(a) on conviction on indictment, to a fine;

(b) on summary conviction, to a fine not exceeding the statutory maximum.

(8) Where an offence under this section is committed by a body corporate, every officer of the body who is in default also commits the offence.

For this purpose—

(a) any person who purports to act as director, manager or secretary of the body is treated as an officer of the body, and

(b) if the body is a company, any shadow director is treated as an officer of the company.

### 520 Company's duties in relation to statement

(1) This section applies where the statement deposited under section 519 states the circumstances connected with the auditor's ceasing to hold office.

(2) The company must within 14 days of the deposit of the statement either—

(a) send a copy of it to every person who under section 423 is entitled to be sent copies of the accounts, or

(b) apply to the court.

(3) If it applies to the court, the company must notify the auditor of the application.

(4) If the court is satisfied that the auditor is using the provisions of section 519 to secure needless publicity for defamatory matter—

(a) it shall direct that copies of the statement need not be sent out, and

(b) it may further order the company's costs (in Scotland, expenses) on the application to be paid in whole or in part by the auditor, even if he is not a party to the application.

The company must within 14 days of the court's decision send to the persons mentioned in subsection (2)(a) a statement setting out the effect of the order.

(5) If no such direction is made the company must send copies of the statement to the persons mentioned in subsection (2)(a) within 14 days of the court's decision or, as the case may be, of the discontinuance of the proceedings.

(6) In the event of default in complying with this section an offence is committed by every officer of the company who is in default.

(7) In proceedings for such an offence it is a defence for the person charged to show that he took all reasonable steps and exercised all due diligence to avoid the commission of the offence.

(8) A person guilty of an offence under this section is liable—

(a) on conviction on indictment, to a fine;

(b) on summary conviction, to a fine not exceeding the statutory maximum.

### 521   Copy of statement to be sent to registrar

(1) Unless within 21 days beginning with the day on which he deposited the statement under section 519 the auditor receives notice of an application to the court under section 520, he must within a further seven days send a copy of the statement to the registrar.

(2) If an application to the court is made under section 520 and the auditor subsequently receives notice under subsection (5) of that section, he must within seven days of receiving the notice send a copy of the statement to the registrar.

(3) An auditor who fails to comply with subsection (1) or (2) commits an offence.

(4) In proceedings for such an offence it is a defence for the person charged to show that he took all reasonable steps and exercised all due diligence to avoid the commission of the offence.

(5) A person guilty of an offence under this section is liable—

(a) on conviction on indictment, to a fine;

(b) on summary conviction, to a fine not exceeding the statutory maximum.

(6) Where an offence under this section is committed by a body corporate, every officer of the body who is in default also commits the offence.

For this purpose—

(a) any person who purports to act as director, manager or secretary of the body is treated as an officer of the body, and

(b) if the body is a company, any shadow director is treated as an officer of the company.

### 522   Duty of auditor to notify appropriate audit authority

(1) Where—

(a) in the case of a major audit, an auditor ceases for any reason to hold office, or

(b) in the case of an audit that is not a major audit, an auditor ceases to hold office before the end of his term of office,

the auditor ceasing to hold office must notify the appropriate audit authority.

(2) The notice must—

(a) inform the appropriate audit authority that he has ceased to hold office, and

(b) be accompanied by a copy of the statement deposited by him at the company's registered office in accordance with section 519.

(3) If the statement so deposited is to the effect that he considers that there are no circumstances in connection with his ceasing to hold office that need to be brought to the attention of members or creditors of the company, the notice must also be accompanied by a statement of the reasons for his ceasing to hold office.

(4) The auditor must comply with this section—

(a) in the case of a major audit, at the same time as he deposits a statement at the company's registered office in accordance with section 519;

(b) in the case of an audit that is not a major audit, at such time (not being earlier than the time mentioned in paragraph (a)) as the appropriate audit authority may require.

(5) A person ceasing to hold office as auditor who fails to comply with this section commits an offence.

(6) If that person is a firm an offence is committed by—

(a) the firm, and

(b) every officer of the firm who is in default.

(7) In proceedings for an offence under this section it is a defence for the person charged to show that he took all reasonable steps and exercised all due diligence to avoid the commission of the offence.

(8) A person guilty of an offence under this section is liable—

(a) on conviction on indictment, to a fine;

(b) on summary conviction, to a fine not exceeding the statutory maximum.

### 523   Duty of company to notify appropriate audit authority

(1) Where an auditor ceases to hold office before the end of his term of office, the company must notify the appropriate audit authority.

(2) The notice must—

(a) inform the appropriate audit authority that the auditor has ceased to hold office, and

(b) be accompanied by—

(i) a statement by the company of the reasons for his ceasing to hold office, or

(ii) if the copy of the statement deposited by the auditor at the company's registered office in accordance with section 519 contains a statement of circumstances in connection with his ceasing to hold office that need to be brought to the attention of members or creditors of the company, a copy of that statement.

(3) The company must give notice under this section not later than 14 days after the date on which the auditor's statement is deposited at the company's registered office in accordance with section 519.

(4) If a company fails to comply with this section, an offence is committed by—

(a) the company, and

(b) every officer of the company who is in default.

(5) In proceedings for such an offence it is a defence for the person charged to show that he took all reasonable steps and exercised all due diligence to avoid the commission of the offence.

(6) A person guilty of an offence under this section is liable—

(a) on conviction on indictment, to a fine;

(b) on summary conviction, to a fine not exceeding the statutory maximum.

### 524  Information to be given to accounting authorities

(1) The appropriate audit authority on receiving notice under section 522 or 523 of an auditor's ceasing to hold office—

(a) must inform the accounting authorities, and

(b) may if it thinks fit forward to those authorities a copy of the statement or statements accompanying the notice.

(2) The accounting authorities are—

(a) the Secretary of State, and

(b) any person authorised by the Secretary of State for the purposes of section 456 (revision of defective accounts: persons authorised to apply to court).

(3) If either of the accounting authorities is also the appropriate audit authority it is only necessary to comply with this section as regards any other accounting authority.

(4) If the court has made an order under section 520(4) directing that copies of the statement need not be sent out by the company, sections 460 and 461 (restriction on further disclosure) apply in relation to the copies sent to the accounting authorities as they apply to information obtained under section 459 (power to require documents etc).

### 525  Meaning of 'appropriate audit authority' and 'major audit'

(1) In sections 522, 523 and 524 'appropriate audit authority' means—

(a) in the case of a major audit (other than one conducted by an Auditor General)—

(i) the Secretary of State, or

(ii) if the Secretary of State has delegated functions under section 1252 to a body whose functions include receiving the notice in question, that body;

(b) in the case of an audit (other than one conducted by an Auditor General) that is not a major audit, the relevant supervisory body,

(c) in the case of an audit conducted by an Auditor General, the Independent Supervisor.

'Supervisory body' and 'Independent Supervisor' have the same meaning as in Part 42 (statutory auditors) (see sections 1217 and 1228).

(2) In sections 522 and this section 'major audit' means a statutory audit conducted in respect of—

(a) a company any of whose securities have been admitted to the official list (within the meaning of Part 6 of the Financial Services and Markets Act 2000 (c. 8)), or

(b) any other person in whose financial condition there is a major public interest.

(3) In determining whether an audit is a major audit within subsection (2)(b), regard shall be had to any guidance issued by any of the authorities mentioned in subsection (1).

*Supplementary*

### 526  Effect of casual vacancies

If an auditor ceases to hold office for any reason, any surviving or continuing auditor or auditors may continue to act.

## Chapter 5  Quoted companies: right of members to raise audit concerns at accounts meeting

### 527  Members' power to require website publication of audit concerns

(1) The members of a quoted company may require the company to publish on a website a statement setting out any matter relating to—

(a) the audit of the company's accounts (including the auditor's report and the conduct of the audit) that are to be laid before the next accounts meeting, or

(b) any circumstances connected with an auditor of the company ceasing to hold office since the previous accounts meeting,

that the members propose to raise at the next accounts meeting of the company.

(2) A company is required to do so once it has received requests to that effect from—

(a) members representing at least 5% of the total voting rights of all the members who have a relevant right to vote (excluding any voting rights attached to any shares in the company held as treasury shares), or

(b) at least 100 members who have a relevant right to vote and hold shares in the company on which there has been paid up an average sum, per member, of at least £100.

See also section 153 (exercise of rights where shares held on behalf of others).

(3) In subsection (2) a 'relevant right to vote' means a right to vote at the accounts meeting.

(4) A request—

(a) may be sent to the company in hard copy or electronic form,

(b) must identify the statement to which it relates,

(c) must be authenticated by the person or persons making it, and

(d) must be received by the company at least one week before the meeting to which it relates.

(5) A quoted company is not required to place on a website a statement under this section if, on an application by the company or another person who claims to be aggrieved, the court is satisfied that the rights conferred by this section are being abused.

(6) The court may order the members requesting website publication to pay the whole or part of the company's costs (in Scotland, expenses) on such an application, even if they are not parties to the application.

### 528   Requirements as to website availability

(1) The following provisions apply for the purposes of section 527 (website publication of members' statement of audit concerns).

(2) The information must be made available on a website that—

(a) is maintained by or on behalf of the company, and

(b) identifies the company in question.

(3) Access to the information on the website, and the ability to obtain a hard copy of the information from the website, must not be conditional on the payment of a fee or otherwise restricted.

(4) The statement—

(a) must be made available within three working days of the company being required to publish it on a website, and

(b) must be kept available until after the meeting to which it relates.

(5) A failure to make information available on a website throughout the period specified in subsection (4)(b) is disregarded if—

(a) the information is made available on the website for part of that period, and

(b) the failure is wholly attributable to circumstances that it would not be reasonable to have expected the company to prevent or avoid.

### 529   Website publication: company's supplementary duties

(1) A quoted company must in the notice it gives of the accounts meeting draw attention to—

(a) the possibility of a statement being placed on a website in pursuance of members' requests under section 527, and

(b) the effect of the following provisions of this section.

(2) A company may not require the members requesting website publication to pay its expenses in complying with that section or section 528 (requirements in connection with website publication).

(3) Where a company is required to place a statement on a website under section 527 it must forward the statement to the company's auditor not later than the time when it makes the statement available on the website.

(4) The business which may be dealt with at the accounts meeting includes any statement that the company has been required under section 527 to publish on a website.

### 530   Website publication: offences

(1) In the event of default in complying with

(a) section 528 (requirements as to website publication), or

(b) section 529 (companies' supplementary duties in relation to request for website publication),

an offence is committed by every officer of the company who is in default.

(2) A person guilty of an offence under this section is liable—

(a) on conviction on indictment, to a fine;

(b) on summary conviction, to a fine not exceeding the statutory maximum.

### 531   Meaning of 'quoted company'

(1) For the purposes of this Chapter a company is a quoted company if it is a quoted company in accordance with section 385 (quoted and unquoted companies for the purposes of Part 15) in relation to the financial year to which the accounts to be laid at the next accounts meeting relate.

(2) The provisions of subsections (4) to (6) of that section (power to amend definition by regulations) apply in relation to the provisions of this Chapter as in relation to the provisions of that Part.

## Chapter 6   Auditors' liability

*Voidness of provisions protecting auditors from liability*

### 532   Voidness of provisions protecting auditors from liability

(1) This section applies to any provision—

(a) for exempting an auditor of a company (to any extent) from any liability that would otherwise attach to him in connection with any negligence, default, breach of duty or breach of trust in relation to the company occurring in the course of the audit of accounts, or

(b) by which a company directly or indirectly provides an indemnity (to any extent) for an auditor of the company, or of an associated company, against any liability attaching to him in connection with any negligence, default, breach of duty or breach of trust in relation to the company of which he is auditor occurring in the course of the audit of accounts.

(2) Any such provision is void, except as permitted by—

(a) section 533 (indemnity for costs of successfully defending proceedings), or

(b) sections 534 to 536 (liability limitation agreements).

(3) This section applies to any provision, whether contained in a company's articles or in any contract with the company or otherwise.

(4) For the purposes of this section companies are associated if one is a subsidiary of the other or both are subsidiaries of the same body corporate.

### *Indemnity for costs of defending proceedings*

### 533   Indemnity for costs of successfully defending proceedings

Section 532 (general voidness of provisions protecting auditors from liability) does not prevent a company from indemnifying an auditor against any liability incurred by him—

(a) in defending proceedings (whether civil or criminal) in which judgment is given in his favour or he is acquitted, or

(b) in connection with an application under section 1157 (power of court to grant relief in case of honest and reasonable conduct) in which relief is granted to him by the court.

### *Liability limitation agreements*

### 534   Liability limitation agreements

(1) A 'liability limitation agreement' is an agreement that purports to limit the amount of a liability owed to a company by its auditor in respect of any negligence, default, breach of duty or breach of trust, occurring in the course of the audit of accounts, of which the auditor may be guilty in relation to the company.

(2) Section 532 (general voidness of provisions protecting auditors from liability) does not affect the validity of a liability limitation agreement that—

(a) complies with section 535 (terms of liability limitation agreement) and of any regulations under that section, and

(b) is authorised by the members of the company (see section 536).

(3) Such an agreement—

(a) is effective to the extent provided by section 537, and

(b) is not subject—

(i) in England and Wales or Northern Ireland, to section 2(2) or 3(2)(a) of the Unfair Contract Terms Act 1977 (c. 50);

(ii) in Scotland, to section 16(1)(b) or 17(1)(a) of that Act.

### 535   Terms of liability limitation agreement

(1) A liability limitation agreement—

(a) must not apply in respect of acts or omissions occurring in the course of the audit of accounts for more than one financial year, and

(b) must specify the financial year in relation to which it applies.

(2) The Secretary of State may by regulations—

(a) require liability limitation agreements to contain specified provisions or provisions of a specified description;

(b) prohibit liability limitation agreements from containing specified provisions or provisions of a specified description.

'Specified' here means specified in the regulations.

(3) Without prejudice to the generality of the power conferred by subsection (2), that power may be exercised with a view to preventing adverse effects on competition.

(4) Subject to the preceding provisions of this section, it is immaterial how a liability limitation agreement is framed.

In particular, the limit on the amount of the auditor's liability need not be a sum of money, or a formula, specified in the agreement.

(5) Regulations under this section are subject to negative resolution procedure.

### 536   Authorisation of agreement by members of the company

(1) A liability limitation agreement is authorised by the members of the company if it has been authorised under this section and that authorisation has not been withdrawn.

(2) A liability limitation agreement between a private company and its auditor may be authorised—

(a) by the company passing a resolution, before it enters into the agreement, waiving the need for approval,

(b) by the company passing a resolution, before it enters into the agreement, approving the agreement's principal terms, or

(c) by the company passing a resolution, after it enters into the agreement, approving the agreement.

(3) A liability limitation agreement between a public company and its auditor may be authorised—

(a) by the company passing a resolution in general meeting, before it enters into the agreement, approving the agreement's principal terms, or

(b) by the company passing a resolution in general meeting, after it enters into the agreement, approving the agreement.

(4) The 'principal terms' of an agreement are terms specifying, or relevant to the determination of—

(a) the kind (or kinds) of acts or omissions covered,

(b) the financial year to which the agreement relates, or

(c) the limit to which the auditor's liability is subject.

(5) Authorisation under this section may be withdrawn by the company passing an ordinary resolution to that effect—

(a) at any time before the company enters into the agreement, or

(b) if the company has already entered into the agreement, before the beginning of the financial year to which the agreement relates.

Paragraph (b) has effect notwithstanding anything in the agreement.

### 537 Effect of liability limitation agreement

(1) A liability limitation agreement is not effective to limit the auditor's liability to less than such amount as is fair and reasonable in all the circumstances of the case having regard (in particular) to—

(a) the auditor's responsibilities under this Part,

(b) the nature and purpose of the auditor's contractual obligations to the company, and

(c) the professional standards expected of him.

(2) A liability limitation agreement that purports to limit the auditor's liability to less than the amount mentioned in subsection (1) shall have effect as if it limited his liability to that amount.

(3) In determining what is fair and reasonable in all the circumstances of the case no account is to be taken of—

(a) matters arising after the loss or damage in question has been incurred, or

(b) matters (whenever arising) affecting the possibility of recovering compensation from other persons liable in respect of the same loss or damage.

### 538 Disclosure of agreement by company

(1) A company which has entered into a liability limitation agreement must make such disclosure in connection with the agreement as the Secretary of State may require by regulations.

(2) The regulations may provide, in particular, that any disclosure required by the regulations shall be made—

(a) in a note to the company's annual accounts (in the case of its individual accounts) or in such manner as is specified in the regulations (in the case of group accounts), or

(b) in the directors' report.

(3) Regulations under this section are subject to negative resolution procedure.

## Chapter 7 Supplementary provisions

### 539 Minor definitions

In this Part—

'e-money issuer' means a person who has permission under Part 4 of the Financial Services and Markets Act 2000 (c. 8) to carry on the activity of issuing electronic money within the meaning of article 9B of the Financial Services and Markets Act 2000 (Regulated Activities) Order 2001 (S.I. 2001/544);

'MiFID investment firm' means an investment firm within the meaning of Article 4.1.1 of Directive 2004/39/EC of the European Parliament and of the Council of 21 April 2004 on markets in financial instruments, other than—

(a) a company to which that Directive does not apply by virtue of Article 2 of that Directive,

(b) a company which is an exempt investment firm within the meaning of regulation 4A(3) of the Financial Services and Markets Act 2000 (Markets in Financial Instruments) Regulations 2007, and

(c) any other company which fulfils all the requirements set out in regulation 4C(3) of those Regulations;

'qualified', in relation to an auditor's report (or a statement contained in an auditor's report), means that the report or statement does not state the auditor's unqualified opinion that the accounts have been properly prepared in accordance with this Act or, in the case of an undertaking not required to prepare accounts in accordance with this Act, under any corresponding legislation under which it is required to prepare accounts;

'turnover', in relation to a company, means the amounts derived from the provision of goods and services falling within the company's ordinary activities, after deduction of—

(a) trade discounts,

(b) value added tax, and

(c) any other taxes based on the amounts so derived;

'UCITS management company' has the meaning given by the Glossary forming part of the Handbook made by the Financial Services Authority under the Financial Services and Markets Act 2000.

# PART 17  A COMPANY'S SHARE CAPITAL

## Chapter 1  Shares and share capital of a company

### *Shares*

### 540  Shares

(1) In the Companies Acts 'share', in relation to a company, means share in the company's share capital.

(2) A company's shares may no longer be converted into stock.

(3) Stock created before the commencement of this Part may be reconverted into shares in accordance with section 620.

(4) In the Companies Acts—

(a) references to shares include stock except where a distinction between share and stock is express or implied, and

(b) references to a number of shares include an amount of stock where the context admits of the reference to shares being read as including stock.

### 541  Nature of shares

The shares or other interest of a member in a company are personal property (or, in Scotland, moveable property) and are not in the nature of real estate (or heritage).

### 542  Nominal value of shares

(1) Shares in a limited company having a share capital must each have a fixed nominal value.

(2) An allotment of a share that does not have a fixed nominal value is void.

(3) Shares in a limited company having a share capital may be denominated in any currency, and different classes of shares may be denominated in different currencies.

But see section 765 (initial authorised minimum share capital requirement for public company to be met by reference to share capital denominated in sterling or euros).

(4) If a company purports to allot shares in contravention of this section, an offence is committed by every officer of the company who is in default.

(5) A person guilty of an offence under this section is liable—

(a) on conviction on indictment, to a fine;

(b) on summary conviction, to a fine not exceeding the statutory maximum.

### 543  Numbering of shares

(1) Each share in a company having a share capital must be distinguished by its appropriate number, except in the following circumstances.

(2) If at any time—

(a) all the issued shares in a company are fully paid up and rank *pari passu* for all purposes, or

(b) all the issued shares of a particular class in a company are fully paid up and rank *pari passu* for all purposes,

none of those shares need thereafter have a distinguishing number so long as it remains fully paid up and ranks *pari passu* for all purposes with all shares of the same class for the time being issued and fully paid up.

### 544  Transferability of shares

(1) The shares or other interest of any member in a company are transferable in accordance with the company's articles.

(2) This is subject to—

(a) the Stock Transfer Act 1963 (c. 18) or the Stock Transfer Act (Northern Ireland) 1963 (c.24 (N.I.)) (which enables securities of certain descriptions to be transferred by a simplified process), and

(b) regulations under Chapter 2 of Part 21 of this Act (which enable title to securities to be evidenced and transferred without a written instrument).

(3) See Part 21 of this Act generally as regards share transfers.

### 545  Companies having a share capital

References in the Companies Acts to a company having a share capital are to a company that has power under its constitution to issue shares.

### 546  Issued and allotted share capital

(1) References in the Companies Acts—

(a) to 'issued share capital' are to shares of a company that have been issued;

(b) to 'allotted share capital' are to shares of a company that have been allotted.

(2) References in the Companies Acts to issued or allotted shares, or to issued or allotted share capital, include shares taken on the formation of the company by the subscribers to the company's memorandum.

*Share capital*

### 547    Called-up share capital

In the Companies Acts—

'called-up share capital', in relation to a company, means so much of its share capital as equals the aggregate amount of the calls made on its shares (whether or not those calls have been paid), together with—

(a) any share capital paid up without being called, and

(b) any share capital to be paid on a specified future date under the articles, the terms of allotment of the relevant shares or any other arrangements for payment of those shares; and

'uncalled share capital' is to be construed accordingly.

### 548    Equity share capital

In the Companies Acts 'equity share capital', in relation to a company, means its issued share capital excluding any part of that capital that, neither as respects dividends nor as respects capital, carries any right to participate beyond a specified amount in a distribution.

## Chapter 2  Allotment of shares: general provisions

*Power of directors to allot shares*

### 549    Exercise by directors of power to allot shares etc.

(1) The directors of a company must not exercise any power of the company—

(a) to allot shares in the company, or

(b) to grant rights to subscribe for, or to convert any security into, shares in the company,

except in accordance with section 550 (private company with single class of shares) or section 551 (authorisation by company).

(2) Subsection (1) does not apply—

(a) to the allotment of shares in pursuance of an employees' share scheme, or

(b) to the grant of a right to subscribe for, or to convert any security into, shares so allotted.

(3) If this section applies in relation to the grant of a right to subscribe for, or to convert any security into, shares, it does not apply in relation to the allotment of shares pursuant to that right.

(4) A director who knowingly contravenes, or permits or authorises a contravention of, this section commits an offence.

(5) A person guilty of an offence under this section is liable—

(a) on conviction on indictment, to a fine;

(b) on summary conviction, to a fine not exceeding the statutory maximum.

(6) Nothing in this section affects the validity of an allotment or other transaction.

### 550    Power of directors to allot shares etc.: private company with only one class of shares

Where a private company has only one class of shares, the directors may exercise any power of the company—

(a) to allot shares of that class, or

(b) to grant rights to subscribe for or to convert any security into such shares,

except to the extent that they are prohibited from doing so by the company's articles.

### 551    Power of directors to allot shares etc.: authorisation by company

(1) The directors of a company may exercise a power of the company—

(a) to allot shares in the company, or

(b) to grant rights to subscribe for or to convert any security into shares in the company,

if they are authorised to do so by the company's articles or by resolution of the company.

(2) Authorisation may be given for a particular exercise of the power or for its exercise generally, and may be unconditional or subject to conditions.

(3) Authorisation must—

(a) state the maximum amount of shares that may be allotted under it, and

(b) specify the date on which it will expire, which must be not more than five years from—

(i) in the case of authorisation contained in the company's articles at the time of its original incorporation, the date of that incorporation;

(ii) in any other case, the date on which the resolution is passed by virtue of which the authorisation is given.

(4) Authorisation may—

(a) be renewed or further renewed by resolution of the company for a further period not exceeding five years, and

(b) be revoked or varied at any time by resolution of the company.

(5) A resolution renewing authorisation must—

    (a) state (or restate) the maximum amount of shares that may be allotted under the authorisation or, as the case may be, the amount remaining to be allotted under it, and

    (b) specify the date on which the renewed authorisation will expire.

(6) In relation to rights to subscribe for or to convert any security into shares in the company, references in this section to the maximum amount of shares that may be allotted under the authorisation are to the maximum amount of shares that may be allotted pursuant to the rights.

(7) The directors may allot shares, or grant rights to subscribe for or to convert any security into shares, after authorisation has expired if—

    (a) the shares are allotted, or the rights are granted, in pursuance of an offer or agreement made by the company before the authorisation expired, and

    (b) the authorisation allowed the company to make an offer or agreement which would or might require shares to be allotted, or rights to be granted, after the authorisation had expired.

(8) A resolution of a company to give, vary, revoke or renew authorisation under this section may be an ordinary resolution, even though it amends the company's articles.

(9) Chapter 3 of Part 3 (resolutions affecting a company's constitution) applies to a resolution under this section.

### Prohibition of commissions, discounts and allowances

### 552   General prohibition of commissions, discounts and allowances

(1) Except as permitted by section 553 (permitted commission), a company must not apply any of its shares or capital money, either directly or indirectly, in payment of any commission, discount or allowance to any person in consideration of his—

    (a) subscribing or agreeing to subscribe (whether absolutely or conditionally) for shares in the company, or

    (b) procuring or agreeing to procure subscriptions (whether absolute or conditional) for shares in the company.

(2) It is immaterial how the shares or money are so applied, whether by being added to the purchase money of property acquired by the company or to the contract price of work to be executed for the company, or being paid out of the nominal purchase money or contract price, or otherwise.

(3) Nothing in this section affects the payment of such brokerage as has previously been lawful.

### 553   Permitted commission

(1) A company may, if the following conditions are satisfied, pay a commission to a person in consideration of his subscribing or agreeing to subscribe (whether absolutely or conditionally) for shares in the company, or procuring or agreeing to procure subscriptions (whether absolute or conditional) for shares in the company.

(2) The conditions are that—

    (a) the payment of the commission is authorised by the company's articles; and

    (b) the commission paid or agreed to be paid does not exceed—

        (i)   10% of the price at which the shares are issued, or

        (ii)   the amount or rate authorised by the articles,

        whichever is the less.

(3) A vendor to, or promoter of, or other person who receives payment in money or shares from, a company may apply any part of the money or shares so received in payment of any commission the payment of which directly by the company would be permitted by this section.

### Registration of allotment

### 554   Registration of allotment

(1) A company must register an allotment of shares as soon as practicable and in any event within two months after the date of the allotment.

(2) This does not apply if the company has issued a share warrant in respect of the shares (see section 779).

(3) If a company fails to comply with this section, an offence is committed by—

    (a) the company, and

    (b) every officer of the company who is in default.

(4) A person guilty of an offence under this section is liable on summary conviction to a fine not exceeding level 3 on the standard scale and, for continued contravention, a daily default fine not exceeding one-tenth of level 3 on the standard scale.

(5) For the company's duties as to the issue of share certificates etc, see Part 21 (certification and transfer of securities).

### Return of allotment

### 555   Return of allotment by limited company

(1) This section applies to a company limited by shares and to a company limited by guarantee and having a share capital.

(2) The company must, within one month of making an allotment of shares, deliver to the registrar for registration a return of the allotment.

(3) The return must—

(a) contain the prescribed information, and

(b) be accompanied by a statement of capital.

(4) The statement of capital must state with respect to the company's share capital at the date to which the return is made up—

(a) the total number of shares of the company,

(b) the aggregate nominal value of those shares,

(c) for each class of shares—

(i) prescribed particulars of the rights attached to the shares,

(ii) the total number of shares of that class, and

(iii) the aggregate nominal value of shares of that class, and

(d) the amount paid up and the amount (if any) unpaid on each share (whether on account of the nominal value of the share or by way of premium).

### 556   Return of allotment by unlimited company allotting new class of shares

(1) This section applies to an unlimited company that allots shares of a class with rights that are not in all respects uniform with shares previously allotted.

(2) The company must, within one month of making such an allotment, deliver to the registrar for registration a return of the allotment.

(3) The return must contain the prescribed particulars of the rights attached to the shares.

(4) For the purposes of this section shares are not to be treated as different from shares previously allotted by reason only that the former do not carry the same rights to dividends as the latter during the twelve months immediately following the former's allotment.

### 557   Offence of failure to make return

(1) If a company makes default in complying with—

section 555 (return of allotment of shares by limited company), or

section 556 (return of allotment of new class of shares by unlimited company),

an offence is committed by every officer of the company who is in default.

(2) A person guilty of an offence under this section is liable—

(a) on conviction on indictment, to a fine;

(b) on summary conviction, to a fine not exceeding the statutory maximum and, for continued contravention, a daily default fine not exceeding one-tenth of the statutory maximum.

(3) In the case of default in delivering to the registrar within one month after the allotment the return required by section 555 or 556—

(a) any person liable for the default may apply to the court for relief, and

(b) the court, if satisfied—

(i) that the omission to deliver the document was accidental or due to inadvertence, or

(ii) that it is just and equitable to grant relief,

(iii) may make an order extending the time for delivery of the document for such period as the court thinks proper.

*Supplementary provisions*

### 558   When shares are allotted

For the purposes of the Companies Acts shares in a company are taken to be allotted when a person acquires the unconditional right to be included in the company's register of members in respect of the shares.

### 559   Provisions about allotment not applicable to shares taken on formation

The provisions of this Chapter have no application in relation to the taking of shares by the subscribers to the memorandum on the formation of the company.

## Chapter 3   Allotment of equity securities: existing shareholders' right of pre-emption

*Introductory*

### 560   Meaning of 'equity securities' and related expressions

(1) In this Chapter—

'equity securities' means—

(a) ordinary shares in the company, or

(b) rights to subscribe for, or to convert securities into, ordinary shares in the company;

'ordinary shares' means shares other than shares that as respects dividends and capital carry a right to participate only up to a specified amount in a distribution.

(2) References in this Chapter to the allotment of equity securities include—

(a) the grant of a right to subscribe for, or to convert any securities into, ordinary shares in the company, and

(b) the sale of ordinary shares in the company that immediately before the sale are held by the company as treasury shares.

*Existing shareholders' right of pre-emption*

### 561   Existing shareholders' right of pre-emption

(1)  A company must not allot equity securities to a person on any terms unless—

(a) it has made an offer to each person who holds ordinary shares in the company to allot to him on the same or more favourable terms a proportion of those securities that is as nearly as practicable equal to the proportion in nominal value held by him of the ordinary share capital of the company, and

(b) the period during which any such offer may be accepted has expired or the company has received notice of the acceptance or refusal of every offer so made.

(2)  Securities that a company has offered to allot to a holder of ordinary shares may be allotted to him, or anyone in whose favour he has renounced his right to their allotment, without contravening subsection (1)(b).

(3)  If subsection (1) applies in relation to the grant of such a right, it does not apply in relation to the allotment of shares in pursuance of that right.

(4)  Shares held by the company as treasury shares are disregarded for the purposes of this section, so that—

(a) the company is not treated as a person who holds ordinary shares, and

(b) the shares are not treated as forming part of the ordinary share capital of the company.

(5)  This section is subject to—

(a) sections 564 to 566 (exceptions to pre-emption right),

(b) sections 567 and 568 (exclusion of rights of pre-emption),

(c) sections 569 to 573 (disapplication of pre-emption rights), and

(d) section 576 (saving for certain older pre-emption procedures).

### 562   Communication of pre-emption offers to shareholders

(1)  This section has effect as to the manner in which offers required by section 561 are to be made to holders of a company's shares.

(2)  The offer may be made in hard copy or electronic form.

(3)  If the holder—

(a) has no registered address in an EEA State and has not given to the company an address in an EEA State for the service of notices on him, or

(b) is the holder of a share warrant,

the offer may be made by causing it, or a notice specifying where a copy of it can be obtained or inspected, to be published in the Gazette.

(4)  The offer must state a period during which it may be accepted and the offer shall not be withdrawn before the end of that period.

(5)  The period must be a period of at least 21 days beginning—

(a) in the case of an offer made in hard copy form, with the date on which the offer is sent or supplied;

(b) in the case of an offer made in electronic form, with the date on which the offer is sent;

(c) in the case of an offer made by publication in the Gazette, with the date of publication.

(6)  The Secretary of State may by regulations made by statutory instrument—

(a) reduce the period specified in subsection (5) (but not to less than 14 days), or

(b) increase that period.

(7)  A statutory instrument containing regulations made under subsection (6) is subject to affirmative resolution procedure.

### 563   Liability of company and officers in case of contravention

(1)  This section applies where there is a contravention of—

section 561 (existing shareholders' right of pre-emption), or

section 562 (communication of pre-emption offers to shareholders).

(2)  The company and every officer of it who knowingly authorised or permitted the contravention are jointly and severally liable to compensate any person to whom an offer should have been made in accordance with those provisions for any loss, damage, costs or expenses which the person has sustained or incurred by reason of the contravention.

(3)  No proceedings to recover any such loss, damage, costs or expenses shall be commenced after the expiration of two years—

(a) from the delivery to the registrar of companies of the return of allotment, or

(b) where equity securities other than shares are granted, from the date of the grant.

*Exceptions to right of pre-emption*

### 564   Exception to pre-emption right: bonus shares

Section 561(1) (existing shareholders' right of pre-emption) does not apply in relation to the allotment of bonus shares.

### 565   Exception to pre-emption right: issue for non-cash consideration

Section 561(1) (existing shareholders' right of pre-emption) does not apply to a particular allotment of equity securities if these are, or are to be, wholly or partly paid up otherwise than in cash.

### 566   Exception to pre-emption right: securities held under employees' share scheme

Section 561 (existing shareholders' right of pre-emption) does not apply to the allotment of securities that would, apart from any renunciation or assignment of the right to their allotment, be held under an employees' share scheme.

*Exclusion of right of pre-emption*

### 567   Exclusion of requirements by private companies

(1)  All or any of the requirements of—
    (a)  section 561 (existing shareholders' right of pre-emption), or
    (b)  section 562 (communication of pre-emption offers to shareholders)
may be excluded by provision contained in the articles of a private company.

(2)  They may be excluded—
    (a)  generally in relation to the allotment by the company of equity securities, or
    (b)  in relation to allotments of a particular description.

(3)  Any requirement or authorisation contained in the articles of a private company that is inconsistent with either of those sections is treated for the purposes of this section as a provision excluding that section.

(4)  A provision to which section 568 applies (exclusion of pre-emption right: corresponding right conferred by articles) is not to be treated as inconsistent with section 561.

### 568   Exclusion of pre-emption right: articles conferring corresponding right

(1)  The provisions of this section apply where, in a case in which section 561 (existing shareholders' right of pre-emption) would otherwise apply—
    (a)  a company's articles contain provision ('pre-emption provision') prohibiting the company from allotting ordinary shares of a particular class unless it has complied with the condition that it makes such an offer as is described in section 561(1) to each person who holds ordinary shares of that class, and
    (b)  in accordance with that provision—
        (i)   the company makes an offer to allot shares to such a holder, and
        (ii)  he or anyone in whose favour he has renounced his right to their allotment accepts the offer.

(2)  In that case, section 561 does not apply to the allotment of those shares and the company may allot them accordingly.

(3)  The provisions of section 562 (communication of pre-emption offers to shareholders) apply in relation to offers made in pursuance of the pre-emption provision of the company's articles.
This is subject to section 567 (exclusion of requirements by private companies).

(4)  If there is a contravention of the pre-emption provision of the company's articles, the company, and every officer of it who knowingly authorised or permitted the contravention, are jointly and severally liable to compensate any person to whom an offer should have been made under the provision for any loss, damage, costs or expenses which the person has sustained or incurred by reason of the contravention.

(5)  No proceedings to recover any such loss, damage, costs or expenses may be commenced after the expiration of two years—
    (a)  from the delivery to the registrar of companies of the return of allotment, or
    (b)  where equity securities other than shares are granted, from the date of the grant.

*Disapplication of pre-emption rights*

### 569   Disapplication of pre-emption rights: private company with only one class of shares

(1)  The directors of a private company that has only one class of shares may be given power by the articles, or by a special resolution of the company, to allot equity securities of that class as if section 561 (existing shareholders' right of pre-emption)—
    (a)  did not apply to the allotment, or
    (b)  applied to the allotment with such modifications as the directors may determine.

(2)  Where the directors make an allotment under this section, the provisions of this Chapter have effect accordingly.

### 570   Disapplication of pre-emption rights: directors acting under general authorisation

(1)  Where the directors of a company are generally authorised for the purposes of section 551 (power of directors to allot shares etc: authorisation by company), they may be given power by the

articles, or by a special resolution of the company, to allot equity securities pursuant to that authorisation as if section 561 (existing shareholders' right of pre-emption)—

    (a) did not apply to the allotment, or

    (b) applied to the allotment with such modifications as the directors may determine.

  (2) Where the directors make an allotment under this section, the provisions of this Chapter have effect accordingly.

  (3) The power conferred by this section ceases to have effect when the authorisation to which it relates—

    (a) is revoked, or

    (b) would (if not renewed) expire.

But if the authorisation is renewed the power may also be renewed, for a period not longer than that for which the authorisation is renewed, by a special resolution of the company.

  (4) Notwithstanding that the power conferred by this section has expired, the directors may allot equity securities in pursuance of an offer or agreement previously made by the company if the power enabled the company to make an offer or agreement that would or might require equity securities to be allotted after it expired.

### 571 Disapplication of pre-emption rights by special resolution

  (1) Where the directors of a company are authorised for the purposes of section 551 (power of directors to allot shares etc.: authorisation by company), whether generally or otherwise, the company may by special resolution resolve that section 561 (existing shareholders' right of preemption)—

    (a) does not apply to a specified allotment of equity securities to be made pursuant to that authorisation, or

    (b) applies to such an allotment with such modifications as may be specified in the resolution.

  (2) Where such a resolution is passed the provisions of this Chapter have effect accordingly.

  (3) A special resolution under this section ceases to have effect when the authorisation to which it relates—

    (a) is revoked, or

    (b) would (if not renewed) expire.

But if the authorisation is renewed the resolution may also be renewed, for a period not longer than that for which the authorisation is renewed, by a special resolution of the company.

  (4) Notwithstanding that any such resolution has expired, the directors may allot equity securities in pursuance of an offer or agreement previously made by the company if the resolution enabled the company to make an offer or agreement that would or might require equity securities to be allotted after it expired.

  (5) A special resolution under this section, or a special resolution to renew such a resolution, must not be proposed unless—

    (a) it is recommended by the directors, and

    (b) the directors have complied with the following provisions.

  (6) Before such a resolution is proposed, the directors must make a written statement setting out—

    (a) their reasons for making the recommendation,

    (b) the amount to be paid to the company in respect of the equity securities to be allotted, and

    (c) the directors' justification of that amount.

  (7) The directors' statement must—

    (a) if the resolution is proposed as a written resolution, be sent or submitted to every eligible member at or before the time at which the proposed resolution is sent or submitted to him;

    (b) if the resolution is proposed at a general meeting, be circulated to the members entitled to notice of the meeting with that notice.

### 572 Liability for false statement in directors' statement

  (1) This section applies in relation to a directors' statement under section 571 (special resolution disapplying pre-emption rights) that is sent, submitted or circulated under subsection (7) of that section.

  (2) A person who knowingly or recklessly authorises or permits the inclusion of any matter that is misleading, false or deceptive in a material particular in such a statement commits an offence.

  (3) A person guilty of an offence under this section is liable—

    (a) on conviction on indictment, to imprisonment for a term not exceeding two years or a fine (or both);

    (b) on summary conviction—

      (i) in England and Wales, to imprisonment for a term not exceeding twelve months or to a fine not exceeding the statutory maximum (or both);

      (ii) in Scotland or Northern Ireland, to imprisonment for a term not exceeding six months, or to a fine not exceeding the statutory maximum (or both).

### 573 Disapplication of pre-emption rights: sale of treasury shares

  (1) This section applies in relation to a sale of shares that is an allotment of equity securities by virtue of section 560(2)(b) (sale of shares held by company as treasury shares).

(2) The directors of a company may be given power by the articles, or by a special resolution of the company, to allot equity securities as if section 561 (existing shareholders' right of pre-emption)—

(a) did not apply to the allotment, or

(b) applied to the allotment with such modifications as the directors may determine.

(3) The provisions of section 570(2) and (4) apply in that case as they apply to a case within subsection (1) of that section.

(4) The company may by special resolution resolve that section 561—

(a) shall not apply to a specified allotment of securities, or

(b) shall apply to the allotment with such modifications as may be specified in the resolution.

(5) The provisions of section 571(2) and (4) to (7) apply in that case as they apply to a case within subsection (1) of that section.

*Supplementary*

### 574   References to holder of shares in relation to offer

(1) In this Chapter, in relation to an offer to allot securities required by—

(a) section 561 (existing shareholders' right of pre-emption), or

(b) any provision to which section 568 applies (articles conferring corresponding right),

a reference (however expressed) to the holder of shares of any description is to whoever was the holder of shares of that description at the close of business on a date to be specified in the offer.

(2) The specified date must fall within the period of 28 days immediately before the date of the offer.

### 575   Saving for other restrictions on offer or allotment

(1) The provisions of this Chapter are without prejudice to any other enactment by virtue of which a company is prohibited (whether generally or in specified circumstances) from offering or allotting equity securities to any person.

(2) Where a company cannot by virtue of such an enactment offer or allot equity securities to a holder of ordinary shares of the company, those shares are disregarded for the purposes of section 561 (existing shareholders' right of pre-emption), so that—

(a) the person is not treated as a person who holds ordinary shares, and

(b) the shares are not treated as forming part of the ordinary share capital of the company.

### 576   Saving for certain older pre-emption requirements

(1) In the case of a public company the provisions of this Chapter do not apply to an allotment of equity securities that are subject to a pre-emption requirement in relation to which section 96(1) of the Companies Act 1985 (c. 6) or Article 106(1) of the Companies (Northern Ireland) Order 1986 (S.I. 1986/1032 (N.I. 6)) applied immediately before the commencement of this Chapter.

(2) In the case of a private company a pre-emption requirement to which section 96(3) of the Companies Act 1985 or Article 106(3) of the Companies (Northern Ireland) Order 1986 applied immediately before the commencement of this Chapter shall have effect, so long as the company remains a private company, as if it were contained in the company's articles.

(3) A pre-emption requirement to which section 96(4) of the Companies Act 1985 or Article 106(4) of the Companies (Northern Ireland) Order 1986 applied immediately before the commencement of this section shall be treated for the purposes of this Chapter as if it were contained in the company's articles.

### 577   Provisions about pre-emption not applicable to shares taken on formation

The provisions of this Chapter have no application in relation to the taking of shares by the subscribers to the memorandum on the formation of the company.

## Chapter 4  Public companies: allotment where issue not fully subscribed

### 578   Public companies: allotment where issue not fully subscribed

(1) No allotment shall be made of shares of a public company offered for subscription unless—

(a) the issue is subscribed for in full, or

(b) the offer is made on terms that the shares subscribed for may be allotted—

(i) in any event, or

(ii) if specified conditions are met (and those conditions are met).

(2) If shares are prohibited from being allotted by subsection (1) and 40 days have elapsed after the first making of the offer, all money received from applicants for shares must be repaid to them forthwith, without interest.

(3) If any of the money is not repaid within 48 days after the first making of the offer, the directors of the company are jointly and severally liable to repay it, with interest at the rate for the time being specified under section 17 of the Judgments Act 1838 (c. 110) from the expiration of the 48th day.

A director is not so liable if he proves that the default in the repayment of the money was not due to any misconduct or negligence on his part.

(4) This section applies in the case of shares offered as wholly or partly payable otherwise than in cash as it applies in the case of shares offered for subscription.

(5) In that case—

    (a) the references in subsection (1) to subscription shall be construed accordingly;

    (b) references in subsections (2) and (3) to the repayment of money received from applicants for shares include—

        (i) the return of any other consideration so received (including, if the case so requires, the release of the applicant from any undertaking), or

        (ii) if it is not reasonably practicable to return the consideration, the payment of money equal to its value at the time it was so received;

    (c) references to interest apply accordingly.

(6) Any condition requiring or binding an applicant for shares to waive compliance with any requirement of this section is void.

### 579 Public companies: effect of irregular allotment where issue not fully subscribed

(1) An allotment made by a public company to an applicant in contravention of section 578 (public companies: allotment where issue not fully subscribed) is voidable at the instance of the applicant within one month after the date of the allotment, and not later.

(2) It is so voidable even if the company is in the course of being wound up.

(3) A director of a public company who knowingly contravenes, or permits or authorises the contravention of, any provision of section 578 with respect to allotment is liable to compensate the company and the allottee respectively for any loss, damages, costs or expenses that the company or allottee may have sustained or incurred by the contravention.

(4) Proceedings to recover any such loss, damages, costs or expenses may not be brought more than two years after the date of the allotment.

## Chapter 5  Payment for shares

### *General rules*

### 580 Shares not to be allotted at a discount

(1) A company's shares must not be allotted at a discount.

(2) If shares are allotted in contravention of this section, the allottee is liable to pay the company an amount equal to the amount of the discount, with interest at the appropriate rate.

### 581 Provision for different amounts to be paid on shares

A company, if so authorised by its articles, may—

    (a) make arrangements on the issue of shares for a difference between the shareholders in the amounts and times of payment of calls on their shares;

    (b) accept from any member the whole or part of the amount remaining unpaid on any shares held by him, although no part of that amount has been called up;

    (c) pay a dividend in proportion to the amount paid up on each share where a larger amount is paid up on some shares than on others.

### 582 General rule as to means of payment

(1) Shares allotted by a company, and any premium on them, may be paid up in money or money's worth (including goodwill and know-how).

(2) This section does not prevent a company—

    (a) from allotting bonus shares to its members, or

    (b) from paying up, with sums available for the purpose, any amounts for the time being unpaid on any of its shares (whether on account of the nominal value of the shares or by way of premium).

(3) This section has effect subject to the following provisions of this Chapter (additional rules for public companies).

### 583 Meaning of payment in cash

(1) The following provisions have effect for the purposes of the Companies Acts.

(2) A share in a company is deemed paid up (as to its nominal value or any premium on it) in cash, or allotted for cash, if the consideration received for the allotment or payment up is a cash consideration.

(3) A 'cash consideration' means—

    (a) cash received by the company,

    (b) a cheque received by the company in good faith that the directors have no reason for suspecting will not be paid,

    (c) a release of a liability of the company for a liquidated sum,

    (d) an undertaking to pay cash to the company at a future date, or

    (e) payment by any other means giving rise to a present or future entitlement (of the company or a person acting on the company's behalf) to a payment, or credit equivalent to payment, in cash.

(4)  The Secretary of State may by order provide that particular means of payment specified in the order are to be regarded as falling within subsection (3)(e).

(5)  In relation to the allotment or payment up of shares in a company—

(a)  the payment of cash to a person other than the company, or

(b)  an undertaking to pay cash to a person other than the company, counts as consideration other than cash.

This does not apply for the purposes of Chapter 3 (allotment of equity securities: existing shareholders' right of pre-emption).

(6)  For the purpose of determining whether a share is or is to be allotted for cash, or paid up in cash, 'cash' includes foreign currency.

(7)  An order under this section is subject to negative resolution procedure.

*Additional rules for public companies*

### 584  Public companies: shares taken by subscribers of memorandum

Shares taken by a subscriber to the memorandum of a public company in pursuance of an undertaking of his in the memorandum, and any premium on the shares, must be paid up in cash.

### 585  Public companies: must not accept undertaking to do work or perform services

(1)  A public company must not accept at any time, in payment up of its shares or any premium on them, an undertaking given by any person that he or another should do work or perform services for the company or any other person.

(2)  If a public company accepts such an undertaking in payment up of its shares or any premium on them, the holder of the shares when they or the premium are treated as paid up (in whole or in part) by the undertaking is liable—

(a)  to pay the company in respect of those shares an amount equal to their nominal value, together with the whole of any premium or, if the case so requires, such proportion of that amount as is treated as paid up by the undertaking; and

(b)  to pay interest at the appropriate rate on the amount payable under paragraph (a).

(3)  The reference in subsection (2) to the holder of shares includes a person who has an unconditional right—

(a)  to be included in the company's register of members in respect of those shares, or

(b)  to have an instrument of transfer of them executed in his favour.

### 586  Public companies: shares must be at least one-quarter paid up

(1)  A public company must not allot a share except as paid up at least as to one-quarter of its nominal value and the whole of any premium on it.

(2)  This does not apply to shares allotted in pursuance of an employees' share scheme.

(3)  If a company allots a share in contravention of this section—

(a)  the share is to be treated as if one-quarter of its nominal value, together with the whole of any premium on it, had been received, and

(b)  the allottee is liable to pay the company the minimum amount which should have been received in respect of the share under subsection (1) (less the value of any consideration actually applied in payment up, to any extent, of the share and any premium on it), with interest at the appropriate rate.

(4)  Subsection (3) does not apply to the allotment of bonus shares, unless the allottee knew or ought to have known the shares were allotted in contravention of this section.

### 587  Public companies: payment by long-term undertaking

(1)  A public company must not allot shares as fully or partly paid up (as to their nominal value or any premium on them) otherwise than in cash if the consideration for the allotment is or includes an undertaking which is to be, or may be, performed more than five years after the date of the allotment.

(2)  If a company allots shares in contravention of subsection (1), the allottee is liable to pay the company an amount equal to the aggregate of their nominal value and the whole of any premium (or, if the case so requires, so much of that aggregate as is treated as paid up by the undertaking), with interest at the appropriate rate.

(3)  Where a contract for the allotment of shares does not contravene subsection (1), any variation of the contract that has the effect that the contract would have contravened the subsection, if the terms of the contract as varied had been its original terms, is void. This applies also to the variation by a public company of the terms of a contract entered into before the company was re-registered as a public company.

(4)  Where—

(a)  a public company allots shares for a consideration which consists of or includes (in accordance with subsection (1)) an undertaking that is to be performed within five years of the allotment, and

(b)  the undertaking is not performed within the period allowed by the contract for the allotment of the shares, the allottee is liable to pay the company, at the end of the period so allowed, an amount equal to the aggregate of the nominal value of the shares and the whole of any premium (or, if the case so requires, so much of that aggregate as is treated as paid up by the undertaking), with interest at the appropriate rate.

(5) References in this section to a contract for the allotment of shares include an ancillary contract relating to payment in respect of them.

*Supplementary provisions*

### 588  Liability of subsequent holders of shares

(1) If a person becomes a holder of shares in respect of which—

(a) there has been a contravention of any provision of this Chapter, and

(b) by virtue of that contravention another is liable to pay any amount under the provision contravened,

that person is also liable to pay that amount (jointly and severally with any other person so liable), subject as follows.

(2) A person otherwise liable under subsection (1) is exempted from that liability if either—

(a) he is a purchaser for value and, at the time of the purchase, he did not have actual notice of the contravention concerned, or

(b) he derived title to the shares (directly or indirectly) from a person who became a holder of them after the contravention and was not liable under subsection (1).

(3) References in this section to a holder, in relation to shares in a company, include any person who has an unconditional right—

(a) to be included in the company's register of members in respect of those shares, or

(b) to have an instrument of transfer of the shares executed in his favour.

(4) This section applies in relation to a failure to carry out a term of a contract as mentioned in section 587(4) (public companies: payment by long-term undertaking) as it applies in relation to a contravention of a provision of this Chapter.

### 589  Power of court to grant relief

(1) This section applies in relation to liability under—

section 585(2) (liability of allottee in case of breach by public company of prohibition on accepting undertaking to do work or perform services),

section 587(2) or (4) (liability of allottee in case of breach by public company of prohibition on payment by long-term undertaking), or

section 588 (liability of subsequent holders of shares),

as it applies in relation to a contravention of those sections.

(2) A person who—

(a) is subject to any such liability to a company in relation to payment in respect of shares in the company, or

(b) is subject to any such liability to a company by virtue of an undertaking given to it in, or in connection with, payment for shares in the company,

may apply to the court to be exempted in whole or in part from the liability.

(3) In the case of a liability within subsection (2)(a), the court may exempt the applicant from the liability only if and to the extent that it appears to the court just and equitable to do so having regard to—

(a) whether the applicant has paid, or is liable to pay, any amount in respect of—

(i) any other liability arising in relation to those shares under any provision of this Chapter or Chapter 6, or

(ii) any liability arising by virtue of any undertaking given in or in connection with payment for those shares;

(b) whether any person other than the applicant has paid or is likely to pay, whether in pursuance of any order of the court or otherwise, any such amount;

(c) whether the applicant or any other person—

(i) has performed in whole or in part, or is likely so to perform any such undertaking, or

(ii) has done or is likely to do any other thing in payment or part payment for the shares.

(4) In the case of a liability within subsection (2)(b), the court may exempt the applicant from the liability only if and to the extent that it appears to the court just and equitable to do so having regard to—

(a) whether the applicant has paid or is liable to pay any amount in respect of liability arising in relation to the shares under any provision of this Chapter or Chapter 6;

(b) whether any person other than the applicant has paid or is likely to pay, whether in pursuance of any order of the court or otherwise, any such amount.

(5) In determining whether it should exempt the applicant in whole or in part from any liability, the court must have regard to the following overriding principles—

(a) a company that has allotted shares should receive money or money's worth at least equal in value to the aggregate of the nominal value of those shares and the whole of any premium or, if the case so requires, so much of that aggregate as is treated as paid up;

(b) subject to that, where a company would, if the court did not grant the exemption, have more than one remedy against a particular person, it should be for the company to decide which remedy it should remain entitled to pursue.

(6) If a person brings proceedings against another ('the contributor') for a contribution in respect of liability to a company arising under any provision of this Chapter or Chapter 6 and it appears to the court that the contributor is liable to make such a contribution, the court may, if and to the extent that it appears to it just and equitable to do so having regard to the respective culpability (in respect of the liability to the company) of the contributor and the person bringing the proceedings—

(a) exempt the contributor in whole or in part from his liability to make such a contribution, or

(b) order the contributor to make a larger contribution than, but for this subsection, he would be liable to make.

### 590    Penalty for contravention of this Chapter

(1) If a company contravenes any of the provisions of this Chapter, an offence is committed by—

(a) the company, and

(b) every officer of the company who is in default.

(2) A person guilty of an offence under this section is liable—

(a) on conviction on indictment, to a fine;

(b) on summary conviction, to a fine not exceeding the statutory maximum.

### 591    Enforceability of undertakings to do work etc

(1) An undertaking given by any person, in or in connection with payment for shares in a company, to do work or perform services or to do any other thing, if it is enforceable by the company apart from this Chapter, is so enforceable notwithstanding that there has been a contravention in relation to it of a provision of this Chapter or Chapter 6.

(2) This is without prejudice to section 589 (power of court to grant relief etc. in respect of liabilities).

### 592    The appropriate rate of interest

(1) For the purposes of this Chapter the 'appropriate rate' of interest is 5% per annum or such other rate as may be specified by order made by the Secretary of State.

(2) An order under this section is subject to negative resolution procedure.

## Chapter 6  Public companies: independent valuation of non-cash consideration

*Non-cash consideration for shares*

### 593    Public company: valuation of non-cash consideration for shares

(1) A public company must not allot shares as fully or partly paid up (as to their nominal value or any premium on them) otherwise than in cash unless—

(a) the consideration for the allotment has been independently valued in accordance with the provisions of this Chapter,

(b) the valuer's report has been made to the company during the six months immediately preceding the allotment of the shares, and

(c) a copy of the report has been sent to the proposed allottee.

(2) For this purpose the application of an amount standing to the credit of—

(a) any of a company's reserve accounts, or

(b) its profit and loss account,

in paying up (to any extent) shares allotted to members of the company, or premiums on shares so allotted, does not count as consideration for the allotment.

Accordingly, subsection (1) does not apply in that case.

(3) If a company allots shares in contravention of subsection (1) and either—

(a) the allottee has not received the valuer's report required to be sent to him, or

(b) there has been some other contravention of the requirements of this section or section 596 that the allottee knew or ought to have known amounted to a contravention,

the allottee is liable to pay the company an amount equal to the aggregate of the nominal value of the shares and the whole of any premium (or, if the case so requires, so much of that aggregate as is treated as paid up by the consideration), with interest at the appropriate rate.

(4) This section has effect subject to—

section 594 (exception to valuation requirement: arrangement with another company), and

section 595 (exception to valuation requirement: merger).

### 594    Exception to valuation requirement: arrangement with another company

(1) Section 593 (valuation of non-cash consideration) does not apply to the allotment of shares by a company ('company A') in connection with an arrangement to which this section applies.

(2) This section applies to an arrangement for the allotment of shares in company A on terms that the whole or part of the consideration for the shares allotted is to be provided by—

(a) the transfer to that company, or

(b) the cancellation,

of all or some of the shares, or of all or some of the shares of a particular class, in another company ('company B').

(3) It is immaterial whether the arrangement provides for the issue to company A of shares, or shares of any particular class, in company B.

(4) This section applies to an arrangement only if under the arrangement it is open to all the holders of the shares in company B (or, where the arrangement applies only to shares of a particular class, to all the holders of shares of that class) to take part in the arrangement.

(5) In determining whether that is the case, the following shall be disregarded—

    (a) shares held by or by a nominee of company A;

    (b) shares held by or by a nominee of a company which is—

        (i) the holding company, or a subsidiary, of company A, or

        (ii) a subsidiary of such a holding company;

    (c) shares held as treasury shares by company B.

(6) In this section—

    (a) 'arrangement' means any agreement, scheme or arrangement (including an arrangement sanctioned in accordance with—

        (i) Part 26 (arrangements and reconstructions), or

        (ii) section 110 of the Insolvency Act 1986 (c. 45) or Article 96 of the Insolvency (Northern Ireland) Order 1989 (S.I. 1989/2405 (N.I. 19)) (liquidator in winding up accepting shares as consideration for sale of company property)), and

    (b) 'company', except in reference to company A, includes any body corporate.

## 595 Exception to valuation requirement: merger

(1) Section 593 (valuation of non-cash consideration) does not apply to the allotment of shares by a company in connection with a proposed merger with another company.

(2) A proposed merger is where one of the companies proposes to acquire all the assets and liabilities of the other in exchange for the issue of shares or other securities of that one to shareholders of the other, with or without any cash payment to shareholders.

(3) In this section 'company', in reference to the other company, includes any body corporate.

## 596 Non-cash consideration for shares: requirements as to valuation and report

(1) The provisions of sections 1150 to 1153 (general provisions as to independent valuation and report) apply to the valuation and report required by section 593 (public company: valuation of non-cash consideration for shares).

(2) The valuer's report must state—

    (a) the nominal value of the shares to be wholly or partly paid for by the consideration in question;

    (b) the amount of any premium payable on the shares;

    (c) the description of the consideration and, as respects so much of the consideration as he himself has valued, a description of that part of the consideration, the method used to value it and the date of the valuation;

    (d) the extent to which the nominal value of the shares and any premium are to be treated as paid up—

        (i) by the consideration;

        (ii) in cash.

(3) The valuer's report must contain or be accompanied by a note by him—

    (a) in the case of a valuation made by a person other than himself, that it appeared to himself reasonable to arrange for it to be so made or to accept a valuation so made,

    (b) whoever made the valuation, that the method of valuation was reasonable in all the circumstances,

    (c) that it appears to the valuer that there has been no material change in the value of the consideration in question since the valuation, and

    (d) that, on the basis of the valuation, the value of the consideration, together with any cash by which the nominal value of the shares or any premium payable on them is to be paid up, is not less than so much of the aggregate of the nominal value and the whole of any such premium as is treated as paid up by the consideration and any such cash.

(4) Where the consideration to be valued is accepted partly in payment up of the nominal value of the shares and any premium and partly for some other consideration given by the company, section 593 and the preceding provisions of this section apply as if references to the consideration accepted by the company included the proportion of that consideration that is properly attributable to the payment up of that value and any premium.

(5) In such a case—

    (a) the valuer must carry out, or arrange for, such other valuations as will enable him to determine that proportion, and

(b) his report must state what valuations have been made under this subsection and also the reason for, and method and date of, any such valuation and any other matters which may be relevant to that determination.

### 597 Copy of report to be delivered to registrar

(1) A company to which a report is made under section 593 as to the value of any consideration for which, or partly for which, it proposes to allot shares must deliver a copy of the report to the registrar for registration.

(2) The copy must be delivered at the same time that the company files the return of the allotment of those shares under section 555 (return of allotment by limited company).

(3) If default is made in complying with subsection (1) or (2), an offence is committed by every officer of the company who is in default.

(4) A person guilty of an offence under this section is liable—

(a) on conviction on indictment, to a fine;

(b) on summary conviction, to a fine not exceeding the statutory maximum and, for continued contravention, a daily default fine not exceeding one-tenth of the statutory maximum.

(5) In the case of default in delivering to the registrar any document as required by this section, any person liable for the default may apply to the court for relief.

(6) The court, if satisfied—

(a) that the omission to deliver the document was accidental or due to inadvertence, or

(b) that it is just and equitable to grant relief,

may make an order extending the time for delivery of the document for such period as the court thinks proper.

*Transfer of non-cash asset in initial period*

### 598 Public company: agreement for transfer of non-cash asset in initial period

(1) A public company formed as such must not enter into an agreement—

(a) with a person who is a subscriber to the company's memorandum,

(b) for the transfer by him to the company, or another, before the end of the company's initial period of one or more non-cash assets, and

(c) under which the consideration for the transfer to be given by the company is at the time of the agreement equal in value to one-tenth or more of the company's issued share capital,

unless the conditions referred to below have been complied with.

(2) The company's 'initial period' means the period of two years beginning with the date of the company being issued with a certificate under section 761 (trading certificate).

(3) The conditions are those specified in—

section 599 (requirement of independent valuation), and

section 601 (requirement of approval by members).

(4) This section does not apply where—

(a) it is part of the company's ordinary business to acquire, or arrange for other persons to acquire, assets of a particular description, and

(b) the agreement is entered into by the company in the ordinary course of that business.

(5) This section does not apply to an agreement entered into by the company under the supervision of the court or of an officer authorised by the court for the purpose.

### 599 Agreement for transfer of non-cash asset: requirement of independent valuation

(1) The following conditions must have been complied with—

(a) the consideration to be received by the company, and any consideration other than cash to be given by the company, must have been independently valued in accordance with the provisions of this Chapter,

(b) the valuer's report must have been made to the company during the six months immediately preceding the date of the agreement, and

(c) a copy of the report must have been sent to the other party to the proposed agreement not later than the date on which copies have to be circulated to members under section 601(3).

(2) The reference in subsection (1)(a) to the consideration to be received by the company is to the asset to be transferred to it or, as the case may be, to the advantage to the company of the asset's transfer to another person.

(3) The reference in subsection (1)(c) to the other party to the proposed agreement is to the person referred to in section 598(1)(a). If he has received a copy of the report under section 601 in his capacity as a member of the company, it is not necessary to send another copy under this section.

(4) This section does not affect any requirement to value any consideration for purposes of section 593 (valuation of non-cash consideration for shares).

### 600  Agreement for transfer of non-cash asset: requirements as to valuation and report

(1) The provisions of sections 1150 to 1153 (general provisions as to independent valuation and report) apply to the valuation and report required by section 599 (public company: transfer of non-cash asset).

(2) The valuer's report must state—

(a) the consideration to be received by the company, describing the asset in question (specifying the amount to be received in cash) and the consideration to be given by the company (specifying the amount to be given in cash), and

(b) the method and date of valuation.

(3) The valuer's report must contain or be accompanied by a note by him—

(a) in the case of a valuation made by a person other than himself, that it appeared to himself reasonable to arrange for it to be so made or to accept a valuation so made,

(b) whoever made the valuation, that the method of valuation was reasonable in all the circumstances,

(c) that it appears to the valuer that there has been no material change in the value of the consideration in question since the valuation, and

(d) that, on the basis of the valuation, the value of the consideration to be received by the company is not less than the value of the consideration to be given by it.

(4) Any reference in section 599 or this section to consideration given for the transfer of an asset includes consideration given partly for its transfer.

(5) In such a case—

(a) the value of any consideration partly so given is to be taken as the proportion of the consideration properly attributable to its transfer,

(b) the valuer must carry out or arrange for such valuations of anything else as will enable him to determine that proportion, and

(c) his report must state what valuations have been made for that purpose and also the reason for and method and date of any such valuation and any other matters which may be relevant to that determination.

### 601  Agreement for transfer of non-cash asset: requirement of approval by members

(1) The following conditions must have been complied with—

(a) the terms of the agreement must have been approved by an ordinary resolution of the company,

(b) the requirements of this section must have been complied with as respects the circulation to members of copies of the valuer's report under section 599, and

(c) a copy of the proposed resolution must have been sent to the other party to the proposed agreement.

(2) The reference in subsection (1)(c) to the other party to the proposed agreement is to the person referred to in section 598(1)(a).

(3) The requirements of this section as to circulation of copies of the valuer's report are as follows—

(a) if the resolution is proposed as a written resolution, copies of the valuer's report must be sent or submitted to every eligible member at or before the time at which the proposed resolution is sent or submitted to him;

(b) if the resolution is proposed at a general meeting, copies of the valuer's report must be circulated to the members entitled to notice of the meeting not later than the date on which notice of the meeting is given.

### 602  Copy of resolution to be delivered to registrar

(1) A company that has passed a resolution under section 601 with respect to the transfer of an asset must, within 15 days of doing so, deliver to the registrar a copy of the resolution together with the valuer's report required by that section.

(2) If a company fails to comply with subsection (1), an offence is committed by—

(a) the company, and

(b) every officer of the company who is in default.

(3) A person guilty of an offence under this section is liable on summary conviction to a fine not exceeding level 3 on the standard scale and, for continued contravention, to a daily default fine not exceeding one-tenth of level 3 on the standard scale.

### 603  Adaptation of provisions in relation to company re-registering as public

The provisions of sections 598 to 602 (public companies: transfer of non-cash assets) apply with the following adaptations in relation to a company re-registered as a public company—

(a) the reference in section 598(1)(a) to a person who is a subscriber to the company's memorandum shall be read as a reference to a person who is a member of the company on the date of re-registration;

(b) the reference in section 598(2) to the date of the company being issued with a certificate under section 761 (trading certificate) shall be read as a reference to the date of re-registration.

### 604   Agreement for transfer of non-cash asset: effect of contravention

(1) This section applies where a public company enters into an agreement in contravention of section 598 and either—

    (a) the other party to the agreement has not received the valuer's report required to be sent to him, or

    (b) there has been some other contravention of the requirements of this Chapter that the other party to the agreement knew or ought to have known amounted to a contravention.

(2) In those circumstances—

    (a) the company is entitled to recover from that person any consideration given by it under the agreement, or an amount equal to the value of the consideration at the time of the agreement, and

    (b) the agreement, so far as not carried out, is void.

(3) If the agreement is or includes an agreement for the allotment of shares in the company, then—

    (a) whether or not the agreement also contravenes section 593 (valuation of non-cash consideration for shares), this section does not apply to it in so far as it is for the allotment of shares, and

    (b) the allottee is liable to pay the company an amount equal to the aggregate of the nominal value of the shares and the whole of any premium (or, if the case so requires, so much of that aggregate as is treated as paid up by the consideration), with interest at the appropriate rate.

*Supplementary provisions*

### 605   Liability of subsequent holders of shares

(1) If a person becomes a holder of shares in respect of which—

    (a) there has been a contravention of section 593 (public company: valuation of non-cash consideration for shares), and

    (b) by virtue of that contravention another is liable to pay any amount under the provision contravened,

that person is also liable to pay that amount (jointly and severally with any other person so liable), unless he is exempted from liability under subsection (3) below.

(2) If a company enters into an agreement in contravention of section 598 (public company: agreement for transfer of non-cash asset in initial period) and—

    (a) the agreement is or includes an agreement for the allotment of shares in the company,

    (b) a person becomes a holder of shares allotted under the agreement, and

    (c) by virtue of the agreement and allotment under it another person is liable to pay an amount under section 604,

the person who becomes the holder of the shares is also liable to pay that amount (jointly and severally with any other person so liable), unless he is exempted from liability under subsection (3) below.

This applies whether or not the agreement also contravenes section 593.

(3) A person otherwise liable under subsection (1) or (2) is exempted from that liability if either—

    (a) he is a purchaser for value and, at the time of the purchase, he did not have actual notice of the contravention concerned, or

    (b) he derived title to the shares (directly or indirectly) from a person who became a holder of them after the contravention and was not liable under subsection (1) or (2).

(4) References in this section to a holder, in relation to shares in a company, include any person who has an unconditional right—

    (a) to be included in the company's register of members in respect of those shares, or

    (b) to have an instrument of transfer of the shares executed in his favour.

### 606   Power of court to grant relief

(1) A person who—

    (a) is liable to a company under any provision of this Chapter in relation to payment in respect of any shares in the company, or

    (b) is liable to a company by virtue of an undertaking given to it in, or in connection with, payment for any shares in the company,

may apply to the court to be exempted in whole or in part from the liability.

(2) In the case of a liability within subsection (1)(a), the court may exempt the applicant from the liability only if and to the extent that it appears to the court just and equitable to do so having regard to—

    (a) whether the applicant has paid, or is liable to pay, any amount in respect of—

        (i) any other liability arising in relation to those shares under any provision of this Chapter or Chapter 5, or

        (ii)  any liability arising by virtue of any undertaking given in or in connection with payment for those shares;

    (b)  whether any person other than the applicant has paid or is likely to pay, whether in pursuance of any order of the court or otherwise, any such amount;

    (c)  whether the applicant or any other person—

        (i)  has performed in whole or in part, or is likely so to perform any such undertaking, or

        (ii)  has done or is likely to do any other thing in payment or part payment for the shares.

(3)  In the case of a liability within subsection (1)(b), the court may exempt the applicant from the liability only if and to the extent that it appears to the court just and equitable to do so having regard to—

    (a)  whether the applicant has paid or is liable to pay any amount in respect of liability arising in relation to the shares under any provision of this Chapter or Chapter 5;

    (b)  whether any person other than the applicant has paid or is likely to pay, whether in pursuance of any order of the court or otherwise, any such amount.

(4)  In determining whether it should exempt the applicant in whole or in part from any liability, the court must have regard to the following overriding principles—

    (a)  that a company that has allotted shares should receive money or money's worth at least equal in value to the aggregate of the nominal value of those shares and the whole of any premium or, if the case so requires, so much of that aggregate as is treated as paid up;

    (b)  subject to this, that where such a company would, if the court did not grant the exemption, have more than one remedy against a particular person, it should be for the company to decide which remedy it should remain entitled to pursue.

(5)  If a person brings proceedings against another ('the contributor') for a contribution in respect of liability to a company arising under any provision of this Chapter or Chapter 5 and it appears to the court that the contributor is liable to make such a contribution, the court may, if and to the extent that it appears to it, just and equitable to do so having regard to the respective culpability (in respect of the liability to the company) of the contributor and the person bringing the proceedings—

    (a)  exempt the contributor in whole or in part from his liability to make such a contribution, or

    (b)  order the contributor to make a larger contribution than, but for this subsection, he would be liable to make.

(6)  Where a person is liable to a company under section 604(2) (agreement for transfer of non-cash asset: effect of contravention), the court may, on application, exempt him in whole or in part from that liability if and to the extent that it appears to the court to be just and equitable to do so having regard to any benefit accruing to the company by virtue of anything done by him towards the carrying out of the agreement mentioned in that subsection.

### 607  Penalty for contravention of this Chapter

(1)  This section applies where a company contravenes—

section 593 (public company allotting shares for non-cash consideration), or

section 598 (public company entering into agreement for transfer of non-cash asset).

(2)  An offence is committed by—

    (a)  the company, and

    (b)  every officer of the company who is in default.

(3)  A person guilty of an offence under this section is liable—

    (a)  on conviction on indictment, to a fine;

    (b)  on summary conviction, to a fine not exceeding the statutory maximum.

### 608  Enforceability of undertakings to do work etc.

(1)  An undertaking given by any person, in or in connection with payment for shares in a company, to do work or perform services or to do any other thing, if it is enforceable by the company apart from this Chapter, is so enforceable notwithstanding that there has been a contravention in relation to it of a provision of this Chapter or Chapter 5.

(2)  This is without prejudice to section 606 (power of court to grant relief etc. in respect of liabilities).

### 609  The appropriate rate of interest

(1)  For the purposes of this Chapter the 'appropriate rate' of interest is 5% per annum or such other rate as may be specified by order made by the Secretary of State.

(2)  An order under this section is subject to negative resolution procedure.

## Chapter 7  Share premiums

*The share premium account*

### 610  Application of share premiums

(1)  If a company issues shares at a premium, whether for cash or otherwise, a sum equal to the aggregate amount or value of the premiums on those shares must be transferred to an account called 'the share premium account'.

(2) Where, on issuing shares, a company has transferred a sum to the share premium account, it may use that sum to write off—

(a) the expenses of the issue of those shares;

(b) any commission paid on the issue of those shares.

(3) The company may use the share premium account to pay up new shares to be allotted to members as fully paid bonus shares.

(4) Subject to subsections (2) and (3), the provisions of the Companies Acts relating to the reduction of a company's share capital apply as if the share premium account were part of its paid up share capital.

(5) This section has effect subject to—

section 611 (group reconstruction relief);

section 612 (merger relief);

section 614 (power to make further provisions by regulations).

(6) In this Chapter 'the issuing company' means the company issuing shares as mentioned in subsection (1) above.

*Relief from requirements as to share premiums*

### 611 Group reconstruction relief

(1) This section applies where the issuing company—

(a) is a wholly-owned subsidiary of another company ('the holding company'), and

(b) allots shares—

(i) to the holding company, or

(ii) to another wholly-owned subsidiary of the holding company,

in consideration for the transfer to the issuing company of non-cash assets of a company ('the transferor company') that is a member of the group of companies that comprises the holding company and all its wholly-owned subsidiaries.

(2) Where the shares in the issuing company allotted in consideration for the transfer are issued at a premium, the issuing company is not required by section 610 to transfer any amount in excess of the minimum premium value to the share premium account.

(3) The minimum premium value means the amount (if any) by which the base value of the consideration for the shares allotted exceeds the aggregate nominal value of the shares.

(4) The base value of the consideration for the shares allotted is the amount by which the base value of the assets transferred exceeds the base value of any liabilities of the transferor company assumed by the issuing company as part of the consideration for the assets transferred.

(5) For the purposes of this section—

(a) the base value of assets transferred is taken as—

(i) the cost of those assets to the transferor company, or

(ii) if less, the amount at which those assets are stated in the transferor company's accounting records immediately before the transfer;

(b) the base value of the liabilities assumed is taken as the amount at which they are stated in the transferor company's accounting records immediately before the transfer.

### 612 Merger relief

(1) This section applies where the issuing company has secured at least a 90% equity holding in another company in pursuance of an arrangement providing for the allotment of equity shares in the issuing company on terms that the consideration for the shares allotted is to be provided—

(a) by the issue or transfer to the issuing company of equity shares in the other company, or

(b) by the cancellation of any such shares not held by the issuing company.

(2) If the equity shares in the issuing company allotted in pursuance of the arrangement in consideration for the acquisition or cancellation of equity shares in the other company are issued at a premium, section 610 does not apply to the premiums on those shares.

(3) Where the arrangement also provides for the allotment of any shares in the issuing company on terms that the consideration for those shares is to be provided—

(a) by the issue or transfer to the issuing company of non-equity shares in the other company, or

(b) by the cancellation of any such shares in that company not held by the issuing company,

relief under subsection (2) extends to any shares in the issuing company allotted on those terms in pursuance of the arrangement.

(4) This section does not apply in a case falling within section 611 (group reconstruction relief).

### 613 Merger relief: meaning of 90% equity holding

(1) The following provisions have effect to determine for the purposes of section 612 (merger relief) whether a company ('company A') has secured at least a 90% equity holding in another company ('company B') in pursuance of such an arrangement as is mentioned in subsection (1) of that section.

(2) Company A has secured at least a 90% equity holding in company B if in consequence of an acquisition or cancellation of equity shares in company B (in pursuance of that arrangement) it holds

equity shares in company B of an aggregate amount equal to 90% or more of the nominal value of that company's equity share capital.

(3) For this purpose—

    (a) it is immaterial whether any of those shares were acquired in pursuance of the arrangement; and

    (b) shares in company B held by the company as treasury shares are excluded in determining the nominal value of company B's share capital.

(4) Where the equity share capital of company B is divided into different classes of shares, company A is not regarded as having secured at least a 90% equity holding in company B unless the requirements of subsection (2) are met in relation to each of those classes of shares taken separately.

(5) For the purposes of this section shares held by—

    (a) a company that is company A's holding company or subsidiary, or

    (b) a subsidiary of company A's holding company, or

    (c) its or their nominees,

are treated as held by company A.

### 614 Power to make further provision by regulations

(1) The Secretary of State may by regulations make such provision as he thinks appropriate—

    (a) for relieving companies from the requirements of section 610 (application of share premiums) in relation to premiums other than cash premiums;

    (b) for restricting or otherwise modifying any relief from those requirements provided by this Chapter.

(2) Regulations under this section are subject to affirmative resolution procedure.

### 615 Relief may be reflected in company's balance sheet

An amount corresponding to the amount representing the premiums, or part of the premiums, on shares issued by a company that by virtue of any relief under this Chapter is not included in the company's share premium account may also be disregarded in determining the amount at which any shares or other consideration provided for the shares issued is to be included in the company's balance sheet.

*Supplementary provisions*

### 616 Interpretation of this Chapter

(1) In this Chapter—

'arrangement' means any agreement, scheme or arrangement (including an arrangement sanctioned in accordance with—

    (a) Part 26 (arrangements and reconstructions), or

    (b) section 110 of the Insolvency Act 1986 (c. 45) or Article 96 of the Insolvency (Northern Ireland) Order 1989 (S.I. 1989/2405 (N.I. 19)) (liquidator in winding up accepting shares as consideration for sale of company property));

'company', except in reference to the issuing company, includes any body corporate;

'equity shares' means shares comprised in a company's equity share capital, and 'non-equity shares' means shares (of any class) that are not so comprised;

'the issuing company' has the meaning given by section 610(6).

(2) References in this Chapter (however expressed) to—

    (a) the acquisition by a company of shares in another company, and

    (b) the issue or allotment of shares to, or the transfer of shares to or by, a company,

include (respectively) the acquisition of shares by, and the issue or allotment or transfer of shares to or by, a nominee of that company.

The reference in section 611 to the transferor company shall be read accordingly.

(3) References in this Chapter to the transfer of shares in a company include the transfer of a right to be included in the company's register of members in respect of those shares.

## Chapter 8 Alteration of share capital

*How share capital may be altered*

### 617 Alteration of share capital of limited company

(1) A limited company having a share capital may not alter its share capital except in the following ways.

(2) The company may—

    (a) increase its share capital by allotting new shares in accordance with this Part, or

    (b) reduce its share capital in accordance with Chapter 10.

(3) The company may—

    (a) sub-divide or consolidate all or any of its share capital in accordance with section 618, or

    (b) reconvert stock into shares in accordance with section 620.

(4) The company may redenominate all or any of its shares in accordance with section 622, and may reduce its share capital in accordance with section 626 in connection with such a redenomination.

(5) Nothing in this section affects—

    (a) the power of a company to purchase its own shares, or to redeem shares, in accordance with Part 18;

    (b) the power of a company to purchase its own shares in pursuance of an order of the court under—

        (i) section 98 (application to court to cancel resolution for re-registration as a private company),

        (ii) section 721(6) (powers of court on objection to redemption or purchase of shares out of capital),

        (iii) section 759 (remedial order in case of breach of prohibition of public offers by private company), or

        (iv) Part 30 (protection of members against unfair prejudice);

    (c) the forfeiture of shares, or the acceptance of shares surrendered in lieu, in pursuance of the company's articles, for failure to pay any sum payable in respect of the shares;

    (d) the cancellation of shares under section 662 (duty to cancel shares held by or for a public company);

    (e) the power of a company—

        (i) to enter into a compromise or arrangement in accordance with Part 26 (arrangements and reconstructions), or

        (ii) to do anything required to comply with an order of the court on an application under that Part.

*Sub-division or consolidation of shares*

### 618    Sub-division or consolidation of shares

(1) A limited company having a share capital may—

    (a) sub-divide its shares, or any of them, into shares of a smaller nominal amount than its existing shares, or

    (b) consolidate and divide all or any of its share capital into shares of a larger nominal amount than its existing shares.

(2) In any sub-division, consolidation or division of shares under this section, the proportion between the amount paid and the amount (if any) unpaid on each resulting share must be the same as it was in the case of the share from which that share is derived.

(3) A company may exercise a power conferred by this section only if its members have passed a resolution authorising it to do so.

(4) A resolution under subsection (3) may authorise a company—

    (a) to exercise more than one of the powers conferred by this section;

    (b) to exercise a power on more than one occasion;

    (c) to exercise a power at a specified time or in specified circumstances.

(5) The company's articles may exclude or restrict the exercise of any power conferred by this section.

### 619    Notice to registrar of sub-division or consolidation

(1) If a company exercises the power conferred by section 618 (sub-division or consolidation of shares) it must within one month after doing so give notice to the registrar, specifying the shares affected.

(2) The notice must be accompanied by a statement of capital.

(3) The statement of capital must state with respect to the company's share capital immediately following the exercise of the power—

    (a) the total number of shares of the company,

    (b) the aggregate nominal value of those shares,

    (c) for each class of shares—

        (i) prescribed particulars of the rights attached to the shares,

        (ii) the total number of shares of that class, and

        (iii) the aggregate nominal value of shares of that class, and

    (d) the amount paid up and the amount (if any) unpaid on each share (whether on account of the nominal value of the share or by way of premium).

(4) If default is made in complying with this section, an offence is committed by—

    (a) the company, and

    (b) every officer of the company who is in default.

(5) A person guilty of an offence under this section is liable on summary conviction to a fine not exceeding level 3 on the standard scale and, for continued contravention, a daily default fine not exceeding one-tenth of level 3 on the standard scale.

*Reconversion of stock into shares*

### 620    Reconversion of stock into shares

(1) A limited company that has converted paid-up shares into stock (before the repeal by this Act of the power to do so) may reconvert that stock into paid-up shares of any nominal value.

(2)  A company may exercise the power conferred by this section only if its members have passed an ordinary resolution authorising it to do so.

(3)  A resolution under subsection (2) may authorise a company to exercise the power conferred by this section—

  (a)  on more than one occasion;

  (b)  at a specified time or in specified circumstances.

### 621   Notice to registrar of reconversion of stock into shares

(1)  If a company exercises a power conferred by section 620 (reconversion of stock into shares) it must within one month after doing so give notice to the registrar, specifying the stock affected.

(2)  The notice must be accompanied by a statement of capital.

(3)  The statement of capital must state with respect to the company's share capital immediately following the exercise of the power—

  (a)  the total number of shares of the company,

  (b)  the aggregate nominal value of those shares,

  (c)  for each class of shares—

    (i)    prescribed particulars of the rights attached to the shares,

    (ii)   the total number of shares of that class, and

    (iii)  the aggregate nominal value of shares of that class, and

  (d)  the amount paid up and the amount (if any) unpaid on each share (whether on account of the nominal value of the share or by way of premium).

(4)  If default is made in complying with this section, an offence is committed by—

  (a)  the company, and

  (b)  very officer of the company who is in default.

(5)  A person guilty of an offence under this section is liable on summary conviction to a fine not exceeding level 3 on the standard scale and, for continued contravention, a daily default fine not exceeding one-tenth of level 3 on the standard scale.

*Redenomination of share capital*

### 622   Redenomination of share capital

(1)  A limited company having a share capital may by resolution redenominate its share capital or any class of its share capital.

'Redenominate' means convert shares from having a fixed nominal value in one currency to having a fixed nominal value in another currency.

(2)  The conversion must be made at an appropriate spot rate of exchange specified in the resolution.

(3)  The rate must be either—

  (a)  a rate prevailing on a day specified in the resolution, or

  (b)  a rate determined by taking the average of rates prevailing on each consecutive day of a period specified in the resolution.

The day or period specified for the purposes of paragraph (a) or (b) must be within the period of 28 days ending on the day before the resolution is passed.

(4)  A resolution under this section may specify conditions which must be met before the redenomination takes effect.

(5)  Redenomination in accordance with a resolution under this section takes effect—

  (a)  on the day on which the resolution is passed, or

  (b)  on such later day as may be determined in accordance with the resolution.

(6)  A resolution under this section lapses if the redenomination for which it provides has not taken effect at the end of the period of 28 days beginning on the date on which it is passed.

(7)  A company's articles may prohibit or restrict the exercise of the power conferred by this section.

(8)  Chapter 3 of Part 3 (resolutions affecting a company's constitution) applies to a resolution under this section.

### 623   Calculation of new nominal values

For each class of share the new nominal value of each share is calculated as follows:

*Step One*

Take the aggregate of the old nominal values of all the shares of that class.

*Step Two*

Translate that amount into the new currency at the rate of exchange specified in the resolution.

*Step Three*

Divide that amount by the number of shares in the class.

### 624   Effect of redenomination

(1)  The redenomination of shares does not affect any rights or obligations of members under the company's constitution, or any restrictions affecting members under the company's constitution.

In particular, it does not affect entitlement to dividends (including entitlement to dividends in a particular currency), voting rights or any liability in respect of amounts unpaid on shares.

(2) For this purpose the company's constitution includes the terms on which any shares of the company are allotted or held.

(3) Subject to subsection (1), references to the old nominal value of the shares in any agreement or statement, or in any deed, instrument or document, shall (unless the context otherwise requires) be read after the resolution takes effect as references to the new nominal value of the shares.

### 625   Notice to registrar of redenomination

(1) If a limited company having a share capital redenominates any of its share capital, it must within one month after doing so give notice to the registrar, specifying the shares redenominated.

(2) The notice must—

(a) state the date on which the resolution was passed, and

(b) be accompanied by a statement of capital.

(3) The statement of capital must state with respect to the company's share capital as redenominated by the resolution—

(a) the total number of shares of the company,

(b) the aggregate nominal value of those shares,

(c) for each class of shares—

(i)   prescribed particulars of the rights attached to the shares,

(ii)   the total number of shares of that class, and

(iii)   the aggregate nominal value of shares of that class, and

(d) the amount paid up and the amount (if any) unpaid on each share (whether on account of the nominal value of the share or by way of premium).

(4) If default is made in complying with this section, an offence is committed by—

(a) the company, and

(b) every officer of the company who is in default.

(5) A person guilty of an offence under this section is liable on summary conviction to a fine not exceeding level 3 on the standard scale and, for continued contravention, a daily default fine not exceeding one-tenth of level 3 on the standard scale.

### 626   Reduction of capital in connection with redenomination

(1) A limited company that passes a resolution redenominating some or all of its shares may, for the purpose of adjusting the nominal values of the redenominated shares to obtain values that are, in the opinion of the company, more suitable, reduce its share capital under this section.

(2) A reduction of capital under this section requires a special resolution of the company.

(3) Any such resolution must be passed within three months of the resolution effecting the redenomination.

(4) The amount by which a company's share capital is reduced under this section must not exceed 10% of the nominal value of the company's allotted share capital immediately after the reduction.

(5) A reduction of capital under this section does not extinguish or reduce any liability in respect of share capital not paid up.

(6) Nothing in Chapter 10 applies to a reduction of capital under this section.

### 627   Notice to registrar of reduction of capital in connection with redenomination

(1) A company that passes a resolution under section 626 (reduction of capital in connection with redenomination) must within 15 days after the resolution is passed give notice to the registrar stating—

(a) the date of the resolution, and

(b) the date of the resolution under section 622 in connection with which it was passed.

This is in addition to the copies of the resolutions themselves that are required to be delivered to the registrar under Chapter 3 of Part 3.

(2) The notice must be accompanied by a statement of capital.

(3) The statement of capital must state with respect to the company's share capital as reduced by the resolution—

(a) the total number of shares of the company,

(b) the aggregate nominal value of those shares,

(c) for each class of shares—

(i)   prescribed particulars of the rights attached to the shares,

(ii)   the total number of shares of that class, and

(iii)   the aggregate nominal value of shares of that class, and

(d) the amount paid up and the amount (if any) unpaid on each share (whether on account of the nominal value of the share or by way of premium).

(4) The registrar must register the notice and the statement on receipt.

(5) The reduction of capital is not effective until those documents are registered.

(6) The company must also deliver to the registrar, within 15 days after the resolution is passed, a statement by the directors confirming that the reduction in share capital is in accordance with section 626(4) (reduction of capital not to exceed 10% of nominal value of allotted shares immediately after reduction).

(7) If default is made in complying with this section, an offence is committed by—

(a) the company, and

(b) every officer of the company who is in default.

(8) A person guilty of an offence under this section is liable—

(a) on conviction on indictment to a fine, and

(b) on summary conviction to a fine not exceeding the statutory maximum.

### 628  Redenomination reserve

(1) The amount by which a company's share capital is reduced under section 626 (reduction of capital in connection with redenomination) must be transferred to a reserve, called 'the redenomination reserve'.

(2) The redenomination reserve may be applied by the company in paying up shares to be allotted to members as fully paid bonus shares.

(3) Subject to that, the provisions of the Companies Acts relating to the reduction of a company's share capital apply as if the redenomination reserve were paid-up share capital of the company.

## Chapter 9  Classes of share and class rights

### *Introductory*

### 629  Classes of shares

(1) For the purposes of the Companies Acts shares are of one class if the rights attached to them are in all respects uniform.

(2) For this purpose the rights attached to shares are not regarded as different from those attached to other shares by reason only that they do not carry the same rights to dividends in the twelve months immediately following their allotment.

### *Variation of class rights*

### 630  Variation of class rights: companies having a share capital

(1) This section is concerned with the variation of the rights attached to a class of shares in a company having a share capital.

(2) Rights attached to a class of a company's shares may only be varied—

(a) in accordance with provision in the company's articles for the variation of those rights, or

(b) where the company's articles contain no such provision, if the holders of shares of that class consent to the variation in accordance with this section.

(3) This is without prejudice to any other restrictions on the variation of the rights.

(4) The consent required for the purposes of this section on the part of the holders of a class of a company's shares is—

(a) consent in writing from the holders of at least three-quarters in nominal value of the issued shares of that class (excluding any shares held as treasury shares), or

(b) a special resolution passed at a separate general meeting of the holders of that class sanctioning the variation.

(5) Any amendment of a provision contained in a company's articles for the variation of the rights attached to a class of shares, or the insertion of any such provision into the articles, is itself to be treated as a variation of those rights.

(6) In this section, and (except where the context otherwise requires) in any provision in a company's articles for the variation of the rights attached to a class of shares, references to the variation of those rights include references to their abrogation.

### 631  Variation of class rights: companies without a share capital

(1) This section is concerned with the variation of the rights of a class of members of a company where the company does not have a share capital.

(2) Rights of a class of members may only be varied—

(a) in accordance with provision in the company's articles for the variation of those rights, or

(b) where the company's articles contain no such provision, if the members of that class consent to the variation in accordance with this section.

(3) This is without prejudice to any other restrictions on the variation of the rights.

(4) The consent required for the purposes of this section on the part of the members of a class is—

(a) consent in writing from at least three-quarters of the members of the class, or

(b) a special resolution passed at a separate general meeting of the members of that class sanctioning the variation.

(5) Any amendment of a provision contained in a company's articles for the variation of the rights of a class of members, or the insertion of any such provision into the articles, is itself to be treated as a variation of those rights.

(6) In this section, and (except where the context otherwise requires) in any provision in a company's articles for the variation of the rights of a class of members, references to the variation of those rights include references to their abrogation.

### 632   Variation of class rights: saving for court's powers under other provisions

Nothing in section 630 or 631 (variation of class rights) affects the power of the court under—

section 98 (application to cancel resolution for public company to be re-registered as private),

Part 26 (arrangements and reconstructions), or

Part 30 (protection of members against unfair prejudice).

### 633   Right to object to variation: companies having a share capital

(1) This section applies where the rights attached to any class of shares in a company are varied under section 630 (variation of class rights: companies having a share capital).

(2) The holders of not less in the aggregate than 15% of the issued shares of the class in question (being persons who did not consent to or vote in favour of the resolution for the variation) may apply to the court to have the variation cancelled.

For this purpose any of the company's share capital held as treasury shares is disregarded.

(3) If such an application is made, the variation has no effect unless and until it is confirmed by the court.

(4) Application to the court—

    (a) must be made within 21 days after the date on which the consent was given or the resolution was passed (as the case may be), and

    (b) may be made on behalf of the shareholders entitled to make the application by such one or more of their number as they may appoint in writing for the purpose.

(5) The court, after hearing the applicant and any other persons who apply to the court to be heard and appear to the court to be interested in the application, may, if satisfied having regard to all the circumstances of the case that the variation would unfairly prejudice the shareholders of the class represented by the applicant, disallow the variation, and shall if not so satisfied confirm it.

The decision of the court on any such application is final.

(6) References in this section to the variation of the rights of holders of a class of shares include references to their abrogation.

### 634   Right to object to variation: companies without a share capital

(1) This section applies where the rights of any class of members of a company are varied under section 631 (variation of class rights: companies without a share capital).

(2) Members amounting to not less than 15% of the members of the class in question (being persons who did not consent to or vote in favour of the resolution for the variation) may apply to the court to have the variation cancelled.

(3) If such an application is made, the variation has no effect unless and until it is confirmed by the court.

(4) Application to the court must be made within 21 days after the date on which the consent was given or the resolution was passed (as the case may be) and may be made on behalf of the members entitled to make the application by such one or more of their number as they may appoint in writing for the purpose.

(5) The court, after hearing the applicant and any other persons who apply to the court to be heard and appear to the court to be interested in the application, may, if satisfied having regard to all the circumstances of the case that the variation would unfairly prejudice the members of the class represented by the applicant, disallow the variation, and shall if not so satisfied confirm it.

The decision of the court on any such application is final.

(6) References in this section to the variation of the rights of a class of members include references to their abrogation.

### 635   Copy of court order to be forwarded to the registrar

(1) The company must within 15 days after the making of an order by the court on an application under section 633 or 634 (objection to variation of class rights) forward a copy of the order to the registrar.

(2) If default is made in complying with this section an offence is committed by—

    (a) the company, and

    (b) every officer of the company who is in default.

(3) A person guilty of an offence under this section is liable on summary conviction to a fine not exceeding level 3 on the standard scale and, for continued contravention, a daily default fine not exceeding one-tenth of level 3 on the standard scale.

*Matters to be notified to the registrar*

### 636   Notice of name or other designation of class of shares

(1) Where a company assigns a name or other designation, or a new name or other designation, to any class or description of its shares, it must within one month from doing so deliver to the registrar a notice giving particulars of the name or designation so assigned.

(2) If default is made in complying with this section, an offence is committed by—
  (a) the company, and
  (b) every officer of the company who is in default.

(3) A person guilty of an offence under this section is liable on summary conviction to a fine not exceeding level 3 on the standard scale and, for continued contravention, a daily default fine not exceeding one-tenth of level 3 on the standard scale.

### 637 Notice of particulars of variation of rights attached to shares

(1) Where the rights attached to any shares of a company are varied, the company must within one month from the date on which the variation is made deliver to the registrar a notice giving particulars of the variation.

(2) If default is made in complying with this section, an offence is committed by—
  (a) the company, and
  (b) every officer of the company who is in default.

(3) A person guilty of an offence under this section is liable on summary conviction to a fine not exceeding level 3 on the standard scale and, for continued contravention, a daily default fine not exceeding one-tenth of level 3 on the standard scale.

### 638 Notice of new class of members

(1) If a company not having a share capital creates a new class of members, the company must within one month from the date on which the new class is created deliver to the registrar a notice containing particulars of the rights attached to that class.

(2) If default is made in complying with this section, an offence is committed by—
  (a) the company, and
  (b) every officer of the company who is in default.

(3) A person guilty of an offence under this section is liable on summary conviction to a fine not exceeding level 3 on the standard scale and, for continued contravention, a daily default fine not exceeding one-tenth of level 3 on the standard scale.

### 639 Notice of name or other designation of class of members

(1) Where a company not having a share capital assigns a name or other designation, or a new name or other designation, to any class of its members, it must within one month from doing so deliver to the registrar a notice giving particulars of the name or designation so assigned.

(2) If default is made in complying with this section, an offence is committed by—
  (a) the company, and
  (b) every officer of the company who is in default.

(3) A person guilty of an offence under this section is liable on summary conviction to a fine not exceeding level 3 on the standard scale and, for continued contravention, a daily default fine not exceeding one-tenth of level 3 on the standard scale.

### 640 Notice of particulars of variation of class rights

(1) If the rights of any class of members of a company not having a share capital are varied, the company must within one month from the date on which the variation is made deliver to the registrar a notice containing particulars of the variation.

(2) If default is made in complying with this section, an offence is committed by—
  (a) the company, and
  (b) every officer of the company who is in default.

(3) A person guilty of an offence under this section is liable on summary conviction to a fine not exceeding level 3 on the standard scale and, for continued contravention, a daily default fine not exceeding one-tenth of level 3 on the standard scale.

## Chapter 10  Reduction of share capital

### *Introductory*

### 641 Circumstances in which a company may reduce its share capital

(1) A limited company having a share capital may reduce its share capital—
  (a) in the case of a private company limited by shares, by special resolution supported by a solvency statement (see sections 642 to 644);
  (b) in any case, by special resolution confirmed by the court (see sections 645 to 651).

(2) A company may not reduce its capital under subsection (1)(a) if as a result of the reduction there would no longer be any member of the company holding shares other than redeemable shares.

(3) Subject to that, a company may reduce its share capital under this section in any way.

(4) In particular, a company may—
  (a) extinguish or reduce the liability on any of its shares in respect of share capital not paid up, or
  (b) either with or without extinguishing or reducing liability on any of its shares—
    (i) cancel any paid-up share capital that is lost or unrepresented by available assets, or
    (ii) repay any paid-up share capital in excess of the company's wants.

(5) A special resolution under this section may not provide for a reduction of share capital to take effect later than the date on which the resolution has effect in accordance with this Chapter.

(6) This Chapter (apart from subsection (5) above) has effect subject to any provision of the company's articles restricting or prohibiting the reduction of the company's share capital.

*Private companies: reduction of capital supported by solvency statement*

### 642 Reduction of capital supported by solvency statement

(1) A resolution for reducing share capital of a private company limited by shares is supported by a solvency statement if—

(a) the directors of the company make a statement of the solvency of the company in accordance with section 643 (a 'solvency statement') not more than 15 days before the date on which the resolution is passed, and

(b) the resolution and solvency statement are registered in accordance with section 644.

(2) Where the resolution is proposed as a written resolution, a copy of the solvency statement must be sent or submitted to every eligible member at or before the time at which the proposed resolution is sent or submitted to him.

(3) Where the resolution is proposed at a general meeting, a copy of the solvency statement must be made available for inspection by members of the company throughout that meeting.

(4) The validity of a resolution is not affected by a failure to comply with subsection (2) or (3).

### 643 Solvency statement

(1) A solvency statement is a statement that each of the directors—

(a) has formed the opinion, as regards the company's situation at the date of the statement, that there is no ground on which the company could then be found to be unable to pay (or otherwise discharge) its debts; and

(b) has also formed the opinion—

(i) if it is intended to commence the winding up of the company within twelve months of that date, that the company will be able to pay (or otherwise discharge) its debts in full within twelve months of the commencement of the winding up; or

(ii) in any other case, that the company will be able to pay (or otherwise discharge) its debts as they fall due during the year immediately following that date.

(2) In forming those opinions, the directors must take into account all of the company's liabilities (including any contingent or prospective liabilities).

(3) The solvency statement must be in the prescribed form and must state—

(a) the date on which it is made, and

(b) the name of each director of the company.

(4) If the directors make a solvency statement without having reasonable grounds for the opinions expressed in it, and the statement is delivered to the registrar, an offence is committed by every director who is in default.

(5) A person guilty of an offence under subsection (4) is liable—

(a) on conviction on indictment, to imprisonment for a term not exceeding two years or a fine (or both);

(b) on summary conviction—

(i) in England and Wales, to imprisonment for a term not exceeding twelve months or to a fine not exceeding the statutory maximum (or both);

(ii) in Scotland or Northern Ireland, to imprisonment for a term not exceeding six months, or to a fine not exceeding the statutory maximum (or both).

### 644 Registration of resolution and supporting documents

(1) Within 15 days after the resolution for reducing share capital is passed the company must deliver to the registrar—

(a) a copy of the solvency statement, and

(b) a statement of capital.

This is in addition to the copy of the resolution itself that is required to be delivered to the registrar under Chapter 3 of Part 3.

(2) The statement of capital must state with respect to the company's share capital as reduced by the resolution—

(a) the total number of shares of the company,

(b) the aggregate nominal value of those shares,

(c) for each class of shares—

(i) prescribed particulars of the rights attached to the shares,

(ii) the total number of shares of that class, and

(iii) the aggregate nominal value of shares of that class, and

(d) the amount paid up and the amount (if any) unpaid on each share (whether on account of the nominal value of the share or by way of premium).

(3) The registrar must register the documents delivered to him under subsection (1) on receipt.

(4) The resolution does not take effect until those documents are registered.

(5) The company must also deliver to the registrar, within 15 days after the resolution is passed, a statement by the directors confirming that the solvency statement was—

(a) made not more than 15 days before the date on which the resolution was passed, and

(b) provided to members in accordance with section 642(2) or (3).

(6) The validity of a resolution is not affected by—

(a) a failure to deliver the documents required to be delivered to the registrar under subsection (1) within the time specified in that subsection, or

(b) a failure to comply with subsection (5).

(7) If the company delivers to the registrar a solvency statement that was not provided to members in accordance with section 642(2) or (3), an offence is committed by every officer of the company who is in default.

(8) If default is made in complying with this section, an offence is committed by—

(a) the company, and

(b) every officer of the company who is in default.

(9) A person guilty of an offence under subsection (7) or (8) is liable—

(a) on conviction on indictment, to a fine;

(b) on summary conviction, to a fine not exceeding the statutory maximum.

### *Reduction of capital confirmed by the court*

### 645 Application to court for order of confirmation

(1) Where a company has passed a resolution for reducing share capital, it may apply to the court for an order confirming the reduction.

(2) If the proposed reduction of capital involves either—

(a) diminution of liability in respect of unpaid share capital, or

(b) the payment to a shareholder of any paid-up share capital,

section 646 (creditors entitled to object to reduction) applies unless the court directs otherwise.

(3) The court may, if having regard to any special circumstances of the case it thinks proper to do so, direct that section 646 is not to apply as regards any class or classes of creditors.

(4) The court may direct that section 646 is to apply in any other case.

### 646 Creditors entitled to object to reduction

(1) Where this section applies (see section 645(2) and (4)), every creditor of the company who at the date fixed by the court is entitled to any debt or claim that, if that date were the commencement of the winding up of the company would be admissible in proof against the company, is entitled to object to the reduction of capital.

(2) The court shall settle a list of creditors entitled to object.

(3) For that purpose the court—

(a) shall ascertain, as far as possible without requiring an application from any creditor, the names of those creditors and the nature and amount of their debts or claims, and

(b) may publish notices fixing a day or days within which creditors not entered on the list are to claim to be so entered or are to be excluded from the right of objecting to the reduction of capital.

(4) If a creditor entered on the list whose debt or claim is not discharged or has not determined does not consent to the reduction, the court may, if it thinks fit, dispense with the consent of that creditor on the company securing payment of his debt or claim.

(5) For this purpose the debt or claim must be secured by appropriating (as the court may direct) the following amount—

(a) if the company admits the full amount of the debt or claim or, though not admitting it, is willing to provide for it, the full amount of the debt or claim;

(b) if the company does not admit, and is not willing to provide for, the full amount of the debt or claim, or if the amount is contingent or not ascertained, an amount fixed by the court after the like enquiry and adjudication as if the company were being wound up by the court.

### 647 Offences in connection with list of creditors

(1) If an officer of the company—

(a) intentionally or recklessly—

(i) conceals the name of a creditor entitled to object to the reduction of capital, or

(ii) misrepresents the nature or amount of the debt or claim of a creditor, or

(b) is knowingly concerned in any such concealment or misrepresentation,

he commits an offence.

(2) A person guilty of an offence under this section is liable—

(a) on conviction on indictment, to a fine;

(b) on summary conviction, to a fine not exceeding the statutory maximum.

### 648 Court order confirming reduction

(1) The court may make an order confirming the reduction of capital on such terms and conditions as it thinks fit.

(2) The court must not confirm the reduction unless it is satisfied, with respect to every creditor of the company who is entitled to object to the reduction of capital that either—

(a) his consent to the reduction has been obtained, or

(b) his debt or claim has been discharged, or has determined or has been secured.

(3) Where the court confirms the reduction, it may order the company to publish (as the court directs) the reasons for reduction of capital, or such other information in regard to it as the court thinks expedient with a view to giving proper information to the public, and (if the court thinks fit) the causes that led to the reduction.

(4) The court may, if for any special reason it thinks proper to do so, make an order directing that the company must, during such period (commencing on or at any time after the date of the order) as is specified in the order, add to its name as its last words the words 'and reduced'.

If such an order is made, those words are, until the end of the period specified in the order, deemed to be part of the company's name.

### 649    Registration of order and statement of capital

(1) The registrar, on production of an order of the court confirming the reduction of a company's share capital and the delivery of a copy of the order and of a statement of capital (approved by the court), shall register the order and statement.

This is subject to section 650 (public company reducing capital below authorised minimum).

(2) The statement of capital must state with respect to the company's share capital as altered by the order—

(a) the total number of shares of the company,

(b) the aggregate nominal value of those shares,

(c) for each class of shares—

(i)   prescribed particulars of the rights attached to the shares,

(ii)  the total number of shares of that class, and

(iii) the aggregate nominal value of shares of that class, and

(d) the amount paid up and the amount (if any) unpaid on each share (whether on account of the nominal value of the share or by way of premium).

(3) The resolution for reducing share capital, as confirmed by the court's order, takes effect—

(a) in the case of a reduction of share capital that forms part of a compromise or arrangement sanctioned by the court under Part 26 (arrangements and reconstructions)—

(i)  on delivery of the order and statement of capital to the registrar, or

(ii) if the court so orders, on the registration of the order and statement of capital;

(b) in any other case, on the registration of the order and statement of capital.

(4) Notice of the registration of the order and statement of capital must be published in such manner as the court may direct.

(5) The registrar must certify the registration of the order and statement of capital.

(6) The certificate—

(a) must be signed by the registrar or authenticated by the registrar's official seal, and

(b) is conclusive evidence—

(i)  that the requirements of this Act with respect to the reduction of share capital have been complied with, and

(ii) that the company's share capital is as stated in the statement of capital.

*Public company reducing capital below authorised minimum*

### 650    Public company reducing capital below authorised minimum

(1) This section applies where the court makes an order confirming a reduction of a public company's capital that has the effect of bringing the nominal value of its allotted share capital below the authorised minimum.

(2) The registrar must not register the order unless either—

(a) the court so directs, or

(b) the company is first re-registered as a private company.

(3) Section 651 provides an expedited procedure for re-registration in these circumstances.

### 651    Expedited procedure for re-registration as a private company

(1) The court may authorise the company to be re-registered as a private company without its having passed the special resolution required by section 97.

(2) If it does so, the court must specify in the order the changes to the company's name and articles to be made in connection with the re-registration.

(3) The company may then be re-registered as a private company if an application to that effect is delivered to the registrar together with—

(a) a copy of the court's order, and

(b) notice of the company's name, and a copy of the company's articles, as altered by the court's order.

(4) On receipt of such an application the registrar must issue a certificate of incorporation altered to meet the circumstances of the case.

(5) The certificate must state that it is issued on re-registration and the date on which it is issued.

(6) On the issue of the certificate—

(a) the company by virtue of the issue of the certificate becomes a private company, and

(b) the changes in the company's name and articles take effect.

(7) The certificate is conclusive evidence that the requirements of this Act as to re-registration have been complied with.

### *Effect of reduction of capital*

### 652  Liability of members following reduction of capital

(1) Where a company's share capital is reduced a member of the company (past or present) is not liable in respect of any share to any call or contribution exceeding in amount the difference (if any) between—

(a) the nominal amount of the share as notified to the registrar in the statement of capital delivered under section 644 or 649, and

(b) the amount paid on the share or the reduced amount (if any) which is deemed to have been paid on it, as the case may be.

(2) This is subject to section 653 (liability to creditor in case of omission from list).

(3) Nothing in this section affects the rights of the contributories among themselves.

### 653  Liability to creditor in case of omission from list of creditors

(1) This section applies where, in the case of a reduction of capital confirmed by the court—

(a) a creditor entitled to object to the reduction of share capital is by reason of his ignorance—

(i) of the proceedings for reduction of share capital, or

(ii) of their nature and effect with respect to his debt or claim, not entered on the list of creditors, and

(b) after the reduction of capital the company is unable to pay the amount of his debt or claim.

(2) Every person who was a member of the company at the date on which the resolution for reducing capital took effect under section 649(3) is liable to contribute for the payment of the debt or claim an amount not exceeding that which he would have been liable to contribute if the company had commenced to be wound up on the day before that date.

(3) If the company is wound up, the court on the application of the creditor in question, and proof of ignorance as mentioned in subsection (1)(a), may if it thinks fit—

(a) settle accordingly a list of persons liable to contribute under this section, and

(b) make and enforce calls and orders on them as if they were ordinary contributories in a winding up.

(4) The reference in subsection (1)(b) to a company being unable to pay the amount of a debt or claim has the same meaning as in section 123 of the Insolvency Act 1986 (c. 45) or Article 103 of the Insolvency (Northern Ireland) Order 1989 (S.I. 1989/2405 (N.I. 19)).

## Chapter 11  Miscellaneous and supplementary provisions

### 654  Treatment of reserve arising from reduction of capital

(1) A reserve arising from the reduction of a company's share capital is not distributable, subject to any provision made by order under this section.

(2) The Secretary of State may by order specify cases in which—

(a) the prohibition in subsection (1) does not apply, and

(b) the reserve is to be treated for the purposes of Part 23 (distributions) as a realised profit.

(3) An order under this section is subject to affirmative resolution procedure.

### 655  Shares no bar to damages against company

A person is not debarred from obtaining damages or other compensation from a company by reason only of his holding or having held shares in the company or any right to apply or subscribe for shares or to be included in the company's register of members in respect of shares.

### 656  Public companies: duty of directors to call meeting on serious loss of capital

(1) Where the net assets of a public company are half or less of its called-up share capital, the directors must call a general meeting of the company to consider whether any, and if so what, steps should be taken to deal with the situation.

(2) They must do so not later than 28 days from the earliest day on which that fact is known to a director of the company.

(3) The meeting must be convened for a date not later than 56 days from that day.

(4) If there is a failure to convene a meeting as required by this section, each of the directors of the company who—

(a) knowingly authorises or permits the failure, or

(b) after the period during which the meeting should have been convened, knowingly authorises or permits the failure to continue,

commits an offence.

(5) A person guilty of an offence under this section is liable—

    (a) on conviction on indictment, to a fine;

    (b) on summary conviction, to a fine not exceeding the statutory maximum.

(6) Nothing in this section authorises the consideration at a meeting convened in pursuance of sub-section (1) of any matter that could not have been considered at that meeting apart from this section.

### 657   General power to make further provision by regulations

(1) The Secretary of State may by regulations modify the following provisions of this Part—

sections 552 and 553 (prohibited commissions, discounts and allowances),

Chapter 5 (payment for shares),

Chapter 6 (public companies: independent valuation of non-cash consideration),

Chapter 7 (share premiums),

sections 622 to 628 (redenomination of share capital),

Chapter 10 (reduction of capital), and

section 656 (public companies: duty of directors to call meeting on serious loss of capital).

(2) The regulations may—

    (a) amend or repeal any of those provisions, or

    (b) make such other provision as appears to the Secretary of State appropriate in place of any of those provisions.

(3) Regulations under this section may make consequential amendments or repeals in other provisions of this Act, or in other enactments.

(4) Regulations under this section are subject to affirmative resolution procedure.

# PART 18   ACQUISITION BY LIMITED COMPANY OF ITS OWN SHARES

## Chapter 1   General provisions

### *Introductory*

### 658   General rule against limited company acquiring its own shares

(1) A limited company must not acquire its own shares, whether by purchase, subscription or otherwise, except in accordance with the provisions of this Part.

(2) If a company purports to act in contravention of this section—

    (a) an offence is committed by—

        (i) the company, and

        (ii) every officer of the company who is in default, and

    (b) the purported acquisition is void.

(3) A person guilty of an offence under this section is liable—

    (a) on conviction on indictment, to imprisonment for a term not exceeding two years or a fine (or both);

    (b) on summary conviction—

        (i) in England and Wales, to imprisonment for a term not exceeding twelve months or a fine not exceeding the statutory maximum (or both);

        (ii) in Scotland or Northern Ireland, to imprisonment for a term not exceeding six months or a fine not exceeding the statutory maximum (or both).

### 659   Exceptions to general rule

(1) A limited company may acquire any of its own fully paid shares otherwise than for valuable consideration.

(2) Section 658 does not prohibit—

    (a) the acquisition of shares in a reduction of capital duly made;

    (b) the purchase of shares in pursuance of an order of the court under—

        (i) section 98 (application to court to cancel resolution for re-registration as a private company),

        (ii) section 721(6) (powers of court on objection to redemption or purchase of shares out of capital),

        (iii) section 759 (remedial order in case of breach of prohibition of public offers by private company), or

        (iv) Part 30 (protection of members against unfair prejudice);

    (c) the forfeiture of shares, or the acceptance of shares surrendered in lieu, in pursuance of the company's articles, for failure to pay any sum payable in respect of the shares.

### *Shares held by company's nominee*

### 660   Treatment of shares held by nominee

(1) This section applies where shares in a limited company—

    (a) are taken by a subscriber to the memorandum as nominee of the company,

(b) are issued to a nominee of the company, or

(c) are acquired by a nominee of the company, partly paid up, from a third person.

(2) For all purposes—

(a) the shares are to be treated as held by the nominee on his own account, and

(b) the company is to be regarded as having no beneficial interest in them.

(3) This section does not apply—

(a) to shares acquired otherwise than by subscription by a nominee of a public company, where—

(i) a person acquires shares in the company with financial assistance given to him, directly or indirectly, by the company for the purpose of or in connection with the acquisition, and

(ii) the company has a beneficial interest in the shares;

(b) to shares acquired by a nominee of the company when the company has no beneficial interest in the shares.

## 661 Liability of others where nominee fails to make payment in respect of shares

(1) This section applies where shares in a limited company—

(a) are taken by a subscriber to the memorandum as nominee of the company,

(b) are issued to a nominee of the company, or

(c) are acquired by a nominee of the company, partly paid up, from a third person.

(2) If the nominee, having been called on to pay any amount for the purposes of paying up, or paying any premium on, the shares, fails to pay that amount within 21 days from being called on to do so, then—

(a) in the case of shares that he agreed to take as subscriber to the memorandum, the other subscribers to the memorandum, and

(b) in any other case, the directors of the company when the shares were issued to or acquired by him,

are jointly and severally liable with him to pay that amount.

(3) If in proceedings for the recovery of an amount under subsection (2) it appears to the court that the subscriber or director—

(a) has acted honestly and reasonably, and

(b) having regard to all the circumstances of the case, ought fairly to be relieved from liability, the court may relieve him, either wholly or in part, from his liability on such terms as the court thinks fit.

(4) If a subscriber to a company's memorandum or a director of a company has reason to apprehend that a claim will or might be made for the recovery of any such amount from him—

(a) he may apply to the court for relief, and

(b) the court has the same power to relieve him as it would have had in proceedings for recovery of that amount.

(5) This section does not apply to shares acquired by a nominee of the company when the company has no beneficial interest in the shares.

### *Shares held by or for public company*

## 662 Duty to cancel shares in public company held by or for the company

(1) This section applies in the case of a public company—

(a) where shares in the company are forfeited, or surrendered to the company in lieu of forfeiture, in pursuance of the articles, for failure to pay any sum payable in respect of the shares;

(b) where shares in the company are surrendered to the company in pursuance of section 102C(1)(b) of the Building Societies Act 1986 (c. 53);

(c) where shares in the company are acquired by it (otherwise than in accordance with this Part or Part 30 (protection of members against unfair prejudice)) and the company has a beneficial interest in the shares;

(d) where a nominee of the company acquires shares in the company from a third party without financial assistance being given directly or indirectly by the company and the company has a beneficial interest in the shares; or

(e) where a person acquires shares in the company, with financial assistance given to him, directly or indirectly, by the company for the purpose of or in connection with the acquisition, and the company has a beneficial interest in the shares.

(2) Unless the shares or any interest of the company in them are previously disposed of, the company must—

(a) cancel the shares and diminish the amount of the company's share capital by the nominal value of the shares cancelled, and

(b) where the effect is that the nominal value of the company's allotted share capital is brought below the authorised minimum, apply for re-registration as a private company, stating the effect of the cancellation.

(3) It must do so no later than—

    (a) in a case within subsection (1)(a) or (b), three years from the date of the forfeiture or surrender;

    (b) in a case within subsection (1)(c) or (d), three years from the date of the acquisition;

    (c) in a case within subsection (1)(e), one year from the date of the acquisition.

(4) The directors of the company may take any steps necessary to enable the company to comply with this section, and may do so without complying with the provisions of Chapter 10 of Part 17 (reduction of capital).

See also section 664 (re-registration as private company in consequence of cancellation).

(5) Neither the company nor, in a case within subsection (1)(d) or (e), the nominee or other shareholder may exercise any voting rights in respect of the shares.

(6) Any purported exercise of those rights is void.

### 663 Notice of cancellation of shares

(1) Where a company cancels shares in order to comply with section 662, it must within one month after the shares are cancelled give notice to the registrar, specifying the shares cancelled.

(2) The notice must be accompanied by a statement of capital.

(3) The statement of capital must state with respect to the company's share capital immediately following the cancellation—

    (a) the total number of shares of the company,

    (b) the aggregate nominal value of those shares,

    (c) for each class of shares—

        (i) prescribed particulars of the rights attached to the shares,

        (ii) the total number of shares of that class, and

        (iii) the aggregate nominal value of shares of that class, and

    (d) the amount paid up and the amount (if any) unpaid on each share (whether on account of the nominal value of the share or by way of premium).

(4) If default is made in complying with this section, an offence is committed by—

    (a) the company, and

    (b) every officer of the company who is in default.

(5) A person guilty of an offence under this section is liable on summary conviction to a fine not exceeding level 3 on the standard scale and, for continued contravention, a daily default fine not exceeding one-tenth of level 3 on the standard scale.

### 664 Re-registration as private company in consequence of cancellation

(1) Where a company is obliged to re-register as a private company to comply with section 662, the directors may resolve that the company should be so re-registered.

Chapter 3 of Part 3 (resolutions affecting a company's constitution) applies to any such resolution.

(2) The resolution may make such changes—

    (a) in the company's name, and

    (b) in the company's articles,

as are necessary in connection with its becoming a private company.

(3) The application for re-registration must contain a statement of the company's proposed name on re-registration.

(4) The application must be accompanied by—

    (a) a copy of the resolution (unless a copy has already been forwarded under Chapter 3 of Part 3),

    (b) a copy of the company's articles as amended by the resolution, and

    (c) a statement of compliance.

(5) The statement of compliance required is a statement that the requirements of this section as to re-registration as a private company have been complied with.

(6) The registrar may accept the statement of compliance as sufficient evidence that the company is entitled to be re-registered as a private company.

### 665 Issue of certificate of incorporation on re-registration

(1) If on an application under section 664 the registrar is satisfied that the company is entitled to be re-registered as a private company, the company shall be re-registered accordingly.

(2) The registrar must issue a certificate of incorporation altered to meet the circumstances of the case.

(3) The certificate must state that it is issued on re-registration and the date on which it is issued.

(4) On the issue of the certificate—

    (a) the company by virtue of the issue of the certificate becomes a private company, and

    (b) the changes in the company's name and articles take effect.

(5) The certificate is conclusive evidence that the requirements of this Act as to re-registration have been complied with.

### 666 Effect of failure to re-register

(1) If a public company that is required by section 662 to apply to be re-registered as a private company fails to do so before the end of the period specified in subsection (3) of that section,

Companies Act 2006    **203**

Chapter 1 of Part 20 (prohibition of public offers by private company) applies to it as if it were a private company.

(2) Subject to that, the company continues to be treated as a public company until it is so reregistered.

### 667 Offence in case of failure to cancel shares or re-register

(1) This section applies where a company, when required to do by section 662—

(a) fails to cancel any shares, or

(b) fails to make an application for re-registration as a private company,

within the time specified in subsection (3) of that section.

(2) An offence is committed by—

(a) the company, and

(b) every officer of the company who is in default.

(3) A person guilty of an offence under this section is liable on summary conviction to a fine not exceeding level 3 on the standard scale and, for continued contravention, a daily default fine not exceeding one-tenth of level 3 on the standard scale.

### 668 Application of provisions to company re-registering as public company

(1) This section applies where, after shares in a private company—

(a) are forfeited in pursuance of the company's articles or are surrendered to the company in lieu of forfeiture,

(b) are acquired by the company (otherwise than by any of the methods permitted by this Part or Part 30 (protection of members against unfair prejudice)), the company having a beneficial interest in the shares,

(c) are acquired by a nominee of the company from a third party without financial assistance being given directly or indirectly by the company, the company having a beneficial interest in the shares, or

(d) are acquired by a person with financial assistance given to him, directly or indirectly, by the company for the purpose of or in connection with the acquisition, the company having a beneficial interest in the shares,

the company is re-registered as a public company.

(2) In that case the provisions of sections 662 to 667 apply to the company as if it had been a public company at the time of the forfeiture, surrender or acquisition, subject to the following modification.

(3) The modification is that the period specified in section 662(3)(a), (b) or (c) (period for complying with obligations under that section) runs from the date of the re-registration of the company as a public company.

### 669 Transfer to reserve on acquisition of shares by public company or nominee

(1) Where—

(a) a public company, or a nominee of a public company, acquires shares in the company, and

(b) those shares are shown in a balance sheet of the company as an asset,

an amount equal to the value of the shares must be transferred out of profits available for dividend to a reserve fund and is not then available for distribution.

(2) Subsection (1) applies to an interest in shares as it applies to shares. As it so applies the reference to the value of the shares shall be read as a reference to the value to the company of its interest in the shares.

*Charges of public company on own shares*

### 670 Public companies: general rule against lien or charge on own shares

(1) A lien or other charge of a public company on its own shares (whether taken expressly or otherwise) is void, except as permitted by this section.

(2) In the case of any description of company, a charge is permitted if the shares are not fully paid up and the charge is for an amount payable in respect of the shares.

(3) In the case of a company whose ordinary business—

(a) includes the lending of money, or

(b) consists of the provision of credit or the bailment (in Scotland, hiring) of goods under a hire-purchase agreement, or both,

a charge is permitted (whether the shares are fully paid or not) if it arises in connection with a transaction entered into by the company in the ordinary course of that business.

(4) In the case of a company that has been re-registered as a public company, a charge is permitted if it was in existence immediately before the application for re-registration.

*Supplementary provisions*

### 671 Interests to be disregarded in determining whether company has beneficial interest

In determining for the purposes of this Chapter whether a company has a beneficial interest in shares, there shall be disregarded any such interest as is mentioned in—

section 672 (residual interest under pension scheme or employees' share scheme),
section 673 (employer's charges and other rights of recovery), or
section 674 (rights as personal representative or trustee).

### 672  Residual interest under pension scheme or employees' share scheme

(1) Where the shares are held on trust for the purposes of a pension scheme or employees' share scheme, there shall be disregarded any residual interest of the company that has not vested in possession.

(2) A 'residual interest' means a right of the company to receive any of the trust property in the event of—

(a)  all the liabilities arising under the scheme having been satisfied or provided for, or

(b)  the company ceasing to participate in the scheme, or

(c)  the trust property at any time exceeding what is necessary for satisfying the liabilities arising or expected to arise under the scheme.

(3)  In subsection (2)—

(a)  the reference to a right includes a right dependent on the exercise of a discretion vested by the scheme in the trustee or another person, and

(b)  the reference to liabilities arising under a scheme includes liabilities that have resulted, or may result, from the exercise of any such discretion.

(4)  For the purposes of this section a residual interest vests in possession—

(a)  in a case within subsection (2)(a), on the occurrence of the event mentioned there (whether or not the amount of the property receivable pursuant to the right is ascertained);

(b)  in a case within subsection (2)(b) or (c), when the company becomes entitled to require the trustee to transfer to it any of the property receivable pursuant to that right.

(5)  Where by virtue of this section shares are exempt from section 660 or 661 (shares held by company's nominee) at the time they are taken, issued or acquired but the residual interest in question vests in possession before they are disposed of or fully paid up, those sections apply to the shares as if they had been taken, issued or acquired on the date on which that interest vests in possession.

(6)  Where by virtue of this section shares are exempt from sections 662 to 668 (shares held by or for public company) at the time they are acquired but the residual interest in question vests in possession before they are disposed of, those sections apply to the shares as if they had been acquired on the date on which the interest vests in possession.

### 673  Employer's charges and other rights of recovery

(1)  Where the shares are held on trust for the purposes of a pension scheme there shall be disregarded—

(a)  any charge or lien on, or set-off against, any benefit or other right or interest under the scheme for the purpose of enabling the employer or former employer of a member of the scheme to obtain the discharge of a monetary obligation due to him from the member;

(b)  any right to receive from the trustee of the scheme, or as trustee of the scheme to retain, an amount that can be recovered or retained—

(i)  under section 61 of the Pension Schemes Act 1993 (c. 48), or otherwise, as reimbursement or partial reimbursement for any contributions equivalent premium paid in connection with the scheme under Part 3 of that Act, or

(ii)  under section 57 of the Pension Schemes (Northern Ireland) Act 1993 (c. 49), or otherwise, as reimbursement or partial reimbursement for any contributions equivalent premium paid in connection with the scheme under Part 3 of that Act.

(2)  Where the shares are held on trust for the purposes of an employees' share scheme, there shall be disregarded any charge or lien on, or set-off against, any benefit or other right or interest under the scheme for the purpose of enabling the employer or former employer of a member of the scheme to obtain the discharge of a monetary obligation due to him from the member.

### 674  Rights as personal representative or trustee

Where the company is a personal representative or trustee, there shall be disregarded any rights that the company has in that capacity including, in particular—

(a)  any right to recover its expenses or be remunerated out of the estate or trust property, and

(b)  any right to be indemnified out of that property for any liability incurred by reason of any act or omission of the company in the performance of its duties as personal representative or trustee.

### 675  Meaning of 'pension scheme'

(1)  In this Chapter 'pension scheme' means a scheme for the provision of benefits consisting of or including relevant benefits for or in respect of employees or former employees.

(2)  In subsection (1) 'relevant benefits' means any pension, lump sum, gratuity or other like benefit given or to be given on retirement or on death or in anticipation of retirement or, in connection with past service, after retirement or death.

### 676  Application of provisions to directors

For the purposes of this Chapter references to 'employer' and 'employee', in the context of a pension scheme or employees' share scheme, shall be read as if a director of a company were employed by it.

## Chapter 2  Financial assistance for purchase of own shares

*Introductory*

### 677  Meaning of 'financial assistance'

(1)  In this Chapter 'financial assistance' means—

(a) financial assistance given by way of gift,

(b) financial assistance given—

(i)  by way of guarantee, security or indemnity (other than an indemnity in respect of the indemnifier's own neglect or default), or

(ii)  by way of release or waiver,

(c) financial assistance given—

(i)  by way of a loan or any other agreement under which any of the obligations of the person giving the assistance are to be fulfilled at a time when in accordance with the agreement any obligation of another party to the agreement remains unfulfilled, or

(ii)  by way of the novation of, or the assignment (in Scotland, assignation) of rights arising under, a loan or such other agreement, or

(d) any other financial assistance given by a company where—

(i)  the net assets of the company are reduced to a material extent by the giving of the assistance, or

(ii)  the company has no net assets.

(2)  'Net assets' here means the aggregate amount of the company's assets less the aggregate amount of its liabilities.

(3)  For this purpose a company's liabilities include—

(a) where the company draws up Companies Act individual accounts, any provision of a kind specified for the purposes of this subsection by regulations under section 396, and

(b) where the company draws up IAS individual accounts, any provision made in those accounts.

*Circumstances in which financial assistance prohibited*

### 678  Assistance for acquisition of shares in public company

(1)  Where a person is acquiring or proposing to acquire shares in a public company, it is not lawful for that company, or a company that is a subsidiary of that company, to give financial assistance directly or indirectly for the purpose of the acquisition before or at the same time as the acquisition takes place.

(2)  Subsection (1) does not prohibit a company from giving financial assistance for the acquisition of shares in it or its holding company if—

(a) the company's principal purpose in giving the assistance is not to give it for the purpose of any such acquisition, or

(b) the giving of the assistance for that purpose is only an incidental part of some larger purpose of the company,

and the assistance is given in good faith in the interests of the company.

(3)  Where—

(a) a person has acquired shares in a company, and

(b) a liability has been incurred (by that or another person) for the purpose of the acquisition,

it is not lawful for that company, or a company that is a subsidiary of that company, to give financial assistance directly or indirectly for the purpose of reducing or discharging the liability if, at the time the assistance is given, the company in which the shares were acquired is a public company.

(4)  Subsection (3) does not prohibit a company from giving financial assistance if—

(a) the company's principal purpose in giving the assistance is not to reduce or discharge any liability incurred by a person for the purpose of the acquisition of shares in the company or its holding company, or

(b) the reduction or discharge of any such liability is only an incidental part of some larger purpose of the company,

and the assistance is given in good faith in the interests of the company.

(5)  This section has effect subject to sections 681 and 682 (unconditional and conditional exceptions to prohibition).

### 679  Assistance by public company for acquisition of shares in its private holding company

(1)  Where a person is acquiring or proposing to acquire shares in a private company, it is not lawful for a public company that is a subsidiary of that company to give financial assistance directly or indirectly for the purpose of the acquisition before or at the same time as the acquisition takes place.

(2)  Subsection (1) does not prohibit a company from giving financial assistance for the acquisition of shares in its holding company if—

    (a)  the company's principal purpose in giving the assistance is not to give it for the purpose of any such acquisition, or

    (b)  the giving of the assistance for that purpose is only an incidental part of some larger purpose of the company,

and the assistance is given in good faith in the interests of the company.

(3)  Where—

    (a)  a person has acquired shares in a private company, and

    (b)  a liability has been incurred (by that or another person) for the purpose of the acquisition,

it is not lawful for a public company that is a subsidiary of that company to give financial assistance directly or indirectly for the purpose of reducing or discharging the liability.

(4)  Subsection (3) does not prohibit a company from giving financial assistance if—

    (a)  the company's principal purpose in giving the assistance is not to reduce or discharge any liability incurred by a person for the purpose of the acquisition of shares in its holding company, or

    (b)  the reduction or discharge of any such liability is only an incidental part of some larger purpose of the company,

and the assistance is given in good faith in the interests of the company.

(5)  This section has effect subject to sections 681 and 682 (unconditional and conditional exceptions to prohibition).

### 680   Prohibited financial assistance an offence

(1)  If a company contravenes section 678(1) or (3) or section 679(1) or (3) (prohibited financial assistance) an offence is committed by—

    (a)  the company, and

    (b)  every officer of the company who is in default.

(2)  A person guilty of an offence under this section is liable—

    (a)  on conviction on indictment, to imprisonment for a term not exceeding two years or a fine (or both);

    (b)  on summary conviction—

       (i)  in England and Wales, to imprisonment for a term not exceeding twelve months or to a fine not exceeding the statutory maximum (or both);

       (ii)  in Scotland or Northern Ireland, to imprisonment for a term not exceeding six months, or to a fine not exceeding the statutory maximum (or both).

### *Exceptions from prohibition*

### 681   Unconditional exceptions

(1)  Neither section 678 nor section 679 prohibits a transaction to which this section applies.

(2)  Those transactions are—

    (a)  a distribution of the company's assets by way of—

       (i)  dividend lawfully made, or

       (ii)  distribution in the course of a company's winding up;

    (b)  an allotment of bonus shares;

    (c)  a reduction of capital under Chapter 10 of Part 17;

    (d)  a redemption of shares under Chapter 3 or a purchase of shares under Chapter 4 of this Part;

    (e)  anything done in pursuance of an order of the court under Part 26 (order sanctioning compromise or arrangement with members or creditors);

    (f)  anything done under an arrangement made in pursuance of section 110 of the Insolvency Act 1986 (c. 45) or Article 96 of the Insolvency (Northern Ireland) Order 1989 (S.I. 1989/2405 (N.I. 19)) (liquidator in winding up accepting shares as consideration for sale of company's property);

    (g)  anything done under an arrangement made between a company and its creditors that is binding on the creditors by virtue of Part 1 of the Insolvency Act 1986 or Part 2 of the Insolvency (Northern Ireland) Order 1989 (S.I. 1989/2405 (N.I. 19)).

### 682   Conditional exceptions

(1)  Neither section 678 nor section 679 prohibits a transaction to which this section applies—

    (a)  if the company giving the assistance is a private company, or

    (b)  if the company giving the assistance is a public company and—

       (i)  the company has net assets that are not reduced by the giving of the assistance, or

       (ii)  to the extent that those assets are so reduced, the assistance is provided out of distributable profits.

(2)  The transactions to which this section applies are—

(a) where the lending of money is part of the ordinary business of the company, the lending of money in the ordinary course of the company's business;

(b) the provision by the company, in good faith in the interests of the company or its holding company, of financial assistance for the purposes of an employees' share scheme;

(c) the provision of financial assistance by the company for the purposes of or in connection with anything done by the company (or another company in the same group) for the purpose of enabling or facilitating transactions in shares in the first-mentioned company or its holding company between, and involving the acquisition of beneficial ownership of those shares by—

    (i) bona fide employees or former employees of that company (or another company in the same group), or

    (ii) spouses or civil partners, widows, widowers or surviving civil partners, or minor children or step-children of any such employees or former employees;

(d) the making by the company of loans to persons (other than directors) employed in good faith by the company with a view to enabling those persons to acquire fully paid shares in the company or its holding company to be held by them by way of beneficial ownership.

(3) The references in this section to 'net assets' are to the amount by which the aggregate of the company's assets exceeds the aggregate of its liabilities.

(4) For this purpose—

(a) the amount of both assets and liabilities shall be taken to be as stated in the company's accounting records immediately before the financial assistance is given, and

(b) 'liabilities' includes any amount retained as reasonably necessary for the purpose of providing for a liability the nature of which is clearly defined and that is either likely to be incurred or certain to be incurred but uncertain as to amount or as to the date on which it will arise.

(5) For the purposes of subsection (2)(c) a company is in the same group as another company if it is a holding company or subsidiary of that company or a subsidiary of a holding company of that company.

### *Supplementary*

### 683   Definitions for this Chapter

(1) In this Chapter—

'distributable profits', in relation to the giving of any financial assistance—

    (i) means those profits out of which the company could lawfully make a distribution equal in value to that assistance, and

    (ii) includes, in a case where the financial assistance consists of or includes, or is treated as arising in consequence of, the sale, transfer or other disposition of a non-cash asset, any profit that, if the company were to make a distribution of that character would be available for that purpose (see section 846); and

'distribution' has the same meaning as in Part 23 (distributions) (see section 829).

(2) In this Chapter—

(a) a reference to a person incurring a liability includes his changing his financial position by making an agreement or arrangement (whether enforceable or unenforceable, and whether made on his own account or with any other person) or by any other means, and

(b) a reference to a company giving financial assistance for the purposes of reducing or discharging a liability incurred by a person for the purpose of the acquisition of shares includes its giving such assistance for the purpose of wholly or partly restoring his financial position to what it was before the acquisition took place.

## Chapter 3   Redeemable shares

### 684   Power of limited company to issue redeemable shares

(1) A limited company having a share capital may issue shares that are to be redeemed or are liable to be redeemed at the option of the company or the shareholder ('redeemable shares'), subject to the following provisions.

(2) The articles of a private limited company may exclude or restrict the issue of redeemable shares.

(3) A public limited company may only issue redeemable shares if it is authorised to do so by its articles.

(4) No redeemable shares may be issued at a time when there are no issued shares of the company that are not redeemable.

### 685   Terms and manner of redemption

(1) The directors of a limited company may determine the terms, conditions and manner of redemption of shares if they are authorised to do so—

(a) by the company's articles, or

(b) by a resolution of the company.

(2) A resolution under subsection (1)(b) may be an ordinary resolution, even though it amends the company's articles.

(3) Where the directors are authorised under subsection (1) to determine the terms, conditions and manner of redemption of shares—

(a) they must do so before the shares are allotted, and

(b) any obligation of the company to state in a statement of capital the rights attached to the shares extends to the terms, conditions and manner of redemption.

(4) Where the directors are not so authorised, the terms, conditions and manner of redemption of any redeemable shares must be stated in the company's articles.

### 686   Payment for redeemable shares

(1) Redeemable shares in a limited company may not be redeemed unless they are fully paid.

(2) The terms of redemption of shares in a limited company may provide that the amount payable on redemption may, by agreement between the company and the holder of the shares, be paid on a date later than the redemption date.

(3) Unless redeemed in accordance with a provision authorised by subsection (2), the shares must be paid for on redemption.

### 687   Financing of redemption

(1) A private limited company may redeem redeemable shares out of capital in accordance with Chapter 5.

(2) Subject to that, redeemable shares in a limited company may only be redeemed out of—

(a) distributable profits of the company, or

(b) the proceeds of a fresh issue of shares made for the purposes of the redemption.

(3) Any premium payable on redemption of shares in a limited company must be paid out of distributable profits of the company, subject to the following provision.

(4) If the redeemable shares were issued at a premium, any premium payable on their redemption may be paid out of the proceeds of a fresh issue of shares made for the purposes of the redemption, up to an amount equal to—

(a) the aggregate of the premiums received by the company on the issue of the shares redeemed, or

(b) the current amount of the company's share premium account (including any sum transferred to that account in respect of premiums on the new shares),

whichever is the less.

(5) The amount of the company's share premium account is reduced by a sum corresponding (or by sums in the aggregate corresponding) to the amount of any payment made under subsection (4).

(6) This section is subject to section 735(4) (terms of redemption enforceable in a winding up).

### 688   Redeemed shares treated as cancelled

Where shares in a limited company are redeemed—

(a) the shares are treated as cancelled, and

(b) the amount of the company's issued share capital is diminished accordingly by the nominal value of the shares redeemed.

### 689   Notice to registrar of redemption

(1) If a limited company redeems any redeemable shares it must within one month after doing so give notice to the registrar, specifying the shares redeemed.

(2) The notice must be accompanied by a statement of capital.

(3) The statement of capital must state with respect to the company's share capital immediately following the redemption—

(a) the total number of shares of the company,

(b) the aggregate nominal value of those shares,

(c) for each class of shares—

(i) prescribed particulars of the rights attached to the shares,

(ii) the total number of shares of that class, and

(iii) the aggregate nominal value of shares of that class, and

(d) the amount paid up and the amount (if any) unpaid on each share (whether on account of the nominal value of the share or by way of premium).

(4) If default is made in complying with this section, an offence is committed by—

(a) the company, and

(b) every officer of the company who is in default.

(5) A person guilty of an offence under this section is liable on summary conviction to a fine not exceeding level 3 on the standard scale and, for continued contravention, a daily default fine not exceeding one-tenth of level 3 on the standard scale.

## Chapter 4  Purchase of own shares

*General provisions*

### 690  Power of limited company to purchase own shares

(1)  A limited company having a share capital may purchase its own shares (including any redeemable shares), subject to—

    (a)  the following provisions of this Chapter, and

    (b)  any restriction or prohibition in the company's articles.

(2)  A limited company may not purchase its own shares if as a result of the purchase there would no longer be any issued shares of the company other than redeemable shares or shares held as treasury shares.

### 691  Payment for purchase of own shares

(1)  A limited company may not purchase its own shares unless they are fully paid.

(2)  Where a limited company purchases its own shares, the shares must be paid for on purchase.

### 692  Financing of purchase of own shares

(1)  A private limited company may purchase its own shares out of capital in accordance with Chapter 5.

(2)  Subject to that—

    (a)  a limited company may only purchase its own shares out of—

        (i)  distributable profits of the company, or

        (ii)  the proceeds of a fresh issue of shares made for the purpose of financing the purchase, and

    (b)  any premium payable on the purchase by a limited company of its own shares must be paid out of distributable profits of the company, subject to subsection (3).

(3)  If the shares to be purchased were issued at a premium, any premium payable on their purchase by the company may be paid out of the proceeds of a fresh issue of shares made for the purpose of financing the purchase, up to an amount equal to—

    (a)  the aggregate of the premiums received by the company on the issue of the shares purchased, or

    (b)  the current amount of the company's share premium account (including any sum transferred to that account in respect of premiums on the new shares),

whichever is the less.

(4)  The amount of the company's share premium account is reduced by a sum corresponding (or by sums in the aggregate corresponding) to the amount of any payment made under subsection (3).

(5)  This section has effect subject to section 735(4) (terms of purchase enforceable in a winding up).

*Authority for purchase of own shares*

### 693  Authority for purchase of own shares

(1)  A limited company may only purchase its own shares—

    (a)  by an off-market purchase, in pursuance of a contract approved in advance in accordance with section 694;

    (b)  by a market purchase, authorised in accordance with section 701.

(2)  A purchase is 'off-market' if the shares either—

    (a)  are purchased otherwise than on a recognised investment exchange, or

    (b)  are purchased on a recognised investment exchange but are not subject to a marketing arrangement on the exchange.

(3)  For this purpose a company's shares are subject to a marketing arrangement on a recognised investment exchange if—

    (a)  they are listed under Part 6 of the Financial Services and Markets Act 2000 (c. 8), or

    (b)  the company has been afforded facilities for dealings in the shares to take place on the exchange—

        (i)  without prior permission for individual transactions from the authority governing that investment exchange, and

        (ii)  without limit as to the time during which those facilities are to be available.

(4)  A purchase is a 'market purchase' if it is made on a recognised investment exchange and is not an off-market purchase by virtue of subsection (2)(b).

(5)  In this section 'recognised investment exchange' means a recognised investment exchange (within the meaning of Part 18 of the Financial Services and Markets Act 2000) other than an overseas exchange (within the meaning of that Part).

*Authority for off-market purchase*

### 694   Authority for off-market purchase

(1)  A company may only make an off-market purchase of its own shares in pursuance of a contract approved prior to the purchase in accordance with this section.

(2)  Either—

(a)  the terms of the contract must be authorised by a special resolution of the company before the contract is entered into, or

(b)  the contract must provide that no shares may be purchased in pursuance of the contract until its terms have been authorised by a special resolution of the company.

(3)  The contract may be a contract, entered into by the company and relating to shares in the company, that does not amount to a contract to purchase the shares but under which the company may (subject to any conditions) become entitled or obliged to purchase the shares.

(4)  The authority conferred by a resolution under this section may be varied, revoked or from time to time renewed by a special resolution of the company.

(5)  In the case of a public company a resolution conferring, varying or renewing authority must specify a date on which the authority is to expire, which must not be later than 18 months after the date on which the resolution is passed.

(6)  A resolution conferring, varying, revoking or renewing authority under this section is subject to—

section 695 (exercise of voting rights), and

section 696 (disclosure of details of contract).

### 695   Resolution authorising off-market purchase: exercise of voting rights

(1)  This section applies to a resolution to confer, vary, revoke or renew authority for the purposes of section 694 (authority for off-market purchase of own shares).

(2)  Where the resolution is proposed as a written resolution, a member who holds shares to which the resolution relates is not an eligible member.

(3)  Where the resolution is proposed at a meeting of the company, it is not effective if—

(a)  any member of the company holding shares to which the resolution relates exercises the voting rights carried by any of those shares in voting on the resolution, and

(b)  the resolution would not have been passed if he had not done so.

(4)  For this purpose—

(a)  a member who holds shares to which the resolution relates is regarded as exercising the voting rights carried by those shares not only if he votes in respect of them on a poll on the question whether the resolution shall be passed, but also if he votes on the resolution otherwise than on a poll;

(b)  any member of the company may demand a poll on that question;

(c)  a vote and a demand for a poll by a person as proxy for a member are the same respectively as a vote and a demand by the member.

### 696   Resolution authorising off-market purchase: disclosure of details of contract

(1)  This section applies in relation to a resolution to confer, vary, revoke or renew authority for the purposes of section 694 (authority for off-market purchase of own shares).

(2)  A copy of the contract (if it is in writing) or a memorandum setting out its terms (if it is not) must be made available to members—

(a)  in the case of a written resolution, by being sent or submitted to every eligible member at or before the time at which the proposed resolution is sent or submitted to him;

(b)  in the case of a resolution at a meeting, by being made available for inspection by members of the company both—

(i)  at the company's registered office for not less than 15 days ending with the date of the meeting, and

(ii)  at the meeting itself.

(3)  A memorandum of contract terms so made available must include the names of the members holding shares to which the contract relates.

(4)  A copy of the contract so made available must have annexed to it a written memorandum specifying such of those names as do not appear in the contract itself.

(5)  The resolution is not validly passed if the requirements of this section are not complied with

### 697   Variation of contract for off-market purchase

(1)  A company may only agree to a variation of a contract authorised under section 694 (authority for off-market purchase) if the variation is approved in advance in accordance with this section.

(2)  The terms of the variation must be authorised by a special resolution of the company before it is agreed to.

(3)  That authority may be varied, revoked or from time to time renewed by a special resolution of the company.

(4) In the case of a public company a resolution conferring, varying or renewing authority must specify a date on which the authority is to expire, which must not be later than 18 months after the date on which the resolution is passed.

(5) A resolution conferring, varying, revoking or renewing authority under this section is subject to—

section 698 (exercise of voting rights), and

section 699 (disclosure of details of variation).

### 698  Resolution authorising variation: exercise of voting rights

(1) This section applies to a resolution to confer, vary, revoke or renew authority for the purposes of section 697 (variation of contract for off-market purchase of own shares).

(2) Where the resolution is proposed as a written resolution, a member who holds shares to which the resolution relates is not an eligible member.

(3) Where the resolution is proposed at a meeting of the company, it is not effective if—

(a) any member of the company holding shares to which the resolution relates exercises the voting rights carried by any of those shares in voting on the resolution, and

(b) the resolution would not have been passed if he had not done so.

(4) For this purpose—

(a) a member who holds shares to which the resolution relates is regarded as exercising the voting rights carried by those shares not only if he votes in respect of them on a poll on the question whether the resolution shall be passed, but also if he votes on the resolution otherwise than on a poll;

(b) any member of the company may demand a poll on that question;

(c) a vote and a demand for a poll by a person as proxy for a member are the same respectively as a vote and a demand by the member.

### 699  Resolution authorising variation: disclosure of details of variation

(1) This section applies in relation to a resolution under section 697 (variation of contract for off-market purchase of own shares).

(2) A copy of the proposed variation (if it is in writing) or a written memorandum giving details of the proposed variation (if it is not) must be made available to members—

(a) in the case of a written resolution, by being sent or submitted to every eligible member at or before the time at which the proposed resolution is sent or submitted to him;

(b) in the case of a resolution at a meeting, by being made available for inspection by members of the company both—

(i) at the company's registered office for not less than 15 days ending with the date of the meeting, and

(ii) at the meeting itself.

(3) There must also be made available as mentioned in subsection (2) a copy of the original contract or, as the case may be, a memorandum of its terms, together with any variations previously made.

(4) A memorandum of the proposed variation so made available must include the names of the members holding shares to which the variation relates.

(5) A copy of the proposed variation so made available must have annexed to it a written memorandum specifying such of those names as do not appear in the variation itself.

(6) The resolution is not validly passed if the requirements of this section are not complied with.

### 700  Release of company's rights under contract for off-market purchase

(1) An agreement by a company to release its rights under a contract approved under section 694 (authorisation of off-market purchase) is void unless the terms of the release agreement are approved in advance in accordance with this section.

(2) The terms of the proposed agreement must be authorised by a special resolution of the company before the agreement is entered into.

(3) That authority may be varied, revoked or from time to time renewed by a special resolution of the company.

(4) In the case of a public company a resolution conferring, varying or renewing authority must specify a date on which the authority is to expire, which must not be later than 18 months after the date on which the resolution is passed.

(5) The provisions of—

section 698 (exercise of voting rights), and

section 699 (disclosure of details of variation),

apply to a resolution authorising a proposed release agreement as they apply to a resolution authorising a proposed variation.

*Authority for market purchase*

### 701  Authority for market purchase

(1) A company may only make a market purchase of its own shares if the purchase has first been authorised by a resolution of the company.

(2) That authority—

   (a) may be general or limited to the purchase of shares of a particular class or description, and

   (b) may be unconditional or subject to conditions.

(3) The authority must—

   (a) specify the maximum number of shares authorised to be acquired, and

   (b) determine both the maximum and minimum prices that may be paid for the shares.

(4) The authority may be varied, revoked or from time to time renewed by a resolution of the company.

(5) A resolution conferring, varying or renewing authority must specify a date on which it is to expire, which must not be later than 18 months after the date on which the resolution is passed.

(6) A company may make a purchase of its own shares after the expiry of the time limit specified if—

   (a) the contract of purchase was concluded before the authority expired, and

   (b) the terms of the authority permitted the company to make a contract of purchase that would or might be executed wholly or partly after its expiration.

(7) A resolution to confer or vary authority under this section may determine either or both the maximum and minimum price for purchase by—

   (a) specifying a particular sum, or

   (b) providing a basis or formula for calculating the amount of the price (but without reference to any person's discretion or opinion).

(8) Chapter 3 of Part 3 (resolutions affecting a company's constitution) applies to a resolution under this section.

*Supplementary provisions*

### 702   Copy of contract or memorandum to be available for inspection

(1) This section applies where a company has entered into—

   (a) a contract approved under section 694 (authorisation of contract for off-market purchase), or

   (b) a contract for a purchase authorised under section 701 (authorisation of market purchase).

(2) The company must keep available for inspection—

   (a) a copy of the contract, or

   (b) if the contract is not in writing, a written memorandum setting out its terms.

(3) The copy or memorandum must be kept available for inspection from the conclusion of the contract until the end of the period of ten years beginning with—

   (a) the date on which the purchase of all the shares in pursuance of the contract is completed, or

   (b) the date on which the contract otherwise determines.

(4) The copy or memorandum must be kept available for inspection—

   (a) at the company's registered office, or

   (b) at a place specified in regulations under section 1136.

(5) The company must give notice to the registrar—

   (a) of the place at which the copy or memorandum is kept available for inspection, and

   (b) of any change in that place,

unless it has at all times been kept at the company's registered office.

(6) Every copy or memorandum required to be kept under this section must be kept open to inspection without charge—

   (a) by any member of the company, and

   (b) in the case of a public company, by any other person.

(7) The provisions of this section apply to a variation of a contract as they apply to the original contract.

### 703   Enforcement of right to inspect copy or memorandum

(1) If default is made in complying with section 702(2), (3) or (4) or default is made for 14 days in complying with section 702(5), or an inspection required under section 702(6) is refused, an offence is committed by—

   (a) the company, and

   (b) every officer of the company who is in default.

(2) A person guilty of an offence under this section is liable on summary conviction to a fine not exceeding level 3 on the standard scale and, for continued contravention, a daily default fine not exceeding one-tenth of level 3 on the standard scale.

(3) In the case of refusal of an inspection required under section 702(6) the court may by order compel an immediate inspection.

### 704   No assignment of company's right to purchase own shares

The rights of a company under a contract authorised under—

   (a) section 694 (authority for off-market purchase), or

(b) section 701 (authority for market purchase)

are not capable of being assigned.

### 705 Payments apart from purchase price to be made out of distributable profits

(1) A payment made by a company in consideration of—

    (a) acquiring any right with respect to the purchase of its own shares in pursuance of a contingent purchase contract approved under section 694 (authorisation of off-market purchase),

    (b) the variation of any contract approved under that section, or

    (c) the release of any of the company's obligations with respect to the purchase of any of its own shares under a contract—

      (i) approved under section 694, or

      (ii) authorised under section 701 (authorisation of market purchase),

must be made out of the company's distributable profits.

(2) If this requirement is not met in relation to a contract, then—

    (a) in a case within subsection (1)(a), no purchase by the company of its own shares in pursuance of that contract may be made under this Chapter;

    (b) in a case within subsection (1)(b), no such purchase following the variation may be made under this Chapter;

    (c) in a case within subsection (1)(c), the purported release is void.

### 706 Treatment of shares purchased

Where a limited company makes a purchase of its own shares in accordance with this Chapter, then—

    (a) if section 724 (treasury shares) applies, the shares may be held and dealt with in accordance with Chapter 6;

    (b) if that section does not apply—

      (i) the shares are treated as cancelled, and

      (ii) the amount of the company's issued share capital is diminished accordingly by the nominal value of the shares cancelled.

### 707 Return to registrar of purchase of own shares

(1) Where a company purchases shares under this Chapter, it must deliver a return to the registrar within the period of 28 days beginning with the date on which the shares are delivered to it.

(2) The return must distinguish—

    (a) shares in relation to which section 724 (treasury shares) applies and shares in relation to which that section does not apply, and

    (b) shares in relation to which that section applies—

      (i) that are cancelled forthwith (under section 729 (cancellation of treasury shares)), and

      (ii) that are not so cancelled.

(3) The return must state, with respect to shares of each class purchased—

    (a) the number and nominal value of the shares, and

    (b) the date on which they were delivered to the company.

(4) In the case of a public company the return must also state—

    (a) the aggregate amount paid by the company for the shares, and

    (b) the maximum and minimum prices paid in respect of shares of each class purchased.

(5) Particulars of shares delivered to the company on different dates and under different contracts may be included in a single return.

In such a case the amount required to be stated under subsection (4)(a) is the aggregate amount paid by the company for all the shares to which the return relates.

(6) If default is made in complying with this section an offence is committed by every officer of the company who is in default.

(7) A person guilty of an offence under this section is liable—

    (a) on conviction on indictment, to a fine;

    (b) on summary conviction to a fine not exceeding the statutory maximum and, for continued contravention, a daily default fine not exceeding one-tenth of the statutory maximum.

### 708 Notice to registrar of cancellation of shares

(1) If on the purchase by a company of any of its own shares in accordance with this Part—

    (a) section 724 (treasury shares) does not apply (so that the shares are treated as cancelled), or

    (b) that section applies but the shares are cancelled forthwith (under section 729 (cancellation of treasury shares)),

the company must give notice of cancellation to the registrar, within the period of 28 days beginning with the date on which the shares are delivered to it, specifying the shares cancelled.

(2) The notice must be accompanied by a statement of capital.

(3) The statement of capital must state with respect to the company's share capital immediately following the cancellation—

(a) the total number of shares of the company,
(b) the aggregate nominal value of those shares,
(c) for each class of shares—
    (i) prescribed particulars of the rights attached to the shares,
    (ii) the total number of shares of that class, and
    (iii) the aggregate nominal value of shares of that class, and
(d) the amount paid up and the amount (if any) unpaid on each share (whether on account of the nominal value of the share or by way of premium).

(4) If default is made in complying with this section, an offence is committed by—
(a) the company, and
(b) every officer of the company who is in default.

(5) A person guilty of an offence under this section is liable on summary conviction to a fine not exceeding level 3 on the standard scale and, for continued contravention, a daily default fine not exceeding one-tenth of level 3 on the standard scale.

## Chapter 5 Redemption or purchase by private company out of capital

### *Introductory*

### 709 Power of private limited company to redeem or purchase own shares out of capital

(1) A private limited company may in accordance with this Chapter, but subject to any restriction or prohibition in the company's articles, make a payment in respect of the redemption or purchase of its own shares otherwise than out of distributable profits or the proceeds of a fresh issue of shares.

(2) References below in this Chapter to payment out of capital are to any payment so made, whether or not it would be regarded apart from this section as a payment out of capital.

### *The permissible capital payment*

### 710 The permissible capital payment

(1) The payment that may, in accordance with this Chapter, be made by a company out of capital in respect of the redemption or purchase of its own shares is such amount as, after applying for that purpose—
(a) any available profits of the company, and
(b) the proceeds of any fresh issue of shares made for the purposes of the redemption or purchase,
is required to meet the price of redemption or purchase.

(2) That is referred to below in this Chapter as 'the permissible capital payment' for the shares.

### 711 Available profits

(1) For the purposes of this Chapter the available profits of the company, in relation to the redemption or purchase of any shares, are the profits of the company that are available for distribution (within the meaning of Part 23).

(2) But the question whether a company has any profits so available, and the amount of any such profits, shall be determined in accordance with section 712 instead of in accordance with sections 836 to 842 in that Part.

### 712 Determination of available profits

(1) The available profits of the company are determined as follows.

(2) First, determine the profits of the company by reference to the following items as stated in the relevant accounts—
(a) profits, losses, assets and liabilities,
(b) provisions of the following kinds—
    (i) where the relevant accounts are Companies Act accounts, provisions of a kind specified for the purposes of this subsection by regulations under section 396;
    (ii) where the relevant accounts are IAS accounts, provisions of any kind;
(c) share capital and reserves (including undistributable reserves).

(3) Second, reduce the amount so determined by the amount of—
(a) any distribution lawfully made by the company, and
(b) any other relevant payment lawfully made by the company out of distributable profits,
after the date of the relevant accounts and before the end of the relevant period.

(4) For this purpose 'other relevant payment lawfully made' includes—
(a) financial assistance lawfully given out of distributable profits in accordance with Chapter 2,
(b) payments lawfully made out of distributable profits in respect of the purchase by the company of any shares in the company, and

   (c) payments of any description specified in section 705 (payments other than purchase price to be made out of distributable profits) lawfully made by the company.

  (5) The resulting figure is the amount of available profits.

  (6) For the purposes of this section 'the relevant accounts' are any accounts that—

   (a) are prepared as at a date within the relevant period, and

   (b) are such as to enable a reasonable judgment to be made as to the amounts of the items mentioned in subsection (2).

  (7) In this section 'the relevant period' means the period of three months ending with the date on which the directors' statement is made in accordance with section 714.

*Requirements for payment out of capital*

### 713 Requirements for payment out of capital

  (1) A payment out of capital by a private company for the redemption or purchase of its own shares is not lawful unless the requirements of the following sections are met—

section 714 (directors' statement and auditor's report);

section 716 (approval by special resolution);

section 719 (public notice of proposed payment);

section 720 (directors' statement and auditor's report to be available for inspection).

  (2) This is subject to any order of the court under section 721 (power of court to extend period for compliance on application by persons objecting to payment).

### 714 Directors' statement and auditor's report

  (1) The company's directors must make a statement in accordance with this section.

  (2) The statement must specify the amount of the permissible capital payment for the shares in question.

  (3) It must state that, having made full inquiry into the affairs and prospects of the company, the directors have formed the opinion—

   (a) as regards its initial situation immediately following the date on which the payment out of capital is proposed to be made, that there will be no grounds on which the company could then be found unable to pay its debts, and

   (b) as regards its prospects for the year immediately following that date, that having regard to—

    (i) their intentions with respect to the management of the company's business during that year, and

    (ii) the amount and character of the financial resources that will in their view be available to the company during that year,

    (iii) the company will be able to continue to carry on business as a going concern (and will accordingly be able to pay its debts as they fall due) throughout that year.

  (4) In forming their opinion for the purposes of subsection (3)(a), the directors must take into account all of the company's liabilities (including any contingent or prospective liabilities).

  (5) The directors' statement must be in the prescribed form and must contain such information with respect to the nature of the company's business as may be prescribed.

  (6) It must in addition have annexed to it a report addressed to the directors by the company's auditor stating that—

   (a) he has inquired into the company's state of affairs,

   (b) the amount specified in the statement as the permissible capital payment for the shares in question is in his view properly determined in accordance with sections 710 to 712, and

   (c) he is not aware of anything to indicate that the opinion expressed by the directors in their statement as to any of the matters mentioned in subsection (3) above is unreasonable in all the circumstances.

### 715 Directors' statement: offence if no reasonable grounds for opinion

  (1) If the directors make a statement under section 714 without having reasonable grounds for the opinion expressed in it, an offence is committed by every director who is in default.

  (2) A person guilty of an offence under this section is liable—

   (a) on conviction on indictment, to imprisonment for a term not exceeding two years or a fine (or both);

   (b) on summary conviction—

    (i) in England and Wales, to imprisonment for a term not exceeding twelve months or a fine not exceeding the statutory maximum (or both);

    (ii) in Scotland or Northern Ireland, to imprisonment for a term not exceeding six months or a fine not exceeding the statutory maximum (or both).

### 716 Payment to be approved by special resolution

  (1) The payment out of capital must be approved by a special resolution of the company.

  (2) The resolution must be passed on, or within the week immediately following, the date on which the directors make the statement required by section 714.

(3) A resolution under this section is subject to—

section 717 (exercise of voting rights), and

section 718 (disclosure of directors' statement and auditors' report).

### 717    Resolution authorising payment: exercise of voting rights

(1) This section applies to a resolution under section 716 (authority for payment out of capital for redemption or purchase of own shares).

(2) Where the resolution is proposed as a written resolution, a member who holds shares to which the resolution relates is not an eligible member.

(3) Where the resolution is proposed at a meeting of the company, it is not effective if—

(a) any member of the company holding shares to which the resolution relates exercises the voting rights carried by any of those shares in voting on the resolution, and

(b) the resolution would not have been passed if he had not done so.

(4) For this purpose—

(a) a member who holds shares to which the resolution relates is regarded as exercising the voting rights carried by those shares not only if he votes in respect of them on a poll on the question whether the resolution shall be passed, but also if he votes on the resolution otherwise than on a poll;

(b) any member of the company may demand a poll on that question;

(c) a vote and a demand for a poll by a person as proxy for a member are the same respectively as a vote and a demand by the member.

### 718    Resolution authorising payment: disclosure of directors' statement and auditor's report

(1) This section applies to a resolution under section 716 (resolution authorising payment out of capital for redemption or purchase of own shares).

(2) A copy of the directors' statement and auditor's report under section 714 must be made available to members—

(a) in the case of a written resolution, by being sent or submitted to every eligible member at or before the time at which the proposed resolution is sent or submitted to him;

(b) in the case of a resolution at a meeting, by being made available for inspection by members of the company at the meeting.

(3) The resolution is ineffective if this requirement is not complied with.

### 719    Public notice of proposed payment

(1) Within the week immediately following the date of the resolution under section 716 the company must cause to be published in the Gazette a notice—

(a) stating that the company has approved a payment out of capital for the purpose of acquiring its own shares by redemption or purchase or both (as the case may be),

(b) specifying—

(i) the amount of the permissible capital payment for the shares in question, and

(ii) the date of the resolution,

(c) stating where the directors' statement and auditor's report required by section 714 are available for inspection, and

(d) stating that any creditor of the company may at any time within the five weeks immediately following the date of the resolution apply to the court under section 721 for an order preventing the payment.

(2) Within the week immediately following the date of the resolution the company must also either—

(a) cause a notice to the same effect as that required by subsection (1) to be published in an appropriate national newspaper, or

(b) give notice in writing to that effect to each of its creditors.

(3) 'An appropriate national newspaper' means a newspaper circulating throughout the part of the United Kingdom in which the company is registered.

(4) Not later than the day on which the company—

(a) first publishes the notice required by subsection (1), or

(b) if earlier, first publishes or gives the notice required by subsection (2),

the company must deliver to the registrar a copy of the directors' statement and auditor's report required by section 714.

### 720    Directors' statement and auditor's report to be available for inspection

(1) The directors' statement and auditor's report must be kept available for inspection throughout the period—

(a) beginning with the day on which the company—

(i) first publishes the notice required by section 719(1), or

(ii) if earlier, first publishes or gives the notice required by section 719(2), and

(b) ending five weeks after the date of the resolution for payment out of capital.

(2) They must be kept available for inspection—

    (a) at the company's registered office, or

    (b) at a place specified in regulations under section 1136.

(3) The company must give notice to the registrar—

    (a) of the place at which the statement and report are kept available for inspection, and

    (b) of any change in that place,

unless they have at all times been kept at the company's registered office.

(4) They must be open to the inspection of any member or creditor of the company without charge.

(5) If default is made for 14 days in complying with subsection (3), or an inspection under subsection (4) is refused, an offence is committed by—

    (a) the company, and

    (b) every officer of the company who is in default.

(6) A person guilty of an offence under this section is liable on summary conviction to a fine not exceeding level 3 on the standard scale and, for continued contravention, a daily default fine not exceeding one-tenth of level 3 on the standard scale.

(7) In the case of a refusal of an inspection required by subsection (4), the court may by order compel an immediate inspection.

*Objection to payment by members or creditors*

### 721 Application to court to cancel resolution

(1) Where a private company passes a special resolution approving a payment out of capital for the redemption or purchase of any of its shares—

    (a) any member of the company (other than one who consented to or voted in favour of the resolution), and

    (b) any creditor of the company,

may apply to the court for the cancellation of the resolution.

(2) The application—

    (a) must be made within five weeks after the passing of the resolution, and

    (b) may be made on behalf of the persons entitled to make it by such one or more of their number as they may appoint in writing for the purpose.

(3) On an application under this section the court may if it thinks fit—

    (a) adjourn the proceedings in order that an arrangement may be made to the satisfaction of the court—

        (i) for the purchase of the interests of dissentient members, or

        (ii) for the protection of dissentient creditors, and

    (b) give such directions and make such orders as it thinks expedient for facilitating or carrying into effect any such arrangement.

(4) Subject to that, the court must make an order either cancelling or confirming the resolution, and may do so on such terms and conditions as it thinks fit.

(5) If the court confirms the resolution, it may by order alter or extend any date or period of time specified—

    (a) in the resolution, or

    (b) in any provision of this Chapter applying to the redemption or purchase to which the resolution relates.

(6) The court's order may, if the court thinks fit—

    (a) provide for the purchase by the company of the shares of any of its members and for the reduction accordingly of the company's capital, and

    (b) make any alteration in the company's articles that may be required in consequence of that provision.

(7) The court's order may, if the court thinks fit, require the company not to make any, or any specified, amendments of its articles without the leave of the court.

### 722 Notice to registrar of court application or order

(1) On making an application under section 721 (application to court to cancel resolution) the applicants, or the person making the application on their behalf, must immediately give notice to the registrar.

This is without prejudice to any provision of rules of court as to service of notice of the application.

(2) On being served with notice of any such application, the company must immediately give notice to the registrar.

(3) Within 15 days of the making of the court's order on the application, or such longer period as the court may at any time direct, the company must deliver to the registrar a copy of the order.

(4) If a company fails to comply with subsection (2) or (3) an offence is committed by—

    (a) the company, and

    (b) every officer of the company who is in default.

(5) A person guilty of an offence under this section is liable on summary conviction to a fine not exceeding level 3 on the standard scale and, for continued contravention, a daily default fine not exceeding one-tenth of level 3 on the standard scale.

*Supplementary provisions*

### 723  When payment out of capital to be made

(1) The payment out of capital must be made—

    (a) no earlier than five weeks after the date on which the resolution under section 716 is passed, and

    (b) no more than seven weeks after that date.

(2) This is subject to any exercise of the court's powers under section 721(5) (power to alter or extend time where resolution confirmed after objection).

## Chapter 6  Treasury shares

### 724  Treasury shares

(1) This section applies where—

    (a) a limited company makes a purchase of its own shares in accordance with Chapter 4,

    (b) the purchase is made out of distributable profits, and

    (c) the shares are qualifying shares.

(2) For this purpose 'qualifying shares' means shares that—

    (a) are included in the official list in accordance with the provisions of Part 6 of the Financial Services and Markets Act 2000 (c. 8),

    (b) are traded on the market known as the Alternative Investment Market established under the rules of London Stock Exchange plc,

    (c) are officially listed in an EEA State, or

    (d) are traded on a regulated market.

In paragraph (a) 'the official list' has the meaning given in section 103(1) of the Financial Services and Markets Act 2000.

(3) Where this section applies the company may—

    (a) hold the shares (or any of them), or

    (b) deal with any of them, at any time, in accordance with section 727 or 729.

(4) Where shares are held by the company, the company must be entered in its register of members as the member holding the shares.

(5) In the Companies Acts references to a company holding shares as treasury shares are to the company holding shares that—

    (a) were (or are treated as having been) purchased by it in circumstances in which this section applies, and

    (b) have been held by the company continuously since they were so purchased (or treated as purchased).

### 725  Treasury shares: maximum holdings

(1) Where a company has shares of only one class, the aggregate nominal value of shares held as treasury shares must not at any time exceed 10% of the nominal value of the issued share capital of the company at that time.

(2) Where the share capital of a company is divided into shares of different classes, the aggregate nominal value of the shares of any class held as treasury shares must not at any time exceed 10% of the nominal value of the issued share capital of the shares of that class at that time.

(3) If subsection (1) or (2) is contravened by a company, the company must dispose of or cancel the excess shares, in accordance with section 727 or 729, before the end of the period of twelve months beginning with the date on which that contravention occurs.

The 'excess shares' means such number of the shares held by the company as treasury shares at the time in question as resulted in the limit being exceeded.

(4) Where a company purchases qualifying shares out of distributable profits in accordance with section 724, a contravention by the company of subsection (1) or (2) above does not render the acquisition void under section 658 (general rule against limited company acquiring its own shares).

### 726  Treasury shares: exercise of rights

(1) This section applies where shares are held by a company as treasury shares.

(2) The company must not exercise any right in respect of the treasury shares, and any purported exercise of such a right is void.

This applies, in particular, to any right to attend or vote at meetings.

(3) No dividend may be paid, and no other distribution (whether in cash or otherwise) of the company's assets (including any distribution of assets to members on a winding up) may be made to the company, in respect of the treasury shares.

(4) Nothing in this section prevents—

(a) an allotment of shares as fully paid bonus shares in respect of the treasury shares, or

(b) the payment of any amount payable on the redemption of the treasury shares (if they are redeemable shares).

(5) Shares allotted as fully paid bonus shares in respect of the treasury shares are treated as if purchased by the company, at the time they were allotted, in circumstances in which section 724(1) (treasury shares) applied.

### 727  Treasury shares: disposal

(1) Where shares are held as treasury shares, the company may at any time—

(a) sell the shares (or any of them) for a cash consideration, or

(b) transfer the shares (or any of them) for the purposes of or pursuant to an employees' share scheme.

(2) In subsection (1)(a) 'cash consideration' means—

(a) cash received by the company, or

(b) a cheque received by the company in good faith that the directors have no reason for suspecting will not be paid, or

(c) a release of a liability of the company for a liquidated sum, or

(d) an undertaking to pay cash to the company on or before a date not more than 90 days after the date on which the company agrees to sell the shares, or

(e) payment by any other means giving rise to a present or future entitlement (of the company or a person acting on the company's behalf) to a payment, or credit equivalent to payment, in cash.

For this purpose 'cash' includes foreign currency.

(3) The Secretary of State may by order provide that particular means of payment specified in the order are to be regarded as falling within subsection (2)(e).

(4) If the company receives a notice under section 979 (takeover offers: right of offeror to buy out minority shareholders) that a person desires to acquire shares held by the company as treasury shares, the company must not sell or transfer the shares to which the notice relates except to that person.

(5) An order under this section is subject to negative resolution procedure.

### 728  Treasury shares: notice of disposal

(1) Where shares held by a company as treasury shares—

(a) are sold, or

(b) are transferred for the purposes of an employees' share scheme,

the company must deliver a return to the registrar not later than 28 days after the shares are disposed of.

(2) The return must state with respect to shares of each class disposed of—

(a) the number and nominal value of the shares, and

(b) the date on which they were disposed of.

(3) Particulars of shares disposed of on different dates may be included in a single return.

(4) If default is made in complying with this section an offence is committed by every officer of the company who is in default.

(5) A person guilty of an offence under this section is liable—

(a) on conviction on indictment, to a fine;

(b) on summary conviction, to a fine not exceeding the statutory maximum and, for continued contravention, a daily default fine not exceeding one-tenth of the statutory maximum.

### 729  Treasury shares: cancellation

(1) Where shares are held as treasury shares, the company may at any time cancel the shares (or any of them).

(2) If shares held as treasury shares cease to be qualifying shares, the company must forthwith cancel the shares.

(3) For this purpose shares are not to be regarded as ceasing to be qualifying shares by virtue only of—

(a) the suspension of their listing in accordance with the applicable rules in the EEA State in which the shares are officially listed, or

(b) the suspension of their trading in accordance with—

(i) in the case of shares traded on the market known as the Alternative Investment Market, the rules of London Stock Exchange plc, and

(ii) in any other case, the rules of the regulated market on which they are traded.

(4) If company cancels shares held as treasury shares, the amount of the company's share capital is reduced accordingly by the nominal amount of the shares cancelled.

(5) The directors may take any steps required to enable the company to cancel its shares under this section without complying with the provisions of Chapter 10 of Part 17 (reduction of share capital).

### 730  Treasury shares: notice of cancellation

(1)  Where shares held by a company as treasury shares are cancelled, the company must deliver a return to the registrar not later than 28 days after the shares are cancelled.

This does not apply to shares that are cancelled forthwith on their acquisition by the company (see section 708).

(2)  The return must state with respect to shares of each class cancelled—

(a)  the number and nominal value of the shares, and

(b)  the date on which they were cancelled.

(3)  Particulars of shares cancelled on different dates may be included in a single return.

(4)  The notice must be accompanied by a statement of capital.

(5)  The statement of capital must state with respect to the company's share capital immediately following the cancellation—

(a)  the total number of shares of the company,

(b)  the aggregate nominal value of those shares,

(c)  for each class of shares—

(i)   prescribed particulars of the rights attached to the shares,

(ii)   the total number of shares of that class, and

(iii)  the aggregate nominal value of shares of that class, and

(d)  the amount paid up and the amount (if any) unpaid on each share (whether on account of the nominal value of the share or by way of premium).

(6)  If default is made in complying with this section, an offence is committed by—

(a)  the company, and

(b)  every officer of the company who is in default.

(7)  A person guilty of an offence under this section is liable on summary conviction to a fine not exceeding level 3 on the standard scale and, for continued contravention, a daily default fine not exceeding one-tenth of level 3 on the standard scale.

### 731  Treasury shares: treatment of proceeds of sale

(1)  Where shares held as treasury shares are sold, the proceeds of sale must be dealt with in accordance with this section.

(2)  If the proceeds of sale are equal to or less than the purchase price paid by the company for the shares, the proceeds are treated for the purposes of Part 23 (distributions) as a realised profit of the company.

(3)  If the proceeds of sale exceed the purchase price paid by the company—

(a)  an amount equal to the purchase price paid is treated as a realised profit of the company for the purposes of that Part, and

(b)  the excess must be transferred to the company's share premium account.

(4)  For the purposes of this section—

(a)  the purchase price paid by the company must be determined by the application of a weighted average price method, and

(b)  if the shares were allotted to the company as fully paid bonus shares, the purchase price paid for them is treated as nil.

### 732  Treasury shares: offences

(1)  If a company contravenes any of the provisions of this Chapter (except section 730 (notice of cancellation)), an offence is committed by—

(a)  the company, and

(b)  every officer of the company who is in default.

(2)  A person guilty of an offence under this section is liable—

(a)  on conviction on indictment, to a fine;

(b)  on summary conviction to a fine not exceeding the statutory maximum.

## Chapter 7  Supplementary provisions

### 733  The capital redemption reserve

(1)  In the following circumstances a company must transfer amounts to a reserve, called the 'capital redemption reserve'.

(2)  Where under this Part shares of a limited company are redeemed or purchased wholly out of the company's profits, the amount by which the company's issued share capital is diminished in accordance with—

(a)  section 688(b) (on the cancellation of shares redeemed), or

(b)  section 706(b)(ii) (on the cancellation of shares purchased),

must be transferred to the capital redemption reserve.

(3)  If—

(a)  the shares are redeemed or purchased wholly or partly out of the proceeds of a fresh issue, and

(b) the aggregate amount of the proceeds is less than the aggregate nominal value of the shares redeemed or purchased,

the amount of the difference must be transferred to the capital redemption reserve.

This does not apply in the case of a private company if, in addition to the proceeds of the fresh issue, the company applies a payment out of capital under Chapter 5 in making the redemption or purchase.

(4) The amount by which a company's share capital is diminished in accordance with section 729(4) (on the cancellation of shares held as treasury shares) must be transferred to the capital redemption reserve.

(5) The company may use the capital redemption reserve to pay up new shares to be allotted to members as fully paid bonus shares.

(6) Subject to that, the provisions of the Companies Acts relating to the reduction of a company's share capital apply as if the capital redemption reserve were part of its paid up share capital.

## 734 Accounting consequences of payment out of capital

(1) This section applies where a payment out of capital is made in accordance with Chapter 5 (redemption or purchase of own shares by private company out of capital).

(2) If the permissible capital payment is less than the nominal amount of the shares redeemed or purchased, the amount of the difference must be transferred to the company's capital redemption reserve.

(3) If the permissible capital payment is greater than the nominal amount of the shares redeemed or purchased—

    (a) the amount of any capital redemption reserve, share premium account or fully paid share capital of the company, and

    (b) any amount representing unrealised profits of the company for the time being standing to the credit of any revaluation reserve maintained by the company,

may be reduced by a sum not exceeding (or by sums not in total exceeding) the amount by which the permissible capital payment exceeds the nominal amount of the shares.

(4) Where the proceeds of a fresh issue are applied by the company in making a redemption or purchase of its own shares in addition to a payment out of capital under this Chapter, the references in subsections (2) and (3) to the permissible capital payment are to be read as referring to the aggregate of that payment and those proceeds.

## 735 Effect of company's failure to redeem or purchase

(1) This section applies where a company—

    (a) issues shares on terms that they are or are liable to be redeemed, or

    (b) agrees to purchase any of its shares.

(2) The company is not liable in damages in respect of any failure on its part to redeem or purchase any of the shares.

This is without prejudice to any right of the holder of the shares other than his right to sue the company for damages in respect of its failure.

(3) The court shall not grant an order for specific performance of the terms of redemption or purchase if the company shows that it is unable to meet the costs of redeeming or purchasing the shares in question out of distributable profits.

(4) If the company is wound up and at the commencement of the winding up any of the shares have not been redeemed or purchased, the terms of redemption or purchase may be enforced against the company.

When shares are redeemed or purchased under this subsection, they are treated as cancelled.

(5) Subsection (4) does not apply if—

    (a) the terms provided for the redemption or purchase to take place at a date later than that of the commencement of the winding up, or

    (b) during the period—

        (i) beginning with the date on which the redemption or purchase was to have taken place, and

        (ii) ending with the commencement of the winding up,

        (iii) the company could not at any time have lawfully made a distribution equal in value to the price at which the shares were to have been redeemed or purchased.

(6) There shall be paid in priority to any amount that the company is liable under subsection (4) to pay in respect of any shares—

    (a) all other debts and liabilities of the company (other than any due to members in their character as such), and

    (b) if other shares carry rights (whether as to capital or as to income) that are preferred to the rights as to capital attaching to the first-mentioned shares, any amount due in satisfaction of those preferred rights.

Subject to that, any such amount shall be paid in priority to any amounts due to members in satisfaction of their rights (whether as to capital or income) as members.

### 736  Meaning of 'distributable profits'

In this Part (except in Chapter 2 (financial assistance): see section 683) 'distributable profits', in relation to the making of any payment by a company, means profits out of which the company could lawfully make a distribution (within the meaning given by section 830) equal in value to the payment.

### 737  General power to make further provision by regulations

(1) The Secretary of State may by regulations modify the provisions of this Part.

(2) The regulations may—

(a) amend or repeal any of the provisions of this Part, or

(b) make such other provision as appears to the Secretary of State appropriate in place of any of the provisions of this Part.

(3) Regulations under this section may make consequential amendments or repeals in other provisions of this Act, or in other enactments.

(4) Regulations under this section are subject to affirmative resolution procedure.

## PART 19  DEBENTURES

### *General provisions*

### 738  Meaning of 'debenture'

In the Companies Acts 'debenture' includes debenture stock, bonds and any other securities of a company, whether or not constituting a charge on the assets of the company.

### 739  Perpetual debentures

(1) A condition contained in debentures, or in a deed for securing debentures, is not invalid by reason only that the debentures are made—

(a) irredeemable, or

(b) redeemable only—

(i) on the happening of a contingency (however remote), or

(ii) on the expiration of a period (however long),

any rule of equity to the contrary notwithstanding.

(2) Subsection (1) applies to debentures whenever issued and to deeds whenever executed.

### 740  Enforcement of contract to subscribe for debentures

A contract with a company to take up and pay for debentures of the company may be enforced by an order for specific performance.

### 741  Registration of allotment of debentures

(1) A company must register an allotment of debentures as soon as practicable and in any event within two months after the date of the allotment.

(2) If a company fails to comply with this section, an offence is committed by—

(a) the company, and

(b) every officer of the company who is in default.

(3) A person guilty of an offence under this section is liable on summary conviction to a fine not exceeding level 3 on the standard scale and, for continued contravention, a daily default fine not exceeding one-tenth of level 3 on the standard scale.

(4) For the duties of the company as to the issue of the debentures, or certificates of debenture stock, see Part 21 (certification and transfer of securities).

### 742  Debentures to bearer (Scotland)

Notwithstanding anything in the statute of the Scots Parliament of 1696, chapter 25, debentures to bearer issued in Scotland are valid and binding according to their terms.

### *Register of debenture holders*

### 743  Register of debenture holders

(1) Any register of debenture holders of a company that is kept by the company must be kept available for inspection—

(a) at the company's registered office, or

(b) at a place specified in regulations under section 1136.

(2) A company must give notice to the registrar of the place where any such register is kept available for inspection and of any change in that place.

(3) No such notice is required if the register has, at all times since it came into existence, been kept available for inspection at the company's registered office.

(4) If a company makes default for 14 days in complying with subsection (2), an offence is committed by—

(a) the company, and

(b) every officer of the company who is in default.

(5) A person guilty of an offence under this section is liable on summary conviction to a fine not exceeding level 3 on the standard scale and, for continued contravention, a daily default fine not exceeding one-tenth of level 3 on the standard scale.

(6) References in this section to a register of debenture holders include a duplicate—

    (a) of a register of debenture holders that is kept outside the United Kingdom, or

    (b) of any part of such a register.

### 744   Register of debenture holders: right to inspect and require copy

(1) Every register of debenture holders of a company must, except when duly closed, be open to the inspection—

    (a) of the registered holder of any such debentures, or any holder of shares in the company, without charge, and

    (b) of any other person on payment of such fee as may be prescribed.

(2) Any person may require a copy of the register, or any part of it, on payment of such fee as may be prescribed.

(3) A person seeking to exercise either of the rights conferred by this section must make a request to the company to that effect.

(4) The request must contain the following information—

    (a) in the case of an individual, his name and address;

    (b) in the case of an organisation, the name and address of an individual responsible for making the request on behalf of the organisation;

    (c) the purpose for which the information is to be used; and

    (d) whether the information will be disclosed to any other person, and if so—

        (i) where that person is an individual, his name and address,

        (ii) where that person is an organisation, the name and address of an individual responsible for receiving the information on its behalf, and

        (iii) the purpose for which the information is to be used by that person.

(5) For the purposes of this section a register is 'duly closed' if it is closed in accordance with provision contained—

    (a) in the articles or in the debentures,

    (b) in the case of debenture stock in the stock certificates, or

    (c) in the trust deed or other document securing the debentures or debenture stock.

The total period for which a register is closed in any year must not exceed 30 days.

(6) References in this section to a register of debenture holders include a duplicate—

    (a) of a register of debenture holders that is kept outside the United Kingdom, or

    (b) of any part of such a register.

### 745   Register of debenture holders: response to request for inspection or copy

(1) Where a company receives a request under section 744 (register of debenture holders: right to inspect and require copy), it must within five working days either—

    (a) comply with the request, or

    (b) apply to the court.

(2) If it applies to the court it must notify the person making the request.

(3) If on an application under this section the court is satisfied that the inspection or copy is not sought for a proper purpose—

    (a) it shall direct the company not to comply with the request, and

    (b) it may further order that the company's costs (in Scotland, expenses) on the application be paid in whole or in part by the person who made the request, even if he is not a party to the application.

(4) If the court makes such a direction and it appears to the court that the company is or may be subject to other requests made for a similar purpose (whether made by the same person or different persons), it may direct that the company is not to comply with any such request.

The order must contain such provision as appears to the court appropriate to identify the requests to which it applies.

(5) If on an application under this section the court does not direct the company not to comply with the request, the company must comply with the request immediately upon the court giving its decision or, as the case may be, the proceedings being discontinued.

### 746   Register of debenture holders: refusal of inspection or default in providing copy

(1) If an inspection required under section 744 (register of debenture holders: right to inspect and require copy) is refused or default is made in providing a copy required under that section, otherwise than in accordance with an order of the court, an offence is committed by—

    (a) the company, and

    (b) every officer of the company who is in default.

(2) A person guilty of an offence under this section is liable on summary conviction to a fine not exceeding level 3 on the standard scale and, for continued contravention, a daily default fine not exceeding one-tenth of level 3 on the standard scale.

(3) In the case of any such refusal or default the court may by order compel an immediate inspection or, as the case may be, direct that the copy required be sent to the person requesting it.

### 747  Register of debenture holders: offences in connection with request for or disclosure of information

(1) It is an offence for a person knowingly or recklessly to make in a request under section 744 (register of debenture holders: right to inspect and require copy) a statement that is misleading, false or deceptive in a material particular.

(2) It is an offence for a person in possession of information obtained by exercise of either of the rights conferred by that section—

(a) to do anything that results in the information being disclosed to another person, or

(b) to fail to do anything with the result that the information is disclosed to another person,

knowing, or having reason to suspect, that person may use the information for a purpose that is not a proper purpose.

(3) A person guilty of an offence under this section is liable—

(a) on conviction on indictment, to imprisonment for a term not exceeding two years or a fine (or both);

(b) on summary conviction—

(i) in England and Wales, to imprisonment for a term not exceeding twelve months or to a fine not exceeding the statutory maximum (or both);

(ii) in Scotland or Northern Ireland, to imprisonment for a term not exceeding six months, or to a fine not exceeding the statutory maximum (or both).

### 748  Time limit for claims arising from entry in register

(1) Liability incurred by a company—

(a) from the making or deletion of an entry in the register of debenture holders, or

(b) from a failure to make or delete any such entry,

is not enforceable more than ten years after the date on which the entry was made or deleted or, as the case may be, the failure first occurred.

(2) This is without prejudice to any lesser period of limitation (and, in Scotland, to any rule that the obligation giving rise to the liability prescribes before the expiry of that period).

### *Supplementary provisions*

### 749  Right of debenture holder to copy of deed

(1) Any holder of debentures of a company is entitled, on request and on payment of such fee as may be prescribed, to be provided with a copy of any trust deed for securing the debentures.

(2) If default is made in complying with this section, an offence is committed by every officer of the company who is in default.

(3) A person guilty of an offence under this section is liable on summary conviction to a fine not exceeding level 3 on the standard scale and, for continued contravention, a daily default fine not exceeding one-tenth of level 3 on the standard scale.

(4) In the case of any such default the court may direct that the copy required be sent to the person requiring it.

### 750  Liability of trustees of debentures

(1) Any provision contained in—

(a) a trust deed for securing an issue of debentures, or

(b) any contract with the holders of debentures secured by a trust deed,

is void in so far as it would have the effect of exempting a trustee of the deed from, or indemnifying him against, liability for breach of trust where he fails to show the degree of care and diligence required of him as trustee, having regard to the provisions of the trust deed conferring on him any powers, authorities or discretions.

(2) Subsection (1) does not invalidate—

(a) a release otherwise validly given in respect of anything done or omitted to be done by a trustee before the giving of the release;

(b) any provision enabling such a release to be given—

(i) on being agreed to by a majority of not less than 75% in value of the debenture holders present and voting in person or, where proxies are permitted, by proxy at a meeting summoned for the purpose, and

(ii) either with respect to specific acts or omissions or on the trustee dying or ceasing to act.

(3) This section is subject to section 751 (saving for certain older provisions).

### 751  Liability of trustees of debentures: saving for certain older provisions

(1) Section 750 (liability of trustees of debentures) does not operate—

(a) to invalidate any provision in force on the relevant date so long as any person—

(i) then entitled to the benefit of the provision, or

(ii) afterwards given the benefit of the provision under subsection (3) below, remains a trustee of the deed in question, or

(b) to deprive any person of any exemption or right to be indemnified in respect of anything done or omitted to be done by him while any such provision was in force.

(2) The relevant date for this purpose is—

(a) 1st July 1948 in a case where section 192 of the Companies Act 1985 (c. 6) applied immediately before the commencement of this section;

(b) 1st July 1961 in a case where Article 201 of the Companies (Northern Ireland) Order 1986 (S.I. 1986/1032 (N.I. 6)) then applied.

(3) While any trustee of a trust deed remains entitled to the benefit of a provision saved by subsection (1) above the benefit of that provision may be given either—

(a) to all trustees of the deed, present and future, or

(b) to any named trustees or proposed trustees of it,

by a resolution passed by a majority of not less than 75% in value of the debenture holders present in person or, where proxies are permitted, by proxy at a meeting summoned for the purpose.

(4) A meeting for that purpose must be summoned in accordance with the provisions of the deed or, if the deed makes no provision for summoning meetings, in a manner approved by the court.

### 752   Power to re-issue redeemed debentures

(1) Where a company has redeemed debentures previously issued, then unless—

(a) provision to the contrary (express or implied) is contained in the company's articles or in any contract made by the company, or

(b) the company has, by passing a resolution to that effect or by some other act, manifested its intention that the debentures shall be cancelled,

the company may re-issue the debentures, either by re-issuing the same debentures or by issuing new debentures in their place.

This subsection is deemed always to have had effect.

(2) On a re-issue of redeemed debentures the person entitled to the debentures has (and is deemed always to have had) the same priorities as if the debentures had never been redeemed.

(3) The re-issue of a debenture or the issue of another debenture in its place under this section is treated as the issue of a new debenture for the purposes of stamp duty.

It is not so treated for the purposes of any provision limiting the amount or number of debentures to be issued.

(4) A person lending money on the security of a debenture re-issued under this section which appears to be duly stamped may give the debenture in evidence in any proceedings for enforcing his security without payment of the stamp duty or any penalty in respect of it, unless he had notice (or, but for his negligence, might have discovered) that the debenture was not duly stamped.

In that case the company is liable to pay the proper stamp duty and penalty.

### 753   Deposit of debentures to secure advances

Where a company has deposited any of its debentures to secure advances from time to time on current account or otherwise, the debentures are not treated as redeemed by reason only of the company's account having ceased to be in debit while the debentures remained so deposited.

### 754   Priorities where debentures secured by floating charge

(1) This section applies where debentures of a company registered in England and Wales or Northern Ireland are secured by a charge that, as created, was a floating charge.

(2) If possession is taken, by or on behalf of the holders of the debentures, of any property comprised in or subject to the charge, and the company is not at that time in the course of being wound up, the company's preferential debts shall be paid out of assets coming to the hands of the persons taking possession in priority to any claims for principal or interest in respect of the debentures.

(3) 'Preferential debts' means the categories of debts listed in Schedule 6 to the Insolvency Act 1986 (c. 45) or Schedule 4 to the Insolvency (Northern Ireland) Order 1989 (S.I. 1989/2405 (N.I. 19)).

For the purposes of those Schedules 'the relevant date' is the date of possession being taken as mentioned in subsection (2).

(4) Payments under this section shall be recouped, as far as may be, out of the assets of the company available for payment of general creditors.

# PART 20   PRIVATE AND PUBLIC COMPANIES

## Chapter 1   Prohibition of public offers by private companies

### 755   Prohibition of public offers by private company

(1) A private company limited by shares or limited by guarantee and having a share capital must not—

(a) offer to the public any securities of the company, or

(b) allot or agree to allot any securities of the company with a view to their being offered to the public.

(2) Unless the contrary is proved, an allotment or agreement to allot securities is presumed to be made with a view to their being offered to the public if an offer of the securities (or any of them) to the public is made—

    (a) within six months after the allotment or agreement to allot, or

    (b) before the receipt by the company of the whole of the consideration to be received by it in respect of the securities.

(3) A company does not contravene this section if—

    (a) it acts in good faith in pursuance of arrangements under which it is to re-register as a public company before the securities are allotted, or

    (b) as part of the terms of the offer it undertakes to re-register as a public company within a specified period, and that undertaking is complied with.

(4) The specified period for the purposes of subsection (3)(b) must be a period ending not later than six months after the day on which the offer is made (or, in the case of an offer made on different days, first made).

(5) In this Chapter 'securities' means shares or debentures.

### 756    Meaning of 'offer to the public'

(1) This section explains what is meant in this Chapter by an offer of securities to the public.

(2) An offer to the public includes an offer to any section of the public, however selected.

(3) An offer is not regarded as an offer to the public if it can properly be regarded, in all the circumstances, as—

    (a) not being calculated to result, directly or indirectly, in securities of the company becoming available to persons other than those receiving the offer, or

    (b) otherwise being a private concern of the person receiving it and the person making it.

(4) An offer is to be regarded (unless the contrary is proved) as being a private concern of the person receiving it and the person making it if—

    (a) it is made to a person already connected with the company and, where it is made on terms allowing that person to renounce his rights, the rights may only be renounced in favour of another person already connected with the company; or

    (b) it is an offer to subscribe for securities to be held under an employees' share scheme and, where it is made on terms allowing that person to renounce his rights, the rights may only be renounced in favour of—

        (i) another person entitled to hold securities under the scheme, or

        (ii) a person already connected with the company.

(5) For the purposes of this section 'person already connected with the company' means—

    (a) an existing member or employee of the company,

    (b) a member of the family of a person who is or was a member or employee of the company,

    (c) the widow or widower, or surviving civil partner, of a person who was a member or employee of the company,

    (d) an existing debenture holder of the company, or

    (e) a trustee (acting in his capacity as such) of a trust of which the principal beneficiary is a person within any of paragraphs (a) to (d).

(6) For the purposes of subsection (5)(b) the members of a person's family are the person's spouse or civil partner and children (including step-children) and their descendants.

### 757    Enforcement of prohibition: order restraining proposed contravention

(1) If it appears to the court—

    (a) on an application under this section, or

    (b) in proceedings under Part 30 (protection of members against unfair prejudice),

that a company is proposing to act in contravention of section 755 (prohibition of public offers by private companies), the court shall make an order under this section.

(2) An order under this section is an order restraining the company from contravening that section.

(3) An application for an order under this section may be made by—

    (a) a member or creditor of the company, or

    (b) the Secretary of State.

### 758    Enforcement of prohibition: orders available to the court after contravention

(1) This section applies if it appears to the court—

    (a) on an application under this section, or

    (b) in proceedings under Part 30 (protection of members against unfair prejudice),

that a company has acted in contravention of section 755 (prohibition of public offers by private companies).

(2)  The court must make an order requiring the company to re-register as a public company unless it appears to the court—

(a) that the company does not meet the requirements for re-registration as a public company, and

(b) that it is impractical or undesirable to require it to take steps to do so.

(3)  If it does not make an order for re-registration, the court may make either or both of the following—

(a) a remedial order (see section 759), or

(b) an order for the compulsory winding up of the company.

(4)  An application under this section may be made by—

(a) a member of the company who—

(i)  was a member at the time the offer was made (or, if the offer was made over a period, at any time during that period), or

(ii)  became a member as a result of the offer,

(b) a creditor of the company who was a creditor at the time the offer was made (or, if the offer was made over a period, at any time during that period), or

(c) the Secretary of State.

### 759  Enforcement of prohibition: remedial order

(1)  A 'remedial order' is an order for the purpose of putting a person affected by anything done in contravention of section 755 (prohibition of public offers by private company) in the position he would have been in if it had not been done.

(2)  The following provisions are without prejudice to the generality of the power to make such an order.

(3)  Where a private company has—

(a) allotted securities pursuant to an offer to the public, or

(b) allotted or agreed to allot securities with a view to their being offered to the public,

a remedial order may require any person knowingly concerned in the contravention of section 755 to offer to purchase any of those securities at such price and on such other terms as the court thinks fit.

(4)  A remedial order may be made—

(a) against any person knowingly concerned in the contravention, whether or not an officer of the company;

(b) notwithstanding anything in the company's constitution (which includes, for this purpose, the terms on which any securities of the company are allotted or held);

(c) whether or not the holder of the securities subject to the order is the person to whom the company allotted or agreed to allot them.

(5)  Where a remedial order is made against the company itself, the court may provide for the reduction of the company's capital accordingly.

### 760  Validity of allotment etc. not affected

Nothing in this Chapter affects the validity of any allotment or sale of securities or of any agreement to allot or sell securities.

## Chapter 2  Minimum share capital requirement for public companies

### 761  Public company: requirement as to minimum share capital

(1)  A company that is a public company (otherwise than by virtue of re-registration as a public company) must not do business or exercise any borrowing powers unless the registrar has issued it with a certificate under this section (a 'trading certificate').

(2)  The registrar shall issue a trading certificate if, on an application made in accordance with section 762, he is satisfied that the nominal value of the company's allotted share capital is not less than the authorised minimum.

(3)  For this purpose a share allotted in pursuance of an employees' share scheme shall not be taken into account unless paid up as to—

(a) at least one-quarter of the nominal value of the share, and

(b) the whole of any premium on the share.

(4)  A trading certificate has effect from the date on which it is issued and is conclusive evidence that the company is entitled to do business and exercise any borrowing powers.

### 762  Procedure for obtaining certificate

(1)  An application for a certificate under section 761 must—

(a) state that the nominal value of the company's allotted share capital is not less than the authorised minimum,

(b) specify the amount, or estimated amount, of the company's preliminary expenses,

(c) specify any amount or benefit paid or given, or intended to be paid or given, to any promoter of the company, and the consideration for the payment or benefit, and

(d) be accompanied by a statement of compliance.

(2) The statement of compliance is a statement that the company meets the requirements for the issue of a certificate under section 761.

(3) The registrar may accept the statement of compliance as sufficient evidence of the matters stated in it.

### 763 The authorised minimum

(1) 'The authorised minimum', in relation to the nominal value of a public company's allotted share capital is—

(a) £50,000, or

(b) the prescribed euro equivalent.

(2) The Secretary of State may by order prescribe the amount in euros that is for the time being to be treated as equivalent to the sterling amount of the authorised minimum.

(3) This power may be exercised from time to time as appears to the Secretary of State to be appropriate.

(4) The amount prescribed shall be determined by applying an appropriate spot rate of exchange to the sterling amount and rounding to the nearest 100 euros.

(5) An order under this section is subject to negative resolution procedure.

(6) This section has effect subject to any exercise of the power conferred by section 764 (power to alter authorised minimum).

### 764 Power to alter authorised minimum

(1) The Secretary of State may by order—

(a) alter the sterling amount of the authorised minimum, and

(b) make a corresponding alteration of the prescribed euro equivalent.

(2) The amount of the prescribed euro equivalent shall be determined by applying an appropriate spot rate of exchange to the sterling amount and rounding to the nearest 100 euros.

(3) An order under this section that increases the authorised minimum may—

(a) require a public company having an allotted share capital of which the nominal value is less than the amount specified in the order to—

(i) increase that value to not less than that amount, or

(ii) re-register as a private company;

(b) make provision in connection with any such requirement for any of the matters for which provision is made by this Act relating to—

(i) a company's registration, re-registration or change of name,

(ii) payment for shares comprised in a company's share capital, and

(iii) offers to the public of shares in or debentures of a company, including provision as to the consequences (in criminal law or otherwise) of a failure to comply with any requirement of the order;

(c) provide for any provision of the order to come into force on different days for different purposes.

(4) An order under this section is subject to affirmative resolution procedure.

### 765 Authorised minimum: application of initial requirement

(1) The initial requirement for a public company to have allotted share capital of a nominal value not less than the authorised minimum, that is—

(a) the requirement in section 761(2) for the issue of a trading certificate, or

(b) the requirement in section 91(1)(a) for re-registration as a public company,

must be met either by reference to allotted share capital denominated in sterling or by reference to allotted share capital denominated in euros (but not partly in one and partly in the other).

(2) Whether the requirement is met is determined in the first case by reference to the sterling amount and in the second case by reference to the prescribed euro equivalent.

(3) No account is to be taken of any allotted share capital of the company denominated in a currency other than sterling or, as the case may be, euros.

(4) If the company could meet the requirement either by reference to share capital denominated in sterling or by reference to share capital denominated in euros, it must elect in its application for a trading certificate or, as the case may be, for re-registration as a public company which is to be the currency by reference to which the matter is determined.

### 766 Authorised minimum: application where shares denominated in different currencies etc.

(1) The Secretary of State may make provision by regulations as to the application of the authorised minimum in relation to a public company that—

(a) has shares denominated in more than one currency,

(b) redenominates the whole or part of its allotted share capital, or

(c) allots new shares.

(2) The regulations may make provision as to the currencies, exchange rates and dates by reference to which it is to be determined whether the nominal value of the company's allotted share capital is less than the authorised minimum.

(3) The regulations may provide that where—

(a) a company has redenominated the whole or part of its allotted share capital, and

(b) the effect of the redenomination is that the nominal value of the company's allotted share capital is less than the authorised minimum,

the company must re-register as a private company.

(4) Regulations under subsection (3) may make provision corresponding to any provision made by sections 664 to 667 (re-registration as private company in consequence of cancellation of shares).

(5) Any regulations under this section have effect subject to section 765 (authorised minimum: application of initial requirement).

(6) Regulations under this section are subject to negative resolution procedure.

### 767 Consequences of doing business etc. without a trading certificate

(1) If a company does business or exercises any borrowing powers in contravention of section 761, an offence is committed by—

(a) the company, and

(b) every officer of the company who is in default.

(2) A person guilty of an offence under subsection (1) is liable—

(a) on conviction on indictment, to a fine;

(b) on summary conviction, to a fine not exceeding the statutory maximum.

(3) A contravention of section 761 does not affect the validity of a transaction entered into by the company, but if a company—

(a) enters into a transaction in contravention of that section, and

(b) fails to comply with its obligations in connection with the transaction within 21 days from being called on to do so,

the directors of the company are jointly and severally liable to indemnify any other party to the transaction in respect of any loss or damage suffered by him by reason of the company's failure to comply with its obligations.

(4) The directors who are so liable are those who were directors at the time the company entered into the transaction.

# PART 21 CERTIFICATION AND TRANSFER OF SECURITIES

## Chapter 1 Certification and transfer of securities: general

### *Share certificates*

### 768 Share certificate to be evidence of title

(1) In the case of a company registered in England and Wales or Northern Ireland, a certificate under the common seal of the company specifying any shares held by a member is prima facie evidence of his title to the shares.

(2) In the case of a company registered in Scotland—

(a) a certificate under the common seal of the company specifying any shares held by a member, or

(b) a certificate specifying any shares held by a member and subscribed by the company in accordance with the Requirements of Writing (Scotland) Act 1995 (c. 7),

is sufficient evidence, unless the contrary is shown, of his title to the shares.

### *Issue of certificates etc on allotment*

### 769 Duty of company as to issue of certificates etc. on allotment

(1) A company must, within two months after the allotment of any of its shares, debentures or debenture stock, complete and have ready for delivery—

(a) the certificates of the shares allotted,

(b) the debentures allotted, or

(c) the certificates of the debenture stock allotted.

(2) Subsection (1) does not apply—

(a) if the conditions of issue of the shares, debentures or debenture stock provide otherwise,

(b) in the case of allotment to a financial institution (see section 778), or

(c) in the case of an allotment of shares if, following the allotment, the company has issued a share warrant in respect of the shares (see section 779).

(3) If default is made in complying with subsection (1) an offence is committed by every officer of the company who is in default.

(4) A person guilty of an offence under subsection (3) is liable on summary conviction to a fine not exceeding level 3 on the standard scale and, for continued contravention, a daily default fine not exceeding one-tenth of level 3 on the standard scale.

*Transfer of securities*

**770 Registration of transfer**

(1) A company may not register a transfer of shares in or debentures of the company unless—

    (a) a proper instrument of transfer has been delivered to it, or

    (b) the transfer—

        (i) is an exempt transfer within the Stock Transfer Act 1982 (c. 41), or

        (ii) is in accordance with regulations under Chapter 2 of this Part.

(2) Subsection (1) does not affect any power of the company to register as shareholder or debenture holder a person to whom the right to any shares in or debentures of the company has been transmitted by operation of law.

**771 Procedure on transfer being lodged**

(1) When a transfer of shares in or debentures of a company has been lodged with the company, the company must either—

    (a) register the transfer, or

    (b) give the transferee notice of refusal to register the transfer, together with its reasons for the refusal,

as soon as practicable and in any event within two months after the date on which the transfer is lodged with it.

(2) If the company refuses to register the transfer, it must provide the transferee with such further information about the reasons for the refusal as the transferee may reasonably request.

This does not include copies of minutes of meetings of directors.

(3) If a company fails to comply with this section, an offence is committed by—

    (a) the company, and

    (b) every officer of the company who is in default.

(4) A person guilty of an offence under this section is liable on summary conviction to a fine not exceeding level 3 on the standard scale and, for continued contravention, a daily default fine not exceeding one-tenth of level 3 on the standard scale.

(5) This section does not apply—

    (a) in relation to a transfer of shares if the company has issued a share warrant in respect of the shares (see section 779);

    (b) in relation to the transmission of shares or debentures by operation of law.

**772 Transfer of shares on application of transferor**

On the application of the transferor of any share or interest in a company, the company shall enter in its register of members the name of the transferee in the same manner and subject to the same conditions as if the application for the entry were made by the transferee.

**773 Execution of share transfer by personal representative**

An instrument of transfer of the share or other interest of a deceased member of a company—

    (a) may be made by his personal representative although the personal representative is not himself a member of the company, and

    (b) is as effective as if the personal representative had been such a member at the time of the execution of the instrument.

**774 Evidence of grant of probate etc.**

The production to a company of any document that is by law sufficient evidence of the grant of—

    (a) probate of the will of a deceased person,

    (b) letters of administration of the estate of a deceased person, or

    (c) confirmation as executor of a deceased person,

shall be accepted by the company as sufficient evidence of the grant.

**775 Certification of instrument of transfer**

(1) The certification by a company of an instrument of transfer of any shares in, or debentures of, the company is to be taken as a representation by the company to any person acting on the faith of the certification that there have been produced to the company such documents as on their face show a prima facie title to the shares or debentures in the transferor named in the instrument.

(2) The certification is not to be taken as a representation that the transferor has any title to the shares or debentures.

(3) Where a person acts on the faith of a false certification by a company made negligently, the company is under the same liability to him as if the certification had been made fraudulently.

(4) For the purposes of this section—

(a) an instrument of transfer is certificated if it bears the words 'certificate lodged' (or words to the like effect);

(b) the certification of an instrument of transfer is made by a company if—

    (i) the person issuing the instrument is a person authorised to issue certificated instruments of transfer on the company's behalf, and

    (ii) the certification is signed by a person authorised to certificate transfers on the company's behalf or by an officer or employee either of the company or of a body corporate so authorised;

(c) a certification is treated as signed by a person if—

    (i) it purports to be authenticated by his signature or initials (whether handwritten or not), and

    (ii) it is not shown that the signature or initials was or were placed there neither by himself nor by a person authorised to use the signature or initials for the purpose of certificating transfers on the company's behalf.

### *Issue of certificates etc. on transfer*

### 776 Duty of company as to issue of certificates etc. on transfer

(1) A company must, within two months after the date on which a transfer of any of its shares, debentures or debenture stock is lodged with the company, complete and have ready for delivery—

(a) the certificates of the shares transferred,

(b) the debentures transferred, or

(c) the certificates of the debenture stock transferred.

(2) For this purpose a 'transfer' means—

(a) a transfer duly stamped and otherwise valid, or

(b) an exempt transfer within the Stock Transfer Act 1982 (c. 41),

but does not include a transfer that the company is for any reason entitled to refuse to register and does not register.

(3) Subsection (1) does not apply—

(a) if the conditions of issue of the shares, debentures or debenture stock provide otherwise,

(b) in the case of a transfer to a financial institution (see section 778), or

(c) in the case of a transfer of shares if, following the transfer, the company has issued a share warrant in respect of the shares (see section 779).

(4) Subsection (1) has effect subject to section 777 (cases where the Stock Transfer Act 1982 applies).

(5) If default is made in complying with subsection (1) an offence is committed by every officer of the company who is in default.

(6) A person guilty of an offence under this section is liable on summary conviction to a fine not exceeding level 3 on the standard scale and, for continued contravention, a daily default fine not exceeding one-tenth of level 3 on the standard scale.

### 777 Issue of certificates etc.: cases within the Stock Transfer Act 1982

(1) Section 776(1) (duty of company as to issue of certificates etc. on transfer) does not apply in the case of a transfer to a person where, by virtue of regulations under section 3 of the Stock Transfer Act 1982, he is not entitled to a certificate or other document of or evidencing title in respect of the securities transferred.

(2) But if in such a case the transferee—

(a) subsequently becomes entitled to such a certificate or other document by virtue of any provision of those regulations, and

(b) gives notice in writing of that fact to the company,

section 776 (duty to company as to issue of certificates etc.) has effect as if the reference in subsection (1) of that section to the date of the lodging of the transfer were a reference to the date of the notice.

### *Issue of certificates etc. on allotment or transfer to financial institution*

### 778 Issue of certificates etc.: allotment or transfer to financial institution

(1) A company—

(a) of which shares or debentures are allotted to a financial institution,

(b) of which debenture stock is allotted to a financial institution, or

(c) with which a transfer for transferring shares, debentures or debenture stock to a financial institution is lodged,

is not required in consequence of that allotment or transfer to comply with section 769(1) or 776(1) (duty of company as to issue of certificates etc.).

(2) A 'financial institution' means—

(a) a recognised clearing house acting in relation to a recognised investment exchange, or

(b) a nominee of—

    (i) a recognised clearing house acting in that way, or

    (ii) a recognised investment exchange,

designated for the purposes of this section in the rules of the recognised investment exchange in question.

(3) Expressions used in subsection (2) have the same meaning as in Part 18 of the Financial Services and Markets Act 2000 (c. 8).

*Share warrants*

### 779   Issue and effect of share warrant to bearer

(1) A company limited by shares may, if so authorised by its articles, issue with respect to any fully paid shares a warrant (a 'share warrant') stating that the bearer of the warrant is entitled to the shares specified in it.

(2) A share warrant issued under the company's common seal or (in the case of a company registered in Scotland) subscribed in accordance with the Requirements of Writing (Scotland) Act 1995 (c. 7) entitles the bearer to the shares specified in it and the shares may be transferred by delivery of the warrant.

(3) A company that issues a share warrant may, if so authorised by its articles, provide (by coupons or otherwise) for the payment of the future dividends on the shares included in the warrant.

### 780   Duty of company as to issue of certificates on surrender of share warrant

(1) A company must, within two months of the surrender of a share warrant for cancellation, complete and have ready for delivery the certificates of the shares specified in the warrant.

(2) Subsection (1) does not apply if the company's articles provide otherwise.

(3) If default is made in complying with subsection (1) an offence is committed by every officer of the company who is in default.

(4) A person guilty of an offence under subsection (3) is liable on summary conviction to a fine not exceeding level 3 on the standard scale and, for continued contravention, a daily default fine not exceeding one-tenth of level 3 on the standard scale.

### 781   Offences in connection with share warrants (Scotland)

(1) If in Scotland a person—

(a) with intent to defraud, forges or alters, or offers, utters, disposes of, or puts off, knowing the same to be forged or altered, any share warrant or coupon, or any document purporting to be a share warrant or coupon issued in pursuance of this Act, or

(b) by means of any such forged or altered share warrant, coupon or document—

(i) demands or endeavours to obtain or receive any share or interest in a company under this Act, or

(ii) demands or endeavours to receive any dividend or money payment in respect of any such share or interest,

(iii) knowing the warrant, coupon or document to be forged or altered,

he commits an offence.

(2) If in Scotland a person without lawful authority or excuse (of which proof lies on him)—

(a) engraves or makes on any plate, wood, stone, or other material, any share warrant or coupon purporting to be—

(i) a share warrant or coupon issued or made by any particular company in pursuance of this Act, or

(ii) a blank share warrant or coupon so issued or made, or

(iii) a part of such a share warrant or coupon, or

(b) uses any such plate, wood, stone, or other material, for the making or printing of any such share warrant or coupon, or of any such blank share warrant or coupon or of any part of such a share warrant or coupon, or

(c) knowingly has in his custody or possession any such plate, wood, stone, or other material,

he commits an offence.

(3) A person guilty of an offence under subsection (1) is liable on summary conviction to imprisonment for a term not exceeding six months or to a fine not exceeding level 5 on the standard scale (or both).

(4) A person guilty of an offence under subsection (2) is liable—

(a) on conviction on indictment, to imprisonment for a term not exceeding seven years or a fine (or both);

(b) on summary conviction, to imprisonment for a term not exceeding six months or a fine not exceeding the statutory maximum (or both).

*Supplementary provisions*

### 782   Issue of certificates etc.: court order to make good default

(1) If a company on which a notice has been served requiring it to make good any default in complying with—

(a) section 769(1) (duty of company as to issue of certificates etc. on allotment),

(b) section 776(1) (duty of company as to issue of certificates etc. on transfer), or

(c) section 780(1) (duty of company as to issue of certificates etc. on surrender of share warrant),

fails to make good the default within ten days after service of the notice, the person entitled to have the certificates or the debentures delivered to him may apply to the court.

(2) The court may on such an application make an order directing the company and any officer of it to make good the default within such time as may be specified in the order.

(3) The order may provide that all costs (in Scotland, expenses) of and incidental to the application are to be borne by the company or by an officer of it responsible for the default.

## Chapter 2  Evidencing and transfer of title to securities without written instrument

### *Introductory*

#### 783  Scope of this Chapter

In this Chapter—

- (a) 'securities' means shares, debentures, debenture stock, loan stock, bonds, units of a collective investment scheme within the meaning of the Financial Services and Markets Act 2000 (c. 8) and other securities of any description;
- (b) references to title to securities include any legal or equitable interest in securities;
- (c) references to a transfer of title include a transfer by way of security;
- (d) references to transfer without a written instrument include, in relation to bearer securities, transfer without delivery.

#### 784  Power to make regulations

(1) The power to make regulations under this Chapter is exercisable by the Treasury and the Secretary of State, either jointly or concurrently.

(2) References in this Chapter to the authority having power to make regulations shall accordingly be read as references to both or either of them, as the case may require.

(3) Regulations under this Chapter are subject to affirmative resolution procedure.

### *Powers exercisable*

#### 785  Provision enabling procedures for evidencing and transferring title

(1) Provision may be made by regulations for enabling title to securities to be evidenced and transferred without a written instrument.

(2) The regulations may make provision—

- (a) for procedures for recording and transferring title to securities, and
- (b) for the regulation of those procedures and the persons responsible for or involved in their operation.

(3) The regulations must contain such safeguards as appear to the authority making the regulations appropriate for the protection of investors and for ensuring that competition is not restricted, distorted or prevented.

(4) The regulations may, for the purpose of enabling or facilitating the operation of the procedures provided for by the regulations, make provision with respect to the rights and obligations of persons in relation to securities dealt with under the procedures.

(5) The regulations may include provision for the purpose of giving effect to—

- (a) the transmission of title to securities by operation of law;
- (b) any restriction on the transfer of title to securities arising by virtue of the provisions of any enactment or instrument, court order or agreement;
- (c) any power conferred by any such provision on a person to deal with securities on behalf of the person entitled.

(6) The regulations may make provision with respect to the persons responsible for the operation of the procedures provided for by the regulations—

- (a) as to the consequences of their insolvency or incapacity, or
- (b) as to the transfer from them to other persons of their functions in relation to those procedures.

#### 786  Provision enabling or requiring arrangements to be adopted

(1) Regulations under this Chapter may make provision—

- (a) enabling the members of a company or of any designated class of companies to adopt, by ordinary resolution, arrangements under which title to securities is required to be evidenced or transferred (or both) without a written instrument; or
- (b) requiring companies, or any designated class of companies, to adopt such arrangements.

(2) The regulations may make such provision—

- (a) in respect of all securities issued by a company, or
- (b) in respect of all securities of a specified description.

(3)  The arrangements provided for by regulations making such provision as is mentioned in sub-section (1)—

    (a)  must not be such that a person who but for the arrangements would be entitled to have his name entered in the company's register of members ceases to be so entitled, and

    (b)  must be such that a person who but for the arrangements would be entitled to exercise any rights in respect of the securities continues to be able effectively to control the exercise of those rights.

(4)  The regulations may—

    (a)  prohibit the issue of any certificate by the company in respect of the issue or transfer of securities,

    (b)  require the provision by the company to holders of securities of statements (at specified intervals or on specified occasions) of the securities held in their name, and

    (c)  make provision as to the matters of which any such certificate or statement is, or is not, evidence.

(5)  In this section—

    (a)  references to a designated class of companies are to a class designated in the regulations or by order under section 787; and

    (b)  'specified' means specified in the regulations.

### 787   Provision enabling or requiring arrangements to be adopted: order-making powers

(1)  The authority having power to make regulations under this Chapter may by order—

    (a)  designate classes of companies for the purposes of section 786 (provision enabling or requiring arrangements to be adopted);

    (b)  provide that, in relation to securities of a specified description—

        (i)  in a designated class of companies, or

        (ii)  in a specified company or class of companies,

        (iii)  specified provisions of regulations made under this Chapter by virtue of that section either do not apply or apply subject to specified modifications.

(2)  In subsection (1) 'specified' means specified in the order.

(3)  An order under this section is subject to negative resolution procedure.

*Supplementary*

### 788   Provision that may be included in regulations

Regulations under this Chapter may—

    (a)  modify or exclude any provision of any enactment or instrument, or any rule of law;

    (b)  apply, with such modifications as may be appropriate, the provisions of any enactment or instrument (including provisions creating criminal offences);

    (c)  require the payment of fees, or enable persons to require the payment of fees, of such amounts as may be specified in the regulations or determined in accordance with them;

    (d)  empower the authority making the regulations to delegate to any person willing and able to discharge them any functions of the authority under the regulations.

### 789   Duty to consult

Before making—

    (a)  regulations under this Chapter, or

    (b)  any order under section 787,

the authority having power to make regulations under this Chapter must carry out such consultation as appears to it to be appropriate.

### 790   Resolutions to be forwarded to registrar

Chapter 3 of Part 3 (resolutions affecting a company's constitution) applies to a resolution passed by virtue of regulations under this Chapter.

# PART 22  INFORMATION ABOUT INTERESTS IN A COMPANY'S SHARES

*Introductory*

### 791   Companies to which this Part applies

This Part applies only to public companies.

### 792   Shares to which this Part applies

(1)  References in this Part to a company's shares are to the company's issued shares of a class carrying rights to vote in all circumstances at general meetings of the company (including any shares held as treasury shares).

(2)  The temporary suspension of voting rights in respect of any shares does not affect the application of this Part in relation to interests in those or any other shares.

*Notice requiring information about interests in shares*

**793  Notice by company requiring information about interests in its shares**

(1)  A public company may give notice under this section to any person whom the company knows or has reasonable cause to believe—

>  (a)  to be interested in the company's shares, or
>  (b)  to have been so interested at any time during the three years immediately preceding the date on which the notice is issued.

(2)  The notice may require the person—

>  (a)  to confirm that fact or (as the case may be) to state whether or not it is the case, and
>  (b)  if he holds, or has during that time held, any such interest, to give such further information as may be required in accordance with the following provisions of this section.

(3)  The notice may require the person to whom it is addressed to give particulars of his own present or past interest in the company's shares (held by him at any time during the three year period mentioned in subsection (1)(b)).

(4)  The notice may require the person to whom it is addressed, where—

>  (a)  his interest is a present interest and another interest in the shares subsists, or
>  (b)  another interest in the shares subsisted during that three year period at a time when his interest subsisted,

to give, so far as lies within his knowledge, such particulars with respect to that other interest as may be required by the notice.

(5)  The particulars referred to in subsections (3) and (4) include—

>  (a)  the identity of persons interested in the shares in question, and
>  (b)  whether persons interested in the same shares are or were parties to—
>>    (i)   an agreement to which section 824 applies (certain share acquisition agreements), or
>>    (ii)  an agreement or arrangement relating to the exercise of any rights conferred by the holding of the shares.

(6)  The notice may require the person to whom it is addressed, where his interest is a past interest, to give (so far as lies within his knowledge) particulars of the identity of the person who held that interest immediately upon his ceasing to hold it.

(7)  The information required by the notice must be given within such reasonable time as may be specified in the notice.

**794  Notice requiring information: order imposing restrictions on shares**

(1)  Where—

>  (a)  a notice under section 793 (notice requiring information about interests in company's shares) is served by a company on a person who is or was interested in shares in the company, and
>  (b)  that person fails to give the company the information required by the notice within the time specified in it,

the company may apply to the court for an order directing that the shares in question be subject to restrictions.

For the effect of such an order see section 797.

(2)  If the court is satisfied that such an order may unfairly affect the rights of third parties in respect of the shares, the court may, for the purpose of protecting those rights and subject to such terms as it thinks fit, direct that such acts by such persons or descriptions of persons and for such purposes as may be set out in the order shall not constitute a breach of the restrictions.

(3)  On an application under this section the court may make an interim order. Any such order may be made unconditionally or on such terms as the court thinks fit.

(4)  Sections 798 to 802 make further provision about orders under this section.

**795  Notice requiring information: offences**

(1)  A person who—

>  (a)  fails to comply with a notice under section 793 (notice requiring information about interests in company's shares), or
>  (b)  in purported compliance with such a notice—
>>    (i)   makes a statement that he knows to be false in a material particular, or
>>    (ii)  recklessly makes a statement that is false in a material particular,

commits an offence.

(2)  A person does not commit an offence under subsection (1)(a) if he proves that the requirement to give information was frivolous or vexatious.

(3)  A person guilty of an offence under this section is liable—

>  (a)  on conviction on indictment, to imprisonment for a term not exceeding two years or a fine (or both);

(b) on summary conviction—

    (i) in England and Wales, to imprisonment for a term not exceeding twelve months or to a fine not exceeding the statutory maximum (or both);

    (ii) in Scotland or Northern Ireland, to imprisonment for a term not exceeding six months, or to a fine not exceeding the statutory maximum (or both).

### 796    Notice requiring information: persons exempted from obligation to comply

(1) A person is not obliged to comply with a notice under section 793 (notice requiring information about interests in company's shares) if he is for the time being exempted by the Secretary of State from the operation of that section.

(2) The Secretary of State must not grant any such exemption unless—

(a) he has consulted the Governor of the Bank of England, and

(b) he (the Secretary of State) is satisfied that, having regard to any undertaking given by the person in question with respect to any interest held or to be held by him in any shares, there are special reasons why that person should not be subject to the obligations imposed by that section.

*Orders imposing restrictions on shares*

### 797    Consequences of order imposing restrictions

(1) The effect of an order under section 794 that shares are subject to restrictions is as follows—

(a) any transfer of the shares is void;

(b) no voting rights are exercisable in respect of the shares;

(c) no further shares may be issued in right of the shares or in pursuance of an offer made to their holder;

(d) except in a liquidation, no payment may be made of sums due from the company on the shares, whether in respect of capital or otherwise.

(2) Where shares are subject to the restriction in subsection (1)(a), an agreement to transfer the shares is void.

This does not apply to an agreement to transfer the shares on the making of an order under section 800 made by virtue of subsection (3)(b) (removal of restrictions in case of court-approved transfer).

(3) Where shares are subject to the restriction in subsection (1)(c) or (d), an agreement to transfer any right to be issued with other shares in right of those shares, or to receive any payment on them (otherwise than in a liquidation), is void.

This does not apply to an agreement to transfer any such right on the making of an order under section 800 made by virtue of subsection (3)(b) (removal of restrictions in case of court-approved transfer).

(4) The provisions of this section are subject—

(a) to any directions under section 794(2) or section 799(3) (directions for protection of third parties), and

(b) in the case of an interim order under section 794(3), to the terms of the order.

### 798    Penalty for attempted evasion of restrictions

(1) This section applies where shares are subject to restrictions by virtue of an order under section 794.

(2) A person commits an offence if he—

(a) exercises or purports to exercise any right—

    (i) to dispose of shares that to his knowledge, are for the time being subject to restrictions, or

    (ii) to dispose of any right to be issued with any such shares, or

(b) votes in respect of any such shares (whether as holder or proxy), or appoints a proxy to vote in respect of them, or

(c) being the holder of any such shares, fails to notify of their being subject to those restrictions a person whom he does not know to be aware of that fact but does know to be entitled (apart from the restrictions) to vote in respect of those shares whether as holder or as proxy, or

(d) being the holder of any such shares, or being entitled to a right to be issued with other shares in right of them, or to receive any payment on them (otherwise than in a liquidation), enters into an agreement which is void under section 797(2) or (3).

(3) If shares in a company are issued in contravention of the restrictions, an offence is committed by—

(a) the company, and

(b) every officer of the company who is in default.

(4) A person guilty of an offence under this section is liable—

(a) on conviction on indictment, to a fine;

(b) on summary conviction, to a fine not exceeding the statutory maximum.

(5) The provisions of this section are subject—

(a) to any directions under—

(b) section 794(2) (directions for protection of third parties), or

(c) section 799 or 800 (relaxation or removal of restrictions), and

(d) in the case of an interim order under section 794(3), to the terms of the order.

**799   Relaxation of restrictions**

(1) An application may be made to the court on the ground that an order directing that shares shall be subject to restrictions unfairly affects the rights of third parties in respect of the shares.

(2) An application for an order under this section may be made by the company or by any person aggrieved.

(3) If the court is satisfied that the application is well-founded, it may, for the purpose of protecting the rights of third parties in respect of the shares, and subject to such terms as it thinks fit, direct that such acts by such persons or descriptions of persons and for such purposes as may be set out in the order do not constitute a breach of the restrictions.

**800   Removal of restrictions**

(1) An application may be made to the court for an order directing that the shares shall cease to be subject to restrictions.

(2) An application for an order under this section may be made by the company or by any person aggrieved.

(3) The court must not make an order under this section unless—

(a) it is satisfied that the relevant facts about the shares have been disclosed to the company and no unfair advantage has accrued to any person as a result of the earlier failure to make that disclosure, or

(b) the shares are to be transferred for valuable consideration and the court approves the transfer.

(4) An order under this section made by virtue of subsection (3)(b) may continue, in whole or in part, the restrictions mentioned in section 797(1)(c) and (d) (restrictions on issue of further shares or making of payments) so far as they relate to a right acquired or offer made before the transfer.

(5) Where any restrictions continue in force under subsection (4)—

(a) an application may be made under this section for an order directing that the shares shall cease to be subject to those restrictions, and

(b) subsection (3) does not apply in relation to the making of such an order.

**801   Order for sale of shares**

(1) The court may order that the shares subject to restrictions be sold, subject to the court's approval as to the sale.

(2) An application for an order under subsection (1) may only be made by the company.

(3) Where the court has made an order under this section, it may make such further order relating to the sale or transfer of the shares as it thinks fit.

(4) An application for an order under subsection (3) may be made—

(a) by the company,

(b) by the person appointed by or in pursuance of the order to effect the sale, or

(c) by any person interested in the shares.

(5) On making an order under subsection (1) or (3) the court may order that the applicant's costs (in Scotland, expenses) be paid out of the proceeds of sale.

**802   Application of proceeds of sale under court order**

(1) Where shares are sold in pursuance of an order of the court under section 801, the proceeds of the sale, less the costs of the sale, must be paid into court for the benefit of the persons who are beneficially interested in the shares.

(2) A person who is beneficially interested in the shares may apply to the court for the whole or part of those proceeds to be paid to him.

(3) On such an application the court shall order the payment to the applicant of—

(a) the whole of the proceeds of sale together with any interest on them, or

(b) if another person had a beneficial interest in the shares at the time of their sale, such proportion of the proceeds and interest as the value of the applicant's interest in the shares bears to the total value of the shares.

This is subject to the following qualification.

(4) If the court has ordered under section 801(5) that the costs (in Scotland, expenses) of an applicant under that section are to be paid out of the proceeds of sale, the applicant is entitled to payment of his costs (or expenses) out of those proceeds before any person interested in the shares receives any part of those proceeds.

*Power of members to require company to act*

**803   Power of members to require company to act**

(1) The members of a company may require it to exercise its powers under section 793 (notice requiring information about interests in shares).

(2) A company is required to do so once it has received requests (to the same effect) from members of the company holding at least 10% of such of the paid-up capital of the company as carries a right to vote at general meetings of the company (excluding any voting rights attached to any shares in the company held as treasury shares).

(3) A request—

    (a) may be in hard copy form or in electronic form,

    (b) must—

        (i) state that the company is requested to exercise its powers under section 793,

        (ii) specify the manner in which the company is requested to act, and

        (iii) give reasonable grounds for requiring the company to exercise those powers in the manner specified, and

    (c) must be authenticated by the person or persons making it.

### 804 Duty of company to comply with requirement

(1) A company that is required under section 803 to exercise its powers under section 793 (notice requiring information about interests in company's shares) must exercise those powers in the manner specified in the requests.

(2) If default is made in complying with subsection (1) an offence is committed by every officer of the company who is in default.

(3) A person guilty of an offence under this section is liable—

    (a) on conviction on indictment, to a fine;

    (b) on summary conviction, to a fine not exceeding the statutory maximum.

### 805 Report to members on outcome of investigation

(1) On the conclusion of an investigation carried out by a company in pursuance of a requirement under section 803 the company must cause a report of the information received in pursuance of the investigation to be prepared. The report must be made available for inspection within a reasonable period (not more than 15 days) after the conclusion of the investigation.

(2) Where—

    (a) a company undertakes an investigation in pursuance of a requirement under section 803, and

    (b) the investigation is not concluded within three months after the date on which the company became subject to the requirement,

the company must cause to be prepared in respect of that period, and in respect of each succeeding period of three months ending before the conclusion of the investigation, an interim report of the information received during that period in pursuance of the investigation.

(3) Each such report must be made available for inspection within a reasonable period (not more than 15 days) after the end of the period to which it relates.

(4) The reports must be retained by the company for at least six years from the date on which they are first made available for inspection and must be kept available for inspection during that time—

    (a) at the company's registered office, or

    (b) at a place specified in regulations under section 1136.

(5) The company must give notice to the registrar—

    (a) of the place at which the reports are kept available for inspection, and

    (b) of any change in that place,

unless they have at all times been kept at the company's registered office.

(6) The company must within three days of making any report prepared under this section available for inspection, notify the members who made the requests under section 803 where the report is so available.

(7) For the purposes of this section an investigation carried out by a company in pursuance of a requirement under section 803 is concluded when—

    (a) the company has made all such inquiries as are necessary or expedient for the purposes of the requirement, and

    (b) in the case of each such inquiry—

        (i) a response has been received by the company, or

        (ii) the time allowed for a response has elapsed.

### 806 Report to members: offences

(1) If default is made for 14 days in complying with section 805(5) (notice to registrar of place at which reports made available for inspection) an offence is committed by—

    (a) the company, and

    (b) every officer of the company who is in default.

(2) A person guilty of an offence under subsection (1) is liable on summary conviction to a fine not exceeding level 3 on the standard scale and, for continued contravention, a daily default fine not exceeding one-tenth of level 3 on the standard scale.

(3) If default is made in complying with any other provision of section 805 (report to members on outcome of investigation), an offence is committed by every officer of the company who is in default.

(4) A person guilty of an offence under subsection (3) is liable—

    (a) on conviction on indictment, to a fine;

    (b) on summary conviction, to a fine not exceeding the statutory maximum.

## 807 Right to inspect and request copy of reports

(1) Any report prepared under section 805 must be open to inspection by any person without charge.

(2) Any person is entitled, on request and on payment of such fee as may be prescribed, to be provided with a copy of any such report or any part of it. The copy must be provided within ten days after the request is received by the company.

(3) If an inspection required under subsection (1) is refused, or default is made in complying with subsection (2), an offence is committed by—

    (a) the company, and

    (b) every officer of the company who is in default.

(4) A person guilty of an offence under this section is liable on summary conviction to a fine not exceeding level 3 on the standard scale and, for continued contravention, a daily default fine not exceeding one-tenth of level 3 on the standard scale.

(5) In the case of any such refusal or default the court may by order compel an immediate inspection or, as the case may be, direct that the copy required be sent to the person requiring it.

*Register of interests disclosed*

## 808 Register of interests disclosed

(1) The company must keep a register of information received by it in pursuance of a requirement imposed under section 793 (notice requiring information about interests in company's shares).

(2) A company which receives any such information must, within three days of the receipt, enter in the register—

    (a) the fact that the requirement was imposed and the date on which it was imposed, and

    (b) the information received in pursuance of the requirement.

(3) The information must be entered against the name of the present holder of the shares in question or, if there is no present holder or the present holder is not known, against the name of the person holding the interest.

(4) The register must be made up so that the entries against the names entered in it appear in chronological order.

(5) If default is made in complying with this section an offence is committed by—

    (a) the company, and

    (b) every officer of the company who is in default.

(6) A person guilty of an offence under this section is liable on summary conviction to a fine not exceeding level 3 on the standard scale and, for continued contravention, a daily default fine not exceeding one-tenth of level 3 on the standard scale.

(7) The company is not by virtue of anything done for the purposes of this section affected with notice of, or put upon inquiry as to, the rights of any person in relation to any shares.

## 809 Register to be kept available for inspection

(1) The register kept under section 808 (register of interests disclosed) must be kept available for inspection—

    (a) at the company's registered office, or

    (b) at a place specified in regulations under section 1136.

(2) A company must give notice to the registrar of companies of the place where the register is kept available for inspection and of any change in that place.

(3) No such notice is required if the register has at all times been kept available for inspection at the company's registered office.

(4) If default is made in complying with subsection (1), or a company makes default for 14 days in complying with subsection (2), an offence is committed by—

    (a) the company, and

    (b) every officer of the company who is in default.

(5) A person guilty of an offence under this section is liable on summary conviction to a fine not exceeding level 3 on the standard scale and, for continued contravention, a daily default fine not exceeding one-tenth of level 3 on the standard scale.

## 810 Associated index

(1) Unless the register kept under section 808 (register of interests disclosed) is kept in such a form as itself to constitute an index, the company must keep an index of the names entered in it.

(2) The company must make any necessary entry or alteration in the index within ten days after the date on which any entry or alteration is made in the register.

(3) The index must contain, in respect of each name, a sufficient indication to enable the information entered against it to be readily found.

(4) The index must be at all times kept available for inspection at the same place as the register.

(5) If default is made in complying with this section, an offence is committed by—

   (a) the company, and

   (b) every officer of the company who is in default.

(6) A person guilty of an offence under this section is liable on summary conviction to a fine not exceeding level 3 on the standard scale and, for continued contravention, a daily default fine not exceeding one-tenth of level 3 on the standard scale.

### 811  Rights to inspect and require copy of entries

(1) The register required to be kept under section 808 (register of interests disclosed), and any associated index, must be open to inspection by any person without charge.

(2) Any person is entitled, on request and on payment of such fee as may be prescribed, to be provided with a copy of any entry in the register.

(3) A person seeking to exercise either of the rights conferred by this section must make a request to the company to that effect.

(4) The request must contain the following information—

   (a) in the case of an individual, his name and address;

   (b) in the case of an organisation, the name and address of an individual responsible for making the request on behalf of the organisation;

   (c) the purpose for which the information is to be used; and

   (d) whether the information will be disclosed to any other person, and if so—

      (i) where that person is an individual, his name and address,

      (ii) where that person is an organisation, the name and address of an individual responsible for receiving the information on its behalf, and

      (iii) the purpose for which the information is to be used by that person.

### 812  Court supervision of purpose for which rights may be exercised

(1) Where a company receives a request under section 811 (register of interests disclosed: right to inspect and require copy), it must—

   (a) comply with the request if it is satisfied that it is made for a proper purpose, and

   (b) refuse the request if it is not so satisfied.

(2) If the company refuses the request, it must inform the person making the request, stating the reason why it is not satisfied.

(3) A person whose request is refused may apply to the court.

(4) If an application is made to the court—

   (a) the person who made the request must notify the company, and

   (b) the company must use its best endeavours to notify any persons whose details would be disclosed if the company were required to comply with the request.

(5) If the court is not satisfied that the inspection or copy is sought for a proper purpose, it shall direct the company not to comply with the request.

(6) If the court makes such a direction and it appears to the court that the company is or may be subject to other requests made for a similar purpose (whether made by the same person or different persons), it may direct that the company is not to comply with any such request.

The order must contain such provision as appears to the court appropriate to identify the requests to which it applies.

(7) If the court does not direct the company not to comply with the request, the company must comply with the request immediately upon the court giving its decision or, as the case may be, the proceedings being discontinued.

### 813  Register of interests disclosed: refusal of inspection or default in providing copy

(1) If an inspection required under section 811 (register of interests disclosed: right to inspect and require copy) is refused or default is made in providing a copy required under that section, otherwise than in accordance with an order of the court, an offence is committed by—

   (a) the company, and

   (b) every officer of the company who is in default.

(2) A person guilty of an offence under this section is liable on summary conviction to a fine not exceeding level 3 on the standard scale and, for continued contravention, a daily default fine not exceeding one-tenth of level 3 on the standard scale.

(3) In the case of any such refusal or default the court may by order compel an immediate inspection or, as the case may be, direct that the copy required be sent to the person requesting it.

### 814  Register of interests disclosed: offences in connection with request for or disclosure of information

(1) It is an offence for a person knowingly or recklessly to make in a request under section 811 (register of interests disclosed: right to inspect or require copy) a statement that is misleading, false or deceptive in a material particular.

(2) It is an offence for a person in possession of information obtained by exercise of either of the rights conferred by that section—

(a) to do anything that results in the information being disclosed to another person, or

(b) to fail to do anything with the result that the information is disclosed to another person,

knowing, or having reason to suspect, that person may use the information for a purpose that is not a proper purpose.

(3) A person guilty of an offence under this section is liable—

(a) on conviction on indictment, to imprisonment for a term not exceeding two years or a fine (or both);

(b) on summary conviction—

(i) in England and Wales, to imprisonment for a term not exceeding twelve months or to a fine not exceeding the statutory maximum (or both);

(ii) in Scotland or Northern Ireland, to imprisonment for a term not exceeding six months, or to a fine not exceeding the statutory maximum (or both).

### 815 Entries not to be removed from register

(1) Entries in the register kept under section 808 (register of interests disclosed) must not be deleted except in accordance with—

section 816 (old entries), or

section 817 (incorrect entry relating to third party).

(2) If an entry is deleted in contravention of subsection (1), the company must restore it as soon as reasonably practicable.

(3) If default is made in complying with subsection (1) or (2), an offence is committed by—

(a) the company, and

(b) every officer of the company who is in default.

(4) A person guilty of an offence under this section is liable on summary conviction to a fine not exceeding level 3 on the standard scale and, for continued contravention of subsection (2), a daily default fine not exceeding one-tenth of level 3 on the standard scale.

### 816 Removal of entries from register: old entries

A company may remove an entry from the register kept under section 808 (register of interests disclosed) if more than six years have elapsed since the entry was made.

### 817 Removal of entries from register: incorrect entry relating to third party

(1) This section applies where in pursuance of an obligation imposed by a notice under section 793 (notice requiring information about interests in company's shares) a person gives to a company the name and address of another person as being interested in shares in the company.

(2) That other person may apply to the company for the removal of the entry from the register.

(3) If the company is satisfied that the information in pursuance of which the entry was made is incorrect, it shall remove the entry.

(4) If an application under subsection (3) is refused, the applicant may apply to the court for an order directing the company to remove the entry in question from the register.

The court may make such an order if it thinks fit.

### 818 Adjustment of entry relating to share acquisition agreement

(1) If a person who is identified in the register kept by a company under section 808 (register of interests disclosed) as being a party to an agreement to which section 824 applies (certain share acquisition agreements) ceases to be a party to the agreement, he may apply to the company for the inclusion of that information in the register.

(2) If the company is satisfied that he has ceased to be a party to the agreement, it shall record that information (if not already recorded) in every place where his name appears in the register as a party to the agreement.

(3) If an application under this section is refused (otherwise than on the ground that the information has already been recorded), the applicant may apply to the court for an order directing the company to include the information in question in the register.

The court may make such an order if it thinks fit.

### 819 Duty of company ceasing to be public company

(1) If a company ceases to be a public company, it must continue to keep any register kept under section 808 (register of interests disclosed), and any associated index, until the end of the period of six years after it ceased to be such a company.

(2) If default is made in complying with this section, an offence is committed by—

(a) the company, and

(b) every officer of the company who is in default.

(3) A person guilty of an offence under this section is liable on summary conviction to a fine not exceeding level 3 on the standard scale and, for continued contravention, a daily default fine not exceeding one-tenth of level 3 on the standard scale.

*Meaning of interest in shares*

### 820   Interest in shares: general

(1)  This section applies to determine for the purposes of this Part whether a person has an interest in shares.

(2)  In this Part—

(a)  a reference to an interest in shares includes an interest of any kind whatsoever in the shares, and

(b)  any restraints or restrictions to which the exercise of any right attached to the interest is or may be subject shall be disregarded.

(3)  Where an interest in shares is comprised in property held on trust, every beneficiary of the trust is treated as having an interest in the shares.

(4)  A person is treated as having an interest in shares if—

(a)  he enters into a contract to acquire them, or

(b)  not being the registered holder, he is entitled—

(i)   to exercise any right conferred by the holding of the shares, or

(ii)  to control the exercise of any such right.

(5)  For the purposes of subsection (4)(b) a person is entitled to exercise or control the exercise of a right conferred by the holding of shares if he—

(a)  has a right (whether subject to conditions or not) the exercise of which would make him so entitled, or

(b)  is under an obligation (whether subject to conditions or not) the fulfilment of which would make him so entitled.

(6)  A person is treated as having an interest in shares if—

(a)  he has a right to call for delivery of the shares to himself or to his order, or

(b)  he has a right to acquire an interest in shares or is under an obligation to take an interest in shares.

This applies whether the right or obligation is conditional or absolute.

(7)  Persons having a joint interest are treated as each having that interest.

(8)  It is immaterial that shares in which a person has an interest are unidentifiable.

### 821   Interest in shares: right to subscribe for shares

(1)  Section 793 (notice by company requiring information about interests in its shares) applies in relation to a person who has, or previously had, or is or was entitled to acquire, a right to subscribe for shares in the company as it applies in relation to a person who is or was interested in shares in that company.

(2)  References in that section to an interest in shares shall be read accordingly.

### 822   Interest in shares: family interests

(1)  For the purposes of this Part a person is taken to be interested in shares in which—

(a)  his spouse or civil partner, or

(b)  any infant child or step-child of his,

is interested.

(2)  In relation to Scotland 'infant' means a person under the age of 18 years.

### 823   Interest in shares: corporate interests

(1)  For the purposes of this Part a person is taken to be interested in shares if a body corporate is interested in them and—

(a)  the body or its directors are accustomed to act in accordance with his directions or instructions, or

(b)  he is entitled to exercise or control the exercise of one-third or more of the voting power at general meetings of the body.

(2)  For the purposes of this section a person is treated as entitled to exercise or control the exercise of voting power if—

(a)  another body corporate is entitled to exercise or control the exercise of that voting power, and

(b)  he is entitled to exercise or control the exercise of one-third or more of the voting power at general meetings of that body corporate.

(3)  For the purposes of this section a person is treated as entitled to exercise or control the exercise of voting power if—

(a)  he has a right (whether or not subject to conditions) the exercise of which would make him so entitled, or

(b)  he is under an obligation (whether or not subject to conditions) the fulfilment of which would make him so entitled.

### 824   Interest in shares: agreement to acquire interests in a particular company

(1)  For the purposes of this Part an interest in shares may arise from an agreement between two or more persons that includes provision for the acquisition by any one or more of them of interests in shares of a particular public company (the 'target company' for that agreement).

(2)  This section applies to such an agreement if—

(a)  the agreement includes provision imposing obligations or restrictions on any one or more of the parties to it with respect to their use, retention or disposal of their interests in the shares of the target company acquired in pursuance of the agreement (whether or not together with any other interests of theirs in the company's shares to which the agreement relates), and

(b)  an interest in the target company's shares is in fact acquired by any of the parties in pursuance of the agreement.

(3)  The reference in subsection (2) to the use of interests in shares in the target company is to the exercise of any rights or of any control or influence arising from those interests (including the right to enter into an agreement for the exercise, or for control of the exercise, of any of those rights by another person).

(4)  Once an interest in shares in the target company has been acquired in pursuance of the agreement, this section continues to apply to the agreement so long as the agreement continues to include provisions of any description mentioned in subsection (2).

This applies irrespective of—

(a)  whether or not any further acquisitions of interests in the company's shares take place in pursuance of the agreement;

(b)  any change in the persons who are for the time being parties to it;

(c)  any variation of the agreement.

References in this subsection to the agreement include any agreement having effect (whether directly or indirectly) in substitution for the original agreement.

(5)  In this section—

(a)  'agreement' includes any agreement or arrangement, and

(b)  references to provisions of an agreement include—

(i)  undertakings, expectations or understandings operative under an arrangement, and

(ii)  any provision whether express or implied and whether absolute or not.

References elsewhere in this Part to an agreement to which this section applies have a corresponding meaning.

(6)  This section does not apply—

(a)  to an agreement that is not legally binding unless it involves mutuality in the undertakings, expectations or understandings of the parties to it; or

(b)  to an agreement to underwrite or sub-underwrite an offer of shares in a company, provided the agreement is confined to that purpose and any matters incidental to it.

**825  Extent of obligation in case of share acquisition agreement**

(1)  For the purposes of this Part each party to an agreement to which section 824 applies is treated as interested in all shares in the target company in which any other party to the agreement is interested apart from the agreement (whether or not the interest of the other party was acquired, or includes any interest that was acquired, in pursuance of the agreement).

(2)  For those purposes an interest of a party to such an agreement in shares in the target company is an interest apart from the agreement if he is interested in those shares otherwise than by virtue of the application of section 824 (and this section) in relation to the agreement.

(3)  Accordingly, any such interest of the person (apart from the agreement) includes for those purposes any interest treated as his under section 822 or 823 (family or corporate interests) or by the application of section 824 (and this section) in relation to any other agreement with respect to shares in the target company to which he is a party.

(4)  A notification with respect to his interest in shares in the target company made to the company under this Part by a person who is for the time being a party to an agreement to which section 824 applies must—

(a)  state that the person making the notification is a party to such an agreement,

(b)  include the names and (so far as known to him) the addresses of the other parties to the agreement, identifying them as such, and

(c)  state whether or not any of the shares to which the notification relates are shares in which he is interested by virtue of section 824 (and this section) and, if so, the number of those shares.

*Other supplementary provisions*

**826  Information protected from wider disclosure**

(1)  Information in respect of which a company is for the time being entitled to any exemption conferred by regulations under section 409(3) (information about related undertakings to be given in notes to accounts: exemption where disclosure harmful to company's business)—

(a)  must not be included in a report under section 805 (report to members on outcome of investigation), and

(b) must not be made available under section 811 (right to inspect and request copy of entries).

(2) Where any such information is omitted from a report under section 805, that fact must be stated in the report.

### 827   Reckoning of periods for fulfilling obligations

Where the period allowed by any provision of this Part for fulfilling an obligation is expressed as a number of days, any day that is not a working day shall be disregarded in reckoning that period.

### 828   Power to make further provision by regulations

(1) The Secretary of State may by regulations amend—

(a) the definition of shares to which this Part applies (section 792),

(b) the provisions as to notice by a company requiring information about interests in its shares (section 793), and

(c) the provisions as to what is taken to be an interest in shares (sections 820 and 821).

(2) The regulations may amend, repeal or replace those provisions and make such other consequential amendments or repeals of provisions of this Part as appear to the Secretary of State to be appropriate.

(3) Regulations under this section are subject to affirmative resolution procedure.

# PART 23   DISTRIBUTIONS

## Chapter 1   Restrictions on when distributions may be made

### *Introductory*

### 829   Meaning of 'distribution'

(1) In this Part 'distribution' means every description of distribution of a company's assets to its members, whether in cash or otherwise, subject to the following exceptions.

(2) The following are not distributions for the purposes of this Part—

(a) an issue of shares as fully or partly paid bonus shares;

(b) the reduction of share capital—

(i)   by extinguishing or reducing the liability of any of the members on any of the company's shares in respect of share capital not paid up, or

(ii)   by repaying paid-up share capital;

(c) the redemption or purchase of any of the company's own shares out of capital (including the proceeds of any fresh issue of shares) or out of unrealised profits in accordance with Chapter 3, 4 or 5 of Part 18;

(d) a distribution of assets to members of the company on its winding up.

### *General rules*

### 830   Distributions to be made only out of profits available for the purpose

(1) A company may only make a distribution out of profits available for the purpose.

(2) A company's profits available for distribution are its accumulated, realised profits, so far as not previously utilised by distribution or capitalisation, less its accumulated, realised losses, so far as not previously written off in a reduction or reorganisation of capital duly made.

(3) Subsection (2) has effect subject to sections 832 and 835 (investment companies etc: distributions out of accumulated revenue profits).

### 831   Net asset restriction on distributions by public companies

(1) A public company may only make a distribution—

(a) if the amount of its net assets is not less than the aggregate of its called-up share capital and undistributable reserves, and

(b) if, and to the extent that, the distribution does not reduce the amount of those assets to less than that aggregate.

(2) For this purpose a company's 'net assets' means the aggregate of the company's assets less the aggregate of its liabilities.

(3) 'Liabilities' here includes—

(a) where the relevant accounts are Companies Act accounts, provisions of a kind specified for the purposes of this subsection by regulations under section 396;

(b) where the relevant accounts are IAS accounts, provisions of any kind.

(4) A company's undistributable reserves are—

(a) its share premium account;

(b) its capital redemption reserve;

(c) the amount by which its accumulated, unrealised profits (so far as not previously utilised by capitalisation) exceed its accumulated, unrealised losses (so far as not previously written off in a reduction or reorganisation of capital duly made);

(d) any other reserve that the company is prohibited from distributing—

    (i)   by any enactment (other than one contained in this Part), or

    (ii)  by its articles.

The reference in paragraph (c) to capitalisation does not include a transfer of profits of the company to its capital redemption reserve.

(5) A public company must not include any uncalled share capital as an asset in any accounts relevant for purposes of this section.

(6) Subsection (1) has effect subject to sections 832 and 835 (investment companies etc.: distributions out of accumulated revenue profits).

*Distributions by investment companies*

### 832  Distributions by investment companies out of accumulated revenue profits

(1) An investment company may make a distribution out of its accumulated, realised revenue profits if the following conditions are met.

(2) It may make such a distribution only if, and to the extent that, its accumulated, realised revenue profits, so far as not previously utilised by a distribution or capitalisation, exceed its accumulated revenue losses (whether realised or unrealised), so far as not previously written off in a reduction or reorganisation of capital duly made.

(3) It may make such a distribution only—

    (a) if the amount of its assets is at least equal to one and a half times the aggregate of its liabilities to creditors, and

    (b) if, and to the extent that, the distribution does not reduce that amount to less than one and a half times that aggregate.

(4) For this purpose a company's liabilities to creditors include—

    (a) in the case of Companies Act accounts, provisions of a kind specified for the purposes of this subsection by regulations under section 396;

    (b) in the case of IAS accounts, provisions for liabilities to creditors.

(5) The following conditions must also be met—

    (a) the company's shares must be listed on a recognised UK investment exchange;

    (b) during the relevant period it must not have—

        (i)   distributed any capital profits otherwise than by way of the redemption or purchase of any of the company's own shares in accordance with Chapter 3 or 4 of Part 18, or

        (ii)  applied any unrealised profits or any capital profits (realised or unrealised) in paying up debentures or amounts unpaid on its issued shares;

    (c) it must have given notice to the registrar under section 833(1) (notice of intention to carry on business as an investment company)—

        (i)   before the beginning of the relevant period, or

        (ii)  as soon as reasonably practicable after the date of its incorporation.

(6) For the purposes of this section—

    (a) 'recognised UK investment exchange' means a recognised investment exchange within the meaning of Part 18 of the Financial Services and Markets Act 2000 (c. 8), other than an overseas investment exchange within the meaning of that Part; and

    (b) the 'relevant period' is the period beginning with—

        (i)   the first day of the accounting reference period immediately preceding that in which the proposed distribution is to be made, or

        (ii)  where the distribution is to be made in the company's first accounting reference period, the first day of that period,

        (iii) and ending with the date of the distribution.

(7) The company must not include any uncalled share capital as an asset in any accounts relevant for purposes of this section.

### 833  Meaning of 'investment company'

(1) In this Part an 'investment company' means a public company that—

    (a) has given notice (which has not been revoked) to the registrar of its intention to carry on business as an investment company, and

    (b) since the date of that notice has complied with the following requirements.

(2) Those requirements are—

    (a) that the business of the company consists of investing its funds mainly in securities, with the aim of spreading investment risk and giving members of the company the benefit of the results of the management of its funds;

    (b) that the condition in section 834 is met as regards holdings in other companies;

    (c) that distribution of the company's capital profits is prohibited by its articles;

    (d) that the company has not retained, otherwise than in compliance with this Part, in respect of any accounting reference period more than 15% of the income it derives from securities.

(3) Subsection (2)(c) does not require an investment company to be prohibited by its articles from redeeming or purchasing its own shares in accordance with Chapter 3 or 4 of Part 18 out of its capital profits.

(4) Notice to the registrar under this section may be revoked at any time by the company on giving notice to the registrar that it no longer wishes to be an investment company within the meaning of this section.

(5) On giving such a notice, the company ceases to be such a company.

### 834   Investment company: condition as to holdings in other companies

(1) The condition referred to in section 833(2)(b) (requirements to be complied with by investment company) is that none of the company's holdings in companies (other than those that are for the time being investment companies) represents more than 15% by value of the company's investments.

(2) For this purpose—
-   (a) holdings in companies that—
    -   (i)   are members of a group (whether or not including the investing company), and
    -   (ii)  are not for the time being investment companies,
    -   (iii) are treated as holdings in a single company; and
-   (b) where the investing company is a member of a group, money owed to it by another member of the group—
    -   (i)   is treated as a security of the latter held by the investing company, and
    -   (ii)  is accordingly treated as, or as part of, the holding of the investing company in the company owing the money.

(3) The condition does not apply—
-   (a) to a holding in a company acquired before 6th April 1965 that on that date represented not more than 25% by value of the investing company's investments, or
-   (b) to a holding in a company that, when it was acquired, represented not more than 15% by value of the investing company's investments,

so long as no addition is made to the holding.

(4) For the purposes of subsection (3)—
-   (a) 'holding' means the shares or securities (whether of one class or more than one class) held in any one company;
-   (b) an addition is made to a holding whenever the investing company acquires shares or securities of that one company, otherwise than by being allotted shares or securities without becoming liable to give any consideration, and if an addition is made to a holding that holding is acquired when the addition or latest addition is made to the holding; and
-   (c) where in connection with a scheme of reconstruction a company issues shares or securities to persons holding shares or securities in a second company in respect of and in proportion to (or as nearly as may be in proportion to) their holdings in the second company, without those persons becoming liable to give any consideration, a holding of the shares or securities in the second company and a corresponding holding of the shares or securities so issued shall be regarded as the same holding.

(5) In this section—

'company' and 'shares' shall be construed in accordance with sections 99 and 288 of the Taxation of Chargeable Gains Act 1992 (c. 12);

'group' means a company and all companies that are its 51% subsidiaries (within the meaning of section 838 of the Income and Corporation Taxes Act 1988 (c. 1)); and

'scheme of reconstruction' has the same meaning as in section 136 of the Taxation of Chargeable Gains Act 1992.

### 835   Power to extend provisions relating to investment companies

(1) The Secretary of State may by regulations extend the provisions of sections 832 to 834 (distributions by investment companies out of accumulated profits), with or without modifications, to other companies whose principal business consists of investing their funds in securities, land or other assets with the aim of spreading investment risk and giving their members the benefit of the results of the management of the assets.

(2) Regulations under this section are subject to affirmative resolution procedure.

## Chapter 2   Justification of distribution by reference to accounts

*Justification of distribution by reference to accounts*

### 836   Justification of distribution by reference to relevant accounts

(1) Whether a distribution may be made by a company without contravening this Part is determined by reference to the following items as stated in the relevant accounts—
-   (a) profits, losses, assets and liabilities;
-   (b) provisions of the following kinds—

> (i)   where the relevant accounts are Companies Act accounts, provisions of a kind specified for the purposes of this subsection by regulations under section 396;
>
> (ii)  where the relevant accounts are IAS accounts, provisions of any kind;

(c)  share capital and reserves (including undistributable reserves).

(2)  The relevant accounts are the company's last annual accounts, except that—

(a)  where the distribution would be found to contravene this Part by reference to the company's last annual accounts, it may be justified by reference to interim accounts, and

(b)  where the distribution is proposed to be declared during the company's first accounting reference period, or before any accounts have been circulated in respect of that period, it may be justified by reference to initial accounts.

(3)  The requirements of—

section 837 (as regards the company's last annual accounts),

section 838 (as regards interim accounts), and

section 839 (as regards initial accounts),

must be complied with, as and where applicable.

(4)  If any applicable requirement of those sections is not complied with, the accounts may not be relied on for the purposes of this Part and the distribution is accordingly treated as contravening this Part.

### *Requirements applicable in relation to relevant accounts*

### 837  Requirements where last annual accounts used

(1)  The company's last annual accounts means the company's individual accounts—

(a)  that were last circulated to members in accordance with section 423 (duty to circulate copies of annual accounts and reports), or

(b)  if in accordance with section 426 the company provided a summary financial statement instead, that formed the basis of that statement.

(2)  The accounts must have been properly prepared in accordance with this Act, or have been so prepared subject only to matters that are not material for determining (by reference to the items mentioned in section 836(1)) whether the distribution would contravene this Part.

(3)  Unless the company is exempt from audit and the directors take advantage of that exemption, the auditor must have made his report on the accounts.

(4)  If that report was qualified—

(a)  the auditor must have stated in writing (either at the time of his report or subsequently) whether in his opinion the matters in respect of which his report is qualified are material for determining whether a distribution would contravene this Part, and

(b)  a copy of that statement must—

> (i)   in the case of a private company, have been circulated to members in accordance with section 423, or
>
> (ii)  in the case of a public company, have been laid before the company in general meeting.

(5)  An auditor's statement is sufficient for the purposes of a distribution if it relates to distributions of a description that includes the distribution in question, even if at the time of the statement it had not been proposed.

### 838  Requirements where interim accounts used

(1)  Interim accounts must be accounts that enable a reasonable judgment to be made as to the amounts of the items mentioned in section 836(1).

(2)  Where interim accounts are prepared for a proposed distribution by a public company, the following requirements apply.

(3)  The accounts must have been properly prepared, or have been so prepared subject to matters that are not material for determining (by reference to the items mentioned in section 836(1)) whether the distribution would contravene this Part.

(4)  'Properly prepared' means prepared in accordance with sections 395 to 397 (requirements for company individual accounts), applying those requirements with such modifications as are necessary because the accounts are prepared otherwise than in respect of an accounting reference period.

(5)  The balance sheet comprised in the accounts must have been signed in accordance with section 414.

(6)  A copy of the accounts must have been delivered to the registrar.

Any requirement of Part 35 of this Act as to the delivery of a certified translation into English of any document forming part of the accounts must also have been met.

### 839  Requirements where initial accounts used

(1)  Initial accounts must be accounts that enable a reasonable judgment to be made as to the amounts of the items mentioned in section 836(1).

(2)  Where initial accounts are prepared for a proposed distribution by a public company, the following requirements apply.

(3)  The accounts must have been properly prepared, or have been so prepared subject to matters that are not material for determining (by reference to the items mentioned in section 836(1)) whether the distribution would contravene this Part.

(4)  'Properly prepared' means prepared in accordance with sections 395 to 397 (requirements for company individual accounts), applying those requirements with such modifications as are necessary because the accounts are prepared otherwise than in respect of an accounting reference period.

(5)  The company's auditor must have made a report stating whether, in his opinion, the accounts have been properly prepared.

(6)  If that report was qualified—

(a)  the auditor must have stated in writing (either at the time of his report or subsequently) whether in his opinion the matters in respect of which his report is qualified are material for determining whether a distribution would contravene this Part, and

(b)  a copy of that statement must—

(i)   in the case of a private company, have been circulated to members in accordance with section 423, or

(ii)  in the case of a public company, have been laid before the company in general meeting.

(7)  A copy of the accounts, of the auditor's report and of any auditor's statement must have been delivered to the registrar.

Any requirement of Part 35 of this Act as to the delivery of a certified translation into English of any of those documents must also have been met.

*Application of provisions to successive distributions etc.*

### 840    Successive distributions etc. by reference to the same accounts

(1)  In determining whether a proposed distribution may be made by a company in a case where—

(a)  one or more previous distributions have been made in pursuance of a determination made by reference to the same relevant accounts, or

(b)  relevant financial assistance has been given, or other relevant payments have been made, since those accounts were prepared,

the provisions of this Part apply as if the amount of the proposed distribution was increased by the amount of the previous distributions, financial assistance and other payments.

(2)  The financial assistance and other payments that are relevant for this purpose are—

(a)  financial assistance lawfully given by the company out of its distributable profits;

(b)  financial assistance given by the company in contravention of section 678 or 679 (prohibited financial assistance) in a case where the giving of that assistance reduces the company's net assets or increases its net liabilities;

(c)  payments made by the company in respect of the purchase by it of shares in the company, except a payment lawfully made otherwise than out of distributable profits;

(d)  payments of any description specified in section 705 (payments apart from purchase price of shares to be made out of distributable profits).

(3)  In this section 'financial assistance' has the same meaning as in Chapter 2 of Part 18 (see section 677).

(4)  For the purpose of applying subsection (2)(b) in relation to any financial assistance—

(a)  'net assets' means the amount by which the aggregate amount of the company's assets exceeds the aggregate amount of its liabilities, and

(b)  'net liabilities' means the amount by which the aggregate amount of the company's liabilities exceeds the aggregate amount of its assets,

taking the amount of the assets and liabilities to be as stated in the company's accounting records immediately before the financial assistance is given.

(5)  For this purpose a company's liabilities include any amount retained as reasonably necessary for the purposes of providing for any liability—

(a)  the nature of which is clearly defined, and

(b)  which is either likely to be incurred or certain to be incurred but uncertain as to amount or as to the date on which it will arise.

## Chapter 3   Supplementary provisions

### *Accounting matters*

### 841    Realised losses and profits and revaluation of fixed assets

(1)  The following provisions have effect for the purposes of this Part.

(2)  The following are treated as realised losses—

(a)  in the case of Companies Act accounts, provisions of a kind specified for the purposes of this paragraph by regulations under section 396 (except revaluation provisions);

(b)  in the case of IAS accounts, provisions of any kind (except revaluation provisions).

(3) A 'revaluation provision' means a provision in respect of a diminution in value of a fixed asset appearing on a revaluation of all the fixed assets of the company, or of all of its fixed assets other than goodwill.

(4) For the purpose of subsections (2) and (3) any consideration by the directors of the value at a particular time of a fixed asset is treated as a revaluation provided—

(a) the directors are satisfied that the aggregate value at that time of the fixed assets of the company that have not actually been revalued is not less than the aggregate amount at which they are then stated in the company's accounts, and

(b) it is stated in a note to the accounts—

(i) that the directors have considered the value of some or all of the fixed assets of the company without actually revaluing them,

(ii) that they are satisfied that the aggregate value of those assets at the time of their consideration was not less than the aggregate amount at which they were then stated in the company's accounts, and

(iii) that accordingly, by virtue of this subsection, amounts are stated in the accounts on the basis that a revaluation of fixed assets of the company is treated as having taken place at that time.

(5) Where—

(a) on the revaluation of a fixed asset, an unrealised profit is shown to have been made, and

(b) on or after the revaluation, a sum is written off or retained for depreciation of that asset over a period,

an amount equal to the amount by which that sum exceeds the sum which would have been so written off or retained for the depreciation of that asset over that period, if that profit had not been made, is treated as a realised profit made over that period.

### 842 Determination of profit or loss in respect of asset where records incomplete

In determining for the purposes of this Part whether a company has made a profit or loss in respect of an asset where—

(a) there is no record of the original cost of the asset, or

(b) a record cannot be obtained without unreasonable expense or delay,

its cost is taken to be the value ascribed to it in the earliest available record of its value made on or after its acquisition by the company.

### 843 Realised profits and losses of long-term insurance business

(1) The provisions of this section have effect for the purposes of this Part as it applies in relation to an authorised insurance company, other than an insurance special purpose vehicle, carrying on long-term business.

(2) An amount included in the relevant part of the company's balance sheet that—

(a) represents a surplus in the fund or funds maintained by it in respect of its long-term business, and

(b) has not been allocated to policy holders or, as the case may be, carried forward unappropriated in accordance with asset identification rules made under section 142(2) of the Financial Services and Markets Act 2000 (c.8),

is treated as a realised profit.

(3) For the purposes of subsection (2)—

(a) the relevant part of the balance sheet is that part of the balance sheet that represents accumulated profit or loss;

(b) a surplus in the fund or funds maintained by the company in respect of its long-term business means an excess of the assets representing that fund or those funds over the liabilities of the company attributable to its long-term business, as shown by an actuarial investigation.

(4) A deficit in the fund or funds maintained by the company in respect of its long term business is treated as a realised loss.

For this purpose a deficit in any such fund or funds means an excess of the liabilities of the company attributable to its long-term business over the assets representing that fund or those funds, as shown by an actuarial investigation.

(5) Subject to subsections (2) and (4), any profit or loss arising in the company's long-term business is to be left out of account.

(6) For the purposes of this section an 'actuarial investigation' means an investigation made into the financial condition of an authorised insurance company in respect of its long-term business–

(a) carried out once in every period of twelve months in accordance with rules made under Part 10 of the Financial Services and Markets Act 2000, or

(b) carried out in accordance with a requirement imposed under section 166 of that Act,

by an actuary appointed as actuary to the company.

(7) In this section 'long-term business' means business that consists of effecting or carrying out contracts of long-term insurance.

This definition must be read with section 22 of the Financial Services and Markets Act 2000, any relevant order under that section and Schedule 2 to that Act.

(8) In this section 'insurance special purpose vehicle' means a special purpose vehicle within the meaning of Article 2.1(p) of Directive 2005/68/EC of the European Parliament and of the Council of 16 November 2005 on reinsurance and amending Council Directives 73/239/EEC, 92/49/EEC as well as Directives 98/78/EC and 2002/83/EC.

### 844 Treatment of development costs

(1) Where development costs are shown or included as an asset in a company's accounts, any amount shown or included in respect of those costs is treated—

    (a) for the purposes of section 830 (distributions to be made out of profits available for the purpose) as a realised loss, and

    (b) for the purposes of section 832 (distributions by investment companies out of accumulated revenue profits) as a realised revenue loss.

This is subject to the following exceptions.

(2) Subsection (1) does not apply to any part of that amount representing an unrealised profit made on revaluation of those costs.

(3) Subsection (1) does not apply if—

    (a) there are special circumstances in the company's case justifying the directors in deciding that the amount there mentioned is not to be treated as required by subsection (1),

    (b) it is stated—

        (i) in the case of Companies Act accounts, in the note required by regulations under section 396 as to the reasons for showing development costs as an asset, or

        (ii) in the case of IAS accounts, in any note to the accounts,

        (iii) that the amount is not to be so treated, and

    (c) the note explains the circumstances relied upon to justify the decision of the directors to that effect.

### Distributions in kind

### 845 Distributions in kind: determination of amount

(1) This section applies for determining the amount of a distribution consisting of or including, or treated as arising in consequence of, the sale, transfer or other disposition by a company of a non-cash asset where—

    (a) at the time of the distribution the company has profits available for distribution, and

    (b) if the amount of the distribution were to be determined in accordance with this section, the company could make the distribution without contravening this Part.

(2) The amount of the distribution (or the relevant part of it) is taken to be—

    (a) in a case where the amount or value of the consideration for the disposition is not less than the book value of the asset, zero;

    (b) in any other case, the amount by which the book value of the asset exceeds the amount or value of any consideration for the disposition.

(3) For the purposes of subsection (1)(a) the company's profits available for distribution are treated as increased by the amount (if any) by which the amount or value of any consideration for the disposition exceeds the book value of the asset.

(4) In this section 'book value', in relation to an asset, means—

    (a) the amount at which the asset is stated in the relevant accounts, or

    (b) where the asset is not stated in those accounts at any amount, zero.

(5) The provisions of Chapter 2 (justification of distribution by reference to accounts) have effect subject to this section.

### 846 Distributions in kind: treatment of unrealised profits

(1) This section applies where—

    (a) a company makes a distribution consisting of or including, or treated as arising in consequence of, the sale, transfer or other disposition by the company of a non-cash asset, and

    (b) any part of the amount at which that asset is stated in the relevant accounts represents an unrealised profit.

(2) That profit is treated as a realised profit—

    (a) for the purpose of determining the lawfulness of the distribution in accordance with this Part (whether before or after the distribution takes place), and

    (b) for the purpose of the application, in relation to anything done with a view to or in connection with the making of the distribution, of any provision of regulations under section 396 under which only realised profits are to be included in or transferred to the profit and loss account.

### Consequences of unlawful distribution

### 847 Consequences of unlawful distribution

(1) This section applies where a distribution, or part of one, made by a company to one of its members is made in contravention of this Part.

(2)  If at the time of the distribution the member knows or has reasonable grounds for believing that it is so made, he is liable—

(a)  to repay it (or that part of it, as the case may be) to the company, or

(b)  in the case of a distribution made otherwise than in cash, to pay the company a sum equal to the value of the distribution (or part) at that time.

(3)  This is without prejudice to any obligation imposed apart from this section on a member of a company to repay a distribution unlawfully made to him.

(4)  This section does not apply in relation to—

(a)  financial assistance given by a company in contravention of section 678 or 679, or

(b)  any payment made by a company in respect of the redemption or purchase by the company of shares in itself.

### *Other matters*

### 848   Saving for certain older provisions in articles

(1)  Where immediately before the relevant date a company was authorised by a provision of its articles to apply its unrealised profits in paying up in full or in part unissued shares to be allotted to members of the company as fully or partly paid bonus shares, that provision continues (subject to any alteration of the articles) as authority for those profits to be so applied after that date.

(2)  For this purpose the relevant date is—

(a)  for companies registered in Great Britain, 22nd December 1980;

(b)  for companies registered in Northern Ireland, 1st July 1983.

### 849   Restriction on application of unrealised profits

A company must not apply an unrealised profit in paying up debentures or any amounts unpaid on its issued shares.

### 850   Treatment of certain older profits or losses

(1)  Where the directors of a company are, after making all reasonable enquiries, unable to determine whether a particular profit made before the relevant date is realised or unrealised, they may treat the profit as realised.

(2)  Where the directors of a company, after making all reasonable enquiries, are unable to determine whether a particular loss made before the relevant date is realised or unrealised, they may treat the loss as unrealised.

(3)  For the purposes of this section the relevant date is—

(a)  for companies registered in Great Britain, 22nd December 1980;

(b)  for companies registered in Northern Ireland, 1st July 1983.

### 851   Application of rules of law restricting distributions

(1)  Except as provided in this section, the provisions of this Part are without prejudice to any rule of law restricting the sums out of which, or the cases in which, a distribution may be made.

(2)  For the purposes of any rule of law requiring distributions to be paid out of profits or restricting the return of capital to members—

(a)  section 845 (distributions in kind: determination of amount) applies to determine the amount of any distribution or return of capital consisting of or including, or treated as arising in consequence of the sale, transfer or other disposition by a company of a non-cash asset; and

(b)  section 846 (distributions in kind: treatment of unrealised profits) applies as it applies for the purposes of this Part.

(3)  In this section references to distributions are to amounts regarded as distributions for the purposes of any such rule of law as is referred to in subsection (1).

### 852   Saving for other restrictions on distributions

The provisions of this Part are without prejudice to any enactment, or any provision of a company's articles, restricting the sums out of which, or the cases in which, a distribution may be made.

### 853   Minor definitions

(1)  The following provisions apply for the purposes of this Part.

(2)  References to profit or losses of any description—

(a)  are to profits or losses of that description made at any time, and

(b)  except where the context otherwise requires, are to profits or losses of a revenue or capital character.

(3)  'Capitalisation', in relation to a company's profits, means any of the following operations (whenever carried out)—

(a)  applying the profits in wholly or partly paying up unissued shares in the company to be allotted to members of the company as fully or partly paid bonus shares, or

(b)  transferring the profits to capital redemption reserve.

(4)  References to 'realised profits' and 'realised losses', in relation to a company's accounts, are to such profits or losses of the company as fall to be treated as realised in accordance with principles

generally accepted at the time when the accounts are prepared, with respect to the determination for accounting purposes of realised profits or losses.

(5) Subsection (4) is without prejudice to—

(a) the construction of any other expression (where appropriate) by reference to accepted accounting principles or practice, or

(b) any specific provision for the treatment of profits or losses of any description as realised.

(6) 'Fixed assets' means assets of a company which are intended for use on a continuing basis in the company's activities.

# PART 24  A COMPANY'S ANNUAL RETURN

### 854  Duty to deliver annual returns

(1) Every company must deliver to the registrar successive annual returns each of which is made up to a date not later than the date that is from time to time the company's return date.

(2) The company's return date is—

(a) the anniversary of the company's incorporation, or

(b) if the company's last return delivered in accordance with this Part was made up to a different date, the anniversary of that date.

(3) Each return must—

(a) contain the information required by or under the following provisions of this Part, and

(b) be delivered to the registrar within 28 days after the date to which it is made up.

### 855  Contents of annual return: general

(1) Every annual return must state the date to which it is made up and contain the following information—

(a) the address of the company's registered office;

(b) the type of company it is and its principal business activities;

(c) the the required particulars (see section 855A) of—

(i) the directors of the company, and

(ii) in the case of a private company with a secretary or a public company, the secretary or joint secretaries;

(d) if any company records are (in accordance with regulations under section 1136) kept at a place other than the company's registered office, the address of that place and the records that are kept there;

(e) [ ];

(f) whether the company was a traded company at any time during the return period.

(2) The information as to the company's type must be given by reference to the classification scheme prescribed for the purposes of this section.

(3) The information as to the company's principal business activities may be given by reference to one or more categories of any prescribed system of classifying business activities.

(4) In this Part—

'return period', in relation to an annual return, means the period beginning immediately after the date to which the last return was made up (or, in the case of the first return, with the incorporation of the company) and ending with the date to which the return is made up; and

'traded company' means a company any of whose shares are shares admitted to trading on a regulated market (so that 'non-traded company' means a company none of whose shares are shares admitted to trading on a regulated market).

### 855A  Required particulars of directors and secretaries

(1) For the purposes of section 855(1)(c) the required particulars of a director are-

(a) where the director is an individual, the particulars required by section 163 to be entered in the register of directors (subject to subsection (2) below); and

(b) where the director is a body corporate or a firm that is a legal person under the law by which it is governed, the particulars required by section 164 to be entered in the register of directors.

(2) The former name of a director who is an individual is a required particular in relation to an annual return only if the director was known by the name for business purposes during the return period.

(3) For the purposes of section 855(1)(c)(ii) the required particulars of a secretary are—

(a) where a secretary is an individual, the particulars required by section 277 to be entered in the register of secretaries (subject to subsection (4) below); and

(b) where a secretary is a body corporate or a firm that is a legal person under the law by which it is governed, the particulars required by section 278(1) to be entered in the register of secretaries.

(4) The former name of a secretary who is an individual is a required particular in relation to an annual return only if the secretary was known by the name for business purposes during the return period.

(5) Where all the partners in a firm are joint secretaries, the required particulars are the particulars that would be required to be entered in the register of secretaries if the firm were a legal person and the firm had been appointed secretary.

**856 Contents of annual return: information about share capital**

(1) The annual return of a company having a share capital must also contain a statement of capital.

(2) The statement of capital must state with respect to the company's share capital at the date to which the return is made up—

(a) the total number of shares of the company,

(b) the aggregate nominal value of those shares,

(c) for each class of shares—

(i) the voting rights attached to the shares,

(ii) the total number of shares of that class, and

(iii) the aggregate nominal value of shares of that class, and

(d) the amount paid up and the amount (if any) unpaid on each share (whether on account of the nominal value of the share or by way of premium).

(3) [...]

(4) [...]

(5) [...]

(6) [...]

**856A Contents of annual return: information about shareholders: non-traded companies**

(1) The annual return of a company that was a non-traded company throughout the return period must also contain the following information.

(2) The return must contain the name (as it appears in the company's register of members) of every person who was a member of the company at any time during the return period. The return must conform to the following requirements for the purpose of enabling the entries relating to any given person to be easily found—

(a) the entries must be listed in alphabetical order by name; or

(b) the return must have annexed to it an index that is sufficient to enable the name of the person in question to be easily found.

(3) The return must also state—

(a) the number of shares of each class held at the end of the date to which the return is made up by each person who was a member of the company at that time,

(b) the number of shares of each class transferred during the return period by or to each person who was a member of the company at any time during that period, and

(c) the dates of registration of those transfers.

(4) If either of the two immediately preceding returns has given the full particulars required by subsections (2) and (3), the return need only give such particulars as relate—

(a) to persons who became, or ceased to be, members during the return period, and

(b) to shares transferred during that period.

**856B Contents of annual return: information about shareholders: traded companies**

(1) The annual return of a company that was a traded company at any time during the return period must also contain the following information.

(2) The return must contain the name and address (as they appear in the company's register of members) of every person who held at least 5% of the issued shares of any class of the company at any time during the return period. The return must conform to the following requirements for the purpose of enabling the entries relating to any given person to be easily found—

(a) the entries must be listed in alphabetical order by name; or

(b) the return must have annexed to it an index that is sufficient to enable the name of the person in question to be easily found.

(3) The return must also state—

(a) the number of shares of each class held at the end of the date to which the return is made up by each person who held at least 5% of the issued shares of any class of the company at that time,

(b) the number of shares of each class transferred during the return period by or to each person who held at least 5% of the issued shares of any class of the company at any time during that period, and

(c) the dates of registration of those transfers.

(4) If either of the two immediately preceding returns has given the full particulars required by subsections (2) and (3), the return need only give such particulars as relate—

(a) to persons who came to hold, or ceased to hold, at least 5% of the issued shares of any class of the company during the return period, and

(b) to shares transferred during that period.

**857 Contents of annual return: power to make further provision by regulations**

(1) The Secretary of State may by regulations make further provision as to the information to be given in a company's annual return.

(2) The regulations may—

(a) amend or repeal the provisions of sections 855 and 856, and

(b) provide for exceptions from the requirements of those sections as they have effect from time to time.

(3) Regulations under this section are subject to negative resolution procedure.

**858 Failure to deliver annual return**

(1) If a company fails to deliver an annual return before the end of the period of 28 days after a return date, an offence is committed by—

(a) the company,

(b) subject to subsection (4)—

(i) every director of the company, and

(ii) in the case of a private company with a secretary or a public company, every secretary of the company, and

(c) every other officer of the company who is in default.

For this purpose a shadow director is treated as a director.

(2) A person guilty of an offence under subsection (1) is liable on summary conviction to a fine not exceeding level 5 on the standard scale and, for continued contravention, a daily default fine not exceeding one-tenth of level 5 on the standard scale.

(3) The contravention continues until such time as an annual return made up to that return date is delivered by the company to the registrar.

(4) It is a defence for a director or secretary charged with an offence under subsection (1)(b) to prove that he took all reasonable steps to avoid the commission or continuation of the offence.

(5) In the case of continued contravention, an offence is also committed by every officer of the company who did not commit an offence under subsection (1) in relation to the initial contravention but is in default in relation to the continued contravention.

A person guilty of an offence under this subsection is liable on summary conviction to a fine not exceeding one-tenth of level 5 on the standard scale for each day on which the contravention continues and he is in default.

**859 [...]**

# PART 25 COMPANY CHARGES

## Chapter 1 Companies registered in England and Wales or in Northern Ireland

### Requirement to register company charges

**860 Charges created by a company**

(1) A company that creates a charge to which this section applies must deliver the prescribed particulars of the charge, together with the instrument (if any) by which the charge is created or evidenced, to the registrar for registration before the end of the period allowed for registration.

(2) Registration of a charge to which this section applies may instead be effected on the application of a person interested in it.

(3) Where registration is effected on the application of some person other than the company, that person is entitled to recover from the company the amount of any fees properly paid by him to the registrar on registration.

(4) If a company fails to comply with subsection (1), an offence is committed by—

(a) the company, and

(b) every officer of it who is in default.

(5) A person guilty of an offence under this section is liable—

(a) on conviction on indictment, to a fine;

(b) on summary conviction, to a fine not exceeding the statutory maximum.

(6) Subsection (4) does not apply if registration of the charge has been effected on the application of some other person.

(7) This section applies to the following charges—

(a) a charge on land or any interest in land, other than a charge for any rent or other periodical sum issuing out of land,

(b) a charge created or evidenced by an instrument which, if executed by an individual, would require registration as a bill of sale,

(c) a charge for the purposes of securing any issue of debentures,

(d) a charge on uncalled share capital of the company,

(e) a charge on calls made but not paid,

(f) a charge on book debts of the company,

(g) a floating charge on the company's property or undertaking,

(h) a charge on a ship or aircraft, or any share in a ship,

(i) a charge on goodwill or on any intellectual property.

### 861 Charges which have to be registered: supplementary

(1) The holding of debentures entitling the holder to a charge on land is not, for the purposes of section 860(7)(a), an interest in the land.

(2) It is immaterial for the purposes of this Chapter where land subject to a charge is situated.

(3) The deposit by way of security of a negotiable instrument given to secure the payment of book debts is not, for the purposes of section 860(7)(f), a charge on those book debts.

(4) For the purposes of section 860(7)(i), 'intellectual property' means—

(a) any patent, trade mark, registered design, copyright or design right;

(b) any licence under or in respect of any such right.

(5) In this Chapter—

'charge' includes mortgage, and

'company' means a company registered in England and Wales or in Northern Ireland.

### 862 Charges existing on property acquired

(1) This section applies where a company acquires property which is subject to a charge of a kind which would, if it had been created by the company after the acquisition of the property, have been required to be registered under this Chapter.

(2) The company must deliver the prescribed particulars of the charge, together with a certified copy of the instrument (if any) by which the charge is created or evidenced, to the registrar for registration.

(3) Subsection (2) must be complied with before the end of the period allowed for registration.

(4) If default is made in complying with this section, an offence is committed by—

(a) the company, and

(b) every officer of it who is in default.

(5) A person guilty of an offence under this section is liable—

(a) on conviction on indictment, to a fine;

(b) on summary conviction, to a fine not exceeding the statutory maximum.

*Special rules about debentures*

### 863 Charge in series of debentures

(1) Where a series of debentures containing, or giving by reference to another instrument, any charge to the benefit of which debenture holders of that series are entitled pari passu is created by a company, it is for the purposes of section 860(1) sufficient if the required particulars, together with the deed containing the charge (or, if there is no such deed, one of the debentures of the series), are delivered to the registrar before the end of the period allowed for registration.

(2) The following are the required particulars—

(a) the total amount secured by the whole series, and

(b) the dates of the resolutions authorising the issue of the series and the date of the covering deed (if any) by which the series is created or defined, and

(c) a general description of the property charged, and

(d) the names of the trustees (if any) for the debenture holders.

(3) Particulars of the date and amount of each issue of debentures of a series of the kind mentioned in subsection (1) must be sent to the registrar for entry in the register of charges.

(4) Failure to comply with subsection (3) does not affect the validity of the debentures issued.

(5) Subsections (2) to (6) of section 860 apply for the purposes of this section as they apply for the purposes of that section, but as if references to the registration of a charge were references to the registration of a series of debentures.

### 864 Additional registration requirement for commission etc. in relation to debentures

(1) Where any commission, allowance or discount has been paid or made either directly or indirectly by a company to a person in consideration of his—

(a) subscribing or agreeing to subscribe, whether absolutely or conditionally, for debentures in a company, or

(b) procuring or agreeing to procure subscriptions, whether absolute or conditional, for such debentures,

the particulars required to be sent for registration under section 860 shall include particulars as to the amount or rate per cent of the commission, discount or allowance so paid or made.

(2) The deposit of debentures as security for a debt of the company is not, for the purposes of this section, treated as the issue of debentures at a discount.

(3) Failure to comply with this section does not affect the validity of the debentures issued.

### 865    Endorsement of certificate on debentures

(1) The company shall cause a copy of every certificate of registration given under section 869 to be endorsed on every debenture or certificate of debenture stock which is issued by the company, and the payment of which is secured by the charge so registered.

(2) But this does not require a company to cause a certificate of registration of any charge so given to be endorsed on any debenture or certificate of debenture stock issued by the company before the charge was created.

(3) If a person knowingly and wilfully authorises or permits the delivery of a debenture or certificate of debenture stock which under this section is required to have endorsed on it a copy of a certificate of registration, without the copy being so endorsed upon it, he commits an offence.

(4) A person guilty of an offence under this section is liable on summary conviction to a fine not exceeding level 3 on the standard scale.

*Charges in other jurisdictions*

### 866    Charges created in, or over property in, jurisdictions outside the United Kingdom

(1) Where a charge is created outside the United Kingdom comprising property situated outside the United Kingdom, the delivery to the registrar of a verified copy of the instrument by which the charge is created or evidenced has the same effect for the purposes of this Chapter as the delivery of the instrument itself.

(2) Where a charge is created in the United Kingdom but comprises property outside the United Kingdom, the instrument creating or purporting to create the charge may be sent for registration under section 860 even if further proceedings may be necessary to make the charge valid or effectual according to the law of the country in which the property is situated.

### 867    Charges created in, or over property in, another United Kingdom jurisdiction

(1) Subsection (2) applies where—

(a) a charge comprises property situated in a part of the United Kingdom other than the part in which the company is registered, and

(b) registration in that other part is necessary to make the charge valid or effectual under the law of that part of the United Kingdom.

(2) The delivery to the registrar of a verified copy of the instrument by which the charge is created or evidenced, together with a certificate stating that the charge was presented for registration in that other part of the United Kingdom on the date on which it was so presented has, for the purposes of this Chapter, the same effect as the delivery of the instrument itself.

*Orders charging land: Northern Ireland*

### 868    Northern Ireland: registration of certain charges etc. affecting land

(1) Where a charge imposed by an order under Article 46 of the 1981 Order or notice of such a charge is registered in the Land Registry against registered land or any estate in registered land of a company, the Registrar of Titles shall as soon as may be cause two copies of the order made under Article 46 of that Order or of any notice under Article 48 of that Order to be delivered to the registrar.

(2) Where a charge imposed by an order under Article 46 of the 1981 Order is registered in the Registry of Deeds against any unregistered land or estate in land of a company, the Registrar of Deeds shall as soon as may be cause two copies of the order to be delivered to the registrar.

(3) On delivery of copies under this section, the registrar shall—

(a) register one of them in accordance with section 869, and

(b) not later than 7 days from that date of delivery, cause the other copy together with a certificate of registration under section 869(5) to be sent to the company against which judgment was given.

(4) Where a charge to which subsection (1) or (2) applies is vacated, the Registrar of Titles or, as the case may be, the Registrar of Deeds shall cause a certified copy of the certificate of satisfaction lodged under Article 132(1) of the 1981 Order to be delivered to the registrar for entry of a memorandum of satisfaction in accordance with section 872.

(5) In this section—

'the 1981 Order' means the Judgments Enforcement (Northern Ireland) Order 1981 (S.I. 1981/226 (N.I. 6));

'the Registrar of Deeds' means the registrar appointed under the Registration of Deeds Act (Northern Ireland) 1970 (c. 25);

'Registry of Deeds' has the same meaning as in the Registration of Deeds Acts;

'Registration of Deeds Acts' means the Registration of Deeds Act (Northern Ireland) 1970 and every statutory provision for the time being in force amending that Act or otherwise relating to the registry of deeds, or the registration of deeds, orders or other instruments or documents in such registry;

'the Land Registry' and 'the Registrar of Titles' are to be construed in accordance with section 1 of the Land Registration Act (Northern Ireland) 1970 (c. 18);

'registered land' and 'unregistered land' have the same meaning as in Part 3 of the Land Registration Act (Northern Ireland) 1970.

*The register of charges*

**869    Register of charges to be kept by registrar**

(1) The registrar shall keep, with respect to each company, a register of all the charges requiring registration under this Chapter.

(2) In the case of a charge to the benefit of which holders of a series of debentures are entitled, the registrar shall enter in the register the required particulars specified in section 863(2).

(3) In the case of a charge imposed by the Enforcement of Judgments Office under Article 46 of the Judgments Enforcement (Northern Ireland) Order 1981, the registrar shall enter in the register the date on which the charge became effective.

(4) In the case of any other charge, the registrar shall enter in the register the following particulars—

  (a) if it is a charge created by a company, the date of its creation and, if it is a charge which was existing on property acquired by the company, the date of the acquisition,

  (b) the amount secured by the charge,

  (c) short particulars of the property charged, and

  (d) the persons entitled to the charge.

(5) The registrar shall give a certificate of the registration of any charge registered in pursuance of this Chapter, stating the amount secured by the charge.

(6) The certificate—

  (a) shall be signed by the registrar or authenticated by the registrar's official seal, and

  (b) is conclusive evidence that the requirements of this Chapter as to registration have been satisfied.

(7) The register kept in pursuance of this section shall be open to inspection by any person.

**870    The period allowed for registration**

(1) The period allowed for registration of a charge created by a company is—

  (a) 21 days beginning with the day after the day on which the charge is created, or

  (b) if the charge is created outside the United Kingdom, 21 days beginning with the day after the day on which the instrument by which the charge is created or evidenced (or a copy of it) could, in due course of post (and if despatched with due diligence) have been received in the United Kingdom.

(2) The period allowed for registration of a charge to which property acquired by a company is subject is—

  (a) 21 days beginning with the day after the day on which the acquisition is completed, or

  (b) if the property is situated and the charge was created outside the United Kingdom, 21 days beginning with the day after the day on which the instrument by which the charge is created or evidenced (or a copy of it) could, in due course of post (and if despatched with due diligence) have been received in the United Kingdom.

(3) The period allowed for registration of particulars of a series of debentures as a result of section 863 is—

  (a) if there is a deed containing the charge mentioned in section 863(1), 21 days beginning with the day after the day on which that deed is executed, or

  (b) if there is no such deed, 21 days beginning with the day after the day on which the first debenture of the series is executed.

**871    Registration of enforcement of security**

(1) If a person obtains an order for the appointment of a receiver or manager of a company's property, or appoints such a receiver or manager under powers contained in an instrument, he shall within 7 days of the order or of the appointment under those powers, give notice of the fact to the registrar.

(2) Where a person appointed receiver or manager of a company's property under powers contained in an instrument ceases to act as such receiver or manager, he shall, on so ceasing, give the registrar notice to that effect.

(3) The registrar must enter a fact of which he is given notice under this section in the register of charges.

(4) A person who makes default in complying with the requirements of this section commits an offence.

(5) A person guilty of an offence under this section is liable on summary conviction to a fine not exceeding level 3 on the standard scale and, for continued contravention, a daily default fine not exceeding one-tenth of level 3 on the standard scale.

**872    Entries of satisfaction and release**

(1) Subsection (2) applies if a statement is delivered to the registrar verifying with respect to a registered charge—

(a) that the debt for which the charge was given has been paid or satisfied in whole or in part, or

(b) that part of the property or undertaking charged has been released from the charge or has ceased to form part of the company's property or undertaking.

(2) The registrar may enter on the register a memorandum of satisfaction in whole or in part, or of the fact part of the property or undertaking has been released from the charge or has ceased to form part of the company's property or undertaking (as the case may be).

(3) Where the registrar enters a memorandum of satisfaction in whole, the registrar shall if required send the company a copy of it.

### 873 Rectification of register of charges

(1) Subsection (2) applies if the court is satisfied—

(a) that the failure to register a charge before the end of the period allowed for registration, or the omission or mis-statement of any particular with respect to any such charge or in a memorandum of satisfaction—

(i) was accidental or due to inadvertence or to some other sufficient cause, or

(ii) is not of a nature to prejudice the position of creditors or shareholders of the company, or

(b) that on other grounds it is just and equitable to grant relief.

(2) The court may, on the application of the company or a person interested, and on such terms and conditions as seem to the court just and expedient, order that the period allowed for registration shall be extended or, as the case may be, that the omission or mis-statement shall be rectified.

*Avoidance of certain charges*

### 874 Consequence of failure to register charges created by a company

(1) If a company creates a charge to which section 860 applies, the charge is void (so far as any security on the company's property or undertaking is conferred by it) against—

(a) a liquidator of the company,

(b) an administrator of the company, and

(c) a creditor of the company,

unless that section is complied with.

(2) Subsection (1) is subject to the provisions of this Chapter.

(3) Subsection (1) is without prejudice to any contract or obligation for repayment of the money secured by the charge; and when a charge becomes void under this section, the money secured by it immediately becomes payable.

*Companies' records and registers*

### 875 Companies to keep copies of instruments creating charges

(1) A company must keep available for inspection a copy of every instrument creating a charge requiring registration under this Chapter, including any document delivered to the company under section 868(3)(b) (Northern Ireland: orders imposing charges affecting land).

(2) In the case of a series of uniform debentures, a copy of one of the debentures of the series is sufficient.

### 876 Company's register of charges

(1) Every limited company shall keep available for inspection a register of charges and enter in it—

(a) all charges specifically affecting property of the company, and

(b) all floating charges on the whole or part of the company's property or undertaking.

(2) The entry shall in each case give a short description of the property charged, the amount of the charge and, except in the cases of securities to bearer, the names of the persons entitled to it.

(3) If an officer of the company knowingly and wilfully authorises or permits the omission of an entry required to be made in pursuance of this section, he commits an offence.

(4) A person guilty of an offence under this section is liable—

(a) on conviction on indictment, to a fine;

(b) on summary conviction, to a fine not exceeding the statutory maximum.

### 877 Instruments creating charges and register of charges to be available for inspection

(1) This section applies to—

(a) documents required to be kept available for inspection under section 875 (copies of instruments creating charges), and

(b) a company's register of charges kept in pursuance of section 876.

(2) The documents and register must be kept available for inspection—

(a) at the company's registered office, or

(b) at a place specified in regulations under section 1136.

(3)  The company must give notice to the registrar—

  (a)  of the place at which the documents and register are kept available for inspection, and

  (b)  of any change in that place,

unless they have at all times been kept at the company's registered office.

(4)  The documents and register shall be open to the inspection—

  (a)  of any creditor or member of the company without charge, and

  (b)  of any other person on payment of such fee as may be prescribed.

(5)  If default is made for 14 days in complying with subsection (3) or an inspection required under subsection (4) is refused, an offence is committed by—

  (a)  the company, and

  (b)  every officer of the company who is in default.

(6)  A person guilty of an offence under this section is liable on summary conviction to a fine not exceeding level 3 on the standard scale and, for continued contravention, a daily default fine not exceeding one-tenth of level 3 on the standard scale.

(7)  If an inspection required under subsection (4) is refused the court may by order compel an immediate inspection.

## Chapter 2  Companies registered in Scotland

*Charges requiring registration*

### 878   Charges created by a company

(1)  A company that creates a charge to which this section applies must deliver the prescribed particulars of the charge, together with a copy certified as a correct copy of the instrument (if any) by which the charge is created or evidenced, to the registrar for registration before the end of the period allowed for registration.

(2)  Registration of a charge to which this section applies may instead be effected on the application of a person interested in it.

(3)  Where registration is effected on the application of some person other than the company, that person is entitled to recover from the company the amount of any fees properly paid by him to the registrar on the registration.

(4)  If a company fails to comply with subsection (1), an offence is committed by—

  (a)  the company, and

  (b)  every officer of the company who is in default.

(5)  A person guilty of an offence under this section is liable—

  (a)  on conviction on indictment, to a fine;

  (b)  on summary conviction, to a fine not exceeding the statutory maximum.

(6)  Subsection (4) does not apply if registration of the charge has been effected on the application of some other person.

(7)  This section applies to the following charges—

  (a)  a charge on land or any interest in such land, other than a charge for any rent or other periodical sum payable in respect of the land,

  (b)  a security over incorporeal moveable property of any of the following categories—

    (i)    goodwill,

    (ii)   a patent or a licence under a patent,

    (iii)  a trademark,

    (iv)   a copyright or a licence under a copyright,

    (v)    a registered design or a licence in respect of such a design,

    (vi)   a design right or a licence under a design right,

    (vii)  the book debts (whether book debts of the company or assigned to it), and

    (viii) uncalled share capital of the company or calls made but not paid,

  (c)  a security over a ship or aircraft or any share in a ship,

  (d)  a floating charge.

### 879   Charges which have to be registered: supplementary

(1)  A charge on land, for the purposes of section 878(7)(a), includes a charge created by a heritable security within the meaning of section 9(8) of the Conveyancing and Feudal Reform (Scotland) Act 1970 (c. 35).

(2)  The holding of debentures entitling the holder to a charge on land is not, for the purposes of section 878(7)(a), deemed to be an interest in land.

(3)  It is immaterial for the purposes of this Chapter where land subject to a charge is situated.

(4)  The deposit by way of security of a negotiable instrument given to secure the payment of book debts is not, for the purposes of section 878(7)(b)(vii), to be treated as a charge on those book debts.

(5)  References in this Chapter to the date of the creation of a charge are—

  (a)  in the case of a floating charge, the date on which the instrument creating the floating charge was executed by the company creating the charge, and

(b) in any other case, the date on which the right of the person entitled to the benefit of the charge was constituted as a real right.

(6) In this Chapter 'company' means an incorporated company registered in Scotland.

### 880  Duty to register charges existing on property acquired

(1) Subsection (2) applies where a company acquires any property which is subject to a charge of any kind as would, if it had been created by the company after the acquisition of the property, have been required to be registered under this Chapter.

(2) The company must deliver the prescribed particulars of the charge, together with a copy (certified to be a correct copy) of the instrument (if any) by which the charge was created or is evidenced, to the registrar for registration before the end of the period allowed for registration.

(3) If default is made in complying with this section, an offence is committed by—

(a) the company, and

(b) every officer of it who is in default.

(4) A person guilty of an offence under this section is liable—

(a) on conviction on indictment, to a fine;

(b) on summary conviction, to a fine not exceeding the statutory maximum.

### 881  Charge by way of ex facie absolute disposition, etc.

(1) For the avoidance of doubt, it is hereby declared that, in the case of a charge created by way of an *ex facie* absolute disposition or assignation qualified by a back letter or other agreement, or by a standard security qualified by an agreement, compliance with section 878(1) does not of itself render the charge unavailable as security for indebtedness incurred after the date of compliance.

(2) Where the amount secured by a charge so created is purported to be increased by a further back letter or agreement, a further charge is held to have been created by the *ex facie* absolute disposition or assignation or (as the case may be) by the standard security, as qualified by the further back letter or agreement.

(3) In that case, the provisions of this Chapter apply to the further charge as if—

(a) references in this Chapter (other than in this section) to a charge were references to the further charge, and

(b) references to the date of the creation of a charge were references to the date on which the further back letter or agreement was executed.

*Special rules about debentures*

### 882  Charge in series of debentures

(1) Where a series of debentures containing, or giving by reference to any other instrument, any charge to the benefit of which the debenture-holders of that series are entitled *pari passu*, is created by a company, it is sufficient for purposes of section 878 if the required particulars, together with a copy of the deed containing the charge (or, if there is no such deed, of one of the debentures of the series) are delivered to the registrar before the end of the period allowed for registration.

(2) The following are the required particulars—

(a) the total amount secured by the whole series,

(b) the dates of the resolutions authorising the issue of the series and the date of the covering deed (if any) by which the security is created or defined,

(c) a general description of the property charged,

(d) the names of the trustees (if any) for the debenture-holders, and

(e) in the case of a floating charge, a statement of any provisions of the charge and of any instrument relating to it which prohibit or restrict or regulate the power of the company to grant further securities ranking in priority to, or *pari passu* with, the floating charge, or which vary or otherwise regulate the order of ranking of the floating charge in relation to subsisting securities.

(3) Where more than one issue is made of debentures in the series, particulars of the date and amount of each issue of debentures of the series must be sent to the registrar for entry in the register of charges.

(4) Failure to comply with subsection (3) does not affect the validity of any of those debentures.

(5) Subsections (2) to (6) of section 878 apply for the purposes of this section as they apply for the purposes of that section but as if for the reference to the registration of the charge there was substituted a reference to the registration of the series of debentures.

### 883  Additional registration requirement for commission etc. in relation to debentures

(1) Where any commission, allowance or discount has been paid or made either directly or indirectly by a company to a person in consideration of his—

(a) subscribing or agreeing to subscribe, whether absolutely or conditionally, for debentures in a company, or

(b) procuring or agreeing to procure subscriptions, whether absolute or conditional, for such debentures,

the particulars required to be sent for registration under section 878 shall include particulars as to the amount or rate per cent. of the commission, discount or allowance so paid or made.

(2) The deposit of debentures as security for a debt of the company is not, for the purposes of this section, treated as the issue of debentures at a discount.

(3) Failure to comply with this section does not affect the validity of the debentures issued.

### *Charges on property outside the United Kingdom*

### 884 Charges on property outside United Kingdom

Where a charge is created in the United Kingdom but comprises property outside the United Kingdom, the copy of the instrument creating or purporting to create the charge may be sent for registration under section 878 even if further proceedings may be necessary to make the charge valid or effectual according to the law of the country in which the property is situated.

### *The register of charges*

### 885 Register of charges to be kept by registrar

(1) The registrar shall keep, with respect to each company, a register of all the charges requiring registration under this Chapter.

(2) In the case of a charge to the benefit of which holders of a series of debentures are entitled, the registrar shall enter in the register the required particulars specified in section 882(2).

(3) In the case of any other charge, the registrar shall enter in the register the following particulars—

(a) if it is a charge created by a company, the date of its creation and, if it is a charge which was existing on property acquired by the company, the date of the acquisition,

(b) the amount secured by the charge,

(c) short particulars of the property charged,

(d) the persons entitled to the charge, and

(e) in the case of a floating charge, a statement of any of the provisions of the charge and of any instrument relating to it which prohibit or restrict or regulate the company's power to grant further securities ranking in priority to, or *pari passu* with, the floating charge, or which vary or otherwise regulate the order of ranking of the floating charge in relation to subsisting securities.

(4) The registrar shall give a certificate of the registration of any charge registered in pursuance of this Chapter, stating—

(a) the name of the company and the person first-named in the charge among those entitled to the benefit of the charge (or, in the case of a series of debentures, the name of the holder of the first such debenture issued), and

(b) the amount secured by the charge.

(5) The certificate—

(a) shall be signed by the registrar or authenticated by the registrar's official seal, and

(b) is conclusive evidence that the requirements of this Chapter as to registration have been satisfied.

(6) The register kept in pursuance of this section shall be open to inspection by any person.

### 886 The period allowed for registration

(1) The period allowed for registration of a charge created by a company is—

(a) 21 days beginning with the day after the day on which the charge is created, or

(b) if the charge is created outside the United Kingdom, 21 days beginning with the day after the day on which a copy of the instrument by which the charge is created or evidenced could, in due course of post (and if despatched with due diligence) have been received in the United Kingdom.

(2) The period allowed for registration of a charge to which property acquired by a company is subject is—

(a) 21 days beginning with the day after the day on which the transaction is settled, or

(b) if the property is situated and the charge was created outside the United Kingdom, 21 days beginning with the day after the day on which a copy of the instrument by which the charge is created or evidenced could, in due course of post (and if despatched with due diligence) have been received in the United Kingdom.

(3) The period allowed for registration of particulars of a series of debentures as a result of section 882 is—

(a) if there is a deed containing the charge mentioned in section 882(1), 21 days beginning with the day after the day on which that deed is executed, or

(b) if there is no such deed, 21 days beginning with the day after the day on which the first debenture of the series is executed.

### 887 Entries of satisfaction and relief

(1) Subsection (2) applies if a statement is delivered to the registrar verifying with respect to any registered charge—

    (a) that the debt for which the charge was given has been paid or satisfied in whole or in part, or

    (b) that part of the property charged has been released from the charge or has ceased to form part of the company's property.

(2) If the charge is a floating charge, the statement must be accompanied by either—

    (a) a statement by the creditor entitled to the benefit of the charge, or a person authorised by him for the purpose, verifying that the statement mentioned in subsection (1) is correct, or

    (b) a direction obtained from the court, on the ground that the statement by the creditor mentioned in paragraph (a) could not be readily obtained, dispensing with the need for that statement.

(3) The registrar may enter on the register a memorandum of satisfaction (in whole or in part) regarding the fact contained in the statement mentioned in subsection (1).

(4) Where the registrar enters a memorandum of satisfaction in whole, he shall, if required, furnish the company with a copy of the memorandum.

(5) Nothing in this section requires the company to submit particulars with respect to the entry in the register of a memorandum of satisfaction where the company, having created a floating charge over all or any part of its property, disposes of part of the property subject to the floating charge.

### 888 Rectification of register of charges

(1) Subsection (2) applies if the court is satisfied—

    (a) that the failure to register a charge before the end of the period allowed for registration, or the omission or mis-statement of any particular with respect to any such charge or in a memorandum of satisfaction—

        (i) was accidental or due to inadvertence or to some other sufficient cause, or

        (ii) is not of a nature to prejudice the position of creditors or shareholders of the company, or

    (b) that on other grounds it is just and equitable to grant relief.

(2) The court may, on the application of the company or a person interested, and on such terms and conditions as seem to the court just and expedient, order that the period allowed for registration shall be extended or, as the case may be, that the omission or mis-statement shall be rectified.

*Avoidance of certain charges*

### 889 Charges void unless registered

(1) If a company creates a charge to which section 878 applies, the charge is void (so far as any security on the company's property or any part of it is conferred by the charge) against—

    (a) the liquidator of the company,

    (b) an administrator of the company, and

    (c) any creditor of the company

unless that section is complied with.

(2) Subsection (1) is without prejudice to any contract or obligation for repayment of the money secured by the charge; and when a charge becomes void under this section the money secured by it immediately becomes payable.

*Companies' records and registers*

### 890 Copies of instruments creating charges to be kept by company

(1) Every company shall cause a copy of every instrument creating a charge requiring registration under this Chapter to be kept available for inspection.

(2) In the case of a series of uniform debentures, a copy of one debenture of the series is sufficient.

### 891 Company's register of charges

(1) Every company shall keep available for inspection a register of charges and enter in it all charges specifically affecting property of the company, and all floating charges on any property of the company.

(2) There shall be given in each case a short description of the property charged, the amount of the charge and, except in the case of securities to bearer, the names of the persons entitled to it.

(3) If an officer of the company knowingly and wilfully authorises or permits the omission of an entry required to be made in pursuance of this section, he commits an offence.

(4) A person guilty of an offence under this section is liable—

    (a) on conviction on indictment, to a fine;

    (b) on summary conviction, to a fine not exceeding the statutory maximum.

### 892 Instruments creating charges and register of charges to be available for inspection

(1) This section applies to—

    (a) documents required to be kept available for inspection under section 890 (copies of instruments creating charges), and

    (b) a company's register of charges kept in pursuance of section 891.

  (2) The documents and register must be kept available for inspection—

    (a) at the company's registered office, or

    (b) at a place specified in regulations under section 1136.

  (3) The company must give notice to the registrar—

    (a) of the place at which the documents and register are kept available for inspection, and

    (b) of any change in that place,

unless they have at all times been kept at the company's registered office.

  (4) The documents and register shall be open to the inspection—

    (a) of any creditor or member of the company without charge, and

    (b) of any other person on payment of such fee as may be prescribed.

  (5) If default is made for 14 days in complying with subsection (3) or an inspection required under subsection (4) is refused, an offence is committed by—

    (a) the company, and

    (b) every officer of the company who is in default.

  (6) A person guilty of an offence under this section is liable on summary conviction to a fine not exceeding level 3 on the standard scale and, for continued contravention, a daily default fine not exceeding one-tenth of level 3 on the standard scale.

  (7) If an inspection required under subsection (4) is refused the court may by order compel an immediate inspection.

## Chapter 3  Powers of the secretary of state

### 893  Power to make provision for effect of registration in special register

  (1) In this section a 'special register' means a register, other than the register of charges kept under this Part, in which a charge to which Chapter 1 or Chapter 2 applies is required or authorised to be registered.

  (2) The Secretary of State may by order make provision for facilitating the making of information-sharing arrangements between the person responsible for maintaining a special register ('the responsible person') and the registrar that meet the requirement in subsection (4).

  'Information-sharing arrangements' are arrangements to share and make use of information held by the registrar or by the responsible person.

  (3) If the Secretary of State is satisfied that appropriate information-sharing arrangements have been made, he may by order provide that—

    (a) the registrar is authorised not to register a charge of a specified description under Chapter 1 or Chapter 2,

    (b) a charge of a specified description that is registered in the special register within a specified period is to be treated as if it had been registered (and certified by the registrar as registered) in accordance with the requirements of Chapter 1 or, as the case may be, Chapter 2, and

    (c) the other provisions of Chapter 1 or, as the case may be, Chapter 2 apply to a charge so treated with specified modifications.

  (4) The information-sharing arrangements must ensure that persons inspecting the register of charges—

    (a) are made aware, in a manner appropriate to the inspection, of the existence of charges in the special register which are treated in accordance with provision so made, and

    (b) are able to obtain information from the special register about any such charge.

  (5) An order under this section may—

    (a) modify any enactment or rule of law which would otherwise restrict or prevent the responsible person from entering into or giving effect to information-sharing arrangements,

    (b) authorise the responsible person to require information to be provided to him for the purposes of the arrangements,

    (c) make provision about—

      (i) the charging by the responsible person of fees in connection with the arrangements and the destination of such fees (including provision modifying any enactment which would otherwise apply in relation to fees payable to the responsible person), and

      (ii) the making of payments under the arrangements by the registrar to the responsible person,

    (d) require the registrar to make copies of the arrangements available to the public (in hard copy or electronic form).

  (6) In this section 'specified' means specified in an order under this section.

  (7) A description of charge may be specified, in particular, by reference to one or more of the following—

    (a) the type of company by which it is created,

    (b) the form of charge which it is,

    (c) the description of assets over which it is granted,

    (d) the length of the period between the date of its registration in the special register and the date of its creation.

(8) Provision may be made under this section relating to registers maintained under the law of a country or territory outside the United Kingdom.

(9) An order under this section is subject to negative resolution procedure.

### 894 General power to make amendments to this Part

(1) The Secretary of State may by regulations under this section—

    (a) amend this Part by altering, adding or repealing provisions,

    (b) make consequential amendments or repeals in this Act or any other enactment (whether passed or made before or after this Act).

(2) Regulations under this section are subject to affirmative resolution procedure.

# PART 26 ARRANGEMENTS AND RECONSTRUCTIONS

## *Application of this Part*

### 895 Application of this Part

(1) The provisions of this Part apply where a compromise or arrangement is proposed between a company and—

    (a) its creditors, or any class of them, or

    (b) its members, or any class of them.

(2) In this Part—

'arrangement' includes a reorganisation of the company's share capital by the consolidation of shares of different classes or by the division of shares into shares of different classes, or by both of those methods; and

'company'—

    (a) in section 900 (powers of court to facilitate reconstruction or amalgamation) means a company within the meaning of this Act, and

    (b) elsewhere in this Part means any company liable to be wound up under the Insolvency Act 1986 (c. 45) or the Insolvency (Northern Ireland) Order 1989 (S.I. 1989/2405 (N.I. 19)).

(3) The provisions of this Part have effect subject to Part 27 (mergers and divisions of public companies) where that Part applies (see sections 902 and 903).

## *Meeting of creditors or members*

### 896 Court order for holding of meeting

(1) The court may, on an application under this section, order a meeting of the creditors or class of creditors, or of the members of the company or class of members (as the case may be), to be summoned in such manner as the court directs.

(2) An application under this section may be made by—

    (a) the company,

    (b) any creditor or member of the company,

    (c) if the company is being wound up, the liquidator, or

    (d) if the company is in administration, the administrator.

(3) Section 323 (representation of corporations at meetings) applies to a meeting of creditors under this section as to a meeting of the company (references to a member of the company being read as references to a creditor).

### 897 Statement to be circulated or made available

(1) Where a meeting is summoned under section 896—

    (a) every notice summoning the meeting that is sent to a creditor or member must be accompanied by a statement complying with this section, and

    (b) every notice summoning the meeting that is given by advertisement must either—

        (i) include such a statement, or

        (ii) state where and how creditors or members entitled to attend the meeting may obtain copies of such a statement.

(2) The statement must—

    (a) explain the effect of the compromise or arrangement, and

    (b) in particular, state—

        (i) any material interests of the directors of the company (whether as directors or as members or as creditors of the company or otherwise), and

        (ii) the effect on those interests of the compromise or arrangement, in so far as it is different from the effect on the like interests of other persons.

(3) Where the compromise or arrangement affects the rights of debenture holders of the company, the statement must give the like explanation as respects the trustees of any deed for securing the issue of the debentures as it is required to give as respects the company's directors.

(4) Where a notice given by advertisement states that copies of an explanatory statement can be obtained by creditors or members entitled to attend the meeting, every such creditor or member is entitled, on making application in the manner indicated by the notice, to be provided by the company with a copy of the statement free of charge.

(5) If a company makes default in complying with any requirement of this section, an offence is committed by—

(a) the company, and

(b) every officer of the company who is in default.

This is subject to subsection (7) below.

(6) For this purpose the following are treated as officers of the company—

(a) a liquidator or administrator of the company, and

(b) a trustee of a deed for securing the issue of debentures of the company.

(7) A person is not guilty of an offence under this section if he shows that the default was due to the refusal of a director or trustee for debenture holders to supply the necessary particulars of his interests.

(8) A person guilty of an offence under this section is liable—

(a) on conviction on indictment, to a fine;

(b) on summary conviction, to a fine not exceeding the statutory maximum.

## 898    Duty of directors and trustees to provide information

(1) It is the duty of—

(a) any director of the company, and

(b) any trustee for its debenture holders,

to give notice to the company of such matters relating to himself as may be necessary for the purposes of section 897 (explanatory statement to be circulated or made available).

(2) Any person who makes default in complying with this section commits an offence.

(3) A person guilty of an offence under this section is liable on summary conviction to a fine not exceeding level 3 on the standard scale.

*Court sanction for compromise or arrangement*

## 899    Court sanction for compromise or arrangement

(1) If a majority in number representing 75% in value of the creditors or class of creditors or members or class of members (as the case may be), present and voting either in person or by proxy at the meeting summoned under section 896, agree a compromise or arrangement, the court may, on an application under this section, sanction the compromise or arrangement.

(2) An application under this section may be made by—

(a) the company,

(b) any creditor or member of the company,

(c) if the company is being wound up, the liquidator, or

(d) if the company is in administration, the administrator.

(3) A compromise or agreement sanctioned by the court is binding on—

(a) all creditors or the class of creditors or on the members or class of members (as the case may be), and

(b) the company or, in the case of a company in the course of being wound up, the liquidator and contributories of the company.

(4) The court's order has no effect until a copy of it has been delivered to the registrar.

(5) Section 323 (representation of corporations at meetings) applies to a meeting of creditors under this section as to a meeting of the company (references to a member of the company being read as references to a creditor).

*Reconstructions and amalgamations*

## 900    Powers of court to facilitate reconstruction or amalgamation

(1) This section applies where application is made to the court under section 899 to sanction a compromise or arrangement and it is shown that—

(a) the compromise or arrangement is proposed for the purposes of, or in connection with, a scheme for the reconstruction of any company or companies, or the amalgamation of any two or more companies, and

(b) under the scheme the whole or any part of the undertaking or the property of any company concerned in the scheme ('a transferor company') is to be transferred to another company ('the transferee company').

(2) The court may, either by the order sanctioning the compromise or arrangement or by a subsequent order, make provision for all or any of the following matters—

(a) the transfer to the transferee company of the whole or any part of the undertaking and of the property or liabilities of any transferor company;

(b) the allotting or appropriation by the transferee company of any shares, debentures, policies or other like interests in that company which under the compromise or arrangement are to be allotted or appropriated by that company to or for any person;

(c) the continuation by or against the transferee company of any legal proceedings pending by or against any transferor company;

(d) the dissolution, without winding up, of any transferor company;

(e) the provision to be made for any persons who, within such time and in such manner as the court directs, dissent from the compromise or arrangement;

(f) such incidental, consequential and supplemental matters as are necessary to secure that the reconstruction or amalgamation is fully and effectively carried out.

(3) If an order under this section provides for the transfer of property or liabilities—

(a) the property is by virtue of the order transferred to, and vests in, the transferee company, and

(b) the liabilities are, by virtue of the order, transferred to and become liabilities of that company.

(4) The property (if the order so directs) vests freed from any charge that is by virtue of the compromise or arrangement to cease to have effect.

(5) In this section—

'property' includes property, rights and powers of every description; and

'liabilities' includes duties.

(6) Every company in relation to which an order is made under this section must cause a copy of the order to be delivered to the registrar within seven days after its making.

(7) If default is made in complying with subsection (6) an offence is committed by—

(a) the company, and

(b) every officer of the company who is in default.

(8) A person guilty of an offence under subsection (7) is liable on summary conviction to a fine not exceeding level 3 on the standard scale and, for continued contravention, a daily default fine not exceeding one-tenth of level 3 on the standard scale.

*Obligations of company with respect to articles etc*

### 901    Obligations of company with respect to articles etc

(1) This section applies—

(a) to any order under section 899 (order sanctioning compromise or arrangement), and

(b) to any order under section 900 (order facilitating reconstruction or amalgamation) that alters the company's constitution.

(2) If the order amends—

(a) the company's articles, or

(b) any resolution or agreement to which Chapter 3 of Part 3 applies (resolution or agreement affecting a company's constitution),

the copy of the order delivered to the registrar by the company under section 899(4) or section 900(6) must be accompanied by a copy of the company's articles, or the resolution or agreement in question, as amended.

(3) Every copy of the company's articles issued by the company after the order is made must be accompanied by a copy of the order, unless the effect of the order has been incorporated into the articles by amendment.

(4) In this section—

(a) references to the effect of the order include the effect of the compromise or arrangement to which the order relates; and

(b) in the case of a company not having articles, references to its articles shall be read as references to the instrument constituting the company or defining its constitution.

(5) If a company makes default in complying with this section an offence is committed by—

(a) the company, and

(b) every officer of the company who is in default.

(6) A person guilty of an offence under this section is liable on summary conviction to a fine not exceeding level 3 on the standard scale.

# PART 27 MERGERS AND DIVISIONS OF PUBLIC COMPANIES

## Chapter 1    Introductory

### 902    Application of this Part

(1) This Part applies where—

(a) a compromise or arrangement is proposed between a public company and—

      (i)   its creditors or any class of them, or

      (ii)  its members or any class of them,

      (iii) for the purposes of, or in connection with, a scheme for the reconstruction of any company or companies or the amalgamation of any two or more companies,

   (b)  the scheme involves—

      (i)   a merger (as defined in section 904), or

      (ii)  a division (as defined in section 919), and

   (c)  the consideration for the transfer (or each of the transfers) envisaged is to be shares in the transferee company (or one or more of the transferee companies) receivable by members of the transferor company (or transferor companies), with or without any cash payment to members.

(2)  In this Part—

   (a)  a 'new company' means a company formed for the purposes of, or in connection with, the scheme, and

   (b)  an 'existing company' means a company other than one formed for the purposes of, or in connection with, the scheme.

(3)  This Part does not apply where the company in respect of which the compromise or arrangement is proposed is being wound up.

### 903  Relationship of this Part to Part 26

(1)  The court must not sanction the compromise or arrangement under Part 26 (arrangements and reconstructions) unless the relevant requirements of this Part have been complied with.

(2)  The requirements applicable to a merger are specified in sections 905 to 914.

Certain of those requirements, and certain general requirements of Part 26, are modified or excluded by the provisions of sections 915 to 918.

(3)  The requirements applicable to a division are specified in sections 920 to 930.

Certain of those requirements, and certain general requirements of Part 26, are modified or excluded by the provisions of sections 931 to 934.

## Chapter 2  Merger

### *Introductory*

### 904  Mergers and merging companies

(1)  The scheme involves a merger where under the scheme—

   (a)  the undertaking, property and liabilities of one or more public companies, including the company in respect of which the compromise or arrangement is proposed, are to be transferred to another existing public company (a 'merger by absorption'), or

   (b)  the undertaking, property and liabilities of two or more public companies, including the company in respect of which the compromise or arrangement is proposed, are to be transferred to a new company, whether or not a public company, (a 'merger by formation of a new company').

(2)  References in this Part to 'the merging companies' are—

   (a)  in relation to a merger by absorption, to the transferor and transferee companies;

   (b)  in relation to a merger by formation of a new company, to the transferor companies.

### *Requirements applicable to merger*

### 905  Draft terms of scheme (merger)

(1)  A draft of the proposed terms of the scheme must be drawn up and adopted by the directors of the merging companies.

(2)  The draft terms must give particulars of at least the following matters—

   (a)  in respect of each transferor company and the transferee company—

      (i)   its name,

      (ii)  the address of its registered office, and

      (iii) whether it is a company limited by shares or a company limited by guarantee and having a share capital;

   (b)  the number of shares in the transferee company to be allotted to members of a transferor company for a given number of their shares (the 'share exchange ratio') and the amount of any cash payment;

   (c)  the terms relating to the allotment of shares in the transferee company;

   (d)  the date from which the holding of shares in the transferee company will entitle the holders to participate in profits, and any special conditions affecting that entitlement;

   (e)  the date from which the transactions of a transferor company are to be treated for accounting purposes as being those of the transferee company;

   (f)  any rights or restrictions attaching to shares or other securities in the transferee company to be allotted under the scheme to the holders of shares or other securities in a transferor company to which any special rights or restrictions attach, or the measures proposed concerning them;

    (g) any amount of benefit paid or given or intended to be paid or given—

        (i)    to any of the experts referred to in section 909 (expert's report), or

        (ii)   to any director of a merging company,

        and the consideration for the payment of benefit.

    (3) The requirements in subsection (2)(b), (c) and (d) are subject to section 915 (circumstances in which certain particulars not required).

### 906    Publication of draft terms (merger)

    (1) The directors of each of the merging companies must deliver a copy of the draft terms to the registrar.

    (2) The registrar must publish in the Gazette notice of receipt by him from that company of a copy of the draft terms.

    (3) That notice must be published at least one month before the date of any meeting of that company summoned for the purpose of approving the scheme.

### 907    Approval of members of merging companies

    (1) The scheme must be approved by a majority in number, representing 75% in value, of each class of members of each of the merging companies, present and voting either in person or by proxy at a meeting.

    (2) This requirement is subject to sections 916, 917 and 918 (circumstances in which meetings of members not required).

### 908    Directors' explanatory report (merger)

    (1) The directors of each of the merging companies must draw up and adopt a report.

    (2) The report must consist of—

    (a) the statement required by section 897 (statement explaining effect of compromise or arrangement), and

    (b) insofar as that statement does not deal with the following matters, a further statement—

        (i)    setting out the legal and economic grounds for the draft terms, and in particular for the share exchange ratio, and

        (ii)   specifying any special valuation difficulties.

    (3) The requirement in this section is subject to section 915 (circumstances in which reports not required).

### 909    Expert's report (merger)

    (1) An expert's report must be drawn up on behalf of each of the merging companies.

    (2) The report required is a written report on the draft terms to the members of the company.

    (3) The court may on the joint application of all the merging companies approve the appointment of a joint expert to draw up a single report on behalf of all those companies.

If no such appointment is made, there must be a separate expert's report to the members of each merging company drawn up by a separate expert appointed on behalf of that company.

    (4) The expert must be a person who—

    (a)  is eligible for appointment as a statutory auditor (see section 1212), and

    (b)  meets the independence requirement in section 936.

    (5) The expert's report must—

    (a)  indicate the method or methods used to arrive at the share exchange ratio;

    (b)  give an opinion as to whether the method or methods used are reasonable in all the circumstances of the case, indicate the values arrived at using each such method and (if there is more than one method) give an opinion on the relative importance attributed to such methods in arriving at the value decided on;

    (c)  describe any special valuation difficulties that have arisen;

    (d)  state whether in the expert's opinion the share exchange ratio is reasonable; and

    (e)  in the case of a valuation made by a person other than himself (see section 935), state that it appeared to him reasonable to arrange for it to be so made or to accept a valuation so made.

    (6) The expert (or each of them) has—

    (a)  the right of access to all such documents of all the merging companies, and

    (b)  the right to require from the companies' officers all such information,

as he thinks necessary for the purposes of making his report.

    (7) The requirement in this section is subject to section 915 (circumstances in which reports not required) and section 918A (agreement to dispense with expert's report).

### 910    Supplementary accounting statement (merger)

    (1) If the last annual accounts of any of the merging companies relate to a financial year ending more than seven months before the first meeting of the company summoned for the purposes of approving the scheme, the directors of that company must prepare a supplementary accounting statement.

(2) That statement must consist of—

    (a) a balance sheet dealing with the state of affairs of the company as at a date not more than three months before the draft terms were adopted by the directors, and

    (b) where the company would be required under section 399 to prepare group accounts if that date were the last day of a financial year, a consolidated balance sheet dealing with the state of affairs of the company and the undertakings that would be included in such a consolidation.

(3) The requirements of this Act (and where relevant Article 4 of the IAS Regulation) as to the balance sheet forming part of a company's annual accounts, and the matters to be included in notes to it, apply to the balance sheet required for an accounting statement under this section, with such modifications as are necessary by reason of its being prepared otherwise than as at the last day of a financial year.

(4) The provisions of section 414 as to the approval and signing of accounts apply to the balance sheet required for an accounting statement under this section.

### 911 Inspection of documents (merger)

(1) The members of each of the merging companies must be able, during the period specified below—

    (a) to inspect at the registered office of that company copies of the documents listed below relating to that company and every other merging company, and

    (b) to obtain copies of those documents or any part of them on request free of charge.

(2) The period referred to above is the period—

    (a) beginning one month before, and

    (b) ending on the date of,

the first meeting of the members, or any class of members, of the company for the purposes of approving the scheme.

(3) The documents referred to above are—

    (a) the draft terms;

    (b) the directors' explanatory report;

    (c) the expert's report;

    (d) the company's annual accounts and reports for the last three financial years ending on or before the first meeting of the members, or any class of members, of the company summoned for the purposes of approving the scheme; and

    (e) any supplementary accounting statement required by section 910.

(4) The requirements of subsection (3)(b) and (c) are subject to section 915 (circumstances in which reports not required).

### 912 Approval of articles of new transferee company (merger)

In the case of a merger by formation of a new company, the articles of the transferee company, or a draft of them, must be approved by ordinary resolution of the transferor company or, as the case may be, each of the transferor companies.

### 913 Protection of holders of securities to which special rights attached (merger)

(1) The scheme must provide that where any securities of a transferor company (other than shares) to which special rights are attached are held by a person otherwise than as a member or creditor of the company, that person is to receive rights in the transferee company of equivalent value.

(2) Subsection (1) does not apply if—

    (a) the holder has agreed otherwise, or

    (b) the holder is, or under the scheme is to be, entitled to have the securities purchased by the transferee company on terms that the court considers reasonable.

### 914 No allotment of shares to transferor company or transferee company (merger)

The scheme must not provide for any shares in the transferee company to be allotted to—

    (a) a transferor company (or its nominee) in respect of shares in the transferor company held by the transferor company itself (or its nominee); or

    (b) the transferee company (or its nominee) in respect of shares in a transferor company held by the transferee company (or its nominee).

*Exceptions where shares of transferor company held by transferee company*

### 915 Circumstances in which certain particulars and reports not required (merger)

(1) This section applies in the case of a merger by absorption where all of the relevant securities of the transferor company (or, if there is more than one transferor company, of each of them) are held by or on behalf of the transferee company.

(2) The draft terms of the scheme need not give the particulars mentioned in section 905(2)(b), (c) or (d) (particulars relating to allotment of shares to members of transferor company).

(3) Section 897 (explanatory statement to be circulated or made available) does not apply.

(4) The requirements of the following sections do not apply—

section 908 (directors' explanatory report),

section 909 (expert's report).

(5) The requirements of section 911 (inspection of documents) so far as relating to any document required to be drawn up under the provisions mentioned in subsection (3) above do not apply.

(6) In this section 'relevant securities', in relation to a company, means shares or other securities carrying the right to vote at general meetings of the company.

### 916    Circumstances in which meeting of members of transferee company not required (merger)

(1) This section applies in the case of a merger by absorption where 90% or more (but not all) of the relevant securities of the transferor company (or, if there is more than one transferor company, of each of them) are held by or on behalf of the transferee company.

(2) It is not necessary for the scheme to be approved at a meeting of the members, or any class of members, of the transferee company if the court is satisfied that the following conditions have been complied with.

(3) The first condition is that publication of notice of receipt of the draft terms by the registrar took place in respect of the transferee company at least one month before the date of the first meeting of members, or any class of members, of the transferor company summoned for the purpose of agreeing to the scheme.

(4) The second condition is that the members of the transferee company were able during the period beginning one month before, and ending on, that date—

(a) to inspect at the registered office of the transferee company copies of the documents listed in section 911(3)(a), (d) and (e) relating to that company and the transferor company (or, if there is more than one transferor company, each of them), and

(b) to obtain copies of those documents or any part of them on request free of charge.

(5) The third condition is that—

(a) one or more members of the transferee company, who together held not less than 5% of the paid-up capital of the company which carried the right to vote at general meetings of the company (excluding any shares in the company held as treasury shares) would have been able, during that period, to require a meeting of each class of members to be called for the purpose of deciding whether or not to agree to the scheme, and

(b) no such requirement was made.

(6) In this section 'relevant securities', in relation to a company, means shares or other securities carrying the right to vote at general meetings of the company.

### 917    Circumstances in which no meetings required (merger)

(1) This section applies in the case of a merger by absorption where all of the relevant securities of the transferor company (or, if there is more than one transferor company, of each of them) are held by or on behalf of the transferee company.

(2) It is not necessary for the scheme to be approved at a meeting of the members, or any class of members, of any of the merging companies if the court is satisfied that the following conditions have been complied with.

(3) The first condition is that publication of notice of receipt of the draft terms by the registrar took place in respect of all the merging companies at least one month before the date of the court's order.

(4) The second condition is that the members of the transferee company were able during the period beginning one month before, and ending on, that date—

(a) to inspect at the registered office of that company copies of the documents listed in section 911(3) relating to that company and the transferor company (or, if there is more than one transferor company, each of them), and

(b) to obtain copies of those documents or any part of them on request free of charge.

(5) The third condition is that—

(a) one or more members of the transferee company, who together held not less than 5% of the paid-up capital of the company which carried the right to vote at general meetings of the company (excluding any shares in the company held as treasury shares) would have been able, during that period, to require a meeting of each class of members to be called for the purpose of deciding whether or not to agree to the scheme, and

(b) no such requirement was made.

(6) In this section 'relevant securities', in relation to a company, means shares or other securities carrying the right to vote at general meetings of the company.

### Other exceptions

### 918    Other circumstances in which meeting of members of transferee company not required (merger)

(1) In the case of any merger by absorption, it is not necessary for the scheme to be approved by the members of the transferee company if the court is satisfied that the following conditions have been complied with.

(2) The first condition is that publication of notice of receipt of the draft terms by the registrar took place in respect of that company at least one month before the date of the first meeting of members, or any class of members, of the transferor company (or, if there is more than one transferor company, any of them) summoned for the purposes of agreeing to the scheme.

(3) The second condition is that the members of that company were able during the period beginning one month before, and ending on, the date of any such meeting—

    (a) to inspect at the registered office of that company copies of the documents specified in section 911(3) relating to that company and the transferor company (or, if there is more than one transferor company, each of them), and

    (b) to obtain copies of those documents or any part of them on request free of charge.

(4) The third condition is that—

    (a) one or more members of that company, who together held not less than 5% of the paid-up capital of the company which carried the right to vote at general meetings of the company (excluding any shares in the company held as treasury shares) would have been able, during that period, to require a meeting of each class of members to be called for the purpose of deciding whether or not to agree to the scheme, and

    (b) no such requirement was made.

### 918A Agreement to dispense with expert's report (merger)

(1) If all members holding shares in, and all persons holding other securities of, the companies involved in the merger, being shares or securities that carry a right to vote in general meetings of the company in question, so agree, the requirement of section 909 (expert's report) does not apply.

(2) For the purposes of this section—

    (a) the members, or holders of other securities, of a company, and

    (b) whether shares or other securities carry a right to vote in general meetings of the company,

    are determined as at the date of the application to the court under section 896.

## Chapter 3  Division

### *Introductory*

### 919 Divisions and companies involved in a division

(1) The scheme involves a division where under the scheme the undertaking, property and liabilities of the company in respect of which the compromise or arrangement is proposed are to be divided among and transferred to two or more companies each of which is either—

    (a) an existing public company, or

    (b) a new company (whether or not a public company).

(2) References in this Part to the companies involved in the division are to the transferor company and any existing transferee companies.

### *Requirements to be complied with in case of division*

### 920 Draft terms of scheme (division)

(1) A draft of the proposed terms of the scheme must be drawn up and adopted by the directors of each of the companies involved in the division.

(2) The draft terms must give particulars of at least the following matters—

    (a) in respect of the transferor company and each transferee company—

        (i) its name,

        (ii) the address of its registered office, and

        (iii) whether it is a company limited by shares or a company limited by guarantee and having a share capital;

    (b) the number of shares in a transferee company to be allotted to members of the transferor company for a given number of their shares (the 'share exchange ratio') and the amount of any cash payment;

    (c) the terms relating to the allotment of shares in a transferee company;

    (d) the date from which the holding of shares in a transferee company will entitle the holders to participate in profits, and any special conditions affecting that entitlement;

    (e) the date from which the transactions of the transferor company are to be treated for accounting purposes as being those of a transferee company;

    (f) any rights or restrictions attaching to shares or other securities in a transferee company to be allotted under the scheme to the holders of shares or other securities in the transferor company to which any special rights or restrictions attach, or the measures proposed concerning them;

    (g) any amount of benefit paid or given or intended to be paid or given—

        (i) to any of the experts referred to in section 924 (expert's report), or

        (ii) to any director of a company involved in the division,

    and the consideration for the payment of benefit.

(3) The draft terms must also—

    (a) give particulars of the property and liabilities to be transferred (to the extent that these are known to the transferor company) and their allocation among the transferee companies;

    (b) make provision for the allocation among and transfer to the transferee companies of any other property and liabilities that the transferor company has acquired or may subsequently acquire; and

    (c) specify the allocation to members of the transferor company of shares in the transferee companies and the criteria upon which that allocation is based.

### 921   Publication of draft terms (division)

(1) The directors of each company involved in the division must deliver a copy of the draft terms to the registrar.

(2) The registrar must publish in the Gazette notice of receipt by him from that company of a copy of the draft terms.

(3) That notice must be published at least one month before the date of any meeting of that company summoned for the purposes of approving the scheme.

(4) The requirements in this section are subject to section 934 (power of court to exclude certain requirements).

### 922   Approval of members of companies involved in the division

(1) The compromise or arrangement must be approved by a majority in number, representing 75% in value, of each class of members of each of the companies involved in the division, present and voting either in person or by proxy at a meeting.

(2) This requirement is subject to sections 931 and 932 (circumstances in which meeting of members not required).

### 923   Directors' explanatory report (division)

(1) The directors of the transferor and each existing transferee company must draw up and adopt a report.

(2) The report must consist of—

    (a) the statement required by section 897 (statement explaining effect of compromise or arrangement), and

    (b) insofar as that statement does not deal with the following matters, a further statement—

      (i) setting out the legal and economic grounds for the draft terms, and in particular for the share exchange ratio and for the criteria on which the allocation to the members of the transferor company of shares in the transferee companies was based, and

      (ii) specifying any special valuation difficulties.

(3) The report must also state—

    (a) whether a report has been made to any transferee company under section 593 (valuation of non-cash consideration for shares), and

    (b) if so, whether that report has been delivered to the registrar of companies.

(4) The requirement in this section is subject to section 933 (agreement to dispense with reports etc).

### 924   Expert's report (division)

(1) An expert's report must be drawn up on behalf of each company involved in the division.

(2) The report required is a written report on the draft terms to the members of the company.

(3) The court may on the joint application of the companies involved in the division approve the appointment of a joint expert to draw up a single report on behalf of all those companies.

If no such appointment is made, there must be a separate expert's report to the members of each company involved in the division drawn up by a separate expert appointed on behalf of that company.

(4) The expert must be a person who—

    (a) is eligible for appointment as a statutory auditor (see section 1212), and

    (b) meets the independence requirement in section 936.

(5) The expert's report must—

    (a) indicate the method or methods used to arrive at the share exchange ratio;

    (b) give an opinion as to whether the method or methods used are reasonable in all the circumstances of the case, indicate the values arrived at using each such method and (if there is more than one method) give an opinion on the relative importance attributed to such methods in arriving at the value decided on;

    (c) describe any special valuation difficulties that have arisen;

    (d) state whether in the expert's opinion the share exchange ratio is reasonable; and

    (e) in the case of a valuation made by a person other than himself (see section 935), state that it appeared to him reasonable to arrange for it to be so made or to accept a valuation so made.

(6) The expert (or each of them) has—

    (a) the right of access to all such documents of the companies involved in the division, and

    (b) the right to require from the companies' officers all such information,

as he thinks necessary for the purposes of making his report.

(7)  The requirement in this section is subject to section 933 (agreement to dispense with reports etc).

### 925  Supplementary accounting statement (division)

(1)  If the last annual accounts of a company involved in the division relate to a financial year ending more than seven months before the first meeting of the company summoned for the purposes of approving the scheme, the directors of that company must prepare a supplementary accounting statement.

(2)  That statement must consist of—

(a)  a balance sheet dealing with the state of affairs of the company as at a date not more than three months before the draft terms were adopted by the directors, and

(b)  where the company would be required under section 399 to prepare group accounts if that date were the last day of a financial year, a consolidated balance sheet dealing with the state of affairs of the company and the undertakings that would be included in such a consolidation.

(3)  The requirements of this Act (and where relevant Article 4 of the IAS Regulation) as to the balance sheet forming part of a company's annual accounts, and the matters to be included in notes to it, apply to the balance sheet required for an accounting statement under this section, with such modifications as are necessary by reason of its being prepared otherwise than as at the last day of a financial year.

(4)  The provisions of section 414 as to the approval and signing of accounts apply to the balance sheet required for an accounting statement under this section.

(5)  The requirement in this section is subject to section 933 (agreement to dispense with reports etc).

### 926  Inspection of documents (division)

(1)  The members of each company involved in the division must be able, during the period specified below—

(a)  to inspect at the registered office of that company copies of the documents listed below relating to that company and every other company involved in the division, and

(b)  to obtain copies of those documents or any part of them on request free of charge.

(2)  The period referred to above is the period—

(a)  beginning one month before, and

(b)  ending on the date of,

the first meeting of the members, or any class of members, of the company for the purposes of approving the scheme.

(3)  The documents referred to above are—

(a)  the draft terms;

(b)  the directors' explanatory report;

(c)  the expert's report;

(d)  the company's annual accounts and reports for the last three financial years ending on or before the first meeting of the members, or any class of members, of the company summoned for the purposes of approving the scheme; and

(e)  any supplementary accounting statement required by section 925.

(4)  The requirements in subsection (3)(b), (c) and (e) are subject to section 933 (agreement to dispense with reports etc) and section 934 (power of court to exclude certain requirements).

### 927  Report on material changes of assets of transferor company (division)

(1)  The directors of the transferor company must report—

(a)  to every meeting of the members, or any class of members, of that company summoned for the purpose of agreeing to the scheme, and

(b)  to the directors of each existing transferee company, any material changes in the property and liabilities of the transferor company between the date when the draft terms were adopted and the date of the meeting in question.

(2)  The directors of each existing transferee company must in turn—

(a)  report those matters to every meeting of the members, or any class of members, of that company summoned for the purpose of agreeing to the scheme, or

(b)  send a report of those matters to every member entitled to receive notice of such a meeting.

(3)  The requirement in this section is subject to section 933 (agreement to dispense with reports etc).

### 928  Approval of articles of new transferee company (division)

The articles of every new transferee company, or a draft of them, must be approved by ordinary resolution of the transferor company.

### 929  Protection of holders of securities to which special rights attached (division)

(1)  The scheme must provide that where any securities of the transferor company (other than shares) to which special rights are attached are held by a person otherwise than as a member or creditor of the company, that person is to receive rights in a transferee company of equivalent value.

(2) Subsection (1) does not apply if—

    (a) the holder has agreed otherwise, or

    (b) the holder is, or under the scheme is to be, entitled to have the securities purchased by a transferee company on terms that the court considers reasonable.

### 930 No allotment of shares to transferor company or to transferee company (division)

The scheme must not provide for any shares in a transferee company to be allotted to—

    (a) the transferor company (or its nominee) in respect of shares in the transferor company held by the transferor company itself (or its nominee); or

    (b) a transferee company (or its nominee) in respect of shares in the transferor company held by the transferee company (or its nominee).

*Exceptions where shares of transferor company held by transferee company*

### 931 Circumstances in which meeting of members of transferor company not required (division)

(1) This section applies in the case of a division where all of the shares or other securities of the transferor company carrying the right to vote at general meetings of the company are held by or on behalf of one or more existing transferee companies.

(2) It is not necessary for the scheme to be approved by a meeting of the members, or any class of members, of the transferor company if the court is satisfied that the following conditions have been complied with.

(3) The first condition is that publication of notice of receipt of the draft terms by the registrar took place in respect of all the companies involved in the division at least one month before the date of the court's order.

(4) The second condition is that the members of every company involved in the division were able during the period beginning one month before, and ending on, that date—

    (a) to inspect at the registered office of their company copies of the documents listed in section 926(3) relating to every company involved in the division, and

    (b) to obtain copies of those documents or any part of them on request free of charge.

(5) The third condition is that—

    (a) one or more members of the transferor company, who together held not less than 5% of the paid-up capital of the company (excluding any shares in the company held as treasury shares) would have been able, during that period, to require a meeting of each class of members to be called for the purpose of deciding whether or not to agree to the scheme, and

    (b) no such requirement was made.

(6) The fourth condition is that the directors of the transferor company have sent—

    (a) to every member who would have been entitled to receive notice of a meeting to agree to the scheme (had any such meeting been called), and

    (b) to the directors of every existing transferee company,

a report of any material change in the property and liabilities of the transferor company between the date when the terms were adopted by the directors and the date one month before the date of the court's order.

*Other exceptions*

### 932 Circumstances in which meeting of members of transferee company not required (division)

(1) In the case of a division, it is not necessary for the scheme to be approved by the members of a transferee company if the court is satisfied that the following conditions have been complied with in relation to that company.

(2) The first condition is that publication of notice of receipt of the draft terms by the registrar took place in respect of that company at least one month before the date of the first meeting of members of the transferor company summoned for the purposes of agreeing to the scheme.

(3) The second condition is that the members of that company were able during the period beginning one month before, and ending on, that date—

    (a) to inspect at the registered office of that company copies of the documents specified in section 926(3) relating to that company and every other company involved in the division, and

    (b) to obtain copies of those documents or any part of them on request free of charge.

(4) The third condition is that—

    (a) one or more members of that company, who together held not less than 5% of the paid-up capital of the company which carried the right to vote at general meetings of the company (excluding any shares in the company held as treasury shares) would have been able, during that period, to require a meeting of each class of members to be called for the purpose of deciding whether or not to agree to the scheme, and

    (b) no such requirement was made.

(5)  The first and second conditions above are subject to section 934 (power of court to exclude certain requirements).

### 933   Agreement to dispense with reports etc (division)

(1)  If all members holding shares in, and all persons holding other securities of, the companies involved in the division, being shares or securities that carry a right to vote in general meetings of the company in question, so agree, the following requirements do not apply.

(2)  The requirements that may be dispensed with under this section are—

    (a)  the requirements of—

        (i)   section 923 (directors' explanatory report),

        (ii)  section 924 (expert's report),

        (iii) section 925 (supplementary accounting statement), and

        (iv)  section 927 (report on material changes in assets of transferor company); and

    (b)  the requirements of section 926 (inspection of documents) so far as relating to any document required to be drawn up under the provisions mentioned in paragraph (a)(i), (ii) or (iii) above.

(3)  For the purposes of this section—

    (a)  the members, or holders of other securities, of a company, and

    (b)  whether shares or other securities carry a right to vote in general meetings of the company,

are determined as at the date of the application to the court under section 896.

### 934   Power of court to exclude certain requirements (division)

(1)  In the case of a division, the court may by order direct that—

    (a)  in relation to any company involved in the division, the requirements of—

        (i)   section 921 (publication of draft terms), and

        (ii)  section 926 (inspection of documents),

    do not apply, and

    (b)  in relation to an existing transferee company, section 932 (circumstances in which meeting of members of transferee company not required) has effect with the omission of the first and second conditions specified in that section,

if the court is satisfied that the following conditions will be fulfilled in relation to that company.

(2)  The first condition is that the members of that company will have received, or will have been able to obtain free of charge, copies of the documents listed in section 926—

    (a)  in time to examine them before the date of the first meeting of the members, or any class of members, of that company summoned for the purposes of agreeing to the scheme, or

    (b)  in the case of an existing transferee company where in the circumstances described in section 932 no meeting is held, in time to require a meeting as mentioned in subsection (4) of that section.

(3)  The second condition is that the creditors of that company will have received or will have been able to obtain free of charge copies of the draft terms in time to examine them—

    (a)  before the date of the first meeting of the members, or any class of members, of the company summoned for the purposes of agreeing to the scheme, or

    (b)  in the circumstances mentioned in subsection (2)(b) above, at the same time as the members of the company.

(4)  The third condition is that no prejudice would be caused to the members or creditors of the transferor company or any transferee company by making the order in question.

## Chapter 4   Supplementary provisions

### *Expert's report and related matters*

### 935   Expert's report: valuation by another person

(1)  Where it appears to an expert—

    (a)  that a valuation is reasonably necessary to enable him to draw up his report, and

    (b)  that it is reasonable for that valuation, or part of it, to be made by (or for him to accept a valuation made by) another person who—

        (i)   appears to him to have the requisite knowledge and experience to make the valuation or that part of it, and

        (ii)  meets the independence requirement in section 936,

    he may arrange for or accept such a valuation, together with a report which will enable him to make his own report under section 909 or 924.

(2)  Where any valuation is made by a person other than the expert himself, the latter's report must state that fact and must also—

    (a)  state the former's name and what knowledge and experience he has to carry out the valuation, and

    (b)  describe so much of the undertaking, property and liabilities as was valued by the other person, and the method used to value them, and specify the date of the valuation.

### 936   Experts and valuers: independence requirement

(1)  A person meets the independence requirement for the purposes of section 909 or 924 (expert's report) or section 935 (valuation by another person) only if—

  (a)  he is not—

    (i)   an officer or employee of any of the companies concerned in the scheme, or

    (ii)  a partner or employee of such a person, or a partnership of which such a person is a partner;

  (b)  he is not—

    (i)   an officer or employee of an associated undertaking of any of the companies concerned in the scheme, or

    (ii)  a partner or employee of such a person, or a partnership of which such a person is a partner; and

  (c)  there does not exist between—

    (i)   the person or an associate of his, and

    (ii)  any of the companies concerned in the scheme or an associated undertaking of such a company,

    a connection of any such description as may be specified by regulations made by the Secretary of State.

(2)  An auditor of a company is not regarded as an officer or employee of the company for this purpose.

(3)  For the purposes of this section—

  (a)  the 'companies concerned in the scheme' means every transferor and existing transferee company;

  (b)  'associated undertaking', in relation to a company, means—

    (i)   a parent undertaking or subsidiary undertaking of the company, or

    (ii)  a subsidiary undertaking of a parent undertaking of the company; and

  (c)  'associate' has the meaning given by section 937.

(4)  Regulations under this section are subject to negative resolution procedure.

### 937   Experts and valuers: meaning of 'associate'

(1)  This section defines 'associate' for the purposes of section 936 (experts and valuers: independence requirement).

(2)  In relation to an individual, 'associate' means—

  (a)  that individual's spouse or civil partner or minor child or step-child,

  (b)  any body corporate of which that individual is a director, and

  (c)  any employee or partner of that individual.

(3)  In relation to a body corporate, 'associate' means—

  (a)  any body corporate of which that body is a director,

  (b)  any body corporate in the same group as that body, and

  (c)  any employee or partner of that body or of any body corporate in the same group.

(4)  In relation to a partnership that is a legal person under the law by which it is governed, 'associate' means—

  (a)  any body corporate of which that partnership is a director,

  (b)  any employee of or partner in that partnership, and

  (c)  any person who is an associate of a partner in that partnership.

(5)  In relation to a partnership that is not a legal person under the law by which it is governed, 'associate' means any person who is an associate of any of the partners.

(6)  In this section, in relation to a limited liability partnership, for 'director' read 'member'.

*Powers of the court*

### 938   Power of court to summon meeting of members or creditors of existing transferee company

(1)  The court may order a meeting of—

  (a)  the members of an existing transferee company, or any class of them, or

  (b)  the creditors of an existing transferee company, or any class of them,

to be summoned in such manner as the court directs.

(2)  An application for such an order may be made by—

  (a)  the company concerned,

  (b)  a member or creditor of the company, or

  (c)  if an administration order is in force in relation to the company, the administrator.

(3)  Section 323 (representation of corporations at meetings) applies to a meeting of creditors under this section as to a meeting of the company (references to a member being read as references to a creditor).

### 939   Court to fix date for transfer of undertaking etc of transferor company

(1)  Where the court sanctions the compromise or arrangement, it must—

(a) in the order sanctioning the compromise or arrangement, or

(b) in a subsequent order under section 900 (powers of court to facilitate reconstruction or amalgamation),

fix a date on which the transfer (or transfers) to the transferee company (or transferee companies) of the undertaking, property and liabilities of the transferor company is (or are) to take place.

(2) Any such order that provides for the dissolution of the transferor company must fix the same date for the dissolution.

(3) If it is necessary for the transferor company to take steps to ensure that the undertaking, property and liabilities are fully transferred, the court must fix a date, not later than six months after the date fixed under subsection (1), by which such steps must be taken.

(4) In that case, the court may postpone the dissolution of the transferor company until that date.

(5) The court may postpone or further postpone the date fixed under subsection (3) if it is satisfied that the steps mentioned cannot be completed by the date (or latest date) fixed under that subsection.

*Liability of transferee companies*

**940   Liability of transferee companies for each other's defaults**

(1) In the case of a division, each transferee company is jointly and severally liable for any liability transferred to any other transferee company under the scheme to the extent that the other company has made default in satisfying that liability. This is subject to the following provisions.

(2) If a majority in number representing 75% in value of the creditors or any class of creditors of the transferor company, present and voting either in person or by proxy at a meeting summoned for the purposes of agreeing to the scheme, so agree, subsection (1) does not apply in relation to the liabilities owed to the creditors or that class of creditors.

(3) A transferee company is not liable under this section for an amount greater than the net value transferred to it under the scheme.

The 'net value transferred' is the value at the time of the transfer of the property transferred to it under the scheme less the amount at that date of the liabilities so transferred.

*Interpretation*

**941   Meaning of 'liabilities' and 'property'**

In this Part—

'liabilities' includes duties;

'property' includes property, rights and powers of every description.

# PART 28   TAKEOVERS ETC.

## Chapter 1   The Takeover Panel

*The Panel and its rules*

**942   The Panel**

(1) The body known as the Panel on Takeovers and Mergers ('the Panel') is to have the functions conferred on it by or under this Chapter.

(2) The Panel may do anything that it considers necessary or expedient for the purposes of, or in connection with, its functions.

(3) The Panel may make arrangements for any of its functions to be discharged by—

(a) a committee or sub-committee of the Panel, or

(b) an officer or member of staff of the Panel, or a person acting as such.

This is subject to section 943(4) and (5).

**943   Rules**

(1) The Panel must make rules giving effect to Articles 3.1, 4.2, 5, 6.1 to 6.3, 7 to 9 and 13 of the Takeovers Directive.

(2) Rules made by the Panel may also make other provision—

(a) for or in connection with the regulation of—

(i) takeover bids,

(ii) merger transactions, and

(iii) transactions (not falling within sub-paragraph (i) or (ii)) that have or may have, directly or indirectly, an effect on the ownership or control of companies;

(b) for or in connection with the regulation of things done in consequence of, or otherwise in relation to, any such bid or transaction;

(c) about cases where—

(i) any such bid or transaction is, or has been, contemplated or apprehended, or

(ii) an announcement is made denying that any such bid or transaction is intended.

(3) The provision that may be made under subsection (2) includes, in particular, provision for a matter that is, or is similar to, a matter provided for by the Panel in the City Code on Takeovers and Mergers as it had effect immediately before the passing of this Act.

(4) In relation to rules made by virtue of section 957 (fees and charges), functions under this section may be discharged either by the Panel itself or by a committee of the Panel (but not otherwise).

(5) In relation to rules of any other description, the Panel must discharge its functions under this section by a committee of the Panel.

(6) Section 1 (meaning of 'company') does not apply for the purposes of this section.

(7) In this section 'takeover bid' includes a takeover bid within the meaning of the Takeovers Directive.

(8) In this Chapter 'the Takeovers Directive' means Directive 2004/25/EC of the European Parliament and of the Council.

(9) A reference to rules in the following provisions of this Chapter is to rules under this section.

### 944    Further provisions about rules

(1) Rules may—
(a) make different provision for different purposes;
(b) make provision subject to exceptions or exemptions;
(c) contain incidental, supplemental, consequential or transitional provision;
(d) authorise the Panel to dispense with or modify the application of rules in particular cases and by reference to any circumstances.

Rules made by virtue of paragraph (d) must require the Panel to give reasons for acting as mentioned in that paragraph.

(2) Rules must be made by an instrument in writing.

(3) Immediately after an instrument containing rules is made, the text must be made available to the public, with or without payment, in whatever way the Panel thinks appropriate.

(4) A person is not to be taken to have contravened a rule if he shows that at the time of the alleged contravention the text of the rule had not been made available as required by subsection (3).

(5) The production of a printed copy of an instrument purporting to be made by the Panel on which is endorsed a certificate signed by an officer of the Panel authorised by it for that purpose and stating—
(a) that the instrument was made by the Panel,
(b) that the copy is a true copy of the instrument, and
(c) that on a specified date the text of the instrument was made available to the public as required by subsection (3),

is evidence (or in Scotland sufficient evidence) of the facts stated in the certificate.

(6) A certificate purporting to be signed as mentioned in subsection (5) is to be treated as having been properly signed unless the contrary is shown.

(7) A person who wishes in any legal proceedings to rely on an instrument by which rules are made may require the Panel to endorse a copy of the instrument with a certificate of the kind mentioned in subsection (5).

### 945    Rulings

(1) The Panel may give rulings on the interpretation, application or effect of rules.

(2) To the extent and in the circumstances specified in rules, and subject to any review or appeal, a ruling has binding effect.

### 946    Directions

Rules may contain provision conferring power on the Panel to give any direction that appears to the Panel to be necessary in order—
(a) to restrain a person from acting (or continuing to act) in breach of rules;
(b) to restrain a person from doing (or continuing to do) a particular thing, pending determination of whether that or any other conduct of his is or would be a breach of rules;
(c) otherwise to secure compliance with rules.

*Information*

### 947    Power to require documents and information

(1) The Panel may by notice in writing require a person—
(a) to produce any documents that are specified or described in the notice;
(b) to provide, in the form and manner specified in the notice, such information as may be specified or described in the notice.

(2) A requirement under subsection (1) must be complied with—
(a) at a place specified in the notice, and
(b) before the end of such reasonable period as may be so specified.

(3) This section applies only to documents and information reasonably required in connection with the exercise by the Panel of its functions.

(4) The Panel may require—
(a) any document produced to be authenticated, or

(b) any information provided (whether in a document or otherwise) to be verified,

in such manner as it may reasonably require.

(5)  The Panel may authorise a person to exercise any of its powers under this section.

(6)  A person exercising a power by virtue of subsection (5) must, if required to do so, produce evidence of his authority to exercise the power.

(7)  The production of a document in pursuance of this section does not affect any lien that a person has on the document.

(8)  The Panel may take copies of or extracts from a document produced in pursuance of this section.

(9)  A reference in this section to the production of a document includes a reference to the production of—

(a) a hard copy of information recorded otherwise than in hard copy form, or

(b) information in a form from which a hard copy can be readily obtained.

(10)  A person is not required by this section to disclose documents or information in respect of which a claim to legal professional privilege (in Scotland, to confidentiality of communications) could be maintained in legal proceedings.

### 948    Restrictions on disclosure

(1)  This section applies to information (in whatever form)—

(a) relating to the private affairs of an individual, or

(b) relating to any particular business,

that is provided to the Panel in connection with the exercise of its functions.

(2)  No such information may, during the lifetime of the individual or so long as the business continues to be carried on, be disclosed without the consent of that individual or (as the case may be) the person for the time being carrying on that business.

(3)  Subsection (2) does not apply to any disclosure of information that—

(a) is made for the purpose of facilitating the carrying out by the Panel of any of its functions,

(b) is made to a person specified in Part 1 of Schedule 2,

(c) is of a description specified in Part 2 of that Schedule, or

(d) is made in accordance with Part 3 of that Schedule.

(4)  The Secretary of State may amend Schedule 2 by order subject to negative resolution procedure.

(5)  An order under subsection (4) must not—

(a) amend Part 1 of Schedule 2 by specifying a person unless the person exercises functions of a public nature (whether or not he exercises any other function);

(b) amend Part 2 of Schedule 2 by adding or modifying a description of disclosure unless the purpose for which the disclosure is permitted is likely to facilitate the exercise of a function of a public nature;

(c) amend Part 3 of Schedule 2 so as to have the effect of permitting disclosures to be made to a body other than one that exercises functions of a public nature in a country or territory outside the United Kingdom.

(6)  Subsection (2) does not apply to—

(a) the disclosure by an authority within subsection (7) of information disclosed to it by the Panel in reliance on subsection (3);

(b) the disclosure of such information by anyone who has obtained it directly or indirectly from an authority within subsection (7).

(7)  The authorities within this subsection are—

(a) the Financial Services Authority;

(b) an authority designated as a supervisory authority for the purposes of Article 4.1 of the Takeovers Directive;

(c) any other person or body that exercises functions of a public nature, under legislation in an EEA State other than the United Kingdom, that are similar to the Panel's functions or those of the Financial Services Authority.

(8)  This section does not prohibit the disclosure of information if the information is or has been available to the public from any other source.

(9)  Nothing in this section authorises the making of a disclosure in contravention of the Data Protection Act 1998 (c. 29).

### 949    Offence of disclosure in contravention of section 948

(1)  A person who discloses information in contravention of section 948 is guilty of an offence, unless—

(a) he did not know, and had no reason to suspect, that the information had been provided as mentioned in section 948(1), or

(b) he took all reasonable steps and exercised all due diligence to avoid the commission of the offence.

(2)  A person guilty of an offence under this section is liable—

(a) on conviction on indictment, to imprisonment for a term not exceeding two years or a fine (or both);

(b) on summary conviction—

    (i)   in England and Wales, to imprisonment for a term not exceeding twelve months or to a fine not exceeding the statutory maximum (or both);

    (ii)  in Scotland or Northern Ireland, to imprisonment for a term not exceeding six months, or to a fine not exceeding the statutory maximum (or both).

(3) Where a company or other body corporate commits an offence under this section, an offence is also committed by every officer of the company or other body corporate who is in default.

### Co-operation

### 950  Panel's duty of co-operation

(1) The Panel must take such steps as it considers appropriate to co-operate with—

(a) the Financial Services Authority;

(b) an authority designated as a supervisory authority for the purposes of Article 4.1 of the Takeovers Directive;

(c) any other person or body that exercises functions of a public nature, under legislation in any country or territory outside the United Kingdom, that appear to the Panel to be similar to its own functions or those of the Financial Services Authority.

(2) Co-operation may include the sharing of information that the Panel is not prevented from disclosing.

### Hearings and appeals

### 951  Hearings and appeals

(1) Rules must provide for a decision of the Panel to be subject to review by a committee of the Panel (the 'Hearings Committee') at the instance of such persons affected by the decision as are specified in the rules.

(2) Rules may also confer other functions on the Hearings Committee.

(3) Rules must provide for there to be a right of appeal against a decision of the Hearings Committee to an independent tribunal (the 'Takeover Appeal Board') in such circumstances and subject to such conditions as are specified in the rules.

(4) Rules may contain—

(a) provision as to matters of procedure in relation to proceedings before the Hearings Committee (including provision imposing time limits);

(b) provision about evidence in such proceedings;

(c) provision as to the powers of the Hearings Committee dealing with a matter referred to it;

(d) provision about enforcement of decisions of the Hearings Committee and the Takeover Appeal Board.

(5) Rules must contain provision—

(a) requiring the Panel, when acting in relation to any proceedings before the Hearings Committee or the Takeover Appeal Board, to do so by an officer or member of staff of the Panel (or a person acting as such);

(b) preventing a person who is or has been a member of the committee mentioned in section 943(5) from being a member of the Hearings Committee or the Takeover Appeal Board;

(c) preventing a person who is a member of the committee mentioned in section 943(5), of the Hearings Committee or of the Takeover Appeal Board from acting as mentioned in paragraph (a).

### Contravention of rules etc

### 952  Sanctions

(1) Rules may contain provision conferring power on the Panel to impose sanctions on a person who has—

(a) acted in breach of rules, or

(b) failed to comply with a direction given by virtue of section 946.

(2) Subsection (3) applies where rules made by virtue of subsection (1) confer power on the Panel to impose a sanction of a kind not provided for by the City Code on Takeovers and Mergers as it had effect immediately before the passing of this Act.

(3) The Panel must prepare a statement (a 'policy statement') of its policy with respect to—

(a) the imposition of the sanction in question, and

(b) where the sanction is in the nature of a financial penalty, the amount of the penalty that may be imposed.

An element of the policy must be that, in making a decision about any such matter, the Panel has regard to the factors mentioned in subsection (4).

(4) The factors are—

(a) the seriousness of the breach or failure in question in relation to the nature of the rule or direction contravened;

(b) the extent to which the breach or failure was deliberate or reckless;

(c) whether the person on whom the sanction is to be imposed is an individual.

(5) The Panel may at any time revise a policy statement.

(6) The Panel must prepare a draft of any proposed policy statement (or revised policy statement) and consult such persons about the draft as the Panel considers appropriate.

(7) The Panel must publish, in whatever way it considers appropriate, any policy statement (or revised policy statement) that it prepares.

(8) In exercising, or deciding whether to exercise, its power to impose a sanction within subsection (2) in the case of any particular breach or failure, the Panel must have regard to any relevant policy statement published and in force at the time when the breach or failure occurred.

## 953   Failure to comply with rules about bid documentation

(1) This section applies where a takeover bid is made for a company that has securities carrying voting rights admitted to trading on a regulated market in the United Kingdom.

(2) Where an offer document published in respect of the bid does not comply with offer document rules, an offence is committed by—

(a) the person making the bid, and

(b) where the person making the bid is a body of persons, any director, officer or member of that body who caused the document to be published.

(3) A person commits an offence under subsection (2) only if—

(a) he knew that the offer document did not comply, or was reckless as to whether it complied, and

(b) he failed to take all reasonable steps to secure that it did comply.

(4) Where a response document published in respect of the bid does not comply with response document rules, an offence is committed by any director or other officer of the company referred to in subsection (1) who—

(a) knew that the response document did not comply, or was reckless as to whether it complied, and

(b) failed to take all reasonable steps to secure that it did comply.

(5) Where an offence is committed under subsection (2)(b) or (4) by a company or other body corporate ('the relevant body')—

(a) subsection (2)(b) has effect as if the reference to a director, officer or member of the person making the bid included a reference to a director, officer or member of the relevant body;

(b) subsection (4) has effect as if the reference to a director or other officer of the company referred to in subsection (1) included a reference to a director, officer or member of the relevant body.

(6) A person guilty of an offence under this section is liable—

(a) on conviction on indictment, to a fine;

(b) on summary conviction, to a fine not exceeding the statutory maximum.

(7) Nothing in this section affects any power of the Panel in relation to the enforcement of its rules.

(8) Section 1 (meaning of 'company') does not apply for the purposes of this section.

(9) In this section—

'designated' means designated in rules;

'offer document' means a document required to be published by rules giving effect to Article 6.2 of the Takeovers Directive;

'offer document rules' means rules designated as rules that give effect to Article 6.3 of that Directive;

'response document' means a document required to be published by rules giving effect to Article 9.5 of that Directive;

'response document rules' means rules designated as rules that give effect to the first sentence of Article 9.5 of that Directive;

'securities' means shares or debentures;

'takeover bid' has the same meaning as in that Directive;

'voting rights' means rights to vote at general meetings of the company in question, including rights that arise only in certain circumstances.

## 954   Compensation

(1) Rules may confer power on the Panel to order a person to pay such compensation as it thinks just and reasonable if he is in breach of a rule the effect of which is to require the payment of money.

(2) Rules made by virtue of this section may include provision for the payment of interest (including compound interest).

## 955   Enforcement by the court

(1) If, on the application of the Panel, the court is satisfied—

(a) that there is a reasonable likelihood that a person will contravene a rule-based requirement, or

(b) that a person has contravened a rule-based requirement or a disclosure requirement,

the court may make any order it thinks fit to secure compliance with the requirement.

(2) In subsection (1) 'the court' means the High Court or, in Scotland, the Court of Session.

(3) Except as provided by subsection (1), no person—

(a) has a right to seek an injunction, or

(b) in Scotland, has title or interest to seek an interdict or an order for specific performance,

to prevent a person from contravening (or continuing to contravene) a rule-based requirement or a disclosure requirement.

(4) In this section—

'contravene' includes fail to comply;

'disclosure requirement' means a requirement imposed under section 947;

'rule-based requirement' means a requirement imposed by or under rules.

### 956 No action for breach of statutory duty etc

(1) Contravention of a rule-based requirement or a disclosure requirement does not give rise to any right of action for breach of statutory duty.

(2) Contravention of a rule-based requirement does not make any transaction void or unenforceable or (subject to any provision made by rules) affect the validity of any other thing.

(3) In this section—

(a) 'contravention' includes failure to comply;

(b) 'disclosure requirement' and 'rule-based requirement' have the same meaning as in section 955.

*Funding*

### 957 Fees and charges

(1) Rules may provide for fees or charges to be payable to the Panel for the purpose of meeting any part of its expenses.

(2) A reference in this section or section 958 to expenses of the Panel is to any expenses that have been or are to be incurred by the Panel in, or in connection with, the discharge of its functions, including in particular—

(a) payments in respect of the expenses of the Takeover Appeal Board;

(b) the cost of repaying the principal of, and of paying any interest on, any money borrowed by the Panel;

(c) the cost of maintaining adequate reserves.

### 958 Levy

(1) For the purpose of meeting any part of the expenses of the Panel, the Secretary of State may by regulations provide for a levy to be payable to the Panel—

(a) by specified persons or bodies, or persons or bodies of a specified description, or

(b) on transactions, of a specified description, in securities on specified markets.

In this subsection 'specified' means specified in the regulations.

(2) The power to specify (or to specify descriptions of) persons or bodies must be exercised in such a way that the levy is payable only by persons or bodies that appear to the Secretary of State—

(a) to be capable of being directly affected by the exercise of any of the functions of the Panel, or

(b) otherwise to have a substantial interest in the exercise of any of those functions.

(3) Regulations under this section may in particular—

(a) specify the rate of the levy and the period in respect of which it is payable at that rate;

(b) make provision as to the times when, and the manner in which, payments are to be made in respect of the levy.

(4) In determining the rate of the levy payable in respect of a particular period, the Secretary of State—

(a) must take into account any other income received or expected by the Panel in respect of that period;

(b) may take into account estimated as well as actual expenses of the Panel in respect of that period.

(5) The Panel must—

(a) keep proper accounts in respect of any amounts of levy received by virtue of this section;

(b) prepare, in relation to each period in respect of which any such amounts are received, a statement of account relating to those amounts in such form and manner as is specified in the regulations.

Those accounts must be audited, and the statement certified, by persons appointed by the Secretary of State.

(6) Regulations under this section—

(a) are subject to affirmative resolution procedure if subsection (7) applies to them;

(b) otherwise, are subject to negative resolution procedure.

(7) This subsection applies to—

(a) the first regulations under this section;

(b) any other regulations under this section that would result in a change in the persons or bodies by whom, or the transactions on which, the levy is payable.

(8) If a draft of an instrument containing regulations under this section would, apart from this subsection, be treated for the purposes of the Standing Orders of either House of Parliament as a hybrid instrument, it is to proceed in that House as if it were not such an instrument.

### 959   Recovery of fees, charges or levy

An amount payable by any person or body by virtue of section 957 or 958 is a debt due from that person or body to the Panel, and is recoverable accordingly.

*Miscellaneous and supplementary*

### 960   Panel as party to proceedings

The Panel is capable (despite being an unincorporated body) of—

(a) bringing proceedings under this Chapter in its own name;

(b) bringing or defending any other proceedings in its own name.

### 961   Exemption from liability in damages

(1) Neither the Panel, nor any person within subsection (2), is to be liable in damages for anything done (or omitted to be done) in, or in connection with, the discharge or purported discharge of the Panel's functions.

(2) A person is within this subsection if—

(a) he is (or is acting as) a member, officer or member of staff of the Panel, or

(b) he is a person authorised under section 947(5).

(3) Subsection (1) does not apply—

(a) if the act or omission is shown to have been in bad faith, or

(b) so as to prevent an award of damages in respect of the act or omission on the ground that it was unlawful as a result of section 6(1) of the Human Rights Act 1998 (c. 42) (acts of public authorities incompatible with Convention rights).

### 962   Privilege against self-incrimination

(1) A statement made by a person in response to—

(a) a requirement under section 947(1), or

(b) an order made by the court under section 955 to secure compliance with such a requirement,

may not be used against him in criminal proceedings in which he is charged with an offence to which this subsection applies.

(2) Subsection (1) applies to any offence other than an offence under one of the following provisions (which concern false statements made otherwise than on oath)—

(a) section 5 of the Perjury Act 1911 (c. 6);

(b) section 44(2) of the Criminal Law (Consolidation) (Scotland) Act 1995 (c. 39);

(c) Article 10 of the Perjury (Northern Ireland) Order 1979 (S.I. 1979/1714 (N.I. 19)).

### 963   Annual reports

(1) After the end of each financial year the Panel must publish a report.

(2) The report must—

(a) set out how the Panel's functions were discharged in the year in question;

(b) include the Panel's accounts for that year;

(c) mention any matters the Panel considers to be of relevance to the discharge of its functions.

### 964   Amendments to Financial Services and Markets Act 2000

(1) The Financial Services and Markets Act 2000 (c. 8) is amended as follows.

(2) Section 143 (power to make rules endorsing the City Code on Takeovers and Mergers etc) is repealed.

(3) In section 144 (power to make price stabilising rules), for subsection (7) substitute—

'(7) "Consultation procedures" means procedures designed to provide an opportunity for persons likely to be affected by alterations to those provisions to make representations about proposed alterations to any of those provisions.'.

(4) In section 349 (exceptions from restrictions on disclosure of confidential information), after subsection (3) insert—

'(3A) Section 348 does not apply to—

(a) the disclosure by a recipient to which subsection (3B) applies of confidential information disclosed to it by the Authority in reliance on subsection (1);

(b) the disclosure of such information by a person obtaining it directly or indirectly from a recipient to which subsection (3B) applies.

(3B) This subsection applies to—
    (a) the Panel on Takeovers and Mergers;
    (b) an authority designated as a supervisory authority for the purposes of Article 4.1 of the Takeovers Directive;
    (c) any other person or body that exercises public functions, under legislation in an EEA State other than the United Kingdom, that are similar to the Authority's functions or those of the Panel on Takeovers and Mergers.'.

(5) In section 354 (Financial Services Authority's duty to co-operate with others), after subsection (1) insert—

'(1A) The Authority must take such steps as it considers appropriate to co-operate with—
    (a) the Panel on Takeovers and Mergers;
    (b) an authority designated as a supervisory authority for the purposes of Article 4.1 of the Takeovers Directive;
    (c) any other person or body that exercises functions of a public nature, under legislation in any country or territory outside the United Kingdom, that appear to the Authority to be similar to those of the Panel on Takeovers and Mergers.'.

(6) In section 417(1)(definitions), insert at the appropriate place—

'"Takeovers Directive" means Directive 2004/25/EC of the European Parliament and of the Council;'.

### 965    Power to extend to Isle of Man and Channel Islands

Her Majesty may by Order in Council direct that any of the provisions of this Chapter extend, with such modifications as may be specified in the Order, to the Isle of Man or any of the Channel Islands.

## Chapter 2  Impediments to takeovers

### *Opting in and opting out*

### 966    Opting in and opting out

(1) A company may by special resolution (an 'opting-in resolution') opt in for the purposes of this Chapter if the following three conditions are met in relation to the company.

(2) The first condition is that the company has voting shares admitted to trading on a regulated market.

(3) The second condition is that—
    (a) the company's articles of association—
        (i)   do not contain any such restrictions as are mentioned in Article 11 of the Takeovers Directive, or
        (ii)  if they do contain any such restrictions, provide for the restrictions not to apply at a time when, or in circumstances in which, they would be disapplied by that Article, and
    (b) those articles do not contain any other provision which would be incompatible with that Article.

(4) The third condition is that—
    (a) no shares conferring special rights in the company are held by—
        (i)   a minister,
        (ii)  a nominee of, or any other person acting on behalf of, a minister, or
        (iii) a company directly or indirectly controlled by a minister, and
    (b) no such rights are exercisable by or on behalf of a minister under any enactment.

(5) A company may revoke an opting-in resolution by a further special resolution (an 'opting-out resolution').

(6) For the purposes of subsection (3), a reference in Article 11 of the Takeovers Directive to Article 7.1 or 9 of that Directive is to be read as referring to rules under section 943(1) giving effect to the relevant Article.

(7) In subsection (4) 'minister' means—
    (a) the holder of an office in Her Majesty's Government in the United Kingdom;
    (b) the Scottish Ministers;
    (c) a Minister within the meaning given by section 7(3) of the Northern Ireland Act 1998 (c. 47);
    (d) the Welsh Ministers;
and for the purposes of that subsection 'minister' also includes the Treasury, the Board of Trade and the Defence Council.

(8) The Secretary of State may by order subject to negative resolution procedure provide that subsection (4) applies in relation to a specified person or body that exercises functions of a public nature as it applies in relation to a minister.

'Specified' means specified in the order.

**967  Further provision about opting-in and opting-out resolutions**

(1) An opting-in resolution or an opting-out resolution must specify the date from which it is to have effect (the 'effective date').

(2) The effective date of an opting-in resolution may not be earlier than the date on which the resolution is passed.

(3) The second and third conditions in section 966 must be met at the time when an opting-in resolution is passed, but the first one does not need to be met until the effective date.

(4) An opting-in resolution passed before the time when voting shares of the company are admitted to trading on a regulated market complies with the requirement in subsection (1) if, instead of specifying a particular date, it provides for the resolution to have effect from that time.

(5) An opting-in resolution passed before the commencement of this section complies with the requirement in subsection (1) if, instead of specifying a particular date, it provides for the resolution to have effect from that commencement.

(6) The effective date of an opting-out resolution may not be earlier than the first anniversary of the date on which a copy of the opting-in resolution was forwarded to the registrar.

(7) Where a company has passed an opting-in resolution, any alteration of its articles of association that would prevent the second condition in section 966 from being met is of no effect until the effective date of an opting-out resolution passed by the company.

*Consequences of opting in*

**968  Effect on contractual restrictions**

(1) The following provisions have effect where a takeover bid is made for an opted-in company.

(2) An agreement to which this section applies is invalid in so far as it places any restriction—

(a) on the transfer to the offeror, or at his direction to another person, of shares in the company during the offer period;

(b) on the transfer to any person of shares in the company at a time during the offer period when the offeror holds shares amounting to not less than 75% in value of all the voting shares in the company;

(c) on rights to vote at a general meeting of the company that decides whether to take any action which might result in the frustration of the bid;

(d) on rights to vote at a general meeting of the company that—

(i)    is the first such meeting to be held after the end of the offer period, and

(ii)   is held at a time when the offeror holds shares amounting to not less than 75% in value of all the voting shares in the company.

(3) This section applies to an agreement—

(a) entered into between a person holding shares in the company and another such person on or after 21st April 2004, or

(b) entered into at any time between such a person and the company,

and it applies to such an agreement even if the law applicable to the agreement (apart from this section) is not the law of a part of the United Kingdom.

(4) The reference in subsection (2)(c) to rights to vote at a general meeting of the company that decides whether to take any action which might result in the frustration of the bid includes a reference to rights to vote on a written resolution concerned with that question.

(5) For the purposes of subsection (2)(c), action which might result in the frustration of a bid is any action of that kind specified in rules under section 943(1) giving effect to Article 9 of the Takeovers Directive.

(6) If a person suffers loss as a result of any act or omission that would (but for this section) be a breach of an agreement to which this section applies, he is entitled to compensation, of such amount as the court considers just and equitable, from any person who would (but for this section) be liable to him for committing or inducing the breach.

(7) In subsection (6) 'the court' means the High Court or, in Scotland, the Court of Session.

(8) A reference in this section to voting shares in the company does not include—

(a) debentures, or

(b) shares that, under the company's articles of association, do not normally carry rights to vote at its general meetings (for example, shares carrying rights to vote that, under those articles, arise only where specified pecuniary advantages are not provided).

**969  Power of offeror to require general meeting to be called**

(1) Where a takeover bid is made for an opted-in company, the offeror may by making a request to the directors of the company require them to call a general meeting of the company if, at the date at which the request is made, he holds shares amounting to not less than 75% in value of all the voting shares in the company.

(2) The reference in subsection (1) to voting shares in the company does not include—

(a) debentures, or

(b) shares that, under the company's articles of association, do not normally carry rights to vote at its general meetings (for example, shares carrying rights to vote that, under those articles, arise only where specified pecuniary advantages are not provided).

(3) Sections 303 to 305 (members' power to require general meetings to be called) apply as they would do if subsection (1) above were substituted for subsections (1) to (3) of section 303, and with any other necessary modifications.

*Supplementary*

### 970   Communication of decisions

(1) A company that has passed an opting-in resolution or an opting-out resolution must notify—
(a) the Panel, and
(b) where the company—
   (i)   has voting shares admitted to trading on a regulated market in an EEA State other than the United Kingdom, or
   (ii)   has requested such admission,
   (iii)   the authority designated by that state as the supervisory authority for the purposes of Article 4.1 of the Takeovers Directive.

(2) Notification must be given within 15 days after the resolution is passed and, if any admission or request such as is mentioned in subsection (1)(b) occurs at a later time, within 15 days after that time.

(3) If a company fails to comply with this section, an offence is committed by—
(a) the company, and
(b) every officer of it who is in default.

(4) A person guilty of an offence under this section is liable on summary conviction to a fine not exceeding level 3 on the standard scale and, for continued contravention, a daily default fine not exceeding one-tenth of level 3 on the standard scale.

### 971   Interpretation of this Chapter

(1) In this Chapter—
'offeror' and 'takeover bid' have the same meaning as in the Takeovers Directive;
'offer period', in relation to a takeover bid, means the time allowed for acceptance of the bid by—
   (a) rules under section 943(1) giving effect to Article 7.1 of the Takeovers Directive, or
   (b) where the rules giving effect to that Article which apply to the bid are those of an EEA State other than the United Kingdom, those rules;
'opted-in company' means a company in relation to which—
   (a) an opting-in resolution has effect, and
   (b) the conditions in section 966(2) and (4) continue to be met;
'opting-in resolution' has the meaning given by section 966(1);
'opting-out resolution' has the meaning given by section 966(5);
'the Takeovers Directive' means Directive 2004/25/EC of the European Parliament and of the Council;
'voting rights' means rights to vote at general meetings of the company in question, including rights that arise only in certain circumstances;
'voting shares' means shares carrying voting rights.

(2) For the purposes of this Chapter—
(a) securities of a company are treated as shares in the company if they are convertible into or entitle the holder to subscribe for such shares;
(b) debentures issued by a company are treated as shares in the company if they carry voting rights.

### 972   Transitory provision

(1) Where a takeover bid is made for an opted-in company, section 368 of the Companies Act 1985 (c. 6) (extraordinary general meeting on members' requisition) and section 378 of that Act (extraordinary and special resolutions) have effect as follows until their repeal by this Act.

(2) Section 368 has effect as if a members' requisition included a requisition of a person who—
(a) is the offeror in relation to the takeover bid, and
(b) holds at the date of the deposit of the requisition shares amounting to not less than 75% in value of all the voting shares in the company.

(3) In relation to a general meeting of the company that—
(a) is the first such meeting to be held after the end of the offer period, and
(b) is held at a time when the offeror holds shares amounting to not less than 75% in value of all the voting shares in the company,
section 378(2) (meaning of 'special resolution') has effect as if '14 days' notice' were substituted for '21 days' notice'.

(4) A reference in this section to voting shares in the company does not include—
(a) debentures, or

(b) shares that, under the company's articles of association, do not normally carry rights to vote at its general meetings (for example, shares carrying rights to vote that, under those articles, arise only where specified pecuniary advantages are not provided).

### 973  Power to extend to Isle of Man and Channel Islands

Her Majesty may by Order in Council direct that any of the provisions of this Chapter extend, with such modifications as may be specified in the Order, to the Isle of Man or any of the Channel Islands.

## Chapter 3  'Squeeze-out' and 'sell-out'

### *Takeover offers*

### 974  Meaning of 'takeover offer'

(1) For the purposes of this Chapter an offer to acquire shares in a company is a 'takeover offer' if the following two conditions are satisfied in relation to the offer.

(2) The first condition is that it is an offer to acquire—
 (a) all the shares in a company, or
 (b) where there is more than one class of shares in a company, all the shares of one or more classes,

other than shares that at the date of the offer are already held by the offeror.

Section 975 contains provision supplementing this subsection.

(3) The second condition is that the terms of the offer are the same—
 (a) in relation to all the shares to which the offer relates, or
 (b) where the shares to which the offer relates include shares of different classes, in relation to all the shares of each class.

Section 976 contains provision treating this condition as satisfied in certain circumstances.

(4) In subsections (1) to (3) 'shares' means shares, other than relevant treasury shares, that have been allotted on the date of the offer (but see subsection (5)).

(5) A takeover offer may include among the shares to which it relates—
 (a) all or any shares that are allotted after the date of the offer but before a specified date;
 (b) all or any relevant treasury shares that cease to be held as treasury shares before a specified date;
 (c) all or any other relevant treasury shares.

(6) In this section—

'relevant treasury shares' means shares that—
 (a) are held by the company as treasury shares on the date of the offer, or
 (b) become shares held by the company as treasury shares after that date but before a specified date;

'specified date' means a date specified in or determined in accordance with the terms of the offer.

(7) Where the terms of an offer make provision for their revision and for acceptances on the previous terms to be treated as acceptances on the revised terms, then, if the terms of the offer are revised in accordance with that provision—
 (a) the revision is not to be regarded for the purposes of this Chapter as the making of a fresh offer, and
 (b) references in this Chapter to the date of the offer are accordingly to be read as references to the date of the original offer.

### 975  Shares already held by the offeror etc.

(1) The reference in section 974(2) to shares already held by the offeror includes a reference to shares that he has contracted to acquire, whether unconditionally or subject to conditions being met.

This is subject to subsection (2).

(2) The reference in section 974(2) to shares already held by the offeror does not include a reference to shares that are the subject of a contract—
 (a) intended to secure that the holder of the shares will accept the offer when it is made, and
 (b) entered into—
  (i) by deed and for no consideration,
  (ii) for consideration of negligible value, or
  (iii) for consideration consisting of a promise by the offeror to make the offer.

(3) In relation to Scotland, this section applies as if the words 'by deed and' in subsection (2)(b)(i) were omitted.

(4) The condition in section 974(2) is treated as satisfied where—
 (a) the offer does not extend to shares that associates of the offeror hold or have contracted to acquire (whether unconditionally or subject to conditions being met), and
 (b) the condition would be satisfied if the offer did extend to those shares.

(For further provision about such shares, see section 977(2).)

### 976    Cases where offer treated as being on same terms

(1)  The condition in section 974(3) (terms of offer to be the same for all shares or all shares of particular classes) is treated as satisfied where subsection (2) or (3) below applies.

(2)  This subsection applies where—

    (a)  shares carry an entitlement to a particular dividend which other shares of the same class, by reason of being allotted later, do not carry,

    (b)  there is a difference in the value of consideration offered for the shares allotted earlier as against that offered for those allotted later,

    (c)  that difference merely reflects the difference in entitlement to the dividend, and

    (d)  the condition in section 974(3) would be satisfied but for that difference.

(3)  This subsection applies where—

    (a)  the law of a country or territory outside the United Kingdom—

        (i)   precludes an offer of consideration in the form, or any of the forms, specified in the terms of the offer ('the specified form'), or

        (ii)  precludes it except after compliance by the offeror with conditions with which he is unable to comply or which he regards as unduly onerous,

    (b)  the persons to whom an offer of consideration in the specified form is precluded are able to receive consideration in another form that is of substantially equivalent value, and

    (c)  the condition in section 974(3) would be satisfied but for the fact that an offer of consideration in the specified form to those persons is precluded.

### 977    Shares to which an offer relates

(1)  Where a takeover offer is made and, during the period beginning with the date of the offer and ending when the offer can no longer be accepted, the offeror—

    (a)  acquires or unconditionally contracts to acquire any of the shares to which the offer relates, but

    (b)  does not do so by virtue of acceptances of the offer,

those shares are treated for the purposes of this Chapter as excluded from those to which the offer relates.

(2)  For the purposes of this Chapter shares that an associate of the offeror holds or has contracted to acquire, whether at the date of the offer or subsequently, are not treated as shares to which the offer relates, even if the offer extends to such shares.

In this subsection 'contracted' means contracted unconditionally or subject to conditions being met.

(3)  This section is subject to section 979(8) and (9).

### 978    Effect of impossibility etc. of communicating or accepting offer

(1)  Where there are holders of shares in a company to whom an offer to acquire shares in the company is not communicated, that does not prevent the offer from being a takeover offer for the purposes of this Chapter if—

    (a)  those shareholders have no registered address in the United Kingdom,

    (b)  the offer was not communicated to those shareholders in order not to contravene the law of a country or territory outside the United Kingdom, and

    (c)  either—

        (i)   the offer is published in the Gazette, or

        (ii)  the offer can be inspected, or a copy of it obtained, at a place in an EEA State or on a website, and a notice is published in the Gazette specifying the address of that place or website.

(2)  Where an offer is made to acquire shares in a company and there are persons for whom, by reason of the law of a country or territory outside the United Kingdom, it is impossible to accept the offer, or more difficult to do so, that does not prevent the offer from being a takeover offer for the purposes of this Chapter.

(3)  It is not to be inferred—

    (a)  that an offer which is not communicated to every holder of shares in the company cannot be a takeover offer for the purposes of this Chapter unless the requirements of paragraphs (a) to (c) of subsection (1) are met, or

    (b)  that an offer which is impossible, or more difficult, for certain persons to accept cannot be a takeover offer for those purposes unless the reason for the impossibility or difficulty is the one mentioned in subsection (2).

*'Squeeze-out'*

### 979    Right of offeror to buy out minority shareholder

(1)  Subsection (2) applies in a case where a takeover offer does not relate to shares of different classes.

(2)  If the offeror has, by virtue of acceptances of the offer, acquired or unconditionally contracted to acquire—

    (a)  not less than 90% in value of the shares to which the offer relates, and

(b) in a case where the shares to which the offer relates are voting shares, not less than 90% of the voting rights carried by those shares,

he may give notice to the holder of any shares to which the offer relates which the offeror has not acquired or unconditionally contracted to acquire that he desires to acquire those shares.

(3) Subsection (4) applies in a case where a takeover offer relates to shares of different classes.

(4) If the offeror has, by virtue of acceptances of the offer, acquired or unconditionally contracted to acquire—

(a) not less than 90% in value of the shares of any class to which the offer relates, and

(b) in a case where the shares of that class are voting shares, not less than 90% of the voting rights carried by those shares,

he may give notice to the holder of any shares of that class to which the offer relates which the offeror has not acquired or unconditionally contracted to acquire that he desires to acquire those shares.

(5) In the case of a takeover offer which includes among the shares to which it relates—

(a) shares that are allotted after the date of the offer, or

(b) relevant treasury shares (within the meaning of section 974) that cease to be held as treasury shares after the date of the offer,

the offeror's entitlement to give a notice under subsection (2) or (4) on any particular date shall be determined as if the shares to which the offer relates did not include any allotted, or ceasing to be held as treasury shares, on or after that date.

(6) Subsection (7) applies where—

(a) the requirements for the giving of a notice under subsection (2) or (4) are satisfied, and

(b) there are shares in the company which the offeror, or an associate of his, has contracted to acquire subject to conditions being met, and in relation to which the contract has not become unconditional.

(7) The offeror's entitlement to give a notice under subsection (2) or (4) shall be determined as if—

(a) the shares to which the offer relates included shares falling within paragraph (b) of subsection (6), and

(b) in relation to shares falling within that paragraph, the words 'by virtue of acceptances of the offer' in subsection (2) or (4) were omitted.

(8) Where—

(a) a takeover offer is made,

(b) during the period beginning with the date of the offer and ending when the offer can no longer be accepted, the offeror—

(i) acquires or unconditionally contracts to acquire any of the shares to which the offer relates, but

(ii) does not do so by virtue of acceptances of the offer, and

(c) subsection (10) applies,

then for the purposes of this section those shares are not excluded by section 977(1) from those to which the offer relates, and the offeror is treated as having acquired or contracted to acquire them by virtue of acceptances of the offer.

(9) Where—

(a) a takeover offer is made,

(b) during the period beginning with the date of the offer and ending when the offer can no longer be accepted, an associate of the offeror acquires or unconditionally contracts to acquire any of the shares to which the offer relates, and

(c) subsection (10) applies,

then for the purposes of this section those shares are not excluded by section 977(2) from those to which the offer relates.

(10) This subsection applies if—

(a) at the time the shares are acquired or contracted to be acquired as mentioned in subsection (8) or (9) (as the case may be), the value of the consideration for which they are acquired or contracted to be acquired ('the acquisition consideration') does not exceed the value of the consideration specified in the terms of the offer, or

(b) those terms are subsequently revised so that when the revision is announced the value of the acquisition consideration, at the time mentioned in paragraph (a), no longer exceeds the value of the consideration specified in those terms.

**980  Further provision about notices given under section 979**

(1) A notice under section 979 must be given in the prescribed manner.

(2) No notice may be given under section 979(2) or (4) after the end of—

(a) the period of three months beginning with the day after the last day on which the offer can be accepted, or

(b) the period of six months beginning with the date of the offer, where that period ends earlier and the offer is one to which subsection (3) below applies.

(3) This subsection applies to an offer if the time allowed for acceptance of the offer is not governed by rules under section 943(1) that give effect to Article 7 of the Takeovers Directive.

In this subsection 'the Takeovers Directive' has the same meaning as in section 943.

(4) At the time when the offeror first gives a notice under section 979 in relation to an offer, he must send to the company—

(a) a copy of the notice, and

(b) a statutory declaration by him in the prescribed form, stating that the conditions for the giving of the notice are satisfied.

(5) Where the offeror is a company (whether or not a company within the meaning of this Act) the statutory declaration must be signed by a director.

(6) A person commits an offence if—

(a) he fails to send a copy of a notice or a statutory declaration as required by subsection (4), or

(b) he makes such a declaration for the purposes of that subsection knowing it to be false or without having reasonable grounds for believing it to be true.

(7) It is a defence for a person charged with an offence for failing to send a copy of a notice as required by subsection (4) to prove that he took reasonable steps for securing compliance with that subsection.

(8) A person guilty of an offence under this section is liable—

(a) on conviction on indictment, to imprisonment for a term not exceeding two years or a fine (or both);

(b) on summary conviction—

(i) in England and Wales, to imprisonment for a term not exceeding twelve months or to a fine not exceeding the statutory maximum (or both) and, for continued contravention, a daily default fine not exceeding one-fiftieth of the statutory maximum;

(ii) in Scotland or Northern Ireland, to imprisonment for a term not exceeding six months, or to a fine not exceeding the statutory maximum (or both) and, for continued contravention, a daily default fine not exceeding one-fiftieth of the statutory maximum.

### 981 Effect of notice under section 979

(1) Subject to section 986 (applications to the court), this section applies where the offeror gives a shareholder a notice under section 979.

(2) The offeror is entitled and bound to acquire the shares to which the notice relates on the terms of the offer.

(3) Where the terms of an offer are such as to give the shareholder a choice of consideration, the notice must give particulars of the choice and state—

(a) that the shareholder may, within six weeks from the date of the notice, indicate his choice by a written communication sent to the offeror at an address specified in the notice, and

(b) which consideration specified in the offer will apply if he does not indicate a choice.

The reference in subsection (2) to the terms of the offer is to be read accordingly.

(4) Subsection (3) applies whether or not any time-limit or other conditions applicable to the choice under the terms of the offer can still be complied with.

(5) If the consideration offered to or (as the case may be) chosen by the shareholder—

(a) is not cash and the offeror is no longer able to provide it, or

(b) was to have been provided by a third party who is no longer bound or able to provide it,

the consideration is to be taken to consist of an amount of cash, payable by the offeror, which at the date of the notice is equivalent to the consideration offered or (as the case may be) chosen.

(6) At the end of six weeks from the date of the notice the offeror must immediately—

(a) send a copy of the notice to the company, and

(b) pay or transfer to the company the consideration for the shares to which the notice relates.

Where the consideration consists of shares or securities to be allotted by the offeror, the reference in paragraph (b) to the transfer of the consideration is to be read as a reference to the allotment of the shares or securities to the company.

(7) If the shares to which the notice relates are registered, the copy of the notice sent to the company under subsection (6)(a) must be accompanied by an instrument of transfer executed on behalf of the holder of the shares by a person appointed by the offeror.

On receipt of that instrument the company must register the offeror as the holder of those shares.

(8) If the shares to which the notice relates are transferable by the delivery of warrants or other instruments, the copy of the notice sent to the company under subsection (6)(a) must be accompanied by a statement to that effect.

On receipt of that statement the company must issue the offeror with warrants or other instruments in respect of the shares, and those already in issue in respect of the shares become void.

(9) The company must hold any money or other consideration received by it under subsection (6)(b) on trust for the person who, before the offeror acquired them, was entitled to the shares in respect of which the money or other consideration was received.

Section 982 contains further provision about how the company should deal with such money or other consideration.

**982    Further provision about consideration held on trust under section 981(9)**

(1)  This section applies where an offeror pays or transfers consideration to the company under section 981(6).

(2)  The company must pay into a separate bank account that complies with subsection (3)—

  (a)  any money it receives under paragraph (b) of section 981(6), and

  (b)  any dividend or other sum accruing from any other consideration it receives under that paragraph.

(3)  A bank account complies with this subsection if the balance on the account—

  (a)  bears interest at an appropriate rate, and

  (b)  can be withdrawn by such notice (if any) as is appropriate.

(4)  If—

  (a)  the person entitled to the consideration held on trust by virtue of section 981(9) cannot be found, and

  (b)  subsection (5) applies,

the consideration (together with any interest, dividend or other benefit that has accrued from it) must be paid into court.

(5)  This subsection applies where—

  (a)  reasonable enquiries have been made at reasonable intervals to find the person, and

  (b)  twelve years have elapsed since the consideration was received, or the company is wound up.

(6)  In relation to a company registered in Scotland, subsections (7) and (8) apply instead of subsection (4).

(7)  If the person entitled to the consideration held on trust by virtue of section 981(9) cannot be found and subsection (5) applies—

  (a)  the trust terminates,

  (b)  the company or (if the company is wound up) the liquidator must sell any consideration other than cash and any benefit other than cash that has accrued from the consideration, and

  (c)  a sum representing—

    (i)  the consideration so far as it is cash,

    (ii)  the proceeds of any sale under paragraph (b), and

    (iii)  any interest, dividend or other benefit that has accrued from the consideration,

    must be deposited in the name of the Accountant of Court in a separate bank account complying with subsection (3) and the receipt for the deposit must be transmitted to the Accountant of Court.

(8)  Section 58 of the Bankruptcy (Scotland) Act 1985 (c. 66) (so far as consistent with this Act) applies (with any necessary modifications) to sums deposited under subsection (7) as it applies to sums deposited under section 57(1)(a) of that Act.

(9)  The expenses of any such enquiries as are mentioned in subsection (5) may be paid out of the money or other property held on trust for the person to whom the enquiry relates.

*'Sell-out'*

**983    Right of minority shareholder to be bought out by offeror**

(1)  Subsections (2) and (3) apply in a case where a takeover offer relates to all the shares in a company.

For this purpose a takeover offer relates to all the shares in a company if it is an offer to acquire all the shares in the company within the meaning of section 974.

(2)  The holder of any voting shares to which the offer relates who has not accepted the offer may require the offeror to acquire those shares if, at any time before the end of the period within which the offer can be accepted—

  (a)  the offeror has by virtue of acceptances of the offer acquired or unconditionally contracted to acquire some (but not all) of the shares to which the offer relates, and

  (b)  those shares, with or without any other shares in the company which he has acquired or contracted to acquire (whether unconditionally or subject to conditions being met)—

    (i)  amount to not less than 90% in value of all the voting shares in the company (or would do so but for section 990(1)), and

    (ii)  carry not less than 90% of the voting rights in the company (or would do so but for section 990(1)).

(3)  The holder of any non-voting shares to which the offer relates who has not accepted the offer may require the offeror to acquire those shares if, at any time before the end of the period within which the offer can be accepted—

  (a)  the offeror has by virtue of acceptances of the offer acquired or unconditionally contracted to acquire some (but not all) of the shares to which the offer relates, and

(b) those shares, with or without any other shares in the company which he has acquired or contracted to acquire (whether unconditionally or subject to conditions being met), amount to not less than 90% in value of all the shares in the company (or would do so but for section 990(1)).

(4) If a takeover offer relates to shares of one or more classes and at any time before the end of the period within which the offer can be accepted—

(a) the offeror has by virtue of acceptances of the offer acquired or unconditionally contracted to acquire some (but not all) of the shares of any class to which the offer relates, and

(b) those shares, with or without any other shares of that class which he has acquired or contracted to acquire (whether unconditionally or subject to conditions being met)—

(i) amount to not less than 90% in value of all the shares of that class, and

(ii) in a case where the shares of that class are voting shares, carry not less than 90% of the voting rights carried by the shares of that class,

the holder of any shares of that class to which the offer relates who has not accepted the offer may require the offeror to acquire those shares.

(5) For the purposes of subsections (2) to (4), in calculating 90% of the value of any shares, shares held by the company as treasury shares are to be treated as having been acquired by the offeror.

(6) Subsection (7) applies where—

(a) a shareholder exercises rights conferred on him by subsection (2), (3) or (4),

(b) at the time when he does so, there are shares in the company which the offeror has contracted to acquire subject to conditions being met, and in relation to which the contract has not become unconditional, and

(c) the requirement imposed by subsection (2)(b), (3)(b) or (4)(b) (as the case may be) would not be satisfied if those shares were not taken into account.

(7) The shareholder is treated for the purposes of section 985 as not having exercised his rights under this section unless the requirement imposed by paragraph (b) of subsection (2), (3) or (4) (as the case may be) would be satisfied if—

(a) the reference in that paragraph to other shares in the company which the offeror has contracted to acquire unconditionally or subject to conditions being met were a reference to such shares which he has unconditionally contracted to acquire, and

(b) the reference in that subsection to the period within which the offer can be accepted were a reference to the period referred to in section 984(2).

(8) A reference in subsection (2)(b), (3)(b), (4)(b), (6) or (7) to shares which the offeror has acquired or contracted to acquire includes a reference to shares which an associate of his has acquired or contracted to acquire.

### 984   Further provision about rights conferred by section 983

(1) Rights conferred on a shareholder by subsection (2), (3) or (4) of section 983 are exercisable by a written communication addressed to the offeror.

(2) Rights conferred on a shareholder by subsection (2), (3) or (4) of that section are not exercisable after the end of the period of three months from—

(a) the end of the period within which the offer can be accepted, or

(b) if later, the date of the notice that must be given under subsection (3) below.

(3) Within one month of the time specified in subsection (2), (3) or (4) (as the case may be) of that section, the offeror must give any shareholder who has not accepted the offer notice in the prescribed manner of—

(a) the rights that are exercisable by the shareholder under that subsection, and

(b) the period within which the rights are exercisable.

If the notice is given before the end of the period within which the offer can be accepted, it must state that the offer is still open for acceptance.

(4) Subsection (3) does not apply if the offeror has given the shareholder a notice in respect of the shares in question under section 979.

(5) An offeror who fails to comply with subsection (3) commits an offence.

If the offeror is a company, every officer of that company who is in default or to whose neglect the failure is attributable also commits an offence.

(6) If an offeror other than a company is charged with an offence for failing to comply with subsection (3), it is a defence for him to prove that he took all reasonable steps for securing compliance with that subsection.

(7) A person guilty of an offence under this section is liable—

(a) on conviction on indictment, to a fine;

(b) on summary conviction, to a fine not exceeding the statutory maximum and, for continued contravention, a daily default fine not exceeding one-fiftieth of the statutory maximum.

### 985   Effect of requirement under section 983

(1) Subject to section 986, this section applies where a shareholder exercises his rights under section 983 in respect of any shares held by him.

(2)  The offeror is entitled and bound to acquire those shares on the terms of the offer or on such other terms as may be agreed.

(3)  Where the terms of an offer are such as to give the shareholder a choice of consideration—

    (a)  the shareholder may indicate his choice when requiring the offeror to acquire the shares, and

    (b)  the notice given to the shareholder under section 984(3)—

        (i)  must give particulars of the choice and of the rights conferred by this subsection, and

        (ii)  may state which consideration specified in the offer will apply if he does not indicate a choice.

The reference in subsection (2) to the terms of the offer is to be read accordingly.

(4)  Subsection (3) applies whether or not any time-limit or other conditions applicable to the choice under the terms of the offer can still be complied with.

(5)  If the consideration offered to or (as the case may be) chosen by the shareholder—

    (a)  is not cash and the offeror is no longer able to provide it, or

    (b)  was to have been provided by a third party who is no longer bound or able to provide it,

the consideration is to be taken to consist of an amount of cash, payable by the offeror, which at the date when the shareholder requires the offeror to acquire the shares is equivalent to the consideration offered or (as the case may be) chosen.

## *Supplementary*

### 986  Applications to the court

(1)  Where a notice is given under section 979 to a shareholder the court may, on an application made by him, order—

    (a)  that the offeror is not entitled and bound to acquire the shares to which the notice relates, or

    (b)  that the terms on which the offeror is entitled and bound to acquire the shares shall be such as the court thinks fit.

(2)  An application under subsection (1) must be made within six weeks from the date on which the notice referred to in that subsection was given.

If an application to the court under subsection (1) is pending at the end of that period, section 981(6) does not have effect until the application has been disposed of.

(3)  Where a shareholder exercises his rights under section 983 in respect of any shares held by him, the court may, on an application made by him or the offeror, order that the terms on which the offeror is entitled and bound to acquire the shares shall be such as the court thinks fit.

(4)  On an application under subsection (1) or (3)—

    (a)  the court may not require consideration of a higher value than that specified in the terms of the offer ('the offer value') to be given for the shares to which the application relates unless the holder of the shares shows that the offer value would be unfair;

    (b)  the court may not require consideration of a lower value than the offer value to be given for the shares.

(5)  No order for costs or expenses may be made against a shareholder making an application under subsection (1) or (3) unless the court considers that—

    (a)  the application was unnecessary, improper or vexatious,

    (b)  there has been unreasonable delay in making the application, or

    (c)  there has been unreasonable conduct on the shareholder's part in conducting the proceedings on the application.

(6)  A shareholder who has made an application under subsection (1) or (3) must give notice of the application to the offeror.

(7)  An offeror who is given notice of an application under subsection (1) or (3) must give a copy of the notice to—

    (a)  any person (other than the applicant) to whom a notice has been given under section 979;

    (b)  any person who has exercised his rights under section 983.

(8)  An offeror who makes an application under subsection (3) must give notice of the application to—

    (a)  any person to whom a notice has been given under section 979;

    (b)  any person who has exercised his rights under section 983.

(9)  Where a takeover offer has not been accepted to the extent necessary for entitling the offeror to give notices under subsection (2) or (4) of section 979 the court may, on an application made by him, make an order authorising him to give notices under that subsection if it is satisfied that—

    (a)  the offeror has after reasonable enquiry been unable to trace one or more of the persons holding shares to which the offer relates,

    (b)  the requirements of that subsection would have been met if the person, or all the persons, mentioned in paragraph (a) above had accepted the offer, and

    (c)  the consideration offered is fair and reasonable.

This is subject to subsection (10).

(10)  The court may not make an order under subsection (9) unless it considers that it is just and equitable to do so having regard, in particular, to the number of shareholders who have been traced but who have not accepted the offer.

## 987  Joint offers

(1)  In the case of a takeover offer made by two or more persons jointly, this Chapter has effect as follows.

(2)  The conditions for the exercise of the rights conferred by section 979 are satisfied—

    (a)  in the case of acquisitions by virtue of acceptances of the offer, by the joint offerors acquiring or unconditionally contracting to acquire the necessary shares jointly;

    (b)  in other cases, by the joint offerors acquiring or unconditionally contracting to acquire the necessary shares either jointly or separately.

(3)  The conditions for the exercise of the rights conferred by section 983 are satisfied—

    (a)  in the case of acquisitions by virtue of acceptances of the offer, by the joint offerors acquiring or unconditionally contracting to acquire the necessary shares jointly;

    (b)  in other cases, by the joint offerors acquiring or contracting (whether unconditionally or subject to conditions being met) to acquire the necessary shares either jointly or separately.

(4)  Subject to the following provisions, the rights and obligations of the offeror under sections 979 to 985 are respectively joint rights and joint and several obligations of the joint offerors.

(5)  A provision of sections 979 to 986 that requires or authorises a notice or other document to be given or sent by or to the joint offerors is complied with if the notice or document is given or sent by or to any of them (but see subsection (6)).

(6)  The statutory declaration required by section 980(4) must be made by all of the joint offerors and, where one or more of them is a company, signed by a director of that company.

(7)  In sections 974 to 977, 979(9), 981(6), 983(8) and 988 references to the offeror are to be read as references to the joint offerors or any of them.

(8)  In section 981(7) and (8) references to the offeror are to be read as references to the joint offerors or such of them as they may determine.

(9)  In sections 981(5)(a) and 985(5)(a) references to the offeror being no longer able to provide the relevant consideration are to be read as references to none of the joint offerors being able to do so.

(10)  In section 986 references to the offeror are to be read as references to the joint offerors, except that—

    (a)  an application under subsection (3) or (9) may be made by any of them, and

    (b)  the reference in subsection (9)(a) to the offeror having been unable to trace one or more of the persons holding shares is to be read as a reference to none of the offerors having been able to do so.

*Interpretation*

## 988  Associates

(1)  In this Chapter 'associate', in relation to an offeror, means—

    (a)  a nominee of the offeror,

    (b)  a holding company, subsidiary or fellow subsidiary of the offeror or a nominee of such a holding company, subsidiary or fellow subsidiary,

    (c)  a body corporate in which the offeror is substantially interested,

    (d)  a person who is, or is a nominee of, a party to a share acquisition agreement with the offeror, or

    (e)  (where the offeror is an individual) his spouse or civil partner and any minor child or step-child of his.

(2)  For the purposes of subsection (1)(b) a company is a fellow subsidiary of another body corporate if both are subsidiaries of the same body corporate but neither is a subsidiary of the other.

(3)  For the purposes of subsection (1)(c) an offeror has a substantial interest in a body corporate if—

    (a)  the body or its directors are accustomed to act in accordance with his directions or instructions, or

    (b)  he is entitled to exercise or control the exercise of one-third or more of the voting power at general meetings of the body.

Subsections (2) and (3) of section 823 (which contain provision about when a person is treated as entitled to exercise or control the exercise of voting power) apply for the purposes of this subsection as they apply for the purposes of that section.

(4)  For the purposes of subsection (1)(d) an agreement is a share acquisition agreement if—

    (a)  it is an agreement for the acquisition of, or of an interest in, shares to which the offer relates,

    (b)  it includes provisions imposing obligations or restrictions on any one or more of the parties to it with respect to their use, retention or disposal of such shares, or their interests in such shares, acquired in pursuance of the agreement (whether or not together with any other shares to which the offer relates or any other interests of theirs in such shares), and

   (c) it is not an excluded agreement (see subsection (5)).
  (5) An agreement is an 'excluded agreement'—
   (a) if it is not legally binding, unless it involves mutuality in the undertakings, expectations or understandings of the parties to it, or
   (b) if it is an agreement to underwrite or sub-underwrite an offer of shares in a company, provided the agreement is confined to that purpose and any matters incidental to it.
  (6) The reference in subsection (4)(b) to the use of interests in shares is to the exercise of any rights or of any control or influence arising from those interests (including the right to enter into an agreement for the exercise, or for control of the exercise, of any of those rights by another person).
  (7) In this section—
   (a) 'agreement' includes any agreement or arrangement;
   (b) references to provisions of an agreement include—
    (i) undertakings, expectations or understandings operative under an arrangement, and
    (ii) any provision whether express or implied and whether absolute or not.

### 989 Convertible securities

  (1) For the purposes of this Chapter securities of a company are treated as shares in the company if they are convertible into or entitle the holder to subscribe for such shares.
  References to the holder of shares or a shareholder are to be read accordingly.
  (2) Subsection (1) is not to be read as requiring any securities to be treated—
   (a) as shares of the same class as those into which they are convertible or for which the holder is entitled to subscribe, or
   (b) as shares of the same class as other securities by reason only that the shares into which they are convertible or for which the holder is entitled to subscribe are of the same class.

### 990 Debentures carrying voting rights

  (1) For the purposes of this Chapter debentures issued by a company to which subsection (2) applies are treated as shares in the company if they carry voting rights.
  (2) This subsection applies to a company that has voting shares, or debentures carrying voting rights, which are admitted to trading on a regulated market.
  (3) In this Chapter, in relation to debentures treated as shares by virtue of subsection (1)—
   (a) references to the holder of shares or a shareholder are to be read accordingly;
   (b) references to shares being allotted are to be read as references to debentures being issued.

### 991 Interpretation

  (1) In this Chapter—
 'the company' means the company whose shares are the subject of a takeover offer;
 'date of the offer' means—
   (a) where the offer is published, the date of publication;
   (b) where the offer is not published, or where any notices of the offer are given before the date of publication, the date when notices of the offer (or the first such notices) are given;
and references to the date of the offer are to be read in accordance with section 974(7) (revision of offer terms) where that applies;
 'non-voting shares' means shares that are not voting shares;
 'offeror' means (subject to section 987) the person making a takeover offer;
 'voting rights' means rights to vote at general meetings of the company, including rights that arise only in certain circumstances;
 'voting shares' means shares carrying voting rights.
  (2) For the purposes of this Chapter a person contracts unconditionally to acquire shares if his entitlement under the contract to acquire them is not (or is no longer) subject to conditions or if all conditions to which it was subject have been met.
 A reference to a contract becoming unconditional is to be read accordingly.

### 992 Matters to be dealt with in directors' report

  (1) Part 7 of the Companies Act 1985 (c.6) (accounts and audit) is amended as follows.
  (2) In Schedule 7 (matters to be dealt with in directors' report), after Part 6 insert—

## 'PART 7 DISCLOSURE REQUIRED BY CERTAIN PUBLICLY-TRADED COMPANIES

**13**

  (1) This Part of this Schedule applies to the directors' report for a financial year if the company had securities carrying voting rights admitted to trading on a regulated market at the end of that year.

(2) The report shall contain detailed information, by reference to the end of that year, on the following matters—

  (a) the structure of the company's capital, including in particular—
    (i) the rights and obligations attaching to the shares or, as the case may be, to each class of shares in the company, and
    (ii) where there are two or more such classes, the percentage of the total share capital represented by each class;

  (b) any restrictions on the transfer of securities in the company, including in particular—
    (i) limitations on the holding of securities, and
    (ii) requirements to obtain the approval of the company, or of other holders of securities in the company, for a transfer of securities;

  (c) in the case of each person with a significant direct or indirect holding of securities in the company, such details as are known to the company of—
    (i) the identity of the person,
    (ii) the size of the holding, and
    (iii) the nature of the holding;

  (d) in the case of each person who holds securities carrying special rights with regard to control of the company—
    (i) the identity of the person, and
    (ii) the nature of the rights;

  (e) where—
    (i) the company has an employees' share scheme, and
    (ii) shares to which the scheme relates have rights with regard to control of the company that are not exercisable directly by the employees,
  how those rights are exercisable;

  (f) any restrictions on voting rights, including in particular—
    (i) limitations on voting rights of holders of a given percentage or number of votes,
    (ii) deadlines for exercising voting rights, and
    (iii) arrangements by which, with the company's cooperation, financial rights carried by securities are held by a person other than the holder of the securities;

  (g) any agreements between holders of securities that are known to the company and may result in restrictions on the transfer of securities or on voting rights;

  (h) any rules that the company has about—
    (i) appointment and replacement of directors, or
    (ii) amendment of the company's articles of association;

  (i) the powers of the company's directors, including in particular any powers in relation to the issuing or buying back by the company of its shares;

  (j) any significant agreements to which the company is a party that take effect, alter or terminate upon a change of control of the company following a takeover bid, and the effects of any such agreements;

  (k) any agreements between the company and its directors or employees providing for compensation for loss of office or employment (whether through resignation, purported redundancy or otherwise) that occurs because of a takeover bid.

(3) For the purposes of sub-paragraph (2)(a) a company's capital includes any securities in the company that are not admitted to trading on a regulated market.

(4) For the purposes of sub-paragraph (2)(c) a person has an indirect holding of securities if—
  (a) they are held on his behalf, or
  (b) he is able to secure that rights carried by the securities are exercised in accordance with his wishes.

(5) Sub-paragraph (2)(j) does not apply to an agreement if—
  (a) disclosure of the agreement would be seriously prejudicial to the company, and
  (b) the company is not under any other obligation to disclose it.

(6) In this paragraph—

"securities" means shares or debentures;

"takeover bid" has the same meaning as in the Takeovers Directive;

"the Takeovers Directive" means Directive 2004/25/EC of the European Parliament and of the Council;

"voting rights" means rights to vote at general meetings of the company in question, including rights that arise only in certain circumstances.'.

(3) In section 234ZZA (requirements of directors' reports), at the end of subsection (1) (contents of Schedule 7) insert—

'Part 7 specifies information to be disclosed by certain publicly-traded companies.'.

(4) After that subsection insert—

'(5)  A directors' report shall also contain any necessary explanatory material with regard to information that is required to be included in the report by Part 7 of Schedule 7.'.

(5)  In section 251 (summary financial statements), after subsection (2ZA) insert—

'(2ZB)  A company that sends to an entitled person a summary financial statement instead of a copy of its directors' report shall—

    (a)  include in the statement the explanatory material required to be included in the directors' report by section 234ZZA(5), or

    (b)  send that material to the entitled person at the same time as it sends the statement.

For the purposes of paragraph (b), subsections (2A) to (2E) apply in relation to the material referred to in that paragraph as they apply in relation to a summary financial statement.'

(6)  The amendments made by this section apply in relation to directors' reports for financial years beginning on or after 20th May 2006.

# PART 29  FRAUDULENT TRADING

## 993  Offence of fraudulent trading

(1)  If any business of a company is carried on with intent to defraud creditors of the company or creditors of any other person, or for any fraudulent purpose, every person who is knowingly a party to the carrying on of the business in that manner commits an offence.

(2)  This applies whether or not the company has been, or is in the course of being, wound up.

(3)  A person guilty of an offence under this section is liable—

    (a)  on conviction on indictment, to imprisonment for a term not exceeding ten years or a fine (or both);

    (b)  on summary conviction—

        (i)  in England and Wales, to imprisonment for a term not exceeding twelve months or a fine not exceeding the statutory maximum (or both);

        (ii)  in Scotland or Northern Ireland, to imprisonment for a term not exceeding six months or a fine not exceeding the statutory maximum (or both).

# PART 30  PROTECTION OF MEMBERS AGAINST UNFAIR PREJUDICE

*Main provisions*

## 994  Petition by company member

(1)  A member of a company may apply to the court by petition for an order under this Part on the ground—

    (a)  that the company's affairs are being or have been conducted in a manner that is unfairly prejudicial to the interests of members generally or of some part of its members (including at least himself), or

    (b)  that an actual or proposed act or omission of the company (including an act or omission on its behalf) is or would be so prejudicial.

(1A)  For the purposes of subsection (1)(a), a removal of the company's auditor from office—

    (a)  on grounds of divergence of opinions on accounting treatments or audit procedures, or

    (b)  on any other improper grounds,

shall be treated as being unfairly prejudicial to the interests of some part of the company's members.

(2)  The provisions of this Part apply to a person who is not a member of a company but to whom shares in the company have been transferred or transmitted by operation of law as they apply to a member of a company.

(3)  In this section, and so far as applicable for the purposes of this section in the other provisions of this Part, 'company' means—

    (a)  a company within the meaning of this Act, or

    (b)  a company that is not such a company but is a statutory water company within the meaning of the Statutory Water Companies Act 1991 (c. 58).

## 995  Petition by Secretary of State

(1)  This section applies to a company in respect of which—

    (a)  the Secretary of State has received a report under section 437 of the Companies Act 1985 (c. 6) (inspector's report);

    (b)  the Secretary of State has exercised his powers under section 447 or 448 of that Act (powers to require documents and information or to enter and search premises);

    (c)  the Secretary of State or the Financial Services Authority has exercised his or its powers under Part 11 of the Financial Services and Markets Act 2000 (c. 8) (information gathering and investigations); or

(d) the Secretary of State has received a report from an investigator appointed by him or the Financial Services Authority under that Part.

(2) If it appears to the Secretary of State that in the case of such a company—

(a) the company's affairs are being or have been conducted in a manner that is unfairly prejudicial to the interests of members generally or of some part of its members, or

(b) an actual or proposed act or omission of the company (including an act or omission on its behalf) is or would be so prejudicial,

he may apply to the court by petition for an order under this Part.

(3) The Secretary of State may do this in addition to, or instead of, presenting a petition for the winding up of the company.

(4) In this section, and so far as applicable for the purposes of this section in the other provisions of this Part, 'company' means any body corporate that is liable to be wound up under the Insolvency Act 1986 (c. 45) or the Insolvency (Northern Ireland) Order 1989 (S.I. 1989/2405 (N.I. 19)).

### 996    Powers of the court under this Part

(1) If the court is satisfied that a petition under this Part is well founded, it may make such order as it thinks fit for giving relief in respect of the matters complained of.

(2) Without prejudice to the generality of subsection (1), the court's order may—

(a) regulate the conduct of the company's affairs in the future;

(b) require the company—

(i)    to refrain from doing or continuing an act complained of, or

(ii)   to do an act that the petitioner has complained it has omitted to do;

(c) authorise civil proceedings to be brought in the name and on behalf of the company by such person or persons and on such terms as the court may direct;

(d) require the company not to make any, or any specified, alterations in its articles without the leave of the court;

(e) provide for the purchase of the shares of any members of the company by other members or by the company itself and, in the case of a purchase by the company itself, the reduction of the company's capital accordingly.

### 997    Application of general rule-making powers

The power to make rules under section 411 of the Insolvency Act 1986 (c. 45) or Article 359 of the Insolvency (Northern Ireland) Order 1989 (S.I. 1989/2405 (N.I. 19)), so far as relating to a winding-up petition, applies for the purposes of a petition under this Part.

*Supplementary provisions*

### 998    Copy of order affecting company's constitution to be delivered to registrar

(1) Where an order of the court under this Part—

(a) alters the company's constitution, or

(b) gives leave for the company to make any, or any specified, alterations to its constitution, the company must deliver a copy of the order to the registrar.

(2) It must do so within 14 days from the making of the order or such longer period as the court may allow.

(3) If a company makes default in complying with this section, an offence is committed by—

(a) the company, and

(b) every officer of the company who is in default.

(4) A person guilty of an offence under this section is liable on summary conviction to a fine not exceeding level 3 on the standard scale and, for continued contravention, a daily default fine not exceeding one-tenth of level 3 on the standard scale.

### 999    Supplementary provisions where company's constitution altered

(1) This section applies where an order under this Part alters a company's constitution.

(2) If the order amends—

(a) a company's articles, or

(b) any resolution or agreement to which Chapter 3 of Part 3 applies (resolution or agreement affecting a company's constitution),

the copy of the order delivered to the registrar by the company under section 998 must be accompanied by a copy of the company's articles, or the resolution or agreement in question, as amended.

(3) Every copy of a company's articles issued by the company after the order is made must be accompanied by a copy of the order, unless the effect of the order has been incorporated into the articles by amendment.

(4) If a company makes default in complying with this section an offence is committed by—

(a) the company, and

(b) every officer of the company who is in default.

(5) A person guilty of an offence under this section is liable on summary conviction to a fine not exceeding level 3 on the standard scale.

# PART 31  DISSOLUTION AND RESTORATION TO THE REGISTER

## Chapter 1  Striking off

### *Registrar's power to strike off defunct company*

**1000  Power to strike off company not carrying on business or in operation**

(1) If the registrar has reasonable cause to believe that a company is not carrying on business or in operation, the registrar may send to the company by post a letter inquiring whether the company is carrying on business or in operation.

(2) If the registrar does not within one month of sending the letter receive any answer to it, the registrar must within 14 days after the expiration of that month send to the company by post a registered letter referring to the first letter, and stating—

(a) that no answer to it has been received, and

(b) that if an answer is not received to the second letter within one month from its date, a notice will be published in the Gazette with a view to striking the company's name off the register.

(3) If the registrar—

(a) receives an answer to the effect that the company is not carrying on business or in operation, or

(b) does not within one month after sending the second letter receive any answer,

the registrar may publish in the Gazette, and send to the company by post, a notice that at the expiration of three months from the date of the notice the name of the company mentioned in it will, unless cause is shown to the contrary, be struck off the register and the company will be dissolved.

(4) At the expiration of the time mentioned in the notice the registrar may, unless cause to the contrary is previously shown by the company, strike its name off the register.

(5) The registrar must publish notice in the Gazette of the company's name having been struck off the register.

(6) On the publication of the notice in the Gazette the company is dissolved.

(7) However—

(a) the liability (if any) of every director, managing officer and member of the company continues and may be enforced as if the company had not been dissolved, and

(b) nothing in this section affects the power of the court to wind up a company the name of which has been struck off the register.

**1001  Duty to act in case of company being wound up**

(1) If, in a case where a company is being wound up—

(a) the registrar has reasonable cause to believe—

(i) that no liquidator is acting, or

(ii) that the affairs of the company are fully wound up, and

(b) the returns required to be made by the liquidator have not been made for a period of six consecutive months,

the registrar must publish in the Gazette and send to the company or the liquidator (if any) a notice that at the expiration of three months from the date of the notice the name of the company mentioned in it will, unless cause is shown to the contrary, be struck off the register and the company will be dissolved.

(2) At the expiration of the time mentioned in the notice the registrar may, unless cause to the contrary is previously shown by the company, strike its name off the register.

(3) The registrar must publish notice in the Gazette of the company's name having been struck off the register.

(4) On the publication of the notice in the Gazette the company is dissolved.

(5) However—

(a) the liability (if any) of every director, managing officer and member of the company continues and may be enforced as if the company had not been dissolved, and

(b) nothing in this section affects the power of the court to wind up a company the name of which has been struck off the register.

**1002  Supplementary provisions as to service of letter or notice**

(1) A letter or notice to be sent under section 1000 or 1001 to a company may be addressed to the company at its registered office or, if no office has been registered, to the care of some officer of the company.

(2) If there is no officer of the company whose name and address are known to the registrar, the letter or notice may be sent to each of the persons who subscribed the memorandum (if their addresses are known to the registrar).

(3) A notice to be sent to a liquidator under section 1001 may be addressed to him at his last known place of business.

*Voluntary striking off*

### 1003   Striking off on application by company

(1)  On application by a company, the registrar of companies may strike the company's name off the register.

(2)  The application—

    (a)  must be made on the company's behalf by its directors or by a majority of them, and

    (b)  must contain the prescribed information.

(3)  The registrar may not strike a company off under this section until after the expiration of three months from the publication by the registrar in the Gazette of a notice—

    (a)  stating that the registrar may exercise the power under this section in relation to the company, and

    (b)  inviting any person to show cause why that should not be done.

(4)  The registrar must publish notice in the Gazette of the company's name having been struck off.

(5)  On the publication of the notice in the Gazette the company is dissolved.

(6)  However—

    (a)  the liability (if any) of every director, managing officer and member of the company continues and may be enforced as if the company had not been dissolved, and

    (b)  nothing in this section affects the power of the court to wind up a company the name of which has been struck off the register.

### 1004   Circumstances in which application not to be made: activities of company

(1)  An application under section 1003 (application for voluntary striking off) on behalf of a company must not be made if, at any time in the previous three months, the company has—

    (a)  changed its name,

    (b)  traded or otherwise carried on business,

    (c)  made a disposal for value of property or rights that, immediately before ceasing to trade or otherwise carry on business, it held for the purpose of disposal for gain in the normal course of trading or otherwise carrying on business, or

    (d)  engaged in any other activity, except one which is—

        (i)   necessary or expedient for the purpose of making an application under that section, or deciding whether to do so,

        (ii)  necessary or expedient for the purpose of concluding the affairs of the company,

        (iii) necessary or expedient for the purpose of complying with any statutory requirement, or

        (iv)  specified by the Secretary of State by order for the purposes of this sub-paragraph.

(2)  For the purposes of this section, a company is not to be treated as trading or otherwise carrying on business by virtue only of the fact that it makes a payment in respect of a liability incurred in the course of trading or otherwise carrying on business.

(3)  The Secretary of State may by order amend subsection (1) for the purpose of altering the period in relation to which the doing of the things mentioned in paragraphs (a) to (d) of that subsection is relevant.

(4)  An order under this section is subject to negative resolution procedure.

(5)  It is an offence for a person to make an application in contravention of this section.

(6)  In proceedings for such an offence it is a defence for the accused to prove that he did not know, and could not reasonably have known, of the existence of the facts that led to the contravention.

(7)  A person guilty of an offence under this section is liable—

    (a)  on conviction on indictment, to a fine;

    (b)  on summary conviction, to a fine not exceeding the statutory maximum.

### 1005   Circumstances in which application not to be made: other proceedings not concluded

(1)  An application under section 1003 (application for voluntary striking off) on behalf of a company must not be made at a time when—

    (a)  an application to the court under Part 26 has been made on behalf of the company for the sanctioning of a compromise or arrangement and the matter has not been finally concluded;

    (b)  a voluntary arrangement in relation to the company has been proposed under Part 1 of the Insolvency Act 1986 (c. 45) or Part 2 of the Insolvency (Northern Ireland) Order 1989 (S.I. 1989/2405 (N.I. 19)) and the matter has not been finally concluded;

    (c)  the company is in administration under Part 2 of that Act or Part 3 of that Order;

    (d)  paragraph 44 of Schedule B1 to that Act or paragraph 45 of Schedule B1 to that Order applies (interim moratorium on proceedings where application to the court for an administration order has been made or notice of intention to appoint administrator has been filed);

(e) the company is being wound up under Part 4 of that Act or Part 5 of that Order, whether voluntarily or by the court, or a petition under that Part for winding up of the company by the court has been presented and not finally dealt with or withdrawn;

(f) there is a receiver or manager of the company's property;

(g) the company's estate is being administered by a judicial factor.

(2) For the purposes of subsection (1)(a), the matter is finally concluded if—

(a) the application has been withdrawn,

(b) the application has been finally dealt with without a compromise or arrangement being sanctioned by the court, or

(c) a compromise or arrangement has been sanctioned by the court and has, together with anything required to be done under any provision made in relation to the matter by order of the court, been fully carried out.

(3) For the purposes of subsection (1)(b), the matter is finally concluded if—

(a) no meetings are to be summoned under section 3 of the Insolvency Act 1986 (c. 45) or Article 16 of the Insolvency (Northern Ireland) Order 1989,

(b) meetings summoned under that section or Article fail to approve the arrangement with no, or the same, modifications,

(c) an arrangement approved by meetings summoned under that section, or in consequence of a direction under section 6(4)(b) of that Act or Article 19(4)(b) of that Order, has been fully implemented, or

(d) the court makes an order under section 6(5) of that Act or Article 19(5) of that Order revoking approval given at previous meetings and, if the court gives any directions under section 6(6) of that Act or Article 19(6) of that Order, the company has done whatever it is required to do under those directions.

(4) It is an offence for a person to make an application in contravention of this section.

(5) In proceedings for such an offence it is a defence for the accused to prove that he did not know, and could not reasonably have known, of the existence of the facts that led to the contravention.

(6) A person guilty of an offence under this section is liable—

(a) on conviction on indictment, to a fine;

(b) on summary conviction, to a fine not exceeding the statutory maximum.

## 1006   Copy of application to be given to members, employees, etc.

(1) A person who makes an application under section 1003 (application for voluntary striking off) on behalf of a company must secure that, within seven days from the day on which the application is made, a copy of it is given to every person who at any time on that day is—

(a) a member of the company,

(b) an employee of the company,

(c) a creditor of the company,

(d) a director of the company,

(e) a manager or trustee of any pension fund established for the benefit of employees of the company, or

(f) a person of a description specified for the purposes of this paragraph by regulations made by the Secretary of State.

Regulations under paragraph (f) are subject to negative resolution procedure.

(2) Subsection (1) does not require a copy of the application to be given to a director who is a party to the application.

(3) The duty imposed by this section ceases to apply if the application is withdrawn before the end of the period for giving the copy application.

(4) A person who fails to perform the duty imposed on him by this section commits an offence. If he does so with the intention of concealing the making of the application from the person concerned, he commits an aggravated offence.

(5) In proceedings for an offence under this section it is a defence for the accused to prove that he took all reasonable steps to perform the duty.

(6) A person guilty of an offence under this section (other than an aggravated offence) is liable—

(a) on conviction on indictment, to a fine;

(b) on summary conviction, to a fine not exceeding the statutory maximum.

(7) A person guilty of an aggravated offence under this section is liable—

(a) on conviction on indictment, to imprisonment for a term not exceeding seven years or a fine (or both);

(b) on summary conviction—

(i) in England and Wales, to imprisonment for a term not exceeding twelve months or to a fine not exceeding the statutory maximum (or both);

(ii) in Scotland or Northern Ireland, to imprisonment for a term not exceeding six months, or to a fine not exceeding the statutory maximum (or both).

**1007    Copy of application to be given to new members, employees, etc.**

(1) This section applies in relation to any time after the day on which a company makes an application under section 1003 (application for voluntary striking off) and before the day on which the application is finally dealt with or withdrawn.

(2) A person who is a director of the company at the end of a day on which a person (other than himself) becomes—

    (a) a member of the company,

    (b) an employee of the company,

    (c) a creditor of the company,

    (d) a director of the company,

    (e) a manager or trustee of any pension fund established for the benefit of employees of the company, or

    (f) a person of a description specified for the purposes of this paragraph by regulations made by the Secretary of State,

must secure that a copy of the application is given to that person within seven days from that day.

Regulations under paragraph (f) are subject to negative resolution procedure.

(3) The duty imposed by this section ceases to apply if the application is finally dealt with or withdrawn before the end of the period for giving the copy application.

(4) A person who fails to perform the duty imposed on him by this section commits an offence.

If he does so with the intention of concealing the making of the application from the person concerned, he commits an aggravated offence.

(5) In proceedings for an offence under this section it is a defence for the accused to prove—

    (a) that at the time of the failure he was not aware of the fact that the company had made an application under section 1003, or

    (b) that he took all reasonable steps to perform the duty.

(6) A person guilty of an offence under this section (other than an aggravated offence) is liable—

    (a) on conviction on indictment, to a fine;

    (b) on summary conviction, to a fine not exceeding the statutory maximum.

(7) A person guilty of an aggravated offence under this section is liable—

    (a) on conviction on indictment, to imprisonment for a term not exceeding seven years or a fine (or both);

    (b) on summary conviction—

        (i) in England and Wales, to imprisonment for a term not exceeding twelve months or to a fine not exceeding the statutory maximum (or both);

        (ii) in Scotland or Northern Ireland, to imprisonment for a term not exceeding six months, or to a fine not exceeding the statutory maximum (or both).

**1008    Copy of application: provisions as to service of documents**

(1) The following provisions have effect for the purposes of—

section 1006 (copy of application to be given to members, employees, etc), and

section 1007 (copy of application to be given to new members, employees, etc).

(2) A document is treated as given to a person if it is—

    (a) delivered to him, or

    (b) left at his proper address, or

    (c) sent by post to him at that address.

(3) For the purposes of subsection (2) and section 7 of the Interpretation Act 1978 (c. 30) (service of documents by post) as it applies in relation to that subsection, the proper address of a person is—

    (a) in the case of a firm incorporated or formed in the United Kingdom, its registered or principal office;

    (b) in the case of a firm incorporated or formed outside the United Kingdom—

        (i) if it has a place of business in the United Kingdom, its principal office in the United Kingdom, or

        (ii) if it does not have a place of business in the United Kingdom, its registered or principal office;

    (c) in the case of an individual, his last known address.

(4) In the case of a creditor of the company a document is treated as given to him if it is left or sent by post to him—

    (a) at the place of business of his with which the company has had dealings by virtue of which he is a creditor of the company, or

    (b) if there is more than one such place of business, at each of them.

**1009    Circumstances in which application to be withdrawn**

(1) This section applies where, at any time on or after the day on which a company makes an application under section 1003 (application for voluntary striking off) and before the day on which the application is finally dealt with or withdrawn—

    (a) the company—

    (i)   changes its name,

    (ii)  trades or otherwise carries on business,

    (iii) makes a disposal for value of any property or rights other than those which it was necessary or expedient for it to hold for the purpose of making, or proceeding with, an application under that section, or

    (iv) engages in any activity, except one to which subsection (4) applies;

(b) an application is made to the court under Part 26 on behalf of the company for the sanctioning of a compromise or arrangement;

(c) a voluntary arrangement in relation to the company is proposed under Part 1 of the Insolvency Act 1986 (c. 45) or Part 2 of the Insolvency (Northern Ireland) Order 1989 (S.I. 1989/2405 (N.I. 19));

(d) an application to the court for an administration order in respect of the company is made under paragraph 12 of Schedule B1 to that Act or paragraph 13 of Schedule B1 to that Order;

(e) an administrator is appointed in respect of the company under paragraph 14 or 22 of Schedule B1 to that Act or paragraph 15 or 23 of Schedule B1 to that Order, or a copy of notice of intention to appoint an administrator of the company under any of those provisions is filed with the court;

(f) there arise any of the circumstances in which, under section 84(1) of that Act or Article 70 of that Order, the company may be voluntarily wound up;

(g) a petition is presented for the winding up of the company by the court under Part 4 of that Act or Part 5 of that Order;

(h) a receiver or manager of the company's property is appointed; or

(i) a judicial factor is appointed to administer the company's estate.

(2) A person who, at the end of a day on which any of the events mentioned in subsection (1) occurs, is a director of the company must secure that the company's application is withdrawn forthwith.

(3) For the purposes of subsection (1)(a), a company is not treated as trading or otherwise carrying on business by virtue only of the fact that it makes a payment in respect of a liability incurred in the course of trading or otherwise carrying on business.

(4) The excepted activities referred to in subsection (1)(a)(iv) are—

(a) any activity necessary or expedient for the purposes of—

    (i)   making, or proceeding with, an application under section 1003 (application for voluntary striking off),

    (ii)  concluding affairs of the company that are outstanding because of what has been necessary or expedient for the purpose of making, or proceeding with, such an application, or

    (iii) complying with any statutory requirement;

(b) any activity specified by the Secretary of State by order for the purposes of this subsection.

An order under paragraph (b) is subject to negative resolution procedure.

(5) A person who fails to perform the duty imposed on him by this section commits an offence.

(6) In proceedings for an offence under this section it is a defence for the accused to prove—

(a) that at the time of the failure he was not aware of the fact that the company had made an application under section 1003, or

(b) that he took all reasonable steps to perform the duty.

(7) A person guilty of an offence under this section is liable—

(a) on conviction on indictment, to a fine;

(b) on summary conviction, to a fine not exceeding the statutory maximum.

**1010    Withdrawal of application**

An application under section 1003 is withdrawn by notice to the registrar.

**1011    Meaning of 'creditor'**

In this Chapter 'creditor' includes a contingent or prospective creditor.

## Chapter 2    Property of dissolved company

### *Property vesting as bona vacantia*

**1012    Property of dissolved company to be bona vacantia**

(1) When a company is dissolved, all property and rights whatsoever vested in or held on trust for the company immediately before its dissolution (including leasehold property, but not including property held by the company on trust for another person) are deemed to be bona vacantia and—

(a) accordingly belong to the Crown, or to the Duchy of Lancaster or to the Duke of Cornwall for the time being (as the case may be), and

(b) vest and may be dealt with in the same manner as other bona vacantia accruing to the Crown, to the Duchy of Lancaster or to the Duke of Cornwall.

(2) Subsection (1) has effect subject to the possible restoration of the company to the register under Chapter 3 (see section 1034).

### 1013    Crown disclaimer of property vesting as bona vacantia

(1) Where property vests in the Crown under section 1012, the Crown's title to it under that section may be disclaimed by a notice signed by the Crown representative, that is to say the Treasury Solicitor, or, in relation to property in Scotland, the Queen's and Lord Treasurer's Remembrancer.

(2) The right to execute a notice of disclaimer under this section may be waived by or on behalf of the Crown either expressly or by taking possession.

(3) A notice of disclaimer must be executed within three years after—

(a) the date on which the fact that the property may have vested in the Crown under section 1012 first comes to the notice of the Crown representative, or

(b) if ownership of the property is not established at that date, the end of the period reasonably necessary for the Crown representative to establish the ownership of the property.

(4) If an application in writing is made to the Crown representative by a person interested in the property requiring him to decide whether he will or will not disclaim, any notice of disclaimer must be executed within twelve months after the making of the application or such further period as may be allowed by the court.

(5) A notice of disclaimer under this section is of no effect if it is shown to have been executed after the end of the period specified by subsection (3) or (4).

(6) A notice of disclaimer under this section must be delivered to the registrar and retained and registered by him.

(7) Copies of it must be published in the Gazette and sent to any persons who have given the Crown representative notice that they claim to be interested in the property.

(8) This section applies to property vested in the Duchy of Lancaster or the Duke of Cornwall under section 1012 as if for references to the Crown and the Crown representative there were respectively substituted references to the Duchy of Lancaster and to the Solicitor to that Duchy, or to the Duke of Cornwall and to the Solicitor to the Duchy of Cornwall, as the case may be.

### 1014    Effect of Crown disclaimer

(1) Where notice of disclaimer is executed under section 1013 as respects any property, that property is deemed not to have vested in the Crown under section 1012.

(2) The following sections contain provisions as to the effect of the Crown disclaimer—

sections 1015 to 1019 apply in relation to property in England and Wales or Northern Ireland;

sections 1020 to 1022 apply in relation to property in Scotland.

*Effect of Crown disclaimer: England and Wales and Northern Ireland*

### 1015    General effect of disclaimer

(1) The Crown's disclaimer operates so as to terminate, as from the date of the disclaimer, the rights, interests and liabilities of the company in or in respect of the property disclaimed.

(2) It does not, except so far as is necessary for the purpose of releasing the company from any liability, affect the rights or liabilities of any other person.

### 1016    Disclaimer of leaseholds

(1) The disclaimer of any property of a leasehold character does not take effect unless a copy of the disclaimer has been served (so far as the Crown representative is aware of their addresses) on every person claiming under the company as underlessee or mortgagee, and either—

(a) no application under section 1017 (power of court to make vesting order) is made with respect to that property before the end of the period of 14 days beginning with the day on which the last notice under this paragraph was served, or

(b) where such an application has been made, the court directs that the disclaimer shall take effect.

(2) Where the court gives a direction under subsection (1)(b) it may also, instead of or in addition to any order it makes under section 1017, make such order as it thinks fit with respect to fixtures, tenant's improvements and other matters arising out of the lease.

(3) In this section the 'Crown representative' means—

(a) in relation to property vested in the Duchy of Lancaster, the Solicitor to that Duchy;

(b) in relation to property vested in the Duke of Cornwall, the Solicitor to the Duchy of Cornwall;

(c) in relation to property in Scotland, the Queen's and Lord Treasurer's Remembrancer;

(d) in relation to other property, the Treasury Solicitor.

### 1017    Power of court to make vesting order

(1) The court may on application by a person who—

(a) claims an interest in the disclaimed property, or

(b) is under a liability in respect of the disclaimed property that is not discharged by the disclaimer, make an order under this section in respect of the property.

(2) An order under this section is an order for the vesting of the disclaimed property in, or its delivery to—

    (a) a person entitled to it (or a trustee for such a person), or

    (b) a person subject to such a liability as is mentioned in subsection (1)(b) (or a trustee for such a person).

(3) An order under subsection (2)(b) may only be made where it appears to the court that it would be just to do so for the purpose of compensating the person subject to the liability in respect of the disclaimer.

(4) An order under this section may be made on such terms as the court thinks fit.

(5) On a vesting order being made under this section, the property comprised in it vests in the person named in that behalf in the order without conveyance, assignment or transfer.

### 1018    Protection of persons holding under a lease

(1) The court must not make an order under section 1017 vesting property of a leasehold nature in a person claiming under the company as underlessee or mortgagee except on terms making that person—

    (a) subject to the same liabilities and obligations as those to which the company was subject under the lease, or

    (b) if the court thinks fit, subject to the same liabilities and obligations as if the lease had been assigned to him.

(2) Where the order relates to only part of the property comprised in the lease, subsection (1) applies as if the lease had comprised only the property comprised in the vesting order.

(3) A person claiming under the company as underlessee or mortgagee who declines to accept a vesting order on such terms is excluded from all interest in the property.

(4) If there is no person claiming under the company who is willing to accept an order on such terms, the court has power to vest the company's estate and interest in the property in any person who is liable (whether personally or in a representative character, and whether alone or jointly with the company) to perform the lessee's covenants in the lease.

(5) The court may vest that estate and interest in such a person freed and discharged from all estates, incumbrances and interests created by the company.

### 1019    Land subject to rentcharge

Where in consequence of the disclaimer land that is subject to a rentcharge vests in any person, neither he nor his successors in title are subject to any personal liability in respect of sums becoming due under the rentcharge, except sums becoming due after he, or some person claiming under or through him, has taken possession or control of the land or has entered into occupation of it.

*Effect of Crown disclaimer: Scotland*

### 1020    General effect of disclaimer

(1) The Crown's disclaimer operates to determine, as from the date of the disclaimer, the rights, interests and liabilities of the company, and the property of the company, in or in respect of the property disclaimed.

(2) It does not (except so far as is necessary for the purpose of releasing the company and its property from liability) affect the rights or liabilities of any other person.

### 1021    Power of court to make vesting order

(1) The court may—

    (a) on application by a person who either claims an interest in disclaimed property or is under a liability not discharged by this Act in respect of disclaimed property, and

    (b) on hearing such persons as it thinks fit,

make an order for the vesting of the property in or its delivery to any persons entitled to it, or to whom it may seem just that the property should be delivered by way of compensation for such liability, or a trustee for him.

(2) The order may be made on such terms as the court thinks fit.

(3) On a vesting order being made under this section, the property comprised in it vests accordingly in the person named in that behalf in the order, without conveyance or assignation for that purpose.

### 1022    Protection of persons holding under a lease

(1) Where the property disclaimed is held under a lease the court must not make a vesting order in favour of a person claiming under the company, whether—

    (a) as sub-lessee, or

    (b) as creditor in a duly registered or (as the case may be) recorded heritable security over a lease,

except on the following terms.

(2) The person must by the order be made subject—

    (a) to the same liabilities and obligations as those to which the company was subject under the lease in respect of the property, or

(b) if the court thinks fit, only to the same liabilities and obligations as if the lease had been assigned to him.

In either event (if the case so requires) the liabilities and obligations must be as if the lease had comprised only the property comprised in the vesting order.

(3)  A sub-lessee or creditor declining to accept a vesting order on such terms is excluded from all interest in and security over the property.

(4)  If there is no person claiming under the company who is willing to accept an order on such terms, the court has power to vest the company's estate and interest in the property in any person liable (either personally or in a representative character, and either alone or jointly with the company) to perform the lessee's obligations under the lease.

(5)  The court may vest that estate and interest in such a person freed and discharged from all interests, rights and obligations created by the company in the lease or in relation to the lease.

(6)  For the purposes of this section a heritable security—

(a) is duly recorded if it is recorded in the Register of Sasines, and

(b) is duly registered if registered in accordance with the Land Registration (Scotland) Act 1979 (c. 33).

### *Supplementary provisions*

### 1023   Liability for rentcharge on company's land after dissolution

(1)  This section applies where on the dissolution of a company land in England and Wales or Northern Ireland that is subject to a rentcharge vests by operation of law in the Crown or any other person ('the proprietor').

(2)  Neither the proprietor nor his successors in title are subject to any personal liability in respect of sums becoming due under the rentcharge, except sums becoming due after the proprietor, or some person claiming under or through him, has taken possession or control of the land or has entered into occupation of it.

(3)  In this section 'company' includes any body corporate.

## Chapter 3   Restoration to the register

### *Administrative restoration to the register*

### 1024   Application for administrative restoration to the register

(1)  An application may be made to the registrar to restore to the register a company that has been struck off the register under section 1000 or 1001 (power of registrar to strike off defunct company).

(2)  An application under this section may be made whether or not the company has in consequence been dissolved.

(3)  An application under this section may only be made by a former director or former member of the company.

(4)  An application under this section may not be made after the end of the period of six years from the date of the dissolution of the company.

For this purpose an application is made when it is received by the registrar.

### 1025   Requirements for administrative restoration

(1)  On an application under section 1024 the registrar shall restore the company to the register if, and only if, the following conditions are met.

(2)  The first condition is that the company was carrying on business or in operation at the time of its striking off.

(3)  The second condition is that, if any property or right previously vested in or held on trust for the company has vested as *bona vacantia*, the Crown representative has signified to the registrar in writing consent to the company's restoration to the register.

(4)  It is the applicant's responsibility to obtain that consent and to pay any costs (in Scotland, expenses) of the Crown representative—

(a) in dealing with the property during the period of dissolution, or

(b) in connection with the proceedings on the application,

that may be demanded as a condition of giving consent.

(5)  The third condition is that the applicant has—

(a) delivered to the registrar such documents relating to the company as are necessary to bring up to date the records kept by the registrar, and

(b) paid any penalties under section 453 or corresponding earlier provisions (civil penalty for failure to deliver accounts) that were outstanding at the date of dissolution or striking off.

(6)  In this section the 'Crown representative' means—

(a) in relation to property vested in the Duchy of Lancaster, the Solicitor to that Duchy;

(b) in relation to property vested in the Duke of Cornwall, the Solicitor to the Duchy of Cornwall;

(c) in relation to property in Scotland, the Queen's and Lord Treasurer's Remembrancer;

(d) in relation to other property, the Treasury Solicitor.

### 1026   Application to be accompanied by statement of compliance

(1) An application under section 1024 (application for administrative restoration to the register) must be accompanied by a statement of compliance.

(2) The statement of compliance required is a statement—

(a) that the person making the application has standing to apply (see subsection (3) of that section), and

(b) that the requirements for administrative restoration (see section 1025) are met.

(3) The registrar may accept the statement of compliance as sufficient evidence of those matters.

### 1027   Registrar's decision on application for administrative restoration

(1) The registrar must give notice to the applicant of the decision on an application under section 1024 (application for administrative restoration to the register).

(2) If the decision is that the company should be restored to the register, the restoration takes effect as from the date that notice is sent.

(3) In the case of such a decision, the registrar must—

(a) enter on the register a note of the date as from which the company's restoration to the register takes effect, and

(b) cause notice of the restoration to be published in the Gazette.

(4) The notice under subsection (3)(b) must state—

(a) the name of the company or, if the company is restored to the register under a different name (see section 1033), that name and its former name,

(b) the company's registered number, and

(c) the date as from which the restoration of the company to the register takes effect.

### 1028   Effect of administrative restoration

(1) The general effect of administrative restoration to the register is that the company is deemed to have continued in existence as if it had not been dissolved or struck off the register.

(2) The company is not liable to a penalty under section 453 or any corresponding earlier provision (civil penalty for failure to deliver accounts) for a financial year in relation to which the period for filing accounts and reports ended—

(a) after the date of dissolution or striking off, and

(b) before the restoration of the company to the register.

(3) The court may give such directions and make such provision as seems just for placing the company and all other persons in the same position (as nearly as may be) as if the company had not been dissolved or struck off the register.

(4) An application to the court for such directions or provision may be made any time within three years after the date of restoration of the company to the register.

### 1029   Application to court for restoration to the register

(1) An application may be made to the court to restore to the register a company—

(a) that has been dissolved under Chapter 9 of Part 4 of the Insolvency Act 1986 (c. 45) or Chapter 9 of Part 5 of the Insolvency (Northern Ireland) Order 1989 (S.I. 1989/2405 (N.I. 19)) (dissolution of company after winding up),

(b) that is deemed to have been dissolved under paragraph 84(6) of Schedule B1 to that Act or paragraph 85(6) of Schedule B1 to that Order (dissolution of company following administration), or

(c) that has been struck off the register—

(i) under section 1000 or 1001 (power of registrar to strike off defunct company), or

(ii) under section 1003 (voluntary striking off),

whether or not the company has in consequence been dissolved.

(2) An application under this section may be made by—

(a) the Secretary of State,

(b) any former director of the company,

(c) any person having an interest in land in which the company had a superior or derivative interest,

(d) any person having an interest in land or other property—

(i) that was subject to rights vested in the company, or

(ii) that was benefited by obligations owed by the company,

(e) any person who but for the company's dissolution would have been in a contractual relationship with it,

(f) any person with a potential legal claim against the company,

(g) any manager or trustee of a pension fund established for the benefit of employees of the company,

(h) any former member of the company (or the personal representatives of such a person),

(i) any person who was a creditor of the company at the time of its striking off or dissolution,

    (j)  any former liquidator of the company,

    (k)  where the company was struck off the register under section 1003 (voluntary striking off), any person of a description specified by regulations under section 1006(1)(f) or 1007(2)(f) (persons entitled to notice of application for voluntary striking off),

or by any other person appearing to the court to have an interest in the matter.

### 1030  When application to the court may be made

(1) An application to the court for restoration of a company to the register may be made at any time for the purpose of bringing proceedings against the company for damages for personal injury.

(2) No order shall be made on such an application if it appears to the court that the proceedings would fail by virtue of any enactment as to the time within which proceedings must be brought.

(3) In making that decision the court must have regard to its power under section 1032(3) (power to give consequential directions etc) to direct that the period between the dissolution (or striking off) of the company and the making of the order is not to count for the purposes of any such enactment.

(4) In any other case an application to the court for restoration of a company to the register may not be made after the end of the period of six years from the date of the dissolution of the company, subject as follows.

(5) In a case where—

    (a)  the company has been struck off the register under section 1000 or 1001 (power of registrar to strike off defunct company),

    (b)  an application to the registrar has been made under section 1024 (application for administrative restoration to the register) within the time allowed for making such an application, and

    (c)  the registrar has refused the application,

an application to the court under this section may be made within 28 days of notice of the registrar's decision being issued by the registrar, even if the period of six years mentioned in subsection (4) above has expired.

(6) For the purposes of this section—

    (a)  'personal injury' includes any disease and any impairment of a person's physical or mental condition; and

    (b)  references to damages for personal injury include—

        (i)  any sum claimed by virtue of section 1(2)(c) of the Law Reform (Miscellaneous Provisions) Act 1934 (c. 41) or section 14(2)(c) of the Law Reform (Miscellaneous Provisions) Act (Northern Ireland) 1937 (1937 c. 9 (N.I.)) (funeral expenses)), and

        (ii)  damages under the Fatal Accidents Act 1976 (c. 30), the Damages (Scotland) Act 1976 (c. 13) or the Fatal Accidents (Northern Ireland) Order 1977 (S.I. 1977/1251 (N.I. 18)).

### 1031  Decision on application for restoration by the court

(1) On an application under section 1029 the court may order the restoration of the company to the register—

    (a)  if the company was struck off the register under section 1000 or 1001 (power of registrar to strike off defunct companies) and the company was, at the time of the striking off, carrying on business or in operation;

    (b)  if the company was struck off the register under section 1003 (voluntary striking off) and any of the requirements of sections 1004 to 1009 was not complied with;

    (c)  if in any other case the court considers it just to do so.

(2) If the court orders restoration of the company to the register, the restoration takes effect on a copy of the court's order being delivered to the registrar.

(3) The registrar must cause to be published in the Gazette notice of the restoration of the company to the register.

(4) The notice must state—

    (a)  the name of the company or, if the company is restored to the register under a different name (see section 1033), that name and its former name,

    (b)  the company's registered number, and

    (c)  the date on which the restoration took effect.

### 1032  Effect of court order for restoration to the register

(1) The general effect of an order by the court for restoration to the register is that the company is deemed to have continued in existence as if it had not been dissolved or struck off the register.

(2) The company is not liable to a penalty under section 453 or any corresponding earlier provision (civil penalty for failure to deliver accounts) for a financial year in relation to which the period for filing accounts and reports ended—

    (a)  after the date of dissolution or striking off, and

    (b)  before the restoration of the company to the register.

(3) The court may give such directions and make such provision as seems just for placing the company and all other persons in the same position (as nearly as may be) as if the company had not been dissolved or struck off the register.

(4) The court may also give directions as to—

    (a) the delivery to the registrar of such documents relating to the company as are necessary to bring up to date the records kept by the registrar,

    (b) the payment of the costs (in Scotland, expenses) of the registrar in connection with the proceedings for the restoration of the company to the register,

    (c) where any property or right previously vested in or held on trust for the company has vested as *bona vacantia*, the payment of the costs (in Scotland, expenses) of the Crown representative—

        (i) in dealing with the property during the period of dissolution, or

        (ii) in connection with the proceedings on the application.

(5) In this section the 'Crown representative' means—

    (a) in relation to property vested in the Duchy of Lancaster, the Solicitor to that Duchy;

    (b) in relation to property vested in the Duke of Cornwall, the Solicitor to the Duchy of Cornwall;

    (c) in relation to property in Scotland, the Queen's and Lord Treasurer's Remembrancer;

    (d) in relation to other property, the Treasury Solicitor.

### 1033　Company's name on restoration

(1) A company is restored to the register with the name it had before it was dissolved or struck off the register, subject to the following provisions.

(2) If at the date of restoration the company could not be registered under its former name without contravening section 66 (name not to be the same as another in the registrar's index of company names), it must be restored to the register—

    (a) under another name specified—

        (i) in the case of administrative restoration, in the application to the registrar, or

        (ii) in the case of restoration under a court order, in the court's order, or

    (b) as if its registered number was also its name.

References to a company's being registered in a name, and to registration in that context, shall be read as including the company's being restored to the register.

(3) If a company is restored to the register under a name specified in the application to the registrar, the provisions of—

section 80 (change of name: registration and issue of new certificate of incorporation), and

section 81 (change of name: effect),

apply as if the application to the registrar were notice of a change of name.

(4) If a company is restored to the register under a name specified in the court's order, the provisions of—

section 80 (change of name: registration and issue of new certificate of incorporation), and

section 81 (change of name: effect),

apply as if the copy of the court order delivered to the registrar were notice of a change a name.

(5) If the company is restored to the register as if its registered number was also its name—

    (a) the company must change its name within 14 days after the date of the restoration,

    (b) the change may be made by resolution of the directors (without prejudice to any other method of changing the company's name),

    (c) the company must give notice to the registrar of the change, and

    (d) sections 80 and 81 apply as regards the registration and effect of the change.

(6) If the company fails to comply with subsection (5)(a) or (c) an offence is committed by—

    (a) the company, and

    (b) every officer of the company who is in default.

(7) A person guilty of an offence under subsection (6) is liable on summary conviction to a fine not exceeding level 5 on the standard scale and, for continued contravention, a daily default fine not exceeding one-tenth of level 5 on the standard scale.

### 1034　Effect of restoration to the register where property has vested as bona vacantia

(1) The person in whom any property or right is vested by section 1012 (property of dissolved company to be *bona vacantia*) may dispose of, or of an interest in, that property or right despite the fact that the company may be restored to the register under this Chapter.

(2) If the company is restored to the register—

    (a) the restoration does not affect the disposition (but without prejudice to its effect in relation to any other property or right previously vested in or held on trust for the company), and

    (b) the Crown or, as the case may be, the Duke of Cornwall shall pay to the company an amount equal to—

        (i) the amount of any consideration received for the property or right or, as the case may be, the interest in it, or

        (ii) the value of any such consideration at the time of the disposition, or, if no consideration was received an amount equal to the value of the property, right or interest disposed of, as at the date of the disposition.

(3) There may be deducted from the amount payable under subsection (2)(b) the reasonable costs of the Crown representative in connection with the disposition (to the extent that they have not been paid as a condition of administrative restoration or pursuant to a court order for restoration).

(4) Where a liability accrues under subsection (2) in respect of any property or right which before the restoration of the company to the register had accrued as *bona vacantia* to the Duchy of Lancaster, the Attorney General of that Duchy shall represent Her Majesty in any proceedings arising in connection with that liability.

(5) Where a liability accrues under subsection (2) in respect of any property or right which before the restoration of the company to the register had accrued as *bona vacantia* to the Duchy of Cornwall, such persons as the Duke of Cornwall (or other possessor for the time being of the Duchy) may appoint shall represent the Duke (or other possessor) in any proceedings arising out of that liability.

(6) In this section the 'Crown representative' means—

(a) in relation to property vested in the Duchy of Lancaster, the Solicitor to that Duchy;

(b) in relation to property vested in the Duke of Cornwall, the Solicitor to the Duchy of Cornwall;

(c) in relation to property in Scotland, the Queen's and Lord Treasurer's Remembrancer;

(d) in relation to other property, the Treasury Solicitor.

# PART 32   COMPANY INVESTIGATIONS: AMENDMENTS

### 1035   Powers of Secretary of State to give directions to inspectors

(1) In Part 14 of the Companies Act 1985 (c. 6) (investigation of companies and their affairs), after section 446 insert—

*'Powers of Secretary of State to give directions to inspectors*

### 446A   General powers to give directions

(1) In exercising his functions an inspector shall comply with any direction given to him by the Secretary of State under this section.

(2) The Secretary of State may give an inspector appointed under section 431, 432(2) or 442(1) a direction—

(a) as to the subject matter of his investigation (whether by reference to a specified area of a company's operation, a specified transaction, a period of time or otherwise), or

(b) which requires the inspector to take or not to take a specified step in his investigation.

(3) The Secretary of State may give an inspector appointed under any provision of this Part a direction requiring him to secure that a specified report under section 437—

(a) includes the inspector's views on a specified matter,

(b) does not include any reference to a specified matter,

(c) is made in a specified form or manner, or

(d) is made by a specified date.

(4) A direction under this section—

(a) may be given on an inspector's appointment,

(b) may vary or revoke a direction previously given, and

(c) may be given at the request of an inspector.

(5) In this section—

(a) a reference to an inspector's investigation includes any investigation he undertakes, or could undertake, under section 433(1) (power to investigate affairs of holding company or subsidiary);

(b) "specified" means specified in a direction under this section.

### 446B   Direction to terminate investigation

(1) The Secretary of State may direct an inspector to take no further steps in his investigation.

(2) The Secretary of State may give a direction under this section to an inspector appointed under section 432(1) or 442(3) only on the grounds that it appears to him that—

(a) matters have come to light in the course of the inspector's investigation which suggest that a criminal offence has been committed, and

(b) those matters have been referred to the appropriate prosecuting authority.

(3) Where the Secretary of State gives a direction under this section, any direction already given to the inspector under section 437(1) to produce an interim report, and any direction given to him under section 446A(3) in relation to such a report, shall cease to have effect.

(4) Where the Secretary of State gives a direction under this section, the inspector shall not make a final report to the Secretary of State unless—

(a) the direction was made on the grounds mentioned in subsection (2) and the Secretary of State directs the inspector to make a final report to him, or

(b) the inspector was appointed under section 432(1) (appointment in pursuance of order of the court).

(5) An inspector shall comply with any direction given to him under this section.

(6) In this section, a reference to an inspector's investigation includes any investigation he undertakes, or could undertake, under section 433(1) (power to investigate affairs of holding company or subsidiary).'.

(2) In section 431 of that Act (inspectors' powers during investigation) in subsection (1) for 'report on them in such manner as he may direct' substitute 'report the result of their investigations to him'.

(3) In section 432 of that Act (other company investigations) in subsection (1) for 'report on them in such manner as he directs' substitute 'report the result of their investigations to him'.

(4) In section 437 of that Act (inspectors' reports)—

(a) in subsection (1) omit the second sentence, and

(b) subsections (1B) and (1C) shall cease to have effect.

(5) In section 442 of that Act (power to investigate company ownership), omit subsection (2).

## 1036  Resignation, removal and replacement of inspectors

After section 446B of the Companies Act 1985 (c. 6) (inserted by section 1035 above) insert—

### 'Resignation, removal and replacement of inspectors

### 446C  Resignation and revocation of appointment

(1) An inspector may resign by notice in writing to the Secretary of State.

(2) The Secretary of State may revoke the appointment of an inspector by notice in writing to the inspector.

### 446D  Appointment of replacement inspectors

(1) Where—

(a) an inspector resigns,

(b) an inspector's appointment is revoked, or

(c) an inspector dies,

the Secretary of State may appoint one or more competent inspectors to continue the investigation.

(2) An appointment under subsection (1) shall be treated for the purposes of this Part (apart from this section) as an appointment under the provision of this Part under which the former inspector was appointed.

(3) The Secretary of State must exercise his power under subsection (1) so as to secure that at least one inspector continues the investigation.

(4) Subsection (3) does not apply if—

(a) the Secretary of State could give any replacement inspector a direction under section 446B (termination of investigation), and

(b) such a direction would (under subsection (4) of that section) result in a final report not being made.

(5) In this section, references to an investigation include any investigation the former inspector conducted under section 433(1) (power to investigate affairs of holding company or subsidiary).'.

## 1037  Power to obtain information from former inspectors etc

(1) After section 446D of the Companies Act 1985 (c. 6) (inserted by section 1036 above) insert—

### 'Power to obtain information from former inspectors etc

### 446E  Obtaining information from former inspectors etc

(1) This section applies to a person who was appointed as an inspector under this Part—

(a) who has resigned, or

(b) whose appointment has been revoked.

(2) This section also applies to an inspector to whom the Secretary of State has given a direction under section 446B (termination of investigation).

(3) The Secretary of State may direct a person to whom this section applies to produce documents obtained or generated by that person during the course of his investigation to—

(a) the Secretary of State, or

(b) an inspector appointed under this Part.

(4) The power under subsection (3) to require production of a document includes power, in the case of a document not in hard copy form, to require the production of a copy of the document—

(a) in hard copy form, or

(b) in a form from which a hard copy can be readily obtained.

(5) The Secretary of State may take copies of or extracts from a document produced in pursuance of this section.

(6) The Secretary of State may direct a person to whom this section applies to inform him of any matters that came to that person's knowledge as a result of his investigation.

(7) A person shall comply with any direction given to him under this section.

(8) In this section—

    (a) references to the investigation of a former inspector or inspector include any investigation he conducted under section 433(1) (power to investigate affairs of holding company or subsidiary), and

    (b) "document" includes information recorded in any form.'.

(2) In section 451A of that Act (disclosure of information by Secretary of State or inspector), in subsection (1)(a) for '446' substitute '446E'.

(3) In section 452(1) of that Act (privileged information) for '446' substitute '446E'.

### 1038   Power to require production of documents

(1) In section 434 of the Companies Act 1985 (c. 6) (production of documents and evidence to inspectors), for subsection (6) substitute—

'(6) In this section "document" includes information recorded in any form.

(7) The power under this section to require production of a document includes power, in the case of a document not in hard copy form, to require the production of a copy of the document—

    (a) in hard copy form, or

    (b) in a form from which a hard copy can be readily obtained.

(8) An inspector may take copies of or extracts from a document produced in pursuance of this section.'.

(2) In section 447 of the Companies Act 1985 (power of Secretary of State to require documents and information), for subsection (9) substitute—

'(9) The power under this section to require production of a document includes power, in the case of a document not in hard copy form, to require the production of a copy of the document—

    (a) in hard copy form, or

    (b) in a form from which a hard copy can be readily obtained.'.

### 1039   Disqualification orders: consequential amendments

In section 8(1A)(b)(i) of the Company Directors Disqualification Act 1986 (c. 46) (disqualification after investigation of company: meaning of 'investigative material')—

    (a) after 'section' insert '437, 446E,', and

    (b) after '448' insert ', 451A'.

# PART 33   UK COMPANIES NOT FORMED UNDER COMPANIES LEGISLATION

## Chapter 1   Companies not formed under companies legislation but authorised to register

### 1040   Companies authorised to register under this Act

(1) This section applies to—

    (a) any company that was in existence on 2nd November 1862 (including any company registered under the Joint Stock Companies Acts), and

    (b) any company formed after that date (whether before or after the commencement of this Act)—

        (i) in pursuance of an Act of Parliament other than this Act or any of the former Companies Acts,

        (ii) in pursuance of letters patent, or

        (iii) that is otherwise duly constituted according to law.

(2) Any such company may on making application register under this Act.

(3) Subject to the following provisions, it may register as an unlimited company, as a company limited by shares or as a company limited by guarantee.

(4) A company having the liability of its members limited by Act of Parliament or letters patent—

    (a) may not register under this section unless it is a joint stock company, and

    (b) may not register under this section as an unlimited company or a company limited by guarantee.

(5) A company that is not a joint stock company may not register under this section as a company limited by shares.

(6) The registration of a company under this section is not invalid by reason that it has taken place with a view to the company's being wound up.

### 1041   Definition of 'joint stock company'

(1) For the purposes of section 1040 (companies authorised to register under this Act) 'joint stock company' means a company—

    (a) having a permanent paid-up or nominal share capital of fixed amount divided into shares, also of fixed amount, or held and transferable as stock, or divided and held partly in one way and partly in the other, and

    (b) formed on the principle of having for its members the holders of those shares or that stock, and no other persons.

    (2) Such a company when registered with limited liability under this Act is deemed a company limited by shares.

### 1042   Power to make provision by regulations

    (1) The Secretary of State may make provision by regulations—

      (a) for and in connection with registration under section 1040 (companies authorised to register under this Act), and

      (b) as to the application to companies so registered of the provisions of the Companies Acts.

    (2) Without prejudice to the generality of that power, regulations under this section may make provision corresponding to any provision formerly made by Chapter 2 of Part 22 of the Companies Act 1985 (c. 6).

    (3) Regulations under this section are subject to negative resolution procedure.

## Chapter 2   Unregistered companies

### 1043   Unregistered companies

    (1) This section applies to bodies corporate incorporated in and having a principal place of business in the United Kingdom, other than—

      (a) bodies incorporated by, or registered under, a public general Act of Parliament;

      (b) bodies not formed for the purpose of carrying on a business that has for its object the acquisition of gain by the body or its individual members;

      (c) bodies for the time being exempted from this section by direction of the Secretary of State;

      (d) open-ended investment companies.

    (2) The Secretary of State may make provision by regulations applying specified provisions of the Companies Acts to all, or any specified description of, the bodies to which this section applies.

    (3) The regulations may provide that the specified provisions of the Companies Acts apply subject to any specified limitations and to such adaptations and modifications (if any) as may be specified.

    (4) This section does not—

      (a) repeal or revoke in whole or in part any enactment, royal charter or other instrument constituting or regulating any body in relation to which provisions of the Companies Acts are applied by regulations under this section, or

      (b) restrict the power of Her Majesty to grant a charter in lieu or supplementary to any such charter.

But in relation to any such body the operation of any such enactment, charter or instrument is suspended in so far as it is inconsistent with any of those provisions as they apply for the time being to that body.

    (5) In this section 'specified' means specified in the regulations.

    (6) Regulations under this section are subject to negative resolution procedure.

## PART 34   OVERSEAS COMPANIES

### *Introductory*

### 1044   Overseas companies

In the Companies Acts an 'overseas company' means a company incorporated outside the United Kingdom.

### 1045   Company contracts and execution of documents by companies

    (1) The Secretary of State may make provision by regulations applying sections 43 to 52 (formalities of doing business and other matters) to overseas companies, subject to such exceptions, adaptations or modifications as may be specified in the regulations.

    (2) Regulations under this section are subject to negative resolution procedure.

### *Registration of particulars*

### 1046   Duty to register particulars

    (1) The Secretary of State may make provision by regulations requiring an overseas company—

      (a) to deliver to the registrar for registration a return containing specified particulars, and

      (b) to deliver to the registrar with the return specified documents.

    (2) The regulations—

      (a) must, in the case of a company other than a Gibraltar company, require the company to register particulars if the company opens a branch in the United Kingdom, and

(b) may, in the case of a Gibraltar company, require the company to register particulars if the company opens a branch in the United Kingdom, and

(c) may, in any case, require the registration of particulars in such other circumstances as may be specified.

(3) In subsection (2)—

'branch' means a branch within the meaning of the Eleventh Company Law Directive (89/666/EEC);

'Gibraltar company' means a company incorporated in Gibraltar.

(4) The regulations may provide that where a company has registered particulars under this section and any alteration is made—

(a) in the specified particulars, or

(b) in any document delivered with the return,

the company must deliver to the registrar for registration a return containing specified particulars of the alteration.

(5) The regulations may make provision—

(a) requiring the return under this section to be delivered for registration to the registrar for a specified part of the United Kingdom, and

(b) requiring it to be so delivered before the end of a specified period.

(6) The regulations may make different provision according to—

(a) the place where the company is incorporated, and

(b) the activities carried on (or proposed to be carried on) by it.

This is without prejudice to the general power to make different provision for different cases.

(7) In this section 'specified' means specified in the regulations.

(8) Regulations under this section are subject to affirmative resolution procedure.

### 1047   Registered name of overseas company

(1) Regulations under section 1046 (duty to register particulars) must require an overseas company that is required to register particulars to register its name.

(2) This may be—

(a) the company's corporate name (that is, its name under the law of the country or territory in which it is incorporated) or

(b) an alternative name specified in accordance with section 1048.

(3) Subject only to subsection (5), an EEA company may always register its corporate name.

(4) In any other case, the following provisions of Part 5 (a company's name) apply in relation to the registration of the name of an overseas company—

(a) section 53 (prohibited names);

(b) sections 54 to 56 (sensitive words and expressions);

(c) section 65 (inappropriate use of indications of company type or legal form);

(d) sections 66 to 74 (similarity to other names);

(e) section 75 (provision of misleading information etc);

(f) section 76 (misleading indication of activities).

(5) The provisions of section 57 (permitted characters etc) apply in every case.

(6) Any reference in the provisions mentioned in subsection (4) or (5) to a change of name shall be read as a reference to registration of a different name under section 1048.

### 1048   Registration under alternative name

(1) An overseas company that is required to register particulars under section 1046 may at any time deliver to the registrar for registration a statement specifying a name, other than its corporate name, under which it proposes to carry on business in the United Kingdom.

(2) An overseas company that has registered an alternative name may at any time deliver to the registrar of companies for registration a statement specifying a different name under which it proposes to carry on business in the United Kingdom (which may be its corporate name or a further alternative) in substitution for the name previously registered.

(3) The alternative name for the time being registered under this section is treated for all purposes of the law applying in the United Kingdom as the company's corporate name.

(4) This does not—

(a) affect the references in this section or section 1047 to the company's corporate name,

(b) affect any rights or obligation of the company, or

(c) render defective any legal proceedings by or against the company.

(5) Any legal proceedings that might have been continued or commenced against the company by its corporate name, or any name previously registered under this section, may be continued or commenced against it by its name for the time being so registered.

*Other requirements*

### 1049   Accounts and reports: general

(1) The Secretary of State may make provision by regulations requiring an overseas company that is required to register particulars under section 1046—

(a) to prepare the like accounts and directors' report, and

(b) to cause to be prepared such an auditor's report, as would be required if the company were formed and registered under this Act.

(2) The regulations may for this purpose apply, with or without modifications, all or any of the provisions of—

Part 15 (accounts and reports), and

Part 16 (audit).

(3) The Secretary of State may make provision by regulations requiring an overseas company to deliver to the registrar copies of—

(a) the accounts and reports prepared in accordance with the regulations, or

(b) the accounts and reports that it is required to prepare and have audited under the law of the country in which it is incorporated.

(4) Regulations under this section are subject to negative resolution procedure.

### 1050   Accounts and reports: credit or financial institutions

(1) This section applies to a credit or financial institution—

(a) that is incorporated or otherwise formed outside the United Kingdom and Gibraltar,

(b) whose head office is outside the United Kingdom and Gibraltar, and

(c) that has a branch in the United Kingdom.

(2) In subsection (1) 'branch' means a place of business that forms a legally dependent part of the institution and conducts directly all or some of the operations inherent in its business.

(3) The Secretary of State may make provision by regulations requiring an institution to which this section applies—

(a) to prepare the like accounts and directors' report, and

(b) to cause to be prepared such an auditor's report, as would be required if the institution were a company formed and registered under this Act.

(4) The regulations may for this purpose apply, with or without modifications, all or any of the provisions of—

Part 15 (accounts and reports), and

Part 16 (audit).

(5) The Secretary of State may make provision by regulations requiring an institution to which this section applies to deliver to the registrar copies of—

(a) accounts and reports prepared in accordance with the regulations, or

(b) accounts and reports that it is required to prepare and have audited under the law of the country in which the institution has its head office.

(6) Regulations under this section are subject to negative resolution procedure.

### 1051   Trading disclosures

(1) The Secretary of State may by regulations make provision requiring overseas companies carrying on business in the United Kingdom—

(a) to display specified information in specified locations,

(b) to state specified information in specified descriptions of document or communication, and

(c) to provide specified information on request to those they deal with in the course of their business.

(2) The regulations—

(a) shall in every case require a company that has registered particulars under section 1046 to disclose the name registered by it under section 1047, and

(b) may make provision as to the manner in which any specified information is to be displayed, stated or provided.

(3) The regulations may make provision corresponding to that made by—

section 83 (civil consequences of failure to make required disclosure), and

section 84 (criminal consequences of failure to make required disclosure).

(4) In this section 'specified' means specified in the regulations.

(5) Regulations under this section are subject to affirmative resolution procedure.

### 1052   Company charges

(1) The Secretary of State may by regulations make provision about the registration of specified charges over property in the United Kingdom of a registered overseas company.

(2) The power in subsection (1) includes power to make provision about—

(a) a registered overseas company that—

(i) has particulars registered in more than one part of the United Kingdom;

(ii) has property in more than one part of the United Kingdom;

(b) the circumstances in which property is to be regarded, for the purposes of the regulations, as being, or not being, in the United Kingdom or in a particular part of the United Kingdom;

(c) the keeping by a registered overseas company of records and registers about specified charges and their inspection;

(d) the consequences of a failure to register a charge in accordance with the regulations;

(e) the circumstances in which a registered overseas company ceases to be subject to the regulations.

(3) The regulations may for this purpose apply, with or without modifications, any of the provisions of Part 25 (company charges).

(4) The regulations may modify any reference in an enactment to Part 25, or to a particular provision of that Part, so as to include a reference to the regulations or to a specified provision of the regulations.

(5) Regulations under this section are subject to negative resolution procedure.

(6) In this section—

'registered overseas company' means an overseas company that has registered particulars under section 1046(1), and

'specified' means specified in the regulations.

## 1053    Other returns etc

(1) This section applies to overseas companies that are required to register particulars under section 1046.

(2) The Secretary of State may make provision by regulations requiring the delivery to the registrar of returns—

(a) by a company to which this section applies that—

(i) is being wound up, or

(ii) becomes or ceases to be subject to insolvency proceedings, or an arrangement or composition or any analogous proceedings;

(b) by the liquidator of a company to which this section applies.

(3) The regulations may specify—

(a) the circumstances in which a return is to be made,

(b) the particulars to be given in it, and

(c) the period within which it is to be made.

(4) The Secretary of State may make provision by regulations requiring notice to be given to the registrar of the appointment in relation to a company to which this section applies of a judicial factor (in Scotland).

(5) The regulations may include provision corresponding to any provision made by section 1154 of this Act (duty to notify registrar of certain appointments).

(6) Regulations under this section are subject to affirmative resolution procedure.

### *Supplementary*

## 1054    Offences

(1) Regulations under this Part may specify the person or persons responsible for complying with any specified requirement of the regulations.

(2) Regulations under this Part may make provision for offences, including provision as to—

(a) the person or persons liable in the case of any specified contravention of the regulations, and

(b) circumstances that are, or are not, to be a defence on a charge of such an offence.

(3) The regulations must not provide—

(a) for imprisonment, or

(b) for the imposition on summary conviction of a fine exceeding level 5 on the standard scale and, for continued contravention, a daily default fine not exceeding one-tenth of level 5 on the standard scale.

(4) In this section 'specified' means specified in the regulations.

## 1055    Disclosure of individual's residential address: protection from disclosure

Where regulations under section 1046 (overseas companies: duty to register particulars) require an overseas company to register particulars of an individual's usual residential address, they must contain provision corresponding to that made by Chapter 8 of Part 10 (directors' residential addresses: protection from disclosure).

## 1056    Requirement to identify persons authorised to accept service of documents

Regulations under section 1046 (overseas companies: duty to register particulars) must require an overseas company to register—

(a) particulars identifying every person resident in the United Kingdom authorised to accept service of documents on behalf of the company, or

(b) a statement that there is no such person.

## 1057    Registrar to whom returns, notices etc to be delivered

(1) This section applies to an overseas company that is required to register or has registered particulars under section 1046 in more than one part of the United Kingdom.

(2) The Secretary of State may provide by regulations that, in the case of such a company, anything authorised or required to be delivered to the registrar under this Part is to be delivered—

    (a) to the registrar for each part of the United Kingdom in which the company is required to register or has registered particulars, or

    (b) to the registrar for such part or parts of the United Kingdom as may be specified in or determined in accordance with the regulations.

(3) Regulations under this section are subject to negative resolution procedure.

### 1058  Duty to give notice of ceasing to have registrable presence

(1) The Secretary of State may make provision by regulations requiring an overseas company—

    (a) if it has registered particulars following the opening of a branch, in accordance with regulations under section 1046(2)(a) or (b), to give notice to the registrar if it closes that branch;

    (b) if it has registered particulars in other circumstances, in accordance with regulations under section 1046(2)(c), to give notice to the registrar if the circumstances that gave rise to the obligation to register particulars cease to obtain.

(2) The regulations must provide for the notice to be given to the registrar for the part of the United Kingdom to which the original return of particulars was delivered.

(3) The regulations may specify the period within which notice must be given.

(4) Regulations under this section are subject to negative resolution procedure.

### 1059  Application of provisions in case of relocation of branch

For the purposes of this Part—

    (a) the relocation of a branch from one part of the United Kingdom to another counts as the closing of one branch and the opening of another;

    (b) the relocation of a branch within the same part of the United Kingdom does not.

# PART 35  THE REGISTRAR OF COMPANIES

### *The registrar*

### 1060  The registrar

(1) There shall continue to be—

    (a) a registrar of companies for England and Wales,

    (b) a registrar of companies for Scotland, and

    (c) a registrar of companies for Northern Ireland.

(2) The registrars shall be appointed by the Secretary of State.

(3) In the Companies Acts 'the registrar of companies' and 'the registrar' mean the registrar of companies for England and Wales, Scotland or Northern Ireland, as the case may require.

(4) References in the Companies Acts to registration in a particular part of the United Kingdom are to registration by the registrar for that part of the United Kingdom.

### 1061  The registrar's functions

(1) The registrar shall continue—

    (a) to perform the functions conferred on the registrar—

        (i)   under the Companies Acts, and

        (ii)  under the enactments listed in subsection (2), and

    (b) to perform such functions on behalf of the Secretary of State, in relation to the registration of companies or other matters, as the Secretary of State may from time to time direct.

(2) The enactments are—

the Joint Stock Companies Acts;

the Newspaper Libel and Registration Act 1881 (c. 60);

the Limited Partnerships Act 1907 (c. 24);

section 53 of the Industrial and Provident Societies Act 1965 (c. 12) or, for Northern Ireland, section 62 of the Industrial and Provident Societies Act (Northern Ireland) 1969 (c. 24 (N.I.));

the Insolvency Act 1986 (c. 45) or, for Northern Ireland, the Insolvency (Northern Ireland) Order 1989 (S.I. 1989/2405 (N.I. 19));

section 12 of the Statutory Water Companies Act 1991 (c. 58);

sections 3, 4, 6, 63 and 64 of, and Schedule 1 to, the Housing Act 1996 (c. 52) or, for Northern Ireland, Articles 3 and 16 to 32 of the Housing (Northern Ireland) Order 1992 (S.I. 1992/1725 (N.I. 15));

sections 2, 4 and 26 of the Commonwealth Development Corporation Act 1999 (c. 20);

Part 6 and section 366 of the Financial Services and Markets Act 2000 (c. 8);

the Limited Liability Partnerships Act 2000 (c. 12);

section 14 of the Insolvency Act 2000 (c. 39) or, for Northern Ireland, Article 11 of the Insolvency (Northern Ireland) Order 2002 (S.I. 2002/ 3152 (N.I. 6));

section 121 of the Land Registration Act 2002 (c. 9);

section 1248 of this Act.

(3) References in this Act to the functions of the registrar are to functions within subsection (1)(a) or (b).

### 1062   The registrar's official seal

The registrar shall have an official seal for the authentication of documents in connection with the performance of the registrar's functions.

### 1063   Fees payable to registrar

(1) The Secretary of State may make provision by regulations requiring the payment to the registrar of fees in respect of—

(a) the performance of any of the registrar's functions, or

(b) the provision by the registrar of services or facilities for purposes incidental to, or otherwise connected with, the performance of any of the registrar's functions.

(2) The matters for which fees may be charged include—

(a) the performance of a duty imposed on the registrar or the Secretary of State,

(b) the receipt of documents delivered to the registrar, and

(c) the inspection, or provision of copies, of documents kept by the registrar.

(3) The regulations may—

(a) provide for the amount of the fees to be fixed by or determined under the regulations;

(b) provide for different fees to be payable in respect of the same matter in different circumstances;

(c) specify the person by whom any fee payable under the regulations is to be paid;

(d) specify when and how fees are to be paid.

(4) Regulations under this section are subject to negative resolution procedure.

(5) In respect of the performance of functions or the provision of services or facilities—

(a) for which fees are not provided for by regulations, or

(b) in circumstances other than those for which fees are provided for by regulations, the registrar may determine from time to time what fees (if any) are chargeable.

(6) Fees received by the registrar are to be paid into the Consolidated Fund.

(7) The Limited Partnerships Act 1907 (c. 24) is amended as follows—

(a) in section 16(1) (inspection of statements registered)—

   (i) omit the words ', and there shall be paid for such inspection such fees as may be appointed by the Board of Trade, not exceeding 5p for each inspection', and

   (ii) omit the words from 'and there shall be paid for such certificate' to the end;

(b) in section 17 (power to make rules)—

   (i) omit the words '(but as to fees with the concurrence of the Treasury)', and

   (ii) omit paragraph (a).

*Certificates of incorporation*

### 1064   Public notice of issue of certificate of incorporation

(1) The registrar must cause to be published—

(a) in the Gazette, or

(b) in accordance with section 1116 (alternative means of giving public notice),

notice of the issue by the registrar of any certificate of incorporation of a company.

(2) The notice must state the name and registered number of the company and the date of issue of the certificate.

(3) This section applies to a certificate of incorporation issued under—

(a) section 80 (change of name),

(b) section 88 (Welsh companies), or

(c) any provision of Part 7 (re-registration),

as well as to the certificate issued on a company's formation.

### 1065   Right to certificate of incorporation

Any person may require the registrar to provide him with a copy of any certificate of incorporation of a company, signed by the registrar or authenticated by the registrar's seal.

*Registered numbers*

### 1066   Company's registered numbers

(1) The registrar shall allocate to every company a number, which shall be known as the company's registered number.

(2) Companies' registered numbers shall be in such form, consisting of one or more sequences of figures or letters, as the registrar may determine.

(3) The registrar may on adopting a new form of registered number make such changes of existing registered numbers as appear necessary.

(4) A change of a company's registered number has effect from the date on which the company is notified by the registrar of the change.

(5) For a period of three years beginning with that date any requirement to disclose the company's registered number imposed by regulations under section 82 or section 1051 (trading disclosures) is satisfied by the use of either the old number or the new.

(6) In this section 'company' includes an overseas company whose particulars have been registered under section 1046, other than a company that appears to the registrar not to be required to register particulars under that section.

### 1067    Registered numbers of branches of overseas company

(1) The registrar shall allocate to every branch of an overseas company whose particulars are registered under section 1046 a number, which shall be known as the branch's registered number.

(2) Branches' registered numbers shall be in such form, consisting of one or more sequences of figures or letters, as the registrar may determine.

(3) The registrar may on adopting a new form of registered number make such changes of existing registered numbers as appear necessary.

(4) A change of a branch's registered number has effect from the date on which the company is notified by the registrar of the change.

(5) For a period of three years beginning with that date any requirement to disclose the branch's registered number imposed by regulations under section 1051 (trading disclosures) is satisfied by the use of either the old number or the new.

### *Delivery of documents to the registrar*

### 1068    Registrar's requirements as to form, authentication and manner of delivery

(1) The registrar may impose requirements as to the form, authentication and manner of delivery of documents required or authorised to be delivered to the registrar under any enactment.

(2) As regards the form of the document, the registrar may—
   (a) require the contents of the document to be in a standard form;
   (b) impose requirements for the purpose of enabling the document to be scanned or copied.

(3) As regards authentication, the registrar may—
   (a) require the document to be authenticated by a particular person or a person of a particular description;
   (b) specify the means of authentication;
   (c) require the document to contain or be accompanied by the name or registered number of the company to which it relates (or both).

(4) As regards the manner of delivery, the registrar may specify requirements as to—
   (a) the physical form of the document (for example, hard copy or electronic form);
   (b) the means to be used for delivering the document (for example, by post or electronic means);
   (c) the address to which the document is to be sent;
   (d) in the case of a document to be delivered by electronic means, the hardware and software to be used, and technical specifications (for example, matters relating to protocol, security, anti-virus protection or encryption).

(5) The registrar must secure that as from 1st January 2007 all documents subject to the Directive disclosure requirements (see section 1078) may be delivered to the registrar by electronic means.

(6) The power conferred by this section does not authorise the registrar to require documents to be delivered by electronic means (see section 1069).

(7) Requirements imposed under this section must not be inconsistent with requirements imposed by any enactment with respect to the form, authentication or manner of delivery of the document concerned.

### 1069    Power to require delivery by electronic means

(1) The Secretary of State may make regulations requiring documents that are authorised or required to be delivered to the registrar to be delivered by electronic means.

(2) Any such requirement to deliver documents by electronic means is effective only if registrar's rules have been published with respect to the detailed requirements for such delivery.

(3) Regulations under this section are subject to affirmative resolution procedure.

### 1070    Agreement for delivery by electronic means

(1) The registrar may agree with a company that documents relating to the company that are required or authorised to be delivered to the registrar—
   (a) will be delivered by electronic means, except as provided for in the agreement, and
   (b) will conform to such requirements as may be specified in the agreement or specified by the registrar in accordance with the agreement.

(2) An agreement under this section may relate to all or any description of documents to be delivered to the registrar.

(3) Documents in relation to which an agreement is in force under this section must be delivered in accordance with the agreement.

### 1071    Document not delivered until received

(1) A document is not delivered to the registrar until it is received by the registrar.

(2) Provision may be made by registrar's rules as to when a document is to be regarded as received.

*Requirements for proper delivery*

### 1072    Requirements for proper delivery

(1) A document delivered to the registrar is not properly delivered unless all the following requirements are met—

    (a) the requirements of the provision under which the document is to be delivered to the registrar as regards—

        (i)   the contents of the document, and

        (ii)  form, authentication and manner of delivery;

    (b) any applicable requirements under—

        section 1068 (registrar's requirements as to form, authentication and manner of delivery),

        section 1069 (power to require delivery by electronic means), or

        section 1070 (agreement for delivery by electronic means);

    (c) any requirements of this Part as to the language in which the document is drawn up and delivered or as to its being accompanied on delivery by a certified translation into English;

    (d) in so far as it consists of or includes names and addresses, any requirements of this Part as to permitted characters, letters or symbols or as to its being accompanied on delivery by a certificate as to the transliteration of any element;

    (e) any applicable requirements under section 1111 (registrar's requirements as to certification or verification);

    (f) any requirement of regulations under section 1082 (use of unique identifiers);

    (g) any requirements as regards payment of a fee in respect of its receipt by the registrar.

(2) A document that is not properly delivered is treated for the purposes of the provision requiring or authorising it to be delivered as not having been delivered, subject to the provisions of section 1073 (power to accept documents not meeting requirements for proper delivery).

### 1073    Power to accept documents not meeting requirements for proper delivery

(1) The registrar may accept (and register) a document that does not comply with the requirements for proper delivery.

(2) A document accepted by the registrar under this section is treated as received by the registrar for the purposes of section 1077 (public notice of receipt of certain documents).

(3) No objection may be taken to the legal consequences of a document's being accepted (or registered) by the registrar under this section on the ground that the requirements for proper delivery were not met.

(4) The acceptance of a document by the registrar under this section does not affect—

    (a) the continuing obligation to comply with the requirements for proper delivery, or

    (b) subject as follows, any liability for failure to comply with those requirements.

(5) For the purposes of—

    (a) section 453 (civil penalty for failure to file accounts and reports), and

    (b) any enactment imposing a daily default fine for failure to deliver the document,

the period after the document is accepted does not count as a period during which there is default in complying with the requirements for proper delivery.

(6) But if, subsequently—

    (a) the registrar issues a notice under section 1094(4) in respect of the document (notice of administrative removal from the register), and

    (b) the requirements for proper delivery are not complied with before the end of the period of 14 days after the issue of that notice,

any subsequent period of default does count for the purposes of those provisions.

### 1074    Documents containing unnecessary material

(1) This section applies where a document delivered to the registrar contains unnecessary material.

(2) 'Unnecessary material' means material that—

    (a) is not necessary in order to comply with an obligation under any enactment, and

    (b) is not specifically authorised to be delivered to the registrar.

(3) For this purpose an obligation to deliver a document of a particular description, or conforming to certain requirements, is regarded as not extending to anything that is not needed for a document of that description or, as the case may be, conforming to those requirements.

(4) If the unnecessary material cannot readily be separated from the rest of the document, the document is treated as not meeting the requirements for proper delivery.

(5)  If the unnecessary material can readily be separated from the rest of the document, the registrar may register the document either—

(a)  with the omission of the unnecessary material, or

(b)  as delivered.

### 1075  Informal correction of document

(1)  A document delivered to the registrar may be corrected by the registrar if it appears to the registrar to be incomplete or internally inconsistent.

(2)  This power is exercisable only—

(a)  on instructions, and

(b)  if the company has given (and has not withdrawn) its consent to instructions being given under this section.

(3)  The following requirements must be met as regards the instructions—

(a)  the instructions must be given in response to an enquiry by the registrar;

(b)  the registrar must be satisfied that the person giving the instructions is authorised to do so—

(i)  by the person by whom the document was delivered, or

(ii)  by the company to which the document relates;

(c)  the instructions must meet any requirements of registrar's rules as to—

(i)  the form and manner in which they are given, and

(ii)  authentication.

(4)  The company's consent to instructions being given under this section (and any withdrawal of such consent)—

(a)  may be in hard copy or electronic form, and

(b)  must be notified to the registrar.

(5)  This section applies in relation to documents delivered under Part 25 (company charges) by a person other than the company as if the references to the company were to the company or the person by whom the document was delivered.

(6)  A document that is corrected under this section is treated, for the purposes of any enactment relating to its delivery, as having been delivered when the correction is made.

(7)  The power conferred by this section is not exercisable if the document has been registered under section 1073 (power to accept documents not meeting requirements for proper delivery).

### 1076  Replacement of document not meeting requirements for proper delivery

(1)  The registrar may accept a replacement for a document previously delivered that—

(a)  did not comply with the requirements for proper delivery, or

(b)  contained unnecessary material (within the meaning of section 1074).

(2)  A replacement document must not be accepted unless the registrar is satisfied that it is delivered by—

(a)  the person by whom the original document was delivered, or

(b)  the company to which the original document relates, and that it complies with the requirements for proper delivery.

(3)  The power of the registrar to impose requirements as to the form and manner of delivery includes power to impose requirements as to the identification of the original document and the delivery of the replacement in a form and manner enabling it to be associated with the original.

(4)  This section does not apply where the original document was delivered under Part 25 (company charges) (but see sections 873 and 888 (rectification of register of charges)).

*Public notice of receipt of certain documents*

### 1077  Public notice of receipt of certain documents

(1)  The registrar must cause to be published—

(a)  in the Gazette, or

(b)  in accordance with section 1116 (alternative means of giving public notice),

notice of the receipt by the registrar of any document that, on receipt, is subject to the Directive disclosure requirements (see section 1078).

(2)  The notice must state the name and registered number of the company, the description of document and the date of receipt.

(3)  The registrar is not required to cause notice of the receipt of a document to be published before the date of incorporation of the company to which the document relates.

### 1078  Documents subject to Directive disclosure requirements

(1)  The documents subject to the 'Directive disclosure requirements' are as follows.

The requirements referred to are those of Article 3 of the First Company Law Directive (68/151/EEC), as amended, extended and applied.

(2)  In the case of every company—

*Constitutional documents*

1. The company's memorandum and articles.

2. Any amendment of the company's articles (including every resolution or agreement required to be embodied in or annexed to copies of the company's articles issued by the company).

3. After any amendment of the company's articles, the text of the articles as amended.

4. Any notice of a change of the company's name.

*Directors*

1. The statement of proposed officers required on formation of the company.

2. Notification of any change among the company's directors.

3. Notification of any change in the particulars of directors required to be delivered to the registrar.

*Accounts, reports and returns*

1. All documents required to be delivered to the registrar under section 441 (annual accounts and reports).

2. The company's annual return.

*Registered office*

Notification of any change of the company's registered office.

*Winding up*

1. Copy of any winding-up order in respect of the company.

2. Notice of the appointment of liquidators.

3. Order for the dissolution of a company on a winding up.

4. Return by a liquidator of the final meeting of a company on a winding up.

(3) In the case of a public company—

*Share capital*

1. Any statement of capital and initial shareholdings.

2. Any return of allotment and the statement of capital accompanying it.

3. Copy of any resolution under section 570 or 571 (disapplication of pre-emption rights).

4. Copy of any report under section 593 or 599 as to the value of a non-cash asset.

5. Statement of capital accompanying notice given under section 625 (notice by company of redenomination of shares).

6. Statement of capital accompanying notice given under section 627 (notice by company of reduction of capital in connection with redenomination of shares).

7. Notice delivered under section 636 (notice of new name of class of shares) or 637 (notice of variation of rights attached to shares).

8. Statement of capital accompanying order delivered under section 649 (order of court confirming reduction of capital).

9. Notification (under section 689) of the redemption of shares and the statement of capital accompanying it.

10. Statement of capital accompanying return delivered under section 708 (notice of cancellation of shares on purchase of own shares) or 730 (notice of cancellation of shares held as treasury shares).

11. Any statement of compliance delivered under section 762 (statement that company meets conditions for issue of trading certificate).

*Mergers and divisions*

1. Copy of any draft of the terms of a scheme required to be delivered to the registrar under section 906 or 921.

2. Copy of any order under section 899 or 900 in respect of a compromise or arrangement to which Part 27 (mergers and divisions of public companies) applies.

(4) Where a private company re-registers as a public company (see section 96)—

(a) the last statement of capital relating to the company received by the registrar under any provision of the Companies Acts becomes subject to the Directive disclosure requirements, and

(b) section 1077 (public notice of receipt of certain documents) applies as if the statement had been received by the registrar when the re-registration takes effect.

(5) In the case of an overseas company, such particulars, returns and other documents required to be delivered under Part 34 as may be specified by the Secretary of State by regulations.

(6) Regulations under subsection (5) are subject to negative resolution procedure.

### 1079    Effect of failure to give public notice

(1) A company is not entitled to rely against other persons on the happening of any event to which this section applies unless—

(a) the event has been officially notified at the material time, or

(b) the company shows that the person concerned knew of the event at the material time.

(2) The events to which this section applies are—

(a) an amendment of the company's articles,

(b) a change among the company's directors,

(c) (as regards service of any document on the company) a change of the company's registered office,

(d) the making of a winding-up order in respect of the company, or

(e) the appointment of a liquidator in a voluntary winding up of the company.

(3) If the material time falls—

(a) on or before the 15th day after the date of official notification, or

(b) where the 15th day was not a working day, on or before the next day that was,

the company is not entitled to rely on the happening of the event as against a person who shows that he was unavoidably prevented from knowing of the event at that time.

(4) 'Official notification' means—

(a) in relation to an amendment of the company's articles, notification in accordance with section 1077 (public notice of receipt by registrar of certain documents) of the amendment and the amended text of the articles;

(b) in relation to anything else stated in a document subject to the Directive disclosure requirements, notification of that document in accordance with that section;

(c) in relation to the appointment of a liquidator in a voluntary winding up, notification of that event in accordance with section 109 of the Insolvency Act 1986 (c. 45) or Article 95 of the Insolvency (Northern Ireland) Order 1989 (S.I.1989/2405 (N.I. 19)).

*The register*

### 1080   The register

(1) The registrar shall continue to keep records of—

(a) the information contained in documents delivered to the registrar under any enactment,

(b) certificates of incorporation issued by the registrar, and

(c) certificates issued by the registrar under section 869(5) or 885(4) (certificates of registration of charge).

(2) The records relating to companies are referred to collectively in the Companies Acts as 'the register'.

(3) Information deriving from documents subject to the Directive disclosure requirements (see section 1078) that are delivered to the registrar on or after 1st January 2007 must be kept by the registrar in electronic form.

(4) Subject to that, information contained in documents delivered to the registrar may be recorded and kept in any form the registrar thinks fit, provided it is possible to inspect it and produce a copy of it.

This is sufficient compliance with any duty of the registrar to keep, file or register the document or to record the information contained in it.

(5) The records kept by the registrar must be such that information relating to a company is associated with that company, in such manner as the registrar may determine, so as to enable all the information relating to the company to be retrieved.

### 1081   Annotation of the register

(1) The registrar must place a note in the register recording—

(a) the date on which a document is delivered to the registrar;

(b) if a document is corrected under section 1075, the nature and date of the correction;

(c) if a document is replaced (whether or not material derived from it is removed), the fact that it has been replaced and the date of delivery of the replacement;

(d) if material is removed—

(i)   what was removed (giving a general description of its contents),

(ii)  under what power, and

(iii) the date on which that was done.

(2) The Secretary of State may make provision by regulations—

(a) authorising or requiring the registrar to annotate the register in such other circumstances as may be specified in the regulations, and

(b) as to the contents of any such annotation.

(3) No annotation is required in the case of a document that by virtue of section 1072(2) (documents not meeting requirements for proper delivery) is treated as not having been delivered.

(4) A note may be removed if it no longer serves any useful purpose.

(5) Any duty or power of the registrar with respect to annotation of the register is subject to the court's power under section 1097 (powers of court on ordering removal of material from the register) to direct—

(a) that a note be removed from the register, or

(b) that no note shall be made of the removal of material that is the subject of the court's order.

(6) Notes placed in the register in accordance with subsection (1), or in pursuance of regulations under subsection (2), are part of the register for all purposes of the Companies Acts.

(7) Regulations under this section are subject to negative resolution procedure.

### 1082   Allocation of unique identifiers

(1) The Secretary of State may make provision for the use, in connection with the register, of reference numbers ('unique identifiers') to identify each person who—

(a) is a director of a company,

(b) is secretary (or a joint secretary) of a company, or

(c) in the case of an overseas company whose particulars are registered under section 1046,

holds any such position as may be specified for the purposes of this section by regulations under that section.

(2) The regulations may—

(a) provide that a unique identifier may be in such form, consisting of one or more sequences of letters or numbers, as the registrar may from time to time determine;

(b) make provision for the allocation of unique identifiers by the registrar;

(c) require there to be included, in any specified description of documents delivered to the registrar, as well as a statement of the person's name—

(i) a statement of the person's unique identifier, or

(ii) a statement that the person has not been allocated a unique identifier;

(d) enable the registrar to take steps where a person appears to have more than one unique identifier to discontinue the use of all but one of them.

(3) The regulations may contain provision for the application of the scheme in relation to persons appointed, and documents registered, before the commencement of this Act.

(4) The regulations may make different provision for different descriptions of person and different descriptions of document.

(5) Regulations under this section are subject to affirmative resolution procedure.

### 1083   Preservation of original documents

(1) The originals of documents delivered to the registrar in hard copy form must be kept for three years after they are received by the registrar, after which they may be destroyed provided the information contained in them has been recorded in the register.

This is subject to section 1087(3) (extent of obligation to retain material not available for public inspection).

(2) The registrar is under no obligation to keep the originals of documents delivered in electronic form, provided the information contained in them has been recorded in the register.

(3) This section applies to documents held by the registrar when this section comes into force as well as to documents subsequently received.

### 1084   Records relating to companies that have been dissolved etc.

(1) This section applies where—

(a) a company is dissolved,

(b) an overseas company ceases to have any connection with the United Kingdom by virtue of which it is required to register particulars under section 1046, or

(c) a credit or financial institution ceases to be within section 1050 (overseas institutions required to file accounts with the registrar).

(2) At any time after two years from the date on which it appears to the registrar that—

(a) the company has been dissolved,

(b) the overseas company has ceased to have any connection with the United Kingdom by virtue of which it is required to register particulars under section 1046, or

(c) the credit or financial institution has ceased to be within section 1050 (overseas institutions required to file accounts with the registrar),

the registrar may direct that records relating to the company or institution may be removed to the Public Record Office or, as the case may be, the Public Record Office of Northern Ireland.

(3) Records in respect of which such a direction is given shall be disposed of under the enactments relating to that Office and the rules made under them.

(4) In subsection (1)(a) 'company' includes a company provisionally or completely registered under the Joint Stock Companies Act 1844 (c. 110).

(5) This section does not extend to Scotland.

*Inspection etc. of the register*

### 1085   Inspection of the register

(1) Any person may inspect the register.

(2) The right of inspection extends to the originals of documents delivered to the registrar in hard copy form if, and only if, the record kept by the registrar of the contents of the document is illegible or unavailable. The period for which such originals are to be kept is limited by section 1083(1).

(3) This section has effect subject to section 1087 (material not available for public inspection).

### 1086   Right to copy of material on the register

(1) Any person may require a copy of any material on the register.

(2) The fee for any such copy of material derived from a document subject to the Directive disclosure requirements (see section 1078), whether in hard copy or electronic form, must not exceed the administrative cost of providing it.

(3) This section has effect subject to section 1087 (material not available for public inspection).

**1087   Material not available for public inspection**

(1) The following material must not be made available by the registrar for public inspection—

(a) the contents of any document sent to the registrar containing views expressed pursuant to section 56 (comments on proposal by company to use certain words or expressions in company name);

(b) protected information within section 242(1) (directors' residential addresses: restriction on disclosure by registrar) or any corresponding provision of regulations under section 1046 (overseas companies);

(c) any application to the registrar under section 1024 (application for administrative restoration to the register) that has not yet been determined or was not successful;

(d) any document received by the registrar in connection with the giving or withdrawal of consent under section 1075 (informal correction of documents);

(e) any application or other document delivered to the registrar under section 1088 (application to make address unavailable for public inspection) and any address in respect of which such an application is successful;

(f) any application or other document delivered to the registrar under section 1095 (application for rectification of register);

(g) any court order under section 1096 (rectification of the register under court order) that the court has directed under section 1097 (powers of court on ordering removal of material from the register) is not to be made available for public inspection;

(h) the contents of—

(i) any instrument creating or evidencing a charge and delivered to the registrar under section 860 (registration of company charges: England and Wales or Northern Ireland), or

(ii) any certified copy of an instrument creating or evidencing a charge and delivered to the registrar under section 878 (registration of company charges: Scotland);

(i) any e-mail address, identification code or password deriving from a document delivered for the purpose of authorising or facilitating electronic filing procedures or providing information by telephone;

(j) the contents of any documents held by the registrar pending a decision of the Regulator of Community Interest Companies under section 36 or 38 of the Companies (Audit, Investigations and Community Enterprise) Act 2004 (c. 27) (decision on eligibility for registration as community interest company) and that the registrar is not later required to record;

(k) any other material excluded from public inspection by or under any other enactment.

(2) A restriction applying by reference to material deriving from a particular description of document does not affect the availability for public inspection of the same information contained in material derived from another description of document in relation to which no such restriction applies.

(3) Material to which this section applies need not be retained by the registrar for longer than appears to the registrar reasonably necessary for the purposes for which the material was delivered to the registrar.

**1088   Application to registrar to make address unavailable for public inspection**

(1) The Secretary of State may make provision by regulations requiring the registrar, on application, to make an address on the register unavailable for public inspection.

(2) The regulations may make provision as to—

(a) who may make an application,

(b) the grounds on which an application may be made,

(c) the information to be included in and documents to accompany an application,

(d) the notice to be given of an application and of its outcome, and

(e) how an application is to be determined.

(3) Provision under subsection (2)(e) may in particular—

(a) confer a discretion on the registrar;

(b) provide for a question to be referred to a person other than the registrar for the purposes of determining the application.

(4) An application must specify the address to be removed from the register and indicate where on the register it is.

(5) The regulations may provide—

(a) that an address is not to be made unavailable for public inspection under this section unless replaced by a service address, and

(b) that in such a case the application must specify a service address.

(6) Regulations under this section are subject to affirmative resolution procedure.

**1089   Form of application for inspection or copy**

(1) The registrar may specify the form and manner in which application is to be made for—

(a) inspection under section 1085, or

(b) a copy under section 1086.

(2) As from 1st January 2007, applications in respect of documents subject to the Directive disclosure requirements may be submitted to the registrar in hard copy or electronic form, as the applicant chooses.

This does not affect the registrar's power under subsection (1) above to impose requirements in respect of other matters.

### 1090 Form and manner in which copies to be provided

(1) The following provisions apply as regards the form and manner in which copies are to be provided under section 1086.

(2) As from 1st January 2007, copies of documents subject to the Directive disclosure requirements must be provided in hard copy or electronic form, as the applicant chooses.

This is subject to the following proviso.

(3) The registrar is not obliged by subsection (2) to provide copies in electronic form of a document that was delivered to the registrar in hard copy form if—

    (a) the document was delivered to the registrar on or before 31st December 1996, or

    (b) the document was delivered to the registrar on or before 31st December 2006 and ten years or more elapsed between the date of delivery and the date of receipt of the first application for a copy on or after 1st January 2007.

(4) Subject to the preceding provisions of this section, the registrar may determine the form and manner in which copies are to be provided.

### 1091 Certification of copies as accurate

(1) Copies provided under section 1086 in hard copy form must be certified as true copies unless the applicant dispenses with such certification.

(2) Copies so provided in electronic form must not be certified as true copies unless the applicant expressly requests such certification.

(3) A copy provided under section 1086, certified by the registrar (whose official position it is unnecessary to prove) to be an accurate record of the contents of the original document, is in all legal proceedings admissible in evidence—

    (a) as of equal validity with the original document, and

    (b) as evidence (in Scotland, sufficient evidence) of any fact stated in the original document of which direct oral evidence would be admissible.

(4) The Secretary of State may make provision by regulations as to the manner in which such a certificate is to be provided in a case where the copy is provided in electronic form.

(5) Except in the case of documents that are subject to the Directive disclosure requirements (see section 1078), copies provided by the registrar may, instead of being certified in writing to be an accurate record, be sealed with the registrar's official seal.

### 1092 Issue of process for production of records kept by the registrar

(1) No process for compelling the production of a record kept by the registrar shall issue from any court except with the permission of the court.

(2) Any such process shall bear on it a statement that it is issued with the permission of the court.

*Correction or removal of material on the register*

### 1093 Registrar's notice to resolve inconsistency on the register

(1) Where it appears to the registrar that the information contained in a document delivered to the registrar is inconsistent with other information on the register, the registrar may give notice to the company to which the document relates—

    (a) stating in what respects the information contained in it appears to be inconsistent with other information on the register, and

    (b) requiring the company to take steps to resolve the inconsistency.

(2) The notice must—

    (a) state the date on which it is issued, and

    (b) require the delivery to the registrar, within 14 days after that date, of such replacement or additional documents as may be required to resolve the inconsistency.

(3) If the necessary documents are not delivered within the period specified, an offence is committed by—

    (a) the company, and

    (b) every officer of the company who is in default.

(4) A person guilty of an offence under subsection (3) is liable on summary conviction to a fine not exceeding level 5 on the standard scale and, for continued contravention, a daily default fine not exceeding one-tenth of level 5 on the standard scale.

### 1094 Administrative removal of material from the register

(1) The registrar may remove from the register anything that there was power, but no duty, to include.

(2) This power is exercisable, in particular, so as to remove—
- (a) unnecessary material within the meaning of section 1074, and
- (b) material derived from a document that has been replaced under—

section 1076 (replacement of document not meeting requirements for proper delivery), or

section 1093 (notice to remedy inconsistency on the register).

(3) This section does not authorise the removal from the register of—
- (a) anything whose registration has had legal consequences in relation to the company as regards—
  - (i) its formation,
  - (ii) a change of name,
  - (iii) its re-registration,
  - (iv) its becoming or ceasing to be a community interest company,
  - (v) a reduction of capital,
  - (vi) a change of registered office,
  - (vii) the registration of a charge, or
  - (viii) its dissolution;
- (b) an address that is a person's registered address for the purposes of section 1140 (service of documents on directors, secretaries and others).

(4) On or before removing any material under this section (otherwise than at the request of the company) the registrar must give notice—
- (a) to the person by whom the material was delivered (if the identity, and name and address of that person are known), or
- (b) to the company to which the material relates (if notice cannot be given under paragraph (a) and the identity of that company is known).

(5) The notice must—
- (a) state what material the registrar proposes to remove, or has removed, and on what grounds, and
- (b) state the date on which it is issued.

### 1095    Rectification of register on application to registrar

(1) The Secretary of State may make provision by regulations requiring the registrar, on application, to remove from the register material of a description specified in the regulations that—
- (a) derives from anything invalid or ineffective or that was done without the authority of the company, or
- (b) is factually inaccurate, or is derived from something that is factually inaccurate or forged.

(2) The regulations may make provision as to—
- (a) who may make an application,
- (b) the information to be included in and documents to accompany an application,
- (c) the notice to be given of an application and of its outcome,
- (d) a period in which objections to an application may be made, and
- (e) how an application is to be determined.

(3) An application must—
- (a) specify what is to be removed from the register and indicate where on the register it is, and
- (b) be accompanied by a statement that the material specified in the application complies with this section and the regulations.

(4) If no objections are made to the application, the registrar may accept the statement as sufficient evidence that the material specified in the application should be removed from the register.

(5) Where anything is removed from the register under this section the registration of which had legal consequences as mentioned in section 1094(3), any person appearing to the court to have a sufficient interest may apply to the court for such consequential orders as appear just with respect to the legal effect (if any) to be accorded to the material by virtue of its having appeared on the register.

(6) Regulations under this section are subject to affirmative resolution procedure.

### 1096    Rectification of the register under court order

(1) The registrar shall remove from the register any material—
- (a) that derives from anything that the court has declared to be invalid or ineffective, or to have been done without the authority of the company, or
- (b) that a court declares to be factually inaccurate, or to be derived from something that is factually inaccurate, or forged, and that the court directs should be removed from the register.

(2) The court order must specify what is to be removed from the register and indicate where on the register it is.

(3) The court must not make an order for the removal from the register of anything the registration of which had legal consequences as mentioned in section 1094(3) unless satisfied—

    (a) that the presence of the material on the register has caused, or may cause, damage to the company, and

    (b) that the company's interest in removing the material outweighs any interest of other persons in the material continuing to appear on the register.

    (4) Where in such a case the court does make an order for removal, it may make such consequential orders as appear just with respect to the legal effect (if any) to be accorded to the material by virtue of its having appeared on the register.

    (5) A copy of the court's order must be sent to the registrar for registration.

    (6) This section does not apply where the court has other, specific, powers to deal with the matter, for example under—

    (a) the provisions of Part 15 relating to the revision of defective accounts and reports, or

    (b) section 873 or 888 (rectification of the register of charges).

### 1097 Powers of court on ordering removal of material from the register

    (1) Where the court makes an order for the removal of anything from the register under section 1096 (rectification of the register), it may give directions under this section.

    (2) It may direct that any note on the register that is related to the material that is the subject of the court's order shall be removed from the register.

    (3) It may direct that its order shall not be available for public inspection as part of the register.

    (4) It may direct—

    (a) that no note shall be made on the register as a result of its order, or

    (b) that any such note shall be restricted to such matters as may be specified by the court.

    (5) The court shall not give any direction under this section unless it is satisfied—

    (a) that—

      (i) the presence on the register of the note or, as the case may be, of an unrestricted note, or

      (ii) the availability for public inspection of the court's order, may cause damage to the company, and

    (b) that the company's interest in non-disclosure outweighs any interest of other persons in disclosure.

### 1098 Public notice of removal of certain material from the register

    (1) The registrar must cause to be published—

    (a) in the Gazette, or

    (b) in accordance with section 1116 (alternative means of giving public notice),

notice of the removal from the register of any document subject to the Directive disclosure requirements (see section 1078) or of any material derived from such a document.

    (2) The notice must state the name and registered number of the company, the description of document and the date of receipt.

*The registrar's index of company names*

### 1099 The registrar's index of company names

    (1) The registrar of companies must keep an index of the names of the companies and other bodies to which this section applies.

  This is 'the registrar's index of company names'.

    (2) This section applies to—

    (a) UK-registered companies;

    (b) any body to which any provision of the Companies Acts applies by virtue of regulations under section 1043 (unregistered companies); and

    (c) overseas companies that have registered particulars with the registrar under section 1046, other than companies that appear to the registrar not to be required to do so.

    (3) This section also applies to—

    (a) limited partnerships registered in the United Kingdom;

    (b) limited liability partnerships incorporated in the United Kingdom;

    (c) European Economic Interest Groupings registered in the United Kingdom;

    (d) open-ended investment companies authorised in the United Kingdom;

    (e) societies registered under the Industrial and Provident Societies Act 1965 (c. 12) or the Industrial and Provident Societies Act (Northern Ireland) 1969 (c. 24 (N.I.)).

    (4) The Secretary of State may by order amend subsection (3)—

    (a) by the addition of any description of body;

    (b) by the deletion of any description of body.

    (5) Any such order is subject to negative resolution procedure.

### 1100 Right to inspect index

Any person may inspect the registrar's index of company names.

**1101    Power to amend enactments relating to bodies other than companies**

(1)  The Secretary of State may by regulations amend the enactments relating to any description of body for the time being within section 1099(3) (bodies other than companies whose names are to be entered in the registrar's index), so as to—

(a)  require the registrar to be provided with information as to the names of bodies registered, incorporated, authorised or otherwise regulated under those enactments, and

(b)  make provision in relation to such bodies corresponding to that made by—

section 66 (company name not to be the same as another in the index), and

sections 67 and 68 (power to direct change of company name in case of similarity to existing name).

(2)  Regulations under this section are subject to affirmative resolution procedure.

*Language requirements: translation*

**1102    Application of language requirements**

(1)  The provisions listed below apply to all documents required to be delivered to the registrar under any provision of—

(a)  the Companies Acts, or

(b)  the Insolvency Act 1986 (c. 45) or the Insolvency (Northern Ireland) Order 1989 (S.I. 1989/2405 (N.I. 19)).

(2)  The Secretary of State may make provision by regulations applying all or any of the listed provisions, with or without modifications, in relation to documents delivered to the registrar under any other enactment.

(3)  The provisions are—

section 1103 (documents to be drawn up and delivered in English),

section 1104 (documents relating to Welsh companies),

section 1105 (documents that may be drawn up and delivered in other languages),

section 1107 (certified translations).

(4)  Regulations under this section are subject to negative resolution procedure.

*Language requirements: translation*

**1103    Documents to be drawn up and delivered in English**

(1)  The general rule is that all documents required to be delivered to the registrar must be drawn up and delivered in English.

(2)  This is subject to—

section 1104 (documents relating to Welsh companies) and

section 1105 (documents that may be drawn up and delivered in other languages).

**1104    Documents relating to Welsh companies**

(1)  Documents relating to a Welsh company may be drawn up and delivered to the registrar in Welsh.

(2)  On delivery to the registrar any such document must be accompanied by a certified translation into English, unless it is—

(a)  of a description excepted from that requirement by regulations made by the Secretary of State, or

(b)  in a form prescribed in Welsh (or partly in Welsh and partly in English) by virtue of section 26 of the Welsh Language Act 1993 (c. 38).

(3)  Where a document is properly delivered to the registrar in Welsh without a certified translation into English, the registrar must obtain such a translation if the document is to be available for public inspection. The translation is treated as if delivered to the registrar in accordance with the same provision as the original.

(4)  A Welsh company may deliver to the registrar a certified translation into Welsh of any document in English that relates to the company and is or has been delivered to the registrar.

(5)  Section 1105 (which requires certified translations into English of documents delivered to the registrar in another language) does not apply to a document relating to a Welsh company that is drawn up and delivered in Welsh.

**1105    Documents that may be drawn up and delivered in other languages**

(1)  Documents to which this section applies may be drawn up and delivered to the registrar in a language other than English, but when delivered to the registrar they must be accompanied by a certified translation into English.

(2)  This section applies to—

(a)  agreements required to be forwarded to the registrar under Chapter 3 of Part 3 (agreements affecting the company's constitution);

(b)  documents required to be delivered under section 400(2)(e) or section 401(2)(f) (company included in accounts of larger group: required to deliver copy of group accounts);

     (c) instruments or copy instruments required to be delivered under Part 25 (company charges);

     (d) documents of any other description specified in regulations made by the Secretary of State.

(3) Regulations under this section are subject to negative resolution procedure.

### 1106   Voluntary filing of translations

(1) A company may deliver to the registrar one or more certified translations of any document relating to the company that is or has been delivered to the registrar.

(2) The Secretary of State may by regulations specify—

     (a) the languages, and

     (b) the descriptions of document,

in relation to which this facility is available.

(3) The regulations must provide that it is available as from 1st January 2007—

     (a) in relation to all the official languages of the European Union, and

     (b) in relation to all documents subject to the Directive disclosure requirements (see section 1078).

(4) The power of the registrar to impose requirements as to the form and manner of delivery includes power to impose requirements as to the identification of the original document and the delivery of the translation in a form and manner enabling it to be associated with the original.

(5) Regulations under this section are subject to negative resolution procedure.

(6) This section does not apply where the original document was delivered to the registrar before this section came into force.

### 1107   Certified translations

(1) In this Part a 'certified translation' means a translation certified to be a correct translation.

(2) In the case of any discrepancy between the original language version of a document and a certified translation—

     (a) the company may not rely on the translation as against a third party, but

     (b) a third party may rely on the translation unless the company shows that the third party had knowledge of the original.

(3) A 'third party' means a person other than the company or the registrar.

*Language requirements: transliteration*

### 1108   Transliteration of names and addresses: permitted characters

(1) Names and addresses in a document delivered to the registrar must contain only letters, characters and symbols (including accents and other diacritical marks) that are permitted.

(2) The Secretary of State may make provision by regulations—

     (a) as to the letters, characters and symbols (including accents and other diacritical marks) that are permitted, and

     (b) permitting or requiring the delivery of documents in which names and addresses have not been transliterated into a permitted form.

(3) Regulations under this section are subject to negative resolution procedure.

### 1109   Transliteration of names and addresses: voluntary transliteration into Roman characters

(1) Where a name or address is or has been delivered to the registrar in a permitted form using other than Roman characters, the company may deliver to the registrar a transliteration into Roman characters.

(2) The power of the registrar to impose requirements as to the form and manner of delivery includes power to impose requirements as to the identification of the original document and the delivery of the transliteration in a form and manner enabling it to be associated with the original.

### 1110   Transliteration of names and addresses: certification

(1) The Secretary of State may make provision by regulations requiring the certification of transliterations and prescribing the form of certification.

(2) Different provision may be made for compulsory and voluntary transliterations.

(3) Regulations under this section are subject to negative resolution procedure.

*Supplementary provisions*

### 1111   Registrar's requirements as to certification or verification

(1) Where a document required or authorised to be delivered to the registrar under any enactment is required—

     (a) to be certified as an accurate translation or transliteration, or

     (b) to be certified as a correct copy or verified,

the registrar may impose requirements as to the person, or description of person, by whom the certificate or verification is to be given.

(2) The power conferred by section 1068 (registrar's requirements as to form, authentication and manner of delivery) is exercisable in relation to the certificate or verification as if it were a separate document.

(3) Requirements imposed under this section must not be inconsistent with requirements imposed by any enactment with respect to the certification or verification of the document concerned.

*Supplementary provisions*

### 1112  General false statement offence

(1) It is an offence for a person knowingly or recklessly—
  (a) to deliver or cause to be delivered to the registrar, for any purpose of the Companies Acts, a document, or
  (b) to make to the registrar, for any such purpose, a statement,
that is misleading, false or deceptive in a material particular.

(2) A person guilty of an offence under this section is liable—
  (a) on conviction on indictment, to imprisonment for a term not exceeding two years or a fine (or both);
  (b) on summary conviction—
    (i) in England and Wales, to imprisonment for a term not exceeding twelve months or to a fine not exceeding the statutory maximum (or both);
    (ii) in Scotland or Northern Ireland, to imprisonment for a term not exceeding six months, or to a fine not exceeding the statutory maximum (or both).

### 1113  Enforcement of company's filing obligations

(1) This section applies where a company has made default in complying with any obligation under the Companies Acts—
  (a) to deliver a document to the registrar, or
  (b) to give notice to the registrar of any matter.

(2) The registrar, or any member or creditor of the company, may give notice to the company requiring it to comply with the obligation.

(3) If the company fails to make good the default within 14 days after service of the notice, the registrar, or any member or creditor of the company, may apply to the court for an order directing the company, and any specified officer of it, to make good the default within a specified time.

(4) The court's order may provide that all costs (in Scotland, expenses) of or incidental to the application are to be borne by the company or by any officers of it responsible for the default.

(5) This section does not affect the operation of any enactment making it an offence, or imposing a civil penalty, for the default.

### 1114  Application of provisions about documents and delivery

(1) In this Part—
  (a) 'document' means information recorded in any form, and
  (b) references to delivering a document include forwarding, lodging, registering, sending, producing or submitting it or (in the case of a notice) giving it.

(2) Except as otherwise provided, this Part applies in relation to the supply to the registrar of information otherwise than in documentary form as it applies in relation to the delivery of a document.

### 1115  Supplementary provisions relating to electronic communications

(1) Registrar's rules may require a company to give any necessary consents to the use of electronic means for communications by the registrar to the company as a condition of making use of any facility to deliver material to the registrar by electronic means.

(2) A document that is required to be signed by the registrar or authenticated by the registrar's seal shall, if sent by electronic means, be authenticated in such manner as may be specified by registrar's rules.

### 1116  Alternative to publication in the Gazette

(1) Notices that would otherwise need to be published by the registrar in the Gazette may instead be published by such means as may from time to time be approved by the registrar in accordance with regulations made by the Secretary of State.

(2) The Secretary of State may make provision by regulations as to what alternative means may be approved.

(3) The regulations may, in particular—
  (a) require the use of electronic means;
  (b) require the same means to be used—
    (i) for all notices or for all notices of specified descriptions, and
    (ii) whether the company is registered in England and Wales, Scotland or Northern Ireland;

    (c) impose conditions as to the manner in which access to the notices is to be made available.

    (4) Regulations under this section are subject to negative resolution procedure.

    (5) Before starting to publish notices by means approved under this section the registrar must publish at least one notice to that effect in the Gazette.

    (6) Nothing in this section prevents the registrar from giving public notice both in the Gazette and by means approved under this section.

    In that case, the requirement of public notice is met when notice is first given by either means.

### 1117   Registrar's rules

    (1) Where any provision of this Part enables the registrar to make provision, or impose requirements, as to any matter, the registrar may make such provision or impose such requirements by means of rules under this section. This is without prejudice to the making of such provision or the imposing of such requirements by other means.

    (2) Registrar's rules—

      (a) may make different provision for different cases, and

      (b) may allow the registrar to disapply or modify any of the rules.

    (3) The registrar must—

      (a) publicise the rules in a manner appropriate to bring them to the notice of persons affected by them, and

      (b) make copies of the rules available to the public (in hard copy or electronic form).

### 1118   Payments into the Consolidated Fund

Nothing in the Companies Acts or any other enactment as to the payment of receipts into the Consolidated Fund shall be read as affecting the operation in relation to the registrar of section 3(1) of the Government Trading Funds Act 1973 (c. 63).

### 1119   Contracting out of registrar's functions

    (1) Where by virtue of an order made under section 69 of the Deregulation and Contracting Out Act 1994 (c. 40) a person is authorised by the registrar to accept delivery of any class of documents that are under any enactment to be delivered to the registrar, the registrar may direct that documents of that class shall be delivered to a specified address of the authorised person.

    Any such direction must be printed and made available to the public (with or without payment).

    (2) A document of that class that is delivered to an address other than the specified address is treated as not having been delivered.

    (3) Registrar's rules are not subordinate legislation for the purposes of section 71 of the Deregulation and Contracting Out Act 1994 (functions excluded from contracting out).

### 1120   Application of this Part to overseas companies

Unless the context otherwise requires, the provisions of this Part apply to an overseas company as they apply to a company as defined in section 1.

# PART 36   OFFENCES UNDER THE COMPANIES ACTS

*Liability of officer in default*

### 1121   Liability of officer in default

    (1) This section has effect for the purposes of any provision of the Companies Acts to the effect that, in the event of contravention of an enactment in relation to a company, an offence is committed by every officer of the company who is in default.

    (2) For this purpose 'officer' includes—

      (a) any director, manager or secretary, and

      (b) any person who is to be treated as an officer of the company for the purposes of the provision in question.

    (3) An officer is 'in default' for the purposes of the provision if he authorises or permits, participates in, or fails to take all reasonable steps to prevent, the contravention.

### 1122   Liability of company as officer in default

    (1) Where a company is an officer of another company, it does not commit an offence as an officer in default unless one of its officers is in default.

    (2) Where any such offence is committed by a company the officer in question also commits the offence and is liable to be proceeded against and punished accordingly.

    (3) In this section 'officer' and 'in default' have the meanings given by section 1121.

### 1123   Application to bodies other than companies

    (1) Section 1121 (liability of officers in default) applies to a body other than a company as it applies to a company.

    (2) As it applies in relation to a body corporate other than a company—

    (a) the reference to a director of the company shall be read as referring—
        (i) where the body's affairs are managed by its members, to a member of the body,
        (ii) in any other case, to any corresponding officer of the body, and
    (b) the reference to a manager or secretary of the company shall be read as referring to any manager, secretary or similar officer of the body.

(3) As it applies in relation to a partnership—
    (a) the reference to a director of the company shall be read as referring to a member of the partnership, and
    (b) the reference to a manager or secretary of the company shall be read as referring to any manager, secretary or similar officer of the partnership.

(4) As it applies in relation to an unincorporated body other than a partnership—
    (a) the reference to a director of the company shall be read as referring—
        (i) where the body's affairs are managed by its members, to a member of the body,
        (ii) in any other case, to a member of the governing body, and
    (b) the reference to a manager or secretary of the company shall be read as referring to any manager, secretary or similar officer of the body.

### 1124   Amendments of the Companies Act 1985

Schedule 3 contains amendments of the Companies Act 1985 (c. 6) relating to offences.

*General provisions*

### 1125   Meaning of 'daily default fine'

(1) This section defines what is meant in the Companies Acts where it is provided that a person guilty of an offence is liable on summary conviction to a fine not exceeding a specified amount 'and, for continued contravention, a daily default fine' not exceeding a specified amount.

(2) This means that the person is liable on a second or subsequent summary conviction of the offence to a fine not exceeding the latter amount for each day on which the contravention is continued (instead of being liable to a fine not exceeding the former amount).

### 1126   Consents required for certain prosecutions

(1) This section applies to proceedings for an offence under any of the following provisions—

section 458, 460 or 949 of this Act (offences of unauthorised disclosure of information);

section 953 of this Act (failure to comply with rules about takeover bid documents);

section 448, 449, 450, 451 or 453A of the Companies Act 1985 (c. 6) (offences in connection with company investigations);

section 798 of this Act or section 455 of the Companies Act 1985 (offence of attempting to evade restrictions on shares).

(2) No such proceedings are to be brought in England and Wales except by or with the consent of—
    (a) in the case of an offence under—
        (i) section 458, 460 or 949 of this Act,
        (ii) section 953 of this Act, or
        (iii) section 448, 449, 450, 451 or 453A of the Companies Act 1985,
        the Secretary of State or the Director of Public Prosecutions;
    (b) in the case of an offence under section 798 of this Act or section 455 of the Companies Act 1985, the Secretary of State.

(3) No such proceedings are to be brought in Northern Ireland except by or with the consent of—
    (a) in the case of an offence under—
        (i) section 458, 460 or 949 of this Act,
        (ii) section 953 of this Act, or
        (iii) section 448, 449, 450, 451 or 453A of the Companies Act 1985,
        the Secretary of State or the Director of Public Prosecutions for Northern Ireland;
    (b) in the case of an offence under section 798 of this Act or section 455 of the Companies Act 1985, the Secretary of State.

### 1127   Summary proceedings: venue

(1) Summary proceedings for any offence under the Companies Acts may be taken—
    (a) against a body corporate, at any place at which the body has a place of business, and
    (b) against any other person, at any place at which he is for the time being.

(2) This is without prejudice to any jurisdiction exercisable apart from this section.

### 1128   Summary proceedings: time limit for proceedings

(1) An information relating to an offence under the Companies Acts that is triable by a magistrates' court in England and Wales may be so tried if it is laid—
    (a) at any time within three years after the commission of the offence, and
    (b) within twelve months after the date on which evidence sufficient in the opinion of the Director of Public Prosecutions or the Secretary of State (as the case may be) to justify the proceedings comes to his knowledge.

(2) Summary proceedings in Scotland for an offence under the Companies Acts—

    (a) must not be commenced after the expiration of three years from the commission of the offence;

    (b) subject to that, may be commenced at any time—

        (i) within twelve months after the date on which evidence sufficient in the Lord Advocate's opinion to justify the proceedings came to his knowledge, or

        (ii) where such evidence was reported to him by the Secretary of State, within twelve months after the date on which it came to the knowledge of the latter.

Section 136(3) of the Criminal Procedure (Scotland) Act 1995 (c. 46) (date when proceedings deemed to be commenced) applies for the purposes of this subsection as for the purposes of that section.

(3) A magistrates' court in Northern Ireland has jurisdiction to hear and determine a complaint charging the commission of a summary offence under the Companies Acts provided that the complaint is made—

    (a) within three years from the time when the offence was committed, and

    (b) within twelve months from the date on which evidence sufficient in the opinion of the Director of Public Prosecutions for Northern Ireland or the Secretary of State (as the case may be) to justify the proceedings comes to his knowledge.

(4) For the purposes of this section a certificate of the Director of Public Prosecutions, the Lord Advocate, the Director of Public Prosecutions for Northern Ireland or the Secretary of State (as the case may be) as to the date on which such evidence as is referred to above came to his notice is conclusive evidence.

### 1129   Legal professional privilege

In proceedings against a person for an offence under the Companies Acts, nothing in those Acts is to be taken to require any person to disclose any information that he is entitled to refuse to disclose on grounds of legal professional privilege (in Scotland, confidentiality of communications).

### 1130   Proceedings against unincorporated bodies

(1) Proceedings for an offence under the Companies Acts alleged to have been committed by an unincorporated body must be brought in the name of the body (and not in that of any of its members).

(2) For the purposes of such proceedings—

    (a) any rules of court relating to the service of documents have effect as if the body were a body corporate, and

    (b) the following provisions apply as they apply in relation to a body corporate—

        (i) in England and Wales, section 33 of the Criminal Justice Act 1925 (c. 86) and Schedule 3 to the Magistrates' Courts Act 1980 (c. 43),

        (ii) in Scotland, sections 70 and 143 of the Criminal Procedure (Scotland) Act 1995 (c. 46),

        (iii) in Northern Ireland, section 18 of the Criminal Justice Act (Northern Ireland) 1945 (c. 15 (N.I.)) and Article 166 of and Schedule 4 to the Magistrates' Courts (Northern Ireland) Order 1981 (S.I. 1981/1675 (N.I. 26)).

(3) A fine imposed on an unincorporated body on its conviction of an offence under the Companies Acts must be paid out of the funds of the body.

### 1131   Imprisonment on summary conviction in England and Wales: transitory provision

(1) This section applies to any provision of the Companies Acts that provides that a person guilty of an offence is liable on summary conviction in England and Wales to imprisonment for a term not exceeding twelve months.

(2) In relation to an offence committed before the commencement of section 154(1) of the Criminal Justice Act 2003 (c. 44), for 'twelve months' substitute 'six months'.

*Production and inspection of documents*

### 1132   Production and inspection of documents where offence suspected

(1) An application under this section may be made—

    (a) in England and Wales, to a judge of the High Court by the Director of Public Prosecutions, the Secretary of State or a chief officer of police;

    (b) in Scotland, to one of the Lords Commissioners of Justiciary by the Lord Advocate;

    (c) in Northern Ireland, to the High Court by the Director of Public Prosecutions for Northern Ireland, the Department of Enterprise, Trade and Investment or a chief superintendent of the Police Service of Northern Ireland.

(2) If on an application under this section there is shown to be reasonable cause to believe—

    (a) that any person has, while an officer of a company, committed an offence in connection with the management of the company's affairs, and

    (b) that evidence of the commission of the offence is to be found in any documents in the possession or control of the company, an order under this section may be made.

(3) The order may—

    (a) authorise any person named in it to inspect the documents in question, or any of them, for the purpose of investigating and obtaining evidence of the offence, or

    (b) require the secretary of the company, or such other officer of it as may be named in the order, to produce the documents (or any of them) to a person named in the order at a place so named.

(4) This section applies also in relation to documents in the possession or control of a person carrying on the business of banking, so far as they relate to the company's affairs, as it applies to documents in the possession or control of the company, except that no such order as is referred to in subsection (3)(b) may be made by virtue of this subsection.

(5) The decision under this section of a judge of the High Court, any of the Lords Commissioners of Justiciary or the High Court is not appealable.

(6) In this section 'document' includes information recorded in any form.

*Supplementary*

### 1133 Transitional provision

The provisions of this Part except section 1132 do not apply to offences committed before the commencement of the relevant provision.

## PART 37 COMPANIES: SUPPLEMENTARY PROVISIONS

*Company records*

### 1134 Meaning of 'company records'

In this Part 'company records' means—

    (a) any register, index, accounting records, agreement, memorandum, minutes or other document required by the Companies Acts to be kept by a company, and

    (b) any register kept by a company of its debenture holders.

### 1135 Form of company records

(1) Company records—

    (a) may be kept in hard copy or electronic form, and

    (b) may be arranged in such manner as the directors of the company think fit,

provided the information in question is adequately recorded for future reference.

(2) Where the records are kept in electronic form, they must be capable of being reproduced in hard copy form.

(3) If a company fails to comply with this section, an offence is committed by every officer of the company who is in default.

(4) A person guilty of an offence under this section is liable on summary conviction to a fine not exceeding level 3 on the standard scale and, for continued contravention, a daily default fine not exceeding one-tenth of level 3 on the standard scale.

(5) Any provision of an instrument made by a company before 12th February 1979 that requires a register of holders of the company's debentures to be kept in hard copy form is to be read as requiring it to be kept in hard copy or electronic form.

### 1136 Regulations about where certain company records to be kept available for inspection

(1) The Secretary of State may make provision by regulations specifying places other than a company's registered office at which company records required to be kept available for inspection under a relevant provision may be so kept in compliance with that provision.

(2) The 'relevant provisions' are—

section 114 (register of members);

section 162 (register of directors);

section 228 (directors' service contracts);

section 237 (directors' indemnities);

section 275 (register of secretaries);

section 358 (records of resolutions etc);

section 702 (contracts relating to purchase of own shares);

section 720 (documents relating to redemption or purchase of own shares out of capital by private company);

section 743 (register of debenture holders);

section 805 (report to members of outcome of investigation by public company into interests in its shares);

section 809 (register of interests in shares disclosed to public company);

section 877 (instruments creating charges and register of charges: England and Wales);

section 892 (instruments creating charges and register of charges: Scotland).

(3) The regulations may specify a place by reference to the company's principal place of business, the part of the United Kingdom in which the company is registered, the place at which the company keeps any other records available for inspection or in any other way.

(4) The regulations may provide that a company does not comply with a relevant provision by keeping company records available for inspection at a place specified in the regulations unless conditions specified in the regulations are met.

(5) The regulations—

    (a) need not specify a place in relation to each relevant provision;

    (b) may specify more than one place in relation to a relevant provision.

(6) A requirement under a relevant provision to keep company records available for inspection is not complied with by keeping them available for inspection at a place specified in the regulations unless all the company's records subject to the requirement are kept there.

(7) Regulations under this section are subject to negative resolution procedure.

### 1137  Regulations about inspection of records and provision of copies

(1) The Secretary of State may make provision by regulations as to the obligations of a company that is required by any provision of the Companies Acts—

    (a) to keep available for inspection any company records, or

    (b) to provide copies of any company records.

(2) A company that fails to comply with the regulations is treated as having refused inspection or, as the case may be, having failed to provide a copy.

(3) The regulations may—

    (a) make provision as to the time, duration and manner of inspection, including the circumstances in which and extent to which the copying of information is permitted in the course of inspection, and

    (b) define what may be required of the company as regards the nature, extent and manner of extracting or presenting any information for the purposes of inspection or the provision of copies.

(4) Where there is power to charge a fee, the regulations may make provision as to the amount of the fee and the basis of its calculation.

(5) Nothing in any provision of this Act or in the regulations shall be read as preventing a company—

    (a) from affording more extensive facilities than are required by the regulations, or

    (b) where a fee may be charged, from charging a lesser fee than that prescribed or none at all.

(6) Regulations under this section are subject to negative resolution procedure.

### 1138  Duty to take precautions against falsification

(1) Where company records are kept otherwise than in bound books, adequate precautions must be taken—

    (a) to guard against falsification, and

    (b) to facilitate the discovery of falsification.

(2) If a company fails to comply with this section, an offence is committed by every officer of the company who is in default.

(3) A person guilty of an offence under this section is liable on summary conviction to a fine not exceeding level 3 on the standard scale and, for continued contravention, a daily default fine not exceeding one-tenth of level 3 on the standard scale.

(4) This section does not apply to the documents required to be kept under—

    (a) section 228 (copy of director's service contract or memorandum of its terms); or

    (b) section 237 (qualifying indemnity provision).

*Service addresses*

### 1139  Service of documents on company

(1) A document may be served on a company registered under this Act by leaving it at, or sending it by post to, the company's registered office.

(2) A document may be served on an overseas company whose particulars are registered under section 1046—

    (a) by leaving it at, or sending it by post to, the registered address of any person resident in the United Kingdom who is authorised to accept service of documents on the company's behalf, or

    (b) if there is no such person, or if any such person refuses service or service cannot for any other reason be effected, by leaving it at or sending by post to any place of business of the company in the United Kingdom.

(3) For the purposes of this section a person's 'registered address' means any address for the time being shown as a current address in relation to that person in the part of the register available for public inspection.

(4)  Where a company registered in Scotland or Northern Ireland carries on business in England and Wales, the process of any court in England and Wales may be served on the company by leaving it at, or sending it by post to, the company's principal place of business in England and Wales, addressed to the manager or other head officer in England and Wales of the company.

Where process is served on a company under this subsection, the person issuing out the process must send a copy of it by post to the company's registered office.

(5)  Further provision as to service and other matters is made in the company communications provisions (see section 1143).

### 1140    Service of documents on directors, secretaries and others

(1)  A document may be served on a person to whom this section applies by leaving it at, or sending it by post to, the person's registered address.

(2)  This section applies to—

(a)  a director or secretary of a company;

(b)  in the case of an overseas company whose particulars are registered under section 1046, a person holding any such position as may be specified for the purposes of this section by regulations under that section;

(c)  a person appointed in relation to a company as—

(i)    a judicial factor (in Scotland),

(ii)   a receiver and manager appointed under section 18 of the Charities Act 1993 (c. 10), or

(iii)  a manager appointed under section 47 of the Companies (Audit, Investigations and Community Enterprise) Act 2004 (c. 27).

(3)  This section applies whatever the purpose of the document in question.

It is not restricted to service for purposes arising out of or in connection with the appointment or position mentioned in subsection (2) or in connection with the company concerned.

(4)  For the purposes of this section a person's 'registered address' means any address for the time being shown as a current address in relation to that person in the part of the register available for public inspection.

(5)  If notice of a change of that address is given to the registrar, a person may validly serve a document at the address previously registered until the end of the period of 14 days beginning with the date on which notice of the change is registered.

(6)  Service may not be effected by virtue of this section at an address—

(a)  if notice has been registered of the termination of the appointment in relation to which the address was registered and the address is not a registered address of the person concerned in relation to any other appointment;

(b)  in the case of a person holding any such position as is mentioned in subsection (2)(b), if the overseas company has ceased to have any connection with the United Kingdom by virtue of which it is required to register particulars under section 1046.

(7)  Further provision as to service and other matters is made in the company communications provisions (see section 1143).

(8)  Nothing in this section shall be read as affecting any enactment or rule of law under which permission is required for service out of the jurisdiction.

### 1141    Service addresses

(1)  In the Companies Acts a 'service address', in relation to a person, means an address at which documents may be effectively served on that person.

(2)  The Secretary of State may by regulations specify conditions with which a service address must comply.

(3)  Regulations under this section are subject to negative resolution procedure.

### 1142    Requirement to give service address

Any obligation under the Companies Acts to give a person's address is, unless otherwise expressly provided, to give a service address for that person.

### *Sending or supplying documents or information*

### 1143    The company communications provisions

(1)  The provisions of sections 1144 to 1148 and Schedules 4 and 5 ('the company communications provisions') have effect for the purposes of any provision of the Companies Acts that authorises or requires documents or information to be sent or supplied by or to a company.

(2)  The company communications provisions have effect subject to any requirements imposed, or contrary provision made, by or under any enactment.

(3)  In particular, in their application in relation to documents or information to be sent or supplied to the registrar, they have effect subject to the provisions of Part 35.

(4)  For the purposes of subsection (2), provision is not to be regarded as contrary to the company communications provisions by reason only of the fact that it expressly authorises a document or information to be sent or supplied in hard copy form, in electronic form or by means of a website.

### 1144   Sending or supplying documents or information

(1) Documents or information to be sent or supplied to a company must be sent or supplied in accordance with the provisions of Schedule 4.

(2) Documents or information to be sent or supplied by a company must be sent or supplied in accordance with the provisions of Schedule 5.

(3) The provisions referred to in subsection (2) apply (and those referred to in subsection (1) do not apply) in relation to documents or information that are to be sent or supplied by one company to another.

### 1145   Right to hard copy version

(1) Where a member of a company or a holder of a company's debentures has received a document or information from the company otherwise than in hard copy form, he is entitled to require the company to send him a version of the document or information in hard copy form.

(2) The company must send the document or information in hard copy form within 21 days of receipt of the request from the member or debenture holder.

(3) The company may not make a charge for providing the document or information in that form.

(4) If a company fails to comply with this section, an offence is committed by the company and every officer of it who is in default.

(5) A person guilty of an offence under this section is liable on summary conviction to a fine not exceeding level 3 on the standard scale and, for continued contravention, a daily default fine not exceeding one-tenth of level 3 on the standard scale.

### 1146   Requirement of authentication

(1) This section applies in relation to the authentication of a document or information sent or supplied by a person to a company.

(2) A document or information sent or supplied in hard copy form is sufficiently authenticated if it is signed by the person sending or supplying it.

(3) A document or information sent or supplied in electronic form is sufficiently authenticated—

    (a) if the identity of the sender is confirmed in a manner specified by the company, or

    (b) where no such manner has been specified by the company, if the communication contains or is accompanied by a statement of the identity of the sender and the company has no reason to doubt the truth of that statement.

(4) Where a document or information is sent or supplied by one person on behalf of another, nothing in this section affects any provision of the company's articles under which the company may require reasonable evidence of the authority of the former to act on behalf of the latter.

### 1147   Deemed delivery of documents and information

(1) This section applies in relation to documents and information sent or supplied by a company.

(2) Where—

    (a) the document or information is sent by post (whether in hard copy or electronic form) to an address in the United Kingdom, and

    (b) the company is able to show that it was properly addressed, prepaid and posted,

it is deemed to have been received by the intended recipient 48 hours after it was posted.

(3) Where—

    (a) the document or information is sent or supplied by electronic means, and

    (b) the company is able to show that it was properly addressed,

it is deemed to have been received by the intended recipient 48 hours after it was sent.

(4) Where the document or information is sent or supplied by means of a website, it is deemed to have been received by the intended recipient—

    (a) when the material was first made available on the website, or

    (b) if later, when the recipient received (or is deemed to have received) notice of the fact that the material was available on the website.

(5) In calculating a period of hours for the purposes of this section, no account shall be taken of any part of a day that is not a working day.

(6) This section has effect subject to—

    (a) in its application to documents or information sent or supplied by a company to its members, any contrary provision of the company's articles;

    (b) in its application to documents or information sent or supplied by a company to its debentures holders, any contrary provision in the instrument constituting the debentures;

    (c) in its application to documents or information sent or supplied by a company to a person otherwise than in his capacity as a member or debenture holder, any contrary provision in an agreement between the company and that person.

### 1148   Interpretation of company communications provisions

(1) In the company communications provisions—

'address' includes a number or address used for the purposes of sending or receiving documents or information by electronic means;

'company' includes any body corporate;

'document' includes summons, notice, order or other legal process and registers.

(2) References in the company communications provisions to provisions of the Companies Acts authorising or requiring a document or information to be sent or supplied include all such provisions, whatever expression is used, and references to documents or information being sent or supplied shall be construed accordingly.

(3) References in the company communications provisions to documents or information being sent or supplied by or to a company include references to documents or information being sent or supplied by or to the directors of a company acting on behalf of the company.

### *Requirements as to independent valuation*

### 1149  Application of valuation requirements

The provisions of sections 1150 to 1153 apply to the valuation and report required by—

section 93 (re-registration as public company: recent allotment of shares for non-cash consideration);

section 593 (allotment of shares of public company in consideration of non-cash asset);

section 599 (transfer of non-cash asset to public company).

### 1150  Valuation by qualified independent person

(1) The valuation and report must be made by a person ('the valuer') who—

(a) is eligible for appointment as a statutory auditor (see section 1212), and

(b) meets the independence requirement in section 1151.

(2) However, where it appears to the valuer to be reasonable for the valuation of the consideration, or part of it, to be made by (or for him to accept a valuation made by) another person who—

(a) appears to him to have the requisite knowledge and experience to value the consideration or that part of it, and

(b) is not an officer or employee of—

(i) the company, or

(ii) any other body corporate that is that company's subsidiary or holding company or a subsidiary of that company's holding company,

or a partner of or employed by any such officer or employee,

he may arrange for or accept such a valuation, together with a report which will enable him to make his own report under this section.

(3) The references in subsection (2)(b) to an officer or employee do not include an auditor.

(4) Where the consideration or part of it is valued by a person other than the valuer himself, the latter's report must state that fact and shall also—

(a) state the former's name and what knowledge and experience he has to carry out the valuation, and

(b) describe so much of the consideration as was valued by the other person, and the method used to value it, and specify the date of that valuation.

### 1151  The independence requirement

(1) A person meets the independence requirement for the purposes of section 1150 only if—

(a) he is not—

(i) an officer or employee of the company, or

(ii) a partner or employee of such a person, or a partnership of which such a person is a partner;

(b) he is not—

(i) an officer or employee of an associated undertaking of the company, or

(ii) a partner or employee of such a person, or a partnership of which such a person is a partner; and

(c) there does not exist between—

(i) the person or an associate of his, and

(ii) the company or an associated undertaking of the company,

a connection of any such description as may be specified by regulations made by the Secretary of State.

(2) An auditor of the company is not regarded as an officer or employee of the company for this purpose.

(3) In this section—

'associated undertaking' means—

(i) a parent undertaking or subsidiary undertaking of the company, or

(ii) a subsidiary undertaking of a parent undertaking of the company; and

'associate' has the meaning given by section 1152.

(4) Regulations under this section are subject to negative resolution procedure.

### 1152  Meaning of 'associate'

(1) This section defines 'associate' for the purposes of section 1151 (valuation: independence requirement).

(2) In relation to an individual, 'associate' means—
  (a) that individual's spouse or civil partner or minor child or step-child,
  (b) any body corporate of which that individual is a director, and
  (c) any employee or partner of that individual.
(3) In relation to a body corporate, 'associate' means—
  (a) any body corporate of which that body is a director,
  (b) any body corporate in the same group as that body, and
  (c) any employee or partner of that body or of any body corporate in the same group.
(4) In relation to a partnership that is a legal person under the law by which it is governed, 'associate' means—
  (a) any body corporate of which that partnership is a director,
  (b) any employee of or partner in that partnership, and
  (c) any person who is an associate of a partner in that partnership.
(5) In relation to a partnership that is not a legal person under the law by which it is governed, 'associate' means any person who is an associate of any of the partners.
(6) In this section, in relation to a limited liability partnership, for 'director' read 'member'.

### 1153  Valuer entitled to full disclosure

(1) A person carrying out a valuation or making a report with respect to any consideration proposed to be accepted or given by a company, is entitled to require from the officers of the company such information and explanation as he thinks necessary to enable him to—
  (a) carry out the valuation or make the report, and
  (b) provide any note required by section 596(3) or 600(3) (note required where valuation carried out by another person).
(2) A person who knowingly or recklessly makes a statement to which this subsection applies that is misleading, false or deceptive in a material particular commits an offence.
(3) Subsection (2) applies to a statement—
  (a) made (whether orally or in writing) to a person carrying out a valuation or making a report, and
  (b) conveying or purporting to convey any information or explanation which that person requires, or is entitled to require, under subsection (1).
(4) A person guilty of an offence under subsection (2) is liable—
  (a) on conviction on indictment, to imprisonment for a term not exceeding two years or a fine (or both);
  (b) on summary conviction—
    (i) in England and Wales, to imprisonment for a term not exceeding twelve months or to a fine not exceeding the statutory maximum (or both);
    (ii) in Scotland or Northern Ireland, to imprisonment for a term not exceeding six months, or to a fine not exceeding the statutory maximum (or both).

### 1154  Duty to notify registrar of certain appointments etc

(1) Notice must be given to the registrar of the appointment in relation to a company of—
  (a) a judicial factor (in Scotland),
  (b) a receiver and manager appointed under section 18 of the Charities Act 1993 (c. 10) or s33 of Charities Act (Northern Ireland) 2008, or
  (c) a manager appointed under section 47 of the Companies (Audit, Investigations and Community Enterprise) Act 2004 (c. 27).
(2) The notice must be given—
  (a) in the case of appointment of a judicial factor, by the judicial factor;
  (b) in the case of appointment of a receiver and manager under section 18 of the Charities Act 1993 (c. 10), by the Charity Commission;
  (bb) in the case of appointment of a receiver or manager under section 33 of the Charities Act (Northern Ireland) 2008 by the Charity Commission for Northern Ireland:
  (c) in the case of appointment of a manager under section 47 of the Companies (Audit, Investigations and Community Enterprise) Act 2004, by the Regulator of Community Interest Companies.
(3) The notice must specify an address at which service of documents (including legal process) may be effected on the person appointed. Notice of a change in the address for service may be given to the registrar by the person appointed.
(4) Where notice has been given under this section of the appointment of a person, notice must also be given to the registrar of the termination of the appointment.
This notice must be given by the person specified in subsection (2).

### 1155  Offence of failure to give notice

(1) If a judicial factor fails to give notice of his appointment in accordance with section 1154 within the period of 14 days after the appointment he commits an offence.

(2)  A person guilty of an offence under this section is liable on summary conviction to a fine not exceeding level 5 on the standard scale and, for continued contravention, a daily default fine not exceeding one-tenth of level 5 on the standard scale.

*Courts and legal proceedings*

### 1156   Meaning of 'the court'

(1)  Except as otherwise provided, in the Companies Acts 'the court' means—

    (a)  in England and Wales, the High Court or (subject to subsection (3)) a county court;

    (b)  in Scotland, the Court of Session or the sheriff court;

    (c)  in Northern Ireland, the High Court.

(2)  The provisions of the Companies Acts conferring jurisdiction on 'the court' as defined above have effect subject to any enactment or rule of law relating to the allocation of jurisdiction or distribution of business between courts in any part of the United Kingdom.

(3)  The Lord Chancellor may, with the concurrence of the Lord Chief Justice, by order—

    (a)  exclude a county court from having jurisdiction under the Companies Acts, and

    (b)  for the purposes of that jurisdiction attach that court's district, or any part of it, to another county court.

(4)  The Lord Chief Justice may nominate a judicial office holder (as defined in section 109(4) of the Constitutional Reform Act 2005 (c. 4)) to exercise his functions under subsection (3).

### 1157   Power of court to grant relief in certain cases

(1)  If in proceedings for negligence, default, breach of duty or breach of trust against—

    (a)  an officer of a company, or

    (b)  a person employed by a company as auditor (whether he is or is not an officer of the company),

it appears to the court hearing the case that the officer or person is or may be liable but that he acted honestly and reasonably, and that having regard to all the circumstances of the case (including those connected with his appointment) he ought fairly to be excused, the court may relieve him, either wholly or in part, from his liability on such terms as it thinks fit.

(2)  If any such officer or person has reason to apprehend that a claim will or might be made against him in respect of negligence, default, breach of duty or breach of trust—

    (a)  he may apply to the court for relief, and

    (b)  the court has the same power to relieve him as it would have had if it had been a court before which proceedings against him for negligence, default, breach of duty or breach of trust had been brought.

(3)  Where a case to which subsection (1) applies is being tried by a judge with a jury, the judge, after hearing the evidence, may, if he is satisfied that the defendant (in Scotland, the defender) ought in pursuance of that subsection to be relieved either in whole or in part from the liability sought to be enforced against him, withdraw the case from the jury and forthwith direct judgment to be entered for the defendant (in Scotland, grant decree of absolvitor) on such terms as to costs (in Scotland, expenses) or otherwise as the judge may think proper.

# PART 38  COMPANIES: INTERPRETATION

*Meaning of 'UK-registered company'*

### 1158   Meaning of 'UK-registered company'

In the Companies Acts 'UK-registered company' means a company registered under this Act.

The expression does not include an overseas company that has registered particulars under section 1046.

*Meaning of 'subsidiary' and related expressions*

### 1159   Meaning of 'subsidiary' etc.

(1)  A company is a 'subsidiary' of another company, its 'holding company', if that other company—

    (a)  holds a majority of the voting rights in it, or

    (b)  is a member of it and has the right to appoint or remove a majority of its board of directors, or

    (c)  is a member of it and controls alone, pursuant to an agreement with other members, a majority of the voting rights in it,

or if it is a subsidiary of a company that is itself a subsidiary of that other company.

(2)  A company is a 'wholly-owned subsidiary' of another company if it has no members except that other and that other's wholly-owned subsidiaries or persons acting on behalf of that other or its wholly-owned subsidiaries.

(3)  Schedule 6 contains provisions explaining expressions used in this section and otherwise supplementing this section.

(4)  In this section and that Schedule 'company' includes any body corporate.

### 1160    Meaning of 'subsidiary' etc.: power to amend

(1)  The Secretary of State may by regulations amend the provisions of section 1159 (meaning of 'subsidiary' etc) and Schedule 6 (meaning of 'subsidiary' etc.: supplementary provisions) so as to alter the meaning of the expressions 'subsidiary', 'holding company' or 'wholly-owned subsidiary'.

(2)  Regulations under this section are subject to negative resolution procedure.

(3)  Any amendment made by regulations under this section does not apply for the purposes of enactments outside the Companies Acts unless the regulations so provide.

(4)  So much of section 23(3) of the Interpretation Act 1978 (c. 30) as applies section 17(2)(a) of that Act (effect of repeal and re-enactment) to deeds, instruments and documents other than enactments does not apply in relation to any repeal and re-enactment effected by regulations under this section.

*Meaning of 'undertaking' and related expressions*

### 1161    Meaning of 'undertaking' and related expressions

(1)  In the Companies Acts 'undertaking' means—

   (a)  a body corporate or partnership, or

   (b)  an unincorporated association carrying on a trade or business, with or without a view to profit.

(2)  In the Companies Acts references to shares—

   (a)  in relation to an undertaking with capital but no share capital, are to rights to share in the capital of the undertaking; and

   (b)  in relation to an undertaking without capital, are to interests—

      (i)  conferring any right to share in the profits or liability to contribute to the losses of the undertaking, or

      (ii)  giving rise to an obligation to contribute to the debts or expenses of the undertaking in the event of a winding up.

(3)  Other expressions appropriate to companies shall be construed, in relation to an undertaking which is not a company, as references to the corresponding persons, officers, documents or organs, as the case may be, appropriate to undertakings of that description.

This is subject to provision in any specific context providing for the translation of such expressions.

(4)  References in the Companies Acts to 'fellow subsidiary undertakings' are to undertakings which are subsidiary undertakings of the same parent undertaking but are not parent undertakings or subsidiary undertakings of each other.

(5)  In the Companies Acts 'group undertaking', in relation to an undertaking, means an undertaking which is—

   (a)  a parent undertaking or subsidiary undertaking of that undertaking, or

   (b)  a subsidiary undertaking of any parent undertaking of that undertaking.

### 1162    Parent and subsidiary undertakings

(1)  This section (together with Schedule 7) defines 'parent undertaking' and 'subsidiary undertaking' for the purposes of the Companies Acts.

(2)  An undertaking is a parent undertaking in relation to another undertaking, a subsidiary undertaking, if—

   (a)  it holds a majority of the voting rights in the undertaking, or

   (b)  it is a member of the undertaking and has the right to appoint or remove a majority of its board of directors, or

   (c)  it has the right to exercise a dominant influence over the undertaking—

      (i)  by virtue of provisions contained in the undertaking's articles, or

      (ii)  by virtue of a control contract, or

   (d)  it is a member of the undertaking and controls alone, pursuant to an agreement with other shareholders or members, a majority of the voting rights in the undertaking.

(3)  For the purposes of subsection (2) an undertaking shall be treated as a member of another undertaking—

   (a)  if any of its subsidiary undertakings is a member of that undertaking, or

   (b)  if any shares in that other undertaking are held by a person acting on behalf of the undertaking or any of its subsidiary undertakings.

(4)  An undertaking is also a parent undertaking in relation to another undertaking, a subsidiary undertaking, if—

   (a)  it has the power to exercise, or actually exercises, dominant influence or control over it, or

   (b)  it and the subsidiary undertaking are managed on a unified basis.

(5)  A parent undertaking shall be treated as the parent undertaking of undertakings in relation to which any of its subsidiary undertakings are, or are to be treated as, parent undertakings; and references to its subsidiary undertakings shall be construed accordingly.

(6)  Schedule 7 contains provisions explaining expressions used in this section and otherwise supplementing this section.

(7) In this section and that Schedule references to shares, in relation to an undertaking, are to allotted shares.

*Other definitions*

### 1163 'Non-cash asset'

(1) In the Companies Acts 'non-cash asset' means any property or interest in property, other than cash. For this purpose 'cash' includes foreign currency.

(2) A reference to the transfer or acquisition of a non-cash asset includes—

(a) the creation or extinction of an estate or interest in, or a right over, any property, and

(b) the discharge of a liability of any person, other than a liability for a liquidated sum.

### 1164 Meaning of 'banking company' and 'banking group'

(1) This section defines 'banking company' and 'banking group' for the purposes of the Companies Acts.

(2) 'Banking company' means a person who has permission under Part 4 of the Financial Services and Markets Act 2000 (c. 8) to accept deposits, other than—

(a) a person who is not a company, and

(b) a person who has such permission only for the purpose of carrying on another regulated activity in accordance with permission under that Part.

(3) The definition in subsection (2) must be read with section 22 of that Act, any relevant order under that section and Schedule 2 to that Act.

(4) References to a banking group are to a group where the parent company is a banking company or where—

(a) the parent company's principal subsidiary undertakings are wholly or mainly credit institutions, and

(b) the parent company does not itself carry on any material business apart from the acquisition, management and disposal of interests in subsidiary undertakings.

'Group' here means a parent undertaking and its subsidiary undertakings.

(5) For the purposes of subsection (4)—

(a) a parent company's principal subsidiary undertakings are the subsidiary undertakings of the company whose results or financial position would principally affect the figures shown in the group accounts, and

(b) the management of interests in subsidiary undertakings includes the provision of services to such undertakings.

### 1165 Meaning of 'insurance company' and related expressions

(1) This section defines 'insurance company', 'authorised insurance company', 'insurance group' and 'insurance market activity' for the purposes of the Companies Acts.

(2) An 'authorised insurance company' means a person (whether incorporated or not) who has permission under Part 4 of the Financial Services and Markets Act 2000 (c. 8) to effect or carry out contracts of insurance.

(3) An 'insurance company' means—

(a) an authorised insurance company, or

(b) any other person (whether incorporated or not) who—

(i) carries on insurance market activity, or

(ii) may effect or carry out contracts of insurance under which the benefits provided by that person are exclusively or primarily benefits in kind in the event of accident to or breakdown of a vehicle.

(4) Neither expression includes a friendly society within the meaning of the Friendly Societies Act 1992 (c. 40).

(5) References to an insurance group are to a group where the parent company is an insurance company or where—

(a) the parent company's principal subsidiary undertakings are wholly or mainly insurance companies, and

(b) the parent company does not itself carry on any material business apart from the acquisition, management and disposal of interests in subsidiary undertakings.

'Group' here means a parent undertaking and its subsidiary undertakings.

(6) For the purposes of subsection (5)—

(a) a parent company's principal subsidiary undertakings are the subsidiary undertakings of the company whose results or financial position would principally affect the figures shown in the group accounts, and

(b) the management of interests in subsidiary undertakings includes the provision of services to such undertakings.

(7) 'Insurance market activity' has the meaning given in section 316(3) of the Financial Services and Markets Act 2000.

(8) References in this section to contracts of insurance and to the effecting or carrying out of such contracts must be read with section 22 of that Act, any relevant order under that section and Schedule 2 to that Act.

### 1166    'Employees' share scheme'

For the purposes of the Companies Acts an employees' share scheme is a scheme for encouraging or facilitating the holding of shares in or debentures of a company by or for the benefit of—

>        (a) the bona fide employees or former employees of—
>             (i)    the company,
>             (ii)   any subsidiary of the company, or
>             (iii)  the company's holding company or any subsidiary of the company's holding company, or
>        (b) the spouses, civil partners, surviving spouses, surviving civil partners, or minor children or step-children of such employees or former employees.

### 1167    Meaning of 'prescribed'

In the Companies Acts 'prescribed' means prescribed (by order or by regulations) by the Secretary of State.

### 1168    Hard copy and electronic form and related expressions

(1) The following provisions apply for the purposes of the Companies Acts.

(2) A document or information is sent or supplied in hard copy form if it is sent or supplied in a paper copy or similar form capable of being read. References to hard copy have a corresponding meaning.

(3) A document or information is sent or supplied in electronic form if it is sent or supplied—

>        (a) by electronic means (for example, by e-mail or fax), or
>        (b) by any other means while in an electronic form (for example, sending a disk by post).

References to electronic copy have a corresponding meaning.

(4) A document or information is sent or supplied by electronic means if it is—

>        (a) sent initially and received at its destination by means of electronic equipment for the processing (which expression includes digital compression) or storage of data, and
>        (b) entirely transmitted, conveyed and received by wire, by radio, by optical means or by other electromagnetic means.

References to electronic means have a corresponding meaning.

(5) A document or information authorised or required to be sent or supplied in electronic form must be sent or supplied in a form, and by a means, that the sender or supplier reasonably considers will enable the recipient—

>        (a) to read it, and
>        (b) to retain a copy of it.

(6) For the purposes of this section, a document or information can be read only if—

>        (a) it can be read with the naked eye, or
>        (b) to the extent that it consists of images (for example photographs, pictures, maps, plans or drawings), it can be seen with the naked eye.

(7) The provisions of this section apply whether the provision of the Companies Acts in question uses the words 'sent' or 'supplied' or uses other words (such as 'deliver', 'provide', 'produce' or, in the case of a notice, 'give') to refer to the sending or supplying of a document or information.

### 1169    Dormant companies

(1) For the purposes of the Companies Acts a company is 'dormant' during any period in which it has no significant accounting transaction.

(2) A 'significant accounting transaction' means a transaction that is required by section 386 to be entered in the company's accounting records.

(3) In determining whether or when a company is dormant, there shall be disregarded—

>        (a) any transaction arising from the taking of shares in the company by a subscriber to the memorandum as a result of an undertaking of his in connection with the formation of the company;
>        (b) any transaction consisting of the payment of—
>             (i)    a fee to the registrar on a change of the company's name,
>             (ii)   a fee to the registrar on the re-registration of the company,
>             (iii)  a penalty under section 453 (penalty for failure to file accounts), or
>             (iv)   a fee to the registrar for the registration of an annual return.

(4) Any reference in the Companies Acts to a body corporate other than a company being dormant has a corresponding meaning.

### 1170    Meaning of 'EEA State' and related expressions

In the Companies Acts—

'EEA State' has the meaning given by Schedule 1 to the Interpretation Act 1978;

'EEA company' and 'EEA undertaking' mean a company or undertaking governed by the law of an EEA State.

## 1171   The former Companies Acts

In the Companies Acts—

'the former Companies Acts' means—

    (a) the Joint Stock Companies Acts, the Companies Act 1862 (c. 89), the Companies (Consolidation) Act 1908 (c. 69), the Companies Act 1929 (c. 23), the Companies Act (Northern Ireland) 1932 (c. 7 (N.I.)), the Companies Acts 1948 to 1983, the Companies Act (Northern Ireland) 1960 (c. 22 (N.I.)), the Companies (Northern Ireland) Order 1986 (S.I. 1986/1032 (N.I. 6)) and the Companies Consolidation (Consequential Provisions) (Northern Ireland) Order 1986 (S.I. 1986/1035 (N.I. 9)), and

    (b) the provisions of the Companies Act 1985 (c. 6) and the Companies Consolidation (Consequential Provisions) Act 1985 (c. 9) that are no longer in force;

'the Joint Stock Companies Acts' means the Joint Stock Companies Act 1856 (c. 47), the Joint Stock Companies Acts 1856, 1857 (20 & 21 Vict. c. 14), the Joint Stock Banking Companies Act 1857 (c. 49), and the Act to enable Joint Stock Banking Companies to be formed on the principle of limited liability (1858 c. 91), but does not include the Joint Stock Companies Act 1844 (c. 110).

*General*

## 1172   References to requirements of this Act

References in the company law provisions of this Act to the requirements of this Act include the requirements of regulations and orders made under it.

## 1173   Minor definitions: general

    (1) In the Companies Acts—

'body corporate' and 'corporation' include a body incorporated outside the United Kingdom, but do not include—

    (a) a corporation sole, or

    (b) a partnership that, whether or not a legal person, is not regarded as a body corporate under the law by which it is governed;

'credit institution' means a credit institution as defined in Article 4.1(a) of Directive 2006/48/EC of the European Parliament and of the Council relating to the taking up and pursuit of the business of credit institutions;

'financial institution' means a financial institution within the meaning of Article 1.1 of the Council Directive on the obligations of branches established in a Member State of credit and financial institutions having their head offices outside that Member State regarding the publication of annual accounting documents (the Bank Branches Directive, 89/117/EEC);

'firm' means any entity, whether or not a legal person, that is not an individual and includes a body corporate, a corporation sole and a partnership or other unincorporated association;

'the Gazette' means—

    (a) as respects companies registered in England and Wales, the London Gazette,

    (b) as respects companies registered in Scotland, the Edinburgh Gazette, and

    (c) as respects companies registered in Northern Ireland, the Belfast Gazette;

'hire-purchase agreement' has the same meaning as in the Consumer Credit Act 1974 (c. 39);

'officer', in relation to a body corporate, includes a director, manager or secretary;

'parent company' means a company that is a parent undertaking (see section 1162 and Schedule 7);

'regulated activity' has the meaning given in section 22 of the Financial Services and Markets Act 2000 (c. 8);

'regulated market' has the same meaning as in Directive 2004/39/EC of the European Parliament and of the Council on markets in financial instruments (see Article 4.1(14));

'working day', in relation to a company, means a day that is not a Saturday or Sunday, Christmas Day, Good Friday or any day that is a bank holiday under the Banking and Financial Dealings Act 1971 (c. 80) in the part of the United Kingdom where the company is registered.

    (2) In relation to an EEA State that has not implemented Directive 2004/39/EC of the European Parliament and of the Council on markets in financial instruments, the following definition of 'regulated market' has effect in place of that in subsection (1)—

'regulated market' has the same meaning as it has in Council Directive 93/22/EEC on investment services in the securities field.

## 1174   Index of defined expressions

Schedule 8 contains an index of provisions defining or otherwise explaining expressions used in the Companies Acts.

## PART 39   COMPANIES: MINOR AMENDMENTS

### 1175   Removal of special provisions about accounts and audit of charitable companies

(1) Part 7 of the Companies Act 1985 (c. 6) and Part 8 of the Companies (Northern Ireland) Order 1986 (accounts and audit) are amended in accordance with Schedule 9 to this Act so as to remove the special provisions about companies that are charities.

(2) In that Schedule—

Part 1 contains repeals and consequential amendments of provisions of the Companies Act 1985;

Part 2 contains repeals and consequential amendments of provisions of the Companies (Northern Ireland) Order 1986.

### 1176   Power of Secretary of State to bring civil proceedings on company's behalf

(1) Section 438 of the Companies Act 1985 (power of Secretary of State to bring civil proceedings on company's behalf) shall cease to have effect.

(2) In section 439 of that Act (expenses of investigating company's affairs)—

(a) in subsection (2) omit ', or is ordered to pay the whole or any part of the costs of proceedings brought under section 438,';

(b) omit subsections (3) and (7) (which relate to section 438);

(c) in subsection (8)—

(i) for 'subsections (2) and (3)' substitute 'subsection (2)', and

(ii) omit '; and any such liability imposed by subsection (2) is (subject as mentioned above) a liability also to indemnify all persons against liability under subsection (3)'.

(3) In section 453(1A) of that Act (investigation of overseas companies: provisions not applicable), omit paragraph (b) (which relates to section 438).

(4) Nothing in this section affects proceedings brought under section 438 before the commencement of this section.

### 1177   Repeal of certain provisions about company directors

The following provisions of Part 10 of the Companies Act 1985 shall cease to have effect—

section 311 (prohibition on tax-free payments to directors);

sections 323 and 327 (prohibition on directors dealing in share options);

sections 324 to 326 and 328 to 329, and Parts 2 to 4 of Schedule 13 (register of directors' interests);

sections 343 and 344 (special procedure for disclosure by banks).

### 1178   Repeal of requirement that certain companies publish periodical statement

The following provisions shall cease to have effect—

section 720 of the Companies Act 1985 (c. 6) (certain companies to publish periodical statement), and

Schedule 23 to that Act (form of statement under section 720).

### 1179   Repeal of requirement that Secretary of State prepare annual report

Section 729 of the Companies Act 1985 (annual report to Parliament by Secretary of State on matters within the Companies Acts) shall cease to have effect.

### 1180   Repeal of certain provisions about company charges

Part 4 of the Companies Act 1989 (c. 40) (registration of company charges), which has not been brought into force, is repealed.

### 1181   Access to constitutional documents of RTE and RTM companies

(1) The Secretary of State may by order—

(a) amend Chapter 1 of Part 1 of the Leasehold Reform, Housing and Urban Development Act 1993 (c. 28) for the purpose of facilitating access to the provisions of the articles or any other constitutional document of RTE companies;

(b) amend Chapter 1 of Part 2 of the Commonhold and Leasehold Reform Act 2002 (c. 15) (leasehold reform) for the purpose of facilitating access to the provisions of the articles or any other constitutional document of RTM companies.

(2) References in subsection (1) to provisions of a company's articles or any other constitutional document include any provisions included in those documents by virtue of any enactment.

(3) An order under this section is subject to negative resolution procedure.

(4) In this section—

'RTE companies' has the same meaning as in Chapter 1 of Part 1 of the Leasehold Reform, Housing and Urban Development Act 1993;

'RTM companies' has the same meaning as in Chapter 1 of Part 2 of the Commonhold and Leasehold Reform Act 2002.

# PART 40   COMPANY DIRECTORS: FOREIGN DISQUALIFICATION ETC.

## *Introductory*

### 1182   Persons subject to foreign restrictions

(1) This section defines what is meant by references in this Part to a person being subject to foreign restrictions.

(2) A person is subject to foreign restrictions if under the law of a country or territory outside the United Kingdom—

    (a) he is, by reason of misconduct or unfitness, disqualified to any extent from acting in connection with the affairs of a company,

    (b) he is, by reason of misconduct or unfitness, required—

        (i) to obtain permission from a court or other authority, or

        (ii) to meet any other condition,

    before acting in connection with the affairs of a company, or

    (c) he has, by reason of misconduct or unfitness, given undertakings to a court or other authority of a country or territory outside the United Kingdom—

        (i) not to act in connection with the affairs of a company, or

        (ii) restricting the extent to which, or the way in which, he may do so.

(3) The references in subsection (2) to acting in connection with the affairs of a company are to doing any of the following—

    (a) being a director of a company,

    (b) acting as receiver of a company's property, or

    (c) being concerned or taking part in the promotion, formation or management of a company.

(4) In this section—

    (a) 'company' means a company incorporated or formed under the law of the country or territory in question, and

    (b) in relation to such a company—

    'director' means the holder of an office corresponding to that of director of a UK company; and 'receiver' includes any corresponding officer under the law of that country or territory.

### 1183   Meaning of 'the court' and 'UK company'

In this Part—

'the court' means—

    (a) in England and Wales, the High Court or a county court;

    (b) in Scotland, the Court of Session or the sheriff court;

    (c) in Northern Ireland, the High Court;

'UK company' means a company registered under this Act.

## *Power to disqualify*

### 1184   Disqualification of persons subject to foreign restrictions

(1) The Secretary of State may make provision by regulations disqualifying a person subject to foreign restrictions from—

    (a) being a director of a UK company,

    (b) acting as receiver of a UK company's property, or

    (c) in any way, whether directly or indirectly, being concerned or taking part in the promotion, formation or management of a UK company.

(2) The regulations may provide that a person subject to foreign restrictions—

    (a) is disqualified automatically by virtue of the regulations, or

    (b) may be disqualified by order of the court on the application of the Secretary of State.

(3) The regulations may provide that the Secretary of State may accept an undertaking (a 'disqualification undertaking') from a person subject to foreign restrictions that he will not do anything which would be in breach of a disqualification under subsection (1).

(4) In this Part—

    (a) a 'person disqualified under this Part' is a person—

        (i) disqualified as mentioned in subsection (2)(a) or (b), or

        (ii) who has given and is subject to a disqualification undertaking;

    (b) references to a breach of a disqualification include a breach of a disqualification undertaking.

(5) The regulations may provide for applications to the court by persons disqualified under this Part for permission to act in a way which would otherwise be in breach of the disqualification.

(6) The regulations must provide that a person ceases to be disqualified under this Part on his ceasing to be subject to foreign restrictions.

(7) Regulations under this section are subject to affirmative resolution procedure.

### 1185    Disqualification regulations: supplementary

(1) Regulations under section 1184 may make different provision for different cases and may in particular distinguish between cases by reference to—

(a) the conduct on the basis of which the person became subject to foreign restrictions;

(b) the nature of the foreign restrictions;

(c) the country or territory under whose law the foreign restrictions were imposed.

(2) Regulations under section 1184(2)(b) or (5) (provision for applications to the court)—

(a) must specify the grounds on which an application may be made;

(b) may specify factors to which the court shall have regard in determining an application.

(3) The regulations may, in particular, require the court to have regard to the following factors—

(a) whether the conduct on the basis of which the person became subject to foreign restrictions would, if done in relation to a UK company, have led a court to make a disqualification order on an application under the Company Directors Disqualification Act 1986 (c. 46) or the Company Directors Disqualification (Northern Ireland) Order 2002 (S.I. 2002/3150 (N.I. 4));

(b) in a case in which the conduct on the basis of which the person became subject to foreign restrictions would not be unlawful if done in relation to a UK company, the fact that the person acted unlawfully under foreign law;

(c) whether the person's activities in relation to UK companies began after he became subject to foreign restrictions;

(d) whether the person's activities (or proposed activities) in relation to UK companies are undertaken (or are proposed to be undertaken) outside the United Kingdom.

(4) Regulations under section 1184(3) (provision as to undertakings given to the Secretary of State) may include provision allowing the Secretary of State, in determining whether to accept an undertaking, to take into account matters other than criminal convictions notwithstanding that the person may be criminally liable in respect of those matters.

(5) Regulations under section 1184(5) (provision for application to court for permission to act) may include provision—

(a) entitling the Secretary of State to be represented at the hearing of the application, and

(b) as to the giving of evidence or the calling of witnesses by the Secretary of State at the hearing of the application.

### 1186    Offence of breach of disqualification

(1) Regulations under section 1184 may provide that a person disqualified under this Part who acts in breach of the disqualification commits an offence.

(2) The regulations may provide that a person guilty of such an offence is liable—

(a) on conviction on indictment, to imprisonment for a term not exceeding two years or a fine (or both);

(b) on summary conviction—

(i) in England and Wales, to imprisonment for a term not exceeding twelve months or to a fine not exceeding the statutory maximum (or both);

(ii) in Scotland or Northern Ireland, to imprisonment for a term not exceeding six months, or to a fine not exceeding the statutory maximum (or both).

(3) In relation to an offence committed before the commencement of section 154(1) of the Criminal Justice Act 2003 (c. 44), for 'twelve months' in subsection (2)(b)(i) substitute 'six months'.

*Power to make persons liable for company's debts*

### 1187    Personal liability for debts of company

(1) The Secretary of State may provide by regulations that a person who, at a time when he is subject to foreign restrictions—

(a) is a director of a UK company, or

(b) is involved in the management of a UK company,

is personally responsible for all debts and other liabilities of the company incurred during that time.

(2) A person who is personally responsible by virtue of this section for debts and other liabilities of a company is jointly and severally liable in respect of those debts and liabilities with—

(a) the company, and

(b) any other person who (whether by virtue of this section or otherwise) is so liable.

(3) For the purposes of this section a person is involved in the management of a company if he is concerned, whether directly or indirectly, or takes part, in the management of the company.

(4) The regulations may make different provision for different cases and may in particular distinguish between cases by reference to—

(a) the conduct on the basis of which the person became subject to foreign restrictions;

(b) the nature of the foreign restrictions;

(c) the country or territory under whose law the foreign restrictions were imposed.

(5) Regulations under this section are subject to affirmative resolution procedure.

*Power to require statements to be sent to the registrar of companies*

### 1188    Statements from persons subject to foreign restrictions

(1) The Secretary of State may make provision by regulations requiring a person who—

    (a) is subject to foreign restrictions, and

    (b) is not disqualified under this Part,

to send a statement to the registrar if he does anything that, if done by a person disqualified under this Part, would be in breach of the disqualification.

(2) The statement must include such information as may be specified in the regulations relating to—

    (a) the person's activities in relation to UK companies, and

    (b) the foreign restrictions to which the person is subject.

(3) The statement must be sent to the registrar within such period as may be specified in the regulations.

(4) The regulations may make different provision for different cases and may in particular distinguish between cases by reference to—

    (a) the conduct on the basis of which the person became subject to foreign restrictions;

    (b) the nature of the foreign restrictions;

    (c) the country or territory under whose law the foreign restrictions were imposed.

(5) Regulations under this section are subject to affirmative resolution procedure.

### 1189    Statements from persons disqualified

(1) The Secretary of State may make provision by regulations requiring a statement or notice sent to the registrar of companies under any of the provisions listed below that relates (wholly or partly) to a person who—

    (a) is a person disqualified under this Part, or

    (b) is subject to a disqualification order or disqualification undertaking under the Company Directors Disqualification Act 1986 (c. 46) or the Company Directors Disqualification (Northern Ireland) Order 2002 (S.I. 2002/3150 (N.I. 4)),

to be accompanied by an additional statement.

(2) The provisions referred to above are—

    (a) section 12 (statement of a company's proposed officers),

    (b) section 167(2) (notice of person having become director), and

    (c) section 276 (notice of a person having become secretary or one of joint secretaries).

(3) The additional statement is a statement that the person has obtained permission from a court, on an application under section 1184(5) or (as the case may be) for the purposes of section 1(1)(a) of the Company Directors Disqualification Act 1986 (c. 46) or Article 3(1) of the Company Directors Disqualification (Northern Ireland) Order 2002 (S.I. 2002/3150 (N.I. 4)), to act in the capacity in question.

(4) Regulations under this section are subject to affirmative resolution procedure.

### 1190    Statements: whether to be made public

(1) Regulations under section 1188 or 1189 (statements required to be sent to registrar) may provide that a statement sent to the registrar of companies under the regulations is to be treated as a record relating to a company for the purposes of section 1080 (the companies register).

(2) The regulations may make provision as to the circumstances in which such a statement is to be, or may be—

    (a) withheld from public inspection, or

    (b) removed from the register.

(3) The regulations may, in particular, provide that a statement is not to be withheld from public inspection or removed from the register unless the person to whom it relates provides such information, and satisfies such other conditions, as may be specified.

(4) The regulations may provide that section 1081 (note of removal of material from the register) does not apply, or applies with such modifications as may be specified, in the case of material removed from the register under the regulations.

(5) In this section 'specified' means specified in the regulations.

### 1191    Offences

(1) Regulations under section 1188 or 1189 may provide that it is an offence for a person—

    (a) to fail to comply with a requirement under the regulations to send a statement to the registrar;

    (b) knowingly or recklessly to send a statement under the regulations to the registrar that is misleading, false or deceptive in a material particular.

(2) The regulations may provide that a person guilty of such an offence is liable—

    (a) on conviction on indictment, to imprisonment for a term not exceeding two years or a fine (or both);

(b) on summary conviction—
  (i)   in England and Wales, to imprisonment for a term not exceeding twelve months or to a fine not exceeding the statutory maximum (or both);
  (ii)  in Scotland or Northern Ireland, to imprisonment for a term not exceeding six months, or to a fine not exceeding the statutory maximum (or both).

(3)  In relation to an offence committed before the commencement of section 154(1) of the Criminal Justice Act 2003 (c. 44), for 'twelve months' in subsection (2)(b)(i) substitute 'six months'.

# PART 41  BUSINESS NAMES

## Chapter 1  Restricted or prohibited names

### *Introductory*

**1192  Application of this Chapter**

(1)  This Chapter applies to any person carrying on business in the United Kingdom.

(2)  The provisions of this Chapter do not prevent—
  (a) an individual carrying on business under a name consisting of his surname without any addition other than a permitted addition, or
  (b) individuals carrying on business in partnership under a name consisting of the surnames of all the partners without any addition other than a permitted addition.

(3)  The following are the permitted additions—
  (a) in the case of an individual, his forename or initial;
  (b) in the case of a partnership—
    (i)   the forenames of individual partners or the initials of those forenames, or
    (ii)  where two or more individual partners have the same surname, the addition of 's' at the end of that surname;
  (c) in either case, an addition merely indicating that the business is carried on in succession to a former owner of the business.

### *Sensitive words or expressions*

**1193  Name suggesting connection with government or public authority**

(1)  A person must not, without the approval of the Secretary of State, carry on business in the United Kingdom under a name that would be likely to give the impression that the business is connected with—
  (a) Her Majesty's Government, any part of the Scottish administration or Her Majesty's Government in Northern Ireland,
  (b) any local authority, or
  (c) any public authority specified for the purposes of this section by regulations made by the Secretary of State.

(2)  For the purposes of this section—
'local authority' means—
  (a) a local authority within the meaning of the Local Government Act 1972 (c. 70), the Common Council of the City of London or the Council of the Isles of Scilly,
  (b) a council constituted under section 2 of the Local Government etc. (Scotland) Act 1994 (c. 39), or
  (c) a district council in Northern Ireland;
'public authority' includes any person or body having functions of a public nature.

(3)  Regulations under this section are subject to affirmative resolution procedure.

(4)  A person who contravenes this section commits an offence.

(5)  Where an offence under this section is committed by a body corporate, an offence is also committed by every officer of the body who is in default.

(6)  A person guilty of an offence under this section is liable on summary conviction to a fine not exceeding level 3 on the standard scale and, for continued contravention, a daily default fine not exceeding one-tenth of level 3 on the standard scale.

**1194  Other sensitive words or expressions**

(1)  A person must not, without the approval of the Secretary of State, carry on business in the United Kingdom under a name that includes a word or expression for the time being specified in regulations made by the Secretary of State under this section.

(2)  Regulations under this section are subject to approval after being made.

(3)  A person who contravenes this section commits an offence.

(4)  Where an offence under this section is committed by a body corporate, an offence is also committed by every officer of the body who is in default.

(5)  A person guilty of an offence under this section is liable on summary conviction to a fine not exceeding level 3 on the standard scale and, for continued contravention, a daily default fine not exceeding one-tenth of level 3 on the standard scale.

### 1195  Requirement to seek comments of government department or other relevant body

(1)  The Secretary of State may by regulations under—

    (a)  section 1193 (name suggesting connection with government or public authority), or

    (b)  section 1194 (other sensitive words or expressions),

require that, in connection with an application for the approval of the Secretary of State under that section, the applicant must seek the view of a specified Government department or other body.

(2)  Where such a requirement applies, the applicant must request the specified department or other body (in writing) to indicate whether (and if so why) it has any objections to the proposed name.

(3)  He must submit to the Secretary of State a statement that such a request has been made and a copy of any response received from the specified body.

(4)  If these requirements are not complied with, the Secretary of State may refuse to consider the application for approval.

(5)  In this section 'specified' means specified in the regulations.

### 1196  Withdrawal of Secretary of State's approval

(1)  This section applies to approval given for the purposes of—

section 1193 (name suggesting connection with government or public authority), or

section 1194 (other sensitive words or expressions).

(2)  If it appears to the Secretary of State that there are overriding considerations of public policy that require such approval to be withdrawn, the approval may be withdrawn by notice in writing given to the person concerned.

(3)  The notice must state the date as from which approval is withdrawn.

*Misleading names*

### 1197  Name containing inappropriate indication of company type or legal form

(1)  The Secretary of State may make provision by regulations prohibiting a person from carrying on business in the United Kingdom under a name consisting of or containing specified words, expressions or other indications—

    (a)  that are associated with a particular type of company or form of organisation, or

    (b)  that are similar to words, expressions or other indications associated with a particular type of company or form of organisation.

(2)  The regulations may prohibit the use of words, expressions or other indications—

    (a)  in a specified part, or otherwise than in a specified part, of a name;

    (b)  in conjunction with, or otherwise than in conjunction with, such other words, expressions or indications as may be specified.

(3)  In this section 'specified' means specified in the regulations.

(4)  Regulations under this section are subject to negative resolution procedure.

(5)  A person who uses a name in contravention of regulations under this section commits an offence.

(6)  Where an offence under this section is committed by a body corporate, an offence is also committed by every officer of the body who is in default.

(7)  A person guilty of an offence under this section is liable on summary conviction to a fine not exceeding level 3 on the standard scale and, for continued contravention, a daily default fine not exceeding one-tenth of level 3 on the standard scale.

### 1198  Name giving misleading indication of activities

(1)  A person must not carry on business in the United Kingdom under a name that gives so misleading an indication of the nature of the activities of the business as to be likely to cause harm to the public.

(2)  A person who uses a name in contravention of this section commits an offence.

(3)  Where an offence under this section is committed by a body corporate, an offence is also committed by every officer of the body who is in default.

(4)  A person guilty of an offence under this section is liable on summary conviction to a fine not exceeding level 3 on the standard scale and, for continued contravention, a daily default fine not exceeding one-tenth of level 3 on the standard scale.

*Supplementary*

### 1199  Savings for existing lawful business names

(1)  This section has effect in relation to—

sections 1192 to 1196 (sensitive words or expressions), and

section 1197 (inappropriate indication of company type or legal form).

(2)  Those sections do not apply to the carrying on of a business by a person who—

    (a)  carried on the business immediately before the date on which this Chapter came into force, and

(b) continues to carry it on under the name that immediately before that date was its lawful business name.

(3) Where—

(a) a business is transferred to a person on or after the date on which this Chapter came into force, and

(b) that person carries on the business under the name that was its lawful business name immediately before the transfer,

those sections do not apply in relation to the carrying on of the business under that name during the period of twelve months beginning with the date of the transfer.

(4) In this section 'lawful business name', in relation to a business, means a name under which the business was carried on without contravening—

(a) section 2(1) of the Business Names Act 1985 (c. 7) or Article 4(1) of the Business Names (Northern Ireland) Order 1986 (S.I. 1986/1033 N.I. 7)), or

(b) after this Chapter has come into force, the provisions of this Chapter.

## Chapter 2  Disclosure required in case of individual or partnership

### *Introductory*

### 1200  Application of this Chapter

(1) This Chapter applies to an individual or partnership carrying on business in the United Kingdom under a business name.

References in this Chapter to 'a person to whom this Chapter applies' are to such an individual or partnership.

(2) For the purposes of this Chapter a 'business name' means a name other than—

(a) in the case of an individual, his surname without any addition other than a permitted addition;

(b) in the case of a partnership—

(i) the surnames of all partners who are individuals, and

(ii) the corporate names of all partners who are bodies corporate,

without any addition other than a permitted addition.

(3) The following are the permitted additions—

(a) in the case of an individual, his forename or initial;

(b) in the case of a partnership—

(i) the forenames of individual partners or the initials of those forenames, or

(ii) where two or more individual partners have the same surname, the addition of 's' at the end of that surname;

(c) in either case, an addition merely indicating that the business is carried on in succession to a former owner of the business.

### 1201  Information required to be disclosed

The 'information required by this Chapter' is—

(a) in the case of an individual, his name;

(b) in the case of a partnership, the name of each member of the partnership;

and in relation to each person so named, an address in the United Kingdom at which service of any document relating in any way to the business will be effective.

### *Disclosure requirements*

### 1202  Disclosure required: business documents etc.

(1) A person to whom this Chapter applies must state the information required by this Chapter, in legible characters, on all—

(a) business letters,

(b) written orders for goods or services to be supplied to the business,

(c) invoices and receipts issued in the course of the business, and

(d) written demands for payment of debts arising in the course of the business.

This subsection has effect subject to section 1203 (exemption for large partnerships if certain conditions met).

(2) A person to whom this Chapter applies must secure that the information required by this Chapter is immediately given, by written notice, to any person with whom anything is done or discussed in the course of the business and who asks for that information.

(3) The Secretary of State may by regulations require that such notices be given in a specified form.

(4) Regulations under this section are subject to negative resolution procedure.

### 1203  Exemption for large partnerships if certain conditions met

(1) Section 1202(1) (disclosure required in business documents) does not apply in relation to a document issued by a partnership of more than 20 persons if the following conditions are met.

(2) The conditions are that—

    (a) the partnership maintains at its principal place of business a list of the names of all the partners,

    (b) no partner's name appears in the document, except in the text or as a signatory, and

    (c) the document states in legible characters the address of the partnership's principal place of business and that the list of the partners' names is open to inspection there.

(3) Where a partnership maintains a list of the partners' names for the purposes of this section, any person may inspect the list during office hours.

(4) Where an inspection required by a person in accordance with this section is refused, an offence is committed by any member of the partnership concerned who without reasonable excuse refused the inspection or permitted it to be refused.

(5) A person guilty of an offence under subsection (4) is liable on summary conviction to a fine not exceeding level 3 on the standard scale and, for continued contravention, a daily default fine not exceeding one-tenth of level 3 on the standard scale.

### 1204    Disclosure required: business premises

(1) A person to whom this Chapter applies must, in any premises—

    (a) where the business is carried on, and

    (b) to which customers of the business or suppliers of goods or services to the business have access,

display in a prominent position, so that it may easily be read by such customers or suppliers, a notice containing the information required by this Chapter.

(2) The Secretary of State may by regulations require that such notices be displayed in a specified form.

(3) Regulations under this section are subject to negative resolution procedure.

*Consequences of failure to make required disclosure*

### 1205    Criminal consequences of failure to make required disclosure

(1) A person who without reasonable excuse fails to comply with the requirements of—

section 1202 (disclosure required: business documents etc.), or

section 1204 (disclosure required: business premises), commits an offence.

(2) Where an offence under this section is committed by a body corporate, an offence is also committed by every officer of the body who is in default.

(3) A person guilty of an offence under this section is liable on summary conviction to a fine not exceeding level 3 on the standard scale and, for continued contravention, a daily default fine not exceeding one-tenth of level 3 on the standard scale.

(4) References in this section to the requirements of section 1202 or 1204 include the requirements of regulations under that section.

### 1206    Civil consequences of failure to make required disclosure

(1) This section applies to any legal proceedings brought by a person to whom this Chapter applies to enforce a right arising out of a contract made in the course of a business in respect of which he was, at the time the contract was made, in breach of section 1202(1) or (2) (disclosure in business documents etc.) or section 1204(1) (disclosure at business premises).

(2) The proceedings shall be dismissed if the defendant (in Scotland, the defender) to the proceedings shows—

    (a) that he has a claim against the claimant (pursuer) arising out of the contract that he has been unable to pursue by reason of the latter's breach of the requirements of this Chapter, or

    (b) that he has suffered some financial loss in connection with the contract by reason of the claimant's (pursuer's) breach of those requirements,

unless the court before which the proceedings are brought is satisfied that it is just and equitable to permit the proceedings to continue.

(3) References in this section to the requirements of this Chapter include the requirements of regulations under this Chapter.

(4) This section does not affect the right of any person to enforce such rights as he may have against another person in any proceedings brought by that person.

## Chapter 3   Supplementary

### 1207    Application of general provisions about offences

The provisions of sections 1121 to 1123 (liability of officer in default) and 1125 to 1131 (general provisions about offences) apply in relation to offences under this Part as in relation to offences under the Companies Acts.

### 1208    Interpretation

In this Part—

    'business' includes a profession;

'initial' includes any recognised abbreviation of a name;
'partnership' means—

(a) a partnership within the Partnership Act 1890 (c. 39), or

(b) a limited partnership registered under the Limited Partnerships Act 1907 (c. 24),

or a firm or entity of a similar character formed under the law of a country or territory outside the United Kingdom;

'surname', in relation to a peer or person usually known by a British title different from his surname, means the title by which he is known.

# PART 42    STATUTORY AUDITORS

## Chapter 1    Introductory

### 1209    Main purposes of Part

The main purposes of this Part are—

(a) to secure that only persons who are properly supervised and appropriately qualified are appointed as statutory auditors, and

(b) to secure that audits by persons so appointed are carried out properly, with integrity and with a proper degree of independence.

### 1210    Meaning of 'statutory auditor' etc

(1) In this Part 'statutory auditor' means—

(a) a person appointed as auditor under Part 16 of this Act,

(b) a person appointed as auditor under section 77 of or Schedule 11 to the Building Societies Act 1986 (c. 53),

(c) a person appointed as auditor of an insurer that is a friendly society under section 72 of or Schedule 14 to the Friendly Societies Act 1992 (c. 40),

(d) [ . . . ]

(e) a person appointed as auditor for the purposes of regulation 5 of the Insurance Accounts Directive (Lloyd's Syndicate and Aggregate Accounts) Regulations 2008 or appointed to report on the 'aggregate accounts' within the meaning of those Regulations,

(f) a person appointed as auditor of an insurance undertaking for the purposes of the Insurance Accounts Directive (Miscellaneous Insurance Undertakings) Regulations 2008,

(g) a person appointed as auditor of a bank for the purposes of the Bank Accounts Directive (Miscellaneous Banks) Regulations 2008,

(h) a person appointed as auditor of a prescribed person under a prescribed enactment authorising or requiring the appointment;

and the expressions 'statutory audit' and 'statutory audit work' are to be construed accordingly.

(2) In this Part 'audited person' means the person in respect of whom a statutory audit is conducted.

(3) In subsection (1)—

'bank' means a person who—

(a) is a credit institution within the meaning given by Article 4.1(a) of Directive 2006/48/EC of the European Parliament and of the Council relating to the taking up and pursuit of the business of credit institutions, and

(b) is a company or a firm as defined in Article 48 of the Treaty establishing the European Community;

'friendly society' means a friendly society within the meaning of the Friendly Societies Act 1992 (c. 40);

(a)–(b) [ . . . ]

'insurer' means a person who is an insurance undertaking within the meaning given by Article 2.1 of Council Directive 1991/674/EEC on the annual accounts and consolidated accounts of insurance undertakings;

'prescribed' means prescribed, or of a description prescribed, by order made by the Secretary of State for the purposes of subsection (1)(h).

(4) An order under this section is subject to negative resolution procedure.

### 1211    Eligibility for appointment as a statutory auditor: overview

A person is eligible for appointment as a statutory auditor only if the person is so eligible—

(a) by virtue of Chapter 2 (individuals and firms), or

(b) by virtue of Chapter 3 (Comptroller and Auditor General, etc).

## Chapter 2    Individuals and firms

*Eligibility for appointment*

### 1212    Individuals and firms: eligibility for appointment as a statutory auditor

(1) An individual or firm is eligible for appointment as a statutory auditor if the individual or firm—

(a) is a member of a recognised supervisory body, and

(b) is eligible for appointment under the rules of that body.

(2) In the cases to which section 1222 applies (individuals retaining only 1967 Act authorisation) a person's eligibility for appointment as a statutory auditor is restricted as mentioned in that section.

### 1213  Effect of ineligibility

(1) No person may act as statutory auditor of an audited person if he is ineligible for appointment as a statutory auditor.

(2) If at any time during his term of office a statutory auditor becomes ineligible for appointment as a statutory auditor, he must immediately—

(a) resign his office (with immediate effect), and

(b) give notice in writing to the audited person that he has resigned by reason of his becoming ineligible for appointment.

(3) A person is guilty of an offence if—

(a) he acts as a statutory auditor in contravention of subsection (1), or

(b) he fails to give the notice mentioned in paragraph (b) of subsection (2) in accordance with that subsection.

(4) A person guilty of an offence under subsection (3) is liable—

(a) on conviction on indictment, to a fine;

(b) on summary conviction, to a fine not exceeding the statutory maximum.

(5) A person is guilty of an offence if—

(a) he has been convicted of an offence under subsection (3)(a) or this subsection, and

(b) he continues to act as a statutory auditor in contravention of subsection (1) after the conviction.

(6) A person is guilty of an offence if—

(a) he has been convicted of an offence under subsection (3)(b) or this subsection, and

(b) he continues, after the conviction, to fail to give the notice mentioned in subsection (2)(b).

(7) A person guilty of an offence under subsection (5) or (6) is liable—

(a) on conviction on indictment, to a fine;

(b) on summary conviction, to a fine not exceeding one-tenth of the statutory maximum for each day on which the act or the failure continues.

(8) In proceedings against a person for an offence under this section it is a defence for him to show that he did not know and had no reason to believe that he was, or had become, ineligible for appointment as a statutory auditor.

*Independence requirement*

### 1214  Independence requirement

(1) A person may not act as statutory auditor of an audited person if one or more of subsections (2), (3) and (4) apply to him.

(2) This subsection applies if the person is—

(a) an officer or employee of the audited person, or

(b) a partner or employee of such a person, or a partnership of which such a person is a partner.

(3) This subsection applies if the person is—

(a) an officer or employee of an associated undertaking of the audited person, or

(b) a partner or employee of such a person, or a partnership of which such a person is a partner.

(4) This subsection applies if there exists, between—

(a) the person or an associate of his, and

(b) the audited person or an associated undertaking of the audited person,

a connection of any such description as may be specified by regulations made by the Secretary of State.

(5) An auditor of an audited person is not to be regarded as an officer or employee of the person for the purposes of subsections (2) and (3).

(6) In this section 'associated undertaking', in relation to an audited person, means—

(a) a parent undertaking or subsidiary undertaking of the audited person, or

(b) a subsidiary undertaking of a parent undertaking of the audited person.

(7) Regulations under subsection (4) are subject to negative resolution procedure.

### 1215  Effect of lack of independence

(1) If at any time during his term of office a statutory auditor becomes prohibited from acting by section 1214(1), he must immediately—

(a) resign his office (with immediate effect), and

(b) give notice in writing to the audited person that he has resigned by reason of his lack of independence.

(2) A person is guilty of an offence if—

(a) he acts as a statutory auditor in contravention of section 1214(1), or

(b) he fails to give the notice mentioned in paragraph (b) of subsection (1) in accordance with that subsection.

(3) A person guilty of an offence under subsection (2) is liable—

(a) on conviction on indictment, to a fine;

(b) on summary conviction, to a fine not exceeding the statutory maximum.

(4) A person is guilty of an offence if—

(a) he has been convicted of an offence under subsection (2)(a) or this subsection, and

(b) he continues to act as a statutory auditor in contravention of section 1214(1) after the conviction.

(5) A person is guilty of an offence if—

(a) he has been convicted of an offence under subsection (2)(b) or this subsection, and

(b) after the conviction, he continues to fail to give the notice mentioned in subsection (1)(b).

(6) A person guilty of an offence under subsection (4) or (5) is liable—

(a) on conviction on indictment, to a fine;

(b) on summary conviction, to a fine not exceeding one-tenth of the statutory maximum for each day on which the act or the failure continues.

(7) In proceedings against a person for an offence under this section it is a defence for him to show that he did not know and had no reason to believe that he was, or had become, prohibited from acting as statutory auditor of the audited person by section 1214(1).

### *Effect of appointment of a partnership*

### 1216 Effect of appointment of a partnership

(1) This section applies where a partnership constituted under the law of—

(a) England and Wales,

(b) Northern Ireland, or

(c) any other country or territory in which a partnership is not a legal person,

is by virtue of this Chapter appointed as statutory auditor of an audited person.

(2) Unless a contrary intention appears, the appointment is an appointment of the partnership as such and not of the partners.

(3) Where the partnership ceases, the appointment is to be treated as extending to—

(a) any appropriate partnership which succeeds to the practice of that partnership, or

(b) any other appropriate person who succeeds to that practice having previously carried it on in partnership.

(4) For the purposes of subsection (3)—

(a) a partnership is to be regarded as succeeding to the practice of another partnership only if the members of the successor partnership are substantially the same as those of the former partnership, and

(b) a partnership or other person is to be regarded as succeeding to the practice of a partnership only if it or he succeeds to the whole or substantially the whole of the business of the former partnership.

(5) Where the partnership ceases and the appointment is not treated under subsection (3) as extending to any partnership or other person, the appointment may with the consent of the audited person be treated as extending to an appropriate partnership, or other appropriate person, who succeeds to—

(a) the business of the former partnership, or

(b) such part of it as is agreed by the audited person is to be treated as comprising the appointment.

(6) For the purposes of this section, a partnership or other person is 'appropriate' if it or he—

(a) is eligible for appointment as a statutory auditor by virtue of this Chapter, and

(b) is not prohibited by section 1214(1) from acting as statutory auditor of the audited person.

### *Supervisory bodies*

### 1217 Supervisory bodies

(1) In this Part a 'supervisory body' means a body established in the United Kingdom (whether a body corporate or an unincorporated association) which maintains and enforces rules as to—

(a) the eligibility of persons for appointment as a statutory auditor, and

(b) the conduct of statutory audit work,

which are binding on persons seeking appointment or acting as a statutory auditor [...] because they are members of that body [...].

(1A) The rules referred to in paragraphs 9(3)(b) (confidentiality of information) and 10C(3)(a) and (b) (bar on appointment as director or other officer) of Schedule 10 must also be binding on persons who—

(a) have sought appointment or acted as a statutory auditor, and

(b) have been members of the body at any time after the commencement of this Part.

(2) In this Part references to the members of a supervisory body are to the persons who, whether or not members of the body, are subject to its rules in seeking appointment or acting as a statutory auditor.

(3) In this Part references to the rules of a supervisory body are to the rules (whether or not laid down by the body itself) which the body has power to enforce and which are relevant for the purposes of this Part.

This includes rules relating to the admission or expulsion of members of the body, so far as relevant for the purposes of this Part.

(4) Schedule 10 has effect with respect to the recognition of supervisory bodies for the purposes of this Part.

### 1218 Exemption from liability for damages

(1) No person within subsection (2) is to be liable in damages for anything done or omitted in the discharge or purported discharge of functions to which this subsection applies.

(2) The persons within this subsection are—
  (a) any recognised supervisory body,
  (b) any officer or employee of a recognised supervisory body, and
  (c) any member of the governing body of a recognised supervisory body.

(3) Subsection (1) applies to the functions of a recognised supervisory body so far as relating to, or to matters arising out of, any of the following—
  (a) rules, practices, powers and arrangements of the body to which the requirements of Part 2 of Schedule 10 apply;
  (b) the obligations with which paragraph 20 of that Schedule requires the body to comply;
  (c) any guidance issued by the body;
  (d) the obligations imposed on the body by or by virtue of this Part.

(4) The reference in subsection (3)(c) to guidance issued by a recognised supervisory body is a reference to any guidance or recommendation which is—
  (a) issued or made by it to all or any class of its members or persons seeking to become members, and
  (b) relevant for the purposes of this Part,
including any guidance or recommendation relating to the admission or expulsion of members of the body, so far as relevant for the purposes of this Part.

(5) Subsection (1) does not apply—
  (a) if the act or omission is shown to have been in bad faith, or
  (b) so as to prevent an award of damages in respect of the act or omission on the ground that it was unlawful as a result of section 6(1) of the Human Rights Act 1998 (c. 42) (acts of public authorities incompatible with Convention rights).

*Professional qualifications*

### 1219 Appropriate qualifications

(1) A person holds an appropriate qualification for the purposes of this Chapter if and only if—
  (a) he holds a recognised professional qualification obtained in the United Kingdom,
  (b) immediately before the commencement of this Chapter, he—
    (i) held an appropriate qualification for the purposes of Part 2 of the Companies Act 1989 (c. 40) (eligibility for appointment as company auditor) by virtue of section 31(1)(a) or (c) of that Act, or
    (ii) was treated as holding an appropriate qualification for those purposes by virtue of section 31(2), (3) or (4) of that Act,
  (c) immediately before the commencement of this Chapter, he—
    (i) held an appropriate qualification for the purposes of Part III of the Companies (Northern Ireland) Order 1990 (S.I. 1990/593 (N.I. 5)) by virtue of Article 34(1)(a) or (c) of that Order, or
    (ii) was treated as holding an appropriate qualification for those purposes by virtue of Article 34(2), (3) or (4) of that Order,
  (d) he is within subsection (2),or
  (e) [...]
  (f) subject to any direction under section 1221(5) , he is regarded for the purposes of this Chapter as holding an approved third country qualification.

(2) A person is within this subsection if—
  (a) before 1st January 1990, he began a course of study or practical training leading to a professional qualification in accountancy offered by a body established in the United Kingdom,
  (b) he obtained that qualification on or after 1st January 1990 and before 1st January 1996, and
  (c) the Secretary of State approves his qualification as an appropriate qualification for the purposes of this Chapter.

(3) The Secretary of State may approve a qualification under subsection (2)(c) only if he is satisfied that, at the time the qualification was awarded, the body concerned had adequate arrangements to ensure that the qualification was awarded only to persons educated and trained to a standard equivalent to that required, at that time, in the case of a recognised professional qualification under Part 2 of the Companies Act 1989 (c. 40) (eligibility for appointment as company auditor).

### 1220   Qualifying bodies and recognised professional qualifications

(1) In this Part a 'qualifying body' means a body established in the United Kingdom (whether a body corporate or an unincorporated association) which offers a professional qualification in accountancy.

(2) In this Part references to the rules of a qualifying body are to the rules (whether or not laid down by the body itself) which the body has power to enforce and which are relevant for the purposes of this Part.

This includes, so far as so relevant, rules relating to—

(a) admission to or expulsion from a course of study leading to a qualification,

(b) the award or deprivation of a qualification, or

(c) the approval of a person for the purposes of giving practical training or the withdrawal of such approval.

(3) Schedule 11 has effect with respect to the recognition for the purposes of this Part of a professional qualification offered by a qualifying body.

### 1221   Approval of third country qualifications

(1) The Secretary of State may declare that the following are to be regarded for the purposes of this Chapter as holding an approved third country qualification—

(a) persons who are qualified to audit accounts under the law of a specified third country, or

(b) persons who hold a specified professional qualification in accountancy obtained in a specified third country.

(1A) A declaration under subsection (1)(a) or (b) must be expressed to be subject to the requirement that any person to whom the declaration relates must pass an aptitude test in accordance with subsection (7A), unless an aptitude test is not required (see subsection (7B)).

(2) A declaration under subsection (1)(b) may be expressed to be subject to the satisfaction of any specified requirement or requirements.

(3) The Secretary of State may make a declaration under subsection (1) only if he is satisfied that—

(a) in the case of a declaration under subsection (1)(a), the fact that the persons in question are qualified to audit accounts under the law of the specified third country, or

(b) in the case of a declaration under subsection (1)(b), the specified professional qualification taken with any requirement or requirements to be specified under subsection (2),

affords an assurance of professional competence equivalent to that afforded by a recognised professional qualification.

(4) The Secretary of State may make a declaration under subsection (1) only if he is satisfied that the treatment that the persons who are the subject of the declaration will receive as a result of it is comparable to the treatment which is, or is likely to be, afforded in the specified third country or a part of it to—

(a) in the case of a declaration under subsection (1)(a), some or all persons who are eligible to be appointed as a statutory auditor, and

(b) in the case of a declaration under subsection (1)(b), some or all persons who hold a corresponding recognised professional qualification.

(5) The Secretary of State may direct that persons holding an approved third country qualification are not to be treated as holding an appropriate qualification for the purposes of this Chapter unless they hold such additional educational qualifications as the Secretary of State may specify for the purpose of ensuring that such persons have an adequate knowledge of the law and practice in the United Kingdom relevant to the audit of accounts.

(6) The Secretary of State may give different directions in relation to different approved third country qualifications.

(7) The Secretary of State may, if he thinks fit, having regard to the considerations mentioned in subsections (3) and (4), withdraw a declaration under subsection (1) in relation to—

(a) persons becoming qualified to audit accounts under the law of the specified third country after such date as he may specify, or

(b) persons obtaining the specified professional qualification after such date as he may specify.

(7A) An aptitude test required for the purposes of subsection (1A)—

(a) must test the person's knowledge of subjects—

(i) that are covered by a recognised professional qualification,

(ii) that are not covered by the professional qualification already held by the person, and

(iii) the knowledge of which is essential for the pursuit of the profession of statutory auditor;

(b) may test the person's knowledge of rules of professional conduct;

(c) must not test the person's knowledge of any other matters.

(7B) No aptitude test is required for the purposes of subsection (1A) if the subjects that are covered by a recognised professional qualification and the knowledge of which is essential for the pursuit of the profession of statutory auditor are covered by the professional qualification already held by the person.

(8) The Secretary of State may, if he thinks fit, having regard to the considerations mentioned in subsections (3) and (4), vary or revoke a requirement specified under subsection (2) from such date as he may specify.

(9) [...]

## 1222    Eligibility of individuals retaining only 1967 Act authorisation

(1) A person whose only appropriate qualification is based on his retention of an authorisation originally granted by the Board of Trade or the Secretary of State under section 13(1) of the Companies Act 1967 (c. 81) is eligible only for appointment as auditor of an unquoted company.

(2) A company is 'unquoted' if, at the time of the person's appointment, neither the company, nor any parent undertaking of which it is a subsidiary undertaking, is a quoted company within the meaning of section 385(2).

(3) References to a person eligible for appointment as a statutory auditor by virtue of this Part in enactments relating to eligibility for appointment as auditor of a person other than a company do not include a person to whom this section applies.

### *Information*

## 1223    Matters to be notified to the Secretary of State

(1) The Secretary of State may require a recognised supervisory body or a recognised qualifying body—

(a) to notify him immediately of the occurrence of such events as he may specify in writing and to give him such information in respect of those events as is so specified;

(b) to give him, at such times or in respect of such periods as he may specify in writing, such information as is so specified.

(2) The notices and information required to be given must be such as the Secretary of State may reasonably require for the exercise of his functions under this Part.

(3) The Secretary of State may require information given under this section to be given in a specified form or verified in a specified manner.

(4) Any notice or information required to be given under this section must be given in writing unless the Secretary of State specifies or approves some other manner.

## 1223A    Notification of matters relevant to other EEA States

(1) A recognised supervisory body must notify the Secretary of State of—

(a) any withdrawal of a notifiable person's eligibility for appointment as a statutory auditor; and

(b) the reasons for the withdrawal.

(2) A recognised supervisory body must also notify the Secretary of State of any reasonable grounds it has for suspecting that—

(a) a person has contravened the law of the United Kingdom, or any other EEA State or part of an EEA State, implementing the Audit Directive, and

(b) the act or omission constituting that contravention took place on the territory of an EEA State other than the United Kingdom.

(3) In this section 'notifiable person' means a member of the recognised supervisory body in question—

(a) who is also an EEA auditor; and

(b) in respect of whom the EEA competent authority is not the recognised supervisory body itself.

## 1224    The Secretary of State's power to call for information

(1) The Secretary of State may by notice in writing require a person within subsection (2) to give him such information as he may reasonably require for the exercise of his functions under this Part.

(2) The persons within this subsection are—

(a) any recognised supervisory body,

(b) any recognised qualifying body, and

(c) any person eligible for appointment as a statutory auditor by virtue of this Chapter.

(3) The Secretary of State may require that any information which he requires under this section is to be given within such reasonable time and verified in such manner as he may specify.

### 1224A   Restrictions on disclosure

(1) This section applies to information (in whatever form)—

    (a) relating to the private affairs of an individual, or

    (b) relating to any particular business,

that is provided to a body to which this section applies in connection with the exercise of its functions under this Part or sections 522 to 524 (notification to appropriate audit authority of resignation or removal of auditor).

(2) This section applies to—

    (a) a recognised supervisory body,

    (b) a recognised qualifying body,

    (c) a body performing functions for the purposes of arrangements within paragraph 23(1) (independent monitoring of certain audits) or paragraph 24(1) (independent investigation of public interest cases) of Schedule 10,

    (d) the Independent Supervisor,

    (e) the Secretary of State, and

    (f) a body designated by the Secretary of State under section 1252 (delegation of the Secretary of State's functions).

(3) No such information may, during the lifetime of the individual or so long as the business continues to be carried on, be disclosed without the consent of that individual or (as the case may be) the person for the time being carrying on that business.

(4) Subsection (3) does not apply to any disclosure of information that—

    (a) is made for the purpose of facilitating the carrying out by the body of any of its functions,

    (b) is made to a person specified in Part 1 of Schedule 11A,

    (c) is of a description specified in Part 2 of that Schedule, or

    (d) is made in accordance with Part 3 of that Schedule.

(5) Subsection (3) does not apply to—

    (a) the disclosure by an EEA competent authority of information disclosed to it by the body in reliance on subsection (4);

    (b) the disclosure of such information by anyone who has obtained it directly or indirectly from an EEA competent authority.

(6) This section does not prohibit the disclosure of information if the information is or has been available to the public from any other source.

(7) Nothing in this section authorises the making of a disclosure in contravention of the Data Protection Act 1998.

### 1224B   Offence of disclosure in contravention of section 1224A

(1) A person who discloses information in contravention of section 1224A (restrictions on disclosure) is guilty of an offence, unless—

    (a) he did not know, and had no reason to suspect, that the information had been provided as mentioned in section 1224A(1), or

    (b) he took all reasonable steps and exercised all due diligence to avoid the commission of the offence.

(2) A person guilty of an offence under this section is liable—

    (a) on conviction on indictment, to imprisonment for a term not exceeding two years or a fine (or both);

    (b) on summary conviction—

        (i) in Scotland, to imprisonment for a term not exceeding 12 months or to a fine not exceeding the statutory maximum, or to both;

        (ii) in England and Wales or Northern Ireland, to imprisonment for a term not exceeding three months or to a fine not exceeding the statutory maximum, or to both.

*Enforcement*

### 1225   Compliance orders

(1) If at any time it appears to the Secretary of State—

    (a) in the case of a recognised supervisory body, that any requirement of Schedule 10 is not satisfied,

    (b) in the case of a recognised professional qualification, that any requirement of Schedule 11 is not satisfied, or

    (c) that a recognised supervisory body or a recognised qualifying body has failed to comply with an obligation to which it is subject under or by virtue of this Part,

he may, instead of revoking the relevant recognition order, make an application to the court under this section.

(2) If on an application under this section the court decides that the requirement in question is not satisfied or, as the case may be, that the body has failed to comply with the obligation in question, it may order the body to take such steps as the court directs for securing that the requirement is satisfied or that the obligation is complied with.

(3) In this section 'the court' means the High Court or, in Scotland, the Court of Session.

## Chapter 3    Auditors general

*Eligibility for appointment*

### 1226    Auditors General: eligibility for appointment as a statutory auditor

(1) In this Part 'Auditor General' means—

    (a) the Comptroller and Auditor General,

    (b) the Auditor General for Scotland,

    (c) the Auditor General for Wales, or

    (d) the Comptroller and Auditor General for Northern Ireland.

(2) An Auditor General is eligible for appointment as a statutory auditor.

(3) Subsection (2) is subject to any suspension notice having effect under section 1234 (notices suspending eligibility for appointment as a statutory auditor).

*Conduct of audits*

### 1227    Individuals responsible for audit work on behalf of Auditors General

An Auditor General must secure that each individual responsible for statutory audit work on behalf of that Auditor General is eligible for appointment as a statutory auditor by virtue of Chapter 2.

*The Independent Supervisor*

### 1228    Appointment of the Independent Supervisor

(1) The Secretary of State must appoint a body ('the Independent Supervisor') to discharge the function mentioned in section 1229(1) ('the supervision function').

(2) An appointment under this section must be made by order.

(3) The order has the effect of making the body appointed under subsection (1) designated under section 5 of the Freedom of Information Act 2000 (c. 36) (further powers to designate public authorities).

(4) A body may be appointed under this section only if it is a body corporate or an unincorporated association which appears to the Secretary of State—

    (a) to be willing and able to discharge the supervision function, and

    (b) to have arrangements in place relating to the discharge of that function which are such as to be likely to ensure that the conditions in subsection (5) are met.

(5) The conditions are—

    (a) that the supervision function will be exercised effectively, and

    (b) where the order is to contain any requirements or other provisions specified under subsection (6), that that function will be exercised in accordance with any such requirements or provisions.

(6) An order under this section may contain such requirements or other provisions relating to the exercise of the supervision function by the Independent Supervisor as appear to the Secretary of State to be appropriate.

(7) An order under this section is subject to negative resolution procedure.

*Supervision of Auditors General*

### 1229    Supervision of Auditors General by the Independent Supervisor

(1) The Independent Supervisor must supervise the performance by each Auditor General of his functions as a statutory auditor.

(2) The Independent Supervisor must discharge that duty by—

    (a) establishing supervision arrangements itself, or

    (b) entering into supervision arrangements with one or more bodies.

(2A) If the Independent Supervisor enters into supervision arrangements with one or more bodies, it must oversee the effective operation of those supervision arrangements.

(3) For this purpose 'supervision arrangements' are arrangements established by the Independent Supervisor or entered into by the Independent Supervisor with a body, for the purposes of this section, in accordance with which the Independent Supervisor or the body does [ . . . ] the following—

    (a) determines standards relating to professional integrity and independence which must be applied by an Auditor General in statutory audit work;

    (b) determines technical standards which must be applied by an Auditor General in statutory audit work and the manner in which those standards are to be applied in practice;

    (c) monitors the performance of statutory audits carried out by an Auditor General;

    (d) investigates any matter arising from the performance by an Auditor General of a statutory audit;

    (e) holds disciplinary hearings in respect of an Auditor General which appear to be desirable following the conclusion of such investigations;

    (f) decides whether (and, if so, what) disciplinary action should be taken against an Auditor General to whom such a hearing related.

(3A) The requirements of paragraphs 9 to 10A and 12 to 15 of Schedule 10 (requirements for recognition of a supervisory body) apply in relation to supervision arrangements as they apply in relation to the rules, practices and arrangements of supervisory bodies.

(4) The Independent Supervisor may enter into supervision arrangements with a body despite any relationship that may exist between the Independent Supervisor and that body.

(5) The Independent Supervisor must notify each Auditor General in writing of any supervision arrangements that it establishes or enters into under this section.

(5A) The Independent Supervisor must, at least once in every calendar year, deliver to the Secretary of State a summary of the results of any inspections conducted for the purposes of subsection (3)(c).

(6) Supervision arrangements within subsection (3)(f) may, in particular, provide for the payment by an Auditor General of a fine to any person.

(7) Any fine received by the Independent Supervisor under supervision arrangements is to be paid into the Consolidated Fund.

### 1230   Duties of Auditors General in relation to supervision arrangements

(1) Each Auditor General must—
- (a) comply with any standards of the kind mentioned in subsection (3)(a) or (b) of section 1229 determined under the supervision arrangements,
- (b) take such steps as may be reasonably required of that Auditor General to enable his performance of statutory audits to be monitored by means of inspections carried out under the supervision arrangements, and
- (c) comply with any decision of the kind mentioned in subsection (3)(f) of that section made under the supervision arrangements.

(2) Each Auditor General must—
- (a) if the Independent Supervisor has established supervision arrangements, pay to the Independent Supervisor;
- (b) if the Independent Supervisor has entered into supervision arrangements with a body, pay to that body,

such proportion of the costs incurred by the Independent Supervisor or body for the purposes of the arrangements as the Independent Supervisor may notify to him in writing.

(3) Expenditure under subsection (2) is—
- (a) in the case of expenditure of the Comptroller and Auditor General, to be regarded as expenditure of the National Audit Office for the purposes of section 4(1) of the National Audit Act 1983 (c. 44);
- (b) in the case of expenditure of the Comptroller and Auditor General for Northern Ireland, to be regarded as expenditure of the Northern Ireland Audit Office for the purposes of Article 6(1) of the Audit (Northern Ireland) Order 1987 (S.I. 1987/460 (N.I. 5)).

(4) In this section 'the supervision arrangements' means the arrangements established or entered into under section 1229.

*Reporting requirement*

### 1231   Reports by the Independent Supervisor

(1) The Independent Supervisor must, at least once in each calendar year, prepare a report on the discharge of its functions.

(2) The Independent Supervisor must give a copy of each report prepared under subsection (1) to—
- (a) the Secretary of State;
- (b) the First Minister in Scotland;
- (c) the First Minister and the deputy First Minister in Northern Ireland;
- (d) the Assembly First Secretary in Wales.

(3) The Secretary of State must lay before each House of Parliament a copy of each report received by him under subsection (2)(a).

(4) In relation to a calendar year during which an appointment of a body as the Independent Supervisor is made or revoked by an order under section 1228, this section applies with such modifications as may be specified in the order.

*Information*

### 1232   Matters to be notified to the Independent Supervisor

(1) The Independent Supervisor may require an Auditor General—
- (a) to notify the Independent Supervisor immediately of the occurrence of such events as it may specify in writing and to give it such information in respect of those events as is so specified;
- (b) to give the Independent Supervisor, at such times or in respect of such periods as it may specify in writing, such information as is so specified.

(2) The notices and information required to be given must be such as the Independent Supervisor may reasonably require for the exercise of the functions conferred on it by or by virtue of this Part.

(3) The Independent Supervisor may require information given under this section to be given in a specified form or verified in a specified manner.

(4) Any notice or information required to be given under this section must be given in writing unless the Independent Supervisor specifies or approves some other manner.

### 1233 The Independent Supervisor's power to call for information

(1) The Independent Supervisor may by notice in writing require an Auditor General to give it such information as it may reasonably require for the exercise of the functions conferred on it by or by virtue of this Part.

(2) The Independent Supervisor may require that any information which it requires under this section is to be given within such reasonable time and verified in such manner as it may specify.

*Enforcement*

### 1234 Suspension notices

(1) The Independent Supervisor may issue—
  (a) a notice (a 'suspension notice') suspending an Auditor General's eligibility for appointment as a statutory auditor in relation to all persons, or any specified person or persons, indefinitely or until a date specified in the notice;
  (b) a notice amending or revoking a suspension notice previously issued to an Auditor General.

(2) In determining whether it is appropriate to issue a notice under subsection (1), the Independent Supervisor must have regard to—
  (a) the Auditor General's performance of the obligations imposed on him by or by virtue of this Part, and
  (b) the Auditor General's performance of his functions as a statutory auditor.

(3) A notice under subsection (1) must—
  (a) be in writing, and
  (b) state the date on which it takes effect (which must be after the period of three months beginning with the date on which it is issued).

(4) Before issuing a notice under subsection (1), the Independent Supervisor must—
  (a) give written notice of its intention to do so to the Auditor General, and
  (b) publish the notice mentioned in paragraph (a) in such manner as it thinks appropriate for bringing it to the attention of any other persons who are likely to be affected.

(5) A notice under subsection (4) must—
  (a) state the reasons for which the Independent Supervisor proposes to act, and
  (b) give particulars of the rights conferred by subsection (6).

(6) A person within subsection (7) may, within the period of three months beginning with the date of service or publication of the notice under subsection (4) or such longer period as the Independent Supervisor may allow, make written representations to the Independent Supervisor and, if desired, oral representations to a person appointed for that purpose by the Independent Supervisor.

(7) The persons within this subsection are—
  (a) the Auditor General, and
  (b) any other person who appears to the Independent Supervisor to be affected.

(8) The Independent Supervisor must have regard to any representations made in accordance with subsection (6) in determining—
  (a) whether to issue a notice under subsection (1), and
  (b) the terms of any such notice.

(9) If in any case the Independent Supervisor considers it appropriate to do so in the public interest it may issue a notice under subsection (1), without regard to the restriction in subsection (3)(b), even if—
  (a) no notice has been given or published under subsection (4), or
  (b) the period of time for making representations in pursuance of such a notice has not expired.

(10) On issuing a notice under subsection (1), the Independent Supervisor must—
  (a) give a copy of the notice to the Auditor General, and
  (b) publish the notice in such manner as it thinks appropriate for bringing it to the attention of persons likely to be affected.

(11) In this section 'specified' means specified in, or of a description specified in, the suspension notice in question.

### 1235 Effect of suspension notices

(1) An Auditor General must not act as a statutory auditor at any time when a suspension notice issued to him in respect of the audited person has effect.

(2) If at any time during an Auditor General's term of office as a statutory auditor a suspension notice issued to him in respect of the audited person takes effect, he must immediately—
  (a) resign his office (with immediate effect), and
  (b) give notice in writing to the audited person that he has resigned by reason of his becoming ineligible for appointment.

(3) A suspension notice does not make an Auditor General ineligible for appointment as a statutory auditor for the purposes of section 1213 (effect of ineligibility: criminal offences).

### 1236  Compliance orders

(1) If at any time it appears to the Independent Supervisor that an Auditor General has failed to comply with an obligation imposed on him by or by virtue of this Part, the Independent Supervisor may make an application to the court under this section.

(2) If on an application under this section the court decides that the Auditor General has failed to comply with the obligation in question, it may order the Auditor General to take such steps as the court directs for securing that the obligation is complied with.

(3) In this section 'the court' means the High Court or, in Scotland, the Court of Session.

*Proceedings*

### 1237  Proceedings involving the Independent Supervisor

(1) If the Independent Supervisor is an unincorporated association, any relevant proceedings may be brought by or against it in the name of any body corporate whose constitution provides for the establishment of the body.

(2) For this purpose 'relevant proceedings' means proceedings brought in or in connection with the exercise of any function by the body as the Independent Supervisor.

(3) Where an appointment under section 1228 is revoked, the revoking order may make such provision as the Secretary of State thinks fit with respect to pending proceedings.

*Grants*

### 1238  Grants to the Independent Supervisor

In section 16 of the Companies (Audit, Investigations and Community Enterprise) Act 2004 (c. 27) (grants to bodies concerned with accounting standards etc), after subsection (2)(k) insert—

'(ka) exercising functions of the Independent Supervisor appointed under Chapter 3 of Part 42 of the Companies Act 2006;'.

## Chapter 4    The register of auditors etc

### 1239  The register of auditors

(1) The Secretary of State must make regulations requiring the keeping of a register of—
  (a) the persons eligible for appointment as a statutory auditor, and
  (b) third country auditors (see Chapter 5) who apply to be registered in the specified manner and in relation to whom specified requirements are met.

(2) The regulations must require each person's entry in the register to contain—
  (a) his name and address,
  (b) in the case of an individual eligible for appointment as a statutory auditor, the specified information relating to any firm on whose behalf he is responsible for statutory audit work,
  (c) in the case of a firm eligible for appointment as a statutory auditor, the specified information relating to the individuals responsible for statutory audit work on its behalf,
  (d) in the case of an individual or firm eligible for appointment as a statutory auditor by virtue of Chapter 2 , the name of the relevant supervisory body,
  (e) in the case of a firm eligible for appointment as a statutory auditor by virtue of Chapter 2 [ . . . ] the information mentioned in subsection (3), and
  (f) in the case of a third country auditor which is a firm, the name and address of each person who is—
    (i)  an owner or shareholder of the firm, or
    (ii)  a member of the firm's administrative or management body,
and may require each person's entry to contain other specified information.

(3) The information referred to in subsection (2)(e) is—
  (a) in relation to a body corporate, except where paragraph (b) applies, the name and address of each person who is a director of the body or holds any shares in it;
  (b) in relation to a limited liability partnership, the name and address of each member of the partnership;
  (c) in relation to a corporation sole, the name and address of the individual for the time being holding the office by the name of which he is the corporation sole;
  (d) in relation to a partnership, the name and address of each partner.

(4) The regulations may provide that different parts of the register are to be kept by different persons.

(5) The regulations may impose such obligations as the Secretary of State thinks fit on—
  (a) recognised supervisory bodies,
  (b) any body designated by order under section 1252 (delegation of Secretary of State's functions),
  (c) persons eligible for appointment as a statutory auditor,

(d) third country auditors,

(e) any person with whom arrangements are made by one or more recognised supervisory bodies, or by any body designated by order under section 1252, with respect to the keeping of the register, or

(f) the Independent Supervisor appointed under section 1228.

(6) The regulations may include—

(a) provision requiring that specified entries in the register be open to inspection at times and places specified or determined in accordance with the regulations;

(b) provision enabling a person to require a certified copy of specified entries in the register;

(c) provision authorising the charging of fees for inspection, or the provision of copies, of such reasonable amount as may be specified or determined in accordance with the regulations.

(7) The Secretary of State may direct in writing that the requirements imposed by the regulations [...], or such of those requirements as are specified in the direction, are not to apply, in whole or in part, in relation to a particular registered third country auditor or class of registered third country auditors.

(8) The obligations imposed by regulations under this section on such persons as are mentioned in subsection (5)(b) or (e) are enforceable on the application of the Secretary of State by injunction or, in Scotland, by an order under section 45 of the Court of Session Act 1988 (c. 36).

(9) In this section 'specified' means specified by regulations under this section.

(10) Regulations under this section are subject to negative resolution procedure.

### 1240    Information to be made available to public

(1) The Secretary of State may make regulations requiring a person eligible for appointment as a statutory auditor, or a member of a specified class of such persons, to keep and make available to the public specified information, including information regarding—

(a) the person's ownership and governance,

(b) the person's internal controls with respect to the quality and independence of its audit work,

(c) the person's turnover, and

(d) the audited persons of whom the person has acted as statutory auditor.

(2) Regulations under this section may—

(a) impose such obligations as the Secretary of State thinks fit on persons eligible for appointment as a statutory auditor;

(b) require the information to be made available to the public in a specified manner.

(3) In this section 'specified' means specified by regulations under this section.

(4) Regulations under this section are subject to negative resolution procedure.

## Chapter 5    Registered third country auditors

*Introductory*

### 1241    Meaning of 'registered third country auditor' and 'UK-traded non-EEA company'

(1) In this Part—

'registered third country auditor' means a third country auditor who is entered in the register kept in accordance with regulations under section 1239(1).

(2) In this Part 'UK-traded non-EEA company' means a body corporate—

(a) which is incorporated or formed under the law of a third country,

(b) whose transferable securities are admitted to trading on a regulated market situated or operating in the United Kingdom, and

(c) which has not been excluded, or is not of a description of bodies corporate which has been excluded, from this definition by an order made by the Secretary of State.

(3) For this purpose—

'regulated market' has the meaning given by Article 4.1(14) of Directive 2004/39/EC of the European Parliament and of the Council on markets in financial instruments;

'transferable securities' has the meaning given by Article 4.1(18) of that Directive.

(4) An order under this section is subject to negative resolution procedure.

*Duties*

### 1242    Duties of registered third country auditors

(1) A registered third country auditor who audits the accounts of a UK-traded non-EEA company must participate in—

(a) arrangements within paragraph 1 of Schedule 12 (arrangements for independent monitoring of audits [...]), and

(b) arrangements within paragraph 2 of that Schedule (arrangements for independent investigation for disciplinary purposes of public interest cases).

(2) A registered third country auditor must—
(a) take such steps as may be reasonably required of it to enable its performance of audits of accounts of UK-traded non-EEA companies to be monitored by means of inspections carried out under the arrangements mentioned in subsection (1)(a), and
(b) comply with any decision as to disciplinary action to be taken against it made under the arrangements mentioned in subsection (1)(b).

(3) Schedule 12 makes further provision with respect to the arrangements in which registered third country auditors are required to participate.

(4) The Secretary of State may direct in writing that subsections (1) to (3) are not to apply, in whole or in part, in relation to a particular registered third country auditor or class of registered third country auditors.

*Information*

**1243   Matters to be notified to the Secretary of State**
(1) The Secretary of State may require a registered third country auditor—
(a) to notify him immediately of the occurrence of such events as he may specify in writing and to give him such information in respect of those events as is so specified;
(b) to give him, at such times or in respect of such periods as he may specify in writing, such information as is so specified.

(2) The notices and information required to be given must be such as the Secretary of State may reasonably require for the exercise of his functions under this Part.

(3) The Secretary of State may require information given under this section to be given in a specified form or verified in a specified manner.

(4) Any notice or information required to be given under this section must be given in writing unless the Secretary of State specifies or approves some other manner.

**1244   The Secretary of State's power to call for information**
(1) The Secretary of State may by notice in writing require a registered third country auditor to give him such information as he may reasonably require for the exercise of his functions under this Part.

(2) The Secretary of State may require that any information which he requires under this section is to be given within such reasonable time and verified in such manner as he may specify.

*Enforcement*

**1245   Compliance orders**
(1) If at any time it appears to the Secretary of State that a registered third country auditor has failed to comply with an obligation imposed on him by or by virtue of this Part, the Secretary of State may make an application to the court under this section.

(2) If on an application under this section the court decides that the auditor has failed to comply with the obligation in question, it may order the auditor to take such steps as the court directs for securing that the obligation is complied with.

(3) In this section 'the court' means the High Court or, in Scotland, the Court of Session.

**1246   Removal of third country auditors from the register of auditors**
(1) The Secretary of State may, by regulations, confer on the person keeping the register in accordance with regulations under section 1239(1) power to remove a third country auditor from the register.

(2) Regulations under this section must require the person keeping the register, in determining whether to remove a third country auditor from the register, to have regard to the auditor's compliance with obligations imposed on him by or by virtue of this Part.

(3) Where provision is made under section 1239(4) (different parts of the register to be kept by different persons), references in this section to the person keeping the register are to the person keeping that part of the register which relates to third country auditors.

(4) Regulations under this section are subject to negative resolution procedure.

**1247   Grants to bodies concerned with arrangements under Schedule 12**
In section 16 of the Companies (Audit, Investigations and Community Enterprise) Act 2004 (c. 27) (grants to bodies concerned with accounting standards etc), after subsection (2)(ka) (inserted by section 1238) insert—

'(kb) establishing, maintaining or carrying out arrangements within paragraph 1 or 2 of Schedule 12 to the Companies Act 2006;'.

## Chapter 6   Supplementary and general

*Power to require second company audit*

**1248   Secretary of State's power to require second audit of a company**
(1) This section applies where a person appointed as statutory auditor of a company was not an appropriate person for any part of the period during which the audit was conducted.

(2) The Secretary of State may direct the company concerned to retain an appropriate person—

    (a) to conduct a second audit of the relevant accounts, or

    (b) to review the first audit and to report (giving his reasons) whether a second audit is needed.

(3) For the purposes of subsections (1) and (2) a person is 'appropriate' if he—

    (a) is eligible for appointment as a statutory auditor or, if the person is an Auditor General, for appointment as statutory auditor of the company, and

    (b) is not prohibited by section 1214(1) (independence requirement) from acting as statutory auditor of the company.

(4) The Secretary of State must send a copy of a direction under subsection (2) to the registrar of companies.

(5) The company is guilty of an offence if—

    (a) it fails to comply with a direction under subsection (2) within the period of 21 days beginning with the date on which it is given, or

    (b) it has been convicted of a previous offence under this subsection and the failure to comply with the direction which led to the conviction continues after the conviction.

(6) The company must—

    (a) send a copy of a report under subsection (2)(b) to the registrar of companies, and

    (b) if the report states that a second audit is needed, take such steps as are necessary for the carrying out of that audit.

(7) The company is guilty of an offence if—

    (a) it fails to send a copy of a report under subsection (2)(b) to the registrar within the period of 21 days beginning with the date on which it receives it,

    (b) in a case within subsection (6)(b), it fails to take the steps mentioned immediately it receives the report, or

    (c) it has been convicted of a previous offence under this subsection and the failure to send a copy of the report, or take the steps, which led to the conviction continues after the conviction.

(8) A company guilty of an offence under this section is liable on summary conviction—

    (a) in a case within subsection (5)(a) or (7)(a) or (b), to a fine not exceeding level 5 on the standard scale, and

    (b) in a case within subsection (5)(b) or (7)(c), to a fine not exceeding one-tenth of level 5 on the standard scale for each day on which the failure continues.

(9) In this section 'registrar of companies' has the meaning given by section 1060.

### 1249 Supplementary provision about second audits

(1) If a person accepts an appointment, or continues to act, as statutory auditor of a company at a time when he knows he is not an appropriate person, the company may recover from him any costs incurred by it in complying with the requirements of section 1248.

For this purpose 'appropriate' is to be construed in accordance with subsection (3) of that section.

(2) Where a second audit is carried out under section 1248, any statutory or other provision applying in relation to the first audit applies also, in so far as practicable, in relation to the second audit.

(3) A direction under section 1248(2) is, on the application of the Secretary of State, enforceable by injunction or, in Scotland, by an order under section 45 of the Court of Session Act 1988 (c. 36).

*False and misleading statements*

### 1250 Misleading, false and deceptive statements

(1) A person is guilty of an offence if—

    (a) for the purposes of or in connection with any application under this Part, or

    (b) in purported compliance with any requirement imposed on him by or by virtue of this Part,

he knowingly or recklessly furnishes information which is misleading, false or deceptive in a material particular.

(2) It is an offence for a person whose name does not appear on the register of auditors kept under regulations under section 1239 in an entry made under subsection (1)(a) of that section to describe himself as a registered auditor or so to hold himself out as to indicate, or be reasonably understood to indicate, that he is a registered auditor.

(3) It is an offence for a person whose name does not appear on the register of auditors kept under regulations under that section in an entry made under subsection (1)(b) of that section to describe himself as a registered third country auditor or so to hold himself out as to indicate, or be reasonably understood to indicate, that he is a registered third country auditor.

(4) It is an offence for a body which is not a recognised supervisory body or a recognised qualifying body to describe itself as so recognised or so to describe itself or hold itself out as to indicate, or be reasonably understood to indicate, that it is so recognised.

(5) A person guilty of an offence under subsection (1) is liable—

    (a) on conviction on indictment, to imprisonment for a term not exceeding two years or to a fine (or both);

(b) on summary conviction—
    (i)  in England and Wales, to imprisonment for a term not exceeding twelve months or to a fine not exceeding the statutory maximum (or both),
    (ii)  in Scotland or Northern Ireland, to imprisonment for a term not exceeding six months or to a fine not exceeding the statutory maximum (or both).

In relation to an offence committed before the commencement of section 154(1) of the Criminal Justice Act 2003 (c. 44), for 'twelve months' in paragraph (b)(i) substitute 'six months'.

(6) Subject to subsection (7), a person guilty of an offence under subsection (2), (3) or (4) is liable on summary conviction—
    (a)  in England and Wales, to imprisonment for a term not exceeding 51 weeks or to a fine not exceeding level 5 on the standard scale (or both),
    (b)  in Scotland or Northern Ireland, to imprisonment for a term not exceeding six months or to a fine not exceeding level 5 on the standard scale (or both).

In relation to an offence committed before the commencement of section 281(5) of the Criminal Justice Act 2003, for '51 weeks' in paragraph (a) substitute 'six months'.

(7) Where a contravention of subsection (2), (3) or (4) involves a public display of the offending description, the maximum fine that may be imposed is an amount equal to level 5 on the standard scale multiplied by the number of days for which the display has continued.

(8) It is a defence for a person charged with an offence under subsection (2), (3) or (4) to show that he took all reasonable precautions and exercised all due diligence to avoid the commission of the offence.

*Fees*

### 1251   Fees

(1) An applicant for a recognition order under this Part must pay such fee in respect of his application as the Secretary of State may by regulations prescribe; and no application is to be regarded as duly made unless this subsection is complied with.

(2) The Secretary of State may by regulations prescribe periodical fees to be paid by—
    (a)  every recognised supervisory body,
    (b)  every recognised qualifying body,
    (c)  every Auditor General, and
    (d)  every registered third country auditor.

(3) Fees received by the Secretary of State by virtue of this Part are to be paid into the Consolidated Fund.

(4) Regulations under this section are subject to negative resolution procedure.

*Duty of Secretary of State to report on inspections*

### 1251A   Duty of the Secretary of State to report on inspections

The Secretary of State must, at least once in every calendar year, publish a report containing a summary of the results of inspections that are delivered to him—
    (a)  by the Independent Supervisor under section 1229(5A);
    (b)  by a recognised supervisory body under paragraph 13(9) of Schedule 10.

*Delegation of Secretary of State's functions*

### 1252   Delegation of the Secretary of State's functions

(1) The Secretary of State may make an order under this section (a 'delegation order') for the purpose of enabling functions of the Secretary of State under this Part to be exercised by a body designated by the order.

(2) The body designated by a delegation order may be either—
    (a)  a body corporate which is established by the order, or
    (b)  subject to section 1253, a body (whether a body corporate or an unincorporated association) which is already in existence ('an existing body').

(3) A delegation order has the effect of making the body designated by the order designated under section 5 of the Freedom of Information Act 2000 (c. 36) (further powers to designate public authorities).

(4) A delegation order has the effect of transferring to the body designated by it all functions of the Secretary of State under this Part—
    (a)  subject to such exceptions and reservations as may be specified in the order, and
    (b)  except—
      (i)  his functions in relation to the body itself, and
      (ii)  his functions under section 1228 (appointment of Independent Supervisor).

(5) A delegation order may confer on the body designated by it such other functions supplementary or incidental to those transferred as appear to the Secretary of State to be appropriate.

(6) Any transfer of functions under the following provisions must be subject to the reservation that the functions remain exercisable concurrently by the Secretary of State—

(a) section 1224 (power to call for information from recognised bodies etc);
(b) section 1244 (power to call for information from registered third country auditors);
(c) section 1254 (directions to comply with international obligations).

(7) Any transfer of—
(a) the function of refusing to make a declaration under section 1221(1) (approval of third Country qualifications) on the grounds referred to in section 1221(4) (lack of comparable treatment), or
(b) the function of withdrawing such a declaration under section 1221(7) on those grounds,
must be subject to the reservation that the function is exercisable only with the consent of the Secretary of State.

(8) A delegation order may be amended or, if it appears to the Secretary of State that it is no longer in the public interest that the order should remain in force, revoked by a further order under this section.

(9) Where functions are transferred or resumed, the Secretary of State may by order confer or, as the case may be, take away such other functions supplementary or incidental to those transferred or resumed as appear to him to be appropriate.

(10) Where a delegation order is made, Schedule 13 has effect with respect to—
(a) the status of the body designated by the order in exercising functions of the Secretary of State under this Part,
(b) the constitution and proceedings of the body where it is established by the order,
(c) the exercise by the body of certain functions transferred to it, and
(d) other supplementary matters.

(11) An order under this section which has the effect of transferring or resuming any functions is subject to affirmative resolution procedure.

(12) Any other order under this section is subject to negative resolution procedure.

### 1253   Delegation of functions to an existing body

(1) The Secretary of State's power to make a delegation order under section 1252 which designates an existing body is exercisable in accordance with this section.

(2) The Secretary of State may make such a delegation order if it appears to him that—
(a) the body is able and willing to exercise the functions that would be transferred by the order, and
(b) the body has arrangements in place relating to the exercise of those functions which are such as to be likely to ensure that the conditions in subsection (3) are met.

(3) The conditions are—
(a) that the functions in question will be exercised effectively, and
(b) where the delegation order is to contain any requirements or other provisions specified under subsection (4), that those functions will be exercised in accordance with any such requirements or provisions.

(4) The delegation order may contain such requirements or other provision relating to the exercise of the functions by the designated body as appear to the Secretary of State to be appropriate.

(5) An existing body—
(a) may be designated by a delegation order under section 1252, and
(b) may accordingly exercise functions of the Secretary of State in pursuance of the order,
despite any involvement of the body in the exercise of any functions under arrangements within paragraph 21 to 22B, 23(1) or 24(1) of Schedule 10 or paragraph 1 or 2 of Schedule 12.

*Cooperation with foreign competent authorities*

### 1253A   Requests to foreign competent authorities

The Secretary of State may request from an EEA competent authority or a third country competent authority such assistance, information or investigation as he may reasonably require in connection with the exercise of his functions under this Part.

### 1253B   Requests from EEA competent authorities

(1) The Secretary of State must take all necessary steps to—
(a) ensure that an investigation is carried out, or
(b) provide any other assistance or information, if requested to do so by an EEA competent authority in accordance with Article 36 of the Audit Directive (cooperation between Member State authorities).

(2) Within 28 days following the date on which he receives the request, the Secretary of State must—
(a) provide the assistance or information required by the EEA competent authority under subsection (1)(b), or
(b) notify the EEA competent authority which made the request of the reasons why he has not done so.

(3) But the Secretary of State need not take steps to comply with a request under subsection (1) if—
(a) he considers that complying with the request may prejudice the sovereignty, security or public order of the United Kingdom;

(b) legal proceedings have been brought in the United Kingdom (whether continuing or not) in relation to the persons and matters to which the request relates; or

(c) disciplinary action has been taken by a recognised supervisory body in relation to the persons and matters to which the request relates.

### 1253C   Notification to competent authorities of other EEA States

(1) The Secretary of State must notify the relevant EEA competent authority if he receives notice from a recognised supervisory body under section 1223A(1) (notification of withdrawal of eligibility for appointment) of the withdrawal of a person's eligibility for appointment as a statutory auditor.

(2) In subsection (1) 'the relevant EEA competent authority' means the EEA competent authority which has approved the person concerned in accordance with the Audit Directive to carry out audits of annual accounts or consolidated accounts required by Community law.

(3) The notification under subsection (1) must include the name of the person concerned and the reasons for the withdrawal of his eligibility for appointment as statutory auditor.

(4) The Secretary of State must notify the relevant EEA competent authority if he has reasonable grounds for suspecting that—

(a) a person has contravened the law of the United Kingdom, or any other EEA State or part of an EEA State, implementing the Audit Directive, and

(b) the act or omission constituting that contravention took place on the territory of an EEA State other than the United Kingdom.,

(5) In subsection (4) 'the relevant EEA competent authority' means the EEA competent authority for the EEA State in which the suspected contravention took place.

(6) The notification under subsection (4) must include the name of the person concerned and the grounds for the Secretary of State's suspicion.

*Transfer of papers to third countries*

### 1253D   Restriction on transfer of audit working papers to third countries

Audit working papers must not be transferred to a third country competent authority by any person other than a statutory auditor acting in accordance with rules imposed under paragraph 16A of Schedule 10 (transfer of papers to third countries).

### 1253E   Working arrangements for transfer of papers

(1) The Secretary of State may enter into arrangements with a third country competent authority relating to the transfer of audit working papers—

(a) from the third country competent authority or third country auditors regulated by that authority to the Secretary of State; and

(b) from statutory auditors to the third country competent authority.

(2) The arrangements must provide that—

(a) the Secretary of State has the rights and duties referred to in subsections (3) to (5) in relation to papers he requests from the third country competent authority or third country auditors, and

(b) the third country competent authority has comparable rights and duties in relation to papers it requests from statutory auditors.

(3) Any request by the Secretary of State for audit working papers from the third country competent authority or a third country auditor must be accompanied by a statement explaining the reasons for the request.

(4) The Secretary of State may use the audit working papers he receives in response to a request only in connection with—

(a) quality assurance functions which meet requirements equivalent to those of Article 29 of the Audit Directive (quality assurance),

(b) investigation or disciplinary functions which meet requirements equivalent to those of Article 30 of the Audit Directive (investigations and penalties), or

(c) public oversight functions which meet requirements equivalent to those of Article 32 of the Audit Directive (principles of public oversight).

(5) The Secretary of State, a person exercising the functions of the Secretary of State and persons employed in discharging those functions must be subject to obligations of professional secrecy in relation to audit papers supplied to the Secretary of State by a third country competent authority or a third country auditor.

### 1253F   Publication of working arrangements

If the Secretary of State enters into working arrangements in accordance with section 1253E, he must publish on a website without undue delay—

(a) the name of the third country competent authority with which he has entered into such arrangements, and

(b) the country or territory in which it is established.

*International obligations*

### 1254   Directions to comply with international obligations

(1) If it appears to the Secretary of State—

    (a) that any action proposed to be taken by a recognised supervisory body or a recognised qualifying body, the Independent Supervisor or a body designated by order under section 1252, would be incompatible with Community obligations or any other international obligations of the United Kingdom, or

    (b) that any action which that body has power to take is required for the purpose of implementing any such obligations,

he may direct the body not to take or, as the case may be, to take the action in question.

(2) A direction may include such supplementary or incidental requirements as the Secretary of State thinks necessary or expedient.

(3) A direction under this section given to the Independent Supervisor or a body designated by order under section 1252 is enforceable on the application of the Secretary of State by injunction or, in Scotland, by an order under section 45 of the Court of Session Act 1988 (c. 36).

*General provision relating to offences*

### 1255   Offences by bodies corporate, partnerships and unincorporated associations

(1) Where an offence under this Part committed by a body corporate is proved to have been committed with the consent or connivance of, or to be attributable to any neglect on the part of, an officer of the body, or a person purporting to act in any such capacity, he as well as the body corporate is guilty of the offence and liable to be proceeded against and punished accordingly.

(2) Where an offence under this Part committed by a partnership is proved to have been committed with the consent or connivance of, or to be attributable to any neglect on the part of, a partner, he as well as the partnership is guilty of the offence and liable to be proceeded against and punished accordingly.

(3) Where an offence under this Part committed by an unincorporated association (other than a partnership) is proved to have been committed with the consent or connivance of, or to be attributable to any neglect on the part of, any officer of the association or any member of its governing body, he as well as the association is guilty of the offence and liable to be proceeded against and punished accordingly.

### 1256   Time limits for prosecution of offences

(1) An information relating to an offence under this Part which is triable by a magistrates' court in England and Wales may be so tried if it is laid at any time within the period of twelve months beginning with the date on which evidence sufficient in the opinion of the Director of Public Prosecutions or the Secretary of State to justify the proceedings comes to his knowledge.

(2) Proceedings in Scotland for an offence under this Part may be commenced at any time within the period of twelve months beginning with the date on which evidence sufficient in the Lord Advocate's opinion to justify proceedings came to his knowledge or, where such evidence was reported to him by the Secretary of State, within the period of twelve months beginning with the date on which it came to the knowledge of the Secretary of State.

(3) For the purposes of subsection (2) proceedings are to be deemed to be commenced on the date on which a warrant to apprehend or cite the accused is granted, if the warrant is executed without undue delay.

(4) A complaint charging an offence under this Part which is triable by a magistrates' court in Northern Ireland may be so tried if it is made at any time within the period of twelve months beginning with the date on which evidence sufficient in the opinion of the Director of Public Prosecutions for Northern Ireland or the Secretary of State to justify the proceedings comes to his knowledge.

(5) This section does not authorise—

    (a) in the case of proceedings in England and Wales, the trial of an information laid,

    (b) in the case of proceedings in Scotland, the commencement of proceedings, or

    (c) in the case of proceedings in Northern Ireland, the trial of a complaint made,

more than three years after the commission of the offence.

(6) For the purposes of this section a certificate of the Director of Public Prosecutions, the Lord Advocate, the Director of Public Prosecutions for Northern Ireland or the Secretary of State as to the date on which such evidence as is referred to above came to his knowledge is conclusive evidence.

(7) Nothing in this section affects proceedings within the time limits prescribed by section 127(1) of the Magistrates' Courts Act 1980 (c. 43), section 331 of the Criminal Procedure (Scotland) Act 1975 or Article 19 of the Magistrates' Courts (Northern Ireland) Order 1981 (S.I. 1981/1675 (N.I. 26)) (the usual time limits for criminal proceedings).

### 1257   Jurisdiction and procedure in respect of offences

(1) Summary proceedings for an offence under this Part may, without prejudice to any jurisdiction exercisable apart from this section, be taken—

(a) against a body corporate or unincorporated association at any place at which it has a place of business, and

(b) against an individual at any place where he is for the time being.

(2) Proceedings for an offence alleged to have been committed under this Part by an unincorporated association must be brought in the name of the association (and not in that of any of its members), and for the purposes of any such proceedings any rules of court relating to the service of documents apply as in relation to a body corporate.

(3) Section 33 of the Criminal Justice Act 1925 (c. 86) and Schedule 3 to the Magistrates' Courts Act 1980 (c. 43) (procedure on charge of offence against a corporation) apply in a case in which an unincorporated association is charged in England and Wales with an offence under this Part as they apply in the case of a corporation.

(4) Section 18 of the Criminal Justice Act (Northern Ireland) 1945 (c. 15 (N.I.)) and Article 166 and Schedule 4 to the Magistrates' Courts (Northern Ireland) Order 1981 (S.I. 1981/1675 (N.I. 26)) (procedure on charge of offence against a corporation) apply in a case in which an unincorporated association is charged in Northern Ireland with an offence under this Part as they apply in the case of a corporation.

(5) In relation to proceedings on indictment in Scotland for an offence alleged to have been committed under this Part by an unincorporated association, section 70 of the Criminal Procedure (Scotland) Act 1995 (proceedings on indictment against bodies corporate) applies as if the association were a body corporate.

(6) A fine imposed on an unincorporated association on its conviction of such an offence must be paid out of the funds of the association.

*Notices etc*

### 1258   Service of notices

(1) This section has effect in relation to any notice, direction or other document required or authorised by or by virtue of this Part to be given to or served on any person other than the Secretary of State.

(2) Any such document may be given to or served on the person in question—

(a) by delivering it to him,

(b) by leaving it at his proper address, or

(c) by sending it by post to him at that address.

(3) Any such document may—

(a) in the case of a body corporate, be given to or served on an officer of that body;

(b) in the case of a partnership, be given to or served on any partner;

(c) in the case of an unincorporated association other than a partnership, be given to or served on any member of the governing body of that association.

(4) For the purposes of this section and section 7 of the Interpretation Act 1978 (c. 30) (service of documents by post) in its application to this section, the proper address of any person is his last known address (whether of his residence or of a place where he carries on business or is employed) and also—

(a) in the case of a person who is eligible under the rules of a recognised supervisory body for appointment as a statutory auditor and who does not have a place of business in the United Kingdom, the address of that body;

(b) in the case of a body corporate or an officer of that body, the address of the registered or principal office of that body in the United Kingdom;

(c) in the case of an unincorporated association other than a partnership or a member of its governing body, its principal office in the United Kingdom.

### 1259   Documents in electronic form

(1) This section applies where—

(a) section 1258 authorises the giving or sending of a notice, direction or other document by its delivery to a particular person ('the recipient'), and

(b) the notice, direction or other document is transmitted to the recipient—

(i) by means of an electronic communications network, or

(ii) by other means but in a form that requires the use of apparatus by the recipient

to render it intelligible.

(2) The transmission has effect for the purposes of this Part as a delivery of the notice, direction or other document to the recipient, but only if the recipient has indicated to the person making the transmission his willingness to receive the notice, direction or other document in the form and manner used.

(3) An indication to a person for the purposes of subsection (2)—

(a) must be given to the person in such manner as he may require,

(b) may be a general indication or an indication that is limited to notices, directions or other documents of a particular description,

(c) must state the address to be used,

(d) must be accompanied by such other information as the person requires for the making of the transmission, and

(e) may be modified or withdrawn at any time by a notice given to the person in such manner as he may require.

(4) In this section 'electronic communications network' has the same meaning as in the Communications Act 2003 (c. 21).

*Interpretation*

### 1260  Meaning of 'associate'

(1) In this Part 'associate', in relation to a person, is to be construed as follows.

(2) In relation to an individual, 'associate' means—

    (a) that individual's spouse, civil partner or minor child or step-child,

    (b) any body corporate of which that individual is a director, and

    (c) any employee or partner of that individual.

(3) In relation to a body corporate, 'associate' means—

    (a) any body corporate of which that body is a director,

    (b) any body corporate in the same group as that body, and

    (c) any employee or partner of that body or of any body corporate in the same group.

(4) In relation to a partnership constituted under the law of Scotland, or any other country or territory in which a partnership is a legal person, 'associate' means—

    (a) any body corporate of which that partnership is a director,

    (b) any employee of or partner in that partnership, and

    (c) any person who is an associate of a partner in that partnership.

(5) In relation to a partnership constituted under the law of England and Wales or Northern Ireland, or the law of any other country or territory in which a partnership is not a legal person, 'associate' means any person who is an associate of any of the partners.

(6) In subsections (2)(b), (3)(a) and (4)(a), in the case of a body corporate which is a limited liability partnership, 'director' is to be read as 'member'.

### 1261  Minor definitions

(1) In this Part, unless a contrary intention appears—

'address' means—

    (a) in relation to an individual, his usual residential or business address;

    (b) in relation to a firm, its registered or principal office in the United Kingdom;

'the Audit Directive' means Directive 2006/43/EC of the European Parliament and of the Council on statutory audits of annual accounts and consolidated accounts, amending Council Directives 78/660/EEC and 83/349/EEC and repealing Council Directive 84/253/EEC, as amended at any time before 1st January 2009;

'audit working papers' means any documents which—

    (a) are or have been held by a statutory auditor or a third country auditor, and

    (b) are related to the conduct of an audit conducted by that auditor;

'company' means any company or other body the accounts of which must be audited in accordance with Part 16;

'director', in relation to a body corporate, includes any person occupying in relation to it the position of a director (by whatever name called) and any person in accordance with whose directions or instructions (not being advice given in a professional capacity) the directors of the body are accustomed to act;

'EEA auditor' means an individual who is approved in accordance with the Audit Directive by an EEA competent authority to carry out audits of annual accounts or consolidated accounts required by Community law;

'EEA competent authority' means a competent authority within the meaning of Article 2.10 of the Audit Directive of an EEA State other than the United Kingdom;

'firm' means any entity, whether or not a legal person, which is not an individual and includes a body corporate, a corporation sole and a partnership or other unincorporated association;

'group', in relation to a body corporate, means the body corporate, any other body corporate which is its holding company or subsidiary and any other body corporate which is a subsidiary of that holding company;

'holding company' and 'subsidiary' are to be read in accordance with section 1159 and Schedule 6;

'officer', in relation to a body corporate, includes a director, a manager, a secretary or, where the affairs of the body are managed by its members, a member;

'parent undertaking' and 'subsidiary undertaking' are to be read in accordance with section 1162 and Schedule 7;

'third country' means a country or territory that is not an EEA State or part of an EEA State;

'third country auditor' means a person, other than a person eligible for appointment as a statutory auditor, who is eligible to conduct audits of the accounts of bodies corporate incorporated or formed under the law of a third country in accordance with the law of that country;

'third country competent authority' means a body established in a third country exercising functions related to the regulation or oversight of auditors.

(2)  For the purposes of this Part a body is to be regarded as 'established in the United Kingdom' if and only if—

(a)  it is incorporated or formed under the law of the United Kingdom or a part of the United Kingdom, or

(b)  its central management and control are exercised in the United Kingdom;

and any reference to a qualification 'obtained in the United Kingdom' is to a qualification obtained from such a body.

(2A)  For the purposes of this Part, Gibraltar shall be treated as if it were an EEA State.

(3)  The Secretary of State may by regulations make such modifications of this Part as appear to him to be necessary or appropriate for the purposes of its application in relation to any firm, or description of firm, which is not a body corporate or a partnership.

(4)  Regulations under subsection (3) are subject to negative resolution procedure.

### 1262  Index of defined expressions

The following Table shows provisions defining or otherwise explaining expressions used in this Part (other than provisions defining or explaining an expression used only in the same section)—

| Expression | Provision |
| --- | --- |
| address | section 1261(1) |
| appropriate qualification | section 1219 |
| associate | section 1260 |
| Audit Directive | section 1261(1) |
| audit working papers | section 1261(1) |
| audited person | section 1210(2) |
| Auditor General | section 1226(1) |
| Company | section 1261(1) |
| delegation order | section 1252(1) |
| director (of a body corporate) | section 1261(1) |
| EEA auditor | section 1261(1) |
| EEA competent authority | section 1261(1) |
| enactment | section 1293 |
| established in the United Kingdom | section 1261(2) |
| firm | section 1261(1) |
| group (in relation to a body corporate) | section 1261(1) |
| holding company | section 1261(1) |
| main purposes of this Part | section 1209 |
| member (of a supervisory body) | section 1217(2) |
| obtained in the United Kingdom s | section 1261(2) |
| officer | section 1261(1) |
| parent undertaking | section 1261(1) |
| qualifying body | section 1220(1) |
| recognised, in relation to a professional qualification | section 1220(3) and Schedule 11 |
| recognised, in relation to a qualifying body | paragraph 1(2) of Schedule 11 |
| recognised, in relation to a supervisory body | section 1217(4) and Schedule 10 |
| registered third country auditor | section 1241(1) |
| rules of a qualifying body | section 1220(2) |
| rules of a supervisory body | section 1217(3) |
| statutory auditor, statutory audit and statutory audit work | section 1210(1) |
| subsidiary | section 1261(1) |
| supervisory body | section 1217(1) |
| subsidiary undertaking | section 1261(1) |
| third country | section 1261(1) |
| third country auditor | section 1261(1) |
| third country competent authority | section 1261(1) |
| UK-traded non-EEA company | section 1241(2) |

*Miscellaneous and general*

### 1263  Power to make provision in consequence of changes affecting accountancy bodies

(1)  The Secretary of State may by regulations make such amendments of enactments as appear to him to be necessary or expedient in consequence of any change of name, merger or transfer of engagements affecting—

(a)  a recognised supervisory body or recognised qualifying body, or

(b)  a body of accountants referred to in, or approved, authorised or otherwise recognised for the purposes of, any other enactment.

(2) Regulations under this section are subject to negative resolution procedure.

### 1264 Consequential amendments

Schedule 14 contains consequential amendments relating to this Part.

## PART 43 TRANSPARENCY OBLIGATIONS AND RELATED MATTERS

### *Introductory*

### 1265 The transparency obligations directive

In Part 6 of the Financial Services and Markets Act 2000 (c. 8) (which makes provision about official listing, prospectus requirements for transferable securities, etc), in section 103(1) (interpretation), at the appropriate place insert—

'"the transparency obligations directive" means Directive 2004/ 109/EC of the European Parliament and of the Council relating to the harmonisation of transparency requirements in relation to information about issuers whose securities are admitted to trading on a regulated market;'.

### *Transparency obligations*

### 1266 Transparency rules

(1) After section 89 of the Financial Services and Markets Act 2000 insert—

### *'Transparency obligations*

### 89A Transparency rules

(1) The competent authority may make rules for the purposes of the transparency obligations directive.

(2) The rules may include provision for dealing with any matters arising out of or related to any provision of the transparency obligations directive.

(3) The competent authority may also make rules—

(a) for the purpose of ensuring that voteholder information in respect of voting shares traded on a UK market other than a regulated market is made public or notified to the competent authority;

(b) providing for persons who hold comparable instruments (see section 89F(1)(c)) in respect of voting shares to be treated, in the circumstances specified in the rules, as holding some or all of the voting rights in respect of those shares.

(4) Rules under this section may, in particular, make provision—

(a) specifying how the proportion of—

(i) the total voting rights in respect of shares in an issuer, or

(ii) the total voting rights in respect of a particular class of shares in an issuer,

held by a person is to be determined;

(b) specifying the circumstances in which, for the purposes of any determination of the voting rights held by a person ("P") in respect of voting shares in an issuer, any voting rights held, or treated by virtue of subsection (3)(b) as held, by another person in respect of voting shares in the issuer are to be regarded as held by P;

(c) specifying the nature of the information which must be included in any notification;

(d) about the form of any notification;

(e) requiring any notification to be given within a specified period;

(f) specifying the manner in which any information is to be made public and the period within which it must be made public;

(g) specifying circumstances in which any of the requirements imposed by rules under this section does not apply.

(5) Rules under this section are referred to in this Part as "transparency rules".

(6) Nothing in sections 89B to 89G affects the generality of the power to make rules under this section.

### 89B Provision of voteholder information

(1) Transparency rules may make provision for voteholder information in respect of voting shares to be notified, in circumstances specified in the rules—

(a) to the issuer, or

(b) to the public,

or to both.

(2) Transparency rules may make provision for voteholder information notified to the issuer to be notified at the same time to the competent authority.

(3) In this Part "voteholder information" in respect of voting shares means information relating to the proportion of voting rights held by a person in respect of the shares.

(4) Transparency rules may require notification of voteholder information relating to a person—

(a) initially, not later than such date as may be specified in the rules for the purposes of the first indent of Article 30.2 of the transparency obligations directive, and

(b) subsequently, in accordance with the following provisions.

(5) Transparency rules under subsection (4)(b) may require notification of voteholder information relating to a person only where there is a notifiable change in the proportion of—

(a) the total voting rights in respect of shares in the issuer, or

(b) the total voting rights in respect of a particular class of share in the issuer, held by the person.

(6) For this purpose there is a "notifiable change" in the proportion of voting rights held by a person when the proportion changes—

(a) from being a proportion less than a designated proportion to a proportion equal to or greater than that designated proportion,

(b) from being a proportion equal to a designated proportion to a proportion greater or less than that designated proportion, or

(c) from being a proportion greater than a designated proportion to a proportion equal to or less than that designated proportion.

(7) In subsection (6) "designated" means designated by the rules.

### 89C    Provision of information by issuers of transferable securities

(1) Transparency rules may make provision requiring the issuer of transferable securities, in circumstances specified in the rules—

(a) to make public information to which this section applies, or

(b) to notify to the competent authority information to which this section applies,

or to do both.

(2) In the case of every issuer, this section applies to—

(a) information required by Article 4 of the transparency obligations directive;

(b) information relating to the rights attached to the transferable securities, including information about the terms and conditions of those securities which could indirectly affect those rights; and

(c) information about new loan issues and about any guarantee or security in connection with any such issue.

(3) In the case of an issuer of debt securities, this section also applies to information required by Article 5 of the transparency obligations directive.

(4) In the case of an issuer of shares, this section also applies to—

(a) information required by Article 5 of the transparency obligations directive;

(b) information required by Article 6 of that directive;

(c) voteholder information—

(i) notified to the issuer, or

(ii) relating to the proportion of voting rights held by the issuer in respect of shares in the issuer;

(d) information relating to the issuer's capital; and

(e) information relating to the total number of voting rights in respect of shares or shares of a particular class.

### 89D    Notification of voting rights held by issuer

(1) Transparency rules may require notification of voteholder information relating to the proportion of voting rights held by an issuer in respect of voting shares in the issuer—

(a) initially, not later than such date as may be specified in the rules for the purposes of the second indent of Article 30.2 of the transparency obligations directive, and

(b) subsequently, in accordance with the following provisions.

(2) Transparency rules under subsection (1)(b) may require notification of voteholder information relating to the proportion of voting rights held by an issuer in respect of voting shares in the issuer only where there is a notifiable change in the proportion of—

(a) the total voting rights in respect of shares in the issuer, or

(b) the total voting rights in respect of a particular class of share in the issuer,

held by the issuer.

(3) For this purpose there is a "notifiable change" in the proportion of voting rights held by a person when the proportion changes—

(a) from being a proportion less than a designated proportion to a proportion equal to or greater than that designated proportion,

(b) from being a proportion equal to a designated proportion to a proportion greater or less than that designated proportion, or

(c) from being a proportion greater than a designated proportion to a proportion equal to or less than that designated proportion.

(4) In subsection (3) "designated" means designated by the rules.

### 89E  Notification of proposed amendment of issuer's constitution

Transparency rules may make provision requiring an issuer of transferable securities that are admitted to trading on a regulated market to notify a proposed amendment to its constitution—

    (a)  to the competent authority, and

    (b)  to the market on which the issuer's securities are admitted,

at times and in circumstances specified in the rules.

### 89F  Transparency rules: interpretation etc

(1)  For the purposes of sections 89A to 89G—

    (a)  the voting rights in respect of any voting shares are the voting rights attached to those shares,

    (b)  a person is to be regarded as holding the voting rights in respect of the shares—

      (i)  if, by virtue of those shares, he is a shareholder within the meaning of Article 2.1(e) of the transparency obligations directive;

      (ii)  if, and to the extent that, he is entitled to acquire, dispose of or exercise those voting rights in one or more of the cases mentioned in Article 10(a) to (h) of the transparency obligations directive;

      (iii)  if he holds, directly or indirectly, a financial instrument which results in an entitlement to acquire the shares and is an Article 13 instrument, and

    (c)  a person holds a "comparable instrument" in respect of voting shares if he holds, directly or indirectly, a financial instrument in relation to the shares which has similar economic effects to an Article 13 instrument (whether or not the financial instrument results in an entitlement to acquire the shares).

(2)  Transparency rules under section 89A(3)(b) may make different provision for different descriptions of comparable instrument.

(3)  For the purposes of sections 89A to 89G two or more persons may, at the same time, each be regarded as holding the same voting rights.

(4)  In those sections—

"Article 13 instrument" means a financial instrument of a type determined by the European Commission under Article 13.2 of the transparency obligations directive;

"UK market" means a market that is situated or operating in the United Kingdom;

"voting shares" means shares of an issuer to which voting rights are attached.

### 89G  Transparency rules: other supplementary provisions

(1)  Transparency rules may impose the same obligations on a person who has applied for the admission of transferable securities to trading on a regulated market without the issuer's consent as they impose on an issuer of transferable securities.

(2)  Transparency rules that require a person to make information public may include provision authorising the competent authority to make the information public in the event that the person fails to do so.

(3)  The competent authority may make public any information notified to the authority in accordance with transparency rules.

(4)  Transparency rules may make provision by reference to any provision of any rules made by the Panel on Takeovers and Mergers under Part 28 of the Companies Act 2006.

(5)  Sections 89A to 89F and this section are without prejudice to any other power conferred by this Part to make Part 6 rules.'.

(2)  The effectiveness for the purposes of section 155 of the Financial Services and Markets Act 2000 (c. 8) (consultation on proposed rules) of things done by the Financial Services Authority before this section comes into force with a view to making transparency rules (as defined in the provisions to be inserted in that Act by subsection (1) above) is not affected by the fact that those provisions were not then in force.

### 1267  Competent authority's power to call for information

In Part 6 of the Financial Services and Markets Act 2000 after the sections inserted by section 1266 above insert—

*'Power of competent authority to call for information*

### 89H  Competent authority's power to call for information

(1)  The competent authority may by notice in writing given to a person to whom this section applies require him—

    (a)  to provide specified information or information of a specified description, or

    (b)  to produce specified documents or documents of a specified description.

(2)  This section applies to—

    (a)  an issuer in respect of whom transparency rules have effect;

    (b)  a voteholder;

    (c)  an auditor of—

     (i)  an issuer to whom this section applies, or

     (ii)  a voteholder;

  (d)  a person who controls a voteholder;

  (e)  a person controlled by a voteholder;

  (f)  a director or other similar officer of an issuer to whom this section applies;

  (g)  a director or other similar officer of a voteholder or, where the affairs of a voteholder are managed by its members, a member of the voteholder.

(3)  This section applies only to information and documents reasonably required in connection with the exercise by the competent authority of functions conferred on it by or under sections 89A to 89G (transparency rules).

(4)  Information or documents required under this section must be provided or produced—

  (a)  before the end of such reasonable period as may be specified, and

  (b)  at such place as may be specified.

(5)  If a person claims a lien on a document, its production under this section does not affect the lien.

### 89I  Requirements in connection with call for information

(1)  The competent authority may require any information provided under section 89H to be provided in such form as it may reasonably require.

(2)  The competent authority may require—

  (a)  any information provided, whether in a document or otherwise, to be verified in such manner as it may reasonably require;

  (b)  any document produced to be authenticated in such manner as it may reasonably require.

(3)  If a document is produced in response to a requirement imposed under section 89H, the competent authority may—

  (a)  take copies of or extracts from the document; or

  (b)  require the person producing the document, or any relevant person, to provide an explanation of the document.

(4)  In subsection (3)(b) "relevant person", in relation to a person who is required to produce a document, means a person who—

  (a)  has been or is a director or controller of that person;

  (b)  has been or is an auditor of that person;

  (c)  has been or is an actuary, accountant or lawyer appointed or instructed by that person; or

  (d)  has been or is an employee of that person.

(5)  If a person who is required under section 89H to produce a document fails to do so, the competent authority may require him to state, to the best of his knowledge and belief, where the document is.

### 89J  Power to call for information: supplementary provisions

(1)  The competent authority may require an issuer to make public any information provided to the authority under section 89H.

(2)  If the issuer fails to comply with a requirement under subsection (1), the competent authority may, after seeking representations from the issuer, make the information public.

(3)  In sections 89H and 89I (power of competent authority to call for information)—

"control" and "controlled" have the meaning given by subsection (4) below;

"specified" means specified in the notice;

"voteholder" means a person who—

  (a)  holds voting rights in respect of any voting shares for the purposes of sections 89A to 89G (transparency rules), or

  (b)  is treated as holding such rights by virtue of rules under section 89A(3)(b).

(4)  For the purposes of those sections a person ("A") controls another person ("B") if—

  (a)  A holds a majority of the voting rights in B,

  (b)  A is a member of B and has the right to appoint or remove a majority of the members of the board of directors (or, if there is no such board, the equivalent management body) of B,

  (c)  A is a member of B and controls alone, pursuant to an agreement with other shareholders or members, a majority of the voting rights in B, or

  (d)  A has the right to exercise, or actually exercises, dominant influence or control over B.

(5)  For the purposes of subsection (4)(b)—

  (a)  any rights of a person controlled by A, and

  (b)  any rights of a person acting on behalf of A or a person controlled by A,

are treated as held by A.'.

### 1268  Powers exercisable in case of infringement of transparency obligation

In Part 6 of the Financial Services and Markets Act 2000 (c. 8), after the sections inserted by section 1267 above insert—

*'Powers exercisable in case of infringement of transparency obligation*

### 89K   Public censure of issuer

(1) If the competent authority finds that an issuer of securities admitted to trading on a regulated market is failing or has failed to comply with an applicable transparency obligation, it may publish a statement to that effect.

(2) If the competent authority proposes to publish a statement, it must give the issuer a warning notice setting out the terms of the proposed statement.

(3) If, after considering any representations made in response to the warning notice, the competent authority decides to make the proposed statement, it must give the issuer a decision notice setting out the terms of the statement.

(4) A notice under this section must inform the issuer of his right to refer the matter to the Tribunal (see section 89N) and give an indication of the procedure on such a reference.

(5) In this section "transparency obligation" means an obligation under—

(a) a provision of transparency rules, or

(b) any other provision made in accordance with the transparency obligations directive.

(6) In relation to an issuer whose home State is a member State other than the United Kingdom, any reference to an applicable transparency obligation must be read subject to section 100A(2).

### 89L   Power to suspend or prohibit trading of securities

(1) This section applies to securities admitted to trading on a regulated market.

(2) If the competent authority has reasonable grounds for suspecting that an applicable transparency obligation has been infringed by an issuer, it may—

(a) suspend trading in the securities for a period not exceeding 10 days,

(b) prohibit trading in the securities, or

(c) make a request to the operator of the market on which the issuer's securities are traded—

(i)  to suspend trading in the securities for a period not exceeding 10 days, or

(ii)  to prohibit trading in the securities.

(3) If the competent authority has reasonable grounds for suspecting that a provision required by the transparency obligations directive has been infringed by a voteholder of an issuer, it may—

(a) prohibit trading in the securities, or

(b) make a request to the operator of the market on which the issuer's securities are traded to prohibit trading in the securities.

(4) If the competent authority finds that an applicable transparency obligation has been infringed, it may require the market operator to prohibit trading in the securities.

(5) In this section "transparency obligation" means an obligation under—

(a) a provision contained in transparency rules, or

(b) any other provision made in accordance with the transparency obligations directive.

(6) In relation to an issuer whose home State is a member State other than the United Kingdom, any reference to an applicable transparency obligation must be read subject to section 100A(2).

### 89M   Procedure under section 89L

(1) A requirement under section 89L takes effect—

(a) immediately, if the notice under subsection (2) states that that is the case;

(b) in any other case, on such date as may be specified in the notice.

(2) If the competent authority—

(a) proposes to exercise the powers in section 89L in relation to a person, or

(b) exercises any of those powers in relation to a person with immediate effect,

it must give that person written notice.

(3) The notice must—

(a) give details of the competent authority's action or proposed action;

(b) state the competent authority's reasons for taking the action in question and choosing the date on which it took effect or takes effect;

(c) inform the recipient that he may make representations to the competent authority within such period as may be specified by the notice (whether or not he had referred the matter to the Tribunal);

(d) inform him of the date on which the action took effect or takes effect;

(e) inform him of his right to refer the matter to the Tribunal (see section 89N) and give an indication of the procedure on such a reference.

(4) The competent authority may extend the period within which representations may be made to it.

(5) If, having considered any representations made to it, the competent authority decides to maintain, vary or revoke its earlier decision, it must give written notice to that effect to the person mentioned in subsection (2).

### 89N   Right to refer matters to the Tribunal

A person—

(a) to whom a decision notice is given under section 89K (public censure), or

(b) to whom a notice is given under section 89M (procedure in connection with suspension or prohibition of trading),

may refer the matter to the Tribunal.'.

*Other matters*

### 1269   Corporate governance rules

In Part 6 of the Financial Services and Markets Act 2000 (c. 8), after the sections inserted by section 1268 above insert—

*'Corporate governance*

### 89O   Corporate governance rules

(1) The competent authority may make rules ("corporate governance rules")—

(a) for the purpose of implementing, enabling the implementation of or dealing with matters arising out of or related to, any Community obligation relating to the corporate governance of issuers who have requested or approved admission of their securities to trading on a regulated market;

(b) about corporate governance in relation to such issuers for the purpose of implementing, or dealing with matters arising out of or related to, any Community obligation.

(2) "Corporate governance", in relation to an issuer, includes—

(a) the nature, constitution or functions of the organs of the issuer;

(b) the manner in which organs of the issuer conduct themselves;

(c) the requirements imposed on organs of the issuer;

(d) the relationship between the different organs of the issuer;

(e) the relationship between the organs of the issuer and the members of the issuer or holders of the issuer's securities.

(3) The burdens and restrictions imposed by rules under this section on foreign-traded issuers must not be greater than the burdens and restrictions imposed on UK-traded issuers by—

(a) rules under this section, and

(b) listing rules.

(4) For this purpose—

"foreign-traded issuer" means an issuer who has requested or approved admission of the issuer's securities to trading on a regulated market situated or operating outside the United Kingdom;

"UK-traded issuer" means an issuer who has requested or approved admission of the issuer's securities to trading on a regulated market situated or operating in the United Kingdom.

(5) This section is without prejudice to any other power conferred by this Part to make Part 6 rules.'.

### 1270   Liability for false or misleading statements in certain publications

In Part 6 of the Financial Services and Markets Act 2000 (c. 8), after section 90 insert—

### '90A   Compensation for statements in certain publications

(1) The publications to which this section applies are—

(a) any reports and statements published in response to a requirement imposed by a provision implementing Article 4, 5 or 6 of the transparency obligations directive, and

(b) any preliminary statement made in advance of a report or statement to be published in response to a requirement imposed by a provision implementing Article 4 of that directive, to the extent that it contains information that it is intended—

(i) will appear in the report or statement, and

(ii) will be presented in the report or statement in substantially the same form as that in which it is presented in the preliminary statement.

(2) The securities to which this section applies are—

(a) securities that are traded on a regulated market situated or operating in the United Kingdom, and

(b) securities that—

(i) are traded on a regulated market situated or operating outside the United Kingdom, and

(ii) are issued by an issuer for which the United Kingdom is the home Member State within the meaning of Article 2.1(i) of the transparency obligations directive.

(3) The issuer of securities to which this section applies is liable to pay compensation to a person who has—

(a) acquired such securities issued by it, and

(b) suffered loss in respect of them as a result of—

(i) any untrue or misleading statement in a publication to which this section applies, or

   (ii) the omission from any such publication of any matter required to be included in it.

  (4) The issuer is so liable only if a person discharging managerial responsibilities within the issuer in relation to the publication—

   (a) knew the statement to be untrue or misleading or was reckless as to whether it was untrue or misleading, or

   (b) knew the omission to be dishonest concealment of a material fact.

  (5) A loss is not regarded as suffered as a result of the statement or omission in the publication unless the person suffering it acquired the relevant securities—

   (a) in reliance on the information in the publication, and

   (b) at a time when, and in circumstances in which, it was reasonable for him to rely on that information.

  (6) Except as mentioned in subsection (8)—

   (a) the issuer is not subject to any other liability than that provided for by this section in respect of loss suffered as a result of reliance by any person on—

    (i) an untrue or misleading statement in a publication to which this section applies, or

    (ii) the omission from any such publication of any matter required to be included in it, and

   (b) a person other than the issuer is not subject to any liability, other than to the issuer, in respect of any such loss.

  (7) Any reference in subsection (6) to a person being subject to a liability includes a reference to another person being entitled as against him to be granted any civil remedy or to rescind or repudiate an agreement.

  (8) This section does not affect—

   (a) the powers conferred by section 382 and 384 (powers of the court to make a restitution order and of the Authority to require restitution);

   (b) liability for a civil penalty;

   (c) liability for a criminal offence.

  (9) For the purposes of this section—

   (a) the following are persons "discharging managerial responsibilities" in relation to a publication—

    (i) any director of the issuer (or person occupying the position of director, by whatever name called),

    (ii) in the case of an issuer whose affairs are managed by its members, any member of the issuer,

    (iii) in the case of an issuer that has no persons within subparagraph (i) or (ii), any senior executive of the issuer having responsibilities in relation to the publication;

   (b) references to the acquisition by a person of securities include his contracting to acquire them or any interest in them.

**90B Power to make further provision about liability for published information**

  (1) The Treasury may by regulations make provision about the liability of issuers of securities traded on a regulated market, and other persons, in respect of information published to holders of securities, to the market or to the public generally.

  (2) Regulations under this section may amend any primary or subordinate legislation, including any provision of, or made under, this Act.'.

**1271 Exercise of powers where UK is host member State**

In Part 6 of the Financial Services and Markets Act 2000 (c. 8), after section 100 insert—

**'100A Exercise of powers where UK is host member state**

  (1) This section applies to the exercise by the competent authority of any power under this Part exercisable in case of infringement of—

   (a) a provision of prospectus rules or any other provision made in accordance with the prospectus directive, or

   (b) a provision of transparency rules or any other provision made in accordance with the transparency obligations directive, in relation to an issuer whose home State is a member State other than the United Kingdom.

  (2) The competent authority may act in such a case only in respect of the infringement of a provision required by the relevant directive. Any reference to an applicable provision or applicable transparency obligation shall be read accordingly.

  (3) If the authority finds that there has been such an infringement, it must give a notice to that effect to the competent authority of the person's home State requesting it—

   (a) to take all appropriate measures for the purpose of ensuring that the person remedies the situation that has given rise to the notice, and

   (b) to inform the authority of the measures it proposes to take or has taken or the reasons for not taking such measures.

(4) The authority may not act further unless satisfied—

(a) that the competent authority of the person's home State has failed or refused to take measures for the purpose mentioned in subsection (3)(a), or

(b) that the measures taken by that authority have proved inadequate for that purpose.

This does not affect exercise of the powers under section 87K(2), 87L(2) or (3) or 89L(2) or (3) (powers to protect market).

(5) If the authority is so satisfied, it must, after informing the competent authority of the person's home State, take all appropriate measures to protect investors.

(6) In such a case the authority must inform the Commission of the measures at the earliest opportunity.'.

### 1272 Transparency obligations and related matters: minor and consequential amendments

(1) Schedule 15 to this Act makes minor and consequential amendments in connection with the provision made by this Part.

(2) In that Schedule—

Part 1 contains amendments of the Financial Services and Markets Act 2000 (c. 8);

Part 2 contains amendments of the Companies (Audit, Investigations and Community Enterprise) Act 2004 (c. 27).

### 1273 Corporate governance regulations

(1) The Secretary of State may make regulations–

(a) for the purpose of implementing, enabling the implementation of or dealing with matters arising out of or related to, any Community obligation relating to the corporate governance of issuers who have requested or approved admission of their securities to trading on a regulated market;

(b) about corporate governance in relation to such issuers for the purpose of implementing, or dealing with matters arising out of or related to, any Community obligation.

(2) 'Corporate governance', in relation to an issuer, includes—

(a) the nature, constitution or functions of the organs of the issuer;

(b) the manner in which organs of the issuer conduct themselves;

(c) the requirements imposed on organs of the issuer;

(d) the relationship between different organs of the issuer;

(e) the relationship between the organs of the issuer and the members of the issuer or holders of the issuer's securities.

(3) The regulations may—

(a) make provision by reference to any specified code on corporate governance that may be issued from time to time by a specified body;

(b) create new criminal offences (subject to subsection (4));

(c) make provision excluding liability in damages in respect of things done or omitted for the purposes of, or in connection with, the carrying on, or purported carrying on, of any specified activities.

'Specified' here means specified in the regulations.

(4) The regulations may not create a criminal offence punishable by a greater penalty than—

(a) on indictment, a fine;

(b) on summary conviction, a fine not exceeding the statutory maximum or (if calculated on a daily basis) £100 a day.

(5) Regulations under this section are subject to negative resolution procedure.

(6) In this section 'issuer', 'securities' and 'regulated market' have the same meaning as in Part 6 of the Financial Services and Markets Act 2000 (c. 8).

# PART 44   MISCELLANEOUS PROVISIONS

*Regulation of actuaries etc*

### 1274 Grants to bodies concerned with actuarial standards etc

(1) Section 16 of the Companies (Audit, Investigations and Community Enterprise) Act 2004 (c. 27) (grants to bodies concerned with accounting standards etc) is amended as follows.

(2) In subsection (2) (matters carried on by bodies eligible for grants) for paragraph (l) substitute—

'(l) issuing standards to be applied in actuarial work;

(m) issuing standards in respect of matters to be contained in reports or other communications required to be produced or made by actuaries or in accordance with standards within paragraph (l);

(n) investigating departures from standards within paragraph (l) or (m);

(o) taking steps to secure compliance with standards within paragraph (l) or (m);

(p) carrying out investigations into public interest cases arising in connection with the performance of actuarial functions by members of professional actuarial bodies;

(q) holding disciplinary hearings relating to members of professional actuarial bodies following the conclusion of investigations within paragraph (p);

(r) deciding whether (and, if so, what) disciplinary action should be taken against members of professional actuarial bodies to whom hearings within paragraph (q) related;

(s) supervising the exercise by professional actuarial bodies of regulatory functions in relation to their members;

(t) overseeing or directing any of the matters mentioned above.'.

(3) In subsection (5) (definitions) at the appropriate places insert—

'"professional actuarial body" means—

(a) the Institute of Actuaries, or

(b) the Faculty of Actuaries in Scotland,

and the "members" of a professional actuarial body include persons who, although not members of the body, are subject to its rules in performing actuarial functions;'

'"regulatory functions", in relation to professional actuarial bodies, means any of the following—

(a) investigatory or disciplinary functions exercised by such bodies in relation to the performance by their members of actuarial functions,

(b) the setting by such bodies of standards in relation to the performance by their members of actuarial functions, and

(c) the determining by such bodies of requirements in relation to the education and training of their members;'.

### 1275 Levy to pay expenses of bodies concerned with actuarial standards etc

(1) Section 17 of the Companies (Audit, Investigations and Community Enterprise) Act 2004 (c. 27) (levy to pay expenses of bodies concerned with accounting standards etc) is amended in accordance with subsections (2) to (5).

(2) In subsection (3)(a) after 'to which' insert ', or persons within subsection (3A) to whom,'.

(3) After subsection (3) insert—

'(3A) The following persons are within this subsection—

(a) the administrators of a public service pension scheme (within the meaning of section 1 of the Pension Schemes Act 1993);

(b) the trustees or managers of an occupational or personal pension scheme (within the meaning of that section).'.

(4) After subsection (4)(b) insert—

'(c) make different provision for different cases.'.

(5) After subsection (12) insert—

'(13) If a draft of any regulations to which subsection (10) applies would, apart from this subsection, be treated for the purposes of the standing orders of either House of Parliament as a hybrid instrument, it is to proceed in that House as if it were not such an instrument.'.

(6) The above amendments have effect in relation to any exercise of the power to make regulations under section 17 of the Companies (Audit, Investigations and Community Enterprise) Act 2004 after this section comes into force, regardless of when the expenses to be met by the levy in respect of which the regulations are made were incurred.

(7) In Schedule 3 to the Pensions Act 2004 (c. 35) (disclosure of information held by the Pensions Regulator), in the entry relating to the Secretary of State, in the second column, for 'or' at the end of paragraph (g) substitute—

'(ga) Section 17 of the Companies (Audit, Investigations and Community Enterprise) Act 2004 (levy to pay expenses of bodies concerned with accounting standards, actuarial standards etc), or'.

### 1276 Application of provisions to Scotland and Northern Ireland

(1) Section 16 of the Companies (Audit, Investigations and Community Enterprise) Act 2004 (grants to bodies concerned with accounting standards etc) is amended as follows.

(2) For subsection (6) (application of section to Scotland) substitute—

'(6) In their application to Scotland, subsection (2)(a) to (t) are to be read as referring only to matters provision relating to which would be outside the legislative competence of the Scottish Parliament.'.

(3) In subsection (2) in paragraph (c), after '1985 (c. 6)' insert 'or the 1986 Order'.

(4) In subsection (5)—

(a) in the definition of 'company' after '1985 (c. 6)' insert 'or the 1986 Order',

(b) in the definition of 'subsidiary' after '1985' insert 'or Article 4 of the 1986 Order', and

(c) after that definition insert—

'"the 1986 Order" means the Companies (Northern Ireland) Order 1986 (S.I. 1986/1032 (N.I. 6)).'.

(5) In section 66 of that Act (extent), in subsection (2) (provisions extending to Northern Ireland, as well as England and Wales and Scotland) for '17' substitute '16 to 18'.

*Information as to exercise of voting rights by institutional investors*

### 1277   Power to require information about exercise of voting rights

(1) The Treasury or the Secretary of State may make provision by regulations requiring institutions to which this section applies to provide information about the exercise of voting rights attached to shares to which this section applies.

(2) This power is exercisable in accordance with—

section 1278 (institutions to which information provisions apply),

section 1279 (shares to which information provisions apply), and

section 1280 (obligations with respect to provision of information).

(3) In this section and the sections mentioned above—

    (a) references to a person acting on behalf of an institution include—

        (i) any person to whom authority has been delegated by the institution to take decisions as to any matter relevant to the subject matter of the regulations, and

        (ii) such other persons as may be specified; and

    (b) 'specified' means specified in the regulations.

(4) The obligation imposed by regulations under this section is enforceable by civil proceedings brought by—

    (a) any person to whom the information should have been provided, or

    (b) a specified regulatory authority.

(5) Regulations under this section may make different provision for different descriptions of institution, different descriptions of shares and for other different circumstances.

(6) Regulations under this section are subject to affirmative resolution procedure.

### 1278   Institutions to which information provisions apply

(1) The institutions to which section 1277 applies are—

    (a) unit trust schemes within the meaning of the Financial Services and Markets Act 2000 (c. 8) in respect of which an order is in force under section 243 of that Act;

    (b) open-ended investment companies incorporated by virtue of regulations under section 262 of that Act;

    (c) companies approved for the purposes of section 842 of the Income and Corporation Taxes Act 1988 (c. 1) (investment trusts);

    (d) pension schemes as defined in section 1(5) of the Pension Schemes Act 1993 (c. 48) or the Pension Schemes (Northern Ireland) Act 1993 (c. 49);

    (e) undertakings authorised under the Financial Services and Markets Act 2000 to carry on long-term insurance business (that is, the activity of effecting or carrying out contracts of long-term insurance within the meaning of the Financial Services and Markets (Regulated Activities) Order 2001 (S.I. 2001/544);

    (f) collective investment schemes that are recognised by virtue of section 270 of that Act (schemes authorised in designated countries or territories).

(2) Regulations under that section may—

    (a) provide that the section applies to other descriptions of institution;

    (b) provide that the section does not apply to a specified description of institution.

(3) The regulations must specify by whom, in the case of any description of institution, the duty imposed by the regulations is to be fulfilled.

### 1279   Shares to which information provisions apply

(1) The shares to which section 1277 applies are shares—

    (a) of a description traded on a specified market, and

    (b) in which the institution has, or is taken to have, an interest.

Regulations under that section may provide that the section does not apply to shares of a specified description.

(2) For this purpose an institution has an interest in shares if the shares, or a depositary certificate in respect of them, are held by it, or on its behalf.

A 'depositary certificate' means an instrument conferring rights (other than options)—

    (a) in respect of shares held by another person, and

    (b) the transfer of which may be effected without the consent of that person.

(3) Where an institution has an interest—

    (a) in a specified description of collective investment scheme (within the meaning of the Financial Services and Markets Act 2000 (c. 8)), or

    (b) in any other specified description of scheme or collective investment vehicle,

it is taken to have an interest in any shares in which that scheme or vehicle has or is taken to have an interest.

(4) For this purpose a scheme or vehicle is taken to have an interest in shares if it would be regarded as having such an interest in accordance with subsection (2) if it was an institution to which section 1277 applied.

### 1280   Obligations with respect to provision of information

(1) Regulations under section 1277 may require the provision of specified information about—

    (a) the exercise or non-exercise of voting rights by the institution or any person acting on its behalf,

    (b) any instructions given by the institution or any person acting on its behalf as to the exercise or non-exercise of voting rights, and

    (c) any delegation by the institution or any person acting on its behalf of any functions in relation to the exercise or non-exercise of voting rights or the giving of such instructions.

(2) The regulations may require information to be provided in respect of specified occasions or specified periods.

(3) Where instructions are given to act on the recommendations or advice of another person, the regulations may require the provision of information about what recommendations or advice were given.

(4) The regulations may require information to be provided—

    (a) in such manner as may be specified, and

    (b) to such persons as may be specified, or to the public, or both.

(5) The regulations may provide—

    (a) that an institution may discharge its obligations under the regulations by referring to information disclosed by a person acting on its behalf, and

    (b) that in such a case it is sufficient, where that other person acts on behalf of more than one institution, that the reference is to information given in aggregated form, that is—

        (i) relating to the exercise or non-exercise by that person of voting rights on behalf of more than one institution, or

        (ii) relating to the instructions given by that person in respect of the exercise or non-exercise of voting rights on behalf of more than one institution, or

        (iii) relating to the delegation by that person of functions in relation to the exercise or non-exercise of voting rights, or the giving of instructions in respect of the exercise or non-exercise of voting rights, on behalf of more than one institution.

(6) References in this section to instructions are to instructions of any description, whether general or specific, whether binding or not and whether or not acted upon.

*Disclosure of information under the Enterprise Act 2002*

### 1281   Disclosure of information under the Enterprise Act 2002

In Part 9 of the Enterprise Act 2002 (c. 40) (information), after section 241 insert—

**'241A Civil proceedings**

(1) A public authority which holds prescribed information to which section 237 applies may disclose that information to any person—

    (a) for the purposes of, or in connection with, prescribed civil proceedings (including prospective proceedings) in the United Kingdom or elsewhere, or

    (b) for the purposes of obtaining legal advice in relation to such proceedings, or

    (c) otherwise for the purposes of establishing, enforcing or defending legal rights that are or may be the subject of such proceedings.

(2) Subsection (1) does not apply to—

    (a) information which comes to a public authority in connection with an investigation under Part 4, 5 or 6 of the 1973 Act or under section 11 of the Competition Act 1980;

    (b) competition information within the meaning of section 351 of the Financial Services and Markets Act 2000;

    (c) information which comes to a public authority in connection with an investigation under Part 3 or 4 or section 174 of this Act;

    (d) information which comes to a public authority in connection with an investigation under the Competition Act 1998 (c. 41).

(3) In subsection (1) 'prescribed' means prescribed by order of the Secretary of State.

(4) An order under this section—

    (a) may prescribe information, or civil proceedings, for the purposes of this section by reference to such factors as appear to the Secretary of State to be appropriate;

    (b) may prescribe for the purposes of this section all information, or civil proceedings, or all information or civil proceedings not falling within one or more specified exceptions;

    (c) must be made by statutory instrument subject to annulment in pursuance of a resolution of either House of Parliament.

(5) Information disclosed under this section must not be used by the person to whom it is disclosed for any purpose other than those specified in subsection (1).'.

*Expenses of winding up*

### 1282   Payment of expenses of winding up

(1) In Chapter 8 of Part 4 of the Insolvency Act 1986 (c. 45) (winding up of companies: provisions of general application), before section 176A (under the heading 'Property subject to floating charge') insert—

**'176ZA    Payment of expenses of winding up (England and Wales)**

(1) The expenses of winding up in England and Wales, so far as the assets of the company available for payment of general creditors are insufficient to meet them, have priority over any claims to property comprised in or subject to any floating charge created by the company and shall be paid out of any such property accordingly.

(2) In subsection (1)—

(a) the reference to assets of the company available for payment of general creditors does not include any amount made available under section 176A(2)(a);

(b) the reference to claims to property comprised in or subject to a floating charge is to the claims of—

(i) the holders of debentures secured by, or holders of, the floating charge, and

(ii) any preferential creditors entitled to be paid out of that property in priority to them.

(3) Provision may be made by rules restricting the application of subsection (1), in such circumstances as may be prescribed, to expenses authorised or approved—

(a) by the holders of debentures secured by, or holders of, the floating charge and by any preferential creditors entitled to be paid in priority to them, or

(b) by the court.

(4) References in this section to the expenses of the winding up are to all expenses properly incurred in the winding up, including the remuneration of the liquidator.'.

(2) In Chapter 8 of Part 5 of the Insolvency (Northern Ireland) Order 1989 (S.I. 1989/2405 (N.I. 19)) (winding up of companies: provisions of general application), before Article 150A (under the heading 'Property subject to floating charge') insert—

**'150ZA    Payment of expenses of winding up**

(1) The expenses of winding up, so far as the assets of the company available for payment of general creditors are insufficient to meet them, have priority over any claims to property comprised in or subject to any floating charge created by the company and shall be paid out of any such property accordingly.

(2) In paragraph (1)—

(a) the reference to assets of the company available for payment of general creditors does not include any amount made available under Article 150A(2)(a);

(b) the reference to claims to property comprised in or subject to a floating charge is to the claims of—

(i) the holders of debentures secured by, or holders of, the floating charge, and

(ii) any preferential creditors entitled to be paid out of that property in priority to them.

(3) Provision may be made by rules restricting the application of paragraph (1), in such circumstances as may be prescribed, to expenses authorised or approved—

(a) by the holders of debentures secured by, or holders of, the floating charge and by any preferential creditors entitled to be paid in priority to them, or

(b) by the Court.

(4) References in this Article to the expenses of the winding up are to all expenses properly incurred in the winding up, including the remuneration of the liquidator.'.

*Commonhold associations*

**1283    Amendment of memorandum or articles of commonhold association**

In paragraph 3(1) of Schedule 3 to the Commonhold and Leasehold Reform Act 2002 (c. 15) (alteration of memorandum or articles by commonhold association to be of no effect until altered version registered with Land Registry) for 'An alteration of the memorandum or articles of association' substitute 'Where a commonhold association alters its memorandum or articles at a time when the land specified in its memorandum is commonhold land, the alteration'.

# PART 45    NORTHERN IRELAND

**1284    Extension of Companies Acts to Northern Ireland**

(1) The Companies Acts as defined by this Act (see section 2) extend to Northern Ireland.

(2) The Companies (Northern Ireland) Order 1986 (S.I. 1986/1032 (N.I. 6)), the Companies Consolidation (Consequential Provisions) (Northern Ireland) Order 1986 (S.I. 1986/1035 (N.I. 9)) and Part 3 of the Companies (Audit, Investigations and Community Enterprise) Order 2005 (S.I. 2005/1967 (N.I. 17)) shall cease to have effect accordingly.

**1285    Extension of GB enactments relating to SEs**

(1) The enactments in force in Great Britain relating to SEs extend to Northern Ireland.

(2) The following enactments shall cease to have effect accordingly—

(a) the European Public Limited-Liability Company Regulations (Northern Ireland) 2004 (SR 2004/417), and

(b) the European Public Limited-Liability Company (Fees) Regulations (Northern Ireland) 2004 (SR 2004/418).

(3)  In this section 'SE' means a European Public Limited-Liability Company (or *Societas Europaea*) within the meaning of Council Regulation 2157/2001/EC of 8 October 2001 on the Statute for a European Company.

### 1286  Extension of GB enactments relating to certain other forms of business organisation

(1)  The enactments in force in Great Britain relating to—

(a)  limited liability partnerships,

(b)  limited partnerships,

(c)  open-ended investment companies, and

(d)  European Economic Interest Groupings,

extend to Northern Ireland.

(2)  The following enactments shall cease to have effect accordingly—

(a)  the Limited Liability Partnerships Act (Northern Ireland) 2002 (c. 12 (N. I.));

(b)  the Limited Partnerships Act 1907 (c. 24) as it formerly had effect in Northern Ireland;

(c)  the Open-Ended Investment Companies Act (Northern Ireland) 2002 (c. 13 (N.I.));

(d)  the European Economic Interest Groupings Regulations (Northern Ireland) 1989 (SR 1989/216).

### 1287  Extension of enactments relating to business names

(1)  The provisions of Part 41 of this Act (business names) extend to Northern Ireland.

(2)  The Business Names (Northern Ireland) Order 1986 (S.I. 1986/1033 (N.I. 7)) shall cease to have effect accordingly.

## PART 46   GENERAL SUPPLEMENTARY PROVISIONS

*Regulations and orders*

### 1288  Regulations and orders: statutory instrument

Except as otherwise provided, regulations and orders under this Act shall be made by statutory instrument.

### 1289  Regulations and orders: negative resolution procedure

Where regulations or orders under this Act are subject to 'negative resolution procedure' the statutory instrument containing the regulations or order shall be subject to annulment in pursuance of a resolution of either House of Parliament.

### 1290  Regulations and orders: affirmative resolution procedure

Where regulations or orders under this Act are subject to 'affirmative resolution procedure' the regulations or order must not be made unless a draft of the statutory instrument containing them has been laid before Parliament and approved by a resolution of each House of Parliament.

### 1291  Regulations and orders: approval after being made

(1)  Regulations or orders under this Act that are subject to 'approval after being made'—

(a)  must be laid before Parliament after being made, and

(b)  cease to have effect at the end of 28 days beginning with the day on which they were made unless during that period they are approved by resolution of each House.

(2)  In reckoning the period of 28 days no account shall be taken of any time during which Parliament is dissolved or prorogued or during which both Houses are adjourned for more than four days.

(3)  The regulations or order ceasing to have effect does not affect—

(a)  anything previously done under them or it, or

(b)  the making of new regulations or a new order.

### 1292  Regulations and orders: supplementary

(1)  Regulations or orders under this Act may—

(a)  make different provision for different cases or circumstances,

(b)  include supplementary, incidental and consequential provision, and

(c)  make transitional provision and savings.

(2)  Any provision that may be made by regulations under this Act may be made by order; and any provision that may be made by order under this Act may be made by regulations.

(3)  Any provision that may be made by regulations or order under this Act for which no Parliamentary procedure is prescribed may be made by regulations or order subject to negative or affirmative resolution procedure.

(4)  Any provision that may be made by regulations or order under this Act subject to negative resolution procedure may be made by regulations or order subject to affirmative resolution procedure.

*Meaning of 'enactment'*

### 1293  Meaning of 'enactment'

In this Act, unless the context otherwise requires, 'enactment' includes—

(a) an enactment contained in subordinate legislation within the meaning of the Interpretation Act 1978 (c. 30),

(b) an enactment contained in, or in an instrument made under, an Act of the Scottish Parliament, and

(c) an enactment contained in, or in an instrument made under, Northern Ireland legislation within the meaning of the Interpretation Act 1978.

*Consequential and transitional provisions*

### 1294   Power to make consequential amendments etc

(1) The Secretary of State or the Treasury may by order make such provision amending, repealing or revoking any enactment to which this section applies as they consider necessary or expedient in consequence of any provision made by or under this Act.

(2) This section applies to—

(a) any enactment passed or made before the passing of this Act,

(b) any enactment contained in this Act or in subordinate legislation made under it, and

(c) any enactment passed or made before the end of the session after that in which this Act is passed.

(3) Without prejudice to the generality of the power conferred by subsection (1), orders under this section may—

(a) make provision extending to other forms of organisation any provision made by or under this Act in relation to companies, or

(b) make provision corresponding to that made by or under this Act in relation to companies,

in either case with such adaptations or other modifications as appear to the Secretary of State or the Treasury to be necessary or expedient.

(4) The references in subsection (3) to provision made by this Act include provision conferring power to make provision by regulations, orders or other subordinate legislation.

(5) Amendments and repeals made under this section are additional, and without prejudice, to those made by or under any other provision of this Act.

(6) Orders under this section are subject to affirmative resolution procedure.

### 1295   Repeals

The enactments specified in Schedule 16, which include enactments that are no longer of practical utility, are repealed to the extent specified.

### 1296   Power to make transitional provision and savings

(1) The Secretary of State or the Treasury may by order make such transitional provision and savings as they consider necessary or expedient in connection with the commencement of any provision made by or under this Act.

(2) An order may, in particular, make such adaptations of provisions brought into force as appear to be necessary or expedient in consequence of other provisions of this Act not yet having come into force.

(3) Transitional provision and savings made under this section are additional, and without prejudice, to those made by or under any other provision of this Act.

(4) Orders under this section are subject to negative resolution procedure.

### 1297   Continuity of the law

(1) This section applies where any provision of this Act re-enacts (with or without modification) an enactment repealed by this Act.

(2) The repeal and re-enactment does not affect the continuity of the law.

(3) Anything done (including subordinate legislation made), or having effect as if done, under or for the purposes of the repealed provision that could have been done under or for the purposes of the corresponding provision of this Act, if in force or effective immediately before the commencement of that corresponding provision, has effect thereafter as if done under or for the purposes of that corresponding provision.

(4) Any reference (express or implied) in this Act or any other enactment, instrument or document to a provision of this Act shall be construed (so far as the context permits) as including, as respects times, circumstances or purposes in relation to which the corresponding repealed provision had effect, a reference to that corresponding provision.

(5) Any reference (express or implied) in any enactment, instrument or document to a repealed provision shall be construed (so far as the context permits), as respects times, circumstances and purposes in relation to which the corresponding provision of this Act has effect, as being or (according to the context) including a reference to the corresponding provision of this Act.

(6) This section has effect subject to any specific transitional provision or saving contained in this Act.

(7) References in this section to this Act include subordinate legislation made under this Act.

(8) In this section 'subordinate legislation' has the same meaning as in the Interpretation Act 1978 (c. 30).

## PART 47  FINAL PROVISIONS

### 1298  Short title
The short title of this Act is the Companies Act 2006.

### 1299  Extent
Except as otherwise provided (or the context otherwise requires), the provisions of this Act extend to the whole of the United Kingdom.

### 1300  Commencement
 (1) The following provisions come into force on the day this Act is passed—

  (a) Part 43 (transparency obligations and related matters), except the amendment in paragraph 11(2) of Schedule 15 of the definition of 'regulated market' in Part 6 of the Financial Services and Markets Act 2000 (c. 8),

  (b) in Part 44 (miscellaneous provisions)—

   section 1274 (grants to bodies concerned with actuarial standards etc.), and

   section 1276 (application of provisions to Scotland and Northern Ireland),

  (c) Part 46 (general supplementary provisions), except section 1295 and Schedule 16 (repeals), and

  (d) this Part.

 (2) The other provisions of this Act come into force on such day as may be appointed by order of the Secretary of State or the Treasury.

# SCHEDULE 1

# CONNECTED PERSONS: REFERENCES TO AN INTEREST IN SHARES OR DEBENTURES

### Introduction

1.–(1) The provisions of this Schedule have effect for the interpretation of references in sections 254 and 255 (directors connected with or controlling a body corporate) to an interest in shares or debentures.

(2) The provisions are expressed in relation to shares but apply to debentures as they apply to shares.

### General provisions

2.–(1) A reference to an interest in shares includes any interest of any kind whatsoever in shares.

(2) Any restraints or restrictions to which the exercise of any right attached to the interest is or may be subject shall be disregarded.

(3) It is immaterial that the shares in which a person has an interest are not identifiable.

(4) Persons having a joint interest in shares are deemed each of them to have that interest.

### Rights to acquire shares

3.–(1) A person is taken to have an interest in shares if he enters into a contract to acquire them.

(2) A person is taken to have an interest in shares if—

 (a) he has a right to call for delivery of the shares to himself or to his order, or

 (b) he has a right to acquire an interest in shares or is under an obligation to take an interest in shares,

whether the right or obligation is conditional or absolute.

(3) Rights or obligations to subscribe for shares are not to be taken for the purposes of sub-paragraph (2) to be rights to acquire or obligations to take an interest in shares.

(4) A person ceases to have an interest in shares by virtue of this paragraph—

 (a) on the shares being delivered to another person at his order—

  (i) in fulfilment of a contract for their acquisition by him, or

  (ii) in satisfaction of a right of his to call for their delivery;

 (b) on a failure to deliver the shares in accordance with the terms of such a contract or on which such a right falls to be satisfied;

 (c) on the lapse of his right to call for the delivery of shares.

### Right to exercise or control exercise of rights

4.–(1) A person is taken to have an interest in shares if, not being the registered holder, he is entitled—

 (a) to exercise any right conferred by the holding of the shares, or

(b) to control the exercise of any such right.

(2) For this purpose a person is taken to be entitled to exercise or control the exercise of a right conferred by the holding of shares if he—

    (a) has a right (whether subject to conditions or not) the exercise of which would make him so entitled, or

    (b) is under an obligation (whether or not so subject) the fulfilment of which would make him so entitled.

(3) A person is not by virtue of this paragraph taken to be interested in shares by reason only that—

    (a) he has been appointed a proxy to exercise any of the rights attached to the shares, or

    (b) he has been appointed by a body corporate to act as its representative at any meeting of a company or of any class of its members.

### Bodies corporate

5.–(1) A person is taken to be interested in shares if a body corporate is interested in them and—

    (a) the body corporate or its directors are accustomed to act in accordance with his directions or instructions, or

    (b) he is entitled to exercise or control the exercise of more than one-half of the voting power at general meetings of the body corporate.

(2) For the purposes of sub-paragraph (1)(b) where—

    (a) a person is entitled to exercise or control the exercise of more than one-half of the voting power at general meetings of a body corporate, and

    (b) that body corporate is entitled to exercise or control the exercise of any of the voting power at general meetings of another body corporate,

the voting power mentioned in paragraph (b) above is taken to be exercisable by that person.

### Trusts

6.–(1) Where an interest in shares is comprised in property held on trust, every beneficiary of the trust is taken to have an interest in shares, subject as follows.

(2) So long as a person is entitled to receive, during the lifetime of himself or another, income from trust property comprising shares, an interest in the shares in reversion or remainder or (as regards Scotland) in fee shall be disregarded.

(3) A person is treated as not interested in shares if and so long as he holds them—

    (a) under the law in force in any part of the United Kingdom, as a bare trustee or as a custodian trustee, or

    (b) under the law in force in Scotland, as a simple trustee.

(4) There shall be disregarded any interest of a person subsisting by virtue of—

    (a) an authorised unit trust scheme (within the meaning of section 237 of the Financial Services and Markets Act 2000 (c. 8));

    (b) a scheme made under section 22 or 22A of the Charities Act 1960 (c. 58), section 25 of the Charities Act (Northern Ireland) 1964 (c. 33 (N.I.)) or section 24 or 25 of the Charities Act 1993 (c. 10), section 44 or 45 of the Charities Act (Northern Ireland) 2008, section 11 of the Trustee Investments Act 1961 (c. 62) or section 42 of the Administration of Justice Act 1982 (c. 53); or

    (c) the scheme set out in the Schedule to the Church Funds Investment Measure 1958 (1958 No. 1).

(5) There shall be disregarded any interest—

    (a) of the Church of Scotland General Trustees or of the Church of Scotland Trust in shares held by them;

    (b) of any other person in shares held by those Trustees or that Trust otherwise than as simple trustees.

'The Church of Scotland General Trustees' are the body incorporated by the order confirmed by the Church of Scotland (General Trustees) Order Confirmation Act 1921 (1921 c. xxv), and 'the Church of Scotland Trust' is the body incorporated by the order confirmed by the Church of Scotland Trust Order Confirmation Act 1932 (1932 c. xxi).

# SCHEDULE 2

# SPECIFIED PERSONS, DESCRIPTIONS OF DISCLOSURES ETC FOR THE PURPOSES OF SECTION 948

## PART 1    SPECIFIED PERSONS

1.–The Secretary of State.

2.–The Department of Enterprise, Trade and Investment for Northern Ireland.

3.–The Treasury.

3A.–The Treasury of the Isle of Man.

4.–The Bank of England.

5.–The Financial Services Authority.

5A.–The Financial Supervision Commission of the Isle of Man.

6.–The Commissioners for Her Majesty's Revenue and Customs.

7.–The Lord Advocate.

7A.–The Attorney General of the Isle of Man.

8.–The Director of Public Prosecutions.

9.–The Director of Public Prosecutions for Northern Ireland.

10.–A constable.

11.–A procurator fiscal.

12.–The Scottish Ministers.

12A.–The members and officers of each of the Departments constituted by section 1(1) of the Government Departments Act 1987 (an Act of Tynwald: c13).'Member' has the same meaning as it has by virtue of section 7(1) of that Act.

## PART 2     SPECIFIED DESCRIPTIONS OF DISCLOSURES

13.–A disclosure for the purpose of enabling or assisting a person authorised under section 457 of this Act (persons authorised to apply to court) to exercise his functions.

Until the coming into force of section 457, the reference to that section is to be read as a reference to section 245C of the Companies Act 1985 (c. 6).

14.–A disclosure for the purpose of enabling or assisting an inspector appointed under Part 14 of the Companies Act 1985 (investigation of companies and their affairs, etc) to exercise his functions.

14A. .–A disclosure for the purpose of enabling or assisting an inspector appointed by the High Court of the Isle of Man under the enactments relating to companies to exercise the functions of the inspector.

15.–A disclosure for the purpose of enabling or assisting a person authorised under section 447 of the Companies Act 1985 (power to require production of documents) or section 84 of the Companies Act 1989 (c. 40) (exercise of powers by officer etc) to exercise his functions.

16.–A disclosure for the purpose of enabling or assisting a person appointed under section 167 of the Financial Services and Markets Act 2000 (c. 8) (general investigations) to conduct an investigation to exercise his functions.

17.–A disclosure for the purpose of enabling or assisting a person appointed under section 168 of the Financial Services and Markets Act 2000 (investigations in particular cases) to conduct an investigation to exercise his functions.

18.–A disclosure for the purpose of enabling or assisting a person appointed under section 169(1) (b) of the Financial Services and Markets Act 2000 (investigation in support of overseas regulator) to conduct an investigation to exercise his functions.

19.–A disclosure for the purpose of enabling or assisting the body corporate responsible for administering the scheme referred to in section 225 of the Financial Services and Markets Act 2000 (the ombudsman scheme) to exercise its functions.

20.–A disclosure for the purpose of enabling or assisting a person appointed under paragraph 4 (the panel of ombudsmen) or 5 (the Chief Ombudsman) of Schedule 17 to the Financial Services and Markets Act 2000 to exercise his functions.

21.–A disclosure for the purpose of enabling or assisting a person appointed under regulations made under section 262(1) and (2)(k) of the Financial Services and Markets Act 2000 (investigations into open-ended investment companies) to conduct an investigation to exercise his functions.

22.–A disclosure for the purpose of enabling or assisting a person appointed under section 284 of the Financial Services and Markets Act 2000 (investigations into affairs of certain collective investment schemes) to conduct an investigation to exercise his functions.

22A.–A disclosure for the purpose of enabling or assisting a person conducting an investigation under—

    (a) section 16 of the Collective Investment Schemes Act 2008 (an Act of Tynwald: c7);

    (b) Schedule 2 to the Financial Services Act 2008 (an Act of Tynwald: c8); or

    (c) Schedule 5 to the Insurance Act 2008 (an Act of Tynwald: c16),

to exercise that person's functions.

23.–A disclosure for the purpose of enabling or assisting the investigator appointed under paragraph 7 of Schedule 1 to the Financial Services and Markets Act 2000 (arrangements for investigation of complaints) to exercise his functions.

24.–A disclosure for the purpose of enabling or assisting a person appointed by the Treasury to hold an inquiry into matters relating to financial services (including an inquiry under section 15 of the Financial Services and Markets Act 2000 (c. 8)) to exercise his functions.

25.–A disclosure for the purpose of enabling or assisting the Secretary of State or the Treasury to exercise any of their functions under any of the following—

    (a) the Companies Acts;

  (b) Part 5 of the Criminal Justice Act 1993 (c. 36) (insider dealing);
  (c) the Insolvency Act 1986 (c. 45);
  (d) the Company Directors Disqualification Act 1986 (c. 46);
  (e) Part 42 of this Act (statutory auditors);
  (f) Part 3 (investigations and powers to obtain information) or 7 (financial markets and insolvency) of the Companies Act 1989 (c. 40);
  (g) the Financial Services and Markets Act 2000.

Until the coming into force of Part 42 of this Act, the reference to it in paragraph (e) is to be read as a reference to Part 2 of the Companies Act 1989.

 25A.–A disclosure for the purpose of enabling or assisting the Financial Supervision Commission of the Isle of Man to exercise any of its functions.

 25B.–A disclosure for the purpose of enabling or assisting an auditor of a permitted person (within the meaning of the Financial Services Act 2008 (an Act of Tynwald)) to exercise the auditor's functions.

 26.–A disclosure for the purpose of enabling or assisting the Scottish Ministers to exercise their functions under the enactments relating to insolvency.

 27.–A disclosure for the purpose of enabling or assisting the Department of Enterprise, Trade and Investment for Northern Ireland to exercise any powers conferred on it by the enactments relating to companies or insolvency.

 27A.–A disclosure for the purpose of enabling or assisting the Treasury of the Isle of Man to exercise its functions under the enactments relating to companies, insurance companies or insolvency.

 28.–A disclosure for the purpose of enabling or assisting a person appointed or authorised by the Department of Enterprise, Trade and Investment for Northern Ireland under the enactments relating to companies or insolvency to exercise his functions.

 29.–A disclosure for the purpose of enabling or assisting the Pensions Regulator to exercise the functions conferred on it by or by virtue of any of the following—
  (a) the Pension Schemes Act 1993 (c. 48);
  (b) the Pensions Act 1995 (c. 26);
  (c) the Welfare Reform and Pensions Act 1999 (c. 30);
  (d) the Pensions Act 2004 (c. 35);
  (e) any enactment in force in Northern Ireland corresponding to any of those enactments.

 29A.–A disclosure for the purpose of enabling or assisting—
  (a) the Insurance and Pensions Authority of the Isle of Man; or
  (b) the Retirement Benefits Schemes Supervisor of the Isle of Man, to exercise its functions under the Retirement Benefits Schemes Act 2000 (an Act of Tynwald: c14).

 30.–A disclosure for the purpose of enabling or assisting the Board of the Pension Protection Fund to exercise the functions conferred on it by or by virtue of Part 2 of the Pensions Act 2004 or any enactment in force in Northern Ireland corresponding to that Part.

 31.–A disclosure for the purpose of enabling or assisting—
  (a) the Bank of England,
  (b) the European Central Bank, or
  (c) the central bank of any country or territory outside the United Kingdom, to exercise its functions.

 32.–A disclosure for the purpose of enabling or assisting the Commissioners for Her Majesty's Revenue and Customs to exercise their functions.

 32A.–A disclosure for the purpose of enabling or assisting the Assessor of Income Tax to exercise the Assessor's functions under enactments of the Isle of Man relating to income tax.

 33.–A disclosure for the purpose of enabling or assisting organs of the Society of Lloyd's (being organs constituted by or under the Lloyd's Act 1982 (c. xiv)) to exercise their functions under or by virtue of the Lloyd's Acts 1871 to 1982.

 34.–A disclosure for the purpose of enabling or assisting the Office of Fair Trading to exercise its functions under any of the following—
  (a) the Fair Trading Act 1973 (c. 41);
  (b) the Consumer Credit Act 1974 (c. 39);
  (c) the Estate Agents Act 1979 (c. 38);
  (d) the Competition Act 1980 (c. 21);
  (e) the Competition Act 1998 (c. 41);
  (f) the Financial Services and Markets Act 2000 (c. 8);
  (g) the Enterprise Act 2002 (c. 40);
  (h) [...]
  (i) the Unfair Terms in Consumer Contracts Regulations 1999 (S.I. 1999/2083) ;
  (j) the Business Protection from Misleading Marketing Regulations 2008;
  (k) the Consumer Protection from Unfair Trading Regulations 2008.

 35.–A disclosure for the purpose of enabling or assisting the Competition Commission to exercise its functions under any of the following—
  (a) the Fair Trading Act 1973;

(b) the Competition Act 1980;

(c) the Competition Act 1998;

(d) the Enterprise Act 2002.

36.–A disclosure with a view to the institution of, or otherwise for the purposes of, proceedings before the Competition Appeal Tribunal.

37.–A disclosure for the purpose of enabling or assisting an enforcer under Part 8 of the Enterprise Act 2002 (enforcement of consumer legislation) to exercise its functions under that Part.

38.–A disclosure for the purpose of enabling or assisting the Charity Commission to exercise its functions.

39.–A disclosure for the purpose of enabling or assisting the Attorney General or the Attorney General of the Isle of Man to exercise his functions in connection with charities.

40.–A disclosure for the purpose of enabling or assisting the National Lottery Commission to exercise its functions under sections 5 to 10 (licensing) and 15 (power of Secretary of State to require information) of the National Lottery etc. Act 1993 (c. 39).

41.–A disclosure by the National Lottery Commission to the National Audit Office for the purpose of enabling or assisting the Comptroller and Auditor General to carry out an examination under Part 2 of the National Audit Act 1983 (c. 44) into the economy, effectiveness and efficiency with which the National Lottery Commission has used its resources in discharging its functions under sections 5 to 10 of the National Lottery etc. Act 1993.

42.–A disclosure for the purpose of enabling or assisting a qualifying body under the Unfair Terms in Consumer Contracts Regulations 1999 (S.I. 1999/ 2083) to exercise its functions under those Regulations.

43.–A disclosure for the purpose of enabling or assisting an enforcement authority under the Consumer Protection (Distance Selling) Regulations 2000 (S.I. 2000/2334) to exercise its functions under those Regulations.

44.–A disclosure for the purpose of enabling or assisting an enforcement authority under the Financial Services (Distance Marketing) Regulations 2004 (S.I. 2004/2095) to exercise its functions under those Regulations.

45.–A disclosure for the purpose of enabling or assisting a local weights and measures authority in England and Wales to exercise its functions under section 230(2) of the Enterprise Act 2002 (c. 40) (notice of intention to prosecute, etc).

46.–A disclosure for the purpose of enabling or assisting the Financial Services Authority to exercise its functions under any of the following—

(a) the legislation relating to friendly societies or to industrial and provident societies;

(b) the Building Societies Act 1986 (c. 53);

(c) Part 7 of the Companies Act 1989 (c. 40) (financial markets and insolvency);

(d) the Financial Services and Markets Act 2000 (c. 8).

47.–A disclosure for the purpose of enabling or assisting the competent authority for the purposes of Part 6 of the Financial Services and Markets Act 2000 (official listing) to exercise its functions under that Part.

48.–A disclosure for the purpose of enabling or assisting a body corporate established in accordance with section 212(1) of the Financial Services and Markets Act 2000 (compensation scheme manager) to exercise its functions.

48A.–A disclosure for the purpose of enabling or assisting the body administering a scheme under section 25 of the Financial Services Act 2008 (an Act of Tynwald) (compensation schemes) to exercise its functions under the scheme.

49.–A disclosure for the purpose of enabling or assisting a recognised investment exchange or a recognised clearing house to exercise its functions as such.

'Recognised investment exchange' and 'recognised clearing house' have the same meaning as in section 285 of the Financial Services and Markets Act 2000.

50.–A disclosure for the purpose of enabling or assisting a person approved under the Uncertificated Securities Regulations 2001 (S.I. 2001/3755) as an operator of a relevant system (within the meaning of those regulations) to exercise his functions.

51.–A disclosure for the purpose of enabling or assisting a body designated under section 326(1) of the Financial Services and Markets Act 2000 (designated professional bodies) to exercise its functions in its capacity as a body designated under that section.

52.–A disclosure with a view to the institution of, or otherwise for the purposes of, civil proceedings arising under or by virtue of the Financial Services and Markets Act 2000.

52A.–A disclosure with a view to the institution of, or otherwise for the purposes of, civil proceedings arising under or by virtue of the Financial Services Act 2008 (an Act of Tynwald).

53.–A disclosure for the purpose of enabling or assisting a body designated by order under section 1252 of this Act (delegation of functions of Secretary of State) to exercise its functions under Part 42 of this Act (statutory auditors).

Until the coming into force of that Part, the references to section 1252 and Part 42 are to be read as references to section 46 of the Companies Act 1989 (c. 40) and Part 2 of that Act respectively.

54.–A disclosure for the purpose of enabling or assisting a recognised supervisory or qualifying body, within the meaning of Part 42 of this Act, to exercise its functions as such. Until the coming into force of that Part, the reference to it is to be read as a reference to Part 2 of the Companies Act 1989.

55.–A disclosure for the purpose of enabling or assisting an official receiver (including the Accountant in Bankruptcy in Scotland and the Official Assignee in Northern Ireland) to exercise his functions under the enactments relating to insolvency.

55A.–A disclosure for the purpose of enabling or assisting an official receiver appointed in the Isle of Man to exercise the official receiver's functions under the enactments relating to insolvency.

56.–A disclosure for the purpose of enabling or assisting the Insolvency Practitioners Tribunal to exercise its functions under the Insolvency Act 1986 (c. 45).

57.–A disclosure for the purpose of enabling or assisting a body that is for the time being a recognised professional body for the purposes of section 391 of the Insolvency Act 1986 (recognised professional bodies) to exercise its functions as such.

58.–A disclosure for the purpose of enabling or assisting an overseas regulatory authority to exercise its regulatory functions.

'Overseas regulatory authority' and 'regulatory functions' have the same meaning as in section 82 of the Companies Act 1989.

59.–A disclosure for the purpose of enabling or assisting the Regulator of Community Interest Companies to exercise functions under the Companies (Audit, Investigations and Community Enterprise) Act 2004 (c. 27).

60.–A disclosure with a view to the institution of, or otherwise for the purposes of, criminal proceedings.

61.–A disclosure for the purpose of enabling or assisting a person authorised by the Secretary of State under Part 2, 3 or 4 of the Proceeds of Crime Act 2002 (c. 29) to exercise his functions.

62.–A disclosure with a view to the institution of, or otherwise for the purposes of, proceedings on an application under section 6, 7 or 8 of the Company Directors Disqualification Act 1986 (c. 46) (disqualification for unfitness).

63.–A disclosure with a view to the institution of, or otherwise for the purposes of, proceedings before the Financial Services and Markets Tribunal.

64.–A disclosure for the purposes of proceedings before the Financial Services Tribunal by virtue of the Financial Services and Markets Act 2000 (Transitional Provisions) (Partly Completed Procedures) Order 2001 (S.I. 2001/3592).

65.–A disclosure for the purposes of proceedings before the Pensions Regulator Tribunal.

66.–A disclosure for the purpose of enabling or assisting a body appointed under section 14 of the Companies (Audit, Investigations and Community Enterprise) Act 2004 (supervision of periodic accounts and reports of issuers of listed securities) to exercise functions mentioned in subsection (2) of that section.

67.–A disclosure with a view to the institution of, or otherwise for the purposes of, disciplinary proceedings relating to the performance by a solicitor, barrister, advocate, foreign lawyer, auditor, accountant, valuer or actuary of his professional duties.

'Foreign lawyer' has the meaning given by section 89(9) of the Courts and Legal Services Act 1990 (c. 41).[1]

68.–A disclosure with a view to the institution of, or otherwise for the purposes of, disciplinary proceedings relating to the performance by a public servant of his duties. 'Public servant' means an officer or employee of the Crown or of any public or other authority for the time being designated for the purposes of this paragraph by the Secretary of State by order subject to negative resolution procedure.

69.–A disclosure for the purpose of the provision of a summary or collection of information framed in such a way as not to enable the identity of any person to whom the information relates to be ascertained.

70.–A disclosure in pursuance of any Community obligation.

## PART 3    OVERSEAS REGULATORY BODIES

71.–A disclosure is made in accordance with this Part of this Schedule if—
    (a) it is made to a person or body within paragraph 72, and
    (b) it is made for the purpose of enabling or assisting that person or body to exercise the functions mentioned in that paragraph.

72.–The persons or bodies that are within this paragraph are those exercising functions of a public nature, under legislation in any country or territory outside the United Kingdom, that appear to the Panel to be similar to its own functions or those of the Financial Services Authority.

---

[1] From a date to be appointed for the words 'solicitor, barrister, advocate' substitute 'relevant lawyer' and for the words ' "Foreign lawyer" has the meaning given by section 89(9) of the Courts and Legal Services Act 1990 (c. 41).' substitute, 'In this paragraph—
    "foreign lawyer" means a person (other than a relevant lawyer) who is a foreign lawyer within the meaning of section 89(9) of the Courts and Legal Services Act 1990;
    "relevant lawyer" means—(a) a person who, for the purposes of the Legal Services Act 2007, is an authorised person in relation to an activity which constitutes a reserved legal activity (within the meaning of that Act), (b) a solicitor or barrister in Northern Ireland, or(c) a solicitor or advocate in Scotland.'. The Legal Services Act 2007 c.29.

73.–In determining whether to disclose information to a person or body in accordance with this Part of this Schedule, the Panel must have regard to the following considerations—

(a) whether the use that the person or body is likely to make of the information is sufficiently important to justify making the disclosure;

(b) whether the person or body has adequate arrangements to prevent the information from being used or further disclosed otherwise than for the purposes of carrying out the functions mentioned in paragraph 72 or any other purposes substantially similar to those for which information disclosed to the Panel could be used or further disclosed.

# SCHEDULE 3

## AMENDMENTS OF REMAINING PROVISIONS OF THE COMPANIES ACT 1985 RELATING TO OFFENCES

### Failure to give information about interests in shares etc

1.–(1) In subsection (3) of section 444 of the Companies Act 1985 (c. 6) (failure to give information requested by Secretary of State relating to interests in shares etc) for 'is liable to imprisonment or a fine, or both' substitute 'commits an offence'.

(2) At the end of that section add—

'(4) A person guilty of an offence under this section is liable—

(a) on conviction on indictment, to imprisonment for a term not exceeding two years or a fine (or both);

(b) on summary conviction—

(i) in England and Wales, to imprisonment for a term not exceeding twelve months or to a fine not exceeding the statutory maximum (or both) and, for continued contravention, a daily default fine not exceeding one-fiftieth of the statutory maximum;

(ii) in Scotland or Northern Ireland, to imprisonment for a term not exceeding six months, or to a fine not exceeding the statutory maximum (or both) and, for continued contravention, a daily default fine not exceeding one-fiftieth of the statutory maximum.'.

2.– [...]

### Wrongful disclosure of information to which section 449 applies

3.–(1) Section 449 of the Companies Act 1985 (wrongful disclosure of information obtained in course of company investigation) is amended as follows.

(2) For subsection (6)(a) and (b) substitute 'is guilty of an offence.'

(3) After subsection (6) insert—

'(6A) A person guilty of an offence under this section is liable—

(a) on conviction on indictment, to imprisonment for a term not exceeding two years or a fine (or both);

(b) on summary conviction—

(i) in England and Wales, to imprisonment for a term not exceeding twelve months or to a fine not exceeding the statutory maximum (or both);

(ii) in Scotland or Northern Ireland, to imprisonment for a term not exceeding six months, or to a fine not exceeding the statutory maximum (or both).'.

(3) Omit subsection (7).

### Destruction, mutilation etc of company documents

4.–(1) For subsection (3) of section 450 of the Companies Act 1985 (offence of destroying, etc company documents) substitute—

'(3) A person guilty of an offence under this section is liable—

(a) on conviction on indictment, to imprisonment for a term not exceeding seven years or a fine (or both);

(b) on summary conviction—

(i) in England and Wales, to imprisonment for a term not exceeding twelve months or to a fine not exceeding the statutory maximum (or both);

(ii) in Scotland or Northern Ireland, to imprisonment for a term not exceeding six months, or to a fine not exceeding the statutory maximum (or both).'.

(2) Omit subsection (4) of that section.

### Provision of false information in purported compliance with section 447

5.–(1) For subsection (2) of section 451 of the Companies Act 1985 (c. 6) (provision of false information in response to requirement under section 447) substitute—

'(2) A person guilty of an offence under this section is liable—

(a) on conviction on indictment, to imprisonment for a term not exceeding two years or a fine (or both);

(b) on summary conviction—

   (i) in England and Wales, to imprisonment for a term not exceeding twelve months or to a fine not exceeding the statutory maximum (or both);

   (ii) in Scotland or Northern Ireland, to imprisonment for a term not exceeding six months, or to a fine not exceeding the statutory maximum (or both).'.

(2) Omit subsection (3) of that section.

### *Obstruction of inspector, etc exercising power to enter and remain on premises*

6.–(1) Section 453A of the Companies Act 1985 (obstruction of inspector etc exercising power to enter and remain on premises) is amended as follows.

(2) For subsection (5)(a) and (b) substitute 'is guilty of an offence.'

(3) After subsection (5) insert—

'(5A) A person guilty of an offence under this section is liable—

   (a) on conviction on indictment, to a fine;

   (b) on summary conviction, to a fine not exceeding the statutory maximum.'.

(4) Omit subsection (6).

### *Attempted evasion of restrictions under Part 15*

7.–(1) In subsection (1) of section 455 of the Companies Act 1985 (attempted evasion of restrictions under Part 15) for 'is liable to a fine if he' substitute 'commits an offence if he'.

(2) In subsection (2) of that section for the words 'the company' to the end substitute 'an offence is committed by—

   (i) the company, and

   (ii) every officer of the company who is in default.'

(3) After that subsection insert—

'(2A) A person guilty of an offence under this section is liable—

   (a) on conviction on indictment, to a fine;

   (b) on summary conviction, to a fine not exceeding the statutory maximum.'.

# SCHEDULE 4

# DOCUMENTS AND INFORMATION SENT OR SUPPLIED TO A COMPANY

## PART 1   INTRODUCTION

### *Application of Schedule*

1.–(1) This Schedule applies to documents or information sent or supplied to a company.

(2) It does not apply to documents or information sent or supplied by another company (see section 1144(3) and Schedule 5).

## PART 2   COMMUNICATIONS IN HARD COPY FORM

### *Introduction*

2. A document or information is validly sent or supplied to a company if it is sent or supplied in hard copy form in accordance with this Part of this Schedule.

### *Method of communication in hard copy form*

3.–(1) A document or information in hard copy form may be sent or supplied by hand or by post to an address (in accordance with paragraph 4).

(2) For the purposes of this Schedule, a person sends a document or information by post if he posts a prepaid envelope containing the document or information.

### *Address for communications in hard copy form*

4. A document or information in hard copy form may be sent or supplied—

   (a) to an address specified by the company for the purpose;

   (b) to the company's registered office;

   (c) to an address to which any provision of the Companies Acts authorises the document or information to be sent or supplied.

## PART 3   COMMUNICATIONS IN ELECTRONIC FORM

### *Introduction*

5. A document or information is validly sent or supplied to a company if it is sent or supplied in electronic form in accordance with this Part of this Schedule.

*Conditions for use of communications in electronic form*

6. A document or information may only be sent or supplied to a company in electronic form if—

    (a) the company has agreed (generally or specifically) that the document or information may be sent or supplied in that form (and has not revoked that agreement), or

    (b) the company is deemed to have so agreed by a provision in the Companies Acts.

*Address for communications in electronic form*

7.–(1) Where the document or information is sent or supplied by electronic means, it may only be sent or supplied to an address—

    (a) specified for the purpose by the company (generally or specifically), or

    (b) deemed by a provision in the Companies Acts to have been so specified.

(2) Where the document or information is sent or supplied in electronic form by hand or by post, it must be sent or supplied to an address to which it could be validly sent if it were in hard copy form.

## PART 4    OTHER AGREED FORMS OF COMMUNICATION

8. A document or information that is sent or supplied to a company otherwise than in hard copy form or electronic form is validly sent or supplied if it is sent or supplied in a form or manner that has been agreed by the company.

# SCHEDULE 5

# COMMUNICATIONS BY A COMPANY

## PART 1    INTRODUCTION

*Application of this Schedule*

1. This Schedule applies to documents or information sent or supplied by a company.

## PART 2    COMMUNICATIONS IN HARD COPY FORM

*Introduction*

2. A document or information is validly sent or supplied by a company if it is sent or supplied in hard copy form in accordance with this Part of this Schedule.

*Method of communication in hard copy form*

3.–(1) A document or information in hard copy form must be—

    (a) handed to the intended recipient, or

    (b) sent or supplied by hand or by post to an address (in accordance with paragraph 4).

(2) For the purposes of this Schedule, a person sends a document or information by post if he posts a prepaid envelope containing the document or information.

*Address for communications in hard copy form*

4.–(1) A document or information in hard copy form may be sent or supplied by the company—

    (a) to an address specified for the purpose by the intended recipient;

    (b) to a company at its registered office;

    (c) to a person in his capacity as a member of the company at his address as shown in the company's register of members;

    (d) to a person in his capacity as a director of the company at his address as shown in the company's register of directors;

    (e) to an address to which any provision of the Companies Acts authorises the document or information to be sent or supplied.

(2) Where the company is unable to obtain an address falling within sub-paragraph (1), the document or information may be sent or supplied to the intended recipient's last address known to the company.

## PART 3    COMMUNICATIONS IN ELECTRONIC FORM

*Introduction*

5. A document or information is validly sent or supplied by a company if it is sent in electronic form in accordance with this Part of this Schedule.

*Agreement to communications in electronic form*

6. A document or information may only be sent or supplied by a company in electronic form—

(a) to a person who has agreed (generally or specifically) that the document or information may be sent or supplied in that form (and has not revoked that agreement), or

(b) to a company that is deemed to have so agreed by a provision in the Companies Acts.

### *Address for communications in electronic form*

7.–(1) Where the document or information is sent or supplied by electronic means, it may only be sent or supplied to an address—

(a) specified for the purpose by the intended recipient (generally or specifically), or

(b) where the intended recipient is a company, deemed by a provision of the Companies Acts to have been so specified.

(2) Where the document or information is sent or supplied in electronic form by hand or by post, it must be—

(a) handed to the intended recipient, or

(b) sent or supplied to an address to which it could be validly sent if it were in hard copy form.

## PART 4    COMMUNICATIONS BY MEANS OF A WEBSITE

### *Use of website*

8. A document or information is validly sent or supplied by a company if it is made available on a website in accordance with this Part of this Schedule.

### *Agreement to use of website*

9. A document or information may only be sent or supplied by the company to a person by being made available on a website if the person—

(a) has agreed (generally or specifically) that the document or information may be sent or supplied to him in that manner, or

(b) is taken to have so agreed under—

(i) paragraph 10 (members of the company etc.), or

(ii) paragraph 11 (debenture holders),

and has not revoked that agreement.

### *Deemed agreement of members of company etc. to use of website*

10.–(1) This paragraph applies to a document or information to be sent or supplied to a person—

(a) as a member of the company, or

(b) as a person nominated by a member in accordance with the company's articles to enjoy or exercise all or any specified rights of the member in relation to the company, or

(c) as a person nominated by a member under section 146 to enjoy information rights.

(2) To the extent that—

(a) the members of the company have resolved that the company may send or supply documents or information to members by making them available on a website, or

(b) the company's articles contain provision to that effect,

a person in relation to whom the following conditions are met is taken to have agreed that the company may send or supply documents or information to him in that manner.

(3) The conditions are that—

(a) the person has been asked individually by the company to agree that the company may send or supply documents or information generally, or the documents or information in question, to him by means of a website, and

(b) the company has not received a response within the period of 28 days beginning with the date on which the company's request was sent.

(4) A person is not taken to have so agreed if the company's request—

(a) did not state clearly what the effect of a failure to respond would be, or

(b) was sent less than twelve months after a previous request made to him for the purposes of this paragraph in respect of the same or a similar class of documents or information.

(5) Chapter 3 of Part 3 (resolutions affecting a company's constitution) applies to a resolution under this paragraph.

### *Deemed agreement of debenture holders to use of website*

11.–(1) This paragraph applies to a document or information to be sent or supplied to a person as holder of a company's debentures.

(2) To the extent that—

(a) the relevant debenture holders have duly resolved that the company may send or supply documents or information to them by making them available on a website, or

(b) the instrument creating the debenture in question contains provision to that effect,

a debenture holder in relation to whom the following conditions are met is taken to have agreed that the company may send or supply documents or information to him in that manner.

(3) The conditions are that—

(a) the debenture holder has been asked individually by the company to agree that the company may send or supply documents or information generally, or the documents or information in question, to him by means of a website, and

(b) the company has not received a response within the period of 28 days beginning with the date on which the company's request was sent.

(4) A person is not taken to have so agreed if the company's request—

(a) did not state clearly what the effect of a failure to respond would be, or

(b) was sent less than twelve months after a previous request made to him for the purposes of this paragraph in respect of the same or a similar class of documents or information.

(4) For the purposes of this paragraph—

(a) the relevant debenture holders are the holders of debentures of the company ranking *pari passu* for all purposes with the intended recipient, and

(b) a resolution of the relevant debenture holders is duly passed if they agree in accordance with the provisions of the instruments creating the debentures.

### *Availability of document or information*

12.–(1) A document or information authorised or required to be sent or supplied by means of a website must be made available in a form, and by a means, that the company reasonably considers will enable the recipient—

(a) to read it, and

(b) to retain a copy of it.

(2) For this purpose a document or information can be read only if—

(a) it can be read with the naked eye, or

(b) to the extent that it consists of images (for example photographs, pictures, maps, plans or drawings), it can be seen with the naked eye.

### *Notification of availability*

13.–(1) The company must notify the intended recipient of—

(a) the presence of the document or information on the website,

(b) the address of the website,

(c) the place on the website where it may be accessed, and

(d) how to access the document or information.

(2) The document or information is taken to be sent—

(a) on the date on which the notification required by this paragraph is sent, or

(b) if later, the date on which the document or information first appears on the website after that notification is sent.

### *Period of availability on website*

14.–(1) The company must make the document or information available on the website throughout—

(a) the period specified by any applicable provision of the Companies Acts, or

(b) if no such period is specified, the period of 28 days beginning with the date on which the notification required under paragraph 13 is sent to the person in question.

(2) For the purposes of this paragraph, a failure to make a document or information available on a website throughout the period mentioned in sub-paragraph (1) shall be disregarded if—

(a) it is made available on the website for part of that period, and

(b) the failure to make it available throughout that period is wholly attributable to circumstances that it would not be reasonable to have expected the company to prevent or avoid.

## PART 5   OTHER AGREED FORMS OF COMMUNICATION

15. A document or information that is sent or supplied otherwise than in hard copy or electronic form or by means of a website is validly sent or supplied if it is sent or supplied in a form or manner that has been agreed by the intended recipient.

## PART 6   SUPPLEMENTARY PROVISIONS

### *Joint holders of shares or debentures*

16.–(1) This paragraph applies in relation to documents or information to be sent or supplied to joint holders of shares or debentures of a company.

(2) Anything to be agreed or specified by the holder must be agreed or specified by all the joint holders.

(3) Anything authorised or required to be sent or supplied to the holder may be sent or supplied either—

(a) to each of the joint holders, or

(b) to the holder whose name appears first in the register of members or the relevant register of debenture holders.

(4)  This paragraph has effect subject to anything in the company's articles.

### Death or bankruptcy of holder of shares

17.–(1)  This paragraph has effect in the case of the death or bankruptcy of a holder of a company's shares.

(2)  Documents or information required or authorised to be sent or supplied to the member may be sent or supplied to the persons claiming to be entitled to the shares in consequence of the death or bankruptcy—

    (a)  by name, or

    (b)  by the title of representatives of the deceased, or trustee of the bankrupt, or by any like description, at the address in the United Kingdom supplied for the purpose by those so claiming.

(3)  Until such an address has been so supplied, a document or information may be sent or supplied in any manner in which it might have been sent or supplied if the death or bankruptcy had not occurred.

(4)  This paragraph has effect subject to anything in the company's articles.

(5)  References in this paragraph to the bankruptcy of a person include—

    (a)  the sequestration of the estate of a person;

    (b)  a person's estate being the subject of a protected trust deed (within the meaning of the Bankruptcy (Scotland) Act 1985 (c. 66)).

In such a case the reference in sub-paragraph (2)(b) to the trustee of the bankrupt is to be read as the permanent or interim trustee (within the meaning of that Act) on the sequestrated estate or, as the case may be, the trustee under the protected deed.

# SCHEDULE 6

# MEANING OF 'SUBSIDIARY' ETC.: SUPPLEMENTARY PROVISIONS

### Introduction

1.  The provisions of this Part of this Schedule explain expressions used in section 1159 (meaning of 'subsidiary' etc.) and otherwise supplement that section.

### Voting rights in a company

2.  In section 1159(1)(a) and (c) the references to the voting rights in a company are to the rights conferred on shareholders in respect of their shares or, in the case of a company not having a share capital, on members, to vote at general meetings of the company on all, or substantially all, matters.

### Right to appoint or remove a majority of the directors

3.–(1)  In section 1159(1)(b) the reference to the right to appoint or remove a majority of the board of directors is to the right to appoint or remove directors holding a majority of the voting rights at meetings of the board on all, or substantially all, matters.

(2)  A company shall be treated as having the right to appoint to a directorship if—

    (a)  a person's appointment to it follows necessarily from his appointment as director of the company, or

    (b)  the directorship is held by the company itself.

(3)  A right to appoint or remove which is exercisable only with the consent or concurrence of another person shall be left out of account unless no other person has a right to appoint or, as the case may be, remove in relation to that directorship.

### Rights exercisable only in certain circumstances or temporarily incapable of exercise

4.–(1)  Rights which are exercisable only in certain circumstances shall be taken into account only—

    (a)  when the circumstances have arisen, and for so long as they continue to obtain, or

    (b)  when the circumstances are within the control of the person having the rights.

(2)  Rights which are normally exercisable but are temporarily incapable of exercise shall continue to be taken into account.

### Rights held by one person on behalf of another

5.  Rights held by a person in a fiduciary capacity shall be treated as not held by him.

6.–(1)  Rights held by a person as nominee for another shall be treated as held by the other.

(2)  Rights shall be regarded as held as nominee for another if they are exercisable only on his instructions or with his consent or concurrence.

### Rights attached to shares held by way of security

7.  Rights attached to shares held by way of security shall be treated as held by the person providing the security—

(a) where apart from the right to exercise them for the purpose of preserving the value of the security, or of realising it, the rights are exercisable only in accordance with his instructions, and

(b) where the shares are held in connection with the granting of loans as part of normal business activities and apart from the right to exercise them for the purpose of preserving the value of the security, or of realising it, the rights are exercisable only in his interests.

### *Rights attributed to holding company*

8.–(1) Rights shall be treated as held by a holding company if they are held by any of its subsidiary companies.

(2) Nothing in paragraph 6 or 7 shall be construed as requiring rights held by a holding company to be treated as held by any of its subsidiaries.

(3) For the purposes of paragraph 7 rights shall be treated as being exercisable in accordance with the instructions or in the interests of a company if they are exercisable in accordance with the instructions of or, as the case may be, in the interests of—

(a) any subsidiary or holding company of that company, or

(b) any subsidiary of a holding company of that company.

### *Disregard of certain rights*

9. The voting rights in a company shall be reduced by any rights held by the company itself.

### *Supplementary*

10. References in any provision of paragraphs 5 to 9 to rights held by a person include rights falling to be treated as held by him by virtue of any other provision of those paragraphs but not rights which by virtue of any such provision are to be treated as not held by him.

## SCHEDULE 7

## PARENT AND SUBSIDIARY UNDERTAKINGS: SUPPLEMENTARY PROVISIONS

### *Introduction*

1. The provisions of this Schedule explain expressions used in section 1162 (parent and subsidiary undertakings) and otherwise supplement that section.

### *Voting rights in an undertaking*

2.–(1) In section 1162(2)(a) and (d) the references to the voting rights in an undertaking are to the rights conferred on shareholders in respect of their shares or, in the case of an undertaking not having a share capital, on members, to vote at general meetings of the undertaking on all, or substantially all, matters.

(2) In relation to an undertaking which does not have general meetings at which matters are decided by the exercise of voting rights the references to holding a majority of the voting rights in the undertaking shall be construed as references to having the right under the constitution of the undertaking to direct the overall policy of the undertaking or to alter the terms of its constitution.

### *Right to appoint or remove a majority of the directors*

3.–(1) In section 1162(2)(b) the reference to the right to appoint or remove a majority of the board of directors is to the right to appoint or remove directors holding a majority of the voting rights at meetings of the board on all, or substantially all, matters.

(2) An undertaking shall be treated as having the right to appoint to a directorship if—

(a) a person's appointment to it follows necessarily from his appointment as director of the undertaking, or

(b) the directorship is held by the undertaking itself.

(3) A right to appoint or remove which is exercisable only with the consent or concurrence of another person shall be left out of account unless no other person has a right to appoint or, as the case may be, remove in relation to that directorship.

### *Right to exercise dominant influence*

4.–(1) For the purposes of section 1162(2)(c) an undertaking shall not be regarded as having the right to exercise a dominant influence over another undertaking unless it has a right to give directions with respect to the operating and financial policies of that other undertaking which its directors are obliged to comply with whether or not they are for the benefit of that other undertaking.

(2) A 'control contract' means a contract in writing conferring such a right which—

(a) is of a kind authorised by the articles of the undertaking in relation to which the right is exercisable, and

(b) is permitted by the law under which that undertaking is established.

(3) This paragraph shall not be read as affecting the construction of section 1162(4)(a).

### *Rights exercisable only in certain circumstances or temporarily incapable of exercise*

5.–(1) Rights which are exercisable only in certain circumstances shall be taken into account only—

(a) when the circumstances have arisen, and for so long as they continue to obtain, or

(b) when the circumstances are within the control of the person having the rights.

(2) Rights which are normally exercisable but are temporarily incapable of exercise shall continue to be taken into account.

### *Rights held by one person on behalf of another*

6. Rights held by a person in a fiduciary capacity shall be treated as not held by him.

7.–(1) Rights held by a person as nominee for another shall be treated as held by the other.

(2) Rights shall be regarded as held as nominee for another if they are exercisable only on his instructions or with his consent or concurrence.

### *Rights attached to shares held by way of security*

8. Rights attached to shares held by way of security shall be treated as held by the person providing the security—

(a) where apart from the right to exercise them for the purpose of preserving the value of the security, or of realising it, the rights are exercisable only in accordance with his instructions, and

(b) where the shares are held in connection with the granting of loans as part of normal business activities and apart from the right to exercise them for the purpose of preserving the value of the security, or of realising it, the rights are exercisable only in his interests.

### *Rights attributed to parent undertaking*

9.–(1) Rights shall be treated as held by a parent undertaking if they are held by any of its subsidiary undertakings.

(2) Nothing in paragraph 7 or 8 shall be construed as requiring rights held by a parent undertaking to be treated as held by any of its subsidiary undertakings.

(3) For the purposes of paragraph 8 rights shall be treated as being exercisable in accordance with the instructions or in the interests of an undertaking if they are exercisable in accordance with the instructions of or, as the case may be, in the interests of any group undertaking.

### *Disregard of certain rights*

10. The voting rights in an undertaking shall be reduced by any rights held by the undertaking itself.

### *Supplementary*

11. References in any provision of paragraphs 6 to 10 to rights held by a person include rights falling to be treated as held by him by virtue of any other provision of those paragraphs but not rights which by virtue of any such provision are to be treated as not held by him.

# SCHEDULE 8

# INDEX OF DEFINED EXPRESSIONS

| | |
|---|---|
| abbreviated accounts (in Part 15) | sections 444(4) and 445(3) |
| accounting reference date and accounting reference period | section 391 |
| accounting standards (in Part 15) | section 464 |
| accounts meeting | section 437(3) |
| acquisition, in relation to a non-cash asset address | section 1163(2) |
| – generally in the Companies Acts | section 1142 |
| – in the company communications provisions | section 1148(1) |
| affirmative resolution procedure, in relation to regulations and orders | section 1290 |
| allotment (time of) | section 558 |
| allotment of equity securities (in Chapter 3 of Part 17) | section 560(2) |
| allotted share capital and allotted shares | section 546(1)(b) and (2) |
| annual accounts (in Part 15) | section 471 |
| annual accounts and reports (in Part 15) | section 471 |
| annual general meeting | section 336 |
| annual return | section 854 |
| appropriate audit authority (in sections 522, 523 and 524) | section 525(1) |

appropriate rate of interest
  – in Chapter 5 of Part 17                                                   section 592
  – in Chapter 6 of Part 17                                                   section 609
approval after being made, in relation to regulations and orders             section 1291
arrangement
  – in Chapter 7 of Part 17                                                   section 616(1)
  – in Part 26                                                                section 895(2)
articles                                                                     section 18
associate (in Chapter 3 of Part 28)                                          section 988
associated bodies corporate and associated company (in Part 10)             section 256
authenticated, in relation to a document or information sent
  or supplied to a company                                                   section 1146
authorised group, of members of a company (in Part 14)                      section 370(3)
authorised insurance company                                                 section 1165(2)
authorised minimum (in relation to share capital of public company)        section 763
available profits (in Chapter 5 of Part 18)                                  sections 711 and 712
banking company and banking group                                           section 1164
body corporate                                                               section 1173(1)
called-up share capital                                                      section 547
capital redemption reserve                                                   section 733
capitalisation in relation to a company's profits (in Part 23)              section 853(3)
cash (in relation to paying up or allotting shares)                         section 583
cause of action, in relation to derivative proceedings
  (in Chapter 2 of Part 11)                                                  section 265(7)
certified translation (in Part 35)                                          section 1107
charge (in Chapter 1 of Part 25)                                            section 861(5)
circulation date, in relation to a written resolution (in Part 13)         section 290
class of shares                                                              section 629
the Companies Acts                                                          section 2
Companies Act accounts                                                      sections 395(1)(a) and
                                                                            403(2)(a)
Companies Act group accounts                                                section 403(2)(a)
Companies Act individual accounts                                           section 395(1)(a)
companies involved in the division (in Part 27)                            section 919(2)
company
  – generally in the Companies Acts                                         section 1
  – in Chapter 7 of Part 17                                                 section 616(1)
  – in Chapter 1 of Part 25                                                 section 861(5)
  – in Chapter 2 of Part 25                                                 section 879(6)
  – in Part 26                                                              section 895(2)
  – in Chapter 3 of Part 28                                                 section 991(1)
  – in the company communications                                          section 1148(1)
    provisions
the company communications provisions                                      section 1143
the company law provisions of this Act                                     section 2(2)
company records (in Part 37)                                               section 1134
connected with, in relation to a director (in                             sections 252 to 254
  Part 10)
constitution, of a company
  – generally in the Companies Acts                                        section 17
  – in Part 10                                                             section 257
controlling, of a body corporate by a director (in Part 10)              section 255
corporation                                                                section 1173(1)
the court                                                                   section 1156
credit institution                                                         section 1173(1)
credit transaction (in Chapter 4 of Part 10)                              section 202
creditor (in Chapter 1 of Part 31)                                        section 1011
daily default fine                                                         section 1125
date of the offer (in Chapter 3 of Part 28)                               section 991(1)
debenture                                                                  section 738
derivative claim (in Chapter 1 of Part 11)                                section 260
derivative proceedings (in Chapter 2 of Part 11)                          section 265
Directive disclosure requirements director                               section 1078
  – generally in the Companies Acts                                       section 250
  – in Chapter 8 of Part 10                                               section 240(3)

– in Chapter 1 of Part 11 — section 260(5)
– in Chapter 2 of Part 11 — section 265(7)
– in Part 14 — section 379(1)
directors' remuneration report — section 420
directors' report — section 415
distributable profits
– in Chapter 2 of Part 18 — section 683(1)
– elsewhere in Part 18 — section 736
distribution
– in Chapter 2 of Part 18 — section 683(1)
– in Part 23 — section 829
division (in Part 27) — section 919
document
– in Part 35 — section 1114(1)
– in the company communications provisions — section 1148(1)
dormant, in relation to a company or other body corporate — section 1169
EEA State and related expressions — section 1170
electronic form, electronic copy, electronic means
– generally in the Companies Acts — section 1168(3) and (4)
– in relation to communications to a company — Part 3 of Schedule 4
– in relation to communications by a company — Part 3 of Schedule 5
eligible members, in relation to a written resolution — section 289
e-money issuer
– in Part 15 — section 474(1)
– in Part 16 — section 539
employees' share scheme — section 1166
employer and employee (in Chapter 1 of Part 18) — section 676
enactment — section 1293
equity securities (in Chapter 3 of Part 17) — section 560(1)
equity share capital — section 548
equity shares (in Chapter 7 of Part 17) — section 616(1)
existing company (in Part 27) — section 902(2)
fellow subsidiary undertakings — section 1161(4)
financial assistance (in Chapter 2 of Part 18) — section 677
financial institution — section 1173(1)
financial year, of a company — section 390
firm — section 1173(1)
fixed assets (in Part 23) — section 853
the former Companies Acts — section 1171
the Gazette — section 1173(1)
group (in Part 15) — section 474(1)
group undertaking — section 1161(5)
hard copy form and hard copy
– generally in the Companies Acts — section 1168(2)
– in relation to communications to a company — Part 2 of Schedule 4
– in relation to communications by a company — Part 2 of Schedule 5
hire-purchase agreement — section 1173(1)
holder of shares (in Chapter 3 of Part 17) — section 574
holding company — section 1159 (and see section 1160 and Schedule 6)
IAS accounts — sections 395(1)(b) and 403(1) and (2)(b)
IAS group accounts — section 403(1) and (2)(b)
IAS individual accounts — section 395(1)(b)
IAS Regulation (in Part 15) — section 474(1)
included in the consolidation, in relation to group accounts (in Part 15) — section 474(1)
individual accounts — section 394
information rights (in Part 9) — section 146(3)
insurance company — section 1165(3)
insurance group — section 1165(5)
insurance market activity — section 1165(7)
interest in shares (for the purposes of Part 22) — sections 820 to 825
international accounting standards (in Part 15) — section 474(1)
investment company (in Part 23) — section 833

| | |
|---|---|
| issued share capital and issued shares | section 546(1)(a) and (2) |
| the issuing company (in Chapter 7 of Part 17) | section 610(6) |
| the Joint Stock Companies Acts | section 1171 |
| liabilities (in Part 27) | section 941 |
| liability, references to incurring, reducing or discharging (in Chapter 2 of Part 18) | section 683(2) |
| limited by guarantee | section 3(3) |
| limited by shares | section 3(2) |
| limited company | section 3 |
| the main register (of members)(in Chapter 3 of Part 8) | section 131(1) |
| major audit (in sections 522 and 525) | section 525(2) |
| market purchase, by a company of its own shares (in Chapter 4 of Part 18) | section 693(4) |
| member, of a company | |
| – generally in the Companies Acts | section 112 |
| – in Chapter 1 of Part 11 | section 260(5) |
| – in Chapter 2 of Part 11 | section 265(7) |
| memorandum of association | section 8 |
| merger (in Part 27) | section 904 |
| merging companies (in Part 27) | section 904(2) |
| merger by absorption (in Part 27) | section 904(1)(a) |
| merger by formation of a new company(in Part 27) | section 904(1)(b) |
| MiFID investment firm | |
| – in Part 15 | section 474(1) |
| – in Part 16 | section 539 |
| negative resolution procedure, in relation to regulations and orders | section 1289 |
| net assets (in Part 7) | section 92 |
| new company (in Part 27) | section 902(2) |
| non-cash asset | section 1163 |
| non traded company (in Part 24) | section 855(4) |
| non-voting shares (in Chapter 3 of Part 28) | section 991(1) |
| number, in relation to shares | section 540(4)(b) |
| off-market purchase, by a company of its own shares (in Chapter 4 of Part 18) | section 693(2) |
| offer period (in Chapter 2 of Part 28) | section 971(1) |
| offer to the public (in Chapter 1 of Part 20) | section 756 |
| offer or | |
| – in Chapter 2 of Part 28 | section 971(1) |
| – in Chapter 3 of Part 28 | section 991(1) |
| officer, in relation to a body corporate | section 1173(1) |
| officer in default | section 1121 |
| official seal, of registrar | section 1062 |
| opted-in company (in Chapter 2 of Part 28) | section 971(1) |
| opting-in resolution (in Chapter 2 of Part 28) | section 966(1) |
| opting-out resolution (in Chapter 2 of Part 28) | section 966(5) |
| ordinary resolution | section 282 |
| ordinary shares (in Chapter 3 of Part 17) | section 560(1) |
| organisation (in Part 14) | section 379(1) |
| other relevant transactions or arrangements (in Chapter 4 of Part 10) | section 210 |
| overseas company | section 1044 |
| overseas branch register | section 129(1) |
| paid up | section 583 |
| the Panel (in Part 28) | section 942 |
| parent company | section 1173(1) |
| parent undertaking | section 1162 (and see Schedule 7) |
| payment for loss of office(in Chapter 4 of Part 10) | section 215 |
| pension scheme (in Chapter 1 of Part 18) | section 675 |
| period for appointing auditors, in relation to a private company | section 485(2) |
| period for filing, in relation to accounts and reports for a financial year | section 442 |
| permissible capital payment (in Chapter 5 of Part 18) | section 710 |
| political donation (in Part 14) | section 364 |
| political expenditure (in Part 14) | section 365 |
| political organisation (in Part 14) | section 363(2) |
| prescribed | section 1167 |

| | |
|---|---|
| private company | section 4 |
| profit and loss account (in Part 15) | section 474(1) and (2) |
| profits and losses (in Part 23) | section 853(2) |
| profits available for distribution(for the purposes of Part 23) | section 830(2) |
| property (in Part 27) | section 941 |
| protected information (in Chapter 8 of Part 10) | section 240 |
| provision for entrenchment, in relation to a company's articles | section 22 |
| public company | section 4 |
| publication, in relation to accounts and reports (in sections 433 to 435) | section 436 |
| qualified, in relation to an auditor's report etc. (in Part 16) | section 539 |
| qualifying shares (in Chapter 6 of Part 18) | section 724(2) |
| qualifying third party indemnity provision (in Chapter 7 of Part 10) | section 234 |
| qualifying pension scheme indemnity provision (in Chapter 7 of Part 10) | section 235 |
| quasi-loan (in Chapter 4 of Part 10) | section 199 |
| quoted company | |
| – in Part 13 | section 361 |
| – in Part 15 | section 385 |
| – in Chapter 5 of Part 16 | section 531 (and section 385) |
| realised profits and losses (in Part 23) | section 853(4) |
| redeemable shares | section 684(1) |
| redenominate | section 622(1) |
| redenomination reserve | section 628 |
| the register | section 1080 |
| register of charges, kept by registrar | |
| – in England and Wales and Northern Ireland | section 869 |
| – in Scotland | section 885 |
| register of directors | section 162 |
| register of directors' residential addresses | section 165 |
| register of members | section 113 |
| register of secretaries | section 275 |
| registered number, of a branch of an overseas company | section 1067 |
| registered number, of a company | section 1066 |
| registered office, of a company | section 86 |
| registrar and registrar of companies | section 1060 |
| registrar's index of company names | section 1099 |
| registrar's rules | section 1117 |
| registration in a particular part of the United Kingdom | section 1060(4) |
| regulated activity | |
| – generally in the Companies Acts | section 1173(1) |
| – in Part 15 | section 474(1) |
| regulated market | section 1173(1) |
| relevant accounts (in Part 23) | section 836(2) |
| requirements for proper delivery (in Part 35) | section 1072 (and see section 1073) |
| requirements of this Act | section 1172 |
| return period (in Part 24) | section 855(4) |
| securities (and related expressions) | |
| – in Chapter 1 of Part 20 | section 755(5) |
| – in Chapter 2 of Part 21 | section 783 |
| senior statutory auditor | section 504 |
| sent or supplied, in relation to documents or information (in the companycommunications provisions) | section 1148(2) and (3) |
| service address | section 1141 |
| service contract, of a director (in Part 10) | section 227 |
| shadow director | section 251 |
| share | |
| – generally in the Companies Acts | section 540 (and see section 1161(2)) |
| – in Part 22 | section 792 |
| – in section 1162 and Schedule 7 | section 1162(7) |
| share capital, company having a | section 545 |
| share exchange ratio | |
| – in Chapter 2 of Part 27 | section 905(2) |

| | |
|---|---|
| – in Chapter 3 of Part 27 | section 920(2) |
| share premium account | section 610(1) |
| share warrant | section 779(1) |
| small companies exemption (in relation to directors' report) | section 415A |
| small companies regime (for accounts) | section 381 |
| solvency statement (in sections 641 to 644) | section 643 |
| special notice, in relation to a resolution | section 312 |
| special resolution | section 283 |
| statutory accounts | section 434(3) |
| subsidiary | section 1159 (and see section 1160 and Schedule 6) |
| subsidiary undertaking | section 1162 (and see Schedule 7) |
| summary financial statement | section 426 |
| takeover bid (in Chapter 2 of Part 28) | section 971(1) |
| takeover offer (in Chapter 3 of Part 28) | section 974 |
| the Takeovers Directive | |
| – in Chapter 1 of Part 28 | section 943(8) |
| – in Chapter 2 of Part 28 | section 971(1) |
| traded company (in Part 24) | section 855(4) |
| trading certificate | section 761(1) |
| transfer, in relation to a non-cash asset | section 1163(2) |
| treasury shares | section 724(5) |
| turnover | |
| – in Part 15 | section 474(1) |
| – in Part 16 | section 539 |
| UCITS management company | |
| – in Part 15 | section 474(1) |
| – in Part 16 | section 539 |
| UK-registered company | section 1158 |
| uncalled share capital | section 547 |
| unconditional, in relation to a contract to acquire shares (in Chapter 3 of Part 28) | section 991(2) |
| undistributable reserves | section 831(4) |
| undertaking | section 1161(1) |
| unique identifier | section 1082 |
| unlimited company | section 3 |
| unquoted company (in Part 15) | section 385 |
| voting rights | |
| – in Chapter 2 of Part 28 | section 971(1) |
| – in Chapter 3 of Part 28 | section 991(1) |
| – in section 1159 and Schedule 6 | paragraph 2 of Schedule 6 |
| – in section 1162 and Schedule 7 | paragraph 2 of Schedule 7 |
| voting shares | |
| – in Chapter 2 of Part 28 | section 971(1) |
| – in Chapter 3 of Part 28 | section 991(1) |
| website, communication by a company by means of | Part 4 of Schedule 5 |
| Welsh company | section 88 |
| wholly-owned subsidiary | section 1159(2) (and see section 1160 and Schedule 6) |
| working day, in relation to a company | section 1173(1) |
| written resolution | section 288 |

# SCHEDULE 9

# REMOVAL OF SPECIAL PROVISIONS ABOUT ACCOUNTS AND AUDIT OF CHARITABLE COMPANIES

## PART 1   THE COMPANIES ACT 1985 (C. 6)

1.–In section 240 (requirements in connection with publication of accounts)—

    (a)  in subsection (1) omit from 'or, as the case may be,' to 'section 249A(2)';

    (b)  in subsection (3)(c) omit from 'and, if no such report' to 'any financial year';

(c) after subsection (3)(c) insert ', and';

(d) omit subsection (3)(e) and the ', and' preceding it;

(e) in the closing words of subsection (3) omit from 'or any report' to 'section 249A(2)'.

2.–In section 245 (voluntary revision of annual accounts or directors' report), in subsection (4)(b) omit 'or reporting accountant'.

3.–In section 249A (exemptions from audit)—

(a) omit subsections (2), (3A) and (4);

(b) in subsection (6) for 'figures for turnover or gross income' substitute 'figure for turnover';

(c) in subsection (6A) omit 'or (2)';

(d) in subsection (7) omit the definition of 'gross income' and the ', and' preceding it.

4.–In section 249B (cases where exemptions not available)—

(a) in the opening words of subsection (1) omit 'or (2)';

(b) in subsection (1C)(b) omit from 'where the company referred to' to 'is not a charity';

(c) in subsection (3) omit 'or (2)';

(d) in subsection (4), in the opening words and in paragraph (a), omit 'or (2)'.

5.–Omit section 249C (report required for purposes of section 249A(2)).

6.–Omit section 249D (the reporting accountant).

7.–In section 249E (effect of exemptions) omit subsection (2).

8.–In section 262A (index of defined expressions) omit the entry for 'reporting accountant'.

### PART 2    THE COMPANIES (NORTHERN IRELAND) ORDER 1986 (S.I. 1986/1032 (N.I. 6))

9.–In Article 248 (requirements in connection with publication of accounts)—

(a) in paragraph (1) omit from 'or, as the case may be,' to 'Article 257A(2)';

(b) in paragraph (3)(c) omit from 'and, if no such report' to 'any such financial year';

(c) after paragraph (3)(c) insert ', and';

(d) omit paragraph (3)(e) and the word ', and' preceding it;

(e) in the closing words of paragraph (3) omit from 'or any report' to 'Article 257A(2)'.

10.–In Article 253 (voluntary revision of annual accounts or directors' report), in paragraph (4)(b) omit 'or reporting accountant'.

11.–In Article 257A (exemptions from audit)—

(a) omit paragraphs (2), (3A) and (4);

(b) in paragraph (6) for 'figures for turnover or gross income' substitute 'figure for turnover';

(c) in paragraph (6A) omit 'or (2)';

(d) in paragraph (7) omit the definition of 'gross income' and the ', and' preceding it.

12.–In Article 257B (cases where exemptions not available)—

(a) in the opening words of paragraph (1) omit 'or (2)';

(b) in paragraph (1C)(b) omit from 'where the company referred to' to 'is not a charity';

(c) in paragraph (3) omit 'or (2)';

(d) in paragraph (4), in the opening words and in sub-paragraph (a), omit 'or (2)'.

13.–Omit Article 257C (report required for purposes of Article 257A(2)).

14.–Omit Article 257D (the reporting accountant).

15.–In Article 257E (effect of exemptions) omit paragraph (2).

16.–In Article 270A (index of defined expressions) omit the entry for 'reporting accountant'.

## SCHEDULE 10

## RECOGNISED SUPERVISORY BODIES

### PART 1    GRANT AND REVOCATION OF RECOGNITION OF A SUPERVISORY BODY

*Application for recognition of supervisory body*

1.–(1) A supervisory body may apply to the Secretary of State for an order declaring it to be a recognised supervisory body for the purposes of this Part of this Act ('a recognition order').

(2) Any such application must be—

(a) made in such manner as the Secretary of State may direct, and

(b) accompanied by such information as the Secretary of State may reasonably require for the purpose of determining the application.

(3) At any time after receiving an application and before determining it the Secretary of State may require the applicant to furnish additional information.

(4) The directions and requirements given or imposed under sub-paragraphs (2) and (3) may differ as between different applications.

(5) The Secretary of State may require any information to be furnished under this paragraph to be in such form or verified in such manner as he may specify.

(6) Every application must be accompanied by—

(a) a copy of the applicant's rules, and

(b) a copy of any guidance issued by the applicant in writing.

(7) The reference in sub-paragraph (6)(b) to guidance issued by the applicant is a reference to any guidance or recommendation—

(a) issued or made by it to all or any class of its members or persons seeking to become members,

(b) relevant for the purposes of this Part, and

(c) intended to have continuing effect, including any guidance or recommendation relating to the admission or expulsion of members of the body, so far as relevant for the purposes of this Part.

### Grant and refusal of recognition

2.–(1) The Secretary of State may, on an application duly made in accordance with paragraph 1 and after being furnished with all such information as he may require under that paragraph, make or refuse to make a recognition order in respect of the applicant.

(2) The Secretary of State may make a recognition order only if it appears to him, from the information furnished by the body and having regard to any other information in his possession, that the requirements of Part 2 of this Schedule are satisfied in the case of that body.

(3) The Secretary of State may refuse to make a recognition order in respect of a body if he considers that its recognition is unnecessary having regard to the existence of one or more other bodies which—

(a) maintain and enforce rules as to the appointment and conduct of statutory auditors, and

(b) have been or are likely to be recognised.

(4) Where the Secretary of State refuses an application for a recognition order he must give the applicant a written notice to that effect—

(a) specifying which requirements, in the opinion of the Secretary of State, are not satisfied, or

(b) stating that the application is refused on the ground mentioned in sub-paragraph (3).

(5) A recognition order must state the date on which it takes effect.

### Revocation of recognition

3.–(1) A recognition order may be revoked by a further order made by the Secretary of State if at any time it appears to him—

(a) that any requirement of Part 2 of this Schedule is not satisfied in the case of the body to which the recognition order relates ('the recognised body'),

(b) that the body has failed to comply with any obligation imposed on it by or by virtue of this Part of this Act, or

(c) that the continued recognition of the body is undesirable having regard to the existence of one or more other bodies which have been or are to be recognised.

(2) An order revoking a recognition order must state the date on which it takes effect, which must be after the period of three months beginning with the date on which the revocation order is made.

(3) Before revoking a recognition order the Secretary of State must—

(a) give written notice of his intention to do so to the recognised body,

(b) take such steps as he considers reasonably practicable for bringing the notice to the attention of the members of the body, and

(c) publish the notice in such manner as he thinks appropriate for bringing it to the attention of any other persons who are in his opinion likely to be affected.

(4) A notice under sub-paragraph (3) must—

(a) state the reasons for which the Secretary of State proposes to act, and

(b) give particulars of the rights conferred by sub-paragraph (5).

(5) A person within sub-paragraph (6) may, within the period of three months beginning with the date of service or publication of the notice under sub-paragraph (3) or such longer period as the Secretary of State may allow, make written representations to the Secretary of State and, if desired, oral representations to a person appointed for that purpose by the Secretary of State.

(6) The persons within this sub-paragraph are—

(a) the recognised body on which a notice is served under sub-paragraph (3),

(b) any member of the body, and

(c) any other person who appears to the Secretary of State to be affected.

(7) The Secretary of State must have regard to any representations made in accordance with sub-paragraph (5) in determining whether to revoke the recognition order.

(8) If in any case the Secretary of State considers it essential to do so in the public interest he may revoke a recognition order without regard to the restriction imposed by sub-paragraph (2), even if—

(a) no notice has been given or published under sub-paragraph (3), or

(b) the period of time for making representations in pursuance of such a notice has not expired.

(9) An order revoking a recognition order may contain such transitional provision as the Secretary of State thinks necessary or expedient.

(10) A recognition order may be revoked at the request or with the consent of the recognised body and any such revocation is not subject to—

    (a) the restrictions imposed by sub-paragraphs (1) and (2), or

    (b) the requirements of sub-paragraphs (3) to (5) and (7).

(11) On making an order revoking a recognition order in respect of a body the Secretary of State must—

    (a) give written notice of the making of the order to the body,

    (b) take such steps as he considers reasonably practicable for bringing the making of the order to the attention of the members of the body, and

    (c) publish a notice of the making of the order in such manner as he thinks appropriate for bringing it to the attention of any other persons who are in his opinion likely to be affected.

### *Transitional provision*

4.–A recognition order made and not revoked under—

    (a) paragraph 2(1) of Schedule 11 to the Companies Act 1989 (c. 40), or

    (b) paragraph 2(1) of Schedule 11 to the Companies (Northern Ireland) Order 1990 (S.I. 1990/593 (N.I. 5)),

before the commencement of this Chapter of this Part of this Act is to have effect after the commencement of this Chapter as a recognition order made under paragraph 2(1) of this Schedule.

### *Orders not statutory instruments*

5.–Orders under this Part of this Schedule shall not be made by statutory instrument.

## PART 2   REQUIREMENTS FOR RECOGNITION OF A SUPERVISORY BODY

### *Holding of appropriate qualification*

6.–(1) The body must have rules to the effect that a person is not eligible for appointment as a statutory auditor unless—

    (a)   in the case of an individual other than an EEA auditor , he holds an appropriate qualification,

    (aa) in the case of an individual who is an EEA auditor—

        (i)   he holds an appropriate qualification,

        (ii)  he has been authorised on or before 5 April 2008 to practise the profession of company auditor pursuant to the European Communities (Recognition of Professional Qualifications) (First General System) Regulations 2005 (S.I. 2005/18) and has fulfilled any requirements imposed pursuant to regulation 6 of those Regulations, or

        (iii) he has passed an aptitude test in accordance with sub-paragraph (2), unless an aptitude test is not required (see sub-paragraph (2A)).

    (b)  in the case of a firm—

        (i)   each individual responsible for statutory audit work on behalf of the firm is eligible for appointment as a statutory auditor, and

        (ii)  the firm is controlled by qualified persons (see paragraph 7 below).

(2) The aptitude test—

    (a) must test the person's knowledge of subjects—

        (i)   that are covered by a recognised professional qualification,

        (ii)  that are not covered by the professional qualification already held by the person, and

        (iii) the knowledge of which is essential for the pursuit of the profession of statutory auditor;

    (b) may test the person's knowledge of rules of professional conduct;

    (c) must not test the person's knowledge of any other matters.

(2A) No aptitude test is required if the subjects that are covered by a recognised professional qualification and the knowledge of which is essential for the pursuit of the profession of statutory auditor are covered by the professional qualification already held by the person.

(3) A firm which has ceased to comply with the conditions mentioned in sub-paragraph (1)(b) may be permitted to remain eligible for appointment as a statutory auditor for a period of not more than three months.

7.–(1) This paragraph explains what is meant in paragraph 6(1)(b) by a firm being 'controlled by qualified persons'.

(2) In this paragraph references to a person being qualified are—

    (a) in relation to an individual, to his holding—

        (i)   an appropriate qualification, or

        (ii)  a corresponding qualification to audit accounts under the law of an EEA State, or part of an EEA State, other than the United Kingdom;

    (b) in relation to a firm, to its—

        (i) being eligible for appointment as a statutory auditor, or

        (ii) being eligible for a corresponding appointment as an auditor under the law of an EEA State , or part of an EEA State, other than the United Kingdom.

(3) A firm is to be treated as controlled by qualified persons if, and only if—

    (a) a majority of the members of the firm are qualified persons, and

    (b) where the firm's affairs are managed by a board of directors, committee or other management body, a majority of that body are qualified persons or, if the body consists of two persons only, at least one of them is a qualified person.

(4) A majority of the members of a firm means—

    (a) where under the firm's constitution matters are decided upon by the exercise of voting rights, members holding a majority of the rights to vote on all, or substantially all, matters;

    (b) in any other case, members having such rights under the constitution of the firm as enable them to direct its overall policy or alter its constitution.

(5) A majority of the members of the management body of a firm means—

    (a) where matters are decided at meetings of the management body by the exercise of voting rights, members holding a majority of the rights to vote on all, or substantially all, matters at such meetings;

    (b) in any other case, members having such rights under the constitution of the firm as enable them to direct its overall policy or alter its constitution.

(6) Paragraphs 5 to 11 of Schedule 7 to this Act (rights to be taken into account and attribution of rights) apply for the purposes of this paragraph.

### *Auditors to be fit and proper persons*

8.–(1) The body must have adequate rules and practices designed to ensure that the persons eligible under its rules for appointment as a statutory auditor are fit and proper persons to be so appointed.

(2) The matters which the body may take into account for this purpose in relation to a person must include—

    (a) any matter relating to any person who is or will be employed by or associated with him for the purposes of or in connection with statutory audit work;

    (b) in the case of a body corporate, any matter relating to—

        (i) any director or controller of the body,

        (ii) any other body corporate in the same group, or

        (iii) any director or controller of any such other body; and

    (c) in the case of a partnership, any matter relating to—

        (i) any of the partners,

        (ii) any director or controller of any of the partners,

        (iii) any body corporate in the same group as any of the partners, or

        (iv) any director or controller of any such other body.

(3) Where the person is a limited liability partnership, in sub-paragraph (2)(b) 'director' is to be read as 'member'.

(4) In sub-paragraph (2)(b) and (c) 'controller', in relation to a body corporate, means a person who either alone or with an associate or associates is entitled to exercise or control the exercise of 15% or more of the rights to vote on all, or substantially all, matters at general meetings of the body or another body corporate of which it is a subsidiary.

### *Professional integrity and independence*

9.–(1) The body must have adequate rules and practices designed to ensure that–

    (a) statutory audit work is conducted properly and with integrity,

    (b) persons are not appointed as statutory auditors in circumstances in which they have an interest likely to conflict with the proper conduct of the audit

    (c) persons appointed as statutory auditors take steps to safeguard their independence from any significant threats to it,

    (d) persons appointed as statutory auditors record any such threats and the steps taken to safeguard the proper conduct of the audit from them, and

    (e) remuneration received or receivable by a statutory auditor in respect of statutory audit work is not—

        (i) influenced or determined by the statutory auditor providing other services to the audited person, or

        (ii) on a contingent fee basis.

(2) The body must participate in arrangements within paragraph 21, and the rules and practices mentioned in sub-paragraph (1) must include provision requiring compliance with any standards for the time being determined under such arrangements.

(3) The body must also have adequate rules and practices designed to ensure that—

    (a) no firm is eligible under its rules for appointment as a statutory auditor unless the firm has arrangements to prevent any person from being able to exert any influence over the way in which a statutory audit is conducted in circumstances in which that influence would be likely to affect the independence or integrity of the audit;

(b) any rule of law relating to the confidentiality of information received in the course of statutory audit work by persons appointed as statutory auditors is complied with; and

(c) a person ceasing to hold office as a statutory auditor makes available to his successor in that office all relevant information which he holds in relation to that office.

(4) The rules referred to in sub-paragraph (3)(b) (confidentiality of information) must apply to persons who are no longer members of the body as they apply to members and any fine imposed in the enforcement of those rules shall be recoverable by the body as a debt due to it from the person obliged to pay it.

### Technical standards

10.–(1) The body must have rules and practices as to—

(a) the technical standards to be applied in statutory audit work, and

(b) the manner in which those standards are to be applied in practice.

(2) The body must participate in arrangements within paragraph 22, and the rules and practices mentioned in sub-paragraph (1) must include provision requiring compliance with any standards for the time being determined under such arrangements.

### Technical standards for group audits

10A.–(1) The body must have rules and practices as to technical standards ensuring that group auditors—

(a) review for the purposes of a group audit the audit work conducted by other persons, and

(b) record that review.

(2) The body must participate in arrangements within paragraph 22, and the rules and practices mentioned in sub-paragraph (1) must include provision requiring compliance with any standards for the time being determined under such arrangements.

(3) The body must also have rules and practices ensuring that group auditors—

(a) retain copies of any documents necessary for the purposes of the review that they have received from third country auditors who are not covered by working arrangements under section 1253E, or

(b) agree with those third country auditors proper and unrestricted access to those documents on request.

(4) The body's rules and practices must ensure that group auditors make those documents available on request to—

(a) the body;

(b) any other body with which the body has entered into arrangements for the purposes of paragraph 23 or 24 (independent arrangements for monitoring and investigation);

(c) the Secretary of State.

(5) The body may provide that the rules and practices referred to in sub-paragraphs (3) and (4) do not apply if, after taking all reasonable steps, a group auditor is unable to obtain the copies of the documents or the access to the documents necessary for the review.

(6) If the body does so provide, its rules and practices must ensure that the group auditor records—

(a) the steps taken to obtain copies of or access to those documents,

(b) the reasons why the copies or access could not be obtained, and

(c) any evidence of those steps or those reasons.

(7) In this paragraph—

'group auditor' means a person appointed as statutory auditor to conduct an audit of group accounts;

'group' has the same meaning as in Part 15 of this Act (see section 474).

### Public interest entity reporting requirements

10B.–(1) The body must have adequate rules and practices designed to ensure that persons appointed as statutory auditors of public interest entities report to the entity's audit committee (if it has one) at least once in each calendar year at any time during which they hold the office of statutory auditor.

(2) The report must include—

(a) a statement in writing confirming the person's independence from the public interest entity;

(b) a description of any services provided by the person to the public interest entity other than in his capacity as statutory auditor;

(c) a description of any significant threats to the person's independence;

(d) an explanation of the steps taken by the person to safeguard his independence from those threats;

(e) a description of any material weaknesses arising from the statutory audit in the public interest entity's internal control in relation to the preparation of accounts; and

(f) any other significant matters arising from the statutory audit.

(3) The body must participate in arrangements within paragraph 22A (arrangements for setting standards), and the rules and practices mentioned in sub-paragraph (1) must include provision requiring compliance with any standards for the time being determined under such arrangements.

(4) In this paragraph, 'audit committee' means a body which performs the functions referred to in Article 41.2 of the Audit Directive or equivalent functions.

### *Public interest entity independence requirements*

10C.–(1) The body must have adequate rules and practices designed to ensure that—

    (a) an individual does not accept an appointment by a public interest entity as statutory auditor if—

        (i) he has been the statutory auditor of the entity for a continuous period of more than seven years, and

        (ii) less than two years have passed since he was last the statutory auditor of the entity;

    (b) where a firm has been appointed by a public interest entity as statutory auditor, an individual may not be a key audit partner if—

        (i) he has been a key audit partner in relation to audits of the entity for a continuous period of more than seven years, and

        (ii) less than two years have passed since he was last the key audit partner in relation to an audit of the entity.

(2) The body must participate in arrangements within paragraph 22B (arrangements for setting standards), and the rules and practices mentioned in sub-paragraph (1) must include provision requiring compliance with any standards for the time being determined under such arrangements.

(3) The body must also have adequate rules and practices designed to ensure that—

    (a) an individual who has been appointed by a public interest entity as statutory auditor may not be appointed as a director or other officer of the entity during a period of two years commencing on the date on which his appointment as statutory auditor ended;

    (b) a key audit partner of a firm which has been appointed by a public interest entity as statutory auditor may not be appointed as a director or other officer of the entity during a period of two years commencing on the date on which his work as key audit partner ended.

(4) The rules referred to in sub-paragraph (3) must apply to persons who are no longer members of the body as they apply to members and any fine imposed in the enforcement of those rules shall be recoverable by the body as a debt due to it from the person obliged to pay it.

(5) An auditor of a public interest entity is not to be regarded as an officer of the entity for the purposes of sub-paragraph (3)(a) and (b).

(6) For the purposes of this paragraph—

    (a) a 'key audit partner' is an individual identified by a firm appointed as statutory auditor as being primarily responsible for the statutory audit; and

    (b) a key audit partner of a firm appointed as statutory auditor of a parent undertaking or a material subsidiary undertaking of a public interest entity is to be treated as if he were a key audit partner of the firm appointed as statutory auditor of the public interest entity.

### *Procedures for maintaining competence*

11.–The body must have rules and practices designed to ensure that persons eligible under its rules for appointment as a statutory auditor continue to maintain an appropriate level of competence in the conduct of statutory audits.

### *Monitoring and enforcement*

12.–(1) The body must—

    (a) have adequate resources for the effective monitoring and enforcement of compliance with its rules, and

    (b) ensure that those resources may not be influenced improperly by the persons monitored.

(1A) The body must—

    (a) have adequate arrangements for the effective monitoring and enforcement of compliance with its rules, and

    (b) ensure that those arrangements operate independently of the persons monitored.

(2) The arrangements for monitoring may make provision for that function to be performed on behalf of the body (and without affecting its responsibility) by any other body or person who is able and willing to perform it.

(3) The arrangements for enforcement must include provision for—

    (a) sanctions which include—

        (i) the withdrawal of eligibility for appointment as a statutory auditor; and

        (ii) any other disciplinary measures necessary to ensure the effective enforcement of the body's rules; and

    (b) the body making available to the public information relating to steps it has taken to ensure the effective enforcement of its rules.

*Independent monitoring of audits of listed companies and other major bodies monitoring*
*of audits*

13.–(1)  The body must—

    (a)  in the case of members of the body who do not perform any statutory audit functions in respect of major audits, have adequate arrangements for enabling the performance by its members of statutory audit functions to be monitored by means of inspections;

    (b)  in the case of members of the body who perform any statutory audit functions in respect of major audits, participate in arrangements within paragraph 23(1); and

    (c)  have rules designed to ensure that members of the body take such steps as may reasonably be required of them to enable their performance of any statutory audit functions to be monitored by means of inspections.

(2)  Any monitoring of members of the body under the arrangements within paragraph 23(1) is to be regarded (so far as their performance of statutory audit functions in respect of major audits is concerned) as monitoring of compliance with the body's rules for the purposes of paragraph 12(1) and (1A).

(3)  The arrangements referred to in sub-paragraph (1)(a) must include an inspection which is conducted in relation to each person eligible for appointment as a statutory auditor at least once every six years.

(4)  The inspection must be conducted by persons who—

    (a)  have an appropriate professional education;

    (b)  have experience of—

        (i)  statutory audit work, or

        (ii)  equivalent work on the audit of accounts under the law of an EEA State, or part of an EEA State, other than the United Kingdom;

    (c)  have received adequate training in the conduct of inspections;

    (d)  do not have any interests likely to conflict with the proper conduct of the inspection.

(5)  The inspection must review one or more statutory audits in which the person to whom the inspection relates has participated.

(6)  The inspection must include an assessment of—

    (a)  the person's compliance with the body's rules established for the purposes of paragraphs 9 (professional integrity and independence), 10 (technical standards), 10A (technical standards for group audits) and 10C (public interest entity independence requirements);

    (b)  the resources allocated by the person to statutory audit work;

    (c)  in the case of an inspection in relation to a firm, its internal quality control system;

    (d)  the remuneration received by the person in respect of statutory audit work.

(7)  An inspection conducted in relation to a firm may be treated as an inspection of all individuals responsible for statutory audit work on behalf of that firm, if the firm has a common quality assurance policy with which each such individual is required to comply.

(8)  The main conclusions of the inspection must be recorded in a report which is made available to—

    (a)  the person to whom the inspection relates, and

    (b)  the body.

(9)  The body must, at least once in every calendar year, deliver to the Secretary of State a summary of the results of inspections conducted under this paragraph.

(10)  In this paragraph—

'major audit' means a statutory audit conducted in respect of—

    (a)  a public interest entity, or

    (b)  any other person in whose financial condition there is a major public interest; 'statutory audit function' means any function performed as a statutory auditor.

### Membership, eligibility and discipline

14.–The rules and practices of the body relating to—

    (a)  the admission and expulsion of members,

    (b)  the grant and withdrawal of eligibility for appointment as a statutory auditor, and

    (c)  the discipline it exercises over its members,

must be fair and reasonable and include adequate provision for appeals.

### Investigation of complaints

15.–(1)  The body must have effective arrangements for the investigation of complaints against–

    (a)  persons who are eligible under its rules for appointment as a statutory auditor, and

    (b)  the body in respect of matters arising out of its functions as a supervisory body.

(2)  The arrangements mentioned in sub-paragraph (1) may make provision for the whole or part of that function to be performed by and to be the responsibility of a body or person independent of the body itself.

### Independent investigation for disciplinary purposes of public interest cases

16.–(1)  The body must–

    (a)  participate in arrangements within paragraph 24(1), and

    (b) have rules and practices designed to ensure that, where the designated persons have decided that any particular disciplinary action should be taken against a member of the body following the conclusion of an investigation under such arrangements, that decision is to be treated as if it were a decision made by the body in disciplinary proceedings against the member.

(2) In sub-paragraph (1) 'the designated persons' means the persons who, under the arrangements, have the function of deciding whether (and if so, what) disciplinary action should be taken against a member of the body in the light of an investigation carried out under the arrangements.

### *Transfer of papers to third countries*

16A.–(1) The body must have adequate rules and practices designed to ensure that persons eligible under its rules for appointment as a statutory auditor deliver audit working papers to a third country competent authority only if—

    (a) the authority has entered into arrangements with the Secretary of State in accordance with section 1253E (working arrangements); and

    (b) the following four conditions are met.

(2) The first condition is that the competent authority has requested the audit working papers for the purposes of an investigation.

(3) The second condition is that the competent authority has given to the Secretary of State notice of its request.

(4) The third condition is that the papers relate to the audit of a body which—

    (a) has issued securities in the country or territory in which the competent authority is established, or

    (b) forms part of a group issuing statutory consolidated accounts in that country or territory.

(5) The fourth condition is that no legal proceedings have been brought (whether continuing or not) in relation to the auditor or audit to which the working papers relate.

(6) The body must also have adequate rules and practices designed to ensure that a person eligible under its rules for appointment as a statutory auditor may refuse to deliver audit working papers to a third country competent authority if the Secretary of State certifies that the delivery of the papers would adversely affect the sovereignty, security or public order of the United Kingdom.

### *Meeting of claims arising out of audit work*

17.–(1) The body must have adequate rules or arrangements designed to ensure that persons eligible under its rules for appointment as a statutory auditor take such steps as may reasonably be expected of them to secure that they are able to meet claims against them arising out of statutory audit work.

(2) This may be achieved by professional indemnity insurance or other appropriate arrangements.

### *Register of auditors and other information to be made available*

18.–The body must have rules requiring persons eligible under its rules for appointment as a statutory auditor to comply with any obligations imposed on them by—

    (a) requirements under section 1224 (Secretary of State's power to call for information);

    (b) regulations under section 1239 (the register of auditors);

    (c) regulations under section 1240 (information to be made available to the public).

### *Taking account of costs of compliance*

19.–The body must have satisfactory arrangements for taking account, in framing its rules, of the cost to those to whom the rules would apply of complying with those rules and any other controls to which they are subject.

### *Promotion and maintenance of standards*

20.–The body must be able and willing—

    (a) to promote and maintain high standards of integrity in the conduct of statutory audit work, and

    (b) to co-operate, by the sharing of information and otherwise, with the Secretary of State and any other authority, body or person having responsibility in the United Kingdom for the qualification, supervision or regulation of auditors.

### *Interpretation*

20A.–In this Part of this Schedule—

'public interest entity' means an issuer—

    (a) whose transferable securities are admitted to trading on a regulated market; and

    (a) the audit of which is a statutory audit (see section 1210(1));

'issuer' and 'regulated market' have the same meaning as in Part 6 of the Financial Services and Markets Act 2000 (see sections 102A to 103); and

'transferable securities' means anything which is a transferable security for the purposes of Directive 2004/39/EC of the European Parliament and of the Council on markets in financial instruments.

## PART 3   ARRANGEMENTS IN WHICH RECOGNISED SUPERVISORY BODIES ARE REQUIRED TO PARTICIPATE

*Arrangements for setting standards relating to professional integrity and independence*

21.–The arrangements referred to in paragraph 9(2) are appropriate arrangements—

  (a) for the determining of standards for the purposes of the rules and practices mentioned in paragraph 9(1), and

  (b) for ensuring that the determination of those standards is done independently of the body.

*Arrangements for setting technical standards*

22.–The arrangements referred to in paragraphs 10(2) and 10A(2) are appropriate arrangements—

  (a) for the determining of standards for the purposes of the rules and practices mentioned in paragraphs 10(1) and 10A(1) respectively, and

  (b) for ensuring that the determination of those standards is done independently of the body.

*Arrangements for setting standards relating to public interest entity reporting requirements*

22A.–The arrangements referred to in paragraph 10B(3) are appropriate arrangements—

  (a) for the determining of standards for the purposes of the rules and practices mentioned in paragraph 10B(1), and

  (b) for ensuring that the determination of those standards is done independently of the body.

*Arrangements for setting standards relating to public interest entity independence requirements*

22B.–The arrangements referred to in paragraph 10C(2) are appropriate arrangements—

  (a) for the determining of standards for the purposes of the rules and practices mentioned in paragraph 10C(1), and

  (b) for ensuring that the determination of those standards is done independently of the body.

*Arrangements for independent monitoring of audits of listed companies and other major bodies*

23.–(1) The arrangements referred to in paragraph 13(1)(b) are appropriate arrangements—

  (a) for enabling the performance by members of the body of statutory audit functions in respect of major audits to be monitored by means of inspections carried out under the arrangements, and

  (b) for ensuring that the carrying out of such monitoring and inspections is done independently of the body.

(1A) Subject to sub-paragraph (1C), the arrangements referred to in sub-paragraph (1) must include provision for an inspection conducted in relation to each person eligible for appointment as a statutory auditor at least once every three years.

(1B) Sub-paragraphs (4) to (9) of paragraph 13 apply in relation to inspections under sub-paragraph (1A) as they apply in relation to inspections under that paragraph.

(1C) The arrangements referred to in sub-paragraph (1) may provide that the body performing the inspections may decide that all or part of the inspection referred to in sub-paragraph (1A) is not required in the case of a member of a supervisory body who performs statutory audit functions in respect of ten or fewer major audits per year.

(1D) If—

  (a) the arrangements make the provision referred to in sub-paragraph (1C), and

  (b) the body performing the inspections decides that all of an inspection is not required in relation to a member,

the supervisory body must ensure that the arrangements referred to in paragraph 13(1)(a) apply in relation to that member, subject to the modification specified in sub-paragraph (1F).

(1E) If—

  (a) the arrangements make the provision referred to in sub-paragraph (1C), and

  (b) the body performing the inspections decides that part of an inspection is not required in relation to a member,

the supervisory body must ensure that the arrangements referred to in paragraph 13(1)(a) apply in relation to that part of the inspection of that member, subject to the modification specified in sub-paragraph (1F).

(1F) For the purposes of sub-paragraphs (1D) and (1E), paragraph 13(3) applies with the substitution of 'three years' for 'six years'.

(2) In this paragraph 'major audit' and 'statutory audit function' have the same meaning as in paragraph 13.

*Arrangements for independent investigation for disciplinary purposes of public interest cases*

24.–(1) The arrangements referred to in paragraph 16(1) are appropriate arrangements—

(a) for the carrying out of investigations into public interest cases arising in connection with the performance of statutory audit functions by members of the body,

(b) for the holding of disciplinary hearings relating to members of the body which appear to be desirable following the conclusion of such investigations,

(c) for requiring such hearings to be held in public except where the interests of justice otherwise require,

(d) for the persons before whom such hearings have taken place to decide whether (and, if so, what) disciplinary action should be taken against the members to whom the hearings related, and

(e) for ensuring that the carrying out of those investigations, the holding of those hearings and the taking of those decisions are done independently of the body.

(2) In this paragraph—

'public interest cases' means matters which raise or appear to raise important issues affecting the public interest;

'statutory audit function' means any function performed as a statutory auditor.

### Supplementary: arrangements to operate independently of body

25.–(1) This paragraph applies for the purposes of—

(a) paragraph 21(b),

(b) paragraph 22(b),

(c) paragraph 23(1)(b), or

(d) paragraph 24(1)(e).

(2) Arrangements are not to be regarded as appropriate for the purpose of ensuring that a thing is done independently of the body unless they are designed to ensure that the body–

(a) will have no involvement in the appointment or selection of any of the persons who are to be responsible for doing that thing, and

(b) will not otherwise be involved in the doing of that thing.

(3) Sub-paragraph (2) imposes a minimum requirement and does not preclude the possibility that additional criteria may need to be satisfied in order for the arrangements to be regarded as appropriate for the purpose in question.

### Supplementary: funding of arrangements

26.–The body must pay any of the costs of maintaining any arrangements within paragraph 21, 22, 23 or 24 which the arrangements provide are to be paid by it.

### Supplementary: scope of arrangement

27.–Arrangements may qualify as arrangements within any of paragraphs 21, 22, 23 and 24 even though the matters for which they provide are more extensive in any respect than those mentioned in the applicable paragraph.

# SCHEDULE 11

# RECOGNISED PROFESSIONAL QUALIFICATIONS

## PART 1   GRANT AND REVOCATION OF RECOGNITION OF A PROFESSIONAL QUALIFICATION

### Application for recognition of professional qualification

1.–(1) A qualifying body may apply to the Secretary of State for an order declaring a qualification offered by it to be a recognised professional qualification for the purposes of this Part of this Act ('a recognition order').

(2) In this Part of this Act 'a recognised qualifying body' means a qualifying body offering a recognised professional qualification.

(3) Any application must be—

(a) made in such manner as the Secretary of State may direct, and

(b) accompanied by such information as the Secretary of State may reasonably require for the purpose of determining the application.

(4) At any time after receiving an application and before determining it the Secretary of State may require the applicant to furnish additional information.

(5) The directions and requirements given or imposed under sub-paragraphs (3) and (4) may differ as between different applications.

(6) The Secretary of State may require any information to be furnished under this paragraph to be in such form or verified in such manner as he may specify.

(7) In the case of examination standards, the verification required may include independent moderation of the examinations over such a period as the Secretary of State considers necessary.

(8) Every application must be accompanied by—
  (a) a copy of the applicant's rules, and
  (b) a copy of any guidance issued by the applicant in writing.
(9) The reference in sub-paragraph (8)(b) to guidance issued by the applicant is a reference to any guidance or recommendation—
  (a) issued or made by it to all or any class of persons holding or seeking to hold a qualification, or approved or seeking to be approved by the body for the purposes of giving practical training,
  (b) relevant for the purposes of this Part of this Act, and
  (c) intended to have continuing effect, including any guidance or recommendation relating to a matter within sub-paragraph (10).
(10) The matters within this sub-paragraph are—
  (a) admission to or expulsion from a course of study leading to a qualification,
  (b) the award or deprivation of a qualification, and
  (c) the approval of a person for the purposes of giving practical training or the withdrawal of such an approval,
so far as relevant for the purposes of this Part of this Act.

### Grant and refusal of recognition

2.–(1) The Secretary of State may, on an application duly made in accordance with paragraph 1 and after being furnished with all such information as he may require under that paragraph, make or refuse to make a recognition order in respect of the qualification in relation to which the application was made.

(2) The Secretary of State may make a recognition order only if it appears to him, from the information furnished by the applicant and having regard to any other information in his possession, that the requirements of Part 2 of this Schedule are satisfied in relation to the qualification.

(3) Where the Secretary of State refuses an application for a recognition order he must give the applicant a written notice to that effect specifying which requirements, in his opinion, are not satisfied.

(4) A recognition order must state the date on which it takes effect.

### Revocation of recognition

3.–(1) A recognition order may be revoked by a further order made by the Secretary of State if at any time it appears to him—
  (a) that any requirement of Part 2 of this Schedule is not satisfied in relation to the qualification to which the recognition order relates, or
  (b) that the qualifying body has failed to comply with any obligation imposed on it by or by virtue of this Part of this Act.
(2) An order revoking a recognition order must state the date on which it takes effect, which must be after the period of three months beginning with the date on which the revocation order is made.
(3) Before revoking a recognition order the Secretary of State must—
  (a) give written notice of his intention to do so to the qualifying body,
  (b) take such steps as he considers reasonably practicable for bringing the notice to the attention of persons holding the qualification or in the course of studying for it, and
  (c) publish the notice in such manner as he thinks appropriate for bringing it to the attention of any other persons who are in his opinion likely to be affected.
(4) A notice under sub-paragraph (3) must—
  (a) state the reasons for which the Secretary of State proposes to act, and
  (b) give particulars of the rights conferred by sub-paragraph (5).
(5) A person within sub-paragraph (6) may, within the period of three months beginning with the date of service or publication or such longer period as the Secretary of State may allow, make written representations to the Secretary of State and, if desired, oral representations to a person appointed for that purpose by the Secretary of State.
(6) The persons within this sub-paragraph are—
  (a) the qualifying body on which a notice is served under sub-paragraph (3),
  (b) any person holding the qualification or in the course of studying for it, and
  (c) any other person who appears to the Secretary of State to be affected.
(7) The Secretary of State must have regard to any representations made in accordance with sub-paragraph (5) in determining whether to revoke the recognition order.
(8) If in any case the Secretary of State considers it essential to do so in the public interest he may revoke a recognition order without regard to the restriction imposed by sub-paragraph (2), even if—
  (a) no notice has been given or published under sub-paragraph (3), or
  (b) the period of time for making representations in pursuance of such a notice has not expired.
(9) An order revoking a recognition order may contain such transitional provision as the Secretary of State thinks necessary or expedient.

(10)  A recognition order may be revoked at the request or with the consent of the qualifying body and any such revocation is not subject to—

    (a)  the restrictions imposed by sub-paragraphs (1) and (2), or

    (b)  the requirements of sub-paragraphs (3) to (5) and (7).

(11)  On making an order revoking a recognition order the Secretary of State must—

    (a)  give written notice of the making of the order to the qualifying body,

    (b)  take such steps as he considers reasonably practicable for bringing the making of the order to the attention of persons holding the qualification or in the course of studying for it, and

    (c)  publish a notice of the making of the order in such manner as he thinks appropriate for bringing it to the attention of any other persons who are in his opinion likely to be affected.

### Transitional provision

4.–A recognition order made and not revoked under—

    (a)  paragraph 2(1) of Schedule 12 to the Companies Act 1989 (c. 40), or

    (b)  paragraph 2(1) of Schedule 12 to the Companies (Northern Ireland) Order 1990 (S.I. 1990/593 (N.I. 5)),

before the commencement of this Chapter of this Part of this Act is to have effect after the commencement of this Chapter as a recognition order made under paragraph 2(1) of this Schedule.

### Orders not statutory instruments

5.–Orders under this Part of this Schedule shall not be made by statutory instrument.

## PART 2    REQUIREMENTS FOR RECOGNITION OF A PROFESSIONAL QUALIFICATION

### Entry requirements

6.–(1)  The qualification must only be open to persons who—

    (a)  have attained university entrance level, or

    (b)  have a sufficient period of professional experience.

(2)  In relation to a person who has not been admitted to a university or other similar establishment in the United Kingdom, 'attaining university entrance level' means—

    (a)  being educated to such a standard as would entitle him to be considered for such admission on the basis of—

        (i)  academic or professional qualifications obtained in the United Kingdom and recognised by the Secretary of State to be of an appropriate standard, or

        (ii)  academic or professional qualifications obtained outside the United Kingdom which the Secretary of State considers to be of an equivalent standard, or

    (b)  being assessed, on the basis of written tests of a kind appearing to the Secretary of State to be adequate for the purpose (with or without oral examination), as of such a standard of ability as would entitle him to be considered for such admission.

(3)  The assessment, tests and oral examination referred to in sub-paragraph (2)(b) may be conducted by—

    (a)  the qualifying body, or

    (b)  some other body approved by the Secretary of State.

(4)  The reference in sub-paragraph (1)(b) to 'a sufficient period of professional experience' is to not less than seven years' experience in a professional capacity in the fields of finance, law and accountancy.

### Requirement for theoretical instruction or professional experience

7.–(1)  The qualification must be restricted to persons who—

    (a)  have completed a course of theoretical instruction in the subjects prescribed for the purposes of paragraph 8, or

    (b)  have a sufficient period of professional experience.

(2)  The reference in sub-paragraph (1)(b) to 'a sufficient period of professional experience' is to not less than seven years' experience in a professional capacity in the fields of finance, law and accountancy.

### Examination

8.–(1)  The qualification must be restricted to persons who have passed an examination (at least part of which is in writing) testing—

    (a)  theoretical knowledge of the subjects prescribed for the purposes of this paragraph by regulations made by the Secretary of State, and

    (b)  ability to apply that knowledge in practice, and requiring a standard of attainment at least equivalent to that required to obtain a degree from a university or similar establishment in the United Kingdom.

(2)  The qualification may be awarded to a person without his theoretical knowledge of a subject being tested by examination if he has passed a university or other examination of equivalent standard in that subject or holds a university degree or equivalent qualification in it.

(3) The qualification may be awarded to a person without his ability to apply his theoretical knowledge of a subject in practice being tested by examination if he has received practical training in that subject which is attested by an examination or diploma recognised by the Secretary of State for the purposes of this paragraph.

(4) Regulations under this paragraph are subject to negative resolution procedure.

### Practical training

9.–(1) The qualification must be restricted to persons who have completed at least three years' practical training of which—

    (a) part was spent being trained in statutory audit work, and

    (b) a substantial part was spent being trained in statutory audit work or other audit work of a description approved by the Secretary of State as being similar to statutory audit work.

(2) For the purpose of sub-paragraph (1) 'statutory audit work' includes the work of a person appointed as the auditor of a person under the law of a country or territory outside the United Kingdom where it appears to the Secretary of State that the law and practice with respect to the audit of accounts is similar to that in the United Kingdom.

(3) The training must be given by persons approved by the body offering the qualification as persons whom the body is satisfied, in the light of undertakings given by them and the supervision to which they are subject (whether by the body itself or some other body or organisation), will provide adequate training.

(4) At least two-thirds of the training must be given by a person—

    (a) eligible for appointment as a statutory auditor, or

    (b) eligible for a corresponding appointment as an auditor under the law of an EEA State, or part of an EEA State, other than the United Kingdom.

### Supplementary provision with respect to a sufficient period of professional experience

10.–(1) Periods of theoretical instruction in the fields of finance, law and accountancy may be deducted from the required period of professional experience, provided the instruction—

    (a) lasted at least one year, and

    (b) is attested by an examination recognised by the Secretary of State for the purposes of this paragraph;

but the period of professional experience may not be so reduced by more than four years.

(2) The period of professional experience together with the practical training required in the case of persons satisfying the requirement in paragraph 7 by virtue of having a sufficient period of professional experience must not be shorter than the course of theoretical instruction referred to in that paragraph and the practical training required in the case of persons satisfying the requirement of that paragraph by virtue of having completed such a course.

### The body offering the qualification

11.–(1) The body offering the qualification must have—

    (a) rules and arrangements adequate to ensure compliance with the requirements of paragraphs 6 to 10, and

    (b) adequate arrangements for the effective monitoring of its continued compliance with those requirements.

(2) The arrangements must include arrangements for monitoring—

    (a) the standard of the body's examinations, and

    (b) the adequacy of the practical training given by the persons approved by it for that purpose.

# SCHEDULE 11A

# SPECIFIED PERSONS, DESCRIPTIONS, DISCLOSURES ETC FOR THE PURPOSES OF SECTION 1224A

## PART 1    SPECIFIED PERSONS

1.–The Secretary of State.

2.–The Department of Enterprise, Trade and Investment for Northern Ireland.

3.–The Treasury.

4.–The Bank of England.

5.–The Financial Services Authority.

6.–The Commissioners for Her Majesty's Revenue and Customs.

7.–The Lord Advocate.

8.–The Director of Public Prosecutions.

9.–The Director of Public Prosecutions for Northern Ireland.

10.–A constable.

11.–A procurator fiscal.

12.–The Scottish Ministers.

13.–A body designated by the Secretary of State under section 1252 (delegation of the Secretary of State's functions).

14.–A recognised supervisory body.

15.–A recognised qualifying body.

16.–A body with which a recognised supervisory body is participating in arrangements for the purposes of paragraph 23 (independent monitoring of audits) or 24 (independent investigation for disciplinary purposes) of Schedule 10 to this Act.

17.–The Independent Supervisor.

## PART 2    SPECIFIED DESCRIPTIONS OF DISCLOSURES

18.–A disclosure for the purpose of enabling or assisting a person authorised under section 457 of this Act (persons authorised to apply to court) to exercise his functions.

19.–A disclosure for the purpose of enabling or assisting an inspector appointed under Part 14 of the Companies Act 1985 (investigation of companies and their affairs, etc) to exercise his functions.

20.–A disclosure for the purpose of enabling or assisting a person authorised under section 447 of the Companies Act 1985 (power to require production of documents) or section 84 of the Companies Act 1989 (c.40) (exercise of powers by officer etc) to exercise his functions.

21.–A disclosure for the purpose of enabling or assisting a person appointed under section 167 of the Financial Services and Markets Act 2000 (c.8) (general investigations) to conduct an investigation to exercise his functions.

22.–A disclosure for the purpose of enabling or assisting a person appointed under section 168 of the Financial Services and Markets Act 2000 (investigations in particular cases) to conduct an investigation to exercise his functions.

23.–A disclosure for the purpose of enabling or assisting a person appointed under section 169(1)(b) of the Financial Services and Markets Act 2000 (investigation in support of overseas regulator) to conduct an investigation to exercise his functions.

24.–A disclosure for the purpose of enabling or assisting the body corporate responsible for administering the scheme referred to in section 225 of the Financial Services and Markets Act 2000 (the ombudsman scheme) to exercise its functions.

25.–A disclosure for the purpose of enabling or assisting a person appointed under paragraph 4 (the panel of ombudsmen) or 5 (the Chief Ombudsman) of Schedule 17 to the Financial Services and Markets Act 2000 to exercise his functions.

26.–A disclosure for the purpose of enabling or assisting a person appointed under regulations made under section 262(1) and (2)(k) of the Financial Services and Markets Act 2000 (investigations into open-ended investment companies) to conduct an investigation to exercise his functions.

27.–A disclosure for the purpose of enabling or assisting a person appointed under section 284 of the Financial Services and Markets Act 2000 (investigations into affairs of certain collective investment schemes) to conduct an investigation to exercise his functions.

28.–A disclosure for the purpose of enabling or assisting the investigator appointed under paragraph 7 of Schedule 1 to the Financial Services and Markets Act 2000 (arrangements for investigation of complaints) to exercise his functions.

29.–A disclosure for the purpose of enabling or assisting a person appointed by the Treasury to hold an inquiry into matters relating to financial services (including an inquiry under section 15 of the Financial Services and Markets Act 2000 (c.8)) to exercise his functions.

30.–A disclosure for the purpose of enabling or assisting the Secretary of State or the Treasury to exercise any of their functions under any of the following—

    (a) the Companies Acts;

    (b) Part 5 of the Criminal Justice Act 1993 (c.36) (insider dealing);

    (c) the Insolvency Act 1986 (c.45);

    (d) the Company Directors Disqualification Act 1986 (c.46);

    (e) Part 42 of this Act (statutory auditors)

    (f) Part 3 (investigations and powers to obtain information) or 7 (financial markets and insolvency) of the Companies Act 1989 (c.40);

    (g) the Financial Services and Markets Act 2000.

31.–A disclosure for the purpose of enabling or assisting the Scottish Ministers to exercise their functions under the enactments relating to insolvency.

32.–A disclosure for the purpose of enabling or assisting the Department of Enterprise, Trade and Investment for Northern Ireland to exercise any powers conferred on it by the enactments relating to companies or insolvency.

33.–A disclosure for the purpose of enabling or assisting a person appointed or authorised by the Department of Enterprise, Trade and Investment for Northern Ireland under the enactments relating to companies or insolvency to exercise his functions.

34.–A disclosure for the purpose of enabling or assisting the Pensions Regulator to exercise the functions conferred on it by or by virtue of any of the following—

(a) the Pension Schemes Act 1993 (c.48);

(b) the Pensions Act 1995 (c.26);

(c) the Welfare Reform and Pensions Act 1999 (c.30);

(d) the Pensions Act 2004 (c.35);

(e) any enactment in force in Northern Ireland corresponding to any of those enactments.

35.–A disclosure for the purpose of enabling or assisting the Board of the Pension Protection Fund to exercise the functions conferred on it by or by virtue of Part 2 of the Pensions Act 2004 or any enactment in force in Northern Ireland corresponding to that Part.

36.–A disclosure for the purpose of enabling or assisting—

(a) the Bank of England,

(b) the European Central Bank, or

(c) the central bank of any country or territory outside the United Kingdom, to exercise its functions.

37.–A disclosure for the purpose of enabling or assisting the Commissioners for Her Majesty's Revenue and Customs to exercise their functions.

38.–A disclosure for the purpose of enabling or assisting organs of the Society of Lloyd's (being organs constituted by or under the Lloyd's Act 1982 (c.xiv)) to exercise their functions under or by virtue of the Lloyd's Acts 1871 to 1982.

39.–A disclosure for the purpose of enabling or assisting the Office of Fair Trading to exercise its functions under any of the following—

(a) the Fair Trading Act 1973 (c.41);

(b) the Consumer Credit Act 1974 (c.39);

(c) the Estate Agents Act 1979 (c.38);

(d) the Competition Act 1980 (c.21);

(e) the Competition Act 1998 (c.41);

(f) the Financial Services and Markets Act 2000 (c.8);

(g) the Enterprise Act 2002 (c.40);

(h) the Control of Misleading Advertisements Regulations 1988 (S.I. 1988/915);

(i) the Unfair Terms in Consumer Contracts Regulations 1999 (S.I. 1999/2083).

40.–A disclosure for the purpose of enabling or assisting the Competition Commission to exercise its functions under any of the following—

(a) the Fair Trading Act 1973;

(b) the Competition Act 1980;

(c) the Competition Act 1998;

(d) the Enterprise Act 2002.

41.–A disclosure with a view to the institution of, or otherwise for the purposes of, proceedings before the Competition Appeal Tribunal.

42.–A disclosure for the purpose of enabling or assisting an enforcer under Part 8 of the Enterprise Act 2002 (enforcement of consumer legislation) to exercise its functions under that Part.

43.–A disclosure for the purpose of enabling or assisting the Takeover Panel to perform any of its functions under Part 28 of this Act (takeovers etc).

44.–A disclosure for the purpose of enabling or assisting the Charity Commission to exercise its functions.

45.–A disclosure for the purpose of enabling or assisting the Attorney General to exercise his functions in connection with charities.

46.–A disclosure for the purpose of enabling or assisting the National Lottery Commission to exercise its functions under sections 5 to 10 (licensing) and 15 (power of Secretary of State to require information) of the National Lottery etc. Act 1993 (c.39).

47.–A disclosure by the National Lottery Commission to the National Audit Office for the purpose of enabling or assisting the Comptroller and Auditor General to carry out an examination under Part 2 of the National Audit Act 1983 (c.44) into the economy, effectiveness and efficiency with which the National Lottery Commission has used its resources in discharging its functions under sections 5 to 10 of the National Lottery etc. Act 1993.

48.–A disclosure for the purpose of enabling or assisting a qualifying body under the Unfair Terms in Consumer Contracts Regulations 1999 (S.I. 1999/2083) to exercise its functions under those Regulations.

49.–A disclosure for the purpose of enabling or assisting an enforcement authority under the Consumer Protection (Distance Selling) Regulations 2000 (S.I. 2000/2334) to exercise its functions under those Regulations.

50.–A disclosure for the purpose of enabling or assisting an enforcement authority under the Financial Services (Distance Marketing) Regulations 2004 (S.I. 2004/2095) to exercise its functions under those Regulations.

51.–A disclosure for the purpose of enabling or assisting a local weights and measures authority in England and Wales to exercise its functions under section 230(2) of the Enterprise Act 2002 (c.40) (notice of intention to prosecute, etc).

52.–A disclosure for the purpose of enabling or assisting the Financial Services Authority to exercise its functions under any of the following—
  (a) the legislation relating to friendly societies or to industrial and provident societies;
  (b) the Building Societies Act 1986 (c.53);
  (c) Part 7 of the Companies Act 1989 (c.40) (financial markets and insolvency);
  (d) the Financial Services and Markets Act 2000 (c.8).

53.–A disclosure for the purpose of enabling or assisting the competent authority for the purposes of Part 6 of the Financial Services and Markets Act 2000 (official listing) to exercise its functions under that Part.

54.–A disclosure for the purpose of enabling or assisting a body corporate established in accordance with section 212(1) of the Financial Services and Markets Act 2000 (compensation scheme manager) to exercise its functions.

55.–A disclosure for the purpose of enabling or assisting a recognised investment exchange or a recognised clearing house to exercise its functions as such. 'Recognised investment exchange' and 'recognised clearing house' have the same meaning as in section 285 of the Financial Services and Markets Act 2000.

56.–A disclosure for the purpose of enabling or assisting a person approved under the Uncertificated Securities Regulations 2001 (S.I. 2001/3755) as an operator of a relevant system (within the meaning of those regulations) to exercise his functions.

57.A disclosure for the purpose of enabling or assisting a body designated under section 326(1) of the Financial Services and Markets Act 2000 (designated professional bodies) to exercise its functions in its capacity as a body designated under that section.

58.–A disclosure with a view to the institution of, or otherwise for the purposes of, civil proceedings arising under or by virtue of the Financial Services and Markets Act 2000.

59.–A disclosure for the purpose of enabling or assisting a body designated by order under section 1252 of this Act (delegation of functions of Secretary of State) to exercise its functions under Part 42 of this Act (statutory auditors).

60.–A disclosure for the purpose of enabling or assisting a recognised supervisory or qualifying body, within the meaning of Part 42 of this Act, to exercise its functions as such.

61.–A disclosure for the purpose of making available to an audited person information relating to a statutory audit of that person's accounts.

62.–A disclosure for the purpose of making available to the public information relating to monitoring or inspections carried out under arrangements within paragraph 23(1) of Schedule 10 to this Act (arrangements for independent monitoring of audits of listed companies and other major bodies), provided such information does not identify any audited person.

63.–A disclosure for the purpose of enabling or assisting an official receiver (including the Accountant in Bankruptcy in Scotland and the Official Assignee in Northern Ireland) to exercise his functions under the enactments relating to insolvency.

64.–A disclosure for the purpose of enabling or assisting the Insolvency Practitioners Tribunal to exercise its functions under the Insolvency Act 1986 (c.45).

65.–A disclosure for the purpose of enabling or assisting a body that is for the time being a recognised professional body for the purposes of section 391 of the Insolvency Act 1986 (recognised professional bodies) to exercise its functions as such.

66.–A disclosure for the purpose of enabling or assisting an overseas regulatory authority to exercise its regulatory functions. 'Overseas regulatory authority' and 'regulatory functions' have the same meaning as in section 82 of the Companies Act 1989.

67.–A disclosure for the purpose of enabling or assisting the Regulator of Community Interest Companies to exercise functions under the Companies (Audit, Investigations and Community Enterprise) Act 2004 (c.27).

68.–A disclosure with a view to the institution of, or otherwise for the purposes of, criminal proceedings.

69.–A disclosure for the purpose of enabling or assisting a person authorised by the Secretary of State under Part 2, 3 or 4 of the Proceeds of Crime Act 2002 (c.29) to exercise his functions.

70.–A disclosure with a view to the institution of, or otherwise for the purposes of, proceedings on an application under section 6, 7 or 8 of the Company Directors Disqualification Act 1986 (c.46) (disqualification for unfitness).

71.–A disclosure with a view to the institution of, or otherwise for the purposes of, proceedings before the Financial Services and Markets Tribunal.

72.–A disclosure for the purposes of proceedings before the Financial Services Tribunal by virtue of the Financial Services and Markets Act 2000 (Transitional Provisions) (Partly Completed Procedures) Order 2001 (S.I. 2001/3592).

73.–A disclosure for the purposes of proceedings before the Pensions Regulator Tribunal.

74.–A disclosure for the purpose of enabling or assisting a body appointed under section 14 of the Companies (Audit, Investigations and Community Enterprise) Act 2004 (supervision of periodic accounts and reports of issuers of listed securities) to exercise functions mentioned in subsection (2) of that section.

75.–A disclosure with a view to the institution of, or otherwise for the purposes of, disciplinary proceedings relating to the performance by a relevant lawyer, foreign lawyer, auditor, accountant, valuer or actuary of his professional duties. In this paragraph—

'foreign lawyer' means a person (other than a relevant lawyer) who is a foreign lawyer within the meaning of section 89(9) of the Courts and Legal Services Act 1990;

'relevant lawyer' means—

    (a) a person who, for the purposes of the Legal Services Act 2007, is an authorised person in relation to an activity which constitutes a reserved legal activity (within the meaning of that Act),

    (b) a solicitor or barrister in Northern Ireland, or

    (c) a solicitor or advocate in Scotland.

76.–A disclosure with a view to the institution of, or otherwise for the purposes of, disciplinary proceedings relating to the performance by a public servant of his duties. 'Public servant' means an officer or employee of the Crown.

77.–A disclosure for the purpose of the provision of a summary or collection of information framed in such a way as not to enable the identity of any person to whom the information relates to be ascertained.

78.–A disclosure in pursuance of any Community obligation.

## PART 3    OVERSEAS REGULATORY BODIES

79.–A disclosure is made in accordance with this Part of this Schedule if it is made to an EEA competent authority in accordance with section 1253B (requests from EEA competent authorities).

80.–A disclosure is made in accordance with this Part of this Schedule if it is—

    (a) a transfer of audit working papers to a third country competent authority in accordance with rules imposed under paragraph 16A of Schedule 10 (transfer of papers to third countries), or

    (b) a disclosure other than a transfer of audit working papers made to a third country competent authority for the purpose of enabling or assisting the authority to exercise its functions.

# SCHEDULE 12

# ARRANGEMENTS IN WHICH REGISTERED THIRD COUNTRY AUDITORS ARE REQUIRED TO PARTICIPATE

*Arrangements for independent monitoring of audits of traded non-Community companies*

1.–(1) The arrangements referred to in section1242(1)(a) are appropriate arrangements—

    (a) for enabling the performance by the registered functions related to the audit of UK-traded non-EEA companies related to the audit of UK-traded non-EEA companies to be monitored by means of inspections carried out under the arrangements, and

    (b) for ensuring that the carrying out of such monitoring and inspections is done independently of the registered third country auditor.

(2) [ ... ]

*Arrangements for independent investigations for disciplinary purposes*

2.–(1) The arrangements referred to in section 1242(1)(b) are appropriate arrangements—

    (a) for the carrying out of investigations into matters arising in connection with the performance of functions related to the audit of UK-traded non-EEA companies by the registered third country auditor,

    (b) for the holding of disciplinary hearings relating to the registered third country auditor which appear to be desirable following the conclusion of such investigations,

    (c) for requiring such hearings to be held in public except where the interests of justice otherwise require,

    (d) for the persons before whom such hearings have taken place to decide whether (and, if so, what) disciplinary action should be taken against the registered third country auditor, and

    (e) for ensuring that the carrying out of those investigations, the holding of those hearings and the taking of those decisions are done independently of the registered third country auditor.

(2) In this paragraph—

'disciplinary action' includes the imposition of a fine.

[ ... ]

*Supplementary: arrangements to operate independently of third country auditor*

3.–(1) This paragraph applies for the purposes of—

    (a) paragraph 1(1)(b), or

(b) paragraph 2(1)(e).

(2) Arrangements are not to be regarded as appropriate for the purpose of ensuring that a thing is done independently of the registered third country auditor unless they are designed to ensure that the registered third country auditor—

(a) will have no involvement in the appointment or selection of any of the persons who are to be responsible for doing that thing, and

(b) will not otherwise be involved in the doing of that thing.

(3) Sub-paragraph (2) imposes a minimum requirement and does not preclude the possibility that additional criteria may need to be satisfied in order for the arrangements to be regarded as appropriate for the purpose in question.

### *Supplementary: funding of arrangements*

4.–(1) The registered third country auditor must pay any of the costs of maintaining any relevant arrangements which the arrangements provide are to be paid by it.

(2) For this purpose 'relevant arrangements' are arrangements within paragraph 1 or 2 in which the registered third country auditor is obliged to participate.

### *Supplementary: scope of arrangements*

5.–Arrangements may qualify as arrangements within either of paragraphs 1 and 2 even though the matters for which they provide are more extensive in any respect than those mentioned in the applicable paragraph.

### *Specification of particular arrangements by the Secretary of State*

6.–(1) If there exist two or more sets of arrangements within paragraph 1 or within paragraph 2, the obligation of a registered third country auditor under section 1242(1)(a) or (b), as the case may be, is to participate in such set of arrangements as the Secretary of State may by order specify.

(2) An order under sub-paragraph (1) is subject to negative resolution procedure.

# SCHEDULE 13

# SUPPLEMENTARY PROVISIONS WITH RESPECT TO DELEGATION ORDER

### *Operation of this Schedule*

1.–(1) This Schedule has effect in relation to a body designated by a delegation order under section 1252 as follows—

(a) paragraphs 2 to 12 have effect in relation to the body where it is established by the order;

(b) paragraphs 2 and 6 to 11 have effect in relation to the body where it is an existing body;

(c) paragraph 13 has effect in relation to the body where it is an existing body that is an unincorporated association.

(2) In their operation in accordance with sub-paragraph (1)(b), paragraphs 2 and 6 apply only in relation to—

(a) things done by or in relation to the body in or in connection with the exercise of functions transferred to it by the delegation order, and

(a) functions of the body which are functions so transferred.

(3) Any power conferred by this Schedule to make provision by order is a power to make provision by an order under section 1252.

### *Status*

2.–The body is not to be regarded as acting on behalf of the Crown and its members, officers and employees are not to be regarded as Crown servants.

### *Name, members and chairman*

3.–(1) The body is to be known by such name as may be specified in the delegation order.

(2) The body is to consist of such persons (not being less than eight) as the Secretary of State may appoint after such consultation as he thinks appropriate.

(3) The chairman of the body is to be such person as the Secretary of State may appoint from among its members.

(4) The Secretary of State may make provision by order as to—

(a) the terms on which the members of the body are to hold and vacate office;

(b) the terms on which a person appointed as chairman is to hold and vacate the office of chairman.

### *Financial provisions*

4.–(1) The body must pay to its chairman and members such remuneration, and such allowances in respect of expenses properly incurred by them in the performance of their duties, as the Secretary of State may determine.

(2) As regards any chairman or member in whose case the Secretary of State so determines, the body must pay or make provision for the payment of—

(a) such pension, allowance or gratuity to or in respect of that person on his retirement or death, or

(b) such contributions or other payment towards the provision of such a pension, allowance or gratuity, as the Secretary of State may determine.

(3) Where—

(a) a person ceases to be a member of the body otherwise than on the expiry of his term of office, and

(b) it appears to the Secretary of State that there are special circumstances which make it right for that person to receive compensation, the body must make a payment to him by way of compensation of such amount as the Secretary of State may determine.

### Proceedings

5.–(1) The delegation order may contain such provision as the Secretary of State considers appropriate with respect to the proceedings of the body.

(2) The delegation order may, in particular—

(a) authorise the body to discharge any functions by means of committees consisting wholly or partly of members of the body;

(b) provide that the validity of proceedings of the body, or of any such committee, is not affected by any vacancy among the members or any defect in the appointment of any member.

### Fees

6.–(1) The body may retain fees payable to it.

(2) The fees must be applied for—

(a) meeting the expenses of the body in discharging its functions, and

(b) any purposes incidental to those functions.

(3) Those expenses include any expenses incurred by the body on such staff, accommodation, services and other facilities as appear to it to be necessary or expedient for the proper performance of its functions.

(4) In prescribing the amount of fees in the exercise of the functions transferred to it the body must prescribe such fees as appear to it sufficient to defray those expenses, taking one year with another.

(5) Any exercise by the body of the power to prescribe fees requires the approval of the Secretary of State.

(6) The Secretary of State may, after consultation with the body, by order vary or revoke any regulations prescribing fees made by the body.

### Legislative functions

7.–(1) Regulations or an order made by the body in the exercise of the functions transferred to it must be made by instrument in writing, but not by statutory instrument.

(2) The instrument must specify the provision of this Part of this Act under which it is made.

(3) The Secretary of State may by order impose such requirements as he thinks necessary or expedient as to the circumstances and manner in which the body must consult on any regulations or order it proposes to make.

(4) Nothing in this Part applies to make regulations or an order made by the body subject to negative resolution procedure or affirmative resolution procedure.

8.–(1) Immediately after an instrument is made it must be printed and made available to the public with or without payment.

(2) A person is not to be taken to have contravened any regulation or order if he shows that at the time of the alleged contravention the instrument containing the regulation or order had not been made available as required by this paragraph.

9.–(1) The production of a printed copy of an instrument purporting to be made by the body on which is endorsed a certificate signed by an officer of the body authorised by it for the purpose and stating—

(a) that the instrument was made by the body,

(b) that the copy is a true copy of the instrument, and

(c) that on a specified date the instrument was made available to the public as required by paragraph 8, is evidence (or, in Scotland, sufficient evidence) of the facts stated in the certificate.

(2) A certificate purporting to be signed as mentioned in sub-paragraph (1) is to be deemed to have been duly signed unless the contrary is shown.

(3) Any person wishing in any legal proceedings to cite an instrument made by the body may require the body to cause a copy of it to be endorsed with such a certificate as is mentioned in this paragraph.

### Report and accounts

10.–(1) The body must, at least once in each calendar year for which the delegation order is in force, make a report to the Secretary of State on—

(a) the discharge of the functions transferred to it, and

    (b) such other matters as the Secretary of State may by order require.

(2) The delegation order may modify sub-paragraph (1) as it has effect in relation to the calendar year in which the order comes into force or is revoked.

(3) The Secretary of State must lay before Parliament copies of each report received by him under this paragraph.

(4) The following provisions of this paragraph apply as follows—

    (a) sub-paragraphs (5) and (6) apply only where the body is established by the order, and

    (b) sub-paragraphs (7) and (8) apply only where the body is an existing body.

(5) The Secretary of State may, with the consent of the Treasury, give directions to the body with respect to its accounts and the audit of its accounts.

(6) A person may only be appointed as auditor of the body if he is eligible for appointment as a statutory auditor.

(7) Unless the body is a company to which section 394 (duty to prepare individual company accounts) applies, the Secretary of State may, with the consent of the Treasury, give directions to the body with respect to its accounts and the audit of its accounts.

(8) Whether or not the body is a company to which section 394 applies, the Secretary of State may direct that any provisions of this Act specified in the directions are to apply to the body, with or without any modifications so specified.

### *Other supplementary provisions*

11.–(1) The transfer of a function to a body designated by a delegation order does not affect anything previously done in the exercise of the function transferred; and the resumption of a function so transferred does not affect anything previously done in exercise of the function resumed.

(2) The Secretary of State may by order make such transitional and other supplementary provision as he thinks necessary or expedient in relation to the transfer or resumption of a function.

(3) The provision that may be made in connection with the transfer of a function includes, in particular, provision—

    (a) for modifying or excluding any provision of this Part of this Act in its application to the function transferred;

    (b) for applying to the body designated by the delegation order, in connection with the function transferred, any provision applying to the Secretary of State which is contained in or made under any other enactment;

    (c) for the transfer of any property, rights or liabilities from the Secretary of State to that body;

    (d) for the carrying on and completion by that body of anything in the process of being done by the Secretary of State when the order takes effect;

    (e) for the substitution of that body for the Secretary of State in any instrument, contract or legal proceedings.

(4) The provision that may be made in connection with the resumption of a function includes, in particular, provision—

    (a) for the transfer of any property, rights or liabilities from that body to the Secretary of State;

    (b) for the carrying on and completion by the Secretary of State of anything in the process of being done by that body when the order takes effect;

    (c) for the substitution of the Secretary of State for that body in any instrument, contract or legal proceedings.

12.–Where a delegation order is revoked, the Secretary of State may by order make provision—

    (a) for the payment of compensation to persons ceasing to be employed by the body established by the delegation order;

    (b) as to the winding up and dissolution of the body.

13.–(1) This paragraph applies where the body is an unincorporated association.

(2) Any relevant proceedings may be brought by or against the body in the name of any body corporate whose constitution provides for the establishment of the body.

(3) In sub-paragraph (2) 'relevant proceedings' means proceedings brought in or in connection with the exercise of any transferred function.

(4) In relation to proceedings brought as mentioned in sub-paragraph (2), any reference in paragraph11(3)(e) or (4)(c) to the body replacing or being replaced by the Secretary of State in any legal proceedings is to be read with the appropriate modifications.

# SCHEDULE 14

# STATUTORY AUDITORS: CONSEQUENTIAL AMENDMENTS

*Companies (Audit, Investigations and Community Enterprise) Act 2004 (c. 27)*

1.–(1) Section 16 of the Companies (Audit, Investigations and Community Enterprise) Act 2004 (c. 27) (grants to bodies concerned with accounting standards etc) is amended as follows.

(2) In subsection (2)—

    (a) in paragraph (f) for 'paragraph 17' to the end substitute 'paragraph 21, 22, 23(1) or 24(1) of Schedule 10 to the Companies Act 2006;',

    (b) in paragraph (g) for 'Part 2 of that Act' substitute 'Part 42 of that Act'.

(3) In subsection (5), in the definition of 'professional accountancy body'—

    (a) in paragraph (a) for 'Part 2 of the Companies Act 1989 (c. 40)' substitute 'Part 42 of the Companies Act 2006', and

    (b) in paragraph (b) for 'section 32' substitute 'section 1220'.

# SCHEDULE 15

# TRANSPARENCY OBLIGATIONS AND RELATED MATTERS: MINOR AND CONSEQUENTIAL AMENDMENTS

## PART 1   AMENDMENTS OF THE FINANCIAL SERVICES AND MARKETS ACT 2000

1.–Part 6 of the Financial Services and Markets Act 2000 (listing and other matters) is amended as follows.

2.–In section 73 (general duty of competent authority), after subsection (1) insert—

'(1A) To the extent that those general functions are functions under or relating to transparency rules, subsection (1)(c) and (f) have effect as if the references to a regulated market were references to a market.'

3.–In section 73A (Part 6 Rules), after subsection (5) insert—

'(6) Transparency rules and corporate governance rules are not listing rules, disclosure rules or prospectus rules, but are Part 6 rules.'

4.–For the cross-heading before section 90 substitute 'Compensation for false or misleading statements etc'.

5.–For the heading to section 90 substitute *'Compensation for statements in listing particulars or prospectus'*.

6.–(1) Section 91 (penalties for breach of Part 6 rules) is amended as follows.

(2) For subsection (1) substitute—

'(1) If the competent authority considers that—

    (a) an issuer of listed securities, or

    (b) an applicant for listing,

has contravened any provision of listing rules, it may impose on him a penalty of such amount as it considers appropriate.

(1ZA) If the competent authority considers that—

    (a) an issuer who has requested or approved the admission of a financial instrument to trading on a regulated market,

    (b) a person discharging managerial responsibilities within such an issuer, or

    (c) a person connected with such a person discharging managerial responsibilities, has contravened any provision of disclosure rules, it may impose on him a penalty of such amount as it considers appropriate.'.

(3) After subsection (1A) insert—

'(1B) If the competent authority considers—

    (a) that a person has contravened—

        (i) a provision of transparency rules or a provision otherwise made in accordance with the transparency obligations directive, or

        (ii) a provision of corporate governance rules, or

    (b) that a person on whom a requirement has been imposed under section 89L (power to suspend or prohibit trading of securities in case of infringement of applicable transparency obligation), has contravened that requirement, it may impose on the person a penalty of such amount as it considers appropriate.'

(4) In subsection (2) for '(1)(a), (1)(b)(i) or (1A)' substitute '(1), (1ZA)(a), (1A) or (1B)'.

7.–In section 96B (persons discharging managerial responsibilities and connected persons)—

    (a) for the heading substitute *'Disclosure rules: persons responsible for compliance'*;

    (b) in subsection (1) for 'For the purposes of this Part' substitute 'for the purposes of the provisions of this Part relating to disclosure rules'.

8.–In section 97(1) (appointment by the competent authority of persons to carry out investigations), for paragraphs (a) and (b) substitute—

    '(a) there may have been a contravention of—

        (i) a provision of this Part or of Part 6 rules, or

      (ii)  a provision otherwise made in accordance with the prospectus directive or the transparency obligations directive;

   (b)  a person who was at the material time a director of a person mentioned in section 91(1), (1ZA)(a), (1A) or (1B) has been knowingly concerned in a contravention by that person of—

      (iii)  a provision of this Part or of Part 6 rules, or

      (iv)  a provision otherwise made in accordance with the prospectus directive or the transparency obligations directive;'.

  9.–In section 99 (fees) after subsection (1B) insert—

'(1C) Transparency rules may require the payment of fees to the competent authority in respect of the continued admission of financial instruments to trading on a regulated market.'.

  10.–(1)  Section 102A (meaning of 'securities' etc) is amended as follows.

  (2)  After subsection (3) insert—

'(3A) "Debt securities" has the meaning given in Article 2.1(b) of the transparency obligations directive.'.

  (3)  In subsection (3) (meaning of 'transferable securities') for 'the investment services directive' substitute 'Directive 2004/39/EC of the European Parliament and of the Council on markets in financial instruments'.

  (4)  In subsection (6) (meaning of 'issuer'), after paragraph (a) insert—

     '(aa)  in relation to transparency rules, means a legal person whose securities are admitted to trading on a regulated market or whose voting shares are admitted to trading on a UK market other than a regulated market, and in the case of depository receipts representing securities, the issuer is the issuer of the securities represented;'.

  11.–(1)  Section 103(1) (interpretation of Part 6) is amended as follows.

  (2)  In the definition of 'regulated market' for 'Article 1.13 of the investment services directive' substitute 'Article 4.1(14) of Directive 2004/39/EC of the European Parliament and of the Council on markets in financial instruments'.

  (3)  At the appropriate place insert—

'"transparency rules" has the meaning given by section 89A(5);

"voteholder information" has the meaning given by section 89B(3);'.

  12.–In section 429(2) (Parliamentary control of statutory instruments: affirmative procedure) of the Financial Services and Markets Act 2000 (c. 8) after 'section' insert '90B or'.

## PART 2   AMENDMENTS OF THE COMPANIES (AUDIT, INVESTIGATIONS AND COMMUNITY ENTERPRISE) ACT 2004

  13.–Chapter 2 of Part 1 of the Companies (Audit, Investigations and Community Enterprise) Act 2004 (accounts and reports) is amended as follows.

  14.–(1)  Section 14 (supervision of periodic accounts and reports of issuers of listed securities) is amended as follows.

  (2)  In subsection (2)(a)—

   (a)  for 'listed' substitute 'transferable';

   (b)  for 'listing' substitute 'Part 6'.

  (3)  In subsection (3)(a)—

   (a)  for 'listed' substitute 'transferable';

   (b)  for 'listing' substitute 'Part 6'.

  (4)  In subsection (7)(b) for 'listed' substitute 'transferable'.

  (5)  In subsection (12)—

   (a)  for 'listed securities' and 'listing rules have' substitute 'Part 6 rules has';

   (b)  for the definition of 'issuer' substitute—

     '"issuer" has the meaning given by section 102A(6) of that Act;';

   (c)  in the definition of 'periodic' for 'listing' substitute 'Part 6';

   (d)  at the end add—

     '" transferable securities" has the meaning given by section 102A(3) of that Act.'.

  15.–(1)  Section 15 (application of certain company law provisions to bodies appointed under section 14) is amended as follows.

  (2)  In subsection (5)(a)—

   (a)  for 'listed' substitute 'transferable';

   (b)  for 'listing' substitute 'Part 6'.

  (3)  In subsection (5B)(a)—

   (a)  for 'listed' substitute 'transferable';

   (b)  for 'listing' substitute 'Part 6'.

  (4)  In subsection (6)(b) for ' "listing rules" and "security" ' substitute ' "Part 6 rules" and "transferable securities" '.

# SCHEDULE 16

# REPEALS

*Company Law repeals Great Britain*

| Short title and chapter | Extent of repeal |
| --- | --- |
| Companies Act 1985 (c. 6) | Sections 1 to 430F. |
| | In section 437– |
| | (a) in subsection (1), the second sentence, and |
| | (b) subsections (1B) and (1C). |
| | Section 438. |
| | In section 439– |
| | (a) in subsection (2), ', or is ordered to pay the whole or any part of the costs of proceedings brought under section 438', |
| | (b) subsections (3) and (7), and |
| | (c) in subsection (8), '; and any such liability imposed by subsection (2) is (subject as mentioned above) a liability also to indemnify all persons against liability under subsection (3)'. |
| | Section 442(2). |
| | Section 446. |
| | In section 448(7), the words 'and liable to a fine.' to the end. |
| | Section 449(7). |
| | Section 450(4). |
| | Section 451(3). |
| | In section 453(1A)– |
| | (a) paragraph (b), and |
| | (b) paragraph (d) and the word 'and' preceding it. |
| | Section 453A(6). |
| | Sections 458 to 461. |
| | Sections 651 to 746. |
| | Schedules 1 to 15B. |
| | Schedules 20 to 25. |
| Insolvency Act 1985 (c. 65) | Schedule 6. |
| Insolvency Act 1986 (c. 45) | In Schedule 13, in Part 1, the entries relating to the following provisions of the Companies Act 1985– |
| | (a) section 13(4), |
| | (b) section 44(7), |
| | (c) section 103(7), |
| | (d) section 131(7), |
| | (e) section 140(2), |
| | (f) section 156(3), |
| | (g) section 173(4), |
| | (h) section 196, |
| | (i) section 380(4), |
| | (j) section 461(6), |

|  | (k)  section 462(5), |
|---|---|
|  | (l)  section 463(2), |
|  | (m) section 463(3), |
|  | (n)  section 464(6), |
|  | (o)  section 657(2), |
|  | (p)  section 658(1), and |
|  | (q)  section 711(2). |
| Building Societies Act 1986 (c. 53) | Section 102C(5). |
| Finance Act 1988 (c. 39) | In section 117(3), from the beginning to 'that section';'. |
|  | In section 117(4), the words 'and (3)'. |
| Water Act 1989 (c. 15) | In Schedule 25, paragraph 71(3). |
| Companies Act 1989 (c. 40) | Sections 1 to 22. |
|  | Section 56(5). |
|  | Sections 57 and 58. |
|  | Section 64(2). |
|  | Section 66(3). |
|  | Section 71. |
|  | Sections 92 to 110. |
|  | Sections 113 to 138. |
|  | Section 139(1) to (3). |
|  | Sections 141 to 143. |
|  | Section 144(1) to (3) and (6). |
|  | Section 207. |
|  | Schedules 1 to 9. |
|  | In Schedule 10, paragraphs 1 to 24. |
|  | Schedules 15 to 17. |
|  | In Schedule 18, paragraphs 32 to 38. |
|  | In Schedule 19, paragraphs 1 to 9 and 11 to 21. |
| Age of Legal Capacity (Scotland) Act 1991 (c. 50) | In Schedule 1, paragraph 39. |
| Water Consolidation (Consequential Provisions) Act 1991 (c. 60) | In Schedule 1, paragraph 40(2). |
| Charities Act 1992 (c. 41) | In Schedule 6, paragraph 11. |
| Charities Act 1993 (c. 10) | In Schedule 6, paragraph 20. |
| Criminal Justice Act 1993 (c. 36) | In Schedule 5, paragraph 4. |
| Welsh Language Act 1993 (c. 38) | Section 30. |
| Pension Schemes Act 1993 (c. 48) | In Schedule 8, paragraph 16. |
| Trade Marks Act 1994 (c. 26) | In Schedule 4, in paragraph 1(2), the reference to the Companies Act 1985. |
| Deregulation and Contracting Out Act 1994 (c. 40) | Section 13(1). |
|  | Schedule 5. |
|  | In Schedule 16, paragraphs 8 to 10. |
| Requirements of Writing (Scotland) Act 1995 (c. 7) | In Schedule 4, paragraphs 51 to 56. |
| Criminal Procedure (Consequential Provisions) (Scotland) Act 1995 (c. 40) | In Schedule 4, paragraph 56(3) and (4). |
| Disability Discrimination Act 1995 (c. 50) | In Schedule 6, paragraph 4. |

*Repeals and revocations relating to Northern Ireland*

| Short title and chapter | Extent of repeal |
| --- | --- |
| Financial Services and Markets Act 2000 (c. 8) | Section 143<br>Section 263 |
| Limited Liability Partnerships Act 2000 (c. 12) | In the Schedule, paragraph 1. |
| Political Parties, Elections and Referendums Act 2000 (c. 41) | Sections 139 and 140.<br>Schedule 19.<br>In Schedule 23, paragraphs 12 and 13. |
| Criminal Justice and Police Act 2001 (c. 16) | Section 45.<br>In Schedule 2, paragraph 17. |
| Enterprise Act 2002 (c. 40) | In Schedule 17, paragraphs 3 to 8. |
| Companies (Audit, Investigations and Community Enterprise) Act 2004 (c. 27) | Sections 7 to 10.<br>Section 11(1).<br>Sections 12 and 13.<br>Sections 19 and 20.<br>Schedule 1.<br>In Schedule 2, paragraphs 5 to 10, 22 to 24 and 26.<br>In Schedule 6, paragraphs 1 to 9. |
| Civil Partnership Act 2004 (c. 33) | In Schedule 27, paragraphs 99 to 105. |
| Constitutional Reform Act 2005 (c. 4) | In Schedule 11, in paragraph 4(3), the reference to the Companies Act 1985. |
| Companies (Northern Ireland) Order 1986 (S.I. 986/1032 (N.I. 6)) | The whole Order. |
| Companies Consolidation (Consequential Provisions) (Northern Ireland) Order 1986 (S.I.1986/1035 (N.I. 9)) | The whole Order. |
| Business Names (Northern Ireland) Order 1986 (S.I. 1986/1033 (N.I. 7)) | The whole Order. |
| Industrial Relations (Northern Ireland) Order 1987 (S.I. 1987/936 N.I. 9)) | Article 3. |
| Finance Act 1988 (c. 39) | In section 117(3), the words from 'and for' to the end. |
| Companies (Northern Ireland) Order 1989 (S.I. 1989/2404 (N.I. 18)) | The whole Order. |
| Insolvency (Northern Ireland) Order 1989 (S.I1989/2405 (N.I. 19)) | In Schedule 7, in the entry relating to Article 166(4), the word 'office'.<br>In Schedule 9, Part I. |
| European Economic Interest Groupings Regulations (Northern Ireland) 1989 (S.R. 1989/216) | The whole Regulations. |
| Companies (Northern Ireland) Order 1990 (S.I. 1990/593 (N.I. 5)) | The whole Order. |
| Companies (No. 2) (Northern Ireland) Order 1990 (S.I. 1990/1504 (N.I. 10)) | Parts II to IV.<br>Part VI.<br>Schedules 1 to 6. |
| Criminal Justice Act 1993 (c. 36) | In Schedule 5, Part 2.<br>Schedule 6. |
| Financial Provisions (Northern Ireland) Order 1993 (S.I. 1993/1252 (N.I. 5)) | Article 15. |

| | |
|---|---|
| Deregulation and Contracting Out Act 1994 (c. 40) | Section 13(2). |
| | Schedule 6. |
| Pensions (Northern Ireland) Order 1995 (S.I. 995/3213 (N.I. 22)) | In Schedule 3, paragraph 7. |
| Deregulation and Contracting Out (Northern Ireland) Order 1996 (S.I. 1996/1632 (N.I. 11)) | Article 11. |
| | Schedule 2. |
| | In Schedule 5, paragraph 4. |
| Youth Justice and Criminal Evidence Act 1999 (c. 23) | In Schedule 4, paragraph 18. |
| Limited Liability Partnerships Act (Northern Ireland) 2002 (c. 12 (N.I.)) | The whole Act |
| Open-Ended Investment Companies Act (Northern Ireland) 2002 (c. 13) | The whole Act |
| Company Directors Disqualification (Northern Ireland) Order 2002 (S.I. 2002/3150 (N.I. 4)) | In Schedule 3, paragraphs 3 to 5. |
| Companies (Audit, Investigations and Community Enterprise) Act 2004 (c. 27) | Section 11(2). |
| | In Schedule 2, paragraphs 11 to 15. |
| Law Reform (Miscellaneous Provisions) (Northern Ireland) Order 2005 (S.I. 2005/1452 (N.I. 7)) | Article 4(2). |
| Companies (Audit, Investigations and Community Enterprise) (Northern Ireland) Order 2005 (S.I. 2005/1967 (N.I. 17)) | The whole Order. |

### *Other repeals*

| | |
|---|---|
| Limited Partnerships Act 1907 (c. 24) | In section 16(1)– |
| | (a) the words ', and there shall be paid for such inspection such fees as may be appointed by the Board of Trade, not exceeding 5p for each inspection', and |
| | (b) the words from 'and there shall be paid for such certificate' to the end. |
| | In section 17– |
| | (a) the words '(but as to fees with the concurrence of the Treasury)', and |
| | (b) paragraph (a). |
| Business Names Act 1985 (c. 7) | The whole Act. |
| Companies Act 1989 (c. 40) | Sections 24 to 25. |
| | Schedules 11 to 13. |
| Criminal Procedure (Consequential Provisions) (Scotland) Act 1995 (c. 40) | In Schedule 4, paragraph 74(2). |
| Companies (Audit, Investigations and Community Enterprise) Act 2004 (c. 27) | Sections 1 to 6. |
| | In Schedule 2, Part 1. |
| Civil Partnership Act 2004 (c. 33) | In Schedule 27, paragraph 128. |

# Company Directors Disqualification Act 1986

(1986, c. 46)

*An Act to consolidate certain enactments relating to the disqualification of persons from being directors of companies, and from being otherwise concerned with a company's affairs.*                    [25 July 1986]

## *Preliminary*

### 1   Disqualification orders: general

(1)  In the circumstances specified below in this Act a court may, and under sections 6 and 9A shall, make against a person a disqualification order, that is to say an order that for a period specified in the order—

    (a)  he shall not be a director of a company, act as receiver of a company's property or in any way, whether directly or indirectly, be concerned or take part in the promotion, formation or management of a company unless (in each case) he has the leave of the court, and

    (b)  he shall not act as an insolvency practitioner.

(2)  In each section of this Act which gives to a court power or, as the case may be, imposes on it the duty to make a disqualification order there is specified the maximum (and, in section 6, the minimum) period of disqualification which may or (as the case may be) must be imposed by means of the order and, unless the court otherwise orders, the period of disqualification so imposed shall begin at the end of the period of 21 days beginning with the date of the order.

(3)  Where a disqualification order is made against a person who is already subject to such an order or to a disqualification undertaking, the periods specified in those orders or, as the case may be, in the order and the undertaking shall run concurrently.

(4)  A disqualification order may be made on grounds which are or include matters other than criminal convictions, notwithstanding that the person in respect of whom it is to be made may be criminally liable in respect of those matters.

### 1A   Disqualification undertakings: general

(1)  In the circumstances specified in sections 7 and 8 the Secretary of State may accept a disqualification undertaking, that is to say an undertaking by any person that, for a period specified in the undertaking, the person—

    (a)  will not be a director of a company, act as receiver of a company's property or in any way, whether directly or indirectly, be concerned or take part in the promotion, formation or management of a company unless (in each case) he has the leave of a court, and

    (b)  will not act as an insolvency practitioner.

(2)  The maximum period which may be specified in a disqualification undertaking is 15 years; and the minimum period which may be specified in a disqualification undertaking under section 7 is two years.

(3)  Where a disqualification undertaking by a person who is already subject to such an undertaking or to a disqualification order is accepted, the periods specified in those undertakings or (as the case may be) the undertaking and the order shall run concurrently.

(4)  In determining whether to accept a disqualification undertaking by any person, the Secretary of State may take account of matters other than criminal convictions, notwithstanding that the person may be criminally liable in respect of those matters.

## *Disqualification for general misconduct in connection with companies*

### 2   Disqualification on conviction of indictable offence

(1)  The court may make a disqualification order against a person where he is convicted of an indictable offence (whether on indictment or summarily) in connection with the promotion, formation, management, liquidation or striking off of a company, with the receivership of a company's property or with his being an administrative receiver of a company.

(2)  'The court' for this purpose means—

    (a)  any court having jurisdiction to wind up the company in relation to which the offence was committed, or

    (b)  the court by or before which the person is convicted of the offence, or

    (c)  in the case of a summary conviction in England and Wales, any other magistrates' court acting in the same local justice area;

and for the purposes of this section the definition of 'indictable offence' in Schedule 1 to the Interpretation Act 1978 applies for Scotland as it does for England and Wales.

(3)  The maximum period of disqualification under this section is—

    (a)  where the disqualification order is made by a court of summary jurisdiction, 5 years, and

    (b)  in any other case, 15 years.

### 3   Disqualification for persistent breaches of companies legislation

(1)  The court may make a disqualification order against a person where it appears to it that he has been persistently in default in relation to provisions of the companies legislation requiring any return,

account or other document to be filed with, delivered or sent, or notice of any matter to be given, to the registrar of companies.

(2) On an application to the court for an order to be made under this section, the fact that a person has been persistently in default in relation to such provisions as are mentioned above may (without prejudice to its proof in any other manner) be conclusively proved by showing that in the 5 years ending with the date of the application he has been adjudged guilty (whether or not on the same occasion) of three or more defaults in relation to those provisions.

(3) A person is to be treated under subsection (2) as being adjudged guilty of a default in relation to any provision of that legislation if—

    (a) he is convicted (whether on indictment or summarily) of an offence consisting in a contravention of or failure to comply with that provision (whether on his own part or on the part of any company), or

    (b) a default order is made against him, that is to say an order under any of the following provisions—

        (i) section 452 of the Companies Act 2006 (order requiring delivery of company accounts),

        (ia) section 456 of that Act (order requiring preparation of revised accounts),

        (ii) section 713 of the Companies Act 1985 (enforcement of company's duty to make returns),

        (iii) section 41 of the Insolvency Act (enforcement of receiver's or manager's duty to make returns), or

        (iv) section 170 of that Act (corresponding provision for liquidator in winding up), in respect of any such contravention of or failure to comply with that provision (whether on his own part or on the part of any company).

(4) In this section 'the court' means any court having jurisdiction to wind up any of the companies in relation to which the offence or other default has been or is alleged to have been committed.

(5) The maximum period of disqualification under this section is 5 years.

## 4 Disqualification for fraud, etc., in winding up

(1) The court may make a disqualification order against a person if, in the course of the winding up of a company, it appears that he—

    (a) has been guilty of an offence for which he is liable (whether he has been convicted or not) under section 993 of the Companies Act 2006 (fraudulent trading), or

    (b) has otherwise been guilty, while an officer or liquidator of the company, receiver of the company's property or administrative receiver of the company, of any fraud in relation to the company or of any breach of his duty as such officer, liquidator, receiver or administrative receiver.

(2) In this section 'the court' means any court having jurisdiction to wind up any of the companies in relation to which the offence or other default has been or is alleged to have been committed; and 'officer' includes a shadow director.

(3) The maximum period of disqualification under this section is 15 years.

## 5 Disqualification on summary conviction

(1) An offence counting for the purposes of this section is one of which a person is convicted (either on indictment or summarily) in consequence of a contravention of, or failure to comply with, any provision of the companies legislation requiring a return, account or other document to be filed with, delivered or sent, or notice of any matter to be given, to the registrar of companies (whether the contravention or failure is on the person's own part or on the part of any company).

(2) Where a person is convicted of a summary offence counting for those purposes, the court by which he is convicted (or, in England and Wales, any other magistrates' court acting in the same local justice area) may make a disqualification order against him if the circumstances specified in the next subsection are present.

(3) Those circumstances are that, during the 5 years ending with the date of the conviction, the person has had made against him, or has been convicted of, in total not less than 3 default orders and offences counting for the purposes of this section; and those offences may include that of which he is convicted as mentioned in subsection (2) and any other offence of which he is convicted on the same occasion.

(4) For the purposes of this section—

    (a) the definition of 'summary offence' in Schedule 1 to the Interpretation Act 1978 applies for Scotland as for England and Wales, and

    (b) 'default order' means the same as in section 3(3)(b).

(5) The maximum period of disqualification under this section is 5 years.

*Disqualification for unfitness*

## 6 Duty of court to disqualify unfit directors of insolvent companies

(1) The court shall make a disqualification order against a person in any case where, on an application under this section, it is satisfied—

(a) that he is or has been a director of a company which has at any time become insolvent (whether while he was a director or subsequently), and

(b) that his conduct as a director of that company (either taken alone or taken together with his conduct as a director of any other company or companies) makes him unfit to be concerned in the management of a company.

(2) For the purposes of this section and the next, a company becomes insolvent if—

(a) the company goes into liquidation at a time when its assets are insufficient for the payment of its debts and other liabilities and the expenses of the winding up,

(b) the company enters administration, or

(c) an administrative receiver of the company is appointed; and references to a person's conduct as a director of any company or companies include, where that company or any of those companies has become insolvent, that person's conduct in relation to any matter connected with or arising out of the insolvency of that company.

(3) In this section and section 7(2), 'the court' means—

(a) where the company in question is being or has been wound up by the court, that court,

(b) where the company in question is being or has been wound up voluntarily, any court which has or (as the case may be) had jurisdiction to wind it up,

(c) where neither paragraph (a) nor (b) applies but an administrator or administrative receiver has at any time been appointed in respect of the company in question, any court which has jurisdiction to wind it up.

(3A) Sections 117 and 120 of the Insolvency Act 1986 (jurisdiction) shall apply for the purposes of subsection (3) as if the references in the definitions of 'registered office' to the presentation of the petition for winding up were references—

(a) in a case within paragraph (b) of that subsection, to the passing of the resolution for voluntary winding up,

(b) in a case within paragraph (c) of that subsection, to the appointment of the administrator or (as the case may be) administrative receiver.

(3B) Nothing in subsection (3) invalidates any proceedings by reason of their being taken in the wrong court; and proceedings—

(a) for or in connection with a disqualification order under this section, or

(b) in connection with a disqualification undertaking accepted under section 7, may be retained in the court in which the proceedings were commenced, although it may not be the court in which they ought to have been commenced.

(3C) In this section and section 7, 'director' includes a shadow director.

(4) Under this section the minimum period of disqualification is 2 years, and the maximum period is 15 years.

## 7 Disqualification order or undertaking; and reporting provisions

(1) If it appears to the Secretary of State that it is expedient in the public interest that a disqualification order under section 6 should be made against any person, an application for the making of such an order against that person may be made—

(a) by the Secretary of State, or

(b) if the Secretary of State so directs in the case of a person who is or has been a director of a company which is being or has been wound up by the court in England and Wales, by the official receiver.

(2) Except with the leave of the court, an application for the making under that section of a disqualification order against any person shall not be made after the end of the period of 2 years beginning with the day on which the company of which that person is or has been a director became insolvent.

(2A) If it appears to the Secretary of State that the conditions mentioned in section 6(1) are satisfied as respects any person who has offered to give him a disqualification undertaking, he may accept the undertaking if it appears to him that it is expedient in the public interest that he should do so (instead of applying, or proceeding with an application, for a disqualification order).

(3) If it appears to the office-holder responsible under this section, that is to say—

(a) in the case of a company which is being wound up by the court in England and Wales, the official receiver,

(b) in the case of a company which is being wound up otherwise, the liquidator,

(c) in the case of a company which is in administration, the administrator, or

(d) in the case of a company of which there is an administrative receiver, that receiver,

that the conditions mentioned in section 6(1) are satisfied as respects a person who is or has been a director of that company, the office-holder shall forthwith report the matter to the Secretary of State.

(4) The Secretary of State or the official receiver may require the liquidator, administrator or administrative receiver of a company, or the former liquidator, administrator or administrative receiver of a company—

(a) to furnish him with such information with respect to any person's conduct as a director of the company, and

(b) to produce and permit inspection of such books, papers and other records relevant to that person's conduct as such a director,

as the Secretary of State or the official receiver may reasonably require for the purpose of determining whether to exercise, or of exercising, any function of his under this section.

## 8  Disqualification after investigation of company

(1) If it appears to the Secretary of State from investigative material that it is expedient in the public interest that a disqualification order should be made against a person who is, or has been, a director or shadow director of a company, he may apply to the court for such an order.

(1A) 'Investigative material' means—

(a) a report made by inspectors under—

(i)   section 437 of the Companies Act 1985;

(ii)  section 167, 168, 169 or 284 of the Financial Services and Markets Act 2000; or

(iii) where the company is an open-ended investment company (within the meaning of that Act) regulations made as a result of section 262(2)(k) of that Act; and

(b) information or documents obtained under—

(i)   section 437, 446E, 447, 448, 451A or 453A of the Companies Act 1985;

(ii)  section 2 of the Criminal Justice Act 1987;

(iii) section 28 of the Criminal Law (Consolidation) (Scotland) Act 1995;

(iv)  section 83 of the Companies Act 1989; or

(v)   section 165, 171, 172, 173 or 175 of the Financial Services and Markets Act 2000.

(2) The court may make a disqualification order against a person where, on an application under this section, it is satisfied that his conduct in relation to the company makes him unfit to be concerned in the management of a company.

(2A) Where it appears to the Secretary of State from such report, information or documents that, in the case of a person who has offered to give him a disqualification undertaking—

(a) the conduct of the person in relation to a company of which the person is or has been a director or shadow director makes him unfit to be concerned in the management of a company, and

(b) it is expedient in the public interest that he should accept the undertaking (instead of applying, or proceeding with an application, for a disqualification order),

he may accept the undertaking.

(3) In this section 'the court' means the High Court or, in Scotland, the Court of Session.

(4) The maximum period of disqualification under this section is 15 years.

## 8A  Variation etc. of disqualification undertaking

(1) The court may, on the application of a person who is subject to a disqualification undertaking—

(a) reduce the period for which the undertaking is to be in force, or

(b) provide for it to cease to be in force.

(2) On the hearing of an application under subsection (1), the Secretary of State shall appear and call the attention of the court to any matters which seem to him to be relevant, and may himself give evidence or call witnesses.

(2A) Subsection (2) does not apply to an application in the case of an undertaking given under section 9B, and in such a case on the hearing of the application whichever of the OFT or a specified regulator (within the meaning of section 9E) accepted the undertaking—

(a) must appear and call the attention of the court to any matters which appear to it or him (as the case may be) to be relevant;

(b) may give evidence or call witnesses.

(3) In this section 'the court'—

(a) in the case of an undertaking given under section 9B means the High Court or (in Scotland) the Court of Session;

(b) in any other case has the same meaning as in section 7(2) or 8 (as the case may be).

## 9  Matters for determining unfitness of directors

(1) Where it falls to a court to determine whether a person's conduct as a director of any particular company or companies makes him unfit to be concerned in the management of a company, the court shall, as respects his conduct as a director of that company or, as the case may be, each of those companies, have regard in particular—

(a) to the matters mentioned in Part I of Schedule 1 to this Act, and

(b) where the company has become insolvent, to the matters mentioned in Part II of that Schedule; and references in that Schedule to the director and the company are to be read accordingly.

(1A) In determining whether he may accept a disqualification undertaking from any person the Secretary of State shall, as respects the person's conduct as a director of any company concerned, have regard in particular—

(a) to the matters mentioned in Part I of Schedule 1 to this Act, and

(b) where the company has become insolvent, to the matters mentioned in Part II of that Schedule;

and references in that Schedule to the director and the company are to be read accordingly.

(2) Section 6(2) applies for the purposes of this section and Schedule 1 as it applies for the purposes of sections 6 and 7 and in this section and that Schedule 'director' includes a shadow director.

(3) Subject to the next subsection, any reference in Schedule 1 to an enactment contained in the Companies Act or the Insolvency Act includes, in relation to any time before the coming into force of that enactment, the corresponding enactment in force at that time.

(4) The Secretary of State may by order modify any of the provisions of Schedule 1; and such an order may contain such transitional provisions as may appear to the Secretary of State necessary or expedient.

(5) The power to make orders under this section is exercisable by statutory instrument subject to annulment in pursuance of a resolution of either House of Parliament.

### *Disqualification for competition infringements*

## 9A  Competition disqualification order

(1) The court must make a disqualification order against a person if the following two conditions are satisfied in relation to him.

(2) The first condition is that an undertaking which is a company of which he is a director commits a breach of competition law.

(3) The second condition is that the court considers that his conduct as a director makes him unfit to be concerned in the management of a company.

(4) An undertaking commits a breach of competition law if it engages in conduct which infringes any of the following—

(a) the Chapter 1 prohibition (within the meaning of the Competition Act 1998) (prohibition on agreements, etc. preventing, restricting or distorting competition);

(b) the Chapter 2 prohibition (within the meaning of that Act) (prohibition on abuse of a dominant position);

(c) Article 81 of the Treaty establishing the European Community (prohibition on agreements, etc. preventing, restricting or distorting competition);

(d) Article 82 of that Treaty (prohibition on abuse of a dominant position).

(5) For the purpose of deciding under subsection (3) whether a person is unfit to be concerned in the management of a company the court—

(a) must have regard to whether subsection (6) applies to him;

(b) may have regard to his conduct as a director of a company in connection with any other breach of competition law;

(c) must not have regard to the matters mentioned in Schedule 1.

(6) This subsection applies to a person if as a director of the company—

(a) his conduct contributed to the breach of competition law mentioned in subsection (2);

(b) his conduct did not contribute to the breach but he had reasonable grounds to suspect that the conduct of the undertaking constituted the breach and he took no steps to prevent it;

(c) he did not know but ought to have known that the conduct of the undertaking constituted the breach.

(7) For the purposes of subsection (6)(a) it is immaterial whether the person knew that the conduct of the undertaking constituted the breach.

(8) For the purposes of subsection (4)(a) or (c) references to the conduct of an undertaking are references to its conduct taken with the conduct of one or more other undertakings.

(9) The maximum period of disqualification under this section is 15 years.

(10) An application under this section for a disqualification order may be made by the OFT or by a specified regulator.

(11) Section 60 of the Competition Act 1998 (c. 41) (consistent treatment of questions arising under United Kingdom and Community law) applies in relation to any question arising by virtue of subsection (4)(a) or (b) above as it applies in relation to any question arising under Part 1 of that Act.

## 9B  Competition undertakings

(1) This section applies if—

(a) the OFT or a specified regulator thinks that in relation to any person an undertaking which is a company of which he is a director has committed or is committing a breach of competition law,

(b) the OFT or the specified regulator thinks that the conduct of the person as a director makes him unfit to be concerned in the management of a company, and

(c) the person offers to give the OFT or the specified regulator (as the case may be) a disqualification undertaking.

(2) The OFT or the specified regulator (as the case may be) may accept a disqualification undertaking from the person instead of applying for or proceeding with an application for a disqualification order.

(3) A disqualification undertaking is an undertaking by a person that for the period specified in the undertaking he will not—

(a) be a director of a company;

(b) act as receiver of a company's property;

(c) in any way, whether directly or indirectly, be concerned or take part in the promotion, formation or management of a company;

(d) act as an insolvency practitioner.

(4) But a disqualification undertaking may provide that a prohibition falling within subsection (3)(a) to (c) does not apply if the person obtains the leave of the court.

(5) The maximum period which may be specified in a disqualification undertaking is 15 years.

(6) If a disqualification undertaking is accepted from a person who is already subject to a disqualification undertaking under this Act or to a disqualification order the periods specified in those undertakings or the undertaking and the order (as the case may be) run concurrently.

(7) Subsections (4) to (8) of section 9A apply for the purposes of this section as they apply for the purposes of that section but in the application of subsection (5) of that section the reference to the court must be construed as a reference to the OFT or a specified regulator (as the case may be).

## 9C  Competition investigations

(1) If the OFT or a specified regulator has reasonable grounds for suspecting that a breach of competition law has occurred it or he (as the case may be) may carry out an investigation for the purpose of deciding whether to make an application under section 9A for a disqualification order.

(2) For the purposes of such an investigation sections 26 to 30 of the Competition Act 1998 (c. 41) apply to the OFT and the specified regulators as they apply to the OFT for the purposes of an investigation under section 25 of that Act.

(3) Subsection (4) applies if as a result of an investigation under this section the OFT or a specified regulator proposes to apply under section 9A for a disqualification order.

(4) Before making the application the OFT or regulator (as the case may be) must—

(a) give notice to the person likely to be affected by the application, and

(b) give that person an opportunity to make representations.

## 9D  Coordination

(1) The Secretary of State may make regulations for the purpose of coordinating the performance of functions under sections 9A to 9C (relevant functions) which are exercisable concurrently by two or more persons.

(2) Section 54(5) to (7) of the Competition Act 1998 (c. 41) applies to regulations made under this section as it applies to regulations made under that section and for that purpose in that section—

(a) references to Part 1 functions must be read as references to relevant functions;

(b) references to a regulator must be read as references to a specified regulator;

(c) a competent person also includes any of the specified regulators.

(3) The power to make regulations under this section must be exercised by statutory instrument subject to annulment in pursuance of a resolution of either House of Parliament.

(4) Such a statutory instrument may—

(a) contain such incidental, supplemental, consequential and transitional provision as the Secretary of State thinks appropriate;

(b) make different provision for different cases.

## 9E  Interpretation

(1) This section applies for the purposes of sections 9A to 9D.

(2) Each of the following is a specified regulator for the purposes of a breach of competition law in relation to a matter in respect of which he or it has a function—

(a) the Office of Communications;

(b) the Gas and Electricity Markets Authority;

(c) the Water Services Regulation Authority;

(d) the Rail Regulator;

(e) the Civil Aviation Authority.

(3) The court is the High Court or (in Scotland) the Court of Session.

(4) Conduct includes omission.

(5) Director includes shadow director.

*Other cases of disqualification*

## 10  Participation in wrongful trading

(1) Where the court makes a declaration under section 213 or 214 of the Insolvency Act that a person is liable to make a contribution to a company's assets, then, whether or not an application for such

an order is made by any person, the court may, if it thinks fit, also make a disqualification order against the person to whom the declaration relates.

(2)  The maximum period of disqualification under this section is 15 years.

## 11  Undischarged bankrupts

(1)  It is an offence for a person to act as director of a company or directly or indirectly to take part in or be concerned in the promotion, formation or management of a company, without the leave of the court, at a time when—

(a)  he is an undischarged bankrupt, or

(b)  a bankruptcy restrictions order is in force in respect of him.

(2)  'The court' for this purpose is the court by which the person was adjudged bankrupt or, in Scotland, sequestration of his estates was awarded.

(3)  In England and Wales, the leave of the court shall not be given unless notice of intention to apply for it has been served on the official receiver; and it is the latter's duty, if he is of opinion that it is contrary to the public interest that the application should be granted, to attend on the hearing of the application and oppose it.

## 12  Failure to pay under county court administration order

(1)  The following has effect where a court under section 429 of the Insolvency Act revokes an administration order under Part VI of the County Courts Act 1984.

(2)  A person to whom that section applies by virtue of the order under section 429(2)(b) shall not, except with the leave of the court which made the order, act as director or liquidator of, or directly or indirectly take part or be concerned in the promotion, formation or management of, a company.[1]

## 12A  Northern Irish disqualification orders

A person subject to a disqualification order under Part II of the Companies (Northern Ireland) Order 1989—

(a)  shall not be a director of a company, act as receiver of a company's property or in any way, whether directly or indirectly, be concerned or take part in the promotion, formation or management of a company unless (in each case) he has the leave of the High Court of Northern Ireland, and

(b)  shall not act as an insolvency practitioner.

## 12B  Northern Irish disqualification undertakings

A person subject to a disqualification undertaking under the Company Directors Disqualification (Northern Ireland) Order 2002—

(a)  shall not be a director of a company, act as receiver of a company's property or in any way, whether directly or indirectly, be concerned or take part in the promotion, formation or management of a company unless (in each case) he has the leave of the High Court of Northern Ireland, and

(b)  shall not act as an insolvency practitioner.

*Consequences of contravention*

## 13  Criminal penalties

If a person acts in contravention of a disqualification order or disqualification undertaking or in contravention of section 12(2), 12A or 12B, or is guilty of an offence under section 11, he is liable—

(a)  on conviction on indictment, to imprisonment for not more than 2 years or a fine, or both; and

(b)  on summary conviction, to imprisonment for not more than 6 months or a fine not exceeding the statutory maximum, or both.

## 14  Offences by body corporate

(1)  Where a body corporate is guilty of an offence of acting in contravention of a disqualification order or disqualification undertaking or in contravention of section 12A or 12B, and it is proved that the offence occurred with the consent or connivance of, or was attributable to any neglect on the part of any director, manager, secretary or other similar officer of the body corporate, or any person who was purporting to act in any such capacity he, as well as the body corporate, is guilty of the offence and liable to be proceeded against and punished accordingly.

(2)  Where the affairs of a body corporate are managed by its members, subsection (1) applies in relation to the acts and defaults of a member in connection with his functions of management as if he were a director of the body corporate.

---

[1]  This section is amended as follows by the Tribunals, Courts and Enforcements Act 2007 c.15 from a date to be appointed. For the title of the section substitute, 'Disabilities on revocation of administration order'. Omit subsection (1). In subsection (2), for the words from 'that section' to '429(2)(b)' substitute 'section 429 of the Insolvency Act applies by virtue of an order under subsection (2) of that section'.

## 15  Personal liability for company's debts where person acts while disqualified

(1)  A person is personally responsible for all the relevant debts of a company if at any time—

    (a)  in contravention of a disqualification order or disqualification undertaking or in contravention of section 11, 12A or 12B of this Act he is involved in the management of the company, or

    (b)  as a person who is involved in the management of the company, he acts or is willing to act on instructions given without the leave of the court by a person whom he knows at that time to be the subject of a disqualification order or disqualification undertaking or a disqualification order under Part II of the Companies (Northern Ireland) Order 1989 or disqualification undertaking under the Company Directors Disqualification (Northern Ireland) Order 2002 or to be an undischarged bankrupt.

(2)  Where a person is personally responsible under this section for the relevant debts of a company, he is jointly and severally liable in respect of those debts with the company and any other person who, whether under this section or otherwise, is so liable.

(3)  For the purposes of this section the relevant debts of a company are—

    (a)  in relation to a person who is personally responsible under paragraph (a) of subsection (1), such debts and other liabilities of the company as are incurred at a time when that person was involved in the management of the company, and

    (b)  in relation to a person who is personally responsible under paragraph (b) of that subsection, such debts and other liabilities of the company as are incurred at a time when that person was acting or was willing to act on instructions given as mentioned in that paragraph.

(4)  For the purposes of this section, a person is involved in the management of a company if he is a director of the company or if he is concerned, whether directly or indirectly, or takes part, in the management of the company.

(5)  For the purposes of this section a person who, as a person involved in the management of a company, has at any time acted on instructions given without the leave of the court by a person whom he knew at that time to be the subject of a disqualification order or disqualification undertaking or a disqualification order under Part II of the Companies (Northern Ireland) Order 1989 or disqualification undertaking under the Company Directors Disqualification (Northern Ireland) Order 2002 or to be an undischarged bankrupt is presumed, unless the contrary is shown, to have been willing at any time thereafter to act on any instructions given by that person.

### *Supplementary provisions*

## 16  Application for disqualification order

(1)  A person intending to apply for the making of a disqualification order by the court having jurisdiction to wind up a company shall give not less than 10 days' notice of his intention to the person against whom the order is sought; and on the hearing of the application the last-mentioned person may appear and himself give evidence or call witnesses.

(2)  An application to a court with jurisdiction to wind up companies for the making against any person of a disqualification order under any of sections 2 to 4 may be made by the Secretary of State or the official receiver, or by the liquidator or any past or present member or creditor of any company in relation to which that person has committed or is alleged to have committed an offence or other default.

(3)  On the hearing of any application under this Act made by a person falling within subsection (4), the applicant shall appear and call the attention of the court to any matters which seem to him to be relevant, and may himself give evidence or call witnesses.

(4)  The following fall within this subsection—

    (a)  the Secretary of State;

    (b)  the official receiver;

    (c)  the OFT;

    (d)  the liquidator;

    (e)  a specified regulator (within the meaning of section 9E).

## 17  Application for leave under an order or undertaking

(1)  Where a person is subject to a disqualification order made by a court having jurisdiction to wind up companies, any application for leave for the purposes of section 1(1)(a) shall be made to that court.

(2)  Where—

    (a)  a person is subject to a disqualification order made under section 2 by a court other than a court having jurisdiction to wind up companies, or

    (b)  a person is subject to a disqualification order made under section 5, any application for leave for the purposes of section 1(1)(a) shall be made to any court which, when the order was made, had jurisdiction to wind up the company (or, if there is more than one such company, any of the companies) to which the offence (or any of the offences) in question related.

(3)  Where a person is subject to a disqualification undertaking accepted at any time under section 7 or 8, any application for leave for the purposes of section 1A(1)(a) shall be made to any court to which, if

the Secretary of State had applied for a disqualification order under the section in question at that time, his application could have been made.

(3A) Where a person is subject to a disqualification undertaking accepted at any time under section 9B any application for leave for the purposes of section 9B(4) must be made to the High Court or (in Scotland) the Court of Session.

(4) But where a person is subject to two or more disqualification orders or undertakings (or to one or more disqualification orders and to one or more disqualification undertakings), any application for leave for the purposes of section 1(1)(a), 1A(1)(a) or 9B(4) shall be made to any court to which any such application relating to the latest order to be made, or undertaking to be accepted, could be made.

(5) On the hearing of an application for leave for the purposes of section 1(1)(a) or 1A(1)(a), the Secretary of State shall appear and call the attention of the court to any matters which seem to him to be relevant, and may himself give evidence or call witnesses.

(6) Subsection (5) does not apply to an application for leave for the purposes of section 1(1)(a) if the application for the disqualification order was made under section 9A.

(7) In such a case and in the case of an application for leave for the purposes of section 9B(4) on the hearing of the application whichever of the OFT or a specified regulator (within the meaning of section 9E) applied for the order or accepted the undertaking (as the case may be)—

(a) must appear and draw the attention of the court to any matters which appear to it or him (as the case may be) to be relevant;

(b) may give evidence or call witnesses.[2]

## 18    Register of disqualification orders and undertakings

(1) The Secretary of State may make regulations requiring officers of courts to furnish him with such particulars as the regulations may specify of cases in which—

(a) a disqualification order is made, or

(b) any action is taken by a court in consequence of which such an order or a disqualification undertaking is varied or ceases to be in force, or

(c) leave is granted by a court for a person subject to such an order to do anything which otherwise the order prohibits him from doing, or

(d) leave is granted by a court for a person subject to such an undertaking to do anything which otherwise the undertaking prohibits him from doing;

and the regulations may specify the time within which, and the form and manner in which, such particulars are to be furnished.

(2) The Secretary of State shall, from the particulars so furnished, continue to maintain the register of orders, and of cases in which leave has been granted as mentioned in subsection (1)(c), which was set up by him under section 29 of the Companies Act 1976 and continued under section 301 of the Companies Act 1985.

(2A) The Secretary of State must include in the register such particulars as he considers appropriate of—

(a) disqualification undertakings accepted by him under section 7 or 8;

(b) disqualification undertakings accepted by the OFT or a specified regulator under section 9B;

(c) cases in which leave has been granted as mentioned in subsection (1)(d).

(3) When an order or undertaking of which entry is made in the register ceases to be in force, the Secretary of State shall delete the entry from the register and all particulars relating to it which have been furnished to him under this section or any previous corresponding provision and, in the case of a disqualification undertaking, any other particulars he has included in the register.

(4) The register shall be open to inspection on payment of such fee as may be specified by the Secretary of State in regulations.

(4A) Regulations under this section may extend the preceding provisions of this section, to such extent and with such modifications as may be specified in the regulations, to disqualification orders made under Part II of the Companies (Northern Ireland) Order 1989 or disqualification undertakings made under the Company Directors Disqualification (Northern Ireland) Order 2002.

(5) Regulations under this section shall be made by statutory instrument subject to annulment in pursuance of a resolution of either House of Parliament.

## 19    Special savings from repealed enactments

Schedule 2 to this Act has effect—

(a) in connection with certain transitional cases arising under sections 93 and 94 of the Companies Act 1981, so as to limit the power to make a disqualification order, or to restrict the duration of an order, by reference to events occurring or things done before those sections came into force,

(b) to preserve orders made under section 28 of the Companies Act 1976 (repealed by the Act of 1981), and

---

[2] The second comma in s. 17(4) has been added editorially.

(c) to preclude any applications for a disqualification order under section 6 or 8, where the relevant company went into liquidation before 28th April 1986.

*Miscellaneous and general*

### 20  Admissibility in evidence of statements

(1) In any proceedings (whether or not under this Act), any statement made in pursuance of a requirement imposed by or under sections 6 to 10, 15 or 19(c) of, or Schedule 1 to, this Act, or by or under rules made for the purposes of this Act under the Insolvency Act, may be used in evidence against any person making or concurring in making the statement.

(2) However, in criminal proceedings in which any such person is charged with an offence to which this subsection applies—

(a) no evidence relating to the statement may be adduced, and

(b) no question relating to it may be asked, by or on behalf of the prosecution, unless evidence relating to it is adduced, or a question relating to it is asked, in the proceedings by or on behalf of that person.

(3) Subsection (2) applies to any offence other than—

(a) an offence which is—

(i) created by rules made for the purposes of this Act under the Insolvency Act, and

(ii) designated for the purposes of this subsection by such rules or by regulations made by the Secretary of State;

(b) an offence which is—

(i) created by regulations made under any such rules, and

(ii) designated for the purposes of this subsection by such regulations;

(c) an offence under section 5 of the Perjury Act 1911 (false statements made otherwise than on oath); or

(d) an offence under section 44(2) of the Criminal Law (Consolidation) (Scotland) Act 1995 (false statements made otherwise than on oath).

(4) Regulations under subsection (3)(a)(ii) shall be made by statutory instrument and, after being made, shall be laid before each House of Parliament.

### 20A  Legal professional privilege

In proceedings against a person for an offence under this Act nothing in this Act is to be taken to require any person to disclose any information that he is entitled to refuse to disclose on grounds of legal professional privilege (in Scotland, confidentiality of communications).

### 21  Interaction with Insolvency Act

(1) References in this Act to the official receiver, in relation to the winding up of a company or the bankruptcy of an individual, are to any person who, by virtue of section 399 of the Insolvency Act, is authorised to act as the official receiver in relation to that winding up or bankruptcy; and, in accordance with section 401(2) of that Act, references in this Act to an official receiver includes a person appointed as his deputy.

(2) Sections 1A, 6 to 10, 13, 14, 15, 19(c) and 20 of, and Schedule 1 to, this Act and sections 1 and 17 of this Act as they apply for the purposes of those provisions are deemed included in Parts I to VII of the Insolvency Act for the purposes of the following sections of that Act—

section 411 (power to make insolvency rules);

section 414 (fees orders);

section 420 (orders extending provisions about insolvent companies to insolvent partnerships);

section 422 (modification of such provisions in their application to recognised banks).

(3) Section 434 of that Act (Crown application) applies to sections 1A, 6 to 10, 13, 14, 15, 19(c) and 20 of, and Schedule 1 to, this Act and sections 1 and 17 of this Act as they apply for the purposes of those provisions as it does to the provisions of that Act which are there mentioned.

(4) For the purposes of summary proceedings in Scotland, section 431 of that Act applies to summary proceedings for an offence under section 11 or 13 of this Act as it applies to summary proceedings for an offence under Parts I to VII of that Act.

### 21A  Bank insolvency

Section 121 of the Banking Act 2009 provides for this Act to apply in relation to bank insolvency as it applies in relation to liquidation.

### 21B  Bank administration

Section 121 of the Banking Act 2009 provides for this Act to apply in relation to bank administration as it applies in relation to liquidation.

### 22  Interpretation

(1) This section has effect with respect to the meaning of expressions used in this Act, and applies unless the context otherwise requires.

(2) The expression 'company'—

(a) in section 11, includes an unregistered company and a company incorporated outside Great Britain which has an established place of business in Great Britain, and

(b) elsewhere, includes any company which may be wound up under Part V of the Insolvency Act.

(3) Section 247 in Part VII of the Insolvency Act (interpretation for the first Group of Parts of that Act) applies as regards references to a company's insolvency and to its going into liquidation; and 'administrative receiver' has the meaning given by section 251 of that Act and references to acting as an insolvency practitioner are to be read in accordance with section 388 of that Act.

(4) 'Director' includes any person occupying the position of director, by whatever name called.

(5) 'Shadow director', in relation to a company, means a person in accordance with whose directions or instructions the directors of the company are accustomed to act (but so that a person is not deemed a shadow director by reason only that the directors act on advice given by him in a professional capacity).

(6) Section 740 of the Companies Act applies as regards the meaning of 'body corporate'; and 'officer' has the meaning given by section 744 of that Act.

(7) In references to legislation other than this Act—

'the Companies Act' means the Companies Act 1985;

'the Companies Acts' has the meaning given by section 2 of the Companies Act 2006; and

'the Insolvency Act' means the Insolvency Act 1986;

and in sections 3(1) and 5(1) of this Act 'the companies legislation' means the Companies Acts, Parts I to VII of the Insolvency Act and, in Part XV of that Act, sections 411, 413, 414, 416 and 417.

(8) Any reference to provisions, or a particular provision, of the Companies Acts or the Insolvency Act includes the corresponding provisions or provision of the former Companies Acts (as defined by section 1171 of the Companies Act 2006) or, as the case may be, the Insolvency Act 1985.

(9) Subject to the provisions of this section, expressions that are defined for the purposes of the Companies Acts have the same meaning in this Act.

(10) Any reference to acting as receiver—

(a) includes acting as manager or as both receiver and manager, but

(b) does not include acting as administrative receiver;

and 'receivership' is to be read accordingly.

### 22A  Application of Act to building societies

(1) This Act applies to building societies as it applies to companies.

(2) References in this Act to a company, or to a director or an officer of a company include, respectively, references to a building society within the meaning of the Building Societies Act 1986 or to a director or officer, within the meaning of that Act, of a building society.

(3) In relation to a building society the definition of 'shadow director' in section 22(5) applies with the substitution of 'building society' for 'company'.

(4) In the application of Schedule 1 to the directors of a building society, references to provisions of the Insolvency Act , the Companies Act 1985 or the Companies Act 2006 include references to the corresponding provisions of the Building Societies Act 1986.

### 22B  Application of Act to incorporated friendly societies.

(1) This Act applies to incorporated friendly societies as it applies to companies.

(2) References in this Act to a company, or to a director or an officer of a company include, respectively, references to an incorporated friendly society within the meaning of the Friendly Societies Act 1992 or to a member of the committee of management or officer, within the meaning of that Act, of an incorporated friendly society.

(3) In relation to an incorporated friendly society every reference to a shadow director shall be omitted.

(4) In the application of Schedule 1 to the members of the committee of management of an incorporated friendly society, references to provisions of the Insolvency Act, the Companies Act 1985 or the Companies Act 2006 include references to the corresponding provisions of the Friendly Societies Act 1992.

### 22C  Application of Act to NHS foundation trusts

(1) This Act applies to NHS foundation trusts as it applies to companies within the meaning of this Act.

(2) References in this Act to a company, or to a director or officer of a company, include, respectively, references to an NHS foundation trust or to a director or officer of the trust; but references to shadow directors are omitted.

(3) In the application of Schedule 1 to the directors of an NHS foundation trust, references to the provisions of the Insolvency Act, the Companies Act 1985 or the Companies Act 2006 include references to the corresponding provisions of Chapter 5 of Part 2 of the National Health Service Act 2006.

### 23  Transitional provisions, savings, repeals.

(1) The transitional provisions and savings in Schedule 3 to this Act have effect, and are without prejudice to anything in the Interpretation Act 1978 with regard to the effect of repeals.

(2)  The enactments specified in the second column of Schedule 4 to this Act are repealed to the extent specified in the third column of that Schedule.

### 24  Extent

(1)  This Act extends to England and Wales and to Scotland.

(2)  Nothing in this Act extends to Northern Ireland.

### 25  Commencement

This Act comes into force simultaneously with the Insolvency Act 1986.

### 26  Citation

This Act may be cited as the Company Directors Disqualification Act 1986.

# SCHEDULES

# SCHEDULE 1

# MATTERS FOR DETERMINING UNFITNESS OF DIRECTORS

## PART I  MATTERS APPLICABLE IN ALL CASES

1. Any misfeasance or breach of any fiduciary or other duty by the director in relation to the company.

2. Any misapplication or retention by the director of, or any conduct by the director giving rise to an obligation to account for, any money or other property of the company.

3. The extent of the director's responsibility for the company entering into any transaction liable to be set aside under Part XVI of the Insolvency Act (provisions against debt avoidance).

4. The extent of the director's responsibility for any failure by the company to comply with any of the following provisions of the Companies Act 1985, namely—

    (a)  section 288 (register of directors and secretaries);

    (b)  section 352 (obligation to keep and enter up register of members);

    (c)  section 353 (location of register of members);

    (d)  section 363 (duty of company to make annual returns);

    (e)  sections 399 and 415 (company's duty to register charges it creates).

4A.  The extent of the director's responsibility for any failure by the company to comply with any of the following provisions of the Companies Act 2006, namely—

    (a)  section 386 (companies to keep accounting records); and

    (b)  section 388 (where and for how long records to be kept).

5. The extent of the director's responsibility for any failure by the directors of the company to comply with the following provisions of the Companies Act 2006—

    (a)  section 394 or 399 (duty to prepare annual accounts);

    (b)  section 414 or 450 (approval and signature of abbreviated accounts); or

    (c)  section 433 (name of signatory to be stated in published copy of accounts).

5A.  In the application of this Part of this Schedule in relation to any person who is a director of an open-ended investment company, any reference to a provision of the Companies Act 1985 or the Companies Act 2006 is to be taken to be a reference to the corresponding provision of the Open-Ended Investment Companies Regulations 2001 or of any rules made under regulation 6 of those Regulations (Financial Services Authority rules).

## PART II  MATTERS APPLICABLE WHERE COMPANY HAS BECOME INSOLVENT

6. The extent of the director's responsibility for the causes of the company becoming insolvent.

7. The extent of the director's responsibility for any failure by the company to supply any goods or services which have been paid for (in whole or in part).

8. The extent of the director's responsibility for the company entering into any transaction or giving any preference, being a transaction or preference—

    (a)  liable to be set aside under section 127 or sections 238 to 240 of the Insolvency Act, or

    (b)  challengeable under section 242 or 243 of that Act or under any rule of law in Scotland.

8A  The extent of the member's and shadow members' responsibility for events leading to a member or shadow member, whether himself or some other member or shadow member, being declared by the court to be liable to make a contribution to the assets of the limited liability partnership under section 214A of the Insolvency Act 1986.

9. The extent of the director's responsibility for any failure by the directors of the company to comply with section 98 of the Insolvency Act (duty to call creditors' meeting in creditors' voluntary winding up).

10. Any failure by the director to comply with any obligation imposed on him by or under any of the following provisions of the Insolvency Act—

    (a) paragraph 47 of Schedule B1 (company's statement of affairs in administration);
    (b) section 47 (statement of affairs to administrative receiver);
    (c) section 66 (statement of affairs in Scottish receivership);
    (d) section 99 (directors' duty to attend meeting; statement of affairs in creditors' voluntary winding up);
    (e) section 131 (statement of affairs in winding up by the court);
    (f) section 234 (duty of anyone with company property to deliver it up);
    (g) section 235 (duty to cooperate with liquidator, etc.).

# SCHEDULE 2

## SAVINGS FROM COMPANIES ACT 1981 SS. 93, 94, AND INSOLVENCY ACT 1985 SCHEDULE 9

### PART 1

1. Sections 2 and 4(1)(b) do not apply in relation to anything done before 15th June 1982 by a person in his capacity as liquidator of a company or as receiver or manager of a company's property.

2. Subject to paragraph 1—

    (a) section 2 applies in a case where a person is convicted on indictment of an offence which he committed (and, in the case of a continuing offence, has ceased to commit) before 15th June 1982; but in such a case a disqualification order under that section shall not be made for a period in excess of 5 years;
    (b) that section does not apply in a case where a person is convicted summarily—
        (i) in England and Wales, if he had consented so to be tried before that date, or
        (ii) in Scotland, if the summary proceedings commenced before that date.

3. Subject to paragraph 1, section 4 applies in relation to an offence committed or other thing done before 15th June 1982; but a disqualification order made on the grounds of such an offence or other thing done shall not be made for a period in excess of 5 years.

4. The powers of a court under section 5 are not exercisable in a case where a person is convicted of an offence which he committed (and, in the case of a continuing offence, had ceased to commit) before 15th June 1982.

5. For purposes of section 3(1) and section 5, no account is to be taken of any offence which was committed, or any default order which was made, before 1st June 1977.

6. An order made under section 28 of the Companies Act 1976 has effect as if made under section 3 of this Act; and an application made before 15th June 1982 for such an order is to be treated as an application for an order under the section last mentioned.

7. Where—

    (a) an application is made for a disqualification order under section 6 of this Act by virtue of paragraph (a) of subsection (2) of that section, and
    (b) the company in question went into liquidation before 28th April 1986 (the coming into force of the provision replaced by section 6).

the court shall not make an order under that section unless it could have made a disqualification order under section 300 of the Companies Act as it had effect immediately before the date specified in sub-paragraph (b) above.

8. An application shall not be made under section 8 of this Act in relation to a report made or information or documents obtained before 28th April 1986.

# SCHEDULE 3

## TRANSITIONAL PROVISIONS AND SAVINGS

1. In this Schedule, "the former enactments" means so much of the Companies Act, and so much of the Insolvency Act, as is repealed and replaced by this Act; and "the appointed day" means the day on which this Act comes into force.

2. So far as anything done or treated as done under or for the purposes of any provision of the former enactments could have been done under or for the purposes of the corresponding provision of this Act, it is not invalidated by the repeal of that provision but has effect as if done under or for the purposes of the corresponding provision; and any order, regulation, rule or other instrument made or having effect under any provision of the former enactments shall, insofar as its effect is preserved by this paragraph, be treated for all purposes as made and having effect under the corresponding provision.

3. Where any period of time specified in a provision of the former enactments is current immediately before the appointed day, this Act has effect as if the corresponding provision had been in force when the period began to run; and (without prejudice to the foregoing) any period of time so specified and current is deemed for the purposes of this Act—

    (a) to run from the date or event from which it was running immediately before the appointed day, and

    (b) to expire (subject to any provision of this Act for its extension) whenever it would have expired if this Act had not been passed;

and any rights, priorities, liabilities, reliefs, obligations, requirements, powers, duties or exemptions dependent on the beginning, duration or end of such a period as above mentioned shall be under this Act as they were or would have been under the former enactments.

4. Where in any provision of this Act there is a reference to another such provision, and the first-mentioned provision operates, or is capable of operating, in relation to things done or omitted, or events occurring or not occurring, in the past (including in particular past acts of compliance with any enactment, failures of compliance, contraventions, offences and convictions of offences) the reference to the other provision is to be read as including a reference to the corresponding provision of the former enactments.

5. Offences committed before the appointed day under any provision of the former enactments may, notwithstanding any repeal by this Act, be prosecuted and punished after that day as if this Act had not passed.

6. A reference in any enactment, instrument or document (whether express or implied, and in whatever phraseology) to a provision of the former enactments (including the corresponding provision of any yet earlier enactment) is to be read, where necessary to retain for the enactment, instrument or document the same force and effect as it would have had but for the passing of this Act, as, or as including, a reference to the corresponding provision by which it is replaced in this Act.

## SCHEDULE 4   REPEALS

| Chapter | Short Title | Extent of repeal |
|---|---|---|
| 1985 c.6 | The Companies Act 1985 | Section 295 to 299. |
| | | Section 301. |
| | | Section 302. |
| | | Schedule 12. |
| | | In Schedule 24, the entries relating to sections 295(7) and 302(1). |
| 1985 c.65 | The Insolvency Act 1985 | Sections 12 to 14. |
| | | Section 16. |
| | | Section 18. |
| | | Section 108(2). |
| | | Schedule 2. |
| | | In Schedule 6, paragraphs 1, 2, 7 and 14. |
| | | In Schedule 9, paragraphs 2 and 3. |

# Companies (Tables A to F) Regulations 1985

(1985 No. 805)

*The Secretary of State, in exercise of the powers conferred by section 454(2) of the Companies Act 1948, and now vested in him S.I. 1970/1537, of the powers conferred by sections 3 and 8 of the Companies Act 1985 and of all other powers enabling him in that behalf, hereby makes the following Regulations—*

1. These Regulations may be cited as the Companies (A to F) Regulations 1985 and shall come into operation on 1 July 1985.

2. The regulations in Table A and the forms in Tables, B, C, D, E and F in the Schedule to these Regulations shall be the regulations and forms of memorandum and articles of association for the purposes of sections 3 and 8 of the Companies Act 1985.

3. The Companies (Alteration of Table A etc) Regulations 1984 are hereby revoked.

# SCHEDULE

# TABLE A

# REGULATIONS FOR MANAGEMENT OF A COMPANY LIMITED BY SHARES

## *Interpretation*

1  In these regulations—

'the Act' means the Companies Act 1985 including any statutory modification or re-enactment thereof for the time being in force and any provisions of the Companies Act 2006 for the time being in force.

'the articles' means the articles of the company.

'clear days' in relation to the period of a notice means that period excluding the day when the notice is given or deemed to be given and the day for which it is given or on which it is to take effect.

'communication' means the same as in the Electronic Communications Act 2000.

'electronic communication' means the same as in the Electronic Communications Act 2000.

'executed' includes any mode of execution.

'office' means the registered office of the company.

'the holder' in relation to shares means the member whose name is entered in the register of members as the holder of the shares.

'the seal' means the common seal of the company.

'secretary' means the secretary of the company or any other person appointed to perform the duties of the secretary of the company, including a joint, assistant or deputy secretary.

'the United Kingdom' means Great Britain and Northern Ireland.

Unless the context otherwise requires, words or expressions contained in these regulations bear the same meaning as in the Act but excluding any statutory modification thereof not in force when these regulations become binding on the company.

## *Share Capital*

2  Subject to the provisions of the Act and without prejudice to any rights attached to any existing shares, any share may be issued with such rights or restrictions as the company may by ordinary resolution determine.

3  Subject to the provisions of the Act, shares may be issued which are to be redeemed or are to be liable to be redeemed at the option of the company or the holder on such terms and in such manner as may be provided by the articles.

4  The company may exercise the powers of paying commissions conferred by the Act. Subject to the provisions of the Act, any such commission may be satisfied by the payment of cash or by the allotment of fully or partly paid shares or partly in one way and partly in the other.

5  Except as required by law, no person shall be recognised by the company as holding any share upon any trust and (except as otherwise provided by the articles or by law) the company shall not be bound by or recognise any interest in any share except an absolute right to the entirety thereof in the holder.

## *Share Certificates*

6  Every member, upon becoming the holder of any shares, shall be entitled without payment to one certificate for all the shares of each class held by him (and, upon transferring a part of his holding of shares of any class, to a certificate for the balance of such holding) or several certificates each for one or more of his shares of any class, to a certificate for the balance of such holding) or several certificates each for one or more of his shares upon payment for every certificate after the first of such reasonable sum as the directors may determine. Every certificate shall be sealed with the seal and shall specify the number, class and distinguishing numbers (if any) of the shares to which it relates and the amount or respective amounts paid up thereon. The company shall not be bound to issue more than one certificate for shares held jointly by several persons and delivery of a certificate to one joint holder shall be a sufficient delivery to all of them.

7  If a share certificate is defaced, worn-out, lost or destroyed, it may be renewed on such terms (if any) as to evidence and indemnity and payment of the expenses reasonably incurred by the company in investigating evidence as the directors may determine but otherwise free of charge, and (in the case of defacement or wearing-out) on delivery up of the old certificate.

## *Lien*

8  The company shall have a first and paramount lien on every share (not being a fully paid share) for all moneys (whether presently payable or not) payable at a fixed time or called in respect of that share. The directors may at any time declare any share to be wholly or in part exempt from the provisions of this regulation. The company's lien on a share shall extend to any amount payable in respect of it.

9 The company may sell in such manner as the directors determine any shares on which the company has a lien if a sum in respect of which the lien exists is presently payable and is not paid within fourteen clear days after notice has been given to the holder of the share or to the person entitled to it in consequence of the death or bankruptcy of the holder, demanding payment and stating that if the notice is not complied with the shares may be sold.

10 To give effect to a sale the directors may authorise some person to execute an instrument of transfer of the shares sold to, or in accordance with the directions of, the purchaser. The title of the transferee to the shares shall not be affected by any irregularity in or invalidity of the proceedings in reference to the sale.

11 The net proceeds of the sale, after payment of the costs, shall be applied in payment of so much of the sum for which the lien exists as is presently payable, and any residue shall (upon surrender to the company for cancellation of the certificate for the shares sold and subject to a like lien for any moneys not presently payable as existed upon the shares before the sale) be paid to the person entitled to the shares at the date of the sale.

## Calls on Shares and Forfeiture

12 Subject to the terms of allotment, the directors may make calls upon the members in respect of any moneys unpaid on their shares (whether in respect of nominal value or premium) and each member shall (subject to receiving at least fourteen clear days' notice specifying when and where payment is to be made) pay to the company as required by the notice the amount called on his shares. A call may, before receipt by the company of any sum due thereunder, be revoked in whole or part and payment of a call may be postponed in whole or part. A person upon whom a call is made shall remain liable for calls made upon him notwithstanding the subsequent transfer of the shares in respect whereof the call was made.

13 A call shall be deemed to have been made at the time when the resolution of the directors authorising the call was passed.

14 The joint holders of a share shall be jointly and severally liable to pay all calls in respect thereof.

15 If a call remains unpaid after it has become due and payable the person from whom it is due and payable shall pay interest on the amount unpaid from the day it became due and payable until it is paid at the rate fixed by the terms of allotment of the share or in the notice of the call or, if no rate is fixed, at the appropriate rate (as defined by the Act) but the directors may waive payment of the interest wholly or in part.

16 An amount payable in respect of a share on allotment or at any fixed date, whether in respect of nominal value or premium or as an instalment of a call, shall be deemed to be a call and if it is not paid the provisions of the articles shall apply as if that amount had become due and payable by virtue of a call.

17 Subject to the terms of allotment, the directors may make arrangements on the issue of shares for a difference between the holders in the amounts and times of payment of calls on their shares.

18 If a call remains unpaid after it has become due and payable the directors may give to the person from whom it is due not less than fourteen clear days' notice requiring payment of the amount unpaid together with any interest which may have accrued. The notice shall name the place where payment is to be made and shall state that if the notice is not complied with the shares in respect of which the call was made will be liable to be forfeited.

19 If the notice is not complied with any share in respect of which it was given may, before the payment required by the notice has been made, be forfeited by a resolution of the directors and the forfeiture shall include all dividends or other moneys payable in respect of the forfeited shares and not paid before the forfeiture.

20 Subject to the provisions of the Act, a forfeited share may be sold, re-alloted or otherwise disposed of on such terms and in such manner as the directors determine either to the person who was before the forfeiture the holder or to any other person and at any time before sale, re-allotment or other disposition, the forfeiture may be cancelled on such terms as the directors think fit. Where for the purposes of its disposal a forfeited share is to be transferred to any person the directors may authorise some person to execute an instrument of transfer of the share to that person.

21 A person any of whose shares have been forfeited shall cease to be a member in respect of them and shall surrender to the company for cancellation the certificate for the shares forfeited but shall remain liable to the company for all moneys which at the date of forfeiture were presently payable by him to the company in respect of those shares with interest at the rate at which interest was payable on those moneys before the forfeiture or, if no interest was so payable, at the appropriate rate (as defined in the Act) from the date of forfeiture until payment but the directors may waive payment wholly or in part or enforce payment without any allowance for the value of the shares at the time of forfeiture or for any consideration received on their disposal.

22 A statutory declaration by a director or the secretary that a share has been forfeited on a specified date shall be conclusive evidence of the facts stated in it as against all persons claiming to be entitled to the share and the declaration shall (subject to the execution of an instrument of transfer if necessary)

constitute a good title to the share and the person to whom the share is disposed of shall not be bound to see to the application of the consideration, if any, nor shall his title to the share be affected by any irregularity in or invalidity of the proceedings in reference to the forfeiture or disposal of the share.

### Transfer of Shares

23  The instrument of transfer of a share may be in any usual form or in any other form which the directors may approve and shall be executed by or on behalf of the transferor and, unless the share is fully paid, by or on behalf of the transferee.

24  The directors may refuse to register the transfer of a share which is not fully paid to a person of whom they do not approve and they may refuse to register the transfer of a share on which the company has a lien. They may also refuse to register a transfer unless—

    (a)  it is lodged at the office or at such other place as the directors may appoint and is accompanied by the certificate for the shares to which it relates and such other evidence as the directors may reasonably require to show the right of the transferor to make the transfer;

    (b)  it is in respect of only one class of shares; and

    (c)  it is in favour of not more than four transferees.

25  If the directors refuse to register a transfer of a share, they shall within two months after the date on which the transfer was lodged with the company send to the transferee notice of the refusal.

26  The registration of transfers of shares or of transfers of any class of shares may be suspended at such times and for such periods (not exceeding thirty days in any year) as the directors may determine.

27  No fee shall be charged for the registration of any instrument of transfer or other document relating to or affecting the title to any share.

28  The company shall be entitled to retain any instrument of transfer which is registered, but any instrument of transfer which the directors refuse to register shall be returned to the person lodging it when notice of the refusal is given.

### Transmission of Shares

29  If a member dies the survivor or survivors where he was a joint holder, and his personal representatives where he was a sole holder or the only survivor of joint holders, shall be the only persons recognised by the company as having any title to his interest; but nothing herein contained shall release the estate of a deceased member from any liability in respect of any share which had been jointly held by him.

30  A person becoming entitled to a share in consequence of the death or bankruptcy of a member may, upon such evidence being produced as the directors may properly require, elect either to become the holder of the share or to have some person nominated by him registered as the transferee. If he elects to become the holder he shall give notice to the company to that effect. If he elects to have another person registered he shall execute an instrument of transfer of the share to that person. All the articles relating to the transfer of shares shall apply to the notice or instrument of transfer as if it were an instrument of transfer executed by the member and the death or bankruptcy of the member had not occurred.

31  A person becoming entitled to a share in consequence of the death or bankruptcy of a member shall have the rights to which he would be entitled if he were the holder of the share, except that he shall not, before being registered as the holder of the share, be entitled in respect of it to attend or vote at any meeting of the company or at any separate meeting of the holders of any class of shares in the company.

### Alteration of Share Capital

32  The company may by ordinary resolution—

    (a)  increase its share capital by new shares of such amount as the resolution prescribes;

    (b)  consolidate and divide all or any of its share capital into shares of larger amount than its existing shares;

    (c)  subject to the provisions of the Act, sub-divide its shares, or any of them, into shares of smaller amount and the resolution may determine that, as between the shares resulting from the sub-division, any of them may have any preference or advantage as compared with the others; and

    (d)  cancel shares which, at the date of the passing of the resolution, have not been taken or agreed to be taken by any person and diminish the amount of its share capital by the amount of the shares so cancelled.

33  Whenever as a result of a consolidation of shares any members would become entitled to fractions of a share, the directors may, on behalf of those members, sell the shares representing the fractions for the best price reasonably obtainable to any person (including, subject to the provisions of the Act, the company) and distribute the net proceeds of sale in due proportion among those members, and the directors may authorise some person to execute an instrument of transfer of the shares to, or in accordance with the directions of, the purchaser. The transferee shall not be bound to see to the application of the purchase money nor shall his title to the shares be affected by any irregularity in or invalidity of the proceedings in reference to the sale.

34  Subject to the provisions of the Act, the company may by special resolution reduce its share capital, any capital redemption reserve and any share premium account in any way.

## Purchase of Own Shares

35  Subject to the provisions of the Act, the company may purchase its own shares (including any redeemable shares) and, if it is a private company, make a payment in respect of the redemption or purchase of its own shares otherwise than out of distributable profits of the company or the proceeds of a fresh issue of shares.

## General Meeting

36  [...]

37  The directors may call general meetings and, on the requisition of members pursuant to the provisions of the Act, shall forthwith proceed to convene a general meeting in accordance with the provisions of the Act. If there are not within the United Kingdom sufficient directors to call a general meeting, any director or any member of the company may call a general meeting.

## Notice of General Meetings

38  General meetings shall be called by at least fourteen clear days' notice but a general meeting may be called by shorter notice if it is so agreed by a majority in number of the members having a right to attend and vote being a majority together holding not less than ninety per cent. in nominal value of the shares giving that right.

The notice shall specify the time and place of the meeting and the general nature of the business to be transacted.

Subject to the provisions of the articles and to any restrictions imposed on any shares, the notice shall be given to all the members, to all persons entitled to a share in consequence of the death or bankruptcy of a member and to the directors and auditors.[1]

39  The accidental omission to give notice of a meeting to, or the non-receipt of notice of a meeting by, any person entitled to receive notice shall not invalidate the proceedings at that meeting.

## Proceedings at General Meetings

40  No business shall be transacted at any meeting unless a quorum is present. Save in the case of a company with a single member two persons entitled to vote upon the business to be transacted, each being a member or a proxy for a member or a duly authorised representative of a corporation, shall be a quorum.[2]

41  If such a quorum is not present within half an hour from the time appointed for the meeting, or if during a meeting such a quorum ceases to be present, the meeting shall stand adjourned to the same day in the next week at the same time and place or to such time and place as the directors may determine.

42  The chairman, if any, of the board of directors or in his absence some other director nominated by the directors shall preside as chairman of the meeting, but if neither the chairman nor such other director (if any) be present within fifteen minutes after the time appointed for holding the meeting and willing to act, the directors present shall elect one of their number to be chairman and, if there is only one director present and willing to act, he shall be chairman.

43  If no director is willing to act as chairman, or if no director is present within fifteen minutes after the time appointed for holding the meeting, the members present and entitled to vote shall choose one of their number to be chairman.

44  A director shall, notwithstanding that he is not a member, be entitled to attend and speak at any general meeting and at any separate meeting of the holders of any class of shares in the company.

45  The chairman may, with the consent of a meeting at which a quorum is present (and shall if so directed by the meeting), adjourn the meeting from time to time and from place to place, but no business shall be transacted at an adjourned meeting other than business which might properly have been transacted at the meeting had the adjournment not taken place. When a meeting is adjourned for fourteen days or more, at least seven clear days' notice shall be given specifying the time and place of the adjourned meeting and the general nature of the business to be transacted. Otherwise it shall not be necessary to give any such notice.

46  A resolution put to the vote of a meeting shall be decided on a show of hands unless before or on the declaration of the result of, the show of hands a poll is duly demanded. Subject to the provisions of the Act, a poll may be demanded—

      (a)  by the chairman; or

---

[1] For a public company limited by shares reg. 38 is as follows:

38  An annual general meeting shall be called by at least twenty-one clear days' notice. All other general meetings shall be called by at least fourteen clear days' notice but a general meeting may be called by shorter notice if it is so agreed—

    (a)  in the case of an annual general meeting, by all the members entitled to attend and vote thereat; and

    (b)  in the case of any other meeting by a majority in number of the members having a right to attend and vote being a majority together holding not less than ninety-five per cent. in nominal value of the shares giving that right.

The notice shall specify the time and place of the meeting and the general nature of the business to be transacted and, in the case of an annual general meeting, shall specify the meeting as such. Subject to the provisions of the articles and to any restrictions imposed on any shares, the notice shall be given to all the members, to all persons entitled to a share in consequence of the death or bankruptcy of a member and to the directors and auditors.

[2] For a public company limited by shares reg. 40 is as follows:

40  No business shall be transacted at any meeting unless a quorum is present. Two persons entitled to vote upon the business to be transacted, each being a member or a proxy for a member or a duly authorised representative of a corporation, shall be a quorum.

(b) by at least two members having the right to vote at the meeting; or

(c) by a member or members representing not less than one-tenth of the total voting rights of all the members having the right to vote at the meeting; or

(d) by a member or members holding shares conferring a right to vote at the meeting being shares on which an aggregate sum has been paid up equal to not less than one-tenth of the total sum paid up on all the shares conferring that right;

and a demand by a person as proxy for a member shall be the same as a demand by the member.

47 Unless a poll is duly demanded a declaration by the chairman that a resolution has been carried or carried unanimously, or by a particular majority, or lost, or not carried by a particular majority and an entry to that effect in the minutes of the meeting shall be conclusive evidence of the fact without proof of the number or proportion of the votes recorded in favour of or against the resolution.

48 The demand for a poll may, before the poll is taken, be withdrawn but only with the consent of the chairman and a demand so withdrawn shall not be taken to have invalidated the result of a show of hands declared before the demand was made.

49 A poll shall be taken as the chairman directs and he may appoint scrutineers (who need not be members) and fix a time and place for declaring the result of the poll. The result of the poll shall be deemed to be the resolution of the meeting at which the poll was demanded.

50 [...]

51 A poll demanded on the election of a chairman or on a question of adjournment shall be taken forthwith. A poll demanded on any other question shall be taken either forthwith or at such time and place as the chairman directs not being more than thirty days after the poll is demanded. The demand for a poll shall not prevent the continuance of a meeting for the transaction of any business other than the question on which the poll was demanded. If a poll is demanded before the declaration of the result of a show of hands and the demand is duly withdrawn, the meeting shall continue as if the demand had not been made.

52 No notice need be given of a poll not taken forthwith if the time and place at which it is to be taken are announced at the meeting at which it is demanded. In any other case at least seven clear days' notice shall be given specifying the time and place at which the poll is to be taken.

53 [...]

### Votes of Members

54 Subject to any rights or restrictions attached to any shares, on a show of hands every member who (being an individual) is present in person or by proxy or (being a corporation) is present by a duly authorised representative or by proxy, unless the proxy (in either case) or the representative is himself a member entitled to vote, shall have one vote and on a poll every member shall have one vote for every share of which he is the holder.

55 In the case of joint holders the vote of the senior who tenders a vote, whether in person or by proxy, shall be accepted to the exclusion of the votes of the other joint holders' and seniority shall be determined by the order in which the names of the holders stand in the register of members.

56 A member in respect of whom an order has been made by any court having jurisdiction (whether in the United Kingdom or elsewhere) in matters concerning mental disorder may vote, whether on a show of hands or on a poll, by his receiver, curator bonis or other person authorised in that behalf appointed by that court, and any such receiver, curator bonis or other person may, on a poll, vote by proxy. Evidence to the satisfaction of the directors of the authority of the person claiming to exercise the right to vote shall be deposited at the office, or at such other place as is specified in accordance with the articles for the deposit of instruments of proxy, not less than 48 hours before the time appointed for holding the meeting or adjourned meeting at which the right to vote is to be exercised and in default the right to vote shall not be exercisable.

57 No member shall vote at any general meeting or at any separate meeting of the holders of any class of shares in the company, either in person or by proxy, in respect of any share held by him unless all moneys presently payable by him in respect of that share have been paid.

58 No objection shall be raised to the qualification of any voter except at the meeting or adjourned meeting at which the vote objected to is tendered, and every vote not disallowed at the meeting shall be valid. Any objection made in due time shall be referred to the chairman whose decision shall be final and conclusive.

59 On a poll votes may be given either personally or by proxy. A member may appoint more than one proxy to attend on the same occasion.

60 The appointment of a proxy shall be executed by or on behalf of the appointor and shall be in the following form (or in a form as near thereto as circumstances allow or in any other form which is usual or which the directors may approve)—

'.......... PLC/Limited ........ I/We, .........., of .........., being a member/members of the above-named company, hereby appoint .......... of .........., or failing him, .......... of .........., as my/our proxy to vote in my/our name[s] and on my/our behalf at the general meeting of the company to be held on .......... 19 .........., and at any adjournment thereof.

Signed on .......... 19 ..........'

61 Where it is desired to afford members an opportunity of instructing the proxy how he shall act the appointment of a proxy shall be in the following form (or in a form as near thereto as circumstances allow or in any other form which is usual or which the directors may approve)—

'.. .. .. .. .. .. PLC/Limited .. .. .. .. .. .. I/We, .. .. .. .. .. .., of .. .. .. .. .. .., being a member/members of the above-named company, hereby appoint .. .. .. .. .. of .. .. .. .. .., or failing him .. .. .. .. .. of .. .. .. .. .. .., as my/our proxy to vote in my/our name[s] and on my/our behalf at the general meeting of the company, to be held on .. .. .. .. .. 19 , .. .. .. .. .. .., and at any adjournment thereof.

This form is to be used in respect of the resolutions mentioned below as follows:

Resolution No. 1 *for *against

Resolution No. 2 *for *against.

*Strike out whichever is not desired.

Unless otherwise instructed, the proxy may vote as he thinks fit or abstain from voting.

Signed this .. .. .. .. .. day of .. .. .. .. .. 19 .. .. .. .. .. .'[3]

62 The appointment of a proxy and any authority under which it is executed or a copy of such authority certified notarially or in some other way approved by the directors may—

(a) in the case of an instrument in writing be deposited at the office or at such other places within the United kingdom as is specified in the notice convening the meeting or in any instrument of proxy sent out by the company in relation to the meeting not less than 48 hours before the time for holding the meeting or adjourned meeting at which the person named in the instrument proposes to vote; or

(aa) in the case of an appointment contained in an electronic communication, where an address has been specified for the purpose of receiving electronic communications-

   (i) in the notice convening the meeting, or

   (ii) in any instrument of proxy sent out by the company in relation to the meeting, or

   (iii) in any invitation contained in an electronic communication to appoint a proxy issued by the company in relation to the meeting,

be received at such address not less than 48 hours before the time for holding the meeting or adjourned meeting at which the person named in the appointment proposes to vote;

(b) in the case of a poll taken more than 48 hours after it is demanded, be deposited or received as aforesaid after the poll has been demanded and not less than 24 hours before the time appointed for the taking of the poll; or

(c) where the poll is not taken forthwith but is taken not more than 48 hours after it was demanded, be delivered at the meeting at which the poll was demanded to the chairman or to the secretary or to any director;

and an appointment of proxy which is not deposited, delivered or received in a manner so permitted shall be invalid.

In this regulation and the next, 'address', in relation to electronic communications, includes any number or address used for the purposes of such communications.

63 A vote given or poll demanded by proxy or by the duly authorised representative of a corporation shall be valid notwithstanding the previous determination of the authority of the person voting or demanding a poll unless notice of the determination was received by the company at the office or at such other place at which the instrument of proxy was duly deposited or, where the appointment of the proxy was contained in an electronic communication, at the address at which such appointment was duly received before the commencement of the meeting or adjourned meeting at which the vote is given or the poll demanded or (in the case of a poll taken otherwise than on the same day as the meeting or adjourned meeting) the time appointed for taking the poll.

---

[3] For a public company limited by shares, regs 60 and 61 are as follows:

60 The appointment of a proxy shall be, executed by or on behalf of the appointor and shall be in the following form (or in a form as near thereto as circumstances allow or in any other form which is usual or which the directors may approve)—

'PLC/Limited

I/We,        , of        , being a member/members of the above-named company, hereby appoint        of        , or failing him, of        , as my/our proxy to vote in my/our name[s] and on my/our behalf at the annual/ any other general meeting of the company to be held on        19, and at any adjournment thereof.

Signed on        19        .'

61 Where it is desired to afford members an opportunity of instructing the proxy how he shall act the appointment of a proxy shall be in the following form (or in a form as near thereto as circumstances allow or in any other form which is usual or which the directors may approve)—

'PLC/Limited

I/We,        , of        , being a member/members of the above-named company, hereby appoint        of        , or failing him, of        , as my/our proxy to vote in my/our name[s] and on my/our behalf at the annual/ any other general meeting of the company to be held on        19        , and at any adjournment thereof.

This form is to be used in respect of the resolutions mentioned below as follows:

Resolution No. 1 *for *against

Resolution No. 2 *for *against

*Strike out whichever is not desired.

Unless otherwise instructed, the proxy may vote as he thinks fit or abstain from voting

Signed this        day of        19        .'

### Number of Directors

64 Unless otherwise determined by ordinary resolution, the number of directors (other than alternate directors) shall not be subject to any maximum but shall be not less than two.

### Alternate Directors

65 Any director (other than an alternate director) may appoint any other director, or any other person approved by resolution of the directors and willing to act, to be an alternate director and may remove from office an alternate director so appointed by him.

66 An alternate director shall be entitled to receive notice of all meetings of directors and of all meetings of committees of directors of which his appointor is a member, to attend and vote at any such meeting at which the director appointing him is not personally present and generally to perform all the functions of his appointor as a director in his absence but shall not be entitled to receive any remuneration from the company for his services as an alternate director. But it shall not be necessary to give notice of such a meeting to an alternate director who is absent from the United Kingdom.

67 An alternate director shall cease to be an alternate director if his appointor ceases to be a director; but, if a director retires by rotation or otherwise but is reappointed or deemed to have been reappointed at the meeting at which he retires, any appointment of an alternate director made by him which was in force immediately prior to his retirement shall continue after his reappointment.

68 Any appointment or removal of an alternate director shall be by notice to the company signed by the director making or revoking the appointment or in any other manner approved by the directors.

69 Save as otherwise provided in the articles, an alternate director shall be deemed for all purposes to be a director and shall alone be responsible for his own acts and defaults and he shall not be deemed to be the agent of the director appointing him.

### Powers of Directors

70 Subject to the provisions of the Act, the memorandum and the articles and to any directions given by special resolution, the business of the company shall be managed by the directors who may exercise all the powers of the company.

71 The directors may, by power of attorney or otherwise, appoint any person to be the agent of the company for such purposes and on such conditions as they determine, including authority for the agent to delegate all or any of his powers.

### Delegation of Directors' Powers

72 The directors may delegate any of their powers to any committee consisting of one or more directors. They may also delegate to any managing director or any director holding any other executive office such of their powers as they consider desirable to be exercised by him. Any such delegation may be made subject to any conditions the directors may impose, and either collaterally with or to the exclusion of their own powers and may be revoked or altered. Subject to any such conditions, the proceedings of a committee with two or more members shall be governed by the articles regulating the proceedings of directors so far as they are capable of applying.

### Appointment and Retirement of Directors

73 [...]

74 [...]

75 [...]

76 No person other than a director retiring by rotation shall be appointed or reappointed a director at any general meeting unless—

  (a) he is recommended by the directors; or
  (b) not less than fourteen nor more than thirty-five clear days before the date appointed for the meeting, notice executed by a member qualified to vote at the meeting has been given to the company of the intention to propose that person for appointment or reappointment stating the particulars which would, if he were so appointed or reappointed, be required to be included in the company's register of directors together with notice executed by that person of his willingness to be appointed or reappointed.

77 Not less than seven nor more than twenty-eight clear days before the date appointed for holding a general meeting notice shall be given to all who are entitled to receive notice of the meeting of any person who is recommended by the directors for appointment or reappointment as a director at the meeting or in respect of whom notice has been duly given to the company of the intention to propose him at the meeting for appointment or reappointment as a director. The notice shall give the particulars of that person which would, if he were so appointed or reappointed, be required to be included in the company's register of directors.

78 The company may by ordinary resolution appoint a person who is willing to act to be a director either to fill a vacancy or as an additional director and may also determine the rotation in which any additional directors are to retire.

79  The directors may appoint a person who is willing to act to be a director, either to fill a vacancy or as an additional director, provided that the appointment does not cause the number of directors to exceed any number fixed by or in accordance with the articles as the maximum number of directors.

80  [...]

4

## Disqualification and Removal of Directors

81  The office of a director shall be vacated if—

(a)  he ceases to be a director by virtue of any provision of the Act or he becomes prohibited by law from being a director; or

(b)  he becomes bankrupt or makes any arrangement or composition with his creditors generally; or

(c)  he is, or may be, suffering from mental disorder and either—

(i)  he is admitted to hospital in pursuance of an application for admission for treatment under the Mental Health Act 1983 or, in Scotland, an application for admission under the Mental Health (Scotland) Act 1960, or

(ii)  an order is made by a court having jurisdiction (whether in the United Kingdom or elsewhere) in matters concerning mental disorder for his detention or for the appointment of a receiver, curator bonis or other person to exercise powers with respect to his property or affairs; or

(d)  he resigns his office by notice to the company; or

(e)  he shall for more than six consecutive months have been absent without permission of the directors from meetings of directors held during that period and the directors resolve that his office be vacated.

## Remuneration of Directors

82  The directors shall be entitled to such remuneration as the company may by ordinary resolution determine and, unless the resolution provides otherwise, the remuneration shall be deemed to accrue from day to day.

## Directors' Expenses

83  The directors may be paid all travelling, hotel, and other expenses properly incurred by them in connection with their attendance at meetings of directors or committees of directors or general meetings or separate meetings of the holders of any class of shares or of debentures of the company or otherwise in connection with the discharge of their duties.

## Directors' Appointments and Interests

84  Subject to the provisions of the Act, the directors may appoint one or more of their number to the office of managing director or to any other executive office under the company and may enter into an agreement or arrangement with any director for his employment by the company or for the provision by him of any services outside the scope of the ordinary duties of a director. Any such appointment, agreement or arrangement may be made upon such terms as the directors determine and they may remunerate any such director for his services as they think fit. Any appointment of a director to an executive office shall terminate if he ceases to be a director but without prejudice to any claim to damages for breach of the contract of service between the director and the company. A managing director and a director holding any other executive office shall not be subject to retirement by rotation.

85  Subject to the provisions of the Act, and provided that he has disclosed to the directors the nature and extent of any material interest of his, a director notwithstanding his office—

---

⁴ For a public company limited by shares, regs 76 to 80 inclusive are as follows:

76 No person other than a director retiring by rotation shall be appointed or reappointed a director at any general meeting unless—

(a)  he is recommended by the directors; or

(b)  not less than fourteen nor more than thirty-five clear days before the date appointed for the meeting, notice executed by a member qualified to vote at the meeting has been given to the company of the intention to propose that person for appointment or reappointment stating the particulars which would, if he were so appointed or reappointed, be required to be included in the company's register of directors together with notice executed by that person of his willingness to be appointed or reappointed.

77 Not less than seven nor more than twenty-eight clear days before the date appointed for holding a general meeting notice shall be given to all who are entitled to receive notice of the meeting of any person (other than a director retiring by rotation at the meeting) who is recommended by the directors for appointment or reappointment as a director at the meeting or in respect of whom notice has been duly given to the company of the intention to propose him at the meeting for appointment or reappointment as a director. The notice shall give the particulars of that person which would, if he were so appointed or reappointed, be required to be included in the company's register of directors.

78 Subject as aforesaid, the company may by ordinary resolution appoint a person who is willing to act to be a director either to fill a vacancy or as an additional director and may also determine the rotation in which any additional directors are to retire.

79 The directors may appoint a person who is willing to act to be a director, either to fill a vacancy or as an additional director, provided that the appointment does not cause the number of directors to exceed any number fixed by or in accordance with the articles as the maximum number of directors. A director so appointed shall hold office only until the next following annual general meeting and shall not be taken into account in determining the directors who are to retire by rotation at the meeting. If not reappointed at such annual general meeting, he shall vacate office at the conclusion thereof.

80 Subject as aforesaid, a director who retires at an annual general meeting may, if willing to act, be reappointed. If he is not reappointed, he shall retain office until the meeting appoints someone in his place, or if it does not do so, until the end of the meeting.

(a) may be a party to, or otherwise interested in, any transaction or arrangement with the company or in which the company or in which the company is otherwise interested; and

(b) may be a director or other officer of, or employed by, or a party to any transaction or arrangement with, or otherwise interested in, any body corporate promoted by the company or in which the company is otherwise interested; and

(c) shall not, by reason of his office, be accountable to the company for any benefit which he derives from any such office or employment or from any such transaction or arrangement or from any interest in any such body corporate and no such transaction or arrangement shall be liable to be avoided on the ground of any such interest or benefit.

86 For the purposes of regulation 85—

(a) a general notice given to the directors that a director is to be regarded as having an interest of the nature and extent specified in the notice in any transaction or arrangement in which a specified person or class of persons is interested shall be deemed to be a disclosure that the director has an interest in any such transaction of the nature and extent so specified; and

(b) an interest of which a director has no knowledge and of which it is unreasonable to expect him to have knowledge shall not be treated as an interest of his.

### *Directors' Gratuities and Pensions*

87 The directors may provide benefits, whether by the payment of gratuities or pensions or by insurance or otherwise, for any director who has held but no longer holds any executive office or employment with the company or with any body corporate which is or has been a subsidiary of the company or a predecessor in business of the company or of any such subsidiary, and for any member of his family (including a spouse and a former spouse) or any person who is or was dependent on him, and may (as well before as after he ceases to hold such office or employment) contribute to any fund and pay premiums for the purchase or provision of any such benefit.

### *Proceedings of Directors*

88 Subject to the provisions of the articles, the directors may regulate their proceedings as they think fit. A director may, and the secretary at the request of a director shall, call a meeting of the directors. It shall not be necessary to give notice of a meeting to a director who is absent from the United Kingdom. Questions arising at a meeting shall be decided by a majority of votes. In the case of an equality of votes, the chairman shall have a second or casting vote. A director who is also an alternate director shall be entitled in the absence of his appointor to a separate vote on behalf of his appointor in addition to his own vote.

89 The quorum for the transaction of the business of the directors may be fixed by the directors and unless so fixed at any other number shall be two. A person who holds office only as an alternate director shall, if his appointor is not present, be counted in the quorum.

90 The continuing directors or a sole continuing director may act notwithstanding any vacancies in their number, but, if the number of directors is less than the number fixed as the quorum, the continuing director may act only for the purpose of filling vacancies or of calling a general meeting.

91 The directors may appoint one of their number to be the chairman of the board of directors and may at any time remove him from that office. Unless he is unwilling to do so, the director so appointed shall preside at every meeting of directors at which he is present. But if there is no director holding that office, or if the director holding it is unwilling to preside or is not present within five minutes after the time appointed for the meeting, the directors present may appoint one of their number to be chairman of the meeting.

92 All acts done by a meeting of directors, or of a committee of directors, or by a person acting as a director shall, notwithstanding that it be afterwards discovered that there was a defect in the appointment of any director or that any of them were disqualified from holding office, or had vacated office, or were not entitled to vote, be as valid as if every such person had been duly appointed and was qualified and had continued to be a director and had been entitled to vote.

93 A resolution in writing signed by all the directors entitled to receive notice of a meeting of directors or of a committee of directors shall be as valid and effectual as it if had been passed at a meeting of directors or (as the case may be) a committee of directors duly convened and held and may consist of several documents in the like form each signed by one or more directors; but a resolution signed by an alternate director need not also be signed by his appointor and, if it is signed by a director who has appointed an alternate director, it need not be signed by the alternate director in that capacity.

94 Save as otherwise provided by the articles, a director shall not vote at a meeting of directors or of a committee of directors on any resolution concerning a matter in which he has, directly or indirectly, an interest or duty which is material and which conflicts or may conflict with the interests of the company unless his interest or duty arises only because the case falls within one or more of the following paragraphs

(a) the resolution relates to the giving to him of a guarantee, security, or indemnity in respect of money lent to, or an obligation incurred by him for the benefit of, the company or any of its subsidiaries;

(b) the resolution relates to the giving to a third party of a guarantee, security, or indemnity in respect of an obligation of the company or any of its subsidiaries for which the director has assumed responsibility in whole or part and whether alone or jointly with others under a guarantee or indemnity or by the giving of security;

(c) his interest arises by virtue of his subscribing or agreeing to subscribe for any shares, debentures, or other securities of the company or any of its subsidiaries, or by virtue of his being, or intending to become, a participant in the underwriting or sub-underwriting of an offer of any such shares, debentures, or other securities by the company or any of its subsidiaries for subscription, purchase or exchange;

(d) the resolution relates in any way to a retirement benefits scheme which has been approved, or is conditional upon approval, by the Board of Inland Revenue for taxation purposes.

For the purposes of this regulation, an interest of a person who is, for any purpose of the Act (excluding any statutory modification thereof not in force when this regulation becomes binding on the company), connected with a director shall be treated as an interest of the director and, in relation to an alternate director, an interest of his appointor shall be treated as an interest of the alternate director without prejudice to any interest which the alternate director has otherwise.

95  A director shall not be counted in the quorum present at a meeting in relation to a resolution on which he is not entitled to vote.

96  The company may by ordinary resolution suspend or relax to any extent, either generally or in respect of any particular matter, any provision of the articles prohibiting a director from voting at a meeting of directors or of a committee of directors.

97  Where proposals are under consideration concerning the appointment of two or more directors to offices or employments with the company or any body corporate in which the company is interested the proposals may be divided and considered in relation to each director separately and (provided he is not for another reason precluded from voting) each of the directors concerned shall be entitled to vote and be counted in the quorum in respect of each resolution except that concerning his own appointment.

98  If a question arises at a meeting of directors or of a committee of directors as to the right of a director to vote, the question may, before the conclusion of the meeting, be referred to the chairman of the meeting and his ruling in relation to any director other than himself shall be final and conclusive.

## Secretary

99  Subject to the provisions of the Act, the secretary shall be appointed by the directors for such term, at such remuneration and upon such conditions as they may think fit; and any secretary so appointed may be removed by them.

## Minutes

100  The directors shall cause minutes to be made in books kept for the purpose—

(a) of all appointments of officers made by the directors; and

(b) of all proceedings at meetings of the company, of the holders of any class of shares in the company, and of the directors, and of committees of directors, including the names of the directors present at each such meeting.

## The Seal

101  The seal shall only be used by the authority of the directors or of a committee of directors authorised by the directors. The directors may determine who shall sign any instrument to which the seal is affixed and unless otherwise so determined it shall be signed by a director and by the secretary or by a second director.

## Dividends

102  Subject to the provisions of the Act, the company may by ordinary resolution declare dividends in accordance with the respective rights of the members, but no dividend shall exceed the amount recommended by the directors.

103  Subject to the provisions of the Act, the directors may pay interim dividends if it appears to them that they are justified by the profits of the company available for distribution. If the share capital is divided into difference classes, the directors may pay interim dividends on shares which confer deferred or non-preferred rights with regard to dividend as well as on shares which confer preferential rights with regard to dividend, but no interim dividend shall be paid on shares carrying deferred or non-preferred rights if, at the time of payment, any preferential dividend is in arrear. The directors may also pay at intervals settled by them any dividend payable at a fixed rate if it appears to them that the profits available for distribution justify the payment. Provided the directors act in good faith they shall not incur any liability to the holders of shares conferring preferred rights for any loss they may suffer by the lawful payment of an interim dividend on any shares having deferred or non-preferred rights.

104  Except as otherwise provided by the rights attached to shares, all dividends shall be declared and paid according to the amounts paid up on the shares on which the dividend is paid. All dividends shall be apportioned and paid proportionately to the amounts paid up on the shares during any portion or portions of the period in respect of which the dividend is paid; but, if any share is issued on terms providing that it shall rank for dividend as from a particular date, that share shall rank for dividend accordingly.

105 A general meeting declaring a dividend may, upon the recommendation of the directors, direct that it shall be satisfied wholly or partly by the distribution of assets and, where any difficulty arises in regard to the distribution, the directors may settle the same and in particular may issue fractional certificates and fix the value for distribution of any assets and may determine that cash shall be paid to any member upon the footing of the value so fixed in order to adjust the rights of members and may vest any assets in trustees.

106 Any dividend or other moneys payable in respect of a share may be paid by cheque sent by post to the registered address of the person entitled or, if two or more persons are the holders of the share or are jointly entitled to it by reason of the death or bankruptcy of the holder, to the registered address of that one of those persons who is first named in the register of members or to such person and to such address as the person or persons entitled may in writing direct. Every cheque shall be made payable to the order of the person or persons entitled or to such other person as the person or persons entitled may in writing direct and payment of the cheque shall be a good discharge to the company. Any joint holder or other person jointly entitled to a share as aforesaid may give receipts for any dividend or other moneys payable in respect of the share.

107 No dividend or other moneys payable in respect of a share shall bear interest against the company unless otherwise provided by the rights attached to the share.

108 Any dividend which has remained unclaimed for twelve years from the date when it became due for payment shall, if the directors so resolve, be forfeited and cease to remain owing by the company.

### Accounts

109 No member shall (as such) have any right of inspecting any accounting records or other book or document of the company except as conferred by statute or authorised by the directors or by ordinary resolution of the company.

### Capitalisation Of Profits

110 The directors may with the authority of an ordinary resolution of the company—

(a) subject as hereinafter provided, resolve to capitalise any undivided profits of the company not required for paying any preferential dividend (whether or not they are available for distribution) or any sum standing to the credit of the company's share premium account or capital redemption reserve;

(b) appropriate the sum resolved to be capitalised to the members who would have been entitled to it if it were distributed by way of dividend and in the same proportions and apply such sum on their behalf either in or towards paying up the amounts, if any, for the time being unpaid on any shares held by them respectively, or in paying up in full unissued shares or debentures of the company of a nominal amount equal to that sum, and allot the shares or debentures credited as fully paid to those members, or as they may direct, in those proportions, or partly in one way and partly in the other: but the share premium account, the capital redemption reserve, and any profits which are not available for distribution may, for the purposes of this regulation, only be applied in paying up unissued to be allotted to members credited as fully paid;

(c) make such provision by the issue of fractional certificates or by payment in cash or otherwise as they determine in the case of shares or debentures becoming distributable under this regulation in fractions; and

(d) authorise any person to enter on behalf of all the members concerned into an agreement with the company providing for the allotment to them respectively, credited as fully paid, of any shares or debentures to which they are entitled upon such capitalisation, any agreement made under such authority being binding on all such members.

### Notices

111 Any notice to be given to or by any person pursuant to the articles (other than a notice calling a meeting of the directors) shall be in writing or shall be given using electronic communications to an address for the time being notified for that purpose to the person giving the notice.
In this regulation, 'address', in relation to electronic communications, includes any number or address used for the purposes of such communications.

112 The company may give any notice to a member either personally or by sending it by post in a prepaid envelope addressed to the member at his registered address or by leaving it at that address or by giving it using electronic communications to an address for the time being notified to the company by the member. In the case of joint holders of a share, all notices shall be given to the joint holder whose name stands first in the register of members in respect of the joint holding and notice so given shall be sufficient notice to all the joint holders. A member whose registered address is not within the United Kingdom at which notices may be given to him, or an address to which notices may be sent using electronic communications, shall be entitled to have notices given to him at that address, but otherwise no such member shall be entitled to receive any notice from the company.
In this regulation and the next, 'address', in relation to electronic communications, includes any number or address used for the purposes of such communications.

113  A member present, either in person or by proxy, at any meeting of the company or of the holders of any class of shares in the company shall be deemed to have received notice of the meeting and, where requisite, of the purposes for which it was called.

114  Every person who becomes entitled to a share shall be bound by any notice in respect of that share which, before his name is entered in the register of members, has been duly given to a person from whom he derives his title.

115  Proof that an envelope containing a notice was properly addressed, prepaid and posted shall be conclusive evidence that that the notice was given. Proof that a notice contained in an electronic communication was sent in accordance with guidance issued by the Institute of Chartered Secretaries and Administrators shall be conclusive evidence that the notice was given. A notice shall, be deemed to be given at the expiration of 48 hours after the envelope containing it was posted or, in the case of a notice contained in an electronic communication, at the expiration of 48 hours after the time it was sent.

116  A notice may be given by the company to the persons entitled to a share in consequence of the death or bankruptcy of a member by sending or delivering it, in any manner authorised by the articles for the giving of notice to a member, addressed to them by name, or by the title of representatives of the deceased, or trustee of the bankrupt or by any like description at the address, if any, within the United Kingdom supplied for that purpose by the persons claiming to be so entitled. Until such an address has been supplied, a notice may be given in any manner in which it might have been given if the death or bankruptcy had not occurred.

## *Winding Up*

117  If the company is wound up, the liquidator may, with the sanction of a special resolution of the company and any other sanction required by the Act, divide among the members in specie the whole or any part of the assets of the company and may, for that purpose, value any assets and determine how the division shall be carried out as between the members or different classes of members. The liquidator may, with the like sanction, vest the whole or any part of the assets in trustees upon such trusts for the benefit of the members as he with the like sanction determines, but no member shall be compelled to accept any assets upon which there is a liability.

## *Indemnity*

118  Subject to the provisions of the Act but without prejudice to any indemnity to which a director may otherwise be entitled, every director or other officer or auditor of the company shall be indemnified out of the assets of the company against any liability incurred by him in defending any proceedings, whether civil or criminal, in which judgment is given in his favour or in which he is acquitted or in connection with any application in which relief is granted to him by the court from liability for negligence, default, breach of duty or breach of trust in relation to the affairs of the company.

# TABLE B

# PRIVATE COMPANY LIMITED BY SHARES

### *Memorandum of Association*

1. The company's name is ' The South Wales Motor Transport Company cyfyngedig'.
2. The company's registered office is to be situated in Wales.
3. The company's objects are the carriage of passengers and goods in motor vehicles between such places as the company may from time to time determine and the doing of all such other things as are incidental or conducive to the attainment of that object.
4. The liability of the members is limited.
5. The company's share capital is £50,000 divided into 50,000 shares of £1 each.

We, the subscribers to this memorandum of association, wish to be formed into a company pursuant to this memorandum; and we agree to take the number of shares shown opposite our respective names.

| Names and Addresses of Subscribers | Number of shares taken by each Subscriber |
|---|---|
| 1.    Thomas Jones, 138 Mountfield Street, Tredegar. | 1 |
|        Mary Evans, 19 Marthyr Road, Aberystwyth | 1 |
|        Total shares taken | 2 |

Dated      19  .
Witness to the above signatures,
Anne Brown, 'Woodlands', Fieldside Road, Bryn Mawr.

# TABLE C

# COMPANY LIMITED BY GUARANTEE AND NOT HAVING A SHARE CAPITAL

### *Memorandum of Association*

1. The company's name is 'The Dundee School Association Limited'.

2. The company's registered office is to be situated in Scotland.

3. The company's objects are the carrying on of a school for boys and girls in Dundee and the doing of all such other things as are incidental or conducive to the attainment of that object.

4. The liability of the members is limited.

5. Every member of the company undertakes to contribute such amount as may be required (not exceeding £100) to the company's assets if it should be wound up while he is a member or within one year after he ceases to be a member, for payment of the company's debts and liabilities contracted before he ceases to be a member, and of the costs, charges and expenses of winding up, and for the adjustment of the rights of the contributories among themselves.

We, the subscribers to this memorandum of association, wish to be formed into a company pursuant to this memorandum.

Names and Addresses of Subscribers.

1. Kenneth Brodie, 14 Bute Street, Dundee.

2. Ian Davis, 2 Burns Avenue, Dundee.

Dated       19   .

Witness to the above signatures.

Anne Brown, 149 Princes Street, Edinburgh.

### *Articles of Association*

A1. References in these Articles to Table A are to that Table so far as it relates to private companies limited by guarantee.

1. Regulations 2 to 35 inclusive, 54, 55, 57, 59, 102 to 108 inclusive, 110, 114, 116 and 117 of Table A, shall not apply to the company but the articles hereinafter contained and, subject to the modifications hereinafter expressed, the remaining regulations of Table A shall constitute the articles of association of the company.

2. In regulation 1 of Table A, the definition of 'the holder' shall be omitted.

3. The subscribers to the memorandum of association of the company and such other persons as are admitted to membership in accordance with the articles shall be members of the company. No person shall be admitted a member of the company unless he is approved by the directors. Every person who wishes to become a member shall deliver to the company an application for membership in such form as the directors require executed by him.

4. A member may at any time withdraw from the company by giving at least seven clear days' notice to the company. Membership shall not be transferable and shall cease on death.

5. In regulation 38 of Table A—

   (a) in paragraph (b) the words "of the total voting rights at the meeting of all the members" shall be substituted for "in nominal value of the shares giving that right" and

   (b) the words "The notice shall be given to all the members and to the directors and auditors" shall be substituted for the last sentence.

6. The words "and at any separate meeting of the holders of any class of shares in the company" shall be omitted from regulation 44 of Table A.

7. Paragraph (d) of regulation 46 of Table A shall be omitted.

8. On a show of hands every member present in person or by proxy shall have one vote. On a poll every member present in person or by proxy shall have one vote.

9. The words "of any class of shares or" shall be omitted from regulation 83 of Table A.

10. In paragraph (c) of regulation 94 of Table A the word "debentures" shall be substituted for the words "shares, debentures or other securities" in both places where they occur.

11. The words "of the holders of any class of shares in the company" shall be omitted from regulation 100 of Table A.

12. The second sentence of regulation 112 of Table A shall be omitted.

13. The words "or of the holders of any class of shares in the company" shall be omitted from regulation 113 of Table A.

# TABLE D

## PART I  A PUBLIC COMPANY LIMITED BY GUARANTEE AND HAVING SHARE CAPITAL

### *Memorandum of Association*

1. The company's name is ' Gwestai Glyndwr, cwmni cyfyngedig cyhoeddus'.
2. The company is to be a public company.
3. The company's registered office is to be situated in Wales.
4. The company's objects are facilitating travelling in Wales by providing hotels and conveyances by sea and by land for the accommodation of travellers and the doing of all such other things as are incidental or conducive to the attainment of those objects.
5. The liability of the members is limited.
6. Every member of the company undertakes to contribute such amount as may be required (not exceeding £100) to the company's assets if it should be wound up while he is a member or within one year after he ceases to be a member, for payment of the company's debts and liabilities contracted before he ceases to be a member, and of the costs, charges and expenses of winding up, and for the adjustment of the rights of the contributories among themselves.
7. The company's share capital is £50,000 divided into 50,000 shares of £1 each.

| We, the subscribers to this memorandum of association, wish to be formed into a company pursuant to this memorandum; and we agree to take the number of shares shown opposite our respective names. Names and Addresses of Subscribers | Number of shares taken by each Subscriber |
| --- | --- |
| 1.    Thomas Jones, 138 Mountfield Street, Tredegar. | 1 |
|        Andrew Smith, 19 Merthyr Road, Aberystwyth | 1 |
|        Total shares taken | 2 |

Dated      19  .

Witness to the above signatures,

Anne Brown, 'Woodlands', Fieldside Road, Bryn Mawr.

## PART II    A PRIVATE COMPANY LIMITED BY GUARANTEE HAVING A SHARE CAPITAL

### *Memorandum of Association*

1. The company's name is 'The Highland Hotel Company Limited'.
2. The company's registered office is to be situated in Scotland.
3. The company's objects are facilitating travelling in the Highlands of Scotland by providing hotels and conveyances by sea and by land for the accommodation of travellers and the doing of all such other things as are incidental or conducive to the attainment of those objects.
4. The liability of the members is limited.
5. Every member of the company undertakes to contribute such amount as may be required (not exceeding £100) to the company's assets if it should be wound up while he is a member or within one year after he ceases to be a member, for payment of the company's debts and liabilities contracted before he ceases to be a member, and of the costs, charges and expenses of winding up, and for the adjustment of the rights of the contributories among themselves.
6. The company's share capital is £50,000 divided into 50,000 shares of £1 each.

We, the subscribers to this memorandum of association, wish to be formed into a company pursuant to this memorandum; and we agree to take the number of shares shown opposite our respective names.

| Names and Addresses of Subscribers | Number of shares taken by each Subscriber |
| --- | --- |
| Kenneth Brodie, 14 Bute Street, Dundee. | 1 |
| Ian Davis, 2 Burns Avenue, Dundee. | 1 |
| Total shares taken | 2 |

Dated      19  .

Witness to the above signatures,

Anne Brown, 149 Princes Street, Edinburgh.

## PART III   A COMPANY (PUBLIC OR PRIVATE) LIMITED BY GUARANTEE AND HAVING A SHARE CAPITAL

*Articles of Association*

1. The regulations of Table A shall constitute the articles of association of the company.

# TABLE E

# AN UNLIMITED COMPANY HAVING A SHARE CAPITAL

*Memorandum of Association*

1. The company's name is 'The Woodford Engineering Company'.
2. The company's registered office is to be situated in England and Wales.
3. The company's objects are the working of certain patented inventions relating to the application of microchip technology to the improvement of food processing, and the doing of all such other things as are incidental or conducive to the attainment of that object.

We, the subscribers to this memorandum of association, wish to be formed into a company pursuant to this memorandum; and we agree to take the number of shares shown opposite our respective names.

| Names and Addresses of Subscribers | Numbers of shares taken by each Subscriber |
| --- | --- |
| Brian Smith, 24 Nibley Road, Wotton-under-Edge, Gloucestershire. | 3 |
| William Green, 278 High Street, Chipping Sodbury, Avon. | 5 |
| Total shares taken | 8 |

Dated     19  .
Witness to the above signatures,
Anne Brown, 108 Park Way, Bristol 8.

*Articles of Association*

1. Regulations 3, 32, 34 and 35 of Table A shall not apply to the company, but the articles hereinafter contained and, subject to the modification hereinafter expressed, the remaining regulations of Table A shall constitute the articles of association of the company.
2. [...]
3. The share capital of the company is £20,000 divided into 20,000 shares of £1 each.
4. The company may by special resolution—
    (a) increase the share capital by such sum to be divided into shares of such amount as the resolution may prescribe;
    (b) consolidate and divide all or any of its share capital into shares of a larger amount than its existing shares;
    (c) subdivide its shares, or any of them, into shares of a smaller amount than its existing shares;
    (d) cancel any shares which at the date of the passing of the resolution have not been taken or agreed to be taken by any person;
    (e) reduce its share capital and any share premium account in any way.

# TABLE F

# A COMPANY LIMITED BY SHARES

*Memorandum of Association*

1. The company's name is 'Western Electronics Public Limited Company'.
2. The company is to be a public company.
3. The company's registered office is to be situated in England and Wales.
4. The company's objects are the manufacture and development of such descriptions of electronic equipment, instruments and appliances as the company may from time to time determine, and the doing of all such other things as are incidental or conducive to the attainment of that object.
5. The liability of the members is limited.
6. The company's share capital is £5,000,000 divided into 5,000,000 shares of £1 each.

We, the subscribers to this memorandum of association, wish to be formed into a company pursuant to this memorandum; and we agree to take the number of shares shown opposite our respective names.

| Names and Addresses of Subscribers | Number of shares taken by each Subscriber |
|---|---|
| James White, 12 Broadmead, Birmingham. | 1 |
| Patrick Smith, 145A Huntley House, London Wall, London, EC2. | 1 |
| Total shares taken | 2 |

Dated    19  .
Witness to the above signatures,
Anne Brown, 13 Hute Street, London WC2.

# The Companies (Model Articles) Regulations 2008

(2008 No. 3229)

*The Secretary of State makes the following Regulations in exercise of the powers conferred by section 19 of the Companies Act 2006*

## 1   Citation and Commencement

These Regulations may be cited as the Companies (Model Articles) Regulations 2008 and come into force on 1st October 2009.

## 2   Model articles for private companies limited by shares

Schedule 1 to these Regulations prescribes the model articles of association for private companies limited by shares.

## 3   Model articles for private companies limited by guarantee

Schedule 2 to these Regulations prescribes the model articles of association for private companies limited by guarantee.

## 4   Model articles for public companies

Schedule 3 to these Regulations prescribes the model articles of association for public companies.

# SCHEDULE 1

# MODEL ARTICLES FOR PRIVATE COMPANIES LIMITED BY SHARES

## PART 1  INTERPRETATION AND LIMITATION OF LIABILITY

### 1   Defined terms

In the articles, unless the context requires otherwise—

'articles' means the company's articles of association;

'bankruptcy' includes individual insolvency proceedings in a jurisdiction other than England and Wales or Northern Ireland which have an effect similar to that of bankruptcy;

'chairman' has the meaning given in article 12;

'chairman of the meeting' has the meaning given in article 39;

'Companies Acts' means the Companies Acts (as defined in section 2 of the Companies Act 2006), in so far as they apply to the company;

'director' means a director of the company, and includes any person occupying the position of director, by whatever name called;

'distribution recipient' has the meaning given in article 31;

'document' includes, unless otherwise specified, any document sent or supplied in electronic form;

'electronic form' has the meaning given in section 1168 of the Companies Act 2006;

'fully paid' in relation to a share, means that the nominal value and any premium to be paid to the company in respect of that share have been paid to the company;

'hard copy form' has the meaning given in section 1168 of the Companies Act 2006;

'holder' in relation to shares means the person whose name is entered in the register of members as the holder of the shares;

'instrument' means a document in hard copy form;

'ordinary resolution' has the meaning given in section 282 of the Companies Act 2006;

'paid' means paid or credited as paid;

'participate', in relation to a directors' meeting, has the meaning given in article 10;

'proxy notice' has the meaning given in article 45;

'shareholder' means a person who is the holder of a share;

'shares' means shares in the company;

'special resolution' has the meaning given in section 283 of the Companies Act 2006;

'subsidiary' has the meaning given in section 1159 of the Companies Act 2006;

'transmittee' means a person entitled to a share by reason of the death or bankruptcy of a shareholder or otherwise by operation of law; and

'writing' means the representation or reproduction of words, symbols or other information in a visible form by any method or combination of methods, whether sent or supplied in electronic form or otherwise.

Unless the context otherwise requires, other words or expressions contained in these articles bear the same meaning as in the Companies Act 2006 as in force on the date when these articles become binding on the company.

## 2 Liability of members

The liability of the members is limited to the amount, if any, unpaid on the shares held by them.

# PART 2 DIRECTORS

*Directors' Powers and responsibilities*

## 3 Directors' general authority

Subject to the articles, the directors are responsible for the management of the company's business, for which purpose they may exercise all the powers of the company.

## 4 Shareholders' reserve power

(1) The shareholders may, by special resolution, direct the directors to take, or refrain from taking, specified action.

(2) No such special resolution invalidates anything which the directors have done before the passing of the resolution.

## 5 Directors may delegate

(1) Subject to the articles, the directors may delegate any of the powers which are conferred on them under the articles—

(a) to such person or committee;

(b) by such means (including by power of attorney);

(c) to such an extent;

(d) in relation to such matters or territories; and

(e) on such terms and conditions;

as they think fit.

(2) If the directors so specify, any such delegation may authorise further delegation of the directors' powers by any person to whom they are delegated.

(3) The directors may revoke any delegation in whole or part, or alter its terms and conditions.

## 6 Committees

(1) Committees to which the directors delegate any of their powers must follow procedures which are based as far as they are applicable on those provisions of the articles which govern the taking of decisions by directors

(2) The directors may make rules of procedure for all or any committees, which prevail over rules derived from the articles if they are not consistent with them.

*Decision-making by directors*

## 7 Directors to take decisions collectively

(1) The general rule about decision-making by directors is that any decision of the directors must be either a majority decision at a meeting or a decision taken in accordance with article 8.

(2) If—

(a) the company only has one director, and

(b) no provision of the articles requires it to have more than one director,

the general rule does not apply, and the director may take decisions without regard to any of the provisions of the articles relating to directors' decision-making.

## 8 Unanimous decisions

(1) A decision of the directors is taken in accordance with this article when all eligible directors indicate to each other by any means that they share a common view on a matter.

(2) Such a decision may take the form of a resolution in writing, copies of which have been signed by each eligible director or to which each eligible director has otherwise indicated agreement in writing.

(3) References in this article to eligible directors are to directors who would have been entitled to vote on the matter had it been proposed as a resolution at a directors' meeting.

(4) A decision may not be taken in accordance with this article if the eligible directors would not have formed a quorum at such a meeting.

### 9   Calling a directors' meeting

(1) Any director may call a directors' meeting by giving notice of the meeting to the directors or by authorising the company secretary (if any) to give such notice.

(2) Notice of any directors' meeting must indicate—

(a) its proposed date and time;

(b) where it is to take place; and

(c) if it is anticipated that directors participating in the meeting will not be in the same place, how it is proposed that they should communicate with each other during the meeting.

(3) Notice of a directors' meeting must be given to each director, but need not be in writing.

(4) Notice of a directors' meeting need not be given to directors who waive their entitlement to notice of that meeting, by giving notice to that effect to the company not more than 7 days after the date on which the meeting is held. Where such notice is given after the meeting has been held, that does not affect the validity of the meeting, or of any business conducted at it.

### 10   Participation in directors' meetings

(1) Subject to the articles, directors participate in a directors' meeting, or part of a directors' meeting, when—

(a) the meeting has been called and takes place in accordance with the articles, and

(b) they can each communicate to the others any information or opinions they have on any particular item of the business of the meeting.

(2) In determining whether directors are participating in a directors' meeting, it is irrelevant where any director is or how they communicate with each other.

(3) If all the directors participating in a meeting are not in the same place, they may decide that the meeting is to be treated as taking place wherever any of them is.

### 11   Quorum for directors' meetings

(1) At a directors' meeting, unless a quorum is participating, no proposal is to be voted on, except a proposal to call another meeting.

(2) The quorum for directors' meetings may be fixed from time to time by a decision of the directors, but it must never be less than two, and unless otherwise fixed it is two.

(3) If the total number of directors for the time being is less than the quorum required, the directors must not take any decision other than a decision—

(a) to appoint further directors, or

(b) to call a general meeting so as to enable the shareholders to appoint further directors.

### 12   Chairing of directors' meetings

(1) The directors may appoint a director to chair their meetings.

(2) The person so appointed for the time being is known as the chairman.

(3) The directors may terminate the chairman's appointment at any time.

(4) If the chairman is not participating in a directors' meeting within ten minutes of the time at which it was to start, the participating directors must appoint one of themselves to chair it.

### 13   Casting vote

(1) If the numbers of votes for and against a proposal are equal, the chairman or other director chairing the meeting has a casting vote.

(2) But this does not apply if, in accordance with the articles, the chairman or other director is not to be counted as participating in the decision-making process for quorum or voting purposes.

### 14   Conflicts of interest

(1) If a proposed decision of the directors is concerned with an actual or proposed transaction or arrangement with the company in which a director is interested, that director is not to be counted as participating in the decision-making process for quorum or voting purposes.

(2) But if paragraph (3) applies, a director who is interested in an actual or proposed transaction or arrangement with the company is to be counted as participating in the decision-making process for quorum and voting purposes.

(3) This paragraph applies when—

(a) the company by ordinary resolution disapplies the provision of the articles which would otherwise prevent a director from being counted as participating in the decision-making process;

(b) the director's interest cannot reasonably be regarded as likely to give rise to a conflict of interest; or

(c) the director's conflict of interest arises from a permitted cause.

(4) For the purposes of this article, the following are permitted causes—

(a) a guarantee given, or to be given, by or to a director in respect of an obligation incurred by or on behalf of the company or any of its subsidiaries;

    (b) subscription, or an agreement to subscribe, for shares or other securities of the company or any of its subsidiaries, or to underwrite, sub-underwrite, or guarantee subscription for any such shares or securities; and

    (c) arrangements pursuant to which benefits are made available to employees and directors or former employees and directors of the company or any of its subsidiaries which do not provide special benefits for directors or former directors.

(5) For the purposes of this article, references to proposed decisions and decision-making processes include any directors' meeting or part of a directors' meeting.

(6) Subject to paragraph (7), if a question arises at a meeting of directors or of a committee of directors as to the right of a director to participate in the meeting (or part of the meeting) for voting or quorum purposes, the question may, before the conclusion of the meeting, be referred to the chairman whose ruling in relation to any director other than the chairman is to be final and conclusive.

(7) If any question as to the right to participate in the meeting (or part of the meeting) should arise in respect of the chairman, the question is to be decided by a decision of the directors at that meeting, for which purpose the chairman is not to be counted as participating in the meeting (or that part of the meeting) for voting or quorum purposes.

### 15   Records of decisions to be kept

The directors must ensure that the company keeps a record, in writing, for at least 10 years from the date of the decision recorded, of every unanimous or majority decision taken by the directors.

### 16   Directors' discretion to make further rules

Subject to the articles, the directors may make any rule which they think fit about how they take decisions, and about how such rules are to be recorded or communicated to directors.

*Appointment of directors*

### 17   Methods of appointing directors

(1) Any person who is willing to act as a director, and is permitted by law to do so, may be appointed to be a director—

    (a) by ordinary resolution, or

    (b) by a decision of the directors.

(2) In any case where, as a result of death, the company has no shareholders and no directors, the personal representatives of the last shareholder to have died have the right, by notice in writing, to appoint a person to be a director.

(3) For the purposes of paragraph (2), where 2 or more shareholders die in circumstances rendering it uncertain who was the last to die, a younger shareholder is deemed to have survived an older shareholder.

### 18   Termination of director's appointment

A person ceases to be a director as soon as—

    (a) that person ceases to be a director by virtue of any provision of the Companies Act 2006 or is prohibited from being a director by law;

    (b) a bankruptcy order is made against that person;

    (c) a composition is made with that person's creditors generally in satisfaction of that person's debts;

    (d) a registered medical practitioner who is treating that person gives a written opinion to the company stating that that person has become physically or mentally incapable of acting as a director and may remain so for more than three months;

    (e) by reason of that person's mental health, a court makes an order which wholly or partly prevents that person from personally exercising any powers or rights which that person would otherwise have;

    (f) notification is received by the company from the director that the director is resigning from office, and such resignation has taken effect in accordance with its terms.

### 19   Directors' remuneration

(1) Directors may undertake any services for the company that the directors decide.

(2) Directors are entitled to such remuneration as the directors determine—

    (a) for their services to the company as directors, and

    (b) for any other service which they undertake for the company.

(3) Subject to the articles, a director's remuneration may—

    (a) take any form, and

    (b) include any arrangements in connection with the payment of a pension, allowance or gratuity, or any death, sickness or disability benefits, to or in respect of that director.

(4) Unless the directors decide otherwise, directors' remuneration accrues from day to day.

(5) Unless the directors decide otherwise, directors are not accountable to the company for any remuneration which they receive as directors or other officers or employees of the company's subsidiaries or of any other body corporate in which the company is interested.

## 20   Directors' expenses

The company may pay any reasonable expenses which the directors properly incur in connection with their attendance at—

 (a)  meetings of directors or committees of directors,

 (b)  general meetings, or

 (c)  separate meetings of the holders of any class of shares or of debentures of the company,

or otherwise in connection with the exercise of their powers and the discharge of their responsibilities in relation to the company.

# PART 3   SHARES AND DISTRIBUTIONS

*Shares*

## 21   All shares to be fully paid up

 (1)  No share is to be issued for less than the aggregate of its nominal value and any premium to be paid to the company in consideration for its issue.

 (2)  This does not apply to shares taken on the formation of the company by the subscribers to the company's memorandum.

## 22   Powers to issue different classes of share

 (1)  Subject to the articles, but without prejudice to the rights attached to any existing share, the company may issue shares with such rights or restrictions as may be determined by ordinary resolution.

 (2)  The company may issue shares which are to be redeemed, or are liable to be redeemed at the option of the company or the holder, and the directors may determine the terms, conditions and manner of redemption of any such shares.

## 23   Company not bound by less than absolute interests

Except as required by law, no person is to be recognised by the company as holding any share upon any trust, and except as otherwise required by law or the articles, the company is not in any way to be bound by or recognise any interest in a share other than the holder's absolute ownership of it and all the rights attaching to it.

## 24   Share certificates

 (1)  The company must issue each shareholder, free of charge, with one or more certificates in respect of the shares which that shareholder holds.

 (2)  Every certificate must specify—

  (a)  in respect of how many shares, of what class, it is issued;

  (b)  the nominal value of those shares;

  (c)  that the shares are fully paid; and

  (d)  any distinguishing numbers assigned to them.

 (3)  No certificate may be issued in respect of shares of more than one class.

 (4)  If more than one person holds a share, only one certificate may be issued in respect of it.

 (5)  Certificates must—

  (a)  have affixed to them the company's common seal, or

  (b)  be otherwise executed in accordance with the Companies Acts.

## 25   Replacement share certificates

 (1)  If a certificate issued in respect of a shareholder's shares is—

  (a)  damaged or defaced, or

  (b)  said to be lost, stolen or destroyed,

that shareholder is entitled to be issued with a replacement certificate in respect of the same shares.

 (2)  A shareholder exercising the right to be issued with such a replacement certificate—

  (a)  may at the same time exercise the right to be issued with a single certificate or separate certificates;

  (b)  must return the certificate which is to be replaced to the company if it is damaged or defaced; and

  (c)  must comply with such conditions as to evidence, indemnity and the payment of a reasonable fee as the directors decide.

## 26   Share transfers

 (1)  Shares may be transferred by means of an instrument of transfer in any usual form or any other form approved by the directors, which is executed by or on behalf of the transferor.

 (2)  No fee may be charged for registering any instrument of transfer or other document relating to or affecting the title to any share.

 (3)  The company may retain any instrument of transfer which is registered.

 (4)  The transferor remains the holder of a share until the transferee's name is entered in the register of members as holder of it.

(5) The directors may refuse to register the transfer of a share, and if they do so, the instrument of transfer must be returned to the transferee with the notice of refusal unless they suspect that the proposed transfer may be fraudulent.

### 27 Transmission of shares

(1) If title to a share passes to a transmittee, the company may only recognise the transmittee as having any title to that share.

(2) A transmittee who produces such evidence of entitlement to shares as the directors may properly require—

    (a) may, subject to the articles, choose either to become the holder of those shares or to have them transferred to another person, and

    (b) subject to the articles, and pending any transfer of the shares to another person, has the same rights as the holder had.

(3) But transmittees do not have the right to attend or vote at a general meeting, or agree to a proposed written resolution, in respect of shares to which they are entitled, by reason of the holder's death or bankruptcy or otherwise, unless they become the holders of those shares.

### 28 Exercise of transmittees' rights

(1) Transmittees who wish to become the holders of shares to which they have become entitled must notify the company in writing of that wish.

(2) If the transmittee wishes to have a share transferred to another person, the transmittee must execute an instrument of transfer in respect of it.

(3) Any transfer made or executed under this article is to be treated as if it were made or executed by the person from whom the transmittee has derived rights in respect of the share, and as if the event which gave rise to the transmission had not occurred.

### 29 Transmittees bound by prior notices

If a notice is given to a shareholder in respect of shares and a transmittee is entitled to those shares, the transmittee is bound by the notice if it was given to the shareholder before the transmittee's name has been entered in the register of members.

*Dividends and other distributions*

### 30 Procedure for declaring dividends

(1) The company may by ordinary resolution declare dividends, and the directors may decide to pay interim dividends.

(2) A dividend must not be declared unless the directors have made a recommendation as to its amount. Such a dividend must not exceed the amount recommended by the directors.

(3) No dividend may be declared or paid unless it is in accordance with shareholders' respective rights.

(4) Unless the shareholders' resolution to declare or directors' decision to pay a dividend, or the terms on which shares are issued, specify otherwise, it must be paid by reference to each shareholder's holding of shares on the date of the resolution or decision to declare or pay it.

(5) If the company's share capital is divided into different classes, no interim dividend may be paid on shares carrying deferred or non-preferred rights if, at the time of payment, any preferential dividend is in arrear.

(6) The directors may pay at intervals any dividend payable at a fixed rate if it appears to them that the profits available for distribution justify the payment.

(7) If the directors act in good faith, they do not incur any liability to the holders of shares conferring preferred rights for any loss they may suffer by the lawful payment of an interim dividend on shares with deferred or non-preferred rights.

### 31 Payment of dividends and other distributions

(1) Where a dividend or other sum which is a distribution is payable in respect of a share, it must be paid by one or more of the following means—

    (a) transfer to a bank or building society account specified by the distribution recipient either in writing or as the directors may otherwise decide;

    (b) sending a cheque made payable to the distribution recipient by post to the distribution recipient at the distribution recipient's registered address (if the distribution recipient is a holder of the share), or (in any other case) to an address specified by the distribution recipient either in writing or as the directors may otherwise decide;

    (c) sending a cheque made payable to such person by post to such person at such address as the distribution recipient has specified either in writing or as the directors may otherwise decide; or

    (d) any other means of payment as the directors agree with the distribution recipient either in writing or by such other means as the directors decide.

(2) In the articles, 'the distribution recipient' means, in respect of a share in respect of which a dividend or other sum is payable—

(a) the holder of the share; or

(b) if the share has two or more joint holders, whichever of them is named first in the register of members; or

(c) if the holder is no longer entitled to the share by reason of death or bankruptcy, or otherwise by operation of law, the transmittee.

## 32   No interest on distributions

The company may not pay interest on any dividend or other sum payable in respect of a share unless otherwise provided by—

(a) the terms on which the share was issued, or

(b) the provisions of another agreement between the holder of that share and the company.

## 33   Unclaimed distributions

(1) All dividends or other sums which are—

(a) payable in respect of shares, and

(b) unclaimed after having been declared or become payable,

may be invested or otherwise made use of by the directors for the benefit of the company until claimed.

(2) The payment of any such dividend or other sum into a separate account does not make the company a trustee in respect of it.

(3) If—

(a) twelve years have passed from the date on which a dividend or other sum became due for payment, and

(b) the distribution recipient has not claimed it,

the distribution recipient is no longer entitled to that dividend or other sum and it ceases to remain owing by the company.

## 34   Non-cash distributions

(1) Subject to the terms of issue of the share in question, the company may, by ordinary resolution on the recommendation of the directors, decide to pay all or part of a dividend or other distribution payable in respect of a share by transferring non-cash assets of equivalent value (including, without limitation, shares or other securities in any company).

(2) For the purposes of paying a non-cash distribution, the directors may make whatever arrangements they think fit, including, where any difficulty arises regarding the distribution—

(a) fixing the value of any assets;

(b) paying cash to any distribution recipient on the basis of that value in order to adjust the rights of recipients; and

(c) vesting any assets in trustees.

## 35   Waiver of distributions

Distribution recipients may waive their entitlement to a dividend or other distribution payable in respect of a share by giving the company notice in writing to that effect, but if—

(a) the share has more than one holder, or

(b) more than one person is entitled to the share, whether by reason of the death or bankruptcy of one or more joint holders, or otherwise,

the notice is not effective unless it is expressed to be given, and signed, by all the holders or persons otherwise entitled to the share.

### *Capitalisation of profits*

## 36   Authority to capitalise and appropriation of capitalised sums

(1) Subject to the articles, the directors may, if they are so authorised by an ordinary resolution—

(a) decide to capitalise any profits of the company (whether or not they are available for distribution) which are not required for paying a preferential dividend, or any sum standing to the credit of the company's share premium account or capital redemption reserve; and

(b) appropriate any sum which they so decide to capitalise (a 'capitalised sum') to the persons who would have been entitled to it if it were distributed by way of dividend (the 'persons entitled') and in the same proportions.

(2) Capitalised sums must be applied—

(a) on behalf of the persons entitled, and

(b) in the same proportions as a dividend would have been distributed to them.

(3) Any capitalised sum may be applied in paying up new shares of a nominal amount equal to the capitalised sum which are then allotted credited as fully paid to the persons entitled or as they may direct.

(4) A capitalised sum which was appropriated from profits available for distribution may be applied in paying up new debentures of the company which are then allotted credited as fully paid to the persons entitled or as they may direct.

(5) Subject to the articles the directors may—

(a) apply capitalised sums in accordance with paragraphs (3) and (4) partly in one way and partly in another;

(b) make such arrangements as they think fit to deal with shares or debentures becoming distributable in fractions under this article (including the issuing of fractional certificates or the making of cash payments); and

(c) authorise any person to enter into an agreement with the company on behalf of all the persons entitled which is binding on them in respect of the allotment of shares and debentures to them under this article.

# PART 4   DECISION-MAKING BY SHAREHOLDERS

*Organisation of general meetings*

## 37   Attendance and speaking at general meetings

(1) A person is able to exercise the right to speak at a general meeting when that person is in a position to communicate to all those attending the meeting, during the meeting, any information or opinions which that person has on the business of the meeting.

(2) A person is able to exercise the right to vote at a general meeting when—

(a) that person is able to vote, during the meeting, on resolutions put to the vote at the meeting, and

(b) that person's vote can be taken into account in determining whether or not such resolutions are passed at the same time as the votes of all the other persons attending the meeting.

(3) The directors may make whatever arrangements they consider appropriate to enable those attending a general meeting to exercise their rights to speak or vote at it.

(4) In determining attendance at a general meeting, it is immaterial whether any two or more members attending it are in the same place as each other.

(5) Two or more persons who are not in the same place as each other attend a general meeting if their circumstances are such that if they have (or were to have) rights to speak and vote at that meeting, they are (or would be) able to exercise them.

## 38   Quorum for general meetings

No business other than the appointment of the chairman of the meeting is to be transacted at a general meeting if the persons attending it do not constitute a quorum.

## 39   Chairing general meetings

(1) If the directors have appointed a chairman, the chairman shall chair general meetings if present and willing to do so.

(2) If the directors have not appointed a chairman, or if the chairman is unwilling to chair the meeting or is not present within ten minutes of the time at which a meeting was due to start—

(a) the directors present, or

(b) (if no directors are present), the meeting,

must appoint a director or shareholder to chair the meeting, and the appointment of the chairman of the meeting must be the first business of the meeting.

(3) The person chairing a meeting in accordance with this article is referred to as 'the chairman of the meeting'.

## 40   Attendance and speaking by directors and non-shareholders

(1) Directors may attend and speak at general meetings, whether or not they are shareholders.

(2) The chairman of the meeting may permit other persons who are not—

(a) shareholders of the company, or

(b) otherwise entitled to exercise the rights of shareholders in relation to general meetings,

to attend and speak at a general meeting.

## 41   Adjournment

(1) If the persons attending a general meeting within half an hour of the time at which the meeting was due to start do not constitute a quorum, or if during a meeting a quorum ceases to be present, the chairman of the meeting must adjourn it.

(2) The chairman of the meeting may adjourn a general meeting at which a quorum is present if—

(a) the meeting consents to an adjournment, or

(b) it appears to the chairman of the meeting that an adjournment is necessary to protect the safety of any person attending the meeting or ensure that the business of the meeting is conducted in an orderly manner.

(3) The chairman of the meeting must adjourn a general meeting if directed to do so by the meeting.

(4) When adjourning a general meeting, the chairman of the meeting must—

(a) either specify the time and place to which it is adjourned or state that it is to continue at a time and place to be fixed by the directors, and

(b) have regard to any directions as to the time and place of any adjournment which have been given by the meeting.

(5) If the continuation of an adjourned meeting is to take place more than 14 days after it was adjourned, the company must give at least 7 clear days' notice of it (that is, excluding the day of the adjourned meeting and the day on which the notice is given)—

(a) to the same persons to whom notice of the company's general meetings is required to be given, and

(b) containing the same information which such notice is required to contain.

(6) No business may be transacted at an adjourned general meeting which could not properly have been transacted at the meeting if the adjournment had not taken place.

### *Voting at general meetings*

### 42   Voting: general

A resolution put to the vote of a general meeting must be decided on a show of hands unless a poll is duly demanded in accordance with the articles.

### 43   Errors and disputes

(1) No objection may be raised to the qualification of any person voting at a general meeting except at the meeting or adjourned meeting at which the vote objected to is tendered, and every vote not disallowed at the meeting is valid.

(2) Any such objection must be referred to the chairman of the meeting, whose decision is final.

### 44   Poll votes

(1) A poll on a resolution may be demanded—

(a) in advance of the general meeting where it is to be put to the vote, or

(b) at a general meeting, either before a show of hands on that resolution or immediately after the result of a show of hands on that resolution is declared.

(2) A poll may be demanded by—

(a) the chairman of the meeting;

(b) the directors;

(c) two or more persons having the right to vote on the resolution; or

(d) a person or persons representing not less than one tenth of the total voting rights of all the shareholders having the right to vote on the resolution.

(3) A demand for a poll may be withdrawn if—

(a) the poll has not yet been taken, and

(b) the chairman of the meeting consents to the withdrawal.

(4) Polls must be taken immediately and in such manner as the chairman of the meeting directs.

### 45   Content of proxy notices

(1) Proxies may only validly be appointed by a notice in writing (a 'proxy notice') which—

(a) states the name and address of the shareholder appointing the proxy;

(b) identifies the person appointed to be that shareholder's proxy and the general meeting in relation to which that person is appointed;

(c) is signed by or on behalf of the shareholder appointing the proxy, or is authenticated in such manner as the directors may determine; and

(d) is delivered to the company in accordance with the articles and any instructions contained in the notice of the general meeting to which they relate.

(2) The company may require proxy notices to be delivered in a particular form, and may specify different forms for different purposes.

(3) Proxy notices may specify how the proxy appointed under them is to vote (or that the proxy is to abstain from voting) on one or more resolutions.

(4) Unless a proxy notice indicates otherwise, it must be treated as—

(a) allowing the person appointed under it as a proxy discretion as to how to vote on any ancillary or procedural resolutions put to the meeting, and

(b) appointing that person as a proxy in relation to any adjournment of the general meeting to which it relates as well as the meeting itself.

### 46   Delivery of proxy notices

(1) A person who is entitled to attend, speak or vote (either on a show of hands or on a poll) at a general meeting remains so entitled in respect of that meeting or any adjournment of it, even though a valid proxy notice has been delivered to the company by or on behalf of that person.

(2) An appointment under a proxy notice may be revoked by delivering to the company a notice in writing given by or on behalf of the person by whom or on whose behalf the proxy notice was given.

(3) A notice revoking a proxy appointment only takes effect if it is delivered before the start of the meeting or adjourned meeting to which it relates.

(4) If a proxy notice is not executed by the person appointing the proxy, it must be accompanied by written evidence of the authority of the person who executed it to execute it on the appointor's behalf.

### 47 Amendments to resolutions

(1) An ordinary resolution to be proposed at a general meeting may be amended by ordinary resolution if—

  (a) notice of the proposed amendment is given to the company in writing by a person entitled to vote at the general meeting at which it is to be proposed not less than 48 hours before the meeting is to take place (or such later time as the chairman of the meeting may determine), and

  (b) the proposed amendment does not, in the reasonable opinion of the chairman of the meeting, materially alter the scope of the resolution.

(2) A special resolution to be proposed at a general meeting may be amended by ordinary resolution, if—

  (a) the chairman of the meeting proposes the amendment at the general meeting at which the resolution is to be proposed, and

  (b) the amendment does not go beyond what is necessary to correct a grammatical or other non-substantive error in the resolution.

(3) If the chairman of the meeting, acting in good faith, wrongly decides that an amendment to a resolution is out of order, the chairman's error does not invalidate the vote on that resolution.

## PART 5   ADMINISTRATIVE ARRANGEMENTS

### 48 Means of communication to be used

(1) Subject to the articles, anything sent or supplied by or to the company under the articles may be sent or supplied in any way in which the Companies Act 2006 provides for documents or information which are authorised or required by any provision of that Act to be sent or supplied by or to the company.

(2) Subject to the articles, any notice or document to be sent or supplied to a director in connection with the taking of decisions by directors may also be sent or supplied by the means by which that director has asked to be sent or supplied with such notices or documents for the time being.

(3) A director may agree with the company that notices or documents sent to that director in a particular way are to be deemed to have been received within a specified time of their being sent, and for the specified time to be less than 48 hours.

### 49 Company seals

(1) Any common seal may only be used by the authority of the directors.

(2) The directors may decide by what means and in what form any common seal is to be used.

(3) Unless otherwise decided by the directors, if the company has a common seal and it is affixed to a document, the document must also be signed by at least one authorised person in the presence of a witness who attests the signature.

(4) For the purposes of this article, an authorised person is—

  (a) any director of the company;

  (b) the company secretary (if any); or

  (c) any person authorised by the directors for the purpose of signing documents to which the common seal is applied.

### 50 No right to inspect accounts and other records

Except as provided by law or authorised by the directors or an ordinary resolution of the company, no person is entitled to inspect any of the company's accounting or other records or documents merely by virtue of being a shareholder.

### 51 Provision for employees on cessation of business

The directors may decide to make provision for the benefit of persons employed or formerly employed by the company or any of its subsidiaries (other than a director or former director or shadow director) in connection with the cessation or transfer to any person of the whole or part of the undertaking of the company or that subsidiary.

*Directors' indemnity and insurance*

### 52 Indemnity

(1) Subject to paragraph (2), a relevant director of the company or an associated company may be indemnified out of the company's assets against—

  (a) any liability incurred by that director in connection with any negligence, default, breach of duty or breach of trust in relation to the company or an associated company,

  (b) any liability incurred by that director in connection with the activities of the company or an associated company in its capacity as a trustee of an occupational pension scheme (as defined in section 235(6) of the Companies Act 2006),

  (c) any other liability incurred by that director as an officer of the company or an associated company.

(2) This article does not authorise any indemnity which would be prohibited or rendered void by any provision of the Companies Acts or by any other provision of law.

(3) In this article—

    (a) companies are associated if one is a subsidiary of the other or both are subsidiaries of the same body corporate, and

    (b) a 'relevant director' means any director or former director of the company or an associated company.

## 53  Insurance

(1) The directors may decide to purchase and maintain insurance, at the expense of the company, for the benefit of any relevant director in respect of any relevant loss.

(2) In this article—

    (a) a 'relevant director' means any director or former director of the company or an associated company,

    (b) a 'relevant loss' means any loss or liability which has been or may be incurred by a relevant director in connection with that director's duties or powers in relation to the company, any associated company or any pension fund or employees' share scheme of the company or associated company, and

    (c) companies are associated if one is a subsidiary of the other or both are subsidiaries of the same body corporate.

# SCHEDULE 2

# MODEL ARTICLES FOR PRIVATE COMPANIES LIMITED BY GUARANTEE

## PART 1  INTERPRETATION AND LIMITATION OF LIABILITY

### 1  Defined terms

In the articles, unless the context requires otherwise—

'articles' means the company's articles of association;

'bankruptcy' includes individual insolvency proceedings in a jurisdiction other than England and Wales or Northern Ireland which have an effect similar to that of bankruptcy;

'chairman' has the meaning given in article 12;

'chairman of the meeting' has the meaning given in article 25;

'Companies Acts' means the Companies Acts (as defined in section 2 of the Companies Act 2006), in so far as they apply to the company;

'director' means a director of the company, and includes any person occupying the position of director, by whatever name called;

'document' includes, unless otherwise specified, any document sent or supplied in electronic form;

'electronic form' has the meaning given in section 1168 of the Companies Act 2006;

'member' has the meaning given in section 112 of the Companies Act 2006;

'ordinary resolution' has the meaning given in section 282 of the Companies Act 2006;

'participate', in relation to a directors' meeting, has the meaning given in article 10;

'proxy notice' has the meaning given in article 31;

'special resolution' has the meaning given in section 283 of the Companies Act 2006;

'subsidiary' has the meaning given in section 1159 of the Companies Act 2006; and

'writing' means the representation or reproduction of words, symbols or other information in a visible form by any method or combination of methods, whether sent or supplied in electronic form or otherwise.

Unless the context otherwise requires, other words or expressions contained in these articles bear the same meaning as in the Companies Act 2006 as in force on the date when these articles become binding on the company.

### 2  Liability of members

The liability of each member is limited to £1, being the amount that each member undertakes to contribute to the assets of the company in the event of its being wound up while he is a member or within one year after he ceases to be a member, for—

    (a) payment of the company's debts and liabilities contracted before he ceases to be a member,

    (b) payment of the costs, charges and expenses of winding up, and

    (c) adjustment of the rights of the contributories among themselves.

## PART 2  DIRECTORS

### *Directors' powers and responsibilities*

### 3  Directors' general authority

Subject to the articles, the directors are responsible for the management of the company's business, for which purpose they may exercise all the powers of the company.

### 4  Members' reserve power

(1) The members may, by special resolution, direct the directors to take, or refrain from taking, specified action.

(2) No such special resolution invalidates anything which the directors have done before the passing of the resolution.

### 5  Directors may delegate

(1) Subject to the articles, the directors may delegate any of the powers which are conferred on them under the articles—

> (a) to such person or committee;
>
> (b) by such means (including by power of attorney);
>
> (c) to such an extent;
>
> (d) in relation to such matters or territories; and
>
> (e) on such terms and conditions;

as they think fit.

(2) If the directors so specify, any such delegation may authorise further delegation of the directors' powers by any person to whom they are delegated.

(3) The directors may revoke any delegation in whole or part, or alter its terms and conditions.

### 6  Committees

(1) Committees to which the directors delegate any of their powers must follow procedures which are based as far as they are applicable on those provisions of the articles which govern the taking of decisions by directors.

(2) The directors may make rules of procedure for all or any committees, which prevail over rules derived from the articles if they are not consistent with them.

*Decision-making by directors*

### 7  Directors to take decisions collectively

(1) The general rule about decision-making by directors is that any decision of the directors must be either a majority decision at a meeting or a decision taken in accordance with article 8.

(2) If—

> (a) the company only has one director, and
>
> (b) no provision of the articles requires it to have more than one director,

the general rule does not apply, and the director may take decisions without regard to any of the provisions of the articles relating to directors' decision-making.

### 8  Unanimous decisions

(1) A decision of the directors is taken in accordance with this article when all eligible directors indicate to each other by any means that they share a common view on a matter.

(2) Such a decision may take the form of a resolution in writing, copies of which have been signed by each eligible director or to which each eligible director has otherwise indicated agreement in writing.

(3) References in this article to eligible directors are to directors who would have been entitled to vote on the matter had it been proposed as a resolution at a directors' meeting.

(4) A decision may not be taken in accordance with this article if the eligible directors would not have formed a quorum at such a meeting.

### 9  Calling a directors' meeting

(1) Any director may call a directors' meeting by giving notice of the meeting to the directors or by authorising the company secretary (if any) to give such notice.

(2) Notice of any directors' meeting must indicate—

> (a) its proposed date and time;
>
> (b) where it is to take place; and
>
> (c) if it is anticipated that directors participating in the meeting will not be in the same place, how it is proposed that they should communicate with each other during the meeting.

(3) Notice of a directors' meeting must be given to each director, but need not be in writing.

(4) Notice of a directors' meeting need not be given to directors who waive their entitlement to notice of that meeting, by giving notice to that effect to the company not more than 7 days after the date on which the meeting is held. Where such notice is given after the meeting has been held, that does not affect the validity of the meeting, or of any business conducted at it.

### 10  Participation in directors' meetings

(1) Subject to the articles, directors participate in a directors' meeting, or part of a directors' meeting, when—

> (a) the meeting has been called and takes place in accordance with the articles, and
>
> (b) they can each communicate to the others any information or opinions they have on any particular item of the business of the meeting.

(2)  In determining whether directors are participating in a directors' meeting, it is irrelevant where any director is or how they communicate with each other.

(3)  If all the directors participating in a meeting are not in the same place, they may decide that the meeting is to be treated as taking place wherever any of them is.

## 11   Quorum for directors' meetings

(1)  At a directors' meeting, unless a quorum is participating, no proposal is to be voted on, except a proposal to call another meeting.

(2)  The quorum for directors' meetings may be fixed from time to time by a decision of the directors, but it must never be less than two, and unless otherwise fixed it is two.

(3)  If the total number of directors for the time being is less than the quorum required, the directors must not take any decision other than a decision—

(a)  to appoint further directors, or

(b)  to call a general meeting so as to enable the members to appoint further directors.

## 12   Chairing of directors' meetings

(1)  The directors may appoint a director to chair their meetings.

(2)  The person so appointed for the time being is known as the chairman.

(3)  The directors may terminate the chairman's appointment at any time.

(4)  If the chairman is not participating in a directors' meeting within ten minutes of the time at which it was to start, the participating directors must appoint one of themselves to chair it.

## 13   Casting vote

(1)  If the numbers of votes for and against a proposal are equal, the chairman or other director chairing the meeting has a casting vote.

(2)  But this does not apply if, in accordance with the articles, the chairman or other director is not to be counted as participating in the decision-making process for quorum or voting purposes.

## 14   Conflicts of interest

(1)  If a proposed decision of the directors is concerned with an actual or proposed transaction or arrangement with the company in which a director is interested, that director is not to be counted as participating in the decision-making process for quorum or voting purposes.

(2)  But if paragraph (3) applies, a director who is interested in an actual or proposed transaction or arrangement with the company is to be counted as participating in the decision-making process for quorum and voting purposes.

(3)  This paragraph applies when—

(a)  the company by ordinary resolution disapplies the provision of the articles which would otherwise prevent a director from being counted as participating in the decision-making process;

(b)  the director's interest cannot reasonably be regarded as likely to give rise to a conflict of interest; or

(c)  the director's conflict of interest arises from a permitted cause.

(4)  For the purposes of this article, the following are permitted causes—

(a)  a guarantee given, or to be given, by or to a director in respect of an obligation incurred by or on behalf of the company or any of its subsidiaries;

(b)  subscription, or an agreement to subscribe, for securities of the company or any of its subsidiaries, or to underwrite, sub-underwrite, or guarantee subscription for any such securities; and

(c)  arrangements pursuant to which benefits are made available to employees and directors or former employees and directors of the company or any of its subsidiaries which do not provide special benefits for directors or former directors.

(5)  For the purposes of this article, references to proposed decisions and decision-making processes include any directors' meeting or part of a directors' meeting.

(6)  Subject to paragraph (7), if a question arises at a meeting of directors or of a committee of directors as to the right of a director to participate in the meeting (or part of the meeting) for voting or quorum purposes, the question may, before the conclusion of the meeting, be referred to the chairman whose ruling in relation to any director other than the chairman is to be final and conclusive.

(7)  If any question as to the right to participate in the meeting (or part of the meeting) should arise in respect of the chairman, the question is to be decided by a decision of the directors at that meeting, for which purpose the chairman is not to be counted as participating in the meeting (or that part of the meeting) for voting or quorum purposes.

## 15   Records of decisions to be kept

The directors must ensure that the company keeps a record, in writing, for at least 10 years from the date of the decision recorded, of every unanimous or majority decision taken by the directors.

## 16   Directors' discretion to make further rules

Subject to the articles, the directors may make any rule which they think fit about how they take decisions, and about how such rules are to be recorded or communicated to directors.

*Appointment of directors*

### 17   Methods of appointing directors

(1) Any person who is willing to act as a director, and is permitted by law to do so, may be appointed to be a director—

    (a) by ordinary resolution, or

    (b) by a decision of the directors.

(2) In any case where, as a result of death, the company has no members and no directors, the personal representatives of the last member to have died have the right, by notice in writing, to appoint a person to be a director.

(3) For the purposes of paragraph (2), where 2 or more members die in circumstances rendering it uncertain who was the last to die, a younger member is deemed to have survived an older member.

### 18   Termination of director's appointment

A person ceases to be a director as soon as—

    (a) that person ceases to be a director by virtue of any provision of the Companies Act 2006 or is prohibited from being a director by law;

    (b) a bankruptcy order is made against that person;

    (c) a composition is made with that person's creditors generally in satisfaction of that person's debts;

    (d) a registered medical practitioner who is treating that person gives a written opinion to the company stating that that person has become physically or mentally incapable of acting as a director and may remain so for more than three months;

    (e) by reason of that person's mental health, a court makes an order which wholly or partly prevents that person from personally exercising any powers or rights which that person would otherwise have;

    (f) notification is received by the company from the director that the director is resigning from office, and such resignation has taken effect in accordance with its terms.

### 19   Directors' remuneration

(1) Directors may undertake any services for the company that the directors decide.

(2) Directors are entitled to such remuneration as the directors determine—

    (a) for their services to the company as directors, and

    (b) for any other service which they undertake for the company.

(3) Subject to the articles, a director's remuneration may—

    (a) take any form, and

    (b) include any arrangements in connection with the payment of a pension, allowance or gratuity, or any death, sickness or disability benefits, to or in respect of that director.

(4) Unless the directors decide otherwise, directors' remuneration accrues from day to day.

(5) Unless the directors decide otherwise, directors are not accountable to the company for any remuneration which they receive as directors or other officers or employees of the company's subsidiaries or of any other body corporate in which the company is interested.

### 20   Directors' expenses

The company may pay any reasonable expenses which the directors properly incur in connection with their attendance at—

    (a) meetings of directors or committees of directors,

    (b) general meetings, or

    (c) separate meetings of the holders of debentures of the company,

or otherwise in connection with the exercise of their powers and the discharge of their responsibilities in relation to the company.

## PART 3   MEMBERS

*Becoming and ceasing to be a member*

### 21   Applications for membership

No person shall become a member of the company unless—

    (a) that person has completed an application for membership in a form approved by the directors, and

    (b) the directors have approved the application.

### 22   Termination of membership

(1) A member may withdraw from membership of the company by giving 7 days' notice to the company in writing.

(2) Membership is not transferable.

(3) A person's membership terminates when that person dies or ceases to exist.

*Organisation of general meetings*

### 23   Attendance and speaking at general meetings

(1)  A person is able to exercise the right to speak at a general meeting when that person is in a position to communicate to all those attending the meeting, during the meeting, any information or opinions which that person has on the business of the meeting.

(2)  A person is able to exercise the right to vote at a general meeting when—

    (a)  that person is able to vote, during the meeting, on resolutions put to the vote at the meeting, and

    (b)  that person's vote can be taken into account in determining whether or not such resolutions are passed at the same time as the votes of all the other persons attending the meeting.

(3)  The directors may make whatever arrangements they consider appropriate to enable those attending a general meeting to exercise their rights to speak or vote at it.

(4)  In determining attendance at a general meeting, it is immaterial whether any two or more members attending it are in the same place as each other.

(5)  Two or more persons who are not in the same place as each other attend a general meeting if their circumstances are such that if they have (or were to have) rights to speak and vote at that meeting, they are (or would be) able to exercise them.

### 24   Quorum for general meetings

No business other than the appointment of the chairman of the meeting is to be transacted at a general meeting if the persons attending it do not constitute a quorum.

### 25   Chairing general meetings

(1)  If the directors have appointed a chairman, the chairman shall chair general meetings if present and willing to do so.

(2)  If the directors have not appointed a chairman, or if the chairman is unwilling to chair the meeting or is not present within ten minutes of the time at which a meeting was due to start—

    (a)  the directors present, or

    (b)  (if no directors are present), the meeting,

must appoint a director or member to chair the meeting, and the appointment of the chairman of the meeting must be the first business of the meeting.

(3)  The person chairing a meeting in accordance with this article is referred to as 'the chairman of the meeting'.

### 26   Attendance and speaking by directors and non-members

(1)  Directors may attend and speak at general meetings, whether or not they are members.

(2)  The chairman of the meeting may permit other persons who are not members of the company to attend and speak at a general meeting.

### 27   Adjournment

(1)  If the persons attending a general meeting within half an hour of the time at which the meeting was due to start do not constitute a quorum, or if during a meeting a quorum ceases to be present, the chairman of the meeting must adjourn it.

(2)  The chairman of the meeting may adjourn a general meeting at which a quorum is present if—

    (a)  the meeting consents to an adjournment, or

    (b)  it appears to the chairman of the meeting that an adjournment is necessary to protect the safety of any person attending the meeting or ensure that the business of the meeting is conducted in an orderly manner.

(3)  The chairman of the meeting must adjourn a general meeting if directed to do so by the meeting.

(4)  When adjourning a general meeting, the chairman of the meeting must—

    (a)  either specify the time and place to which it is adjourned or state that it is to continue at a time and place to be fixed by the directors, and

    (b)  have regard to any directions as to the time and place of any adjournment which have been given by the meeting.

(5)  If the continuation of an adjourned meeting is to take place more than 14 days after it was adjourned, the company must give at least 7 clear days' notice of it (that is, excluding the day of the adjourned meeting and the day on which the notice is given)—

    (a)  to the same persons to whom notice of the company's general meetings is required to be given, and

    (b)  containing the same information which such notice is required to contain.

(6)  No business may be transacted at an adjourned general meeting which could not properly have been transacted at the meeting if the adjournment had not taken place.

*Voting at general meetings*

### 28   Voting: general

A resolution put to the vote of a general meeting must be decided on a show of hands unless a poll is duly demanded in accordance with the articles.

### 29   Errors and disputes

(1)  No objection may be raised to the qualification of any person voting at a general meeting except at the meeting or adjourned meeting at which the vote objected to is tendered, and every vote not disallowed at the meeting is valid.

(2)  Any such objection must be referred to the chairman of the meeting whose decision is final.

### 30   Poll votes

(1)  A poll on a resolution may be demanded—
   (a)  in advance of the general meeting where it is to be put to the vote, or
   (b)  at a general meeting, either before a show of hands on that resolution or immediately after the result of a show of hands on that resolution is declared.

(2)  A poll may be demanded by—
   (a)  the chairman of the meeting;
   (b)  the directors;
   (c)  two or more persons having the right to vote on the resolution; or
   (d)  a person or persons representing not less than one tenth of the total voting rights of all the members having the right to vote on the resolution.

(3)  A demand for a poll may be withdrawn if—
   (a)  the poll has not yet been taken, and
   (b)  the chairman of the meeting consents to the withdrawal.

(4)  Polls must be taken immediately and in such manner as the chairman of the meeting directs.

### 31   Content of proxy notices

(1)  Proxies may only validly be appointed by a notice in writing (a 'proxy notice') which—
   (a)  states the name and address of the member appointing the proxy;
   (b)  identifies the person appointed to be that member's proxy and the general meeting in relation to which that person is appointed;
   (c)  is signed by or on behalf of the member appointing the proxy, or is authenticated in such manner as the directors may determine; and
   (d)  is delivered to the company in accordance with the articles and any instructions contained in the notice of the general meeting to which they relate.

(2)  The company may require proxy notices to be delivered in a particular form, and may specify different forms for different purposes.

(3)  Proxy notices may specify how the proxy appointed under them is to vote (or that the proxy is to abstain from voting) on one or more resolutions.

(4)  Unless a proxy notice indicates otherwise, it must be treated as—
   (a)  allowing the person appointed under it as a proxy discretion as to how to vote on any ancillary or procedural resolutions put to the meeting, and
   (b)  appointing that person as a proxy in relation to any adjournment of the general meeting to which it relates as well as the meeting itself.

### 32   Delivery of proxy notices

(1)  A person who is entitled to attend, speak or vote (either on a show of hands or on a poll) at a general meeting remains so entitled in respect of that meeting or any adjournment of it, even though a valid proxy notice has been delivered to the company by or on behalf of that person.

(2)  An appointment under a proxy notice may be revoked by delivering to the company a notice in writing given by or on behalf of the person by whom or on whose behalf the proxy notice was given.

(3)  A notice revoking a proxy appointment only takes effect if it is delivered before the start of the meeting or adjourned meeting to which it relates.

(4)  If a proxy notice is not executed by the person appointing the proxy, it must be accompanied by written evidence of the authority of the person who executed it to execute it on the appointor's behalf.

### 33   Amendments to resolutions

(1)  An ordinary resolution to be proposed at a general meeting may be amended by ordinary resolution if—
   (a)  notice of the proposed amendment is given to the company in writing by a person entitled to vote at the general meeting at which it is to be proposed not less than 48 hours before the meeting is to take place (or such later time as the chairman of the meeting may determine), and
   (b)  the proposed amendment does not, in the reasonable opinion of the chairman of the meeting, materially alter the scope of the resolution.

(2)  A special resolution to be proposed at a general meeting may be amended by ordinary resolution, if—

> (a)  the chairman of the meeting proposes the amendment at the general meeting at which the resolution is to be proposed, and
>
> (b)  the amendment does not go beyond what is necessary to correct a grammatical or other non-substantive error in the resolution.

(3)  If the chairman of the meeting, acting in good faith, wrongly decides that an amendment to a resolution is out of order, the chairman's error does not invalidate the vote on that resolution.

## PART 4   ADMINISTRATIVE ARRANGEMENTS

### 34  Means of communication to be used

(1)  Subject to the articles, anything sent or supplied by or to the company under the articles may be sent or supplied in any way in which the Companies Act 2006 provides for documents or information which are authorised or required by any provision of that Act to be sent or supplied by or to the company.

(2)  Subject to the articles, any notice or document to be sent or supplied to a director in connection with the taking of decisions by directors may also be sent or supplied by the means by which that director has asked to be sent or supplied with such notices or documents for the time being.

(3)  A director may agree with the company that notices or documents sent to that director in a particular way are to be deemed to have been received within a specified time of their being sent, and for the specified time to be less than 48 hours.

### 35  Company seals

(1)  Any common seal may only be used by the authority of the directors.

(2)  The directors may decide by what means and in what form any common seal is to be used.

(3)  Unless otherwise decided by the directors, if the company has a common seal and it is affixed to a document, the document must also be signed by at least one authorised person in the presence of a witness who attests the signature.

(4)  For the purposes of this article, an authorised person is—

> (a)  any director of the company;
>
> (b)  the company secretary (if any); or
>
> (c)  any person authorised by the directors for the purpose of signing documents to which the common seal is applied.

### 36  No right to inspect accounts and other records

Except as provided by law or authorised by the directors or an ordinary resolution of the company, no person is entitled to inspect any of the company's accounting or other records or documents merely by virtue of being a member.

### 37  Provision for employees on cessation of business

The directors may decide to make provision for the benefit of persons employed or formerly employed by the company or any of its subsidiaries (other than a director or former director or shadow director) in connection with the cessation or transfer to any person of the whole or part of the undertaking of the company or that subsidiary.

*Directors' indemnity and insurance*

### 38  Indemnity

(1)  Subject to paragraph (2), a relevant director of the company or an associated company may be indemnified out of the company's assets against—

> (a)  any liability incurred by that director in connection with any negligence, default, breach of duty or breach of trust in relation to the company or an associated company,
>
> (b)  any liability incurred by that director in connection with the activities of the company or an associated company in its capacity as a trustee of an occupational pension scheme (as defined in section 235(6) of the Companies Act 2006),
>
> (c)  any other liability incurred by that director as an officer of the company or an associated company.

(2)  This article does not authorise any indemnity which would be prohibited or rendered void by any provision of the Companies Acts or by any other provision of law.

(3)  In this article—

> (a)  companies are associated if one is a subsidiary of the other or both are subsidiaries of the same body corporate, and
>
> (b)  a 'relevant director' means any director or former director of the company or an associated company.

### 39  Insurance

(1)  The directors may decide to purchase and maintain insurance, at the expense of the company, for the benefit of any relevant director in respect of any relevant loss.

(2) In this article—

 (a) a 'relevant director' means any director or former director of the company or an associated company,

 (b) a 'relevant loss' means any loss or liability which has been or may be incurred by a relevant director in connection with that director's duties or powers in relation to the company, any associated company or any pension fund or employees' share scheme of the company or associated company, and

 (c) companies are associated if one is a subsidiary of the other or both are subsidiaries of the same body corporate.

# SCHEDULE 3

# MODEL ARTICLES FOR PUBLIC COMPANIES

## PART 1 INTERPRETATION AND LIMITATION OF LIABILITY

### 1 Defined terms

In the articles , unless the context requires otherwise—

'alternate' or 'alternate director' has the meaning given in article 25;

'appointor' has the meaning given in article 25;

'articles' means the company's articles of association;

'bankruptcy' includes individual insolvency proceedings in a jurisdiction other than England and Wales or Northern Ireland which have an effect similar to that of bankruptcy;

'call' has the meaning given in article 54;

'call notice' has the meaning given in article 54;

'certificate' means a paper certificate (other than a share warrant) evidencing a person's title to specified shares or other securities;

'certificated' in relation to a share, means that it is not an uncertificated share or a share in respect of which a share warrant has been issued and is current;

'chairman' has the meaning given in article 12;

'chairman of the meeting' has the meaning given in article 31;

'Companies Acts' means the Companies Acts (as defined in section 2 of the Companies Act 2006), in so far as they apply to the company;

'company's lien' has the meaning given in article 52;

'director' means a director of the company, and includes any person occupying the position of director, by whatever name called;

'distribution recipient' has the meaning given in article 72;

'document' includes, unless otherwise specified, any document sent or supplied in electronic form;

'electronic form' has the meaning given in section 1168 of the Companies Act 2006;

'fully paid' in relation to a share, means that the nominal value and any premium to be paid to the company in respect of that share have been paid to the company;

'hard copy form' has the meaning given in section 1168 of the Companies Act 2006;

'holder' in relation to shares means the person whose name is entered in the register of members as the holder of the shares, or, in the case of a share in respect of which a share warrant has been issued (and not cancelled), the person in possession of that warrant;

'instrument' means a document in hard copy form;

'lien enforcement notice' has the meaning given in article 53;

'member' has the meaning given in section 112 of the Companies Act 2006;

'ordinary resolution' has the meaning given in section 282 of the Companies Act 2006;

'paid' means paid or credited as paid;

'participate', in relation to a directors' meeting, has the meaning given in article 9;

'partly paid' in relation to a share means that part of that share's nominal value or any premium at which it was issued has not been paid to the company;

'proxy notice' has the meaning given in article 38;

'securities seal' has the meaning given in article 47;

'shares' means shares in the company;

'special resolution' has the meaning given in section 283 of the Companies Act 2006;

'subsidiary' has the meaning given in section 1159 of the Companies Act 2006;

'transmittee' means a person entitled to a share by reason of the death or bankruptcy of a shareholder or otherwise by operation of law;

'uncertificated' in relation to a share means that, by virtue of legislation (other than section 778 of the Companies Act 2006) permitting title to shares to be evidenced and transferred without a certificate, title to that share is evidenced and may be transferred without a certificate; and 'writing' means the representation or reproduction of words, symbols or other information in a visible form by any method or combination of methods, whether sent or supplied in electronic form or otherwise.

Unless the context otherwise requires, other words or expressions contained in these articles bear the same meaning as in the Companies Act 2006 as in force on the date when these articles become binding on the company.

## 2  Liability of members

The liability of the members is limited to the amount, if any, unpaid on the shares held by them.

# PART 2  DIRECTORS

## *Directors' powers and responsibilities*

### 3  Directors' general authority

Subject to the articles, the directors are responsible for the management of the company's business, for which purpose they may exercise all the powers of the company.

### 4  Members' reserve power

(1) The members may, by special resolution, direct the directors to take, or refrain from taking, specified action.

(2) No such special resolution invalidates anything which the directors have done before the passing of the resolution.

### 5  Directors may delegate

(1) Subject to the articles, the directors may delegate any of the powers which are conferred on them under the articles—

    (a) to such person or committee;

    (b) by such means (including by power of attorney);

    (c) to such an extent;

    (d) in relation to such matters or territories; and

    (e) on such terms and conditions;

as they think fit.

(2) If the directors so specify, any such delegation may authorise further delegation of the directors' powers by any person to whom they are delegated.

(3) The directors may revoke any delegation in whole or part, or alter its terms and conditions.

### 6  Committees

(1) Committees to which the directors delegate any of their powers must follow procedures which are based as far as they are applicable on those provisions of the articles which govern the taking of decisions by directors.

(2) The directors may make rules of procedure for all or any committees, which prevail over rules derived from the articles if they are not consistent with them.

## *Decision-making by directors*

### 7  Directors to take decisions collectively

Decisions of the directors may be taken—

    (a) at a directors' meeting, or

    (b) in the form of a directors' written resolution.

### 8  Calling a directors' meeting

(1) Any director may call a directors' meeting.

(2) The company secretary must call a directors' meeting if a director so requests.

(3) A directors' meeting is called by giving notice of the meeting to the directors.

(4) Notice of any directors' meeting must indicate—

    (a) its proposed date and time;

    (b) where it is to take place; and

    (c) if it is anticipated that directors participating in the meeting will not be in the same place, how it is proposed that they should communicate with each other during the meeting.

(5) Notice of a directors' meeting must be given to each director, but need not be in writing.

(6) Notice of a directors' meeting need not be given to directors who waive their entitlement to notice of that meeting, by giving notice to that effect to the company not more than 7 days after the date on which the meeting is held. Where such notice is given after the meeting has been held, that does not affect the validity of the meeting, or of any business conducted at it.

### 9  Participation in directors' meetings

(1) Subject to the articles, directors participate in a directors' meeting, or part of a directors' meeting, when—

    (a) the meeting has been called and takes place in accordance with the articles, and

(b) they can each communicate to the others any information or opinions they have on any particular item of the business of the meeting.

(2) In determining whether directors are participating in a directors' meeting, it is irrelevant where any director is or how they communicate with each other.

(3) If all the directors participating in a meeting are not in the same place, they may decide that the meeting is to be treated as taking place wherever any of them is.

### 10   Quorum for directors' meetings

(1) At a directors' meeting, unless a quorum is participating, no proposal is to be voted on, except a proposal to call another meeting.

(2) The quorum for directors' meetings may be fixed from time to time by a decision of the directors, but it must never be less than two, and unless otherwise fixed it is two.

### 11   Meetings where total number of directors less than quorum

(1) This article applies where the total number of directors for the time being is less than the quorum for directors' meetings.

(2) If there is only one director, that director may appoint sufficient directors to make up a quorum or call a general meeting to do so.

(3) If there is more than one director—

(a) a directors' meeting may take place, if it is called in accordance with the articles and at least two directors participate in it, with a view to appointing sufficient directors to make up a quorum or calling a general meeting to do so, and

(b) if a directors' meeting is called but only one director attends at the appointed date and time to participate in it, that director may appoint sufficient directors to make up a quorum or call a general meeting to do so.

### 12   Chairing directors' meetings

(1) The directors may appoint a director to chair their meetings.

(2) The person so appointed for the time being is known as the chairman.

(3) The directors may appoint other directors as deputy or assistant chairmen to chair directors' meetings in the chairman's absence.

(4) The directors may terminate the appointment of the chairman, deputy or assistant chairman at any time.

(5) If neither the chairman nor any director appointed generally to chair directors' meetings in the chairman's absence is participating in a meeting within ten minutes of the time at which it was to start, the participating directors must appoint one of themselves to chair it.

### 13   Voting at directors' meetings: general rules

(1) Subject to the articles, a decision is taken at a directors' meeting by a majority of the votes of the participating directors.

(2) Subject to the articles, each director participating in a directors' meeting has one vote.

(3) Subject to the articles, if a director has an interest in an actual or proposed transaction or arrangement with the company—

(a) that director and that director's alternate may not vote on any proposal relating to it, but

(b) this does not preclude the alternate from voting in relation to that transaction or arrangement on behalf of another appointor who does not have such an interest.

### 14   Chairman's casting vote at directors' meetings

(1) If the numbers of votes for and against a proposal are equal, the chairman or other director chairing the meeting has a casting vote.

(2) But this does not apply if, in accordance with the articles, the chairman or other director is not to be counted as participating in the decision-making process for quorum or voting purposes.

### 15   Alternates voting at directors' meetings

A director who is also an alternate director has an additional vote on behalf of each appointor who is—

(a) not participating in a directors' meeting, and

(b) would have been entitled to vote if they were participating in it.

### 16   Conflicts of interest

(1) If a directors' meeting, or part of a directors' meeting, is concerned with an actual or proposed transaction or arrangement with the company in which a director is interested, that director is not to be counted as participating in that meeting, or part of a meeting, for quorum or voting purposes.

(2) But if paragraph (3) applies, a director who is interested in an actual or proposed transaction or arrangement with the company is to be counted as participating in a decision at a directors' meeting, or part of a directors' meeting, relating to it for quorum and voting purposes.

(3) This paragraph applies when—

(a) the company by ordinary resolution disapplies the provision of the articles which would otherwise prevent a director from being counted as participating in, or voting at, a directors' meeting;

(b) the director's interest cannot reasonably be regarded as likely to give rise to a conflict of interest; or

(c) the director's conflict of interest arises from a permitted cause.

(4) For the purposes of this article, the following are permitted causes—

(a) a guarantee given, or to be given, by or to a director in respect of an obligation incurred by or on behalf of the company or any of its subsidiaries;

(b) subscription, or an agreement to subscribe, for shares or other securities of the company or any of its subsidiaries, or to underwrite, sub-underwrite, or guarantee subscription for any such shares or securities; and

(c) arrangements pursuant to which benefits are made available to employees and directors or former employees and directors of the company or any of its subsidiaries which do not provide special benefits for directors or former directors.

(5) Subject to paragraph (6), if a question arises at a meeting of directors or of a committee of directors as to the right of a director to participate in the meeting (or part of the meeting) for voting or quorum purposes, the question may, before the conclusion of the meeting, be referred to the chairman whose ruling in relation to any director other than the chairman is to be final and conclusive.

(6) If any question as to the right to participate in the meeting (or part of the meeting) should arise in respect of the chairman, the question is to be decided by a decision of the directors at that meeting, for which purpose the chairman is not to be counted as participating in the meeting (or that part of the meeting) for voting or quorum purposes.

## 17   Proposing directors' written resolutions

(1) Any director may propose a directors' written resolution.

(2) The company secretary must propose a directors' written resolution if a director so requests.

(3) A directors' written resolution is proposed by giving notice of the proposed resolution to the directors.

(4) Notice of a proposed directors' written resolution must indicate—

(a) the proposed resolution, and

(b) the time by which it is proposed that the directors should adopt it.

(5) Notice of a proposed directors' written resolution must be given in writing to each director.

(6) Any decision which a person giving notice of a proposed directors' written resolution takes regarding the process of adopting that resolution must be taken reasonably in good faith.

## 18   Adoption of directors' written resolutions

(1) A proposed directors' written resolution is adopted when all the directors who would have been entitled to vote on the resolution at a directors' meeting have signed one or more copies of it, provided that those directors would have formed a quorum at such a meeting.

(2) It is immaterial whether any director signs the resolution before or after the time by which the notice proposed that it should be adopted.

(3) Once a directors' written resolution has been adopted, it must be treated as if it had been a decision taken at a directors' meeting in accordance with the articles.

(4) The company secretary must ensure that the company keeps a record, in writing, of all directors' written resolutions for at least ten years from the date of their adoption.

## 19   Directors' discretion to make further rules

Subject to the articles, the directors may make any rule which they think fit about how they take decisions, and about how such rules are to be recorded or communicated to directors.

*Appointment of directors*

## 20   Methods of appointing directors

Any person who is willing to act as a director, and is permitted by law to do so, may be appointed to be a director—

(a) by ordinary resolution, or

(b) by a decision of the directors.

## 21   Retirement of directors by rotation

(1) At the first annual general meeting all the directors must retire from office.

(2) At every subsequent annual general meeting any directors—

(a) who have been appointed by the directors since the last annual general meeting, or

(b) who were not appointed or reappointed at one of the preceding two annual general meetings, must retire from office and may offer themselves for reappointment by the members.

## 22   Termination of director's appointment

A person ceases to be a director as soon as—

(a) that person ceases to be a director by virtue of any provision of the Companies Act 2006 or is prohibited from being a director by law;

(b) a bankruptcy order is made against that person;

(c) a composition is made with that person's creditors generally in satisfaction of that person's debts;

(d) a registered medical practitioner who is treating that person gives a written opinion to the company stating that that person has become physically or mentally incapable of acting as a director and may remain so for more than three months;

(e) by reason of that person's mental health, a court makes an order which wholly or partly prevents that person from personally exercising any powers or rights which that person would otherwise have;

(f) notification is received by the company from the director that the director is resigning from office as director, and such resignation has taken effect in accordance with its terms.

### 23   Directors' remuneration

(1) Directors may undertake any services for the company that the directors decide.

(2) Directors are entitled to such remuneration as the directors determine—

(a) for their services to the company as directors, and

(b) for any other service which they undertake for the company.

(3) Subject to the articles, a director's remuneration may—

(a) take any form, and

(b) include any arrangements in connection with the payment of a pension, allowance or gratuity, or any death, sickness or disability benefits, to or in respect of that director.

(4) Unless the directors decide otherwise, directors' remuneration accrues from day to day.

(5) Unless the directors decide otherwise, directors are not accountable to the company for any remuneration which they receive as directors or other officers or employees of the company's subsidiaries or of any other body corporate in which the company is interested.

### 24   Directors' expenses

The company may pay any reasonable expenses which the directors properly incur in connection with their attendance at—

(a) meetings of directors or committees of directors,

(b) general meetings, or

(c) separate meetings of the holders of any class of shares or of debentures of the company,

or otherwise in connection with the exercise of their powers and the discharge of their responsibilities in relation to the company.

*Alternate directors*

### 25   Appointment and removal of alternates

(1) Any director (the 'appointor') may appoint as an alternate any other director, or any other person approved by resolution of the directors, to—

(a) exercise that director's powers, and

(b) carry out that director's responsibilities,

in relation to the taking of decisions by the directors in the absence of the alternate's appointor.

(2) Any appointment or removal of an alternate must be effected by notice in writing to the company signed by the appointor, or in any other manner approved by the directors.

(3) The notice must—

(a) identify the proposed alternate, and

(b) in the case of a notice of appointment, contain a statement signed by the proposed alternate that the proposed alternate is willing to act as the alternate of the director giving the notice.

### 26   Rights and responsibilities of alternate directors

(1) An alternate director has the same rights, in relation to any directors' meeting or directors' written resolution, as the alternate's appointor.

(2) Except as the articles specify otherwise, alternate directors—

(a) are deemed for all purposes to be directors;

(b) are liable for their own acts and omissions;

(c) are subject to the same restrictions as their appointors; and

(d) are not deemed to be agents of or for their appointors.

(3) A person who is an alternate director but not a director—

(a) may be counted as participating for the purposes of determining whether a quorum is participating (but only if that person's appointor is not participating), and

(b) may sign a written resolution (but only if it is not signed or to be signed by that person's appointor).

No alternate may be counted as more than one director for such purposes.

(4) An alternate director is not entitled to receive any remuneration from the company for serving as an alternate director except such part of the alternate's appointor's remuneration as the appointor may direct by notice in writing made to the company.

### 27   Termination of alternate directorship
An alternate director's appointment as an alternate terminates—

      (a) when the alternate's appointor revokes the appointment by notice to the company in writing specifying when it is to terminate;

      (b) on the occurrence in relation to the alternate of any event which, if it occurred in relation to the alternate's appointor, would result in the termination of the appointor's appointment as a director;

      (c) on the death of the alternate's appointor; or

      (d) when the alternate's appointor's appointment as a director terminates, except that an alternate's appointment as an alternate does not terminate when the appointor retires by rotation at a general meeting and is then re-appointed as a director at the same general meeting.

## PART 3   DECISION-MAKING BY MEMBERS

*Organisation of general meetings*

### 28   Members can call general meeting if not enough directors
If—

      (a) the company has fewer than two directors, and

      (b) the director (if any) is unable or unwilling to appoint sufficient directors to make up a quorum or to call a general meeting to do so,

then two or more members may call a general meeting (or instruct the company secretary to do so) for the purpose of appointing one or more directors.

### 29   Attendance and speaking at general meetings
(1) A person is able to exercise the right to speak at a general meeting when that person is in a position to communicate to all those attending the meeting, during the meeting, any information or opinions which that person has on the business of the meeting.

(2) A person is able to exercise the right to vote at a general meeting when—

      (a) that person is able to vote, during the meeting, on resolutions put to the vote at the meeting, and

      (b) that person's vote can be taken into account in determining whether or not such resolutions are passed at the same time as the votes of all the other persons attending the meeting.

(3) The directors may make whatever arrangements they consider appropriate to enable those attending a general meeting to exercise their rights to speak or vote at it.

(4) In determining attendance at a general meeting, it is immaterial whether any two or more members attending it are in the same place as each other.

(5) Two or more persons who are not in the same place as each other attend a general meeting if their circumstances are such that if they have (or were to have) rights to speak and vote at that meeting, they are (or would be) able to exercise them.

### 30   Quorum for general meetings
No business other than the appointment of the chairman of the meeting is to be transacted at a general meeting if the persons attending it do not constitute a quorum.

### 31   Chairing general meetings
(1) If the directors have appointed a chairman, the chairman shall chair general meetings if present and willing to do so.

(2) If the directors have not appointed a chairman, or if the chairman is unwilling to chair the meeting or is not present within ten minutes of the time at which a meeting was due to start—

      (a) the directors present, or

      (b) (if no directors are present), the meeting,

must appoint a director or member to chair the meeting, and the appointment of the chairman of the meeting must be the first business of the meeting.

(3) The person chairing a meeting in accordance with this article is referred to as 'the chairman of the meeting'.

### 32   Attendance and speaking by directors and non-members
(1) Directors may attend and speak at general meetings, whether or not they are members.

(2) The chairman of the meeting may permit other persons who are not—

      (a) members of the company, or

      (b) otherwise entitled to exercise the rights of members in relation to general meetings,

to attend and speak at a general meeting.

### 33  Adjournment

(1)  If the persons attending a general meeting within half an hour of the time at which the meeting was due to start do not constitute a quorum, or if during a meeting a quorum ceases to be present, the chairman of the meeting must adjourn it.

(2)  The chairman of the meeting may adjourn a general meeting at which a quorum is present if—

(a)  the meeting consents to an adjournment, or

(b)  it appears to the chairman of the meeting that an adjournment is necessary to protect the safety of any person attending the meeting or ensure that the business of the meeting is conducted in an orderly manner.

(3)  The chairman of the meeting must adjourn a general meeting if directed to do so by the meeting.

(4)  When adjourning a general meeting, the chairman of the meeting must—

(a)  either specify the time and place to which it is adjourned or state that it is to continue at a time and place to be fixed by the directors, and

(b)  have regard to any directions as to the time and place of any adjournment which have been given by the meeting.

(5)  If the continuation of an adjourned meeting is to take place more than 14 days after it was adjourned, the company must give at least 7 clear days' notice of it (that is, excluding the day of the adjourned meeting and the day on which the notice is given)—

(a)  to the same persons to whom notice of the company's general meetings is required to be given, and

(b)  containing the same information which such notice is required to contain.

(6)  No business may be transacted at an adjourned general meeting which could not properly have been transacted at the meeting if the adjournment had not taken place.

### *Voting at general meetings*

### 34  Voting: general

A resolution put to the vote of a general meeting must be decided on a show of hands unless a poll is duly demanded in accordance with the articles.

### 35  Errors and disputes

(1)  No objection may be raised to the qualification of any person voting at a general meeting except at the meeting or adjourned meeting at which the vote objected to is tendered, and every vote not disallowed at the meeting is valid.

(2)  Any such objection must be referred to the chairman of the meeting whose decision is final.

### 36  Demanding a poll

(1)  A poll on a resolution may be demanded—

(a)  in advance of the general meeting where it is to be put to the vote, or

(b)  at a general meeting, either before a show of hands on that resolution or immediately after the result of a show of hands on that resolution is declared.

(2)  A poll may be demanded by—

(a)  the chairman of the meeting;

(b)  the directors;

(c)  two or more persons having the right to vote on the resolution; or

(d)  a person or persons representing not less than one tenth of the total voting rights of all the members having the right to vote on the resolution.

(3)  A demand for a poll may be withdrawn if—

(a)  the poll has not yet been taken, and

(b)  the chairman of the meeting consents to the withdrawal.

### 37  Procedure on a poll

(1)  Subject to the articles, polls at general meetings must be taken when, where and in such manner as the chairman of the meeting directs.

(2)  The chairman of the meeting may appoint scrutineers (who need not be members) and decide how and when the result of the poll is to be declared.

(3)  The result of a poll shall be the decision of the meeting in respect of the resolution on which the poll was demanded.

(4)  A poll on—

(a)  the election of the chairman of the meeting, or

(b)  a question of adjournment,

must be taken immediately.

(5)  Other polls must be taken within 30 days of their being demanded.

(6)  A demand for a poll does not prevent a general meeting from continuing, except as regards the question on which the poll was demanded.

(7) No notice need be given of a poll not taken immediately if the time and place at which it is to be taken are announced at the meeting at which it is demanded.

(8) In any other case, at least 7 days' notice must be given specifying the time and place at which the poll is to be taken.

## 38   Content of proxy notices

(1) Proxies may only validly be appointed by a notice in writing (a 'proxy notice') which—

    (a) states the name and address of the member appointing the proxy;

    (b) identifies the person appointed to be that member's proxy and the general meeting in relation to which that person is appointed;

    (c) is signed by or on behalf of the member appointing the proxy, or is authenticated in such manner as the directors may determine; and

    (d) is delivered to the company in accordance with the articles and any instructions contained in the notice of the general meeting to which they relate.

(2) The company may require proxy notices to be delivered in a particular form, and may specify different forms for different purposes.

(3) Proxy notices may specify how the proxy appointed under them is to vote (or that the proxy is to abstain from voting) on one or more resolutions.

(4) Unless a proxy notice indicates otherwise, it must be treated as—

    (a) allowing the person appointed under it as a proxy discretion as to how to vote on any ancillary or procedural resolutions put to the meeting, and

    (b) appointing that person as a proxy in relation to any adjournment of the general meeting to which it relates as well as the meeting itself.

## 39   Delivery of proxy notices

(1) Any notice of a general meeting must specify the address or addresses ('proxy notification address') at which the company or its agents will receive proxy notices relating to that meeting, or any adjournment of it, delivered in hard copy or electronic form.

(2) A person who is entitled to attend, speak or vote (either on a show of hands or on a poll) at a general meeting remains so entitled in respect of that meeting or any adjournment of it, even though a valid proxy notice has been delivered to the company by or on behalf of that person.

(3) Subject to paragraphs (4) and (5), a proxy notice must be delivered to a proxy notification address not less than 48 hours before the general meeting or adjourned meeting to which it relates.

(4) In the case of a poll taken more than 48 hours after it is demanded, the notice must be delivered to a proxy notification address not less than 24 hours before the time appointed for the taking of the poll.

(5) In the case of a poll not taken during the meeting but taken not more than 48 hours after it was demanded, the proxy notice must be delivered—

    (a) in accordance with paragraph (3), or

    (b) at the meeting at which the poll was demanded to the chairman, secretary or any director.

(6) An appointment under a proxy notice may be revoked by delivering a notice in writing given by or on behalf of the person by whom or on whose behalf the proxy notice was given to a proxy notification address.

(7) A notice revoking a proxy appointment only takes effect if it is delivered before—

    (a) the start of the meeting or adjourned meeting to which it relates, or

    (b) (in the case of a poll not taken on the same day as the meeting or adjourned meeting) the time appointed for taking the poll to which it relates.

(8) If a proxy notice is not signed by the person appointing the proxy, it must be accompanied by written evidence of the authority of the person who executed it to execute it on the appointor's behalf.

## 40   Amendments to resolutions

(1) An ordinary resolution to be proposed at a general meeting may be amended by ordinary resolution if—

    (a) notice of the proposed amendment is given to the company secretary in writing by a person entitled to vote at the general meeting at which it is to be proposed not less than 48 hours before the meeting is to take place (or such later time as the chairman of the meeting may determine), and

    (b) the proposed amendment does not, in the reasonable opinion of the chairman of the meeting, materially alter the scope of the resolution.

(2) A special resolution to be proposed at a general meeting may be amended by ordinary resolution, if—

    (a) the chairman of the meeting proposes the amendment at the general meeting at which the resolution is to be proposed, and

    (b) the amendment does not go beyond what is necessary to correct a grammatical or other non-substantive error in the resolution.

(3) If the chairman of the meeting, acting in good faith, wrongly decides that an amendment to a resolution is out of order, the chairman's error does not invalidate the vote on that resolution.

*Restrictions on members' rights*

### 41  No voting of shares on which money owed to company

No voting rights attached to a share may be exercised at any general meeting, at any adjournment of it, or on any poll called at or in relation to it, unless all amounts payable to the company in respect of that share have been paid.

*Application of rules to class meetings*

### 42  Class meetings

The provisions of the articles relating to general meetings apply, with any necessary modifications, to meetings of the holders of any class of shares.

## PART 4    SHARES AND DISTRIBUTIONS

*Issue of shares*

### 43  Powers to issue different classes of share

(1)  Subject to the articles, but without prejudice to the rights attached to any existing share, the company may issue shares with such rights or restrictions as may be determined by ordinary resolution.

(2)  The company may issue shares which are to be redeemed, or are liable to be redeemed at the option of the company or the holder, and the directors may determine the terms, conditions and manner of redemption of any such shares.

### 44  Payment of commissions on subscription for shares

(1)  The company may pay any person a commission in consideration for that person—
   (a)  subscribing, or agreeing to subscribe, for shares, or
   (b)  procuring, or agreeing to procure, subscriptions for shares.

(2)  Any such commission may be paid—
   (a)  in cash, or in fully paid or partly paid shares or other securities, or partly in one way and partly in the other, and
   (b)  in respect of a conditional or an absolute subscription.

*Interests in shares*

### 45  Company not bound by less than absolute interests

Except as required by law, no person is to be recognised by the company as holding any share upon any trust, and except as otherwise required by law or the articles, the company is not in any way to be bound by or recognise any interest in a share other than the holder's absolute ownership of it and all the rights attaching to it.

*Share certificates*

### 46  Certificates to be issued except in certain cases

(1)  The company must issue each member with one or more certificates in respect of the shares which that member holds.

(2)  This article does not apply to—
   (a)  uncertificated shares;
   (b)  shares in respect of which a share warrant has been issued; or
   (c)  shares in respect of which the Companies Acts permit the company not to issue a certificate.

(3)  Except as otherwise specified in the articles, all certificates must be issued free of charge.

(4)  No certificate may be issued in respect of shares of more than one class.

(5)  If more than one person holds a share, only one certificate may be issued in respect of it.

### 47  Contents and execution of share certificates

(1)  Every certificate must specify—
   (a)  in respect of how many shares, of what class, it is issued;
   (b)  the nominal value of those shares;
   (c)  the amount paid up on them; and
   (d)  any distinguishing numbers assigned to them.

(2)  Certificates must—
   (a)  have affixed to them the company's common seal or an official seal which is a facsimile of the company's common seal with the addition on its face of the word 'Securities' (a 'securities seal'), or
   (b)  be otherwise executed in accordance with the Companies Acts.

### 48  Consolidated share certificates

(1)  When a member's holding of shares of a particular class increases, the company may issue that member with—
   (a)  a single, consolidated certificate in respect of all the shares of a particular class which that member holds, or

(b) a separate certificate in respect of only those shares by which that member's holding has increased.

(2) When a member's holding of shares of a particular class is reduced, the company must ensure that the member is issued with one or more certificates in respect of the number of shares held by the member after that reduction. But the company need not (in the absence of a request from the member) issue any new certificate if—

(a) all the shares which the member no longer holds as a result of the reduction, and

(b) none of the shares which the member retains following the reduction,

were, immediately before the reduction, represented by the same certificate.

(3) A member may request the company, in writing, to replace—

(a) the member's separate certificates with a consolidated certificate, or

(b) the member's consolidated certificate with two or more separate certificates representing such proportion of the shares as the member may specify.

(4) When the company complies with such a request it may charge such reasonable fee as the directors may decide for doing so.

(5) A consolidated certificate must not be issued unless any certificates which it is to replace have first been returned to the company for cancellation.

### 49  Replacement share certificates

(1) If a certificate issued in respect of a member's shares is—

(a) damaged or defaced, or

(b) said to be lost, stolen or destroyed,

that member is entitled to be issued with a replacement certificate in respect of the same shares.

(2) A member exercising the right to be issued with such a replacement certificate—

(a) may at the same time exercise the right to be issued with a single certificate or separate certificates;

(b) must return the certificate which is to be replaced to the company if it is damaged or defaced; and

(c) must comply with such conditions as to evidence, indemnity and the payment of a reasonable fee as the directors decide.

*Shares not held in certificated form*

### 50  Uncertificated shares

(1) In this article, 'the relevant rules' means—

(a) any applicable provision of the Companies Acts about the holding, evidencing of title to, or transfer of shares other than in certificated form, and

(b) any applicable legislation, rules or other arrangements made under or by virtue of such provision.

(2) The provisions of this article have effect subject to the relevant rules.

(3) Any provision of the articles which is inconsistent with the relevant rules must be disregarded, to the extent that it is inconsistent, whenever the relevant rules apply.

(4) Any share or class of shares of the company may be issued or held on such terms, or in such a way, that—

(a) title to it or them is not, or must not be, evidenced by a certificate, or

(b) it or they may or must be transferred wholly or partly without a certificate.

(5) The directors have power to take such steps as they think fit in relation to—

(a) the evidencing of and transfer of title to uncertificated shares (including in connection with the issue of such shares);

(b) any records relating to the holding of uncertificated shares;

(c) the conversion of certificated shares into uncertificated shares; or

(d) the conversion of uncertificated shares into certificated shares.

(6) The company may by notice to the holder of a share require that share—

(a) if it is uncertificated, to be converted into certificated form, and

(b) if it is certificated, to be converted into uncertificated form,

to enable it to be dealt with in accordance with the articles.

(7) If—

(a) the articles give the directors power to take action, or require other persons to take action, in order to sell, transfer or otherwise dispose of shares, and

(b) uncertificated shares are subject to that power, but the power is expressed in terms which assume the use of a certificate or other written instrument,

the directors may take such action as is necessary or expedient to achieve the same results when exercising that power in relation to uncertificated shares.

(8) In particular, the directors may take such action as they consider appropriate to achieve the sale, transfer, disposal, forfeiture, re-allotment or surrender of an uncertificated share or otherwise to enforce a lien in respect of it.

(9) Unless the directors otherwise determine, shares which a member holds in uncertificated form must be treated as separate holdings from any shares which that member holds in certificated form.

(10) A class of shares must not be treated as two classes simply because some shares of that class are held in certificated form and others are held in uncertificated form.

### 51 Share warrants

(1) The directors may issue a share warrant in respect of any fully paid share.

(2) Share warrants must be—

(a) issued in such form, and

(b) executed in such manner,

as the directors decide.

(3) A share represented by a share warrant may be transferred by delivery of the warrant representing it.

(4) The directors may make provision for the payment of dividends in respect of any share represented by a share warrant.

(5) Subject to the articles, the directors may decide the conditions on which any share warrant is issued. In particular, they may—

(a) decide the conditions on which new warrants are to be issued in place of warrants which are damaged or defaced, or said to have been lost, stolen or destroyed;

(b) decide the conditions on which bearers of warrants are entitled to attend and vote at general meetings;

(c) decide the conditions subject to which bearers of warrants may surrender their warrant so as to hold their shares in certificated or uncertificated form instead; and

(d) vary the conditions of issue of any warrant from time to time,

and the bearer of a warrant is subject to the conditions and procedures in force in relation to it, whether or not they were decided or specified before the warrant was issued.

(6) Subject to the conditions on which the warrants are issued from time to time, bearers of share warrants have the same rights and privileges as they would if their names had been included in the register as holders of the shares represented by their warrants.

(7) The company must not in any way be bound by or recognise any interest in a share represented by a share warrant other than the absolute right of the bearer of that warrant to that warrant.

### *Partly paid shares*

### 52 Company's lien over partly paid shares

(1) The company has a lien ( 'the company's lien') over every share which is partly paid for any part of—

(a) that share's nominal value, and

(b) any premium at which it was issued,

which has not been paid to the company, and which is payable immediately or at some time in the future, whether or not a call notice has been sent in respect of it.

(2) The company's lien over a share—

(a) takes priority over any third party's interest in that share, and

(b) extends to any dividend or other money payable by the company in respect of that share and (if the lien is enforced and the share is sold by the company) the proceeds of sale of that share.

(3) The directors may at any time decide that a share which is or would otherwise be subject to the company's lien shall not be subject to it, either wholly or in part.

### 53 Enforcement of the company's lien

(1) Subject to the provisions of this article, if—

(a) a lien enforcement notice has been given in respect of a share, and

(b) the person to whom the notice was given has failed to comply with it,

the company may sell that share in such manner as the directors decide.

(2) A lien enforcement notice—

(a) may only be given in respect of a share which is subject to the company's lien, in respect of which a sum is payable and the due date for payment of that sum has passed;

(b) must specify the share concerned;

(c) must require payment of the sum payable within 14 days of the notice;

(d) must be addressed either to the holder of the share or to a person entitled to it by reason of the holder's death, bankruptcy or otherwise; and

(e) must state the company's intention to sell the share if the notice is not complied with.

(3) Where shares are sold under this article—

(a) the directors may authorise any person to execute an instrument of transfer of the shares to the purchaser or a person nominated by the purchaser, and

(b) the transferee is not bound to see to the application of the consideration, and the transferee's title is not affected by any irregularity in or invalidity of the process leading to the sale.

(4) The net proceeds of any such sale (after payment of the costs of sale and any other costs of enforcing the lien) must be applied—

(a) first, in payment of so much of the sum for which the lien exists as was payable at the date of the lien enforcement notice,

(b) second, to the person entitled to the shares at the date of the sale, but only after the certificate for the shares sold has been surrendered to the company for cancellation or a suitable indemnity has been given for any lost certificates, and subject to a lien equivalent to the company's lien over the shares before the sale for any money payable in respect of the shares after the date of the lien enforcement notice.

(5) A statutory declaration by a director or the company secretary that the declarant is a director or the company secretary and that a share has been sold to satisfy the company's lien on a specified date—

(a) is conclusive evidence of the facts stated in it as against all persons claiming to be entitled to the share, and

(b) subject to compliance with any other formalities of transfer required by the articles or by law, constitutes a good title to the share.

## 54   Call notices

(1) Subject to the articles and the terms on which shares are allotted, the directors may send a notice (a 'call notice') to a member requiring the member to pay the company a specified sum of money (a 'call') which is payable in respect of shares which that member holds at the date when the directors decide to send the call notice.

(2) A call notice—

(a) may not require a member to pay a call which exceeds the total sum unpaid on that member's shares (whether as to the share's nominal value or any amount payable to the company by way of premium);

(b) must state when and how any call to which it relates it is to be paid; and

(c) may permit or require the call to be paid by instalments.

(3) A member must comply with the requirements of a call notice, but no member is obliged to pay any call before 14 days have passed since the notice was sent.

(4) Before the company has received any call due under a call notice the directors may—

(a) revoke it wholly or in part, or

(b) specify a later time for payment than is specified in the notice,

by a further notice in writing to the member in respect of whose shares the call is made.

## 55   Liability to pay calls

(1) Liability to pay a call is not extinguished or transferred by transferring the shares in respect of which it is required to be paid.

(2) Joint holders of a share are jointly and severally liable to pay all calls in respect of that share.

(3) Subject to the terms on which shares are allotted, the directors may, when issuing shares, provide that call notices sent to the holders of those shares may require them—

(a) to pay calls which are not the same, or

(b) to pay calls at different times.

## 56   When call notice need not be issued

(1) A call notice need not be issued in respect of sums which are specified, in the terms on which a share is issued, as being payable to the company in respect of that share (whether in respect of nominal value or premium)—

(a) on allotment;

(b) on the occurrence of a particular event; or

(c) on a date fixed by or in accordance with the terms of issue.

(2) But if the due date for payment of such a sum has passed and it has not been paid, the holder of the share concerned is treated in all respects as having failed to comply with a call notice in respect of that sum, and is liable to the same consequences as regards the payment of interest and forfeiture.

## 57   Failure to comply with call notice: automatic consequences

(1) If a person is liable to pay a call and fails to do so by the call payment date—

(a) the directors may issue a notice of intended forfeiture to that person, and

(b) until the call is paid, that person must pay the company interest on the call from the call payment date at the relevant rate.

(2) For the purposes of this article—

(a) the 'call payment date' is the time when the call notice states that a call is payable, unless the directors give a notice specifying a later date, in which case the 'call payment date' is that later date;

     (b) the 'relevant rate' is—

         (i)   the rate fixed by the terms on which the share in respect of which the call is due was allotted;

        (ii)  such other rate as was fixed in the call notice which required payment of the call, or has otherwise been determined by the directors; or

      (iii)  if no rate is fixed in either of these ways, 5 per cent per annum.

(3) The relevant rate must not exceed by more than 5 percentage points the base lending rate most recently set by the Monetary Policy Committee of the Bank of England in connection with its responsibilities under Part 2 of the Bank of England Act 1998.

(4) The directors may waive any obligation to pay interest on a call wholly or in part.

### 58   Notice of intended forfeiture

A notice of intended forfeiture—

    (a) may be sent in respect of any share in respect of which a call has not been paid as required by a call notice;

    (b) must be sent to the holder of that share or to a person entitled to it by reason of the holder's death, bankruptcy or otherwise;

    (c) must require payment of the call and any accrued interest by a date which is not less than 14 days after the date of the notice;

    (d) must state how the payment is to be made; and

    (e) must state that if the notice is not complied with, the shares in respect of which the call is payable will be liable to be forfeited.

### 59   Directors' power to forfeit shares

If a notice of intended forfeiture is not complied with before the date by which payment of the call is required in the notice of intended forfeiture, the directors may decide that any share in respect of which it was given is forfeited, and the forfeiture is to include all dividends or other moneys payable in respect of the forfeited shares and not paid before the forfeiture.

### 60   Effect of forfeiture

(1) Subject to the articles, the forfeiture of a share extinguishes—

    (a) all interests in that share, and all claims and demands against the company in respect of it, and

    (b) all other rights and liabilities incidental to the share as between the person whose share it was prior to the forfeiture and the company.

(2) Any share which is forfeited in accordance with the articles—

    (a) is deemed to have been forfeited when the directors decide that it is forfeited;

    (b) is deemed to be the property of the company; and

    (c) may be sold, re-allotted or otherwise disposed of as the directors think fit.

(3) If a person's shares have been forfeited—

    (a) the company must send that person notice that forfeiture has occurred and record it in the register of members;

    (b) that person ceases to be a member in respect of those shares;

    (c) that person must surrender the certificate for the shares forfeited to the company for cancellation;

    (d) that person remains liable to the company for all sums payable by that person under the articles at the date of forfeiture in respect of those shares, including any interest (whether accrued before or after the date of forfeiture); and

    (e) the directors may waive payment of such sums wholly or in part or enforce payment without any allowance for the value of the shares at the time of forfeiture or for any consideration received on their disposal.

(4) At any time before the company disposes of a forfeited share, the directors may decide to cancel the forfeiture on payment of all calls and interest due in respect of it and on such other terms as they think fit.

### 61   Procedure following forfeiture

(1) If a forfeited share is to be disposed of by being transferred, the company may receive the consideration for the transfer and the directors may authorise any person to execute the instrument of transfer.

(2) A statutory declaration by a director or the company secretary that the declarant is a director or the company secretary and that a share has been forfeited on a specified date—

    (a) is conclusive evidence of the facts stated in it as against all persons claiming to be entitled to the share, and

    (b) subject to compliance with any other formalities of transfer required by the articles or by law, constitutes a good title to the share.

(3) A person to whom a forfeited share is transferred is not bound to see to the application of the consideration (if any) nor is that person's title to the share affected by any irregularity in or invalidity of the process leading to the forfeiture or transfer of the share.

(4) If the company sells a forfeited share, the person who held it prior to its forfeiture is entitled to receive from the company the proceeds of such sale, net of any commission, and excluding any amount which—

      (a) was, or would have become, payable, and

      (b) had not, when that share was forfeited, been paid by that person in respect of that share,

but no interest is payable to such a person in respect of such proceeds and the company is not required to account for any money earned on them.

## 62  Surrender of shares

(1) A member may surrender any share—

      (a) in respect of which the directors may issue a notice of intended forfeiture;

      (b) which the directors may forfeit; or

      (c) which has been forfeited.

(2) The directors may accept the surrender of any such share.

(3) The effect of surrender on a share is the same as the effect of forfeiture on that share.

(4) A share which has been surrendered may be dealt with in the same way as a share which has been forfeited.

### *Transfer and transmission of shares*

## 63  Transfers of certificated shares

(1) Certificated shares may be transferred by means of an instrument of transfer in any usual form or any other form approved by the directors, which is executed by or on behalf of—

      (a) the transferor, and

      (b) (if any of the shares is partly paid) the transferee.

(2) No fee may be charged for registering any instrument of transfer or other document relating to or affecting the title to any share.

(3) The company may retain any instrument of transfer which is registered.

(4) The transferor remains the holder of a certificated share until the transferee's name is entered in the register of members as holder of it.

(5) The directors may refuse to register the transfer of a certificated share if—

      (a) the share is not fully paid;

      (b) the transfer is not lodged at the company's registered office or such other place as the directors have appointed;

      (c) the transfer is not accompanied by the certificate for the shares to which it relates, or such other evidence as the directors may reasonably require to show the transferor's right to make the transfer, or evidence of the right of someone other than the transferor to make the transfer on the transferor's behalf;

      (d) the transfer is in respect of more than one class of share; or

      (e) the transfer is in favour of more than four transferees.

(6) If the directors refuse to register the transfer of a share, the instrument of transfer must be returned to the transferee with the notice of refusal unless they suspect that the proposed transfer may be fraudulent.

## 64  Transfer of uncertificated shares

A transfer of an uncertificated share must not be registered if it is in favour of more than four transferees.

## 65  Transmission of shares

(1) If title to a share passes to a transmittee, the company may only recognise the transmittee as having any title to that share.

(2) Nothing in these articles releases the estate of a deceased member from any liability in respect of a share solely or jointly held by that member.

## 66  Transmittees' rights

(1) A transmittee who produces such evidence of entitlement to shares as the directors may properly require—

      (a) may, subject to the articles, choose either to become the holder of those shares or to have them transferred to another person, and

      (b) subject to the articles, and pending any transfer of the shares to another person, has the same rights as the holder had.

(2) But transmittees do not have the right to attend or vote at a general meeting in respect of shares to which they are entitled, by reason of the holder's death or bankruptcy or otherwise, unless they become the holders of those shares

## 67  Exercise of transmittees' rights

(1) Transmittees who wish to become the holders of shares to which they have become entitled must notify the company in writing of that wish.

(2)  If the share is a certificated share and a transmittee wishes to have it transferred to another person, the transmittee must execute an instrument of transfer in respect of it.

(3)  If the share is an uncertificated share and the transmittee wishes to have it transferred to another person, the transmittee must—

(a)  procure that all appropriate instructions are given to effect the transfer, or

(b)  procure that the uncertificated share is changed into certificated form and then execute an instrument of transfer in respect of it.

(4)  Any transfer made or executed under this article is to be treated as if it were made or executed by the person from whom the transmittee has derived rights in respect of the share, and as if the event which gave rise to the transmission had not occurred.

### 68   Transmittees bound by prior notices

If a notice is given to a member in respect of shares and a transmittee is entitled to those shares, the transmittee is bound by the notice if it was given to the member before the transmittee's name has been entered in the register of members.

*Consolidation of shares*

### 69   Procedure for disposing of fractions of shares

(1)  This article applies where—

(a)  there has been a consolidation or division of shares, and

(b)  as a result, members are entitled to fractions of shares.

(2)  The directors may—

(a)  sell the shares representing the fractions to any person including the company for the best price reasonably obtainable;

(b)  in the case of a certificated share, authorise any person to execute an instrument of transfer of the shares to the purchaser or a person nominated by the purchaser; and

(c)  distribute the net proceeds of sale in due proportion among the holders of the shares.

(3)  Where any holder's entitlement to a portion of the proceeds of sale amounts to less than a minimum figure determined by the directors, that member's portion may be distributed to an organisation which is a charity for the purposes of the law of England and Wales, Scotland or Northern Ireland.

(4)  The person to whom the shares are transferred is not obliged to ensure that any purchase money is received by the person entitled to the relevant fractions.

(5)  The transferee's title to the shares is not affected by any irregularity in or invalidity of the process leading to their sale.

*Distributions*

### 70   Procedure for declaring dividends

(1)  The company may by ordinary resolution declare dividends, and the directors may decide to pay interim dividends.

(2)  A dividend must not be declared unless the directors have made a recommendation as to its amount. Such a dividend must not exceed the amount recommended by the directors.

(3)  No dividend may be declared or paid unless it is in accordance with members' respective rights.

(4)  Unless the members' resolution to declare or directors' decision to pay a dividend, or the terms on which shares are issued, specify otherwise, it must be paid by reference to each member's holding of shares on the date of the resolution or decision to declare or pay it.

(5)  If the company's share capital is divided into different classes, no interim dividend may be paid on shares carrying deferred or non-preferred rights if, at the time of payment, any preferential dividend is in arrear.

(6)  The directors may pay at intervals any dividend payable at a fixed rate if it appears to them that the profits available for distribution justify the payment.

(7)  If the directors act in good faith, they do not incur any liability to the holders of shares conferring preferred rights for any loss they may suffer by the lawful payment of an interim dividend on shares with deferred or non-preferred rights.

### 71   Calculation of dividends

(1)  Except as otherwise provided by the articles or the rights attached to shares, all dividends must be—

(a)  declared and paid according to the amounts paid up on the shares on which the dividend is paid, and

(b)  apportioned and paid proportionately to the amounts paid up on the shares during any portion or portions of the period in respect of which the dividend is paid.

(2)  If any share is issued on terms providing that it ranks for dividend as from a particular date, that share ranks for dividend accordingly.

(3)  For the purposes of calculating dividends, no account is to be taken of any amount which has been paid up on a share in advance of the due date for payment of that amount.

## 72   Payment of dividends and other distributions

(1)  Where a dividend or other sum which is a distribution is payable in respect of a share, it must be paid by one or more of the following means—

    (a)  transfer to a bank or building society account specified by the distribution recipient either in writing or as the directors may otherwise decide;

    (b)  sending a cheque made payable to the distribution recipient by post to the distribution recipient at the distribution recipient's registered address (if the distribution recipient is a holder of the share), or (in any other case) to an address specified by the distribution recipient either in writing or as the directors may otherwise decide;

    (c)  sending a cheque made payable to such person by post to such person at such address as the distribution recipient has specified either in writing or as the directors may otherwise decide; or

    (d)  any other means of payment as the directors agree with the distribution recipient either in writing or by such other means as the directors decide.

(2)  In the articles, 'the distribution recipient' means, in respect of a share in respect of which a dividend or other sum is payable—

    (a)  the holder of the share; or

    (b)  if the share has two or more joint holders, whichever of them is named first in the register of members; or

    (c)  if the holder is no longer entitled to the share by reason of death or bankruptcy, or otherwise by operation of law, the transmittee.

## 73   Deductions from distributions in respect of sums owed to the company

(1)  If—

    (a)  a share is subject to the company's lien, and

    (b)  the directors are entitled to issue a lien enforcement notice in respect of it,

they may, instead of issuing a lien enforcement notice, deduct from any dividend or other sum payable in respect of the share any sum of money which is payable to the company in respect of that share to the extent that they are entitled to require payment under a lien enforcement notice.

(2)  Money so deducted must be used to pay any of the sums payable in respect of that share.

(3)  The company must notify the distribution recipient in writing of—

    (a)  the fact and amount of any such deduction;

    (b)  any non-payment of a dividend or other sum payable in respect of a share resulting from any such deduction; and

    (c)  how the money deducted has been applied.

## 74   No interest on distributions

The company may not pay interest on any dividend or other sum payable in respect of a share unless otherwise provided by—

    (a)  the terms on which the share was issued, or

    (b)  the provisions of another agreement between the holder of that share and the company.

## 75   Unclaimed distributions

(1)  All dividends or other sums which are—

    (a)  payable in respect of shares, and

    (b)  unclaimed after having been declared or become payable,

may be invested or otherwise made use of by the directors for the benefit of the company until claimed.

(2)  The payment of any such dividend or other sum into a separate account does not make the company a trustee in respect of it.

(3)  If—

    (a)  twelve years have passed from the date on which a dividend or other sum became due for payment, and

    (b)  the distribution recipient has not claimed it,

the distribution recipient is no longer entitled to that dividend or other sum and it ceases to remain owing by the company.

## 76   Non-cash distributions

(1)  Subject to the terms of issue of the share in question, the company may, by ordinary resolution on the recommendation of the directors, decide to pay all or part of a dividend or other distribution payable in respect of a share by transferring non-cash assets of equivalent value (including, without limitation, shares or other securities in any company).

(2)  If the shares in respect of which such a non-cash distribution is paid are uncertificated, any shares in the company which are issued as a non-cash distribution in respect of them must be uncertificated.

(3)  For the purposes of paying a non-cash distribution, the directors may make whatever arrangements they think fit, including, where any difficulty arises regarding the distribution—

    (a)  fixing the value of any assets;

     (b) paying cash to any distribution recipient on the basis of that value in order to adjust the rights of recipients; and

     (c) vesting any assets in trustees.

## 77   Waiver of distributions

Distribution recipients may waive their entitlement to a dividend or other distribution payable in respect of a share by giving the company notice in writing to that effect, but if—

     (a) the share has more than one holder, or

     (b) more than one person is entitled to the share, whether by reason of the death or bankruptcy of one or more joint holders, or otherwise,

the notice is not effective unless it is expressed to be given, and signed, by all the holders or persons otherwise entitled to the share.

### *Capitalisation of profits*

## 78   Authority to capitalise and appropriation of capitalised sums

(1)  Subject to the articles, the directors may, if they are so authorised by an ordinary resolution—

     (a) decide to capitalise any profits of the company (whether or not they are available for distribution) which are not required for paying a preferential dividend, or any sum standing to the credit of the company's share premium account or capital redemption reserve; and

     (b) appropriate any sum which they so decide to capitalise (a 'capitalised sum') to the persons who would have been entitled to it if it were distributed by way of dividend (the 'persons entitled') and in the same proportions.

(2)  Capitalised sums must be applied—

     (a) on behalf of the persons entitled, and

     (b) in the same proportions as a dividend would have been distributed to them.

(3)  Any capitalised sum may be applied in paying up new shares of a nominal amount equal to the capitalised sum which are then allotted credited as fully paid to the persons entitled or as they may direct.

(4)  A capitalised sum which was appropriated from profits available for distribution may be applied—

     (a) in or towards paying up any amounts unpaid on existing shares held by the persons entitled, or

     (b) in paying up new debentures of the company which are then allotted credited as fully paid to the persons entitled or as they may direct.

(5)  Subject to the articles the directors may—

     (a) apply capitalised sums in accordance with paragraphs (3) and (4) partly in one way and partly in another;

     (b) make such arrangements as they think fit to deal with shares or debentures becoming distributable in fractions under this article (including the issuing of fractional certificates or the making of cash payments); and

     (c) authorise any person to enter into an agreement with the company on behalf of all the persons entitled which is binding on them in respect of the allotment of shares and debentures to them under this article.

# PART 5   MISCELLANEOUS PROVISIONS

### *Communications*

## 79   Means of communication to be used

(1)  Subject to the articles, anything sent or supplied by or to the company under the articles may be sent or supplied in any way in which the Companies Act 2006 provides for documents or information which are authorised or required by any provision of that Act to be sent or supplied by or to the company.

(2)  Subject to the articles, any notice or document to be sent or supplied to a director in connection with the taking of decisions by directors may also be sent or supplied by the means by which that director has asked to be sent or supplied with such notices or documents for the time being.

(3)  A director may agree with the company that notices or documents sent to that director in a particular way are to be deemed to have been received within a specified time of their being sent, and for the specified time to be less than 48 hours.

## 80   Failure to notify contact details

(1)  If—

     (a) the company sends two consecutive documents to a member over a period of at least 12 months, and

     (b) each of those documents is returned undelivered, or the company receives notification that it has not been delivered,

that member ceases to be entitled to receive notices from the company.

(2) A member who has ceased to be entitled to receive notices from the company becomes entitled to receive such notices again by sending the company—

    (a) a new address to be recorded in the register of members, or

    (b) if the member has agreed that the company should use a means of communication other than sending things to such an address, the information that the company needs to use that means of communication effectively.

*Administrative arrangements*

### 81   Company seals

(1) Any common seal may only be used by the authority of the directors.

(2) The directors may decide by what means and in what form any common seal or securities seal is to be used.

(3) Unless otherwise decided by the directors, if the company has a common seal and it is affixed to a document, the document must also be signed by at least one authorised person in the presence of a witness who attests the signature.

(4) For the purposes of this article, an authorised person is—

    (a) any director of the company;

    (b) the company secretary; or

    (c) any person authorised by the directors for the purpose of signing documents to which the common seal is applied.

(5) If the company has an official seal for use abroad, it may only be affixed to a document if its use on that document, or documents of a class to which it belongs, has been authorised by a decision of the directors.

(6) If the company has a securities seal, it may only be affixed to securities by the company secretary or a person authorised to apply it to securities by the company secretary.

(7) For the purposes of the articles, references to the securities seal being affixed to any document include the reproduction of the image of that seal on or in a document by any mechanical or electronic means which has been approved by the directors in relation to that document or documents of a class to which it belongs.

### 82   Destruction of documents

(1) The company is entitled to destroy—

    (a) all instruments of transfer of shares which have been registered, and all other documents on the basis of which any entries are made in the register of members, from six years after the date of registration;

    (b) all dividend mandates, variations or cancellations of dividend mandates, and notifications of change of address, from two years after they have been recorded;

    (c) all share certificates which have been cancelled from one year after the date of the cancellation;

    (d) all paid dividend warrants and cheques from one year after the date of actual payment; and

    (e) all proxy notices from one year after the end of the meeting to which the proxy notice relates.

(2) If the company destroys a document in good faith, in accordance with the articles, and without notice of any claim to which that document may be relevant, it is conclusively presumed in favour of the company that—

    (a) entries in the register purporting to have been made on the basis of an instrument of transfer or other document so destroyed were duly and properly made;

    (b) any instrument of transfer so destroyed was a valid and effective instrument duly and properly registered;

    (c) any share certificate so destroyed was a valid and effective certificate duly and properly cancelled; and

    (d) any other document so destroyed was a valid and effective document in accordance with its recorded particulars in the books or records of the company.

(3) This article does not impose on the company any liability which it would not otherwise have if it destroys any document before the time at which this article permits it to do so.

(4) In this article, references to the destruction of any document include a reference to its being disposed of in any manner.

### 83   No right to inspect accounts and other records

Except as provided by law or authorised by the directors or an ordinary resolution of the company, no person is entitled to inspect any of the company's accounting or other records or documents merely by virtue of being a member.

### 84   Provision for employees on cessation of business

The directors may decide to make provision for the benefit of persons employed or formerly employed by the company or any of its subsidiaries (other than a director or former director or shadow director) in connection with the cessation or transfer to any person of the whole or part of the undertaking of the company or that subsidiary.

*Directors' indemnity and insurance*

## 85 Indemnity

(1) Subject to paragraph (2), a relevant director of the company or an associated company may be indemnified out of the company's assets against—

    (a) any liability incurred by that director in connection with any negligence, default, breach of duty or breach of trust in relation to the company or an associated company,

    (b) any liability incurred by that director in connection with the activities of the company or an associated company in its capacity as a trustee of an occupational pension scheme (as defined in section 235(6) of the Companies Act 2006),

    (c) any other liability incurred by that director as an officer of the company or an associated company.

(2) This article does not authorise any indemnity which would be prohibited or rendered void by any provision of the Companies Acts or by any other provision of law.

(3) In this article—

    (a) companies are associated if one is a subsidiary of the other or both are subsidiaries of the same body corporate, and

    (b) a 'relevant director' means any director or former director of the company or an associated company.

## 86 Insurance

(1) The directors may decide to purchase and maintain insurance, at the expense of the company, for the benefit of any relevant director in respect of any relevant loss.

(2) In this article—

    (a) a 'relevant director' means any director or former director of the company or an associated company,

    (b) a 'relevant loss' means any loss or liability which has been or may be incurred by a relevant director in connection with that director's duties or powers in relation to the company, any associated company or any pension fund or employees' share scheme of the company or associated company, and

    (c) companies are associated if one is a subsidiary of the other or both are subsidiaries of the same body corporate.

# Company and Business Names

## Company and Business Names Regulations 1981

(1981 No. 1685)

*The Secretary of State, in exercise of his powers under sections 31 and 32 of the Companies Act 1981 hereby makes the following Regulations:—*

1. These Regulations may be cited as the Company and Business Names Regulations 1981 and shall come into operation on 26th February 1982.

2. In these Regulations unless the context otherwise requires, 'the Act' means the Companies Act 1981.

3. The words and expressions state in column (1) of the Schedule hereto (together with the plural and the possessive forms of those words and expressions are hereby specified as words and expressions for the registration of which as or as part of a company's corporate name the approval of the Secretary of State is required by section 22(2)(b) of the Act or for the use of which as or as part of a business name his approval is required by section 28(2)(b) of the Act.

4. Subject to Regulation 5 each Government department or other body stated in column (2) of the Schedule hereto is hereby specified as the relevant body for the purposes of section 31(2) and (3) of the Act in relation to the word or expression (and the plural and the possessive forms of that word or expression) opposite to it in column (1).

5. Where two Government departments or other bodies are specified in the alternative in Column (2) of the Schedule hereto the second alternative is to be treated as specified,

    (a) in the case of the corporate name of a company,

        (i) if the company has not yet been registered and its principal or only place of business in Great Britain is to be in Scotland or, if it will have no place of business in Great Britain, its proposed registered office is in Scotland, and

        (ii) if the company is already registered and its principal or only place of business in Great Britain is in Scotland or, if it has no place of business in Great Britain, its registered office is in Scotland, and

    (b) in the case of a business name, if the principal or only place of the business carried on or to be carried on in Great Britain is or is to be in Scotland,

and the first alternative is to be treated as specified in any other case.

### SCHEDULE

### SPECIFICATION OF WORDS, EXPRESSIONS AND RELEVANT BODIES

| Column (1) | Column (2) |
| --- | --- |
| Word or expression | Relevant body |
| Abortion | Department of Health and Social Security |
| Apothecary | Worshipful Society of Apothecaries of London or Pharmaceutical Society of Great Britain |
| Association | |
| Assurance | |
| Assurer | |
| Authority | |
| Benevolent | |
| Board | |
| [...] | |

| Column (1) | Column (2) |
|---|---|
| British | |
| [...] | |
| Chamber (or Chambers) of Business (or their Welsh equivalents, Siambr Fusnes; Siambrau Busnes) | |
| Chamber (or Chambers) of Commerce (or their Welsh equivalents, Siambr Fasnach; Siambrau Masnach) | |
| Chamber (or Chambers) of Commerce and Industry (or their Welsh equivalents, Siambr Masnach a Diwydiant; Siambrau Masnach a Diwydiant) | |
| Chamber (or Chambers) of Commerce, Training and Enterprise (or their Welsh equivalents, Siambr Masnach, Hyfforddiant a Menter; Siambrau Masnach, Hyfforddiant a Menter) | |
| Chamber (or Chambers) of Enterprise (or their Welsh equivalents, Siambr Fenter; siambrau Menter) | |
| Chamber (or Chambers) of Industry (or their Welsh equivalents, Siambr Ddiwydiant;Siambrau Diwydiant) | |
| Chamber (or Chambers) of Trade (or their Welsh equivalents, Siambr Fasnach; Siambrau Masnach) | |
| Chamber (or Chambers) of Trade and Industry (or their Welsh equivalents, Siambr Masnach a Diwydiant; Siambrau Masnach a Diwydiant) | |
| Chamber (or Chambers) of Training (or their Welsh equivalents, Siambr Hyfforddiant; Siambrau Hyfforddiant) | |
| Chamber (or Chambers) of Training and Enterprise (or their Welsh equivalents, Siambr Hyfforddiant a Menter; Siambrau Hyfforddiant a Menter) | |
| Charitable | Charity Commission or the Scottish Ministers |
| Charity | Charity Commission or the Scottish Ministers |
| Charter | |
| Chemist | |
| Chemistry | |
| Contact Lens | General Optical Council |
| Co-operative | |
| Council | |
| Dental | General Dental Council |
| Dentistry | General Dental Council |
| District Nurse | Nursing and Midwifery Council |
| Duke | Home Office or the Scottish Ministers |
| England | |
| English | |
| European | |
| Federation | |
| Friendly Society | |
| Foundation | |
| Fund | |
| Giro | |
| Government | |
| Great Britain | |
| Group | |
| Health Centre | Department of Health and Social Security |
| Health Service | Department of Health and Social Security |
| Health Visitor | Nursing and Midwifery Council |
| Her Majesty | Home Office or the Scottish Ministers |
| His Majesty | Home Office or the Scottish Ministers |
| Holding | |
| HPSS | |

| Column (1) | Column (2) |
| --- | --- |
| HSC | |
| Industrial and Provident Society | |
| Institute | |
| Institution | |
| Insurance | |
| Insurer | |
| International | |
| Ireland | |
| Irish | |
| King | Home Office or the Scottish Home and Health Department |
| Midwife | Nursing and Midwifery Council |
| Midwifery | Nursing and Midwifery Council |
| National | |
| NHS | Department of Health |
| Nurse | Nursing and Midwifery Council |
| Nursing | Nursing and Midwifery Council |
| [...] | |
| Patent | |
| Patentee | |
| Police | Home Office or the Scottish Ministers |
| Polytechnic | Department for Innovation, Universities and Skills |
| Post Office | |
| Pregnancy Termination | Department of Health and Social Security |
| Prince | Home Office or the Scottish Ministers |
| Princess | Home Office or the Scottish Ministers |
| Queen | Home Office or the Scottish Ministers |
| Reassurance | |
| Reassurer | |
| Register | |
| Registered | |
| Reinsurance | |
| Reinsurer | |
| Royal | Home Office or Scottish Ministers |
| Royale | Home Office or the Scottish Ministers |
| Royalty | Home Office or the Scottish Ministers |
| Scotland | |
| Scottish | |
| Sheffield | |
| Society | |
| Special School | Department for Children, Schools and Families |
| Stock Exchange | |
| Trade Union | |
| Trust | |
| United Kingdom | |
| University | The Privy Council |
| Wales | |
| Welsh | |
| Windsor | Home Office of the Scottish Ministers |

**Note:** The reference in Column (2) to the Home Office shall be treated as a reference to the Lord Chancellor's Department in relation to the following entries in Column (1)—

    (a)  Duke,

    (b)  Her Majesty,

    (c)  His Majesty,

(d) King,

(e) Prince,

(f) Princess,

(g) Queen,

(h) Royal,

(i) Royale,

(j) Royalty, and

(k) Windsor.

# The Companies (Trading Disclosures) Regulations 2008

**(2008 No. 495)**

*The Secretary of State makes the following Regulations in exercise of the powers conferred by sections 82, 84, 1292(1)(a) and 1294 of the Companies Act 2006.*

*In accordance with sections 82(5), 1290 and 1294(6) of the Companies Act 2006, a draft of this instrument was laid before Parliament and approved by a resolution of each House of Parliament.*

## 1 Citation, commencement and interpretation

(1) These Regulations may be cited as the Companies (Trading Disclosures) Regulations 2008 and come into force on 1st October 2008.

(2) In these Regulations—

(a) 'the Act' means the Companies Act 2006;

(b) 'company record' means—

(i) any register, index, accounting records, agreement, memorandum, minutes or other document required by the Companies Acts to be kept by a company; and

(ii) any register kept by a company of its debenture holders;

(c) 'inspection place' means any location, other than a company's registered office, at which a company keeps available for inspection any company record which it is required under the Companies Acts to keep available for inspection;

(d) a reference to any type of document is a reference to a document of that type in hard copy, electronic or any other form; and

(e) in relation to a company, a reference to 'its websites' includes a reference to any part of a website relating to that company which that company has caused or authorised to appear.

## 2 Legibility of displays and disclosures

Any display or disclosure of information required by these Regulations must be in characters that can be read with the naked eye.

## 3 Requirement to display registered name at registered office and inspection place

(1) A company shall display its registered name at—

(a) its registered office; and

(b) any inspection place.

(2) But paragraph (1) does not apply to any company which has at all times since its incorporation been dormant.

(3) Paragraph (1) shall also not apply to the registered office or an inspection place of a company where—

(a) in respect of that company, a liquidator, administrator or administrative receiver has been appointed; and

(b) the registered office or inspection place is also a place of business of that liquidator, administrator or administrative receiver.

## 4 Requirement to display registered name at other business locations

(1) This regulation applies to a location other than a company's registered office or any inspection place.

(2) A company shall display its registered name at any such location at which it carries on business.

(3) But paragraph (2) shall not apply to a location which is primarily used for living accommodation.

(4) Paragraph (2) shall also not apply to any location at which business is carried on by a company where—

(a) in respect of that company, a liquidator, administrator or administrative receiver has been appointed; and

(b) the location is also a place of business of that liquidator, administrator or administrative receiver.

(5) Paragraph (2) shall also not apply to any location at which business is carried on by a company of which every director who is an individual is a relevant director.

(6)  In this regulation—
    (a)  'administrative receiver' has the meaning given—
        (i)   in England and Wales or Scotland, by section 251 of the Insolvency Act 1986, and
        (ii)  in Northern Ireland, by Article 5 of the Insolvency (Northern Ireland) Order 1989;
    (b)  'credit reference agency' has the meaning given in section 243(7) of the Act;
    (c)  'protected information' has the meaning given in section 240 of the Act; and
    (d)  'relevant director' means an individual in respect of whom the registrar is required by regulations made pursuant to section 243(4) of the Act to refrain from disclosing protected information to a credit reference agency.

## 5   Manner of display of registered name

(1)  This regulation applies where a company is required to display its registered name at any office, place or location.

(2)  The registered name shall be so positioned that it may be easily seen by any visitor to that office, place or location.

(3)  The registered name shall be displayed continuously but where any such office, place or location is shared by six or more companies, each such company is only required to display its registered name for at least fifteen continuous seconds at least once in every three minutes.

## 6   Registered name to appear in communications

(1)  Every company shall disclose its registered name on—
    (a)  its business letters, notices and other official publications;
    (b)  its bills of exchange, promissory notes, endorsements and order forms;
    (c)  cheques purporting to be signed by or on behalf of the company;
    (d)  orders for money, goods or services purporting to be signed by or on behalf of the company;
    (e)  its bills of parcels, invoices and other demands for payment, receipts and letters of credit;
    (f)  its applications for licences to carry on a trade or activity; and
    (g)  all other forms of its business correspondence and documentation.

(2)  Every company shall disclose its registered name on its websites.

## 7   Further particulars to appear in business letters, order forms and websites

(1)  Every company shall disclose the particulars set out in paragraph (2) on—
    (a)  its business letters;
    (b)  its order forms; and
    (c)  its websites.

(2)  The particulars are—
    (a)  the part of the United Kingdom in which the company is registered;
    (b)  the company's registered number;
    (c)  the address of the company's registered office;
    (d)  in the case of a limited company exempt from the obligation to use the word 'limited' as part of its registered name under section 60 of the Act , the fact that it is a limited company;
    (e)  in the case of a community interest company which is not a public company, the fact that it is a limited company; and
    (f)  in the case of an investment company within the meaning of section 833 of the Act, the fact that it is such a company.

(3)  If, in the case of a company having a share capital, there is a disclosure as to the amount of share capital on—
    (a)  its business letters;
    (b)  its order forms; or
    (c)  its websites,
that disclosure must be to paid up share capital.

## 8   Disclosure of names of directors

(1)  Where a company's business letter includes the name of any director of that company, other than in the text or as a signatory, the letter must disclose the name of every director of that company.

(2)  In paragraph (1), 'name' has the following meanings—
    (a)  in the case of a director who is an individual, 'name' has the meaning given in section 163(2) of the Act; and
    (b)  in the case of a director who is a body corporate or a firm that is a legal person under the law by which it is governed, 'name' means corporate name or firm name.

## 9   Disclosures relating to registered office and inspection place

(1)  A company shall disclose—
    (a)  the address of its registered office;
    (b)  any inspection place; and
    (c)  the type of company records which are kept at that office or place,

to any person it deals with in the course of business who makes a written request to the company for that information.

(2) The company shall send a written response to that person within five working days of the receipt of that request.

### 10   Offence

(1) Where a company fails, without reasonable excuse, to comply with any requirement in regulations 2 to 9, an offence is committed by—

    (a) the company; and

    (b) every officer of the company who is in default.

(2) A person guilty of an offence under paragraph (1) is liable on summary conviction to—

    (a) a fine not exceeding level 3 on the standard scale; and

    (b) for continued contravention, a daily default fine not exceeding one-tenth of level 3 on the standard scale.

(3) For the purposes of this regulation a shadow director is to be treated as an officer of the company.

### 11   Revocation

(1) The Companies (Registrar, Languages and Trading Disclosures) Regulations 2006 are amended as follows.

(2) Revoke regulation 6 and Schedules 1 and 2.

# Partnership Law

## Partnership Act 1890

**(1890 c.39 53 and 54 Vict)**

*An Act to declare and amend the Law of Partnership.*                    [14th August 1890]

*Nature of Partnership*

**1   Definition of partnership.**

   (1)   Partnership is the relation which subsists between persons carrying on a business in common with a view of profit.

   (2)   But the relation between members of any company or association which is—

     (a)   Registered as a company under the Companies Act 1862, or any other Act of Parliament for the time being in force and relating to the registration of joint stock companies; or

     (b)   Formed or incorporated by or in pursuance of any other Act of Parliament or letters patent, or Royal Charter [...];

is not a partnership within the meaning of this Act.

**2   Rules for determining existence of partnership.**

In determining whether a partnership does or does not exist, regard shall be had to the following rules:

   (1)   Joint tenancy, tenancy in common, joint property, common property, or part ownership does not of itself create a partnership as to anything so held or owned, whether the tenants or owners do or do not share any profits made by the use thereof.

   (2)   The sharing of gross returns does not of itself create a partnership, whether the persons sharing such returns have or have not a joint or common right or interest in any property from which or from the use of which the returns are derived.

   (3)   The receipt by a person of a share of the profits of a business is *primâ facie* evidence that he is a partner in the business, but the receipt of such a share, or of a payment contingent on or varying with the profits of a business, does not of itself make him a partner in the business; and in particular—

     (a)   The receipt by a person of a debt or other liquidated amount by instalments or otherwise out of the accruing profits of a business does not of itself make him a partner in the business or liable as such:

     (b)   A contract for the remuneration of a servant or agent of a person engaged in a business by a share of the profits of the business does not of itself make the servant or agent a partner in the business or liable as such:

     (c)   A person being the widow, widower, surviving civil partner or child of a deceased partner, and receiving by way of annuity a portion of the profits made in the business in which the deceased person was a partner, is not by reason only of such receipt a partner in the business or liable as such:

     (d)   The advance of money by way of loan to a person engaged or about to engage in any business on a contract with that person that the lender shall receive a rate of interest varying with the profits, or shall receive a share of the profits arising from carrying on the business, does not of itself make the lender a partner with the person or persons carrying on the business or liable as such. Provided that the contract is in writing, and signed by or on behalf of all the parties thereto:

     (e)   A person receiving by way of annuity or otherwise a portion of the profits of a business in consideration of the sale by him of the goodwill of the business is not by reason only of such receipt a partner in the business or liable as such.

**3   Postponement of rights of person lending or selling in consideration of share of profits in case of insolvency.**

In the event of any person to whom money has been advanced by way of loan upon such a contract as is mentioned in the last foregoing section, or of any buyer of a goodwill in consideration of a share of the profits of the business, being adjudged a bankrupt, entering into an arrangement to pay his creditors less than 100p in the pound, or dying in insolvent circumstances, the lender of the loan shall not be entitled to recover anything in respect of his loan, and the seller of the goodwill shall not be entitled to recover anything in respect of the share of profits contracted for, until the claims of the other creditors of the borrower or buyer for valuable consideration in money or money's worth have been satisfied.

### 4   Meaning of firm.

(1) Persons who have entered into partnership with one another are for the purposes of this Act called collectively a firm, and the name under which their business is carried on is called the firm-name.

(2) In Scotland a firm is a legal person distinct from the partners of whom it is composed, but an individual partner may be charged on a decree or diligence directed against the firm, and on payment of the debts is entitled to relief *pro ratâ* from the firm and its other members.

### *Relations of Partners to persons dealing with them*

### 5   Power of partner to bind the firm.

Every partner is an agent of the firm and his other partners for the purpose of the business of the partnership; and the acts of every partner who does any act for carrying on in the usual way business of the kind carried on by the firm of which he is a member bind the firm and his partners, unless the partner so acting has in fact no authority to act for the firm in the particular matter, and the person with whom he is dealing either knows that he has no authority, or does not know or believe him to be a partner.

### 6   Partners bound by acts on behalf of firm.

An act or instrument relating to the business of the firm done or executed in the firm-name, or in any other manner showing an intention to bind the firm, by any person thereto authorised, whether a partner or not, is binding on the firm and all the partners.

Provided that this section shall not affect any general rule of law relating to the execution of deeds or negotiable instruments.

### 7   Partner using credit of firm for private purposes.

Where one partner pledges the credit of the firm for a purpose apparently not connected with the firm's ordinary course of business, the firm is not bound, unless he is in fact specially authorised by the other partners; but this section does not affect any personal liability incurred by an individual partner.

### 8   Effect of notice that firm will not be bound by acts of partner.

If it has been agreed between the partners that any restriction shall be placed on the power of any one or more of them to bind the firm, no act done in contravention of the agreement is binding on the firm with respect to persons having notice of the agreement.

### 9   Liability of partners.

Every partner in a firm is liable jointly with the other partners, and in Scotland severally also, for all debts and obligations of the firm incurred while he is a partner; and after his death his estate is also severally liable in a due course of administration for such debts and obligations, so far as they remain unsatisfied, but subject in England or Ireland to the prior payment of his separate debts.

### 10   Liability of the firm for wrongs.

Where, by any wrongful act or omission of any partner acting in the ordinary course of the business of the firm, or with the authority of his co-partners, loss or injury is caused to any person not being a partner in the firm, or any penalty is incurred, the firm is liable therefor to the same extent as the partner so acting or omitting to act.

### 11   Misapplication of money or property received for or in custody of the firm.

In the following cases; namely—

(a) Where one partner acting within the scope of his apparent authority receives the money or property of a third person and misapplies it; and

(b) Where a firm in the course of its business receives money or property of a third person, and the money or property so received is misapplied by one or more of the partners while it is in the custody of the firm;

the firm is liable to make good the loss.

### 12   Liability for wrongs joint and several.

Every partner is liable jointly with his co-partners and also severally for everything for which the firm while he is a partner therein becomes liable under either of the two last preceding sections.

### 13   Improper employment of trust-property for partnership purposes.

If a partner, being a trustee, improperly employs trust-property in the business or on the account of the partnership, no other partner is liable for the trust property to the persons beneficially interested therein:

Provided as follows:—

(1) This section shall not affect any liability incurred by any partner by reason of his having notice of a breach of trust; and

(2)  Nothing in this section shall prevent trust money from being followed and recovered from the firm if still in its possession or under its control.

## 14   Persons liable by 'holding out'.

(1)  Every one who by words spoken or written or by conduct represents himself, or who knowingly suffers himself to be represented, as a partner in a particular firm, is liable as a partner to any one who has on the faith of any such representation given credit to the firm, whether the representation has or has not been made or communicated to the person so giving credit by or with the knowledge of the apparent partner making the representation or suffering it to be made.

(2)  Provided that where after a partner's death the partnership business is continued in the old firm's name, the continued use of that name or of the deceased partner's name as part thereof shall not of itself make his executors or administrators estate or effects liable for any partnership debts contracted after his death.

## 15   Admissions and representations of partners.

An admission or representation made by any partner concerning the partnership affairs, and in the ordinary course of its business, is evidence against the firm.

## 16   Notice to acting partner to be notice to the firm.

Notice to any partner who habitually acts in the partnership business of any matter relating to partnership affairs operates as notice to the firm, except in the case of a fraud on the firm committed by or with the consent of that partner.

## 17   Liabilities of incoming and outgoing partners.

(1)  A person who is admitted as a partner into an existing firm does not thereby become liable to the creditors of the firm for anything done before he became a partner.

(2)  A partner who retires from a firm does not thereby cease to be liable for partnership debts or obligations incurred before his retirement.

(3)  A retiring partner may be discharged from any existing liabilities, by an agreement to that effect between himself and the members of the firm as newly constituted and the creditors, and this agreement may be either expressed or inferred as a fact from the course of dealing between the creditors and the firm as newly constituted.

## 18   Revocation of continuing guaranty by change in firm.

A continuing guaranty or cautionary obligation given either to a firm or to a third person in respect of the transactions of a firm is, in the absence of agreement to the contrary, revoked as to future transactions by any change in the constitution of the firm to which, or of the firm in respect of the transactions of which, the guaranty or obligation was given.

*Relations of Partners to one another*

## 19   Variation by consent of terms of partnership.

The mutual rights and duties of partners, whether ascertained by agreement or defined by this Act, may be varied by the consent of all the partners, and such consent may be either express or inferred from a course of dealing.

## 20   Partnership property.

(1)  All property and rights and interests in property originally brought into the partnership stock or acquired, whether by purchase or otherwise, on account of the firm, or for the purposes and in the course of the partnership business, are called in this Act partnership property, and must be held and applied by the partners exclusively for the purposes of the partnership and in accordance with the partnership agreement.

(2)  Provided that the legal estate or interest in any land, or in Scotland the title to and interest in any heritable estate, which belongs to the partnership shall devolve according to the nature and tenure thereof, and the general rules of law thereto applicable, but in trust, so far as necessary, for the persons beneficially interested in the land under this section.

(3)  Where co-owners of an estate or interest in any land, or in Scotland of any heritable estate, not being itself partnership property, are partners as to profits made by the use of that land or estate, and purchase other land or estate out of the profits to be used in like manner, the land or estate so purchased belongs to them, in the absence of an agreement to the contrary, not as partners, but as co-owners for the same respective estates and interests as are held by them in the land or estate first mentioned at the date of the purchase.

## 21   Property bought with partnership money.

Unless the contrary intention appears, property bought with money belonging to the firm is deemed to have been bought on account of the firm.

## 22   [...]

### 23 Procedure against partnership property for a partner's separate judgment debt.

(1) A writ of execution shall not issue against any partnership property except on a judgment against the firm.

(2) The High Court, or a judge thereof, [...] a county court, may, on the application by summons of any judgment creditor of a partner, make an order charging that partner's interest in the partnership property and profits with payment of the amount of the judgment debt and interest thereon, and may by the same or a subsequent order appoint a receiver of that partner's share of profits (whether already declared or accruing), and of any other money which may be coming to him in respect of the partnership, and direct all accounts and inquiries, and give all other orders and directions which might have been directed or given if the charge had been made in favour of the judgment creditor by the partner, or which the circumstances of the case may require.

(3) The other partner or partners shall be at liberty at any time to redeem the interest charged, or in case of a sale being directed, to purchase the same.

(4) [...]

(5) This section shall not apply to Scotland.

### 24 Rules as to interests and duties of partners subject to special agreement.

The interests of partners in the partnership property and their rights and duties in relation to the partnership shall be determined, subject to any agreement express or implied between the partners, by the following rules:—

(1) All the partners are entitled to share equally in the capital and profits of the business, and must contribute equally towards the losses whether of capital or otherwise sustained by the firm.

(2) The firm must indemnify every partner in respect of payments made and personal liabilities incurred by him—

    (a) In the ordinary and proper conduct of the business of the firm; or,

    (b) In or about anything necessarily done for the preservation of the business or property of the firm.

(3) A partner making, for the purpose of the partnership, any actual payment or advance beyond the amount of capital which he has agreed to subscribe, is entitled to interest at the rate of five per cent. per annum from the date of the payment or advance.

(4) A partner is not entitled, before the ascertainment of profits, to interest on the capital subscribed by him.

(5) Every partner may take part in the management of the partnership business.

(6) No partner shall be entitled to remuneration for acting in the partnership business.

(7) No person may be introduced as a partner without the consent of all existing partners.

(8) Any difference arising as to ordinary matters connected with the partnership business may be decided by a majority of the partners, but no change may be made in the nature of the partnership business without the consent of all existing partners.

(9) The partnership books are to be kept at the place of business of the partnership (or the principal place, if there is more than one), and every partner may, when he thinks fit, have access to and inspect and copy any of them.

### 25 Expulsion of partner.

No majority of the partners can expel any partner unless a power to do so has been conferred by express agreement between the partners.

### 26 Retirement from partnership at will.

(1) Where no fixed term has been agreed upon for the duration of the partnership, any partner may determine the partnership at any time on giving notice of his intention so to do to all the other partners.

(2) Where the partnership has originally been constituted by deed, a notice in writing, signed by the partner giving it, shall be sufficient for this purpose.

### 27 Where partnership for term is continued over, continuance on old terms presumed.

(1) Where a partnership entered into for a fixed term is continued after the term has expired, and without any express new agreement, the rights and duties of the partners remain the same as they were at the expiration of the term, so far as is consistent with the incidents of a partnership at will.

(2) A continuance of the business by the partners or such of them as habitually acted therein during the term, without any settlement or liquidation of the partnership affairs, is presumed to be a continuance of the partnership.

### 28 Duty of partners to render accounts, &c.

Partners are bound to render true accounts and full information of all things affecting the partnership to any partner or his legal representatives.

**29   Accountability of partners for private profits.**

(1)  Every partner must account to the firm for any benefit derived by him without the consent of the other partners from any transaction concerning the partnership, or from any use by him of the partnership property name or business connexion.

(2)  This section applies also to transactions undertaken after a partnership has been dissolved by the death of a partner, and before the affairs thereof have been completely wound up, either by any surviving partner or by the representatives of the deceased partner.

**30   Duty of partner not to compete with firm.**

If a partner, without the consent of the other partners, carries on any business of the same nature as and competing with that of the firm, he must account for and pay over to the firm all profits made by him in that business.

**31   Rights of assignee of share in partnership.**

(1)  An assignment by any partner of his share in the partnership, either absolute or by way of mortgage or redeemable charge, does not, as against the other partners, entitle the assignee, during the continuance of the partnership, to interfere in the management or administration of the partnership business or affairs, or to require any accounts of the partnership transactions, or to inspect the partnership books, but entitles the assignee only to receive the share of profits to which the assigning partner would otherwise be entitled, and the assignee must accept the account of profits agreed to by the partners.

(2)  In case of a dissolution of the partnership, whether as respects all the partners or as respects the assigning partner, the assignee is entitled to receive the share of the partnership assets to which the assigning partner is entitled as between himself and the other partners, and, for the purpose of ascertaining that share, to an account as from the date of the dissolution.

*Dissolution of Partnership, and its consequences*

**32   Dissolution by expiration or notice.**

Subject to any agreement between the partners, a partnership is dissolved—
  (a)  If entered into for a fixed term, by the expiration of that term:
  (b)  If entered into for a single adventure or undertaking, by the termination of that adventure or undertaking:
  (c)  If entered into for an undefined time, by any partner giving notice to the other or others of his intention to dissolve the partnership.

In the last-mentioned case the partnership is dissolved as from the date mentioned in the notice as the date of dissolution, or, if no date is so mentioned, as from the date of the communication of the notice.

**33   Dissolution by bankruptcy, death, or charge.**

(1)  Subject to any agreement between the partners, every partnership is dissolved as regards all the partners by the death or bankruptcy of any partner.

(2)  A partnership may, at the option of the other partners, be dissolved if any partner suffers his share of the partnership property to be charged under this Act for his separate debt.

**34   Dissolution by illegality of partnership.**

A partnership is in every case dissolved by the happening of any event which makes it unlawful for the business of the firm to be carried on or for the members of the firm to carry it on in partnership.

**35   Dissolution by the Court.**

On application by a partner the Court may decree a dissolution of the partnership in any of the following cases:
  (a)  [...]
  (b)  When a partner, other than the partner suing, becomes in any other way permanently incapable of performing his part of the partnership contract:
  (c)  When a partner, other than the partner suing, has been guilty of such conduct as, in the opinion of the Court, regard being had to the nature of the business, is calculated to prejudicially affect the carrying on of the business:
  (d)  When a partner, other than the partner suing, wilfully or persistently commits a breach of the partnership agreement, or otherwise so conducts himself in matters relating to the partnership business that it is not reasonably practicable for the other partner or partners to carry on the business in partnership with him:
  (e)  When the business of the partnership can only be carried on at a loss:
  (f)  Whenever in any case circumstances have arisen which, in the opinion of the Court, render it just and equitable that the partnership be dissolved.

**36   Rights of persons dealing with firm against apparent members of firm.**

(1)  Where a person deals with a firm after a change in its constitution he is entitled to treat all apparent members of the old firm as still being members of the firm until he has notice of the change.

(2) An advertisement in the London Gazette as to a firm whose principal place of business is in England or Wales, in the Edinburgh Gazette as to a firm whose principal place of business is in Scotland, and in the Belfast Gazette as to a firm whose principal place of business is in Ireland, shall be notice as to persons who had not dealings with the firm before the date of the dissolution or change so advertised.

(3) The estate of a partner who dies, or who becomes bankrupt, or of a partner who, not having been known to the person dealing with the firm to be a partner, retires from the firm, is not liable for partnership debts contracted after the date of the death, bankruptcy, or retirement respectively.

### 37    Right of partners to notify dissolution.

On the dissolution of a partnership or retirement of a partner any partner may publicly notify the same, and may require the other partner or partners to concur for that purpose in all necessary or proper acts, if any, which cannot be done without his or their concurrence.

### 38    Continuing authority of partners for purposes of winding up.

After the dissolution of a partnership the authority of each partner to bind the firm, and the other rights and obligations of the partners, continue notwithstanding the dissolution so far as may be necessary to wind up the affairs of the partnership, and to complete transactions begun but unfinished at the time of the dissolution, but not otherwise.

Provided that the firm is in no case bound by the acts of a partner who has become bankrupt; but this proviso does not affect the liability of any person who has after the bankruptcy represented himself or knowingly suffered himself to be represented as a partner of the bankrupt.

### 39    Rights of partners as to application of partnership property.

On the dissolution of a partnership every partner is entitled, as against the other partners in the firm, and all persons claiming through them in respect of their interests as partners, to have the property of the partnership applied in payment of the debts and liabilities of the firm, and to have the surplus assets after such payment applied in payment of what may be due to the partners respectively after deducting what may be due from them as partners to the firm; and for that purpose any partner or his representatives may on the termination of the partnership apply to the Court to wind up the business and affairs of the firm.

### 40    Apportionment of premium where partnership prematurely dissolved.

Where one partner has paid a premium to another on entering into a partnership for a fixed term, and the partnership is dissolved before the expiration of that term otherwise than by the death of a partner, the Court may order the repayment of the premium, or of such part thereof as it thinks just, having regard to the terms of the partnership contract and to the length of time during which the partnership has continued; unless

   (a) the dissolution is, in the judgment of the Court, wholly or chiefly due to the misconduct of the partner who paid the premium, or
   (b) the partnership has been dissolved by an agreement containing no provision for a return of any part of the premium.

### 41    Rights where partnership dissolved for fraud or misrepresentation.

Where a partnership contract is rescinded on the ground of the fraud or misrepresentation of one of the parties thereto, the party entitled to rescind is, without prejudice to any other right, entitled—

   (a) to a lien on, or right of retention of, the surplus of the partnership assets, after satisfying the partnership liabilities, for any sum of money paid by him for the purchase of a share in the partnership and for any capital contributed by him, and is
   (b) to stand in the place of the creditors of the firm for any payments made by him in respect of the partnership liabilities, and
   (c) to be indemnified by the person guilty of the fraud or making the representation against all the debts and liabilities of the firm.

### 42    Right of out-going partner in certain cases to share profits made after dissolution.

(1) Where any member of a firm has died or otherwise ceased to be a partner, and the surviving or continuing partners carry on the business of the firm with its capital or assets without any final settlement of accounts as between the firm and the outgoing partner or his estate, then, in the absence of any agreement to the contrary, the outgoing partner or his estate is entitled at the option of himself or his representatives to such share of the profits made since the dissolution as the Court may find to be attributable to the use of his share of the partnership assets, or to interest at the rate of five per cent. per annum on the amount of his share of the partnership assets.

(2) Provided that where by the partnership contract an option is given to surviving or continuing partners to purchase the interest of a deceased or outgoing partner, and that option is duly exercised, the estate of the deceased partner, or the outgoing partner or his estate, as the case may be, is not entitled to any further or other share of profits; but if any partner assuming to act in exercise of the option does not in all material respects comply with the terms thereof, he is liable to account under the foregoing provisions of this section.

### 43    Retiring or deceased partner's share to be a debt.

Subject to any agreement between the partners, the amount due from surviving or continuing partners to an outgoing partner or the representatives of a deceased partner in respect of the outgoing or deceased partner's share is a debt accruing at the date of the dissolution or death.

### 44    Rule for distribution of assets on final settlement of accounts.

In settling accounts between the partners after a dissolution of partnership, the following rules shall, subject to any agreement, be observed:

(a) Losses, including losses and deficiencies of capital, shall be paid first out of profits, next out of capital, and lastly, if necessary, by the partners individually in the proportion in which they were entitled to share profits:

(b) The assets of the firm including the sums, if any, contributed by the partners to make up losses or deficiencies of capital, shall be applied in the following manner and order:

1.    In paying the debts and liabilities of the firm to persons who are not partners therein:

2.    In paying to each partner rateably what is due from the firm to him for advances as distinguished from capital:

3.    In paying to each partner rateably what is due from the firm to him in respect of capital:

4.    The ultimate residue, if any, shall be divided among the partners in the proportion in which profits are divisible.

*Supplemental*

### 45    Definitions of 'court' and 'business'.

In this Act, unless the contrary intention appears,—

The expression 'court' includes every court and judge having jurisdiction in the case:

The expression 'business' includes every trade, occupation, or profession.

### 46    Saving for rules of equity and common law.

The rules of equity and of common law applicable to partnership shall continue in force except so far as they are inconsistent with the express provisions of this Act.

### 47    Provision as to bankruptcy in Scotland.

(1) In the application of this Act to Scotland the bankruptcy of a firm or of an individual shall mean sequestration under the Bankruptcy (Scotland) Acts, and also in the case of an individual the issue against him of a decree of cessio bonorum.

(2) Nothing in this Act shall alter the rules of the law of Scotland relating to the bankruptcy of a firm or of the individual partners thereof.

### 48    [...]

### 49    [...]

### 50    Short title.

This Act may be cited as the Partnership Act 1890.

# Limited Liability Partnerships Act 2000

(2000 c. 12)

*An Act to make provision for limited liability partnerships.*                    [20th July 2000]

*Be it enacted by the Queen's most Excellent Majesty, by and with the advice and consent of the Lords Spiritual and Temporal, and Commons, in this present Parliament assembled, and by the authority of the same, as follows:—*

*Introductory*

### 1    Limited liability partnerships

(1) There shall be a new form of legal entity to be known as a limited liability partnership.

(2) A limited liability partnership is a body corporate (with legal personality separate from that of its members) which is formed by being incorporated under this Act; and—

(a) in the following provisions of this Act (except in the phrase 'oversea limited liability partnership'), and

(b) in any other enactment (except where provision is made to the contrary or the context otherwise requires),

references to a limited liability partnership are to such a body corporate.

(3) A limited liability partnership has unlimited capacity.

(4) The members of a limited liability partnership have such liability to contribute to its assets in the event of its being wound up as is provided for by virtue of this Act.

(5) Accordingly, except as far as otherwise provided by this Act or any other enactment, the law relating to partnerships does not apply to a limited liability partnership.

(6) The Schedule (which makes provision about the names and registered offices of limited liability partnerships) has effect.

*Incorporation*

## 2 Incorporation document etc

(1) For a limited liability partnership to be incorporated—

    (a) two or more persons associated for carrying on a lawful business with a view to profit must have subscribed their names to an incorporation document,

    (b) there must have been delivered to the registrar either the incorporation document or a copy authenticated in a manner approved by him, and

    (c) there must have been so delivered a statement in a form approved by the registrar, made by either a solicitor engaged in the formation of the limited liability partnership or anyone who subscribed his name to the incorporation document, that the requirement imposed by paragraph (a) has been complied with.

(2) The incorporation document must—

    (a) be in a form approved by the registrar (or as near to such a form as circumstances allow),

    (b) state the name of the limited liability partnership,

    (c) state whether the registered office of the limited liability partnership is to be situated in England and Wales, in Wales or in Scotland,

    (d) state the address of that registered office,

    (e) state the name and address of each of the persons who are to be members of the limited liability partnership on incorporation, and

    (f) either specify which of those persons are to be designated members or state that every person who from time to time is a member of the limited liability partnership is a designated member.

(2A) Where a confidentiality order, made under section 723B of the Companies Act 1985 as applied to a limited liability partnerships, is in force in respect of any individual named as a member of a limited liability partnership under subsection (2) that subsection shall have effect as if the reference to the address of the individual were a reference to the address for the time being notified by him under the Limited Liability Partnerships (Particulars of Usual Residential Address)(Confidentiality Orders) Regulations 2002 to any limited liability partnership of which he is a member or if he is not such a member either the address specified in his application for a confidentiality order or the address last notified by him under such a confidentiality order as the case may be.

(2B) Where the incorporation document or a copy of such delivered under this section includes an address specified in reliance on subsection (2A) there shall be delivered with it or the copy of it a statement in a form approved by the registrar containing particulars of the usual residential address of the member whose address is so specified.

(3) If a person makes a false statement under subsection (1)(c) which he—

    (a) knows to be false, or

    (b) does not believe to be true,

he commits an offence.

(4) A person guilty of an offence under subsection (3) is liable—

    (a) on summary conviction, to imprisonment for a period not exceeding six months or a fine not exceeding the statutory maximum, or to both, or

    (b) on conviction on indictment, to imprisonment for a period not exceeding two years or a fine, or to both.

## 3 Incorporation by registration

(1) When the requirements imposed by paragraphs (b) and (c) of subsection (1) of section 2 have been complied with, the registrar shall retain the incorporation document or copy delivered to him and, unless the requirement imposed by paragraph (a) of that subsection has not been complied with, he shall—

    (a) register the incorporation document or copy, and

    (b) give a certificate that the limited liability partnership is incorporated by the name specified in the incorporation document.

(2) The registrar may accept the statement delivered under paragraph (c) of subsection (1) of section 2 as sufficient evidence that the requirement imposed by paragraph (a) of that subsection has been complied with.

(3) The certificate shall either be signed by the registrar or be authenticated by his official seal.

(4) The certificate is conclusive evidence that the requirements of section 2 are complied with and that the limited liability partnership is incorporated by the name specified in the incorporation document.

*Membership*

## 4 Members

(1) On the incorporation of a limited liability partnership its members are the persons who subscribed their names to the incorporation document (other than any who have died or been dissolved).

(2) Any other person may become a member of a limited liability partnership by and in accordance with an agreement with the existing members.

(3) A person may cease to be a member of a limited liability partnership (as well as by death or dissolution) in accordance with an agreement with the other members or, in the absence of agreement with the other members as to cessation of membership, by giving reasonable notice to the other members.

(4) A member of a limited liability partnership shall not be regarded for any purpose as employed by the limited liability partnership unless, if he and the other members were partners in a partnership, he would be regarded for that purpose as employed by the partnership.

## 5 Relationship of members etc

(1) Except as far as otherwise provided by this Act or any other enactment, the mutual rights and duties of the members of a limited liability partnership, and the mutual rights and duties of a limited liability partnership and its members, shall be governed—

    (a) by agreement between the members, or between the limited liability partnership and its members, or

    (b) in the absence of agreement as to any matter, by any provision made in relation to that matter by regulations under section 15(c).

(2) An agreement made before the incorporation of a limited liability partnership between the persons who subscribe their names to the incorporation document may impose obligations on the limited liability partnership (to take effect at any time after its incorporation).

## 6 Members as agents

(1) Every member of a limited liability partnership is the agent of the limited liability partnership.

(2) But a limited liability partnership is not bound by anything done by a member in dealing with a person if—

    (a) the member in fact has no authority to act for the limited liability partnership by doing that thing, and

    (b) the person knows that he has no authority or does not know or believe him to be a member of the limited liability partnership.

(3) Where a person has ceased to be a member of a limited liability partnership, the former member is to be regarded (in relation to any person dealing with the limited liability partnership) as still being a member of the limited liability partnership unless—

    (a) the person has notice that the former member has ceased to be a member of the limited liability partnership, or

    (b) notice that the former member has ceased to be a member of the limited liability partnership has been delivered to the registrar.

(4) Where a member of a limited liability partnership is liable to any person (other than another member of the limited liability partnership) as a result of a wrongful act or omission of his in the course of the business of the limited liability partnership or with its authority, the limited liability partnership is liable to the same extent as the member.

## 7 Ex-members

(1) This section applies where a member of a limited liability partnership has either ceased to be a member or—

    (a) has died,

    (b) has become bankrupt or had his estate sequestrated or has been wound up,

    (c) has granted a trust deed for the benefit of his creditors, or

    (d) has assigned the whole or any part of his share in the limited liability partnership (absolutely or by way of charge or security).

(2) In such an event the former member or—

    (a) his personal representative,

    (b) his trustee in bankruptcy or permanent or interim trustee (within the meaning of the Bankruptcy (Scotland) Act 1985) or liquidator,

    (c) his trustee under the trust deed for the benefit of his creditors, or

    (d) his assignee,

may not interfere in the management or administration of any business or affairs of the limited liability partnership.

(3) But subsection (2) does not affect any right to receive an amount from the limited liability partnership in that event.

## 8 Designated members

(1) If the incorporation document specifies who are to be designated members—

    (a) they are designated members on incorporation, and

    (b) any member may become a designated member by and in accordance with an agreement with the other members,

and a member may cease to be a designated member in accordance with an agreement with the other members.

(2)  But if there would otherwise be no designated members, or only one, every member is a designated member.

(3)  If the incorporation document states that every person who from time to time is a member of the limited liability partnership is a designated member, every member is a designated member.

(4)  A limited liability partnership may at any time deliver to the registrar—

(a)  notice that specified members are to be designated members, or

(b)  notice that every person who from time to time is a member of the limited liability partnership is a designated member,

and, once it is delivered, subsection (1)(apart from paragraph (a)) and subsection (2), or subsection (3), shall have effect as if that were stated in the incorporation document.

(5)  A notice delivered under subsection (4)—

(a)  shall be in a form approved by the registrar, and

(b)  shall be signed by a designated member of the limited liability partnership or authenticated in a manner approved by the registrar.

(6)  A person ceases to be a designated member if he ceases to be a member.

## 9   Registration of membership changes

(1)  A limited liability partnership must ensure that—

(a)  where a person becomes or ceases to be a member or designated member, notice is delivered to the registrar within fourteen days, and

(b)  where there is any change in the name or address of a member, notice is delivered to the registrar within 28 days.

(2)  Where all the members from time to time of a limited liability partnership are designated members, subsection (1)(a) does not require notice that a person has become or ceased to be a designated member as well as a member.

(3)  A notice delivered under subsection (1)—

(a)  shall be in a form approved by the registrar, and

(b)  shall be signed by a designated member of the limited liability partnership or authenticated in a manner approved by the registrar,

and, if it relates to a person becoming a member or designated member, shall contain a statement that he consents to becoming a member or designated member signed by him or authenticated in a manner approved by the registrar.

(3A)  Where a confidentiality order under section 723B of the Companies Act 1985 as applied to limited liability partnerships is made in respect of an existing member, the limited liability partnership must ensure that there is delivered within 28 days to the registrar notice in a form approved by the registrar containing the address for the time being notified to it by the member under the Limited Liability Partnerships (Particulars of Usual Residential Address)(Confidentiality Orders) Regulations 2002.

(3B)  Where such a confidentiality order is in force in respect of a member the requirement in subsection (1)(b) to notify a change in the address of a member shall be read in relation to that member as a requirement to deliver to the registrar, within 28 days, notice of—

(a)  any change in the usual residential address of that member; and

(b)  any change in the address for the time being notified to the limited liability partnership by the member under the Limited Liability Partnerships (Particulars of Usual Residential Address)(Confidentiality Orders) Regulations 2002,

and the registrar may approve different forms for the notification of each kind of address.

(4)  If a limited liability partnership fails to comply with subsection (1), the partnership and every designated member commits an offence.

(5)  But it is a defence for a designated member charged with an offence under subsection (4) to prove that he took all reasonable steps for securing that subsection (1) was complied with.

(6)  A person guilty of an offence under subsection (4) is liable on summary conviction to a fine not exceeding level 5 on the standard scale.

*Taxation*

## 10   Income tax and chargeable gains

(1)  In the Income and Corporation Taxes Act 1988, after section 118 insert—

*'Limited liability partnerships*

### 118ZA   Treatment of limited liability partnerships

For the purposes of the Tax Acts, a trade, profession or business carried on by a limited liability partnership with a view to profit shall be treated as carried on in partnership by its members (and not by the limited liability partnership as such); and, accordingly, the property of the limited liability partnership shall be treated for those purposes as partnership property.

### 118ZB   Restriction on relief

Sections 117 and 118 have effect in relation to a member of a limited liability partnership as in relation to a limited partner, but subject to sections 118ZC and 118ZD.

### 118ZC   Member's contribution to trade

(1) Subsection (3) of section 117 does not have effect in relation to a member of a limited liability partnership.

(2) But, for the purposes of that section and section 118, such a member's contribution to a trade at any time ("the relevant time") is the greater of—

    (a) the amount subscribed by him, and

    (b) the amount of his liability on a winding up.

(3) The amount subscribed by a member of a limited liability partnership is the amount which he has contributed to the limited liability partnership as capital, less so much of that amount (if any) as—

    (a) he has previously, directly or indirectly, drawn out or received back,

    (b) he so draws out or receives back during the period of five years beginning with the relevant time,

    (c) he is or may be entitled so to draw out or receive back at any time when he is a member of the limited liability partnership, or

    (d) he is or may be entitled to require another person to reimburse to him.

(4) The amount of the liability of a member of a limited liability partnership on a winding up is the amount which—

    (a) he is liable to contribute to the assets of the limited liability partnership in the event of its being wound up, and

    (b) he remains liable so to contribute for the period of at least five years beginning with the relevant time (or until it is wound up, if that happens before the end of that period).

### 118ZD   Carry forward of unrelieved losses.

(1) Where amounts relating to a trade carried on by a member of a limited liability partnership are, in any one or more chargeable periods, prevented from being given or allowed by section 117 or 118 as it applies otherwise than by virtue of this section (his "total unrelieved loss"), subsection (2) applies in each subsequent chargeable period in which—

    (a) he carries on the trade as a member of the limited liability partnership, and

    (b) any of his total unrelieved loss remains outstanding.

(2) Sections 380, 381, 393A(1) and 403 (and sections 117 and 118 as they apply in relation to those sections) shall have effect in the subsequent chargeable period as if—

    (a) any loss sustained or incurred by the member in the trade in that chargeable period were increased by an amount equal to so much of his total unrelieved loss as remains outstanding in that period, or

    (b) (if no loss is so sustained or incurred) a loss of that amount were so sustained or incurred.

(3) To ascertain whether any (and, if so, how much) of a member's total unrelieved loss remains outstanding in the subsequent chargeable period, deduct from the amount of his total unrelieved loss the aggregate of—

    (a) any relief given under any provision of the Tax Acts (otherwise than as a result of subsection (2)) in respect of his total unrelieved loss in that or any previous chargeable period, and

    (b) any amount given or allowed in respect of his total unrelieved loss as a result of subsection (2) in any previous chargeable period (or which would have been so given or allowed had a claim been made).'

(3) In the Taxation of Chargeable Gains Act 1992, after section 59 insert—

### '59A   Limited liability partnerships.

(1) Where a limited liability partnership carries on a trade or business with a view to profit—

    (a) assets held by the limited liability partnership shall be treated for the purposes of tax in respect of chargeable gains as held by its members as partners, and

    (b) any dealings by the limited liability partnership shall be treated for those purposes as dealings by its members in partnership (and not by the limited liability partnership as such),

and tax in respect of chargeable gains accruing to the members of the limited liability partnership on the disposal of any of its assets shall be assessed and charged on them separately.

(2) Where subsection (1) ceases to apply in relation to a limited liability partnership with the effect that tax is assessed and charged—

    (a) on the limited liability partnership (as a company) in respect of chargeable gains accruing on the disposal of any of its assets, and

    (b) on the members in respect of chargeable gains accruing on the disposal of any of their capital interests in the limited liability partnership,

it shall be assessed and charged on the limited liability partnership as if subsection (1) had never applied in relation to it.

(3) Neither the commencement of the application of subsection (1) nor the cessation of its application in relation to a limited liability partnership is to be taken as giving rise to the disposal of any assets by it or any of its members.'

(4) After section 156 of that Act insert—

### '156A   Cessation of trade by limited liability partnership.

(1)   Where, immediately before the time of cessation of trade, a member of a limited liability partnership holds an asset, or an interest in an asset, acquired by him for a consideration treated as reduced under section 152 or 153, he shall be treated as if a chargeable gain equal to the amount of the reduction accrued to him immediately before that time.

(2)   Where, as a result of section 154(2), a chargeable gain on the disposal of an asset, or an interest in an asset, by a member of a limited liability partnership has not accrued before the time of cessation of trade, the member shall be treated as if the chargeable gain accrued immediately before that time.

(3)   In this section "the time of cessation of trade", in relation to a limited liability partnership, means the time when section 59A(1) ceases to apply in relation to the limited liability partnership.'

### 11   Inheritance tax.

In the Inheritance Tax Act 1984, after section 267 insert—

### '267A   Limited liability partnerships.

For the purposes of this Act and any other enactments relating to inheritance tax—

    (a)   property to which a limited liability partnership is entitled, or which it occupies or uses, shall be treated as property to which its members are entitled, or which they occupy or use, as partners,

    (b)   any business carried on by a limited liability partnership shall be treated as carried on in partnership by its members,

    (c)   incorporation, change in membership or dissolution of a limited liability partnership shall be treated as formation, alteration or dissolution of a partnership, and

    (d)   any transfer of value made by or to a limited liability partnership shall be treated as made by or to its members in partnership (and not by or to the limited liability partnership as such).'

### 12   Stamp duty.

(1)   Stamp duty shall not be chargeable on an instrument by which property is conveyed or transferred by a person to a limited liability partnership in connection with its incorporation within the period of one year beginning with the date of incorporation if the following two conditions are satisfied.

(2)   The first condition is that at the relevant time the person—

    (a)   is a partner in a partnership comprised of all the persons who are or are to be members of the limited liability partnership (and no-one else), or

    (b)   holds the property conveyed or transferred as nominee or bare trustee for one or more of the partners in such a partnership.

(3)   The second condition is that—

    (a)   the proportions of the property conveyed or transferred to which the persons mentioned in subsection (2)(a) are entitled immediately after the conveyance or transfer are the same as those to which they were entitled at the relevant time, or

    (b)   none of the differences in those proportions has arisen as part of a scheme or arrangement of which the main purpose, or one of the main purposes, is avoidance of liability to any duty or tax.

(4)   For the purposes of subsection (2) a person holds property as bare trustee for a partner if the partner has the exclusive right (subject only to satisfying any outstanding charge, lien or other right of the trustee to resort to the property for payment of duty, taxes, costs or other outgoings) to direct how the property shall be dealt with.

(5)   In this section 'the relevant time' means—

    (a)   if the person who conveyed or transferred the property to the limited liability partnership acquired the property after its incorporation, immediately after he acquired the property, and

    (b)   in any other case, immediately before its incorporation.

(6)   An instrument in respect of which stamp duty is not chargeable by virtue of subsection (1) shall not be taken to be duly stamped unless—

    (a)   it has, in accordance with section 12 of the Stamp Act 1891, been stamped with a particular stamp denoting that it is not chargeable with any duty or that it is duly stamped, or

    (b)   it is stamped with the duty to which it would be liable apart from that subsection.

### 13   Class 4 national insurance contributions.

In section 15 of the Social Security Contributions and Benefits Act 1992 and section 15 of the Social Security Contributions and Benefits (Northern Ireland) Act 1992 (Class 4 contributions), after subsection (3) insert—

'(3A)   Where income tax is (or would be) charged on a member of a limited liability partnership in respect of profits or gains arising from the carrying on of a trade or profession by the limited liability partnership, Class 4 contributions shall be payable by him if they would be payable were the trade or profession carried on in partnership by the members.'

*Regulations*

## 14   Insolvency and winding up.

(1)   Regulations shall make provision about the insolvency and winding up of limited liability partnerships by applying or incorporating, with such modifications as appear appropriate, Parts I to IV, VI and VII of the Insolvency Act 1986.

(2)   Regulations may make other provision about the insolvency and winding up of limited liability partnerships, and provision about the insolvency and winding up of oversea limited liability partnerships, by—

(a)   applying or incorporating, with such modifications as appear appropriate, any law relating to the insolvency or winding up of companies or other corporations which would not otherwise have effect in relation to them, or

(b)   providing for any law relating to the insolvency or winding up of companies or other corporations which would otherwise have effect in relation to them not to apply to them or to apply to them with such modifications as appear appropriate.

(3)   In this Act 'oversea limited liability partnership' means a body incorporated or otherwise established outside Great Britain and having such connection with Great Britain, and such other features, as regulations may prescribe.

## 15   Application of company law etc.

Regulations may make provision about limited liability partnerships and oversea limited liability partnerships (not being provision about insolvency or winding up) by—

(a)   applying or incorporating, with such modifications as appear appropriate, any law relating to companies or other corporations which would not otherwise have effect in relation to them,

(b)   providing for any law relating to companies or other corporations which would otherwise have effect in relation to them not to apply to them or to apply to them with such modifications as appear appropriate, or

(c)   applying or incorporating, with such modifications as appear appropriate, any law relating to partnerships.

## 16   Consequential amendments.

(1)   Regulations may make in any enactment such amendments or repeals as appear appropriate in consequence of this Act or regulations made under it.

(2)   The regulations may, in particular, make amendments and repeals affecting companies or other corporations or partnerships.

## 17   General.

(1)   In this Act 'regulations' means regulations made by the Secretary of State by statutory instrument.

(2)   Regulations under this Act may in particular—

(a)   make provision for dealing with non-compliance with any of the regulations (including the creation of criminal offences),

(b)   impose fees (which shall be paid into the Consolidated Fund), and

(c)   provide for the exercise of functions by persons prescribed by the regulations.

(3)   Regulations under this Act may—

(a)   contain any appropriate consequential, incidental, supplementary or transitional provisions or savings, and

(b)   make different provision for different purposes.

(4)   No regulations to which this subsection applies shall be made unless a draft of the statutory instrument containing the regulations (whether or not together with other provisions) has been laid before, and approved by a resolution of, each House of Parliament.

(5)   Subsection (4) applies to—

(a)   regulations under section 14(2) not consisting entirely of the application or incorporation (with or without modifications) of provisions contained in or made under the Insolvency Act 1986,

(b)   regulations under section 15 not consisting entirely of the application or incorporation (with or without modifications) of provisions contained in or made under Part I, Chapter VIII of Part V, Part VII, Parts XI to XIII, Parts XVI to XVIII, Part XX or Parts XXIV to XXVI of the Companies Act 1985,

(c)   regulations under section 14 or 15 making provision about oversea limited liability partnerships, and

(d)   regulations under section 16.

(6)   A statutory instrument containing regulations under this Act shall (unless a draft of it has been approved by a resolution of each House of Parliament) be subject to annulment in pursuance of a resolution of either House of Parliament.

*Supplementary*

## 18  Interpretation.

In this Act—

'address', in relation to a member of a limited liability partnership, means—

    (a)  if an individual, his usual residential address, and

    (b)  if a corporation or Scottish firm, its registered or principal office,

'business' includes every trade, profession and occupation,

'designated member' shall be construed in accordance with section 8,

'enactment' includes subordinate legislation (within the meaning of the Interpretation Act 1978),

'incorporation document' shall be construed in accordance with section 2,

'limited liability partnership' has the meaning given by section 1(2),

'member' shall be construed in accordance with section 4,

'modifications' includes additions and omissions,

'name', in relation to a member of a limited liability partnership, means—

    (a)  if an individual, his forename and surname (or, in the case of a peer or other person usually known by a title, his title instead of or in addition to either or both his forename and surname), and

    (b)  if a corporation or Scottish firm, its corporate or firm name,

'oversea limited liability partnership' has the meaning given by section 14(3),

'the registrar' means—

    (a)  if the registered office of the limited liability partnership is, or is to be, situated in England and Wales or in Wales, the registrar or other officer performing under the Companies Act 1985 the duty of registration of companies in England and Wales, and

    (b)  if its registered office is, or is to be, situated in Scotland, the registrar or other officer performing under that Act the duty of registration of companies in Scotland, and

'regulations' has the meaning given by section 17(1).

## 19  Commencement, extent and short title.

(1)  The preceding provisions of this Act shall come into force on such day as the Secretary of State may by order made by statutory instrument appoint; and different days may be appointed for different purposes.

(2)  The Secretary of State may by order made by statutory instrument make any transitional provisions and savings which appear appropriate in connection with the coming into force of any provision of this Act.

(3)  For the purposes of the Scotland Act 1998 this Act shall be taken to be a pre-commencement enactment within the meaning of that Act.

(4)  Apart from sections 10 to 13 (and this section), this Act does not extend to Northern Ireland.

(5)  This Act may be cited as the Limited Liability Partnerships Act 2000.

# SCHEDULE

# NAMES AND REGISTERED OFFICES

## PART I   NAMES

### *Index of names*

1.  *In section 714(1) of the Companies Act 1985 (index of names), after paragraph(d) insert—*

    '(da)   limited liability partnerships incorporated under the Limited Liability Partnerships Act 2000.'[1]

### *Name to indicate status*

2.—(1)  The name of a limited liability partnership must end with—

    (a)  the expression 'limited liability partnership', or

    (b)  the abbreviation 'llp' or 'LLP'.

(2)  But if the incorporation document for a limited liability partnership states that the registered office is to be situated in Wales, its name must end with—

    (a)  one of the expressions 'limited liability partnership' and 'partneriaeth atebolrwydd cyfyngedig', or

    (b)  one of the abbreviations 'llp', 'LLP', 'pac' and 'PAC'.

---

[1]  Para 1 is repealed with effect from 1 October 2009.

### Registration of names

**3.**—(1) A limited liability partnership shall not be registered by a name—

(a) which includes, otherwise than at the end of the name, either of the expressions 'limited liability partnership' and 'partneriaeth atebolrwydd cyfyngedig' or any of the abbreviations 'llp', 'LLP', 'pac' and 'PAC',

(b) which is the same as a name appearing in the index kept under section 714(1) of the Companies Act 1985,

(c) the use of which by the limited liability partnership would in the opinion of the Secretary of State constitute a criminal offence, or

(d) which in the opinion of the Secretary of State is offensive.

(2) Except with the approval of the Secretary of State, a limited liability partnership shall not be registered by a name which—

(a) in the opinion of the Secretary of State would be likely to give the impression that it is connected in any way with Her Majesty's Government or with any local authority, or

(b) includes any word or expression for the time being specified in regulations under section 29 of the Companies Act 1985 (names needing approval),

and in paragraph (a) 'local authority' means any local authority within the meaning of the Local Government Act 1972 or the Local Government etc. (Scotland) Act 1994, the Common Council of the City of London or the Council of the Isles of Scilly.

### Change of name

**4.**—(1) A limited liability partnership may change its name at any time.

(2) Where a limited liability partnership has been registered by a name which—

(a) is the same as or, in the opinion of the Secretary of State, too like a name appearing at the time of registration in the index kept under section 714(1) of the Companies Act 1985, or

(b) is the same as or, in the opinion of the Secretary of State, too like a name which should have appeared in the index at that time,

the Secretary of State may within twelve months of that time in writing direct the limited liability partnership to change its name within such period as he may specify.

(3) If it appears to the Secretary of State—

(a) that misleading information has been given for the purpose of the registration of a limited liability partnership by a particular name, or

(b) that undertakings or assurances have been given for that purpose and have not been fulfilled,

he may, within five years of the date of its registration by that name, in writing direct the limited liability partnership to change its name within such period as he may specify.

(4) If in the Secretary of State's opinion the name by which a limited liability partnership is registered gives so misleading an indication of the nature of its activities as to be likely to cause harm to the public, he may in writing direct the limited liability partnership to change its name within such period as he may specify.

(5) But the limited liability partnership may, within three weeks from the date of the direction apply to the court to set it aside and the court may set the direction aside or confirm it and, if it confirms it, shall specify the period within which it must be complied with.

(6) In sub-paragraph (5) 'the court' means—

(a) if the registered office of the limited liability partnership is situated in England and Wales or in Wales, the High Court, and

(b) if it is situated in Scotland, the Court of Session.

(7) Where a direction has been given under sub-paragraph (2), (3) or (4) specifying a period within which a limited liability partnership is to change its name, the Secretary of State may at any time before that period ends extend it by a further direction in writing.

(8) If a limited liability partnership fails to comply with a direction under this paragraph—

(a) the limited liability partnership, and

(b) any designated member in default,

commits an offence.

(9) A person guilty of an offence under sub-paragraph (8) is liable on summary conviction to a fine not exceeding level 3 on the standard scale.

### Notification of change of name

**5.**—(1) Where a limited liability partnership changes its name it shall deliver notice of the change to the registrar.

(2) A notice delivered under sub-paragraph (1)—

(a) shall be in a form approved by the registrar, and

(b) shall be signed by a designated member of the limited liability partnership or authenticated in a manner approved by the registrar.

(3) Where the registrar receives a notice under sub-paragraph (2) he shall (unless the new name is one by which a limited liability partnership may not be registered)—

(a) enter the new name in the index kept under section 714(1) of the Companies Act 1985, and

(b) issue a certificate of the change of name.

(4) The change of name has effect from the date on which the certificate is issued.

### Effect of change of name

**6.** A change of name by a limited liability partnership does not—

(a) affect any of its rights or duties,

(b) render defective any legal proceedings by or against it,

and any legal proceedings that might have been commenced or continued against it by its former name may be commenced or continued against it by its new name.

### Improper use of 'limited liability partnership' etc.

**7.**—(1) If any person carries on a business under a name or title which includes as the last words—

(a) the expression 'limited liability partnership' or 'partneriaeth atebolrwydd cyfyngedig', or

(b) any contraction or imitation of either of those expressions,

that person, unless a limited liability partnership or oversea limited liability partnership, commits an offence.

(2) A person guilty of an offence under sub-paragraph (1) is liable on summary conviction to a fine not exceeding level 3 on the standard scale.

### Similarity of names

**8.** In determining for the purposes of this Part whether one name is the same as another there are to be disregarded—

(1) the definite article as the first word of the name,

(2) any of the following (or their Welsh equivalents or abbreviations of them or their Welsh equivalents) at the end of the name—

'limited liability partnership',

'company',

'and company',

'company limited',

'and company limited',

'limited',

'unlimited',

'public limited company',

'community interest company',

'community interest public limited company',

'investment company with variable capital', and

'open-ended investment company', and

(3) type and case of letters, accents, spaces between letters and punctuation marks, and 'and' and '&' are to be taken as the same.

## PART II   REGISTERED OFFICES

### Situation of registered office

**9.**—(1) A limited liability partnership shall—

(a) at all times have a registered office situated in England and Wales or in Wales, or

(b) at all times have a registered office situated in Scotland,

to which communications and notices may be addressed.

(2) On the incorporation of a limited liability partnership the situation of its registered office shall be that stated in the incorporation document.

(3) Where the registered office of a limited liability partnership is situated in Wales, but the incorporation document does not state that it is to be situated in Wales (as opposed to England and Wales), the limited liability partnership may deliver notice to the registrar stating that its registered office is to be situated in Wales.

(4) A notice delivered under sub-paragraph (3)—

(a) shall be in a form approved by the registrar, and

(b) shall be signed by a designated member of the limited liability partnership or authenticated in a manner approved by the registrar.

### Change of registered office

**10.**—(1) A limited liability partnership may change its registered office by delivering notice of the change to the registrar.

(2)  A notice delivered under sub-paragraph (1)—

    (a)  shall be in a form approved by the registrar, and

    (b)  shall be signed by a designated member of the limited liability partnership or authenticated in a manner approved by the registrar.

# Limited Liability Partnerships Regulations 2001

**(2001 No. 1090)**

*Whereas a draft of these Regulations has been approved by a resolution of each House of Parliament pursuant to section 17(4) of the Limited Liability Partnerships Act 2000;*

*Now, therefore, the Secretary of State, in exercise of the powers conferred on him by sections 14, 15, 16 and 17 of the Limited Liability Partnerships Act 2000 and all other powers enabling him in that behalf hereby makes the following Regulations:*

## PART I    CITATION, COMMENCEMENT AND INTERPRETATION

### 1    Citation and commencement

These Regulations may be cited as the Limited Liability Partnerships Regulations 2001 and shall come into force on 6th April 2001.

### 2    Interpretation

In these Regulations—

'the 1985 Act' means the Companies Act 1985;

'the 1986 Act' means the Insolvency Act 1986;

'the 2000 Act' means the Financial Services and Markets Act 2000;

'devolved', in relation to the provisions of the 1986 Act, means the provisions of the 1986 Act which are listed in Schedule 4 and, in their application to Scotland, concern wholly or partly, matters which are set out in Section C.2 of Schedule 5 to the Scotland Act 1998 as being exceptions to the reservations made in that Act in the field of insolvency;

'limited liability partnership agreement', in relation to a limited liability partnership, means any agreement express or implied between the members of the limited liability partnership or between the limited liability partnership and the members of the limited liability partnership which determines the mutual rights and duties of the members, and their rights and duties in relation to the limited liability partnership;

'the principal Act' means the Limited Liability Partnerships Act 2000; and

'shadow member', in relation to limited liability partnerships, means a person in accordance with whose directions or instructions the members of the limited liability partnership are accustomed to act (but so that a person is not deemed a shadow member by reason only that the members of the limited partnership act on advice given by him in a professional capacity).

## PART II    ACCOUNTS AND AUDIT

**3**  [...]

## PART III    COMPANIES ACT 1985 AND COMPANY DIRECTORS DISQUALIFICATION ACT 1986

### 4    Application of the remainder of the provisions of the 1985 Act and of the provisions of the Company Directors Disqualification Act 1986 to limited liability partnerships

(1)  The provisions of the 1985 Act specified in the first column of Part I of Schedule 2 to these Regulations shall apply to limited liability partnerships, except where the context otherwise requires, with the following modifications—

    (a)  references to a company shall include references to a limited liability partnership;

    (b)  references to the Companies Acts shall include references to the principal Act and regulations made thereunder;

    (c)  references to the Insolvency Act 1986 shall include references to that Act as it applies to limited liability partnerships by virtue of Part IV of these Regulations;

    (d)  references in a provision of the 1985 Act to other provisions of that Act shall include references to those other provisions as they apply to limited liability partnerships by virtue of these Regulations;

(e) references to the memorandum of association of a company shall include references to the incorporation document of a limited liability partnership;

(f) references to a shadow director shall include references to a shadow member;

(g) references to a director of a company or to an officer of a company shall include references to a member of a limited liability partnership;

(h) the modifications, if any, specified in the second column of Part I of Schedule 2 opposite the provision specified in the first column; and

(i) such further modifications as the context requires for the purpose of giving effect to that legislation as applied by these Regulations.

(2) The provisions of the Company Director Disqualification Act 1986 shall apply to limited liability partnerships, except where the context otherwise requires, with the following modifications—

(a) references to a company shall include references to a limited liability partnership;

(b) references to the Companies Acts shall include references to the principal Act and regulations made thereunder and references to the companies legislation shall include references to the principal Act, regulations made thereunder and to any enactment applied by regulations to limited liability partnerships;

(d) references to the Insolvency Act 1986 shall include references to that Act as it applies to limited liability partnerships by virtue of Part IV of these Regulations;

(e) references to the memorandum of association of a company shall include references to the incorporation document of a limited liability partnership;

(f) references to a shadow director shall include references to a shadow member;

(g) references to a director of a company or to an officer of a company shall include references to a member of a limited liability partnership;

(h) the modifications, if any, specified in the second column of Part II of Schedule 2 opposite the provision specified in the first column; and

(i) such further modifications as the context requires for the purpose of giving effect to that legislation as applied by these Regulations.

## PART IV   WINDING UP AND INSOLVENCY

### 5   Application of the 1986 Act to limited liability partnerships

(1) Subject to paragraphs (2) and (3), the following provisions of the 1986 Act, shall apply to limited liability partnerships—

(a) Parts I, II, III, IV, VI and VII of the First Group of Parts (company insolvency; companies winding up),

(b) the Third Group of Parts (miscellaneous matters bearing on both company and individual insolvency; general interpretation; final provisions).

(2) The provisions of the 1986 Act referred to in paragraph (1) shall apply to limited liability partnerships, except where the context otherwise requires, with the following modifications—

(a) references to a company shall include references to a limited liability partnership;

(b) references to a director or to an officer of a company shall include references to a member of a limited liability partnership;

(c) references to a shadow director shall include references to a shadow member;

(d) references to the 1985 Act, the Company Directors Disqualification Act 1986, the Companies Act 1989 or to any provisions of those Acts or to any provisions of the 1986 Act shall include references to those Acts or provisions as they apply to limited liability partnerships by virtue of the principal Act;

(e) references to the memorandum of association of a company and to the articles of association of a company shall include references to the limited liability partnership agreement of a limited liability partnership;

(f) the modifications set out in Schedule 3 to these Regulations; and

(g) such further modifications as the context requires for the purpose of giving effect to that legislation as applied by these Regulations.

(3) In the application of this regulation to Scotland, the provisions of the 1986 Act referred to in paragraph (1) shall not include the provisions listed in Schedule 4 to the extent specified in that Schedule.

## PART V   FINANCIAL SERVICES AND MARKETS

### 6   Application of provisions contained in Parts XV and XXIV of the 2000 Act to limited liability partnerships

(1) Subject to paragraph (2), sections 215(3),(4) and (6), 356, 359(1) to (4), 361 to 365, 367, 370 and 371 of the 2000 Act shall apply to limited liability partnerships.

(2) The provisions of the 2000 Act referred to in paragraph (1) shall apply to limited liability partnerships, except where the context otherwise requires, with the following modifications—

(a) references to a company shall include references to a limited liability partnership;

(b) references to body shall include references to a limited liability partnership; and

(c) references to the 1985 Act, the 1986 Act or to any of the provisions of those Acts shall include references to those Acts or provisions as they apply to limited liability partnerships by virtue of the principal Act.

# PART VI    DEFAULT PROVISION

## 7    Default provision for limited liability partnerships

The mutual rights and duties of the members and the mutual rights and duties of the limited liability partnership and the members shall be determined, subject to the provisions of the general law and to the terms of any limited liability partnership agreement, by the following rules:

(1) All the members of a limited liability partnership are entitled to share equally in the capital and profits of the limited liability partnership.

(2) The limited liability partnership must indemnify each member in respect of payments made and personal liabilities incurred by him—

(a) in the ordinary and proper conduct of the business of the limited liability partnership; or

(b) in or about anything necessarily done for the preservation of the business or property of the limited liability partnership.

(3) Every member may take part in the management of the limited liability partnership.

(4) No member shall be entitled to remuneration for acting in the business or management of the limited liability partnership.

(5) No person may be introduced as a member or voluntarily assign an interest in a limited liability partnership without the consent of all existing members.

(6) Any difference arising as to ordinary matters connected with the business of the limited liability partnership may be decided by a majority of the members, but no change may be made in the nature of the business of the limited liability partnership without the consent of all the members.

(7) The books and records of the limited liability partnership are to be made available for inspection at the registered office of the limited liability partnership or at such other place as the members think fit and every member of the limited liability partnership may when he thinks fit have access to and inspect and copy any of them.

(8) Each member shall render true accounts and full information of all things affecting the limited liability partnership to any member or his legal representatives.

(9) If a member, without the consent of the limited liability partnership, carries on any business of the same nature as and competing with the limited liability partnership, he must account for and pay over to the limited liability partnership all profits made by him in that business.

(10) Every member must account to the limited liability partnership for any benefit derived by him without the consent of the limited liability partnership from any transaction concerning the limited liability partnership, or from any use by him of the property of the limited liability partnership, name or business connection.

## 8    Expulsion

No majority of the members can expel any member unless a power to do so has been conferred by express agreement between the members.

# PART VII    MISCELLANEOUS

## 9    General and consequential amendments

(1) Subject to paragraph (2), the enactments mentioned in Schedule 5 shall have effect subject to the amendments specified in that Schedule.

(2) In the application of this regulation to Scotland—

(a) paragraph 15 of Schedule 5 which amends section 110 of the 1986 Act shall not extend to Scotland; and

(b) paragraph 22 of Schedule 5 which applies to limited liability partnerships the culpable officer provisions in existing primary legislation shall not extend to Scotland insofar as it relates to matters which have not been reserved by Schedule 5 to the Scotland Act 1998.

## 10    Application of subordinate legislation

(1) The subordinate legislation specified in Schedule 6 shall apply as from time to time in force to limited liability partnerships and—

(a) in the case of the subordinate legislation listed in Part I of that Schedule with such modifications as the context requires for the purpose of giving effect to the provisions of the Companies Act 1985 which are applied by these Regulations;

(b) in the case of the subordinate legislation listed in Part II of that Schedule with such modifications as the context requires for the purpose of giving effect to the provisions of the Insolvency Act 1986 which are applied by these Regulations; and

(c) in the case of the subordinate legislation listed in Part III of that Schedule with such modifications as the context requires for the purpose of giving effect to the provisions of the
Business Names Act 1985 and the Company Directors Disqualification Act 1986 which are
applied by these Regulations.

(2) In the case of any conflict between any provision of the subordinate legislation applied by paragraph (1) and any provision of these Regulations, the latter shall prevail.

# SCHEDULE 1

[...]

# SCHEDULE 2

## PART I   MODIFICATIONS TO PROVISIONS OF THE 1985 ACT APPLIED TO LIMITED LIABILITY PARTNERSHIPS

| Provisions | Modifications |
| --- | --- |
| *Formalities of Carrying on Business* | |
| 24 (minimum membership for carrying on business) | In the first paragraph omit the words 'other than a private company limited by shares or by guarantee,'. |
| 36 (company contracts England and Wales) | |
| 36A (execution of documents England and Wales) | In subsection (4) for 'a director and the secretary of a company, or by two directors of a company,' substitute 'two members of a limited liability partnership'. |
| | In subsection (6) for 'a director and the secretary of a company, or by two directors of the company' substitute 'two members of a limited liability partnership'. |
| 36C (pre-incorporation contracts, deeds and obligations) | |
| 37 (bills of exchange and promissory notes) | |
| 38 (execution of deeds abroad) | |
| 39 (power of company to have official seal for use abroad) | In subsection (1), omit the words 'whose objects require or comprise the transaction of business in foreign countries may, if authorised by its articles' and before the word 'have' insert the word 'may'. |
| 41 (authentication of documents) | For 'director, secretary or other authorised officer' substitute 'member'. |
| 42 (events affecting a company's status) | |
| subsection (1) | In subsection (1), for 'other persons' substitute 'persons other than members of the limited liability partnership'. |
| subsection (1)(b) | In subsection (1)(b) omit the words 'or articles'. |
| subsection (1)(c) | Omit subsection (1)(c). |
| *Miscellaneous provisions about shares and debentures* | |
| 183 (transfer and registration) | |
| subsection (1) | Subsection (1), omit the words 'shares in or'. |
| | For the words 'company's articles' substitute 'limited liability partnership agreement.' |
| subsection (2) | Subsection (2), omit the words 'shareholder or' together with the words 'shares in or'. |
| subsection (3) | Omit subsection (3). |
| subsection (4) | Omit subsection (4). |
| subsection (5) | Omit the words 'shares or'. |
| 184 (certification of transfers) | |
| subsection (1) | Subsection (1), omit the words 'shares in or' together with the words 'shares or'. |
| 185 (duty of company as to issue of certificates) | |
| subsection (1) | Subsection (1), omit the words 'shares,' in each of the four places that it occurs. |
| subsection (3) | Omit subsection (3). |
| subsection (4) | Omit the words 'shares or' together with the words 'shares,'. |

| Provisions | Modifications |
|---|---|
| *Debentures* | |
| 190 (register of debenture holders) | |
| 191 (right to inspect register) | |
| subsection (1) | In subsection (1), paragraph (a), for the words 'or any holder of shares in the company' substitute 'or any member of the limited liability partnership'. |
| subsection (2) | In subsection (2), delete 'or holder of shares'. |
| subsection (6) | In subsection (6), delete the words 'in the articles or'. |
| 192 (liability of trustees of debentures) | |
| 193 (perpetual debentures) | |
| 194 (power to re-issue redeemed debentures) | |
| subsection (1)(a) | In subsection (1)(a), omit the words 'in the articles or'. |
| subsection (1)(b) | In subsection (1)(b), for 'passing a resolution' substitute 'making a determination'. |
| 195 (contract to subscribe for debentures) | |
| 196 (payment of debts out of assets subject to floating charge (England and Wales)) | |
| *Officers and registered office* | |
| 287 (registered office) | For section 287 there shall be substituted: |
| | '(1) The change of registered office takes effect upon the notice of change of registered office (delivered to the registrar in accordance with paragraph 10 of the Schedule to the Limited Liability Partnerships Act 2000), being registered by the registrar, but until the end of the period of 14 days beginning with the date on which it is registered a person may validly serve any document on the limited liability partnership at its previous registered office. |
| | (2) Where a limited liability partnership unavoidably ceases to perform at its registered office any duty to keep at its registered office any register, index or other document or to mention the address of its registered office in any document in circumstances in which it was not practicable to give prior notice to the registrar of a change in the situation of the registered office, but— |
| |     (a) resumes performance of that duty at other premises as soon as practicable, and |
| |     (b) gives notice accordingly to the registrar of a change in the situation of its registered office within 14 days of doing so it shall not be treated as having failed to comply with that duty'. |
| 288 (register of directors and secretaries) | For section 288 there shall be substituted: |
| | 'Where a person becomes a member or designated member of a limited liability partnership the notice to be delivered to the registrar under section 9(1)(a) of the Limited Liability Partnerships Act 2000 shall contain the following particulars with respect to that person: |
| | (1) name, which |
| |     (a) in the case of an individual means his forename and surname (or, in the case of a peer or other person usually known by a title, his title instead of or in addition to either or both his forename and surname), and |
| |     (b) if a corporation or a Scottish firm, its corporate or firm name; and |
| | (2) address, which |
| |     (a) in the case of an individual means his usual residential address; and |
| |     (b) if a corporation or a Scottish firm, its registered or principal office; and |
| | (3) in the case of an individual, the date of his birth.' |
| *Company Identification* | |
| 348 (company name to appear outside place of business) | |
| 349 (company's name to appear in its correspondence) | |
| 350 (company seal) | |

| Provisions | Modifications |
|---|---|
| 351 (particulars in correspondence etc.) | In subsection (1) for paragraph (c) substitute the words 'in the case of a limited liability partnership, whose name ends with the abbreviation 'llp', 'LLP', 'pac' or 'PAC', the fact that it is a limited liability partnership or a partneriaeth atebolrwydd cyfyngedig.'<br><br>Also in subsection (1) delete paragraph (d) and delete subsection (2). |
| *Annual Return* | |
| 363 (duty to deliver annual returns) | Section 363 of the 1985 Act shall apply to a limited liability partnership being modified so as to read as follows:<br><br>'(1) Every limited liability partnership shall deliver to the registrar successive annual returns each of which is made up to a date not later than the date which is from time to time the 'return date' of the limited liability partnership, that is—<br><br>(a) the anniversary of the incorporation of the limited liability partnership, or<br><br>(b) if the last return delivered by the limited liability partnership in accordance with this section was made up to a different date, the anniversary of that date.<br><br>(2) Each return shall—<br><br>(a) be in a form approved by the registrar,<br><br>(b) contain the information required by section 364, and<br><br>(c) be signed by a designated member of the limited liability partnership.<br><br>(3) If a limited liability partnership fails to deliver an annual return in accordance with this section before the end of the period of 28 days after the return date, the limited liability partnership is guilty of an offence and liable on summary conviction to a fine not exceeding level 5 on the standard scale. The contravention continues until such time as an annual return made up to that return date and complying with the requirements of subsection (2)(except as to date of delivery) is delivered by the limited liability partnership to the registrar.<br><br>(4) Where a limited liability partnership is guilty of an offence under subsection (3) every designated member of the limited liability partnership is similarly liable unless he shows that he took all reasonable steps to avoid the commission of or the continuance of the offence.' |
| 364 (contents of annual return: general) | For section 364 substitute the following—<br><br>'Every annual return shall state the date to which it is made up and shall contain the following information—<br><br>(a) the address of the registered office of the limited liability partnership,<br><br>(b) the names and usual residential addresses of the members of the limited liability partnership and, if some only of them are designated members, which of them are designated members, and<br><br>(c) if any register of debenture holders (or a duplicate of any such register or a part of it) is not kept at the registered office of the limited liability partnership, the address of the place where it is kept.' |
| *Auditors* | |
| *Registration of charges* | |
| The following references are to sections of the 1985 Act which were replaced by section 92 of the Companies Act 1989. They will apply to limited liability partnerships until the said section 92 is commenced. | |
| 395 (certain charges void if not registered) | |
| 396 (charges which have to be registered) | In subsection (1) delete paragraphs (b) and (g). |
| 397 (formalities of registration (debentures)) | In subsection (1), paragraph (b) for the word 'resolutions' substitute 'determinations of the limited liability partnership'. |
| 398 (verification of charge on property outside United Kingdom) | |
| 399 (company's duty to register charges it creates) | |
| 400 (charges existing on property acquired) | |
| 401 (register of charges to be kept by registrar of companies) | |

| Provisions | Modifications |
| --- | --- |
| 402 (endorsement of certificate on debentures) | |
| 403 (entries of satisfaction and release) | In subsection (1A), after 'of the company' insert 'or designated member, administrator or administrative receiver of the limited liability partnership'. |
| 404 (rectification of register of charges) | In subsection (1), omit the words 'or shareholders'. |
| 405 (registration of enforcement of security) | |
| 406 (companies to keep copies of instruments creating charges) | |
| 407 (company's register of charges) | In subsection (1), for 'limited company' substitute 'company (including limited liability partnership)'. |
| 408 (right to inspect instruments which create charges etc.) | In subsection (1) delete 'in general meeting'. |
| 410 (charges void unless registered) | In subsection (4) delete paragraph (b) and sub-paragraph (ii) of paragraph (c). |
| | In subsection (5) for 'an incorporated company' substitute 'a limited liability partnership'. |
| 411 (charges on property outside the United Kingdom) | |
| 412 (negotiable instrument to secure book debts) | |
| 413 (charges associated with debentures) | In subsection (2)(b), for the word 'resolutions' substitute 'determinations of the limited liability partnership'. |
| 414 (charge by way of ex facie absolute disposition, etc.) | |
| 415 (company's duty to register charges created by it) | |
| 416 (duty to register charges existing on property acquired) | |
| 417 (register of charges to be kept by registrar of companies) | |
| 418 (certificate of registration to be issued) | |
| 419 (entries of satisfaction and relief) | In subsection (1A), after the words 'of the company' insert 'or a designated member, liquidator, receiver or administrative receiver of the limited liability partnership'. |
| 420 (rectification of the register) | Omit the words 'or shareholders'. |
| 421 (copies of instruments creating charges to be kept by the company) | |
| 422 (company's register of charges) | |
| 423 (right to inspect copies of instruments, and the company's register) | In subsection (1) delete 'in general meeting'. |
| *Arrangements and Reconstructions* | |
| 425 (power of company to compromise with creditors and members) | |
| subsection (3) | Omit the words 'and a copy of every such order shall be annexed to every copy of the company's memorandum issued after the order has been made or, in the case of a company not having a memorandum, of every copy so issued of the instrument constituting the company or defining its constitution.' For the semi-colon after the word 'registration' substitute a full stop. |
| subsection (6) | Omit subsection (6). |
| 426 (information as to compromise to be circulated) | |
| subsection (2) | Omit the words 'as directors or'. |
| 427 (provisions for facilitating company reconstruction or amalgamation) | |

| Provisions | Modifications |
|---|---|
| subsection (3) | In paragraph (b) for the words 'policies or other like interests' substitute 'policies, other like interests or, in the case of a limited liablity partnership, property or interests in the limited liability partnership'. |
| subsection (6) | For the words ' 'company' includes only a company as defined in section 735(1)' substitute "company' includes only a company as defined in section 735(1) or a limited liability partnership'. |

*Investigation of companies and their affairs: Requisition of documents*

| | |
|---|---|
| 431 (investigation of a company on its own application or that of its members) | For subsection (2) substitute the following: '(2) —The appointment may be made on the application of the limited liability partnership or on the application of not less than one-fifth in number of those who appear from notifications made to the registrar of companies to be currently members of the limited liability partnership.' |
| 432 (other company investigations) | |
| subsection (4) | For the words 'but to whom shares in the company have been transferred or transmitted by operation of law' substitute 'but to whom a member's share in the limited liability partnership has been transferred or transmitted by operation of law.' |
| 433 (inspectors' powers during investigation) | |
| 434 (production of documents and evidence to inspectors) | |
| 436 (obstruction of inspectors treated as contempt of court) | |
| 437 (inspectors' reports) | |
| 438 (power to bring civil proceedings on company's behalf) | |
| 439 (expenses of investigating a company's affairs) | |
| subsection (5) | Omit paragraph (b) together with the word 'or' at the end of paragraph (a). |
| 441 (inspectors' report to be evidence) | |
| 447 (Secretary of State's power torequire production of documents) | |
| 447A (Information provided: evidence | |
| 448 (entry and search of premises) | |
| 448A (protection in relation to certain disclosures: information provided to Secretary of State) | |
| 449 (provision for security of information obtained) | |
| 451 (punishment for furnishing false information) | |
| 451A (disclosure of information by Secretary of State or inspector) | In subsection (1), for the words 'sections 434 to 446' substitute 'sections 434 to 441'. Omit subsection (5). |
| 452 (privileged information) | In subsection (1) for the words 'sections 431 to 446' substitute 'sections 431 to 441'. |
| 453A (power to enter and remain on premises) | In subsection (7) for the words ' sections 431,432 or 442' substitute 'section 431 or 432' |
| 453B (power to enter and remain on premises) | |
| 453C (failure to comply with certain requirements) | In subsection (1A) for the words 'sections 434, 443 or 446' substitute 'section 434'. |

*Fraudulent Trading*

| | |
|---|---|
| 458 (punishment for fraudulent trading) | |

*Protection of company's members against unfair prejudice*

| Provisions | Modifications |
|---|---|
| 459 (order on application of company member) | At the beginning of subsection (1), insert the words 'Subject to subsection (1A)'. After subsection (1) insert as subsection (1A): |
| | 'The members of a limited liability partnership may by unanimous agreement exclude the right contained in subsection 459(1) for such period as shall be agreed. The agreement referred to in this subsection shall be recorded in writing.' |
| | Omit subsections (2) and (3). |
| 460 (order on application of Secretary of State) | Omit subsection (2). |
| 461 (provisions as to orders and petitions under this Part) | In subsection (2)(d) for the words 'the shares of any members of the company by other members or by the company itself and, in the case of a purchase by the company itself, the reduction of the company's capital accordingly' substitute the words 'the shares of any members in the limited liability partnership by other members or by the limited liability partnership itself.' |
| | In subsection (3) for the words 'memorandum or articles' substitute the words 'limited liability partnership agreement'. |
| | For the existing words of subsection (4) substitute the words 'Any alteration in the limited liability partnership agreement made by virtue of an order under this Part is of the same effect as if duly agreed by the members of the limited liability partnership and the provisions of this Act apply to the limited liability partnership agreement as so altered accordingly.' |
| | Omit subsection (5). |

*Floating charges and Receivers (Scotland)*

| Provisions | Modifications |
|---|---|
| 464 (ranking of floating charges) | In subsection (1), for the words 'section 462' substitute 'the law of Scotland'. |
| 466 (alteration of floating charges) | Omit subsections (1), (2), (3) and (6). |
| 486 (interpretation for Part XVIII generally) | For the current definition of 'company' substitute |
| | '"company" means a limited liability partnership;' |
| | Omit the definition of 'Register of Sasines'. |
| 487 (extent of Part XVIII) | |

*Matters arising subsequent to winding up*

| Provisions | Modifications |
|---|---|
| 651 (power of court to declare dissolution of company void) | |
| 652 (registrar may strike defunct company off the register) | In subsection (6) paragraph (a) omit the word 'director'. |
| 652A (registrar may strike private company off the register on application) | In this section the references to 'a private company' shall include a reference to 'a limited liability partnership'. |
| subsection (1) | In subsection (1) the following shall be substituted for the existing wording |
| | 'On application by two or more designated members of a limited liability partnership, the registrar of companies may strike the limited liability partnership's name off the register'. |
| | Omit subsection 2(a) and in subsection 2(b) after the word 'be' insert the word 'made'. |
| | In subsection (6), omit the word 'director'. |
| 652B (duties in connection with making an application under section 652A) | In paragraph (a) of subsection (5) for 'no meetings are' substitute 'no meeting is'. |
| | In paragraph (b) of subsection (5) for 'meetings summoned under that section fail' substitute 'the meeting summoned under that section fails'. |
| | In paragraph (c) of subsection (5) for 'meetings' substitute 'a meeting'. |
| | In paragraph (d) of subsection (5) for 'at previous meetings' substitute 'at a previous meeting'. |
| 652C (directors' duties following application under section 652A) | In subsection (2), for the words 'is a director of the company' substitute 'is a designated member of the limited liability partnership'. |
| | In subsection (2) omit paragraph (d). |
| | In subsection (5) for the words 'is a director of the company' substitute 'is a designated member of the limited liability partnership'. |
| | In subsection (6), omit paragraph (d). |
| 652D (sections 652B and 652C: supplementary provisions) | |

| Provisions | Modifications |
|---|---|
| 652E (sections 652B and 652C: enforcement) | |
| 652F (other offences connected with section 652A) | |
| 653 (objection to striking off by person aggrieved) | |
| 654 (property of dissolved company to be bona vacantia) | |
| 655 (effect on section 654 of company's revival after dissolution) | |
| 656 (crown disclaimer of property vesting as bona vacantia) | |
| 657 (effect of crown disclaimer under section 656) | |
| 658 (liability for rentcharge on company's land after dissolution) | |
| *Oversea Limited Liability Partnerships* | |
| 693 (obligation to state name and other particulars) | For the wording of subsection (1) there shall be substituted the following words: 'Every oversea limited liability partnership shall— (a) in every prospectus inviting subscriptions for its debentures in Great Britain, state the country in which the limited liability partnership is incorporated, (b) conspicuously exhibit on every place where it carries on business in Great Britain the name of the limited liability partnership and the country in which it is incorporated, (c) cause the name of the limited liability partnership and the country in which it is incorporated to be stated in legible characters in all bill heads, letter paper, and in all notices and other official publications and communications of the limited liability partnership.' For subsection (2) there shall be substituted the following words 'For the purposes of this section "oversea limited liability partnership" means a body incorporated or otherwise established outside Great Britain whose name under its law of incorporation or establishment includes the words "limited liability partnership."' Subsections (3) and (4) shall be omitted. |
| *The Registrar of Companies: His functions and offices* | |
| 704 (registration offices) | |
| 705 (companies' registered numbers) | Omit subsection (5). |
| 706 (delivery to the registrar of documents in legible form) | In subsection (2)(a), omit the words from 'and, if the document is delivered' to the end of that paragraph. |
| 707A (the keeping of company records by the registrar) | Omit subsection (4). |
| 707B (delivery to the registrar using electronic communications) | In subsection (3), omit the 'or' at the end of paragraph (a) and omit paragraph (b). |
| 708 (fees payable to the registrar) | |
| 709 (inspection of records kept by the registrar) | |
| 710 (certificate of incorporation) | |
| 710A (provision and authentication by registrar of documents in non-legible form) | |
| 710B (documents relating to Welsh companies) | In subsection (7), omit the words '272(5) and 273(7) and paragraph 7(3) of Part II of Schedule 9'. |
| 711 (public notice by registrar of receipt and issue of certain documents) | In subsection (1) delete 'or articles' in paragraph (b) and delete paragraphs (d) to ( j), (l), (m) and (s) to (z). |
| 713 (enforcement of company's duty to make returns) | In subsection (1), in the penultimate line for 'any officer' substitute 'any designated member'. In subsections (2) and (3) for 'officers' substitute 'designated members'. |
| 714 (registrar's index of company and corporate names) | |

| Provisions | Modifications |
| --- | --- |
| 715A (interpretation) | |
| *Miscellaneous and supplementary provisions* | |
| 721 (production and inspection of books where offence suspected) | In subsection (2)(b), for the words 'the secretary of the company or such other' substitute 'such'. |
| 722 (form of company registers, etc.) | |
| 723 (use of computers for company records) | Omit subsection (2). |
| 723A (obligations of company as to inspections of registers, & etc.) | |
| 725 (service of documents) | In subsection (2), for the words 'other head officer' substitute 'a designated member'. |
| 726 (costs and expenses in actions by certain limited companies) | References to a 'limited company' shall include references to a 'limited liability partnership'. |
| 727 (power of court to grant relief in certain cases) | In subsection (1) delete the words 'an officer of a company or' and 'officer or'. In subsection (2), delete the words 'officer or'. |
| 728 (enforcement of High Court orders) | |
| 729 (annual report by Secretary of State) | |
| 730 (punishment of offences) | |
| 731 (summary proceedings) | |
| 732 (prosecution by public authorities) | Delete the references to sections 210, 324, 329 and 455. Omit subsection (2) paragraphs (a) and (c). In subsection (2)(b), for the words 'either one of those two persons' substitute 'either the Secretary of State, the Director of Public Prosecutions'. Omit subsection (3). |
| 733 (offences by bodies corporate) | |
| subsection (1) | In subsection (1), delete the references to section 210 and 216(3). |
| subsection (2) | In subsection (2), omit the word 'secretary'. |
| subsection (3) | Omit subsection (3). |
| 734 (criminal proceedings against unincorporated bodies) | |
| *Interpretation* | |
| 735A (relationship of this Act to the Insolvency Act) | In subsection (1), delete all the references to provisions of the 1985 Act other than the references to sections 425(6)(a), 460(2) and 728. |
| 736 ('subsidiary', 'holding company', and 'wholly-owned subsidiary') | |
| subsection (1) | For subsection (1) there shall be substituted the following words: '(1) Subject to subsection (1A), a company is a subsidiary of a limited liability partnership, its 'holding company', if that limited liability partnership— (a) holds a majority of the voting rights in it, or (b) is a member of it and has the right to appoint or remove a majority of its board of directors, or (c) is a member of it and controls alone, pursuant to an agreement with other shareholders or members, a majority of the voting rights in it, or if it is a subsidiary of a company or limited liability partnership which is itself a subsidiary of that other company.' |
| subsection (1A) | Insert as subsection (1A)— '(1A) A limited liability partnership is a subsidiary of a company or a subsidiary of another limited liability partnership, (such company or limited liability partnership being referred to in this section as its 'holding company') if that company or limited liability partnership— (a) holds a majority of the voting rights in it; (b) is a member of it and has the right to appoint or remove a majority of other members; or (c) is a member of it and controls, alone or pursuant to an agreement with other members, a majority of voting rights in it, or if it is a subsidiary of a company or limited liability partnership which is itself a subsidiary of that holding company'. |

| Provisions | Modifications |
|---|---|
| subsection (2) | For subsection (2) substitute 'A company or a limited liability partnership is a "wholly-owned subsidiary" of another company or limited liability partnership if it has no members except that other and that other's wholly-owned subsidiaries or persons acting on behalf of that other or its wholly-owned subsidiaries.' |
| 736A (provisions supplementing section 736) | After subsection (1) insert a new subsection (1A) in the following form—<br><br>'(1A) In section 736(1A)(a) and (c) the references to the voting rights in a limited liability partnership are to the rights conferred on members in respect of their interest in the limited liability partnership to vote on those matters which are to be decided upon by a vote of the members of the limited liability partnership.'<br><br>After subsection (2) insert the new subsection (2A) in the following form—<br><br>'(2A) In section 736(1A)(b) the reference to the right to appoint or remove a majority of the members of the limited liability partnership is to the right to appoint or remove members holding a majority of the voting rights referred to in subsection (1A) and for this purpose—<br><br>    (a)  a person shall be treated as having the right to appoint a member if<br><br>        (i)  a person's appointment as member results directly from his appointment as a director or member of the holding company, or<br><br>        (ii)  the member of the limited liability partnership is the company or limited liability partnership which is the holding company; and<br><br>    (b)  a right to appoint or remove which is exercisable only with the consent or concurrence of another person shall be left out of account.'<br><br>In subsection (7) after the words 'Rights attached to shares' insert the words 'or to a member's interest in a limited liability partnership'.<br><br>In subsection (8) after the words 'held by a company', in both places where they occur, insert 'or a limited liability partnership'.<br><br>In subsection (9) after the words 'in the interest of company' insert 'or a limited liability partnership' and after the words 'that company' in both places where they occur insert<br><br>'or limited liability partnership'.<br><br>In subsection (10) after the words 'a company' insert the words 'or a limited liability partnership' and after the words 'by the company' insert the words<br><br>'or the limited liability partnership'.<br><br>In subsection (12) for the existing words substitute 'In this section 'company' includes a body corporate other than a limited liability partnership.' |
| 739 ( 'non-cash asset') | |
| 740 ( 'body corporate' and 'corporation') | |
| 741 ( 'director' and 'shadow director') | Omit subsection (3). |
| 743A (meaning of 'office copy' in Scotland) | |
| 744 (expressions used generally in this Act) | Delete the definitions of expressions not used in provisions which apply to limited liability partnerships and insert the following definitions—<br><br>'"limited liability partnership" has the meaning given it in section 1(2) of the Limited Liability Partnerships Act 2000.'<br><br>'shadow member' has the same meaning as it has in the Limited Liability Partnerships Regulations 2000. |
| 744A (index of defined expressions) | Delete the references to expressions not used in provisions which apply to limited liability partnerships including, in particular, the following expressions:<br><br>Allotment (and related expressions)<br><br>Section 738<br><br>Annual general meeting<br><br>Section 366<br><br>Authorised minimum |

| Provisions | Modifications |
|---|---|
| | Section 118 |
| | Called up share capital |
| | Section 737(1) |
| | Capital redemption reserve Section 170(1) |
| | Elective resolution |
| | Section 379A |
| | Employees' share scheme |
| | Section 743 |
| | Existing company |
| | Section 735(1) |
| | Extraordinary general meeting |
| | Section 368 |
| | Extraordinary resolution |
| | Section 378(1) |
| | The former Companies Acts |
| | Section 735(1) |
| | The Joint Stock Companies Acts |
| | Section 735(3) |
| | Overseas branch register |
| | Section 362 |
| | Paid up (and related expressions) |
| | Section 738 |
| | Registered office (of a company) |
| | Section 287 |
| | Resolution for reducing share capital |
| | Section 135(3) |
| | Share premium account |
| | Section 130(1) |
| | Share warrant |
| | Section 188 |
| | Special notice (in relation to a resolution) |
| | Section 379 |
| | Special resolution |
| | Section 378(2) |
| | Uncalled share capital |
| | Section 737(2) |
| | Undistributable reserves |
| | Section 264(3) |
| | Unlimited company |
| | Section 1(2) |
| | Unregistered company |
| | Section 718 |
| Schedule 15C (security of information obtained: specified persons) | |
| Schedule 15D (security of information obtained: specified disclosures) | |
| SCHEDULE 24 (PUNISHMENT OF OFFENCES UNDER THIS ACT) | Delete the references to those sections which are not applied to limited liability partnerships including, in particular, the following sections: |
| | Section 6(3) company failing to deliver to the registrar notice or other document, following alteration of its objects; |
| | Section 18(3) company failing to register change in memorandum or articles; |

| Provisions | Modifications |
| --- | --- |
| | Section 19(2) company failing to send to one of its members a copy of the memorandum or articles, when so required by the member; |
| | Section 20(2) where company's memorandum altered, company issuing copy of the memorandum without the alteration; |
| | Section 28(5) company failing to change name on direction of Secretary of State; |
| | Section 31(5) company altering its memorandum or articles, so ceasing to be exempt from having 'limited' after its name; |
| | Section 31(6) company failing to change name, on Secretary of State's direction, so as to have 'limited' (or Welsh equivalent) at the end; |
| | Section 32(4) company failing to comply with the Secretary of State's direction to change its name, on grounds that the name is misleading; |
| | Section 33 trading under misleading name (use of 'public limited company' or Welsh equivalent when not so entitled); purporting to be a private company; |
| | Section 34 trading or carrying on business with improper use of 'limited' or 'cyfyngedig'; |
| | Section 54(10) public company failing to give notice, or copy of court order, to registrar, concerning application to re-register as private company; |
| | Section 80(9) directors exercising company's power of allotment without the authority required by section 80(1); |
| | Section 81(2) private company offering shares to the public, or allotting shares with a view to their being so offered; |
| | Section 82(5) allotting shares or debentures before third day after issue of prospectus; |
| | Section 86(6) company failing to keep money in separate bank account, where received in pursuance of prospectus stating that stock exchange listing is to be applied for; |
| | Section 87(4) offeror of shares for sale failing to keep proceeds in separate bank account; |
| | Section 88(5) officer of company failing to deliver return of allotments, etc. to the registrar; |
| | Section 95(6) knowingly or recklessly authorising or permitting misleading, false or deceptive material in statement by directors under section 95(5); |
| | Section 97(4) company failing to deliver to registrar the prescribed form disclosing amount or rate of share commission; |
| | Section 110(2) making misleading, false or deceptive statement in connection with valuation under section 103 or 104; |
| | Section 111(3) officer of company failing to deliver copy of asset valuation report to registrar; |
| | Section 111(4) company failing to deliver to registrar copy of resolution under Section 104(4), with respect to transfer of an asset as consideration for allotment; |
| | Section 114 contravention of any of the provisions of sections 99 to 104, 106; |
| | Section 117(7) company doing business or exercising borrowing powers contrary to section 117; |
| | Section 122(2) company failing to give notice to registrar of reorganisation of share capital; |
| | Section 123(4) company failing to give notice to registrar of increase of share capital; |
| | Section 127(5) company failing to forward to registrar copy of court order, when application made to cancel resolution varying shareholders' rights; |
| | Section 128(5) company failing to send to registrar statement or notice required by section 128 (particulars of shares carrying special rights); |
| | Section 129(4) company failing to deliver to registrar statement or notice required by section 129 (registration of newly created class rights); |
| | Section 141 officer of company concealing name of creditor entitled to object to reduction of capital, or wilfully misrepresenting the nature or amount of debt or claim, etc.; |

| Provisions | Modifications |
| --- | --- |
| | Section 142(2) director authorising or permitting non-compliance with section 142 (requirement to convene company meeting to consider serious loss of capital); |
| | Section 143(2) company acquiring its own shares in breach of section 143; |
| | Section 149(2) company failing to cancel its own shares acquired by itself, as required by section 146(2); or failing to apply for re-registration as private company as so required in the case there mentioned; |
| | Section 151(3) company giving financial assistance towards acquisition of its own shares; |
| | Section 156(6) company failing to register statutory declaration under section 155; |
| | Section 156(7) director making statutory declaration under section 155, without having reasonable grounds for opinion expressed in it; |
| | Section 169(6) default by company's officer in delivering to registrar the return required by section 169 (disclosure by company of purchase of its own shares); |
| | Section 169(7) company failing to keep copy of contract, etc., at registered office; refusal of inspection to person demanding it; |
| | Section 173(6) director making statutory declaration under section 173 without having reasonable grounds for the opinion expressed in the declaration; |
| | Section 175(7) refusal of inspection of statutory declaration and auditor's report under section 173, etc.; |
| | Section 176(4) company failing to give notice to registrar of application to court under section 176, or to register court order; |
| | Section 183(6) company failing to send notice of refusal to register a transfer of shares or debentures; |
| | Section 185(5) company default in compliance with section 185(1) (certificates to be made ready following allotment or transfer of shares, etc.); |
| | Section 189(1) offences of fraud and forgery in connection with share warrants in Scotland; |
| | Section 189(2) unauthorised making of, or using or possessing apparatus for making share warrants in Scotland; |
| | Section 210(3) failure to discharge obligation of disclosure under Part VI; other forms of non-compliance with that Part; |
| | Section 211(10) company failing to keep register of interests disclosed under Part IV; other contraventions of section 211; |
| | Section 214(5) company failing to exercise powers under section 212, when so required by the members; |
| | Section 215(8) company default in compliance with section 215 (company report of investigation of shareholdings on members' requisition); |
| | Section 216(3) failure to comply with company notice under section 212; |
| | Making false statement in response etc.; |
| | Section 217(7) company failing to notify a person that he has been named as a shareholder; on removal of name from register, failing to alter associated index; |
| | Section 218(3) improper removal of entry from register of interests disclosed; |
| | company failing to restore entry improperly removed; |
| | Section 219(3) refusal of inspection of register or report under Part VI; failure to send copy when required; |
| | Section 232(4) default by director or officer of a company in giving notice of matters relating to himself for purposes of Schedule 6 Part I; |
| | Section 234(5) non-compliance with Part VII as to directors' report and its content; |
| | directors individually liable; |
| | Section 234A(4) laying, circulating or delivering directors' report without required signature; |
| | Section 241(2) failure to lay accounts and reports before the company in general meeting before the end of the period allowed for doing this; |
| | Section 251(6) failure to comply with requirements in relation to summary financial statements; |

| Provisions | Modifications |
|---|---|
| | Section 288(4) default in complying with section 288 (keeping register of directors and secretaries, refusal of inspection); |
| | Section 291(5) acting as director of a company without having the requisite share qualification; |
| | Section 294(3) director failing to give notice of his attaining retirement age; |
| | acting as director under appointment invalid due to his attaining it; |
| | Section 305(3) company default in complying with section 305 (directors' name to appear on company correspondence, etc.); |
| | Section 306(4) failure to state that liability of proposed director or manager is unlimited; failure to give notice of that fact to person accepting office; |
| | Section 314(3) director failing to comply with section 314; |
| | Section 317(7) director failing to disclose interest in contract; |
| | Section 318(8) company in default in complying with section 318(1) or (5); |
| | Section 322B(4) terms of unwritten contract between sole member of a private company limited by shares or by guarantee and the company not set out in a written memorandum or recorded in minutes of a directors' meeting; |
| | Section 323(2) director dealing in options to buy or sell company's listed shares or debentures; |
| | Section 324(7) director failing to notify interest in company's shares; making false statement in purported notification; |
| | Section 326(2), (3), (4) and (5) various defaults in connection with company register of directors' interests; |
| | Section 328(6) director failing to notify company that members of his family etc. have or have exercised options to buy shares or debentures; making false statement in purported notification; |
| | Section 329(3) company failing to notify investment exchange of acquisition of its securities by a director; |
| | Section 342(1) director or relevant company authorising or permitting company to enter into transaction or arrangement, knowing or suspecting it to contravene section 330; |
| | Section 342(2) relevant company entering into transaction or arrangement for a director in contravention of section 330; |
| | Section 342(3) procuring a relevant company to enter into transaction or arrangement known to be contrary to section 330; |
| | Section 343(8) company failing to maintain register of transactions etc. made with and for directors and not disclosed in company accounts; failing to make register available at registered office or at company meeting; |
| | Section 352(5) company default in complying with section 352 (requirement to keep register of members and their particulars); |
| | Section 352A(3) company default in complying with section 352A (statement that company has only one member); |
| | Section 353(4) company failing to send notice to registrar as to place where register of members is kept; |
| | Section 354(4) company failing to keep index of members; |
| | Section 356(5) refusal of inspection of members' register; failure to send copy on requisition; |
| | Section 364(4) company without share capital failing to complete and register annual return in due time; |
| | Section 366(4) company default in holding annual general meeting; |
| | Section 367(3) company default in complying with Secretary of State's direction to hold a company meeting; |
| | Section 367(5) company failing to register resolution that meeting held under section 367 is to be its annual general meeting; |
| | Section 372(4) failure to give notice, to member entitled to vote at company meeting, that he may do so by proxy; |
| | Section 372(6) officer of company authorising or permitting issue of irregular invitations to appoint proxies; |

| Provisions | Modifications |
|---|---|
| | Section 376(7) officer of company in default as to circulation of members' resolutions for company meeting; |
| | Section 380(5) company failing to comply with section 380 (copies of certain resolutions etc. to be sent to registrar of companies); |
| | Section 380(6) company failing to include copy of resolution to which section 380 applies in articles; failing to forward copy to member on request; |
| | Section 381B(2) director or secretary of company failing to notify auditors of proposed written resolution; |
| | Section 382(5) company failing to keep minutes of proceedings at company and board meetings, etc.; |
| | Section 382B(2) failure of sole member to provide the company with a written record of a decision; |
| | Section 383(4) refusal of inspection of minutes of general meeting; failure to send copy of minutes on member's request; |
| | Section 389(10) person acting as a company auditor knowing himself to be disqualified: failing to give notice vacating office when he becomes disqualified; |
| | Section 429(6) offeror failing to send copy of notice or making statutory declaration knowing it to be false etc.; |
| | Section 430A(6) offeror failing to give rights to minority shareholder; |
| | Section 444(3) failing to give Secretary of State, when required to do so, information about interests in shares etc.; giving false information; |
| | Section 455(1) exercising a right to dispose of, or vote in respect of, shares which are subject to restrictions under Part XV; failing to give notice in respect of shares so subject; entering into agreement void under section 454(2), (3); |
| | Section 455(2) issuing shares in contravention of restrictions under Part XV; |
| | Section 461(5) failure to register office copy of court order under Part XVII altering, or giving leave to alter, company's memorandum; |
| | Section 697(1) oversea company failing to comply with any of sections 691 to 693 or 696; |
| | Section 697(2) oversea company contravening section 694(6)(carrying on business under its corporate name after Secretary of State's direction); |
| | Section 697(3) oversea company failing to comply with section 695A or Schedule 21A; |
| | Section 703(1) oversea company failing to comply with requirements as to accounts and reports; |
| | Section 703D(5) oversea company failing to deliver particulars of charge to registrar; |
| | Section 703R(1) company failing to register winding up or commencement of insolvency proceedings etc.; |
| | Section 703R(2) liquidator failing to register appointment, termination of winding up or striking off of company; |
| | Section 720(4) insurance company etc. failing to send twice yearly statement in form of Schedule 23; |
| | Schedule 14, Pt II, paragraph 1(3) company failing to give notice of location of overseas branch register, etc.; |
| | Schedule 14, Pt II, paragraph 4(2) company failing to transmit to its registered office in Great Britain copies of entries in overseas branch register or to keep duplicate of overseas branch register.; |
| | Schedule 21C, Pt I, paragraph 7 credit or financial institution failing to deliver accounting documents; |
| | Schedule 21C, Pt II, paragraph 15 credit or financial institution failing to deliver accounts and reports; |
| | Schedule 21D, Pt I, paragraph 5 company failing to deliver accounting documents; |
| | Schedule 21D, Pt I, Paragraph 13 company failing to deliver accounts and reports. |

## PART II   MODIFICATIONS TO THE COMPANY DIRECTORS DISQUALIFICATION ACT 1986

| | |
|---|---|
| Part II of Schedule I | After paragraph 8 insert—<br><br>'**8A** The extent of the member's and shadow members' responsibility for events leading to a member or shadow member, whether himself or some other member or shadow member, being declared by the court to be liable to make a contribution to the assets of the limited liability partnership under section 214A of the Insolvency Act 1986.' |

# SCHEDULE 3

# MODIFICATIONS TO THE 1986 ACT

| Provisions | Modifications |
|---|---|
| Section 1 (those who may propose an arrangement) | |
| subsection (1) | For 'The directors of a company' substitute 'A limited liability partnership' and delete 'to the company and'. |
| subsection (3) | At the end add 'but where a proposal is so made it must also be made to the limited liability partnership'. |
| Section 1A (moratorium) | |
| Subsection (1) | For 'the directors of an eligible company intend' substitute 'an eligible limited liability partnership intends'<br><br>For 'they' substitute 'it'. |
| The following modifications to sections 2 to 7 apply where a proposal under section 1 has been made by the limited liability partnership. | |
| Section 2 (procedure where the nominee is not the liquidator or administrator) | |
| subsection (1) | For 'the directors do' substitute 'the limited liability partnership does' |
| subsection (2) | In paragraph (a) for 'meetings of the company and of it creditors' substitute 'a meeting of the creditors of the limited liability partnership';<br><br>In paragraph (b) for the first 'meetings' substitute 'a meeting' and for the second 'meetings' substitute 'meeting'. |
| subsection (3) | For 'the person intending to make the proposal' substitute 'the designated members of the limited liability partnership'. |
| subsection (4) | For 'the person intending to make the proposal' substitute 'the designated members of the limited liability partnership'. |
| Section 3 (summoning of meetings) | |
| subsection (1) | For 'such meetings as are mentioned in section 2(2)' substitute 'a meeting of creditors' and for 'those meetings' substitute 'that meeting'. |
| subsection (2) | Delete subsection (2). |
| Section 4 (decisions of meetings) | |
| subsection (1) | For 'meetings' substitute 'meeting'. |
| subsection (5) | For 'each of the meetings' substitute 'the meeting'. |
| new subsection (5A) | Insert a new subsection (5A) as follows—<br><br>'(5A) If modifications to the proposal are proposed at the meeting the chairman of the meeting shall, before the conclusion of the meeting, ascertain from the limited liability partnership whether or not it accepts the proposed modifications; and if at that conclusion the limited liability partnership has failed to respond to a proposed modification it shall be presumed not to have agreed to it.' |
| subsection (6) | For 'either' substitute 'the'; after 'the result of the meeting', in the first place where it occurs, insert '(including, where modifications to the proposal were proposed at the meeting, the response to those proposed modifications made by the limited liability partnership)'; and at the end add 'and to the limited liability partnership'. |
| Section 4A (approval of arrangement) | |
| subsection (2) | Omit '(a)'<br><br>For 'both meetings' substitute 'the meeting'<br><br>Omit the words from 'or' to 'that section' |

| Provisions | Modifications |
| --- | --- |
| subsection (3) | Omit |
| subsection (4) | Omit |
| subsection (5) | Omit |
| subsection (6) | Omit |
| Section 5 (effect of approval) | |
| [...] | |
| subsection (4) | For 'each of the reports' substitute 'the report'. |
| Section 6 (challenge of decisions) | |
| subsection (1) | For 'meetings' substitute 'meeting' and for 'either of the meetings' substitute 'the meeting'. |
| subsection (2) | For 'either of the meetings' substitute 'the meeting' and after paragraph (aa) add a new paragraph (ab) as follows— |
| | '(ab) any member of the limited liability partnership; and'. |
| | Omit the word 'and' at the end of paragraph (b) and omit paragraph (c). |
| subsection (3) | For 'each of the reports' substitute 'the report'. |
| subsection (4) | For subsection (4) substitute the following— |
| | '(4) Where on such an application the court is satisfied as to either of the grounds mentioned in subsection (1), it may do one or both of the following, namely— |
| | (a) revoke or suspend the approval given by the meeting; |
| | (b) give a direction to any person for the summoning of a further meeting to consider any revised proposal the limited liability partnership may make or, in a case falling within subsection (1)(b), a further meeting to consider the original proposal.'. |
| subsection (5) | For [...] 'meetings' substitute 'a meeting', [...] and for 'person who made the original proposal' substitute 'limited liability partnership'. |
| Section 6A (false representations, etc) | |
| subsection (1) | Omit 'members or' |
| Section 7 (implementation of proposal) | |
| [...] | |
| subsection (2) | In paragraph (a) omit 'one or both of' and for 'meetings' substitute 'meeting' |

The following modifications to sections 2 and 3 apply where a proposal under section 1 has been made, where an administration order is in force in relation to the limited liability partnership, by the administrator or, where the limited liability partnership is being wound up, by the liquidator.

| | |
| --- | --- |
| Section 2 (procedure where the nominee is not the liquidator or administrator) | |
| subsection (2) | In paragraph (a) for 'meetings of the company' substitute 'meetings of the members of the limited liability partnership'. |
| Section 3 (summoning of meetings) | |
| subsection (2) | For 'meetings of the company' substitute 'a meeting of the members of the limited liability partnership'. |
| Section 73 (alternative modes of winding up) | |
| subsection (1) | Delete ',within the meaning given to that expression by section 735 of the Companies Act,'. |
| Section 74 (liability as contributories of present and past members) | |
| For section 74 there shall be substituted the following— | |
| | '74. When a limited liability partnership is wound up every present and past member of the limited liability partnership who has agreed with the other members or with the limited liability partnership that he will, in circumstances which have arisen, be liable to contribute to the assets of the limited liability partnership in the event that the limited liability partnership goes into liquidation is liable, to the extent that he has so agreed, to contribute to its assets to any amount sufficient for payment of its debts and liabilities, and the expenses of the winding up, and for the adjustment of the rights of the contributories among themselves. |

| Provisions | Modifications |
|---|---|
| | However, a past member shall only be liable if the obligation arising from such agreement survived his ceasing to be a member of the limited liability partnership.' |
| Section 75 to 78 | Delete sections 75 to 78. |
| Section 79 (meaning of 'contributory') | |
| subsection (1) | In subsection (1) for 'every person' substitute |
| | '(a) every present member of the limited liability partnership and (b) every past member of the limited liability partnership'. |
| subsection (2) | After 'section 214 (wrongful trading)' insert |
| | 'or |
| | 214A (adjustment of withdrawals)'. |
| subsection (3) | Delete subsection (3). |
| Section 83 (companies registered under Companies Act, Part XXII, Chapter II) | |
| | Delete section 83. |
| Section 84 (circumstances in which company may be wound up voluntarily) | |
| subsection (1) | For subsection (1) substitute the following— |
| | '(1) A limited liability partnership may be wound up voluntarily when it determines that it is to be wound up voluntarily.' |
| subsection (2) | Omit subsection (2). |
| subsection (2A) | For 'company passes a resolution for voluntary winding up' substitute 'limited liability partnership determines that it is to be wound up voluntarily' and for 'resolution' where it appears for the second time substitute 'determination' |
| subsection (2B) | For 'resolution for voluntary winding up may be passed only ' substitute 'determination to wind up voluntarily may only be made' limited liability partnership determines that it is to be wound up voluntarily' and in sub-paragraph (b) for 'passing of the resolution' substitute 'making of the determination' |
| subsection (3) | For subsection (3) substitute the following— |
| | '(3) Within 15 days after a limited liability partnership has determined that it be wound up there shall be forwarded to the registrar of companies either a printed copy or else a copy in some other form approved by the registrar of the determination.' |
| subsection (5) | After subsection ((4) insert a new subsection (5) |
| | '((5) If a limited liability partnership fails to comply with this regulation the limited liability partnership and every designated member of it who is in default is liable on summary conviction to a fine not exceeding level 3 on the standard scale.' |
| Section 85 (notice of resolution to wind up) | |
| subsection (1) | For subsection (1) substitute the following— |
| | '(1) When a limited liability partnership has determined that it shall be wound up voluntarily, it shall within 14 days after the making of the determination give notice of the determination by advertisement in the Gazette.' |
| Section 86 (commencement of winding up) | |
| | Substitute the following new section— |
| | '86. A voluntary winding up is deemed to commence at the time when the limited liability partnership determines that it be wound up voluntarily.'. |
| Section 87 (effect on business and status of company) | |
| subsection (2) | In subsection (2), for 'articles' substitute 'limited liability partnership agreement'. |
| Section 88 (avoidance of share transfers, etc. after winding-up resolution) | |
| | For 'shares' substitute 'the interest of any member in the property of the limited liability partnership'. |

| Provisions | Modifications |
| --- | --- |
| Section 89 (statutory declaration of solvency) | |
| | For 'director(s)' wherever it appears in section 89 substitute 'designated member(s)'; |
| subsection (2) | For paragraph (a) substitute the following— |
| | '(a) it is made within the 5 weeks immediately preceding the date when the limited liability partnership determined that it be wound up voluntarily or on that date but before the making of the determination, and'. |
| subsection (3) | For 'the resolution for winding up is passed' substitute 'the limited liability partnership determined that it be wound up voluntarily'. |
| subsection (5) | For 'in pursuance of a resolution passed' substitute 'voluntarily'. |
| Section 90 (distinction between 'members' and 'creditors' voluntary winding up) | |
| | For 'directors' substitute 'designated members'. |
| Section 91 (appointment of liquidator) | |
| subsection (1) | Delete 'in general meeting'. |
| subsection (2) | For the existing wording substitute |
| | '(2) On the appointment of a liquidator the powers of the members of the limited liability partnership shall cease except to the extent that a meeting of the members of the limited liability partnership summoned for the purpose or the liquidator sanctions their continuance.' |
| | After subsection (2) insert— |
| | '(3) Subsections (3) and (4) of section 92 shall apply for the purposes of this section as they apply for the purposes of that section.' |
| Section 92 (power to fill vacancy in office of liquidator) | |
| subsection (1) | For 'the company in general meeting' substitute 'a meeting of the members of the limited liability partnership summoned for the purpose'. |
| subsection (2) | For 'a general meeting' substitute 'a meeting of the members of the limited liability partnership'. |
| subsection (3) | In subsection (3), for 'articles' substitute 'limited liability partnership agreement'. |
| new subsection (4) | Add a new subsection (4) as follows— |
| | '(4) The quorum required for a meeting of the members of the limited liability partnership shall be any quorum required by the limited liability partnership agreement for meetings of the members of the limited liability partnership and if no requirement for a quorum has been agreed upon the quorum shall be 2 members.' |
| Section 93 (general company meeting at each year's end) | |
| subsection (1) | For 'a general meeting of the company' substitute 'a meeting of the members of the limited liability partnership'. |
| new subsection (4) | Add a new subsection (4) as follows— |
| | '(4) subsections (3) and (4) of section 92 shall apply for the purposes of this section as they apply for the purposes of that section.' |
| Section 94 (final meeting prior to dissolution) | |
| subsection (1) | For 'a general meeting of the company' substitute 'a meeting of the members of the limited liability partnership'. |
| new subsection (5A) | Add a new subsection (5A) as follows— |
| | '(5A) Subsections (3) and (4) of section 92 shall apply for the purposes of this section as they apply for the purposes of that section.' |
| subsection (6) | For 'a general meeting of the company' substitute 'a meeting of the members of the limited liability partnership'. |
| Section 95 (effect of company's insolvency) | |
| subsection (1) | For 'directors' substitute 'designated members'. |
| subsection (7) | For subsection (7) substitute the following— |
| | '(7) In this section 'the relevant period' means the period of 6 months immediately preceding the date on which the limited liability partnership determined that it be wound up voluntarily.' |

| Provisions | Modifications |
|---|---|
| Section 96 (conversion to creditors' voluntary winding up) | |
| paragraph (a) | For 'directors' substitute 'designated members'. |
| paragraph (b) | Substitute a new paragraph (b) as follows— |
| | '(b) the creditors' meeting was the meeting mentioned in section 98 in the next Chapter;'. |
| Section 98 (meeting of creditors) | |
| subsection (1) | For paragraph (a) substitute the following— |
| | '(a) cause a meeting of its creditors to be summoned for a day not later than the 14th day after the day on which the limited liability partnership determines that it be wound up voluntarily;'. |
| subsection (5) | For 'were sent the notices summoning the company meeting at which it was resolved that the company be wound up voluntarily' substitute 'the limited liability partnership determined that it be wound up voluntarily'. |
| Section 99 (directors to lay statement of affairs before creditors) | |
| subsection (1) | For 'the directors of the company' substitute 'the designated members' and for 'the director so appointed' substitute 'the designated member so appointed'. |
| subsection (2) | For 'directors' substitute 'designated members'. |
| subsection (3) | For 'directors' substitute 'designated members' and for 'director' substitute 'designated member'. |
| Section 100 (appointment of liquidator) | |
| subsection (1) | For 'The creditors and the company at their respective meetings mentioned in section 98' substitute 'The creditors at their meeting mentioned in section 98 and the limited liability partnership'. |
| subsection (3) | Delete 'director,'. |
| Section 101 (appointment of liquidation committee) | |
| subsection (2) | For subsection (2) substitute the following— |
| | '(2) If such a committee is appointed, the limited liability partnership may, when it determines that it be wound up voluntarily or at any time thereafter, appoint such number of persons as they think fit to act as members of the committee, not exceeding 5.' |
| Section 105 (meetings of company and creditors at each year's end) | |
| subsection (1) | For 'a general meeting of the company' substitute 'a meeting of the members of the limited liability partnership'. |
| new subsection (5) | Add a new subsection (5) as follows— |
| | '(5) Subsections (3) and (4) of section 92 shall apply for the purposes of this section as they apply for the purposes of that section.' |
| Section 106 (final meeting prior to dissolution) | |
| subsection (1) | For 'a general meeting of the company' substitute 'a meeting of the members of the limited liability partnership'. |
| new subsection (5A) | After subsection (5) insert a new subsection (5A) as follows— |
| | '(5A) Subsections (3) and (4) of section 92 shall apply for the purposes of this section as they apply for the purposes of that section.' |
| subsection (6) | For 'a general meeting of the company' substitute 'a meeting of the members of the limited liability partnership'. |
| Section 110 (acceptance of shares, etc., as consideration for sale of company property) | |
| | For the existing section substitute the following: |
| | '(1) This section applies, in the case of a limited liability partnership proposed to be, or being, wound up voluntarily, where the whole or part of the limited liability partnership's business or property is proposed to be transferred or sold to another company whether or not it is a company within the meaning of the Companies Act ( "the transferee company") or to a limited liability partnership ( "the transferee limited liability partnership"). |

| Provisions | Modifications |
|---|---|
| | (2) With the requisite sanction, the liquidator of the limited liability partnership being, or proposed to be, wound up ("the transferor limited liability partnership") may receive, in compensation or part compensation for the transfer or sale, shares, policies or other like interests in the transferee company or the transferee limited liability partnership for distribution among the members of the transferor limited liability partnership. |
| | (3) The sanction required under subsection (2) is— |
| | (a) in the case of a members' voluntary winding up, that of a determination of the limited liability partnership at a meeting of the members of the limited liability partnership conferring either a general authority on the liquidator or an authority in respect of any particular arrangement, (subsections (3) and (4) of section 92 to apply for this purpose as they apply for the purposes of that section), and |
| | (b) in the case of a creditor's voluntary winding up, that of either court or the liquidation committee. |
| | (4) Alternatively to subsection (2), the liquidator may (with the sanction) enter into any other arrangement whereby the members of the transferor limited liability partnership may, in lieu of receiving cash, shares, policies or other like interests (or in addition thereto), participate in the profits, or receive any other benefit from the transferee company or the transferee limited liability partnership. |
| | (5) A sale or arrangement in pursuance of this section is binding on members of the transferor limited liability partnership. |
| | (6) A determination by the limited liability partnership is not invalid for the purposes of this section by reason that it is made before or concurrently with a determination by the limited liability partnership that it be wound up voluntarily or for appointing liquidators; but, if an order is made within a year for winding up the limited liability partnership by the court, the determination by the limited liability partnership is not valid unless sanctioned by the court.' |
| Section 111 (dissent from arrangement under section 110) | |
| subsections (1)—(3) | For subsections (1)–(3) substitute the following— |
| | '(1) This section applies in the case of a voluntary winding up where, for the purposes of section 110(2) or (4), a determination of the limited liability partnership has provided the sanction requisite for the liquidator under that section. |
| | (2) If a member of the transferor limited liability partnership who did not vote in favour of providing the sanction required for the liquidator under section 110 expresses his dissent from it in writing addressed to the liquidator and left at the registered office of the limited liability partnership within 7 days after the date on which that sanction was given, he may require the liquidator either to abstain from carrying the arrangement so sanctioned into effect or to purchase his interest at a price to be determined by agreement or arbitration under this section. |
| | (3) If the liquidator elects to purchase the member's interest, the purchase money must be paid before the limited liability partnership is dissolved and be raised by the liquidator in such manner as may be determined by the limited liability partnership.' |
| subsection (4) | Omit subsection (4). |
| Section 117 (high court and county court jurisdiction) | |
| subsection (2) | Delete 'Where the amount of a company's share capital paid up or credited as paid up does not exceed £120,000, then (subject to this section)'. |
| subsection (3) | Delete subsection (3). |
| Section 120 (court of session and sheriff court jurisdiction) | |
| subsection (3) | Delete 'Where the amount of a company's share capital paid up or credited as paid up does not exceed £120,000,'. |
| subsection (5) | Delete subsection (5). |
| Section 122 (circumstances in which company may be wound up by the court) | |
| subsection (1) | For subsection (1) substitute the following— |
| | '(1) A limited liability partnership may be wound up by the court if— |

| Provisions | Modifications |
| --- | --- |
| | (a) the limited liability partnership has determined that the limited liability partnership be wound up by the court, |
| | (b) the limited liability partnership does not commence its business within a year from its incorporation or suspends its business for a whole year, |
| | (c) the number of members is reduced below two, |
| | (d) the limited liability partnership is unable to pay its debts, or |
| | (e) the court is of the opinion that it is just and equitable that the limited liability partnership should be wound up.' |
| Section 124 (application for winding up) | |
| subsections (2), (3) and (4)(a) | Delete these subsections. |
| subsection (3A) | For '122(1)(fa)' substitute '122(1)(da)' |
| Section 124A (petition for winding-up on grounds of public interest) | |
| subsection (1) | Omit paragraph (b) and (bb) |
| Section 126 (power to stay or restrain proceedings against company) | |
| subsection (2) | Delete subsection (2). |
| Section 127 (avoidance of property dispositions, etc.) | |
| subsection (1) | For 'any transfer of shares' substitute 'any transfer by a member of the limited liability partnership of his interest in the property of the limited liability partnership'. |
| Section 129 (commencement of winding up by the court) | |
| subsection (1) | For 'a resolution has been passed by the company' substitute 'a determination has been made' and for 'at the time of the passing of the resolution' substitute 'at the time of that determination'. |
| Section 130 (consequences of winding-up order) | |
| subsection (3) | Delete subsection (3). |
| Section 148 (settlement of list of contributories and application of assets) | |
| subsection (1) | Delete ', with power to rectify the register of members in all cases where rectification is required in pursuance of the Companies Act or this Act,'. |
| Section 149 (debts due from contributory to company) | |
| subsection (1) | Delete 'the Companies Act or'. |
| subsection (2) | Delete subsection (2). |
| subsection (3) | Delete 'whether limited or unlimited,'. |
| Section 160 (delegation of powers to liquidator (England and Wales)) | |
| subsection (1) | In subsection (1)(b) delete 'and the rectifying of the register of members'. |
| subsection (2) | For subsection (2) substitute the following— |
| | '(2) But the liquidator shall not make any call without the special leave of the court or the sanction of the liquidation committee.' |
| Section 165 (voluntary winding up) | |
| subsection (2) | In paragraph (a) for 'an extraordinary resolution of the company' substitute 'a determination by a meeting of the members of the limited liability partnership'. |
| subsection (4) | For paragraph (c) substitute the following— |
| | '(c) summon meetings of the members of the limited liability partnership for the purpose of obtaining their sanction or for any other purpose he may think fit.' |
| new subsection (4A) | Insert a new subsection (4A) as follows— |
| | '(4A) Subsections (3) and (4) of section 92 shall apply for the purposes of this section as they apply for the purposes of that section.' |

| Provisions | Modifications |
| --- | --- |
| Section 166 (creditors' voluntary winding up) | |
| subsection (5) | In paragraph (b) for 'directors' substitute 'designated members'. |
| Section 171 (removal, etc. (voluntary winding up)) | |
| subsection (2) | For paragraph (a) substitute the following— |
| | '(a) in the case of a members' voluntary winding up, by a meeting of the members of the limited liability partnership summoned specially for that purpose, or'. |
| subsection (6) | In paragraph (a) for 'final meeting of the company' substitute 'final meeting of the members of the limited liability partnership' and in paragraph (b) for 'final meetings of the company' substitute 'final meetings of the members of the limited liability partnership'. |
| new subsection (7) | Insert a new subsection (7) as follows— |
| | '(7) Subsections (3) and (4) of section 92 are to apply for the purposes of this section as they apply for the purposes of that section.' |
| Section 173 (release (voluntary winding up)) | |
| subsection (2) | In paragraph (a) for 'a general meeting of the company' substitute 'a meeting of the members of the limited liability partnership'. |
| Section 183 (effect of execution or attachment (England and Wales)) | |
| subsection (2) | Delete paragraph (a). |
| Section 184 (duties of sheriff (England and Wales)) | |
| subsection (1) | For 'a resolution for voluntary winding up has been passed' substitute 'the limited liability partnership has determined that it be wound up voluntarily'. |
| subsection (4) | Delete 'or of a meeting having been called at which there is to be proposed a resolution for voluntary winding up,' and 'or a resolution is passed (as the case may be)'. |
| Section 187 (power to make over assets to employees) | |
| | Delete section 187. |
| Section 194 (resolutions passed at adjourned meetings) | |
| | After 'contributories' insert 'or of the members of a limited liability partnership'. |
| Section 195 (meetings to ascertain wishes of creditors or contributories) | |
| subsection (3) | Delete 'the Companies Act or'. |
| Section 206 (fraud, etc. in anticipation of winding up) | |
| subsection (1) | For 'passes a resolution for voluntary winding up' substitute 'makes a determination that it be wound up voluntarily'. |
| Section 207 (transactions in fraud of creditors) | |
| subsection (1) | For 'passes a resolution for voluntary winding up' substitute 'makes a determination that it be wound up voluntarily'. |
| Section 210 (material omissions from statement relating to company's affairs) | |
| subsection (2) | For 'passed a resolution for voluntary winding up' substitute 'made a determination that it be wound up voluntarily'. |
| Section 214 (wrongful trading) | |
| subsection (2) | Delete from 'but the court shall not' to the end of the subsection. |
| After section 214 | |
| | Insert the following new section 214A |
| | '214A Adjustment of withdrawals |
| | (1) This section has effect in relation to a person who is or has been a member of a limited liability partnership where, in the course of the winding up of that limited liability partnership, it appears that subsection (2) of this section applies in relation to that person. |

| Provisions | Modifications |
|---|---|
| | (2) This subsection applies in relation to a person if— |
| | (a) within the period of two years ending with the commencement of the winding up, he was a member of the limited liability partnership who withdrew property of the limited liability partnership, whether in the form of a share of profits, salary, repayment of or payment of interest on a loan to the limited liability partnership or any other withdrawal of property, and |
| | (b) it is proved by the liquidator to the satisfaction of the court that at the time of the withdrawal he knew or had reasonable ground for believing that the limited liability partnership— |
| | (i) was at the time of the withdrawal unable to pay its debts within the meaning of section 123, or |
| | (ii) would become so unable to pay its debts after the assets of the limited liability partnership had been depleted by that withdrawal taken together with all other withdrawals (if any) made by any members contemporaneously with that withdrawal or in contemplation when that withdrawal was made. |
| | (3) Where this section has effect in relation to any person the court, on the application of the liquidator, may declare that that person is to be liable to make such contribution (if any) to the limited liability partnership's assets as the court thinks proper. |
| | (4) The court shall not make a declaration in relation to any person the amount of which exceeds the aggregate of the amounts or values of all the withdrawals referred to in subsection (2) made by that person within the period of two years referred to in that subsection. |
| | (5) The court shall not make a declaration under this section with respect to any person unless that person knew or ought to have concluded that after each withdrawal referred to in subsection (2) there was no reasonable prospect that the limited liability partnership would avoid going into insolvent liquidation. |
| | (6) For the purposes of subsection (5) the facts which a member ought to know or ascertain and the conclusions which he ought to reach are those which would be known, ascertained, or reached by a reasonably diligent person having both: |
| | (a) the general knowledge, skill and experience that may reasonably be expected of a person carrying out the same functions as are carried out by that member in relation to the limited liability partnership, and |
| | (b) the general knowledge, skill and experience that that member has. |
| | (7) For the purposes of this section a limited liability partnership goes into insolvent liquidation if it goes into liquidation at a time when its assets are insufficient for the payment of its debts and other liabilities and the expenses of the winding up. |
| | (8) In this section 'member' includes a shadow member. |
| | (9) This section is without prejudice to section 214.' |
| Section 215 (proceedings under ss 213, 214) | |
| subsection (1) | Omit the word 'or' between the words '213' and '214' and insert after '214' 'or 214A'. |
| subsection (2) | For 'either section' substitute 'any of those sections'. |
| subsection (4) | For 'either section' substitute 'any of those sections'. |
| subsection (5) | For 'Sections 213 and 214' substitute 'Sections 213, 214 or 214A'. |
| Section 218 (prosecution of delinquent officers and members of company) | |
| subsection (1) | For 'officer, or any member, of the company' substitute 'member of the limited liability partnership'. |
| subsections (3), (4) and (6) | For 'officer of the company, or any member of it,' substitute 'officer or member of the limited liability partnership'. |
| [...] | |
| Section 247 ('insolvency' and 'go into liquidation') | |
| subsection (2) | For 'passes a resolution for voluntary winding up' substitute 'makes a determination that it be wound up voluntarily' and for 'passing such a resolution' substitute 'making such a determination'. |
| subsection (3) | For 'resolution for a voluntary winding up' substitute 'determination to wind up voluntarily' |

| Provisions | Modifications |
| --- | --- |
| Section 249 ( 'connected with a company') | For the existing words substitute<br><br>'For the purposes of any provision in this Group of Parts, a person is connected with a company (including a limited liability partnership) if—<br><br>(a) he is a director or shadow director of a company or an associate of such a director or shadow director (including a member or a shadow member of a limited liability partnership or an associate of such a member or shadow member); or<br><br>(b) he is an associate of the company or of the limited liability partnership.' |
| Section 250 ( 'member' of a company) | |
| | Delete section 250. |
| Section 251 (expressions used generally) | |
| | Delete the word 'and' appearing after the definition of 'the rules' and insert the word 'and' after the definition of 'shadow director'.<br><br>After the definition of 'shadow director' insert the following—<br><br>'"shadow member", in relation to a limited liability partnership, means a person in accordance with whose directions or instructions the members of the limited liability partnership are accustomed to act (but so that a person is not deemed a shadow member by reason only that the members of the limited liability partnership act on advice given by him in a professional capacity);'. |
| Section 386 (categories of preferential debts) | |
| subsection (1) | In subsection (1), omit the words 'or an individual'. |
| subsection (2) | In subsection (2), omit the words 'or the individual'. |
| Section 387 ( 'the relevant date') | |
| subsection (3) | In paragraph (c) for 'passing of the resolution for the winding up of the company' substitute 'making of the determination by the limited liability partnership that it be wound up voluntarily'. |
| subsection (5) | Omit subsection (5). |
| subsection (6) | Omit subsection (6). |
| Section 388 (meaning of 'act as insolvency practitioner') | |
| subsection (2) | Omit subsection (2). |
| subsection (3) | Omit subsection (3). |
| subsection (4) | Delete '"company' means a company within the meaning given by section 735(1) of the Companies Act or a company which may be wound up under Part V of this Act (unregistered companies);' and delete '"interim trustee" and "permanent trustee" mean the same as the Bankruptcy (Scotland) Act 1985'. |
| Section 389 (acting without qualification an offence) | |
| subsection (1) | Omit the words 'or an individual'. |
| Section 389A (authorisation of nominees and supervisors) | |
| subsection (1) | Omit 'or Part VIII' |
| Section 402 (official petitioner) | Delete section 402. |
| Section 412 (individual insolvency rules (England and Wales)) | Delete section 412. |
| Section 415 (Fees orders (individual insolvency proceedings in England and Wales)) | Delete section 415. |
| Section 416 (monetary limits (companies winding up)) | |
| subsection (1) | In subsection (1), omit the words 'section 117(2)(amount of company's share capital determining whether county court has jurisdiction to wind it up);' and the words 'section 120(3)(the equivalent as respects sheriff court jurisdiction in Scotland);'. |
| subsection (3) | In subsection (3), omit the words '117(2), 120(3) or'. |
| Section 418 (monetary limits (bankruptcy)) | Delete section 418. |

| Provisions | Modifications |
|---|---|
| Section 420 (insolvent partnerships) | |
| | Delete section 420. |
| Section 421 (insolvent estates of deceased persons) | |
| | Delete section 421. |
| Section 422 (recognised banks, etc.) | |
| | Delete section 422. |
| Section 426A (disqualification from Parliament (England and Wales)) | Omit |
| Section 426B (devolution) | Omit |
| Section 426C (irrelevance of privilege) | Omit |
| Section 427 (parliamentary disqualification) | Delete section 427. |
| Section 429 (disabilities on revocation or administration order against an individual) | |
| | Delete section 429. |
| Section 432 (offences by bodies corporate) | |
| subsection (2) | Delete 'secretary or'. |
| Section 435 (meaning of 'associate') | |
| new subsection (3A) | Insert a new subsection (3A) as follows— |
| | '(3A) A member of a limited liability partnership is an associate of that limited liability partnership and of every other member of that limited liability partnership and of the husband or wife or relative of every other member of that limited liability partnership.' |
| subsection (11) | For subsection (11) there shall be substituted |
| | '(11) In this section "company" includes any body corporate (whether incorporated in Great Britain or elsewhere); and references to directors and other officers of a company and to voting power at any general meeting of a company have effect with any necessary modifications.' |
| Section 436 (expressions used generally) | |
| | The following expressions and definitions shall be added to the section— |
| | 'designated member' has the same meaning as it has in the Limited Liability Partnerships Act 2000; |
| | 'limited liability partnership' means a limited liability partnership formed and registered under the Limited Liability Partnerships Act 2000; |
| | 'limited liability partnership agreement', in relation to a limited liability partnership, means any agreement, express or implied, made between the members of the limited liability partnership or between the limited liability partnership and the members of the limited liability partnership which determines the mutual rights and duties of the members, and their rights and duties in relation to the limited liability partnership. |
| Section 437 (transitional provisions, and savings) | Delete section 437. |
| Section 440 (extent (Scotland)) | |
| subsection (2) | In subsection (2), omit paragraph (b). |
| Section 441 (extent (Northern Ireland)) | |
| | Delete section 441. |
| Section 442 (extent (other territories)) | |
| | Delete section 442. |
| Schedule A1 | |
| Paragraph 6 | |
| Sub-paragraph (1) | For 'directors of a company wish' substitute "limited liability partnership wishes'. For 'they' substitute 'the designated members of the limited liability partnership'. |

| Provisions | Modifications |
| --- | --- |
| Sub-paragraph (2) | For 'directors' substitute 'the designated members of the limited liability partnership'. |
| | In sub-paragraph (c), for 'meetings of the company and' substitute 'a meeting of'. |
| Paragraph 7 | |
| Sub-paragraph (1) | For 'directors of a company' substitute 'designated members of the limited liability partnership'. |
| Sub-paragraph (1) | In sub-paragraph (e)(iii), for 'meetings of the company and' substitute 'a meeting of'. |
| Paragraph 8 | |
| sub-paragraph (2) | For 'meetings' substitute 'meeting'. |
| | For 'are' substitute 'is'. |
| | Omit the words in parenthesis. |
| sub-paragraph (3) | For 'either of those meetings' substitute 'the meeting'. |
| | For 'those meetings were' substitute 'that meeting was'. |
| | Omit the words in parenthesis. |
| sub-paragraph (4) | For 'either' substitute 'the'. |
| sub-paragraph (6)(c) | For 'one or both of the meetings' substitute 'the meeting'. |
| Paragraph 9 | |
| sub-paragraph (1) | For 'directors' substitute 'designated members of the limited liability partnership'. |
| sub-paragraph (2) | For 'directors' substitute 'designated members of the limited liability partnership'. |
| Paragraph 12 | |
| sub-paragraph (1)(b) | Omit. |
| sub-paragraph (1)(c) | For 'resolution may be passed' substitute 'determination that it may be wound up may be made'. |
| sub-paragraph (2) | For 'transfer of shares' substitute 'any transfer by a member of the limited liability partnership of his interest in the property of the limited liability partnership'. |
| Paragraph 20 | |
| sub-paragraph (8) | For 'directors' substitute 'designated members of the limited liability partnership'. |
| sub-paragraph (9) | For 'directors' substitute 'designated members of the limited liability partnership'. |
| Paragraph 24 | |
| sub-paragraph (2) | For 'directors' substitute 'designated members of the limited liability partnership'. |
| Paragraph 25 | |
| sub-paragraph (2)(c) | For 'directors' substitute 'designated members of the limited liability partnership'. |
| Paragraph 26 | |
| sub-paragraph (1) | Omit 'director'. |
| Paragraph 29 | |
| sub-paragraph (1) | For 'meetings of the company and its creditors' substitute 'a meeting of the creditors of the limited liability partnership'. |
| Paragraph 30 | |
| sub-paragraph (1) | For 'meetings' substitute 'meeting'. |
| new sub-paragraph (2A) | Insert new sub-paragraph (2A) as follows— |
| | '(2A) If modifications to the proposal are proposed at the meeting the chairman of the meeting shall, before the conclusion of the meeting, ascertain from the limited liability partnership whether or not it accepts the proposed modifications; and if at that conclusion the limited liability partnership has failed to respond to a proposed modification it shall be presumed not to have agreed to it.'. |
| sub-paragraph (3) | For 'either' substitute 'the'. |
| | After 'the result of the meeting' in the first place where it occurs insert '(including, where modifications to the proposal were proposed at the meeting, the response to those proposed modifications made by the limited liability partnership)'. |
| | At the end add 'and to the limited liability partnership'. |

| Provisions | Modifications |
| --- | --- |
| Paragraph 31 | |
| sub-paragraph (1) | For 'meetings' substitute 'meeting'. |
| sub-paragraph (7) | For 'directors of the company' substitute 'designated members of the limited liability partnership'. |
| | For 'meetings (or either of them)' substitute 'meeting'. |
| | For 'directors' substitute 'limited liability partnership'. |
| | For 'those meetings' substitute 'that meeting'. |
| Paragraph 32 | |
| sub-paragraph (2) | For sub-paragraphs (a) and (b) substitute 'with the day on which the meeting summoned under paragraph 29 is first held.' |
| Paragraph 36 | |
| sub-paragraph (2) | For sub-paragraph (2) substitute— |
| | '(2) The decision has effect if, in accordance with the rules, it has been taken by the creditors' meeting summoned under paragraph 29.' |
| sub-paragraph (3) | Omit. |
| sub-paragraph (4) | Omit. |
| sub-paragraph (5) | Omit. |
| Paragraph 37 | |
| sub-paragraph (5) | For 'each of the reports of the meetings' substitute 'the report of the meeting'. |
| Paragraph 38 | |
| sub-paragraph (1)(a) | For 'one or both of the meetings' substitute 'the meeting'. |
| sub-paragraph (1)(b) | For 'either of those meetings' substitutes 'the meeting'. |
| sub-paragraph (2)(a) | For 'either of those meetings' substitutes 'the meeting'. |
| | After sub-paragraph (2)(a) insert new (aa) as follows— |
| | '(aa) any member of the limited liability partnership;' |
| sub-paragraph (2)(b) | Omit 'creditors'. |
| sub-paragraph (3)(a) | For 'each of the reports' substitute 'the report'. |
| sub-paragraph (3)(b) | Omit 'creditors'. |
| sub-paragraph (4)(a)(ii) | Omit 'in question'. |
| sub-paragraph (4)(b)(I) | For 'further meetings' substitute 'a further meeting' and for 'directors' substitute 'limited liability partnership'. |
| sub-paragraph (4)(b)(ii) | Omit 'company or (as the case may be) creditors'. |
| sub-paragraph (5) | For 'directors do' substitute 'limited liability partnerships does'. |
| Paragraph 39 | |
| sub-paragraph (1) | For 'one or both of the meetings' substitute 'the meeting'. |
| Schedule B1 | |
| Paragraph 2 | |
| sub-paragraph (c) | For 'company or its directors' substitute 'limited liability partnership'. |
| Paragraph 8 | |
| sub-paragraph (1)(a) | For 'resolution for voluntary winding up' substitute 'determination to wind up voluntarily'. |
| Paragraph 9 | Omit. |
| Paragraph 12 | |
| sub-paragraph (1)(b) | Omit. |
| Paragraph 22 | For sub-paragraph (1) substitute— |
| | '(1) A limited liability partnership may appoint an administrator.' |
| | Omit sub-paragraph (2). |
| Paragraph 23 | |
| sub-paragraph (1)(b) | Omit 'or its directors'. |
| Paragraph 42 | |
| sub-paragraph (2) | For 'resolution may be passed for the winding up of' substitute 'determination to wind up voluntarily may be made by'. |
| Paragraph 61 | For paragraph 61 substitute— |
| | '61. The administrator has power to prevent any person from taking part in the management of the business of the limited liability partnership and to appoint any person to be a manager of that business.' |

| Provisions | Modifications |
| --- | --- |
| Paragraph 62 | At the end add the following— |
| | Subsections (3) and (4) of section 92 shall apply for the purposes of this paragraph as they apply for the purposes of that section... |
| Paragraph 83 | |
| sub-paragraph (6)(b) | For 'resolution for voluntary winding up' substitute 'determination to wind up voluntarily'. |
| sub-paragraph (8)(b) | For 'passing of the resolution for voluntary winding up' substitute 'determination to wind up voluntarily'. |
| sub-paragraph (8)(e) | For 'passing of the resolution for voluntary winding up' substitute 'determination to wind up voluntarily'. |
| Paragraph 87 | |
| sub-paragraph (2)(b) | Insert at the end 'or'. |
| sub-paragraph (2)(c) | Omit 'or'. |
| sub-paragraph (2)(d) | Omit the words from '(d)' to 'company'. |
| Paragraph 89 | |
| sub-paragraph (2)(b) | Insert at the end 'or'. |
| sub-paragraph (2)(c) | Omit 'or'. |
| sub-paragraph (2)(d) | Omit the words from '(d)' to 'company'. |
| Paragraph 91 | |
| sub-paragraph (1)(c) | Omit. |
| Paragraph 94 | Omit. |
| Paragraph 95 | For 'to 94' substitute 'and 93'. |
| Paragraph 97 | |
| sub-paragraph (1)(a) | Omit 'or directors'. |
| Paragraph 103 | |
| sub-paragraph (5) | Omit. |
| Paragraph 105 | Omit. |
| Schedule 1 | |
| Paragraph 19 | For paragraph 19 substitute the following— |
| | '19. Power to enforce any rights the limited liability partnership has against the members under the terms of the limited liability partnership agreement.' |
| Schedule 10 | |
| Section 6A(1) | In the entry relating to section 6A omit 'members' or'. |
| Section 85(2) | In the entry relating to section 85(2) for 'resolution for voluntary winding up' substitute 'making of determination for voluntary winding up'. |
| Section 89(4) | In the entry relating to section 89(4) for 'Director' substitute 'Designated member'. |
| Section 93(3) | In the entry relating to section 93(3) for 'general meeting of the company' substitute 'meeting of members of the limited liability partnership'. |
| Section 99(3) | In the entries relating to section 99(3) for 'director' and 'directors' where they appear substitute 'designated member' or 'designated members' as appropriate. |
| Section 105(3) | In the entry relating to section 105(3) for 'company general meeting' substitute 'meeting of the members of the limited liability partnership'. |
| Section 106(6) | In the entry relating to section 106(6) for 'final meeting of the company' substitute 'final meeting of the members of the limited liability partnership'. |
| Sections 353(1) to 362 | Delete the entries relating to sections 353(1) to 362 inclusive. |
| Section 429(5) | Delete the entry relating to section 429(5). |
| Schedule A1, paragraph 9(2) | For 'Directors' substitute 'Designated Members'. |
| Schedule A1, paragraph 20(9) | For 'Directors' substitute 'Designated Members'. |
| Schedule B1 paragraph 27(4) | Omit 'or directors'. |
| Schedule B1 paragraph 29(7) | Omit 'or directors'. |
| Schedule B1 paragraph 32 | Omit 'or directors'. |

# SCHEDULE 4

The provisions listed in this Schedule are not applied to Scotland to the extent specified below:

Sections 50 to 52;

Section 53(1) and (2), to the extent that those subsections do not relate to the requirement for a copy of the instrument and notice being forwarded to the registrar of companies;

Section 53(4)(6) and (7);

Section 54(1), (2), (3)(to the extent that that subsection does not relate to the requirement for a copy of the interlocutor to be sent to the registrar of companies), and subsections (5), (6) and (7);

Sections 55 to 58;

Section 60, other than subsection (1);

Section 61, including subsections (6) and (7) to the extent that those subsections do not relate to anything to be done or which may be done to or by the registrar of companies;

Section 62, including subsection (5) to the extent that that subsection does not relate to anything to be done or which may be done to or by the registrar of companies;

Sections 63 to 66;

Section 67, including subsections (1) and (8) to the extent that those subsections do not relate to anything to be done or which may be done to the registrar of companies;

Section 68;

Section 69, including subsections (1) and (2) to the extent that those subsections do not relate to anything to be done or which may be done by the registrar of companies;

Sections 70 and 71;

Subsection 84(3), to the extent that it does not concern the copy of the resolution being forwarded to the registrar of companies within 15 days;

Sections 91 to 93;

Section 94, including subsections (3) and (4) to the extent that those subsections do not relate to the liquidator being required to send to the registrar of companies a copy of the account and a return of the final meeting;

Section 95;

Section 97;

Sections 100 to 102;

Sections 104 to 105;

Section 106, including subsections (3), (4) and (5) to the extent that those subsections do not relate to the liquidator being required to send to the registrar of companies a copy of the account of winding up and a return of the final meeting/quorum;

Sections 109 to 111;

Section 112, including subsection (3) to the extent that that subsection does not relate to the liquidator being required to send to the registrar a copy of the order made by the court;

Sections 113 to 115;

Sections 126 to 128;

Section 130(1) to the extent that that subsection does not relate to a copy of the order being forwarded by the court to the registrar;

Section 131;

Sections 133 to 135;

Sections 138 to 140;

Sections 142 to 146;

Section 147, including subsection (3) to the extent that that subsection does not relate to a copy of the order being forwarded by the company to the registrar;

Section 162 to the extent that that section concerns the matters set out in Section C.2 of Schedule 5 to the Scotland Act 1998 as being exceptions to the insolvency reservation;

Sections 163 to 167;

Section 169;

Section 170, including subsection (2) to the extent that that subsection does not relate to an application being made by the registrar to make good the default;

Section 171;

Section 172, including subsection (8) to the extent that that subsection does not relate to the liquidator being required to give notice to the registrar;

Sections 173 and 174;

Section 177;

Sections 185 to 189;

Sections 191 to 194;

Section 196 to the extent that that section applies to the specified devolved functions of Part IV of the Insolvency Act 1986;

Section 199;

Section 200 to the extent that it applies to the specified devolved functions of Part IV of the First Group of Parts of the 1986 Act;

Sections 206 to 215;

Section 218 subsections (1), (2), (4) and (6);

Section 231 to 232 to the extent that the sections apply to administrative receivers, liquidators and provisional liquidators;

Section 233, to the extent that that section applies in the case of the appointment of an administrative receiver, of a voluntary arrangement taking effect, of a company going into liquidation or where a provisional liquidator is appointed;

Section 234 to the extent that that section applies to situations other than those where an administration order applies;

Section 235 to the extent that that section applies to situations other than those where an administration order applies;

Sections 236 to 237 to the extent that those sections apply to situations other than administration orders and winding up;

Sections 242 to 243;

Section 244 to the extent that that section applies in circumstances other than a company which is subject to an administration order;

Section 245;

Section 251, to the extent that that section contains definitions which apply only to devolved matters;

Section 416(1) and (4), to the extent that those subsections apply to section 206(1)(a) and (b) in connection with the offence provision relating to the winding up of a limited liability partnership;

Schedule 2;

Schedule 3;

Schedule 4;

Schedule 8, to the extent that that Schedule does not apply to voluntary arrangements or administrations within the meaning of Parts I and II of the 1986 Act.

In addition, Schedule 10, which concerns punishment of offences under the Insolvency Act 1986, lists various sections of the Insolvency Act 1986 which create an offence. The following sections, which are listed in Schedule 10, are devolved in their application to Scotland:

Section 51(4);

Section 51(5);

Sections 53(2) to 62(5) to the extent that those subsections relate to matters other than delivery to the registrar of companies;

Section 64(2);

Section 65(4);

Section 66(6);

Section 67(8) to the extent that that subsection relates to matters other than delivery to the registrar of companies;

Section 93(3);

Section 94(4) to the extent that that subsection relates to matters other than delivery to the registrar of companies;

Section 94(6);

Section 95(8);

Section 105(3);

Section 106(4) to the extent that that subsection relates to matters other than delivery to the registrar of companies;

Section 106(6);

Section 109(2);

Section 114(4);

Section 131(7);

Section 164;

Section 166(7);

Section 188(2);

Section 192(2);

Sections 206 to 211; and

Section 235(5) to the extent that it relates to matters other than administration orders.

# SCHEDULE 5

## GENERAL AND CONSEQUENTIAL AMENDMENTS IN OTHER LEGISLATION

### *The Bills of Sale Act (1878) Amendment Act 1882 c. 43*

**1.** In section 17, after 'incorporated company' insert 'or by any limited liability partnership' and after 'such company' insert 'or a limited liability partnership'.

### The Third Parties (Rights Against Insurers) Act 1930 c. 25

**2.** After section 3, insert—

#### '3A Application to limited liability partnerships

(1) This Act applies to limited liability partnerships as it applies to companies.

(2) In its application to limited liability partnerships, references to a resolution for a voluntary winding-up being passed are references to a determination for a voluntary winding-up being made.'

### The Corporate Bodies' Contracts Act 1960 c. 46

**3.** In section 2, insert at the end 'or to a limited liability partnership'.

### The Criminal Justice Act 1967 c. 80

**4.** In section 9(8)(d), insert at the end—

'and in paragraph (d) of this subsection references to the secretary, in relation to a limited liability partnership, are to any designated member of the limited liability partnership.'

### The Solicitors Act 1974 c. 47

**5.** In section 87, after the definition of 'non-contentious business', insert—

'"officer", in relation to a limited liability partnership, means a member of the limited liability partnership;'.

### The Sex Discrimination Act 1975 c. 65

**6.** In section 11, insert at the end—

'(6) This section applies to a limited liability partnership as it applies to a firm; and, in its application to a limited liability partnership, references to a partner in a firm are references to a member of the limited liability partnership.'

### The Race Relations Act 1976 c. 74

**7.** In section 10, insert at the end—

'(5) This section applies to a limited liability partnership as it applies to a firm; and, in its application to a limited liability partnership, references to a partner in a firm are references to a member of the limited liability partnership.'

### The Betting and Gaming Duties Act 1981 c. 63

**8.** After section 32, insert—

#### '32A Application to limited liability partnerships

(1) This Act applies to limited liability partnerships as it applies to companies.

(2) In its application to a limited liability partnership, references to a director of a company are references to a member of the limited liability partnership.'

### The Companies Act 1985 c. 6

**9.** In section 26, in subsection (1), after paragraph (bb) insert—

'(bbb) which includes, at any place in the name, the expression "limited liability partnership" or its Welsh equivalent ( "partneriaeth atebolrwydd cyfyngedig");'.

### The Business Names Act 1985 c. 7.

**10.** In section 1, in subsection (1), insert at the end—

'(d) in the case of a limited liability partnership, does not consist of its corporate name without any addition other than one so permitted.'

**11.**—(1) Section 4 is amended as follows.

(2) In subsection (1)(a), for 'subject to subsection (3)' substitute 'subject to subsections (3) and (3A)', omit the word 'and' at the end of sub-paragraph (iii) and after that sub-paragraph insert—

'(iiia) In the case of a limited liability partnership, its corporate name and the name of each member, and'.

(3) In subsection (2), for 'the subsection next following' substitute 'subsection (3) or (3A)'.

(4) After subsection (3) insert—

'(3A) Subsection (1)(a) does not apply in relation to any document issued by a limited liability partnership with more than 20 members which maintains at its principal place of business a list of the names of all the members if—

(a) none of the names of the members appears in the document otherwise than in the text or as a signatory; and

(b) the document states in legible characters the address of the principal place of business of the limited liability partnership and that the list of the members' names is open to inspection at that place.'

(5) After subsection (4) insert—

'(4A) Where a limited liability partnership maintains a list of the members' names for the purposes of subsection (3A), any person may inspect the list during office hours.'

(6) In subsection (7), after 'subsection (4)' insert 'or (4A)' and after 'any partner of the partnership concerned' insert ',or any member of the limited liability partnership concerned,'.

### The Administration of Justice Act 1985 c. 61

**12.** In section 9(8), after the definition of 'multi-national partnership', insert—

'"officer", in relation to a limited liability partnership, means a member of the limited liability partnership;'.

**13.** In section 39(1), after the definition of 'the Council', insert—

'"director", in relation to a limited liability partnership, means a member of the limited liability partnership;'.

**14.** In paragraph 1(3) of Schedule 2, insert at the end

'and references in this Schedule to a director, in relation to a limited liability partnership, are references to a member of the limited liability partnership.'

### The Insolvency Act 1986 c. 45

**15.**—(1) Section 110 is amended as follows.

(2) In subsection (1), after 'sold' insert '(a)' and at the end insert—

'or (b) to a limited liability partnership (the "transferee limited liability partnership").'

(3) In subsection (2), for the words 'sale,' onwards substitute

'sale—

    (a) in the case of the transferee company, shares, policies or other like interests in the transferee company for distribution among the members of the transferor company, or

    (b) in the case of the transferee limited liability partnership, membership in the transferee limited liability partnership for distribution among the members of the transferor company.'

(4) In subsection (4), for the words 'company may,' onwards substitute

'company may—

    (a) in the case of the transferee company, in lieu of receiving cash, shares, policies or other like interests (or in addition thereto) participate in the profits of, or receive any other benefit from, the transferee company, or

    (b) in the case of the transferee limited liability partnership, in lieu of receiving cash or membership (or in addition thereto), participate in some other way in the profits of, or receive any other benefit from, the transferee limited liability partnership.'

### The Building Societies Act 1986 c. 53

**16.** In paragraph 1(2) of Schedule 21, after 'In this Schedule—', insert—

'"director", in relation to a limited liability partnership, means a member of the limited liability partnership;'.

### The Courts and Legal Services Act 1990 c. 41

**17.** In section 119(1), after the definition of 'multi-national partnership' insert—

'"officer", in relation to a limited liability partnership, means a member of the limited liability partnership;'.

### The Employment Rights Act 1996 c. 18

**18.**—(1) Section 166 is amended as follows.

(2) In subsection (5), omit the word 'and' at the end of paragraph (a), and insert at the end of paragraph (b)

'and

    (c) where the employer is a limited liability partnership, if (but only if) subsection (8) is satisfied.'

(3) After subsection (7) insert—

'(8) This subsection is satisfied in the case of an employer which is a limited liability partnership—

    (a) if a winding-up order, an administration order or a determination for a voluntary winding-up has been made with respect to the limited liability partnership,

    (b) if a receiver or (in England and Wales only) a manager of the undertaking of the limited liability partnership has been duly appointed, or (in England and Wales only) possession has been taken, by or on behalf of the holders of any debentures secured by a floating charge, of any property of the limited liability partnership comprised in or subject to the charge, or

    (c) if a voluntary arrangement proposed in the case of the limited liability partnership for the purpose of Part I of the Insolvency Act 1986 has been approved under that Part of that Act.'

**19.**—(1) Section 183 is amended as follows.

(2) In subsection (1), omit the word 'and' at the end of paragraph (a), and insert at the end of paragraph (b)

'and

(c) where the employer is a limited liability partnership, if (but only if) subsection (4) is satisfied.'

(3) After subsection (3) insert—

'(4) This subsection is satisfied in the case of an employer which is a limited liability partnership—

   (a) if a winding-up order, an administration order or a determination for a voluntary winding-up has been made with respect to the limited liability partnership,

   (b) if a receiver or (in England and Wales only) a manager of the undertaking of the limited liability partnership has been duly appointed, or (in England and Wales only) possession has been taken, by or on behalf of the holders of any debentures secured by a floating charge, of any property of the limited liability partnership comprised in or subject to the charge, or

   (c) if a voluntary arrangement proposed in the case of the limited liability partnership for the purposes of Part I of the Insolvency Act 1986 has been approved under that Part of that Act.'

### The Contracts (Rights of Third Parties) Act 1999 c. 31

**20.** In section 6, after subsection (2) insert—

'(2A) Section 1 confers no rights on a third party in the case of any incorporation document of a limited liability partnership or any limited liability partnership agreement as defined in the Limited Liability Partnerships Regulations 2001 (S.I. No. 2001/    ).'

### The Financial Services and Markets Act 2000 c. 8

**21.** In each of sections 177(2), 221(2) and 232(2) insert at the end—

'and "officer", in relation to a limited liability partnership, means a member of the limited liability partnership.'

### Culpable officer provisions

**22.** — (1) A culpable officer provision applies in the case of a limited liability partnership as if the reference in the provision to a director (or a person purporting to act as a director) were a reference to a member (or a person purporting to act as a member) of the limited liability partnership.

(2) A culpable officer provision is a provision in any Act or subordinate legislation (within the meaning of the Interpretation Act 1978) to the effect that where—

   (a) a body corporate is guilty of a particular offence, and

   (b) the offence is proved to have been committed with the consent or connivance of, or to be attributable to the neglect on the part of, (among others) a director of the body corporate,

he (as well as the body corporate) is guilty of the offence.

# SCHEDULE 6

# APPLICATION OF SUBORDINATE LEGISLATION

## PART I    REGULATIONS MADE UNDER THE 1985 ACT

**1.** [...]

**2.** [...]

**3.** [...]

**4.** The Companies (Inspection and Copying of Registers, Indices and Documents) Regulations 1991

**5.** The Companies (Registers and other Records) Regulations 1985

**6.** [...]

**7.** The Companies Act 1985 (Power to Enter and Remain on Premises: Procedural) Regulations 2005

## PART II    REGULATIONS MADE UNDER THE 1986 ACT

**1.** Insolvency Practitioners Regulations 1990

**2.** The Insolvency Practitioners (Recognised Professional Bodies) Order 1986

**3.** The Insolvency Rules 1986 and the Insolvency (Scotland) Rules 1986 (except in so far as they relate to the exceptions to the reserved matters specified in section C.2 of Part II of Schedule 5 to the Scotland Act 1998)

**4.** The Insolvency Fees Order 1986

**5.** The Co-operation of Insolvency Courts (Designation of Relevant Countries and Territories) Order 1986

**6.** The Co-operation of Insolvency Courts (Designation of Relevant Countries and Territories) Order 1996

7. The Co-operation of Insolvency Courts (Designation of Relevant Country) Order 1998
8. Insolvency Proceedings (Monetary Limits) Order 1986
9. Insolvency Practitioners Tribunal (Conduct of Investigations) Rules 1986
10. Insolvency Regulations 1994
11. Insolvency (Amendment) Regulations 2000

## PART III   REGULATIONS MADE UNDER OTHER LEGISLATION
1. Company and Business Names Regulations 1981
2. The Companies (Disqualification Orders) Regulations 1986
3. The Insolvent Companies (Disqualification of Unfit Directors) Proceedings Rules 1987
4. The Contracting Out (Functions of the Official Receiver) Order 1995
5. The Uncertificated Securities Regulations 1995
6. The Insolvent Companies (Reports on Conduct of Directors) Rules 1996
7. The Insolvent Companies (Reports on Conduct of Directors) (Scotland) Rules 1996

# 4

# Insolvency Law

## Insolvency Act 1986

(c. 45)

*An Act to consolidate the enactments relating to company insolvency and winding up (including the winding up of companies that are not insolvent, and of unregistered companies); enactments relating to the insolvency and bankruptcy of individuals; and other enactments bearing on those two subject matters, including the functions and qualification of insolvency practitioners, the public administration of insolvency, the penalisation and redress of malpractice and wrongdoing, and the avoidance of certain transactions at an undervalue*                                                        [25th July 1986]

## THE FIRST GROUP OF PARTS

## COMPANY INSOLVENCY; COMPANIES WINDING UP

## PART I

## COMPANY VOLUNTARY ARRANGEMENTS

### *The Proposal*

**1  Those who may propose an arrangement**

(1)  The directors of a company (other than one which is in administration or being wound up) may make a proposal under this Part to the company and to its creditors for a composition in satisfaction of its debts or a scheme of arrangement of its affairs (from here on referred to, in either case, as a 'voluntary arrangement').

(2)  A proposal under this Part is one which provides for some person ('the nominee') to act in relation to the voluntary arrangement either as trustee or otherwise for the purpose of supervising its implementation; and the nominee must be a person who is qualified to act as an insolvency practitioner or authorised to act as nominee, in relation to the voluntary arrangement.

(3)  Such a proposal may also be made—

    (a)  where the company is in administration, by the administrator,

    (b)  where the company is being wound up, by the liquidator.

(4)  In this Part 'company' means—

    (a)  a company within the meaning of section 735(1) of the Companies Act 1985,

    (b)  a company incorporated in an EEA State other than the United Kingdom; or

    (c)  a company not incorporated in an EEA State but having its centre of main interests in a member State other than Denmark.

(5)  In subsection (4), in relation to a company, 'centre of main interests' has the same meaning as in the EC Regulation and, in the absence of proof to the contrary, is presumed to be the place of its registered office (within the meaning of that Regulation).

(6)  If a company incorporated outside the United Kingdom has a principal place of business in Northern Ireland, no proposal under this Part shall be made in relation to it unless it also has a principal place of business in England and Wales or Scotland (or both in England and Wales or Scotland).

**1A  Moratorium**

(1)  Where the directors of an eligible company intend to make a proposal for a voluntary arrangement, they may take steps to obtain a moratorium for the company.

(2)  The provisions of Schedule A1 to this Act have effect with respect to—

    (a)  companies eligible for a moratorium under this section,

    (b)  the procedure for obtaining such a moratorium,

    (c)  the effects of such a moratorium, and

(d) the procedure applicable (in place of sections 2 to 6 and 7) in relation to the approval and implementation of a voluntary arrangement where such a moratorium is or has been in force.

## 2  Procedure where nominee is not the liquidator or administrator

(1)  This section applies where the nominee under section 1 is not the liquidator or administrator of the company and the directors do not propose to take steps to obtain a moratorium under section 1A for the company.

(2)  The nominee shall, within 28 days (or such longer period as the court may allow) after he is given notice of the proposal for a voluntary arrangement, submit a report to the court stating—

(a)  whether, in his opinion, the proposed voluntary arrangement has a reasonable prospect of being approved and implemented,

(aa)  whether, in his opinion, meetings of the company and of its creditors should be summoned to consider the proposal, and

(b)  if in his opinion such meetings should be summoned, the date on which, and time and place at which, he proposes the meetings should be held.

(3)  For the purposes of enabling the nominee to prepare his report, the person intending to make the proposal shall submit to the nominee—

(a)  a document setting out the terms of the proposed voluntary arrangement, and

(b)  a statement of the company's affairs containing—

(i)  such particulars of its creditors and of its debts and other liabilities and of its assets as may be prescribed, and

(ii)  such other information as may be prescribed.

(4)  The court may—

(a)  on an application made by the person intending to make the proposal, in a case where the nominee has failed to submit the report required by this section or has died, or

(b)  on an application made by that person or the nominee, in a case where it is impracticable or inappropriate for the nominee to continue to act as such,

direct that the nominee be replaced as such by another person qualified to act as an insolvency practitioner, or authorised to act as nominee, in relation to the voluntary arrangement.

## 3  Summoning of meetings

(1)  Where the nominee under section 1 is not the liquidator or administrator, and it has been report to the court that such meetings as are mentioned in section 2(2) should be summoned, the person making the report shall (unless the court otherwise directs) summon those meetings for the time, date and place proposed in the report.

(2)  Where the nominee is the liquidator or administrator, he shall summon meetings of the company and of its creditors to consider the proposal for such a time, date and place as he thinks fit.

(3)  The persons to be summoned to a creditors' meeting under this section are every creditor of the company of whose claim and address the person summoning the meeting is aware.

### *Consideration and implementation of proposal*

## 4  Decisions of meetings

(1)  The meetings summoned under section 3 shall decide whether to approve the proposed voluntary arrangement (with or without modifications).

(2)  The modifications may include one conferring the functions proposed to be conferred on the nominee on another person qualified to act as an insolvency practitioner or authorised to act as nominee, in relation to the voluntary arrangement.

But they shall not include any modification by virtue of which the proposal ceases to be a proposal such as is mentioned in section 1.

(3)  A meeting so summoned shall not approve any proposal or modification which affects the right of a secured creditor of the company to enforce his security, except with the concurrence of the creditor concerned.

(4)  Subject as follows, a meeting so summoned shall not approve any proposal or modification under which—

(a)  any preferential debt of the company is to be paid otherwise than in priority to such of its debts as are not preferential debts, or

(b)  a preferential creditor of the company is to be paid an amount in respect of a preferential debt that bears to that debt a smaller proportion than is borne to another preferential debt by the amount that is to be paid in respect of that other debt.

However, the meeting may approve such a proposal or modification with the concurrence of the preferential creditor concerned.

(5)  Subject as above, each of the meetings shall be conducted in accordance with the rules.

(6)  After the conclusion of either meeting in accordance with the rules, the chairman of the meeting shall report the result of the meeting to the court, and, immediately after reporting to the court, shall give notice of the result of the meeting to such persons as may be prescribed.

(7) References in this section to preferential debts and preferential creditors are to be read in accordance with section 386 in Part XII of this Act.

## 4A   Approval of arrangement

(1) This section applies to a decision, under section 4, with respect to the approval of a proposed voluntary arrangement.

(2) The decision has effect if, in accordance with the rules—

    (a) it has been taken by both meetings summoned under section 3, or

    (b) (subject to any order made under subsection (4)) it has been taken by the creditors' meeting summoned under that section.

(3) If the decision taken by the creditors' meeting differs from that taken by the company meeting, a member of the company may apply to the court.

(4) An application under subsection (3) shall not be made after the end of the period of 28 days beginning with—

    (a) the day on which the decision was taken by the creditors' meeting, or

    (b) where the decision of the company meeting was taken on a later day, that day.

(5) Where a member of a regulated company, within the meaning given by paragraph 44 of Schedule A1, applies to the court under subsection (3), the Financial Services Authority is entitled to be heard on the application.

(6) On an application under subsection (3), the court may—

    (a) order the decision of the company meeting to have effect instead of the decision of the creditors' meeting, or

    (b) make such other order as it thinks fit.

## 5   Effect of approval

(1) This section applies where a decision approving a voluntary arrangement has effect under section 4A.

(2) The [...] voluntary arrangement—

    (a) takes effect as if made by the company at the creditors' meeting, and

    (b) binds every person who in accordance with the rules—

        (i) was entitled to vote at that meeting (whether or not he was present or represented at it), or

        (ii) would have been so entitled if he had had notice of it,

as if he were a party to the voluntary arrangement.

(2A) If—

    (a) when the arrangement ceases to have effect any amount payable under the arrangement to a person bound by virtue of subsection (2)(b)(ii) has not been paid, and

    (b) the arrangement did not come to an end prematurely,

the company shall at that time become liable to pay to that person the amount payable under the arrangement.

(3) Subject as follows, if the company is being wound up or is in administration, the court may do one or both of the following, namely—

    (a) by order stay or sist all proceedings in the winding up or provide for the appointment of the administrator to cease to have effect;

    (b) give such directions with respect to the conduct of the winding up or the administration as it thinks appropriate for facilitating the implementation of the [...] voluntary arrangement.

(4) The court shall not make an order under subsection (3)(a)—

    (a) at any time before the end of the period of 28 days beginning with the first day on which each of the reports required by section 4(6) has been made to the court, or

    (b) at any time when an application under the next section or an appeal in respect of such an application is pending, or at any time in the period within which such an appeal may be brought.

(5) Where the company is in energy administration, the court shall not make an order or give a direction under subsection (3) unless—

    (a) the court has given the Secretary of State or the Gas and Electricity Markets Authority a reasonable opportunity of making representations to it about the proposed order or direction; and

    (b) the order or direction is consistent with the objective of the energy administration.

(6) In subsection (5) 'in energy administration' and 'objective of the energy administration' are to be construed in accordance with Schedule B1 to this Act, as applied by Part 1 of Schedule 20 to the Energy Act 2004.

## 6   Challenge of decisions

(1) Subject to this section, an application to the court may be made, by any of the persons specified below, on one or both of the following grounds, namely—

    (a) that a voluntary arrangement which has effect under section 4A unfairly prejudices the interests of a creditor, member or contributory of the company;

(b)  that there has been some material irregularity at or in relation to either of the meetings.

(2)  The persons who may apply under subsection (1) are—

(a)  a person entitled, in accordance with the rules, to vote at either of the meetings;

(aa)  a person who would have been entitled, in accordance with the rules, to vote at the creditors' meeting if he had had notice of it

(b)  the nominee or any person who has replaced him under section 2(4) or 4(2); and

(c)  if the company is being wound up or is in administration, the liquidator or administrator.

(2A)  Subject to this section, where a voluntary arrangement in relation to a company in energy administration is approved at the meetings summoned under section 3, an application to the court may be made—

(a)  by the Secretary of State, or

(b)  with the consent of the Secretary of State, by the Gas and Electricity Markets Authority,

on the ground that the voluntary arrangement is not consistent with the achievement of the objective of the energy administration.

(3)  An application under this section shall not be made

(a)  after the end of the period of 28 days beginning with the first day on which each of the reports required by section 4(6) has been made to the court or

(b)  in the case of a person who was not given notice of the creditors' meeting, after the end of the period of 28 days beginning with the day on which he became aware that the meeting had taken place,

but (subject to that) an application made by a person within subsection (2)(aa) on the ground that the voluntary arrangement prejudices his interests may be made after the arrangement has ceased to have effect, unless it came to an end prematurely.

(4)  Where on such an application the court is satisfied as to either of the grounds mentioned in subsection (1) or, in the case of an application under subsection (2A), as to the ground mentioned in that subsection, it may do one or both of the following, namely—

(a)  revoke or suspend any decision approving the voluntary arrangement which has effect under section 4A or, in a case falling within subsection (1)(b), any decision taken by the meeting in question which has effect under that section;

(b)  give a direction to any person for the summoning of further meetings to consider any revised proposal the person who made the original proposal may make or, in the case falling within subsection (1)(b), a further company or (as the case may be) creditors' meeting to reconsider the original proposal.

(5)  Where at any time after giving a direction under subsection (4)(b) for the summoning of meetings to consider a revised proposal the court is satisfied that the person who made the original proposal does not intend to submit a revised proposal, the court shall revoke the direction and revoke or suspend any decision approving the voluntary arrangement which has effect under section 4A.

(6)  In a case where the court, on an application under this section with respect to any meeting—

(a)  gives a direction under subsection (4)(b), or

(b)  revokes or suspends an approval under subsection (4)(a) or (5),

the court may give such supplemental directions as it thinks fit and, in particular, directions with respect to things done under the voluntary arrangement since it took effect.

(7)  Except in pursuance of the preceding provisions of this section, a decision taken at a meeting summoned under section 3 is not invalidated by any irregularity at or in relation to the meeting.

(8)  In this section 'in energy administration' and 'objective of the energy administration' are to be construed in accordance with Schedule B1 to this Act, as applied by Part 1 of Schedule 20 to the Energy Act 2004.

## 6A  False representations, etc

(1)  If, for the purpose of obtaining the approval of the members or creditors of a company to a proposal for a voluntary arrangement, a person who is an officer of the company—

(a)  makes any false representation, or

(b)  fraudulently does, or omits to do, anything,

he commits an offence.

(2)  Subsection (1) applies even if the proposal is not approved.

(3)  For purposes of this section 'officer' includes a shadow director.

(4)  A person guilty of an offence under this section is liable to imprisonment or a fine, or both.

## 7  Implementation of proposal

(1)  This section applies where a voluntary arrangement has effect under section 4A.

(2)  The person who is for the time being carrying out in relation to the voluntary arrangement the functions conferred—

(a)  on the nominee by virtue of the approval given at one or both of the meetings summoned under section 3

(b)  by virtue of section 2(4) or 4(2) on a person other than the nominee,

shall be known as the supervisor of the voluntary arrangement.

(3)  If any of the company's creditors or any other person is dissatisfied by any act, omission or decision of the supervisor, he may apply to the court; and on the application the court may—

    (a)  confirm, reverse or modify any act or decision of the supervisor,

    (b)  give him directions, or

    (c)  make such other order as it thinks fit.

(4)  The supervisor—

    (a)  may apply to the court for directions in relation to any particular matter arising under the voluntary arrangement, and

    (b)  is included among the persons who may apply to the court for the winding up of the company or for an administration order to be made in relation to it.

(5)  The court may, whenever—

    (a)  it is expedient to appoint a person to carry out the functions of the supervisor, and

    (b)  it is inexpedient, difficult or impracticable for an appointment to be made without the assistance of the court,

make an order appointing a person who is qualified to act as an insolvency practitioner or authorised to act as supervisor, in relation to the voluntary arrangement, either in substitution for the existing supervisor or to fill a vacancy.

(6)  The power conferred by subsection (5) is exercisable so as to increase the number of persons exercising the functions of supervisor or, where there is more than one person exercising those functions, so as to replace one or more of those persons.

## 7A   Prosecution of delinquent officers of company

(1)  This section applies where a moratorium under section 1A has been obtained for a company or the approval of a voluntary arrangement in relation to a company has taken effect under section 4A or paragraph 36 of Schedule A1.

(2)  If it appears to the nominee or supervisor that any past or present officer of the company has been guilty of any offence in connection with the moratorium or, as the case may be, voluntary arrangement for which he is criminally liable, the nominee or supervisor shall forthwith—

    (a)  report the matter to the appropriate authority, and

    (b)  provide the appropriate authority with such information and give the authority such access to and facilities for inspecting and taking copies of documents (being information or documents in the possession or under the control of the nominee or supervisor and relating to the matter in question) as the authority requires.

In this subsection, 'the appropriate authority' means—

    (i)  in the case of a company registered in England and Wales, the Secretary of State, and

    (ii)  in the case of a company registered in Scotland, the Lord Advocate.

(3)  Where a report is made to the Secretary of State under subsection (2), he may, for the purpose of investigating the matter reported to him and such other matters relating to the affairs of the company as appear to him to require investigation, exercise any of the powers which are exercisable by inspectors appointed under section 431 or 432 of the Companies Act to investigate a company's affairs.

(4)  For the purpose of such an investigation any obligation imposed on a person by any provision of the Companies Act to produce documents or give information to, or otherwise to assist, inspectors so appointed is to be regarded as an obligation similarly to assist the Secretary of State in his investigation.

(5)  An answer given by a person to a question put to him in exercise of the powers conferred by subsection (3) may be used in evidence against him.

(6)  However, in criminal proceedings in which that person is charged with an offence to which this subsection applies—

    (a)  no evidence relating to the answer may be adduced, and

    (b)  no question relating to it may be asked,

by or on behalf of the prosecution, unless evidence relating to it is adduced, or a question relating to it is asked, in the proceedings by or on behalf of that person.

(7)  Subsection (6) applies to any offence other than—

    (a)  an offence under section 2 or 5 of the Perjury Act 1911 (false statements made on oath otherwise than in judicial proceedings or made otherwise than on oath), or

    (b)  an offence under section 44(1) or (2) of the Criminal Law (Consolidation)(Scotland) Act 1995 (false statements made on oath or otherwise than on oath).

(8)  Where a prosecuting authority institutes criminal proceedings following any report under subsection (2), the nominee or supervisor, and every officer and agent of the company past and present (other than the defendant or defender), shall give the authority all assistance in connection with the prosecution which he is reasonably able to give.

For this purpose—

'agent' includes any banker or solicitor of the company and any person employed by the company as auditor, whether that person is or is not an officer of the company,

'prosecuting authority' means the Director of Public Prosecutions, the Lord Advocate or the Secretary of State.

(9)  The court may, on the application of the prosecuting authority, direct any person referred to in subsection (8) to comply with that subsection if he has failed to do so.

**7B  Arrangements coming to an end prematurely**

For the purposes of this Part, a voluntary arrangement the approval of which has taken effect under section 4A or paragraph 36 of Schedule A1 comes to an end prematurely if, when it ceases to have effect, it has not been fully implemented in respect of all persons bound by the arrangement by virtue of section 5(2)(b)(i) or, as the case may be, paragraph 37(2)(b)(i) of Schedule A1.

# PART II

# ADMINISTRATION

**8  Administration**

Schedule B1 to this Act (which makes provision about the administration of companies) shall have effect.

**9–27**  [...]

# PART III

# RECEIVERSHIP

## Chapter I

### Receivers and managers (England and Wales)

*Preliminary and general provisions*

**28  Extent of this Chapter**

This Chapter does not apply to receivers appointed under Chapter II of this Part (Scotland).

**29  Definitions**

(1)  It is hereby declared that, except where the context otherwise requires—

(a)  any reference in the Companies Act or this Act to a receiver or manager of the property of a company, or to a receiver of it, includes a receiver or manager, or (as the case may be) a receiver of part only of that property and a receiver only of the income arising from the property or from part of it; and

(b)  any reference in the Companies Act or this Act to the appointment of a receiver or manager under powers contained in an instrument includes an appointment made under powers which, by virtue of any enactment, are implied in and have effect as if contained in an instrument.

(2)  In this Chapter 'administrative receiver' means—

(a)  a receiver or manager of the whole (or substantially the whole) of a company's property appointed by or on behalf of the holders of any debentures of the company secured by a charge which, as created, was a floating charge, or by such a charge and one or more other securities; or

(b)  a person who would be such a receiver or manager but for the appointment of some other person as the receiver of part of the company's property.

**30  Disqualification of body corporate from acting as receiver**

A body corporate is not qualified for appointment as receiver of the property of a company, and any body corporate which acts as such a receiver is liable to a fine.

**31  Disqualification of bankrupt or person in respect of who a debt relief order is made**

(1)  A person commits an offence if he acts as receiver or manager of the property of a company on behalf of debenture holders while—

(a)  he is an undischarged bankrupt,

(aa)  a moratorium period under a debt relief order applies in relation to him; or

(b)  a bankruptcy restrictions order or a debt relief restrictions order is in force in respect of him.

(2)  A person guilty of an offence under subsection (1) shall be liable to imprisonment, a fine or both.

(3)  This section does not apply to a receiver or manager acting under an appointment made by the court.

### 32   Power for court to appoint official receiver

Where application is made to the court to appoint a receiver on behalf of the debenture holders or other creditors of a company which is being wound up by the court, the official receiver may be appointed.

*Receivers and managers appointed out of court*

### 33   Time from which appointment is effective

(1)   The appointment of a person as a receiver or manager of a company's property under powers contained in an instrument—

(a)   is of no effect unless it is accepted by that person before the end of the business day next following that on which the instrument of appointment is received by him or on his behalf, and

(b)   subject to this, is deemed to be made at the time at which the instrument of appointment is so received.

(2)   This section applies to the appointment of two or more persons as joint receivers or managers of a company's property under powers contained in an instrument, subject to such modifications as may be prescribed by the rules.

### 34   Liability for invalid appointment

Where the appointment of a person as the receiver or manager of a company's property under powers contained in an instrument is discovered to be invalid (whether by virtue of the invalidity of the instrument or otherwise), the court may order the person by whom or on whose behalf the appointment was made to indemnify the person appointed against any liability which arises solely by reason of the invalidity of the appointment.

### 35   Application to court for directions

(1)   A receiver or manager of the property of a company appointed under powers contained in an instrument, or the persons by whom or on whose behalf a receiver or manager has been so appointed, may apply to the court for directions in relation to any particular matter arising in connection with the performance of the functions of the receiver or manager.

(2)   On such an application, the court may give such directions, or may make such order declaring the rights of persons before the court or otherwise, as it thinks just.

### 36   Court's power to fix remuneration

(1)   The court may, on an application made by the liquidator of a company, by order fix the amount to be paid by way of remuneration to a person who, under powers contained in an instrument, has been appointed receiver or manager of the company's property.

(2)   The court's power under subsection (1), where no previous order has been made with respect thereto under the subsection—

(a)   extends to fixing the remuneration for any period before the making of the order or the application for it,

(b)   is exercisable notwithstanding that the receiver or manager has died or ceased to act before the making of the order or the application, and

(c)   where the receiver or manager has been paid or has retained for his remuneration for any period before the making of the order any amount in excess of that so fixed for that period, extends to requiring him or his personal representatives to account for the excess or such part of it as may be specified in the order.

But the power conferred by paragraph (c) shall not be exercised as respects any period before the making of the application for the order under this section, unless in the court's opinion there are special circumstances making it proper for the power to be exercised.

(3)   The court may from time to time on an application made either by the liquidator or by the receiver or manager, vary or amend an order made under subsection (1).

### 37   Liability for contracts, etc

(1)   A receiver or manager appointed under powers contained in an instrument (other than an administrative receiver) is, to the same extent as if he had been appointed by order of the court—

(a)   personally liable on any contract entered into by him in the performance of his functions (except in so far as the contract otherwise provides) and on any contract of employment adopted by him in the performance of those functions, and

(b)   entitled in respect of that liability to indemnity out of the assets.

(2)   For the purposes of subsection (1)(a), the receiver or manager is not to be taken to have adopted a contract of employment by reason of anything done or omitted to be done with 14 days after his appointment.

(3)   Subsection (1) does not limit any right to indemnity which the receiver or manager would have apart from it, nor limit his liability on contracts entered into without authority, nor confer any right to indemnity in respect of that liability.

(4)   Where at any time the receiver or manager so appointed vacates office—

(a) his remuneration and any expenses properly incurred by him, and

(b) any indemnity to which he is entitled out of the assets of the company,

shall be charged on and paid out of any property of the company which is in his custody or under his control at that time in priority to any charge or other security held by the person by or on whose behalf he was appointed.

## 38 Receivership accounts to be delivered to registrar

(1) Except in the case of an administrative receiver, every receiver or manager of a company's property who has been appointed under powers contained in an instrument shall deliver to the registrar of companies for registration the requisite accounts of his receipts and payments.

(2) The accounts shall be delivered within one month (or such longer period as the registrar may allow) after the expiration of 12 months from the date of his appointment and of every subsequent period of 6 months, and also within one month after he ceases to act as receiver or manager.

(3) The requisite accounts shall be an abstract in the prescribed form showing—

(a) receipts and payments during the relevant period of 12 or 6 months, or

(b) where the receiver or manager ceases to act, receipts and payments during the period from the end of the period of 12 or 6 months to which the last preceding abstract related (or, if no preceding abstract has been delivered under this section, from the date of his appointment) up to the date of his so ceasing, and the aggregate amount of receipts and payments during all preceding periods since his appointment.

(4) In this section 'prescribed' means prescribed by regulations made by statutory instrument by the Secretary of State.

(5) A receiver or manager who makes default in complying with this section is liable to a fine and, for continued contravention, to a daily default fine.

*Provisions applicable to every receivership*

## 39 Notification that receiver or manager appointed

(1) Where a receiver or manager of the property of a company has been appointed—

(a) every invoice, order for goods or services, business letter or order form (whether in hard copy, electronic or any other form) issued by or on behalf of the company or the receiver or manager or the liquidator of the company; and

(b) all the company's websites,

must contain a statement that a receiver or manager has been appointed.

(2) If default is made in complying with this section, the company and any of the following persons, who knowingly and wilfully authorises or permits the default, namely, any officer of the company, any liquidator of the company and any receiver or manager, is liable to a fine.

## 40 Payment of debts out of assets subject to floating charge

(1) The following applies in the case of a company, where a receiver is appointed on behalf of the holders of any debentures of the company secured by a charge which, as created, was a floating charge.

(2) If the company is not at the time in course of being wound up, its preferential debts (within the meaning given to that expression by section 386 in Part XII) shall be paid out of the assets coming to the hands of the receiver in priority to any claims for principal or interest in respect of the debentures.

(3) Payments made under this section shall be recouped, as far as may be, out of the assets of the company available for payment of general creditors.

## 41 Enforcement of duty to make returns

(1) If a receiver or manager of a company's property—

(a) having made default in filing, delivering or making any return, account or other document, or in giving any notice, which a receiver or manager is by law required to file, deliver, make or give, fails to make good the default within 14 days after the service on him of a notice requiring him to do so, or

(b) having been appointed under powers contained in an instrument, has, after being required at any time by the liquidator of the company to do so, failed to render proper accounts of his receipts and payments and to vouch them and pay over to the liquidator the amount properly payable to him,

the court may, on an application made for the purpose, make an order directing the receiver or manager (as the case may be) to make good the default within such time as may be specified in the order.

(2) In the case of the default mentioned in subsection (1)(a), application to the court may be made by any member or creditor of the company or by the registrar of companies; and in the case of the default mentioned in subsection (1)(b), the application shall be made by the liquidator.

In either case the court's order may provide that all costs of and incidental to the application shall be borne by the receiver or manager, as the case may be.

(3) Nothing in this section prejudices the operation of any enactment imposing penalties on receivers in respect of any such default as is mentioned in subsection (1).

*Administrative receivers: general*

### 42    General powers

(1)  The powers conferred on the administrative receiver of a company by the debentures by virtue of which he was appointed are deemed to include (except in so far as they are inconsistent with any of the provisions of those debentures) the powers specified in Schedule 1 to this Act.

(2)  In the application of Schedule 1 to the administrative receiver of a company—

(a)  the words 'he' and 'him' refer to the administrative receiver, and

(b)  references to the property of the company are to the property of which he is or, but for the appointment of some other person as the receiver of part of the company's property, would be the receiver or manager.

(3)  A person dealing with the administrative receiver in good faith and for value is not concerned to inquire whether the receiver is acting within his powers.

### 43    Power to dispose of charged property, etc

(1)  Where, on an application by the administrative receiver, the court is satisfied that the disposal (with or without other assets) of any relevant property which is subject to a security would be likely to promote a more advantageous realisation of the company's assets than would otherwise be effected, the court may by order authorise the administrative receiver to dispose of the property as if it were not subject to the security.

(2)  Subsection (1) does not apply in the case of any security held by the person by or on whose behalf the administrative receiver was appointed, or of any security to which a security so held has priority.

(3)  It shall be a condition of an order under this section that—

(a)  the net proceeds of the disposal, and

(b)  where those proceeds are less than such amount as may be determined by the court to be the net amount which would be realised on a sale of the property in the open market by a willing vendor, such sums as may be required to make good the deficiency,

shall be applied towards discharging the sums secured by the security.

(4)  Where a condition imposed in pursuance of subsection (3) relates to two or more securities, that condition shall require the net proceeds of the disposal and, where paragraph (b) of that subsection applies, the sums mentioned in that paragraph to be applied towards discharging the sums secured by those securities in the order of their priorities.

(5)  An office copy of an order under this section shall, within 14 days of the making of the order, be sent by the administrative receiver to the registrar of companies.

(6)  If the administrative receiver without reasonable excuse fails to comply with subsection (5), he is liable to a fine and, for continued contravention, to a daily default fine.

(7)  In this section 'relevant property', in relation to the administrative receiver, means the property of which he is or, but for the appointment of some other person as the receiver of part of the company's property, would be the receiver or manager.

### 44    Agency and liability for contracts

(1)  The administrative receiver of a company—

(a)  is deemed to be the company's agent, unless and until the company goes into liquidation;

(b)  is personally liable on any contract entered into by him in the carrying out of his functions (except in so far as the contract otherwise provides) and , to the extent of any qualifying liability, on any contract of employment adopted by him in the carrying out of those functions; and

(c)  is entitled in respect of that liability to an indemnity out of the assets of the company.

(2)  For the purposes of subsection (1)(b) the administrative receiver is not to be taken to have adopted a contract of employment by reason of anything done or omitted to be done within 14 days after his appointment.

(2A)  For the purposes of subsection (1)(b), a liability under a contract of employment is a qualifying liability if—

(a)  it is a liability to pay a sum by way of wages or salary or contribution to an occupational pension scheme,

(b)  it is incurred while the administrative receiver is in office, and

(c)  it is in respect of services rendered wholly or partly after the adoption of the contract.

(2B)  Where a sum payable in respect of a liability which is a qualifying liability for the purposes of subsection (1)(b) is payable in respect of services rendered partly before and partly after the adoption of the contract, liability under subsection (1)(b) shall only extend to so much of the sum as is payable in respect of services rendered after the adoption of the contract.

(2C)  For the purposes of subsections (2A) and (2B)—

(a)  wages or salary payable in respect of a period of holiday or absence from work through sickness or other good cause are deemed to be wages or (as the case may be) salary in respect of services rendered in that period, and

(b) a sum payable in lieu of holiday is deemed to be wages or (as the case may be) salary in respect of services rendered in the period by reference to which the holiday entitlement arose.

(2D) In subsection (2C)(a), the reference to wages or salary payable in respect of a period of holiday includes any sums which, if they had been paid, would have been treated for the purposes of the enactments relating to social security as earnings in respect of that period.

(3) This section does not limit any right to indemnity which the administrative receiver would have apart from it, nor limit his liability on contracts entered into or adopted without authority, nor confer any right to indemnity in respect of that liability.

### 45    Vacation of office

(1) An administrative receiver of a company may at any time be removed from office by order of the court (but not otherwise) and may resign his office by giving notice of his resignation in the prescribed manner to such persons as may be prescribed.

(2) An administrative receiver shall vacate office if he ceases to be qualified to act as an insolvency practitioner in relation to the company.

(3) Where at any time an administrative receiver vacates office—

(a) his remuneration and any expenses properly incurred by him, and

(b) any indemnity to which he is entitled out of the assets of the company,

shall be charged on and paid out of any property of the company which is in his custody or under his control at that time in priority to any security held by the person by or on whose behalf he was appointed.

(4) Where an administrative receiver vacates office otherwise than by death, he shall, within 14 days after his vacation of office, send a notice to that effect to the registrar of companies.

(5) If an administrative receiver without reasonable excuse fails to comply with subsection (4), he is liable to a fine *and, for continued contravention, to a daily default fine*[1]

*Administrative receivers: ascertainment and investigation of company's affairs*

### 46    Information to be given by administrative receiver

(1) Where an administrative receiver is appointed, he shall—

(a) forthwith send to the company and publish in the prescribed manner a notice of his appointment, and

(b) within 28 days after his appointment, unless the court otherwise directs, send such a notice to all the creditors of the company (so far as he is aware of their addresses).

(2) This section and the next do not apply in relation to the appointment of an administrative receiver to act—

(a) with an existing administrative receiver, or

(b) in place of an administrative receiver dying or ceasing to act,

except that, where they apply to an administrative receiver who dies or ceases to act before they have been fully complied with, the references in this section and the next to the administrative receiver include (subject to the next subsection) his successor and any continuing administrative receiver.

(3) If the company is being wound up, this section and the next apply notwithstanding that the administrative receiver and the liquidator are the same person, but with any necessary modifications arising from that fact.

(4) If the administrative receiver without reasonable excuse fails to comply with this section, he is liable to a fine and, for continued contravention, to a daily default fine.

### 47    Statement of affairs to be submitted

(1) Where an administrative receiver is appointed, he shall forthwith require some or all of the persons mentioned below to make out and submit to him a statement in the prescribed form as to the affairs of the company.

(2) A statement submitted under this section shall be verified by affidavit by the persons required to submit it and shall show—

(a) particulars of the company's assets, debts and liabilities;

(b) the names and addresses of its creditors;

(c) the securities held by them respectively;

(d) the dates when the securities were respectively given; and

(e) such further or other information as may be prescribed.

(3) The persons referred to in subsection (1) are—

(a) those who are or have been officers of the company;

(b) those who have taken part in the company's formation at any time within one year before the date of the appointment of the administrative receiver;

(c) those who are in the company's employment, or have been in its employment within that year, and are in the administrative receiver's opinion capable of giving the information required;

(d) those who are or have been within that year officers of or in the employment of a company which is, or within that year was, an officer of the company.

---

[1] The words in italics repealed by the Companies Act 1989 c 40 from a date to be appointed.

In this subsection 'employment' includes employment under a contract for services.

(4) Where any persons are required under this section to submit a statement of affairs to the administrative receiver, they shall do so (subject to the next subsection) before the end of the period of 21 days beginning with the day after that on which the prescribed notice of the requirement is given to them by the administrative receiver.

(5) The administrative receiver, if he thinks fit, may—

(a) at any time release a person from an obligation imposed on him under subsection (1) or (2), or

(b) either when giving notice under subsection (4) or subsequently, extend the period so mentioned;

and where the administrative receiver has refused to exercise a power conferred by this subsection, the court, if it thinks fit, may exercise it.

(6) If a person without reasonable excuse fails to comply with any obligation imposed under this section, he is liable to a fine and, for continued contravention, to a daily default fine.

### 48   Report by administrative receiver

(1) Where an administrative receiver is appointed, he shall, within 3 months (or such longer period as the court may allow) after his appointment, send to the registrar of companies, to any trustees for secured creditors of the company and (so far as he is aware of their addresses) to all such creditors a report as to the following matters, namely—

(a) the events leading up to his appointment, so far as he is aware of them;

(b) the disposal or proposed disposal by him of any property of the company and the carrying on or proposed carrying on by him of any business of the company;

(c) the amounts of principal and interest payable to the debenture holders by whom or on whose behalf he was appointed and the amounts payable to preferential creditors; and

(d) the amount (if any) likely to be available for the payment of other creditors.

(2) The administrative receiver shall also, within 3 months (or such longer period as the court may allow) after his appointment, either—

(a) send a copy of the report (so far as he is aware of their addresses) to all unsecured creditors of the company; or

(b) publish in the prescribed manner a notice stating an address to which unsecured creditors of the company should write for copies of the report to be sent to them free of charge,

and (in either case), unless the court otherwise directs, lay a copy of the report before a meeting of the company's unsecured creditors summoned for the purpose on not less than 14 days' notice.

(3) The court shall not give a direction under subsection (2) unless—

(a) the report states the intention of the administrative receiver to apply for the direction, and

(b) a copy of the report is sent to the persons mentioned in paragraph (a) of that subsection, or a notice is published as mentioned in paragraph (b) of that subsection, not less than 14 days before the hearing of the application.

(4) Where the company has gone or goes into liquidation, the administrative receiver—

(a) shall, within 7 days after his compliance with subsection (1) or, if later, the nomination or appointment of the liquidator, send a copy of the report to the liquidator, and

(b) where he does so within the time limited for compliance with subsection (2), is not required to comply with that subsection.

(5) A report under this section shall include a summary of the statement of affairs made out and submitted to the administrative receiver under section 47 and of his comments (if any) upon it.

(6) Nothing in this section is to be taken as requiring any such report to include any information the disclosure of which would seriously prejudice the carrying out by the administrative receiver of his functions.

(7) Section 46(2) applies for the purposes of this section also.

(8) If the administrative receiver without reasonable excuse fails to comply with this section, he is liable to a fine and, for continued contravention, to a daily default fine.

### 49   Committee of creditors

(1) Where a meeting of creditors is summoned under section 48, the meeting may, if it thinks fit, establish a committee ('the creditors' committee') to exercise the functions conferred on it by or under this Act.

(2) If such a committee is established, the committee may, on giving not less than 7 days' notice, require the administrative receiver to attend before it at any reasonable time and furnish it with such information relating to the carrying out by him of his functions as it may reasonably require.

## Chapter II

## Receivers (Scotland)

### 50   Extent of this Chapter

This Chapter extends to Scotland only.

### 51  Power to appoint receiver

(1)  It is competent under the law of Scotland for the holder of a floating charge over all or any part of the property (including uncalled capital), which may from time to time be comprised in the property and undertaking of an incorporated company (whether a company within the meaning of the Companies Act or not) which the Court of Session has jurisdiction to wind up, to appoint a receiver of such part of the property of the company as is subject to the charge.

(2)  It is competent under the law of Scotland for the court, on the application of the holder of such a floating charge, to appoint a receiver of such part of the property of the company as is subject to the charge.

(2A)  Subsections (1) and (2) are subject to section 72A.

(3)  The following are disqualified from being appointed as receiver—

    (a)  a body corporate;

    (b)  an undischarged bankrupt; and

    (ba)  a person subject to a bankruptcy restriction order

    (c)  a firm according to the law of Scotland.

(4)  A body corporate or a firm according to the law of Scotland which acts as a receiver is liable to a fine.

(5)  An undischarged bankrupt or a person subject to bankruptcy restriction order who so acts is liable to imprisonment or a fine, or both.

(6)  In this section, 'receiver' includes joint receivers; and
'bankruptcy restrictions order' means—

    (a)  a bankruptcy restrictions order made under section 56A of the Bankruptcy (Scotland) Act 1985 (c.66);

    (b)  a bankruptcy restrictions undertaking entered into under section 56G of that Act;

    (c)  a bankruptcy restrictions order made under paragraph 1 of Schedule 4A to this Act; or

    (d)  a bankruptcy restrictions undertaking entered into under paragraph 7 of that Schedule.

### 52  Circumstances justifying appointment

(1)  A receiver may be appointed under section 51(1) by the holder of the floating charge on the occurrence of any event which, by the provisions of the instrument creating the charge, entitles the holder of the charge to make that appointment and, in so far as not otherwise provided for by the instrument, on the occurrence of any of the following events, namely—

    (a)  the expiry of a period of 21 days after the making of a demand for payment of the whole or any part of the principal sum secured by the charge, without payment having been made;

    (b)  the expiry of a period of 2 months during the whole of which interest due and payable under the charge has been in arrears;

    (c)  the making of an order or the passing of a resolution to wind up the company;

    (d)  the appointment of a receiver by virtue of any other floating charge created by the company.

(2)  A receiver may be appointed by the court under section 51(2) on the occurrence of any event which, by the provisions of the instrument creating the floating charge, entitles the holder of the charge to make that appointment and, in so far as not otherwise provided for by the instrument, on the occurrence of any of the following events, namely—

    (a)  where the court, on the application of the holder of the charge, pronounces itself satisfied that the position of the holder of the charge is likely to be prejudiced if no such appointment is made;

    (b)  any of the events referred to in paragraphs (a) to (c) of subsection (1).

### 53  Mode of appointment by holder of charge

(1)  The appointment of a receiver by the holder of the floating charge under section 51(1) shall be by means of an instrument subscribed in accordance with the Requirements of Writing (Scotland) Act 1995 ('the instrument of appointment'), a copy (certified in the prescribed manner to be a correct copy) whereof shall be delivered by or on behalf of the person making the appointment to the registrar of companies for registration within 7 days of its execution and shall be accompanied by a notice in the prescribed form.

(2)  If any person without reasonable excuse makes default in complying with the requirements of subsection (1), he is liable to a fine *and, for continued contravention, to a daily default fine*.

(3)  [...].

(4)  If the receiver is to be appointed by the holders of a series of secured debentures, the instrument of appointment may be executed on behalf of the holders of the floating charge by any person authorised by resolution of the debenture-holders to execute the instrument.

(5)  On receipt of the certified copy of the instrument of appointment in accordance with subsection (1), the registrar shall, on payment of the prescribed fee, enter the particulars of the appointment in the register of charges.

(6)  The appointment of a person as a receiver by an instrument of appointment in accordance with subsection (1)—

(a) is of no effect unless it is accepted by that person before the end of the business day next following that on which the instrument of appointment is received by him or on his behalf, and

(b) subject to paragraph (a), is deemed to be made on the day on and at the time at which the instrument of appointment is so received, as evidenced by a written docquet by that person or on his behalf;

and this subsection applies to the appointment of joint receivers subject to such modifications as may be prescribed.

(7) On the appointment of a receiver under this section, the floating charge by virtue of which he was appointed attaches to the property then subject to the charge; and such attachment has effect as if the charge was a fixed security over the property to which it has attached.[2]

### 54   Appointment by court

(1) Application for the appointment of a receiver by the court under section 51(2) shall be by petition to the court, which shall be served on the company.

(2) On such an application, the court shall, if it thinks fit, issue an interlocutor making the appointment of the receiver.

(3) A copy (certified by the clerk of the court to be a correct copy) of the court's interlocutor making the appointment shall be delivered by or on behalf of the petitioner to the registrar of companies for registration, accompanied by a notice in the prescribed form, within 7 days of the date of the interlocutor or much longer period as the court may allow.

If any person without reasonable excuse makes default in complying with the requirements of this subsection, he is liable to a fine *and, for continued contravention, to a daily default fine*.

(4) On receipt of the certified copy interlocutor in accordance with subsection (3), the registrar shall, on payment of the prescribed fee, enter the particulars of the appointment in the register of charges.

(5) The receiver is to be regarded as having been appointed on the date of his being appointed by the court.

(6) On the appointment of a receiver under this section, the floating charge by virtue of which he was appointed attaches to the property then subject to the charge; and such attachment has effect as if the charge were a fixed security over the property to which it has attached.

(7) In making rules of court for the purposes of this section, the Court of Session shall have regard to the need for special provision for cases which appear to the court to require to be dealt with as a matter of urgency.[3]

### 55   Powers of receiver

(1) Subject to the next subsection, a receiver has in relation to such part of the property of the company as is attached by the floating charge by virtue of which he was appointed, the powers, if any, given to him by the instrument creating that charge.

(2) In addition, the receiver has under this Chapter the powers as respects that property (in so far as these are not inconsistent with any provision contained in that instrument) which are specified in Schedule 2 to this Act.

(3) Subsections (1) and (2) apply—

(a) subject to the rights of any person who has effectually executed diligence on all or any part of the property of the company prior to the appointment of the receiver, and

(b) subject to the rights of any person who holds over all or any part of the property of the company a fixed security or floating charge having priority, over, or ranking pari passu with, the floating charge by virtue of which the receiver was appointed.

(4) A person dealing with a receiver in good faith and for value is not concerned to enquire whether the receiver is acting within his powers.

### 56   Precedence among receivers

(1) Where there are two or more floating charges subsisting over all or any part of the property of the company, a receiver may be appointed under this Chapter by virtue of each such charge; but a receiver appointed by, or on the application of, the holder of a floating charge having priority of ranking over any other floating charge by virtue of which a receiver has been appointed has the powers given to a receiver by section 55 and Schedule 2 to the exclusion of any other receiver.

(2) Where two or more floating charges rank with one another equally, and two or more receivers have been appointed by virtue of such charges, the receivers so appointed are deemed to have been appointed as joint receivers.

(3) Receivers appointed, or deemed to have been appointed, as joint receivers shall act jointly unless the instrument of appointment or respective instruments of appointment otherwise provide.

(4) Subject to subsection (5) below, the powers of a receiver appointed by, or on the application of, the holder of a floating charge are suspended by, and as from the date of, the appointment of a receiver by, or on the application of, the holder of a floating charge having priority of ranking over that charge to

---

[2]   The words in italics repealed by the Companies Act 1989 c 40 from a date to be appointed.
[3]   The words in italics repealed by the Companies Act 1989 c 40 from a date to be appointed.

such extent as may be necessary to enable the receiver second mentioned to exercise his powers under section 55 and Schedule 2; and any powers so suspended take effect again when the floating charge having priority of ranking ceases to attach to the property then subject to the charge, whether such cessation is by virtue of section 62(6) or otherwise.

(5)  The suspension of the powers of a receiver under subsection (4) does not have the effect of requiring him to release any part of the property (including any letters or documents) of the company from his control until he receives from the receiver superseding him a valid indemnity (subject to the limit of the value of such part of the property of the company as is subject to the charge by virtue of which he was appointed) in respect of any expenses, charges and liabilities he may have incurred in the performance of his functions as receiver.

(6)  The suspension of the powers of a receiver under subsection (4) does not cause the floating charge by virtue of which he was appointed to cease to attach to the property to which it attached by virtue of section 53(7) or 54(6).

(7)  Nothing in this section prevents the same receiver being appointed by virtue of two or more floating charges.

## 57  Agency and liability of receiver for contracts

(1)  A receiver is deemed to be the agent of the company in relation to such property of the company as is attached by the floating charge by virtue of which he was appointed.

(1A)  Without prejudice to subsection (1), a receiver is deemed to be the agent of the company in relation to any contract of employment adopted by him in the carrying out of his functions.

(2)  A receiver (including a receiver whose powers are subsequently suspended under section 56) is personally liable on any contract entered into by him in the performance of his functions, except in so far as the contract otherwise provides, and , to the extent of any qualifying liability,on any contract of employment adopted by him in the carrying out of those functions.

(2A)  For the purposes of subsection (2), a liability under a contract of employment is a qualifying liability if—

    (a)  it is a liability to pay a sum by way of wages or salary or contribution to an occupational pension scheme,

    (b)  it is incurred while the receiver is in office, and

    (c)  it is in respect of services rendered wholly or partly after the adoption of the contract.

(2B)  Where a sum payable in respect of a liability which is a qualifying liability for the purposes of subsection (2) is payable in respect of services rendered partly before and partly after the adoption of the contract, liability under that subsection shall only extend to so much of the sum as is payable in respect of services rendered after the adoption of the contract.

(2C)  For the purposes of subsections (2A) and (2B)—

    (a)  wages or salary payable in respect of a period of holiday or absence from work through sickness or other good cause are deemed to be wages or (as the case may be) salary in respect of services rendered in that period, and

    (b)  a sum payable in lieu of holiday is deemed to be wages or (as the case may be) salary in respect of services rendered in the period by reference to which the holiday entitlement arose.

(2D)  In subsection (2C)(a), the reference to wages or salary payable in respect of a period of holiday includes any sums which, if they had been paid, would have been treated for the purposes of the enactments relating to social security as earnings in respect of that period.

(3)  A receiver who is personally liable by virtue of subsection (2) is entitled to be indemnified out of the property in respect of which he was appointed.

(4)  Any contract entered into by or on behalf of the company prior to the appointment of a receiver continues in force (subject to its terms) notwithstanding that appointment, but the receiver does not by virtue only of his appointment incur any personal liability on any such contract.

(5)  For the purposes of subsection (2), a receiver is not to be taken to have adopted a contract of employment by reason of anything done or omitted to be done within 14 days after his appointment.

(6)  This section does not limit any right to indemnity which the receiver would have apart from it, nor limit his liability on contracts entered into or adopted without authority, nor confer any right to indemnity in respect of that liability.

(7)  Any contract entered into by a receiver in the performance of his functions continues in force (subject to its terms) although the powers of the receiver are subsequently suspended under section 56.

## 58  Remuneration of receiver

(1)  The remuneration to be paid to a receiver is to be determined by agreement between the receiver and the holder of the floating charge by virtue of which he was appointed.

(2)  Where the remuneration to be paid to the receiver has not been determined under subsection (1), or where it has been so determined but is disputed by any of the persons mentioned in paragraphs (a) to (d) below, it may be fixed instead by the Auditor of the Court of Session on application made to him by—

> (a) the receiver;
>
> (b) the holder of any floating charge or fixed security over all or any part of the property of the company;
>
> (c) the company; or
>
> (d) the liquidator of the company.

(3) Where the receiver has been paid or has retained for his remuneration for any period before the remuneration has been fixed by the Auditor of the Court of Session under subsection (2) any amount in excess of the remuneration so fixed for that period, the receiver or his personal representatives shall account for the excess.

## 59   Priority of debts

(1) Where a receiver is appointed and the company is not at the time of the appointment in course of being wound up, the debts which fall under subsection (2) of this section shall be paid out of any assets coming to the hands of the receiver in priority to any claim for principal or interest by the holder of the floating charge by virtue of which the receiver was appointed.

(2) Debts falling under this subsection are preferential debts (within the meaning given by section 386 in Part XII) which, by the end of a period of 6 months after advertisement by the receiver for claims in the Edinburgh Gazette and in a newspaper circulating in the district where the company carries on business either—

> (i)  have been intimated to him, or
>
> (ii) have become known to him.

(3) Any payments made under this section shall be recouped as far as may be out of the assets of the company available for payment of ordinary creditors.

## 60   Distribution of moneys

(1) Subject to the next section, and to the rights of any of the following categories of persons (which rights shall, except to the extent otherwise provided in any instrument, have the following order of priority), namely—

> (a) the holder of any fixed security which is over property subject to the floating charge and which ranks prior to, or pari passu with, the floating charge;
>
> (b) all persons who have effectually executed diligence on any part of the property of the company which is subject to the charge by virtue of which the receiver was appointed;
>
> (c) creditors in respect of all liabilities, charges and expenses incurred by or on behalf of the receiver;
>
> (d) the receiver in respect of his liabilities, expenses and remuneration, and any indemnity to which he is entitled out of the property of the company; and
>
> (e) the preferential creditors entitled to payment under section 59,

the receiver shall pay moneys received by him to the holder of the floating charge by virtue of which the receiver was appointed in or towards satisfaction of the debt secured by the floating charge.

(2) Any balance of moneys remaining after the provisions of subsection (1) and section 61 below have been satisfied shall be paid in accordance with their respective rights and interests to the following persons, as the case may require—

> (a) any other receiver;
>
> (b) the holder of a fixed security which is over property subject to the floating charge;
>
> (c) the company or its liquidator, as the case may be.

(3) Where any question arises as to the person entitled to a payment under this section, or where a receipt or a discharge of a security cannot be obtained in respect of any such payment, the receiver shall consign the amount of such payment in any joint stock bank of issue in Scotland in name of the Accountant of Court for behoof of the person or persons entitled thereto.

## 61   Disposal of interest in property

(1) Where the receiver sells or disposes, or is desirous of selling or disposing, or any property or interest in property of the company which is subject to the floating charge by virtue of which the receiver was appointed and which is—

> (a) subject to any security or interest of, or burden or encumbrance in favour of, a creditor the ranking of which is prior to, or pari passu with, or postponed to the floating charge, or
>
> (b) property or an interest in property affected or attached by effectual diligence executed by any person,

and the receiver is unable to obtain the consent of such creditor or, as the case may be, such person to such a sale or disposal, the receiver may apply to the court for authority to sell or dispose of the property or interest in property free of such security, interest, burden, encumbrance or diligence

(1A) For the purposes of subsection (1) above, an inhibition which takes effect after the creation of the floating charge by virtue of which the receiver was appointed is not an effectual diligence.

*(1B) For the purposes of subsection (1) above, an arrestment is an effectual diligence only where it is executed before the floating charge, by virtue of which the receiver was appointed, attaches to the property comprised in the company's property and undertaking.*

(2) Subject to the next subsection, on such an application the court may, if it thinks fit, authorise the sale or disposal of the property or interest in question free of such security, interest, burden, encumbrance or diligence, and such authorisation may be on such terms or conditions as the court thinks fit.

(3) In the case of an application where a fixed security over the property or interest in question which ranks prior to the floating charge has not been met or provided for in full, the court shall not authorise the sale or disposal of the property or interest in question unless it is satisfied that the sale or disposal would be like to provide a more advantageous realisation of the company's assets than would otherwise be effected.

(4) It shall be a condition of an authorisation to which subsection (3) applies that—

    (a) the net proceeds of the disposal, and

    (b) where those proceeds are less than such amount as may be determined by the court to be the net amount which would be realised on a sale of the property or interest in the open market by a willing seller, such sums as may be required to make good the deficiency,

shall be applied towards discharging the sums secured by the fixed security.

(5) Where a condition imposed in pursuance of subsection (4) relates to two or more such fixed securities, that condition shall require the net proceeds of the disposal and, where paragraph (b) of that subsection applies, the sums mentioned in that paragraph to be applied towards discharging the sums secured by those fixed securities in the order of their priorities.

(6) A copy of an authorisation under subsection (2) certified by the clerk of court shall, within 14 days of the granting of the authorisation, be sent by the receiver to the registrar of companies.

(7) If the receiver without reasonable excuse fails to comply with subsection (6), he is liable to a fine and, for continued contravention, to a daily default fine.

(8) Where any sale or disposal is effected in accordance with the authorisation of the court under subsection (2), the receiver shall grant to the purchaser or disponee an appropriate document of transfer or conveyance of the property or interest in question, and that document has the effect, or, where recording, intimation or registration of that document is a legal requirement for completion of title to the property or interest, then that recording, intimation or registration (as the case may be) has the effect, of—

    (a) disencumbering the property or interest of the security, interest, burden or encumbrance affecting it, and

    (b) freeing the property or interest from the diligence executed upon it.

(9) Nothing in this section prejudices the right of any creditor of the company to rank for his debt in the winding up of the company.[4]

## 62  Cessation of appointment of receiver

(1) A receiver may be removed from office by the court under subsection (3) below and may resign his office by giving notice of his resignation in the prescribed manner to such persons as may be prescribed.

(2) A receiver shall vacate office if he ceases to be qualified to act as an insolvency practitioner in relation to the company.

(3) Subject to the next subsection, a receiver may, on application to the court by the holder of the floating charge by virtue of which he was appointed, be removed by the court on cause shown.

(4) Where at any time a receiver vacates office—

    (a) his remuneration and any expenses properly incurred by him, and

    (b) any indemnity to which he is entitled out of the property of the company,

shall be paid out of the property of the company which is subject to the floating charge and shall have priority as provided for in section 60(1).

(5) When a receiver ceases to act as such otherwise than by death he shall, and, when a receiver is removed by the court, the holder of the floating charge by virtue of which he was appointed shall, within 14 days of the cessation or removal (as the case may be) given the registrar of companies notice to that effect, and the registrar shall enter the notice in the register of charges.

If the receiver or the holder of the floating charge (as the case may require) makes default in complying with the requirements of this subsection, he is liable to a fine and, *for continued contravention, to a daily default fine.*

(6) If by the expiry of a period of one month following upon the removal of the receiver or his ceasing to act as such no other receiver has been appointed, the floating charge by virtue of which the receiver was appointed—

    (a) thereupon ceases to attach to the property then subject to the charge, and

    (b) again subsists as a floating charge;

and for the purposes of calculating the period of one month under this subsection no account shall be taken of any period during which the company is in administration, under Part II of this Act [...].[5]

## 63  Powers of court

(1) The court on the application of—

---

[4] Section 61(1B) inserted by Bankruptcy and Due Diligence etc (Scotland) Act 2007 from a date to be appointed.

[5] The words in italics repealed by the Companies Act 1989 c 40 from a date to be appointed.

(a) the holder of a floating charge by virtue of which a receiver was appointed, or

(b) a receiver appointed under section 51,

may give directions to the receiver in respect of any matter arising in connection with the performance by him of his functions.

(2) Where the appointment of a person as a receiver by the holder of a floating charge is discovered to be invalid (whether by virtue of the invalidity of the instrument or otherwise), the court may order the holder of the floating charge to indemnify the person appointed against any liability which arises solely by reason of the invalidity of the appointment.

### 64  Notification that receiver appointed

(1) Where a receiver has been appointed—

(a) every invoice, order for goods or services, business letter or order form (whether in hard copy, electronic or any other form) issued by or on behalf of the company or the receiver or the liquidator of the company; and

(b) all the company's websites,

must contain a statement that a receiver has been appointed.

(2) If default is made in complying with the requirements of this section, the company and any of the following persons who knowingly and wilfully authorises or permits the default, namely any officer of the company, any liquidator of the company and any receiver, is liable to a fine.

### 65  Information to be given by receiver

(1) Where a receiver is appointed, he shall—

(a) forthwith send to the company and publish notice of his appointment, and

(b) within 28 days after his appointment, unless the court otherwise directs, send such notice to all the creditors of the company (so far as he is aware of their addresses).

(2) This section and the next do not apply in relation to the appointment of a receiver to act—

(a) with an existing receiver, or

(b) in place of a receiver who has died or ceased to act,

except that, where they apply to a receiver who dies or ceases to act before they have been fully complied with, the references in this section and the next to the receiver include (subject to subsection (3) of this section) his successor and any continuing receiver.

(3) If the company is being wound up, this section and the next apply notwithstanding that the receiver and the liquidator are the same person, but with any necessary modifications arising from that fact.

(4) If a person without reasonable excuse fails to comply with this section, he is liable to a fine and, for continued contravention, to a daily default fine.

### 66  Company's statement of affairs

(1) Where a receiver of a company is appointed, the receiver shall forthwith require some or all of the persons mentioned in subsection (3) below to make out and submit to him a statement in the prescribed form as to the affairs of the company.

(2) A statement submitted under this section shall be verified by affidavit by the persons required to submit it and shall show—

(a) particulars of the company's assets, debts and liabilities;

(b) the names and addresses of its creditors;

(c) the securities held by them respectively;

(d) the dates when the securities were respectively given; and

(e) such further or other information as may be prescribed.

(3) The persons referred to in subsection (1) are—

(a) those who are or have been officers of the company;

(b) those who have taken part in the company's formation at any time within one year before the date of the appointment of the receiver;

(c) those who are in the company's employment or have been in its employment within that year, and are in the receiver's opinion capable of giving the information required;

(d) those who are or have been within that year officers of or in the employment of a company which is, or within that year was, an officer of the company.

In this subsection 'employment' includes employment under a contract for services.

(4) Where any persons are required under this section to submit a statement of affairs to the receiver they shall do so (subject to the next subsection) before the end of the period of 21 days beginning with the day after that on which the prescribed notice of the requirement is given to them by the receiver.

(5) The receiver, if he thinks fit, may—

(a) at any time release a person from an obligation imposed on him under subsection (1) or (2), or

(b) either when giving the notice mentioned in subsection (4) or subsequently extend the period so mentioned,

and where the receiver has refused to exercise a power conferred by this subsection, the court, if it thinks fit, may exercise it.

(6) If a person without reasonable excuse fails to comply with any obligation imposed under this section, he is liable to a fine and, for continued contravention to a daily default fine.

## 67   Report by receiver

(1) Where a receiver is appointed under section 51, he shall within 3 months (or such longer period as the court may allow) after his appointment, send to the registrar of companies, to the holder of the floating charge by virtue of which he was appointed and to any trustees for secured creditors of the company and (so far as he is aware of their addresses) to all such creditors a report as to the following matters, namely—

(a) the events leading up to his appointment, so far as he is aware of them;

(b) the disposal or proposed disposal by him of any property of the company and the carrying on or proposed carrying on by him of any business of the company;

(c) the amounts of principal and interest payable to the holder of the floating charge by virtue of which he was appointed and the amounts payable to preferential creditors; and

(d) the amount (if any) likely to be available for the payment of other creditors.

(2) The receiver shall also, within 3 months (or such longer period as the court may allow) after his appointment, either—

(a) send a copy of the report (so far as he is aware of their addresses) to all unsecured creditors of the company, or

(b) publish in the prescribed manner a notice stating an address to which unsecured creditors of the company should write for copies of the report to be sent to them free of charge,

and (in either case), unless the court otherwise directs, lay a copy of the report before a meeting of the company's unsecured creditors summoned for the purpose on not less than 14 days' notice.

(3) The court shall not give a direction under subsection (2) unless—

(a) the report states the intention of the receiver to apply for the direction, and

(b) a copy of the report is sent to the persons mentioned in paragraph (a) of that subsection, or a notice is published as mentioned in paragraph (b) of that subsection, not less than 14 days before the hearing of the application.

(4) Where the company has gone or goes into liquidation, the receiver—

(a) shall, within 7 days after his compliance with subsection (1) or, if later, the nomination or appointment of the liquidator, send a copy of the report to the liquidator, and

(b) where he does so within the time limited for compliance with subsection (2), is not required to comply with that subsection.

(5) A report under this section shall include a summary of the statement of affairs made out and submitted under section 66 and of his comments (if any) on it.

(6) Nothing in this section shall be taken as requiring any such report to include any information the disclosure of which would seriously prejudice the carrying out by the receiver of his functions.

(7) Section 65(2) applies for the purposes of this section also.

(8) If a person without reasonable excuse fails to comply with this section, he is liable to a fine and, for continued contravention, to a daily default fine.

(9) In this section 'secured creditor', in relation to a company, means a creditor of the company who holds in respect of his debt a security over property of the company, and 'unsecured creditor' shall be construed accordingly.

## 68   Committee of creditors

(1) Where a meeting of creditors is summoned under section 67, the meeting may, if it thinks fit, establish a committee ('the creditors' committee') to exercise the functions conferred on it by or under this Act.

(2) If such a committee is established, the committee may on giving not less than 7 days' notice require the receiver to attend before it at any reasonable time and furnish it with such information relating to the carrying out by him of his functions as it may reasonably require.

## 69   Enforcement of receiver's duty to make returns, etc

(1) If any receiver—

(a) having made default in filing, delivering or making any return, account or other document, or in giving any notice, which a receiver is by law required to file, deliver, make or give, fails to make good the default within 14 days after the service on him of a notice requiring him to do so; or

(b) has, after being required at any time by the liquidator of the company so to do, failed to render proper accounts of his receipts and payments and to vouch the same and to pay over to the liquidator the amount properly payable to him,

the court may, on an application made for the purpose, make an order directing the receiver to make good the default within such time as may be specified in the order.

(2) In the case of any such default as is mentioned in subsection (1)(a), an application for the purposes of this section may be made by any member or creditor of the company or by the registrar of companies; and, in the case of any such default as is mentioned in subsection (1)(b), the application shall be

made by the liquidator; and, in either case, the order may provide that all expenses of and incidental to the application shall be borne by the receiver.

(3) Nothing in this section prejudices the operation of any enactments imposing penalties on receivers in respect of any such default as is mentioned in subsection (1).

**70 Interpretation for Chapter II**

(1) In this Chapter, unless the contrary intention appears, the following expressions have the following meanings respectively assigned to them—

'company' means an incorporated company (whether or not a company within the meaning of the Companies Act) which the Court of Session has jurisdiction to wind up;

'fixed security', in relation to any property of a company, means any security, other than a floating charge or a charge having the nature of a floating charge, which on the winding up of the company in Scotland would be treated as an effective security over that property, and (without prejudice to that generality) includes a security over that property, being a heritable security within the meaning of the Conveyancing and Feudal Reform (Scotland) Act 1970;

'instrument of appointment' has the meaning given by section 53(1);

'prescribed' means prescribed by regulations made under this Chapter by the Secretary of State;

'receiver' means a receiver of such part of the property of the company as is subject to the floating charge by virtue of which he has been appointed under section 51;

'register of charges' means the register kept by the registrar of companies for the purposes of Chapter II of Part XII of the Companies Act;

'secured debenture' means a bond, debenture, debenture stock or other security which, either itself or by reference to any other instrument, creates a floating charge over all or any part of the property of the company, but does not include a security which creates no charge other than a fixed security; and

'series of secured debentures' means two or more secured debentures created as a series by the company in such a manner that the holders thereof are entitled pari passu to the benefit of the floating charge.

(2) Where a floating charge, secured debenture or series of secured debentures has been created by the company, then, except where the context otherwise requires, any reference in this Chapter to the holder of the floating charge shall—

(a) where the floating charge, secured debenture or series of secured debentures provides for a receiver to be appointed by any person or body, be construed as a reference to that person or body;

(b) where, in the case of a series of secured debentures, no such provision has been made therein but—

  (i) there are trustees acting for the debenture-holders under and in accordance with a trust deed, be construed as a reference to those trustees, and

  (ii) where no such trustees are acting, be construed as a reference to—

(aa) a majority in nominal value of those present or represented by proxy and voting at a meeting of debenture-holders at which the holders of at least one-third in nominal value of the outstanding debentures of the series are present or so represented, or

(bb) where no such meeting is held, the holders of at least one-half in nominal value of the outstanding debentures of the series.

(3) Any reference in this Chapter to a floating charge, secured debenture, series of secured debentures or instrument creating a charge includes, except where the context otherwise requires, a reference to that floating charge, debenture, series of debentures or instrument as varied by any instrument.

(4) References in this Chapter to the instrument by which a floating charge was created are, in the case of a floating charge created by words in a bond or other written acknowledgement, references to the bond or, as the case may be, the other written acknowledgement.

**71 Prescription of forms, etc; regulations**

(1) The notice referred to in section 62(5), and the notice referred to in section 65(1)(a) shall be in such form as may be prescribed.

(2) Any power conferred by this Chapter on the Secretary of State to make regulations is exercisable by statutory instrument; and a statutory instrument made in the exercise of the power so conferred to prescribe a fee is subject to annulment in pursuance of a resolution of either House of Parliament.

# Chapter III

## Receivers' powers in Great Britain as a whole

**72 Cross-border operation of receivership provisions**

(1) A receiver appointed under the law of either part of Great Britain in respect of the whole or any part of any property or undertaking of a company and in consequence of the company having created a charge which, as created, was a floating charge may exercise his powers in the other part of Great Britain so far as their exercise is not inconsistent with the law applicable there.

(2) In subsection (1) 'receiver' includes a manager and a person who is appointed both receiver and manager.

## Chapter IV

## Prohibition of appointment of administrative receiver

### 72A   Floating charge holder not to appoint administrative receiver

(1) The holder of a qualifying floating charge in respect of a company's property may not appoint an administrative receiver of the company.

(2) In Scotland, the holder of a qualifying floating charge in respect of a company's property may not appoint or apply to the court for the appointment of a receiver who on appointment would be an administrative receiver of property of the company.

(3) In subsections (1) and (2)—
'holder of a qualifying floating charge in respect of a company's property' has the same meaning as in paragraph 14 of Schedule B1 to this Act, and
'administrative receiver' has the meaning given by section 251.

(4) This section applies—
  (a) to a floating charge created on or after a date appointed by the Secretary of State by order made by statutory instrument, and
  (b) in spite of any provision of an agreement or instrument which purports to empower a person to appoint an administrative receiver (by whatever name).

(5) An order under subsection (4)(a) may—
  (a) make provision which applies generally or only for a specified purpose;
  (b) make different provision for different purposes;
  (c) make transitional provision.

(6) This section is subject to the exceptions specified in sections 72B to 72GA .

### 72B   First exception: capital market

(1) Section 72A does not prevent the appointment of an administrative receiver in pursuance of an agreement which is or forms part of a capital market arrangement if—
  (a) a party incurs or, when the agreement was entered into was expected to incur, a debt of at least £50 million under the arrangement, and
  (b) the arrangement involves the issue of a capital market investment.

(2) In subsection (1)—
'capital market arrangement' means an arrangement of a kind described in paragraph 1 of Schedule 2A, and
'capital market investment' means an investment of a kind described in paragraph 2 or 3 of that Schedule.

### 72C   Second exception: public-private partnership

(1) Section 72A does not prevent the appointment of an administrative receiver of a project company of a project which—
  (a) is a public-private partnership project, and
  (b) includes step-in rights.

(2) In this section 'public-private partnership project' means a project—
  (a) the resources for which are provided partly by one or more public bodies and partly by one or more private persons, or
  (b) which is designed wholly or mainly for the purpose of assisting a public body to discharge a function.

(3) In this section—
'step-in rights' has the meaning given by paragraph 6 of Schedule 2A, and
'project company' has the meaning given by paragraph 7 of that Schedule.

### 72D   Third exception: utilities

(1) Section 72A does not prevent the appointment of an administrative receiver of a project company of a project which—
  (a) is a utility project, and
  (b) includes step-in rights.

(2) In this section—
  (a) 'utility project' means a project designed wholly or mainly for the purpose of a regulated business,
  (b) 'regulated business' means a business of a kind listed in paragraph 10 of Schedule 2A,
  (c) 'step-in rights' has the meaning given by paragraph 6 of that Schedule, and
  (d) 'project company' has the meaning given by paragraph 7 of that Schedule.

### 72DA  Exception in respect of urban regeneration projects

(1) Section 72A does not prevent the appointment of an administrative receiver of a project company of a project which—

  (a) is designed wholly or mainly to develop land which at the commencement of the project is wholly or partly in a designated disadvantaged area outside Northern Ireland, and

  (b) includes step-in rights.

(2) In subsection (1) 'develop' means to carry out—

  (a) building operations,

  (b) any operation for the removal of substances or waste from land and the levelling of the surface of the land, or

  (c) engineering operations in connection with the activities mentioned in paragraph (a) or (b).

(3) In this section—

'building' includes any structure or erection, and any part of a building as so defined, but does not include plant and machinery comprised in a building,

'building operations' includes—

  (a) demolition of buildings,

  (b) filling in of trenches,

  (c) rebuilding,

  (d) structural alterations of, or additions to, buildings and

  (e) other operations normally undertaken by a person carrying on business as a builder,

'designated disadvantaged area' means an area designated as a disadvantaged area under section 92 of the Finance Act 2001,

'engineering operations' includes the formation and laying out of means of access to highways,

'project company' has the meaning given by paragraph 7 of Schedule 2A,

'step-in rights' has the meaning given by paragraph 6 of that Schedule,

'substance' means any natural or artificial substance whether in solid or liquid form or in the form of a gas or vapour, and

'waste' includes any waste materials, spoil, refuse or other matter deposited on land.

### 72E  Fourth exception: project finance

(1) Section 72A does not prevent the appointment of an administrative receiver of a project company of a project which—

  (a) is a financed project, and

  (b) includes step-in rights.

(2) In this section—

  (a) a project is 'financed' if under an agreement relating to the project a project company incurs, or when the agreement is entered into is expected to incur, a debt of at least £50 million for the purposes of carrying out the project,

  (b) 'project company' has the meaning given by paragraph 7 of Schedule 2A, and

  (c) 'step-in rights' has the meaning given by paragraph 6 of that Schedule.

### 72F  Fifth exception: financial market

Section 72A does not prevent the appointment of an administrative receiver of a company by virtue of—

  (a) a market charge within the meaning of section 173 of the Companies Act 1989 (c 40),

  (b) a system-charge within the meaning of the Financial Markets and Insolvency Regulations 1996 (SI 1996/1469),

  (c) a collateral security charge within the meaning of the Financial Markets and Insolvency (Settlement Finality) Regulations 1999 (SI 1999/2979).

### 72G  Sixth exception: registered social landlord

Section 72A does not prevent the appointment of an administrative receiver of a company which is registered as a social landlord under Part I of the Housing Act 1996 (c 52) or under Part 3 of the Housing (Scotland) Act 2001 (asp 10).

### 72GA  Exception in relation to protected railway companies etc

Section 72A does not prevent the appointment of an administrative receiver of—

  (a) a company holding an appointment under Chapter I of Part II of the Water Industry Act 1991,

  (b) a protected railway company within the meaning of section 59 of the Railways Act 1993 (including that section as it has effect by virtue of section 19 of the Channel Tunnel Rail Link Act 1996, or

  (c) a licence company within the meaning of section 26 of the Transport Act 2000.

### 72H  Sections 72A to 72G: supplementary

(1) Schedule 2A (which supplements sections 72B to 72G) shall have effect.

(2) The Secretary of State may by order—

  (a) insert into this Act provision creating an additional exception to section 72A(1) or (2);

(b) provide for a provision of this Act which creates an exception to section 72A(1) or (2) to cease to have effect;

(c) amend section 72A in consequence of provision made under paragraph (a) or (b);

(d) amend any of sections 72B to 72G;

(e) amend Schedule 2A.

(3) An order under subsection (2) must be made by statutory instrument.

(4) An order under subsection (2) may make—

(a) provision which applies generally or only for a specified purpose;

(b) different provision for different purposes;

(c) consequential or supplementary provision;

(d) transitional provision.

(5) An order under subsection (2)—

(a) in the case of an order under subsection (2)(e), shall be subject to annulment in pursuance of a resolution of either House of Parliament,

(b) in the case of an order under subsection (2)(d) varying the sum specified in section 72B(1)(a) or 72E(2)(a)(whether or not the order also makes consequential or transitional provision), shall be subject to annulment in pursuance of a resolution of either House of Parliament, and

(c) in the case of any other order under subsection (2)(a) to (d), may not be made unless a draft has been laid before and approved by resolution of each House of Parliament.

# PART IV

# WINDING UP OF COMPANIES REGISTERED UNDER THE COMPANIES ACTS

## Chapter I

### Preliminary

*Modes of winding up*

### 73  Alternative modes of winding up

(1) The winding up of a company, within the meaning given to that expression by section 735 of the Companies Act, may be either voluntary (Chapters II, III, IV and V in this Part) or by the court (Chapter VI).

(2) This Chapter, and Chapters VII to X, relate to winding up generally, except where otherwise stated.

*Contributories*

### 74  Liability as contributories of present and past members

(1) When a company is wound up, every present and past member is liable to contribute to its assets to any amount sufficient for payment of its debts and liabilities, and the expenses of the winding up, and for the adjustment of the rights of the contributories among themselves.

(2) This is subject as follows—

(a) a past member is not liable to contribute if he has ceased to be a member for one year or more before the commencement of the winding up;

(b) a past member is not liable to contribute in respect of any debt or liability of the company contracted after he ceased to be a member;

(c) a past member is not liable to contribute, unless it appears to the court that the existing members are unable to satisfy the contributions required to be made by them in pursuance of the Companies Act and this Act;

(d) in the case of a company limited by shares, no contribution is required from any member exceeding the amount (if any) unpaid on the shares in respect of which he is liable as a present or past member;

(e) nothing in the Companies Act or this Act invalidates any provision contained in a policy of insurance or other contract whereby the liability of individual members on the policy or contract is restricted, or whereby the funds of the company are alone made liable in respect of the policy or contract;

(f) a sum due to any member of the company (in his character of a member) by way of dividends, profits or otherwise is not deemed to be a debt of the company, payable to that member in a case of competition between himself and any other creditor not a member of the company, but any such sum may be taken into account for the purpose of the final adjustment of the rights of the contributories among themselves.

(3) In the case of a company limited by guarantee, no contribution is required from any member exceeding the amount undertaken to be contributed by him to the company's assets in the event of its being wound up; but if it is a company with a share capital, every member of it is liable (in addition to the amount so undertaken to be contributed to the assets), to contribute to the extent of any sums unpaid on shares held by him.

### 75   Directors, etc with unlimited liability

(1) In the winding up of a limited company, any director or manager (whether past or present) whose liability is under the Companies Act unlimited is liable, in addition to his liability (if any) to contribute as an ordinary member, to make a further contribution as if he were at the commencement of the winding up a member of an unlimited company.

(2) However—
- (a) a past director or manager is not liable to make such further contribution if he has ceased to hold office for a year or more before the commencement of the winding up;
- (b) a past director or manager is not liable to make such further contribution in respect of any debt or liability of the company contracted after he ceased to hold office;
- (c) subject to the company's articles, a director or manager is not liable to make such further contribution unless the court deems it necessary to require that contribution in order to satisfy the company's debts and liabilities, and the expenses of the winding up.

### 76   Liability of past directors and shareholders

(1) This section applies where a company is being wound up and—
- (a) it has under Chapter VII of Part V of the Companies Act (redeemable shares; purchase by a company of its own shares) made a payment out of capital in respect of the redemption or purchase of any of its own shares (the payment being referred to below as 'the relevant payment'), and
- (b) the aggregate amount of the company's assets and the amounts paid by way of contribution to its assets (apart from this section) is not sufficient for payment of its debts and liabilities, and the expenses of the winding up.

(2) If the winding up commenced within one year of the date on which the relevant payment was made, then—
- (a) the person from whom the shares were redeemed or purchased, and
- (b) the directors who signed the statutory declaration made in accordance with section 173(3) of the Companies Act for purposes of the redemption or purchase (except a director who shows that he had reasonable grounds for forming the opinion set out in the declaration,

are, so as to enable that insufficiency to be met, liable to contribute to the following extent to the company's assets.

(3) A person from whom any of the shares were redeemed or purchased is liable to contribute an amount not exceeding so much of the relevant payment as was made by the company in respect of his shares; and the directors are jointly and severally liable with that person to contribute that amount.

(4) A person who has contributed any amount to the assets in pursuance of this section may apply to the court for an order directing any other person jointly and severally liable in respect of that amount to pay him such amount as the court thinks just and equitable.

(5) Sections 74 and 75 do not apply in relation to liability accruing by virtue of this section.

(6) This section is deemed included in Chapter VII of Part V of the Companies Act for the purposes of the Secretary of State's power to make regulations under section 179 of that Act.

### 77   Limited company formerly unlimited

(1) This section applies in the case of a company being wound up which was at some former time registered as unlimited but has re-registered—
- (a) as a public company under section 43 of the Companies Act (or the former corresponding provision, section 5 of the Companies Act 1980), or
- (b) as a limited company under section 51 of the Companies Act (or the former corresponding provision, section 44 of the Companies Act 1967).

(2) Notwithstanding section 74(2)(a) above, a past member of the company who was a member of it at the time of re-registration, if the winding up commences within the period of 3 years beginning with the day on which the company was re-registered, is liable to contribute to the assets of the company in respect of debts and liabilities contracted before that time.

(3) If no persons who were members of the company at that time are existing members of it, a person who at that time was a present or past member is liable to contribute as above notwithstanding that the existing members have satisfied the contributions required to be made by them under the Companies Act and this Act

This applies subject to section 74(2)(a) above and to subsection (2) of this section, but notwithstanding section 74(2)(c).

(4) Notwithstanding section 74(2)(d) and (3), there is no limit on the amount which a person who, at that time, was a past or present member of the company is liable to contribute as above.

## 78    Unlimited company formerly limited

(1)  This section applies in the case of a company being wound up which was at some former time registered as limited but has been re-registered as unlimited under section 49 of the Companies Act (or the former corresponding provision, section 43 of the Companies Act 1967).

(2)  A person who, at the time when the application for the company to be re-registered was lodged, was a past member of the company and did not after that again become a member of it is not liable to contribute to the assets of the company more than he would have been liable to contribute had the company not been re-registered.

## 79    Meaning of 'contributory'

(1)  In this Act and the Companies Act the expression 'contributory' means every person liable to contribute to the assets of a company in the event of its being wound up, and for the purposes of all proceedings for determining, and all proceedings prior to the final determination of, the persons who are to be deemed contributories, includes any person alleged to be a contributory.

(2)  The reference in subsection (1) to persons liable to contribute to the assets does not include a person so liable by virtue of a declaration by the court under section 213 (imputed responsibility for company's fraudulent trading) or section 214 (wrongful trading) in Chapter X of this Part.

(3)  A reference in a company's articles to a contributory does not (unless the context requires) include a person who is a contributory only by virtue of section 76.

This section is deemed included in Chapter VII of Part V of the Companies Act for the purposes of the Secretary of State's power to make regulations under section 179 of that Act.

## 80    Nature of contributory's liability

The liability of a contributory creates a debt (in England and Wales in the nature of a speciality) accruing due from him at the time when his liability commenced, but payable at the times when calls are made for enforcing the liability.

## 81    Contributories in case of death of a member

(1)  If a contributory dies either before or after he has been placed on the list of contributories, his personal representatives, and the heirs and legatees of heritage of his heritable estate in Scotland, are liable in a due course of administration to contribute to the assets of the company in discharge of his liability and are contributories accordingly.

(2)  Where the personal representatives are placed on the list of contributories, the heirs or legatees of heritage need not be added, but they may be added as and when the court thinks fit.

(3)  If in England and Wales the personal representatives make default in paying any money ordered to be paid by them, proceedings may be taken for administering the estate of the deceased contributory and for compelling payment out of it of the money due.

## 82    Effect of contributory's bankruptcy

(1)  The following applies if a contributory becomes bankrupt, either before or after he has been placed on the list of contributories.

(2)  His trustee in bankruptcy represents him for all purposes of the winding up, and is a contributory accordingly.

(3)  The trustee may be called on to admit to proof against the bankrupt's estate, or otherwise allow to be paid out of the bankrupt's assets in due course of law, any money due from the bankrupt in respect of his liability to contribute to the company's assets.

(4)  There may be proved against the bankrupt's estate the estimated value of his liability to future calls as well as calls already made.

## 83    Companies registered under Companies Act, Part XXII, Chapter II

(1)  The following applies in the event of a company being wound up which has been registered under section 680 of the Companies Act (or previous corresponding provisions in the Companies Act 1948 or earlier Acts).

(2)  Every person is a contributory, in respect of the company's debts and liabilities contracted before registration, who is liable—

(a)  to pay, or contribute to the payment of, any debt or liability so contracted, or

(b)  to pay, or contribute to the payment of, any sum for the adjustment of the rights of the members among themselves in respect of any such debt or liability, or

(c)  to pay, or contribute to the amount of, the expenses of winding up the company, so far as relates to the debts or liabilities above mentioned.

(3)  Every contributory is liable to contribute to the assets of the company, in the course of the winding up, all sums due from him in respect of any such liability.

(4)  In the event of the death, bankruptcy or insolvency of any contributory, provisions of this Act, with respect to the personal representatives, to the heirs and legatees of heritage of the heritable estate in Scotland of deceased contributories and to the trustees of bankrupt or insolvent contributories respectively, apply.

## Chapter II

## Voluntary winding up (introductory and general)

*Resolutions for, and commencement of, voluntary winding up*

### 84   Circumstances in which company may be wound up voluntarily

(1)  A company may be wound up voluntarily—

    (a)  when the period (if any) fixed for the duration of the company by the articles expires, or the event (if any) occurs, on the occurrence of which the articles provide that the company is to be dissolved, and the company in general meeting has passed a resolution requiring it be wound up voluntarily;

    (b)  if the company resolves by special resolution that it be wound up voluntarily;

    (c)  if the company resolves by extraordinary resolution to the effect that it cannot by reason of its liabilities continue its business, and that it is advisable to wind up.

(2)  In this Act the expression 'a resolution for voluntary winding up' means a resolution passed under any of the paragraphs of subsection (1).

(2A)  Before a company passes a resolution for voluntary winding up it must give written notice of the resolution to the holder of any qualifying floating charge to which section 72A applies.

(2B)  Where notice is given under subsection (2A) a resolution for voluntary winding up may be passed only—

    (a)  after the end of the period of five business days beginning with the day on which the notice was given, or

    (b)  if the person to whom the notice was given has consented in writing to the passing of the resolution.

(3)  A resolution passed under paragraph (a) of subsection (1), as well as a special resolution under paragraph (b) and an extraordinary resolution under paragraph (c), is subject to section 380 of the Companies Act (copy of resolution to be forwarded to registrar of companies within 15 days).

(4)  This section has effect subject to section 43 of the Commonhold and Leasehold Reform Act 2002.

### 85   Notice of resolution to wind up

(1)  When a company has passed a resolution for voluntary winding up, it shall, within 14 days after the passing of the resolution, give notice of the resolution by advertisement in the Gazette.

(2)  If default is made in complying with this section, the company and every officer of it who is in default is liable to a fine and, for continued contravention, to a daily default fine.

For purposes of this subsection the liquidator is deemed an officer of the company.

### 86   Commencement of winding up

A voluntary winding up is deemed to commence at the time of the passing of the resolution for voluntary winding up.

*Consequences of resolution to wind up*

### 87   Effect on business and status of company

(1)  In case of a voluntary winding up, the company shall from the commencement of the winding up cease to carry on its business, except so far as may be required for its beneficial winding up.

(2)  However, the corporate state and corporate powers of the company, notwithstanding anything to the contrary in its articles, continue until the company is dissolved.

### 88   Avoidance of share transfers, etc after winding-up resolution

Any transfer of shares, not being a transfer made to or with the sanction of the liquidator, and any alteration in the status of the company's members, made after the commencement of a voluntary winding up, is void.

*Declaration of solvency*

### 89   Statutory declaration of solvency.

(1)  Where it is proposed to wind up a company voluntarily, the directors (or, in the case of a company having more than two directors, the majority of them) may at a directors' meeting make a statutory declaration to the effect that they have made a full inquiry into the company's affairs and that, having done so, they have formed the opinion that the company will be able to pay its debts in full, together with interest at the official rate (as defined in section 251), within such period, not exceeding 12 months from the commencement of the winding up, as may be specified in the declaration.

(2)  Such a declaration by the directors has no effect for purposes of this Act unless—

    (a)  it is made within the 5 weeks immediately preceding the date of the passing of the resolution for winding up, or on that date but before the passing of the resolution, and

    (b)  it embodies a statement of the company's assets and liabilities as at the latest practicable date before the making of the declaration.

(3)  The declaration shall be delivered to the registrar of companies before the expiration of 15 days immediately following the date on which the resolution for winding up is passed.

(4)  A director making a declaration under this section without having reasonable grounds for the opinion that the company will be able to pay its debts in full, together with interest at the official rate, within the period specified is liable to imprisonment or a fine, or both.

(5)  If the company is wound up in pursuance of a resolution passed within 5 weeks after the making of the declaration, and its debts (together with interest at the official rate) are not paid or provided for in full within the period specified, it is to be presumed (unless the contrary is shown) that the director did not have reasonable grounds for his opinion.

(6)  If a declaration required by subsection (3) to be delivered to the registrar is not so delivered within the time prescribed by that subsection, the company and every officer in default is liable to a fine and, for continued contravention, to a daily default fine.

### 90  Distinction between 'members'' and 'creditors'' voluntary winding up

A winding up in the case of which a directors' statutory declaration under section 89 has been made is a 'members' voluntary winding up'; and a winding up in the case of which such a declaration has not been made is a 'creditors' voluntary winding up'.

## Chapter III

## Members' voluntary winding up

### 91  Appointment of liquidator

(1)  In a members' voluntary winding up, the company in general meeting shall appoint one or more liquidators for the purpose of winding up the company's affairs and distributing its assets.

(2)  On the appointment of a liquidator all the powers of the directors cease, except so far as the company in general meeting or the liquidator sanctions their continuance.

### 92  Power to fill vacancy in office of liquidator

(1)  If a vacancy occurs by death resignation or otherwise in the office of liquidator appointed by the company, the company in general meeting may, subject to any arrangement with its creditors, fill the vacancy.

(2)  For that purpose a general meeting may be convened by any contributory or, if there were more liquidators than one, by the continuing liquidators.

(3)  The meeting shall be held in manner provided by this Act or by the articles, or in such manner as may, on application by any contributory or by the continuing liquidators, be determined by the court.

### 93  General company meeting at each year's end

(1)  Subject to sections 96 and 102, in the event of the winding up continuing for more than one year, the liquidator shall summon a general meeting of the company at the end of the first year from the commencement of the winding up, and of each succeeding year, or at the first convenient date within 3 months from the end of the year or such longer period as the Secretary of State may allow.

(2)  The liquidator shall lay before the meeting an account of his acts and dealings, and of the conduct of the winding up, during the preceding year.

(3)  If the liquidator fails to comply with this section, he is liable to a fine.

### 94  Final meeting prior to dissolution

(1)  As soon as the company's affairs are fully wound up, the liquidator shall make up an account of the winding up showing how it has been conducted and the company's property has been disposed of, and thereupon shall call a general meeting of the company for the purpose of laying before it the account, and giving an explanation of it.

(2)  The meeting shall be called by advertisement in the Gazette, specifying its time, place and object and published at least one month before the meeting.

(3)  Within one week after the meeting, the liquidator shall send to the registrar of companies a copy of the account, and shall make a return to him of the holding of the meeting and of its date.

(4)  If the copy is not sent or the return is not made in accordance with subsection (3), the liquidator is liable to a fine and, for continued contravention, to a daily default fine.

(5)  If a quorum is not present at the meeting, the liquidator shall, in lieu of the return mentioned above, make a return that the meeting was duly summoned and that no quorum was present; and upon such a return being made, the provisions of subsection (3) as to the making of the return are deemed complied with.

(6)  If the liquidator fails to call a general meeting of the company as required by subsection (1), he is liable to a fine.

### 95  Effect of company's insolvency

(1)  This section applies where the liquidator is of the opinion that the company will be unable to pay its debts in full (together with interest at the official rate) within the period stated in the directors' declaration under section 89.

(2) The liquidator shall—

(a) summon a meeting of creditors for a day not later than the 28th day after the day on which he formed that opinion;

(b) send notices of the creditors' meeting to the creditors by post not less than 7 days before the day on which that meeting is to be held;

(c) cause notice of the creditors' meeting to be advertised once in the Gazette and once at least in 2 newspapers circulating in the relevant locality (that is to say the locality in which the company's principal place of business in Great Britain was situated during the relevant period); and

(d) during the period before the day on which the creditors' meeting is to be held, furnish creditors free of charge with such information concerning the affairs of the company as they may reasonably require;

and the notice of the creditors' meeting shall state the duty imposed by paragraph (d) above.

(3) The liquidator shall also—

(a) make out a statement in the prescribed form as to the affairs of the company;

(b) lay that statement before the creditors' meeting; and

(c) attend and preside at that meeting.

(4) The statement as to the affairs of the company shall be verified by affidavit by the liquidator and shall show—

(a) particulars of the company's assets, debts and liabilities;

(b) the names and addresses of the company's creditors;

(c) the securities held by them respectively;

(d) the dates when the securities were respectively given; and

(e) such further or other information as may be prescribed.

(5) Where the company's principal place of business in Great Britain was situated in different localities at different times during the relevant period, the duty imposed by subsection (2)(c) applies separately in relation to each of those localities.

(6) Where the company had no place of business in Great Britain during the relevant period, references in subsections (2)(c) and (5) to the company's principal place of business in Great Britain are replaced by references to its registered office.

(7) In this section 'the relevant period' means the period of 6 months immediately preceding the day on which were sent the notices summoning the company meeting at which it was resolved that the company be wound up voluntarily.

(8) If the liquidator without reasonable excuse fails to comply with this section, he is liable to a fine.

### 96 Conversion to creditors' voluntary winding up

As from the day on which the creditors' meeting is held under section 95, this Act has effect as if—

(a) the directors' declaration under section 89 had not been made; and

(b) the creditors' meeting and the company meeting at which it was resolved that the company be wound up voluntarily were the meetings mentioned in section 98 in the next Chapter;

and accordingly the winding up becomes a creditors' voluntary winding up.

## Chapter IV

## Creditors' voluntary winding up

### 97 Application of this Chapter

(1) Subject as follows, this Chapter applies in relation to a creditors' voluntary winding up.

(2) Sections 98 and 99 do not apply where, under section 96 in Chapter III, a members' voluntary winding up has become a creditors' voluntary winding up.

### 98 Meeting of creditors

(1) The company shall—

(a) cause a meeting of its creditors to be summoned for a day not later than the 14th day after the day on which there is to be held the company meeting at which the resolution for voluntary winding up is to be proposed;

(b) cause the notices of the creditors' meeting to be sent by post to the creditors not less than 7 days before the day on which that meeting is to be held; and

(c) cause notice of the creditors' meeting to be advertised once in the Gazette and once at least in two newspapers circulating in the relevant locality (that is to say the locality in which the company's principal place of business in Great Britain was situated during the relevant period).

(2) The notice of the creditors' meeting shall state either—

(a) the name and address of a person qualified to act as an insolvency practitioner in relation to the company who, during the period before the day on which that meeting is to be held, will furnish creditors free of charge with such information concerning the company's affairs as they may reasonably require; or

(b) a place in the relevant locality where, on the two business days falling next before the day on which that meeting is to be held, a list of the names and addresses of the company's creditors will be available for inspection free of charge.

(3) Where the company's principal place of business in Great Britain was situated in different localities at different times during the relevant period, the duties imposed by subsections (1)(c) and (2)(b) above apply separately in relation to each of those localities.

(4) Where the company had no place of business in Great Britain during the relevant period, references in subsections (1)(c) and (3) to the company's principal place of business in Great Britain are replaced by references to its registered office.

(5) In this section 'the relevant period' means the period of 6 months immediately preceding the day on which were sent the notices summoning the company meeting at which it was resolved that the company be wound up voluntarily.

(6) If the company without reasonable excuse fails to comply with subsection (1) or (2), it is guilty of an offence and liable to a fine.

## 99  Directors to lay statement of affairs before creditors

(1) The directors of the company shall—

(a) make out a statement in the prescribed form as to the affairs of the company;

(b) cause that statement to be laid before the creditors' meeting under section 98; and

(c) appoint one of their number to preside at that meeting;

and it is the duty of the director so appointed to attend the meeting and preside over it.

(2) The statement as to the affairs of the company shall be verified by affidavit by some or all of the directors and shall show—

(a) particulars of the company's assets, debts and liabilities;

(b) the names and addresses of the company's creditors;

(c) the securities held by them respectively;

(d) the dates when the securities were respectively given; and

(e) such further or other information as may be prescribed.

(3) If—

(a) the directors without reasonable excuse fail to comply with subsection (1) or (2); or

(b) any director without reasonable excuse fails to comply with subsection (1), so far as requiring him to attend and preside at the creditors' meeting,

the directors are or (as the case may be) the director is guilty of an offence and liable to a fine.

## 100  Appointment of liquidator

(1) The creditors and the company at their respective meetings mentioned in section 98 may nominate a person to be liquidator for the purpose of winding up the company's affairs and distributing its assets.

(2) The liquidator shall be the person nominated by the creditors or, where no person has been so nominated, the person (if any) nominated by the company.

(3) In the case of different persons being nominated, any director, member or creditor of the company may, within 7 days after the date on which the nomination was made by the creditors, apply to the court for an order either—

(a) directing that the person nominated as liquidator by the company shall be liquidator instead of or jointly with the person nominated by the creditors, or

(b) appointing some other person to be liquidator instead of the person nominated by the creditors.

(4) *The court shall grant an application under subsection (3) made by the holder of a qualifying floating charge in respect of the company's property (within the meaning of paragraph 14 of Schedule B1) unless the court thinks it right to refuse the application because of the particular circumstances of the case.*[6]

## 101  Appointment of liquidation committee

(1) The creditors at the meeting to be held under section 98 or at any subsequent meeting may, if they think fit, appoint a committee ('the liquidation committee') of not more than 5 persons to exercise the functions conferred on it by or under this Act.

(2) If such a committee is appointed, the company may, either at the meeting at which the resolution for voluntary winding up is passed or at any time subsequently in general meeting, appoint such number of persons as they think fit to act as members of the committee, not exceeding 5.

(3) However, the creditors may, if they think fit, resolve that all or any of the persons so appointed by the company ought not to be members of the liquidation committee; and if the creditors so resolve—

(a) the persons mentioned in the resolution are not then, unless the court otherwise directs, qualified to act as members of the committee; and

---

[6] Subsection (4) inserted by the Enterprise Act 2002 c 40 from a date to be appointed.

(b) on any application to the court under this provision the court may, if it thinks fit, appoint other persons to act as such members in place of the persons mentioned in the resolution.

(4) In Scotland, the liquidation committee has, in addition to the powers and duties conferred and imposed on it by this Act, such of the powers and duties of commissioners on a bankrupt estate as may be conferred and imposed on liquidation committees by the rules.

### 102 Creditors' meeting where winding up converted under s 96

Where, in the case of a winding up which was under section 96 in Chapter III, converted to a creditors' voluntary winding up, a creditors' meeting is held in accordance with section 95, any appointment made or committee established by that meeting is deemed to have been made or established by a meeting held in accordance with section 98 in this Chapter.

### 103 Cesser of directors' powers

On the appointment of a liquidator, all the powers of the directors cease, except so far as the liquidation committee (or, if there is no such committee, the creditors) sanction their continuance.

### 104 Vacancy in office of liquidator

If a vacancy occurs, by death, resignation or otherwise, in the office of a liquidator (other than a liquidator appointed by, or by the direction of, the court), the creditors may fill the vacancy.

### 105 Meetings of company and creditors at each year's end

(1) If the winding up continues for more than one year, the liquidator shall summon a general meeting of the company and a meeting of the creditors at the end of the first year from the commencement of the winding up, and of each succeeding year, or at the first convenient date within 3 months from the end of the year or such longer period as the Secretary of State may allow.

(2) The liquidator shall lay before each of the meetings an account of his acts and dealings and of the conduct of the winding up during the preceding year.

(3) If the liquidator fails to comply with this section, he is liable to a fine.

(4) Where under section 96 a members' voluntary winding up has become a creditors' voluntary winding up, and the creditors' meeting under section 95 is held 3 months or less before the end of the first year from the commencement of the winding up, the liquidator is not required by this section to summon a meeting of creditors at the end of that year.

### 106 Final meeting prior to dissolution

(1) As soon as the company's affairs are fully wound up, the liquidator shall make up an account of the winding up, showing how it has been conducted and the company's property has been disposed of, and thereupon shall call a general meeting of the company and a meeting of the creditors for the purpose of laying the account before the meetings and giving an explanation of it.

(2) Each such meeting shall be called by advertisement in the Gazette specifying the time, place and object of the meeting, and published at least one month before it.

(3) Within one week after the date of the meetings (or, if they are not held on the same date, after the date of the later one) the liquidator shall send to the registrar of companies a copy of the account, and shall make a return to him of the holding of the meetings and of their dates.

(4) If the copy is not sent or the return is not made in accordance with subsection (3), the liquidator is liable to a fine and, for continued contravention, to a daily default fine.

(5) However, if a quorum is not present at either such meeting, the liquidator shall, in lieu of the return required by subsection (3), make a return that the meeting was duly summoned and that no quorum was present; and upon such return being made the provisions of that subsection as to the making of the return are, in respect of that meeting, deemed complied with.

(6) If the liquidator fails to call a general meeting of the company or a meeting of the creditors as required by this section, he is liable to a fine.

## Chapter V

## Provisions applying to both kinds of voluntary winding up

### 107 Distribution of company's property

Subject to the provisions of this Act as to preferential payments, the company's property in a voluntary winding up shall on the winding up be applied in satisfaction of the company's liabilities pari passu and, subject to that application, shall (unless the articles otherwise provide) be distributed among the members according to their rights and interests in the company.

### 108 Appointment or removal of liquidator by the court

(1) If from any cause whatever there is not liquidator acting, the court may appoint a liquidator.

(2) The court may, on cause shown, remove a liquidator and appoint another.

### 109  Notice by liquidator of his appointment

(1)  The liquidator shall, within 14 days after his appointment, publish in the Gazette and deliver to the registrar of companies for registration a notice of his appointment in the form prescribed by statutory instrument made by the Secretary of State.

(2)  If the liquidator fails to comply with this section, he is liable to a fine and, for continued contravention, to a daily default fine.

### 110  Acceptance of shares, etc, as consideration for sale of company property

(1)  This section applies, in the case of a company proposed to be, or being, wound up voluntarily, where the whole or part of the company's business or property is proposed to be transferred or sold (a) to another company ('the transferee company'), whether or not the latter is a company within the meaning of the Companies Act , or (b) to a limited liability partnership (the 'transferee limited liability partnership').

(2)  With the requisite sanction, the liquidator of the company being, or proposed to be, wound up ('the transferor company') may receive, in compensation or part compensation for the transfer or sale–

  (a)  in the case of the transferee company, shares, policies or other like interests in the company for distribution among the members of the transferor company, or

  (b)  in the case of the transferee limited liability partnership, membership in the limited liability partnership for distribution among the members of the transferor company.

(3)  The sanction requisite under subsection (2) is—

  (a)  in the case of a members' voluntary winding up, that of a special resolution of the company, conferring either a general authority on the liquidator or an authority in respect of any particular arrangement, and

  (b)  in the case of a creditors' voluntary winding up, that of either the court or the liquidation committee.

(4)  Alternatively to subsection (2), the liquidator may-

  (a)  in the case of the transferee company, in lieu of receiving cash, shares, policies or other like interests (or in addition thereto) participate in the profits of, or receive any other benefit from, the company, or

  (b)  in the case of the transferee limited liability partnership, in lieu of receiving cash, or membership (or in addition thereto) participate in some other way in the profits of, or receive any other benefit from, the limited liability partnership.

(5)  A sale or arrangement in pursuance of this section is binding on members of the transferor company.

(6)  A special resolution is not invalid for purposes of this section by reason that it is passed before or concurrently with a resolution for voluntary winding up or for appointing liquidators; but, if an order is made within a year for winding up the company by the court, the special resolution is not valid unless sanctioned by the court.

### 110  Acceptance of shares, etc, as consideration for sale of company property

(1)  This section applies, in the case of a company proposed to be, or being, wound up voluntarily, where the whole or part of the company's business or property is proposed to be transferred or sold

  (a)  to another company ('the transferee company'), whether or not the latter is a company within the meaning of the Companies Act, or

  (b)  to a limited liability partnership (the 'transferee limited liability partnership').

(2)  With the requisite sanction, the liquidator of the company being, or proposed to be, wound up ('the transferor company') may receive, in compensation or part compensation for the transfer or sale—

  (a)  in the case of the transferee company, shares, policies or other like interests in the transferee company for distribution among the members of the transferor company, or

  (b)  in the case of the transferee limited liability partnership, membership in the transferee limited liability partnership for distribution among the members of the transferor company.

(3)  The sanction requisite under subsection (2) is—

  (a)  in the case of a members' voluntary winding up, that of a special resolution of the company, conferring either a general authority on the liquidator or an authority in respect of any particular arrangement, and

  (b)  in the case of a creditors' voluntary winding up, that of either the court or the liquidation committee.

(4)  Alternatively to subsection (2), the liquidator may (with that sanction) enter into any other arrangement whereby the members of the transferor company may—

  (a)  in the case of the transferee company, in lieu of receiving cash, shares, policies or other like interests (or in addition thereto) participate in the profits of, or receive any other benefit from, the transferee company, or

  (b)  in the case of the transferee limited liability partnership, in lieu of receiving cash or membership (or in addition thereto), participate in some other way in the profits of, or receive any other benefit from, the transferee limited liability partnership.

(5) A sale or arrangement in pursuance of this section is binding on members of the transferor company.

(6) A special resolution is not invalid for purposes of this section by reason that it is passed before or concurrently with a resolution for voluntary winding up or for appointing liquidators; but, if an order is made within a year for winding up the company by the court, the special resolution is not valid unless sanctioned by the court.

### 111  Dissent from arrangement under s 110

(1) This section applies in the case of a voluntary winding up where, for the purposes of section 110(2) or (4), there has been passed a special resolution of the transferor company providing the sanction requisite for the liquidator under that section.

(2) If a member of the transferor company who did not vote in favour of the special resolution expresses his dissent from it in writing, addressed to the liquidator and left at the company's registered office within 7 days after the passing of the resolution, he may require the liquidator either to abstain from carrying the resolution into effect or to purchase his interest at a price to be determined by agreement or by arbitration under this section.

(3) If the liquidator elects to purchase the member's interest, the purchase money must be paid before the company is dissolved and be raised by the liquidator in such manner as may be determined by special resolution.

(4) For purposes of an arbitration under this section, the provisions of the Companies Clauses Consolidation Act 1845 or, in the case of a winding up in Scotland, the Companies Clauses Consolidation (Scotland) Act 1845 with respect to the settlement of disputes by arbitration are incorporated with this Act, and—

(a) in the construction of those provisions this Act is deemed the special Act and 'the company' means the transferor company, and

(b) any appointment by the incorporated provisions directed to be made under the hand of the secretary or any two of the directors may be made in writing by the liquidator (or, if there is more than one liquidator, then any two or more of them).

### 112  Reference of questions to court

(1) The liquidator or any contributory or creditor may apply to the court to determine any question arising in the winding up of a company, or to exercise, as respects the enforcing of calls or any other matter, all or any of the powers which the court might exercise if the company were being wound up by the court.

(2) The court, if satisfied that the determination of the question or the required exercise of power will be just and beneficial, may accede wholly or partially to the application on such terms and conditions as it thinks fit, or may make such other order on the application as it thinks just.

(3) A copy of an order made by virtue of this section staying the proceedings in the winding up shall forthwith be forwarded by the company, or otherwise as may be prescribed, to the registrar of companies, who shall enter it in his records relating to the company.

### 113  Court's power to control proceedings (Scotland)

If the court, on the application of the liquidator in the winding up of a company registered in Scotland, so directs, no action or proceeding shall be proceeded with or commenced against the company except by leave of the court and subject to such terms as the court may impose.

### 114  No liquidator appointed or nominated by company

(1) This section applies where, in the case of a voluntary winding up, no liquidator has been appointed or nominated by the company.

(2) The powers of the directors shall not be exercised, except with the sanction of the court or (in the case of a creditors' voluntary winding up) so far as may be necessary to secure compliance with sections 98 (creditors' meeting) and 99 (statement of affairs), during the period before the appointment or nomination of a liquidator of the company.

(3) Subsection (2) does not apply in relation to the powers of the directors—

(a) to dispose of perishable goods and other goods the value of which is likely to diminish if they are not immediately disposed of, and

(b) to do all such other things as may be necessary for the protection of the company's assets.

(4) If the directors of the company without reasonable excuse fail to comply with this section, they are liable to a fine.

### 115  Expenses of voluntary winding up

All expenses properly incurred in the winding up, including the remuneration of the liquidator, are payable out of the company's assets in priority to all other claims.

### 116  Saving for certain rights

The voluntary winding up of a company does not bar the right of any creditor or contributory to have it wound up by the court; but in the case of an application by a contributory the court must be satisfied that the rights of the contributories will be prejudiced by a voluntary winding up.

## Chapter VI

## Winding up by the court

### *Jurisdiction (England and Wales)*

**117   High Court and county court jurisdiction**

(1)   The High Court has jurisdiction to wind up any company registered in England and Wales.

(2)   Where the amount of a company's share capital paid up or credited as paid up does not exceed £120,000, then (subject to this section) the county court of the district in which the company's registered office is situated has concurrent jurisdiction with the High Court to wind up the company.

(3)   The money sum for the time being specified in subsection (2) is subject to increase or reduction by order under section 416 in Part XV.

(4)   The Lord Chancellor may, with the concurrence of the Lord Chief Justice, by order in a statutory instrument exclude a county court from having winding-up jurisdiction, and for the purposes of that jurisdiction may attach its district, or any part thereof, to any other county court, and may by statutory instrument revoke or vary any such order.

In exercising the powers of this section, the Lord Chancellor shall provide that a county court is not to have winding-up jurisdiction unless it has for the time being jurisdiction for the purposes of Parts VIII to XI of this Act (individual insolvency).

(5)   Every court in England and Wales having winding-up jurisdiction has for the purposes of that jurisdiction all the powers of the High Court; and every prescribed officer of the court shall perform any duties which an officer of the High Court may discharge by order of a judge of that court or otherwise in relation to winding up.

(6)   For the purposes of this section, a company's 'registered office' is the place which has longest been its registered office during the 6 months immediately preceding the presentation of the petition for winding up.

(7)   This section is subject to Article 3 of the EC Regulation (jurisdiction under EC Regulation).

(8)   The Lord Chief Justice may nominate a judicial office holder (as defined in section 109(4) of the Constitutional Reform Act 2005) to exercise his functions under this section.

**118   Proceedings taken in wrong court**

(1)   Nothing in section 117 invalidates a proceeding by reason of its being taken in the wrong court.

(2)   The winding up of a company by the court in England and Wales, or any proceedings in the winding up, may be retained in the court in which the proceedings were commenced, although it may not be the court in which they ought to have been commenced.

**119   Proceedings in county court; case stated for High Court**

(1)   If any question arises in any winding-up proceedings in a county court which all the parties to the proceedings, or which one of them and the judge of the court, desire to have determined in the first instance in the High Court, the judge shall state the facts in the form of a special case for the opinion of the High Court.

(2)   Thereupon the special case and the proceedings (or such of them as may be required) shall be transmitted to the High Court for the purposes of the determination.

### *Jurisdiction (Scotland)*

**120   Court of Session and sheriff court jurisdiction**

(1)   The Court of Session has jurisdiction to wind up any company registered in Scotland.

(2)   When the Court of Session is in vacation, the jurisdiction conferred on that court by this section may (subject to the provisions of this Part) be exercised by the judge acting as vacation judge [...]

(3)   Where the amount of a company's share capital paid up or credited as paid up does not exceed £120,000, the sheriff court of the sheriffdom in which the company's registered office is situated has concurrent jurisdiction with the Court of Session to wind up the company; but—

(a)   the Court of Session may, if it thinks expedient having regard to the amount of the company's assets to do so—

(i)   remit to a sheriff court any petition presented to the Court of Session for winding up such a company, or

(ii)   require such a petition presented to a sheriff court to be remitted to the Court of Session; and

(b)   the Court of Session may require any such petition as above mentioned presented to one sheriff court to be remitted to another sheriff court; and

(c)   in a winding up in the sheriff court the sheriff may submit a stated case for the opinion of the Court of Session on any question of law arising in that winding up.

(4)  For purposes of this section, the expression 'registered office' means the place which has longest been the company's registered office during the 6 months immediately preceding the presentation of the petition for winding up.

(5)  The money sum for the time being specified in subsection (3) is subject to increase or reduction by order under section 416 in Part XV.

(6)  This section is subject to Article 3 of the EC Regulation (jurisdiction under EC Regulation).

### 121   Power to remit winding up to Lord Ordinary

(1)  The Court of Session may, by Act of Sederunt, make provision for the taking of proceedings in a winding up before one of the Lords Ordinary; and, where provision is so made, the Lord Ordinary has, for the purposes of the winding up all the powers and jurisdiction of the court.

(2)  However, the Lord Ordinary may report to the Inner House any matter which may arise in the course of a winding up.

*Grounds and effect of winding-up petition*

### 122   Circumstances in which company may be wound up by the court

(1)  A company may be wound up by the court if—
  (a)  the company has by special resolution resolved that the company be wound up by the court,
  (b)  being a public company which was registered as such on its original incorporation, the company has not been issued with a a trading certificate under section 761 of the Companies Act 2006 (requirement as to minimum share capital)and more than a year has expired since it was so registered,
  (c)  it is an old public company, within the meaning of the Consequential Provisions Act,
  (d)  the company does not commence its business within a year from its incorporation or suspends its business for a whole year;
  (e)  except in the case of a private company limited by shares or by guarantee, the number of members is reduced below 2,
  (f)  the company is unable to pay its debts,
  (fa) at the time at which a moratorium for the company under section 1A comes to an end, no voluntary arrangement approved under Part I has effect in relation to the company,
  (g)  the court is of the opinion that it is just and equitable that the company should be wound up.

(2)  In Scotland, a company which the Court of Session has jurisdiction to wind up may be wound up by the Court if there is subsisting a floating charge over property comprised in the company's property and undertaking, and the court is satisfied that the security of the creditor entitled to the benefit of the floating charge is in jeopardy.

For this purpose a creditor's security is deemed to be in jeopardy if the Court is satisfied that events have occurred or are about to occur which render it unreasonable in the creditor's interests that the company should retain power to dispose of the property which is subject to the floating charge.

### 123   Definition of inability to pay debts

(1)  A company is deemed unable to pay its debts—
  (a)  if a creditor (by assignment or otherwise) to whom the company is indebted in a sum exceeding £750 then due has served on the company, by leaving it at the company's registered office, a written demand (in the prescribed form) requiring the company to pay the sum so due and the company has for 3 weeks thereafter neglected to pay the sum or to secure or compound for it to the reasonable satisfaction of the creditor, or
  (b)  if, in England and Wales, execution or other process issued on a judgment, decree or order of any court in favour of a creditor of the company is returned unsatisfied in whole or in part, or
  (c)  if, in Scotland, the induciae of a charge for payment on an extract decree, or an extract registered bond, or an extract registered protest, have expired without payment being made, or
  (d)  if, in Northern Ireland, a certificate of unenforceability has been granted in respect of a judgment against the company, or
  (e)  if it is proved to the satisfaction of the court that the company is unable to pay its debts as they fall due.

(2)  A company is also deemed unable to pay its debts if it is proved to the satisfaction of the court that the value of the company's assets is less than the amount of its liabilities, taking into account its contingent and prospective liabilities.

(3)  The money sum for the time being specified in subsection (1)(a) is subject to increase or reduction by order under section 416 in Part XV.

### 124   Application for winding up

(1)  Subject to the provisions of this section, an application to the court for the winding up of a company shall be by petition presented either by the company, or the directors, or by any creditor or

creditors (including any contingent or prospective creditor or creditors), contributory or contributories, or by a liquidator (within the meaning of Article 2(b) of the EC Regulation) appointed in proceedings by virtue of Article 3(1) of the EC Regulation or a temporary administrator (within the meaning of Article 38 of the EC Regulation)or by the designated officer for a magistrates' court in the exercise of the power conferred by section 87A of the Magistrates' Courts Act 1980 (enforcement of fines imposed on companies), or by all or any of those parties, together or separately.

(2) Except as mentioned below, a contributory is not entitled to present a winding-up petition unless either—

    (a) the number of members is reduced below 2, or

    (b) the shares in respect of which he is a contributory, or some of them, either were originally allotted to him, or have been held by him, and registered in his name, for at least 6 months during the 18 months before the commencement of the winding up, or have devolved on him through the death of a former holder.

(3) A person who is liable under section 76 to contribute to a company's assets in the event of its being wound up may petition on either of the grounds set out in section 122(1)(f) and (g), and subsection (2) above does not then apply; but unless the person is a contributory otherwise than under section 76, he may not in his character as contributory petition on any other ground.

This subsection is deemed included in Chapter VII of Part V of the Companies Act (redeemable shares; purchase by a company of its own shares) for the purposes of the Secretary of State's power to make regulations under section 179 of that Act.

(3A) A winding-up petition on the ground set out in section 122(1)(fa) may only be presented by one or more creditors.

(4) A winding-up petition may be presented by the Secretary of State—

    (a) if the ground of the petition is that in section 122(1)(b) or (c), or

    (b) in a case falling within section 124A or 124B below.

(4AA) A winding up petition may be presented by the Financial Services Authority in a case falling within section 124C(1) or (2).

(4A) A winding-up petition may be presented by the Regulator of Community Interest Companies in a case falling within section 50 of the Companies (Audit, Investigations and Community Enterprise) Act 2004.

(5) Where a company is being wound up voluntarily in England and Wales, a winding-up petition may be presented by the official receiver attached to the court as well as by any other person authorised in that behalf under the other provisions of this section; but the court shall not make a winding-up order on the petition unless it is satisfied that the voluntary winding up cannot be continued with due regard to the interests of the creditors or contributories.

### 124A    Petition for winding up on grounds of public interest

(1) Where it appears to the Secretary of State from—

    (a) any report made or information obtained under Part XIV (except section 448A) of the Companies Act 1985 (company investigations, &c.),

    (b) any report made by inspectors under—

        (i) section 167, 168, 169 or 284 of the Financial Services and Markets Act 2000, or

        (ii) where the company is an open-ended investment company (within the meaning of that Act), regulations made as a result of section 262(2)(k) of that Act;

    (bb) any information or documents obtained under section 165, 171, 172, 173 or 175 of that Act,

    (c) any information obtained under section 2 of the Criminal Justice Act 1987 or section 28 of the Criminal Law (Consolidation)(Scotland) Act 1995(fraud investigations), or

    (d) any information obtained under section 83 of the Companies Act 1989 (powers exercisable for purpose of assisting overseas regulatory authorities),

that it is expedient in the public interest that a company should be wound up, he may present a petition for it to be wound up if the court thinks it just and equitable for it to be so.

(2) This section does not apply if the company is already being wound up by the court.

### 124B    Petition for winding up of SE

('(1)) Where—

    (a) an SE whose registered office is in Great Britain is not in compliance with Article 7 of Council Regulation (EC) No 2157/2001 on the Statute for a European company (the 'EC Regulation') (location of head office and registered office), and

    (b) it appears to the Secretary of State that the SE should be wound up, he may present a petition for it to be wound up if the court thinks it is just and equitable for it to be so.

(2) This section does not apply if the SE is already being wound up by the court.

(3) In this section 'SE' has the same meaning as in the EC Regulation.

### 124C    Petition for winding up of SCE

(1) Where, in the case of an SCE whose registered office is in Great Britain—

(a) there has been such a breach as is mentioned in Article 73(1) of Council Regulation (EC) No 1435/2003 on the Statute for a European Cooperative Society (SCE)(the 'European Cooperative Society Regulation')(winding up by the court or other competent authority), and

(b) it appears to the Financial Services Authority that the SCE should be wound up,

the Authority may present a petition for the SCE to be wound up if the court thinks it is just and equitable for it to be so.

(2) Where, in the case of an SCE whose registered office is in Great Britain—

(a) the SCE is not in compliance with Article 6 of the European Cooperative Society Regulation (location of head office and registered office, and

(b) it appears to the Financial Service Authority that the SCE should be wound up,

the Authority may present a petition for the SCE to be wound up if the court thinks it is just and equitable for it to be so.

(3) This section does not apply if the SCE is already being wound up by the court.

(4) In this section 'SCE' has the same meaning as in the European Cooperative Society Regulation.

### 125   Powers of court on hearing of petition

(1) On hearing a winding-up petition the court may dismiss it, or adjourn the hearing conditionally or unconditionally, or make an interim order, or any other order that it thinks fit; but the court shall not refuse to make a winding-up order on the ground only that the company's assets have been mortgaged to an amount equal to or in excess of those assets, or that the company has no assets.

(2) If the petition is presented by members of the company as contributories on the ground that it is just and equitable that the company should be wound up, the court, if it is of opinion—

(a) that the petitioners are entitled to relief either by winding up the company or by some other means, and

(b) that in the absence of any other remedy it would be just and equitable that the company should be wound up,

shall make a winding-up order; but this does not apply if the court is also of the opinion both that some other remedy is available to the petitioners and that they are acting unreasonably in seeking to have the company wound up instead of pursuing that other remedy.

### 126   Power to stay or restrain proceedings against company

(1) At any time after the presentation of a winding-up petition, and before a winding-up order has been made, the company, or any creditor or contributory, may—

(a) where any action or proceeding against the company is pending in the High Court or Court of Appeal in England and Wales or Northern Ireland, apply to the court in which the action or proceeding is pending for a stay of proceedings therein, and

(b) where any other action or proceeding is pending against the company, apply to the court having jurisdiction to wind up the company to restrain further proceedings in the action or proceeding;

and the court to which the application is so made may (as the case may be) stay, sist or restrain the proceedings accordingly on such terms as it thinks fit.

(2) In the case of a company registered under section 680 of the Companies Act (pre-1862 companies; companies formed under legislation other than the Companies Acts) or the previous corresponding legislation, where the application to stay, sist or restrain is by a creditor, this section extends to actions and proceedings against any contributory of the company.

### 127   Avoidance of property dispositions, etc

(1) In a winding up by the court, any disposition of the company's property, and any transfer of shares, or alteration in the status of the company's members, made after the commencement of the winding up is, unless the court otherwise orders, void.

(2) This section has no effect in respect of anything done by an administrator of a company while a winding-up petition is suspended under paragraph 40 of Schedule B1.

### 128   Avoidance of attachments, etc

(1) Where a company registered in England and Wales is being wound up by the court, any attachment, sequestration, distress or execution put in force against the estate or effects of the company after the commencement of the winding up is void.

(2) This section, so far as relates to any estate or effects of the company situated in England and Wales, applies in the case of a company registered in Scotland as it applies in the case of a company registered in England and Wales.

*Commencement of winding up*

### 129   Commencement of winding up by the court

(1) If, before the presentation of a petition for the winding up of a company by the court, a resolution has been passed by the company for voluntary winding up, the winding up of the company is deemed to have commenced at the time of the passing of the resolution; and unless the court, on proof

of fraud or mistake, directs otherwise, all proceedings taken in the voluntary winding up are deemed to have been validly taken.

(1A) Where the court makes a winding-up order by virtue of paragraph 13(1)(e) of Schedule B1, the winding up is deemed to commence on the making of the order.

(2) In any other case, the winding up of a company by the court is deemed to commence at the time of the presentation of the petition for winding up.

### 130  Consequences of winding-up order

(1) On the making of a winding-up order, a copy of the order must forthwith be forwarded by the company (or otherwise as may be prescribed) to the registrar of companies, who shall enter it in his records relating to the company.

(2) When a winding-up order has been made or a provisional liquidator has been appointed, no action or proceeding shall be proceeded with or commenced against the company or its property, except by leave of the court and subject to such terms as the court may impose.

(3) When an order has been made for winding up a company registered under section 680 of the Companies Act, no action or proceeding shall be commenced or proceeded with against the company or its property or any contributory of the company, in respect of any debt of the company, except by leave of the court, and subject to such terms as the court may impose.

(4) An order for winding up a company operates in favour of all the creditors and of all contributories of the company as if made on the joint petition of a creditor and of a contributory.

*Investigation procedures*

### 131  Company's statement of affairs

(1) Where the court has made a winding-up order or appointed a provisional liquidator, the official receiver may require some or all of the persons mentioned in subsection (3) below to make out and submit to him a statement in the prescribed form as to the affairs of the company.

(2) The statement shall be verified by affidavit by the persons required to submit it and shall show—

   (a) particulars of the company's assets, debts and liabilities;
   (b) the names and addresses of the company's creditors;
   (c) the securities held by them respectively;
   (d) the dates when the securities were respectively given; and
   (e) such further or other information as may be prescribed or as the official receiver may require

(3) The persons referred to in subsection (1) are—

   (a) those who are or have been officers of the company;
   (b) those who have taken part in the formation of the company at any time within one year before the relevant date;
   (c) those who are in the company's employment, or have been in its employment within that year, and are in the official receiver's opinion capable of giving the information required;
   (d) those who are or have been within that year officers of, or in the employment of, a company which is, or within that year was, an officer of the company.

(4) Where any persons are required under this section to submit a statement of affairs to the official receiver, they shall do so (subject to the next subsection) before the end of the period of 21 days beginning with the day after that on which the prescribed notice of the requirement is given to them by the official receiver.

(5) The official receiver, if he thinks fit, may—

   (a) at any time release a person from an obligation imposed on him under subsection (1) or (2) above; or
   (b) either when giving the notice mentioned in subsection (4) or subsequently, extend the period so mentioned;

and where the official receiver has refused to exercise a power conferred by this subsection, the court, if it thinks fit, may exercise it.

(6) In this section—

'employment' includes employment under a contract for services; and

'the relevant date' means—

   (a) in a case where a provisional liquidator is appointed, the date of his appointment; and
   (b) in a case where no such appointment is made, the date of the winding-up order.

(7) If a person without reasonable excuse fails to comply with any obligation imposed under this section, he is liable to a fine and, for continued contravention, to a daily default fine.

(8) In the application of this section to Scotland references to the official receiver are to the liquidator or, in a case where a provisional liquidator is appointed, the provisional liquidator.

### 132  Investigation by official receiver

(1) Where a winding-up order is made by the court in England and Wales, it is the duty of the official receiver to investigate—

(a)  if the company has failed, the causes of the failure; and

(b)  generally, the promotion, formation, business, dealings and affairs of the company,

and to make such report (if any) to the court as he thinks fit.

(2)  The report is, in any proceedings, prima facie evidence of the facts stated in it.

### 133  Public examination of officers

(1)  Where a company is being wound up by the court, the official receiver or, in Scotland, the liquidator may at any time before the dissolution of the company apply to the court for the public examination of any person who—

(a)  is or has been an officer of the company; or

(b)  has acted as liquidator or administrator of the company or as receiver or manager or, in Scotland, receiver of its property; or

(c)  not being a person falling within paragraph (a) or (b), is or has been concerned, or has taken part, in the promotion, formation or management of the company.

(2)  Unless the court otherwise orders, the official receiver or, in Scotland, the liquidator shall make an application under subsection (1) if he is requested in accordance with the rules to do so by—

(a)  one-half, in value, of the company's creditors; or

(b)  three-quarters, in value, of the company's contributories.

(3)  On an application under subsection (1), the court shall direct that a public examination of the person to whom the application relates shall be held on a day appointed by the court; and that person shall attend on that day and be publicly examined as to the promotion, formation or management of the company or as to the conduct of its business and affairs, or his conduct or dealings in relation to the company.

(4)  The following may take part in the public examination of a person under this section and may question that person concerning the matters mentioned in subsection (3), namely—

(a)  the official receiver;

(b)  the liquidator of the company;

(c)  any person who has been appointed as special manager of the company's property or business;

(d)  any creditor of the company who has tendered a proof or, in Scotland, submitted a claim in the winding up;

(e)  any contributory of the company.

### 134  Enforcement of s 133

(1)  If a person without reasonable excuse fails at any time to attend his public examination under section 133, he is guilty of a contempt of court and liable to be punished accordingly.

(2)  In a case where a person without reasonable excuse fails at any time to attend his examination under section 133 or there are reasonable grounds for believing that a person has absconded, or is about to abscond, with a view to avoiding or delaying his examination under that section, the court may cause a warrant to be issued to a constable or prescribed officer of the court—

(a)  for the arrest of that person; and

(b)  for the seizure of any books, papers, records, money or goods in that person's possession.

(3)  In such a case the court may authorise the person arrested under the warrant to be kept in custody, and anything seized under such a warrant to be held, in accordance with the rules, until such time as the court may order.

*Appointment of liquidator*

### 135  Appointment and powers of provisional liquidator

(1)  Subject to the provisions of this section, the court may, at any time after the presentation of a winding-up petition, appoint a liquidator provisionally.

(2)  In England and Wales, the appointment of a provisional liquidator may be made at any time before the making of a winding-up order; and either the official receiver or any other fit person may be appointed.

(3)  In Scotland, such an appointment may be made at any time before the first appointment of liquidators.

(4)  The provisional liquidator shall carry out such functions as the court may confer on him.

(5)  When a liquidator is provisionally appointed by the court, his powers may be limited by the order appointing him.

### 136  Functions of official receiver in relation to office of liquidator

(1)  The following provisions of this section have effect, subject to section 140 below, on a winding-up order being made by the court in England and Wales.

(2)  The official receiver, by virtue of his office, becomes the liquidator of the company and continues in office until another person becomes liquidator under the provisions of this Part.

(3)  The official receiver is, by virtue of his office, the liquidator during any vacancy.

(4)  At any time when he is the liquidator of the company, the official receiver may summon separate meetings of the company's creditors and contributories for the purpose of choosing a person to be liquidator of the company in place of the official receiver.

(5)  It is the duty of the official receiver—

    (a)  as soon as practicable in the period of 12 weeks beginning with the day on which the winding-up order was made, to decide whether to exercise his power under sub-section (4) to summon meetings, and

    (b)  if in pursuance of paragraph (a) he decides not to exercise that power, to give notice of his decision, before the end of that period, to the court and to the company's creditors and contributories, and

    (c)  (whether or not he has decided to exercise that power) to exercise his power to summon meetings under subsection (4) if he is at any time requested, in accordance with rules, to do so by one-quarter, in value, of the company's creditors;

and accordingly, where the duty imposed by paragraph (c) arises before the official receiver has performed a duty imposed by paragraph (a) or (b), he is not required to perform the latter duty.

(6)  A notice given under subsection (5)(b) to the company's creditors shall contain an explanation of the creditors' power under subsection (5)(c) to require the official receiver to summon meetings of the company's creditors and contributories.

## 137  Appointment by Secretary of State

(1)  In a winding up by the court in England and Wales the official receiver may, at any time when he is the liquidator of the company, apply to the Secretary of State for the appointment of a person as liquidator in his place.

(2)  If meetings are held in pursuance of a decision under section 136(5)(a), but no person is chosen to be liquidator as a result of those meetings, it is the duty of the official receiver to decide whether to refer the need for an appointment to the Secretary of State.

(3)  On an application under subsection (1), or a reference made in pursuance of a decision under subsection (2), the Secretary of State shall either make an appointment or decline to make one.

(4)  Where a liquidator has been appointed by the Secretary of State under subsection (3), the liquidator shall give notice of his appointment to the company's creditors or, if the court so allows, shall advertise his appointment in accordance with the directions of the court.

(5)  In that notice or advertisement the liquidator shall—

    (a)  state whether he proposes to summon a general meeting of the company's creditors under section 141 below for the purpose of determining (together with any meeting of contributories) whether a liquidation committee should be established under that section, and

    (b)  if he does not propose to summon such a meeting, set out the power of the company's creditors under that section to require him to summon one.

## 138  Appointment of liquidator in Scotland

(1)  Where a winding-up order is made by the court in Scotland, a liquidator shall be appointed by the court at the time when the order is made.

(2)  The liquidator so appointed (here referred to as 'the interim liquidator') continues in office until another person becomes liquidator in his place under this section or the next.

(3)  The interim liquidator shall (subject to the next subsection) as soon as practicable in the period of 28 days beginning with the day on which the winding-up order was made or such longer period as the court may allow, summon separate meetings of the company's creditors and contributories for the purpose of choosing a person (who may be the person who is the interim liquidator) to be liquidator of the company in place of the interim liquidator.

(4)  If it appears to the interim liquidator, in any case where a company is being wound up on grounds including its inability to pay its debts, that it would be inappropriate to summon under subsection (3) a meeting of the company's contributories, he may summon only a meeting of the company's creditors for the purpose mentioned in that subsection.

(5)  If one or more meetings are held in pursuance of this section but no person is appointed or nominated by the meeting or meetings, the interim liquidator shall make a report to the court which shall appoint either the interim liquidator or some other person to be liquidator of the company.

(6)  A person who becomes liquidator of the company in place of the interim liquidator shall, unless he is appointed by the court, forthwith notify the court of that fact.

## 139  Choice of liquidator at meetings of creditors and contributories

(1)  This section applies where a company is being wound up by the court and separate meetings of the company's creditors and contributories are summoned for the purpose of choosing a person to be liquidator of the company.

(2)  The creditors and the contributories at their respective meetings may nominate a person to be liquidator.

(3)  The liquidator shall be the person nominated by the creditors or, where no person has been so nominated, the person (if any) nominated by the contributories.

(4) In the case of different persons being nominated, any contributory or creditor may, within 7 days after the date on which the nomination was made by the creditors, apply to the court for an order either—

    (a) appointing the person nominated as liquidator by the contributories to be a liquidator instead of, or jointly with, the person nominated by the creditors; or

    (b) appointing some other person to be liquidator instead of the person nominated by the creditors.

### 140 Appointment by the court following administration or voluntary arrangement

(1) Where a winding-up order is made immediately upon the appointment of an administrator ceasing to have effect, the court may appoint as liquidator of the company the person whose appointment as administrator has ceased to have effect.

(2) Where a winding-up order is made at a time when there is a supervisor of a voluntary arrangement approved in relation to the company under Part I, the court may appoint as liquidator of the company the person who is the supervisor at the time when the winding-up order is made.

(3) Where the court makes an appointment under this section, the official receiver does not become the liquidator as otherwise provided by section 136(2), and he has no duty under section 136(5)(a) or (b) in respect of the summoning of creditors' or contributories' meetings.

*Liquidation committees*

### 141 Liquidation committee (England and Wales)

(1) Where a winding-up order has been made by the court in England and Wales and separate meetings of creditors and contributories have been summoned for the purpose of choosing a person to be liquidator, those meetings may establish a committee ('the liquidation committee') to exercise the functions conferred on it by or under this Act.

(2) The liquidator (not being the official receiver) may at any time, if he thinks fit, summon separate general meetings of the company's creditors and contributories for the purpose of determining whether such a committee should be established and, if it is so determined, of establishing it.

The liquidator (not being the official receiver) shall summon such a meeting if he is requested, in accordance with the rules, to do so by one-tenth, in value, of the company's creditors.

(3) Where meetings are summoned under this section, or for the purpose of choosing a person to be liquidator, and either the meeting of creditors or the meeting of contributories decides that a liquidation committee should be established, but the other meeting does not so decide or decides that a committee should not be established, the committee shall be established in accordance with the rules, unless the court otherwise orders.

(4) The liquidation committee is not to be able or required to carry out its functions at any time when the official receiver is liquidator; but at any such time its functions are vested in the Secretary of State except to the extent that the rules otherwise provide.

(5) Where there is for the time being no liquidation committee, and the liquidator is a person other than the official receiver, the functions of such a committee are vested in the Secretary of State except to the extent that the rules otherwise provide.

### 142 Liquidation committee (Scotland)

(1) Where a winding-up order has been made by the court in Scotland and separate meetings of creditors and contributories have been summoned for the purpose of choosing a person to be liquidator or, under section 138(4), only a meeting of creditors has been summoned for that purpose, those meetings or (as the case may be) that meeting may establish a committee ('the liquidation committee') to exercise the functions conferred on it by or under this Act.

(2) The liquidator may at any time, if he thinks fit, summon separate general meetings of the company's creditors and contributories for the purpose of determining whether such a committee should be established and, if it is so determined, of establishing it.

(3) The liquidator, if appointed by the court otherwise than under section 139(4)(a), is required to summon meetings under subsection (2) if he is requested, in accordance with the rules, to do so by one-tenth, in value, of the company's creditors.

(4) Where meetings are summoned under this section, or for the purpose of choosing a person to be liquidator, and either the meeting of creditors or the meeting of contributories decides that a liquidation committee should be established, but the other meeting does not so decide or decides that a committee should not be established, the committee shall be established in accordance with the rules, unless the court otherwise orders.

(5) Where in the case of any winding up there is for the time being no liquidation committee, the functions of such a committee are vested in the court except to the extent that the rules otherwise provide.

(6) In addition to the powers and duties conferred and imposed on it by this Act, a liquidation committee has such of the powers and duties of commissioners in a sequestration as may be conferred and imposed on such committees by the rules.

*The liquidator's functions*

### 143   General functions in winding up by the court

(1)   The functions of the liquidator of a company which is being wound up by the court are to secure that the assets of the company are got in, realised and distributed to the company's creditors and, if there is a surplus, to the persons entitled to it.

(2)   It is the duty of the liquidator of a company which is being wound up by the court in England and Wales, if he is not the official receiver—

  (a)  to furnish the official receiver with such information,

  (b)  to produce to the official receiver, and permit inspection by the official receiver of, such books, papers and other records, and

  (c)  to give the official receiver such other assistance,

as the official receiver may reasonably require for the purposes of carrying out his functions in relation to the winding up.

### 144   Custody of company's property

(1)   When a winding-up order has been made, or where a provisional liquidator has been appointed, the liquidator or the provisional liquidator (as the case may be) shall take into his custody or under his control all the property and things in action to which the company is or appears to be entitled.

(2)   In a winding up by the court in Scotland, if and so long as there is no liquidator, all the property of the company is deemed to be in the custody of the court.

### 145   Vesting of company property in liquidator

(1)   When a company is being wound up by the court, the court may on the application of the liquidator by order direct that all or any part of the property of whatsoever description belonging to the company or held by trustees on its behalf shall vest in the liquidator by his official name; and thereupon the property to which the order relates vests accordingly.

(2)   The liquidator may, after giving such indemnity (if any) as the court may direct, bring or defend in his official name any action or other legal proceeding which relates to that property or which it is necessary to bring or defend for the purpose of effectually winding up the company and recovering its property.

### 146   Duty to summon final meeting

(1)   Subject to the next subsection, if it appears to the liquidator of a company which is being wound up by the court that the winding up of the company is for practical purposes complete and the liquidator is not the official receiver, the liquidator shall summon a final general meeting of the company's creditors which—

  (a)  shall receive the liquidator's report of the winding up, and

  (b)  shall determine whether the liquidator should have his release under section 174 in Chapter VII of this Part.

(2)   The liquidator may, if he thinks fit, give the notice summoning the final general meeting at the same time as giving notice of any final distribution of the company's property but, if summoned for an earlier date, that meeting shall be adjourned (and, if necessary, further adjourned) until a date on which the liquidator is able to report to the meeting that the winding up of the company is for practical purposes complete.

(3)   In the carrying out of his functions in the winding up it is the duty of the liquidator to retain sufficient sums from the company's property to cover the expenses of summoning and holding the meeting required by this section.

*General powers of court*

### 147   Power to stay or sist winding up

(1)   The court may at any time after an order for winding up, on the application either of the liquidator or the official receiver or any creditor or contributory, and on proof to the satisfaction of the court that all proceedings in the winding up ought to be stayed or sisted, make an order staying or sisting the proceedings, either altogether or for a limited time, on such terms and conditions as the court thinks fit.

(2)   The court may, before making an order, require the official receiver to furnish to it a report with respect to any facts or matters which are in his opinion relevant to the application.

(3)   A copy of every order made under this section shall forthwith be forwarded by the company, or otherwise as may be prescribed, to the registrar of companies, who shall enter it in his records relating to the company.

### 148   Settlement of list of contributories and application of assets

(1)   As soon as may be after making a winding-up order, the court shall settle a list of contributories, with power to rectify the register of members in all cases where rectification is required in pursuance of the Companies Act or this Act, and shall cause the company's assets to be collected, and applied in discharge of its liabilities.

(2) If it appears to the court that it will not be necessary to make calls on or adjust the rights of con-tributories, the court may dispense with the settlement of a list of contributories.

(3) In settling the list, the court shall distinguish between persons who are contributories in their own right and persons who are contributories as being representatives of or liable for the debts of others.

### 149 Debts due from contributory to company

(1) The court may, at any time after making a winding-up order, make an order on any contribu-tory for the time being on the list of contributories to pay, in manner directed by the order, any money due from him (or from the estate of the person who he represents) to the company, exclusive of any money payable by him or the estate by virtue of any call in pursuance of the Companies Act or this Act.

(2) The court in making such an order may—

(a) in the case of an unlimited company, allow to the contributory by way of set-off any money due to him or the estate which he represents from the company on any independent dealing or contract with the company, but not any money due to him as a member of the company in respect of any dividend or profit, and

(b) in the case of a limited company, make to any director or manager whose liability is unlim-ited or to his estate the like allowance.

(3) In the case of any company, whether limited or unlimited, when all the creditors are paid in full (together with interest at the official rate) any money due on any account whatever to a contributory from the company may be allowed to him by way of set-off against any subsequent call.

### 150 Power to make calls

(1) The court may, at any time after making a winding-up order, and either before or after it has ascertained the sufficiency of the company's assets, make calls on all or any of the contributories for the time being settled on the list of the contributories to the extent of their liability, for payment of any money which the court considers necessary to satisfy the company's debts and liabilities, and the expenses of winding up, and for the adjustment of the rights of the contributories among themselves, and make an order for payment of any calls so made.

(2) In making a call the court may take into consideration the probability that some of the contribu-tories may partly or wholly fail to pay it.

### 151 Payment into bank of money due to company

(1) The court may order any contributory, purchaser or other person from whom money is due to the company to pay the amount due into the Bank of England (or any branch of it) to the account of the liquidator instead of to the liquidator, and such an order may be enforced in the same manner as if it had directed payment to the liquidator.

(2) All money and securities paid or delivered into the Bank of England (or branch) in the event of a winding up by the court are subject in all respects to the orders of the court.

### 152 Order on contributory to be conclusive evidence

(1) An order made by the court on a contributory is conclusive evidence that the money (if any) thereby appearing to be due or ordered to be paid is due, but subject to any right of appeal.

(2) All other pertinent matters stated in the order are to be taken as truly stated as against all per-sons and in all proceedings except proceedings in Scotland against the heritable estate of a deceased contributory; and in that case the order is only prima facie evidence for the purpose of charging his heritable estate, unless his heirs or legatees of heritage were on the list of contributories at the time of the order being made.

### 153 Power to exclude creditors not proving in time

The court may fix a time or times within which creditors are to prove their debts or claims or to be excluded from the benefit of any distribution made before those debts are proved.

### 154 Adjustment of rights of contributories

The court shall adjust the rights of the contributories among themselves and distribute any surplus among the persons entitled to it.

### 155 Inspection of books by creditors, etc

(1) The court may, at any time after making a winding-up order, make such order for inspection of the company's books and papers by creditors and contributories as the court thinks just; and any books and papers in the company's possession may be inspected by creditors and contributories accordingly, but not further or otherwise.

(2) Nothing in this section excludes or restricts any statutory rights of a government department or person acting under the authority of a government department.

(3) For the purposes of subsection (2) above, references to a government department shall be con-strued as including references to any part of the Scottish Administration.

### 156 Payment of expenses of winding up

The court may, in the event of the assets being insufficient to satisfy the liabilities, make an order as to the payment out of the assets of the expenses incurred in the winding up in such order of priority as the court thinks just.

### 157   Attendance at company meetings (Scotland)

In the winding up by the court of a company registered in Scotland, the court has power to require the attendance of any officer of the company at any meeting of creditors or of contributories, or of a liquidation committee, for the purpose of giving information as to the trade, dealings, affairs or property of the company.

### 158   Power to arrest absconding contributory

The court, at any time either before or after making a winding-up order, on proof of probable cause for believing that a contributory is about to quit the United Kingdom or otherwise to abscond or to remove or conceal any of his property for the purpose of evading payment of calls, may cause the contributory to be arrested and his books and papers and moveable personal property to be seized and him and them to be kept safely until such time as the court may order.

### 159   Powers of court to be cumulative

Powers conferred by this Act and the Companies Act on the court are in addition to, and not in restriction of, any existing powers of instituting proceedings against a contributory or debtor of the company, or the estate of any contributory or debtor, for the recovery of any call or other sums.

### 160   Delegation of powers to liquidator (England and Wales)

(1)   Provision may be made by rules for enabling or requiring all or any of the powers and duties conferred and imposed on the court in England and Wales by the Companies Act and this Act in respect of the following matters—

    (a) the holding and conducting of meetings to ascertain the wishes of creditors and contributories,

    (b) the settling of lists of contributories and the rectifying of the register of members where required, and the collection and application of the assets,

    (c) the payment, delivery, conveyance, surrender or transfer of money, property, books or papers to the liquidator,

    (d) the making of calls,

    (e) the fixing of a time within which debts and claims must be proved,

to be exercised or performed by the liquidator as an officer of the court, and subject to the court's control.

(2)   But the liquidator shall not, without the special leave of the court, rectify the register of members, and shall not make any call without either that special leave or the sanction of the liquidation committee.

*Enforcement of, and appeal from, orders*

### 161   Orders for calls on contributories (Scotland)

(1)   In Scotland, where an order, interlocutor or decree has been made for winding up a company by the court, it is competent to the court, on production by the liquidators of a list certified by them of the names of the contributories liable in payment of any calls, and of the amount due by each contributory, and of the date when that amount became due, to pronounce forthwith a decree against those contributories for payment of the sums so certified to be due, with interest from that date until payment (at 5 per cent. per annum) in the same way and to the same effect as if they had severally consented to registration for execution, on a charge of 6 days, of a legal obligation to pay those calls and interest.

(2)   The decree may be extracted immediately, and no suspension of it is competent, except on caution or consignation, unless with special leave of the court.

### 162   Appeals from orders in Scotland

(1)   Subject to the provision of this section and to rules of court, an appeal from any order or decision made or given in the winding up of a company by the court in Scotland under this Act lies in the same manner and subject to the same conditions as an appeal from an order or decision of the court in cases within its ordinary jurisdiction.

(2)   In regard to orders of judgments pronounced by the judge acting as vacation judge [...]—

    (a) none of the orders specified in Part I of Schedule 3 to this Act are subject to review, reduction, suspension or stay of execution, and

    (b) every other order or judgment (except as mentioned below) may be submitted to review by the Inner House by reclaiming motion enrolled within 14 days from the date of the order or judgment.

(3)   However, an order being one of those specified in Part II of that Schedule shall, from the date of the order and notwithstanding that it has been submitted to review as above, be carried out and receive effect until the Inner House have disposed of the matter.

(4)   In regard to orders or judgments pronounced in Scotland by a Lord Ordinary before whom proceedings in a winding up are being taken, any such order or judgment may be submitted to review by the Inner House by reclaiming motion enrolled within 14 days from its date; but should it not be so submitted to review during session, the provisions of this section in regard to orders or judgments pronounced by the judge acting as vacation judge apply.

(5) Nothing in this section affects provisions of the Companies Act or this Act in reference to decrees in Scotland for payment of calls in the winding up of companies, whether voluntary or by the court.

# Chapter VII

# Liquidators

*Preliminary*

### 163 Style and title of liquidators

The liquidator of a company shall be described—

    (a) where a person other than the official receiver is liquidator, by the style of 'the liquidator' of the particular company, or

    (b) where the official receiver is liquidator, by the style of 'the official receiver and liquidator' of the particular company;

and in neither case shall he be described by an individual name.

### 164 Corrupt inducement affecting appointment

A person who gives, or agrees or offers to give, to any member or creditor of a company any valuable consideration with a view to securing his own appointment or nomination, or to securing or preventing the appointment or nomination of some person other than himself, as the company's liquidator is liable to a fine.

*Liquidator's powers and duties*

### 165 Voluntary winding up

(1) This section has effect where a company is being wound up voluntarily, but subject to section 166 below in the case of a creditor's voluntary winding up.

(2) The liquidator may—

    (a) in the case of a members' voluntary winding up, with the sanction of an extraordinary resolution of the company, and

    (b) in the case of a creditor's voluntary winding up, with the sanction of the court or the liquidation committee (or, if there is no such committee, a meeting of the company's creditors),

exercise any of the powers specified in Part I of Schedule 4 to this Act (payment of debts, compromise of claims, etc.).

(3) The liquidator may, without sanction exercise either of the powers specified in Part II of that Schedule (institution and defence of proceedings; carrying on the business of the company) and any of the general powers specified in Part III of that Schedule.

(4) The liquidator may—

    (a) exercise the court's power of settling a list of contributories (which list is prima facie evidence of the liability of the persons named in it to be contributories),

    (b) exercise the court's power of making calls,

    (c) summon general meetings of the company for the purpose of obtaining its sanction by special or extraordinary resolution or for any other purpose he may think fit.

(5) The liquidator shall pay the company's debts and adjust the rights of the contributories among themselves.

(6) Where the liquidator in exercise of the powers conferred on him by this Act disposes of any property of the company to a person who is connected with the company (within the meaning of section 249 in Part VII), he shall, if there is for the time being a liquidation committee, give notice to the committee of that exercise of his powers.

### 166 Creditors' voluntary winding up

(1) This section applies where, in the case of a creditors' voluntary winding up, a liquidator has been nominated by the company.

(1A) The exercise by the liquidator of the power specified in paragraph 6 of Schedule 4 to this Act (power to sell any of the company's property) shall not be challengeable on the ground of any prior inhibition.

(2) The powers conferred on the liquidator by section 165 shall not be exercised, except with the sanction of the court, during the period before the holding of the creditors' meeting under section 98 in Chapter IV.

(3) Subsection (2) does not apply in relation to the power of the liquidator—

    (a) to take into his custody or under his control all the property to which the company is or appears to be entitled;

    (b) to dispose of perishable goods and other goods the value of which is likely to diminish if they are not immediately disposed of; and

    (c) to do all such other things as may be necessary for the protection of the company's assets.

(4) The liquidator shall attend the creditors' meeting held under section 98 and shall report to the meeting on any exercise by him of his powers (whether or not under this section or under section 112 or 165).

(5) If default is made—

(a) by the company in complying with subsection (1) or (2) of section 98, or

(b) by the directors in complying with subsection (1) or (2) of section 99,

the liquidator shall, within 7 days of the relevant day, apply to the court for directions as to the manner in which that default is to be remedied.

(6) 'The relevant day' means the day on which the liquidator was nominated by the company or the day on which he first became aware of the default, whichever is the later.

(7) If the liquidator without reasonable excuse fails to comply with this section, he is liable to a fine.

### 167   Winding up by the court

(1) Where a company is being wound up by the court, the liquidator may—

(a) with the sanction of the court or the liquidation committee, exercise any of the powers specified in Parts I and II of Schedule 4 to this Act (payment of debts; compromise of claims, etc., institution and defence of proceedings; carrying on of the business of the company), and

(b) with or without that sanction, exercise any of the general powers specified in Part III of that Schedule.

(2) Where the liquidator (not being the official receiver), in exercise of the powers conferred on him by this Act—

(a) disposes of any property of the company to a person who is connected with the company (within the meaning of section 249 in Part VII) or

(b) employs a solicitor to assist him in the carrying out of his functions,

he shall, if there is for the time being a liquidation committee, give notice to the committee of that exercise of his powers.

(3) The exercise by the liquidator in a winding up by the court of the powers conferred by this section is subject to the control of the court, and any creditor or contributory may apply to the court with respect to any exercise or proposed exercise of any of those powers.

### 168   Supplementary powers (England and Wales)

(1) This section applies in the case of a company which is being wound up by the court in England and Wales.

(2) The liquidator may summon general meetings of the creditors or contributories for the purpose of ascertaining their wishes; and it is his duty to summon meetings at such times as the creditors or contributories by resolution (either at the meeting appointing the liquidator or otherwise) may direct, or whenever requested in writing to do so by one-tenth in value of the creditors or contributories (as the case may be).

(3) The liquidator may apply to the court (in the prescribed manner) for directions in relation to any particular matter arising in the winding up.

(4) Subject to the provisions of this Act, the liquidator shall use his own discretion in the management of the assets and their distribution among the creditors.

(5) If any person is aggrieved by an act or decision of the liquidator, that person may apply to the court; and the court may confirm, reverse or modify the act or decision complained of, and make such order in the case as it thinks just.

(5A) Where at any time after a winding-up petition has been presented to the court against any person (including an insolvent partnership or other body which may be wound up under Part V of the Act as an unregistered company), whether by virtue of the provisions of the Insolvent Partnerships Order 1994 or not, the attention of the court is drawn to the fact that the person in question is a member of an insolvent partnership, the court may make an order as to the future conduct of the insolvency proceedings and any such order may apply any provisions of that Order with any necessary modifications.

(5B) Any order or directions under subsection (5A) may be made or given on the application of the official receiver, any responsible insolvency practitioner, the trustee of the partnership or any other interested person and may include provisions as to the administration of the joint estate of the partnership, and in particular how it and the separate estate of any member are to be administered.

(5C) Where the court makes an order for the winding up of an insolvent partnership under—

(a) section 72(1)(a) of the Financial Services Act 1986;

(b) section 92(1)(a) of the Banking Act 1987; or

(c) section 367(3)(a) of the Financial Services and Markets Act 2000,

the court may make an order as to the future conduct of the winding up proceedings, and any such order may apply any provisions of the Insolvent Partnerships Order 1994 with any necessary modifications.

### 169   Supplementary powers (Scotland)

(1) In the case of a winding up in Scotland, the court may provide by order that the liquidator may, where there is no liquidation committee, exercise any of the following powers, namely—

(a) to bring or defend any action or other legal proceeding in the name and on behalf of the company, or

(b) to carry on the business of the company so far as may be necessary for its beneficial winding up,

without the sanction or intervention of the court.

(2) In a winding up by the court in Scotland, the liquidator has (subject to the rules) the same powers as a trustee on a bankrupt estate.

### 170    Enforcement of liquidator's duty to make returns, etc

(1) If a liquidator who has made any default—

(a) in filing, delivering or making any return, account or other document, or

(b) in giving any notice which he is by law required to file, deliver, make or give,

fails to make good the default within 14 days after the service on him of a notice requiring him to do so, the court has the following powers.

(2) On an application made by any creditor or contributory of the company, or by the registrar of companies, the court may make an order directing the liquidator to make good the default within such time as may be specified in the order.

(3) The court's order may provide that all costs of and incidental to the application shall be borne by the liquidator.

(4) Nothing in this section prejudices the operation of any enactment imposing penalties on a liquidator in respect of any such default as is mentioned above.

*Removal; vacation of office*

### 171    Removal, etc (voluntary winding up)

(1) This section applies with respect to the removal from office and vacation of office of the liquidator of a company which is being wound up voluntarily.

(2) Subject to the next subsection, the liquidator may be removed from office only by an order of the court or—

(a) in the case of a members' voluntary winding up, by a general meeting of the company summoned specially for that purpose, or

(b) in the case of a creditors' voluntary winding up, by a general meeting of the company's creditors summoned specially for that purpose in accordance with the rules.

(3) Where the liquidator was appointed by the court under section 108 in Chapter V, a meeting such as is mentioned in subsection (2) above shall be summoned for the purpose of replacing him only if he thinks fit or the court so directs or the meeting is requested, in accordance with the rules—

(a) in the case of a members' voluntary winding up, by members representing not less than one-half of the total voting rights of all the members having at the date of the request a right to vote at the meeting, or

(b) in the case of a creditors' voluntary winding up, by not less than one-half, in value, of the company's creditors.

(4) A liquidator shall vacate office if he ceases to be a person who is qualified to act as an insolvency practitioner in relation to the company.

(5) A liquidator may, in the prescribed circumstances, resign his office by giving notice of his resignation to the registrar of companies.

(6) Where—

(a) in the case of a members' voluntary winding up, a final meeting of the company has been held under section 94 in Chapter III, or

(b) in the case of a creditors' voluntary winding up, final meetings of the company and of the creditors have been held under section 106 in Chapter IV,

the liquidator whose report was considered at the meeting or meetings shall vacate office as soon as he has complied with subsection (3) of that section and has given notice to the registrar of companies that the meeting or meetings have been held and of the decisions (if any) of the meeting or meetings.

### 172    Removal, etc (winding up by the court)

(1) This section applies with respect to the removal from office and vacation of office of the liquidator of a company which is being wound up by the court, or of a provisional liquidator.

(2) Subject as follows, the liquidator may be removed from office only by an order of the court or by a general meeting of the company's creditors summoned specially for that purpose in accordance with the rules; and a provisional liquidator may be removed from office only by an order of the court.

(3) Where—

(a) the official receiver is liquidator otherwise than in succession under section 136(3) to a person who held office as a result of a nomination by a meeting of the company's creditors or contributories, or

(b) the liquidator was appointed by the court otherwise than under section 139(4)(a) or 140(1), or was appointed by the Secretary of State, a general meeting of the company's creditors shall be summoned for the purpose of replacing him only if he thinks fit, or the court so directs, or the meeting is requested, in accordance with the rules, by not less than one-quarter, in value, of the creditors.

(4) If appointed by the Secretary of State, the liquidator may be removed from office by a direction of the Secretary of State.

(5) A liquidator or provisional liquidator, not being the official receiver, shall vacate office if he ceases to be a person who is qualified to act as an insolvency practitioner in relation to the company.

(6) A liquidator may, in the prescribed circumstances, resign his office by giving notice of his resignation to the court.

(7) Where an order is made under section 204 (early dissolution in Scotland) for the dissolution of the company, the liquidator shall vacate office when the dissolution of the company takes effect in accordance with that section.

(8) Where a final meeting has been held under section 146 (liquidator's report on completion of winding up), the liquidator whose report was considered at the meeting shall vacate office as soon as he has given notice to the court and the registrar of companies that the meeting has been held and of the decisions (if any) of the meeting.

*Release of liquidator*

### 173   Release (voluntary winding up)

(1) This section applies with respect to the release of the liquidator of a company which is being wound up voluntarily.

(2) A person who has ceased to be a liquidator shall have his release with effect from the following time, that is to say—

    (a) in the case of a person who has been removed from office by a general meeting of the company or by a general meeting of the company's creditors that has not resolved against his release or who has died, the time at which notice is given to the registrar of companies in accordance with the rules that that person has ceased to hold office;

    (b) in the case of a person who has been removed from office by a general meeting of the company's creditors that has resolved against his release, or by the court, or who has vacated office under section 171(4) above, such time as the Secretary of State may, on the application of that person, determine;

    (c) in the case of a person who has resigned, such time as may be prescribed;

    (d) in the case of a person who has vacated office under subsection (6)(a) of section 171, the time at which he vacated office;

    (e) in the case of a person who has vacated office under subsection (6)(b) of that section—

        (i) if the final meeting of the creditors referred to in that subsection has resolved against that person's release, such time as the Secretary of State may, on an application by that person, determine, and

        (ii) if that meeting has not resolved against that person's release, the time at which he vacated office.

(3) In the application of subsection (2) to the winding up of a company registered in Scotland, the references to a determination by the Secretary of State as to the time from which a person who has ceased to be liquidator shall have his release are to be read as references to such a determination by the Accountant of Court.

(4) Where a liquidator has his release under subsection (2), he is, with effect from the time specified in that subsection, discharged from all liability both in respect of acts or omissions of his in the winding up and otherwise in relation to his conduct as liquidator.

But nothing in this section prevents the exercise, in relation to a person who has had his release under subsection (2), of the court's powers under section 212 of this Act (summary remedy against delinquent directors, liquidators, etc.).

### 174   Release (winding up by the court)

(1) This section applies with respect to the release of the liquidator of a company which is being wound up by the court, or of a provisional liquidator.

(2) Where the official receiver has ceased to be liquidator and a person becomes liquidator in his stead, the official receiver has his release with effect from the following time, that is to say—

    (a) in a case where that person was nominated by a general meeting of creditors or contributories, or was appointed by the Secretary of State, the time at which the official receiver gives notice to the court that he has been replaced;

    (b) in a case where that person is appointed by the court, such time as the court may determine.

(3) If the official receiver while he is a liquidator gives notice to the Secretary of State that the winding up is for practical purposes complete, he has his release with effect from such time as the Secretary of State may determine.

(4) A person other than the official receiver who has ceased to be a liquidator has his release with effect from the following time, that is to say—

(a) in the case of a person who has been removed from office by a general meeting of creditors that has not resolved against his release or who has died, the time at which notice is given to the court in accordance with the rules that that person has ceased to hold office;

(b) in the case of a person who has been removed from office by a general meeting of creditors that has resolved against his release, or by the court or the Secretary of State, or who has vacated office under section 172(5) or (7), such time as the Secretary of State may, on an application by that person, determine;

(c) in the case of a person who has resigned, such time as may be prescribed;

(d) in the case of a person who has vacated office under section 172(8)—

   (i) if the final meeting referred to in that subsection has resolved against that person's release, such time as the Secretary of State may, on an application by that person, determine, and

   (ii) if that meeting has not so resolved, the time at which that person vacated office.

(5) A person who has ceased to hold office as a provisional liquidator has his release with effect from such time as the court may, on an application by him, determine.

(6) Where the official receiver or a liquidator or provisional liquidator has his release under this section, he is, with effect from the time specified in the preceding provisions of this section, discharged from all liability both in respect of acts or omissions of his in the winding up and otherwise in relation to his conduct as liquidator or provisional liquidator.

But nothing in this section prevents the exercise, in relation to a person who has had his release under this section, of the court's powers under section 212 (summary remedy against delinquent directors, liquidators, etc.).

(7) In the application of this section to a case where the order for winding up has been made by the court in Scotland, the references to a determination by the Secretary of State as to the time from which a person who has ceased to be liquidator has his release are to such a determination by the Accountant of Court.

## Chapter VIII

## Provisions of general application in winding up

### *Preferential debts*

### 175  Preferential debts (general provision)

(1) In a winding up the company's preferential debts (within the meaning given by section 386 in Part XII) shall be paid in priority to all other debts.

(2) Preferential debts—

(a) rank equally among themselves after the expenses of the winding up and shall be paid in full, unless the assets are insufficient to meet them, in which case they abate in equal proportions; and

(b) so far as the assets of the company available for payment of general creditors are insufficient to meet them, have priority over the claims of holders of debentures secured by, or holders of, any floating charge created by the company, and shall be paid accordingly out of any property comprised in or subject to that charge.

### 176  Preferential charge on goods distrained

(1) This section applies where a company is being wound up by the court in England and Wales, and is without prejudice to section 128 (avoidance of attachments, etc.).

(2) Where any person (whether or not a landlord or person entitled to rent) has distrained upon the goods or effects of the company in the period of 3 months ending with the date of the winding-up order, those goods or effects, or the proceeds of their sale, shall be charged for the benefit of the company with the preferential debts of the company to the extent that the company's property is for the time being insufficient for meeting them.

(3) Where by virtue of a charge under subsection (2) any person surrenders any goods or effects to a company or makes a payment to a company, that person ranks, in respect of the amount of the proceeds of sale of those goods or effects by the liquidator or (as the case may be) the amount of the payment, as a preferential creditor of the company, except as against so much of the company's property as is available for the payment of preferential creditors by virtue of the surrender or payment.

### *Property subject to floating charge*

### 176ZA Payment of expenses of winding up (England and Wales)

(1) The expenses of winding up in England and Wales, so far as the assets of the company available for payment of general creditors are insufficient to meet them, have priority over any claims to property comprised in or subject to any floating charge created by the company and shall be paid out of any such property accordingly.

(2) In subsection (1)—

    (a) the reference to assets of the company available for payment of general creditors does not include any amount made available under section 176A(2)(a);

    (b) the reference to claims to property comprised in or subject to a floating charge is to the claims of—

        (i) the holders of debentures secured by, or holders of, the floating charge, and

        (ii) any preferential creditors entitled to be paid out of that property in priority to hem.

(3) Provision may be made by rules restricting the application of subsection (1), in such circumstances as may be prescribed, to expenses authorised or approved—

    (a) by the holders of debentures secured by, or holders of, the floating charge and by any preferential creditors entitled to be paid in priority to them, or

    (b) by the court.

(4) References in this section to the expenses of the winding up are to all expenses properly incurred in the winding up, including the remuneration of the liquidator.

## 176A  Share of assets for unsecured creditors

(1) This section applies where a floating charge relates to property of a company—

    (a) which has gone into liquidation,

    (b) which is in administration,

    (c) of which there is a provisional liquidator, or

    (d) of which there is a receiver.

(2) The liquidator, administrator or receiver—

    (a) shall make a prescribed part of the company's net property available for the satisfaction of unsecured debts, and

    (b) shall not distribute that part to the proprietor of a floating charge except in so far as it exceeds the amount required for the satisfaction of unsecured debts.

(3) Subsection (2) shall not apply to a company if—

    (a) the company's net property is less than the prescribed minimum, and

    (b) the liquidator, administrator or receiver thinks that the cost of making a distribution to unsecured creditors would be disproportionate to the benefits.

(4) Subsection (2) shall also not apply to a company if or in so far as it is disapplied by—

    (a) a voluntary arrangement in respect of the company, or

    (b) a compromise or arrangement agreed under Part 26 of the Companies Act 2006 (reconstructions and arrangements).

(5) Subsection (2) shall also not apply to a company if—

    (a) the liquidator, administrator or receiver applies to the court for an order under this subsection on the ground that the cost of making a distribution to unsecured creditors would be disproportionate to the benefits, and

    (b) the court orders that subsection (2) shall not apply.

(6) In subsections (2) and (3) a company's net property is the amount of its property which would, but for this section, be available for satisfaction of claims of holders of debentures secured by, or holders of, any floating charge created by the company.

(7) An order under subsection (2) prescribing part of a company's net property may, in particular, provide for its calculation—

    (a) as a percentage of the company's net property, or

    (b) as an aggregate of different percentages of different parts of the company's net property.

(8) An order under this section—

    (a) must be made by statutory instrument, and

    (b) shall be subject to annulment pursuant to a resolution of either House of Parliament.

(9) In this section—

'floating charge' means a charge which is a floating charge on its creation and which is created after the first order under subsection (2)(a) comes into force, and

'prescribed' means prescribed by order by the Secretary of State.

(10) An order under this section may include transitional or incidental provision.

### Special managers

## 177  Power to appoint special manager

(1) Where a company has gone into liquidation or a provisional liquidator has been appointed, the court may, on an application under this section, appoint any person to be the special manager of the business or property of the company.

(2) The application may be made by the liquidator or provisional liquidator in any case where it appears to him that the nature of the business or property of the company, or the interests of the company's creditors or contributories or members generally, require the appointment of another to manage the company's business or property.

(3) The special manager has such powers as may be entrusted to him by the court.

(4)　The court's power to entrust powers to the special manager includes power to direct that any provision of this Act that has effect in relation to the provisional liquidator or liquidator of a company shall have the like effect in relation to the special manager for the purposes of the carrying out by him of any of the functions of the provisional liquidator or liquidator.

(5)　The special manager shall—

(a)　give such security or, in Scotland, caution, as may be prescribed;

(b)　prepare and keep such accounts as may be prescribed; and

(c)　produce those accounts in accordance with the rules to the Secretary of State or to such other persons as may be prescribed.

### *Disclaimer (England and Wales only)*

### 178　Power to disclaim onerous property

(1)　This and the next two sections apply to a company that is being wound up in England and Wales.

(2)　Subject as follows, the liquidator may, by the giving of the prescribed notice, disclaim any onerous property and may do so notwithstanding that he has taken possession of it, endeavoured to sell it, or otherwise exercised rights of ownership in relation to it.

(3)　The following is onerous property for the purposes of this section—

(a)　any unprofitable contract, and

(b)　any other property of the company which is unsaleable or not readily saleable or is such that it may give rise to a liability to pay money or perform any other onerous act.

(4)　A disclaimer under this section—

(a)　operates so as to determine, as from the date of the disclaimer, the rights, interests and liabilities of the company in or in respect of the property disclaimed; but

(b)　does not, except so far as is necessary for the purpose of releasing the company from any liability, affect the rights or liabilities of any other person.

(5)　A notice of disclaimer shall not be given under this section in respect of any property if—

(a)　a person interested in the property has applied in writing to the liquidator or one of his predecessors as liquidator requiring the liquidator or that predecessor to decide whether he will disclaim or not, and

(b)　the period of 28 days beginning with the day on which that application was made, or such longer period as the court may allow, has expired without a notice of disclaimer having been given under this section in respect of that property.

(6)　Any person sustaining loss or damage in consequence of the operation of a disclaimer under this section is deemed a creditor of the company to the extent of the loss or damage and accordingly may prove for the loss or damage in the winding up.

### 179　Disclaimer of leaseholds

(1)　The disclaimer under section 178 of any property of a leasehold nature does not take effect unless a copy of the disclaimer has been served (so far as the liquidator is aware of their addresses) on every person claiming under the company as underlessee or mortgagee and either—

(a)　no application under section 181 below is made with respect to that property before the end of the period of 14 days beginning with the day on which the last notice served under this subsection was served; or

(b)　where such an application has been made, the court directs that the disclaimer shall take effect.

(2)　Where the court gives a direction under subsection (1)(b) it may also, instead of or in addition to any order it makes under section 181, make such orders with respect to fixtures, tenant's improvements and other matters arising out of the lease as it thinks fit.

### 180　Land subject to rentcharge

(1)　The following applies where, in consequence of the disclaimer under section 178 of any land subject to a rentcharge, that land vests by operation of law in the Crown or any other person (referred to in the next subsection as 'the proprietor').

(2)　The proprietor and the successors in title of the proprietor are not subject to any personal liability in respect of any sums becoming due under the rentcharge except sums becoming due after the proprietor, or some person claiming under or through the proprietor, has taken possession or control of the land or has entered into occupation of it.

### 181　Powers of court (general)

(1)　This section and the next apply where the liquidator has disclaimed property under section 178.

(2)　An application under this section may be made to the court by—

(a)　any person who claims an interest in the disclaimed property, or

(b)　any person who is under any liability in respect of the disclaimed property, not being a liability discharged by the disclaimer.

(3)　Subject as follows, the court may on the application make an order, on such terms as it thinks fit, for the vesting of the disclaimed property in, or for its delivery to—

(a) a person entitled to it or a trustee for such a person, or

(b) a person subject to such a liability as is mentioned in subsection (2)(b) or a trustee for such a person.

(4) The court shall not make an order under subsection (3)(b) except where it appears to the court that it would be just to do so for the purpose of compensating the person subject to the liability in respect of the disclaimer.

(5) The effect of any order under this section shall be taken into account in assessing for the purpose of section 178(6) the extent of any loss or damage sustained by any person in consequence of the disclaimer.

(6) An order under this section vesting property in any person need not be completed by conveyance, assignment or transfer.

### 182   Powers of court (leaseholds)

(1) The court shall not make an order under section 181 vesting property of a leasehold nature in any person claiming under the company as underlessee or mortgagee except on terms making that person—

(a) subject to the same liabilities and obligations as the company was subject to under the lease at the commencement of the winding up, or

(b) if the court thinks fit, subject to the same liabilities and obligations as that person would be subject to if the lease had been assigned to him at the commencement of the winding up.

(2) For the purposes of an order under section 181 relating to only part of any property comprised in a lease, the requirements of subsection (1) apply as if the lease comprised only the property to which the order relates.

(3) Where subsection (1) applies and no person claiming under the company as underlessee or mortgagee is willing to accept an order under section 181 on the terms required by virtue of that subsection, the court may, by order under that section, vest the company's estate or interest in the property in any person who is liable (whether personally or in a representative capacity, and whether alone or jointly with the company) to perform the lessee's covenants in the lease.

The court may vest that estate and interest in such a person freed and discharged from all estates, incumbrances and interests created by the company.

(4) Where subsection (1) applies and a person claiming under the company as underlessee or mortgagee declines to accept an order under section 181, that person is excluded from all interest in the property.

*Execution, attachment and the Scottish equivalents*

### 183   Effect of execution or attachment (England and Wales)

(1) Where a creditor has issued execution against the goods or land of a company or has attached any debt due to it, and the company is subsequently wound up, he is not entitled to retain the benefit of the execution or attachment against the liquidator unless he has completed the execution or attachment before the commencement of the winding up.

(2) However—

(a) if a creditor has had notice of a meeting having been called at which a resolution for voluntary winding up is to be proposed, the date on which he had notice is substituted, for the purpose of subsection (1), for the date of commencement of the winding up;

(b) a person who purchases in good faith under a sale by the enforcement officer or other officer charged with the execution of the writ any goods of a company on which execution has been levied in all cases acquires a good title to them against the liquidator; and

(c) the rights conferred by subsection (1) on the liquidator may be set aside by the court in favour of the creditor to such extent and subject to such terms as the court thinks fit.

(3) For purposes of this Act—

(a) an execution against goods is completed by seizure and sale, or by making of a charging order under section 1 of the Charging Orders Act 1979;

(b) an attachment of a debt is completed by receipt of the debt; and

(c) an execution against land is completed by seizure, by the appointment of a receiver, or by the making of a charging order under section 1 of the Act above-mentioned.

(4) In this section 'goods' includes all chattels personal; and 'enforcement officer' means an individual who is authorised to act as an enforcement officer under the Courts Act 2003.

(5) This section does not apply in the case of a winding up in Scotland.

### 184   Duties of officers charged with execution of writs and other processes (England and Wales)

(1) The following applies where a company's goods are taken in execution and, before their sale or the completion of the execution (by the receipt or recovery of the full amount of the levy), notice is served on the enforcement officer, or other officer, charged with execution of the writ or other process, that a provisional liquidator has been appointed or that a winding-up order has been made, or that a resolution for voluntary winding up has been passed.

(2) The enforcement officer or other officer shall, on being so required, deliver the goods and any money seized or received in part satisfaction of the execution to the liquidator; but the costs of execution are a first charge on the goods or money so delivered, and the liquidator may sell the goods, or a sufficient part of them for the purpose of satisfying the charge.

(3) If under an execution in respect of a judgement for a sum exceeding £500 a company's goods are sold or money is paid in order to avoid sale, the enforcement officer or other officer shall deduct the costs of the execution from the proceeds of sale or the money paid and retain the balance for 14 days.

(4) If within that time notice is served on the enforcement officer or other officer of a petition for the winding up of the company having been presented, or of a meeting having been called at which there is to be proposed a resolution for voluntary winding up, and an order is made or a resolution passed (as the case may be), the enforcement officer or other officer shall pay the balance to the liquidator, who is entitled to retain it as against the execution creditor.

(5) The rights conferred by this section on the liquidator may be set aside by the court in favour of the creditor to such extent and subject to such terms as the court thinks fit.

(6) In this section, 'goods' includes all chattels personal; and 'enforcement officer' means an individual who is authorised to act as an enforcement officer under the Courts Act 2003.

(7) The money sum for the time being specified in subsection (3) is subject to increase or reduction by order under section 416 in Part XV.

(8) This section does not apply in the case of a winding up in Scotland.

### 185  Effect of diligence (Scotland)

(1) In the winding up of a company registered in Scotland, the following provisions of the Bankruptcy (Scotland) Act 1985—

    (a) subsections (1) to (6) *(8A) to (8F) and (10)* of section 37 (effect of sequestration on diligence); and

    (b) subsections (3), (4), (7) and (8) of section 39 (realisation of estate),

apply so far as consistent with this Act, in like manner as they apply in the sequestration of a debtor's estate, with the substitutions specified below and with any other necessary modifications.

(2) The substitutions to be made in those sections of the Act of 1985 are as follows—

    (a) for references to the debtor, substitute references to the company;

    (b) for references to the sequestration, substitute references to the winding up;

    (c) for references to the date of sequestration, substitute references to the commencement of the winding up of the company; and

    (d) for references to the [...] trustee, substitute references to the liquidator.

(3) In this section, 'the commencement of the winding up of the company' means, where it is being wound up by the court, the day on which the winding-up order is made.

(4) This section, so far as relating to any estate or effects of the company situated in Scotland, applies in the case of a company registered in England and Wales as in the case of one registered in Scotland.[7]

*Miscellaneous matters*

### 186  Rescission of contracts by the court

(1) The court may, on the application of a person who is, as against the liquidator, entitled to the benefit or subject to the burden of a contract made with the company, make an order rescinding the contract on such terms as to payment by or to either party of damages for the non-performance of the contract, or otherwise as the court thinks just.

(2) Any damages payable under the order to such a person may be proved by him as a debt in the winding up.

### 187  Power to make over assets to employees

(1) On the winding up of a company (whether by the court or voluntarily), the liquidator may, subject to the following provisions of this section, make any payment which the company has, before the commencement of the winding up, decided to make under section 719 of the Companies Act (power to provide for employees or former employees on cessation or transfer of business).

(2) The power which a company may exercise by virtue only of that section may be exercised by the liquidator after the winding up has commenced if, after the company's liabilities have been fully satisfied and provision has been made for the expenses of the winding up, the exercise of that power has been sanctioned by such a resolution of the company as would be required of the company itself by section 719(3) before that commencement, if paragraph (b) of that subsection were omitted and any other requirement applicable to its exercise by the company had been met.

(3) Any payment which may be made by a company under this section (that is, a payment after the commencement of its winding up) may be made out of the company's assets which are available to the members on the winding up.

---

[7] The words in italics inserted by the Bankruptcy and Diligence etc (Scotland) Act 2007 from a date to be appointed.

(4) On a winding up by the court, the exercise by the liquidator of his powers under this section is subject to the court's control, and any creditor or contributory may apply to the court with respect to any exercise or proposed exercise of the power.

(5) Subsections (1) and (2) above have effect notwithstanding anything in any rule of law or in section 107 of this Act (property of company after satisfaction of liabilities to be distributed among members).

### 188   Notification that company is in liquidation

(1) When a company is being wound up, whether by the court or voluntarily—

    (a) every invoice, order for goods or services, business letter or order form (whether in hard copy, electronic or any other form) issued by or on behalf of the company, or a liquidator of the company or a receiver or manager of the company's property, [...] and

    (b) all the company's websites,

must contain a statement that the company is being wound up.

(2) If default is made in complying with this section, the company and any of the following persons who knowingly and wilfully authorises or permits the default, namely, any officer of the company, any liquidator of the company and any receiver or manager, is liable to a fine.

### 189   Interest on debts

(1) In a winding up interest is payable in accordance with this section on any debt proved in the winding up, including so much of any such debt as represents interest on the remainder.

(2) Any surplus remaining after the payment of the debts proved in a winding up shall, before being applied for any other purpose, be applied in paying interest on those debts in respect of the periods during which they have been outstanding since the company went into liquidation.

(3) All interest under this section ranks equally, whether or not the debts on which it is payable rank equally.

(4) The rate of interest payable under this section in respect of any debt ('the official rate' for the purposes of any provision of this Act in which that expression is used) is whichever is the greater of—

    (a) the rate specified in section 17of the Judgments Act 1838 on the day on which the company went into liquidation, and

    (b) the rate applicable to that debt apart from the winding up.

(5) In the application of this section to Scotland—

    (a) references to a debt proved in a winding up have effect as references to a claim accepted in a winding up, and

    (b) the reference to section 17 of the Judgments Act 1838 has effect as a reference to the rules.

### 190   Documents exempt from stamp duty

(1) In the case of a winding up by the court, or of a creditors' voluntary winding up, the following has effect as regards exemption from duties chargeable under the enactments relating to stamp duties.

(2) If the company is registered in England and Wales, the following documents are exempt from stamp duty—

    (a) every assurance relating solely to freehold or leasehold property, or to any estate, right or interest in, any real or personal property, which forms part of the company's assets and which, after the execution of the assurance, either at law of in equity, is or remains part of those assets, and

    (b) every writ, order, certificate, or other instrument or writing relating solely to the property of any company which is being wound up as mentioned in subsection (1), or to any proceeding under such a winding up.

'Assurance' here includes deed, conveyance, assignment and surrender.

(3) If the company is registered in Scotland, the following documents are exempt from stamp duty—

    (a) every conveyance relating solely to property which forms part of the company's assets and which, after the execution of the conveyance, is or remains the company's property for the benefit of its creditors,

    (b) any articles of roup of sale, submission and every other instrument and writing whatsoever relating solely to the company's property, and

    (c) every deed or writing forming part of the proceedings in the winding up.

'Conveyance' here includes assignation, instrument, discharge, writing and deed.

### 191   Company's books to be evidence

Where a company is being wound up, all books and papers of the company and of the liquidators are, as between the contributories of the company, prima facie evidence of the truth of all matters purporting to be recorded in them.

### 192   Information as to pending liquidations

(1) If the winding up of a company is not concluded within one year after its commencement, the liquidator shall, at such intervals as may be prescribed, until the winding up is concluded, send to the

registrar of companies a statement in the prescribed form and containing the prescribed particulars with respect to the proceedings in, and position of, the liquidation.

(2) If a liquidator fails to comply with this section, he is liable to a fine and, for continued contravention, to a daily default fine.

### 193   Unclaimed dividends (Scotland)

(1) The following applies where a company registered in Scotland has been wound up, and is about to be dissolved.

(2) The liquidator shall lodge in an appropriate bank or institution as defined in section 73(1) of the Bankruptcy (Scotland) Act 1985 (not being a bank or institution in or of which the liquidator is acting partner, manager, agent or cashier) in the name of the Accountant of Court the whole unclaimed dividends and unapplied or undistributable balances, and the deposit receipts shall be transmitted to the Accountant of Court.

(3) The provisions of section 58 of the Bankruptcy (Scotland) Act 1985 (so far as consistent with this Act and the Companies Act) apply with any necessary modifications to sums lodged in a bank or institution under this section as they apply to sums deposited under section 57 of the Act first mentioned.

### 194   Resolutions passed at adjourned meetings

Where a resolution is passed at an adjourned meeting of a company's creditors or contributories, the resolution is treated for all purposes as having been passed on the date on which it was in fact passed, and not as having been passed on any earlier date.

### 195   Meetings to ascertain wishes of creditors or contributories

(1) The court may—
   (a) as to all matters relating to the winding up of a company, have regard to the wishes of the creditors or contributories (as proved to it by any sufficient evidence), and
   (b) if it thinks fit, for the purpose of ascertaining those wishes, direct meetings of the creditors or contributories to be called, held and conducted in such manner as the court directs, and appoint a person to act as chairman of any such meeting and report the result of it to the court.

(2) In the case of creditors, regard shall be had to the value of each creditor's debt.

(3) In the case of contributories, regard shall be had to the number of votes conferred on each contributory by the Companies Act or the articles.

### 196   Judicial notice of court documents

In all proceedings under this Part, all courts, judges and persons judicially acting, and all officers, judicial or ministerial, of any court, or employed in enforcing the process of any court shall take judicial notice—
   (a) of the signature of any officer of the High Court or of a county court in England and Wales, or of the Court of Session or a sheriff court in Scotland, or of the High Court in Northern Ireland, and also
   (b) of the official seal or stamp of the several offices of the High Court in England and Wales or Northern Ireland, or of the Court of Session, appended to or impressed on any document made, issued or signed under the provisions of this Act or the Companies Act, or any official copy of such a document.

### 197   Commission for receiving evidence

(1) When a company is wound up in England and Wales or in Scotland, the court may refer the whole or any part of the examination of witnesses—
   (a) to a specified county court in England and Wales, or
   (b) to the sheriff principal for a specified sheriffdom in Scotland, or
   (c) to the High Court in Northern Ireland or a specified Northern Ireland County Court,
('specified' meaning specified in the order of the winding-up court).

(2) Any person exercising jurisdiction as a judge of the court to which the reference is made (or, in Scotland, the sheriff principal to whom it is made) shall then, by virtue of this section, be a commissioner for the purpose of taking the evidence of those witnesses.

(3) The judge or sheriff principal has in the matter referred the same power of summoning and examining witnesses, of requiring the production and delivery of documents, of punishing defaults by witnesses, and of allowing costs and expenses to witnesses, as the court which made the winding-up order.

These powers are in addition to any which the judge or sheriff principal might lawfully exercise apart from this section.

(4) The examination so taken shall be returned or reported to the court which made the order in such manner as that court requests.

(5) This section extends to Northern Ireland.

### 198   Court order for examination of persons in Scotland

(1) The court may direct the examination in Scotland of any person for the time being in Scotland (whether a contributory of the company or not), in regard to the trade, dealings, affairs or property of

any company in course of being wound up, or of any person being a contributory of the company, so far as the company may be interested by reason of his being a contributory.

(2)  The order or commission to take the examination shall be directed to the sheriff principal of the sheriffdom in which the person to be examined is residing or happens to be for the time; and the sheriff principal shall summon the person to appear before him at a time and place to be specified in the summons for examination on oath as a witness or as a haver, and to produce any books or papers called for which are in his possession or power.

(3)  The sheriff principal may take the examination either orally or on written interrogatories, and shall report the same in writing in the usual form to the court, and shall transmit with the report the books and papers produced, if the originals are required and specified by the order or commission, or otherwise copies or extracts authenticated by the sheriff.

(4)  If a person so summoned fails to appear at the time and place specified, or refuses to be examined or to make the production required, the sheriff principal shall proceed against him as a witness or haver duly cited; and failing to appear or refusing to give evidence or make production may be proceeded against by the law of Scotland.

(5)  The sheriff principal is entitled to such fees, and the witness is entitled to such allowances, as sheriffs principal when acting as commissioners under appointment from the Court of Session and as witnesses and havers are entitled to in the like cases according to the law and practice of Scotland.

(6)  If any objection is stated to the sheriff principal by the witness, either on the ground of his incompetency as a witness, or as to the production required, or on any other ground, the sheriff principal may, if he thinks fit, report the objection to the court, and suspend the examination of the witness until it has been disposed of by the court.

### 199  Costs of application for leave to proceed (Scottish companies)

Where a petition or application for leave to proceed with an action or proceeding against a company which is being wound up in Scotland is unopposed and is granted by the court, the costs of the petition or application shall, unless the court otherwise directs, be added to the amount of the petitioner's or applicant's claim against the company.

### 200  Affidavits etc in United Kingdom and overseas

(1)  An affidavit required to be sworn under or for the purposes of this Part may be sworn in the United Kingdom, or elsewhere in Her Majesty's dominions, before any court, judge or person lawfully authorised to take and receive affidavits, or before any of Her Majesty's consuls or vice-consuls in any place outside Her dominions.

(2)  All courts, judges, justices, commissioners and persons acting judicially shall take judicial notice of the seal or stamp or signature (as the case may be) of any such court, judge, person, consul or vice-consul attached, appended or subscribed to any such affidavit, or to any other document to be used for the purposes of this Part.

## Chapter IX

## Dissolution of companies after winding up

### 201  Dissolution (voluntary winding up)

(1)  This section applies, in the case of a company wound up voluntarily, where the liquidator has sent to the registrar of companies his final account and return under section 94 (members' voluntary) or section 106 (creditors' voluntary).

(2)  The registrar on receiving the account and return shall forthwith register them; and on the expiration of 3 months from the registration of the return the company is deemed to be dissolved.

(3)  However, the court may, on the application of the liquidator or any other person who appears to the court to be interested, make an order deferring the date at which the dissolution of the company is to take effect for such time as the court thinks fit.

(4)  It is the duty of the person on whose application an order of the court under this section is made within 7 days after the making of the order to deliver to the registrar a copy of the order for registration; and if that person fails to do so he is liable to a fine and, for continued contravention, to a daily default fine.

### 202  Early dissolution (England and Wales)

(1)  This section applies where an order for the winding up of a company has been made by the court in England and Wales.

(2)  The official receiver, if—

(a)  he is the liquidator of the company, and

(b)  it appears to him—

(i)   that the realisable assets of the company are insufficient to cover the expenses of the winding up, and

(ii)  that the affairs of the company do not require any further investigation,

may at any time apply to the registrar of companies for the early dissolution of the company.

(3) Before making that application, the official receiver shall give not less than 28 days' notice of his intention to do so to the company's creditors and contributories and, if there is an administrative receiver of the company, to that receiver.

(4) With the giving of that notice the official receiver ceases (subject to any directions under the next section) to be required to perform any duties imposed on him in relation to the company, its creditors or contributories by virtue of any provision of this Act, apart from a duty to make an application under subsection (2) of this section.

(5) On the receipt of the official receivers' application under subsection (2) the registrar shall forthwith register it and, at the end of the period of 3 months beginning with the day of the registration of the application, the company shall be dissolved.

However, the Secretary of State may, on the application of the official receiver or any other person who appears to the Secretary of State to be interested, give directions under section 203 at any time before the end of that period.

### 203  Consequence of notice under s 202

(1) Where a notice has been given under section 202(3), the official receiver or any creditor or contributory of the company, or the administrative receiver of the company (if there is one) may apply to the Secretary of State for directions under this section.

(2) The grounds on which that application may be made are—

    (a) that the realisable assets of the company are sufficient to cover the expenses of the winding up;

    (b) that the affairs of the company do require further investigation; or

    (c) that for any other reason the early dissolution of the company is inappropriate.

(3) Directions under this section—

    (a) are directions making such provision as the Secretary of State thinks fit for enabling the winding up of the company to proceed as if no notice had been given under section 202(3), and

    (b) may, in the case of an application under section 202(5), include a direction deferring the date at which the dissolution of the company is to take effect for such period as the Secretary of State thinks fit.

(4) An appeal to the court lies from any decision of the Secretary of State on an application for directions under this section.

(5) It is the duty of the person on whose application any directions are given under this section, or in whose favour an appeal with respect to an application for such directions is determined, within 7 days after the giving of the directions or the determination of the appeal, to deliver to the registrar of companies for registration such a copy of the directions or determination as is prescribed.

(6) If a person without reasonable excuse fails to deliver a copy as required by subsection (5), he is liable to a fine and, for continued contravention, to a daily default fine.

### 204  Early dissolution (Scotland)

(1) This section applies where a winding-up order has been made by the court in Scotland.

(2) If after a meeting or meetings under section 138 (appointment of liquidator in Scotland) it appears to the liquidator that the realisable assets of the company are insufficient to cover the expenses of the winding up, he may apply to the court for an order that the company be dissolved.

(3) Where the liquidator makes that application, if the court is satisfied that the realisable assets of the company are insufficient to cover the expenses of the winding up and it appears to the court appropriate to do so, the court shall make an order that the company be dissolved in accordance with this section.

(4) A copy of the order shall within 14 days from its date be forwarded by the liquidator to the registrar of companies, who shall forthwith register it; and, at the end of the period of 3 months beginning with the day of the registration of the order, the company shall be dissolved.

(5) The court may, on an application by any person who appears to the court to have an interest, order that the date at which the dissolution of the company is to take effect shall be deferred for such period as the court thinks fit.

(6) It is the duty of the person on whose application an order is made under subsection (5), within 7 days after the making of the order, to deliver to the registrar of companies such a copy of the order as is prescribed.

(7) If the liquidator without reasonable excuse fails to comply with the requirements of subsection (4), he is liable to a fine and, for continued contravention, to a daily default fine.

(8) If a person without reasonable excuse fails to deliver a copy as required by subsection (6), he is liable to a fine and, for continued contravention, to a daily default fine.

### 205  Dissolution otherwise than under ss 202–204

(1) This section applies where the registrar of companies receives—

    (a) a notice served for the purposes of section 172(8) (final meeting of creditors and vacation of office by liquidator), or

(b) a notice, from the official receiver that the winding up of a company by the court is complete.

(2) The registrar shall, on receipt of the notice, forthwith register it; and, subject, as follows, at the end of the period of 3 months beginning with the day of the registration of the notice, the company shall be dissolved.

(3) The Secretary of State may, on the application of the official receiver or any other person who appears to the Secretary of State to be interested, give a direction deferring the date at which the dissolution of the company is to take effect for such period as the Secretary of State thinks fit.

(4) An appeal to the court lies from any decision of the Secretary of State on an application for a direction under subsection (3).

(5) Subsection (3) does not apply in a case where the winding-up order was made by the court in Scotland, but in such a case the court may, on an application by any person appearing to the court to have an interest, order that the date at which the dissolution of the company is to take effect shall be deferred for such period as the court thinks fit.

(6) It is the duty of the person—

(a) on whose application a direction is given under subsection (3);

(b) in whose favour an appeal with respect to an application for such a direction is determined; or

(c) on whose application an order is made under subsection (5),

within 7 days after the giving of the direction, the determination of the appeal or the making of the order, to deliver to the registrar for registration such a copy of the direction, determination or order as is prescribed.

(7) If a person without reasonable excuse fails to deliver a copy as required by subsection (6), he is liable to a fine and, for continued contravention, to a daily default fine.

# Chapter X

## Malpractice before and during liquidation; penalisation of companies and company officers; investigations and prosecutions

*Offences of fraud, deception, etc.*

### 206  Fraud, etc in anticipation of winding up

(1) When a company is ordered to be wound up by the court, or passes a resolution for voluntary winding up, any person, being a past or present officer of the company, is deemed to have committed an offence if, within the 12 months immediately preceding the commencement of the winding up, he has—

(a) concealed any part of the company's property to the value of £500 or more, or concealed any debt due to or from the company, or

(b) fraudulently removed any part of the company's property to the value of £500 or more, or

(c) concealed, destroyed, mutilated or falsified any book or paper affecting or relating to the company's property or affairs, or

(d) made any false entry in any book or paper affecting or relating to the company's property or affairs, or

(e) fraudulently parted with, altered or made any omission in any document affecting or relating to the company's property or affairs, or

(f) pawned, pledged or disposed of any property of the company which has been obtained on credit and has not been paid for (unless the pawning, pledging or disposal was in the ordinary way of the company's business).

(2) Such a person is deemed to have committed an offence if within the period above mentioned he has been privy to the doing by others of any of the things mentioned in paragraphs (c), (d) and (e) of subsection (1); and he commits an offence if, at any time after the commencement of the winding up, he does any of the things mentioned in paragraphs (a) to (f) of that subsection, or is privy to the doing by others of any of the things mentioned in paragraphs (c) to (e) of it.

(3) For purposes of this section, 'officer' includes a shadow director.

(4) It is a defence—

(a) for a person charged under paragraph (a) or (f) of subsection (1)(or under subsection (2) in respect of the things mentioned in either of those two paragraphs) to prove that he had no intent to defraud, and

(b) for a person charged under paragraph (c) or (d) of subsection (1)(or under subsection (2) in respect of the things mentioned in either of those two paragraphs) to prove that he had no intent to conceal the state of affairs of the company or to defeat the law.

(5) Where a person pawns, pledges or disposes of any property in circumstances which amount to an offence under subsection (1)(f), every person who takes in pawn or pledge, or otherwise receives,

the property knowing it to be pawned, pledged or disposed of in such circumstances, is guilty of an offence.

(6) A person guilty of an offence under this section is liable to imprisonment or a fine, or both.

(7) The money sums specified in paragraphs (a) and (b) of subsection (1) are subject to increase or reduction by order under section 416 in Part XV.

### 207    Transactions in fraud of creditors

(1) When a company is ordered to be wound up by the court or passes a resolution for voluntary winding up, a person is deemed to have committed an offence if he, being at the time an officer of the company—

(a) has made or caused to be made any gift or transfer of, or charge on, or has caused or connived at the levying of any execution against, the company's property, or

(b) has concealed or removed any part of the company's property since, or within 2 months before, the date of any unsatisfied judgment or order for the payment of money obtained against the company.

(2) A person is not guilty of an offence under this section—

(a) by reason of conduct constituting an offence under subsection (1)(a) which occurred more than 5 years before the commencement of the winding up, or

(b) if he proves that, at the time of the conduct constituting the offence, he had no intent to defraud the company's creditors.

(3) A person guilty of an offence under this section is liable to imprisonment or a fine, or both.

### 208    Misconduct in course of winding up

(1) When a company is being wound up, whether by the court or voluntarily, any person, being a past or present officer of the company, commits an offence if he—

(a) does not to the best of his knowledge and belief fully and truly discover to the liquidator all the company's property, and how and to whom and for what consideration and when the company disposed of any part of that property (except such part as has been disposed of in the ordinary way of the company's business), or

(b) does not deliver up to the liquidator (or as he directs) all such part of the company's property as is in his custody or under his control, and which he is required by law to deliver up, or

(c) does not deliver up to the liquidator (or as he directs) all books and papers in his custody or under his control belonging to the company and which he is required by law to deliver up, or

(d) knowing or believing that a false debt has been proved by any person in the winding up, fails to inform the liquidator as soon as practicable, or

(e) after the commencement of the winding up, prevents the production of any book or paper affecting or relating to the company's property or affairs.

(2) Such a person commits an offence if after the commencement of the winding up he attempts to account for any part of the company's property by fictitious losses or expenses; and he is deemed to have committed that offence if he has so attempted at any meeting of the company's creditors within the 12 months immediately preceding the commencement of the winding up.

(3) For purposes of this section, 'officer' includes a shadow director.

(4) It is a defence—

(a) for a person charged under paragraph (a), (b) or (c) of subsection (1) to prove that he had no intent to defraud, and

(b) for a person charged under paragraph (e) of that subsection to prove that he had no intent to conceal the state of affairs of the company or to defeat the law.

(5) A person guilty of an offence under this section is liable to imprisonment or a fine, or both.

### 209    Falsification of company's books

(1) When a company is being wound up, an officer or contributory of the company commits an offence if he destroys, mutilates, alters or falsifies any books, papers or securities, or makes or is privy to the making of any false or fraudulent entry in any register, book of account or document belonging to the company with intent to defraud or deceive any person.

(2) A person guilty of an offence under this section is liable to imprisonment or a fine, or both.

### 210    Material omissions from statement relating to company's affairs

(1) When a company is being wound up, whether by the court or voluntarily, any person, being a past or present officer of the company, commits an offence if he makes any material omission in any statement relating to the company's affairs.

(2) When a company has been ordered to be wound up by the court, or has passed a resolution for voluntary winding up, any such person is deemed to have committed that offence if, prior to the winding up, he has made any material omission in any such statement.

(3) For purposes of this section, 'officer' includes a shadow director.

(4) It is a defence for a person charged under this section to prove that he had no intent to defraud.

(5) A person guilty of an offence under this section is liable to imprisonment or a fine, or both.

### 211  False representations to creditors

(1) When a company is being wound up, whether by the court or voluntarily, any person, being a past or present officer of the company—

    (a) commits an offence if he makes any false representation or commits any other fraud for the purpose of obtaining the consent of the company's creditors or any of them to an agreement with reference to the company's affairs or to the winding up, and

    (b) is deemed to have committed that offence if, prior to the winding up, he has made any false representation, or committed any other fraud, for that purpose.

(2) For purposes of this section, 'officer' includes a shadow director.

(3) A person guilty of an offence under this section is liable to imprisonment or a fine, or both.

### *Penalisation of directors and officers*

### 212  Summary remedy against delinquent directors, liquidators, etc

(1) This section applies if in the course of the winding up of a company it appears that a person who—

    (a) is or has been an officer of the company,

    (b) has acted as liquidator [...] or administrative receiver of the company, or

    (c) not being a person falling within paragraph (a) or (b), is or has been concerned, or has taken part, in the promotion, formation or management of the company,

has misapplied or retained, or become accountable for, any money or other property of the company, or been guilty of any misfeasance or breach of any fiduciary or other duty in relation to the company.

(2) The reference in subsection (1) to any misfeasance or breach of any fiduciary or other duty in relation to the company includes, in the case of a person who has acted as liquidator [...] of the company, any misfeasance or breach of any fiduciary or other duty in connection with the carrying out of his functions as liquidator [...] of the company.

(3) The court may, on the application of the official receiver or the liquidator, or of any creditor or contributory, examine into the conduct of the person falling within subsection (1) and compel him—

    (a) to repay, restore or account for the money or property or any part of it, with interest at such rate as the court thinks just, or

    (b) to contribute such sum to the company's assets by way of compensation in respect of the misfeasance or breach of fiduciary or other duty as the court thinks just.

(4) The power to make an application under subsection (3) in relation to a person who has acted as liquidator [...] of the company is not exercisable, except with the leave of the court, after he has had his release.

(5) The power of a contributory to make an application under subsection (3) is not exercisable except with the leave of the court, but is exercisable notwithstanding that he will not benefit from any order the court may make on the application.

### 213  Fraudulent trading

(1) If in the course of the winding up of a company it appears that any business of the company has been carried on with intent to defraud creditors of the company or creditors of any other person, or for any fraudulent purpose, the following has effect.

(2) The court, on the application of the liquidator may declare that any persons who were knowingly parties to the carrying on of the business in the manner above-mentioned are to be liable to make such contributions (if any) to the company's assets as the court thinks proper.

### 214  Wrongful trading

(1) Subject to subsection (3) below, if in the course of the winding up of a company it appears that subsection (2) of this section applies in relation to a person who is or has been a director of the company, the court, on the application of the liquidator, may declare that that person is to be liable to make such contribution (if any) to the company's assets as the court thinks proper.

(2) This subsection applies in relation to a person if—

    (a) the company has gone into insolvent liquidation,

    (b) at some time before the commencement of the winding up of the company, that person knew or ought to have concluded that there was no reasonable prospect that the company would avoid going into insolvent liquidation, and

    (c) that person was a director of the company at that time;

but the court shall not make a declaration under this section in any case where the time mentioned in paragraph (b) above was before 28th April 1986.

(3) The court shall not make a declaration under this section with respect to any person if it is satisfied that after the condition specified in subsection (2)(b) was first satisfied in relation to him that person took every step with a view to minimising the potential loss to the company's creditors as (assuming him to have known that there was no reasonable prospect that the company would avoid going into solvent liquidation) he ought to have taken.

(4) For the purposes of subsections (2) and (3), the facts which a director of a company ought to know or ascertain, the conclusions which he ought to reach and the steps which he ought to take are those which would be known or ascertained, or reached or taken, by a reasonably diligent person having both—

(a) the general knowledge, skill and experience that may reasonably be expected of a person carrying out the same functions as are carried out by that director in relation to the company, and

(b) the general knowledge, skill and experience that that director has.

(5) The reference in subsection (4) to the functions carried out in relation to a company by a director of the company includes any functions which he does not carry out but which have been entrusted to him.

(6) For the purposes of this section a company goes into insolvent liquidation if it goes into liquidation at a time when its assets are insufficient for the payment of its debts and other liabilities and the expenses of the winding up.

(7) In this section 'director' includes a shadow director.

(8) This section is without prejudice to section 213.

### 215  Proceedings under ss 213, 214

(1) On the hearing of an application under section 213 or 214, the liquidator may himself give evidence or call witnesses.

(2) Where under either section the court makes a declaration, it may give such further directions as it thinks proper for giving effect to the declaration; and in particular, the court may—

(a) provide for the liability of any person under the declaration to be a charge on any debt or obligation due from the company to him, or on any mortgage or charge or any interest in a mortgage or charge on assets of the company held by or vested in him, or any person on his behalf, or any person claiming as assignee from or through the person liable or any person acting on his behalf, and

(b) from time to time make such further order as may be necessary for enforcing any charge imposed under this subsection.

(3) For the purposes of subsection (2), 'assignee'—

(a) includes a person to whom or in whose favour, by the directions of the person made liable, the debt, obligation, mortgage or charge was created, issued or transferred or the interest created, but

(b) does not include an assignee for valuable consideration (not including consideration by way of marriage or the formation of a civil partnership) given in good faith and without notice of any of the matters on the ground of which the declaration is made.

(4) Where the court makes a declaration under either section in relation to a person who is a creditor of the company, it may direct that the whole or any part of any debt owed by the company to that person and any interest thereon shall rank in priority after all other debts owed by the company and after any interest on those debts.

(5) Sections 213 and 214 have effect notwithstanding that the person concerned may be criminally liable in respect of matters on the ground of which the declaration under the section is to be made.

### 216  Restriction on re-use of company names

(1) This section applies to a person where a company ('the liquidating company') has gone into insolvent liquidation on or after the appointed day and he was a director or shadow director of the company at any time in the period of 12 months ending with the day before it went into liquidation.

(2) For the purposes of this section, a name is a prohibited name in relation to such a person if—

(a) it is a name by which the liquidating company was known at any time in that period of 12 months, or

(b) it is a name which is so similar to a name falling within paragraph (a) as to suggest an association with that company.

(3) Except with leave of the court or in such circumstances as may be prescribed, a person to whom this section applies shall not at any time in the period of 5 years beginning with the day on which the liquidating company went into liquidation—

(a) be a director of any other company that is known by a prohibited name, or

(b) in any way, whether directly or indirectly, be concerned or take part in the promotion, formation or management of any such company, or

(c) in any way, whether directly or indirectly, be concerned or take part in the carrying on of a business carried on (otherwise than by a company) under a prohibited name.

(4) If a person acts in contravention of this section, he is liable to imprisonment or a fine, or both.

(5) In subsection (3) 'the court' means any court having jurisdiction to wind up companies; and on an application for leave under that subsection, the Secretary of State or the official receiver may appear and call the attention of the court to any matters which seem to him to be relevant.

(6) References in this section, in relation to any time, to a name by which a company is known are to the name of the company at that time or to any name under which the company carries on business at that time.

(7) For the purposes of this section a company goes into insolvent liquidation if it goes into liquidation at a time when its assets are insufficient for the payment of its debts and other liabilities and the expenses of the winding up.

(8) In this section 'company' includes a company which may be wound up under Part V of this Act.

## 217 Personal liability for debts, following contravention of s 216

(1) A person is personally responsible for all the relevant debts of a company if at any time—

   (a) in contravention of section 216, he is involved in the management of the company, or

   (b) as a person who is involved in the management of the company, he acts or is willing to act on instructions given (without the leave of the court) by a person whom he knows at that time to be in contravention in relation to the company of section 216.

(2) Where a person is personally responsible under this section for the relevant debts of a company, he is jointly and severally liable in respect of those debts with the company and any other person who, whether under this section or otherwise, is so liable.

(3) For the purposes of this section the relevant debts of a company are—

   (a) in relation to a person who is personally responsible under paragraph (a) of subsection (1), such debts and other liabilities of the company as are incurred at a time when that person was involved in the management of the company, and

   (b) in relation to a person who is personally responsible under paragraph (b) of that subsection, such debts and other liabilities of the company as are incurred at a time when that person was acting or was willing to act on instructions given as mentioned in that paragraph.

(4) For the purposes of this section, a person is involved in the management of a company if he is a director of the company or if he is concerned, whether directly or indirectly, or takes part, in the management of the company.

(5) For the purposes of this section a person who, as a person involved in the management of a company, has at any time acted on instructions given (without the leave of the court) by a person whom he knew at that time to be in contravention in relation to the company of section 216 is presumed, unless the contrary is shown, to have been willing at any time thereafter to act on any instructions given by that person.

(6) In this section 'company' includes a company which may be wound up under Part V.

*Investigation and prosecution of malpractice*

## 218 Prosecution of delinquent officers and members of company

(1) If it appears to the court in the course of a winding up by the court that any past or present officer, or any member, of the company has been guilty of any offence in relation to the company for which he is criminally liable, the court may (either on the application of a person interested in the winding up or of its own motion) direct the liquidator to refer the matter

   (a) in the case of a winding up in England and Wales, to the Secretary of State, and

   (b) in the case of a winding up in Scotland, to the Lord Advocate

(2) [...]

(3) If in the case of a winding up by the court in England and Wales it appears to the liquidator, not being the official receiver, that any past or present officer of the company, or any member of it, has been guilty of an offence in relation to the company for which he is criminally liable, the liquidator shall report the matter to the official receiver.

(4) If it appears to the liquidator in the course of a voluntary winding up that any past or present officer of the company, or any member of it, has been guilty of an offence in relation to the company for which he is criminally liable, he shall forthwith report the matter—

   (a) in the case of a winding up in England and Wales, to the Secretary of State, and

   (b) in the case of a winding up in Scotland, to the Lord Advocate,

and shall furnish to the Secretary of State or (as the case may be) the Lord Advocate such information and give to him such access to and facilities for inspecting and taking copies of documents (being information or documents in the possession or under the control of the liquidator and relating to the matter in question) as the Secretary of State or (as the case may be) the Lord Advocate requires.

(5) Where a report is made to the Secretary of State under subsection (4) he may, for the purpose of investigating the matter reported to him and such other matters relating to the affairs of the company as appear to him to require investigation, exercise any of the powers which are exercisable by inspectors appointed under section 431 or 432 of the Companies Act to investigate a company's affairs.

(6) If it appears to the court in the course of a voluntary winding up that—

   (a) any past or present officer of the company, or any member of it, has been guilty as above-mentioned, and

   (b) no report with respect to the matter has been made by the liquidator [...] under subsection (4), the court may (on the application of any person interested in the winding up or of its own motion) direct the liquidator to make such a report.

On a report being made accordingly, this section has effect as though the report had been made in pursuance of subsection (4).

### 219   Obligations arising under s 218

(1) For the purpose of an investigation by the Secretary of State in consequence of a report made to him under section 218(4), any obligation imposed on a person by any provision of the Companies Act to produce documents or give information to, or otherwise to assist, inspectors appointed as mentioned in section 218(5)is to be regarded as an obligation similarly to assist the Secretary of State in his investigation.

(2) An answer given by a person to a question put to him in exercise of the powers conferred by section 218(5) may be used in evidence against him.

(2A) However, in criminal proceedings in which that person is charged with an offence to which this subsection applies—

(a) no evidence relating to the answer may be adduced, and

(b) no question relating to it may be asked,

by or on behalf of the prosecution, unless evidence relating to it is adduced, or a question relating to it is asked, in the proceedings by or on behalf of that person.

(2B) Subsection (2A) applies to any offence other than—

(a) an offence under section 2 or 5 of the Perjury Act 1911 (false statements made on oath otherwise than in judicial proceedings or made otherwise than on oath), or

(b) an offence under section 44(1) or (2) of the Criminal Law (Consolidation)(Scotland) Act 1995 (false statements made on oath or otherwise than on oath).

(3) Where criminal proceedings are instituted by the Director of Public Prosecutions, the Lord Advocate or the Secretary of State following any report or reference under section 218, it is the duty of the liquidator and every officer and agent of the company past and present (other than the defendant or defender) to give to the Director of Public Prosecutions, the Lord Advocate or the Secretary of State (as the case may be) all assistance in connection with the prosecution which he is reasonably able to give.

For this purpose 'agent' includes any banker or solicitor of the company and any person employed by the company as auditor, whether that person is or is not an officer of the company.

(4) If a person fails or neglects to give assistance in the manner required by subsection (3), the court may, on the application of the Director of Public Prosecutions, the Lord Advocate or the Secretary of State (as the case may be) direct the person to comply with that subsection; and if the application is made with respect to a liquidator, the court may (unless it appears that the failure or neglect to comply was due to the liquidator not having in his hands sufficient assets of the company to enable him to do so) direct that the costs shall be borne by the liquidator personally.

# PART V

# WINDING UP OF UNREGISTERED COMPANIES

### 220   Meaning of 'unregistered company'

(1) For the purposes of this Part, the expression 'unregistered company' includes , any association and any company, with the following exceptions—

(a) [...]

(b) a company registered in any part of the United Kingdom under the Joint Stock Companies Acts or under the legislation (past or present) relating to companies in Great Britain.

(2) On such day as the Treasury appoints by order under section 4(3) of the Trustee Savings Banks Act 1985, the words in subsection (1) from 'any trustee' to 'banks' cease to have effect and are hereby repealed.

### 221   Winding up of unregistered companies

(1) Subject to the provisions of this Part, any unregistered company may be wound up under this Act; and all the provisions of this Act and the Companies Act about winding up apply to an unregistered company with the exceptions and additions mentioned in the following subsections.

(2) If an unregistered company has a principal place of business situated in Northern Ireland, it shall not be wound up under this Part unless it has a principal place of business situated in England and Wales or Scotland, or in both England and Wales and Scotland.

(3) For the purpose of determining a court's winding-up jurisdiction, an unregistered company is deemed—

(a) to be registered in England and Wales or Scotland, according as its principal place of business is situated in England and Wales or Scotland, or

(b) if it has a principal place of business situated in both countries, to be registered in both countries;

and the principal place of business situated in that part of Great Britain in which proceedings are being instituted is, for all purposes of the winding up, deemed to be the registered office of the company.

(4)  No unregistered company shall be wound up under this Act voluntarily , except in accordance with the EC Regulation.

(5)  The circumstances in which an unregistered company may be wound up are as follows—

    (a)  if the company is dissolved, or has ceased to carry on business, or is carrying on business only for the purpose of winding up its affairs;

    (b)  if the company is unable to pay its debts;

    (c)  if the court is of opinion that it is just and equitable that the company should be wound up.

(6)  A petition for winding up a trustee savings bank may be presented by the Trustee Savings Banks Central Board or by a commissioner appointed under section 35 of the Trustee Savings Banks Act 1981 as well as by any person authorised under Part IV of this Act to present a petition for the winding up of a company.

On such day as the Treasury appoints by order under section 4(3) of the Trustee Savings Banks Act 1985, this subsection ceases to have effect and is hereby repealed.

(7)  In Scotland, an unregistered company which the Court of Session has jurisdiction to wind up may be wound up by the court if there is subsisting a floating charge over property comprised in the company's property and undertaking, and the court is satisfied that the security of the creditor entitled to the benefit of the floating charge is in jeopardy.

For this purpose a creditor's security is deemed to be in jeopardy if the court is satisfied that events have occurred or are about to occur which render it unreasonable in the creditor's interests that the company should retain power to dispose of the property which is subject to the floating charge.

### 222  Inability to pay debts: unpaid creditor for £750 or more

(1)  An unregistered company is deemed (for the purposes of section 221) unable to pay its debts if there is a creditor, by assignment or otherwise, to whom the company is indebted in a sum exceeding £750 then due and—

    (a)  the creditor has served on the company, by leaving at its principal place of business, or by delivering to the secretary or some director, manager or principal officer of the company, or by otherwise serving in such manner as the court may approve or direct, a written demand in the prescribed form requiring the company to pay the sum due, and

    (b)  the company has for 3 weeks after the service of the demand neglected to pay the sum or to secure or compound for it to the creditor's satisfaction.

(2)  The money sum for the time being specified in subsection (1) is subject to increase or reduction by regulations under section 417 in Part XV; but no increase in the sum so specified affects any case in which the winding-up petition was presented before the coming into force of the increase.

### 223  Inability to pay debts: debt remaining unsatisfied after action brought

An unregistered company is deemed (for the purposes of section 221) unable to pay its debts if an action or other proceeding has been instituted against any member for any debt or demand due, or claimed to be due, from the company, or from him in his character of member, and—

    (a)  notice in writing of the institution of the action or proceeding has been served on the company by leaving it at the company's principal place of business (or by delivering it to the secretary, or some director, manager or principal officer of the company, or by otherwise serving it in such manner as the court may approve or direct), and

    (b)  the company has not within 3 weeks after service of the notice paid, secured or compounded for the debt or demand, or procured the action or proceeding to be stayed or sisted, or indemnified the defendant or defender to his reasonable satisfaction against the action or proceeding, and against all costs, damages and expenses to be incurred by him because of it.

### 224  Inability to pay debts: other cases

(1)  An unregistered company is deemed (for purposes of section 221) unable to pay its debts—

    (a)  if in England and Wales execution or other process issued on a judgment, decree or order obtained in any court in favour of a creditor against the company, or any member of it as such, or any person authorised to be sued as nominal defendant on behalf of the company, is returned unsatisfied;

    (b)  if in Scotland the induciae of a charge for payment on an extract decree, or an extract registered bond, or an extract registered protest, have expired without payment being made;

    (c)  if in Northern Ireland a certificate of unenforceability has been granted in respect of any judgment, decree or order obtained as mentioned in paragraph (a);

    (d)  if it is otherwise proved to the satisfaction of the court that the company is unable to pay its debts as they fall due.

(2)  An unregistered company is also deemed unable to pay its debts if it is proved to the satisfaction of the court that the value of the company's assets is less than the amount of its liabilities, taking into account its contingent and prospective liabilities.

### 225  Oversea company may be wound up though dissolved

(1)  Where a company incorporated outside Great Britain which has been carrying on business in Great Britain ceases to carry on business in Great Britain, it may be wound up as an unregistered company under this Act, notwithstanding that it has been dissolved or otherwise ceased to exist as a company under or by virtue of the laws of the country under which it was incorporated.

(2)  This section is subject to the EC Regulation.

### 226  Contributories in winding up of unregistered company

(1)  In the event of an unregistered company being wound up, every person is deemed a contributory who is liable to pay or contribute to the payment of any debt or liability of the company, or to pay or contribute to the payment of any sum for the adjustment of the rights of members among themselves, or to pay or contribute to the payment of the expenses of winding up the company.

(2)  Every contributory is liable to contribute to the company's assets all sums due from him in respect of any such liability as is mentioned above.

(3)  In the case of an unregistered company engaged in or formed for working mines within the stannaries, a past member is not liable to contribute to the assets if he has ceased to be a member for 2 years or more either before the mine ceased to be worked or before the date of the winding-up order.

(4)  In the event of the death, bankruptcy or insolvency of any contributory, the provisions of this Act with respect to the personal representatives, to the heirs and legatees of heritage of the heritable estate in Scotland of deceased contributories, and to the trustees of bankrupt or insolvent contributories, respectively apply.

### 227  Power of court to stay, sist or restrain proceedings

The provisions of this Part with respect to staying, sisting or restraining actions and proceedings against a company at any time after the presentation of a petition for winding up and before the making of a winding-up order extend, in the case of an unregistered company, where the application to stay, sist or restrain is presented by a creditor, to actions and proceedings against any contributory of the company.

### 228  Actions stayed on winding-up order

Where an order has been made for winding up an unregistered company, no action or proceeding shall be proceeded with or commenced against any contributory of the company in respect of any debt of the company, except by leave of the court, and subject to such terms as the court may impose.

### 229  Provisions of this Part to be cumulative

(1)  The provisions of this Part with respect to unregistered companies are in addition to and not in restriction of any provisions in Part IV with respect to winding up companies by the court; and the court or liquidator may exercise any powers or do any act in the case of unregistered companies which might be exercised or done by it or him in winding up companies formed and registered under the Companies Act.

(2)  However, an unregistered company is not, except in the event of its being wound up, deemed to be a company under the Companies Act, and then only to the extent provided by this Part of this Act.

# PART VI

# MISCELLANEOUS PROVISIONS APPLYING TO COMPANIES WHICH ARE INSOLVENT OR IN LIQUIDATION

*Office-holders*

### 230  Holders of office to be qualified insolvency practitioners

(1)  [...]

(2)  Where an administrative receiver of a company is appointed, he must be a person who is so qualified.

(3)  Where a company goes into liquidation, the liquidator must be a person who is so qualified.

(4)  Where a provisional liquidator is appointed, he must be a person who is so qualified.

(5)  Subsections (3) and (4) are without prejudice to any enactment under which the official receiver is to be, or may be, liquidator or provisional liquidator.

### 231  Appointment to office of two or more persons

(1)  This section applies if an appointment or nomination of any person to the office of [...] administrative receiver, liquidator or provisional liquidator—

    (a)  relates to more than one person, or

    (b)  has the effect that the office is to be held by more than one person.

(2)  The appointment or nomination shall declare whether any act required or authorised under any enactment to be done by the [...] administrative receiver, liquidator or provisional liquidator is to be done by all or any one or more of the persons for the time being holding the office in question.

## 232   Validity of office-holder's acts

The acts of an individual as [...] administrative receiver, liquidator or provisional liquidator of a company are valid notwithstanding any defect in his appointment, nomination or qualifications.

### *Management by administrators, liquidators, etc.*

## 233   Supplies of gas, water, electricity, etc

(1) This section applies in the case of a company where—

    (a)   the company enters administration,(b) a public supply of electricity,

    (ba) a moratorium under section 1A is in force, or

    (c)   a voluntary arrangement approved under Part I, has taken effect, or

    (d)   the company goes into liquidation, or

    (e)   a provisional liquidator is appointed;

and 'the office-holder' means the administrator, the administrative receiver, the nominee, the supervisor of the voluntary arrangement, the liquidator or the provisional liquidator, as the case may be.

(2) If a request is made by or with the concurrence of the office-holder for the giving, after the effective date, of any of the supplies mentioned in the next subsection, the supplier—

    (a)   may make it a condition of the giving of the supply that the office-holder personally guarantees the payment of any charges in respect of the supply, but

    (b)   shall not make it a condition of the giving of the supply, or do anything which has the effect of making it a condition of the giving of the supply, that any outstanding charges in respect of a supply given to the company before the effective date are paid.

(3) The supplies referred to in subsection (2) are—

    (a) a supply of gas by a gas supplier within the meaning of Part I of the Gas Act 1986;

    (b) a supply of electricity by an electricity supplier within the meaning of Part I of the Electricity Act 1989;

    (c) a supply of water by a water undertaker or, in Scotland, Scottish Water,

    (d) a supply of communications services by a provider of a public electronic communications service.

(4) 'The effective date' for the purposes of this section is whichever is applicable of the following dates—

    (a)   the date on which the company entered administration

    (b)   the date on which the administrative receiver was appointed (or, if he was appointed in succession to another administrative receiver, the date on which the first of his predecessors was appointed),

    (ba) the date on which the moratorium came into force

    (c)   the date on which the voluntary arrangement took effect,

    (d)   the date on which the company went into liquidation,

    (e)   the date on which the provisional liquidator was appointed.

(5) The following applies to expressions used in subsection (3)—

    (a)   [...]

    (b)   [...]

    (c)   [...]

    (d)   'communications services' do not include electronic communications services to the extent that they are used to broadcast or otherwise transmit programme services (within the meaning of the Communications Act 2003).

## 234   Getting in the company's property

(1) This section applies in the case of a company where—

    (a) the company enters administration,

    (b) an administrative receiver is appointed, or

    (c) the company goes into liquidation, or

    (d) a provisional liquidator is appointed;

and 'the office-holder' means the administrator, the administrative receiver, the liquidator or the provisional liquidator, as the case may be.

(2) Where any person has in his possession or control any property, books, papers or records to which the company appears to be entitled, the court may require that person forthwith (or within such period as the court may direct) to pay, deliver, convey, surrender or transfer the property, books, papers or records to the office-holder.

(3) Where the office-holder—

    (a) seizes or disposes of any property which is not property of the company, and

    (b) at the time of seizure or disposal believes, and has reasonable grounds for believing, that he is entitled (whether in pursuance of an order of the court or otherwise) to seize or dispose of that property,

the next subsection has effect.

(4) In that case the office-holder—

    (a) is not liable to any person in respect of any loss or damage resulting from the seizure or disposal except in so far as that loss or damage is caused by the office-holder's own negligence, and

    (b) has a lien on the property, or the proceeds of its sale, for such expenses as were incurred in connection with the seizure or disposal.

### 235 Duty to co-operate with office-holder

(1) This section applies as does section 234; and it also applies, in the case of a company in respect of which a winding-up order has been made by the court in England and Wales, as if references to the office-holder included the official receiver, whether or not he is the liquidator.

(2) Each of the persons mentioned in the next subsection shall—

    (a) give to the office-holder such information concerning the company and its promotion, formation, business, dealings, affairs or property as the office-holder may at any time after the effective date reasonably require, and

    (b) attend on the office-holder at such times as the latter may reasonably require.

(3) The persons referred to above are—

    (a) those who are or have at any time been officers of the company,

    (b) those who have taken part in the formation of the company at any time within one year before the effective date,

    (c) those who are in the employment of the company, or have been in its employment (including employment under a contract for services) within that year, and are in the office-holder's opinion capable of giving information which he requires,

    (d) those who are, or have within that year been, officers of, or in the employment (including employment under a contract for services) of, another company which is, or within that year was, an officer of the company in question, and

    (e) in the case of a company being wound up by the court, any person who has acted as administrator, administrative receiver or liquidator of the company.

(4) For the purposes of subsections (2) and (3), 'the effective date' is whichever is applicable of the following dates—

    (a) the date on which the company entered administration,

    (b) the date on which the administrative receiver was appointed or, if he was appointed in succession to another administrative receiver, the date on which the first of his predecessors was appointed,

    (c) the date on which the provisional liquidator was appointed, and

    (d) the date on which the company went into liquidation.

(5) If a person without reasonable excuse fails to comply with any obligation imposed by this section, he is liable to a fine and, for continued contravention, to a daily default fine.

### 236 Inquiry into company's dealings, etc

(1) This section applies as does section 234; and it also applies in the case of a company in respect of which a winding-up order has been made by the court in England and Wales as if references to the office-holder included the official receiver, whether or not he is the liquidator.

(2) The court may, on the application of the office-holder, summon to appear before it—

    (a) any officer of the company,

    (b) any person known or suspected to have in his possession any property of the company or supposed to be indebted to the company, or

    (c) any person whom the court thinks capable of giving information concerning the promotion, formation, business, dealings, affairs or property of the company.

(3) The court may require any such person as is mentioned in subsection (2)(a) to (c) to submit an affidavit to the court containing an account of his dealings with the company or to produce any books, papers or other records in his possession or under his control relating to the company or the matters mentioned in paragraph (c) of the subsection.

(4) The following applies in a case where—

    (a) a person without reasonable excuse fails to appear before the court when he is summoned to do so under this section, or

    (b) there are reasonable grounds for believing that a person has absconded, or is about to abscond, with a view to avoiding his appearance before the court under this section.

(5) The court may, for the purpose of bringing that person and anything in his possession before the court, cause a warrant to be issued to a constable or prescribed officer of the court—

    (a) for the arrest of that person, and

    (b) for the seizure of any books, papers, records, money or goods in that person's possession.

(6) The court may authorise a person arrested under such a warrant to be kept in custody, and anything seized under such a warrant to be held, in accordance with the rules, until that person is brought before the court under the warrant or until such other time as the court may order.

### 237    Court's enforcement powers under s 236

(1)  If it appears to the court, on consideration of any evidence obtained under section 236 or this section, that any person has in his possession any property of the company, the court may, on the application of the office-holder, order that person to deliver the whole or any part of the property to the office-holder at such time, in such manner and on such terms as the court thinks fit.

(2)  If it appears to the court, on consideration of any evidence so obtained, that any person is indebted to the company, the court may, on the application of the office-holder, order that person to pay to the office holder, at such time and in such manner as the court may direct, the whole or any part of the amount due, whether in full discharge of the debt or otherwise, as the court thinks fit.

The court may, if it thinks fit, order that any person who if within the jurisdiction of the court would be liable to be summoned to appear before it under section 236 or this section shall be examined in any part of the United Kingdom where he may for the time being be, or in a place outside the United Kingdom.

(4)  Any person who appears or is brought before the court under section 236 or this section may be examined on oath, either orally or (except in Scotland) by interrogatories, concerning the company or the matters mentioned in section 236(2)(c).

*Adjustment of prior transactions (administration and liquidation)*

### 238    Transactions at an undervalue (England and Wales)

(1)  This section applies in the case of a company where—
  (a)  the company enters administration,
  (b)  the company goes into liquidation;
and 'the office-holder' means the administrator or the liquidator, as the case may be.

(2)  Where the company has at a relevant time (defined in section 240) entered into a transaction with any person at an undervalue, the office-holder may apply to the court for an order under this section.

(3)  Subject as follows, the court shall, on such an application, make such order as it thinks fit for restoring the position to what it would have been if the company had not entered into that transaction.

(4)  For the purposes of this section and section 241, a company enters into a transaction with a person at an undervalue if—
  (a)  the company makes a gift to that person or otherwise enters into a transaction with that person on terms that provide for the company to receive no consideration, or
  (b)  the company enters into a transaction with that person for a consideration the value of which, in money or money's worth, is significantly less than the value, in money or money's worth, of the consideration provided by the company.

(5)  The court shall not make an order under this section in respect of a transaction at an undervalue if it is satisfied—
  (a)  that the company which entered into the transaction did so in good faith and for the purpose of carrying on its business, and
  (b)  that at the time it did so there were reasonable grounds for believing that the transaction would benefit the company.

### 239    Preferences (England and Wales)

(1)  This section applies as does section 238.

(2)  Where the company has at a relevant time (defined in the next section) given a preference to any person, the office-holder may apply to the court for an order under this section.

(3)  Subject as follows, the court shall, on such an application, make such order as it thinks fit for restoring the position to what it would have been if the company had not given that preference.

(4)  For the purposes of this section and section 241, a company gives a preference to a person if—
  (a)  that person is one of the company's creditors or a surety or guarantor for any of the company's debts or other liabilities, and
  (b)  the company does anything or suffers anything to be done which (in either case) has the effect of putting that person into a position which, in the event of the company going into insolvent liquidation, will be better than the position he would have been in if that thing had not been done.

(5)  The court shall not make an order under this section in respect of a preference given to any person unless the company which gave the preference was influenced in deciding to give it by a desire to produce in relation to that person the effect mentioned in subsection (4)(b).

(6)  A company which has given a preference to a person connected with the company (otherwise than by reason only of being its employee) at the time the preference was given is presumed, unless the contrary is shown, to have been influenced in deciding to give it by such a desire as is mentioned in subsection (5).

(7)  The fact that something has been done in pursuance of the order of a court does not, without more, prevent the doing or suffering of that thing from constituting the giving of a preference.

**240 'Relevant time' under ss 238, 239**

(1) Subject to the next subsection, the time at which a company enters into a transaction at an undervalue or gives a preference is a relevant time if the transaction is entered into, or the preference given—

(a) in the case of a transaction at an undervalue or of a preference which is given to a person who is connected with the company (otherwise than by reason only of being its employee), at a time in the period of 2 years ending with the onset of insolvency (which expression is defined below),

(b) in the case of a preference which is not such a transaction and is not so given, at a time in the period of 6 months ending with the onset of insolvency, [...]

(c) in either case, at a time between the making of an administration application in respect of the company and the making of an administration order on that application, and

(d) in either case, at a time between the filing with the court of a copy of notice of intention to appoint an administrator under paragraph 14 or 22 of Schedule B1 and the making of an appointment under that paragraph.

(2) Where a company enters into a transaction at an undervalue or gives a preference at a time mentioned in subsection (1)(a) or (b), that time is not a relevant time for the purposes of section 238 or 239 unless the company—

(a) is at that time unable to pay its debts within the meaning of section 123 in Chapter VI of Part IV, or

(b) becomes unable to pay its debts within the meaning of that section in consequence of the transaction or preference;

but the requirements of this subsection are presumed to be satisfied, unless the contrary is shown, in relation to any transaction at an undervalue which is entered into by a company with a person who is connected with the company.

(3) For the purposes of subsection (1), the onset of insolvency is—

(a) in a case where section 238 or 239 applies by reason of an administrator of a company being appointed by administration order, the date on which the administration application is made,

(b) in a case where section 238 or 239 applies by reason of an administrator of a company being appointed under paragraph 14 or 22 of Schedule B1 following filing with the court of a copy of a notice of intention to appoint under that paragraph, the date on which the copy of the notice is filed,

(c) in a case where section 238 or 239 applies by reason of an administrator of a company being appointed otherwise than as mentioned in paragraph (a) or (b), the date on which the appointment takes effect,

(d) in a case where section 238 or 239 applies by reason of a company going into liquidation either following conversion of administration into winding up by virtue of Article 37 of the EC Regulation or at the time when the appointment of an administrator ceases to have effect, the date on which the company entered administration (or, if relevant, the date on which the application for the administration order was made or a copy of the notice of intention to appoint was filed), and

(e) in a case where section 238 or 239 applies by reason of a company going into liquidation at any other time, the date of the commencement of the winding up.

**241 Orders under ss 238, 239**

(1) Without prejudice to the generality of sections 238(3) and 239(3), an order under either of those sections with respect to a transaction or preference entered into or given by a company may (subject to the next subsection)—

(a) require any property transferred as part of the transaction, or in connection with the giving of the preference, to be vested in the company,

(b) require any property to be so vested if it represents in any person's hands the application either of the proceeds of sale of property so transferred or of money so transferred,

(c) release or discharge (in whole or in part) any security given by the company,

(d) require any person to pay, in respect of benefits received by him from the company, such sums to the office-holder as the court may direct,

(e) provide for any surety or guarantor whose obligations to any person were released or discharged (in whole or in part) under the transaction, or by the giving of the preference, to be under such new or revived obligations to that person as the court thinks appropriate,

(f) provide for security to be provided for the discharge of any obligation imposed by or arising under the order, for such an obligation to be charged on any property and for the security or charge to have the same priority as a security or charge released or discharged (in whole or in part) under the transaction or by the giving of the preference, and

(g) provide for the extent to which any person whose property is vested by the order in the company, or on whom obligations are imposed by the order, is to be able to prove in the winding up of the company for debts or other liabilities which arose from, or were released or discharged (in whole or in part) under or by, the transaction or the giving of the preference.

(2)  An order under section 238 or 239 may affect the property of, or impose any obligation on, any person whether or not he is the person with whom the company in question entered into the transaction or (as the case may be) the person to whom the preference was given; but such an order—

(a) shall not prejudice any interest in property which was acquired from a person other than the company and was acquired in good faith and for value, or prejudice any interest deriving from such an interest, and

(b) shall not require a person who received a benefit from the transaction or preference in good faith and for value to pay a sum to the office-holder, except where that person was a party to the transaction or the payment is to be in respect of a preference given to that person at a time when he was a creditor of the company.

(2A)  Where a person has acquired an interest in property from a person other than the company in question, or has received a benefit from the transaction or preference, and at the time of that acquisition or receipt—

(a) he had notice of the relevant surrounding circumstances and of the relevant proceedings, or

(b) he was connected with, or was an associate of, either the company in question or the person with whom that company entered into the transaction or to whom that company gave the preference,

then, unless the contrary is shown, it shall be presumed for the purposes of paragraph (a) or (as the case may be) paragraph (b) of subsection (2) that the interest was acquired or the benefit was received otherwise than in good faith.

(3)  For the purposes of subsection (2A)(a), the relevant surrounding circumstances are (as the case may require)—

(a) the fact that the company in question entered into the transaction at an undervalue; or

(b) the circumstances which amounted to the giving of the preference by the company in question;

and subsections (3A) to (3C) have effect to determine whether, for those purposes, a person has notice of the relevant proceedings.

(3A)  Where section 238 or 239 applies by reason of a company's entering administration, a person has notice of the relevant proceedings if he has notice that—

(a) an administration application has been made,

(b) an administration order has been made,

(c) a copy of a notice of intention to appoint an administrator under paragraph 14 or 22 of Schedule B1 has been filed, or

(d) notice of the appointment of an administrator has been filed under paragraph 18 or 29 of that Schedule.

(3B)  Where section 238 or 239 applies by reason of a company's going into liquidation at the time when the appointment of an administrator of the company ceases to have effect, a person has notice of the relevant proceedings if he has notice that—

(a) an administration application has been made,

(b) an administration order has been made,

(c) a copy of a notice of intention to appoint an administrator under paragraph 14 or 22 of Schedule B1 has been filed,

(d) notice of the appointment of an administrator has been filed under paragraph 18 or 29 of that Schedule, or

(e) the company has gone into liquidation.

(3C)  In a case where section 238 or 239 applies by reason of the company in question going into liquidation at any other time, a person has notice of the relevant proceedings if he has notice—

(a) where the company goes into liquidation on the making of a winding-up order, of the fact that the petition on which the winding-up order is made has been presented or of the fact that the company has gone into liquidation;

(b) in any other case, of the fact that the company has gone into liquidation.

(4)  The provisions of sections 238 to 241 apply without prejudice to the availability of any other remedy, even in relation to a transaction or preference which the company had no power to enter into or give.

## 242  Gratuitous alienations (Scotland)

(1)  Where this subsection applies and—

(a) the winding up of a company has commenced, an alienation by the company is challengeable by—

(i) any creditor who is a creditor by virtue of a debt incurred on or before the date of such commencement, or

(ii) the liquidator;

(b) a company enters administration, an alienation by the company is challengeable by the administrator.

(2) Subsection (1) applies where—

(a) by the alienation, whether before or after 1st April 1986 (the coming into force of section 75 of the Bankruptcy (Scotland) Act 1985), any part of the company's property is transferred or any claim or right of the company is discharged or renounced, and

(b) the alienation takes place on a relevant day.

(3) For the purposes of subsection (2)(b), the day on which an alienation takes place is the day on which it becomes completely effectual; and in that subsection 'relevant day' means, if the alienation has the effect of favouring—

(a) a person who is an associate (within the meaning of the Bankruptcy (Scotland) Act 1985) of the company, a day not earlier than 5 years before the date on which—

(i) the winding up of the company commences, or

(ii) as the case may be, the company enters administration; or

(b) any other person, a day not earlier than 2 years before that date.

(4) On a challenge being brought under subsection (1), the court shall grant decree of reduction or for such restoration of property to the company's assets or other redress as may be appropriate; but the court shall not grant such a decree if the person seeking to uphold the alienation establishes—

(a) that immediately, or at any other time, after the alienation the company's assets were greater than its liabilities, or

(b) that the alienation was made for adequate consideration, or

(c) that the alienation—

(i) was a birthday, Christmas or other conventional gift, or

(ii) was a gift made, for a charitable purpose, to a person who is not an associate of the company,

which, having regard to all the circumstances, it was reasonable for the company to make:

Provided that this subsection is without prejudice to any right or interest acquired in good faith and for value from or through the transferee in the alienation.

(5) In subsection (4) above, 'charitable purpose' means any charitable, benevolent or philanthropic purpose, whether or not it is charitable within the meaning of any rule of law.

(6) For the purposes of the foregoing provisions of this section, an alienation in implementation of a prior obligation is deemed to be one for which there was no consideration or no adequate consideration to the extent that the prior obligation was undertaken for no consideration or no adequate consideration.

(7) A liquidator and an administrator have the same right as a creditor has under any rule of law to challenge an alienation of a company made for no consideration or no adequate consideration.

(8) This section applies to Scotland only.

## 243  Unfair preferences (Scotland)

(1) Subject to subsection (2) below, subsection (4) below applies to a transaction entered into by a company, whether before or after 1st April 1986, which has the effect of creating a preference in favour of a creditor to the prejudice of the general body of creditors, being a preference created not earlier than 6 months before the commencement of the winding up of the company or the company enters administration.

(2) Subsection (4) below does not apply to any of the following transactions—

(a) a transaction in the ordinary course of trade or business;

(b) a payment in cash for a debt which when it was paid had become payable, unless the transaction was collusive with the purpose of prejudicing the general body of creditors;

(c) a transaction whereby the parties to it undertake reciprocal obligations (whether the performance by the parties of their respective obligations occurs at the same time or at different times) unless the transaction was collusive as aforesaid;

(d) the granting of a mandate by a company authorising an arrestee to pay over the arrested funds or part thereof to the arrester where—

(i) there has been a decree for payment or a warrant for summary diligence, and

(ii) the decree or warrant has been preceded by an arrestment on the dependence of the action or followed by an arrestment in execution.

(3) For the purposes of subsection (1) above, the day on which a preference was created is the day on which the preference became completely effectual.

(4) A transaction to which this subsection applies is challengeable by—

(a) in the case of a winding up—

(i) any creditor who is a creditor by virtue of a debt incurred on or before the date of commencement of the winding up, or

(ii) the liquidator; and

(b) where the company has entered administration, the administrator.

(5) On a challenge being brought under subsection (4) above, the court, if satisfied that the transaction challenged is a transaction to which this section applies, shall grant decree of reduction or for such restoration of property to the company's assets or other redress as may be appropriate;

Provided that this subsection is without prejudice to any right or interest acquired in good faith and for value from or through the creditor in whose favour the preference was created.

(6) A liquidator and an administrator have the same right as a creditor has under any rule of law to challenge a preference created by a debtor.

(7) This section applies to Scotland only.

### 244  Extortionate credit transactions

(1) This section applies as does section 238, and where the company is, or has been, a party to a transaction for, or involving, the provision of credit to the company.

(2) The court may, on the application of the office-holder, make an order with respect to the transaction if the transaction is or was extortionate and was entered into in the period of 3 years ending with the day on which the company entered administration or went into liquidation.

(3) For the purposes of this section a transaction is extortionate if, having regard to the risk accepted by the person providing the credit—

    (a) the terms of it are or were such as to require grossly exorbitant payments to be made (whether unconditionally or in certain contingencies) in respect of the provision of the credit, or

    (b) it otherwise grossly contravened ordinary principles of fair dealing;

and it shall be presumed, unless the contrary is proved, that a transaction with respect to which an application is made under this section is or, as the case may be, was extortionate.

(4) An order under this section with respect to any transaction may contain such one or more of the following as the court thinks fit, that is to say—

    (a) provision setting aside the whole or part of any obligation created by the transaction,

    (b) provision otherwise varying the terms of the transaction or varying the terms on which any security for the purposes of the transaction is held,

    (c) provision requiring any person who is or was a party to the transaction to pay to the office-holder any sums paid to that person, by virtue of the transaction, by the company,

    (d) provision requiring any person to surrender to the office-holder any property held by him as security for the purposes of the transaction,

    (e) provision directing accounts to be taken between any persons.

(5) The powers conferred by this section are exercisable in relation to any transaction concurrently with any powers exercisable in relation to that transaction as a transaction at an undervalue or under section 242 (gratuitous alienations in Scotland).

### 245  Avoidance of certain floating charges

(1) This section applies as does section 238, but applies to Scotland as well as to England and Wales.

(2) Subject as follows, a floating charge on the company's undertaking or property created at a relevant time is invalid except to the extent of the aggregate of—

    (a) the value of so much of the consideration for the creation of the charge as consists of money paid, or goods or services supplied, to the company at the same time as, or after, the creation of the charge,

    (b) the value of so much of that consideration as consists of the discharge or reduction, at the same time as, or after, the creation of the charge, of any debt of the company, and

    (c) the amount of such interest (if any) as is payable on the amount falling within paragraph (a) or (b) in pursuance of any agreement under which the money was so paid, the goods or services were so supplied or the debt was so discharged or reduced.

(3) Subject to the next subsection, the time at which a floating charge is created by a company is a relevant time for the purposes of this section if the charge is created—

    (a) in the case of a charge which is created in favour of a person who is connected with the company, at a time in the period of 2 years ending with the onset of insolvency,

    (b) in the case of a charge which is created in favour of any other person, at a time in the period of 12 months ending with the onset of insolvency, [...]

    (c) in either case, at a time between the making of an administration application in respect of the company and the making of an administration order on that application, or

    (d) in either case, at a time between the filing with the court of a copy of notice of intention to appoint an administrator under paragraph 14 or 22 of Schedule B1 and the making of an appointment under that paragraph.

(4) Where a company creates a floating charge at a time mentioned in subsection (3)(b) and the person in favour of whom the charge is created is not connected with the company, that time is not a relevant time for the purposes of this section unless the company—

    (a) is at that time unable to pay its debts within the meaning of section 123 in Chapter VI of Part IV, or

    (b) becomes unable to pay its debts within the meaning of that section in consequence of the transaction under which the charge is created.

(5) For the purposes of subsection (3), the onset of insolvency is—

    (a) in a case where this section applies by reason of an administrator of a company being appointed by administration order, the date on which the administration application is made,

(b) in a case where this section applies by reason of an administrator of a company being appointed under paragraph 14 or 22 of Schedule B1 following filing with the court of a copy of notice of intention to appoint under that paragraph, the date on which the copy of the notice is filed,

(c) in a case where this section applies by reason of an administrator of a company being appointed otherwise than as mentioned in paragraph (a) or (b), the date on which the appointment takes effect, and

(d) in a case where this section applies by reason of a company going into liquidation, the date of the commencement of the winding up.

(6) For the purposes of subsection (2)(a) the value of any goods or services supplied by way of consideration for a floating charge is the amount in money which at the time they were supplied could reasonably have been expected to be obtained for supplying the goods or services in the ordinary course of business and on the same terms (apart from the consideration) as those on which they were supplied to the company.

### 246 Unenforceability of liens on books, etc

(1) This section applies in the case of a company where—

(a) the company enters administration,

(b) the company goes into liquidation, or

(c) a provisional liquidator is appointed;

and 'the office-holder' means the administrator, the liquidator or the provisional liquidator, as the case may be.

(2) Subject as follows, a lien or other right to retain possession of any of the books, papers or other records of the company is unenforceable to the extent that its enforcement would deny possession of any books, papers or other records to the office-holder.

(3) This does not apply to a lien on documents which give a title to property and are held as such.

# PART VII

# INTERPRETATION FOR FIRST GROUP OF PARTS

### 247 'Insolvency' and 'go into liquidation'

(1) In this Group of Parts, except in so far as the context otherwise requires, 'insolvency', in relation to a company, includes the approval of a voluntary arrangement under Part I, or the appointment of an administrator or administrative receiver.

(2) For the purposes of any provision in this Group of Parts, a company goes into liquidation if it passes a resolution for voluntary winding up or an order for its winding up is made by the court at a time when it has not already gone into liquidation by passing such a resolution.

(3) The reference to a resolution for voluntary winding up in subsection (2) includes a reference to a resolution which is deemed to occur by virtue of—

(a) paragraph 83(6)(b) of Schedule B1, or

(b) an order made following conversion of administration or a voluntary arrangement into winding up by virtue of Article 37 of the EC Regulation.

### 248 'Secured creditor', etc

In this Group of Parts, except in so far as the context otherwise requires—

(a) 'secured creditor', in relation to a company, means a creditor of the company who holds in respect of his debt a security over property of the company, and 'unsecured creditor' is to be read accordingly; and

(b) 'security' means—

(i) in relation to England and Wales, any mortgage, charge, lien or other security, and

(ii) in relation to Scotland, any security (whether heritable or moveable), any floating charge and any right of lien or preference and any right of retention (other than a right of compensation or set off).

### 249 'Connected' with a company

For the purposes of any provision in this Group of Parts, a person is connected with a company if—

(a) he is a director or shadow director of the company or an associate of such a director or shadow director, or

(b) he is an associate of the company,

and 'associate' has the meaning given by section 435 in Part XVIII of this Act.

### 250 'Member' of a company

For the purposes of any provision in this Group of Parts, a person who is not a member of a company but to whom shares in the company have been transferred, or transmitted by operation of law, is to be regarded as a member of the company, and references to a member or members are to be read accordingly.

### 251  Expressions used generally

In this Group of Parts, except in so far as the context otherwise requires—

'administative receiver' means—

(a) an administrative receiver as defined by section 29(2) in Chapter I of Part III, or

(b) a receiver appointed under section 51 in Chapter II of that Part in a case where the whole (or substantially the whole) of the company's property is attached by the floating charge;

'business day' means any day other than a Saturday, a Sunday, Christmas Day, Good Friday or a day which is a bank holiday in any part of Great Britain;

'chattel leasing agreement' means an agreement for the bailment or, in Scotland, the hiring of goods which is capable of subsisting for more than 3 months;

'contributory' has the meaning given by section 79;

'director' includes any person occupying the position of director, by whatever name called;

'floating charge' means a charge which, as created, was a floating charge an includes a floating charge within section 462 of the Companies Act (Scottish floating charges);

'office copy', in relation to Scotland, means a copy certified by the clerk of court;

'the official rate', in relation to interest, means the rate payable under section 189(4);

'prescribed' means prescribed by the rules;

'receiver', in the expression 'receiver or manager', does not include a receiver appointed under section 51 in Chapter II of Part III;

'retention of title agreement' means an agreement for the sale of goods to a company, being an agreement—

(a) which does not constitute a charge on the goods, but

(b) under which, if the seller is not paid and the company is wound up, the seller will have priority over all other creditors of the company as respects the goods or any property representing the goods;

'the rules' means rules under section 411 in Part XV; and

'shadow director', in relation to a company, means a person in accordance with whose directions or instructions the directors of the company are accustomed to act (but so that a person is not deemed a shadow director by reason only that the directors act on advice given by him in a professional capacity);

and any expression for whose interpretation provision is made by Part XXVI of the Companies Act, other than an expression defined above in this section, is to be construed in accordance with that provision.

# PART 7A DEBT RELIEF ORDERS

*Preliminary*

### 251A  Debt relief orders

(1) An individual who is unable to pay his debts may apply for an order under this Part ('a debt relief order') to be made in respect of his qualifying debts.

(2) In this Part 'qualifying debt' means (subject to subsection (3)) a debt which—

(a) is for a liquidated sum payable either immediately or at some certain future time; and

(b) is not an excluded debt.

(3) A debt is not a qualifying debt to the extent that it is secured.

(4) In this Part 'excluded debt' means a debt of any description prescribed for the purposes of this subsection.

*Applications for a debt relief order*

### 251B  Making of application

(1) An application for a debt relief order must be made to the official receiver through an approved intermediary.

(2) The application must include—

(a) a list of the debts to which the debtor is subject at the date of the application, specifying the amount of each debt (including any interest, penalty or other sum that has become payable in relation to that debt on or before that date) and the creditor to whom it is owed;

(b) details of any security held in respect of any of those debts; and

(c) such other information about the debtor's affairs (including his creditors, debts and liabilities and his income and assets) as may be prescribed.

(3) The rules may make further provision as to—

(a) the form of an application for a debt relief order;

(b) the manner in which an application is to be made; and

(c) information and documents to be supplied in support of an application.

(4) For the purposes of this Part an application is not to be regarded as having been made until—

    (a) the application has been submitted to the official receiver; and

    (b) any fee required in connection with the application by an order under section 415 has been paid to such person as the order may specify.

### 251C    Duty of official receiver to consider and determine application

(1) This section applies where an application for a debt relief order is made.

(2) The official receiver may stay consideration of the application until he has received answers to any queries raised with the debtor in relation to anything connected with the application.

(3) The official receiver must determine the application by—

    (a) deciding whether to refuse the application;

    (b) if he does not refuse it, by making a debt relief order in relation to the specified debts he is satisfied were qualifying debts of the debtor at the application date;

but he may only refuse the application if he is authorised or required to do so by any of the following provisions of this section.

(4) The official receiver may refuse the application if he considers that—

    (a) the application does not meet all the requirements imposed by or under section 251B;

    (b) any queries raised with the debtor have not been answered to the satisfaction of the official receiver within such time as he may specify when they are raised;

    (c) the debtor has made any false representation or omission in making the application or on supplying any information or documents in support of it.

(5) The official receiver must refuse the application if he is not satisfied that—

    (a) the debtor is an individual who is unable to pay his debts;

    (b) at least one of the specified debts was a qualifying debt of the debtor at the application date;

    (c) each of the conditions set out in Part 1 of Schedule 4ZA is met.

(6) The official receiver may refuse the application if he is not satisfied that each condition specified in Part 2 of Schedule 4ZA is met.

(7) If the official receiver refuses an application he must give reasons for his refusal to the debtor in the prescribed manner.

(8) In this section 'specified debt' means a debt specified in the application.

### 251D    Presumptions applicable to the determination of an application

(1) The following presumptions are to apply to the determination of an application for a debt relief order.

(2) The official receiver must presume that the debtor is an individual who is unable to pay his debts at the determination date if—

    (a) that appears to the official receiver to be the case at the application date from the information supplied in the application and he has no reason to believe that the information supplied is incomplete or inaccurate; and

    (b) he has no reason to believe that, by virtue of a change in the debtor's financial circumstances since the application date, the debtor may be able to pay his debts.

(3) The official receiver must presume that a specified debt (of the amount specified in the application and owed to the creditor so specified) is a qualifying debt at the application date if—

    (a) that appears to him to be the case from the information supplied in the application; and

    (b) he has no reason to believe that the information supplied is incomplete or inaccurate.

(4) The official receiver must presume that the condition specified in paragraph 1 of Schedule 4ZA is met if—

    (a) that appears to him to be the case from the information supplied in the application;

    (b) any prescribed verification checks relating to the condition have been made; and

    (c) he has no reason to believe that the information supplied is incomplete or inaccurate.

(5) The official receiver must presume that any other condition specified in Part 1 or 2 of Schedule 4ZA is met if—

    (a) that appears to him to have been the case as at the application date from the information supplied in the application and he has no reason to believe that the information supplied is incomplete or inaccurate;

    (b) any prescribed verification checks relating to the condition have been made; and

    (c) he has no reason to believe that, by virtue of a change in circumstances since the application date, the condition may no longer be met.

(6) References in this section to information supplied in the application include information supplied to the official receiver in support of the application.

(7) In this section 'specified debt' means a debt specified in the application.

### Making and effect of debt relief order

### 251E    Making of debt relief orders

(1) This section applies where the official receiver makes a debt relief order on determining an application under section 251C.

(2) The order must be made in the prescribed form.

(3) The order must include a list of the debts which the official receiver is satisfied were qualifying debts of the debtor at the application date, specifying the amount of the debt at that time and the creditor to whom it was then owed.

(4) The official receiver must—

(a) give a copy of the order to the debtor; and

(b) make an entry for the order in the register containing the prescribed information about the order or the debtor.

(5) The rules may make provision as to other steps to be taken by the official receiver or the debtor on the making of the order.

(6) Those steps may include in particular notifying each creditor to whom a qualifying debt specified in the order is owed of—

(a) the making of the order and its effect,

(b) the grounds on which a creditor may object under section 251K, and

(c) any other prescribed information.

(7) In this Part the date on which an entry relating to the making of a debt relief order is first made in the register is referred to as 'the effective date'.

### 251F   Effect of debt relief order on other debt management arrangements

(1) This section applies if—

(a) a debt relief order is made, and

(b) immediately before the order is made, other debt management arrangements are in force in respect of the debtor.

(2) The other debt management arrangements cease to be in force when the debt relief order is made.

(3) In this section 'other debt management arrangements' means—

(a) an administration order under Part 6 of the County Courts Act 1984;

(b) an enforcement restriction order under Part 6A of that Act;

(c) a debt repayment plan arranged in accordance with a debt management scheme that is approved under Chapter 4 of Part 5 of the Tribunals, Courts and Enforcement Act 2007.

### 251G   Moratorium from qualifying debts

(1) A moratorium commences on the effective date for a debt relief order in relation to each qualifying debt specified in the order ('a specified qualifying debt').

(2) During the moratorium, the creditor to whom a specified qualifying debt is owed—

(a) has no remedy in respect of the debt, and

(b) may not–

(i) commence a creditor's petition in respect of the debt, or

(ii) otherwise commence any action or other legal proceedings against the debtor for the debt,

except with the permission of the court and on such terms as the court may impose.

(3) If on the effective date a creditor to whom a specified qualifying debt is owed has any such petition, action or other proceeding as mentioned in subsection (2)(b) pending in any court, the court may—

(a) stay the proceedings on the petition, action or other proceedings (as the case may be), or

(b) allow them to continue on such terms as the court thinks fit.

(4) In subsection (2)(a) and (b) references to the debt include a reference to any interest, penalty or other sum that becomes payable in relation to that debt after the application date.

(5) Nothing in this section affects the right of a secured creditor of the debtor to enforce his security.

### 251H   The moratorium period

(1) The moratorium relating to the qualifying debts specified in a debt relief order continues for the period of one year beginning with the effective date for the order, unless—

(a) the moratorium terminates early; or

(b) the moratorium period is extended by the official receiver under this section or by the court under section 251M.

(2) The official receiver may only extend the moratorium period for the purpose of—

(a) carrying out or completing an investigation under section 251K;

(b) taking any action he considers necessary (whether as a result of an investigation or otherwise) in relation to the order; or

(c) in a case where he has decided to revoke the order, providing the debtor with the opportunity to make arrangements for making payments towards his debts.

(3) The official receiver may not extend the moratorium period for the purpose mentioned in subsection (2)(a) without the permission of the court.

(4) The official receiver may not extend the moratorium period beyond the end of the period of three months beginning after the end of the initial period of one year mentioned in subsection (1).

(5) The moratorium period may be extended more than once, but any extension (whether by the official receiver or by the court) must be made before the moratorium would otherwise end.

(6) References in this Part to a moratorium terminating early are to its terminating before the end of what would otherwise be the moratorium period, whether on the revocation of the order or by virtue of any other enactment.

### 251I   Discharge from qualifying debts

(1) Subject as follows, at the end of the moratorium applicable to a debt relief order the debtor is discharged from all the qualifying debts specified in the order (including all interest, penalties and other sums which may have become payable in relation to those debts since the application date).

(2) Subsection (1) does not apply if the moratorium terminates early.

(3) Subsection (1) does not apply in relation to any qualifying debt which the debtor incurred in respect of any fraud or fraudulent breach of trust to which the debtor was a party.

(4) The discharge of the debtor under subsection (1) does not release any other person from–
    (a) any liability (whether as partner or co-trustee of the debtor or otherwise) from which the debtor is released by the discharge; or
    (b) any liability as surety for the debtor or as a person in the nature of such a surety.

(5) If the order is revoked by the court under section 251M after the end of the moratorium period, the qualifying debts specified in the order shall (so far as practicable) be treated as though subsection (1) had never applied to them.

### *Duties of debtor*

### 251J   Providing assistance to official receiver etc

(1) The duties in this section apply to a debtor at any time after the making of an application by him for a debt relief order.

(2) The debtor must—
    (a) give to the official receiver such information as to his affairs,
    (b) attend on the official receiver at such times, and
    (c) do all such other things,
as the official receiver may reasonably require for the purpose of carrying out his functions in relation to the application or, as the case may be, the debt relief order made as a result of the application.

(3) The debtor must notify the official receiver as soon as reasonably practicable if he becomes aware of—
    (a) any error in, or omission from, the information supplied to the official receiver in, or in support of, the application;
    (b) any change in his circumstances between the application date and the determination date that would affect (or would have affected) the determination of the application.

(4) The duties under subsections (2) and (3) apply after (as well as before) the determination of the application, for as long as the official receiver is able to exercise functions of the kind mentioned in subsection (2).

(5) If a debt relief order is made as a result of the application, the debtor must notify the official receiver as soon as reasonably practicable if—
    (a) there is an increase in his income during the moratorium period applicable to the order;
    (b) he acquires any property or any property is devolved upon him during that period;
    (c) he becomes aware of any error in or omission from any information supplied by him to the official receiver after the determination date.

(6) A notification under subsection (3) or (5) must give the prescribed particulars (if any) of the matter being notified.

### *Objections, investigations and revocation*

### 251K   Objections and investigations

(1) Any person specified in a debt relief order as a creditor to whom a specified qualifying debt is owed may object to—
    (a) the making of the order;
    (b) the inclusion of the debt in the list of the debtor's qualifying debts; or
    (c) the details of the debt specified in the order.

(2) An objection under subsection (1) must be—
    (a) made during the moratorium period relating to the order and within the prescribed period for objections;
    (b) made to the official receiver in the prescribed manner;
    (c) based on a prescribed ground;
    (d) supported by any information and documents as may be prescribed;

and the prescribed period mentioned in paragraph (a) must not be less than 28 days after the creditor in question has been notified of the making of the order.

(3)  The official receiver must consider every objection made to him under this section.

(4)  The official receiver may—

(a)  as part of his consideration of an objection, or

(b)  on his own initiative,

carry out an investigation of any matter that appears to the official receiver to be relevant to the making of any decision mentioned in subsection (5) in relation to a debt relief order or the debtor.

(5)  The decisions to which an investigation may be directed are—

(a)  whether the order should be revoked or amended under section 251L;

(b)  whether an application should be made to the court under section 251M; or

(c)  whether any other steps should be taken in relation to the debtor.

(6)  The power to carry out an investigation under this section is exercisable after (as well as during) the moratorium relating to the order.

(7)  The official receiver may require any person to give him such information and assistance as he may reasonably require in connection with an investigation under this section.

(8)  Subject to anything prescribed in the rules as to the procedure to be followed in carrying out an investigation under this section, an investigation may be carried out by the official receiver in such manner as he thinks fit.

### 251L    Power of official receiver to revoke or amend a debt relief order

(1)  The official receiver may revoke or amend a debt relief order during the applicable moratorium period in the circumstances provided for by this section.

(2)  The official receiver may revoke the order on the ground that—

(a)  any information supplied to him by the debtor—

(i)   in, or in support of, the application, or

(ii)  after the determination date,

was incomplete, incorrect or otherwise misleading;

(b)  the debtor has failed to comply with a duty under section 251J;

(c)  a bankruptcy order has been made in relation to the debtor; or

(d)  the debtor has made a proposal under Part 8 (or has notified the official receiver of his intention to do so).

(3)  The official receiver may revoke the order on the ground that he should not have been satisfied—

(a)  that the debts specified in the order were qualifying debts of the debtor as at the application date;

(b)  that the conditions specified in Part 1 of Schedule 4ZA were met;

(c)  that the conditions specified in Part 2 of that Schedule were met or that any failure to meet such a condition did not prevent his making the order.

(4)  The official receiver may revoke the order on the ground that either or both of the conditions in paragraphs 7 and 8 of Schedule 4ZA (monthly surplus income and property) are not met at any time after the order was made.

For this purpose those paragraphs are to be read as if references to the determination date were references to the time in question.

(5)  Where the official receiver decides to revoke the order, he may revoke it either—

(a)  with immediate effect, or

(b)  with effect from such date (not more than three months after the date of the decision) as he may specify.

(6)  In considering when the revocation should take effect the official receiver must consider (in the light of the grounds on which the decision to revoke was made and all the other circumstances of the case) whether the debtor ought to be given the opportunity to make arrangements for making payments towards his debts.

(7)  If the order has been revoked with effect from a specified date the official receiver may, if he thinks it appropriate to do so at any time before that date, revoke the order with immediate effect.

(8)  The official receiver may amend a debt relief order for the purpose of correcting an error in or omission from anything specified in the order.

(9)  But subsection (8) does not permit the official receiver to add any debts that were not specified in the application for the debt relief order to the list of qualifying debts.

(10)  The rules may make further provision as to the procedure to be followed by the official receiver in the exercise of his powers under this section.

*Role of the court*

### 251M    Powers of court in relation to debt relief orders

(1)  Any person may make an application to the court if he is dissatisfied by any act, omission or decision of the official receiver in connection with a debt relief order or an application for such an order.

(2)  The official receiver may make an application to the court for directions or an order in relation to any matter arising in connection with a debt relief order or an application for such an order.

(3)  The matters referred to in subsection (2) include, among other things, matters relating to the debtor's compliance with any duty arising under section 251J.

(4)  An application under this section may, subject to anything in the rules, be made at any time.

(5)  The court may extend the moratorium period applicable to a debt relief order for the purposes of determining an application under this section.

(6)  On an application under this section the court may dismiss the application or do one or more of the following—

   (a)  quash the whole or part of any act or decision of the official receiver;
   (b)  give the official receiver directions (including a direction that he reconsider any matter in relation to which his act or decision has been quashed under paragraph (a));
   (c)  make an order for the enforcement of any obligation on the debtor arising by virtue of a duty under section 251J;
   (d)  extend the moratorium period applicable to the debt relief order;
   (e)  make an order revoking or amending the debt relief order;
   (f)  make an order under section 251N; or
   (g)  make such other order as the court thinks fit.

(7)  An order under subsection (6)(e) for the revocation of a debt relief order—

   (a)  may be made during the moratorium period applicable to the debt relief order or at any time after that period has ended;
   (b)  may be made on the court's own motion if the court has made a bankruptcy order in relation to the debtor during that period;
   (c)  may provide for the revocation of the order to take effect on such terms and at such a time as the court may specify.

(8)  An order under subsection (6)(e) for the amendment of a debt relief order may not add any debts that were not specified in the application for the debt relief order to the list of qualifying debts.

### 251N    Inquiry into debtor's dealings and property

(1)  An order under this section may be made by the court on the application of the official receiver.

(2)  An order under this section is an order summoning any of the following persons to appear before the court—

   (a)  the debtor;
   (b)  the debtor's spouse or former spouse or the debtor's civil partner or former civil partner;
   (c)  any person appearing to the court to be able to give information or assistance concerning the debtor or his dealings, affairs and property.

(3)  The court may require a person falling within subsection (2)(c)—

   (a)  to provide a written account of his dealings with the debtor; or
   (b)  to produce any documents in his possession or under his control relating to the debtor or to the debtor's dealings, affairs or property.

(4)  Subsection (5) applies where a person fails without reasonable excuse to appear before the court when he is summoned to do so by an order under this section.

(5)  The court may cause a warrant to be issued to a constable or prescribed officer of the court—

   (a)  for the arrest of that person, and
   (b)  for the seizure of any records or other documents in that person's possession.

(6)  The court may authorise a person arrested under such a warrant to be kept in custody, and anything seized under such a warrant to be held, in accordance with the rules, until that person is brought before the court under the warrant or until such other time as the court may order.

*Offences*

### 251O    False representations and omissions

(1)  A person who makes an application for a debt relief order is guilty of an offence if he knowingly or recklessly makes any false representation or omission in making the application or providing any information or documents to the official receiver in support of the application.

(2)  A person who makes an application for a debt relief order is guilty of an offence if—

   (a)  he intentionally fails to comply with a duty under section 251J(3) in connection with the application; or
   (b)  he knowingly or recklessly makes any false representation or omission in providing any information to the official receiver in connection with such a duty or otherwise in connection with the application.

(3)  It is immaterial for the purposes of an offence under subsection (1) or (2) whether or not a debt relief order is made as a result of the application.

(4)  A person in respect of whom a debt relief order is made is guilty of an offence if—

   (a)  he intentionally fails to comply with a duty under section 251J(5) in connection with the order; or

(b) he knowingly or recklessly makes any false representation or omission in providing information to the official receiver in connection with such a duty or otherwise in connection with the performance by the official receiver of functions in relation to the order.

(5) It is immaterial for the purposes of an offence under subsection (4)—

(a) whether the offence is committed during or after the moratorium period; and

(b) whether or not the order is revoked after the conduct constituting the offence takes place.

### 251P    Concealment or falsification of documents

(1) A person in respect of whom a debt relief order is made is guilty of an offence if, during the moratorium period in relation to that order—

(a) he does not provide, at the request of the official receiver, all his books, papers and other records of which he has possession or control and which relate to his affairs;

(b) he prevents the production to the official receiver of any books, papers or other records relating to his affairs;

(c) he conceals, destroys, mutilates or falsifies, or causes or permits the concealment, destruction, mutilation or falsification of, any books, papers or other records relating his affairs;

(d) he makes, or causes or permits the making of, any false entries in any book, document or record relating to his affairs; or

(e) he disposes of, or alters or makes any omission in, or causes or permits the disposal, altering or making of any omission in, any book, document or record relating to his affairs.

(2) A person in respect of whom a debt relief order is made is guilty of an offence if—

(a) he did anything falling within paragraphs (c) to (e) of subsection (1) during the period of 12 months ending with the application date; or

(b) he did anything falling within paragraphs (b) to (e) of subsection (1) after that date but before the effective date.

(3) A person is not guilty of an offence under this section if he proves that, in respect of the conduct constituting the offence, he had no intent to defraud or to conceal the state of his affairs.

(4) In its application to a trading record subsection (2)(a) has effect as if the reference to 12 months were a reference to two years.

(5) In subsection (4) 'trading record' means a book, document or record which shows or explains the transactions or financial position of a person's business, including—

(a) a periodic record of cash paid and received,

(b) a statement of periodic stock-taking, and

(c) except in the case of goods sold by way of retail trade, a record of goods sold and purchased which identifies the buyer and seller or enables them to be identified.

(6) It is immaterial for the purposes of an offence under this section whether or not the debt relief order in question is revoked after the conduct constituting the offence takes place (but no offence is committed under this section by virtue of conduct occurring after the order is revoked).

### 251Q    Fraudulent disposal of property

(1) A person in respect of whom a debt relief order is made is guilty of an offence if he made or caused to be made any gift or transfer of his property during the period between—

(a) the start of the period of two years ending with the application date; and

(b) the end of the moratorium period.

(2) The reference in subsection (1) to making a transfer of any property includes causing or conniving at the levying of any execution against that property.

(3) A person is not guilty of an offence under this section if he proves that, in respect of the conduct constituting the offence, he had no intent to defraud or to conceal the state of his affairs.

(4) For the purposes of subsection (3) a person is to be taken to have proved that he had no such intent if—

(a) sufficient evidence is adduced to raise an issue as to whether he had such intent; and

(b) the contrary is not proved beyond reasonable doubt.

(5) It is immaterial for the purposes of this section whether or not the debt relief order in question is revoked after the conduct constituting an offence takes place (but no offence is committed by virtue of conduct occurring after the order is revoked).

### 251R    Fraudulent dealing with property obtained on credit

(1) A person in respect of whom a debt relief order is made is guilty of an offence if during the relevant period he disposed of any property which he had obtained on credit and, at the time he disposed of it, had not paid for it.

(2) Any other person is guilty of an offence if during the relevant period he acquired or received property from a person in respect of whom a debt relief order was made (the 'debtor') knowing or believing—

(a) that the debtor owed money in respect of the property, and

(b) that the debtor did not intend, or was unlikely to be able, to pay the money he so owed.

(3) In subsections (1) and (2) 'relevant period' means the period between—

(a) the start of the period of two years ending with the application date; and

(b) the determination date.

(4) A person is not guilty of an offence under subsection (1) or (2) if the disposal, acquisition or receipt of the property was in the ordinary course of a business carried on by the debtor at the time of the disposal, acquisition or receipt.

(5) In determining for the purposes of subsection (4) whether any property is disposed of, acquired or received in the ordinary course of a business carried on by the debtor, regard may be had, in particular, to the price paid for the property.

(6) A person is not guilty of an offence under subsection (1) if he proves that, in respect of the conduct constituting the offence, he had no intent to defraud or to conceal the state of his affairs.

(7) In this section references to disposing of property include pawning or pledging it; and references to acquiring or receiving property shall be read accordingly.

(8) It is immaterial for the purposes of this section whether or not the debt relief order in question is revoked after the conduct constituting an offence takes place (but no offence is committed by virtue of conduct occurring after the order is revoked).

### 251S   Obtaining credit or engaging in business

(1) A person in respect of whom a debt relief order is made is guilty of an offence if, during the relevant period—

(a) he obtains credit (either alone or jointly with any other person) without giving the person from whom he obtains the credit the relevant information about his status; or

(b) he engages directly or indirectly in any business under a name other than that in which the order was made without disclosing to all persons with whom he enters into any business transaction the name in which the order was made.

(2) For the purposes of subsection (1)(a) the relevant information about a person's status is the information that—

(a) a moratorium is in force in relation to the debt relief order,

(b) a debt relief restrictions order is in force in respect of him, or

(c) both a moratorium and a debt relief restrictions order is in force,

as the case may be.

(3) In subsection (1) 'relevant period' means—

(a) the moratorium period relating to the debt relief order, or

(b) the period for which a debt relief restrictions order is in force in respect of the person in respect of whom the debt relief order is made,

as the case may be.

(4) Subsection (1)(a) does not apply if the amount of the credit is less than the prescribed amount (if any).

(5) The reference in subsection (1)(a) to a person obtaining credit includes the following cases—

(a) where goods are bailed to him under a hire-purchase agreement, or agreed to be sold to him under a conditional sale agreement;

(b) where he is paid in advance (in money or otherwise) for the supply of goods or services.

### 251T   Offences: supplementary

(1) Proceedings for an offence under this Part may only be instituted by the Secretary of State or by or with the consent of the Director of Public Prosecutions.

(2) It is not a defence in proceedings for an offence under this Part that anything relied on, in whole or in part, as constituting the offence was done outside England and Wales.

(3) A person guilty of an offence under this Part is liable to imprisonment or a fine, or both (but see section 430).

*Supplementary*

### 251U   Approved intermediaries

(1) In this Part 'approved intermediary' means an individual for the time being approved by a competent authority to act as an intermediary between a person wishing to make an application for a debt relief order and the official receiver.

(2) In this section 'competent authority' means a person or body for the time being designated by the Secretary of State for the purposes of granting approvals under this section.

(3) Designation as a competent authority may be limited so as to permit the authority only to approve persons of a particular description.

(4) The Secretary of State may by regulations make provision as to—

(a) the procedure for designating persons or bodies as competent authorities;

(b) descriptions of individuals who are ineligible to be approved under this section;

(c) the procedure for granting approvals under this section;

(d) the withdrawal of designations or approvals under this section;

and provision made under paragraph (a) or (c) may include provision requiring the payment of fees.

(5) The rules may make provision about the activities to be carried out by an approved intermediary in connection with an application for a debt relief order, which may in particular include—

(a) assisting the debtor in making the application;

(b) checking that the application has been properly completed;

(c) sending the application to the official receiver.

(6) The rules may also make provision about other activities to be carried out by approved intermediaries.

(7) An approved intermediary may not charge a debtor any fee in connection with an application for a debt relief order.

(8) An approved intermediary is not liable to any person in damages for anything done or omitted to be done when acting (or purporting to act) as an approved intermediary in connection with a particular application by a debtor for a debt relief order.

(9) Subsection (8) does not apply if the act or omission was in bad faith.

(10) Regulations under subsection (4) shall be made by statutory instrument subject to annulment in pursuance of a resolution of either House of Parliament.

### 251V   Debt relief restrictions orders and undertakings

Schedule 4ZB (which makes provision about debt relief restrictions orders and debt relief restrictions undertakings) has effect.

### 251W   Register of debt relief orders etc

The Secretary of State must maintain a register of matters relating to—

(a) debt relief orders;

(b) debt relief restrictions orders; and

(c) debt relief restrictions undertakings.

### 251X   Interpretation

(1) In this Part—

'the application date', in relation to a debt relief order or an application for a debt relief order, means the date on which the application for the order is made to the official receiver;

'approved intermediary' has the meaning given in section 251U(1);

'debt relief order' means an order made by the official receiver under this Part;

'debtor' means—

(a) in relation to an application for a debt relief order, the applicant; and

(b) in relation to a debt relief order, the person in relation to whom the order is made;

'debt relief restrictions order' and 'debt relief restrictions undertaking' means an order made, or an undertaking accepted, under Schedule 4ZB;

'the determination date', in relation to a debt relief order or an application for a debt relief order, means the date on which the application for the order is determined by the official receiver;

'the effective date' has the meaning given in section 251E(7);

'excluded debt' is to be construed in accordance with section 251A;

'moratorium' and 'moratorium period' are to be construed in accordance with sections 251G and 251H;

'qualifying debt', in relation to a debtor, has the meaning given in section 251A(2);

'the register' means the register maintained under section 251W;

'specified qualifying debt' has the meaning given in section 251G(1).

(2) In this Part references to a creditor specified in a debt relief order as the person to whom a qualifying debt is owed by the debtor include a reference to any person to whom the right to claim the whole or any part of the debt has passed, by assignment or operation of law, after the date of the application for the order.

# THE SECOND GROUP OF PARTS

# INSOLVENCY OF INDIVIDUALS; BANKRUPTCY

# PART VIII

# INDIVIDUAL VOLUNTARY ARRANGEMENTS

*Moratorium for insolvent debtor*

### 252   Interim order of court

(1) In the circumstances specified below, the court may in the case of a debtor (being an individual) make an interim order under this section.

(2)  An interim order has the effect that, during the period for which it is in force—

    (a)   no bankruptcy petition relating to the debtor may be presented or proceeded with,

    (aa)  no landlord or other person to whom rent is payable may exercise any right of forfeiture by peaceable re-entry in relation to premises let to the debtor in respect of a failure by the debtor to comply with any term or condition of his tenancy of such premises, except with the leave of the court and

    (b)   no other proceedings, and no execution or other legal process, may be commenced or continued and no distress may be levied against the debtor or his property except with leave of the court.

### 253   Application for interim order

(1)  Application to the court for an interim order may be made where the debtor intends to make a proposal under this Part, that is, a proposal to his creditors for a composition in satisfaction of his debts or a scheme of arrangement of his affairs (from here on referred to, in either case, as a 'voluntary arrangement').

(2)  The proposal must provide for some person ('the nominee') to act in relation to the voluntary arrangement either as trustee or otherwise for the purpose of supervising its implementation and the nominee must be a person who is qualified to act as an insolvency practitioner, or authorised to act as nominee, in relation to the voluntary arrangement.

(3)  Subject as follows, the application may be made—

    (a)   if the debtor is an undischarged bankrupt, by the debtor, the trustee of his estate, or the official receiver, and

    (b)   in any other case, by the debtor.

(4)  An application shall not be made under subsection (3)(a) unless the debtor has given notice of the proposal to the official receiver and, if there is one, the trustee of his estate.

(5)  An application shall not be made while a bankruptcy petition presented by the debtor is pending, if the court has, under section 273 below, appointed an insolvency practitioner to inquire into the debtor's affairs and report.

### 254   Effect of application

(1)  At any time when an application under section 253 for an interim order is pending

    (a)   no landlord or other person to whom rent is payable may exercise any right of forfeiture by peaceable re-entry in relation to premises let to the debtor in respect of a failure by the debtor to comply with any term or condition of his tenancy of such premises, except with the leave of the court, and

    (b)   the court may forbid the levying of any distress on the debtor's property or its subsequent sale, or both, and stay any action, execution or other legal process against the property or person of the debtor.

(2)  Any court in which proceedings are pending against an individual may, on proof that an application under that section has been made in respect of that individual, either stay the proceedings or allow them to continue on such terms as it thinks fit.

### 255   Cases in which interim order can be made

(1)  The court shall not make an interim order on an application under section 253 unless it is satisfied—

    (a)   that the debtor intends to make a proposal under this Part;

    (b)   that on the day of the making of the application the debtor was an undischarged bankrupt or was able to petition for his own bankruptcy;

    (c)   that no previous application has been made by the debtor for an interim order in the period of 12 months ending with that day; and

    (d)   that the nominee under the debtor's proposal [...] is willing to act in relation to the proposal.

(2)  The court may make an order if it thinks that it would be appropriate to do so for the purpose of facilitating the consideration and implementation of the debtor's proposal.

(3)  Where the debtor is an undischarged bankrupt, the interim order may contain provision as to the conduct of the bankruptcy, and the administration of the bankrupt's estate, during the period for which the order is in force.

(4)  Subject as follows, the provision contained in an interim order by virtue of subsection (3) may include provision staying proceedings in the bankruptcy or modifying any provision in this Group of Parts, and any provision of the rules in their application to the debtor's bankruptcy.

(5)  An interim order shall not, in relation to a bankrupt, make provision relaxing or removing any of the requirements of provisions in this Group of Parts, or of the rules, unless the court is satisfied that that provision is unlikely to result in any significant diminution in, or in the value of, the debtor's estate for the purposes of the bankruptcy.

(6)  Subject to the following provisions of this Part, an interim order made on an application under section 253 ceases to have effect at the end of the period of 14 days beginning with the day after the making of the order.

### 256 Nominee's report on debtor's proposal

(1) Where an interim order has been made on an application under section 253, the nominee shall, before the order ceases to have effect, submit a report to the court stating—

    (a)  sonable prospect of being approved and implemented,

    (aa)  whether, in his opinion, a meeting of the debtor's creditors should be summoned to consider the debtors' proposal, and

    (b)  if in his opinion such a meeting should be summoned, the date on which, and time and place at which, he proposes the meeting should be held.

(2) For the purpose of enabling the nominee to prepare his report the debtor shall submit to the nominee—

    (a)  a document setting out the terms of the voluntary arrangement which the debtor is proposing, and

    (b)  a statement of his affairs containing—

        (i)  such particulars of his creditors and of his debts and other liabilities and of his assets as may be prescribed, and

        (ii)  such other information as may be prescribed.

(3) The court may—

    (a)  on an application made by the debtor in a case where the nominee has failed to submit the report required by this section or has died, or

    (b)  on an application made by the debtor or the nominee in a case where it is impracticable or inappropriate for the nominee to continue to act as such,

direct that the nominee shall be replaced as such by another person qualified to act as an insolvency practitioner, or authorised to act as nominee, in relation to the voluntary arrangement.

(3A) The court may, on an application made by the debtor in a case where the nominee has failed to submit the report required by this section, direct that the interim order shall continue, or (if it has ceased to have effect) be renewed, for such further period as the court may specify in the direction.

(4) The court may, on the application of the nominee, extend the period for which the interim order has effect so as to enable the nominee to have more time to prepare his report.

(5) If the court is satisfied on receiving the nominee's report that a meeting of the debtor's creditors should be summoned to consider the debtor's proposal, the court shall direct that the period for which the interim order has effect shall be extended, for such further period as it may specify in the direction, for the purpose of enabling the debtor's proposal to be considered by his creditors in accordance with the following provisions of this Part.

(6) The court may discharge the interim order if it is satisfied, on the application of the nominee—

    (a)  that the debtor has failed to comply with his obligations under subsection (2), or

    (b)  that for any other reason it would be inappropriate for a meeting of the debtor's creditors to be summoned to consider the debtor's proposal.

*Procedure where no interim order made*

### 256A Debtor's proposal and nominee's report

(1) This section applies where a debtor (being an individual)—

    (a)  intends to make a proposal under this Part (but an interim order has not been made in relation to the proposal and no application for such an order is pending), and

    (b)  if he is an undischarged bankrupt, has given notice of the proposal to the official receiver and, if there is one, the trustee of his estate,

unless a bankruptcy petition presented by the debtor is pending and the court has, under section 273, appointed an insolvency practitioner to inquire into the debtor's affairs and report.

(2) For the purpose of enabling the nominee to prepare a report to the court, the debtor shall submit to the nominee—

    (a)  a document setting out the terms of the voluntary arrangement which the debtor is proposing, and

    (b)  a statement of his affairs containing—

        (i)  such particulars of his creditors and of his debts and other liabilities and of his assets as may be prescribed, and

        (ii)  such other information as may be prescribed.

(3) If the nominee is of the opinion that the debtor is an undischarged bankrupt, or is able to petition for his own bankruptcy, the nominee shall, within 14 days (or such longer period as the court may allow) after receiving the document and statement mentioned in subsection (2), submit a report to the court stating—

    (a)  whether, in his opinion, the voluntary arrangement which the debtor is proposing has a reasonable prospect of being approved and implemented,

    (b)  whether, in his opinion, a meeting of the debtor's creditors should be summoned to consider the debtor's proposal, and

(c) if in his opinion such a meeting should be summoned, the date on which, and time and place at which, he proposes the meeting should be held.

(4) The court may—

(a) on an application made by the debtor in a case where the nominee has failed to submit the report required by this section or has died, or

(b) on an application made by the debtor or the nominee in a case where it is impracticable or inappropriate for the nominee to continue to act as such,

direct that the nominee shall be replaced as such by another person qualified to act as an insolvency practitioner, or authorised to act as nominee, in relation to the voluntary arrangement.

(5) The court may, on an application made by the nominee, extend the period within which the nominee is to submit his report.

## *Creditors' meeting*

### 257  Summoning of creditors' meeting

(1) Where it has been reported to the court under section 256 or 256A that a meeting of the debtor's creditors should be summoned, the nominee (or his replacement under section 256(3) or 256A(4)) shall, unless the court otherwise directs, summon that meeting for the time, date and place proposed in his report.

(2) The persons to be summoned to the meeting are every creditor of the debtor of whose claim and address the person summoning the meeting is aware.

(3) For this purpose the creditors of a debtor who is an undischarged bankrupt include—

(a) every person who is a creditor of the bankrupt in respect of a bankruptcy debt, and

(b) every person who would be such a creditor if the bankruptcy had commenced on the date on which notice of the meeting is given.

## *Consideration and implementation of debtor's proposal*

### 258  Decisions of creditor's meeting

(1) A creditors' meeting summoned under section 257 shall decide whether to approve the proposed voluntary arrangement.

(2) The meeting may approve the proposed voluntary arrangement with modifications, but shall not do so unless the debtor consents to each modification.

(3) The modifications subject to which the proposed voluntary arrangement may be approved may include one conferring the functions proposed to be conferred on the nominee on another person qualified to act as an insolvency practitioner or authorised to act as nominee, in relation to the voluntary arrangement.

But they shall not include any modification by virtue of which the proposal ceases to be a proposal under this Part.

(4) The meeting shall not approve any proposal or modification which affects the right of a secured creditor of the debtor to enforce his security, except with the concurrence of the creditor concerned.

(5) Subject as follows, the meeting shall not approve any proposal or modification under which—

(a) any preferential debt of the debtor is to be paid otherwise than in priority to such of his debts as are not preferential debts, or

(b) a preferential creditor of the debtor is to be paid an amount in respect of a preferential debt that bears to that debt a smaller proportion than is borne to another preferential debt by the amount that is to be paid in respect of that other debt.

However, the meeting may approve such a proposal or modification with the concurrence of the preferential creditor concerned.

(6) Subject as above, the meeting shall be conducted in accordance with the rules.

(7) In this section 'preferential debt' has the meaning given by section 386 in Part XII; and 'preferential creditor' is to be construed accordingly.

### 259  Report of decisions to court

(1) After the conclusion in accordance with the rules of the meeting summoned under section 257, the chairman of the meeting shall report the result of it to the court and, immediately after so reporting, shall give notice of the result of the meeting to such persons as may be prescribed.

(2) If the report is that the meeting has declined (with or without modifications) to approve the debtor's proposal, the court may discharge any interim order which is in force in relation to the debtor.

### 260  Effect of approval

(1) This section has effect where the meeting summoned under section 257 approves the proposed voluntary arrangement (with or without modifications).

(2) The approved arrangement—

(a) takes effect as if made by the debtor at the meeting, and

(b) binds every person who in accordance with the rules—

(i) was entitled to vote at the meeting (whether or not he was present or represented at it), or

(ii)  would have been so entitled if he had had notice of it,

as if he were a party to the arrangement.

(2A) If—

(a)  when the arrangement ceases to have effect any amount payable under the arrangement to a person bound by virtue of subsection (2)(b)(ii) has not been paid, and

(b)  the arrangement did not come to an end prematurely,

the debtor shall at that time become liable to pay to that person the amount payable under the arrangement.

(3)  The Deeds of Arrangement Act 1914 does not apply to the approved voluntary arrangement.

(4)  Any interim order in force in relation to the debtor immediately before the end of the period of 28 days beginning with the day on which the report with respect to the creditors' meeting was made to the court under section 259 ceases to have effect at the end of that period.

This subsection applies except to such extent as the court may direct for the purposes of any application under section 262 below.

(5)  Where proceedings on a bankruptcy petition have been stayed by an interim order which ceases to have effect under subsection (4), that petition is deemed, unless the court otherwise orders, to have been dismissed.

## 261  Additional effect on undischarged bankrupt

(1)  This section applies where—

(a)  the creditors' meeting summoned under section 257 approves the proposed voluntary arrangement (with or without modifications), and

(b)  the debtor is an undischarged bankrupt.

(2)  Where this section applies the court shall annul the bankruptcy order on an application made—

(a)  by the bankrupt, or

(b)  where the bankrupt has not made an application within the prescribed period, by the official receiver.

(3)  An application under subsection (2) may not be made—

(a)  during the period specified in section 262(3)(a) during which the decision of the creditors' meeting can be challenged by application under section 262,

(b)  while an application under that section is pending, or

(c)  while an appeal in respect of an application under that section is pending or may be brought.

(4)  Where this section applies the court may give such directions about the conduct of the bankruptcy and the administration of the bankrupt's estate as it thinks appropriate for facilitating the implementation of the approved voluntary arrangement.

## 262  Challenge of meeting's decision

(1)  Subject to this section, an application to the court may be made, by any of the persons specified below, on one or both of the following grounds, namely—

(a)  that a voluntary arrangement approved by a creditors' meeting summoned under section 257 unfairly prejudices the interests of a creditor of the debtor;

(b)  that there has been some material irregularity at or in relation to such a meeting.

(2)  The persons who may apply under this section are—

(a)  the debtor;

(b)  a person who—

(i)  was entitled, in accordance with the rules, to vote at the creditors' meeting, or

(ii)  would have been so entitled if he had had notice of it

(c)  the nominee (or his replacement under section 256(3), 256A(4) or 258(3)); and

(d)  if the debtor is an undischarged bankrupt, the trustee of his estate or the official receiver.

(3)  An application under this section shall not be made

(a)  after the end of the period of 28 days beginning with the day on which the report of the creditors' meeting was made to the court under section 259 or

(b)  in the case of a person who was not given notice of the creditors' meeting, after the end of the period of 28 days beginning with the day on which he became aware that the meeting had taken place,

but (subject to that) an application made by a person within subsection (2)(b)(ii) on the ground that the arrangement prejudices his interests may be made after the arrangement has ceased to have effect, unless it has come to an end prematurely.

(4)  Where on an application under this section the court is satisfied as to either of the grounds mentioned in subsection (1), it may do one or both of the following, namely—

(a)  revoke or suspend any approval given by the meeting;

(b)  give a direction to any person for the summoning of a further meeting of the debtor's creditors to consider any revised proposal he may make or, in a case falling within subsection (1)(b), to reconsider his original proposal.

(5) Where at any time after giving a direction under subsection (4)(b) for the summoning of a meeting to consider a revised proposal the court is satisfied that the debtor does not intend to submit such a proposal, the court shall revoke the direction and revoke or suspend any approval given at the previous meeting.

(6) Where the court gives a direction under subsection (4)(b), it may also give a direction continuing or, as the case may require, renewing, for such period as may be specified in the direction, the effect in relation to the debtor of any interim order.

(7) In any case where the court, on an application made under this section with respect to a creditors' meeting, gives a direction under subsection (4)(b) or revokes or suspends an approval under subsection (4)(a) or (5), the court may give such supplemental directions as it thinks fit and, in particular, directions with respect to—

    (a) things done since the meeting under any voluntary arrangement approved by the meeting, and

    (b) such things done since the meeting as could not have been done if any interim order had been in force in relation to the debtor when they were done.

(8) Except in pursuance of the preceding provisions of this section, an approval given at a creditors' meeting summoned under section 257 is not invalidated by any irregularity at or in relation to the meeting.

### 262A  False representations etc

(1) If for the purpose of obtaining the approval of his creditors to a proposal for a voluntary arrangement, the debtor—

    (a) makes any false representation, or

    (b) fraudulently does, or omits to do, anything,

he commits an offence.

(2) Subsection (1) applies even if the proposal is not approved.

(3) A person guilty of an offence under this section is liable to imprisonment or a fine, or both.

### 262B  Prosecution of delinquent debtors

(1) This section applies where a voluntary arrangement approved by a creditors' meeting summoned under section 257 has taken effect.

(2) If it appears to the nominee or supervisor that the debtor has been guilty of any offence in connection with the arrangement for which he is criminally liable, he shall forthwith—

    (a) report the matter to the Secretary of State, and

    (b) provide the Secretary of State with such information and give the Secretary of State such access to and facilities for inspecting and taking copies of documents (being information or documents in his possession or under his control and relating to the matter in question) as the Secretary of State requires.

(3) Where a prosecuting authority institutes criminal proceedings following any report under subsection (2), the nominee or, as the case may be, supervisor shall give the authority all assistance in connection with the prosecution which he is reasonably able to give.

For this purpose, 'prosecuting authority' means the Director of Public Prosecutions or the Secretary of State.

(4) The court may, on the application of the prosecuting authority, direct a nominee or supervisor to comply with subsection (3) if he has failed to do so.

### 262C  Arrangements coming to an end prematurely

For the purposes of this Part, a voluntary arrangement approved by a creditors' meeting summoned under section 257 comes to an end prematurely if, when it ceases to have effect, it has not been fully implemented in respect of all persons bound by the arrangement by virtue of section 260(2)(b)(i).

### 263  Implementation and supervision of approved voluntary arrangement

(1) This section applies where a voluntary arrangement approved by a creditors' meeting summoned under section 257 has taken effect.

(2) The person who is for the time being carrying out, in relation to the voluntary arrangement, the functions conferred by virtue of the approval on the nominee (or his replacement under section 256(3), 256A(4) or 258(3)) shall be known as the supervisor of the voluntary arrangement.

(3) If the debtor, any of his creditors or any other person is dissatisfied by any act, omission or decision of the supervisor, he may apply to the court; and on such an application the court may—

    (a) confirm, reverse or modify any act or decision of the supervisor,

    (b) give him directions, or

    (c) make such other order as it thinks fit.

(4) The supervisor may apply to the court for directions in relation to any particular matter arising under the voluntary arrangement.

(5) The court may, whenever—

    (a) it is expedient to appoint a person to carry out the functions of the supervisor, and

(b) it is inexpedient, difficult or impracticable for an appointment to be made without the assistance of the court,

make an order appointing a person who is qualified to act as an insolvency practitioner or authorised to
act as supervisor, in relation to the voluntary arrangement, either in substitution for the existing supervisor or to fill a vacancy.

This is without prejudice to section 41(2) of the Trustee Act 1925 (power of court to appoint trustees
of deeds of arrangement).

(6) The power conferred by subsection (5) is exercisable so as to increase the number of persons
exercising the functions of the supervisor or, where there is more than one person exercising those functions, so as to replace one or more of those persons.

### *Fast-track voluntary arrangement*

### 263A   Availability

Section 263B applies where an individual debtor intends to make a proposal to his creditors for a voluntary arrangement and—

(a) the debtor is an undischarged bankrupt,
(b) the official receiver is specified in the proposal as the nominee in relation to the voluntary
arrangement, and
(c) no interim order is applied for under section 253.

### 263B   Decision

(1) The debtor may submit to the official receiver—

(a) a document setting out the terms of the voluntary arrangement which the debtor is proposing, and
(b) a statement of his affairs containing such particulars as may be prescribed of his creditors,
debts, other liabilities and assets and such other information as may be prescribed.

(2) If the official receiver thinks that the voluntary arrangement proposed has a reasonable prospect of being approved and implemented, he may make arrangements for inviting creditors to decide
whether to approve it.

(3) For the purposes of subsection (2) a person is a 'creditor' only if—

(a) he is a creditor of the debtor in respect of a bankruptcy debt, and
(b) the official receiver is aware of his claim and his address.

(4) Arrangements made under subsection (2)—

(a) must include the provision to each creditor of a copy of the proposed voluntary arrangement,
(b) must include the provision to each creditor of information about the criteria by reference to
which the official receiver will determine whether the creditors approve or reject the proposed voluntary arrangement, and
(c) may not include an opportunity for modifications to the proposed voluntary arrangement to
be suggested or made.

(5) Where a debtor submits documents to the official receiver under subsection (1) no application under section 253 for an interim order may be made in respect of the debtor until the official
receiver has—

(a) made arrangements as described in subsection (2), or
(b) informed the debtor that he does not intend to make arrangements (whether because he
does not think the voluntary arrangement has a reasonable prospect of being approved and
implemented or because he declines to act).

### 263C   Result

As soon as is reasonably practicable after the implementation of arrangements under section 263B(2)
the official receiver shall report to the court whether the proposed voluntary arrangement has been
approved or rejected.

### 263D   Approval of voluntary arrangement

(1) This section applies where the official receiver reports to the court under section 263C that a
proposed voluntary arrangement has been approved.

(2) The voluntary arrangement—

(a) takes effect,
(b) binds the debtor, and
(c) binds every person who was entitled to participate in the arrangements made under section
263B(2).

(3) The court shall annul the bankruptcy order in respect of the debtor on an application made by
the official receiver.

(4) An application under subsection (3) may not be made—

(a) during the period specified in section 263F(3) during which the voluntary arrangement can
be challenged by application under section 263F(2),
(b) while an application under that section is pending, or
(c) while an appeal in respect of an application under that section is pending or may be brought.

(5) The court may give such directions about the conduct of the bankruptcy and the administration of the bankrupt's estate as it thinks appropriate for facilitating the implementation of the approved voluntary arrangement.

(6) The Deeds of Arrangement Act 1914 (c 47) does not apply to the voluntary arrangement.

(7) A reference in this Act or another enactment to a voluntary arrangement approved under this Part includes a reference to a voluntary arrangement which has effect by virtue of this section.

### 263E  Implementation

Section 263 shall apply to a voluntary arrangement which has effect by virtue of section 263D(2) as it applies to a voluntary arrangement approved by a creditors' meeting.

### 263F  Revocation

(1) The court may make an order revoking a voluntary arrangement which has effect by virtue of section 263D(2) on the ground—

(a) that it unfairly prejudices the interests of a creditor of the debtor, or

(b) that a material irregularity occurred in relation to the arrangements made under section 263B(2).

(2) An order under subsection (1) may be made only on the application of—

(a) the debtor,

(b) a person who was entitled to participate in the arrangements made under section 263B(2),

(c) the trustee of the bankrupt's estate, or

(d) the official receiver.

(3) An application under subsection (2) may not be made after the end of the period of 28 days beginning with the date on which the official receiver makes his report to the court under section 263C.

(4) But a creditor who was not made aware of the arrangements under section 263B(2) at the time when they were made may make an application under subsection (2) during the period of 28 days beginning with the date on which he becomes aware of the voluntary arrangement.

### 263G  Offences

(1) Section 262A shall have effect in relation to obtaining approval to a proposal for a voluntary arrangement under section 263D.

(2) Section 262B shall have effect in relation to a voluntary arrangement which has effect by virtue of section 263D(2) (for which purposes the words 'by a creditors' meeting summoned under section 257' shall be disregarded).

# PART IX

# BANKRUPTCY

## Chapter I

## Bankruptcy petitions; bankruptcy orders

### *Preliminary*

### 264  Who may present a bankruptcy petition

(1) A petition for a bankruptcy order to be made against an individual may be presented to the court in accordance with the following provisions of this Part—

(a)  by one of the individual's creditors or jointly by more than one of them,

(b)  by the individual himself,

(ba)  by a temporary administrator (within the meaning of Article 38 of the EC Regulation),

(bb)  by a liquidator (within the meaning of Article 2(b) of the EC Regulation) appointed in proceedings by virtue of Article 3(1) of the EC Regulation,

(c)  by the supervisor of, or any person (other than the individual) who is for the time being bound by, a voluntary arrangement proposed by the individual and approved under Part VIII, *or*

(d)  *where a criminal bankruptcy order has been made against the individual, by the Official Petitioner or by any person specified in the order in pursuance of section 39(3)(b) of the Powers of Criminal Courts Act 1973.*

(2) Subject to those provisions, the court may make a bankruptcy order on any such petition.[8]

### 265  Conditions to be satisfied in respect of debtor

(1) A bankruptcy petition shall not be presented to the court under section 264(1)(a) or (b) unless the debtor—

(a) is domiciled in England and Wales,

---

[8] The words in italics repealed by the Criminal Justice Act 1988 c 33 from a date to be appointed.

(b) is personally present in England and Wales on the day on which the petition is presented, or

(c) at any time in the period of 3 years ending with that day—

   (i) has been ordinarily resident, or has had a place of residence, in England and Wales, or

   (ii) has carried on business in England and Wales.

(2) The reference in subsection (1)(c) to an individual carrying on business includes—

   (a) the carrying on of business by a firm or partnership of which the individual is a member, and

   (b) the carrying on of business by an agent or manager for the individual or for such a firm or partnership.

(3) This section is subject to Article 3 of the EC Regulation.

### 266   Other preliminary conditions

(1) Where a bankruptcy petition relating to an individual is presented by a person who is entitled to present a petition under two or more paragraphs of section 264(1), the petition is to be treated for the purposes of this Part as a petition under such one of those paragraphs as may be specified in the petition.

(2) A bankruptcy petition shall not be withdrawn without the leave of the court.

(3) The court has a general power, if it appears to it appropriate to do so on the grounds that there has been a contravention of the rules or for any other reason, to dismiss a bankruptcy petition or to stay proceedings on such a petition; and, where it stays proceedings on a petition, it may do so on such terms and conditions as it thinks fit.

*(4) Without prejudice to subsection (3), where a petition under section 264(1)(a), (b) or (c) in respect of an individual is pending at a time when a criminal bankruptcy order is made against him, or is presented after such an order has been so made, the court may on the application of the Official Petitioner dismiss the petition if it appears to it appropriate to do so.*[9]

### *Creditor's petition*

### 267   Grounds of creditor's petition

(1) A creditor's petition must be in respect of one or more debts owed by the debtor, and the petitioning creditor or each of the petitioning creditors must be a person to whom the debt or (as the case may be) at least one of the debts is owed.

(2) Subject to the next three sections, a creditor's petition may be presented to the court in respect of a debt or debts only if, at the time the petition is presented—

   (a) the amount of the debt, or the aggregate amount of the debts, is equal to or exceeds the bankruptcy level,

   (b) the debt, or each of the debts, is for a liquidated sum payable to the petitioning creditor, or one or more of the petitioning creditors, either immediately or at some certain, future time, and is unsecured,

   (c) the debt, or each of the debts, is a debt which the debtor appears either to be unable to pay or to have no reasonable prospect of being able to pay, and

   (d) there is no outstanding application to set aside a statutory demand served (under section 268 below) in respect of the debt or any of the debts.

*(3) A debt is not to be regarded for the purposes of subsection (2) as a debt for a liquidated sum by reason only that the amount of the debt is specified in a criminal bankruptcy order.*

(4) 'The bankruptcy level' is £750 but the Secretary of State may by order in a statutory instrument substitute any amount specified in the order for that amount or (as the case may be) for the amount which by virtue of such an order is for the time being the amount of the bankruptcy level.

(5) An order shall not be made under subsection (4) unless a draft of it has been laid before, and approved by a resolution of, each House of Parliament.[10]

### 268   Definition of 'inability to pay', etc ; the statutory demand

(1) For the purposes of section 267(2)(c), the debtor appears to be unable to pay a debt if, but only if, the debt is payable immediately and either—

   (a) the petitioning creditor to whom the debt is owed has served on the debtor a demand (known as 'the statutory demand') in the prescribed form requiring him to pay the debt or to secure or compound for it to the satisfaction of the creditor, at least 3 weeks have elapsed since the demand was served and the demand has been neither complied with nor set aside in accordance with the rules, or

   (b) execution or other process issued in respect of the debt on a judgment or order of any court in favour of the petitioning creditor, or one or more of the petitioning creditors to whom the debt is owed, has been returned unsatisfied in whole or in part.

(2) For the purposes of section 267(2)(c) the debtor appears to have no reasonable prospect of being able to pay a debt if, but only if, the debt is not immediately payable and—

---

[9] The words in italics repealed by the Criminal Justice Act 1988 c 33 from a date to be appointed.

[10] The words in italics repealed by the Criminal Justice Act 1988 c 33 from a date to be appointed.

    (a) the petitioning creditor to whom it is owed has served on the debtor a demand (also known as 'the statutory demand') in the prescribed form requiring him to establish to the satisfaction of the creditor that there is a reasonable prospect that the debtor will be able to pay the debt when it falls due,

    (b) at least 3 weeks have elapsed since the demand was served, and

    (c) the demand has been neither complied with nor set aside in accordance with the rules.

### 269    Creditor with security

(1) A debt which is the debt, or one of the debts, in respect of which a creditor's petition is presented need not be unsecured if either—

    (a) the petition contains a statement by the person having the right to enforce the security that he is willing, in the event of a bankruptcy order being made, to give up his security for the benefit of all the bankrupt's creditors, or

    (b) the petition is expressed not to be made in respect of the secured part of the debt and contains a statement by that person of the estimated value at the date of the petition of the security for the secured part of the debt.

(2) In a case falling within subsection (1)(b) the secured and unsecured parts of the debt are to be treated for the purposes of sections 267 to 270 as separate debts.

### 270    Expedited petition

In the case of a creditor's petition presented wholly or partly in respect of a debt which is the subject of a statutory demand under section 268, the petition may be presented before the end of the 3-week period there mentioned if there is a serious possibility that the debtor's property or the value of any of his property will be significantly diminished during that period and the petition contains a statement to that effect.

### 271    Proceedings on creditor's petition

(1) The court shall not make a bankruptcy order on a creditor's petition unless it is satisfied that the debt, or one of the debts, in respect of which the petition was presented is either—

    (a) a debt which, having been payable at the date of the petition or having since become payable, has been neither paid nor secured or compounded for, or

    (b) a debt which the debtor has no reasonable prospect of being able to pay when it falls due.

(2) In a case in which the petition contains such a statement as is required by section 270, the court shall not make a bankruptcy order until at least 3 weeks have elapsed since the service of any statutory demand under section 268.

(3) The court may dismiss the petition if it is satisfied that the debtor is able to pay all his debts or is satisfied—

    (a) that the debtor has made an offer to secure or compound for a debt in respect of which the petition is presented,

    (b) that the acceptance of that offer would have required the dismissal of the petition, and

    (c) that the offer has been unreasonably refused;

and, in determining for the purposes of this subsection whether the debtor is able to pay all his debts, the court shall take into account his contingent and prospective liabilities.

(4) In determining for the purposes of this section what constitutes a reasonable prospect that a debtor will be able to pay a debt when it falls due, it is to be assumed that the prospect given by the facts and other matters known to the creditor at the time he entered into the transaction resulting in the debt was a reasonable prospect.

(5) Nothing in sections 267 to 271 prejudices the power of the court, in accordance with the rules, to authorise a creditor's petition to be amended by the omission of any creditor or debt and to be proceeded with as if things done for the purposes of those sections had been done only by or in relation to the remaining creditors or debts.

*Debtor's petition*

### 272    Grounds of debtor's petition

(1) A debtor's petition may be presented to the court only on the grounds that the debtor is unable to pay his debts.

(2) The petition shall be accompanied by a statement of the debtor's affairs containing—

    (a) such particulars of the debtor's creditors and of his debts and other liabilities and of his assets as may be prescribed, and

    (b) such other information as may be prescribed.

### 273    Appointment of insolvency practitioner by the court

(1) Subject to the next section, on the hearing of a debtor's petition the court shall not make a bankruptcy order if it appears to the court—

    (a) that if a bankruptcy order were made the aggregate amount of the bankruptcy debts, so far as unsecured, would be less than the small bankruptcies level,

    (b) that if a bankruptcy order were made, the value of the bankrupt's estate would be equal to or more than the minimum amount,

(c) that within the period of 5 years ending with the presentation of the petition the debtor has neither been adjudged bankrupt nor made a composition with his creditors in satisfaction of his debts or a scheme of arrangement of his affairs, and

(d) that it would be appropriate to appoint a person to prepare a report under section 274.

'The minimum amount' and 'the small bankruptcies level' means such amounts as may for the time being be prescribed for the purposes of this section.

(2) Where on the hearing of the petition, it appears to the court as mentioned in subsection (1), the court shall appoint a person who is qualified to act as an insolvency practitioner in relation to the debtor—

(a) to prepare a report under the next section, and

(b) subject to section 258(3) in Part VIII, to act in relation to any voluntary arrangement to which the report relates either as trustee or otherwise for the purpose of supervising its implementation.

## 274  Action on report of insolvency practitioner

(1) A person appointed under section 273 shall inquire into the debtor's affairs and, within such period as the court may direct, shall submit a report to the court stating whether the debtor is willing, for the purposes of Part VIII, to make a proposal for a voluntary arrangement.

(2) A report which states that the debtor is willing as above mentioned shall also state—

(a) whether, in the opinion of the person making the report, a meeting of the debtor's creditors should be summoned to consider the proposal, and

(b) if in that person's opinion such a meeting should be summoned, the date on which, and time and place at which, he proposes the meeting should be held.

(3) On considering a report under this section the court may—

(a) without any application, make an interim order under section 252, if it thinks that it is appropriate to do so for the purposes of facilitating the consideration and implementation of the debtor's proposal, or

(b) if it thinks it would be inappropriate to make such an order, make a bankruptcy order.

(4) An interim order made by virtue of this section ceases to have effect at the end of such period as the court may specify for the purpose of enabling the debtor's proposal to be considered by his creditors in accordance with the applicable provisions of Part VIII.

(5) Where it has been reported to the court under this section that a meeting of the debtor's creditors should be summoned, the person making the report shall, unless the court otherwise directs, summon that meeting for the time, date and place proposed in his report.

The meeting is then deemed to have been summoned under section 257 in Part VIII, and subsections (2) and (3) of that section, and sections 258 to 263 apply accordingly.

## 274A  Debtor who meets conditions for a debt relief order

(1) This section applies where, on the hearing of a debtor's petition—

(a) it appears to the court that a debt relief order would be made in relation to the debtor if, instead of presenting the petition, he had made an application under Part 7A; and

(b) the court does not appoint an insolvency practitioner under section 273.

(2) If the court thinks it would be in the debtor's interests to apply for a debt relief order instead of proceeding on the petition, the court may refer the debtor to an approved intermediary (within the meaning of Part 7A) for the purposes of making an application for a debt relief order.

(3) Where a reference is made under subsection (2) the court shall stay proceedings on the petition on such terms and conditions as it thinks fit; but if following the reference a debt relief order is made in relation to the debtor the court shall dismiss the petition.

## 275  Summary administration

[...]

*Other cases for special consideration*

## 276  Default in connection with voluntary arrangement

(1) The court shall not make a bankruptcy order on a petition under section 264(1)(c)(supervisor of, or person bound by, voluntary arrangement proposed and approved) unless it is satisfied—

(a) that the debtor has failed to comply with his obligations under the voluntary arrangement, or

(b) that information which was false or misleading in any material particular or which contained material omissions—

(i) was contained in any statement of affairs or other document supplied by the debtor under Part VIII to any person, or

(ii) was otherwise made available by the debtor to his creditors at or in connection with a meeting summoned under that Part, or

(c) that the debtor has failed to do all such things as may for the purposes of the voluntary arrangement have been reasonably required of him by the supervisor of the arrangement.

(2) Where a bankruptcy order is made on a petition under section 264(1)(c), any expenses properly incurred as expenses of the administration of the voluntary arrangement in question shall be a first charge on the bankrupt's estate.

### 277   Petition based on criminal bankruptcy order

(1) Subject to section 266(3), the court shall make a bankruptcy order on a petition under section 264(1)(d) on production of a copy of the criminal bankruptcy order on which the petition is based.

This does not apply if it appears to the court that the criminal bankruptcy order has been rescinded on appeal.

(2) Subject to the provisions of this Part, the fact that an appeal is pending against any conviction by virtue of which a criminal bankruptcy order was made does not affect any proceedings on a petition under section 264(1)(d) based on that order.

(3) For the purposes of this section, an appeal against a conviction is pending—

(a) in any case, until the expiration of the period of 28 days beginning with the date of conviction;

(b) if notice of appeal to the Court of Appeal is given during that period and during that period the appellant notifies the official receiver of it, until the determination of the appeal and thereafter for so long as an appeal to the House of Lords is pending within the meaning of section 40(5) of the Powers of Criminal Courts Act 1973.

(4) For the purposes of subsection (3)(b) an appeal to the Supreme Court shall be treated as pending until any application for leave to appeal is disposed of and, if leave to appeal is granted, until the appeal is disposed of; and for the purposes of this subsection an application for leave to appeal shall be treated as disposed of at the expiration of the time within which it may be made, if it is not made within that time.[11]

### Commencement and duration of bankruptcy; discharge

### 278   Commencement and continuance

The bankruptcy of an individual against whom a bankruptcy order has been made—

(a) commences with the day on which the order is made, and

(b) continues until the individual is discharged under the following provisions of this Chapter.

### 279   Duration

(1) A bankrupt is discharged from bankruptcy at the end of the period of one year beginning with the date on which the bankruptcy commences.

(2) If before the end of that period the official receiver files with the court a notice stating that investigation of the conduct and affairs of the bankrupt under section 289 is unnecessary or concluded, the bankrupt is discharged when the notice is filed.

(3) On the application of the official receiver or the trustee of a bankrupt's estate, the court may order that the period specified in subsection (1) shall cease to run until—

(a) the end of a specified period, or

(b) the fulfillment of a specified condition.

(4) The court may make an order under subsection (3) only if satisfied that the bankrupt has failed or is failing to comply with an obligation under this Part.

(5) In subsection (3)(b) 'condition' includes a condition requiring that the court be satisfied of something.

(6) In the case of an individual who is adjudged bankrupt on a petition under section 264(1)(d)—

(a) subsections (1) to (5) shall not apply, and

(b) the bankrupt is discharged from bankruptcy by an order of the court under section 280.

(7) This section is without prejudice to any power of the court to annul a bankruptcy order.

### 280   Discharge by order of the court

(1) An application for an order of the court discharging an individual from bankruptcy in a case falling within section 279(6) may be made by the bankrupt at any time after the end of the period of 5 years beginning with the date on which the bankruptcy commences.

(2) On an application under this section the court may—

(a) refuse to discharge the bankrupt from bankruptcy,

(b) make an order discharging him absolutely, or

(c) make an order discharging him subject to such conditions with respect to any income which may subsequently become due to him, or with respect to property devolving upon him, or acquired by him, after his discharge, as may be specified in the order.

(3) The court may provide for an order falling within subsection (2)(b) or (c) to have immediate effect or to have its effect suspended for such period, or until the fulfillment of such conditions (including a condition requiring the court to be satisfied as to any matter), as may be specified in the order.

[11] This section is repealed by the Criminal Justice Act 1988 c 33 from a date to be appointed. In subsection (3)(b) the words 'Supreme Court' are to be substituted for 'House of Lords' and 'subsection 4' is to be substituted for 'section 40(5) of the Powers of Criminal Courts Act 1973', and subsection 4 is added by the Constitutional Reform Act 2005 c 4 from a date to be appointed.

### 281    Effect of discharge

(1)  Subject as follows, where a bankrupt is discharged, the discharge releases him from all the bankruptcy debts, but has no effect—

(a)  on the functions (so far as they remain to be carried out) of the trustee of his estate, or

(b)  on the operation, for the purposes of the carrying out of those functions, of the provisions of this Part;

and, in particular, discharge does not affect the right of any creditor of the bankrupt to prove in the bankruptcy for any debt from which the bankrupt is released.

(2)  Discharge does not affect the right of any secured creditor of the bankrupt to enforce his security for the payment of a debt from which the bankrupt is released.

(3)  Discharge does not release the bankrupt from any bankruptcy debt which he incurred in respect of, or forbearance in respect of which was secured by means of, any fraud or fraudulent breach of trust to which he was a party.

(4)  Discharge does not release the bankrupt from any liability in respect of a fine imposed for an offence or from any liability under a recognisance except, in the case of a penalty imposed for an offence under an enactment relating to the public revenue or of a recognisance, with the consent of the Treasury.

(4A)  In subsection (4) the reference to a fine includes a reference to a confiscation order under Part 2, 3 or 4 of the Proceeds of Crime Act 2002.

(5)  Discharge does not, except to such extent and on such conditions as the court may direct, release the bankrupt from any bankruptcy debt which—

(a)  consists in a liability to pay damages for negligence, nuisance or breach of a statutory, contractual or other duty, or to pay damages by virtue of Part I of the Consumer Protection Act 1987, being in either case damages in respect of personal injuries to any person, or

(b)  arises under any order made in family proceedings or under a maintenance calculation made under the Child Support Act 1991[.. ]

(6)  Discharge does not release the bankrupt from such other bankruptcy debts, not being debts provable in his bankruptcy, as are prescribed.

(7)  Discharge does not release any person other than the bankrupt from any liability (whether as partner or co-trustee of the bankrupt or otherwise) from which the bankrupt is released by the discharge, or from any liability as surety for the bankrupt or as a person in the nature of such a surety.

(8)  In this section—

'family proceedings' means—

(a)  family proceedings within the meaning of the Magistrates' Courts Act 1980 and any proceedings which would be such proceedings but for section 65(1)(ii) of that Act (proceedings for variation of order for periodical payments); and

(b)  family proceedings within the meaning of Part V of the Matrimonial and Family Proceedings Act 1984.

'fine' means the same as in the Magistrates' Courts Act 1980; and

'personal injuries' includes death and any disease or other impairment of a person's physical or mental condition.

### 281A    Post-discharge restrictions

Schedule 4A to this Act (bankruptcy restrictions order and bankruptcy restrictions undertaking) shall have effect.

### 282    Court's power to annul bankruptcy order

(1)  The court may annul a bankruptcy order if it at any time appears to the court—

(a)  that, on any grounds existing at the time the order was made, the order ought not to have been made, or

(b)  that, to the extent required by the rules, the bankruptcy debts and the expenses of the bankruptcy have all, since the making of the order, been either paid or secured for to the satisfaction of the court.

(2)  *The court may annul a bankruptcy order made against an individual on a petition under paragraph (a), (b) or (c) of section 264(1) if it at any time appears to the court, on an application by the Official Petitioner—*

(a)  *that the petition was pending at a time when a criminal bankruptcy order was made against the individual or was presented after such an order was so made, and*

(b)  *no appeal is pending (within the meaning of section 277) against the individual's conviction of any offence by virtue of which the criminal bankruptcy order was made;*

*and the court shall annul a bankruptcy order made on a petition under section 264(1)(d) if it at any time appears to the court that the criminal bankruptcy order on which the petition was based has been rescinded in consequence of an appeal.*

(3)  The court may annul a bankruptcy order whether or not the bankrupt has been discharged from the bankruptcy.

(4)  Where the court annuls a bankruptcy order (whether under this section or under section 261or 263D in Part VIII)—

(a) any sale or other disposition of property, payment made or other thing duly done, under any provision in this Group of Parts, by or under the authority of the official receiver or a trustee of the bankrupt's estate or by the court is valid, but

(b) if any of the bankrupt's estate is then vested, under any such provision, in such a trustee, it shall vest in such person as the court may appoint or, in default of any such appointment, revert to the bankrupt on such terms (if any) as the court may direct;

and the court may include in its order such supplemental provisions as may be authorised by the rules.

(5) [...][12]

# Chapter II

# Protection of bankrupt's estate and investigation of his affairs

### 283 Definition of bankrupt's estate

(1) Subject as follows, a bankrupt's estate for the purposes of any of this Group of Parts comprises—

(a) all property belonging to or vested in the bankrupt at the commencement of the bankruptcy, and

(b) any property which by virtue of any of the following provisions of this Part is comprised in that estate or is treated as falling with the preceding paragraph.

(2) Subsection (1) does not apply to—

(a) such tools, books, vehicles and other items of equipment as are necessary to the bankrupt for use personally by him in his employment, business or vocation;

(b) such clothing, bedding, furniture, household equipment and provisions as are necessary for satisfying the basic domestic needs of the bankrupt and his family.

This subsection is subject to section 308 in Chapter IV (certain excluded property reclaimable by trustee).

(3) Subsection (1) does not apply to—

(a) property held by the bankrupt on trust for any other person, or

(b) the right of nomination to a vacant ecclesiastical benefice.

(3A) Subject to section 308A in Chapter IV, subsection (1) does not apply to—

(a) a tenancy which is an assured tenancy or an assured agricultural occupancy, within the meaning of Part I of the Housing Act 1988, and the terms of which inhibit an assignment as mentioned in section 127(5) of the Rent Act 1977, or

(b) a protected tenancy, within the meaning of the Rent Act 1977, in respect of which, by virtue of any provision of Part IX of that Act, no premium can lawfully be required as a condition of assignment, or

(c) a tenancy of a dwelling-house by virtue of which the bankrupt is, within the meaning of the Rent (Agriculture) Act 1976, a protected occupier of the dwelling-house, and the terms of which inhibit an assignment as mentioned in section 127(5) of the Rent Act 1977, or

(d) a secure tenancy, within the meaning of Part IV of the Housing Act 1985, which is not capable of being assigned, except in the cases mentioned in section 91(3) of that Act.

(4) References in any of this Group of Parts to property, in relation to a bankrupt, include references to any power exercisable by him over or in respect of property except in so far as the power is exercisable over or in respect of property not for the time being comprised in the bankrupt's estate and—

(a) is so exercisable at a time after either the official receiver has had his release in respect of that estate under section 299(2) in chapter III or a meeting summoned by the trustee of that estate under section 331 in Chapter IV has been held, or

(b) cannot be so exercised for the benefit of the bankrupt;

and a power exercisable over or in respect of property is deemed for the purposes of any of this Group of Parts to vest in the person entitled to exercise it at the time of the transaction or event by virtue of which it is exercisable by that person (whether or not it becomes so exercisable at that time).

(5) For the purposes of any such provision in this Group of Parts, property comprised in a bankrupt's estate is so comprised subject to the rights of any person other than the bankrupt (whether as a secured creditor of the bankrupt or otherwise) in relation thereto, but disregarding—

(a) any rights in relation to which a statement such as is required by section 269(1)(a) was made in the petition on which the bankrupt was adjudged bankrupt, and

(b) any rights which have been otherwise given up in accordance with the rules.

(6) This section has effect subject to the provisions of any enactment not contained in this Act under which any property is to be excluded from a bankrupt's estate.

### 283A Bankrupt's home ceasing to form part of estate

(1) This section applies where property comprised in the bankrupt's estate consists of an interest in a dwelling-house which at the date of the bankruptcy was the sole or principal residence of—

---

[12] The words in italics repealed by the Criminal Justice Act 1988 c 33 from a date to be appointed.

(a) the bankrupt,

(b) the bankrupt's spouse or civil partner, or

(c) a former spouse or former civil partner of the bankrupt.

(2) At the end of the period of three years beginning with the date of the bankruptcy the interest mentioned in subsection (1) shall—

(a) cease to be comprised in the bankrupt's estate, and

(b) vest in the bankrupt (without conveyance, assignment or transfer).

(3) Subsection (2) shall not apply if during the period mentioned in that subsection—

(a) the trustee realises the interest mentioned in subsection (1),

(b) the trustee applies for an order for sale in respect of the dwelling-house,

(c) the trustee applies for an order for possession of the dwelling-house,

(d) the trustee applies for an order under section 313 in Chapter IV in respect of that interest, or

(e) the trustee and the bankrupt agree that the bankrupt shall incur a specified liability to his estate (with or without the addition of interest from the date of the agreement) in consideration of which the interest mentioned in subsection (1) shall cease to form part of the estate.

(4) Where an application of a kind described in subsection (3)(b) to (d) is made during the period mentioned in subsection (2) and is dismissed, unless the court orders otherwise the interest to which the application relates shall on the dismissal of the application—

(a) cease to be comprised in the bankrupt's estate, and

(b) vest in the bankrupt (without conveyance, assignment or transfer).

(5) If the bankrupt does not inform the trustee or the official receiver of his interest in a property before the end of the period of three months beginning with the date of the bankruptcy, the period of three years mentioned in subsection (2)—

(a) shall not begin with the date of the bankruptcy, but

(b) shall begin with the date on which the trustee or official receiver becomes aware of the bankrupt's interest.

(6) The court may substitute for the period of three years mentioned in subsection (2) a longer period—

(a) in prescribed circumstances, and

(b) in such other circumstances as the court thinks appropriate.

(7) The rules may make provision for this section to have effect with the substitution of a shorter period for the period of three years mentioned in subsection (2) in specified circumstances (which may be described by reference to action to be taken by a trustee in bankruptcy).

(8) The rules may also, in particular, make provision—

(a) requiring or enabling the trustee of a bankrupt's estate to give notice that this section applies or does not apply;

(b) about the effect of a notice under paragraph (a);

(c) requiring the trustee of a bankrupt's estate to make an application to the Chief Land Registrar.

(9) Rules under subsection (8)(b) may, in particular—

(a) disapply this section;

(b) enable a court to disapply this section;

(c) make provision in consequence of a disapplication of this section;

(d) enable a court to make provision in consequence of a disapplication of this section;

(e) make provision (which may include provision conferring jurisdiction on a court or tribunal) about compensation.

**284    Restrictions on dispositions of property**

(1) Where a person is adjudged bankrupt, any disposition of property made by that person in the period to which this section applies is void except to the extent that it is or was made with the consent of the court, or is or was subsequently ratified by the court.

(2) Subsection (1) applies to a payment (whether in cash or otherwise) as it applies to a disposition of property and, accordingly, where any payment is void by virtue of that subsection, the person paid shall hold the sum paid for the bankrupt as part of his estate.

(3) This section applies to the period beginning with the day of the presentation of the petition for the bankruptcy order and ending with the vesting, under Chapter IV of this Part, of the bankrupt's estate in a trustee.

(4) The preceding provisions of this section do not give a remedy against any person—

(a) in respect of any property or payment which he received before the commencement of the bankruptcy in good faith, for value and without notice that the petition had been presented, or

(b) in respect of any interest in property which derives from an interest in respect of which there is, by virtue of this subsection, no remedy.

(5) Where after the commencement of his bankruptcy the bankrupt has incurred a debt to a banker or other person by reason of the making of a payment which is void under this section, that debt is

deemed for the purposes of any of this Group of Parts to have been incurred before the commencement of the bankruptcy unless—

    (a)  that banker or person had notice of the bankruptcy before the debt was incurred, or

    (b)  it is not reasonably practicable for the amount of the payment to be recovered from the person to whom it was made.

(6)  A disposition of property is void under this section notwithstanding that the property is not or, as the case may be, would not be comprised in the bankrupt's estate; but nothing in this section affects any disposition made by a person of property held by him on trust for any other person.

### 285  Restriction on proceedings and remedies

(1)  At any time when proceedings on a bankruptcy petition are pending or an individual has been adjudged bankrupt the court may stay any action, execution or other legal process against the property or person of the debtor or, as the case may be, of the bankrupt.

(2)  Any court in which proceedings are pending against any individual may, on proof that a bankruptcy petition has been presented in respect of that individual or that he is an undischarged bankrupt, either stay the proceedings or allow them to continue on such terms as it thinks fit.

(3)  After the making of a bankruptcy order no person who is a creditor of the bankrupt in respect of a debt provable in the bankruptcy shall—

    (a)  have any remedy against the property or person of the bankrupt in respect of that debt, or

    (b)  before the discharge of the bankrupt, commence any action or other legal proceedings against the bankrupt except with the leave of the court and on such terms as the court may impose.

This is subject to sections 346 (enforcement procedures) and 347 (limited right to distress).

(4)  Subject as follows, subsection (3) does not affect the right of a secured creditor of the bankrupt to enforce his security.

(5)  Where any goods of an undischarged bankrupt are held by any person by way of pledge, pawn or other security, the official receiver may, after giving notice in writing of his intention to do so, inspect the goods.

Where such a notice has been given to any person, that person is not entitled, without leave of the court, to realise his security unless he has given the trustee of the bankrupt's estate a reasonable opportunity of inspecting the goods and of exercising the bankrupt's right of redemption.

(6)  References in this section to the property or goods of the bankrupt are to any of his property or goods, whether or not comprised in his estate.

### 286  Power to appoint interim receiver

(1)  The court may, if it is shown to be necessary for the protection of the debtor's property, at any time after the presentation of a bankruptcy petition and before making a bankruptcy order, appoint the official receiver to be interim receiver of the debtor's property.

(2)  Where the court has, on a debtor's petition, appointed an insolvency practitioner under section 273 and it is shown to the court as mentioned in subsection (1) of this section, the court may, without making a bankruptcy order, appoint that practitioner, instead of the official receiver, to be interim receiver of the debtor's property.

(3)  The court may by an order appointing any person to be an interim receiver direct that his powers shall be limited or restricted in any respect; but, save as so directed, an interim receiver has, in relation to the debtor's property, all the rights, powers, duties and immunities of a receiver and manager under the next section.

(4)  An order of the court appointing any person to be an interim receiver shall require that person to take immediate possession of the debtor's property or, as the case may be, the part of it to which his powers as interim receiver are limited.

(5)  Where an interim receiver has been appointed, the debtor shall give him such inventory of his property and such other information, and shall attend on the interim receiver at such times, as the latter may for the purpose of carrying out his functions under this section reasonably require.

(6)  Where an interim receiver is appointed, section 285(3) applies for the period between the appointment and the making of a bankruptcy order on the petition, or the dismissal of the petition, as if the appointment were the making of such an order.

(7)  A person ceases to be interim receiver of a debtor's property if the bankruptcy petition relating to the debtor is dismissed, if a bankruptcy order is made on the petition or if the court by order otherwise terminates the appointment.

(8)  References in this section to the debtor's property are to all his property, whether or not it would be comprised in his estate if he were adjudged bankrupt.

### 287  Receivership pending appointment of trustee

(1)  Between the making of a bankruptcy order and the time at which the bankrupt's estate vests in a trustee under Chapter IV of this Part, the official receiver is the receiver and (subject to section 370 (special manager)) the manager of the bankrupt's estate and is under a duty to act as such.

(2)  The function of the official receiver while acting as receiver or manager of the bankrupt's estate under this section is to protect the estate; and for this purpose—

    (a)  he has the same powers as if he were a receiver or manager appointed by the High Court, and

    (b)  he is entitled to sell or otherwise dispose of any perishable goods comprised in the estate and any other goods so comprised the value of which is likely to diminish if they are not disposed of.

(3)  The official receiver while acting as receiver or manager of the estate under this section—

    (a)  shall take all such steps as he thinks fit for protecting any property which may be claimed for the estate by the trustee of that estate,

    (b)  is not, except in pursuance of directions given by the Secretary of State, required to do anything that involves his incurring expenditure,

    (c)  may, if he thinks fit (and shall, if so directed by the court) at any time summon a general meeting of the bankrupt's creditors.

(4)  Where—

    (a)  the official receiver acting as receiver or manager of the estate under this section seizes or disposes of any property which is not comprised in the estate, and

    (b)  at the time of the seizure or disposal the official receiver believes, and has reasonable grounds for believing, that he is entitled (whether in pursuance of an order of the court or otherwise) to seize or dispose of that property,

the official receiver is not to be liable to any person in respect of any loss or damage resulting from the seizure or disposal except in so far as that loss or damage is caused by his negligence; and he has a lien on the property, or the proceeds of its sale, for such of the expenses of the bankruptcy as were incurred in connection with the seizure or disposal.

(5)  This section does not apply where by virtue of section 297 (appointment of trustee; special cases) the bankrupt's estate vests in a trustee immediately on the making of the bankruptcy order.

### 288  Statement of affairs

(1)  Where a bankruptcy order has been made otherwise than on a debtor's petition, the bankrupt shall submit a statement of his affairs to the official receiver before the end of the period of 21 days beginning with the commencement of the bankruptcy.

(2)  The statement of affairs shall contain—

    (a)  such particulars of the bankrupt's creditors and of his debts and other liabilities and of his assets as may be prescribed, and

    (b)  such other information as may be prescribed.

(3)  The official receiver may, if he thinks fit—

    (a)  release the bankrupt from his duty under subsection (1), or

    (b)  extend the period specified in that subsection;

and where the official receiver has refused to exercise a power conferred by this section, the court, if it thinks fit, may exercise it.

(4)  A bankrupt who—

    (a)  without reasonable excuse fails to comply with the obligation imposed by his section, or

    (b)  without reasonable excuse submits a statement of affairs that does not comply with the prescribed requirements,

is guilty of a contempt of court and liable to be punished accordingly (in addition to any other punishment to which he may be subject).

### 289  Investigatory duties of official receiver

(1)  The official receiver shall—

    (a)  investigate the conduct and affairs of each bankrupt (including his conduct and affairs before the making of the bankruptcy order), and

    (b)  make such report (if any) to the court as the official receiver thinks fit.

(2)  Subsection (1) shall not apply to a case in which the official receiver thinks an investigation under that subsection unnecessary.

(3)  Where a bankrupt makes an application for discharge under section 280—

    (a)  the official receiver shall make a report to the court about such matters as may be prescribed, and

    (b)  the court shall consider the report before determining the application.

(4)  A report by the official receiver under this section shall in any proceedings be prima facie evidence of the facts stated in it.

### 290  Public examination of bankrupt

(1)  Where a bankruptcy order has been made, the official receiver may at any time before the discharge of the bankrupt apply to the court for the public examination of the bankrupt.

(2)  Unless the court otherwise orders, the official receiver shall make an application under subsection (1) if notice requiring him to do so is given to him, in accordance with the rules, by one of the

bankrupt's creditors with the concurrence of not less than one-half, in value, of those creditors (including the creditor giving notice).

(3) On an application under subsection (1), the court shall direct that a public examination of the bankrupt shall be held on a day appointed by the court; and the bankrupt shall attend on that day and be publicly examined as to his affairs, dealings and property.

(4) The following may take part in the public examination of the bankrupt and may question him concerning his affairs, dealings and property and the causes of his failure, namely—

    (a) the official receiver and, in the case of an individual adjudged bankrupt on a petition under section 264(1)(d), the Official Petitioner,

    (b) the trustee of the bankrupt's estate, if his appointment has taken effect,

    (c) any person who has been appointed as special manager of the bankrupt's estate or business,

    (d) any creditor of the bankrupt who has tendered a proof in the bankruptcy.

(5) If a bankrupt without reasonable excuse fails at any time to attend his public examination under this section he is guilty of a contempt of court and liable to be punished accordingly (in addition to any other punishment to which he may be subject).

### 291 Duties of bankrupt in relation to official receiver

(1) Where a bankruptcy order has been made, the bankrupt is under a duty—

    (a) to deliver possession of his estate to the official receiver, and

    (b) to deliver up to the official receiver all books, papers and other records of which he has possession or control and which relate to his estate and affairs (including any which would be privileged from disclosure in any proceedings).

(2) In the case of any part of the bankrupt's estate which consists of things possession of which cannot be delivered to the official receiver, and in the case of any property that may be claimed for the bankrupt's estate by the trustee, it is the bankrupt's duty to do all such things as may reasonably be required by the official receiver for the protection of those things or that property.

(3) Subsections (1) and (2) do not apply where by virtue of section 297 below the bankrupt's estate vests in a trustee immediately on the making of the bankruptcy order.

(4) The bankrupt shall give the official receiver such inventory of his estate and such other information, and shall attend on the official receiver at such times, as the official receiver may reasonably require—

    (a) for a purpose of this Chapter, or

    (b) in connection with the making of a bankruptcy restrictions order.

(5) Subsection (4) applies to a bankrupt after his discharge.

(6) If the bankrupt without reasonable excuse fails to comply with any obligation imposed by this section, he is guilty of a contempt of court and liable to be punished accordingly (in addition to any other punishment to which he may be subject).

# Chapter III

## Trustees in bankruptcy

*Tenure of office as trustee*

### 292 Power to make appointments

(1) The power to appoint a person as trustee of a bankrupt's estate (whether the first such trustee or a trustee appointed to fill any vacancy) is exercisable—

    (a) [...] by a general meeting of the bankrupt's creditors;

    (b) under section 295(2), 296(2) or 300(6) below in this Chapter, by the Secretary of State; or

    (c) under section 297, by the court.

(2) No person may be appointed as trustee of a bankrupt's estate unless he is, at the time of the appointment, qualified to act as an insolvency practitioner in relation to the bankrupt.

(3) Any power to appoint a person as trustee of a bankrupt's estate includes power to appoint two or more persons as joint trustees; but such an appointment must make provision as to the circumstances in which the trustees must act together and the circumstances in which one or more of them may act for the others.

(4) The appointment of any person as trustee takes effect only if that person accepts the appointment in accordance with the rules. Subject to this, the appointment of any person as trustee takes effect at the time specified in his certificate of appointment.

(5) This section is without prejudice to the provisions of this Chapter under which the official receiver is, in certain circumstances, to be trustee of the estate.

### 293 Summoning of meeting to appoint first trustee

(1) Where a bankruptcy order has been made [...] it is the duty of the official receiver, as soon as practicable in the period of 12 weeks beginning with the day on which the order was made, to decide whether to summon a general meeting of the bankrupt's creditors for the purpose of appointing a trustee of the bankrupt's estate.

*This section does not apply where the bankruptcy order was made on a petition under section 264(1)(d) (criminal bankruptcy); and it is subject to the provision made in sections 294(3) and 297(6) below.*

(2) Subject to the next section, if the official receiver decides not to summon such a meeting, he shall, before the end of the period of 12 weeks above mentioned, given notice of his decision to the court and to every creditor of the bankrupt who is known to the official receiver or is identified in the bankrupt's statement of affairs.

(3) As from the giving to the court of a notice under subsection (2), the official receiver is the trustee of the bankrupt's estate.[13]

### 294    Power of creditors to requisition meeting

(1) Where in the case of any bankruptcy—

(a) the official receiver has not yet summoned, or has decided not to summon, a general meeting of the bankrupt's creditors for the purpose of appointing the trustee, [...]

(b) [...]

any creditor of the bankrupt may request the official receiver to summon such a meeting for that purpose.

(2) If such a request appears to the official receiver to be made with the concurrence of not less than one-quarter, in value, of the bankrupt's creditors (including the creditor making the request), it is the duty of the official receiver to summon the requested meeting.

(3) Accordingly, where the duty imposed by subsection (2) has arisen, the official receiver is required neither to reach a decision for the purposes of section 293(1) nor (if he has reached one) to serve any notice under section 293(2).

### 295    Failure of meeting to appoint trustee

(1) If a meeting summoned under section 293 or 294 is held but no appointment of a person as trustee is made, it is the duty of the official receiver to decide whether to refer the need for an appointment to the Secretary of State.

(2) On a reference made in pursuance of that decision, the Secretary of State shall either make an appointment or decline to make one.

(3) If—

(a) the official receiver decides not to refer the need for an appointment to the Secretary of State, or

(b) on such a reference the Secretary of State declines to make an appointment,

the official receiver shall give notice of his decision or, as the case may be, of the Secretary of State's decision to the court.

(4) As from the giving of notice under subsection (3) in a case in which no notice has been given under section 293(2), the official receiver shall be trustee of the bankrupt's estate.

### 296    Appointment of trustee by Secretary of State

(1) At any time when the official receiver is the trustee of a bankrupt's estate by virtue of any provision of this Chapter (other than section 297(1) below) he may apply to the Secretary of State for the appointment of a person as trustee instead of the official receiver.

(2) On an application under subsection (1) the Secretary of State shall either make an appointment or decline to make one.

(3) Such an application may be made notwithstanding that the Secretary of State has declined to make an appointment either on a previous application under subsection (1) or on a reference under section 295 or under section 300(4) below.

(4) Where the trustee of a bankrupt's estate has been appointed by the Secretary of State (whether under this section or otherwise), the trustee shall give notice to the bankrupt's creditors of his appointment or, if the court so allows, shall advertise his appointment in accordance with the court's directions.

(5) In that notice or advertisement the trustee shall—

(a) state whether he proposes to summon a general meeting of the bankrupt's creditors for the purpose of establishing a creditor's committee under section 301, and

(b) if he does not propose to summon such a meeting, set out the power of the creditors under this Part to require him to summon one.

### 297    Special cases

(1) *Where a bankruptcy order is made on a petition under section 264(1)(d)(criminal bankruptcy), the official receiver shall be trustee of the bankrupt's estate.*

(2) [...]

(3) [...]

(4) Where a bankruptcy order is made in a case in which an insolvency practitioner's report has been submitted to the court under section 274 [...], the court, if it thinks fit, may on making the order appoint the person who made the report as trustee.

---

[13] The words in italics repealed by the Criminal Justice Act 1988 c 33 from a date to be appointed.

(5) Where a bankruptcy order is made (whether or not on a petition under section 264(1)(c)) at a time when there is a supervisor of a voluntary arrangement approved in relation to the bankrupt under Part VIII, the court, if it thinks fit, may on making the order appoint the supervisor of the arrangement as trustee.

(6) Where an appointment is made under subsection (4) or (5) of this section, the official receiver is not under the duty imposed by section 293(1)(to decide whether or not to summon a meeting of creditors).

(7) Where the trustee of a bankrupt's estate has been appointed by the court, the trustee shall give notice to the bankrupt's creditors of his appointment or, if the court so allows, shall advertise his appointment in accordance with the directions of the court.

(8) In that notice or advertisement he shall—
- (a) state whether he proposes to summon a general meeting of the bankrupt's creditors for the purpose of establishing a creditor's committee under section 301 below, and
- (b) if he does not propose to summon such a meeting, set out the power of the creditors under this Part to require him to summon one.[14]

### 298  Removal of trustee; vacation of office

(1) Subject as follows, the trustee of a bankrupt's estate may be removed from office only by an order of the court or by a general meeting of the bankrupt's creditors summoned specially for that purpose in accordance with the rules.

(2) Where the official receiver is trustee by virtue of section 297(1), he shall not be removed from office under this section.

(3) [...]

(4) Where the official receiver is trustee by virtue of section 293(3) or 295(4) or a trustee is appointed by the Secretary of State or (otherwise than under section 297(5)) by the court, a general meeting of the bankrupt's creditors shall be summoned for the purpose of replacing the trustee only if—
- (a) the trustee thinks fit, or
- (b) the court so directs, or
- (c) the meeting is requested by one of the bankrupt's creditors with the concurrence of not less than one-quarter, in value, of the creditors (including the creditor making the request).

(5) If the trustee was appointed by the Secretary of State, he may be removed by a direction of the Secretary of State.

(6) The trustee (not being the official receiver) shall vacate office if he ceases to be a person who is for the time being qualified to act as an insolvency practitioner in relation to the bankrupt.

(7) The trustee may, in the prescribed circumstances, resign his office by giving notice of his resignation to the court.

(8) The trustee shall vacate office on giving notice to the court that a final meeting has been held under section 331 in Chapter IV and of the decision (if any) of that meeting.

(9) The trustee shall vacate office if the bankruptcy order is annulled.

### 299  Release of trustee

(1) Where the official receiver has ceased to be the trustee of a bankrupt's estate and a person is appointed in his stead, the official receiver shall have his release with effect from the following time, that is to say—
- (a) where that person is appointed by a general meeting of the bankrupt's creditors or by the Secretary of State, the time at which the official receiver gives notice to the court that he has been replaced, and
- (b) where that person is appointed by the court, such time as the court may determine.

(2) If the official receiver while he is the trustee gives notice to the Secretary of State that the administration of the bankrupt's estate in accordance with Chapter IV of this Part is for practical purposes complete, he shall have his release with effect from such time as the Secretary of State may determine.

(3) A person other than the official receiver who has ceased to be the trustee shall have his release with effect from the following time, that is to say—
- (a) in the case of a person who has been removed from office by a general meeting of the bankrupt's creditors that has not resolved against his release or who has died, the time at which notice is given to the court in accordance with the rules that that person has ceased to hold office;
- (b) in the case of a person who has been removed from office by a general meeting of the bankrupt's creditors that has resolved against his release, or by the court, or by the Secretary of State, or who has vacated office under section 298(6), such time as the Secretary of State may, on an application by that person, determine;
- (c) in the case of a person who has resigned, such time as may be prescribed;
- (d) in the case of a person who has vacated office under section 298(8)—

---

[14] The words in italics repealed by the Criminal Justice Act 1988 c 3 from a date to be appointed.

(i)   if the final meeting referred to in that subsection has resolved against that person's release, such time as the Secretary of State may, on an application by that person, determine; and

(ii)   if that meeting has not so resolved, the time at which the person vacated office.

(4)   Where a bankruptcy order is annulled, the trustee at the time of the annulment has his release with effect from such time as the court may determine.

(5)   Where the official receiver or the trustee has his release under this section, he shall, with effect from the time specified in the preceding provisions of this section, be discharged from all liability both in respect of acts or omissions of his in the administration of the estate and otherwise in relation to his conduct as trustee.

But nothing in this section prevents the exercise, in relation to a person who has had his release under this section, of the court's powers under section 304.

### 300   Vacancy in office as trustee

(1)   This section applies where the appointment of any person as trustee of a bankrupt's estate fails to take effect or, such an appointment having taken effect, there is otherwise a vacancy in the office of trustee.

(2)   The official receiver shall be trustee until the vacancy is filled.

(3)   The official receiver may summon a general meeting of the bankrupt's creditors for the purpose of filling the vacancy and shall summon such a meeting if required to do so in pursuance of section 314(7)(creditor's requisition).

(4)   If at the end of the period of 28 days beginning with the day on which the vacancy first came to the official receiver's attention he has not summoned, and is not proposing to summon, a general meeting of creditors for the purpose of filling the vacancy, he shall refer the need for an appointment to the Secretary of State.

(5)   [...]

(6)   On a reference to the Secretary of State under subsection (4)[...] the Secretary of State shall either make an appointment or decline to make one.

(7)   If on a reference under subsection (4)[...] no appointment is made, the official receiver shall continue to be trustee of the bankrupt's estate, but without prejudice to his power to make a further reference.

(8)   References in this section to a vacancy include a case where it is necessary, in relation to any property which is or may be comprised in a bankrupt's estate, to revive the trusteeship of that estate after the holding of a final meeting summoned under section 331 or the giving by the official receiver of notice under section 299(2).

*Control of trustee*

### 301   Creditors' committee

(1)   Subject as follows, a general meeting of a bankrupt's creditors (whether summoned under the preceding provisions of this Chapter or otherwise) may, in accordance with the rules, establish a committee (known as 'the creditors' committee') to exercise the functions conferred on it by or under this Act.

(2)   A general meeting of the bankrupt's creditors shall not establish such a committee, or confer any functions on such a committee, at any time when the official receiver is the trustee of the bankrupt's estate, except in connection with an appointment made by that meeting of a person to be trustee instead of the official receiver.

### 302   Exercise by Secretary of State of functions of creditors' committee

(1)   The creditors' committee is not to be able or required to carry out its functions at any time when the official receiver is trustee of the bankrupt's estate; but at any such time the functions of the committee under this Act shall be vested in the Secretary of State, except to the extent that the rules otherwise provide.

(2)   Where in the case of any bankruptcy there is for the time being no creditors' committee and the trustee of the bankrupt's estate is a person other than the official receiver, the functions of such a committee shall be vested in the Secretary of State, except to the extent that the rules otherwise provide.

### 303   General control of trustee by the court

(1)   If a bankrupt or any of his creditors or any other person is dissatisfied by any act, omission or decision of a trustee of the bankrupt's estate, he may apply to the court; and on such an application the court may confirm, reverse or modify any act or decision of the trustee, may give him directions or may make such other order as it thinks fit.

(2)   The trustee of a bankrupt's estate may apply to the court for directions in relation to any particular matter arising under the bankruptcy.

(2A)   Where at any time after a bankruptcy petition has been presented to the court against any person, whether under the provisions of the Insolvent Partnerships Order 1994 or not, the attention of the court is drawn to the fact that the person in question is a member of an insolvent partnership, the court may make an order as to the future conduct of the insolvency proceedings and any such order may apply any provisions of that Order with any necessary modifications.

(2B) Where a bankruptcy petition has been presented against more than one individual in the circumstances mentioned in subsection (2A) above, the court may give such directions for consolidating the proceedings, or any of them, as it thinks just.

(2C) Any order or directions under subsection (2A) or (2B) may be made or given on the application of the official receiver, any responsible insolvency practitioner, the trustee of the partnership or any other interested person and may include provisions as to the administration of the joint estate of the partnership, and in particular how it and the separate estate of any member are to be administered.

### 304  Liability of trustee
(1)  Where on an application under this section the court is satisfied—
- (a) that the trustee of a bankrupt's estate has misapplied or retained, or become accountable for, any money or other property comprised in the bankrupt's estate, or
- (b) that a bankrupt's estate has suffered any loss in consequence of any misfeasance or breach of fiduciary or other duty by a trustee of the estate in the carrying out of his functions,

the court may order the trustee, for the benefit of the estate, to repay, restore or account for money or other property (together with interest at such rate as the court thinks just) or, as the case may require, to pay such sum by way of compensation in respect of the misfeasance or breach of fiduciary or other duty as the court thinks just.

This is without prejudice to any liability arising apart from this section.

(2)  An application under this section may be made by the official receiver, the Secretary of State, a creditor of the bankrupt or (whether or not there is, or is likely to be, a surplus for the purposes of section 330(5) (final distribution)) the bankrupt himself.

But the leave of the court is required for the making of an application if it is to be made by the bankrupt or if it is to be made after the trustee has had his release under section 299.

(3)  Where—
- (a) the trustee seizes or disposes of any property which is not comprised in the bankrupts estate, and
- (b) at the time of the seizure or disposal the trustee believes, and has reasonable grounds for believing, that he is entitled (whether in pursuance of an order of the court or otherwise) to seize or dispose of that property,

the trustee is not liable to any person (whether under this section or otherwise) in respect of any loss or damage resulting from the seizure or disposal except in so far as that loss or damage is caused by the negligence of the trustee; and he has a lien on the property, or the proceeds of its sale, for such of the expenses of the bankruptcy as were incurred in connection with the seizure or disposal.

# Chapter IV

## Administration by trustee

### *Preliminary*

### 305  General functions of trustee
(1)  This Chapter applies in relation to any bankruptcy where either—
- (a) the appointment of a person as trustee of a bankrupt's estate takes effect, or
- (b) the official receiver becomes trustee of a bankrupt's estate.

(2)  The function of the trustee is to get in, realise and distribute the bankrupt's estate in accordance with the following provisions of this Chapter; and in the carrying out of that function and in the management of the bankrupt's estate the trustee is entitled, subject to those provisions, to use his own discretion.

(3)  It is the duty of the trustee, if he is not the official receiver—
- (a) to furnish the official receiver with such information,
- (b) to produce to the official receiver, and permit inspection by the official receiver of, such books, papers and other records, and
- (c) to give the official receiver such other assistance,

as the official receiver may reasonably require for the purpose of enabling him to carry out his functions in relation to the bankruptcy.

(4)  The official name of the trustee shall be 'the trustee of the estate of ............, a bankrupt' (inserting the name of the bankrupt); but he may be referred to as 'the trustee in bankruptcy' of the particular bankrupt.

### *Acquisition, control and realisation of bankrupt's estate*

### 306  Vesting of bankrupt's estate in trustee
(1)  The bankrupt's estate shall vest in the trustee immediately on his appointment taking effect or, in the case of the official receiver, on his becoming trustee.

(2)  Where any property which is, or is to be, comprised in the bankrupt's estate vests in the trustee (whether under this section or under any other provision of this Part), it shall so vest without any conveyance, assignment or transfer.

### 306A  Property subject to restraint order

(1)  This section applies where—
- (a)  property is excluded from the bankrupt's estate by virtue of section 417(2)(a) of the Proceeds of Crime Act 2002 (property subject to a restraint order),
- (b)  an order under section 50, 128, 198 of that Act has not been made in respect of the property, and
- (c)  the restraint order is discharged.

(2)  On the discharge of the restraint order the property vests in the trustee as part of the bankrupt's estate.

(3)  But subsection (2) does not apply to the proceeds of property realised by a management receiver under section 49(2)(d) or 197(2)(d) of that Act (realisation of property to meet receiver's remuneration and expenses).

### 306B  Property in respect of which receivership or administration order made

(1)  This section applies where—
- (a)  property is excluded from the bankrupt's estate by virtue of section 417(2)(b), (c) or (d) of the Proceeds of Crime Act 2002 (property in respect of which an order for the appointment of a receiver or administrator under certain provisions of that Act is in force),
- (b)  a confiscation order is made under section 6, 92 or 156 of that Act,
- (c)  the amount payable under the confiscation order is fully paid, and
- (d)  any of the property remains in the hands of the receiver or administrator (as the case may be).

(2)  The property vests in the trustee as part of the bankrupt's estate.

### 306C  Property subject to certain orders where confiscation order discharged or quashed

(1)  This section applies where—
- (a)  property is excluded from the bankrupt's estate by virtue of section 417(2)(a), (b), (c) or (d) of the Proceeds of Crime Act 2002 (property in respect of which a restraint order or an order for the appointment of a receiver or administrator under that Act is in force),
- (b)  a confiscation order is made under section 6, 92 or 156 of that Act, and
- (c)  the confiscation order is discharged under section 30, 114 or 180 of that Act (as the case may be) or quashed under that Act or in pursuance of any enactment relating to appeals against conviction or sentence.

(2)  Any such property in the hands of a receiver appointed under Part 2 or 4 of that Act or an administrator appointed under Part 3 of that Act vests in the trustee as part of the bankrupt's estate.

(3)  But subsection (2) does not apply to the proceeds of property realised by a management receiver under section 49(2)(d) or 197(2)(d) of that Act (realisation of property to meet receiver's remuneration and expenses).

### 307  After-acquired property

(1)  Subject to this section and section 309, the trustee may by notice in writing claim for the bankrupt's estate any property which has been acquired by, or has devolved upon, the bankrupt since the commencement of the bankruptcy.

(2)  A notice under this section shall not be served in respect of—
- (a)   any property falling within subsection (2) or (3) of section 283 in Chapter II,
- (aa)  any property vesting in the bankrupt by virtue of section 283A in Chapter II,
- (b)   any property which by virtue of any other enactment is excluded from the bankrupt's estate, or
- (c)   without prejudice to section 280(2)(c)(order of court on application for discharge), any property which is acquired by, or devolves upon, the bankrupt after his discharge.

(3)  Subject to the next subsection, upon the service on the bankrupt of a notice under this section the property to which the notice relates shall vest in the trustee as part of the bankrupt's estate; and the trustee's title to that property has relation back to the time at which the property was acquired by, or devolved upon, the bankrupt.

(4)  Where, whether before or after service of a notice under this section—
- (a)  a person acquires property in good faith, for value and without notice of the bankruptcy, or
- (b)  a banker enters into a transaction in good faith and without such notice,

the trustee is not in respect of that property or transaction entitled by virtue of this section to any remedy against that person or banker, or any person whose title to any property derives from that person or banker.

(5)  References in this section to property do not include any property which, as part of the bankrupt's income, may be the subject of an income payments order under section 310.

### 308    Vesting in trustee of certain items of excess value

(1) Subject to section 309, where—

(a) property is excluded by virtue of section 283(2) (tools of trade, household effects, etc.) from the bankrupt's estate, and

(b) it appears to the trustee that the realisable value of the whole or any part of that property exceeds the cost of a reasonable replacement for that property or that part of it,

the trustee may by notice in writing claim that property or, as the case may be, that part of it, for the bankrupt's estate.

(2) Upon the service on the bankrupt of a notice under this section, the property to which the notice relates vests in the trustee as part of the bankrupt's estate; and, except against a purchaser in good faith, for value and without notice of the bankruptcy, the trustee's title to that property has relation back to the commencement of the bankruptcy.

(3) The trustee shall apply funds comprised in the estate to the purchase by or on behalf of the bankrupt of a reasonable replacement for any property vested in the trustee under this section; and the duty imposed by this subsection has priority over the obligation of the trustee to distribute the estate.

(4) For the purposes of this section property is a reasonable replacement for other property if it is reasonably adequate for meeting the needs met by the other property.

### 308A    Vesting in trustee of certain tenancies

Upon the service on the bankrupt by the trustee of a notice in writing under this section, any tenancy—

(a) which is excluded by virtue of section 283(3A) from the bankrupt's estate, and

(b) to which the notice relates,

vests in the trustee as part of the bankrupt's estate; and, except against a purchaser in good faith, for value and without notice of the bankruptcy, the trustee's title to that tenancy has relation back to the commencement of the bankruptcy.

### 309    Time-limit for notice under s 307 or 308

(1) Except with the leave of the court, a notice shall not be served—

(a) under section 307, after the end of the period of 42 days beginning with the day on which it first came to the knowledge of the trustee that property in question had been acquired by, or had devolved upon, the bankrupt;

(b) under section 308 or section 308A, after the end of the period of 42 days beginning with the day on which the property or tenancy in question first came to the knowledge of the trustee.

(2) For the purposes of this section—

(a) any thing which comes to the knowledge of the trustee is deemed in relation to any successor of his as trustee to have come to the knowledge of the sucessor at the same time; and

(b) any thing which comes (otherwise than under paragraph (a)) to the knowledge of a person before he is the trustee is deemed to come to his knowledge on his appointment taking effect or, in the case of the official receiver, on his becoming trustee.

### 310    Income payments orders

(1) The court may [...] make an order ('an income payments order') claiming for the bankrupt's estate so much of the income of the bankrupt during the period for which the order is in force as may be specified in the order.

(1A) An income payments order may be made only on an application instituted—

(a) by the trustee, and

(b) before the discharge of the bankrupt.

(2) The court shall not make an income payments order the effect of which would be to reduce the income of the bankrupt when taken together with any payments to which subsection (8) applies below what appears to the court to be necessary for meeting the reasonable domestic needs of the bankrupt and his family.

(3) An income payments order shall, in respect of any payment of income to which it is to apply, either—

(a) require the bankrupt to pay the trustee an amount equal to so much of that payment as is claimed by the order, or

(b) require the person making the payment to pay so much of it as is so claimed to the trustee, instead of to the bankrupt.

(4) Where the court makes an income payments order it may, if it thinks fit, discharge or vary any attachment of earnings order that is for the time being in force to secure payments by the bankrupt.

(5) Sums received by the trustee under an income payments order form part of the bankrupt's estate.

(6) An income payments order must specify the period during which it is to have effect; and that period—

(a) may end after the discharge of the bankrupt, but

(b) may not end after the period of three years beginning with the date on which the order is made.

(6A)  An income payments order may (subject to subsection (6)(b)) be varied on the application of the trustee or the bankrupt (whether before or after discharge).

(7)  For the purposes of this section the income of the bankrupt comprises every payment in the nature of income which is from time to time made to him or to which he from time to time becomes entitled, including any payment in respect of the carrying on of any business or in respect of any office or employment and (despite anything in section 11 or 12 of the Welfare Reform and Pensions Act 1999) any payment under a pension scheme but excluding any payment to which subsection (8) applies.

(8)  This subsection applies to—
    (a)  payments by way of guaranteed minimum pension; and
    (b)  payments giving effect to the bankrupt's protected rights as a member of a pension scheme.

(9)  In this section, 'guaranteed minimum pension' and 'protected rights' have the same meaning as in the Pension Schemes Act 1993.

### 310A  Income payments agreement

(1)  In this section 'income payments agreement' means a written agreement between a bankrupt and his trustee or between a bankrupt and the official receiver which provides—
    (a)  that the bankrupt is to pay to the trustee or the official receiver an amount equal to a speci-fied part or proportion of the bankrupt's income for a specified period, or
    (b)  that a third person is to pay to the trustee or the official receiver a specified proportion of money due to the bankrupt by way of income for a specified period.

(2)  A provision of an income payments agreement of a kind specified in subsection (1)(a) or (b) may be enforced as if it were a provision of an income payments order.

(3)  While an income payments agreement is in force the court may, on the application of the bank-rupt, his trustee or the official receiver, discharge or vary an attachment of earnings order that is for the time being in force to secure payments by the bankrupt.

(4)  The following provisions of section 310 shall apply to an income payments agreement as they apply to an income payments order—
    (a)  subsection (5)(receipts to form part of estate), and
    (b)  subsections (7) to (9)(meaning of income).

(5)  An income payments agreement must specify the period during which it is to have effect; and that period—
    (a)  may end after the discharge of the bankrupt, but
    (b)  may not end after the period of three years beginning with the date on which the agreement is made.

(6)  An income payments agreement may (subject to subsection (5)(b)) be varied—
    (a)  by written agreement between the parties, or
    (b)  by the court on an application made by the bankrupt, the trustee or the official receiver.

(7)  The court—
    (a)  may not vary an income payments agreement so as to include provision of a kind which could not be included in an income payments order, and
    (b)  shall grant an application to vary an income payments agreement if and to the extent that the court thinks variation necessary to avoid the effect mentioned in section 310(2).

### 311  Acquisition by trustee of control

(1)  The trustee shall take possession of all books, papers and other records which relate to the bankrupt's estate or affairs and which belong to him or are in his possession or under his control (includ-ing any which would be privileged from disclosure in any proceedings).

(2)  In relation to, and for the purpose of acquiring or retaining possession of, the bankrupt's estate, the trustee is in the same position as if her were a receiver of property appointed by the High Court; and the court may, on his application, enforce such acquisition or retention accordingly.

(3)  Where any part of the bankrupt's estate consists of stock or shares in a company, shares in a ship or any other property transferable in the books of a company, office or person, the trustee may exercise the right to transfer the property to the same extent as the bankrupt might have exercised it if he had not become bankrupt.

(4)  Where any part of the estate consists of things in action, they are deemed to have been assigned to the trustee; but notice of the deemed assignment need not be given except in so far as it is necessary, in a case where the deemed assignment is from the bankrupt himself for protecting the priority of the trustee.

(5)  Where any goods comprised in the estate are held by any person by way of pledge, pawn or other security and no notice has been served in respect of those goods by the official receiver under subsection (5) of section 285 (restriction on realising security), the trustee may serve such a notice in respect of the goods; and whether or not a notice has been served under this subsection or that subsec-tion, the trustee may, if he thinks fit, exercise the bankrupt's right of redemption in respect of any such goods.

(6)  A notice served by the trustee under subsection (5) has the same effect as a notice served by the official receiver under section 285(5).

### 312   Obligation to surrender control to trustee

(1)  The bankrupt shall deliver up to the trustee possession of any property, books, papers or other records of which he has possession or control and of which the trustee is required to take possession. This is without prejudice to the general duties of the bankrupt under section 333 in this Chapter.

(2)  If any of the following is in possession of any property, books, papers or other records of which the trustee is required to take possession, namely—

   (a)  the official receiver,

   (b)  a person who has ceased to be trustee of the bankrupt's estate, or

   (c)  a person who has been the supervisor of a voluntary arrangement approved in relation to the bankrupt under Part VIII,

the official receiver or, as the case may be, that person shall deliver up possession of the property, books, papers or records to the trustee.

(3)  Any banker or agent of the bankrupt or any other person who holds any property to the account of, or for, the bankrupt shall pay or deliver to the trustee all property in his possession or under his control which forms part of the bankrupt's estate and which he is not by law entitled to retain as against the bankrupt or trustee.

(4)  If any person without reasonable excuse fails to comply with any obligation imposed by this section, he is guilty of a contempt of court and liable to be punished accordingly (in addition to any other punishment to which he may be subject).

### 313   Charge on bankrupt's home

(1)  Where any property consisting of an interest in a dwelling house which is occupied by the bankrupt or by his spouse or former spouse or by his civil partner or former civil partner is comprised in the bankrupt's estate and the trustee is, for any reason, unable for the time being to realise that property, the trustee may apply to the court for an order imposing a charge on the property for the benefit of the bankrupt's estate.

(2)  If on an application under this section the court imposes a charge on any property, the benefit of that charge shall be comprised in the bankrupt's estate and is enforceable ,up to the charged value from time to time, for the payment of any amount which is payable otherwise than to the bankrupt out of the estate and of interest on that amount at the prescribed rate.

(2A)  In subsection (2) the charged value means—

   (a)  the amount specified in the charging order as the value of the bankrupt's interest in the property at the date of the order, plus

   (b)  interest on that amount from the date of the charging order at the prescribed rate.

(2B)  In determining the value of an interest for the purposes of this section the court shall disregard any matter which it is required to disregard by the rules.

(3)  An order under this section made in respect of property vested in the trustee shall provide, in accordance with the rules, for the property to cease to be comprised in the bankrupt's estate and, subject to the charge (and any prior charge), to vest in the bankrupt.

(4)  Subsections (1) and (2) and (4) , 5 and (6) of section 3 of the Charging Orders Act 1979 (supplemental provisions with respect to charging orders) have effect in relation to orders under this section as in relation to charging orders under that Act.

(5)  But an order under section 3(5) of that Act may not vary a charged value.[15]

### 313A   Low value home: application for sale, possession or charge

(1)  This section applies where—

   (a)  property comprised in the bankrupt's estate consists of an interest in a dwelling-house which at the date of the bankruptcy was the sole or principal residence of—

      (i)  the bankrupt,

      (ii)  the bankrupt's spouse or civil partner, or

      (iii)  a former spouse or former civil partner of the bankrupt, and

   (b)  the trustee applies for an order for the sale of the property, for an order for possession of the property or for an order under section 313 in respect of the property.

(2)  The court shall dismiss the application if the value of the interest is below the amount prescribed for the purposes of this subsection.

(3)  In determining the value of an interest for the purposes of this section the court shall disregard any matter which it is required to disregard by the order which prescribes the amount for the purposes of subsection (2).

### 314   Powers of trustee

(1)  The trustee may—

   (a)  with the permission of the creditor's committee or the court, exercise any of the powers specified in Part I of Schedule 5 to this Act, and

   (b)  without that permission, exercise any of the general powers specified in Part II of that Schedule.

---

[15]  Subsection (4) amended by the Tribunals Courts and Enforcement Act 2007 c 5 from a date to be appointed.

(2) With the permission of the creditors' committee or the court, the trustee may appoint the bankrupt—

    (a) to superintend the management of his estate or any part of it,

    (b) to carry on his business (if any) for the benefit of his creditors, or

    (c) in any other respect to assist in administering the estate in such manner and on such terms as the trustee may direct.

(3) A permission given for the purposes of subsection (1)(a) or (2) shall not be a general permission but shall relate to a particular exercise of the power in question; and a person dealing with the trustee in good faith and for value is not to be concerned to enquire whether any permission required in either case has been given.

(4) Where the trustee has done anything without the permission required by subsection (1)(a) or (2), the court or the creditor's committee may, for the purpose of enabling him to meet his expenses out of the bankrupt's estate, ratify what the trustee has done.

But the committee shall not do so unless it is satisfied that the trustee has acted in a case or urgency and has sought its ratification without undue delay.

(5) Part III of Schedule 5 to this Act has effect with respect to the things which the trustee is able to do for the purposes of, or in connection with, the exercise of any of his powers under any of his Group of Parts.

(6) Where the trustee (not being the official receiver) in exercise of the powers conferred on him by any provision in this Group of Parts—

    (a) disposes of any property comprised in the bankrupt's estate to an associate of the bankrupt, or

    (b) employs a solicitor,

he shall, if there is for the time being a creditor's committee, give notice to the committee of that exercise of his powers.

(7) Without prejudice to the generality of subsection (5) and Part III of Schedule 5, the trustee may, if he thinks fit, at any time summon a general meeting of the bankrupt's creditors.

Subject to the preceding provisions in this Group of Parts, he shall summon such a meeting if he is requested to do so by a creditor of the bankrupt and the request is made with the concurrence of not less than one-tenth, in value, of the bankrupt's creditors (including the creditor making the request).

(8) Nothing in this Act is to be construed as restricting the capacity of the trustee to exercise any of his powers outside England and Wales.

*Disclaimer of onerous property*

### 315 Disclaimer (general power)

(1) Subject as follows, the trustee may, by the giving of the prescribed notice, disclaim any onerous property and may do so notwithstanding that he has taken possession of it, endeavoured to sell it or otherwise exercised rights of ownership in relation to it.

(2) The following is onerous property for the purposes of this section, that is to say—

    (a) any unprofitable contract, and

    (b) any other property comprised in the bankrupt's estate which is unsaleable or not readily saleable, or is such that it may give rise to a liability to pay money or perform any other onerous act.

(3) A disclaimer under this section—

    (a) operates so as to determine, as from the date of the disclaimer, the rights, interests and liabilities of the bankrupt and his estate in or in respect of the property disclaimed, and

    (b) discharges the trustee from all personal liability in respect of that property as from the commencement of his trusteeship,

but does not, except so far as is necessary for the purpose of releasing the bankrupt, the bankrupt's estate and the trustee from any liability, affect the rights or liabilities of any other person.

(4) A notice of disclaimer shall not be given under this section in respect of any property that has been claimed for the estate under section 307 (after-acquired property) or 308 (personal property of bankrupt exceeding reasonable replacement value) or 308A, except with the leave of the court.

(5) Any person sustaining loss or damage in consequence of the operation of a disclaimer under this section is deemed to be a creditor of the bankrupt to the extent of the loss or damage and accordingly may prove for the loss or damage as a bankruptcy debt.

### 316 Notice requiring trustee's decision

(1) Notice of disclaimer shall not be given under section 315 in respect of any property if—

    (a) a person interested in the property has applied in writing to the trustee or one of his predecessors as trustee requiring the trustee or that predecessor to decide whether he will disclaim or not, and

    (b) the period of 28 days beginning with the day on which that application was made has expired without a notice of disclaimer having been given under section 315 in respect of that property.

(2) The trustee is deemed to have adopted any contract which by virtue of this section he is not entitled to disclaim.

### 317 Disclaimer of leaseholds

(1) The disclaimer of any property of a leasehold nature does not take effect unless a copy of the disclaimer has been served (so far as the trustee is aware of their addresses) on every person claiming under the bankrupt as underlessee or mortgagee and either—

    (a) no application under section 320 below is made with respect to the property before the end of the period of 14 days beginning with the day on which the last notice served under this subsection was served, or

    (b) where such an application has been made, the court directs that the disclaimer is to take effect.

(2) Where the court gives a direction under subsection (1)(b) it may also, instead of or in addition to any order it makes under section 320, make such orders with respect to fixtures, tenant's improvements and other matters arising out of the lease as it thinks fit.

### 318 Disclaimer of dwelling house

Without prejudice to section 317, the disclaimer of any property in a dwelling house does not take effect unless a copy of the disclaimer has been served (so far as the trustee is aware of their addresses) on every person in occupation of or claiming a right to occupy the dwelling house and either—

    (a) no application under section 320 is made with respect to the property before the end of the period of 14 days beginning with the day on which the last notice served under this section was served, or

    (b) where such an application has been made, the court directs that the disclaimer is to take effect.

### 319 Disclaimer of land subject to rentcharge

(1) The following applies where, in consequence of the disclaimer under section 315 of any land subject to a rentcharge, that land vests by operation of law in the Crown or any other person (referred to in the next subsection as 'the proprietor').

(2) The proprietor, and the successors in title of the proprietor, are not subject to any personal liability in respect of any sums becoming due under the rentcharge, except sums becoming due after the proprietor, or some person claiming under or through the proprietor, has taken possession or control of the land or has entered into occupation of it.

### 320 Court order vesting disclaimed property

(1) This section and the next apply where the trustee has disclaimed property under section 315.

(2) An application may be made to the court under this section by—

    (a) any person who claims an interest in the disclaimed property,

    (b) any person who is under any liability in respect of the disclaimed property, not being a liability discharged by the disclaimer, or

    (c) where the disclaimed property is property in a dwelling house, any person who at the time when the bankruptcy petition was presented was in occupation of or entitled to occupy the dwelling house.

(3) Subject as follows in this section and the next, the court may, on an application under this section, make an order on such terms as it thinks fit for the vesting of the disclaimed property in, or for its delivery to—

    (a) a person entitled to it or a trustee for such a person,

    (b) a person subject to such a liability as is mentioned in subsection (2)(b) or a trustee for such a person, or

    (c) where the disclaimed property is property in a dwelling house, any person who at the time when the bankruptcy petition was presented was in occupation of or entitled to occupy the dwelling house.

(4) The court shall not make an order by virtue of subsection (3)(b) except where it appears to the court that it would be just to do so for the purpose of compensating the person subject to the liability in respect of the disclaimer.

(5) The effect of any order under this section shall be taken into account in assessing for the purposes of section 315(5) the extent of any loss or damage sustained by any person in consequence of the disclaimer.

(6) An order under this section vesting property in any person need not be completed by any conveyance, assignment or transfer.

### 321 Order under s 320 in respect of leaseholds

(1) The court shall not make an order under section 320 vesting property of a leasehold nature in any person, except on terms making that person—

    (a) subject to the same liabilities and obligations as the bankrupt was subject to under the lease on the day the bankruptcy petition was presented, or

(b) if the court thinks fit, subject to the same liabilities and obligations as that person would be subject to if the lease had been assigned to him on that day.

(2) For the purposes of an order under section 320 relating to only part of any property comprised in a lease, the requirements of subsection (1) apply as if the lease comprised only the property to which the order relates.

(3) Where subsection (1) applies and no person is willing to accept an order under section 320 on the terms required by that subsection, the court may (by order under section 320) vest the estate or interest in the bankrupt in the property in any person who is liable (whether personally or in a representative capacity and whether alone or jointly with the bankrupt) to perform the lessee's covenants in the lease.

The court may by virtue of this subsection vest that estate and interest in such a person freed and discharged from all estates, incumbrances and interests created by the bankrupt.

(4) Where subsection (1) applies and a person declines to accept any order under section 320, that person shall be excluded from all interest in the property.

### *Distribution of bankrupt's estate*

### 322    Proof of debts

(1) Subject to this section and the next, the proof of any bankruptcy debt by a secured or unsecured creditor of the bankrupt and the admission or rejection of any proof shall take place in accordance with the rules.

(2) Where a bankruptcy debt bears interest, that interest is provable as part of the debt except in so far as it is payable in respect of any period after the commencement of the bankruptcy.

(3) The trustee shall estimate the value of any bankruptcy debt which, by reason of its being subject to any contingency or contingencies or for any other reason, does not bear a certain value.

(4) Where the value of a bankruptcy debt is estimated by the trustee under subsection (3) or, by virtue of section 303 in Chapter III, by the court, the amount provable in the bankruptcy in respect of the debt is the amount of the estimate.

### 323    Mutual credit and set-off

(1) This section applies where before the commencement of the bankruptcy there have been mutual credits, mutual debts or other mutual dealings between the bankruptcy and any creditor of the bankrupt proving or claiming to prove for a bankruptcy debt.

(2) An account shall be taken of what is due from each party to the other in respect of the mutual dealings and the sums due from one party shall be set off against the sums due from the other.

(3) Sums due from the bankrupt to another party shall not be included in the account taken under subsection (2) if that other party had notice at the time they became due that a bankruptcy petition relating to the bankrupt was pending.

(4) Only the balance (if any) of the account taken under subsection (2) is provable as a bankruptcy debt or, as the case may be, to be paid to the trustee as part of the bankrupt's estate.

### 324    Distribution by means of dividend

(1) Whenever the trustee has sufficient funds in hand for the purpose he shall, subject to the retention of such sums as may be necessary for the expenses of the bankruptcy, declare and distribute dividends among the creditors in respect of the bankruptcy debts which they have respectively proved.

(2) The trustee shall give notice of his intention to declare and distribute a dividend.

(3) Where the trustee has declared a dividend, he shall give notice of the dividend and of how it is proposed to distribute it; and a notice given under this subsection shall contain the prescribed particulars of the bankrupt's estate.

(4) In the calculation and distribution of a dividend the trustee shall make provision—

(a) for any bankruptcy debts which appear to him to be due to persons who, by reason of the distance of their place of residence, may not have had sufficient time to tender and establish their proofs,

(b) for any bankruptcy debts which are the subject of claims which have not yet been determined, and

(c) for disputed proofs and claims.

### 325    Claims by unsatisfied creditors

(1) A creditor who has not proved his debt before the declaration of any dividend is not entitled to disturb, by reason that he has not participated in it, the distribution of that dividend or any other dividend declared before his debt was proved, but—

(a) when he has proved that debt he is entitled to be paid, out of any money for the time being available for the payment of any further dividend, any dividend or dividends which he has failed to receive; and

(b) any dividend or dividends payable under paragraph (a) shall be paid before that money is applied to the payment of any such further dividend.

(2) No action lies against the trustee for a dividend, but if the trustee refuses to pay a dividend the court may, if it thinks fit, order him to pay it and also to pay, out of his own money—

(a) interest on the dividend, at the rate for the time being specified in section 17 of the Judgments Act 1838, from the time it was withheld, and

(b) the costs of the proceedings in which the order to pay is made.

### 326 Distribution of property in specie

(1) Without prejudice to sections 315 to 319 (disclaimer), the trustee may, with the permission of the creditors' committee, divide in its existing form amongst the bankrupt's creditors, according to its estimated value, any property which from its peculiar nature or other special circumstances cannot be readily or advantageously sold.

(2) A permission given for the purposes of subsection (1) shall not be a general permission but shall relate to a particular proposed exercise of the power in question; and a person dealing with the trustee in good faith and for value is not to be concerned to enquire whether any permission required by subsection (1) has been given.

(3) Where the trustee has done anything without the permission required by subsection (1), the court or the creditors' committee may, for the purpose of enabling him to meet his expenses out of the bankrupt's estate, ratify what the trustee has done.

But the committee shall not do so unless it is satisfied that the trustee acted in a case of urgency and has sought its ratification without undue delay.

### 327 *Distribution in criminal bankruptcy*

*Where the bankruptcy order was made on a petition under section 264(1)(d)(criminal bankruptcy), no distribution shall be made under sections 324 to 326 so long as an appeal is pending (within the meaning of section 277) against the bankrupt's conviction of any offence by virtue of which the criminal bankruptcy order on which the petition was based was made.*[16]

### 328 Priority of debts

(1) In the distribution of the bankrupt's estate, his preferential debts (within the meaning given by section 386 in Part XII) shall be paid in priority to other debts.

(2) Preferential debts rank equally between themselves after the expenses of the bankruptcy and shall be paid in full unless the bankrupt's estate is insufficient for meeting them, in which case they abate in equal proportions between themselves.

(3) Debts which are neither preferential debts nor debts to which the next section applies also rank equally between themselves and, after the preferential debts, shall be paid in full unless the bankrupt's estate is insufficient for meeting them, in which case they abate in equal proportions between themselves.

(4) Any surplus remaining after the payment of the debts that are preferential or rank equally under subsection (3) shall be applied in paying interest on those debts in respect of the periods during which they have been outstanding since the commencement of the bankruptcy; and interest on preferential debts ranks equally with interest on debts other than preferential debts.

(5) The rate of interest payable under subsection (4) in respect of any debt is whichever is the greater of the following—

(a) the rate specified in section 17 of the Judgments Act 1838 at the commencement of the bankruptcy, and

(b) the rate applicable to that debt apart from the bankruptcy.

(6) This section and the next are without prejudice to any provision of this Act or any other Act under which the payment of any debt or the making of any other payment is, in the event of bankruptcy, to have a particular priority or to be postponed.

### 329 Debts to spouse

(1) This section applies to bankruptcy debts owed in respect of credit provided by a person who (whether or not the bankrupt's spouse or civil partner at the time the credit was provided) was the bankrupt's spouse or civil partner at the commencement of the bankruptcy.

(2) Such debts—

(a) rank in priority after the debts and interest required to be paid in pursuance of section 328(3) and (4), and

(b) are payable with interest at the rate specified in section 328(5) in respect of the period during which they have been outstanding since the commencement of the bankruptcy;

and the interest payable under paragraph (b) has the same priority as the debts on which it is payable.

### 330 Final distribution

(1) When the trustee has realised all the bankrupt's estate or so much of it as can, in the trustee's opinion, be realised without needlessly protracting the trusteeship, he shall give notice in the prescribed manner either—

---

[16] Section 327 is repealed by the Criminal Justice Act 1988 c 3 from a date to be appointed.

     (a) of his intention to declare a final dividend, or

     (b) that no dividend, or further dividend, will be declared.

  (2) The notice under subsection (1) shall contain the prescribed particulars and shall require claims against the bankrupt's estate to be established by a date ('the final date') specified in the notice.

  (3) The court may, on the application of any person, postpone the final date.

  (4) After the final date, the trustee shall—

     (a) defray any outstanding expenses of the bankruptcy out of the bankrupt's estate, and

     (b) if he intends to declare a final dividend, declare and distribute that dividend without regard to the claim of any person in respect of a debt not already proved in the bankruptcy.

  (5) If a surplus remains after payment in full and with interest of all the bankrupt's creditors and the payment of the expenses of the bankruptcy, the bankrupt is entitled to the surplus.

  (6) Subsection (5) is subject to Article 35 of the EC Regulation (surplus in secondary proceedings to be transferred to main proceedings).

## 331   Final meeting

  (1) Subject as follows in this section and the next, this section applies where—

     (a) it appears to the trustee that the administration of the bankrupt's estate in accordance with this Chapter is for practical purposes complete, and

     (b) the trustee is not the official receiver.

  (2) The trustee shall summon a final general meeting of the bankrupt's creditors which—

     (a) shall receive the trustee's report of his administration of the bankrupt's estate, and

     (b) shall determine whether the trustee should have his release under section 299 in Chapter III.

  (3) The trustee may, if he thinks fit, give the notice summoning the final general meeting at the same time as giving notice under section 330(1); but, if summoned for an earlier date, that meeting shall be adjourned (and, if necessary, further adjourned) until a date on which the trustee is able to report to the meeting that the administration of the bankrupt's estate is for practical purposes complete.

  (4) In the administration of the estate it is the trustee's duty to retain sufficient sums from the estate to cover the expenses of summoning and holding the meeting required by this section.

## 332   Saving for bankrupt's home

  (1) This section applies where—

     (a) there is comprised in the bankrupt's estate property consisting of an interest in a dwelling house which is occupied by the bankrupt or by his spouse or former spouse or by his civil partner or former civil partner, and

     (b) the trustee has been unable for any reason to realise that property.

  (2) The trustee shall not summon a meeting under section 331 unless either—

     (a) the court has made an order under section 313 imposing a charge on that property for the benefit of the bankrupt's estate, or

     (b) the court has declined, on an application under that section, to make such an order, or

     (c) the Secretary of State has issued a certificate to the trustee stating that it would be inappropriate or inexpedient for such an application to be made in the case in question.

### *Supplemental*

## 333   Duties of bankrupt in relation to trustee

  (1) The bankrupt shall—

     (a) give to the trustee such information as to his affairs,

     (b) attend on the trustee at such times, and

     (c) do all such other things,

as the trustee may for the purposes of carrying out his functions under any of this Group of Parts reasonably require.

  (2) Where at any time after the commencement of the bankruptcy any property is acquired by, or devolves upon, the bankrupt or there is an increase of the bankrupt's income, the bankrupt shall, within the prescribed period, give the trustee notice of the property or, as the case may be, of the increase.

  (3) Subsection (1) applies to a bankrupt after his discharge.

  (4) If the bankrupt without reasonable excuse fails to comply with any obligation imposed by this section, he is guilty of a contempt of court and liable to be punished accordingly (in addition to any other punishment to which he may be subject).

## 334   Stay of distribution in case of second bankruptcy

  (1) This section and the next apply where a bankruptcy order is made against an undischarged bankrupt; and in both sections—

     (a) 'the later bankruptcy' means the bankruptcy arising from that order,

     (b) 'the earlier bankruptcy' means the bankruptcy (or, as the case may be, most recent bankruptcy) from which the bankrupt has not been discharged at the commencement of the later bankruptcy, and

(c) 'the existing trustee' means the trustee (if any) of the bankrupt's estate for the purposes of the earlier bankruptcy.

(2) Where the existing trustee has been given the prescribed notice of the presentation of the petition of the later bankruptcy, any distribution or other disposition by him of anything to which the next subsection applies, if made after the giving of the notice, is void except to the extent that it was made with the consent of the court or is or was subsequently ratified by the court.

This is without prejudice to section 284 (restrictions on dispositions of property following bankruptcy order).

(3) This subsection applies to—

(a) any property which is vested in the existing trustee under section 307(3)(after-acquired property);

(b) any money paid to the existing trustee in pursuance of an income payments order under section 310; and

(c) any property or money, which is, or in the hands of the existing trustee represents, the proceeds of sale or application of property or money falling within paragraph (a) or (b) of this subsection.

### 335  Adjustment between earlier and later bankruptcy estates

(1) With effect from the commencement of the later bankruptcy anything to which section 334(3) applies which, immediately before the commencement of that bankruptcy, is comprised in the bankrupt's estate for the purposes of the earlier bankruptcy is to be treated as comprised in the bankrupt's estate for the purposes of the later bankruptcy and, until there is a trustee of that estate, is to be dealt with by the existing trustee in accordance with the rules.

(2) Any sums which in pursuance of an income payments order under section 310 are payable after the commencement of the later bankruptcy to the existing trustee shall form part of the bankrupt's estate for the purposes of the later bankruptcy; and the court may give such consequential directions for the modification of the order as it thinks fit.

(3) Anything comprised in a bankrupt's estate by virtue of subsection (1) or (2) is so comprised subject to a first charge in favour of the existing trustee for any bankruptcy expenses incurred by him in relation thereto.

(4) Except as provided above and in section 334, property which is, or by virtue of section 308 (personal property of bankrupt exceeding reasonable replacement value) or section 308A (vesting in trustee of certain tenancies) is capable of being, comprised in the bankrupt's estate for the purposes of the earlier bankruptcy, or of any bankruptcy prior to it, shall not be comprised in his estate for the purposes of the later bankruptcy.

(5) The creditors of the bankrupt in the earlier bankruptcy and the creditors of the bankrupt in any bankruptcy prior to the earlier one, are not to be creditors of his in the later bankruptcy in respect of the same debts; but the existing trustee may prove in the later bankruptcy for—

(a) the unsatisfied balance of the debts (including any debt under this subsection) provable against the bankrupt's estate in the earlier bankruptcy;

(b) any interest payable on that balance; and

(c) any unpaid expenses of the earlier bankruptcy.

(6) Any amount provable under subsection (5) ranks in priority after all the other debts provable in the later bankruptcy and after interest on those debts and, accordingly, shall not be paid unless those debts and that interest have first been paid in full.

# Chapter V

# Effect of bankruptcy on certain rights transactions, etc.

*Rights under trusts of land*

### 335A  Rights under trusts of land

(1) Any application by a trustee of a bankrupt's estate under section 14 of the Trusts of Land and Appointment of Trustees Act 1996 (powers of court in relation to trusts of land) for an order under that section for the sale of land shall be made to the court having jurisdiction in relation to the bankruptcy.

(2) On such an application the court shall make such order as it thinks just and reasonable having regard to—

(a) the interests of the bankrupt's creditors;

(b) where the application is made in respect of land which includes a dwelling house which is or has been the home of the bankrupt or the bankrupt's spouse or civil partner or former spouse or former civil partner—

(i) the conduct of the spouse, civil partner, former spouse or former civil partner, so far as contributing to the bankruptcy,

(ii) the needs and financial resources of the spouse, civil partner, former spouse or former civil partner, and

(iii) the needs of any children; and

(c) all the circumstances of the case other than the needs of the bankrupt.

(3) Where such an application is made after the end of the period of one year beginning with the first vesting under Chapter IV of this Part of the bankrupt's estate in a trustee, the court shall assume, unless the circumstances of the case are exceptional, that the interests of the bankrupt's creditors outweigh all other considerations.

(4) The powers conferred on the court by this section are exercisable on an application whether it is made before or after the commencement of this section.

*Rights of occupation*

### 336 Rights of occupation etc of bankrupt's spouse or civil partner

(1) Nothing occurring in the initial period of the bankruptcy (that is to say, the period beginning with the day of the presentation of the petition for the bankruptcy order and ending with the vesting of the bankrupt's estate in a trustee) is to be taken as having given rise to any home rights under Part IV of the Family Law Act 1996 in relation to a dwelling house comprised in the bankrupt's estate.

(2) Where a spouse's or civil partner's home rights under the Act of 1996 are a charge on the estate or interest of the other spouse or civil partner, or of trustees for the other spouse or civil partner, and the other spouse or civil partner is adjudged bankrupt—

(a) the charge continues to subsist notwithstanding the bankruptcy and, subject to the provisions of that Act, binds the trustee of the bankrupt's estate and persons deriving title under the trustee, and

(b) any application for an order under section 33 of that Act shall be made to the court having jurisdiction in relation to the bankruptcy.

(3) [...]

(4) On such an application as is mentioned in subsection (2) [...] the court shall make such order under section 33 of the Act of 1996 [...] as it thinks just and reasonable having regard to—

(a) the interests of the bankrupt's creditors,

(b) the conduct of the spouse or former spouse or civil partner or former civil partner, so far as contributing to the bankruptcy,

(c) the needs and financial resources of the spouse or former spouse or civil partner or former civil partner,

(d) the needs of any children, and

(e) all the circumstances of the case other than the needs of the bankrupt.

(5) Where such an application is made after the end of the period of one year beginning with the first vesting under Chapter IV of this Part of the bankrupt's estate in a trustee, the court shall assume, unless the circumstances of the case are exceptional, that the interests of the bankrupt's creditors outweigh all other considerations.

### 337 Rights of occupation of bankrupt

(1) This section applies where—

(a) a person who is entitled to occupy a dwelling house by virtue of a beneficial estate or interest is adjudged bankrupt, and

(b) any persons under the age of 18 with whom that person had at some time occupied that dwelling house had their home with that person at the time when the bankruptcy petition was presented and at the commencement of the bankruptcy.

(2) Whether or not the bankrupt's spouse or civil partner (if any) has home rights under Part IV of the Family Law Act 1996—

(a) the bankrupt has the following rights as against the trustee of his estate—

(i) if in occupation, a right not to be evicted or excluded from the dwelling house or any part of it, except with the leave of the court,

(ii) if not in occupation, a right with the leave of the court to enter into and occupy the dwelling house, and

(b) the bankrupt's rights are a charge, having the like priority as an equitable interest created immediately before the commencement of the bankruptcy, on so much of his estate or interest in the dwelling house as vests in the trustee.

(3) The Act of 1996 has effect, with the necessary modifications, as if—

(a) the rights conferred by paragraph (a) of subsection (2) were home rights under that Act,

(b) any application for such leave as is mentioned in that paragraph were an application for an order under section 33 of that Act, and

(c) any charge under paragraph (b) of that subsection on the estate or interest of the trustee were a charge under that Act on the estate or interest of a spouse or civil partner.

(4) Any application for leave such as is mentioned in subsection (2)(a) or otherwise by virtue of this section for an order under section 33 of the Act of 1996 shall be made to the court having jurisdiction in relation to the bankruptcy.

(5) On such an application the court shall make such order under section 33 of the Act of 1996 as it thinks just and reasonable having regard to the interests of the creditors, to the bankrupt's financial resources, to the needs of the children and to all the circumstances of the case other than the needs of the bankrupt.

(6) Where such an application is made after the end of the period of one year beginning with the first vesting (under Chapter IV of this Part) of the bankrupt's estate in a trustee, the court shall assume, unless the circumstances of the case are exceptional, that the interests of the bankrupt's creditors outweigh all other considerations.

### 338 Payments in respect of premises occupied by bankrupt

Where any premises comprised in a bankrupt's estate are occupied by him (whether by virtue of the preceding section or otherwise) on condition that he makes payments towards satisfying any liability arising under a mortgage of the premises or otherwise towards the outgoings of the premises, the bankrupt does not, by virtue of those payments, acquire any interest in the premises.

*Adjustment of prior transactions, etc*

### 339 Transactions at an undervalue

(1) Subject as follows in this section and sections 341 and 342, where an individual is adjudged bankrupt and he has at a relevant time (defined in section 341) entered into a transaction with any person at an undervalue, the trustee of the bankrupt's estate may apply to the court for an order under this section.

(2) The court shall, on such an application, make such order as it thinks fit for restoring the position to what it would have been if that individual had not entered into that transaction.

(3) For the purposes of this section and sections 341 and 342, an individual enters into a transaction with a person at an undervalue if—

(a) he makes a gift to that person or he otherwise enters into a transaction with that person on terms that provide for him to receive no consideration,

(b) he enters into a transaction with that person in consideration of marriage or the formation of a civil partnership, or

(c) he enters into a transaction with that person for a consideration the value of which, in money or money's worth, is significantly less than the value, in money or money's worth, of the consideration provided by the individual.

### 340 Preferences

(1) Subject as follows in this and the next two sections, where an individual is adjudged bankrupt and he has at a relevant time (defined in section 341) given a preference to any person, the trustee of the bankrupt's estate may apply to the court for an order under this section.

(2) The court shall, on such an application, make such order as it thinks fit for restoring the position to what it would have been if that individual had not given that preference.

(3) For the purposes of this and the next two sections, an individual gives a preference to a person if—

(a) that person is one of the individual's creditors or a surety or guarantor for any of his debts or other liabilities, and

(b) the individual does anything or suffers anything to be done which (in either case) has the effect of putting that person into a position which, in the event of the individual's bankruptcy, will be better than the position he would have been in if that thing had not been done.

(4) The court shall not make an order under this section in respect of a preference given to any person unless the individual who gave the preference was influenced in deciding to give it by a desire to produce in relation to that person the effect mentioned in subsection (3)(b) above.

(5) An individual who has given a preference to a person who, at the time the preference was given, was an associate of his (otherwise than by reason only of being his employee) is presumed, unless the contrary is shown, to have been influenced in deciding to give it by such a desire as is mentioned in subsection (4).

(6) The fact that something has been done in pursuance of the order of a court does not, without more, prevent the doing or suffering of that thing from constituting the giving of a preference.

### 341 'Relevant time' under ss 339, 340

(1) Subject as follows, the time at which an individual enters into a transaction at an undervalue or gives a preference is a relevant time if the transaction is entered into or the preference given—

(a) in the case of a transaction at an undervalue, at a time in the period of 5 years ending with the day of the presentation of the bankruptcy petition on which the individual is adjudged bankrupt,

(b) in the case of a preference which is not a transaction at an undervalue and is given to a person who is an associate of the individual (otherwise than by reason only of being his employee), at a time in the period of 2 years ending with that day, and

(c) in any other case of a preference which is not a transaction at an undervalue, at a time in the period of 6 months ending with that day.

(2) Where an individual enters into a transaction at an undervalue or gives a preference at a time mentioned in paragraph (a), (b) or (c) of subsection (1)(not being, in the case of a transaction at an undervalue, a time less than 2 years before the end of the period mentioned in paragraph (a)), that time is not a relevant time for the purposes of sections 339 and 340 unless the individual—

(a) is insolvent at that time, or

(b) becomes insolvent in consequence of the transaction or preference;

but the requirements of this subsection are presumed to be satisfied, unless the contrary is shown, in relation to any transaction at an undervalue which is entered into by an individual with a person who is an associate of his (otherwise than by reason only of being his employee).

(3) For the purposes of subsection (2), an individual is insolvent if—

(a) he is unable to pay his debts as they fall due, or

(b) the value of his assets is less than the amount of his liabilities, taking into account his contingent and prospective liabilities.

*(4) A transaction entered into or preference given by a person who is subsequently adjudged bankrupt on a petition under section 264(1)(d)(criminal bankruptcy) is to be treated as having been entered into or given at a relevant time for the purposes of sections 339 and 340 if it was entered into or given at any time on or after the date specified for the purposes of this subsection in the criminal bankruptcy order on which the petition was based.*

*(5) No order shall be made under section 339 or 340 by virtue of subsection (4) of this section where an appeal is pending (within the meaning of section 277) against the individual's conviction of any offence by virtue of which the criminal bankruptcy order was made.*[17]

## 342  Orders under ss 339, 340

(1) Without prejudice to the generality of section 339(2) or 340(2), an order under either of those sections with respect to a transaction or preference entered into or given by an individual who is subsequently adjudged bankrupt may (subject as follows)—

(a) require any property transferred as part of the transaction, or in connection with the giving of the preference, to be vested in the trustee of the bankrupt's estate as part of that estate;

(b) require any property to be so vested it if represents in any person's hands the application either of the proceeds of sale of property so transferred or of money so transferred;

(c) release or discharge (in whole or in part) any security given by the individual;

(d) require any person to pay, in respect of benefits received by him from the individual, such sums to the trustee of his estate as the court may direct;

(e) provide for any surety or guarantor whose obligations to any person were released or discharged (in whole or in part) under the transaction or by the giving of the preference to be under such new or revived obligations to that person as the court thinks appropriate;

(f) provide for security to be provided for the discharge of any obligation imposed by or arising under the order, for such an obligation to be charged on any property and for the security or charge to have the same priority as a security or charge released or discharged (in whole or in part) under the transaction or by the giving of the preference; and

(g) provide for the extent to which any person whose property is vested by the order in the trustee of the bankrupt's estate, or on whom obligations are imposed by the order, is to be able to prove in the bankruptcy for debts or other liabilities which arose from, or were released or discharged (in whole or in part) under or by, the transaction or the giving of the preference.

(2) An order under section 339 or 340 may affect the property of, or impose any obligation on, any person whether or not he is the person with whom the individual in question entered into the transaction or, as the case may be the person to whom the preference was given; but such an order—

(a) shall not prejudice any interest in property which was acquired from a person other than that individual and was acquired in good faith and for value, or prejudice any interest deriving from such an interest, and

(b) shall not require a person who received a benefit from the transaction or preference in good faith and for value to pay a sum to the trustee of the bankrupt's estate except where he was a party to the transaction or the payment is to be in respect of a preference given to that person at a time when he was a creditor of that individual.

(2A) Where a person has acquired an interest in property from a person other than the individual in question, or has received a benefit from the transaction or preference, and at the time of that acquisition or receipt—

(a) he had notice of the relevant surrounding circumstances and of the relevant proceedings, or

(b) he was an associate of, or was connected with, either the individual in question or the person with whom that individual entered into the transaction or to whom that individual gave the preference,

---

[17] Subsections (4) and (5) repealed by the Criminal Justice Act 1988 c 33 from a date to be appointed.

then, unless the contrary is shown, it shall be presumed for the purposes of paragraph (a) or (as the case may be) paragraph (b) of subsection (2) that the interest was acquired or the benefit was received otherwise than in good faith.

(3) Any sums required to be paid to the trustee in accordance with an order under section 339 or 340 shall be comprised in the bankrupt's estate.

(4) For the purposes of subsection (2A)(a), the relevant surrounding circumstances are (as the case may require)—

    (a) the fact that the individual in question entered into the transaction at an undervalue; or

    (b) the circumstances which amounted to the giving of the preference by the individual in question.

(5) For the purposes of subsection (2A)(a), a person has notice of the relevant proceedings if he has notice—

    (a) of the fact that the petition on which the individual in question is adjudged bankrupt has been presented; or

    (b) of the fact that the individual in question has been adjudged bankrupt.

(6) Section 249 in Part VII of this Act shall apply for the purposes of subsection (2A)(b) as it applies for the purposes of the first Group of Parts.

### 342A Recovery of excessive pension contributions

(1) Where an individual who is adjudged bankrupt—

    (a) has rights under an approved pension arrangement, or

    (b) has excluded rights under an unapproved pension arrangement,

the trustee of the bankrupt's estate may apply to the court for an order under this section.

(2) If the court is satisfied—

    (a) that the rights under the arrangement are to any extent, and whether directly or indirectly, the fruits of relevant contributions, and

    (b) that the making of any of the relevant contributions ('the excessive contributions') has unfairly prejudiced the individual's creditors,

the court may make such order as it thinks fit for restoring the position to what it would have been had the excessive contributions not been made.

(3) Subsection (4) applies where the court is satisfied that the value of the rights under the arrangement is, as a result of rights of the individual under the arrangement or any other pension arrangement having at any time become subject to a debit under section 29(1)(a) of the Welfare Reform and Pensions Act 1999 (debits giving effect to pension-sharing), less than it would otherwise have been.

(4) Where this subsection applies—

    (a) any relevant contributions which were represented by the rights which became subject to the debit shall, for the purposes of subsection (2), be taken to be contributions of which the rights under the arrangement are the fruits, and

    (b) where the relevant contributions represented by the rights under the arrangement (including those so represented by virtue of paragraph (a)) are not all excessive contributions, relevant contributions which are represented by the rights under the arrangement otherwise than by virtue of paragraph (a) shall be treated as excessive contributions before any which are so represented by virtue of that paragraph.

(5) In subsections (2) to (4) 'relevant contributions' means contributions to the arrangement or any other pension arrangement—

    (a) which the individual has at any time made on his own behalf, or

    (b) which have at any time been made on his behalf.

(6) The court shall, in determining whether it is satisfied under subsection (2)(b), consider in particular—

    (a) whether any of the contributions were made for the purpose of putting assets beyond the reach of the individual's creditors or any of them, and

    (b) whether the total amount of any contributions—

        (i) made by or on behalf of the individual to pension arrangements, and

        (ii) represented (whether directly or indirectly) by rights under approved pension arrangements or excluded rights under unapproved pension arrangements,

    is an amount which is excessive in view of the individual's circumstances when those contributions were made.

(7) For the purposes of this section and sections 342B and 342C ('the recovery provisions'), rights of an individual under an unapproved pension arrangement are excluded rights if they are rights which are excluded from his estate by virtue of regulations under section 12 of the Welfare Reform and Pensions Act 1999.

(8) In the recovery provisions—

'approved pension arrangement' has the same meaning as in section 11 of the Welfare Reform and Pensions Act 1999;

'unapproved pension arrangement' has the same meaning as in section 12 of that Act.

**342B    Orders under section 342A**

(1) Without prejudice to the generality of section 342A(2), an order under section 342A may include provision—

    (a) requiring the person responsible for the arrangement to pay an amount to the individual's trustee in bankruptcy,

    (b) adjusting the liabilities of the arrangement in respect of the individual,

    (c) adjusting any liabilities of the arrangement in respect of any other person that derive, directly or indirectly, from rights of the individual under the arrangement,

    (d) for the recovery by the person responsible for the arrangement (whether by deduction from any amount which that person is ordered to pay or otherwise) of costs incurred by that person in complying in the bankrupt's case with any requirement under section 342C(1) or in giving effect to the order.

(2) In subsection (1), references to adjusting the liabilities of the arrangement in respect of a person include (in particular) reducing the amount of any benefit or future benefit to which that person is entitled under the arrangement.

(3) In subsection (1)(c), the reference to liabilities of the arrangement does not include liabilities in respect of a person which result from giving effect to an order or provision falling within section 28(1) of the Welfare Reform and Pensions Act 1999 (pension sharing orders and agreements).

(4) The maximum amount which the person responsible for an arrangement may be required to pay by an order under section 342A is the lesser of—

    (a) the amount of the excessive contributions, and

    (b) the value of the individual's rights under the arrangement (if the arrangement is an approved pension arrangement) or of his excluded rights under the arrangement (if the arrangement is an unapproved pension arrangement).

(5) An order under section 342A which requires the person responsible for an arrangement to pay an amount ('the restoration amount') to the individual's trustee in bankruptcy must provide for the liabilities of the arrangement to be correspondingly reduced.

(6) For the purposes of subsection (5), liabilities are correspondingly reduced if the difference between—

    (a) the amount of the liabilities immediately before the reduction, and

    (b) the amount of the liabilities immediately after the reduction,

is equal to the restoration amount.

(7) An order under section 342A in respect of an arrangement—

    (a) shall be binding on the person responsible for the arrangement, and

    (b) overrides provisions of the arrangement to the extent that they conflict with the provisions of the order.

**342C    Orders under section 342A: supplementary**

(1) The person responsible for—

    (a) an approved pension arrangement under which a bankrupt has rights,

    (b) an unapproved pension arrangement under which a bankrupt has excluded rights, or

    (c) a pension arrangement under which a bankrupt has at any time had rights,

shall, on the bankrupt's trustee in bankruptcy making a written request, provide the trustee with such information about the arrangement and rights as the trustee may reasonably require for, or in connection with, the making of applications under section 342A.

(2) Nothing in—

    (a) any provision of section 159 of the Pension Schemes Act 1993 or section 91 of the Pensions Act 1995 (which prevent assignment and the making of orders that restrain a person from receiving anything which he is prevented from assigning),

    (b) any provision of any enactment (whether passed or made before or after the passing of the Welfare Reform and Pensions Act 1999) corresponding to any of the provisions mentioned in paragraph (a), or

    (c) any provision of the arrangement in question corresponding to any of those provisions,

applies to a court exercising its powers under section 342A.

(3) Where any sum is required by an order under section 342A to be paid to the trustee in bankruptcy, that sum shall be comprised in the bankrupt's estate.

(4) Regulations may, for the purposes of the recovery provisions, make provision about the calculation and verification of—

    (a) any such value as is mentioned in section 342B(4)(b);

    (b) any such amounts as are mentioned in section 342B(6)(a) and (b).

(5) The power conferred by subsection (4) includes power to provide for calculation or verification—

    (a) in such manner as may, in the particular case, be approved by a prescribed person; or

    (b) in accordance with guidance from time to time prepared by a prescribed person.

(6) References in the recovery provisions to the person responsible for a pension arrangement are to—

    (a) the trustees, managers or provider of the arrangement, or

(b) the person having functions in relation to the arrangement corresponding to those of a trustee, manager or provider.

(7) In this section and sections 342A and 342B—

'prescribed' means prescribed by regulations;

'the recovery provisions' means this section and sections 342A and 342B;

'regulations' means regulations made by the Secretary of State.

(8) Regulations under the recovery provisions may—

(a) make different provision for different cases;

(b) contain such incidental, supplemental and transitional provisions as appear to the Secretary of State necessary or expedient.

(9) Regulations under the recovery provisions shall be made by statutory instrument subject to annulment in pursuance of a resolution of either House of Parliament.

### 342D  Recovery of excessive contributions in pension-sharing cases

(1) For the purposes of sections 339, 341 and 342, a pension-sharing transaction shall be taken—

(a) to be a transaction, entered into by the transferor with the transferee, by which the appropriate amount is transferred by the transferor to the transferee; and

(b) to be capable of being a transaction entered into at an undervalue only so far as it is a transfer of so much of the appropriate amount as is recoverable.

(2) For the purposes of sections 340 to 342, a pension-sharing transaction shall be taken—

(a) to be something (namely a transfer of the appropriate amount to the transferee) done by the transferor; and

(b) to be capable of being a preference given to the transferee only so far as it is a transfer of so much of the appropriate amount as is recoverable.

(3) If on an application under section 339 or 340 any question arises as to whether, or the extent to which, the appropriate amount in the case of a pension-sharing transaction is recoverable, the question shall be determined in accordance with subsections (4) to (8).

(4) The court shall first determine the extent (if any) to which the transferor's rights under the shared arrangement at the time of the transaction appear to have been (whether directly or indirectly) the fruits of contributions ('personal contributions')—

(a) which the transferor has at any time made on his own behalf, or

(b) which have at any time been made on the transferor's behalf,

to the shared arrangement or any other pension arrangement.

(5) Where it appears that those rights were to any extent the fruits of personal contributions, the court shall then determine the extent (if any) to which those rights appear to have been the fruits of personal contributions whose making has unfairly prejudiced the transferor's creditors ('the unfair contributions').

(6) If it appears to the court that the extent to which those rights were the fruits of the unfair contributions is such that the transfer of the appropriate amount could have been made out of rights under the shared arrangement which were not the fruits of the unfair contributions, then the appropriate amount is not recoverable.

(7) If it appears to the court that the transfer could not have been wholly so made, then the appropriate amount is recoverable to the extent to which it appears to the court that the transfer could not have been so made.

(8) In making the determination mentioned in subsection (5) the court shall consider in particular—

(a) whether any of the personal contributions were made for the purpose of putting assets beyond the reach of the transferor's creditors or any of them, and

(b) whether the total amount of any personal contributions represented, at the time the pension-sharing transaction was made, by rights under pension arrangements is an amount which is excessive in view of the transferor's circumstances when those contributions were made.

(9) In this section and sections 342E and 342F—

'appropriate amount', in relation to a pension-sharing transaction, means the appropriate amount in relation to that transaction for the purposes of section 29(1) of the Welfare Reform and Pensions Act 1999 (creation of pension credits and debits);

'pension-sharing transaction' means an order or provision falling within section 28(1) of the Welfare Reform and Pensions Act 1999 (orders and agreements which activate pension-sharing);

'shared arrangement', in relation to a pension sharing transaction, means the pension arrangement to which the transaction relates;

'transferee', in relation to a pension-sharing transaction, means the person for whose benefit the transaction is made;

'transferor', in relation to a pension-sharing transaction, means the person to whose rights the transaction relates.

**342E    Orders under section 339 or 340 in respect of pension-sharing transactions**

(1) This section and section 342F apply if the court is making an order under section 339 or 340 in a case where—

    (a) the transaction or preference is, or is any part of, a pension-sharing transaction, and

    (b) the transferee has rights under a pension arrangement ('the destination arrangement', which may be the shared arrangement or any other pension arrangement) that are derived, directly or indirectly, from the pension-sharing transaction.

(2) Without prejudice to the generality of section 339(2) or 340(2), or of section 342, the order may include provision—

    (a) requiring the person responsible for the destination arrangement to pay an amount to the transferor's trustee in bankruptcy,

    (b) adjusting the liabilities of the destination arrangement in respect of the transferee,

    (c) adjusting any liabilities of the destination arrangement in respect of any other person that derive, directly or indirectly, from rights of the transferee under the destination arrangement,

    (d) for the recovery by the person responsible for the destination arrangement (whether by deduction from any amount which that person is ordered to pay or otherwise) of costs incurred by that person in complying in the transferor's case with any requirement under section 342F(1) or in giving effect to the order,

    (e) for the recovery, from the transferor's trustee in bankruptcy, by the person responsible for a pension arrangement, of costs incurred by that person in complying in the transferor's case with any requirement under section 342F(2) or (3).

(3) In subsection (2), references to adjusting the liabilities of the destination arrangement in respect of a person include (in particular) reducing the amount of any benefit or future benefit to which that person is entitled under the arrangement.

(4) The maximum amount which the person responsible for the destination arrangement may be required to pay by the order is the smallest of—

    (a) so much of the appropriate amount as, in accordance with section 342D, is recoverable,

    (b) so much (if any) of the amount of the unfair contributions (within the meaning given by section 342D(5)) as is not recoverable by way of an order under section 342A containing provision such as is mentioned in section 342B(1)(a), and

    (c) the value of the transferee's rights under the destination arrangement so far as they are derived, directly or indirectly, from the pension-sharing transaction.

(5) If the order requires the person responsible for the destination arrangement to pay an amount ('the restoration amount') to the transferor's trustee in bankruptcy it must provide for the liabilities of the arrangement to be correspondingly reduced.

(6) For the purposes of subsection (5), liabilities are correspondingly reduced if the difference between—

    (a) the amount of the liabilities immediately before the reduction, and

    (b) the amount of the liabilities immediately after the reduction,

is equal to the restoration amount.

(7) The order—

    (a) shall be binding on the person responsible for the destination arrangement, and

    (b) overrides provisions of the destination arrangement to the extent that they conflict with the provisions of the order.

**342F    Orders under section 339 or 340 in pension-sharing cases: supplementary**

(1) On the transferor's trustee in bankruptcy making a written request to the person responsible for the destination arrangement, that person shall provide the trustee with such information about—

    (a) the arrangement,

    (b) the transferee's rights under it, and

    (c) where the destination arrangement is the shared arrangement, the transferor's rights under it,

as the trustee may reasonably require for, or in connection with, the making of applications under sections 339 and 340.

(2) Where the shared arrangement is not the destination arrangement, the person responsible for the shared arrangement shall, on the transferor's trustee in bankruptcy making a written request to that person, provide the trustee with such information about—

    (a) the arrangement, and

    (b) the transferor's rights under it,

as the trustee may reasonably require for, or in connection with, the making of applications under sections 339 and 340.

(3) On the transferor's trustee in bankruptcy making a written request to the person responsible for any intermediate arrangement, that person shall provide the trustee with such information about—

    (a) the arrangement, and

    (b) the transferee's rights under it,

as the trustee may reasonably require for, or in connection with, the making of applications under sections 339 and 340.

(4) In subsection (3) 'intermediate arrangement' means a pension arrangement, other than the shared arrangement or the destination arrangement, in relation to which the following conditions are fulfilled—

    (a) there was a time when the transferee had rights under the arrangement that were derived (directly or indirectly) from the pension-sharing transaction, and

    (b) the transferee's rights under the destination arrangement (so far as derived from the pension-sharing transaction) are to any extent derived (directly or indirectly) from the rights mentioned in paragraph (a).

(5) Nothing in—

    (a) any provision of section 159 of the Pension Schemes Act 1993 or section 91 of the Pensions Act 1995 (which prevent assignment and the making of orders which restrain a person from receiving anything which he is prevented from assigning),

    (b) any provision of any enactment (whether passed or made before or after the passing of the Welfare Reform and Pensions Act 1999) corresponding to any of the provisions mentioned in paragraph (a), or

    (c) any provision of the destination arrangement corresponding to any of those provisions,

applies to a court exercising its powers under section 339 or 340.

(6) Regulations may, for the purposes of sections 339 to 342, sections 342D and 342E and this section, make provision about the calculation and verification of—

    (a) any such value as is mentioned in section 342E(4)(c);

    (b) any such amounts as are mentioned in section 342E(6)(a) and (b).

(7) The power conferred by subsection (6) includes power to provide for calculation or verification—

    (a) in such manner as may, in the particular case, be approved by a prescribed person; or

    (b) in accordance with guidance from time to time prepared by a prescribed person.

(8) In section 342E and this section, references to the person responsible for a pension arrangement are to—

    (a) the trustees, managers or provider of the arrangement, or

    (b) the person having functions in relation to the arrangement corresponding to those of a trustee, manager or provider.

(9) In this section—

'prescribed' means prescribed by regulations;

'regulations' means regulations made by the Secretary of State.

(10) Regulations under this section may—

    (a) make different provision for different cases;

    (b) contain such incidental, supplemental and transitional provisions as appear to the Secretary of State necessary or expedient.

(11) Regulations under this section shall be made by statutory instrument subject to annulment in pursuance of a resolution of either House of Parliament.

### 343   Extortionate credit transactions

(1) This section applies where a person is adjudged bankrupt who is or has been a party to a transaction for, or involving, the provision to him of credit.

(2) The court may, on the application of the trustee of the bankrupt's estate, make an order with respect to the transaction if the transaction is or was extortionate and was not entered into more than 3 years before the commencement of the bankruptcy.

(3) For the purposes of this section a transaction is extortionate if, having regard to the risk accepted by the person providing the credit—

    (a) the terms of it are or were such as to require grossly exorbitant payments to be made (whether unconditionally or in certain contingencies) in respect of the provision of the credit, or

    (b) it otherwise grossly contravened ordinary principles of fair dealing;

and it shall be presumed, unless the contrary is proved, that a transaction, with respect to which an application is made under this section is or, as the case may be, was extortionate.

(4) An order under this section with respect to any transaction may contain such one or more of the following as the court thinks fit, that is to say—

    (a) provision setting aside the whole or part of any obligation created by the transaction;

    (b) provision otherwise varying the terms of the transaction or varying the terms on which any security for the purposes of the transaction is held;

    (c) provision requiring any person who is or was party to the transaction to pay to the trustee any sums paid to that person, by virtue of the transaction, by the bankrupt;

    (d) provision requiring any person to surrender to the trustee any property held by him as security for the purposes of the transaction;

    (e) provision directing accounts to be taken between any persons.

(5) Any sums or property required to be paid or surrendered to the trustee in accordance with an order under this section shall be comprised in the bankrupt's estate.

(6) Neither the trustee of a bankrupt's estate nor an undischarged bankrupt is entitled to make an application under section 139(1)(a) of the Consumer Credit Act 1974 (re-opening of extortionate credit agreements) for any agreement by which credit is or has been provided to the bankrupt to be re-opened.

But the powers conferred by this section are exercisable in relation to any transaction concurrently with any powers exercisable under this Act in relation to that transaction as a transaction at an undervalue.

### 344 Avoidance of general assignment of book debts

(1) The following applies where a person engaged in any business makes a general assignment to another person of his existing or future book debts, or any class of them, and is subsequently adjudged bankrupt.

(2) The assignment is void against the trustee of the bankrupt's estate as regards book debts which were not paid before the presentation of the bankruptcy petition, unless the assignment has been registered under the Bills of Sale Act 1878.

(3) For the purposes of subsections (1) and (2)—
  (a) 'assignment' includes an assignment by way of security or charge on book debts, and
  (b) 'general assignment' does not include—
    (i) an assignment of book debts due at the date of the assignment from specified debtors or of debts becoming due under specified contracts, or
    (ii) an assignment of book debts included either in a transfer of a business made in good faith and for value or in an assignment of assets for the benefit of creditors generally.

(4) For the purposes of registration under the Act of 1878 an assignment of book debts is to be treated as if it were a bill of sale given otherwise than by way of security for the payment of a sum of money; and the provisions of that Act with respect to the registration of bills of sale apply accordingly with such necessary modifications as may be made by rules under that Act.

### 345 Contracts to which bankrupt is a party

(1) The following applies where a contract has been made with a person who is subsequently adjudged bankrupt.

(2) The court may, on the application of any other party to the contract, make an order discharging obligations under the contract on such terms as to payment by the applicant or the bankrupt of damages for non-performance or otherwise as appear to the court to be equitable.

(3) Any damages payable by the bankrupt by virtue of an order of the court under this section are provable as a bankruptcy debt.

(4) Where an undischarged bankrupt is a contractor in respect of any contract jointly with any person, that person may sue or be sued in respect of the contract without the joinder of the bankrupt.

### 346 Enforcement procedures

(1) Subject to section 285 in Chapter II (restriction on proceedings and remedies) and to the following provisions of this section, where the creditor of any person who is adjudged bankrupt has, before the commencement of the bankruptcy—
  (a) issued execution against the goods or land of that person, or
  (b) attached a debt due to that person from another person,
that creditor is not entitled, as against the official receiver or trustee of the bankrupt's estate, to retain the benefit of the execution or attachment, or any sums paid to avoid it, unless the execution or attachment was completed, or the sums were paid, before the commencement of the bankruptcy.

(2) Subject as follows, where any goods of a person have been taken in execution, then, if before the completion of the execution notice is given to the enforcement officer or other officer charged with the execution that that person has been adjudged bankrupt—
  (a) the enforcement officer or other officer shall on request deliver to the official receiver or trustee of the bankrupt's estate the goods and any money seized or recovered in part satisfaction of the execution, but
  (b) the costs of the execution are a first charge on the goods or money so delivered and the official receiver or trustee may sell the goods or a sufficient part of them for the purpose of satisfying the charge.

(3) Subject to subsection (6) below, where—
  (a) under an execution in respect of a judgment for a sum exceeding such sum as may be prescribed for the purposes of this subsection, the goods of any person are sold or money is paid in order to avoid a sale, and
  (b) before the end of the period of 14 days beginning with the day of the sale or payment the enforcement officer or other officer charged with the execution is given notice that a bankruptcy petition has been presented in relation to that person, and
  (c) a bankruptcy order is or has been made on that petition,

the balance of the proceeds of sale or money paid, after deducting the costs of execution, shall (in priority to the claim of the execution creditor) be comprised in the bankrupt's estate.

(4)  Accordingly, in the case of an execution in respect of a judgment for a sum exceeding the sum prescribed for the purposes of subsection (3), the enforcement officer or other officer charged with the execution—

(a) shall not dispose of the balance mentioned in subsection (3) at any time within the period of 14 days so mentioned or while there is pending a bankruptcy petition of which he has been given notice under that subsection, and

(b) shall pay that balance, where by virtue of that subsection it is comprised, in the bankrupt's estate, to the official receiver or (if there is one) to the trustee or that estate.

(5)  For the purposes of this section—

(a) an execution against goods is completed by seizure and sale or by the making of a charging order under section 1 of the Charging Orders Act 1979;

(b) an execution against land is completed by seizure, by the appointment of a receiver or by the making of a charging order under that section;

(c) an attachment of a debt is completed by the receipt of the debt.

(6)  The rights conferred by subsections (1) to (3) on the official receiver or the trustee may, to such extent and on such terms as it thinks fit, be set aside by the court in favour of the creditor who has issued the execution or attached the debt.

(7)  Nothing in this section entitles the trustee of a bankrupt's estate to claim goods from a person who has acquired them in good faith under a sale by an enforcement officer or other officer charged with an execution.

(8)  Neither subsection (2) nor subsection (3) applies in relation to any execution against property which has been acquired by or has devolved upon the bankrupt since the commencement of the bankruptcy, unless, at the time the execution is issued or before it is completed—

(a) the property has been or is claimed for the bankrupt's estate under section 307 (after-acquired property), and

(b) a copy of the notice given under that section has been or is served on the enforcement officer or other officer charged with the execution.

(9)  In this section 'enforcement officer' means an individual who is authorised to act as an enforcement officer under the Courts Act 2003.

### 347  Distress, etc

(1)  *The right of any landlord or other person to whom rent is payable to distrain upon the goods and effects of an undischarged bankrupt for rent due to him from the bankrupt is available* (subject to sections 252(2)(b) and 254(1) above and subsection (5) below) against goods and effects comprised in the bankrupt's estate, but only for 6 months' rent accrued due before the commencement of the bankruptcy.

(2)  *Where a landlord or other person to whom rent is payable has distrained for rent upon the goods and effects* of an individual to whom a bankruptcy petition relates and a bankruptcy order is subsequently made on that petition, any amount recovered by way of *that distress* which—

(a) is in excess of the amount which by virtue of subsection (1) would have been recoverable after the commencement of the bankruptcy, or

(b) is in respect of rent for a period or part of a period after *the distress was levied,*

shall be held for the bankrupt as a part of his estate.

(3)  Where any person (whether or not a landlord or person entitled to rent) has distrained upon the goods or effects of an individual who is adjudged bankrupt before the end of the period of 3 months beginning with the distraint, so much of those goods or effects, or of the proceeds of their sale, as is not held for the bankrupt under subsection (2) shall be charged for the benefit of the bankrupt's estate with the preferential debts of the bankrupt to the extent that the bankrupt's estate is for the time being insufficient for meeting those debts.

(4)  Where by virtue of any charge under subsection (3) any person surrenders any goods or effects to the trustee of a bankrupt's estate or makes a payment to such a trustee, that person ranks, in respect of the amount of the proceeds of the sale of those goods or effects by the trustee or, as the case may be, the amount of the payment, as a preferential creditor of the bankrupt, except as against so much of the bankrupt's estate as is available for the payment of preferential creditors by virtue of the surrender or payment.

(5)  *A landlord or other person to whom rent is payable is not at any time after the discharge of a bankrupt entitled to distrain upon* any goods or effects comprised in the bankrupt's estate.

(6)  *Where in the case of any execution—*

(a) *a landlord is (apart from this section) entitled under section 1 of the Landlord and Tenant Act 1709 or section 102 of the County Courts Act 1984 (claims for rent where goods seized in execution) to claim for an amount not exceeding one year's rent, and*

(b) *the person against whom the execution is levied is adjudged bankrupt before the notice of claim is served on the enforcement officer, or other officer charged with the execution, the right of the landlord to claim under that section is restricted to a right to claim for an amount not exceeding 6 months' rent and does not extend to any rent payable in respect of a period after the notice of claim is so served.*

*(7) Nothing in subsection (6) imposes any liability on an enforcement officer or other officer charged with an execution to account to the official receiver or the trustee of a bankrupt's estate for any sums paid by him to a landlord at any time before the enforcement officer or other officer was served with notice of the bankruptcy order in question.*

*But this subsection is without prejudice to the liability of the landlord.*

(8) Subject to sections 252(2)(b) and 254(1) above nothing in this Group of Parts affects any right to distrain otherwise than for rent; and any such right is at any time exercisable without restriction against property comprised in a bankrupt's estate, even if that right is expressed by any enactment to be exercisable in like manner as a right to distrain for rent.

(9) Any right to distrain against property comprised in a bankrupt's estate is exercisable notwithstanding that the property has vested in the trustee.

(10) The provisions of this section are without prejudice to a landlord's right in a bankruptcy to prove for any bankruptcy debt in respect of rent.

*(11) In this section 'enforcement officer' means an individual who is authorised to act as an enforcement officer under the Courts Act 2003.*[18]

### 348  Apprenticeships, etc

(1) This section applies where—
- (a) a bankruptcy order is made in respect of an individual to whom another individual was an apprentice or articled clerk at the time when the petition on which the order was made was presented, and
- (b) the bankrupt or the apprentice or clerk gives notice to the trustee terminating the apprenticeship or articles.

(2) Subject to subsection (6) below, the indenture of apprenticeship or, as the case may be, the articles of agreement shall be discharged with effect from the commencement of the bankruptcy.

(3) If any money has been paid by or on behalf of the apprentice or clerk to the bankrupt as a fee, the trustee may, on an application made by or on behalf of the apprentice or clerk, pay such sum to the apprentice or clerk as to the trustee thinks reasonable, having regard to—
- (a) the amount of the fee,
- (b) the proportion of the period in respect of which the fee was paid that has been served by the apprentice or clerk before the commencement of the bankruptcy, and
- (c) the other circumstances of the case.

(4) The power of the trustee to make a payment under subsection (3) has priority over his obligation to distribute the bankrupt's estate.

(5) Instead of making a payment under subsection (3), the trustee may, if it appears to him expedient to do so on an application made by or on behalf of the apprentice or clerk, transfer the indenture or articles to a person other than the bankrupt.

(6) Where a transfer is made under subsection (5), subsection (2) has effect only as between the apprentice or clerk and the bankrupt.

### 349  Unenforceability of liens on books, etc

(1) Subject as follows, a lien or other right to retain possession of any of the books, papers or other records of a bankrupt is unenforceable to the extent that its enforcement would deny possession of any books, papers or other records to the official receiver or the trustee of the bankrupt's estate.

(2) Subsection (1) does not apply to a lien on documents which give a title to property and are held as such.

### 349A  Arbitration agreements to which bankrupt is party

(1) This section applies where a bankrupt had become party to a contract containing an arbitration agreement before the commencement of his bankruptcy.

(2) If the trustee in bankruptcy adopts the contract, the arbitration agreement is enforceable by or against the trustee in relation to matters arising from or connected with the contract.

(3) If the trustee in bankruptcy does not adopt the contract and a matter to which the arbitration agreement applies requires to be determined in connection with or for the purposes of the bankruptcy proceedings—

---

[18] This section is to be amended by the Tribunals Courts and Enforcement Act 2007 c 15 from a date to be appointed as follows:

In subsection (1) for the words in italics substitute 'CRAR (the power of commercial rent arrears recovery under section 72(1) of the Tribunals, Courts and Enforcement Act 2007) is exercisable where the tenant is an undischarged bankrupt'.

In subsection (2) for the words in italics substitute 'Where CRAR has been exercised to recover rent from' and 'CRAR'.

In subsection 2(b) for the words in italics substitute 'goods were taken control of under CRAR'.

In subsection (5) for the words in italics substitute 'CRAR is not exercisable at any time after the discharge of a bankrupt against'.

Omit subsections (6), (7) and (11).

(a) the trustee with the consent of the creditors' committee, or

(b) any other party to the agreement,

may apply to the court which may, if it thinks fit in all the circumstances of the case, order that the matter be referred to arbitration in accordance with the arbitration agreement.

(4) In this section—

'arbitration agreement' has the same meaning as in Part I of the Arbitration Act 1996; and

'the court' means the court which has jurisdiction in the bankruptcy proceedings.

# Chapter VI

## Bankruptcy offences

### *Preliminary*

### 350   Scheme of this Chapter

(1) Subject to section 360(3) below, this Chapter applies where the court has made a bankruptcy order on a bankruptcy petition.

(2) This Chapter applies whether or not the bankruptcy order is annulled, but proceedings for an offence under this Chapter shall not be instituted after the annulment.

(3) Without prejudice to his liability in respect of a subsequent bankruptcy, the bankrupt is not guilty of an offence under this Chapter in respect of anything done after his discharge; but nothing in this Group of Parts prevents the institution of proceedings against a discharged bankrupt for an offence committed before his discharge.

(3A) Subsection (3) is without prejudice to any provision of this Chapter which applies to a person in respect of whom a bankruptcy restrictions order is in force.

(4) It is not a defence in proceedings for an offence under this Chapter that anything relied on, in whole or in part, as constituting that offence was done outside England and Wales.

(5) Proceedings for an offence under this Chapter or under the rules shall not be instituted except by the Secretary of State or by or with the consent of the Director of Public Prosecutions.

(6) A person guilty of any offence under this Chapter is liable to imprisonment or a fine, or both.

### 351   Definitions

In the following provisions of this Chapter—

(a) references to property comprised in the bankrupt's estate or to property possession of which is required to be delivered up to the official receiver or the trustee of the bankrupt's estate include any property which would be such property if a notice in respect of it were given under section 307 (after-acquired property) , section 308 (personal property and effects of bankrupt having more than replacement value) or section 308A (vesting in trustee of certain tenancies);

(b) 'the initial period' means the period between the presentation of the bankruptcy petition and the commencement of the bankruptcy; and

(c) a reference to a number of months or years before petition is to that period ending with the presentation of the bankruptcy petition.

### 352   Defence of innocent intention

Where in the case of an offence under any provision of this Chapter it is stated that this section applies, a person is not guilty of the offence if he proves that, at the time of the conduct constituting the offence, he had no intent to defraud or to conceal the state of his affairs.

### *Wrongdoing by the bankrupt before and after bankruptcy*

### 353   Non-disclosure

(1) The bankrupt is guilty of an offence if—

(a) he does not to the best of his knowledge and belief disclose all the property comprised in his estate to the official receiver or the trustee, or

(b) he does not inform the official receiver or the trustee of any disposal of any property which but for the disposal would be so comprised, stating how, when, to whom and for what consideration the property was disposed of.

(2) Subsection (1)(b) does not apply to any disposal in the ordinary course of a business carried on by the bankrupt or to any payment of the ordinary expenses of the bankrupt or his family.

(3) Section 352 applies to this offence.

### 354   Concealment of property

(1) The bankrupt is guilty of an offence if—

(a) he does not deliver up possession to the official receiver or trustee, or as the official receiver or trustee may direct, of such part of the property comprised in his estate as is in his possession or under his control and possession of which he is required by law so to deliver up,

(b) he conceals any debt due to or from him or conceals any property the value of which is not less than the prescribed amount and possession of which he is required to deliver up to the official receiver or trustee, or

(c) in the 12 months before petition, or in the initial period, he did anything which would have been an offence under paragraph (b) above if the bankruptcy order had been made immediately before he did it.

Section 352 applies to this offence.

(2) The bankrupt is guilty of an offence if he removes, or in the initial period removed, any property the value of which was not less than the prescribed amount and possession of which he has or would have been required to deliver up to the official receiver or the trustee.

Section 352 applies to this offence.

(3) The bankrupt is guilty of an offence if he without reasonable excuse fails, on being required to do so by the official receiver , the trustee or the court—

(a) to account for the loss of any substantial part of his property incurred in the 12 months before petition or in the initial period, or

(b) to give a satisfactory explanation of the manner in which such a loss was incurred.

## 355   Concealment of books and papers; falsification

(1) The bankrupt is guilty of an offence if he does not deliver up possession to the official receiver or the trustee, or as the official receiver or trustee may direct, of all books, papers and other records of which he has possession or control and which relate to his estate or his affairs.

Section 352 applies to this offence.

(2) The bankrupt is guilty of an offence if—

(a) he prevents, or in the initial period prevented, the production of any books, papers or records relating to his estate or affairs;

(b) he conceals destroys, mutilates or falsifies, or causes or permits the concealment, destruction, mutilation or falsification of, any books, papers or other records relating to his estate or affairs;

(c) he makes, or causes or permits the making of, any false entries in any book, document or record relating to his estate or affairs; or

(d) in the 12 months before petition, or in the initial period, he did anything which would have been an offence under paragraph (b) or (c) above if the bankruptcy order had been made before he did it.

Section 352 applies to this offence.

(3) The bankrupt is guilty of an offence if—

(a) he disposes of, or alters or makes any omission in, or causes or permits the disposal, altering or making of any omission in, any book, document or record relating to his estate or affairs, or

(b) in the 12 months before petition, or in the initial period, he did anything which would have been an offence under paragraph (a) if the bankruptcy order had been made before he did it.

Section 352 applies to this offence.

(4) In their application to a trading record subsections (2)(d) and (3)(b) shall have effect as if the reference to 12 months were a reference to two years.

(5) In subsection (4) 'trading record' means a book, document or record which shows or explains the transactions or financial position of a person's business, including—

(a) a periodic record of cash paid and received,

(b) a statement of periodic stock-taking, and

(c) except in the case of goods sold by way of retail trade, a record of goods sold and purchased which identifies the buyer and seller or enables them to be identified.

## 356   False statements

(1) The bankrupt is guilty of an offence if he makes or has made any material omission in any statement made under any provision in this Group of Parts and relating to his affairs.

Section 352 applies to this offence.

(2) The bankrupt is guilty of an offence if—

(a) knowing or believing that a false debt has been proved by any person under the bankruptcy, he fails to inform the trustee as soon as practicable; or

(b) he attempts to account for any part of his property by fictitious losses or expenses; or

(c) at any meeting of his creditors in the 12 months before petition or (whether or not such a meeting) at any time in the initial period, he did anything which would have been an offence under paragraph (b) if the bankruptcy order had been made before he did it; or

(d) he is, or at any time has been, guilty of any false representation or other fraud for the purpose of obtaining the consent of his creditors, or any of them, to an agreement with reference to his affairs or to his bankruptcy.

### 357 Fraudulent disposal of property

(1) The bankrupt is guilty of an offence if he makes or causes to be made, or has in the period of 5 years ending with the commencement of the bankruptcy made or caused to be made, any gift or transfer of, or any charge on, his property.

Section 352 applies to this offence.

(2) The reference to making a transfer of or charge on any property includes causing or conniving at the levying of any execution against that property.

(3) The bankrupt is guilty of an offence if he conceals or removes, or has at any time before the commencement of the bankruptcy concealed or removed, any part of his property after, or within 2 months before, the date on which a judgment or order for the payment of money has been obtained against him, being a judgment or order which was not satisfied before the commencement of the bankruptcy.

Section 352 applies to this offence.

### 358 Absconding

The bankrupt is guilty of an offence if—

    (a) he leaves, or attempts or makes preparations to leave, England and Wales with any property the value of which is not less than the prescribed amount and possession of which he is required to deliver up to the official receiver or the trustee, or

    (b) in the 6 months before petition, or in the initial period, he did anything which would have been an offence under paragraph (a) if the bankruptcy order had been made immediately before he did it.

Section 352 applies to this offence.

### 359 Fraudulent dealing with property obtained on credit

(1) The bankrupt is guilty of an offence if, in the 12 months before petition, or in the initial period, he disposed of any property which he had obtained on credit and, at the time he disposed of it, had not paid for.

Section 352 applies to this offence.

(2) A person is guilty of an offence if, in the 12 months before petition or in the initial period, he acquired or received property from the bankrupt knowing or believing—

    (a) that the bankrupt owed money in respect of the property, and

    (b) that the bankrupt did not intend, or was unlikely to be able, to pay the money he so owed.

(3) A person is not guilty of an offence under subsection (1) or (2) if the disposal, acquisition or receipt of the property was in the ordinary course of a business carried on by the bankrupt at the time of the disposal, acquisition or receipt.

(4) In determining for the purposes of this section whether any property is disposed of, acquired or received in the ordinary course of a business carried on by the bankrupt, regard may be had, in particular, to the price paid for the property.

(5) In this section references to disposing of property include pawning or pledging it; and references to acquiring or receiving property shall be read accordingly.

### 360 Obtaining credit; engaging in business

(1) The bankrupt is guilty of an offence if—

    (a) either alone or jointly with any other person, he obtains credit to the extent of the prescribed amount or more without giving the person from whom he obtains it the relevant information about his status; or

    (b) he engages (whether directly or indirectly) in any business under a name other than that in which he was adjudged bankrupt without disclosing to all persons with whom he enters into any business transaction the name in which he was so adjudged.

(2) The reference to the bankrupt obtaining credit includes the following cases—

    (a) where goods are bailed to him under a hire-purchase agreement, or agreed to be sold to him under a conditional sale agreement, and

    (b) where he is paid in advance (whether in money or otherwise) for the supply of goods or services.

(3) A person whose estate has been sequestrated in Scotland, or who has been adjudged bankrupt in Northern Ireland, is guilty of an offence if, before his discharge, he does anything in England and Wales which would be an offence under subsection (1) if he were an undischarged bankrupt and the sequestration of his estate or the adjudication in Northern Ireland were an adjudication under this Part.

(4) For the purposes of subsection (1)(a), the relevant information about the status of the person in question is the information that he is an undischarged bankrupt or, as the case may be, that his estate has been sequestrated in Scotland and that he has not been discharged.

(5) This section applies to the bankrupt after discharge while a bankruptcy restrictions order is in force in respect of him.

(6) For the purposes of subsection (1)(a) as it applies by virtue of subsection (5), the relevant information about the status of the person in question is the information that a bankruptcy restrictions order is in force in respect of him.

**361    Failure to keep proper accounts of business**

[...]

**362    Gambling**

[...]

## Chapter VII

## Powers of court in bankruptcy

### 363    General control of court

(1)  Every bankruptcy is under the general control of the court and, subject to the provisions in this Group of Parts, the court has full power to decide all questions of priorities and all other questions, whether of law or fact, arising in any bankruptcy.

(2)  Without prejudice to any other provision in this Group of Parts, an undischarged bankrupt or a discharged bankrupt whose estate is still being administered under Chapter IV of this Part shall do all such things as he may be directed to do by the court for the purposes of his bankruptcy or, as the case may be, the administration of that estate.

(3)  The official receiver or the trustee of a bankrupt's estate may at any time apply to the court for a direction under subsection (2).

(4)  If any person without reasonable excuse fails to comply with any obligation imposed on him by subsection (2), he is guilty of a contempt of court and liable to be punished accordingly (in addition to any other punishment to which may be subject).

### 364    Power of arrest

(1)  In the cases specified in the next subsection the court may cause a warrant to be issued to a constable or prescribed officer of the court—

(a) for the arrest of a debtor to whom a bankruptcy petition relates or of an undischarged bankrupt, or of a discharged bankrupt whose estate is still being administered under Chapter IV of this Part, and

(b) for the seizure of any books, papers, records, money or goods in the possession of a person arrested under the warrant,

and may authorise a person arrested under such a warrant to be kept in custody, and anything seized under such a warrant to be held, in accordance with the rules, until such time as the court may order.

(2)  The powers conferred by subsection (1) are exercisable in relation to a debtor or undischarged or discharged bankrupt if, at any time after the presentation of the bankruptcy petition relating to him or the making of the bankruptcy order against him, it appears to the court—

(a) that there are reasonable grounds for believing that he has absconded, or is about to abscond, with a view to avoiding or delaying the payment of any of his debts or his appearance to a bankruptcy petition or to avoiding, delaying or disrupting any proceedings in bankruptcy against him or any examination of his affairs, or

(b) that he is about to remove his goods with a view to preventing or delaying possession being taken of them by the official receiver or the trustee of his estate, or

(c) that there are reasonable grounds for believing that he has concealed or destroyed, or is about to conceal or destroy, any of his goods or any books, papers or records which might be of use to his creditors in the course of his bankruptcy or in connection with the administration of his estate, or

(d) that he has, without the leave of the official receiver or the trustee of his estate, removed any goods in his possession which exceed in value such sums as may be prescribed for the purposes of this paragraph or

(e) that he has failed, without reasonable excuse, to attend any examination ordered by the court.

### 365    Seizure of bankrupt's property

(1)  At any time after a bankruptcy order has been made, the court may, on the application of the official receiver or the trustee of the bankrupt's estate, issue a warrant authorising the person to whom it is directed to seize any property comprised in the bankrupt's estate which is, or any books, papers or records relating to the bankrupt's estate or affairs which are, in the possession or under the control of the bankrupt or any other person who is required to deliver the property, books, papers or records to the official receiver or trustee.

(2)  Any person executing a warrant under this section may, for the purpose of seizing any property comprised in the bankrupt's estate or any books, papers or records relating to the bankrupt's estate or affairs, break open any premises where the bankrupt or anything that may be seized under the warrant is or is believed to be and any receptacle of the bankrupt which contains or is believed to contain anything that may be so seized.

(3) If, after a bankruptcy order has been made, the court is satisfied that any property comprised in the bankrupt's estate is, or any books, papers or records relating to the bankrupt's estate or affairs are, concealed in any premises not belonging to him, it may issue a warrant authorising any constable or prescribed officer of the court to search those premises for the property, books, papers or records.

(4) A warrant under subsection (3) shall not be executed except in the prescribed manner and in accordance with its terms.

### 366   Inquiry into bankrupt's dealings and property

(1) At any time after a bankruptcy order has been made the court may, on the application of the official receiver or the trustee of the bankrupt's estate, summon to appear before it—

    (a) the bankrupt or the bankrupt's spouse or former spouse or civil partner or former civil partner,

    (b) any person known or believed to have any property comprised in the bankrupt's estate in his possession or to be indebted to the bankrupt,

    (c) any person appearing to the court to be able to give information concerning the bankrupt or the bankrupt's dealings, affairs or property.

The court may require any such person as is mentioned in paragraph (b) or (c) to submit an affidavit to the court containing an account of his dealings with the bankrupt or to produce any documents in his possession or under his control relating to the bankrupt or the bankrupt's dealings, affairs or property.

(2) Without prejudice to section 364, the following applies in a case where—

    (a) a person without reasonable excuse fails to appear before the court when he is summoned to do so under this section, or

    (b) there are reasonable grounds for believing that a person has absconded, or is about to abscond, with a view to avoiding his appearance before the court under this section.

(3) The court may, for the purpose of bringing that person and anything in his possession before the court, cause a warrant to be issued to a constable or prescribed officer of the court—

    (a) for the arrest of that person, and

    (b) for the seizure of any books, papers, records, money or goods in that person's possession.

(4) The court may authorise a person arrested under such a warrant to be kept in custody, and anything seized under such a warrant to be held, in accordance with the rules, until that person is brought before the court under the warrant or until such other times as the court may order.

### 367   Court's enforcement powers under s 366

(1) If it appears to the court, on consideration of any evidence obtained under section 366 or this section, that any person has in his possession any property comprised in the bankrupt's estate, the court may, on the application of the official receiver or the trustee of the bankrupt's estate, order that person to deliver the whole or any part of the property to the official receiver or the trustee at such time, in such manner and on such terms as the court thinks fit.

(2) If it appears to the court, on consideration of any evidence obtained under section 366 or this section, that any person is indebted to the bankrupt, the court may, on the application of the official receiver or the trustee of the bankrupt's estate, order that person to pay to the official receiver or trustee, at such time and in such manner as the court may direct, the whole or part of the amount due, whether in full discharge of the debt or otherwise as the court thinks fit.

(3) The court may, if it thinks fit, order that any person who if within the jurisdiction of the court would be liable to be summoned to appear before it under section 366 shall be examined in any part of the United Kingdom where he may be for the time being, or in any place outside the United Kingdom.

(4) Any person who appears or is brought before the court under section 366 or this section may be examined on oath, either orally or by interrogatories, concerning the bankrupt or the bankrupt's dealings, affairs and property.

### 368   Provision corresponding to s 366, where interim receiver appointed

Sections 366 and 367 apply where an interim receiver has been appointed under section 286 as they apply where a bankruptcy order has been made, as if—

    (a) references to the official receiver or the trustee were to the interim receiver, and

    (b) references to the bankrupt and to his estate were (respectively) to the debtor and his property.

### 369   Order for production of documents by inland revenue

(1) For the purposes of an examination under section 290 (public examination of bankrupt) or proceedings under sections 366 to 368, the court may, on the application of the official receiver or the trustee of the bankrupt's estate, order an inland revenue official to produce to the court—

    (a) any return, account or accounts submitted (whether before or after the commencement of the bankruptcy) by the bankrupt to any inland revenue official,

    (b) any assessment or determination made (whether before or after the commencement of the bankruptcy) in relation to the bankrupt by any inland revenue official, or

    (c) any correspondence (whether before or after the commencement of the bankruptcy) between the bankrupt and any inland revenue official.

(2) Where the court has made an order under subsection (1) for the purposes of any examination or proceedings, the court may, at any time after the document to which the order relates is produced to it, by order authorised the disclosure of the document, or of any part of its contents, to the official receiver, the trustee of the bankrupt's estate or the bankrupt's creditors.

(3) The court shall not address an order under subsection (1) to an inland revenue official unless it is satisfied that that official is dealing, or has dealt, with the affairs of the bankrupt.

(4) Where any document to which an order under subsection (1) relates is not in the possession of the official to whom the order is addressed, it is the duty of that official to take all reasonable steps to secure possession of it and, if he fails to do so, to report the reasons for his failure to the court.

(5) Where any document to which an order under subsection (1) relates is in the possession of an inland revenue official other than the one to whom the order is addressed, it is the duty of the official in possession of the document, at the request of the official to whom the order is addressed, to deliver it to the official making the request.

(6) In this section 'inland revenue official' means any inspector or collector of taxes appointed by the Commissioners of Inland Revenue or any person appointed by the Commissioners to serve in any other capacity.

(7) This section does not apply for the purposes of an examination under sections 366 and 367 which takes places by virtue of section 368 (interim receiver).

### 370    Power to appoint special manager

(1) The court may, on an application under this section, appoint any person to be the special manager—

 (a) of a bankrupt's estate, or

 (b) of the business of an undischarged bankrupt, or

 (c) of the property or business of a debtor in whose case the official receiver has been appointed interim receiver under section 286.

(2) An application under this section may be made by the official receiver or the trustee of the bankrupt's estate in any case where it appears to the official receiver or trustee that the nature of the estate, property or business, or the interests of the creditors generally, require the appointment of another person to manage the estate, property or business.

(3) A special manager appointed under this section has such powers as may be entrusted to him by the court.

(4) The power of the court under subsection (3) to entrust powers to a special manager includes power to direct that any provision in this Group of Parts that has effect in relation to the official receiver, interim receiver or trustee shall have the like effect in relation to the special manager for the purposes of the carrying out by the special manager of any of the functions of the official receiver, interim receiver or trustee.

(5) A special manager appointed under this section shall—

 (a) give such security as may be prescribed,

 (b) prepare and keep such accounts as may be prescribed, and

 (c) produce those accounts in accordance with the rules to the Secretary of State or to such other persons as may be prescribed.

### 371    Re-direction of bankrupt's letters, etc

(1) Where a bankruptcy order has been made, the court may from time to time, on the application of the official receiver or the trustee of the bankrupt's estate, order a postal operator (within the meaning of the Postal Services Act 2000) to re-direct and send or deliver to the official receiver or trustee or otherwise any postal packet (within the meaning of that Act) which would otherwise be sent or delivered by the operator concerned to the bankrupt at such place or places as may be specified in the order.

(2) An order under this section has effect for such period, not exceeding 3 months, as may be specified in the order.

# PART X

# INDIVIDUAL INSOLVENCY: GENERAL PROVISIONS

### 372    Supplies of gas, water, electricity, etc

(1) This section applies where on any day ('the relevant day')—

 (a) a bankruptcy order is made against an individual or an interim receiver of an individual's property is appointed, or

 (b) a voluntary arrangement proposed by an individual is approved under Part VIII, or

 (c) a deed of arrangement is made for the benefit of an individual's creditors;

and in this section 'the office-holder' means the official receiver, the trustee in bankruptcy, the interim receiver, the supervisor of the voluntary arrangement or the trustee under the deed of arrangement, as the case may be.

(2)  If a request falling within the next subsection is made for the giving after the relevant day of any of the supplies mentioned in subsection (4), the supplier—

    (a) may make it a condition of the giving of the supply that the office-holder personally guarantees the payment of any charges in respect of the supply, but

    (b) shall not make it a condition of the giving of the supply, or do anything which has the effect of making it a condition of the giving of the supply, that any outstanding charges in respect of a supply given to the individual before the relevant day are paid.

(3)  A request falls within this subsection if it is made—

    (a) by or with the concurrence of the office-holder, and

    (b) for the purposes of any business which is or has been carried on by the individual, by a firm or partnership of which the individual is or was a member, or by an agent or manager for the individual or for such a firm or partnership.

(4)  The supplies referred to in subsection (2) are—

    (a) a supply of gas by a gas supplier within the meaning of Part I of the Gas Act 1986;

    (b) a supply of electricity by an electricity supplier within the meaning of Part I of the Electricity Act 1989;

    (c) a supply of water by a water undertaker,

    (d) a supply of communications services by a provider of a public electronic communications service.

(5)  The following applies to expressions used in subsection (4)—

    (a) [...]

    (b) [...]

    (c) 'communications services' do not include electronic communications services to the extent that they are used to broadcast or otherwise transmit programme services (within the meaning of the Communications Act 2003).

## 373  Jurisdiction in relation to insolvent individuals

(1)  The High Court and the county courts have jurisdiction throughout England and Wales for the purposes of the Parts in this Group.

(2)  For the purposes of those Parts, a county court has, in addition to its ordinary jurisdiction, all the powers and jurisdiction of the High Court; and the orders of the court may be enforced accordingly in the prescribed manner.

(3)  Jurisdiction for the purposes of those Parts is exercised—

    (a) by the High Court in relation to the proceedings, which, in accordance with the rules, are allocated to the London insolvency district, and

    (b) by each county court in relation to the proceedings which are so allocated to the insolvency district of that court.

(4)  Subsection (3) is without prejudice to the transfer of proceedings from one court to another in the manner prescribed by the rules; and nothing in that subsection invalidates any proceedings on the grounds that they were initiated or continued in the wrong court.

## 374  Insolvency districts

(1)  The Lord Chancellor may , with the concurrence of the Lord Chief Justice, by order designate the areas which are for the time being to be comprised, for the purposes of the Parts in this Group, in the London insolvency district and the insolvency district of each county court; and an order under this section may—

    (a) exclude any county court from having jurisdiction for the purposes of those Parts, or

    (b) confer jurisdiction for those purposes on any county court which has not previously had that jurisdiction.

(2)  An order under this section may contain such incidental, supplemental and transitional provisions as may appear to the Lord Chancellor and the Lord Chief Justice necessary or expedient.

(3)  An order under this section shall be made by statutory instrument and, after being made, shall be laid before each House of Parliament.

(4)  Subject to any order under this section—

    (a) the district which, immediately before the appointed day, is the London bankruptcy district becomes, on that day, the London insolvency district;

    (b) any district which immediately before that day is the bankruptcy district of a county court becomes, on that day, the insolvency district of that court, and

    (c) any county court which immediately before that day is excluded from having jurisdiction in bankruptcy is excluded, on and after that day, from having jurisdiction for the purposes of the Parts in this Group.

(5)  The Lord Chief Justice may nominate a judicial office holder (as defined in section 109(4) of the Constitutional Reform Act 2005) to exercise his functions under this section.

## 375  Appeals etc from courts exercising insolvency jurisdiction

(1)  Every court having jurisdiction for the purposes of the Parts in this Group may review, rescind or vary any order made by it in the exercise of that jurisdiction.

(2) An appeal from a decision made in the exercise of jurisdiction for the purposes of those Parts by a county court or by a registrar in bankruptcy of the High Court lies to a single judge of the High Court; and an appeal from a decision of that judge on such an appeal lies […].

(3) A county court is not, in the exercise of its jurisdiction for the purposes of those Parts, to be subject to be restrained by the order of any other court, and no appeal lies from its decision in the exercise of that jurisdiction except as provided by this section.

### 376  Time-limits

Where by any provision in this Group of Parts or by the rules the time for doing anything is limited, the court may extend the time, either before or after it has expired, on such terms, if any, as it thinks fit.

### 377  Formal defects

The acts of a person as the trustee of a bankrupt's estate or as a special manager, and the acts of the creditors' committee established for any bankruptcy, are valid notwithstanding any defect in the appointment, election or qualifications of the trustee or manager or, as the case may be, of any member of the committee.

### 378  Exemption from stamp duty

Stamp duty shall not be charged on—

(a) any document, being a deed, conveyance, assignment, surrender, admission or other assurance relating solely to property which is comprised in a bankrupt's estate and which, after the execution of that document, is or remains at law or in equity the property of the bankrupt or of the trustee of that estate,

(b) any writ, order, certificate or other instrument relating solely to the property of a bankrupt or to any bankruptcy proceedings.

### 379  Annual report

As soon as practicable after the end of 1986 and each subsequent calendar year, the Secretary of State shall prepare and lay before each House of Parliament a report about the operation during that year of so much of this Act as is comprised in this Group of Parts, and about proceedings in the course of that year under the Deeds of Arrangement Act 1914.

# PART XI

# INTERPRETATION FOR SECOND GROUP OF PARTS

### 380  Introductory

The next five sections have effect for the interpretation of the provisions of this Act which are comprised in this Group of Parts; and where a definition is provided for a particular expression, it applies except so far as the context otherwise requires.

### 381  'Bankrupt' and associated terminology

(1) 'Bankrupt' means an individual who has been adjudged bankrupt and, in relation to a bankruptcy order, it means the individual adjudged bankrupt by that order.

(2) 'Bankruptcy order' means an order adjudging an individual bankrupt.

(3) 'Bankruptcy petition' means a petition to the court for a bankruptcy order.

### 382  'Bankruptcy debt', etc

(1) 'Bankruptcy debt', in relation to a bankrupt, means (subject to the next subsection) any of the following—

(a) any debt or liability to which he is subject at the commencement of the bankruptcy,

(b) any debt or liability to which he may become subject after the commencement of the bankruptcy (including after his discharge from bankruptcy) by reason of any obligation incurred before the commencement of the bankruptcy,

(c) *any amount specified in pursuance of section 39(3)(c) of the Powers of Criminal Courts Act 1973 in any criminal bankruptcy order made against him before the commencement of the bankruptcy, and*

(d) any interest provable as mentioned in section 322(2) in Chapter IV of Part IX.

(2) In determining for the purposes of any provision in this Group of Parts whether any liability in tort is a bankruptcy debt, the bankrupt is deemed to become subject to that liability by reason of an obligation incurred at the time when the cause of action accrued.

(3) For the purposes of references in this Group of Parts to a debt or liability, it is immaterial whether the debt or liability is present or future, whether it is certain or contingent or whether its amount is fixed or liquidated, or is capable of being ascertained by fixed rules or as a matter of opinion; and references in this Group of Parts to owing a debt are to be read accordingly.

(4) In this Group of Parts, except in so far as the context otherwise requires, 'liability' means (subject to subsection (3) above) a liability to pay money or money's worth, including any liability under an

enactment, any liability for breach of trust, any liability in contract, tort or bailment and any liability arising out of an obligation to make restitution.[19]

### 383 'Creditor', 'security', etc

(1) 'Creditor'—

    *(a) in relation to a bankrupt, means a person to whom any of the bankruptcy debts is owed (being, in the case of an amount falling within paragraph (c) of the definition in section 382(1) or 'bankruptcy debt', the person in respect of whom that amount is specified in the criminal bankruptcy order in question), and*

    (b) in relation to an individual to whom a bankruptcy petition relates, means a person who would be a creditor in the bankruptcy if a bankruptcy order were made on that petition.

(2) Subject to the next two subsections and any provision of the rules requiring a creditor to give up his security for the purposes of proving a debt, a debt is secured for the purposes of this Group of Parts to the extent that the person to whom the debt is owed holds any security for the debt (whether a mortgage, charge, lien or other security) over any property of the person by whom the debt is owed.

(3) Where a statement such as is mentioned in section 269(1)(a) in Chapter I of Part IX has been made by a secured creditor for the purposes of any bankruptcy petition and a bankruptcy order is subsequently made on that petition, the creditor is deemed for the purposes of the Parts in this Group to have given up the security specified in the statement.

(4) In subsection (2) the reference to a security does not include a lien on books, papers or other records, except to the extent that they consist of documents which give a title to property and are held as such.[20]

### 384 'Prescribed' and 'the rules'

(1) Subject to the next subsection and sections 342C(7) and 342F(9) in Chapter V of Part IX, 'prescribed' means prescribed by the rules; and 'the rules' means rules made under section 412 in Part XV.

(2) References in this Group of Parts to the amount prescribed for the purposes of any of the following provisions—

    section 251S(4)

    section 273;

    section 313A;

    section 346(3);

    section 354(1) and (2);

    section 358;

    section 360(1);

    section 361(2); [...]

    section 364(2)(d),

    paragraphs 6 to 8 of Schedule 4ZA

and references in those provisions to the prescribed amount are to be read in accordance with section 418 in Part XV and orders made under that section.

### 385 Miscellaneous definitions

(1) The following definitions have effect—

'the court', in relation to any matter, means the court to which, in accordance with section 373 in Part X and the rules, proceedings with respect to that matter are allocated or transferred;

'creditor's petition' means a bankruptcy petition under section 264(1)(a);

*'criminal bankruptcy order' means an order under section 39(1) of the Powers of Criminal Courts Act 1973;*

'debt' is to be construed in accordance with section 382(3);

'the debtor'—

    (za) in relation to a debt relief order or an application for such an order, has the same meaning as in Part 7A,

    (a) in relation to a proposal for the purposes of Part VIII, means the individual making or intending to make that proposal, and

    (b) in relation to a bankruptcy petition, means the individual to whom the petition relates;

'debtor's petition' means a bankruptcy petition presented by the debtor himself under section 264(1)(b);

'debt relief order' means an order made by the official receiver under Part 7A;

'dwelling house' includes any building or part of a building which is occupied as a dwelling and any yard, garden, garage or outhouse belonging to the dwelling house and occupied with it;

'estate', in relation to a bankrupt is to be construed in accordance with section 283 in Chapter II of Part IX;

'family', in relation to a bankrupt, means the persons (if any) who are living with him and are dependent on him;

---

[19] Subsection 1(c) repealed by the Criminal Justice Act 1988 c 33 from a date to be appointed.

[20] Subsection 1(a) repealed by the Criminal Justice Act 1988 c 33 from a date to be appointed.

'insolvency administration order' means an order for the administration in bankruptcy of the insolvent estate of a deceased debtor (being an individual at the date of his death);

'insolvency administration petition' means a petition for an insolvency administration order;

'secured' and related expressions are to be construed in accordance with section 383;

'the Rules' means the Insolvency Rules 1986. and

'the trustee', in relation to a bankruptcy and the bankrupt, means the trustee of the bankrupt's estate.

(2) References in this Group of Parts to a person's affairs include his business, if any.[21]

# THE THIRD GROUP OF PARTS

# MISCELLANEOUS MATTERS BEARING ON BOTH COMPANY AND INDIVIDUAL INSOLVENCY; GENERAL INTERPRETATION; FINAL PROVISIONS

# PART XII

# PREFERENTIAL DEBTS IN COMPANY AND INDIVIDUAL INSOLVENCY

## 386   Categories of preferential debts

(1) A reference in this Act to the preferential debts of a company or an individual is to the debts listed in Schedule 6 to this Act (contributions to occupational pension schemes; remuneration, &c. of employees; levies on coal and steel production); and references to preferential creditors are to be read accordingly.

(2) In that Schedule 'the debtor' means the company or the individual concerned.

(3) Schedule 6 is to be read with Schedule 4 to the Pension Schemes Act 1993 (occupational pension scheme contributions).

## 387   'The relevant date'

(1) This section explains references in Schedule 6 to the relevant date (being the date which determines the existence and amount of a preferential debt).

(2) For the purposes of section 4 in Part I (meetings to consider company voluntary arrangement), the relevant date in relation to a company which is not being wound up is—

(a) if the company is in administration, the date on which it entered administration, and

(b) if the company is not in administration, the date on which the voluntary arrangement takes effect.

(2A) For the purposes of paragraph 31 of Schedule A1 (meetings to consider company voluntary arrangement where a moratorium under section 1A is in force), the relevant date in relation to a company is the date of filing.

(3) In relation to a company which is being wound up, the following applies—

(a) if the winding up is by the court, and the winding-up order was made immediately upon the discharge of an administration order, the relevant date is the date on which the company entered administration;

(aa) if the winding up is by the court and the winding-up order was made following conversion of administration into winding up by virtue of Article 37 of the EC Regulation, the relevant date is the date on which the company entered administration;

(ab) if the company is deemed to have passed a resolution for voluntary winding up by virtue of an order following conversion of administration into winding up under Article 37 of the EC Regulation, the relevant date is the date on which the company entered administration;

(b) if the case does not fall within paragraph (a), (aa) or (ab) and the company—

(i) is being wound up by the court, and

(ii) had not commenced to be wound up voluntarily before the date of the making of the winding-up order,

the relevant date is the date of the appointment (or first appointment) of a provisional liquidator or, if no such appointment has been made, the date of the winding-up order;

(ba) if the case does not fall within paragraph (a), (aa), (ab) or (b) and the company is being wound up following administration pursuant to paragraph 83 of Schedule B1, the relevant date is the date on which the company entered administration;

(c) if the case does not fall within paragraph (a), (aa), (ab), (b) or (ba), the relevant date is the date of the passing of the resolution for the winding up of the company.

---

[21] The words in italics repealed by the Criminal Justice Act 1988 c 33 from a date to be appointed.

(3A)  In relation to a company which is in administration (and to which no other provision of this section applies) the relevant date is the date on which the company enters administration.

(4)  In relation to a company in receivership (where section 40 or, as the case may be, section 59 applies), the relevant date is—

    (a)  in England and Wales, the date of the appointment of the receiver by debenture-holders, and

    (b)  in Scotland, the date of the appointment of the receiver under section 53(6) or (as the case may be) 54(5).

(5)  For the purposes of section 258 in Part VIII (individual voluntary arrangements), the relevant date is, in relation to a debtor who is not an undischarged bankrupt

    (a)  where an interim order has been made under section 252 with respect to his proposal, the date of that order, and

    (b)  in any other case, the date on which the voluntary arrangement takes effect.

(6)  In relation to a bankrupt, the following applies—

    (a)  where at the time the bankruptcy order was made there was an interim receiver appointed under section 286, the relevant date is the date on which the interim receiver was first appointed after the presentation of the bankruptcy petition;

    (b)  otherwise, the relevant date is the date of the making of the bankruptcy order.

# PART XIII

## INSOLVENCY PRACTITIONERS AND THEIR QUALIFICATION

*Restrictions on unqualified persons acting as liquidator, trustee in bankruptcy, etc.*

### 388  Meaning of 'act as insolvency practitioner'

(1)  A person acts as an insolvency practitioner in relation to a company by acting—

    (a)  as its liquidator, provisional liquidator, administrator or administrative receiver, or

    (b)  where a voluntary arrangement in relation to the company is proposed or approved under Part I, as nominee or supervisor

(2)  A person acts as an insolvency practitioner in relation to an individual by acting—

    (a)  as his trustee in bankruptcy or interim receiver of his property or as permanent or interim trustee in the sequestration of his estate; or

    (b)  as trustee under a deed which is a deed of arrangement made for the benefit of his creditors or, in Scotland, a trust deed for his creditor; or

    (c)  where a voluntary arrangement in relation to the individual is proposed or approved under Part VIII, as nominee or supervisor

    (d)  in the case of a deceased individual to the administration of whose estate this section applies by virtue of an order under section 421 (application of provisions of this Act to insolvent estates of deceased persons), as administrator of that estate.

(2A)  A person acts as an insolvency practitioner in relation to an insolvent partnership by acting—

    (a)  as its liquidator, provisional liquidator or administrator, or

    (b)  as trustee of the partnership under article 11 of the Insolvent Partnerships Order 1994, or

    (c)  where a voluntary arrangement in relation to the insolvent partnership is proposed or approved under Part I of the Act, as nominee or supervisor.

(2B)  In relation to a voluntary arrangement proposed under Part I or VIII, a person acts as nominee if he performs any of the functions conferred on nominees under the Part in question.

(3)  References in this section to an individual include, except in so far as the context otherwise requires, references […] to any debtor within the meaning of the Bankruptcy (Scotland) Act 1985.

(4)  In this section—

'administrative receiver' has the meaning given by section 251 in Part VII;

'company' means a company within the meaning given by section 735(1) of the 1985 Act, a company which may be wound up under Part XXI of that Act or a building society within the meaning of the Building Societies Act 1986.

'interim trustee' and 'permanent trustee' mean the same as in the Bankruptcy (Scotland) Act 1985.

(5)  Nothing in this section applies to anything done by—

    (a)  the official receiver; or

    (b)  the Accountant in Bankruptcy (within the meaning of the Bankruptcy (Scotland) Act 1985).

(6)  Nothing in this section applies to anything done (whether in the United Kingdom or elsewhere) in relation to insolvency proceedings under the EC Regulation in a member State other than the United Kingdom.

### 389 Acting without qualification an offence

(1) A person who acts as an insolvency practitioner in relation to a company or an individual at a time when he is not qualified to do so is liable to imprisonment or a fine, or to both.

(1A) This section is subject to section 389A

(2) This section does not apply to the official receiver or the Accountant in Bankruptcy (within the meaning of the Bankruptcy (Scotland) Act 1985).

### 389A Authorisation of nominees and supervisors

(1) Section 389 does not apply to a person acting, in relation to a voluntary arrangement proposed or approved under Part I or Part VIII, as nominee or supervisor if he is authorised so to act.

(2) For the purposes of subsection (1) and those Parts, an individual to whom subsection (3) does not apply is authorised to act as nominee or supervisor in relation to such an arrangement if—

    (a) he is a member of a body recognised for the purpose by the Secretary of State, and

    (b) there is in force security (in Scotland, caution) for the proper performance of his functions and that security or caution meets the prescribed requirements with respect to his so acting in relation to the arrangement.

(3) This subsection applies to a person if—

    (a) he has been adjudged bankrupt or sequestration of his estate has been awarded and (in either case) he has not been discharged,

    (b) he is subject to a disqualification order made or a disqualification undertaking accepted under the Company Directors Disqualification Act 1986 or to a disqualification order made under Part II of the Companies (Northern Ireland) Order 1989 or a disqualification undertaking accepted under the Company Directors Disqualification (Northern Ireland) Order 2002 or

    (c) he is a patient within the meaning of Part VII of the Mental Health Act 1983 or section 329(1) of the Mental Health (Care and Treatment)(Scotland) Act 2003.

(4) The Secretary of State may by order declare a body which appears to him to fall within subsection (5) to be a recognised body for the purposes of subsection (2)(a).

(5) A body may be recognised if it maintains and enforces rules for securing that its members—

    (a) are fit and proper persons to act as nominees or supervisors, and

    (b) meet acceptable requirements as to education and practical training and experience.

(6) For the purposes of this section, a person is a member of a body only if he is subject to its rules when acting as nominee or supervisor (whether or not he is in fact a member of the body).

(7) An order made under subsection (4) in relation to a body may be revoked by a further order if it appears to the Secretary of State that the body no longer falls within subsection (5).

(8) An order of the Secretary of State under this section has effect from such date as is specified in the order; and any such order revoking a previous order may make provision for members of the body in question to continue to be treated as members of a recognised body for a specified period after the revocation takes effect.

### 389B Official receiver as nominee or supervisor

(1) The official receiver is authorised to act as nominee or supervisor in relation to a voluntary arrangement approved under Part VIII provided that the debtor is an undischarged bankrupt when the arrangement is proposed.

(2) The Secretary of State may by order repeal the proviso in subsection (1).

(3) An order under subsection (2)—

    (a) must be made by statutory instrument, and

    (b) shall be subject to annulment in pursuance of a resolution of either House of Parliament.

*The requisite qualification, and the means of obtaining it*

### 390 Persons not qualified to act as insolvency practitioners

(1) A person who is not an individual is not qualified to act as an insolvency practitioner.

(2) A person is not qualified to act as an insolvency practitioner at any time unless at that time—

    (a) he is authorised so to act by virtue of membership of a professional body recognised under section 391 below, being permitted so to act by or under the rules of that body, or

    (b) he holds an authorisation granted by a competent authority under section 393.

(3) A person is not qualified to act as an insolvency practitioner in relation to another person at any time unless—

    (a) there is in force at that time security or, in Scotland, caution for the proper performance of his functions, and

    (b) that security or caution meets the prescribed requirements with respect to his so acting in relation to that other person.

(4) A person is not qualified to act as an insolvency practitioner at any time if at that time—

    (a) he has been adjudged bankrupt or sequestration of his estate has been awarded and (in either case) he has not been discharged,

    (aa) a moratorium period under a debt relief order applies in relation of him,

(b) he is subject to a disqualification order made or a disqualification undertaking accepted under the Company Directors Disqualification Act 1986 or to a disqualification order made under Part II of the Companies (Northern Ireland) Order 1989 or to a disqualification undertaking accepted under the Company Directors Disqualification (Northern Ireland) Order 2002, or

(c) he is a patient within the meaning of Part VII of the Mental Health Act 1983 or section 329(1) of the Mental Health (Care and Treatment)(Scotland) Act 2003 or has had a guardian appointed to him under the Adults with Incapacity (Scotland) Act 2000 (asp 4).

(5) A person is not qualified to act as an insolvency practitioner while a bankruptcy restrictions order or a debt relief restrictions order is in force in respect of him.

### 391 Recognised professional bodies

(1) The Secretary of State may by order declare a body which appears to him to fall within subsection (2) below to be a recognised professional body for the purposes of this section.

(2) A body may be recognised if it regulates the practice of a profession and maintains and enforces rules for securing that such of its members as are permitted by or under the rules to act as insolvency practitioners—

(a) are fit and proper persons so to act, and

(b) meet acceptable requirements as to education and practical training and experience.

(3) References to members of a recognised professional body are to persons who, whether members of that body or not, are subject to its rules in the practice of the profession in question.

The reference in section 390(2) above to membership of a professional body recognised under this section is to be read accordingly.

(4) An order made under subsection (1) in relation to a professional body may be revoked by a further order if it appears to the Secretary of State that the body no longer falls within subsection (2).

(5) An order of the Secretary of State under this section has effect from such date as is specified in the order; and any such order revoking a previous order may make provision whereby members of the body in question continue to be treated as authorised to act as insolvency practitioners for a specified period after the revocation takes effect.

### 392 Authorisation by competent authority

(1) Application may be made to a competent authority for authorisation to act as an insolvency practitioner.

(2) The competent authorities for this purpose are—

(a) in relation to a case of any description specified in directions given by the Secretary of State, the body or person so specified in relation to cases of that description, and

(b) in relation to a case not falling within paragraph (a), the Secretary of State.

(3) The application—

(a) shall be made in such manner as the competent authority may direct,

(b) shall contain or be accompanied by such information as that authority may reasonably require for the purpose of determining the application, and

(c) shall be accompanied by the prescribed fee;

and the authority may direct that notice of the making of the application shall be published in such manner as may be specified in the direction.

(4) At any time after receiving the application and before determining it the authority may require the applicant to furnish additional information.

(5) Directions and requirements given or imposed under subsection (3) or (4) may differ as between different applications.

(6) Any information to be furnished to the competent authority under this section shall, if it so requires, be in such form or verified in such manner as it may specify.

(7) An application may be withdrawn before it is granted or refused.

(8) Any sums received under this section by a competent authority other than the Secretary of State may be retained by the authority; and any sums so received by the Secretary of State shall be paid into the Consolidated Fund.

(9) Subsection (3)(c) shall not have effect in respect of an application made to the Secretary of State (but this subsection is without prejudice to section 415A).

### 393 Grant, refusal and withdrawal of authorisation

(1) The competent authority may, on an application duly made in accordance with section 392 and after being furnished with all such information as it may require under that section, grant or refuse the application.

(2) The authority shall grant the application if it appears to it from the information furnished by the applicant and having regard to such other information, if any, as it may have—

(a) that the applicant is a fit and proper person to act as an insolvency practitioner, and

(b) that the applicant meets the prescribed requirements with respect to education and practical training and experience.

(3) An authorisation granted under this section, if not previously withdrawn, continues in force for such period not exceeding the prescribed maximum as may be specified in the authorisation.

(4) An authorisation so granted may be withdrawn by the competent authority if it appears to it—

    (a) that the holder of the authorisation is no longer a fit and proper person to act as an insolvency practitioner, or

    (b) without prejudice to paragraph (a), that the holder—

        (i) has failed to comply with any provision of this Part or of any regulations made under this Part or Part XV, or

        (ii) in purported compliance with any such provision, has furnished the competent authority with false, inaccurate or misleading information.

(5) An authorisation granted under this section may be withdrawn by the competent authority at the request or with the consent of the holder of the authorisation.

### 394  Notices

(1) Where a competent authority grants an authorisation under section 393, it shall give written notice of that fact to the applicant, specifying the date on which the authorisation takes effect.

(2) Where the authority proposes to refuse an application, or to withdraw an authorisation under section 393(4), it shall give the applicant or holder of the authorisation written notice of its intention to do so, setting out particulars of the grounds on which it proposes to act.

(3) In the case of a proposed withdrawal the notice shall state the date on which it is proposed that the withdrawal should take effect.

(4) A notice under subsection (2) shall give particulars of the rights exercisable under the next two sections by a person on whom the notice is served.

### 395  Right to make representations

(1) A person on whom a notice is served under section 394(2) may within 14 days after the date of service make written representations to the competent authority.

(2) The competent authority shall have regard to any representations so made in determining whether to refuse the application or withdraw the authorisation, as the case may be.

### 396  Reference to Tribunal

(1) The Insolvency Practitioners Tribunal ('the Tribunal') continues in being; and the provisions of Schedule 7 apply to it.

(2) Where a person is served with a notice under section 394(2), he may—

    (a) at any time within 28 days after the date of service of the notice, or

    (b) at any time after the making by him of representations under section 395 and before the end of the period of 28 days after the date of the service on him of a notice by the competent authority that the authority does not propose to alter its decision in consequence of the representations,

give written notice to the authority requiring the case to be referred to the Tribunal.

(3) Where a requirement is made under subsection (2), then, unless the competent authority—

    (a) has decided or decides to grant the application or, as the case may be, not to withdraw the authorisation, and

    (b) within 7 days after the date of the making of the requirement, gives written notice of that decision to the person by whom the requirement was made,

it shall refer the case to the Tribunal.

### 397  Action of Tribunal on reference

(1) On a reference under section 396 the Tribunal shall—

    (a) investigate the case, and

    (b) make a report to the competent authority stating what would in their opinion be the appropriate decision in the matter and the reasons for that opinion,

and it is the duty of the competent authority to decide the matter accordingly.

(2) The Tribunal shall send a copy of the report to the applicant or, as the case may be, the holder of the authorisation; and the competent authority shall serve him with a written notice of the decision made by it in accordance with the report.

(3) The competent authority may, if he thinks fit, publish the report of the Tribunal.

### 398  Refusal or withdrawal without reference to Tribunal

Where in the case of any proposed refusal or withdrawal of an authorisation either—

    (a) the period mentioned in section 396(2)(a) has expired without the making of any requirement under that subsection or of any representations under section 395, or

    (b) the competent authority has given a notice such as is mentioned in section 396(2)(b) and the period so mentioned has expired without the making of any such requirement,

the competent authority may give written notice of the refusal or withdrawal to the person concerned in accordance with the proposal in the notice given under section 394(2).

# PART XIV

# PUBLIC ADMINISTRATION (ENGLAND AND WALES)

*Official receivers*

### 399   Appointment, etc of official receivers

(1)  For the purposes of this Act the official receiver, in relation to any bankruptcy , winding up or individual voluntary arrangement, debt relief order or application for such an order, is any person who by virtue of the following provisions of this section or section 401 below is authorised to act as the official receiver in relation to that bankruptcy, winding up or individual voluntary arrangement, debt relief order or application for such an order.

(2)  The Secretary of State may (subject to the approval of the Treasury as to numbers) appoint persons to the office of official receiver, and a person appointed to that office (whether under this section or section 70 of the Bankruptcy Act 1914)—

(a)  shall be paid out of money provided by Parliament such salary as the Secretary of State may with the concurrence of the Treasury direct,

(b)  shall hold office on such other terms and conditions as the Secretary of State may with the concurrence of the Treasury direct, and

(c)  may be removed from office by a direction of the Secretary of State.

(3)  Where a person holds the office of official receiver, the Secretary of State shall from time to time attach him either to the High Court or to a county court having jurisdiction for the purposes of the second Group of Parts of this Act.

(4)  Subject to any directions under subsection (6) below, an official receiver attached to a particular court is the person authorised to act as the official receiver in relation to every bankruptcy, winding up or individual voluntary arrangement falling within the jurisdiction of that court.

(5)  The Secretary of State shall ensure that there is, at all times, at least one official receiver attached to the High Court and at least one attached to each county court having jurisdiction for the purposes of the second Group of Parts; but he may attach the same official receiver to two or more different courts.

(6)  The Secretary of State may give directions with respect to the disposal of the business of official receivers, and such directions may, in particular—

(a)  authorise an official receiver attached to one court to act as the official receiver in relation to any case or description of cases falling within the jurisdiction of another court;

(b)  provide, where there is more than one official receiver authorised to act as the official receiver in relation to cases falling within the jurisdiction of any court, for the distribution of their business between or among themselves.

(7)  A person who at the coming into force of section 222 of the Insolvency Act 1985 (replaced by this section) is an official receiver attached to a court shall continue in office after the coming into force of that section as an official receiver attached to that court under this section.

### 400   Functions and status of official receivers

(1)  In addition to any functions conferred on him by this Act, a person holding the office of official receiver shall carry out such other functions as may from time to time be conferred on him by the Secretary of State.

(2)  In the exercise of the functions of his office a person holding the office of official receiver shall act under the general directions of the Secretary of State and shall also be an officer of the court in relation to which he exercises those functions.

(3)  Any property vested in his official capacity in a person holding the office of official receiver shall, on his dying, ceasing to hold office or being otherwise succeeded in relation to the bankruptcy or winding up in question by another official receiver, vest in his successor without any conveyance, assignment or transfer.

### 401   Deputy official receivers and staff

(1)  The Secretary of State may, if he thinks it expedient to do so in order to facilitate the disposal of the business of the official receiver attached to any court, appoint an officer of his department to act as deputy to that official receiver.

(2)  Subject to any directions given by the Secretary of State under section 399 or 400, a person appointed to act as deputy to an official receiver has, on such conditions and for such period as may be specified in the terms of his appointment, the same status and functions as the official receiver to whom he is appointed deputy.

Accordingly, references in this Act (except section 399(1) to (5)) to an official receiver include a person appointed to act as his deputy.

(3)  An appointment made under subsection (1) may be terminated at any time by the Secretary of State.

(4)  The Secretary of State may, subject to the approval of the Treasury as to numbers and remuneration and as to the other terms and conditions of the appointments, appoint officers of his department to assist official receivers in the carrying out of their functions.

### The Official Petitioner

### 402  Official Petitioner

(1)  *There continues to be an officer known as the Official Petitioner for the purposes of discharging, in relation to cases in which a criminal bankruptcy order is made, the functions assigned to him by or under this Act; and the Director of Public Prosecutions continues, by virtue of his office, to be the Official Petitioner.*

(2)  *The functions of the Official Petitioner include the following—*

(a)  *to consider whether, in a case in which a criminal bankruptcy order is made, it is in the public interest that he should himself present a petition under section 264(1)(d) of this Act;*

(b)  *to present such a petition in any case where he determines that it is in the public interest for him to do so;*

(c)  *to make payments, in such cases as he may determine, towards expenses incurred by other persons in connection with proceedings in pursuance of such a petition; and*

(d)  *to exercise, so far as he considers it in the public interest to do so, any of the powers conferred on him by or under this Act.*

(3)  *Any functions of the Official Petitioner may be discharged on his behalf by any person acting with his authority.*

(4)  *Neither the Official Petitioner nor any person acting with his authority is liable to any action or proceeding in respect of anything done or omitted to be done in the discharge, or purported discharge, of the functions of the Official Petitioner.*

(5)  *In this section 'criminal bankruptcy order' means an order under section 39(1) of the Powers of Criminal Courts Act 1973.*[22]

### Insolvency Service finance, accounting and investment

### 403  Insolvency Services Account

(1)  All money received by the Secretary of State in respect of proceedings under this Act as it applies to England and Wales shall be paid into the Insolvency Services Account kept by the Secretary of State with the Bank of England; and all payments out of money standing to the credit of the Secretary of State in that account shall be made by the Bank of England in such manner as he may direct.

(2)  Whenever the cash balance standing to the credit of the Insolvency Services Account is in excess of the amount which in the opinion of the Secretary of State is required for the time being to answer demands in respect of bankrupts' estates or companies' estates, the Secretary of State shall—

(a)  notify the excess to the National Debt Commissioners, and

(b)  pay into the Insolvency Services Investment Account ('the Investment Account') kept by the Commissioners with the Bank of England the whole or any part of the excess as the Commissioners may require for investment in accordance with the following provisions of this Part.

(3)  Whenever any part of the money so invested is, in the opinion of the Secretary of State, required to answer any demand in respect of bankrupt's estates or companies' estates, he shall notify to the National Debt Commissioners the amount so required and the Commissioners—

(a)  shall thereupon repay to the Secretary of State such sum as may be required to the credit of the Insolvency Services Account, and

(b)  for that purpose may direct the sale of such part of the securities in which the money has been invested as may be necessary.

### 404  Investment Account

Any money standing to the credit of the Investment Account (including any money received by the National Debt Commissioners by way of interest on or proceeds of any investment under this section) may be invested by the Commissioners, in accordance with such directions as may be given by the Treasury, in any manner for the time being specified in Part II of Schedule 1 to the Trustee Investments Act 1961.

### 405  Application of income in Investment Account; adjustment of balances
[...]

### 406  Interest on money received by liquidators or trustees in bankruptcy and invested

Where under rules made by virtue of paragraph 16 of Schedule 8 to this Act (investment of money received by company liquidators) or paragraph 21 of Schedule 9 to this Act (investment of money received by trustee in bankruptcy) a company or a bankrupt's estate has become entitled to any sum by

---

[22] Section 402 is repealed by the Criminal Justice Act 1988 c 33 from a date to be appointed.

way of interest, the Secretary of State shall certify that sum and the amount of tax payable on it to the National Debt Commissioners; and the Commissioners shall pay, out of the Investment Account—

    (a) into the Insolvency Services Account, the sum so certified less the amount of tax so certified, and

    (b) to the Commissioners of Inland Revenue, the amount of tax so certified.

### 407 Unclaimed dividends and undistributed balances

(1) The Secretary of State shall from time to time pay into the Consolidated Fund out of the Insolvency Services Account so much of the sums standing to the credit of that Account as represents—

    (a) dividends which were declared before such date as the Treasury may from time to time determine and have not been claimed, and

    (b) balances ascertained before that date which are too small to be divided among the persons entitled to them.

(2) For the purposes of this section the sums standing to the credit of the Insolvency Services Account are deemed to include any sums paid out of that Account and represented by any sums or securities standing to the credit of the Investment Account.

(3) The Secretary of State may require the National Debt Commissioners to pay out of the Investment Account into the Insolvency Services Account the whole or part of any sum which he is required to pay out of that account under subsection (1); and the Commissioners may direct the sale of such securities standing to the credit of the Investment Account as may be necessary for that purpose.

### 408 Adjustment of balances

(1) The Treasury may direct the payment out of the Consolidated Fund of sums into—

    (a) the Insolvency Services Account;

    (b) the Investment Account.

(2) The Treasury shall certify to the House of Commons the reason for any payment under subsection (1).

(3) The Secretary of State may pay sums out of the Insolvency Services Account into the Consolidated Fund.

(4) The National Debt Commissioners may pay sums out of the Investment Account into the Consolidated Fund.

### 409 Annual financial statement and audit

(1) The National Debt Commissioners shall for each year ending on 31st March prepare a statement of the sums credited and debited to the Investment Account in such form and manner as the Treasury may direct and shall transmit it to the Comptroller and Auditor General before the end of November next following the year.

(2) The Secretary of State shall for each year ending 31st March prepare a statement of the sums received or paid by him under section 403 above in such form and manner as the Treasury may direct and shall transmit each statement to the Comptroller and Auditor General before the end of November next following the year.

(3) Every such statement shall include such additional information as the Treasury may direct.

(4) The Comptroller and Auditor General shall examine, certify and report on every such statement and shall lay copies of it, and of his report, before Parliament.

*Supplementary*

### 410 Extent of this Part

This part of this Act extends to England and Wales only.

# PART XV

# SUBORDINATE LEGISLATION

*General insolvency rules*

### 411 Company insolvency rules

(1) Rules may be made—

    (a) in relation to England and Wales, by the Lord Chancellor with the concurrence of the Secretary of State and, in the case of rules that affect court procedure, with the concurrence of the Lord Chief Justice or

    (b) in relation to Scotland, by the Secretary of State,

for the purpose of giving effect to Parts I to VII of this Act or the EC Regulation.

(1A) Rules may also be made for the purpose of giving effect to Part 2 of the Banking Act 2009 (bank insolvency orders); and rules for that purpose shall be made—

    (a) in relation to England and Wales, by the Lord Chancellor with the concurrence of—

        (i) the Treasury, and

    (ii) in the case of rules that affect court procedure, the Lord Chief Justice, or

   (b) in relation to Scotland, by the Treasury.

  (1B) Rules may also be made for the purpose of giving effect to Part 3 of the Banking Act 2009 (bank administration); and rules for that purpose shall be made—

   (a) in relation to England and Wales, by the Lord Chancellor with the concurrence of—

    (i) the Treasury, and

    (ii) in the case of rules that affect court procedure, the Lord Chief Justice, or

   (b) in relation to Scotland, by the Treasury.

  (2) Without prejudice to the generality of subsection (1) and (1A) or (1B), or to any provision of those Parts by virtue of which rules under this section may be made with respect to any matter, rules under this section may contain—

   (a) any such provision as is specified in Schedule 8 to this Act or corresponds to provision contained immediately before the coming into force of section 106 of the Insolvency Act 1985 in rules made, or having effect as if made, under section 663(1) or (2) of the Companies Act (old winding-up rules), and

   (b) such incidental, supplemental and transitional provisions as may appear to the Lord Chancellor or, as the case may be, the Secretary of State or the Treasury necessary or expedient.

  (2A) For the purposes of subsection (2), a reference in Schedule 8 to this Act to doing anything under or for the purposes of a provision of this Act includes a reference to doing anything under or for the purposes of the EC Regulation (in so far as the provision of this Act relates to a matter to which the EC Regulation applies).

  (2B) Rules under this section for the purpose of giving effect to the EC Regulation may not create an offence of a kind referred to in paragraph 1(1)(d) of Schedule 2 to the European Communities Act 1972.

  (2C) For the purposes of subsection (2), a reference in Schedule 8 to this Act to doing anything under or for the purposes of a provision of this Act includes a reference to doing anything under or for the purposes of Part 2 of the Banking Act 2009.

  (2D) For the purposes of subsection (2), a reference in Schedule 8 to this Act to doing anything under or for the purposes of a provision of this Act includes a reference to doing anything under or for the purposes of Part 3 of the Banking Act 2009.

  (3) In Schedule 8 to this Act 'liquidator' includes a provisional liquidator or bank liquidator or administrator; and references above in this section to Parts I to VII of this Act or Part 2 or 3 of the Banking Act 2009 are to be read as including the Companies Act so far as relating to, and to matters connected with or arising out of, the insolvency or winding up of companies.

  (4) Rules under this section shall be made by statutory instrument subject to annulment in pursuance of a resolution of either House of Parliament.

  (5) Regulations made by the Secretary of State or the Treasury under a power conferred by rules under this section shall be made by statutory instrument and, after being made, shall be laid before each House of Parliament.

  (6) Nothing in this section prejudices any power to make rules of court.

  (7) The Lord Chief Justice may nominate a judicial office holder (as defined in section 109(4) of the Constitutional Reform Act 2005) to exercise his functions under this section.

### 412 Individual insolvency rules (England and Wales)

  (1) The Lord Chancellor may, with the concurrence of the Secretary of State and, in the case of rules that affect court procedure, with the concurrence of the Lord Chief Justice, make rules for the purpose of giving effect to Parts 7A to 11 of this Act or the EC Regulation.

  (2) Without prejudice to the generality of subsection (1), or to any provision of those Parts by virtue of which rules under this section may be made with respect to any matter, rules under this section may contain—

   (a) any such provision as is specified in Schedule 9 to this Act or corresponds to provision contained immediately before the appointed day in rules made under section 132 of the Bankruptcy Act 1914; and

   (b) such incidental, supplemental and transitional provisions as may appear to the Lord Chancellor necessary or expedient.

  (2A) For the purposes of subsection (2), a reference in Schedule 9 to this Act to doing anything under or for the purposes of a provision of this Act includes a reference to doing anything under or for the purposes of the EC Regulation (in so far as the provision of this Act relates to a matter to which the EC Regulation applies).

  (2B) Rules under this section for the purpose of giving effect to the EC Regulation may not create an offence of a kind referred to in paragraph 1(1)(d) of Schedule 2 to the European Communities Act 1972.

  (3) Rules under this section shall be made by statutory instrument subject to annulment in pursuance of a resolution of either House of Parliament.

(4) Regulations made by the Secretary of State under a power conferred by rules under this section shall be made by statutory instrument and, after being made, shall be laid before each House of Parliament.

(5) Nothing in this section prejudices any power to make rules of court.

(6) The Lord Chief Justice may nominate a judicial office holder (as defined in section 109(4) of the Constitutional Reform Act 2005) to exercise his functions under this section.

### 413   Insolvency Rules Committee

(1) The committee established under section 10 of the Insolvency Act 1976 (advisory committee on bankruptcy and winding-up rules) continues to exist for the purpose of being consulted under this section.

(2) The Lord Chancellor shall consult the committee before making any rules under section 411 or 412 other than rules which contain a statement that the only provision made by the rules is provision applying rules made under section 411, with or without modifications, for the purposes of provision made by section any of sections 23 to 26 of the Water Industry Act 1991 or Schedule 3 to that Act or by any of sections 59 to 65 of, or Schedule 6 or 7 to, the Railways Act 1993.

(3) Subject to the next subsection, the committee shall consist of—

(a) a judge of the High Court attached to the Chancery Division;
(b) a circuit judge;
(c) a registrar in bankruptcy of the High Court;
(d) the registrar of a county court;
(e) a practising barrister;
(f) a practising solicitor; and
(g) a practising accountant;

and the appointment of any person as a member of the committee shall be made in accordance with subsection (3A) or (3B).

(3A) The Lord Chief Justice must appoint the persons referred to in paragraphs (a) to (d) of subsection (3), after consulting the Lord Chancellor.

(3B) The Lord Chancellor must appoint the persons referred to in paragraphs (e) to (g) of subsection (3), after consulting the Lord Chief Justice.

(4) The Lord Chancellor may appoint as additional members of the committee any persons appearing to him to have qualifications or experience that would be of value to the committee in considering any matter with which it is concerned.

(5) The Lord Chief Justice may nominate a judicial office holder (as defined in section 109(4) of the Constitutional Reform Act 2005) to exercise his functions under this section.

*Fees orders*

### 414   Fees orders (company insolvency proceedings)

(1) There shall be paid in respect of—

(a) proceedings under any of Parts I to VII of this Act, and
(b) the performance by the official receiver or the Secretary of State of functions under those Parts,

such fees as the competent authority may with the sanction of the Treasury by order direct.

(2) That authority is—

(a) in relation to England and Wales, the Lord Chancellor, and
(b) in relation to Scotland, the Secretary of State.

(3) The Treasury may by order direct by whom and in what manner the fees are to be collected and accounted for.

(4) The Lord Chancellor may, with the sanction of the Treasury, by order provide for sums to be deposited, by such persons, in such manner and in such circumstances as may be specified in the order, by way of security for fees payable by virtue of this section.

(5) An order under this section may contain such incidental, supplemental and transitional provisions as may appear to the Lord Chancellor, the Secretary of State or (as the case may be) the Treasury necessary or expedient.

(6) An order under this section shall be made by statutory instrument and, after being made, shall be laid before each House of Parliament.

(7) Fees payable by virtue of this section shall be paid into the Consolidated Fund.

(8) References in subsection (1) to Parts I to VII of this Act are to be read as including the Companies Act so far as relating to, and to matters connected with or arising out of, the insolvency or winding up of companies.

(8A) This section applies in relation to Part 2 of the Banking Act 2009 (bank insolvency) as in relation to Parts I to VII of this Act.

(8B) This section applies in relation to Part 3 of the Banking Act 2009 (bank administration) as in relation to Parts I to VII of this Act.

(9) Nothing in this section prejudices any power to make rules of court; and the application of this section to Scotland is without prejudice to section 2 of the Courts of Law Fees (Scotland) Act 1895.

**415  Fees orders (individual insolvency proceedings in England and Wales)**

(1)  There shall be paid in respect of—

(za)  the costs of persons acting as approved intermediaries under Part 7A,

(a)  proceedings under Parts 7A to 11 of this Act, and

(b)  the performance by the official receiver or the Secretary of State of functions under those Parts,

such fees as the Lord Chancellor may with the sanction of the Treasury by order direct.

(2)  The Treasury may by order direct by whom and in what manner the fees are to be collected and accounted for.

(3)  The Lord Chancellor may, with the sanction of the Treasury, by order provide for sums to be deposited, by such persons, in such manner and in such circumstances as may be specified in the order, by way of security for—

(a)  fees payable by virtue of this section, and

(b)  fees payable to any person who has prepared an insolvency practitioner's report under section 274 in Chapter I of Part IX.

(4)  An order under this section may contain such incidental, supplemental and transitional provisions as may appear to the Lord Chancellor or, as the case may be, the Treasury, necessary or expedient.

(5)  An order under this section shall be made by statutory instrument and, after being made, shall be laid before each House of Parliament.

(6)  Fees payable by virtue of this section shall be paid into the Consolidated Fund.

(7)  Nothing in this section prejudices any power to make rules of court.

**415A  Fees orders (general)**

(A1)  The Secretary of State—

(a)  may by order require a person or body to pay a fee in connection with the grant or maintenance of a designation of that person or body as a competent authority under section 251U, and

(b)  may refuse to grant, or may withdraw, any such designation where a fee is not paid.

(1)  The Secretary of State—

(a)  may by order require a body to pay a fee in connection with the grant or maintenance of recognition of the body under section 391, and

(b)  may refuse recognition, or revoke an order of recognition under section 391(1) by a further order, where a fee is not paid.

(2)  The Secretary of State—

(a)  may by order require a person to pay a fee in connection with the grant or maintenance of authorisation of the person under section 393, and

(b)  may disregard an application or withdraw an authorisation where a fee is not paid.

(3)  The Secretary of State may by order require the payment of fees in respect of—

(a)  the operation of the Insolvency Services Account;

(b)  payments into and out of that Account.

(4)  The following provisions of section 414 apply to fees under this section as they apply to fees under that section—

(a)  subsection (3) (manner of payment),

(b)  subsection (5) (additional provision),

(c)  subsection (6) (statutory instrument),

(d)  subsection (7) (payment into Consolidated Fund), and

(e)  subsection (9) (saving for rules of court).

**416  Monetary limits (companies winding up)**

(1)  The Secretary of State may by order in a statutory instrument increase or reduce any of the money sums for the time being specified in the following provisions in the first Group of Parts—

section 117(2)(amount of company's share capital determining whether county court has jurisdiction to wind it up);

section 120(3)(the equivalent as respects sheriff court jurisdiction in Scotland);

section 123(1)(a)(minimum debt for service of demand on company by unpaid creditor);

section 184(3)(minimum value of judgment, affecting sheriff's duties on levying execution);

section 206(1)(a) and (b)(minimum value of company property concealed or fraudulently removed, affecting criminal liability of company's officer).

(2)  An order under this section may contain such transitional provisions as may appear to the Secretary of State necessary or expedient.

(3)  No order under this section increasing or reducing any of the money sums for the time being specified in section 117(2), 120(3) or 123(1)(a) shall be made unless a draft of the order has been laid before and approved by a resolution of each House of Parliament.

(4)  A statutory instrument containing an order under this section, other than an order to which subsection (3) applies, is subject to annulment in pursuance of a resolution of either House of Parliament.

### 417   Money sum in s 222

The Secretary of State may by regulations in a statutory instrument increase or reduce the money sum for the time being specified in section 222(1)(minimum debt for service of demand on unregistered company by unpaid creditor); but such regulations shall not be made unless a draft of the statutory instrument containing them has been approved by resolution of each House of Parliament.

### 417A   Money sums (company moratorium)

(1) The Secretary of State may by order increase or reduce any of the money sums for the time being specified in the following provisions of Schedule A1 to this Act—

paragraph 17(1)(maximum amount of credit which company may obtain without disclosure of moratorium);

paragraph 41(4)(minimum value of company property concealed or fraudulently removed, affecting criminal liability of company's officer).

(2) An order under this section may contain such transitional provisions as may appear to the Secretary of State necessary or expedient.

(3) An order under this section shall be made by statutory instrument subject to annulment in pursuance of a resolution of either House of Parliament.

### 418   Monetary limits (bankruptcy)

(1) The Secretary of State may by order prescribe amounts for the purposes of the following provisions in the second Group of Parts—

section 251S(4) (maximum amount of credit which a person in respect of whom a debt relief order is made may obtain without disclosure of his status);

section 273 (minimum value of debtor's estate determining whether immediate bankruptcy order should be made; small bankruptcies level);

section 313A (value of property below which application for sale, possession or charge to be dismissed);

section 346(3)(minimum amount of judgment, determining whether amount recovered on sale of debtor's goods is to be treated as part of his estate in bankruptcy);

section 354(1) and (2)(minimum amount of concealed debt, or value or property concealed or removed, determining criminal liability under the section);

section 358 (minimum value of property taken by a bankrupt out of England and Wales, determining his criminal liability);

section 360(1)(maximum amount of credit which bankrupt may obtain without disclosure of his status);

section 361(2)(exemption of bankrupt from criminal liability for failure to keep proper accounts, if unsecured debts not more than the prescribed minimum);

section 364(2)(d)(minimum value of goods removed by the bankrupt, determining his liability to arrest);

paragraphs 6 to 8 of Schedule 4ZA (maximum amount of a person's debts, monthly surplus income and property for purposes of obtaining a debt relief order);

and references in the second Group of Parts to the amount prescribed for the purposes of any of those provisions, and references in those provisions to the prescribed amount, are to be construed accordingly.

(2) An order under this section may contain such transitional provisions as may appear to the Secretary of State necessary or expedient.

(3) An order under this section shall be made by statutory instrument subject to annulment in pursuance of a resolution of either House of Parliament.

*Insolvency practice*

### 419   Regulations for purposes of Part XIII

(1) The Secretary of State may make regulations for the purpose of giving effect to Part XIII of this Act; and 'prescribed' in that Part means prescribed by regulations made by the Secretary of State.

(2) Without prejudice to the generality of subsection (1) or to any provision of that Part by virtue of which regulations may be made with respect to any matter, regulations under this section may contain—

(a) provision as to the matters to be taken into account in determining whether a person is a fit and proper person to act as an insolvency practitioner;

(b) provision prohibiting a person from so acting in prescribed cases, being cases in which a conflict of interest will or may arise;

(c) provision imposing requirements with respect to—

(i) the preparation and keeping by a person who acts as an insolvency practitioner of prescribed books, accounts and other records, and

(ii) the production of those books, accounts and records to prescribed persons;

(d) provision conferring power on prescribed persons—

(i) to require any person who acts or has acted as an insolvency practitioner to answer any inquiry in relation to a case in which he is so acting or has so acted, and

(ii) to apply to a court to examine such a person or any other person on oath concerning such a case;

(e) provision making non-compliance with any of the regulations a criminal offence; and

(f) such incidental, supplemental and transitional provisions as may appear to the Secretary of State necessary or expedient.

(3) Any power conferred by Part XIII of this Part to make regulations, rules or orders is exercisable by statutory instrument subject to annulment by resolution of either House of Parliament.

(4) Any rule or regulation under Part XIII or this Part may make different provision with respect to different cases or descriptions of cases, including different provision for different areas.

*Other order-making powers*

## 420 Insolvent partnerships

(1) The Lord Chancellor may, by order made with the concurrence of the Secretary of State and the Lord Chief Justice, provide that such provisions of this Act as may be specified in the order shall apply in relation to insolvent partnerships with such modifications as may be so specified.

(1A) An order under this section may make provision in relation to the EC Regulation.

(1B) But provision made by virtue of this section in relation to the EC Regulation may not create an offence of a kind referred to in paragraph 1(1)(d) of Schedule 2 to the European Communities Act 1972.

(2) An order under this section may make different provision for different cases and may contain such incidental, supplemental and transitional provisions as may appear to the Lord Chancellor and the Lord Chief Justice necessary or expedient.

(3) An order under this section shall be made by statutory instrument subject to annulment in pursuance of a resolution of either House of Parliament.

(4) The Lord Chief Justice may nominate a judicial office holder (as defined in section 109(4) of the Constitutional Reform Act 2005) to exercise his functions under this section.

## 421 Insolvent estates of deceased persons

(1) The Lord Chancellor may, by order made with the concurrence of the Secretary of State and the Lord Chief Justice, provide that such provisions of this Act as may be specified in the order shall apply in relation to the administration of the insolvent estates of deceased persons with such modifications as may be so specified.

(1A) An order under this section may make provision in relation to the EC Regulation.

(1B) But provision made by virtue of this section in relation to the EC Regulation may not create an offence of a kind referred to in paragraph 1(1)(d) of Schedule 2 to the European Communities Act 1972.

(2) An order under this section may make different provision for different cases and may contain such incidental, supplemental and transitional provisions as may appear to the Lord Chancellor and the Lord Chief Justice necessary or expedient.

(3) An order under this section shall be made by statutory instrument subject to annulment in pursuance of a resolution of either House of Parliament.

(4) For the purposes of this section the estate of a deceased person is insolvent if, when realised, it will be insufficient to meet in full all the debts and other liabilities to which it is subject.

(5) The Lord Chief Justice may nominate a judicial office holder (as defined in section 109(4) of the Constitutional Reform Act 2005) to exercise his functions under this section.

## 421A Insolvent estates: joint tenancies

(1) This section applies where—

(a) an insolvency administration order has been made in respect of the insolvent estate of a deceased person,

(b) the petition for the order was presented after the commencement of this section and within the period of five years beginning with the day on which he died, and

(c) immediately before his death he was beneficially entitled to an interest in any property as joint tenant.

(2) For the purpose of securing that debts and other liabilities to which the estate is subject are met, the court may, on an application by the trustee appointed pursuant to the insolvency administration order, make an order under this section requiring the survivor to pay to the trustee an amount not exceeding the value lost to the estate.

(3) In determining whether to make an order under this section, and the terms of such an order, the court must have regard to all the circumstances of the case, including the interests of the deceased's creditors and of the survivor; but, unless the circumstances are exceptional, the court must assume that the interests of the deceased's creditors outweigh all other considerations.

(4) The order may be made on such terms and conditions as the court thinks fit.

(5) Any sums required to be paid to the trustee in accordance with an order under this section shall be comprised in the estate.

(6) The modifications of this Act which may be made by an order under section 421 include any modifications which are necessary or expedient in consequence of this section.

(7) In this section, 'survivor' means the person who, immediately before the death, was beneficially entitled as joint tenant with the deceased or, if the person who was so entitled dies after the making of the insolvency administration order, his personal representatives.

(8) If there is more than one survivor—

(a) an order under this section may be made against all or any of them, but

(b) no survivor shall be required to pay more than so much of the value lost to the estate as is properly attributable to him.

(9) In this section—

'insolvency administration order' has the same meaning as in any order under section 421 having effect for the time being,

'value lost to the estate' means the amount which, if paid to the trustee, would in the court's opinion restore the position to what it would have been if the deceased had been adjudged bankrupt immediately before his death.

### 422 Formerly authorised banks

(1) The Secretary of State may by order made with the concurrence of the Treasury and after consultation with the Financial Services Authority provide that specified provisions in the first Group of Parts shall apply with specified modifications in relation to any person who—

(a) has a liability in respect of a deposit which he accepted in accordance with the Banking Act 1979 (c 37) or 1987 (c 22), but

(b) does not have permission under Part IV of the Financial Services and Markets Act 2000 (c 8) (regulated activities) to accept deposits.

(1A) Subsection (1)(b) shall be construed in accordance with—

(a) section 22 of the Financial Services and Markets Act 2000 (classes of regulated activity and categories of investment),

(b) any relevant order under that section, and

(c) Schedule 2 to that Act (regulated activities).

(1A) [...].

(2) An order under this section may make different provision for different cases and may contain such incidental, supplemental and transitional provisions as may appear to the Secretary of State necessary or expedient.

(3) An order under this section shall be made by statutory instrument subject to annulment in pursuance of a resolution of either House of Parliament.

# PART XVI

# PROVISIONS AGAINST DEBT AVOIDANCE (ENGLAND AND WALES ONLY)

### 423 Transactions defrauding creditors

(1) This section relates to transactions entered into at an undervalue; and a person enters into such a transaction with another person if—

(a) he makes a gift to the other person or he otherwise enters into a transaction with the other on terms that provide for him to receive no consideration;

(b) he enters into a transaction with the other in consideration of marriage or the formation of a civil partnership; or

(c) he enters into a transaction with the other for a consideration the value of which, in money or money's worth, is significantly less than the value, in money or money's worth, of the consideration provided by himself.

(2) Where a person has entered into such a transaction, the court may, if satisfied under the next subsection, make such order as it thinks fit for—

(a) restoring the position to what it would have been if the transaction had not been entered into, and

(b) protecting the interests of persons who are victims of the transaction.

(3) In the case of a person entering into such a transaction, an order shall only be made if the court is satisfied that it was entered into by him for the purpose—

(a) of putting assets beyond the reach of a person who is making, or may at some time make, a claim against him, or

(b) of otherwise prejudicing the interests of such a person in relation to the claim which he is making or may make.

(4) In this section 'the court' means the High Court or—

(a) if the person entering into the transaction is an individual, any other court which would have jurisdiction in relation to a bankruptcy petition relating to him;

(b) if that person is a body capable of being wound up under Part IV or V of this Act, any other court having jurisdiction to wind it up.

(5) In relation to a transaction at an undervalue, references here and below to a victim of the transaction are to a person who is, or is capable of being, prejudiced by it; and in the following two sections the person entering into the transaction is referred to as 'the debtor'.

### 424    Those who may apply for an order under s 423

(1) An application for an order under section 423 shall not be made in relation to a transaction except—

(a) in a case where the debtor has been adjudged bankrupt or is a body corporate which is being wound up or is in administration, by the official receiver, by the trustee of the bankrupt's estate or the liquidator or administrator of the body corporate or (with the leave of the court) by a victim of the transaction;

(b) in a case where a victim of the transaction is bound by a voluntary arrangement approved under Part I or Part VIII of this Act, by the supervisor of the voluntary arrangement or by any person who (whether or not so bound) is such a victim; or

(c) in any other case, by a victim of the transaction.

(2) An application made under any of the paragraphs of subsection (1) is to be treated as made on behalf of every victim of the transaction.

### 425    Provision which may be made by order under s 423

(1) Without prejudice to the generality of section 423, an order made under that section with respect to a transaction may (subject as follows)—

(a) require any property transferred as part of the transaction to be vested in any person, either absolutely or for the benefit of all the persons on whose behalf the application for the order is treated as made;

(b) require any property to be so vested if it represents, in any person's hands, the application either of the proceeds of sale of property so transferred or of the money so transferred;

(c) release or discharge (in whole or in part) any security given by the debtor;

(d) require any person to pay to any other person in respect of benefits received from the debtor such sums as the court may direct;

(e) provide for any surety or guarantor whose obligations to any person were released or discharged (in whole or in part) under the transaction to be under such new or revived obligations as the court thinks appropriate;

(f) provide for security to be provided for the discharge of any obligation imposed by or arising under the order, for such an obligation to be charged on any property and for such security or charge to have the same priority as a security or charge released or discharged (in whole or in part) under the transaction.

(2) An order under section 423 may affect the property of, or impose any obligation on, any person whether or not he is the person with whom the debtor entered into the transaction; but such an order—

(a) shall not prejudice any interest in property which was acquired from a person other than the debtor and was acquired in good faith, for value and without notice of the relevant circumstances, or prejudice any interest deriving from such an interest, and

(b) shall not require a person who received a benefit from the transaction in good faith, for value and without notice of the relevant circumstances to pay any sum unless he was a party to the transaction.

(3) For the purposes of this section the relevant circumstances in relation to a transaction are the circumstances by virtue of which an order under section 423 may be made in respect of the transaction.

(4) In this section 'security' means any mortgage, charge, lien or other security.

# PART XVII

# MISCELLANEOUS AND GENERAL

### 426    Co-operation between courts exercising jurisdiction in relation to insolvency

(1) An order made by a court in any part of the United Kingdom in the exercise of jurisdiction in relation to insolvency law shall be enforced in any other part of the United Kingdom as if it were made by a court exercising the corresponding jurisdiction in that other part.

(2) However, without prejudice to the following provisions of this section, nothing in subsection (1) requires a court in any part of the United Kingdom to enforce, in relation to property situated in that part, any order made by a court in any other part of the United Kingdom.

(3) The Secretary of State, with the concurrence in relation to property situated in England and Wales of the Lord Chancellor, may by order make provision for securing that a trustee or assignee under the insolvency law of any part of the United Kingdom has, with such modifications as may be specified in the order, the same rights in relation to any property situated in another part of the United Kingdom as he would have in the corresponding circumstances if he were a trustee or assignee under the insolvency law of that other part.

(4) The courts having jurisdiction in relation to insolvency law in any part of the United Kingdom shall assist the courts having the corresponding jurisdiction in any other part of the United Kingdom or any relevant country or territory.

(5) For the purposes of subsection (4) a request made to a court in any part of the United Kingdom by a court in any other part of the United Kingdom or in a relevant country or territory is authority for the court to which the request is made to apply, in relation to any matters specified in the request, the insolvency law which is applicable by either court in relation to comparable matters falling within its jurisdiction.

In exercising its discretion under this subsection, a court shall have regard in particular to the rules of private international law.

(6) Where a person who is a trustee or assignee under the insolvency law of any part of the United Kingdom claims property situated in any other part of the United Kingdom (whether by virtue of an order under subsection (3) or otherwise), the submission of that claim to the court exercising jurisdiction in relation to insolvency law in that other part shall be treated in the same manner as a request made by a court for the purpose of subsection (4).

(7) Section 38 of the Criminal Law Act 1977 (execution of warrant of arrest throughout the United Kingdom) applies to a warrant which, in exercise of any jurisdiction in relation to insolvency law, is issued in any part of the United Kingdom for the arrest of a person as it applies to a warrant issued in that part of the United Kingdom for the arrest of a person charged with an offence.

(8) Without prejudice to any power to make rules of court, any power to make provision by subordinate legislation for the purpose of giving effect in relation to companies or individuals to the insolvency law of any part of the United Kingdom includes power to make provision for the purpose of giving effect in that part to any provision made by or under the preceding provisions of this section.

(9) An order under subsection (3) shall be made by statutory instrument subject to annulment in pursuance of a resolution of either House of Parliament.

(10) In this section 'insolvency law' means—

    (a) in relation to England and Wales, provision extending to England and Wales and made by or under this Act or sections 1A 6 to 10, 12 to 15, 19(c) and 20 (with Schedule 1) of the Company Directors Disqualification Act 1986 and sections 1 to 17 of that Act as they apply for the purposes of those provisions of that Act;

    (b) in relation to Scotland, provision extending to Scotland and made by or under this Act, sections 1A 6 to 10,12 to 15 19(c) and 20 (with Schedule 1) of the Company Directors Disqualification Act 1986 and sections 1 to 17 of that Act as they apply for the purposes of those provisions of that Act, Part XVIII of the Companies Act or the Bankruptcy (Scotland) Act 1985;

    (c) in relation to Northern Ireland, provision made by or under the Insolvency (Northern Ireland) Order 1989or the Company Directors Disqualification (Northern Ireland) Order 2002;

    (d) in relation to any relevant country or territory, so much of the law of that country or territory as corresponds to provisions falling within any of the foregoing paragraphs;

and references in this subsection to any enactment include, in relation to any time before the coming into force of that enactment the corresponding enactment in force at that time.

(11) In this section 'relevant country or territory' means—

    (a) any of the Channel Islands or the Isle of Man, or

    (b) any country or territory designated for the purposes of this section by the Secretary of State by order made by statutory instrument.

(12) In the application of this section to Northern Ireland—

    (a) for any reference to the Secretary of State there is substituted a reference to the Department of Economic Development in Northern Ireland;

    (b) in subsection (3) for the words 'another part of the United Kingdom' and the words 'that other part' there is substituted the words 'Northern Ireland';

    (c) for subsection (9) there is substituted the following subsection—

'(9) An order made under subsection (3) by the Department of Economic Development in Northern Ireland shall be a statutory rule for the purposes of the Statutory Rules (Northern Ireland) Order 1979 and shall be subject to negative resolution within the meaning of section 41(6) of the Interpretation Act (Northern Ireland) 1954.'.

(13) Section 129 of the Banking Act 2009 provides for provisions of that Act about bank insolvency to be 'insolvency law' for the purposes of this section.

(14)  Section 165 of the Banking Act 2009 provides for provisions of that Act about bank administration to be 'insolvency law' for the purposes of this section.

### 426A    Disqualification from Parliament (England and Wales)

(1)  A person in respect of whom a bankruptcy restrictions order or a debt relief restrictions order has effect shall be disqualified—

    (a)  from membership of the House of Commons,

    (b)  from sitting or voting in the House of Lords, and

    (c)  from sitting or voting in a committee of the House of Lords or a joint committee of both Houses.

(2)  If a member of the House of Commons becomes disqualified under this section, his seat shall be vacated.

(3)  If a person who is disqualified under this section is returned as a member of the House of Commons, his return shall be void.

(4)  No writ of summons shall be issued to a member of the House of Lords who is disqualified under this section.

(5)  If a court makes a bankruptcy restrictions order or interim order or a debt relief restrictions order or an interim debt relief restrictions order in respect of a member of the House of Commons or the House of Lords the court shall notify the Speaker of that House.

(6)  If the Secretary of State accepts a bankruptcy restrictions undertaking or a debt relief restrictions undertaking made by a member of the House of Commons or the House of Lords, the Secretary of State shall notify the Speaker of that House.

### 426B    Devolution

(1)  If a court makes a bankruptcy restrictions order or interim order in respect of a member of the Scottish Parliament, the Northern Ireland Assembly or the National Assembly for Wales, or makes a debt relief restrictions order or interim debt relief restrictions order in respect of such a member the court shall notify the presiding officer of that body.

(2)  If the Secretary of State accepts a bankruptcy restrictions undertaking or a debt relief restrictions undertaking made by a member of the Scottish Parliament, the Northern Ireland Assembly or the National Assembly for Wales, the Secretary of State shall notify the presiding officer of that body.

### 426C    Irrelevance of privilege

(1)  An enactment about insolvency applies in relation to a member of the House of Commons or the House of Lords irrespective of any Parliamentary privilege.

(2)  In this section 'enactment' includes a provision made by or under—

    (a)  an Act of the Scottish Parliament, or

    (b)  Northern Ireland legislation.

### 427    Disqualification from Parliament (Scotland and Northern Ireland)

(1)  Where a court in [...] Northern Ireland adjudges an individual bankrupt or a court in Scotland awards sequestrian of an individual's estate, the individual is disqualified—

    (a)  for sitting or voting in the House of Lords,

    (b)  for being elected to, or sitting or voting in, the House of Commons, and

    (c)  for sitting or voting in a committee of either House.

(2)  Where an individual is disqualified under this section, the disqualification ceases—

    (a)  except where the adjudication is annulled or the award recalled or reduced without the individual having been first discharged, on the discharge of the individual, and

    (b)  in the excepted case, on the annulment, recall or reduction, as the case may be.

(3)  No writ of summons shall be issued to any lord of Parliament who is for the time being disqualified under this section for sitting and voting in the House of Lords.

(4)  Where a member of the House of Commons who is disqualified under this section continues to be so disqualified until the end of the period of 6 months beginning with the day of the adjudication or award, his seat shall be vacated at the end of that period.

(5)  A court which makes an adjudication or award such as is mentioned is subsection (1) in relation to any lord of Parliament or member of the House of Commons shall forthwith certify the adjudication or award to the Speaker of the House of Lords or, as the case may be, to the Speaker of the House of Commons.

(6)  Where a court has certified an adjudication or award to the Speaker of the House of Commons under subsection (5), then immediately after it becomes apparent which of the following certificates is applicable, the court shall certify to the Speaker of the House of Commons—

    (a)  that the period of 6 months beginning with the day of the adjudication or award has expired without the adjudication or award having been annulled, recalled or reduced, or

    (b)  that the adjudication or award has been annulled, recalled or reduced before the end of that period.

(6A) Subsections (4) to (6) have effect in relation to a member of the Scottish Parliament but as if—

    (a) references to the House of Commons were to the Parliament and references to the Speaker were to the Presiding Officer, and

    (b) in subsection (4), for 'under this section' there were substituted 'under section 15(1)(b) of the Scotland Act 1998 by virtue of this section'.

(6B) Subsections (4) to (6) have effect in relation to a member of the National Assembly for Wales but as if—

    (a) references to the House of Commons were to the Assembly and references to the Speaker were to the presiding officer, and

    (b) in subsection (4), for 'under this section' there were substituted 'under section 16(2) of the Government of Wales Act 2006 by virtue of this section'.

*(6C) Subsection (1), as applied to a member of the Northern Ireland Assembly by virtue of section 36(4) of the Northern Ireland Act 1998, has effect as if 'or Northern Ireland' were omitted; and subsections (4) to (6) have effect in relation to such a member as if—*

    *(a) references to the House of Commons were to the Assembly and references to the Speaker were to the Presiding Officer; and*

    *(b) in subsection (4), for 'under this section' there were substituted 'under section 36(4) of the Northern Ireland Act 1998 by virtue of this section'.*

(7) [...][23]

### 428   Exemptions from Restrictive Trade Practices Act

(1) [...]

(2) [...]

(3) In this section 'insolvency services' means the services of persons acting as insolvency practitioners or carrying out under the law of Northern Ireland functions corresponding to those mentioned in section 388(1) or (2) in Part XIII, in their capacity as such [...]

### 429   Disabilities on revocation of administration order against an individual

*(1) The following applies where a person fails to make any payment which he is required to make by virtue of an administration order under Part VI of the County Courts Act 1984.*

*(2) The court which is administering that person's estate under the order may, if it thinks fit—*

    *(a) revoke the administration order, and*

    *(b) make an order directing that this section and section 12 of the Company Directors Disqualification Act 1986 shall apply to the person for such period, not exceeding one year, as may be specified in the order.*

*(3) A person* to whom this section so applies shall not—

    (a) either alone or jointly with another person, obtain credit to the extent of the amount prescribed for the purposes of section 360(1)(a) or more, or

    (b) enter into any transaction in the course of or for the purposes of any business in which he is directly or indirectly engaged,

without disclosing to the person from whom he obtains the credit, or (as the case may be) with whom the transaction is entered into, the fact that this section applies to him.

(4) The reference in subsection (3) to *a person* obtaining credit includes—

    (a) a case where goods are bailed or hired to him under a hire-purchase agreement or agreed to be sold to him under a conditional sale agreement, and

    (b) a case where he is paid in advance (whether in money or otherwise) for the supply of goods or services.

(5) *A person* who contravenes this section is guilty of an offence and liable to imprisonment or a fine, or both.[24]

---

## 430  Provision introducing Schedule of punishments

(1)  Schedule 10 to this Act has effect with respect to the way in which offences under this Act are punishable on conviction.

(2)  In relation to an offence under a provision of this Act specified in the first column of the Schedule (the general nature of the offence being described in the second column), the third column shows whether the offence is punishable on conviction on indictment, or on summary conviction, or either in the one way or the other.

(3)  The fourth column of the Schedule shows, in relation to an offence, the maximum punishment by way of fine or imprisonment under this Act which may be imposed on a person convicted of the offence in the way specified in relation to it in the third column (that is to say, on indictment or summarily) a reference to a period of years or months being to a term of imprisonment of that duration.

(4)  The fifth column shows (in relation to an offence for which there is an entry in that column) that a person convicted of the offence after continued contravention is liable to a daily default fine; that is to say, he is liable on a second or subsequent conviction of the offence to the fine specified in that column for each day on which the contravention is continued (instead of the penalty specified for the offence in the fourth column of the Schedule).

(5)  For the purpose of any enactment in this Act whereby an officer of a company who is in default is liable to a fine or penalty, the expression 'officer who is in default' means any officer of the company who knowingly and wilfully authorises or permits the default, refusal or contravention mentioned in the enactment.

## 431  Summary proceedings

(1)  Summary proceedings for any offence under any of Parts I to VII of this Act may (without prejudice to any jurisdiction exercisable apart from this subsection) be taken against a body corporate at any place at which the body has a place of business, and against any other person at any place at which he is for the time being.

(2)  Notwithstanding anything in section 127(1) of the Magistrates' Courts Act 1980, an information relating to such an offence which is triable by a magistrates' court in England and Wales may be so tried if it is laid at any time within 3 years after the commission of the offence and within 12 months after the date on which evidence sufficient in the opinion of the Director of Public Prosecutions or the Secretary of State (as the case may be) to justify the proceedings comes to his knowledge.

(3)  Summary proceedings in Scotland for such an offence shall not be commenced after the expiration of 3 years from the commission of the offence.

Subject to this (and notwithstanding anything in section 136 of the Criminal Procedure (Scotland) Act 1995), such proceedings may (in Scotland) be commenced at any time within 12 months after the date on which evidence sufficient in the Lord Advocate's opinion to justify the proceedings came to his knowledge or, where such evidence was reported to him by the Secretary of State, within 12 months after the date on which it came to the knowledge of the latter; and subsection (3) of that section applies for the purpose of this subsection as it applies for the purpose of that section.

(4)  For purposes of this section, a certificate of the Director of Public Prosecutions, the Lord Advocate or the Secretary of State (as the case may be) as to the date on which such evidence as is referred to above came to his knowledge is conclusive evidence.

## 432  Offences by bodies corporate

(1)  This section applies to offences under this Act other than those excepted by subsection (4).

(2)  Where a body corporate is guilty of an offence to which this section applies and the offence is proved to have been committed with the consent or connivance of, or to be attributable to any neglect on the part of, any director, manager, secretary or other similar officer of the body corporate or any person who was purporting to act in any such capacity he, as well as the body corporate, is guilty of the offence and liable to be proceeded against and punished accordingly.

(3)  Where the affairs of a body corporate are managed by its members, subsection (2) applies in relation to the acts and defaults of a member in connection with his functions of management as if he were a director of the body corporate.

(4)  The offences excepted from this section are those under sections 30, 39, 51, 53, 54, 62, 64, 66, 85, 89, 164, 188, 201, 206, 207, 208, 209, 210 and 211 and those under paragraphs 16(2), 17(3)(a), 18(3)(a), 19(3)(a), 22(1) and 23(1)(a) of Schedule A1.

## 433  Admissibility in evidence of statements of affairs, etc

(1)  In any proceedings (whether or not under this Act)—

(a)  a statement of affairs prepared for the purposes of any provision of this Act which is derived from the Insolvency Act 1985,

(aa)  a statement made in pursuance of a requirement imposed by or under Part 2 of the Banking Act 2009 (bank insolvency),

(ab)  a statement made in pursuance of a requirement imposed by or under Part 3 of that Act (bank administration), and

(b) any other statement made in pursuance of a requirement imposed by or under any such provision or by or under rules made under this Act,

may be used in evidence against any person making or concurring in making the statement.

(2)  However, in criminal proceedings in which any such person is charged with an offence to which this subsection applies—

(a) no evidence relating to the statement may be adduced, and

(b) no question relating to it may be asked,

by or on behalf of the prosecution, unless evidence relating to it is adduced, or a question relating to it is asked, in the proceedings by or on behalf of that person.

(3)  Subsection (2) applies to any offence other than—

(a) an offence under section 22(6), 47(6), 48(8), 66(6), 67(8), 95(8), 98(6), 99(3)(a), 131(7), 192(2), 208(1)(a) or (d) or (2), 210, 235(5), 353(1), 354(1)(b) or (3) or 356(1) or (2)(a) or (b) or paragraph 4(3)(a) of Schedule 7;

(b) an offence which is—

(i)  created by rules made under this Act, and

(ii)  designated for the purposes of this subsection by such rules or by regulations made by the Secretary of State;

(c) an offence which is—

(i)  created by regulations made under any such rules, and

(ii)  designated for the purposes of this subsection by such regulations;

(d) an offence under section 1, 2 or 5 of the Perjury Act 1911 (false statements made on oath or made otherwise than on oath); or

(e) an offence under section 44(1) or (2) of the Criminal Law (Consolidation)(Scotland) Act 1995 (false statements made on oath or otherwise than on oath).

(4)  Regulations under subsection (3)(b)(ii) shall be made by statutory instrument and, after being made, shall be laid before each House of Parliament.

### 434   Crown application

For the avoidance of doubt it is hereby declared that provisions of this Act which derive from the Insolvency Act 1985 bind the Crown so far as affecting or relating to the following matters, namely—

(a) remedies against, or against the property of, companies or individuals;

(b) priorities of debts;

(c) transactions at an undervalue or preferences;

(d) voluntary arrangements approved under Part I or Part VIII, and

(e) discharge from bankruptcy.

# PART 17A

## SUPPLEMENTARY PROVISIONS

### 434A   Introductory

The provisions of this Part have effect for the purposes of—

(a) the First Group of Parts, and

(b) sections 411, 413, 414, 416 and 417 in Part 15.

### 434B   Representation of corporations at meetings

(1)  If a corporation is a creditor or debenture-holder, it may by resolution of its directors or other governing body authorise a person or persons to act as its representative or representatives—

(a) at any meeting of the creditors of a company held in pursuance of this Act or of rules made under it, or

(b) at any meeting of a company held in pursuance of the provisions contained in a debenture or trust deed.

(2)  Where the corporation authorises only one person, that person is entitled to exercise the same powers on behalf of the corporation as the corporation could exercise if it were an individual creditor or debenture-holder.

(3)  Where the corporation authorises more than one person, any one of them is entitled to exercise the same powers on behalf of the corporation as the corporation could exercise if it were an individual creditor or debenture-holder.

(4)  Where the corporation authorises more than one person and more than one of them purport to exercise a power under subsection (3)—

(a) if they purport to exercise the power in the same way, the power is treated as exercised in that way;

(b) if they do not purport to exercise the power in the same way, the power is treated as not exercised.

### 434C   Legal professional privilege

In proceedings against a person for an offence under this Act nothing in this Act is to be taken to require any person to disclose any information that he is entitled to refuse to disclose on grounds of legal professional privilege (in Scotland, confidentiality of communications).

# PART XVIII

# INTERPRETATION

### 435   Meaning of 'associate'

(1)  For the purposes of this Act any question whether a person is an associate of another person is to be determined in accordance with the following provisions of this section (any provision that a person is an associate of another person being taken to mean that they are associates of each other).

(2)  A person is an associate of an individual if that person is—

   (a)  the individual's husband or wife or civil partner,

   (b)  a relative of—

      (i)   the individual, or

      (ii)  the individual's husband or wife or civil partner, or

   (c)  the husband or wife or civil partner of a relative of—

      (i)   the individual, or

      (ii)  the individual's husband or wife or civil partner.

(3)  A person is an associate of any person with whom he is in partnership, and of the husband or wife or civil partner or a relative of any individual with whom he is in partnership; and a Scottish firm is an associate of any person who is a member of the firm.

(4)  A person is an associate of any person whom he employs or by whom he is employed.

(5)  A person in his capacity as trustee of a trust other than—

   (a)  a trust arising under any of the second Group of Parts or the Bankruptcy (Scotland) Act 1985, or

   (b)  a pension scheme or an employees' share scheme (within the meaning of the Companies Act),

is an associate of another person if the beneficiaries of the trust include, or the terms of the trust confer a power that may be exercised for the benefit of, that other person or an associate of that other person.

(6)  A company is an associate of another company—

   (a)  if the same person has control of both, or a person has control of one and persons who are his associates, or he and persons who are his associates, have control of the other, or

   (b)  if a group of two or more persons has control of each company, and the groups either consist of the same persons or could be regarded as consisting of the same persons by treating (in one or more cases) a member of either group as replaced by a person of whom he is an associate.

(7)  A company is an associate of another person if that person has control of it or if that person and persons who are his associates together have control of it.

(8)  For the purposes of this section a person is a relative of an individual if he is that individual's brother, sister, uncle, aunt, nephew, niece, lineal ancestor or lineal descendant, treating—

   (a)  any relationship of the half blood as a relationship of the whole blood and the stepchild or adopted child of any person as his child, and

   (b)  an illegitimate child as the legitimate child of his mother and reputed father;

and references in this section to a husband or wife include a former husband or wife and a reputed husband or wife and references to a civil partner include a former civil partner and a reputed civil partner.

(9)  For the purposes of this section any director or other officer of a company is to be treated as employed by that company.

(10)  For the purposes of this section a person is to be taken as having control of a company if—

   (a)  the directors of the company or of another company which has control of it (or any of them) are accustomed to act in accordance with his directions or instructions, or

   (b)  he is entitled to exercise, or control the exercise of, one third or more of the voting power at any general meeting of the company of or another company which has control of it;

and where two or more persons together satisfy either of the above conditions, they are to be taken as having control of the company.

(11)  In this section 'company' includes any body corporate (whether incorporated in Great Britain or elsewhere); and references to directors and other officers of a company and to voting power at any general meeting of a company have effect with any necessary modifications.

### 436   Expressions used generally

In this Act, except in so far as the context otherwise requires (and subject to Parts VII and XI)—

   'the appointed day' means the day of which this Act comes into force under section 443;

'associate' has the meaning given by section 435;

'business' includes a trade or profession;

'the Companies Act' means the Companies Act 1985;

'the Companies Acts' means the Companies Acts (as defined in section 2 of the Companies Act 2006) as they have effect in Great Britain;

'conditional sale agreement' and 'hire-purchase agreement' have the same meanings as in the Consumer Credit Act 1974;

*'distress' includes use of the procedure in Schedule 12 to the Tribunals, Courts and Enforcement Act 2007, and references to levying distress, seizing goods and related expressions shall be construed accordingly;*

'the EC Regulation' means Council Regulation (EC) No. 1346/2000;

'EEA State' means a state that is a Contracting Party to the Agreement on the European Economic Area signed at Oporto on 2nd May 1992 as adjusted by the Protocol signed at Brussels on 17th March 1993;

'modifications' includes additions, alterations and omissions and cognate expressions shall be construed accordingly;

'property' includes money, goods, things in action, land and every description of property wherever situated and also obligations and every description of interest, whether present or future or vested or contingent, arising out of, or incidental to, property;

'records' includes computer records and other non-documentary records;

'subordinate legislation' has the same meaning as in the Interpretation Act 1978; and

'transaction' includes a gift, agreement or arrangement, and references to entering into a transaction shall be construed accordingly.[25]

### 436A   Proceedings under EC Regulations: modified definition of property

In the application of this Act to proceedings by virtue of Article 3 of the EC Regulation, a reference to property is a reference to property which may be dealt with in the proceedings.

# PART XIX

# FINAL PROVISIONS

### 437   Transitional provisions, and savings

The transitional provisions and savings set out in Schedule 11 to this Act shall have effect, the Schedule comprising the following Parts—

Part I: company insolvency and winding up (matters arising before appointed day, and continuance of proceedings in certain cases as before that day);

Part II: individual insolvency (matters so arising, and continuance of bankruptcy proceedings in certain cases as before that day);

Part III: transactions entered into before the appointed day and capable of being affected by orders of the court under Part XVI of this Act;

Part IV: insolvency practitioners acting as such before the appointed day; and

Part V: general transitional provisions and savings required consequentially on, and in connection with, the repeal and replacement by this Act and the Company Directors Disqualification Act 1986 of provisions of the Companies Act, the greater part of the Insolvency Act 1985 and other enactments.

### 438   Repeals

The enactments specified in the second column of Schedule 12 to this Act are repealed to the extent specified in the third column of that Schedule.

### 439   Amendment of enactments

(1)  The Companies Act is amended as shown in Parts I and II of Schedule 13 to this Act, being amendments consequential on this Act and the Company Directors Disqualification Act 1986.

(2)  The enactments specified in the first column of Schedule 14 to this Act (being enactments which refer, or otherwise relate, to those which are repealed and replaced by this Act or the Company Directors Disqualification Act 1986) are amended as shown in the second column of that Schedule.

(3)  The Lord Chancellor may by order make such consequential modifications of any provision contained in any subordinate legislation made before the appointed day and such transitional provisions in connection with those modifications as appear to him necessary or expedient in respect of—

(a)  any reference in that subordinate legislation to the Bankruptcy Act 1914;

(b)  any reference in that subordinate legislation to any enactment repealed by Part III or IV or Schedule 10 to the Insolvency Act 1985; or

(c)  any reference in that subordinate legislation to any matter provided for under the Act of 1914 or under any enactment so repealed.

---

[25] The words in italics inserted by the Tribunals, Courts and Enforcement Act 2007 c 15 from a date to be appointed.

(4)  An order under this section shall be made by statutory instrument subject to annulment in pursuance of a resolution of either House of Parliament.

### 440   Extent (Scotland)

(1)  Subject to the next subsection, provisions of this Act contained in the first Group of Parts extend to Scotland except where otherwise stated.

(2)  The following provisions of this Act do not extend to Scotland—

(a)  in the first Group of Parts—

section 43;

sections 238 to 241; and

section 246;

(b)  the second Group of Parts;

(c)  in the third Group of Parts—

sections 399 to 402,

sections 412, 413, 415, 418, 420 and 421,

sections 423 to 425, and

section 429(1) and (2) *and 2A*; and

(d)  in the Schedules—

Parts II and III of Schedule 11; and

Schedules 12 and 14 so far as they repeal or amend enactments which extend to England and Wales only.[26]

### 441   Extent (Northern Ireland)

(1)  The following provisions of this Act extend to Northern Ireland—

(a)  sections 197, 426, 427 and 428; and

(b)  so much of section 439 and Schedule 14 as relates to enactments which extend to Northern Ireland.

(2)  Subject as above, and to any provision expressly relating to companies incorporated elsewhere than in Great Britain, nothing in this Act extends to Northern Ireland or applies to or in relation to companies registered or incorporated in Northern Ireland.

### 442   Extent (other territories)

Her Majesty may, by Order in Council, direct that such of the provisions of this Act as are specified in the Order, being provisions formerly contained in the Insolvency Act 1985, shall extend to any of the Channel Islands or any colony with such modifications as may be so specified.

### 443   Commencement

This Act comes into force on the day appointed under section 236(2) of the Insolvency Act 1985 for the coming into force of Part III of that Act (individual insolvency and bankruptcy), immediately after that Part of that Act comes into force for England and Wales.

### 444   Citation

This Act may be cited as the Insolvency Act 1986.

# SCHEDULES

# SCHEDULE A1

# MORATORIUM WHERE DIRECTORS PROPOSE VOLUNTARY ARRANGEMENT

## PART I

## INTRODUCTORY

### *Interpretation*

**1** In this Schedule—

'the beginning of the moratorium' has the meaning given by paragraph 8(1),

'the date of filing' means the date on which the documents for the time being referred to in paragraph 7(1) are filed or lodged with the court,

'hire-purchase agreement' includes a conditional sale agreement, a chattel leasing agreement and a retention of title agreement,

---

[26] Subsection inserted by the Tribunals, Courts and Enforcement Act 200 c 15 from a date to be appointed.

'market contract' and 'market charge' have the meanings given by Part VII of the Companies Act 1989,
[...]
'moratorium' means a moratorium under section 1A,
'the nominee' includes any person for the time being carrying out the functions of a nominee under this Schedule,
[...]
'the settlement finality regulations' means the Financial Markets and Insolvency (Settlement Finality) Regulations 1999,
'system-charge' has the meaning given by the Financial Markets and Insolvency Regulations 1996.

*Eligible companies*

2 (1) A company is eligible for a moratorium if it meets the requirements of paragraph 3, unless—
   (a) it is excluded from being eligible by virtue of paragraph 4, or
   (b) it falls within sub-paragraph (2).
(2) A company falls within this sub-paragraph if—
   (a) it effects or carries out contracts of insurance, but is not exempt from the general prohibition, within the meaning of section 19 of the Financial Services and Markets Act 2000, in relation to that activity,
   (b) it has permission under Part IV of that Act to accept deposits,
   (bb) it has a liability in respect of a deposit which it accepted in accordance with the Banking Act 1979 (c 37) or 1987 (c 22),
   (c) it is a party to a market contract [...]or any of its property is subject to a market charge [...] or a system-charge, or
   (d) it is a participant (within the meaning of the settlement finality regulations) or any of its property is subject to a collateral security charge (within the meaning of those regulations).
(3) Paragraphs (a), (b) and (bb) of sub-paragraph (2) must be read with—
   (a) section 22 of the Financial Services and Markets Act 2000;
   (b) any relevant order under that section; and
   (c) Schedule 2 to that Act.
3 (1) A company meets the requirements of this paragraph if the qualifying conditions are met—
   (a) in the year ending with the date of filing, or
   (b) in the financial year of the company which ended last before that date.
(2) For the purposes of sub-paragraph (1)—
   (a) the qualifying conditions are met by a company in a period if, in that period, it satisfies two or more of the requirements for being a small company specified for the time being in section 382(3) of the Companies Act 2006, and
   (b) a company's financial year is to be determined in accordance with that Act.
(3) Section 382 (4), (5) and (6) of that Act apply for the purposes of this paragraph as they apply for the purposes of that section.
(4) A company does not meet the requirements of this paragraph if it is a parent company of a group of companies which does not qualify as a small group or a medium-sized group in relation to the financial year of the company which ended last before the date of filing.
(5) For the purposes of sub-paragraph (4)—
   (a) 'group' has the same meaning as in Part 15 of the Companies Act 2006 (see section 474(1) of that Act); and
   (b) a group qualifies as small in relation to a financial year if it so qualifies under section 383(2) to (7) of that Act, and qualifies as medium-sized in relation to a financial year if it so qualifies under section 466(2) to (7) of that Act.
4 (1) A company is excluded from being eligible for a moratorium if, on the date of filing—
   (a) the company is in administration,
   (b) the company is being wound up,
   (c) there is an administrative receiver of the company,
   (d) a voluntary arrangement has effect in relation to the company,
   (e) there is a provisional liquidator of the company,
   (f) a moratorium has been in force for the company at any time during the period of 12 months ending with the date of filing and—
      (i) no voluntary arrangement had effect at the time at which the moratorium came to an end, or
      (ii) a voluntary arrangement which had effect at any time in that period has come to an end prematurely, or
   (fa) an administrator appointed under paragraph 22 of Schedule B1 has held office in the period of 12 months ending with the date of filing,
   (g) a voluntary arrangement in relation to the company which had effect in pursuance of a proposal under section 1(3) has come to an end prematurely and, during the period of 12 months ending with the date of filing, an order under section 5(3)(a) has been made.

(2) Sub-paragraph (1)(b) does not apply to a company which, by reason of a winding-up order made after the date of filing, is treated as being wound up on that date.

### Capital market arrangement

**4A** A company is also excluded from being eligible for a moratorium if, on the date of filing, it is a party to an agreement which is or forms part of a capital market arrangement under which—

    (i)   a party has incurred, or when the agreement was entered into was expected to incur, a debt of at least £10 million under the arrangement, and

    (ii)   the arrangement involves the issue of a capital market investment.

### Public private partnership

**4B** A company is also excluded from being eligible for a moratorium if, on the date of filing, it is a project company of a project which—

    (i)   is a public-private partnership project, and

    (ii)   includes step-in rights.

### Liability under an arrangement

**4C** (1) A company is also excluded from being eligible for a moratorium if, on the date of filing, it has incurred a liability under an agreement of £10 million or more.

(2) Where the liability in sub-paragraph (1) is a contingent liability under or by virtue of a guarantee or an indemnity or security provided on behalf of another person, the amount of that liability is the full amount of the liability in relation to which the guarantee, indemnity or security is provided.

(3) In this paragraph—

    (a)   the reference to 'liability' includes a present or future liability whether, in either case, it is certain or contingent,

    (b)   the reference to 'liability' includes a reference to a liability to be paid wholly or partly in foreign currency (in which case the sterling equivalent shall be calculated as at the time when the liability is incurred).

### Interpretation of capital market arrangement

**4D** (1) For the purposes of paragraph 4A an arrangement is a capital market arrangement if—

    (a)   it involves a grant of security to a person holding it as trustee for a person who holds a capital market investment issued by a party to the arrangement, or

    (b)   at least one party guarantees the performance of obligations of another party, or

    (c)   at least one party provides security in respect of the performance of obligations of another party, or

    (d)   the arrangement involves an investment of a kind described in articles 83 to 85 of the Financial Services and Markets Act 2000 (Regulated Activities) Order 2001 (SI 2001/544)(options, futures and contracts for differences).

(2) For the purposes of sub-paragraph (1)—

    (a)   a reference to holding as trustee includes a reference to holding as nominee or agent,

    (b)   a reference to holding for a person who holds a capital market investment includes a reference to holding for a number of persons at least one of whom holds a capital market investment, and

    (c)   a person holds a capital market investment if he has a legal or beneficial interest in it.

(3) In paragraph 4A, 4C, 4J and this paragraph—

'agreement' includes an agreement or undertaking effected by—

    (a)   contract,

    (b)   deed, or

    (c)   any other instrument intended to have effect in accordance with the law of England and Wales, Scotland or another jurisdiction, and

'party' to an arrangement includes a party to an agreement which—

    (a)   forms part of the arrangement,

    (b)   provides for the raising of finance as part of the arrangement, or

    (c)   is necessary for the purposes of implementing the arrangement.

### Capital market investment

**4E** (1) For the purposes of paragraphs 4A and 4D, an investment is a capital market investment if—

    (a)   it is within article 77 of the Financial Services and Markets Act 2000 (Regulated Activities) Order 2001 (SI 2001/544)(debt instruments) and

    (b)   it is rated, listed or traded or designed to be rated, listed or traded.

(2) In sub-paragraph (1)—

'listed' means admitted to the official list within the meaning given by section 103(1) of the Financial Services and Markets Act 2000 (c 8)(interpretation),

'rated' means rated for the purposes of investment by an internationally recognised rating agency,

'traded' means admitted to trading on a market established under the rules of a recognised investment exchange or on a foreign market.

(3) In sub-paragraph (2)—

'foreign market' has the same meaning as 'relevant market' in article 67(2) of the Financial Services and Markets Act 2000 (Financial Promotion) Order 2001 (SI 2001/1335)(foreign markets),

'recognised investment exchange' has the meaning given by section 285 of the Financial Services and Markets Act 2000 (recognised investment exchange).

**4F** (1) For the purposes of paragraphs 4A and 4D an investment is also a capital market investment if it consists of a bond or commercial paper issued to one or more of the following—

    (a) an investment professional within the meaning of article 19(5) of the Financial Services and Markets Act 2000 (Financial Promotion) Order 2001,

    (b) a person who is, when the agreement mentioned in paragraph 4A is entered into, a certified high net worth individual in relation to a communication within the meaning of article 48(2) of that order,

    (c) a person to whom article 49(2) of that order applies (high net worth company, &c.),

    (d) a person who is, when the agreement mentioned in paragraph 4A is entered into, a certified sophisticated investor in relation to a communication within the meaning of article 50(1) of that order, and

    (e) a person in a State other than the United Kingdom who under the law of that State is not prohibited from investing in bonds or commercial paper.

(2) For the purposes of sub-paragraph (1)—

    (a) in applying article 19(5) of the Financial Services and Markets Act 2000 (Financial Promotion) Order 2001 for the purposes of sub-paragraph (1)(a)—

        (i) in article 19(5)(b), ignore the words after 'exempt person',

        (ii) in article 19(5)(c)(i), for the words from 'the controlled activity' to the end substitute 'a controlled activity', and

        (iii) in article 19(5)(e) ignore the words from 'where the communication' to the end, and

    (b) in applying article 49(2) of that order for the purposes of sub-paragraph (1)(c), ignore article 49(2)(e).

(3) In sub-paragraph (1)—

'bond' shall be construed in accordance with article 77 of the Financial Services and Markets Act 2000 (Regulated Activities) Order 2001 (SI 2001/544), and

'commercial paper' has the meaning given by article 9(3) of that order.

### Debt

**4G** The debt of at least £10 million referred to in paragraph 4A—

    (a) may be incurred at any time during the life of the capital market arrangement, and

    (b) may be expressed wholly or partly in a foreign currency (in which case the sterling equivalent shall be calculated as at the time when the arrangement is entered into).

### Interpretation of project company

**4H** (1) For the purposes of paragraph 4B a company is a 'project company' of a project if—

    (a) it holds property for the purpose of the project,

    (b) it has sole or principal responsibility under an agreement for carrying out all or part of the project,

    (c) it is one of a number of companies which together carry out the project,

    (d) it has the purpose of supplying finance to enable the project to be carried out, or

    (e) it is the holding company of a company within any of paragraphs (a) to (d).

(2) But a company is not a 'project company' of a project if—

    (a) it performs a function within sub-paragraph (1)(a) to (d) or is within sub-paragraph (1)(e), but

    (b) it also performs a function which is not—

        (i) within sub-paragraph (1)(a) to (d),

        (ii) related to a function within sub-paragraph (1)(a) to (d), or

        (iii) related to the project.

(3) For the purposes of this paragraph a company carries out all or part of a project whether or not it acts wholly or partly through agents.

### Public-private partnership project

**4I** (1) In paragraph 4B 'public-private partnership project' means a project—

    (a) the resources for which are provided partly by one or more public bodies and partly by one or more private persons, or

    (b) which is designed wholly or mainly for the purpose of assisting a public body to discharge a function.

(2) In sub-paragraph (1) 'resources' includes—

    (a) funds (including payment for the provision of services or facilities),

(b) assets,

(c) professional skill,

(d) the grant of a concession or franchise, and

(e) any other commercial resource.

(3) In sub-paragraph (1) 'public body' means—

(a) a body which exercises public functions,

(b) a body specified for the purposes of this paragraph by the Secretary of State, and

(c) a body within a class specified for the purposes of this paragraph by the Secretary of State.

(4) A specification under sub-paragraph (3) may be—

(a) general, or

(b) for the purpose of the application of paragraph 4B to a specified case.

### *Step-in rights*

**4J** (1) For the purposes of paragraph 4B a project has 'step-in rights' if a person who provides finance in connection with the project has a conditional entitlement under an agreement to—

(i) assume sole or principal responsibility under an agreement for carrying out all or part of the project, or

(ii) make arrangements for carrying out all or part of the project.

(2) In sub-paragraph (1) a reference to the provision of finance includes a reference to the provision of an indemnity.

### *'Person'*

**4K** For the purposes of paragraphs 4A to 4J, a reference to a person includes a reference to a partnership or another unincorporated group of persons.

**5** The Secretary of State may by regulations modify the qualifications for eligibility of a company for a moratorium.

# PART II

# OBTAINING A MORATORIUM

### *Nominee's statement*

**6** (1) Where the directors of a company wish to obtain a moratorium, they shall submit to the nominee—

(a) a document setting out the terms of the proposed voluntary arrangement,

(b) a statement of the company's affairs containing—

(i) such particulars of its creditors and of its debts and other liabilities and of its assets as may be prescribed, and

(ii) such other information as may be prescribed, and

(c) any other information necessary to enable the nominee to comply with sub-paragraph (2) which he requests from them.

(2) The nominee shall submit to the directors a statement in the prescribed form indicating whether or not, in his opinion—

(a) the proposed voluntary arrangement has a reasonable prospect of being approved and implemented,

(b) the company is likely to have sufficient funds available to it during the proposed moratorium to enable it to carry on its business, and

(c) meetings of the company and its creditors should be summoned to consider the proposed voluntary arrangement.

(3) In forming his opinion on the matters mentioned in sub-paragraph (2), the nominee is entitled to rely on the information submitted to him under sub-paragraph (1) unless he has reason to doubt its accuracy.

(4) The reference in sub-paragraph (2)(b) to the company's business is to that business as the company proposes to carry it on during the moratorium.

### *Documents to be submitted to court*

**7** (1) To obtain a moratorium the directors of a company must file (in Scotland, lodge) with the court—

(a) a document setting out the terms of the proposed voluntary arrangement,

(b) a statement of the company's affairs containing—

(i) such particulars of its creditors and of its debts and other liabilities and of its assets as may be prescribed, and

(ii) such other information as may be prescribed,

(c) a statement that the company is eligible for a moratorium,

   (d) a statement from the nominee that he has given his consent to act, and
   (e) a statement from the nominee that, in his opinion—
     (i) the proposed voluntary arrangement has a reasonable prospect of being approved and implemented,
     (ii) the company is likely to have sufficient funds available to it during the proposed moratorium to enable it to carry on its business, and
     (iii) meetings of the company and its creditors should be summoned to consider the proposed voluntary arrangement.

(2) Each of the statements mentioned in sub-paragraph (1)(b) to (e), except so far as it contains the particulars referred to in paragraph (b)(i), must be in the prescribed form.

(3) The reference in sub-paragraph (1)(e)(ii) to the company's business is to that business as the company proposes to carry it on during the moratorium.

(4) The Secretary of State may by regulations modify the requirements of this paragraph as to the documents required to be filed (in Scotland, lodged) with the court in order to obtain a moratorium.

### Duration of moratorium

**8** (1) A moratorium comes into force when the documents for the time being referred to in paragraph 7(1) are filed or lodged with the court and references in this Schedule to 'the beginning of the moratorium' shall be construed accordingly.

(2) A moratorium ends at the end of the day on which the meetings summoned under paragraph 29(1) are first held (or, if the meetings are held on different days, the later of those days), unless it is extended under paragraph 32.

(3) If either of those meetings has not first met before the end of the period of 28 days beginning with the day on which the moratorium comes into force, the moratorium ends at the end of the day on which those meetings were to be held (or, if those meetings were summoned to be held on different days, the later of those days), unless it is extended under paragraph 32.

(4) If the nominee fails to summon either meeting within the period required by paragraph 29(1), the moratorium ends at the end of the last day of that period.

(5) If the moratorium is extended (or further extended) under paragraph 32, it ends at the end of the day to which it is extended (or further extended).

(6) Sub-paragraphs (2) to (5) do not apply if the moratorium comes to an end before the time concerned by virtue of—
   (a) paragraph 25(4)(effect of withdrawal by nominee of consent to act),
   (b) an order under paragraph 26(3), 27(3) or 40 (challenge of actions of nominee or directors), or
   (c) a decision of one or both of the meetings summoned under paragraph 29.

(7) If the moratorium has not previously come to an end in accordance with sub-paragraphs (2) to (6), it ends at the end of the day on which a decision under paragraph 31 to approve a voluntary arrangement takes effect under paragraph 36.

(8) The Secretary of State may by order increase or reduce the period for the time being specified in sub-paragraph (3).

### Notification of beginning of moratorium

**9** (1) When a moratorium comes into force, the directors shall notify the nominee of that fact forthwith.

(2) If the directors without reasonable excuse fail to comply with sub-paragraph (1), each of them is liable to imprisonment or a fine, or both.

**10** (1) When a moratorium comes into force, the nominee shall, in accordance with the rules—
   (a) advertise that fact forthwith, and
   (b) notify the registrar of companies, the company and any petitioning creditor of the company of whose claim he is aware of that fact.

(2) In sub-paragraph (1)(b), 'petitioning creditor' means a creditor by whom a winding-up petition has been presented before the beginning of the moratorium, as long as the petition has not been dismissed or withdrawn.

(3) If the nominee without reasonable excuse fails to comply with sub-paragraph (1)(a) or (b), he is liable to a fine.

### Notification of end of moratorium

**11** (1) When a moratorium comes to an end, the nominee shall, in accordance with the rules—
   (a) advertise that fact forthwith, and
   (b) notify the court, the registrar of companies, the company and any creditor of the company of whose claim he is aware of that fact.

(2) If the nominee without reasonable excuse fails to comply with sub-paragraph (1)(a) or (b), he is liable to a fine.

## PART III

## EFFECTS OF MORATORIUM

*Effect on creditors, etc.*

**12** (1) During the period for which a moratorium is in force for a company—

(a) no petition may be presented for the winding up of the company,

(b) no meeting of the company may be called or requisitioned except with the consent of the nominee or the leave of the court and subject (where the court gives leave) to such terms as the court may impose,

(c) no resolution may be passed or order made for the winding up of the company,

(d) no administration application may be made in respect of the company,

(da) no administrator of the company may be appointed under paragraph 14 or 22 of Schedule B1,

(e) no administrative receiver of the company may be appointed,

(f) no landlord or other person to whom rent is payable may exercise any right of forfeiture by peaceable re-entry in relation to premises let to the company in respect of a failure by the company to comply with any term or condition of its tenancy of such premises, except with the leave of the court and subject to such terms as the court may impose,

(g) no other steps may be taken to enforce any security over the company's property, or to repossess goods in the company's possession under any hire-purchase agreement, except with the leave of the court and subject to such terms as the court may impose, and

(h) no other proceedings and no execution or other legal process may be commenced or continued, and no distress may be levied, against the company or its property except with the leave of the court and subject to such terms as the court may impose.

(2) Where a petition, other than an excepted petition, for the winding up of the company has been presented before the beginning of the moratorium, section 127 shall not apply in relation to any disposition of property, transfer of shares or alteration in status made during the moratorium or at a time mentioned in paragraph 37(5)(a).

(3) In the application of sub-paragraph (1)(h) to Scotland, the reference to execution being commenced or continued includes a reference to diligence being carried out or continued, and the reference to distress being levied is omitted.

(4) Paragraph (a) of sub-paragraph (1) does not apply to an excepted petition and, where such a petition has been presented before the beginning of the moratorium or is presented during the moratorium, paragraphs (b) and (c) of that sub-paragraph do not apply in relation to proceedings on the petition.

(5) For the purposes of this paragraph, 'excepted petition' means a petition under—

(a) section 124A or 124B of this Act,

(b) section 72 of the Financial Services Act 1986 on the ground mentioned in subsection (1)(b) of that section, or

(c) section 92 of the Banking Act 1987 on the ground mentioned in subsection (1)(b) of that section.

(d) section 367 of the Financial Services and Markets Act 2000 on the ground mentioned in subsection (3)(b) of that section.

**13** (1) This paragraph applies where there is an uncrystallised floating charge on the property of a company for which a moratorium is in force.

(2) If the conditions for the holder of the charge to give a notice having the effect mentioned in sub-paragraph (4) are met at any time, the notice may not be given at that time but may instead be given as soon as practicable after the moratorium has come to an end.

(3) If any other event occurs at any time which (apart from this sub-paragraph) would have the effect mentioned in sub-paragraph (4), then—

(a) the event shall not have the effect in question at that time, but

(b) if notice of the event is given to the company by the holder of the charge as soon as is practicable after the moratorium has come to an end, the event is to be treated as if it had occurred when the notice was given.

(4) The effect referred to in sub-paragraphs (2) and (3) is—

(a) causing the crystallisation of the floating charge, or

(b) causing the imposition, by virtue of provision in the instrument creating the charge, of any restriction on the disposal of any property of the company.

(5) Application may not be made for leave under paragraph 12(1)(g) or (h) with a view to obtaining—

(a) the crystallisation of the floating charge, or

(b) the imposition, by virtue of provision in the instrument creating the charge, of any restriction on the disposal of any property of the company.

**14** Security granted by a company at a time when a moratorium is in force in relation to the company may only be enforced if, at that time, there were reasonable grounds for believing that it would benefit the company.

### *Effect on company*

**15** (1) Paragraphs 16 to 23 apply in relation to a company for which a moratorium is in force.

(2) The fact that a company enters into a transaction in contravention of any of paragraphs 16 to 22 does not—

(a) make the transaction void, or

(b) make it to any extent unenforceable against the company.

### *Company invoices, etc.*

**16** (1) Every invoice, order for goods or services, business letter or order form (whether in hard copy, electronic or any other form) issued by or on behalf of the company, and all the company's websites, must also contain the nominee's name and a statement that the moratorium is in force for the company.

(2) If default is made in complying with sub-paragraph (1), the company and (subject to sub-paragraph (3)) any officer of the company is liable to a fine.

(3) An officer of the company is only liable under sub-paragraph (2) if, without reasonable excuse, he authorises or permits the default.

### *Obtaining credit during moratorium*

**17** (1) The company may not obtain credit to the extent of £250 or more from a person who has not been informed that a moratorium is in force in relation to the company.

(2) The reference to the company obtaining credit includes the following cases—

(a) where goods are bailed (in Scotland, hired) to the company under a hire-purchase agreement, or agreed to be sold to the company under a conditional sale agreement, and

(b) where the company is paid in advance (whether in money or otherwise) for the supply of goods or services.

(3) Where the company obtains credit in contravention of sub-paragraph (1)—

(a) the company is liable to a fine, and

(b) if any officer of the company knowingly and wilfully authorised or permitted the contravention, he is liable to imprisonment or a fine, or both.

(4) The money sum specified in sub-paragraph (1) is subject to increase or reduction by order under section 417A in Part XV.

### *Disposals and payments*

**18** (1) Subject to sub-paragraph (2), the company may only dispose of any of its property if—

(a) there are reasonable grounds for believing that the disposal will benefit the company, and

(b) the disposal is approved by the committee established under paragraph 35(1) or, where there is no such committee, by the nominee.

(2) Sub-paragraph (1) does not apply to a disposal made in the ordinary way of the company's business.

(3) If the company makes a disposal in contravention of sub-paragraph (1) otherwise than in pursuance of an order of the court—

(a) the company is liable to a fine, and

(b) if any officer of the company authorised or permitted the contravention, without reasonable excuse, he is liable to imprisonment or a fine, or both.

**19** (1) Subject to sub-paragraph (2), the company may only make any payment in respect of any debt or other liability of the company in existence before the beginning of the moratorium if—

(a) there are reasonable grounds for believing that the payment will benefit the company, and

(b) the payment is approved by the committee established under paragraph 35(1) or, where there is no such committee, by the nominee.

(2) Sub-paragraph (1) does not apply to a payment required by paragraph 20(6).

(3) If the company makes a payment in contravention of sub-paragraph (1) otherwise than in pursuance of an order of the court—

(a) the company is liable to a fine, and

(b) if any officer of the company authorised or permitted the contravention, without reasonable excuse, he is liable to imprisonment or a fine, or both.

### *Disposal of charged property, etc.*

**20** (1) This paragraph applies where—

(a) any property of the company is subject to a security, or

(b) any goods are in the possession of the company under a hire-purchase agreement.

(2) If the holder of the security consents, or the court gives leave, the company may dispose of the property as if it were not subject to the security.

(3) If the owner of the goods consents, or the court gives leave, the company may dispose of the goods as if all rights of the owner under the hire-purchase agreement were vested in the company.

(4) Where property subject to a security which, as created, was a floating charge is disposed of under sub-paragraph (2), the holder of the security has the same priority in respect of any property of the company directly or indirectly representing the property disposed of as he would have had in respect of the property subject to the security.

(5) Sub-paragraph (6) applies to the disposal under sub-paragraph (2) or (as the case may be) sub-paragraph (3) of—

(a) any property subject to a security other than a security which, as created, was a floating charge, or

(b) any goods in the possession of the company under a hire-purchase agreement.

(6) It shall be a condition of any consent or leave under sub-paragraph (2) or (as the case may be) sub-paragraph (3) that—

(a) the net proceeds of the disposal, and

(b) where those proceeds are less than such amount as may be agreed, or determined by the court, to be the net amount which would be realised on a sale of the property or goods in the open market by a willing vendor, such sums as may be required to make good the deficiency,

shall be applied towards discharging the sums secured by the security or payable under the hire-purchase agreement.

(7) Where a condition imposed in pursuance of sub-paragraph (6) relates to two or more securities, that condition requires—

(a) the net proceeds of the disposal, and

(b) where paragraph (b) of sub-paragraph (6) applies, the sums mentioned in that paragraph,

to be applied towards discharging the sums secured by those securities in the order of their priorities.

(8) Where the court gives leave for a disposal under sub-paragraph (2) or (3), the directors shall, within 14 days after leave is given, send an office copy of the order giving leave to the registrar of companies.

(9) If the directors without reasonable excuse fail to comply with sub-paragraph (8), they are liable to a fine.

**21** (1) Where property is disposed of under paragraph 20 in its application to Scotland, the company shall grant to the disponee an appropriate document of transfer or conveyance of the property, and

(a) that document, or

(b) where any recording, intimation or registration of the document is a legal requirement for completion of title to the property, that recording, intimation or registration,

has the effect of disencumbering the property of, or (as the case may be) freeing the property from, the security.

(2) Where goods in the possession of the company under a hire-purchase agreement are disposed of under paragraph 20 in its application to Scotland, the disposal has the effect of extinguishing, as against the disponee, all rights of the owner of the goods under the agreement.

**22** (1) If the company—

(a) without any consent or leave under paragraph 20, disposes of any of its property which is subject to a security otherwise than in accordance with the terms of the security,

(b) without any consent or leave under paragraph 20, disposes of any goods in the possession of the company under a hire-purchase agreement otherwise than in accordance with the terms of the agreement, or

(c) fails to comply with any requirement imposed by paragraph 20 or 21,

it is liable to a fine.

(2) If any officer of the company, without reasonable excuse, authorises or permits any such disposal or failure to comply, he is liable to imprisonment or a fine, or both.

### *Market contracts, etc.*

**23** (1) If the company enters into any transaction to which this paragraph applies—

(a) the company is liable to a fine, and

(b) if any officer of the company, without reasonable excuse, authorised or permitted the company to enter into the transaction, he is liable to imprisonment or a fine, or both.

(2) A company enters into a transaction to which this paragraph applies if it—

(a) enters into a market contract, [...]

(b) gives a transfer order,

(c) grants a market charge [...] or a system-charge, or

(d) provides any collateral security.

(3) The fact that a company enters into a transaction in contravention of this paragraph does not—

(a) make the transaction void, or

(b) make it to any extent unenforceable by or against the company.

(4) Where during the moratorium a company enters into a transaction to which this paragraph applies, nothing done by or in pursuance of the transaction is to be treated as done in contravention of paragraphs 12(1)(g), 14 or 16 to 22.

(5) Paragraph 20 does not apply in relation to any property which is subject to a market charge, [...] a system-charge or a collateral security charge.

(6) In this paragraph, 'transfer order', 'collateral security' and 'collateral security charge' have the same meanings as in the settlement finality regulations.

# PART IV

## NOMINEES

### *Monitoring of company's activities*

**24** (1) During a moratorium, the nominee shall monitor the company's affairs for the purpose of forming an opinion as to whether—

    (a) the proposed voluntary arrangement or, if he has received notice of proposed modifications under paragraph 31(7), the proposed arrangement with those modifications has a reasonable prospect of being approved and implemented, and

    (b) the company is likely to have sufficient funds available to it during the remainder of the moratorium to enable it to continue to carry on its business.

(2) The directors shall submit to the nominee any information necessary to enable him to comply with sub-paragraph (1) which he requests from them.

(3) In forming his opinion on the matters mentioned in sub-paragraph (1), the nominee is entitled to rely on the information submitted to him under sub-paragraph (2) unless he has reason to doubt its accuracy.

(4) The reference in sub-paragraph (1)(b) to the company's business is to that business as the company proposes to carry it on during the remainder of the moratorium.

### *Withdrawal of consent to act*

**25** (1) The nominee may only withdraw his consent to act in the circumstances mentioned in this paragraph.

(2) The nominee must withdraw his consent to act if, at any time during a moratorium—

    (a) he forms the opinion that—

        (i)   the proposed voluntary arrangement or, if he has received notice of proposed modifications under paragraph 31(7), the proposed arrangement with those modifications no longer has a reasonable prospect of being approved or implemented, or

        (ii)  the company will not have sufficient funds available to it during the remainder of the moratorium to enable it to continue to carry on its business,

    (b) he becomes aware that, on the date of filing, the company was not eligible for a moratorium, or

    (c) the directors fail to comply with their duty under paragraph 24(2).

(3) The reference in sub-paragraph (2)(a)(ii) to the company's business is to that business as the company proposes to carry it on during the remainder of the moratorium.

(4) If the nominee withdraws his consent to act, the moratorium comes to an end.

(5) If the nominee withdraws his consent to act he must, in accordance with the rules, notify the court, the registrar of companies, the company and any creditor of the company of whose claim he is aware of his withdrawal and the reason for it.

(6) If the nominee without reasonable excuse fails to comply with sub-paragraph (5), he is liable to a fine.

### *Challenge of nominee's actions, etc.*

**26** (1) If any creditor, director or member of the company, or any other person affected by a moratorium, is dissatisfied by any act, omission or decision of the nominee during the moratorium, he may apply to the court.

(2) An application under sub-paragraph (1) may be made during the moratorium or after it has ended.

(3) On an application under sub-paragraph (1) the court may—

    (a) confirm, reverse or modify any act or decision of the nominee,

    (b) give him directions, or

    (c) make such other order as it thinks fit.

(4) An order under sub-paragraph (3) may (among other things) bring the moratorium to an end and make such consequential provision as the court thinks fit.

**27** (1) Where there are reasonable grounds for believing that—

    (a) as a result of any act, omission or decision of the nominee during the moratorium, the company has suffered loss, but

(b) the company does not intend to pursue any claim it may have against the nominee,

any creditor of the company may apply to the court.

(2) An application under sub-paragraph (1) may be made during the moratorium or after it has ended.

(3) On an application under sub-paragraph (1) the court may—

    (a) order the company to pursue any claim against the nominee,

    (b) authorise any creditor to pursue such a claim in the name of the company, or

    (c) make such other order with respect to such a claim as it thinks fit,

unless the court is satisfied that the act, omission or decision of the nominee was in all the circumstances reasonable.

(4) An order under sub-paragraph (3) may (among other things)—

    (a) impose conditions on any authority given to pursue a claim,

    (b) direct the company to assist in the pursuit of a claim,

    (c) make directions with respect to the distribution of anything received as a result of the pursuit of a claim,

    (d) bring the moratorium to an end and make such consequential provision as the court thinks fit.

(5) On an application under sub-paragraph (1) the court shall have regard to the interests of the members and creditors of the company generally.

### Replacement of nominee by court

**28** (1) The court may—

    (a) on an application made by the directors in a case where the nominee has failed to comply with any duty imposed on him under this Schedule or has died, or

    (b) on an application made by the directors or the nominee in a case where it is impracticable or inappropriate for the nominee to continue to act as such,

direct that the nominee be replaced as such by another person qualified to act as an insolvency practitioner, or authorised to act as nominee, in relation to the voluntary arrangement.

(2) A person may only be appointed as a replacement nominee under this paragraph if he submits to the court a statement indicating his consent to act.

# PART V

## CONSIDERATION AND IMPLEMENTATION OF VOLUNTARY ARRANGEMENT

### Summoning of meetings

**29** (1) Where a moratorium is in force, the nominee shall summon meetings of the company and its creditors for such a time, date (within the period for the time being specified in paragraph 8(3)) and place as he thinks fit.

(2) The persons to be summoned to a creditors' meeting under this paragraph are every creditor of the company of whose claim the nominee is aware.

### Conduct of meetings

**30** (1) Subject to the provisions of paragraphs 31 to 35, the meetings summoned under paragraph 29 shall be conducted in accordance with the rules.

(2) A meeting so summoned may resolve that it be adjourned (or further adjourned).

(3) After the conclusion of either meeting in accordance with the rules, the chairman of the meeting shall report the result of the meeting to the court, and, immediately after reporting to the court, shall give notice of the result of the meeting to such persons as may be prescribed.

### Approval of voluntary arrangement

**31** (1) The meetings summoned under paragraph 29 shall decide whether to approve the proposed voluntary arrangement (with or without modifications).

(2) The modifications may include one conferring the functions proposed to be conferred on the nominee on another person qualified to act as an insolvency practitioner, or authorised to act as nominee, in relation to the voluntary arrangement.

(3) The modifications shall not include one by virtue of which the proposal ceases to be a proposal such as is mentioned in section 1.

(4) A meeting summoned under paragraph 29 shall not approve any proposal or modification which affects the right of a secured creditor of the company to enforce his security, except with the concurrence of the creditor concerned.

(5) Subject to sub-paragraph (6), a meeting so summoned shall not approve any proposal or modification under which—

    (a) any preferential debt of the company is to be paid otherwise than in priority to such of its
        debts as are not preferential debts, or
    (b) a preferential creditor of the company is to be paid an amount in respect of a preferential
        debt that bears to that debt a smaller proportion than is borne to another preferential debt
        by the amount that is to be paid in respect of that other debt.

    (6) The meeting may approve such a proposal or modification with the concurrence of the preferential creditor concerned.

    (7) The directors of the company may, before the beginning of the period of seven days which ends with the meetings (or either of them) summoned under paragraph 29 being held, give notice to the nominee of any modifications of the proposal for which the directors intend to seek the approval of those meetings.

    (8) References in this paragraph to preferential debts and preferential creditors are to be read in accordance with section 386 in Part XII of this Act.

### Extension of moratorium

    **32** (1) Subject to sub-paragraph (2), a meeting summoned under paragraph 29 which resolves that it be adjourned (or further adjourned) may resolve that the moratorium be extended (or further extended), with or without conditions.

    (2) The moratorium may not be extended (or further extended) to a day later than the end of the period of two months which begins—
    (a) where both meetings summoned under paragraph 29 are first held on the same day, with
        that day,
    (b) in any other case, with the day on which the later of those meetings is first held.

    (3) At any meeting where it is proposed to extend (or further extend) the moratorium, before a decision is taken with respect to that proposal, the nominee shall inform the meeting—
    (a) of what he has done in order to comply with his duty under paragraph 24 and the cost of his
        actions for the company, and
    (b) of what he intends to do to continue to comply with that duty if the moratorium is extended
        (or further extended) and the expected cost of his actions for the company.

    (4) Where, in accordance with sub-paragraph (3)(b), the nominee informs a meeting of the expected cost of his intended actions, the meeting shall resolve whether or not to approve that expected cost.

    (5) If a decision not to approve the expected cost of the nominee's intended actions has effect under paragraph 36, the moratorium comes to an end.

    (6) A meeting may resolve that a moratorium which has been extended (or further extended) be brought to an end before the end of the period of the extension (or further extension).

    (7) The Secretary of State may by order increase or reduce the period for the time being specified in sub-paragraph (2).

    **33** (1) The conditions which may be imposed when a moratorium is extended (or further extended) include a requirement that the nominee be replaced as such by another person qualified to act as an insolvency practitioner, or authorised to act as nominee, in relation to the voluntary arrangement.

    (2) A person may only be appointed as a replacement nominee by virtue of sub-paragraph (1) if he submits to the court a statement indicating his consent to act.

    (3) At any meeting where it is proposed to appoint a replacement nominee as a condition of extending (or further extending) the moratorium—
    (a) the duty imposed by paragraph 32(3)(b) on the nominee shall instead be imposed on the
        person proposed as the replacement nominee, and
    (b) paragraphs 32(4) and (5) and 36(1)(e) apply as if the references to the nominee were to
        that person.

    **34** (1) If a decision to extend, or further extend, the moratorium takes effect under paragraph 36, the nominee shall, in accordance with the rules, notify the registrar of companies and the court.

    (2) If the moratorium is extended, or further extended, by virtue of an order under paragraph 36(5), the nominee shall, in accordance with the rules, send an office copy of the order to the registrar of companies.

    (3) If the nominee without reasonable excuse fails to comply with this paragraph, he is liable to a fine.

### Moratorium committee

    **35** (1) A meeting summoned under paragraph 29 which resolves that the moratorium be extended (or further extended) may, with the consent of the nominee, resolve that a committee be established to exercise the functions conferred on it by the meeting.

    (2) The meeting may not so resolve unless it has approved an estimate of the expenses to be incurred by the committee in the exercise of the proposed functions.

    (3) Any expenses, not exceeding the amount of the estimate, incurred by the committee in the exercise of its functions shall be reimbursed by the nominee.

    (4) The committee shall cease to exist when the moratorium comes to an end.

*Effectiveness of decisions*

**36** (1) Sub-paragraph (2) applies to references to one of the following decisions having effect, that is, a decision, under paragraph 31, 32 or 35, with respect to—

(a) the approval of a proposed voluntary arrangement,

(b) the extension (or further extension) of a moratorium,

(c) the bringing of a moratorium to an end,

(d) the establishment of a committee, or

(e) the approval of the expected cost of a nominee's intended actions.

(2) The decision has effect if, in accordance with the rules—

(a) it has been taken by both meetings summoned under paragraph 29, or

(b) (subject to any order made under sub-paragraph (5)) it has been taken by the creditors' meeting summoned under that paragraph.

(3) If a decision taken by the creditors' meeting under any of paragraphs 31, 32 or 35 with respect to any of the matters mentioned in sub-paragraph (1) differs from one so taken by the company meeting with respect to that matter, a member of the company may apply to the court.

(4) An application under sub-paragraph (3) shall not be made after the end of the period of 28 days beginning with—

(a) the day on which the decision was taken by the creditors' meeting, or

(b) where the decision of the company meeting was taken on a later day, that day.

(5) On an application under sub-paragraph (3), the court may—

(a) order the decision of the company meeting to have effect instead of the decision of the creditors' meeting, or

(b) make such other order as it thinks fit.

*Effect of approval of voluntary arrangement*

**37** (1) This paragraph applies where a decision approving a voluntary arrangement has effect under paragraph 36.

(2) The approved voluntary arrangement—

(a) takes effect as if made by the company at the creditors' meeting, and

(b) binds every person who in accordance with the rules—

(i) was entitled to vote at that meeting (whether or not he was present or represented at it), or

(ii) would have been so entitled if he had had notice of it,

as if he were a party to the voluntary arrangement.

(3) If—

(a) when the arrangement ceases to have effect any amount payable under the arrangement to a person bound by virtue of sub-paragraph (2)(b)(ii) has not been paid, and

(b) the arrangement did not come to an end prematurely,

the company shall at that time become liable to pay to that person the amount payable under the arrangement.

(4) Where a petition for the winding up of the company, other than an excepted petition within the meaning of paragraph 12, was presented before the beginning of the moratorium, the court shall dismiss the petition.

(5) The court shall not dismiss a petition under sub-paragraph (4)—

(a) at any time before the end of the period of 28 days beginning with the first day on which each of the reports of the meetings required by paragraph 30(3) has been made to the court, or

(b) at any time when an application under paragraph 38 or an appeal in respect of such an application is pending, or at any time in the period within which such an appeal may be brought.

*Challenge of decisions*

**38** (1) Subject to the following provisions of this paragraph, any of the persons mentioned in sub-paragraph (2) may apply to the court on one or both of the following grounds—

(a) that a voluntary arrangement approved at one or both of the meetings summoned under paragraph 29 and which has taken effect unfairly prejudices the interests of a creditor, member or contributory of the company,

(b) that there has been some material irregularity at or in relation to either of those meetings.

(2) The persons who may apply under this paragraph are—

(a) a person entitled, in accordance with the rules, to vote at either of the meetings,

(b) a person who would have been entitled, in accordance with the rules, to vote at the creditors' meeting if he had had notice of it, and

(c) the nominee.

(3) An application under this paragraph shall not be made—

(a) after the end of the period of 28 days beginning with the first day on which each of the reports required by paragraph 30(3) has been made to the court, or

(b) in the case of a person who was not given notice of the creditors' meeting, after the end of the period of 28 days beginning with the day on which he became aware that the meeting had taken place,

but (subject to that) an application made by a person within sub-paragraph (2)(b) on the ground that the arrangement prejudices his interests may be made after the arrangement has ceased to have effect, unless it came to an end prematurely.

(4) Where on an application under this paragraph the court is satisfied as to either of the grounds mentioned in sub-paragraph (1), it may do any of the following—

    (a) revoke or suspend—

        (i) any decision approving the voluntary arrangement which has effect under paragraph 36, or

        (ii) in a case falling within sub-paragraph (1)(b), any decision taken by the meeting in question which has effect under that paragraph,

    (b) give a direction to any person—

        (i) for the summoning of further meetings to consider any revised proposal for a voluntary arrangement which the directors may make, or

        (ii) in a case falling within sub-paragraph (1)(b), for the summoning of a further company or (as the case may be) creditors' meeting to reconsider the original proposal.

(5) Where at any time after giving a direction under sub-paragraph (4)(b)(i) the court is satisfied that the directors do not intend to submit a revised proposal, the court shall revoke the direction and revoke or suspend any decision approving the voluntary arrangement which has effect under paragraph 36.

(6) Where the court gives a direction under sub-paragraph (4)(b), it may also give a direction continuing or, as the case may require, renewing, for such period as may be specified in the direction, the effect of the moratorium.

(7) Sub-paragraph (8) applies in a case where the court, on an application under this paragraph—

    (a) gives a direction under sub-paragraph (4)(b), or

    (b) revokes or suspends a decision under sub-paragraph (4)(a) or (5).

(8) In such a case, the court may give such supplemental directions as it thinks fit and, in particular, directions with respect to—

    (a) things done under the voluntary arrangement since it took effect, and

    (b) such things done since that time as could not have been done if a moratorium had been in force in relation to the company when they were done.

(9) Except in pursuance of the preceding provisions of this paragraph, a decision taken at a meeting summoned under paragraph 29 is not invalidated by any irregularity at or in relation to the meeting.

### Implementation of voluntary arrangement

**39** (1) This paragraph applies where a voluntary arrangement approved by one or both of the meetings summoned under paragraph 29 has taken effect.

(2) The person who is for the time being carrying out in relation to the voluntary arrangement the functions conferred—

    (a) by virtue of the approval of the arrangement, on the nominee, or

    (b) by virtue of paragraph 31(2), on a person other than the nominee,

shall be known as the supervisor of the voluntary arrangement.

(3) If any of the company's creditors or any other person is dissatisfied by any act, omission or decision of the supervisor, he may apply to the court.

(4) On an application under sub-paragraph (3) the court may—

    (a) confirm, reverse or modify any act or decision of the supervisor,

    (b) give him directions, or

    (c) make such other order as it thinks fit.

(5) The supervisor—

    (a) may apply to the court for directions in relation to any particular matter arising under the voluntary arrangement, and

    (b) is included among the persons who may apply to the court for the winding up of the company or for an administration order to be made in relation to it.

(6) The court may, whenever—

    (a) it is expedient to appoint a person to carry out the functions of the supervisor, and

    (b) it is inexpedient, difficult or impracticable for an appointment to be made without the assistance of the court,

make an order appointing a person who is qualified to act as an Insolvency practitioner, or authorised to act as supervisor, in relation to the voluntary arrangement, either in substitution for the existing supervisor or to fill a vacancy.

(7) The power conferred by sub-paragraph (6) is exercisable so as to increase the number of persons exercising the functions of supervisor or, where there is more than one person exercising those functions, so as to replace one or more of those persons.

## PART VI

## MISCELLANEOUS

### *Challenge of directors' actions*

**40** (1) This paragraph applies in relation to acts or omissions of the directors of a company during a moratorium.

(2) A creditor or member of the company may apply to the court for an order under this paragraph on the ground—

(a) that the company's affairs, business and property are being or have been managed by the directors in a manner which is unfairly prejudicial to the interests of its creditors or members generally, or of some part of its creditors or members (including at least the petitioner), or

(b) that any actual or proposed act or omission of the directors is or would be so prejudicial.

(3) An application for an order under this paragraph may be made during or after the moratorium.

(4) On an application for an order under this paragraph the court may—

(a) make such order as it thinks fit for giving relief in respect of the matters complained of,

(b) adjourn the hearing conditionally or unconditionally, or

(c) make an interim order or any other order that it thinks fit.

(5) An order under this paragraph may in particular—

(a) regulate the management by the directors of the company's affairs, business and property during the remainder of the moratorium,

(b) require the directors to refrain from doing or continuing an act complained of by the petitioner, or to do an act which the petitioner has complained they have omitted to do,

(c) require the summoning of a meeting of creditors or members for the purpose of considering such matters as the court may direct,

(d) bring the moratorium to an end and make such consequential provision as the court thinks fit.

(6) In making an order under this paragraph the court shall have regard to the need to safeguard the interests of persons who have dealt with the company in good faith and for value.

(7) Sub-paragraph (8) applies where—

(a) the appointment of an administrator has effect in relation to the company and that appointment was in pursuance of—

(i)   an administration application made, or

(ii)  a notice of intention to appoint filed,

before the moratorium came into force, or

(b) the company is being wound up in pursuance of a petition presented before the moratorium came into force.

(8) No application for an order under this paragraph may be made by a creditor or member of the company; but such an application may be made instead by the administrator or (as the case may be) the liquidator.

### *Offences*

**41** (1) This paragraph applies where a moratorium has been obtained for a company.

(2) If, within the period of 12 months ending with the day on which the moratorium came into force, a person who was at the time an officer of the company—

(a) did any of the things mentioned in paragraphs (a) to (f) of sub-paragraph (4), or

(b) was privy to the doing by others of any of the things mentioned in paragraphs (c), (d) and (e) of that sub-paragraph,

he is to be treated as having committed an offence at that time.

(3) If, at any time during the moratorium, a person who is an officer of the company—

(a) does any of the things mentioned in paragraphs (a) to (f) of sub-paragraph (4), or

(b) is privy to the doing by others of any of the things mentioned in paragraphs (c), (d) and (e) of that sub-paragraph,

he commits an offence.

(4) Those things are—

(a) concealing any part of the company's property to the value of £500 or more, or concealing any debt due to or from the company, or

(b) fraudulently removing any part of the company's property to the value of £500 or more, or

(c) concealing, destroying, mutilating or falsifying any book or paper affecting or relating to the company's property or affairs, or

(d) making any false entry in any book or paper affecting or relating to the company's property or affairs, or

(e) fraudulently parting with, altering or making any omission in any document affecting or relating to the company's property or affairs, or

     (f)  pawning, pledging or disposing of any property of the company which has been obtained on credit and has not been paid for (unless the pawning, pledging or disposal was in the ordinary way of the company's business).

   (5)  For the purposes of this paragraph, 'officer' includes a shadow director.

   (6)  It is a defence—

     (a)  for a person charged under sub-paragraph (2) or (3) in respect of the things mentioned in paragraph (a) or (f) of sub-paragraph (4) to prove that he had no intent to defraud, and

     (b)  for a person charged under sub-paragraph (2) or (3) in respect of the things mentioned in paragraph (c) or (d) of sub-paragraph (4) to prove that he had no intent to conceal the state of affairs of the company or to defeat the law.

   (7)  Where a person pawns, pledges or disposes of any property of a company in circumstances which amount to an offence under sub-paragraph (2) or (3), every person who takes in pawn or pledge, or otherwise receives, the property knowing it to be pawned, pledged or disposed of in circumstances which—

     (a)  would, if a moratorium were obtained for the company within the period of 12 months beginning with the day on which the pawning, pledging or disposal took place, amount to an offence under sub-paragraph (2), or

     (b)  amount to an offence under sub-paragraph (3),

commits an offence.

   (8)  A person guilty of an offence under this paragraph is liable to imprisonment or a fine, or both.

   (9)  The money sums specified in paragraphs (a) and (b) of sub-paragraph (4) are subject to increase or reduction by order under section 417A in Part XV.

   **42**  (1)  If, for the purpose of obtaining a moratorium, or an extension of a moratorium, for a company, a person who is an officer of the company—

     (a)  makes any false representation, or

     (b)  fraudulently does, or omits to do, anything,

he commits an offence.

   (2)  Sub-paragraph (1) applies even if no moratorium or extension is obtained.

   (3)  For the purposes of this paragraph, 'officer' includes a shadow director.

   (4)  A person guilty of an offence under this paragraph is liable to imprisonment or a fine, or both.

### Void provisions in floating charge documents

   **43**  (1)  A provision in an instrument creating a floating charge is void if it provides for—

     (a)  obtaining a moratorium, or

     (b)  anything done with a view to obtaining a moratorium (including any preliminary decision or investigation),

to be an event causing the floating charge to crystallise or causing restrictions which would not otherwise apply to be imposed on the disposal of property by the company or a ground for the appointment of a receiver.

   (2)  In sub-paragraph (1), 'receiver' includes a manager and a person who is appointed both receiver and manager.

### Functions of the Financial Services Authority

   **44**  (1)  This Schedule has effect in relation to a moratorium for a regulated company with the modifications in sub-paragraphs (2) to (16) below.

   (2)  Any notice or other document required by virtue of this Schedule to be sent to a creditor of a regulated company must also be sent to the Authority.

   (3)  The Authority is entitled to be heard on any application to the court for leave under paragraph 20(2) or 20(3)(disposal of charged property, etc.).

   (4)  Where paragraph 26(1)(challenge of nominee's actions, etc.) applies, the persons who may apply to the court include the Authority.

   (5)  If a person other than the Authority applies to the court under that paragraph, the Authority is entitled to be heard on the application.

   (6)  Where paragraph 27(1)(challenge of nominee's actions, etc.) applies, the persons who may apply to the court include the Authority.

   (7)  If a person other than the Authority applies to the court under that paragraph, the Authority is entitled to be heard on the application.

   (8)  The persons to be summoned to a creditors' meeting under paragraph 29 include the Authority.

   (9)  A person appointed for the purpose by the Authority is entitled to attend and participate in (but not to vote at)—

     (a)  any creditors' meeting summoned under that paragraph,

     (b)  any meeting of a committee established under paragraph 35 (moratorium committee).

   (10)  The Authority is entitled to be heard on any application under paragraph 36(3)(effectiveness of decisions).

   (11)  Where paragraph 38(1)(challenge of decisions) applies, the persons who may apply to the court include the Authority.

(12)  If a person other than the Authority applies to the court under that paragraph, the Authority is entitled to be heard on the application.

(13)  Where paragraph 39(3)(implementation of voluntary arrangement) applies, the persons who may apply to the court include the Authority.

(14)  If a person other than the Authority applies to the court under that paragraph, the Authority is entitled to be heard on the application.

(15)  Where paragraph 40(2)(challenge of directors' actions) applies, the persons who may apply to the court include the Authority.

(16)  If a person other than the Authority applies to the court under that paragraph, the Authority is entitled to be heard on the application.

(17)  This paragraph does not prejudice any right the Authority has (apart from this paragraph) as a creditor of a regulated company.

(18)  In this paragraph—

'the Authority' means the Financial Services Authority, and

'regulated company' means a company which—

(a)  is, or has been, an authorised person within the meaning given by section 31 of the Financial Services and Markets Act 2000,

(b)  is, or has been, an appointed representative within the meaning given by section 39 of that Act, or

(c)  is carrying on, or has carried on, a regulated activity, within the meaning given by section 22 of that Act, in contravention of the general prohibition within the meaning given by section 19 of that Act.

### *Subordinate legislation*

**45**  (1)  Regulations or an order made by the Secretary of State under this Schedule may make different provision for different cases.

(2)  Regulations so made may make such consequential, incidental, supplemental and transitional provision as may appear to the Secretary of State necessary or expedient.

(3)  Any power of the Secretary of State to make regulations under this Schedule may be exercised by amending or repealing any enactment contained in this Act (including one contained in this Schedule) or contained in the Company Directors Disqualification Act 1986.

(4)  Regulations (except regulations under paragraph 5) or an order made by the Secretary of State under this Schedule shall be made by statutory instrument subject to annulment in pursuance of a resolution of either House of Parliament.

(5)  Regulations under paragraph 5 of this Schedule are to be made by statutory instrument and shall only be made if a draft containing the regulations has been laid before and approved by resolution of each House of Parliament.

# SCHEDULE B1

# ADMINISTRATION

## ARRANGEMENT OF SCHEDULE

## NATURE OF ADMINISTRATION

### *Administration*

**1**  (1)  For the purposes of this Act 'administrator' of a company means a person appointed under this Schedule to manage the company's affairs, business and property.

(2)  For the purposes of this Act—

(a)  a company is 'in administration' while the appointment of an administrator of the company has effect,

(b)  a company 'enters administration' when the appointment of an administrator takes effect,

(c)  a company ceases to be in administration when the appointment of an administrator of the company ceases to have effect in accordance with this Schedule, and

(d)  a company does not cease to be in administration merely because an administrator vacates office (by reason of resignation, death or otherwise) or is removed from office.

**2**  A person may be appointed as administrator of a company—

(a)  by administration order of the court under paragraph 10,

(b)  by the holder of a floating charge under paragraph 14, or

(c)  by the company or its directors under paragraph 22.

### *Purpose of administration*

**3**  (1)  The administrator of a company must perform his functions with the objective of—

(a) rescuing the company as a going concern, or

(b) achieving a better result for the company's creditors as a whole than would be likely if the company were wound up (without first being in administration), or

(c) realising property in order to make a distribution to one or more secured or preferential creditors.

(2) Subject to sub-paragraph (4), the administrator of a company must perform his functions in the interests of the company's creditors as a whole.

(3) The administrator must perform his functions with the objective specified in sub-paragraph (1)(a) unless he thinks either—

(a) that it is not reasonably practicable to achieve that objective, or

(b) that the objective specified in sub-paragraph (1)(b) would achieve a better result for the company's creditors as a whole.

(4) The administrator may perform his functions with the objective specified in sub-paragraph (1)(c) only if—

(a) he thinks that it is not reasonably practicable to achieve either of the objectives specified in sub-paragraph (1)(a) and (b), and

(b) he does not unnecessarily harm the interests of the creditors of the company as a whole.

**4** The administrator of a company must perform his functions as quickly and efficiently as is reasonably practicable.

### *Status of administrator*

**5** An administrator is an officer of the court (whether or not he is appointed by the court).

### *General restrictions*

**6** A person may be appointed as administrator of a company only if he is qualified to act as an insolvency practitioner in relation to the company.

**7** A person may not be appointed as administrator of a company which is in administration (subject to the provisions of paragraphs 90 to 97 and 100 to 103 about replacement and additional administrators).

**8** (1) A person may not be appointed as administrator of a company which is in liquidation by virtue of—

(a) a resolution for voluntary winding up, or

(b) a winding-up order.

(2) Sub-paragraph (1)(a) is subject to paragraph 38.

(3) Sub-paragraph (1)(b) is subject to paragraphs 37 and 38.

**9** (1) A person may not be appointed as administrator of a company which—

(a) has a liability in respect of a deposit which it accepted in accordance with the Banking Act 1979 (c 37) or 1987 (c 22), but

(b) is not an authorised deposit taker.

(2) A person may not be appointed as administrator of a company which effects or carries out contracts of insurance.

(3) But sub-paragraph (2) does not apply to a company which—

(a) is exempt from the general prohibition in relation to effecting or carrying out contracts of insurance, or

(b) is an authorised deposit taker effecting or carrying out contracts of insurance in the course of a banking business.

(4) In this paragraph—

'authorised deposit taker' means a person with permission under Part IV of the Financial Services and Markets Act 2000 (c 8) to accept deposits, and

'the general prohibition' has the meaning given by section 19 of that Act.

(5) This paragraph shall be construed in accordance with—

(a) section 22 of the Financial Services and Markets Act 2000 (classes of regulated activity and categories of investment),

(b) any relevant order under that section, and

(c) Schedule 2 to that Act (regulated activities).

## APPOINTMENT OF ADMINISTRATOR BY COURT

### *Administration order*

**10** An administration order is an order appointing a person as the administrator of a company.

### *Conditions for making order*

**11** The court may make an administration order in relation to a company only if satisfied—

(a) that the company is or is likely to become unable to pay its debts, and

(b) that the administration order is reasonably likely to achieve the purpose of administration.

### Administration application

**12** (1) An application to the court for an administration order in respect of a company (an 'administration application') may be made only by—

    (a) the company,

    (b) the directors of the company,

    (c) one or more creditors of the company,

    (d) the designated officer for a magistrates' court in the exercise of the power conferred by section 87A of the Magistrates' Courts Act 1980 (c 43)(fine imposed on company), or

    (e) a combination of persons listed in paragraphs (a) to (d).

(2) As soon as is reasonably practicable after the making of an administration application the applicant shall notify—

    (a) any person who has appointed an administrative receiver of the company,

    (b) any person who is or may be entitled to appoint an administrative receiver of the company,

    (c) any person who is or may be entitled to appoint an administrator of the company under paragraph 14, and

    (d) such other persons as may be prescribed.

(3) An administration application may not be withdrawn without the permission of the court.

(4) In sub-paragraph (1) 'creditor' includes a contingent creditor and a prospective creditor.

(5) Sub-paragraph (1) is without prejudice to section 7(4)(b).

### Powers of court

**13** (1) On hearing an administration application the court may—

    (a) make the administration order sought;

    (b) dismiss the application;

    (c) adjourn the hearing conditionally or unconditionally;

    (d) make an interim order;

    (e) treat the application as a winding-up petition and make any order which the court could make under section 125;

    (f) make any other order which the court thinks appropriate.

(2) An appointment of an administrator by administration order takes effect—

    (a) at a time appointed by the order, or

    (b) where no time is appointed by the order, when the order is made.

(3) An interim order under sub-paragraph (1)(d) may, in particular—

    (a) restrict the exercise of a power of the directors or the company;

    (b) make provision conferring a discretion on the court or on a person qualified to act as an insolvency practitioner in relation to the company.

(4) This paragraph is subject to paragraph 39.

## APPOINTMENT OF ADMINISTRATOR BY HOLDER OF FLOATING CHARGE

### Power to appoint

**14** (1) The holder of a qualifying floating charge in respect of a company's property may appoint an administrator of the company.

(2) For the purposes of sub-paragraph (1) a floating charge qualifies if created by an instrument which—

    (a) states that this paragraph applies to the floating charge,

    (b) purports to empower the holder of the floating charge to appoint an administrator of the company,

    (c) purports to empower the holder of the floating charge to make an appointment which would be the appointment of an administrative receiver within the meaning given by section 29(2), or

    (d) purports to empower the holder of a floating charge in Scotland to appoint a receiver who on appointment would be an administrative receiver.

(3) For the purposes of sub-paragraph (1) a person is the holder of a qualifying floating charge in respect of a company's property if he holds one or more debentures of the company secured—

    (a) by a qualifying floating charge which relates to the whole or substantially the whole of the company's property,

    (b) by a number of qualifying floating charges which together relate to the whole or substantially the whole of the company's property, or

    (c) by charges and other forms of security which together relate to the whole or substantially the whole of the company's property and at least one of which is a qualifying floating charge.

### Restrictions on power to appoint

**15** (1) A person may not appoint an administrator under paragraph 14 unless—
    (a) he has given at least two business days' written notice to the holder of any prior floating charge which satisfies paragraph 14(2), or
    (b) the holder of any prior floating charge which satisfies paragraph 14(2) has consented in writing to the making of the appointment.
    (2) One floating charge is prior to another for the purposes of this paragraph if—
    (a) it was created first, or
    (b) it is to be treated as having priority in accordance with an agreement to which the holder of each floating charge was party.
    (3) Sub-paragraph (2) shall have effect in relation to Scotland as if the following were substituted for paragraph (a)—
    '(a) it has priority of ranking in accordance with section 464(4)(b) of the Companies Act 1985 (c 6),'.

**16** An administrator may not be appointed under paragraph 14 while a floating charge on which the appointment relies is not enforceable.

**17** An administrator of a company may not be appointed under paragraph 14 if—
    (a) a provisional liquidator of the company has been appointed under section 135, or
    (b) an administrative receiver of the company is in office.

### Notice of appointment

**16** (1) A person who appoints an administrator of a company under paragraph 14 shall file with the court—
    (a) a notice of appointment, and
    (b) such other documents as may be prescribed.
    (2) The notice of appointment must include a statutory declaration by or on behalf of the person who makes the appointment—
    (a) that the person is the holder of a qualifying floating charge in respect of the company's property,
    (b) that each floating charge relied on in making the appointment is (or was) enforceable on the date of the appointment, and
    (c) that the appointment is in accordance with this Schedule.
    (3) The notice of appointment must identify the administrator and must be accompanied by a statement by the administrator—
    (a) that he consents to the appointment,
    (b) that in his opinion the purpose of administration is reasonably likely to be achieved, and
    (c) giving such other information and opinions as may be prescribed.
    (4) For the purpose of a statement under sub-paragraph (3) an administrator may rely on information supplied by directors of the company (unless he has reason to doubt its accuracy).
    (5) The notice of appointment and any document accompanying it must be in the prescribed form.
    (6) A statutory declaration under sub-paragraph (2) must be made during the prescribed period.
    (7) A person commits an offence if in a statutory declaration under sub-paragraph (2) he makes a statement—
    (a) which is false, and
    (b) which he does not reasonably believe to be true.

### Commencement of appointment

**19** The appointment of an administrator under paragraph 14 takes effect when the requirements of paragraph 18 are satisfied.

**20** A person who appoints an administrator under paragraph 14—
    (a) shall notify the administrator and such other persons as may be prescribed as soon as is reasonably practicable after the requirements of paragraph 18 are satisfied, and
    (b) commits an offence if he fails without reasonable excuse to comply with paragraph (a).

### Invalid appointment: indemnity

**21** (1) This paragraph applies where—
    (a) a person purports to appoint an administrator under paragraph 14, and
    (b) the appointment is discovered to be invalid.
    (2) The court may order the person who purported to make the appointment to indemnify the person appointed against liability which arises solely by reason of the appointment's invalidity.

## APPOINTMENT OF ADMINISTRATOR BY COMPANY OR DIRECTORS

### *Power to appoint*

**22** (1)  A company may appoint an administrator.

(2)  The directors of a company may appoint an administrator.

### *Restrictions on power to appoint*

(1)  This paragraph applies where an administrator of a company is appointed—

   (a)  under paragraph 22, or

   (b)  on an administration application made by the company or its directors.

(2)  An administrator of the company may not be appointed under paragraph 22 during the period of 12 months beginning with the date on which the appointment referred to in sub-paragraph (1) ceases to have effect.

**24** (1)  If a moratorium for a company under Schedule A1 ends on a date when no voluntary arrangement is in force in respect of the company, this paragraph applies for the period of 12 months beginning with that date.

(2)  This paragraph also applies for the period of 12 months beginning with the date on which a voluntary arrangement in respect of a company ends if—

   (a)  the arrangement was made during a moratorium for the company under Schedule A1, and

   (b)  the arrangement ends prematurely (within the meaning of section 7B).

(3)  While this paragraph applies, an administrator of the company may not be appointed under paragraph 22.

**25**  An administrator of a company may not be appointed under paragraph 22 if—

   (a)  a petition for the winding up of the company has been presented and is not yet disposed of,

   (b)  an administration application has been made and is not yet disposed of, or

   (c)  an administrative receiver of the company is in office.

### *Notice of intention to appoint*

**26** (1)  A person who proposes to make an appointment under paragraph 22 shall give at least five business days' written notice to—

   (a)  any person who is or may be entitled to appoint an administrative receiver of the company, and

   (b)  any person who is or may be entitled to appoint an administrator of the company under paragraph 14.

(2)  A person who proposes to make an appointment under paragraph 22 shall also give such notice as may be prescribed to such other persons as may be prescribed.

(3)  A notice under this paragraph must—

   (a)  identify the proposed administrator, and

   (b)  be in the prescribed form.

**27** (1)  A person who gives notice of intention to appoint under paragraph 26 shall file with the court as soon as is reasonably practicable a copy of—

   (a)  the notice, and

   (b)  any document accompanying it.

(2)  The copy filed under sub-paragraph (1) must be accompanied by a statutory declaration made by or on behalf of the person who proposes to make the appointment—

   (a)  that the company is or is likely to become unable to pay its debts,

   (b)  that the company is not in liquidation, and

   (c)  that, so far as the person making the statement is able to ascertain, the appointment is not prevented by paragraphs 23 to 25, and

   (d)  to such additional effect, and giving such information, as may be prescribed.

(3)  A statutory declaration under sub-paragraph (2) must—

   (a)  be in the prescribed form, and

   (b)  be made during the prescribed period.

(4)  A person commits an offence if in a statutory declaration under sub-paragraph (2) he makes a statement—

   (a)  which is false, and

   (b)  which he does not reasonably believe to be true.

**28** (1)  An appointment may not be made under paragraph 22 unless the person who makes the appointment has complied with any requirement of paragraphs 26 and 27 and—

   (a)  the period of notice specified in paragraph 26(1) has expired, or

   (b)  each person to whom notice has been given under paragraph 26(1) has consented in writing to the making of the appointment.

(2)  An appointment may not be made under paragraph 22 after the period of ten business days beginning with the date on which the notice of intention to appoint is filed under paragraph 27(1).

### Notice of appointment

**29** (1)  A person who appoints an administrator of a company under paragraph 22 shall file with the court—

(a)  a notice of appointment, and

(b)  such other documents as may be prescribed.

(2)  The notice of appointment must include a statutory declaration by or on behalf of the person who makes the appointment—

(a)  that the person is entitled to make an appointment under paragraph 22,

(b)  that the appointment is in accordance with this Schedule, and

(c)  that, so far as the person making the statement is able to ascertain, the statements made and information given in the statutory declaration filed with the notice of intention to appoint remain accurate.

(3)  The notice of appointment must identify the administrator and must be accompanied by a statement by the administrator—

(a)  that he consents to the appointment,

(b)  that in his opinion the purpose of administration is reasonably likely to be achieved, and

(c)  giving such other information and opinions as may be prescribed.

(4)  For the purpose of a statement under sub-paragraph (3) an administrator may rely on information supplied by directors of the company (unless he has reason to doubt its accuracy).

(5)  The notice of appointment and any document accompanying it must be in the prescribed form.

(6)  A statutory declaration under sub-paragraph (2) must be made during the prescribed period.

(7)  A person commits an offence if in a statutory declaration under sub-paragraph (2) he makes a statement—

(a)  which is false, and

(b)  which he does not reasonably believe to be true.

**30**  In a case in which no person is entitled to notice of intention to appoint under paragraph 26(1) (and paragraph 28 therefore does not apply)—

(a)  the statutory declaration accompanying the notice of appointment must include the statements and information required under paragraph 27(2), and

(b)  paragraph 29(2)(c) shall not apply.

### Commencement of appointment

**31**  The appointment of an administrator under paragraph 22 takes effect when the requirements of paragraph 29 are satisfied.

**32**  A person who appoints an administrator under paragraph 22—

(a)  shall notify the administrator and such other persons as may be prescribed as soon as is reasonably practicable after the requirements of paragraph 29 are satisfied, and

(b)  commits an offence if he fails without reasonable excuse to comply with paragraph (a).

**33**  If before the requirements of paragraph 29 are satisfied the company enters administration by virtue of an administration order or an appointment under paragraph 14—

(a)  the appointment under paragraph 22 shall not take effect, and

(b)  paragraph 32 shall not apply.

### Invalid appointment: indemnity

**34** (1)  This paragraph applies where—

(a)  a person purports to appoint an administrator under paragraph 22, and

(b)  the appointment is discovered to be invalid.

(2)  The court may order the person who purported to make the appointment to indemnify the person appointed against liability which arises solely by reason of the appointment's invalidity.

## ADMINISTRATION APPLICATION – SPECIAL CASES

### Application by holder of floating charge

**35** (1)  This paragraph applies where an administration application in respect of a company—

(a)  is made by the holder of a qualifying floating charge in respect of the company's property, and

(b)  includes a statement that the application is made in reliance on this paragraph.

(2)  The court may make an administration order—

(a)  whether or not satisfied that the company is or is likely to become unable to pay its debts, but

(b)  only if satisfied that the applicant could appoint an administrator under paragraph 14.

### Intervention by holder of floating charge

**36** (1)  This paragraph applies where—

(a)  an administration application in respect of a company is made by a person who is not the holder of a qualifying floating charge in respect of the company's property, and

(b) the holder of a qualifying floating charge in respect of the company's property applies to the court to have a specified person appointed as administrator (and not the person specified by the administration applicant).

(2) The court shall grant an application under sub-paragraph (1)(b) unless the court thinks it right to refuse the application because of the particular circumstances of the case.

### Application where company in liquidation

**37** (1) This paragraph applies where the holder of a qualifying floating charge in respect of a company's property could appoint an administrator under paragraph 14 but for paragraph 8(1)(b).

(2) The holder of the qualifying floating charge may make an administration application.

(3) If the court makes an administration order on hearing an application made by virtue of sub-paragraph (2)—

(a) the court shall discharge the winding-up order,

(b) the court shall make provision for such matters as may be prescribed,

(c) the court may make other consequential provision,

(d) the court shall specify which of the powers under this Schedule are to be exercisable by the administrator, and

(e) this Schedule shall have effect with such modifications as the court may specify.

**38** (1) The liquidator of a company may make an administration application.

(2) If the court makes an administration order on hearing an application made by virtue of sub-paragraph (1)—

(a) the court shall discharge any winding-up order in respect of the company,

(b) the court shall make provision for such matters as may be prescribed,

(c) the court may make other consequential provision,

(d) the court shall specify which of the powers under this Schedule are to be exercisable by the administrator, and

(e) this Schedule shall have effect with such modifications as the court may specify.

### Effect of administrative receivership

**39** (1) Where there is an administrative receiver of a company the court must dismiss an administration application in respect of the company unless—

(a) the person by or on behalf of whom the receiver was appointed consents to the making of the administration order,

(b) the court thinks that the security by virtue of which the receiver was appointed would be liable to be released or discharged under sections 238 to 240 (transaction at undervalue and preference) if an administration order were made,

(c) the court thinks that the security by virtue of which the receiver was appointed would be avoided under section 245 (avoidance of floating charge) if an administration order were made, or

(d) the court thinks that the security by virtue of which the receiver was appointed would be challengeable under section 242 (gratuitous alienations) or 243 (unfair preferences) or under any rule of law in Scotland.

(2) Sub-paragraph (1) applies whether the administrative receiver is appointed before or after the making of the administration application.

## EFFECT OF ADMINISTRATION

### Dismissal of pending winding-up petition

**40** (1) A petition for the winding up of a company—

(a) shall be dismissed on the making of an administration order in respect of the company, and

(b) shall be suspended while the company is in administration following an appointment under paragraph 14.

(2) Sub-paragraph (1)(b) does not apply to a petition presented under—

(a) section 124A (public interest), or

(aa) section 124B (SEs),

(b) section 367 of the Financial Services and Markets Act 2000 (c 8)(petition by Financial Services Authority).

(3) Where an administrator becomes aware that a petition was presented under a provision referred to in sub-paragraph (2) before his appointment, he shall apply to the court for directions under paragraph 63.

### 41 Dismissal of administrative or other receiver

**41** (1) When an administration order takes effect in respect of a company any administrative receiver of the company shall vacate office.

(2) Where a company is in administration, any receiver of part of the company's property shall vacate office if the administrator requires him to.

(3) Where an administrative receiver or receiver vacates office under sub-paragraph (1) or (2)—

    (a) his remuneration shall be charged on and paid out of any property of the company which was in his custody or under his control immediately before he vacated office, and

    (b) he need not take any further steps under section 40 or 59.

(4) In the application of sub-paragraph (3)(a)—

    (a) 'remuneration' includes expenses properly incurred and any indemnity to which the administrative receiver or receiver is entitled out of the assets of the company,

    (b) the charge imposed takes priority over security held by the person by whom or on whose behalf the administrative receiver or receiver was appointed, and

    (c) the provision for payment is subject to paragraph 43.

### Moratorium on insolvency proceedings

**42** (1) This paragraph applies to a company in administration.

(2) No resolution may be passed for the winding up of the company.

(3) No order may be made for the winding up of the company.

(4) Sub-paragraph (3) does not apply to an order made on a petition presented under—

    (a) section 124A (public interest), or

    (aa) section 124B (SEs),

    (b) section 367 of the Financial Services and Markets Act 2000 (c 8) (petition by Financial Services Authority).

(5) If a petition presented under a provision referred to in sub-paragraph (4) comes to the attention of the administrator, he shall apply to the court for directions under paragraph 63.

### Moratorium on other legal process

**43** (1) This paragraph applies to a company in administration.

(2) No step may be taken to enforce security over the company's property except—

    (a) with the consent of the administrator, or

    (b) with the permission of the court.

(3) No step may be taken to repossess goods in the company's possession under a hire-purchase agreement except—

    (a) with the consent of the administrator, or

    (b) with the permission of the court.

(4) A landlord may not exercise a right of forfeiture by peaceable re-entry in relation to premises let to the company except—

    (a) with the consent of the administrator, or

    (b) with the permission of the court.

(5) In Scotland, a landlord may not exercise a right of irritancy in relation to premises let to the company except—

    (a) with the consent of the administrator, or

    (b) with the permission of the court.

(6) No legal process (including legal proceedings, execution, distress and diligence) may be instituted or continued against the company or property of the company except—

    (a) with the consent of the administrator, or

    (b) with the permission of the court.

(6A) An administrative receiver of the company may not be appointed

(7) Where the court gives permission for a transaction under this paragraph it may impose a condition on or a requirement in connection with the transaction.

(8) In this paragraph 'landlord' includes a person to whom rent is payable.

### Interim moratorium

**44** (1) This paragraph applies where an administration application in respect of a company has been made and—

    (a) the application has not yet been granted or dismissed, or

    (b) the application has been granted but the administration order has not yet taken effect.

(2) This paragraph also applies from the time when a copy of notice of intention to appoint an administrator under paragraph 14 is filed with the court until—

    (a) the appointment of the administrator takes effect, or

    (b) the period of five business days beginning with the date of filing expires without an administrator having been appointed.

(3) Sub-paragraph (2) has effect in relation to a notice of intention to appoint only if it is in the prescribed form.

(4) This paragraph also applies from the time when a copy of notice of intention to appoint an administrator is filed with the court under paragraph 27(1) until—

    (a) the appointment of the administrator takes effect, or

    (b) the period specified in paragraph 28(2) expires without an administrator having been appointed.

(5) The provisions of paragraphs 42 and 43 shall apply (ignoring any reference to the consent of the administrator).

(6) If there is an administrative receiver of the company when the administration application is made, the provisions of paragraphs 42 and 43 shall not begin to apply by virtue of this paragraph until the person by or on behalf of whom the receiver was appointed consents to the making of the administration order.

(7) This paragraph does not prevent or require the permission of the court for—

    (a) the presentation of a petition for the winding up of the company under a provision mentioned in paragraph 42(4),

    (b) the appointment of an administrator under paragraph 14,

    (c) the appointment of an administrative receiver of the company, or

    (d) the carrying out by an administrative receiver (whenever appointed) of his functions.

### *Publicity*

**45** (1) While a company is in administration, every business document issued by or on behalf of the company or the administrator, and all the company's websites, must state—

    (a) the name of the administrator, and

    (b) that the affairs, business and property of the company are being managed by the administrator.

(2) Any of the following persons commits an offence if without reasonable excuse the person authorises or permits a contravention of sub-paragraph (1)—

    (a) the administrator,

    (b) an officer of the company, and

    (c) the company.

(3) In sub-paragraph (1) 'business document' means—

    (a) an invoice,

    (b) an order for goods or services,

    (c) a business letter, and

    (d) an order form,

whether in hard copy, electronic or any other form.

## PROCESS OF ADMINISTRATION

### *Announcement of administrator's appointment*

**46** (1) This paragraph applies where a person becomes the administrator of a company.

(2) As soon as is reasonably practicable the administrator shall—

    (a) send a notice of his appointment to the company, and

    (b) publish a notice of his appointment in the prescribed manner.

(3) As soon as is reasonably practicable the administrator shall—

    (a) obtain a list of the company's creditors, and

    (b) send a notice of his appointment to each creditor of whose claim and address he is aware.

(4) The administrator shall send a notice of his appointment to the registrar of companies before the end of the period of 7 days beginning with the date specified in sub-paragraph (6).

(5) The administrator shall send a notice of his appointment to such persons as may be prescribed before the end of the prescribed period beginning with the date specified in sub-paragraph (6).

(6) The date for the purpose of sub-paragraphs (4) and (5) is—

    (a) in the case of an administrator appointed by administration order, the date of the order,

    (b) in the case of an administrator appointed under paragraph 14, the date on which he receives notice under paragraph 20, and

    (c) in the case of an administrator appointed under paragraph 22, the date on which he receives notice under paragraph 32.

(7) The court may direct that sub-paragraph (3)(b) or (5)—

    (a) shall not apply, or

    (b) shall apply with the substitution of a different period.

(8) A notice under this paragraph must—

    (a) contain the prescribed information, and

    (b) be in the prescribed form.

(9) An administrator commits an offence if he fails without reasonable excuse to comply with a requirement of this paragraph.

### *Statement of company's affairs*

**47** (1) As soon as is reasonably practicable after appointment the administrator of a company shall by notice in the prescribed form require one or more relevant persons to provide the administrator with a statement of the affairs of the company.

(2) The statement must—

    (a) be verified by a statement of truth in accordance with Civil Procedure Rules,

(b) be in the prescribed form,

(c) give particulars of the company's property, debts and liabilities,

(d) give the names and addresses of the company's creditors,

(e) specify the security held by each creditor,

(f) give the date on which each security was granted, and

(g) contain such other information as may be prescribed.

(3) In sub-paragraph (1) 'relevant person' means—

(a) a person who is or has been an officer of the company,

(b) a person who took part in the formation of the company during the period of one year ending with the date on which the company enters administration,

(c) a person employed by the company during that period, and

(d) a person who is or has been during that period an officer or employee of a company which is or has been during that year an officer of the company.

(4) For the purpose of sub-paragraph (3) a reference to employment is a reference to employment through a contract of employment or a contract for services.

(5) In Scotland, a statement of affairs under sub-paragraph (1) must be a statutory declaration made in accordance with the Statutory Declarations Act 1835 (c 62) (and sub-paragraph (2)(a) shall not apply).

**48** (1) A person required to submit a statement of affairs must do so before the end of the period of 11 days beginning with the day on which he receives notice of the requirement.

(2) The administrator may—

(a) revoke a requirement under paragraph 47(1), or

(b) extend the period specified in sub-paragraph (1) (whether before or after expiry).

(3) If the administrator refuses a request to act under sub-paragraph (2)—

(a) the person whose request is refused may apply to the court, and

(b) the court may take action of a kind specified in sub-paragraph (2).

(4) A person commits an offence if he fails without reasonable excuse to comply with a requirement under paragraph 47(1).

### Administrator's proposals

**49** (1) The administrator of a company shall make a statement setting out proposals for achieving the purpose of administration.

(2) A statement under sub-paragraph (1) must, in particular—

(a) deal with such matters as may be prescribed, and

(b) where applicable, explain why the administrator thinks that the objective mentioned in paragraph 3(1)(a) or (b) cannot be achieved.

(3) Proposals under this paragraph may include—

(a) a proposal for a voluntary arrangement under Part I of this Act (although this paragraph is without prejudice to section 4(3));

(b) a proposal for a compromise or arrangement to be sanctioned under Part 26 of the Companies Act 2006 (arrangements and reconstructions)

(4) The administrator shall send a copy of the statement of his proposals—

(a) to the registrar of companies,

(b) to every creditor of the company of whose claim and address he is aware, and

(c) to every member of the company of whose address he is aware.

(5) The administrator shall comply with sub-paragraph (4)—

(a) as soon as is reasonably practicable after the company enters administration, and

(b) in any event, before the end of the period of eight weeks beginning with the day on which the company enters administration.

(6) The administrator shall be taken to comply with sub-paragraph (4)(c) if he publishes in the prescribed manner a notice undertaking to provide a copy of the statement of proposals free of charge to any member of the company who applies in writing to a specified address.

(7) An administrator commits an offence if he fails without reasonable excuse to comply with sub-paragraph (5).

(8) A period specified in this paragraph may be varied in accordance with paragraph 107.

### Creditors' meeting

**50** (1) In this Schedule 'creditors' meeting' means a meeting of creditors of a company summoned by the administrator—

(a) in the prescribed manner, and

(b) giving the prescribed period of notice to every creditor of the company of whose claim and address he is aware.

(2) A period prescribed under sub-paragraph (1)(b) may be varied in accordance with paragraph 107.

(3) A creditors' meeting shall be conducted in accordance with the rules.

### Requirement for initial creditors' meeting

**51** (1) Each copy of an administrator's statement of proposals sent to a creditor under paragraph 49(4)(b) must be accompanied by an invitation to a creditors' meeting (an 'initial creditors' meeting').

(2)  The date set for an initial creditors' meeting must be—

(a)  as soon as is reasonably practicable after the company enters administration, and

(b)  in any event, within the period of ten weeks beginning with the date on which the company enters administration.

(3)  An administrator shall present a copy of his statement of proposals to an initial creditors' meeting.

(4)  A period specified in this paragraph may be varied in accordance with paragraph 107.

(5)  An administrator commits an offence if he fails without reasonable excuse to comply with a requirement of this paragraph.

**52** (1) Paragraph 51(1) shall not apply where the statement of proposals states that the administrator thinks—

(a)  that the company has sufficient property to enable each creditor of the company to be paid in full,

(b)  that the company has insufficient property to enable a distribution to be made to unsecured creditors other than by virtue of section 176A(2)(a), or

(c)  that neither of the objectives specified in paragraph 3(1)(a) and (b) can be achieved.

(2)  But the administrator shall summon an initial creditors' meeting if it is requested—

(a)  by creditors of the company whose debts amount to at least 10% of the total debts of the company,

(b)  in the prescribed manner, and

(c)  in the prescribed period.

(3)  A meeting requested under sub-paragraph (2) must be summoned for a date in the prescribed period.

(4)  The period prescribed under sub-paragraph (3) may be varied in accordance with paragraph 107.

### Business and result of initial creditors' meeting

**53** (1) An initial creditors' meeting to which an administrator's proposals are presented shall consider them and may—

(a)  approve them without modification, or

(b)  approve them with modification to which the administrator consents.

(2)  After the conclusion of an initial creditors' meeting the administrator shall as soon as is reasonably practicable report any decision taken to—

(a)  the court,

(b)  the registrar of companies, and

(c)  such other persons as may be prescribed.

(3)  An administrator commits an offence if he fails without reasonable excuse to comply with sub-paragraph (2).

### Revision of administrator's proposals

**54** (1) This paragraph applies where—

(a)  an administrator's proposals have been approved (with or without modification) at an initial creditors' meeting,

(b)  the administrator proposes a revision to the proposals, and

(c)  the administrator thinks that the proposed revision is substantial.

(2)  The administrator shall—

(a)  summon a creditors' meeting,

(b)  send a statement in the prescribed form of the proposed revision with the notice of the meeting sent to each creditor,

(c)  send a copy of the statement, within the prescribed period, to each member of the company of whose address he is aware, and

(d)  present a copy of the statement to the meeting.

(3)  The administrator shall be taken to have complied with sub-paragraph (2)(c) if he publishes a notice undertaking to provide a copy of the statement free of charge to any member of the company who applies in writing to a specified address.

(4)  A notice under sub-paragraph (3) must be published—

(a)  in the prescribed manner, and

(b)  within the prescribed period.

(5)  A creditors' meeting to which a proposed revision is presented shall consider it and may—

(a)  approve it without modification, or

(b)  approve it with modification to which the administrator consents.

(6) After the conclusion of a creditors' meeting the administrator shall as soon as is reasonably practicable report any decision taken to—

    (a) the court,

    (b) the registrar of companies, and

    (c) such other persons as may be prescribed.

(7) An administrator commits an offence if he fails without reasonable excuse to comply with sub-paragraph (6).

### *Failure to obtain approval of administrator's proposals*

**55** (1) This paragraph applies where an administrator reports to the court that—

    (a) an initial creditors' meeting has failed to approve the administrator's proposals presented to it, or

    (b) a creditors' meeting has failed to approve a revision of the administrator's proposals presented to it.

(2) The court may—

    (a) provide that the appointment of an administrator shall cease to have effect from a specified time;

    (b) adjourn the hearing conditionally or unconditionally;

    (c) make an interim order;

    (d) make an order on a petition for winding up suspended by virtue of paragraph 40(1)(b);

    (e) make any other order (including an order making consequential provision) that the court thinks appropriate.

### *Further creditors' meetings*

**56** (1) The administrator of a company shall summon a creditors' meeting if—

    (a) it is requested in the prescribed manner by creditors of the company whose debts amount to at least 10% of the total debts of the company, or

    (b) he is directed by the court to summon a creditors' meeting.

(2) An administrator commits an offence if he fails without reasonable excuse to summon a creditors' meeting as required by this paragraph.

### *Creditors' committee*

**57** (1) A creditors' meeting may establish a creditors' committee.

(2) A creditors' committee shall carry out functions conferred on it by or under this Act.

(3) A creditors' committee may require the administrator—

    (a) to attend on the committee at any reasonable time of which he is given at least seven days' notice, and

    (b) to provide the committee with information about the exercise of his functions.

### *Correspondence instead of creditors' meeting*

**58** (1) Anything which is required or permitted by or under this Schedule to be done at a creditors' meeting may be done by correspondence between the administrator and creditors—

    (a) in accordance with the rules, and

    (b) subject to any prescribed condition.

(2) A reference in this Schedule to anything done at a creditors' meeting includes a reference to anything done in the course of correspondence in reliance on sub-paragraph (1).

(3) A requirement to hold a creditors' meeting is satisfied by conducting correspondence in accordance with this paragraph.

## FUNCTIONS OF ADMINISTRATOR

### *General powers*

**59** (1) The administrator of a company may do anything necessary or expedient for the management of the affairs, business and property of the company.

(2) A provision of this Schedule which expressly permits the administrator to do a specified thing is without prejudice to the generality of sub-paragraph (1).

(3) A person who deals with the administrator of a company in good faith and for value need not inquire whether the administrator is acting within his powers.

**60** The administrator of a company has the powers specified in Schedule 1 to this Act.

**61** The administrator of a company—

    (a) may remove a director of the company, and

    (b) may appoint a director of the company (whether or not to fill a vacancy).

**62** The administrator of a company may call a meeting of members or creditors of the company.

**63** The administrator of a company may apply to the court for directions in connection with his functions.

**64** (1)  A company in administration or an officer of a company in administration may not exercise a management power without the consent of the administrator.

(2)  For the purpose of sub-paragraph (1)—

(a)  'management power' means a power which could be exercised so as to interfere with the exercise of the administrator's powers,

(b)  it is immaterial whether the power is conferred by an enactment or an instrument, and

(c)  consent may be general or specific.

### Distribution

**65** (1)  The administrator of a company may make a distribution to a creditor of the company.

(2)  Section 175 shall apply in relation to a distribution under this paragraph as it applies in relation to a winding up.

(3)  A payment may not be made by way of distribution under this paragraph to a creditor of the company who is neither secured nor preferential unless the court gives permission.

**66**  The administrator of a company may make a payment otherwise than in accordance with paragraph 65 or paragraph 13 of Schedule 1 if he thinks it likely to assist achievement of the purpose of administration.

### General duties

**67**  The administrator of a company shall on his appointment take custody or control of all the property to which he thinks the company is entitled.

**68** (1)  Subject to sub-paragraph (2), the administrator of a company shall manage its affairs, business and property in accordance with—

(a)  any proposals approved under paragraph 53,

(b)  any revision of those proposals which is made by him and which he does not consider substantial, and

(c)  any revision of those proposals approved under paragraph 54.

(2)  If the court gives directions to the administrator of a company in connection with any aspect of his management of the company's affairs, business or property, the administrator shall comply with the directions.

(3)  The court may give directions under sub-paragraph (2) only if—

(a)  no proposals have been approved under paragraph 53,

(b)  the directions are consistent with any proposals or revision approved under paragraph 53 or 54,

(c)  the court thinks the directions are required in order to reflect a change in circumstances since the approval of proposals or a revision under paragraph 53 or 54, or

(d)  the court thinks the directions are desirable because of a misunderstanding about proposals or a revision approved under paragraph 53 or 54.

### Administrator as agent of company

**69**  In exercising his functions under this Schedule the administrator of a company acts as its agent.

### Charged property: floating charge

**70** (1)  The administrator of a company may dispose of or take action relating to property which is subject to a floating charge as if it were not subject to the charge.

(2)  Where property is disposed of in reliance on sub-paragraph (1) the holder of the floating charge shall have the same priority in respect of acquired property as he had in respect of the property disposed of.

(3)  In sub-paragraph (2) 'acquired property' means property of the company which directly or indirectly represents the property disposed of.

### Charged property: non-floating charge

**71** (1)  The court may by order enable the administrator of a company to dispose of property which is subject to a security (other than a floating charge) as if it were not subject to the security.

(2)  An order under sub-paragraph (1) may be made only—

(a)  on the application of the administrator, and

(b)  where the court thinks that disposal of the property would be likely to promote the purpose of administration in respect of the company.

(3)  An order under this paragraph is subject to the condition that there be applied towards discharging the sums secured by the security—

(a)  the net proceeds of disposal of the property, and

(b)  any additional money required to be added to the net proceeds so as to produce the amount determined by the court as the net amount which would be realised on a sale of the property at market value.

(4)  If an order under this paragraph relates to more than one security, application of money under sub-paragraph (3) shall be in the order of the priorities of the securities.

**740**   Insolvency Act 1986

(5) An administrator who makes a successful application for an order under this paragraph shall send a copy of the order to the registrar of companies before the end of the period of 14 days starting with the date of the order.

(6) An administrator commits an offence if he fails to comply with sub-paragraph (5) without reasonable excuse.

### Hire-purchase property

**72** (1) The court may by order enable the administrator of a company to dispose of goods which are in the possession of the company under a hire-purchase agreement as if all the rights of the owner under the agreement were vested in the company.

(2) An order under sub-paragraph (1) may be made only—

    (a) on the application of the administrator, and

    (b) where the court thinks that disposal of the goods would be likely to promote the purpose of administration in respect of the company.

(3) An order under this paragraph is subject to the condition that there be applied towards discharging the sums payable under the hire-purchase agreement—

    (a) the net proceeds of disposal of the goods, and

    (b) any additional money required to be added to the net proceeds so as to produce the amount determined by the court as the net amount which would be realised on a sale of the goods at market value.

(4) An administrator who makes a successful application for an order under this paragraph shall send a copy of the order to the registrar of companies before the end of the period of 14 days starting with the date of the order.

(5) An administrator commits an offence if he fails without reasonable excuse to comply with sub-paragraph (4).

### Protection for secured or preferential creditor

**73** (1) An administrator's statement of proposals under paragraph 49 may not include any action which—

    (a) affects the right of a secured creditor of the company to enforce his security,

    (b) would result in a preferential debt of the company being paid otherwise than in priority to its non-preferential debts, or

    (c) would result in one preferential creditor of the company being paid a smaller proportion of his debt than another.

(2) Sub-paragraph (1) does not apply to—

    (a) action to which the relevant creditor consents,

    (b) a proposal for a voluntary arrangement under Part I of this Act (although this sub-paragraph is without prejudice to section 4(3)),

    (c) a proposal for a compromise or arrangement to be sanctioned underPart 26 of the Companies Act 2006 (arrangements and reconstructions); or

    (d) a proposal for a cross-border merger within the meaning of regulation 2 of the Companies (Cross-Border Mergers) Regulations 2007.

(3) The reference to a statement of proposals in sub-paragraph (1) includes a reference to a statement as revised or modified.

### Challenge to administrator's conduct of company

**74** (1) A creditor or member of a company in administration may apply to the court claiming that—

    (a) the administrator is acting or has acted so as unfairly to harm the interests of the applicant (whether alone or in common with some or all other members or creditors), or

    (b) the administrator proposes to act in a way which would unfairly harm the interests of the applicant (whether alone or in common with some or all other members or creditors).

(2) A creditor or member of a company in administration may apply to the court claiming that the administrator is not performing his functions as quickly or as efficiently as is reasonably practicable.

(3) The court may—

    (a) grant relief;

    (b) dismiss the application;

    (c) adjourn the hearing conditionally or unconditionally;

    (d) make an interim order;

    (e) make any other order it thinks appropriate.

(4) In particular, an order under this paragraph may—

    (a) regulate the administrator's exercise of his functions;

    (b) require the administrator to do or not do a specified thing;

    (c) require a creditors' meeting to be held for a specified purpose;

    (d) provide for the appointment of an administrator to cease to have effect;

    (e) make consequential provision.

(5) An order may be made on a claim under sub-paragraph (1) whether or not the action complained of—

(a) is within the administrator's powers under this Schedule;

(b) was taken in reliance on an order under paragraph 71 or 72.

(6) An order may not be made under this paragraph if it would impede or prevent the implementation of—

(a) a voluntary arrangement approved under Part I,

(b) a compromise or arrangement sanctioned under Part 26 of the Companies Act 2006 (arrangements and reconstructions),

(c) proposals or a revision approved under paragraph 53 or 54 more than 28 days before the day on which the application for the order under this paragraph is made; or

(d) a cross-border merger within the meaning of regulation 2 of the Companies (Cross-Border Mergers) Regulations 2007.

### Misfeasance

**75** (1) The court may examine the conduct of a person who—

(a) is or purports to be the administrator of a company, or

(b) has been or has purported to be the administrator of a company.

(2) An examination under this paragraph may be held only on the application of—

(a) the official receiver,

(b) the administrator of the company,

(c) the liquidator of the company,

(d) a creditor of the company, or

(e) a contributory of the company.

(3) An application under sub-paragraph (2) must allege that the administrator—

(a) has misapplied or retained money or other property of the company,

(b) has become accountable for money or other property of the company,

(c) has breached a fiduciary or other duty in relation to the company, or

(d) has been guilty of misfeasance.

(4) On an examination under this paragraph into a person's conduct the court may order him—

(a) to repay, restore or account for money or property;

(b) to pay interest;

(c) to contribute a sum to the company's property by way of compensation for breach of duty or misfeasance.

(5) In sub-paragraph (3) 'administrator' includes a person who purports or has purported to be a company's administrator.

(6) An application under sub-paragraph (2) may be made in respect of an administrator who has been discharged under paragraph 98 only with the permission of the court.

## ENDING ADMINISTRATION

### Automatic end of administration

**76** (1) The appointment of an administrator shall cease to have effect at the end of the period of one year beginning with the date on which it takes effect.

(2) But—

(a) on the application of an administrator the court may by order extend his term of office for a specified period, and

(b) an administrator's term of office may be extended for a specified period not exceeding six months by consent.

**77** (1) An order of the court under paragraph 76—

(a) may be made in respect of an administrator whose term of office has already been extended by order or by consent, but

(b) may not be made after the expiry of the administrator's term of office.

(2) Where an order is made under paragraph 76 the administrator shall as soon as is reasonably practicable notify the registrar of companies.

(3) An administrator who fails without reasonable excuse to comply with sub-paragraph (2) commits an offence.

**78** (1) In paragraph 76(2)(b) 'consent' means consent of—

(a) each secured creditor of the company, and

(b) if the company has unsecured debts, creditors whose debts amount to more than 50% of the company's unsecured debts, disregarding debts of any creditor who does not respond to an invitation to give or withhold consent.

(2) But where the administrator has made a statement under paragraph 52(1)(b) 'consent' means—

(a) consent of each secured creditor of the company, or

(b) if the administrator thinks that a distribution may be made to preferential creditors, consent of—

    (i) each secured creditor of the company, and

    (ii) preferential creditors whose debts amount to more than 50% of the preferential debts of the company, disregarding debts of any creditor who does not respond to an invitation to give or withhold consent.

(3) Consent for the purposes of paragraph 76(2)(b) may be—

    (a) written, or

    (b) signified at a creditors' meeting.

(4) An administrator's term of office—

    (a) may be extended by consent only once,

    (b) may not be extended by consent after extension by order of the court, and

    (c) may not be extended by consent after expiry.

(5) Where an administrator's term of office is extended by consent he shall as soon as is reasonably practicable—

    (a) file notice of the extension with the court, and

    (b) notify the registrar of companies.

(6) An administrator who fails without reasonable excuse to comply with sub-paragraph (5) commits an offence.

### ourt ending administration on application of administrator

**79** (1) On the application of the administrator of a company the court may provide for the appointment of an administrator of the company to cease to have effect from a specified time.

(2) The administrator of a company shall make an application under this paragraph if—

    (a) he thinks the purpose of administration cannot be achieved in relation to the company,

    (b) he thinks the company should not have entered administration, or

    (c) a creditors' meeting requires him to make an application under this paragraph.

(3) The administrator of a company shall make an application under this paragraph if—

    (a) the administration is pursuant to an administration order, and

    (b) the administrator thinks that the purpose of administration has been sufficiently achieved in relation to the company.

(4) On an application under this paragraph the court may—

    (a) adjourn the hearing conditionally or unconditionally;

    (b) dismiss the application;

    (c) make an interim order;

    (d) make any order it thinks appropriate (whether in addition to, in consequence of or instead of the order applied for).

### Termination of administration where objective achieved

**80** (1) This paragraph applies where an administrator of a company is appointed under paragraph 14 or 22.

(2) If the administrator thinks that the purpose of administration has been sufficiently achieved in relation to the company he may file a notice in the prescribed form—

    (a) with the court, and

    (b) with the registrar of companies.

(3) The administrator's appointment shall cease to have effect when the requirements of sub-paragraph (2) are satisfied.

(4) Where the administrator files a notice he shall within the prescribed period send a copy to every creditor of the company of whose claim and address he is aware.

(5) The rules may provide that the administrator is taken to have complied with sub-paragraph (4) if before the end of the prescribed period he publishes in the prescribed manner a notice undertaking to provide a copy of the notice under sub-paragraph (2) to any creditor of the company who applies in writing to a specified address.

(6) An administrator who fails without reasonable excuse to comply with sub-paragraph (4) commits an offence.

### Court ending administration on application of creditor

**81** (1) On the application of a creditor of a company the court may provide for the appointment of an administrator of the company to cease to have effect at a specified time.

(2) An application under this paragraph must allege an improper motive—

    (a) in the case of an administrator appointed by administration order, on the part of the applicant for the order, or

    (b) in any other case, on the part of the person who appointed the administrator.

(3) On an application under this paragraph the court may—

    (a) adjourn the hearing conditionally or unconditionally;

(b) dismiss the application;

(c) make an interim order;

(d) make any order it thinks appropriate (whether in addition to, in consequence of or instead of the order applied for).

### Public interest winding-up

**82** (1) This paragraph applies where a winding-up order is made for the winding up of a company in administration on a petition presented under—

(a) section 124A (public interest), or

(aa) section 124B (SEs),

(b) section 367 of the Financial Services and Markets Act 2000 (c 8)(petition by Financial Services Authority).

(2) This paragraph also applies where a provisional liquidator of a company in administration is appointed following the presentation of a petition under any of the provisions listed in sub-paragraph (1).

(3) The court shall order—

(a) that the appointment of the administrator shall cease to have effect, or

(b) that the appointment of the administrator shall continue to have effect.

(4) If the court makes an order under sub-paragraph (3)(b) it may also—

(a) specify which of the powers under this Schedule are to be exercisable by the administrator, and

(b) order that this Schedule shall have effect in relation to the administrator with specified modifications.

### Moving from administration to creditors' voluntary liquidation

**83** (1) This paragraph applies in England and Wales where the administrator of a company thinks—

(a) that the total amount which each secured creditor of the company is likely to receive has been paid to him or set aside for him, and

(b) that a distribution will be made to unsecured creditors of the company (if there are any).

(2) This paragraph applies in Scotland where the administrator of a company thinks—

(a) that each secured creditor of the company will receive payment in respect of his debt, and

(b) that a distribution will be made to unsecured creditors (if there are any).

(3) The administrator may send to the registrar of companies a notice that this paragraph applies.

(4) On receipt of a notice under sub-paragraph (3) the registrar shall register it.

(5) If an administrator sends a notice under sub-paragraph (3) he shall as soon as is reasonably practicable—

(a) file a copy of the notice with the court, and

(b) send a copy of the notice to each creditor of whose claim and address he is aware.

(6) On the registration of a notice under sub-paragraph (3)—

(a) the appointment of an administrator in respect of the company shall cease to have effect, and

(b) the company shall be wound up as if a resolution for voluntary winding up under section 84 were passed on the day on which the notice is registered.

(7) The liquidator for the purposes of the winding up shall be—

(a) a person nominated by the creditors of the company in the prescribed manner and within the prescribed period, or

(b) if no person is nominated under paragraph (a), the administrator.

(8) In the application of Part IV to a winding up by virtue of this paragraph—

(a) section 85 shall not apply,

(b) section 86 shall apply as if the reference to the time of the passing of the resolution for voluntary winding up were a reference to the beginning of the date of registration of the notice under sub-paragraph (3),

(c) section 89 does not apply,

(d) sections 98, 99 and 100 shall not apply,

(e) section 129 shall apply as if the reference to the time of the passing of the resolution for voluntary winding up were a reference to the beginning of the date of registration of the notice under sub-paragraph (3), and

(f) any creditors' committee which is in existence immediately before the company ceases to be in administration shall continue in existence after that time as if appointed as a liquidation committee under section 101.

### Moving from administration to dissolution

**84** (1) If the administrator of a company thinks that the company has no property which might permit a distribution to its creditors, he shall send a notice to that effect to the registrar of companies.

(2) The court may on the application of the administrator of a company disapply sub-paragraph (1) in respect of the company.

(3) On receipt of a notice under sub-paragraph (1) the registrar shall register it.

(4) On the registration of a notice in respect of a company under sub-paragraph (1) the appointment of an administrator of the company shall cease to have effect.

(5) If an administrator sends a notice under sub-paragraph (1) he shall as soon as is reasonably practicable—

(a) file a copy of the notice with the court, and

(b) send a copy of the notice to each creditor of whose claim and address he is aware.

(6) At the end of the period of three months beginning with the date of registration of a notice in respect of a company under sub-paragraph (1) the company is deemed to be dissolved.

(7) On an application in respect of a company by the administrator or another interested person the court may—

(a) extend the period specified in sub-paragraph (6),

(b) suspend that period, or

(c) disapply sub-paragraph (6).

(8) Where an order is made under sub-paragraph (7) in respect of a company the administrator shall as soon as is reasonably practicable notify the registrar of companies.

(9) An administrator commits an offence if he fails without reasonable excuse to comply with sub-paragraph (5).

### Discharge of administration order where administration ends

**85** (1) This paragraph applies where—

(a) the court makes an order under this Schedule providing for the appointment of an administrator of a company to cease to have effect, and

(b) the administrator was appointed by administration order.

(2) The court shall discharge the administration order.

### Notice to Companies Registrar where administration ends

**86** (1) This paragraph applies where the court makes an order under this Schedule providing for the appointment of an administrator to cease to have effect.

(2) The administrator shall send a copy of the order to the registrar of companies within the period of 14 days beginning with the date of the order.

(3) An administrator who fails without reasonable excuse to comply with sub-paragraph (2) commits an offence.

# REPLACING ADMINISTRATOR

### Resignation of administrator

**87** (1) An administrator may resign only in prescribed circumstances.

(2) Where an administrator may resign he may do so only—

(a) in the case of an administrator appointed by administration order, by notice in writing to the court,

(b) in the case of an administrator appointed under paragraph 14, by notice in writing to the holder of the floating charge by virtue of which the appointment was made,

(c) in the case of an administrator appointed under paragraph 22(1), by notice in writing to the company, or

(d) in the case of an administrator appointed under paragraph 22(2), by notice in writing to the directors of the company.

### Removal of administrator from office

**88** The court may by order remove an administrator from office.

### Administrator ceasing to be qualified

**89** (1) The administrator of a company shall vacate office if he ceases to be qualified to act as an insolvency practitioner in relation to the company.

(2) Where an administrator vacates office by virtue of sub-paragraph (1) he shall give notice in writing—

(a) in the case of an administrator appointed by administration order, to the court,

(b) in the case of an administrator appointed under paragraph 14, to the holder of the floating charge by virtue of which the appointment was made,

(c) in the case of an administrator appointed under paragraph 22(1), to the company, or

(d) in the case of an administrator appointed under paragraph 22(2), to the directors of the company.

(3) An administrator who fails without reasonable excuse to comply with sub-paragraph (2) commits an offence.

### Supplying vacancy in office of administrator

**90** Paragraphs 91 to 95 apply where an administrator—

(a) dies,

(b) resigns,

(c) is removed from office under paragraph 88, or

(d) vacates office under paragraph 89.

**91** (1) Where the administrator was appointed by administration order, the court may replace the administrator on an application under this sub-paragraph made by—

(a) a creditors' committee of the company,

(b) the company,

(c) the directors of the company,

(d) one or more creditors of the company, or

(e) where more than one person was appointed to act jointly or concurrently as the administrator, any of those persons who remains in office.

(2) But an application may be made in reliance on sub-paragraph (1)(b) to (d) only where—

(a) there is no creditors' committee of the company,

(b) the court is satisfied that the creditors' committee or a remaining administrator is not taking reasonable steps to make a replacement, or

(c) the court is satisfied that for another reason it is right for the application to be made.

**92** Where the administrator was appointed under paragraph 14 the holder of the floating charge by virtue of which the appointment was made may replace the administrator.

**93** (1) Where the administrator was appointed under paragraph 22(1) by the company it may replace the administrator.

(2) A replacement under this paragraph may be made only—

(a) with the consent of each person who is the holder of a qualifying floating charge in respect of the company's property, or

(b) where consent is withheld, with the permission of the court.

**94** (1) Where the administrator was appointed under paragraph 22(2) the directors of the company may replace the administrator.

(2) A replacement under this paragraph may be made only—

(a) with the consent of each person who is the holder of a qualifying floating charge in respect of the company's property, or

(b) where consent is withheld, with the permission of the court.

**95** The court may replace an administrator on the application of a person listed in paragraph 91(1) if the court—

(a) is satisfied that a person who is entitled to replace the administrator under any of paragraphs 92 to 94 is not taking reasonable steps to make a replacement, or

(b) that for another reason it is right for the court to make the replacement.

### Substitution of administrator: competing floating charge-holder

**96** (1) This paragraph applies where an administrator of a company is appointed under paragraph 14 by the holder of a qualifying floating charge in respect of the company's property.

(2) The holder of a prior qualifying floating charge in respect of the company's property may apply to the court for the administrator to be replaced by an administrator nominated by the holder of the prior floating charge.

(3) One floating charge is prior to another for the purposes of this paragraph if—

(a) it was created first, or

(b) it is to be treated as having priority in accordance with an agreement to which the holder of each floating charge was party.

(4) Sub-paragraph (3) shall have effect in relation to Scotland as if the following were substituted for paragraph (a)—

'(a) it has priority of ranking in accordance with section 464(4)(b) of the Companies Act 1985 (c 6),'.

### Substitution of administrator appointed by company or directors: creditors' meeting

**97** (1) This paragraph applies where—

(a) an administrator of a company is appointed by a company or directors under paragraph 22, and

(b) there is no holder of a qualifying floating charge in respect of the company's property.

(2) A creditors' meeting may replace the administrator.

(3) A creditors' meeting may act under sub-paragraph (2) only if the new administrator's written consent to act is presented to the meeting before the replacement is made.

### Vacation of office: discharge from liability

**98** (1) Where a person ceases to be the administrator of a company (whether because he vacates office by reason of resignation, death or otherwise, because he is removed from office or because his appointment ceases to have effect) he is discharged from liability in respect of any action of his as administrator.

(2) The discharge provided by sub-paragraph (1) takes effect—

(a) in the case of an administrator who dies, on the filing with the court of notice of his death,

(b) in the case of an administrator appointed under paragraph 14 or 22, at a time appointed by resolution of the creditors' committee or, if there is no committee, by resolution of the creditors, or

(c) in any case, at a time specified by the court.

(3) For the purpose of the application of sub-paragraph (2)(b) in a case where the administrator has made a statement under paragraph 52(1)(b), a resolution shall be taken as passed if (and only if) passed with the approval of—

(a) each secured creditor of the company, or

(b) if the administrator has made a distribution to preferential creditors or thinks that a distribution may be made to preferential creditors—

(i)    each secured creditor of the company, and

(ii)   preferential creditors whose debts amount to more than 50% of the preferential debts of the company, disregarding debts of any creditor who does not respond to an invitation to give or withhold approval.

(4) Discharge—

(a) applies to liability accrued before the discharge takes effect, and

(b) does not prevent the exercise of the court's powers under paragraph 75.

### *Vacation of office: charges and liabilities*

**99** (1) This paragraph applies where a person ceases to be the administrator of a company (whether because he vacates office by reason of resignation, death or otherwise, because he is removed from office or because his appointment ceases to have effect).

(2) In this paragraph—

'the former administrator' means the person referred to in sub-paragraph (1), and

'cessation' means the time when he ceases to be the company's administrator.

(3) The former administrator's remuneration and expenses shall be—

(a) charged on and payable out of property of which he had custody or control immediately before cessation, and

(b) payable in priority to any security to which paragraph 70 applies.

(4) A sum payable in respect of a debt or liability arising out of a contract entered into by the former administrator or a predecessor before cessation shall be—

(a) charged on and payable out of property of which the former administrator had custody or control immediately before cessation, and

(b) payable in priority to any charge arising under sub-paragraph (3).

(5) Sub-paragraph (4) shall apply to a liability arising under a contract of employment which was adopted by the former administrator or a predecessor before cessation; and for that purpose—

(a) action taken within the period of 14 days after an administrator's appointment shall not be taken to amount or contribute to the adoption of a contract,

(b) no account shall be taken of a liability which arises, or in so far as it arises, by reference to anything which is done or which occurs before the adoption of the contract of employment, and

(c) no account shall be taken of a liability to make a payment other than wages or salary.

(6) In sub-paragraph (5)(c) 'wages or salary' includes—

(a) a sum payable in respect of a period of holiday (for which purpose the sum shall be treated as relating to the period by reference to which the entitlement to holiday accrued),

(b) a sum payable in respect of a period of absence through illness or other good cause,

(c) a sum payable in lieu of holiday,

(d) in respect of a period, a sum which would be treated as earnings for that period for the purposes of an enactment about social security, and

(e) a contribution to an occupational pension scheme.

# GENERAL

### *Joint and concurrent administrators*

**100** (1) In this Schedule—

(a) a reference to the appointment of an administrator of a company includes a reference to the appointment of a number of persons to act jointly or concurrently as the administrator of a company, and

(b) a reference to the appointment of a person as administrator of a company includes a reference to the appointment of a person as one of a number of persons to act jointly or concurrently as the administrator of a company.

(2) The appointment of a number of persons to act as administrator of a company must specify—

(a) which functions (if any) are to be exercised by the persons appointed acting jointly, and

(b) which functions (if any) are to be exercised by any or all of the persons appointed.

**101** (1) This paragraph applies where two or more persons are appointed to act jointly as the administrator of a company.

(2) A reference to the administrator of the company is a reference to those persons acting jointly.

(3) But a reference to the administrator of a company in paragraphs 87 to 99 of this Schedule is a reference to any or all of the persons appointed to act jointly.

(4) Where an offence of omission is committed by the administrator, each of the persons appointed to act jointly—

(a) commits the offence, and

(b) may be proceeded against and punished individually.

(5) The reference in paragraph 45(1)(a) to the name of the administrator is a reference to the name of each of the persons appointed to act jointly.

(6) Where persons are appointed to act jointly in respect of only some of the functions of the administrator of a company, this paragraph applies only in relation to those functions.

**102** (1) This paragraph applies where two or more persons are appointed to act concurrently as the administrator of a company.

(2) A reference to the administrator of a company in this Schedule is a reference to any of the persons appointed (or any combination of them).

**103** (1) Where a company is in administration, a person may be appointed to act as administrator jointly or concurrently with the person or persons acting as the administrator of the company.

(2) Where a company entered administration by administration order, an appointment under sub-paragraph (1) must be made by the court on the application of—

(a) a person or group listed in paragraph 12(1)(a) to (e), or

(b) the person or persons acting as the administrator of the company.

(3) Where a company entered administration by virtue of an appointment under paragraph 14, an appointment under sub-paragraph (1) must be made by—

(a) the holder of the floating charge by virtue of which the appointment was made, or

(b) the court on the application of the person or persons acting as the administrator of the company.

(4) Where a company entered administration by virtue of an appointment under paragraph 22(1), an appointment under sub-paragraph (1) above must be made either by the court on the application of the person or persons acting as the administrator of the company or—

(a) by the company, and

(b) with the consent of each person who is the holder of a qualifying floating charge in respect of the company's property or, where consent is withheld, with the permission of the court.

(5) Where a company entered administration by virtue of an appointment under paragraph 22(2), an appointment under sub-paragraph (1) must be made either by the court on the application of the person or persons acting as the administrator of the company or—

(a) by the directors of the company, and

(b) with the consent of each person who is the holder of a qualifying floating charge in respect of the company's property or, where consent is withheld, with the permission of the court.

(6) An appointment under sub-paragraph (1) may be made only with the consent of the person or persons acting as the administrator of the company.

### Presumption of validity

**104** An act of the administrator of a company is valid in spite of a defect in his appointment or qualification.

### Majority decision of directors

**105** A reference in this Schedule to something done by the directors of a company includes a reference to the same thing done by a majority of the directors of a company.

### Penalties

**106** (1) A person who is guilty of an offence under this Schedule is liable to a fine (in accordance with section 430 and Schedule 10).

(2) A person who is guilty of an offence under any of the following paragraphs of this Schedule is liable to a daily default fine (in accordance with section 430 and Schedule 10)—

(a) paragraph 20,

(b) paragraph 32,

(c) paragraph 46,

(d) paragraph 48,

(e) paragraph 49,

(f) paragraph 51,

(g) paragraph 53,

(h) paragraph 54,

(i) paragraph 56,

(j) paragraph 71,

(k) paragraph 72,

(l) paragraph 77,
(m) paragraph 78,
(n) paragraph 80,
(o) paragraph 84,
(p) paragraph 86, and
(q) paragraph 89.

*Extension of time limit*

**107** (1) Where a provision of this Schedule provides that a period may be varied in accordance with this paragraph, the period may be varied in respect of a company—

(a) by the court, and
(b) on the application of the administrator.

(2) A time period may be extended in respect of a company under this paragraph—

(a) more than once, and
(b) after expiry.

**108** (1) A period specified in paragraph 49(5), 50(1)(b) or 51(2) may be varied in respect of a company by the administrator with consent.

(2) In sub-paragraph (1) 'consent' means consent of—

(a) each secured creditor of the company, and
(b) if the company has unsecured debts, creditors whose debts amount to more than 50% of the company's unsecured debts, disregarding debts of any creditor who does not respond to an invitation to give or withhold consent.

(3) But where the administrator has made a statement under paragraph 52(1)(b) 'consent' means—

(a) consent of each secured creditor of the company, or
(b) if the administrator thinks that a distribution may be made to preferential creditors, consent of—

(i) each secured creditor of the company, and
(ii) preferential creditors whose debts amount to more than 50% of the total preferential debts of the company, disregarding debts of any creditor who does not respond to an invitation to give or withhold consent.

(4) Consent for the purposes of sub-paragraph (1) may be—

(a) written, or
(b) signified at a creditors' meeting.

(5) The power to extend under sub-paragraph (1)—

(a) may be exercised in respect of a period only once,
(b) may not be used to extend a period by more than 28 days,
(c) may not be used to extend a period which has been extended by the court, and
(d) may not be used to extend a period after expiry.

**109** Where a period is extended under paragraph 107 or 108, a reference to the period shall be taken as a reference to the period as extended.

*Amendment of provision about time*

**110** (1) The Secretary of State may by order amend a provision of this Schedule which—

(a) requires anything to be done within a specified period of time,
(b) prevents anything from being done after a specified time, or
(c) requires a specified minimum period of notice to be given.

(2) An order under this paragraph—

(a) must be made by statutory instrument, and
(b) shall be subject to annulment in pursuance of a resolution of either House of Parliament.

*Interpretation*

**111** (1) In this Schedule—

'administrative receiver' has the meaning given by section 251,

'administrator' has the meaning given by paragraph 1 and, where the context requires, includes a reference to a former administrator,

[...]

'correspondence' includes correspondence by telephonic or other electronic means,

'creditors' meeting' has the meaning given by paragraph 50,

'enters administration' has the meaning given by paragraph 1,

'floating charge' means a charge which is a floating charge on its creation,

'in administration' has the meaning given by paragraph 1,

'hire-purchase agreement' includes a conditional sale agreement, a chattel leasing agreement and a retention of title agreement,

'holder of a qualifying floating charge' in respect of a company's property has the meaning given by paragraph 14, 'market value' means the amount which would be realised on a sale of property in the open market by a willing vendor,

'the purpose of administration' means an objective specified in paragraph 3, and

'unable to pay its debts' has the meaning given by section 123.

(1A) In this Schedule, 'company' means—

(a) a company within the meaning of section 735(1) of the Companies Act 1985,

(b) a company incorporated in an EEA State other than the United Kingdom, or

(c) a company not incorporated in an EEA State but having its centre of main interests in a member State other than Denmark.

(1B) In sub-paragraph (1A), in relation to a company, 'centre of main interests' has the same meaning as in the EC Regulation and, in the absence of proof to the contrary, is presumed to be the place of its registered office (within the meaning of that Regulation).

(2) A reference in this Schedule to a thing in writing includes a reference to a thing in electronic form.

(3) In this Schedule a reference to action includes a reference to inaction.

### *Non-UK companies*

**111A** A company incorporated outside the United Kingdom that has a principal place of business in Northern Ireland may not enter administration under this Schedule unless it also has a principal place of business in England and Wales or Scotland (or both in England and Wales and in Scotland).

### *Scotland*

**112** In the application of this Schedule to Scotland—

(a) a reference to filing with the court is a reference to lodging in court, and

(b) a reference to a charge is a reference to a right in security.

**113** Where property in Scotland is disposed of under paragraph 70 or 71, the administrator shall grant to the disponee an appropriate document of transfer or conveyance of the property, and—

(a) that document, or

(b) recording, intimation or registration of that document (where recording, intimation or registration of the document is a legal requirement for completion of title to the property),

has the effect of disencumbering the property of or, as the case may be, freeing the property from, the security.

**114** In Scotland, where goods in the possession of a company under a hire-purchase agreement are disposed of under paragraph 72, the disposal has the effect of extinguishing as against the disponee all rights of the owner of the goods under the agreement.

**115** (1) In Scotland, the administrator of a company may make, in or towards the satisfaction of the debt secured by the floating charge, a payment to the holder of a floating charge which has attached to the property subject to the charge.

(2) In Scotland, where the administrator thinks that the company has insufficient property to enable a distribution to be made to unsecured creditors other than by virtue of section 176A(2)(a), he may file a notice to that effect with the registrar of companies.

(3) On delivery of the notice to the registrar of companies, any floating charge granted by the company shall, unless it has already so attached, attach to the property which is subject to the charge and that attachment shall have effect as if each floating charge is a fixed security over the property to which it has attached.

**116** In Scotland, the administrator in making any payment in accordance with paragraph 115 shall make such payment subject to the rights of any of the following categories of persons (which rights shall, except to the extent provided in any instrument, have the following order of priority)—

(a) the holder of any fixed security which is over property subject to the floating charge and which ranks prior to, or pari passu with, the floating charge,

(b) creditors in respect of all liabilities and expenses incurred by or on behalf of the administrator,

(c) the administrator in respect of his liabilities, expenses and remuneration and any indemnity to which he is entitled out of the property of the company,

(d) the preferential creditors entitled to payment in accordance with paragraph 65,

(e) the holder of the floating charge in accordance with the priority of that charge in relation to any other floating charge which has attached, and

(f) the holder of a fixed security, other than one referred to in paragraph (a), which is over property subject to the floating charge.

# SCHEDULE 1

## POWERS OF ADMINISTRATOR OR ADMINISTRATIVE RECEIVER

**1** Power to take possession of, collect and get in the property of the company and, for that purpose, to take such proceedings as may seem to him expedient.

**2** Power to sell or otherwise dispose of the property of the company by public auction or private contract or, in Scotland, to sell, [..] hire out or otherwise dispose of the property of the company by public group or private bargain.

**3** Power to raise or borrow money and grant security therefor over the property of the company.

**4** Power to appoint a solicitor or accountant or other professionally qualified person to assist him in the performance of his functions.

**5** Power to bring or defend any action or other legal proceedings in the name and on behalf of the company.

**6** Power to refer to arbitration any question affecting the company.

**7** Power to effect and maintain insurances in respect of the business and property of the company.

**8** Power to use the company's seal.

**9** Power to do all acts and to execute in the name and on behalf of the company any deed, receipt or other document.

**10** Power to draw, accept, make and endorse any bill of exchange or promissory note in the name and on behalf of the company.

**11** Power to appoint any agent to do any business which he is unable to do himself or which can more conveniently be done by an agent and power to employ and dismiss employees.

**12** Power to do all such things (including the carrying out of works) as may be necessary for the realisation of the property of the company.

**13** Power to make any payment which is necessary or incidental to the performance of his functions.

**14** Power to carry on the business of the company.

**15** Power to establish subsidiaries of the company.

**16** Power to transfer to subsidiaries of the company the whole or any part of the business and property of the company.

**17** Power to grant or accept a surrender of a lease or tenancy of any of the property of the company, and to take a lease or tenancy of any property required or convenient for the business of the company.

**18** Power to make any arrangement or compromise on behalf of the company.

**19** Power to call up any uncalled capital of the company.

**20** Power to rank and claim in the bankruptcy, insolvency, sequestration or liquidation of any person indebted to the company and to receive dividends, and to accede to trust deeds for the creditors of any such person.

**21** Power to present or defend a petition for the winding up of the company.

**22** Power to change the situation of the company's registered office.

**23** Power to do all other things incidental to the exercise of the foregoing powers.

# SCHEDULE 2

## POWERS OF A SCOTTISH RECEIVER (ADDITIONAL TO THOSE CONFERRED ON HIM BY THE INSTRUMENT OF CHARGE)

**1** Power to take possession of, collect and get in the property from the company or a liquidator thereof or any other person, and for that purpose, to take such proceedings as may seem to him expedient.

**2** Power to sell, [...] hire out or otherwise dispose of the property by public roup or private bargain and with or without advertisement.

**3** Power to raise or borrow money and grant security therefor over the property.

**4** Power to appoint a solicitor or accountant or other professionally qualified person to assist him in the performance of his functions.

**5** Power to bring or defend any action or other legal proceedings in the name and on behalf of the company.

**6** Power to refer to arbitration all questions affecting the company.

**7** Power to effect and maintain insurances in respect of the business and property of the company.

**8** Power to use the company's seal.

**9** Power to do all acts and to execute in the name and on behalf of the company any deed, receipt or other document.

**10** Power to draw, accept, make and endorse any bill of exchange or promissory note in the name and on behalf of the company.

**11** Power to appoint any agent to do any business which he is unable to do himself or which can more conveniently be done by an agent, and power to employ and dismiss employees.

**12** Power to do all such things (including the carrying out of works), as may be necessary for the realisation of the property.

**13** Power to make any payment which is necessary or incidental to the performance of his functions.

**14** Power to carry on the business of the company or any part of it.

**15** Power to grant or accept a surrender of a lease or tenancy of any of the property, and to take a lease or tenancy of any property required or convenient for the business of the company.

**16** Power to make any arrangement or compromise on behalf of the company.

**17** Power to call up any uncalled capital of the company.

**18** Power to establish subsidiaries of the company.

**19** Power to transfer to subsidiaries of the company the business of the company or any part of it and any of the property.

**20** Power to rank and claim in the bankruptcy, insolvency, sequestration or liquidation of any person or company indebted to the company and to receive dividends, and to accede to trust deeds for creditors of any such person.

**21** Power to present or defend a petition for the winding up of the company.

**22** Power to change the situation of the company's registered office.

**23** Power to do all other things incidental to the exercise of the powers mentioned in section 55(1) of this Act or above in this Schedule.

## SCHEDULE 2A

## EXCEPTIONS TO PROHIBITION ON APPOINTMENT OF ADMINISTRATIVE RECEIVER: SUPPLEMENTARY PROVISIONS

### Capital market arrangement

**1** (1) For the purposes of section 72B an arrangement is a capital market arrangement if—

(a) it involves a grant of security to a person holding it as trustee for a person who holds a capital market investment issued by a party to the arrangement, or

(aa) it involves a grant of security to—

(i) a party to the arrangement who issues a capital market investment, or

(ii) a person who holds the security as trustee for a party to the arrangement in connection with the issue of a capital market investment, or

(ab) it involves a grant of security to a person who holds the security as trustee for a party to the arrangement who agrees to provide finance to another party, or

(b) at least one party guarantees the performance of obligations of another party, or

(c) at least one party provides security in respect of the performance of obligations of another party, or

(d) the arrangement involves an investment of a kind described in articles 83 to 85 of the Financial Services and Markets Act 2000 (Regulated Activities) Order 2001 (SI 2001/544)(options, futures and contracts for differences).

(2) For the purposes of sub-paragraph (1)—

(a) a reference to holding as trustee includes a reference to holding as nominee or agent,

(b) a reference to holding for a person who holds a capital market investment includes a reference to holding for a number of persons at least one of whom holds a capital market investment, and

(c) a person holds a capital market investment if he has a legal or beneficial interest in it ; and

(d) the reference to the provision of finance includes the provision of an indemnity

(3) In section 72B(1) and this paragraph 'party' to an arrangement includes a party to an agreement which—

(a) forms part of the arrangement,

(b) provides for the raising of finance as part of the arrangement, or

(c) is necessary for the purposes of implementing the arrangement.

### Capital market investment

**2** (1) For the purposes of section 72B an investment is a capital market investment if it—

(a) is within article 77 of the Financial Services and Markets Act 2000 (Regulated Activities) Order 2001 (SI 2001/544)(debt instruments), and

(b) is rated, listed or traded or designed to be rated, listed or traded.

(2) In sub-paragraph (1)—

'rated' means rated for the purposes of investment by an internationally recognised rating agency,

'listed' means admitted to the official list within the meaning given by section 103(1) of the Financial Services and Markets Act 2000 (c 8)(interpretation), and

'traded' means admitted to trading on a market established under the rules of a recognised investment exchange or on a foreign market.

(3) In sub-paragraph (2)—

'recognised investment exchange' has the meaning given by section 285 of the Financial Services and Markets Act 2000 (recognised investment exchange), and

'foreign market' has the same meaning as 'relevant market' in article 67(2) of the Financial Services and Markets Act 2000 (Financial Promotion) Order 2001 (SI 2001/1335)(foreign markets).

**3** (1) An investment is also a capital market investment for the purposes of section 72B if it consists of a bond or commercial paper issued to one or more of the following—

(a) an investment professional within the meaning of article 19(5) of the Financial Services and Markets Act 2000 (Financial Promotion) Order 2001,

(b) a person who is, when the agreement mentioned in section 72B(1) is entered into, a certified high net worth individual in relation to a communication within the meaning of article 48(2) of that order,

(c) a person to whom article 49(2) of that order applies (high net worth company, &c.),

(d) a person who is, when the agreement mentioned in section 72B(1) is entered into, a certified sophisticated investor in relation to a communication within the meaning of article 50(1) of that order, and

(e) a person in a State other than the United Kingdom who under the law of that State is not prohibited from investing in bonds or commercial paper.

(2) In sub-paragraph (1)—

'bond' shall be construed in accordance with article 77 of the Financial Services and Markets Act 2000 (Regulated Activities) Order 2001 (SI 2001/544), and

'commercial paper' has the meaning given by article 9(3) of that order.

(3) For the purposes of sub-paragraph (1)—

(a) in applying article 19(5) of the Financial Promotion Order for the purposes of sub-paragraph (1)(a)—

(i) in article 19(5)(b), ignore the words after 'exempt person',

(ii) in article 19(5)(c)(i), for the words from 'the controlled activity' to the end substitute 'a controlled activity', and

(iii) in article 19(5)(e) ignore the words from 'where the communication' to the end, and

(b) in applying article 49(2) of that order for the purposes of sub-paragraph (1)(c), ignore article 49(2)(e).

#### *'Agreement'*

**4** For the purposes of sections 72B and 72E and this Schedule 'agreement' includes an agreement or undertaking effected by—

(a) contract,

(b) deed, or

(c) any other instrument intended to have effect in accordance with the law of England and Wales, Scotland or another jurisdiction.

#### *Debt*

**5** The debt of at least £50 million referred to in section 72B(1)(a) or 72E(2)(a)—

(a) may be incurred at any time during the life of the capital market arrangement or financed project, and

(b) may be expressed wholly or partly in foreign currency (in which case the sterling equivalent shall be calculated as at the time when the arrangement is entered into or the project begins).

#### *Step-in rights*

**6** (1) For the purposes of sections 72C to 72E a project has 'step-in rights' if a person who provides finance in connection with the project has a conditional entitlement under an agreement to—

(a) assume sole or principal responsibility under an agreement for carrying out all or part of the project, or

(b) make arrangements for carrying out all or part of the project.

(2) In sub-paragraph (1) a reference to the provision of finance includes a reference to the provision of an indemnity.

#### *Project company*

**7** (1) For the purposes of sections 72C to 72E a company is a 'project company' of a project if—

(a) it holds property for the purpose of the project,

(b) it has sole or principal responsibility under an agreement for carrying out all or part of the project,

(c) it is one of a number of companies which together carry out the project,

(d) it has the purpose of supplying finance to enable the project to be carried out, or

(e) it is the holding company of a company within any of paragraphs (a) to (d).

(2) But a company is not a 'project company' of a project if—

(a) it performs a function within sub-paragraph (1)(a) to (d) or is within sub-paragraph (1)(e), but

(b) it also performs a function which is not—

    (i) within sub-paragraph (1)(a) to (d),

    (ii) related to a function within sub-paragraph (1)(a) to (d), or

    (iii) related to the project.

(3) For the purposes of this paragraph a company carries out all or part of a project whether or not it acts wholly or partly through agents.

## 'Resources'

**8** In section 72C 'resources' includes—

(a) funds (including payment for the provision of services or facilities),

(b) assets,

(c) professional skill,

(d) the grant of a concession or franchise, and

(e) any other commercial resource.

## 'Public body'

**9** (1) In section 72C 'public body' means—

(a) a body which exercises public functions,

(b) a body specified for the purposes of this paragraph by the Secretary of State, and

(c) a body within a class specified for the purposes of this paragraph by the Secretary of State.

(2) A specification under sub-paragraph (1) may be—

(a) general, or

(b) for the purpose of the application of section 72C to a specified case.

## Regulated business

**10** (1) For the purposes of section 72D a business is regulated if it is carried on—

(a) in reliance on a licence granted to a person under section 7 of the Telecommunications Act 1984 (c 12)(telecommunications service),

(b) in reliance on a licence under section 7 or 7A of the Gas Act 1986 (c 44)(transport and supply of gas),

(c) in reliance on a licence granted by virtue of section 41C of that Act (power to prescribe additional licensable activity),

(d) in reliance on a licence under section 6 of the Electricity Act 1989 (c 29)(supply of electricity),

(e) by a water undertaker,

(f) by a sewerage undertaker,

(g) by a universal service provider within the meaning given by section 4(3) and (4) of the Postal Services Act 2000 (c 26),

(h) by the Post Office company within the meaning given by section 62 of that Act (transfer of property),

(i) by a relevant subsidiary of the Post Office Company within the meaning given by section 63 of that Act (government holding),

(j) in reliance on a licence under section 8 of the Railways Act 1993 (c 43)(railway services),

(k) in reliance on a licence exemption under section 7 of that Act (subject to sub-paragraph (2) below),

(l) by the operator of a system of transport which is deemed to be a railway for a purpose of Part I of that Act by virtue of section 81(2) of that Act (tramways, &c.), [...]

(m) by the operator of a vehicle carried on flanged wheels along a system within paragraph (l) or

(n) in reliance on a European licence granted pursuant to a provision contained in any instrument made for the purpose of implementing Council Directive 1995/18/EC dated 19th June 1995 on the licensing of railway undertakings, as amended by Directive 2001/13/EC dated 26th February 2001 and Directive 2004/49/EC dated 29th April 2004, both of the European Parliament and of the Council, or pursuant to any action taken by an EEA State for that purpose.

(2) Sub-paragraph (1)(k) does not apply to the operator of a railway asset on a railway unless on some part of the railway there is a permitted line speed exceeding 40 kilometres per hour.

(2A) For the purposes of section 72D a business is also regulated to the extent that it consists in the provision of a public electronic communications network or a public electronic communications service.

(2B) In sub-paragraph (1)(n), an 'EEA State' means a member State, Norway, Iceland or Liechtenstein.

## 'Person'

**11** A reference to a person in this Schedule includes a reference to a partnership or another unincorporated group of persons.

# SCHEDULE 3

# ORDERS IN COURSE OF WINDING UP PRONOUNCED IN VACATION (SCOTLAND)

## PART I

### ORDERS WHICH ARE TO BE FINAL

Orders under section 153, as to the time for proving debts and claims.

Orders under section 195 as to meetings for ascertaining wishes of creditors or contributories.

Orders under section 198, as to the examination of witnesses in regard to the property or affairs of a company.

## PART II

### ORDERS WHICH ARE TO TAKE EFFECT UNTIL MATTER DISPOSED OF BY INNER HOUSE

Orders under section 126(1), 130(2) or (3), 147, 227 or 228, restraining or permitting the commencement or the continuance of legal proceedings.

Orders under section 135(5),limiting the powers of provisional liquidators.

Orders under section 108, appointing a liquidator to fill a vacancy.

Orders under section 167 or 169, sanctioning the exercise of any powers by a liquidator, other than the powers specified in paragraphs 1, 2 and 3 of Schedule 4 to this Act.

Orders under section 158, as to the arrest and detention of an absconding contributory and his property.

# SCHEDULE 4

# POWERS OF LIQUIDATOR IN A WINDING UP

## PART I

### POWERS EXERCISABLE WITH SANCTION

**1** Power to pay any class of creditors in full.

**2** Power to make any compromise or arrangement with creditors or persons claiming to be creditors, or having or alleging themselves to have any claim (present or future, certain or contingent, ascertained or sounding only in damages) against the company, or whereby the company may be rendered liable.

**3** Power to compromise, on such terms as may be agreed—

(a) all calls and liabilities to calls, all debts and liabilities capable of resulting in debts, and all claims (present or future, certain or contingent, ascertained or sounding only in damages) subsisting or supposed to subsist between the company and a contributory or alleged contributory or other debtor or person apprehending liability to the company, and

(b) all questions in any way relating to or affecting the assets or the winding up of the company,

and take any security for the discharge of any such call, debt, liability or claim and give a complete discharge in respect of it.

**3A.** Power to bring legal proceedings under section 213, 214, 238, 239, 242, 243 or 423.

## PART II

### POWERS EXERCISABLE WITHOUT SANCTION IN VOLUNTARY WINDING UP, WITH SANCTION IN WINDING UP BY THE COURT

**4** Power to bring or defend any action or other legal proceeding in the name and on behalf of the company.

**5** Power to carry on the business of the company so far as may be necessary for its beneficial winding up.

## PART III

## POWERS EXERCISABLE WITHOUT SANCTION IN ANY WINDING UP

**6** Power to sell any of the company's property by public auction or private contract with power to transfer the whole of it to any person or to sell the same in parcels.

**7** Power to do all acts and execute, in the name and on behalf of the company, all deeds, receipts and other documents and for that purpose to use, when necessary, the company's seal.

**8** Power to prove, rank and claim in the bankruptcy, insolvency or sequestration of any contributory for any balance against his estate, and to receive dividends in the bankruptcy, insolvency or sequestration in respect of that balance, as a separate debt due from the bankrupt or insolvent, and rateably with the other separate creditors.

**9** Power to draw, accept, make and indorse any bill of exchange or promissory note in the name and on behalf of the company, with the same effect with respect to the company's liability as if the bill or note had been drawn, accepted, made or indorsed by or on behalf of the company in the course of its business.

**10** Power to raise on the security of the assets of the company any money requisite.

**11** Power to take out in his official name letters of administration to any deceased contributory, and to do in his official name any other act necessary for obtaining payment of any money due from a contributory or his estate which cannot conveniently be done in the name of the company.

In all such cases the money due is deemed, for the purpose of enabling the liquidator to take out the letters of administration or recover the money, to be due to the liquidator himself.

**12** Power to appoint an agent to do any business which the liquidator is unable to do himself.

**13** Power to do all such other things as may be necessary for winding up the company's affairs and distributing its assets.

## SCHEDULE 4A

## BANKRUPTCY RESTRICTIONS ORDER AND UNDERTAKING

### *Bankruptcy restrictions order*

**1** (1) A bankruptcy restrictions order may be made by the court.

(2) An order may be made only on the application of—
   (a) the Secretary of State, or
   (b) the official receiver acting on a direction of the Secretary of State.

### *Grounds for making order*

**2** (1) The court shall grant an application for a bankruptcy restrictions order if it thinks it appropriate having regard to the conduct of the bankrupt (whether before or after the making of the bankruptcy order).

(2) The court shall, in particular, take into account any of the following kinds of behaviour on the part of the bankrupt—
   (a) failing to keep records which account for a loss of property by the bankrupt, or by a business carried on by him, where the loss occurred in the period beginning 2 years before petition and ending with the date of the application;
   (b) failing to produce records of that kind on demand by the official receiver or the trustee;
   (c) entering into a transaction at an undervalue;
   (d) giving a preference;
   (e) making an excessive pension contribution;
   (f) a failure to supply goods or services which were wholly or partly paid for which gave rise to a claim provable in the bankruptcy;
   (g) trading at a time before commencement of the bankruptcy when the bankrupt knew or ought to have known that he was himself to be unable to pay his debts;
   (h) incurring, before commencement of the bankruptcy, a debt which the bankrupt had no reasonable expectation of being able to pay;
   (i) failing to account satisfactorily to the court, the official receiver or the trustee for a loss of property or for an insufficiency of property to meet bankruptcy debts;
   (j) carrying on any gambling, rash and hazardous speculation or unreasonable extravagance which may have materially contributed to or increased the extent of the bankruptcy or which took place between presentation of the petition and commencement of the bankruptcy;

    (k) neglect of business affairs of a kind which may have materially contributed to or increased the extent of the bankruptcy;

    (l) fraud or fraudulent breach of trust;

    (m) failing to cooperate with the official receiver or the trustee.

    (3) The court shall also, in particular, consider whether the bankrupt was an undischarged bankrupt at some time during the period of six years ending with the date of the bankruptcy to which the application relates.

    (4) For the purpose of sub-paragraph (2)—

'before petition' shall be construed in accordance with section 351(c),

'excessive pension contribution' shall be construed in accordance with section 342A,

'preference' shall be construed in accordance with section 340, and

'undervalue' shall be construed in accordance with section 339.

### Timing of application for order

**3** (1) An application for a bankruptcy restrictions order in respect of a bankrupt must be made—

    (a) before the end of the period of one year beginning with the date on which the bankruptcy commences, or

    (b) with the permission of the court.

    (2) The period specified in sub-paragraph (1)(a) shall cease to run in respect of a bankrupt while the period set for his discharge is suspended under section 279(3).

### Duration of order

**4** (1) A bankruptcy restrictions order—

    (a) shall come into force when it is made, and

    (b) shall cease to have effect at the end of a date specified in the order.

    (2) The date specified in a bankruptcy restrictions order under sub-paragraph (1)(b) must not be—

    (a) before the end of the period of two years beginning with the date on which the order is made, or

    (b) after the end of the period of 15 years beginning with that date.

### Interim bankruptcy restrictions order

**5** (1) This paragraph applies at any time between—

    (a) the institution of an application for a bankruptcy restrictions order, and

    (b) the determination of the application.

    (2) The court may make an interim bankruptcy restrictions order if the court thinks that—

    (a) there are prima facie grounds to suggest that the application for the bankruptcy restrictions order will be successful, and

    (b) it is in the public interest to make an interim order.

    (3) An interim order may be made only on the application of—

    (a) the Secretary of State, or

    (b) the official receiver acting on a direction of the Secretary of State.

    (4) An interim order—

    (a) shall have the same effect as a bankruptcy restrictions order, and

    (b) shall come into force when it is made.

    (5) An interim order shall cease to have effect—

    (a) on the determination of the application for the bankruptcy restrictions order,

    (b) on the acceptance of a bankruptcy restrictions undertaking made by the bankrupt, or

    (c) if the court discharges the interim order on the application of the person who applied for it or of the bankrupt.

**6** (1) This paragraph applies to a case in which both an interim bankruptcy restrictions order and a bankruptcy restrictions order are made.

    (2) Paragraph 4(2) shall have effect in relation to the bankruptcy restrictions order as if a reference to the date of that order were a reference to the date of the interim order.

### Bankruptcy restrictions undertaking

**7** (1) A bankrupt may offer a bankruptcy restrictions undertaking to the Secretary of State.

    (2) In determining whether to accept a bankruptcy restrictions undertaking the Secretary of State shall have regard to the matters specified in paragraph 2(2) and (3).

**8** A reference in an enactment to a person in respect of whom a bankruptcy restrictions order has effect (or who is 'the subject of' a bankruptcy restrictions order) includes a reference to a person in respect of whom a bankruptcy restrictions undertaking has effect.

**9** (1) A bankruptcy restrictions undertaking—

    (a) shall come into force on being accepted by the Secretary of State, and

    (b) shall cease to have effect at the end of a date specified in the undertaking.

    (2) The date specified under sub-paragraph (1)(b) must not be—

(a) before the end of the period of two years beginning with the date on which the undertaking is accepted, or

(b) after the end of the period of 15 years beginning with that date.

(3) On an application by the bankrupt the court may—

(a) annul a bankruptcy restrictions undertaking;

(b) provide for a bankruptcy restrictions undertaking to cease to have effect before the date specified under sub-paragraph (1)(b).

### *Effect of annulment of bankruptcy order*

**10** Where a bankruptcy order is annulled under section 282(1)(a) or (2)—

(a) any bankruptcy restrictions order, interim order or undertaking which is in force in respect of the bankrupt shall be annulled,

(b) no new bankruptcy restrictions order or interim order may be made in respect of the bankrupt, and

(c) no new bankruptcy restrictions undertaking by the bankrupt may be accepted.

**11** Where a bankruptcy order is annulled under section 261, 263D or 282(1)(b)—

(a) the annulment shall not affect any bankruptcy restrictions order, interim order or undertaking in respect of the bankrupt,

(b) the court may make a bankruptcy restrictions order in relation to the bankrupt on an application instituted before the annulment,

(c) the Secretary of State may accept a bankruptcy restrictions undertaking offered before the annulment, and

(d) an application for a bankruptcy restrictions order or interim order in respect of the bankrupt may not be instituted after the annulment.

### *Registration*

**12** The Secretary of State shall maintain a register of—

(a) bankruptcy restrictions orders,

(b) interim bankruptcy restrictions orders, and

(c) bankruptcy restrictions undertakings.

# SCHEDULE 4ZA

# CONDITIONS FOR MAKING A DEBT RELIEF ORDER

## PART 1

## CONDITIONS WHICH MUST BE MET

### *Connection with England and Wales*

**1** (1) The debtor—

(a) is domiciled in England and Wales on the application date; or

(b) at any time during the period of three years ending with that date—

(i) was ordinarily resident, or had a place of residence, in England and Wales; or

(ii) carried on business in England and Wales.

(2) The reference in sub-paragraph (1)(b)(ii) to the debtor carrying on business includes—

(a) the carrying on of business by a firm or partnership of which he is a member;

(b) the carrying on of business by an agent or manager for him or for such a firm or partnership.

### *Debtor's previous insolvency history*

**2** The debtor is not, on the determination date—

(a) an undischarged bankrupt;

(b) subject to an interim order or voluntary arrangement under Part 8; or

(c) subject to a bankruptcy restrictions order or a debt relief restrictions order.

**3** A debtor's petition for the debtor's bankruptcy under Part 9—

(a) has not been presented by the debtor before the determination date;

(b) has been so presented, but proceedings on the petition have been finally disposed of before that date; or

(c) has been so presented and proceedings in relation to the petition remain before the court at that date, but the court has referred the debtor under section 274A(2) for the purposes of making an application for a debt relief order.

**4** A creditor's petition for the debtor's bankruptcy under Part 9—

(a) has not been presented against the debtor at any time before the determination date;

(b) has been so presented, but proceedings on the petition have been finally disposed of before that date; or

(c) has been so presented and proceedings in relation to the petition remain before the court at that date, but the person who presented the petition has consented to the making of an application for a debt relief order.

**5** A debt relief order has not been made in relation to the debtor in the period of six years ending with the determination date.

### *Limit on debtor's overall indebtedness*

**6** (1) The total amount of the debtor's debts on the determination date, other than unliquidated debts and excluded debts, does not exceed the prescribed amount.

(2) For this purpose an unliquidated debt is a debt that is not for a liquidated sum payable to a creditor either immediately or at some future certain time.

### *Limit on debtor's monthly surplus income*

**7** (1) The debtor's monthly surplus income (if any) on the determination date does not exceed the prescribed amount.

(2) For this purpose 'monthly surplus income' is the amount by which a person's monthly income exceeds the amount necessary for the reasonable domestic needs of himself and his family.

(3) The rules may—
(a) make provision as to how the debtor's monthly surplus income is to be determined;
(b) provide that particular descriptions of income are to be excluded for the purposes of this paragraph.

### *Limit on value of debtor's property*

**8** (1) The total value of the debtor's property on the determination date does not exceed the prescribed amount.

(2) The rules may—
(a) make provision as to how the value of a person's property is to be determined;
(b) provide that particular descriptions of property are to be excluded for the purposes of this paragraph.

## PART 2

## OTHER CONDITIONS

**9** (1) The debtor has not entered into a transaction with any person at an undervalue during the period between—
(a) the start of the period of two years ending with the application date; and
(b) the determination date.

(2) For this purpose a debtor enters into a transaction with a person at an undervalue if—
(a) he makes a gift to that person or he otherwise enters into a transaction with that person on terms that provide for him to receive no consideration;
(b) he enters into a transaction with that person in consideration of marriage or the formation of a civil partnership; or
(c) he enters into a transaction with that person for a consideration the value of which, in money or money's worth, is significantly less than the value, in money or money's worth, of the consideration provided by the individual.

**10** (1) The debtor has not given a preference to any person during the period between—
(a) the start of the period of two years ending with the application date; and
(b) the determination date.

(2) For this purpose a debtor gives a preference to a person if—
(a) that person is one of the debtor's creditors to whom a qualifying debt is owed or is a surety or guarantor for any such debt, and
(b) the debtor does anything or suffers anything to be done which (in either case) has the effect of putting that person into a position which, in the event that a debt relief order is made in relation to the debtor, will be better than the position he would have been in if that thing had not been done.

## SCHEDULE 4ZB

## DEBT RELIEF RESTRICTIONS ORDERS AND UNDERTAKINGS

### *Debt relief restrictions order*

**1** (1) A debt relief restrictions order may be made by the court in relation to a person in respect of whom a debt relief order has been made.

(2) An order may be made only on the application of—
- (a) the Secretary of State, or
- (b) the official receiver acting on a direction of the Secretary of State.

### Grounds for making order

**2** (1) The court shall grant an application for a debt relief restrictions order if it thinks it appropriate to do so having regard to the conduct of the debtor (whether before or after the making of the debt relief order).

(2) The court shall, in particular, take into account any of the following kinds of behaviour on the part of the debtor—
- (a) failing to keep records which account for a loss of property by the debtor, or by a business carried on by him, where the loss occurred in the period beginning two years before the application date for the debt relief order and ending with the date of the application for the debt relief restrictions order;
- (b) failing to produce records of that kind on demand by the official receiver;
- (c) entering into a transaction at an undervalue in the period beginning two years before the application date for the debt relief order and ending with the date of the determination of that application;
- (d) giving a preference in the period beginning two years before the application date for the debt relief order and ending with the date of the determination of that application;
- (e) making an excessive pension contribution;
- (f) a failure to supply goods or services that were wholly or partly paid for;
- (g) trading at a time, before the date of the determination of the application for the debt relief order, when the debtor knew or ought to have known that he was himself to be unable to pay his debts;
- (h) incurring, before the date of the determination of the application for the debt relief order, a debt which the debtor had no reasonable expectation of being able to pay;
- (i) failing to account satisfactorily to the court or the official receiver for a loss of property or for an insufficiency of property to meet his debts;
- (j) carrying on any gambling, rash and hazardous speculation or unreasonable extravagance which may have materially contributed to or increased the extent of his inability to pay his debts before the application date for the debt relief order or which took place between that date and the date of the determination of the application for the debt relief order;
- (k) neglect of business affairs of a kind which may have materially contributed to or increased the extent of his inability to pay his debts;
- (l) fraud or fraudulent breach of trust;
- (m) failing to co-operate with the official receiver.

(3) The court shall also, in particular, consider whether the debtor was an undischarged bankrupt at some time during the period of six years ending with the date of the application for the debt relief order.

(4) For the purposes of sub-paragraph (2)—
'excessive pension contribution' shall be construed in accordance with section 342A;
'preference' shall be construed in accordance with paragraph 10(2) of Schedule 4ZA;
'undervalue' shall be construed in accordance with paragraph 9(2) of that Schedule.

### Timing of application for order

**3** An application for a debt relief restrictions order in respect of a debtor may be made—
- (a) at any time during the moratorium period relating to the debt relief order in question, or
- (b) after the end of that period, but only with the permission of the court.

### Duration of order

**4** (1) A debt relief restrictions order—
- (a) comes into force when it is made, and
- (b) ceases to have effect at the end of a date specified in the order.

(2) The date specified in a debt relief restrictions order under sub-paragraph (1)(b) must not be—
- (a) before the end of the period of two years beginning with the date on which the order is made, or
- (b) after the end of the period of 15 years beginning with that date.

### Interim debt relief restrictions order

**5** (1) This paragraph applies at any time between—
- (a) the institution of an application for a debt relief restrictions order, and
- (b) the determination of the application.

(2) The court may make an interim debt relief restrictions order if the court thinks that—
- (a) there are prima facie grounds to suggest that the application for the debt relief restrictions order will be successful, and
- (b) it is in the public interest to make an interim debt relief restrictions order.

(3) An interim debt relief restrictions order may only be made on the application of—

    (a) the Secretary of State, or

    (b) the official receiver acting on a direction of the Secretary of State.

(4) An interim debt relief restrictions order—

    (a) has the same effect as a debt relief restrictions order, and

    (b) comes into force when it is made.

(5) An interim debt relief restrictions order ceases to have effect—

    (a) on the determination of the application for the debt relief restrictions order,

    (b) on the acceptance of a debt relief restrictions undertaking made by the debtor, or

    (c) if the court discharges the interim debt relief restrictions order on the application of the person who applied for it or of the debtor.

**6** (1) This paragraph applies to a case in which both an interim debt relief restrictions order and a debt relief restrictions order are made.

(2) Paragraph 4(2) has effect in relation to the debt relief restrictions order as if a reference to the date of that order were a reference to the date of the interim debt relief restrictions order.

### Debt relief restrictions undertaking

**7** (1) A debtor may offer a debt relief restrictions undertaking to the Secretary of State.

(2) In determining whether to accept a debt relief restrictions undertaking the Secretary of State shall have regard to the matters specified in paragraph 2(2) and (3).

**8** A reference in an enactment to a person in respect of whom a debt relief restrictions order has effect (or who is 'the subject of' a debt relief restrictions order) includes a reference to a person in respect of whom a debt relief restrictions undertaking has effect.

**9** (1) A debt relief restrictions undertaking—

    (a) comes into force on being accepted by the Secretary of State, and

    (b) ceases to have effect at the end of a date specified in the undertaking.

(2) The date specified under sub-paragraph (1)(b) must not be—

    (a) before the end of the period of two years beginning with the date on which the undertaking is accepted, or

    (b) after the end of the period of 15 years beginning with that date.

(3) On an application by the debtor the court may—

    (a) annul a debt relief restrictions undertaking;

    (b) provide for a debt relief restrictions undertaking to cease to have effect before the date specified under sub-paragraph (1)(b).

### Effect of revocation of debt relief order

**10** Unless the court directs otherwise, the revocation at any time of a debt relief order does not—

    (a) affect the validity of any debt relief restrictions order, interim debt relief restrictions order or debt relief restrictions undertaking which is in force in respect of the debtor;

    (b) prevent the determination of any application for a debt relief restrictions order, or an interim debt relief restrictions order, in relation to the debtor that was instituted before that time;

    (c) prevent the acceptance of a debt relief restrictions undertaking that was offered before that time; or

    (d) prevent the institution of an application for a debt relief restrictions order or interim debt relief restrictions order in respect of the debtor, or the offer or acceptance of a debt relief restrictions undertaking by the debtor, after that time.

# SCHEDULE 5

# POWERS OF TRUSTEE IN BANKRUPTCY

## PART I

## POWERS EXERCISABLE WITH SANCTION

**1** Power to carry on any business of the bankrupt so far as may be necessary for winding it up beneficially and so far as the trustee is able to do so without contravening any requirement imposed by or under any enactment.

**2** Power to bring, institute or defend any action or legal proceedings relating to the property comprised in the bankrupt's estate.

**2A** Power to bring legal proceedings under section 339, 340 or 423.

**3** Power to accept as the consideration for the sale of any property comprised in the bankrupt's estate a sum of money payable at a future time subject to such stipulations as to security or otherwise as the creditors' committee or the court thinks fit.

**4** Power to mortgage or pledge any part of the property comprised in the bankrupt's estate for the purpose of raising money for the payment of his debts.

**5** Power, where any right, option or other power forms part of the bankrupt's estate, to make payments or incur liabilities with a view to obtaining, for the benefit of the creditors, any property which is the subject of the right, option or power.

**6** Power to refer to arbitration, or compromise on such terms as may be agreed on, any debts, claims or liabilities subsisting or supposed to subsist between the bankrupt and any person who may have incurred any liability to the bankrupt.

**7** Power to make such compromise or other arrangement as may be thought expedient with creditors, or persons claiming to be creditors, in respect of bankruptcy debts.

**8** Power to make such compromise or other arrangement as ay be thought expedient with respect to any claim arising out of or incidental to the bankrupt's estate made or capable of being made on the trustee by any person or by the trustee on any person.

## PART II

### GENERAL POWERS

**9** Power to sell any part of the property for the time being comprised in the bankrupt's estate, including the goodwill and book debts of any business.

**10** Power to give receipts for any money received by him, being receipts which effectually discharge the person paying the money from all responsibility in respect of its application.

**11** Power to prove, rank, claim and draw a dividend in respect of such debts due to the bankrupt as are comprised in his estate.

**12** Power to exercise in relation to any property comprised in the bankrupt's estate any powers the capacity to exercise which is vested in him under Parts VIII to XI of this Act.

**13** Power to deal with any property comprised in the estate to which the bankrupt is beneficially entitled as tenant in tail in the same manner as the bankrupt might have dealt with it.

## PART III

### ANCILLARY POWERS

**14** For the purposes of, or in connection with, the exercise of any of his powers under Parts VIII to XI of this Act, the trustee may, by his official name—

(a)  hold property of every description,

(b)  make contracts,

(c)  sue and be sued,

(d)  enter into engagements binding on himself and, in respect of the bankrupt's estate, on his successors in office,

(e)  employ an agent,

(f)  execute any power of attorney, deed or other instrument;

and he may do any other act which is necessary or expedient for the purposes of or in connection with the exercise of those powers.

## SCHEDULE 6

## THE CATEGORIES OF PREFERENTIAL DEBTS

*Category 1: Depts due to Inland Revenue*

**1.–2.** [...]

*Category 2: Depts due to Customs and Excise*

**3.–5C** [...]

*Category 3: Social security contributions*

**6.–7.** [...]

*Category 4: Contributions to occupational pension schemes, etc.*

**8** Any sum which is owed by the debtor and is a sum to which Schedule 4 to the Pension Schemes Act 1993 applies (contributions to occupational pension schemes and state scheme premiums).

*Category 5: Remuneration, etc., of employees*

**9** So much of any amount which—

(a) is owed by the debtor to a person who is or has been an employee of the debtor, and

(b) is payable by way of remuneration in respect of the whole or any part of the period of 4 months next before the relevant date,

as does not exceed so much as may be prescribed by order made by the Secretary of State.

**10** An amount owed by way of accrued holiday remuneration, in respect of any period of employment before the relevant date, to a person whose employment by the debtor has been terminated, whether before, on or after that date.

**11** So much of any sum owed in respect of money advanced for the purpose as has been applied for the payment of a debt which, if it had not been paid, would have been a debt falling within paragraph 9 or 10.

**12** So much of any amount which—

(a) is ordered (whether before or after the relevant date) to be paid by the debtor under the Reserve Forces (Safeguard of Employment) Act 1985, and

(b) is so ordered in respect of a default made by the debtor before that date in the discharge of his obligations under that Act,

as does not exceed such amount as may be prescribed by order made by the Secretary of State.

### *Interpretation for Category 5*

**13** (1) For the purposes of paragraphs 9 to 12, a sum is payable by the debtor to a person by way of remuneration in respect of any period if—

(a) it is paid as wages or salary (whether payable for time or for piece work or earned wholly or partly by way of commission) in respect of services rendered to the debtor in that period, or

(b) it is an amount falling within the following sub-paragraph and is payable by the debtor in respect of that period.

(2) An amount falls within this sub-paragraph if it is—

(a) a guarantee payment under Part III of the Employment Rights Act 1996 (employee without work to do);

(b) any payment for time off under section 53 (time off to look for work or arrange training) or section 56 (time off for ante-natal care) of that Act or under section 169 of the Trade Union and Labour Relations (Consolidation) Act 1992 (time off for carrying out trade union duties etc.);

(c) remuneration on suspension on medical grounds, or on maternity grounds, under Part VII of the Employment Rights Act 1996; or

(d) remuneration under a protective award under section 189 of the Trade Union and Labour Relations (Consolidation) Act 1992 (redundancy dismissal with compensation).

**14** (1) This paragraph relates to a case in which a person's employment has been terminated by or in consequence of his employer going into liquidation or being adjudged bankrupt or (his employer being a company not in liquidation) by or in consequence of—

(a) a receiver being appointed as mentioned in section 40 of this Act (debenture-holders secured by floating charge), or

(b) the appointment of a receiver under section 53(6) or 54(5) of this Act (Scottish company with property subject to floating charge), or

(c) the taking of possession by debenture-holders (so secured), as mentioned in section 754 of the Companies Act 2006.

(2) For the purposes of paragraphs 9 to 12, holiday remuneration is deemed to have accrued to that person in respect of any period of employment if, by virtue of his contract of employment or of any enactment that remuneration would have accrued in respect of that period if his employment had continued until he became entitled to be allowed the holiday.

(3) The reference in sub-paragraph (2) to any enactment includes an order or direction made under an enactment.

**15** Without prejudice to paragraphs 13 and 14—

(a) any remuneration payable by the debtor to a person in respect of a period of holiday or of absence from work through sickness or other good cause is deemed to be wages or (as the case may be) salary in respect of services rendered to the debtor in that period, and

(b) references here and in those paragraphs to remuneration in respect of a period of holiday include any sums which, if they had been paid, would have been treated for the purposes of the enactments relating to social security as earnings in respect of that period.

### *Category 6: Levies on coal and steel production*

**15A** Any sums due at the relevant date from the debtor in respect of—

(a) the levies on the production of coal and steel referred to in Articles 49 and 50 of the ECSC Treaty, or

(b) any surcharge for delay provided for in Article 50(3) of that Treaty and Article 6 of Decision 3/52 of the High Authority of the Coal and Steel Community.

### *Orders*

**16** An order under paragraph 9 or 12—

(a) may contain such transitional provisions as may appear to the Secretary of State necessary or expedient;

(b) shall be made by statutory instrument subject to annulment in pursuance of a resolution of either House of Parliament.

# SCHEDULE 7

## INSOLVENCY PRACTITIONERS TRIBUNAL

### *Panels of members*

**1** (1) The Secretary of State shall draw up and from time to time revise—

    (a) a panel of persons who

        (i) satisfy the judicial-appointment eligibility condition on a 5-year basis;

        (ii) are advocates or solicitors in Scotland of at least 5 years' standing, and are nominated for the purpose by the Lord Chancellor or the Lord President of the Court of Session, and

    (b) a panel of persons who are experienced in insolvency matters;

and the members of the Tribunal shall be selected from those panels in accordance with this Schedule.

(2) The power to revise the panels includes power to terminate a person's membership of either of them, and is accordingly to that extent subject to section 7 of the Tribunals and Inquiries Act 1992 (which makes it necessary to obtain the concurrence of the Lord Chancellor and the Lord President of the Court of Session to dismissals in certain cases).

### *Remuneration of members*

**2** The Secretary of State may out of money provided by Parliament pay to members of the Tribunal such remuneration as he may with the approval of the Treasury determine; and such expenses of the Tribunal as the Secretary of State and the Treasury may approve shall be defrayed by the Secretary of State out of money so provided.

### *Sittings of Tribunal*

**3** (1) For the purposes of carrying out their functions in relation to any cases referred to them, the Tribunal may sit either as a single tribunal or in two or more divisions.

(2) The functions of the Tribunal in relation to any case referred to them shall be exercised by three members consisting of—

    (a) a chairman selected by the Secretary of State from the panel drawn up under paragraph 1(1)(a) above, and

    (b) two other members selected by the Secretary of State from the panel drawn up under paragraph 1(1)(b).

### *Procedure of Tribunal*

**4** (1) Any investigation by the Tribunal shall be so conducted as to afford a reasonable opportunity for representations to be made to the Tribunal by or on behalf of the person whose case is the subject of the investigation.

(2) For the purposes of any such investigation, the Tribunal—

    (a) may be summons require any person to attend, at such time and place as is specified in the summons, to give evidence or to produce any books, papers and other records in his possession or under his control which the Tribunal consider it necessary for the purposes of the investigation to examine, and

    (b) may take evidence on oath, and for the purpose administer oaths, or may, instead of administering an oath, require the person examined to make and subscribe a declaration of the truth of the matter respecting which he is examined;

but no person shall be required, in obedience to such a summons, to go more than ten miles from his place of residence, unless the necessary expenses of his attendance are paid or tendered to him.

(3) Every person who—

    (a) without reasonable excuse fails to attend in obedience to a summons issued under this paragraph, or refuses to give evidence, or

    (b) intentionally alters, suppresses, conceals or destroys or refuses to produce any document which he may be required to produce for the purpose of an investigation by the Tribunal,

is liable to a fine.

(4) Subject to the provisions of this paragraph, the Secretary of State may make rules for regulating the procedure on any investigation by the Tribunal.

(5) In their application to Scotland, sub-paragraphs (2) and (3) above have effect as if for any reference to a summons there were substituted a reference to a notice in writing.

# SCHEDULE 8

## PROVISIONS CAPABLE OF INCLUSION IN COMPANY INSOLVENCY RULES

### *Courts*

**1** Provision for supplementing, in relation to the insolvency or winding up of companies, any provision made by or under section 117 of this Act (jurisdiction in relation to winding up).

**2** (1) Provision for regulating the practice and procedure of any court exercising jurisdiction for the purposes of Parts I to VII of this Act or the Companies Act so far as relating to, and to matters connected with or arising out of, the insolvency or winding up of companies, being any provision that could be made by rules of court.

(2) Rules made by virtue of this paragraph about the consequence of failure to comply with practice or procedure may, in particular, include provision about the termination of administration.

### *Notices, etc.*

**3** Provision requiring notice of any proceedings in connection with or arising out of the insolvency or winding up of a company to be given or published in the manner prescribed by the rules.

**4** Provision with respect to the form, manner of serving, contents and proof of any petition, application, order, notice, statement or other document required to be presented, made, given, published or prepared under any enactment or subordinate legislation relating to, or to matters connected with or arising out of, the insolvency or winding up of companies.

**5** Provision specifying the persons to whom any notice is to be given.

### *Registration of voluntary arrangements*

**6** Provision for the registration of voluntary arrangements approved under Part I of this Act, including provision for the keeping and inspection of a register.

### *Provisional liquidator*

**7** Provision as to the manner in which a provisional liquidator appointed under section 135 is to carry out his functions.

### *Conduct of insolvency*

**8** Provision with respect to the certification of any person as, and as to the proof that a person is, the liquidator, administrator or administrative receiver of a company.

**9** The following provision with respect to meetings of a company's creditors, contributories or members—

    (a) provision as to the manner of summoning a meeting (including provision as to how any power to require a meeting is to be exercised, provision as to the manner of determining the value of any debt or contribution for the purposes of any such power and provision making the exercise of any such power subject to the deposit of a sum sufficient to cover the expenses likely to be incurred in summoning and holding a meeting);

    (b) provision specifying the time and place at which a meeting may be held and the period of notice required for a meeting;

    (c) provision as to the procedure to be followed at a meeting (including the manner in which decisions may be reached by a meeting and the manner in which the value of any vote at a meeting is to be determined);

    (d) provision for requiring a person who is or has been an officer of the company to attend a meeting;

    (e) provision creating, in the prescribed circumstances, a presumption that a meeting has been duly summoned and held;

    (f) provision as to the manner of proving the decisions of a meeting.

**10** (1) Provision as to the functions, membership and proceedings of a committee established under section 49, 68, 101, 141 or 142 of, or paragraph 57 of Schedule B1 to, this Act.

(2) The following provision with respect to the establishment of a committee under section 101, 141 or 142 of this Act, that is to say—

    (a) provision for resolving differences between a meeting of the company's creditors and a meeting of its contributories or members;

    (b) provision authorising the establishment of the committee without a meeting of contributories in a case where a company is being wound up on grounds including its inability to pay its debts; and

    (c) provision modifying the requirements of this Act with respect to the establishment of the committee in a case where a winding-up order has been made immediately upon the discharge of an administration order.

**11** Provision as to the manner in which any requirement that may be imposed on a person under any of Parts I to VII of this Act by the official receiver, the liquidator, administrator or administrative receiver of a company or a special manager appointed under section 177 is to be so imposed.

**12** Provision as to the debts that may be proved in a winding up, as to the manner and conditions of proving a debt and as to the manner and expenses of establishing the value of any debt or security.

**13** Provision with respect to the manner of the distribution of the property of a company that is being wound up, including provision with respect to unclaimed funds and dividends.

**14** Provision which, with or without modifications, applies in relation to the winding up of companies any enactment contained in Parts VIII to XI of this Act or in the Bankruptcy (Scotland) Act 1985.

**14A** Provision about the application of section 176A of this Act which may include, in particular—

    (a) provision enabling a receiver to institute winding up proceedings;

    (b) provision requiring a receiver to institute winding up proceedings.

### Administration

**14B** Provision which—

    (a) applies in relation to administration, with or without modifications, a provision of Parts IV to VII of this Act, or

    (b) serves a purpose in relation to administration similar to a purpose that may be served by the rules in relation to winding up by virtue of a provision of this Schedule.

### Financial provisions

**15** Provision as to the amount, or manner of determining the amount, payable to the liquidator, administrator or administrative receiver of a company or a special manager appointed under section 177, by way of remuneration for the carrying out of functions in connection with or arising out of the insolvency or winding up of a company.

**16** Provision with respect to the manner in which moneys received by the liquidator of a company in the course of carrying out his functions as such are to be invested or otherwise handled and with respect to the payment of interest on sums which, in pursuance of rules made by virtue of this paragraph, have been paid into the Insolvency Services Account.

**17** Provision as to the fees, costs, charges and other expenses that may be treated as the expenses of a winding up.

**18** Provision as to the fees, costs, charges and other expenses that may be treated as properly incurred by the administrator or administrative receiver of a company.

**19** Provision as to the fees, costs, charges and other expenses that may be incurred for any of the purposes of Part I of this Act or in the administration of any voluntary arrangement approved under that Part.

### Information and records

**20** Provision requiring registrars and other officers of courts having jurisdiction in England and Wales in relation to, or to matters connected with or arising out of, the insolvency or winding up of companies—

    (a) to keep books and other records with respect to the exercise of that jurisdiction, and

    (b) to make returns to the Secretary of State of the business of those courts.

**21** Provision requiring a creditor, member or contributory, or such a committee as is mentioned in paragraph 10 above, to be supplied (on payment in prescribed cases of the prescribed fee) with such information and with copies of such documents as may be prescribed.

**22** Provision as to the manner in which public examinations under section 133 and 134 of this Act and proceedings under sections 236 and 237 are to be conducted, as to the circumstances in which records of such examinations or proceedings are to be made available to prescribed persons and as to the costs of such examinations and proceedings.

**23** Provision imposing requirements with respect to—

    (a) the preparation and keeping by the liquidator, administrator or administrative receiver of a company, or by the supervisor of a voluntary arrangement approved under Part I of this Act, of prescribed books, accounts and other records;

    (b) the production of those books, accounts and records for inspection by prescribed persons;

    (c) the auditing of accounts kept by the liquidator, administrator or administrative receiver of a company, or the supervisor of such a voluntary arrangement; and

    (d) the issue by the administrator or administrative receiver of a company of such a certificate as is mentioned in section 22(3)(b) of the Value Added Tax Act 1983 (refund of tax in cases of bad debts) and the supply of copies of the certificate to creditors of the company.

24 Provision requiring the person who is the supervisor of a voluntary arrangement approved under Part I, when it appears to him that the voluntary arrangement has been fully implemented and that nothing remains to be done by him under the arrangement—

(a) to give notice of that fact to persons bound by the voluntary arrangement, and

(b) to report to those persons on the carrying out of the functions conferred on the supervisor of the arrangement.

25 Provision as to the manner in which the liquidator of a company is to act in relation to the books, papers and other records of the company, including provision authorising their disposal.

26 Provision imposing requirements in connection with the carrying out of functions under section 7(3) of the Company Directors Disqualification Act 1986 (including, in particular, requirements with respect to the making of periodic returns).

### General

27 Provision conferring power on the Secretary of State or the Treasury to make regulations with respect to so much of any matter that may be provided for in the rules as relates to the carrying out of the functions of the liquidator, administrator or administrative receiver of a company.

28 Provision conferring a discretion on the court.

29 Provision conferring power on the court to make orders for the purpose of securing compliance with obligations imposed by or under section 47, 66, 131, 143(2) or 235 of, or paragraph 47 of Schedule B1 to, this Act or section 7(4) of the Company Directors Disqualification Act 1986.

30 Provision making non-compliance with any of the rules a criminal offence.

31 Provision making different provision for different cases or descriptions of cases, including different provisions for different areas.

# SCHEDULE 9

# PROVISIONS CAPABLE OF INCLUSION IN INDIVIDUAL INSOLVENCY RULES

### Courts

1 Provision with respect to the arrangement and disposition of the business under Parts 7A to 11 of this Act of courts having jurisdiction for the purpose of those Parts, including provision for the allocation of proceedings under those Parts to particular courts and for the transfer of such proceedings from one court to another.

2 Provision for enabling a registrar in bankruptcy of the High Court or a registrar of a county court having jurisdiction for the purposes of those Parts to exercise such of the jurisdiction conferred for those purposes on the High Court or, as the case may be, that county court as may be prescribed.

3 Provision for regulating the practice and procedure of any court exercising jurisdiction for the purposes of those Parts, being any provision that could be made by rules of court.

4 Provision conferring rights of audience, in courts exercising jurisdiction for the purposes of those Parts, on the official receiver and on solicitors.

### Notices, etc.

5 Provision requiring notice of any proceedings under Parts 7A to 11 of this Act or of any matter relating to or arising out of a proposal under Part VIII or a bankruptcy to be given or published in the prescribed manner.

6 Provision with respect to the form, manner of serving, contents and proof of any petition, application, order, notice, statement or other document required to be presented, made, given, published or prepared under any enactment contained in Parts 7A to 11 or subordinate legislation under those Parts or Part XV (including provision requiring prescribed matters to be verified by affidavit).

7 Provision specifying the persons to whom any notice under Parts VIII to XI is to be given.

### Debt relief orders

7A. Provision as to the manner in which the official receiver is to carry out his functions under Part 7A.

7B. Provision as to the manner in which any requirement that may be imposed by the official receiver on a person under Part 7A is to take effect.

7C. Provision modifying the application of Part 7A in relation to an individual who has died at a time when a moratorium period under a debt relief order applies in relation to him.

### Debt relief restrictions orders and undertakings

7D. Provision about debt relief restrictions orders, interim orders and undertakings, including provision about evidence.

### Register of debt relief orders and debt relief restrictions orders etc

**7E** Provision about the register required to be maintained by section 251W and the information to be contained in it, including provision

    (a) enabling the amalgamation of the register with another register;

    (b) enabling inspection of the register by the public.

### Registration of voluntary arrangements

**8** Provision for the registration of voluntary arrangements approved under Part VIII of this Act, including provision for the keeping and inspection of a register.

### Official receiver acting on voluntary arrangement

**8A** Provision about the official receiver acting as nominee or supervisor in relation to a voluntary arrangement under Part VIII of this Act, including—

    (a) provision requiring the official receiver to act in specified circumstances;

    (b) provision about remuneration;

    (c) provision prescribing terms or conditions to be treated as forming part of a voluntary arrangement in relation to which the official receiver acts as nominee or supervisor;

    (d) provision enabling those terms or conditions to be varied or excluded, in specified circumstances or subject to specified conditions, by express provision in an arrangement.

### Interim receiver

**9** Provision as to the manner in which an interim receiver appointed under section 286 is to carry out his functions, including any such provision as is specified in relation to the trustee of a bankrupt's estate in paragraph 21 or 27 below.

### Receiver or manager

**10** Provision as to the manner in which the official receiver is to carry out his functions as receiver or manager of a bankrupt's estate under section 287, including any such provision as is specified in relation to the trustee of a bankrupt's estate in paragraph 21 or 27 below.

### Administration of individual insolvency

**11** Provision with respect to the certification of the appointment of any person as trustee of a bankrupt's estate and as to the proof of that appointment.

**12** The following provision with respect to meetings of creditors—

    (a) provision as to the manner of summoning a meeting (including provision as to how any power to require a meeting is to be exercised, provision as to the manner of determining the value of any debt for the purposes of any such power and provision making the exercise of any such power subject to the deposit of a sum sufficient to cover the expenses likely to be incurred in summoning and holding a meeting);

    (b) provision specifying the time and place at which a meeting may be held and the period of notice required for a meeting;

    (c) provision as to the procedure to be followed at such a meeting (including the manner in which decisions may be reached by a meeting and the manner in which the value of any vote at a meeting is to be determined);

    (d) provision for requiring a bankrupt or debtor to attend a meeting;

    (e) provision creating, in the prescribed circumstances, a presumption that a meeting has been duly summoned and held; and

    (f) provision as to the manner of proving the decisions of a meeting.

**13** Provision as to the functions, membership and proceedings of a creditors' committee established under section 301.

**14** Provision as to the manner in which any requirement that may be imposed on a person under Parts VIII to XI of this Act by the official receiver, the trustee of a bankrupt's estate or a special manager appointed under section 370 is to be so imposed and, in the case of any requirement imposed under section 305(3)(information etc. to be given by the trustee to the official receiver), provision conferring power on the court to make orders for the purpose of securing compliance with that requirement.

**15** Provision as to the manner in which any requirement imposed by virtue of section 310(3)(compliance with income payments order) is to take effect.

**16** Provision as to the terms and conditions that may be included in a charge under section 313 (dwelling house forming part of bankrupt's estate).

**17** Provision as to the debts that may be proved in any bankruptcy, as to the manner and conditions of proving a debt and as to the manner and expenses of establishing the value of any debt or security.

**18** Provision with respect to the manner of the distribution of a bankrupt's estate, including provision with respect to unclaimed funds and dividends.

**19** Provision modifying the application of Parts VIII to XI of this Act in relation to a debtor or bankrupt who has died.

### Financial provisions

**20** Provision as to the amount, or manner of determining the amount, payable to an interim receiver, the trustee of a bankrupt's estate or a special manager appointed under section 370 by way of remuneration for the performance of functions in connection with or arising out of the bankruptcy of any person.

**21** Provision with respect to the manner in which moneys received by the trustee of a bankrupt's estate in the course of carrying out his functions as such are to be invested or otherwise handled and with respect to the payment of interest on sums which, in pursuance of rules made by virtue of this paragraph, have been paid into the Insolvency Services Account.

**22** Provision as to the fees, costs, charges and other expenses that may be treated as the expenses of a bankruptcy.

**23** Provision as to the fees, costs, charges and other expenses that may be incurred for any of the purposes of Part VIII of this Act or in the administration of any voluntary arrangement approved under that Part.

### Information and records

**24** Provision requiring registrars and other officers of courts having jurisdiction for the purposes of Parts VIII to XI—

    (a) to keep books and other records with respect to the exercise of that jurisdiction and of jurisdiction under the Deeds of Arrangement Act 1914, and

    (b) to make returns to the Secretary of State of the business of those courts.

**25** Provision requiring a creditor or a committee established under section 301 to be supplied (on payment in prescribed cases of the prescribed fee) with such information and with copies of such documents as may be prescribed.

**26** Provision as to the manner in which public examinations under section 290 and proceedings under sections 366 to 368 are to be conducted, as to the circumstances in which records of such examinations and proceedings are to be made available to prescribed persons and as to the costs of such examinations and proceedings.

**27** Provision imposing requirements with respect to—

    (a) the preparation and keeping by the trustee of a bankrupt's estate, or the supervisor of a voluntary arrangement approved under Part VIII, of prescribed books, accounts and other records;

    (b) the production of those books, accounts and records for inspection by prescribed persons; and

    (c) the auditing of accounts kept by the trustee of a bankrupt's estate or the supervisor of such a voluntary arrangement.

**28** Provision requiring the person who is the supervisor of a voluntary arrangement approved under Part VIII, when it appears to him that the voluntary arrangement has been fully implemented and that nothing remains to be done by him under it—

    (a) to give notice of that fact to persons bound by the voluntary arrangement, and

    (b) to report to those persons on the carrying out of the functions conferred on the supervisor of it.

**29** Provision as to the manner in which the trustee of a bankrupt's estate is to act in relation to the books, papers and other records of the bankrupt, including provision authorising their disposal.

### Bankruptcy restrictions orders and undertakings

**29A** Provision about bankruptcy restrictions orders, interim orders and undertakings, including—

    (a) provision about evidence;

    (b) provision enabling the amalgamation of the register mentioned in paragraph 12 of Schedule 4A with another register;

    (c) provision enabling inspection of that register by the public.

### General

**30** Provision conferring power on the Secretary of State to make regulations with respect to so much of any matter that may be provided for in the rules as relates to the carrying out of the functions of an interim receiver appointed under section 286, of the official receiver while acting as a receiver or manager under section 287 or of a trustee of a bankrupt's estate.

**31** Provision conferring a discretion on the court.

**32** Provision making non-compliance with any of the rule a criminal offence.

**33** Provision making different provision for different cases including different provision for different areas.

# SCHEDULE 10

## PUNISHMENT OF OFFENCES UNDER THIS ACT

| Section of Act creating offence | General nature of offence | Mode of prosecution | Punishment | Daily default fine (where applicable) |
|---|---|---|---|---|
| 6A(1). | False representation or fraud for purpose of obtaining members' or creditors' approval of proposed voluntary arrangement. | 1. On indictment. | 7 years or a fine, or both. | |
| | | 2. Summary. | 6 months or the statutory maximum, or both. | |
| ... | | | | |
| 30 | Body corporate acting as receiver. | 1. On indictment | A fine. | |
| | | 2. Summary. | The statutory maximum. | |
| 31 | Bankrupt or person in respect of whom a debt relief order is made acting as receiver or manager. | 1. On indictment | 2 years or a fine, or both. | |
| | | 2. Summary. | 6 months or the statutory maximum, or both. | |
| 38(5) | Receiver failing to deliver accounts to registrar. | Summary. | One-fifth of the statutory maximum. | One-fiftieth of the statutory maximum. |
| 39(2) | Company and others failing to state in correspondence that receiver appointed. | Summary. | One-fifth of the statutory maximum. | |
| 43(6) | Administrative receiver failing to file office copy of order permitting disposal of charged property. | Summary. | One-fifth of the statutory maximum. | One-fiftieth of the statutory maximum. |
| 45(5) | Administrative receiver failing to file notice of vacation of office. | Summary. | One-fifth of the statutory maximum. | One-fiftieth of the statutory maximum. |
| 46(4) | Administrative receiver failing to give notice of his appointment. | Summary. | One-fifth of the statutory maximum. | One-fiftieth of the statutory maximum. |
| 47(6) | Failure to comply with provisions relating to statement of affairs, where administrative receiver appointed. | 1. On indictment | A fine. | One-tenth of the statutory maximum. |
| | | 2. Summary. | The statutory maximum. | |
| 48(8) | Administrative receiver failing to comply with requirements as to his report. | Summary. | One-fifth of the statutory maximum. | One-fiftieth of the statutory maximum. |
| 51(4) | Body corporate or Scottish firm acting as receiver. | 1. On indictment | A fine. | |
| | | 2. Summary. | The statutory maximum. | |
| 51(5) | Undischarged bankrupt acting as receiver (Scotland). | 1. On indictment | 2 years or a fine, or both. | |
| | | 2. Summary. | 6 months or the statutory maximum, or both. | |
| 53(2) | Failing to deliver to registrar copy of instrument of appointment of receiver. | Summary. | One-fifth of the statutory maximum. | One-fiftieth of the statutory maximum. |
| 54(3) | Failing to deliver to registrar the court's interlocutor appointing receiver. | Summary. | One-fifth of the statutory maximum. | One-fiftieth of the statutory maximum. |
| 61(7) | Receiver failing to send to registrar certified copy of court order authorising disposal of charged property. | Summary. | One-fifth of the statutory maximum. | One-fiftieth of the statutory maximum. |
| 62(5) | Failing to give notice to registrar of cessation or removal of receiver. | Summary. | One-fifth of the statutory maximum. | One-fiftieth of the statutory maximum. |

| Section of Act creating offence | General nature of offence | Mode of prosecution | Punishment | Daily default fine (where applicable) |
|---|---|---|---|---|
| 64(2) | Company and others failing to state on correspondence etc. that receiver appointed. | Summary. | One-fifth of the statutory maximum. | |
| 65(4) | Receiver failing to send or publish notice of his appointment. | Summary. | One-fifth of the statutory maximum. | One-fiftieth of the statutory maximum. |
| 66(6) | Failing to comply with provisions concerning statement of affairs, where receiver appointed. | 1. On indictment<br>2. Summary. | A fine.<br>The statutory maximum. | One-tenth of the statutory maximum. |
| 67(8) | Receiver failing to comply with requirements as to his report. | Summary. | One-fifth of the statutory maximum. | One-fiftieth of the statutory maximum. |
| 85(2) | Company failing to give notice in Gazette of resolution for voluntary winding up. | Summary. | One-fifth of the statutory maximum. | One-fiftieth of the statutory maximum. |
| 89(4) | Director making statutory declaration of company's solvency without reasonable grounds for his opinion. | 1. On indictment<br>2. Summary. | 2 years or a fine, or both.<br>6 months or the statutory maximum. | |
| 89(6) | Declaration under section 89 not delivered to registrar within prescribed time. | Summary. | One-fifth of the statutory maximum. | One-fiftieth of the statutory maximum. |
| 93(3) | Liquidator failing to summon general meeting of company at each year's end. | Summary. | One-fifth of the statutory maximum. | |
| 94(4) | Liquidator failing to send a registrar a copy of account of winding up and return of final meeting. | Summary. | One-fifth of the statutory maximum. | One-fiftieth of the statutory maximum. |
| 94(6) | Liquidator failing to call final meeting. | Summary. | One-fifth of the statutory maximum. | |
| 95(8) | Liquidator failing to comply with s. 95, where company insolvent. | Summary. | The statutory maximum. | |
| 98(6) | Company failing to comply with s. 98 in respect of summoning and giving notice of creditors' meeting. | 1. On indictment<br>2. Summary. | A fine.<br>The statutory maximum. | |
| 99(3) | Directors failing to attend and lay statement in prescribed from before creditors' meeting. | 1. On indictment<br>2. Summary. | A fine.<br>The statutory maximum. | |
| 105(3) | Liquidator failing to summon company general meeting and creditors' meeting at each year's end. | Summary. | One-fifth of the statutory maximum. | |
| 106(4) | Liquidator failing to send to registrar account of winding up and return of final meetings. | Summary. | One-fifth of the statutory maximum. | One-fiftieth of the statutory maximum. |
| 106(6) | Liquidator failing to call final meeting of company or creditors. | Summary. | One-fifth of the statutory maximum. | |
| 109(2) | Liquidator failing to publish notice of his appointment. | Summary. | One-fifth of the statutory maximum. | One-fiftieth of the statutory maximum. |
| 114(4) | Directors exercising powers in breach of s. 114, where no liquidator. | Summary. | The statutory maximum. | |
| 131(7) | Failing to comply with requirements as to statement of affairs, where liquidator appointed. | 1. On indictment<br>2. Summary. | A fine.<br>The statutory maximum. | One-tenth of the statutory maximum. |

| Section of Act creating offence | General nature of offence | Mode of prosecution | Punishment | Daily default fine (where applicable) |
|---|---|---|---|---|
| 164 | Giving, offering etc. corrupt inducement affecting appointment of liquidator. | 1. On indictment<br>2. Summary. | A fine.<br>The statutory maximum. | |
| 166(7) | Liquidator failing to comply with requirements of s. 166 in creditors' voluntary winding up. | Summary. | The statutory maximum. | |
| 188(2) | Default in compliance with s. 188 as to notification that company being wound up. | Summary. | One-fifth of the statutory maximum. | |
| 192(2) | Liquidator failing to notify registrar as to progress of winding up. | Summary. | One-fifth of the statutory maximum. | One-fiftieth of the statutory maximum. |
| 201(4) | Failing to deliver to registrar office copy of court order deferring dissolution. | Summary. | One-fifth of the statutory maximum. | One-fiftieth of the statutory maximum. |
| 203(6) | Failing to deliver to registrar copy of directions or result of appeal under s. 203. | Summary. | One-fifth of the statutory maximum. | One-fiftieth of the statutory maximum. |
| 204(7) | Liquidator failing to deliver to registrar copy of court order for early dissolution. | Summary. | One-fifth of the statutory maximum. | One-fiftieth of the statutory maximum. |
| 204(8) | Failing to deliver to registrar copy of court order deferring early dissolution. | Summary. | One-fifth of the statutory maximum. | One-fiftieth of the statutory maximum. |
| 205(7) | Failing to deliver to registrar copy of Secretary of State's directions or court order deferring dissolution. | Summary. | One-fifth of the statutory maximum. | One-fiftieth of the statutory maximum. |
| 206(1) | Fraud etc. in anticipation of winding up. | 1. On indictment<br>2. Summary. | 7 years or a fine, or both.<br>6 months or the statutory maximum, or both. | |
| 206(2) | Privity to fraud in anticipation of winding up; fraud, or privity to fraud, after commencement of winding up. | 1. On indictment<br>2. Summary. | 7 years or a fine, or both.<br>6 months or the statutory maximum, or both. | |
| 206(5) | Knowingly taking in pawn or pledge, or otherwise receiving, company property. | 1. On indictment<br>2. Summary. | 7 years or a fine, or both.<br>6 months or the statutory maximum, or both. | |
| 207 | Officer of company entering into transaction in fraud of company's creditors. | 1. On indictment<br>2. Summary. | 2 years or a fine, or both.<br>6 months or the statutory maximum, or both. | |
| 208 | Officer of company misconducting himself in course of winding up. | 1. On indictment<br>2. Summary. | 7 years or a fine, or both.<br>6 months or the statutory maximum, or both. | |
| 209 | Officer or contributory destroying, falsifying, etc. company's books. | 1. On indictment<br>2. Summary. | 7 years or a fine, or both.<br>6 months or the statutory maximum, or both. | |
| 210 | Officer of company making material omission from statement relating to company's affairs. | 1. On indictment<br>2. Summary. | 7 years or a fine, or both.<br>6 months or the statutory maximum, or both. | |
| 211 | False representation or fraud for purpose of obtaining creditors' consent to an agreement in connection with winding up. | 1. On indictment<br>2. Summary. | 7 years or a fine, or both.<br>6 months or the statutory maximum, or both. | |
| 216(4) | Contravening restrictions on re-use of name of company in insolvent liquidation. | 1. On indictment<br>2. Summary. | 2 years or a fine, or both.<br>6 months or the statutory maximum, or both. | |
| 235(5) | Failing to co-operate with office-holder. | 1. On indictment<br>2. Summary. | A fine.<br>The statutory maximum | One-tenth of the statutory maximum. |

| Section of Act creating offence | General nature of offence | Mode of prosecution | Punishment | Daily default fine (where applicable) |
|---|---|---|---|---|
| 251O(1) | False representations or omissions in making an application for a debt relief order. | 1. On indictment<br>2. Summary | 7 years or a fine, or both.<br>12 months or the statutory maximum, or both. | |
| 251O(2)(a) | Failing to comply with duty in connection with an application for a debt relief order. | 1. On indictment<br>2. Summary | 2 years or a fine, or both.<br>12 months or the statutory maximum, or both. | |
| 251O(2)(b) | False representations or omissions in connection with duty in relation to an application for a debt relief order. | 1. On indictment<br>2. Summary | 7 years or a fine, or both.<br>12 months or the statutory maximum, or both. | |
| 251O(4)(a) | Failing to comply with duty in connection with a debt relief order. | 1. On indictment<br>2. Summary | 2 years or a fine, or both.<br>12 months or the statutory maximum, or both. | |
| 251O(4)(b) | False representations or omissions in connection with a duty in relation to a debt relief order. | 1. On indictment<br>2. Summary | 7 years or a fine, or both.<br>12 months or the statutory maximum, or both. | |
| 251P(1) | Failing to deliver books, records and papers to official receiver, concealing or destroying them or making false entries in them by person in respect of whom a debt relief order is made. | 1. On indictment<br>2. Summary | 7 years or a fine, or both.<br>12 months or the statutory maximum, or both. | |
| 251P(2) | Person in respect of whom debt relief order is made doing anything falling within paragraphs (c) to (e) of section 251P(1) during the period of 12 months ending with the application date or doing anything falling within paragraphs (b) to (e) of section 251P(1) after that date but before the effective date. | 1. On indictment<br>2. Summary | 7 years or a fine, or both.<br>12 months or the statutory maximum, or both. | |
| 251Q(1) | Fraudulent disposal of property by person in respect of whom a debt relief order is made. | 1. On indictment<br>2. Summary | 2 years or a fine, or both.<br>12 months or the statutory maximum, or both. | |
| 251R(1) | Disposal of property that is not paid for by person in respect of whom a debt relief order is made. | 1. On indictment<br>2. Summary | 7 years or a fine, or both.<br>12 months or the statutory maximum, or both. | |
| 251R(2) | Obtaining property in respect of which money is owed by a person in respect of whom a debt relief order is made. | 1. On indictment<br>2. Summary | 7 years or a fine, or both.<br>12 months or the statutory maximum, or both. | |
| 251S(1) | Person in respect of whom a debt relief order is made obtaining credit or engaging in business without disclosing his status or name. | 1. On indictment<br>2. Summary | 2 years or a fine, or both.<br>12 months or the statutory maximum, or both.' | |
| 262A(1). | False representation or fraud for purpose of obtaining creditors' approval of proposed voluntary arrangement. | 1. On indictment<br>2. Summary. | 7 years or a fine, or both.<br>6 months or the statutory maximum, or both. | |
| 353(1) | Bankrupt failing to disclose property or disposals to official receiver or trustee. | 1. On indictment<br>2. Summary. | 7 years or a fine, or both.<br>6 months or the statutory maximum, or both. | |

| Section of Act creating offence | General nature of offence | Mode of prosecution | Punishment | Daily default fine (where applicable) |
|---|---|---|---|---|
| 354(1) | Bankrupt failing to deliver property to, or concealing property from, official receiver or trustee. | 1. On indictment<br>2. Summary. | 7 years or a fine, or both.<br>6 months or the statutory maximum, or both. | |
| 354(2) | Bankrupt removing property which he is required to deliver to official receiver or trustee. | 1. On indictment<br>2. Summary. | 7 years or a fine, or both.<br>6 months or the statutory maximum, or both. | |
| 354(3) | Bankrupt failing to account for loss of substantial part of property. | 1. On indictment<br>2. Summary. | 2 years or a fine, or both.<br>6 months or the statutory maximum, or both. | |
| 355(1) | Bankrupt failing to deliver books, papers and records to official receiver or trustee. | 1. On indictment<br>2. Summary. | 7 years or a fine, or both.<br>6 months or the statutory maximum, or both. | |
| 355(2) | Bankrupt concealing, destroying etc. books, papers or records, or making false entries in them. | 1. On indictment<br>2. Summary. | 7 years or a fine, or both.<br>6 months or the statutory maximum, or both. | |
| 355(3) | Bankrupt disposing of, or altering, books, papers or records relating to his estate or affairs. | 1. On indictment<br>2. Summary. | 7 years or a fine, or both.<br>6 months or the statutory maximum, or both. | |
| 356(1) | Bankrupt making material omission in statement relating to his affairs. | 1. On indictment<br>2. Summary. | 7 years or a fine, or both.<br>6 months or the statutory maximum, or both. | |
| 356(2) | Bankrupt making false statement, or failing to inform trustee, where false debt proved. | 1. On indictment<br>2. Summary. | 7 ears or a fine, or both.<br>6 months or the statutory maximum, or both. | |
| 357 | Bankrupt fraudulently disposing or property. | 1. On indictment<br>2. Summary. | 2 years or a fine, or both.<br>6 months or the statutory maximum, or both. | |
| 358 | Bankrupt absconding with property he is required to deliver to official receiver or trustee. | 1. On indictment<br>2. Summary. | 2 years or a fine, or both.<br>6 months or the statutory maximum, or both. | |
| 359(1) | Bankrupt disposing of property obtained on credit and not paid for. | 1. On indictment<br>2. Summary. | 7 years or a fine, or both.<br>6 months or the statutory maximum, or both. | |
| 359(2) | Obtaining property in respect of which money is owed by a bankrupt. | 1. On indictment<br>2. Summary. | 7 years or a fine, or both.<br>6 months or the statutory maximum, or both. | |
| 360(1) | Bankrupt obtaining credit or engaging in business without disclosing his status or name in which he was made bankrupt. | 1. On indictment<br>2. Summary. | 2 years or a fine, or both.<br>6 months or the statutory maximum, or both. | |
| 360(3) | Person made bankrupt in Scotland or Northern Ireland obtaining credit, etc. in England and Wales. | 1. On indictment<br>2. Summary. | 2 years or a fine, or both.<br>6 months or the statutory maximum, or both. | |
| 389 | Acting as insolvency practitioner when not qualified. | 1. On indictment<br>2. Summary. | 2 years or a fine, or both.<br>6 months or the statutory maximum, or both. | |
| 429(5) | Contravening s. 429 in respect of disabilities imposed by county court on revocation of administration order. | 1. On indictment<br>2. Summary. | 2 years or a fine, or both.<br>6 months or the statutory maximum, or both. | |
| Sch A1, para 9(2). | Directors failing to notify nominee of beginning of moratorium. | 1. On indictment<br>2. Summary. | 2 years or a fine, or both.<br>6 months or the statutory maximum, or both. | |
| Sch A1, para 10(3). | Nominee failing to advertise or notify beginning of moratorium. | Summary. | One-fifth of the statutory maximum. | |

| Section of Act creating offence | General nature of offence | Mode of prosecution | Punishment | Daily default fine (where applicable) |
|---|---|---|---|---|
| Sch A1, para 11(2). | Nominee failing to advertise or notify end of moratorium. | Summary. | One-fifth of the statutory maximum. | |
| Sch A1, para 16(2). | Company and officers failing to state in correspondence etc. that moratorium in force. | Summary. | One-fifth of the statutory maximum. | |
| Sch A1, para 17(3)(a). | Company obtaining credit without disclosing existence of moratorium. | 1. On indictment<br>2. Summary. | A fine.<br>The statutory maximum. | |
| Sch A1, para 17(3)(b). | Obtaining credit for company without disclosing existence of moratorium. | 1. On indictment<br>2. Summary. | 2 years or a fine, or both.<br>6 months or the statutory maximum, or both. | |
| Sch A1, para 18(3)(a). | Company disposing of property otherwise than in ordinary way of business. | 1. On indictment<br>2. Summary. | A fine.<br>The statutory maximum. | |
| Sch A1, para 18(3)(b). | Authorising or permitting disposal of company property. | 1. On indictment<br>2. Summary. | 2 years or a fine, or both.<br>6 months or the statutory maximum, or both. | |
| Sch A1, para 19(3)(a). | Company making payments in respect of liabilities existing before beginning of moratorium. | 1. On indictment<br>2. Summary. | A fine.<br>The statutory maximum. | |
| Sch A1, para 19(3)(b). | Authorising or permitting such a payment. | 1. On indictment<br>2. Summary. | 2 years or a fine, or both.<br>6 months or the statutory maximum, or both. | |
| Sch A1, para 20(9). | Directors failing to send to registrar office copy of court order permitting disposal of charged property. | Summary. | One-fifth of the statutory maximum. | |
| Sch A1, para 22(1). | Company disposing of charged property. | 1. On indictment<br>2. Summary. | A fine.<br>The statutory maximum. | |
| Sch A1, para 22(2). | Authorising or permitting such a disposal. | 1. On indictment<br>2. Summary. | 2 years or a fine, or both.<br>6 months or the statutory maximum, or both. | |
| Sch A1, para 23(1)(a). | Company entering into market contract, etc. | 1. On indictment<br>2. Summary. | A fine.<br>The statutory maximum. | |
| Sch A1, para 23(1)(b). | Authorising or permitting company to do so. | 1. On indictment<br>2. Summary. | 2 years or a fine, or both.<br>6 months or the statutory maximum, or both. | |
| Sch A1, para 25(6). | Nominee failing to give notice of withdrawal of consent to act. | Summary. | One-fifth of the statutory maximum. | |
| Sch A1, para 34(3). | Nominee failing to give notice of extension of moratorium. | Summary. | One-fifth of the statutory maximum. | |
| Sch A1, para 41(2). | Fraud or privity to fraud in anticipation of moratorium. | 1. On indictment<br>2. Summary. | 7 years or a fine, or both.<br>6 months or the statutory maximum, or both. | |
| Sch A1, para 41(3). | Fraud or privity to fraud in anticipation of moratorium. | 1. On indictment<br>2. Summary. | 7 years or a fine, or both.<br>6 months or the statutory maximum, or both. | |
| Sch A1, para 41(7). | Knowingly taking in pawn or pledge, or otherwise receiving, company property. | 1. On indictment<br>2. Summary. | 7 years or a fine, or both.<br>6 months or the statutory maximum, or both. | |
| Sch A1, para 42(1). | False representation or fraud for purpose of obtaining or extending moratorium. | 1. On indictment<br>2. Summary. | 7 years or a fine, or both.<br>6 months or the statutory maximum, or both. | |

| Section of Act creating offence | General nature of offence | Mode of prosecution | Punishment | Daily default fine (where applicable) |
|---|---|---|---|---|
| Sch B1, para 18(7). | Making false statement in statutory declaration where administrator appointed by holder of floating charge. | 1. On indictment.<br>2. Summary. | 2 years, or a fine or both.<br>6 months, or the statutory maximum or both. | |
| Sch B1, para 20. | Holder of floating charge failing to notify administrator or others of commencement of appointment. | 1. On indictment.<br>2. Summary. | 2 years, or a fine or both.<br>6 months, or the statutory maximum or both. | One-tenth of the statutory maximum. |
| Sch B1, para 27(4). | Making false statement in statutory declaration where appointment of administrator proposed by company or directors. | 1. On indictment.<br>2. Summary. | 2 years, or a fine or both.<br>6 months, or the statutory maximum or both. | |
| Sch B1, para 29(7). | Making false statement in statutory declaration where administrator appointed by company or directors. | 1. On indictment.<br>2. Summary. | 2 years, or a fine or both.<br>6 months, or the statutory maximum or both. | |
| Sch B1, para 32. | Company or directors failing to notify administrator or others of commencement of appointment. | 1. On indictment.<br>2. Summary. | 2 years, or a fine or both.<br>6 months, or the statutory maximum or both. | One-tenth of the statutory maximum. |
| Sch B1, para 45(2). | Administrator, company or officer failing to state in business document that administrator appointed. | Summary. | One-fifth of the statutory maximum. | |
| Sch B1, para 46(9). | Administrator failing to give notice of his appointment. | Summary. | One-fifth of the statutory maximum. | One-fiftieth of the statutory maximum. |
| Sch B1, para 48(4). | Failing to comply with provisions about statement of affairs where administrator appointed. | 1. On indictment.<br>2. Summary. | A fine.<br>The statutory maximum. | One-tenth of the statutory maximum. |
| Sch B1, para 49(7). | Administrator failing to send out statement of his proposals. | Summary. | One-fifth of the statutory maximum. | One-fiftieth of the statutory maximum. |
| Sch B1, para 51(5). | Administrator failing to arrange initial creditors' meeting. | Summary. | One-fifth of the statutory maximum. | One-fiftieth of the statutory maximum. |
| Sch B1, para 53(3). | Administrator failing to report decision taken at initial creditors' meeting. | Summary. | One-fifth of the statutory maximum. | One-fiftieth of the statutory maximum. |
| Sch B1, para 54(7). | Administrator failing to report decision taken at creditors' meeting summoned to consider revised proposal. | Summary. | One-fifth of the statutory maximum. | One-fiftieth of the statutory maximum. |
| Sch B1, para 56(2). | Administrator failing to summon creditors' meeting. | Summary. | One-fifth of the statutory maximum. | One-fiftieth of the statutory maximum. |
| Sch B1, para 71(6). | Administrator failing to file court order enabling disposal of charged property. | Summary. | One-fifth of the statutory maximum. | One-fiftieth of the statutory maximum. |
| Sch B1, para 72(5). | Administrator failing to file court order enabling disposal of hire-purchase property. | Summary. | One-fifth of the statutory maximum. | One-fiftieth of the statutory maximum. |
| Sch B1, para 77(3). | Administrator failing to notify Registrar of Companies of automatic end of administration. | Summary. | One-fifth of the statutory maximum. | One-fiftieth of the statutory maximum. |
| Sch B1, para 78(6). | Administrator failing to give notice of extension by consent of term of office. | Summary. | One-fifth of the statutory maximum. | One-fiftieth of the statutory maximum. |
| Sch B1, para 80(6). | Administrator failing to give notice of termination of administration where objective achieved. | Summary. | One-fifth of the statutory maximum. | One-fiftieth of the statutory maximum. |

| Section of Act creating offence | General nature of offence | Mode of prosecution | Punishment | Daily default fine (where applicable) |
|---|---|---|---|---|
| Sch B1, para 84(9). | Administrator failing to comply with provisions where company moves to dissolution. | Summary. | One-fifth of the statutory maximum. | One-fiftieth of the statutory maximum. |
| Sch B1, para 86(3). | Administrator failing to notify Registrar of Companies where court terminates administration. | Summary. | One-fifth of the statutory maximum. | One-fiftieth of the statutory maximum. |
| Sch B1, para 89(3). | Administrator failing to give notice on ceasing to be qualified. | Summary. | One-fifth of the statutory maximum. | One-fiftieth of the statutory maximum. |
| Sch 7, para 4(3). | Failure to attend and give evidence to Insolvency Practitioners Tribunal; suppressing, concealing, etc. relevant documents.. | Summary. | Level 3 on the standard scale within the meaning given by section 75 of the Criminal Justice Act 1982. | |

# SCHEDULE 11

# TRANSITIONAL PROVISIONS AND SAVINGS

## PART I

## COMPANY INSOLVENCY AND WINDING UP

### *Administration orders*

**1** (1) Where any right to appoint an administrative receiver of a company is conferred by any debentures or floating charge created before the appointed day, the conditions precedent to the exercise of that right are deemed to include the presentation of a petition applying for an administration order to be made in relation to the company.

(2) 'Administrative receiver' here has the meaning assigned by section 251.

### *Receivers and managers (England and Wales)*

**2** (1) In relation to any receiver or manager of a company's property who was appointed before the appointed day, the new law does not apply; and the relevant provisions of the former law continue to have effect.

(2) 'The new law' here means Chapter I of Part III, and Part VI, of this Act; and 'the former law' means the Companies Act and so much of this Act as replaces provisions of that Act (without the amendments in paragraphs 15 to 17 of Schedule 6 to the Insolvency Act 1985, or the associated repeals by that Act), and any provision of the Insolvency Act 1985 which was in force before the appointed day.

(3) This paragraph is without prejudice to the power conferred by this Act under which rules under section 411 may make transitional provision in connection with the coming into force of those rules; and such provision may apply those rules in relation to the receiver or manager of a company's property notwithstanding that he was appointed before the coming into force of the rules or section 411.

### *Receivers (Scotland)*

**3** (1) In relation to any receiver appointed under section 467 of the Companies Act before the appointed day, the new law does not apply and the relevant provisions of the former law continue to have effect.

(2) 'The new law' here means Chapter II of Part III, and Part VI, of this Act; and 'the former law' means the Companies Act and so much of this Act as replaces provisions of that Act (without the amendments in paragraphs 18 to 22 of Schedule 6 to the Insolvency Act 1985 or the associated repeals made by the Act), and any provision of the Insolvency Act 1985 which was in force before the appointed day.

(3) This paragraph is without prejudice to the power conferred by this Act under which rules under section 411 may make transitional provision in connection with the coming into force of those rules; and such provision may apply those rules in relation to a receiver appointed under section 467 notwithstanding that he was appointed before the coming into force of the rules or section 411.

### *Winding up already in progress*

**4** (1) In relation to any winding up which has commenced, or is treated as having commenced, before the appointed day, the new law does not apply, and the former law continues to have effect, subject to the following paragraphs.

(2) 'The new law' here means any provisions in the first Group of Parts of this Act which replace sections 66 to 87 and 89 to 105 of the Insolvency Act 1985; and 'the former law' means Parts XX and XXI of the Companies Act (without the amendments in paragraphs 23 to 52 of Schedule 6 to the Insolvency Act 1985, or the associated repeals made by the Act).

### *Statement of affairs*

**5** (1) Where a winding up by the court in England and Wales has commenced, or is treated as having commenced, before the appointed day, the official receiver or (on appeal from a refusal by him) the court may, at any time on or after that day—

    (a) release a person from an obligation imposed on him by or under section 528 of the Companies Act (statement or affairs), or

    (b) extend the period specified in subsection (6) of that section.

(2) Accordingly, on and after the appointed day, section 528(6) has effect in relation to a winding up to which this paragraph applies with the omission of the words from 'or within' onwards.

### *Provisions relating to liquidator*

**6** (1) This paragraph applies as regards the liquidator in the case of winding up by the court in England and Wales commenced, or treated as having commenced, before the appointed day.

(2) The official receiver may, at any time when he is liquidator of the company, apply to the Secretary of State for the appointment of a liquidator in his (the official receiver's) place; and on any such application the Secretary of State shall either make an appointment or decline to make one.

(3) Where immediately before the appointed day the liquidator of the company has not made an application under section 545 of the Companies Act (release of liquidators), then—

    (a) except where the Secretary of State otherwise directs, sections 146(1) and (2) and 172(8) of this Act apply, and section 545 does not apply, in relation to any liquidator of that company who holds office on or at any time after the appointed day and is not the official receiver;

    (b) section 146(3) applies in relation to the carrying out at any time after that day by any liquidator of the company of any of his functions; and

    (c) a liquidator in relation to whom section 172(8) has effect by virtue of this paragraph has his release with effect from the time specified in section 174(4)(d) of this Act.

(4) Subsection (6) of section 174 of this Act has effect for the purposes of sub-paragraph (3)(c) above as it has for the purposes of that section, but as if the reference to section 212 were to section 631 of the Companies Act.

(5) The liquidator may employ a solicitor to assist him in the carrying out of his functions without the permission of the committee of inspection; but if he does so employ a solicitor he shall inform the committee of inspection that he has done so.

### *Winding up under supervision of the court*

**7** The repeals in Part II of Schedule 10 the Insolvency Act 1985 of references (in the Companies Act and elsewhere) to a winding up under the supervision of the court do not affect the operation of the enactments in which the references are contained in relation to any case in which an order under section 606 of the Companies Act (power to order winding up under supervision) was made before the appointed day.

### *Saving for power to make rules*

**8** (1) Paragraphs 4 to 7 are without prejudice to the power conferred by this Act under which rules made under section 411 may make transitional provision in connection with the coming into force of those rules.

(2) Such provision may apply those rules in relation to a winding up notwithstanding that the winding up commenced, or is treated as having commenced, before the coming into force of the rules or section 411.

### *Setting aside of preferences and other transactions*

**9** (1) Where a provision in Part VI of this Act applies in relation to a winding up or in relation to a case in which an administration order has been made, a preference given, floating charge created or other transaction entered into before the appointed day shall not be set aside under the provision except to the extent that it could have been set aside under the law in force immediately before that day, assuming for this purpose that any relevant administration order had been winding-up order.

(2) The references above to setting aside a preference, floating charge or other transaction include the making of an order which varies or reverses any effect of a preference, floating charge or other transaction.

# PART II

## INDIVIDUAL INSOLVENCY

### *Bankruptcy (general)*

**10** (1) Subject to the following provisions of this Part of this Schedule, so much of this Act as replaces Part III of the Insolvency Act 1985 does not apply in relation to any case in which a petition in bankruptcy was presented, or a receiving order or adjudication in bankruptcy was made, before the appointed day.

(2) In relation to any such case as is mentioned above, the enactments specified in Schedule 8 to that Act, so far as they relate to bankruptcy, and those specified in Parts III and IV of Schedule 10 to that Act, so far as they so relate, have effect without the amendments and repeals specified in those Schedules.

(3) Where any subordinate legislation made under an enactment referred to in sub-paragraph (2) is in force immediately before the appointed day, that subordinate legislation continues to have effect on and after that day in relation to any such case as is mentioned in sub-paragraph (1).

**11** (1) In relation to any such case as is mentioned in paragraph 10(1) the references in any enactment or subordinate legislation to a petition, order or other matter which is provided for under the Bankruptcy Act 1914 and corresponds to a petition, order or other matter provided for under provisions of this Act replacing Part III of the Insolvency Act 1985 continue on and after the appointed day to have effect as references to the petition, order or matter provided for by the Act of 1914; but otherwise those references have effect on and after that day as references to the petition, order or matter provided for by those provisions of this Act.

(2) Without prejudice to sub-paragraph (1), in determining for the purposes of section 279 of this Act (period of bankruptcy) or paragraph 13 below whether any person was an undischarged bankrupt at a time before the appointed day, an adjudication in bankruptcy and an annulment of a bankruptcy under the Act of 1914 are to be taken into account in the same way, respectively, as a bankruptcy order under the provisions of this Act replacing Part III of the Insolvency Act 1985 and the annulment under section 282 of this Act of such an order.

**12** Transactions entered into before the appointed day have effect on and after that day as if references to acts of bankruptcy in the provisions for giving effect to those transactions continued to be references to acts of bankruptcy within the meaning of the Bankruptcy Act 1914, but as if such acts included failure to comply with a statutory demand served under section 268 of this Act.

### *Discharge from old bankruptcy*

**13** (1) Where a person—

(a) was adjudged bankrupt before the appointed day or is adjudged bankrupt on or after that day on a petition presented before that day, and

(b) that person was not an undischarged bankrupt at any time in the period of 15 years ending with the adjudication,

that person is deemed (if not previously discharged) to be discharged from his bankruptcy for the purposes of the Bankruptcy Act 1914 at the end of the discharge period.

(2) Subject to sub-paragraph (3) below, the discharge period for the purposes of this paragraph is—

(a) in the case of a person adjudged bankrupt before the appointed day, the period of 3 years beginning with that day, and

(b) in the case of a person who is adjudged bankrupt on or after that day on a petition presented before that day, the period of 3 years beginning with the date of the adjudication.

(3) Where the court exercising jurisdiction in relation to a bankruptcy to which this paragraph applies is satisfied, on the application of the official receiver, that the bankrupt has failed, or is failing, to comply with any of his obligations under the Bankruptcy Act 1914, any rules made under that Act or any such rules as are mentioned in paragraph 19(1) below, the court may order that the discharge period shall cease to run for such period, or until the fulfillment of such conditions (including a condition requiring the court to be satisfied as to any matter) as may be specified in the order.

### *Provisions relating to trustee*

**14** (1) This paragraph applies as regards the trustee in the case of a person adjudged bankrupt before the appointed day, or adjudged bankrupt on or after that day on a petition presented before that day.

(2) The official receiver may at any time when he is the trustee of the bankrupt's estate apply to the Secretary of State for the appointment of a person as trustee instead of the official receiver; and on any such application the Secretary of State shall either make an appointment or decline to make one.

(3) Where on the appointed day the trustee of a bankrupt's estate has not made an application under section 93 of the Bankruptcy Act 1914 (release of trustee), then—

    (a) except where the Secretary of State otherwise directs, sections 298(8), 304 and 331(1) to (3) of this Act apply, and section 93 of the Act of 1914 does not apply, in relation to any trustee of the bankrupt's estate who holds office on or at any time after the appointed day and is not the official receiver;

    (b) section 331(4) of this Act applies in relation to the carrying out at any time on or after the appointed day by the trustee of the bankrupt's estate of any of his functions; and

    (c) a trustee in relation to whom section 298(8) of this Act has effect by virtue of this paragraph has his release with effect from the time specified in section 299(3)(d).

(4) Subsection (5) of this section 299 has effect for the purposes of sub-paragraph (3)(c) as it has for the purposes of that section 8.

(5) In the application of subsection (3) of section 331 in relation to a case by virtue of this paragraph, the reference in that subsection to section 330(1) has effect as a reference to section 67 of the Bankruptcy Act 1914.

(6) The trustee of the bankrupt's estate may employ a solicitor to assist him in the carrying out of his functions without the permission of the committee of inspection; but if he does so employ a solicitor, he shall inform the committee of inspection that he has done so.

### Copyright

**15** (1) Where a person who is adjudged bankrupt on a petition presented on or after the appointed day is liable, by virtue of a transaction entered into before that day, to pay royalties or a share of the profits to any person in respect of any copyright or interest in copyright comprised in the bankrupt's estate, section 60 of the Bankruptcy Act 1914 (limitation on trustee's powers in relation to copyright) applies in relation to the trustee of that estate as it applies in relation to a trustee in bankruptcy under the Act of 1914.

### Second bankruptcy

**16** (1) Sections 334 and 335 of this Act apply with the following modifications where the earlier bankruptcy (within the meaning of section 334) is a bankruptcy in relation to which the Act of 1914 applies instead of the second Group of Parts in this Act, that is to say—

    (a) references to property vested in the existing trustee under section 307(3) of this Act have effect as references to such property vested in that trustee as was acquired by or devolved on the bankrupt after the commencement (within the meaning of the Act of 1914) of the earlier bankruptcy; and

    (b) references to an order under section 310 of this Act have effect as references to an order under section 51 of the Act of 1914.

(2) Section 39 of the Act of 1914 (second bankruptcy) does not apply where a person is an undischarged bankrupt under that Act is adjudged bankrupt under this Act.

### Setting aside of preferences and other transactions

**17** (1) A performance given, assignment made or other transaction entered into before the appointed day shall not be set aside under any of sections 339 to 344 of this Act except to the extent that it could have been set aside under the law in force immediately before that day.

(2) References in sub-paragraph (1) to setting aside a preference, assignment or other transaction include the making of any order which varies or reverses any effect of a preference, assignment or other transaction.

### Bankruptcy offences

**18** (1) Where a bankruptcy order is made under this Act on or after the appointed day, a person is not guilty of an offence under Chapter VI of Part IX in respect of anything done before that day; but, notwithstanding the repeal by the Insolvency Act 1985 of the Bankruptcy Act 1914, is guilty of an offence under the Act of 1914 in respect of anything done before the appointed day which would have been an offence under that Act if the making of the bankruptcy order had been the making of a receiving order under that Act.

(2) Subsection (5) of section 350 of this Act applies (instead of sections 157(2), 158(2), 161 and 165 of the Act of 1914) in relation to proceedings for an offence under that Act which are instituted (whether by virtue of sub-paragraph (1) or otherwise) after the appointed day.

### Power to make rules

**19** (1) The preceding provisions of this Part of this Schedule are without prejudice to the power conferred by this Act under which rules under section 412 may make transitional provision in connection with the coming into force of those rules; and such provision may apply those rules in relation to a bankruptcy notwithstanding that it arose from a petition presented before either the coming into force of the rules or the appointed day.

(2) Rules under section 412 may provide for such notices served before the appointed day as may be prescribed to be treated for the purposes of this Act as statutory demands served under section 268.

# PART III

## TRANSITIONAL EFFECT OF PART XVI

**20** (1) A transaction entered into before the appointed day shall not be set aside under Part XVI of this Act except to the extent that it could have been set aside under the law in force immediately before that day.

(2) References above to setting aside a transaction include the making of any order which varies or reverses any effect of a transaction.

# PART IV

## INSOLVENCY PRACTITIONERS

**21** Where an individual began to act as an insolvency practitioner in relation to any person before the appointed day, nothing in section 390(2) or (3) prevents that individual from being qualified to act as an insolvency practitioner in relation to that person.

# PART V

## GENERAL TRANSITIONAL PROVISIONS AND SAVINGS

### Interpretation for this Part

**22** In this Part of this Schedule, 'the former enactments' means so much of the Companies Act as is repealed and replaced by this Act, the Insolvency Act 1985 and the other enactments repealed by this Act.

### General saving for past acts and events

**23** So far as anything done or treated as done under or for the purposes of any provision of the former enactments could have been done under or for the purposes of the corresponding provision of this Act, it is not invalidated by the repeal of that provision by has effect as if done under or for the purposes of the corresponding provision; and any order, regulation, rule or other instrument made or having effect under any provision of the former enactments shall, insofar as its effect is preserved by this paragraph, be treated for all purposes as made and having effect under the corresponding provision.

### Periods of time

**24** Where any period of time specified in a provision of the former enactments is current immediately before the appointed day, this Act has effect as if the corresponding provision had been in force when the period began to run; and (without prejudice to the foregoing) any period of time so specified and current is deemed for the purposes of this Act—

(a) to run from the date or event from which it was running immediately before the appointed day, and

(b) to expire (subject to any provision of this Act for its extension) whenever it would have expired if this Act had not been passed;

and any rights, priorities, liabilities, reliefs, obligations, requirements, powers, duties or exemptions dependent on the beginning, duration or end of such period as above mentioned shall be under this Act as they were or would have been under the former enactments.

### Internal cross-references in this Act

**25** Where in any provision of this Act there is a reference to another such provision, and the first-mentioned provision operates, or is capable of operating, in relation to things done or omitted, or events occurring or not occurring, in the past (including in particular past act of compliance with any enactment, failures of compliance, contraventions, offences and convictions of offences), the reference to the other provision is to be read as including a reference to the corresponding provision of the former enactments.

### Punishment of offences

**26** (1) Offences committed before the appointed day under any provision of the former enactments may, notwithstanding any repeal by this Act, be prosecuted and punished after that day as if this Act had not passed.

(2) A contravention of any provision of the former enactments committed before the appointed day shall not be visited with any severer punishment under or by virtue of this Act than would have been applicable under that provision at the time of the contravention; but where an offence for the continuance of which a penalty was provided has been committed under any provision of the former enactments, proceedings may be taken under this Act in respect of the continuance of the offence on and after the appointed day in the like manner as if the offence had been committed under the corresponding provision of this Act.

### References elsewhere to the former enactments

**27** (1) A reference in any enactment, instrument or document (whether express or implied, and in whatever phraseology) to a provision of the former enactments (including the corresponding provision of any yet earlier enactment) is to be read, where necessary to retain for the enactment, instrument or document the same force and effect as it would have had but for the passing of this Act, as, or as including, a reference to the corresponding provision by which it is replaced in this Act.

(2) The generality of the preceding sub-paragraph is not affected by any specific conversion of references made by this Act, nor by the inclusion in any provision of this Act of a reference (whether express or implied, and in whatever phraseology) to the provision of the former enactments corresponding to that provision, or to a provision of the former enactments which is replaced by a corresponding provision of this Act.

### Saving for power to repeal provisions in section 51

**28** The Secretary of State may by order in a statutory instrument repeal subsections (3) to (5) of section 51 of this Act and the entries in Schedule 10 relating to subsections (4) and (5) of that section.

### Saving for Interpretation Act 1978 ss. 16, 17

**29** Nothing in this Schedule is to be taken as prejudicing sections 16 and 17 of the Interpretation Act 1978 (savings from, and effect of, repeals); and for the purposes of section 17(2) of that Act (construction of references to enactments repealed and replaced, etc.), so much of section 18 of the Insolvency Act 1985 as is replaced by a provision of this Act is deemed to have been repealed by this Act and not by the Company Directors Disqualification Act 1986.

## SCHEDULE 12

## ENACTMENTS REPEALED

| Chapter | Short title | Extent of repeal |
|---|---|---|
| 1970 c 8. | The Insolvency Services (Accounting and Investment) Act 1970. | The whole Act. |
| 1976 c 60 | The Insolvency Act 1976. | Section 3. |
| 1985 c 6. | The Companies Act 1985. | In section 463(4), the words 'Subject to section 617'. |
| | | Sections 467 to 485. |
| | | In section 486, in the definition of 'company' the words 'other than in Chapter II of this Part'; and the definitions of 'instrument of appointment', 'prescribed', 'receiver' and 'register of charges'. |
| | | Sections 488 to 650. |
| | | Sections 659 to 664. |
| | | Sections 665 to 674. |
| | | Section 709(4). |
| | | Section 710(4). |
| | | Section 724. |
| | | Schedule 16. |
| | | In Schedule 24, the entries relating to section 467; all entries thereafter up to and including section 641(2); and the entry relating to section 710(4). |
| 1985 c 65. | The Insolvency Act 1985. | Sections 1 to 11. |
| | | Section 15. |
| | | Section 17. |
| | | Section 19. |
| | | Sections 20 to 107. |
| | | Section 108(1) and (3) to (7). |

| Chapter | Short title | Extent of repeal |
|---------|-------------|------------------|
| | | Sections 109 to 211. |
| | | Sections 212 to 214. |
| | | Section 216. |
| | | Section 217(1) to (3). |
| | | Sections 221 to 234. |
| | | In section 235, subsections (2) to (5). |
| | | In section 236, subsections (3) to (5). |
| | | In Schedule 1, paragraphs 1 to 4, and sub-paragraph (4) of paragraph 5. |
| | | Schedules 3 to 5. |
| | | In Schedule 6, paragraphs 5, 6, 9, 15 to 17, 20 to 22, 25 to 44 and 48 to 52. |
| | | Schedule 7. |
| | | In Schedule 9, paragraphs 1 and 4 to 24. |
| | | Schedule 10. |
| 1985 c 66. | The Bankruptcy (Scotland) Act 1985. | In Schedule 7, paragraphs 19 to 22. |
| 1986 c 44. | The Gas Act 1986. | In Schedule 7, paragraph 31. |

# SCHEDULE 13

# CONSEQUENTIAL AMENDMENTS OF COMPANIES ACT 1985

## PART I

## INTERNAL AND OTHER SECTION REFERENCES AMENDED OR RE-AMENDED

| Section of Act | Consequential amendment or re-amendment |
|----------------|------------------------------------------|
| […] | |
| Section 153(3) | In paragraph (f), for 'section 582' substitute 'section 110 of the Insolvency Act'. |
| | In paragraph (g), for 'Chapter II of Part II of the Insolvency Act 1985' substitute 'Part I of the Insolvency Act'. |
| […] | |
| Section 441(1) | For 'section 13 of the Insolvency Act 1985' substitute 'section 8 of the Company Directors Disqualification Act 1986'. |
| […] | |
| Section 733 | In subsection (1), omit '295(7)'. |

## PART II

## AMENDMENT OF PART XXVI (INTERPRETATION)

In Part XXVI of the Companies Act, after section 735, insert the following section—

**'735A   Relationship of this Act to Insolvency Act**

(1)  In this Act "the Insolvency Act" means the Insolvency Act 1986; and in the following provisions of this Act, namely, sections 375(1)(b), 425(6)(a), 440, 449(1)(a) and (d), 460(2), 675, 676, 677, 699(1), 728 and Schedule 21, paragraph 6(1), the words "this Act" are to be read as including Part I to VII of that Act, sections 411, 413, 414, 416 and 417 in Part XV of that Act, and also the Company Directors Disqualification Act 1986.

(2)  In sections 704(5), 706(1), 707(1), 708(1)(a) and (4), 710(5), 713(1), 729 and 732(3) references to the Companies Acts include Parts I to VII of the Insolvency Act, sections 411, 413, 414, 416 and 417 in Part XV of that Act, and also the Company Directors Disqualification Act 1986.

(3)  Subsections (1) and (2) apply unless the contrary intention appears.'

# SCHEDULE 14

## CONSEQUENTIAL AMENDMENTS OF OTHER ENACTMENTS

| Enactment | Amendment |
| --- | --- |
| **Deeds of Arrangement Act 1914 (c 47):** | |
| Section 3(1) | For 'Part III of the Insolvency Act 1985' substitute 'Parts VIII to XI of the Insolvency Act 1986'. |
| Section 3(4) | The same amendment. |
| Section 11(1) and (2) | In each subsection, the same amendment. |
| Section 15(1) | For 'section 207 of the Insolvency Act 1985' substitute 'section 412 of the Insolvency Act 1986'. |
| Section 16 | The same amendment as of section 3(1). |
| Section 23 | The same amendment. |
| Section 30(1) | For the definition of 'property' substitute—' "property" has the meaning given by section 436 of the Insolvency Act 1986'. |
| **Law of Property Act 1925 (c 20):** | |
| Section 52(2)(b) | For 'section 91 or 161 of the Insolvency Act 1985' substitute 'sections 178 to 180 or sections 315 to 319 of the Insolvency Act 1986'. |
| [...] | |
| **Third Parties (Rights against Insurers) Act 1930 (c 25):** | |
| Section 1 | In subsection (1)(b), for the words from 'a composition' to 'that Chapter' substitute 'a voluntary arrangement proposed for the purposes of Part I of the Insolvency Act 1986 being approved under that Part'. In subsection (2), for '228 of the Insolvency Act 1985' substitute '421 of the Insolvency Act 1986'. In subsection (3), the same amendment. |
| Section 2 | In subsection (1), the same amendment as of section 1(2). In subsection (1A), for the words from 'composition or scheme' to the end of the subsection substitute 'voluntary arrangement proposed for the purposes of, and approved under Part I or Part VIII of the Insolvency Act 1986'. |
| Section 4 | In paragraph (b), the same amendment as of section 1(2). |
| [...] | |
| **Agricultural Marketing Act 1958 (c 47):** | |
| Schedule 2 | For paragraph 4 substitute—'4.—(1) A scheme shall provide for the winding up of the board, and for that purpose may apply Part V of the Insolvency Act 1986 (winding up of unregistered companies), subject to the following modifications. (2) For the purpose of sections 221, 222 and 224 of the Act of 1986, the principal place of business of the board is deemed to be the office of the board the address of which is registered by the Minister under paragraph 3 above. (3) Section 223 does not apply. (4) Section 224 applies as if the words 'or any member of it as such' were omitted. (5) A petition for winding up the board may be presented by the Minister as well as by any person authorised under Part IV of the Insolvency Act 1986 to present a petition for winding up a company'. |
| **Charities Act 1960 (c 58):** | |
| Section 30(1) | For 'Companies Act 1985' substitute 'Insolvency Act 1986'. |
| [...] | |
| **Industrial and Provident Societies Act 1965 (c 12):** | |
| Section 55 | For 'Companies Act 1985' substitute 'Insolvency Act 1986'. |
| **Medicines Act 1968 (c 67):** | |
| Section 72(4) | For the words from 'composition or scheme' to the end of the subsection substitute 'voluntary arrangement proposed for the purposes of, and approved under, Part VIII of the Insolvency Act 1986'. |
| [...] | |
| **Conveyancing and Feudal Reform (Scotland) Act 1970 (c 35):** | |

| Enactment | Amendment |
|---|---|
| [...] | |
| Section 5(2) | For '156 of the Insolvency Act 1985' substitute '310 of the Insolvency Act 1986'; and for 'the said section 156' substitute 'the said section 310'. |
| [...] | |
| Land Charges Act 1972 (c 61): | |
| Section 16(2) | For '207 of the Insolvency Act 1985' substitute '412 of the Insolvency Act 1986'; and for 'Part III' substitute 'Parts VIII to XI'. |
| Matrimonial Causes Act 1973 (c 18): | |
| Section 39 | For 'section 174 of the Insolvency Act 1985' substitute 'section 339 or 340 of the Insolvency Act 1986'. |
| Powers of Criminal Courts Act 1973 (c 62): | |
| Section 39(3) | In paragraph (d), for '174(10) of the Insolvency Act 1985' substitute '341(4) of the Insolvency Act 1986'. |
| Friendly Societies Act 1974 (c 46): | |
| Section 87(2) | For 'Companies Act 1985' substitute 'Insolvency Act 1986'. |
| [...] | |
| Recess Elections Act 1975 (c 66): | |
| Section 1(2) | In the definition of 'certificate of vacancy', for '214(6)(a) of the Insolvency Act 1985' substitute '427(6)(a) of the Insolvency Act 1986'. |
| Policyholders Protection Act 1975 (c 75): | |
| Section 5(1)(a) | For 'Companies Act 1985' substitute 'Insolvency Act 1986'. |
| Section 15(1) | For '532 of the Companies Act 1985' substitute 'Insolvency Act 1986'. |
| Section 16(1)(b) | The same amendment as of section 5(1)(a). |
| Development Land Tax Act 1976 (c 24): | |
| Section 33(1) | For '538 of the Companies Act 1985' substitute '145 of the Insolvency Act 1986'. |
| Restrictive Trade Practices Act 1976 (c 34): | |
| Schedule 1 | For paragraph 9A (inserted by Insolvency Act 1985, section 217(4)) substitute—'9A. Insolvency services within the meaning of section 428 of the Insolvency Act 1986'. |
| [...] | |
| Credit Unions Act 1979 (c 34): | |
| Section 6(1) | For '517(1)(e) of the Companies Act 1985' substitute '122(1)(e) of the Insolvency Act 1986'; and for '517(1)(e) of the Act of 1985' substitute '122(1)(e) of the Act of 1986'. |
| Banking Act 1979 (c 37): | |
| Section 6(3) | In paragraph (b), for 'Part XXI of the Companies Act 1985' substitute 'Part V of the Insolvency Act 1986'. |
| Section 18 | In subsection (1), for 'Companies Act 1985' substitute 'Insolvency Act 1986'; and in paragraph (a) of the subsection for '518' substitute '123'. |
| | In subsection (2), for 'Companies Act 1985' substitute 'Insolvency Act 1986'; and for 'Part XXI' substitute 'Part V'. |
| | In subsection (4)—in paragraph (a), for 'Companies Act 1985' substitute 'Insolvency Act 1986';in paragraph (b), for '518 of the said Act of 1985' substitute '123 of the said Act 1986'; and in paragraph (c), for 'Part XXI of the said Act of 1985' substitute 'Part V of the said Act 1986'. |
| Enactment | Amendment |
| Section 19 | In subsection (2), for paragraph (ba) substitute— |
| | '(ba) in connection with any proceedings under any provision of— |
| | (i)Part XVIII or XX of the Companies Act 1985, or |
| | (ii)Parts I to VII of the Insolvency Act 1986 (other than sections 236 and 237)'. |

| Enactment | Amendment |
|---|---|
| | In subsection (8), for paragraphs (a) and (aa) substitute— |
| | '(a) for the references in subsection (2) to Part XVIII or XX of the Companies Act 1985 and Parts I to VII of the Insolvency Act 1986, there shall be substituted references to Parts V, VI and IX of the Companies Act (Northern Ireland) 1960 (the reference to sections 236 and 237 of the Act of 1986 being disregarded)'. |
| Section 28 | |
| | In subsection (3), in paragraph (c), for '83 of the Insolvency Act 1985' substitute '95 of the Insolvency Act 1986'. |
| | In subsection (4), in paragraph (a), for 'Part XXI of the Companies Act 1985' substitute 'Part V of the Insolvency Act 1986'. |
| | In subsection (6)(b), for sub-paragraphs (ii) to (iv) substitute— |
| | '(ii) to be a member of a liquidation committee established under Part IV or V of the Insolvency Act 1986; |
| | (iii) to be a member of a creditors committee appointed under section 301 of that Act; and |
| | (iv) to be a commissioner under section 30 or the Bankruptcy (Scotland) Act 1985'; |
| | (v) to be a member of a committee of inspection appointed for the purposes of Part V or Part IX of the Companies Act (Northern Ireland) 1960; |
| | and (in the passage following sub-paragraph (iv)) for 'such a commitee as is mentioned in paragraph (b)(ii) or (iv) above' substitute 'a liquidation committee, creditors' committee or committee of inspection'. |
| | In subsection (7), in paragraph (b), for the words from 'section 116(4)' to the end of the paragraph substitute 'section 261(1) of the Insolvency Act 1986 to any person in whom the property of the firm is vested under section 282(4) of that Act'. |
| Section 31(7) | For paragraph (a) substitute - |
| | '(a) for England and Wales, under sections 411 and 412 of the Insolvency Act 1986'; |
| | and in paragraph (b) for 'the said section 106' substitute 'section 411 of that Act'. |
| British Aerospace Act 1980 (c 26): | |
| Section 9(1) | In paragraph (a), for 'Companies Act 1985' substitute 'Insolvency Act 1986'. |
| Public Passenger Vehicles Act 1981 (c 14): | |
| Section 19(3) | In paragraph (a), for 'Chapter III of Part II of the Insolvency Act 1985' substitute 'Part II of the Insolvency Act 1986'. |
| [...] | |
| Supreme Court Act 1981 (c 54): | |
| Section 40A(2) | For 'section 179 of the Insolvency Act 1985' substitute 'section 346 of the Insolvency Act 1986'; and for '621 of the Companies Act 1985' substitute '183 of the Insolvency Act 1986'. |
| Trustee Savings Banks Act 1981 (c 65): | |
| Section 31 | In paragraph (b), for '666 to 669 of the Companies Act 1985' substitute '221 to 224 of the Insolvency Act 1986'. |
| Section 54(2) | For '666(6) of the Companies Act 1985' substitute '221(6) of the Insolvency Act 1986'. |
| Iron and Steel Act 1982 (c 25): | |
| Schedule 4 | In paragraph 3(3) after 'Companies Act 1985' insert 'or the Insolvency Act 1986'. |
| Civil Jurisdiction and Judgments Act 1982 (c 27): | |
| Section 18(3) | In paragraph (ba), for '213 of the Insolvency Act 1985' substitute '426 of the Insolvency Act 1986'. |
| Schedule 5 | In paragraph (1), for 'Companies Act 1985' substitute 'Insolvency Act 1986'. |
| Insurance Companies Act 1982 (c 50): | |
| Section 53 | For 'Companies Act'(the first time) substitute 'Insolvency Act 1986'; and for 'Companies Act'(the second time) substitute 'that Act of 1986'. |

| Enactment | Amendment |
|---|---|
| Section 54 | In subsection (1), for 'the Companies Act'(the first time) substitute 'Part IV or V of the Insolvency Act 1986'; and in paragraph (a), for '518 or sections 667 to 669' substitute '123 or sections 222 to 224'. In subsection (4) for 'Companies Act'(the first time) substitute 'Insolvency Act 1986'. |
| Section 55 | In subsection (5) for 'subsection (3) of section 540 of the Companies Act' substitute 'section 168(2) of the Insolvency Act 1986'. |
| | In subsection (6), for '631 of the Companies Act' substitute '212 of the Insolvency Act 1986'. |
| Section 56 | In subsection (4), for 'Section 90(5) of the Insolvency Act 1985' substitute 'Section 177(5) of the Insolvency Act 1986'; and for 'section 90 of the said Act of 1985' substitute 'section 177 of the said Act of 1986'. |
| | In subsection (7), for 'section 539(1) of the Companies Act' substitute 'section 167 of, and Schedule 4 to, the Insolvency Act 1986'. |
| Section 59 | In subsection (1), for '106 of the Insolvency Act 1985' substitute '411 of the Insolvency Act 1986'. |
| | In subsection (2), for '106 of the Insolvency Act 1985' substitute '411 of the Insolvency Act 1986'; and for 'section 89 of, and Schedule 4 to, the Insolvency Act 1985' substitute 'sections 175 and 176 of, and Schedule 6 to, the Insolvency Act 1986'. |
| Section 96(1) | In the definition of 'insolvent', for '517 and 518 or section 666 of the Companies Act' substitute '122 and 123 or section 221 of the Insolvency Act 1986'. |
| [...] | |
| Telecommunications Act 1984 (c 12): | |
| Section 68(1) | In paragraph (a), for 'Companies Act 1985' substitute 'Insolvency Act 1986'. |
| County Courts Act 1984 (c 28): | |
| Section 98 | For subsection (3) substitute— |
| | '(3) The provisions of this section have effect subject to those of sections 183, 184 and 346 of the Insolvency Act 1986'. |
| Section 102 | For subsection (8) substitute— |
| | '(8) Nothing in this section affects section 346 of the Insolvency Act 1986'. |
| Section 109(2) | For '179 of the Insolvency Act 1985' substitute '346 of the Insolvency Act 1986' |
| Finance Act 1985 (c 54): | |
| Section 79 | Omit the word 'altogether'; and after 'Companies Act 1985' insert 'sections 110 and 111 of the Insolvency Act 1986'. |
| Housing Act 1985 (c 68): | |
| Schedule 18 | In paragraphs 3(4) and 5(3), for '228 of the Insolvency Act 1985' substitute '421 of the Insolvency Act 1986'. |

# Financial Services

## Financial Services and Markets Act 2000

**(c. 8)**

*An Act to make provision about the regulation of financial services and markets; to provide for the transfer of certain statutory functions relating to building societies, friendly societies, industrial and provident societies and certain other mutual societies; and for connected purposes.* [14th June 2000]

## PART I

## THE REGULATOR

### 1 The Financial Services Authority

(1) The body corporate known as the Financial Services Authority ('the Authority') is to have the functions conferred on it by or under this Act.

(2) The Authority must comply with the requirements as to its constitution set out in Schedule 1.

(3) Schedule 1 also makes provision about the status of the Authority and the exercise of certain of its functions.

(4) Section 249 of the Banking Act 2009 provides for references to functions of the Authority (whether generally or under this Act) to include references to functions conferred on the Authority by that Act (subject to any order under that section).

*The Authority's general duties*

### 2 The Authority's general duties

(1) In discharging its general functions the Authority must, so far as is reasonably possible, act in a way—
 (a) which is compatible with the regulatory objectives; and
 (b) which the Authority considers most appropriate for the purpose of meeting those objectives.

(2) The regulatory objectives are—
 (a) market confidence;
 (b) public awareness;
 (c) the protection of consumers; and
 (d) the reduction of financial crime.

(3) In discharging its general functions the Authority must have regard to—
 (a) the need to use its resources in the most efficient and economic way;
 (b) the responsibilities of those who manage the affairs of authorised persons;
 (c) the principle that a burden or restriction which is imposed on a person, or on the carrying on of an activity, should be proportionate to the benefits, considered in general terms, which are expected to result from the imposition of that burden or restriction;
 (d) the desirability of facilitating innovation in connection with regulated activities;
 (e) the international character of financial services and markets and the desirability of maintaining the competitive position of the United Kingdom;
 (f) the need to minimise the adverse effects on competition that may arise from anything done in the discharge of those functions;
 (g) the desirability of facilitating competition between those who are subject to any form of regulation by the Authority.

(4) The Authority's general functions are—
 (a) its function of making rules under this Act (considered as a whole);
 (b) its function of preparing and issuing codes under this Act (considered as a whole);
 (c) its functions in relation to the giving of general guidance (considered as a whole); and
 (d) its function of determining the general policy and principles by reference to which it performs particular functions.

(5) 'General guidance' has the meaning given in section 158(5).

*The regulatory objectives*

### 3  Market confidence

(1) The market confidence objective is: maintaining confidence in the financial system.

(2) 'The financial system' means the financial system operating in the United Kingdom and includes—

    (a) financial markets and exchanges;

    (b) regulated activities; and

    (c) other activities connected with financial markets and exchanges.

### 4  Public awareness

(1) The public awareness objective is: promoting public understanding of the financial system.

(2) It includes, in particular—

    (a) promoting awareness of the benefits and risks associated with different kinds of investment or other financial dealing; and

    (b) the provision of appropriate information and advice.

(3) 'The financial system' has the same meaning as in section 3.

### 5  The protection of consumers

(1) The protection of consumers objective is: securing the appropriate degree of protection for consumers.

(2) In considering what degree of protection may be appropriate, the Authority must have regard to—

    (a) the differing degrees of risk involved in different kinds of investment or other transaction;

    (b) the differing degrees of experience and expertise that different consumers may have in relation to different kinds of regulated activity;

    (c) the needs that consumers may have for advice and accurate information; and

    (d) the general principle that consumers should take responsibility for their decisions.

(3) 'Consumers' means persons—

    (a) who are consumers for the purposes of section 138; or

    (b) who, in relation to regulated activities carried on otherwise than by authorised persons, would be consumers for those purposes if the activities were carried on by authorised persons.

### 6  The reduction of financial crime

(1) The reduction of financial crime objective is: reducing the extent to which it is possible for a business carried on—

    (a) by a regulated person, or

    (b) in contravention of the general prohibition,

to be used for a purpose connected with financial crime.

(2) In considering that objective the Authority must, in particular, have regard to the desirability of—

    (a) regulated persons being aware of the risk of their businesses being used in connection with the commission of financial crime;

    (b) regulated persons taking appropriate measures (in relation to their administration and employment practices, the conduct of transactions by them and otherwise) to prevent financial crime, facilitate its detection and monitor its incidence;

    (c) regulated persons devoting adequate resources to the matters mentioned in paragraph (b).

(3) 'Financial crime' includes any offence involving—

    (a) fraud or dishonesty;

    (b) misconduct in, or misuse of information relating to, a financial market; or

    (c) handling the proceeds of crime.

(4) 'Offence' includes an act or omission which would be an offence if it had taken place in the United Kingdom.

(5) 'Regulated person' means an authorised person, a recognised investment exchange or a recognised clearing house.

*Corporate governance*

### 7  Duty of Authority to follow principles of good governance

In managing its affairs, the Authority must have regard to such generally accepted principles of good corporate governance as it is reasonable to regard as applicable to it.

*Arrangements for consulting practitioners and consumers*

### 8  The Authority's general duty to consult

The Authority must make and maintain effective arrangements for consulting practitioners and consumers on the extent to which its general policies and practices are consistent with its general duties under section 2.

**9   The Practitioner Panel**

(1)   Arrangements under section 8 must include the establishment and maintenance of a panel of persons (to be known as 'the Practitioner Panel') to represent the interests of practitioners.

(2)   The Authority must appoint one of the members of the Practitioner Panel to be its chairman.

(3)   The Treasury's approval is required for the appointment or dismissal of the chairman.

(4)   The Authority must have regard to any representations made to it by the Practitioner Panel.

(5)   The Authority must appoint to the Practitioner Panel such—

(a)   individuals who are authorised persons,

(b)   persons representing authorised persons,

(c)   persons representing recognised investment exchanges, and

(d)   persons representing recognised clearing houses,

as it considers appropriate.

**10   The Consumer Panel**

(1)   Arrangements under section 8 must include the establishment and maintenance of a panel of persons (to be known as 'the Consumer Panel') to represent the interests of consumers.

(2)   The Authority must appoint one of the members of the Consumer Panel to be its chairman.

(3)   The Treasury's approval is required for the appointment or dismissal of the chairman.

(4)   The Authority must have regard to any representations made to it by the Consumer Panel.

(5)   The Authority must appoint to the Consumer Panel such consumers, or persons representing the interests of consumers, as it considers appropriate.

(5A)   The Secretary of State may direct the Authority to appoint as a member of the Consumer Panel a person specified by the Secretary of State who—

(a)   is a non-executive member of the National Consumer Council, and

(b)   is nominated for the purposes of this subsection by the National Consumer Council after consultation with the Authority.

(5B)   Only one person may, at any time, be a member of the Consumer Panel appointed in accordance with a direction under subsection (5A); but that does not prevent the Authority appointing as a member of the Consumer Panel any person who is also a member of the National Consumer Council.

(5C)   A person appointed in accordance with a direction under subsection (5A) ceases to be a member of the Panel on ceasing to be a non-executive member of the National Consumer Council.

(6)   The Authority must secure that the membership of the Consumer Panel is such as to give a fair degree of representation to those who are using, or are or may be contemplating using, services otherwise than in connection with businesses carried on by them.

(7)   'Consumers' means persons, other than authorised persons—

(a)   who are consumers for the purposes of section 138; or

(b)   who, in relation to regulated activities carried on otherwise than by authorised persons, would be consumers for those purposes if the activities were carried on by authorised persons.

**11   Duty to consider representations by the Panels**

(1)   This section applies to a representation made, in accordance with arrangements made under section 8, by the Practitioner Panel or by the Consumer Panel.

(2)   The Authority must consider the representation.

(3)   If the Authority disagrees with a view expressed, or proposal made, in the representation, it must give the Panel a statement in writing of its reasons for disagreeing.

*Reviews*

**12   Reviews**

(1)   The Treasury may appoint an independent person to conduct a review of the economy, efficiency and effectiveness with which the Authority has used its resources in discharging its functions.

(2)   A review may be limited by the Treasury to such functions of the Authority (however described) as the Treasury may specify in appointing the person to conduct it.

(3)   A review is not to be concerned with the merits of the Authority's general policy or principles in pursuing regulatory objectives or in exercising functions under Part VI.

(4)   On completion of a review, the person conducting it must make a written report to the Treasury—

(a)   setting out the result of the review; and

(b)   making such recommendations (if any) as he considers appropriate.

(5)   A copy of the report must be—

(a)   laid before each House of Parliament; and

(b)   published in such manner as the Treasury consider appropriate.

(6)   Any expenses reasonably incurred in the conduct of a review are to be met by the Treasury out of money provided by Parliament.

(7)   'Independent' means appearing to the Treasury to be independent of the Authority.

### 13   Right to obtain documents and information

(1)  A person conducting a review under section 12—

   (a)  has a right of access at any reasonable time to all such documents as he may reasonably require for purposes of the review; and

   (b)  may require any person holding or accountable for any such document to provide such information and explanation as are reasonably necessary for that purpose.

(2)  Subsection (1) applies only to documents in the custody or under the control of the Authority.

(3)  An obligation imposed on a person as a result of the exercise of powers conferred by subsection (1) is enforceable by injunction or, in Scotland, by an order for specific performance under section 45 of the Court of Session Act 1988.

*Inquiries*

### 14   Cases in which the Treasury may arrange independent inquiries

(1)  This section applies in two cases.

(2)  The first is where it appears to the Treasury that—

   (a)  events have occurred in relation to—

      (i)   a collective investment scheme, or

      (ii)  a person who is, or was at the time of the events, carrying on a regulated activity (whether or not as an authorised person),

   which posed or could have posed a grave risk to the financial system or caused or risked causing significant damage to the interests of consumers; and

   (b)  those events might not have occurred, or the risk or damage might have been reduced, but for a serious failure in—

      (i)   the system established by this Act, or by any previous statutory provision, for the regulation of such schemes or of such persons and their activities; or

      (ii)  the operation of that system.

(3)  The second is where it appears to the Treasury that—

   (a)  events have occurred in relation to listed securities or an issuer of listed securities which caused or could have caused significant damage to holders of listed securities; and

   (b)  those events might not have occurred but for a serious failure in

      (i)   the regulatory system established by Part 6 or by any previous statutory provision concerned with the official listing of securities; or

      (ii)  the operation of that system.

(4)  If the Treasury consider that it is in the public interest that there should be an independent inquiry into the events and the circumstances surrounding them, they may arrange for an inquiry to be held under section 15(5) 'Consumers' means persons—

   (a)  who are consumers for the purposes of section 138; or

   (b)  who, in relation to regulated activities carried on otherwise than by authorised persons, would be consumers for those purposes if the activities were carried on by authorised persons.

(5A)  'Event' does not include any event occurring before 1st December 2001 (but no such limitation applies to the reference in subsection (4) to surrounding circumstances).

(6)  'The financial system' has the same meaning as in section 3.

(7)  'Listed securities' means anything which has been admitted to the official list under Part VI.

### 15   Power to appoint person to hold an inquiry

(1)  If the Treasury decide to arrange for an inquiry to be held under this section, they may appoint such person as they consider appropriate to hold the inquiry.

(2)  The Treasury may, by a direction to the appointed person, control—

   (a)  the scope of the inquiry;

   (b)  the period during which the inquiry is to be held;

   (c)  the conduct of the inquiry; and

   (d)  the making of reports.

(3)  A direction may, in particular—

   (a)  confine the inquiry to particular matters;

   (b)  extend the inquiry to additional matters;

   (c)  require the appointed person to discontinue the inquiry or to take only such steps as are specified in the direction;

   (d)  require the appointed person to make such interim reports as are so specified.

### 16   Powers of appointed person and procedure

(1)  The person appointed to hold an inquiry under section 15 may—

   (a)  obtain such information from such persons and in such manner as he thinks fit;

   (b)  make such inquiries as he thinks fit; and

   (c)  determine the procedure to be followed in connection with the inquiry.

(2) The appointed person may require any person who, in his opinion, is able to provide any information, or produce any document, which is relevant to the inquiry to provide any such information or produce any such document.

(3) For the purposes of an inquiry, the appointed person has the same powers as the court in respect of the attendance and examination of witnesses (including the examination of witnesses abroad) and in respect of the production of documents.

(4) 'Court' means—

    (a) the High Court; or

    (b) in Scotland, the Court of Session.

## 17  Conclusion of inquiry

(1) On completion of an inquiry under section 15, the person holding the inquiry must make a written report to the Treasury—

    (a) setting out the result of the inquiry; and

    (b) making such recommendations (if any) as he considers appropriate.

(2) The Treasury may publish the whole, or any part, of the report and may do so in such manner as they consider appropriate.

(3) Subsection (4) applies if the Treasury propose to publish a report but consider that it contains material—

    (a) which relates to the affairs of a particular person whose interests would, in the opinion of the Treasury, be seriously prejudiced by publication of the material; or

    (b) the disclosure of which would be incompatible with an international obligation of the United Kingdom.

(4) The Treasury must ensure that the material is removed before publication.

(5) The Treasury must lay before each House of Parliament a copy of any report or part of a report published under subsection (2).

(6) Any expenses reasonably incurred in holding an inquiry are to be met by the Treasury out of money provided by Parliament.

## 18  Obstruction and contempt

(1) If a person ('A')—

    (a) fails to comply with a requirement imposed on him by a person holding an inquiry under section 15, or

    (b) otherwise obstructs such an inquiry,

the person holding the inquiry may certify the matter to the High Court (or, in Scotland, the Court of Session).

(2) The court may enquire into the matter.

(3) If, after hearing—

    (a) any witnesses who may be produced against or on behalf of A, and

    (b) any statement made by or on behalf of A,

the court is satisfied that A would have been in contempt of court if the inquiry had been proceedings before the court, it may deal with him as if he were in contempt.

# PART II

# REGULATED AND PROHIBITED ACTIVITIES

*The general prohibition*

## 19  The general prohibition

(1) No person may carry on a regulated activity in the United Kingdom, or purport to do so, unless he is—

    (a) an authorised person; or

    (b) an exempt person.

(2) The prohibition is referred to in this Act as the general prohibition.

*Requirement for permission*

## 20  Authorised persons acting without permission

(1) If an authorised person carries on a regulated activity in the United Kingdom, or purports to do so, otherwise than in accordance with permission—

    (a) given to him by the Authority under Part IV, or

    (b) resulting from any other provision of this Act,

he is to be taken to have contravened a requirement imposed on him by the Authority under this Act.

(2) The contravention does not—

    (a) make a person guilty of an offence;

(b) make any transaction void or unenforceable; or

(c) (subject to subsection (3)) give rise to any right of action for breach of statutory duty.

(3) In prescribed cases the contravention is actionable at the suit of a person who suffers loss as a result of the contravention, subject to the defences and other incidents applying to actions for breach of statutory duty.

*Financial promotion*

### 21   Restrictions on financial promotion

(1) A person ('A') must not, in the course of business, communicate an invitation or inducement to engage in investment activity.

(2) But subsection (1) does not apply if—

(a) A is an authorised person; or

(b) the content of the communication is approved for the purposes of this section by an authorised person.

(3) In the case of a communication originating outside the United Kingdom, subsection (1) applies only if the communication is capable of having an effect in the United Kingdom.

(4) The Treasury may by order specify circumstances in which a person is to be regarded for the purposes of subsection (1) as—

(a) acting in the course of business;

(b) not acting in the course of business.

(5) The Treasury may by order specify circumstances (which may include compliance with financial promotion rules) in which subsection (1) does not apply.

(6) An order under subsection (5) may, in particular, provide that subsection (1) does not apply in relation to communications—

(a) of a specified description;

(b) originating in a specified country or territory outside the United Kingdom;

(c) originating in a country or territory which falls within a specified description of country or territory outside the United Kingdom; or

(d) originating outside the United Kingdom.

(7) The Treasury may by order repeal subsection (3).

(8) 'Engaging in investment activity' means—

(a) entering or offering to enter into an agreement the making or performance of which by either party constitutes a controlled activity; or

(b) exercising any rights conferred by a controlled investment to acquire, dispose of, underwrite or convert a controlled investment.

(9) An activity is a controlled activity if—

(a) it is an activity of a specified kind or one which falls within a specified class of activity; and

(b) it relates to an investment of a specified kind, or to one which falls within a specified class of investment.

(10) An investment is a controlled investment if it is an investment of a specified kind or one which falls within a specified class of investment.

(11) Schedule 2 (except paragraph 26) applies for the purposes of subsections (9) and (10) with references to section 22 being read as references to each of those subsections.

(12) Nothing in Schedule 2, as applied by subsection (11), limits the powers conferred by subsection (9) or (10).

(13) 'Communicate' includes causing a communication to be made.

(14) 'Investment' includes any asset, right or interest.

(15) 'Specified' means specified in an order made by the Treasury.

*Regulated activities*

### 22   The classes of activity and categories of investment

(1) An activity is a regulated activity for the purposes of this Act if it is an activity of a specified kind which is carried on by way of business and—

(a) relates to an investment of a specified kind; or

(b) in the case of an activity of a kind which is also specified for the purposes of this paragraph, is carried on in relation to property of any kind.

(2) Schedule 2 makes provision supplementing this section.

(3) Nothing in Schedule 2 limits the powers conferred by subsection (1).

(4) 'Investment' includes any asset, right or interest.

(5) 'Specified' means specified in an order made by the Treasury.

*Offences*

### 23   Contravention of the general prohibition

(1) A person who contravenes the general prohibition is guilty of an offence and liable—

(a) on summary conviction, to imprisonment for a term not exceeding six months or a fine not exceeding the statutory maximum, or both;

(b) on conviction on indictment, to imprisonment for a term not exceeding two years or a fine, or both.

(2) In this Act 'an authorisation offence' means an offence under this section.

(3) In proceedings for an authorisation offence it is a defence for the accused to show that he took all reasonable precautions and exercised all due diligence to avoid committing the offence.

### 24  False claims to be authorised or exempt

(1) A person who is neither an authorised person nor, in relation to the regulated activity in question, an exempt person is guilty of an offence if he—

(a) describes himself (in whatever terms) as an authorised person;

(b) describes himself (in whatever terms) as an exempt person in relation to the regulated activity; or

(c) behaves, or otherwise holds himself out, in a manner which indicates (or which is reasonably likely to be understood as indicating) that he is—

(i) an authorised person; or

(ii) an exempt person in relation to the regulated activity.

(2) In proceedings for an offence under this section it is a defence for the accused to show that he took all reasonable precautions and exercised all due diligence to avoid committing the offence.

(3) A person guilty of an offence under this section is liable on summary conviction to imprisonment for a term not exceeding six months or a fine not exceeding level 5 on the standard scale, or both.

(4) But where the conduct constituting the offence involved or included the public display of any material, the maximum fine for the offence is level 5 on the standard scale multiplied by the number of days for which the display continued.

### 25  Contravention of section 21

(1) A person who contravenes section 21(1) is guilty of an offence and liable—

(a) on summary conviction, to imprisonment for a term not exceeding six months or a fine not exceeding the statutory maximum, or both;

(b) on conviction on indictment, to imprisonment for a term not exceeding two years or a fine, or both.

(2) In proceedings for an offence under this section it is a defence for the accused to show—

(a) that he believed on reasonable grounds that the content of the communication was prepared, or approved for the purposes of section 21, by an authorised person; or

(b) that he took all reasonable precautions and exercised all due diligence to avoid committing the offence.

### *Enforceability of agreements*

### 26  Agreements made by unauthorised persons

(1) An agreement made by a person in the course of carrying on a regulated activity in contravention of the general prohibition is unenforceable against the other party.

(2) The other party is entitled to recover—

(a) any money or other property paid or transferred by him under the agreement; and

(b) compensation for any loss sustained by him as a result of having parted with it.

(3) 'Agreement' means an agreement—

(a) made after this section comes into force; and

(b) the making or performance of which constitutes, or is part of, the regulated activity in question.

(4) This section does not apply if the regulated activity is accepting deposits.

### 27  Agreements made through unauthorised persons

(1) An agreement made by an authorised person ('the provider')—

(a) in the course of carrying on a regulated activity (not in contravention of the general prohibition), but

(b) in consequence of something said or done by another person ('the third party') in the course of a regulated activity carried on by the third party in contravention of the general prohibition,

is unenforceable against the other party.

(2) The other party is entitled to recover—

(a) any money or other property paid or transferred by him under the agreement; and

(b) compensation for any loss sustained by him as a result of having parted with it.

(3) 'Agreement' means an agreement—

(a) made after this section comes into force; and

(b) the making or performance of which constitutes, or is part of, the regulated activity in question carried on by the provider.

(4) This section does not apply if the regulated activity is accepting deposits.

## 28    Agreements made unenforceable by section 26 or 27

(1) This section applies to an agreement which is unenforceable because of section 26 or 27.

(2) The amount of compensation recoverable as a result of that section is—

(a) the amount agreed by the parties; or

(b) on the application of either party, the amount determined by the court.

(3) If the court is satisfied that it is just and equitable in the circumstances of the case, it may allow—

(a) the agreement to be enforced; or

(b) money and property paid or transferred under the agreement to be retained.

(4) In considering whether to allow the agreement to be enforced or (as the case may be) the money or property paid or transferred under the agreement to be retained the court must—

(a) if the case arises as a result of section 26, have regard to the issue mentioned in subsection (5); or

(b) if the case arises as a result of section 27, have regard to the issue mentioned in subsection (6).

(5) The issue is whether the person carrying on the regulated activity concerned reasonably believed that he was not contravening the general prohibition by making the agreement.

(6) The issue is whether the provider knew that the third party was (in carrying on the regulated activity) contravening the general prohibition.

(7) If the person against whom the agreement is unenforceable—

(a) elects not to perform the agreement, or

(b) as a result of this section, recovers money paid or other property transferred by him under the agreement,

he must repay any money and return any other property received by him under the agreement.

(8) If property transferred under the agreement has passed to a third party, a reference in section 26 or 27 or this section to that property is to be read as a reference to its value at the time of its transfer under the agreement.

(9) The commission of an authorisation offence does not make the agreement concerned illegal or invalid to any greater extent than is provided by section 26 or 27.

## 29    Accepting deposits in breach of general prohibition

(1) This section applies to an agreement between a person ('the depositor') and another person ('the deposit-taker') made in the course of the carrying on by the deposit-taker of accepting deposits in contravention of the general prohibition.

(2) If the depositor is not entitled under the agreement to recover without delay any money deposited by him, he may apply to the court for an order directing the deposit-taker to return the money to him.

(3) The court need not make such an order if it is satisfied that it would not be just and equitable for the money deposited to be returned, having regard to the issue mentioned in subsection (4).

(4) The issue is whether the deposit-taker reasonably believed that he was not contravening the general prohibition by making the agreement.

(5) 'Agreement' means an agreement—

(a) made after this section comes into force; and

(b) the making or performance of which constitutes, or is part of, accepting deposits.

## 30    Enforceability of agreements resulting from unlawful communications

(1) In this section—

'unlawful communication' means a communication in relation to which there has been a contravention of section 21(1);

'controlled agreement' means an agreement the making or performance of which by either party constitutes a controlled activity for the purposes of that section; and

'controlled investment' has the same meaning as in section 21.

(2) If in consequence of an unlawful communication a person enters as a customer into a controlled agreement, it is unenforceable against him and he is entitled to recover—

(a) any money or other property paid or transferred by him under the agreement; and

(b) compensation for any loss sustained by him as a result of having parted with it.

(3) If in consequence of an unlawful communication a person exercises any rights conferred by a controlled investment, no obligation to which he is subject as a result of exercising them is enforceable against him and he is entitled to recover—

(a) any money or other property paid or transferred by him under the obligation; and

(b) compensation for any loss sustained by him as a result of having parted with it.

(4) But the court may allow—

(a) the agreement or obligation to be enforced, or

(b) money or property paid or transferred under the agreement or obligation to be retained,

if it is satisfied that it is just and equitable in the circumstances of the case.

(5)  In considering whether to allow the agreement or obligation to be enforced or (as the case may be) the money or property paid or transferred under the agreement to be retained the court must have regard to the issues mentioned in subsections (6) and (7).

(6)  If the applicant made the unlawful communication, the issue is whether he reasonably believed that he was not making such a communication.

(7)  If the applicant did not make the unlawful communication, the issue is whether he knew that the agreement was entered into in consequence of such a communication.

(8)  'Applicant' means the person seeking to enforce the agreement or obligation or retain the money or property paid or transferred.

(9)  Any reference to making a communication includes causing a communication to be made.

(10)  The amount of compensation recoverable as a result of subsection (2) or (3) is—

    (a)  the amount agreed between the parties; or

    (b)  on the application of either party, the amount determined by the court.

(11)  If a person elects not to perform an agreement or an obligation which (by virtue of subsection (2) or (3)) is unenforceable against him, he must repay any money and return any other property received by him under the agreement.

(12)  If (by virtue of subsection (2) or (3)) a person recovers money paid or property transferred by him under an agreement or obligation, he must repay any money and return any other property received by him as a result of exercising the rights in question.

(13)  If any property required to be returned under this section has passed to a third party, references to that property are to be read as references to its value at the time of its receipt by the person required to return it.

# PART III

# AUTHORISATION AND EXEMPTION

## *Authorisation*

### 31  Authorised persons

(1)  The following persons are authorised for the purposes of this Act—

    (a)  a person who has a Part IV permission to carry on one or more regulated activities;

    (b)  an EEA firm qualifying for authorisation under Schedule 3;

    (c)  a Treaty firm qualifying for authorisation under Schedule 4;

    (d)  a person who is otherwise authorised by a provision of, or made under, this Act.

(2)  In this Act 'authorised person' means a person who is authorised for the purposes of this Act.

### 32  Partnerships and unincorporated associations

(1)  If a firm is authorised—

    (a)  it is authorised to carry on the regulated activities concerned in the name of the firm; and

    (b)  its authorisation is not affected by any change in its membership.

(2)  If an authorised firm is dissolved, its authorisation continues to have effect in relation to any individual or firm which succeeds to the business of the dissolved firm.

(3)  For the purposes of this section, an individual or firm is to be regarded as succeeding to the business of a dissolved firm only if succession is to the whole or substantially the whole of the business of the former firm.

(4)  'Firm' means—

    (a)  a partnership; or

    (b)  an unincorporated association of persons.

(5)  'Partnership' does not include a partnership which is constituted under the law of any place outside the United Kingdom and is a body corporate.

## *Ending of authorisation*

### 33  Withdrawal of authorisation by the Authority

(1)  This section applies if—

    (a)  an authorised person's Part IV permission is cancelled; and

    (b)  as a result, there is no regulated activity for which he has permission.

(2)  The Authority must give a direction withdrawing that person's status as an authorised person.

### 34  EEA firms

(1)  An EEA firm ceases to qualify for authorisation under Part II of Schedule 3 if it ceases to be an EEA firm as a result of—

    (a)  having its EEA authorisation withdrawn; or

    (b)  ceasing to have an EEA right in circumstances in which EEA authorisation is not required.

(2) At the request of an EEA firm, the Authority may give a direction cancelling its authorisation under Part II of Schedule 3.

(3) If an EEA firm has a Part IV permission, it does not cease to be an authorised person merely because it ceases to qualify for authorisation under Part II of Schedule 3.

### 35　Treaty firms

(1) A Treaty firm ceases to qualify for authorisation under Schedule 4 if its home State authorisation is withdrawn.

(2) At the request of a Treaty firm, the Authority may give a direction cancelling its Schedule 4 authorisation.

(3) If a Treaty firm has a Part IV permission, it does not cease to be an authorised person merely because it ceases to qualify for authorisation under Schedule 4.

### 36　Persons authorised as a result of paragraph 1(1) of Schedule 5

(1) At the request of a person authorised as a result of paragraph 1(1) of Schedule 5, the Authority may give a direction cancelling his authorisation as such a person.

(2) If a person authorised as a result of paragraph 1(1) of Schedule 5 has a Part IV permission, he does not cease to be an authorised person merely because he ceases to be a person so authorised.

*Exercise of EEA rights by UK firms*

### 37　Exercise of EEA rights by UK firms

Part III of Schedule 3 makes provision in relation to the exercise outside the United Kingdom of EEA rights by UK firms.

*Exemption*

### 38　Exemption orders

(1) The Treasury may by order ('an exemption order') provide for—

(a) specified persons, or

(b) persons falling within a specified class,

to be exempt from the general prohibition.

(2) But a person cannot be an exempt person as a result of an exemption order if he has a Part IV permission.

(3) An exemption order may provide for an exemption to have effect—

(a) in respect of all regulated activities;

(b) in respect of one or more specified regulated activities;

(c) only in specified circumstances;

(d) only in relation to specified functions;

(e) subject to conditions.

(4) 'Specified' means specified by the exemption order.

### 39　Exemption of appointed representatives

(1) If a person (other than an authorised person)—

(a) is a party to a contract with an authorised person ('his principal') which—

　(i) permits or requires him to carry on business of a prescribed description, and

　(ii) complies with such requirements as may be prescribed, and

(b) is someone for whose activities in carrying on the whole or part of that business his principal has accepted responsibility in writing,

he is exempt from the general prohibition in relation to any regulated activity comprised in the carrying on of that business for which his principal has accepted responsibility.

(1A) But a person is not exempt as a result of subsection (1)—

(a) if his principal is an investment firm or a credit institution, and

(b) so far as the business for which his principal has accepted responsibility is investment services business,

unless he is entered on the applicable register.

(1B) The 'applicable register' is—

(a) in the case of a person established in an EEA State (other than the United Kingdom) which permits investment firms authorised by the competent authority of that State to appoint tied agents, the register of tied agents maintained in that State pursuant to Article 23 of the markets in financial instruments directive;

(b) in the case of a person established in an EEA State which does not permit investment firms authorised as mentioned in paragraph (a) to appoint tied agents—

　(i) if his principal has his relevant office in the United Kingdom, the record maintained by the Authority by virtue of section 347(1)(ha), and

　(ii) if his principal is established in an EEA State (other than the United Kingdom) which permits investment firms authorised by the competent authority of the State to appoint tied agents, the register of tied agents maintained by that State pursuant to Article 23 of the markets in financial instruments directive; and (c) in any other case, the record maintained by the Authority by virtue of section 347(1)(ha).

(2) A person who is exempt as a result of subsection (1) is referred to in this Act as an appointed representative.

(3) The principal of an appointed representative is responsible, to the same extent as if he had expressly permitted it, for anything done or omitted by the representative in carrying on the business for which he has accepted responsibility.

(4) In determining whether an authorised person has complied with a provision contained in or made under this Act, or with a provision contained in any directly applicable Community regulation made under the markets in financial instruments directive, anything which a relevant person has done or omitted as respects business for which the authorised person has accepted responsibility is to be treated as having been done or omitted by the authorised person.

(5) 'Relevant person' means a person who at the material time is or was an appointed representative by virtue of being a party to a contract with the authorised person.

(6) Nothing in subsection (4) is to cause the knowledge or intentions of an appointed representative to be attributed to his principal for the purpose of determining whether the principal has committed an offence, unless in all the circumstances it is reasonable for them to be attributed to him.

(7) A person carries on 'investment services business' if—

   (a) the business includes providing services or carrying on activities of the kind mentioned in Article 4.1.25 of the markets in financial instruments directive, and

   (b) as a result of providing such services or carrying on such activities he is a tied agent or would be if he were established in an EEA State.

(8) In this section—

'competent authority' has the meaning given in Article 4.1.22 of the markets in financial instruments directive;

'credit institution' means—

   (a) a credit institution authorised under the banking consolidation directive, or

   (b) an institution which would satisfy the requirements for authorisation as a credit institution under that directive if it had its relevant office in an EEA State;

'relevant office' means—

   (a) in relation to a body corporate, its registered office or, if it has no registered office, its head office, and

   (b) in relation to a person other than a body corporate, the person's head office.

### 39A   Certain tied agents operating outside United Kingdom

(1) This section applies to an authorised person whose relevant office is in the United Kingdom if—

   (a) he is a party to a contract with a person (other than an authorised person) who is established—

      (i)   in the United Kingdom, or

      (ii)  in an EEA State which does not permit investment firms authorised by the competent authority of the State to appoint tied agents; and

   (b) the contract is a relevant contract.

(2) A contract is a 'relevant contract' if it satisfies conditions A to C.

(3) Condition A is that the contract permits or requires the person mentioned in subsection (1)(a) (the 'agent') to carry on investment services business.

(4) Condition B is that either—

   (a) it is a condition of the contract that such business may only be carried on by the agent in an EEA State other than the United Kingdom; or

   (b) in a case not falling within paragraph (a), the Authority is satisfied that no such business is, or is likely to be, carried on by the agent in the United Kingdom.

(5) Condition C is that the business is of a description that, if carried on in the United Kingdom, would be prescribed for the purposes of section 39(1)(a)(i).

(6) An authorised person to whom this section applies who—

   (a) enters into or continues to perform a relevant contract with an agent which does not comply with the applicable requirements,

   (b) enters into or continues to perform a relevant contract without accepting or having accepted responsibility in writing for the agent's activities in carrying on investment services business,

   (c) enters into a relevant contract with an agent who is not entered on the record maintained by the Authority by virtue of section 347(1)(ha), or

   (d) continues to perform a relevant contract with an agent when he knows or ought to know that the agent is not entered on that record,

is to be taken for the purposes of this Act to have contravened a requirement imposed on him by or under this Act.

(7) The 'applicable requirements' are the requirements prescribed for the purposes of subsection (1)(a)(ii) of section 39 which have effect in the case of a person to whom subsection (1A) of that section applies.

(8) A person carries on 'investment services business' if—

    (a) his business includes providing services or carrying on activities of the kind mentioned in Article 4.1.25 of the markets in financial instruments directive, and

    (b) as a result of providing such services or carrying on such activities he is a tied agent.

(9) In this section—

'competent authority' has the meaning given in Article 4.1.22 of the markets in financial instruments directive;

'relevant office' means—

    (a) in relation to a body corporate, its registered office or, if it has no registered office, its head office, and

    (b) in relation to a person other than a body corporate, the person's head office.

# PART IV

# PERMISSION TO CARRY ON REGULATED ACTIVITIES

### *Application for permission*

## 40   Application for permission

(1) An application for permission to carry on one or more regulated activities may be made to the Authority by—

    (a) an individual;

    (b) a body corporate;

    (c) a partnership; or

    (d) an unincorporated association.

(2) An authorised person may not apply for permission under this section if he has a permission—

    (a) given to him by the Authority under this Part, or

    (b) having effect as if so given,

which is in force.

(3) An EEA firm may not apply for permission under this section to carry on a regulated activity which it is, or would be, entitled to carry on in exercise of an EEA right, whether through a United Kingdom branch or by providing services in the United Kingdom.

(4) A permission given by the Authority under this Part or having effect as if so given is referred to in this Act as 'a Part IV permission'.

## 41   The threshold conditions

(1) 'The threshold conditions', in relation to a regulated activity, means the conditions set out in Schedule 6.

(2) In giving or varying permission, or imposing or varying any requirement, under this Part the Authority must ensure that the person concerned will satisfy, and continue to satisfy, the threshold conditions in relation to all of the regulated activities for which he has or will have permission.

(3) But the duty imposed by subsection (2) does not prevent the Authority, having due regard to that duty, from taking such steps as it considers are necessary, in relation to a particular authorised person, in order to secure its regulatory objective of the protection of consumers.

### *Permission*

## 42   Giving permission

(1) 'The applicant' means an applicant for permission under section 40.

(2) The Authority may give permission for the applicant to carry on the regulated activity or activities to which his application relates or such of them as may be specified in the permission.

(3) If the applicant—

    (a) in relation to a particular regulated activity, is exempt from the general prohibition as a result of section 39(1) or an order made under section 38(1), but

    (b) has applied for permission in relation to another regulated activity,

the application is to be treated as relating to all the regulated activities which, if permission is given, he will carry on.

(4) If the applicant—

    (a) in relation to a particular regulated activity, is exempt from the general prohibition as a result of section 285(2) or (3), but

    (b) has applied for permission in relation to another regulated activity,

the application is to be treated as relating only to that other regulated activity.

(5) If the applicant—

    (a) is a person to whom, in relation to a particular regulated activity, the general prohibition does not apply as a result of Part XIX, but

    (b) has applied for permission in relation to another regulated activity, the application is to be treated as relating only to that other regulated activity.

(6) If it gives permission, the Authority must specify the permitted regulated activity or activities, described in such manner as the Authority considers appropriate.

(7) The Authority may—

    (a) incorporate in the description of a regulated activity such limitations (for example as to circumstances in which the activity may, or may not, be carried on) as it considers appropriate;

    (b) specify a narrower or wider description of regulated activity than that to which the application relates;

    (c) give permission for the carrying on of a regulated activity which is not included among those to which the application relates.

### 43  Imposition of requirements

(1) A Part IV permission may include such requirements as the Authority considers appropriate.

(2) A requirement may, in particular, be imposed—

    (a) so as to require the person concerned to take specified action; or

    (b) so as to require him to refrain from taking specified action.

(3) A requirement may extend to activities which are not regulated activities.

(4) A requirement may be imposed by reference to the person's relationship with—

    (a) his group; or

    (b) other members of his group.

(5) A requirement expires at the end of such period as the Authority may specify in the permission.

(6) But subsection (5) does not affect the Authority's powers under section 44 or 45.

*Variation and cancellation of Part IV permission*

### 44  Variation etc at request of authorised person

(1) The Authority may, on the application of an authorised person with a Part IV permission, vary the permission by—

    (a) adding a regulated activity to those for which it gives permission;

    (b) removing a regulated activity from those for which it gives permission;

    (c) varying the description of a regulated activity for which it gives permission;

    (d) cancelling a requirement imposed under section 43; or

    (e) varying such a requirement.

(2) The Authority may, on the application of an authorised person with a Part IV permission, cancel the permission.

(3) The Authority may refuse an application under this section if it appears to it—

    (a) that the interests of consumers, or potential consumers, would be adversely affected if the application were to be granted; and

    (b) that it is desirable in the interests of consumers, or potential consumers, for the application to be refused.

(4) If, as a result of a variation of a Part IV permission under this section, there are no longer any regulated activities for which the authorised person concerned has permission, the Authority must, once it is satisfied that it is no longer necessary to keep the permission in force, cancel it.

(5) The Authority's power to vary a Part IV permission under this section extends to including any provision in the permission as varied that could be included if a fresh permission were being given in response to an application under section 40.

### 45  Variation etc on the Authority's own initiative

(1) The Authority may exercise its power under this section in relation to an authorised person if it appears to it that—

    (a) he is failing, or is likely to fail, to satisfy the threshold conditions;

    (b) he has failed, during a period of at least 12 months, to carry on a regulated activity for which he has a Part IV permission; or

    (c) it is desirable to exercise that power in order to protect the interests of consumers or potential consumers (whether of the services of the authorised person or of the services of other authorised persons).

(2) The Authority's power under this section is the power to vary a Part IV permission in any of the ways mentioned in section 44(1) or to cancel it.

(2A) Without prejudice to the generality of subsections (1) and (2), the Authority may, in relation to an authorised person who is an investment firm, exercise its power under this section to cancel the Part IV permission of the firm if it appears to it that—

    (a) the firm has failed, during a period of at least six months, to carry on a regulated activity which is an investment service or activity for which it has a Part IV permission;

    (b) the firm obtained the Part IV permission by making a false statement or by other irregular means;

    (c) the firm no longer satisfies the requirements for authorisation pursuant to Chapter I of Title II of the markets in financial instruments directive, or pursuant to or contained in any

Community legislation made under that Chapter, in relation to a regulated activity which is an investment service or activity for which it has a Part IV permission; or

(d) the firm has seriously and systematically infringed the operating conditions pursuant to Chapter II of Title II of the markets in financial instruments directive, or pursuant to or contained in any Community legislation made under that Chapter, in relation to a regulated activity which is an investment service or activity for which it has a Part IV permission.

(2B) For the purposes of subsection (2A) a regulated activity is an investment service or activity if it falls within the definition of 'investment services and activities' in section 417(1).

(3) If, as a result of a variation of a Part IV permission under this section, there are no longer any regulated activities for which the authorised person concerned has permission, the Authority must, once it is satisfied that it is no longer necessary to keep the permission in force, cancel it.

(4) The Authority's power to vary a Part IV permission under this section extends to including any provision in the permission as varied that could be included if a fresh permission were being given in response to an application under section 40.

(5) The Authority's power under this section is referred to in this Part as its own-initiative power.

### 46 Variation of permission on acquisition of control

(1) This section applies if it appears to the Authority that—

(a) a person has acquired control over a UK authorised person who has a Part IV permission; but

(b) there are no grounds for exercising its own-initiative power.

(2) If it appears to the Authority that the likely effect of the acquisition of control on the authorised person, or on any of its activities, is uncertain the Authority may vary the authorised person's permission by—

(a) imposing a requirement of a kind that could be imposed under section 43 on giving permission; or

(b) varying a requirement included in the authorised person's permission under that section.

(3) Any reference to a person having acquired control is to be read in accordance with Part XII.

### 47 Exercise of power in support of overseas regulator

(1) The Authority's own-initiative power may be exercised in respect of an authorised person at the request of, or for the purpose of assisting, a regulator who is—

(a) outside the United Kingdom; and

(b) of a prescribed kind.

(2) Subsection (1) applies whether or not the Authority has powers which are exercisable in relation to the authorised person by virtue of any provision of Part XIII.

(3) If a request to the Authority for the exercise of its own-initiative power has been made by a regulator who is—

(a) outside the United Kingdom,

(b) of a prescribed kind, and

(c) acting in pursuance of provisions of a prescribed kind,

the Authority must, in deciding whether or not to exercise that power in response to the request, consider whether it is necessary to do so in order to comply with a Community obligation.

(4) In deciding in any case in which the Authority does not consider that the exercise of its own-initiative power is necessary in order to comply with a Community obligation, it may take into account in particular—

(a) whether in the country or territory of the regulator concerned, corresponding assistance would be given to a United Kingdom regulatory authority;

(b) whether the case concerns the breach of a law, or other requirement, which has no close parallel in the United Kingdom or involves the assertion of a jurisdiction not recognised by the United Kingdom;

(c) the seriousness of the case and its importance to persons in the United Kingdom;

(d) whether it is otherwise appropriate in the public interest to give the assistance sought.

(5) The Authority may decide not to exercise its own-initiative power, in response to a request, unless the regulator concerned undertakes to make such contribution towards the cost of its exercise as the Authority considers appropriate.

(6) Subsection (5) does not apply if the Authority decides that it is necessary for it to exercise its own-initiative power in order to comply with a Community obligation.

(7) In subsections (4) and (5) 'request' means a request of a kind mentioned in subsection (1).

### 48 Prohibitions and restrictions

(1) This section applies if the Authority—

(a) on giving a person a Part IV permission, imposes an assets requirement on him; or

(b) varies an authorised person's Part IV permission so as to alter an assets requirement imposed on him or impose such a requirement on him.

(2) A person on whom an assets requirement is imposed is referred to in this section as 'A'.

(3) 'Assets requirement' means a requirement under section 43—

    (a) prohibiting the disposal of, or other dealing with, any of A's assets (whether in the United Kingdom or elsewhere) or restricting such disposals or dealings; or

    (b) that all or any of A's assets, or all or any assets belonging to consumers but held by A or to his order, must be transferred to and held by a trustee approved by the Authority.

(4) If the Authority—

    (a) imposes a requirement of the kind mentioned in subsection (3)(a), and

    (b) gives notice of the requirement to any institution with whom A keeps an account,

the notice has the effects mentioned in subsection (5).

(5) Those effects are that—

    (a) the institution does not act in breach of any contract with A if, having been instructed by A (or on his behalf) to transfer any sum or otherwise make any payment out of A's account, it refuses to do so in the reasonably held belief that complying with the instruction would be incompatible with the requirement; and

    (b) if the institution complies with such an instruction, it is liable to pay to the Authority an amount equal to the amount transferred from, or otherwise paid out of, A's account in contravention of the requirement.

(6) If the Authority imposes a requirement of the kind mentioned in subsection (3)(b), no assets held by a person as trustee in accordance with the requirement may, while the requirement is in force, be released or dealt with except with the consent of the Authority.

(7) If, while a requirement of the kind mentioned in subsection (3)(b) is in force, A creates a charge over any assets of his held in accordance with the requirement, the charge is (to the extent that it confers security over the assets) void against the liquidator and any of A's creditors.

(8) Assets held by a person as trustee ('T') are to be taken to be held by T in accordance with a requirement mentioned in subsection (3)(b) only if—

    (a) A has given T written notice that those assets are to be held by T in accordance with the requirement; or

    (b) they are assets into which assets to which paragraph (a) applies have been transposed by T on the instructions of A.

(9) A person who contravenes subsection (6) is guilty of an offence and liable on summary conviction to a fine not exceeding level 5 on the standard scale.

(10) 'Charge' includes a mortgage (or in Scotland a security over property).

(11) Subsections (6) and (8) do not affect any equitable interest or remedy in favour of a person who is a beneficiary of a trust as a result of a requirement of the kind mentioned in subsection (3)(b).

*Connected persons*

### 49  Persons connected with an applicant

(1) In considering—

    (a) an application for a Part IV permission, or

    (b) whether to vary or cancel a Part IV permission,

the Authority may have regard to any person appearing to it to be, or likely to be, in a relationship with the applicant or person given permission which is relevant.

(2) Before—

    (a) giving permission in response to an application made by a person who is connected with an EEA firm, or

    (b) varying any permission given by the Authority to such a person, where the effect of the variation is to grant permission for the purposes of a single market directive other than the one for the purposes of which the existing permission was granted,

the Authority must consult the firm's home state regulator.

(2A) But subsection (2) does not apply to the extent that the permission relates to—

    (a) an insurance mediation activity (within the meaning given by paragraph 2(5) of Schedule 6); or

    (b) a regulated activity involving a regulated mortgage contract , a regulated home reversion plan or a regulated home purchase plan.

(3) A person ('A') is connected with an EEA firm if—

    (a) A is a subsidiary undertaking of the firm; or

    (b) A is a subsidiary undertaking of a parent undertaking of the firm.

*Additional permissions*

### 50  Authority's duty to consider other permissions etc

(1) 'Additional Part IV permission' means a Part IV permission which is in force in relation to an EEA firm, a Treaty firm or a person authorised as a result of paragraph 1(1) of Schedule 5.

(2) If the Authority is considering whether, and if so how, to exercise its own-initiative power under this Part in relation to an additional Part IV permission, it must take into account—

    (a) the home State authorisation of the authorised person concerned;

(b) any relevant directive; and

(c) relevant provisions of the Treaty.

*Procedure*

**51 Applications under this Part**

(1) An application for a Part IV permission must—

(a) contain a statement of the regulated activity or regulated activities which the applicant proposes to carry on and for which he wishes to have permission; and

(b) give the address of a place in the United Kingdom for service on the applicant of any notice or other document which is required or authorised to be served on him under this Act.

(2) An application for the variation of a Part IV permission must contain a statement—

(a) of the desired variation; and

(b) of the regulated activity or regulated activities which the applicant proposes to carry on if his permission is varied.

(3) Any application under this Part must—

(a) be made in such manner as the Authority may direct; and

(b) contain, or be accompanied by, such other information as the Authority may reasonably require.

(4) At any time after receiving an application and before determining it, the Authority may require the applicant to provide it with such further information as it reasonably considers necessary to enable it to determine the application.

(5) Different directions may be given, and different requirements imposed, in relation to different applications or categories of application.

(6) The Authority may require an applicant to provide information which he is required to provide under this section in such form, or to verify it in such a way, as the Authority may direct.

**52 Determination of applications**

(1) An application under this Part must be determined by the Authority before the end of the period of six months beginning with the date on which it received the completed application.

(2) The Authority may determine an incomplete application if it considers it appropriate to do so; and it must in any event determine such an application within twelve months beginning with the date on which it received the application.

(3) The applicant may withdraw his application, by giving the Authority written notice, at any time before the Authority determines it.

(4) If the Authority grants an application for, or for variation of, a Part IV permission, it must give the applicant written notice.

(5) The notice must state the date from which the permission, or the variation, has effect.

(6) If the Authority proposes—

(a) to give a Part IV permission but to exercise its power under section 42(7)(a) or (b) or 43(1), or

(b) to vary a Part IV permission on the application of an authorised person but to exercise its power under any of those provisions (as a result of section 44(5)),

it must give the applicant a warning notice.

(7) If the Authority proposes to refuse an application made under this Part, it must (unless subsection (8) applies) give the applicant a warning notice.

(8) This subsection applies if it appears to the Authority that—

(a) the applicant is an EEA firm; and

(b) the application is made with a view to carrying on a regulated activity in a manner in which the applicant is, or would be, entitled to carry on that activity in the exercise of an EEA right whether through a United Kingdom branch or by providing services in the United Kingdom.

(9) If the Authority decides—

(a) to give a Part IV permission but to exercise its power under section 42(7)(a) or (b) or 43(1),

(b) to vary a Part IV permission on the application of an authorised person but to exercise its power under any of those provisions (as a result of section 44(5)), or

(c) to refuse an application under this Part,

it must give the applicant a decision notice.

**53 Exercise of own-initiative power: procedure**

(1) This section applies to an exercise of the Authority's own-initiative power to vary an authorised person's Part IV permission.

(2) A variation takes effect—

(a) immediately, if the notice given under subsection (4) states that that is the case;

(b) on such date as may be specified in the notice; or

(c) if no date is specified in the notice, when the matter to which the notice relates is no longer open to review.

(3) A variation may be expressed to take effect immediately (or on a specified date) only if the Authority, having regard to the ground on which it is exercising its own-initiative power, reasonably considers that it is necessary for the variation to take effect immediately (or on that date).

(4) If the Authority proposes to vary the Part IV permission, or varies it with immediate effect, it must give the authorised person written notice.

(5) The notice must—

(a) give details of the variation;

(b) state the Authority's reasons for the variation and for its determination as to when the variation takes effect;

(c) inform the authorised person that he may make representations to the Authority within such period as may be specified in the notice (whether or not he has referred the matter to the Tribunal);

(d) inform him of when the variation takes effect; and

(e) inform him of his right to refer the matter to the Tribunal.

(6) The Authority may extend the period allowed under the notice for making representations.

(7) If, having considered any representations made by the authorised person, the Authority decides—

(a) to vary the permission in the way proposed, or

(b) if the permission has been varied, not to rescind the variation,

it must give him written notice.

(8) If, having considered any representations made by the authorised person, the Authority decides—

(a) not to vary the permission in the way proposed,

(b) to vary the permission in a different way, or

(c) to rescind a variation which has effect,

it must give him written notice.

(9) A notice given under subsection (7) must inform the authorised person of his right to refer the matter to the Tribunal.

(10) A notice under subsection (8)(b) must comply with subsection (5).

(11) If a notice informs a person of his right to refer a matter to the Tribunal, it must give an indication of the procedure on such a reference.

(12) For the purposes of subsection (2)(c), whether a matter is open to review is to be determined in accordance with section 391(8).

### 54 Cancellation of Part IV permission: procedure

(1) If the Authority proposes to cancel an authorised person's Part IV permission otherwise than at his request, it must give him a warning notice.

(2) If the Authority decides to cancel an authorised person's Part IV permission otherwise than at his request, it must give him a decision notice.

*References to the Tribunal*

### 55 Right to refer matters to the Tribunal

(1) An applicant who is aggrieved by the determination of an application made under this Part may refer the matter to the Tribunal.

(2) An authorised person who is aggrieved by the exercise of the Authority's own-initiative power may refer the matter to the Tribunal.

# PART V

# PERFORMANCE OF REGULATED ACTIVITIES

*Prohibition orders*

### 56 Prohibition orders

(1) Subsection (2) applies if it appears to the Authority that an individual is not a fit and proper person to perform functions in relation to a regulated activity carried on by an authorised person.

(2) The Authority may make an order ('a prohibition order') prohibiting the individual from performing a specified function, any function falling within a specified description or any function.

(3) A prohibition order may relate to—

(a) a specified regulated activity, any regulated activity falling within a specified description or all regulated activities;

(b) authorised persons generally or any person within a specified class of authorised person.

(4) An individual who performs or agrees to perform a function in breach of a prohibition order is guilty of an offence and liable on summary conviction to a fine not exceeding level 5 on the standard scale.

(5) In proceedings for an offence under subsection (4) it is a defence for the accused to show that he took all reasonable precautions and exercised all due diligence to avoid committing the offence.

(6) An authorised person must take reasonable care to ensure that no function of his, in relation to the carrying on of a regulated activity, is performed by a person who is prohibited from performing that function by a prohibition order.

(7) The Authority may, on the application of the individual named in a prohibition order, vary or revoke it.

(8) This section applies to the performance of functions in relation to a regulated activity carried on by—

(a) a person who is an exempt person in relation to that activity, and

(b) a person to whom, as a result of Part XX, the general prohibition does not apply in relation to that activity,

as it applies to the performance of functions in relation to a regulated activity carried on by an authorised person.

(9) 'Specified' means specified in the prohibition order.

### 57 Prohibition orders: procedure and right to refer to Tribunal

(1) If the Authority proposes to make a prohibition order it must give the individual concerned a warning notice.

(2) The warning notice must set out the terms of the prohibition.

(3) If the Authority decides to make a prohibition order it must give the individual concerned a decision notice.

(4) The decision notice must—

(a) name the individual to whom the prohibition order applies;

(b) set out the terms of the order; and

(c) be given to the individual named in the order.

(5) A person against whom a decision to make a prohibition order is made may refer the matter to the Tribunal.

### 58 Applications relating to prohibitions: procedure and right to refer to Tribunal

(1) This section applies to an application for the variation or revocation of a prohibition order.

(2) If the Authority decides to grant the application, it must give the applicant written notice of its decision.

(3) If the Authority proposes to refuse the application, it must give the applicant a warning notice.

(4) If the Authority decides to refuse the application, it must give the applicant a decision notice.

(5) If the Authority gives the applicant a decision notice, he may refer the matter to the Tribunal.

*Approval*

### 59 Approval for particular arrangements

(1) An authorised person ('A') must take reasonable care to ensure that no person performs a controlled function under an arrangement entered into by A in relation to the carrying on by A of a regulated activity, unless the Authority approves the performance by that person of the controlled function to which the arrangement relates.

(2) An authorised person ('A') must take reasonable care to ensure that no person performs a controlled function under an arrangement entered into by a contractor of A in relation to the carrying on by A of a regulated activity, unless the Authority approves the performance by that person of the controlled function to which the arrangement relates.

(3) 'Controlled function' means a function of a description specified in rules.

(4) The Authority may specify a description of function under subsection (3) only if, in relation to the carrying on of a regulated activity by an authorised person, it is satisfied that the first, second or third condition is met.

(5) The first condition is that the function is likely to enable the person responsible for its performance to exercise a significant influence on the conduct of the authorised person's affairs, so far as relating to the regulated activity.

(6) The second condition is that the function will involve the person performing it in dealing with customers of the authorised person in a manner substantially connected with the carrying on of the regulated activity.

(7) The third condition is that the function will involve the person performing it in dealing with property of customers of the authorised person in a manner substantially connected with the carrying on of the regulated activity.

(8) Neither subsection (1) nor subsection (2) applies to an arrangement which allows a person to perform a function if the question of whether he is a fit and proper person to perform the function is

reserved under any of the single market directives to an authority in a country or territory outside the United Kingdom.

(9) In determining whether the first condition is met, the Authority may take into account the likely consequences of a failure to discharge that function properly.

(10) 'Arrangement'—

    (a) means any kind of arrangement for the performance of a function of A which is entered into by A or any contractor of his with another person; and

    (b) includes, in particular, that other person's appointment to an office, his becoming a partner or his employment (whether under a contract of service or otherwise).

(11) 'Customer', in relation to an authorised person, means a person who is using, or who is or may be contemplating using, any of the services provided by the authorised person.

## 60 Applications for approval

(1) An application for the Authority's approval under section 59 may be made by the authorised person concerned.

(2) The application must—

    (a) be made in such manner as the Authority may direct; and

    (b) contain, or be accompanied by, such information as the Authority may reasonably require.

(3) At any time after receiving the application and before determining it, the Authority may require the applicant to provide it with such further information as it reasonably considers necessary to enable it to determine the application.

(4) The Authority may require an applicant to present information which he is required to give under this section in such form, or to verify it in such a way, as the Authority may direct.

(5) Different directions may be given, and different requirements imposed, in relation to different applications or categories of application.

(6) 'The authorised person concerned' includes a person who has applied for permission under Part IV and will be the authorised person concerned if permission is given.

## 61 Determination of applications

(1) The Authority may grant an application made under section 60 only if it is satisfied that the person in respect of whom the application is made ('the candidate') is a fit and proper person to perform the function to which the application relates.

(2) In deciding that question, the Authority may have regard (among other things) to whether the candidate, or any person who may perform a function on his behalf—

    (a) has obtained a qualification,

    (b) has undergone, or is undergoing, training, or

    (c) possesses a level of competence,

required by general rules in relation to persons performing functions of the kind to which the application relates.

(3) The Authority must, before the end of the period of three months beginning with the date on which it receives an application made under section 60 ('the period for consideration'), determine whether—

    (a) to grant the application; or

    (b) to give a warning notice under section 62(2).

(4) If the Authority imposes a requirement under section 60(3), the period for consideration stops running on the day on which the requirement is imposed but starts running again—

    (a) on the day on which the required information is received by the Authority; or

    (b) if the information is not provided on a single day, on the last of the days on which it is received by the Authority.

(5) A person who makes an application under section 60 may withdraw his application by giving written notice to the Authority at any time before the Authority determines it, but only with the consent of—

    (a) the candidate; and

    (b) the person by whom the candidate is to be retained to perform the function concerned, if not the applicant.

## 62 Applications for approval: procedure and right to refer to Tribunal

(1) If the Authority decides to grant an application made under section 60 ('an application'), it must give written notice of its decision to each of the interested parties.

(2) If the Authority proposes to refuse an application, it must give a warning notice to each of the interested parties.

(3) If the Authority decides to refuse an application, it must give a decision notice to each of the interested parties.

(4) If the Authority decides to refuse an application, each of the interested parties may refer the matter to the Tribunal.

(5) 'The interested parties', in relation to an application, are—

    (a) the applicant;

(b) the person in respect of whom the application is made ('A'); and

(c) the person by whom A's services are to be retained, if not the applicant.

### 63   Withdrawal of approval

(1) The Authority may withdraw an approval given under section 59 if it considers that the person in respect of whom it was given is not a fit and proper person to perform the function to which the approval relates.

(2) When considering whether to withdraw its approval, the Authority may take into account any matter which it could take into account if it were considering an application made under section 60 in respect of the performance of the function to which the approval relates.

(3) If the Authority proposes to withdraw its approval, it must give each of the interested parties a warning notice.

(4) If the Authority decides to withdraw its approval, it must give each of the interested parties a decision notice.

(5) If the Authority decides to withdraw its approval, each of the interested parties may refer the matter to the Tribunal.

(6) 'The interested parties', in relation to an approval, are—

(a) the person on whose application it was given ('A');

(b) the person in respect of whom it was given ('B'); and

(c) the person by whom B's services are retained, if not A.

*Conduct*

### 64   Conduct: statements and codes

(1) The Authority may issue statements of principle with respect to the conduct expected of approved persons.

(2) If the Authority issues a statement of principle under subsection (1), it must also issue a code of practice for the purpose of helping to determine whether or not a person's conduct complies with the statement of principle.

(3) A code issued under subsection (2) may specify—

(a) descriptions of conduct which, in the opinion of the Authority, comply with a statement of principle;

(b) descriptions of conduct which, in the opinion of the Authority, do not comply with a statement of principle;

(c) factors which, in the opinion of the Authority, are to be taken into account in determining whether or not a person's conduct complies with a statement of principle.

(4) The Authority may at any time alter or replace a statement or code issued under this section.

(5) If a statement or code is altered or replaced, the altered or replacement statement or code must be issued by the Authority.

(6) A statement or code issued under this section must be published by the Authority in the way appearing to the Authority to be best calculated to bring it to the attention of the public.

(7) A code published under this section and in force at the time when any particular conduct takes place may be relied on so far as it tends to establish whether or not that conduct complies with a statement of principle.

(8) Failure to comply with a statement of principle under this section does not of itself give rise to any right of action by persons affected or affect the validity of any transaction.

(9) A person is not to be taken to have failed to comply with a statement of principle if he shows that, at the time of the alleged failure, it or its associated code of practice had not been published.

(10) The Authority must, without delay, give the Treasury a copy of any statement or code which it publishes under this section.

(11) The power under this section to issue statements of principle and codes of practice—

(a) includes power to make different provision in relation to persons, cases or circumstances of different descriptions; and

(b) is to be treated for the purposes of section 2(4)(a) as part of the Authority's rule-making functions.

(12) The Authority may charge a reasonable fee for providing a person with a copy of a statement or code published under this section.

(13) 'Approved person' means a person in relation to whom the Authority has given its approval under section 59.

### 65   Statements and codes: procedure

(1) Before issuing a statement or code under section 64, the Authority must publish a draft of it in the way appearing to the Authority to be best calculated to bring it to the attention of the public.

(2) The draft must be accompanied by—

(a) a cost benefit analysis; and

(b) notice that representations about the proposal may be made to the Authority within a specified time.

(3) Before issuing the proposed statement or code, the Authority must have regard to any representations made to it in accordance with subsection (2)(b).

(4) If the Authority issues the proposed statement or code it must publish an account, in general terms, of—

    (a) the representations made to it in accordance with subsection (2)(b); and

    (b) its response to them.

(5) If the statement or code differs from the draft published under subsection (1) in a way which is, in the opinion of the Authority, significant—

    (a) the Authority must (in addition to complying with subsection (4)) publish details of the difference; and

    (b) those details must be accompanied by a cost benefit analysis.

(6) Neither subsection (2)(a) nor subsection (5)(b) applies if the Authority considers—

    (a) that, making the appropriate comparison, there will be no increase in costs; or

    (b) that, making that comparison, there will be an increase in costs but the increase will be of minimal significance.

(7) Subsections (1) to (6) do not apply if the Authority considers that the delay involved in complying with them would prejudice the interests of consumers.

(8) A statement or code must state that it is issued under section 64.

(9) The Authority may charge a reasonable fee for providing a copy of a draft published under subsection (1).

(10) This section also applies to a proposal to alter or replace a statement or code.

(11) 'Cost benefit analysis' means an estimate of the costs together with an analysis of the benefits that will arise—

    (a) if the proposed statement or code is issued; or

    (b) if subsection (5)(b) applies, from the statement or code that has been issued.

(12) 'The appropriate comparison' means—

    (a) in relation to subsection (2)(a), a comparison between the overall position if the statement or code is issued and the overall position if it is not issued;

    (b) in relation to subsection (5)(b), a comparison between the overall position after the issuing of the statement or code and the overall position before it was issued.

## 66  Disciplinary powers

(1) The Authority may take action against a person under this section if—

    (a) it appears to the Authority that he is guilty of misconduct; and

    (b) the Authority is satisfied that it is appropriate in all the circumstances to take action against him.

(2) A person is guilty of misconduct if, while an approved person—

    (a) he has failed to comply with a statement of principle issued under section 64; or

    (b) he has been knowingly concerned in a contravention by the relevant authorised person of a requirement imposed on that authorised person by or under this Act or by any directly applicable Community regulation made under the markets in financial instruments directive.

(3) If the Authority is entitled to take action under this section against a person, it may—

    (a) impose a penalty on him of such amount as it considers appropriate; or

    (b) publish a statement of his misconduct.

(4) The Authority may not take action under this section after the end of the period of two years beginning with the first day on which the Authority knew of the misconduct, unless proceedings in respect of it against the person concerned were begun before the end of that period.

(5) For the purposes of subsection (4)—

    (a) the Authority is to be treated as knowing of misconduct if it has information from which the misconduct can reasonably be inferred; and

    (b) proceedings against a person in respect of misconduct are to be treated as begun when a warning notice is given to him under section 67(1).

(6) 'Approved person' has the same meaning as in section 64.

(7) 'Relevant authorised person', in relation to an approved person, means the person on whose application approval under section 59 was given.

## 67  Disciplinary measures: procedure and right to refer to Tribunal

(1) If the Authority proposes to take action against a person under section 66, it must give him a warning notice.

(2) A warning notice about a proposal to impose a penalty must state the amount of the penalty.

(3) A warning notice about a proposal to publish a statement must set out the terms of the statement.

(4) If the Authority decides to take action against a person under section 66, it must give him a decision notice.

(5) A decision notice about the imposition of a penalty must state the amount of the penalty.

(6) A decision notice about the publication of a statement must set out the terms of the statement.

(7) If the Authority decides to take action against a person under section 66, he may refer the matter to the Tribunal.

### 68   Publication

After a statement under section 66 is published, the Authority must send a copy of it to the person concerned and to any person to whom a copy of the decision notice was given.

### 69   Statement of policy

(1) The Authority must prepare and issue a statement of its policy with respect to—

(a) the imposition of penalties under section 66; and

(b) the amount of penalties under that section.

(2) The Authority's policy in determining what the amount of a penalty should be must include having regard to—

(a) the seriousness of the misconduct in question in relation to the nature of the principle or requirement concerned;

(b) the extent to which that misconduct was deliberate or reckless; and

(c) whether the person on whom the penalty is to be imposed is an individual.

(3) The Authority may at any time alter or replace a statement issued under this section.

(4) If a statement issued under this section is altered or replaced, the Authority must issue the altered or replacement statement.

(5) The Authority must, without delay, give the Treasury a copy of any statement which it publishes under this section.

(6) A statement issued under this section must be published by the Authority in the way appearing to the Authority to be best calculated to bring it to the attention of the public.

(7) The Authority may charge a reasonable fee for providing a person with a copy of the statement.

(8) In exercising, or deciding whether to exercise, its power under section 66 in the case of any particular misconduct, the Authority must have regard to any statement of policy published under this section and in force at the time when the misconduct in question occurred.

### 70   Statements of policy: procedure

(1) Before issuing a statement under section 69, the Authority must publish a draft of the proposed statement in the way appearing to the Authority to be best calculated to bring it to the attention of the public.

(2) The draft must be accompanied by notice that representations about the proposal may be made to the Authority within a specified time.

(3) Before issuing the proposed statement, the Authority must have regard to any representations made to it in accordance with subsection (2).

(4) If the Authority issues the proposed statement it must publish an account, in general terms, of—

(a) the representations made to it in accordance with subsection (2); and

(b) its response to them.

(5) If the statement differs from the draft published under subsection (1) in a way which is, in the opinion of the Authority, significant, the Authority must (in addition to complying with subsection (4)) publish details of the difference.

(6) The Authority may charge a reasonable fee for providing a person with a copy of a draft published under subsection (1).

(7) This section also applies to a proposal to alter or replace a statement.

*Breach of statutory duty*

### 71   Actions for damages

(1) A contravention of section 56(6) or 59(1) or (2) is actionable at the suit of a private person who suffers loss as a result of the contravention, subject to the defences and other incidents applying to actions for breach of statutory duty.

(2) In prescribed cases, a contravention of that kind which would be actionable at the suit of a private person is actionable at the suit of a person who is not a private person, subject to the defences and other incidents applying to actions for breach of statutory duty.

(3) 'Private person' has such meaning as may be prescribed.

# PART VI

# OFFICIAL LISTING

*The competent authority*

### 72   The competent authority

(1) On the coming into force of this section, the functions conferred on the competent authority by this Part are to be exercised by the Authority.

(2) Schedule 7 modifies this Act in its application to the Authority when it acts as the competent authority.

(3) But provision is made by Schedule 8 allowing some or all of those functions to be transferred by the Treasury so as to be exercisable by another person.

### 73  General duty of the competent authority

(1) In discharging its general functions the competent authority must have regard to—

    (a)  the need to use its resources in the most efficient and economic way;

    (b)  the principle that a burden or restriction which is imposed on a person should be proportionate to the benefits, considered in general terms, which are expected to arise from the imposition of that burden or restriction;

    (c)  the desirability of facilitating innovation in respect of listed securities and in respect of financial instruments which have otherwise been admitted to trading on a regulated market or for which a request for admission to trading on such a market has been made;

    (d)  the international character of capital markets and the desirability of maintaining the competitive position of the United Kingdom;

    (e)  the need to minimise the adverse effects on competition of anything done in the discharge of those functions;

    (f)  the desirability of facilitating competition in relation to listed securities and in relation to financial instruments which have otherwise been admitted to trading on a regulated market or for which a request for admission to trading on such a market has been made.

(1A) To the extent that those general functions are functions under or relating to transparency rules, subsection (1)(c) and (f) have effect as if the references to a regulated market were references to a market.

(2) The competent authority's general functions are—

    (a)  its function of making rules under this Part (considered as a whole);

    (b)  its functions in relation to the giving of general guidance in relation to this Part (considered as a whole);

    (c)  its function of determining the general policy and principles by reference to which it performs particular functions under this Part.

### 73A  Part 6 Rules

(1) The competent authority may make rules ('Part 6 rules') for the purposes of this Part.

(2) Provisions of Part 6 rules expressed to relate to the official list are referred to in this Part as 'listing rules'.

(3) Provisions of Part 6 rules expressed to relate to disclosure of information in respect of financial instruments which have been admitted to trading on a regulated market or for which a request for admission to trading on such a market has been made, are referred to in this Part as 'disclosure rules'.

(4) Provisions of Part 6 rules expressed to relate to transferable securities are referred to in this Part as 'prospectus rules'.

(5) In relation to prospectus rules, the purposes of this Part include the purposes of the prospectus directive.

(6) Transparency rules and corporate governance rules are not listing rules, disclosure rules or prospectus rules, but are Part 6 rules.

*The official list*

### 74  The official list

(1) The competent authority must maintain the official list.

(2) The competent authority may admit to the official list such securities and other things as it considers appropriate.

(3) But—

    (a)  nothing may be admitted to the official list except in accordance with this Part; and

    (b)  the Treasury may by order provide that anything which falls within a description or category specified in the order may not be admitted to the official list.

(4)  [...]

(5)  In the following provisions of this Part—

[...]

'listing' means being included in the official list in accordance with this Part.

*Listing*

### 75  Applications for listing

(1) Admission to the official list may be granted only on an application made to the competent authority in such manner as may be required by listing rules.

(2) No application for listing may be entertained by the competent authority unless it is made by, or with the consent of, the issuer of the securities concerned.

(3) No application for listing may be entertained by the competent authority in respect of securities which are to be issued by a body of a prescribed kind.

(4) The competent authority may not grant an application for listing unless it is satisfied that—

(a) the requirements of listing rules (so far as they apply to the application), and

(b) any other requirements imposed by the authority in relation to the application,

are complied with.

(5) An application for listing may be refused if, for a reason relating to the issuer, the competent authority considers that granting it would be detrimental to the interests of investors.

(6) An application for listing securities which are already officially listed in another EEA State may be refused if the issuer has failed to comply with any obligations to which he is subject as a result of that listing.

### 76 Decision on application

(1) The competent authority must notify the applicant of its decision on an application for listing—

(a) before the end of the period of six months beginning with the date on which the application is received; or

(b) if within that period the authority has required the applicant to provide further information in connection with the application, before the end of the period of six months beginning with the date on which that information is provided.

(2) If the competent authority fails to comply with subsection (1), it is to be taken to have decided to refuse the application.

(3) If the competent authority decides to grant an application for listing, it must give the applicant written notice.

(4) If the competent authority proposes to refuse an application for listing, it must give the applicant a warning notice.

(5) If the competent authority decides to refuse an application for listing, it must give the applicant a decision notice.

(6) If the competent authority decides to refuse an application for listing, the applicant may refer the matter to the Tribunal.

(7) If securities are admitted to the official list, their admission may not be called in question on the ground that any requirement or condition for their admission has not been complied with.

### 77 Discontinuance and suspension of listing

(1) The competent authority may, in accordance with listing rules, discontinue the listing of any securities if satisfied that there are special circumstances which preclude normal regular dealings in them.

(2) The competent authority may, in accordance with listing rules, suspend the listing of any securities.

(2A) The competent authority may discontinue under subsection (1) or suspend under subsection (2) the listing of any securities on its own initiative or on the application of the issuer of those securities.

(3) If securities are suspended under subsection (2) they are to be treated, for the purposes of sections 96 and 99, as still being listed.

(4) This section applies to securities whenever they were admitted to the official list.

(5) If the competent authority discontinues or suspends the listing of any securities on its own initiative, the issuer may refer the matter to the Tribunal.

### 78 Discontinuance or suspension: procedure

(1) A discontinuance or suspension by the competent authority on its own initiative takes effect—

(a) immediately, if the notice under subsection (2) states that that is the case;

(b) in any other case, on such date as may be specified in that notice.

(2) If on its own initiative the competent authority—

(a) proposes to discontinue or suspend the listing of securities, or

(b) discontinues or suspends the listing of securities with immediate effect,

it must give the issuer of the securities written notice.

(3) The notice must—

(a) give details of the discontinuance or suspension;

(b) state the competent authority's reasons for the discontinuance or suspension and for choosing the date on which it took effect or takes effect;

(c) inform the issuer of the securities that he may make representations to the competent authority within such period as may be specified in the notice (whether or not he has referred the matter to the Tribunal);

(d) inform him of the date on which the discontinuance or suspension took effect or will take effect; and

(e) inform him of his right to refer the matter to the Tribunal.

(4) The competent authority may extend the period within which representations may be made to it.

(5) If, having considered any representations made by the issuer of the securities, the competent authority decides—

    (a) to discontinue or suspend the listing of the securities, or

    (b) if the discontinuance or suspension has taken effect, not to cancel it,

the competent authority must give the issuer of the securities written notice.

(6) A notice given under subsection (5) must inform the issuer of the securities of his right to refer the matter to the Tribunal.

(7) If a notice informs a person of his right to refer a matter to the Tribunal, it must give an indication of the procedure on such a reference.

(8) If the competent authority decides—

    (a) not to discontinue or suspend the listing of the securities, or

    (b) if the discontinuance or suspension has taken effect, to cancel it,

the competent authority must give the issuer of the securities written notice.

(9) The effect of cancelling a discontinuance is that the securities concerned are to be readmitted, without more, to the official list.

(10) If the competent authority has suspended the listing of securities on its own initiative and proposes to refuse an application by the issuer of the securities for the cancellation of the suspension, it must give him a warning notice.

(11) The competent authority must, having considered any representations made in response to the warning notice—

    (a) if it decides to refuse the application, give the issuer of the securities a decision notice;

    (b) if it grants the application, give him written notice of its decision.

(12) If the competent authority decides to refuse an application for the cancellation of the suspension of listed securities, the applicant may refer the matter to the Tribunal.

(13) 'Discontinuance' means a discontinuance of listing under section 77(1).

(14) 'Suspension' means a suspension of listing under section 77(2).

## 78A  Discontinuance or suspension at the request of the issuer: procedure

(1) A discontinuance or suspension by the competent authority on the application of the issuer of the securities takes effect—

    (a) immediately, if the notice under subsection (2) states that this is the case;

    (b) in any other case, on such date as may be specified in that notice.

(2) If the competent authority discontinues or suspends the listing of securities on the application of the issuer of the securities it must give him written notice.

(3) The notice must—

    (a) give details of the discontinuance or suspension;

    (b) inform the issuer of the securities of the date on which the discontinuance or suspension took effect or will take effect; and

    (c) inform the issuer of his right to apply for the cancellation of the suspension.

(4) If the competent authority proposes to refuse an application by the issuer of the securities for the discontinuance or suspension of the listing of the securities, it must give him a warning notice.

(5) The competent authority must, having considered any representations made in response to the warning notice, if it decides to refuse the application, give the issuer of the securities a decision notice.

(6) If the competent authority decides to refuse an application by the issuer of the securities for the discontinuance or suspension of the listing of the securities, the issuer may refer the matter to the Tribunal.

(7) If the competent authority has suspended the listing of securities on the application of the issuer of the securities and proposes to refuse an application by the issuer for the cancellation of the suspension, it must give him a warning notice.

(8) The competent authority must, having considered any representations made in response to the warning notice—

    (a) if it decides to refuse the application for the cancellation of the suspension, give the issuer of the securities a decision notice;

    (b) if it grants the application, give him written notice of its decision.

(9) If the competent authority decides to refuse an application for the cancellation of the suspension of listed securities, the applicant may refer the matter to the Tribunal.

(10) 'Discontinuance' means a discontinuance of listing under section 77(1).

(11) 'Suspension' means a suspension of listing under section 77(2).

*Listing particulars*

## 79  Listing particulars and other documents

(1) Listing rules may provide that securities [...] of a kind specified in the rules may not be admitted to the official list unless—

    (a) listing particulars have been submitted to, and approved by, the competent authority and published; or

    (b) in such cases as may be specified by listing rules, such document (other than listing particulars or a prospectus of a kind required by listing rules) as may be so specified has been published.

(2) 'Listing particulars' means a document in such form and containing such information as may be specified in listing rules.

(3) For the purposes of this Part, the persons responsible for listing particulars are to be determined in accordance with regulations made by the Treasury.

(3A) Listing rules made under subsection (1) may not specify securities of a kind for which an approved prospectus is required as a result of section 85.

(4) Nothing in this section affects the competent authority's general power to make listing rules.

### 80 General duty of disclosure in listing particulars

(1) Listing particulars submitted to the competent authority under section 79 must contain all such information as investors and their professional advisers would reasonably require, and reasonably expect to find there, for the purpose of making an informed assessment of—

(a) the assets and liabilities, financial position, profits and losses, and prospects of the issuer of the securities; and

(b) the rights attaching to the securities.

(2) That information is required in addition to any information required by—

(a) listing rules, or

(b) the competent authority,

as a condition of the admission of the securities to the official list.

(3) Subsection (1) applies only to information—

(a) within the knowledge of any person responsible for the listing particulars; or

(b) which it would be reasonable for him to obtain by making enquiries.

(4) In determining what information subsection (1) requires to be included in listing particulars, regard must be had (in particular) to—

(a) the nature of the securities and their issuer;

(b) the nature of the persons likely to consider acquiring them;

(c) the fact that certain matters may reasonably be expected to be within the knowledge of professional advisers of a kind which persons likely to acquire the securities may reasonably be expected to consult; and

(d) any information available to investors or their professional advisers as a result of requirements imposed on the issuer of the securities by a recognised investment exchange, by listing rules or by or under any other enactment.

### 81 Supplementary listing particulars

(1) If at any time after the preparation of listing particulars which have been submitted to the competent authority under section 79 and before the commencement of dealings in the securities concerned following their admission to the official list—

(a) there is a significant change affecting any matter contained in those particulars the inclusion of which was required by—

(i) section 80,

(ii) listing rules, or

(iii) the competent authority, or

(b) a significant new matter arises, the inclusion of information in respect of which would have been so required if it had arisen when the particulars were prepared,

the issuer must, in accordance with listing rules, submit supplementary listing particulars of the change or new matter to the competent authority, for its approval and, if they are approved, publish them.

(2) 'Significant' means significant for the purpose of making an informed assessment of the kind mentioned in section 80(1).

(3) If the issuer of the securities is not aware of the change or new matter in question, he is not under a duty to comply with subsection (1) unless he is notified of the change or new matter by a person responsible for the listing particulars.

(4) But it is the duty of any person responsible for those particulars who is aware of such a change or new matter to give notice of it to the issuer.

(5) Subsection (1) applies also as respects matters contained in any supplementary listing particulars previously published under this section in respect of the securities in question.

### 82 Exemptions from disclosure

(1) The competent authority may authorise the omission from listing particulars of any information, the inclusion of which would otherwise be required by section 80 or 81, on the ground—

(a) that its disclosure would be contrary to the public interest;

(b) that its disclosure would be seriously detrimental to the issuer; or

(c) in the case of securities of a kind specified in listing rules, that its disclosure is unnecessary for persons of the kind who may be expected normally to buy or deal in securities of that kind.

(2) But—

(a) no authority may be granted under subsection (1)(b) in respect of essential information; and

(b) no authority granted under subsection (1)(b) extends to any such information.

(3) The Secretary of State or the Treasury may issue a certificate to the effect that the disclosure of any information (including information that would otherwise have to be included in listing particulars for which they are themselves responsible) would be contrary to the public interest.

(4) The competent authority is entitled to act on any such certificate in exercising its powers under subsection (1)(a).

(5) This section does not affect any powers of the competent authority under listing rules made as a result of section 101(2).

(6) 'Essential information' means information which a person considering acquiring securities of the kind in question would be likely to need in order not to be misled about any facts which it is essential for him to know in order to make an informed assessment.

(7) 'Listing particulars' includes supplementary listing particulars.

**83**  [...]

### *Prospectuses*

## 84  Matters which may be dealt with by prospectus rules

(1) Prospectus rules may make provision as to—

    (a) the required form and content of a prospectus (including a summary);

    (b) the cases in which a summary need not be included in a prospectus;

    (c) the languages which may be used in a prospectus (including a summary);

    (d) the determination of the persons responsible for a prospectus;

    (e) the manner in which applications to the competent authority for the approval of a prospectus are to be made.

(2) Prospectus rules may also make provision as to—

    (a) the period of validity of a prospectus;

    (b) the disclosure of the maximum price or of the criteria or conditions according to which the final offer price is to be determined, if that information is not contained in a prospectus;

    (c) the disclosure of the amount of the transferable securities which are to be offered to the public or of the criteria or conditions according to which that amount is to be determined, if that information is not contained in a prospectus;

    (d) the required form and content of other summary documents (including the languages which may be used in such a document);

    (e) the ways in which a prospectus that has been approved by the competent authority may be made available to the public;

    (f) the disclosure, publication or other communication of such information as the competent authority may reasonably stipulate;

    (g) the principles to be observed in relation to advertisements in connection with an offer of transferable securities to the public or admission of transferable securities to trading on a regulated market and the enforcement of those principles;

    (h) the suspension of trading in transferable securities where continued trading would be detrimental to the interests of investors;

    (i) elections under section 87 or under Article 2.1 (m)(iii) of the prospectus directive as applied for the purposes of this Part by section 102C.

(3) Prospectus rules may also make provision as to—

    (a) access to the register of investors maintained under section 87R; and

    (b) the supply of information from that register.

(4) Prospectus rules may make provision for the purpose of dealing with matters arising out of or related to any provision of the prospectus directive.

(5) In relation to cases where the home State in relation to an issuer of transferable securities is an EEA State other than the United Kingdom, prospectus rules may make provision for the recognition of elections made in relation to such securities under the law of that State in accordance with Article 1.3 or 2.1(m)(iii) of the prospectus directive.

(6) In relation to a document relating to transferable securities issued by an issuer incorporated in a non-EEA State and drawn up in accordance with the law of that State, prospectus rules may make provision as to the approval of that document as a prospectus.

(7) Nothing in this section affects the competent authority's general power to make prospectus rules.

## 85  Prohibition of dealing etc in transferable securities without approved prospectus

(1) It is unlawful for transferable securities to which this subsection applies to be offered to the public in the United Kingdom unless an approved prospectus has been made available to the public before the offer is made.

(2) It is unlawful to request the admission of transferable securities to which this subsection applies to trading on a regulated market situated or operating in the United Kingdom unless an approved prospectus has been made available to the public before the request is made.

(3)  A person who contravenes subsection (1) or (2) is guilty of an offence and liable—
  (a)  on summary conviction, to imprisonment for a term not exceeding 3 months or a fine not exceeding the statutory maximum or both;
  (b)  on conviction on indictment, to imprisonment for a term not exceeding 2 years or a fine or both.

(4)  A contravention of subsection (1) or (2) is actionable, at the suit of a person who suffers loss as a result of the contravention, subject to the defences and other incidents applying to actions for breach of statutory duty.

(5)  Subsection (1) applies to all transferable securities other than—
  (a)  those listed in Schedule 11A;
  (b)  such other transferable securities as may be specified in prospectus rules.

(6)  Subsection (2) applies to all transferable securities other than—
  (a)  those listed in Part 1 of Schedule 11A;
  (b)  such other transferable securities as may be specified in prospectus rules.

(7)  'Approved prospectus' means, in relation to transferable securities to which this section applies, a prospectus approved by the competent authority of the home State in relation to the issuer of the securities.

## 86  Exempt offers to the public

(1)  A person does not contravene section 85(1) if—
  (a)  the offer is made to or directed at qualified investors only;
  (b)  the offer is made to or directed at fewer than 100 persons, other than qualified investors, per EEA State;
  (c)  the minimum consideration which may be paid by any person for transferable securities acquired by him pursuant to the offer is at least 50,000 euros (or an equivalent amount);
  (d)  the transferable securities being offered are denominated in amounts of at least 50,000 euros (or equivalent amounts); or
  (e)  the total consideration for the transferable securities being offered cannot exceed 100,000 euros (or an equivalent amount).

(2)  Where—
  (a)  a person who is not a qualified investor ('the client') has engaged a qualified investor falling within Article 2.1(e)(i) of the prospectus directive to act as his agent, and
  (b)  the terms on which the qualified investor is engaged enable him to make decisions concerning the acceptance of offers of transferable securities on the client's behalf without reference to the client,
an offer made to or directed at the qualified investor is not to be regarded for the purposes of subsection (1) as also having been made to or directed at the client.

(3)  For the purposes of subsection (1)(b), the making of an offer of transferable securities to—
  (a)  trustees of a trust,
  (b)  members of a partnership in their capacity as such, or
  (c)  two or more persons jointly,
is to be treated as the making of an offer to a single person.

(4)  In determining whether subsection (1)(e) is satisfied in relation to an offer ('offer A'), offer A is to be taken together with any other offer of transferable securities of the same class made by the same person which—
  (a)  was open at any time within the period of 12 months ending with the date on which offer A is first made; and
  (b)  had previously satisfied subsection (1)(e).

(5)  For the purposes of this section, an amount (in relation to an amount denominated in euros) is an 'equivalent amount' if it is an amount of equal value denominated wholly or partly in another currency or unit of account.

(6)  The equivalent is to be calculated at the latest practicable date before (but in any event not more than 3 working days before) the date on which the offer is first made.

(7)  'Qualified investor' means—
  (a)  an entity falling within Article 2.1(e)(i), (ii) or (iii) of the prospectus directive;
  (b)  an investor registered on the register maintained by the competent authority under section 87R;
  (c)  an investor authorised by an EEA State other than the United Kingdom to be considered as a qualified investor for the purposes of the prospectus directive.

## 87  Election to have prospectus

(1)  A person who proposes—
  (a)  to issue transferable securities to which this section applies,
  (b)  to offer to the public transferable securities to which this section applies, or
  (c)  to request the admission to a regulated market of transferable securities to which this section applies,

may elect, in accordance with prospectus rules, to have a prospectus in relation to the securities.

(2) If a person makes such an election, the provisions of this Part and of prospectus rules apply in relation to those transferable securities as if, in relation to an offer of the securities to the public or the admission of the securities to trading on a regulated market, they were transferable securities for which an approved prospectus would be required as a result of section 85.

(3) Listing rules made under section 79 do not apply to securities which are the subject of an election.

(4) The transferable securities to which this section applies are those which fall within any of the following paragraphs of Schedule 11A—

(a) paragraph 2,
(b) paragraph 4,
(c) paragraph 8, or
(d) paragraph 9,

where the United Kingdom is the home State in relation to the issuer of the securities.

### 87A Criteria for approval of prospectus by competent authority

(1) The competent authority may not approve a prospectus unless it is satisfied that—

(a) the United Kingdom is the home State in relation to the issuer of the transferable securities to which it relates,
(b) the prospectus contains the necessary information, and
(c) all of the other requirements imposed by or in accordance with this Part or the prospectus directive have been complied with (so far as those requirements apply to a prospectus for the transferable securities in question).

(2) The necessary information is the information necessary to enable investors to make an informed assessment of—

(a) the assets and liabilities, financial position, profits and losses, and prospects of the issuer of the transferable securities and of any guarantor; and
(b) the rights attaching to the transferable securities.

(3) The necessary information must be presented in a form which is comprehensible and easy to analyse.

(4) The necessary information must be prepared having regard to the particular nature of the transferable securities and their issuer.

(5) The prospectus must include a summary (unless the transferable securities in question are ones in relation to which prospectus rules provide that a summary is not required).

(6) The summary must, briefly and in non-technical language, convey the essential characteristics of, and risks associated with, the issuer, any guarantor and the transferable securities to which the prospectus relates.

(7) Where the prospectus for which approval is sought does not include the final offer price or the amount of transferable securities to be offered to the public, the applicant must inform the competent authority in writing of that information as soon as that element is finalised.

(8) 'Prospectus' (except in subsection (5)) includes a supplementary prospectus.

### 87B Exemptions from disclosure

(1) The competent authority may authorise the omission from a prospectus of any information, the inclusion of which would otherwise be required, on the ground—

(a) that its disclosure would be contrary to the public interest;
(b) that its disclosure would be seriously detrimental to the issuer, provided that the omission would be unlikely to mislead the public with regard to any facts or circumstances which are essential for an informed assessment of the kind mentioned in section 87A(2); or
(c) that the information is only of minor importance for a specific offer to the public or admission to trading on a regulated market and unlikely to influence an informed assessment of the kind mentioned in section 87A(2).

(2) The Secretary of State or the Treasury may issue a certificate to the effect that the disclosure of any information would be contrary to the public interest.

(3) The competent authority is entitled to act on any such certificate in exercising its powers under subsection (1)(a).

(4) This section does not affect any powers of the competent authority under prospectus rules.

(5) 'Prospectus' includes a supplementary prospectus.

### 87C Consideration of application for approval

(1) The competent authority must notify the applicant of its decision on an application for approval of a prospectus before the end of the period for consideration.

(2) The period for consideration—

(a) begins with the first working day after the date on which the application is received; but
(b) if the competent authority gives a notice under subsection (4), is to be treated as beginning with the first working day after the date on which the notice is complied with.

(3) The period for consideration is—
    (a) except in the case of a new issuer, 10 working days; or
    (b) in that case, 20 working days.

(4) The competent authority may by notice in writing require a person who has applied for approval of a prospectus to provide—
    (a) specified documents or documents of a specified description, or
    (b) specified information or information of a specified description.

(5) No notice under subsection (4) may be given after the end of the period, beginning with the first working day after the date on which the application is received, of—
    (a) except in the case of a new issuer, 10 working days; or
    (b) in that case, 20 working days.

(6) Subsection (4) applies only to information and documents reasonably required in connection with the exercise by the competent authority of its functions in relation to the application.

(7) The competent authority may require any information provided under this section to be provided in such form as it may reasonably require.

(8) The competent authority may require—
    (a) any information provided, whether in a document or otherwise, to be verified in such manner, or
    (b) any document produced to be authenticated in such manner,
as it may reasonably require.

(9) The competent authority must notify the applicant of its decision on an application for approval of a supplementary prospectus before the end of the period of 7 working days beginning with the date on which the application is received; and subsections (4) and (6) to (8) apply to such an application as they apply to an application for approval of a prospectus.

(10) The competent authority's failure to comply with subsection (1) or (9) does not constitute approval of the application in question.

(11) 'New issuer' means an issuer of transferable securities which—
    (a) does not have transferable securities admitted to trading on any regulated market; and
    (b) has not previously offered transferable securities to the public.

### 87D   Procedure for decision on application for approval

(1) If the competent authority approves a prospectus, it must give the applicant written notice.

(2) If the competent authority proposes to refuse to approve a prospectus, it must give the applicant written notice.

(3) The notice must state the competent authority's reasons for the proposed refusal.

(4) If the competent authority decides to refuse to approve a prospectus, it must give the applicant written notice.

(5) The notice must—
    (a) give the competent authority's reasons for refusing the application; and
    (b) inform the applicant of his right to refer the matter to the Tribunal.

(6) If the competent authority refuses to approve a prospectus, the applicant may refer the matter to the Tribunal.

(7) In this section 'prospectus' includes a supplementary prospectus.

### 87E   Transfer by competent authority of application for approval

(1) The competent authority may transfer an application for the approval of a prospectus or a supplementary prospectus to the competent authority of another EEA State ('the transferee authority').

(2) Before doing so, the competent authority must obtain the agreement of the transferee authority.

(3) The competent authority must inform the applicant of the transfer within 3 working days beginning with the first working day after the date of the transfer.

(4) On making a transfer under subsection (1), the competent authority ceases to have functions under this Part in relation to the application transferred.

### 87F   Transfer to competent authority of application for approval

(1) Where the competent authority agrees to the transfer to it of an application for the approval of a prospectus made to the competent authority of another EEA State—
    (a) the United Kingdom is to be treated for the purposes of this Part as the home State in relation to the issuer of the transferable securities to which the prospectus relates, and
    (b) this Part applies to the application as if it had been made to the competent authority but with the modification in subsection (2).

(2) Section 87C applies as if the date of the transfer were the date on which the application was received by the competent authority.

### 87G   Supplementary prospectus

(1) Subsection (2) applies if, during the relevant period, there arises or is noted a significant new factor, material mistake or inaccuracy relating to the information included in a prospectus approved by the competent authority.

(2) The person on whose application the prospectus was approved must, in accordance with prospectus rules, submit a supplementary prospectus containing details of the new factor, mistake or inaccuracy to the competent authority for its approval.

(3) The relevant period begins when the prospectus is approved and ends—

    (a) with the closure of the offer of the transferable securities to which the prospectus relates; or

    (b) when trading in those securities on a regulated market begins.

(4) 'Significant' means significant for the purposes of making an informed assessment of the kind mentioned in section 87A(2).

(5) Any person responsible for the prospectus who is aware of any new factor, mistake or inaccuracy which may require the submission of a supplementary prospectus in accordance with subsection (2) must give notice of it to—

    (a) the issuer of the transferable securities to which the prospectus relates, and

    (b) the person on whose application the prospectus was approved.

(6) A supplementary prospectus must provide sufficient information to correct any mistake or inaccuracy which gave rise to the need for it.

(7) Subsection (1) applies also to information contained in any supplementary prospectus published under this section.

### 87H Prospectus approved in another EEA State

(1) A prospectus approved by the competent authority of an EEA State other than the United Kingdom is not an approved prospectus for the purposes of section 85 unless that authority has provided the competent authority with—

    (a) a certificate of approval;

    (b) a copy of the prospectus as approved; and

    (c) if requested by the competent authority, a translation of the summary of the prospectus.

(2) A document is not a certificate of approval unless it states that the prospectus—

    (a) has been drawn up in accordance with the prospectus directive; and

    (b) has been approved, in accordance with that directive, by the competent authority providing the certificate.

(3) A document is not a certificate of approval unless it states whether (and, if so, why) the competent authority providing it authorised, in accordance with the prospectus directive, the omission from the prospectus of information which would otherwise have been required to be included.

(4) 'Prospectus' includes a supplementary prospectus.

### 87I Provision of information to host Member State

(1) The competent authority must, if requested to do so, supply the competent authority of a specified EEA State with—

    (a) a certificate of approval;

    (b) a copy of the specified prospectus (as approved by the competent authority); and

    (c) a translation of the summary of the specified prospectus (if the request states that one has been requested by the other competent authority).

(2) Only the following may make a request under this section—

    (a) the issuer of the transferable securities to which the specified prospectus relates;

    (b) a person who wishes to offer the transferable securities to which the specified prospectus relates to the public in an EEA State other than (or as well as) the United Kingdom;

    (c) a person requesting the admission of the transferable securities to which the specified prospectus relates to a regulated market situated or operating in an EEA State other than (or as well as) the United Kingdom.

(3) A certificate of approval must state that the prospectus—

    (a) has been drawn up in accordance with this Part and the prospectus directive; and

    (b) has been approved, in accordance with those provisions, by the competent authority.

(4) A certificate of approval must state whether (and, if so, why) the competent authority authorised, in accordance with section 87B, the omission from the prospectus of information which would otherwise have been required to be included.

(5) The competent authority must comply with a request under this section—

    (a) if the prospectus has been approved before the request is made, within 3 working days beginning with the date of the request; or

    (b) if the request is submitted with an application for the approval of the prospectus, on the first working day after the date on which it approves the prospectus.

(6) 'Prospectus' includes a supplementary prospectus.

(7) 'Specified' means specified in a request made for the purposes of this section.

### 87J Requirements imposed as condition of approval

(1) As a condition of approving a prospectus, the competent authority may by notice in writing—

    (a) require the inclusion in the prospectus of such supplementary information necessary for investor protection as the competent authority may specify;

(b) require a person controlling, or controlled by, the applicant to provide specified information or documents;

(c) require an auditor or manager of the applicant to provide specified information or documents;

(d) require a financial intermediary commissioned to assist either in carrying out the offer to the public of the transferable securities to which the prospectus relates or in requesting their admission to trading on a regulated market, to provide specified information or documents.

(2) 'Specified' means specified in the notice.

(3) 'Prospectus' includes a supplementary prospectus.

### 87K   Power to suspend or prohibit offer to the public

(1) This section applies where a person ('the offeror') has made an offer of transferable securities to the public in the United Kingdom ('the offer').

(2) If the competent authority has reasonable grounds for suspecting that an applicable provision has been infringed, it may—

(a) require the offeror to suspend the offer for a period not exceeding 10 working days;

(b) require a person not to advertise the offer, or to take such steps as the authority may specify to suspend any existing advertisement of the offer, for a period not exceeding 10 working days.

(3) If the competent authority has reasonable grounds for suspecting that it is likely that an applicable provision will be infringed, it may require the offeror to withdraw the offer.

(4) If the competent authority finds that an applicable provision has been infringed, it may require the offeror to withdraw the offer.

(5) 'An applicable provision' means—

(a) a provision of this Part,

(b) a provision contained in prospectus rules,

(c) any other provision made in accordance with the prospectus directive,

applicable in relation to the offer.

### 87L   Power to suspend or prohibit admission to trading on a regulated market

(1) This section applies where a person has requested the admission of transferable securities to trading on a regulated market situated or operating in the United Kingdom.

(2) If the competent authority has reasonable grounds for suspecting that an applicable provision has been infringed and the securities have not yet been admitted to trading on the regulated market in question, it may—

(a) require the person requesting admission to suspend the request for a period not exceeding 10 working days;

(b) require a person not to advertise the securities to which it relates, or to take such steps as the authority may specify to suspend any existing advertisement in connection with those securities, for a period not exceeding 10 working days.

(3) If the competent authority has reasonable grounds for suspecting that an applicable provision has been infringed and the securities have been admitted to trading on the regulated market in question, it may—

(a) require the market operator to suspend trading in the securities for a period not exceeding 10 working days;

(b) require a person not to advertise the securities, or to take such steps as the authority may specify to suspend any existing advertisement in connection with those securities, for a period not exceeding 10 working days.

(4) If the competent authority finds that an applicable provision has been infringed, it may require the market operator to prohibit trading in the securities on the regulated market in question.

(5) 'An applicable provision' means—

(a) a provision of this Part,

(b) a provision contained in prospectus rules,

(c) any other provision made in accordance with the prospectus directive,

applicable in relation to the admission of the transferable securities to trading on the regulated market in question.

### 87M   Public censure of issuer

(1) If the competent authority finds that—

(a) an issuer of transferable securities,

(b) a person offering transferable securities to the public, or

(c) a person requesting the admission of transferable securities to trading on a regulated market,

is failing or has failed to comply with his obligations under an applicable provision, it may publish a statement to that effect.

(2) If the competent authority proposes to publish a statement, it must give the person a warning notice setting out the terms of the proposed statement.

(3) If, after considering any representations made in response to the warning notice, the competent authority decides to make the proposed statement, it must give the person a decision notice setting out the terms of the statement.

(4) 'An applicable provision' means—

(a) a provision of this Part,

(b) a provision contained in prospectus rules,

(c) any other provision made in accordance with the prospectus directive,

applicable to a prospectus in relation to the transferable securities in question.

(5) 'Prospectus' includes a supplementary prospectus.

### 87N Right to refer matters to the Tribunal

(1) A person to whom a decision notice is given under section 87M may refer the matter to the Tribunal.

(2) A person to whom a notice is given under section 87O may refer the matter to the Tribunal.

### 87O Procedure under sections 87K and 87L

(1) A requirement under section 87K or 87L takes effect—

(a) immediately, if the notice under subsection (2) states that that is the case;

(b) in any other case, on such date as may be specified in that notice.

(2) If the competent authority—

(a) proposes to exercise the powers in section 87K or 87L in relation to a person, or

(b) exercises any of those powers in relation to a person with immediate effect,

it must give that person written notice.

(3) The notice must—

(a) give details of the competent authority's action or proposed action;

(b) state the competent authority's reasons for taking the action in question and choosing the date on which it took effect or takes effect;

(c) inform the recipient that he may make representations to the competent authority within such period as may be specified by the notice (whether or not he has referred the matter to the Tribunal);

(d) inform him of the date on which the action took effect or takes effect; and

(e) inform him of his right to refer the matter to the Tribunal.

(4) The competent authority may extend the period within which representations may be made to it.

(5) If, having considered any representations made to it, the competent authority decides to maintain, vary or revoke its earlier decision, it must give written notice to that effect to the person mentioned in subsection (2).

(6) A notice given under subsection (5) must inform that person, where relevant, of his right to refer the matter to the Tribunal.

(7) If a notice informs a person of his right to refer a matter to the Tribunal, it must give an indication of the procedure on such a reference.

(8) If a notice under this section relates to the exercise of the power conferred by section 87L(3), the notice must also be given to the person at whose request the transferable securities were admitted to trading on the regulated market.

### 87P Exercise of powers at request of competent authority of another EEA State

(1) This section applies if—

(a) the competent authority of an EEA State other than the United Kingdom has approved a prospectus,

(b) the transferable securities to which the prospectus relates have been offered to the public in the United Kingdom or their admission to trading on a regulated market has been requested, and

(c) that competent authority makes a request that the competent authority assist it in the performance of its functions under the law of that State in connection with the prospectus directive.

(2) For the purpose of complying with the request mentioned in subsection (1)(c), the powers conferred by sections 87K and 87L may be exercised as if the prospectus were one which had been approved by the competent authority.

(3) Section 87N does not apply to an exercise of those powers as a result of this section.

(4) Section 87O does apply to such an exercise of those powers but with the omission of subsections (3)(e), (6) and (7).

### 87Q Right of investor to withdraw

(1) Where a person agrees to buy or subscribe for transferable securities in circumstances where the final offer price or the amount of transferable securities to be offered to the public is not included in the prospectus, he may withdraw his acceptance before the end of the withdrawal period.

(2) The withdrawal period—

  (a) begins with the investor's acceptance; and

  (b) ends at the end of the second working day after the date on which the competent authority is informed of the information in accordance with section 87A(7).

 (3) Subsection (1) does not apply if the prospectus contains—

  (a) in the case of the amount of transferable securities to be offered to the public, the criteria or conditions (or both) according to which that element will be determined, or

  (b) in the case of price, the criteria or conditions (or both) according to which that element will be determined or the maximum price.

 (4) Where a supplementary prospectus has been published and, prior to the publication, a person agreed to buy or subscribe for transferable securities to which it relates, he may withdraw his acceptance before the end of the period of 2 working days beginning with the first working day after the date on which the supplementary prospectus was published.

### 87R   Register of investors

 (1) The competent authority must establish and maintain, in accordance with this section and prospectus rules, a register of investors for the purposes of section 86.

 (2) An individual may not be entered in the register unless—

  (a) he is resident in the United Kingdom; and

  (b) he meets at least two of the criteria mentioned in Article 2.2 of the prospectus directive.

 (3) A company may not be entered in the register unless—

  (a) it falls within the meaning of 'small and medium-sized enterprises' in Article 2.1 of the prospectus directive; and

  (b) its registered office is in the United Kingdom.

 (4) A person who does not fall within subsection (2) or (3) may not be entered in the register.

*Sponsors*

### 88   Sponsors

 (1) Listing rules may require a person to make arrangements with a sponsor for the performance by the sponsor of such services in relation to him as may be specified in the rules.

 (2) 'Sponsor' means a person approved by the competent authority for the purposes of the rules.

 (3) Listing rules made by virtue of subsection (1) may—

  (a) provide for the competent authority to maintain a list of sponsors;

  (b) specify services which must be performed by a sponsor;

  (c) impose requirements on a sponsor in relation to the provision of services or specified services;

  (d) specify the circumstances in which a person is qualified for being approved as a sponsor.

 (4) If the competent authority proposes—

  (a) to refuse a person's application for approval as a sponsor, or

  (b) to cancel a person's approval as a sponsor otherwise that at his request,

it must give him a warning notice.

 (5) If, after considering any representations made in response to the warning notice, the competent authority decides—

  (a) to grant the application for approval, or

  (b) not to cancel the approval,

it must give the person concerned, and any person to whom a copy of the warning notice was given, written notice of its decision.

 (6) If, after considering any representations made in response to the warning notice, the competent authority decides—

  (a) to refuse to grant the application for approval, or

  (b) to cancel the approval,

it must give the person concerned a decision notice.

 (7) A person to whom a decision notice is given under this section may refer the matter to the Tribunal.

### 89   Public censure of sponsor

 (1) Listing rules may make provision for the competent authority, if it considers that a sponsor has contravened a requirement imposed on him by rules made as a result of section 88(3)(c), to publish a statement to that effect.

 (2) If the competent authority proposes to publish a statement it must give the sponsor a warning notice setting out the terms of the proposed statement.

 (3) If, after considering any representations made in response to the warning notice, the competent authority decides to make the proposed statement, it must give the sponsor a decision notice setting out the terms of the statement.

 (4) A sponsor to whom a decision notice is given under this section may refer the matter to the Tribunal.

### 89A  Transparency rules

(1) The competent authority may make rules for the purposes of the transparency obligations directive.

(2) The rules may include provision for dealing with any matters arising out of or related to any provision of the transparency obligations directive.

(3) The competent authority may also make rules—

  (a) for the purpose of ensuring that voteholder information in respect of voting shares traded on a UK market other than a regulated market is made public or notified to the competent authority;

  (b) providing for persons who hold comparable instruments (see section 89F(1)(c)) in respect of voting shares to be treated, in the circumstances specified in the rules, as holding some or all of the voting rights in respect of those shares.

(4) Rules under this section may, in particular, make provision—

  (a) specifying how the proportion of—

    (i)  the total voting rights in respect of shares in an issuer, or

    (ii) the total voting rights in respect of a particular class of shares in an issuer,

    held by a person is to be determined;

  (b) specifying the circumstances in which, for the purposes of any determination of the voting rights held by a person ('P') in respect of voting shares in an issuer, any voting rights held, or treated by virtue of subsection (3)(b) as held, by another person in respect of voting shares in the issuer are to be regarded as held by P;

  (c) specifying the nature of the information which must be included in any notification;

  (d) about the form of any notification;

  (e) requiring any notification to be given within a specified period;

  (f) specifying the manner in which any information is to be made public and the period within which it must be made public;

  (g) specifying circumstances in which any of the requirements imposed by rules under this section does not apply.

(5) Rules under this section are referred to in this Part as 'transparency rules'.

(6) Nothing in sections 89B to 89G affects the generality of the power to make rules under this section.

### 89B  Provision of voteholder information

(1) Transparency rules may make provision for voteholder information in respect of voting shares to be notified, in circumstances specified in the rules—

  (a) to the issuer, or

  (b) to the public,

or to both.

(2) Transparency rules may make provision for voteholder information notified to the issuer to be notified at the same time to the competent authority.

(3) In this Part 'voteholder information' in respect of voting shares means information relating to the proportion of voting rights held by a person in respect of the shares.

(4) Transparency rules may require notification of voteholder information relating to a person—

  (a) initially, not later than such date as may be specified in the rules for the purposes of the first indent of Article 30.2 of the transparency obligations directive, and

  (b) subsequently, in accordance with the following provisions.

(5) Transparency rules under subsection (4)(b) may require notification of voteholder information relating to a person only where there is a notifiable change in the proportion of—

  (a) the total voting rights in respect of shares in the issuer, or

  (b) the total voting rights in respect of a particular class of share in the issuer,

held by the person.

(6) For this purpose there is a 'notifiable change' in the proportion of voting rights held by a person when the proportion changes—

  (a) from being a proportion less than a designated proportion to a proportion equal to or greater than that designated proportion,

  (b) from being a proportion equal to a designated proportion to a proportion greater or less than that designated proportion, or

  (c) from being a proportion greater than a designated proportion to a proportion equal to or less than that designated proportion.

(7) In subsection (6) 'designated' means designated by the rules.

### 89C  Provision of information by issuers of transferable securities

(1) Transparency rules may make provision requiring the issuer of transferable securities, in circumstances specified in the rules—

  (a) to make public information to which this section applies, or

  (b) to notify to the competent authority information to which this section applies,

or to do both.

(2) In the case of every issuer, this section applies to—

(a) information required by Article 4 of the transparency obligations directive;

(b) information relating to the rights attached to the transferable securities, including information about the terms and conditions of those securities which could indirectly affect those rights; and

(c) information about new loan issues and about any guarantee or security in connection with any such issue.

(3) In the case of an issuer of debt securities, this section also applies to information required by Article 5 of the transparency obligations directive.

(4) In the case of an issuer of shares, this section also applies to—

(a) information required by Article 5 of the transparency obligations directive;

(b) information required by Article 6 of that directive;

(c) voteholder information—

(i) notified to the issuer, or

(ii) relating to the proportion of voting rights held by the issuer in respect of shares in the issuer;

(d) information relating to the issuer's capital; and

(e) information relating to the total number of voting rights in respect of shares or shares of a particular class.

### 89D  Notification of voting rights held by issuer

(1) Transparency rules may require notification of voteholder information relating to the proportion of voting rights held by an issuer in respect of voting shares in the issuer—

(a) initially, not later than such date as may be specified in the rules for the purposes of the second indent of Article 30.2 of the transparency obligations directive, and

(b) subsequently, in accordance with the following provisions.

(2) Transparency rules under subsection (1)(b) may require notification of voteholder information relating to the proportion of voting rights held by an issuer in respect of voting shares in the issuer only where there is a notifiable change in the proportion of—

(a) the total voting rights in respect of shares in the issuer, or

(b) the total voting rights in respect of a particular class of share in the issuer,

held by the issuer.

(3) For this purpose there is a 'notifiable change' in the proportion of voting rights held by a person when the proportion changes—

(a) from being a proportion less than a designated proportion to a proportion equal to or greater than that designated proportion,

(b) from being a proportion equal to a designated proportion to a proportion greater or less than that designated proportion, or

(c) from being a proportion greater than a designated proportion to a proportion equal to or less than that designated proportion.

(4) In subsection (3) 'designated' means designated by the rules.

### 89E  Notification of proposed amendment of issuer's constitution

Transparency rules may make provision requiring an issuer of transferable securities that are admitted to trading on a regulated market to notify a proposed amendment to its constitution—

(a) to the competent authority, and

(b) to the market on which the issuer's securities are admitted,

at times and in circumstances specified in the rules.

### 89F  Transparency rules: interpretation etc

(1) For the purposes of sections 89A to 89G—

(a) the voting rights in respect of any voting shares are the voting rights attached to those shares,

(b) a person is to be regarded as holding the voting rights in respect of the shares—

(i) if, by virtue of those shares, he is a shareholder within the meaning of Article 2.1(e) of the transparency obligations directive;

(ii) if, and to the extent that, he is entitled to acquire, dispose of or exercise those voting rights in one or more of the cases mentioned in Article 10(a) to (h) of the transparency obligations directive;

(iii) if he holds, directly or indirectly, a financial instrument which results in an entitlement to acquire the shares and is an Article 13 instrument, and

(c) a person holds a 'comparable instrument' in respect of voting shares if he holds, directly or indirectly, a financial instrument in relation to the shares which has similar economic effects to an Article 13 instrument (whether or not the financial instrument results in an entitlement to acquire the shares).

(2) Transparency rules under section 89A(3)(b) may make different provision for different descriptions of comparable instrument.

(3) For the purposes of sections 89A to 89G two or more persons may, at the same time, each be regarded as holding the same voting rights.

(4) In those sections—

'Article 13 instrument' means a financial instrument of a type determined by the European Commission under Article 13.2 of the transparency obligations directive;

'financial instrument' has the meaning given in Article 4.1(17) of Directive 2004/39/EC on markets in financial instruments;

'UK market' means a market that is situated or operating in the United Kingdom;

'voting shares' means shares of an issuer to which voting rights are attached.

### 89G   Transparency rules: other supplementary provisions

(1) Transparency rules may impose the same obligations on a person who has applied for the admission of transferable securities to trading on a regulated market without the issuer's consent as they impose on an issuer of transferable securities.

(2) Transparency rules that require a person to make information public may include provision authorising the competent authority to make the information public in the event that the person fails to do so.

(3) The competent authority may make public any information notified to the authority in accordance with transparency rules.

(4) Transparency rules may make provision by reference to any provision of any rules made by the Panel on Takeovers and Mergers under Part 28 of the Companies Act 2006.

(5) Sections 89A to 89F and this section are without prejudice to any other power conferred by this Part to make Part 6 rules.

### 89H   Competent authority's power to call for information

(1) The competent authority may by notice in writing given to a person to whom this section applies require him—

(a) to provide specified information or information of a specified description, or

(b) to produce specified documents or documents of a specified description.

(2) This section applies to—

(a) an issuer in respect of whom transparency rules have effect;

(b) a voteholder;

(c) an auditor of—

(i) an issuer to whom this section applies, or

(ii) a voteholder;

(d) a person who controls a voteholder;

(e) a person controlled by a voteholder;

(f) a director or other similar officer of an issuer to whom this section applies;

(g) a director or other similar officer of a voteholder or, where the affairs of a voteholder are managed by its members, a member of the voteholder.

(3) This section applies only to information and documents reasonably required in connection with the exercise by the competent authority of functions conferred on it by or under sections 89A to 89G (transparency rules).

(4) Information or documents required under this section must be provided or produced—

(a) before the end of such reasonable period as may be specified, and

(b) at such place as may be specified.

(5) If a person claims a lien on a document, its production under this section does not affect the lien.

### 89I   Requirements in connection with call for information

(1) The competent authority may require any information provided under section 89H to be provided in such form as it may reasonably require.

(2) The competent authority may require—

(a) any information provided, whether in a document or otherwise, to be verified in such manner as it may reasonably require;

(b) any document produced to be authenticated in such manner as it may reasonably require.

(3) If a document is produced in response to a requirement imposed under section 89H, the competent authority may—

(a) take copies of or extracts from the document; or

(b) require the person producing the document, or any relevant person, to provide an explanation of the document.

(4) In subsection (3)(b) 'relevant person', in relation to a person who is required to produce a document, means a person who—

(a) has been or is a director or controller of that person;

(b) has been or is an auditor of that person;

(c) has been or is an actuary, accountant or lawyer appointed or instructed by that person; or

(d) has been or is an employee of that person.

(5) If a person who is required under section 89H to produce a document fails to do so, the competent authority may require him to state, to the best of his knowledge and belief, where the document is.

### 89J Power to call for information: supplementary provisions

(1) The competent authority may require an issuer to make public any information provided to the authority under section 89H.

(2) If the issuer fails to comply with a requirement under subsection (1), the competent authority may, after seeking representations from the issuer, make the information public.

(3) In sections 89H and 89I (power of competent authority to call for information)—

'control' and 'controlled' have the meaning given by subsection (4) below;

'specified' means specified in the notice;

'voteholder' means a person who—

(a) holds voting rights in respect of any voting shares for the purposes of sections 89A to 89G (transparency rules), or

(b) is treated as holding such rights by virtue of rules under section 89A(3)(b).

(4) For the purposes of those sections a person ('A') controls another person ('B') if—

(a) A holds a majority of the voting rights in B,

(b) A is a member of B and has the right to appoint or remove a majority of the members of the board of directors (or, if there is no such board, the equivalent management body) of B,

(c) A is a member of B and controls alone, pursuant to an agreement with other shareholders or members, a majority of the voting rights in B, or

(d) A has the right to exercise, or actually exercises, dominant influence or control over B.

(5) For the purposes of subsection (4)(b)—

(a) any rights of a person controlled by A, and

(b) any rights of a person acting on behalf of A or a person controlled by A,

are treated as held by A.

### 89K Public censure of issuer

(1) If the competent authority finds that an issuer of securities admitted to trading on a regulated market is failing or has failed to comply with an applicable transparency obligation, it may publish a statement to that effect.

(2) If the competent authority proposes to publish a statement, it must give the issuer a warning notice setting out the terms of the proposed statement.

(3) If, after considering any representations made in response to the warning notice, the competent authority decides to make the proposed statement, it must give the issuer a decision notice setting out the terms of the statement.

(4) A notice under this section must inform the issuer of his right to refer the matter to the Tribunal (see section 89N) and give an indication of the procedure on such a reference.

(5) In this section 'transparency obligation' means an obligation under–

(a) a provision of transparency rules, or

(b) any other provision made in accordance with the transparency obligations directive.

(6) In relation to an issuer whose home State is a member State other than the United Kingdom, any reference to an applicable transparency obligation must be read subject to section 100A(2).

### 89L Power to suspend or prohibit trading of securities

(1) This section applies to securities admitted to trading on a regulated market.

(2) If the competent authority has reasonable grounds for suspecting that an applicable transparency obligation has been infringed by an issuer, it may—

(a) suspend trading in the securities for a period not exceeding 10 days,

(b) prohibit trading in the securities, or

(c) make a request to the operator of the market on which the issuer's securities are traded—

(i) to suspend trading in the securities for a period not exceeding 10 days, or

(ii) to prohibit trading in the securities.

(3) If the competent authority has reasonable grounds for suspecting that a provision required by the transparency obligations directive has been infringed by a voteholder of an issuer, it may—

(a) prohibit trading in the securities, or

(b) make a request to the operator of the market on which the issuer's securities are traded to prohibit trading in the securities.

(4) If the competent authority finds that an applicable transparency obligation has been infringed, it may require the market operator to prohibit trading in the securities.

(5) In this section 'transparency obligation' means an obligation under—

(a) a provision contained in transparency rules, or

(b) any other provision made in accordance with the transparency obligations directive.

(6) In relation to an issuer whose home State is a member State other than the United Kingdom, any reference to an applicable transparency obligation must be read subject to section 100A(2).

### 89M　Procedure under section 89L

(1)　A requirement under section 89L takes effect—

(a)　immediately, if the notice under subsection (2) states that that is the case;

(b)　in any other case, on such date as may be specified in the notice.

(2)　If the competent authority—

(a)　proposes to exercise the powers in section 89L in relation to a person, or

(b)　exercises any of those powers in relation to a person with immediate effect,

it must give that person written notice.

(3)　The notice must—

(a)　give details of the competent authority's action or proposed action;

(b)　state the competent authority's reasons for taking the action in question and choosing the date on which it took effect or takes effect;

(c)　inform the recipient that he may make representations to the competent authority within such period as may be specified by the notice (whether or not he had referred the matter to the Tribunal);

(d)　inform him of the date on which the action took effect or takes effect;

(e)　inform him of his right to refer the matter to the Tribunal (see section 89N) and give an indication of the procedure on such a reference.

(4)　The competent authority may extend the period within which representations may be made to it.

(5)　If, having considered any representations made to it, the competent authority decides to maintain, vary or revoke its earlier decision, it must give written notice to that effect to the person mentioned in subsection (2).

### 89N　Right to refer matters to the Tribunal

A person—

(a)　to whom a decision notice is given under section 89K (public censure), or

(b)　to whom a notice is given under section 89M (procedure in connection with suspension or prohibition of trading),

may refer the matter to the Tribunal.

### 89O　Corporate governance rules

(1)　The competent authority may make rules ('corporate governance rules')—

(a)　for the purpose of implementing, enabling the implementation of or dealing with matters arising out of or related to, any Community obligation relating to the corporate governance of issuers who have requested or approved admission of their securities to trading on a regulated market;

(b)　about corporate governance in relation to such issuers for the purpose of implementing, or dealing with matters arising out of or related to, any Community obligation.

(2)　'Corporate governance', in relation to an issuer, includes—

(a)　the nature, constitution or functions of the organs of the issuer;

(b)　the manner in which organs of the issuer conduct themselves;

(c)　the requirements imposed on organs of the issuer;

(d)　the relationship between the different organs of the issuer;

(e)　the relationship between the organs of the issuer and the members of the issuer or holders of the issuer's securities.

(3)　The burdens and restrictions imposed by rules under this section on foreign-traded issuers must not be greater than the burdens and restrictions imposed on UK-traded issuers by—

(a)　rules under this section, and

(b)　listing rules.

(4)　For this purpose—

'foreign-traded issuer' means an issuer who has requested or approved admission of the issuer's securities to trading on a regulated market situated or operating outside the United Kingdom;

'UK-traded issuer' means an issuer who has requested or approved admission of the issuer's securities to trading on a regulated market situated or operating in the United Kingdom.

(5)　This section is without prejudice to any other power conferred by this Part to make Part 6 rules.

*Compensation*

### 90　Compensation for statements in listing particulars or prospectus

(1)　Any person responsible for listing particulars is liable to pay compensation to a person who has—

(a)　acquired securities to which the particulars apply; and

(b)　suffered loss in respect of them as a result of—

(i)　any untrue or misleading statement in the particulars; or

(ii)　the omission from the particulars of any matter required to be included by section 80 or 81.

(2) Subsection (1) is subject to exemptions provided by Schedule 10.

(3) If listing particulars are required to include information about the absence of a particular matter, the omission from the particulars of that information is to be treated as a statement in the listing particulars that there is no such matter.

(4) Any person who fails to comply with section 81 is liable to pay compensation to any person who has—

> (a) acquired securities of the kind in question; and
>
> (b) suffered loss in respect of them as a result of the failure.

(5) Subsection (4) is subject to exemptions provided by Schedule 10.

(6) This section does not affect any liability which may be incurred apart from this section.

(7) References in this section to the acquisition by a person of securities include references to his contracting to acquire them or any interest in them.

(8) No person shall, by reason of being a promoter of a company or otherwise, incur any liability for failing to disclose information which he would not be required to disclose in listing particulars in respect of a company's securities—

> (a) if he were responsible for those particulars; or
>
> (b) if he is responsible for them, which he is entitled to omit by virtue of section 82.

(9) The reference in subsection (8) to a person incurring liability includes a reference to any other person being entitled as against that person to be granted any civil remedy or to rescind or repudiate an agreement.

(10) 'Listing particulars', in subsection (1) and Schedule 10, includes supplementary listing particulars.

(11) This section applies in relation to a prospectus as it applies to listing particulars, with the following modifications—

> (a) references in this section or in Schedule 10 to listing particulars, supplementary listing particulars or sections 80, 81 or 82 are to be read, respectively, as references to a prospectus, supplementary prospectus and sections 87A, 87G and 87B;
>
> (b) references in Schedule 10 to admission to the official list are to be read as references to admission to trading on a regulated market;
>
> (c) in relation to a prospectus, 'securities' means 'transferable securities'.

(12) A person is not to be subject to civil liability solely on the basis of a summary in a prospectus unless the summary is misleading, inaccurate or inconsistent when read with the rest of the prospectus; and, in this subsection, a summary includes any translation of it.

### 90A   Compensation for statements in certain publications

(1) The publications to which this section applies are—

> (a) any reports and statements published in response to a requirement imposed by a provision implementing Article 4, 5 or 6 of the transparency obligations directive, and
>
> (b) any preliminary statement made in advance of a report or statement to be published in response to a requirement imposed by a provision implementing Article 4 of that directive, to the extent that it contains information that it is intended—
>
> > (i) will appear in the report or statement, and
> >
> > (ii) will be presented in the report or statement in substantially the same form as that in which it is presented in the preliminary statement.

(2) The securities to which this section applies are—

> (a) securities that are traded on a regulated market situated or operating in the United Kingdom, and
>
> (b) securities that—
>
> > (i) are traded on a regulated market situated or operating outside the United Kingdom, and
> >
> > (ii) are issued by an issuer for which the United Kingdom is the home Member State within the meaning of Article 2.1(i) of the transparency obligations directive.

(3) The issuer of securities to which this section applies is liable to pay compensation to a person who has—

> (a) acquired such securities issued by it, and
>
> (b) suffered loss in respect of them as a result of—
>
> > (i) any untrue or misleading statement in a publication to which this section applies, or
> >
> > (ii) the omission from any such publication of any matter required to be included in it.

(4) The issuer is so liable only if a person discharging managerial responsibilities within the issuer in relation to the publication—

> (a) knew the statement to be untrue or misleading or was reckless as to whether it was untrue or misleading, or
>
> (b) knew the omission to be dishonest concealment of a material fact.

(5) A loss is not regarded as suffered as a result of the statement or omission in the publication unless the person suffering it acquired the relevant securities—

   (a) in reliance on the information in the publication, and
   (b) at a time when, and in circumstances in which, it was reasonable for him to rely on that information.
(6) Except as mentioned in subsection (8)—
   (a) the issuer is not subject to any other liability than that provided for by this section in respect of loss suffered as a result of reliance by any person on—
      (i) an untrue or misleading statement in a publication to which this section applies, or
      (ii) the omission from any such publication of any matter required to be included in it, and
   (b) a person other than the issuer is not subject to any liability, other than to the issuer, in respect of any such loss.
(7) Any reference in subsection (6) to a person being subject to a liability includes a reference to another person being entitled as against him to be granted any civil remedy or to rescind or repudiate an agreement.
(8) This section does not affect—
   (a) the powers conferred by section 382 and 384 (powers of the court to make a restitution order and of the Authority to require restitution);
   (b) liability for a civil penalty;
   (c) liability for a criminal offence.
(9) For the purposes of this section—
   (a) the following are persons 'discharging managerial responsibilities' in relation to a publication—
      (i) any director of the issuer (or person occupying the position of director, by whatever name called),
      (ii) in the case of an issuer whose affairs are managed by its members, any member of the issuer,
      (iii) in the case of an issuer that has no persons within subparagraph (i) or (ii), any senior executive of the issuer having responsibilities in relation to the publication;
   (b) references to the acquisition by a person of securities include his contracting to acquire them or any interest in them.

### 90B  Power to make further provision about liability for published information
(1) The Treasury may by regulations make provision about the liability of issuers of securities traded on a regulated market, and other persons, in respect of information published to holders of securities, to the market or to the public generally.
(2) Regulations under this section may amend any primary or subordinate legislation, including any provision of, or made under, this Act.

*Penalties*

### 91  Penalties for breach of Part 6 rules
(1) If the competent authority considers that—
   (a) an issuer of listed securities, or
   (b) an applicant for listing,
has contravened any provision of listing rules, it may impose on him a penalty of such amount as it considers appropriate.
(1ZA) If the competent authority considers that—
   (a) an issuer who has requested or approved the admission of a financial instrument to trading on a regulated market,
   (b) a person discharging managerial responsibilities within such an issuer, or
   (c) a person connected with such a person discharging managerial responsibilities,
has contravened any provision of disclosure rules, it may impose on him a penalty of such amount as it considers appropriate.
(1A) If the competent authority considers that—
   (a) an issuer of transferable securities,
   (b) a person offering transferable securities to the public or requesting their admission to trading on a regulated market,
   (c) an applicant for the approval of a prospectus in relation to transferable securities,
   (d) a person on whom a requirement has been imposed under section 87K or 87L, or
   (e) any other person to whom a provision of the prospectus directive applies,
has contravened a provision of this Part or of prospectus rules, or a provision otherwise made in accordance with the prospectus directive or a requirement imposed on him under such a provision, it may impose on him a penalty of such amount as it considers appropriate.
(1B) If the competent authority considers—
   (a) that a person has contravened—
      (i) a provision of transparency rules or a provision otherwise made in accordance with the transparency obligations directive, or

>>> (ii) a provision of corporate governance rules, or
>> (b) that a person on whom a requirement has been imposed under section 89L (power to suspend or prohibit trading of securities in case of infringement of applicable transparency obligation), has contravened that requirement,

it may impose on the person a penalty of such amount as it considers appropriate.

(2) If, in the case of a contravention by a person referred to in subsection (1), (1ZA)(a), (1A) or (1B) ('P'), the competent authority considers that another person who was at the material time a director of P was knowingly concerned in the contravention, it may impose upon him a penalty of such amount as it considers appropriate.

(3) If the competent authority is entitled to impose a penalty on a person under this section in respect of a particular matter it may, instead of imposing a penalty on him in respect of that matter, publish a statement censuring him.

(4) Nothing in this section prevents the competent authority from taking any other steps which it has power to take under this Part.

(5) A penalty under this section is payable to the competent authority.

(6) The competent authority may not take action against a person under this section after the end of the period of two years beginning with the first day on which it knew of the contravention unless proceedings against that person, in respect of the contravention, were begun before the end of that period.

(7) For the purposes of subsection (6)—
>> (a) the competent authority is to be treated as knowing of a contravention if it has information from which the contravention can reasonably be inferred; and
>> (b) proceedings against a person in respect of a contravention are to be treated as begun when a warning notice is given to him under section 92.

## 92 Procedure

(1) If the competent authority proposes to take action against a person under section 91, it must give him a warning notice.

(2) A warning notice about a proposal to impose a penalty must state the amount of the proposed penalty.

(3) A warning notice about a proposal to publish a statement must set out the terms of the proposed statement.

(4) If the competent authority decides to take action against a person under section 91, it must give him a decision notice.

(5) A decision notice about the imposition of a penalty must state the amount of the penalty.

(6) A decision notice about the publication of a statement must set out the terms of the statement.

(7) If the competent authority decides to take action against a person under section 91, he may refer the matter to the Tribunal.

## 93 Statement of policy

(1) The competent authority must prepare and issue a statement ('its policy statement') of its policy with respect to—
>> (a) the imposition of penalties under section 91; and
>> (b) the amount of penalties under that section.

(2) The competent authority's policy in determining what the amount of a penalty should be must include having regard to—
>> (a) the seriousness of the contravention in question in relation to the nature of the requirement contravened;
>> (b) the extent to which that contravention was deliberate or reckless; and
>> (c) whether the person on whom the penalty is to be imposed is an individual.

(3) The competent authority may at any time alter or replace its policy statement.

(4) If its policy statement is altered or replaced, the competent authority must issue the altered or replacement statement.

(5) In exercising, or deciding whether to exercise, its power under section 91 in the case of any particular contravention, the competent authority must have regard to any policy statement published under this section and in force at the time when the contravention in question occurred.

(6) The competent authority must publish a statement issued under this section in the way appearing to the competent authority to be best calculated to bring it to the attention of the public.

(7) The competent authority may charge a reasonable fee for providing a person with a copy of the statement.

(8) The competent authority must, without delay, give the Treasury a copy of any policy statement which it publishes under this section.

## 94 Statements of policy: procedure

(1) Before issuing a statement under section 93, the competent authority must publish a draft of the proposed statement in the way appearing to the competent authority to be best calculated to bring it to the attention of the public.

(2) The draft must be accompanied by notice that representations about the proposal may be made to the competent authority within a specified time.

(3) Before issuing the proposed statement, the competent authority must have regard to any representations made to it in accordance with subsection (2).

(4) If the competent authority issues the proposed statement it must publish an account, in general terms, of—

    (a) the representations made to it in accordance with subsection (2); and

    (b) its response to them.

(5) If the statement differs from the draft published under subsection (1) in a way which is, in the opinion of the competent authority, significant, the competent authority must (in addition to complying with subsection (4)) publish details of the difference.

(6) The competent authority may charge a reasonable fee for providing a person with a copy of a draft published under subsection (1).

(7) This section also applies to a proposal to alter or replace a statement.

### *Competition*

### 95   Competition scrutiny

(1) The Treasury may by order provide for—

    (a) regulating provisions, and

    (b) the practices of the competent authority in exercising its functions under this Part ('practices'),

to be kept under review.

(2) Provision made as a result of subsection (1) must require the person responsible for keeping regulating provisions and practices under review to consider—

    (a) whether any regulating provision or practice has a significantly adverse effect on competition; or

    (b) whether two or more regulating provisions or practices taken together have, or a particular combination of regulating provisions and practices has, such an effect.

(3) An order under this section may include provision corresponding to that made by any provision of Chapter III of Part X.

(4) Subsection (3) is not to be read as in any way restricting the power conferred by subsection (1).

(5) Subsections (6) to (8) apply for the purposes of provision made by or under this section.

(6) Regulating provisions or practices have a significantly adverse effect on competition if—

    (a) they have, or are intended or likely to have, that effect; or

    (b) the effect that they have, or are intended or likely to have, is to require or encourage behaviour which has, or is intended or likely to have, a significantly adverse effect on competition.

(7) If regulating provisions or practices have, or are intended or likely to have, the effect of requiring or encouraging exploitation of the strength of a market position they are to be taken to have, or be intended or be likely to have, an adverse effect on competition.

(8) In determining whether any of the regulating provisions or practices have, or are intended or likely to have, a particular effect, it may be assumed that the persons to whom the provisions concerned are addressed will act in accordance with them.

(9) 'Regulating provisions' means—

    (a) Part 6 rules

    (b) general guidance given by the competent authority in connection with its functions under this Part.

### 96   Obligations of issuers of listed securities

(1) Listing rules may—

    (a) specify requirements to be complied with by issuers of listed securities; and

    (b) make provision with respect to the action that may be taken by the competent authority in the event of non-compliance.

(2) If the rules require an issuer to publish information, they may include provision authorising the competent authority to publish it in the event of his failure to do so.

(3) This section applies whenever the listed securities were admitted to the official list.

### 96A   Disclosure of information requirements

(1) Disclosure rules must include provision specifying the disclosure of information requirements to be complied with by—

    (a) issuers who have requested or approved admission of their financial instruments to trading on a regulated market in the United Kingdom;

    (b) persons acting on behalf of or for the account of such issuers;

    (c) persons discharging managerial responsibilities within an issuer—

        (i) who is registered in the United Kingdom and who has requested or approved admission of its shares to trading on a regulated market; or

(ii) who is not registered in the United Kingdom or any other EEA State but who has requested or approved admission of its shares to trading on a regulated market and who is required to file annual information in relation to the shares in the United Kingdom in accordance with Article 10 of the prospectus directive;

(d) persons connected to such persons discharging managerial responsibilities.

(2) The rules must in particular—

(a) require an issuer to publish specified inside information;

(b) require an issuer to publish any significant change concerning information it has already published in accordance with paragraph (a);

(c) allow an issuer to delay the publication of inside information in specified circumstances;

(d) require an issuer (or a person acting on his behalf or for his account) who discloses inside information to a third party to publish that information without delay in specified circumstances;

(e) require an issuer (or person acting on his behalf or for his account) to draw up a list of those persons working for him who have access to inside information relating directly or indirectly to that issuer; and

(f) require persons discharging managerial responsibilities within an issuer falling within subsection (1)(c)(i) or (ii), and persons connected to such persons discharging managerial responsibilities, to disclose transactions conducted on their own account in shares of the issuer, or derivatives or any other financial instrument relating to those shares.

(3) Disclosure rules may make provision with respect to the action that may be taken by the competent authority in respect of non-compliance.

## 96B  Disclosure rules: persons responsible for compliance

(1) For the purposes of the provisions of this Part relating to disclosure rules , a 'person discharging managerial responsibilities within an issuer' means—

(a) a director of an issuer falling within section 96A(1)(c)(i) or (ii); or

(b) a senior executive of such an issuer who—

(i) has regular access to inside information relating, directly or indirectly, to the issuer, and

(ii) has power to make managerial decisions affecting the future development and business prospects of the issuer.

(2) A person 'connected' with a person discharging managerial responsibilities within an issuer means—

(a) a 'connected person' within the meaning in section 346 of the Companies Act 1985 (reading that section as if any reference to a director of a company were a reference to a person discharging managerial responsibilities within an issuer);

(b) a relative of a person discharging managerial responsibilities within an issuer, who, on the date of the transaction in question, has shared the same household as that person for at least 12 months;

(c) a body corporate in which—

(i) a person discharging managerial responsibilities within an issuer, or

(ii) any person connected with him by virtue of subsection (a) or (b),

is a director or a senior executive who has the power to make management decisions affecting the future development and business prospects of that body corporate.

## 96C  Suspension of trading

(1) The competent authority may, in accordance with disclosure rules, suspend trading in a financial instrument.

(2) If the competent authority does so, the issuer of that financial instrument may refer the matter to the Tribunal.

(3) The provisions relating to suspension of listing of securities in section 78 apply to the suspension of trading in a financial instrument and the references to listing and securities are to be read as references to trading and financial instruments respectively for the purposes of this section.

## 97  Appointment by competent authority of persons to carry out investigations

(1) Subsection (2) applies if it appears to the competent authority that there are circumstances suggesting that—

(a) there may have been a contravention of—

(i) a provision of this Part or of Part 6 rules, or

(ii) a provision otherwise made in accordance with the prospectus directive or the transparency obligations directive;

(b) a person who was at the material time a director of a person mentioned in section 91(1), (1ZA)(a), (1A) or (1B) has been knowingly concerned in a contravention by that person of—

(i) a provision of this Part or of Part 6 rules, or

(ii) a provision otherwise made in accordance with the prospectus directive or the transparency obligations directive;

(c) [...]

(d) there may have been a contravention of section 83, 85, 87G or 98.

(2) The competent authority may appoint one or more competent persons to conduct an investigation on its behalf.

(3) Part XI applies to an investigation under subsection (2) as if—

(a) the investigator were appointed under section 167(1);

(b) references to the investigating authority in relation to him were to the competent authority;

(c) references to the offences mentioned in section 168 were to those mentioned in subsection (1)(d);

(d) references to an authorised person were references to the person under investigation.

**98** [...]

**99  Fees**

(1) Listing rules may require the payment of fees to the competent authority in respect of—

(a) applications for listing;

(b) the continued inclusion of securities in the official list;

(c) applications under section 88 for approval as a sponsor; and

(d) continued inclusion of sponsors in the list of sponsors.

(1A) Disclosure rules may require the payment of fees to the competent authority in respect of the continued admission of financial instruments to trading on a regulated market.

(1B) Prospectus rules may require the payment of fees to the competent authority in respect of—

(a) applications for approval of a prospectus or a supplementary prospectus;

(b) applications for inclusion in the register of investors;

(c) the continued inclusion of investors in that register;

(d) access to that register.

(1C) Transparency rules may require the payment of fees to the competent authority in respect of the continued admission of financial instruments to trading on a regulated market.

(2) In exercising its powers under subsection (1), the competent authority may set such fees as it considers will (taking account of the income it expects as the competent authority) enable it—

(a) to meet expenses incurred in carrying out its functions under this Part or for any incidental purpose;

(b) to maintain adequate reserves; and

(c) in the case of the Authority, to repay the principal of, and pay any interest on, any money which it has borrowed and which has been used for the purpose of meeting expenses incurred in relation to—

(i) its assumption of functions from the London Stock Exchange Limited in relation to the official list; and

(ii) its assumption of functions under this Part.

(3) In fixing the amount of any fee which is to be payable to the competent authority, no account is to be taken of any sums which it receives, or expects to receive, by way of penalties imposed by it under this Part.

(4) Subsection (2)(c) applies whether expenses were incurred before or after the coming into force of this Part.

(5) Any fee which is owed to the competent authority under any provision made by or under this Part may be recovered as a debt due to it.

**100  Penalties**

(1) In determining its policy with respect to the amount of penalties to be imposed by it under this Part, the competent authority must take no account of the expenses which it incurs, or expects to incur, in discharging its functions under this Part.

(2) The competent authority must prepare and operate a scheme for ensuring that the amounts paid to it by way of penalties imposed under this Part are applied for the benefit of issuers of securities admitted to the official list and issuers who have requested or approved the admission of financial instruments to trading on a regulated market.

(3) The scheme may, in particular, make different provision with respect to different classes of issuer.

(4) Up to date details of the scheme must be set out in a document ('the scheme details').

(5) The scheme details must be published by the competent authority in the way appearing to it to be best calculated to bring them to the attention of the public.

(6) Before making the scheme, the competent authority must publish a draft of the proposed scheme in the way appearing to it to be best calculated to bring it to the attention of the public.

(7) The draft must be accompanied by notice that representations about the proposals may be made to the competent authority within a specified time.

(8) Before making the scheme, the competent authority must have regard to any representations made to it under subsection (7).

(9) If the competent authority makes the proposed scheme, it must publish an account, in general terms, of—

(a) the representations made to it in accordance with subsection (7); and

(b) its response to them.

(10) If the scheme differs from the draft published under subsection (6) in a way which is, in the opinion of the competent authority, significant the competent authority must (in addition to complying with subsection (9)) publish details of the difference.

(11) The competent authority must, without delay, give the Treasury a copy of any scheme details published by it.

(12) The competent authority may charge a reasonable fee for providing a person with a copy of—

(a) a draft published under subsection (6);

(b) scheme details.

(13) Subsections (6) to (10) and (12) apply also to a proposal to alter or replace the scheme.

## 100A   Exercise of powers where UK is host member state

(1) This section applies to the exercise by the competent authority of any power under this Part exercisable in case of infringement of—

(a) a provision of prospectus rules or any other provision made in accordance with the prospectus directive, or

(b) a provision of transparency rules or any other provision made in accordance with the transparency obligations directive,

in relation to an issuer whose home State is a member State other than the United Kingdom.

(2) The competent authority may act in such a case only in respect of the infringement of a provision required by the relevant directive. Any reference to an applicable provision or applicable transparency obligation shall be read accordingly.

(3) If the authority finds that there has been such an infringement, it must give a notice to that effect to the competent authority of the person's home State requesting it—

(a) to take all appropriate measures for the purpose of ensuring that the person remedies the situation that has given rise to the notice, and

(b) to inform the authority of the measures it proposes to take or has taken or the reasons for not taking such measures.

(4) The authority may not act further unless satisfied—

(a) that the competent authority of the person's home State has failed or refused to take measures for the purpose mentioned in subsection (3)(a), or

(b) that the measures taken by that authority have proved inadequate for that purpose.

This does not affect exercise of the powers under section 87K(2), 87L(2) or (3) or 89L(2) or (3) (powers to protect market).

(5) If the authority is so satisfied, it must, after informing the competent authority of the person's home State, take all appropriate measures to protect investors.

(6) In such a case the authority must inform the Commission of the measures at the earliest opportunity.

## 101   Listing rules: general provisions

(1) Part 6 rules may make different provision for different cases.

(2) Part 6 rules may authorise the competent authority to dispense with or modify the application of the rules in particular cases and by reference to any circumstances.

(3) Part 6 rules must be made by an instrument in writing.

(4) Immediately after an instrument containing Part 6 rules is made, it must be printed and made available to the public with or without payment.

(5) A person is not to be taken to have contravened any Part 6 rule if he shows that at the time of the alleged contravention the instrument containing the rule had not been made available as required by subsection (4).

(6) The production of a printed copy of an instrument purporting to be made by the competent authority on which is endorsed a certificate signed by an officer of the authority authorised by it for that purpose and stating—

(a) that the instrument was made by the authority,

(b) that the copy is a true copy of the instrument, and

(c) that on a specified date the instrument was made available to the public as required by subsection (4),

is evidence (or in Scotland sufficient evidence) of the facts stated in the certificate.

(7) A certificate purporting to be signed as mentioned in subsection (6) is to be treated as having been properly signed unless the contrary is shown.

(8) A person who wishes in any legal proceedings to rely on a rule-making instrument may require the Authority to endorse a copy of the instrument with a certificate of the kind mentioned in subsection (6).

*Miscellaneous*

## 102 Exemption from liability in damages

(1) Neither the competent authority nor any person who is, or is acting as, a member, officer or member of staff of the competent authority is to be liable in damages for anything done or omitted in the discharge, or purported discharge, of the authority's functions.

(2) Subsection (1) does not apply—

    (a) if the act or omission is shown to have been in bad faith; or

    (b) so as to prevent an award of damages made in respect of an act or omission on the ground that the act or omission was unlawful as a result of section 6(1) of the Human Rights Act 1998.

## 102A Meaning of 'securities' etc

(1) This section applies for the purposes of this Part.

(2) 'Securities' means (except in section 74(2) and the expression 'transferable securities') anything which has been, or may be, admitted to the official list.

(3) 'Transferable securities' means anything which is a transferable security for the purposes of Directive 2004/39/EC of the European Parliament and of the Council on markets in financial instruments , other than money-market instruments for the purposes of that directive which have a maturity of less than 12 months .

(3A) 'Debt securities' has the meaning given in Article 2.1(b) of the transparency obligations directive.

(4) 'Financial instrument' has (except in section 89F) the meaning given in Article 1.3 of Directive 2003/6/EC of the European Parliament and of the Council of 28 January 2003 on insider dealing and market manipulation (as modified by Article 69 of Directive 2004/39/EC on markets in financial instruments).

(5) 'Non-equity transferable securities' means all transferable securities that are not equity securities; and for this purpose 'equity securities' has the meaning given in Article 2.1(b) of the prospectus directive.

(6) 'Issuer' —

    (a) in relation to an offer of transferable securities to the public or admission of transferable securities to trading on a regulated market for which an approved prospectus is required as a result of section 85, means a legal person who issues or proposes to issue the transferable securities in question,

    (aa) in relation to transparency rules, means a legal person whose securities are admitted to trading on a regulated market or whose voting shares are admitted to trading on a UK market other than a regulated market, and in the case of depository receipts representing securities, the issuer is the issuer of the securities represented;

    (b) in relation to anything else which is or may be admitted to the official list, has such meaning as may be prescribed by the Treasury, and

    (c) in any other case, means a person who issues financial instruments.

## 102B Meaning of 'offer of transferable securities to the public' etc

(1) For the purposes of this Part there is an offer of transferable securities to the public if there is a communication to any person which presents sufficient information on—

    (a) the transferable securities to be offered, and

    (b) the terms on which they are offered,

to enable an investor to decide to buy or subscribe for the securities in question.

(2) For the purposes of this Part, to the extent that an offer of transferable securities is made to a person in the United Kingdom it is an offer of transferable securities to the public in the United Kingdom.

(3) The communication may be made—

    (a) in any form;

    (b) by any means.

(4) Subsection (1) includes the placing of securities through a financial intermediary.

(5) Subsection (1) does not include a communication in connection with trading on—

    (a) a regulated market;

    (b) a multilateral trading facility; or

    (c) a market prescribed by an order under section 130A(3).

(6) 'Multilateral trading facility' means a multilateral system, operated by an investment firm [...] or a market operator, which brings together multiple third-party buying and selling interests in financial instruments in accordance with non-discretionary rules so as to result in a contract .

## 102C Meaning of 'home State' in relation to transferable securities

In this Part, in relation to an issuer of transferable securities, the 'home-State' is the EEA State which is the 'home Member State' for the purposes of the prospectus directive (which is to be determined in accordance with Article 2.1(m) of that directive).

### 103 Interpretation of this Part

(1) In this Part, save where the context otherwise requires—

'disclosure rules' has the meaning given in section 73A;

'inside information' has the meaning given in section 118C;

'listed securities' means anything which has been admitted to the official list;

'listing' has the meaning given in section 74(5);

'listing particulars' has the meaning given in section 79(2);

'listing rules' has the meaning given in section 73A;

'market operator' means a person who manages or operates the business of a regulated market;

'offer of transferable securities to the public' has the meaning given in section 102B;

'the official list' means the list maintained by the competent authority as that list has effect for the time being;

'Part 6 rules' has the meaning given in section 73A;

'the prospectus directive' means Directive 2003/71/EC of the European Parliament and of the Council of 4 November 2003 on the prospectus to be published when securities are offered to the public or admitted to trading;

'prospectus rules' has the meaning given in section 73A;

'regulated market' has the meaning given in Article 4.1(14) of Directive 2004/39/EC of the European Parliament and of the Council on markets in financial instruments ;

'supplementary prospectus' has the meaning given in section 87G;

'the transparency obligations directive' means Directive 2004/ 109/EC of the European Parliament and of the Council relating to the harmonisation of transparency requirements in relation to information about issuers whose securities are admitted to trading on a regulated market;

'transparency rules' has the meaning given by section 89A(5);

'voteholder information' has the meaning given by section 89B(3);

'working day' means any day other that a Saturday, a Sunday, Christmas Day, Good Friday or a day which is a bank holiday under the Banking and Financial Dealings Act 1971 (c 80) in any part of the United Kingdom.

(2) In relation to any function conferred on the competent authority by this Part, any reference in this Part to the competent authority is to be read as a reference to the person by whom that function is for the time being exercisable.

(3) If, as a result of an order under Schedule 8, different functions conferred on the competent authority by this Part are exercisable by different persons, the powers conferred by section 91 are exercisable by such person as may be determined in accordance with the provisions of the order.

# PART VII

# CONTROL OF BUSINESS TRANSFERS

### 104 Control of business transfers

No insurance business transfer scheme or banking business transfer scheme is to have effect unless an order has been made in relation to it under section 111(1).

### 105 Insurance business transfer schemes

(1) A scheme is an insurance business transfer scheme if it—

(a) satisfies one of the conditions set out in subsection (2);

(b) results in the business transferred being carried on from an establishment of the transferee in an EEA State; and

(c) is not an excluded scheme.

(2) The conditions are that—

(a) the whole or part of the business carried on in one or more member States by a UK authorised person who has permission to effect or carry out contracts of insurance ('the authorised person concerned') is to be transferred to another body ('the transferee');

(b) the whole or part of the business, so far as it consists of reinsurance, carried on in the United Kingdom through an establishment there by an EEA firm falling within paragraph 5(d) of Schedule 3 and qualifying for authorisation under that Schedule ('the authorised person concerned') is to be transferred to another body ('the transferee');

(c) the whole or part of the business carried on in the United Kingdom by an authorised person who is neither a UK authorised person nor an EEA firm but who has permission to effect or carry out contracts of insurance ('the authorised person concerned') is to be transferred to another body ('the transferee').

(3) A scheme is an excluded scheme for the purposes of this section if it falls within any of the following cases:

Case 1
Where the authorised person concerned is a friendly society.

Case 2
Where—
- (a)  the authorised person concerned is a UK authorised person;
- (aa)  the authorised person concerned is not a reinsurance undertaking (within the meaning of Article 2.1(c) of the reinsurance directive);
- (b)  the business to be transferred under the scheme is business which consists of the effecting or carrying out of contracts of reinsurance in one or more EEA States other than the United Kingdom; and
- (c)  the scheme has been approved by a court in an EEA State other than the United Kingdom or by the host state regulator.

Case 3
Where—
- (a)  the authorised person concerned is a UK authorised person;
- (b)  the business to be transferred under the scheme is carried on in one or more countries or territories (none of which is an EEA State) and does not include policies of insurance [...] against risks arising in an EEA State; and
- (c)  the scheme has been approved by a court in a country or territory other than an EEA State or by the authority responsible for the supervision of that business in a country or territory in which it is carried on.

Case 4
Where—
- (a)  the business to be transferred under the scheme is the whole of the business of the authorised person concerned;
- (b)  all the policyholders are controllers of the firm or of firms within the same group as the firm which is the transferee, and
- (c)  all of the policyholders who will be affected by the transfer have consented to it.

Case 5
Where—
- (a)  the business of the authorised person concerned consists solely of the effecting or carrying out of contracts of reinsurance;
- (b)  the business to be transferred is the whole or part of that business;
- (c)  the scheme does not fall within Case 4;
- (d)  all of the policyholders who will be affected by the transfer have consented to it; and
- (e)  a certificate has been obtained under paragraph 2 of Schedule 12 in relation to the proposed transfer.

(4)  The parties to a scheme which falls within Case 2, 3, 4 or 5 may apply to the court for an order sanctioning the scheme as if it were an insurance business transfer scheme.

(5)  If the scheme involves a compromise or arrangement falling within Part 27 of the Companies Act 2006 (mergers and divisions of public companies), the provisions of that Part (and Part 26 of that Act) apply accordingly but this does not affect the operation of this Part in relation to the scheme.

(6)  Sections 425 to 427 of that Act (or Articles 418 to 420 of that Order) have effect as modified by section 427A of that Act (or Article 420A of that Order) in relation to that compromise or arrangement.

(7)  But subsection (6) does not affect the operation of this Part in relation to the scheme.

(8)  'UK authorised person' means a body which is an authorised person and which—
- (a)  is incorporated in the United Kingdom; or
- (b)  is an unincorporated association formed under the law of any part of the United Kingdom.

(9)  'Establishment' means, in relation to a person, his head office or a branch of his.

## 106   Banking business transfer schemes

(1)  A scheme is a banking business transfer scheme if it—
- (a)  satisfies one of the conditions set out in subsection (2);
- (b)  is one under which the whole or part of the business to be transferred includes the accepting of deposits; and
- (c)  is not an excluded scheme.

(2)  The conditions are that—
- (a)  the whole or part of the business carried on by a UK authorised person who has permission to accept deposits ('the authorised person concerned') is to be transferred to another body ('the transferee');
- (b)  the whole or part of the business carried on in the United Kingdom by an authorised person who is not a UK authorised person but who has permission to accept deposits ('the authorised person concerned') is to be transferred to another body which will carry it on in the United Kingdom ('the transferee').

(3) A scheme is an excluded scheme for the purposes of this section if—

(a) the authorised person concerned is a building society or a credit union; or

(b) the scheme is a compromise or arrangement to which Part 27 of the Companies Act 2006 (mergers and divisions of public companies) applies.

(4) For the purposes of subsection (2)(a) it is immaterial whether or not the business to be transferred is carried on in the United Kingdom.

(5) 'UK authorised person' has the same meaning as in section 105.

(6) 'Building society' has the meaning given in the Building Societies Act 1986.

(7) 'Credit union' means a credit union within the meaning of—

(a) the Credit Unions Act 1979;

(b) the Credit Unions (Northern Ireland) Order 1985.

### 106A  Reclaim fund business transfer scheme

(1) A scheme is a reclaim fund business transfer scheme if, under the scheme, the whole or part of the business carried on by a reclaim fund is to be transferred to one or more other reclaim funds.

(2) 'Reclaim fund' has the meaning given by section 5(1) of the Dormant Bank and Building Society Accounts Act 2008.

### 107  Application for order sanctioning transfer scheme

(1) An application may be made to the court for an order sanctioning an insurance business transfer scheme or a banking business transfer scheme a banking business transfer scheme or a reclaim fund business transfer scheme.

(2) An application may be made by—

(a) the authorised person concerned;

(b) the transferee; or

(c) both.

(3) The application must be made—

(a) if the authorised person concerned and the transferee are registered or have their head offices in the same jurisdiction, to the court in that jurisdiction;

(b) if the authorised person concerned and the transferee are registered or have their head offices in different jurisdictions, to the court in either jurisdiction;

(c) if the transferee is not registered in the United Kingdom and does not have his head office there, to the court which has jurisdiction in relation to the authorised person concerned.

(4) 'Court' means—

(a) the High Court; or

(b) in Scotland, the Court of Session.

### 108  Requirements on applicants

(1) The Treasury may by regulations impose requirements on applicants under section 107.

(2) The court may not determine an application under that section if the applicant has failed to comply with a prescribed requirement.

(3) The regulations may, in particular, include provision—

(a) as to the persons to whom, and periods within which, notice of an application must be given;

(b) enabling the court to waive a requirement of the regulations in prescribed circumstances.

### 109  Scheme reports

(1) An application under section 107 in respect of an insurance business transfer scheme must be accompanied by a report on the terms of the scheme ('a scheme report').

(2) A scheme report may be made only by a person—

(a) appearing to the Authority to have the skills necessary to enable him to make a proper report; and

(b) nominated or approved for the purpose by the Authority.

(3) A scheme report must be made in a form approved by the Authority.

### 110  Right to participate in proceedings

On an application under section 107, the following are also entitled to be heard—

(a) the Authority, and

(b) any person (including an employee of the authorised person concerned or of the transferee) who alleges that he would be adversely affected by the carrying out of the scheme.

### 111  Sanction of the court for business transfer schemes

(1) This section sets out the conditions which must be satisfied before the court may make an order under this section sanctioning an insurance business transfer scheme or a banking business transfer scheme a banking business transfer scheme or a reclaim fund business transfer scheme.

(2) The court must be satisfied that—

(a) in the case of an insurance business transfer scheme or a banking business transfer scheme the appropriate certificates have been obtained (as to which see Parts I and II of Schedule 12);

(aa) in the case of a reclaim fund business transfer scheme, the appropriate certificate has been obtained (as to which see Part 2A of that Schedule);

(b) the transferee has the authorisation required (if any) to enable the business, or part, which is to be transferred to be carried on in the place to which it is to be transferred (or will have it before the scheme takes effect).

(3) The court must consider that, in all the circumstances of the case, it is appropriate to sanction the scheme.

## 112    Effect of order sanctioning business transfer scheme

(1) If the court makes an order under section 111(1), it may by that or any subsequent order make such provision (if any) as it thinks fit—

(a) for the transfer to the transferee of the whole or any part of the undertaking concerned and of any property or liabilities of the authorised person concerned;

(b) for the allotment or appropriation by the transferee of any shares, debentures, policies or other similar interests in the transferee which under the scheme are to be allotted or appropriated to or for any other person;

(c) for the continuation by (or against) the transferee of any pending legal proceedings by (or against) the authorised person concerned;

(d) with respect to such incidental, consequential and supplementary matters as are, in its opinion, necessary to secure that the scheme is fully and effectively carried out.

(2) An order under subsection (1)(a) may—

(a) transfer property or liabilities whether or not the authorised person concerned otherwise has the capacity to effect the transfer in question;

(b) make provision in relation to property which was held by the authorised person concerned as trustee;

(c) make provision as to future or contingent rights or liabilities of the authorised person concerned, including provision as to the construction of instruments (including wills) under which such rights or liabilities may arise;

(d) make provision as to the consequences of the transfer in relation to any occupational pension scheme (within the meaning of section 150(5) of the Finance Act 2004) operated by or on behalf of the authorised person concerned.

(2A) Subsection (2)(a) is to be taken to include power to make provision in an order—

(a) for the transfer of property or liabilities which would not otherwise be capable of being transferred or assigned;

(b) for a transfer of property or liabilities to take effect as if there were—

(i) no such requirement to obtain a person's consent or concurrence, and

(ii) no such contravention, liability or interference with any interest or right, as there would otherwise be (in the case of a transfer apart from this section) by reason of any provision falling within subsection (2B).

(2B) A provision falls within this subsection to the extent that it has effect (whether under an enactment or agreement or otherwise) in relation to the terms on which the authorised person concerned is entitled to the property or subject to the liabilities in question.

(2C) Nothing in subsection (2A) or (2B) is to be read as limiting the scope of subsection (1)

(3) If an order under subsection (1) makes provision for the transfer of property or liabilities—

(a) the property is transferred to and vests in, and

(b) the liabilities are transferred to and become liabilities of,

the transferee as a result of the order.

(4) But if any property or liability included in the order is governed by the law of any country or territory outside the United Kingdom, the order may require the authorised person concerned, if the transferee so requires, to take all necessary steps for securing that the transfer to the transferee of the property or liability is fully effective under the law of that country or territory.

(5) Property transferred as the result of an order under subsection (1) may, if the court so directs, vest in the transferee free from any charge which is (as a result of the scheme) to cease to have effect.

(6) An order under subsection (1) which makes provision for the transfer of property is to be treated as an instrument of transfer for the purposes of section 770(1) of the Companies Act 2006 (registration of transfer of shares or debentures) and any other enactment requiring the delivery of an instrument of transfer for the registration of property.

(7) [...]

(8) If the court makes an order under section 111(1) in relation to an insurance business transfer scheme, it may by that or any subsequent order make such provision (if any) as it thinks fit—

(a) for dealing with the interests of any person who, within such time and in such manner as the court may direct, objects to the scheme;

(b) for the dissolution, without winding up, of the authorised person concerned;

(c) for the reduction, on such terms and subject to such conditions (if any) as it thinks fit, of the benefits payable under—

(i)   any description of policy, or

(ii)   policies generally,

entered into by the authorised person concerned and transferred as a result of the scheme.

(9)  If, in the case of an insurance business transfer scheme, the authorised person concerned is not an EEA firm, it is immaterial for the purposes of subsection (1)(a), (c) or (d) or subsection (2), (2A), (3) or (4) that the law applicable to any of the contracts of insurance included in the transfer is the law of an EEA State other than the United Kingdom.

(10)  The transferee must, if an insurance or banking business transfer scheme is sanctioned by the court, deposit two office copies of the order made under subsection (1) with the Authority within 10 days of the making of the order.

(11)  But the Authority may extend that period.

(12)  'Property' includes property, rights and powers of any description.

(13)  'Liabilities' includes duties.

(14)  'Shares' and 'debentures' have the same meaning as in the Companies Acts (see sections 540 and 738 of the Companies Act 2006).

(15)  'Charge' includes a mortgage (or, in Scotland, a security over property).

### 112A   Rights to terminate etc

(1)  Subsection (2) applies where (apart from that subsection) a person would be entitled, in consequence of anything done or likely to be done by or under this Part in connection with an insurance business transfer scheme or a banking business transfer scheme—

(a)  to terminate, modify, acquire or claim an interest or right; or

(b)  to treat an interest or right as terminated or modified.

(2)  The entitlement—

(a)  is not enforceable in relation to that interest or right until after an order has been made under section 112(1) in relation to the scheme; and

(b)  is then enforceable in relation to that interest or right only insofar as the order contains provision to that effect.

(3)  Nothing in subsection (1) or (2) is to be read as limiting the scope of section 112(1).

### 113   Appointment of actuary in relation to reduction of benefits

(1)  This section applies if an order has been made under section 111(1).

(2)  The court making the order may, on the application of the Authority, appoint an independent actuary—

(a)  to investigate the business transferred under the scheme; and

(b)  to report to the Authority on any reduction in the benefits payable under policies entered into by the authorised person concerned that, in the opinion of the actuary, ought to be made.

### 114   Rights of certain policyholders

(1)  This section applies in relation to an insurance business transfer scheme if—

(a)  the authorised person concerned is an authorised person other than an EEA firm qualifying for authorisation under Schedule 3;

(b)  the court has made an order under section 111 in relation to the scheme; and

(c)  an EEA State other than the United Kingdom is, as regards any policy included in the transfer which evidences a contract of insurance (other than a contract of reinsurance), the State of the commitment or the EEA State in which the risk is situated ('the EEA State concerned').

(2)  The court must direct that notice of the making of the order, or the execution of any instrument, giving effect to the transfer must be published by the transferee in the EEA State concerned.

(3)  A notice under subsection (2) must specify such period as the court may direct as the period during which the policyholder may exercise any right which he has to cancel the policy.

(4)  The order or instrument mentioned in subsection (2) does not bind the policyholder if—

(a)  the notice required under that subsection is not published; or

(b)  the policyholder cancels the policy during the period specified in the notice given under that subsection.

(5)  The law of the EEA State concerned governs—

(a)  whether the policyholder has a right to cancel the policy; and

(b)  the conditions, if any, subject to which any such right may be exercised.

(6)  Paragraph 6 of Schedule 12 applies for the purposes of this section as it applies for the purposes of that Schedule.

### 114A   Notice of transfer of reinsurance contracts

(1)  This section applies in relation to an insurance business transfer scheme if—

(a)  the authorised person concerned is an authorised person other than an EEA firm qualifying for authorisation under Schedule 3;

(b)  the court has made an order under section 111 in relation to the scheme; and

(c)  an EEA State other than the United Kingdom is, as regards any policy included in the transfer which evidences a contract of reinsurance, the State in which the establishment of the policyholder to which the policy relates is situated at the date when the contract was entered into ('the EEA State concerned').

(2) The court may direct that notice of the making of the order, or the execution of any instrument, giving effect to the transfer must be published by the transferee in the EEA State concerned.

*Business transfers outside the United Kingdom*

## 115   Certificates for purposes of insurance business transfers overseas
Part III of Schedule 12 makes provision about certificates which the Authority may issue in relation to insurance business transfers taking place outside the United Kingdom.

## 116   Effect of insurance business transfers authorised in other EEA States
(1) This section applies if, as a result of an authorised transfer, an EEA firm falling within paragraph 5(d) or (da) of Schedule 3 transfers to another body all its rights and obligations under any UK policies.

(2) This section also applies if, as a result of an authorised transfer, any of the following transfers to another body all its rights and obligations under any UK policies—

(a) an undertaking authorised in an EEA State other than the United Kingdom under Article 51 of the life assurance consolidation directive;

(b) an undertaking authorised in an EEA State other than the United Kingdom under Article 23 of the first non-life insurance directive;

(c) an undertaking, whose head office is not within the EEA, authorised under the law of an EEA State other than the United Kingdom to carry out reinsurance activities in its territory (as mentioned in Article 49 of the reinsurance directive).

(3) If appropriate notice of the execution of an instrument giving effect to the transfer is published, the instrument has the effect in law—

(a) of transferring to the transferee all the transferor's rights and obligations under the UK policies to which the instrument applies, and

(b) if the instrument so provides, of securing the continuation by or against the transferee of any legal proceedings by or against the transferor which relate to those rights and obligations.

(4) No agreement or consent is required before subsection (3) has the effects mentioned.

(5) 'Authorised transfer' means—

(a) in subsection (1), a transfer authorised in the home State of the EEA firm in accordance with—

(i) Article 14 of the life assurance consolidation directive; [...]

(ii) Article 12 of the third non-life directive; or

(iii) Article 18 of the reinsurance directive; and

(b) in subsection (2), a transfer authorised in an EEA State other than the United Kingdom in accordance with—

(i) Article 53 of the life assurance consolidation directive; [...]

(ii) Article 28a of the first non-life directive ; or

(iii) the provisions in the law of that EEA State which provide for the authorisation of transfers of all or part of a portfolio of contracts of an undertaking authorised to carry out reinsurance activities in its territory (as mentioned in Article 49 of the reinsurance directive).

(6) 'UK policy' means—

(a) in the case of an authorised transfer within the meaning of paragraph (a)(i) or (ii) or (b)(i) or (ii) of subsection (5), a policy evidencing a contract of insurance (other than a contract of reinsurance) to which the applicable law is the law of a part of the United Kingdom;

(b) in the case of an authorised transfer within the meaning of paragraph (a)(iii) or (b)(iii) of that subsection, a policy evidencing a contract of reinsurance to which the applicable law is the law of a part of the United Kingdom.

(7) 'Appropriate notice' means—

(a) if the UK policy evidences a contract of insurance in relation to which an EEA State other than the United Kingdom is the State of the commitment, notice given in accordance with the law of that State;

(b) if the UK policy evidences a contract of insurance where the risk is situated in an EEA State other than the United Kingdom, notice given in accordance with the law of that EEA State;

(c) in any other case, notice given in accordance with the applicable law.

(8) Paragraph 6 of Schedule 12 applies for the purposes of this section as it applies for the purposes of that Schedule.

*Modifications*

## 117   Power to modify this Part
The Treasury may by regulations—

(a) provide for prescribed provisions of this Part to have effect in relation to prescribed cases with such modifications as may be prescribed;

(b) make such amendments to any provision of this Part as they consider appropriate for the more effective operation of that or any other provision of this Part.

# PART VIII

# PENALTIES FOR MARKET ABUSE

*Market abuse*

### 118    Market abuse

(1) For the purposes of this Act, market abuse is behaviour (whether by one person alone or by two or more persons jointly or in concert) which—

(a) occurs in relation to—

(i) qualifying investments admitted to trading on a prescribed market,

(ii) qualifying investments in respect of which a request for admission to trading on such a market has been made, or

(iii) in the case of subsection (2) or (3) behaviour, investments which are related investments in relation to such qualifying investments, and

(b) falls within any one or more of the types of behaviour set out in subsections (2) to (8).

(2) The first type of behaviour is where an insider deals, or attempts to deal, in a qualifying investment or related investment on the basis of inside information relating to the investment in question.

(3) The second is where an insider discloses inside information to another person otherwise than in the proper course of the exercise of his employment, profession or duties.

(4) The third is where the behaviour (not falling within subsection (2) or (3))—

(a) is based on information which is not generally available to those using the market but which, if available to a regular user of the market, would be, or would be likely to be, regarded by him as relevant when deciding the terms on which transactions in qualifying investments should be effected, and

(b) is likely to be regarded by a regular user of the market as a failure on the part of the person concerned to observe the standard of behaviour reasonably expected of a person in his position in relation to the market.

(5) The fourth is where the behaviour consists of effecting transactions or orders to trade (otherwise than for legitimate reasons and in conformity with accepted market practices on the relevant market) which—

(a) give, or are likely to give, a false or misleading impression as to the supply of, or demand for, or as to the price of, one or more qualifying investments, or

(b) secure the price of one or more such investments at an abnormal or artificial level.

(6) The fifth is where the behaviour consists of effecting transactions or orders to trade which employ fictitious devices or any other form of deception or contrivance.

(7) The sixth is where the behaviour consists of the dissemination of information by any means which gives, or is likely to give, a false or misleading impression as to a qualifying investment by a person who knew or could reasonably be expected to have known that the information was false or misleading.

(8) The seventh is where the behaviour (not falling within subsection (5), (6) or (7))—

(a) is likely to give a regular user of the market a false or misleading impression as to the supply of, demand for or price or value of, qualifying investments, or

(b) would be, or would be likely to be, regarded by a regular user of the market as behaviour that would distort, or would be likely to distort, the market in such an investment,

and the behaviour is likely to be regarded by a regular user of the market as a failure on the part of the person concerned to observe the standard of behaviour reasonably expected of a person in his position in relation to the market.

(9) Subsections (4) and (8) and the definition of 'regular user' in section 130A(3) cease to have effect on 31 December 2009 and subsection (1)(b) is then to be read as no longer referring to those subsections.

### 118A    Supplementary provision about certain behaviour

(1) Behaviour is to be taken into account for the purposes of this Part only if it occurs—

(a) in the United Kingdom, or

(b) in relation to—

(i) qualifying investments which are admitted to trading on a prescribed market situated in, or operating in, the United Kingdom,

(ii) qualifying investments for which a request for admission to trading on such a prescribed market has been made, or

(iii) in the case of section 118(2) and (3), investments which are related investments in relation to such qualifying investments.

(2) For the purposes of subsection (1), as it applies in relation to section 118(4) and (8), a prescribed market accessible electronically in the United Kingdom is to be treated as operating in the United Kingdom.

(3) For the purposes of section 118(4) and (8), the behaviour that is to be regarded as occurring in relation to qualifying investments includes behaviour which—

(a) occurs in relation to anything that is the subject matter, or whose price or value is expressed by reference to the price or value of the qualifying investments, or

(b) occurs in relation to investments (whether or not they are qualifying investments) whose subject matter is the qualifying investments.

(4) For the purposes of section 118(7), the dissemination of information by a person acting in the capacity of a journalist is to be assessed taking into account the codes governing his profession unless he derives, directly or indirectly, any advantage or profits from the dissemination of the information.

(5) Behaviour does not amount to market abuse for the purposes of this Act if—

(a) it conforms with a rule which includes a provision to the effect that behaviour conforming with the rule does not amount to market abuse,

(b) it conforms with the relevant provisions of Commission Regulation (EC) No 2273/2003 of 22 December 2003 implementing Directive 2003/6/EC of the European Parliament and of the Council as regards exemptions for buy-back programmes and stabilisation of financial instruments, or

(c) it is done by a person acting on behalf of a public authority in pursuit of monetary policies or policies with respect to exchange rates or the management of public debt or foreign exchange reserves.

(6) Subsections (2) and (3) cease to have effect on 31 December 2009.

## 118B   Insiders

For the purposes of this Part an insider is any person who has inside information—

(a) as a result of his membership of an administrative, management or supervisory body of an issuer of qualifying investments,

(b) as a result of his holding in the capital of an issuer of qualifying investments,

(c) as a result of having access to the information through the exercise of his employment, profession or duties,

(d) as a result of his criminal activities, or

(e) which he has obtained by other means and which he knows, or could reasonably be expected to know, is inside information.

## 118C   Inside information

(1) This section defines 'inside information' for the purposes of this Part.

(2) In relation to qualifying investments, or related investments, which are not commodity derivatives, inside information is information of a precise nature which—

(a) is not generally available,

(b) relates, directly or indirectly, to one or more issuers of the qualifying investments or to one or more of the qualifying investments, and

(c) would, if generally available, be likely to have a significant effect on the price of the qualifying investments or on the price of related investments.

(3) In relation to qualifying investments or related investments which are commodity derivatives, inside information is information of a precise nature which—

(a) is not generally available,

(b) relates, directly or indirectly, to one or more such derivatives, and

(c) users of markets on which the derivatives are traded would expect to receive in accordance with any accepted market practices on those markets.

(4) In relation to a person charged with the execution of orders concerning any qualifying investments or related investments, inside information includes information conveyed by a client and related to the client's pending orders which—

(a) is of a precise nature,

(b) is not generally available,

(c) relates, directly or indirectly, to one or more issuers of qualifying investments or to one or more qualifying investments, and

(d) would, if generally available, be likely to have a significant effect on the price of those qualifying investments or the price of related investments.

(5) Information is precise if it—

(a) indicates circumstances that exist or may reasonably be expected to come into existence or an event that has occurred or may reasonably be expected to occur, and

(b) is specific enough to enable a conclusion to be drawn as to the possible effect of those circumstances or that event on the price of qualifying investments or related investments.

(6) Information would be likely to have a significant effect on price if and only if it is information of a kind which a reasonable investor would be likely to use as part of the basis of his investment decisions.

(7) For the purposes of subsection (3)(c), users of markets on which investments in commodity derivatives are traded are to be treated as expecting to receive information relating directly or indirectly to one or more such derivatives in accordance with any accepted market practices, which is—

    (a) routinely made available to the users of those markets, or

    (b) required to be disclosed in accordance with any statutory provision, market rules, or contracts or customs on the relevant underlying commodity market or commodity derivatives market.

(8) Information which can be obtained by research or analysis conducted by, or on behalf of, users of a market is to be regarded, for the purposes of this Part, as being generally available to them.

*The code*

### 119 The code

(1) The Authority must prepare and issue a code containing such provisions as the Authority considers will give appropriate guidance to those determining whether or not behaviour amounts to market abuse.

(2) The code may among other things specify—

    (a) descriptions of behaviour that, in the opinion of the Authority, amount to market abuse;

    (b) descriptions of behaviour that, in the opinion of the Authority, do not amount to market abuse;

    (c) factors that, in the opinion of the Authority, are to be taken into account in determining whether or not behaviour amounts to market abuse.

    (d) descriptions of behaviour that are accepted market practices in relation to one or more specified markets;

    (e) descriptions of behaviour that are not accepted market practices in relation to one or more specified markets.

(2A) In determining, for the purposes of subsections (2)(d) and (2)(e) or otherwise, what are and what are not accepted market practices, the Authority must have regard to the factors and procedures laid down in Articles 2 and 3 respectively of Commission Directive 2004/72/EC of 29 April 2004 implementing Directive 2003/6/EC of the European Parliament and of the Council.

(3) The code may make different provision in relation to persons, cases or circumstances of different descriptions.

(4) The Authority may at any time alter or replace the code.

(5) If the code is altered or replaced, the altered or replacement code must be issued by the Authority.

(6) A code issued under this section must be published by the Authority in the way appearing to the Authority to be best calculated to bring it to the attention of the public.

(7) The Authority must, without delay, give the Treasury a copy of any code published under this section.

(8) The Authority may charge a reasonable fee for providing a person with a copy of the code.

### 120 Provisions included in the Authority's code by reference to the City Code

(1) The Authority may include in a code issued by it under section 119 ('the Authority's code') provision to the effect that in its opinion behaviour conforming with the City Code—

    (a) does not amount to market abuse;

    (b) does not amount to market abuse in specified circumstances; or

    (c) does not amount to market abuse if engaged in by a specified description of person.

(2) But the Treasury's approval is required before any such provision may be included in the Authority's code.

(3) If the Authority's code includes provision of a kind authorised by subsection (1), the Authority must keep itself informed of the way in which the Panel on Takeovers and Mergers interprets and administers the relevant provisions of the City Code.

(4) 'City Code' means the City Code on Takeovers and Mergers issued by the Panel as it has effect at the time when the behaviour occurs.

(5) 'Specified' means specified in the Authority's code.

### 121 Codes: procedure

(1) Before issuing a code under section 119, the Authority must publish a draft of the proposed code in the way appearing to the Authority to be best calculated to bring it to the attention of the public.

(2) The draft must be accompanied by—

    (a) a cost benefit analysis; and

    (b) notice that representations about the proposal may be made to the Authority within a specified time.

(3) Before issuing the proposed code, the Authority must have regard to any representations made to it in accordance with subsection (2)(b).

(4) If the Authority issues the proposed code it must publish an account, in general terms, of—

    (a) the representations made to it in accordance with subsection (2)(b); and

    (b) its response to them.

(5) If the code differs from the draft published under subsection (1) in a way which is, in the opinion of the Authority, significant—

    (a) the Authority must (in addition to complying with subsection (4)) publish details of the difference; and

    (b) those details must be accompanied by a cost benefit analysis.

(6) Subsections (1) to (5) do not apply if the Authority considers that there is an urgent need to publish the code.

(7) Neither subsection (2)(a) nor subsection (5)(b) applies if the Authority considers—

    (a) that, making the appropriate comparison, there will be no increase in costs; or

    (b) that, making that comparison, there will be an increase in costs but the increase will be of minimal significance.

(8) The Authority may charge a reasonable fee for providing a person with a copy of a draft published under subsection (1).

(9) This section also applies to a proposal to alter or replace a code.

(10) 'Cost benefit analysis' means an estimate of the costs together with an analysis of the benefits that will arise—

    (a) if the proposed code is issued; or

    (b) if subsection (5)(b) applies, from the code that has been issued.

(11) 'The appropriate comparison' means—

    (a) in relation to subsection (2)(a), a comparison between the overall position if the code is issued and the overall position if it is not issued;

    (b) in relation to subsection (5)(b), a comparison between the overall position after the issuing of the code and the overall position before it was issued.

## 122    Effect of the code

(1) If a person behaves in a way which is described (in the code in force under section 119 at the time of the behaviour) as behaviour that, in the Authority's opinion, does not amount to market abuse that behaviour of his is to be taken, for the purposes of this Act, as not amounting to market abuse.

(2) Otherwise, the code in force under section 119 at the time when particular behaviour occurs may be relied on so far as it indicates whether or not that behaviour should be taken to amount to market abuse.

*Power to impose penalties*

## 123    Power to impose penalties in cases of market abuse

(1) If the Authority is satisfied that a person ('A')—

    (a) is or has engaged in market abuse, or

    (b) by taking or refraining from taking any action has required or encouraged another person or persons to engage in behaviour which, if engaged in by A, would amount to market abuse,

it may impose on him a penalty of such amount as it considers appropriate.

(2) But the Authority may not impose a penalty on a person if, having considered any representations made to it in response to a warning notice, there are reasonable grounds for it to be satisfied that—

    (a) he believed, on reasonable grounds, that his behaviour did not fall within paragraph (a) or (b) of subsection (1), or

    (b) he took all reasonable precautions and exercised all due diligence to avoid behaving in a way which fell within paragraph (a) or (b) of that subsection.

(3) If the Authority is entitled to impose a penalty on a person under this section it may, instead of imposing a penalty on him, publish a statement to the effect that he has engaged in market abuse.

*Statement of policy*

## 124    Statement of policy

(1) The Authority must prepare and issue a statement of its policy with respect to—

    (a) the imposition of penalties under section 123; and

    (b) the amount of penalties under that section.

(2) The Authority's policy in determining what the amount of a penalty should be must include having regard to—

    (a) whether the behaviour in respect of which the penalty is to be imposed had an adverse effect on the market in question and, if it did, how serious that effect was;

    (b) the extent to which that behaviour was deliberate or reckless; and

    (c) whether the person on whom the penalty is to be imposed is an individual.

(3) A statement issued under this section must include an indication of the circumstances in which the Authority is to be expected to regard a person as—

(a) having a reasonable belief that his behaviour did not amount to market abuse; or

(b) having taken reasonable precautions and exercised due diligence to avoid engaging in market abuse.

(4) The Authority may at any time alter or replace a statement issued under this section.

(5) If a statement issued under this section is altered or replaced, the Authority must issue the altered or replacement statement.

(6) In exercising, or deciding whether to exercise, its power under section 123 in the case of any particular behaviour, the Authority must have regard to any statement published under this section and in force at the time when the behaviour concerned occurred.

(7) A statement issued under this section must be published by the Authority in the way appearing to the Authority to be best calculated to bring it to the attention of the public.

(8) The Authority may charge a reasonable fee for providing a person with a copy of a statement published under this section.

(9) The Authority must, without delay, give the Treasury a copy of any statement which it publishes under this section.

### 125 Statement of policy: procedure

(1) Before issuing a statement of policy under section 124, the Authority must publish a draft of the proposed statement in the way appearing to the Authority to be best calculated to bring it to the attention of the public.

(2) The draft must be accompanied by notice that representations about the proposal may be made to the Authority within a specified time.

(3) Before issuing the proposed statement, the Authority must have regard to any representations made to it in accordance with subsection (2).

(4) If the Authority issues the proposed statement it must publish an account, in general terms, of—

(a) the representations made to it in accordance with subsection (2); and

(b) its response to them.

(5) If the statement differs from the draft published under subsection (1) in a way which is, in the opinion of the Authority, significant, the Authority must (in addition to complying with subsection (4)) publish details of the difference.

(6) The Authority may charge a reasonable fee for providing a person with a copy of a draft published under subsection (1).

(7) This section also applies to a proposal to alter or replace a statement.

*Procedure*

### 126 Warning notices

(1) If the Authority proposes to take action against a person under section 123, it must give him a warning notice.

(2) A warning notice about a proposal to impose a penalty must state the amount of the proposed penalty.

(3) A warning notice about a proposal to publish a statement must set out the terms of the proposed statement.

### 127 Decision notices and right to refer to Tribunal

(1) If the Authority decides to take action against a person under section 123, it must give him a decision notice.

(2) A decision notice about the imposition of a penalty must state the amount of the penalty.

(3) A decision notice about the publication of a statement must set out the terms of the statement.

(4) If the Authority decides to take action against a person under section 123, that person may refer the matter to the Tribunal.

*Miscellaneous*

### 128 Suspension of investigations

(1) If the Authority considers it desirable or expedient because of the exercise or possible exercise of a power relating to market abuse, it may direct a recognised investment exchange or recognised clearing house—

(a) to terminate, suspend or limit the scope of any inquiry which the exchange or clearing house is conducting under its rules; or

(b) not to conduct an inquiry which the exchange or clearing house proposes to conduct under its rules.

(2) A direction under this section—

(a) must be given to the exchange or clearing house concerned by notice in writing; and

(b) is enforceable, on the application of the Authority, by injunction or, in Scotland, by an order under section 45 of the Court of Session Act 1988.

(3) The Authority's powers relating to market abuse are its powers—

(a) to impose penalties under section 123; or

(b) to appoint a person to conduct an investigation under section 168 in a case falling within subsection (2)(d) of that section.

## 129   Power of court to impose penalty in cases of market abuse

(1) The Authority may on an application to the court under section 381 or 383 request the court to consider whether the circumstances are such that a penalty should be imposed on the person to whom the application relates.

(2) The court may, if it considers it appropriate, make an order requiring the person concerned to pay to the Authority a penalty of such amount as it considers appropriate.

## 130   Guidance

(1) The Treasury may from time to time issue written guidance for the purpose of helping relevant authorities to determine the action to be taken in cases where behaviour occurs which is behaviour—

(a) with respect to which the power in section 123 appears to be exercisable; and

(b) which appears to involve the commission of an offence under section 397 of this Act or Part V of the Criminal Justice Act 1993 (insider dealing).

(2) The Treasury must obtain the consent of the Attorney General and the Secretary of State before issuing any guidance under this section.

(3) In this section 'relevant authorities'—

(a) in relation to England and Wales, means the Secretary of State, the Authority, the Director of the Serious Fraud Office and the Director of Public Prosecutions;

(b) in relation to Northern Ireland, means the Secretary of State, the Authority, the Director of the Serious Fraud Office and the Director of Public Prosecutions for Northern Ireland.

(4) Subsections (1) to (3) do not apply to Scotland.

(5) In relation to Scotland, the Lord Advocate may from time to time, after consultation with the Treasury, issue written guidance for the purpose of helping the Authority to determine the action to be taken in cases where behaviour mentioned in subsection (1) occurs.

## 130A   Interpretation and supplementary provision

(1) The Treasury may by order specify (whether by name or description)—

(a) the markets which are prescribed markets for the purposes of specified provisions of this Part, and

(b) the investments that are qualifying investments in relation to the prescribed markets.

(2) An order may prescribe different investments or descriptions of investment in relation to different markets or descriptions of market.

(3) In this Part—

'accepted market practices' means practices that are reasonably expected in the financial market or markets in question and are accepted by the Authority or, in the case of a market situated in another EEA State, the competent authority of that EEA State within the meaning of Directive 2003/6/EC of the European Parliament and of the Council of 28 January 2003 on insider dealing and market manipulation (market abuse),

'behaviour' includes action or inaction,

'dealing', in relation to an investment, means acquiring or disposing of the investment whether as principal or agent or directly or indirectly, and includes agreeing to acquire or dispose of the investment, and entering into and bringing to an end a contract creating it,

'investment' is to be read with section 22 and Schedule 2,

'regular user', in relation to a particular market, means a reasonable person who regularly deals on that market in investments of the kind in question,

'related investment', in relation to a qualifying investment, means an investment whose price or value depends on the price or value of the qualifying investment.

(4) Any reference in this Act to a person engaged in market abuse is to a person engaged in market abuse either alone or with one or more other persons.

## 131   Effect on transactions

The imposition of a penalty under this Part does not make any transaction void or unenforceable.

## 131A   Protected Disclosures

(1) A disclosure which satisfies the following three conditions is not to be taken to breach any restriction on the disclosure of information (however imposed).

(2) The first condition is that the information or other matter—

(a) causes the person making the disclosure (the discloser) to know or suspect, or

(b) gives him reasonable grounds for knowing or suspecting, that another person has engaged in market abuse.

(3) The second condition is that the information or other matter disclosed came to the discloser in the course of his trade, profession, business or employment.

(4) The third condition is that the disclosure is made to the Authority or to a nominated officer as soon as is practicable after the information or other matter comes to the discloser.

(5) A disclosure to a nominated officer is a disclosure which is made to a person nominated by the discloser's employer to receive disclosures under this section, and is made in the course of the discloser's employment and in accordance with the procedure established by the employer for the purpose.

(6) For the purposes of this section, references to a person's employer include any body, association or organisation (including a voluntary organisation) in connection with whose activities the person exercises a function (whether or not for gain or reward) and references to employment must be construed accordingly.

# PART IX

# HEARINGS AND APPEALS

### 132  The Financial Services and Markets Tribunal

(1) For the purposes of this Act, there is to be a tribunal known as the Financial Services and Markets Tribunal (but referred to in this Act as 'the Tribunal').

(2) The Tribunal is to have the functions conferred on it by or under this Act.

(3) The Lord Chancellor may by rules make such provision as appears to him to be necessary or expedient in respect of the conduct of proceedings before the Tribunal.

(4) Schedule 13 is to have effect as respects the Tribunal and its proceedings (but does not limit the Lord Chancellor's powers under this section).

### 133  Proceedings: general provision

(1) A reference to the Tribunal under this Act must be made before the end of—

    (a) the period of 28 days beginning with the date on which the decision notice or supervisory notice in question is given; or

    (b) such other period as may be specified in rules made under section 132.

(2) Subject to rules made under section 132, the Tribunal may allow a reference to be made after the end of that period.

(3) On a reference the Tribunal may consider any evidence relating to the subject-matter of the reference, whether or not it was available to the Authority at the material time.

(4) On a reference the Tribunal must determine what (if any) is the appropriate action for the Authority to take in relation to the matter referred to it.

(5) On determining a reference, the Tribunal must remit the matter to the Authority with such directions (if any) as the Tribunal considers appropriate for giving effect to its determination.

(6) In determining a reference made as a result of a decision notice, the Tribunal may not direct the Authority to take action which the Authority would not, as a result of section 388(2), have had power to take when giving the decision notice.

(7) In determining a reference made as a result of a supervisory notice, the Tribunal may not direct the Authority to take action which would have otherwise required the giving of a decision notice.

(8) The Tribunal may, on determining a reference, make recommendations as to the Authority's regulating provisions or its procedures.

(9) The Authority must not take the action specified in a decision notice—

    (a) during the period within which the matter to which the decision notice relates may be referred to the Tribunal; and

    (b) if the matter is so referred, until the reference, and any appeal against the Tribunal's determination, has been finally disposed of.

(10) The Authority must act in accordance with the determination of, and any direction given by, the Tribunal.

(11) An order of the Tribunal may be enforced—

    (a) as if it were an order of a county court; or

    (b) in Scotland, as if it were an order of the Court of Session.

(12) 'Supervisory notice' has the same meaning as in section 395.

*Legal assistance before the Tribunal*

### 134  Legal assistance scheme

(1) The Lord Chancellor may by regulations establish a scheme governing the provision of legal assistance in connection with proceedings before the Tribunal.

(2) If the Lord Chancellor establishes a scheme under subsection (1), it must provide that a person is eligible for assistance only if—

    (a) he falls within subsection (3); and

    (b) he fulfils such other criteria (if any) as may be prescribed as a result of section 135(1)(d).

(3) A person falls within this subsection if he is an individual who has referred a matter to the Tribunal under section 127(4).

(4) In this Part of this Act 'the legal assistance scheme' means any scheme in force under subsection (1).

### 135 Provisions of the legal assistance scheme

(1) The legal assistance scheme may, in particular, make provision as to—

    (a) the kinds of legal assistance that may be provided;

    (b) the persons by whom legal assistance may be provided;

    (c) the manner in which applications for legal assistance are to be made;

    (d) the criteria on which eligibility for legal assistance is to be determined;

    (e) the persons or bodies by whom applications are to be determined;

    (f) appeals against refusals of applications;

    (g) the revocation or variation of decisions;

    (h) its administration and the enforcement of its provisions.

(2) Legal assistance under the legal assistance scheme may be provided subject to conditions or restrictions, including conditions as to the making of contributions by the person to whom it is provided.

### 136 Funding of the legal assistance scheme

(1) The Authority must pay to the Lord Chancellor such sums at such times as he may, from time to time, determine in respect of the anticipated or actual cost of legal assistance provided in connection with proceedings before the Tribunal under the legal assistance scheme.

(2) In order to enable it to pay any sum which it is obliged to pay under subsection (1), the Authority must make rules requiring the payment to it by authorised persons or any class of authorised person of specified amounts or amounts calculated in a specified way.

(3) Sums received by the Lord Chancellor under subsection (1) must be paid into the Consolidated Fund.

(4) The Lord Chancellor must, out of money provided by Parliament fund the cost of legal assistance provided in connection with proceedings before the Tribunal under the legal assistance scheme.

(5) Subsection (6) applies if, as respects a period determined by the Lord Chancellor, the amount paid to him under subsection (1) as respects that period exceeds the amount he has expended in that period under subsection (4).

(6) The Lord Chancellor must—

    (a) repay, out of money provided by Parliament, the excess to the Authority; or

    (b) take the excess into account on the next occasion on which he makes a determination under subsection (1).

(7) The Authority must make provision for any sum repaid to it under subsection (6)(a)—

    (a) to be distributed among—

        (i) the authorised persons on whom a levy was imposed in the period in question as a result of rules made under subsection (2); or

        (ii) such of those persons as it may determine;

    (b) to be applied in order to reduce any amounts which those persons, or such of them as it may determine, are or will be liable to pay to the Authority, whether under rules made under subsection (2) or otherwise; or

    (c) to be partly so distributed and partly so applied.

(8) If the Authority considers that it is not practicable to deal with any part of a sum repaid to it under subsection (6)(a) in accordance with provision made by it as a result of subsection (7), it may, with the consent the Lord Chancellor, apply or dispose of that part of that sum in such manner as it considers appropriate.

(9) 'Specified' means specified in the rules.

*Appeals*

### 137 Appeal on a point of law

(1) A party to a reference to the Tribunal may with permission appeal—

    (a) to the Court of Appeal, or

    (b) in Scotland, to the Court of Session,

on a point of law arising from a decision of the Tribunal disposing of the reference.

(2) 'Permission' means permission given by the Tribunal or by the Court of Appeal or (in Scotland) the Court of Session.

(3) If, on an appeal under subsection (1), the court considers that the decision of the Tribunal was wrong in law, it may—

    (a) remit the matter to the Tribunal for rehearing and determination by it; or

    (b) itself make a determination.

(4) An appeal may not be brought from a decision of the Court of Appeal under subsection (3) except with the leave of—

    (a) the Court of Appeal; or

    (b) the *House of Lords.*

(5) An appeal lies, with the leave of the Court of Session or the *House of Lords*, from any decision of the Court of Session under this section, and such leave may be given on such terms as to costs, expenses or otherwise as the Court of Session or the *House of Lords* may determine.

(6) Rules made under section 132 may make provision for regulating or prescribing any matters incidental to or consequential on an appeal under this section.[1]

# PART X

# RULES AND GUIDANCE

## Chapter I

### Rule-making powers

**138   General rule-making power**

(1) The Authority may make such rules applying to authorised persons—

    (a) with respect to the carrying on by them of regulated activities, or

    (b) with respect to the carrying on by them of activities which are not regulated activities,

as appear to it to be necessary or expedient for the purpose of protecting the interests of consumers.

(1A) The Authority may also make such rules applying to authorised persons who are investment firms or credit institutions, with respect to the provision by them of a relevant ancillary service, as appear to the Authority to be necessary or expedient for the purpose of protecting the interests of consumers.

(1B) 'Credit institution' means—

    (a) a credit institution authorised under the banking consolidation directive, or

    (b) an institution which would satisfy the requirements for authorisation as a credit institution under that directive if it had its registered office (or if it does not have a registered office, its head office) in an EEA State.

(1C) 'Relevant ancillary service' means any service of a kind mentioned in Section B of Annex I to the markets in financial instruments directive the provision of which does not involve the carrying on of a regulated activity.

(2) Rules made under this section are referred to in this Act as the Authority's general rules.

(3) The Authority's power to make general rules is not limited by any other power which it has to make regulating provisions.

(4) The Authority's general rules may make provision applying to authorised persons even though there is no relationship between the authorised persons to whom the rules will apply and the persons whose interests will be protected by the rules.

(5) General rules may contain requirements which take into account, in the case of an authorised person who is a member of a group, any activity of another member of the group.

(6) General rules may not—

    (a) make provision prohibiting an EEA firm from carrying on, or holding itself out as carrying on, any activity which it has permission conferred by Part II of Schedule 3 to carry on in the United Kingdom;

    (b) make provision, as respects an EEA firm, about any matter responsibility for which is, under any of the single market directives, reserved to the firm's home state regulator.

(7) 'Consumers' means persons—

    (a) who use, have used, or are or may be contemplating using, any of the services provided by—

        (i) authorised persons in carrying on regulated activities;

        (ia) authorised persons who are investment firms or credit institutions in providing a relevant ancillary service; or

        (ii) persons acting as appointed representatives;

    (b) who have rights or interests which are derived from, or are otherwise attributable to, the use of any such services by other persons; or

    (c) who have rights or interests which may be adversely affected by the use of any such services by persons acting on their behalf or in a fiduciary capacity in relation to them.

(8) If an authorised person is carrying on a regulated activity in his capacity as a trustee, the persons who are, have been or may be beneficiaries of the trust are to be treated as persons who use, have used or are or may be contemplating using services provided by the authorised person in his carrying on of that activity.

(9) For the purposes of subsection (7) a person who deals with an authorised person in the course of the authorised person's carrying on of a regulated activity is to be treated as using services provided by the authorised person in carrying on those activities.

---

[1] In subsections (4)(b) and (5) the words 'House of Lords' are to be substituted with 'Supreme Court' under the Constitutional Reform Act 2005 c 4 from a date to be appointed.

## 139  Miscellaneous ancillary matters

(1) Rules relating to the handling of money held by an authorised person in specified circumstances ('clients' money') may—

    (a) make provision which results in that clients' money being held on trust in accordance with the rules;

    (b) treat two or more accounts as a single account for specified purposes (which may include the distribution of money held in the accounts);

    (c) authorise the retention by the authorised person of interest accruing on the clients' money; and

    (d) make provision as to the distribution of such interest which is not to be retained by him.

(2) An institution with which an account is kept in pursuance of rules relating to the handling of clients' money does not incur any liability as constructive trustee if money is wrongfully paid from the account, unless the institution permits the payment—

    (a) with knowledge that it is wrongful; or

    (b) having deliberately failed to make enquiries in circumstances in which a reasonable and honest person would have done so.

(3) In the application of subsection (1) to Scotland, the reference to money being held on trust is to be read as a reference to its being held as agent for the person who is entitled to call for it to be paid over to him or to be paid on his direction or to have it otherwise credited to him.

(4) Rules may—

    (a) confer rights on persons to rescind agreements with, or withdraw offers to, authorised persons within a specified period; and

    (b) make provision, in respect of authorised persons and persons exercising those rights, for the restitution of property and the making or recovery of payments where those rights are exercised.

(5) 'Rules' means general rules.

(6) 'Specified' means specified in the rules.

## 140  Restriction on managers of certain collective investment schemes

(1) The Authority may make rules prohibiting an authorised person who has permission to act as

    (a) the manager of an authorised unit trust scheme

    (b) the management company of an authorised UCITS open-ended investment company,

from carrying on a specified activity.

(2) Such rules may specify an activity which is not a regulated activity.

(3) In this section—

    (a) 'authorised UCITS open-ended investment company' means an authorised open-ended investment company to which the UCITS directive applies; and

    (b) 'management company' has the meaning given by Article 1a.2 of the UCITS directive.

## 141  Insurance business rules

(1) The Authority may make rules prohibiting an authorised person who has permission to effect or carry out contracts of insurance from carrying on a specified activity.

(2) Such rules may specify an activity which is not a regulated activity.

(3) The Authority may make rules in relation to contracts entered into by an authorised person in the course of carrying on business which consists of the effecting or carrying out of contracts of long-term insurance.

(4) Such rules may, in particular—

    (a) restrict the descriptions of property or indices of the value of property by reference to which the benefits under such contracts may be determined;

    (b) make provision, in the interests of the protection of policyholders, for the substitution of one description of property, or index of value, by reference to which the benefits under a contract are to be determined for another such description of property or index.

(5) Rules made under this section are referred to in this Act as insurance business rules.

## 142  Insurance business: regulations supplementing Authority's rules

(1) The Treasury may make regulations for the purpose of preventing a person who is not an authorised person but who—

    (a) is a parent undertaking of an authorised person who has permission to effect or carry out contracts of insurance, and

    (b) falls within a prescribed class,

from doing anything to lessen the effectiveness of asset identification rules.

(2) 'Asset identification rules' means rules made by the Authority which require an authorised person who has permission to effect or carry out contracts of insurance to identify assets which belong to him and which are maintained in respect of a particular aspect of his business.

(3) The regulations may, in particular, include provision—

    (a) prohibiting the payment of dividends;

(b) prohibiting the creation of charges;

(c) making charges created in contravention of the regulations void.

(4) The Treasury may by regulations provide that, in prescribed circumstances, charges created in contravention of asset identification rules are void.

(5) A person who contravenes regulations under subsection (1) is guilty of an offence and liable on summary conviction to a fine not exceeding level 5 on the standard scale.

(6) 'Charges' includes mortgages (or in Scotland securities over property).

**143**   [...]

*Specific rules*

### 144   Price stabilising rules

(1) The Authority may make rules ('price stabilising rules') as to—

(a) the circumstances and manner in which,

(b) the conditions subject to which, and

(c) the time when or the period during which,

action may be taken for the purpose of stabilising the price of investments of specified kinds.

(2) Price stabilising rules—

(a) are to be made so as to apply only to authorised persons;

(b) may make different provision in relation to different kinds of investment.

(3) The Authority may make rules which, for the purposes of section 397(5)(b), treat a person who acts or engages in conduct—

(a) for the purpose of stabilising the price of investments, and

(b) in conformity with such provisions corresponding to price stabilising rules and made by a body or authority outside the United Kingdom as may be specified in the rules under this subsection,

as acting, or engaging in that conduct, for that purpose and in conformity with price stabilising rules.

(4) The Treasury may by order impose limitations on the power to make rules under this section.

(5) Such an order may, in particular—

(a) specify the kinds of investment in relation to which price stabilising rules may make provision;

(b) specify the kinds of investment in relation to which rules made under subsection (3) may make provision;

(c) provide for price stabilising rules to make provision for action to be taken for the purpose of stabilising the price of investments only in such circumstances as the order may specify;

(d) provide for price stabilising rules to make provision for action to be taken for that purpose only at such times or during such periods as the order may specify.

(6) If provisions specified in rules made under subsection (3) are altered, the rules continue to apply to those provisions as altered, but only if before the alteration the Authority has notified the body or authority concerned (and has not withdrawn its notification) that it is satisfied with its consultation procedures.

(7) 'Consultation procedures' means procedures designed to provide an opportunity for persons likely to be affected by alterations to those provisions to make representations about proposed alterations to any of those provisions.

### 145   Financial promotion rules

(1) The Authority may make rules applying to authorised persons about the communication by them, or their approval of the communication by others, of invitations or inducements—

(a) to engage in investment activity; or

(b) to participate in a collective investment scheme.

(2) Rules under this section may, in particular, make provision about the form and content of communications.

(3) Subsection (1) applies only to communications which—

(a) if made by a person other than an authorised person, without the approval of an authorised person, would contravene section 21(1);

(b) may be made by an authorised person without contravening section 238(1).

(3A) But subsection (3) does not prevent the Authority from making rules under subsection (1) in relation to a communication that would not contravene section 21(1) if made by a person other than an authorised person, without the approval of an authorised person, if the conditions set out in subsection (3B) are satisfied.

(3B) Those conditions are—

(a) that the communication would not contravene subsection (1) of section 21 because it is a communication to which that subsection does not apply as a result of an order under subsection (5) of that section;

(b) that the Authority considers that any of the requirements of—

(i) paragraphs 1 to 8 of Article 19 of the markets in financial instruments directive; or

   (ii)  any implementing measure made under paragraph 10 of that Article,
        apply to the communication; and
   (c)  that the Authority considers that the rules are necessary to secure that the communication
        satisfies such of the requirements mentioned in paragraph (b) as the Authority considers
        apply to the communication.
   (4)  'Engage in investment activity' has the same meaning as in section 21.
   (5)  The Treasury may by order impose limitations on the power to make rules under this section.

## 146   Money laundering rules

The Authority may make rules in relation to the prevention and detection of money laundering in connection with the carrying on of regulated activities by authorised persons.

## 147   Control of information rules

   (1)  The Authority may make rules ('control of information rules') about the disclosure and use of
information held by an authorised person ('A').
   (2)  Control of information rules may—
   (a)  require the withholding of information which A would otherwise have to disclose to a per-
        son ('B') for or with whom A does business in the course of carrying on any regulated or other
        activity;
   (b)  specify circumstances in which A may withhold information which he would otherwise have
        to disclose to B;
   (c)  require A not to use for the benefit of B information A holds which A would otherwise have
        to use in that way;
   (d)  specify circumstances in which A may decide not to use for the benefit of B information A
        holds which A would otherwise have to use in that way.

*Modification or waiver*

## 148   Modification or waiver of rules

   (1)  [...]
   (2)  The Authority may, on the application or with the consent of a person who is subject to rules
made by the Authority, direct that all or any of those rules (other than rules made under section 247
(trust scheme rules) or section 248 (scheme particulars rules))—
   (a)  are not to apply to that person; or
   (b)  are to apply to him with such modifications as may be specified in the direction.
   (3)  An application must be made in such manner as the Authority may direct.
   (4)  The Authority may not give a direction unless it is satisfied that—
   (a)  compliance by the [...] person with the rules, or with the rules as unmodified, would be unduly
        burdensome or would not achieve the purpose for which the rules were made; and
   (b)  the direction would not result in undue risk to persons whose interests the rules are intended
        to protect.
   (5)  A direction may be given subject to conditions.
   (6)  Unless it is satisfied that it is inappropriate or unnecessary to do so, a direction must be
published by the Authority in such a way as it thinks most suitable for bringing the direction to the
attention of—
   (a)  those likely to be affected by it; and
   (b)  others who may be likely to make an application for a similar direction.
   (7)  In deciding whether it is satisfied as mentioned in subsection (6), the Authority must—
   (a)  take into account whether the direction relates to a rule contravention of which is actionable
        in accordance with section 150;
   (b)  consider whether its publication would prejudice, to an unreasonable degree, the commer-
        cial interests of the [...] person concerned or any other member of his immediate group; and
   (c)  consider whether its publication would be contrary to an international obligation of the
        United Kingdom.
   (8)  For the purposes of paragraphs (b) and (c) of subsection (7), the Authority must consider
whether it would be possible to publish the direction without either of the consequences mentioned in
those paragraphs by publishing it without disclosing the identity of the [...] person concerned.
   (9)  The Authority may—
   (a)  revoke a direction; or
   (b)  vary it on the application, or with the consent, of the [...] person to whom it relates.
   (10)  'Direction' means a direction under subsection (2).
   (11)  'Immediate group', in relation to a person ('A'), means—
   (a)  A;
   (b)  a parent undertaking of A;
   (c)  a subsidiary undertaking of A;
   (d)  a subsidiary undertaking of a parent undertaking of A;
   (e)  a parent undertaking of a subsidiary undertaking of A.

*Contravention of rules*

### 149    Evidential provisions

(1) If a particular rule so provides, contravention of the rule does not give rise to any of the consequences provided for by other provisions of this Act.

(2) A rule which so provides must also provide—

(a) that contravention may be relied on as tending to establish contravention of such other rule as may be specified; or

(b) that compliance may be relied on as tending to establish compliance with such other rule as may be specified.

(3) A rule may include the provision mentioned in subsection (1) only if the Authority considers that it is appropriate for it also to include the provision required by subsection (2).

### 150    Actions for damages

(1) A contravention by an authorised person of a rule is actionable at the suit of a private person who suffers loss as a result of the contravention, subject to the defences and other incidents applying to actions for breach of statutory duty.

(2) If rules so provide, subsection (1) does not apply to contravention of a specified provision of those rules.

(3) In prescribed cases, a contravention of a rule which would be actionable at the suit of a private person is actionable at the suit of a person who is not a private person, subject to the defences and other incidents applying to actions for breach of statutory duty.

(4) In subsections (1) and (3) 'rule' does not include—

(a) Part 6 rules; or

(b) a rule requiring an authorised person to have or maintain financial resources.

(5) 'Private person' has such meaning as may be prescribed.

### 151    Limits on effect of contravening rules

(1) A person is not guilty of an offence by reason of a contravention of a rule made by the Authority.

(2) No such contravention makes any transaction void or unenforceable.

*Procedural provisions*

### 152    Notification of rules to the Treasury

(1) If the Authority makes any rules, it must give a copy to the Treasury without delay.

(2) If the Authority alters or revokes any rules, it must give written notice to the Treasury without delay.

(3) Notice of an alteration must include details of the alteration.

### 153    Rule-making instruments

(1) Any power conferred on the Authority to make rules is exercisable in writing.

(2) An instrument by which rules are made by the Authority ('a rule-making instrument') must specify the provision under which the rules are made.

(3) To the extent to which a rule-making instrument does not comply with subsection (2), it is void.

(4) A rule-making instrument must be published by the Authority in the way appearing to the Authority to be best calculated to bring it to the attention of the public.

(5) The Authority may charge a reasonable fee for providing a person with a copy of a rule-making instrument.

(6) A person is not to be taken to have contravened any rule made by the Authority if he shows that at the time of the alleged contravention the rule-making instrument concerned had not been made available in accordance with this section.

### 154    Verification of rules

(1) The production of a printed copy of a rule-making instrument purporting to be made by the Authority—

(a) on which is endorsed a certificate signed by a member of the Authority's staff authorised by it for that purpose, and

(b) which contains the required statements,

is evidence (or in Scotland sufficient evidence) of the facts stated in the certificate.

(2) The required statements are—

(a) that the instrument was made by the Authority;

(b) that the copy is a true copy of the instrument; and

(c) that on a specified date the instrument was made available to the public in accordance with section 153(4).

(3) A certificate purporting to be signed as mentioned in subsection (1) is to be taken to have been properly signed unless the contrary is shown.

(4) A person who wishes in any legal proceedings to rely on a rule-making instrument may require the Authority to endorse a copy of the instrument with a certificate of the kind mentioned in subsection (1).

### 155  Consultation

(1) If the Authority proposes to make any rules, it must publish a draft of the proposed rules in the way appearing to it to be best calculated to bring them to the attention of the public.

(2) The draft must be accompanied by—

    (a) a cost benefit analysis;

    (b) an explanation of the purpose of the proposed rules;

    (c) an explanation of the Authority's reasons for believing that making the proposed rules is compatible with its general duties under section 2; and

    (d) notice that representations about the proposals may be made to the Authority within a specified time.

(3) In the case of a proposal to make rules under a provision mentioned in subsection (9), the draft must also be accompanied by details of the expected expenditure by reference to which the proposal is made.

(4) Before making the proposed rules, the Authority must have regard to any representations made to it in accordance with subsection (2)(d).

(5) If the Authority makes the proposed rules, it must publish an account, in general terms, of—

    (a) the representations made to it in accordance with subsection (2)(d); and

    (b) its response to them.

(6) If the rules differ from the draft published under subsection (1) in a way which is, in the opinion of the Authority, significant—

    (a) the Authority must (in addition to complying with subsection (5)) publish details of the difference; and

    (b) those details must be accompanied by a cost benefit analysis.

(7) Subsections (1) to (6) do not apply if the Authority considers that the delay involved in complying with them would be prejudicial to the interests of consumers.

(8) Neither subsection (2)(a) nor subsection (6)(b) applies if the Authority considers—

    (a) that, making the appropriate comparison, there will be no increase in costs; or

    (b) that, making that comparison, there will be an increase in costs but the increase will be of minimal significance.

(9) Neither subsection (2)(a) nor subsection (6)(b) requires a cost benefit analysis to be carried out in relation to rules made under—

    (a) section 136(2);

    (b) subsection (1) of section 213 as a result of subsection (4) of that section;

    (c) section 234;

    (d) paragraph 17 of Schedule 1.

(10) 'Cost benefit analysis' means an estimate of the costs together with an analysis of the benefits that will arise—

    (a) if the proposed rules are made; or

    (b) if subsection (6) applies, from the rules that have been made.

(11) 'The appropriate comparison' means—

    (a) in relation to subsection (2)(a), a comparison between the overall position if the rules are made and the overall position if they are not made;

    (b) in relation to subsection (6)(b), a comparison between the overall position after the making of the rules and the overall position before they were made.

(12) The Authority may charge a reasonable fee for providing a person with a copy of a draft published under subsection (1).

### 156  General supplementary powers

(1) Rules made by the Authority may make different provision for different cases and may, in particular, make different provision in respect of different descriptions of authorised person, activity or investment.

(2) Rules made by the Authority may contain such incidental, supplemental, consequential and transitional provision as the Authority considers appropriate.

## Chapter II

## Guidance

### 157  Guidance

(1) The Authority may give guidance consisting of such information and advice as it considers appropriate—

    (a) with respect to the operation of this Act and of any rules made under it;

(b)  with respect to any matters relating to functions of the Authority;

(c)  for the purpose of meeting the regulatory objectives;

(d)  with respect to any other matters about which it appears to the Authority to be desirable to give information or advice.

(2)  The Authority may give financial or other assistance to persons giving information or advice of a kind which the Authority could give under this section.

(3)  If the Authority proposes to give guidance to regulated persons generally, or to a class of regulated person, in relation to rules to which those persons are subject, subsections (1), (2) and (4) to (10) of section 155 apply to the proposed guidance as they apply to proposed rules unless the Authority considers that the delay in complying with them would be prejudicial to the interests of consumers.

(4)  The Authority may—

(a)  publish its guidance;

(b)  offer copies of its published guidance for sale at a reasonable price; and

(c)  if it gives guidance in response to a request made by any person, make a reasonable charge for that guidance.

(5)  In this Chapter (except in section 158A), references to guidance given by the Authority include references to any recommendation made by the Authority to persons generally, to regulated persons generally or to any class of regulated person.

(6)  'Regulated person' means any—

(a)  authorised person;

(b)  person who is otherwise subject to rules made by the Authority.

### 158  Notification of guidance to the Treasury

(1)  On giving any general guidance, the Authority must give the Treasury a copy of the guidance without delay.

(2)  If the Authority alters any of its general guidance, it must give written notice to the Treasury without delay.

(3)  The notice must include details of the alteration.

(4)  If the Authority revokes any of its general guidance, it must give written notice to the Treasury without delay.

(5)  'General guidance' means guidance given by the Authority under section 157 which is—

(a)  given to persons generally, to regulated persons generally or to a class of regulated person;

(b)  intended to have continuing effect; and

(c)  given in writing or other legible form.

(6)  'Regulated person' has the same meaning as in section 157.

### 158A  Guidance on outsourcing by investment firms and credit institutions

(1)  Without prejudice to the generality of section 157, the Authority must give guidance in the terms required by Article 15(3) of Commission Directive 2006/73/EC of 10 August 2006 (requirement to publish statement of policy on outsourcing of investment services by investment firms and credit institutions).

(2)  Subsections (1), (2)(b) and (d), (4), (5), (6)(a) and (7) of section 155 apply to guidance which the Authority is required to give under this section as they apply to proposed rules.

(3)  The Authority must publish its guidance under this section.

(4)  The Authority may offer copies of the published guidance for sale at a reasonable price.

(5)  Subsections (1) to (4) of section 158 apply to guidance under this section as they apply to general guidance (as defined by section 158(5)).

## Chapter III

## Competition scrutiny

### 159  Interpretation

(1)  In this Chapter—

'OFT' means the Office of Fair Trading

'practices', in relation to the Authority, means practices adopted by the Authority in the exercise of functions under this Act;

'regulating provisions' means any—

(a)  rules;

(b)  general guidance (as defined by section 158(5) or guidance under section158A);

(c)  statement issued by the Authority under section 64;

(d)  code issued by the Authority under section 64 or 119.

(2)  For the purposes of this Chapter, regulating provisions or practices have a significantly adverse effect on competition if—

(a)  they have, or are intended or likely to have, that effect; or

(b) the effect that they have, or are intended or likely to have, is to require or encourage behaviour which has, or is intended or likely to have, a significantly adverse effect on competition.

(3) If regulating provisions or practices have, or are intended or likely to have, the effect of requiring or encouraging exploitation of the strength of a market position they are to be taken, for the purposes of this Chapter, to have an adverse effect on competition.

(4) In determining under this Chapter whether any of the regulating provisions have, or are likely to have, a particular effect, it may be assumed that the persons to whom the provisions concerned are addressed will act in accordance with them.

### 160  Reports by OFT

(1) The OFT must keep the regulating provisions and the Authority's practices under review.

(2) If at any time the OFT considers that—

(a) a regulating provision or practice has a significantly adverse effect on competition, or

(b) two or more regulating provisions or practices taken together, or a particular combination of regulating provisions and practices, have such an effect,

The OFT must make a report to that effect.

(3) If at any time the OFT considers that—

(a) a regulating provision or practice does not have a significantly adverse effect on competition, or

(b) two or more regulating provisions or practices taken together, or a particular combination of regulating provisions and practices, do not have any such effect,

the OFT may make a report to that effect.

(4) A report under subsection (2) must include details of the adverse effect on competition.

(5) If the OFT makes a report under subsection (2) The OFT must—

(a) send a copy of it to the Treasury, the Competition Commission and the Authority; and

(b) publish it in the way appearing to it to be best calculated to bring it to the attention of the public.

(6) If the OFT makes a report under subsection (3)—

(a) the OFT must send a copy of it to the Treasury, the Competition Commission and the Authority; and

(b) the OFT may publish it.

(7) Before publishing a report under this section the OFT must, so far as practicable, exclude any matter which relates to the private affairs of a particular individual the publication of which, in the opinion of the OFT, would or might seriously and prejudicially affect his interests.

(8) Before publishing such a report the OFT must, so far as practicable, exclude any matter which relates to the affairs of a particular body the publication of which, in the opinion of the OFT, would or might seriously and prejudicially affect its interests.

(9) Subsections (7) and (8) do not apply in relation to copies of a report which the OFT is required to send under subsection (5)(a) or (6)(a).

(10) For the purposes of the law of defamation, absolute privilege attaches to any report of the OFT under this section.

### 161  Power of OFT to request information

(1) For the purpose of investigating any matter with a view to its consideration under section 160, the OFT may exercise the powers conferred on it by this section.

(2) The OFT may by notice in writing require any person to produce to it or to a person appointed by him for the purpose, at a time and place specified in the notice, any document which—

(a) is specified or described in the notice; and

(b) is a document in that person's custody or under his control.

(3) The OFT may by notice in writing—

(a) require any person carrying on any business to provide it with such information as may be specified or described in the notice; and

(b) specify the time within which, and the manner and form in which, any such information is to be provided.

(4) A requirement may be imposed under subsection (2) or (3)(a) only in respect of documents or information which relate to any matter relevant to the investigation.

(5) If a person ('the defaulter') refuses, or otherwise fails, to comply with a notice under this section, the OFT may certify that fact in writing to the court and the court may enquire into the case.

(6) If, after hearing any witness who may be produced against or on behalf of the defaulter and any statement which may be offered in defence, the court is satisfied that the defaulter did not have a reasonable excuse for refusing or otherwise failing to comply with the notice, the court may deal with the defaulter as if he were in contempt.

(7) 'Court' means—

(a) the High Court; or

(b) in relation to Scotland, the Court of Session.

### 162 Consideration by Competition Commission

(1) If the OFT—

(a) makes a report under section 160(2), or

(b) asks the Commission to consider a report that he has made under section 160(3),

the Commission must investigate the matter.

(2) The Commission must then make its own report on the matter unless it considers that, as a result of a change of circumstances, no useful purpose would be served by a report.

(3) If the Commission decides in accordance with subsection (2) not to make a report, it must make a statement setting out the change of circumstances which resulted in that decision.

(4) A report made under this section must state the Commission's conclusion as to whether—

(a) the regulating provision or practice which is the subject of the report has a significantly adverse effect on competition; or

(b) the regulating provisions or practices, or combination of regulating provisions and practices, which are the subject of the report have such an effect.

(5) A report under this section stating the Commission's conclusion that there is a significantly adverse effect on competition must also—

(a) state whether the Commission considers that that effect is justified; and

(b) if it states that the Commission considers that it is not justified, state its conclusion as to what action, if any, ought to be taken by the Authority.

(6) Subsection (7) applies whenever the Commission is considering, for the purposes of this section, whether a particular adverse effect on competition is justified.

(7) The Commission must ensure, so far as that is reasonably possible, that the conclusion it reaches is compatible with the functions conferred, and obligations imposed, on the Authority by or under this Act.

(8) A report under this section must contain such an account of the Commission's reasons for its conclusions as is expedient, in the opinion of the Commission, for facilitating proper understanding of them.

(9) Schedule 14 supplements this section.

(10) If the Commission makes a report under this section it must send a copy to the Treasury, the Authority and the OFT.

### 163 Role of the Treasury

(1) This section applies if the Competition Commission makes a report under section 162(2) which states its conclusion that there is a significantly adverse effect on competition.

(2) If the Commission's conclusion, as stated in the report, is that the adverse effect on competition is not justified, the Treasury must give a direction to the Authority requiring it to take such action as may be specified in the direction.

(3) But subsection (2) does not apply if the Treasury consider—

(a) that, as a result of action taken by the Authority in response to the Commission's report, it is unnecessary for them to give a direction; or

(b) that the exceptional circumstances of the case make it inappropriate or unnecessary for them to do so.

(4) In considering the action to be specified in a direction under subsection (2), the Treasury must have regard to any conclusion of the Commission included in the report because of section 162(5)(b).

(5) Subsection (6) applies if—

(a) the Commission's conclusion, as stated in its report, is that the adverse effect on competition is justified; but

(b) the Treasury consider that the exceptional circumstances of the case require them to act.

(6) The Treasury may give a direction to the Authority requiring it to take such action—

(a) as they consider to be necessary in the light of the exceptional circumstances of the case; and

(b) as may be specified in the direction.

(7) The Authority may not be required as a result of this section to take any action—

(a) that it would not have power to take in the absence of a direction under this section; or

(b) that would otherwise be incompatible with any of the functions conferred, or obligations imposed, on it by or under this Act.

(8) Subsection (9) applies if the Treasury are considering—

(a) whether subsection (2) applies and, if so, what action is to be specified in a direction under that subsection; or

(b) whether to give a direction under subsection (6).

(9) The Treasury must—

(a) do what they consider appropriate to allow the Authority, and any other person appearing to the Treasury to be affected, an opportunity to make representations; and

(b) have regard to any such representations.

(10) If, in reliance on subsection (3)(a) or (b), the Treasury decline to act under subsection (2), they must make a statement to that effect, giving their reasons.

(11)  If the Treasury give a direction under this section they must make a statement giving—
   (a)  details of the direction; and
   (b)  if the direction is given under subsection (6), their reasons for giving it.
(12)  The Treasury must—
   (a)  publish any statement made under this section in the way appearing to them best calculated to bring it to the attention of the public; and
   (b)  lay a copy of it before Parliament.

## 164　The Competition Act 1998

(1)  The Chapter I prohibition does not apply to an agreement the parties to which consist of or include—
   (a)  an authorised person, or
   (b)  a person who is otherwise subject to the Authority's regulating provisions,
to the extent to which the agreement consists of provisions the inclusion of which in the agreement is encouraged by any of the Authority's regulating provisions.

(2)  The Chapter I prohibition does not apply to the practices of an authorised person or a person who is otherwise subject to the regulating provisions to the extent to which the practices are encouraged by any of the Authority's regulating provisions.

(3)  The Chapter II prohibition does not apply to conduct of—
   (a)  an authorised person, or
   (b)  a person who is otherwise subject to the Authority's regulating provisions,
to the extent to which the conduct is encouraged by any of the Authority's regulating provisions.

(4)  'The Chapter I prohibition' means the prohibition imposed by section 2(1) of the Competition Act 1998.

(5)  'The Chapter II prohibition' means the prohibition imposed by section 18(1) of that Act.

# PART XI

# INFORMATION GATHERING AND INVESTIGATIONS

*Powers to gather information*

## 165　Authority's power to require information

(1)  The Authority may, by notice in writing given to an authorised person, require him—
   (a)  to provide specified information or information of a specified description; or
   (b)  to produce specified documents or documents of a specified description.
(2)  The information or documents must be provided or produced—
   (a)  before the end of such reasonable period as may be specified; and
   (b)  at such place as may be specified.
(3)  An officer who has written authorisation from the Authority to do so may require an authorised person without delay—
   (a)  to provide the officer with specified information or information of a specified description; or
   (b)  to produce to him specified documents or documents of a specified description.
(4)  This section applies only to information and documents reasonably required in connection with the exercise by the Authority of functions conferred on it by or under this Act.
(5)  The Authority may require any information provided under this section to be provided in such form as it may reasonably require.
(6)  The Authority may require—
   (a)  any information provided, whether in a document or otherwise, to be verified in such manner, or
   (b)  any document produced to be authenticated in such manner,
as it may reasonably require.
(7)  The powers conferred by subsections (1) and (3) may also be exercised to impose requirements on—
   (a)  a person who is connected with an authorised person;
   (b)  an operator, trustee or depositary of a scheme recognised under section 270 or 272 who is not an authorised person;
   (c)  a recognised investment exchange or recognised clearing house.
(8)  'Authorised person' includes a person who was at any time an authorised person but who has ceased to be an authorised person.
(9)  'Officer' means an officer of the Authority and includes a member of the Authority's staff or an agent of the Authority.
(10)  'Specified' means—
   (a)  in subsections (1) and (2), specified in the notice; and
   (b)  in subsection (3), specified in the authorisation.

(11)  For the purposes of this section, a person is connected with an authorised person ('A') if he is or has at any relevant time been—

(a)  a member of A's group;

(b)  a controller of A;

(c)  any other member of a partnership of which A is a member; or

(d)  in relation to A, a person mentioned in Part I of Schedule 15.

## 166  Reports by skilled persons

(1)  The Authority may, by notice in writing given to a person to whom subsection (2) applies, require him to provide the Authority with a report on any matter about which the Authority has required or could require the provision of information or production of documents under section 165.

(2)  This subsection applies to—

(a)  an authorised person ('A'),

(b)  any other member of A's group,

(c)  a partnership of which A is a member, or

(d)  a person who has at any relevant time been a person falling within paragraph (a), (b) or (c), who is, or was at the relevant time, carrying on a business.

(3)  The Authority may require the report to be in such form as may be specified in the notice.

(4)  The person appointed to make a report required by subsection (1) must be a person—

(a)  nominated or approved by the Authority; and

(b)  appearing to the Authority to have the skills necessary to make a report on the matter concerned.

(5)  It is the duty of any person who is providing (or who at any time has provided) services to a person to whom subsection (2) applies in relation to a matter on which a report is required under subsection (1) to give a person appointed to provide such a report all such assistance as the appointed person may reasonably require.

(6)  The obligation imposed by subsection (5) is enforceable, on the application of the Authority, by an injunction or, in Scotland, by an order for specific performance under section 45 of the Court of Session Act 1988.

*Appointment of investigators*

## 167  Appointment of persons to carry out general investigations

(1)  If it appears to the Authority or the Secretary of State ('the investigating authority') that there is good reason for doing so, the investigating authority may appoint one or more competent persons to conduct an investigation on its behalf into—

(a)  the nature, conduct or state of the business of a recognised investment exchange or an authorised person or of an appointed representative;

(b)  a particular aspect of that business; or

(c)  the ownership or control of a recognised investment exchange or an authorised person.

(2)  If a person appointed under subsection (1) thinks it necessary for the purposes of his investigation, he may also investigate the business of a person who is or has at any relevant time been—

(a)  a member of the group of which the person under investigation ('A') is part; or

(b)  a partnership of which A is a member.

(3)  If a person appointed under subsection (1) decides to investigate the business of any person under subsection (2) he must give that person written notice of his decision.

(4)  The power conferred by this section may be exercised in relation to a former authorised person (or appointed representative) but only in relation to—

(a)  business carried on at any time when he was an authorised person (or appointed representative); or

(b)  the ownership or control of a former authorised person at any time when he was an authorised person.

(5)  'Business' includes any part of a business even if it does not consist of carrying on regulated activities.

(6)  References in subsection (1) to a recognised investment exchange do not include references to an overseas investment exchange (as defined by section 313(1)).

## 168  Appointment of persons to carry out investigations in particular cases

(1)  Subsection (3) applies if it appears to an investigating authority that there are circumstances suggesting that—

(a)  a person may have contravened any regulation made under section 142; or

(b)  a person may be guilty of an offence under section 177, 191, 346 or 398(1) or under Schedule 4.

(2)  Subsection (3) also applies if it appears to an investigating authority that there are circumstances suggesting that—

(a)  an offence under section 24(1) or 397 or under Part V of the Criminal Justice Act 1993 may have been committed;

(b) there may have been a breach of the general prohibition;

(c) there may have been a contravention of section 21 or 238; or

(d) market abuse may have taken place.

(3) The investigating authority may appoint one or more competent persons to conduct an investigation on its behalf.

(4) Subsection (5) applies if it appears to the Authority that there are circumstances suggesting that—

(a) a person may have contravened section 20;

(b) a person may be guilty of an offence under prescribed regulations relating to money laundering;

(ba) a person may be guilty of an offence under Schedule 7 to the Counter-Terrorism Act 2008 (terrorist financing or money laundering);

(c) an authorised person may have contravened a rule made by the Authority;

(d) an individual may not be a fit and proper person to perform functions in relation to a regulated activity carried on by an authorised or exempt person;

(e) an individual may have performed or agreed to perform a function in breach of a prohibition order;

(f) an authorised or exempt person may have failed to comply with section 56(6);

(g) an authorised person may have failed to comply with section 59(1) or (2);

(h) a person in relation to whom the Authority has given its approval under section 59 may not be a fit and proper person to perform the function to which that approval relates; [...]

(i) a person may be guilty of misconduct for the purposes of section 66; or

(j) a person may have contravened any provision made by or under this Act for the purpose of implementing the markets in financial instruments directive or by any directly applicable Community regulation made under that directive.

(5) The Authority may appoint one or more competent persons to conduct an investigation on its behalf.

(6) 'Investigating authority' means the Authority or the Secretary of State.

### Assistance to overseas regulators

**169    Investigations etc in support of overseas regulator**

(1) At the request of an overseas regulator, the Authority may—

(a) exercise the power conferred by section 165; or

(b) appoint one or more competent persons to investigate any matter.

(2) An investigator has the same powers as an investigator appointed under section 168(3)(as a result of subsection (1) of that section).

(3) If the request has been made by a competent authority in pursuance of any Community obligation the Authority must, in deciding whether or not to exercise its investigative power, consider whether its exercise is necessary to comply with any such obligation.

(4) In deciding whether or not to exercise its investigative power, the Authority may take into account in particular—

(a) whether in the country or territory of the overseas regulator concerned, corresponding assistance would be given to a United Kingdom regulatory authority;

(b) whether the case concerns the breach of a law, or other requirement, which has no close parallel in the United Kingdom or involves the assertion of a jurisdiction not recognised by the United Kingdom;

(c) the seriousness of the case and its importance to persons in the United Kingdom;

(d) whether it is otherwise appropriate in the public interest to give the assistance sought.

(5) The Authority may decide that it will not exercise its investigative power unless the overseas regulator undertakes to make such contribution towards the cost of its exercise as the Authority considers appropriate.

(6) Subsections (4) and (5) do not apply if the Authority considers that the exercise of its investigative power is necessary to comply with a Community obligation.

(7) If the Authority has appointed an investigator in response to a request from an overseas regulator, it may direct the investigator to permit a representative of that regulator to attend, and take part in, any interview conducted for the purposes of the investigation.

(8) A direction under subsection (7) is not to be given unless the Authority is satisfied that any information obtained by an overseas regulator as a result of the interview will be subject to safeguards equivalent to those contained in Part XXIII.

(9) The Authority must prepare a statement of its policy with respect to the conduct of interviews in relation to which a direction under subsection (7) has been given.

(10) The statement requires the approval of the Treasury.

(11) If the Treasury approve the statement, the Authority must publish it.

(12) No direction may be given under subsection (7) before the statement has been published.

(13) 'Overseas regulator' has the same meaning as in section 195.

(14) 'Investigative power' means one of the powers mentioned in subsection (1).

(15) 'Investigator' means a person appointed under subsection (1)(b).

*Conduct of investigations*

**170   Investigations: general**

(1) This section applies if an investigating authority appoints one or more competent persons ('investigators') under section 167 or 168(3) or (5) to conduct an investigation on its behalf.

(2) The investigating authority must give written notice of the appointment of an investigator to the person who is the subject of the investigation ('the person under investigation').

(3) Subsections (2) and (9) do not apply if —

(a) the investigator is appointed as a result of section 168(1) or (4) and the investigating authority believes that the notice required by subsection (2) or (9) would be likely to result in the investigation being frustrated; or

(b) the investigator is appointed as a result of subsection (2) of section 168.

(4) A notice under subsection (2) must—

(a) specify the provisions under which, and as a result of which, the investigator was appointed; and

(b) state the reason for his appointment.

(5) Nothing prevents the investigating authority from appointing a person who is a member of its staff as an investigator.

(6) An investigator must make a report of his investigation to the investigating authority.

(7) The investigating authority may, by a direction to an investigator, control—

(a) the scope of the investigation;

(b) the period during which the investigation is to be conducted;

(c) the conduct of the investigation; and

(d) the reporting of the investigation.

(8) A direction may, in particular—

(a) confine the investigation to particular matters;

(b) extend the investigation to additional matters;

(c) require the investigator to discontinue the investigation or to take only such steps as are specified in the direction;

(d) require the investigator to make such interim reports as are so specified.

(9) If there is a change in the scope or conduct of the investigation and, in the opinion of the investigating authority, the person subject to investigation is likely to be significantly prejudiced by not being made aware of it, that person must be given written notice of the change.

(10) 'Investigating authority', in relation to an investigator, means—

(a) the Authority, if the Authority appointed him;

(b) the Secretary of State, if the Secretary of State appointed him.

**171   Powers of persons appointed under section 167**

(1) An investigator may require the person who is the subject of the investigation ('the person under investigation') or any person connected with the person under investigation—

(a) to attend before the investigator at a specified time and place and answer questions; or

(b) otherwise to provide such information as the investigator may require.

(2) An investigator may also require any person to produce at a specified time and place any specified documents or documents of a specified description.

(3) A requirement under subsection (1) or (2) may be imposed only so far as the investigator concerned reasonably considers the question, provision of information or production of the document to be relevant to the purposes of the investigation.

(3A) Where the investigation relates to a recognised investment exchange, an investigator has the additional powers conferred by sections 172 and 173 (and for this purpose references in those sections to an investigator are to be read accordingly).

(4) For the purposes of this section and section 172, a person is connected with the person under investigation ('A') if he is or has at any relevant time been—

(a) a member of A's group;

(b) a controller of A;

(c) a partnership of which A is a member; or

(d) in relation to A, a person mentioned in Part I or II of Schedule 15.

(5) 'Investigator' means a person conducting an investigation under section 167.

(6) 'Specified' means specified in a notice in writing.

(7) The reference in subsection (3A) to a recognised investment exchange does not include a reference to an overseas investment exchange (as defined by section 313(1)).

**172   Additional power of persons appointed as a result of section 168(1) or (4)**

(1) An investigator has the powers conferred by section 171.

(2) An investigator may also require a person who is neither the subject of the investigation ('the person under investigation') nor a person connected with the person under investigation—

    (a) to attend before the investigator at a specified time and place and answer questions; or

    (b) otherwise to provide such information as the investigator may require for the purposes of the investigation.

(3) A requirement may only be imposed under subsection (2) if the investigator is satisfied that the requirement is necessary or expedient for the purposes of the investigation.

(4) 'Investigator' means a person appointed as a result of subsection (1) or (4) of section 168.

(5) 'Specified' means specified in a notice in writing.

### 173    Powers of persons appointed as a result of section 168(2)

(1) Subsections (2) to (4) apply if an investigator considers that any person ('A') is or may be able to give information which is or may be relevant to the investigation.

(2) The investigator may require A—

    (a) to attend before him at a specified time and place and answer questions; or

    (b) otherwise to provide such information as he may require for the purposes of the investigation.

(3) The investigator may also require A to produce at a specified time and place any specified documents or documents of a specified description which appear to the investigator to relate to any matter relevant to the investigation.

(4) The investigator may also otherwise require A to give him all assistance in connection with the investigation which A is reasonably able to give.

(5) 'Investigator' means a person appointed under subsection (3) of section 168 (as a result of subsection (2) of that section).

### 174    Admissibility of statements made to investigators

(1) A statement made to an investigator by a person in compliance with an information requirement is admissible in evidence in any proceedings, so long as it also complies with any requirements governing the admissibility of evidence in the circumstances in question.

(2) But in criminal proceedings in which that person is charged with an offence to which this subsection applies or in proceedings in relation to action to be taken against that person under section 123—

    (a) no evidence relating to the statement may be adduced, and

    (b) no question relating to it may be asked,

by or on behalf of the prosecution or (as the case may be) the Authority, unless evidence relating to it is adduced, or a question relating to it is asked, in the proceedings by or on behalf of that person.

(3) Subsection (2) applies to any offence other than one—

    (a) under section 177(4) or 398;

    (b) under section 5 of the Perjury Act 1911 (false statements made otherwise than on oath);

    (c) under section 44(2) of the Criminal Law (Consolidation)(Scotland) Act 1995 (false statements made otherwise than on oath); or

    (d) under Article 10 of the Perjury (Northern Ireland) Order 1979.

(4) 'Investigator' means a person appointed under section 167 or 168(3) or (5).

(5) 'Information requirement' means a requirement imposed by an investigator under section 171, 172, 173 or 175.

### 175    Information and documents: supplemental provisions

(1) If the Authority or an investigator has power under this Part to require a person to produce a document but it appears that the document is in the possession of a third person, that power may be exercised in relation to the third person.

(2) If a document is produced in response to a requirement imposed under this Part, the person to whom it is produced may—

    (a) take copies or extracts from the document; or

    (b) require the person producing the document, or any relevant person, to provide an explanation of the document.

(3) If a person who is required under this Part to produce a document fails to do so, the Authority or an investigator may require him to state, to the best of his knowledge and belief, where the document is.

(4) A lawyer may be required under this Part to furnish the name and address of his client.

(5) No person may be required under this Part to disclose information or produce a document in respect of which he owes an obligation of confidence by virtue of carrying on the business of banking unless—

    (a) he is the person under investigation or a member of that person's group;

    (b) the person to whom the obligation of confidence is owed is the person under investigation or a member of that person's group;

    (c) the person to whom the obligation of confidence is owed consents to the disclosure or production; or

(d) the imposing on him of a requirement with respect to such information or document has been specifically authorised by the investigating authority.

(6) If a person claims a lien on a document, its production under this Part does not affect the lien.

(7) 'Relevant person', in relation to a person who is required to produce a document, means a person who—

    (a) has been or is or is proposed to be a director or controller of that person;

    (b) has been or is an auditor of that person;

    (c) has been or is an actuary, accountant or lawyer appointed or instructed by that person; or

    (d) has been or is an employee of that person.

(8) 'Investigator' means a person appointed under section 167 or 168(3) or (5).

### 176 Entry of premises under warrant

(1) A justice of the peace may issue a warrant under this section if satisfied on information on oath given by or on behalf of the Secretary of State, the Authority or an investigator that there are reasonable grounds for believing that the first, second or third set of conditions is satisfied.

(2) The first set of conditions is—

    (a) that a person on whom an information requirement has been imposed has failed (wholly or in part) to comply with it; and

    (b) that on the premises specified in the warrant—

        (i) there are documents which have been required; or

        (ii) there is information which has been required.

(3) The second set of conditions is—

    (a) that the premises specified in the warrant are premises of an authorised person or an appointed representative;

    (b) that there are on the premises documents or information in relation to which an information requirement could be imposed; and

    (c) that if such a requirement were to be imposed—

        (i) it would not be complied with; or

        (ii) the documents or information to which it related would be removed, tampered with or destroyed.

(4) The third set of conditions is—

    (a) that an offence mentioned in section 168 for which the maximum sentence on conviction on indictment is two years or more has been (or is being) committed by any person;

    (b) that there are on the premises specified in the warrant documents or information relevant to whether that offence has been (or is being) committed;

    (c) that an information requirement could be imposed in relation to those documents or information; and

    (d) that if such a requirement were to be imposed—

        (i) it would not be complied with; or

        (ii) the documents or information to which it related would be removed, tampered with or destroyed.

(5) A warrant under this section shall authorise a constable—

    (a) to enter the premises specified in the warrant;

    (b) to search the premises and take possession of any documents or information appearing to be documents or information of a kind in respect of which a warrant under this section was issued ('the relevant kind') or to take, in relation to any such documents or information, any other steps which may appear to be necessary for preserving them or preventing interference with them;

    (c) to take copies of, or extracts from, any documents or information appearing to be of the relevant kind;

    (d) to require any person on the premises to provide an explanation of any document or information appearing to be of the relevant kind or to state where it may be found; and

    (e) to use such force as may be reasonably necessary.

(6) In England and Wales, sections 15(5) to (8) and section 16 of the Police and Criminal Evidence Act 1984 (execution of search warrants and safeguards) apply to warrants issued under this section.

(7) In Northern Ireland, Articles 17(5) to (8) and 18 of the Police and Criminal Evidence (Northern Ireland) Order 1989 apply to warrants issued under this section.

(8) Any document of which possession is taken under this section may be retained—

    (a) for a period of three months; or

    (b) if within that period proceedings to which the document is relevant are commenced against any person for any criminal offence, until the conclusion of those proceedings.

(9) In the application of this section to Scotland—

    (a) for the references to a justice of the peace substitute references to a justice of the peace or a sheriff; and

    (b) for the references to information on oath substitute references to evidence on oath.

(10) 'Investigator' means a person appointed under section 167 or 168(3) or (5).

(11) 'Information requirement' means a requirement imposed—

(a) by the Authority under section 87C, 87J, 165 or 175; or

(b) by an investigator under section 171, 172, 173 or 175.

*Offences*

### 177  Offences

(1) If a person other than the investigator ('the defaulter') fails to comply with a requirement imposed on him under this Part the person imposing the requirement may certify that fact in writing to the court.

(2) If the court is satisfied that the defaulter failed without reasonable excuse to comply with the requirement, it may deal with the defaulter (and in the case of a body corporate, any director or officer) as if he were in contempt ; and 'officer', in relation to a limited liability partnership, means a member of the limited liability partnership.

(3) A person who knows or suspects that an investigation is being or is likely to be conducted under this Part is guilty of an offence if—

(a) he falsifies, conceals, destroys or otherwise disposes of a document which he knows or suspects is or would be relevant to such an investigation, or

(b) he causes or permits the falsification, concealment, destruction or disposal of such a document,

unless he shows that he had no intention of concealing facts disclosed by the documents from the investigator.

(4) A person who, in purported compliance with a requirement imposed on him under this Part—

(a) provides information which he knows to be false or misleading in a material particular, or

(b) recklessly provides information which is false or misleading in a material particular,

is guilty of an offence.

(5) A person guilty of an offence under subsection (3) or (4) is liable—

(a) on summary conviction, to imprisonment for a term not exceeding six months or a fine not exceeding the statutory maximum, or both;

(b) on conviction on indictment, to imprisonment for a term not exceeding two years or a fine, or both.

(6) Any person who intentionally obstructs the exercise of any rights conferred by a warrant under section 176 is guilty of an offence and liable on summary conviction to imprisonment for a term not exceeding *three months* or a fine not exceeding level 5 on the standard scale, or both.

(7) 'Court' means—

(a) the High Court;

(b) in Scotland, the Court of Session.[2]

# PART XII

# CONTROL OVER AUTHORISED PERSONS

*Notices of acquisitions of control over UK authorised persons*

### 178  Obligation to notify the Authority: acquisitions of control

(1) A person who decides to acquire or increase control over a UK authorised person must give the Authority notice in writing before making the acquisition.

(2) For the purposes of calculations relating to this section, the holding of shares or voting power by a person ('A1') includes any shares or voting power held by another ('A2') if A1 and A2 are acting in concert.

(3) In this Part, a notice given under this section is a 'section 178 notice' and a person giving notice is a 'section 178 notice-giver'.

### 179  Requirements for section 178 notices

(1) A section 178 notice must be in such form, include such information and be accompanied by such documents as the Authority may reasonably require.

(2) The Authority must publish a list of its requirements as to the form, information and accompanying documents for a section 178 notice.

---

[2] In subsection (6) the words 'three months' are to be substituted with '51 weeks' under the Criminal Justice Act 2003 c 44 from a date to be appointed.

(3) The Authority may impose different requirements for different cases and may vary or waive requirements in particular cases.

### 180   Acknowledgment of receipt

(1) The Authority must acknowledge receipt of a completed section 178 notice in writing before the end of the second working day following receipt.

(2) If the Authority receives an incomplete section 178 notice it must inform the section 178 notice-giver as soon as reasonably practicable.

*Acquiring control and other changes of holding*

### 181   Acquiring control

(1) For the purposes of this Part, a person ('A') acquires control over a UK authorised person ('B') if any of the cases in subsection (2) begin to apply.

(2) The cases are where A holds—

  (a) 10% or more of the shares in B or in a parent undertaking of B ('P');

  (b) 10% or more of the voting power in B or P; or

  (c) shares or voting power in B or P as a result of which A is able to exercise significant influence over the management of B.

### 182   Increasing control

(1) For the purposes of this Part, a person ('A') increases control over a UK authorised person ('B') whenever—

  (a) the percentage of shares which A holds in B or in a parent undertaking of B ('P') increases by any of the steps mentioned in subsection (2);

  (b) the percentage of voting power A holds in B or P increases by any of the steps mentioned in subsection (2); or

  (c) A becomes a parent undertaking of B.

(2) The steps are—

  (a) from less than 20% to 20% or more;

  (b) from less than 30% to 30% or more;

  (c) from less than 50% to 50% or more.

### 183   Reducing or ceasing to have control

(1) For the purposes of this Part, a person ('A') reduces control over a UK authorised person ('B') whenever—

  (a) the percentage of shares which A holds in B or in a parent undertaking of B ('P') decreases by any of the steps mentioned in subsection (2);

  (b) the percentage of voting power which A holds in B or P decreases by any of the steps mentioned in subsection (2); or

  (c) A ceases to be a parent undertaking of B.

(2) The steps are—

  (a) from 50% or more to less than 50%;

  (b) from 30% or more to less than 30%;

  (c) from 20% or more to less than 20%.

(3) For the purposes of this Part, a person ('A') ceases to have control over a UK authorised person ('B') if A ceases to be in the position of holding—

  (a) 10% or more of the shares in B or in a parent undertaking of B ('P');

  (b) 10% or more of the voting power in B or P; or

  (c) shares or voting power in B or P as a result of which A is able to exercise significant influence over the management of B.

### 184   Disregarded holdings

(1) For the purposes of sections 181 to 183, shares and voting power that a person holds in a UK authorised person ('B') or in a parent undertaking of B ('P') are disregarded in the following circumstances.

(2) Shares held only for the purposes of clearing and settling within a short settlement cycle are disregarded.

(3) Shares held by a custodian or its nominee in a custodian capacity are disregarded, provided that the custodian or nominee is only able to exercise voting power represented by the shares in accordance with instructions given in writing.

(4) Shares representing no more than 5% of the total voting power in B or P held by an investment firm are disregarded, provided that it—

  (a) holds the shares in the capacity of a market maker (as defined in article 4.1(8) of the markets in financial instruments directive);

  (b) is authorised by its home state regulator under the markets in financial instruments directive; and

  (c) neither intervenes in the management of B or P nor exerts any influence on B or P to buy the shares or back the share price.

(5) Shares held by a credit institution or investment firm in its trading book are disregarded, provided that—

    (a) the shares represent no more than 5% of the total voting power in B or P; and

    (b) the credit institution or investment firm ensures that the voting power is not used to intervene in the management of B or P.

(6) Shares held by a credit institution or an investment firm are disregarded, provided that—

    (a) the shares are held as a result of performing the investment services and activities of—

        (i) underwriting a share issue; or

        (ii) placing shares on a firm commitment basis in accordance with Annex I, section A.6 of the markets in financial instruments directive; and

    (b) the credit institution or investment firm—

        (i) does not exercise voting power represented by the shares or otherwise intervene in the management of the issuer; and

        (ii) retains the holding for a period of less than one year.

(7) Where a management company (as defined in Article 1a.2 of the UCITS directive) and its parent undertaking both hold shares or voting power, each may disregard holdings of the other, provided that each exercises its voting power independently of the other.

(8) But subsection (7) does not apply if the management company—

    (a) manages holdings for its parent undertaking or an undertaking in respect of which the parent undertaking is a controller;

    (b) has no discretion as to the exercise of the voting power attached to such holdings; and

    (c) may only exercise the voting power in relation to such holdings under direct or indirect instruction from—

        (i) the parent undertaking; or

        (ii) an undertaking in respect of which of the parent undertaking is a controller.

(9) Where an investment firm and its parent undertaking both hold shares or voting power, the parent undertaking may disregard holdings managed by the investment firm on a client by client basis and the investment firm may disregard holdings of the parent undertaking, provided that the investment firm—

    (a) has permission to provide portfolio management;

    (b) exercises its voting power independently from the parent undertaking; and

    (c) may only exercise the voting power under instructions given in writing, or has appropriate mechanisms in place for ensuring that individual portfolio management services are conducted independently of any other services.

*Assessment procedure*

## 185  Assessment: general

(1) Where the Authority receives a section 178 notice, it must—

    (a) determine whether to approve the acquisition to which it relates unconditionally; or

    (b) propose to—

        (i) approve the acquisition subject to conditions (see section 187); or

        (ii) object to the acquisition.

(2) The Authority must—

    (a) consider the suitability of the section 178 notice-giver and the financial soundness of the acquisition in order to ensure the sound and prudent management of the UK authorised person;

    (b) have regard to the likely influence that the section 178 notice-giver will have on the UK authorised person; and

    (c) disregard the economic needs of the market.

(3) The Authority may only object to an acquisition—

    (a) if there are reasonable grounds for doing so on the basis of the matters set out in section 186; or

    (b) if the information provided by the section 178 notice-giver is incomplete.

## 186  Assessment criteria

The matters specified in section 185(3)(a) are—

    (a) the reputation of the section 178 notice-giver;

    (b) the reputation and experience of any person who will direct the business of the UK authorised person as a result of the proposed acquisition;

    (c) the financial soundness of the section 178 notice-giver, in particular in relation to the type of business that the UK authorised person pursues or envisages pursuing;

    (d) whether the UK authorised person will be able to comply with its prudential requirements (including the threshold conditions in relation to all of the regulated activities for which it has or will have permission);

    (e) if the UK authorised person is to become part of a group as a result of the acquisition, whether that group has a structure which makes it possible to—

        (i) exercise effective supervision;

(ii) exchange information among regulators; and

(iii) determine the allocation of responsibility among regulators; and

(f) whether there are reasonable grounds to suspect that in connection with the proposed acquisition—

(i) money laundering or terrorist financing (within the meaning of Article 1 of Directive 2005/60/EC of the European Parliament and of the Council of 26th October 2005 on the prevention of the use of the financial system for the purpose of money laundering and terrorist financing) is being or has been committed or attempted; or

(ii) the risk of such activity could increase.

### 187 Approval with conditions

(1) The Authority may impose conditions on its approval of an acquisition.

(2) The Authority may only impose conditions where, if it did not impose those conditions, it would propose to object to the acquisition.

(3) The Authority may not impose conditions requiring a particular level of holding to be acquired.

(4) The Authority may vary or cancel the conditions.

### 188 Assessment: consultation with EC competent authorities

(1) The Authority must consult any appropriate home state regulator before making a determination under section 185 and, in doing so, must comply with such requirements as to consultation as may be prescribed.

(2) Where the Authority makes a determination under section 185, it must indicate any views or reservations received from any home state regulator it consults in accordance with subsection (1).

(3) The Authority must cooperate with any equivalent consultation by a host state regulator in relation to a UK authorised person.

(4) In order to comply with an obligation under subsection (1) or (3), the Authority must provide the regulator with—

(a) any relevant information that it requests; and

(b) any information that the Authority considers that it needs.

### 189 Assessment: Procedure

(1) The Authority must act under section 185 within a period of 60 working days beginning with the day on which the Authority acknowledges receipt of the section 178 notice ('the assessment period').

(2) The assessment period may be interrupted, no more than once, in accordance with section 190.

(3) The Authority must inform the section 178 notice-giver in writing of—

(a) the duration of the assessment period;

(b) its expiry date; and

(c) any change to the expiry date by virtue of section 190.

(4) The Authority must, within two working days of acting under section 185 (and in any event no later than the expiry date of the assessment period)—

(a) notify the section 178 notice-giver that it has determined to approve the acquisition unconditionally; or

(b) give a warning notice stating that it proposes to—

(i) approve the acquisition subject to conditions; or

(ii) object to the acquisition.

(5) Where the Authority gives a warning notice stating that it proposes to approve the acquisition subject to conditions—

(a) it must, in the warning notice, specify those conditions; and

(b) the conditions take effect as interim conditions.

(6) The Authority is treated as having approved the acquisition if, at the expiry of the assessment period, it has neither—

(a) given notice under subsection (4); nor

(b) informed the section 178 notice-giver that the section 178 notice is incomplete.

(7) If the Authority decides to approve an acquisition subject to conditions or to object to an acquisition it must give the section 178 notice-giver a decision notice.

(8) Following receipt of a decision notice under this section, the section 178 notice-giver may refer the Authority's decision to the Tribunal.

### 190 Requests for further information

(1) The Authority may, no later than the 50th working day of the assessment period, in writing ask the section 178 notice-giver to provide any further information necessary to complete its assessment.

(2) On the first occasion that the Authority asks for further information, the assessment period is interrupted from the date of the request until the date the Authority receives the requested information ('the interruption period').

(3) But the interruption period may not exceed 20 working days, unless subsection (4) applies.

(4) The interruption period may not exceed 30 working days if the notice-giver—

(a) is situated or regulated outside the European Community; or

(b) is not subject to supervision under—

(i)   the UCITS directive;

(ii)  the insurance directives;

(iii) the markets in financial instruments directive;

(iv)  the reinsurance directive; or

(v)   the banking consolidation directive.

(5) The Authority may make further requests for information (but a further request does not result in a further interruption of the assessment period).

(6) The Authority must acknowledge in writing receipt of further information before the end of the second working day following receipt.

### 191   Duration of approval

(1) Approval of an acquisition (whether granted unconditionally or subject to conditions) is effective for such period as the Authority may specify in writing.

(2) Where the Authority has specified a period under subsection (1), it may extend the period.

(3) Where the Authority has not specified a period, the approval is effective for one year beginning with the date—

(a) of the notice given under section 189(4)(a) or (b)(i);

(b) on which the Authority is treated as having given approval under section 189(6); or

(c) of a decision on a reference to the Tribunal which results in the person receiving approval.

### *Enforcement procedures*

### 191A   Objection by the Authority

(1) The Authority may object to a person's control over a UK authorised person in any of the circumstances specified in subsection (2).

(2) The circumstances are that the Authority reasonably believes that—

(a) the person acquired or increased control without giving notice under section 178(1) in circumstances where notice was required;

(b) the person is in breach of a condition imposed under section 187; or

(c) there are grounds for objecting to control on the basis of the matters in section 186.

(3) The Authority—

(a) must take into account whether influence exercised by the person is likely to operate to the detriment of the sound and prudent management of the UK authorised person; and

(b) may take into account whether the person has co-operated with any information requests made or requirements imposed by the Authority.

(4) If the Authority proposes to object to a person's control over a UK authorised person, it must give that person a warning notice.

(5) The Authority must consult any appropriate home state regulator before giving a warning notice under this section and, in doing so, must comply with such requirements as to consultation as may be prescribed.

(6) If the Authority decides to object to a person's control over a UK authorised person, it must give that person a decision notice.

(7) A person to whom the Authority gives a decision notice under this section may refer the matter to the Tribunal.

### 191B   Restriction notices

(1) The Authority may give notice in writing (a 'restriction notice') to a person in the following circumstances.

(2) The circumstances are that—

(a) the person has control over a UK authorised person by virtue of holding shares or voting power; and

(b) in relation to the shares or voting power, the Authority has given the person a warning notice or a decision notice under section 189 or 191A or a final notice which confirms a decision notice given under section 189 or 191A.

(3) In a restriction notice, the Authority may direct that shares or voting power to which the notice relates are, until further notice, subject to one or more of the following restrictions—

(a) except by court order, an agreement to transfer or a transfer of any such shares or voting power or, in the case of unissued shares, any agreement to transfer or transfer of the right to be issued with them, is void;

(b) no voting power is to be exercisable;

(c) no further shares are to be issued in pursuance of any right of the holder of any such shares or voting power or in pursuance of any offer made to their holder;

(d) except in a liquidation, no payment is to be made of any sums due from the body corporate on any such shares, whether in respect of capital or otherwise.

(4) A restriction notice takes effect—

(a) immediately; or

(b) on such date as may be specified in the notice.

(5) A restriction notice does not extinguish rights which would be enjoyable but for the notice.

(6) A copy of the restriction notice must be served on—

(a) the UK authorised person in question; and

(b) in the case of shares or voting power held in a parent undertaking of a UK authorised person, the parent undertaking.

(7) A person to whom the Authority gives a restriction notice may refer the matter to the Tribunal.

### 191C   Orders for sale of shares

(1) The court may, on the application of the Authority, order the sale of shares or the disposition of voting power in the following circumstances.

(2) The circumstances are that—

(a) a person has control over a UK authorised person by virtue of holding the shares or voting power; and

(b) the acquisition or continued holding of the shares or voting power by that person is in contravention of a final notice which confirms a decision notice given under section 189 or section 191A.

(3) Where the court orders the sale of shares or disposition of voting power it may—

(a) if a restriction notice has been given in relation to the shares or voting power, order that the restrictions cease to apply; and

(b) make any further order.

(4) Where the court makes an order under this section, it must take into account the level of holding that the person would have been entitled to acquire, or to continue to hold, without contravening the final notice.

(5) If shares are sold or voting power disposed of in pursuance of an order under this section, any proceeds, less the costs of the sale or disposition, must be paid into court for the benefit of the persons beneficially interested in them; and any such person may apply to the court for payment of a whole or part of the proceeds.

(6) The jurisdiction conferred by this section may be exercised by the High Court and the Court of Session.

*Notice of reductions of control of UK authorised persons*

### 191D   Obligation to notify the Authority: dispositions of control

(1) A person who decides to reduce or cease to have control over a UK authorised person must give the Authority notice in writing before making the disposition.

(2) For the purposes of calculations relating to this section, the holding of shares or voting power by a person ('A1') includes any shares or voting power held by another ('A2') if A1 and A2 are acting in concert.

### 191E   Requirements for notices under section 191D

(1) A notice under section 191D must be in such form, include such information and be accompanied by such documents as the Authority may reasonably require.

(2) The Authority must publish a list of its requirements as to the form, information and accompanying documents for a notice under section 191D.

(3) The Authority may impose different requirements for different cases and may vary or waive requirements in particular cases.

*Offences*

### 191F   Offences under this Part

(1) A person who fails to comply with an obligation to notify the Authority under section 178(1) or 191D(1) is guilty of an offence.

(2) A person who gives notice to the Authority under section 178(1) and makes the acquisition to which the notice relates before the expiry date of the assessment period is guilty of an offence unless the Authority has approved the acquisition or given a warning notice under section 189(4)(b)(i).

(3) A person who contravenes an interim condition in a warning notice given under section 189(4)(b)(i) or a condition in a decision notice given under section 189(7) or a final notice which confirms a decision notice under that section is guilty of an offence.

(4) A person who makes an acquisition in contravention of a warning notice given under section 189(4)(b)(ii) or a decision notice given under section 189(7) or a final notice which confirms a decision notice under that section is guilty of an offence.

(5) A person who makes an acquisition after the Authority's approval for the acquisition has ceased to be effective by virtue of section 191 is guilty of an offence.

(6) A person who provides information to the Authority which is false in a material particular is guilty of an offence.

(7) A person who breaches a direction contained in a restriction notice given under section 191B is guilty of an offence.

(8) A person guilty of an offence under subsection (1) to (3) or (5) to (7) is liable—

    (a) on summary conviction to a fine not exceeding the statutory maximum; or

    (b) on conviction on indictment, to a fine.

(9) A person guilty of an offence under subsection (4) is liable—

    (a) on summary conviction, to a fine not exceeding the statutory maximum; or

    (b) on conviction on indictment, to imprisonment for a term not exceeding two years or a fine, or both.

*Interpretation*

### 191G  Interpretation

(1) In this Part—

'acquisition' means the acquisition of control or of an increase in control over a UK authorised person;

'credit institution' means—

    (a) a credit institution authorised under the banking consolidation directive; or

    (b) an institution which would satisfy the requirements for authorisation as a credit institution under that directive if it had its registered office (or if it does not have a registered office, its head office) in an EEA State;

'shares' has the same meaning as in section 422;

'UK authorised person' means an authorised person who—

    (a) is a body incorporated in, or an unincorporated association formed under the law of, any part of the United Kingdom; and

    (b) is not a person authorised as a result of paragraph 1 of Schedule 5; and

'voting power' has the same meaning as in section 422.

(2) For the purposes of this Part, a 'working day' is a day other than—

    (a) a Saturday or a Sunday; or

    (b) a day which is a bank holiday in England and Wales under the Banking and Financial Dealings Act 1971.

*Miscellaneous*

### 192  Power to change definitions of control etc

The Treasury may by order—

    (a) provide for exemptions from the obligations to notify imposed by sections 178 and 191D;

    (b) amend section 181 by varying, or removing, any of the cases in which a person is treated as acquiring control over a UK authorised person or by adding a case;

    (c) amend section 182 by varying, or removing, any of the cases in which a person is treated as increasing control over a UK authorised person or by adding a case;

    (d) amend section 183 by varying, or removing, any of the cases in which a person is treated as reducing or ceasing to have control over a UK authorised person or by adding a case;

    (e) amend section 422 by varying, or removing, any of the cases in which a person is treated as being a controller of a person or by adding a case.

# PART XIII

## INCOMING FIRMS: INTERVENTION BY AUTHORITY

*Interpretation*

### 193  Interpretation of this Part

(1) In this Part—

'additional procedure' means the procedure described in section 199;

'incoming firm' means—

    (a) an EEA firm which is exercising, or has exercised, its right to carry on a regulated activity in the United Kingdom in accordance with Schedule 3; or

    (b) a Treaty firm which is exercising, or has exercised, its right to carry on a regulated activity in the United Kingdom in accordance with Schedule 4; and

'power of intervention' means the power conferred on the Authority by section 196.

(2) In relation to an incoming firm which is an EEA firm, expressions used in this Part and in Schedule 3 have the same meaning in this Part as they have in that Schedule.

### 194  General grounds on which power of intervention is exercisable

(1) The Authority may exercise its power of intervention in respect of an incoming firm if it appears to it that—

(a) the firm has contravened, or is likely to contravene, a requirement which is imposed on it by or under this Act (in a case where the Authority is responsible for enforcing compliance in the United Kingdom);

(b) the firm has, in purported compliance with any requirement imposed by or under this Act, knowingly or recklessly given the Authority information which is false or misleading in a material particular; or

(c) it is desirable to exercise the power in order to protect the interests of actual or potential customers.

(2) Subsection (3) applies to an incoming EEA firm falling within sub-paragraph (a) or (b) of paragraph 5 of Schedule 3 which is exercising an EEA right to carry on any Consumer Credit Act business in the United Kingdom.

(3) The Authority may exercise its power of intervention in respect of the firm if the OFT has informed the Authority that—

(a) the firm,

(b) any of the firm's employees, agents or associates (whether past or present), or

(c) if the firm is a body corporate, a controller of the firm or an associate of such a controller,

has done any of the things specified in paragraph (a) to (e) of section 25(2A) Consumer Credit Act 1974.

(4) 'Associate', 'Consumer Credit Act business' and 'controller' have the same meaning as in section 203.

### 194A   Contravention by relevant EEA firm with UK branch of requirement under markets in financial instruments directive: Authority primarily responsible for securing compliance

(1) This section applies if—

(a) a relevant EEA firm has a branch in the United Kingdom; and

(b) the Authority ascertains that the firm has contravened, or is contravening, a requirement falling within subsection (3) (in a case to which Article 62.2 of the markets in financial instruments directive applies).

(2) 'Relevant EEA firm' means an EEA firm falling within paragraph 5(a) or (b) of Schedule 3 which is exercising in the United Kingdom an EEA right deriving from the markets in financial instruments directive.

(3) A requirement falls within this subsection if it is imposed on the firm—

(a) by any provision of or made under this Act which implements the markets in financial instruments directive; or

(b) by any directly applicable Community regulation made under that directive.

(4) The Authority must give the firm written notice which—

(a) requires the firm to put an end to the contravention;

(b) states that the Authority's power of intervention will become exercisable in relation to the firm if the firm continues the contravention; and

(c) indicates any requirements that the Authority proposes to impose on the firm in exercise of its power of intervention in the event of the power becoming exercisable.

(5) The Authority may exercise its power of intervention in respect of the firm if—

(a) a reasonable time has expired since the giving of the notice under subsection (4);

(b) the firm has failed to put an end to the contravention within that time; and

(c) the Authority has informed the firm's home state regulator of its intention to exercise its power of intervention in respect of the firm.

(6) Subsection (5) applies whether or not the Authority's power of intervention is also exercisable as a result of section 194.

(7) If the Authority exercises its power of intervention in respect of a relevant EEA firm by virtue of subsection (5), it must at the earliest opportunity inform the firm's home state regulator and the Commission of—

(a) the fact that the Authority has exercised that power in respect of the firm; and

(b) any requirements it has imposed on the firm in exercise of the power.

### 195   Exercise of power in support of overseas regulator

(1) The Authority may exercise its power of intervention in respect of an incoming firm at the request of, or for the purpose of assisting, an overseas regulator.

(2) Subsection (1) applies whether or not the Authority's power of intervention is also exercisable as a result of section 194.

(3) 'An overseas regulator' means an authority in a country or territory outside the United Kingdom—

(a) which is a home state regulator; or

(b) which exercises any function of a kind mentioned in subsection (4).

(4) The functions are—

(a) a function corresponding to any function of the Authority under this Act;

(b) a function corresponding to any function exercised by the competent authority under Part VI;

(c) a function corresponding to any function exercised by the Secretary of State under the Companies Acts (as defined in section 2 of the Companies Act 2006);

(d) a function in connection with—

    (i) the investigation of conduct of the kind prohibited by Part V of the Criminal Justice Act 1993 (insider dealing); or

    (ii) the enforcement of rules (whether or not having the force of law) relating to such conduct;

(e) a function prescribed by regulations made for the purposes of this subsection which, in the opinion of the Treasury, relates to companies or financial services.

(5) If—

(a) a request to the Authority for the exercise of its power of intervention has been made by a home state regulator in pursuance of a Community obligation, or

(b) a home state regulator has notified the Authority that an EEA firm's EEA authorisation has been withdrawn,

the Authority must, in deciding whether or not to exercise its power of intervention, consider whether exercising it is necessary in order to comply with a Community obligation.

(6) In deciding in any case in which the Authority does not consider that the exercise of its power of intervention is necessary in order to comply with a Community obligation, it may take into account in particular—

(a) whether in the country or territory of the overseas regulator concerned, corresponding assistance would be given to a United Kingdom regulatory authority;

(b) whether the case concerns the breach of a law, or other requirement, which has no close parallel in the United Kingdom or involves the assertion of a jurisdiction not recognised by the United Kingdom;

(c) the seriousness of the case and its importance to persons in the United Kingdom;

(d) whether it is otherwise appropriate in the public interest to give the assistance sought.

(7) The Authority may decide not to exercise its power of intervention, in response to a request, unless the regulator concerned undertakes to make such contribution to the cost of its exercise as the Authority considers appropriate.

(8) Subsection (7) does not apply if the Authority decides that it is necessary for it to exercise its power of intervention in order to comply with a Community obligation.

## 195A   Contravention by relevant EEA firm of requirement under markets in financial instruments directive: home state regulator primarily responsible for securing compliance

(1) This section applies if the Authority has clear and demonstrable grounds for believing that a relevant EEA firm has contravened, or is contravening, a requirement falling within subsection (2) (in a case to which Article 62.1 or 62.3 of the markets in financial instruments directive applies).

(2) A requirement falls within this subsection if it is imposed on the firm—

(a) by or under any provision adopted in the firm's home state for the purpose of implementing the markets in financial instruments directive; or

(b) by any directly applicable Community regulation made under that directive.

(3) The Authority must notify the firm's home state regulator of the situation mentioned in subsection (1).

(4) The notice under subsection (3) must—

(a) request that the home state regulator take all appropriate measures for the purpose of ensuring that the firm puts an end to the contravention;

(b) state that the Authority's power of intervention is likely to become exercisable in relation to the firm if the firm continues the contravention; and

(c) indicate any requirements that the Authority proposes to impose on the firm in exercise of its power of intervention in the event of the power becoming exercisable.

(5) The Authority may exercise its power of intervention in respect of the firm if—

(a) a reasonable time has expired since the giving of the notice under subsection (3); and

(b) conditions A to C are satisfied.

(6) Condition A is that—

(a) the firm's home state regulator has failed or refused to take measures for the purpose mentioned in subsection (4)(a); or

(b) any measures taken by the home state regulator have proved inadequate for that purpose.

(7) Condition B is that the firm is acting in a manner which is clearly prejudicial to the interests of investors in the United Kingdom or the orderly functioning of the markets.

(8) Condition C is that the Authority has informed the firm's home state regulator of its intention to exercise its power of intervention in respect of the firm.

(9) Subsection (5) applies whether or not the Authority's power of intervention is also exercisable as a result of section 194 or 195.

(10) If the Authority exercises its power of intervention in respect of a relevant EEA firm by virtue of subsection (5), it must at the earliest opportunity inform the Commission of—

(a) the fact that the Authority has exercised that power in respect of the firm; and

(b) any requirements it has imposed on the firm in exercise of the power.

(11) In this section—

'home state' , in relation to a relevant EEA firm, means—

(a) in the case of a firm which is a body corporate, the EEA State in which the firm has its registered office or, if it has no registered office, its head office; and

(b) in any other case, the EEA State in which the firm has its head office;

'relevant EEA firm' has the same meaning as in section 194A

### 196  The power of intervention

If the Authority is entitled to exercise its power of intervention in respect of an incoming firm under this Part, it may impose any requirement in relation to the firm which it could impose if—

(a) the firm's permission was a Part IV permission; and

(b) the Authority was entitled to exercise its power under that Part to vary that permission.

*Exercise of power of intervention*

### 197  Procedure on exercise of power of intervention

(1) A requirement takes effect—

(a) immediately, if the notice given under subsection (3) states that that is the case;

(b) on such date as may be specified in the notice; or

(c) if no date is specified in the notice, when the matter to which it relates is no longer open to review.

(2) A requirement may be expressed to take effect immediately (or on a specified date) only if the Authority, having regard to the ground on which it is exercising its power of intervention, considers that it is necessary for the requirement to take effect immediately (or on that date).

(3) If the Authority proposes to impose a requirement under section 196 on an incoming firm, or imposes such a requirement with immediate effect, it must give the firm written notice.

(4) The notice must—

(a) give details of the requirement;

(b) inform the firm of when the requirement takes effect;

(c) state the Authority's reasons for imposing the requirement and for its determination as to when the requirement takes effect;

(d) inform the firm that it may make representations to the Authority within such period as may be specified in the notice (whether or not it has referred the matter to the Tribunal); and

(e) inform it of its right to refer the matter to the Tribunal.

(5) The Authority may extend the period allowed under the notice for making representations.

(6) If, having considered any representations made by the firm, the Authority decides—

(a) to impose the requirement proposed, or

(b) if it has been imposed, not to rescind the requirement,

it must give it written notice.

(7) If, having considered any representations made by the firm, the Authority decides—

(a) not to impose the requirement proposed,

(b) to impose a different requirement from that proposed, or

(c) to rescind a requirement which has effect,

it must give it written notice.

(8) A notice given under subsection (6) must inform the firm of its right to refer the matter to the Tribunal.

(9) A notice under subsection (7)(b) must comply with subsection (4).

(10) If a notice informs a person of his right to refer a matter to the Tribunal, it must give an indication of the procedure on such a reference.

### 198  Power to apply to court for injunction in respect of certain overseas insurance companies

(1) This section applies if the Authority has received a request made in respect of an incoming EEA firm in accordance with—

(a) Article 20.5 of the first non-life insurance directive;

(b) Article 37.5 of the life assurance consolidation directive.

(c) Article 42.4 of the reinsurance directive.

(2) The court may, on an application made to it by the Authority with respect to the firm, grant an injunction restraining (or in Scotland an interdict prohibiting) the firm disposing of or otherwise dealing with any of its assets.

(3) If the court grants an injunction, it may by subsequent orders make provision for such incidental, consequential and supplementary matters as it considers necessary to enable the Authority to perform any of its functions under this Act.

(4) 'The court' means—
  (a) the High Court; or
  (b) in Scotland, the Court of Session.

## 199  Additional procedure for EEA firms in certain cases

(1)  This section applies if it appears to the Authority that its power of intervention is exercisable in relation to an EEA firm exercising EEA rights in the United Kingdom ('an incoming EEA firm') in respect of the contravention of a relevant requirement.

(2)  A requirement is relevant if—
  (a) it is imposed by the Authority under this Act; and
  (b) as respects its contravention, any of the single market directives provides that a procedure of the kind set out in the following provisions of this section (so far as they are relevant in the firm's case) is to apply.

(3)  The Authority must, in writing, require the firm to remedy the situation.

(3A) If the firm falls within paragraph 5(da) of Schedule 3, the Authority must at the same time as it gives notice to the firm under subsection (3) refer its findings to the firm's home state regulator.

(3B) Subsections (4) to (8) apply to an incoming EEA firm other than a firm falling within paragraph 5(da) of Schedule 3.

(4)  If the firm fails to comply with the requirement under subsection (3) within a reasonable time, the Authority must give a notice to that effect to the firm's home state regulator requesting it—
  (a) to take all appropriate measures for the purpose of ensuring that the firm remedies the situation which has given rise to the notice; and
  (b) to inform the Authority of the measures it proposes to take or has taken or the reasons for not taking such measures.

(5)  Except as mentioned in subsection (6), the Authority may not exercise its power of intervention before informing the firm's home state regulator unless satisfied—
  (a) that the firm's home state regulator has failed or refused to take measures for the purpose mentioned in subsection (4)(a); or
  (b) that the measures taken by the home state regulator have proved inadequate for that purpose.

(6)  If the Authority decides that it should exercise its power of intervention in respect of the incoming EEA firm as a matter of urgency in order to protect the interests of consumers, it may exercise that power—
  (a) before complying with subsections (3) and (4); or
  (b) where it has complied with those subsections, before it is satisfied as mentioned in subsection (5).

(7)  In such a case the Authority must at the earliest opportunity inform the firm's home state regulator and the Commission.

(8)  If—
  (a) the Authority has (by virtue of subsection (6)) exercised its power of intervention before complying with subsections (3) and (4) or before it is satisfied as mentioned in subsection (5), and
  (b) the Commission decides under any of the single market directives (other than the markets in financial instruments directive) that the Authority must rescind or vary any requirement imposed in the exercise of its power of intervention,
the Authority must in accordance with the decision rescind or vary the requirement.

(9)  In the case of a firm falling within paragraph 5(da) of Schedule 3, the Authority may not exercise its power of intervention before informing the firm's home state regulator and unless satisfied—
  (a) that the firm's home state regulator has failed or refused to take all appropriate measures for the purpose of ensuring that the firm remedies
the situation which gave rise to the notice under subsection (3); or
  (b) that the measures taken by the home state regulator have proved inadequate for that purpose.

### Supplemental

## 200  Rescission and variation of requirements

(1)  The Authority may rescind or vary a requirement imposed in exercise of its power of intervention on its own initiative or on the application of the person subject to the requirement.

(2)  The power of the Authority on its own initiative to rescind a requirement is exercisable by written notice given by the Authority to the person concerned, which takes effect on the date specified in the notice.

(3)  Section 197 applies to the exercise of the power of the Authority on its own initiative to vary a requirement as it applies to the imposition of a requirement.

(4)  If the Authority proposes to refuse an application for the variation or rescission of a requirement, it must give the applicant a warning notice.

(5) If the Authority decides to refuse an application for the variation or rescission of a requirement—

    (a) the Authority must give the applicant a decision notice; and

    (b) that person may refer the matter to the Tribunal.

### 201 Effect of certain requirements on other persons

If the Authority, in exercising its power of intervention, imposes on an incoming firm a requirement of a kind mentioned in subsection (3) of section 48, the requirement has the same effect in relation to the firm as it would have in relation to an authorised person if it had been imposed on the authorised person by the Authority acting under section 45.

### 202 Contravention of requirement imposed under this Part

(1) Contravention of a requirement imposed by the Authority under this Part does not—

    (a) make a person guilty of an offence;

    (b) make any transaction void or unenforceable; or

    (c) (subject to subsection (2)) give rise to any right of action for breach of statutory duty.

(2) In prescribed cases the contravention is actionable at the suit of a person who suffers loss as a result of the contravention, subject to the defences and other incidents applying to actions for breach of statutory duty.

*Powers of Office of Fair Trading*

### 203 Power to prohibit the carrying on of Consumer Credit Act business.

(1) If it appears to the Office of Fair Trading ('the OFT') that subsection (4) has been, or is likely to be, contravened as respects a consumer credit EEA firm, it may by written notice given to the firm impose on the firm a consumer credit prohibition.

(2) If it appears to the OFT that a restriction imposed under section 204 on an EEA consumer credit firm has not been complied with, it may by written notice given to the firm impose a consumer credit prohibition.

(3) 'Consumer credit prohibition' means a prohibition on carrying on, or purporting to carry on, in the United Kingdom any Consumer Credit Act business which consists of or includes carrying on one or more listed activities.

(4) This subsection is contravened as respects a firm if—

    (a) the firm or any of its employees, agents or associates (whether past or present), or

    (b) if the firm is a body corporate, any controller of the firm or an associate of any such controller,

does any of the things specified in paragraphs (a) to (e) of section 25(2A) of the Consumer Credit Act 1974.

(5) A consumer credit prohibition may be absolute or may be imposed—

    (a) for such period,

    (b) until the occurrence of such event, or

    (c) until such conditions are complied with,

as may be specified in the notice given under subsection (1) or (2).

(6) Any period, event or condition so specified may be varied by the OFT on the application of the firm concerned.

(7) A consumer credit prohibition may be withdrawn by written notice served by the OFT on the firm concerned, and any such notice takes effect on such date as is specified in the notice.

(8) Schedule 16 has effect as respects consumer credit prohibitions and restrictions under section 204.

(9) A firm contravening a prohibition under this section is guilty of an offence and liable—

    (a) on summary conviction, to a fine not exceeding the statutory maximum;

    (b) on conviction on indictment, to a fine.

(10) In this section and section 204—

'a consumer credit EEA firm' means an *authorised payment institution (as defined by regulation 2(1) of the Payment Services Regulations 2009) which is exercising passport rights in the United Kingdom and is carrying on Consumer Credit Act business;*

'Consumer Credit Act business' means consumer credit business, consumer hire business or ancillary credit business;

'consumer credit business', 'consumer hire business' and 'ancillary credit business' have the same meaning as in the Consumer Credit Act 1974;

'listed activity' *means an activity listed in the Annex to the payment services directive and any activity carried on in accordance with Article 16 of that directive;*

'associate' has the same meaning as in section 25(2A) of the Consumer Credit Act 1974;

'controller' has the meaning given by section 189(1) of that Act.[3]

---

[3] The words in italics substituted by the Payment Services Regulations 2009/209. In force from 1 November 2009.

**204   Power to restrict the carrying on of Consumer Credit Act business**

(1) In this section 'restriction' means a direction that a consumer credit EEA firm may not carry on in the United Kingdom, otherwise than in accordance with such condition or conditions as may be specified in the direction, any Consumer Credit Act business which—

(a) consists of or includes carrying on any listed activity; and

(b) is specified in the direction.

(2) If it appears to the OFT that the situation as respects a consumer credit EEA firm is such that the powers conferred by section 203(1) are exercisable, the Director may, instead of imposing a prohibition, impose such restriction as appears to it desirable.

(3) A restriction—

(a) may be withdrawn, or

(b) may be varied with the agreement of the firm concerned,

by written notice served by the OFT on the firm, and any such notice takes effect on such date as is specified in the notice.

(4) A firm contravening a restriction is guilty of an offence and liable—

(a) on summary conviction, to a fine not exceeding the statutory maximum;

(b) on conviction on indictment, to a fine.

# PART XIV

# DISCIPLINARY MEASURES

**205   Public censure**

If the Authority considers that an authorised person has contravened a requirement imposed on him by or under this Act, or by any directly applicable Community regulation made under the markets in financial instruments directive, the Authority may publish a statement to that effect.

**206   Financial penalties**

(1) If the Authority considers that an authorised person has contravened a requirement imposed on him by or under this Act, or by any directly applicable Community regulation made under the markets in financial instruments directive, it may impose on him a penalty, in respect of the contravention, of such amount as it considers appropriate.

(2) The Authority may not in respect of any contravention both require a person to pay a penalty under this section and withdraw his authorisation under section 33.

(3) A penalty under this section is payable to the Authority.

**207   Proposal to take disciplinary measures**

(1) If the Authority proposes—

(a) to publish a statement in respect of an authorised person (under section 205), or

(b) to impose a penalty on an authorised person (under section 206),

it must give the authorised person a warning notice.

(2) A warning notice about a proposal to publish a statement must set out the terms of the statement.

(3) A warning notice about a proposal to impose a penalty, must state the amount of the penalty.

**208   Decision notice**

(1) If the Authority decides—

(a) to publish a statement under section 205 (whether or not in the terms proposed), or

(b) to impose a penalty under section 206 (whether or not of the amount proposed),

it must without delay give the authorised person concerned a decision notice.

(2) In the case of a statement, the decision notice must set out the terms of the statement.

(3) In the case of a penalty, the decision notice must state the amount of the penalty.

(4) If the Authority decides to—

(a) publish a statement in respect of an authorised person under section 205, or

(b) impose a penalty on an authorised person under section 206,

the authorised person may refer the matter to the Tribunal.

**209   Publication**

After a statement under section 205 is published, the Authority must send a copy of it to the authorised person and to any person on whom a copy of the decision notice was given under section 393(4).

**210   Statements of policy**

(1) The Authority must prepare and issue a statement of its policy with respect to—

(a) the imposition of penalties under this Part; and

(b) the amount of penalties under this Part.

(2) The Authority's policy in determining what the amount of a penalty should be must include having regard to—

   (a) the seriousness of the contravention in question in relation to the nature of the requirement contravened;

   (b) the extent to which that contravention was deliberate or reckless; and

   (c) whether the person on whom the penalty is to be imposed is an individual.

(3) The Authority may at any time alter or replace a statement issued under this section.

(4) If a statement issued under this section is altered or replaced, the Authority must issue the altered or replacement statement.

(5) The Authority must, without delay, give the Treasury a copy of any statement which it publishes under this section.

(6) A statement issued under this section must be published by the Authority in the way appearing to the Authority to be best calculated to bring it to the attention of the public.

(7) In exercising, or deciding whether to exercise, its power under section 206 in the case of any particular contravention, the Authority must have regard to any statement published under this section and in force at the time when the contravention in question occurred.

(8) The Authority may charge a reasonable fee for providing a person with a copy of the statement.

### 211  Statements of policy: procedure

(1) Before issuing a statement under section 210, the Authority must publish a draft of the proposed statement in the way appearing to the Authority to be best calculated to bring it to the attention of the public.

(2) The draft must be accompanied by notice that representations about the proposal may be made to the Authority within a specified time.

(3) Before issuing the proposed statement, the Authority must have regard to any representations made to it in accordance with subsection (2).

(4) If the Authority issues the proposed statement it must publish an account, in general terms, of—

   (a) the representations made to it in accordance with subsection (2); and

   (b) its response to them.

(5) If the statement differs from the draft published under subsection (1) in a way which is, in the opinion of the Authority, significant, the Authority must (in addition to complying with subsection (4)) publish details of the difference.

(6) The Authority may charge a reasonable fee for providing a person with a copy of a draft published under subsection (1).

(7) This section also applies to a proposal to alter or replace a statement.

# PART XV

# THE FINANCIAL SERVICES COMPENSATION SCHEME

*The scheme manager*

### 212  The scheme manager

(1) The Authority must establish a body corporate ('the scheme manager') to exercise the functions conferred on the scheme manager by or under this Part.

(2) The Authority must take such steps as are necessary to ensure that the scheme manager is, at all times, capable of exercising those functions.

(3) The constitution of the scheme manager must provide for it to have—

   (a) a chairman; and

   (b) a board (which must include the chairman) whose members are the scheme manager's directors.

(4) The chairman and other members of the board must be persons appointed, and liable to removal from office, by the Authority (acting, in the case of the chairman, with the approval of the Treasury).

(5) But the terms of their appointment (and in particular those governing removal from office) must be such as to secure their independence from the Authority in the operation of the compensation scheme.

(6) The scheme manager is not to be regarded as exercising functions on behalf of the Crown.

(7) The scheme manager's board members, officers and staff are not to be regarded as Crown servants.

*The scheme*

### 213  The compensation scheme

(1) The Authority must by rules establish a scheme for compensating persons in cases where relevant persons are unable, or are likely to be unable, to satisfy claims against them.

(2) The rules are to be known as the Financial Services Compensation Scheme (but are referred to in this Act as 'the compensation scheme').

(3) The compensation scheme must, in particular, provide for the scheme manager—

    (a) to assess and pay compensation, in accordance with the scheme, to claimants in respect of claims made in connection with regulated activities carried on (whether or not with permission) by relevant persons; and

    (b) to have power to impose levies on authorised persons, or any class of authorised person, for the purpose of meeting its expenses (including in particular expenses incurred, or expected to be incurred, in paying compensation, borrowing or insuring risks).

(4) The compensation scheme may provide for the scheme manager to have power to impose levies on authorised persons, or any class of authorised person, for the purpose of recovering the cost (whenever incurred) of establishing the scheme.

(5) In making any provision of the scheme by virtue of subsection (3)(b), the Authority must take account of the desirability of ensuring that the amount of the levies imposed on a particular class of authorised person reflects, so far as practicable, the amount of the claims made, or likely to be made, in respect of that class of person.

(6) An amount payable to the scheme manager as a result of any provision of the scheme made by virtue of subsection (3)(b) or (4) may be recovered as a debt due to the scheme manager.

(7) Sections 214 to 217 make further provision about the scheme but are not to be taken as limiting the power conferred on the Authority by subsection (1) *(except where limitations are expressly stated)*.

(8) In those sections 'specified' means specified in the scheme.

(9) In this Part (except in sections 219, 220 or 224) 'relevant person' means a person who was—

    (a) an authorised person at the time the act or omission giving rise to the claim against him took place; or

    (b) an appointed representative at that time.

(10) But a person who, at that time—

    (a) qualified for authorisation under Schedule 3, and

    (b) fell within a prescribed category,

is not to be regarded as a relevant person in relation to any activities for which he had permission as a result of any provision of, or made under, that Schedule unless he had elected to participate in the scheme in relation to those activities at that time.[4]

### *Provisions of the scheme*

## 214 General

(1) The compensation scheme may, in particular, make provision—

    (a) as to the circumstances in which a relevant person is to be taken (for the purposes of the scheme) to be unable, or likely to be unable, to satisfy claims made against him;

    (b) for the establishment of different funds for meeting different kinds of claim;

    (c) for the imposition of different levies in different cases;

    (d) limiting the levy payable by a person in respect of a specified period;

    (e) for repayment of the whole or part of a levy in specified circumstances;

    (f) for a claim to be entertained only if it is made by a specified kind of claimant;

    (g) for a claim to be entertained only if it falls within a specified kind of claim;

    (h) as to the procedure to be followed in making a claim;

    (i) for the making of interim payments before a claim is finally determined;

    (j) limiting the amount payable on a claim to a specified maximum amount or a maximum amount calculated in a specified manner;

    (k) for payment to be made, in specified circumstances, to a person other than the claimant.

(1A) Rules by virtue of subsection (1)(h) may, in particular, allow the scheme manager to treat persons who are or may be entitled to claim under the scheme as if they had done so.

(1B) A reference in any enactment or instrument to a claim or claimant under this Part includes a reference to a deemed claim or claimant in accordance with subsection (1A).

(1C) Rules by virtue of subsection (1)(j) may, in particular, allow, or be subject to rules which allow, the scheme manager to settle a class of claim by payment of sums fixed without reference to, or by modification of, the normal rules for calculation of maximum entitlement for individual claims.

(2) Different provision may be made with respect to different kinds of claim.

(3) The scheme may provide for the determination and regulation of matters relating to the scheme by the scheme manager.

(4) The scheme, or particular provisions of the scheme, may be made so as to apply only in relation to—

    (a) activities carried on,

    (b) claimants,

    (c) matters arising, or

    (d) events occurring,

---

[4] The words in italics added by the Banking Act 2009 c 1 from a date to be appointed.

in specified territories, areas or localities.

(5) The scheme may provide for a person who—

(a) qualifies for authorisation under Schedule 3, and

(b) falls within a prescribed category,

to elect to participate in the scheme in relation to some or all of the activities for which he has permission as a result of any provision of, or made under, that Schedule.

(6) The scheme may provide for the scheme manager to have power—

(a) in specified circumstances,

(b) but only if the scheme manager is satisfied that the claimant is entitled to receive a payment in respect of his claim—

(i)    under a scheme which is comparable to the compensation scheme, or

(ii)   as the result of a guarantee given by a government or other authority,

to make a full payment of compensation to the claimant and recover the whole or part of the amount of that payment from the other scheme or under that guarantee.

### 214A   Contingency funding

*(1) The Treasury may make regulations ('contingency fund regulations') permitting the scheme manager to impose levies under section 213 for the purpose of maintaining contingency funds from which possible expenses may be paid.*

*(2) Contingency fund regulations may make provision about the establishment and management of contingency funds; in particular, the regulations may make provision about—*

*(a) the number and size of funds;*

*(b) the circumstances and timing of their establishment;*

*(c) the classes of person from whom contributions to the funds may be levied;*

*(d) the amount and timing of payments into and out of funds (which may include provision for different levies for different classes of person);*

*(e) refunds;*

*(f) the ways in which funds' contents may be invested (including (i) the extent of reliance on section 223A, and (ii) the application of investment income);*

*(g) the purposes for which funds may be applied, but only so as to determine whether a fund is to be used (i) for the payment of compensation, (ii) for the purposes of co-operating with a bank liquidator in accordance with section 99 of the Banking Act 2009, or (iii) for contributions under section 214B;*

*(h) procedures to be followed in connection with funds, including the keeping of records and the provision of information.*

*(3) The compensation scheme may include provision about contingency funds provided that it is not inconsistent with contingency fund regulations.*[5]

### 214B   Contribution to costs of special resolution regime

(1) This section applies where—

(a) a stabilisation power under Part 1 of the Banking Act 2009 has been exercised in respect of a bank, building society or credit union (within the meaning of that Part), and

(b) the Treasury think that the bank, building society or credit union was, or but for the exercise of the stabilisation power would have become, unable to satisfy claims against it.

(2) Where this section applies—

(a) the Treasury may require the scheme manager to make payments in connection with the exercise of the stabilisation power, and

(b) payments shall be treated as expenditure under the scheme for all purposes (including levies, contingency funds and borrowing).

(3) The Treasury shall make regulations—

(a) specifying what expenses the scheme manager may be required to incur under subsection (2),

(b) providing for independent verification of the nature and amount of expenses incurred in connection with the exercise of the stabilisation power (which may include provision about appointment and payment of an auditor), and

(c) providing for the method by which amounts to be paid are to be determined.

(4) The regulations must ensure that payments required do not exceed the amount of compensation that would have been payable under the scheme if the stabilisation power had not been exercised and the bank had been unable to satisfy claims against it; and for that purpose the amount of compensation that would have been payable does not include—

(a) amounts that would have been likely, at the time when the stabilisation power was exercised, to be recovered by the scheme from the bank, or

(b) any compensation actually paid to an eligible depositor of the bank.

[5] Section 214A inserted by the Banking Act 2009 c 1 from a date to be appointed.

(5) The regulations must provide for the appointment of an independent valuer (who may be the person appointed as valuer under section 54 of the Banking Act 2009 in respect of the exercise of the stabilisation power) to calculate the amounts referred to in subsection (4)(a); and the regulations—

    (a) must provide for the valuer to be appointed by the Treasury or by a person designated by the Treasury,

    (b) must include provision enabling the valuer to reconsider a decision,

    (c) must provide a right of appeal to a court or tribunal,

    (d) must provide for payment of the valuer,

    (e) may replicate or apply a provision of section 54 or 55, and

    (f) may apply or include any provision that is or could be made under that section.

(6) Payments required to be made by the scheme by virtue of section 61 of the Banking Act 2009 (special resolution regime: compensation) shall be treated for the purposes of subsection (4) as if required to be made under this section.

(7) The regulations may include provision for payments (including payments under those provisions of the Banking Act 2009) to be made—

    (a) before verification in accordance with subsection (3)(b), and

    (b) before the calculation of the limit imposed by subsection (4), by reference to estimates of that limit and subject to any necessary later adjustment.

(8) The regulations may include provision—

    (a) about timing;

    (b) about procedures to be followed;

    (c) for discretionary functions to be exercised by a specified body or by persons of a specified class;

    (d) about the resolution of disputes (which may include provision conferring jurisdiction on a court or tribunal).

(9) The compensation scheme may include provision about payments under and levies in connection with this section, provided that it is not inconsistent with this section or regulations under it.

## 215   Rights of the scheme in insolvency

(1) The compensation scheme may make provision—

    (a) about the effect of a payment of compensation under the scheme on rights or obligations arising out of matters in connection with which the compensation was paid;

    (b) giving the scheme manager a right of recovery in respect of those rights or obligations.

(2) Such a right of recovery conferred by the scheme does not, in the event of a person's insolvency, exceed such right (if any) as the claimant would have had in that event.

(3) If a person other than the scheme manager makes an administration application under Schedule B1 to the 1986 Act or presents a petition under Article 22 of the 1989 Order in relation to a company or partnership which is a relevant person, the scheme manager has the same rights as are conferred on the Authority by section 362.

(3A) In subsection (3) the reference to making an administration application includes a reference to—

    (a) appointing an administrator under paragraph 14 or 22 of Schedule B1 to the 1986 Act, or

    (b) filing with the court a copy of notice of intention to appoint an administrator under either of those paragraphs.

(4) If a person other than the scheme manager presents a petition for the winding up of a body which is a relevant person, the scheme manager has the same rights as are conferred on the Authority by section 371.

(5) If a person other than the scheme manager presents a bankruptcy petition to the court in relation to an individual who, or an entity which, is a relevant person, the scheme manager has the same rights as are conferred on the Authority by section 374.

(6) Insolvency rules may be made for the purpose of integrating any procedure for which provision is made as a result of subsection (1) into the general procedure on the administration of a company or partnership or on a winding-up, bankruptcy or sequestration.

(7) 'Bankruptcy petition' means a petition to the court—

    (a) under section 264 of the 1986 Act or Article 238 of the 1989 Order for a bankruptcy order to be made against an individual;

    (b) under section 5 of the 1985 Act for the sequestration of the estate of an individual; or

    (c) under section 6 of the 1985 Act for the sequestration of the estate belonging to or held for or jointly by the members of an entity mentioned in subsection (1) of that section.

(8) 'Insolvency rules' are—

    (a) for England and Wales, rules made under sections 411 and 412 of the 1986 Act;

    (b) for Scotland, rules made by order by the Treasury, after consultation with the Scottish Ministers, for the purposes of this section; and

    (c) for Northern Ireland, rules made under Article 359 of the 1989 Order and section 55 of the Judicature (Northern Ireland) Act 1978.

(9) 'The 1985 Act', 'the 1986 Act', 'the 1989 Order' and 'court' have the same meaning as in Part XXIV.

### 216   Continuity of long-term insurance policies

(1) The compensation scheme may, in particular, include provision requiring the scheme manager to make arrangements for securing continuity of insurance for policyholders, or policyholders of a specified class, of relevant long-term insurers.

(2) 'Relevant long-term insurers' means relevant persons who—

   (a) have permission to effect or carry out contracts of long-term insurance; and

   (b) are unable, or likely to be unable, to satisfy claims made against them.

(3) The scheme may provide for the scheme manager to take such measures as appear to him to be appropriate—

   (a) for securing or facilitating the transfer of a relevant long-term insurer's business so far as it consists of the carrying out of contracts of long-term insurance, or of any part of that business, to another authorised person;

   (b) for securing the issue by another authorised person to the policyholders concerned of policies in substitution for their existing policies.

(4) The scheme may also provide for the scheme manager to make payments to the policyholders concerned—

   (a) during any period while he is seeking to make arrangements mentioned in subsection (1);

   (b) if it appears to him that it is not reasonably practicable to make such arrangements.

(5) A provision of the scheme made by virtue of section 213(3)(b) may include power to impose levies for the purpose of meeting expenses of the scheme manager incurred in—

   (a) taking measures as a result of any provision of the scheme made by virtue of subsection (3);

   (b) making payments as a result of any such provision made by virtue of subsection (4).

### 217   Insurers in financial difficulties

(1) The compensation scheme may, in particular, include provision for the scheme manager to have power to take measures for safeguarding policyholders, or policyholders of a specified class, of relevant insurers.

(2) 'Relevant insurers' means relevant persons who—

   (a) have permission to effect or carry out contracts of insurance; and

   (b) are in financial difficulties.

(3) The measures may include such measures as the scheme manager considers appropriate for—

   (a) securing or facilitating the transfer of a relevant insurer's business so far as it consists of the carrying out of contracts of insurance, or of any part of that business, to another authorised person;

   (b) giving assistance to the relevant insurer to enable it to continue to effect or carry out contracts of insurance.

(4) The scheme may provide—

   (a) that if measures of a kind mentioned in subsection (3)(a) are to be taken, they should be on terms appearing to the scheme manager to be appropriate, including terms reducing, or deferring payment of, any of the things to which any of those who are eligible policyholders in relation to the relevant insurer are entitled in their capacity as such;

   (b) that if measures of a kind mentioned in subsection (3)(b) are to be taken, they should be conditional on the reduction of, or the deferment of the payment of, the things to which any of those who are eligible policyholders in relation to the relevant insurer are entitled in their capacity as such;

   (c) for ensuring that measures of a kind mentioned in subsection (3)(b) do not benefit to any material extent persons who were members of a relevant insurer when it began to be in financial difficulties or who had any responsibility for, or who may have profited from, the circumstances giving rise to its financial difficulties, except in specified circumstances;

   (d) for requiring the scheme manager to be satisfied that any measures he proposes to take are likely to cost less than it would cost to pay compensation under the scheme if the relevant insurer became unable, or likely to be unable, to satisfy claims made against him.

(5) The scheme may provide for the Authority to have power—

   (a) to give such assistance to the scheme manager as it considers appropriate for assisting the scheme manager to determine what measures are practicable or desirable in the case of a particular relevant insurer;

   (b) to impose constraints on the taking of measures by the scheme manager in the case of a particular relevant insurer;

   (c) to require the scheme manager to provide it with information about any particular measures which the scheme manager is proposing to take.

(6) The scheme may include provision for the scheme manager to have power—

   (a) to make interim payments in respect of eligible policyholders of a relevant insurer;

   (b) to indemnify any person making payments to eligible policyholders of a relevant insurer.

(7) A provision of the scheme made by virtue of section 213(3)(b) may include power to impose levies for the purpose of meeting expenses of the scheme manager incurred in—

    (a) taking measures as a result of any provision of the scheme made by virtue of subsection (1);

    (b) making payments or giving indemnities as a result of any such provision made by virtue of subsection (6).

(8) 'Financial difficulties' and 'eligible policyholders' have such meanings as may be specified.

### *Annual report*

### 218  Annual report

(1) At least once a year, the scheme manager must make a report to the Authority *and the Treasury* on the discharge of its functions.

(2) The report must—

    (a) include a statement setting out the value of each of the funds established by the compensation scheme; and

    (b) comply with any requirements specified in rules made by the Authority *or in contingency fund regulations*.

(3) The scheme manager must publish each report in the way it considers appropriate.[6]

### 218A  Authority's power to require information

(1) The Authority may make rules enabling the Authority to require authorised persons to provide information, which may then be made available to the scheme manager by the Authority.

(2) A requirement may be imposed only if the Authority thinks the information is of a kind that may be of use to the scheme manager in connection with functions in respect of the scheme.

(3) A requirement under this section may apply—

    (a) to authorised persons generally or only to specified persons or classes of person;

    (b) to the provision of information at specified periods, in connection with specified events or in other ways.

(4) In addition to requirements under this section, a notice under section 165 may relate to information or documents which the Authority thinks are reasonably required by the scheme manager in connection with the performance of functions in respect of the scheme; and section 165(4) is subject to this subsection.

(5) Rules under subsection (1) shall be prepared, made and treated in the same way as (and may be combined with) the Authority's general rules.

### *Information and documents*

### 219  Scheme manager's power to require information

(1) The scheme manager may, by notice in writing given to the relevant person in respect of whom a claim is made under the scheme or to a person otherwise involved, require that person—

    (a) to provide specified information or information of a specified description; or

    (b) to produce specified documents or documents of a specified description.

(1A) A requirement may be imposed only—

    (a) on a person (P) against whom a claim has been made under the scheme,

    (b) on a person (P) who is unable or likely to be unable to satisfy claims under the scheme against P,

    (c) on a person ('the Third Party') whom the scheme manager thinks was knowingly involved in matters giving rise to a claim against another person (P) under the scheme, or

    (d) on a person ('the Third Party') whom the scheme manager thinks was knowingly involved in matters giving rise to the actual or likely inability of another person (P) to satisfy claims under the scheme.

(1B) For the purposes of subsection (1A)(b) and (d) whether P is unable or likely to be unable to satisfy claims shall be determined in accordance with provision to be made by the scheme (which may, in particular—

    (a) apply or replicate, with or without modifications, a provision of an enactment;

    (b) confer discretion on a specified person).

(2) The information or documents must be provided or produced—

    (a) before the end of such reasonable period as may be specified; and

    (b) in the case of information, in such manner or form as may be specified.

(3) This section applies only to information and documents the provision or production of which the scheme manager considers to be necessary (or likely to be necessary) for the fair determination of claims which have been or may be made against P.

(3A) Where a stabilisation power under Part 1 of the Banking Act 2009 has been exercised in respect of a bank, the scheme manager may by notice in writing require the bank or the Bank of England to

---

[6] The words in italics added by the Banking Act 2009 c 1 from a date to be appointed.

provide information that the scheme manager requires for the purpose of applying regulations under section 214B(3) above.

(4) If a document is produced in response to a requirement imposed under this section, the scheme manager may—

(a) take copies or extracts from the document; or

(b) require the person producing the document to provide an explanation of the document.

(5) If a person who is required under this section to produce a document fails to do so, the scheme manager may require the person to state, to the best of his knowledge and belief, where the document is.

(6) If P is insolvent, no requirement may be imposed under this section on a person to whom section 220 or 224 applies.

(7) If a person claims a lien on a document, its production under this Part does not affect the lien.

(8) [...]

(9) 'Specified' means specified in the notice given under subsection (1).

(10) [...]

### 220 Scheme manager's power to inspect information held by liquidator etc

(1) For the purpose of assisting the scheme manager to discharge its functions in relation to a claim made in respect of an insolvent relevant person, a person to whom this section applies must permit a person authorised by the scheme manager to inspect relevant documents.

(2) A person inspecting a document under this section may take copies of, or extracts from, the document.

(3) This section applies to—

(a) the administrative receiver, administrator, liquidator, or bank liquidator or trustee in bankruptcy of an insolvent relevant person;

(b) the permanent trustee, within the meaning of the Bankruptcy (Scotland) Act 1985, on the estate of an insolvent relevant person.

(4) This section does not apply to a liquidator, administrator or trustee in bankruptcy who is—

(a) the Official Receiver;

(b) the Official Receiver for Northern Ireland; or

(c) the Accountant in Bankruptcy.

(5) 'Relevant person' has the same meaning as in section 224.

### 221 Powers of court where information required

(1) If a person ('the defaulter')—

(a) fails to comply with a requirement imposed under section 219, or

(b) fails to permit documents to be inspected under section 220,

the scheme manager may certify that fact in writing to the court and the court may enquire into the case.

(2) If the court is satisfied that the defaulter failed without reasonable excuse to comply with the requirement (or to permit the documents to be inspected), it may deal with the defaulter (and, in the case of a body corporate, any director or officer) as if he were in contempt; and 'officer', in relation to a limited liability partnership, means a member of the limited liability partnership..

(3) 'Court' means—

(a) the High Court;

(b) in Scotland, the Court of Session.

### 221A Delegation of functions

(1) The scheme manager may arrange for any of its functions to be discharged on its behalf by another person (a 'scheme agent').

(2) Before entering into arrangements the scheme manager must be satisfied that the scheme agent—

(a) is competent to discharge the function, and

(b) has been given sufficient directions to enable the agent to take any decisions required in the course of exercising the function in accordance with policy determined by the scheme manager.

(3) Arrangements may include provision for payments to be made by the scheme manager to the scheme agent (which payments are management expenses of the scheme manager).

*Miscellaneous*

### 222 Statutory immunity

(1) Neither the scheme manager nor any person who is, or is acting as, its board member, officer, scheme agent or member of staff is to be liable in damages for anything done or omitted in the discharge, or purported discharge, of the scheme manager's functions.

(2) Subsection (1) does not apply—

(a) if the act or omission is shown to have been in bad faith; or

(b) so as to prevent an award of damages made in respect of an act or omission on the ground that the act or omission was unlawful as a result of section 6(1) of the Human Rights Act 1998.

### 223   Management expenses

(1) The amount which the scheme manager may recover, from the sums levied under the scheme, as management expenses attributable to a particular period may not exceed such amount as may be fixed by the scheme as the limit applicable to that period.

(2) In calculating the amount of any levy to be imposed by the scheme manager, no amount may be included to reflect management expenses unless the limit mentioned in subsection (1) has been fixed by the scheme.

(3) 'Management expenses' means expenses incurred, or expected to be incurred, by the scheme manager in connection with its functions under this Act other than those incurred—

   (a) in paying compensation;
   (b) as a result of any provision of the scheme made by virtue of section 216(3) or (4) or 217(1) or (6);
   (c) under section 214B.

### 223A   Investing in National Loans Fund

(1) Sums levied for the purpose of maintaining a contingency fund may be paid to the Treasury.

(2) The Treasury may receive sums under subsection (1) and may set terms and conditions of receipts.

(3) Sums received shall be treated as if raised under section 12 of the National Loans Act 1968 (and shall therefore be invested as part of the National Loans Fund).

(4) Interest accruing on the invested sums may be credited to the contingency fund (subject to any terms and conditions set under subsection (2)).

(5) The Treasury shall comply with any request of the scheme manager to arrange for the return of sums for the purpose of making payments out of a contingency fund (subject to any terms and conditions set under subsection (2)).

### 223B   Borrowing from National Loans Fund

(1) The scheme manager may request a loan from the National Loans Fund for the purpose of funding expenses incurred or expected to be incurred under the scheme.

(2) The Treasury may arrange for money to be paid out of the National Loans Fund in pursuance of a request under subsection (1).

(3) The Treasury shall determine—

   (a) the rate of interest on a loan, and
   (b) other terms and conditions.

(4) The Treasury may make regulations—

   (a) about the amounts that may be borrowed under this section;
   (b) permitting the scheme manager to impose levies under section 213 for the purpose of meeting expenses in connection with loans under this section (and the regulations may have effect despite any provision of this Act);
   (c) about the classes of person on whom those levies may be imposed;
   (d) about the amounts and timing of those levies.

(5) The compensation scheme may include provision about borrowing under this section provided that it is not inconsistent with regulations under this section.

### 223C   Payments in error

(1) Payments made by the scheme manager in error may be provided for in setting a levy by virtue of section 213, 214A, 214B or 223B.

(2) This section does not apply to payments made in bad faith.

### 224   Scheme manager's power to inspect documents held by Official Receiver etc

(1) If, as a result of the insolvency or bankruptcy of a relevant person, any documents have come into the possession of a person to whom this section applies, he must permit any person authorised by the scheme manager to inspect the documents for the purpose of establishing—

   (a) the identity of persons to whom the scheme manager may be liable to make a payment in accordance with the compensation scheme; or
   (b) the amount of any payment which the scheme manager may be liable to make.

(2) A person inspecting a document under this section may take copies or extracts from the document.

(3) In this section 'relevant person' means a person who was—

   (a) an authorised person at the time the act or omission which may give rise to the liability mentioned in subsection (1)(a) took place; or

(b) an appointed representative at that time.

(4) But a person who, at that time—

(a) qualified for authorisation under Schedule 3, and

(b) fell within a prescribed category,

is not to be regarded as a relevant person for the purposes of this section in relation to any activities for which he had permission as a result of any provision of, or made under, that Schedule unless he had elected to participate in the scheme in relation to those activities at that time.

(5) This section applies to—

(a) the Official Receiver;

(b) the Official Receiver for Northern Ireland; and

(c) the Accountant in Bankruptcy.

### 224A  Functions under the Banking Act 2009

A reference in this Part to functions of the scheme manager (including a reference to functions conferred by or under this Part) includes a reference to functions conferred by or under the Banking Act 2009.

# PART XVI

# THE OMBUDSMAN SCHEME

### *The scheme*

### 225  The scheme and the scheme operator

(1) This Part provides for a scheme under which certain disputes may be resolved quickly and with minimum formality by an independent person.

(2) The scheme is to be administered by a body corporate ('the scheme operator').

(3) The scheme is to be operated under a name chosen by the scheme operator but is referred to in this Act as 'the ombudsman scheme'.

(4) Schedule 17 makes provision in connection with the ombudsman scheme and the scheme operator.

### 226  Compulsory jurisdiction

(1) A complaint which relates to an act or omission of a person ('the respondent') in carrying on an activity to which compulsory jurisdiction rules apply is to be dealt with under the ombudsman scheme if the conditions mentioned in subsection (2) are satisfied.

(2) The conditions are that—

(a) the complainant is eligible and wishes to have the complaint dealt with under the scheme;

(b) the respondent was an authorised person or a payment service provider within the meaning of the Payment Services Regulations 2009 at the time of the act or omission to which the complaint relates; and

(c) the act or omission to which the complaint relates occurred at a time when compulsory jurisdiction rules were in force in relation to the activity in question.

(3) 'Compulsory jurisdiction rules' means rules—

(a) made by the Authority for the purposes of this section; and

(b) specifying the activities to which they apply.

(4) Only activities which are regulated activities, or which could be made regulated activities by an order under section 22, may be specified.

(5) Activities may be specified by reference to specified categories (however described).

(6) A complainant is eligible, in relation to the compulsory jurisdiction of the ombudsman scheme, if he falls within a class of person specified in the rules as eligible.

(7) The rules—

(a) may include provision for persons other than individuals to be eligible; but

(b) may not provide for authorised persons to be eligible except in specified circumstances or in relation to complaints of a specified kind.

(8) The jurisdiction of the scheme which results from this section is referred to in this Act as the 'compulsory jurisdiction'.

### 226A  Consumer credit jurisdiction

(1) A complaint which relates to an act or omission of a person ('the respondent') is to be dealt with under the ombudsman scheme if the conditions mentioned in subsection (2) are satisfied.

(2) The conditions are that—

(a) the complainant is eligible and wishes to have the complaint dealt with under the scheme;

(b) the complaint falls within a description specified in consumer credit rules;

(c) at the time of the act or omission the respondent was the licensee under a standard licence or was authorised to carry on an activity by virtue of section 34A of the Consumer Credit Act 1974;

(d) the act or omission occurred in the course of a business being carried on by the respondent which was of a type mentioned in subsection (3);

(e) at the time of the act or omission that type of business was specified in an order made by the Secretary of State; and

(f) the complaint cannot be dealt with under the compulsory jurisdiction.

(3) The types of business referred to in subsection (2)(d) are—

(a) a consumer credit business;

(b) a consumer hire business;

(c) a business so far as it comprises or relates to credit brokerage;

(d) a business so far as it comprises or relates to debt-adjusting;

(e) a business so far as it comprises or relates to debt-counselling;

(f) a business so far as it comprises or relates to debt-collecting;

(g) a business so far as it comprises or relates to debt administration;

(h) a business so far as it comprises or relates to the provision of credit information services;

(i) a business so far as it comprises or relates to the operation of a credit reference agency.

(4) A complainant is eligible if—

(a) he is—

(i) an individual; or

(ii) a surety in relation to a security provided to the respondent in connection with the business mentioned in subsection (2)(d); and

(b) he falls within a class of person specified in consumer credit rules.

(5) The approval of the Treasury is required for an order under subsection (2)(e).

(6) The jurisdiction of the scheme which results from this section is referred to in this Act as the 'consumer credit jurisdiction'.

(7) In this Act 'consumer credit rules' means rules made by the scheme operator with the approval of the Authority for the purposes of the consumer credit jurisdiction.

(8) Consumer credit rules under this section may make different provision for different cases.

(9) Expressions used in the Consumer Credit Act 1974 have the same meaning in this section as they have in that Act

### 227 Voluntary jurisdiction

(1) A complaint which relates to an act or omission of a person ('the respondent') in carrying on an activity to which voluntary jurisdiction rules apply is to be dealt with under the ombudsman scheme if the conditions mentioned in subsection (2) are satisfied.

(2) The conditions are that—

(a) the complainant is eligible and wishes to have the complaint dealt with under the scheme;

(b) at the time of the act or omission to which the complaint relates, the respondent was participating in the scheme;

(c) at the time when the complaint is referred under the scheme, the respondent has not withdrawn from the scheme in accordance with its provisions;

(d) the act or omission to which the complaint relates occurred at a time when voluntary jurisdiction rules were in force in relation to the activity in question; and

(e) the complaint cannot be dealt with under the compulsory jurisdiction or the consumer credit jurisdiction.

(3) 'Voluntary jurisdiction rules' means rules—

(a) made by the scheme operator for the purposes of this section; and

(b) specifying the activities to which they apply.

(4) The only activities which may be specified in the rules are activities which are, or could be, specified in compulsory jurisdiction rules.

(5) Activities may be specified by reference to specified categories (however described).

(6) The rules require the Authority's approval.

(7) A complainant is eligible, in relation to the voluntary jurisdiction of the ombudsman scheme, if he falls within a class of person specified in the rules as eligible.

(8) The rules may include provision for persons other than individuals to be eligible.

(9) A person qualifies for participation in the ombudsman scheme if he falls within a class of person specified in the rules in relation to the activity in question.

(10) Provision may be made in the rules for persons other than authorised persons to participate in the ombudsman scheme.

(11) The rules may make different provision in relation to complaints arising from different activities.

(12) The jurisdiction of the scheme which results from this section is referred to in this Act as the 'voluntary jurisdiction'.

(13) In such circumstances as may be specified in voluntary jurisdiction rules, a complaint—

(a) which relates to an act or omission occurring at a time before the rules came into force, and

(b) which could have been dealt with under a scheme which has to any extent been replaced by the voluntary jurisdiction, is to be dealt with under the ombudsman scheme even though paragraph (b) or (d) of subsection (2) would otherwise prevent that.

(14)  In such circumstances as may be specified in voluntary jurisdiction rules, a complaint is to be dealt with under the ombudsman scheme even though—

    (a)  paragraph (b) or (d) of subsection (2) would otherwise prevent that, and

    (b)  the complaint is not brought within the scheme as a result of subsection (13),

but only if the respondent has agreed that complaints of that kind were to be dealt with under the scheme.

*Determination of complaints*

### 228  Determination under the compulsory jurisdiction and to the consumer credit jurisdiction

(1)  This section applies only in relation to the compulsory jurisdiction.

(2)  A complaint is to be determined by reference to what is, in the opinion of the ombudsman, fair and reasonable in all the circumstances of the case.

(3)  When the ombudsman has determined a complaint he must give a written statement of his determination to the respondent and to the complainant.

(4)  The statement must—

    (a)  give the ombudsman's reasons for his determination;

    (b)  be signed by him; and

    (c)  require the complainant to notify him in writing, before a date specified in the statement, whether he accepts or rejects the determination.

(5)  If the complainant notifies the ombudsman that he accepts the determination, it is binding on the respondent and the complainant and final.

(6)  If, by the specified date, the complainant has not notified the ombudsman of his acceptance or rejection of the determination he is to be treated as having rejected it.

(7)  The ombudsman must notify the respondent of the outcome.

(8)  A copy of the determination on which appears a certificate signed by an ombudsman is evidence (or in Scotland sufficient evidence) that the determination was made under the scheme.

(9)  Such a certificate purporting to be signed by an ombudsman is to be taken to have been duly signed unless the contrary is shown.

### 229  Awards

(1)  This section applies only in relation to the compulsory jurisdiction and to the consumer credit jurisdiction.

(2)  If a complaint which has been dealt with under the scheme is determined in favour of the complainant, the determination may include—

    (a)  an award against the respondent of such amount as the ombudsman considers fair compensation for loss or damage (of a kind falling within subsection (3)) suffered by the complainant ('a money award');

    (b)  a direction that the respondent take such steps in relation to the complainant as the ombudsman considers just and appropriate (whether or not a court could order those steps to be taken).

(3)  A money award may compensate for—

    (a)  financial loss; or

    (b)  any other loss, or any damage, of a specified kind.

(4)  The Authority may specify for the purposes of the compulsory jurisdiction the maximum amount which may be regarded as fair compensation for a particular kind of loss or damage specified under subsection (3)(b).

(4A)  The scheme operator may specify for the purposes of the consumer credit jurisdiction the maximum amount which may be regarded as fair compensation for a particular kind of loss or damage specified under subsection (3)(b).

(5)  A money award may not exceed the monetary limit; but the ombudsman may, if he considers that fair compensation requires payment of a larger amount, recommend that the respondent pay the complainant the balance.

(6)  The monetary limit is such amount as may be specified.

(7)  Different amounts may be specified in relation to different kinds of complaint.

(8)  A money award—

    (a)  may provide for the amount payable under the award to bear interest at a rate and as from a date specified in the award; and

    (b)  is enforceable by the complainant in accordance with Part III of Schedule 17 or (as the case may be) Part 3A of that Schedule.

(9)  Compliance with a direction under subsection (2)(b)—

    (a)  is enforceable by an injunction; or

    (b)  in Scotland, is enforceable by an order under section 45 of the Court of Session Act 1988.

(10)  Only the complainant may bring proceedings for an injunction or proceedings for an order.

(11) 'Specified' means—

    (a) for the purposes of the compulsory jurisdiction, specified in compulsory jurisdiction rules;

    (b) for the purposes of the consumer credit jurisdiction, specified in consumer credit rules.

(12) Consumer credit rules under this section may make different provision for different cases.

## 230  Costs

(1) The scheme operator may by rules ('costs rules') provide for an ombudsman to have power, on determining a complaint under the compulsory jurisdiction or the consumer credit jurisdiction, to award costs in accordance with the provisions of the rules.

(2) Costs rules require the approval of the Authority.

(3) Costs rules may not provide for the making of an award against the complainant in respect of the respondent's costs.

(4) But they may provide for the making of an award against the complainant in favour of the scheme operator, for the purpose of providing a contribution to resources deployed in dealing with the complaint, if in the opinion of the ombudsman—

    (a) the complainant's conduct was improper or unreasonable; or

    (b) the complainant was responsible for an unreasonable delay.

(5) Costs rules may authorise an ombudsman making an award in accordance with the rules to order that the amount payable under the award bears interest at a rate and as from a date specified in the order.

(6) An amount due under an award made in favour of the scheme operator is recoverable as a debt due to the scheme operator.

(7) Any other award made against the respondent is to be treated as a money award for the purposes of paragraph 16 of Schedule 17 or (as the case may be) paragraph 16D of that Schedule.

### *Information*

## 231  Ombudsman's power to require information

(1) An ombudsman may, by notice in writing given to a party to a complaint, require that party—

    (a) to provide specified information or information of a specified description; or

    (b) to produce specified documents or documents of a specified description.

(2) The information or documents must be provided or produced—

    (a) before the end of such reasonable period as may be specified; and

    (b) in the case of information, in such manner or form as may be specified.

(3) This section applies only to information and documents the production of which the ombudsman considers necessary for the determination of the complaint.

(4) If a document is produced in response to a requirement imposed under this section, the ombudsman may—

    (a) take copies or extracts from the document; or

    (b) require the person producing the document to provide an explanation of the document.

(5) If a person who is required under this section to produce a document fails to do so, the ombudsman may require him to state, to the best of his knowledge and belief, where the document is.

(6) If a person claims a lien on a document, its production under this Part does not affect the lien.

(7) 'Specified' means specified in the notice given under subsection (1).

## 232  Powers of court where information required

(1) If a person ('the defaulter') fails to comply with a requirement imposed under section 231, the ombudsman may certify that fact in writing to the court and the court may enquire into the case.

(2) If the court is satisfied that the defaulter failed without reasonable excuse to comply with the requirement, it may deal with the defaulter (and, in the case of a body corporate, any director or officer) as if he were in contempt ; and 'officer', in relation to a limited liability partnership, means a member of the limited liability partnership.

(3) 'Court' means—

    (a) the High Court;

    (b) in Scotland, the Court of Session.

## 233  Data protection

In section 31 of the Data Protection Act 1998 (regulatory activity), after subsection (4), insert—

'(4A) Personal data processed for the purpose of discharging any function which is conferred by or under Part XVI of the Financial Services and Markets Act 2000 on the body established by the Financial Services Authority for the purposes of that Part are exempt from the subject information provisions in any case to the extent to which the application of those provisions to the data would be likely to prejudice the proper discharge of the function.'

### *Funding*

## 234  Industry funding

(1) For the purpose of funding—

    (a) the establishment of the ombudsman scheme (whenever any relevant expense is incurred), and

(b) its operation in relation to the compulsory jurisdiction,

the Authority may make rules requiring the payment to it or to the scheme operator, by authorised persons or any class of authorised person or any payment service provider within the meaning of the Payment Services Regulations 2009 of specified amounts (or amounts calculated in a specified way).

(2) 'Specified' means specified in the rules.

### 234A   Funding by consumer credit licensees etc

(1) For the purpose of funding—

   (a) the establishment of the ombudsman scheme so far as it relates to the consumer credit jurisdiction (whenever any relevant expense is incurred), and

   (b) its operation in relation to the consumer credit jurisdiction,

the scheme operator may from time to time with the approval of the Authority determine a sum which is to be raised by way of contributions under this section.

(2) A sum determined under subsection (1) may include a component to cover the costs of the collection of contributions to that sum ('collection costs') under this section.

(3) The scheme operator must notify the OFT of every determination under subsection (1).

(4) The OFT must give general notice of every determination so notified.

(5) The OFT may by general notice impose requirements on—

   (a) licensees to whom this section applies, or

   (b) persons who make applications to which this section applies,

to pay contributions to the OFT for the purpose of raising sums determined under subsection (1).

(6) The amount of the contribution payable by a person under such a requirement—

   (a) shall be the amount specified in or determined under the general notice; and

   (b) shall be paid before the end of the period or at the time so specified or determined.

(7) A general notice under subsection (5) may—

   (a) impose requirements only on descriptions of licensees or applicants specified in the notice;

   (b) provide for exceptions from any requirement imposed on a description of licensees or applicants;

   (c) impose different requirements on different descriptions of licensees or applicants;

   (d) make provision for refunds in specified circumstances.

(8) Contributions received by the OFT must be paid to the scheme operator.

(9) As soon as practicable after the end of—

   (a) each financial year of the scheme operator, or

   (b) if the OFT and the scheme operator agree that this paragraph is to apply instead of paragraph (a) for the time being, each period agreed by them,

the scheme operator must pay to the OFT an amount representing the extent to which collection costs are covered in accordance with subsection (2) by the total amount of the contributions paid by the OFT to it during the year or (as the case may be) the agreed period.

(10) Amounts received by the OFT from the scheme operator are to be retained by it for the purpose of meeting its costs.

(11) The Secretary of State may by order provide that the functions of the OFT under this section are for the time being to be carried out by the scheme operator.

(12) An order under subsection (11) may provide that while the order is in force this section shall have effect subject to such modifications as may be set out in the order.

(13) The licensees to whom this section applies are licensees under standard licences which cover to any extent the carrying on of a type of business specified in an order under section 226A(2)(e).

(14) The applications to which this section applies are applications for—

   (a) standard licences covering to any extent the carrying on of a business of such a type;

   (b) the renewal of standard licences on terms covering to any extent the carrying on of a business of such a type.

(15) Expressions used in the Consumer Credit Act 1974 have the same meaning in this section as they have in that Act.

# PART XVII

## COLLECTIVE INVESTMENT SCHEMES

### Chapter I

### Interpretation

### 235   Collective investment schemes

(1) In this Part 'collective investment scheme' means any arrangements with respect to property of any description, including money, the purpose or effect of which is to enable persons taking part in the

arrangements (whether by becoming owners of the property or any part of it or otherwise) to participate in or receive profits or income arising from the acquisition, holding, management or disposal of the property or sums paid out of such profits or income.

(2) The arrangements must be such that the persons who are to participate ('participants') do not have day-to-day control over the management of the property, whether or not they have the right to be consulted or to give directions.

(3) The arrangements must also have either or both of the following characteristics—

    (a) the contributions of the participants and the profits or income out of which payments are to be made to them are pooled;

    (b) the property is managed as a whole by or on behalf of the operator of the scheme.

(4) If arrangements provide for such pooling as is mentioned in subsection (3)(a) in relation to separate parts of the property, the arrangements are not to be regarded as constituting a single collective investment scheme unless the participants are entitled to exchange rights in one part for rights in another.

(5) The Treasury may by order provide that arrangements do not amount to a collective investment scheme—

    (a) in specified circumstances; or

    (b) if the arrangements fall within a specified category of arrangement.

### 236 Open-ended investment companies

(1) In this Part 'an open-ended investment company' means a collective investment scheme which satisfies both the property condition and the investment condition.

(2) The property condition is that the property belongs beneficially to, and is managed by or on behalf of, a body corporate ('BC') having as its purpose the investment of its funds with the aim of—

    (a) spreading investment risk; and

    (b) giving its members the benefit of the results of the management of those funds by or on behalf of that body.

(3) The investment condition is that, in relation to BC, a reasonable investor would, if he were to participate in the scheme—

    (a) expect that he would be able to realize, within a period appearing to him to be reasonable, his investment in the scheme (represented, at any given time, by the value of shares in, or securities of, BC held by him as a participant in the scheme); and

    (b) be satisfied that his investment would be realized on a basis calculated wholly or mainly by reference to the value of property in respect of which the scheme makes arrangements.

(4) In determining whether the investment condition is satisfied, no account is to be taken of any actual or potential redemption or repurchase of shares or securities under—

    (a) Chapter VII of Part V of the Companies Act 1985;

    (b) Chapter VII of Part VI of the Companies (Northern Ireland) Order 1986;

    (c) corresponding provisions in force in another EEA State; or

    (d) provisions in force in a country or territory other than an EEA state which the Treasury have, by order, designated as corresponding provisions.

(5) The Treasury may by order amend the definition of 'an open-ended investment company' for the purposes of this Part.

### 237 Other definitions

(1) In this Part 'unit trust scheme' means a collective investment scheme under which the property is held on trust for the participants.

(2) In this Part—

'trustee', in relation to a unit trust scheme, means the person holding the property in question on trust for the participants;

'depositary', in relation to—

    (a) a collective investment scheme which is constituted by a body incorporated by virtue of regulations under section 262, or

    (b) any other collective investment scheme which is not a unit trust scheme,

means any person to whom the property subject to the scheme is entrusted for safekeeping;

'the operator', in relation to a unit trust scheme with a separate trustee, means the manager and in relation to an open-ended investment company, means that company;

'units' means the rights or interests (however described) of the participants in a collective investment scheme.

(3) In this Part—

'an authorised unit trust scheme' means a unit trust scheme which is authorised for the purposes of this Act by an authorisation order in force under section 243;

'an authorised open-ended investment company' means a body incorporated by virtue of regulations under section 262 in respect of which an authorisation order is in force under any provision made in such regulations by virtue of subsection (2)(l) of that section;

'a recognised scheme' means a scheme recognised under section 264, 270 or 272.

## Chapter II

## Restrictions on promotion

### 238  Restrictions on promotion

(1)  An authorised person must not communicate an invitation or inducement to participate in a collective investment scheme.

(2)  But that is subject to the following provisions of this section and to section 239.

(3)  Subsection (1) applies in the case of a communication originating outside the United Kingdom only if the communication is capable of having an effect in the United Kingdom.

(4)  Subsection (1) does not apply in relation to—

(a)  an authorised unit trust scheme;

(b)  a scheme constituted by an authorised open-ended investment company; or

(c)  a recognised scheme.

(5)  Subsection (1) does not apply to anything done in accordance with rules made by the Authority for the purpose of exempting from that subsection the promotion otherwise than to the general public of schemes of specified descriptions.

(6)  The Treasury may by order specify circumstances in which subsection (1) does not apply.

(7)  An order under subsection (6) may, in particular, provide that subsection (1) does not apply in relation to communications—

(a)  of a specified description;

(b)  originating in a specified country or territory outside the United Kingdom;

(c)  originating in a country or territory which falls within a specified description of country or territory outside the United Kingdom; or

(d)  originating outside the United Kingdom.

(8)  The Treasury may by order repeal subsection (3).

(9)  'Communicate' includes causing a communication to be made.

(10)  'Promotion otherwise than to the general public' includes promotion in a way designed to reduce, so far as possible, the risk of participation by persons for whom participation would be unsuitable.

(11)  'Participate', in relation to a collective investment scheme, means become a participant (within the meaning given by section 235(2)) in the scheme.

### 239  Single property schemes

(1)  The Treasury may by regulations make provision for exempting single property schemes from section 238(1).

(2)  For the purposes of subsection (1) a single property scheme is a scheme which has the characteristics mentioned in subsection (3) and satisfies such other requirements as are prescribed by the regulations conferring the exemption.

(3)  The characteristics are—

(a)  that the property subject to the scheme (apart from cash or other assets held for management purposes) consists of—

(i)  a single building (or a single building with ancillary buildings) managed by or on behalf of the operator of the scheme, or

(ii)  a group of adjacent or contiguous buildings managed by him or on his behalf as a single enterprise,

with or without ancillary land and with or without furniture, fittings or other contents of the building or buildings in question; and

(b)  that the units of the participants in the scheme are either dealt in on a recognised investment exchange or offered on terms such that any agreement for their acquisition is conditional on their admission to dealings on such an exchange.

(4)  If regulations are made under subsection (1), the Authority may make rules imposing duties or liabilities on the operator and (if any) the trustee or depositary of a scheme exempted by the regulations.

(5)  The rules may include, to such extent as the Authority thinks appropriate, provision for purposes corresponding to those for which provision can be made under section 248 in relation to authorised unit trust schemes.

### 240  Restriction on approval of promotion

(1)  An authorised person may not approve for the purposes of section 21 the content of a communication relating to a collective investment scheme if he would be prohibited by section 238(1) from effecting the communication himself or from causing it to be communicated.

(2)  For the purposes of determining in any case whether there has been a contravention of section 21(1), an approval given in contravention of subsection (1) is to be regarded as not having been given.

**241    Actions for damages**
If an authorised person contravenes a requirement imposed on him by section 238 or 240, section 150 applies to the contravention as it applies to a contravention mentioned in that section.

## Chapter III

## Authorised unit trust schemes

### *Applications for authorisation*

**242    Applications for authorisation of unit trust schemes**
    (1) Any application for an order declaring a unit trust scheme to be an authorised unit trust scheme must be made to the Authority by the manager and trustee, or proposed manager and trustee, of the scheme.
    (2) The manager and trustee (or proposed manager and trustee) must be different persons.
    (3) The application—
      (a) must be made in such manner as the Authority may direct; and
      (b) must contain or be accompanied by such information as the Authority may reasonably require for the purpose of determining the application.
    (4) At any time after receiving an application and before determining it, the Authority may require the applicants to provide it with such further information as it reasonably considers necessary to enable it to determine the application.
    (5) Different directions may be given, and different requirements imposed, in relation to different applications.
    (6) The Authority may require applicants to present information which they are required to give under this section in such form, or to verify it in such a way, as the Authority may direct.

**243    Authorisation orders**
    (1) If, on an application under section 242 in respect of a unit trust scheme, the Authority—
      (a) is satisfied that the scheme complies with the requirements set out in this section,
      (b) is satisfied that the scheme complies with the requirements of the trust scheme rules, and
      (c) has been provided with a copy of the trust deed and a certificate signed by a solicitor to the effect that it complies with such of the requirements of this section or those rules as relate to its contents,
the Authority may make an order declaring the scheme to be an authorised unit trust scheme.
    (2) If the Authority makes an order under subsection (1), it must give written notice of the order to the applicant.
    (3) In this Chapter 'authorisation order' means an order under subsection (1).
    (4) The manager and the trustee must be persons who are independent of each other.
    (5) The manager and the trustee must each—
      (a) be a body corporate incorporated in the United Kingdom or another EEA State, and
      (b) have a place of business in the United Kingdom,
and the affairs of each must be administered in the country in which it is incorporated.
    (6) If the manager is incorporated in another EEA State, the scheme must not be one which satisfies the requirements prescribed for the purposes of section 264.
    (7) The manager and the trustee must each be an authorised person and the manager must have permission to act as manager and the trustee must have permission to act as trustee.
    (8) The name of the scheme must not be undesirable or misleading.
    (9) The purposes of the scheme must be reasonably capable of being successfully carried into effect.
    (10) The participants must be entitled to have their units redeemed in accordance with the scheme at a price—
      (a) related to the net value of the property to which the units relate; and
      (b) determined in accordance with the scheme.
    (11) But a scheme is to be treated as complying with subsection (10) if it requires the manager to ensure that a participant is able to sell his units on an investment exchange at a price not significantly different from that mentioned in that subsection.

**244    Determination of applications**
    (1) An application under section 242 must be determined by the Authority before the end of the period of six months beginning with the date on which it receives the completed application.
    (2) The Authority may determine an incomplete application if it considers it appropriate to do so; and it must in any event determine such an application within twelve months beginning with the date on which it first receives the application.
    (3) The applicant may withdraw his application, by giving the Authority written notice, at any time before the Authority determines it.

*Applications refused*

## 245 Procedure when refusing an application

(1) If the Authority proposes to refuse an application made under section 242 it must give each of the applicants a warning notice.

(2) If the Authority decides to refuse the application—

    (a) it must give each of the applicants a decision notice; and

    (b) either applicant may refer the matter to the Tribunal.

*Certificates*

## 246 Certificates

(1) If the manager or trustee of a unit trust scheme which complies with the conditions necessary for it to enjoy the rights conferred by any relevant Community instrument so requests, the Authority may issue a certificate to the effect that the scheme complies with those conditions.

(2) Such a certificate may be issued on the making of an authorisation order in respect of the scheme or at any subsequent time.

*Rules*

## 247 Trust scheme rules

(1) The Authority may make rules ('trust scheme rules') as to—

    (a) the constitution, management and operation of authorised unit trust schemes;

    (b) the powers, duties, rights and liabilities of the manager and trustee of any such scheme;

    (c) the rights and duties of the participants in any such scheme; and

    (d) the winding up of any such scheme.

(2) Trust scheme rules may, in particular, make provision—

    (a) as to the issue and redemption of the units under the scheme;

    (b) as to the expenses of the scheme and the means of meeting them;

    (c) for the appointment, removal, powers and duties of an auditor for the scheme;

    (d) for restricting or regulating the investment and borrowing powers exercisable in relation to the scheme;

    (e) requiring the keeping of records with respect to the transactions and financial position of the scheme and for the inspection of those records;

    (f) requiring the preparation of periodical reports with respect to the scheme and the provision of those reports to the participants and to the Authority; and

    (g) with respect to the amendment of the scheme.

(3) Trust scheme rules may make provision as to the contents of the trust deed, including provision requiring any of the matters mentioned in subsection (2) to be dealt with in the deed.

(4) But trust scheme rules are binding on the manager, trustee and participants independently of the contents of the trust deed and, in the case of the participants, have effect as if contained in it.

(5) If—

    (a) a modification is made of the statutory provisions in force in Great Britain or Northern Ireland relating to companies,

    (b) the modification relates to the rights and duties of persons who hold the beneficial title to any shares in a company without also holding the legal title, and

    (c) it appears to the Treasury that, for the purpose of assimilating the law relating to authorised unit trust schemes to the law relating to companies as so modified, it is expedient to modify the rule-making powers conferred on the Authority by this section,

the Treasury may by order make such modifications of those powers as they consider appropriate.

## 248 Scheme particulars rules

(1) The Authority may make rules ('scheme particulars rules') requiring the manager of an authorised unit trust scheme—

    (a) to submit scheme particulars to the Authority; and

    (b) to publish scheme particulars or make them available to the public on request.

(2) 'Scheme particulars' means particulars in such form, containing such information about the scheme and complying with such requirements, as are specified in scheme particulars rules.

(3) Scheme particulars rules may require the manager of an authorised unit trust scheme to submit, and to publish or make available, revised or further scheme particulars if there is a significant change affecting any matter—

    (a) which is contained in scheme particulars previously published or made available; and

    (b) whose inclusion in those particulars was required by the rules.

(4) Scheme particulars rules may require the manager of an authorised unit trust scheme to submit, and to publish or make available, revised or further scheme particulars if—

    (a) a significant new matter arises; and

(b) the inclusion of information in respect of that matter would have been required in previous particulars if it had arisen when those particulars were prepared.

(5) Scheme particulars rules may provide for the payment, by the person or persons who in accordance with the rules are treated as responsible for any scheme particulars, of compensation to any qualifying person who has suffered loss as a result of—

(a) any untrue or misleading statement in the particulars; or

(b) the omission from them of any matter required by the rules to be included.

(6) 'Qualifying person' means a person who—

(a) has become or agreed to become a participant in the scheme; or

(b) although not being a participant, has a beneficial interest in units in the scheme.

(7) Scheme particulars rules do not affect any liability which any person may incur apart from the rules.

### 249  Disqualification of auditor for breach of trust scheme rules

(1) If it appears to the Authority that an auditor has failed to comply with a duty imposed on him by trust scheme rules, it may disqualify him from being the auditor for any authorised unit trust scheme or authorised open-ended investment company.

(2) Subsections (2) to (5) of section 345 have effect in relation to disqualification under subsection (1) as they have effect in relation to disqualification under subsection (1) of that section.

### 250  Modification or waiver of rules

(1) In this section 'rules' means—

(a) trust scheme rules; or

(b) scheme particulars rules.

(2) The Authority may, on the application or with the consent of any person to whom any rules apply, direct that all or any of the rules—

(a) are not to apply to him as respects a particular scheme; or

(b) are to apply to him, as respects a particular scheme, with such modifications as may be specified in the direction.

(3) The Authority may, on the application or with the consent of the manager and trustee of a particular scheme acting jointly, direct that all or any of the rules—

(a) are not to apply to the scheme; or

(b) are to apply to the scheme with such modifications as may be specified in the direction.

(4) Subsections (3) to (9) and (11) of section 148 have effect in relation to a direction under subsection (2) as they have effect in relation to a direction under section 148(2) but with the following modifications—

(a) [...]

(b) any reference to the person (except in subsection (4)(a)) is to be read as a reference to the person mentioned in subsection (2); and

(c) subsection (7)(b) is to be read, in relation to a participant of the scheme, as if the word 'commercial' were omitted.

(5) Subsections (3) to (9) and (11) of section 148 have effect in relation to a direction under subsection (3) as they have effect in relation to a direction under section 148(2) but with the following modifications—

(a) subsection (4)(a) is to be read as if the words 'by the [...] person' were omitted;

(b) subsections (7)(b) and (11) are to be read as if references to the [...] person were references to each of the manager and the trustee of the scheme;

(c) subsection (7)(b) is to be read, in relation to a participant of the scheme, as if the word 'commercial' were omitted;

(d) subsection (8) is to be read as if the reference to the [...] person concerned were a reference to the scheme concerned and to its manager and trustee; and

(e) subsection (9) is to be read as if the reference to the [...] person were a reference to the manager and trustee of the scheme acting jointly.

### *Alterations*

### 251  Alteration of schemes and changes of manager or trustee

(1) The manager of an authorised unit trust scheme must give written notice to the Authority of any proposal to alter the scheme or to replace its trustee.

(2) Any notice given in respect of a proposal to alter the scheme involving a change in the trust deed must be accompanied by a certificate signed by a solicitor to the effect that the change will not affect the compliance of the deed with the trust scheme rules.

(3) The trustee of an authorised unit trust scheme must give written notice to the Authority of any proposal to replace the manager of the scheme.

(4) Effect is not to be given to any proposal of which notice has been given under subsection (1) or (3) unless—

(a) the Authority, by written notice, has given its approval to the proposal; or

(b) one month, beginning with the date on which the notice was given, has expired without the manager or trustee having received from the Authority a warning notice under section 252 in respect of the proposal.

(5) The Authority must not approve a proposal to replace the manager or the trustee of an authorised unit trust scheme unless it is satisfied that, if the proposed replacement is made, the scheme will continue to comply with the requirements of section 243(4) to (7).

### 252   Procedure when refusing approval of change of manager or trustee

(1) If the Authority proposes to refuse approval of a proposal to replace the trustee or manager of an authorised unit trust scheme, it must give a warning notice to the person by whom notice of the proposal was given under section 251(1) or (3).

(2) If the Authority proposes to refuse approval of a proposal to alter an authorised unit trust scheme it must give separate warning notices to the manager and the trustee of the scheme.

(3) To be valid the warning notice must be received by that person before the end of one month beginning with the date on which notice of the proposal was given.

(4) If, having given a warning notice to a person, the Authority decides to refuse approval—
(a) it must give him a decision notice; and
(b) he may refer the matter to the Tribunal.

*Exclusion clauses*

### 253   Avoidance of exclusion clauses

Any provision of the trust deed of an authorised unit trust scheme is void in so far as it would have the effect of exempting the manager or trustee from liability for any failure to exercise due care and diligence in the discharge of his functions in respect of the scheme.

*Ending of authorisation*

### 254   Revocation of authorisation order otherwise than by consent

(1) An authorisation order may be revoked by an order made by the Authority if it appears to the Authority that—
(a) one or more of the requirements for the making of the order are no longer satisfied;
(b) the manager or trustee of the scheme concerned has contravened a requirement imposed on him by or under this Act;
(c) the manager or trustee of the scheme has, in purported compliance with any such requirement, knowingly or recklessly given the Authority information which is false or misleading in a material particular;
(d) no regulated activity is being carried on in relation to the scheme and the period of that inactivity began at least twelve months earlier; or
(e) none of paragraphs (a) to (d) applies, but it is desirable to revoke the authorisation order in order to protect the interests of participants or potential participants in the scheme.

(2) For the purposes of subsection (1)(e), the Authority may take into account any matter relating to—
(a) the scheme;
(b) the manager or trustee;
(c) any person employed by or associated with the manager or trustee in connection with the scheme;
(d) any director of the manager or trustee;
(e) any person exercising influence over the manager or trustee;
(f) any body corporate in the same group as the manager or trustee;
(g) any director of any such body corporate;
(h) any person exercising influence over any such body corporate.

### 255   Procedure

(1) If the Authority proposes to make an order under section 254 revoking an authorisation order ('a revoking order'), it must give separate warning notices to the manager and the trustee of the scheme.

(2) If the Authority decides to make a revoking order, it must without delay give each of them a decision notice and either of them may refer the matter to the Tribunal.

### 256   Requests for revocation of authorisation order

(1) An authorisation order may be revoked by an order made by the Authority at the request of the manager or trustee of the scheme concerned.

(2) If the Authority makes an order under subsection (1), it must give written notice of the order to the manager and trustee of the scheme concerned.

(3) The Authority may refuse a request to make an order under this section if it considers that—
(a) the public interest requires that any matter concerning the scheme should be investigated before a decision is taken as to whether the authorisation order should be revoked; or

(b) revocation would not be in the interests of the participants or would be incompatible with a Community obligation.

(4) If the Authority proposes to refuse a request under this section, it must give separate warning notices to the manager and the trustee of the scheme.

(5) If the Authority decides to refuse the request, it must without delay give each of them a decision notice and either of them may refer the matter to the Tribunal.

*Powers of intervention*

## 257 Directions

(1) The Authority may give a direction under this section if it appears to the Authority that—

(a) one or more of the requirements for the making of an authorisation order are no longer satisfied;

(b) the manager or trustee of an authorised unit trust scheme has contravened, or is likely to contravene, a requirement imposed on him by or under this Act;

(c) the manager or trustee of such a scheme has, in purported compliance with any such requirement, knowingly or recklessly given the Authority information which is false or misleading in a material particular; or

(d) none of paragraphs (a) to (c) applies, but it is desirable to give a direction in order to protect the interests of participants or potential participants in such a scheme.

(2) A direction under this section may—

(a) require the manager of the scheme to cease the issue or redemption, or both the issue and redemption, of units under the scheme;

(b) require the manager and trustee of the scheme to wind it up.

(3) If the authorisation order is revoked, the revocation does not affect any direction under this section which is then in force.

(4) A direction may be given under this section in relation to a scheme in the case of which the authorisation order has been revoked if a direction under this section was already in force at the time of revocation.

(5) If a person contravenes a direction under this section, section 150 applies to the contravention as it applies to a contravention mentioned in that section.

(6) The Authority may, either on its own initiative or on the application of the manager or trustee of the scheme concerned, revoke or vary a direction given under this section if it appears to the Authority—

(a) in the case of revocation, that it is no longer necessary for the direction to take effect or continue in force;

(b) in the case of variation, that the direction should take effect or continue in force in a different form.

## 258 Applications to the court

(1) If the Authority could give a direction under section 257, it may also apply to the court for an order—

(a) removing the manager or the trustee, or both the manager and the trustee, of the scheme; and

(b) replacing the person or persons removed with a suitable person or persons nominated by the Authority.

(2) The Authority may nominate a person for the purposes of subsection (1)(b) only if it is satisfied that, if the order was made, the requirements of section 243(4) to (7) would be complied with.

(3) If it appears to the Authority that there is no person it can nominate for the purposes of subsection (1)(b), it may apply to the court for an order—

(a) removing the manager or the trustee, or both the manager and the trustee, of the scheme; and

(b) appointing an authorised person to wind up the scheme.

(4) On an application under this section the court may make such order as it thinks fit.

(5) The court may, on the application of the Authority, rescind any such order as is mentioned in subsection (3) and substitute such an order as is mentioned in subsection (1).

(6) The Authority must give written notice of the making of an application under this section to the manager and trustee of the scheme concerned.

(7) The jurisdiction conferred by this section may be exercised by—

(a) the High Court;

(b) in Scotland, the Court of Session.

## 259 Procedure on giving directions under section 257 and varying them on Authority's own initiative

(1) A direction takes effect—

(a) immediately, if the notice given under subsection (3) states that that is the case;

(b) on such date as may be specified in the notice; or

(c) if no date is specified in the notice, when the matter to which it relates is no longer open to review.

(2) A direction may be expressed to take effect immediately (or on a specified date) only if the Authority, having regard to the ground on which it is exercising its power under section 257, considers that it is necessary for the direction to take effect immediately (or on that date).

(3) If the Authority proposes to give a direction under section 257, or gives such a direction with immediate effect, it must give separate written notice to the manager and the trustee of the scheme concerned.

(4) The notice must—

(a) give details of the direction;

(b) inform the person to whom it is given of when the direction takes effect;

(c) state the Authority's reasons for giving the direction and for its determination as to when the direction takes effect;

(d) inform the person to whom it is given that he may make representations to the Authority within such period as may be specified in it (whether or not he has referred the matter to the Tribunal); and

(e) inform him of his right to refer the matter to the Tribunal.

(5) If the direction imposes a requirement under section 257(2)(a), the notice must state that the requirement has effect until—

(a) a specified date; or

(b) a further direction.

(6) If the direction imposes a requirement under section 257(2)(b), the scheme must be wound up—

(a) by a date specified in the notice; or

(b) if no date is specified, as soon as practicable.

(7) The Authority may extend the period allowed under the notice for making representations.

(8) If, having considered any representations made by a person to whom the notice was given, the Authority decides—

(a) to give the direction in the way proposed, or

(b) if it has been given, not to revoke the direction,

it must give separate written notice to the manager and the trustee of the scheme concerned.

(9) If, having considered any representations made by a person to whom the notice was given, the Authority decides—

(a) not to give the direction in the way proposed,

(b) to give the direction in a way other than that proposed, or

(c) to revoke a direction which has effect,

it must give separate written notice to the manager and the trustee of the scheme concerned.

(10) A notice given under subsection (8) must inform the person to whom it is given of his right to refer the matter to the Tribunal.

(11) A notice under subsection (9)(b) must comply with subsection (4).

(12) If a notice informs a person of his right to refer a matter to the Tribunal, it must give an indication of the procedure on such a reference.

(13) This section applies to the variation of a direction on the Authority's own initiative as it applies to the giving of a direction.

(14) For the purposes of subsection (1)(c), whether a matter is open to review is to be determined in accordance with section 391(8).

### 260  Procedure: refusal to revoke or vary direction

(1) If on an application under section 257(6) for a direction to be revoked or varied the Authority proposes—

(a) to vary the direction otherwise than in accordance with the application, or

(b) to refuse to revoke or vary the direction,

it must give the applicant a warning notice.

(2) If the Authority decides to refuse to revoke or vary the direction—

(a) it must give the applicant a decision notice; and

(b) the applicant may refer the matter to the Tribunal.

### 261  Procedure: revocation of direction and grant of request for variation

(1) If the Authority decides on its own initiative to revoke a direction under section 257 it must give separate written notices of its decision to the manager and trustee of the scheme.

(2) If on an application under section 257(6) for a direction to be revoked or varied the Authority decides to revoke the direction or vary it in accordance with the application, it must give the applicant written notice of its decision.

(3) A notice under this section must specify the date on which the decision takes effect.

(4)  The Authority may publish such information about the revocation or variation, in such way, as it considers appropriate.

## Chapter IV

## Open-ended investment companies

### 262  Open-ended investment companies

(1)  The Treasury may by regulations make provision for—

    (a)  facilitating the carrying on of collective investment by means of open-ended investment companies;

    (b)  regulating such companies.

(2)  The regulations may, in particular, make provision—

    (a)  for the incorporation and registration in Great Britain of bodies corporate;

    (b)  for a body incorporated by virtue of the regulations to take such form as may be determined in accordance with the regulations;

    (c)  as to the purposes for which such a body may exist, the investments which it may issue and otherwise as to its constitution;

    (d)  as to the management and operation of such a body and the management of its property;

    (e)  as to the powers, duties, rights and liabilities of such a body and of other persons, including—

        (i)  the directors or sole director of such a body;

        (ii)  its depositary (if any);

        (iii)  its shareholders, and persons who hold the beneficial title to shares in it without holding the legal title;

        (iv)  its auditor; and

        (v)  any persons who act or purport to act on its behalf;

    (f)  as to the merger of one or more such bodies and the division of such a body;

    (g)  for the appointment and removal of an auditor for such a body;

    (h)  as to the winding up and dissolution of such a body;

    (i)  for such a body, or any director or depositary of such a body, to be required to comply with directions given by the Authority;

    (j)  enabling the Authority to apply to a court for an order removing and replacing any director or depositary of such a body;

    (k)  for the carrying out of investigations by persons appointed by the Authority or the Secretary of State;

    (l)  corresponding to any provision made in relation to unit trust schemes by Chapter III of this Part.

(3)  Regulations under this section may—

    (a)  impose criminal liability;

    (b)  confer functions on the Authority;

    (c)  in the case of provision made by virtue of subsection (2)(l), authorise the making of rules by the Authority;

    (d)  confer jurisdiction on any court or on the Tribunal;

    (e)  provide for fees to be charged by the Authority in connection with the carrying out of any of its functions under the regulations (including fees payable on a periodical basis);

    (f)  modify, exclude or apply (with or without modifications) any primary or subordinate legislation (including any provision of, or made under, this Act);

    (g)  make consequential amendments, repeals and revocations of any such legislation;

    (h)  modify or exclude any rule of law.

(4)  The provision that may be made by virtue of subsection (3)(f) includes provision extending or adapting any power to make subordinate legislation.

(5)  Regulations under this section may, in particular—

    (a)  revoke the Open-Ended Investment Companies (Investment Companies with Variable Capital) Regulations 1996; and

    (b)  provide for things done under or in accordance with those regulations to be treated as if they had been done under or in accordance with regulations under this section.

### 263  Amendment of section 716 Companies Act 1985

In section 716(1) of the Companies Act 1985 (prohibition on formation of companies with more than 20 members unless registered under the Act etc.), after 'this Act,' insert 'is incorporated by virtue of regulations made under section 262 of the Financial Services and Markets Act 2000'.[7]

---

[7]  This section is to be repealed by the Companies Act 2006 c 46 from a date to be appointed.

## Chapter V

## Recognised overseas schemes

### Schemes constituted in other EEA States

**264   Schemes constituted in other EEA States**

(1)  A collective investment scheme constituted in another EEA State is a recognised scheme if—

(a)  it satisfies such requirements as are prescribed for the purposes of this section; and

(b)  not less than two months before inviting persons in the United Kingdom to become participants in the scheme, the operator of the scheme gives notice to the Authority of his intention to do so, specifying the way in which the invitation is to be made.

(2)  But this section does not make the scheme a recognised scheme if within two months of receiving the notice under subsection (1) the Authority notifies—

(a)  the operator of the scheme, and

(b)  the authorities of the State in question who are responsible for the authorisation of collective investment schemes,

that the way in which the invitation is to be made does not comply with the law in force in the United Kingdom.

(3)  The notice to be given to the Authority under subsection (1)—

(a)  must be accompanied by a certificate from the authorities mentioned in subsection (2)(b) to the effect that the scheme complies with the conditions necessary for it to enjoy the rights conferred by any relevant Community instrument;

(b)  must contain the address of a place in the United Kingdom for the service on the operator of notices or other documents required or authorised to be served on him under this Act; and

(c)  must contain or be accompanied by such other information and documents as may be prescribed.

(4)  A notice given by the Authority under subsection (2) must—

(a)  give the reasons for which the Authority considers that the law in force in the United Kingdom will not be complied with; and

(b)  specify a reasonable period (which may not be less than 28 days) within which any person to whom it is given may make representations to the Authority.

(5)  For the purposes of this section a collective investment scheme is constituted in another EEA State if—

(a)  it is constituted under the law of that State by a contract or under a trust and is managed by a body corporate incorporated under that law; or

(b)  it takes the form of an open-ended investment company incorporated under that law.

(6)  The operator of a recognised scheme may give written notice to the Authority that he desires the scheme to be no longer recognised by virtue of this section.

(7)  On the giving of notice under subsection (6), the scheme ceases to be a recognised scheme.

**265   Representations and references to the Tribunal**

(1)  This section applies if any representations are made to the Authority, before the period for making representations has ended, by a person to whom a notice was given by the Authority under section 264(2).

(2)  The Authority must, within a reasonable period, decide in the light of those representations whether or not to withdraw its notice.

(3)  If the Authority withdraws its notice the scheme is a recognised scheme from the date on which the notice is withdrawn.

(4)  If the Authority decides not to withdraw its notice, it must give a decision notice to each person to whom the notice under section 264(2) was given.

(5)  The operator of the scheme to whom the decision notice is given may refer the matter to the Tribunal.

**266   Disapplication of rules**

(1)  Apart from—

(a)  financial promotion rules, and

(b)  rules under section 283(1),

rules made by the Authority under this Act do not apply to the operator, trustee or depositary of a scheme in relation to the carrying on by him of regulated activities for which he has permission in that capacity.

(1A)  But subsection (1) does not affect the application of rules to an operator of a scheme if the operator is an EEA firm falling within paragraph 5(f) of Schedule 3 who qualifies for authorisation under that Schedule.

(2)  'Scheme' means a scheme which is a recognised scheme by virtue of section 264.

### 267   Power of Authority to suspend promotion of scheme

(1)  Subsection (2) applies if it appears to the Authority that the operator of a scheme has communicated an invitation or inducement in relation to the scheme in a manner contrary to financial promotion rules.

(2)  The Authority may direct that—

(a)  the exemption from subsection (1) of section 238 provided by subsection (4)(c) of that section is not to apply in relation to the scheme; and

(b)  subsection (5) of that section does not apply with respect to things done in relation to the scheme.

(3)  A direction under subsection (2) has effect—

(a)  for a specified period;

(b)  until the occurrence of a specified event; or

(c)  until specified conditions are complied with.

(4)  The Authority may, either on its own initiative or on the application of the operator of the scheme concerned, vary a direction given under subsection (2) if it appears to the Authority that the direction should take effect or continue in force in a different form.

(5)  The Authority may, either on its own initiative or on the application of the operator of the recognised scheme concerned, revoke a direction given under subsection (2) if it appears to the Authority—

(a)  that the conditions specified in the direction have been complied with; or

(b)  that it is no longer necessary for the direction to take effect or continue in force.

(6)  If an event is specified, the direction ceases to have effect (unless revoked earlier) on the occurrence of that event.

(7)  For the purposes of this section and sections 268 and 269—

(a)  the scheme's home State is the EEA State in which the scheme is constituted (within the meaning given by section 264);

(b)  the competent authorities in the scheme's home State are the authorities in that State who are responsible for the authorisation of collective investment schemes.

(8)  'Scheme' means a scheme which is a recognised scheme by virtue of section 264.

(9)  'Specified', in relation to a direction, means specified in it.

### 268   Procedure on giving directions under section 267 and varying them on Authority's own initiative

(1)  A direction under section 267 takes effect—

(a)  immediately, if the notice given under subsection (3)(a) states that that is the case;

(b)  on such date as may be specified in the notice; or

(c)  if no date is specified in the notice, when the matter to which it relates is no longer open to review.

(2)  A direction may be expressed to take effect immediately (or on a specified date) only if the Authority, having regard to its reasons for exercising its power under section 267, considers that it is necessary for the direction to take effect immediately (or on that date).

(3)  If the Authority proposes to give a direction under section 267, or gives such a direction with immediate effect, it must—

(a)  give the operator of the scheme concerned written notice; and

(b)  inform the competent authorities in the scheme's home State of its proposal or (as the case may be) of the direction.

(4)  The notice must—

(a)  give details of the direction;

(b)  inform the operator of when the direction takes effect;

(c)  state the Authority's reasons for giving the direction and for its determination as to when the direction takes effect;

(d)  inform the operator that he may make representations to the Authority within such period as may be specified in it (whether or not he has referred the matter to the Tribunal); and

(e)  inform him of his right to refer the matter to the Tribunal.

(5)  The Authority may extend the period allowed under the notice for making representations.

(6)  Subsection (7) applies if, having considered any representations made by the operator, the Authority decides—

(a)  to give the direction in the way proposed, or

(b)  if it has been given, not to revoke the direction.

(7)  The Authority must—

(a)  give the operator of the scheme concerned written notice; and

(b)  inform the competent authorities in the scheme's home State of the direction.

(8)  Subsection (9) applies if, having considered any representations made by a person to whom the notice was given, the Authority decides—

(a)  not to give the direction in the way proposed,

(b) to give the direction in a way other than that proposed, or

(c) to revoke a direction which has effect.

(9) The Authority must—

(a) give the operator of the scheme concerned written notice; and

(b) inform the competent authorities in the scheme's home State of its decision.

(10) A notice given under subsection (7)(a) must inform the operator of his right to refer the matter to the Tribunal.

(11) A notice under subsection (9)(a) given as a result of subsection (8)(b) must comply with subsection (4).

(12) If a notice informs a person of his right to refer a matter to the Tribunal, it must give an indication of the procedure on such a reference.

(13) This section applies to the variation of a direction on the Authority's own initiative as it applies to the giving of a direction.

(14) For the purposes of subsection (1)(c), whether a matter is open to review is to be determined in accordance with section 391(8).

### 269  Procedure on application for variation or revocation of direction

(1) If, on an application under subsection (4) or (5) of section 267, the Authority proposes—

(a) to vary a direction otherwise than in accordance with the application, or

(b) to refuse the application,

it must give the operator of the scheme concerned a warning notice.

(2) If, on such an application, the Authority decides—

(a) to vary a direction otherwise than in accordance with the application, or

(b) to refuse the application,

it must give the operator of the scheme concerned a decision notice.

(3) If the application is refused, the operator of the scheme may refer the matter to the Tribunal.

(4) If, on such an application, the Authority decides to grant the application it must give the operator of the scheme concerned written notice.

(5) If the Authority decides on its own initiative to revoke a direction given under section 267 it must give the operator of the scheme concerned written notice.

(6) The Authority must inform the competent authorities in the scheme's home State of any notice given under this section.

*Schemes authorised in designated countries or territories*

### 270  Schemes authorised in designated countries or territories

(1) A collective investment scheme which is not a recognised scheme by virtue of section 264 but is managed in, and authorised under the law of, a country or territory outside the United Kingdom is a recognised scheme if—

(a) that country or territory is designated for the purposes of this section by an order made by the Treasury;

(b) the scheme is of a class specified by the order;

(c) the operator of the scheme has given written notice to the Authority that he wishes it to be recognised; and

(d) either—

(i) the Authority, by written notice, has given its approval to the scheme's being recognised; or

(ii) two months, beginning with the date on which notice was given under paragraph (c), have expired without the operator receiving a warning notice from the Authority under section 271.

(2) The Treasury may not make an order designating any country or territory for the purposes of this section unless satisfied—

(a) that the law and practice under which relevant collective investment schemes are authorised and supervised in that country or territory affords to investors in the United Kingdom protection at least equivalent to that provided for them by or under this Part in the case of comparable authorised schemes; and

(b) that adequate arrangements exist, or will exist, for co-operation between the authorities of the country or territory responsible for the authorisation and supervision of relevant collective investment schemes and the Authority.

(3) 'Relevant collective investment schemes' means collective investment schemes of the class or classes to be specified by the order.

(4) 'Comparable authorised schemes' means whichever of the following the Treasury consider to be the most appropriate, having regard to the class or classes of scheme to be specified by the order—

(a) authorised unit trust schemes;

(b) authorised open-ended investment companies;

(c) both such unit trust schemes and such companies.

(5) If the Treasury are considering whether to make an order designating a country or territory for the purposes of this section—

(a) the Treasury must ask the Authority for a report—

(i) on the law and practice of that country or territory in relation to the authorisation and supervision of relevant collective investment schemes,

(ii) on any existing or proposed arrangements for co-operation between it and the authorities responsible in that country or territory for the authorisation and supervision of relevant collective investment schemes,

having regard to the Treasury's need to be satisfied as mentioned in subsection (2);

(b) the Authority must provide the Treasury with such a report; and

(c) the Treasury must have regard to it in deciding whether to make the order.

(6) The notice to be given by the operator under subsection (1)(c)—

(a) must contain the address of a place in the United Kingdom for the service on the operator of notices or other documents required or authorised to be served on him under this Act; and

(b) must contain or be accompanied by such information and documents as may be specified by the Authority.

## 271  Procedure

(1) If the Authority proposes to refuse approval of a scheme's being a recognised scheme by virtue of section 270, it must give the operator of the scheme a warning notice.

(2) To be valid the warning notice must be received by the operator before the end of two months beginning with the date on which notice was given under section 270(1)(c).

(3) If, having given a warning notice, the Authority decides to refuse approval—

(a) it must give the operator of the scheme a decision notice; and

(b) the operator may refer the matter to the Tribunal.

### *Individually recognised overseas schemes*

## 272  Individually recognised overseas schemes

(1) The Authority may, on the application of the operator of a collective investment scheme which—

(a) is managed in a country or territory outside the United Kingdom,

(b) does not satisfy the requirements prescribed for the purposes of section 264,

(c) is not managed in a country or territory designated for the purposes of section 270 or, if it is so managed, is of a class not specified by the designation order, and

(d) appears to the Authority to satisfy the requirements set out in the following provisions of this section,

make an order declaring the scheme to be a recognised scheme.

(2) Adequate protection must be afforded to participants in the scheme.

(3) The arrangements for the scheme's constitution and management must be adequate.

(4) The powers and duties of the operator and, if the scheme has a trustee or depositary, of the trustee or depositary must be adequate.

(5) In deciding whether the matters mentioned in subsection (3) or (4) are adequate, the Authority must have regard to—

(a) any rule of law, and

(b) any matters which are, or could be, the subject of rules,

applicable in relation to comparable authorised schemes.

(6) 'Comparable authorised schemes' means whichever of the following the Authority considers the most appropriate, having regard to the nature of scheme in respect of which the application is made—

(a) authorised unit trust schemes;

(b) authorised open-ended investment companies;

(c) both such unit trust schemes and such companies.

(7) The scheme must take the form of an open-ended investment company or (if it does not take that form) the operator must be a body corporate.

(8) The operator of the scheme must—

(a) if an authorised person, have permission to act as operator;

(b) if not an authorised person, be a fit and proper person to act as operator.

(9) The trustee or depositary (if any) of the scheme must—

(a) if an authorised person, have permission to act as trustee or depositary;

(b) if not an authorised person, be a fit and proper person to act as trustee or depositary.

(10) The operator and the trustee or depositary (if any) of the scheme must be able and willing to co-operate with the Authority by the sharing of information and in other ways.

(11) The name of the scheme must not be undesirable or misleading.

(12) The purposes of the scheme must be reasonably capable of being successfully carried into effect.

(13)  The participants must be entitled to have their units redeemed in accordance with the scheme at a price related to the net value of the property to which the units relate and determined in accordance with the scheme.

(14)  But a scheme is to be treated as complying with subsection (13) if it requires the operator to ensure that a participant is able to sell his units on an investment exchange at a price not significantly different from that mentioned in that subsection.

(15)  Subsection (13) is not to be read as imposing a requirement that the participants must be entitled to have their units redeemed (or sold as mentioned in subsection (14)) immediately following a demand to that effect.

### 273  Matters that may be taken into account

For the purposes of subsections (8)(b) and (9)(b) of section 272, the Authority may take into account any matter relating to—

    (a)  any person who is or will be employed by or associated with the operator, trustee or depositary in connection with the scheme;

    (b)  any director of the operator, trustee or depositary;

    (c)  any person exercising influence over the operator, trustee or depositary;

    (d)  any body corporate in the same group as the operator, trustee or depositary;

    (e)  any director of any such body corporate;

    (f)  any person exercising influence over any such body corporate.

### 274  Applications for recognition of individual schemes

(1)  An application under section 272 for an order declaring a scheme to be a recognised scheme must be made to the Authority by the operator of the scheme.

(2)  The application—

    (a)  must be made in such manner as the Authority may direct;

    (b)  must contain the address of a place in the United Kingdom for the service on the operator of notices or other documents required or authorised to be served on him under this Act;

    (c)  must contain or be accompanied by such information as the Authority may reasonably require for the purpose of determining the application.

(3)  At any time after receiving an application and before determining it, the Authority may require the applicant to provide it with such further information as it reasonably considers necessary to enable it to determine the application.

(4)  Different directions may be given, and different requirements imposed, in relation to different applications.

(5)  The Authority may require an applicant to present information which he is required to give under this section in such form, or to verify it in such a way, as the Authority may direct.

### 275  Determination of applications

(1)  An application under section 272 must be determined by the Authority before the end of the period of six months beginning with the date on which it receives the completed application.

(2)  The Authority may determine an incomplete application if it considers it appropriate to do so; and it must in any event determine such an application within twelve months beginning with the date on which it first receives the application.

(3)  If the Authority makes an order under section 272(1), it must give written notice of the order to the applicant.

### 276  Procedure when refusing an application

(1)  If the Authority proposes to refuse an application made under section 272 it must give the applicant a warning notice.

(2)  If the Authority decides to refuse the application—

    (a)  it must give the applicant a decision notice; and

    (b)  the applicant may refer the matter to the Tribunal.

### 277  Alteration of schemes and changes of operator, trustee or depositary

(1)  The operator of a scheme recognised by virtue of section 272 must give written notice to the Authority of any proposed alteration to the scheme.

(2)  Effect is not to be given to any such proposal unless—

    (a)  the Authority, by written notice, has given its approval to the proposal; or

    (b)  one month, beginning with the date on which notice was given under subsection (1), has expired without the Authority having given written notice to the operator that it has decided to refuse approval.

(3)  At least one month before any replacement of the operator, trustee or depositary of such a scheme, notice of the proposed replacement must be given to the Authority—

    (a)  by the operator, trustee or depositary (as the case may be); or

    (b)  by the person who is to replace him.

*Schemes recognised under sections 270 and 272*

### 278   Rules as to scheme particulars

The Authority may make rules imposing duties or liabilities on the operator of a scheme recognised under section 270 or 272 for purposes corresponding to those for which rules may be made under section 248 in relation to authorised unit trust schemes.

### 279   Revocation of recognition

The Authority may direct that a scheme is to cease to be recognised by virtue of section 270 or revoke an order under section 272 if it appears to the Authority—

(a) that the operator, trustee or depositary of the scheme has contravened a requirement imposed on him by or under this Act;

(b) that the operator, trustee or depositary of the scheme has, in purported compliance with any such requirement, knowingly or recklessly given the Authority information which is false or misleading in a material particular;

(c) in the case of an order under section 272, that one or more of the requirements for the making of the order are no longer satisfied; or

(d) that none of paragraphs (a) to (c) applies, but it is undesirable in the interests of the participants or potential participants that the scheme should continue to be recognised.

### 280   Procedure

(1) If the Authority proposes to give a direction under section 279 or to make an order under that section revoking a recognition order, it must give a warning notice to the operator and (if any) the trustee or depositary of the scheme.

(2) If the Authority decides to give a direction or make an order under that section—

(a) it must without delay give a decision notice to the operator and (if any) the trustee or depositary of the scheme; and

(b) the operator or the trustee or depositary may refer the matter to the Tribunal.

### 281   Directions

(1) In this section a 'relevant recognised scheme' means a scheme recognised under section 270 or 272.

(2) If it appears to the Authority that—

(a) the operator, trustee or depositary of a relevant recognised scheme has contravened, or is likely to contravene, a requirement imposed on him by or under this Act,

(b) the operator, trustee or depositary of such a scheme has, in purported compliance with any such requirement, knowingly or recklessly given the Authority information which is false or misleading in a material particular,

(c) one or more of the requirements for the recognition of a scheme under section 272 are no longer satisfied, or

(d) none of paragraphs (a) to (c) applies, but the exercise of the power conferred by this section is desirable in order to protect the interests of participants or potential participants in a relevant recognised scheme who are in the United Kingdom,

it may direct that the scheme is not to be a recognised scheme for a specified period or until the occurrence of a specified event or until specified conditions are complied with.

### 282   Procedure on giving directions under section 281 and varying them otherwise than as requested

(1) A direction takes effect—

(a) immediately, if the notice given under subsection (3) states that that is the case;

(b) on such date as may be specified in the notice; or

(c) if no date is specified in the notice, when the matter to which it relates is no longer open to review.

(2) A direction may be expressed to take effect immediately (or on a specified date) only if the Authority, having regard to the ground on which it is exercising its power under section 281, considers that it is necessary for the direction to take effect immediately (or on that date).

(3) If the Authority proposes to give a direction under section 281, or gives such a direction with immediate effect, it must give separate written notice to the operator and (if any) the trustee or depositary of the scheme concerned.

(4) The notice must—

(a) give details of the direction;

(b) inform the person to whom it is given of when the direction takes effect;

(c) state the Authority's reasons for giving the direction and for its determination as to when the direction takes effect;

(d) inform the person to whom it is given that he may make representations to the Authority within such period as may be specified in it (whether or not he has referred the matter to the Tribunal); and

(e)  inform him of his right to refer the matter to the Tribunal.

(5)  The Authority may extend the period allowed under the notice for making representations.

(6)  If, having considered any representations made by a person to whom the notice was given, the Authority decides—

(a)  to give the direction in the way proposed, or

(b)  if it has been given, not to revoke the direction,

it must give separate written notice to the operator and (if any) the trustee or depositary of the scheme concerned.

(7)  If, having considered any representations made by a person to whom the notice was given, the Authority decides—

(a)  not to give the direction in the way proposed,

(b)  to give the direction in a way other than that proposed, or

(c)  to revoke a direction which has effect,

it must give separate written notice to the operator and (if any) the trustee or depositary of the scheme concerned.

(8)  A notice given under subsection (6) must inform the person to whom it is given of his right to refer the matter to the Tribunal.

(9)  A notice under subsection (7)(b) must comply with subsection (4).

(10)  If a notice informs a person of his right to refer a matter to the Tribunal, it must give an indication of the procedure on such a reference.

(11)  This section applies to the variation of a direction on the Authority's own initiative as it applies to the giving of a direction.

(12)  For the purposes of subsection (1)(c), whether a matter is open to review is to be determined in accordance with section 391(8).

*Facilities and information in UK*

### 283  Facilities and information in UK

(1)  The Authority may make rules requiring operators of recognised schemes to maintain in the United Kingdom, or in such part or parts of it as may be specified, such facilities as the Authority thinks desirable in the interests of participants and as are specified in rules.

(2)  The Authority may by notice in writing require the operator of any recognised scheme to include such explanatory information as is specified in the notice in any communication of his which—

(a)  is a communication of an invitation or inducement of a kind mentioned in section 21(1); and

(b)  names the scheme.

(3)  In the case of a communication originating outside the United Kingdom, subsection (2) only applies if the communication is capable of having an effect in the United Kingdom.

# Chapter VI

# Investigations

### 284  Power to investigate

(1)  An investigating authority may appoint one or more competent persons to investigate on its behalf—

(a)  the affairs of, or of the manager or trustee of, any authorised unit trust scheme,

(b)  the affairs of, or of the operator, trustee or depositary of, any recognised scheme so far as relating to activities carried on in the United Kingdom, or

(c)  the affairs of, or of the operator, trustee or depositary of, any other collective investment scheme except a body incorporated by virtue of regulations under section 262,

if it appears to the investigating authority that it is in the interests of the participants or potential participants to do so or that the matter is of public concern.

(2)  A person appointed under subsection (1) to investigate the affairs of, or of the manager, trustee, operator or depositary of, any scheme (scheme 'A'), may also, if he thinks it necessary for the purposes of that investigation, investigate—

(a)  the affairs of, or of the manager, trustee, operator or depositary of, any other such scheme as is mentioned in subsection (1) whose manager, trustee, operator or depositary is the same person as the manager, trustee, operator or depositary of scheme A;

(b)  the affairs of such other schemes and persons (including bodies incorporated by virtue of regulations under section 262 and the directors and depositaries of such bodies) as may be prescribed.

(3)  If the person appointed to conduct an investigation under this section ('B') considers that a person ('C') is or may be able to give information which is relevant to the investigation, B may require C—

(a)  to produce to B any documents in C's possession or under his control which appear to B to be relevant to the investigation,

    (b) to attend before B, and

    (c) otherwise to give B all assistance in connection with the investigation which C is reasonably able to give,

and it is C's duty to comply with that requirement.

(4) Subsections (5) to (9) of section 170 apply if an investigating authority appoints a person under this section to conduct an investigation on its behalf as they apply in the case mentioned in subsection (1) of that section.

(5) Section 174 applies to a statement made by a person in compliance with a requirement imposed under this section as it applies to a statement mentioned in that section.

(6) Subsections (2) to (4) and (6) of section 175 and section 177 have effect as if this section were contained in Part XI.

(7) Subsections (1) to (9) of section 176 apply in relation to a person appointed under subsection (1) as if—

    (a) references to an investigator were references to a person so appointed;

    (b) references to an information requirement were references to a requirement imposed under section 175 or under subsection (3) by a person so appointed;

    (c) the premises mentioned in subsection (3)(a) were the premises of a person whose affairs are the subject of an investigation under this section or of an appointed representative of such a person.

(8) No person may be required under this section to disclose information or produce a document in respect of which he owes an obligation of confidence by virtue of carrying on the business of banking unless subsection (9) or (10) applies.

(9) This subsection applies if—

    (a) the person to whom the obligation of confidence is owed consents to the disclosure or production; or

    (b) the imposing on the person concerned of a requirement with respect to information or a document of a kind mentioned in subsection (8) has been specifically authorised by the investigating authority.

(10) This subsection applies if the person owing the obligation of confidence or the person to whom it is owed is—

    (a) the manager, trustee, operator or depositary of any collective investment scheme which is under investigation;

    (b) the director of a body incorporated by virtue of regulations under section 262 which is under investigation;

    (c) any other person whose own affairs are under investigation.

(11) 'Investigating authority' means the Authority or the Secretary of State.

# PART XVIII

# RECOGNISED INVESTMENT EXCHANGES AND CLEARING HOUSES

## Chapter I

## Exemption

### *General*

### 285 Exemption for recognised investment exchanges and clearing houses

(1) In this Act—

    (a) 'recognised investment exchange' means an investment exchange in relation to which a recognition order is in force; and

    (b) 'recognised clearing house' means a clearing house in relation to which a recognition order is in force.

(2) A recognised investment exchange is exempt from the general prohibition as respects any regulated activity—

    (a) which is carried on as a part of the exchange's business as an investment exchange; or

    (b) which is carried on for the purposes of, or in connection with, the provision of clearing services by the exchange.

(3) A recognised clearing house is exempt from the general prohibition as respects any regulated activity which is carried on for the purposes of, or in connection with, the provision of clearing services by the clearing house.

### 286   Qualification for recognition

(1)   The Treasury may make regulations setting out the requirements—

    (a)   which must be satisfied by an investment exchange or clearing house if it is to qualify as a body in respect of which the Authority may make a recognition order under this Part; and

    (b)   which, if a recognition order is made, it must continue to satisfy if it is to remain a recognised body.

(2)   But if regulations contain provision as to the default rules of an investment exchange or clearing house, or as to proceedings taken under such rules by such a body, they require the approval of the Secretary of State.

(3)   'Default rules' means rules of an investment exchange or clearing house which provide for the taking of action in the event of a person's appearing to be unable, or likely to become unable, to meet his obligations in respect of one or more market contracts connected with the exchange or clearing house.

(4)   'Market contract' means—

    (a)   a contract to which Part VII of the Companies Act 1989 applies as a result of section 155 of that Act or a contract to which Part V of the Companies (No. 2)(Northern Ireland) Order 1990 applies as a result of Article 80 of that Order; and

    (b)   such other kind of contract as may be prescribed.

(4A)   If regulations under subsection (1) require an investment exchange to make information available to the public in accordance with—

    (a)   Article 29.1 of the markets in financial instruments directive and the Commission Regulation, or

    (b)   Article 44.1 of that directive and that Regulation,

the regulations may authorise the Authority to waive the requirement in the circumstances specified in the relevant provisions.

(4B)   The 'relevant provisions' for the purposes of subsection (4A) are—

    (a)   in a case falling within paragraph (a) of that subsection, Article 29.2 of the markets in financial instruments directive and the Commission Regulation, and

    (b)   in a case falling within paragraph (b) of that subsection, Article 44.2 of that directive and that Regulation.

(4C)   If regulations under subsection (1) require an investment exchange to make information available to the public in accordance with—

    (a)   Article 30.1 of the markets in financial instruments directive and the Commission Regulation, or

    (b)   Article 45.1 of that directive and that Regulation,

the regulations may authorise the Authority to defer the requirement in the circumstances specified, and subject to the requirements contained, in the relevant provisions.

(4D)   The 'relevant provisions' for the purposes of subsection (4C) are—

    (a)   in a case falling within paragraph (a) of that subsection, Article 30.2 of the markets in financial instruments directive and the Commission Regulation, and

    (b)   in a case falling within paragraph (b) of that subsection, Article 45.2 of that directive and that Regulation.

(4E)   'The Commission Regulation' means Commission Regulation 1287/2006 of 10 August 2006.

(5)   Requirements resulting from this section are referred to in this Part as 'recognition requirements'.

(6)   In the case of an investment exchange, requirements resulting from this section are in addition to requirements which must be satisfied by the exchange as a result of section 290(1A) before the Authority may make a recognition order declaring the exchange to be a recognised investment exchange.

### *Applications for recognition*

### 287   Application by an investment exchange

(1)   Any body corporate or unincorporated association may apply to the Authority for an order declaring it to be a recognised investment exchange for the purposes of this Act.

(2)   The application must be made in such manner as the Authority may direct and must be accompanied by—

    (a)   a copy of the applicant's rules;

    (b)   a copy of any guidance issued by the applicant;

    (c)   the required particulars; and

    (d)   such other information as the Authority may reasonably require for the purpose of determining the application.

(3)   The required particulars are—

    (a)   particulars of any arrangements which the applicant has made, or proposes to make, for the provision of clearing services in respect of transactions effected on the exchange;

    (b)   if the applicant proposes to provide clearing services in respect of transactions other than those effected on the exchange, particulars of the criteria which the applicant will apply when determining to whom it will provide those services.

### 288   Application by a clearing house

(1) Any body corporate or unincorporated association may apply to the Authority for an order declaring it to be a recognised clearing house for the purposes of this Act.

(2) The application must be made in such manner as the Authority may direct and must be accompanied by—

   (a) a copy of the applicant's rules;

   (b) a copy of any guidance issued by the applicant;

   (c) the required particulars; and

   (d) such other information as the Authority may reasonably require for the purpose of determining the application.

(3) The required particulars are—

   (a) if the applicant makes, or proposes to make, clearing arrangements with a recognised investment exchange, particulars of those arrangements;

   (b) if the applicant proposes to provide clearing services for persons other than recognised investment exchanges, particulars of the criteria which it will apply when determining to whom it will provide those services.

### 289   Applications: supplementary

(1) At any time after receiving an application and before determining it, the Authority may require the applicant to provide such further information as it reasonably considers necessary to enable it to determine the application.

(2) Information which the Authority requires in connection with an application must be provided in such form, or verified in such manner, as the Authority may direct.

(3) Different directions may be given, or requirements imposed, by the Authority with respect to different applications.

### 290   Recognition orders

(1) If it appears to the Authority that the applicant satisfies the recognition requirements applicable in its case, the Authority may make a recognition order declaring the applicant to be—

   (a) a recognised investment exchange, if the application is made under section 287;

   (b) a recognised clearing house, if it is made under section 288.

(1A) In the case of an application for an order declaring the applicant to be a recognised investment exchange, the reference in subsection (1) to the recognition requirements applicable in its case includes a reference to requirements contained in any directly applicable Community regulation made under the markets in financial instruments directive.

(1B) In the case mentioned in subsection (1A), the application must be determined by the Authority before the end of the period of six months beginning with the date on which it receives the completed application.

(1C) Subsection (1B) does not apply in the case of an application by an overseas applicant.

(2) The Treasury's approval of the making of a recognition order is required under section 307.

(3) In considering an application, the Authority may have regard to any information which it considers is relevant to the application.

(4) A recognition order must specify a date on which it is to take effect.

(5) Section 298 has effect in relation to a decision to refuse to make a recognition order—

   (a) as it has effect in relation to a decision to revoke such an order; and

   (b) as if references to a recognised body were references to the applicant.

(6) Subsection (5) does not apply in a case in which the Treasury have failed to give their approval under section 307.

### 290A   Refusal of recognition on ground of excessive regulatory provision

(1) The Authority must not make a recognition order if it appears to the Authority that an existing or proposed regulatory provision of the applicant in connection with—

   (a) the applicant's business as an investment exchange, or

   (b) the provision by the applicant of clearing services,

imposes or will impose an excessive requirement on the persons affected (directly or indirectly) by it.

(2) The reference in section 290(1) (making of recognition order) to satisfying the applicable recognition requirements shall be read accordingly.

(3) Expressions used in subsection (1) above that are defined for the purposes of section 300A (power of Authority to disallow excessive regulatory provision) have the same meaning as in that section.

(4) The provisions of section 300A(3) and (4) (determination whether regulatory provision excessive) apply for the purposes of this section as for the purposes of section 300A.

(5) Section 298 has effect in relation to a decision under this section to refuse a recognition order—

   (a) as it has effect in relation to a decision to revoke such an order, and

   (b) as if references to a recognised body were references to the applicant.

(6) This section does not apply to an application for recognition as an overseas investment exchange or overseas clearing house.

### 291 Liability in relation to recognised body's regulatory functions

(1) A recognised body and its officers and staff are not to be liable in damages for anything done or omitted in the discharge of the recognised body's regulatory functions unless it is shown that the act or omission was in bad faith.

(2) But subsection (1) does not prevent an award of damages made in respect of an act or omission on the ground that the act or omission was unlawful as a result of section 6(1) of the Human Rights Act 1998.

(3) 'Regulatory functions' means the functions of the recognised body so far as relating to, or to matters arising out of, the obligations to which the body is subject under or by virtue of this Act.

### 292 Overseas investment exchanges and overseas clearing houses

(1) An application under section 287 or 288 by an overseas applicant must contain the address of a place in the United Kingdom for the service on the applicant of notices or other documents required or authorised to be served on it under this Act.

(2) If it appears to the Authority that an overseas applicant satisfies the requirements of subsection (3) it may make a recognition order declaring the applicant to be—

    (a) a recognised investment exchange;

    (b) a recognised clearing house.

(3) The requirements are that—

    (a) investors are afforded protection equivalent to that which they would be afforded if the body concerned were required to comply with recognition requirements other than any such requirements which are expressed in regulations under section 286 not to apply for the purposes of this paragraph;

    (b) there are adequate procedures for dealing with a person who is unable, or likely to become unable, to meet his obligations in respect of one or more market contracts connected with the investment exchange or clearing house;

    (c) the applicant is able and willing to co-operate with the Authority by the sharing of information and in other ways;

    (d) adequate arrangements exist for co-operation between the Authority and those responsible for the supervision of the applicant in the country or territory in which the applicant's head office is situated.

(4) In considering whether it is satisfied as to the requirements mentioned in subsection (3)(a) and (b), the Authority is to have regard to—

    (a) the relevant law and practice of the country or territory in which the applicant's head office is situated;

    (b) the rules and practices of the applicant.

(5) In relation to an overseas applicant and a body or association declared to be a recognised investment exchange or recognised clearing house by a recognition order made by virtue of subsection (2)—

    (a) the reference in section 313(2) to recognition requirements is to be read as a reference to matters corresponding to the matters in respect of which provision is made in the recognition requirements;

    (b) sections 296(1) and 297(2) have effect as if the requirements mentioned in section 296(1)(a) and section 297(2)(a) were those of subsection (3)(a), (b), and (c) of this section;

    (c) section 297(2) has effect as if the grounds on which a recognition order may be revoked under that provision included the ground that in the opinion of the Authority arrangements of the kind mentioned in subsection (3)(d) no longer exist.

### 292A Publication of information by recognised investment exchange

(1) A recognised investment exchange must as soon as practicable after a recognition order is made in respect of it publish such particulars of the ownership of the exchange as the Authority may reasonably require.

(2) The particulars published under subsection (1) must include particulars of the identity and scale of interests of the persons who are in a position to exercise significant influence over the management of the exchange, whether directly or indirectly.

(3) If an ownership transfer takes place in relation to a recognised investment exchange, the exchange must as soon as practicable after becoming aware of the transfer publish such particulars relating to the transfer as the Authority may reasonably require.

(4) 'Ownership transfer', in relation to an exchange, means a transfer of ownership which gives rise to a change in the persons who are in a position to exercise significant influence over the management of the exchange, whether directly or indirectly.

(5) A recognised investment exchange must publish such particulars of any decision it makes to suspend or remove a financial instrument from trading on a regulated market operated by it as the Authority may reasonably require.

(6) The Authority may determine the manner of publication under subsections (1), (3) and (5) and the timing of publication under subsection (5).

(7) This section does not apply to an overseas investment exchange.

*Supervision*

### 293   Notification requirements

(1) The Authority may make rules requiring a recognised body to give it—

 (a) notice of such events relating to the body as may be specified; and

 (b) such information in respect of those events as may be specified.

(2) The rules may also require a recognised body to give the Authority, at such times or in respect of such periods as may be specified, such information relating to the body as may be specified.

(3) An obligation imposed by the rules extends only to a notice or information which the Authority may reasonably require for the exercise of its functions under this Act.

(4) The rules may require information to be given in a specified form and to be verified in a specified manner.

(5) If a recognised body—

 (a) alters or revokes any of its rules or guidance, or

 (b) makes new rules or issues new guidance,

it must give written notice to the Authority without delay.

(6) If a recognised investment exchange makes a change—

 (a) in the arrangements it makes for the provision of clearing services in respect of transactions effected on the exchange, or

 (b) in the criteria which it applies when determining to whom it will provide clearing services,

it must give written notice to the Authority without delay.

(7) If a recognised clearing house makes a change—

 (a) in the recognised investment exchanges for whom it provides clearing services, or

 (b) in the criteria which it applies when determining to whom (other than recognised investment exchanges) it will provide clearing services,

it must give written notice to the Authority without delay.

(8) Subsections (5) to (7) do not apply to an overseas investment exchange or an overseas clearing house.

(9) 'Specified' means specified in the Authority's rules.

### 293A   Information: compliance of recognised investment exchanges with directly applicable Community regulations

The Authority may require a recognised investment exchange to give the Authority such information as it reasonably requires in order to satisfy itself that the exchange is complying with any directly applicable Community regulation made under the markets in financial instruments directive.

### 294   Modification or waiver of rules

(1) The Authority may, on the application or with the consent of a recognised body, direct that rules made under section 293 or 295—

 (a) are not to apply to the body; or

 (b) are to apply to the body with such modifications as may be specified in the direction.

(2) An application must be made in such manner as the Authority may direct.

(3) Subsections (4) to (6) apply to a direction given under subsection (1).

(4) The Authority may not give a direction unless it is satisfied that—

 (a) compliance by the recognised body with the rules, or with the rules as unmodified, would be unduly burdensome or would not achieve the purpose for which the rules were made; and

 (b) the direction would not result in undue risk to persons whose interests the rules are intended to protect.

(5) A direction may be given subject to conditions.

(6) The Authority may—

 (a) revoke a direction; or

 (b) vary it on the application, or with the consent, of the recognised body to which it relates.

### 295   Notification: overseas investment exchanges and overseas clearing houses

(1) At least once a year, every overseas investment exchange and overseas clearing house must provide the Authority with a report.

(2) The report must contain a statement as to whether any events have occurred which are likely—

 (a) to affect the Authority's assessment of whether it is satisfied as to the requirements set out in section 292(3); or

 (b) to have any effect on competition.

(3) The report must also contain such information as may be specified in rules made by the Authority.

(4) The investment exchange or clearing house must provide the Treasury and the OFT with a copy of the report.

### 296  Authority's power to give directions

(1) This section applies if it appears to the Authority that a recognised body—

    (a) has failed, or is likely to fail, to satisfy the recognition requirements; or

    (b) has failed to comply with any other obligation imposed on it by or under this Act.

(1A) This section also applies in the case of a recognised body which is a recognised investment exchange if it appears to the Authority that the body has failed, or is likely to fail, to comply with any obligation imposed on it by any directly applicable Community regulation made under the markets in financial instruments directive.

(2) The Authority may direct the body to take specified steps for the purpose of securing the body's compliance with—

    (a) the recognition requirements; or

    (b) any obligation of the kind in question.

(2A) In the case of a recognised investment exchange other than an overseas investment exchange, those steps may include—

    (a) the granting to the Authority of access to the premises of the exchange for the purpose of inspecting—

        (i) those premises; or

        (ii) any documents on the premises which appear to the Authority to be relevant for the purpose mentioned in subsection (2);

    (b) the suspension of the carrying on of any regulated activity by the exchange for the period specified in the direction.

(3) A direction under this section is enforceable, on the application of the Authority, by an injunction or, in Scotland, by an order for specific performance under section 45 of the Court of Session Act 1988.

(4) The fact that a rule made by a recognised body has been altered in response to a direction given by the Authority does not prevent it from being subsequently altered or revoked by the recognised body.

### 297  Revoking recognition

(1) A recognition order may be revoked by an order made by the Authority at the request, or with the consent, of the recognised body concerned.

(2) If it appears to the Authority that a recognised body—

    (a) is failing, or has failed, to satisfy the recognition requirements, or

    (b) is failing, or has failed, to comply with any other obligation imposed on it by or under this Act,

it may make an order revoking the recognition order for that body even though the body does not wish the order to be made.

(2A) If it appears to the Authority that a recognised body which is a recognised investment exchange—

    (a) has not carried on the business of an investment exchange during the period of twelve months beginning with the day on which the recognition order took effect in relation to it,

    (b) has not carried on the business of an investment exchange at any time during the period of six months ending with the relevant day, or

    (c) has failed, or is likely to fail, to comply with any obligation imposed on it by a directly applicable Community regulation made under the markets in financial instruments directive,

it may make an order revoking the recognition order for that body even though the body does not wish the order to be made.

(2B) The 'relevant day', for the purposes of paragraph (b) of subsection (2A), is the day on which the power to make an order under that subsection is exercised.

(2C) Subsection (2A) does not apply to an overseas investment exchange.

(3) An order under this section ('a revocation order') must specify the date on which it is to take effect.

(4) In the case of a revocation order made under subsection (2) or (2A), the specified date must not be earlier than the end of the period of three months beginning with the day on which the order is made.

(5) A revocation order may contain such transitional provisions as the Authority thinks necessary or expedient.

### 298  Directions and revocation: procedure

(1) Before giving a direction under section 296, or making a revocation order under section 297(2) or (2A), the Authority must—

    (a) give written notice of its intention to do so to the recognised body concerned;

    (b) take such steps as it considers reasonably practicable to bring the notice to the attention of members (if any) of that body; and

(c) publish the notice in such manner as it thinks appropriate for bringing it to the attention of other persons who are, in its opinion, likely to be affected.

(2) A notice under subsection (1) must—

(a) state why the Authority intends to give the direction or make the order; and

(b) draw attention to the right to make representations conferred by subsection (3).

(3) Before the end of the period for making representations—

(a) the recognised body,

(b) any member of that body, and

(c) any other person who is likely to be affected by the proposed direction or revocation order,

may make representations to the Authority.

(4) The period for making representations is—

(a) two months beginning—

(i) with the date on which the notice is served on the recognised body; or

(ii) if later, with the date on which the notice is published; or

(b) such longer period as the Authority may allow in the particular case.

(5) In deciding whether to—

(a) give a direction, or

(b) make a revocation order,

the Authority must have regard to any representations made in accordance with subsection (3).

(6) When the Authority has decided whether to give a direction under section 296 or to make the proposed revocation order, it must—

(a) give the recognised body written notice of its decision; and

(b) if it has decided to give a direction or make an order, take such steps as it considers reasonably practicable for bringing its decision to the attention of members of the body or of other persons who are, in the Authority's opinion, likely to be affected.

(7) If the Authority considers it essential to do so, it may give a direction under section 296—

(a) without following the procedure set out in this section; or

(b) if the Authority has begun to follow that procedure, regardless of whether the period for making representations has expired.

(8) If the Authority has, in relation to a particular matter, followed the procedure set out in subsections (1) to (5), it need not follow it again if, in relation to that matter, it decides to take action other than that specified in its notice under subsection (1).

### 299    Complaints about recognised bodies

(1) The Authority must make arrangements for the investigation of any relevant complaint about a recognised body.

(2) 'Relevant complaint' means a complaint which the Authority considers is relevant to the question of whether the body concerned should remain a recognised body.

### 300    Extension of functions of Tribunal

(1) If the Treasury are satisfied that the condition mentioned in subsection (2) is satisfied, they may by order confer functions on the Tribunal with respect to disciplinary proceedings—

(a) of one or more investment exchanges in relation to which a recognition order under section 290 is in force or of such investment exchanges generally, or

(b) of one or more clearing houses in relation to which a recognition order under that section is in force or of such clearing houses generally.

(2) The condition is that it is desirable to exercise the power conferred under subsection (1) with a view to ensuring that—

(a) decisions taken in disciplinary proceedings with respect to which functions are to be conferred on the Tribunal are consistent with—

(i) decisions of the Tribunal in cases arising under Part VIII; and

(ii) decisions taken in other disciplinary proceedings with respect to which the Tribunal has functions as a result of an order under this section; or

(b) the disciplinary proceedings are in accordance with the Convention rights.

(3) An order under this section may modify or exclude any provision made by or under this Act with respect to proceedings before the Tribunal.

(4) 'Disciplinary proceedings' means proceedings under the rules of an investment exchange or clearing house in relation to market abuse by persons subject to the rules.

(5) 'The Convention rights' has the meaning given in section 1 of the Human Rights Act 1998.

### 300A    Power of Authority to disallow excessive regulatory provision

(1) This section applies where a recognised body proposes to make any regulatory provision in connection with its business as an investment exchange or the provision by it of clearing services.

(2) If it appears to the Authority—

(a) that the proposed provision will impose a requirement on persons affected (directly or indirectly) by it, and

(b) that the requirement is excessive,

the Authority may direct that the proposed provision must not be made.

(3) A requirement is excessive if—

(a) it is not required under Community law or any enactment or rule of law in the United Kingdom, and

(b) either—

(i)   it is not justified as pursuing a reasonable regulatory objective, or

(ii)  it is disproportionate to the end to be achieved.

(4) In considering whether a requirement is excessive the Authority must have regard to all the relevant circumstances, including—

(a) the effect of existing legal and other requirements,

(b) the global character of financial services and markets and the international mobility of activity,

(c) the desirability of facilitating innovation, and

(d) the impact of the proposed provision on market confidence.

(5) In this section 'requirement' includes any obligation or burden.

(6) Any provision made in contravention of a direction under this section is of no effect.

### 300B   Duty to notify proposal to make regulatory provision

(1) A recognised body that proposes to make any regulatory provision must give written notice of the proposal to the Authority without delay.

(2) The Authority may by rules under section 293 (notification requirements)—

(a) specify descriptions of regulatory provision in relation to which, or circumstances in which, the duty in subsection (1) above does not apply, or

(b) provide that the duty applies only to specified descriptions of regulatory provision or in specified circumstances.

(3) The Authority may also by rules under that section—

(a) make provision as to the form and contents of the notice required, and

(b) require the body to provide such information relating to the proposal as may be specified in the rules or as the Authority may reasonably require.

### 300C   Restriction on making provision before Authority decides whether to act

(1) Where notice of a proposal to make regulatory provision is required to be given to the Authority under section 300B, the provision must not be made—

(a) before that notice is given, or

(b) subject to the following provisions of this section, before the end of the initial period.

(2) The initial period is—

(a) the period of 30 days beginning with the day on which the Authority receives notice of the proposal, or

(b) if any consultation period announced by the body in relation to the proposal ends after that 30-day period, the end of the consultation period.

(3) If before the end of the initial period the Authority notifies the body that it is calling in the proposal, the provisions of section 300D (consideration by Authority whether to disallow proposed provision) apply as to when the provision may be made.

(4) If—

(a) before the end of the initial period the Authority notifies the body that it is not calling in the proposal, or

(b) the initial period ends without the Authority having notified the body that it is calling in the proposal,

the body may then make the proposed provision.

(5) Any provision made in contravention of this section is of no effect.

### 300D   Consideration by Authority whether to disallow proposed provision

(1) This section applies where the Authority notifies a recognised body that it is calling in a proposal to make regulatory provision.

(2) The Authority must publish a notice—

(a) giving details of the proposed provision,

(b) stating that it has called in the proposal in order to consider whether to disallow it, and

(c) specifying a period during which representations with respect to that question may be made to it.

(3) The Authority may extend the period for making representations.

(4) The Authority must notify the body of its decision whether to disallow the provision not later than 30 days after the end of the period for making representations, and must publish the decision and the reasons for it.

(5) The body must not make the provision unless and until—

(a) the Authority notifies it of its decision not to disallow it, or

(b) the 30-day period specified in subsection (4) ends without the Authority having notified any decision.

(6) If the Authority notifies the body of its decision to disallow the provision and that decision is questioned in legal proceedings—

    (a) the body must not make the provision until those proceedings, and any proceedings on appeal, are finally determined,

    (b) if the Authority's decision is quashed and the matter is remitted to it for reconsideration, the court may give directions as to the period within which the Authority is to complete its reconsideration, and

    (c) the body must not make the provision until—

        (i) the Authority notifies it of its decision on reconsideration not to disallow the provision, or

        (ii) the period specified by the court ends without the Authority having notified any decision.

(7) Any provision made in contravention of subsection (5) or (6) is of no effect.

### 300E    Power to disallow excessive regulatory provision: supplementary

(1) In sections 300A to 300D—

    (a) 'regulatory provision' means any rule, guidance, arrangements, policy or practice, and

    (b) references to making provision shall be read accordingly as including, as the case may require, issuing guidance, entering into arrangements or adopting a policy or practice.

(2) For the purposes of those sections a variation of a proposal is treated as a new proposal.

(3) Those sections do not apply to an overseas investment exchange or overseas clearing house.

*Other matters*

### 301    Supervision of certain contracts

(1) The Secretary of State and the Treasury, acting jointly, may by regulations provide for—

    (a) Part VII of the Companies Act 1989 (financial markets and insolvency), and

    (b) Part V of the Companies (No. 2)(Northern Ireland) Order 1990,

to apply to relevant contracts as it applies to contracts connected with a recognised body.

(2) 'Relevant contracts' means contracts of a prescribed description in relation to which settlement arrangements are provided by a person for the time being included in a list ('the list') maintained by the Authority for the purposes of this section.

(3) Regulations may be made under this section only if the Secretary of State and the Treasury are satisfied, having regard to the extent to which the relevant contracts concerned are contracts of a kind dealt in by persons supervised by the Authority, that it is appropriate for the arrangements mentioned in subsection (2) to be supervised by the Authority.

(4) The approval of the Treasury is required for—

    (a) the conditions set by the Authority for admission to the list; and

    (b) the arrangements for admission to, and removal from, the list.

(5) If the Treasury withdraw an approval given by them under subsection (4), all regulations made under this section and then in force are to be treated as suspended.

(6) But if—

    (a) the Authority changes the conditions or arrangements (or both), and

    (b) the Treasury give a fresh approval under subsection (4),

the suspension of the regulations ends on such date as the Treasury may, in giving the fresh approval, specify.

(7) The Authority must—

    (a) publish the list as for the time being in force; and

    (b) provide a certified copy of it to any person who wishes to refer to it in legal proceedings.

(8) A certified copy of the list is evidence (or in Scotland sufficient evidence) of the contents of the list.

(9) A copy of the list which purports to be certified by or on behalf of the Authority is to be taken to have been duly certified unless the contrary is shown.

(10) Regulations under this section may, in relation to a person included in the list—

    (a) apply (with such exceptions, additions and modifications as appear to the Secretary of State and the Treasury to be necessary or expedient) such provisions of, or made under, this Act as they consider appropriate;

    (b) provide for the provisions of Part VII of the Companies Act 1989 and Part V of the Companies (No. 2)(Northern Ireland) Order 1990 to apply (with such exceptions, additions or modifications as appear to the Secretary of State and the Treasury to be necessary or expedient).

# Chapter 1A

# Control over recognised investment exchange

### 301A    Obligation to notify the Authority: acquisitions of control

(1) A person who decides to acquire or increase control over a recognised investment exchange must give the Authority notice in writing before making the acquisition.

(2) A person who acquires or increases control over a recognised investment exchange in circumstances where notice is not required under subsection (1) must give the Authority notice in writing before the end of 14 days beginning with—

    (a) the day the person acquired or increased the control; or

    (b) if later, the day on which the person first became aware that the control had been acquired or increased.

(3) For the purposes of calculations relating to this section, the holding of shares or voting power by a person ('A1') includes any shares or voting power held by another ('A2') if A1 and A2 are acting in concert.

(4) A notice given under this section is a 'section 301A notice' and a person giving notice is a 'section 301A notice-giver'.

### 301B   Requirements for section 301A notices

(1) A section 301A notice must be in such form, include such information and be accompanied by such documents as the Authority may reasonably require.

(2) The Authority must publish a list of its requirements as to the form, information and accompanying documents for a section 301A notice.

(3) The Authority may impose different requirements for different cases and may vary or waive requirements in particular cases.

### 301C   Acknowledgment of receipt

(1) The Authority must acknowledge receipt of a section 301A notice in writing before the end of the second working day following receipt.

(2) If the Authority receives an incomplete section 301A notice it must inform the section 301A notice-giver as soon as reasonably practicable.

*Acquiring and increasing control*

### 301D   Acquiring and increasing control

(1) For the purposes of this Chapter, a person ('A') acquires control over a recognised investment exchange ('B') if any of the cases in subsection (2) begin to apply.

(2) The cases are where A holds—

    (a) 20% or more of the shares in B or in a parent undertaking of B ('P');

    (b) 20% or more of the voting power in B or P; or

    (c) shares or voting power in B or P as a result of which A is able to exercise significant influence over the management of B.

(3) For the purposes of this Chapter, a person ('A') increases control over a recognised investment exchange ('B') whenever—

    (a) the percentage of shares which A holds in B or in a parent undertaking of B ('P') increases from less than 50% to 50% or more;

    (b) the percentage of voting power A holds in B or P increases from less than 50% to 50% or more; or

    (c) A becomes a parent undertaking of B.

### 301E   *Disregarded holdings*

(1) For the purpose of section 301D, shares and voting power that a person holds in a recognised investment exchange ('B') or in a parent undertaking of B ('P') are disregarded in the following circumstances.

(2) Shares held only for the purposes of clearing and settling within a short settlement cycle are disregarded.

(3) Shares held by a custodian or its nominee in a custodian capacity are disregarded, provided that the custodian or nominee is only able to exercise voting power represented by the shares in accordance with instructions given in writing.

(4) Shares representing no more than 5% of the total voting power in B or P held by an investment firm are disregarded, provided that it—

    (a) holds the shares in the capacity of a market maker (as defined in article 4.1(8) of the markets in financial instruments directive);

    (b) is authorised by its home state regulator under the markets in financial instruments directive; and

    (c) neither intervenes in the management of B or P nor exerts any influence on B or P to buy the shares or back the share price.

(5) Shares held by a credit institution or investment firm in its trading book are disregarded, provided that—

    (a) the shares represent no more than 5% of the total voting power in B or P; and

    (b) the credit institution or investment firm ensures that the voting power is not exercised nor otherwise used to intervene in the management of B or P.

(6) Shares held by a credit institution or an investment firm are disregarded, provided that—

(a) the shares are held as a result of performing the investment services and activities of—
   (i)   underwriting a share issue; or
   (ii)  placing shares on a firm commitment basis in accordance with Annex I, section A.6 of the markets in financial instruments directive; and
(b) the credit institution or investment firm—
   (i)   does not exercise voting power represented by the shares or otherwise intervene in the management of the issuer; and
   (ii)  retains the holding for a period of less than one year.

(7) Where a management company (as defined in Article 1a.2 of the UCITS directive) and its parent undertaking both hold shares or voting power, each may disregard holdings of the other, provided that each exercises its voting power independently of the other.

(8) But subsection (7) does not apply if the management company—
(a) manages holdings for its parent undertaking or an undertaking in respect of which the parent undertaking is a controller;
(b) has no discretion as to the exercise of the voting power attached to such holdings; and
(c) may only exercise the voting power in relation to such holdings under direct or indirect instruction from—
   (i)   the parent undertaking; or
   (ii)  an undertaking in respect of which of the parent undertaking is a controller.

(9) Where an investment firm and its parent undertaking both hold shares or voting power, the parent undertaking may disregard holdings managed by the investment firm on a client by client basis and the investment firm may disregard holdings of the parent undertaking, provided that the investment firm—
(a) has permission to provide portfolio management;
(b) exercises its voting power independently from the parent undertaking; and
(c) may only exercise the voting power under instructions given in writing, or has appropriate mechanisms in place for ensuring that individual portfolio management services are conducted independently of any other services.

### *Assessment procedure*

### 301F   Assessment: general
(1) Where the Authority receives a section 301A notice, it must—
(a) determine whether to approve the acquisition to which it relates; or
(b) propose to object to the acquisition.
(2) In making its determination the Authority must—
(a) consider the suitability of the section 301A notice-giver and the financial soundness of the acquisition in order to ensure the sound and prudent management of the recognised investment exchange in question; and
(b) have regard to the likely influence that the section 301A notice-giver will have on the recognised investment exchange.
(3) The Authority may only object to an acquisition if it is not satisfied that the approval requirement is met.
(4) The approval requirement is that the acquisition in question by the notice-giver does not pose a threat to the sound and prudent management of any financial market operated by the recognised investment exchange.

### 301G   Assessment: Procedure
(1) The Authority must act under section 301F within a period three months from the date the Authority receives the completed section 301A notice ('the assessment period').
(2) The Authority must inform the section 301A notice-giver in writing of—
(a) the duration of the assessment period; and
(b) its expiry date.
(3) The Authority must, within two working days of acting under section 301F (and in any event no later than the expiry date of the assessment period)—
(a) notify the section 301A notice-giver that it has determined to approve the acquisition; or
(b) in the case of a proposed objection to an acquisition, give a warning notice.
(4) The Authority is treated as having approved the acquisition if, at the expiry of the assessment period, it has neither—
(a) given notice under subsection (3); nor
(b) informed the section 301A notice-giver that the notice is incomplete.
(5) If the Authority decides to object to an acquisition it must give the section 301A notice-giver a decision notice.
(6) Following receipt of a decision notice under this section, the section 301A notice-giver may refer the Authority's decision to the Tribunal.

### 301H   Duration of approval
(1) Approval of an acquisition is effective for such period as the Authority may specify in writing.

(2) Where the Authority has specified a period under subsection (1), it may extend the period.

(3) Where the Authority has not specified a period, the approval is effective for one year beginning with the date—

(a) of the notice given under section 301G(3)(a);

(b) on which the Authority is treated as having given approval under section 301G(5); or

(c) of a decision on a reference to the Tribunal which results in the person receiving approval.

*Enforcement procedures*

### 301I   Objections by the Authority

(1) The Authority may object to a person's control over a recognised investment exchange in any of the circumstances specified in subsection (2).

(2) The circumstances are that the Authority reasonably believes that—

(a) the person acquired or increased control without giving notice under section 301A in circumstances where notice was required; and

(b) there are grounds for objecting to control on the basis of the approval requirement in section 301F(4).

(3) If the Authority proposes to object to a person's control over a recognised investment exchange, it must give that person a warning notice.

(4) If the Authority decides to object to a person's control over a UK authorised person, it must give that person a decision notice.

(5) A person to whom the Authority gives a decision notice under this section may refer the matter to the Tribunal.

### 301J   Restriction notices

(1) The Authority may give notice in writing (a 'restriction notice') to a person in the following circumstances.

(2) The circumstances are that—

(a) the person has control over a recognised investment exchange by virtue of holding shares or voting power; and

(b) in relation to the shares or voting power, the Authority has given the person a warning notice or a decision notice under section 301G or 301I or a final notice which confirms a decision notice given under section 301G or 301I.

(3) In a restriction notice, the Authority may direct that shares or voting power to which the notice relates are, until further notice, subject to one or more of the following restrictions—

(a) except by court order, an agreement to transfer or a transfer of any such shares or voting power or, in the case of unissued shares, any agreement to transfer or transfer of the right to be issued with them, is void;

(b) no voting power is to be exercisable;

(c) no further shares are to be issued in pursuance of any right of the holder of any such shares or voting power or in pursuance of any offer made to their holder;

(d) except in a liquidation, no payment is to be made of any sums due from the body corporate on any such shares, whether in respect of capital or otherwise.

(4) A restriction notice takes effect—

(a) immediately; or

(b) on such date as may be specified in the notice.

(5) A restriction notice does not extinguish rights which would be enjoyable but for the notice.

(6) A copy of the restriction notice must be served on—

(a) the recognised investment exchange in question; and

(b) in the case of shares or voting power held in a parent undertaking of a recognised investment exchange, the parent undertaking.

(7) A person to whom the Authority gives a restriction notice may refer the matter to the Tribunal.

### 301K   Orders for sale of shares

(1) The court may, on the application of the Authority, order the sale of shares or the disposition of voting power in the following circumstances.

(2) The circumstances are that—

(a) a person has control over a recognised investment exchange by virtue of holding the shares or voting power; and

(b) the acquisition or continued holding of the shares or voting power by that person is in contravention of a final notice which confirms a decision notice given under section 301G or section 301I.

(3) Where the court orders the sale of shares or disposition of voting power it may—

(a) if a restriction notice has been given in relation to the shares or voting power, order that the restrictions cease to apply; and

(b) make any further order.

(4) Where the court makes an order under this section, it must take into account the level of holding that the person would have been entitled to acquire, or to continue to hold, without contravening the final notice.

(5) If shares are sold or voting power disposed of in pursuance of an order under this section, any proceeds, less the costs of the sale or disposition, must be paid into court for the benefit of the persons beneficially interested in them; and any such person may apply to the court for payment of a whole or part of the proceeds.

(6) The jurisdiction conferred by this section may be exercised by the High Court and the Court of Session.

*Offences*

### 301L  Offences under this Chapter

(1) A person who fails to comply with an obligation to notify the Authority under section 301A(1) or (2) is guilty of an offence.

(2) A person who gives notice to the Authority under section 301A(1) and makes the acquisition to which the notice relates before the expiry date of the assessment period is guilty of an offence unless the Authority has approved the acquisition.

(3) A person who makes an acquisition in contravention of a warning notice or a decision notice given under section 301G or a final notice which confirms a decision notice under that section is guilty of an offence.

(4) A person who makes an acquisition after the Authority's approval for the acquisition has ceased to be effective by virtue of section 301H is guilty of an offence.

(5) A person who provides information to the Authority which is false in a material particular is guilty of an offence.

(6) A person who breaches a direction contained in a restriction notice given under section 301J is guilty of an offence.

(7) A person guilty of an offence under subsection (1), (2) or (4) to (6) is liable—
  (a) on summary conviction to a fine not exceeding the statutory maximum; or
  (b) on conviction on indictment, to a fine.

(8) A person guilty of an offence under subsection (3) is liable—
  (a) on summary conviction, to a fine not exceeding the statutory maximum; or
  (b) on conviction on indictment, to imprisonment for a term not exceeding two years or a fine, or both.

(9) It is a defence for a person charged with an offence under subsection (1) in relation to section 301A(2) to show that the person had, at the time of the alleged offence, no knowledge of the act or circumstances by virtue of which the duty to notify the Authority arose.

*Interpretation*

### 301M  Interpretation

(1) In this Chapter—
'acquisition' means the acquisition of control or of an increase in control over a recognised investment exchange;
'credit institution' means—
  (a) a credit institution authorised under the banking consolidation directive; or
  (b) an institution which would satisfy the requirements for authorisation as a credit institution under that directive if it had its registered office (or if it does not have a registered office, its head office) in an EEA State; and
'shares' and 'voting power' have the same meaning as in section 422.

(2) For the purposes of this Chapter, a 'working day' is a day other than—
  (a) a Saturday or a Sunday; or
  (b) a day which is a bank holiday in England and Wales under the Banking and Financial Dealings Act 1971.'

# Chapter II

## Competition scrutiny

### 302  Interpretation

(1) In this Chapter and Chapter III—
'practices' means—
  (a) in relation to a recognised investment exchange, the practices of the exchange in its capacity as such; and
  (b) in relation to a recognised clearing house, the practices of the clearing house in respect of its clearing arrangements;

'regulatory provisions' means—

    (a) the rules of an investment exchange or a clearing house;

    (b) any guidance issued by an investment exchange or clearing house;

    (c) in the case of an investment exchange, the arrangements and criteria mentioned in section 287(3)(a) and (b);

    (d) in the case of a clearing house, the arrangements and criteria mentioned in section 288(3).

(2) For the purposes of this Chapter, regulatory provisions or practices have a significantly adverse effect on competition if—

    (a) they have, or are intended or likely to have, that effect; or

    (b) the effect that they have, or are intended or likely to have, is to require or encourage behaviour which has, or is intended or likely to have, a significantly adverse effect on competition.

(3) If regulatory provisions or practices have, or are intended or likely to have, the effect of requiring or encouraging exploitation of the strength of a market position they are to be taken, for the purposes of this Chapter, to have an adverse effect on competition.

(4) In determining under this Chapter whether any regulatory provisions have, or are intended or likely to have, a particular effect, it may be assumed that persons to whom the provisions concerned are addressed will act in accordance with them.

### *Role of Office of Fair Trading*

### 303  Initial report by OFT

(1) The Authority must send to the Treasury and to the OFT a copy of any regulatory provisions with which it is provided on an application for recognition under section 287 or 288.

(2) The Authority must send to the OFT such information in its possession as a result of the application for recognition as it considers will assist The OFT in discharging its functions in connection with the application.

(3) The OFT must issue a report as to whether—

    (a) a regulatory provision of which a copy has been sent to it under subsection (1) has a significantly adverse effect on competition; or

    (b) a combination of regulatory provisions so copied to it have such an effect.

(4) If the OFT's conclusion is that one or more provisions have a significantly adverse effect on competition, it must state its reasons for that conclusion.

(5) When the OFT issues a report under subsection (3), the OFT must send a copy of it to the Authority, the Competition Commission and the Treasury.

(6) In the case of an application for recognition under section 287, the OFT must issue its report under subsection (3) before the end of the period of 12 weeks beginning with the date on which it receives the copy sent to it under subsection (1).

(7) Subsection (6) does not apply if the application is made by an overseas investment exchange.

### 304  Further reports by the OFT

(1) The OFT must keep under review the regulatory provisions and practices of recognised bodies.

(2) If at any time the OFT considers that—

    (a) a regulatory provision or practice has a significantly adverse effect on competition, or

    (b) regulatory provisions or practices, or a combination of regulating provisions and practices have such an effect,

the OFT must make a report.

(3) If at any time the OFT considers that—

    (a) a regulatory provision or practice does not have a significantly adverse effect on competition, or

    (b) regulatory provisions or practices, or a combination of regulatory provisions and practices do not have any such effect,

the OFT may make a report to that effect.

(4) A report under subsection (2) must contain details of the adverse effect on competition.

(5) If the OFT makes a report under subsection (2), the OFT must—

    (a) send a copy of it to the Treasury, to the Competition Commission and to the Authority; and

    (b) publish it in the way appearing to it to be best calculated to bring it to the attention of the public.

(6) If the OFT makes a report under subsection (3)

    (a) the OFT must send a copy of it to the Treasury, to the Competition Commission and to the Authority; and

    (b) the OFT may publish it.

(7) Before publishing a report under this section, the OFT must, so far as practicable, exclude any matter which relates to the private affairs of a particular individual the publication of which, in the opinion of the OFT, would or might seriously and prejudicially affect his interests.

(8) Before publishing such a report, the OFT must exclude any matter which relates to the affairs of a particular body the publication of which, in the opinion of the OFT, would or might seriously and prejudicially affect its interests.

(9) Subsections (7) and (8) do not apply to the copy of a report which the OFT is required to send to the Treasury, the Competition Commission and the Authority under subsection (5)(a) or (6)(a).

(10) For the purposes of the law of defamation, absolute privilege attaches to any report of the OFT under this section.

### 305  Investigations by OFT

(1) For the purpose of investigating any matter with a view to its consideration under section 303 or 304, the OFT may exercise the powers conferred on it by this section.

(2) The OFT may by notice in writing require any person to produce to it or to a person appointed by it for the purpose, at a time and place specified in the notice, any document which—

    (a) is specified or described in the notice; and

    (b) is a document in that person's custody or under his control.

(3) The OFT may by notice in writing—

    (a) require any person carrying on any business to provide it with such information as may be specified or described in the notice; and

    (b) specify the time within which, and the manner and form in which, any such information is to be provided.

(4) A requirement may be imposed under subsection (2) or (3)(a) only in respect of documents or information which relate to any matter relevant to the investigation.

(5) If a person ('the defaulter') refuses, or otherwise fails, to comply with a notice under this section, the OFT may certify that fact in writing to the court and the court may enquire into the case.

(6) If, after hearing any witness who may be produced against or on behalf of the defaulter and any statement which may be offered in defence, the court is satisfied that the defaulter did not have a reasonable excuse for refusing or otherwise failing to comply with the notice, the court may deal with the defaulter as if he were in contempt.

(7) In this section, 'the court' means—

    (a) the High Court; or

    (b) in Scotland, the Court of Session.

*Role of Competition Commission*

### 306  Consideration by Competition Commission

(1) If subsection (2) or (3) applies, the Commission must investigate the matter which is the subject of the OFT's report.

(2) This subsection applies if the OFT sends to the Competition Commission a report—

    (a) issued by the OFT under section 303(3) which concludes that one or more regulatory provisions have a significantly adverse effect on competition, or

    (b) made by the OFT under section 304(2).

(3) This subsection applies if the OFT asks the Commission to consider a report—

    (a) issued by the OFT under section 303(3) which concludes that one or more regulatory provisions do not have a significantly adverse effect on competition, or

    (b) made by the OFT under section 304(3).

(4) The Commission must then make its own report on the matter unless it considers that, as a result of a change of circumstances, no useful purpose would be served by a report.

(5) If the Commission decides in accordance with subsection (4) not to make a report, it must make a statement setting out the change of circumstances which resulted in that decision.

(6) A report made under this section must state the Commission's conclusion as to whether—

    (a) the regulatory provision or practice which is the subject of the report has a significantly adverse effect on competition, or

    (b) the regulatory provisions or practices or combination of regulatory provisions and practices which are the subject of the report have such an effect.

(7) A report under this section stating the Commission's conclusion that there is a significantly adverse effect on competition must also—

    (a) state whether the Commission considers that that effect is justified; and

    (b) if it states that the Commission considers that it is not justified, state its conclusion as to what action, if any, the Treasury ought to direct the Authority to take.

(8) Subsection (9) applies whenever the Commission is considering, for the purposes of this section, whether a particular adverse effect on competition is justified.

(9) The Commission must ensure, so far as that is reasonably possible, that the conclusion it reaches is compatible with the obligations imposed on the recognised body concerned by or under this Act.

(10) A report under this section must contain such an account of the Commission's reasons for its conclusions as is expedient, in the opinion of the Commission, for facilitating proper understanding of them.

(11) The provisions of Schedule 14 (except paragraph 2(b)) apply for the purposes of this section as they apply for the purposes of section 162.

(12) If the Commission makes a report under this section it must send a copy to the Treasury, the Authority and the OFT.

(13) Subsection (14) applies if—

   (a) the case relates to an application for recognition under section 287, other than an application by an overseas applicant; and

   (b) subsection (2)(a) or (3)(a) of this section applies.

(14) The Commission must—

   (a) make a report under this section, or a statement under subsection (5), before the end of the period of 12 weeks beginning with the date on which it receives a copy of the OFT's report under section 303(3); and

   (b) if it makes a statement under subsection (5), send a copy to the Authority and the Treasury.

*Role of the Treasury*

### 307    Recognition orders: role of the Treasury

(1) Subsection (2) applies if, on an application for a recognition order—

   (a) the OFT makes a report under section 303 but does not ask the Competition Commission to consider it under section 306;

   (b) the Competition Commission concludes—

      (i)   that the applicant's regulatory provisions do not have a significantly adverse effect on competition; or

      (ii)  that if those provisions do have that effect, the effect is justified.

(2) The Treasury may refuse to approve the making of the recognition order only if they consider that the exceptional circumstances of the case make it inappropriate for them to give their approval.

(3) Subsection (4) applies if, on an application for a recognition order, the Competition Commission concludes—

   (a) that the applicant's regulatory provisions have a significantly adverse effect on competition; and

   (b) that that effect is not justified.

(4) The Treasury must refuse to approve the making of the recognition order unless they consider that the exceptional circumstances of the case make it inappropriate for them to refuse their approval.

(5) Subsection (6) applies in the case of an application for recognition under section 287, other than an application by an overseas applicant.

(6) The Treasury must decide whether to approve the application before the end of the period of 10 days beginning with—

   (a) in a case falling within subsection (2)(a) or (3)(a) of section 306, the date on which they receive a copy of the report under that section or, if no such report was made, of the statement under subsection (5) of that section;

   (b) in any other case, the date on which they receive a copy of the report from the OFT under section 303.

### 308    Directions by the Treasury

(1) This section applies if the Competition Commission makes a report under section 306(4)(other than a report on an application for a recognition order) which states the Commission's conclusion that there is a significantly adverse effect on competition.

(2) If the Commission's conclusion, as stated in the report, is that the adverse effect on competition is not justified, the Treasury must give a remedial direction to the Authority.

(3) But subsection (2) does not apply if the Treasury consider—

   (a) that, as a result of action taken by the Authority or the recognised body concerned in response to the Commission's report, it is unnecessary for them to give a direction; or

   (b) that the exceptional circumstances of the case make it inappropriate or unnecessary for them to do so.

(4) In considering the action to be specified in a remedial direction, the Treasury must have regard to any conclusion of the Commission included in the report because of section 306(7)(b).

(5) Subsection (6) applies if—

   (a) the Commission's conclusion, as stated in its report, is that the adverse effect on competition is justified; but

   (b) the Treasury consider that the exceptional circumstances of the case require them to act.

(6) The Treasury may give a direction to the Authority requiring it to take such action—

   (a) as they consider to be necessary in the light of the exceptional circumstances of the case; and

   (b) as may be specified in the direction.

(7) If the action specified in a remedial direction is the giving by the Authority of a direction—

   (a) the direction to be given must be compatible with the recognition requirements applicable to the recognised body in relation to which it is given; and

(b) subsections (3) and (4) of section 296 apply to it as if it were a direction given under that section.

(8) 'Remedial direction' means a direction requiring the Authority—

(a) to revoke the recognition order for the body concerned; or

(b) to give such directions to the body concerned as may be specified in it.

### 309   Statements by the Treasury

(1) If, in reliance on subsection (3)(a) or (b) of section 308, the Treasury decline to act under subsection (2) of that section, they must make a statement to that effect, giving their reasons.

(2) If the Treasury give a direction under section 308 they must make a statement giving—

(a) details of the direction; and

(b) if the direction is given under subsection (6) of that section, their reasons for giving it.

(3) The Treasury must—

(a) publish any statement made under this section in the way appearing to them best calculated to bring it to the attention of the public; and

(b) lay a copy of it before Parliament.

### 310   Procedure on exercise of certain powers by the Treasury

(1) Subsection (2) applies if the Treasury are considering—

(a) whether to refuse their approval under section 307;

(b) whether section 308(2) applies; or

(c) whether to give a direction under section 308(6).

(2) The Treasury must—

(a) take such steps as they consider appropriate to allow the exchange or clearing house concerned, and any other person appearing to the Treasury to be affected, an opportunity to make representations—

(i) about any report made by the OFT under section 303 or 304 or by the Competition Commission under section 306;

(ii) as to whether, and if so how, the Treasury should exercise their powers under section 307 or 308; and

(b) have regard to any such representations.

## Chapter III

## Exclusion from the Competition Act 1998

### 311   The Chapter I prohibition

(1) The Chapter I prohibition does not apply to an agreement for the constitution of a recognised body to the extent to which the agreement relates to the regulatory provisions of that body.

(2) If the conditions set out in subsection (3) are satisfied, the Chapter I prohibition does not apply to an agreement for the constitution of—

(a) an investment exchange which is not a recognised investment exchange, or

(b) a clearing house which is not a recognised clearing house,

to the extent to which the agreement relates to the regulatory provisions of that body.

(3) The conditions are that—

(a) the body has applied for a recognition order in accordance with the provisions of this Act; and

(b) the application has not been determined.

(4) The Chapter I prohibition does not apply to a recognised body's regulatory provisions.

(5) The Chapter I prohibition does not apply to a decision made by a recognised body to the extent to which the decision relates to any of that body's regulatory provisions or practices.

(6) The Chapter I prohibition does not apply to practices of a recognised body.

(7) The Chapter I prohibition does not apply to an agreement the parties to which consist of or include—

(a) a recognised body, or

(b) a person who is subject to the rules of a recognised body,

to the extent to which the agreement consists of provisions the inclusion of which is required or encouraged by any of the body's regulatory provisions or practices.

(8) If a recognised body's recognition order is revoked, this section is to have effect as if that body had continued to be recognised until the end of the period of six months beginning with the day on which the revocation took effect.

(9) 'The Chapter I prohibition' means the prohibition imposed by section 2(1) of the Competition Act 1998.

(10) Expressions used in this section which are also used in Part I of the Competition Act 1998 are to be interpreted in the same way as for the purposes of that Part of that Act.

### 312 The Chapter II prohibition

(1) The Chapter II prohibition does not apply to—

(a) practices of a recognised body;

(b) the adoption or enforcement of such a body's regulatory provisions;

(c) any conduct which is engaged in by such a body or by a person who is subject to the rules of such a body to the extent to which it is encouraged or required by the regulatory provisions of the body.

(2) The Chapter II prohibition means the prohibition imposed by section 18(1) of the Competition Act 1998.

### 312A Exercise of passport rights by EEA market operator

(1) An EEA market operator may, in pursuance of the right under the applicable provision, make arrangements in the United Kingdom to facilitate access to, or use of, a specified regulated market or specified multilateral trading facility operated by it if—

(a) the operator has given its home state regulator notice of its intention to make such arrangements; and

(b) the home state regulator has given the Authority notice of the operator's intention.

(2) In making arrangements under subsection (1), the operator is exempt from the general prohibition as respects any regulated activity which is carried on as a part of its business of operating the market or facility in question, or in connection with, or for the purposes of, that business.

(3) 'Specified' means specified in the notice referred to in subsection (1)(a).

(4) This section does not apply to an overseas investment exchange.

### 312B Removal of passport rights from EEA market operator

(1) The Authority may prohibit an EEA market operator from making or, as the case may be, continuing arrangements in the United Kingdom, in pursuance of the applicable provision, to facilitate access to, or use of, a regulated market or multilateral trading facility operated by the operator if—

(a) the Authority has clear and demonstrable grounds for believing that the operator has contravened a relevant requirement, and

(b) the Authority has first complied with subsections (3) to (9).

(2) A requirement is relevant if it is imposed—

(a) by the operator's home state regulator in the implementation of the markets in financial instruments directive or any Community legislation made under that directive;

(b) by provision implementing that directive, or any Community legislation made under it, in the operator's home state; or

(c) by any directly applicable Community regulation made under that directive.

(3) The Authority must notify the operator and its home state regulator of its finding under subsection (1)(a).

(4) The notice to the home state regulator under subsection (3) must—

(a) request that the home state regulator take all appropriate measures for the purpose of ensuring that the operator puts an end to the contravention; and

(b) state that the Authority proposes to exercise the power under subsection (1) if the operator continues the contravention.

(5) The Authority may not exercise the power under subsection (1) unless satisfied—

(a) either—

(i) that the home state regulator has failed or refused to take measures for the purpose mentioned in subsection (4)(a); or

(ii) that the measures taken by the home state regulator have proved inadequate for that purpose; and

(b) that the operator is acting in a manner which is clearly prejudicial to the interests of investors in the United Kingdom or the orderly functioning of the financial markets.

(6) If the Authority is satisfied as mentioned in subsection (5), it must give written notice to—

(a) the operator, and

(b) the home state regulator,

of its intention to exercise the power under subsection (1).

(7) A notice under subsection (6) must—

(a) state why the Authority intends to exercise its power under subsection (1), and

(b) in the case of the notice to the operator, inform the operator that it may make representations to the Authority before the end of the representation period.

(8) The representation period is—

(a) the period of two months beginning with the date on which the notice is given to the operator; or

(b) such longer period as the Authority may allow in a particular case.

(9) If, having considered any representations made by the operator, the Authority decides to exercise the power under subsection (1), it must—

(a) notify the operator in writing that it will be prohibited from making or, as the case may be, continuing the arrangements mentioned in that subsection from the date specified in the notice; and

(b) notify the home state regulator of the action to be taken in relation to the operator.

(10) If the Authority exercises the power under subsection (1) it must at the earliest opportunity notify the Commission of the action taken in relation to the operator.

(11) The exemption conferred on an operator by section 312A(2) ceases to apply if the Authority exercises the power under subsection (1) in relation to the operator.

(12) The right to make the arrangements mentioned in subsection (1) may be reinstated in relation to the operator (together with the exemption mentioned in subsection (11)) if the Authority is satisfied that the contravention which led to the Authority exercising the power under subsection (1) has been remedied.

### 312C   Exercise of passport rights by recognised investment exchange

(1) Subject to subsection (4), a recognised investment exchange may, in pursuance of the right under the applicable provision, make arrangements in an EEA State (other than the United Kingdom) to facilitate access to, or use of, a regulated market or multilateral trading facility operated by the exchange ('the relevant arrangements').

(2) The exchange must give the Authority written notice of its intention to make the relevant arrangements which—

(a) describes the arrangements, and

(b) identifies the EEA State in which it intends to make them.

(3) The Authority must, within one month of receiving a notice under subsection (2), send a copy of it to the host state regulator.

(4) The exchange may not make the relevant arrangements until the Authority has complied with subsection (3).

(5) Subsection (6) applies if the Authority receives a request for information—

(a) under the second sub-paragraph of Article 31.6 of the markets in financial instruments directive (in the case of relevant arrangements relating to a multilateral trading facility), or

(b) under the third sub-paragraph of Article 42.6 of that directive (in the case of relevant arrangements relating to a regulated market),

from the host state regulator.

(6) The Authority must, as soon as reasonably practicable, comply with the request.

(7) 'Host state regulator' means the competent authority (within the meaning of Article 4.1.22 of the markets in financial instruments directive) of the EEA State in which the exchange intends to make, or has made, the relevant arrangements.

(8) This section does not apply to an overseas investment exchange.

### 312D   Interpretation of Chapter 3A

In this Chapter—

'the applicable provision' means—

(a) in the case of arrangements relating to a multilateral trading facility, Article 31.5 of the markets in financial instruments directive; and

(b) in the case of arrangements relating to a regulated market, the first sub-paragraph of Article 42.6 of that directive;

'EEA market operator' means a person who is a market operator (within the meaning of Article 4.1.13 of the markets in financial instruments directive) whose home state is an EEA State other than the United Kingdom;

'home state', in relation to an EEA market operator, means the EEA State in which it has its registered office, or if it has no registered office, its head office;

'home state regulator' means the competent authority (within the meaning of Article 4.1.22 of the markets in financial instruments directive) of the EEA State which is the home state in relation to the EEA market operator concerned.

## Chapter IV

*Interpretation*

### 313   Interpretation of Part XVIII

(1) In this Part—

'application' means an application for a recognition order made under section 287 or 288;

'applicant' means a body corporate or unincorporated association which has applied for a recognition order;

'OFT' means the Office of Fair Trading

'multilateral trading facility' has the meaning given in Article 4.1.15 of the markets in financial instruments directive

'overseas applicant' means a body corporate or association which has neither its head office nor its registered office in the United Kingdom and which has applied for a recognition order;

'overseas investment exchange' means a body corporate or association which has neither its head office nor its registered office in the United Kingdom and in relation to which a recognition order is in force;

'overseas clearing house' means a body corporate or association which has neither its head office nor its registered office in the United Kingdom and in relation to which a recognition order is in force;

'recognised body' means a recognised investment exchange or a recognised clearing house;

'recognised clearing house' has the meaning given in section 285;

'recognised investment exchange' has the meaning given in section 285;

'recognition order' means an order made under section 290 or 292;

'recognition requirements' has the meaning given by section 286;

'regulated market' has the meaning given in Article 4.1.14 of the markets in financial instruments directive;

'remedial direction' has the meaning given in section 308(8);

'revocation order' has the meaning given in section 297.

(2) References in this Part to rules of an investment exchange (or a clearing house) are to rules made, or conditions imposed, by the investment exchange (or the clearing house) with respect to—

    (a) recognition requirements;

    (b) admission of persons to, or their exclusion from the use of, its facilities; or

    (c) matters relating to its constitution.

(3) References in this Part to guidance issued by an investment exchange are references to guidance issued, or any recommendation made, in writing or other legible form and intended to have continuing effect, by the investment exchange to—

    (a) all or any class of its members or users, or

    (b) persons seeking to become members of the investment exchange or to use its facilities,

with respect to any of the matters mentioned in subsection (2)(a) to (c).

(4) References in this Part to guidance issued by a clearing house are to guidance issued, or any recommendation made, in writing or other legible form and intended to have continuing effect, by the clearing house to—

    (a) all or any class of its members, or

    (b) persons using or seeking to use its services,

with respect to the provision by it or its members of clearing services.

### 313A Authority's power to require suspension or removal of financial instruments from trading

(1) The Authority may, for the purpose of protecting—

    (a) the interests of investors, or

    (b) the orderly functioning of the financial markets,

require an institution to suspend or remove a financial instrument from trading.

(2) If the Authority exercises the power conferred by subsection (1), the institution concerned or, if any, the issuer of the financial instrument concerned may refer the matter to the Tribunal.

(3) In this section, 'trading' includes trading otherwise than on a regulated market or a multilateral trading facility.

### 313B Suspension or removal of financial instruments from trading: procedure

(1) A requirement imposed on an institution under section 313A (a 'relevant requirement') takes effect—

    (a) immediately, if the notice given under subsection (2) states that this is the case;

    (b) in any other case, on such date as may be specified in the notice.

(2) If the Authority proposes to impose a relevant requirement on an institution, or imposes such a requirement with immediate effect, it must give written notice to—

    (a) the institution, and

    (b) if any, the issuer of the financial instrument in question.

(3) The notice must—

    (a) give details of the relevant requirement;

    (b) state the Authority's reasons for imposing the requirement and choosing the date on which it took effect or takes effect;

    (c) inform the recipient that he may make representations to the Authority within such period as may be specified by the notice (whether or not he has referred the matter to the Tribunal);

    (d) inform him of the date on which the requirement took effect or takes effect; and

    (e) inform him of his right to refer the matter to the Tribunal and give an indication of the procedure on such a reference.

(4) The Authority may extend the period within which representations may be made to it.

(5) If, having considered any representations made to it by the institution or any issuer, the Authority decides—

    (a) to impose the relevant requirement proposed, or

(b) if it has been imposed, not to revoke it, it must give the institution and any issuer written notice.

(6) If, having considered any representations made to it by the institution or any issuer, the Authority decides—

(a) not to impose the relevant requirement proposed, or

(b) to revoke a requirement which has been imposed,

it must give the institution and any issuer written notice.

(7) A notice given under subsection (5) must inform the recipient of his right to refer the matter to the Tribunal.

(8) Subsections (9) and (10) apply if—

(a) the Authority has imposed a relevant requirement on an institution, and

(b) the institution or any issuer of the financial instrument in question has applied for the revocation of the requirement.

(9) If the Authority decides to grant the application, it must give the institution and any issuer written notice of its decision.

(10) If the Authority proposes to refuse the application, it must give the institution and any issuer a warning notice.

(11) If, having considered any representations made in response to the warning notice, the Authority decides to refuse the application, it must give the institution and any issuer a decision notice.

(12) If the Authority gives a decision notice under subsection (11), the recipient may refer the matter to the Tribunal.

### 313C    Notification in relation to suspension or removal of a financial instrument from trading

(1) If the Authority exercises the power under section 313A(1) in relation to a financial instrument traded on a regulated market, it must as soon as reasonably practicable—

(a) publish its decision in such manner as it considers appropriate, and

(b) inform the competent authorities of all other EEA States of its decision.

(2) If the Authority receives notice from a recognised investment exchange that the exchange has suspended or removed a financial instrument from trading on a regulated market operated by it, the Authority must inform the competent authorities of all other EEA States of the action taken by the exchange.

(3) Subsections (4) and (5) apply if the Authority receives notice from the competent authority of another EEA State that that authority, pursuant to Article 41.2 of the markets in financial instruments directive—

(a) has required the suspension of a financial instrument from trading, or

(b) has required the removal of a financial instrument from trading.

(4) In the case of a notice under subsection (3)(a), the Authority—

(a) must require each recognised investment exchange to suspend the instrument from trading on any regulated market operated by the exchange, and

(b) must require each institution operating a multilateral trading facility to suspend the instrument from trading on that facility,

unless such a step would be likely to cause significant damage to the interests of investors or the orderly functioning of the financial markets.

(5) In the case of a notice under subsection (3)(b), the Authority—

(a) must require each recognised investment exchange to remove the instrument from trading on any regulated market operated by the exchange, and

(b) must require each institution operating a multilateral trading facility to remove the instrument from trading on that facility,

unless such a step would be likely to cause significant damage to the interests of investors or the orderly functioning of the financial markets.

(6) 'Competent authority' has the meaning given in Article 4.1.22 of the markets in financial instruments directive.

### 313D    Interpretation of Part 18A

In this Part—

'financial instrument' has the meaning given in Article 4.1.17 of the markets in financial instruments directive;

'institution' means—

(a) a recognised investment exchange, other than an overseas investment exchange (within the meaning of Part 18);

(b) an investment firm;

(c) a credit institution authorised under the banking consolidation directive, when carrying on investment services and activities; or

(d) an institution which would satisfy the requirements for authorisation as a credit institution under that directive if it had its registered office (or if it does not have a registered office, its head office) in an EEA State, but does not include an EEA firm qualifying for authorisation under Schedule 3;

'issuer', in relation to a financial instrument, means the person who issued the instrument;

'multilateral trading facility' has the meaning given in Article 4.1.15 of the markets in financial instruments directive;

'regulated market' has the meaning given in Article 4.1.14 of the markets in financial instruments directive.

# PART XIX

## LLOYD'S

### *General*

### 314 Authority's general duty

(1) The Authority must keep itself informed about—

(a) the way in which the Council supervises and regulates the market at Lloyd's; and

(b) the way in which regulated activities are being carried on in that market.

(2) The Authority must keep under review the desirability of exercising—

(a) any of its powers under this Part;

(b) any powers which it has in relation to the Society as a result of section 315.

### *The Society*

### 315 The Society: authorisation and permission

(1) The Society is an authorised person.

(2) The Society has permission to carry on a regulated activity of any of the following kinds—

(a) arranging deals in contracts of insurance written at Lloyd's ('the basic market activity');

(b) arranging deals in participation in Lloyd's syndicates ('the secondary market activity'); and

(c) an activity carried on in connection with, or for the purposes of, the basic or secondary market activity.

(3) For the purposes of Part IV, the Society's permission is to be treated as if it had been given on an application for permission under that Part.

(4) The power conferred on the Authority by section 45 may be exercised in anticipation of the coming into force of the Society's permission (or at any other time).

(5) The Society is not subject to any requirement of this Act concerning the registered office of a body corporate.

### *Power to apply Act to Lloyd's underwriting*

### 316 Direction by Authority

(1) The general prohibition or (if the general prohibition is not applied under this section) a core provision applies to the carrying on of an insurance market activity by—

(a) a member of the Society, or

(b) the members of the Society taken together,

only if the Authority so directs.

(2) A direction given under subsection (1) which applies a core provision is referred to in this Part as 'an insurance market direction'.

(3) In subsection (1)—

'core provision' means a provision of this Act mentioned in section 317; and

'insurance market activity' means a regulated activity relating to contracts of insurance written at Lloyd's.

(4) In deciding whether to give a direction under subsection (1), the Authority must have particular regard to—

(a) the interests of policyholders and potential policyholders;

(b) any failure by the Society to satisfy an obligation to which it is subject as a result of a provision of the law of another EEA State which—

(i) gives effect to any of the insurance directives; and

(ii) is applicable to an activity carried on in that State by a person to whom this section applies;

(c) the need to ensure the effective exercise of the functions which the Authority has in relation to the Society as a result of section 315.

(5) A direction under subsection (1) must be in writing.

(6) A direction under subsection (1) applying the general prohibition may apply it in relation to different classes of person.

(7) An insurance market direction—

(a) must specify each core provision, class of person and kind of activity to which it applies;

    (b) may apply different provisions in relation to different classes of person and different kinds of activity.

    (8) A direction under subsection (1) has effect from the date specified in it, which may not be earlier than the date on which it is made.

    (9) A direction under subsection (1) must be published in the way appearing to the Authority to be best calculated to bring it to the attention of the public.

    (10) The Authority may charge a reasonable fee for providing a person with a copy of the direction.

    (11) The Authority must, without delay, give the Treasury a copy of any direction which it gives under this section.

### 317 The core provisions

    (1) The core provisions are Parts V, X, XI, XII, XIV, XV, XVI, XXII and XXIV, sections 384 to 386 and Part XXVI.

    (2) References in an applied core provision to an authorised person are (where necessary) to be read as references to a person in the class to which the insurance market direction applies.

    (3) An insurance market direction may provide that a core provision is to have effect, in relation to persons to whom the provision is applied by the direction, with modifications.

### 318 Exercise of powers through Council

    (1) The Authority may give a direction under this subsection to the Council or to the Society (acting through the Council) or to both.

    (2) A direction under subsection (1) is one given to the body concerned—

        (a) in relation to the exercise of its powers generally with a view to achieving, or in support of, a specified objective; or

        (b) in relation to the exercise of a specified power which it has, whether in a specified manner or with a view to achieving, or in support of, a specified objective.

    (3) 'Specified' means specified in the direction.

    (4) A direction under subsection (1) may be given—

        (a) instead of giving a direction under section 316(1); or

        (b) if the Authority considers it necessary or expedient to do so, at the same time as, or following, the giving of such a direction.

    (5) A direction may also be given under subsection (1) in respect of underwriting agents as if they were among the persons mentioned in section 316(1).

    (6) A direction under this section—

        (a) does not, at any time, prevent the exercise by the Authority of any of its powers;

        (b) must be in writing.

    (7) A direction under subsection (1) must be published in the way appearing to the Authority to be best calculated to bring it to the attention of the public.

    (8) The Authority may charge a reasonable fee for providing a person with a copy of the direction.

    (9) The Authority must, without delay, give the Treasury a copy of any direction which it gives under this section.

### 319 Consultation

    (1) Before giving a direction under section 316 or 318, the Authority must publish a draft of the proposed direction.

    (2) The draft must be accompanied by—

        (a) a cost benefit analysis; and

        (b) notice that representations about the proposed direction may be made to the Authority within a specified time.

    (3) Before giving the proposed direction, the Authority must have regard to any representations made to it in accordance with subsection (2)(b).

    (4) If the Authority gives the proposed direction it must publish an account, in general terms, of—

        (a) the representations made to it in accordance with subsection (2)(b); and

        (b) its response to them.

    (5) If the direction differs from the draft published under subsection (1) in a way which is, in the opinion of the Authority, significant—

        (a) the Authority must (in addition to complying with subsection (4)) publish details of the difference; and

        (b) those details must be accompanied by a cost benefit analysis.

    (6) Subsections (1) to (5) do not apply if the Authority considers that the delay involved in complying with them would be prejudicial to the interests of consumers.

    (7) Neither subsection (2)(a) nor subsection (5)(b) applies if the Authority considers—

        (a) that, making the appropriate comparison, there will be no increase in costs; or

        (b) that, making that comparison, there will be an increase in costs but the increase will be of minimal significance.

(8) The Authority may charge a reasonable fee for providing a person with a copy of a draft published under subsection (1).

(9) When the Authority is required to publish a document under this section it must do so in the way appearing to it to be best calculated to bring it to the attention of the public.

(10) 'Cost benefit analysis' means an estimate of the costs together with an analysis of the benefits that will arise—

    (a) if the proposed direction is given; or

    (b) if subsection (5)(b) applies, from the direction that has been given.

(11) 'The appropriate comparison' means—

    (a) in relation to subsection (2)(a), a comparison between the overall position if the direction is given and the overall position if it is not given;

    (b) in relation to subsection (5)(b), a comparison between the overall position after the giving of the direction and the overall position before it was given.

### *Former underwriting members*

### 320 Former underwriting members

(1) A former underwriting member may carry out each contract of insurance that he has underwritten at Lloyd's whether or not he is an authorised person.

(2) If he is an authorised person, any Part IV permission that he has does not extend to his activities in carrying out any of those contracts.

(3) The Authority may impose on a former underwriting member such requirements as appear to it to be appropriate for the purpose of protecting policyholders against the risk that he may not be able to meet his liabilities.

(4) A person on whom a requirement is imposed may refer the matter to the Tribunal.

### 321 Requirements imposed under section 320

(1) A requirement imposed under section 320 takes effect—

    (a) immediately, if the notice given under subsection (2) states that that is the case;

    (b) in any other case, on such date as may be specified in that notice.

(2) If the Authority proposes to impose a requirement on a former underwriting member ('A') under section 320, or imposes such a requirement on him which takes effect immediately, it must give him written notice.

(3) The notice must—

    (a) give details of the requirement;

    (b) state the Authority's reasons for imposing it;

    (c) inform A that he may make representations to the Authority within such period as may be specified in the notice (whether or not he has referred the matter to the Tribunal);

    (d) inform him of the date on which the requirement took effect or will take effect; and

    (e) inform him of his right to refer the matter to the Tribunal.

(4) The Authority may extend the period allowed under the notice for making representations.

(5) If, having considered any representations made by A, the Authority decides—

    (a) to impose the proposed requirement, or

    (b) if it has been imposed, not to revoke it,

it must give him written notice.

(6) If the Authority decides—

    (a) not to impose a proposed requirement, or

    (b) to revoke a requirement that has been imposed,

it must give A written notice.

(7) If the Authority decides to grant an application by A for the variation or revocation of a requirement, it must give him written notice of its decision.

(8) If the Authority proposes to refuse an application by A for the variation or revocation of a requirement it must give him a warning notice.

(9) If the Authority, having considered any representations made in response to the warning notice, decides to refuse the application, it must give A a decision notice.

(10) A notice given under—

    (a) subsection (5), or

    (b) subsection (9) in the case of a decision to refuse the application,

must inform A of his right to refer the matter to the Tribunal.

(11) If the Authority decides to refuse an application for a variation or revocation of the requirement, the applicant may refer the matter to the Tribunal.

(12) If a notice informs a person of his right to refer a matter to the Tribunal, it must give an indication of the procedure on such a reference.

### 322 Rules applicable to former underwriting members

(1) The Authority may make rules imposing such requirements on persons to whom the rules apply as appear to it to be appropriate for protecting policyholders against the risk that those persons may not be able to meet their liabilities.

(2)  The rules may apply to—
   (a)  former underwriting members generally; or
   (b)  to a class of former underwriting member specified in them.

(3)  Section 319 applies to the making of proposed rules under this section as it applies to the giving of a proposed direction under section 316.

(4)  Part X (except sections 152 to 154) does not apply to rules made under this section.

*Transfers of business done at Lloyd's*

## 323  Transfer schemes

The Treasury may by order provide for the application of any provision of Part VII (with or without modification) in relation to schemes for the transfer of the whole or any part of the business carried on by one or more members of the Society or former underwriting members.

*Supplemental*

## 324  Interpretation of this Part

(1)  In this Part—

'arranging deals', in relation to the investments to which this Part applies, has the same meaning as in paragraph 3 of Schedule 2;

'former underwriting member' means a person ceasing to be an underwriting member of the Society on, or at any time after, 24 December 1996; and

'participation in Lloyd's syndicates', in relation to the secondary market activity, means the investment described in sub-paragraph (1) of paragraph 21 of Schedule 2.

(2)  A term used in this Part which is defined in Lloyd's Act 1982 has the same meaning as in that Act.

# PART XX

# PROVISION OF FINANCIAL SERVICES BY MEMBERS OF THE PROFESSIONS

## 325  Authority's general duty

(1)  The Authority must keep itself informed about—
   (a)  the way in which designated professional bodies supervise and regulate the carrying on of exempt regulated activities by members of the professions in relation to which they are established;
   (b)  the way in which such members are carrying on exempt regulated activities.

(2)  In this Part—

'exempt regulated activities' means regulated activities which may, as a result of this Part, be carried on by members of a profession which is supervised and regulated by a designated professional body without breaching the general prohibition; and

'members', in relation to a profession, means persons who are entitled to practise the profession in question and, in practising it, are subject to the rules of the body designated in relation to that profession, whether or not they are members of that body.

(3)  The Authority must keep under review the desirability of exercising any of its powers under this Part.

(4)  Each designated professional body must co-operate with the Authority, by the sharing of information and in other ways, in order to enable the Authority to perform its functions under this Part.

## 326  Designation of professional bodies

(1)  The Treasury may by order designate bodies for the purposes of this Part.

(2)  A body designated under subsection (1) is referred to in this Part as a designated professional body.

(3)  The Treasury may designate a body under subsection (1) only if they are satisfied that—
   (a)  the basic condition, and
   (b)  one or more of the additional conditions,
are met in relation to it.

(4)  The basic condition is that the body has rules applicable to the carrying on by members of the profession in relation to which it is established of regulated activities which, if the body were to be designated, would be exempt regulated activities.

(5)  The additional conditions are that—
   (a)  the body has power under any enactment to regulate the practice of the profession;
   (b)  being a member of the profession is a requirement under any enactment for the exercise of particular functions or the holding of a particular office;
   (c)  the body has been recognised for the purpose of any enactment other than this Act and the recognition has not been withdrawn;

(d) the body is established in an EEA State other than the United Kingdom and in that State—

    (i) the body has power corresponding to that mentioned in paragraph (a);

    (ii) there is a requirement in relation to the body corresponding to that mentioned in paragraph (b); or

    (iii) the body is recognised in a manner corresponding to that mentioned in paragraph (c).

(6) 'Enactment' includes an Act of the Scottish Parliament, Northern Ireland legislation and subordinate legislation (whether made under an Act, an Act of the Scottish Parliament or Northern Ireland legislation).

(7) 'Recognised' means recognised by—

(a) a Minister of the Crown;

(b) the Scottish Ministers;

(c) a Northern Ireland Minister;

(d) a Northern Ireland department or its head.

## 327   Exemption from the general prohibition

(1) The general prohibition does not apply to the carrying on of a regulated activity by a person ('P') if—

(a) the conditions set out in subsections (2) to (7) are satisfied; and

(b) there is not in force—

    (i) a direction under section 328, or

    (ii) an order under section 329,

    which prevents this subsection from applying to the carrying on of that activity by him.

(2) P must be—

(a) a member of a profession; or

(b) controlled or managed by one or more such members.

(3) P must not receive from a person other than his client any pecuniary reward or other advantage, for which he does not account to his client, arising out of his carrying on of any of the activities.

(4) The manner of the provision by P of any service in the course of carrying on the activities must be incidental to the provision by him of professional services.

(5) P must not carry on, or hold himself out as carrying on, a regulated activity other than—

(a) one which rules made as a result of section 332(3) allow him to carry on; or

(b) one in relation to which he is an exempt person.

(6) The activities must not be of a description, or relate to an investment of a description, specified in an order made by the Treasury for the purposes of this subsection.

(7) The activities must be the only regulated activities carried on by P (other than regulated activities in relation to which he is an exempt person).

(8) 'Professional services' means services—

(a) which do not constitute carrying on a regulated activity, and

(b) the provision of which is supervised and regulated by a designated professional body.

## 328   Directions in relation to the general prohibition

(1) The Authority may direct that section 327(1) is not to apply to the extent specified in the direction.

(2) A direction under subsection (1)—

(a) must be in writing;

(b) may be given in relation to different classes of person or different descriptions of regulated activity.

(3) A direction under subsection (1) must be published in the way appearing to the Authority to be best calculated to bring it to the attention of the public.

(4) The Authority may charge a reasonable fee for providing a person with a copy of the direction.

(5) The Authority must, without delay, give the Treasury a copy of any direction which it gives under this section.

(6) The Authority may exercise the power conferred by subsection (1) only if it is satisfied either—

(a) that it is desirable to do so in order to protect the interests of clients; or

(b) that it is necessary to do so in order to comply with a Community obligation imposed by the insurance mediation directive.

(7) In considering whether it is so satisfied of a matter in specified in subsection 6 (a), the Authority must have regard amongst other things to the effectiveness of any arrangements made by any designated professional body—

(a) for securing compliance with rules made under section 332(1);

(b) for dealing with complaints against its members in relation to the carrying on by them of exempt regulated activities;

(c) in order to offer redress to clients who suffer, or claim to have suffered, loss as a result of misconduct by its members in their carrying on of exempt regulated activities;

(d) for co-operating with the Authority under section 325(4).

(8) In this Part 'clients' means—

(a) persons who use, have used or are or may be contemplating using, any of the services provided by a member of a profession in the course of carrying on exempt regulated activities;

(b) persons who have rights or interests which are derived from, or otherwise attributable to, the use of any such services by other persons; or

(c) persons who have rights or interests which may be adversely affected by the use of any such services by persons acting on their behalf or in a fiduciary capacity in relation to them.

(9) If a member of a profession is carrying on an exempt regulated activity in his capacity as a trustee, the persons who are, have been or may be beneficiaries of the trust are to be treated as persons who use, have used or are or may be contemplating using services provided by that person in his carrying on of that activity.

### 329  Orders in relation to the general prohibition

(1) Subsection (2) applies if it appears to the Authority that a person to whom, as a result of section 327(1), the general prohibition does not apply is not a fit and proper person to carry on regulated activities in accordance with that section.

(2) The Authority may make an order disapplying section 327(1) in relation to that person to the extent specified in the order.

(3) The Authority may, on the application of the person named in an order under subsection (1), vary or revoke it.

(4) 'Specified' means specified in the order.

(5) If a partnership is named in an order under this section, the order is not affected by any change in its membership.

(6) If a partnership named in an order under this section is dissolved, the order continues to have effect in relation to any partnership which succeeds to the business of the dissolved partnership.

(7) For the purposes of subsection (6), a partnership is to be regarded as succeeding to the business of another partnership only if—

(a) the members of the resulting partnership are substantially the same as those of the former partnership; and

(b) succession is to the whole or substantially the whole of the business of the former partnership.

### 330  Consultation

(1) Before giving a direction under section 328(1), the Authority must publish a draft of the proposed direction.

(2) The draft must be accompanied by—

(a) a cost benefit analysis; and

(b) notice that representations about the proposed direction may be made to the Authority within a specified time.

(3) Before giving the proposed direction, the Authority must have regard to any representations made to it in accordance with subsection (2)(b).

(4) If the Authority gives the proposed direction it must publish an account, in general terms, of—

(a) the representations made to it in accordance with subsection (2)(b); and

(b) its response to them.

(5) If the direction differs from the draft published under subsection (1) in a way which is, in the opinion of the Authority, significant—

(a) the Authority must (in addition to complying with subsection (4)) publish details of the difference; and

(b) those details must be accompanied by a cost benefit analysis.

(6) Subsections (1) to (5) do not apply if the Authority considers that the delay involved in complying with them would prejudice the interests of consumers.

(7) Neither subsection (2)(a) nor subsection (5)(b) applies if the Authority considers—

(a) that, making the appropriate comparison, there will be no increase in costs; or

(b) that, making that comparison, there will be an increase in costs but the increase will be of minimal significance.

(8) The Authority may charge a reasonable fee for providing a person with a copy of a draft published under subsection (1).

(9) When the Authority is required to publish a document under this section it must do so in the way appearing to it to be best calculated to bring it to the attention of the public.

(10) 'Cost benefit analysis' means an estimate of the costs together with an analysis of the benefits that will arise—

(a) if the proposed direction is given; or

(b) if subsection (5)(b) applies, from the direction that has been given.

(11) 'The appropriate comparison' means—

(a) in relation to subsection (2)(a), a comparison between the overall position if the direction is given and the overall position if it is not given;

(b) in relation to subsection (5)(b), a comparison between the overall position after the giving of the direction and the overall position before it was given.

**331   Procedure on making or varying orders under section 329**

(1) If the Authority proposes to make an order under section 329, it must give the person concerned a warning notice.

(2) The warning notice must set out the terms of the proposed order.

(3) If the Authority decides to make an order under section 329, it must give the person concerned a decision notice.

(4) The decision notice must—

(a) name the person to whom the order applies;

(b) set out the terms of the order; and

(c) be given to the person named in the order.

(5) Subsections (6) to (8) apply to an application for the variation or revocation of an order under section 329.

(6) If the Authority decides to grant the application, it must give the applicant written notice of its decision.

(7) If the Authority proposes to refuse the application, it must give the applicant a warning notice.

(8) If the Authority decides to refuse the application, it must give the applicant a decision notice.

(9) A person—

(a) against whom the Authority have decided to make an order under section 329, or

(b) whose application for the variation or revocation of such an order the Authority had decided to refuse,

may refer the matter to the Tribunal.

(10) The Authority may not make an order under section 329 unless—

(a) the period within which the decision to make to the order may be referred to the Tribunal has expired and no such reference has been made; or

(b) if such a reference has been made, the reference has been determined.

**332   Rules in relation to persons to whom the general prohibition does not apply**

(1) The Authority may make rules applicable to persons to whom, as a result of section 327(1), the general prohibition does not apply.

(2) The power conferred by subsection (1) is to be exercised for the purpose of ensuring that clients are aware that such persons are not authorised persons.

(3) A designated professional body must make rules—

(a) applicable to members of the profession in relation to which it is established who are not authorised persons; and

(b) governing the carrying on by those members of regulated activities (other than regulated activities in relation to which they are exempt persons).

(4) Rules made in compliance with subsection (3) must be designed to secure that, in providing a particular professional service to a particular client, the member carries on only regulated activities which arise out of, or are complementary to, the provision by him of that service to that client.

(5) Rules made by a designated professional body under subsection (3) require the approval of the Authority.

**333   False claims to be a person to whom the general prohibition does not apply**

(1) A person who—

(a) describes himself (in whatever terms) as a person to whom the general prohibition does not apply, in relation to a particular regulated activity, as a result of this Part, or

(b) behaves, or otherwise holds himself out, in a manner which indicates (or which is reasonably likely to be understood as indicating) that he is such a person,

is guilty of an offence if he is not such a person.

(2) In proceedings for an offence under this section it is a defence for the accused to show that he took all reasonable precautions and exercised all due diligence to avoid committing the offence.

(3) A person guilty of an offence under this section is liable on summary conviction to imprisonment for a term not exceeding six months or a fine not exceeding level 5 on the standard scale, or both.

(4) But where the conduct constituting the offence involved or included the public display of any material, the maximum fine for the offence is level 5 on the standard scale multiplied by the number of days for which the display continued.

# PART XXI

# MUTUAL SOCIETIES

## *Friendly societies*

### 334  The Friendly Societies Commission

(1)  The Treasury may by order provide—

(a)  for any functions of the Friendly Societies Commission to be transferred to the Authority;

(b)  for any functions of the Friendly Societies Commission which have not been, or are not being, transferred to the Authority to be transferred to the Treasury.

(2)  If the Treasury consider it appropriate to do so, they may by order provide for the Friendly Societies Commission to cease to exist on a day specified in or determined in accordance with the order.

(3)  The enactments relating to friendly societies which are mentioned in Part I of Schedule 18 are amended as set out in that Part.

(4)  Part II of Schedule 18—

(a)  removes certain restrictions on the ability of incorporated friendly societies to form subsidiaries and control corporate bodies; and

(b)  makes connected amendments.

### 335  The Registry of Friendly Societies

(1)  The Treasury may by order provide—

(a)  for any functions of the Chief Registrar of Friendly Societies, or of an assistant registrar of friendly societies for the central registration area, to be transferred to the Authority;

(b)  for any of their functions which have not been, or are not being, transferred to the Authority to be transferred to the Treasury.

(2)  The Treasury may by order provide—

(a)  for any functions of the central office of the registry of friendly societies to be transferred to the Authority;

(b)  for any functions of that office which have not been, or are not being, transferred to the Authority to be transferred to the Treasury.

(3)  The Treasury may by order provide—

(a)  for any functions of the assistant registrar of friendly societies for Scotland to be transferred to the Authority;

(b)  for any functions of the assistant registrar which have not been, or are not being, transferred to the Authority to be transferred to the Treasury.

(4)  If the Treasury consider it appropriate to do so, they may by order provide for—

(a)  the office of Chief Registrar of Friendly Societies,

(b)  the office of assistant registrar of friendly societies for the central registration area,

(c)  the central office, or

(d)  the office of assistant registrar of friendly societies for Scotland,

to cease to exist on a day specified in or determined in accordance with the order.

## *Building societies*

### 336  The Building Societies Commission

(1)  The Treasury may by order provide—

(a)  for any functions of the Building Societies Commission to be transferred to the Authority;

(b)  for any functions of the Building Societies Commission which have not been, or are not being, transferred to the Authority to be transferred to the Treasury.

(2)  If the Treasury consider it appropriate to do so, they may by order provide for the Building Societies Commission to cease to exist on a day specified in or determined in accordance with the order.

(3)  The enactments relating to building societies which are mentioned in Part III of Schedule 18 are amended as set out in that Part.

### 337  The Building Societies Investor Protection Board

The Treasury may by order provide for the Building Societies Investor Protection Board to cease to exist on a day specified in or determined in accordance with the order.

## *Industrial and provident societies and credit unions*

### 338  Industrial and provident societies and credit unions

(1)  The Treasury may by order provide for the transfer to the Authority of any functions conferred by—

(a)  the Industrial and Provident Societies Act 1965;

(b)  the Industrial and Provident Societies Act 1967;

(c)  the Friendly and Industrial and Provident Societies Act 1968;

(d) the Industrial and Provident Societies Act 1975;

(e) the Industrial and Provident Societies Act 1978;

(f) the Credit Unions Act 1979.

(2) The Treasury may by order provide for the transfer to the Treasury of any functions under those enactments which have not been, or are not being, transferred to the Authority.

(3) The enactments relating to industrial and provident societies which are mentioned in Part IV of Schedule 18 are amended as set out in that Part.

(4) The enactments relating to credit unions which are mentioned in Part V of Schedule 18 are amended as set out in that Part.

*Supplemental*

### 339 Supplemental provisions

(1) The additional powers conferred by section 428 on a person making an order under this Act include power for the Treasury, when making an order under section 334, 335, 336 or 338 which transfers functions, to include provision—

    (a) for the transfer of any functions of a member of the body, or servant or agent of the body or person, whose functions are transferred by the order;

    (b) for the transfer of any property, rights or liabilities held, enjoyed or incurred by any person in connection with transferred functions;

    (c) for the carrying on and completion by or under the authority of the person to whom functions are transferred of any proceedings, investigations or other matters commenced, before the order takes effect, by or under the authority of the person from whom the functions are transferred;

    (d) amending any enactment relating to transferred functions in connection with their exercise by, or under the authority of, the person to whom they are transferred;

    (e) for the substitution of the person to whom functions are transferred for the person from whom they are transferred, in any instrument, contract or legal proceedings made or begun before the order takes effect.

(2) The additional powers conferred by section 428 on a person making an order under this Act include power for the Treasury, when making an order under section 334(2), 335(4), 336(2) or 337, to include provision—

    (a) for the transfer of any property, rights or liabilities held, enjoyed or incurred by any person in connection with the office or body which ceases to have effect as a result of the order;

    (b) for the carrying on and completion by or under the authority of such person as may be specified in the order of any proceedings, investigations or other matters commenced, before the order takes effect, by or under the authority of the person whose office, or the body which, ceases to exist as a result of the order;

    (c) amending any enactment which makes provision with respect to that office or body;

    (d) for the substitution of the Authority, the Treasury or such other body as may be specified in the order in any instrument, contract or legal proceedings made or begun before the order takes effect.

(3) On or after the making of an order under any of sections 334 to 338 ('the original order'), the Treasury may by order make any incidental, supplemental, consequential or transitional provision which they had power to include in the original order.

(4) A certificate issued by the Treasury that property vested in a person immediately before an order under this Part takes effect has been transferred as a result of the order is conclusive evidence of the transfer.

(5) Subsections (1) and (2) are not to be read as affecting in any way the powers conferred by section 428.


# PART XXII


# AUDITORS AND ACTUARIES

*Appointment*

### 340 Appointment

(1) Rules may require an authorised person, or an authorised person falling within a specified class—

    (a) to appoint an auditor, or

    (b) to appoint an actuary,

if he is not already under an obligation to do so imposed by another enactment.

(2) Rules may require an authorised person, or an authorised person falling within a specified class—

    (a) to produce periodic financial reports; and

(b) to have them reported on by an auditor or an actuary.

(3) Rules may impose such other duties on auditors of, or actuaries acting for, authorised persons as may be specified.

(4) Rules under subsection (1) may make provision—

 (a) specifying the manner in which and time within which an auditor or actuary is to be appointed;

 (b) requiring the Authority to be notified of an appointment;

 (c) enabling the Authority to make an appointment if no appointment has been made or notified;

 (d) as to remuneration;

 (e) as to the term of office, removal and resignation of an auditor or actuary.

(5) An auditor or actuary appointed as a result of rules under subsection (1), or on whom duties are imposed by rules under subsection (3)—

 (a) must act in accordance with such provision as may be made by rules; and

 (b) is to have such powers in connection with the discharge of his functions as may be provided by rules.

(6) In subsections (1) to (3) 'auditor' or 'actuary' means an auditor, or actuary, who satisfies such requirements as to qualifications, experience and other matters (if any) as may be specified.

(7) 'Specified' means specified in rules.

*Information*

### 341 Access to books etc

(1) An appointed auditor of, or an appointed actuary acting for, an authorised person—

 (a) has a right of access at all times to the authorised person's books, accounts and vouchers; and

 (b) is entitled to require from the authorised person's officers such information and explanations as he reasonably considers necessary for the performance of his duties as auditor or actuary.

(2) 'Appointed' means appointed under or as a result of this Act.

### 342 Information given by auditor or actuary to the Authority

(1) This section applies to a person who is, or has been, an auditor of an authorised person appointed under or as a result of a statutory provision.

(2) This section also applies to a person who is, or has been, an actuary acting for an authorised person and appointed under or as a result of a statutory provision.

(3) An auditor or actuary does not contravene any duty to which he is subject merely because he gives to the Authority—

 (a) information on a matter of which he has, or had, become aware in his capacity as auditor of, or actuary acting for, the authorised person, or

 (b) his opinion on such a matter,

if he is acting in good faith and he reasonably believes that the information or opinion is relevant to any functions of the Authority.

(4) Subsection (3) applies whether or not the auditor or actuary is responding to a request from the Authority.

(5) The Treasury may make regulations prescribing circumstances in which an auditor or actuary must communicate matters to the Authority as mentioned in subsection (3).

(6) It is the duty of an auditor or actuary to whom any such regulations apply to communicate a matter to the Authority in the circumstances prescribed by the regulations.

(7) The matters to be communicated to the Authority in accordance with the regulations may include matters relating to persons other than the authorised person concerned.

### 343 Information given by auditor or actuary to the Authority: persons with close links

(1) This section applies to a person who—

 (a) is, or has been, an auditor of an authorised person appointed under or as a result of a statutory provision; and

 (b) is, or has been, an auditor of a person ('CL') who has close links with the authorised person.

(2) This section also applies to a person who—

 (a) is, or has been, an actuary acting for an authorised person and appointed under or as a result of a statutory provision; and

 (b) is, or has been, an actuary acting for a person ('CL') who has close links with the authorised person.

(3) An auditor or actuary does not contravene any duty to which he is subject merely because he gives to the Authority—

 (a) information on a matter concerning the authorised person of which he has, or had, become aware in his capacity as auditor of, or actuary acting for, CL, or

(b)  his opinion on such a matter,

if he is acting in good faith and he reasonably believes that the information or opinion is relevant to any functions of the Authority.

(4)  Subsection (3) applies whether or not the auditor or actuary is responding to a request from the Authority.

(5)  The Treasury may make regulations prescribing circumstances in which an auditor or actuary must communicate matters to the Authority as mentioned in subsection (3).

(6)  It is the duty of an auditor or actuary to whom any such regulations apply to communicate a matter to the Authority in the circumstances prescribed by the regulations.

(7)  The matters to be communicated to the Authority in accordance with the regulations may include matters relating to persons other than the authorised person concerned.

(8)  CL has close links with the authorised person concerned ('A') if CL is—

(a)  a parent undertaking of A;

(b)  a subsidiary undertaking of A;

(c)  a parent undertaking of a subsidiary undertaking of A; or

(d)  a subsidiary undertaking of a parent undertaking of A.

(9)  'Subsidiary undertaking' includes all the instances mentioned in Article 1(1) and (2) of the Seventh Company Law Directive in which an entity may be a subsidiary of an undertaking.

### 344  Duty of auditor or actuary resigning etc to give notice

(1)  This section applies to an auditor or actuary to whom section 342 applies.

(2)  He must without delay notify the Authority if he—

(a)  is removed from office by an authorised person;

(b)  resigns before the expiry of his term of office with such a person; or

(c)  is not re-appointed by such a person.

(3)  If he ceases to be an auditor of, or actuary acting for, such a person, he must without delay notify the Authority—

(a)  of any matter connected with his so ceasing which he thinks ought to be drawn to the Authority's attention; or

(b)  that there is no such matter.

*Disqualification*

### 345  Disqualification

(1)  If it appears to the Authority that an auditor or actuary to whom section 342 applies has failed to comply with a duty imposed on him under this Act, it may disqualify him from being the auditor of, or (as the case may be) from acting as an actuary for, any authorised person or any particular class of authorised person.

(2)  If the Authority proposes to disqualify a person under this section it must give him a warning notice.

(3)  If it decides to disqualify him it must give him a decision notice.

(4)  The Authority may remove any disqualification imposed under this section if satisfied that the disqualified person will in future comply with the duty in question.

(5)  A person who has been disqualified under this section may refer the matter to the Tribunal.

*Offence*

### 346  Provision of false or misleading information to auditor or actuary

(1)  An authorised person who knowingly or recklessly gives an appointed auditor or actuary information which is false or misleading in a material particular is guilty of an offence and liable—

(a)  on summary conviction, to imprisonment for a term not exceeding six months or a fine not exceeding the statutory maximum, or both;

(b)  on conviction on indictment, to imprisonment for a term not exceeding two years or a fine, or both.

(2)  Subsection (1) applies equally to an officer, controller or manager of an authorised person.

(3)  'Appointed' means appointed under or as a result of this Act.

# PART XXIII

# PUBLIC RECORD, DISCLOSURE OF INFORMATION AND CO-OPERATION

*The public record*

### 347  The record of authorised persons etc

(1)  The Authority must maintain a record of every—

(a)  person who appears to the Authority to be an authorised person;
(b)  authorised unit trust scheme;
(c)  authorised open-ended investment company;
(d)  recognised scheme;
(e)  recognised investment exchange;
(f)  recognised clearing house;
(g)  individual to whom a prohibition order relates;
(h)  approved person; [...]
(ha)  a person to whom subsection 2A applies; and
(i)  person falling within such other class (if any) as the Authority may determine.

(2)  The record must include such information as the Authority considers appropriate and at least the following information—

(a)  in the case of a person appearing to the Authority to be an authorised person—
(i)  information as to the services which he holds himself out as able to provide; and
(ii)  any address of which the Authority is aware at which a notice or other document may be served on him;
(b)  in the case of an authorised unit trust scheme, the name and address of the manager and trustee of the scheme;
(c)  in the case of an authorised open-ended investment company, the name and address of—
(i)  the company;
(ii)  if it has only one director, the director; and
(iii)  its depositary (if any);
(d)  in the case of a recognised scheme, the name and address of—
(i)  the operator of the scheme; and
(ii)  any representative of the operator in the United Kingdom;
(e)  in the case of a recognised investment exchange or recognised clearing house, the name and address of the exchange or clearing house;
(f)  in the case of an individual to whom a prohibition order relates—
(i)  his name; and
(ii)  details of the effect of the order;
(g)  in the case of a person who is an approved person—
(i)  his name;
(ii)  the name of the relevant authorised person;
(iii)  if the approved person is performing a controlled function under an arrangement with a contractor of the relevant authorised person, the name of the contractor.

(2A)  This subsection applies to—
(a)  an appointed representative to whom subsection (1A) of section 39 applies for whom the applicable register (as defined by subsection (1B) of that section) is the record maintained by virtue of subsection (1)(ha) above;
(b)  a person mentioned in subsection (1)(a) of section 39A if—
(i)  the contract with an authorised person to which he is party complies with the applicable requirements (as defined by subsection (7) of that section), and
(ii)  the authorised person has accepted responsibility in writing for the person's activities in carrying on investment services business (as defined by subsection (8) of that section); and
(c)  any person not falling within paragraph (a) or (b) in respect of whom the Authority considers that a record must be maintained for the purpose of securing compliance with Article 23.3 of the markets in financial instruments directive (registration of tied agents).

(3)  If it appears to the Authority that a person in respect of whom there is an entry in the record as a result of one of the paragraphs of subsection (1) has ceased to be a person to whom that paragraph applies, the Authority may remove the entry from the record.

(4)  But if the Authority decides not to remove the entry, it must—
(a)  make a note to that effect in the record; and
(b)  state why it considers that the person has ceased to be a person to whom that paragraph applies.

(5)  The Authority must—
(a)  make the record available for inspection by members of the public in a legible form at such times and in such place or places as the Authority may determine; and
(b)  provide a certified copy of the record, or any part of it, to any person who asks for it—
(i)  on payment of the fee (if any) fixed by the Authority; and
(ii)  in a form (either written or electronic) in which it is legible to the person asking for it.

(6)  The Authority may—
(a)  publish the record, or any part of it;
(b)  exploit commercially the information contained in the record, or any part of that information.

(7) 'Authorised unit trust scheme', 'authorised open-ended investment company' and 'recognised scheme' have the same meaning as in Part XVII, and associated expressions are to be read accordingly.

(8) 'Approved person' means a person in relation to whom the Authority has given its approval under section 59 and 'controlled function' and 'arrangement' have the same meaning as in that section.

(9) 'Relevant authorised person' has the meaning given in section 66.

*Disclosure of information*

### 348    Restrictions on disclosure of confidential information by Authority etc

(1) Confidential information must not be disclosed by a primary recipient, or by any person obtaining the information directly or indirectly from a primary recipient, without the consent of—

(a) the person from whom the primary recipient obtained the information; and

(b) if different, the person to whom it relates.

(2) In this Part 'confidential information' means information which—

(a) relates to the business or other affairs of any person;

(b) was received by the primary recipient for the purposes of, or in the discharge of, any functions of the Authority, the competent authority for the purposes of Part VI or the Secretary of State under any provision made by or under this Act; and

(c) is not prevented from being confidential information by subsection (4).

(3) It is immaterial for the purposes of subsection (2) whether or not the information was received—

(a) by virtue of a requirement to provide it imposed by or under this Act;

(b) for other purposes as well as purposes mentioned in that subsection.

(4) Information is not confidential information if—

(a) it has been made available to the public by virtue of being disclosed in any circumstances in which, or for any purposes for which, disclosure is not precluded by this section; or

(b) it is in the form of a summary or collection of information so framed that it is not possible to ascertain from it information relating to any particular person.

(5) Each of the following is a primary recipient for the purposes of this Part—

(a) the Authority;

(b) any person exercising functions conferred by Part VI on the competent authority;

(c) the Secretary of State;

(d) a person appointed to make a report under section 166;

(e) any person who is or has been employed by a person mentioned in paragraphs (a) to (c);

(f) any auditor or expert instructed by a person mentioned in those paragraphs.

(6) In subsection (5)(f) 'expert' includes—

(a) a competent person appointed by the competent authority under section 97;

(b) a competent person appointed by the Authority or the Secretary of State to conduct an investigation under Part XI;

(c) any body or person appointed under paragraph 6 of Schedule 1 to perform a function on behalf of the Authority.

### 349    Exceptions from section 348

(1) Section 348 does not prevent a disclosure of confidential information which is—

(a) made for the purpose of facilitating the carrying out of a public function; and

(b) permitted by regulations made by the Treasury under this section.

(2) The regulations may, in particular, make provision permitting the disclosure of confidential information or of confidential information of a prescribed kind—

(a) by prescribed recipients, or recipients of a prescribed description, to any person for the purpose of enabling or assisting the recipient to discharge prescribed public functions;

(b) by prescribed recipients, or recipients of a prescribed description, to prescribed persons, or persons of prescribed descriptions, for the purpose of enabling or assisting those persons to discharge prescribed public functions;

(c) by the Authority to the Treasury or the Secretary of State for any purpose;

(d) by any recipient if the disclosure is with a view to or in connection with prescribed proceedings.

(3) The regulations may also include provision—

(a) making any permission to disclose confidential information subject to conditions (which may relate to the obtaining of consents or any other matter);

(b) restricting the uses to which confidential information disclosed under the regulations may be put.

(3A) Section 348 does not apply to—

(a) the disclosure by a recipient to which subsection (3B) applies of confidential information disclosed to it by the Authority in reliance on subsection (1);

(b) the disclosure of such information by a person obtaining it directly or indirectly from a recipient to which subsection (3B) applies.

(3B) This subsection applies to—

    (a) the Panel on Takeovers and Mergers;

    (b) an authority designated as a supervisory authority for the purposes of Article 4.1 of the Takeovers Directive;

    (c) any other person or body that exercises public functions, under legislation in an EEA State other than the United Kingdom, that are similar to the Authority's functions or those of the Panel on Takeovers and Mergers.

(4) In relation to confidential information, each of the following is a 'recipient'—

    (a) a primary recipient;

    (b) a person obtaining the information directly or indirectly from a primary recipient.

(5) 'Public functions' includes—

    (a) functions conferred by or in accordance with any provision contained in any enactment or subordinate legislation;

    (b) functions conferred by or in accordance with any provision contained in the Community Treaties or any Community instrument;

    (c) similar functions conferred on persons by or under provisions having effect as part of the law of a country or territory outside the United Kingdom;

    (d) functions exercisable in relation to prescribed disciplinary proceedings.

(6) 'Enactment' includes—

    (a) an Act of the Scottish Parliament;

    (b) Northern Ireland legislation.

(7) 'Subordinate legislation' has the meaning given in the Interpretation Act 1978 and also includes an instrument made under an Act of the Scottish Parliament or under Northern Ireland legislation.

(8) [...]

### 350   Disclosure of information by the Inland Revenue

(1) No obligation as to secrecy imposed by statute or otherwise prevents the disclosure of Revenue information to—

    (a) the Authority, or

    (b) the Secretary of State,

if the disclosure is made for the purpose of assisting in the investigation of a matter under section 168 or with a view to the appointment of an investigator under that section.

(2) A disclosure may only be made under subsection (1) by or under the authority of the Commissioners of Inland Revenue.

(3) Section 348 does not apply to Revenue information.

(4) Information obtained as a result of subsection (1) may not be used except—

    (a) for the purpose of deciding whether to appoint an investigator under section 168;

    (b) in the conduct of an investigation under section 168;

    (c) in criminal proceedings brought against a person under this Act or the Criminal Justice Act 1993 as a result of an investigation under section 168;

    (d) for the purpose of taking action under this Act against a person as a result of an investigation under section 168;

    (e) in proceedings before the Tribunal as a result of action taken as mentioned in paragraph (d).

(5) Information obtained as a result of subsection (1) may not be disclosed except—

    (a) by or under the authority of the Commissioners of Inland Revenue;

    (b) in proceedings mentioned in subsection (4)(c) or (e) or with a view to their institution.

(6) Subsection (5) does not prevent the disclosure of information obtained as a result of subsection (1) to a person to whom it could have been disclosed under subsection (1).

(7) 'Revenue information' means information held by a person which it would be an offence under section 182 of the Finance Act 1989 for him to disclose.

### 351   Competition information

(1)–(3) [...]

(4) Section 348 does not apply to competition information.

(5) 'Competition information' means information which—

    (a) relates to the affairs of a particular individual or body;

    (b) is not otherwise in the public domain; and

    (c) was obtained under or by virtue of a competition provision.

(6) 'Competition provision' means any provision of—

    (a) an order made under section 95;

    (b) Chapter III of Part X; or

    (c) Chapter II of Part XVIII.

(7) [...]

### 352   Offences

(1) A person who discloses information in contravention of section 348 or 350(5) is guilty of an offence.

(2) A person guilty of an offence under subsection (1) is liable—

    (a) on summary conviction, to imprisonment for a term not exceeding three months or a fine not exceeding the statutory maximum, or both;

    (b) on conviction on indictment, to imprisonment for a term not exceeding two years or a fine, or both.

(3) A person is guilty of an offence if, in contravention of any provision of regulations made under section 349, he uses information which has been disclosed to him in accordance with the regulations.

(4) A person is guilty of an offence if, in contravention of subsection (4) of section 350, he uses information which has been disclosed to him in accordance with that section.

(5) A person guilty of an offence under subsection (3) or (4) is liable on summary conviction to imprisonment for a term not exceeding *three months* or a fine not exceeding level 5 on the standard scale, or both.

(6) In proceedings for an offence under this section it is a defence for the accused to prove—

    (a) that he did not know and had no reason to suspect that the information was confidential information or that it had been disclosed in accordance with section 350;

    (b) that he took all reasonable precautions and exercised all due diligence to avoid committing the offence.[8]

### 353 Removal of other restrictions on disclosure

(1) The Treasury may make regulations permitting the disclosure of any information, or of information of a prescribed kind—

    (a) by prescribed persons for the purpose of assisting or enabling them to discharge prescribed functions under this Act or any rules or regulations made under it;

    (b) by prescribed persons, or persons of a prescribed description, to the Authority for the purpose of assisting or enabling the Authority to discharge prescribed functions.

    (c) by the scheme operator to the Office of Fair Trading for the purpose of assisting or enabling that Office to discharge prescribed functions under the Consumer Credit Act 1974.

(2) Regulations under this section may not make any provision in relation to the disclosure of confidential information by primary recipients or by any person obtaining confidential information directly or indirectly from a primary recipient.

(3) If a person discloses any information as permitted by regulations under this section the disclosure is not to be taken as a contravention of any duty to which he is subject.

*Co-operation*

### 354 Authority's duty to co-operate with others

(1) The Authority must take such steps as it considers appropriate to co-operate with other persons (whether in the United Kingdom or elsewhere) who have functions—

    (a) similar to those of the Authority; or

    (b) in relation to the prevention or detection of financial crime.

(1A) The Authority must take such steps as it considers appropriate to cooperate with—

    (a) the Panel on Takeovers and Mergers;

    (b) an authority designated as a supervisory authority for the purposes of Article 4.1 of the Takeovers Directive;

    (c) any other person or body that exercises functions of a public nature, under legislation in any country or territory outside the United Kingdom, that appear to the Authority to be similar to those of the Panel on Takeovers and Mergers.

(2) Co-operation may include the sharing of information which the Authority is not prevented from disclosing.

(3) 'Financial crime' has the same meaning as in section 6.

## PART XXIV

## INSOLVENCY

*Interpretation*

### 355 Interpretation of this Part

(1) In this Part—

'the 1985 Act' means the Bankruptcy (Scotland) Act 1985;

'the 1986 Act' means the Insolvency Act 1986;

---

[8] In subsection (5) the words 'three months' are to be substituted with '51 weeks' under the Criminal Justice Act 2003 c 44 from a date to be appointed.

'the 1989 Order' means the Insolvency (Northern Ireland) Order 1989;

'body' means a body of persons—

    (a) over which the court has jurisdiction under any provision of, or made under, the 1986 Act (or the 1989 Order); but

    (b) which is not a building society, a friendly society or an industrial and provident society; and

'court' means—

    (a) the court having jurisdiction for the purposes of the 1985 Act or the 1986 Act; or

    (b) in Northern Ireland, the High Court.

    (2) In this Part 'insurer' has such meaning as may be specified in an order made by the Treasury.

## *Voluntary arrangements*

### 356 Authority's powers to participate in proceedings: company voluntary arrangements

    (1) Where a voluntary arrangement has effect under Part I of the 1986 Act in respect of a company or insolvent partnership which is an authorised person, the Authority may apply to the court under section 6 or 7 of that Act.

    (2) Where a voluntary arrangement has been approved under Part II of the 1989 Order in respect of a company or insolvent partnership which is an authorised person, the Authority may apply to the court under Article 19 or 20 of that Order.

    (3) If a person other than the Authority makes an application to the court in relation to the company or insolvent partnership under any of those provisions, the Authority is entitled to be heard at any hearing relating to the application.

### 357 Authority's powers to participate in proceedings: individual voluntary arrangements

    (1) The Authority is entitled to be heard on an application by an individual who is an authorised person under section 253 of the 1986 Act (or Article 227 of the 1989 Order).

    (2) Subsections (3) to (6) apply if such an order is made on the application of such a person.

    (3) A person appointed for the purpose by the Authority is entitled to attend any meeting of creditors of the debtor summoned under section 257 of the 1986 Act (or Article 231 of the 1989 Order).

    (4) Notice of the result of a meeting so summoned is to be given to the Authority by the chairman of the meeting.

    (5) The Authority may apply to the court—

    (a) under section 262 of the 1986 Act (or Article 236 of the 1989 Order); or

    (b) under section 263 of the 1986 Act (or Article 237 of the 1989 Order).

    (6) If a person other than the Authority makes an application to the court under any provision mentioned in subsection (5), the Authority is entitled to be heard at any hearing relating to the application.

### 358 Authority's powers to participate in proceedings: trust deeds for creditors in Scotland

    (1) This section applies where a trust deed has been granted by or on behalf of a debtor who is an authorised person.

    (2) The trustee must, as soon as practicable after he becomes aware that the debtor is an authorised person, send to the Authority—

    (a) in every case, a copy of the trust deed;

    (b) where any other document or information is sent to every creditor known to the trustee in pursuance of paragraph 5(1)(c) of Schedule 5 to the 1985 Act, a copy of such document or information.

    (3) Paragraph 7 of that Schedule applies to the Authority as if it were a qualified creditor who has not been sent a copy of the notice as mentioned in paragraph 5(1)(c) of the Schedule.

    (4) The Authority must be given the same notice as the creditors of any meeting of creditors held in relation to the trust deed.

    (5) A person appointed for the purpose by the Authority is entitled to attend and participate in (but not to vote at) any such meeting of creditors as if the Authority were a creditor under the deed.

    (6) This section does not affect any right the Authority has as a creditor of a debtor who is an authorised person.

    (7) Expressions used in this section and in the 1985 Act have the same meaning in this section as in that Act.

## *Administration orders*

### 359 Administration order

    (1) The Authority may make an administration application under Schedule B1 to the 1986 Act (or present a petition under Article 22 of the 1989 Order) in relation to a company or insolvent partnership which—

    (a) is, or has been, an authorised person;

    (b) is, or has been, an appointed representative; or

(c) is carrying on, or has carried on, a regulated activity in contravention of the general prohibition.

(2) Subsection (3) applies in relation to a petition presented by the Authority by virtue of this section.

(3) Any of the following shall be treated for the purpose of paragraph 11(a) of Schedule B1 to the 1986 Act (or Article 21(1)(a) of the 1989 Order) as unable to pay its debts—

(a) a company or partnership in default on an obligation to pay a sum due and payable under an agreement, [...]

(b) an authorised deposit taker in default on an obligation to pay a sum due and payable in respect of a relevant deposit , and

(c) an authorised reclaim fund in default on an obligation to pay a sum payable as a result of a claim made by virtue of section 1(2)(b) or 2(2)(b) of the Dormant Bank and Building Society Accounts Act 2008.

(4) In this section—

'agreement' means an agreement the making or performance of which constitutes or is part of a regulated activity carried on by the company or partnership,

'authorised deposit taker' means a person with a Part IV permission to accept deposits (but not a person who has a Part IV permission to accept deposits only for the purpose of carrying on another regulated activity in accordance with that permission),

'authorised reclaim fund' means a reclaim fund within the meaning given by section 5(1) of the Dormant Bank and Building Society Accounts Act 2008 that is authorised for the purposes of this Act;

'company' means a company—

(a) in respect of which an administrator may be appointed under Schedule B1 to the 1986 Act, or

(b) to which Article 21 of the 1989 Order applies, and

'relevant deposit' shall, ignoring any restriction on the meaning of deposit arising from the identity of the person making the deposit, be construed in accordance with—

(a) section 22,

(b) any relevant order under that section, and

(c) Schedule 2.

(5) The definition of 'authorised deposit taker' in subsection (4) shall be construed in accordance with—

(a) section 22,

(b) any relevant order under that section, and

(c) Schedule 2.

### 360   Insurers

(1) The Treasury may by order provide that such provisions of Part II of the 1986 Act (or Part III of the 1989 Order) as may be specified are to apply in relation to insurers with such modifications as may be specified.

(2) An order under this section—

(a) may provide that such provisions of this Part as may be specified are to apply in relation to the administration of insurers in accordance with the order with such modifications as may be specified; and

(b) requires the consent of the Secretary of State.

(3) 'Specified' means specified in the order.

### 361   Administrator's duty to report to Authority

(1) This section applies where a company or partnership is—

(a) in administration within the meaning of Schedule B1 to the 1986 Act, or

(b) the subject of an administration order under Part III of the 1989 Order.

(2) If the administrator thinks that the company or partnership is carrying on or has carried on a regulated activity in contravention of the general prohibition, he must report to the Authority without delay.

(3) Subsection (2) does not apply where the administration arises out of an administration order made on an application made or petition presented by the Authority.

### 362   Authority's powers to participate in proceedings

(1) This section applies if a person other than the Authority makes an administration application under Schedule B1 to the 1986 Act (or presents a petition under Article 22 of the 1989 Order) in relation to a company or partnership which—

(a) is, or has been, an authorised person;

(b) is, or has been, an appointed representative; or

(c) is carrying on, or has carried on, a regulated activity in contravention of the general prohibition.

(1A) This section also applies in relation to—

    (a) the appointment under paragraph 14 or 22 of Schedule B1 to the 1986 Act of an administrator of a company of a kind described in subsection (1)(a) to (c), or

    (b) the filing with the court of a copy of notice of intention to appoint an administrator under either of those paragraphs.

(2) The Authority is entitled to be heard—

    (a) at the hearing of the administration application or petition; and

    (b) at any other hearing of the court in relation to the company or partnership under Part II of the 1986 Act (or Part III of the 1989 Order).

(3) Any notice or other document required to be sent to a creditor of the company or partnership must also be sent to the Authority.

(4) The Authority may apply to the court under section 27 of the 1986 Act (or Article 39 of the 1989 Order); and on such an application, section 27(1)(a)(or Article 39(1)(a)) has effect with the omission of the words '(including at least himself)'.

(4A) In respect of an application under subsection (4)—

    (a) paragraph 74(1)(a) and (b) shall have effect as if for the words 'harm the interests of the applicant (whether alone or in common with some or all other members or creditors)' there were substituted the words 'harm the interests of some or all members or creditors', and

    (b) Article 39 of the 1989 Order shall have effect with the omission of the words '(including at least himself').

(5) A person appointed for the purpose by the Authority is entitled—

    (a) to attend any meeting of creditors of the company or partnership summoned under any enactment;

    (b) to attend any meeting of a committee established paragraph 57 of Schedule B1 to the 1986 Act (or Article 38 of the 1989 Order); and

    (c) to make representations as to any matter for decision at such a meeting.

(6) If, during the course of the administration of a company, a compromise or arrangement is proposed between the company and its creditors, or any class of them, the Authority may apply to the court under section 896 or 899 of the Companies Act 2006.

### 362A   Administrator appointed by company or directors

(1) This section applies in relation to a company of a kind described in section 362(1)(a) to (c).

(2) An administrator of the company may not be appointed under paragraph 22 of Schedule B1 to the 1986 Act without the consent of the Authority.

(3) Consent under subsection (2)—

    (a) must be in writing, and

    (b) must be filed with the court along with the notice of intention to appoint under paragraph 27 of that Schedule.

(4) In a case where no notice of intention to appoint is required—

    (a) subsection (3)(b) shall not apply, but

    (b) consent under subsection (2) must accompany the notice of appointment filed under paragraph 29 of that Schedule.

*Receivership*

### 363   Authority's powers to participate in proceedings

(1) This section applies if a receiver has been appointed in relation to a company which—

    (a) is, or has been, an authorised person;

    (b) is, or has been, an appointed representative; or

    (c) is carrying on, or has carried on, a regulated activity in contravention of the general prohibition.

(2) The Authority is entitled to be heard on an application made under section 35 or 63 of the 1986 Act (or Article 45 of the 1989 Order).

(3) The Authority is entitled to make an application under section 41(1)(a) or 69(1)(a) of the 1986 Act (or Article 51(1)(a) of the 1989 Order).

(4) A report under section 48(1) or 67(1) of the 1986 Act (or Article 58(1) of the 1989 Order) must be sent by the person making it to the Authority.

(5) A person appointed for the purpose by the Authority is entitled—

    (a) to attend any meeting of creditors of the company summoned under any enactment;

    (b) to attend any meeting of a committee established under section 49 or 68 of the 1986 Act (or Article 59 of the 1989 Order); and

    (c) to make representations as to any matter for decision at such a meeting.

### 364   Receiver's duty to report to Authority

If—

    (a) a receiver has been appointed in relation to a company, and

(b) it appears to the receiver that the company is carrying on, or has carried on, a regulated activity in contravention of the general prohibition,

the receiver must report the matter to the Authority without delay.

*Voluntary winding up*

### 365 Authority's powers to participate in proceedings

(1) This section applies in relation to a company which—

(a) is being wound up voluntarily;

(b) is an authorised person; and

(c) is not an insurer effecting or carrying out contracts of long-term insurance.

(2) The Authority may apply to the court under section 112 of the 1986 Act (or Article 98 of the 1989 Order) in respect of the company.

(3) The Authority is entitled to be heard at any hearing of the court in relation to the voluntary winding up of the company.

(4) Any notice or other document required to be sent to a creditor of the company must also be sent to the Authority.

(5) A person appointed for the purpose by the Authority is entitled—

(a) to attend any meeting of creditors of the company summoned under any enactment;

(b) to attend any meeting of a committee established under section 101 of the 1986 Act (or Article 87 of the 1989 Order); and

(c) to make representations as to any matter for decision at such a meeting.

(6) The voluntary winding up of the company does not bar the right of the Authority to have it wound up by the court.

(7) If, during the course of the winding up of the company, a compromise or arrangement is proposed between the company and its creditors, or any class of them, the Authority may apply to the court under section 896 or 899 of the Companies Act 2006.

### 366 Insurers effecting or carrying out long-term contracts or insurance

(1) An insurer effecting or carrying out contracts of long-term insurance may not be wound up voluntarily without the consent of the Authority.

(2) If notice of a general meeting of such an insurer is given, specifying the intention to propose a resolution for voluntary winding up of the insurer, a director of the insurer must notify the Authority as soon as practicable after he becomes aware of it.

(3) A person who fails to comply with subsection (2) is guilty of an offence and liable on summary conviction to a fine not exceeding level 5 on the standard scale.

(4) A winding up resolution may not be passed—

(a) as a written resolution (in accordance with Chapter 2 of Part 13 of the Companies Act 2006), or

(b) at a meeting called in accordance with section 307(4) to (6) or 337(2) of that Act (agreement of members to calling of meeting at short notice).

(5) A copy of a winding-up resolution forwarded to the registrar of companies in accordance with section 30 Companies Act 2006 must be accompanied by a certificate issued by the Authority stating that it consents to the voluntary winding up of the insurer.

(6) If subsection (5) is complied with, the voluntary winding up is to be treated as having commenced at the time the resolution was passed.

(7) If subsection (5) is not complied with, the resolution has no effect.

(8) 'Winding-up resolution' means a resolution for voluntary winding up of an insurer effecting or carrying out contracts of long-term insurance.

*Winding up by the court*

### 367 Winding-up petitions

(1) The Authority may present a petition to the court for the winding up of a body which—

(a) is, or has been, an authorised person;

(b) is, or has been, an appointed representative; or

(c) is carrying on, or has carried on, a regulated activity in contravention of the general prohibition.

(2) In subsection (1) 'body' includes any partnership.

(3) On such a petition, the court may wind up the body if—

(a) the body is unable to pay its debts within the meaning of section 123 or 221 of the 1986 Act (or Article 103 or 185 of the 1989 Order); or

(b) the court is of the opinion that it is just and equitable that it should be wound up.

(4) If a body is in default on an obligation to pay a sum due and payable under an agreement, it is to be treated for the purpose of subsection (3)(a) as unable to pay its debts.

(5) 'Agreement' means an agreement the making or performance of which constitutes or is part of a regulated activity carried on by the body concerned.

(6) Subsection (7) applies if a petition is presented under subsection (1) for the winding up of a partnership—

> (a) on the ground mentioned in subsection (3)(b); or
>
> (b) in Scotland, on a ground mentioned in subsection (3)(a) or (b).

(7) The court has jurisdiction, and the 1986 Act (or the 1989 Order) has effect, as if the partnership were an unregistered company as defined by section 220 of that Act (or Article 184 of that Order).

## 368 Winding-up petitions: EEA and Treaty firms

The Authority may not present a petition to the court under section 367 for the winding up of—

> (a) an EEA firm which qualifies for authorisation under Schedule 3, or
>
> (b) a Treaty firm which qualifies for authorisation under Schedule 4,

unless it has been asked to do so by the home state regulator of the firm concerned.

## 369 Insurers: service of petition etc on Authority

(1) If a person other than the Authority presents a petition for the winding up of an authorised person with permission to effect or carry out contracts of insurance, the petitioner must serve a copy of the petition on the Authority.

(2) If a person other than the Authority applies to have a provisional liquidator appointed under section 135 of the 1986 Act (or Article 115 of the 1989 Order) in respect of an authorised person with permission to effect or carry out contracts of insurance, the applicant must serve a copy of the application on the Authority.

## 369A Reclaim funds: service of petition etc on Authority

(1) If a person other than the Authority presents a petition for the winding up of an authorised reclaim fund, the petitioner must serve a copy of the petition on the Authority.

(2) If a person other than the Authority applies to have a provisional liquidator appointed under section 135 of the 1986 Act (or Article 115 of the 1989 Order) in respect of an authorised reclaim fund, the applicant must serve a copy of the application on the Authority.

(3) In this section 'authorised reclaim fund' means a reclaim fund within the meaning given by section 5(1) of the Dormant Bank and Building Society Accounts Act 2008 that is authorised for the purposes of this Act.

## 370 Liquidator's duty to report to Authority

If—

> (a) a company is being wound up voluntarily or a body is being wound up on a petition presented by a person other than the Authority, and
>
> (b) it appears to the liquidator that the company or body is carrying on, or has carried on, a regulated activity in contravention of the general prohibition,

the liquidator must report the matter to the Authority without delay.

## 371 Authority's powers to participate in proceedings

(1) This section applies if a person other than the Authority presents a petition for the winding up of a body which—

> (a) is, or has been, an authorised person;
>
> (b) is, or has been, an appointed representative; or
>
> (c) is carrying on, or has carried on, a regulated activity in contravention of the general prohibition.

(2) The Authority is entitled to be heard—

> (a) at the hearing of the petition; and
>
> (b) at any other hearing of the court in relation to the body under or by virtue of Part IV or V of the 1986 Act (or Part V or VI of the 1989 Order).

(3) Any notice or other document required to be sent to a creditor of the body must also be sent to the Authority.

(4) A person appointed for the purpose by the Authority is entitled—

> (a) to attend any meeting of creditors of the body;
>
> (b) to attend any meeting of a committee established for the purposes of Part IV or V of the 1986 Act under section 101 of that Act or under section 141 or 142 of that Act;
>
> (c) to attend any meeting of a committee established for the purposes of Part V or VI of the 1989 Order under Article 87 of that Order or under Article 120 of that Order; and
>
> (d) to make representations as to any matter for decision at such a meeting.

(5) If, during the course of the winding up of a company, a compromise or arrangement is proposed between the company and its creditors, or any class of them, the Authority may apply to the court under section 896 or 899 of the Companies Act 2006.

*Bankruptcy*

## 372 Petitions

(1) The Authority may present a petition to the court—

(a) under section 264 of the 1986 Act (or Article 238 of the 1989 Order) for a bankruptcy order to be made against an individual; or

(b) under section 5 of the 1985 Act for the sequestration of the estate of an individual.

(2) But such a petition may be presented only on the ground that—

(a) the individual appears to be unable to pay a regulated activity debt; or

(b) the individual appears to have no reasonable prospect of being able to pay a regulated activity debt.

(3) An individual appears to be unable to pay a regulated activity debt if he is in default on an obligation to pay a sum due and payable under an agreement.

(4) An individual appears to have no reasonable prospect of being able to pay a regulated activity debt if—

(a) the Authority has served on him a demand requiring him to establish to the satisfaction of the Authority that there is a reasonable prospect that he will be able to pay a sum payable under an agreement when it falls due;

(b) at least three weeks have elapsed since the demand was served; and

(c) the demand has been neither complied with nor set aside in accordance with rules.

(5) A demand made under subsection (4)(a) is to be treated for the purposes of the 1986 Act (or the 1989 Order) as if it were a statutory demand under section 268 of that Act (or Article 242 of that Order).

(6) For the purposes of a petition presented in accordance with subsection (1)(b)—

(a) the Authority is to be treated as a qualified creditor; and

(b) a ground mentioned in subsection (2) constitutes apparent insolvency.

(7) 'Individual' means an individual—

(a) who is, or has been, an authorised person; or

(b) who is carrying on, or has carried on, a regulated activity in contravention of the general prohibition.

(8) 'Agreement' means an agreement the making or performance of which constitutes or is part of a regulated activity carried on by the individual concerned.

(9) 'Rules' means—

(a) in England and Wales, rules made under section 412 of the 1986 Act;

(b) in Scotland, rules made by order by the Treasury, after consultation with the Scottish Ministers, for the purposes of this section; and

(c) in Northern Ireland, rules made under Article 359 of the 1989 Order.

### 373 Insolvency practitioner's duty to report to Authority

(1) If—

(a) a bankruptcy order or sequestration award is in force in relation to an individual by virtue of a petition presented by a person other than the Authority, and

(b) it appears to the insolvency practitioner that the individual is carrying on, or has carried on, a regulated activity in contravention of the general prohibition,

the insolvency practitioner must report the matter to the Authority without delay.

(2) 'Bankruptcy order' means a bankruptcy order under Part IX of the 1986 Act (or Part IX of the 1989 Order).

(3) 'Sequestration award' means an award of sequestration under section 12 of the 1985 Act.

(4) 'Individual' includes an entity mentioned in section 374(1)(c).

### 374 Authority's powers to participate in proceedings

(1) This section applies if a person other than the Authority presents a petition to the court—

(a) under section 264 of the 1986 Act (or Article 238 of the 1989 Order) for a bankruptcy order to be made against an individual;

(b) under section 5 of the 1985 Act for the sequestration of the estate of an individual; or

(c) under section 6 of the 1985 Act for the sequestration of the estate belonging to or held for or jointly by the members of an entity mentioned in subsection (1) of that section.

(2) The Authority is entitled to be heard—

(a) at the hearing of the petition; and

(b) at any other hearing in relation to the individual or entity under—

(i) Part IX of the 1986 Act;

(ii) Part IX of the 1989 Order; or

(iii) the 1985 Act.

(3) A copy of the report prepared under section 274 of the 1986 Act (or Article 248 of the 1989 Order) must also be sent to the Authority.

(4) A person appointed for the purpose by the Authority is entitled—

(a) to attend any meeting of creditors of the individual or entity;

(b) to attend any meeting of a committee established under section 301 of the 1986 Act (or Article 274 of the 1989 Order);

(c) to attend any meeting of commissioners held under paragraph 17 or 18 of Schedule 6 to the 1985 Act; and

(d) to make representations as to any matter for decision at such a meeting.

(5) 'Individual' means an individual who—

(a) is, or has been, an authorised person; or

(b) is carrying on, or has carried on, a regulated activity in contravention of the general prohibition.

(6) 'Entity' means an entity which—

(a) is, or has been, an authorised person; or

(b) is carrying on, or has carried on, a regulated activity in contravention of the general prohibition.

### *Provisions against debt avoidance*

### 375 Authority's right to apply for an order

(1) The Authority may apply for an order under section 423 of the 1986 Act (or Article 367 of the 1989 Order) in relation to a debtor if—

(a) at the time the transaction at an undervalue was entered into, the debtor was carrying on a regulated activity (whether or not in contravention of the general prohibition); and

(b) a victim of the transaction is or was party to an agreement entered into with the debtor, the making or performance of which constituted or was part of a regulated activity carried on by the debtor.

(2) An application made under this section is to be treated as made on behalf of every victim of the transaction to whom subsection (1)(b) applies.

(3) Expressions which are given a meaning in Part XVI of the 1986 Act (or Article 367, 368 or 369 of the 1989 Order) have the same meaning when used in this section.

### *Supplemental provisions concerning insurers*

### 376 Continuation of contracts of long-term insurance where insurer in liquidation

(1) This section applies in relation to the winding up of an insurer which effects or carries out contracts of long-term insurance.

(2) Unless the court otherwise orders, the liquidator must carry on the insurer's business so far as it consists of carrying out the insurer's contracts of long-term insurance with a view to its being transferred as a going concern to a person who may lawfully carry out those contracts.

(3) In carrying on the business, the liquidator—

(a) may agree to the variation of any contracts of insurance in existence when the winding up order is made; but

(b) must not effect any new contracts of insurance.

(4) If the liquidator is satisfied that the interests of the creditors in respect of liabilities of the insurer attributable to contracts of long-term insurance effected by it require the appointment of a special manager, he may apply to the court.

(5) On such an application, the court may appoint a special manager to act during such time as the court may direct.

(6) The special manager is to have such powers, including any of the powers of a receiver or manager, as the court may direct.

(7) Section 177(5) of the 1986 Act (or Article 151(5) of the 1989 Order) applies to a special manager appointed under subsection (5) as it applies to a special manager appointed under section 177 of the 1986 Act (or Article 151 of the 1989 Order).

(8) If the court thinks fit, it may reduce the value of one or more of the contracts of long-term insurance effected by the insurer.

(9) Any reduction is to be on such terms and subject to such conditions (if any) as the court thinks fit.

(10) The court may, on the application of an official, appoint an independent actuary to investigate the insurer's business so far as it consists of carrying out its contracts of long-term insurance and to report to the official—

(a) on the desirability or otherwise of that part of the insurer's business being continued; and

(b) on any reduction in the contracts of long-term insurance effected by the insurer that may be necessary for successful continuation of that part of the insurer's business.

(11) 'Official' means—

(a) the liquidator;

(b) a special manager appointed under subsection (5); or

(c) the Authority.

(12) The liquidator may make an application in the name of the insurer and on its behalf under Part VII without obtaining the permission that would otherwise be required by section 167 of, and Schedule 4 to, the 1986 Act (or Article 142 of, and Schedule 2 to, the 1989 Order).

### 377   Reducing the value of contracts instead of winding up

(1)  This section applies in relation to an insurer which has been proved to be unable to pay its debts.

(2)  If the court thinks fit, it may reduce the value of one or more of the insurer's contracts instead of making a winding up order.

(3)  Any reduction is to be on such terms and subject to such conditions (if any) as the court thinks fit.

### 378   Treatment of assets on winding up

(1)  The Treasury may by regulations provide for the treatment of the assets of an insurer on its winding up.

(2)  The regulations may, in particular, provide for—

  (a)  assets representing a particular part of the insurer's business to be available only for meeting liabilities attributable to that part of the insurer's business;

  (b)  separate general meetings of the creditors to be held in respect of liabilities attributable to a particular part of the insurer's business.

### 379   Winding-up rules

(1)  Winding-up rules may include provision—

  (a)  for determining the amount of the liabilities of an insurer to policyholders of any class or description for the purpose of proof in a winding up; and

  (b)  generally for carrying into effect the provisions of this Part with respect to the winding up of insurers.

(2)  Winding-up rules may, in particular, make provision for all or any of the following matters—

  (a)  the identification of assets and liabilities;

  (b)  the apportionment, between assets of different classes or descriptions, of—

    (i)   the costs, charges and expenses of the winding up; and

    (ii)  any debts of the insurer of a specified class or description;

  (c)  the determination of the amount of liabilities of a specified description;

  (d)  the application of assets for meeting liabilities of a specified description;

  (e)  the application of assets representing any excess of a specified description.

(3)  'Specified' means specified in winding-up rules.

(4)  'Winding-up rules' means rules made under section 411 of the 1986 Act (or Article 359 of the 1989 Order).

(5)  Nothing in this section affects the power to make winding-up rules under the 1986 Act or the 1989 Order.

# PART XXV

# INJUNCTIONS AND RESTITUTION

*Injunctions*

### 380   Injunctions

(1)  If, on the application of the Authority or the Secretary of State, the court is satisfied—

  (a)  that there is a reasonable likelihood that any person will contravene a relevant requirement, or

  (b)  that any person has contravened a relevant requirement and that there is a reasonable likelihood that the contravention will continue or be repeated,

the court may make an order restraining (or in Scotland an interdict prohibiting) the contravention.

(2)  If on the application of the Authority or the Secretary of State the court is satisfied—

  (a)  that any person has contravened a relevant requirement, and

  (b)  that there are steps which could be taken for remedying the contravention,

the court may make an order requiring that person, and any other person who appears to have been knowingly concerned in the contravention, to take such steps as the court may direct to remedy it.

(3)  If, on the application of the Authority or the Secretary of State, the court is satisfied that any person may have—

  (a)  contravened a relevant requirement, or

  (b)  been knowingly concerned in the contravention of such a requirement,

it may make an order restraining (or in Scotland an interdict prohibiting) him from disposing of, or otherwise dealing with, any assets of his which it is satisfied he is reasonably likely to dispose of or otherwise deal with.

(4)  The jurisdiction conferred by this section is exercisable by the High Court and the Court of Session.

(5)  In subsection (2), references to remedying a contravention include references to mitigating its effect.

(6)  'Relevant requirement'—

(a) in relation to an application by the Authority, means a requirement—
    (i) which is imposed by or under this Act or by any directly applicable Community regulation made under the markets in financial instruments directive; or
    (ii) which is imposed by or under any other Act and whose contravention constitutes an offence which the Authority has power to prosecute under this Act;
(b) in relation to an application by the Secretary of State, means a requirement which is imposed by or under this Act and whose contravention constitutes an offence which the Secretary of State has power to prosecute under this Act.

(7) In the application of subsection (6) to Scotland—
(a) in paragraph (a)(ii) for 'which the Authority has power to prosecute under this Act' substitute 'mentioned in paragraph (a) or (b) of section 402(1)'; and
(b) in paragraph (b) omit 'which the Secretary of State has power to prosecute under this Act'.

## 381  Injunctions in cases of market abuse

(1) If, on the application of the Authority, the court is satisfied—
(a) that there is a reasonable likelihood that any person will engage in market abuse, or
(b) that any person is or has engaged in market abuse and that there is a reasonable likelihood that the market abuse will continue or be repeated,
the court may make an order restraining (or in Scotland an interdict prohibiting) the market abuse.

(2) If on the application of the Authority the court is satisfied—
(a) that any person is or has engaged in market abuse, and
(b) that there are steps which could be taken for remedying the market abuse,
the court may make an order requiring him to take such steps as the court may direct to remedy it.

(3) Subsection (4) applies if, on the application of the Authority, the court is satisfied that any person—
(a) may be engaged in market abuse; or
(b) may have been engaged in market abuse.

(4) The court make an order restraining (or in Scotland an interdict prohibiting) the person concerned from disposing of, or otherwise dealing with, any assets of his which it is satisfied that he is reasonably likely to dispose of, or otherwise deal with.

(5) The jurisdiction conferred by this section is exercisable by the High Court and the Court of Session.

(6) In subsection (2), references to remedying any market abuse include references to mitigating its effect.

### *Restitution orders*

## 382  Restitution orders

(1) The court may, on the application of the Authority or the Secretary of State, make an order under subsection (2) if it is satisfied that a person has contravened a relevant requirement, or been knowingly concerned in the contravention of such a requirement, and—
(a) that profits have accrued to him as a result of the contravention; or
(b) that one or more persons have suffered loss or been otherwise adversely affected as a result of the contravention.

(2) The court may order the person concerned to pay to the Authority such sum as appears to the court to be just having regard—
(a) in a case within paragraph (a) of subsection (1), to the profits appearing to the court to have accrued;
(b) in a case within paragraph (b) of that subsection, to the extent of the loss or other adverse effect;
(c) in a case within both of those paragraphs, to the profits appearing to the court to have accrued and to the extent of the loss or other adverse effect.

(3) Any amount paid to the Authority in pursuance of an order under subsection (2) must be paid by it to such qualifying person or distributed by it among such qualifying persons as the court may direct.

(4) On an application under subsection (1) the court may require the person concerned to supply it with such accounts or other information as it may require for any one or more of the following purposes—
(a) establishing whether any and, if so, what profits have accrued to him as mentioned in paragraph (a) of that subsection;
(b) establishing whether any person or persons have suffered any loss or adverse effect as mentioned in paragraph (b) of that subsection and, if so, the extent of that loss or adverse effect; and
(c) determining how any amounts are to be paid or distributed under subsection (3).

(5) The court may require any accounts or other information supplied under subsection (4) to be verified in such manner as it may direct.

(6) The jurisdiction conferred by this section is exercisable by the High Court and the Court of Session.

(7) Nothing in this section affects the right of any person other than the Authority or the Secretary of State to bring proceedings in respect of the matters to which this section applies.

(8) 'Qualifying person' means a person appearing to the court to be someone—

(a) to whom the profits mentioned in subsection (1)(a) are attributable; or

(b) who has suffered the loss or adverse effect mentioned in subsection (1)(b).

(9) 'Relevant requirement'—

(a) in relation to an application by the Authority, means a requirement—

(i) which is imposed by or under this Act or by any directly applicable Community regulation made under the markets in financial instruments directive; or

(ii) which is imposed by or under any other Act and whose contravention constitutes an offence which the Authority has power to prosecute under this Act;

(b) in relation to an application by the Secretary of State, means a requirement which is imposed by or under this Act and whose contravention constitutes an offence which the Secretary of State has power to prosecute under this Act.

(10) In the application of subsection (9) to Scotland—

(a) in paragraph (a)(ii) for 'which the Authority has power to prosecute under this Act' substitute 'mentioned in paragraph (a) or (b) of section 402(1); and

(b) in paragraph (b) omit 'which the Secretary of State has power to prosecute under this Act'.

### 383    Restitution orders in cases of market abuse

(1) The court may, on the application of the Authority, make an order under subsection (4) if it is satisfied that a person ('the person concerned')—

(a) has engaged in market abuse, or

(b) by taking or refraining from taking any action has required or encouraged another person or persons to engage in behaviour which, if engaged in by the person concerned, would amount to market abuse,

and the condition mentioned in subsection (2) is fulfilled.

(2) The condition is—

(a) that profits have accrued to the person concerned as a result; or

(b) that one or more persons have suffered loss or been otherwise adversely affected as a result.

(3) But the court may not make an order under subsection (4) if it is satisfied that—

(a) the person concerned believed, on reasonable grounds, that his behaviour did not fall within paragraph (a) or (b) of subsection (1); or

(b) he took all reasonable precautions and exercised all due diligence to avoid behaving in a way which fell within paragraph (a) or (b) of subsection (1).

(4) The court may order the person concerned to pay to the Authority such sum as appears to the court to be just having regard—

(a) in a case within paragraph (a) of subsection (2), to the profits appearing to the court to have accrued;

(b) in a case within paragraph (b) of that subsection, to the extent of the loss or other adverse effect;

(c) in a case within both of those paragraphs, to the profits appearing to the court to have accrued and to the extent of the loss or other adverse effect.

(5) Any amount paid to the Authority in pursuance of an order under subsection (4) must be paid by it to such qualifying person or distributed by it among such qualifying persons as the court may direct.

(6) On an application under subsection (1) the court may require the person concerned to supply it with such accounts or other information as it may require for any one or more of the following purposes—

(a) establishing whether any and, if so, what profits have accrued to him as mentioned in subsection (2)(a);

(b) establishing whether any person or persons have suffered any loss or adverse effect as mentioned in subsection (2)(b) and, if so, the extent of that loss or adverse effect; and

(c) determining how any amounts are to be paid or distributed under subsection (5).

(7) The court may require any accounts or other information supplied under subsection (6) to be verified in such manner as it may direct.

(8) The jurisdiction conferred by this section is exercisable by the High Court and the Court of Session.

(9) Nothing in this section affects the right of any person other than the Authority to bring proceedings in respect of the matters to which this section applies.

(10) 'Qualifying person' means a person appearing to the court to be someone—

(a) to whom the profits mentioned in paragraph (a) of subsection (2) are attributable; or

    (b) who has suffered the loss or adverse effect mentioned in paragraph (b) of that
        subsection.

*Restitution required by Authority*

### 384  Power of Authority to require restitution

    (1)  The Authority may exercise the power in subsection (5) if it is satisfied that an authorised person ('the person concerned') has contravened a relevant requirement, or been knowingly concerned in the contravention of such a requirement, and—
        (a) that profits have accrued to him as a result of the contravention; or
        (b) that one or more persons have suffered loss or been otherwise adversely affected as a result
            of the contravention.
    (2)  The Authority may exercise the power in subsection (5) if it is satisfied that a person ('the person concerned')—
        (a) has engaged in market abuse, or
        (b) by taking or refraining from taking any action has required or encouraged another person
            or persons to engage in behaviour which, if engaged in by the person concerned, would
            amount to market abuse,
and the condition mentioned in subsection (3) is fulfilled,
    (3)  The condition is—
        (a) that profits have accrued to the person concerned as a result of the market abuse; or
        (b) that one or more persons have suffered loss or been otherwise adversely affected as a result
            of the market abuse.
    (4)  But the Authority may not exercise that power as a result of subsection (2) if, having considered any representations made to it in response to a warning notice, there are reasonable grounds for it to be satisfied that—
        (a) the person concerned believed, on reasonable grounds, that his behaviour did not fall within
            paragraph (a) or (b) of that subsection; or
        (b) he took all reasonable precautions and exercised all due diligence to avoid behaving in a way
            which fell within paragraph (a) or (b) of that subsection.
    (5)  The power referred to in subsections (1) and (2) is a power to require the person concerned, in accordance with such arrangements as the Authority considers appropriate, to pay to the appropriate person or distribute among the appropriate persons such amount as appears to the Authority to be just having regard—
        (a) in a case within paragraph (a) of subsection (1) or (3), to the profits appearing to the
            Authority to have accrued;
        (b) in a case within paragraph (b) of subsection (1) or (3), to the extent of the loss or other
            adverse effect;
        (c) in a case within paragraphs (a) and (b) of subsection (1) or (3), to the profits appearing to
            the Authority to have accrued and to the extent of the loss or other adverse effect.
    (6)  'Appropriate person' means a person appearing to the Authority to be someone—
        (a) to whom the profits mentioned in paragraph (a) of subsection (1) or (3) are
            attributable; or
        (b) who has suffered the loss or adverse effect mentioned in paragraph (b) of subsection (1)
            or (3).
    (7)  'Relevant requirement' means—
        (a) a requirement imposed by or under this Act or by any directly applicable Community regula-
            tion made under the markets in financial instruments directive ; and
        (b) a requirement which is imposed by or under any other Act and whose contravention
            constitutes an offence in relation to which this Act confers power to prosecute on the
            Authority.
    (8)  In the application of subsection (7) to Scotland, in paragraph (b) for 'in relation to which this Act confers power to prosecute on the Authority' substitute 'mentioned in paragraph (a) or (b) of section 402(1)'.

### 385  Warning notices

    (1)  If the Authority proposes to exercise the power under section 384(5) in relation to a person, it must give him a warning notice.
    (2)  A warning notice under this section must specify the amount which the Authority proposes to require the person concerned to pay or distribute as mentioned in section 384(5).

### 386  Decision notices

    (1)  If the Authority decides to exercise the power under section 384(5), it must give a decision notice to the person in relation to whom the power is exercised.
    (2)  The decision notice must—
        (a) state the amount that he is to pay or distribute as mentioned in section 384(5);

(b) identify the person or persons to whom that amount is to be paid or among whom that amount is to be distributed; and

(c) state the arrangements in accordance with which the payment or distribution is to be made.

(3) If the Authority decides to exercise the power under section 384(5), the person in relation to whom it is exercised may refer the matter to the Tribunal.

# PART XXVI

## NOTICES

### *Warning notices*

**387 Warning notices**

(1) A warning notice must—

(a) state the action which the Authority proposes to take;

(b) be in writing;

(c) give reasons for the proposed action;

(d) state whether section 394 applies; and

(e) if that section applies, describe its effect and state whether any secondary material exists to which the person concerned must be allowed access under it.

(2) The warning notice must specify a reasonable period (which may not be less than 28 days) within which the person to whom it is given may make representations to the Authority.

(3) The Authority may extend the period specified in the notice.

(4) The Authority must then decide, within a reasonable period, whether to give the person concerned a decision notice.

### *Decision notices*

**388 Decision notices**

(1) A decision notice must—

(a) be in writing;

(b) give the Authority's reasons for the decision to take the action to which the notice relates;

(c) state whether section 394 applies;

(d) if that section applies, describe its effect and state whether any secondary material exists to which the person concerned must be allowed access under it; and

(e) give an indication of—

(i) any right to have the matter referred to the Tribunal which is given by this Act; and

(ii) the procedure on such a reference.

(2) If the decision notice was preceded by a warning notice, the action to which the decision notice relates must be action under the same Part as the action proposed in the warning notice.

(3) The Authority may, before it takes the action to which a decision notice ('the original notice') relates, give the person concerned a further decision notice which relates to different action in respect of the same matter.

(4) The Authority may give a further decision notice as a result of subsection (3) only if the person to whom the original notice was given consents.

(5) If the person to whom a decision notice is given under subsection (3) had the right to refer the matter to which the original decision notice related to the Tribunal, he has that right as respects the decision notice under subsection (3).

### *Conclusion of proceedings*

**389 Notices of discontinuance**

(1) If the Authority decides not to take—

(a) the action proposed in a warning notice, or

(b) the action to which a decision notice relates,

it must give a notice of discontinuance to the person to whom the warning notice or decision notice was given.

(2) But subsection (1) does not apply if the discontinuance of the proceedings concerned results in the granting of an application made by the person to whom the warning or decision notice was given.

(3) A notice of discontinuance must identify the proceedings which are being discontinued.

**390 Final notices**

(1) If the Authority has given a person a decision notice and the matter was not referred to the Tribunal within the period mentioned in section 133(1), the Authority must, on taking the action to

which the decision notice relates, give the person concerned and any person to whom the decision notice was copied a final notice.

(2) If the Authority has given a person a decision notice and the matter was referred to the Tribunal, the Authority must, on taking action in accordance with any directions given by—

(a) the Tribunal, or

(b) the court under section 137,

give that person and any person to whom the decision notice was copied a final notice.

(3) A final notice about a statement must—

(a) set out the terms of the statement;

(b) give details of the manner in which, and the date on which, the statement will be published.

(4) A final notice about an order must—

(a) set out the terms of the order;

(b) state the date from which the order has effect.

(5) A final notice about a penalty must—

(a) state the amount of the penalty;

(b) state the manner in which, and the period within which, the penalty is to be paid;

(c) give details of the way in which the penalty will be recovered if it is not paid by the date stated in the notice.

(6) A final notice about a requirement to make a payment or distribution in accordance with section 384(5) must state—

(a) the persons to whom,

(b) the manner in which, and

(c) the period within which,

it must be made.

(7) In any other case, the final notice must—

(a) give details of the action being taken;

(b) state the date on which the action is to be taken.

(8) The period stated under subsection (5)(b) or (6)(c) may not be less than 14 days beginning with the date on which the final notice is given.

(9) If all or any of the amount of a penalty payable under a final notice is outstanding at the end of the period stated under subsection (5)(b), the Authority may recover the outstanding amount as a debt due to it.

(10) If all or any of a required payment or distribution has not been made at the end of a period stated in a final notice under subsection (6)(c), the obligation to make the payment is enforceable, on the application of the Authority, by injunction or, in Scotland, by an order under section 45 of the Court of Session Act 1988.

*Publication*

### 391   Publication

(1) Neither the Authority nor a person to whom a warning notice or decision notice is given or copied may publish the notice or any details concerning it.

(2) A notice of discontinuance must state that, if the person to whom the notice is given consents, the Authority may publish such information as it considers appropriate about the matter to which the discontinued proceedings related.

(3) A copy of a notice of discontinuance must be accompanied by a statement that, if the person to whom the notice is copied consents, the Authority may publish such information as it considers appropriate about the matter to which the discontinued proceedings related, so far as relevant to that person.

(4) The Authority must publish such information about the matter to which a final notice relates as it considers appropriate.

(5) When a supervisory notice takes effect, the Authority must publish such information about the matter to which the notice relates as it considers appropriate.

(6) But the Authority may not publish information under this section if publication of it would, in its opinion, be unfair to the person with respect to whom the action was taken or prejudicial to the interests of consumers.

(7) Information is to be published under this section in such manner as the Authority considers appropriate.

(8) For the purposes of determining when a supervisory notice takes effect, a matter to which the notice relates is open to review if—

(a) the period during which any person may refer the matter to the Tribunal is still running;

(b) the matter has been referred to the Tribunal but has not been dealt with;

(c) the matter has been referred to the Tribunal and dealt with but the period during which an appeal may be brought against the Tribunal's decision is still running; or

(d) such an appeal has been brought but has not been determined.

    (9) 'Notice of discontinuance' means a notice given under section 389.

    (10) 'Supervisory notice' has the same meaning as in section 395.

    (11) 'Consumers' means persons who are consumers for the purposes of section 138.

### *Third party rights and access to evidence*

### 392  Application of sections 393 and 394

Sections 393 and 394 apply to—

    (a) a warning notice given in accordance with section 54(1), 57(1), 63(3), 67(1), 88(4)(b), 89(2), 92(1), 126(1), 207(1), 255(1), 280(1), 331(1), 345(2)(whether as a result of subsection (1) of that section or section 249(1)) or 385(1) or 412(B)(4) or (8);

    (b) a decision notice given in accordance with section 54(2), 57(3), 63(4), 67(4), 88(6)(b), 89(3), 92(4), 127(1), 208(1), 255(2), 280(2), 331(3), 345(3)(whether as a result of subsection (1) of that section or section 249(1)) or 386(1) or 412(B)(5) or (9).

### 393  Third party rights

    (1) If any of the reasons contained in a warning notice to which this section applies relates to a matter which—

    (a) identifies a person ('the third party') other than the person to whom the notice is given, and

    (b) in the opinion of the Authority, is prejudicial to the third party,

a copy of the notice must be given to the third party.

    (2) Subsection (1) does not require a copy to be given to the third party if the Authority—

    (a) has given him a separate warning notice in relation to the same matter; or

    (b) gives him such a notice at the same time as it gives the warning notice which identifies him.

    (3) The notice copied to a third party under subsection (1) must specify a reasonable period (which may not be less than 28 days) within which he may make representations to the Authority.

    (4) If any of the reasons contained in a decision notice to which this section applies relates to a matter which—

    (a) identifies a person ('the third party') other than the person to whom the decision notice is given, and

    (b) in the opinion of the Authority, is prejudicial to the third party,

a copy of the notice must be given to the third party.

    (5) If the decision notice was preceded by a warning notice, a copy of the decision notice must (unless it has been given under subsection (4)) be given to each person to whom the warning notice was copied.

    (6) Subsection (4) does not require a copy to be given to the third party if the Authority—

    (a) has given him a separate decision notice in relation to the same matter; or

    (b) gives him such a notice at the same time as it gives the decision notice which identifies him.

    (7) Neither subsection (1) nor subsection (4) requires a copy of a notice to be given to a third party if the Authority considers it impracticable to do so.

    (8) Subsections (9) to (11) apply if the person to whom a decision notice is given has a right to refer the matter to the Tribunal.

    (9) A person to whom a copy of the notice is given under this section may refer to the Tribunal—

    (a) the decision in question, so far as it is based on a reason of the kind mentioned in subsection (4); or

    (b) any opinion expressed by the Authority in relation to him.

    (10) The copy must be accompanied by an indication of the third party's right to make a reference under subsection (9) and of the procedure on such a reference.

    (11) A person who alleges that a copy of the notice should have been given to him, but was not, may refer to the Tribunal the alleged failure and—

    (a) the decision in question, so far as it is based on a reason of the kind mentioned in subsection (4); or

    (b) any opinion expressed by the Authority in relation to him.

    (12) Section 394 applies to a third party as it applies to the person to whom the notice to which this section applies was given, in so far as the material which the Authority must disclose under that section relates to the matter which identifies the third party.

    (13) A copy of a notice given to a third party under this section must be accompanied by a description of the effect of section 394 as it applies to him.

    (14) Any person to whom a warning notice or decision notice was copied under this section must be given a copy of a notice of discontinuance applicable to the proceedings to which the warning notice or decision notice related.

### 394  Access to Authority material

    (1) If the Authority gives a person ('A') a notice to which this section applies, it must—

(a) allow him access to the material on which it relied in taking the decision which gave rise to the obligation to give the notice;

(b) allow him access to any secondary material which, in the opinion of the Authority, might undermine that decision.

(2) But the Authority does not have to allow A access to material under subsection (1) if the material is excluded material or it—

(a) relates to a case involving a person other than A; and

(b) was taken into account by the Authority in A's case only for purposes of comparison with other cases.

(3) The Authority may refuse access A to particular material which it would otherwise have to allow him access to if, in its opinion, allowing him access to the material—

(a) would not be in the public interest; or

(b) would not be fair, having regard to—

(i) the likely significance of the material to A in relation to the matter in respect of which he has been given a notice to which this section applies; and

(ii) the potential prejudice to the commercial interests of a person other than A which would be caused by the material's disclosure.

(4) If the Authority does not allow A access to material because it is excluded material consisting of a protected item, it must give A written notice of—

(a) the existence of the protected item; and

(b) the Authority's decision not to allow him access to it.

(5) If the Authority refuses under subsection (3) to allow A access to material, it must give him written notice of—

(a) the refusal; and

(b) the reasons for it.

(6) 'Secondary material' means material, other than material falling within paragraph (a) of subsection (1) which—

(a) was considered by the Authority in reaching the decision mentioned in that paragraph; or

(b) was obtained by the Authority in connection with the matter to which the notice to which this section applies relates but which was not considered by it in reaching that decision.

(7) 'Excluded material' means material which—

(a) is material the disclosure of which for the purposes of or in connection with any legal proceedings is prohibited by section 17 of the Regulation of Investigatory Powers Act 2000; or

[...]

(c) is a protected item (as defined in section 413).

### *The Authority's procedures*

### 395   **The Authority's procedures**

(1) The Authority must determine the procedure that it proposes to follow in relation to the giving of—

(a) supervisory notices; and

(b) warning notices and decision notices.

(2) That procedure must be designed to secure, among other things, that the decision which gives rise to the obligation to give any such notice is taken by a person not directly involved in establishing the evidence on which that decision is based.

(3) But the procedure may permit a decision which gives rise to an obligation to give a supervisory notice to be taken by a person other than a person mentioned in subsection (2) if—

(a) the Authority considers that, in the particular case, it is necessary in order to protect the interests of consumers; and

(b) the person taking the decision is of a level of seniority laid down by the procedure.

(4) A level of seniority laid down by the procedure for the purposes of subsection (3)(b) must be appropriate to the importance of the decision.

(5) The Authority must issue a statement of the procedure.

(6) The statement must be published in the way appearing to the Authority to be best calculated to bring it to the attention of the public.

(7) The Authority may charge a reasonable fee for providing a person with a copy of the statement.

(8) The Authority must, without delay, give the Treasury a copy of any statement which it issues under this section.

(9) When giving a supervisory notice, or a warning notice or decision notice, the Authority must follow its stated procedure.

(10) If the Authority changes the procedure in a material way, it must publish a revised statement.

(11) The Authority's failure in a particular case to follow its procedure as set out in the latest published statement does not affect the validity of a notice given in that case.

(12) But subsection (11) does not prevent the Tribunal from taking into account any such failure in considering a matter referred to it.

(13) 'Supervisory notice' means a notice given in accordance with section—

(a)  53(4), (7) or (8)(b);

(b)  78(2) or (5);

(bza)  78A(2) or (8)(b);

(ba)  96C;

(bb)  87O(2) or (5);

(bc)  191B(1);

(c)  197(3), (6) or (7)(b);

(d)  259(3), (8) or (9)(b);

(e)  268(3), (7)(a) or (9)(a)(as a result of subsection (8)(b));

(f)  282(3), (6) or (7)(b);

(fa)  301J (1);

(g)  321(2) or (5).

### 396  Statements under section 395: consultation

(1) Before issuing a statement of procedure under section 395, the Authority must publish a draft of the proposed statement in the way appearing to the Authority to be best calculated to bring it to the attention of the public.

(2) The draft must be accompanied by notice that representations about the proposal may be made to the Authority within a specified time.

(3) Before issuing the proposed statement of procedure, the Authority must have regard to any representations made to it in accordance with subsection (2).

(4) If the Authority issues the proposed statement of procedure it must publish an account, in general terms, of—

(a)  the representations made to it in accordance with subsection (2); and

(b)  its response to them.

(5) If the statement of procedure differs from the draft published under subsection (1) in a way which is, in the opinion of the Authority, significant, the Authority must (in addition to complying with subsection (4)) publish details of the difference.

(6) The Authority may charge a reasonable fee for providing a person with a copy of a draft published under subsection (1).

(7) This section also applies to a proposal to revise a statement of policy.

# PART XXVII

# OFFENCES

## *Miscellaneous offences*

### 397  Misleading statements and practices

(1) This subsection applies to a person who—

(a)  makes a statement, promise or forecast which he knows to be misleading, false or deceptive in a material particular;

(b)  dishonestly conceals any material facts whether in connection with a statement, promise or forecast made by him or otherwise; or

(c)  recklessly makes (dishonestly or otherwise) a statement, promise or forecast which is misleading, false or deceptive in a material particular.

(2) A person to whom subsection (1) applies is guilty of an offence if he makes the statement, promise or forecast or conceals the facts for the purpose of inducing, or is reckless as to whether it may induce, another person (whether or not the person to whom the statement, promise or forecast is made)—

(a)  to enter or offer to enter into, or to refrain from entering or offering to enter into, a relevant agreement; or

(b)  to exercise, or refrain from exercising, any rights conferred by a relevant investment.

(3) Any person who does any act or engages in any course of conduct which creates a false or misleading impression as to the market in or the price or value of any relevant investments is guilty of an offence if he does so for the purpose of creating that impression and of thereby inducing another person to acquire, dispose of, subscribe for or underwrite those investments or to refrain from doing so or to exercise, or refrain from exercising, any rights conferred by those investments.

(4) In proceedings for an offence under subsection (2) brought against a person to whom subsection (1) applies as a result of paragraph (a) of that subsection, it is a defence for him to show that the statement, promise or forecast was made in conformity with

(a) price stabilising rules or control of information rules.

(b) control of information rules; or

(c) the relevant provisions of Commission Regulation (EC) No 2273/2003 of 22 December 2003 implementing Directive 2003/6/EC of the European Parliament and of the Council as regards exemptions for buy-back programmes and stabilisation of financial instruments.

(5) In proceedings brought against any person for an offence under subsection (3) it is a defence for him to show—

(a) that he reasonably believed that his act or conduct would not create an impression that was false or misleading as to the matters mentioned in that subsection;

(b) that he acted or engaged in the conduct—

(i) for the purpose of stabilising the price of investments; and

(ii) in conformity with price stabilising rules;

(c) that he acted or engaged in the conduct in conformity with control of information rules; or

(a) that he acted or engaged in the conduct in conformity with the relevant provisions of Commission Regulation (EC) No 2273/2003 of 22 December 2003 implementing Directive 2003/6/EC of the European Parliament and of the Council as regards exemptions for buy-back programmes and stabilisation of financial instruments.[9]

(6) Subsections (1) and (2) do not apply unless—

(a) the statement, promise or forecast is made in or from, or the facts are concealed in or from, the United Kingdom or arrangements are made in or from the United Kingdom for the statement, promise or forecast to be made or the facts to be concealed;

(b) the person on whom the inducement is intended to or may have effect is in the United Kingdom; or

(c) the agreement is or would be entered into or the rights are or would be exercised in the United Kingdom.

(7) Subsection (3) does not apply unless—

(a) the act is done, or the course of conduct is engaged in, in the United Kingdom; or

(b) the false or misleading impression is created there.

(8) A person guilty of an offence under this section is liable—

(a) on summary conviction, to imprisonment for a term not exceeding six months or a fine not exceeding the statutory maximum, or both;

(b) on conviction on indictment, to imprisonment for a term not exceeding seven years or a fine, or both.

(9) 'Relevant agreement' means an agreement—

(a) the entering into or performance of which by either party constitutes an activity of a specified kind or one which falls within a specified class of activity; and

(b) which relates to a relevant investment.

(10) 'Relevant investment' means an investment of a specified kind or one which falls within a prescribed class of investment.

(11) Schedule 2 (except paragraphs 25 and 26) applies for the purposes of subsections (9) and (10) with references to section 22 being read as references to each of those subsections.

(12) Nothing in Schedule 2, as applied by subsection (11), limits the power conferred by subsection (9) or (10).

(13) 'Investment' includes any asset, right or interest.

(14) 'Specified' means specified in an order made by the Treasury.

### 398   Misleading the Authority: residual cases

(1) A person who, in purported compliance with any requirement imposed by or under this Act, knowingly or recklessly gives the Authority information which is false or misleading in a material particular is guilty of an offence.

(2) Subsection (1) applies only to a requirement in relation to which no other provision of this Act creates an offence in connection with the giving of information.

(3) A person guilty of an offence under this section is liable—

(a) on summary conviction, to a fine not exceeding the statutory maximum;

(b) on conviction on indictment, to a fine.

### 399   Misleading the OFT

Section 44 of the Competition Act 1998 (offences connected with the provision of false or misleading information) applies in relation to any function of the OFT under this Act as if it were a function under Part I of that Act.

---

[9] Possible drafting error, inserted (a) falls after (c), Financial Services and Markets Act 2000 (Market Abuse) Regulations 2005/381 reg 8(3).

*Bodies corporate and partnerships*

### 400 Offences by bodies corporate etc

(1) If an offence under this Act committed by a body corporate is shown—

(a) to have been committed with the consent or connivance of an officer, or

(b) to be attributable to any neglect on his part,

the officer as well as the body corporate is guilty of the offence and liable to be proceeded against and punished accordingly.

(2) If the affairs of a body corporate are managed by its members, subsection (1) applies in relation to the acts and defaults of a member in connection with his functions of management as if he were a director of the body.

(3) If an offence under this Act committed by a partnership is shown—

(a) to have been committed with the consent or connivance of a partner, or

(b) to be attributable to any neglect on his part,

the partner as well as the partnership is guilty of the offence and liable to be proceeded against and punished accordingly.

(4) In subsection (3) 'partner' includes a person purporting to act as a partner.

(5) 'Officer', in relation to a body corporate, means—

(a) a director, member of the committee of management, chief executive, manager, secretary or other similar officer of the body, or a person purporting to act in any such capacity; and

(b) an individual who is a controller of the body.

(6) If an offence under this Act committed by an unincorporated association (other than a partnership) is shown—

(a) to have been committed with the consent or connivance of an officer of the association or a member of its governing body, or

(b) to be attributable to any neglect on the part of such an officer or member,

that officer or member as well as the association is guilty of the offence and liable to be proceeded against and punished accordingly.

(7) Regulations may provide for the application of any provision of this section, with such modifications as the Treasury consider appropriate, to a body corporate or unincorporated association formed or recognised under the law of a territory outside the United Kingdom.

*Institution of proceedings*

### 401 Proceedings for offences

(1) In this section 'offence' means an offence under this Act or subordinate legislation made under this Act.

(2) Proceedings for an offence may be instituted in England and Wales only—

(a) by the Authority or the Secretary of State; or

(b) by or with the consent of the Director of Public Prosecutions.

(3) Proceedings for an offence may be instituted in Northern Ireland only—

(a) by the Authority or the Secretary of State; or

(b) by or with the consent of the Director of Public Prosecutions for Northern Ireland.

(4) Except in Scotland, proceedings for an offence under section 203 may also be instituted by the OFT.

(5) In exercising its power to institute proceedings for an offence, the Authority must comply with any conditions or restrictions imposed in writing by the Treasury.

(6) Conditions or restrictions may be imposed under subsection (5) in relation to—

(a) proceedings generally; or

(b) such proceedings, or categories of proceedings, as the Treasury may direct.

### 402 Power of the Authority to institute proceedings for certain other offences

(1) Except in Scotland, the Authority may institute proceedings for an offence under—

(a) Part V of the Criminal Justice Act 1993 (insider dealing);

(b) prescribed regulations relating to money laundering-; or.

(c) Schedule 7 to the Counter-Terrorism Act 2008 (terrorist financing or money laundering).

(2) In exercising its power to institute proceedings for any such offence, the Authority must comply with any conditions or restrictions imposed in writing by the Treasury.

(3) Conditions or restrictions may be imposed under subsection (2) in relation to—

(a) proceedings generally; or

(b) such proceedings, or categories of proceedings, as the Treasury may direct.

### 403 Jurisdiction and procedure in respect of offences

(1) A fine imposed on an unincorporated association on its conviction of an offence is to be paid out of the funds of the association.

(2) Proceedings for an offence alleged to have been committed by an unincorporated association must be brought in the name of the association (and not in that of any of its members).

(3) Rules of court relating to the service of documents are to have effect as if the association were a body corporate.

(4) In proceedings for an offence brought against an unincorporated association—

(a) section 33 of the Criminal Justice Act 1925 and Schedule 3 to the Magistrates' Courts Act 1980 (procedure) apply as they do in relation to a body corporate;

(b) section 70 of the Criminal Procedure (Scotland) Act 1995 (procedure) applies as if the association were a body corporate;

(c) section 18 of the Criminal Justice (Northern Ireland) Act 1945 and Schedule 4 to the Magistrates' Courts (Northern Ireland) Order 1981 (procedure) apply as they do in relation to a body corporate.

(5) Summary proceedings for an offence may be taken—

(a) against a body corporate or unincorporated association at any place at which it has a place of business;

(b) against an individual at any place where he is for the time being.

(6) Subsection (5) does not affect any jurisdiction exercisable apart from this section.

(7) 'Offence' means an offence under this Act.

# PART XXVIII

## MISCELLANEOUS

### *Schemes for reviewing past business*

**404   Schemes for reviewing past business**

(1) Subsection (2) applies if the Treasury are satisfied that there is evidence suggesting—

(a) that there has been a widespread or regular failure on the part of authorised persons to comply with rules relating to a particular kind of activity; and

(b) that, as a result, private persons have suffered (or will suffer) loss in respect of which authorised persons are (or will be) liable to make payments ('compensation payments').

(2) The Treasury may by order ('a scheme order') authorise the Authority to establish and operate a scheme for—

(a) determining the nature and extent of the failure;

(b) establishing the liability of authorised persons to make compensation payments; and

(c) determining the amounts payable by way of compensation payments.

(3) An authorised scheme must be made so as to comply with specified requirements.

(4) A scheme order may be made only if—

(a) the Authority has given the Treasury a report about the alleged failure and asked them to make a scheme order;

(b) the report contains details of the scheme which the Authority propose to make; and

(c) the Treasury are satisfied that the proposed scheme is an appropriate way of dealing with the failure.

(5) A scheme order may provide for specified provisions of or made under this Act to apply in relation to any provision of, or determination made under, the resulting authorised scheme subject to such modifications (if any) as may be specified.

(6) For the purposes of this Act, failure on the part of an authorised person to comply with any provision of an authorised scheme is to be treated (subject to any provision made by the scheme order concerned) as a failure on his part to comply with rules.

(7) The Treasury may prescribe circumstances in which loss suffered by a person ('A') acting in a fiduciary or other prescribed capacity is to be treated, for the purposes of an authorised scheme, as suffered by a private person in relation to whom A was acting in that capacity.

(8) This section applies whenever the failure in question occurred.

(9) 'Authorised scheme' means a scheme authorised by a scheme order.

(10) 'Private person' has such meaning as may be prescribed.

(11) 'Specified' means specified in a scheme order.

### *Third countries*

**405   Directions**

(1) For the purpose of implementing a third country decision, the Treasury may direct the Authority to—

(a) refuse an application for permission under Part IV made by a body incorporated in, or formed under the law of, any part of the United Kingdom;

(b) defer its decision on such an application either indefinitely or for such period as may be specified in the direction;

(c) give a notice of objection to a person who has served a notice of control to the effect that he proposes to acquire a 50% stake in a UK authorised person; or

(d) give a notice of objection to a person who has acquired a 50% stake in a UK authorised person without having served the required notice of control.

(2) A direction may also be given in relation to—

(a) any person falling within a class specified in the direction;

(b) future applications, notices of control or acquisitions.

(3) The Treasury may revoke a direction at any time.

(4) But revocation does not affect anything done in accordance with the direction before it was revoked.

(5) 'Third country decision' means a decision of the Council or the Commission under—

(a) Article 15(3) of the markets in financial instruments directive;

(b) [...]

(c) Article 29b(4) of the first non-life insurance directive; or

(d) Article 59(4) of the life assurance consolidation directive.

### 406   Interpretation of section 405

(1) For the purposes of section 405, a person ('the acquirer') acquires a 50% stake in a UK authorised person ('A') on first falling within any of the cases set out in subsection (2).

(2) The cases are where the acquirer—

(a) holds 50% or more of the shares in A;

(b) holds 50% or more of the shares in a parent undertaking ('P') of A;

(c) is entitled to exercise, or control the exercise of, 50% or more of the voting power in A; or

(d) is entitled to exercise, or control the exercise of, 50% or more of the voting power in P.

(3) In subsection (2) 'the acquirer' means—

(a) the acquirer;

(b) any of the acquirer's associates; or

(c) the acquirer and any of his associates.

(4) 'Associate', 'shares' and 'voting power' have the same meaning as in section 422.

### 407   Consequences of a direction under section 405

(1) If the Authority refuses an application for permission as a result of a direction under section 405(1)(a)—

(a) subsections (7) to (9) of section 52 do not apply in relation to the refusal; but

(b) the Authority must notify the applicant of the refusal and the reasons for it.

(2) If the Authority defers its decision on an application for permission as a result of a direction under section 405(1)(b)—

(a) the time limit for determining the application mentioned in section 52(1) or (2) stops running on the day of the deferral and starts running again (if at all) on the day the period specified in the direction (if any) ends or the day the direction is revoked; and

(b) the Authority must notify the applicant of the deferral and the reasons for it.

(3) If the Authority gives a notice of objection to a person as a result of a direction under section 405(1)(c) or (d)—

(a) sections 189 and 191 have effect as if the notice was a notice of objection within the meaning of Part XII; and

(b) the Authority must state in the notice the reasons for it.

### 408   EFTA firms

(1) If a third country decision has been taken, the Treasury may make a determination in relation to an EFTA firm which is a subsidiary undertaking of a parent undertaking which is governed by the law of the country to which the decision relates.

(2) 'Determination' means a determination that the firm concerned does not qualify for authorisation under Schedule 3 even if it satisfies the conditions in paragraph 13 or 14 of that Schedule.

(3) A determination may also be made in relation to any firm falling within a class specified in the determination.

(4) The Treasury may withdraw a determination at any time.

(5) But withdrawal does not affect anything done in accordance with the determination before it was withdrawn.

(6) If the Treasury make a determination in respect of a particular firm, or withdraw such a determination, they must give written notice to that firm.

(7) The Treasury must publish notice of any determination (or the withdrawal of any determination)—

(a) in such a way as they think most suitable for bringing the determination (or withdrawal) to the attention of those likely to be affected by it; and

(b) on, or as soon as practicable after, the date of the determination (or withdrawal).

(8) 'EFTA firm' means a firm, institution or undertaking which—

    (a) is an EEA firm as a result of paragraph 5(a), (b) or (d) of Schedule 3; and

    (b) is incorporated in, or formed under the law of, an EEA State which is not a member State.

(9) 'Third country decision' has the same meaning as in section 405.

## 409　Gibraltar

(1) The Treasury may by order—

    (a) modify Schedule 3 so as to provide for Gibraltar firms of a specified description to qualify for authorisation under that Schedule in specified circumstances;

    (b) modify Schedule 3 so as to make provision in relation to the exercise by UK firms of rights under the law of Gibraltar which correspond to EEA rights;

    (c) modify Schedule 4 so as to provide for Gibraltar firms of a specified description to qualify for authorisation under that Schedule in specified circumstances;

    (d) modify section 264 so as to make provision in relation to collective investment schemes constituted under the law of Gibraltar;

    (e) provide for the Authority to be able to give notice under section 264(2) on grounds relating to the law of Gibraltar;

    (f) provide for this Act to apply to a Gibraltar recognised scheme as if the scheme were a scheme recognised under section 264.

(2) The fact that a firm may qualify for authorisation under Schedule 3 as a result of an order under subsection (1) does not prevent it from applying for a Part IV permission.

(3) 'Gibraltar firm' means a firm which has its head office in Gibraltar or is otherwise connected with Gibraltar.

(4) 'Gibraltar recognised scheme' means a collective investment scheme—

    (a) constituted in an EEA State other than the United Kingdom, and

    (b) recognised in Gibraltar under provisions which appear to the Treasury to give effect to the provisions of a relevant Community instrument.

(5) 'Specified' means specified in the order.

(6) 'UK firm' and 'EEA right' have the same meaning as in Schedule 3.

### *International obligations*

## 410　International obligations

(1) If it appears to the Treasury that any action proposed to be taken by a relevant person would be incompatible with Community obligations or any other international obligations of the United Kingdom, they may direct that person not to take that action.

(2) If it appears to the Treasury that any action which a relevant person has power to take is required for the purpose of implementing any such obligations, they may direct that person to take that action.

(3) A direction under this section—

    (a) may include such supplemental or incidental requirements as the Treasury consider necessary or expedient; and

    (b) is enforceable, on an application made by the Treasury, by injunction or, in Scotland, by an order for specific performance under section 45 of the Court of Session Act 1988.

(4) 'Relevant person' means—

    (a) the Authority;

    (b) any person exercising functions conferred by Part VI on the competent authority;

    (c) any recognised investment exchange (other than one which is an overseas investment exchange);

    (d) any recognised clearing house (other than one which is an overseas clearing house);

    (e) a person included in the list maintained under section 301; or

    (f) the scheme operator of the ombudsman scheme.

### *Tax treatment of levies and repayments*

## 411　[...]

### *Gaming contracts*

## 412　Gaming contracts

(1) No contract to which this section applies is void or unenforceable because of—

    (a) [...]Article 170 of the Betting, Gaming, Lotteries and Amusements (Northern Ireland) Order 1985; or

    (b) [...]

(2) This section applies to a contract if—

    (a) it is entered into by either or each party by way of business;

    (b) the entering into or performance of it by either party constitutes an activity of a specified kind or one which falls within a specified class of activity; and

(c) it relates to an investment of a specified kind or one which falls within a specified class of investment.

(3) Part II of Schedule 2 applies for the purposes of subsection (2)(c), with the references to section 22 being read as references to that subsection.

(4) Nothing in Part II of Schedule 2, as applied by subsection (3), limits the power conferred by subsection (2)(c).

(5) 'Investment' includes any asset, right or interest.

(6) 'Specified' means specified in an order made by the Treasury.

### 412A  Approval and monitoring of trade-matching and reporting systems

(1) A relevant system is an approved relevant system if it is approved by the Authority under subsection (2) for the purposes of Article 25.5 of the markets in financial instruments directive; and references in this section and section 412B to an 'approved relevant system' are to be read accordingly.

(2) The Authority must approve a relevant system if, on an application by the operator of the system, it is satisfied that the arrangements established by the system for reporting transactions comply with Article 12(1) of Commission Regulation 1287/2006 of 10 August 2006 ('the Regulation').

(3) Section 51(3) and (4) applies to an application under this section as it applies to an application under Part 4.

(4) If, at any time after approving a relevant system under subsection (2), the Authority is not satisfied as mentioned in that subsection, it may suspend or withdraw the approval.

(5) The Authority must keep under review the arrangements established by an approved relevant system for reporting transactions for the purpose of ensuring that the arrangements comply with Article 12(1) of the Regulation; and for the purposes of this subsection the Authority must have regard to information provided to it under subsections (6) and (7).

(6) The operator of an approved relevant system must make reports to the Authority at specified intervals containing specified information relating to—

(a) the system,

(b) the reports made by the system in accordance with Article 25 of the markets in financial instruments directive and the Regulation, and

(c) the transactions to which those reports relate.

'Specified' means specified by the Authority.

(7) The Authority may by written notice require the operator of an approved relevant system to provide such additional information as may be specified in the notice, by such reasonable time as may be so specified, about any of the matters mentioned in subsection (6).

(8) The recipient of a notice under subsection (7) must provide the information by the time specified in the notice.

(9) In this section and section 412B, 'relevant system' means a trade-matching or reporting system of a kind described in Article 12 of the Regulation.

### 412B  Procedure for approval and suspension or withdrawal of approval

(1) If the Authority approves a relevant system, it must give the operator of the system written notice specifying the date from which the approval has effect.

(2) If the Authority proposes to refuse to approve a relevant system, it must give the operator of the system a warning notice.

(3) If the Authority decides to refuse to approve a relevant system, it must give the operator of the system a decision notice.

(4) If the Authority proposes to suspend or withdraw its approval in relation to an approved relevant system, it must give the operator of the system a warning notice.

(5) If the Authority decides to suspend or withdraw its approval in relation to an approved relevant system, it must give the operator of the system a decision notice specifying the date from which the suspension or withdrawal is to take effect.

(6) Subsections (7) to (9) apply if—

(a) the Authority has suspended its approval in relation to an approved relevant system, and

(b) the operator of the system has applied for the suspension to be cancelled.

(7) The Authority must grant the application if it is satisfied as mentioned in section 412A(2); and in such a case the Authority must give written notice to the operator that the suspension is to be cancelled from the date specified in the notice.

(8) If the Authority proposes to refuse the application, it must give the operator a warning notice.

(9) If the Authority decides to refuse the application, it must give the operator a decision notice.

(10) A person who receives a decision notice under subsection (3), (5) or (9) may refer the matter to the Tribunal.

### *Limitation on powers to require documents*

### 413  Protected items

(1) A person may not be required under this Act to produce, disclose or permit the inspection of protected items.

(2) 'Protected items' means—

    (a) communications between a professional legal adviser and his client or any person representing his client which fall within subsection (3);

    (b) communications between a professional legal adviser, his client or any person representing his client and any other person which fall within subsection (3)(as a result of paragraph (b) of that subsection);

    (c) items which—

      (i) are enclosed with, or referred to in, such communications;

      (ii) fall within subsection (3); and

      (iii) are in the possession of a person entitled to possession of them.

(3) A communication or item falls within this subsection if it is made—

    (a) in connection with the giving of legal advice to the client; or

    (b) in connection with, or in contemplation of, legal proceedings and for the purposes of those proceedings.

(4) A communication or item is not a protected item if it is held with the intention of furthering a criminal purpose.

### *Service of notices*

### 414  Service of notices

(1) The Treasury may by regulations make provision with respect to the procedure to be followed, or rules to be applied, when a provision of or made under this Act requires a notice, direction or document of any kind to be given or authorises the imposition of a requirement.

(2) The regulations may, in particular, make provision—

    (a) as to the manner in which a document must be given;

    (b) as to the address to which a document must be sent;

    (c) requiring, or allowing, a document to be sent electronically;

    (d) for treating a document as having been given, or as having been received, on a date or at a time determined in accordance with the regulations;

    (e) as to what must, or may, be done if the person to whom a document is required to be given is not an individual;

    (f) as to what must, or may, be done if the intended recipient of a document is outside the United Kingdom.

(3) Subsection (1) applies however the obligation to give a document is expressed (and so, in particular, includes a provision which requires a document to be served or sent).

(4) Section 7 of the Interpretation Act 1978 (service of notice by post) has effect in relation to provisions made by or under this Act subject to any provision made by regulations under this section.

### *Jurisdiction*

### 415  Jurisdiction in civil proceedings

(1) Proceedings arising out of any act or omission (or proposed act or omission) of—

    (a) the Authority,

    (b) the competent authority for the purposes of Part VI,

    (c) the scheme manager, or

    (d) the scheme operator,

in the discharge or purported discharge of any of its functions under this Act may be brought before the High Court or the Court of Session.

(2) The jurisdiction conferred by subsection (1) is in addition to any other jurisdiction exercisable by those courts.

### *Removal of certain unnecessary provisions*

### 416  Provisions relating to industrial assurance and certain other enactments

(1) The following enactments are to cease to have effect—

    (a) the Industrial Assurance Act 1923;

    (b) the Industrial Assurance and Friendly Societies Act 1948;

    (c) theInsurance Brokers (Registration) Act 1977.

(2) The Industrial Assurance (Northern Ireland) Order 1979 is revoked.

(3) The following bodies are to cease to exist—

    (a) the Insurance Brokers Registration Council;

    (b) the Policyholders Protection Board;

    (c) the Deposit Protection Board;

    (d) the Board of Banking Supervision.

(4) If the Treasury consider that, as a consequence of any provision of this section, it is appropriate to do so, they may by order make any provision of a kind that they could make under this Act (and in

particular any provision of a kind mentioned in section 339) with respect to anything done by or under any provision of Part XXI.

(5) Subsection (4) is not to be read as affecting in any way any other power conferred on the Treasury by this Act.

# PART XXIX

# INTERPRETATION

### 417 Definitions

(1) In this Act—

'appointed representative' has the meaning given in section 39(2);

'auditors and actuaries rules' means rules made under section 340;

'authorisation offence' has the meaning given in section 23(2);

'authorised open-ended investment company' has the meaning given in section 237(3);

'authorised person' has the meaning given in section 31(2);

'the Authority' means the Financial Services Authority;

'body corporate' includes a body corporate constituted under the law of a country or territory outside the United Kingdom;

'chief executive'—

(a) in relation to a body corporate whose principal place of business is within the United Kingdom, means an employee of that body who, alone or jointly with one or more others, is responsible under the immediate authority of the directors, for the conduct of the whole of the business of that body; and

(b) in relation to a body corporate whose principal place of business is outside the United Kingdom, means the person who, alone or jointly with one or more others, is responsible for the conduct of its business within the United Kingdom;

'claim', in relation to the Financial Services Compensation Scheme under Part XV, is to be construed in accordance with section 214(1B);

'collective investment scheme' has the meaning given in section 235;

'the Commission' means the European Commission (except in provisions relating to the Competition Commission);

'the compensation scheme' has the meaning given in section 213(2);

'control of information rules' has the meaning given in section 147(1);

'director', in relation to a body corporate, includes—

(a) a person occupying in relation to it the position of a director (by whatever name called); and

(b) a person in accordance with whose directions or instructions (not being advice given in a professional capacity) the directors of that body are accustomed to act;

'documents' includes information recorded in any form and, in relation to information recorded otherwise than in legible form, references to its production include references to producing a copy of the information in legible form or in a form from which it can readily be produced in visible and legible form;

'electronic commerce directive' means Directive 2000/31/EC of the European Parliament and the Council of 8 June 2000 on certain legal aspects of information society services, in particular electronic commerce, in the Internal Market (Directive on electronic commerce);

'exempt person', in relation to a regulated activity, means a person who is exempt from the general prohibition in relation to that activity as a result of an exemption order made under section 38(1) or as a result of section 39(1) or 285(2) or (3);

'financial promotion rules' means rules made under section 145;

'friendly society' means an incorporated or registered friendly society;

'general prohibition' has the meaning given in section 19(2);

'general rules' has the meaning given in section 138(2);

'incorporated friendly society' means a society incorporated under the Friendly Societies Act 1992;

'industrial and provident society' means a society registered or deemed to be registered under the Industrial and Provident Societies Act 1965 or the Industrial and Provident Societies Act (Northern Ireland) 1969;

'information society service' means an information society service within the meaning of Article 2(a) of the electronic commerce directive;

'investment services and activities' has the meaning given in Article 4.1.2 of the markets in financial instruments directive, read with—

(a) Chapter VI of Commission Regulation 1287/2006 of 10 August 2006, and

(b) Article 52 of Commission Directive 2006/73/EC of 10 August 2006;

'market abuse' has the meaning given in section 118;

'Minister of the Crown' has the same meaning as in the Ministers of the Crown Act 1975;

'money laundering rules' means rules made under section 146;

'notice of control' (except in Chapter 1A of Part 18) has the meaning given in section 178(5);

'the ombudsman scheme' has the meaning given in section 225(3);

'open-ended investment company' has the meaning given in section 236;

'Part IV permission' has the meaning given in section 40(4);

'partnership' includes a partnership constituted under the law of a country or territory outside the United Kingdom;

'prescribed'(where not otherwise defined) means prescribed in regulations made by the Treasury;

'price stabilising rules' means rules made under section 144;

'private company' has the meaning given in section 1(3) of the Companies Act 1985 or in Article 12(3) of the Companies (Northern Ireland) Order 1986;

'prohibition order' has the meaning given in section 56(2);

'recognised clearing house' and 'recognised investment exchange' have the meaning given in section 285;

'registered friendly society' means a society which is—

    (a) a friendly society within the meaning of section 7(1)(a) of the Friendly Societies Act 1974; and

    (b) registered within the meaning of that Act;

'regulated activity' has the meaning given in section 22;

'regulating provisions' has the meaning given in section 159(1);

'regulatory objectives' means the objectives mentioned in section 2;

'regulatory provisions' has the meaning given in section 302;

'rule' means a rule made by the Authority under this Act;

'rule-making instrument' has the meaning given in section 153;

'the scheme manager' has the meaning given in section 212(1);

'the scheme operator' has the meaning given in section 225(2);

'scheme particulars rules' has the meaning given in section 248(1);

'Seventh Company Law Directive' means the European Council Seventh Company Law

'Takeovers Directive' means Directive 2004/25/EC of the European Parliament and of the Council;

'threshold conditions', in relation to a regulated activity, has the meaning given in section 41;

'the Treaty' means the treaty establishing the European Community;

'trust scheme rules' has the meaning given in section 247(1);

'UK authorised person' has the meaning given in section 178(4); and

'unit trust scheme' has the meaning given in section 237.

(2) In the application of this Act to Scotland, references to a matter being actionable at the suit of a person are to be read as references to the matter being actionable at the instance of that person.

(3) For the purposes of any provision of this Act (other than a provision of Part 6) authorising or requiring a person to do anything within a specified number of days no account is to be taken of any day which is a public holiday in any part of the United Kingdom.

(4) For the purposes of this Act—

    (a) an information society service is provided from an EEA State if it is provided from an establishment in that State;

    (b) an establishment, in connection with an information society service, is the place at which the provider of the service (being a national of an EEA State or a company or firm as mentioned in Article 48 of the Treaty) effectively pursues an economic activity for an indefinite period;

    (c) the presence or use in a particular place of equipment or other technical means of providing an information society service does not, of itself, constitute that place as an establishment of the kind mentioned in paragraph (b);

    (d) where it cannot be determined from which of a number of establishments a given information society service is provided, that service is to be regarded as provided from the establishment where the provider has the centre of his activities relating to the service.

## 418 Carrying on regulated activities in the United Kingdom

(1) In the five cases described in this section, a person who—

    (a) is carrying on a regulated activity, but

    (b) would not otherwise be regarded as carrying it on in the United Kingdom,

is, for the purposes of this Act, to be regarded as carrying it on in the United Kingdom.

(2) The first case is where—

    (a) his registered office (or if he does not have a registered office his head office) is in the United Kingdom;

    (b) he is entitled to exercise rights under a single market directive as a UK firm; and

    (c) he is carrying on in another EEA State a regulated activity to which that directive applies.

(3) The second case is where—

    (a) his registered office (or if he does not have a registered office his head office) is in the United Kingdom;

    (b) he is the manager of a scheme which is entitled to enjoy the rights conferred by an instrument which is a relevant Community instrument for the purposes of section 264; and

(c) persons in another EEA State are invited to become participants in the scheme.

(4) The third case is where—

(a) his registered office (or if he does not have a registered office his head office) is in the United Kingdom;

(b) the day-to-day management of the carrying on of the regulated activity is the responsibility of—

(i) his registered office (or head office); or

(ii) another establishment maintained by him in the United Kingdom.

(5) The fourth case is where—

(a) his head office is not in the United Kingdom; but

(b) the activity is carried on from an establishment maintained by him in the United Kingdom.

(5A) The fifth case is any other case where the activity—

(a) consists of the provision of an information society service to a person or persons in one or more EEA States; and

(b) is carried on from an establishment in the United Kingdom.

(6) For the purposes of subsections (2) to (5A) it is irrelevant where the person with whom the activity is carried on is situated.

### 419 Carrying on regulated activities by way of business

(1) The Treasury may by order make provision—

(a) as to the circumstances in which a person who would otherwise not be regarded as carrying on a regulated activity by way of business is to be regarded as doing so;

(b) as to the circumstances in which a person who would otherwise be regarded as carrying on a regulated activity by way of business is to be regarded as not doing so.

(2) An order under subsection (1) may be made so as to apply—

(a) generally in relation to all regulated activities;

(b) in relation to a specified category of regulated activity; or

(c) in relation to a particular regulated activity.

(3) An order under subsection (1) may be made so as to apply—

(a) for the purposes of all provisions;

(b) for a specified group of provisions; or

(c) for a specified provision.

(4) 'Provision' means a provision of, or made under, this Act.

(5) Nothing in this section is to be read as affecting the provisions of section 428(3).

### 420 Parent and subsidiary undertaking

(1) In this Act, except in relation to an incorporated friendly society, 'parent undertaking' and 'subsidiary undertaking' have the same meaning as in the Companies Acts (see section 1162 of, and Schedule 7 to, the Companies Act 2006

(2) But—

(a) 'parent undertaking' also includes an individual who would be a parent undertaking for the purposes of those provisions if he were taken to be an undertaking (and 'subsidiary undertaking' is to be read accordingly);

(b) 'subsidiary undertaking' also includes, in relation to a body incorporated in or formed under the law of an EEA State other than the United Kingdom, an undertaking which is a subsidiary undertaking within the meaning of any rule of law in force in that State for purposes connected with implementation of the Seventh Company Law Directive (and 'parent undertaking' is to be read accordingly).

(3) In this Act 'subsidiary undertaking', in relation to an incorporated friendly society, means a body corporate of which the society has control within the meaning of section 13(9)(a) or (aa) of the Friendly Societies Act 1992 (and 'parent undertaking' is to be read accordingly).

### 421 Group

(1) In this Act 'group', in relation to a person ('A'), means A and any person who is—

(a) a parent undertaking of A;

(b) a subsidiary undertaking of A;

(c) a subsidiary undertaking of a parent undertaking of A;

(d) a parent undertaking of a subsidiary undertaking of A;

(e) an undertaking in which A or an undertaking mentioned in paragraph (a), (b), (c) or (d) has a participating interest;

(f) if A or an undertaking mentioned in paragraph (a) or (d) is a building society, an associated undertaking of the society; or

(g) if A or an undertaking mentioned in paragraph (a) or (d) is an incorporated friendly society, a body corporate of which the society has joint control (within the meaning of section 13(9)(c) or (cc) of the Friendly Societies Act 1992).

(2) 'Participating interest' has the same meaning as in s421A; but also includes an interest held by an individual which would be a participating interest for the purposes of those provisions if he were taken to be an undertaking.

(3) 'Associated undertaking' has the meaning given in section 119(1) of the Building Societies Act 1986.

### 421A  Meaning of 'participating interest'

(1) In section 421 a 'participating interest' means an interest held by an undertaking in the shares of another undertaking which it holds on a long-term basis for the purpose of securing a contribution to its activities by the exercise of control or influence arising from or related to that interest.

(2) A holding of 20% or more of the shares of an undertaking is presumed to be a participating interest unless the contrary is shown.

(3) The reference in subsection (1) to an interest in shares includes—

(a) an interest which is convertible into an interest in shares, and

(b) an option to acquire shares or any such interest;

and an interest or option falls within paragraph (a) or (b) notwithstanding that the shares to which it relates are, until the conversion or the exercise of the option, unissued.

(4) For the purposes of this section an interest held on behalf of an undertaking shall be treated as held by it.

(5) In this section 'undertaking' has the same meaning as in the Companies Acts (see section 1161(1) of the Companies Act 2006).

### 422  Controller

(1) In this Act 'controller', in relation to an undertaking ('B'), means a person ('A') who falls within any of the cases in subsection (2).

(2) The cases are where A holds—

(a) 10% or more of the shares in B or in a parent undertaking of B ('P');

(b) 10% or more of the voting power in B or P; or

(c) shares or voting power in B or P as a result of which A is able to exercise significant influence over the management of B.

(3) For the purposes of calculations relating to this section, the holding of shares or voting power by a person ('A1') includes any shares or voting power held by another ('A2') if A1 and A2 are acting in concert.

(4) In this section 'shares' —

(a) in relation to an undertaking with a share capital, means allotted shares;

(b) in relation to an undertaking with capital but no share capital, means rights to share in the capital of the undertaking;

(c) in relation to an undertaking without capital, means interests—

(i) conferring any right to share in the profits, or liability to contribute to the losses, of the undertaking; or

(ii) giving rise to an obligation to contribute to the debts or expenses of the undertaking in the event of a winding up.

(5) In this section 'voting power' —

(a) includes, in relation to a person ('H')—

(i) voting power held by a third party with whom H has concluded an agreement, which obliges H and the third party to adopt, by concerted exercise of the voting power they hold, a lasting common policy towards the management of the undertaking in question;

(ii) voting power held by a third party under an agreement concluded with H providing for the temporary transfer for consideration of the voting power in question;

(iii) voting power attaching to shares which are lodged as collateral with H, provided that H controls the voting power and declares an intention to exercise it;

(iv) voting power attaching to shares in which H has a life interest;

(v) voting power which is held, or may be exercised within the meaning of subparagraphs (i) to (iv), by a subsidiary undertaking of H;

(vi) voting power attaching to shares deposited with H which H has discretion to exercise in the absence of specific instructions from the shareholders;

(vii) voting power held in the name of a third party on behalf of H;

(viii) voting power which H may exercise as a proxy where H has discretion about the exercise of the voting power in the absence of specific instructions from the shareholders; and

(b) in relation to an undertaking which does not have general meetings at which matters are decided by the exercise of voting rights, means the right under the constitution of the undertaking to direct the overall policy of the undertaking or alter the terms of its constitution.

### 422A  Disregarded holdings

(1) For the purposes of section 422, shares and voting power that a person holds in an undertaking ('B') or in a parent undertaking of B ('P') are disregarded in the following circumstances.

(2) Shares held only for the purposes of clearing and settling within a short settlement cycle are disregarded.

(3) Shares held by a custodian or its nominee in a custodian capacity are disregarded, provided that the custodian or nominee is only able to exercise voting power attached to the shares in accordance with instructions given in writing.

(4) Shares representing no more than 5% of the total voting power in B or P held by an investment firm are disregarded, provided that it—

    (a) holds the shares in the capacity of a market maker (as defined in article 4.1(8) of the markets in financial instruments directive);

    (b) is authorised by its home state regulator under the markets in financial instruments directive; and

    (c) neither intervenes in the management of B or P nor exerts any influence on B or P to buy the shares or back the share price.

(5) Shares held by a credit institution or investment firm in its trading book are disregarded, provided that—

    (a) the shares represent no more than 5% of the total voting power in B or P; and

    (b) the credit institution or investment firm ensures that the voting power is not used to intervene in the management of B or P.

(6) Shares held by a credit institution or an investment firm are disregarded, provided that—

    (a) the shares are held as a result of performing the investment services and activities of—

        (i) underwriting shares; or

        (ii) placing shares on a firm commitment basis in accordance with Annex I, section A.6 of the markets in financial instruments directive; and

    (b) the credit institution or investment firm—

        (i) does not exercise voting power represented by the shares or otherwise intervene in the management of the issuer; and

        (ii) retains the holding for a period of less than one year.

(7) Where a management company (as defined in Article 1a.2 of the UCITS directive) and its parent undertaking both hold shares or voting power, each may disregard holdings of the other, provided that each exercises its voting power independently of the other.

(8) But subsection (7) does not apply if the management company—

    (a) manages holdings for its parent undertaking or an undertaking in respect of which the parent undertaking is a controller;

    (b) has no discretion to exercise the voting power attached to such holdings; and

    (c) may only exercise the voting power in relation to such holdings under direct or indirect instruction from—

        (i) its parent undertaking; or

        (ii) an undertaking in respect of which of the parent undertaking is a controller.

(9) Where an investment firm and its parent undertaking both hold shares or voting power, the parent undertaking may disregard holdings managed by the investment firm on a client by client basis and the investment firm may disregard holdings of the parent undertaking, provided that the investment firm—

    (a) has permission to provide portfolio management;

    (b) exercises its voting power independently from the parent undertaking; and

    (c) may only exercise the voting power under instructions given in writing, or has appropriate mechanisms in place for ensuring that individual portfolio management services are conducted independently of any other services.

(10) In this section 'credit institution' means—

    (a) a credit institution authorised under the banking consolidation directive; or

    (b) an institution which would satisfy the requirements for authorisation as a credit institution under that directive if it had its registered office (or if it does not have a registered office, its head office) in an EEA State.

### 423 Manager

(1) In this Act, except in relation to a unit trust scheme or a registered friendly society, 'manager' means an employee who—

    (a) under the immediate authority of his employer is responsible, either alone or jointly with one or more other persons, for the conduct of his employer's business; or

    (b) under the immediate authority of his employer or of a person who is a manager by virtue of paragraph (a) exercises managerial functions or is responsible for maintaining accounts or other records of his employer.

(2) If the employer is not an individual, references in subsection (1) to the authority of the employer are references to the authority—

    (a) in the case of a body corporate, of the directors;

    (b) in the case of a partnership, of the partners; and

    (c) in the case of an unincorporated association, of its officers or the members of its governing body.

(3) 'Manager', in relation to a body corporate, means a person (other than an employee of the body) who is appointed by the body to manage any part of its business and includes an employee of the body corporate (other than the chief executive) who, under the immediate authority of a director or chief executive of the body corporate, exercises managerial functions or is responsible for maintaining accounts or other records of the body corporate.

### 424  Insurance

(1) In this Act, references to—

    (a) contracts of insurance,

    (b) reinsurance,

    (c) contracts of long-term insurance,

    (d) contracts of general insurance,

are to be read with section 22 and Schedule 2.

(2) In this Act 'policy' and 'policyholder', in relation to a contract of insurance, have such meaning as the Treasury may by order specify.

(3) The law applicable to a contract of insurance, the effecting of which constitutes the carrying on of a regulated activity, is to be determined, if it is of a prescribed description, in accordance with regulations made by the Treasury.

### 424A  Investment firm

(1) In this Act, 'investment firm' has the meaning given in Article 4.1.1 of the markets in financial instruments directive.

(2) Subsection (1) is subject to subsections (3) to (5).

(3) References in this Act to an 'investment firm' include references to a person who would be an investment firm (within the meaning of Article 4.1.1 of the markets in financial instruments directive) if—

    (a) in the case of a body corporate, his registered office or, if he has no registered office, his head office, and

    (b) in the case of a person other than a body corporate, his head office,

were in an EEA State.

(4) But subsection (3) does not apply if the person in question is one to whom the markets in financial instruments directive would not apply by virtue of Article 2 of that directive.

(5) References in this Act to an 'investment firm' do not include references to—

    (a) a person to whom the markets in financial instruments directive does not apply by virtue of Article 2 of the directive; or

    (b) a person whose home Member State (within the meaning of Article 4.1.20 of the markets in financial instruments directive) is an EEA State and to whom, by reason of the fact that the State has given effect to Article 3 of that directive, that directive does not apply by virtue of that Article.

### 425  Expressions relating to authorisation elsewhere in the single market

(1) In this Act—

    (a) 'banking consolidation directive', 'life assurance consolidation directive', 'EEA authorisation', 'EEA firm', 'EEA right', 'EEA State', 'first non-life insurance directive', 'insurance directives', 'reinsurance directive', 'insurance mediation directive', 'markets in financial instruments directive', 'single market directives', 'tied agent' and 'UCITS directive' have the meaning given in Schedule 3; and

    (b) 'home state regulator', in relation to an EEA firm, has the meaning given in Schedule 3.

(2) In this Act—

    (a) 'home state authorisation' has the meaning given in Schedule 4;

    (a) 'Treaty firm' has the meaning given in Schedule 4; and

    (c) 'home state regulator', in relation to a Treaty firm, has the meaning given in Schedule 4.

# PART XXX

# SUPPLEMENTAL

### 426  Consequential and supplementary provision

(1) A Minister of the Crown may by order make such incidental, consequential, transitional or supplemental provision as he considers necessary or expedient for the general purposes, or any particular purpose, of this Act or in consequence of any provision made by or under this Act or for giving full effect to this Act or any such provision.

(2) An order under subsection (1) may, in particular, make provision—

    (a) for enabling any person by whom any powers will become exercisable, on a date set by or under this Act, by virtue of any provision made by or under this Act to take before that date any steps which are necessary as a preliminary to the exercise of those powers;

(b) for applying (with or without modifications) or amending, repealing or revoking any provision of or made under an Act passed before this Act or in the same Session;

(c) dissolving any body corporate established by any Act passed, or instrument made, before the passing of this Act;

(d) for making savings, or additional savings, from the effect of any repeal or revocation made by or under this Act.

(3) Amendments made under this section are additional, and without prejudice, to those made by or under any other provision of this Act.

(4) No other provision of this Act restricts the powers conferred by this section.

### 427   Transitional provisions

(1) Subsections (2) and (3) apply to an order under section 426 which makes transitional provisions or savings.

(2) The order may, in particular—

(a) if it makes provision about the authorisation and permission of persons who before commencement were entitled to carry on any activities, also include provision for such persons not to be treated as having any authorisation or permission (whether on an application to the Authority or otherwise);

(b) make provision enabling the Authority to require persons of such descriptions as it may direct to re-apply for permissions having effect by virtue of the order;

(c) make provision for the continuation as rules of such provisions (including primary and subordinate legislation) as may be designated in accordance with the order by the Authority, including provision for the modification by the Authority of provisions designated;

(d) make provision about the effect of requirements imposed, liabilities incurred and any other things done before commencement, including provision for and about investigations, penalties and the taking or continuing of any other action in respect of contraventions;

(e) make provision for the continuation of disciplinary and other proceedings begun before commencement, including provision about the decisions available to bodies before which such proceedings take place and the effect of their decisions;

(f) make provision as regards the Authority's obligation to maintain a record under section 347 as respects persons in relation to whom provision is made by the order.

(3) The order may—

(a) confer functions on the Treasury, the Secretary of State, the Authority, the scheme manager, the scheme operator, members of the panel established under paragraph 4 of Schedule 17, the Competition Commission or the OFT;

(b) confer jurisdiction on the Tribunal;

(c) provide for fees to be charged in connection with the carrying out of functions conferred under the order;

(d) modify, exclude or apply (with or without modifications) any primary or subordinate legislation (including any provision of, or made under, this Act).

(4) In subsection (2) 'commencement' means the commencement of such provisions of this Act as may be specified by the order.

### 428   Regulations and orders

(1) Any power to make an order which is conferred on a Minister of the Crown by this Act and any power to make regulations which is conferred by this Act is exercisable by statutory instrument.

(2) The Lord Chancellor's power to make rules under section 132 is exercisable by statutory instrument.

(3) Any statutory instrument made under this Act may—

(a) contain such incidental, supplemental, consequential and transitional provision as the person making it considers appropriate; and

(b) make different provision for different cases.

### 429   Parliamentary control of statutory instruments

(1) No order is to be made under—

(a) section 144(4), 192(b) or (e), 236(5), 404 or 419, or

(b) paragraph 1 of Schedule 8,

unless a draft of the order has been laid before Parliament and approved by a resolution of each House.

(2) No regulations are to be made under section section 90B, 214A, 214B or 262 unless a draft of the regulations has been laid before Parliament and approved by a resolution of each House.

(3) An order to which, if it is made, subsection (4) or (5) will apply is not to be made unless a draft of the order has been laid before Parliament and approved by a resolution of each House.

(4) This subsection applies to an order under section 21 if—

(a) it is the first order to be made, or to contain provisions made, under section 21(4);

(b) it varies an order made under section 21(4) so as to make section 21(1) apply in circumstances in which it did not previously apply;

(c) it is the first order to be made, or to contain provision made, under section 21(5);

(d) it varies a previous order made under section 21(5) so as to make section 21(1) apply in circumstances in which it did not, as a result of that previous order, apply;

(e) it is the first order to be made, or to contain provisions made, under section 21(9) or (10);

(f) it adds one or more activities to those that are controlled activities for the purposes of section 21; or

(g) it adds one or more investments to those which are controlled investments for the purposes of section 21.

(5) This subsection applies to an order under section 38 if—

(a) it is the first order to be made, or to contain provisions made, under that section; or

(b) it contains provisions restricting or removing an exemption provided by an earlier order made under that section.

(6) An order containing a provision to which, if the order is made, subsection (7) will apply is not to be made unless a draft of the order has been laid before Parliament and approved by a resolution of each House.

(7) This subsection applies to a provision contained in an order if—

(a) it is the first to be made in the exercise of the power conferred by subsection (1) of section 326 or it removes a body from those for the time being designated under that subsection; or

(b) it is the first to be made in the exercise of the power conferred by subsection (6) of section 327 or it adds a description of regulated activity or investment to those for the time being specified for the purposes of that subsection.

(8) Any other statutory instrument made under this Act, apart from one made under section 431(2) or to which paragraph 26 of Schedule 2 applies, shall be subject to annulment in pursuance of a resolution of either House of Parliament.

### 430  Extent

(1) This Act, except Chapter IV of Part XVII, extends to Northern Ireland.

(2) Except where Her Majesty by Order in Council provides otherwise, the extent of any amendment or repeal made by or under this Act is the same as the extent of the provision amended or repealed.

(3) Her Majesty may by Order in Council provide for any provision of or made under this Act relating to a matter which is the subject of other legislation which extends to any of the Channel Islands or the Isle of Man to extend there with such modifications (if any) as may be specified in the Order.

### 431  Commencement

(1) The following provisions come into force on the passing of this Act—

(a) this section;

(b) sections 428, 430 and 433;

(c) paragraphs 1 and 2 of Schedule 21.

(2) The other provisions of this Act come into force on such day as the Treasury may by order appoint; and different days may be appointed for different purposes.

### 432  Minor and consequential amendments, transitional provisions and repeals

(1) Schedule 20 makes minor and consequential amendments.

(2) Schedule 21 makes transitional provisions.

(3) The enactments set out in Schedule 22 are repealed.

### 433  Short title

This Act may be cited as the Financial Services and Markets Act 2000.

# SCHEDULES

# SCHEDULE 1

## THE FINANCIAL SERVICES AUTHORITY

### PART I

### GENERAL

*Interpretation*

1  (1) In this Schedule—

'the 1985 Act' means the Companies Act 1985;

'non-executive committee' means the committee maintained under paragraph 3;

'functions', in relation to the Authority, means functions conferred on the Authority by or under any provision of this Act.

(2) For the purposes of this Schedule, the following are the Authority's legislative functions—

    (a) making rules;

    (b) issuing codes under section 64 or 119;

    (c) issuing statements under section 64, 69, 124 or 210;

    (d) giving directions under section 316, 318 or 328;

    (e) issuing general guidance (as defined by section 158(5) or guidance under s158A).

## Constitution

**2**  (1) The constitution of the Authority must continue to provide for the Authority to have—

    (a) a chairman; and

    (b) a governing body.

(2) The governing body must include the chairman.

(3) The chairman and other members of the governing body must be appointed, and be liable to removal from office, by the Treasury.

(4) The validity of any act of the Authority is not affected—

    (a) by a vacancy in the office of chairman; or

    (b) by a defect in the appointment of a person as a member of the governing body or as chairman.

## Non-executive members of the governing body

**3**  (1) The Authority must secure—

    (a) that the majority of the members of its governing body are non-executive members; and

    (b) that a committee of its governing body, consisting solely of the non-executive members, is set up and maintained for the purposes of discharging the functions conferred on the committee by this Schedule.

(2) The members of the non-executive committee are to be appointed by the Authority.

(3) The non-executive committee is to have a chairman appointed by the Treasury from among its members.

## Functions of the non-executive committee

**4**  (1) In this paragraph 'the committee' means the non-executive committee

(2) The non-executive functions are functions of the Authority but must be discharged by the committee.

(3) The non-executive functions are—

    (a) keeping under review the question whether the Authority is, in discharging its functions in accordance with decisions of its governing body, using its resources in the most efficient and economic way;

    (b) keeping under review the question whether the Authority's internal financial controls secure the proper conduct of its financial affairs; and

    (c) determining the remuneration of—

        (i)   the chairman of the Authority's governing body; and

        (ii)  the executive members of that body.

(4) The function mentioned in sub-paragraph (3)(b) and those mentioned in sub-paragraph (3)(c) may be discharged on behalf of the committee by a sub-committee.

(5) Any sub-committee of the committee—

    (a) must have as its chairman the chairman of the committee; but

    (b) may include persons other than members of the committee.

(6) The committee must prepare a report on the discharge of its functions for inclusion in the Authority's annual report to the Treasury under paragraph 10.

(7) The committee's report must relate to the same period as that covered by the Authority's report.

## Arrangements for discharging functions

**5**  (1) The Authority may make arrangements for any of its functions to be discharged by a committee, sub-committee, officer or member of staff of the Authority

(2) But—

    (a) in exercising the legislative functions mentioned in paragraph 1(2)(a) to (d), the Authority must act through its governing body; and

    (b) the legislative function mentioned in paragraph 1(2)(e) may not be discharged by an officer or member of staff of the Authority.

(3) Sub-paragraph (1) does not apply to the non-executive functions.

## *Monitoring and enforcement*

**6** (1) The Authority must maintain arrangements designed to enable it to determine whether persons on whom requirements are imposed by or under this Act or by any directly applicable Community regulation made under the markets in financial instruments directive, are complying with them

(2) Those arrangements may provide for functions to be performed on behalf of the Authority by any body or person who, in its opinion, is competent to perform them.

(3) The Authority must also maintain arrangements for enforcing the provisions of, or made under, this Act or of any directly applicable Community regulation made under the markets in financial instruments directive.

(4) Sub-paragraph (2) does not affect the Authority's duty under sub-paragraph (1).

## *Arrangements for the investigation of complaints*

**7** (1) The Authority must—

(a) make arrangements ('the complaints scheme') for the investigation of complaints arising in connection with the exercise of, or failure to exercise, any of its functions (other than its legislative functions); and

(b) appoint an independent person ('the investigator') to be responsible for the conduct of investigations in accordance with the complaints scheme.

(2) The complaints scheme must be designed so that, as far as reasonably practicable, complaints are investigated quickly.

(3) The Treasury's approval is required for the appointment or dismissal of the investigator.

(4) The terms and conditions on which the investigator is appointed must be such as, in the opinion of the Authority, are reasonably designed to secure—

(a) that he will be free at all times to act independently of the Authority; and

(b) that complaints will be investigated under the complaints scheme without favouring the Authority.

(5) Before making the complaints scheme, the Authority must publish a draft of the proposed scheme in the way appearing to the Authority best calculated to bring it to the attention of the public.

(6) The draft must be accompanied by notice that representations about it may be made to the Authority within a specified time.

(7) Before making the proposed complaints scheme, the Authority must have regard to any representations made to it in accordance with sub-paragraph (6).

(8) If the Authority makes the proposed complaints scheme, it must publish an account, in general terms, of—

(a) the representations made to it in accordance with sub-paragraph (6); and

(b) its response to them.

(9) If the complaints scheme differs from the draft published under sub-paragraph (5) in a way which is, in the opinion of the Authority, significant the Authority must (in addition to complying with sub-paragraph (8)) publish details of the difference.

(10) The Authority must publish up-to-date details of the complaints scheme including, in particular, details of—

(a) the provision made under paragraph 8(5); and

(b) the powers which the investigator has to investigate a complaint.

(11) Those details must be published in the way appearing to the Authority to be best calculated to bring them to the attention of the public.

(12) The Authority must, without delay, give the Treasury a copy of any details published by it under this paragraph.

(13) The Authority may charge a reasonable fee for providing a person with a copy of—

(a) a draft published under sub-paragraph (5);

(b) details published under sub-paragraph (10).

(14) Sub-paragraphs (5) to (9) and (13)(a) also apply to a proposal to alter or replace the complaints scheme.

## *Investigation of complaints*

**8** (1) The Authority is not obliged to investigate a complaint in accordance with the complaints scheme which it reasonably considers would be more appropriately dealt with in another way (for example by referring the matter to the Tribunal or by the institution of other legal proceedings).

(2) The complaints scheme must provide—

(a) for reference to the investigator of any complaint which the Authority is investigating; and

(b) for him—

(i) to have the means to conduct a full investigation of the complaint;

(ii) to report on the result of his investigation to the Authority and the complainant; and

(iii) to be able to publish his report (or any part of it) if he considers that it (or the part) ought to be brought to the attention of the public.

(3) If the Authority has decided not to investigate a complaint, it must notify the investigator.

(4) If the investigator considers that a complaint of which he has been notified under sub-paragraph (3) ought to be investigated, he may proceed as if the complaint had been referred to him under the complaints scheme.

(5) The complaints scheme must confer on the investigator the power to recommend, if he thinks it appropriate, that the Authority—

(a) makes a compensatory payment to the complainant,

(b) remedies the matter complained of,

or takes both of those steps.

(6) The complaints scheme must require the Authority, in a case where the investigator—

(a) has reported that a complaint is well-founded, or

(b) has criticised the Authority in his report,

to inform the investigator and the complainant of the steps which it proposes to take in response to the report.

(7) The investigator may require the Authority to publish the whole or a specified part of the response.

(8) The investigator may appoint a person to conduct the investigation on his behalf but subject to his direction.

(9) Neither an officer nor an employee of the Authority may be appointed under sub-paragraph (8).

(10) Sub-paragraph (2) is not to be taken as preventing the Authority from making arrangements for the initial investigation of a complaint to be conducted by the Authority.

### *Records*

9 The Authority must maintain satisfactory arrangements for—

(a) recording decisions made in the exercise of its functions; and

(b) the safe-keeping of those records which it considers ought to be preserved.

### *Annual report*

10 (1) At least once a year the Authority must make a report to the Treasury on—

(a) the discharge of its functions;

(b) the extent to which, in its opinion, the regulatory objectives have been met;

(c) its consideration of the matters mentioned in section 2(3); and

(d) such other matters as the Treasury may from time to time direct.

(2) The report must be accompanied by—

(a) the report prepared by the non-executive committee under paragraph 4(6); and

(b) such other reports or information, prepared by such persons, as the Treasury may from time to time direct.

(3) The Treasury must lay before Parliament a copy of each report received by them under this paragraph.

(4) The Treasury may—

(a) require the Authority to comply with any provisions of the Companies Act 2006 about accounts and their audit which would not otherwise apply to it; or

(b) direct that any such provision of that Act is to apply to the Authority with such modifications as are specified in the direction.

(5) Compliance with any requirement imposed under sub-paragraph (4)(a) or (b) is enforceable by injunction or, in Scotland, an order under section 45(b) of the Court of Session Act 1988.

(6) Proceedings under sub-paragraph (5) may be brought only by the Treasury.

### *Annual public meeting*

11 (1) Not later than three months after making a report under paragraph 10, the Authority must hold a public meeting ('the annual meeting') for the purposes of enabling that report to be considered

(2) The Authority must organise the annual meeting so as to allow—

(a) a general discussion of the contents of the report which is being considered; and

(b) a reasonable opportunity for those attending the meeting to put questions to the Authority about the way in which it discharged, or failed to discharge, its functions during the period to which the report relates.

(3) But otherwise the annual meeting is to be organised and conducted in such a way as the Authority considers appropriate.

(4) The Authority must give reasonable notice of its annual meeting.

(5) That notice must—

(a) give details of the time and place at which the meeting is to be held;

(b) set out the proposed agenda for the meeting;

(c) indicate the proposed duration of the meeting;

(d) give details of the Authority's arrangements for enabling persons to attend; and

(e) be published by the Authority in the way appearing to it to be most suitable for bringing the notice to the attention of the public.

(6) If the Authority proposes to alter any of the arrangements which have been included in the notice given under sub-paragraph (4) it must—

(a) give reasonable notice of the alteration; and

(b) publish that notice in the way appearing to the Authority to be best calculated to bring it to the attention of the public.

### Report of annual meeting

**12** Not later than one month after its annual meeting, the Authority must publish a report of the proceedings of the meeting

## PART II

## STATUS

**13** In relation to any of its functions—

(a) the Authority is not to be regarded as acting on behalf of the Crown; and

(b) its members, officers and staff are not to be regarded as Crown servants.

### Exemption from requirement of 'limited' in Authority's name

**14** The Authority is to continue to be exempt from the requirements of the 1985 Act relating to the use of 'limited' as part of its name

**15** If the Secretary of State is satisfied that any action taken by the Authority makes it inappropriate for the exemption given by paragraph 14 to continue he may, after consulting the Treasury, give a direction removing it

## PART III

## PENALTIES AND FEES

### Penalties

**16** (1) In determining its policy with respect to the amounts of penalties to be imposed by it under this Act, the Authority must take no account of the expenses which it incurs, or expects to incur, in discharging its functions

(2) The Authority must prepare and operate a scheme for ensuring that the amounts paid to the Authority by way of penalties imposed under this Act are applied for the benefit of authorised persons.

(3) The scheme may, in particular, make different provision with respect to different classes of authorised person.

(4) Up to date details of the scheme must be set out in a document ('the scheme details').

(5) The scheme details must be published by the Authority in the way appearing to it to be best calculated to bring them to the attention of the public.

(6) Before making the scheme, the Authority must publish a draft of the proposed scheme in the way appearing to the Authority to be best calculated to bring it to the attention of the public.

(7) The draft must be accompanied by notice that representations about the proposals may be made to the Authority within a specified time.

(8) Before making the scheme, the Authority must have regard to any representations made to it in accordance with sub-paragraph (7).

(9) If the Authority makes the proposed scheme, it must publish an account, in general terms, of—

(a) the representations made to it in accordance with sub-paragraph (7); and

(b) its response to them.

(10) If the scheme differs from the draft published under sub-paragraph (6) in a way which is, in the opinion of the Authority, significant the Authority must (in addition to complying with sub-paragraph (9)) publish details of the difference.

(11) The Authority must, without delay, give the Treasury a copy of any scheme details published by it.

(12)  The Authority may charge a reasonable fee for providing a person with a copy of—

(a)  a draft published under sub-paragraph (6);

(b)  scheme details.

(13)  Sub-paragraphs (6) to (10) and (12)(a) also apply to a proposal to alter or replace the complaints scheme.

### Fees

**17**  (1)  The Authority may make rules providing for the payment to it of such fees, in connection with the discharge of any of its functions under or as a result of this Act, as it considers will (taking account of its expected income from fees and charges provided for by any other provision of this Act) enable it—

(a)  to meet expenses incurred in carrying out its functions or for any incidental purpose;

(b)  to repay the principal of, and pay any interest on, any money which it has borrowed and which has been used for the purpose of meeting expenses incurred in relation to its assumption of functions under this Act or the Bank of England Act 1998; and

(c)  to maintain adequate reserves.

(2)  In fixing the amount of any fee which is to be payable to the Authority, no account is to be taken of any sums which the Authority receives, or expects to receive, by way of penalties imposed by it under this Act.

(3)  Sub-paragraph (1)(b) applies whether expenses were incurred before or after the coming into force of this Act or the Bank of England Act 1998.

(4)  Any fee which is owed to the Authority under any provision made by or under this Act may be recovered as a debt due to the Authority.

### Services for which fees may not be charged

**18**  The power conferred by paragraph 17 may not be used to require—

(a)  a fee to be paid in respect of the discharge of any of the Authority's functions under paragraphs 13, 14, 19 or 20 of Schedule 3; or

(b)  a fee to be paid by any person whose application for approval under section 59 has been granted.

# PART IV

# MISCELLANEOUS

### Exemption from liability in damages

**19**  (1)  Neither the Authority nor any person who is, or is acting as, a member, officer or member of staff of the Authority is to be liable in damages for anything done or omitted in the discharge, or purported discharge, of the Authority's functions

(2)  Neither the investigator appointed under paragraph 7 nor a person appointed to conduct an investigation on his behalf under paragraph 8(8) is to be liable in damages for anything done or omitted in the discharge, or purported discharge, of his functions in relation to the investigation of a complaint.

(3)  Neither sub-paragraph (1) nor sub-paragraph (2) applies—

(a)  if the act or omission is shown to have been in bad faith; or

(b)  so as to prevent an award of damages made in respect of an act or omission on the ground that the act or omission was unlawful as a result of section 6(1) of the Human Rights Act 1998.

**19A**  For the purposes of this Act anything done by an accredited financial investigator within the meaning of the Proceeds of Crime Act 2002 who is—

(a)  a member of the staff of the Authority, or

(b)  a person appointed by the Authority under section 97, 167 or 168 to conduct an investigation,

must be treated as done in the exercise or discharge of a function of the Authority.

### Disqualification for membership of House of Commons

**20**  In Part III of Schedule 1 to the House of Commons Disqualification Act 1975 (disqualifying offices), insert at the appropriate place—

'Member of the governing body of the Financial Services Authority.'

### Disqualification for membership of Northern Ireland Assembly

**21**  In Part III of Schedule 1 to the Northern Ireland Assembly Disqualification Act 1975 (disqualifying offices), insert at the appropriate place—

'Member of the governing body of the Financial Services Authority'.

# SCHEDULE 2

# REGULATED ACTIVITIES

## PART I

### REGULATED ACTIVITIES: GENERAL

#### General

**1**  The matters with respect to which provision may be made under section 22(1) in respect of activities include, in particular, those described in general terms in this Part of this Schedule

#### Dealing in investments

**2**  (1) Buying, selling, subscribing for or underwriting investments or offering or agreeing to do so, either as a principal or as an agent

(2)  In the case of an investment which is a contract of insurance, that includes carrying out the contract.

#### Arranging deals in investments

**3**  Making, or offering or agreeing to make—

   (a) arrangements with a view to another person buying, selling, subscribing for or underwriting a particular investment;

   (b) arrangements with a view to a person who participates in the arrangements buying, selling, subscribing for or underwriting investments.

#### Deposit taking

**4**  Accepting deposits

#### Safekeeping and administration of assets

**5**  (1) Safeguarding and administering assets belonging to another which consist of or include investments or offering or agreeing to do so

(2)  Arranging for the safeguarding and administration of assets belonging to another, or offering or agreeing to do so.

#### Managing investments

**6**  Managing, or offering or agreeing to manage, assets belonging to another person where—

   (a) the assets consist of or include investments; or

   (b) the arrangements for their management are such that the assets may consist of or include investments at the discretion of the person managing or offering or agreeing to manage them.

#### Investment advice

**7**  Giving or offering or agreeing to give advice to persons on—

   (a) buying, selling, subscribing for or underwriting an investment; or

   (b) exercising any right conferred by an investment to acquire, dispose of, underwrite or convert an investment.

#### Establishing collective investment schemes

**8**  Establishing, operating or winding up a collective investment scheme, including acting as—

   (a) trustee of a unit trust scheme;

   (b) depositary of a collective investment scheme other than a unit trust scheme; or

   (c) sole director of a body incorporated by virtue of regulations under section 262.

#### Using computer-based systems for giving investment instructions

**9**  (1) Sending on behalf of another person instructions relating to an investment by means of a computer-based system which enables investments to be transferred without a written instrument

(2)  Offering or agreeing to send such instructions by such means on behalf of another person.

(3)  Causing such instructions to be sent by such means on behalf of another person.

(4)  Offering or agreeing to cause such instructions to be sent by such means on behalf of another person.

# PART 1A

## REGULATED ACTIVITIES: RECLAIM FUNDS

### Activities of reclaim funds

**9A**  (1)  The matters with respect to which provision may be made under section 22(1) in respect of activities include, in particular, any of the activities of a reclaim fund.

(2)  'Reclaim fund' has the meaning given by section 5(1) of the Dormant Bank and Building Society Accounts Act 2008.

# PART II

## INVESTMENTS

### General

**10**  The matters with respect to which provision may be made under section 22(1) in respect of investments include, in particular, those described in general terms in this Part of this Schedule

### Securities

**11**  (1) Shares or stock in the share capital of a company

(2)  'Company' includes—

    (a) any body corporate (wherever incorporated), and

    (b) any unincorporated body constituted under the law of a country or territory outside the United Kingdom,

other than an open-ended investment company.

### Instruments creating or acknowledging indebtedness

**12**  Any of the following—

    (a) debentures;

    (b) debenture stock;

    (c) loan stock;

    (d) bonds;

    (e) certificates of deposit;

    (f) any other instruments creating or acknowledging a present or future indebtedness.

### Government and public securities

**13**  (1) Loan stock, bonds and other instruments—

    (a) creating or acknowledging indebtedness; and

    (b) issued by or on behalf of a government, local authority or public authority.

(2)  'Government, local authority or public authority' means—

    (a) the government of the United Kingdom, of Northern Ireland, or of any country or territory outside the United Kingdom;

    (b) a local authority in the United Kingdom or elsewhere;

    (c) any international organisation the members of which include the United Kingdom or another member State.

### Instruments giving entitlement to investments

**14**  (1) Warrants or other instruments entitling the holder to subscribe for any investment

(2)  It is immaterial whether the investment is in existence or identifiable.

### Certificates representing securities

**15**  Certificates or other instruments which confer contractual or property rights—

    (a) in respect of any investment held by someone other than the person on whom the rights are conferred by the certificate or other instrument; and

    (b) the transfer of which may be effected without requiring the consent of that person.

### Units in collective investment schemes

**16**  (1) Shares in or securities of an open-ended investment company

(2)  Any right to participate in a collective investment scheme.

### Options

**17**  Options to acquire or dispose of property

### Futures

**18**  Rights under a contract for the sale of a commodity or property of any other description under which delivery is to be made at a future date

### *Contracts for differences*

**19** Rights under—

(a) a contract for differences; or

(b) any other contract the purpose or pretended purpose of which is to secure a profit or avoid a loss by reference to fluctuations in—

(i) the value or price of property of any description; or

(ii) an index or other factor designated for that purpose in the contract.

### *Contracts of insurance*

**20** Rights under a contract of insurance, including rights under contracts falling within head C of Schedule 2 to the Friendly Societies Act 1992

### *Participation in Lloyd's syndicates*

**21** (1) The underwriting capacity of a Lloyd's syndicate

(2) A person's membership (or prospective membership) of a Lloyd's syndicate.

### *Deposits*

**22** Rights under any contract under which a sum of money (whether or not denominated in a currency) is paid on terms under which it will be repaid, with or without interest or a premium, and either on demand or at a time or in circumstances agreed by or on behalf of the person making the payment and the person receiving it

### *Loans secured on land*

**23** (1) Rights under any contract under which—

(a) one person provides another with credit; and

(b) the obligation of the borrower to repay is secured on land.

(2) 'Credit' includes any cash loan or other financial accommodation.

(3) 'Cash' includes money in any form.

### *Other finance arrangements involving land*

**23A** (1) Rights under any arrangement for the provision of finance under which the person providing the finance either—

(a) acquires a major interest in land from the person to whom the finance is provided, or

(b) disposes of a major interest in land to that person,

as part of the arrangement.

(2) References in sub-paragraph (1) to a 'major interest' in land are to—

(a) in relation to land in England or Wales—

(i) an estate in fee simple absolute, or

(ii) a term of years absolute,

whether subsisting at law or in equity;

(b) in relation to land in Scotland—

(i) the interest of an owner of land, or

(ii) the tenant's right over or interest in a property subject to a lease;

(c) in relation to land in Northern Ireland—

(i) any freehold estate, or

(ii) any leasehold estate,

whether subsisting at law or in equity.

(3) It is immaterial for the purposes of sub-paragraph (1) whether either party acquires or (as the case may be) disposes of the interest in land—

(a) directly, or

(b) indirectly.

### *Rights in investments*

**24** Any right or interest in anything which is an investment as a result of any other provision made under section 22(1)

## PART III

## SUPPLEMENTAL PROVISIONS

### *The order-making power*

**25** (1) An order under section 22(1) may—

(a) provide for exemptions;

(b) confer powers on the Treasury or the Authority;

(c) authorise the making of regulations or other instruments by the Treasury for purposes of, or connected with, any relevant provision;

(d) authorise the making of rules or other instruments by the Authority for purposes of, or connected with, any relevant provision;

(e) make provision in respect of any information or document which, in the opinion of the Treasury or the Authority, is relevant for purposes of, or connected with, any relevant provision;

(f) make such consequential, transitional or supplemental provision as the Treasury consider appropriate for purposes of, or connected with, any relevant provision.

(2) Provision made as a result of sub-paragraph (1)(f) may amend any primary or subordinate legislation, including any provision of, or made under, this Act.

(3) 'Relevant provision' means any provision—

(a) of section 22 or this Schedule; or

(b) made under that section or this Schedule.

### *Parliamentary control*

**26** (1) This paragraph applies to the first order made under section 22(1)

(2) This paragraph also applies to any subsequent order made under section 22(1) which contains a statement by the Treasury that, in their opinion, the effect (or one of the effects) of the proposed order would be that an activity which is not a regulated activity would become a regulated activity.

(3) An order to which this paragraph applies—

(a) must be laid before Parliament after being made; and

(b) ceases to have effect at the end of the relevant period unless before the end of that period the order is approved by a resolution of each House of Parliament (but without that affecting anything done under the order or the power to make a new order).

(4) 'Relevant period' means a period of twenty-eight days beginning with the day on which the order is made.

(5) In calculating the relevant period no account is to be taken of any time during which Parliament is dissolved or prorogued or during which both Houses are adjourned for more than four days.

### *Interpretation*

**27** (1) In this Schedule—

'buying' includes acquiring for valuable consideration;

'offering' includes inviting to treat;

'property' includes currency of the United Kingdom or any other country or territory; and

'selling' includes disposing for valuable consideration.

(2) In sub-paragraph (1) 'disposing' includes—

(a) in the case of an investment consisting of rights under a contract—

(i) surrendering, assigning or converting those rights; or

(ii) assuming the corresponding liabilities under the contract;

(b) in the case of an investment consisting of rights under other arrangements, assuming the corresponding liabilities under the contract or arrangements;

(c) in the case of any other investment, issuing or creating the investment or granting the rights or interests of which it consists.

(3) In this Schedule references to an instrument include references to any record (whether or not in the form of a document).

# SCHEDULE 3

# EEA PASSPORT RIGHTS

## PART I

## DEFINED TERMS

### *The single market directives*

**1** 'The single market directives' means—

(a) the banking consolidation directive;

(c) the insurance directives;

(ca) the reinsurance directive;

(d) the markets in financial instruments directive ; and

(e) the insurance mediation directive;

(f) the UCITS directive.

**2** 'The banking consolidation directive' means Directive 2006/48/EC of the European Parliament and of the Council of 14 June 2006 relating to the taking up and pursuit of the business of credit institutions.

### The insurance directives

**3** (1) 'The insurance directives' means the first, second and third non-life insurance directives and the life assurance consolidation directive.

(2) 'First non-life insurance directive' means the Council Directive of 24 July 1973 on the co-ordination of laws, regulations and administrative provisions relating to the taking up and pursuit of the business of direct insurance other than life assurance (No. 73/239/EEC).

(3) 'Second non-life insurance directive' means the Council Directive of 22 June 1988 on the co-ordination of laws, etc, and laying down provisions to facilitate the effective exercise of freedom to provide services and amending Directive 73/239/EEC (No. 88/357/EEC).

(4) 'Third non-life insurance directive' means the Council Directive of 18 June 1992 on the co-ordination of laws, etc, and amending Directives 73/239/EEC and 88/357/EEC (No. 92/49/EEC).

(8) 'Life assurance consolidation directive' means Directive 2002/83/EC of the European Parliament and of the Council of 5th November 2002 concerning life assurance.

### The reinsurance directive

**3A** 'The reinsurance directive' means Directive 2005/68/EC of the European Parliament and of the Council of 16 November 2005 on reinsurance and amending Council Directives 73/239/EEC, 92/49/EEC as well as Directives 98/78/EC and 2002/83/EC.

**4** [...]

### The insurance mediation directive

**4A** 'The insurance mediation directive' means the European Parliament and Council Directive of 9th December 2002 on insurance mediation (No. 2002/92/EC).

### The UCITS directive

**4B** 'The UCITS directive' means the Council Directive of 20 December 1985 on the coordination of laws, regulations and administrative provisions relating to undertakings for collective investment in transferable securities (No. 85/611/EEC).

### The markets in financial instruments directive

**4C** 'The markets in financial instruments directive' means Directive 2004/39/EC of the European Parliament and of the Council of 21 April 2004 on markets in financial instruments.

### EEA firm

**5** 'EEA firm' means any of the following if it does not have its relevant office in the United Kingdom—
- (a) an investment firm (as defined in Article 4.1.1 of the markets in financial instruments directive) which is authorised (within the meaning of Article 5) by its home state regulator;
- (b) a credit institution (as defined in Article 4.1 of the banking consolidation directive) which is authorised (within the meaning of Article 4.2) by its home state regulator,
- (c) a financial institution (as defined in Article 4.5 of the banking consolidation directive) which is a subsidiary of the kind mentioned in Article 24 and which fulfils the conditions in that Article;
- (d) an undertaking pursuing the activity of direct insurance (within the meaning of Article 2 of the life assurance consolidation directive or Article 1 of the first non-life insurance directive) which has received authorisation under Article 4 of the life assurance consolidation directive or Article 6 of the first non-life insurance directive from its home state regulator ;
- (da) an undertaking pursuing the activity of reinsurance (within the meaning of Article 2.1(a) of the reinsurance directive) which has received authorisation under (or is deemed to be authorised in accordance with) Article 3 of the reinsurance directive from its home state regulator;
- (e) an insurance intermediary (as defined in Article 2.5 of the insurance mediation directive), or a reinsurance intermediary (as defined in Article 2.6) which is registered with its home state regulator under Article 3; or
- (f) a management company (as defined in Article 1a.2 of the UCITS directive) which is authorised (within the meaning of Article 5) by its home state regulator.

**5A** In paragraph 5, 'relevant office' means—
- (a) in relation to a firm falling within sub-paragraph (e) of that paragraph which has a registered office, its registered office;
- (b) in relation to any other firm, its head office.

**6** 'EEA authorisation' means—
- (a) in relation to an EEA firm falling within paragraph 5(e), registration with its home state regulator under Article 3 of the insurance mediation directive;

(b) in relation to any other EEA firm, authorisation granted to an EEA firm by its home state regulator for the purpose of the relevant single market directive.

### *EEA right*

7 'EEA right' means the entitlement of a person to establish a branch, or provide services, in an EEA State other than that in which he has his relevant office—
    (a) in accordance with the Treaty as applied in the EEA; and
    (b) subject to the conditions of the relevant single market directive.

7A In paragraph 7, 'relevant office' means—
    (a) in relation to a person who has a registered office and whose entitlement is subject to the conditions of the insurance mediation directive, his registered office;
    (b) in relation to any other person, his head office.

8 'EEA State' has the meaning given by Schedule 1 to the Interpretation Act 1978.

### *Home state regulator*

9 'Home state regulator' means the competent authority (within the meaning of the relevant single market directive) of an EEA State (other than the United Kingdom) in relation to the EEA firm concerned.

### *UK firm*

10 'UK firm' means a person whose relevant office is in the UK and who has an EEA right to carry on activity in an EEA State other than the United Kingdom .

10A In paragraph 10, 'relevant office' means–
    (a) in relation to a firm whose EEA right derives from the insurance mediation directive and which has a registered office, its registered office;
    (b) in relation to any other firm, its head office.

### *UK investment firm*

10B 'UK investment firm' means a UK firm—
    (a) which is an investment firm, and
    (b) whose EEA right derives from the markets in financial instruments directive.

### *Host state regulator*

11 'Host state regulator' means the competent authority (within the meaning of the relevant single market directive) of an EEA State (other than the United Kingdom) in relation to a UK firm's exercise of EEA rights there.

### *Tied agent*

11A 'Tied agent' has the meaning given in Article 4.1.25 of the markets in financial instruments directive.

# PART II

## EXERCISE OF PASSPORT RIGHTS BY EEA FIRMS

### *Firms qualifying for authorisation*

12 (1) Once an EEA firm which is seeking to establish a branch in the United Kingdom in exercise of an EEA right satisfies the establishment conditions, it qualifies for authorisation.

(2) Once an EEA firm which is seeking to provide services in the United Kingdom in exercise of an EEA right satisfies the service conditions, it qualifies for authorisation.

(3) If an EEA firm falling within paragraph 5(a) is seeking to use a tied agent established in the United Kingdom in connection with the exercise of an EEA right deriving from the markets in financial instruments directive, this Part of this Schedule applies as if the firm were seeking to establish a branch in the United Kingdom.

(4) But if—
    (a) an EEA firm already qualifies for authorisation by virtue of sub-paragraph (1); and
    (b) the EEA right which it is exercising derives from the markets in financial instruments directive,
sub-paragraph (3) does not require the firm to satisfy the establishment conditions in respect of its use of the tied agent in question.

(5) An EEA firm which falls within paragraph 5(da) which establishes a branch in the United Kingdom, or provides services in the United Kingdom, in exercise of an EEA right qualifies for authorisation.

(6) Sub-paragraphs (1) and (2) do not apply to an EEA firm falling within paragraph 5(da).

### *Establishment*

13 (1) If the firm falls within paragraph 5(a), (b), (c), (d) or (f), the establishment conditions are that—

    (a) the Authority has received notice ('a consent notice') from the firm's home state regulator that it has given the firm consent to establish a branch in the United Kingdom;

    (b) the consent notice—

       (i)   is given in accordance with the relevant single market directive;

       (ii)  identifies the activities to which consent relates; and

       (iii) includes such other information as may be prescribed; [...]

    (ba) in the case of a firm falling within paragraph 5(a), the Authority has given the firm notice for the purposes of this paragraph or two months have elapsed beginning with the date when the home state regulator gave the consent notice; and

    (c) in the case of a firm falling within paragraph 5(b), (c), (d) or (f), the firm has been informed of the applicable provisions or two months have elapsed beginning with the date when the Authority received the consent notice.

(1A) If the firm falls within paragraph 5(e), the establishment conditions are that—

    (a) the firm has given its home state regulator notice of its intention to establish a branch in the United Kingdom;

    (b) the Authority has received notice ('a regulator's notice') from the firm's home state regulator that the firm intends to establish a branch in the United Kingdom;

    (c) the firm's home state regulator has informed the firm that the regulator's notice has been sent to the Authority; and

    (d) one month has elapsed beginning with the date on which the firm's home state regulator informed the firm that the regulator's notice has been sent to the Authority.

(2) If the Authority has received a consent notice, it must—

    (a) prepare for the firm's supervision;

    (b) except if the firm falls within paragraph 5(a), notify the firm of the applicable provisions (if any); and

    (c) if the firm falls within paragraph 5(d), notify its home state regulator of the applicable provisions (if any).

(3) A notice under sub-paragraph (2)(b) or (c) must be given before the end of the period of two months beginning with the day on which the Authority received the consent notice.

(4) For the purposes of this paragraph—

'applicable provisions' means the host state rules with which the firm is required to comply when carrying on a permitted activity through a branch in the United Kingdom;

'host state rules' means rules—

    (a) made in accordance with the relevant single market directive; and

    (b) which are the responsibility of the United Kingdom (both as to implementation and as to supervision of compliance) in accordance with that directive; and

'permitted activity' means an activity identified in the consent notice or regulator's notice, as the case may be.

### *Services*

**14** (1) The service conditions are that—

    (a) the firm has given its home state regulator notice of its intention to provide services in the United Kingdom ('a notice of intention');

    (b) if the firm falls within paragraph 5(a), (d), (e) or (f) , the Authority has received notice ('a regulator's notice') from the firm's home state regulator containing such information as may be prescribed; [...]

    (ba) if the firm falls within paragraph 5(b) and is seeking to provide services in exercise of the right under Article 31.5 of the markets in financial instruments directive, the Authority has received notice ('a regulator's notice') from the firm's home state regulator stating that the firm intends to exercise that right in the United Kingdom;

    (c) if the firm falls within paragraph 5(d) or (e), its home state regulator has informed it that the regulator's notice has been sent to the Authority; and

    (d) if the firm falls within paragraph 5(e), one month has elapsed beginning with the date on which the firm's home state regulator informed the firm that the regulator's notice has been sent to the Authority.

(2) If the Authority has received a regulator's notice or, where none is required by sub-paragraph (1), has been informed of the firm's intention to provide services in the United Kingdom, it must , unless the firm falls within paragraph 5(e)—

    (a) prepare for the firm's supervision; and

    (b) notify the firm of the applicable provisions (if any).

(2A) Sub-paragraph (2)(b) does not apply in the case of a firm falling within paragraph 5(a).

(3) A notice under sub-paragraph (2)(b) must be given before the end of the period of two months beginning on the day on which the Authority received the regulator's notice, or was informed of the firm's intention.

(4) For the purposes of this paragraph—

'applicable provisions' means the host state rules with which the firm is required to comply when carrying on a permitted activity by providing services in the United Kingdom;

'host state rules' means rules—

(a) made in accordance with the relevant single market directive; and

(b) which are the responsibility of the United Kingdom (both as to implementation and as to supervision of compliance) in accordance with that directive; and

'permitted activity' means an activity identified in—

(a) the regulator's notice; or

(b) where none is required by sub-paragraph (1), the notice of intention.

### Grant of permission

**15**   (1) On qualifying for authorisation as a result of paragraph 12(1), (2) or (3), a firm has, in respect of each permitted activity which is a regulated activity, permission to carry it on through its United Kingdom branch (if it satisfies the establishment conditions) or by providing services in the United Kingdom (if it satisfies the service conditions).

(1A) Sub-paragraph (1) is to be read subject to paragraph 15A(3).

(2) The permission is to be treated as being on terms equivalent to those appearing from the consent notice, regulator's notice or notice of intention.

(3) Sections 21 and 39(1) of the Consumer Credit Act 1974 (business requiring a licence under that Act) do not apply in relation to the carrying on of a permitted activity which is Consumer Credit Act business by a firm which qualifies for authorisation as a result of paragraph 12 , unless the Office of Fair Trading has exercised the power conferred on it by section 203 in relation to the firm.

(4) 'Consumer Credit Act business' has the same meaning as in section 203.

(5) A firm which qualifies for authorisation as a result of paragraph 12(5) has, in respect of each permitted activity which is a regulated activity, permission to carry it on through its United Kingdom branch or by providing services in the United Kingdom.

(6) The permission is to be treated as being on terms equivalent to those appearing in the authorisation granted to the firm under Article 3 of the reinsurance directive by its home state regulator ('its home authorisation').

(7) For the purposes of sub-paragraph (5), 'permitted activity' means an activity which the firm is permitted to carry on under its home authorisation.

### Power to restrict permission of management companies

**15A**   (1) Sub-paragraph (2) applies if—

(a) a firm falling within paragraph 5(f) qualifies for authorisation as a result of paragraph 12(1) (establishment conditions satisfied); but

(b) the Authority determines that the way in which the firm intends to invite persons in the United Kingdom to become participants in any collective investment scheme which that firm manages does not comply with the law in force in the United Kingdom.

(2) The Authority may give a notice to the firm and the firm's home state regulator of the Authority's determination under sub-paragraph (1)(b).

(3) Paragraph 15(1) does not give a firm to which the Authority has given (and not withdrawn) a notice under sub-paragraph (2) permission to carry on through the firm's United Kingdom branch the regulated activity of dealing in units in the collective investment schemes which the firm manages.

(4) Any notice given under sub-paragraph (2) must be given before the end of the period of two months beginning with the day on which the Authority received the consent notice.

(5) Sections 264(4) and 265(1), (2) and (4) apply to a notice given under sub-paragraph (2) as they apply to a notice given by the Authority under section 264(2).

(6) If a decision notice is given to the firm under section 265(4), by virtue of sub-paragraph (5), the firm may refer the matter to the Tribunal.

(7) In sub-paragraph (3)—

(a) 'units' has the meaning given by section 237(2); and

(b) the reference to 'dealing in' units in a collective investment scheme must be read with–

(i) section 22;

(ii) any relevant order under that section; and

(iii) Schedule 2.

### Effect of carrying on regulated activity when not qualified for authorisation

**16**   (1) This paragraph applies to an EEA firm which is not qualified for authorisation under paragraph 12.

(2) Section 26 does not apply to an agreement entered into by the firm.

(3) Section 27 does not apply to an agreement in relation to which the firm is a third party for the purposes of that section.

(4) Section 29 does not apply to an agreement in relation to which the firm is the deposit-taker.

### *Continuing regulation of EEA firms*

17 Regulations may—

    (a) modify any provision of this Act which is an applicable provision (within the meaning of paragraph 13 or 14) in its application to an EEA firm qualifying for authorisation;

    (b) make provision as to any change (or proposed change) of a prescribed kind relating to an EEA firm or to an activity that it carries on in the United Kingdom and as to the procedure to be followed in relation to such cases;

    (c) provide that the Authority may treat an EEA firm's notification that it is to cease to carry on regulated activity in the United Kingdom as a request for cancellation of its qualification for authorisation under this Schedule.

### *Giving up right to authorisation*

18 Regulations may provide that in prescribed circumstances an EEA firm falling within paragraph 5(c) may, on following the prescribed procedure—

    (a) have its qualification for authorisation under this Schedule cancelled; and

    (b) seek to become an authorised person by applying for a Part IV permission.

19 (1) Subject to sub-paragraphs (5ZA) and (5A), a UK firm may not exercise an EEA right to establish a branch unless three conditions are satisfied.

(2) The first is that the firm has given the Authority, in the specified way, notice of its intention to establish a branch ('a notice of intention') which—

    (a) identifies the activities which it seeks to carry on through the branch; and

    (b) includes such other information as may be specified.

(3) Subject to sub-paragraph (5B), the activities identified in a notice of intention may include activities which are not regulated activities.

(4) The second is that the Authority has given notice in specified terms ('a consent notice') to the host state regulator.

(5) The third is—

    (a) if the EEA right in question derives from the insurance mediation directive, that one month has elapsed beginning with the date on which the firm received notice, in accordance with sub-paragraph (11), that the Authority has given a consent notice;

    (b) in any other case, that either—

        (i) the host state regulator has notified the firm (or, where the EEA right in question derives from any of the insurance directives, the Authority) of the applicable provisions; or

        (ii) two months have elapsed beginning with the date on which the Authority gave the consent notice.

(5ZA) This paragraph does not apply to a UK firm having an EEA right which is subject to the conditions of the reinsurance directive.

(5A) If—

    (a) the EEA right in question derives from the insurance mediation directive, and

    (b) the EEA State in which the firm intends to establish a branch has not notified the Commission, in accordance with Article 6(2) of that directive, of its wish to be informed of the intention of any UK firm to establish a branch in its territory,

the second and third conditions do not apply (and so the firm may establish the branch to which its notice of intention relates as soon as the first condition is satisfied).

(5B) If the firm is a UK investment firm, a notice of intention may not include ancillary services unless such services are to be provided in connection with the carrying on of one or more investment services and activities.

(5C) In sub-paragraph (5B) 'ancillary services' has the meaning given in Article 4.1.3 of the markets in financial instruments directive.

(6) If the firm's EEA right derives from the banking consolidation directive, the UCITS directive or, in the case of a credit institution authorised under the banking consolidation directive, the markets in financial instruments directive and the first condition is satisfied, the Authority must give a consent notice to the host state regulator unless it has reason to doubt the adequacy of the firm's resources or its administrative structure.

(7) If the firm's EEA right derives from any of the insurance directives and the first condition is satisfied, the Authority must give a consent notice unless it has reason—

    (a) to doubt the adequacy of the firm's resources or its administrative structure, or

    (b) to question the reputation, qualifications or experience of the directors or managers of the firm or the person proposed as the branch's authorised agent for the purposes of those directives,

in relation to the business to be conducted through the proposed branch.

(7A) If—

    (a) the firm's EEA right derives from the insurance mediation directive,

    (b) the first condition is satisfied, and

    (c) the second condition applies,

the Authority must give a consent notice, and must do so within one month beginning with the date on which it received the firm's notice of intention.

(7B) If the firm is a UK investment firm and the first condition is satisfied, the Authority must give a consent notice to the host state regulator within three months beginning with the date on which it received the firm's notice of intention unless the Authority has reason to doubt the adequacy of the firm's resources or its administrative structure.

(8) If the Authority proposes to refuse to give a consent notice it must give the firm concerned a warning notice.

(9) If the firm's EEA right derives from any of the insurance directives and the host state regulator has notified it of the applicable provisions, the Authority must inform the firm of those provisions.

(10) Rules may specify the procedure to be followed by the Authority in exercising its functions under this paragraph.

(11) If the Authority gives a consent notice it must give written notice that it has done so to the firm concerned.

(12) If the Authority decides to refuse to give a consent notice—

    (a) it must, within the relevant period , give the person who gave that notice a decision notice to that effect; and

    (b) that person may refer the matter to the Tribunal.

(12A) In sub-paragraph (12), 'the relevant period' means—

    (a) if the firm's EEA right derives from the UCITS directive, two months beginning with the date on which the Authority received the notice of intention;

    (b) in any other case, three months beginning with that date.

(13) In this paragraph, 'applicable provisions' means the host state rules with which the firm will be required to comply when conducting business through the proposed branch in the EEA State concerned.

(14) In sub-paragraph (13), 'host state rules' means rules—

    (a) made in accordance with the relevant single market directive; and

    (b) which are the responsibility of the EEA State concerned (both as to implementation and as to supervision of compliance) in accordance with that directive.

(15) 'Specified' means specified in rules.

### Services

**20** (1) Subject to sub-paragraph (4D), a UK firm may not exercise an EEA right to provide services unless the firm has given the Authority, in the specified way, notice of its intention to provide services ('a notice of intention') which—

    (a) identifies the activities which it seeks to carry out by way of provision of services; and

    (b) includes such other information as may be specified.

(2) Subject to sub-paragraph (2A), the activities identified in a notice of intention may include activities which are not regulated activities.

(2A) If the firm is a UK investment firm, a notice of intention may not include ancillary services unless such services are to be provided in connection with the carrying on of one or more investment services and activities.

(2B) In sub-paragraph (2A) 'ancillary services' has the meaning given in Article 4.1.3 of the markets in financial instruments directive.

(3) If the firm's EEA right derives from the banking consolidation directive, the markets in financial instruments directive or the UCITS directive, the Authority must, within one month of receiving a notice of intention, send a copy of it to the host state regulator with such other information as may be specified.

(3A) If the firm's EEA right derives from any of the insurance directives, the Authority must, within one month of receiving the notice of intention—

    (a) give notice in specified terms ('a consent notice') to the host state regulator; or

    (b) give written notice to the firm of—

        (i) its refusal to give a consent notice; and

        (ii) its reasons for that refusal.

(3B) If the firm's EEA right derives from the insurance mediation directive and the EEA State in which the firm intends to provide services has notified the Commission, in accordance with Article 6(2) of that directive, of its wish to be informed of the intention of any UK firm to provide services in its territory—

    (a) the Authority must, within one month of receiving the notice of intention, send a copy of it to the host state regulator;

    (b) the Authority, when it sends the copy in accordance with sub-paragraph (a), must give written notice to the firm concerned that it has done so; and

    (c) the firm concerned must not provide the services to which its notice of intention relates until one month, beginning with the date on which it receives the notice under sub-paragraph (b), has elapsed.

(4) When the Authority sends the copy under sub-paragraph (3) or gives a consent notice, it must give written notice to the firm concerned.

(4A) If the firm is given notice under sub-paragraph (3A)(b), it may refer the matter to the Tribunal.

(4B) If the firm's EEA right derives from any of the insurance directives or from the markets in financial instruments directive , it must not provide the services to which its notice of intention relates until it has received written notice under sub-paragraph (4).

(4BA) If the firm's EEA right derives from the markets in financial instruments directive, the Authority must comply as soon as reasonably practicable with a request for information under the second sub-paragraph of Article 31.6 of that directive from the host state regulator.

(4C) Rules may specify the procedure to be followed by the Authority under this paragraph.

(4D) This paragraph does not apply to a UK firm having an EEA right which is subject to the conditions of the reinsurance directive.

(6) 'Specified' means specified in rules.

### Tied agents

**20A**   (1) If a UK investment firm is seeking to use a tied agent established in an EEA State (other than the United Kingdom) in connection with the exercise of an EEA right deriving from the markets in financial instruments directive, this Part of this Schedule applies as if the firm were seeking to establish a branch in that State.

(2)  But if—

(a) a UK investment firm has already established a branch in an EEA State other than the United Kingdom in accordance with paragraph 19; and

(b) the EEA right which it is exercising derives from the markets in financial instruments directive,

paragraph 19 does not apply in respect of its use of the tied agent in question.

### Offence relating to exercise of passport rights

**21**   (1) If a UK firm which is not an authorised person contravenes the prohibition imposed by—

(a) sub-paragraph (1) of paragraph 19, or

(b) sub-paragraph (1), (3B)(c) or (4B) of paragraph 20,

it is guilty of an offence.

(2)  A firm guilty of an offence under sub-paragraph (1) is liable—

(a) on summary conviction, to a fine not exceeding the statutory maximum; or

(b) on conviction on indictment, to a fine.

(3)  In proceedings for an offence under sub-paragraph (1), it is a defence for the firm to show that it took all reasonable precautions and exercised all due diligence to avoid committing the offence.

### Continuing regulation of UK firms

**22**   (1) Regulations may make such provision as the Treasury consider appropriate in relation to a UK firm's exercise of EEA rights, and may in particular provide for the application (with or without modification) of any provision of, or made under, this Act in relation to an activity of a UK firm.

(2)  Regulations may—

(a) make provision as to any change (or proposed change) of a prescribed kind relating to a UK firm or to an activity that it carries on and as to the procedure to be followed in relation to such cases;

(b) make provision with respect to the consequences of the firm's failure to comply with a provision of the regulations.

(3)  Where a provision of the kind mentioned in sub-paragraph (2) requires the Authority's consent to a change (or proposed change)—

(a) consent may be refused only on prescribed grounds; and

(b) if the Authority decides to refuse consent, the firm concerned may refer the matter to the Tribunal.

**23**   (1) Sub-paragraphs (2) and (2A) apply if a UK firm—

(a) has a Part IV permission; and

(b) is exercising an EEA right to carry on any Consumer Credit Act business in an EEA State other than the United Kingdom.

(2)  The Authority may exercise its power under section 45 in respect of the firm if the Office of Fair Trading has informed the Authority that—

(a) the firm,

(b) any of the firm's employees, agents or associates (whether past or present), or

(c) if the firm is a body corporate, a controller of the firm or an associate of such a controller,

has done any of the things specified in paragraphs (a) to (e) of section 25(2A) of the Consumer Credit Act 1974.

(2A) The Authority may also exercise its power under section 45 in respect of the firm if the Office of Fair Trading has informed the Authority that it has concerns about any of the following—

(a) the firm's skills, knowledge and experience in relation to Consumer Credit Act businesses;

(b) such skills, knowledge and experience of other persons who are participating in any Consumer Credit Act business being carried on by the firm;

(c) practices and procedures that the firm is implementing in connection with any such business.

(3) 'Associate', 'Consumer Credit Act business' and 'controller' have the same meaning as in section 203.

24   (1) Sub-paragraph (2) applies if a UK firm—

(a) is not required to have a Part IV permission in relation to the business which it is carrying on; and

(b) is exercising the right conferred by Article 24 of the banking consolidation directive to carry on that business in an EEA State other than the United Kingdom.

(2) If requested to do so by the host state regulator in the EEA State in which the UK firm's business is being carried on, the Authority may impose any requirement in relation to the firm which it could impose if—

(a) the firm had a Part IV permission in relation to the business which it is carrying on; and

(b) the Authority was entitled to exercise its power under that Part to vary that permission.

### Information to be included in the public record

25   The Authority must include in the record that it maintains under section 347 in relation to any UK firm whose EEA right derives from the insurance mediation directive information as to each EEA State in which the UK firm, in accordance with such a right—

(a) has established a branch; or

(b) is providing services.

# SCHEDULE 4

# TREATY RIGHTS

### Definitions

1   In this Schedule—

'consumers' means persons who are consumers for the purposes of section 138;

'Treaty firm' means a person—

(a) whose head office is situated in an EEA State (its 'home state') other than the United Kingdom; and

(b) which is recognised under the law of that State as its national; and

'home state regulator', in relation to a Treaty firm, means the competent authority of the firm's home state for the purpose of its home state authorisation (as to which see paragraph 3(1)(a)).

### Firms qualifying for authorisation

2   Once a Treaty firm which is seeking to carry on a regulated activity satisfies the conditions set out in paragraph 3(1), it qualifies for authorisation

### Exercise of Treaty rights

3   (1) The conditions are that—

(a) the firm has received authorisation ('home state authorisation') under the law of its home state to carry on the regulated activity in question ('the permitted activity');

(b) the relevant provisions of the law of the firm's home state—

(i) afford equivalent protection; or

(ii) satisfy the conditions laid down by a Community instrument for the co-ordination or approximation of laws, regulations or administrative provisions of member States relating to the carrying on of that activity; and

(c) the firm has no EEA right to carry on that activity in the manner in which it is seeking to carry it on.

(2) A firm is not to be regarded as having home state authorisation unless its home state regulator has so informed the Authority in writing.

(3) Provisions afford equivalent protection if, in relation to the firm's carrying on of the permitted activity, they afford consumers protection which is at least equivalent to that afforded by or under this Act in relation to that activity.

(4) A certificate issued by the Treasury that the provisions of the law of a particular EEA State afford equivalent protection in relation to the activities specified in the certificate is conclusive evidence of that fact.

*Permission*

**4** (1) On qualifying for authorisation under this Schedule, a Treaty firm has permission to carry on each permitted activity through its United Kingdom branch or by providing services in the United Kingdom

(2) The permission is to be treated as being on terms equivalent to those to which the firm's home state authorisation is subject.

(3) If, on qualifying for authorisation under this Schedule, a firm has a Part IV permission which includes permission to carry on a permitted activity, the Authority must give a direction cancelling the permission so far as it relates to that activity.

(4) The Authority need not give a direction under sub-paragraph (3) if it considers that there are good reasons for not doing so.

*Notice to Authority*

**5** (1) Sub-paragraph (2) applies to a Treaty firm which—

(a) qualifies for authorisation under this Schedule, but

(b) is not carrying on in the United Kingdom the regulated activity, or any of the regulated activities, which it has permission to carry on there.

(2) At least seven days before it begins to carry on such a regulated activity, the firm must give the Authority written notice of its intention to do so.

(3) If a Treaty firm to which sub-paragraph (2) applies has given notice under that sub-paragraph, it need not give such a notice if it again becomes a firm to which that sub-paragraph applies.

(4) Subsections (1), (3) and (6) of section 51 apply to a notice under sub-paragraph (2) as they apply to an application for a Part IV permission.

*Offences*

**6** (1) A person who contravenes paragraph 5(2) is guilty of an offence.

(2) In proceedings against a person for an offence under sub-paragraph (1) it is a defence for him to show that he took all reasonable precautions and exercised all due diligence to avoid committing the offence.

(3) A person is guilty of an offence if in, or in connection with, a notice given by him under paragraph 5(2) he—

(a) provides information which he knows to be false or misleading in a material particular; or

(b) recklessly provides information which is false or misleading in a material particular.

(4) A person guilty of an offence under this paragraph is liable—

(a) on summary conviction, to a fine not exceeding the statutory maximum;

(b) on conviction on indictment, to a fine.

# SCHEDULE 5

## PERSONS CONCERNED IN COLLECTIVE INVESTMENT SCHEMES

*Authorisation*

**1** (1) A person who for the time being is an operator, trustee or depositary of a recognised collective investment scheme is an authorised person

(2) 'Recognised' means recognised by virtue of section 264.

(3) An authorised open-ended investment company is an authorised person.

(4) A body—

(a) incorporated by virtue of regulations made under section 1 of the Open-Ended Investment Companies Act (Northern Ireland) 2002 in respect of which an authorisation order is in force, and

(b) to which the UCITS directive applies,

is an authorised person.

(5) 'Authorisation order' means an order made under (or having effect as made under) any provision of those regulations which is made by virtue of section 1(2)(1) of that Act (provision corresponding to Chapter 3 of Part 17 of the Act).

*Permission*

**2** (1) A person authorised as a result of paragraph 1(1) has permission to carry on, so far as it is a regulated activity—

(a) any activity, appropriate to the capacity in which he acts in relation to the scheme, of the kind described in paragraph 8 of Schedule 2;

(b) any activity in connection with, or for the purposes of, the scheme.

(2) A person authorised as a result of paragraph 1(3) or (4) has permission to carry on, so far as it is a regulated activity—

    (a) the operation of the scheme;

    (b) any activity in connection with, or for the purposes of, the operation of the scheme.

# SCHEDULE 6

# THRESHOLD CONDITIONS

## PART I

## PART IV PERMISSION

### *Legal status*

**1** (1) If the regulated activity concerned is the effecting or carrying out of contracts of insurance the authorised person must be a body corporate (other than a limited liability partnership), a registered friendly society or a member of Lloyd's

(2) If the person concerned appears to the Authority to be seeking to carry on, or to be carrying on, a regulated activity constituting accepting deposits or issuing electronic money, it must be—

    (a) a body corporate; or

    (b) a partnership.

### *Location of offices*

**2** (1) Subject to paragraphs 2A and 3, if the person concerned is a body corporate constituted under the law of any part of the United Kingdom—

    (a) its head office, and

    (b) if it has a registered office, that office,

must be in the United Kingdom.

(2) If the person concerned has its head office in the United Kingdom but is not a body corporate, it must carry on business in the United Kingdom.

(2A) If—

    (a) the regulated activity concerned is any of the investment services and activities, and

    (b) the person concerned is a body corporate with no registered office,

sub-paragraph (2B) applies in place of sub-paragraph (1).

(2B) If the person concerned has its head office in the United Kingdom, it must carry on business in the United Kingdom.

(3) If the regulated activity concerned is an insurance mediation activity, sub-paragraph (1) does not apply.

(4) If the regulated activity concerned is an insurance mediation activity, the person concerned—

    (a) if he is a body corporate constituted under the law of any part of the United Kingdom, must have its registered office, or if it has no registered office, its head office, in the United Kingdom;

    (b) if he is a natural person, is to be treated for the purposes of sub-paragraph (2), as having his head office in the United Kingdom if his residence is situated there.

(5) 'Insurance mediation activity' means any of the following activities—

    (a) dealing in rights under a contract of insurance as agent; (b) arranging deals in rights under a contract of insurance;

    (c) assisting in the administration and performance of a contract of insurance;

    (d) advising on buying or selling rights under a contract of insurance;

    (e) agreeing to do any of the activities specified in sub-paragraph (a) to (d).

(6) Paragraph (5) must be read with—

    (a) section 22;

    (b) any relevant order under that section; and

    (c) Schedule 2.

### *Appointment of claims representatives*

**2A** (1) If it appears to the Authority that—

    (a) the regulated activity that the person concerned is carrying on, or is seeking to carry on, is the effecting or carrying out of contracts of insurance, and

    (b) contracts of insurance against damage arising out of or in connection with the use of motor vehicles on land (other than carrier's liability) are being, or will be, effected or carried out by the person concerned,

that person must have a claims representative in each EEA State other than the United Kingdom.

(2) For the purposes of sub-paragraph (1)(b), contracts of reinsurance are to be disregarded.

(3) A claims representative is a person with responsibility for handling and settling claims arising from accidents of the kind mentioned in Article 1(2) of the fourth motor insurance directive.

(4) In this paragraph 'fourth motor insurance directive' means Directive 2000/26/EC of the European Parliament and of the Council of 16th May 2000 on the approximation of the laws of the Member States relating to insurance against civil liability in respect of the use of motor vehicles and amending Council Directives 73/239/EEC and 88/357/EEC

### Close links

**3**  (1) If the person concerned ('A') has close links with another person ('CL') the Authority must be satisfied—

    (a) that those links are not likely to prevent the Authority's effective supervision of A; and

    (b) if it appears to the Authority that CL is subject to the laws, regulations or administrative provisions of a territory which is not an EEA State ('the foreign provisions'), that neither the foreign provisions, nor any deficiency in their enforcement, would prevent the Authority's effective supervision of A.

(2) A has close links with CL if—

    (a) CL is a parent undertaking of A;

    (b) CL is a subsidiary undertaking of A;

    (c) CL is a parent undertaking of a subsidiary undertaking of A;

    (d) CL is a subsidiary undertaking of a parent undertaking of A;

    (e) CL owns or controls 20% or more of the voting rights or capital of A; or

    (f) A owns or controls 20% or more of the voting rights or capital of CL.

(3) 'Subsidiary undertaking' includes all the instances mentioned in Article 1(1) and (2) of the Seventh Company Law Directive in which an entity may be a subsidiary of an undertaking.

### Adequate resources

**4**  (1) The resources of the person concerned must, in the opinion of the Authority, be adequate in relation to the regulated activities that he seeks to carry on, or carries on

(2) In reaching that opinion, the Authority may—

    (a) take into account the person's membership of a group and any effect which that membership may have; and

    (b) have regard to—

        (i) the provision he makes and, if he is a member of a group, which other members of the group make in respect of liabilities (including contingent and future liabilities); and

        (ii) the means by which he manages and, if he is a member of a group, which other members of the group manage the incidence of risk in connection with his business.

### Suitability

**5**  The person concerned must satisfy the Authority that he is a fit and proper person having regard to all the circumstances, including—

    (a) his connection with any person;

    (b) the nature of any regulated activity that he carries on or seeks to carry on; and

    (c) the need to ensure that his affairs are conducted soundly and prudently.

## PART II

## AUTHORISATION

### Authorisation under Schedule 3

**6**  In relation to an EEA firm qualifying for authorisation under Schedule 3, the conditions set out in paragraphs 1 and 3 to 5 apply, so far as relevant, to—

    (a) an application for permission under Part IV;

    (b) exercise of the Authority's own-initiative power under section 45 in relation to a Part IV permission.

### Authorisation under Schedule 4

**7**  In relation to a person who qualifies for authorisation under Schedule 4, the conditions set out in paragraphs 1 and 3 to 5 apply, so far as relevant, to—

    (a) an application for an additional permission;

    (b) the exercise of the Authority's own-initiative power under section 45 in relation to additional permission.

## PART III

## ADDITIONAL CONDITIONS

**8**    (1) If this paragraph applies to the person concerned, he must, for the purposes of such provisions of this Act as may be specified, satisfy specified additional conditions

(2)  This paragraph applies to a person who—

(a)  has his head office outside the EEA; and

(b)  appears to the Authority to be seeking to carry on a regulated activity relating to insurance business.

(3)  'Specified' means specified in, or in accordance with, an order made by the Treasury.

**9**    The Treasury may by order—

(a)  vary or remove any of the conditions set out in Parts I and II;

(b)  add to those conditions.

# SCHEDULE 7

# THE AUTHORITY AS COMPETENT AUTHORITY FOR PART VI

### General

**1**    This Act applies in relation to the Authority when it is exercising functions under Part VI as the competent authority subject to the following modifications.

### The Authority's general functions

**2**    In section 2—

(a)  subsection (4)(a) does not apply to the Part 6 rule;

(b)  subsection (4)(c) does not apply to general guidance given in relation to Part VI; and

(c)  subsection (4)(d) does not apply to functions under Part VI.

### Duty to consult

**3**    Section 8 does not apply

### Rules

**4**    (1) Sections 149, 153, 154 and 156 do not apply

(2)  Section 155 has effect as if—

(a)  the reference in subsection (2)(c) to the general duties of the Authority under section 2 were a reference to its duty under section 73; and

(b)  section 99 were included in the provisions referred to in subsection (9).

### Statements of policy

**5**    (1) Paragraph 5 of Schedule 1 has effect as if the requirement to act through the Authority's governing body applied also to the exercise of its functions of publishing statements under section 93

(2)  Paragraph 1 of Schedule 1 has effect as if section 93 were included in the provisions referred to in sub-paragraph (2)(d).

### Penalties

**6**    Paragraph 16 of Schedule 1 does not apply in relation to penalties under Part VI (for which separate provision is made by section 100)

### Fees

**7**    Paragraph 17 of Schedule 1 does not apply in relation to fees payable under Part VI (for which separate provision is made by section 99)

### Exemption from liability in damages

**8**    Schedule 1 has effect as if—

(a)  sub-paragraph (1) of paragraph 19 were omitted (similar provision being made in relation to the competent authority by section 102); and

(b)  for the words from the beginning to '(a)' in sub-paragraph (3) of that paragraph, there were substituted 'Sub-paragraph (2) does not apply'.

# SCHEDULE 8

## TRANSFER OF FUNCTIONS UNDER PART VI

### *The power to transfer*

**1** (1) The Treasury may by order provide for any function conferred on the competent authority which is exercisable for the time being by a particular person to be transferred so as to be exercisable by another person

(2)  An order may be made under this paragraph only if—

    (a)  the person from whom the relevant functions are to be transferred has agreed in writing that the order should be made;

    (b)  the Treasury are satisfied that the manner in which, or efficiency with which, the functions are discharged would be significantly improved if they were transferred to the transferee; or

    (c)  the Treasury are satisfied that it is otherwise in the public interest that the order should be made.

### *Supplemental*

**2**  (1) An order under this Schedule does not affect anything previously done by any person ('the previous authority') in the exercise of functions which are transferred by the order to another person ('the new authority')

(2)  Such an order may, in particular, include provision—

    (a)  modifying or excluding any provision of Part VI, IX or XXVI in its application to any such functions;

    (b)  for reviews similar to that made, in relation to the Authority, by section 12;

    (c)  imposing on the new authority requirements similar to those imposed, in relation to the Authority, by sections 152, 155 and 354;

    (d)  as to the giving of guidance by the new authority;

    (e)  for the delegation by the new authority of the exercise of functions under Part VI and as to the consequences of delegation;

    (f)  for the transfer of any property, rights or liabilities relating to any such functions from the previous authority to the new authority;

    (g)  for the carrying on and completion by the new authority of anything in the process of being done by the previous authority when the order takes effect;

    (h)  for the substitution of the new authority for the previous authority in any instrument, contract or legal proceedings;

    (i)  for the transfer of persons employed by the previous authority to the new authority and as to the terms on which they are to transfer;

    (j)  making such amendments to any primary or subordinate legislation (including any provision of, or made under, this Act) as the Treasury consider appropriate in consequence of the transfer of functions effected by the order.

(3)  Nothing in this paragraph is to be taken as restricting the powers conferred by section 428.

**3**  If the Treasury have made an order under paragraph 1 ('the transfer order') they may, by a separate order made under this paragraph, make any provision of a kind that could have been included in the transfer order

# SCHEDULE 9

# [...]

# SCHEDULE 10

## COMPENSATION: EXEMPTIONS

### *Statements believed to be true*

**1**   (1) In this paragraph 'statement' means—

    (a)  any untrue or misleading statement in listing particulars; or

    (b)  the omission from listing particulars of any matter required to be included by section 80 or 81.

(2)  A person does not incur any liability under section 90(1) for loss caused by a statement if he satisfies the court that, at the time when the listing particulars were submitted to the competent authority, he reasonably believed (having made such enquiries, if any, as were reasonable) that—

    (a)  the statement was true and not misleading, or

(b) the matter whose omission caused the loss was properly omitted,

and that one or more of the conditions set out in sub-paragraph (3) are satisfied.

(3) The conditions are that—

(a) he continued in his belief until the time when the securities in question were acquired;

(b) they were acquired before it was reasonably practicable to bring a correction to the attention of persons likely to acquire them;

(c) before the securities were acquired, he had taken all such steps as it was reasonable for him to have taken to secure that a correction was brought to the attention of those persons;

(d) he continued in his belief until after the commencement of dealings in the securities following their admission to the official list and they were acquired after such a lapse of time that he ought in the circumstances to be reasonably excused.

### Statements by experts

2 (1) In this paragraph 'statement' means a statement included in listing particulars which—

(a) purports to be made by, or on the authority of, another person as an expert; and

(b) is stated to be included in the listing particulars with that other person's consent.

(2) A person does not incur any liability under section 90(1) for loss in respect of any securities caused by a statement if he satisfies the court that, at the time when the listing particulars were submitted to the competent authority, he reasonably believed that the other person—

(a) was competent to make or authorise the statement, and

(b) had consented to its inclusion in the form and context in which it was included,

and that one or more of the conditions set out in sub-paragraph (3) are satisfied.

(3) The conditions are that—

(a) he continued in his belief until the time when the securities were acquired;

(b) they were acquired before it was reasonably practicable to bring the fact that the expert was not competent, or had not consented, to the attention of persons likely to acquire the securities in question;

(c) before the securities were acquired he had taken all such steps as it was reasonable for him to have taken to secure that that fact was brought to the attention of those persons;

(d) he continued in his belief until after the commencement of dealings in the securities following their admission to the official list and they were acquired after such a lapse of time that he ought in the circumstances to be reasonably excused.

### Corrections of statements

3 (1) In this paragraph 'statement' has the same meaning as in paragraph 1

(2) A person does not incur liability under section 90(1) for loss caused by a statement if he satisfies the court—

(a) that before the securities in question were acquired, a correction had been published in a manner calculated to bring it to the attention of persons likely to acquire the securities; or

(b) that he took all such steps as it was reasonable for him to take to secure such publication and reasonably believed that it had taken place before the securities were acquired.

(3) Nothing in this paragraph is to be taken as affecting paragraph 1.

### Corrections of statements by experts

4 (1) In this paragraph 'statement' has the same meaning as in paragraph 2

(2) A person does not incur liability under section 90(1) for loss caused by a statement if he satisfies the court—

(a) that before the securities in question were acquired, the fact that the expert was not competent or had not consented had been published in a manner calculated to bring it to the attention of persons likely to acquire the securities; or

(b) that he took all such steps as it was reasonable for him to take to secure such publication and reasonably believed that it had taken place before the securities were acquired.

(3) Nothing in this paragraph is to be taken as affecting paragraph 2.

### Official statements

5 A person does not incur any liability under section 90(1) for loss resulting from—

(a) a statement made by an official person which is included in the listing particulars, or

(b) a statement contained in a public official document which is included in the listing particulars,

if he satisfies the court that the statement is accurately and fairly reproduced.

### False or misleading information known about

6 A person does not incur any liability under section 90(1) or (4) if he satisfies the court that the person suffering the loss acquired the securities in question with knowledge—

(a) that the statement was false or misleading,

(b) of the omitted matter, or

(c) of the change or new matter,

as the case may be.

### *Belief that supplementary listing particulars not called for*

**7**    A person does not incur any liability under section 90(4) if he satisfies the court that he reasonably believed that the change or new matter in question was not such as to call for supplementary listing particulars

### *Meaning of 'expert'*

**8**    'Expert' includes any engineer, valuer, accountant or other person whose profession, qualifications or experience give authority to a statement made by him

### *Meaning of 'approved exchange'*

**9**    'Approved exchange' has such meaning as may be prescribed.

# SCHEDULE 11

# [...]

# SCHEDULE 11A

# TRANSFERABLE SECURITIES

## PART I

**1**    Units (within the meaning in section 237(2)) in an open-ended collective investment scheme.

**2**    Non-equity transferable securities issued by

(a) the government of an EEA State;

(b) a local or regional authority of an EEA State;

(c) a public international body of which an EEA State is a member;

(d) the European Central Bank;

(e) the central bank of an EEA State.

**3**    Shares in the share capital of the central bank of an EEA State.

**4**    Transferable securities unconditionally and irrevocably guaranteed by the government, or a local or regional authority, of an EEA State.

**5**    (1) Non-equity transferable securities, issued in a continuous or repeated manner by a credit institution, which satisfy the conditions in sub-paragraph (2).

(2) The conditions are that the transferable securities—

(a) are not subordinated, convertible or exchangeable;

(b) do not give a right to subscribe to or acquire other types of securities and are not linked to a derivative instrument;

(c) materialise reception of repayable deposits; and

(d) are covered by a deposit guarantee under directive 94/19/EC of the European Parliament and of the Council on deposit-guarantee schemes.

**6**    Non-fungible shares of capital—

(a) the main purpose of which is to provide the holder with a right to occupy any immoveable property, and

(b) which cannot be sold without that right being given up.

## PART II

**7**    (1) Transferable securities issued by a body specified in sub-paragraph (2) if, and only if, the proceeds of the offer of the transferable securities to the public will be used solely for the purposes of the issuer's objectives.

(2) The bodies are

(a) a charity within the meaning of—

(i) section 96(1) of the Charities Act 1993 (c 10), or

(ii) section 35 of the Charities Act (Northern Ireland) 1964 (c 33 (N.I.));

(b) a body entered in the Scottish Charity Register;

(c) a housing association within the meaning of—

(i) section 5(1) of the Housing Act 1985 (c 68),

(ii) section 1 of the Housing Associations Act 1985 (c 69), or

(iii) Article 3 of the Housing (Northern Ireland) Order 1992 (S.I. 1992/1725 (N.I. 15));

    (d) an industrial and provident society registered in accordance with—

        (i) section 1(2)(b) of the Industrial and Provident Societies Act 1965 (c 12), or

        (ii) section 1(2)(b) of the Industrial and Provident Societies Act (Northern Ireland) 1969 (c 24 (N.I.));

    (e) a non-profit making association or body recognised by an EEA State with objectives similar to those of a body falling within any of sub-paragraphs (a) to (d).

**8** (1) Non-equity transferable securities, issued in a continuous or repeated manner by a credit institution, which satisfy the conditions in sub-paragraph (2).

(2) The conditions are—

    (a) that the total consideration of the offer is less than 50,000,000 euros (or an equivalent amount); and

    (b) those mentioned in paragraph 5(2)(a) and (b).

(3) In determining whether sub-paragraph (2)(a) is satisfied in relation to an offer ('offer A'), offer A is to be taken together with any other offer of transferable securities of the same class made by the same person which—

    (a) was open at any time within the period of 12 months ending with the date on which offer A is first made; and

    (b) had previously satisfied sub-paragraph (2)(a).

(4) For the purposes of this paragraph, an amount (in relation to an amount denominated in euros) is an 'equivalent amount' if it is an amount of equal value denominated wholly or partly in another currency or unit of account.

(5) The equivalent is to be calculated at the latest practicable date before (but in any event not more than 3 working days before) the date on which the offer is first made.

(6) 'Credit institution' means a credit institution as defined in Article 4(1)(a) of the banking consolidation directive.

**9** (1) Transferable securities included in an offer where the total consideration of the offer is less than 2,500,000 euros (or an equivalent amount).

(2) Sub-paragraphs (3) to (5) of paragraph 8 apply for the purposes of this paragraph but with the references in sub-paragraph (3) to 'sub-paragraph (2)(a)' being read as references to 'paragraph 9(1)'.

# SCHEDULE 12

## TRANSFER SCHEMES: CERTIFICATES

### PART I

### INSURANCE BUSINESS TRANSFER SCHEMES

**1** (1) For the purposes of section 111(2) the appropriate certificates, in relation to an insurance business transfer scheme, are—

    (a) a certificate under paragraph 2;

    (b) if sub-paragraph (2) applies, a certificate under paragraph 3;

    (c) if sub-paragraph (3) applies, a certificate under paragraph 4;

    (d) if sub-paragraph (4) applies, a certificate under paragraph 5;

    (e) if sub paragraph (5) applies a certificate under paragraph 5A.

(2) This sub-paragraph applies if—

    (a) the authorised person concerned is a UK authorised person which has received authorisation under Article 4 of the life assurance consolidation directive or Article 6 of the first life insurance directive or of the first non-life insurance directive from the Authority; and

    (b) the establishment from which the business is to be transferred under the proposed insurance business transfer scheme is in an EEA State other than the United Kingdom.

(3) This sub-paragraph applies if—

    (a) the authorised person concerned has received authorisation under Article 4 or Article 51 of the life assurance consolidation directive

    (b) the proposed transfer relates to business which consists of the effecting or carrying out of contracts of long-term insurance; and

    (c) as regards any policy which is included in the proposed transfer and which evidences a contract of insurance (other than reinsurance), an EEA State other than the United Kingdom is the State of the commitment.

(4) This sub-paragraph applies if—

(a) the authorised person concerned has received authorisation under Article 6 or Article 23 of the first non-life insurance directive from the Authority;

(b) the business to which the proposed insurance business transfer scheme relates is business which consists of the effecting or carrying out of contracts of general insurance; and

(c) as regards any policy which is included in the proposed transfer and which evidences a contract of insurance (other than reinsurance), the risk is situated in an EEA State other than the United Kingdom.

(5) This sub-paragraph applies if—

(a) the authorised person concerned has received authorisation under Article 23 of the first non-life insurance directive or Article 51 of the life assurance consolidation directive from the Authority; and

(b) the proposed transfer is to a branch or agency, in an EEA State other than the United Kingdom, authorised under the same Article.

### *Certificates as to margin of solvency*

**2** (1) A certificate under this paragraph is to be given—

(a) by the relevant authority; or

(b) in a case in which there is no relevant authority, by the Authority.

(2) A certificate given under sub-paragraph (1)(a) is one certifying that, taking the proposed transfer into account—

(a) the transferee possesses, or will possess before the scheme takes effect, the necessary margin of solvency; or

(b) there is no necessary margin of solvency applicable to the transferee.

(3) A certificate under sub-paragraph (1)(b) is one certifying that the Authority has received from the authority which it considers to be the authority responsible for supervising persons who effect or carry out contracts of insurance in the place to which the business is to be transferred that, taking the proposed transfer into account—

(a) the transferee possesses or will possess before the scheme takes effect the margin of solvency required under the law applicable in that place; or

(b) there is no such margin of solvency applicable to the transferee .

(4) 'Necessary margin of solvency' means the margin of solvency required in relation to the transferee, taking the proposed transfer into account, under the law which it is the responsibility of the relevant authority to apply.

(5) 'Margin of solvency' means the excess of the value of the assets of the transferee over the amount of its liabilities.

(6) 'Relevant authority' means—

(a) if the transferee is an EEA firm falling within paragraph 5(d) or (da) of Schedule 3, its home state regulator;

(aa) if the transferee is a non-EEA branch, the competent authorities of the EEA State in which the transferee is situated or, where appropriate, the competent authorities of an EEA State which supervises the state of solvency of the entire business of the transferee's agencies and branches within the EEA in accordance with Article 26 of the first non-life insurance directive or Article 56 of the life assurance consolidation directive;

(b) if the transferee is a Swiss general insurer, the authority responsible in Switzerland for supervising persons who effect or carry out contracts of insurance;

(c) if the transferee is an authorised person not falling within paragraph (a), (aa) or (b), the Authority.

(7) In sub-paragraph (6), any reference to a transferee of a particular description includes a reference to a transferee who will be of that description if the proposed scheme takes effect.

(7A) 'Competent authorities' has the same meaning as in the insurance directives. (8) 'Swiss general insurer' means a body—

(a) whose head office is in Switzerland;

(b) which has permission to carry on regulated activities consisting of the effecting and carrying out of contracts of general insurance; and

(c) whose permission is not restricted to the effecting or carrying out of contracts of reinsurance.

(9) 'Non-EEA branch' means a branch or agency which has received authorisation under Article 23 of the first non-life insurance directive or Article 51 of the life assurance consolidation directive.

### *Certificates as to consent*

**3** A certificate under this paragraph is one given by the Authority and certifying that the host State regulator has been notified of the proposed scheme and that—

(a) that regulator has responded to the notification; or

(b) that it has not responded but the period of three months beginning with the notification has elapsed.

### *Certificates as to long-term business*

**4**    A certificate under this paragraph is one given by the Authority and certifying that the authority responsible for supervising persons who effect or carry out contracts of insurance in the State of the commitment has been notified of the proposed scheme and that—

(a)  that authority has consented to the proposed scheme; or

(b)  the period of three months beginning with the notification has elapsed and that authority has not refused its consent.

### *Certificates as to general business*

**5**    A certificate under this paragraph is one given by the Authority and certifying that the authority responsible for supervising persons who effect or carry out contracts of insurance in the EEA State in which the risk is situated has been notified of the proposed scheme and that—

(a)  that authority has consented to the proposed scheme; or

(b)  the period of three months beginning with the notification has elapsed and that authority has not refused its consent.

### *Certificates as to legality and as to consent*

**5A**    (1) The certificates under this paragraph are to be given—

(a)  in the case of the certificate under sub-paragraph (2), by the Authority;

(b)  in the case of the certificate under sub-paragraph (3), by the relevant authority.

(2)  A certificate given under this sub-paragraph is one certifying that the relevant authority has been notified of the proposed scheme and that—

(a)  the relevant authority has consented to the proposed scheme; or

(b)  the period of three months beginning with the notification has elapsed and that relevant authority has not refused its consent.

(3)  A certificate given under this sub-paragraph is one certifying that the law of the EEA State in which the transferee is set up permits such a transfer.

(4)  'Relevant authority' means the competent authorities (within the meaning of the insurance directives) of the EEA State in which the transferee is set up.

### *Interpretation of Part I*

**6**    (1) 'State of the commitment', in relation to a commitment entered into at any date, means—

(a)  if the policyholder is an individual, the State in which he had his habitual residence at that date;

(b)  if the policyholder is not an individual, the State in which the establishment of the policyholder to which the commitment relates was situated at that date.

(2)  'Commitment' means a commitment represented by contracts of insurance of a prescribed class.

(3)  References to the EEA State in which a risk is situated are—

(a)  if the insurance relates to a building or to a building and its contents (so far as the contents are covered by the same policy), to the EEA State in which the building is situated;

(b)  if the insurance relates to a vehicle of any type, to the EEA State of registration;

(c)  in the case of policies of a duration of four months or less covering travel or holiday risks (whatever the class concerned), to the EEA State in which the policyholder took out the policy;

(d)  in a case not covered by paragraphs (a) to (c)—

(i)   if the policyholder is an individual, to the EEA State in which he has his habitual residence at the date when the contract is entered into; and

(ii)  otherwise, to the EEA State in which the establishment of the policyholder to which the policy relates is situated at that date.

(4)  If the insurance relates to a vehicle dispatched from one EEA State to another, in respect of the period of 30 days beginning with the day on which the purchaser accepts delivery a reference to the EEA State in which a risk is situated is a reference to the State of destination (and not, as provided by sub-paragraph (3)(b), to the State of registration).

## PART II

## BANKING BUSINESS TRANSFER SCHEMES

**7**    (1) For the purposes of section 111(2) the appropriate certificates, in relation to a banking business transfer scheme, are—

(a)  a certificate under paragraph 8; and

(b)  if sub-paragraph (2) applies, a certificate under paragraph 9.

(2)  This sub-paragraph applies if the authorised person concerned or the transferee is an EEA firm falling within paragraph 5(b) of Schedule 3.

### Certificates as to financial resources

**8**  (1) A certificate under this paragraph is one given by the relevant authority and certifying that, taking the proposed transfer into account, the transferee possesses, or will possess before the scheme takes effect, adequate financial resources

(2) 'Relevant authority' means—

(a)  if the transferee is a person with a Part IV permission or with permission under Schedule 4, the Authority;

(b)  if the transferee is an EEA firm falling within paragraph 5(b) of Schedule 3, its home state regulator;

(c)  if the transferee does not fall within paragraph (a) or (b), the authority responsible for the supervision of the transferee's business in the place in which the transferee has its head office.

(3) In sub-paragraph (2), any reference to a transferee of a particular description of person includes a reference to a transferee who will be of that description if the proposed banking business transfer scheme takes effect.

### Certificates as to consent of home state regulator

**9**  A certificate under this paragraph is one given by the Authority and certifying that the home State regulator of the authorised person concerned or of the transferee has been notified of the proposed scheme and that—

(a)  the home State regulator has responded to the notification; or

(b)  the period of three months beginning with the notification has elapsed.

## PART 2A

## RECLAIM FUND BUSINESS TRANSFER SCHEMES

### Certificate as to financial resources

**9A**  For the purposes of section 111(2) the appropriate certificate, in relation to a reclaim fund business transfer scheme, is a certificate given by the Authority certifying that, taking the proposed transfer into account, the transferee possesses, or will possess before the scheme takes effect, adequate financial resources.

## PART III

## INSURANCE BUSINESS TRANSFERS EFFECTED OUTSIDE THE UNITED KINGDOM

**10**  (1) This paragraph applies to a proposal to execute under provisions corresponding to Part VII in a country or territory other than the United Kingdom an instrument transferring all the rights and obligations of the transferor under general or long-term insurance policies, or under such descriptions of such policies as may be specified in the instrument, to the transferee if any of the conditions in sub-paragraphs (2), (3) or (4) is met in relation to it

(2) The transferor is an EEA firm falling within paragraph 5(d) or (da) of Schedule 3 and the transferee is an authorised person whose margin of solvency is supervised by the Authority.

(3) The transferor is a company authorised in an EEA State other than the United Kingdom under Article 51 of the life assruance consolidation directive or Article 23 of the first non-life insurance directive and the transferee is a UK authorised person which has received authorisation under Article 4 of the life assurance consolidation directive or Article 6 of the first non-life insurance directive .

(4) The transferor is a Swiss general insurer and the transferee is a UK authorised person which has received authorisation under Article 4 of the life assurance consolidation directive or Article 6 of the first non-life insurance directive.

(5) In relation to a proposed transfer to which this paragraph applies, the Authority may, if it is satisfied that the transferee possesses the necessary margin of solvency, issue a certificate to that effect.

(6) 'Necessary margin of solvency' means the margin of solvency which the transferee, taking the proposed transfer into account, is required by the Authority to maintain.

(7) 'Swiss general insurer' has the same meaning as in paragraph 2.

(8) 'General policy' means a policy evidencing a contract which, if it had been effected by the transferee, would have constituted the carrying on of a regulated activity consisting of the effecting of contracts of general insurance.

(9) 'Long-term policy' means a policy evidencing a contract which, if it had been effected by the transferee, would have constituted the carrying on of a regulated activity consisting of the effecting of contracts of long-term insurance.

# SCHEDULE 13

# THE FINANCIAL SERVICES AND MARKETS TRIBUNAL

## PART I

## GENERAL

### *Interpretation*

1   In this Schedule—
'panel of chairmen' means the panel established under paragraph 3(1);
'lay panel' means the panel established under paragraph 3(4);
'rules' means rules made by the Lord Chancellor under section 132.

## PART II

## THE TRIBUNAL

### *President*

2. — (1) The Lord Chancellor must appoint one of the members of the panel of chairmen to preside over the discharge of the Tribunal's functions.

(2)  The member so appointed is to be known as the President of the Financial Services and Markets Tribunal (but is referred to in this Act as 'the President').

(3)  The Lord Chancellor may appoint one of the members of the panel of chairmen to be Deputy President.

(4)  The Deputy President is to have such functions in relation to the Tribunal as the President may assign to him.

(5)  The Lord Chancellor may not appoint a person to be the President or Deputy President unless that person—

(a)  satisfies the judicial-appointment eligibility condition on a 7-year basis;

(b)  is an advocate or solicitor in Scotland of at least 7 years standing; or

(c)  is—

(i)   a member of the Bar of Northern Ireland of at least 7 years standing; or

(ii)  a solicitor of the Supreme Court of Northern Ireland of at least 7 years standing.

(6)  If the President (or Deputy President) ceases to be a member of the panel of chairmen, he also ceases to be the President (or Deputy President).

(7)  The functions of the President may, if he is absent or is otherwise unable to act, be discharged—

(a)  by the Deputy President; or

(b)  if there is no Deputy President or he too is absent or otherwise unable to act, by a person appointed for that purpose from the panel of chairmen by the Lord Chancellor.

(8)  The Lord Chancellor may appoint a person under sub-paragraph (7)(b) only after consulting the following—

(a)  the Lord Chief Justice of England and Wales;

(b)  the Lord President of the Court of Session;

(c)  the Lord Chief Justice of Northern Ireland.

(9)  The Lord Chief Justice of England and Wales may nominate a judicial office holder (as defined in section 109(4) of the Constitutional Reform Act 2005) to exercise his functions under this paragraph.

(10)  The Lord President of the Court of Session may nominate a judge of the Court of Session who is a member of the First or Second Division of the Inner House of that Court to exercise his functions under this paragraph.

(11)  The Lord Chief Justice of Northern Ireland may nominate any of the following to exercise his functions under this paragraph—

(a)  the holder of one of the offices listed in Schedule 1 to the Justice (Northern Ireland) Act 2002;

(b)  a Lord Justice of Appeal (as defined in section 88 of that Act).

### *Panels*

3   (1) The Lord Chancellor must appoint a panel of persons for the purposes of serving as chairmen of the Tribunal

(2)  A person is qualified for membership of the panel of chairmen if—

(a)  he satisfies the judicial-appointment eligibility condition on a 5-year basis;

(b) he is an advocate or solicitor in Scotland of at least 5 years' standing; or

(c) he is—

    (i)   a member of the Bar of Northern Ireland of at least 5 years' standing; or

    (ii)   a solicitor of the Supreme Court of Northern Ireland of at least 5 years' standing.

(3) The panel of chairmen must include at least one member who is a person of the kind mentioned in sub-paragraph (2)(b).

(4) The Lord Chancellor must also appoint a panel of persons who appear to him to be qualified by experience or otherwise to deal with matters of the kind that may be referred to the Tribunal.

### *Terms of office etc*

**4** (1) Subject to the provisions of this Schedule, each member of the panel of chairmen and the lay panel is to hold and vacate office in accordance with the terms of his appointment

(2) The Lord Chancellor may remove a member of either panel (including the President) on the ground of incapacity or misbehaviour.

(2A) The Lord Chancellor may remove a person under sub-paragraph (2) only with the concurrence of appropriate senior judge.

(2B) The appropriate senior judge is the Lord Chief Justice of England and Wales, unless—

(a) the person to be removed exercises functions wholly or mainly in Scotland, in which case it is the Lord President of the Court of Session, or

(b) the person to be removed exercises functions wholly or mainly in Northern Ireland, in which case it is the Lord Chief Justice of Northern Ireland.

(3) A member of either panel—

(a) may at any time resign office by notice in writing to the Lord Chancellor;

(b) is eligible for re-appointment if he ceases to hold office.

### *Remuneration and expenses*

**5** The Lord Chancellor may pay to any person, in respect of his service—

(a) as a member of the Tribunal (including service as the President or Deputy President), or

(b) as a person appointed under paragraph 7(4),

such remuneration and allowances as he may determine.

### *Staff*

**6** (1) The Lord Chancellor may appoint such staff for the Tribunal as he may determine

(2) The remuneration of the Tribunal's staff is to be defrayed by the Lord Chancellor.

(3) Such expenses of the Tribunal as the Lord Chancellor may determine are to be defrayed by the Lord Chancellor.

## PART III

## CONSTITUTION OF TRIBUNAL

**7** (1) On a reference to the Tribunal, the persons to act as members of the Tribunal for the purposes of the reference are to be selected from the panel of chairmen or the lay panel in accordance with arrangements made by the President for the purposes of this paragraph ('the standing arrangements').

(2) The standing arrangements must provide for at least one member to be selected from the panel of chairmen.

(3) If while a reference is being dealt with, a person serving as member of the Tribunal in respect of the reference becomes unable to act, the reference may be dealt with by—

(a) the other members selected in respect of that reference; or

(b) if it is being dealt with by a single member, such other member of the panel of chairmen as may be selected in accordance with the standing arrangements for the purposes of the reference.

(4) If it appears to the Tribunal that a matter before it involves a question of fact of special difficulty, it may appoint one or more experts to provide assistance.

## PART IV

## TRIBUNAL PROCEDURE

**8** For the purpose of dealing with references, or any matter preliminary or incidental to a reference, the Tribunal must sit at such times and in such place or places as the Lord Chancellor may, after consulting the President of the Financial Services and Markets Tribunal direct

**9** Rules made by the Lord Chancellor under section 132 may, in particular, include provision—

(a) as to the manner in which references are to be instituted;

(b) for the holding of hearings in private in such circumstances as may be specified in the rules;

(c) as to the persons who may appear on behalf of the parties;

(d) for a member of the panel of chairmen to hear and determine interlocutory matters arising on a reference;

(e) for the suspension of decisions of the Authority which have taken effect;

(f) as to the withdrawal of references;

(g) as to the registration, publication and proof of decisions and orders.

### Practice directions

**10** The President of the Tribunal may give directions as to the practice and procedure to be followed by the Tribunal in relation to references to it

### Evidence

**11** (1) The Tribunal may by summons require any person to attend, at such time and place as is specified in the summons, to give evidence or to produce any document in his custody or under his control which the Tribunal considers it necessary to examine

(2) The Tribunal may—

(a) take evidence on oath and for that purpose administer oaths; or

(b) instead of administering an oath, require the person examined to make and subscribe a declaration of the truth of the matters in respect of which he is examined.

(3) A person who without reasonable excuse—

(a) refuses or fails—

(i) to attend following the issue of a summons by the Tribunal, or

(ii) to give evidence, or

(b) alters, suppresses, conceals or destroys, or refuses to produce a document which he may be required to produce for the purposes of proceedings before the Tribunal,

is guilty of an offence.

(4) A person guilty of an offence under sub-paragraph (3)(a) is liable on summary conviction to a fine not exceeding the statutory maximum.

(5) A person guilty of an offence under sub-paragraph (3)(b) is liable—

(a) on summary conviction, to a fine not exceeding the statutory maximum;

(b) on conviction on indictment, to imprisonment for a term not exceeding two years or a fine or both.

### Decisions of Tribunal

**12** (1) A decision of the Tribunal may be taken by a majority

(2) The decision must—

(a) state whether it was unanimous or taken by a majority;

(b) be recorded in a document which—

(i) contains a statement of the reasons for the decision; and

(ii) is signed and dated by the member of the panel of chairmen dealing with the reference.

(3) The Tribunal must—

(a) inform each party of its decision; and

(b) as soon as reasonably practicable, send to each party and, if different, to any authorised person concerned, a copy of the document mentioned in sub-paragraph (2).

(4) The Tribunal must send the Treasury a copy of its decision.

### Costs

**13** (1) If the Tribunal considers that a party to any proceedings on a reference has acted vexatiously, frivolously or unreasonably it may order that party to pay to another party to the proceedings the whole or part of the costs or expenses incurred by the other party in connection with the proceedings

(2) If, in any proceedings on a reference, the Tribunal considers that a decision of the Authority which is the subject of the reference was unreasonable it may order the Authority to pay to another party to the proceedings the whole or part of the costs or expenses incurred by the other party in connection with the proceedings.

# SCHEDULE 14

## ROLE OF THE COMPETITION COMMISSION

### *Provision of information by Treasury*

**1**  (1) The Treasury's powers under this paragraph are to be exercised only for the purpose of assisting the Commission in carrying out an investigation under section 162

(2)  The Treasury may give to the Commission—

(a) any information in their possession which relates to matters falling within the scope of the investigation; and

(b) other assistance in relation to any such matters.

(3)  In carrying out an investigation under section 162, the Commission must have regard to any information given to it under this paragraph.

### *Consideration of matters arising on a report*

**2**  In considering any matter arising from a report made by the OFT under section 160, the Commission must have regard to—

(a) any representations made to it in connection with the matter by any person appearing to the Commission to have a substantial interest in the matter; and

(b) any cost benefit analysis prepared by the Authority (at any time) in connection with the regulatory provision or practice, or any of the regulatory provisions or practices, which are the subject of the report.

### *Investigations under section 162: application of Enterprise Act 2002*

**2A**  (1) The following sections of Part 3 of the Enterprise Act 2002 shall apply, with the modifications mentioned in sub-paragraphs (2) and (3), for the purposes of any investigation by the Commission under section 162 of this Act as they apply for the purposes of references under that Part—

(a) section 109 (attendance of witnesses and production of documents etc.);

(b) section 110 (enforcement of powers under section 109: general);

(c) section 111 (penalties);

(d) section 112 (penalties: main procedural requirements);

(e) section 113 (payments and interest by instalments);

(f) section 114 (appeals in relation to penalties);

(g) section 115 (recovery of penalties); and

(h) section 116 (statement of policy).

(2)  Section 110 shall, in its application by virtue of sub-paragraph (1), have effect as if—

(a) subsection (2) were omitted; and

(b) in subsection (9) the words from 'or section' to 'section 65(3)')' were omitted.

(3)  Section 111(5)(b) shall, in its application by virtue of sub-paragraph (1), have effect as if for sub-paragraph (ii) there were substituted—

'(ii)  if earlier, the day on which the report of the Commission on the investigation concerned is made or, if the Commission decides not to make a report, the day on which the Commission makes the statement required by section 162(3) of the Financial Services and Markets Act 2000.'

(4)  Section 117 of the Enterprise Act 2002 (false or misleading information) shall apply in relation to functions of the Commission in connection with an investigation under section 162 of this Act as it applies in relation to its functions under Part 3 of that Act but as if, in subsections (1)(a) and (2), the words ' the OFT, OFCOM,' and 'or the Secretary of State' were omitted.

(5)  Provisions of Part 3 of the Enterprise Act 2002 which have effect for the purposes of sections 109 to 117 of that Act (including, in particular, provisions relating to offences and the making of orders) shall, for the purposes of the application of those sections by virtue of sub-paragraph (1) or (4) above, have effect in relation to those sections as applied by virtue of those sub-paragraphs.

(6)  Accordingly, corresponding provisions of this Act shall not have effect in relation to those sections as applied by virtue of those sub-paragraphs.

### *Section 162: modification of Schedule 7 to the Competition Act 1998*

**2B**  For the purposes of its application in relation to the function of the Commission of deciding in accordance with section 162(2) of this Act not to make a report, paragraph 15(7) of Schedule 7 to the Competition Act 1998 (power of the Chairman to act on his own while a group is being constituted) has effect as if, after paragraph (a), there were inserted

'; or

(aa) in the case of an investigation under section 162 of the Financial Services and Markets Act 2000, decide not to make a report in accordance with subsection (2) of that section (decision not to make a report where no useful purpose would be served).'

*Reports under section 162: further provision*

**2C** (1) For the purposes of section 163 of this Act, a conclusion contained in a report of the Commission is to be disregarded if the conclusion is not that of at least two-thirds of the members of the group constituted in connection with the investigation concerned in pursuance of paragraph 15 of Schedule 7 to the Competition Act 1998.

(2) If a member of a group so constituted disagrees with any conclusions contained in a report made under section 162 of this Act as the conclusions of the Commission, the report shall, if the member so wishes, include a statement of his disagreement and of his reasons for disagreeing.

(3) For the purposes of the law relating to defamation, absolute privilege attaches to any report made by the Commission under section 162.

*Publication of reports*

**4** (1) If the Commission makes a report under section 162, it must publish it in such a way as appears to it to be best calculated to bring it to the attention of the public

(2) Before publishing the report the Commission must, so far as practicable, exclude any matter which relates to the private affairs of a particular individual the publication of which, in the opinion of the Commission, would or might seriously and prejudicially affect his interests.

(3) Before publishing the report the Commission must, so far as practicable, also exclude any matter which relates to the affairs of a particular body the publication of which, in the opinion of the Commission, would or might seriously and prejudicially affect its interests.

(4) Sub-paragraphs (2) and (3) do not apply in relation to copies of a report which the Commission is required to send under section 162(10).

# SCHEDULE 15

# INFORMATION AND INVESTIGATIONS: CONNECTED PERSONS

## PART I

## RULES FOR SPECIFIC BODIES

*Corporate bodies*

**1** If the authorised person ('BC') is a body corporate, a person who is or has been—
(a) an officer or manager of BC or of a parent undertaking of BC;
(b) an employee of BC;
(c) an agent of BC or of a parent undertaking of BC.

*Partnerships*

**2** If the authorised person ('PP') is a partnership, a person who is or has been a member, manager, employee or agent of PP

*Unincorporated associations*

**3** If the authorised person ('UA') is an unincorporated association of persons which is neither a partnership nor an unincorporated friendly society, a person who is or has been an officer, manager, employee or agent of UA

*Friendly societies*

**4** (1) If the authorised person ('FS') is a friendly society, a person who is or has been an officer, manager or employee of FS

(2) In relation to FS, 'officer' and 'manager' have the same meaning as in section 119(1) of the Friendly Societies Act 1992.

*Building societies*

**5** (1) If the authorised person ('BS') is a building society, a person who is or has been an officer or employee of BS

(2) In relation to BS, 'officer' has the same meaning as it has in section 119(1) of the Building Societies Act 1986.

*Individuals*

**6** If the authorised person ('IP') is an individual, a person who is or has been an employee or agent of IP.

*Application to sections 171 and 172*

7   For the purposes of sections 171 and 172, if the person under investigation is not an authorised person the references in this Part of this Schedule to an authorised person are to be taken to be references to the person under investigation.

# PART II

# ADDITIONAL RULES

8   A person who is, or at the relevant time was, the partner, manager, employee, agent, appointed representative, banker, auditor, actuary or solicitor of—
- (a) the person under investigation ('A');
- (b) a parent undertaking of A;
- (c) a subsidiary undertaking of A;
- (d) a subsidiary undertaking of a parent undertaking of A; or
- (e) a parent undertaking of a subsidiary undertaking of A.

# SCHEDULE 16

# PROHIBITIONS AND RESTRICTIONS IMPOSED BY DIRECTOR GENERAL OF FAIR TRADING

*Preliminary*

1   In this Schedule—
'appeal period' has the same meaning as in the Consumer Credit Act 1974;
'prohibition' means a consumer credit prohibition under section 203;
'restriction' means a restriction under section 204.

*Notice of prohibition or restriction*

2   (1) This paragraph applies if the OFT proposes, in relation to a firm—
- (a) to impose a prohibition;
- (b) to impose a restriction; or
- (c) to vary a restriction otherwise than with the agreement of the firm.

(2) The OFT must by notice—
- (a) inform the firm of its proposal, stating its reasons; and
- (b) invite the firm to submit representations in accordance with paragraph 4.

(3) If the OFT imposes the prohibition or restriction or varies the restriction, the OFT may give directions authorising the firm to carry into effect agreements made before the coming into force of the prohibition, restriction or variation.

(4) A prohibition, restriction or variation is not to come into force before the end of the appeal period.

(5) If the OFT imposes a prohibition or restriction or varies a restriction, the OFT it must serve a copy of the prohibition, restriction or variation—
- (a) on the Authority; and
- (b) on the *home state competent authority*.[10]

*Application to revoke prohibition or restriction*

3   (1) This paragraph applies if the OFT proposes to refuse an application made by a firm for the revocation of a prohibition or restriction.

(2) The OFT must by notice—
- (a) inform the firm of the proposed refusal, stating its reasons; and
- (b) invite the firm to submit representations in accordance with paragraph 4.

*Representations to the OFT*

4   (1) If this paragraph applies to an invitation to submit representations, the OFT must invite the firm, within 21 days after the notice containing the invitation is given to it or such longer period as the OFT may allow—
- (a) to submit its representations in writing to OFT; and
- (b) to give notice to OFT, if the firm thinks fit, that it wishes to make representations orally.

(2) If notice is given under sub-paragraph (1)(b), the OFT must arrange for the oral representations to be heard.

(3) The OFT must give the firm notice of its determination.

---

[10] The words in italics substituted by the Payment Services Regulations 2009/209. In force from 1 November 2009.

*Appeals*

5  Section 41 of the Consumer Credit Act 1974 (appeals to the Secretary of State) has effect as if—

  (a) the following determinations were mentioned in column 1 of the table set out at the end of that section—

    (i)  imposition of a prohibition or restriction or the variation of a restriction; and

    (ii)  refusal of an application for the revocation of a prohibition or restriction; and

  (b) the firm concerned were mentioned in column 2 of that table in relation to those determinations.

# SCHEDULE 17

# THE OMBUDSMAN SCHEME

## PART I

## GENERAL

### *Interpretation*

1  In this Schedule—

'ombudsman' means a person who is a member of the panel; and

'the panel' means the panel established under paragraph 4.

## PART II

## THE SCHEME OPERATOR

### *Establishment by the Authority*

2  (1) The Authority must establish a body corporate to exercise the functions conferred on the scheme operator by or under this Act

(2) The Authority must take such steps as are necessary to ensure that the scheme operator is, at all times, capable of exercising those functions.

### *Constitution*

3  (1) The constitution of the scheme operator must provide for it to have—

  (a) a chairman; and

  (b) a board (which must include the chairman) whose members are the scheme operator's directors.

(2) The chairman and other members of the board must be persons appointed, and liable to removal from office, by the Authority (acting, in the case of the chairman, with the approval of the Treasury).

(3) But the terms of their appointment (and in particular those governing removal from office) must be such as to secure their independence from the Authority in the operation of the scheme.

(4) The function of making voluntary jurisdiction rules under section 227 the function of making consumer credit rules, the function of making determinations under section 234A(1) and the functions conferred by paragraphs 4, 5, 7, 9 or 14 may be exercised only by the board.

(5) The validity of any act of the scheme operator is unaffected by—

  (a) a vacancy in the office of chairman; or

  (b) a defect in the appointment of a person as chairman or as a member of the board.

### *The panel of ombudsmen*

4  (1) The scheme operator must appoint and maintain a panel of persons, appearing to it to have appropriate qualifications and experience, to act as ombudsmen for the purposes of the scheme

(2) A person's appointment to the panel is to be on such terms (including terms as to the duration and termination of his appointment and as to remuneration) as the scheme operator considers—

  (a) consistent with the independence of the person appointed; and

  (b) otherwise appropriate.

### *The Chief Ombudsman*

5  (1) The scheme operator must appoint one member of the panel to act as Chief Ombudsman

(2) The Chief Ombudsman is to be appointed on such terms (including terms as to the duration and termination of his appointment) as the scheme operator considers appropriate.

*Status*

**6** (1) The scheme operator is not to be regarded as exercising functions on behalf of the Crown

(2) The scheme operator's board members, officers and staff are not to be regarded as Crown servants.

(3) Appointment as Chief Ombudsman or to the panel or as a deputy ombudsman does not confer the status of Crown servant.

*Annual reports*

**7** (1) At least once a year—

(a) the scheme operator must make a report to the Authority on the discharge of its functions; and

(b) the Chief Ombudsman must make a report to the Authority on the discharge of his functions.

(2) Each report must distinguish between functions in relation to the scheme's compulsory jurisdiction and functions in relation to its consumer credit jurisdiction and in relation to its voluntary jurisdiction.

(3) Each report must also comply with any requirements specified in rules made by the Authority.

(4) The scheme operator must publish each report in the way it considers appropriate.

*Guidance*

**8** The scheme operator may publish guidance consisting of such information and advice as it considers appropriate and may charge for it or distribute it free of charge

*Budget*

**9** (1) The scheme operator must, before the start of each of its financial years, adopt an annual budget which has been approved by the Authority

(2) The scheme operator may, with the approval of the Authority, vary the budget for a financial year at any time after its adoption.

(3) The annual budget must include an indication of—

(a) the distribution of resources deployed in the operation of the scheme, and

(b) the amounts of income of the scheme operator arising or expected to arise from the operation of the scheme,

distinguishing between the scheme's compulsory consumer credit and voluntary jurisdiction.

*Exemption from liability in damages*

**10** (1) No person is to be liable in damages for anything done or omitted in the discharge, or purported discharge, of any functions under this Act in relation to the compulsory jurisdiction or to the consumer credit jurisdiction

(2) Sub-paragraph (1) does not apply—

(a) if the act or omission is shown to have been in bad faith; or

(b) so as to prevent an award of damages made in respect of an act or omission on the ground that the act or omission was unlawful as a result of section 6(1) of the Human Rights Act 1998.

*Privilege*

**11** For the purposes of the law relating to defamation, proceedings in relation to a complaint which is subject to the compulsory jurisdiction or to the consumer credit jurisdiction are to be treated as if they were proceedings before a court

# PART III

## THE COMPULSORY JURISDICTION

*Introduction*

**12** This Part of this Schedule applies only in relation to the compulsory jurisdiction

*Authority's procedural rules*

**13** (1) The Authority must make rules providing that a complaint is not to be entertained unless the complainant has referred it under the ombudsman scheme before the applicable time limit (determined in accordance with the rules) has expired

(2) The rules may provide that an ombudsman may extend that time limit in specified circumstances.

(3) The Authority may make rules providing that a complaint is not to be entertained (except in specified circumstances) if the complainant has not previously communicated its substance to the respondent and given him a reasonable opportunity to deal with it.

(4) The Authority may make rules requiring an authorised person or a payment service provider within the meaning of the Payment Services Regulations 2009 who may become subject to the compulsory jurisdiction as a respondent to establish such procedures as the Authority considers appropriate for the resolution of complaints which—

    (a) may be referred to the scheme; and

    (b) arise out of activity to which the Authority's powers under Part X do not apply.

### The scheme operator's rules

**14** (1) The scheme operator must make rules, to be known as 'scheme rules', which are to set out the procedure for reference of complaints and for their investigation, consideration and determination by an ombudsman

    (2) Scheme rules may, among other things—

        (a) specify matters which are to be taken into account in determining whether an act or omission was fair and reasonable;

        (b) provide that a complaint may, in specified circumstances, be dismissed without consideration of its merits;

        (c) provide for the reference of a complaint, in specified circumstances and with the consent of the complainant, to another body with a view to its being determined by that body instead of by an ombudsman;

        (d) make provision as to the evidence which may be required or admitted, the extent to which it should be oral or written and the consequences of a person's failure to produce any information or document which he has been required (under section 231 or otherwise) to produce;

        (e) allow an ombudsman to fix time limits for any aspect of the proceedings and to extend a time limit;

        (f) provide for certain things in relation to the reference, investigation or consideration (but not determination) of a complaint to be done by a member of the scheme operator's staff instead of by an ombudsman;

        (g) make different provision in relation to different kinds of complaint.

    (3) The circumstances specified under sub-paragraph (2)(b) may include the following—

        (a) the ombudsman considers the complaint frivolous or vexatious;

        (b) legal proceedings have been brought concerning the subject-matter of the complaint and the ombudsman considers that the complaint is best dealt with in those proceedings; or

        (c) the ombudsman is satisfied that there are other compelling reasons why it is inappropriate for the complaint to be dealt with under the ombudsman scheme.

    (4) If the scheme operator proposes to make any scheme rules it must publish a draft of the proposed rules in the way appearing to it to be best calculated to bring them to the attention of persons appearing to it to be likely to be affected.

    (5) The draft must be accompanied by a statement that representations about the proposals may be made to the scheme operator within a time specified in the statement.

    (6) Before making the proposed scheme rules, the scheme operator must have regard to any representations made to it under sub-paragraph (5).

    (7) The consent of the Authority is required before any scheme rules may be made.

### Fees

**15** (1) Scheme rules may require a respondent to pay to the scheme operator such fees as may be specified in the rules

    (2) The rules may, among other things—

        (a) provide for the scheme operator to reduce or waive a fee in a particular case;

        (b) set different fees for different stages of the proceedings on a complaint;

        (c) provide for fees to be refunded in specified circumstances;

        (d) make different provision for different kinds of complaint.

### Enforcement of money awards

**16** A money award, including interest, which has been registered in accordance with scheme rules may—

    (a) if a county court so orders in England and Wales, be recovered *by execution issued from the county court* (or otherwise) as if it were payable under an order of that court;

    (b) be enforced in Northern Ireland as a money judgment under the Judgments Enforcement (Northern Ireland) Order 1981;

    (c) be enforced in Scotland by the sheriff, as if it were a judgment or order of the sheriff and whether or not the sheriff could himself have granted such judgment or order.[11]

---

[11] In paragraph 16(a) the words 'by execution issued from the county court' are to be substituted with 'under section 85 of the County Courts Act 1984' under the Tribunals, Courts and Enforcement Act 2007 c 15 from a date to be appointed.

*Introduction*

**16A**   This Part of this Schedule applies only in relation to the consumer credit jurisdiction.

*Procedure for complaints etc.*

**16B**   (1) Consumer credit rules—
- (a) must provide that a complaint is not to be entertained unless the complainant has referred it under the ombudsman scheme before the applicable time limit (determined in accordance with the rules) has expired;
- (b) may provide that an ombudsman may extend that time limit in specified circumstances;
- (c) may provide that a complaint is not to be entertained (except in specified circumstances) if the complainant has not previously communicated its substance to the respondent and given him a reasonable opportunity to deal with it;
- (d) may make provision about the procedure for the reference of complaints and for their investigation, consideration and determination by an ombudsman.

(2) Sub-paragraphs (2) and (3) of paragraph 14 apply in relation to consumer credit rules under sub-paragraph (1) of this paragraph as they apply in relation to scheme rules under that paragraph.

(3) Consumer credit rules may require persons falling within sub-paragraph (6) to establish such procedures as the scheme operator considers appropriate for the resolution of complaints which may be referred to the scheme.

(4) Consumer credit rules under sub-paragraph (3) may make different provision in relation to persons of different descriptions or to complaints of different descriptions.

(5) Consumer credit rules under sub-paragraph (3) may authorise the scheme operator to dispense with or modify the application of such rules in particular cases where the scheme operator—
- (a) considers it appropriate to do so; and
- (b) is satisfied that the specified conditions (if any) are met.

(6) A person falls within this sub-paragraph if he is licensed by a standard licence (within the meaning of the Consumer Credit Act 1974) to carry on to any extent a business of a type specified in an order under section 226A(2)(e) of this Act.

*Fees*

**16C**   (1) Consumer credit rules may require a respondent to pay to the scheme operator such fees as may be specified in the rules.

(2) Sub-paragraph (2) of paragraph 15 applies in relation to consumer credit rules under this paragraph as it applies in relation to scheme rules under that paragraph.

*Enforcement of money awards*

**16D**   A money award, including interest, which has been registered in accordance with consumer credit rules may—
- (a) if a county court so orders in England and Wales, be recovered by execution issued from the county court (or otherwise) as if it were payable under an order of that court;
- (b) be enforced in Northern Ireland as a money judgment under the Judgments Enforcement (Northern Ireland) Order 1981;
- (c) be enforced in Scotland as if it were a decree of the sheriff and whether or not the sheriff could himself have granted such a decree.

*Procedure for consumer credit rules*

**16E**   (1) If the scheme operator makes any consumer credit rules, it must give a copy of them to the Authority without delay.

(2) If the scheme operator revokes any such rules, it must give written notice to the Authority without delay.

(3) The power to make such rules is exercisable in writing.

(4) Immediately after the making of such rules, the scheme operator must arrange for them to be printed and made available to the public.

(5) The scheme operator may charge a reasonable fee for providing a person with a copy of any such rules.

*Verification of consumer credit rules*

**16F**   (1) The production of a printed copy of consumer credit rules purporting to be made by the scheme operator—
- (a) on which there is endorsed a certificate signed by a member of the scheme operator's staff authorised by the scheme operator for that purpose, and
- (b) which contains the required statements,

is evidence (or in Scotland sufficient evidence) of the facts stated in the certificate.

(2) The required statements are—
- (a) that the rules were made by the scheme operator;
- (b) that the copy is a true copy of the rules; and

(c) that on a specified date the rules were made available to the public in accordance with paragraph 16E(4).

(3) A certificate purporting to be signed as mentioned in sub-paragraph (1) is to be taken to have been duly signed unless the contrary is shown.

### *Consultation*

**16G** (1) If the scheme operator proposes to make consumer credit rules, it must publish a draft of the proposed rules in the way appearing to it to be best calculated to bring the draft to the attention of the public.

(2) The draft must be accompanied by—

(a) an explanation of the proposed rules; and

(b) a statement that representations about the proposals may be made to the scheme operator within a specified time.

(3) Before making any consumer credit rules, the scheme operator must have regard to any representations made to it in accordance with sub-paragraph (2)(b).

(4) If consumer credit rules made by the scheme operator differ from the draft published under sub-paragraph (1) in a way which the scheme operator considers significant, the scheme operator must publish a statement of the difference.

## PART IV

## THE VOLUNTARY JURISDICTION

### *Introduction*

**17** This Part of this Schedule applies only in relation to the voluntary jurisdiction

### *Terms of reference to the scheme*

**18** (1) Complaints are to be dealt with and determined under the voluntary jurisdiction on standard terms fixed by the scheme operator with the approval of the Authority

(2) Different standard terms may be fixed with respect to different matters or in relation to different cases.

(3) The standard terms may, in particular—

(a) require the making of payments to the scheme operator by participants in the scheme of such amounts, and at such times, as may be determined by the scheme operator;

(b) make provision as to the award of costs on the determination of a complaint.

(4) The scheme operator may not vary any of the standard terms or add or remove terms without the approval of the Authority.

(5) The standard terms may include provision to the effect that (unless acting in bad faith) none of the following is to be liable in damages for anything done or omitted in the discharge or purported discharge of functions in connection with the voluntary jurisdiction—

(a) the scheme operator;

(b) any member of its governing body;

(c) any member of its staff;

(d) any person acting as an ombudsman for the purposes of the scheme.

### *Delegation by and to other schemes*

**19** (1) The scheme operator may make arrangements with a relevant body—

(a) for the exercise by that body of any part of the voluntary jurisdiction of the ombudsman scheme on behalf of the scheme; or

(b) for the exercise by the scheme of any function of that body as if it were part of the voluntary jurisdiction of the scheme.

(2) A 'relevant body' is one which the scheme operator is satisfied—

(a) is responsible for the operation of a broadly comparable scheme (whether or not established by statute) for the resolution of disputes; and

(b) in the case of arrangements under sub-paragraph (1)(a), will exercise the jurisdiction in question in a way compatible with the requirements imposed by or under this Act in relation to complaints of the kind concerned.

(3) Such arrangements require the approval of the Authority.

### *Voluntary jurisdiction rules: procedure*

**20** (1) If the scheme operator makes voluntary jurisdiction rules, it must give a copy to the Authority without delay

(2) If the scheme operator revokes any such rules, it must give written notice to the Authority without delay.

(3) The power to make voluntary jurisdiction rules is exercisable in writing.

(4) Immediately after making voluntary jurisdiction rules, the scheme operator must arrange for them to be printed and made available to the public.

(5) The scheme operator may charge a reasonable fee for providing a person with a copy of any voluntary jurisdiction rules.

### Verification of the rules

**21** (1) The production of a printed copy of voluntary jurisdiction rules purporting to be made by the scheme operator—

(a) on which is endorsed a certificate signed by a member of the scheme operator's staff authorised by the scheme operator for that purpose, and

(b) which contains the required statements,

is evidence (or in Scotland sufficient evidence) of the facts stated in the certificate.

(2) The required statements are—

(a) that the rules were made by the scheme operator;

(b) that the copy is a true copy of the rules; and

(c) that on a specified date the rules were made available to the public in accordance with paragraph 20(4).

(3) A certificate purporting to be signed as mentioned in sub-paragraph (1) is to be taken to have been duly signed unless the contrary is shown.

### Consultation

**22** (1) If the scheme operator proposes to make voluntary jurisdiction rules, it must publish a draft of the proposed rules in the way appearing to it to be best calculated to bring them to the attention of the public

(2) The draft must be accompanied by—

(a) an explanation of the proposed rules; and

(b) a statement that representations about the proposals may be made to the scheme operator within a specified time.

(3) Before making any voluntary jurisdiction rules, the scheme operator must have regard to any representations made to it in accordance with sub-paragraph (2)(b).

(4) If voluntary jurisdiction rules made by the scheme operator differ from the draft published under sub-paragraph (1) in a way which the scheme operator considers significant, the scheme operator must publish a statement of the difference.

# SCHEDULE 18

# MUTUALS

## PART I

## FRIENDLY SOCIETIES

### The Friendly Societies Act 1974 (c 46)

**1** Omit sections 4 (provision for separate registration areas) and 10 (societies registered in one registration area carrying on business in another)

**2** In section 7 (societies which may be registered), in subsection (2)(b), for 'in the central registration area or in Scotland' substitute 'in the United Kingdom, the Channel Islands or the Isle of Man'

**3** In section 11 (additional registration requirements for societies with branches), omit 'and where any such society has branches in more than one registration area, section 10 above shall apply to that society'

**4** In section 99(4)(punishment of fraud etc and recovery of property misapplied), omit 'in the central registration area'

### The Friendly Societies Act 1992 (c 40)

**5** Omit sections 31 to 36A (authorisation of friendly societies business)

**6** In section 37 (restrictions on combinations of business), omit subsections (1), (1A) and (7A) to (9)

**7** Omit sections 38 to 43 (restrictions on business of certain authorised societies)

**8** Omit sections 44 to 50 (regulation of friendly societies business)

## PART II

## FRIENDLY SOCIETIES: SUBSIDIARIES AND CONTROLLED BODIES

*Interpretation*

**9**   In this Part of this Schedule—

'the 1992 Act' means the Friendly Societies Act 1992; and

'section 13' means section 13 of that Act.

*Qualifying bodies*

**10**   (1) Subsections (2) to (5) of section 13 (incorporated friendly societies allowed to form or acquire control or joint control only of qualifying bodies) cease to have effect

(2)  As a result, omit—

  (a)  subsections (8) and (11) of that section, and

  (b)  Schedule 7 to the 1992 Act (activities which may be carried on by a subsidiary of, or body jointly controlled by, an incorporated friendly society).

*Bodies controlled by societies*

**11**   In section 13(9)(defined terms), after paragraph (a) insert—

  '(aa)  an incorporated friendly society also has control of a body corporate if the body corporate is itself a body controlled in one of the ways mentioned in paragraph (a)(i), (ii) or (iii) by a body corporate of which the society has control;'.

*Joint control by societies*

**12**   In section 13(9), after paragraph (c) insert—

  '(cc) an incorporated friendly society also has joint control of a body corporate if—

    (i)   a subsidiary of the society has joint control of the body corporate in a way mentioned in paragraph (c)(i), (ii) or (iii);

    (ii)  a body corporate of which the society has joint control has joint control of the body corporate in such a way; or

    (iii) the body corporate is controlled in a way mentioned in paragraph (a)(i), (ii) or (iii) by a body corporate of which the society has joint control;'.

*Acquisition of joint control*

**13**   In section 13(9), in the words following paragraph (d), after 'paragraph (c)' insert 'or (cc)'

*Amendment of Schedule 8 to the 1992 Act*

**14**   (1) Schedule 8 to the 1992 Act (provisions supplementing section 13) is amended as follows

(2)  Omit paragraph 3(2).

(3)  After paragraph 3 insert—

  '**3A** (1) A body is to be treated for the purposes of section 13(9) as having the right to appoint to a directorship if—

    (a)  a person's appointment to the directorship follows necessarily from his appointment as an officer of that body; or

    (b)  the directorship is held by the body itself.

  (2)  A body ('B') and some other person ('P') together are to be treated, for the purposes of section 13(9), as having the right to appoint to a directorship if—

    (a)  P is a body corporate which has directors and a person's appointment to the directorship follows necessarily from his appointment both as an officer of B and a director of P;

    (b)  P is a body corporate which does not have directors and a person's appointment to the directorship follows necessarily from his appointment both as an officer of B and as a member of P's managing body; or

    (c)  the directorship is held jointly by B and P.

  (3)  For the purposes of section 13(9), a right to appoint (or remove) which is exercisable only with the consent or agreement of another person must be left out of account unless no other person has a right to appoint (or remove) in relation to that directorship.

  (4)  Nothing in this paragraph is to be read as restricting the effect of section 13(9).'

(5)  In paragraph 9 (exercise of certain rights under instruction by, or in the interests of, incorporated friendly society) insert at the end 'or in the interests of any body over which the society has joint control'.

*Consequential amendments*

**15**   (1) Section 52 of the 1992 Act is amended as follows.

(2)  In subsection (2), omit paragraph (d).

(3)  In subsection (3), for '(4) below' substitute '(2)'.

(4)  For subsection (4) substitute—

'(4) A court may not make an order under subsection (5) unless it is satisfied that one or more of the conditions mentioned in subsection (2) are satisfied.'

(5)  In subsection (5), omit the words from 'or, where' to the end.

### *References in other enactments*

**16**  References in any provision of, or made under, any enactment to subsidiaries of, or bodies jointly controlled by, an incorporated friendly society are to be read as including references to bodies which are such subsidiaries or bodies as a result of any provision of this Part of this Schedule

## PART III

## BUILDING SOCIETIES

### *The Building Societies Act 1986 (c 53)*

**17**  Omit section 9 (initial authorisation to raise funds and borrow money).

**18**  Omit Schedule 3 (supplementary provisions about authorisation).

## PART IV

## INDUSTRIAL AND PROVIDENT SOCIETIES

### *The Industrial and Provident Societies Act 1965 (c 12)*

**19**  Omit section 8 (provision for separate registration areas for Scotland and for England, Wales and the Channel Islands).

**20**  Omit section 70 (scale of fees to be paid in respect of transactions and inspection of documents).

## PART V

## CREDIT UNIONS

### *The Credit Unions Act 1979 (c 34)*

**21**  In section 6 (minimum and maximum number of members), omit subsections (2) to (6).

**22**  In section 11 (loans), omit subsections (2) and (6).

**23**  Omit sections 11B (loans approved by credit unions), 11C (grant of certificates of approval) and 11D (withdrawal of certificates of approval).

**24**  In section 12, omit subsections (4) and (5).

**25**  In section 14, omit subsections (2), (3), (5) and (6).

**26**  In section 28 (offences), omit subsection (2).

## SCHEDULE 19

## [...]

## SCHEDULE 20

## MINOR AND CONSEQUENTIAL AMENDMENTS

### *The House of Commons Disqualification Act 1975 (c 24)*

**1**  In Part III of Schedule 1 to the House of Commons Disqualification Act 1975 (disqualifying offices)—

(a)  omit—

'Any member of the Financial Services Tribunal in receipt of remuneration';
and

(b)  at the appropriate place, insert—

'Any member, in receipt of remuneration, of a panel of persons who may be selected to act as members of the Financial Services and Markets Tribunal'.

### *The Northern Ireland Assembly Disqualification Act 1975 (c 25)*

**2**   In Part III of Schedule 1 to the Northern Ireland Assembly Disqualification Act 1975 (disqualifying offices)—

   (a) omit—
   'Any member of the Financial Services Tribunal in receipt of remuneration';
   and
   (b) at the appropriate place, insert—
   'Any member, in receipt of remuneration, of a panel of persons who may be selected to act as members of the Financial Services and Markets Tribunal'.

### *The Civil Jurisdiction and Judgments Act 1982 (c 27)*

**3**   In paragraph 10 of Schedule 5 to the Civil Jurisdiction and Judgments Act 1982 (proceedings excluded from the operation of Schedule 4 to that Act), for 'section 188 of the Financial Services Act 1986' substitute 'section 415 of the Financial Services and Markets Act 2000'

### *The Income and Corporation Taxes Act 1988 (c 1)*

**4**   (1) The Income and Corporation Taxes Act 1988 is amended as follows
   (2) In section 76 (expenses of management: insurance companies), in subsection (8), omit the definitions of—
   'the 1986 Act';
   'authorised person';
   'investment business';
   'investor';
   'investor protection scheme';
   'prescribed'; and
   'recognised self-regulating organisation'.
   (3) In section 468 (authorised unit trusts), in subsections (6) and (8), for '78 of the Financial Services Act 1986' substitute '243 of the Financial Services and Markets Act 2000'.
   (4) [...]
   (5) In section 728 (information in relation to transfers of securities), in subsection (7)(a), for 'Financial Services Act 1986' substitute 'Financial Services and Markets Act 2000'.
   (6) [...]

### *The Finance Act 1991 (c 31)*

**5**   (1) The Finance Act 1991 is amended as follows
   (2) In section 47 (investor protection schemes), omit subsections (1), (2) and (4).
   (3) In section 116 (investment exchanges and clearing houses: stamp duty), in subsection (4)(b), for 'Financial Services Act 1986' substitute 'Financial Services and Markets Act 2000'.

### *The Tribunals and Inquiries Act 1992 (c 53)*

**6**   (1) The Tribunals and Inquiries Act 1992 is amended as follows
   (2) In Schedule 1 (tribunals under supervision of the Council on Tribunals), for the entry relating to financial services and paragraph 18, substitute—

| | |
|---|---|
| 'Financial services and markets | 18. The Financial Services and Markets Tribunal.' |

### *The Judicial Pensions and Retirement Act 1993 (c 8)*

**7**   (1) The Judicial Pensions and Retirement Act 1993 is amended as follows
   (2) In Schedule 1 (offices which may be qualifying offices), in Part II, after the entry relating to the President or chairman of the Transport Tribunal insert—
   'President or Deputy President of the Financial Services and Markets Tribunal'
   (3) In Schedule 5 (relevant offices in relation to retirement provisions)—
   (a) omit the entry—
   'Member of the Financial Services Tribunal appointed by the Lord Chancellor';
   and
   (b) at the end insert—
   'Member of the Financial Services and Markets Tribunal'.

# SCHEDULE 21

## TRANSITIONAL PROVISIONS AND SAVINGS

### *Self-regulating organisations*

**1** (1) No new application under section 9 of the 1986 Act (application for recognition) may be entertained

(2) No outstanding application made under that section before the passing of this Act may continue to be entertained.

(3) After the date which is the designated date for a recognised self-regulating organisation—

  (a) the recognition order for that organisation may not be revoked under section 11 of the 1986 Act (revocation of recognition);

  (b) no application may be made to the court under section 12 of the 1986 Act (compliance orders) with respect to that organisation.

(4) The powers conferred by section 13 of the 1986 Act (alteration of rules for protection of investors) may not be exercised.

(5) 'Designated date' means such date as the Treasury may by order designate.

(6) Sub-paragraph (3) does not apply to a recognised self-regulating organisation in respect of which a notice of intention to revoke its recognition order was given under section 11(3) of the 1986 Act before the passing of this Act if that notice has not been withdrawn.

(7) Expenditure incurred by the Authority in connection with the winding up of any body which was, immediately before the passing of this Act, a recognised self-regulating organisation is to be treated as having been incurred in connection with the discharge by the Authority of functions under this Act.

(8) 'Recognised self-regulating organisation' means an organisation which, immediately before the passing of this Act, was such an organisation for the purposes of the 1986 Act.

(9) 'The 1986 Act' means the Financial Services Act 1986.

### *Self-regulating organisations for friendly societies*

**2** (1) No new application under paragraph 2 of Schedule 11 to the 1986 Act (application for recognition) may be entertained

(2) No outstanding application made under that paragraph before the passing of this Act may continue to be entertained.

(3) After the date which is the designated date for a recognised self-regulating organisation for friendly societies—

  (a) the recognition order for that organisation may not be revoked under paragraph 5 of Schedule 11 to the 1986 Act (revocation of recognition);

  (b) no application may be made to the court under paragraph 6 of that Schedule (compliance orders) with respect to that organisation.

(4) 'Designated date' means such date as the Treasury may by order designate.

(5) Sub-paragraph (3) does not apply to a recognised self-regulating organisation for friendly societies in respect of which a notice of intention to revoke its recognition order was given under section 11(3) of the 1986 Act (as applied by paragraph 5(2) of that Schedule) before the passing of this Act if that notice has not been withdrawn.

(6) Expenditure incurred by the Authority in connection with the winding up of any body which was, immediately before the passing of this Act, a recognised self-regulating organisation for friendly societies is to be treated as having been incurred in connection with the discharge by the Authority of functions under this Act.

(7) 'Recognised self-regulating organisation for friendly societies' means an organisation which, immediately before the passing of this Act, was such an organisation for the purposes of the 1986 Act.

(8) 'The 1986 Act' means the Financial Services Act 1986.

# SCHEDULE 22

## REPEALS

| Chapter | Short title | Extent of repeal |
| --- | --- | --- |
| 1923 c 8. | The Industrial Assurance Act 1923. | The whole Act. |
| 1948 c 39. | The Industrial Assurance and Friendly Societies Act 1948. | The whole Act. |
| 1965 c 12. | The Industrial and Provident Societies Act 1965. | Section 8. |
|  |  | Section 70. |
| 1974 c 46. | The Friendly Societies Act 1974. | Section 4. |

| | | Section 10. |
|---|---|---|
| | | In section 11, from 'and where' to 'that society'. |
| | | In section 99(4), 'in the central registration area'. |
| 1975 c 24. | The House of Commons Disqualification Act 1975. | In Schedule 1, in Part III, 'Any member of the Financial Services Tribunal in receipt of remuneration'. |
| 1975 c 25. | The Northern Ireland Assembly Dis-qualification Act 1975. | In Schedule 1, in Part III, 'Any member of the Financial Services Tribunal in receipt of remuneration'. |
| 1977 c 46. | The Insurance Brokers (Registration) Act 1977. | The whole Act. |
| 1979 c 34. | The Credit Unions Act 1979. | Section 6(2) to (6). |
| | | Section 11(2) and (6). |
| | | Sections 11B, 11C and 11D. |
| | | Section 12(4) and (5). |
| | | In section 14, subsections (2), (3), (5) and (6). |
| | | Section 28(2). |
| 1986 c 53. | The Building Societies Act 1986. | Section 9. |
| | | Schedule 3. |
| 1988 c 1. | The Income and Corporation Taxes Act 1988. | In section 76, in subsection (8), the definitions of 'the 1986 Act', 'authorised person', 'investment business', 'investor', 'investor protection scheme', 'prescribed' and 'recognised self-regulating organisation'. |
| 1991 c 31. | The Finance Act 1991. | In section 47, subsections (1), (2) and (4). |
| 1992 c 40. | The Friendly Societies Act 1992. | In section 13, subsections (2) to (5), (8) and (11). |
| | | Sections 31 to 36. |
| | | In section 37, subsections (1), (1A) and (7A) to (9). |
| | | Sections 38 to 50. |
| | | In section 52, subsection (2)(d) and, in subsection (5), the words from 'or where' to the end. |
| | | Schedule 7. |
| | | In Schedule 8, paragraph 3(2). |
| 1993 c 8. | The Judicial Pensions and Retirement Act 1993. | In Schedule 5, 'Member of the Financial Services Tribunal appointed by the Lord Chancellor'. |

# The Financial Services and Markets Act 2000 (Regulated Activities) Order 2001

(2001 No. 544)

*The Treasury, in exercise of the powers conferred on them by sections 22(1) and (5), 426 and 428(3) of, and paragraph 25 of Schedule 2 to, the Financial Services and Markets Act 2000, hereby make the following Order:*

## PART I

## GENERAL

### 1   Citation

This Order may be cited as the Financial Services and Markets Act 2000 (Regulated Activities) Order 2001.

### 2   Commencement

(1) Except as provided by paragraph (2), this Order comes into force on the day on which section 19 of the Act comes into force.

(2) This Order comes into force—

(a) for the purposes of articles 59, 60 and 87 (funeral plan contracts) on 1st January 2002; and

(b) for the purposes of articles 61 to 63, 88, 90 and 91 (regulated mortgage contracts) on such a day as the Treasury may specify.

(3) Any day specified under paragraph (2)(b) must be caused to be notified in the London, Edinburgh and Belfast Gazettes published not later than one week before that day.

## 3 Interpretation

(1) In this Order—

'the Act' means the Financial Services and Markets Act 2000;

'annuities on human life' does not include superannuation allowances and annuities payable out of any fund applicable solely to the relief and maintenance of persons engaged, or who have been engaged, in any particular profession, trade or employment, or of the dependants of such persons;

'buying' includes acquiring for valuable consideration;

'close relative' in relation to a person means—

    (a) his spouse or civil partner;

    (b) his children and step children, his parents and step-parents, his brothers and sisters and his step-brothers and step-sisters; and

    (c) the spouse or civil partner of any person within sub-paragraph (b);

'the Commission Regulation' means Commission Regulation 1287/2006 of 10 August 2006

'contract of general insurance' means any contract falling within Part I of Schedule 1;

'contract of insurance' means any contract of insurance which is a contract of long-term insurance or a contract of general insurance, and includes—

    (a) fidelity bonds, performance bonds, administration bonds, bail bonds, customs bonds or similar contracts of guarantee, where these are—

        (i) effected or carried out by a person not carrying on a banking business;

        (ii) not effected merely incidentally to some other business carried on by the person effecting them; and

        (iii) effected in return for the payment of one or more premiums;

    (b) tontines;

    (c) capital redemption contracts or pension fund management contracts, where these are effected or carried out by a person who—

        (i) does not carry on a banking business; and

        (ii) otherwise carries on a regulated activity of the kind specified by article 10(1) or (2);

    (d) contracts to pay annuities on human life;

    (e) contracts of a kind referred to in article 1(2)(e) of the first life insurance directive (collective insurance etc.); and

    (f) contracts of a kind referred to in article 1(3) of the first life insurance directive (social insurance);

but does not include a funeral plan contract (or a contract which would be a funeral plan contract but for the exclusion in article 60);

'contract of long-term insurance' means any contract falling within Part II of Schedule 1;

'contractually based investment' means—

    (a) rights under a qualifying contract of insurance;

    (b) any investment of the kind specified by any of articles 83, 84, 85 and 87; or

    (c) any investment of the kind specified by article 89 so far as relevant to an investment falling within (a) or (b);

'credit institution' means—

    (a) a credit institution authorised under the banking consolidation directive other than an institution to which Article 2.1 of the markets in financial instruments directive (the text of which is set out in Schedule 3) applies, or

    (b) an institution which would satisfy the requirements for authorisation as a credit institution under that directive (other than an institution to which Article 2.1 of the markets in financial instruments directive would apply) if it had its registered office (or if it does not have a registered office, its head office) in an EEA State;

'deposit' has the meaning given by article 5;

'electronic money' means monetary value, as represented by a claim on the issuer, which is—

    (a) stored on an electronic device;

    (b) issued on receipt of funds; and

    (c) accepted as a means of payment by persons other than the issuer;

'financial instrument' means any instrument listed in Section C of Annex I to the markets in financial instruments directive (the text of which is set out in Part 1 of Schedule 2) read with Chapter VI of the Commission Regulation (the text of which is set out in Part 2 of Schedule 2);

'funeral plan contract' has the meaning given by article 59;

'home Member State', in relation to an investment firm, has the meaning given by Article 4.1.20 of the markets in financial instruments directive, and in relation to a credit institution, has the meaning given by Article 4.7 of the banking consolidation directive;

'home purchase provider' has the meaning given by article 63F(3);

'home purchaser' has the meaning given by article 63F(3);

'instrument' includes any record whether or not in the form of a document;

'investment firm' means a person whose regular occupation or business is the provision or performance of investment services and activities on a professional basis but does not include—

    (a) a person to whom the markets in financial instruments directive does not apply by virtue of Article 2 of that directive (the text of which is set out in Schedule 3);

    (b) a person whose home Member State is an EEA State other than the United Kingdom and to whom, by reason of the fact that the State has given effect to Article 3 of that directive, that directive does not apply by virtue of that Article;

    (c) a person who does not have a home Member State and to whom (if he had his registered office in an EEA State, or, being a person other than a body corporate or a body corporate not having a registered office, if he had his head office in an EEA State) the markets in financial instruments directive would not apply by virtue of Article 2 of that directive;

'investment services and activities' means—

    (a) any service provided to third parties listed in Section A of Annex I to the markets in financial instruments directive (the text of which is set out in Part 3 of Schedule 2) read with Article 52 of Commission Directive 2006/73/EC of 10 August 2006 (the text of which is set out in Part 4 of Schedule 2), or

    (b) any activity listed in Section A of Annex I to that directive,

relating to any financial instrument;

'joint enterprise' means an enterprise into which two or more persons ('the participators') enter for commercial purposes related to a business or businesses (other than the business of engaging in a regulated activity) carried on by them; and, where a participator is a member of a group, each other member of the group is also to be regarded as a participator in the enterprise;

'local authority' means—

    (a) in England and Wales, a local authority within the meaning of the Local Government Act 1972 , the Greater London Authority, the Common Council of the City of London or the Council of the Isles of Scilly;

    (b) in Scotland, a local authority within the meaning of the Local Government (Scotland) Act 1973;

    (c) in Northern Ireland, a district council within the meaning of the Local Government Act (Northern Ireland) 1972;

'management company' has the meaning given by Article 1a.2 of the UCITS directive as amended by Directive 2001/107/EC;

'managing agent' means a person who is permitted by the Council of Lloyd's in the conduct of his business as an underwriting agent to perform for a member of Lloyd's one or more of the following functions—

    (a) underwriting contracts of insurance at Lloyd's;

    (b) reinsuring such contracts in whole or in part;

    (c) paying claims on such contracts;

'market operator' means a market operator within the meaning of Article 4.1.13 of the markets in financial instruments directive, or a person who would be a market operator if he had his registered office, or if he does not have a registered office his head office, in an EEA State, but does not include—

    (a) a person to whom the markets in financial instruments directive does not apply by virtue of Article 2 of that directive (the text of which is set out in Schedule 3);

    (b) a person who does not have a home Member State to whom (if he had his registered office, or if he does not have a registered office his head office, in an EEA State) the markets in financial instruments directive would not apply by virtue of Article 2 of that directive;

'multilateral trading facility' means—

    (a) a multilateral trading facility (within the meaning of Article 4.1.15 of the markets in financial instruments directive) operated by an investment firm, a credit institution or a market operator, or

    (b) a facility which—

        (i) is operated by an investment firm, a credit institution or market operator which does not have a home Member State, and

        (ii) if its operator had a home Member State, would be a multilateral trading facility within the meaning of Article 4.1.15 of the markets in financial instruments directive;

'occupational pension scheme' has the meaning given by section 1 of the Pensions Schemes Act 1993 but with paragraph (b) of the definition omitted;

'overseas person' means a person who—

    (a) carries on activities of the kind specified by any of articles 14, 21, 25, 37, 40, 45, 51, 52 and 53 or, so far as relevant to any of those articles, article 64 (or activities of a kind which would be so specified but for the exclusion in article 72); but

    (b) does not carry on any such activities, or offer to do so, from a permanent place of business maintained by him in the United Kingdom;

'pension fund management contract' means a contract to manage the investments of pension funds (other than funds solely for the benefit of the officers or employees of the person effecting or carrying out the contract and their dependants or, in the case of a company, partly for the benefit of officers and employees and their dependants of its subsidiary or holding company or a subsidiary of its holding company); and for the purposes of this definition, 'subsidiary' and 'holding company' are to be construed in accordance with section 736 of the Companies Act 1985 or article 4 of the Companies (Northern Ireland) Order 1986;

'personal pension scheme' means any scheme or arrangement which is comprised in one or more instruments or agreements and which has, or is capable of having, effect in relation to one or more descriptions or categories of employment so as to provide benefits, in the form of pensions or otherwise, payable on termination of service, or on death or retirement, to or in respect of earners with qualifying service in an employment of any such description or category;

'plan provider' has the meaning given by paragraph (3) of article 63B, read with paragraphs (7) and (8) of that article;

'property' includes currency of the United Kingdom or any other country or territory;

'qualifying contract of insurance' means a contract of long-term insurance which is not—

(a) a reinsurance contract; nor

(b) a contract in respect of which the following conditions are met—

(i) the benefits under the contract are payable only on death or in respect of incapacity due to injury, sickness or infirmity;

(ii) [...]

(iii) the contract has no surrender value, or the consideration consists of a single premium and the surrender value does not exceed that premium; and

(iv) the contract makes no provision for its conversion or extension in a manner which would result in it ceasing to comply with any of the above conditions;

'regulated home purchase plan' has the meaning given by article 63F(3);

'regulated home reversion plan' has the meaning given by article 63B(3);

'regulated mortgage contract' has the meaning given by article 61(3);

'relevant investment' means—

(a) rights under a qualifying contract of insurance;

(b) rights under any other contract of insurance;

(c) any investment of the kind specified by any of articles 83, 84, 85 and 87; or

(d) any investment of the kind specified by article 89 so far as relevant to an investment falling within (a) or (c);

'reversion seller' has the meaning given by article 63B(3);

'security' means (except where the context otherwise requires) any investment of the kind specified by any of articles 76 to 82 or, so far as relevant to any such investment, article 89;

'selling', in relation to any investment, includes disposing of the investment for valuable consideration, and for these purposes 'disposing' includes—

(a) in the case of an investment consisting of rights under a contract—

(i) surrendering, assigning or converting those rights; or

(ii) assuming the corresponding liabilities under the contract;

(b) in the case of an investment consisting of rights under other arrangements, assuming the corresponding liabilities under the arrangements; and

(c) in the case of any other investment, issuing or creating the investment or granting the rights or interests of which it consists;

'stakeholder pension scheme' has the meaning given by section 1 of the Welfare Reform and Pensions Act 1999 in relation to Great Britain and has the meaning given by article 3 of the Welfare Reform and Pensions (Northern Ireland) Order 1999 in relation to Northern Ireland;

'syndicate' means one or more persons, to whom a particular syndicate number has been assigned by or under the authority of the Council of Lloyd's, carrying out or effecting contracts of insurance written at Lloyd's;

'voting shares', in relation to a body corporate, means shares carrying voting rights attributable to share capital which are exercisable in all circumstances at any general meeting of that body corporate.

(2) For the purposes of this Order, a transaction is entered into through a person if he enters into it as agent or arranges, in a manner constituting the carrying on of an activity of the kind specified by article 25(1), 25A(1), 25B(1) or 25C(1), for it to be entered into by another person as agent or principal.

(3) For the purposes of this Order, a contract of insurance is to be treated as falling within Part II of Schedule 1, notwithstanding the fact that it contains related and subsidiary provisions such that it might also be regarded as falling within Part I of that Schedule, if its principal object is that of a contract falling within Part II and it is effected or carried out by an authorised person who has permission to effect or carry out contracts falling within paragraph I of Part II of Schedule 1.

# PART II

# SPECIFIED ACTIVITIES

## Chapter I   General

### 4   Specified activities: general

(1)  The following provisions of this Part specify kinds of activity for the purposes of section 22 of the Act (and accordingly any activity of one of those kinds, which is carried on by way of business, and relates to an investment of a kind specified by any provision of Part III and applicable to that activity, is a regulated activity for the purposes of the Act).

(2)  The kinds of activity specified by articles 51 and 52 are also specified for the purposes of section 22(1)(b) of the Act (and accordingly any activity of one of those kinds, when carried on by way of business, is a regulated activity when carried on in relation to property of any kind).

(3)  Subject to paragraph (4), each provision specifying a kind of activity is subject to the exclusions applicable to that provision (and accordingly any reference in this Order to an activity of the kind specified by a particular provision is to be read subject to any such exclusions).

(4)  Where an investment firm or credit institution—

  (a)  provides or performs investment services and activities on a professional basis, and

  (b)  in doing so would be treated as carrying on an activity of a kind specified by a provision of this Part but for an exclusion in any of articles 15, 16, 19, 22, 23, 29, 38, 67, 68, 69, 70 and 72E,

that exclusion is to be disregarded and, accordingly, the investment firm or credit institution is to be treated as carrying on an activity of the kind specified by the provision in question.

(4A)  Where a person, other than a person specified by Article 1.2 of the insurance mediation directive (the text of which is set out in Part 1 of Schedule 4)—

  (a)  for remuneration, takes up or pursues insurance mediation or reinsurance mediation in relation to a risk or commitment located in an EEA State, and

  (b)  in doing so would be treated as carrying on an activity of a kind specified by a provision of this Part but for an exclusion in any of articles 30, 66 and 67,

that exclusion is to be disregarded (and accordingly that person is to be treated as carrying on an activity of the kind specified by the provision in question).

(5)  In this article—

[…]

'insurance mediation' has the meaning given by Article 2.3 of the insurance mediation directive, the text of which is set out in Part II of Schedule 4;

'reinsurance mediation' has the meaning given by Article 2.4 of the insurance mediation directive, the text of which is set out in Part III of Schedule 4.

## Chapter II   Accepting deposits

### *The activity*

### 5   Accepting deposits

(1)  Accepting deposits is a specified kind of activity if—

  (a)  money received by way of deposit is lent to others; or

  (b)  any other activity of the person accepting the deposit is financed wholly, or to a material extent, out of the capital of or interest on money received by way of deposit.

(2)  In paragraph (1), 'deposit' means a sum of money, other than one excluded by any of articles 6 to 9A, paid on terms—

  (a)  under which it will be repaid, with or without interest or premium, and either on demand or at a time or in circumstances agreed by or on behalf of the person making the payment and the person receiving it; and

  (b)  which are not referable to the provision of property (other than currency) or services or the giving of security.

(3)  For the purposes of paragraph (2), money is paid on terms which are referable to the provision of property or services or the giving of security if, and only if—

  (a)  it is paid by way of advance or part payment under a contract for the sale, hire or other provision of property or services, and is repayable only in the event that the property or services is or are not in fact sold, hired or otherwise provided;

  (b)  it is paid by way of security for the performance of a contract or by way of security in respect of loss which may result from the non-performance of a contract; or

(c) without prejudice to sub-paragraph (b), it is paid by way of security for the delivery up or return of any property, whether in a particular state of repair or otherwise.

*Exclusions*

## 6 Sums paid by certain persons

(1) A sum is not a deposit for the purposes of article 5 if it is—
  (a) paid by any of the following persons—
    (i) the Bank of England, the central bank of an EEA State other than the United Kingdom, or the European Central Bank;
    (ii) an authorised person who has permission to accept deposits, or to effect or carry out contracts of insurance;
    (iii) an EEA firm falling within paragraph 5(b), (c) or (d) of Schedule 3 to the Act (other than one falling within paragraph (ii) above);
    (iv) the National Savings Bank;
    (v) a municipal bank, that is to say a company which was, immediately before the coming into force of this article, exempt from the prohibition in section 3 of the Banking Act 1987 by virtue of section 4(1) of, and paragraph 4 of Schedule 2 to, that Act;
    (vi) Keesler Federal Credit Union;
    (vii) a body of persons certified as a school bank by the National Savings Bank or by an authorised person who has permission to accept deposits;
    (viii) a local authority;
    (xi) any body which by virtue of any enactment has power to issue a precept to a local authority in England and Wales or a requisition to a local authority in Scotland, or to the expenses of which, by virtue of any enactment, a local authority in the United Kingdom is or can be required to contribute (and in this paragraph, 'enactment' includes an enactment comprised in, or in an instrument made under, an Act of the Scottish Parliament);
    (x) the European Community, the European Atomic Energy Community or the European Coal and Steel Community;
    (xi) the European Investment Bank;
    (xii) the International Bank for Reconstruction and Development;
    (xiii) the International Finance Corporation;
    (xiv) the International Monetary Fund;
    (xv) the African Development Bank;
    (xvi) the Asian Development Bank;
    (xvii) the Caribbean Development Bank;
    (xviii) the Inter-American Development Bank;
    (xix) the European Bank for Reconstruction and Development;
    (xx) the Council of Europe Development Bank;
  (b) paid by a person other than one mentioned in sub-paragraph (a) in the course of carrying on a business consisting wholly or to a significant extent of lending money;
  (c) paid by one company to another at a time when both are members of the same group or when the same individual is a majority shareholder controller of both of them; or
  (d) paid by a person who, at the time when it is paid, is a close relative of the person receiving it or who is, or is a close relative of, a director or manager of that person or who is, or is a close relative of, a controller of that person.

(2) For the purposes of paragraph (1)(c), an individual is a majority shareholder controller of a company if he is a controller of the company by virtue of paragraph (a), (c), (e) or (g) of section 422(2) of the Act, and if in his case the greatest percentage of those referred to in those paragraphs is 50 or more.

(3) In the application of sub-paragraph (d) of paragraph (1) to a sum paid by a partnership, that sub-paragraph is to have effect as if, for the reference to the person paying the sum, there were substituted a reference to each of the partners.

## 7 Sums received by solicitors etc

(1) A sum is not a deposit for the purposes of article 5 if it is received by a practising solicitor acting in the course of his profession.

(2) In paragraph (1), 'practising solicitor' means—
  (a) a solicitor who is qualified to act as such under section 1 of the Solicitors Act 1974 , article 4 of the Solicitors (Northern Ireland) Order 1976 or section 4 of the Solicitors (Scotland) Act 1980;
  (b) a recognised body;
  (c) a registered foreign lawyer in the course of providing professional services as a member of a multi-national partnership;
  (d) a registered European lawyer; or

(e) a partner of a registered European lawyer who is providing professional services in accordance with—

    (i) rules made under section 31 of the Solicitors Act 1974;

    (ii) regulations made under article 26 of the Solicitors (Northern Ireland) Order 1976; or

    (iii) rules made under section 34 of the Solicitors (Scotland) Act 1980.

(3) In this article—

(a) 'a recognised body' means a body recognised by—

    (i) the Council of the Law Society under section 9 of the Administration of Justice Act 1985;

    (ii) the Incorporated Law Society of Northern Ireland under article 26A of the Solicitors (Northern Ireland) Order 1976 ; or

    (iii) the Council of the Law Society of Scotland under section 34 of the Solicitors (Scotland) Act 1980;

(b) 'registered foreign lawyer' has the meaning given by section 89 of the Courts and Legal Services Act 1990 or, in Scotland, section 65 of the Solicitors (Scotland) Act 1980 ;

(c) 'multi-national partnership' has the meaning given by section 89 of the Courts and Legal Services Act 1990 but, in Scotland, is a reference to a 'multi-national practice' within the meaning of section 60A of the Solicitors (Scotland) Act 1980; and

(d) 'registered European lawyer' has the meaning given by regulation 2(1) of the European Communities (Lawyer's Practice) Regulations 2000 or regulation 2(1) of the European Communities (Lawyer's Practice) (Scotland) Regulation 2000 .

## 8 Sums received by persons authorised to deal etc

A sum is not a deposit for the purposes of article 5 if it is received by a person who is—

(a) an authorised person with permission to carry on an activity of the kind specified by any of articles 14, 21, 25, 37, 51 and 52, or

(b) an exempt person in relation to any such activity,

in the course of, or for the purpose of, carrying on any such activity (or any activity which would be such an activity but for any exclusion made by this Part) with or on behalf of the person by or on behalf of whom the sum is paid.

## 9 Sums received in consideration for the issue of debt securities

(1) Subject to paragraph (2), a sum is not a deposit for the purposes of article 5 if it is received by a person as consideration for the issue by him of any investment of the kind specified by article 77 or 78.

(2) The exclusion in paragraph (1) does not apply to the receipt by a person of a sum as consideration for the issue by him of commercial paper unless—

(a) the commercial paper is issued to persons—

    (i) whose ordinary activities involve them in acquiring, holding, managing or disposing of investments (as principal or agent) for the purposes of their businesses; or

    (ii) who it is reasonable to expect will acquire, hold, manage or dispose of investments (as principal or agent) for the purposes of their businesses; and

(b) the redemption value of the commercial paper is not less than £100,000 (or an amount of equivalent value denominated wholly or partly in a currency other than sterling), and no part of the commercial paper may be transferred unless the redemption value of that part is not less than £100,000 (or such an equivalent amount).

(3) In paragraph (2), 'commercial paper' means an investment of the kind specified by article 77 or 78 having a maturity of less than one year from the date of issue.

## 9A Sums received in exchange for electronic money

A sum is not a deposit for the purposes of article 5 if it is immediately exchanged for electronic money.

## 9AA Information society services

Article 5 is subject to the exclusion in article 72A (information society services).

# Chapter IIa Electronic money

*The activity*

## 9B Issuing electronic money

Issuing electronic money is a specified kind of activity.

*Exclusions*

## 9C Persons certified as small issuers etc.

(1) There is excluded from article 9B the issuing of electronic money by a person to whom the Authority has given a certificate under this article (provided the certificate has not been revoked).

(2) An application for a certificate may be made by—

(a) a body corporate, or

(b) a partnership,

(other than a credit institution as defined in Article 4(1)(a) of the banking consolidation directive) which has its head office in the United Kingdom.

(3) The authority must, on the application of such a person ('A'), give A a certificate if it appears to the Authority that paragraph (4), (5) or (6) applies.

(4) This paragraph applies if—

(a) A does not issue electronic money except on terms that the electronic device on which the monetary value is stored is subject to a maximum storage amount of not more than 150 euro; and

(b) A's total liabilities with respect to the issuing of electronic money do not (or will not) usually exceed 5 million euro and do not (or will not) ever exceed 6 million euro.

(5) This paragraph applies if—

(a) the condition in paragraph (4)(a) is met;

(b) A's total liabilities with respect to the issuing of electronic money do not (or will not) exceed 10 million euro; and

(c) electronic money issued by A is accepted as a means of payment only by—

(i) subsidiaries of A which perform operational or other ancillary functions related to electronic money issued or distributed by A; or

(ii) other members of the same group as A (other than subsidiaries of A).

(6) This paragraph applies if—

(a) the conditions in paragraphs (4)(a) and (5)(b) are met; and

(b) electronic money issued by A is accepted as a means of payment, in the course of business, by not more than one hundred persons where—

(i) those persons accept such electronic money only at locations within the same premises or limited local area; or

(ii) those persons have a close financial or business relationship with A, such as a common marketing or distribution scheme.

(7) For the purposes of paragraph (6)(b)(i), locations are to be treated as situated within the same premises or limited local area if they are situated within—

(a) a shopping centre, airport, railway station, bus station, or campus of a university, polytechnic, college, school or similar educational establishment; or

(b) an area which does not exceed four square kilometres;

but sub-paragraphs (a) and (b) are illustrative only and are not to be treated as limiting the scope of paragraph (6)(b)(i).

(8) For the purposes of paragraph (6)(b)(ii), persons are not to be treated as having a close financial or business relationship with A merely because they participate in arrangements for the acceptance of electronic money issued by A.

(9) In this article, references to amounts in euro include references to equivalent amounts in sterling.

(10) A person to whom a certificate has been given under this article (and whose certificate has not been revoked) is referred to in this Chapter as a 'certified person'.

## 9D  Applications for certificates

The following provisions of the Act apply to applications to the Authority for certificates under 9C (and the determination of such applications) as they apply to applications for Part IV permissions (and the determination of such applications)—

(a) section 51(1)(b) and (3) to (6);

(b) section 52, except subsections (6), (8) and (9)(a) and (b); and

(c) section 55(1).

## 9E  Revocation of certificate on Authority's own initiative

(1) The Authority may revoke a certificate given to a person ('A') under article 9C if—

(a) it appears to it that A does not meet the relevant conditions, or has failed to meet the relevant conditions at any time since the certificate was given; or

(b) the person to whom the certificate was given has contravened any rule or requirement to which he is subject as a result of article 9G.

(2) For the purposes of paragraph (1), A meets the relevant conditions at any time if, at that time, paragraph (4), (5) or (6) of article 9C applies.

(3) Sections 54 and 55(2) of the Act apply to the revocation of a certificate under paragraph (1) as they apply to the cancellation of a Part IV permission on the Authority's own initiative, as if references in those sections to an authorised person were references to a certified person.

## 9F  Revocation of certificate on request

(1) A certified person ('B') may apply to the Authority for his certificate to be revoked, and the Authority must then revoke the certificate and give B written notice that it has done so.

(2) An application under paragraph (1) must be made in such manner as the Authority may direct.

(3) If—

(a) B has made an application under Part IV of the Act for permission to carry on a regulated activity of the kind specified by article 9B (or for variation of an existing permission so as to add a regulated activity of that kind), and

(b) on making an application for revocation of his certificate under paragraph (1), he requests that the revocation be conditional on the granting of his application under Part IV of the Act,

the revocation of B's certificate is to be conditional on the granting of his application under Part IV of the Act.

### 9G Obtaining information from certified persons etc

(1) The Authority may make rules requiring certified persons to provide information to the Authority about their activities so far as relating to the issuing of electronic money, including the amount of their liabilities with respect to the issuing of electronic money.

(2) Section 148 of the Act (modification or waiver of rules) applies in relation to rules made under paragraph (1) as if references in that section to an authorised person were references to a certified person.

(3) Section 150 of the Act (actions for damages) applies in relation to a rule made under paragraph (1) as if the reference in subsection (1) of that section to an authorised person were a reference to a certified person.

(4) The Authority may, by notice in writing given to a certified person, require him—

(a) to provide specified information or information of a specified description; or

(b) to produce specified documents or documents of a specified description.

(5) Paragraph (4) applies only to information or documents reasonably required for the purposes of determining whether the certified person meets, or has met, the relevant conditions.

(6) Subsections (2), (5) and (6) of section 165 of the Act (Authority's power to require information) apply to a requirement imposed under paragraph (4) as they apply to a requirement imposed under that section.

(7) Section 166 of the Act (reports by skilled persons) has effect as if—

(a) the reference in subsection (1) of that section to section 165 included a reference to paragraph (4) above; and

(b) the reference in section 166(2)(a) of the Act to an authorised person included a reference to a certified person.

(8) Subsection (4) of section 168 of the Act (appointment of persons to carry out investigations in particular cases) has effect as if it provided for subsection (5) of that section to apply if it appears to the Authority that there are circumstances suggesting that a certified person may not meet, or may not have met, the relevant conditions.

(9) Sections 175 (information and documents: supplemental provisions), 176 (entry of premises under warrant) and 177 (offences) of the Act apply to a requirement imposed under paragraph (4) as they apply to a requirement imposed under section 165 of the Act (the reference in section 176(3)(a) to an authorised person being read as a reference to a certified person).

(10) In this article—

(a) 'specified', in paragraph (4), means specified in the notice mentioned in that paragraph;

(b) a certified person ('A') meets the relevant conditions at any time if, at that time, paragraph (4), (5) or (6) of article 9C applies.

*Supplemental*

### 9H Rules prohibiting the issue of electronic money at a discount

(1) The Authority may make rules applying to authorised persons with permission to carry on an activity of the kind specified by article 9B, prohibiting the issue of electronic money having a monetary value greater than the funds received.

(2) Section 148 of the Act (modification or waiver of rules) applies in relation to rules made under paragraph (1).

### 9I False claims to be a certified person

A person who is not a certified person is to be treated as guilty of an offence under section 24 of the Act (false claims to be authorised or exempt) if he—

(a) describes himself (in whatever terms) as a certified person;

(b) behaves, or otherwise holds himself out, in a manner which indicates (or which is reasonably likely to be understood as indicating) that he is a certified person.

### 9J Exclusion of electronic money from the compensation scheme

The compensation scheme established under Part XV of the Act is not to provide for the compensation of persons in respect of claims made in connection with any activity of the kind specified by article 9B.

### 9K Record of certified persons

The record maintained by the Authority under section 347 of the Act (public record of authorised persons etc.) must include every certified person.

## Chapter III  Insurance

*The activities*

### 10  Effecting and carrying out contracts of insurance

(1) Effecting a contract of insurance as principal is a specified kind of activity.

(2) Carrying out a contract of insurance as principal is a specified kind of activity.

*Exclusions*

### 11  Community co-insurers

(1) There is excluded from article 10(1) or (2) the effecting or carrying out of a contract of insurance by an EEA firm falling within paragraph 5(d) of Schedule 3 to the Act—

    (a) other than through a branch in the United Kingdom; and

    (b) pursuant to a Community co-insurance operation in which the firm is participating otherwise than as the leading insurer.

(2) In paragraph (1), 'Community co-insurance operation' and 'leading insurer' have the same meaning as in the Council Directive of 30 May 1978 on the co-ordination of laws, regulations and administrative provisions relating to Community co-insurance (No. 78/473/EEC).

### 12  Breakdown insurance

(1) There is excluded from article 10(1) or (2) the effecting or carrying out, by a person who does not otherwise carry on an activity of the kind specified by that article, of a contract of insurance which—

    (a) is a contract under which the benefits provided by that person ('the provider') are exclusively or primarily benefits in kind in the event of accident to or breakdown of a vehicle; and

    (b) contains the terms mentioned in paragraph (2).

(2) Those terms are that—

    (a) the assistance takes either or both of the forms mentioned in paragraph (3)(a) and (b);

    (b) the assistance is not available outside the United Kingdom and the Republic of Ireland except where it is provided without the payment of additional premium by a person in the country concerned with whom the provider has entered into a reciprocal agreement; and

    (c) assistance provided in the case of an accident or breakdown occurring in the United Kingdom or the Republic of Ireland is, in most circumstances, provided by the provider's servants.

(3) The forms of assistance are—

    (a) repairs to the relevant vehicle at the place where the accident or breakdown has occurred; this assistance may also include the delivery of parts, fuel, oil, water or keys to the relevant vehicle;

    (b) removal of the relevant vehicle to the nearest or most appropriate place at which repairs may be carried out, or to—

        (i) the home, point of departure or original destination within the United Kingdom of the driver and passengers, provided the accident or breakdown occurred within the United Kingdom;

        (ii) the home, point of departure or original destination within the Republic of Ireland of the driver and passengers, provided the accident or breakdown occurred within the Republic of Ireland or within Northern Ireland;

        (iii) the home, point of departure or original destination within Northern Ireland of the driver and passengers, provided the accident or breakdown occurred within the Republic of Ireland;

and this form of assistance may include the conveyance of the driver or passengers of the relevant vehicle, with the vehicle, or (where the vehicle is to be conveyed only to the nearest or most appropriate place at which repairs may be carried out) separately, to the nearest location from which they may continue their journey by other means.

(4) A contract does not fail to meet the condition in paragraph (1)(a) solely because the provider may reimburse the person entitled to the assistance for all or part of any sums paid by him in respect of assistance either because he failed to identify himself as a person entitled to the assistance or because he was unable to get in touch with the provider in order to claim the assistance.

(5) In this article—

'the assistance' means the benefits to be provided under a contract of the kind mentioned in paragraph (1);

'breakdown' means an event—

    (a) which causes the driver of the relevant vehicle to be unable to start a journey in the vehicle or involuntarily to bring the vehicle to a halt on a journey because of some malfunction of the vehicle or failure of it to function, and

    (b) after which the journey cannot reasonably be commenced or continued in the relevant vehicle;

'the relevant vehicle' means the vehicle (including a trailer or caravan) in respect of which the assistance is required.

### 12A   Information society services

Article 10 is subject to the exclusion in article 72A (information society services), as qualified by paragraph (2) of that article.

*Supplemental*

### 13   Application of sections 327 and 332 of the Act to insurance market activities

(1)  In sections 327(5) and (7) and 332(3)(b) of the Act (exemption from the general prohibition for members of the professions, and rules in relation to such persons), the references to 'a regulated activity' and 'regulated activities' do not include—

    (a) any activity of the kind specified by article 10(1) or (2), where—
        (i)   P is a member of the Society; and
        (ii)  by virtue of section 316 of the Act (application of the Act to Lloyd's underwriting), the general prohibition does not apply to the carrying on by P of that activity; or

    (b) any activity of the kind specified by article 10(2), where—
        (i)   P is a former underwriting member; and
        (ii)  the contract of insurance in question is one underwritten by P at Lloyd's.

(2)  In paragraph (1)—
'member of the Society' has the same meaning as in Lloyd's Act 1982 ; and
'former underwriting member' has the meaning given by section 324(1) of the Act.

## Chapter IV   Dealing in investments as principal

*The activity*

### 14   Dealing in investments as principal

(1)  Buying, selling, subscribing for or underwriting securities or contractually based investments (other than investments of the kind specified by article 87, or article 89 so far as relevant to that article) as principal is a specified kind of activity.

(2)  Paragraph (1) does not apply to the kind of activity to which article 25D applies.

*Exclusions*

### 15   Absence of holding out etc

(1)  Subject to paragraph (3), a person ('A') does not carry on an activity of the kind specified by article 14 by entering into a transaction which relates to a security or is the assignment (or, in Scotland, the assignation) of a qualifying contract of insurance (or an investment of the kind specified by article 89, so far as relevant to such a contract), unless—

    (a) A holds himself out as willing, as principal, to buy, sell or subscribe for investments of the kind to which the transaction relates at prices determined by him generally and continuously rather than in respect of each particular transaction;

    (b) A holds himself out as engaging in the business of buying investments of the kind to which the transaction relates, with a view to selling them;

    (c) A holds himself out as engaging in the business of underwriting investments of the kind to which the transaction relates; or

    (d) A regularly solicits members of the public with the purpose of inducing them, as principals or agents, to enter into transactions constituting activities of the kind specified by article 14, and the transaction is entered into as a result of his having solicited members of the public in that manner.

(2)  In paragraph (1)(d), 'members of the public' means any persons other than—

    (a) authorised persons or persons who are exempt persons in relation to activities of the kind specified by article 14;

    (b) members of the same group as A;

    (c) persons who are or who propose to become participators with A in a joint enterprise;

    (d) any person who is solicited by A with a view to the acquisition by A of 20 per cent or more of the voting shares in a body corporate;

    (e) if A (either alone or with members of the same group as himself) holds more than 20 per cent of the voting shares in a body corporate, any person who is solicited by A with a view to—
        (i)   the acquisition by A of further shares in the body corporate; or
        (ii)  the disposal by A of shares in the body corporate to the person solicited or to a member of the same group as the person solicited;

    (f) any person who—
        (i)   is solicited by A with a view to the disposal by A of shares in a body corporate to the person solicited or to a member of the same group as that person; and

        (ii)   either alone or with members of the same group holds 20 per cent or more of the voting shares in the body corporate;

    (g)  any person whose head office is outside the United Kingdom, who is solicited by an approach made or directed to him at a place outside the United Kingdom and whose ordinary business involves him in carrying on activities of the kind specified by any of articles 14, 21, 25, 37, 40, 45, 51, 52 and 53 or (so far as relevant to any of those articles) article 64, or would do so apart from any exclusion from any of those articles made by this Order.

(3)  This article does not apply where A enters into the transaction as bare trustee or, in Scotland, as nominee for another person and is acting on that other person's instructions (but the exclusion in article 66(1) applies if the conditions set out there are met).

(4)  This article is subject article 4(4).

## 16  Dealing in contractually based investments

(1)  A person who is not an authorised person does not carry on an activity of the kind specified by article 14 by entering into a transaction relating to a contractually based investment—

    (a)  with or through an authorised person, or an exempt person acting in the course of a business comprising a regulated activity in relation to which he is exempt; or

    (b)  through an office outside the United Kingdom maintained by a party to the transaction, and with or through a person whose head office is situated outside the United Kingdom and whose ordinary business involves him in carrying on activities of the kind specified by any of articles 14, 21, 25, 37, 40, 45, 51, 52 and 53 or, so far as relevant to any of those articles, article 64 (or would do so apart from any exclusion from any of those articles made by this Order).

(2)  This article is subject to article 4(4).

## 17  Acceptance of instruments creating or acknowledging indebtedness

(1)  A person does not carry on an activity of the kind specified by article 14 by accepting an instrument creating or acknowledging indebtedness in respect of any loan, credit, guarantee or other similar financial accommodation or assurance which he has made, granted or provided.

(2)  The reference in paragraph (1) to a person accepting an instrument includes a reference to a person becoming a party to an instrument otherwise than as a debtor or a surety.

## 18  Issue by a company of its own shares etc

(1)  There is excluded from article 14 the issue by a company of its own shares or share warrants, and the issue by any person of his own debentures or debenture warrants.

(2)  In this article—

    (a)  'company' means any body corporate other than an open-ended investment company;

    (b)  'shares' and 'debentures' include any investment of the kind specified by article 76 or 77;

    (c)  'share warrants' and 'debenture warrants' mean any investment of the kind specified by article 79 which relates to shares in the company concerned or, as the case may be, debentures issued by the person concerned.

## 18A  Dealing by a company in its own shares

(1)  A company does not carry on an activity of the kind specified by article 14 by purchasing its own shares where section 162A of the Companies Act 1985 (Treasury shares) applies to the shares purchased.

(2)  A company does not carry on an activity of the kind specified by article 14 by dealing in its own shares held as treasury shares, in accordance with section 162D of that Act (Treasury shares: disposal and cancellation).

(3)  In this article 'shares held as treasury shares' has the same meaning as in that Act.

## 19  Risk management

(1)  A person ('B') does not carry on an activity of the kind specified by article 14 by entering as principal into a transaction with another person ('C') if—

    (a)  the transaction relates to investments of the kind specified by any of articles 83 to 85 (or article 89 so far as relevant to any of those articles);

    (b)  neither B nor C is an individual;

    (c)  the sole or main purpose for which B enters into the transaction (either by itself or in combination with other such transactions) is that of limiting the extent to which a relevant business will be affected by any identifiable risk arising otherwise than as a result of the carrying on of a regulated activity; and

    (d)  the relevant business consists mainly of activities other than—

        (i)   regulated activities; or

        (ii)  activities which would be regulated activities but for any exclusion made by this Part.

(2)  In paragraph (1), 'relevant business' means a business carried on by—

    (a)  B;

    (b)  a member of the same group as B; or

(c) where B and another person are, or propose to become, participators in a joint enterprise, that other person.

(3) This article is subject to article 4(4).

## 20 Other exclusions

Article 14 is also subject to the exclusions in articles 66 (trustees etc.), 68 (sale of goods and supply of services), 69 (groups and joint enterprises), 70 (sale of body corporate), 71 (employee share schemes) and 72 (overseas persons) and 72A (information society services).

## Chapter V  Dealing in investments as agent

### *The activity*

### 21 Dealing in investments as agent

(1) Buying, selling, subscribing for or underwriting securities or contractually based investments (other than investments of the kind specified by article 87, or article 89 so far as relevant to that article) as agent is a specified kind of activity.

(2) Paragraph (1) does not apply to a kind of activity to which article 25D applies.

### *Exclusions*

### 22 Deals with or through authorised persons

(1) A person who is not an authorised person does not carry on an activity of the kind specified by article 21 by entering into a transaction as agent for another person ('the client') with or through an authorised person if—

(a) the transaction is entered into on advice given to the client by an authorised person; or

(b) it is clear, in all the circumstances, that the client, in his capacity as an investor, is not seeking and has not sought advice from the agent as to the merits of the client's entering into the transaction (or, if the client has sought such advice, the agent has declined to give it but has recommended that the client seek such advice from an authorised person).

(2) But the exclusion in paragraph (1) does not apply if—

(a) the transaction relates to a contract of insurance; or

(b) the agent receives from any person other than the client any pecuniary reward or other advantage, for which he does not account to the client, arising out of his entering into the transaction.

(3) This article is subject to article 4(4).

### 23 Risk management

(1) A person ('B') does not carry on an activity of the kind specified by article 21 by entering as agent for a relevant person into a transaction with another person ('C') if—

(a) the transaction relates to investments of the kind specified by any of articles 83 to 85 (or article 89 so far as relevant to any of those articles);

(b) neither B nor C is an individual;

(c) the sole or main purpose for which B enters into the transaction (either by itself or in combination with other such transactions) is that of limiting the extent to which a relevant business will be affected by any identifiable risk arising otherwise than as a result of the carrying on of a regulated activity; and

(d) the relevant business consists mainly of activities other than—

(i) regulated activities; or

(ii) activities which would be regulated activities but for any exclusion made by this Part.

(2) In paragraph (1), 'relevant person' means—

(a) a member of the same group as B; or

(b) where B and another person are, or propose to become, participators in a joint enterprise, that other person;

and 'relevant business' means a business carried on by a relevant person.

(3) This article is subject to article 4(4).

### 24 Other exclusions

Article 21 is also subject to the exclusions in articles 67 (profession or non-investment business), 68 (sale of goods and supply of services), 69 (groups and joint enterprises), 70 (sale of body corporate), 71 (employee share schemes) and 72 (overseas persons) 72A (information society services), 72B (activities carried on by a provider of relevant goods or services) and 72D (large risks contracts where risk is situated outside the EEA).

## Chapter VI  Arranging deals in investments
### *The activities*

**25  Arranging deals in investments**

(1)  Making arrangements for another person (whether as principal or agent) to buy, sell, subscribe for or underwrite a particular investment which is—

  (a)  a security,

  (b)  a relevant investment, or

  (c)  an investment of the kind specified by article 86, or article 89 so far as relevant to that article,

is a specified kind of activity.

(2)  Making arrangements with a view to a person who participates in the arrangements buying, selling, subscribing for or underwriting investments falling within paragraph (1)(a), (b) or (c) (whether as principal or agent) is also a specified kind of activity.

(3)  Paragraphs (1) and (2) do not apply to a kind of activity to which article 25D applies.

**25A  Arranging regulated mortgage contracts**

(1)  Making arrangements—

  (a)  for another person to enter into a regulated mortgage contract as borrower; or

  (b)  for another person to vary the terms of a regulated mortgage contract entered into by him as borrower after the coming into force of article 61, in such a way as to vary his obligations under that contract,

is a specified kind of activity.

(2)  Making arrangements with a view to a person who participates in the arrangements entering into a regulated mortgage contract as borrower is also a specified kind of activity.

(3)  In this article 'borrower' has the meaning given by article 61(3)(a)(i).

**25B  Arranging regulated home reversion plans**

(1)  Making arrangements—

  (a)  for another person to enter into a regulated home reversion plan as reversion seller or as plan provider; or

  (b)  for another person to vary the terms of a regulated home reversion plan, entered into on or after 6th April 2007 by him as reversion seller or as plan provider, in such a way as to vary his obligations under that plan,

is a specified kind of activity.

(2)  Making arrangements with a view to a person who participates in the arrangements entering into a regulated home reversion plan as reversion seller or as plan provider is also a specified kind of activity.

**25C  Arranging regulated home purchase plans**

(1)  Making arrangements—

  (a)  for another person to enter into a regulated home purchase plan as home purchaser; or

  (b)  for another person to vary the terms of a regulated home purchase plan, entered into on or after 6th April 2007 by him as home purchaser, in such a way as to vary his obligations under that plan,

is a specified kind of activity.

(2)  Making arrangements with a view to a person who participates in the arrangements entering into a regulated home purchase plan as home purchaser is also a specified kind of activity.

**25D  Operating a multilateral trading facility**

(1)  The operation of a multilateral trading facility on which MiFID instruments are traded is a specified kind of activity.

(2)  In paragraph (1), 'MiFID instrument' means any investment—

  (a)  of the kind specified by article 76, 77, 78, 79, 80, 81, 83, 84 or 85; or

  (b)  of the kind specified by article 89 so far as relevant to an investment falling within sub-paragraph (a),

that is a financial instrument.

### *Exclusions*

**26  Arrangements not causing a deal**

There are excluded from articles 25(1), 25A(1), 25B(1) and 25(C)1 arrangements which do not or would not bring about the transaction to which the arrangements relate.

**27  Enabling parties to communicate**

A person does not carry on an activity of the kind specified by article 25(2) 25A(2), 25B(2) or 25C(2) merely by providing means by which one party to a transaction (or potential transaction) is able to communicate with other such parties.

### 28 Arranging transactions to which the arranger is a party

(1) There are excluded from article 25(1) any arrangements for a transaction into which the person making the arrangements enters or is to enter as principal or as agent for some other person.

(2) There are excluded from article 25(2) any arrangements which a person makes with a view to transactions into which he enters or is to enter as principal or as agent for some other person.

(3) But the exclusions in paragraphs (1) and (2) do not apply to arrangements made for or with a view to a transaction which relates to a contract of insurance, unless the person making the arrangements either—

    (a) is the only policyholder; or

    (b) as a result of the transaction, would become the only policyholder.

### 28A Arranging contracts or plans to which the arranger is a party

(1) There are excluded from articles 25A(1), 25B(1) and 25C(1) any arrangements—

    (a) for a contract or plan into which the person making the arrangements enters or is to enter; or

    (b) for a variation of a contract or plan to which that person is (or is to become) a party.

(2) There are excluded from articles 25A(2), 25B(2) and 25C(2) any arrangements which a person makes with a view to contracts or plans into which he enters or is to enter.

### 29 Arranging deals with or through authorised persons

(1) There are excluded from article 25(1) and (2), 25A(1) and (2), 25B(1) and (2) and 25C(1) and (2) arrangements made by a person ('A') who is not an authorised person for or with a view to a transaction which is or is to be entered into by a person ('the client') with or though an authorised person if—

    (a) the transaction is or is to be entered into on advice to the client by an authorised person; or

    (b) it is clear, in all the circumstances, that the client, in his capacity as an investor, borrower, reversion seller, plan provider or (as the case may be) home purchaser is not seeking and has not sought advice from A as to the merits of the client's entering into the transaction (or, if the client has sought such advice, A has declined to give it but has recommended that the client seek such advice from an authorised person).

(2) But the exclusion in paragraph (1) does not apply if—

    (a) the transaction relates, or would relate, to a contract of insurance; or

    (b) A receives from any person other than the client any pecuniary reward or other advantage, for which he does not account to the client, arising out of his making the arrangements.

(3) This article is subject to article 4(4).

### 29A Arrangements made in the course of administration by authorised person

(1) A person who is not an authorised person ('A') does not carry on an activity of the kind specified by article 25A(1)(b) as a result of—

    (a) anything done by an authorised person ('B') in relation to a regulated mortgage contract which B is administering pursuant to an arrangement of the kind mentioned in article 62(a); or

    (b) anything A does in connection with the administration of a regulated mortgage contract in circumstances falling within article 62(b).

(2) A person who is not an authorised person ('A') does not carry on an activity of the kind specified by article 25B(1)(b) as a result of—

    (a) anything done by an authorised person ('B') in relation to a regulated home reversion plan which B is administering pursuant to an arrangement of the kind mentioned in article 63C(a); or

    (b) anything A does in connection with the administration of a regulated home reversion plan in circumstances falling within article 63C(b).

(3) A person who is not an authorised person ('A') does not carry on an activity of the kind specified by article 25C(1)(b) as a result of—

    (a) anything done by an authorised person ('B') in relation to a regulated home purchase plan which B is administering pursuant to an arrangement of the kind mentioned in article 63G(a); or

    (b) anything A does in connection with the administration of a regulated home purchase plan in circumstances falling within article 63G(b).

### 30 Arranging transactions in connection with lending on the security of insurance policies

(1) There are excluded from article 25(1) and (2) arrangements made by a money-lender under which either—

    (a) a relevant authorised person or a person acting on his behalf will introduce to the money-lender persons with whom the relevant authorised person has entered, or proposes to enter, into a relevant transaction, or will advise such persons to approach the money-lender, with a view to the money-lender lending money on the security of any contract effected pursuant to a relevant transaction; or

    (b)  a relevant authorised person gives an assurance to the money-lender as to the amount which, on the security of any contract effected pursuant to a relevant transaction, will or may be received by the money-lender should the money-lender lend money to a person introduced to him pursuant to the arrangements.

(2)  In paragraph (1)—

'money-lender' means a person who is—

    (a)  a money-lending company within the meaning of section 338 of the Companies Act 1985;

    (b)  a body corporate incorporated under the law of, or of any part of, the United Kingdom relating to building societies; or

    (c)  a person whose ordinary business includes the making of loans or the giving of guarantees in connection with loans;

'relevant authorised person' means an authorised person who has permission to effect contracts of insurance or to sell investments of the kind specified by article 89, so far as relevant to such contracts;

'relevant transaction' means the effecting of a contract of insurance or the sale of an investment of the kind specified by article 89, so far as relevant to such contracts.

(3)  This article is subject to article 4(4A)

## 31  Arranging the acceptance of debentures in connection with loans

(1)  There are excluded from article 25(1) and (2) arrangements under which a person accepts or is to accept, whether as principal or agent, an instrument creating or acknowledging indebtedness in respect of any loan, credit, guarantee or other similar financial accommodation or assurance which is, or is to be, made, granted or provided by that person or his principal.

(2)  The reference in paragraph (1) to a person accepting an instrument includes a reference to a person becoming a party to an instrument otherwise than as a debtor or a surety.

## 32  Provision of finance

There are excluded from article 25(2) arrangements having as their sole purpose the provision of finance to enable a person to buy, sell, subscribe for or underwrite investments.

## 33  Introducing

There are excluded from article 25(2), 25A(2), 25B(2) and 25C(2) arrangements where—

    (a)  they are arrangements under which persons ('clients') will be introduced to another person;

    (b)  the person to whom introductions are to be made is—

        (i)  an authorised person;

        (ii)  an exempt person acting in the course of a business comprising a regulated activity in relation to which he is exempt; or

        (iii)  a person who is not unlawfully carrying on regulated activities in the United Kingdom and whose ordinary business involves him in engaging in an activity of the kind specified by any of articles 14, 21, 25, 25A, 25B, 25C 37, 39A, 40, 45, 51, 52, 53, 53A, 53B and 53C (or, so far as relevant to any of those articles, article 64), or would do so apart from any exclusion from any of those articles made by this Order[...]

    (c)  the introduction is made with a view to the provision of independent advice or the independent exercise of discretion in relation to investments generally or in relation to any class of investments to which the arrangements relate; and

    (d)  the arrangements are made with a view to a person entering into a transaction which does not relate to a contract of insurance.

## 33A  Introducing to authorised persons etc

(1)  There are excluded from article 25A(2) arrangements where—

    (a)  they are arrangements under which a client is introduced to a person ('N') who is—

        (i)  an authorised person who has permission to carry on a regulated activity of the kind specified by any of articles 25A, 53A, and 61(1),

        (ii)  an appointed representative who may carry on a regulated activity of the kind specified by either of articles 25A and 53A without contravening the general prohibition, or

        (iii)  an overseas person who carries on activities specified by any of articles 25A, 53A and 61(1); and

    (b)  the conditions mentioned in paragraph (2) are satisfied.

(1A) There are excluded from article 25B(2) arrangements where—

    (a)  they are arrangements under which a client is introduced to a person ('N') who is—

        (i)  an authorised person who has permission to carry on a regulated activity of the kind specified by any of articles 25B, 53B and 63B(1),

        (ii)  an appointed representative who may carry on a regulated activity of the kind specified by either of articles 25B and 53B without contravening the general prohibition, or

        (iii)  an overseas person who carries on activities specified by any of articles 25B, 53B and 63B(1); and

(b) the conditions mentioned in paragraph (2) are satisfied.

(1B) There are excluded from article 25C(2) arrangements where—

(a) they are arrangements under which a client is introduced to a person ('N') who is—

(i) an authorised person who has permission to carry on a regulated activity of the kind specified by any of articles 25C, 53C and 63F(1),

(ii) an appointed representative who may carry on a regulated activity of the kind specified by either of articles 25C and 53C without contravening the general prohibition, or

(iii) an overseas person who carries on activities specified by any of articles 25C, 53C and 63F(1); and

(b) the conditions mentioned in paragraph (2) are satisfied.

(2) Those conditions are—

(a) that the person making the introduction ('P') does not receive any money, other than money payable to P on his own account, paid by the client for or in connection with any transaction which the client enters into with or through N as a result of the introduction; and

(b) that before making the introduction P discloses to the client such of the information mentioned in paragraph (3) as applies to P.

(3) That information is—

(a) that P is a member of the same group as N;

(b) details of any payment which P will receive from N, by way of fee or commission, for introducing the client to N;

(c) an indication of any other reward or advantage received or to be received by P that arises out of his introducing clients to N.

(4) In this article, 'client' means—

(a) for the purposes of paragraph (1), a borrower within the meaning given by article 61(3)(a)(i), or a person who is or may be contemplating entering into a regulated mortgage contract as such a borrower;

(b) for the purposes of paragraph (1A), a reversion seller, a plan provider or a person who is or may be contemplating entering into a regulated home reversion plan as a reversion seller or as a plan provider;

(c) for the purposes of paragraph (1B), a home purchaser or a person who is or may be contemplating entering into a regulated home purchase plan as a home purchaser.

## 34 Arrangements for the issue of shares etc

(1) There are excluded from article 25(1) and (2)—

(a) arrangements made by a company for the purposes of issuing its own shares or share warrants; and

(b) arrangements made by any person for the purposes of issuing his own debentures or debenture warrants;

and for the purposes of article 25(1) and (2), a company is not, by reason of issuing its own shares or share warrants, and a person is not, by reason of issuing his own debentures or debenture warrants, to be treated as selling them.

(2) In paragraph (1), 'company', 'shares', 'debentures', 'share warrants' and 'debenture warrants' have the meanings given by article 18(2).

## 35 International securities self-regulating organisations

(1) There are excluded from article 25(1) and (2) any arrangements made for the purposes of carrying out the functions of a body or association which is approved under this article as an international securities self-regulating organisation, whether the arrangements are made by the organisation itself or by a person acting on its behalf.

(2) The Treasury may approve as an international securities self-regulating organisation any body corporate or unincorporated association with respect to which the conditions mentioned in paragraph (3) appear to them to be met if, having regard to such matters affecting international trade, overseas earnings and the balance of payments or otherwise as they consider relevant, it appears to them that to do so would be desirable and not result in any undue risk to investors.

(3) The conditions are that—

(a) the body or association does not have its head office in the United Kingdom;

(b) the body or association is not eligible for recognition under section 287 or 288 of the Act (applications by investment exchanges and clearing houses) on the ground that (whether or not it has applied, and whether or not it would be eligible on other grounds) it is unable to satisfy the requirements of one or both of paragraphs (a) and (b) of section 292(3) of the Act (requirements for overseas investment exchanges and overseas clearing houses);

(c) the body or association is able and willing to co-operate with the Authority by the sharing of information and in other ways;

(d) adequate arrangements exist for co-operation between the Authority and those responsible for the supervision of the body or association in the country or territory in which its head office is situated;

(e) the body or association has a membership composed of persons falling within any of the following categories, that is to say, authorised persons, exempt persons, and persons whose head offices are outside the United Kingdom and whose ordinary business involves them in engaging in activities which are activities of a kind specified by this Order (or would be apart from any exclusion made by this Part); and

(f) the body or association facilitates and regulates the activity of its members in the conduct of international securities business.

(4) In paragraph (3)(f), 'international securities business' means the business of buying, selling, subscribing for or underwriting investments (or agreeing to do so), either as principal or agent, where—

(a) the investments are securities or relevant investments and are of a kind which, by their nature, and the manner in which the business is conducted, may be expected normally to be bought or dealt in by persons sufficiently expert to understand the risks involved; and

(b) either the transaction is international or each of the parties may be expected to be indifferent to the location of the other;

and, for the purposes of this definition, it is irrelevant that the investments may ultimately be bought otherwise than in the course of such business by persons not so expert.

(5) Any approval under this article is to be given by notice in writing; and the Treasury may by a further notice in writing withdraw any such approval if for any reason it appears to them that it is not appropriate to it to continue in force.

## 36 Other exclusions

(1) Article 25 is also subject to the exclusions in articles 66 (trustees etc.), 67 (profession or non-investment business), 68 (sale of goods and supply of services), 69 (groups and joint enterprises), 70 (sale of body corporate), 71 (employee share schemes) and 72 (overseas persons), 72A (information society services), 72B (activities carried on by a provider of relevant goods or services), 72C (provision of information about contracts of insurance on an incidental basis) and 72D (large risks contracts where risk situated outside the EEA) .

(2) Articles 25A, 25B and 25C is also subject to the exclusions in articles 66 (trustees etc.), 67 (profession or non-investment business), 72 (overseas persons) and 72A (information society services).

(3) Article 25D is also subject to the exclusion in article 72 (overseas persons).

## Chapter VII  Managing investments

### *The activity*

## 37 Managing investments

Managing assets belonging to another person, in circumstances involving the exercise of discretion, is a specified kind of activity if—

(a) the assets consist of or include any investment which is a security or a contractually based investment; or

(b) the arrangements for their management are such that the assets may consist of or include such investments, and either the assets have at any time since 29th April 1988 done so, or the arrangements have at any time (whether before or after that date) been held out as arrangements under which the assets would do so.

### *Exclusions*

## 38 Attorneys

(1) A person does not carry on an activity of the kind specified by article 37 if—

(a) he is a person appointed to manage the assets in question under a power of attorney; and

(b) all routine or day-to-day decisions, so far as relating to investments of a kind mentioned in article 37(a), are taken on behalf of that person by—

(i) an authorised person with permission to carry on activities of the kind specified by article 37; or

(ii) a person who is an exempt person in relation to activities of that kind.

(2) This article is subject to article 4(4)

## 39 Other exclusions

Article 37 is also subject to the exclusions in articles 66 (trustees etc.), 68 (sale of goods and supply of services) and 69 (groups and joint enterprises), 72A (information society services) and 72C (provision of information about contracts of insurance on an incidental basis).

## Chapter VIIA  Assisting in the administration and performance of a contract of insurance

### *The activity*

**39A  Assisting in the administration and performance of a contract of insurance**
Assisting in the administration and performance of a contract of insurance is a specified kind of activity.

### *Exclusions*

**39B  Claims management on behalf of an insurer etc**
 (1)  A person does not carry on an activity of the kind specified by article 39A if he acts in the course of carrying on the activity of—
  (a)  expert appraisal;
  (b)  loss adjusting on behalf of a relevant insurer; or
  (c)  managing claims on behalf of a relevant insurer,
and that activity is carried on in the course of carrying on any profession or business.
 (2)  In this article—
  (a)  'relevant insurer' means—
   (i)  a person who has Part IV permission to carry on an activity of the kind specified by article 10;
   (ii)  a person to whom the general prohibition does not apply by virtue of section 316(1)(a) of the Act (members of the Society of Lloyd's);
   (iii)  an EEA firm falling within paragraph 5(d) of Schedule 3 to the Act (insurance under-taking); or
   (iv)  a relevant reinsurer;
  (b)  'relevant reinsurer' means a person whose main business consists of accepting risks ceded by—
   (i)  a person falling within sub-paragraph (i), (ii) or (iii) of the definition of 'relevant insurer'; [...]
   (ii)  an EEA firm falling within paragraph 5(da) of Schedule 3 to the Act (reinsurance under-taking); or
   (iii)  a person established outside the United Kingdom and not falling within paragraph (ii) who carries on an activity of the kind specified by article 10 by way of business.

**39C  Other exclusions**
Article 39A is also subject to the exclusions in articles 66 (trustees etc.), 67 (profession or non-invest-ment business), 72A (information society services), 72B (activities carried on by a provider of relevant goods or services), 72C (provision of information about contracts of insurance on an incidental basis) and 72D (large risks contracts where risk situated outside the EEA).

## Chapter VIII  Safeguarding and administering investments

### *The activity*

**40  Safeguarding and administering investments**
 (1)  The activity consisting of both—
  (a)  the safeguarding of assets belonging to another, and
  (b)  the administration of those assets,
or arranging for one or more other persons to carry on that activity, is a specified kind of activity if the condition in sub-paragraph (a) or (b) of paragraph (2) is met.
 (2)  The condition is that—
  (a)  the assets consist of or include any investment which is a security or a contractually based investment; or
  (b)  the arrangements for their safeguarding and administration are such that the assets may consist of or include such investments, and either the assets have at any time since 1st June 1997 done so, or the arrangements have at any time (whether before or after that date) been held out as ones under which such investments would be safeguarded and administered.
 (3)  For the purposes of this article—
  (a)  it is immaterial that title to the assets safeguarded and administered is held in uncertificated form;
  (b)  it is immaterial that the assets safeguarded and administered may be transferred to another person, subject to a commitment by the person safeguarding and administering them, or arranging for their safeguarding and administration, that they will be replaced by equiva-lent assets at some future date or when so requested by the person to whom they belong.

*Exclusions*

## 41   Acceptance of responsibility by third party

(1)   There are excluded from article 40 any activities which a person carries on pursuant to arrangements which—

    (a)   are ones under which a qualifying custodian undertakes to the person to whom the assets belong a responsibility in respect of the assets which is no less onerous than the qualifying custodian would have if the qualifying custodian were safeguarding and administering the assets; and

    (b)   are operated by the qualifying custodian in the course of carrying on in the United Kingdom an activity of the kind specified by article 40.

(2)   In paragraph (1), 'qualifying custodian' means a person who is—

    (a)   an authorised person who has permission to carry on an activity of the kind specified by article 40, or

    (b)   an exempt person acting in the course of a business comprising a regulated activity in relation to which he is exempt.

## 42   Introduction to qualifying custodians

(1)   There are excluded from article 40 any arrangements pursuant to which introductions are made by a person ('P') to a qualifying custodian with a view to the qualifying custodian providing in the United Kingdom a service comprising an activity of the kind specified by article 40, where the qualifying person (or other person who is to safeguard and administer the assets in question) is not connected with P.

(2)   For the purposes of paragraph (1)—

    (a)   'qualifying custodian' has the meaning given by article 41(2); and

    (b)   a person is connected with P if either he is a member of the same group as P, or P is remunerated by him.

## 43   Activities not constituting administration

The following activities do not constitute the administration of assets for the purposes of article 40—

    (a)   providing information as to the number of units or the value of any assets safeguarded;

    (b)   converting currency;

    (c)   receiving documents relating to an investment solely for the purpose of onward transmission to, from or at the direction of the person to whom the investment belongs.

## 44   Other exclusions

Article 40 is also subject to the exclusions in articles 66 (trustees etc.), 67 (profession or non-investment business), 68 (sale of goods and supply of services), 69 (groups and joint enterprises) and 71 (employee share schemes), 72A (information society service) and 72C (provision of information about contracts of insurance on an incidental basis).

# Chapter IX   Sending dematerialised instructions

*The activities*

## 45   Sending dematerialised instructions

(1)   Sending, on behalf of another person, dematerialised instructions relating to a security or a contractually based investment is a specified kind of activity, where those instructions are sent by means of a relevant system in respect of which an Operator is approved under the 2001 Regulations.

(2)   Causing dematerialised instructions relating to a security or a contractually based investment to be sent on behalf of another person by means of such a system is also a specified kind of activity where the person causing them to be sent is a system-participant.

(3)   In this Chapter—

    (a)   'the 2001 Regulations' means the Uncertified Securities Regulations 2001; and

    (b)   'dematerialised instruction', 'Operator', 'settlement bank' and 'system-participant' have the meaning given by regulation 3 of the 2001 Regulations.

*Exclusions*

## 46   Instructions on behalf of participating issuers

There is excluded from article 45 the act of sending, or causing to be sent, a dematerialised instruction where the person on whose behalf the instruction is sent or caused to be sent is a participating issuer within the meaning of the 2001 Regulations.

## 47   Instructions on behalf of settlement banks

There is excluded from article 45 the act of sending, or causing to be sent, a dematerialised instruction where the person on whose behalf the instruction is sent or caused to be sent is a settlement bank in its capacity as such.

### 48   Instructions in connection with takeover offers

(1)  There is excluded from article 45 of the act of sending, or causing to be sent, a dematerialised instruction where the person on whose behalf the instruction is sent or caused to be sent is an offeror making a takeover offer.

(2)  In this article—

(a)  'offeror' means, in the case of a takeover offer made by two or more persons jointly, the joint offers or any of them;

(b)  'takeover offer' means—

(i)  an offer to acquire shares (which in this sub-paragraph has the same meaning as in section 974 of the Companies Act 2006) in a body corporate incorporated in the United Kingdom which is a takeover offer within the meaning of Chapter 3 Part 28 of that Act [...] (or would be such an offer if that Part of that Act applied in relation to any body corporate);

(ii)  an offer to acquire all or substantially all the shares, or all the shares of a particular class, in a body corporate incorporated outside the United Kingdom; or

(iii)  an offer made to all the holders of shares, or shares of a particular class, in a body corporate to acquire a specified proportion of those shares;

but in determining whether an offer falls within paragraph (ii) there are to be disregarded any shares which the offeror or any associate of his (within the meaning of section 988 of the Companies Act 2006) holds or has contracted to acquire; and in determining whether an offer falls within paragraph (iii) the offeror, any such associate and any person whose shares the offeror or any such associate has contracted to acquire is not to be regarded as a holder of shares.

### 49   Instructions in the course of providing a network

There is excluded from article 45 the act of sending, or causing to be sent, a dematerialised instruction as a necessary part of providing a network, the purpose of which is to carry dematerialised instructions which are at all time properly authenticated (within the meaning of the 2001 Regulations).

### 50   Other exclusions

Article 45 is also subject to the exclusions in articles 66 (trustees etc.) and 69 (groups and joint enterprises) and 72A (information society services).

## Chapter X   Collective investment schemes

### *The activities*

### 51   Establishing etc. a collective investment scheme

(1)  The following are specified kinds of activity—

(a)  establishing, operating or winding up a collective investment scheme;

(b)  acting as trustee of an authorised unit trust scheme;

(c)  acting as the depositary or sole director of an open-ended investment company.

(2)  In this article, 'trustee', 'authorised unit trust scheme' and 'depositary' have the meaning given by section 237 of the Act.

### *Exclusion*

### 51A   Information society services

Article 51 is subject to the exclusion in article 72A (information society services).

## Chapter XI   [...] Pension schemes

### *The activities*

### 52   Establishing etc a pension scheme

The following are specified kinds of activity—

(a)  establishing, operating or winding up a stakeholder pension scheme;

(b)  establishing, operating or winding up a personal pension scheme.

## Chapter XIa   Promoting basic advice on stakeholder products

### *The activity*

### 52A   Information society services

Article 52 is subject to the exclusion in article 72A (information society services).

### 52B   Providing basic advice on stakeholder products

(1)  Providing basic advice to a retail consumer on a stakeholder product is a specified kind of activity.

(2)  For the purposes of paragraph (1), a person ('P') provides basic advice when—

    (a) he asks a retail consumer questions to enable him to assess whether a stakeholder product is appropriate for that consumer; and

    (b) relying on the information provided by the retail consumer P assesses that a stakeholder product is appropriate for the retail consumer and—

        (i) describes that product to that consumer;

        (ii) gives a recommendation of that product to that consumer; and

    (c) the retail consumer has indicated to P that he has understood the description and the recommendation in sub-paragraph (b).

  (3) In this article—

'retail consumer' means any person who is advised by P on the merits of opening or buying a stakeholder product in the course of a business carried on by P and who does not receive the advice in the course of a business carried on by him;

'stakeholder product' means—

    (a) an account which qualifies as a stakeholder child trust fund within the meaning given by the Child Trust Funds Regulations 2004;

    (b) rights under a stakeholder pension scheme;

    (c) an investment of a kind specified in regulations made by the Treasury.

## Chapter XII    Advising on investments

### *The activity*

### 53    Advising on investments

Advising a person is a specified kind of activity if the advice is—

    (a) given to the person in his capacity as an investor or potential investor, or in his capacity as agent for an investor or a potential investor; and

    (b) advice on the merits of his doing any of the following (whether as principal or agent)—

        (i) buying, selling, subscribing for or underwriting a particular investment which is a security or a relevant investment, or

        (ii) exercising any right conferred by such an investment to buy, sell, subscribe for or underwrite such an investment.

### 53A    Advising on regulated mortgage contracts

  (1) Advising a person is a specified kind of activity if the advice—

    (a) is given to the person in his capacity as a borrower or potential borrower; and

    (b) is advice on the merits of his doing any of the following—

        (i) entering into a particular regulated mortgage contract, or

        (ii) varying the terms of a regulated mortgage contract entered into by him after the coming into force of article 61 in such a way as to vary his obligations under that contract.

  (2) In this article, 'borrower' has the meaning given by article 61(3)(a)(i).

### 53B    Advising on regulated home reversion plans

Advising a person is a specified kind of activity if the advice—

    (a) is given to the person in his capacity as—

        (i) a reversion seller or potential reversion seller, or

        (ii) a plan provider or potential plan provider; and

    (b) is advice on the merits of his doing either of the following—

        (i) entering into a particular regulated home reversion plan, or

        (ii) varying the terms of a regulated home reversion plan, entered into on or after 6th April 2007 by him, in such a way as to vary his obligations under that plan.

### 53C    Advising on regulated home purchase plans

Advising a person is a specified kind of activity if the advice—

    (a) is given to the person in his capacity as a home purchaser or potential home purchaser; and

    (b) is advice on the merits of his doing either of the following—

        (i) entering into a particular regulated home purchase plan, or

        (ii) varying the terms of a regulated home purchase plan, entered into on or after 6th April 2007 by him, in such a way as to vary his obligations under that plan.

### *Exclusions*

### 54    Advice given in newspapers etc

  (1) There is excluded from articles 53, 53A, 53B and 53C the giving of advice in writing or other legible form if the advice is contained in a newspaper, journal, magazine, or other periodical publication, or is given by way of a service comprising regularly updated news or information, if the principal purpose of the publication or service, taken as a whole and including any advertisements or other promotional material contained in it, is neither—

 (a) that of giving advice of a kind mentioned in article 53, 53A, 53B or 53C (as the case may be; nor

 (b) that of leading or enabling persons

  (i) to buy, sell, subscribe for or underwrite securities or relevant investments, or (as the case may be),

  (ii) to enter as borrower into regulated mortgage contracts, or vary the terms of regulated mortgage contracts entered into by them as borrower;

  (iii) to enter as reversion seller or plan provider into regulated home reversion plans, or vary the terms of regulated home reversion plans entered into by them as reversion seller or plan provider,

  (iv) to enter as home purchaser into regulated home purchase plans, or vary the terms of regulated home purchase plans entered into by them as home purchaser;

(2) There is also excluded from articles 53, 53A, 53B and 53C the giving of advice in any service consisting of the broadcast or transmission of television or radio programmes, if the principal purpose of the service, taken as a whole and including any advertisements or other promotional material contained in it, is neither of those mentioned in paragraph (1)(a) and (b).

(3) The Authority may, on the application of the proprietor of any such publication or service as is mentioned in paragraph (1) or (2), certify that it is of the nature described in that paragraph, and may revoke any such certificate if it considers that it is no longer justified.

(4) A certificate given under paragraph (3) and not revoked is conclusive evidence of the matters certified.

### 54A Advice given in the course of administration by authorised person

(1) A person who is not an authorised person ('A') does not carry on an activity of the kind specified by article 53A by reason of—

 (a) anything done by an authorised person ('B') in relation to a regulated mortgage contract which B is administering pursuant to arrangements of the kind mentioned in article 62(a); or

 (b) anything A does in connection with the administration of a regulated mortgage contract in circumstances falling within article 62(b).

(2) A person who is not an authorised person ('A') does not carry on an activity of the kind specified by article 53B by reason of—

 (a) anything done by an authorised person ('B') in relation to a regulated home reversion plan which B is administering pursuant to arrangements of the kind mentioned in article 63C(a); or

 (b) anything A does in connection with the administration of a regulated home reversion plan in circumstances falling within article 63C(b).

(3) A person who is not an authorised person ('A') does not carry on an activity of the kind specified by article 53C by reason of—

 (a) anything done by an authorised person ('B') in relation to a regulated home purchase plan which B is administering pursuant to arrangements of the kind mentioned in article 63G(a); or

 (b) anything A does in connection with the administration of a regulated home purchase plan in circumstances falling within article 63G(b).

### 55 Other exclusions

(1) Article 53 is also subject to the exclusions in articles 66 (trustees etc.), 67, (profession or non-investment business), 68 (sale of goods and supply of services), 69 (groups and joint enterprises), 70 (sale of body corporate) and 72 (overseas persons), 72A (information society services), 72B (activities carried on by a provider of relevant goods or services) and 72D (large risk contracts where risk is situated outside the EEA).

(2) Articles 53A, 53B and 53C are also subject to the exclusions in articles 66 (trustees etc.), 67 (profession or non-investment business) and 72A (information society services).

## Chapter XIII Lloyd's

*The activities*

### 56 Advice on syndicate participation at Lloyd's

Advising a person to become, or continue or cease to be, a member of a particular Lloyd's syndicate is a specified kind of activity.

### 57 Managing the underwriting capacity of a Lloyd's syndicate

Managing the underwriting capacity of a Lloyd's syndicate as a managing agent at Lloyd's is a specified kind of activity.

**58   Arranging deals in contracts of insurance written at Lloyd's**

The arranging, by the society incorporated by Lloyd's Act 1871 by the name of Lloyd's, of deals in contracts of insurance written at Lloyd's, is a specified kind of activity.

*Exclusion*

**58A   Information society services**

Articles 56 to 58 are subject to the exclusion in article 72A (information society services).

## Chapter XIV   Funeral plan contracts

### *The activity*

**59   Funeral plan contracts**

(1)  Entering as provider into a funeral plan contract is a specified kind of activity.

(2)  A 'funeral plan contract' is a contract (other than one excluded by article 60) under which—

(a)  a person ('the customer') makes one or more payments to another person ('the provider'); and

(b)  the provider undertakes to provide, or secure that another person provides, a funeral in the United Kingdom for the customer (or some other person who is living at the date when the contract is entered into) on his death;

unless, at the time of entering into the contract, the customer and the provider intend or expect the funeral to occur within one month.

### *Exclusions*

**60   Plans covered by insurance or trust arrangements**

(1)  There is excluded from article 59 any contract under which—

(a)  the provider undertakes to secure that sums paid by the customer under the contract will be applied towards a contract of whole life insurance on the life of the customer (or other person for whom the funeral is to be provided), effected and carried out by an authorised person who has permission to effect and carry out such contracts of insurance, for the purpose of providing the funeral; or

(b)  the provider undertakes to secure that sums paid by the customer under the contract will be held on trust for the purpose of providing the funeral, and that the following requirements are or will be met with respect to the trust—

(i)   the trust must be established by a written instrument;

(ii)  more than half of the trustees must be unconnected with the provider;

(iii) the trustees must appoint, or have appointed, an independent fund manager who is an authorised person who has permission to carry on an activity of the kind specified by article 37, and who is a person who is unconnected with the provider, to manage the assets of the trust;

(iv)  annual accounts must be prepared, and audited by a person who is eligible for appointment as a statutory auditor under Part 42 of the Companies Act 2006, with respect to the assets and liabilities of the trust; and

(v)   the assets and liabilities of the trust must, at least once every three years, be determined, calculated and verified by an actuary who is a Fellow of the Institute of Actuaries or of the Faculty of Actuaries.

(2)  For the purposes of paragraph (1)(b)(ii) and (iii), a person is unconnected with the provider if he is a person other than—

(a)  the provider;

(b)  a member of the same group as the provider;

(c)  a director, other officer or employee of the provider, or of any member of the same group as the provider;

(d)  a partner of the provider;

(e)  a close relative of a person falling within sub-paragraph (a), (c) or (d); or

(f)  an agent of any person falling within sub-paragraphs (a) to (e).

**60A   Information society services**

Article 59 is subject to the exclusion in article 72A (information society services).

## Chapter XV   Regulated mortgage contracts

### *The activities*

**61   Regulated mortgage contracts**

(1)  Entering into a regulated mortgage contract as lender is a specified kind of activity.

(2)  Administering a regulated mortgage contract is also a specified kind of activity, where the contract was entered into by way of business after the coming into force of this article.

(3)  In this Chapter—

(a) a contract is a 'regulated mortgage contract' if, at the time it is entered into, the following conditions are met—

    (i) the contract is one under which a person ('the lender') provides credit to an individual or to trustees ('the borrower');

    (ii) the contract provides for the obligation of the borrower to repay to be secured by a first legal mortgage on land (other than timeshare accommodation) in the United Kingdom;

    (iii) at least 40% of that land is used, or is intended to be used, as or in connection with a dwelling by the borrower or (in the case of credit provided to trustees) by an individual who is a beneficiary of the trust, or by a related person;

but such a contract is not a regulated mortgage contract if it is a regulated home purchase plan;

(b) 'administering' a regulated mortgage contract means either or both of—

    (i) notifying the borrower of changes in interest rates or payments due under the contract, or of other matters of which the contract requires him to be notified; and

    (ii) taking any necessary steps for the purposes of collecting or recovering payments due under the contract from the borrower;

but a person is not to be treated as administering a regulated mortgage contract merely because he has, or exercises, a right to take action for the purposes of enforcing the contract (or to require that such action is or is not taken);

(c) 'credit' includes a cash loan, and any other form of financial accommodation.

(4) For the purposes of paragraph 3(a) —

(a) a 'first legal mortgage' means a legal mortgage ranking in priority ahead of all other mortgages (if any) affecting the land in question, where 'mortgage' includes charge and (in Scotland) a heritable security;

(b) the area of any land which comprises a building or other structure containing two or more storeys is to be taken to be the aggregate of the floor areas of each of those storeys;

(c) 'related person', in relation to the borrower or (in the case of credit provided to trustees) a beneficiary of the trust, means—

    (i) that person's spouse or civil partner;

    (ii) a person (whether or not of the opposite sex) whose relationship with that person has the characteristics of the relationship between husband and wife; or

    (iii) that person's parent, brother, sister, child, grandparent or grandchild; and

(d) 'timeshare accommodation' has the meaning given by section 1 of the Timeshare Act 1992.

## *Exclusions*

### 62 Arranging administration by authorised person

A person who is not an authorised person does not carry on an activity of the kind specified by article 61(2) in relation to a regulated mortgage contract where he—

(a) arranges for another person, being an authorised person with permission to carry on an activity of that kind, to administer the contract; or

(b) administers the contract himself during a period of not more than one month beginning with the day on which any such arrangement comes to an end.

### 63 Administration pursuant to agreement with authorised person

A person who is not an authorised person does not carry on an activity of the kind specified by article 61(2) in relation to a regulated mortgage contract where he administers the contract pursuant to an agreement with an authorised person who has permission to carry on an activity of that kind.

### 63A Other exclusions

Article 61 is also subject to the exclusions in articles 66 (trustees etc.), 72 (overseas persons) and 72A (information society services).

## Chapter XVa    Regulated home reversion plans

### *The activities*

### 63B Entering into and administering regulated home reversion plans

(1) Entering into a regulated home reversion plan as plan provider is a specified kind of activity.

(2) Administering a regulated home reversion plan is also a specified kind of activity where the plan was entered into on or after 6th April 2007.

(3) In this Chapter—

(a) a 'regulated home reversion plan' is an arrangement comprised in one or more instruments or agreements, in relation to which the following conditions are met at the time it is entered into—

   (i) the arrangement is one under which a person (the 'plan provider') buys all or part of a qualifying interest in land (other than timeshare accommodation) in the United Kingdom from an individual or trustees (the 'reversion seller');

   (ii) the reversion seller (if he is an individual) or an individual who is a beneficiary of the trust (if the reversion seller is a trustee), or a related person, is entitled under the arrangement to occupy at least 40% of the land in question as or in connection with a dwelling, and intends to do so; and

   (iii) the arrangement specifies one or more qualifying termination events, on the occurrence of which that entitlement will end;

  (b) 'administering' a regulated home reversion plan means any of—

   (i) notifying the reversion seller of changes in payments due under the plan, or of other matters of which the plan requires him to be notified;

   (ii) taking any necessary steps for the purposes of making payments to the reversion seller under the plan; and

   (iii) taking any necessary steps for the purposes of collecting or recovering payments due under the plan from the reversion seller,

  but a person is not to be treated as administering a regulated home reversion plan merely because he has, or exercises, a right to take action for the purposes of enforcing the plan (or to require that such action is or is not taken).

 (4) For the purposes of paragraph (3)—

  (a) the reference to a 'qualifying interest' in land—

   (i) in relation to land in England or Wales, is to an estate in fee simple absolute or a term of years absolute, whether subsisting at law or in equity;

   (ii) in relation to land in Scotland, is to the interest of an owner in land or the tenant's right over or interest in a property subject to a lease;

   (iii) in relation to land in Northern Ireland, is to any freehold estate or any leasehold estate, whether subsisting at law or in equity;

  (b) 'timeshare accommodation' has the meaning given by section 1 of the Timeshare Act 1992;

  (c) 'related person' in relation to the reversion seller or, where the reversion seller is a trustee, a beneficiary of the trust, means—

   (i) that person's spouse or civil partner;

   (ii) a person (whether or not of the opposite sex) whose relationship with that person has the characteristics of the relationship between husband and wife; or

   (iii) that person's parent, brother, sister, child, grandparent or grandchild; and

  (d) 'qualifying termination event', in relation to a person's entitlement to occupy land, means—

   (i) the person becomes a resident of a care home;

   (ii) the person dies;

   (iii) the end of a specified period of at least twenty years beginning with the day on which the reversion seller entered into the arrangement.

 (5) For the purposes of paragraph (3)(a)(ii), the area of any land which comprises a building or other structure containing two or more storeys is to be taken to be the aggregate of the floor areas of each of those storeys.

 (6) For the purposes of the definition of 'qualifying termination event' in paragraph (4), 'care home' —

  (a) in relation to England and Wales, has the meaning given by section 3 of the Care Standards Act 2000;

  (b) in relation to Scotland, means accommodation provided by a 'care home' within the meaning of section 2(3)of the Regulation of Care (Scotland) Act 2001;

  (c) in relation to Northern Ireland, means—

   (i) a residential care home within the meaning of article 10 of the Health and Personal Social Services (Quality, Improvement and Regulation) (Northern Ireland) Order 2003; or

   (ii) a nursing home within the meaning of article 11 of that Order.

 (7) In this Order—

  (a) references to entering into a regulated home reversion plan as plan provider include acquiring any obligations or rights (including his interest in land) of the plan provider, under such a plan; but

  (b) in relation to a person who acquires any such obligations or rights, an activity is a specified kind of activity for the purposes of articles 25B(1)(b) and 53B(b)(ii) and paragraph (2) only if the plan was entered into by the plan provider (rather than the obligations or rights acquired) on or after 6th April 2007.

 (8) Accordingly, references in this Order to a plan provider, other than in paragraph (7), include a person who acquires any such obligations or rights.

*Exclusions*

### 63C  Arranging administration by authorised person

A person who is not an authorised person does not carry on an activity of the kind specified by article 63B(2) in relation to a regulated home reversion plan where he—

(a) arranges for another person, being an authorised person with permission to carry on an activity of that kind, to administer the plan; or

(b) administers the plan himself during a period of not more than one month beginning with the day on which any such arrangement comes to an end.

### 63D  Administration pursuant to agreement with authorised person

A person who is not an authorised person does not carry on an activity of the kind specified by article 63B(2) in relation to a regulated home reversion plan where he administers the plan pursuant to an agreement with an authorised person who has permission to carry on an activity of that kind.

### 63E  Other exclusions

Article 63B is also subject to the exclusions in articles 66 (trustees etc.), 72 (overseas persons) and 72A (information society services).

## Chapter XVb   Regulated home purchase plans

*The activities*

### 63F  Entering into and administering regulated home purchase plans

(1) Entering into a regulated home purchase plan as home purchase provider is a specified kind of activity.

(2) Administering a regulated home purchase plan is also a specified kind of activity where the plan was entered into by way of business on or after 6th April 2007.

(3) In this Chapter—

(a) a 'regulated home purchase plan' is an arrangement comprised in one or more instruments or agreements, in relation to which the following conditions are met at the time it is entered into—

(i) the arrangement is one under which a person (the 'home purchase provider') buys a qualifying interest or an undivided share of a qualifying interest in land (other than timeshare accommodation) in the United Kingdom;

(ii) where an undivided share of a qualifying interest in land is bought, the interest is held on trust for the home purchase provider and the individual or trustees mentioned in paragraph (iii) as beneficial tenants in common;

(iii) the arrangement provides for the obligation of an individual or trustees (the 'home purchaser') to buy the interest bought by the home purchase provider over the course of or at the end of a specified period; and

(iv) the home purchaser (if he is an individual) or an individual who is a beneficiary of the trust (if the home purchaser is a trustee), or a related person, is entitled under the arrangement to occupy at least 40% of the land in question as or in connection with a dwelling during that period, and intends to do so;

(b) 'administering' a regulated home purchase plan means either or both of—

(i) notifying the home purchaser of changes in payments due under the plan, or of other matters of which the plan requires him to be notified; and

(ii) taking any necessary steps for the purposes of collecting or recovering payments due under the plan from the home purchaser;

but a person is not to be treated as administering a regulated home purchase plan merely because he has, or exercises, a right to take action for the purposes of enforcing the plan or to require that such action is or is not taken.

(4) Article 63B(4)(a) to (c) applies for the purposes of paragraph (3)(a) with references to the 'reversion seller' being read as references to the 'home purchaser'.

(5) Article 63B(5) applies for the purposes of paragraph (3)(a)(iv) with the reference to 'paragraph (3)(a)(ii)' being read as a reference to 'paragraph (3)(a)(iv)'.

*Exclusions*

### 63G  Arranging administration by authorised person

A person who is not an authorised person does not carry on an activity of the kind specified by article 63F(2) in relation to a regulated home purchase plan where he—

(a) arranges for another person, being an authorised person with permission to carry on an activity of that kind, to administer the plan; or

(b) administers the plan himself during a period of not more than one month beginning with the day on which any such arrangement comes to an end.

**63H Administration pursuant to agreement with authorised person**

A person who is not an authorised person does not carry on an activity of the kind specified by article 63F(2) in relation to a regulated home purchase plan where he administers the plan pursuant to an agreement with an authorised person who has permission to carry on an activity of that kind.

**63I Other exclusions**

Article 63F is also subject to the exclusions in articles 66 (trustees etc.), 72 (overseas persons) and 72A (information society services).

## Chapter XVI Agreeing to carry on activities

### *The activity*

**64 Agreeing to carry on specified kinds of activity**

Agreeing to carry on an activity of the kind specified by any other provision of this Part (other than article 5, 9B, 10, 25D, 51 or 52) is a specified kind of activity.

### *Exclusion*

**65 Overseas persons**

Article 64 is subject to the exclusion in article 72 (overseas persons) and 72A (information society services).

## Chapter XVII Exclusions applying to several specified kinds of activity

**66 Trustees, nominees and personal representatives**

(1) A person ('X') does not carry on an activity of the kind specified by article 14 where he enters into a transaction as bare trustee or, in Scotland, as nominee for another person ('Y') and—

    (a) X is acting on Y's instructions; and

    (b) X does not hold himself out as providing a service of buying and selling securities or contractually based investments.

(2) Subject to paragraph (7), there are excluded from article 25(1) and (2), 25A(1) and (2), 25B(1) and (2) and 25C(1) and (2) arrangements made by a person acting as trustee or personal representative for or with a view to a transaction which is or is to be entered into—

    (a) by that person and a fellow trustee or personal representative (acting in their capacity as such); or

    (b) by a beneficiary under the trust, will or intestacy.

(3) Subject to paragraph (7), there is excluded from article 37 any activity carried on by a person acting as trustee or personal representative, unless—

    (a) he holds himself out as providing a service comprising an activity of the kind specified by article 37; or

    (b) the assets in question are held for the purposes of an occupational pension scheme, and, by virtue of article 4 of the Financial Services and Markets Act 2000 (Carrying on Regulated Activities by Way of Business) Order 2001, he is to be treated as carrying on that activity by way of business.

(3A) Subject to paragraph (7), there is excluded from article 39A any activity carried on by a person acting as trustee or personal representative, unless he holds himself out as providing a service comprising an activity of the kind specified by article 39A.

(4) Subject to paragraph (7), there is excluded from article 40 any activity carried on by a person acting as trustee or personal representative, unless he holds himself out as providing a service comprising an activity of the kind specified by article 40.

(4A) There is excluded from article 40 any activity carried on by a person acting as trustee which consists of arranging for one or more other persons to safeguard and administer trust assets where—

    (a) that other person is a qualifying custodian; or

    (b) that safeguarding and administration is also arranged by a qualifying custodian.

In this paragraph, 'qualifying custodian' has the meaning given by article 41(2).

(5) A person does not, by sending or causing to be sent a dematerialised instruction (within the meaning of article 45), carry on an activity of the kind specified by that article if the instruction relates to an investment which that person holds as trustee or personal representative.

(6) Subject to paragraph (7), there is excluded from articles 53, 53A, 53B and 53C the giving of advice by a person acting as trustee or personal representative where he gives the advice to—

    (a) a fellow trustee or personal representative for the purposes of the trust or the estate; or

    (b) a beneficiary under the trust, will or intestacy concerning his interest in the trust fund or estate.

(6A) Subject to paragraph (7), a person acting as trustee or personal representative does not carry on an activity of the kind specified by article 61(1) or (2) where the borrower under the regulated mortgage contract in question is a beneficiary under the trust, will or intestacy.

(6B) Subject to paragraph (7), a person acting as trustee or personal representative does not carry on an activity of the kind specified by article 63B(1) or (2) where the reversion seller under the regulated home reversion plan in question is a beneficiary under the trust, will or intestacy.

(6C) Subject to paragraph (7), a person acting as trustee or personal representative does not carry on an activity of the kind specified by article 63F(1) or (2) where the home purchaser under the regulated home purchase plan in question is a beneficiary under the trust, will or intestacy.

(7) Paragraphs (2), (3), (3A), (4) and (6), (6A), (6B) and (6C) do not apply if the person carrying on the activity is remunerated for what he does in addition to any remuneration he receives as trustee or personal representative, and for these purposes a person is not to be regarded as receiving additional remuneration merely because his remuneration is calculated by reference to time spent.

(8) This article is subject to article 4(4A).

## 67 Activities carried on in the course of a profession or non-investment business

(1) There is excluded from articles 21, 25(1) and (2), 25A, 25B, 25C, 39A, 40 and 53, 53A, 53B and 53C any activity which—

(a) is carried on in the course of carrying on any profession or business which does not otherwise consist of the carrying on of regulated activities in the United Kingdom ; and

(b) may reasonably be regarded as a necessary part of other services provided in the course of that profession or business.

(2) But the exclusion in paragraph (1) does not apply if the activity in question is remunerated separately from the other services.

(3) This article is subject to article 4(4) and 4(A).

## 68 Activities carried on in connection with the sale of goods or supply of services

(1) Subject to paragraphs (9), (10) and (11), this article concerns certain activities carried on for the purposes of or in connection with the sale of goods or supply of services by a supplier to a customer, where—

'supplier' means a person whose main business is to sell goods or supply services and not to carry on any activities of the kind specified by any of articles 14, 21, 25, 37, 39A, 40, 45, 51, 52 and 53 and, where the supplier is a member of a group, also means any other member of that group; and

'customer' means a person, other than an individual, to whom a supplier sells goods or supplies services, or agrees to do so, and, where the customer is a member of a group, also means any other member of that group;

and in this article 'related sale or supply' means a sale of goods or supply of services to the customer otherwise than by the supplier, but for or in connection with the same purpose as the sale or supply mentioned above.

(2) There is excluded from article 14 any transaction entered into by a supplier with a customer, if the transaction is entered into for the purposes of or in connection with the sale of goods or supply of services, or a related sale or supply.

(3) There is excluded from article 21 any transaction entered into by a supplier as agent for a consumer, if the transaction is entered into for the purposes of or in connection with the sale of goods or supply of services, or a related sale or supply, and provided that—

(a) where the investment to which the transaction relates is a security, the supplier does not hold himself out (other than to the customer) as engaging in the business of buying securities of the kind to which the transaction relates with a view to selling them, and does not regularly solicit members of the public for the purpose of inducing them (as principals or agents) to buy, sell, subscribe for or underwrite securities;

(b) where the investment to which the transaction relates is a contractually based investment, the supplier enters into the transaction—

(i) with or through an authorised person, or an exempt person acting in the course of a business comprising a regulated activity in relation to which he is exempt; or

(ii) through an office outside the United Kingdom maintained by a party to the transaction, and with or through a person whose head office is situated outside the United Kingdom and whose ordinary business involves him in carrying on activities of the kind specified by any of articles 14, 21, 25, 37, 40, 45, 51, 52 and 53 or, so far as relevant to any of those articles, article 64, or would do so apart from any exclusion from any of those articles made by this Order.

(4) In paragraph (3)(a), 'members of the public' has the meaning given by article 15(2), references to 'A' being read as references to the supplier.

(5) There are excluded from article 25(1) and (2) arrangements made by a supplier for, or with a view to, a transaction which is or is to be entered into by a customer for the purposes of or in connection with the sale of goods or supply of services, or a related sale or supply.

(6) There is excluded from article 37 any activity carried on by a supplier where the assets in question—

    (a) are those of a customer; and

    (b) are managed for the purposes of or in connection with the sale of goods or supply of services, or a related sale or supply.

(7) There is excluded from article 40 any activity carried on by a supplier where the assets in question are or are to be safeguarded and administered for the purposes of or in connection with the sale of goods or supply of services, or a related sale or supply.

(8) There is excluded from article 53 the giving of advice by a supplier to a customer for the purposes of or in connection with the sale of goods or supply of services, or a related sale or supply, or to a person with whom the customer proposes to enter into a transaction for the purposes of or in connection with such a sale or supply or related sale or supply.

(9) Paragraphs (2), (3) and (5) do not apply in the case of a transaction for the sale or purchase of a [...] contract of insurance, an investment of the kind specified by article 81, or an investment of the kind specified by article 89 so far as relevant to such a contract or such an investment.

(10) Paragraph (6) does not apply where the assets managed consist of qualifying contracts of insurance, investments of the kind specified by article 81, or investments of the kind specified by article 89 so far as relevant to such contracts or such investments.

(11) Paragraph (8) does not apply in the case of advice in relation to an investment which is a contract of insurance, is of the kind specified by article 81, or is of the kind specified by article 89 so far as relevant to such a contract or such an investment.

(12) This article is subject to article 4(4).

## 69  Groups and joint enterprises

(1) There is excluded from article 14 any transaction into which a person enters as principal with another person if that other person is also acting as principal and—

    (a) they are members of the same group; or

    (b) they are, or propose to become, participators in a joint enterprise and the transaction is entered into for the purposes of or in connection with that enterprise.

(2) There is excluded from article 21 any transaction into which a person enters as agent for another person if that other person is acting as principal, and the condition in paragraph (1)(a) or (b) is met, provided that—

    (a) where the investment to which the transaction relates is a security, the agent does not hold himself out (other than to members of the same group or persons who are or propose to become participators with him in a joint enterprise) as engaging in the business of buying securities of the kind to which the transaction relates with a view to selling them, and does not regularly solicit members of the public for the purpose of inducing them (as principals or agents) to buy, sell, subscribe for or underwrite securities;

    (b) where the investment to which the transaction relates is a contractually based investment, the agent enters into the transaction—

        (i) with or through an authorised person, or an exempt person acting in the course of a business comprising a regulated activity in relation to which he is exempt; or

        (ii) through an office outside the United Kingdom maintained by a party to the transaction, and with or through a person whose head office is situated outside the United Kingdom and whose ordinary business involves him in carrying on activities of the kind specified by any of articles 14, 21, 25, 37, 40, 45, 51, 52 and 53 or, so far as relevant to any of those articles, article 64, or would do so apart from any exclusion from any of those articles made by this Order.

(3) In paragraph (2)(a), 'members of the public' has the meaning given by article 15(2), references to 'A' being read as references to the agent.

(4) There are excluded from article 25(1) and (2) arrangements made by a person if—

    (a) he is a member of a group and the arrangements in question are for, or with a view to, a transaction which is or is to be entered into, as principal, by another member of the same group; or

    (b) he is or proposes to become a participator in a joint enterprise, and the arrangements in question are for, or with a view to, a transaction which is or is to be entered into, as principal, by another person who is or proposes to become a participator in that enterprise, for the purposes of or in connection with that enterprise.

(5) There is excluded from article 37 any activity carried on by a person if—

    (a) he is a member of a group and the assets in question belong to another member of the same group; or

    (b) he is or proposes to become a participator in a joint enterprise with the person to whom the assets belong, and the assets are managed for the purposes of or in connection with that enterprise.

(6) There is excluded from article 40 any activity carried on by a person if—

(a)  he is a member of a group and the assets in question belong to another member of the same group; or

(b)  he is or proposes to become a participator in a joint enterprise, and the assets in question—

   (i)  belong to another person who is or proposes to become a participator in that joint enterprise; and

   (ii)  are or are to be safeguarded and administered for the purposes of or in connection with that enterprise.

(7)  A person who is a member of a group does not carry on an activity of the kind specified by article 45 where he sends a dematerialised instruction, or causes one to be sent, on behalf of another member of the same group, if the investment to which the instruction relates is one in respect of which a member of the same group is registered as holder in the appropriate register of securities, or will be so registered as a result of the instruction.

(8)  In paragraph (7), 'dematerialised instruction' and 'register of securities' have the meaning given by regulation 3 of the Uncertificated Securities Regulations 2001.

(9)  There is excluded from article 53 the giving of advice by a person if—

(a)  he is a member of a group and gives the advice in question to another member of the same group; or

(b)  he is, or proposes to become, a participator in a joint enterprise and the advice in question is given to another person who is, or proposes to become, a participator in that enterprise for the purposes of or in connection with that enterprise.

(10)  Paragraph (2) does not apply to a transaction for the sale or purchase of a contract of insurance.

(11)  Paragraph (4) does not apply to arrangements for, or with a view to, a transaction for the sale or purchase of a contract of insurance.

(12)  Paragraph (9) does not apply where the advice relates to a transaction for the sale or purchase of a contract of insurance.

(13)  This article is subject to article 4(4).

## 70  Activities carried on in connection with the sale of a body corporate

(1)  A person does not carry on an activity of the kind specified by article 14 by entering as principal into a transaction if—

(a)  the transaction is one to acquire or dispose of shares in a body corporate other than an open-ended investment company, or is entered into for the purposes of such an acquisition or disposal; and

(b)  either—

   (i)  the conditions set out in paragraph (2) are met; or

   (ii)  those conditions are not met, but the object of the transaction may nevertheless reasonably be regarded as being the acquisition of day to day control of the affairs of the body corporate.

(2)  The conditions mentioned in paragraph (1)(b) are that—

(a)  the shares consist of or include 50 per cent or more of the voting shares in the body corporate; or

(b)  the shares, together with any already held by the person acquiring them, consist of or include at least that percentage of such shares; and

(c)  in either case, the acquisition or disposal is between parties each of whom is a body corporate, a partnership, a single individual or a group of connected individuals.

(3)  In paragraph (2)(c), 'a group of connected individuals' means—

(a)  in relation to a party disposing of shares in a body corporate, a single group of persons each of whom is—

   (i)  a director or manager of the body corporate;

   (ii)  a close relative of any such director or manager;

   (iii)  a person acting as trustee for any person falling within paragraph (i) or (ii); and

(b)  in relation to a party acquiring shares in a body corporate, a single group of persons each of whom is—

   (i)  a person who is or is to be a director or manager of the body corporate;

   (ii)  a close relative of any such person; or

   (iii)  a person acting as trustee for any person falling within paragraph (i) or (ii).

(4)  A person does not carry on an activity of the kind specified by article 21 by entering as agent into a transaction of the kind described in paragraph (1).

(5)  There are excluded from article 25(1) and (2) arrangements made for, or with a view to, a transaction of the kind described in paragraph (1).

(6)  There is excluded from article 53 the giving of advice in connection with a transaction (or proposed transaction) of the kind described in paragraph (1).

(7)  Paragraphs (4), (5) and (6) do not apply in the case of a transaction for the sale or purchase of a contract of insurance.

(8)  This article is subject to article 4(4).

## 71  Activities carried on in connection with employee share schemes

(1)  A person ('C'), a member of the same group as C or a relevant trustee does not carry on an activity of the kind specified by article 14 by entering as principal into a transaction the purpose of which is to enable or facilitate—

   (a)  transactions in shares in, or debentures issued by, C between, or for the benefit of, any of the persons mentioned in paragraph (2); or

   (b)  the holding of such shares or debentures by, or for the benefit of, such persons.

(2)  The persons referred to in paragraph (1) are—

   (a)  the bona fide employees or former employees of C or of another member of the same group as C;

   (b)  the wives, husbands, widows, widowers, civil partners, surviving civil partners or children or step-children under the age of eighteen of such employees or former employees.

(3)  C, a member of the same group as C or a relevant trustee does not carry on an activity of the kind specified by article 21 by entering as agent into a transaction of the kind described in paragraph (1).

(4)  There are excluded from article 25(1) or (2) arrangements made by C, a member of the same group as C or a relevant trustee if the arrangements in question are for, or with a view to, a transaction of the kind described in paragraph (1).

(5)  There is excluded from article 40 any activity if the assets in question are, or are to be, safeguarded and administered by C, a member of the same group as C or a relevant trustee for the purpose of enabling or facilitating transactions of the kind described in paragraph (1).

(6)  In this article—

   (a)  'shares' and 'debentures' include—

      (i)  any investment of the kind specified by article 76 or 77;

      (ii)  any investment of the kind specified by article 79 or 80 so far as relevant to articles 76 and 77; and

      (iii)  any investment of the kind specified by article 89 so far as relevant to investments of the kind mentioned in paragraph (i) or (ii);

   (b)  'relevant trustee' means a person who, in pursuance of the arrangements made for the purpose mentioned in paragraph (1), holds, as trustee, shares in or debentures issued by C.

## 72  Overseas persons

(1)  An overseas person does not carry on an activity of the kind specified by article 14 or 25D by—

   (a)  entering into a transaction as principal with or though an authorised person, or an exempt person acting in the course of a business comprising a regulated activity in relation to which he is exempt; or

   (b)  entering into a transaction as principal with a person in the United Kingdom, if the transaction is the result of a legitimate approach.

(2)  An overseas person does not carry on an activity of the kind specified by article 21 or 25D by—

   (a)  entering into a transaction as agent for any person with or through an authorised person or an exempt person acting in the course of a business comprising a regulated activity in relation to which he is exempt; or

   (b)  entering into a transaction with another party ('X') as agent for any person ('Y'), other than with or through an authorised person or such an exempt person, unless—

      (i)  either X or Y is in the United Kingdom; and

      (ii)  the transaction is the result of an approach (other than a legitimate approach) made by or on behalf of, or to, whichever of X or Y is in the United Kingdom.

(3)  There are excluded from article 25(1) or 25D arrangements made by an overseas person with an authorised person, or an exempt person acting in the course of a business comprising a regulated activity in relation to which he is exempt.

(4)  There are excluded from article 25(2) or 25D arrangements made by an overseas person with a view to transactions which are, as respects transactions in the United Kingdom, confined to—

   (a)  transactions entered into by authorised persons as principal or agent; and

   (b)  transactions entered into by exempt persons, as principal or agent, in the course of business comprising regulated activities in relation to which they are exempt.

(5)  There is excluded from article 53 the giving of advice by an overseas person as a result of a legitimate approach.

(5A)  An overseas person does not carry on an activity of the kind specified by article 25A(1)(a), 25B(1)(a) or 25C(1)(a) if each person who may be contemplating entering into the relevant type of agreement in the relevant capacity is non-resident.

(5B)  There are excluded from articles 25A(1)(b), 25B(1)(b) and 25C(1)(b) arrangements made by an overseas person to vary the terms of a qualifying agreement.

(5C) There are excluded from articles 25A(2), 25B(2) and 25C(2), arrangements made by an overseas person which are made solely with a view to non-resident persons who participate in those arrangements entering, in the relevant capacity, into the relevant type of agreement.

(5D) An overseas person does not carry on an activity of the kind specified in article 61(1), 63B(1) or 63F(1) by entering into a qualifying agreement.

(5E) An overseas person does not carry on an activity of the kind specified in article 61(2), 63B(2) or 63F(2) where he administers a qualifying agreement.

(5F) In paragraphs (5A) to (5E)—

(a) 'non-resident' means not normally resident in the United Kingdom;

(b) 'qualifying agreement' means—

(i) in relation to articles 25A and 61, a regulated mortgage contract where the borrower (or each borrower) is non-resident when he enters into it;

(ii) in relation to articles 25B and 63B, a regulated home reversion plan where the reversion seller (or each reversion seller) is non-resident when he enters into it;

(iii) in relation to articles 25C and 63F, a regulated home purchase plan where the home purchaser (or each home purchaser) is non-resident when he enters into it;

(c) 'the relevant capacity' means—

(i) in the case of a regulated mortgage contract, as borrower;

(ii) in the case of a regulated home reversion plan, as reversion seller or plan provider;

(iii) in the case of a regulated home purchase plan, as home purchaser;

(d) 'the relevant type of agreement' means—

(i) in relation to article 25A, a regulated mortgage contract;

(ii) in relation to article 25B, a regulated home reversion plan;

(iii) in relation to article 25C, a regulated home purchase plan.

(6) There is excluded from article 64 any agreement made by an overseas person to carry on an activity of the kind specified by article 25(1) or (2), 37, 39A, 40 or 45 if the agreement is the result of a legitimate approach.

(7) In this article, 'legitimate approach' means—

(a) an approach made to the overseas person which has not been solicited by him in any way, or has been solicited by him in a way which does not contravene section 21 of the Act; or

(b) an approach made by or on behalf of the overseas person in a way which does not contravene that section.

(8) Paragraphs (1) to (5) do not apply where the overseas person is an investment firm or credit institution—

(a) who is providing or performing investment services and activities on a professional basis; and

(b) whose home Member State is the United Kingdom.

**72A Information society services**

(1) There is excluded from this Part any activity consisting of the provision of an information society service from an EEA State other than the United Kingdom.

(2) The exclusion in paragraph (1) does not apply to the activity of effecting or carrying out a contract of insurance as principal, where—

(a) the activity is carried on by an undertaking which has received official authorisation in accordance with Article 4 of the life assurance consolidation directive or the first non-life insurance directive, and

(b) the insurance falls within the scope of any of the insurance directives.

**72B Activities carried on by a provider of relevant goods or services**

(1) In this article—

'connected contract of insurance' means a contract of insurance which—

(a) is not a contract of long-term insurance;

(b) has a total duration (or would have a total duration were any right to renew conferred by the contract exercised) of five years or less;

(c) has an annual premium (or, where the premium is paid otherwise than by way of annual premium, the equivalent of an annual premium) of 500 euro or less, or the equivalent amount in sterling or other currency;

(d) covers the risk of—

(i) breakdown, loss of, or damage to, non-motor goods supplied by the provider; or

(ii) damage to, or loss of, baggage and other risks linked to the travel booked with the provider ('travel risks') in circumstances where—

(aa) the travel booked with the provider relates to attendance at an event organised or managed by that provider and the party seeking insurance is not an individual (acting in his private capacity) or a small business; or

(bb) the travel booked with the provider is only the hire of an aircraft, vehicle or vessel which does not provide sleeping accommodation.

    (e)   does not cover any liability risks (except, in the case of a contract which covers travel risks, where that cover is ancillary to the main cover provided by the contract);

    (f)   is complementary to the non-motor goods being supplied or service being provided by the provider; and

    (g)   is of such a nature that the only information that a person requires in order to carry on an activity of the kind specified by article 21, 25, 39A or 53 in relation to it is the cover provided by the contract;

'non-motor goods' means goods which are not mechanically propelled road vehicles;

'provider' means a person who supplies non-motor goods or provides services related to travel in the course of carrying on a profession or business which does not otherwise consist of the carrying on of regulated activities. For these purposes, the transfer of possession of an aircraft, vehicle or vessel under an agreement for hire which is not—

    (a)   a hire-purchase agreement within the meaning of section 189(1) of the Consumer Credit Act 1974, or

    (b)   any other agreement which contemplates that the property in those goods will also pass at some time in the future,

is the provision of a service related to travel, not a supply of goods.

'small business' means—

    (a)   subject to paragraph (b) a sole trader, body corporate, partnership or an unincorporated association which had a turnover in the last financial year of less than £1,000,000;

    (b)   where the business concerned is a member of a group within the meaning of section 262(1) of the Companies Act 1985 (and after the repeal of that section within the meaning of section 474(1) of the Companies Act 2006), reference to its turnover means the combined turnover of the group.

'turnover' means the amounts derived from the provision of goods and services falling within the business's ordinary activities, after deduction of trade discounts, value added tax and any other taxes based on the amounts so derived.

    (2)  There is excluded from article 21 any transaction for the sale or purchase of a connected contract of insurance into which a provider enters as agent.

    (3)  There are excluded from article 25(1) and (2) any arrangements made by a provider for, or with a view to, a transaction for the sale or purchase of a connected contract of insurance.

    (4)  There is excluded from article 39A any activity carried on by a provider where the contract of insurance in question is a connected contract of insurance.

    (5)  There is excluded from article 53 the giving of advice by a provider in relation to a transaction for the sale or purchase of a connected contract of insurance.

    (6)  For the purposes of this article, a contract of insurance which covers travel risks is not to be treated as a contract of long-term insurance, notwithstanding the fact that it contains related and subsidiary provisions such that it might be regarded as a contract of long-term insurance, if the cover to which those provisions relate is ancillary to the main cover provided by the contract.

### 72C  Provision of information on an incidental basis

    (1)  There is excluded from articles 25(1) and (2) the making of arrangements for, or with a view to, a transaction for the sale or purchase of a contract of insurance or an investment of the kind specified by article 89, so far as relevant to such a contract, where that activity meets the conditions specified in paragraph (4).

    (2)  There is excluded from articles 37 and 40 any activity—

    (a)   where the assets in question are rights under a contract of insurance or an investment of the kind specified by article 89, so far as relevant to such a contract; and

    (b)   which meets the conditions specified in paragraph (4).

    (3)  There is excluded from article 39A any activity which meets the conditions specified in paragraph (4).

    (4)  The conditions specified in this paragraph are that the activity—

    (a)   consists of the provision of information to the policyholder or potential policyholder;

    (b)   is carried on by a person in the course of carrying on a profession or business which does not otherwise consist of the carrying on of regulated activities; and

    (c)   may reasonably be regarded as being incidental to that profession or business.

### 72D  Large risks contracts where risk situated outside the EEA

    (1)  There is excluded from articles 21, 25(1) and (2), 39A and 53 any activity which is carried on in relation to a large risks contract of insurance, to the extent that the risk or commitment covered by the contract is not situated in an EEA State.

    (2)  In this article, a 'large risks contract of insurance' is a contract of insurance the principal object of which is to cover—

    (a)   risks falling within paragraph 4 (railway rolling stock), 5 (aircraft), 6 (ships), 7 (goods in transit), 11 (aircraft liability) or 12 (liability of ships) of Part 1 of Schedule 1;

     (b) risks falling within paragraph 14 (credit) or 15 (suretyship) of that Part provided that the risks relate to a business carried on by the policyholder; or

     (c) risks falling within paragraph 3 (land vehicles), 8 (fire and natural forces), 9 (damage to property), 10 (motor vehicle liability), 13 (general liability) or 16 (miscellaneous financial loss) of that Part provided that the risks relate to a business carried on by the policyholder and that the condition specified in paragraph (3) is met in relation to that business.

    (3) The condition specified in this paragraph is that at least two of the three following criteria were met in the most recent financial year for which information is available—

     (a) the balance sheet total of the business (within the meaning of section 247(5) of the Companies Act 1985 or article 255(5) of the Companies (Northern Ireland) Order 1986) exceeded 6.2 million euro,

     (b) the net turnover (within the meaning given to 'turnover' by section 262(1) of that Act or article 270(1) of that Order) exceeded 12.8 million euro,

     (c) the number of employees (within the meaning given by section 247(6) of that Act or article 255(6) of that Order) exceeded 250,

and for a financial year which is a company's financial year but not in fact a year, the net turnover of the policyholder shall be proportionately adjusted.

    (4) For the purposes of paragraph (3), where the policyholder is a member of a group for which consolidated accounts (within the meaning of the Seventh Company Law Directive) are drawn up, the question whether the condition specified by that paragraph is met is to be determined by reference to those accounts.

### 72E  Business Angel-led Enterprise Capital Funds

    (1) A body corporate of a type specified in paragraph (7) does not carry on the activity of the kind specified by article 21 by entering as agent into a transaction on behalf of the participants of a Business Angel-led Enterprise Capital Fund.

    (2) There are excluded from article 25(1) and (2) arrangements, made by a body corporate of a type specified in paragraph (7), for or with a view to a transaction which is or is to be entered into by or on behalf of the participants in a Business Angel-led Enterprise Capital Fund.

    (3) There is excluded from article 37 any activity, carried on by a body corporate of a type specified in paragraph (7), which consists in the managing of assets belonging to the participants in a Business Angel-led Enterprise Capital Fund.

    (4) There is excluded from article 40 any activity, carried on by a body corporate of a type specified in paragraph (7), in respect of assets belonging to the participants in a Business Angel-led Enterprise Capital Fund.

    (5) A body corporate of a type specified in paragraph (7) does not carry on the activity of the kind specified in article 51(1)(a) where it carries on the activity of establishing, operating or winding up a Business Angel-led Enterprise Capital Fund.

    (6) A body corporate of a type specified in paragraph (7) does not carry on the activity of the kind specified in article 53 where it is advising the participants in a Business Angel-led Enterprise Capital Fund on investments to be made by or on behalf of the participants of that Business Angel-led Enterprise Capital Fund.

    (7) The type of body corporate specified is a limited company—

     (i) which operates a Business Angel-led Enterprise Capital Fund; and

     (ii) the members of which are participants in the Business Angel-led Enterprise Capital Fund operated by that limited company and between them have invested at least 50 per cent of the total investment in that Business Angel-led Enterprise Capital Fund excluding any investment made by the Secretary of State.

    (8) For the purposes of paragraph (7), 'a limited company' means a body corporate with limited liability which is a company or firm formed in accordance with the law of an EEA State and having its registered office, central administration or principal place of business within the territory of an EEA State.

    (9) Nothing in this article has the effect of excluding a body corporate from the application of the Money Laundering Regulations 2007, in so far as those Regulations would have applied to it but for this article.

    (10) Nothing in this article has the effect of excluding a body corporate from the application of section 397 of the Act (misleading statements and practices), in so far as that section would have applied to it but for this article.

    (11) This article is subject to article 4(4).

### 72F  Interpretation

    (1) For the purposes of this article and of article 72E—

'Business Angel-led Enterprise Capital Fund' means a collective investment scheme which—

    (a) is established for the purpose of enabling participants to participate in or receive profits or income arising from the acquisition, holding, management or disposal of investments falling within one or more of—

     (i) article 76, being shares in an unlisted company;

      (ii) article 77, being instruments creating or acknowledging indebtedness in respect of an unlisted company; and

      (iii) article 79, being warrants or other instruments entitling the holder to subscribe for shares in an unlisted company;

  (b) has only the following as its participants—

      (i)   the Secretary of State;

      (ii) a body corporate of a type specified in article 72E(7); and

      (iii) one or more persons each of whom at the time they became a participant was—

         (aa) a sophisticated investor;

         (bb) a high net worth individual;

         (cc) a high net worth company;

         (dd) a high net worth unincorporated association;

         (ee) a trustee of a high value trust; or

         (ff)  a self-certified sophisticated investor;

  (c) is prevented, by the arrangements by which it is established, from—

      (i)  acquiring investments, other than those falling within paragraphs (i) to (iii) of sub-paragraph (a); and

      (ii) acquiring investments falling within paragraphs (i) to (iii) of sub-paragraph (a) in an unlisted company, where the aggregated cost of those investments exceeds £2 million, unless that acquisition is necessary to prevent or reduce the dilution of an existing share-holding in that unlisted company;

'high net worth company' means a body corporate which—

  (a) falls within article 49(2)(a) of the Financial Services and Markets Act 2000 (Financial Promotion) Order 2001[2] (high net worth companies, unincorporated associations etc.); and

  (b) has executed a document (in a manner which binds the company) in the following terms:

'This company is a high net worth company and falls within article 49(2)(a) of the Financial Services and Markets Act 2000 (Financial Promotion) Order 2001. We understand that any Business Angel-led Enterprise Capital Fund (within the meaning of article 72F of the Financial Services and Markets Act 2000 (Regulated Activities) Order 2001), in which this company participates, or any person who operates that Business Angel-led Enterprise Capital Fund, in which this company participates, will not be authorised under the Financial Services and Markets Act 2000 (and so will not have to satisfy the threshold conditions set out in Part I of Schedule 6 to that Act and will not be subject to Financial Services Authority rules such as those on holding client money). We understand that this means that redress through the Financial Services Authority, the Financial Ombudsman Scheme or the Financial Services Compensation Scheme will not be available. We also understand the risks associated in investing in a Business Angel-led Enterprise Capital Fund and are aware that it is open to us to seek advice from someone who is authorised under the Financial Services and Markets Act 2000 and who specialises in advising on this kind of investment.'

'high net worth individual' means an individual who—

  (a) is a 'certified high net worth individual' within the meaning of article 48(2) of the Financial Services and Markets Act 2000 (Financial Promotion) Order 2001 (certified high net worth individuals); and

  (b) has signed a statement in the following terms:

'I declare that I am a certified high net worth individual within the meaning of article 48(2) of the Financial Services and Markets Act 2000 (Financial Promotion) Order 2001 and that I understand that any Business Angel-led Enterprise Capital Fund (within the meaning of article 72F of the Financial Services and Markets Act 2000 (Regulated Activities) Order 2001), in which I participate, or any person who operates that Business Angel-led Enterprise Capital Fund, in which I participate, will not be authorised under the Financial Services and Markets Act 2000 (and so will not have to satisfy the threshold conditions set out in Part I of Schedule 6 to that Act and will not be subject to Financial Services Authority rules such as those on holding client money). I understand that this means that redress through the Financial Services Authority, the Financial Ombudsman Scheme or the Financial Services Compensation Scheme will not be available. I also understand the risks associated in investing in a Business Angel-led Enterprise Capital Fund and am aware that it is open to me to seek advice from someone who is authorised under the Financial Services and Markets Act 2000 and who specialises in advising on this kind of investment.';

'high net worth unincorporated association' means an unincorporated association—

  (a) which falls within article 49(2)(b) of the Financial Services and Markets Act 2000 (Financial Promotion) Order 2001; and

  (b) on behalf of which an officer of that association or a member of its governing body has signed a statement in the following terms:

'This unincorporated association is a high net worth unincorporated association and falls within article 49(2)(b) of the Financial Services and Markets Act 2000 (Financial Promotion) Order 2001. I understand that any Business Angel-led Enterprise Capital Fund (within the meaning of article 72F of the Financial Services and Markets Act 2000 (Regulated Activities) Order 2001), in which this association participates, or any person who operates that Business Angel-led Enterprise Capital Fund, in which this association participates, will not be authorised under the Financial Services and Markets Act 2000 (and so will not have to satisfy the threshold conditions set out in Part I of Schedule 6 to that Act and will not be subject to Financial Services Authority rules such as those on holding client money). I understand that this means that redress through the Financial Services Authority, the Financial Ombudsman Scheme or the Financial Services Compensation Scheme will not be available. I also understand the risks associated in investing in a Business Angel-led Enterprise Capital Fund and am aware that it is open to the association to seek advice from someone who is authorised under the Financial Services and Markets Act 2000 and who specialises in advising on this kind of investment.';

 'high value trust' means a trust—

  (a) where the aggregate value of the cash and investments which form a part of the trust's assets (before deducting the amount of its liabilities) is £10 million or more;

  (b) on behalf of which a trustee has signed a statement in the following terms:

'This trust is a high value trust. I understand that any Business Angel-led Enterprise Capital Fund (within the meaning of article 72F of the Financial Services and Markets Act 2000 (Regulated Activities) Order 2001), in which this trust participates, or any person who operates that Business Angel-led Enterprise Capital Fund, in which this trust participates, will not be authorised under the Financial Services and Markets Act 2000 (and so will not have to satisfy the threshold conditions set out in Part I of Schedule 6 to that Act and will not be subject to Financial Services Authority rules such as those on holding client money). I understand that this means that redress through the Financial Services Authority, the Financial Ombudsman Scheme or the Financial Services Compensation Scheme will not be available. I also understand the risks associated in investing in a Business Angel-led Enterprise Capital Fund and am aware that it is open to the trust to seek advice from someone who is authorised under the Financial Services and Markets Act 2000 and who specialises in advising on this kind of investment.';

 'self-certified sophisticated investor' means an individual who—

  (a) is a 'self-certified sophisticated investor' within the meaning of article 50A of the Financial Services and Markets Act 2000 (Financial Promotion) Order 2001[4];

  (b) has signed a statement in the following terms:

'I declare that I am a self-certified sophisticated investor within the meaning of article 50A of the Financial Services and Markets Act 2000 (Financial Promotion) Order 2001 and that I understand that any Business Angel-led Enterprise Capital Fund (within the meaning of article 72F of the Financial Services and Markets Act 2000 (Regulated Activities) Order 2001), in which I participate, or any person who operates that Business Angel-led Enterprise Capital Fund, in which I participate, will not be authorised under the Financial Services and Markets Act 2000 (and so will not have to satisfy the threshold conditions set out in Part I of Schedule 6 to that Act and will not be subject to Financial Services Authority rules such as those on holding client money). I understand that this means that redress through the Financial Services Authority, the Financial Ombudsman Scheme or the Financial Services Compensation Scheme will not be available. I also understand the risks associated in investing in a Business Angel-led Enterprise Capital Fund and am aware that it is open to me to seek advice from someone who is authorised under the Financial Services and Markets Act 2000 and who specialises in advising on this kind of investment.';

 'sophisticated investor' means an individual who—

  (a) is a 'certified sophisticated investor' within the meaning of article 50(1) of the Financial Services and Markets Act 2000 (Financial Promotion) Order 2001; and

  (b) has signed a statement in the following terms:

'I declare that I am a certified sophisticated investor within the meaning of article 50(1) of the Financial Services and Markets Act 2000 (Financial Promotion) Order 2001 and that I understand that any Business Angel-led Enterprise Capital Fund (within the meaning of article 72F of the Financial Services and Markets Act 2000 (Regulated Activities) Order 2001), in which I participate, or any person who operates that Business Angel-led Enterprise Capital Fund, in which I participate, will not be authorised under the Financial Services and Markets Act 2000 (and so will not have to satisfy the threshold conditions set out in Part I of Schedule 6 to that Act and will not be subject to Financial Services Authority rules such as those on holding client money). I understand that this means that redress through the Financial Services Authority, the Financial Ombudsman Scheme or the Financial Services Compensation Scheme will not be available. I also understand the risks associated in investing in a Business Angel-led Enterprise Capital Fund and am aware that it is open to me to seek advice from someone who is authorised under the Financial Services and Markets Act 2000 and who specialises in advising on this kind of investment.';

 'unlisted company' has the meaning given by article 3 of the Financial Services and Markets Act 2000 (Financial Promotion) Order 2001.

 (2) References in this Article and in Article 72E to a participant in a Business Angel-led Enterprise Capital Fund, doing things on behalf of such a participant and property belonging to such a participant are, respectively, references to that participant in that capacity, to doing things on behalf of that participant in that capacity or to the property of that participant held in that capacity.

# PART III

## SPECIFIED INVESTMENTS

### 73  Investments: general
The following kinds of investment are specified for the purposes of section 22 of the Act.

### 74  Deposits
A deposit.

### 74A  Electronic money
Electronic money.

### 75  Contracts of insurance
Rights under a contract of insurance.

### 76  Shares etc
(1) Shares or stock in the share capital of—
(a) any body corporate (wherever incorporated), and
(b) any unincorporated body constituted under the law of a country or territory outside the United Kingdom.
(2) Paragraph (1) includes—
(a) any shares of a class defined as deferred shares for the purposes of section 119 of the Building Societies Act 1986; and
(b) any transferable shares in a body incorporated under the law of, or any part of, the United Kingdom relating to industrial and provident societies or credit unions, or in a body constituted under the law of another EEA State for purposes equivalent to those of such a body.
(3) But subject to paragraph (2) there are excluded from paragraph (1) shares or stock in the share capital of—
(a) an open-ended investment company;
(b) a building society incorporated under the law of, or any part of, the United Kingdom;
(c) a body incorporated under the law of, or any part of, the United Kingdom relating to industrial and provident societies or credit unions;
(d) any body constituted under the law of an EEA State for purposes equivalent to those of a body falling within sub-paragraph (b) or (c).

### 77  Instruments creating or acknowledging indebtedness
(1) Subject to paragraph (2), such of the following as do not fall within article 78—
(a) debentures;
(b) debenture stock;
(c) loan stock;
(d) bonds;
(e) certificates of deposit;
(f) any other instrument creating or acknowledging indebtedness.
(2) If and to the extent that they would otherwise fall within paragraph (1), there are excluded from that paragraph—
(a) an instrument acknowledging or creating indebtedness for, or for money borrowed to defray, the consideration payable under a contract for the supply of goods or services;
(b) a cheque or other bill of exchange, a banker's draft or a letter of credit (but not a bill of exchange accepted by a banker);
(c) a banknote, a statement showing a balance on a current, deposit or savings account, a lease or other disposition of property, or a heritable security; and
(d) a contract of insurance.
(3) An instrument excluded from paragraph (1) of article 78 by paragraph (2)(b) of that article is not thereby to be taken to fall within paragraph (1) of this article.

### 78  Government and public securities
(1) Subject to paragraph (2), loan stock, bonds and other instruments creating or acknowledging indebtedness, issued by or on behalf of any of the following—
(a) the government of the United Kingdom;
(b) the Scottish Administration;
(c) the Executive Committee of the Northern Ireland Assembly;
(d) the National Assembly for Wales;
(e) the government of any country or territory outside the United Kingdom;
(f) a local authority in the United Kingdom or elsewhere; or
(g) a body the members of which comprise—
(i) states including the United Kingdom or another EEA State; or

        (ii)  bodies whose members comprise states including the United Kingdom or another EEA State.

  (2)  There are excluded from paragraph (1)—

    (a)  so far as applicable, the instruments mentioned in article 77(2)(a) to (d);

    (b)  any instrument creating or acknowledging indebtedness in respect of—

        (i)  money received by the Director of Savings as deposits or otherwise in connection with the business of the National Savings Bank;

        (ii)  money raised under the National Loans Act 1968 under the auspices of the Director of Savings or treated as so raised by virtue of section 11(3) of the National Debt Act 1972.

### 79   Instruments giving entitlements to investments

  (1)  Warrants and other instruments entitling the holder to subscribe for any investment of the kind specified by article 76, 77 or 78.

  (2)  It is immaterial whether the investment to which the entitlement relates is in existence or identifiable.

  (3)  An investment of the kind specified by this article is not to be regarded as falling within article 83, 84 or 85.

### 80   Certificates representing certain securities

  (1)  Subject to paragraph (2), certificates or other instruments which confer contractual or property rights (other than rights consisting of an investment of the kind specified by article 83)—

    (a)  in respect of any investment of the kind specified by any of articles 76 to 79, being an investment held by a person other than the person on whom the rights are conferred by the certificate or instrument; and

    (b)  the transfer of which may be effected without the consent of that person.

  (2)  There is excluded from paragraph (1) any certificate or other instrument which confers rights in respect of two or more investments issued by different persons, or in respect of two or more different investments of the kind specified by article 78 and issued by the same person.

### 81   Units in a collective investment scheme

Units in a collective investment scheme (within the meaning of Part XVII of the Act).

### 82   Rights under a pension scheme

  (1)  Rights under a stakeholder pension scheme.

  (2)  Rights under a personal pension scheme.

### 83   Options

Options to acquire or dispose of—

    (a)  a security or contractually based investment (other than one of a kind specified by this article);

    (b)  currency of the United Kingdom or any other country or territory;

    (c)  palladium, platinum, gold or silver;

    (d)  an option to acquire or dispose of an investment of the kind specified by this article by virtue of paragraph (a), (b) or (c); or

    (e)  subject to paragraph (4), an option to acquire or dispose of an option to which paragraphs 5, 6, 7 or 10 of section C of Annex I to the markets in financial instruments directive (the text of which is set out in Part 1 Schedule 2 applies.

  (2)  Subject to paragraph (4), options—

    (a)  to which paragraph (1) does not apply;

    (b)  which relate to commodities;

    (c)  which may be settled physically; and

    (d)  either—

        (i)  to which paragraph 5 or 6 of Section C of Annex I to the markets in financial instruments directive, the text of which is set out in Part 1 of Schedule 2, applies, or

        (ii)  which in accordance with Article 38 of the Commission Regulation (the text of which is set out in Part 2 of Schedule 2) are to be considered as having the characteristics of other derivative financial instruments and not being for commercial purposes, and to which paragraph 7 of Section C of Annex I to the markets in financial instruments directive applies.

  (3)  Subject to paragraph (4), options—

    (a)  to which paragraph (1) does not apply; (b) which may be settled physically; and

    (c)  to which paragraph 10 of Section C of Annex I to the markets in financial instruments directive (read with the Commission Regulation) applies.

  (4)  Paragraphs (1)(e), (2) and (3) only apply to options in relation to which—

    (a)  an investment firm or credit institution is providing or performing investment services and activities on a professional basis,

(b) a management company is providing, in accordance with Article 5(3) of the UCITS directive, the investment service specified in paragraph 4 or 5 of Section A, or the ancillary service specified in paragraph 1 of Section B, of Annex I to the markets in financial instruments directive, or

(c) a market operator is providing the investment service specified in paragraph 8 of Section A of Annex I to the markets in financial instruments directive.

(5) Expressions used in paragraphs (1)(e), (2) and (3) and in the markets in financial instruments directive have the same meaning as in that directive.

## 84  Futures

(1) Subject to paragraph (2), rights under a contract for the sale of a commodity or property of any other description under which delivery is to be made at a future date and at a price agreed on when the contract is made.

(1A) Subject to paragraph (1D), futures—

(a) to which paragraph (1) does not apply;

(b) which relate to commodities;

(c) which may be settled physically; and

(d) to which paragraph 5 or 6 of Section C of Annex I to the markets in financial instruments directive applies.

(1B) Subject to paragraph (1D), futures and forwards—

(a) to which paragraph (1) does not apply;

(b) which relate to commodities;

(c) which may be settled physically;

(d) which in accordance with Article 38 of the Commission Regulation (the text of which is set out in in Part 2 of Schedule 2 are to be considered as having the characteristics of other derivative financial instruments and not being for commercial purposes; and

(e) to which paragraph 7 of Section C of Annex I to the markets in financial instruments directive applies.

(1C) Subject to paragraph (1D), futures—

(a) to which paragraph (1) does not apply;

(b) which may be settled physically; and

(c) to which paragraph 10 of Section C of Annex I to the markets in financial instruments directive (read with the Commission Regulation) applies.

(1D) Paragraph (1A), (1B) and (1C) only apply to futures or forwards in relation to which—

(a) an investment firm or credit institution is providing or performing investment services and activities on a professional basis,

(b) a management company is providing, in accordance with Article 5(3) of the UCITS directive, the investment service specified in paragraph 4 or 5 of Section A, or the ancillary service specified in paragraph 1 of Section B, of Annex I to the markets in financial instruments directive, or

(c) a market operator is providing the investment service specified in paragraph 8 of Section A of Annex I to the markets in financial instruments directive.

(1E) Expressions used in paragraphs (1A) to (1C) and in the markets in financial instruments directive have the same meaning as in that directive.

(2) There are excluded from paragraph (1) rights under any contract which is made for commercial and not investment purposes.

(3) A contract is to be regarded as made for investment purposes if it is made or traded on a recognised investment exchange, or is made otherwise than on a recognised investment exchange but is expressed to be as traded on such an exchange or on the same terms as those on which an equivalent contract would be made on such an exchange.

(4) A contract not falling within paragraph (3) is to be regarded as made for commercial purposes if under the terms of the contract delivery is to be made within seven days, unless it can be shown that there existed an understanding that (notwithstanding the express terms of the contract) delivery would not be made within seven days.

(5) The following are indications that a contract not falling within paragraph (3) or (4) is made for commercial purposes and the absence of them is an indication that it is made for investment purposes—

(a) one or more of the parties is a producer of the commodity or other property, or uses it in his business;

(b) the seller delivers or intends to deliver the property or the purchaser takes or intends to take delivery of it.

(6) It is an indication that a contract is made for commercial purposes that the prices, the lot, the delivery date or other terms are determined by the parties for the purposes of the particular contract and not by reference (or not solely by reference) to regularly published prices, to standard lots or delivery dates or to standard terms.

1056    The Financial Services and Markets Act 2000 (Regulated Activities) Order 2001

(7) The following are indications that a contract is made for investment purposes—

    (a) it is expressed to be as traded on an investment exchange;

    (b) performance of the contract is ensured by an investment exchange or a clearing house;

    (c) there are arrangements for the payment or provision of margin.

(8) For the purposes of paragraph (1), a price is to be taken to be agreed on when a contract is made—

    (a) notwithstanding that it is left to be determined by reference to the price at which a contract is to be entered into on a market or exchange or could be entered into at a time and place specified in the contract; or

    (b) in a case where the contract is expressed to be by reference to a standard lot and quality, notwithstanding that provision is made for a variation in the price to take account of any variation in quantity or quality on delivery.

## 85  Contracts for differences etc

(1) Subject to paragraph (2), rights under—

    (a) a contract for differences; or

    (b) any other contract the purpose or pretended purpose of which is to secure a profit or avoid a loss by reference to fluctuations in—

        (i) the value or price of property of any description; or

        (ii) an index or other factor designated for that purpose in the contract.

(2) There are excluded from paragraph (1)—

    (a) rights under a contract if the parties intend that the profit is to be secured or the loss is to be avoided by one or more of the parties taking delivery of any property to which the contract relates;

    (b) rights under a contract under which money is received by way of deposit on terms that any interest or other return to be paid on the sum deposited will be calculated by reference to fluctuations in an index or other factor;

    (c) rights under any contract under which—

        (i) money is received by the Director of Savings as deposits or otherwise in connection with the business of the National Savings Bank; or

        (ii) money is raised under the National Loans Act 1968 under the auspices of the Director of Savings or treated as so raised by virtue of section 11(3) of the National Debt Act 1972;

    (d) rights under a qualifying contract of insurance.

(3) Subject to paragraph (4), derivative instruments for the transfer of credit risk—

    (a) to which neither article 83 nor paragraph (1) applies; and

    (b) to which paragraph 8 of Section C of Annex I to the markets in financial instruments directive applies.

(4) Paragraph (3) only applies to derivatives in relation to which—

    (a) an investment firm or credit institution is providing or performing investment services and activities on a professional basis,

    (b) a management company is providing, in accordance with Article 5(3) of the UCITS directive, the investment service specified in paragraph 4 or 5 of Section A, or the ancillary service specified in paragraph 1 of Section B, of Annex I to the markets in financial instruments directive, or

    (c) a market operator is providing the investment service specified in paragraph 8 of Section A of Annex I to the markets in financial instruments directive.

(5) 'Derivative instruments for the transfer of credit risk' has the same meaning as in the markets in financial instruments directive.

## 86  Lloyd's syndicate capacity and syndicate membership

(1) The underwriting capacity of a Lloyd's syndicate.

(2) A person's membership (or prospective membership) of a Lloyd's syndicate.

## 87  Funeral plan contracts

Rights under a funeral plan contract.

## 88  Regulated mortgage contracts

Rights under a regulated mortgage contract.

## 88A  Regulated home reversion plans

Rights under a regulated home reversion pan.

## 88B  Regulated home purchase plan

Rights under a regulated home purchase plan.

## 89  Rights to or interests in investments

(1) Subject to paragraphs (2) to (4), any right to or interest in anything which is specified by any other provision of this Part (other than article 88, 88A or 88B).

(2) Paragraph (1) does not include interests under the trusts of an occupational pension scheme.

(3) Paragraph (1) does not include—

    (a) rights to or interests in a contract of insurance of the kind referred to in paragraph (1)(a) of article 60; or

    (b) interests under a trust of the kind referred to in paragraph (1)(b) of that article.

(4) Paragraph (1) does not include anything which is specified by any other provision of this Part.

# PART IV

# CONSEQUENTIAL PROVISIONS

*Regulated mortgage contracts: consequential provisions*

### 90  Consequential amendments of the Consumer Credit Act 1974

(1) The Consumer Credit Act 1974 is amended as follows.

(2) In section 16 (exempt agreements), after subsection (6B) insert—

'(6C) This Act does not regulate a consumer credit agreement if—

    (a) it is secured by a land mortgage; and

    (b) entering into that agreement as lender is a regulated activity for the purposes of the Financial Services and Markets Act 2000.

(6D) But section 126, and any other provision so far as it relates to section 126, applies to an agreement which would (but for subsection (6C)) be a regulated agreement.

(6E) Subsection (6C) must be read with—

    (a) section 22 of the Financial Services and Markets Act 2000 (regulated activities: power to specify classes of activity and categories of investment);

    (b) any order for the time being in force under that section; and

    (c) Schedule 2 to that Act.'.

(3) In section 43 (advertisements), after subsection (3) insert—

'(3A) An advertisement does not fall within subsection (1)(a) in so far as it is a communication of an invitation or inducement to engage in investment activity within the meaning of section 21 of the Financial Services and Markets Act 2000, other than an exempt generic communication.

(3B) An "exempt generic communication" is a communication to which subsection (1) of section 21 of the Financial Services and Markets Act 2000 does not apply, as a result of an order under subsection (5) of that section, because it does not identify a person as providing an investment or as carrying on an activity to which the communication relates.'.

(4) In section 52 (quotations), after subsection (2) insert—

'(3) In this section, "quotation" does not include—

    (a) any document which is a communication of an invitation or inducement to engage in investment activity within the meaning of section 21 of the Financial Services and Markets Act 2000; or

    (b) any document (other than one falling within paragraph (a)) provided by an authorised person (within the meaning of that Act) in connection with an agreement which would or might be an exempt agreement as a result of section 16(6C).'.

(5) In section 53 (duty to display information), after 'land' insert '(other than credit provided under an agreement which is an exempt agreement as a result of section 16(6C))'.

(6) In section 137 (extortionate credit bargains), in subsection (2)(a), after 'any agreement' insert '(other than an agreement which is an exempt agreement as a result of section 16(6C))'.

(7) In section 151 (advertisements for the purposes of ancillary credit business), after subsection (2) insert—

'(2A) An advertisement does not fall within subsection (1) or (2) in so far as it is a communication of an invitation or inducement to engage in investment activity within the meaning of section 21 of the Financial Services and Markets Act 2000, other than an exempt generic communication (as defined in section 43(3B)).'.

### 91  Consequential amendments of subordinate legislation under the Consumer Credit Act 1974

(1) In the Consumer Credit (Advertisements) Regulations 1989 , after paragraph (2) of regulation 9 (application of Regulations) insert—

'(3) These Regulations do not apply to any advertisement in so far as it is a communication of an invitation or inducement to engage in investment activity within the meaning of section 21 of the Financial Services and Markets Act 2000, other than an exempt generic communication.

(4) An "exempt generic communication" is a communication to which subsection (1) of section 21 of the Financial Services and Markets Act 2000 does not apply, as a result of an order under subsection

(5) of that section, because it does not identify a person as providing an investment or as carrying on an activity to which the communication relates.'.

(2) In the Consumer Credit (Content of Quotations) and Consumer Credit (Advertisements) (Amendment) Regulations 1999 , in the definition of 'quotation' in paragraph (1) of regulation 2 (interpretation of Part II)—

(a) omit 'or' at the end of sub-paragraph (c); and

(b) after sub-paragraph (d) insert—

'(e) any document which is a communication of an invitation or inducement to engage in investment activity within the meaning of section 21 of the Financial Services and Markets Act 2000; or

(f) any document (other than one falling within sub-paragraph (e)), provided by an authorised person (within the meaning of that Act) in connection with an agreement which would or might be an exempt agreement as a result of section 16(6C) of the Act.'.

# PART V

# UNAUTHORISED PERSONS CARRYING ON INSURANCE MEDIATION ACTIVITIES

### 92 Interpretation

In this Part—

'designated professional body' means a body which is for the time being designated by the Treasury under section 326 of the Act (designation of professional bodies);

'insurance mediation activity' means any regulated activity of the kind specified by article 21, 25(1) or (2), 39A or 53, or, so far as relevant to any of those articles, article 64, which is carried on in relation to a contract of insurance;

'the record' means the record maintained by the Authority under section 347 of the Act (public record of authorised persons etc.);

'recorded insurance intermediary' has the meaning given by article 93(4);

'a relevant member', in relation to a designated professional body, means a member (within the meaning of section 325(2) of the Act) of the profession in relation to which that designated professional body is established, or a person who is controlled or managed by one or more such members.

### 93 Duty to maintain a record of unauthorised persons carrying on insurance mediation activities

(1) Subject to articles 95 and 96, the Authority must include in the record every person who—

(a) as a result of information obtained by virtue of its rules or by virtue of a direction given, or requirement imposed, under section 51(3) of the Act (procedure for applications under Part IV), appears to the Authority to fall within paragraph (2); or

(b) as a result of information obtained by virtue of article 94, appears to the Authority to fall within paragraph (3).

(2) A person falls within this paragraph if he is, or has entered into a contract by virtue of which he will be, an appointed representative who carries on any insurance mediation activity.

(3) A person falls within this paragraph if—

(a) he is a relevant member of a designated professional body who carries on, or is proposing to carry on, any insurance mediation activity; and

(b) the general prohibition does not (or will not) apply to the carrying on of those activities by virtue of section 327 of the Act (exemption from the general prohibition).

(4) In this Part, 'recorded insurance intermediary' means a person who is included in the record by virtue of paragraph (1).

(5) The record must include—

(a) in the case of any recorded insurance intermediary, its address; and

(b) in the case of a recorded insurance intermediary which is not an individual, the name of the individuals who are responsible for the management of the business carried on by the intermediary, so far as it relates to insurance mediation activities.

### 94 Members of designated professional bodies

(1) A designated professional body must, by notice in writing, inform the Authority of—

(a) the name,

(b) the address, and

(c) in the case of a relevant member which is not an individual, the name of the individuals who are responsible for the management of the business carried on by the member, so far as it relates to insurance mediation activities,

of any relevant member who falls within paragraph (2).

(2) A relevant member of a designated professional body falls within this paragraph if, in accordance with the rules of that body, he carries on, or proposes to carry on any insurance mediation activity but does not have, and does not propose to apply for, Part IV permission on the basis that the general prohibition does not (or will not) apply to the carrying on of that activity by virtue of section 327 of the Act.

(3) A designated professional body must also, by notice in writing, inform the Authority of any change in relation to the matters specified in sub-paragraphs (a) to (c) of paragraph (1).

(4) A designated professional body must inform the Authority when a relevant member to whom paragraph (2) applies ceases, for whatever reason, to carry on insurance mediation activities.

(5) The Authority may give directions to a designated professional body as to the manner in which the information referred to in paragraphs (1), (3) and (4) must be provided.

## 95   Exclusion from record where not fit and proper to carry on insurance mediation activities

(1) If it appears to the Authority that a person who falls within article 93(2) (appointed representatives) ('AR') is not a fit and proper person to carry on insurance mediation activities, it may decide not to include him in the record or, if that person is already included in the record, to remove him from the record.

(2) Where the Authority proposes to make a determination under paragraph (1), it must give AR a warning notice.

(3) If the Authority makes a determination under paragraph (1), it must give AR a decision notice.

(4) If the Authority gives AR a decision notice under paragraph (3), AR may refer the matter to the Tribunal.

(5) The Authority may, on the application of AR, revoke a determination under paragraph (1).

(6) If the Authority decides to grant the application, it must give AR written notice of its decision.

(7) If the Authority proposes to refuse the application, it must give AR a warning notice.

(8) If the Authority decides to refuse the application, it must give AR a decision notice.

(9) If the Authority gives AR a decision notice under paragraph (8), AR may refer the matter to the Tribunal.

(10) Sections 393 and 394 of the Act (third party rights and access to Authority material) apply to a warning notice given in accordance with paragraph (2) or (7) and to a decision notice given in accordance with paragraph (3) or (8).

## 96   Exclusion from the record where Authority has exercised its powers under Part XX of the Act

(1) If a person who appears to the Authority to fall within article 93(3) (member of a designated professional body) falls within paragraph (2) or (3), the Authority must not include him in the record or, if that person is already included in the record, must remove him from the record.

(2) A person falls within this paragraph if, by virtue of a direction given by the Authority under section 328(1) of the Act (directions in relation to the general prohibition), section 327(1) of the Act does not apply in relation to the carrying on by him of any insurance mediation activity.

(3) A person falls within this paragraph if the Authority has made an order under section 329(2) of the Act (orders in relation to the general prohibition) disapplying section 327(1) of the Act in relation to the carrying on by him of any insurance mediation activity.

# PART VI

# MISCELLANEOUS

## 97   Disapplication of section 49(2) of the Act

In section 49 of the Act (persons connected with an applicant for Part 4 permission), after subsection (2) insert—

'(2A) But subsection (2) does not apply to the extent that the permission relates to—

(a) an insurance mediation activity (within the meaning given by paragraph 2(5) of Schedule 6); or

(b) a regulated activity involving a regulated mortgage contract.'.

# SCHEDULE 1

# CONTRACTS OF INSURANCE

## PART I

## CONTRACTS OF GENERAL INSURANCE

### 1 Accident

Contracts of insurance providing fixed pecuniary benefits or benefits in the nature of indemnity (or a combination of both) against risks of the person insured or, in the case of a contract made by virtue of section 140, 140A or 140B of the Local Government Act 1972 (or, in Scotland, section 86(1) of the Local Government (Scotland) Act 1973), a person for whose benefit the contract is made—

    (a)  sustaining injury as the result of an accident or of an accident of a specified class; or

    (b)  dying as a result of an accident or of an accident of a specified class; or

    (c)  becoming incapacitated in consequence of disease or of disease of a specified class,

including contracts relating to industrial injury and occupational disease but excluding contracts falling within paragraph 2 of Part I of, or paragraph IV of Part II of, this Schedule.

### 2 Sickness

Contracts of insurance providing fixed pecuniary benefits or benefits in the nature of indemnity (or a combination of both) against risks of loss to the persons insured attributable to sickness or infirmity but excluding contracts falling within paragraph IV of Part II of this Schedule.

### 3 Land vehicles

Contracts of insurance against loss of or damage to vehicles used on land, including motor vehicles but excluding railway rolling stock.

### 4 Railway rolling stock

Contract of insurance against loss of or damage to railway rolling stock.

### 5 Aircraft

Contracts of insurance upon aircraft or upon the machinery, tackle, furniture or equipment of aircraft.

### 6 Ships

Contracts of insurance upon vessels used on the sea or on inland water, or upon the machinery, tackle, furniture or equipment of such vessels.

### 7 Goods in transit

Contracts of insurance against loss of or damage to merchandise, baggage and all other goods in transit, irrespective of the form of transport.

### 8 Fire and natural forces

Contracts of insurance against loss of or damage to property (other than property to which paragraphs 3 to 7 relate) due to fire, explosion, storm, natural forces other than storm, nuclear energy or land subsidence.

### 9 Damage to property

Contracts of insurance against loss of or damage to property (other than property to which paragraphs 3 to 7 relate) due to hail or frost or any other event (such as theft) other than those mentioned in paragraph 8.

### 10 Motor vehicle liability

Contracts of insurance against damage arising out of or in connection with the use of motor vehicles on land, including third-party risks and carrier's liability.

### 11 Aircraft liability

Contracts of insurance against damage arising out of or in connection with the use of aircraft, including third-party risks and carrier's liability.

### 12 Liability of ships

Contracts of insurance against damage arising out of or in connection with the use of vessels on the sea or on inland water, including third party risks and carrier's liability.

### 13 General liability

Contracts of insurance against risks of the persons insured incurring liabilities to third parties, the risks in question not being risks to which paragraph 10, 11 or 12 relates.

### 14  Credit

Contracts of insurance against risks of loss to the persons insured arising from the insolvency of debtors of theirs or from the failure (otherwise than through insolvency) of debtors of theirs to pay their debts when due.

### 15  Suretyship

(1) Contracts of insurance against the risks of loss to the persons insured arising from their having to perform contracts of guarantee entered into by them.

(2) Fidelity bonds, performance bonds, administration bonds, bail bonds or customs bonds or similar contracts of guarantee, where these are—

- (a) effected or carried out by a person not carrying on a banking business;
- (b) not effected merely incidentally to some other business carried on by the person effecting them; and
- (c) effected in return for the payment of one or more premiums.

### 16  Miscellaneous financial loss

Contracts of insurance against any of the following risks, namely—

- (a) risks of loss to the persons insured attributable to interruptions of the carrying on of business carried on by them or to reduction of the scope of business so carried on;
- (b) risks of loss to the persons insured attributable to their incurring unforeseen expense (other than loss such as is covered by contracts falling within paragraph 18);
- (c) risks which do not fall within sub-paragraph (a) or (b) and which are not of a kind such that contracts of insurance against them fall within any other provision of this Schedule.

### 17  Legal expenses

Contracts of insurance against risks of loss to the persons insured attributable to their incurring legal expenses (including costs of litigation).

### 18  Assistance

Contracts of insurance providing either or both of the following benefits, namely—

- (a) assistance (whether in cash or in kind) for persons who get into difficulties while travelling, while away from home or while away from their permanent residence; or
- (b) assistance (whether in cash or in kind) for persons who get into difficulties otherwise than as mentioned in sub-paragraph (a).

# PART II

## CONTRACTS OF LONG-TERM INSURANCE

### I  Life and annuity

Contracts of insurance on human life or contracts to pay annuities on human life, but excluding (in each case) contracts within paragraph III.

### II  Marriage and birth

Contract of insurance to provide a sum on marriage or the formation of a civil partnership or on the birth of a child, being contracts expressed to be in effect for a period of more than one year.

### III  Linked long term

Contracts of insurance on human life or contracts to pay annuities on human life where the benefits are wholly or party to be determined by references to the value of, or the income from, property of any description (whether or not specified in the contracts) or by reference to fluctuations in, or in an index of, the value of property of any description (whether or not so specified).

### IV  Permanent health

Contracts of insurance providing specified benefits against risks of persons becoming incapacitated in consequence of sustaining injury as a result of an accident or of an accident of a specified class or of sickness or infirmity, being contracts that—

- (a) are expressed to be in effect for a period of not less than five years, or until the normal retirement age for the persons concerned, or without limit of time; and
- (b) either are not expressed to be terminable by the insurer, or are expressed to be so terminable only in special circumstances mentioned in the contract.

### V  Tontines

Tontines.

### VI  Capital redemption contracts

Capital redemption contracts, where effected or carried out by a person who does not carry on a banking business, and otherwise carries on a regulated activity of the kind specified by article 10(1) or (2).

### VII Pension fund management

(a) Pension fund management contracts, and

(b) pension fund management contracts which are combined with contracts of insurance covering either conservation of capital or payment of a minimum interest,

where effected or carried out by a person who does not carry on a banking business, and otherwise carries on a regulated activity of the kind specified by article 10(1) or (2).

### VIII Collective insurance etc.

Contracts of a kind referred to in article 1(2)(e) of the first life insurance directive.

### IX Social insurance

Contracts of a kind referred to in article 1(3) of the first life insurance directive.

# SCHEDULE 2

# SECTIONS A AND C OF ANNEX I TO THE MARKETS IN FINANCIAL INSTRUMENTS DIRECTIVE AND RELATED COMMUNITY SUBORDINATE LEGISLATION

## PART 1

## SECTION C OF ANNEX 1 TO THE MARKETS IN FINANCIAL INSTRUMENTS DIRECTIVE

### *Financial Instruments*

1  Transferable securities.

2  Money-market instruments.

3  Units in collective investment undertakings

4  Options, futures, swaps, forward rate agreements and any other derivative contracts relating to securities, currencies, interest rates or yields, or other derivatives instruments, financial indices or financial measures which may be settled physically or in cash;

5  Options, futures, swaps, forward rate agreements and any other derivative contracts relating to commodities that must be settled in cash or may be settled in cash at the option of one of the parties (otherwise than by reason of a default or other termination event);

6  Options, futures, swaps, and any other derivative contracts relating to commodities that can be physically settled provided that they are traded on a regulated market and/or an MTF;

7  Options, futures, swaps, forwards and any other derivative contracts relating to commodities, that can be physically settled not otherwise mentioned in C.6 and not being for commercial purposes, which have the characteristics of other derivative financial instruments, having regard to whether, inter alia, they are cleared and settled through recognised clearing houses or are subject to regular margin calls;

8  Derivative instruments for the transfer of credit risk;

9  Financial contracts for differences;

10  Options, futures, swaps, forward rate agreements and any other derivative contracts relating to climatic variables, freight rates, emission allowances or inflation rates or other official economic statistics that must be settled in cash or may be settled in cash at the option of one of the parties (otherwise than by reason of a default or other termination event), as well as any other derivative contracts relating to assets, rights, obligations, indices and measures not otherwise mentioned in this Section, which have the characteristics of other derivative financial instruments, having regard to whether, inter alia, they are traded on a regulated market or an MTF, are cleared and settled through recognised clearing houses or are subject to regular margin calls.

## PART 2

## CHAPTER VI OF THE COMMISSION REGULATION

### *Derivative financial instruments*

### *Article 38  Characteristics of other derivative financial instruments*

1  For the purposes of Section C(7) of Annex I to Directive 2004/39/EC, a contract which is not a spot contract within the meaning of paragraph 2 of this Article and which is not covered by paragraph 4 shall be considered as having the characteristics of other derivative financial instruments and not being for commercial purposes if it satisfies the following conditions:

(a) it meets one of the following sets of criteria:

    (i) it is traded on a third country trading facility that performs a similar function to a regulated market or an MTF;

    (ii) it is expressly stated to be traded on, or is subject to the rules of, a regulated market, an MTF or such a third country trading facility;

    (iii) it is expressly stated to be equivalent to a contract traded on a regulated market, MTF or such a third country trading facility;

(b) it is cleared by a clearing house or other entity carrying out the same functions as a central counterparty, or there are arrangements for the payment or provision of margin in relation to the contract;

(c) it is standardised so that, in particular, the price, the lot, the delivery date or other terms are determined principally by reference to regularly published prices, standard lots or standard delivery dates.

**2**  A spot contract for the purposes of paragraph 1 means a contract for the sale of a commodity, asset or right, under the terms of which delivery is scheduled to be made within the longer of the following periods:

(a) two trading days;

(b) the period generally accepted in the market for that commodity, asset or right as the standard delivery period.

However, a contract is not a spot contract if, irrespective of its explicit terms, there is an understanding between the parties to the contract that delivery of the underlying is to be postponed and not to be performed within the period mentioned in the first subparagraph.

**3**  For the purposes of Section C(10) of Annex I to Directive 2004/39/EC, a derivative contract relating to an underlying referred to in that Section or in Article 39 shall be considered to have the characteristics of other derivative financial instruments if one of the following conditions is satisfied:

(a) that contract is settled in cash or may be settled in cash at the option of one or more of the parties, otherwise than by reason of a default or other termination event;

(b) that contract is traded on a regulated market or an MTF;

(c) the conditions laid down in paragraph 1 are satisfied in relation to that contract.

**4**  A contract shall be considered to be for commercial purposes for the purposes of Section C(7) of Annex I to Directive 2004/39/EC, and as not having the characteristics of other derivative financial instruments for the purposes of Sections C(7) and (10) of that Annex, if it is entered into with or by an operator or administrator of an energy transmission grid, energy balancing mechanism or pipeline network, and it is necessary to keep in balance the supplies and uses of energy at a given time.

### Article 39   Derivatives within Section C(10) of Annex I to Directive 2004/39/EC

In addition to derivative contracts of a kind referred to in Section C(10) of Annex I to Directive 2004/39/EC, a derivative contract relating to any of the following shall fall within that Section if it meets the criteria set out in that Section and in Article 38(3):

(a) telecommunications bandwidth;

(b) commodity storage capacity;

(c) transmission or transportation capacity relating to commodities, whether cable, pipeline or other means;

(d) an allowance, credit, permit, right or similar asset which is directly linked to the supply, distribution or consumption of energy derived from renewable resources;

(e) a geological, environmental or other physical variable;

(f) any other asset or right of a fungible nature, other than a right to receive a service, that is capable of being transferred;

(g) an index or measure related to the price or value of, or volume of transactions in any asset, right, service or obligation.

# PART 3

## SECTION A OF ANNEX I TO THE MARKETS IN FINANCIAL INSTRUMENTS DIRECTIVE

### Investment services and activities

**1**  Reception and transmission of orders in relation to one or more financial instruments.

**2**  Execution of orders on behalf of clients.

**3**  Dealing on own account.

**4**  Portfolio management.

**5**  Investment advice.

**6**  Underwriting of financial instruments and/or placing of financial instruments on a firm commitment basis.

7 Placing of financial instruments without a firm commitment basis.

8 Operation of Multilateral Trading Facilities.

# PART 4

## ARTICLE 52 OF COMMISSION DIRECTIVE 2006/73/EC

### *Article 52  Investment advice*

For the purposes of the definition of 'investment advice' in Article 4(1)(4) of Directive 2004/39/EC, a personal recommendation is a recommendation that is made to a person in his capacity as an investor or potential investor, or in his capacity as an agent for an investor or potential investor.

That recommendation must be presented as suitable for that person, or must be based on a consideration of the circumstances of that person, and must constitute a recommendation to take one of the following sets of steps:

(a) to buy, sell, subscribe for, exchange, redeem, hold or underwrite a particular financial instrument;

(b) to exercise or not to exercise any right conferred by a particular financial instrument to buy, sell, subscribe for, exchange, or redeem a financial instrument.

A recommendation is not a personal recommendation if it is issued exclusively through distribution channels or to the public.

# SCHEDULE 3

## ARTICLE 2 OF THE MARKETS IN FINANCIAL INSTRUMENTS DIRECTIVE

### *Article 2  Exemptions*

1 This Directive shall not apply to:

(a) insurance undertakings as defined in Article 1 of Directive 73/239/EEC or assurance undertakings as defined in Article 1 of Directive 2002/83/EC or undertakings carrying on the reinsurance and retrocession activities referred to in Directive 64/225/EEC;

(b) persons which provide investment services exclusively for their parent undertakings, for their subsidiaries or for other subsidiaries of their parent undertakings;

(c) persons providing an investment service where that service is provided in an incidental manner in the course of a professional activity and that activity is regulated by legal or regulatory provisions or a code of ethics governing the profession which do not exclude the provision of that service;

(d) persons who do not provide any investment services or activities other than dealing on own account unless they are market makers or deal on own account outside a regulated market or an MTF on an organised, frequent and systematic basis by providing a system accessible to third parties in order to engage in dealings with them;

(e) persons which provide investment services consisting exclusively in the administration of employee-participation schemes;

(f) persons which provide investment services which only involve both administration of employee-participation schemes and the provision of investment services exclusively for their parent undertakings, for their subsidiaries or for other subsidiaries of their parent undertakings;

(g) the members of the European System of Central Banks and other national bodies performing similar functions and other public bodies charged with or intervening in the management of the public debt;

(h) collective investment undertakings and pension funds whether coordinated at Community level or not and the depositaries and managers of such undertakings;

(i) persons dealing on own account in financial instruments, or providing investment services in commodity derivatives or derivative contracts included in Annex I, Section C10 to the clients of their main business, provided this is an ancillary activity to their main business, when considered on a group basis, and that main business is not the provision of investment services within the meaning of this Directive or banking services under Directive 2000/12/EC;

(j) persons providing investment advice in the course of providing another professional activity not covered by this Directive provided that the provision of such advice is not specifically remunerated;

(k) persons whose main business consists of dealing on own account in commodities and/or commodity derivatives. This exception shall not apply where the persons that deal on own account in commodities and/or commodity derivatives are part of a group the main business of which is the provision of other investment services within the meaning of this Directive or banking services under Directive 2000/12/EC;

(l) firms which provide investment services and/or perform investment activities consisting exclusively in dealing on own account on markets in financial futures or options or other derivatives and on cash markets for the sole purpose of hedging positions on derivatives markets or which deal for the accounts of other members of those markets or make prices for them and which are guaranteed by clearing members of the same markets, where responsibility for ensuring the performance of contracts entered into by such firms is assumed by clearing members of the same markets;

(m) associations set up by Danish and Finnish pensions funds with the sole aim of managing the assets of pension funds that are members of those associations;

(n) 'agenti di cambio' whose activities and functions are governed by Article 201 of Italian Legislative Decree No 58 of 24 February 1998.

2   The rights conferred by this Directive shall not extend to the provision of services as counterparty in transactions carried out by public bodies dealing with public debt or by members of the European System of Central Banks performing their tasks as provided for by the Treaty and the Statute of the European System of Central Banks and of the European Central Bank or performing equivalent functions under national provisions.

3   In order to take account of developments on financial markets, and to ensure the uniform application of this Directive, the Commission, acting in accordance with the procedure referred to in Article 64(2), may, in respect of exemptions (c), (i) and (k) define the criteria for determining when an activity is to be considered as ancillary to the main business on a group level as well as for determining when an activity is provided in an incidental manner.

# SCHEDULE 4

# RELEVANT TEXT OF THE INSURANCE MEDIATION DIRECTIVE

## PART I

### ARTICLE 1.2

This Directive shall not apply to persons providing mediation services for insurance contracts if all the following conditions are met:

(a) the insurance contract only requires knowledge of the insurance cover that is provided;
(b) the insurance contract is not a life assurance contract;
(c) the insurance contract does not cover any liability risks;
(d) the principal professional activity of the person is other than insurance mediation;
(e) the insurance is complementary to the product or service supplied by any provider, where such insurance covers:
  (i) the risk of breakdown, loss of or damage to goods supplied by that provider; or
  (ii) damage to or loss of baggage and other risks linked to the travel booked with that provider, even if the insurance covers life assurance or liability risks, provided that the cover is ancillary to the main cover for the risks linked to that travel;
(f) the amount of the annual premium does not exceed EUR 500 and the total duration of the insurance contract, including any renewals, does not exceed five years.

## PART II

### ARTICLE 2.3

'Insurance mediation' means the activities of introducing, proposing or carrying out other work preparatory to the conclusion of contracts of insurance, or of concluding such contracts, or of assisting in the administration and performance of such contracts, in particular in the event of a claim.

These activities when undertaken by an insurance undertaking or an employee of an insurance undertaking who is acting under the responsibility of the insurance undertaking shall not be considered as insurance mediation.

The provision of information on an incidental basis in the context of another professional activity provided that the purpose of that activity is not to assist the customer in concluding or performing an insurance contract, the management of claims of an insurance undertaking on a professional basis, and loss adjusting and expert appraisal of claims shall also not be considered as insurance mediation.

## PART III

## ARTICLE 2.4

'Reinsurance mediation' means the activities of introducing, proposing or carrying out other work preparatory to the conclusion of contracts of reinsurance, or of concluding such contracts, or of assisting in the administration and performance of such contracts, in particular in the event of a claim.

These activities when undertaken by a reinsurance undertaking or an employee of a reinsurance undertaking who is acting under the responsibility of the reinsurance undertaking are not considered as reinsurance mediation.

The provision of information on an incidental basis in the context of another professional activity provided that the purpose of that activity is not to assist the customer in concluding or performing a reinsurance contract, the management of claims of a reinsurance undertaking on a professional basis, and loss adjusting and expert appraisal of claims shall also not be considered as reinsurance mediation.

# The Financial Services and Markets Act 2000 (Professions) (Non-Exempt Activities) Order 2001

(2001 No. 1227)

*Whereas:*

*(1) This Order contains the first provision to be made in exercise of the power conferred by section 327(6) of the Financial Services and Markets Act 2000 ;*

*(2) In accordance with section 429(6) and (7) of that Act, a draft of this Order has been laid before, and approved by a resolution of, each House of Parliament;*

*Now, therefore, the Treasury, in exercise of the powers conferred on them by sections 327(6) and 428(3) of that Act, hereby make the following Order:-*

### Citation and commencement

**1** (1) This Order may be cited as the Financial Services and Markets Act 2000 (Professions) (Non-Exempt Activities) Order 2001.

(2) Subject to paragraph (3), this Order comes into force on the day on which section 19 of the Act comes into force.

(3) This Order comes into force—

(a) for the purposes of article 4(g), on 1st January 2002; and

(b) for the purposes of article 6A, on such day as the Treasury may specify.

(4) Any day specified under paragraph (3)(b) must be caused to be notified in the London, Edinburgh and Belfast Gazettes published not later than one week before that day.

### Interpretation

**2** (1) In this Order—

'the Act' means the Financial Services and Markets Act 2000;

'contract of insurance' has the meaning given by article 3(1) of the Regulated Activities Order;

'contractually based investment' has the meaning given by article 3(1) of the Regulated Activities Order;

'home purchase provider' has the meaning given by article 63F(3) of the Regulated Activities Order;

'home purchaser' has the meaning given by article 63F of the Regulated Activities Order;

'occupational pension scheme' and 'personal pension scheme' have the meaning given by section 1 of the Pension Schemes Act 1993 ;

'plan provider' has the meaning given by paragraph (3) of article 63B of the Regulated Activities Order, read with paragraphs (7) and (8) of that article;

'record of insurance intermediaries' means the record maintained bt the Authority under section 347 of the Act (the public record) by virtue of article 93 of the Regulated Activities Order (recorded insurance intermediaries);

'the Regulated Activities Order' means the Financial Services and Markets Act 2000 (Regulated Activities) Order 2001 ;

'regulated home purchase plan' has the meaning given by article 63F(3) of the Regulated Activities Order;

'regulated home reversion plan' has the meaning given by article 63B(3) of the Regulated Activities Order;

'regulated mortgage contract' has the meaning given by article 61 of the Regulated Activities Order;

'relevant investment' has the meaning given by article 3(1) of the Regulated Activities Order

'reversion seller' has the meaning given by article 63B(3) of the Regulated Activities Order;

'security' has the meaning given by article 3(1) of the Regulated Activities Order;

'syndicate' has the meaning given by article 3(1) of the Regulated Activities Order.

(2) For the purposes of this Order, a person is a member of a personal pension scheme if he is a person to or in respect of whom benefits are or may become payable under the scheme.

## Activities to which exemption from the general prohibition does not apply

**3** The activities in articles 4 to 8 are specified for the purposes of section 327(6) of the Act.

**4** An activity of the kind specified by any of the following provisions of the Regulated Activities Order—

- (a) article 5 (accepting deposits);
- (aa) article 9B (issuing electronic money);
- (b) article 10 (effecting and carrying out contracts of insurance);
- (c) article 14 (dealing in investments as principal);
- (d) article 51 (establishing etc. a collective investment scheme);
- (e) article 52 (establishing etc. a [...] pension scheme);
- (ea) article 52B (providing basic stakeholder products)
- (f) article 57 (managing the underwriting capacity of a Lloyd's syndicate);
- (g) article 59 (funeral plan contracts);
- (h) [...]

**4A** An activity of the kind specified by article 21 or 25 of the Regulated Activities order (dealing in investments as agent or arranging deals in investments) in so far as it—

- (a) relates to a transaction for the sale or purchase of rights under a contract of insurance; and
- (b) is carried on by a person who is not included in the record of insurance intermediaries.

**5** (1) An activity of the kind specified by article 37 of the Regulated Activities Order (managing investments) in so far as it consists of buying or subscribing for a security or contractually based investment.

(2) Paragraph (1) does not apply—

- (a) if all routine or day to day decisions, so far as relating to that activity, are taken by an authorised person with permission to carry on that activity or by a person who is an exempt person in relation to such an activity; or
- (b) to an activity undertaken in accordance with the advice of an authorised person with permission to give advice in relation to such an activity or a person who is an exempt person in relation to the giving of such advice.

**5A** An activity of the kind specified by article 39A of the Regulated Activities Order (assisting in the administration and performance of a contract of insurance) if it is carried on by a person who is not included in the record of insurance intermediaries.

**6** (1) An activity of the kind specified by article 53 of the Regulated Activities Order (advising on investments) where the advice in question falls within paragraph (2), (3) or (5).

(2) Subject to paragraph (4), advice falls within this paragraph in so far as—

- (a) it is given to an individual (or his agent) other than where the individual acts—
  - (i) in connection with the carrying on of a business of any kind by himself or by an undertaking of which he is, or would become as a result of the transaction to which the advice relates, a controller; or
  - (ii) in his capacity as a trustee of an occupational pension scheme;
- (b) it consists of a recommendation to buy or subscribe for a particular security or contractually based investment; and
- (c) the transaction to which the advice relates would be made—
  - (i) with a person acting in the course of carrying on the business of buying, selling, subscribing for or underwriting the security or contractually based investment, whether as principal or agent;
  - (ii) on an investment exchange or any other market to which that investment is admitted for dealing; or
  - (iii) in response to an invitation to subscribe for such an investment which is, or is to be, admitted for dealing on an investment exchange or any other market.

(3) Subject to paragraph (4), advice falls within this paragraph in so far as it consists of a recommendation to a member of a personal pension scheme (or his agent) to dispose of any rights or interests which the member has in or under the scheme.

(4) Advice does not fall within paragraph (2) or (3) if it endorses a corresponding recommendation given to the individual (or, as the case may be, the member) by an authorised person with permission to give advice in relation to the proposed transaction or a person who is an exempt person in relation to the giving of such advice.

(5) Advice falls within this paragraph in so far as—

- (a) it relates to a transaction for the sale or purchase of rights under a contract of insurance; and

(b) it is given by a person who is not included in the record of insurance intermediaries.

**6A**   (1) An activity of the kind specified by article 53A of the Regulated Activities Order (advising on regulated mortgage contracts) where the advice in question falls within paragraph (2).

(2) Subject to paragraph (3), advice falls within this paragraph in so far as—

(a) it consists of a recommendation, given to an individual, to enter as borrower into a regulated mortgage contract with a particular person; and

(b) in entering into a regulated mortgage contract that person would be carrying on an activity of the kind specified by article 61(1) of the Regulated Activities Order (regulated mortgage contracts).

(3) Advice does not fall within paragraph (2) if it endorses a corresponding recommendation given to the individual by an authorised person with permission to carry on an activity of the kind specified by article 53A of the Regulated Activities Order or a person who is an exempt person in relation to an activity of that kind.

**6B**   (1) An activity of the kind specified by article 61(1) or (2) of the Regulated Activities Order (regulated mortgage contracts).

(2) Paragraph (1) does not apply to an activity carried on by a person in his capacity as a trustee or personal representative where the borrower under the regulated mortgage contract in question is a beneficiary under the trust, will or intestacy.

**6C**   (1) An activity of the kind specified by article 53B of the Regulated Activities Order (advising on regulated home reversion plans) where the advice in question falls within paragraph (2).

(2) Subject to paragraph (3), advice falls within this paragraph in so far as—

(a) it consists of a recommendation, given to an individual to enter as reversion seller or plan provider into a regulated home reversion plan with a particular person; and

(b) in entering into a regulated home reversion plan that person would be carrying on an activity of the kind specified by article 63B(1) of the Regulated Activities Order (regulated home reversion plans).

(3) Advice does not fall within paragraph (2) if it endorses a corresponding recommendation given to the individual by an authorised person with permission to carry on an activity of the kind specified by article 53B of the Regulated Activities Order or a person who is an exempt person in relation to an activity of that kind.

**6D**   (1) An activity of the kind specified by article 63B(1) or (2) of the Regulated Activities Order (regulated home reversion plans).

(2) Paragraph (1) does not apply to an activity carried on by a person in his capacity as a trustee or personal representative where the reversion seller under the regulated home reversion plan in question is a beneficiary under the trust, will or intestacy.

**6E**   (1) An activity of the kind specified by article 53C of the Regulated Activities Order (advising on regulated home purchase plans) where the advice in question falls within paragraph (2).

(2) Subject to paragraph (3), advice falls within this paragraph in so far as—

(a) it consists of a recommendation, given to an individual to enter as home purchaser into a regulated home purchase plan with a particular person; and

(b) in entering into a regulated home purchase plan that person would be carrying on an activity of the kind specified by article 63F(1) of the Regulated Activities Order (regulated home purchase plans).

(3) Advice does not fall within paragraph (2) if it endorses a corresponding recommendation given to the individual by an authorised person with permission to carry on an activity of the kind specified by article 53C of the Regulated Activities Order or a person who is an exempt person in relation to an activity of that kind.

**6F**   (1) An activity of the kind specified by article 63F(1) or (2) of the Regulated Activities Order (regulated home purchase plans).

(2) Paragraph (1) does not apply to an activity carried on by a person in his capacity as a trustee or personal representative where the home purchaser under the regulated home purchase plan in question is a beneficiary under the trust, will or intestacy.

**7**   (1) Advising a person to become a member of a particular Lloyd's syndicate.

(2) Paragraph (1) does not apply to advice which endorses that of an authorised person with permission to give such advice or a person who is an exempt person in relation to the giving of such advice.

**8**   Agreeing to carry on any of the activities mentioned in articles 4 to 7 other than the activities mentioned in article 4(a), (aa), (b), (d) and (e).

# Sale of Goods

## Sale of Goods Act 1979

(c. 54)

*An Act to consolidate the law relating to the sale of goods.*          [6th December 1979]

## PART I

## CONTRACTS TO WHICH ACT APPLIES

**1  Contracts to which Act applies**

(1) This Act applies to contracts of sale of goods made on or after (but not to those made before) 1 January 1894.

(2) In relation to contracts made on certain dates, this Act applies subject to the modification of certain of its sections as mentioned in Schedule 1 below.

(3) Any such modification is indicated in the section concerned by a reference to Schedule 1 below.

(4) Accordingly, where a section does not contain such a reference, this Act applies in relation to the contract concerned without such modification of the section.

## PART II

## FORMATION OF THE CONTRACT

### *Contract of sale*

**2  Contract of sale**

(1) A contract of sale of goods is a contract by which the seller transfers or agrees to transfer the property in goods to the buyer for a money consideration, called the price.

(2) There may be a contract of sale between one part owner and another.

(3) A contract of sale may be absolute or conditional.

(4) Where under a contract of sale the property in the goods is transferred from the seller to the buyer the contract is called a sale.

(5) Where under a contract of sale the transfer of the property in the goods is to take place at a future time or subject to some condition later to be fulfilled the contract is called an agreement to sell.

(6) An agreement to sell becomes a sale when the time elapses or the conditions are fulfilled subject to which the property in the goods is to be transferred.

**3  Capacity to buy and sell**

(1) Capacity to buy and sell is regulated by the general law concerning capacity to contract and to transfer and acquire property.

(2) Where necessaries are sold and delivered to a minor or to a person who by reason of [...] drunkenness is incompetent to contract, he must pay a reasonable price for them.

(3) In subsection (2) above 'necessaries' means goods suitable to the condition in life of the minor or other person concerned and to his actual requirements at the time of the sale and delivery.

### *Formalities of contract*

**4  How contract of sale is made**

(1) Subject to this and any other Act, a contract of sale may be made in writing (either with or without seal), or by word of mouth, or partly in writing and partly by word of mouth, or may be implied from the conduct of the parties.

(2) Nothing in this section affects the law relating to corporations.

*Subject matter of contract*

### 5 Existing or future goods

(1) The goods which form the subject of a contract of sale may be either existing goods, owned or possessed by the seller, or goods to be manufactured or acquired by him after the making of the contract of sale, in this Act called future goods.

(2) There may be a contract for the sale of goods the acquisition of which by the seller depends on a contingency which may or may not happen.

(3) Where by a contract of sale the seller purports to effect a present sale of future goods, the contract operates as an agreement to sell the goods.

### 6 Goods which have perished

Where there is a contract for the sale of specific goods, and the goods without the knowledge of the seller have perished at the time when the contract is made, the contract is void.

### 7 Goods perishing before sale but after agreement to sell

Where there is an agreement to sell specific goods and subsequently the goods, without any fault on the part of the seller or buyer, perish before the risk passes to the buyer, the agreement is avoided.

*The price*

### 8 Ascertainment of price

(1) The price in a contract of sale may be fixed by the contract, or may be left to be fixed in a manner agreed by the contract, or may be determined by the course of dealing between the parties.

(2) Where the price is not determined as mentioned in sub-section (1) above the buyer must pay a reasonable price.

(3) What is a reasonable price is a question of fact dependent on the circumstances of each particular case.

### 9 Agreement to sell at valuation

(1) Where there is an agreement to sell goods on the terms that the price is to be fixed by the valuation of a third party, and he cannot or does not make the valuation, the agreement is avoided; but if the goods or any part of them have been delivered to and appropriated by the buyer he must pay a reasonable price for them.

(2) Where the third party is prevented from making the valuation by the fault of the seller or buyer, the party not at fault may maintain an action for damages against the party at fault.

*Implied terms etc*

### 10 Stipulations about time

(1) Unless a different intention appears from the terms of the contract, stipulations as to time of payment are not of the essence of a contract of sale.

(2) Whether any other stipulation as to time is or is not of the essence of the contract depends on the terms of the contract.

(3) In a contract of sale 'month' prima facie means calendar month.

### 11 When condition to be treated as warranty

(1) This section does not apply to Scotland.

(2) Where a contract of sale is subject to a condition to be fulfilled by the seller, the buyer may waive the condition, or may elect to treat the breach of the condition as a breach of warranty and not as a ground for treating the contract as repudiated.

(3) Whether a stipulation in a contract of sale is a condition, the breach of which may give rise to a right to treat the contract as repudiated, or a warranty, the breach of which may give rise to a claim for damages but not to a right to reject the goods and treat the contract as repudiated, depends in each case on the construction of the contract; and a stipulation may be a condition, though called a warranty in the contract.

(4) Subject to section 35A below where a contract of sale is not severable and the buyer has accepted the goods or part of them, the breach of a condition to be fulfilled by the seller can only be treated as a breach of warranty, and not as a ground for rejecting the goods and treating the contract as repudiated, unless there is an express or implied term of the contract to that effect.

(5) [...]

(6) Nothing in this section affects a condition or warranty whose fulfilment is excused by law by reason of impossibility or otherwise.

(7) Paragraph 2 of Schedule 1 below applies in relation to a contract made before 22 April 1967 or (in the application of this Act to Northern Ireland) 28 July 1967.

### 12 Implied terms about title, etc

(1) In a contract of sale, other than one to which subsection (3) below applies, there is an implied term on the part of the seller that in the case of a sale he has a right to sell the goods, and in the case of an agreement to sell he will have such a right at the time when the property is to pass.

(2) In a contract of sale, other than one to which subsection (3) below applies, there is also an implied term that—

    (a) the goods are free, and will remain free until the time when the property is to pass, from any charge or encumbrance not disclosed or known to the buyer before the contract is made, and

    (b) the buyer will enjoy quiet possession of the goods except so far as it may be disturbed by the owner or other person entitled to the benefit of any charge or encumbrance so disclosed or known.

(3) This subsection applies to a contract of sale in the case of which there appears from the contract or is to be inferred from its circumstances an intention that the seller should transfer only such title as he or a third person may have.

(4) In a contract to which subsection (3) above applies there is an implied term that all charges or encumbrances known to the seller and not known to the buyer have been disclosed to the buyer before the contract is made.

(5) In a contract to which subsection (3) above applies there is also an implied term that none of the following will disturb the buyer's quiet possession of the goods, namely—

    (a) the seller;

    (b) in a case where the parties to the contract intend that the seller should transfer only such title as a third person may have, that person;

    (c) anyone claiming through or under the seller or that third person otherwise than under a charge or encumbrance disclosed or known to the buyer before the contract is made.

(5A) As regards England and Wales and Northern Ireland, the term implied by subsection (1) above is a condition and the terms implied by subsections (2), (4) and (5) above are warranties.

(6) Paragraph 3 of Schedule 1 below applies in relation to a contract made before 18 May 1973.

## 13   Sale by description

(1) Where there is a contract for the sale of goods by description, there is an implied term that the goods will correspond with the description.

(1A) As regards England and Wales and Northern Ireland, the term implied by subsection (1) above is a condition.

(2) If the sale is by sample as well as by description it is not sufficient that the bulk of the goods corresponds with the sample if the goods do not also correspond with the description.

(3) A sale of goods is not prevented from being a sale by description by reason only that, being exposed for sale or hire, they are selected by the buyer.

(4) Paragraph 4 of Schedule 1 below applies in relation to a contract made before 18 May 1973.

## 14   Implied terms about quality or fitness

(1) Except as provided by this section and section 15 below and subject to any other enactment, there is no implied term about the quality or fitness for any particular purpose of goods supplied under a contract of sale.

(2) Where the seller sells goods in the course of a business, there is an implied term that the goods supplied under the contract are of satisfactory quality.

(2A) For the purposes of this Act, goods are of satisfactory quality if they meet the standard that a reasonable person would regard as satisfactory, taking account of any description of the goods, the price (if relevant) and all the other relevant circumstances.

(2B) For the purposes of this Act, the quality of goods includes their state and condition and the following (among others) are in appropriate cases aspects of the quality of goods—

    (a) fitness for all the purposes for which goods of the kind in question are commonly supplied,

    (b) appearance and finish,

    (c) freedom from minor defects,

    (d) safety, and

    (e) durability.

(2C) The term implied by subsection (2) above does not extend to any matter making the quality of goods unsatisfactory—

    (a) which is specifically drawn to the buyer's attention before the contract is made,

    (b) where the buyer examines the goods before the contract is made, which that examination ought to reveal, or

    (c) in the case of a contract for sale by sample, which would have been apparent on a reasonable examination of the sample.

(2D) If the buyer deals as consumer or, in Scotland, if a contract of sale is a consumer contract, the relevant circumstances mentioned in subsection (2A) above include any public statements on the specific characteristics of the goods made about them by the seller, the producer or his representative, particularly in advertising or on labelling.

(2E) A public statement is not by virtue of subsection (2D) above a relevant circumstance for the purposes of subsection (2A) above in the case of a contract of sale, if the seller shows that—

(a) at the time the contract was made, he was not, and could not reasonably have been, aware of the statement,

(b) before the contract was made, the statement had been withdrawn in public or, to the extent that it contained anything which was incorrect or misleading, it had been corrected in public, or

(c) the decision to buy the goods could not have been influenced by the statement.

(2F) Subsections (2D) and (2E) above do not prevent any public statement from being a relevant circumstance for the purposes of subsection (2A) above (whether or not the buyer deals as consumer or, in Scotland, whether or not the contract of sale is a consumer contract) if the statement would have been such a circumstance apart from those subsections.

(3) Where the seller sells goods in the course of a business and the buyer, expressly or by implication, makes known—

(a) to the seller, or

(b) where the purchase price or part of it is payable by instalments and the goods were previously sold by a credit-broker to the seller, to that credit-broker,

any particular purpose for which the goods are being bought, there is an implied term that the goods supplied under the contract are reasonably fit for that purpose, whether or not that is a purpose for which such goods are commonly supplied, except where the circumstances show that the buyer does not rely, or that it is unreasonable for him to rely, on the skill or judgment of the seller or credit-broker.

(4) An implied term about quality or fitness for a particular purpose may be annexed to a contract of sale by usage.

(5) The preceding provisions of this section apply to a sale by a person who in the course of a business is acting as agent for another as they apply to a sale by a principal in the course of a business, except where that other is not selling in the course of a business and either the buyer knows that fact or reasonable steps are taken to bring it to the notice of the buyer before the contract is made.

(6) As regards England and Wales and Northern Ireland, the terms implied by subsections (2) and (3) above are conditions.

(7) Paragraph 5 of Schedule 1 below applies in relation to a contract made on or after 18 May 1973 and before the appointed day, and paragraph 6 in relation to one made before 18 May 1973.

(8) In subsection (7) above and paragraph 5 of Schedule 1 below references to the appointed day are to the day appointed for the purposes of those provisions by an order of the Secretary of State made by statutory instrument.

### *Sale by sample*

### 15   Sale by sample

(1) A contract of sale is a contract for sale by sample where there is an express or implied term to that effect in the contract.

(2) In the case of a contract for sale by sample there is an implied term—

(a) that the bulk will correspond with the sample in quality;

(b) [...]

(c) that the goods will be free from any defect, making their quality unsatisfactory, which would not be apparent on reasonable examination of the sample.

(3) As regards England and Wales and Northern Ireland, the term implied by subsection (2) above is a condition.

(4) Paragraph 7 of Schedule 1 below applies in relation to a contract made before 18 May 1973.

### *Miscellaneous*

### 15A   Modification of remedies for breach of condition in non-consumer cases

(1) Where in the case of a contract of sale—

(a) the buyer would, apart from this subsection, have the right to reject goods by reason of a breach on the part of the seller of a term implied by section 13, 14 or 15 above, but

(b) the breach is so slight that it would be unreasonable for him to reject them,

then, if the buyer does not deal as consumer, the breach is not to be treated as a breach of condition but may be treated as a breach of warranty.

(2) This section applies unless a contrary intention appears in, or is to be implied from, the contract.

(3) It is for the seller to show that a breach fell within subsection (1)(b) above.

(4) This section does not apply to Scotland.

### 15B   Remedies for breach of contract as respects Scotland

(1) Where in a contract of sale the seller is in breach of any term of the contract (express or implied), the buyer shall be entitled—

(a) to claim damages, and

(b) if the breach is material, to reject any goods delivered under the contract and treat it as repudiated.

(2) Where a contract of sale is a consumer contract, then, for the purposes of subsection (1)(b) above, breach by the seller of any term (express or implied)—

(a) as to the quality of the goods or their fitness for a purpose,

(b) if the goods are, or are to be, sold by description, that the goods will correspond with the description,

(c) if the goods are, or are to be, sold by reference to a sample, that the bulk will correspond with the sample in quality,

shall be deemed to be a material breach.

(3) This section applies to Scotland only.

# PART III

# EFFECTS OF THE CONTRACT

*Transfer of property as between seller and buyer*

### 16  Goods must be ascertained

Subject to section 20A below where there is a contract for the sale of unascertained goods no property in the goods is transferred to the buyer unless and until the goods are ascertained.

### 17  Property passes when intended to pass

(1) Where there is a contract for the sale of specific or ascertained goods the property in them is transferred to the buyer at such time as the parties to the contract intend it to be transferred.

(2) For the purpose of ascertaining the intention of the parties regard shall be had to the terms of the contract, the conduct of the parties and the circumstances of the case.

### 18  Rules for ascertaining intention

Unless a different intention appears, the following are rules for ascertaining the intention of the parties as to the time at which the property in the goods is to pass to the buyer.

*Rule 1.* —Where there is an unconditional contract for the sale of specific goods in a deliverable state the property in the goods passes to the buyer when the contract is made, and it is immaterial whether the time of payment or the time of delivery, or both, be postponed.

*Rule 2.* —Where there is a contract for the sale of specific goods and the seller is bound to do something to the goods for the purpose of putting them into a deliverable state, the property does not pass until the thing is done and the buyer has notice that it has been done.

*Rule 3.*—Where there is a contract for the sale of specific goods in a deliverable state but the seller is bound to weigh, measure, test, or do some other act or thing with reference to the goods for the purpose of ascertaining the price, the property does not pass until the act or thing is done and the buyer has notice that it has been done.

*Rule 4.*—When goods are delivered to the buyer on approval or on sale or return or other similar terms the property in the goods passes to the buyer:—

(a) when he signifies his approval or acceptance to the seller or does any other act adopting the transaction;

(b) if he does not signify his approval or acceptance to the seller but retains the goods without giving notice of rejection, then, if a time has been fixed for the return of the goods, on the expiration of that time, and, if no time has been fixed, on the expiration of a reasonable time.

*Rule 5.*— (1) Where there is a contract for the sale of unascertained or future goods by description, and goods of that description and in a deliverable state are unconditionally appropriated to the contract, either by the seller with the assent of the buyer or by the buyer with the assent of the seller, the property in the goods then passes to the buyer; and the assent may be express or implied, and may be given either before or after the appropriation is made.

(2) Where, in pursuance of the contract, the seller delivers the goods to the buyer or to a carrier or other bailee or custodier (whether named by the buyer or not) for the purpose of transmission to the buyer, and does not reserve the right of disposal, he is to be taken to have unconditionally appropriated the goods to the contract.

(3) Where there is a contract for the sale of a specified quantity of unascertained goods in a deliverable state forming part of a bulk which is identified either in the contract or by subsequent agreement between the parties and the bulk is reduced to (or to less than) that quantity, then, if the buyer under that contract is the only buyer to whom goods are then due out of the bulk—

(a) the remaining goods are to be taken as appropriated to that contract at the time when the bulk is so reduced; and

(b) the property in those goods then passes to that buyer.

(4) Paragraph (3) above applies also (with the necessary modifications) where a bulk is reduced to (or to less than) the aggregate of the quantities due to a single buyer under separate contracts relating to that bulk and he is the only buyer to whom goods are then due out of that bulk.

## 19   Reservation of right of disposal

(1)   Where there is a contract for the sale of specific goods or where goods are subsequently appropriated to the contract, the seller may, by the terms of the contract or appropriation, reserve the right of disposal of the goods until certain conditions are fulfilled; and in such a case, notwithstanding the delivery of the goods to the buyer, or to a carrier or other bailee or custodier for the purpose of transmission to the buyer, the property in the goods does not pass to the buyer until the conditions imposed by the seller are fulfilled.

(2)   Where goods are shipped, and by the bill of lading the goods are deliverable to the order of the seller or his agent, the seller is prima facie to be taken to reserve the right of disposal.

(3)   Where the seller of goods draws on the buyer for the price, and transmits the bill of exchange and bill of lading to the buyer together to secure acceptance or payment of the bill of exchange, the buyer is bound to return the bill of lading if he does not honour the bill of exchange, and if he wrongfully retains the bill of lading the property in the goods does not pass to him.

## 20   Passing of risk

(1)   Unless otherwise agreed, the goods remain at the seller's risk until the property in them is transferred to the buyer, but when the property in them is transferred to the buyer the goods are at the buyer's risk whether delivery has been made or not.

(2)   But where delivery has been delayed through the fault of either buyer or seller the goods are at the risk of the party at fault as regards any loss which might not have occurred but for such fault.

(3)   Nothing in this section affects the duties or liabilities of either seller or buyer as a bailee or custodier of the goods of the other party.

(4)   In a case where the buyer deals as consumer or, in Scotland, where there is a consumer contract in which the buyer is a consumer, subsections (1) to (3) above must be ignored and the goods remain at the seller's risk until they are delivered to the consumer.

## 20A   Undivided shares in goods forming part of a bulk

(1)   This section applies to a contract for the sale of a specified quantity of unascertained goods if the following conditions are met—

    (a)   the goods or some of them form part of a bulk which is identified either in the contract or by subsequent agreement between the parties; and

    (b)   the buyer has paid the price for some or all of the goods which are the subject of the contract and which form part of the bulk.

(2)   Where this section applies, then (unless the parties agree otherwise), as soon as the conditions specified in paragraphs (a) and (b) of subsection (1) above are met or at such later time as the parties may agree—

    (a)   property in an undivided share in the bulk is transferred to the buyer, and

    (b)   the buyer becomes an owner in common of the bulk.

(3)   Subject to subsection (4) below, for the purposes of this section, the undivided share of a buyer in a bulk at any time shall be such share as the quantity of goods paid for and due to the buyer out of the bulk bears to the quantity of goods in the bulk at that time.

(4)   Where the aggregate of the undivided shares of buyers in a bulk determined under subsection (3) above would at any time exceed the whole of the bulk at that time, the undivided share in the bulk of each buyer shall be reduced proportionately so that the aggregate of the undivided shares is equal to the whole bulk.

(5)   Where a buyer has paid the price for only some of the goods due to him out of a bulk, any delivery to the buyer out of the bulk shall, for the purposes of this section, be ascribed in the first place to the goods in respect of which payment has been made.

(6)   For the purposes of this section payment of part of the price for any goods shall be treated as payment for a corresponding part of the goods.

## 20B   Deemed consent by co-owner to dealings in bulk goods

(1)   A person who has become an owner in common of a bulk by virtue of section 20A above shall be deemed to have consented to—

    (a)   any delivery of goods out of the bulk to any other owner in common of the bulk, being goods which are due to him under his contract;

    (b)   any dealing with or removal, delivery or disposal of goods in the bulk by any other person who is an owner in common of the bulk in so far as the goods fall within that co-owner's undivided share in the bulk at the time of the dealing, removal, delivery or disposal.

(2)   No cause of action shall accrue to anyone against a person by reason of that person having acted in accordance with paragraph (a) or (b) of subsection (1) above in reliance on any consent deemed to have been given under that subsection.

(3)   Nothing in this section or section 20A above shall—

    (a)   impose an obligation on a buyer of goods out of a bulk to compensate any other buyer of goods out of that bulk for any shortfall in the goods received by that other buyer;

(b) affect any contractual arrangement between buyers of goods out of a bulk for adjustments between themselves; or

(c) affect the rights of any buyer under his contract.

### *Transfer of title*

### 21   Sale by person not the owner

(1)  Subject to this Act, where goods are sold by a person who is not their owner, and who does not sell them under the authority or with the consent of the owner, the buyer acquires no better title to the goods than the seller had, unless the owner of the goods is by his conduct precluded from denying the seller's authority to sell.

(2)  Nothing in this Act affects—

(a)  the provisions of the Factors Acts or any enactment enabling the apparent owner of goods to dispose of them as if he were their true owner;

(b)  the validity of any contract of sale under any special common law or statutory power of sale or under the order of a court of competent jurisdiction.

### 22   Market overt

(1)  [...]

(2)  This section does not apply to Scotland.

(3)  Paragraph 8 of Schedule 1 below applies in relation to a contract under which goods were sold before 1 January 1968 or (in the application of this Act to Northern Ireland) 29 August 1967.

### 23   Sale under voidable title

When the seller of goods has a voidable title to them, but his title has not been avoided at the time of the sale, the buyer acquires a good title to the goods, provided he buys them in good faith and without notice of the seller's defect of title.

### 24   Seller in possession after sale

Where a person having sold goods continues or is in possession of the goods, or of the documents of title to the goods, the delivery or transfer by that person, or by a mercantile agent acting for him, of the goods or documents of title under any sale, pledge, or other disposition thereof, to any person receiving the same in good faith and without notice of the previous sale, has the same effect as if the person making the delivery or transfer were expressly authorised by the owner of the goods to make the same.

### 25   Buyer in possession after sale

(1)  Where a person having bought or agreed to buy goods obtains, with the consent of the seller, possession of the goods or the documents of title to the goods, the delivery or transfer by that person, or by a mercantile agent acting for him, of the goods or documents of title, under any sale, pledge, or other disposition thereof, to any person receiving the same in good faith and without notice of any lien or other right of the original seller in respect of the goods, has the same effect as if the person making the delivery or transfer were a mercantile agent in possession of the goods or documents of title with the consent of the owner.

(2)  For the purposes of subsection (1) above—

(a)  the buyer under a conditional sale agreement is to be taken not to be a person who has bought or agreed to buy goods, and

(b)  'conditional sale agreement' means an agreement for the sale of goods which is a consumer credit agreement within the meaning of the Consumer Credit Act 1974 under which the purchase price or part of it is payable by instalments, and the property in the goods is to remain in the seller (notwithstanding that the buyer is to be in possession of the goods) until such conditions as to the payment of instalments or otherwise as may be specified in the agreement are fulfilled.

(3)  Paragraph 9 of Schedule 1 below applies in relation to a contract under which a person buys or agrees to buy goods and which is made before the appointed day.

(4)  In subsection (3) above and paragraph 9 of Schedule 1 below references to the appointed day are to the day appointed for the purposes of those provisions by an order of the Secretary of State made by statutory instrument.

### 26   Supplementary to sections 24 and 25

In sections 24 and 25 above 'mercantile agent' means a mercantile agent having in the customary course of his business as such agent authority either—

(a)  to sell goods, or

(b)  to consign goods for the purpose of sale, or

(c)  to buy goods, or

(d)  to raise money on the security of goods.

# PART IV

## PERFORMANCE OF THE CONTRACT

### 27   Duties of seller and buyer

It is the duty of the seller to deliver the goods, and of the buyer to accept and pay for them, in accordance with the terms of the contract of sale.

### 28   Payment and delivery are concurrent conditions

Unless otherwise agreed, delivery of the goods and payment of the price are concurrent conditions, that is to say, the seller must be ready and willing to give possession of the goods to the buyer in exchange for the price and the buyer must be ready and willing to pay the price in exchange for possession of the goods.

### 29   Rules about delivery

(1)  Whether it is for the buyer to take possession of the goods or for the seller to send them to the buyer is a question depending in each case on the contract, express or implied, between the parties.

(2)  Apart from any such contract, express or implied, the place of delivery is the seller's place of business if he has one, and if not, his residence; except that, if the contract is for the sale of specific goods, which to the knowledge of the parties when the contract is made are in some other place, then that place is the place of delivery.

(3)  Where under the contract of sale the seller is bound to send the goods to the buyer, but no time for sending them is fixed, the seller is bound to send them within a reasonable time.

(4)  Where the goods at the time of sale are in the possession of a third person, there is no delivery by seller to buyer unless and until the third person acknowledges to the buyer that he holds the goods on his behalf; but nothing in this section affects the operation of the issue or transfer of any document of title to goods.

(5)  Demand or tender of delivery may be treated as ineffectual unless made at a reasonable hour; and what is a reasonable hour is a question of fact.

(6)  Unless otherwise agreed, the expenses of and incidental to putting the goods into a deliverable state must be borne by the seller.

### 30   Delivery of wrong quantity

(1)  Where the seller delivers to the buyer a quantity of goods less than he contracted to sell, the buyer may reject them, but if the buyer accepts the goods so delivered he must pay for them at the contract rate.

(2)  Where the seller delivers to the buyer a quantity of goods larger than he contracted to sell, the buyer may accept the goods included in the contract and reject the rest, or he may reject the whole.

(2A) A buyer who does not deal as consumer may not—

    (a)  where the seller delivers a quantity of goods less than he contracted to sell, reject the goods under subsection (1) above, or

    (b)  where the seller delivers a quantity of goods larger than he contracted to sell, reject the whole under subsection (2) above,

if the shortfall or, as the case may be, excess is so slight that it would be unreasonable for him to do so.

(2B) It is for the seller to show that a shortfall or excess fell within subsection (2A) above.

(2C) Subsections (2A) and (2B) above do not apply to Scotland.

(2D) Where the seller delivers a quantity of goods—

    (a)  less than he contracted to sell, the buyer shall not be entitled to reject the goods under subsection (1) above,

    (b)  larger than he contracted to sell, the buyer shall not be entitled to reject the whole under subsection (2) above,

unless the shortfall or excess is material.

(2E) Subsection (2D) above applies to Scotland only.

(3)  Where the seller delivers to the buyer a quantity of goods larger than he contracted to sell and the buyer accepts the whole of the goods so delivered he must pay for them at the contract rate.

(4)  [...]

(5)  This section is subject to any usage of trade, special agreement, or course of dealing between the parties.

### 31   Instalment deliveries

(1)  Unless otherwise agreed, the buyer of goods is not bound to accept delivery of them by instalments.

(2)  Where there is a contract for the sale of goods to be delivered by stated instalments, which are to be separately paid for, and the seller makes defective deliveries in respect of one or more instalments, or the buyer neglects or refuses to take delivery of or pay for one or more instalments, it is a question in

each case depending on the terms of the contract and the circumstances of the case whether the breach of contract is a repudiation of the whole contract or whether it is a severable breach giving rise to a claim for compensation but not to a right to treat the whole contract as repudiated.

### 32   Delivery to carrier

(1) Where, in pursuance of a contract of sale, the seller is authorised or required to send the goods to the buyer, delivery of the goods to a carrier (whether named by the buyer or not) for the purpose of transmission to the buyer is prima facie deemed to be a delivery of the goods to the buyer.

(2) Unless otherwise authorised by the buyer, the seller must make such contract with the carrier on behalf of the buyer as may be reasonable having regard to the nature of the goods and the other circumstances of the case; and if the seller omits to do so, and the goods are lost or damaged in course of transit, the buyer may decline to treat the delivery to the carrier as a delivery to himself or may hold the seller responsible in damages.

(3) Unless otherwise agreed, where goods are sent by the seller to the buyer by a route involving sea transit, under circumstances in which it is usual to insure, the seller must give such notice to the buyer as may enable him to insure them during their sea transit; and if the seller fails to do so, the goods are at his risk during such sea transit.

(4) In a case where the buyer deals as consumer or, in Scotland, where there is a consumer contract in which the buyer is a consumer, subsections (1) to (3) above must be ignored, but if in pursuance of a contract of sale the seller is authorised or required to send the goods to the buyer, delivery of the goods to the carrier is not delivery of the goods to the buyer.

### 33   Risk where goods are delivered at distant place

Where the seller of goods agrees to deliver them at his own risk at a place other than that where they are when sold, the buyer must nevertheless (unless otherwise agreed) take any risk of deterioration in the goods necessarily incident to the course of transit.

### 34   Buyer's right of examining the goods

Unless otherwise agreed, when the seller tenders delivery of goods to the buyer, he is bound on request to afford the buyer a reasonable opportunity of examining the goods for the purpose of ascertaining whether they are in conformity with the contract and, in the case of a contract for sale by sample, of comparing the bulk with the sample.

### 35   Acceptance

(1) The buyer is deemed to have accepted the goods subject to subsection (2) below—
   (a) when he intimates to the seller that he has accepted them, or
   (b) when the goods have been delivered to him and he does any act in relation to them which is inconsistent with the ownership of the seller.

(2) Where goods are delivered to the buyer, and he has not previously examined them, he is not deemed to have accepted them under subsection (1) above until he has had a reasonable opportunity of examining them for the purpose—
   (a) of ascertaining whether they are in conformity with the contract, and
   (b) in the case of a contract for sale by sample, of comparing the bulk with the sample.

(3) Where the buyer deals as consumer or (in Scotland) the contract of sale is a consumer contract, the buyer cannot lose his right to rely on subsection (2) above by agreement, waiver or otherwise.

(4) The buyer is also deemed to have accepted the goods when after the lapse of a reasonable time he retains the goods without intimating to the seller that he has rejected them.

(5) The questions that are material in determining for the purposes of subsection (4) above whether a reasonable time has elapsed include whether the buyer has had a reasonable opportunity of examining the goods for the purpose mentioned in subsection (2) above.

(6) The buyer is not by virtue of this section deemed to have accepted the goods merely because—
   (a) he asks for, or agrees to, their repair by or under an arrangement with the seller, or
   (b) the goods are delivered to another under a sub-sale or other disposition.

(7) Where the contract is for the sale of goods making one or more commercial units, a buyer accepting any goods included in a unit is deemed to have accepted all the goods making the unit; and in this subsection 'commercial unit' means a unit division of which would materially impair the value of the goods or the character of the unit.

(8) Paragraph 10 of Schedule 1 below applies in relation to a contract made before 22 April 1967 or (in the application of this Act to Northern Ireland) 28 July 1967.

### 35A   Right of partial rejection

(1) If the buyer—
   (a) has the right to reject the goods by reason of a breach on the part of the seller that affects some or all of them, but
   (b) accepts some of the goods, including, where there are any goods unaffected by the breach, all such goods,

he does not by accepting them lose his right to reject the rest.

(2) In the case of a buyer having the right to reject an instalment of goods, subsection (1) above applies as if references to the goods were references to the goods comprised in the instalment.

(3) For the purposes of subsection (1) above, goods are affected by a breach if by reason of the breach they are not in conformity with the contract.

(4) This section applies unless a contrary intention appears in, or is to be implied from, the contract.

### 36 Buyer not bound to return rejected goods

Unless otherwise agreed, where goods are delivered to the buyer, and he refuses to accept them, having the right to do so, he is not bound to return them to the seller, but it is sufficient if he intimates to the seller that he refuses to accept them.

### 37 Buyer's liability for not taking delivery of goods

(1) When the seller is ready and willing to deliver the goods, and requests the buyer to take delivery, and the buyer does not within a reasonable time after such request take delivery of the goods, he is liable to the seller for any loss occasioned by his neglect or refusal to take delivery, and also for a reasonable charge for the care and custody of the goods.

(2) Nothing in this section affects the rights of the seller where the neglect or refusal of the buyer to take delivery amounts to a repudiation of the contract.

# PART V

# RIGHTS OF UNPAID SELLER AGAINST THE GOODS

## *Preliminary*

### 38 Unpaid seller defined

(1) The seller of goods is an unpaid seller within the meaning of this Act—

  (a) when the whole of the price has not been paid or tendered;

  (b) when a bill of exchange or other negotiable instrument has been received as conditional payment, and the condition on which it was received has not been fulfilled by reason of the dishonour of the instrument or otherwise.

(2) In this Part of this Act 'seller' includes any person who is in the position of a seller, as, for instance, an agent of the seller to whom the bill of lading has been indorsed, or a consignor or agent who has himself paid (or is directly responsible for) the price.

### 39 Unpaid seller's rights

(1) Subject to this and any other Act, notwithstanding that the property in the goods may have passed to the buyer, the unpaid seller of goods, as such, has by implication of law—

  (a) a lien on the goods or right to retain them for the price while he is in possession of them;

  (b) in case of the insolvency of the buyer, a right of stopping the goods in transit after he has parted with the possession of them;

  (c) a right of re-sale as limited by this Act.

(2) Where the property in goods has not passed to the buyer, the unpaid seller has (in addition to his other remedies) a right of withholding delivery similar to and co-extensive with his rights of lien or retention and stoppage in transit where the property has passed to the buyer.

### 40 [...]

...

### 41 Seller's lien

(1) Subject to this Act, the unpaid seller of goods who is in possession of them is entitled to retain possession of them until payment or tender of the price in the following cases:—

  (a) where the goods have been sold without any stipulation as to credit;

  (b) where the goods have been sold on credit but the term of credit has expired;

  (c) where the buyer becomes insolvent.

(2) The seller may exercise his lien or right of retention notwithstanding that he is in possession of the goods as agent or bailee or custodier for the buyer.

### 42 Part delivery

Where an unpaid seller has made part delivery of the goods, he may exercise his lien or right of retention on the remainder, unless such part delivery has been made under such circumstances as to show an agreement to waive the lien or right of retention.

### 43 Termination of lien

(1) The unpaid seller of goods loses his lien or right of retention in respect of them—

  (a) when he delivers the goods to a carrier or other bailee or custodier for the purpose of transmission to the buyer without reserving the right of disposal of the goods;

    (b) when the buyer or his agent lawfully obtains possession of the goods;

    (c) by waiver of the lien or right of retention.

    (2) An unpaid seller of goods who has a lien or right of retention in respect of them does not lose his lien or right of retention by reason only that he has obtained judgment or decree for the price of the goods.

### Stoppage in transit

### 44  Right of stoppage in transit

Subject to this Act, when the buyer of goods becomes insolvent the unpaid seller who has parted with the possession of the goods has the right of stopping them in transit, that is to say, he may resume possession of the goods as long as they are in course of transit, and may retain them until payment or tender of the price.

### 45  Duration of transit

    (1) Goods are deemed to be in course of transit from the time when they are delivered to a carrier or other bailee or custodier for the purpose of transmission to the buyer, until the buyer or his agent in that behalf takes delivery of them from the carrier or other bailee or custodier.

    (2) If the buyer or his agent in that behalf obtains delivery of the goods before their arrival at the appointed destination, the transit is at an end.

    (3) If, after the arrival of the goods at the appointed destination, the carrier or other bailee or custodier acknowledges to the buyer or his agent that he holds the goods on his behalf and continues in possession of them as bailee or custodier for the buyer or his agent, the transit is at an end, and it is immaterial that a further destination for the goods may have been indicated by the buyer.

    (4) If the goods are rejected by the buyer, and the carrier or other bailee or custodier continues in possession of them, the transit is not deemed to be at an end, even if the seller has refused to receive them back.

    (5) When goods are delivered to a ship chartered by the buyer it is a question depending on the circumstances of the particular case whether they are in the possession of the master as a carrier or as agent to the buyer.

    (6) Where the carrier or other bailee or custodier wrongfully refuses to deliver the goods to the buyer or his agent in that behalf, the transit is deemed to be at an end.

    (7) Where part delivery of the goods has been made to the buyer or his agent in that behalf, the remainder of the goods may be stopped in transit, unless such part delivery has been made under such circumstances as to show an agreement to give up possession of the whole of the goods.

### 46  How stoppage in transit is effected

    (1) The unpaid seller may exercise his right of stoppage in transit either by taking actual possession of the goods or by giving notice of his claim to the carrier or other bailee or custodier in whose possession the goods are.

    (2) The notice may be given either to the person in actual possession of the goods or to his principal.

    (3) If given to the principal, the notice is ineffective unless given at such time and under such circumstances that the principal, by the exercise of reasonable diligence, may communicate it to his servant or agent in time to prevent a delivery to the buyer.

    (4) When notice of stoppage in transit is given by the seller to the carrier or other bailee or custodier in possession of the goods, he must re-deliver the goods to, or according to the directions of, the seller; and the expenses of the re-delivery must be borne by the seller.

### Re-sale etc. by buyer

### 47  Effect of sub-sale etc by buyer

    (1) Subject to this Act, the unpaid seller's right of lien or retention or stoppage in transit is not affected by any sale or other disposition of the goods which the buyer may have made, unless the seller has assented to it.

    (2) Where a document of title to goods has been lawfully transferred to any person as buyer or owner of the goods, and that person transfers the document to a person who take it in good faith and for valuable consideration, then—

        (a) if the last-mentioned transfer was by way of sale the unpaid seller's right of lien or retention or stoppage in transit is defeated; and

        (b) if the last-mentioned transfer was made by way of pledge or other disposition for value, the unpaid seller's right of lien or retention or stoppage in transit can only be exercised subject to the rights of the transferee.

### Rescission: and re-sale by seller

### 48  Rescission: and re-sale by seller

    (1) Subject to this section, a contract of sale is not rescinded by the mere exercise by an unpaid seller of his right of lien or retention or stoppage in transit.

(2) Where an unpaid seller who has exercised his right of lien or retention or stoppage in transit re-sells the goods, the buyer acquires a good title to them as against the original buyer.

(3) Where the goods are of a perishable nature, or where the unpaid seller gives notice to the buyer of his intention to re-sell, and the buyer does not within a reasonable time pay or tender the price, the unpaid seller may re-sell the goods and recover from the original buyer damages for any loss occasioned by his breach of contract.

(4) Where the seller expressly reserves the right of re-sale in case the buyer should make default, and on the buyer making default re-sells the goods, the original contract of sale is rescinded but without prejudice to any claim the seller may have for damages.

# PART 5A

## ADDITIONAL RIGHTS OF BUYER IN CONSUMER CASES

### 48A  Introductory

(1) This section applies if—
  (a) the buyer deals as consumer or, in Scotland, there is a consumer contract in which the buyer is a consumer, and
  (b) the goods do not conform to the contract of sale at the time of delivery.

(2) If this section applies, the buyer has the right—
  (a) under and in accordance with section 48B below, to require the seller to repair or replace the goods, or
  (b) under and in accordance with section 48C below—
    (i) to require the seller to reduce the purchase price of the goods to the buyer by an appropriate amount, or
    (ii) to rescind the contract with regard to the goods in question.

(3) For the purposes of subsection (1)(b) above goods which do not conform to the contract of sale at any time within the period of six months starting with the date on which the goods were delivered to the buyer must be taken not to have so conformed at that date.

(4) Subsection (3) above does not apply if—
  (a) it is established that the goods did so conform at that date;
  (b) its application is incompatible with the nature of the goods or the nature of the lack of conformity.

### 48B  Repair or replacement of the goods

(1) If section 48A above applies, the buyer may require the seller—
  (a) to repair the goods, or
  (b) to replace the goods.

(2) If the buyer requires the seller to repair or replace the goods, the seller must—
  (a) repair or, as the case may be, replace the goods within a reasonable time but without causing significant inconvenience to the buyer;
  (b) bear any necessary costs incurred in doing so (including in particular the cost of any labour, materials or postage).

(3) The buyer must not require the seller to repair or, as the case may be, replace the goods if that remedy is—
  (a) impossible, or
  (b) disproportionate in comparison to the other of those remedies, or
  (c) disproportionate in comparison to an appropriate reduction in the purchase price under paragraph (a), or rescission under paragraph (b), of section 48C(1) below.

(4) One remedy is disproportionate in comparison to the other if the one imposes costs on the seller which, in comparison to those imposed on him by the other, are unreasonable, taking into account—
  (a) the value which the goods would have if they conformed to the contract of sale,
  (b) the significance of the lack of conformity, and
  (c) whether the other remedy could be effected without significant inconvenience to the buyer.

(5) Any question as to what is a reasonable time or significant inconvenience is to be determined by reference to—
  (a) the nature of the goods, and
  (b) the purpose for which the goods were acquired.

### 48C  Reduction of purchase price or rescission of contract

(1) If section 48A above applies, the buyer may—
  (a) require the seller to reduce the purchase price of the goods in question to the buyer by an appropriate amount, or
  (b) rescind the contract with regard to those goods,
if the condition in subsection (2) below is satisfied.

(2) The condition is that—

    (a) by virtue of section 48B(3) above the buyer may require neither repair nor replacement of the goods; or

    (b) the buyer has required the seller to repair or replace the goods, but the seller is in breach of the requirement of section 48B(2)(a) above to do so within a reasonable time and without significant inconvenience to the buyer.

(3) For the purposes of this Part, if the buyer rescinds the contract, any reimbursement to the buyer may be reduced to take account of the use he has had of the goods since they were delivered to him.

### 48D  Relation to other remedies etc

(1) If the buyer requires the seller to repair or replace the goods the buyer must not act under subsection (2) until he has given the seller a reasonable time in which to repair or replace (as the case may be) the goods.

(2) The buyer acts under this subsection if—

    (a) in England and Wales or Northern Ireland he rejects the goods and terminates the contract for breach of condition;

    (b) in Scotland he rejects any goods delivered under the contract and treats it as repudiated;

    (c) he requires the goods to be replaced or repaired (as the case may be).

### 48E  Powers of the court

(1) In any proceedings in which a remedy is sought by virtue of this Part the court, in addition to any other power it has, may act under this section.

(2) On the application of the buyer the court may make an order requiring specific performance or, in Scotland, specific implement by the seller of any obligation imposed on him by virtue of section 48B above.

(3) Subsection (4) applies if—

    (a) the buyer requires the seller to give effect to a remedy under section 48B or 48C above or has claims to rescind under section 48C, but

    (b) the court decides that another remedy under section 48B or 48C is appropriate.

(4) The court may proceed—

    (a) as if the buyer had required the seller to give effect to the other remedy, or if the other remedy is rescission under section 48C

    (b) as if the buyer had claimed to rescind the contract under that section.

(5) If the buyer has claimed to rescind the contract the court may order that any reimbursement to the buyer is reduced to take account of the use he has had of the goods since they were delivered to him.

(6) The court may make an order under this section unconditionally or on such terms and conditions as to damages, payment of the price and otherwise as it thinks just.

### 48F  Conformity with the contract

For the purposes of this Part, goods do not conform to a contract of sale if there is, in relation to the goods, a breach of an express term of the contract or a term implied by section 13, 14 or 15 above.

# PART VI

# ACTIONS FOR BREACH OF THE CONTRACT

*Seller's remedies*

### 49  Action for price

(1) Where, under a contract of sale, the property in the goods has passed to the buyer and he wrongfully neglects or refuses to pay for the goods according to the terms of the contract, the seller may maintain an action against him for the price of the goods.

(2) Where, under a contract of sale, the price is payable on a day certain irrespective of delivery and the buyer wrongfully neglects or refuses to pay such price, the seller may maintain an action for the price, although the property in the goods has not passed and the goods have not been appropriated to the contract.

(3) Nothing in this section prejudices the right of the seller in Scotland to recover interest on the price from the date of tender of the goods, or from the date on which the price was payable, as the case may be.

### 50  Damages for non-acceptance

(1) Where the buyer wrongfully neglects or refuses to accept and pay for the goods, the seller may maintain an action against him for damages for non-acceptance.

(2) The measure of damages is the estimated loss directly and naturally resulting, in the ordinary course of events, from the buyer's breach of contract.

(3) Where there is an available market for the goods in question the measure of damages is prima facie to be ascertained by the difference between the contract price and the market or current price at the time or times when the goods ought to have been accepted or (if no time was fixed for acceptance) at the time of the refusal to accept.

*Buyer's remedies*

### 51 Damages for non-delivery

(1) Where the seller wrongfully neglects or refuses to deliver the goods to the buyer, the buyer may maintain an action against the seller for damages for non-delivery.

(2) The measure of damages is the estimated loss directly and naturally resulting, in the ordinary course of events, from the seller's breach of contract.

(3) Where there is an available market for the goods in question the measure of damages is prima facie to be ascertained by the difference between the contract price and the market or current price of the goods at the time or times when they ought to have been delivered or (if no time was fixed) at the time of the refusal to deliver.

### 52 Specific performance

(1) In any action for breach of contract to deliver specific or ascertained goods the court may, if it thinks fit, on the plaintiff's application, by its judgment or decree direct that the contract shall be performed specifically, without giving the defendant the option of retaining the goods on payment of damages.

(2) The plaintiff's application may be made at any time before judgment or decree.

(3) The judgment or decree may be unconditional, or on such terms and conditions as to damages, payment of the price and otherwise as seem just to the court.

(4) The provisions of this section shall be deemed to be supplementary to, and not in derogation of, the right of specific implement in Scotland.

### 53 Remedy for breach of warranty

(1) Where there is a breach of warranty by the seller, or where the buyer elects (or is compelled) to treat any breach of a condition on the part of the seller as a breach of warranty, the buyer is not by reason only of such breach of warranty entitled to reject the goods; but he may—

(a) set up against the seller the breach of warranty in diminution or extinction of the price, or

(b) maintain an action against the seller for damages for the breach of warranty.

(2) The measure of damages for breach of warranty is the estimated loss directly and naturally resulting, in the ordinary course of events, from the breach of warranty.

(3) In the case of breach of warranty of quality such loss is prima facie the difference between the value of the goods at the time of delivery to the buyer and the value they would have had if they had fulfilled the warranty.

(4) The fact that the buyer has set up the breach of warranty in diminution or extinction of the price does not prevent him from maintaining an action for the same breach of warranty if he has suffered further damage.

(5) This section does not apply to Scotland.

### 53A Measure of damages as respects Scotland

(1) The measure of damages for the seller's breach of contract is the estimated loss directly and naturally resulting, in the ordinary course of events, from the breach.

(2) Where the seller's breach consists of the delivery of goods which are not of the quality required by the contract and the buyer retains the goods, such loss as aforesaid is prima facie the difference between the value of the goods at the time of delivery to the buyer and the value they would have had if they had fulfilled the contract.

(3) This section applies to Scotland only.

*Interest, etc.*

### 54 Interest, etc

Nothing in this Act affects the right of the buyer or the seller to recover interest or special damages in any case where by law interest or special damages may be recoverable, or to recover money paid where the consideration for the payment of it has failed.

# PART VII

# SUPPLEMENTARY

### 55 Exclusion of implied terms

(1) Where a right, duty or liability would arise under a contract of sale of goods by implication of law, it may (subject to the Unfair Contract Terms Act 1977) be negatived or varied by express agreement, or by the course of dealing between the parties, or by such usage as binds both parties to the contract.

(2) An express term does not negative a term implied by this Act unless inconsistent with it.

(3) Paragraph 11 of Schedule 1 below applies in relation to a contract made on or after 18 May 1973 and before 1 February 1978, and paragraph 12 in relation to one made before 18 May 1973.

## 56 Conflict of laws

Paragraph 13 of Schedule 1 below applies in relation to a contract made on or after 18 May 1973 and before 1 February 1978, so as to make provision about conflict of laws in relation to such a contract.

## 57 Auction sales

(1) Where goods are put up for sale by auction in lots, each lot is prima facie deemed to be the subject of a separate contract of sale.

(2) A sale by auction is complete when the auctioneer announces its completion by the fall of the hammer, or in other customary manner; and until the announcement is made any bidder may retract his bid.

(3) A sale by auction may be notified to be subject to a reserve or upset price, and a right to bid may also be reserved expressly by or on behalf of the seller.

(4) Where a sale by auction is not notified to be subject to a right to bid by or on behalf of the seller, it is not lawful for the seller to bid himself or to employ any person to bid at the sale, or for the auctioneer knowingly to take any bid from the seller or any such person.

(5) A sale contravening subsection (4) above may be treated as fraudulent by the buyer.

(6) Where, in respect of a sale by auction, a right to bid is expressly reserved (but not otherwise) the seller or any one person on his behalf may bid at the auction.

## 58 Payment into court in Scotland

In Scotland where a buyer has elected to accept goods which he might have rejected, and to treat a breach of contract as only giving rise to a claim for damages, he may, in an action by the seller for the price, be required, in the discretion of the court before which the action depends, to consign or pay into court the price of the goods, or part of the price, or to give other reasonable security for its due payment.

## 59 Reasonable time a question of fact

Where a reference is made in this Act to a reasonable time the question what is a reasonable time is a question of fact.

## 60 Rights etc enforceable by action

Where a right, duty or liability is declared by this Act, it may (unless otherwise provided by this Act) be enforced by action.

## 61 Interpretation

(1) In this Act, unless the context or subject matter otherwise requires,—

'action' includes counterclaim and set-off, and in Scotland condescendence and claim and compensation;

'bulk' means a mass or collection of goods of the same kind which—

    (a) is contained in a defined space or area; and

    (b) is such that any goods in the bulk are interchangeable with any other goods therein of the same number or quantity;

'business' includes a profession and the activities of any government department (including a Northern Ireland department) or local or public authority;

'buyer' means a person who buys or agrees to buy goods;

'consumer contract' has the same meaning as in section 25(1) of the Unfair Contract Terms Act 1977; and for the purposes of this Act the onus of proving that a contract is not to be regarded as a consumer contract shall lie on the seller;

'contract of sale' includes an agreement to sell as well as a sale;

'credit-broker' means a person acting in the course of a business of credit brokerage carried on by him, that is a business of effecting introductions of individuals desiring to obtain credit—

    (a) to persons carrying on any business so far as it relates to the provision of credit, or

    (b) to other persons engaged in credit brokerage;

'defendant' includes in Scotland defender, respondent, and claimant in a multiplepoinding;

'delivery' means voluntary transfer of possession from one person to another except that in relation to sections 20A and 20B above it includes such appropriation of goods to the contract as results in property in the goods being transferred to the buyer;

'document of title to goods' has the same meaning as it has in the Factors Acts;

'Factors Acts' means the Factors Act 1889, the Factors (Scotland) 1890, and any enactment amending or substituted for the same;

'fault' means wrongful act or default;

'future goods' means goods to be manufactured or acquired by the seller after the making of the contract of sale;

'goods' includes all personal chattels other than things in action and money, and in Scotland all corporeal moveables except money; and in particular 'goods' includes emblements, industrial growing crops, and things attached to or forming part of the land which are agreed to be severed before sale or under the contract of sale; and includes an undivided share in goods;

'plaintiff' includes pursuer, complainer, claimant in a multiple-poinding and defendant or defender counter-claiming;

'producer' means the manufacturer of goods, the importer of goods into the European Economic Area or any person purporting to be a producer by placing his name, trade mark or other distinctive sign on the goods;

'property' means the general property in goods, and not merely a special property;

[...]

'repair' means, in cases where there is a lack of conformity in goods for the purposes of section 48F of this Act, to bring the goods into conformity with the contract;

'sale' includes a bargain and sale as well as a sale and delivery;

'seller' means a person who sells or agrees to sell goods;

'specific goods' means goods identified and agreed on at the time a contract of sale is made and includes an undivided share, specified as a fraction or percentage, of goods identified and agreed on as aforesaid;

'warranty'(as regards England and Wales and Northern Ireland) means an agreement with reference to goods which are the subject of a contract of sale, but collateral to the main purpose of such contract, the breach of which gives rise to a claim for damages, but not to a right to reject the goods and treat the contract as repudiated.

(2) [...]

(3) A thing is deemed to be done in good faith within the meaning of this Act when it is in fact done honestly, whether it is done negligently or not.

(4) A person is deemed to be insolvent within the meaning of this Act if he has either ceased to pay his debts in the ordinary course of business or he cannot pay his debts as they become due. [...]

(5) Goods are in a deliverable state within the meaning of this Act when they are in such a state that the buyer would under the contract be bound to take delivery of them.

(5A) References in this Act to dealing as consumer are to be construed in accordance with Part I of the Unfair Contract Terms Act 1977; and, for the purposes of this Act, it is for a seller claiming that the buyer does not deal as consumer to show that he does not.

(6) As regards the definition of 'business' in subsection (1) above, paragraph 14 of Schedule 1 below applies in relation to a contract made on or after 18 May 1973 and before 1 February 1978, and paragraph 15 in relation to one made before 18 May 1973.

### 62   Savings: rules of law etc

(1) The rules in bankruptcy relating to contracts of sale apply to those contracts, notwithstanding anything in this Act.

(2) The rules of the common law, including the law merchant, except in so far as they are inconsistent with the provisions of this Act, and in particular the rules relating to the law of principal and agent and the effect of fraud, misrepresentation, duress or coercion, mistake, or other invalidating cause, apply to contracts for the sale of goods.

(3) Nothing in this Act or the Sale of Goods 1893 affects the enactments relating to bills of sale, or any enactment relating to the sale of goods which is not expressly repealed or amended by this Act or that.

(4) The provisions of this Act about contracts of sale do not apply to a transaction in the form of a contract of sale which is intended to operate by way of mortgage, pledge, charge, or other security.

(5) Nothing in this Act prejudices or affects the landlord's right of hypothec or sequentration for rent in Scotland.

### 63   Consequential amendments, repeals and savings

(1) Without prejudice to section 17 of the Interpretation Act 1978 (repeal and re-enactment), the enactments mentioned in Schedule 2 below have effect subject to the amendments there specified (being amendments consequential on this Act).

(2) The enactments mentioned in Schedule 3 below are repealed to the extent specified in column 3, but subject to the savings in Schedule 4 below.

(3) The savings in Schedule 4 below have effect.

### 64   Short title and commencement

(1) This Act may be cited as the Sale of Goods Act 1979.

(2) This Act comes into force on 1 January 1980.

# SCHEDULES

# SCHEDULE 1

# MODIFICATION OF ACT FOR CERTAIN CONTRACTS

## *Preliminary*

**1**   (1) This Schedule modifies this Act as it applies to contracts of sale of goods made on certain dates.

(2)  In this Schedule references to sections are to those of this Act and references to contracts are to contracts of sale of goods.

(3)  Nothing in this Schedule affects a contract made before 1 January 1894.

## *Section 11: condition treated as warranty*

**2**   In relation to a contract made before 22 April 1967 or (in the application of this Act to Northern Ireland) 28 July 1967, in section 11(4) after 'or part of them,' insert 'or where the contract is for specific goods, the property in which has passed to the buyer,'.

## *Section 12: implied terms about title etc.*

**3**   In relation to a contract made before 18 May 1973 substitute the following for section 12:—

## '12   Implied terms about title, etc

In a contract of sale, unless the circumstances of the contract are such as to show a different intention, there is—

   (a) an implied condition on the part of the seller that in the case of a sale he has a right to sell the goods, and in the case of an agreement to sell he will have such a right at the time when the property is to pass;

   (b) an implied warranty that the buyer will have and enjoy quiet possession of the goods;

   (c) an implied warranty that the goods will be free from any charge or encumbrance in favour of any third party, not declared or known to the buyer before or at the time when the contract is made.'

## *Section 13: sale by description*

**4**   In relation to a contract made before 18 May 1973, omit section 13(3).

## *Section 14: quality or fitness (i)*

**5**   In relation to a contract made on or after 18 May 1973 and before the appointed day, substitute the following for section 14:—

## '14   Implied terms about quality or fitness

(1)  Except as provided by this section and section 15 below and subject to any other enactment, there is no implied condition or warranty about the quality or fitness for any particular purpose of goods supplied under a contract of sale.

(2)  Where the seller sells goods in the course of a business, there is an implied condition that the goods supplied under the contract are of merchantable quality, except that there is no such condition—

   (a) as regards defects specifically drawn to the buyer's attention before the contract is made; or

   (b) if the buyer examines the goods before the contract is made, as regards defects which that examination ought to reveal.

(3)  Where the seller sells goods in the course of a business and the buyer, expressly or by implication, makes known to the seller any particular purpose for which the goods are being bought, there is an implied condition that the goods supplied under the contract are reasonably fit for that purpose, whether or not that is a purpose for which such goods are commonly supplied, except where the circumstances show that the buyer does not rely, or that it is unreasonable for him to rely, on the seller's skill or judgment.

(4)  An implied condition or warranty about quality or fitness for a particular purpose may be annexed to a contract of sale by usage.

(5)  The preceding provisions of this section apply to a sale by a person who in the course of a business is acting as agent for another as they apply to a sale by a principal in the course of a business, except where that other is not selling in the course of a business and either the buyer knows that fact or reasonable steps are taken to bring it to the notice of the buyer before the contract is made.

(6)  Goods of any kind are of merchantable quality within the meaning of subsection (2) above if they are as fit for the purpose or purposes for which goods of that kind are commonly bought as it is reasonable to expect having regard to any description applied to them, the price (if relevant) and all the other relevant circumstances.

(7) In the application of subsection (3) above to an agreement for the sale of goods under which the purchase price or part of it is payable by instalments any reference to the seller includes a reference to the person by whom any antecedent negotiations are conducted; and section 58(3) and (5) of the Hire-Purchase Act 1965, section 54(3) and (5) of the Hire-Purchase (Scotland) Act 1965 and section 65(3) and (5) of theHire-Purchase Act (Northern Ireland) 1966 (meaning of antecedent negotiations and related expressions) apply in relation to this subsection as in relation to each of those Acts, but as if a reference to any such agreement were included in the references in subsection (3) of each of those sections to the agreements there mentioned.'

### Section 14: quality or fitness (ii)

6   In relation to a contract made before 18 May 1973 substitute the following for section 14:—

### '14   Implied terms about quality or fitness

(1)   Subject to this and any other Act, there is no implied condition or warranty about the quality or fitness for any particular purpose of goods supplied under a contract of sale.

(2)   Where the buyer, expressly or by implication, makes known to the seller the particular purpose for which the goods are required, so as to show that the buyer relies on the seller's skill or judgment, and the goods are of a description which it is in the course of the seller's business to supply (whether he is the manufacturer or not), there is an implied condition that the goods will be reasonably fit for such purpose, except that in the case of a contract for the sale of a specified article under its patent or other trade name there is no implied condition as to its fitness for any particular purpose.

(3)   Where goods are bought by description from a seller who deals in goods of that description (whether he is the manufacturer or not), there is an implied condition that the goods will be of merchantable quality; but if the buyer has examined the goods, there is no implied condition as regards defects which such examination ought to have revealed.

(4)   An implied condition or warranty about quality or fitness for a particular purpose may be annexed by the usage of trade.

(5)   An express condition or warranty does not negative a condition or warranty implied by this Act unless inconsistent with it.'

### Section 15: sale by sample

7   In relation to a contract made before 18 May 1973, omit section 15(3).

### Section 22: market overt

8   In relation to a contract under which goods were sold before 1 January 1968 or (in the application of this Act to Northern Ireland) 29 August 1967, add the following paragraph at the end of section 22(1):—

'Nothing in this subsection affects the law relating to the sale of horses.'

### Section 25: buyer in possession

9   In relation to a contract under which a person buys or agrees to buy goods and which is made before the appointed day, omit section 25(2).

### Section 35: acceptance

10   In relation to a contract made before 22 April 1967 or (in the application of this Act to Northern Ireland) 28 July 1967, in section 35(1) omit '(except where section 34 above otherwise provides)'.

### Section 55: exclusion of implied terms (i)

11   In relation to a contract made on or after 18 May 1973 and before 1 February 1978 substitute the following for section 55:—

### '55   Exclusion of implied terms

(1)   Where a right, duty or liability would arise under a contract of sale of goods by implication of law, it may be negatived or varied by express agreement, or by the course of dealing between the parties, or by such usage as binds both parties to the contract, but the preceding provision has effect subject to the following provisions of this section.

(2)   An express condition or warranty does not negative a condition or warranty implied by this Act unless inconsistent with it.

(3)   In the case of a contract of sale of goods, any term of that or any other contract exempting from all or any of the provisions of section 12 above is void.

(4)   In the case of a contract of sale of goods, any term of that or any other contract exempting from all or any of the provisions of section 13, 14 or 15 above is void in the case of a consumer sale and is, in any other case, not enforceable to the extent that it is shown that it would not be fair or reasonable to allow reliance on the term.

(5)   In determining for the purposes of subsection (4) above whether or not reliance on any such term would be fair or reasonable regard shall be had to all the circumstances of the case and in particular to the following matters—

(a) the strength of the bargaining positions of the seller and buyer relative to each other, taking into account, among other things, the availability of suitable alternative products and sources of supply;

(b) whether the buyer received an inducement to agree to the term or in accepting it had an opportunity of buying the goods or suitable alternatives without it from any source of supply;

(c) whether the buyer knew or ought reasonably to have known of the existence and extent of the term (having regard, among other things, to any custom of the trade and any previous course of dealing between the parties);

(d) where the term exempts from all or any of the provisions of section 13, 14 or 15 above if some condition is not complied with, whether it was reasonable at the time of the contract to expect that compliance with that condition would be practicable;

(e) whether the goods were manufactured, processed, or adapted to the special order of the buyer.

(6) Subsection (5) above does not prevent the court from holding, in accordance with any rule of law, that a term which purports to exclude or restrict any of the provisions of section 13, 14 or 15 above is not a term of the contract.

(7) In this section 'consumer sale' means a sale of goods (other than a sale by auction or by competitive tender) by a seller in the course of a business where the goods—

(a) are of a type ordinarily bought for private use or consumption; and

(b) are sold to a person who does not buy or hold himself out as buying them in the course of a business.

(8) The onus of proving that a sale falls to be treated for the purposes of this section as not being a consumer sale lies on the party so contending.

(9) Any reference in this section to a term exempting from all or any of the provisions of any section of this Act is a reference to a term which purports to exclude or restrict, or has the effect of excluding or restricting, the operation of all or any of the provisions of that section, or the exercise of a right conferred by any provision of that section, or any liability of the seller for breach of a condition or warranty implied by any provision of that section.

(10) It is hereby declared that any reference in this section to a term of a contract includes a reference to a term which although not contained in a contract is incorporated in the contract by another term of the contract.

(11) Nothing in this section prevents the parties to a contract for the international sale of goods from negativing or varying any right, duty or liability which would otherwise arise by implication of law under sections 12 to 15 above.

(12) In subsection (11) above 'contract for the international sale of goods' means a contract of sale of goods made by parties whose places of business (or, if they have none, habitual residences) are in the territories of different States (the Channel Islands and the Isle of Man being treated for this purpose as different States from the United Kingdom) and in the case of which one of the following conditions is satisfied:—

(a) the contract involves the sale of goods which are at the time of the conclusion of the contract in the course of carriage or will be carried from the territory of one State to the territory of another; or

(b) the acts constituting the offer and acceptance have been effected in the territories of different States; or

(c) delivery of the goods is to be made in the territory of a State other than that within whose territory the acts constituting the offer and the acceptance have been effected.'

### Section 55: exclusion of implied terms (ii)

**12**　In relation to a contract made before 18 May 1973 substitute the following for section 55:—

### '55　Exclusion of implied terms

Where a right, duty or liability would arise under a contract of sale by implication of law, it may be negatived or varied by express agreement, or by the course of dealing between the parties, or by such usage as binds both parties to the contract.'

### Section 56: conflict of laws

**13**　(1) In relation to a contract made on or after 18 May 1973 and before 1 February 1978 substitute for section 56 the section set out in sub-paragraph (3) below.

(2) In relation to a contract made otherwise than as mentioned in sub-paragraph (1) above, ignore section 56 and this paragraph.

(3) The section mentioned in sub-paragraph (1) above is as follows:—

### '56　Conflict of laws

(1) Where the proper law of a contract for the sale of goods would, apart from a term that it should be the law of some other country or a term to the like effect, be the law of any part of the United Kingdom, or where any such contract contains a term which purports to substitute, or has the effect of substituting,

provisions of the law of some other country for all or any of the provisions of sections 12 to 15 and 55 above, those sections shall, notwithstanding that term but subject to subsection (2) below, apply to the contract.

(2) Nothing in subsection (1) above prevents the parties to a contract for the international sale of goods from negativing or varying any right, duty or liability which would otherwise arise by implication of law under sections 12 to 15 above.

(3) In subsection (2) above 'contract for the international sale of goods' means a contract of sale of goods made by parties whose places of business (or, if they have none, habitual residences) are in the territories of different States (the Channel Islands and the Isle of Man being treated for this purpose as different States from the United Kingdom) and in the case of which one of the following conditions is satisfied:—

(a) the contract involves the sale of goods which are at the time of the conclusion of the contract in the course of carriage or will be carried from the territory of one State to the territory of another; or

(b) the acts constituting the offer and acceptance have been effected in the territories of different States; or

(c) delivery of the goods is to be made in the territory of a State other than that within whose territory the acts constituting the offer and the acceptance have been effected.'

### *Section 61(1): definition of 'business'(i)*

**14**  In relation to a contract made on or after 18 May 1973 and before 1 February 1978, in the definition of 'business' in section 61(1) for 'or local or public authority' substitute ', local authority or statutory undertaker'.

### *Section 61(1): definition of 'business'(ii)*

**15**  In relation to a contract made before 18 May 1973 omit the definition of 'business' in section 61(1).

# SCHEDULE 2

# CONSEQUENTIAL AMENDMENTS

[...]

# SCHEDULE 3

# REPEALS

[...]

# SCHEDULE 4

# SAVINGS

### *Preliminary*

**1**  In this Schedule references to the 1893 Act are to the Sale of Goods Act 1893.

### *Orders*

**2**  An order under section 14(8) or 25(4) above may make provision that it is to have effect only as provided by the order (being provision corresponding to that which could, apart from this Act, have been made by an order under section 192(4) of the Consumer Credit Act 1974 bringing into operation an amendment or repeal making a change corresponding to that made by the order under section 14(8) or 25(4) above).

### *Offences*

**3**  Where an offence was committed in relation to goods before 1 January 1969 or (in the application of this Act to Northern Ireland) 1 August 1969, the effect of a conviction in respect of the offence is not affected by the repeal by this Act of section 24 of the 1893 Act.

### *1893 Act, section 26*

**4**  The repeal by this Act of provisions of the 1893 Act does not extend to the following provisions of that Act in so far as they are needed to give effect to or interpret section 26 of that Act, namely, the definitions of 'goods' and 'property' in section 62(1), section 62(2) and section 63 (which was repealed subject to savings by the Statute Law Revision Act 1908).

### *Things done before 1 January 1894*

**5**   The repeal by this Act of section 60 of and the Schedule to the 1893 Act (which effected repeals and which were themselves repealed subject to savings by the Statute Law Revision Act 1908) does not affect those savings, and accordingly does not affect things done or acquired before 1 January 1894.

**6**   In so far as the 1893 Act applied (immediately before the operation of the repeals made by this Act) to contracts made before 1 January 1894 (when the 1893 Act came into operation), the 1893 Act shall continue so to apply notwithstanding this Act.

## Unfair Contract Terms Act 1977

(c. 50)

*An Act to impose further limits on the extent to which under the law of England and Wales and Northern Ireland civil liability for breach of contract, or for negligence or other breach of duty, can be avoided by means of contract terms and otherwise, and under the law of Scotland civil liability can be avoided by means of contract terms.*                                                   [26th October 1977]

# PART I

# AMENDMENT OF LAW FOR ENGLAND AND WALES AND NORTHERN IRELAND

### *Introductory*

**1   Scope of Part I**

(1)   For the purposes of this Part of this Act, 'negligence' means the breach—

    (a)   of any obligation, arising from the express or implied terms of a contract, to take reasonable care or exercise reasonable skill in the performance of the contract;

    (b)   of any common law duty to take reasonable care or exercise reasonable skill (but not any stricter duty);

    (c)   of the common duty of care imposed by the Occupiers' Liability Act 1957 or the Occupiers' Liability Act (Northern Ireland) 1957.

(2)   This Part of this Act is subject to Part 111; and in relation to contracts, the operation of sections 2 to 4 and 7 is subject to the exceptions made by Schedule 1.

(3)   In the case of both contract and tort, sections 2 to 7 apply (except where the contrary is stated in section 6(4)) only to business liability, that is liability for breach of obligations or duties arising—

    (a)   from things done or to be done by a person in the course of a business (whether his own business or another's); or

    (b)   from the occupation of premises used for business purposes of the occupier;

and references to liability are to be read accordingly but liability of an occupier of premises for breach of an obligation or duty towards a person obtaining access to the premises for recreational or educational purposes, being liability for loss or damage suffered by reason of the dangerous state of the premises, is not a business liability of the occupier unless granting that person such access for the purposes concerned falls within the business purposes of the occupier.

(4)   In relation to any breach of duty or obligation, it is, immaterial for any purpose of this Part of this Act whether the breach was inadvertent or intentional, or whether liability for it arises directly or vicariously.

### *Avoidance of liability for negligence, breach of contract, etc*

**2   Negligence liability**

(1)   A person cannot by reference to any contract term or to a notice given to persons generally or to particular persons exclude or restrict his liability for death or personal injury resulting from negligence.

(2)   In the case of other loss or damage, a person cannot so exclude or restrict his liability for negligence except in so far as the term or notice satisfies the requirement of reasonableness.

(3)   Where a contract term or notice purports to exclude or restrict liability for negligence a person's agreement to or awareness of it is not of itself to be taken as indicating his voluntary acceptance of any risk.

### 3  Liability arising in contract

(1)  This section applies as between contracting parties where one of them deals as consumer or on the other's written standard terms of business.

(2)  As against that party, the other cannot by reference to any contract term—

(a)  when himself in breach of contract, exclude or restrict any liability of his in respect of the breach; or

(b)  claim to be entitled—

(i)  to render a contractual performance substantially different from that which was reasonably expected of him, or

(ii)  in respect of the whole or any part of his contractual obligation, to render no performance at all,

except in so far as (in any of the cases mentioned above in this subsection) the contract term satisfies the requirement of reasonableness.

### 4  Unreasonable indemnity clauses

(1)  A person dealing as consumer cannot by reference to any contract term be made to indemnify another person (whether a party to the contract or not) in respect of liability that may be incurred by the other for negligence or breach of contract, except in so far as the contract term satisfies the requirement of reasonableness.

(2)  This section applies whether the liability in question—

(a)  is directly that of the person to be indemnified or is incurred by him vicariously;

(b)  is to the person dealing as consumer or to someone else.

*Liability arising from sale or supply of goods*

### 5  'Guarantee' of consumer goods

(1)  In the case of goods of a type ordinarily supplied for private use or consumption, where loss or damage—

(a)  arises from the goods proving defective while in consumer use; and

(b)  results from the negligence of a person concerned in the manufacture or distribution of the goods,

liability for the loss or damage cannot be excluded or restricted by reference to any contract term or notice contained in or operating by reference to a guarantee of the goods.

(2)  For these purposes—

(a)  goods are to be regarded as 'in consumer use' when a person is using them, or has them in his possession for use, otherwise than exclusively for the purposes of a business; and

(b)  anything in writing is a guarantee if it contains or purports to contain some promise or assurance (however worded or presented) that defects will be made good by complete or partial replacement, or by repair, monetary compensation or otherwise.

(3)  This section does not apply as between the parties to a contract under or in pursuance of which possession or ownership of the goods passed.

### 6  Sale and hire purchase

(1)  Liability for breach of the obligations arising from—

(a)  section 12 of the Sale of Goods Act 1979 (seller's implied undertakings as to title, etc.);

(b)  section 8 of the Supply of Goods (Implied Terms) Act 1973 (the corresponding thing in relation to hire-purchase),

cannot be excluded or restricted by reference to any contract term.

(2)  As against a person dealing as consumer, liability for breach of the obligations arising from—

(a)  section 13, 14, or 15 of the 1979 Act (seller's implied undertakings as to conformity of goods with description or sample, or as to their quality or fitness for a particular purpose);

(b)  section 9, 10 or 11 of the 1973 Act (the corresponding things in relation to hire-purchase),

cannot be excluded or restricted by reference to any contract term.

(3)  As against a person dealing otherwise than as consumer, the liability specified in subsection (2) above can be excluded or restricted by reference to a contract term, but only in so far as the term satisfies the requirement of reasonableness.

(4)  The liabilities referred to in this section are not only the business liabilities defined by section 1(3), but include those arising under any contract of sale of goods or hire-purchase agreement.

### 7  Miscellaneous contracts under which goods pass

(1)  Where the possession or ownership of goods passes under or in pursuance of a contract not governed by the law of sale of goods or hire-purchase, subsections (2) to (4) below apply as regards the effect (if any) to be given to contract terms excluding or restricting liability for breach of obligation arising by implication of law from the nature of the contract.

(2)  As against a person dealing as consumer, liability in respect of the goods' correspondence with description or sample, or their quality or fitness for any particular purpose, cannot be excluded or restricted by reference to any such term.

(3) As against a person dealing otherwise than as consumer, that liability can be excluded or restricted by reference to such a term, but only in so far as the term satisfies the requirement of reasonableness.

(3A) Liability for breach of the obligations arising under section 2 of the Supply of Goods and Services Act 1982 (implied terms about title etc. in certain contracts for the transfer of the property in goods) cannot be excluded or restricted by reference to any such term.

(4) Liability in respect of—

(a) the right to transfer ownership of the goods, or give possession; or

(b) the assurance of quiet possession to a person taking goods in pursuance of the contract,

cannot (in a case to which subsection (3A) above does not apply), be excluded or restricted by reference to any such term except in so far as the term satisfies the requirement of reasonableness.

(5) [...]

### Other provisions about contracts

## 8 [...]

## 9 Effect of breach

(1) Where for reliance upon it a contract term has to satisfy the requirement of reasonableness, it may be found to do so and be given effect accordingly notwithstanding that the contract has been terminated either by breach or by a party electing to treat it as repudiated.

(2) Where on a breach the contract is nevertheless affirmed by a party entitled to treat it as repudiated, this does not of itself exclude the requirement of reasonableness in relation to any contract term.

## 10 Evasion by means of secondary contract

A person is not bound by any contract term prejudicing or taking away rights of his which arise under, or in connection with the performance of, another contract, so far as those rights extend to the enforcement of another's liability which this Part of this Act prevents that other from excluding or restricting.

### Explanatory provisions

## 11 The 'reasonableness' test

(1) In relation to a contract term, the requirement of reasonableness for the purposes of this Part of this Act, section 3 of the Misrepresentation Act 1967 and section 3 of the Misrepresentation Act (Northern Ireland) 1967 is that the term shall have been a fair and reasonable one to be included having regard to the circumstances which were, or ought reasonably to have been, known to or in the contemplation of the parties when the contract was made.

(2) In determining for the purposes of section 6 or 7 above whether a contract term satisfies the requirement of reasonableness, regard shall be had in particular to the matters specified in Schedule 2 to this Act; but this subsection does not prevent the court or arbitrator from holding, in accordance with any rule of law, that a term which purports to exclude or restrict any relevant liability is not a term of the contract.

(3) In relation to a notice (not being a notice having contractual effect), the requirement of reasonableness under this Act is that it should be fair and reasonable to allow reliance on it, having regard to all the circumstances obtaining when the liability arose or (but for the notice) would have arisen.

(4) Where by reference to a contract term or notice a person seeks to restrict liability to a specified sum of money, and the question arises (under this or any other Act) whether the term or notice satisfies the requirement of reasonableness, regard shall be had in particular (but without prejudice to subsection (2) above in the case of contract terms) to—

(a) the resources which he could expect to be available to him for the purpose of meeting the liability should it arise; and

(b) how far it was open to him to cover himself by insurance.

(5) It is for those claiming that a contract term or notice satisfies the requirement of reasonableness to show that it does.

## 12 'Dealing as a consumer'

(1) A party to a contract 'deals as consumer' in relation to another party if—

(a) he neither makes the contract in the course of a business nor holds himself out as doing so; and

(b) the other party does make the contract in the course of a business; and

(c) in the case of a contract governed by the law of sale of goods or hire-purchase, or by section 7 of this Act, the goods passing under or in pursuance of the contract are of a type ordinarily supplied for private use or consumption.

(1A) But if the first party mentioned in subsection (1) is an individual paragraph (c) of that subsection must be ignored.

(2) But the buyer is not in any circumstances to be regarded as dealing as consumer—

(a) if he is an individual and the goods are second hand goods sold at public auction at which individuals have the opportunity of attending the sale in person;

(b) if he is not an individual and the goods are sold by auction or by competitive tender.

(3) Subject to this, it is for those claiming that a party does not deal as consumer to show that he does not.

## 13  Varieties of exemption clause

(1) To the extent that this Part of this Act prevents the exclusion or restriction of any liability it also prevents—

    (a) making the liability or its enforcement subject to restrictive or onerous conditions;

    (b) excluding or restricting any right or remedy in respect of the liability, or subjecting a person to any prejudice in consequence of his pursuing any such right or remedy;

    (c) excluding or restricting rules of evidence or procedure;

and (to that extent) sections 2 and 5 to 7 also prevent excluding or restricting liability by reference to terms and notices which exclude or restrict the relevant obligation or duty.

(2) But an agreement in writing to submit present or future differences to arbitration is not to be treated under this Part of this Act as excluding or restricting any liability.

## 14  Interpretation of Part I

In this Part of this Act—

'business' includes a profession and the activities of any government department or local or public authority;

'goods' has the same meaning as in the Sale of Goods Act 1979;

'hire-purchase agreement' has the same meaning as in the Consumer Credit Act 1974;

'negligence' has the meaning given by section 1(1);

'notice' includes an announcement, whether or not in writing, and any other communication or pretended communication; and

'personal injury' includes any disease and any impairment of physical or mental condition.

# PART II

# AMENDMENT OF LAW FOR SCOTLAND

## 15  Scope of Part II

(1) This Part of this Act [...] is subject to Part III of this Act and does not affect the validity, of any discharge or indemnity given by a person in consideration of the receipt by him of compensation in settlement of any claim which he has.

(2) Subject to subsection (3) below, sections 16 to 18 of this Act apply to any contract only to the extent that the contract—

    (a) relates to the transfer of the ownership or possession of goods from one person to another (with or without work having been done on them);

    (b) constitutes a contract of service or apprenticeship;

    (c) relates to services of whatever kind, including (without prejudice to the foregoing generality) carriage, deposit and pledge, care and custody, mandate, agency, loan and services relating to the use of land;

    (d) relates to the liability of an occupier of land to persons entering upon or using that land;

    (e) relates to a grant of any right or permission to enter upon or use land not amounting to an estate or interest in the land.

(3) Notwithstanding anything in subsection (2) above, sections 16 to 18—

    (a) do not apply to any contract to the extent that the contract—

        (i) is a contract of insurance (including a contract to pay annuity on human life);

        (ii) relates to the formation, constitution or dissolution of any body corporate or unincorporated association or partnership;

    (b) apply to—

    a contract of marine salvage or towage;

    a charter party of a ship or hovercraft;

    a contract for the carriage of goods by ship or hovercraft; or,

    a contract to which subsection (4) below relates,

only to the extent that—

        (i) both parties deal or hold themselves out as dealing in the course of a business (and then only in so far as the contract purports to exclude or restrict liability for breach of duty in respect of death or personal injury); or

        (ii) the contract is a consumer contract (and then only in favour of the consumer).

(4) This subsection relates to a contract in pursuance of which goods are carried by ship or hovercraft and which either—

    (a) specifies ship or hovercraft as the means of carriage over part of the journey to be covered; or

    (b) makes no provision as to the means of carriage and does not exclude ship or hovercraft as that means,

in so far as the contract operates for and in relation to the carriage of the goods by that means.

## 16   Liability for breach of duty

(1) Subject to subsection (1A) below, where a term of a contract, or a provision of a notice given to persons generally or to particular persons, purports to exclude or restrict liability for breach of duty arising in the course of any business or from the occupation of any premises used for business purposes of the occupier, that term or provision—

> (a) shall be void in any case where such exclusion or restriction is in respect of death or personal injury;
>
> (b) shall, in any other case, have no effect if it was not fair and reasonable to incorporate the term in the contract or, as the case may be, if it is not fair and reasonable to allow reliance on the provision.

(1A) Nothing in paragraph (b) of subsection (1) above shall be taken as implying that a provision of a notice has effect in circumstances where, apart from that paragraph, it would not have effect.

(2) Subsection (1)(*a*) above does not affect the validity of any discharge and indemnity given by a person, on or in connection with an award to him of compensation for pneumoconiosis attributable to employment in the coal industry, in respect of any further claim arising from his contracting that disease.

(3) Where under subsection (1) above a term of a contract or a provision of a notice is void or has no effect, the fact that a person agreed to, or was aware of, the term or provision shall not of itself be sufficient evidence that he knowingly and voluntarily assumed any risk.

## 17   Control of unreasonable exemptions in consumer or standard form contracts

(1) Any term of a contract which is a consumer contract or a standard form contract shall have no effect for the purpose of enabling a party to the contract—

> (a) who is in breach of a contractual obligation, to exclude or restrict any liability of his to the consumer or customer in respect of the breach;
>
> (b) in respect of a contractual obligation, to render no performance, or to render a performance substantially different from that which the consumer or customer reasonably expected from the contract;

if it was not fair and reasonable to incorporate the term in the contract.

(2) In this section 'customer' means a party to a standard form contract who deals on the basis of written standard terms of business of the other party to the contract who himself deals in the course of a business.

## 18   Unreasonable indemnity clauses in consumer contracts

(1) Any term of a contract which is a consumer contract shall have no effect for the purpose of making the consumer indemnify another person (whether a party to the contract or not) in respect of liability which that other person may incur as a result of breach of duty or breach of contract, if it was not fair and reasonable to incorporate the term in the contract.

(2) In this section 'liability' means liability arising in the course of any business or from the occupation of any premises used for business purposes of the occupier.

## 19   'Guarantee' of consumer goods

(1) This section applies to a guarantee—

> (a) in relation to goods which are of a type ordinarily supplied for private use or consumption; and
>
> (b) which is not a guarantee given by one party to the other party to a contract under or in pursuance of which the ownership or possession of the goods to which the guarantee relates is transferred.

(2) A term of a guarantee to which this section applies shall be void in so far as it purports to exclude or restrict liability for loss or damage (including death or personal injury)—

> (a) arising from the goods proving defective while—
>
> > (i)   in use otherwise than exclusively for the purposes of a business; or
> >
> > (ii)  in the possession of a person for such use; and
>
> (b) resulting from the breach of duty of a person concerned in the manufacture or distribution of the goods.

(3) For the purposes of this section, any document is a guarantee if it contains or purports to contain some promise or assurance (however worded or presented) that defects will be made good by complete or partial replacement, or by repair, monetary compensation otherwise.

## 20   Obligations implied by law in sale and hire-purchase contracts

(1) Any term of a contract which purports to exclude or restrict liability for breach of the obligations arising from—

> (a) section 12 of the Sale of Goods Act 1979 (seller's implied undertakings as to title etc.);
>
> (b) section 8 of the Supply of Goods (Implied Terms) Act 1973 (implied terms as to title in hire-purchase agreements),

shall be void.

(2) Any term of a contract which purports to exclude or restrict liability for breach of the obligations arising from—

(a) section 13, 14 or 15 of the said Act of 1979 (seller's implied undertakings as to conformity of goods with description or sample, or as to their quality or fitness for a particular purpose);

(b) section 9, 10 or 11 of the said Act of 1973 (the corresponding provisions in relation to hire-purchase),

shall—

(i) in the case of a consumer contract, be void against the consumer;

(ii) in any other case, have no effect if it was not fair and reasonable to incorporate the term in the contract.

### 21   Obligations implied by law in other contracts for the supply of goods

(1) Any term of a contract to which this section applies purporting to exclude or restrict liability for breach of an obligation—

(a) such as is referred to in subsection (3)(a) below—

(i) in the case of a consumer contract, shall be void against the consumer, and

(ii) in any other case, shall have no effect if it was not fair and reasonable to incorporate the term in the contract;

(b) such as is referred to in subsection (3)(b) below, shall have no effect if it was not fair and reasonable to incorporate the term in the contract.

(2) This section applies to any contract to the extent that it relates to any such matter as is referred to in section 15(2)(a) of this Act, but does not apply to—

(a) a contract of sale of goods or a hire-purchase agreement; or

(b) a charterparty of a ship or hovercraft unless it is a consumer contract (and then only in favour of the consumer).

(3) An obligation referred to in this subsection is an obligation incurred under a contract in the course of a business and arising by implication of law from the nature of the contract which relates—

(a) to the correspondence of goods with description or sample, or to the quality or fitness of goods for any particular purpose; or

(b) to any right to transfer ownership or possession of goods, or to the enjoyment of quiet possession of goods.

(3A) Notwithstanding anything in the foregoing provisions of this section, any term of a contract which purports to exclude or restrict liability for breach of the obligations arising under section 11B of the Supply of Goods and Services Act 1982 (implied terms about title, freedom from encumbrances and quiet possession in certain contracts for the transfer of property in goods) shall be void.

(4) [...]

### 22   Consequence of breach

For the avoidance of doubt, where any provision of this Part of this Act requires that the incorporation of a term in a contract must be fair and reasonable for that term to have effect—

(a) if that requirement is satisfied, the term may be given effect to notwithstanding that the contract has been terminated in consequence of breach of that contract;

(b) for the term to be given effect to, that requirement must be satisfied even where a party who is entitled to rescind the contract elects not to rescind it.

### 23   Evasion by means of secondary contract

Any term of any contract shall be void which purports to exclude or restrict, or has the effect of excluding or restricting—

(a) the exercise, by a party to any other contract, of any right or remedy which arises in respect of that other contract in consequence of breach of duty, or of obligation, liability for which could not by virtue of the provisions of this Part of this Act be excluded or restricted by a term of that other contract;

(b) the application of the provisions of this Part of this Act in respect of that or any other contract.

### 24   The 'reasonableness' test

(1) In determining for the purposes of this Part of this Act whether it was fair and reasonable to incorporate a term in a contract, regard shall be had only to the circumstances which were, or ought reasonably to have been, known to or in the contemplation of the parties to the contract at the time the contract was made.

(2) In determining for the purposes of section 20 or 21 of this Act whether it was fair and reasonable to incorporate a term in a contract, regard shall be had in particular to the matters specified in

Schedule 2 to this Act; but this subsection shall not prevent a court or arbiter from holding, in accordance with any rule of law, that a term which purports to exclude or restrict any relevant liability is not a term of the contract.

(2A) In determining for the purposes of this Part of this Act whether it is fair and reasonable to allow reliance on a provision of a notice (not being a notice having contractual effect), regard shall be had to all the circumstances obtaining when the liability arose or (but for the provision) would have arisen.

(3) Where a term in a contract or a provision of a notice purports to restrict liability to a specified sum of money, and the question arises for the purposes of this Part of this Act whether it was fair and reasonable to incorporate the term in the contract or whether it is fair and reasonable to allow reliance on the provision, then, without prejudice to subsection (2) above in the case of a term in a contract, regard shall be had in particular to—

    (a) the resources which the party seeking to rely on that term or provision could expect to be available to him for the purpose of meeting the liability should it arise;

    (b) how far it was open to that party to cover himself by insurance.

(4) The onus of proving that it was fair and reasonable to incorporate a term in a contract or that it is fair and reasonable to allow reliance on a provision of a notice shall lie on the party so contending.

## 25  Interpretation of Part II

(1) In this Part of this Act—

'breach of duty' means the breach —

    (a) of any obligation, arising from the express or implied terms of a contract, to take reasonable care or exercise reasonable skill in the performance of the contract;

    (b) of any common law duty to take reasonable care or exercise reasonable skill;

    (c) of the duty of reasonable care imposed by section 2(1) of the Occupiers' Liability (Scotland) Act 1960;

'business' includes a profession and the activities of any government department or local or public authority;

'consumer' has the meaning assigned to that expression in the definition in this section of 'consumer contract';

'consumer contract' means subject to subsections (1A) and (1B) below a contract […] in which —

    (a) one party to the contract deals, and the other party to the contract ('the consumer') does not deal or hold himself out as dealing, in the course of a business, and

    (b) in the case of a contract such as is mentioned in section 15(2)(a) of this Act, the goods are of a type ordinarily supplied for private use or consumption;

and for the purposes of this Part of this Act the onus of proving that a contract is not to be regarded as a consumer contract shall lie on the party so contending;

'goods' has the same meaning as in the Sale of Goods Act 1979;

'hire-purchase agreement' has the same meaning as in section 189(1) of the Consumer Credit Act 1974;

'notice' includes an announcement, whether or not in writing, and any other communication or pretended communication

'personal injury' includes any disease and any impairment of physical or mental condition.

(1A) Where the consumer is an individual, paragraph (b) in the definition of 'consumer contract' in subsection (1) must be disregarded.

(1B) The expression of 'consumer contract' does not include a contract in which—

    (a) the buyer is an individual and the goods are second hand goods sold by public auction at which individuals have the opportunity of attending in person; or

    (b) the buyer is not an individual and the goods are sold by auction or competitive tender.

(2) In relation to any breach of duty or obligation, it is immaterial for any purpose of this Part of this Act whether the act or omission giving rise to that breach was inadvertent or intentional, or whether liability for it arises directly or vicariously.

(3) In this Part of this Act, any reference to excluding or restricting any liability includes—

    (a) making the liability or its enforcement subject to any restrictive or onerous conditions;

    (b) excluding or restricting any right or remedy in respect of the liability, or subjecting a person to any prejudice in consequence of his pursuing any such right or remedy;

    (c) excluding or restricting any rule of evidence or procedure;

but does not include an agreement to submit any question to arbitration.

(4) […]

(5) In sections 15 and 16 and 19 to 21 of this Act, any reference to excluding or restricting liability for breach of an obligation or duty shall include a reference to excluding or restricting the obligation or duty itself.

# PART III

# PROVISIONS APPLYING TO WHOLE OF UNITED KINGDOM

## *Miscellaneous*

### 26  International supply contracts

(1)  The limits imposed by this Act on the extent to which a person may exclude or restrict liability by reference to a contract term do not apply to liability arising under such a contract as is described in subsection (3) below.

(2)  The terms of such a contract are not subject to any requirement of reasonableness under section 3 or 4: and nothing in Part 11 of this Act shall require the incorporation of the terms of such a contract to be fair and reasonable for them to have effect.

(3)  Subject to subsection (4), that description of contract is one whose characteristics are the following—

    (a)  either it is a contract of sale of goods or it is one under or in pursuance of which the possession or ownership of goods passes; and

    (b)  it is made by parties whose places of business (or, if they have none, habitual residences) are in the territories of different States (the Channel Islands and the Isle of Man being treated for this purpose as different States from the United Kingdom).

(4)  A contract falls within subsection (3) above only if either—

    (a)  the goods in question are, at the time of the conclusion of the contract, in the course of carriage, or will be carried, from the territory of one State to the territory of another; or

    (b)  the acts constituting the offer and acceptance have been done in the territories of different States; or

    (c)  the contract provides for the goods to be delivered to the territory of a State other than that within whose territory those acts were done.

### 27  Choice of law clauses

(1)  Where the law applicable to a contract is the law of any part of the United Kingdom only by choice of the parties (and apart from that choice would be the law of some country outside the United Kingdom) sections 2 to 7 and 16 to 21 of this Act do not operate as part of the law applicable to the contract.

(2)  This Act has effect notwithstanding any contract term which applies or purports to apply the law of some country outside the United Kingdom, where (either or both)—

    (a)  the term appears to the court, or arbitrator or arbiter to have been imposed wholly or mainly for the purpose of enabling the party imposing it to evade the operation of this Act; or

    (b)  in the making of the contract one of the parties dealt as consumer, and he was then habitually resident in the United Kingdom, and the essential steps necessary for the making of the contract were taken there, whether by him or by others on his behalf.

(3)  In the application of subsection (2) above to Scotland, for paragraph (b) there shall be substituted—

    '(b)  the contract is a consumer contract as defined in Part 11 of this Act, and the consumer at the date when the contract was made was habitually resident in the United Kingdom, and the essential steps necessary for the making of the contract were taken there, whether by him or by others on his behalf.'.

### 28  Temporary provision for sea carriage passengers

(1)  This section applies to a contract for carriage by sea of a passenger or of a passenger and his luggage where the provisions of the Athens Convention (with or without modification) do not have, in relation to the contract, the force of law in the United Kingdom.

(2)  In a case where—

    (a)  the contract is not made in the United Kingdom, and

    (b)  neither the place of departure nor the place of destination under it is in the United Kingdom,

a person is not precluded by this Act from excluding or restricting liability for loss or damage, being loss or damage for which the provisions of the Convention would, if they had the force of law in relation to the contract, impose liability on him.

(3)  In any other case, a person is not precluded by this Act from excluding or restricting liability for that loss or damage—

    (a)  in so far as the exclusion or restriction would have been effective in that case had the provisions of the Convention had the force of law in relation to the contract; or

    (b)  in such circumstances and to such extent as may be prescribed, by reference to a prescribed term of the contract.

(4)  For the purposes of subsection (3)(a), the values which shall be taken to be the official values in the United Kingdom of the amounts (expressed in gold francs) by reference to which liability under the

provisions of the Convention is limited shall be such amounts in sterling as the Secretary of State may from time to time by order made by statutory instrument specify.

(5) In this section,—

    (a) the references to excluding or restricting liability include doing any of those things in relation to the liability which are mentioned in section 13 or section 25(3) and (5); and

    (b) 'the Athens Convention' means the Athens Convention relating to the Carriage of Passengers and their Luggage by Sea, 1974;and

    (c) 'prescribed' means prescribed by the Secretary of State by regulations made by statutory instrument;

and a statutory instrument containing the regulations shall be subject to annulment in pursuance of a resolution of either House of Parliament.

## 29  Saving for other relevant legislation

(1) Nothing in this Act removes or restricts the effect of, or prevents reliance upon, any contractual provision which—

    (a) is authorised or required by the express terms or necessary implication of an enactment; or

    (b) being made with a view to compliance with an international agreement to which the United Kingdom is a party, does not operate more restrictively than is contemplated by the agreement.

(2) A contract term is to be taken—

    (a) for the purposes of Part I of this Act, as satisfying the requirement of reasonableness; and

    (b) for those of Part 11, to have been fair and reasonable to incorporate,

if it is incorporated or approved by, or incorporated pursuant to a decision or ruling of, a competent authority acting in the exercise of any statutory jurisdiction or function and is not a term in a contract to which the competent authority is itself a party.

(3) In this section—

'competent authority' means any court, arbitrator or arbiter, government department or public authority;

'enactment' means any legislation (including subordinate legislation) of the United Kingdom or Northern Ireland and any instrument having effect by virtue of such legislation; and

'statutory' means conferred by an enactment.

## 30  [...]

### *General*

## 31  Commencement; amendments; repeals

(1) This Act comes into force on 1st February 1978.

(2) Nothing in this Act applies to contracts made before the date on which it comes into force; but subject to this, it applies to liability for any loss or damage which is suffered on or after that date.

(3) [...]

(4) [...]

## 32  Citation and extent

(1) This Act may be cited as the Unfair Contract Terms Act 1977.

(2) Part I of this Act extends to England and Wales and to Northern Ireland; but it does not extend to Scotland.

(3) Part II of this Act extends to Scotland only.

(4) This Part of this Act extends to the whole of the United Kingdom.

# SCHEDULES

Section 1(2).            # SCHEDULE 1

## SCOPE OF SECTIONS 2 TO 4 AND 7

**1**  Sections 2 to 4 of this Act do not extend to—

    (a) any contract of insurance (including a contract to pay an annuity on human life);

    (b) any contract so far as it relates to the creation or transfer of an interest in land, or to the termination of such an interest, whether by extinction, merger, surrender, forfeiture or otherwise;

    (c) any contract so far as it relates to the creation or transfer of a right or interest in any patent, trade mark, copyright or design right, registered design, technical or commercial information or other intellectual property, or relates to the termination of any such right or interest;

(d) any contract so far as it relates—
  (i) to the formation or dissolution of a company (which means any body corporate or unincorporated association and includes a partnership), or
  (ii) to its constitution or the rights or obligations of its corporators or members;
(e) any contract so far as it relates to the creation or transfer of securities or of any right or interest in securities.

2 Section 2(1) extends to—
(a) any contract of marine salvage or towage;
(b) any charterparty of a ship or hovercraft; and
(c) any contract for the carriage of goods by ship or hovercraft;

but subject to this sections 2 to 4 and 7 do not extend to any such contract except in favour of a person dealing as consumer.

3 Where goods are carried by ship or hovercraft in pursuance of a contract which either—
(a) specifies that as the means of carriage over part of the journey to be covered, or
(b) makes no provision as to the means of carriage and does not exclude that means,

then sections 2(2), 3 and 4 do not, except in favour of a person dealing as consumer, extend to the contract as it operates for and in relation to the carriage of the goods by that means.

4 Section 2(1) and (2) do not extend to a contract of employment, except in favour of the employee.

5 Section 2(1) does not affect the validity of any discharge and indemnity given by a person, on or in connection with an award to him of compensation for pneumoconiosis attributable to employment in the coal industry, in respect of any further claim arising from his contracting that disease.

# SCHEDULE 2

## 'GUIDELINES' FOR APPLICATION OF REASONABLENESS TEST

The matters to which regard is to be had in particular for the purposes of sections 6(3), 7(3) and (4), 20 and 21 are any of the following which appear to be relevant—
(a) the strength of the bargaining positions of the parties relative to each other, taking into account (among other things) alternative means by which the customer's requirements could have been met;
(b) whether the customer received an inducement to agree to the term, or in accepting it had an opportunity of entering into a similar contract with other persons, but without having a similar term;
(c) whether the customer knew or ought reasonably to have known of the existence and the extent of the term (having regard, among other things, to any custom of the trade and any previous course of dealing between the parties);
(d) where the term excludes or restricts any relevant liability if some condition was not complied with, whether it was reasonable at the time of the contract to expect that compliance with that condition would be practicable;
(e) whether the goods were manufactured, processed or adapted to the special order of the customer.

# SCHEDULE 3

## AMENDMENTS OF ENACTMENTS
[...]

# SCHEDULE 4

## REPEALS
[...]

# The Unfair Terms in Consumer Contracts Regulations 1999

**(1999 No. 2083)**

*Whereas the Secretary of State is a Minister designated for the purposes of section 2(2) of the European Communities Act 1972 in relation to measures relating to consumer protection:*

*Now, the Secretary of State, in exercise of the powers conferred upon him by section 2(2) of that Act, hereby makes the following Regulations:—*

## 1 Citation and commencement

These Regulations may be cited as the Unfair Terms in Consumer Contracts Regulations 1999 and shall come into force on 1st October 1999.

## 2 Revocation

The Unfair Terms in Consumer Contracts Regulations 1994 are hereby revoked.

## 3 Interpretation

(1) In these Regulations—

'the Community' means the European Community;

'consumer' means any natural person who, in contracts covered by these Regulations, is acting for purposes which are outside his trade, business or profession;

'court' in relation to England and Wales and Northern Ireland means a county court or the High Court, and in relation to Scotland, the Sheriff or the Court of Session;

'Director' means the Director General of Fair Trading;

'EEA Agreement' means the Agreement on the European Economic Area signed at Oporto on 2nd May 1992 as adjusted by the protocol signed at Brussels on 17th March 1993

'Member State' means a State which is a contracting party to the EEA Agreement;

'notified' means notified in writing;

'qualifying body' means a person specified in Schedule 1;

'seller or supplier' means any natural or legal person who, in contracts covered by these Regulations, is acting for purposes relating to his trade, business or profession, whether publicly owned or privately owned;

'unfair terms' means the contractual terms referred to in regulation 5.

(1A) The references—

(a) in regulation 4(1) to a seller or a supplier, and

(b) in regulation 8(1) to a seller or supplier,

Include references to a distance supplier and intermediary.

(1B) In paragraph (1A) and regulation 5(6)—

'distance supplier' means—

(a) a supplier under a distance contract within the meaning of the Financial Services (Distance Marketing) Regulations 2004, or

(b) a supplier of unsolicited financial services within regulation 15 of those Regulations; and

'intermediary' has the same meaning as in those Regulations.

(2) In the application of these Regulations to Scotland for references to an 'injunction' or an 'interim injunction' there shall be substituted references to an 'interdict' or 'interim interdict' respectively.

## 4 Terms to which these Regulations apply

(1) These Regulations apply in relation to unfair terms in contracts concluded between a seller or a supplier and a consumer.

(2) These Regulations do not apply to contractual terms which reflect—

(a) mandatory statutory or regulatory provisions (including such provisions under the law of any Member State or in Community legislation having effect in the United Kingdom without further enactment);

(b) the provisions or principles of international conventions to which the Member States or the Community are party.

## 5 Unfair Terms

(1) A contractual term which has not been individually negotiated shall be regarded as unfair if, contrary to the requirement of good faith, it causes a significant imbalance in the parties' rights and obligations arising under the contract, to the detriment of the consumer.

(2) A term shall always be regarded as not having been individually negotiated where it has been drafted in advance and the consumer has therefore not been able to influence the substance of the term.

(3) Notwithstanding that a specific term or certain aspects of it in a contract has been individually negotiated, these Regulations shall apply to the rest of a contract if an overall assessment of it indicates that it is a pre-formulated standard contract.

(4) It shall be for any seller or supplier who claims that a term was individually negotiated to show that it was.

(5) Schedule 2 to these Regulations contains an indicative and non-exhaustive list of the terms which may be regarded as unfair.

(6) Any contractual term providing that a consumer bears the burden of proof in respect of showing whether a distance supplier or an intermediary complied with any or all of the obligations placed upon him resulting from the Directive and any rule or enactment implementing it shall always be regarded as unfair.

(7) In paragraph (6)—

'the Directive' means Directive 2002/65/EC of the European Parliament and of the Council of 23 September 2002 concerning the distance marketing of consumer financial services and amending Council Directive 90/619/EEC and Directives 97/7/EC; and

'rule' means a rule made by the Financial Services Authority under the Financial Services and Markets Act 2000 or by a designated professional body within the meaning of section s326(2) of that Act.

### 6  Assessment of unfair terms

(1)  Without prejudice to regulation 12, the unfairness of a contractual term shall be assessed, taking into account the nature of the goods or services for which the contract was concluded and by referring, at the time of conclusion of the contract, to all the circumstances attending the conclusion of the contract and to all the other terms of the contract or of another contract on which it is dependent.

(2)  In so far as it is in plain intelligible language, the assessment of fairness of a term shall not relate—

    (a)  to the definition of the main subject matter of the contract, or

    (b)  to the adequacy of the price or remuneration, as against the goods or services supplied in exchange.

### 7  Written contracts

(1)  A seller or supplier shall ensure that any written term of a contract is expressed in plain, intelligible language.

(2)  If there is doubt about the meaning of a written term, the interpretation which is most favourable to the consumer shall prevail but this rule shall not apply in proceedings brought under regulation 12.

### 8  Effect of unfair term

(1)  An unfair term in a contract concluded with a consumer by a seller or supplier shall not be binding on the consumer.

(2)  The contract shall continue to bind the parties if it is capable of continuing in existence without the unfair term.

### 9  Choice of law clauses

These Regulations shall apply notwithstanding any contract term which applies or purports to apply the law of a non-Member State, if the contract has a close connection with the territory of the Member States.

### 10  Complaints – consideration by Director

(1)  It shall be the duty of the Director to consider any complaint made to him that any contract term drawn up for general use is unfair, unless—

    (a)  the complaint appears to the Director to be frivolous or vexatious; or

    (b)  a qualifying body has notified the Director that it agrees to consider the complaint.

(2)  The Director shall give reasons for his decision to apply or not to apply, as the case may be, for an injunction under regulation 12 in relation to any complaint which these Regulations require him to consider.

(3)  In deciding whether or not to apply for an injunction in respect of a term which the Director considers to be unfair, he may, if he considers it appropriate to do so, have regard to any undertakings given to him by or on behalf of any person as to the continued use of such a term in contracts concluded with consumers.

### 11  Complaints – consideration by qualifying bodies

(1)  If a qualifying body specified in Part One of Schedule 1 notifies the Director that it agrees to consider a complaint that any contract term drawn up for general use is unfair, it shall be under a duty to consider that complaint.

(2)  Regulation 10(2) and (3) shall apply to a qualifying body which is under a duty to consider a complaint as they apply to the Director.

### 12  Injunctions to prevent continued use of unfair terms

(1)  The Director or, subject to paragraph (2), any qualifying body may apply for an injunction (including an interim injunction) against any person appearing to the Director or that body to be using, or recommending use of, an unfair term drawn up for general use in contracts concluded with consumers.

(2)  A qualifying body may apply for an injunction only where—

    (a)  it has notified the Director of its intention to apply at least fourteen days before the date on which the application is made, beginning with the date on which the notification was given; or

    (b)  the Director consents to the application being made within a shorter period.

(3)  The court on an application under this regulation may grant an injunction on such terms as it thinks fit.

(4)  An injunction may relate not only to use of a particular contract term drawn up for general use but to any similar term, or a term having like effect, used or recommended for use by any person.

## 13  Powers of the Director and qualifying bodies to obtain documents and information

(1) The Director may exercise the power conferred by this regulation for the purpose of—

  (a) facilitating his consideration of a complaint that a contract term drawn up for general use is unfair; or

  (b) ascertaining whether a person has complied with an undertaking or court order as to the continued use, or recommendation for use, of a term in contracts concluded with consumers.

(2) A qualifying body specified in Part One of Schedule 1 may exercise the power conferred by this regulation for the purpose of—

  (a) facilitating its consideration of a complaint that a contract term drawn up for general use is unfair; or

  (b) ascertaining whether a person has complied with—

    (i)  an undertaking given to it or to the court following an application by that body, or

    (ii)  a court order made on an application by that body,

as to the continued use, or recommendation for use, of a term in contracts concluded with consumers.

(3) The Director may require any person to supply to him, and a qualifying body specified in Part One of Schedule 1 may require any person to supply to it—

  (a) a copy of any document which that person has used or recommended for use, at the time the notice referred to in paragraph (4) below is given, as a pre-formulated standard contract in dealings with consumers;

  (b) information about the use, or recommendation for use, by that person of that document or any other such document in dealings with consumers.

(4) The power conferred by this regulation is to be exercised by a notice in writing which may—

  (a) specify the way in which and the time within which it is to be complied with; and

  (b) be varied or revoked by a subsequent notice.

(5) Nothing in this regulation compels a person to supply any document or information which he would be entitled to refuse to produce or give in civil proceedings before the court.

(6) If a person makes default in complying with a notice under this regulation, the court may, on the application of the Director or of the qualifying body, make such order as the court thinks fit for requiring the default to be made good, and any such order may provide that all the costs or expenses of and incidental to the application shall be borne by the person in default or by any officers of a company or other association who are responsible for its default.

## 14  Notification of undertakings and orders to Director

A qualifying body shall notify the Director—

  (a) of any undertaking given to it by or on behalf of any person as to the continued use of a term which that body considers to be unfair in contracts concluded with consumers;

  (b) of the outcome of any application made by it under regulation 12, and of the terms of any undertaking given to, or order made by, the court;

  (c) of the outcome of any application made by it to enforce a previous order of the court.

## 15  Publication, information and advice

(1) The Director shall arrange for the publication in such form and manner as he considers appropriate, of—

  (a) details of any undertaking or order notified to him under regulation 14;

  (b) details of any undertaking given to him by or on behalf of any person as to the continued use of a term which the Director considers to be unfair in contracts concluded with consumers;

  (c) details of any application made by him under regulation 12, and of the terms of any undertaking given to, or order made by, the court;

  (d) details of any application made by the Director to enforce a previous order of the court.

(2) The Director shall inform any person on request whether a particular term to which these Regulations apply has been—

  (a) the subject of an undertaking given to the Director or notified to him by a qualifying body; or

  (b) the subject of an order of the court made upon application by him or notified to him by a qualifying body;

and shall give that person details of the undertaking or a copy of the order, as the case may be, together with a copy of any amendments which the person giving the undertaking has agreed to make to the term in question.

(3) The Director may arrange for the dissemination in such form and manner as he considers appropriate of such information and advice concerning the operation of these Regulations as may appear to him to be expedient to give to the public and to all persons likely to be affected by these Regulations.

## 16  The functions of the Financial Services Authority

The functions of the Financial Services Authority under these Regulations shall be treated as functions of the Financial Services Authority under the Financial Services and Markets Act 2000.

# SCHEDULE 1

## QUALIFYING BODIES

### PART ONE

1   The Information Commissioner.
2   The Gas and Electricity Markets Authority.
3   The Director General of Electricity Supply for Northern Ireland.
4   The Director General of Gas for Northern Ireland.
5   The Office of Communications.
6   The Water Services Regulation Authority.
7   The Rail Regulator.
8   Every weights and measures authority in Great Britain.
9   The Department of Enterprise, Trade and Investment in Northern Ireland.
10   The Financial Services Authority

### PART TWO

11   Consumers' Association.

# SCHEDULE 2

## INDICATIVE AND NON-EXHAUSTIVE LIST OF TERMS WHICH MAY BE REGARDED AS UNFAIR

1   Terms which have the object or effect of—
  (a) excluding or limiting the legal liability of a seller or supplier in the event of the death of a consumer or personal injury to the latter resulting from an act or omission of that seller or supplier;
  (b) inappropriately excluding or limiting the legal rights of the consumer vis-à-vis the seller or supplier or another party in the event of total or partial non-performance or inadequate performance by the seller or supplier of any of the contractual obligations, including the option of offsetting a debt owed to the seller or supplier against any claim which the consumer may have against him;
  (c) making an agreement binding on the consumer whereas provision of services by the seller or supplier is subject to a condition whose realisation depends on his own will alone;
  (d) permitting the seller or supplier to retain sums paid by the consumer where the latter decides not to conclude or perform the contract, without providing for the consumer to receive compensation of an equivalent amount from the seller or supplier where the latter is the party cancelling the contract;
  (e) requiring any consumer who fails to fulfil his obligation to pay a disproportionately high sum in compensation;
  (f) authorising the seller or supplier to dissolve the contract on a discretionary basis where the same facility is not granted to the consumer, or permitting the seller or supplier to retain the sums paid for services not yet supplied by him where it is the seller or supplier himself who dissolves the contract;
  (g) enabling the seller or supplier to terminate a contract of indeterminate duration without reasonable notice except where there are serious grounds for doing so;
  (h) automatically extending a contract of fixed duration where the consumer does not indicate otherwise, when the deadline fixed for the consumer to express his desire not to extend the contract is unreasonably early;
  (i) irrevocably binding the consumer to terms with which he had no real opportunity of becoming acquainted before the conclusion of the contract;
  (j) enabling the seller or supplier to alter the terms of the contract unilaterally without a valid reason which is specified in the contract;
  (k) enabling the seller or supplier to alter unilaterally without a valid reason any characteristics of the product or service to be provided;
  (l) providing for the price of goods to be determined at the time of delivery or allowing a seller of goods or supplier of services to increase their price without in both cases giving the consumer the corresponding right to cancel the contract if the final price is too high in relation to the price agreed when the contract was concluded;

(m) giving the seller or supplier the right to determine whether the goods or services supplied are in conformity with the contract, or giving him the exclusive right to interpret any term of the contract;

(n) limiting the seller's or supplier's obligation to respect commitments undertaken by his agents or making his commitments subject to compliance with a particular formality;

(o) obliging the consumer to fulfil all his obligations where the seller or supplier does not perform his;

(p) giving the seller or supplier the possibility of transferring his rights and obligations under the contract, where this may serve to reduce the guarantees for the consumer, without the latter's agreement;

(q) excluding or hindering the consumer's right to take legal action or exercise any other legal remedy, particularly by requiring the consumer to take disputes exclusively to arbitration not covered by legal provisions, unduly restricting the evidence available to him or imposing on him a burden of proof which, according to the applicable law, should lie with another party to the contract.

2   Scope of paragraphs 1(g), (j) and (l)

(a) Paragraph 1(g) is without hindrance to terms by which a supplier of financial services reserves the right to terminate unilaterally a contract of indeterminate duration without notice where there is a valid reason, provided that the supplier is required to inform the other contracting party or parties thereof immediately.

(b) Paragraph 1(j) is without hindrance to terms under which a supplier of financial services reserves the right to alter the rate of interest payable by the consumer or due to the latter, or the amount of other charges for financial services without notice where there is a valid reason, provided that the supplier is required to inform the other contracting party or parties thereof at the earliest opportunity and that the latter are free to dissolve the contract immediately.

Paragraph 1(j) is also without hindrance to terms under which a seller or supplier reserves the right to alter unilaterally the conditions of a contract of indeterminate duration, provided that he is required to inform the consumer with reasonable notice and that the consumer is free to dissolve the contract.

(c) Paragraphs 1(g), (j) and (l) do not apply to:

transactions in transferable securities, financial instruments and other products or services where the price is linked to fluctuations in a stock exchange quotation or index or a financial market rate that the seller or supplier does not control;

contracts for the purchase or sale of foreign currency, traveller's cheques or international money orders denominated in foreign currency;

(d) Paragraph 1(l) is without hindrance to price indexation clauses, where lawful, provided that the method by which prices vary is explicitly described.